Bill James presents. . .

STATS
Minor League Handbook
2001

STATS, Inc.
and
Howe Sportsdata

STATS INC.™
PUBLISHING

HOWE SPORTSDATA
A SERVICE OF **SPORTSTICKER**®

Published by STATS Publishing
A division of Sports Team Analysis & Tracking Systems, Inc.

Cover by Ryan Balock, Marc Elman and Chuck Miller

Cover photo by Diamond Images®

First Edition: November, 2000

Printed in the United States of America

ISBN 1-884064-85-X

Acknowledgments

Publishing the 10th edition of the *STATS Minor League Handbook* is a collective effort. The STATS team is successfully anchored by CEO John Dewan and President Alan Leib, and lending invaluable assistance to the guys at the top is Jennifer Manicki. Sue Dewan and Bob Meyerhoff oversee our Research & Development/Special Projects efforts. Sue works on special projects and Bob directs a group composed of Athan Arvanitis, Jim Osborne, Craig Rolling, Joe Sclafani and Andy Tumpowsky. Arthur Ashley provides programming and project support for the development group. Tom Schmitt leads the Technical Operations Department, which includes: Roger Liss, Angie Melecio, Dean Peterson, Brian Spisak and Yingmin Wang.

Marc Elman oversees the Publications Department that produced this book and all our other sports titles. Getting the numbers programmed appropriately fell into the hands of Tim Coletta with help from Jim Henzler. Chuck Miller painstakingly manipulated the many columns and graphs that are key to the book's design. Tony Nistler and Thom Henninger oversaw editorial responsibilities, with help from Taylor Bechtold, Marc Carl and Norm DeNosaquo. Getting the word out about the *STATS Minor League Handbook* and other STATS publications requires the hard work of Ryan Balock, Mike Janosi, Antoinette Kelly and Mike Sarkis. Ryan designed this book's cover.

We couldn't get the book out without our Operations Department. Managing the collection of these numbers is Allan Spear. His troup includes Jeremy Alpert, Scott Berg, Michelle Blanco, Les Briesemeister, Jon Caplin, Jeff Chernow, Mike Hammer, Derek Kenar, Tony Largo, Jon Passman, Jeff Schinski, Matt Senter, Bill Stephens, Joe Stillwell and Chris Witt. Special thanks to Jeff, who oversees the accuracy of our baseball data.

The efforts of our Commercial, Fantasy, Interactive and Sales departments help pay most of our bills at STATS. Vince Smith heads our Commercial staff, made up of Ethan D. Cooperson, Stefan Kretschmann and Nick Stamm. Steve Byrd oversees the Fantasy Department, which consists of Bill Burke, Sean Bush, Jim Corelis, Consilia DiBartolo, Mike Dreckmann, Dan Ford, Brian Hogan, Walter Lis, Marc Moeller, Jim Pollard, Eric Robin, Jeff Smith, Jake Stein, John Strougal, Michael Trakan, Zach Williams and Rick Wilton. Robert Schur directs an Interactive group that includes Li Chen, Karen Christensen, Walt Cohen, Jake Costello, Chuck Durvis, Jay Fleck, Gregg Kosieniak, Scott Kraatz, Joe Lindholm, Patrick Markey, Will McCleskey, Oscar Palacios, Pat Quinn, John Sasman, Mindy Singer, David Thiel and Brian Tolleson. Jim Capuano heads Sales with the help of Greg Kirkorsky.

Keeping us in the game is the Financial/Administrative/Human Resources/Legal Department. Howard Lanin facilitates the financial and administrative concerns of the company with assistance from Kim Bartlett, Mary Ellen Gomez and Susan Zamecheck. Betty Moy contributes in finance and keeps our headquarters running smoothly. Tracy Lickton is in charge of human resources and is assisted by Megan Bennett, while Carol Savier aids with legal matters.

Our Research Department for Fox Sports in Los Angeles is headed by Don Zminda, and his team of sports researchers includes: Mike Berger, Matt Brown, Eric Corwin, Khalid El-Bayoumy, Eddie Garcia, Tracey Graham, Ryan Gunn, Don Hartack, Matt Jenkins, Fred King, Sam Lubeck, Barry Rubinowitz, Meghan Sheehan, Stephanie Sluke, Paul Sobaje, Aneel Trivedi and Randy Williams.

—Chuck Miller

This book is dedicated to
STATS 2000 Co-Rookies of the Year:

Madison Christine Sasman (1/2/00)
Abigail Serena Liss (6/23/00)

Table of Contents

Introduction

Except for those baseball fans who follow the game's minor league prospects, few Americans had heard of Ben Sheets before he blanked Cuba on three hits to lead the U.S. team to the gold medal in Sydney. Sheets was just one of many promising prospects who shared Olympic glory, and they include Kurt Ainsworth, Chris George, Roy Oswalt, Jon Rauch, Brent Abernathy, Sean Burroughs, Gookie Dawkins and Adam Everett.

As much as this was a victory for the nation's Olympic team, the gold medal in baseball also is a reason to celebrate the minor leagues. For decades the minors have been the training grounds for the big leaguers of the past and present. And through the years, minor league ball has become synonymous with small-town America, where baseball is a bargain, the games are interspersed with silly promotions and lovable, dorky mascots, and fans can enjoy quaint minor league parks.

It's an annual STATS tradition to celebrate minor league ball with the release of the *STATS Minor League Handbook*. You're holding the 10th edition, which contains the complete career stats for every player who appeared in Double-A and Triple-A ball during the 2000 season. The exceptions are players who reached the major leagues in 2000. Those players appear in our companion book, the *STATS Major League Handbook 2001*.

For players in Class-A and Rookie leagues, we supply complete 2000 statistical lines in the section that follows the career register of Double-A and Triple-A players. A year ago, this section in the *Handbook's* ninth edition housed many of the young pitchers on the Olympic team. Undoubtedly, there are future Olympians and major league stars who are in this section after playing Class-A or Rookie ball in 2000.

As always, the *Handbook* has much more than just the year-by-year stats of minor league players. This 10th edition includes lefty/righty and home/road breakdowns for all Double-A and Triple-A regulars. In addition, you will find Major League Equivalencies for the top Double-A and Triple-A hitters in each organization. The MLEs, developed by Bill James, translate a hitter's minor league numbers into what they would have looked like in the majors. Adjustments are made for home park (both major and minor league parks), league and level of competition.

Also found within these pages are team and league totals for each of professional baseball's 16 minor leagues. League information provides insight into the impact a player's surroundings has on his performance. On top of that, we provide leader boards for all minor league levels, from short-season leagues to Triple-A.

Our annual celebration of the minor leagues closes with a statistical look at the U.S. Olympic team. This bonus section includes box scores and final stats, plus a stat line for all other minor leaguers who represented their homeland at the 2000 Games.

—Thom Henninger

Career Register

Any player who appeared in Double-A or Triple-A in 2000 gets a profile in this section. The exception is if he also played in the major leagues, in which case his statistics are in our companion book, the *STATS Major League Handbook*. Another exception is Nick Johnson from the New York Yankees' system. He missed all of the 2000 season because of a hand injury, but he has been added to the register because we anticipate a solid return in 2001.

The profiles have complete major and minor league records for all qualifying players. Most of the statistical abbreviations are common and will be used throughout the book. Here's a quick review:

For all players, **Pos** = games played by position in 2000; **Ht** = Height; **Wt** = Weight; **Age** = age as of June 30, 2001.

For hitters, **G** = games; **AB** = at-bats; **H** = hits; **2B** = doubles; **3B** = triples; **HR** = home runs; **TB** = total bases; **R** = runs; **RBI** = runs batted in; **TBB** = total bases on balls; **IBB** = intentional bases on balls; **SO** = strikeouts; **HBP** = times hit by pitches; **SH** = sacrifice hits; **SF** = sacrifice flies; **SB** = stolen bases; **CS** = times caught stealing; **SB%** = stolen base percentage; **GDP** = times grounded into double plays; **Avg** = batting average; **OBP** = on-base percentage; **SLG** = slugging percentage.

For pitchers, **G** = games pitched; **GS** = games started; **CG** = complete games; **GF** = games finished; **IP** = innings pitched; **BFP** = batters facing pitcher; **H** = hits allowed; **R** = runs allowed; **ER** = earned runs allowed; **HR** = home runs allowed; **SH** = sacrifice hits allowed; **SF** = sacrifice flies allowed; **HB** = hits batsmen; **TBB** = total bases on balls; **IBB** = intentional bases on balls; **SO** = strikeouts; **WP** = wild pitches; **Bk** = balks; **W** = wins; **L** = losses; **Pct.** = winning percentage; **ShO** = shutouts; **Sv** = saves; **ERA** = earned run average.

Class-A (A+, A, A-) and Rookie (R+, R) have separate classifications to distinguish the level of competition.

Chuck Abbott

Bats: Right **Throws:** Right **Pos:** 2B-84; SS-17; 3B-2; PH-1   **Ht:** 6'1" **Wt:** 180 **Born:** 1/26/75 **Age:** 26

Year Team	Lg Org	G	AB	H	2B	3B	HR	TB	R	RBI	TBB	IBB	SO	HBP	SH	SF	SB	CS	SB%	GDP	Avg	OBP	SLG
1996 Boise	A- Ana	70	268	53	9	2	0	66	41	20	24	0	59	5	4	4	11	5	.69	8	.198	.272	.246
1997 Cedar Rapds	A Ana	133	520	120	21	5	7	172	86	54	62	0	170	3	6	2	31	12	.72	7	.231	.315	.331
1998 Midland	AA Ana	132	525	138	21	9	2	183	74	62	38	0	135	4	8	4	16	9	.64	18	.263	.315	.349
1999 Erie	AA Ana	125	444	106	13	1	6	139	70	46	47	1	138	2	6	2	9	10	.47	10	.239	.313	.313
2000 Edmonton	AAA Ana	5	15	3	1	0	0	4	0	4	0	0	5	0	0	0	0	0	—	0	.200	.200	.267
Erie	AA Ana	97	330	82	14	3	5	117	39	39	22	0	96	4	7	2	3	3	.50	11	.248	.302	.355
5 Min. YEARS		562	2102	502	79	20	20	681	310	225	193	1	603	18	31	14	70	39	.64	54	.239	.306	.324

Brent Abernathy

Bats: Right **Throws:** Right **Pos:** 2B-114; DH-5   **Ht:** 6'1" **Wt:** 185 **Born:** 9/23/77 **Age:** 23

Year Team	Lg Org	G	AB	H	2B	3B	HR	TB	R	RBI	TBB	IBB	SO	HBP	SH	SF	SB	CS	SB%	GDP	Avg	OBP	SLG
1997 Hagerstown	A Tor	99	379	117	27	2	1	151	69	26	30	0	32	6	6	2	22	13	.63	6	.309	.363	.398
1998 Dunedin	A+ Tor	124	485	159	36	1	3	206	85	65	44	0	38	1	12	6	35	13	.73	11	.328	.381	.425
1999 Knoxville	AA Tor	136	577	168	42	1	13	251	108	62	55	1	47	6	5	7	34	15	.69	11	.291	.355	.435
2000 Syracuse	AAA Tor	92	358	106	21	2	4	143	47	35	26	1	32	1	3	3	14	13	.52	7	.296	.343	.399
Durham	AAA TB	27	91	24	6	0	1	33	14	15	11	0	11	4	3	5	9	2	.82	0	.264	.351	.363
4 Min. YEARS		478	1890	574	132	6	22	784	323	203	166	2	160	18	29	23	114	56	.67	35	.304	.361	.415

Dennis Abreu

Bats: Right **Throws:** Right **Pos:** 2B-60; SS-14; PH-7; PR-6; OF-5; DH-3; 3B-1   **Ht:** 6'0" **Wt:** 180 **Born:** 4/22/78 **Age:** 23

Year Team	Lg Org	G	AB	H	2B	3B	HR	TB	R	RBI	TBB	IBB	SO	HBP	SH	SF	SB	CS	SB%	GDP	Avg	OBP	SLG
1996 Cubs	R ChC	56	192	60	5	0	0	65	32	15	21	0	20	2	7	1	35	9	.80	6	.313	.384	.339
1997 Rockford	A ChC	126	483	155	19	3	1	183	71	37	45	2	99	7	5	1	36	26	.58	8	.321	.386	.379
1998 Daytona	A+ ChC	127	535	139	21	5	2	176	87	58	31	0	133	3	8	0	23	14	.62	14	.260	.304	.329
1999 Daytona	A+ ChC	105	374	96	10	2	2	116	44	30	13	0	69	3	2	1	29	9	.76	10	.257	.286	.310
2000 Daytona	A+ ChC	39	118	38	4	0	2	48	18	10	4	1	24	3	2	0	8	5	.62	4	.322	.360	.407
West Tenn	AA ChC	52	166	40	8	1	2	56	24	13	9	0	36	3	3	0	7	5	.58	4	.241	.292	.337
5 Min. YEARS		505	1868	528	67	11	9	644	276	163	123	3	381	21	27	3	138	68	.67	46	.283	.333	.345

Winston Abreu

Pitches: Right **Bats:** Right **Pos:** RP-13; SP-4   **Ht:** 6'2" **Wt:** 155 **Born:** 4/5/77 **Age:** 24

Year Team	Lg Org	G	GS	CG	GF	IP	BFP	H	R	ER	HR	SH	SF	HB	TBB	IBB	SO	WP	Bk	W	L	Pct.	ShO	Sv	ERA
1994 Braves	R Atl	13	11	0	1	57.1	257	57	35	26	2	0	5	4	24	0	53	3	4	0	8	.000	0	0	4.08
1995 Danville	R+ Atl	13	13	1	0	74	277	54	29	19	5	0	4	1	13	0	90	2	0	6	3	.667	0	0	2.31
1996 Macon	A Atl	12	12	0	0	60	247	51	29	20	4	1	0	1	25	1	60	3	1	4	3	.571	0	0	3.00
1998 Eugene	A- Atl	17	10	0	3	45.1	206	39	36	32	6	0	2	5	31	0	52	6	0	0	4	.000	0	0	6.35
1999 Macon	AA Atl	14	14	0	0	69.1	272	41	17	13	3	0	2	4	26	0	95	7	1	7	2	.778	0	0	1.69
Myrtle Bch	A+ Atl	13	12	0	0	68.2	290	53	26	25	7	2	4	0	41	0	76	3	1	3	2	.600	0	0	3.28
2000 Greenville	AA Atl	1	1	0	0	4	17	4	1	1	0	0	0	0	3	0	5	0	0	0	1	.000	0	0	2.25
Braves	R Atl	2	2	0	0	3	14	2	1	1	1	0	0	1	2	0	2	0	0	0	0	—	0	0	3.00
Macon	A Atl	11	1	0	8	28.2	103	11	6	6	2	0	0	1	6	0	48	1	0	2	1	.667	0	3	1.88
Richmond	AAA Atl	3	0	0	0	9	42	7	8	7	2	1	1	1	10	0	5	0	0	0	1	.000	0	0	7.00
6 Min. YEARS		99	76	1	12	419.1	1725	319	188	150	32	4	18	17	181	1	486	25	7	22	25	.468	0	3	3.22

Scott Ackerman

Bats: Right **Throws:** Right **Pos:** C-94; DH-8; PH-1   **Ht:** 6'1" **Wt:** 215 **Born:** 4/23/79 **Age:** 22

Year Team	Lg Org	G	AB	H	2B	3B	HR	TB	R	RBI	TBB	IBB	SO	HBP	SH	SF	SB	CS	SB%	GDP	Avg	OBP	SLG
1997 Expos	R Mon	43	142	34	6	1	2	48	17	18	14	0	26	1	2	0	3	4	.43	1	.239	.312	.338
1998 Expos	R Mon	18	57	15	1	0	1	19	9	7	9	0	12	1	1	0	0	2	.00	0	.263	.373	.333
1999 Cape Fear	A Mon	67	224	60	14	0	6	92	30	31	16	1	58	2	1	3	5	2	.71	4	.268	.318	.411
2000 Cape Fear	A Mon	54	210	59	8	0	8	91	27	41	12	0	35	0	0	1	1	2	.33	11	.281	.318	.433
Jupiter	A+ Mon	48	182	51	5	0	2	62	14	25	15	2	22	1	2	1	1	0	1.00	0	.280	.337	.341
Harrisburg	AA Mon	1	3	0	0	0	0	0	0	0	0	0	0	0	0	0	0	0	—	0	.000	.000	.000
4 Min. YEARS		231	818	219	34	1	19	312	97	122	66	3	153	5	6	5	10	10	.50	24	.268	.324	.381

Willie Adams

Pitches: Right **Bats:** Right **Pos:** RP-22   **Ht:** 6'7" **Wt:** 215 **Born:** 10/8/72 **Age:** 28

Year Team	Lg Org	G	GS	CG	GF	IP	BFP	H	R	ER	HR	SH	SF	HB	TBB	IBB	SO	WP	Bk	W	L	Pct.	ShO	Sv	ERA
1993 Madison	A Oak	5	5	0	0	18.2	84	21	10	7	2	1	1	0	8	0	22	1	1	0	2	.000	0	0	3.38
1994 Modesto	A+ Oak	11	5	0	6	45.1	181	41	17	17	7	2	0	0	10	0	42	2	3	7	1	.875	0	2	3.38
Huntsville	AA Oak	10	10	0	0	60.2	256	58	32	29	3	2	3	5	23	2	33	1	1	4	3	.571	0	0	4.30
1995 Huntsville	AA Oak	13	13	0	0	80.2	330	75	33	27	8	2	1	2	17	0	72	1	0	6	5	.545	0	0	3.01
Edmonton	AAA Oak	11	10	1	1	68	288	73	35	33	7	2	2	6	15	5	40	3	0	2	5	.286	0	0	4.37
1996 Edmonton	AAA Oak	19	19	3	0	112	466	95	49	47	12	1	1	6	39	2	80	4	0	10	4	.714	1	0	3.78
1997 Edmonton	AAA Oak	13	12	0	0	75.1	345	105	57	54	13	2	4	2	19	3	58	3	1	5	4	.556	0	0	6.45
1998 Athletics	R Oak	2	2	0	0	3.2	17	3	2	1	0	0	0	1	1	0	3	0	0	0	0	.000	0	0	2.45
Edmonton	AAA Oak	2	2	0	0	3.2	20	8	5	5	2	0	0	0	1	0	1	0	0	0	0	—	0	0	12.27
1999 Sarasota	A+ Bos	2	2	0	0	13.2	58	14	5	3	1	0	0	1	1	0	6	0	0	1	1	.500	0	0	1.98
Trenton	AA Bos	2	2	0	0	11.2	53	17	6	6	2	0	0	0	2	0	6	0	0	1	1	.500	0	0	4.63
Pawtucket	AAA Bos	11	11	1	0	64.2	290	82	46	37	7	2	3	3	10	0	37	2	0	4	5	.444	1	0	5.15

Year Team	Lg Org	G	GS	CG	GF	IP	BFP	H	R	ER	HR	SH	SF	HB	TBB	IBB	SO	WP	Bk	W	L	Pct.	ShO	Sv	ERA
2000 Pawtucket	AAA Bos	22	0	0	15	26.1	124	38	18	16	4	2	0	1	7	2	21	0	0	0	2	.000	0	4	5.47
1996 Oakland	AL	12	12	1	0	76.1	329	76	39	34	11	3	2	5	23	3	68	2	0	3	4	.429	1	0	4.01
1997 Oakland	AL	13	12	0	0	58.1	282	73	53	53	9	3	5	4	32	2	37	2	0	3	5	.375	0	0	8.18
8 Min. YEARS		123	93	5	22	584.1	2512	630	315	282	63	16	15	27	153	14	421	19	9	40	34	.541	2	6	4.34
2 Maj. YEARS		25	24	1	0	134.2	611	149	92	87	20	6	7	9	55	5	105	4	0	6	9	.400	1	0	5.81

Jon Adkins

Pitches: Right **Bats:** Left **Pos:** SP-10; RP-4 **Ht:** 6'0" **Wt:** 200 **Born:** 8/30/77 **Age:** 23

Year Team	Lg Org	G	GS	CG	GF	IP	BFP	H	R	ER	HR	SH	SF	HB	TBB	IBB	SO	WP	Bk	W	L	Pct.	ShO	Sv	ERA
1999 Modesto	A+ Oak	26	15	0	2	102	460	113	65	54	6	4	6	9	30	1	93	8	0	9	5	.643	0	1	4.76
2000 Athletics	R Oak	4	2	0	1	15	68	15	6	5	1	0	0	1	3	0	17	0	0	1	1	.500	0	0	3.00
Sacramento	AAA Oak	1	1	0	0	4	19	6	4	4	2	0	0	1	1	0	2	0	0	1	0	1.000	0	0	9.00
Modesto	A+ Oak	9	7	1	0	49.2	203	41	17	10	1	1	2	1	17	0	38	2	0	5	2	.714	0	0	1.81
2 Min. YEARS		40	25	1	3	170.2	750	175	92	73	10	5	8	11	51	1	150	10	0	15	9	.625	0	1	3.85

Tim Adkins

Pitches: Left **Bats:** Left **Pos:** SP-19; RP-9 **Ht:** 6'0" **Wt:** 195 **Born:** 5/12/74 **Age:** 27

Year Team	Lg Org	G	GS	CG	GF	IP	BFP	H	R	ER	HR	SH	SF	HB	TBB	IBB	SO	WP	Bk	W	L	Pct.	ShO	Sv	ERA
1992 Blue Jays	R Tor	11	10	0	1	57.2	230	50	15	11	2	1	1	1	11	0	49	3	1	6	2	.750	0	0	1.72
1993 St.Cathrnes	A- Tor	16	15	1	0	96.2	404	80	43	38	5	2	3	2	45	0	91	5	1	5	6	.455	1	0	3.54
1994 Hagerstown	A Tor	35	0	0	7	70.2	299	64	37	29	2	6	4	2	33	1	75	4	0	3	3	.500	0	2	3.69
1995 Dunedin	A+ Tor	45	0	0	37	48	215	36	29	20	2	3	2	1	33	0	49	7	0	7	4	.636	0	17	3.75
1996 Dunedin	A+ Tor	39	11	0	14	103.1	475	88	68	45	4	3	1	8	73	1	91	2	2	7	9	.438	0	2	3.92
1997 Dunedin	A+ Tor	39	0	0	10	49.2	252	52	43	26	1	2	3	3	58	0	55	9	2	1	1	.500	0	3	4.71
1998 Dunedin	A+ Tor	19	0	0	10	24.1	114	32	18	16	2	0	1	3	10	0	18	3	0	0	1	.000	0	1	5.92
1999 Bridgeport	IND —	26	21	1	1	140.2	614	152	74	62	17	7	2	6	49	0	100	3	0	8	6	.571	1	0	3.97
2000 Bridgeport	IND —	19	19	3	0	133.2	543	127	55	51	10	5	1	4	25	0	74	3	2	10	5	.667	0	0	3.43
Norwich	AA NYY	9	0	0	1	7	33	9	3	3	0	1	0	0	3	0	8	0	0	1	0	1.000	0	0	3.86
9 Min. YEARS		258	76	5	81	731.2	3179	690	385	301	45	30	18	30	340	2	610	39	8	48	37	.565	2	25	3.70

Brandon Agamennone

Pitches: Right **Bats:** Right **Pos:** SP-15; RP-15 **Ht:** 6'2" **Wt:** 190 **Born:** 11/6/75 **Age:** 25

Year Team	Lg Org	G	GS	CG	GF	IP	BFP	H	R	ER	HR	SH	SF	HB	TBB	IBB	SO	WP	Bk	W	L	Pct.	ShO	Sv	ERA
1998 Vermont	A- Mon	9	3	0	0	31.2	124	38	6	5	1	0	1	1	11	0	30	0	0	3	1	.750	0	0	1.42
Cape Fear	A Mon	6	6	1	0	35.1	134	24	15	12	2	0	1	2	6	0	29	0	0	2	0	1.000	1	0	3.06
1999 Jupiter	A+ Mon	16	9	0	0	65.2	268	51	31	23	4	2	4	3	15	0	41	1	2	4	2	.667	0	0	3.15
Harrisburg	AA Mon	22	4	0	11	52.1	210	44	19	18	5	3	0	2	14	0	41	2	0	5	2	.714	0	5	3.10
2000 Harrisburg	AA Mon	30	15	0	8	96	411	102	58	44	10	4	8	3	26	2	55	6	0	8	7	.533	0	4	4.13
3 Min. YEARS		83	37	1	19	281	1147	240	129	102	22	9	14	11	72	2	196	9	2	22	12	.647	1	9	3.27

Stevenson Agosto

Pitches: Left **Bats:** Left **Pos:** RP-39; SP-3 **Ht:** 5'11" **Wt:** 170 **Born:** 9/2/75 **Age:** 25

Year Team	Lg Org	G	GS	CG	GF	IP	BFP	H	R	ER	HR	SH	SF	HB	TBB	IBB	SO	WP	Bk	W	L	Pct.	ShO	Sv	ERA
1994 Angels	R Ana	13	1	0	7	26.1	125	27	18	13	1	3	1	3	14	0	26	6	1	0	2	.000	0	1	4.44
1995 Angels	R Ana	1	1	0	0	5	22	3	5	3	0	2	1	1	2	0	2	3	0	0	1	.000	0	0	5.40
Boise	A- Ana	13	11	0	1	52.1	224	39	20	17	1	0	3	5	30	2	34	12	0	6	2	.750	0	0	2.92
1996 Cedar Rapds	A Ana	28	28	1	0	156.2	680	143	91	77	12	7	6	7	86	2	121	8	7	8	10	.444	0	0	4.42
1997 Lk Elsinore	A+ Ana	24	21	1	0	137	603	155	91	81	23	2	2	3	50	0	91	11	3	5	8	.385	1	0	5.32
Rancho Cuca	A+ SD	3	3	1	0	22	89	18	7	7	2	3	0	0	6	0	18	1	0	2	0	1.000	1	0	2.86
1998 Rancho Cuca	A+ SD	23	23	0	0	108	505	132	83	73	14	4	6	3	68	0	91	15	4	5	8	.385	0	0	6.08
1999 Mobile	AA SD	40	1	0	5	81	371	81	61	53	13	2	7	1	59	1	59	10	1	3	3	.500	0	0	5.89
2000 St. Pete	A+ TB	13	0	0	1	16.2	90	22	17	10	0	0	2	1	16	0	18	2	0	0	1	.000	0	0	5.40
Orlando	AA TB	28	3	0	5	51	210	37	18	14	4	1	1	2	24	1	38	2	0	2	2	.500	0	1	2.47
Durham	AAA TB	1	0	0	0	4	12	0	0	0	0	0	0	0	1	0	3	0	0	0	0	—	0	0	0.00
7 Min. YEARS		187	92	3	19	660	2931	657	411	348	70	24	29	26	356	6	501	70	16	31	37	.456	2	2	4.75

Pat Ahearne

Pitches: Right **Bats:** Right **Pos:** SP-26; RP-3 **Ht:** 6'3" **Wt:** 195 **Born:** 12/10/69 **Age:** 31

Year Team	Lg Org	G	GS	CG	GF	IP	BFP	H	R	ER	HR	SH	SF	HB	TBB	IBB	SO	WP	Bk	W	L	Pct.	ShO	Sv	ERA
1992 Lakeland	A+ Det	1	1	0	0	4.2	17	4	2	1	0	0	0	0	0	0	4	0	0	0	0	—	0	0	1.93
1993 Lakeland	A+ Det	25	24	2	0	147.1	650	160	87	73	8	7	4	6	48	0	51	3	1	6	15	.286	0	0	4.46
1994 Trenton	AA Det	30	13	2	3	108.2	467	126	55	48	8	1	6	5	25	1	57	5	0	7	5	.583	0	0	3.98
1995 Toledo	AAA Det	25	23	1	0	139.2	599	165	83	73	11	2	5	5	37	3	54	2	0	7	9	.438	1	0	4.70
1996 Norfolk	AAA NYM	5	4	0	0	25.1	108	26	14	13	1	3	0	1	9	1	14	0	1	1	2	.333	0	0	4.62
Duluth-Sup	IND —	1	1	0	0	4.1	24	10	6	6	3	0	0	0	1	0	1	1	0	0	0	—	0	0	12.46
San Antonio	AA LA	8	8	0	0	45.1	208	59	34	29	3	2	2	1	18	0	21	4	0	2	4	.333	0	0	5.76
Vero Beach	A+ LA	6	6	1	0	47	179	38	16	11	2	2	1	1	5	0	26	2	0	3	1	.600	1	0	2.11
1997 Albuquerque	AAA LA	20	8	0	3	60.2	280	82	43	33	9	4	2	1	20	1	44	2	0	2	4	.333	0	0	4.90
San Antonio	AA LA	14	14	3	0	84	364	109	48	42	1	6	2	2	13	0	45	4	0	4	5	.444	0	0	4.50
1998 Bridgeport	IND —	5	5	0	0	28	123	29	14	8	3	1	1	1	5	0	16	1	0	2	2	.500	0	0	2.57
1999 Bridgeport	IND —	7	7	1	0	46.1	188	35	17	13	4	1	1	0	14	0	43	4	0	6	0	1.000	1	0	2.53
New Haven	AA Sea	17	17	4	0	124	493	114	41	36	6	3	1	3	27	0	80	2	0	8	3	.727	2	0	2.61
2000 Tacoma	AAA Sea	29	26	1	0	168	725	190	92	72	17	5	2	1	53	5	92	5	1	13	8	.619	0	0	3.86

Year Team	Lg Org	HOW MUCH HE PITCHED						WHAT HE GAVE UP									THE RESULTS					
		G	GS	CG	GF	IP	BFP	H	R	ER	HR	SH	SF	HB	TBB	IBB	SO	WP	Bk	W	L	Pct.	ShO	Sv	ERA
1995 Detroit	AL	4	3	0	0	10	55	20	13	13	2	0	0		5	1	4	1	0	0	2	.000	0		11.70
9 Min. YEARS		193	157	15	6	1033.1	4425	1147	550	458	69	37	27	27	275	11	548	35	3	61	59	.508	5	0	3.99

Paul Ah Yat

Pitches: Left **Bats:** Right **Pos:** SP-18; RP-1 **Ht:** 6'1" **Wt:** 192 **Born:** 10/13/74 **Age:** 26

Year Team	Lg Org	HOW MUCH HE PITCHED						WHAT HE GAVE UP									THE RESULTS					
		G	GS	CG	GF	IP	BFP	H	R	ER	HR	SH	SF	HB	TBB	IBB	SO	WP	Bk	W	L	Pct.	ShO	Sv	ERA
1996 Erie	A- Pit	26	0	0	4	27.2	114	24	15	10	1	1	0	0	6	0	34	0	0	1	1	.500	0	1	3.25
1997 Augusta	A Pit	29	9	0	5	90	366	82	34	29	7	3	0	3	16	1	119	4	0	5	1	.833	0	0	2.90
Lynchburg	A+ Pit	6	6	3	0	48	182	37	8	7	2	2	0	1	4	0	38	1	0	5	1	.833	1	0	1.31
1998 Lynchburg	A+ Pit	14	14	4	0	102.1	410	95	40	31	9	1	3	4	13	2	77	2	0	6	3	.667	3	0	2.73
Carolina	AA Pit	13	13	1	0	84.1	362	84	43	34	10	1	3	2	21	0	60	6	0	5	5	.500	0	0	3.63
1999 Altoona	AA Pit	16	15	0	0	95.1	398	86	41	32	6	4	4	3	30	0	90	4	1	8	4	.667	0	0	3.02
Nashville	AAA Pit	13	11	1	1	64.2	291	75	45	41	10	3	2	4	24	1	41	1	1	4	3	.571	0	0	5.71
2000 Nashville	AAA Pit	19	18	0	1	110.2	468	110	55	50	14	1	5	3	36	0	60	6	0	3	9	.250	0	0	4.07
5 Min. YEARS		136	86	9	11	623	2591	593	281	234	59	16	17	20	150	4	519	24	2	37	27	.578	4	1	3.38

Kurt Ainsworth

Pitches: Right **Bats:** Right **Pos:** SP-28 **Ht:** 6'3" **Wt:** 185 **Born:** 9/9/78 **Age:** 22

Year Team	Lg Org	HOW MUCH HE PITCHED						WHAT HE GAVE UP									THE RESULTS					
		G	GS	CG	GF	IP	BFP	H	R	ER	HR	SH	SF	HB	TBB	IBB	SO	WP	Bk	W	L	Pct.	ShO	Sv	ERA
1999 Salem-Keizr	A- SF	10	10	1	0	44.2	187	34	18	8	1	3	2	3	18	0	64	3	0	3	3	.500	0	0	1.61
2000 Shreveport	AA SF	28	28	0	0	158	667	138	67	58	12	4	5	3	63	3	130	7	1	10	9	.526	0	0	3.30
2 Min. YEARS		38	38	1	0	202.2	854	172	85	66	13	7	7	6	81	3	194	10	1	13	12	.520	0	0	2.93

Kurt Airoso

Bats: Right **Throws:** Right **Pos:** OF-87; DH-8; PH-7; PR-2 **Ht:** 6'2" **Wt:** 190 **Born:** 2/12/75 **Age:** 26

Year Team	Lg Org	BATTING														BASERUNNING				PERCENTAGES		
		G	AB	H	2B	3B	HR	TB	R	RBI	TBB	IBB	SO	HBP	SH	SF	SB	CS	SB%	GDP	Avg	OBP	SLG
1996 Jamestown	A- Det	27	78	22	5	2	3	37	12	12	10	0	31	2	0	2	3	1	.75	1	.282	.370	.474
1997 Lakeland	A+ Det	22	62	12	1	2	0	17	12	7	11	0	23	1	1	0	0	0	—	2	.194	.324	.274
Tigers	R Det	4	10	0	0	0	0	0	1	0	3	0	3	1	0	0	0	0	—	0	.000	.286	.000
W Michigan	A Det	14	37	11	5	0	0	16	6	2	6	0	15	0	0	1	0	0	—	0	.297	.386	.432
1998 Lakeland	A+ Det	109	386	112	24	0	15	181	69	61	67	0	106	5	1	1	7	3	.70	5	.290	.401	.469
1999 Jacksnville	AA Det	134	536	146	28	6	10	216	95	72	89	1	113	5	0	6	10	3	.77	8	.272	.377	.403
2000 Jacksnville	AA Det	98	326	78	14	1	4	106	43	41	49	0	69	5	2	3	6	1	.86	7	.239	.345	.325
5 Min. YEARS		408	1435	381	77	11	31	573	238	195	235	1	360	19	4	13	26	8	.76	25	.266	.373	.399

Chad Akers

Bats: Right **Throws:** Right **Pos:** 3B-71; 2B-24; DH-8; OF-5; PH-2; PR-2; P-1 **Ht:** 5'8" **Wt:** 170 **Born:** 5/30/72 **Age:** 29

Year Team	Lg Org	BATTING														BASERUNNING				PERCENTAGES		
		G	AB	H	2B	3B	HR	TB	R	RBI	TBB	IBB	SO	HBP	SH	SF	SB	CS	SB%	GDP	Avg	OBP	SLG
1993 Billings	R+ Cin	65	247	66	14	3	2	92	54	35	24	0	26	8	1	3	14	7	.67	4	.267	.348	.372
1994 Chston-WV	A Cin	133	490	135	23	4	4	172	65	35	52	1	49	2	2	3	41	16	.72	14	.276	.346	.351
1995 Winston-Sal	A+ Cin	103	361	94	14	1	2	116	41	29	27	1	49	1	7	3	25	8	.76	7	.260	.311	.321
1996 Fargo-Mh	IND —	83	330	90	11	0	5	116	84	41	57	2	32	10	2	4	13	12	.52	8	.273	.392	.352
1997 Fargo-Mh	IND —	84	368	117	14	6	4	155	75	43	25	0	41	4	2	5	27	4	.87	6	.318	.363	.421
1998 Fargo-Mh	IND —	83	358	111	30	5	8	175	79	44	29	0	39	2	3	1	12	5	.71	9	.310	.364	.489
1999 Atlantic Ct	IND —	59	243	66	18	3	5	105	42	32	29	1	30	4	3	3	16	4	.80	2	.272	.338	.432
New Haven	AA Sea	1	0	0	0	0	0	0	1	0	0	0	0	0	0	0	0	0	—	0	—	—	—
Tacoma	AAA Sea	48	192	60	9	3	1	78	31	14	18	1	25	1	1	2	7	3	.70	3	.313	.371	.406
2000 Tacoma	AAA Sea	103	389	106	31	5	6	165	56	34	24	0	41	6	4	3	13	5	.72	7	.272	.322	.424
8 Min. YEARS		762	2978	845	164	27	37	1174	528	307	278	6	332	38	22	27	168	64	.72	59	.284	.350	.394

Juan Alcala

Bats: Right **Throws:** Right **Pos:** C-16; DH-9; OF-2; PH-2 **Ht:** 6'2" **Wt:** 160 **Born:** 4/15/78 **Age:** 23

Year Team	Lg Org	BATTING														BASERUNNING				PERCENTAGES		
		G	AB	H	2B	3B	HR	TB	R	RBI	TBB	IBB	SO	HBP	SH	SF	SB	CS	SB%	GDP	Avg	OBP	SLG
1997 Mariners	R Sea	29	92	21	5	0	1	29	15	7	7	0	26	0	0	2	0	0	—	2	.228	.283	.315
Everett	A- Sea	9	33	5	1	0	0	6	3	1	1	0	15	0	0	0	1	0	1.00	1	.152	.176	.182
1998 Everett	A- Sea	29	104	17	2	1	1	24	6	7	5	0	25	0	0	0	1	1	.50	2	.163	.202	.231
1999 Tacoma	AAA Sea	1	1	0	0	0	0	0	0	0	0	0	0	0	0	0	0	0	—	0	.000	.000	.000
Everett	A- Sea	17	58	12	4	0	1	19	4	8	0	0	17	0	1	0	1	0	1.00	0	.207	.207	.328
Lancaster	A+ Sea	8	14	1	1	0	0	2	1	0	2	1	7	0	0	0	0	0	—	0	.071	.133	.143
2000 Wisconsin	A Sea	23	69	19	6	0	1	28	9	14	4	0	16	1	0	2	1	0	1.00	2	.275	.316	.406
New Haven	AA Sea	2	9	2	0	0	0	2	1	0	0	0	2	0	0	0	0	0	1.00	0	.222	.222	.222
Tacoma	AAA Sea	3	10	3	1	0	0	4	1	1	0	0	2	0	1	0	0	0	—	0	.300	.300	.400
4 Min. YEARS		121	390	80	20	1	4	114	39	40	18	0	110	1	4	2	5	1	.83	7	.205	.241	.292

Chad Alexander

Bats: Right **Throws:** Right **Pos:** OF-105; DH-14; PH-2; PR-1; P-1 **Ht:** 6'1" **Wt:** 190 **Born:** 5/22/74 **Age:** 27

Year Team	Lg Org	BATTING														BASERUNNING				PERCENTAGES		
		G	AB	H	2B	3B	HR	TB	R	RBI	TBB	IBB	SO	HBP	SH	SF	SB	CS	SB%	GDP	Avg	OBP	SLG
1995 Auburn	A- Hou	71	278	81	15	5	5	121	45	43	25	1	37	7	1	5	7	1	.88	11	.291	.359	.435
Quad City	A Hou	7	7	2	0	0	0	2	2	1	0	0	0	0	0	0	0	0	—	0	.286	.286	.286
1996 Quad City	A Hou	118	435	115	25	4	13	187	86	69	57	4	108	2	0	3	16	11	.59	11	.264	.350	.430

Year Team	Lg Org	G	AB	H	2B	3B	HR	TB	R	RBI	TBB	IBB	SO	HBP	SH	SF	SB	CS	SB%	GDP	Avg	OBP	SLG
1997 Kissimmee	A+ Hou	129	469	127	31	6	4	182	67	46	56	1	91	4	2	3	11	8	.58	15	.271	.352	.388
1998 Jackson	AA Hou	128	416	119	33	2	13	195	77	45	71	0	80	5	3	3	6	7	.46	8	.286	.394	.469
New Orleans	AAA Hou	2	5	2	0	0	0	2	1	2	0	0	2	0	0	0	0	0	—	0	.400	.400	.400
1999 New Orleans	AAA Hou	28	96	23	5	0	2	34	7	8	6	0	22	0	0	2	0	1	.00	3	.240	.279	.354
Jackson	AA Hou	84	317	98	27	3	9	158	42	44	34	1	58	3	0	3	9	5	.64	4	.309	.378	.498
2000 Tacoma	AAA Sea	120	440	119	27	2	12	186	58	55	39	1	70	2	1	6	6	3	.67	14	.270	.329	.423
6 Min. YEARS		682	2463	686	163	22	58	1067	367	313	288	8	468	23	7	25	55	36	.60	66	.279	.356	.433

Jose Alguacil

Bats: Left **Throws:** Right **Pos:** 2B-23; SS-14; 3B-8; PR-3; DH-2; PH-2; OF-1   **Ht:** 6'2" **Wt:** 200 **Born:** 8/9/72 **Age:** 28

Year Team	Lg Org	G	AB	H	2B	3B	HR	TB	R	RBI	TBB	IBB	SO	HBP	SH	SF	SB	CS	SB%	GDP	Avg	OBP	SLG
1993 Giants	R SF	42	145	35	6	1	1	46	28	13	6	0	23	1	3	1	8	1	.89	3	.241	.275	.317
1994 Clinton	A SF	74	245	71	13	0	1	87	40	25	13	0	42	5	11	1	6	6	.50	2	.290	.337	.355
Everett	A- SF	45	169	36	7	0	0	43	24	7	10	1	41	8	3	0	18	4	.82	4	.213	.289	.254
1995 Burlington	A SF	38	136	30	2	0	0	32	15	5	7	0	27	2	3	0	13	1	.93	2	.221	.269	.235
Shreveport	AA SF	1	4	1	0	0	0	1	1	1	0	0	1	0	0	0	1	0	1.00	0	.250	.250	.250
San Jose	A+ SF	58	225	53	10	3	0	69	30	17	14	0	44	4	8	2	11	6	.65	2	.236	.290	.307
1996 Shreveport	AA SF	13	24	5	0	0	0	5	2	0	3	0	9	1	0	0	0	0	—	0	.208	.321	.208
San Jose	A+ SF	79	272	72	11	3	1	92	53	31	24	1	53	7	10	2	18	7	.72	8	.265	.338	.338
1997 San Jose	A+ SF	122	392	81	15	2	7	121	53	42	32	2	98	10	10	1	13	13	.50	4	.207	.283	.309
1998 Bakersfield	A+ SF	61	228	57	11	2	2	78	25	23	11	0	45	8	7	0	3	0	1.00	6	.250	.308	.342
Shreveport	AA SF	43	97	20	3	1	1	28	13	6	9	1	15	1	5	0	3	2	.60	2	.206	.280	.289
1999 Canton	IND —	8	30	6	1	0	0	7	6	0	4	0	8	0	1	0	2	0	1.00	0	.200	.294	.233
Sonoma Cty	IND —	67	253	72	15	2	1	94	37	33	23	0	30	8	5	1	12	4	.75	7	.285	.361	.372
2000 Charlotte	AAA CWS	3	9	0	0	0	0	0	0	0	0	0	1	0	0	0	0	0	—	0	.000	.000	.000
Winston-Sal	A+ CWS	40	138	37	9	2	0	50	18	18	7	0	19	2	5	1	10	3	.77	3	.268	.311	.362
Birmingham	AA CWS	9	19	1	0	0	0	1	1	0	3	0	3	0	0	0	2	0	1.00	1	.053	.182	.053
8 Min. YEARS		703	2386	577	103	16	14	754	346	221	166	5	459	57	71	9	120	47	.72	44	.242	.306	.316

Jeff Allen

Bats: Right **Throws:** Right **Pos:** OF-122; PH-6; DH-1; PR-1   **Ht:** 6'1" **Wt:** 190 **Born:** 6/8/76 **Age:** 25

Year Team	Lg Org	G	AB	H	2B	3B	HR	TB	R	RBI	TBB	IBB	SO	HBP	SH	SF	SB	CS	SB%	GDP	Avg	OBP	SLG
1998 Salem-Keizr	A- SF	60	215	63	10	5	11	116	47	47	33	3	64	5	1	2	10	5	.67	2	.293	.396	.540
1999 Bakersfield	A+ SF	130	480	127	32	3	10	195	80	65	47	0	130	10	0	4	24	5	.83	12	.265	.340	.406
2000 Shreveport	AA SF	128	447	106	23	2	7	154	40	52	26	0	97	4	3	5	8	10	.44	9	.237	.282	.345
3 Min. YEARS		318	1142	296	65	10	28	465	167	164	106	3	291	19	4	11	42	20	.68	23	.259	.329	.407

Luke Allen

Bats: Left **Throws:** Right **Pos:** 3B-86; 1B-2; DH-2; PH-1   **Ht:** 6'2" **Wt:** 208 **Born:** 8/4/78 **Age:** 22

Year Team	Lg Org	G	AB	H	2B	3B	HR	TB	R	RBI	TBB	IBB	SO	HBP	SH	SF	SB	CS	SB%	GDP	Avg	OBP	SLG
1997 Great Falls	R+ LA	67	258	89	12	6	7	134	50	40	19	1	53	0	1	0	12	11	.52	3	.345	.390	.519
1998 San Berndno	A+ LA	105	399	119	25	6	4	168	51	46	30	0	93	3	7	4	18	11	.62	4	.298	.349	.421
San Antonio	AA LA	23	78	26	3	1	3	40	9	10	6	1	16	0	1	0	1	2	.33	0	.333	.381	.513
1999 San Antonio	AA LA	137	533	150	16	12	14	232	90	82	44	0	102	1	2	2	14	8	.64	8	.281	.336	.435
2000 San Antonio	AA LA	90	339	90	15	5	7	136	55	60	40	3	71	1	0	5	14	5	.74	10	.265	.340	.401
4 Min. YEARS		422	1607	474	71	30	35	710	255	238	139	5	335	5	11	11	59	37	.61	25	.295	.351	.442

Rich Almanzar

Bats: Right **Throws:** Right **Pos:** 2B-54; PR-5; DH-1; PH-1   **Ht:** 5'10" **Wt:** 165 **Born:** 4/3/76 **Age:** 25

Year Team	Lg Org	G	AB	H	2B	3B	HR	TB	R	RBI	TBB	IBB	SO	HBP	SH	SF	SB	CS	SB%	GDP	Avg	OBP	SLG
1995 Lakeland	A+ Det	42	140	43	9	0	1	55	29	14	18	0	20	4	5	0	11	9	.55	5	.307	.401	.393
Fayettevlle	A Det	80	308	76	12	1	0	90	47	16	29	0	32	7	9	0	39	15	.72	5	.247	.326	.292
1996 Lakeland	A+ Det	124	471	144	22	2	1	173	81	36	49	0	49	8	12	3	53	19	.74	5	.306	.379	.367
1997 Jacksnville	AA Det	103	387	94	20	2	5	133	55	35	37	0	43	3	11	0	20	6	.77	11	.243	.314	.344
1998 Toledo	AAA Det	104	306	64	16	1	1	85	36	16	28	0	30	3	4	2	11	7	.61	6	.209	.280	.278
1999 Iowa	AAA ChC	33	93	20	2	3	1	31	13	4	6	0	7	0	2	0	6	1	.86	4	.215	.263	.333
West Tenn	AA ChC	42	151	46	7	0	2	59	27	16	18	0	19	1	2	0	13	7	.65	0	.305	.382	.391
2000 Norwich	AA NYY	58	183	40	8	0	0	48	18	9	26	1	14	4	5	0	9	6	.60	6	.219	.329	.262
6 Min. YEARS		586	2039	527	96	9	11	674	306	146	211	1	214	30	50	5	162	70	.70	44	.258	.336	.331

Edwin Almonte

Pitches: Right **Bats:** Right **Pos:** RP-27; SP-13   **Ht:** 6'3" **Wt:** 200 **Born:** 12/17/76 **Age:** 24

Year Team	Lg Org	G	GS	CG	GF	IP	BFP	H	R	ER	HR	SH	SF	HB	TBB	IBB	SO	WP	Bk	W	L	Pct.	ShO	Sv	ERA
1998 White Sox	R CWS	5	0	0	0	9.2	37	6	5	1	0	0	1	0	1	0	8	0	0	0	0		0	0	0.93
Bristol	R+ CWS	8	3	0	0	26.2	113	29	14	10	3	0	1	1	4	0	26	2	0	3	0	1.000	0	0	3.38
1999 Burlington	A CWS	37	5	2	16	115.2	480	107	48	39	5	2	1	2	28	4	85	6	1	9	12	.429	0	5	3.03
2000 Winston-Sal	A+ CWS	33	7	0	10	77	320	66	32	27	2	3	1		20	0	73	4	0	3	1	.750	0	2	3.16
Birmingham	AA CWS	7	6	0	0	39.2	159	45	22	20	5	0	1	1	9	0	21	2	0	1	3	.250	0	0	4.54
3 Min. YEARS		90	21	2	28	268.2	1109	253	121	97	15	5	4	10	62	4	213	14	2	16	16	.500	0	7	3.25

Erick Almonte

Bats: Right Throws: Right Pos: SS-129; PR-3; PH-1   Ht: 6'2" Wt: 180 Born: 2/1/78 Age: 23

Year Team	Lg Org	G	AB	H	2B	3B	HR	TB	R	RBI	TBB	IBB	SO	HBP	SH	SF	SB	CS	SB%	GDP	Avg	OBP	SLG
1997 Yankees	R NYY	52	180	51	4	4	3	72	32	31	21	1	27	0	1	2	8	2	.80	5	.283	.355	.400
1998 Greensboro	A NYY	120	450	94	13	0	6	125	53	33	29	0	121	3	7	2	6	2	.75	17	.209	.260	.278
1999 Yankees	R NYY	9	30	9	2	0	2	17	5	9	3	0	10	0	0	2	1	0	1.00	1	.300	.343	.567
Tampa	A+ NYY	61	230	59	8	2	5	86	36	25	18	0	49	2	5	2	3	1	.75	6	.257	.313	.374
2000 Norwich	AA NYY	131	454	123	18	4	15	194	56	77	35	0	129	3	12	2	12	2	.86	3	.271	.326	.427
4 Min. YEARS		373	1344	336	45	10	31	494	182	175	106	1	336	8	25	10	30	7	.81	32	.250	.307	.368

Hector Almonte

Pitches: Right Bats: Right Pos: RP-28; SP-3   Ht: 6'2" Wt: 190 Born: 10/17/75 Age: 25

Year Team	Lg Org	G	GS	CG	GF	IP	BFP	H	R	ER	HR	SH	SF	HB	TBB	IBB	SO	WP	Bk	W	L	Pct.	ShO	Sv	ERA
1997 Marlins	R Fla	8	0	0	7	23.2	89	12	3	2	0	0	1	2	6	0	25	1	0	2	0	1.000	0	3	0.76
Kane County	A Fla	8	1	0	3	14	59	11	6	6	1	1	2	1	6	0	10	2	0	1	0	1.000	0	1	3.86
1998 Kane County	A Fla	43	0	0	41	43.1	200	51	22	19	5	1	1	1	19	0	51	3	2	1	5	.167	0	21	3.95
1999 Portland	AA Fla	47	0	0	41	44.1	202	42	14	14	1	8	1	2	26	3	42	4	0	1	4	.200	0	23	2.84
2000 Calgary	AAA Fla	18	0	0	13	19.1	98	36	24	24	7	1	0	0	9	0	16	2	1	0	4	.000	0	3	11.17
Marlins	R Fla	1	1	0	0	2	8	3	1	1	0	0	0	0	1	0	2	0	0	0	0	—	0	0	4.50
Brevard Cty	A+ Fla	8	2	0	3	15.1	61	11	6	4	2	1	0	2	5	0	16	1	0	1	1	.500	0	0	2.35
Portland	AA Fla	4	0	0	4	5	25	5	2	2	1	0	0	0	4	0	6	0	0	0	1	.000	0	3	3.60
1999 Florida	NL	15	0	0	6	15	67	20	7	7	1	1	1	0	6	2	8	2	0	0	2	.000	0	0	4.20
4 Min. YEARS		137	4	0	112	167	742	171	78	72	17	12	5	8	76	3	168	13	3	5	16	.238	0	54	3.88

Wady Almonte

Bats: Right Throws: Right Pos: OF-71; PR-1; P-1   Ht: 6'0" Wt: 200 Born: 4/20/75 Age: 26

Year Team	Lg Org	G	AB	H	2B	3B	HR	TB	R	RBI	TBB	IBB	SO	HBP	SH	SF	SB	CS	SB%	GDP	Avg	OBP	SLG
1994 Orioles	R Bal	42	120	24	2	0	2	32	11	9	8	0	22	1	1	0	1	2	.33	0	.200	.256	.267
1995 Bluefield	R+ Bal	51	189	58	12	1	6	90	37	30	9	2	49	1	0	2	6	5	.55	4	.307	.338	.476
1996 Orioles	R Bal	1	3	1	0	0	0	1	2	1	1	0	0	0	0	0	1	0	1.00	0	.333	.500	.333
Frederick	A+ Bal	85	287	82	12	2	12	134	45	44	21	2	59	6	4	1	1	5	.17	12	.286	.346	.467
1997 Bowie	AA Bal	69	222	46	7	2	6	75	25	25	27	0	64	5	0	1	2	4	.33	6	.207	.306	.338
Frederick	A+ Bal	57	202	52	13	2	10	99	34	36	16	4	59	4	1	3	4	1	.80	8	.257	.320	.490
1998 Bowie	AA Bal	7	21	1	0	0	1	4	2	2	4	0	9	1	0	0	0	0	—	2	.048	.231	.190
1999 Bowie	AA Bal	124	482	141	27	4	17	227	68	83	31	1	72	7	0	5	10	10	.50	12	.293	.341	.471
2000 Rochester	AAA Bal	73	229	60	18	5	1	91	25	33	11	0	34	1	3	1	3	5	.38	7	.262	.298	.397
7 Min. YEARS		509	1755	465	91	16	55	753	249	263	128	9	368	26	9	13	28	32	.47	51	.265	.322	.429

Garvin Alston

Pitches: Right Bats: Right Pos: RP-28   Ht: 6'1" Wt: 185 Born: 12/8/71 Age: 29

Year Team	Lg Org	G	GS	CG	GF	IP	BFP	H	R	ER	HR	SH	SF	HB	TBB	IBB	SO	WP	Bk	W	L	Pct.	ShO	Sv	ERA
1992 Bend	A- Col	14	12	0	0	73	320	71	40	32	1	5	5	9	29	0	73	7	8	5	4	.556	0	0	3.95
1993 Central Val	A+ Col	25	24	1	0	117	538	124	81	71	11	6	6	6	70	0	90	10	2	5	9	.357	0	0	5.46
1994 Central Val	A+ Col	37	13	0	20	87	382	91	51	35	9	5	0	6	42	1	83	5	2	5	9	.357	0	8	3.62
New Haven	AA Col	4	0	0	1	4.1	22	5	6	6	1	0	0	0	3	0	8	0	0	0	0	—	0	1	12.46
1995 New Haven	AA Col	47	0	0	20	66.2	271	47	24	21	1	4	2	3	26	3	73	4	0	4	4	.500	0	6	2.84
1996 Colo Sprngs	AAA Col	35	0	0	26	34.1	171	47	23	22	3	1	0	1	27	0	36	2	0	1	4	.200	0	14	5.77
1998 Colo Sprngs	AAA Col	44	0	0	17	67	313	85	53	48	12	1	2	1	32	3	69	2	2	2	4	.333	0	5	6.45
1999 Albuquerque	AAA LA	5	0	0	2	10.2	46	12	6	6	1	1	0	1	4	0	5	1	0	1	2	.333	0	0	5.06
2000 Albuquerque	AAA LA	10	0	0	2	25	107	23	12	11	2	0	3	2	12	0	19	3	0	2	0	1.000	0	0	3.96
Wichita	AA KC	18	0	0	10	30.2	137	30	23	22	5	1	0	5	9	3	24	3	0	1	1	.500	0	0	6.46
1996 Colorado	NL	6	0	0	4	6	30	9	6	6	1	0	2	1	3	0	5	1	0	1	0	1.000	0	0	9.00
8 Min. YEARS		239	49	1	98	515.2	2307	535	319	274	46	24	18	36	254	10	480	37	14	28	38	.424	0	34	4.78

Carlos Alvarado

Pitches: Right Bats: Right Pos: RP-23; SP-8   Ht: 6'3" Wt: 213 Born: 1/24/78 Age: 23

Year Team	Lg Org	G	GS	CG	GF	IP	BFP	H	R	ER	HR	SH	SF	HB	TBB	IBB	SO	WP	Bk	W	L	Pct.	ShO	Sv	ERA
1995 Pirates	R Pit	2	0	0	3	15		1	2	2	0	0	1	0	5	0	2	3	0	0	0	—	0	0	6.00
1996 Pirates	R Pit	11	1	0	4	27.1	125	32	20	15	1	1	1	2	10	0	31	2	2	1	1	.500	0	0	4.94
1997 Augusta	A Pit	29	20	0	2	113	499	114	58	41	4	3	8	11	45	0	109	9	4	6	5	.545	0	0	3.27
1998 Augusta	A Pit	14	10	0	0	50	209	48	20	20	2	2	2	1	24	0	50	6	0	4	1	.800	0	0	3.60
Lynchburg	A+ Pit	13	10	0	0	59.1	274	69	48	37	10	4	2	3	24	0	52	6	0	3	5	.375	0	0	5.61
1999 Lynchburg	A+ Pit	20	18	0	0	90.2	400	89	52	46	4	0	1	2	46	0	75	8	4	4	6	.400	0	0	4.57
2000 Lynchburg	A+ Pit	15	7	0	2	49.1	216	50	30	23	2	2	2	1	25	0	37	5	0	0	5	.000	0	0	4.20
Altoona	AA Pit	16	1	0	4	30.2	140	31	16	14	2	2	2	1	18	1	27	2	0	3	0	1.000	0	1	4.11
6 Min. YEARS		120	67	0	13	423.1	1878	434	246	198	25	14	19	21	197	1	383	41	10	21	23	.477	0	1	4.21

Damien Alvarado

Bats: Left Throws: Right Pos: C-16; DH-11; PH-3; 3B-2   Ht: 6'0" Wt: 190 Born: 3/14/78 Age: 23

Year Team	Lg Org	G	AB	H	2B	3B	HR	TB	R	RBI	TBB	IBB	SO	HBP	SH	SF	SB	CS	SB%	GDP	Avg	OBP	SLG
2000 Tacoma	AAA Sea	1	0	0	0	0	0	0	0	0	1	0	0	0	0	0	0	0	—	0	—	1.000	—
Mariners	R Sea	7	18	2	0	0	0	2	2	2	5	0	4	1	1	0	0	0	—	0	.111	.333	.111
Wisconsin	A Sea	23	61	13	3	0	1	19	7	7	17	0	10	2	2	0	0	0	—	0	.213	.400	.311
1 Min. YEARS		31	79	15	3	0	1	21	9	9	23	0	14	3	3	0	0	0	—	0	.190	.390	.266

Rafael Alvarez

Bats: Left   **Throws:** Left   **Pos:** OF-73; PH-19; DH-11; PR-2   **Ht:** 5'11"   **Wt:** 192   **Born:** 1/22/77   **Age:** 24

		BATTING															BASERUNNING				PERCENTAGES		
Year Team	Lg Org	G	AB	H	2B	3B	HR	TB	R	RBI	TBB	IBB	SO	HBP	SH	SF	SB	CS	SB%	GDP	Avg	OBP	SLG
1994 Twins	R Min	32	101	32	5	0	2	43	15	10	18	0	14	1	2	0	4	2	.67	4	.317	.425	.426
1995 Fort Wayne	A Min	99	374	106	17	5	5	148	62	36	34	1	53	2	2	4	15	11	.58	5	.283	.343	.396
1996 Fort Myers	A+ Min	6	22	3	0	0	0	3	1	1	1	0	7	0	0	1	0	1	.00	0	.136	.167	.136
Fort Wayne	A Min	119	473	143	30	7	4	199	61	58	43	5	55	3	2	1	11	9	.55	5	.302	.363	.421
1997 Salt Lake	AAA Min	17	48	13	1	1	0	16	10	5	6	0	9	0	1	0	5	0	1.00	1	.271	.352	.333
New Britain	AA Min	16	47	12	0	0	2	18	5	7	5	0	9	1	1	0	1	4	.20	0	.255	.340	.383
Fort Myers	A+ Min	47	122	33	9	1	1	47	13	15	17	0	27	0	3	1	6	2	.75	1	.270	.357	.385
1998 Fort Myers	A+ Min	110	391	114	20	2	4	150	54	38	45	8	51	1	5	3	19	8	.70	5	.292	.364	.384
1999 Salt Lake	AAA Min	6	16	6	1	0	0	7	3	2	0	0	1	0	0	0	0	0	—	1	.375	.375	.438
Fort Myers	A+ Min	83	304	89	22	4	10	149	47	58	38	4	48	4	1	3	8	4	.67	8	.293	.375	.490
2000 New Britain	AA Min	97	274	71	15	2	7	111	35	46	35	2	65	4	0	2	3	1	.75	8	.259	.349	.405
7 Min. YEARS		632	2172	622	120	22	35	891	306	276	242	20	339	16	17	15	72	42	.63	38	.286	.360	.410

Victor Alvarez

Pitches: Left   **Bats:** Left   **Pos:** SP-12; RP-3   **Ht:** 5'10"   **Wt:** 150   **Born:** 11/8/76   **Age:** 24

		HOW MUCH HE PITCHED						WHAT HE GAVE UP												THE RESULTS					
Year Team	Lg Org	G	GS	CG	GF	IP	BFP	H	R	ER	HR	SH	SF	HB	TBB	IBB	SO	WP	Bk	W	L	Pct.	ShO	Sv	ERA
1997 Great Falls	R+ LA	12	8	0	3	48.1	212	49	30	18	0	0	4	3	17	0	50	2	3	4	1	.800	0	0	3.35
1999 Vero Beach	A+ LA	12	12	1	0	73	280	56	21	16	4	1	1	2	16	0	57	1	1	4	4	.500	0	0	1.97
San Antonio	AA LA	9	9	0	0	56.1	234	58	27	23	5	3	1	2	10	0	43	1	0	4	3	.571	0	0	3.67
2000 Vero Beach	A+ LA	4	4	0	0	22.2	94	17	14	13	6	0	0	0	11	0	20	1	0	1	1	.500	0	0	5.16
San Antonio	AA LA	11	8	0	0	48.1	218	44	27	21	3	5	3	7	30	1	43	0	0	0	3	.000	0	0	3.91
3 Min. YEARS		48	41	1	3	248.2	1038	224	119	91	18	9	9	14	84	1	213	5	4	13	12	.520	0	0	3.29

Jose Amado

Bats: Right   **Throws:** Right   **Pos:** 1B-55; DH-25; 3B-10; PH-1   **Ht:** 6'1"   **Wt:** 180   **Born:** 2/7/75   **Age:** 26

		BATTING															BASERUNNING				PERCENTAGES		
Year Team	Lg Org	G	AB	H	2B	3B	HR	TB	R	RBI	TBB	IBB	SO	HBP	SH	SF	SB	CS	SB%	GDP	Avg	OBP	SLG
1995 Everett	A- Sea	57	215	57	15	1	8	98	33	33	24	6	19	6	0	5	15	5	.75	4	.265	.348	.456
1996 Wisconsin	A Sea	61	232	67	13	0	5	95	43	36	20	1	20	8	2	3	6	5	.55	5	.289	.361	.409
Lansing	A KC	57	212	74	18	1	5	109	39	47	17	2	17	8	1	2	8	4	.67	6	.349	.414	.514
1997 Lansing	A KC	61	234	80	25	1	4	119	49	45	24	1	18	4	0	6	10	2	.83	8	.342	.403	.509
1998 Wilmington	A+ KC	70	236	62	17	1	4	93	34	28	24	2	28	10	1	2	6	5	.55	11	.263	.353	.394
1999 Wichita	AA KC	121	459	133	29	2	13	205	71	93	54	4	37	3	0	6	5	3	.63	15	.290	.364	.447
2000 Wichita	AA KC	88	318	93	17	0	5	125	41	56	39	1	26	7	0	4	6	2	.75	9	.292	.378	.393
6 Min. YEARS		515	1906	566	134	6	44	844	310	338	202	17	165	46	4	28	56	26	.68	58	.297	.373	.443

John Ambrose

Pitches: Right   **Bats:** Right   **Pos:** RP-58   **Ht:** 6'5"   **Wt:** 180   **Born:** 11/1/74   **Age:** 26

		HOW MUCH HE PITCHED						WHAT HE GAVE UP												THE RESULTS					
Year Team	Lg Org	G	GS	CG	GF	IP	BFP	H	R	ER	HR	SH	SF	HB	TBB	IBB	SO	WP	Bk	W	L	Pct.	ShO	Sv	ERA
1994 White Sox	R CWS	11	10	1	0	46.2	195	34	21	19	4	1	2	6	24	0	43	4	3	1	2	.333	0	0	3.66
Hickory	A CWS	3	1	0	1	12.2	58	16	11	10	1	0	1	0	6	0	7	0	0	1	1	.500	0	1	7.11
1995 Hickory	A CWS	14	14	0	0	73	314	65	41	32	6	2	3	3	35	0	49	9	2	4	8	.333	0	0	3.95
South Bend	A CWS	3	3	1	0	16.2	77	18	13	10	2	1	0	0	10	0	15	2	0	1	1	.500	0	0	5.40
1997 Winston-Sal	A+ CWS	27	27	1	0	149.2	688	136	102	91	17	5	9	8	117	2	137	16	5	8	13	.381	1	0	5.47
1998 Birmingham	AA CWS	31	22	0	3	140.2	641	156	90	81	18	2	4	13	69	2	103	14	2	9	12	.429	0	0	5.18
1999 Arkansas	AA StL	34	16	0	17	106.2	483	108	65	56	11	6	5	5	68	0	78	10	0	4	12	.250	0	9	4.73
2000 Arkansas	AA StL	45	0	0	28	49	226	48	31	23	3	2	1	3	32	3	49	8	0	3	4	.429	0	15	4.22
Memphis	AAA StL	13	0	0	0	19.2	97	24	12	12	1	0	3	0	20	0	8	4	0	1	1	.500	0	1	5.49
6 Min. YEARS		181	93	3	52	614.2	2779	605	386	334	63	19	28	38	381	7	489	67	12	32	54	.372	1	26	4.89

Jesus Ametller

Bats: Left   **Throws:** Right   **Pos:** 2B-9; PH-4; DH-3   **Ht:** 5'8"   **Wt:** 175   **Born:** 7/25/74   **Age:** 26

		BATTING															BASERUNNING				PERCENTAGES		
Year Team	Lg Org	G	AB	H	2B	3B	HR	TB	R	RBI	TBB	IBB	SO	HBP	SH	SF	SB	CS	SB%	GDP	Avg	OBP	SLG
1997 Pr William	A+ StL	60	215	58	10	2	3	81	26	26	15	1	12	0	4	0	3	1	.75	5	.270	.317	.377
1998 Pr William	A+ StL	101	358	112	29	0	1	144	52	38	2	0	29	3	6	5	4	6	.40	8	.313	.318	.402
1999 Arkansas	AA StL	116	397	122	26	2	10	182	53	53	5	0	21	4	1	5	2	1	.67	13	.307	.319	.458
Memphis	AAA StL	2	4	1	0	0	0	1	0	0	0	0	0	0	0	0	0	0	—	0	.250	.250	.250
2000 Memphis	AAA StL	10	28	6	2	0	0	8	2	2	0	0	3	0	0	1	0	1	.00	2	.214	.207	.286
Arkansas	AA StL	5	16	4	1	0	0	5	1	2	0	0	1	0	0	0	0	0	—	2	.250	.250	.313
4 Min. YEARS		294	1018	303	68	4	14	421	134	121	22	1	66	7	11	11	9	9	.50	28	.298	.314	.414

Adan Amezcua

Bats: Right   **Throws:** Right   **Pos:** C-32; DH-21; PH-3   **Ht:** 6'1"   **Wt:** 195   **Born:** 3/9/74   **Age:** 27

		BATTING															BASERUNNING				PERCENTAGES		
Year Team	Lg Org	G	AB	H	2B	3B	HR	TB	R	RBI	TBB	IBB	SO	HBP	SH	SF	SB	CS	SB%	GDP	Avg	OBP	SLG
1993 Astros	R Hou	48	145	43	13	3	0	62	14	24	12	0	19	1	0	1	1	0	1.00	4	.297	.352	.428
1994 Auburn	A- Hou	32	99	26	9	0	0	35	12	9	4	0	21	4	1	1	0	1	.00	2	.263	.315	.354
1995 Quad City	A Hou	46	142	35	8	2	4	59	13	12	5	0	28	1	1	1	2	3	.40	4	.246	.275	.415
1996 Kissimmee	A+ Hou	88	264	75	16	1	0	93	24	29	25	0	42	3	8	3	0	1	.00	4	.284	.349	.352
1997 Kissimmee	A+ Hou	9	20	8	3	0	0	11	3	5	3	1	3	0	0	1	0	0	—	0	.400	.458	.550
1998 Jackson	AA Hou	23	73	15	2	0	2	23	6	6	3	0	11	0	0	0	1	1	.50	2	.205	.237	.315
Kissimmee	A+ Hou	72	262	72	19	1	8	117	40	35	22	0	43	7	1	2	2	0	1.00	8	.275	.345	.447

Year Team	Lg Org	G	AB	H	2B	3B	HR	TB	R	RBI	TBB	IBB	SO	HBP	SH	SF	SB	CS	SB%	GDP	Avg	OBP	SLG
2000 Bowie	AA Bal	17	51	16	4	0	1	23	4	6	3	0	9	0	0	0	1	0	1.00	0	.314	.352	.451
Rochester	AAA Bal	38	132	31	5	1	1	41	9	14	14	0	25	0	1	1	0	0	—	7	.235	.306	.311
7 Min. YEARS		373	1188	321	79	8	16	464	125	140	91	1	201	16	12	10	7	6	.54	30	.270	.328	.391

Mike Amrhein

Bats: Right Throws: Right Pos: C-58; 1B-35; PH-6; DH-5; PR-1
Ht: 6'2" Wt: 215 Born: 6/14/75 Age: 26

Year Team	Lg Org	G	AB	H	2B	3B	HR	TB	R	RBI	TBB	IBB	SO	HBP	SH	SF	SB	CS	SB%	GDP	Avg	OBP	SLG
1997 Williamsprt	A- ChC	62	237	66	11	1	1	82	17	31	10	1	19	2	0	4	0	2	.00	11	.278	.308	.346
1998 Rockford	A ChC	121	457	145	34	1	9	208	61	87	30	1	47	8	3	3	7	4	.64	20	.317	.367	.455
1999 Daytona	A+ ChC	127	449	125	27	1	10	184	55	58	31	1	67	13	3	6	1	1	.50	14	.278	.339	.410
2000 West Tenn	AA ChC	104	352	100	18	0	9	145	45	49	35	2	40	14	2	2	0	3	.00	10	.284	.370	.412
4 Min. YEARS		414	1495	436	90	3	29	619	178	225	106	5	173	37	8	15	8	10	.44	55	.292	.350	.414

Jason Anderson

Pitches: Left Bats: Left Pos: RP-47
Ht: 6'2" Wt: 185 Born: 4/6/76 Age: 25

Year Team	Lg Org	G	GS	CG	GF	IP	BFP	H	R	ER	HR	SH	SF	HB	TBB	IBB	SO	WP	Bk	W	L	Pct.	ShO	Sv	ERA
1997 Sou Oregon	A- Oak	14	9	0	1	52.1	238	63	38	29	4	3	0	5	19	0	38	8	2	3	3	.500	0	0	4.99
1998 Modesto	A+ Oak	28	24	1	2	145.2	612	147	67	56	5	5	4	2	53	0	110	5	1	9	4	.692	1	0	3.46
Huntsville	AA Oak	3	3	1	0	17	80	16	15	10	2	1	0	2	11	1	14	1	1	1	1	.500	1	0	5.29
1999 Visalia	A+ Oak	4	4	0	0	25	110	32	9	7	1	0	2	0	7	0	17	1	0	2	1	.667	0	0	2.52
Midland	AA Oak	23	23	0	0	111	531	148	103	85	15	6	7	10	47	0	74	5	3	4	9	.308	0	0	6.89
2000 Midland	AA Oak	28	0	0	9	41	192	47	36	22	3	1	4	1	20	3	17	3	0	0	4	.000	0	1	4.83
Visalia	A+ Oak	19	0	0	6	29.2	137	36	26	23	3	2	1	2	12	0	19	0	0	3	3	.500	0	2	6.98
4 Min. YEARS		119	63	2	18	421.2	1900	489	294	232	33	18	16	24	169	4	289	23	7	22	25	.468	2	3	4.95

Ryan Anderson

Pitches: Left Bats: Left Pos: SP-20
Ht: 6'10" Wt: 215 Born: 7/12/79 Age: 21

Year Team	Lg Org	G	GS	CG	GF	IP	BFP	H	R	ER	HR	SH	SF	HB	TBB	IBB	SO	WP	Bk	W	L	Pct.	ShO	Sv	ERA
1998 Wisconsin	A Sea	22	22	0	0	111.1	474	86	47	40	4	3	3	10	67	0	152	4	3	6	5	.545	0	0	3.23
1999 New Haven	AA Sea	24	24	0	0	134	606	131	77	67	9	2	5	8	86	1	162	9	3	9	13	.409	0	0	4.50
2000 Tacoma	AAA Sea	20	20	1	0	104	439	83	51	46	8	0	1	3	55	0	146	7	3	5	8	.385	1	0	3.98
3 Min. YEARS		66	66	1	0	349.1	1519	300	175	153	21	5	9	21	208	1	460	20	9	20	26	.435	1	0	3.94

Jeff Andra

Pitches: Left Bats: Left Pos: SP-24
Ht: 6'5" Wt: 210 Born: 9/9/75 Age: 25

Year Team	Lg Org	G	GS	CG	GF	IP	BFP	H	R	ER	HR	SH	SF	HB	TBB	IBB	SO	WP	Bk	W	L	Pct.	ShO	Sv	ERA
1997 Salem-Keizr	A- SF	8	8	0	0	44.1	185	39	21	10	3	1	1	1	10	0	58	4	0	3	1	.750	0	0	2.03
San Jose	A+ SF	6	6	0	0	29.2	142	36	25	23	2	3	0	4	11	0	29	2	2	1	4	.200	0	0	6.98
1998 San Jose	A+ SF	15	15	2	0	86.2	358	75	36	32	2	4	0	2	28	0	80	5	1	8	2	.800	1	0	3.32
1999 San Jose	A+ SF	13	7	0	0	50	217	54	28	25	3	2	2	0	19	1	54	3	1	4	2	.667	0	0	4.50
2000 Shreveport	AA SF	17	17	0	0	91.1	403	106	51	39	6	7	5	1	35	2	64	1	0	6	6	.500	0	0	3.84
Fresno	AAA SF	7	7	0	0	33	171	49	35	32	9	1	1	1	24	0	16	1	0	0	3	.000	0	0	8.73
4 Min. YEARS		66	60	2	0	335	1476	359	196	161	25	18	9	9	127	3	301	16	4	22	18	.550	1	0	4.33

Alex Andreopoulos

Bats: Left Throws: Right Pos: C-81; DH-21; 1B-2; PH-2
Ht: 5'10" Wt: 190 Born: 8/19/72 Age: 28

Year Team	Lg Org	G	AB	H	2B	3B	HR	TB	R	RBI	TBB	IBB	SO	HBP	SH	SF	SB	CS	SB%	GDP	Avg	OBP	SLG
1995 Helena	R+ Mil	3	9	5	0	0	2	11	3	7	4	0	0	0	0	0	0	0	—	0	.556	.692	1.222
Beloit	A Mil	60	163	49	9	0	1	61	32	20	35	1	16	3	3	1	5	3	.63	2	.301	.431	.374
1996 Stockton	A+ Mil	87	291	88	17	2	5	124	52	41	40	2	33	5	2	4	10	3	.77	5	.302	.391	.426
1997 El Paso	AA Mil	7	26	4	1	0	0	5	1	3	1	0	2	0	0	0	0	0	—	1	.154	.185	.192
Tucson	AAA Mil	10	15	6	1	0	0	7	3	1	0	0	1	0	0	0	0	0	—	0	.400	.400	.467
1998 El Paso	AA Mil	113	377	121	35	1	10	188	72	93	54	4	31	9	2	5	2	3	.40	9	.321	.413	.499
1999 Louisville	AAA Mil	71	201	53	8	0	5	76	19	31	25	4	21	2	3	1	1	0	1.00	5	.264	.349	.378
2000 Huntsville	AA Mil	5	10	2	1	0	0	3	1	2	1	0	2	0	0	0	0	0	—	0	.200	.250	.300
Aberdeen	IND —	100	350	95	20	1	10	147	51	52	50	3	34	5	0	2	8	2	.80	11	.271	.369	.420
6 Min. YEARS		456	1442	423	92	4	33	622	234	250	210	14	140	24	10	14	26	11	.70	33	.293	.389	.431

Jeff Andrews

Pitches: Right Bats: Right Pos: RP-24; SP-13
Ht: 6'3" Wt: 190 Born: 9/1/74 Age: 26

Year Team	Lg Org	G	GS	CG	GF	IP	BFP	H	R	ER	HR	SH	SF	HB	TBB	IBB	SO	WP	Bk	W	L	Pct.	ShO	Sv	ERA
1997 South Bend	A Ari	23	4	0	7	55	237	52	37	32	4	2	1	2	27	1	32	3	0	1	5	.167	0	0	5.24
Lethbridge	R+ Ari	9	9	1	0	49.2	219	52	27	18	3	1	0	3	10	0	50	3	0	3	3	.500	0	0	3.26
1998 South Bend	A Ari	20	17	0	2	123	524	130	62	39	4	4	3	2	28	2	68	7	1	3	8	.273	0	0	2.85
1999 High Desert	A+ Ari	6	3	0	2	25	119	36	19	12	1	0	2	0	7	0	8	0	0	1	1	.500	0	0	4.32
High Desert	A+ Ari	6	6	0	0	29.2	143	41	27	21	5	0	1	2	13	0	25	1	0	0	3	.000	0	0	6.37
2000 El Paso	AA Ari	35	8	0	21	73	323	87	47	43	8	5	5	3	24	3	40	1	1	3	8	.273	0	7	5.30
El Paso	AA Ari	21	8	0	4	60.2	292	88	54	51	12	2	4	3	30	0	35	3	1	3	4	.429	0	0	7.57
Tucson	AAA Ari	16	5	0	2	38	182	47	31	28	2	2	4	1	26	1	21	3	1	1	2	.333	0	0	6.63
4 Min. YEARS		136	60	1	38	454	2039	536	304	244	37	14	20	16	165	7	279	21	4	15	34	.306	0	7	4.84

Luis Andujar

Pitches: Right **Bats:** Right **Pos:** RP-35

Ht: 6'2" **Wt:** 215 **Born:** 11/22/72 **Age:** 28

Year Team	Lg Org	G	GS	CG	GF	IP	BFP	H	R	ER	HR	SH	SF	HB	TBB	IBB	SO	WP	Bk	W	L	Pct.	ShO	Sv	ERA
1991 White Sox	R CWS	10	10	1	0	62.1	255	60	27	17	0	1	2	4	10	0	52	3	1	4	4	.500	1	0	2.45
1992 South Bend	A CWS	32	15	1	11	120.1	516	109	49	39	5	2	0	6	47	0	91	5	1	6	5	.545	1	3	2.92
1993 Sarasota	A+ CWS	18	11	2	4	86	345	67	26	19	2	7	0	3	28	0	72	1	0	6	6	.500	0	1	1.99
Birmingham	AA CWS	6	6	0	0	39.2	169	31	9	8	3	3	1	5	18	0	48	1	0	5	0	1.000	0	0	1.82
1994 White Sox	R CWS	2	0	0	0	6	22	3	1	0	0	0	0	1	1	0	6	0	0	1	0	1.000	0	0	0.00
Birmingham	AA CWS	15	15	0	0	76.2	344	90	50	43	5	1	2	8	25	0	64	5	0	3	7	.300	0	0	5.05
1995 Birmingham	AA CWS	27	27	2	0	167.1	689	147	64	53	10	1	5	7	44	0	146	3	1	14	8	.636	1	0	2.85
1996 White Sox	R CWS	1	1	0	0	6	22	3	0	0	0	0	0	1	0	0	3	0	0	1	0	1.000	0	0	0.00
Nashville	AAA CWS	8	7	1	0	38	171	50	26	25	4	0	2	2	8	0	24	1	1	1	4	.200	0	0	5.92
Syracuse	AAA Tor	2	2	0	0	12	55	17	7	3	1	0	2	0	2	0	10	0	0	0	0	—	0	0	2.25
1997 Syracuse	AAA Tor	13	5	1	7	39	169	37	25	24	6	2	2	3	14	1	29	1	1	1	6	.143	0	1	5.54
1998 Syracuse	AAA Tor	20	0	0	14	34	130	23	9	8	5	2	0	4	6	0	24	2	1	3	2	.600	0	8	2.12
Calgary	AAA CWS	13	9	0	0	50.1	226	62	38	35	8	0	1	5	15	1	46	0	0	3	3	.500	0	0	6.26
1999 Charlotte	AAA CWS	52	0	0	35	60	252	62	21	20	3	4	4	3	13	0	59	3	0	4	5	.444	0	16	3.00
2000 Las Vegas	AAA SD	10	0	0	4	15.1	73	18	13	11	6	0	2	2	4	0	8	1	0	2	1	.667	0	0	6.46
Nashville	AAA Pit	25	0	0	11	38.1	179	46	25	23	5	3	0	0	18	2	29	1	0	1	4	.200	0	3	5.40
1995 Chicago	AL	5	5	0	0	30.1	128	26	12	11	4	0	0	1	14	2	9	0	0	2	1	.667	0	0	3.26
1996 Chicago	AL	5	5	0	0	23	113	32	22	21	4	1	2	0	15	0	6	0	0	0	2	.000	0	0	8.22
Toronto	AL	3	2	0	0	14.1	57	14	8	8	4	0	2	1	1	0	5	1	0	1	1	.500	0	0	5.02
1997 Toronto	AL	17	8	0	5	50	244	76	45	36	9	3	4	0	21	1	28	2	0	0	6	.000	0	0	6.48
1998 Toronto	AL	5	0	0	3	5.2	30	12	6	6	0	0	0	0	2	0	1	1	0	0	0	—	0	0	9.53
10 Min. YEARS		254	108	8	86	851.1	3617	825	390	328	63	26	23	54	253	4	711	27	6	55	55	.500	3	32	3.47
4 Maj. YEARS		35	20	0	8	123.1	572	160	93	82	21	4	8	2	53	3	49	4	0	3	10	.231	0	0	5.98

Juan Aracena

Pitches: Right **Bats:** Right **Pos:** RP-49; SP-2

Ht: 6'0" **Wt:** 150 **Born:** 12/17/76 **Age:** 24

Year Team	Lg Org	G	GS	CG	GF	IP	BFP	H	R	ER	HR	SH	SF	HB	TBB	IBB	SO	WP	Bk	W	L	Pct.	ShO	Sv	ERA
1996 Burlington	R+ Cle	13	5	0	3	42.2	197	61	38	26	4	0	0	1	7	0	28	5	3	3	4	.429	0	0	5.48
1997 Burlington	R+ Cle	19	0	0	3	38.2	176	45	32	21	4	1	1	0	16	0	31	3	2	1	4	.200	0	2	4.89
1998 Columbus	A Cle	5	0	0	3	6.2	38	15	10	10	0	0	1	0	6	1	4	5	0	0	1	.000	0	0	13.50
Watertown	A- Cle	18	0	0	17	25.1	103	21	8	8	2	1	0	0	7	1	22	1	0	1	4	.200	0	6	2.84
1999 Columbus	A Cle	32	0	0	36	35.2	138	32	13	13	7	1	0	1	3	0	30	1	0	2	0	1.000	0	18	3.28
Kinston	A+ Cle	5	0	0	2	7	28	7	2	2	0	1	0	0	1	0	7	1	0	1	1	.500	0	0	2.57
Frederick	A+ Bal	2	0	0	2	2	7	2	1	0	0	0	0	0	0	0	0	0	0	0	0	—	0	0	0.00
2000 Bowie	AA Bal	33	0	0	22	36.1	168	39	24	24	4	0	1	0	25	5	26	1	0	3	2	.600	0	1	5.94
Frederick	A+ Bal	11	0	0	11	9.2	44	9	9	6	3	0	0	0	5	0	12	2	0	1	1	.500	0	2	5.59
Binghamton	AA NYM	7	2	0	1	10.1	64	24	20	17	5	0	0	0	9	0	11	0	0	0	2	.000	0	1	14.81
5 Min. YEARS		145	7	0	99	214.1	963	255	157	127	29	4	3	2	79	7	167	19	5	12	19	.387	0	37	5.33

Angel Aragon

Pitches: Right **Bats:** Right **Pos:** RP-52; SP-2

Ht: 6'1" **Wt:** 238 **Born:** 12/19/73 **Age:** 27

Year Team	Lg Org	G	GS	CG	GF	IP	BFP	H	R	ER	HR	SH	SF	HB	TBB	IBB	SO	WP	Bk	W	L	Pct.	ShO	Sv	ERA
1997 Sioux Falls	IND —	33	3	1	18	68	304	77	33	24	4	4	2	4	27	3	43	5	0	4	3	.571	0	3	3.18
1998 Clinton	A SD	42	7	0	14	91.1	400	100	57	45	7	3	4	3	36	3	77	8	0	6	8	.429	0	1	4.43
1999 Rancho Cuca	A+ SD	53	0	0	36	68.2	291	55	33	27	3	4	3	6	28	3	76	6	1	2	7	.222	0	19	3.54
2000 Mobile	AA SD	54	2	0	20	76.2	338	84	46	44	9	5	1	1	30	3	61	8	0	3	6	.333	0	5	5.17
4 Min. YEARS		182	12	1	88	304.2	1333	316	169	140	23	16	10	14	121	12	257	27	1	15	24	.385	0	28	4.14

Luis Arroyo

Pitches: Left **Bats:** Left **Pos:** RP-38

Ht: 6'0" **Wt:** 174 **Born:** 9/29/73 **Age:** 27

Year Team	Lg Org	G	GS	CG	GF	IP	BFP	H	R	ER	HR	SH	SF	HB	TBB	IBB	SO	WP	Bk	W	L	Pct.	ShO	Sv	ERA
1992 Padres	R SD	17	9	0	3	57.2	259	65	45	27	0	1	6	2	21	0	55	4	12	4	4	.500	0	0	4.21
1993 Waterloo	A SD	17	16	1	0	95.2	424	99	59	48	11	7	6	6	46	1	59	5	3	5	7	.417	0	0	4.52
1994 Springfield	A SD	16	16	1	0	99.2	434	86	50	38	8	5	2	1	47	4	76	4	4	8	2	.800	0	0	3.43
Rancho Cuca	A+ SD	10	10	0	0	54.1	243	62	33	29	6	1	1	3	30	0	34	2	0	3	4	.429	0	0	4.80
1995 Rancho Cuca	A+ SD	26	24	0	0	128.2	599	158	97	75	9	8	6	12	62	6	102	7	3	7	10	.412	0	0	5.25
1996 St. Lucie	A+ NYM	22	0	0	4	42	170	36	17	14	1	0	3	1	15	1	28	3	0	1	0	1.000	0	2	3.00
1997 Binghamton	AA NYM	7	0	0	1	14.2	60	14	6	5	2	2	1	0	6	0	9	0	1	0	0	—	0	0	3.07
St. Lucie	A+ NYM	36	2	0	11	56	231	37	21	13	2	3	1	3	23	2	57	1	3	3	3	.500	0	1	2.09
1998 Norfolk	AAA NYM	8	0	0	5	8	41	11	7	6	1	0	1	1	7	0	7	0	0	0	1	.000	0	0	6.75
Binghamton	AA NYM	57	0	0	16	66.1	280	59	30	19	1	5	2	1	26	3	78	4	1	1	5	.167	0	3	2.58
1999 Knoxville	AA Tor	5	0	0	2	6.2	22	2	1	1	0	0	0	0	0	0	7	0	0	0	0	—	0	1	1.35
Syracuse	AAA Tor	9	0	0	3	12.2	65	18	13	12	1	1	1	0	9	1	10	1	1	0	1	.000	0	0	8.53
Portland	AA Fla	9	0	0	1	13.2	71	14	11	5	2	2	0	0	8	4	10	0	0	1	0	.000	0	1	3.29
Calgary	AAA Fla	22	0	0	8	33.1	157	42	33	24	6	2	2	3	17	0	26	0	1	2	1	.667	0	0	6.48
2000 Calgary	AAA Fla	7	0	0	2	15.2	71	16	11	10	3	1	2	0	8	0	9	0	1	1	1	.500	0	0	5.74
Portland	AA Fla	31	0	0	14	57	249	50	26	24	2	6	0	2	33	1	47	1	1	3	2	.600	0	0	3.79
9 Min. YEARS		299	77	2	71	762	3366	769	460	350	55	44	34	36	358	23	614	32	31	38	42	.475	0	7	4.13

J.D. Arteaga

Pitches: Left **Bats:** Left **Pos:** RP-20; SP-15

Ht: 6'3" **Wt:** 227 **Born:** 8/2/74 **Age:** 26

Year Team	Lg Org	G	GS	CG	GF	IP	BFP	H	R	ER	HR	SH	SF	HB	TBB	IBB	SO	WP	Bk	W	L	Pct.	ShO	Sv	ERA
1997 Pittsfield	A- NYM	12	3	0	2	30.1	129	32	15	9	0	1	0	1	4	0	29	1	0	4	2	.667	0	0	2.67
Capital Cty	A NYM	1	1	0	0	6	20	3	0	0	0	0	0	0	0	0	4	0	0	1	0	1.000	0	0	0.00

Year Team	Lg Org	G	GS	CG	GF	IP	BFP	H	R	ER	HR	SH	SF	HB	TBB	IBB	SO	WP	Bk	W	L	Pct.	ShO	Sv	ERA
1998 St. Lucie	A+ NYM	15	2	0	1	37.1	154	37	15	12	1	4	0	0	7	0	28	1	1	2	0	1.000	0	0	2.89
Binghamton	AA NYM	21	18	0	0	119	495	122	48	37	8	6	5	5	25	1	97	2	0	8	7	.533	0	0	2.80
1999 St. Lucie	A+ NYM	1	1	0	0	5	19	3	2	2	1	0	1	0	2	0	0	0	0	0	1	.000	0	0	3.60
Mets	R NYM	2	1	0	0	4	15	4	3	3	1	0	0	0	0	0	3	0	0	0	0	—	0	0	6.75
Binghamton	AA NYM	11	3	0	1	28.1	133	32	21	18	3	0	2	2	14	0	24	0	0	3	1	.750	0	0	5.72
2000 Norfolk	AAA NYM	1	1	0	0	5.2	23	4	1	1	0	0	0	0	2	0	1	0	0	1	0	1.000	0	0	1.59
Binghamton	AA NYM	34	14	2	2	112.1	490	125	60	43	6	7	5	6	25	0	76	1	0	10	7	.588	1	1	3.45
4 Min. YEARS		98	44	2	6	348	1478	362	165	125	20	18	13	14	79	1	262	5	1	29	18	.617	1	1	3.23

Chris Ashby

Bats: Right **Throws:** Right **Pos:** OF-121; 1B-21; PH-12   **Ht:** 6'3" **Wt:** 196 **Born:** 12/15/74 **Age:** 26

Year Team	Lg Org	G	AB	H	2B	3B	HR	TB	R	RBI	TBB	IBB	SO	HBP	SH	SF	SB	CS	SB%	GDP	Avg	OBP	SLG
1993 Yankees	R NYY	49	175	37	12	0	0	49	24	23	32	0	45	6	0	2	5	3	.63	6	.211	.349	.280
Greensboro	A NYY	1	4	3	0	0	0	3	2	0	0	0	0	1	0	0	0	0	—	0	.750	.800	.750
1994 Yankees	R NYY	45	163	55	8	1	5	80	28	38	21	0	20	1	1	3	2	0	1.00	4	.337	.410	.491
Greensboro	A NYY	6	16	2	1	0	0	3	0	2	2	0	6	0	0	0	0	0	—	1	.125	.222	.188
1995 Greensboro	A NYY	88	288	79	23	1	9	131	45	45	61	2	68	6	2	2	3	3	.50	9	.274	.409	.455
1996 Tampa	A+ NYY	100	325	80	28	0	6	126	55	46	71	1	78	5	1	1	16	4	.80	5	.246	.388	.388
1997 Norwich	AA NYY	136	457	114	20	1	24	208	92	82	80	2	95	6	0	3	10	7	.59	14	.249	.366	.455
1998 Columbus	AAA NYY	5	11	1	0	0	0	1	0	1	3	0	6	0	0	0	0	0	—	0	.091	.286	.091
Norwich	AA NYY	126	438	125	24	0	11	182	65	53	65	3	99	7	0	4	17	3	.85	12	.285	.383	.416
1999 Norwich	AA NYY	29	108	27	5	1	3	43	11	16	11	0	20	3	0	2	3	4	.43	3	.250	.341	.398
Columbus	AAA NYY	70	206	55	13	1	9	97	46	32	21	0	39	2	1	0	6	3	.67	5	.267	.341	.471
2000 Albuquerque	AAA LA	134	465	138	34	3	7	199	98	59	55	1	74	2	1	1	16	11	.59	10	.297	.373	.428
8 Min. YEARS		789	2656	716	168	8	74	1122	466	397	422	9	550	39	6	18	78	38	.67	69	.270	.375	.422

Scott Atchison

Pitches: Right **Bats:** Right **Pos:** SP-23   **Ht:** 6'2" **Wt:** 180 **Born:** 3/29/76 **Age:** 25

Year Team	Lg Org	G	GS	CG	GF	IP	BFP	H	R	ER	HR	SH	SF	HB	TBB	IBB	SO	WP	Bk	W	L	Pct.	ShO	Sv	ERA
1999 Wisconsin	A Sea	15	13	0	0	81.2	326	67	34	31	4	2	2	3	25	1	85	4	1	4	5	.444	0	0	3.42
2000 Tacoma	AAA Sea	5	5	0	0	26	103	22	11	11	3	0	0	0	6	0	18	0	0	1	1	.500	0	0	3.81
Lancaster	A+ Sea	18	18	1	0	97.2	436	117	58	40	10	2	4	4	21	0	77	2	0	5	5	.500	0	0	3.69
2 Min. YEARS		38	36	1	0	205.1	865	206	103	82	17	4	6	7	52	1	180	6	1	10	11	.476	0	0	3.59

Justin Atchley

Pitches: Left **Bats:** Left **Pos:** SP-19; RP-11   **Ht:** 6'3" **Wt:** 215 **Born:** 9/5/73 **Age:** 27

Year Team	Lg Org	G	GS	CG	GF	IP	BFP	H	R	ER	HR	SH	SF	HB	TBB	IBB	SO	WP	Bk	W	L	Pct.	ShO	Sv	ERA
1995 Billings	R+ Cin	13	13	0	0	77	327	91	33	30	4	2	1	2	20	2	65	2	1	10	0	1.000	0	0	3.51
1996 Chston-WV	A Cin	17	16	0	1	91	392	98	42	35	7	4	2	1	23	0	78	0	1	3	3	.500	0	1	3.46
Winston-Sal	A+ Cin	12	12	0	0	69	290	74	48	39	13	3	3	2	16	0	50	2	0	3	3	.500	0	0	5.09
1997 Chattanooga	AA Cin	13	13	1	0	67	289	75	45	35	8	2	5	1	14	0	48	5	0	4	2	.667	0	0	4.70
1999 Chattanooga	AA Cin	17	17	0	0	97.1	416	114	48	37	9	1	6	1	22	1	70	1	1	4	9	.308	0	0	3.42
Indianapolis	AAA Cin	5	4	0	1	23.1	106	39	14	14	5	0	0	0	2	0	6	0	0	2	1	.667	0	0	5.40
2000 Louisville	AAA Cin	30	19	0	5	122.1	547	168	83	80	19	2	5	3	26	1	69	8	0	8	6	.571	0	0	5.89
5 Min. YEARS		107	94	1	7	547	2367	659	313	270	65	14	22	10	123	4	386	18	3	34	24	.586	0	3	4.44

Jeff Austin

Pitches: Right **Bats:** Right **Pos:** SP-25; RP-4   **Ht:** 6'0" **Wt:** 185 **Born:** 10/19/76 **Age:** 24

Year Team	Lg Org	G	GS	CG	GF	IP	BFP	H	R	ER	HR	SH	SF	HB	TBB	IBB	SO	WP	Bk	W	L	Pct.	ShO	Sv	ERA
1999 Wilmington	A+ KC	18	18	0	0	112.1	473	108	52	47	10	5	3	2	39	0	97	5	0	7	2	.778	0	0	3.77
Wichita	AA KC	6	6	0	0	34.1	155	40	19	17	1	0	1	2	11	1	21	4	0	3	1	.750	0	0	4.46
2000 Wichita	AA KC	6	6	1	0	43	168	33	16	14	3	0	2	5	4	0	31	2	0	2	2	.500	0	0	2.93
Omaha	AAA KC	23	19	1	1	126.2	551	150	85	63	16	3	7	4	35	1	57	8	1	7	9	.438	1	0	4.48
2 Min. YEARS		53	49	2	1	316.1	1347	331	172	141	30	8	13	13	89	2	206	19	1	19	14	.576	1	0	4.01

Robert Averette

Pitches: Right **Bats:** Right **Pos:** SP-26   **Ht:** 6'2" **Wt:** 195 **Born:** 9/30/76 **Age:** 24

Year Team	Lg Org	G	GS	CG	GF	IP	BFP	H	R	ER	HR	SH	SF	HB	TBB	IBB	SO	WP	Bk	W	L	Pct.	ShO	Sv	ERA
1997 Billings	R+ Cin	2	1	0	1	2.2	11	3	0	0	0	0	0	0	1	1	3	0	0	0	0	—	0	0	0.00
Chston-WV	A Cin	11	3	0	2	26.1	131	42	28	23	3	3	1	0	12	0	20	2	0	2	2	.500	0	1	7.86
1998 Chston-WV	A Cin	14	14	3	0	84	355	84	38	26	2	6	3	2	26	2	68	4	1	5	4	.556	0	0	2.79
Chattanooga	AA Cin	14	14	0	0	81	355	97	51	46	6	2	3	3	36	2	32	2	0	5	8	.385	0	0	5.11
1999 Rockford	A Cin	19	19	2	0	125.2	521	117	54	36	2	4	3	4	40	3	98	9	0	9	5	.643	2	0	2.58
Chattanooga	AA Cin	6	6	1	0	36.1	164	42	22	21	1	0	1	2	19	0	15	0	0	2	1	.667	0	0	5.20
2000 Louisville	AAA Cin	2	2	0	0	9.2	49	9	10	9	1	1	1	0	10	0	4	0	0	1	0	1.000	0	0	8.38
Chattanooga	AA Cin	19	19	5	0	136.1	555	126	51	37	6	2	1	4	28	3	87	7	1	12	6	.667	2	0	2.44
Carolina	AA Col	5	5	0	0	31	131	25	12	11	3	1	0	1	10	0	29	2	0	1	3	.250	0	0	3.19
4 Min. YEARS		92	83	11	3	533	2272	545	266	209	24	19	13	16	182	9	356	26	2	36	30	.545	4	1	3.53

Steve Avery

Pitches: Left **Bats:** Left **Pos:** SP-19

Ht: 6'4" **Wt:** 205 **Born:** 4/14/70 **Age:** 31

Year Team	Lg Org	G	GS	CG	GF	IP	BFP	H	R	ER	HR	SH	SF	HB	TBB	IBB	SO	WP	Bk	W	L	Pct.	ShO	Sv	ERA
1988 Pulaski	R+ Atl	10	10	3	0	66	249	38	16	11	2	1	1	1	19	0	80	5	1	7	1	.875	2	0	1.50
1989 Durham	A+ Atl	13	13	3	0	86.2	337	59	22	14	5	5	0	1	20	1	90	4	1	6	4	.600	1	0	1.45
Greenville	AA Atl	13	13	1	0	84.1	341	68	32	26	3	4	1	1	34	0	75	4	0	6	3	.667	0	0	2.77
1990 Richmond	AAA Atl	13	13	3	0	82.1	343	85	35	32	7	6	2	2	21	0	69	5	0	5	5	.500	0	0	3.50
1996 Greenville	AA Atl	1	1	0	0	0.2	2	0	0	0	0	0	0	0	0	0	0	0	0	0	0	—	0	0	0.00
1997 Sarasota	A+ Bos	1	1	0	0	3	11	2	0	0	0	0	0	1	0	0	3	0	0	0	0	—	0	0	0.00
Red Sox	R Bos	1	1	0	0	6	25	5	3	1	1	0	0	0	0	0	8	0	0	0	0	—	0	0	1.50
Pawtucket	AAA Bos	1	1	0	0	5	19	1	0	0	0	0	0	0	3	0	1	0	0	1	0	1.000	0	0	0.00
1998 Pawtucket	AAA Bos	3	3	0	0	11.1	53	9	9	7	2	3	2	1	9	0	6	0	0	0	2	.000	0	0	5.56
2000 Macon	A Atl	2	2	0	0	6	25	6	5	1	2	0	0	0	1	0	7	0	0	1	0	1.000	0	0	1.50
Greenville	AA Atl	6	6	0	0	29	147	43	32	28	6	1	5	0	22	1	17	2	0	0	5	.000	0	0	8.69
Myrtle Bch	A+ Atl	7	7	1	0	47	195	40	11	8	2	2	1	0	25	0	32	1	0	3	3	.500	0	0	1.53
Richmond	AAA Atl	4	4	0	0	21	101	23	25	22	3	1	1	0	17	0	8	1	0	1	3	.250	0	0	9.43
1990 Atlanta	NL	21	20	1	1	99	466	121	79	62	7	14	4	2	45	2	75	5	1	3	11	.214	1	0	5.64
1991 Atlanta	NL	35	35	3	0	210.1	868	189	89	79	21	8	4	3	65	0	137	4	1	18	8	.692	1	0	3.38
1992 Atlanta	NL	35	35	2	0	233.2	969	216	95	83	14	12	8	0	71	3	129	7	3	11	11	.500	2	0	3.20
1993 Atlanta	NL	35	35	3	0	223.1	891	216	81	73	14	12	8	0	43	5	125	3	1	18	6	.750	1	0	2.94
1994 Atlanta	NL	24	24	1	0	151.2	628	127	71	68	15	4	6	4	55	4	122	5	2	8	3	.727	0	0	4.04
1995 Atlanta	NL	29	29	3	0	173.1	724	165	92	90	22	6	4	6	52	4	141	3	0	7	13	.350	1	0	4.67
1996 Atlanta	NL	24	23	1	0	131	567	146	70	65	10	7	3	4	40	8	86	5	0	7	10	.412	0	0	4.47
1997 Boston	AL	22	18	0	1	96.2	453	127	76	69	15	1	4	2	49	0	51	4	0	6	7	.462	0	0	6.42
1998 Boston	AL	34	23	0	4	123.2	546	128	74	69	14	3	0	4	64	0	57	7	0	10	7	.588	0	0	5.02
1999 Cincinnati	NL	19	19	0	0	96	426	75	62	55	11	3	6	1	78	0	51	4	1	6	7	.462	0	0	5.16
7 Min. YEARS		75	75	11	0	448.1	1848	379	190	150	33	23	13	6	172	2	396	21	2	29	27	.518	3	0	3.01
10 Maj. YEARS		278	261	14	6	1538.2	6538	1510	789	713	143	70	47	26	562	26	974	47	9	94	83	.531	6	0	4.17

Corey Avrard

Pitches: Right **Bats:** Right **Pos:** RP-57

Ht: 6'4" **Wt:** 190 **Born:** 12/6/76 **Age:** 24

Year Team	Lg Org	G	GS	CG	GF	IP	BFP	H	R	ER	HR	SH	SF	HB	TBB	IBB	SO	WP	Bk	W	L	Pct.	ShO	Sv	ERA
1995 Savannah	A StL	13	13	0	0	54.1	228	38	25	24	4	1	4	0	33	2	51	6	0	1	6	.143	0	0	3.98
1996 Peoria	A StL	21	21	2	0	110.1	489	105	73	52	6	6	2	8	58	0	103	5	0	5	9	.357	0	0	4.24
1997 Peoria	A StL	20	20	0	0	93.1	437	97	76	66	5	4	4	4	69	1	94	9	0	4	5	.444	0	0	6.36
Pr William	A+ StL	8	8	0	0	40.1	190	30	28	24	1	0	0	2	44	0	50	4	1	0	3	.000	0	0	5.36
1998 Pr William	A+ StL	31	11	0	6	80	345	67	54	45	9	2	6	3	50	0	52	5	0	4	5	.444	0	0	5.06
1999 Potomac	A+ StL	28	0	0	11	32.2	157	32	19	16	2	1	1	4	26	1	40	7	0	2	2	.500	0	2	4.41
Arkansas	AA StL	25	0	0	13	26	109	15	12	9	2	1	2	0	14	1	31	5	0	1	1	.500	0	6	3.12
2000 Arkansas	AA StL	57	0	0	33	71	323	64	46	43	10	5	6	1	53	4	57	10	0	0	6	.000	0	14	5.45
6 Min. YEARS		203	73	2	63	508	2278	448	336	279	39	20	25	22	347	9	478	51	1	17	37	.315	0	20	4.94

Bobby Ayala

Pitches: Right **Bats:** Right **Pos:** RP-34

Ht: 6'3" **Wt:** 215 **Born:** 7/8/69 **Age:** 31

Year Team	Lg Org	G	GS	CG	GF	IP	BFP	H	R	ER	HR	SH	SF	HB	TBB	IBB	SO	WP	Bk	W	L	Pct.	ShO	Sv	ERA
1988 Reds	R Cin	20	0	0	15	33	153	34	23	14	0	3	3	3	12	0	24	1	0	0	4	.000	0	3	3.82
1989 Greensboro	A Cin	22	19	1	1	105.1	467	97	73	48	7	2	3	4	50	0	70	10	2	5	8	.385	0	0	4.10
1990 Cedar Rapds	A Cin	18	7	3	3	53.1	215	40	24	20	6	2	1	4	18	0	59	6	0	3	2	.600	1	1	3.38
Chston-WV	A Cin	21	4	2	8	74	287	48	23	20	2	2	1	3	21	1	73	0	0	6	1	.857	1	2	2.43
1991 Chattanooga	AA Cin	39	8	1	16	90.2	404	79	52	47	10	4	3	4	58	4	92	10	1	3	1	.750	0	4	4.67
1992 Chattanooga	AA Cin	27	27	3	0	162.2	690	152	75	64	14	8	2	11	58	0	154	9	0	12	6	.667	3	0	3.54
1993 Indianapols	AAA Cin	5	5	0	0	27	123	36	19	17	1	3	0	1	12	1	19	1	0	0	2	.000	0	0	5.67
1996 Port City	AA Sea	2	1	0	0	1.2	7	0	0	0	0	0	0	0	1	0	2	0	0	0	0	—	0	0	0.00
Tacoma	AAA Sea	1	1	0	0	1	4	0	0	0	0	0	0	0	1	0	1	0	0	0	0	—	0	0	0.00
2000 Iowa	AAA ChC	10	0	0	1	13.2	60	12	7	7	1	0	0	0	7	0	17	0	0	1	2	.333	0	0	4.61
Albuquerque	AAA LA	24	0	0	22	27.1	120	29	16	15	2	1	2	2	11	1	31	3	0	2	0	1.000	0	9	4.94
1992 Cincinnati	NL	5	5	0	0	29	127	33	15	14	1	2	0	1	13	2	23	0	0	2	1	.667	0	0	4.34
1993 Cincinnati	NL	43	9	0	8	98	450	106	72	61	16	9	2	7	45	4	65	5	0	7	10	.412	0	3	5.60
1994 Seattle	AL	46	0	0	40	56.2	236	42	25	18	2	1	2	0	26	0	76	2	0	4	3	.571	0	18	2.86
1995 Seattle	AL	63	0	0	50	71	320	73	42	35	9	2	3	6	30	4	77	3	0	6	5	.545	0	19	4.44
1996 Seattle	AL	50	0	0	26	67.1	285	65	45	44	10	2	2	2	25	3	61	2	0	6	5	.545	0	0	5.88
1997 Seattle	AL	71	0	0	33	96.2	403	91	45	41	14	3	6	3	41	3	92	6	0	10	5	.667	0	8	3.82
1998 Seattle	AL	62	0	0	36	75.1	351	100	66	61	9	8	6	1	26	4	68	4	0	1	10	.091	0	8	7.29
1999 Montreal	NL	53	0	0	17	66	300	60	36	27	6	4	3	4	34	1	64	4	0	1	6	.143	0	2	3.68
Chicago	NL	13	0	0	4	16	65	11	7	5	4	1	0	2	5	1	15	1	0	0	1	.000	0	0	2.81
8 Min. YEARS		189	72	10	66	589.2	2530	527	312	252	43	25	15	32	249	7	542	40	3	32	26	.552	5	19	3.85
8 Maj. YEARS		406	14	0	214	576	2537	581	353	306	71	32	24	26	245	22	541	27	0	37	44	.457	0	59	4.78

Julio Ayala

Pitches: Left **Bats:** Left **Pos:** SP-14; RP-11

Ht: 6'2" **Wt:** 203 **Born:** 4/20/75 **Age:** 26

Year Team	Lg Org	G	GS	CG	GF	IP	BFP	H	R	ER	HR	SH	SF	HB	TBB	IBB	SO	WP	Bk	W	L	Pct.	ShO	Sv	ERA
1996 Everett	A- Sea	12	6	0	2	44	185	43	20	17	2	2	1	4	10	0	28	2	2	1	3	.250	0	0	3.48
1997 Wisconsin	A Sea	36	9	0	13	103	443	114	47	42	4	2	1	4	30	4	81	7	2	11	3	.786	0	3	3.67
1998 Lancaster	A+ Sea	25	25	1	0	139.2	634	166	91	69	14	5	8	1	44	1	129	15	2	10	7	.588	0	0	4.45
2000 Lancaster	A+ Sea	14	3	0	1	26.1	124	34	19	15	4	0	0	4	5	0	20	2	0	4	1	.800	0	0	5.13
New Haven	AA Sea	11	11	1	0	63.1	259	55	21	19	4	2	3	0	23	0	41	3	0	7	1	.875	0	0	2.70
4 Min. YEARS		98	54	2	16	376.1	1645	412	198	162	28	11	13	13	112	5	299	29	6	33	15	.688	1	0	3.87

Mike Ayers

Pitches: Left **Bats:** Left **Pos:** RP-49   **Ht:** 5'10" **Wt:** 206 **Born:** 12/23/73 **Age:** 27

Year Team	Lg Org	G	GS	CG	GF	IP	BFP	H	R	ER	HR	SH	SF	HB	TBB	IBB	SO	WP	Bk	W	L	Pct.	ShO	Sv	ERA
1996 Augusta	A Pit	27	0	0	7	30.1	134	33	21	14	1	2	2	0	8	0	31	4	0	3	0	1.000	0	0	4.15
1997 Lynchburg	A+ Pit	39	0	0	13	63	288	54	38	35	8	4	2	6	44	6	62	4	0	5	4	.556	0	4	5.00
1998 Augusta	A Pit	4	0	0	1	5.2	37	11	13	11	0	0	1	0	6	1	6	3	0	0	1	.000	0	0	17.47
Lynchburg	A+ Pit	34	0	0	15	40.1	188	53	36	34	5	1	2	5	17	0	31	2	1	3	3	.500	0	0	7.59
1999 Lynchburg	A+ Pit	27	0	0	14	36.2	153	34	13	11	1	2	2	1	16	0	28	4	0	1	2	.333	0	2	2.70
Altoona	AA Pit	11	0	0	3	17	70	10	4	3	1	1	1	0	11	0	16	5	0	0	0	—	0	0	1.59
2000 Altoona	AA Pit	38	0	0	12	58.1	250	47	30	21	2	5	1	1	29	2	49	4	0	3	2	.600	0	1	3.24
Nashville	AAA Pit	11	0	0	6	15.2	74	22	11	10	5	0	0	0	6	0	11	1	0	0	0	—	0	1	5.74
5 Min. YEARS		191	0	0	71	267	1194	264	166	139	23	15	11	13	137	9	234	27	1	15	12	.556	0	8	4.69

Jesus Azuaje

Bats: Right **Throws:** Right **Pos:** SS-52; 2B-9; PR-1   **Ht:** 5'10" **Wt:** 177 **Born:** 1/16/73 **Age:** 28

Year Team	Lg Org	G	AB	H	2B	3B	HR	TB	R	RBI	TBB	IBB	SO	HBP	SH	SF	SB	CS	SB%	GDP	Avg	OBP	SLG
1993 Burlington	R+ Cle	62	254	71	10	1	7	104	46	41	22	0	53	0	0	3	19	2	.90	4	.280	.333	.409
Kinston	A+ Cle	3	11	5	2	0	0	7	1	0	2	0	1	0	0	0	0	2	.00	0	.455	.538	.636
1994 Columbus	A Cle	118	450	127	20	1	7	170	77	57	69	0	72	5	6	0	21	7	.75	6	.282	.384	.378
1995 Norfolk	AAA NYM	5	14	6	1	0	0	7	1	0	2	0	2	0	0	0	1	1	.50	0	.429	.500	.500
Binghamton	AA NYM	24	86	17	5	0	0	22	10	8	11	0	25	2	3	0	1	1	.50	1	.198	.303	.256
St. Lucie	A+ NYM	91	306	73	5	1	2	86	35	20	36	1	55	7	11	0	14	9	.61	5	.239	.332	.281
1996 Capital Cty	A NYM	1	3	2	1	0	0	3	1	1	0	0	0	0	0	0	1	0	—	0	.667	.500	1.000
Binghamton	AA NYM	86	249	59	16	0	2	81	36	26	45	1	33	1	3	1	5	6	.45	5	.237	.355	.325
1997 Binghamton	AA NYM	100	331	92	15	1	6	127	50	37	45	1	42	8	8	4	11	9	.55	13	.278	.374	.384
Norfolk	AAA NYM	22	49	15	3	0	1	21	11	6	7	1	8	2	0	0	1	0	1.00	3	.306	.414	.429
1998 Norfolk	AAA NYM	10	33	7	3	0	0	10	1	1	2	0	6	0	1	0	0	0	—	3	.212	.257	.303
Binghamton	AA NYM	110	384	106	22	1	7	151	66	52	52	0	48	4	7	5	15	1	.94	8	.276	.364	.393
1999 Huntsville	AA Mil	119	391	110	21	0	10	161	63	60	70	4	26	11	0	7	34	8	.81	13	.281	.399	.412
2000 Toledo	AAA Det	61	235	51	9	0	4	72	32	13	23	0	17	4	1	2	3	2	.60	9	.217	.295	.306
8 Min. YEARS		812	2796	741	133	5	46	1022	430	322	386	8	388	44	42	23	125	48	.72	69	.265	.360	.366

Brandon Backe

Bats: Right **Throws:** Right **Pos:** OF-77; SS-38; 2B-1; 3B-1; PH-1   **Ht:** 6'0" **Wt:** 182 **Born:** 4/5/78 **Age:** 23

Year Team	Lg Org	G	AB	H	2B	3B	HR	TB	R	RBI	TBB	IBB	SO	HBP	SH	SF	SB	CS	SB%	GDP	Avg	OBP	SLG
1998 Hudson Val	A- TB	11	26	6	2	0	0	8	3	1	2	0	7	1	0	0	0	0	—	0	.231	.310	.308
Princeton	R+ TB	27	92	23	5	1	0	30	14	7	12	0	31	1	0	1	1	1	.50	1	.250	.340	.326
1999 Chston-SC	A TB	84	272	63	11	2	9	105	43	40	35	1	81	6	6	3	3	5	.38	8	.232	.329	.386
St. Pete	A+ TB	41	132	26	6	1	1	37	21	11	21	0	34	3	6	2	0	3	.00	4	.197	.316	.280
2000 St. Pete	A+ TB	112	376	93	25	6	1	133	38	34	31	2	99	10	4	5	3	6	.33	8	.247	.318	.354
Orlando	AA TB	4	8	2	0	0	0	2	1	0	2	0	4	0	0	0	0	2	.00	0	.250	.400	.250
3 Min. YEARS		279	906	213	49	10	11	315	120	93	103	3	253	21	16	11	7	17	.29	21	.235	.324	.348

Mike Bacsik

Pitches: Left **Bats:** Left **Pos:** SP-27   **Ht:** 6'3" **Wt:** 190 **Born:** 11/11/77 **Age:** 23

Year Team	Lg Org	G	GS	CG	GF	IP	BFP	H	R	ER	HR	SH	SF	HB	TBB	IBB	SO	WP	Bk	W	L	Pct.	ShO	Sv	ERA
1996 Burlington	R+ Cle	13	13	1	0	69.2	276	49	23	17	3	0	2	1	14	0	61	3	1	4	2	.667	0	0	2.20
1997 Columbus	A Cle	28	28	0	0	139	622	163	94	84	16	7	3	9	47	1	100	12	2	4	14	.222	0	0	5.44
1998 Kinston	A+ Cle	27	27	1	0	165.2	667	147	64	53	17	5	4	4	37	3	128	4	0	10	9	.526	0	0	2.88
1999 Akron	AA Cle	26	26	1	0	149.1	647	164	84	77	24	5	5	7	47	0	84	4	0	11	11	.500	0	0	4.64
2000 Kinston	A+ Cle	11	11	0	0	65	269	72	36	33	4	1	2	2	8	0	56	0	0	3	6	.333	0	0	4.57
Akron	AA Cle	11	11	1	0	71.1	287	61	23	22	3	4	1	3	15	0	44	3	0	7	1	.875	0	0	2.78
Buffalo	AAA Cle	5	5	0	0	29	124	31	20	18	7	0	2	0	7	0	9	0	0	0	3	.000	0	0	5.59
5 Min. YEARS		121	121	4	0	689	2892	687	344	304	74	22	19	26	175	4	482	26	3	39	46	.459	1	0	3.97

Brooks Badeaux

Bats: Both **Throws:** Right **Pos:** 2B-78; SS-12; 3B-12; PH-3; PR-2; DH-1   **Ht:** 5'10" **Wt:** 175 **Born:** 10/20/76 **Age:** 24

Year Team	Lg Org	G	AB	H	2B	3B	HR	TB	R	RBI	TBB	IBB	SO	HBP	SH	SF	SB	CS	SB%	GDP	Avg	OBP	SLG
1998 Hudson Val	A- TB	68	267	80	9	4	1	100	48	36	29	0	47	3	7	2	11	4	.73	4	.300	.372	.375
1999 St. Pete	A+ TB	96	342	97	6	1	0	105	68	19	57	1	44	2	5	0	2	7	.22	4	.284	.389	.307
Orlando	AA TB	3	2	1	0	0	1	4	1	1	0	0	0	0	0	0	0	0	—	0	.500	.500	2.000
2000 Orlando	AA TB	73	260	68	8	6	1	91	37	27	34	1	29	5	5	1	2	2	.50	5	.262	.357	.350
Durham	AAA TB	33	98	32	2	1	0	36	11	3	9	0	21	0	1	0	1	1	1.00	1	.327	.383	.367
3 Min. YEARS		273	969	278	25	12	3	336	165	86	129	2	141	10	18	3	16	13	.55	14	.287	.375	.347

Benito Baez

Pitches: Left **Bats:** Left **Pos:** RP-37   **Ht:** 6'0" **Wt:** 160 **Born:** 5/6/77 **Age:** 24

Year Team	Lg Org	G	GS	CG	GF	IP	BFP	H	R	ER	HR	SH	SF	HB	TBB	IBB	SO	WP	Bk	W	L	Pct.	ShO	Sv	ERA
1995 Athletics	R Oak	14	11	0	0	70	303	64	35	26	2	2	2	4	28	0	83	2	0	5	1	.833	0	0	3.34
1996 W Michigan	A Oak	32	20	0	4	129.2	557	123	60	50	6	5	6	2	52	1	92	4	1	8	4	.667	0	4	3.47
1997 Visalia	A+ Oak	16	15	1	0	96.2	393	83	40	38	8	1	2	1	28	0	87	0	1	5	5	.500	0	0	3.54
Huntsville	AA Oak	15	7	0	2	42.1	206	64	47	43	8	2	4	1	22	1	27	3	2	2	4	.333	0	0	9.14
1998 Huntsville	AA Oak	34	17	0	11	122.2	579	161	92	79	12	3	5	4	64	0	83	7	1	3	8	.273	0	0	5.80

Year Team	Lg Org	G	GS	CG	GF	IP	BFP	H	R	ER	HR	SH	SF	HB	TBB	IBB	SO	WP	Bk	W	L	Pct.	ShO	Sv	ERA
1999 Midland	AA Oak	37	0	0	9	54.1	243	68	35	33	5	3	7	0	15	2	51	2	2	5	1	.833	0	3	5.47
Vancouver	AAA Oak	11	0	0	4	18	76	18	7	7	2	0	0	0	7	0	19	1	1	0	2	.000	0	1	3.50
2000 Midland	AA Oak	37	0	0	9	53.1	246	61	35	29	4	1	1	1	27	3	50	4	0	5	4	.556	0	0	4.89
6 Min. YEARS		196	70	2	39	587	2603	642	351	305	47	17	27	15	243	7	492	23	8	33	29	.532	0	8	4.68

Danys Baez

Pitches: Right **Bats:** Right **Pos:** SP-27   **Ht:** 6'3" **Wt:** 225 **Born:** 9/10/77 **Age:** 23

Year Team	Lg Org	G	GS	CG	GF	IP	BFP	H	R	ER	HR	SH	SF	HB	TBB	IBB	SO	WP	Bk	W	L	Pct.	ShO	Sv	ERA
2000 Kinston	A+ Cle	9	9	0	0	49.2	221	45	29	26	5	3	1	6	20	0	56	4	1	2	2	.500	0	0	4.71
Akron	AA Cle	18	18	0	0	102.2	426	98	46	42	6	5	6	5	32	0	77	7	0	4	9	.308	0	0	3.68
1 Min. YEARS		27	27	0	0	152.1	647	143	75	68	11	8	7	11	52	0	133	11	1	6	11	.353	0	0	4.02

Kevin Baez

Bats: Right **Throws:** Right **Pos:** SS-61; 3B-34; 2B-25; DH-3; PH-3   **Ht:** 5'11" **Wt:** 175 **Born:** 1/10/67 **Age:** 34

Year Team	Lg Org	G	AB	H	2B	3B	HR	TB	R	RBI	TBB	IBB	SO	HBP	SH	SF	SB	CS	SB%	GDP	Avg	OBP	SLG
1988 Little Fall	A- NYM	70	218	58	7	1	1	70	23	19	32	1	30	2	2	3	7	3	.70	3	.266	.361	.321
1989 Columbia	A NYM	123	426	108	25	1	5	150	59	44	58	3	53	6	9	3	11	9	.55	5	.254	.349	.352
1990 Jackson	AA NYM	106	327	76	11	0	2	93	29	29	37	4	44	2	11	2	3	4	.43	7	.232	.313	.284
1991 Tidewater	AAA NYM	65	210	36	8	0	0	44	18	13	12	1	32	1	4	4	0	1	.00	5	.171	.226	.210
1992 Tidewater	AAA NYM	109	352	83	16	1	2	107	30	33	13	1	57	4	5	5	1	1	.50	9	.236	.267	.304
1993 Norfolk	AAA NYM	63	209	54	11	1	2	73	23	21	20	1	29	1	2	1	0	2	.00	3	.258	.325	.349
1994 Rochester	AAA Bal	110	359	85	17	1	2	110	50	42	40	0	52	2	5	5	2	7	.22	13	.237	.313	.306
1995 Toledo	AAA Det	116	376	87	13	2	4	116	30	37	22	1	57	1	10	2	1	6	.14	13	.231	.274	.309
1996 Toledo	AAA Det	98	302	74	12	3	11	125	34	44	24	0	53	2	5	4	3	0	1.00	6	.245	.301	.414
1997 Salt Lake	AAA Min	112	383	105	25	3	5	151	38	54	29	0	74	4	3	6	3	4	.43	7	.274	.327	.394
1998 Chattanoops	AA Cin	49	180	46	10	0	0	56	30	22	26	1	27	1	1	2	0	1	.00	6	.256	.349	.311
Indianapols	AAA Cin	49	137	36	5	0	1	44	21	12	19	0	26	0	2	1	0	1	.00	6	.263	.350	.321
1999 Indianapols	AAA Cin	20	40	12	3	0	0	15	4	7	11	0	4	0	1	0	1	0	1.00	2	.300	.451	.375
Norfolk	AAA NYM	60	175	46	5	0	1	54	15	26	17	1	21	2	0	3	2	0	1.00	2	.263	.330	.309
2000 Norfolk	AAA NYM	122	407	113	27	0	5	155	52	50	51	1	50	6	4	8	4	11	.27	8	.278	.360	.381
1990 New York	NL	5	12	2	1	0	0	3	0	0	0	0	0	0	0	0	0	0	—	2	.167	.167	.250
1992 New York	NL	6	13	2	0	0	0	2	0	0	0	0	0	0	0	0	0	0	—	1	.154	.154	.154
1993 New York	NL	52	126	23	9	0	0	32	10	7	13	1	17	0	4	0	0	0	—	1	.183	.259	.254
13 Min. YEARS		1272	4101	1019	195	13	41	1363	456	453	411	15	609	37	65	49	38	50	.43	95	.248	.319	.332
3 Maj. YEARS		63	151	27	10	0	0	37	10	7	13	1	17	0	4	0	0	0	—	4	.179	.244	.245

Cory Bailey

Pitches: Right **Bats:** Right **Pos:** RP-55   **Ht:** 6'1" **Wt:** 200 **Born:** 1/24/71 **Age:** 30

Year Team	Lg Org	G	GS	CG	GF	IP	BFP	H	R	ER	HR	SH	SF	HB	TBB	IBB	SO	WP	Bk	W	L	Pct.	ShO	Sv	ERA
1991 Red Sox	R Bos	1	0	1	0	2	9	2	1	0	0	0	0	0	1	0	1	0	0	0	0	—	0	1	0.00
Elmira	A- Bos	28	0	0	25	39	151	19	10	8	2	1	0	3	12	0	54	2	0	2	4	.333	0	15	1.85
1992 Lynchburg	A+ Bos	49	0	0	43	66.1	272	43	20	18	3	6	2	2	30	2	87	5	0	5	7	.417	0	23	2.44
1993 Pawtucket	AAA Bos	52	0	0	40	65.2	264	48	21	21	1	2	1	2	31	3	59	5	1	4	5	.444	0	20	2.88
1994 Pawtucket	AAA Bos	53	0	0	43	61.1	264	44	25	22	4	4	0	1	38	2	52	7	0	4	3	.571	0	19	3.23
1995 Louisville	AAA StL	55	0	0	40	59.1	258	51	30	30	6	6	2	0	30	4	49	7	0	5	3	.625	0	25	4.55
1996 Louisville	AAA StL	22	0	0	8	34	151	29	22	22	1	3	1	0	20	5	27	4	1	2	4	.333	0	1	5.82
1997 Okla City	AAA Tex	42	0	0	33	50.1	219	49	20	19	1	3	1	0	23	7	38	4	0	3	4	.429	0	15	3.40
Phoenix	AAA SF	13	0	0	11	17.1	70	16	4	3	0	1	1	0	6	1	14	1	0	4	0	1.000	0	3	1.56
1998 Fresno	AAA SF	57	0	0	25	94.2	375	79	31	26	4	1	2	3	18	4	76	4	2	7	2	.778	0	10	2.47
1999 Fresno	AAA SF	43	0	0	39	46.1	200	47	24	17	7	2	0	0	17	0	52	3	1	2	1	.667	0	18	3.30
2000 Nashville	AAA Pit	55	0	0	41	72.2	318	76	32	28	2	4	5	1	35	10	62	8	1	2	4	.333	0	12	3.47
1993 Boston	AL	11	0	0	5	15.2	66	12	7	6	0	1	1	0	12	3	11	2	1	0	1	.000	0	0	3.45
1994 Boston	AL	5	0	0	2	4.1	24	10	6	6	2	0	0	0	3	1	4	0	0	0	1	.000	0	0	12.46
1995 St. Louis	NL	3	0	0	0	3.2	15	2	3	3	0	0	0	0	2	1	5	1	0	0	0	—	0	0	7.36
1996 St. Louis	NL	51	0	0	12	57	251	57	21	19	1	2	1	1	30	3	38	3	0	5	2	.714	0	0	3.00
1997 San Francisco	NL	7	0	0	4	9.2	45	15	9	9	1	0	1	0	4	0	5	0	0	0	1	.000	0	0	8.38
1998 San Francisco	NL	5	0	0	1	3.1	13	2	1	1	1	0	0	0	1	0	2	0	0	0	0	—	0	0	2.70
10 Min. YEARS		470	0	0	349	609	2551	503	240	214	31	33	16	11	261	38	571	50	6	40	37	.519	0	162	3.16
6 Maj. YEARS		82	0	0	24	93.2	414	98	47	44	5	3	3	1	52	8	65	6	1	5	5	.500	0	0	4.23

Rod Bair

Bats: Right **Throws:** Right **Pos:** OF-25; DH-2   **Ht:** 5'11" **Wt:** 195 **Born:** 10/29/74 **Age:** 26

Year Team	Lg Org	G	AB	H	2B	3B	HR	TB	R	RBI	TBB	IBB	SO	HBP	SH	SF	SB	CS	SB%	GDP	Avg	OBP	SLG
1996 Portland	A- Col	56	221	48	11	2	4	75	34	33	17	2	29	7	5	4	9	4	.69	2	.217	.289	.339
1997 Salem	A+ Col	16	44	12	3	0	0	15	5	6	0	0	6	2	3	1	2	0	1.00	1	.273	.298	.341
Asheville	A Col	91	356	100	20	1	8	146	50	51	13	1	51	11	3	1	9	6	.60	11	.281	.325	.410
1998 Salem	A+ Col	114	425	127	42	5	8	203	62	60	24	3	64	13	0	5	12	6	.67	11	.299	.351	.478
1999 Carolina	AA Col	125	472	143	34	6	13	228	70	81	28	0	78	16	0	6	14	12	.54	11	.303	.358	.483
2000 Carolina	AA Col	27	89	15	6	0	1	24	13	6	12	1	16	5	0	1	1	2	.33	2	.169	.299	.270
5 Min. YEARS		429	1607	445	116	14	34	691	234	237	94	7	244	54	11	18	47	30	.61	38	.277	.334	.430

Jason Baker

Pitches: Right **Bats:** Right **Pos:** SP-18; RP-6 **Ht:** 6'4" **Wt:** 195 **Born:** 11/21/74 **Age:** 26

Year Team	Lg Org	G	GS	CG	GF	IP	BFP	H	R	ER	HR	SH	SF	HB	TBB	IBB	SO	WP	Bk	W	L	Pct.	ShO	Sv	ERA
1993 Expos	R Mon	7	7	0	0	32	132	26	14	8	0	1	3	1	11	0	24	6	0	1	1	.500	0	0	2.25
1994 Vermont	A- Mon	13	13	0	0	61.2	279	55	44	33	4	0	2	5	40	0	21	20	1	6	5	.545	0	0	4.82
1995 Vermont	A- Mon	14	14	0	0	72	317	59	40	33	2	1	0	5	47	1	57	11	0	6	5	.545	0	0	4.13
1996 Delmarva	A Mon	27	27	2	0	160.1	688	127	70	50	6	3	3	16	77	0	147	22	0	9	7	.563	0	0	2.81
1997 Expos	R Mon	2	2	0	0	7	28	4	0	0	0	0	0	1	3	0	8	0	0	0	0	—	0	0	0.00
Wst Plm Bch	A+ Mon	15	14	1	0	72	326	90	55	48	10	4	3	2	31	0	47	11	2	3	4	.429	1	0	6.00
1998 Harrisburg	AA Mon	25	20	0	2	103.2	476	95	69	65	18	1	3	8	71	1	88	11	1	4	10	.286	0	0	5.64
1999 Ottawa	AAA Mon	11	0	0	7	12.2	69	18	12	12	1	1	0	0	14	0	9	4	0	1	0	1.000	0	0	8.53
Harrisburg	AA Mon	23	1	0	7	31.1	150	29	22	21	4	2	2	1	28	0	24	1	0	1	3	.250	0	2	6.03
2000 Omaha	AAA KC	7	6	0	1	36	161	40	28	25	9	0	2	2	14	0	18	4	0	1	3	.250	0	0	6.25
Wichita	AA KC	17	12	0	1	69	323	87	50	48	8	1	2	6	35	0	49	6	0	4	5	.444	0	0	6.26
8 Min. YEARS		161	116	3	18	657.2	2949	630	404	343	62	14	20	47	371	2	492	96	4	36	43	.456	1	2	4.69

Ryan Balfe

Bats: Both **Throws:** Right **Pos:** OF-108; DH-11; 1B-7; PH-7; 3B-2 **Ht:** 6'1" **Wt:** 180 **Born:** 11/11/75 **Age:** 25

Year Team	Lg Org	G	AB	H	2B	3B	HR	TB	R	RBI	TBB	IBB	SO	HBP	SH	SF	SB	CS	SB%	GDP	Avg	OBP	SLG
1994 Bristol	R+ Det	43	121	26	3	0	1	32	12	11	23	0	38	1	1	1	2	4	.33	1	.215	.342	.264
1995 Fayettevlle	A Det	113	398	104	20	2	10	158	53	49	48	0	85	9	0	1	1	1	.50	11	.261	.353	.397
1996 Lakeland	A+ Det	92	347	97	21	1	11	153	48	66	24	2	66	5	0	3	3	0	1.00	13	.280	.332	.441
1997 Tigers	R Det	2	7	4	0	0	1	7	2	1	1	0	1	0	0	0	0	0	—	0	.571	.625	1.000
Lakeland	A+ Det	86	312	84	13	2	13	140	40	48	24	3	75	3	1	6	1	1	.50	7	.269	.322	.449
1998 Mobile	AA SD	23	69	16	5	1	2	29	9	11	8	0	10	0	0	0	1	0	1.00	3	.232	.312	.420
1999 Mobile	AA SD	111	400	112	31	3	11	182	69	70	50	4	95	4	0	3	0	1	.00	18	.280	.363	.455
2000 Mobile	AA SD	130	462	121	21	4	12	186	61	66	46	2	120	9	0	4	3	3	.50	12	.262	.338	.403
7 Min. YEARS		600	2116	564	114	13	61	887	294	322	224	11	490	31	2	18	11	10	.52	65	.267	.343	.419

Jeff Ball

Bats: Right **Throws:** Right **Pos:** OF-31; PH-17; DH-15; 1B-7; 3B-5; 2B-1 **Ht:** 5'10" **Wt:** 185 **Born:** 4/17/69 **Age:** 32

Year Team	Lg Org	G	AB	H	2B	3B	HR	TB	R	RBI	TBB	IBB	SO	HBP	SH	SF	SB	CS	SB%	GDP	Avg	OBP	SLG
1990 Auburn	A- Hou	70	263	76	18	1	5	111	40	38	22	1	35	4	3	5	20	5	.80	4	.289	.347	.422
1991 Osceola	A+ Hou	118	392	96	15	3	5	132	53	51	49	4	74	10	3	4	20	8	.71	9	.245	.341	.337
1992 Jackson	AA Hou	93	278	53	14	1	5	84	27	24	20	1	58	10	2	1	5	3	.63	9	.191	.269	.302
1993 Quad City	A Hou	112	389	114	28	2	14	188	68	76	58	3	63	7	1	5	40	19	.68	11	.293	.390	.483
1994 Jackson	AA Hou	111	358	113	30	3	13	188	65	57	34	3	74	5	5	3	9	8	.53	9	.316	.380	.525
1995 Tucson	AAA Hou	110	362	106	25	2	4	147	58	56	25	3	66	7	4	5	11	5	.69	13	.293	.346	.406
1996 Tucson	AAA Hou	116	429	139	31	2	19	231	64	73	34	1	83	1	0	1	10	8	.56	12	.324	.374	.538
1997 Phoenix	AAA SF	126	470	151	38	3	18	249	90	103	58	5	84	5	1	7	10	4	.71	12	.321	.396	.530
1998 Fresno	AAA SF	124	456	135	29	0	21	227	81	80	55	6	86	8	0	1	5	2	.71	18	.296	.381	.498
1999 Vancouver	AAA Oak	96	346	107	22	2	8	157	50	51	37	0	57	3	7	4	7	2	.78	19	.309	.377	.454
2000 Fresno	AAA SF	72	223	54	8	1	5	79	32	11	15	1	45	5	1	0	1	1	.50	9	.242	.305	.354
1998 San Francisco	NL	2	4	1	0	0	0	1	0	0	0	0	0	0	0	0	0	0	—	0	.250	.250	.250
11 Min. YEARS		1148	3966	1144	258	20	117	1793	628	620	407	28	725	65	27	36	138	65	.68	124	.288	.361	.452

Willie Banks

Pitches: Right **Bats:** Right **Pos:** SP-9 **Ht:** 6'1" **Wt:** 200 **Born:** 2/27/69 **Age:** 32

Year Team	Lg Org	G	GS	CG	GF	IP	BFP	H	R	ER	HR	SH	SF	HB	TBB	IBB	SO	WP	Bk	W	L	Pct.	ShO	Sv	ERA
1987 Elizabethtn	R+ Min	13	13	0	0	65.2	332	73	71	51	3	3	4	3	62	0	71	28	3	1	8	.111	0	0	6.99
1988 Kenosha	A Min	24	24	0	0	125.2	580	109	73	52	3	2	5	4	107	2	113	14	2	10	10	.500	0	0	3.72
1989 Visalia	A+ Min	27	27	7	0	174	723	122	70	50	5	2	7	10	85	0	173	22	1	12	9	.571	4	0	2.59
Orlando	AA Min	1	1	0	0	7	30	10	4	4	0	0	0	0	0	0	9	2	0	1	0	1.000	0	0	5.14
1990 Orlando	AA Min	28	28	1	0	162.2	737	161	93	71	15	1	8	7	98	0	114	6	1	7	9	.438	0	0	3.93
1991 Portland	AAA Min	25	24	1	0	146.1	653	156	81	74	6	2	4	6	76	1	63	14	1	9	8	.529	1	0	4.55
1992 Portland	AAA Min	11	11	2	0	75	310	62	20	16	2	2	1	0	34	0	41	5	2	6	1	.857	1	0	1.92
1997 Columbus	AAA NYY	33	24	1	5	154	662	164	87	73	18	3	3	4	45	0	130	7	0	14	5	.737	0	3	4.27
2000 Norfolk	AAA NYM	9	9	0	0	51.1	224	56	32	29	5	0	0	2	25	2	20	5	1	2	4	.333	0	0	5.08
1991 Minnesota	AL	5	3	0	2	17.1	85	21	15	11	1	0	0	0	12	0	16	3	0	1	1	.500	0	0	5.71
1992 Minnesota	AL	16	12	0	2	71	324	80	46	45	6	2	5	2	37	0	37	5	1	4	4	.500	0	0	5.70
1993 Minnesota	AL	31	30	0	1	171.1	754	186	91	77	17	4	4	3	78	2	138	9	5	11	12	.478	0	0	4.04
1994 Chicago	NL	23	23	1	0	138.1	598	139	88	83	16	5	2	2	56	3	91	8	1	8	12	.400	1	0	5.40
1995 Chicago	NL	10	0	0	2	11.2	73	27	23	20	5	1	1	0	12	4	9	3	0	0	1	.000	0	0	15.43
Los Angeles	NL	6	6	0	0	29	138	36	21	13	2	1	1	1	16	2	23	4	1	2	0	1.000	0	0	4.03
Florida	NL	9	9	0	0	50	219	43	27	24	7	4	1	1	30	1	30	2	0	2	3	.400	0	0	4.32
1997 New York	AL	5	1	0	1	14	57	9	3	3	0	2	0	1	6	0	13	1	0	3	0	1.000	0	0	1.93
1998 New York	AL	9	0	0	5	14.1	77	20	16	16	4	2	0	1	12	2	8	1	0	1	1	.500	0	0	10.05
Arizona	NL	33	0	0	8	43.2	188	34	21	15	2	4	1	1	25	2	32	4	1	1	2	.333	0	1	3.09
8 Min. YEARS		171	161	12	6	961.2	4251	913	531	420	57	15	32	36	532	5	734	103	11	62	54	.534	6	3	3.93
7 Maj. YEARS		147	84	1	21	560.2	2513	595	351	307	60	25	15	12	284	16	392	39	9	31	38	.449	1	1	4.93

Travis Baptist

Pitches: Left **Bats:** Left **Pos:** RP-18; SP-16 **Ht:** 6'0" **Wt:** 195 **Born:** 12/30/71 **Age:** 29

Year Team	Lg Org	G	GS	CG	GF	IP	BFP	H	R	ER	HR	SH	SF	HB	TBB	IBB	SO	WP	Bk	W	L	Pct.	ShO	Sv	ERA
1991 Medcine Hat	R+ Tor	14	14	1	0	85.1	379	100	52	39	5	2	2	1	21	0	48	4	1	4	4	.500	1	0	4.11
1992 Myrtle Bch	A Tor	19	19	2	0	118	455	81	24	19	2	6	2	4	22	0	97	5	4	11	2	.846	1	0	1.45

15

Year Team	Lg Org	G	GS	CG	GF	IP	BFP	H	R	ER	HR	SH	SF	HB	TBB	IBB	SO	WP	Bk	W	L	Pct.	ShO	Sv	ERA
1993 Knoxville	AA Tor	7	7	0	0	33	139	37	17	15	2	2	3	2	7	0	24	3	0	1	3	.250	0	0	4.09
1994 Syracuse	AAA Tor	24	22	1	0	122.2	539	145	80	62	20	3	4	0	33	2	42	6	1	8	8	.500	0	0	4.55
1995 Syracuse	AAA Tor	15	13	0	0	79	356	83	56	38	12	2	3	2	32	2	52	4	1	3	4	.429	0	0	4.33
1996 Syracuse	AAA Tor	30	21	2	1	141	633	187	91	85	15	5	10	2	48	2	77	7	2	7	6	.538	0	0	5.43
1997 New Britain	AA Min	36	3	0	7	60.2	247	49	27	23	6	8	1	2	26	2	50	4	0	5	6	.455	0	0	3.41
Salt Lake	AAA Min	7	6	1	0	47.2	194	47	16	11	3	0	1	1	9	0	28	2	1	4	1	.800	1	0	2.08
1998 Salt Lake	AAA Min	21	21	1	0	135.2	559	128	53	47	12	3	0	4	41	1	98	7	1	8	5	.615	0	0	3.12
1999 Salt Lake	AAA Min	17	6	0	5	38.2	174	46	24	23	6	0	0	1	17	0	23	3	0	1	3	.250	0	1	5.35
Pawtucket	AAA Bos	17	3	0	2	42.1	195	49	27	25	5	1	0	1	19	0	30	2	0	4	2	.667	0	0	5.31
2000 Nashville	AAA Pit	34	16	3	6	133	578	146	85	83	17	8	4	7	51	3	93	11	2	4	10	.286	0	0	5.62
1998 Minnesota	AL	13	0	0	4	27	123	34	18	17	5	0	6	0	11	1	11	0	0	0	1	.000	0	0	5.67
10 Min. YEARS		241	151	11	21	1037	4448	1098	552	470	105	40	30	27	326	12	662	58	14	60	54	.526	3	1	4.08

Josh Bard

Bats: Both **Throws:** Right **Pos:** C-94; PH-3; DH-2 **Ht:** 6'3" **Wt:** 205 **Born:** 3/30/78 **Age:** 23

Year Team	Lg Org	G	AB	H	2B	3B	HR	TB	R	RBI	TBB	IBB	SO	HBP	SH	SF	SB	CS	SB%	GDP	Avg	OBP	SLG
2000 Salem	A+ Col	93	309	88	17	0	2	111	40	25	32	1	33	1	1	2	3	1	.75	6	.285	.352	.359
Colo Sprngs	AAA Col	4	17	4	0	0	0	4	0	1	0	0	2	0	0	0	0	0	—	0	.235	.235	.235
1 Min. YEARS		97	326	92	17	0	2	115	40	26	32	1	35	1	1	2	3	1	.75	6	.282	.346	.353

Richie Barker

Pitches: Right **Bats:** Right **Pos:** RP-20 **Ht:** 6'2" **Wt:** 220 **Born:** 10/29/72 **Age:** 28

Year Team	Lg Org	G	GS	CG	GF	IP	BFP	H	R	ER	HR	SH	SF	HB	TBB	IBB	SO	WP	Bk	W	L	Pct.	ShO	Sv	ERA
1994 Huntington	R+ ChC	17	0	0	6	39.1	187	36	35	26	3	2	2	7	25	0	22	2	3	2	4	.333	0	0	5.95
1995 Rockford	A ChC	32	0	0	15	43.2	196	45	20	18	2	1	0	2	20	1	23	5	0	2	0	1.000	0	1	3.71
1996 Daytona	A+ ChC	17	0	0	7	27	135	34	23	17	0	2	1	2	18	0	14	10	0	4	0	1.000	0	0	5.67
Rockford	A ChC	19	0	0	9	33	156	42	24	19	2	1	4	0	15	0	23	3	0	1	1	.500	0	1	5.18
1997 Daytona	A+ ChC	29	1	0	10	51	220	49	27	19	3	2	1	3	15	1	38	7	1	2	1	.667	0	1	3.35
Orlando	AA ChC	19	0	0	7	30	121	25	17	11	5	0	1	2	7	0	19	2	0	0	1	.000	0	0	3.30
1998 West Tenn	AA ChC	51	0	0	42	53.2	227	51	22	16	3	4	0	2	17	0	23	1	1	2	5	.286	0	2	2.68
Iowa	AAA ChC	16	0	0	5	22.1	106	31	14	12	2	2	0	0	5	1	21	4	0	3	1	.750	0	0	4.84
1999 Iowa	AAA ChC	55	2	0	25	74	326	72	37	35	7	3	1	6	30	2	52	7	1	4	4	.500	0	7	4.26
2000 Eugene	A- ChC	10	0	0	9	11	43	6	5	4	2	0	0	1	4	0	11	0	0	1	0	1.000	0	4	3.27
Iowa	AAA ChC	10	0	0	2	13	70	20	12	11	0	0	0	1	9	0	10	3	1	0	1	.000	0	1	7.62
1999 Chicago	NL	5	0	0	1	5	25	6	4	4	0	0	0	1	4	1	3	1	0	0	0	—	0	0	7.20
7 Min. YEARS		275	3	0	137	398	1787	411	236	188	29	17	10	26	165	5	256	44	7	20	19	.513	0	33	4.25

Andy Barkett

Bats: Left **Throws:** Left **Pos:** 1B-63; OF-23; DH-5; PH-3 **Ht:** 6'1" **Wt:** 205 **Born:** 9/5/74 **Age:** 26

Year Team	Lg Org	G	AB	H	2B	3B	HR	TB	R	RBI	TBB	IBB	SO	HBP	SH	SF	SB	CS	SB%	GDP	Avg	OBP	SLG
1995 Butte	R+ Tex	45	162	54	11	5	5	90	33	51	33	2	39	3	0	4	1	0	1.00	1	.333	.446	.556
Chston-SC	A Tex	21	78	17	6	0	0	23	7	12	10	0	27	0	0	3	0	3	.00	3	.218	.297	.295
1996 Charlotte	A+ Tex	115	392	112	22	3	6	158	57	54	57	2	59	5	0	4	3	1	.75	6	.286	.380	.403
1997 Tulsa	AA Tex	130	471	141	34	8	8	215	82	65	63	2	86	5	1	2	1	3	.25	15	.299	.386	.456
1998 Tulsa	AA Tex	43	157	42	11	1	2	61	23	31	27	0	22	1	0	1	0	0	—	2	.268	.376	.389
Oklahoma	AAA Tex	80	255	80	17	5	4	119	38	36	35	2	43	0	0	3	3	4	.43	6	.314	.392	.467
1999 Oklahoma	AAA Tex	132	486	149	32	5	10	221	70	76	44	4	71	6	0	5	7	7	.50	18	.307	.368	.455
2000 Oklahoma	AAA Tex	13	45	8	2	0	0	10	4	1	2	0	6	0	0	0	0	0	—	0	.178	.213	.222
Richmond	AAA Atl	75	260	63	17	1	6	100	22	38	16	1	37	2	2	3	4	2	.67	6	.242	.288	.385
6 Min. YEARS		654	2306	666	152	28	41	997	336	364	287	13	390	22	3	25	19	20	.49	57	.289	.369	.432

Brian Barkley

Pitches: Left **Bats:** Left **Pos:** SP-12; RP-8 **Ht:** 6'2" **Wt:** 185 **Born:** 12/8/75 **Age:** 25

Year Team	Lg Org	G	GS	CG	GF	IP	BFP	H	R	ER	HR	SH	SF	HB	TBB	IBB	SO	WP	Bk	W	L	Pct.	ShO	Sv	ERA
1994 Red Sox	R Bos	4	3	0	0	18.2	71	11	7	2	1	1	0	0	4	0	14	2	1	0	1	.000	0	0	0.96
1995 Sarasota	A+ Bos	24	24	2	0	146.2	611	147	66	53	5	2	3	5	37	3	70	4	1	8	10	.444	2	0	3.25
1996 Trenton	AA Bos	22	21	0	0	119.2	535	126	79	76	17	6	5	5	56	4	89	7	2	8	6	.571	0	0	5.72
1997 Trenton	AA Bos	29	29	4	0	178.2	797	208	113	98	18	3	6	3	79	0	121	3	2	12	9	.571	0	0	4.94
1998 Pawtucket	AAA Bos	23	23	1	0	139.1	609	161	81	76	22	3	10	7	50	4	88	5	2	7	9	.438	0	0	4.91
1999 Sarasota	A+ Bos	1	0	0	0	3	12	2	0	0	0	0	0	0	1	0	2	0	0	1	0	1.000	0	0	0.00
Trenton	AA Bos	7	7	0	0	35.1	135	32	10	10	2	2	0	2	6	0	18	0	0	5	0	1.000	0	0	2.55
Pawtucket	AAA Bos	3	3	0	0	14	63	11	9	8	2	1	1	1	7	0	5	1	0	0	1	.000	0	0	5.14
2000 Red Sox	R Bos	1	0	0	0	2	8	2	0	0	0	0	0	0	1	0	1	0	0	0	0	—	0	0	0.00
Trenton	AA Bos	17	12	2	0	69.1	313	85	44	40	1	3	4	4	29	0	65	1	1	5	5	.500	0	0	5.19
Pawtucket	AAA Bos	2	0	0	1	4	15	3	2	2	0	1	0	1	0	0	1	0	0	0	0	—	0	0	4.50
1998 Boston	AL	6	0	0	0	11	59	16	13	12	2	0	2	1	9	1	2	1	0	0	0	—	0	0	9.82
7 Min. YEARS		133	122	9	1	730.2	3169	788	411	365	68	19	30	27	271	11	474	23	9	46	43	.517	2	0	4.50

Brian Barnes

Pitches: Left **Bats:** Left **Pos:** RP-47; SP-3 **Ht:** 5'9" **Wt:** 170 **Born:** 3/25/67 **Age:** 34

Year Team	Lg Org	G	GS	CG	GF	IP	BFP	H	R	ER	HR	SH	SF	HB	TBB	IBB	SO	WP	Bk	W	L	Pct.	ShO	Sv	ERA
1989 Jamestown	A- Mon	2	2	0	0	9	33	4	1	1	0	0	0	0	3	0	15	1	1	1	0	1.000	0	0	1.00
Wst Plm Bch	A+ Mon	7	7	4	0	50	187	25	9	4	0	3	1	0	16	0	67	4	0	4	3	.571	3	0	0.72
Indianapls	AAA Mon	1	1	0	0	6	24	5	1	1	0	0	0	0	2	0	5	0	0	1	0	1.000	0	0	1.50

(pitcher — continued)

Year Team	Lg Org	G	GS	CG	GF	IP	BFP	H	R	ER	HR	SH	SF	HB	TBB	IBB	SO	WP	Bk	W	L	Pct.	ShO	Sv	ERA
1990 Jacksnville	AA Mon	29	28	3	0	201.1	828	144	78	62	12	7	5	9	87	2	213	8	1	13	7	.650	1	0	2.77
1991 Wst Plm Bch	A+ Mon	2	2	0	0	7	27	3	0	0	0	0	0	0	4	0	6	3	0	0	0	—	0	0	0.00
Indianapols	AAA Mon	2	2	0	0	11	44	6	2	2	0	1	0	1	8	0	10	0	0	2	0	1.000	0	0	1.64
1992 Indianapols	AAA Mon	13	13	2	0	83	338	69	35	34	8	1	2	1	30	1	77	2	2	4	4	.500	1	0	3.69
1994 Charlotte	AAA Cle	13	0	0	2	18.1	80	17	10	8	2	0	0	1	8	2	23	1	0	0	1	.000	0	1	3.93
Albuquerque	AAA LA	9	9	0	0	47	221	57	38	33	9	0	1	1	23	2	44	1	0	5	1	.833	0	0	6.32
1995 Pawtucket	AAA Bos	21	18	2	0	106.1	454	107	62	50	12	0	2	4	30	0	90	5	1	7	5	.583	0	0	4.23
1996 Jacksnville	AA Det	13	12	1	0	74.2	320	74	37	31	8	6	1	4	25	1	74	3	0	4	6	.400	1	0	3.74
Toledo	AAA Det	14	13	2	0	88	373	85	49	39	8	0	1	4	29	0	70	6	1	6	6	.500	0	0	3.99
1997 Toledo	AAA Det	32	18	0	4	115.1	540	143	100	86	16	1	6	8	57	6	86	9	0	7	10	.412	0	0	6.71
1998 Memphis	AAA StL	35	21	0	6	140.2	593	138	66	56	15	3	4	7	39	1	154	5	0	7	5	.583	0	0	3.58
1999 Memphis	AAA StL	36	10	0	7	90	393	104	55	55	16	4	3	3	33	1	88	0	0	3	3	.571	0	0	5.50
2000 Calgary	AAA Fla	26	3	0	5	36.2	182	54	32	32	3	1	5	3	24	1	15	3	0	1	3	.250	0	1	7.85
Greenville	AA Atl	24	0	0	18	39	165	37	7	6	1	7	3	1	9	1	45	1	0	2	2	.500	0	11	1.38
11 Min. YEARS		279	159	14	42	1123.1	4802	1072	582	500	110	35	36	46	427	18	1082	57	6	68	56	.548	6	13	4.01
1990 Montreal	NL	4	4	1	0	28	115	25	10	9	2	2	0	0	7	0	23	2	0	1	1	.500	0	0	2.89
1991 Montreal	NL	28	27	1	0	160	684	135	82	75	16	9	5	6	84	2	117	5	1	5	8	.385	0	0	4.22
1992 Montreal	NL	21	17	0	2	100	417	77	34	33	9	5	1	3	46	1	65	1	2	6	6	.500	0	0	2.97
1993 Montreal	NL	52	8	0	8	100	442	105	53	49	9	8	3	0	48	2	60	5	1	2	6	.250	0	3	4.41
1994 Cleveland	AL	6	0	0	2	13.1	67	12	10	8	2	0	1	0	15	2	5	0	0	0	1	.000	0	0	5.40
Los Angeles	NL	5	0	0	5	5	29	10	4	4	1	0	0	0	4	1	5	2	0	0	0	—	0	0	7.20
5 Maj. YEARS		116	56	2	13	406.1	1754	364	193	178	39	24	10	9	204	8	275	15	4	14	22	.389	0	3	3.94

Larry Barnes

Bats: Left **Throws:** Left **Pos:** 1B-94; OF-6; DH-3 **Ht:** 6'1" **Wt:** 195 **Born:** 7/23/74 **Age:** 26

Year Team	Lg Org	G	AB	H	2B	3B	HR	TB	R	RBI	TBB	IBB	SO	HBP	SH	SF	SB	CS	SB%	GDP	Avg	OBP	SLG
1995 Angels	R Ana	56	197	61	8	3	3	84	42	37	27	0	40	5	1	2	12	5	.71	1	.310	.403	.426
1996 Cedar Rapds	A Ana	131	489	155	36	5	27	282	84	112	58	5	101	6	1	6	9	6	.60	8	.317	.392	.577
1997 Lk Elsinore	A+ Ana	115	446	128	32	2	13	203	68	71	43	4	84	5	1	5	3	4	.43	6	.287	.353	.455
1998 Lk Elsinore	A+ Ana	51	183	45	11	2	7	81	32	33	22	2	49	1	0	0	2	0	1.00	3	.246	.330	.443
Midland	AA Ana	69	245	67	16	4	6	109	29	35	28	3	54	1	2	2	4	2	.67	5	.273	.348	.445
1999 Erie	AA Ana	130	497	142	25	9	20	245	73	100	49	7	99	5	0	16	14	3	.82	7	.286	.346	.493
2000 Edmonton	AAA Ana	103	397	102	22	11	7	167	56	54	48	5	81	0	0	3	3	6	.33	4	.257	.335	.421
6 Min. YEARS		655	2454	700	150	36	83	1171	384	442	275	26	508	23	5	34	47	26	.64	34	.285	.358	.477

Marty Barnett

Pitches: Right **Bats:** Right **Pos:** RP-19; SP-3 **Ht:** 6'3" **Wt:** 213 **Born:** 3/10/74 **Age:** 27

Year Team	Lg Org	G	GS	CG	GF	IP	BFP	H	R	ER	HR	SH	SF	HB	TBB	IBB	SO	WP	Bk	W	L	Pct.	ShO	Sv	ERA
1995 Batavia	A- Phi	10	10	0	0	49.1	228	67	45	34	3	2	4	5	10	1	32	9	3	1	6	.143	0	0	6.20
1997 Piedmont	A Phi	6	6	0	0	37	154	34	16	13	1	1	2	2	11	0	28	1	0	2	1	.667	0	0	3.16
Clearwater	A+ Phi	17	15	1	0	97.2	411	102	50	40	10	1	1	0	29	0	62	6	2	5	6	.455	0	0	3.69
1998 Reading	AA Phi	5	5	0	0	24.2	116	31	17	17	5	0	1	2	13	0	21	0	1	0	3	.000	0	0	6.20
Clearwater	A+ Phi	7	6	0	0	27.1	128	34	23	19	4	0	0	1	14	0	13	2	1	1	0	1.000	0	0	6.26
1999 Reading	AA Phi	35	0	0	19	53.1	226	43	19	15	2	2	0	0	24	2	33	1	1	2	3	.400	0	7	2.53
Durham	AAA TB	16	0	0	6	28	124	30	17	17	2	1	3	1	14	1	19	4	0	1	0	1.000	0	0	5.46
2000 Durham	AAA TB	16	3	0	2	30	158	43	29	28	3	4	2	2	27	0	24	2	0	3	3	.500	0	0	8.40
Norwich	AA NYY	6	0	0	4	7	32	8	6	5	1	0	0	0	3	1	6	1	0	0	0	—	0	0	6.43
5 Min. YEARS		118	45	1	31	354.1	1577	392	222	188	31	11	13	13	145	5	238	26	8	14	23	.378	0	7	4.78

Jim Baron

Pitches: Left **Bats:** Left **Pos:** RP-13; SP-2 **Ht:** 6'3" **Wt:** 222 **Born:** 2/22/74 **Age:** 27

Year Team	Lg Org	G	GS	CG	GF	IP	BFP	H	R	ER	HR	SH	SF	HB	TBB	IBB	SO	WP	Bk	W	L	Pct.	ShO	Sv	ERA
1992 Padres	R SD	14	0	0	3	25	117	24	28	23	0	1	4	1	25	0	18	10	6	2	0	1.000	0	0	8.28
1993 Padres	R SD	13	8	1	2	48.2	220	38	33	24	0	1	3	6	38	0	36	5	1	1	3	.250	0	1	4.44
1994 Springfield	A SD	25	23	0	0	105.2	515	121	83	75	14	2	3	7	76	2	73	14	3	6	6	.500	0	0	6.39
1995 Rancho Cuca	A+ SD	3	0	0	1	2.2	22	7	8	5	1	1	0	0	6	0	3	2	0	0	0	—	0	0	16.88
Clinton	A SD	11	9	1	1	50.2	232	65	42	35	4	3	2	1	16	2	31	4	0	0	8	.000	0	0	6.22
Idaho Falls	R+ SD	27	1	0	5	43	201	51	31	27	2	0	2	1	19	1	43	8	0	2	3	.400	0	0	5.65
1996 Rancho Cuca	A+ SD	54	0	0	17	87	383	87	44	29	9	2	3	1	35	0	85	7	2	6	3	.667	0	1	3.00
1997 Las Vegas	AAA SD	4	0	0	2	4	21	8	5	5	2	0	0	0	3	0	3	0	0	0	0	—	0	0	11.25
Mobile	AA SD	19	1	0	4	33.2	152	35	21	17	3	2	0	3	13	1	30	3	0	2	4	.333	0	0	4.54
Rancho Cuca	A+ SD	14	14	0	0	85.1	371	89	50	32	2	4	7	2	28	1	64	4	1	1	7	.125	1	0	3.38
1998 Norwich	AA NYY	23	12	4	6	96.2	403	99	35	25	2	2	0	2	20	0	69	4	0	6	4	.600	1	0	2.33
Columbus	AAA NYY	8	7	1	1	44.1	196	54	32	30	7	0	2	1	19	0	28	3	0	1	5	.167	0	0	6.09
1999 Altoona	AA Pit	29	20	0	3	145	618	141	73	64	13	6	8	4	44	2	75	6	5	9	9	.500	0	0	3.97
2000 Norfolk	AAA NYM	2	2	0	0	7.1	50	26	15	12	1	0	0	1	4	1	3	1	0	0	1	.000	0	0	14.73
Binghamton	AA NYM	13	0	0	3	21.1	88	23	8	8	2	1	0	0	3	0	21	0	1	1	0	1.000	0	0	3.38
9 Min. YEARS		259	97	7	48	800.1	3589	868	508	411	62	25	36	28	349	10	582	71	19	37	53	.411	1	2	4.62

Manny Barrios

Pitches: Right **Bats:** Right **Pos:** RP-47 **Ht:** 6'0" **Wt:** 185 **Born:** 9/21/74 **Age:** 26

Year Team	Lg Org	G	GS	CG	GF	IP	BFP	H	R	ER	HR	SH	SF	HB	TBB	IBB	SO	WP	Bk	W	L	Pct.	ShO	Sv	ERA
1994 Quad City	A Hou	43	0	0	11	65	295	73	44	43	4	5	2	7	23	4	63	8	2	0	6	.000	0	4	5.95
1995 Quad City	A Hou	50	0	0	48	52	219	44	16	13	1	2	1	4	17	1	55	1	0	1	5	.167	0	23	2.25
1996 Jackson	AA Hou	60	0	0	53	68.1	298	60	29	18	4	4	2	3	29	5	69	3	0	6	4	.600	0	23	2.37
1997 New Orleans	AAA Hou	57	0	0	17	82.2	350	70	32	30	5	10	4	1	34	9	77	2	0	4	8	.333	0	0	3.27
1998 Albuquerque	AAA LA	20	2	0	7	36	170	47	25	24	7	1	2	0	15	0	33	4	0	3	3	.250	0	0	6.00
Charlotte	AAA Fla	18	1	0	6	24.1	98	19	10	10	3	0	0	1	9	2	22	0	0	2	0	1.000	0	0	3.70

17

Year Team	Lg Org	HOW MUCH HE PITCHED						WHAT HE GAVE UP												THE RESULTS					
		G	GS	CG	GF	IP	BFP	H	R	ER	HR	SH	SF	HB	TBB	IBB	SO	WP	Bk	W	L	Pct.	ShO	Sv	ERA
1999 Indianapols	AAA Cin	49	8	0	9	90.1	399	94	60	53	8	3	2	7	35	0	73	9	2	2	7	.222	0	0	5.28
2000 Scranton-WB	AAA Phi	47	0	0	21	64	288	71	35	35	6	2	1	2	31	3	60	5	0	6	5	.545	0	4	4.92
1997 Houston	NL	2	0	0	0	3	18	6	4	4	0	0	0	0	3	0	3	0	0	0	0	—	0	0	12.00
1998 Florida	NL	2	0	0	0	2.2	13	4	1	1	1	0	0	0	2	0	1	0	0	0	0	—	0	0	3.38
Los Angeles	NL	1	0	0	1	1	4	0	0	0	0	0	0	0	2	0	0	0	0	0	0	—	0	0	0.00
7 Min. YEARS		344	11	0	172	482.2	2117	478	251	226	38	27	13	27	193	24	452	32	4	22	38	.367	0	54	4.21
2 Maj. YEARS		5	0	0	1	6.2	35	10	5	5	1	0	0	0	7	0	4	0	0	0	0	—	0	0	6.75

Blake Barthol

Bats: Right **Throws:** Right **Pos:** C-67; DH-4; PH-2; 1B-1; PR-1   **Ht:** 6'0" **Wt:** 200 **Born:** 4/7/73 **Age:** 28

Year Team	Lg Org	BATTING													BASERUNNING				PERCENTAGES		
		G	AB	H	2B	3B	HR	TB	R	RBI	TBB	IBB	SO	HBP	SH	SF	SB	CS	SB%	GDP	Avg	OBP	SLG
1995 Portland	A- Col	56	191	45	10	2	1	62	20	25	22	0	32	4	1	3	5	2	.71	5	.236	.323	.325
1996 Salem	A+ Col	109	375	107	17	2	13	167	58	67	36	0	48	12	6	1	12	5	.71	5	.285	.366	.445
1997 New Haven	AA Col	109	325	79	12	2	6	113	42	39	31	0	76	10	11	2	5	3	.63	6	.243	.326	.348
1998 Salem	A+ Col	122	441	128	37	2	11	202	56	68	46	5	94	7	4	5	5	3	.63	2	.290	.363	.458
1999 Carolina	AA Col	96	322	90	18	3	8	138	41	27	32	2	62	7	5	1	0	1	.00	8	.280	.356	.429
2000 New Haven	AA Sea	74	248	74	9	1	7	106	43	30	26	1	44	2	2	2	1	1	.50	13	.298	.367	.427
6 Min. YEARS		566	1902	523	103	12	46	788	260	256	193	8	356	42	29	14	28	15	.65	39	.275	.352	.414

Jayson Bass

Bats: Left **Throws:** Left **Pos:** OF-27; DH-12; PH-12   **Ht:** 6'3" **Wt:** 205 **Born:** 6/22/74 **Age:** 27

Year Team	Lg Org	BATTING													BASERUNNING				PERCENTAGES		
		G	AB	H	2B	3B	HR	TB	R	RBI	TBB	IBB	SO	HBP	SH	SF	SB	CS	SB%	GDP	Avg	OBP	SLG
1993 Bristol	R+ Det	35	119	25	6	2	4	47	21	13	14	0	42	2	0	0	2	2	.50	0	.210	.304	.395
1994 Jamestown	A- Det	48	162	44	9	4	5	76	23	18	22	1	52	2	0	0	4	3	.57	2	.272	.366	.469
1995 Fayettevlle	A Det	108	368	79	15	6	10	136	47	48	37	1	111	3	1	1	14	3	.82	3	.215	.291	.370
1996 Fayettevlle	A Det	104	295	68	12	3	11	119	44	43	54	3	118	2	3	2	19	10	.66	2	.231	.351	.403
1997 Lakeland	A+ Det	108	376	97	18	4	13	162	58	53	41	5	130	2	0	4	17	7	.71	4	.258	.331	.431
1998 Lancaster	A+ Sea	110	392	113	26	6	21	214	80	84	40	2	102	4	0	2	31	12	.72	3	.288	.358	.546
1999 New Haven	AA Sea	123	431	114	23	5	21	210	79	67	72	1	160	3	0	5	34	14	.71	3	.265	.370	.487
2000 West Tenn	AA ChC	50	145	46	7	0	4	65	27	17	22	1	20	4	0	2	4	5	.44	4	.317	.416	.448
8 Min. YEARS		686	2288	586	116	30	89	1029	379	343	302	14	735	22	4	16	125	56	.69	21	.256	.346	.450

Jayson Bass

Bats: Both **Throws:** Right **Pos:** OF-90; PH-16; DH-5; PR-1   **Ht:** 6'0" **Wt:** 180 **Born:** 6/2/76 **Age:** 25

Year Team	Lg Org	BATTING													BASERUNNING				PERCENTAGES		
		G	AB	H	2B	3B	HR	TB	R	RBI	TBB	IBB	SO	HBP	SH	SF	SB	CS	SB%	GDP	Avg	OBP	SLG
1994 Braves	R Atl	49	173	25	8	0	0	33	14	4	15	0	33	2	0	1	5	8	.38	2	.145	.220	.191
1995 Danville	R+ Atl	64	268	60	17	4	0	85	38	17	28	2	61	4	0	2	24	8	.75	2	.224	.305	.317
1996 Danville	R+ Atl	57	207	50	11	6	2	79	41	23	34	0	32	6	1	5	22	5	.81	1	.242	.357	.382
Macon	A Atl	5	22	8	0	0	1	11	2	1	0	0	5	1	0	0	3	1	.75	0	.364	.391	.500
1997 Durham	A+ Atl	75	277	71	20	4	4	111	48	34	29	1	57	2	2	0	8	4	.67	6	.256	.331	.401
1998 Danville	A+ Atl	10	38	6	1	1	0	9	3	1	0	0	12	1	0	0	2	1	.67	0	.158	.179	.237
Greenville	AA Atl	86	233	53	10	1	5	80	27	18	37	1	60	1	6	2	11	6	.65	2	.227	.333	.343
1999 Myrtle Bch	A+ Atl	44	164	36	7	3	2	55	20	19	15	1	45	2	2	1	8	3	.73	1	.220	.291	.335
Richmond	AAA Atl	59	153	32	4	1	1	41	20	10	19	0	46	2	2	2	9	2	.82	5	.209	.301	.268
2000 Greenville	AA Atl	31	65	9	0	1	1	14	9	4	8	1	18	2	0	1	5	2	.71	0	.138	.250	.215
Lehigh Val	IND —	56	212	63	5	4	8	100	39	27	31	0	48	0	1	0	11	10	.52	1	.297	.387	.472
Altoona	AA Pit	19	45	11	0	1	0	13	7	5	5	0	8	0	0	1	3	0	1.00	1	.244	.314	.289
7 Min. YEARS		555	1857	424	83	26	24	631	268	163	221	6	425	23	13	15	111	50	.69	21	.228	.316	.340

Fletcher Bates

Bats: Both **Throws:** Right **Pos:** OF-94; PH-15; DH-1   **Ht:** 6'1" **Wt:** 193 **Born:** 3/24/74 **Age:** 27

Year Team	Lg Org	BATTING													BASERUNNING				PERCENTAGES		
		G	AB	H	2B	3B	HR	TB	R	RBI	TBB	IBB	SO	HBP	SH	SF	SB	CS	SB%	GDP	Avg	OBP	SLG
1994 Mets	R NYM	52	183	39	5	3	5	65	23	29	33	0	49	0	1	4	4	3	.57	1	.213	.327	.355
St. Lucie	A+ NYM	7	24	6	1	1	1	12	2	4	1	0	5	0	0	0	0	0	—	0	.250	.280	.500
1995 Pittsfield	A- NYM	75	276	90	14	9	6	140	52	37	41	0	72	4	1	3	17	9	.65	1	.326	.417	.507
Binghamton	AA NYM	2	8	0	0	0	0	0	1	0	1	0	6	0	0	0	0	0	—	0	.000	.111	.000
1996 Capital Cty	A NYM	132	491	127	21	13	15	219	84	72	64	4	162	3	4	3	16	6	.73	3	.259	.346	.446
1997 St. Lucie	A+ NYM	70	253	76	19	11	11	150	49	38	33	6	66	4	0	2	7	6	.54	4	.300	.387	.593
Binghamton	AA NYM	68	245	63	14	2	12	117	44	34	26	0	71	1	1	2	9	3	.75	2	.257	.328	.478
1998 Portland	AA Fla	140	537	147	23	5	11	213	67	60	46	2	118	2	1	1	19	6	.76	4	.274	.333	.397
1999 Portland	AA Fla	139	537	136	28	9	9	209	72	55	39	1	109	2	4	8	18	6	.75	10	.253	.302	.389
2000 El Paso	AA Ari	109	355	98	24	5	10	162	52	62	35	1	73	1	1	3	13	9	.59	4	.276	.340	.456
7 Min. YEARS		794	2909	782	149	58	80	1287	446	391	319	14	731	17	13	26	103	48	.68	29	.269	.342	.442

Jason Bates

Bats: Both **Throws:** Right **Pos:** 2B-13; SS-2   **Ht:** 5'10" **Wt:** 192 **Born:** 1/5/71 **Age:** 30

Year Team	Lg Org	BATTING													BASERUNNING				PERCENTAGES		
		G	AB	H	2B	3B	HR	TB	R	RBI	TBB	IBB	SO	HBP	SH	SF	SB	CS	SB%	GDP	Avg	OBP	SLG
1992 Bend	A- Col	70	255	73	10	3	6	107	57	31	56	1	55	5	2	4	18	4	.82	5	.286	.419	.420
1993 Colo Sprngs	AAA Col	122	449	120	21	2	13	184	76	62	45	4	99	10	3	3	9	8	.53	8	.267	.345	.410
1994 Colo Sprngs	AAA Col	125	458	131	19	5	10	190	68	76	60	4	57	4	2	5	4	6	.40	11	.286	.370	.415
1997 Colo Sprngs	AAA Col	35	135	32	6	1	3	49	21	18	13	0	36	2	1	1	1	3	.25	1	.237	.311	.363
1998 Colo Sprngs	AAA Col	49	182	59	9	1	5	85	37	20	17	0	31	1	1	1	2	2	.33	4	.324	.383	.467
2000 Rochester	AAA Bal	15	53	9	1	0	0	10	6	1	3	0	13	0	2	0	1	0	1.00	1	.170	.214	.189

Year Team	Lg Org	G	AB	H	2B	3B	HR	TB	R	RBI	TBB	IBB	SO	HBP	SH	SF	SB	CS	SB%	GDP	Avg	OBP	SLG
1995 Colorado	NL	116	322	86	17	4	8	135	42	46	42	3	70	2	2	0	3	6	.33	4	.267	.355	.419
1996 Colorado	NL	88	160	33	8	1	1	46	19	9	23	1	34	2	1	1	2	1	.67	7	.206	.312	.288
1997 Colorado	NL	62	121	29	10	0	3	48	17	11	15	1	27	3	0	0	0	1	.00	3	.240	.338	.397
1998 Colorado	NL	53	74	14	3	0	0	17	10	3	8	1	21	0	0	0	0	0	—	4	.189	.268	.230
6 Min. YEARS		416	1532	424	66	12	37	625	265	208	194	9	291	22	11	14	34	23	.60	30	.277	.363	.408
4 Maj. YEARS		319	677	162	38	5	12	246	88	69	88	6	152	7	3	1	5	8	.38	18	.239	.332	.363

Eric Battersby

Bats: Both **Throws:** Left **Pos:** 1B-124; OF-4; PR-1   **Ht:** 6'1" **Wt:** 205 **Born:** 2/28/76 **Age:** 25

Year Team	Lg Org	G	AB	H	2B	3B	HR	TB	R	RBI	TBB	IBB	SO	HBP	SH	SF	SB	CS	SB%	GDP	Avg	OBP	SLG
1998 White Sox	R CWS	43	136	51	15	3	5	87	34	27	29	0	32	0	1	2	4	2	.67	0	.375	.479	.640
1999 Burlington	A CWS	132	472	137	27	2	18	222	78	93	83	1	90	4	0	9	13	2	.87	8	.290	.394	.470
2000 Birmingham	AA CWS	127	411	98	20	3	8	148	59	43	55	1	84	3	1	4	6	8	.43	8	.238	.330	.360
3 Min. YEARS		302	1019	286	62	8	31	457	171	163	167	2	206	7	2	15	23	12	.66	16	.281	.381	.448

Howard Battle

Bats: Right **Throws:** Right **Pos:** 1B-11; 3B-2; DH-2   **Ht:** 6'0" **Wt:** 197 **Born:** 3/25/72 **Age:** 29

Year Team	Lg Org	G	AB	H	2B	3B	HR	TB	R	RBI	TBB	IBB	SO	HBP	SH	SF	SB	CS	SB%	GDP	Avg	OBP	SLG
1990 Medcine Hat	R+ Tor	61	233	62	17	1	5	96	25	32	15	2	38	2	0	0	5	2	.71	2	.266	.316	.412
1991 Myrtle Bch	A Tor	138	520	147	33	4	20	248	82	86	49	2	88	3	0	4	15	7	.68	1	.283	.345	.477
1992 Dunedin	A+ Tor	136	520	132	27	3	17	216	76	85	49	3	89	5	1	5	6	8	.43	5	.254	.321	.415
1993 Knoxville	AA Tor	141	521	145	21	5	7	197	66	70	45	3	94	7	1	7	12	9	.57	8	.278	.342	.378
1994 Syracuse	AAA Tor	139	517	143	26	8	14	227	72	75	40	4	82	3	1	7	26	2	.93	15	.277	.328	.439
1995 Syracuse	AAA Tor	118	443	111	17	4	8	160	43	48	39	2	73	3	1	2	10	11	.48	7	.251	.314	.361
1996 Scranton-WB	AAA Phi	115	391	89	24	1	8	139	37	44	21	0	53	2	2	6	3	8	.27	15	.228	.267	.355
1997 San Antonio	AA LA	16	33	8	1	0	0	9	2	1	0	0	7	2	1	0	0	0	—	0	.242	.286	.273
Albuquerque	AAA LA	50	139	33	3	2	3	49	14	16	6	0	23	0	0	2	1	2	.33	3	.237	.265	.353
1998 Birmingham	AA CWS	12	39	7	4	0	1	14	6	5	4	0	7	0	0	2	0	0	—	0	.179	.244	.359
Greenville	AA Atl	79	291	96	27	2	10	157	41	50	35	2	51	2	0	3	3	2	.60	12	.330	.402	.540
1999 Richmond	AAA Atl	121	454	129	29	1	24	232	80	74	33	2	66	3	0	5	2	3	.40	12	.284	.333	.511
2000 Louisville	AAA Cin	14	56	10	0	0	0	10	6	3	4	0	10	0	0	0	0	0	—	2	.179	.207	.179
1995 Toronto	AL	9	15	3	0	0	0	3	3	0	4	0	8	0	0	0	1	0	1.00	0	.200	.368	.200
1996 Philadelphia	NL	5	5	0	0	0	0	0	0	0	2	0	2	0	0	0	0	0	—	0	.000	.000	.000
1999 Atlanta	NL	15	17	6	0	0	1	9	2	5	2	0	3	0	0	0	0	0	—	1	.353	.421	.529
11 Min. YEARS		1140	4157	1112	229	31	117	1754	550	589	338	20	681	32	7	39	83	54	.61	82	.268	.325	.422
3 Maj. YEARS		29	37	9	0	0	1	12	5	5	6	0	13	0	0	0	1	0	1.00	1	.243	.349	.324

Rick Bauer

Pitches: Right **Bats:** Right **Pos:** SP-26; RP-3   **Ht:** 6'5" **Wt:** 210 **Born:** 1/10/77 **Age:** 24

Year Team	Lg Org	G	GS	CG	GF	IP	BFP	H	R	ER	HR	SH	SF	HB	TBB	IBB	SO	WP	Bk	W	L	Pct.	ShO	Sv	ERA
1997 Bluefield	R+ Bal	13	13	0	0	72.1	294	58	31	23	1	0	4	4	20	0	67	8	0	8	3	.727	0	0	2.86
Delmarva	A Bal	1	0	0	1	2	7	0	0	0	0	0	0	0	1	0	2	0	0	0	0	—	0	1	0.00
1998 Delmarva	A Bal	22	22	1	0	118	505	127	69	62	11	5	2	8	44	0	81	6	0	5	8	.385	1	0	4.73
1999 Frederick	A+ Bal	26	26	4	0	152	662	159	85	77	17	3	11	12	54	2	123	11	1	10	9	.526	0	0	4.56
2000 Frederick	A+ Bal	3	3	0	0	19	79	20	13	11	1	0	1	0	6	0	15	2	0	0	1	.000	0	0	5.21
Bowie	AA Bal	26	23	1	1	129	583	154	89	76	16	3	3	12	39	1	87	4	0	6	8	.429	1	0	5.30
4 Min. YEARS		91	87	6	2	492.1	2130	518	287	249	46	11	21	36	164	3	375	31	1	29	29	.500	1	2	4.55

Juan Bautista

Bats: Right **Throws:** Right **Pos:** SS-31; 3B-15; DH-15; OF-13; PH-10; 2B-9; PR-6   **Ht:** 6'0" **Wt:** 170 **Born:** 6/24/75 **Age:** 26

Year Team	Lg Org	G	AB	H	2B	3B	HR	TB	R	RBI	TBB	IBB	SO	HBP	SH	SF	SB	CS	SB%	GDP	Avg	OBP	SLG
1993 Albany	A Bal	88	295	70	17	2	0	91	24	28	14	0	72	7	3	4	11	3	.79	11	.237	.284	.308
1994 Orioles	R Bal	21	65	10	2	2	0	16	4	3	2	0	19	1	1	0	3	1	.75	3	.154	.191	.246
1995 Bowie	AA Bal	13	38	4	2	0	0	6	3	0	3	0	5	2	1	0	1	0	1.00	3	.105	.209	.158
High Desert	A+ Bal	99	374	98	13	4	11	152	54	51	18	0	74	7	6	3	22	9	.71	6	.262	.306	.406
1996 Bowie	AA Bal	129	441	103	18	3	3	136	35	33	21	1	102	5	8	2	15	12	.56	6	.234	.275	.308
1997 Orioles	R Bal	3	9	1	0	0	0	1	3	0	1	0	2	2	0	0	1	1	.50	0	.111	.333	.111
Bowie	AA Bal	21	68	17	1	0	0	18	9	3	5	0	17	0	1	1	1	2	.33	2	.250	.297	.265
Birmingham	AA CWS	12	46	11	3	0	0	14	6	4	3	0	15	0	1	0	1	0	1.00	2	.239	.286	.304
1998 Birmingham	AA CWS	120	420	107	13	1	5	137	46	34	18	1	98	4	6	3	6	12	.33	18	.255	.290	.326
1999 Tulsa	AA Tex	127	471	116	14	3	8	160	60	45	25	0	114	4	7	6	18	9	.67	12	.246	.294	.340
2000 Tulsa	AA Tex	50	172	43	10	1	5	70	24	25	13	0	29	1	1	1	8	6	.57	5	.250	.305	.407
Oklahoma	AAA Tex	7	25	6	1	0	0	7	3	1	0	0	6	0	1	0	1	1	.50	2	.240	.240	.280
New Orleans	AAA Hou	33	78	16	4	0	0	20	9	5	3	0	18	2	1	0	3	2	.60	2	.205	.253	.256
8 Min. YEARS		733	2502	602	98	16	32	828	280	232	126	2	571	38	36	14	90	59	.60	74	.241	.286	.331

Ray Beasley

Pitches: Left **Bats:** Right **Pos:** RP-52   **Ht:** 5'11" **Wt:** 168 **Born:** 10/26/76 **Age:** 24

Year Team	Lg Org	G	GS	CG	GF	IP	BFP	H	R	ER	HR	SH	SF	HB	TBB	IBB	SO	WP	Bk	W	L	Pct.	ShO	Sv	ERA
1996 Danville	R+ Atl	27	0	0	21	36.2	145	28	8	7	0	1	1	1	10	0	47	1	1	1	2	.333	0	12	1.72
Eugene	A- Atl	3	0	0	0	4	19	4	2	0	0	0	0	0	2	0	7	0	0	0	0	—	0	0	0.00
1997 Macon	A Atl	49	0	0	30	71.1	294	52	28	21	4	4	3	5	26	2	102	2	0	3	4	.429	0	8	2.65
1998 Danville	A+ Atl	54	0	0	20	55.2	241	54	26	22	3	3	2	3	24	4	55	2	1	6	8	.429	0	8	3.56
Richmond	AAA Atl	2	0	0	1	6	28	8	3	3	0	2	0	0	2	0	8	0	0	0	0	—	0	0	4.50

19

Year Team	Lg Org	G	GS	CG	GF	IP	BFP	H	R	ER	HR	SH	SF	HB	TBB	IBB	SO	WP	Bk	W	L	Pct.	ShO	Sv	ERA
		HOW MUCH HE PITCHED						WHAT HE GAVE UP												THE RESULTS					
1999 Greenville	AA Atl	50	0	0	22	81.2	349	84	45	42	8	2	4	3	26	5	71	3	1	7	4	.636	0	3	4.63
2000 Richmond	AAA Atl	4	0	0	2	5	26	11	9	4	2	0	0	0	2	0	2	0	0	0	2	.000	0	0	7.20
Greenville	AA Atl	48	0	0	16	59	255	54	25	20	2	5	1	1	25	3	64	4	0	3	4	.429	0	3	3.05
5 Min. YEARS		237	0	0	112	319.1	1357	295	146	119	19	17	11	13	117	14	356	12	3	20	24	.455	0	34	3.35

Matt Beaumont

Pitches: Left **Bats:** Left **Pos:** SP-22; RP-10   **Ht:** 6'3" **Wt:** 210 **Born:** 4/22/73 **Age:** 28

Year Team	Lg Org	G	GS	CG	GF	IP	BFP	H	R	ER	HR	SH	SF	HB	TBB	IBB	SO	WP	Bk	W	L	Pct.	ShO	Sv	ERA
		HOW MUCH HE PITCHED						WHAT HE GAVE UP												THE RESULTS					
1994 Boise	A- Ana	12	10	0	0	64	268	52	27	25	2	4	2	7	22	1	77	3	0	3	3	.500	0	0	3.52
1995 Lk Elsinore	A+ Ana	27	26	0	0	175.1	724	162	80	64	15	1	6	7	57	1	149	1	1	16	9	.640	0	0	3.29
1996 Midland	AA Ana	28	28	2	0	161.2	746	198	124	105	20	4	6	12	71	0	132	5	0	7	16	.304	0	0	5.85
1997 Midland	AA Ana	4	3	0	0	9.2	62	24	27	27	5	0	0	0	10	0	11	1	0	0	2	.000	0	0	25.14
Lk Elsinore	A+ Ana	1	1	0	0	1.1	7	2	1	1	0	0	0	0	1	0	1	0	1	0	0	—	0	0	6.75
1998 Midland	AA Ana	34	18	1	6	128.2	583	124	81	60	10	5	4	10	67	1	107	3	3	9	12	.429	0	1	4.20
1999 Erie	AA Ana	32	12	0	6	106.2	474	97	46	56	13	5	3	7	59	0	76	3	3	5	6	.455	0	1	4.73
2000 Edmonton	AAA Ana	2	1	0	1	7.1	40	11	10	10	1	0	0	1	9	0	4	1	0	0	0	—	0	0	12.27
Erie	AA Ana	30	21	0	3	118.1	539	95	62	50	11	4	1	17	92	0	84	4	1	5	10	.333	0	0	3.80
7 Min. YEARS		170	120	3	16	773	3443	765	476	398	77	23	22	61	388	3	641	21	9	45	58	.437	0	2	4.63

Greg Beck

Pitches: Right **Bats:** Right **Pos:** RP-47; SP-1   **Ht:** 6'3" **Wt:** 215 **Born:** 10/21/72 **Age:** 28

Year Team	Lg Org	G	GS	CG	GF	IP	BFP	H	R	ER	HR	SH	SF	HB	TBB	IBB	SO	WP	Bk	W	L	Pct.	ShO	Sv	ERA
		HOW MUCH HE PITCHED						WHAT HE GAVE UP												THE RESULTS					
1994 Helena	R+ Mil	18	2	0	11	43.2	191	42	26	21	4	3	2	2	20	1	41	3	0	4	3	.571	0	4	4.33
1995 Beloit	A Mil	35	5	0	12	74.1	331	73	46	39	2	1	6	2	35	2	91	7	2	5	2	.714	0	2	4.72
1996 Stockton	A+ Mil	28	28	0	0	152.1	695	197	119	104	18	8	7	12	53	1	96	7	0	9	11	.450	0	0	6.14
1997 Stockton	A+ Mil	27	1	0	11	55	222	33	16	15	4	2	1	3	23	2	46	2	0	4	4	.500	0	0	2.45
El Paso	AA Mil	18	6	0	3	48.1	232	75	46	35	8	2	3	5	15	2	37	5	1	1	5	.167	0	0	6.52
1998 El Paso	AA Mil	30	15	0	4	98	452	135	80	73	14	2	3	8	24	2	76	7	0	9	7	.563	0	0	6.70
Louisville	AAA Mil	10	8	1	0	46	204	49	31	29	8	3	2	2	16	0	37	2	0	4	3	.571	0	0	5.67
1999 Louisville	AAA Mil	1	0	0	0	0.1	4	3	3	3	1	0	0	0	0	0	0	0	0	0	0	—	0	0	81.00
Huntsville	AA Mil	26	25	0	1	151.2	648	157	79	75	24	5	7	8	48	1	93	12	0	10	9	.526	0	0	4.45
2000 Huntsville	AA Mil	48	1	0	14	83.2	367	97	51	46	8	2	4	4	26	5	60	2	0	3	6	.333	0	2	4.95
7 Min. YEARS		241	91	1	56	753.1	3346	861	497	440	91	28	35	46	260	16	577	47	3	49	50	.495	0	8	5.26

Brian Becker

Bats: Right **Throws:** Right **Pos:** 1B-129; DH-3   **Ht:** 6'7" **Wt:** 237 **Born:** 5/26/75 **Age:** 26

Year Team	Lg Org	G	AB	H	2B	3B	HR	TB	R	RBI	TBB	IBB	SO	HBP	SH	SF	SB	CS	SB%	GDP	Avg	OBP	SLG
		BATTING															BASERUNNING				PERCENTAGES		
1996 Devil Rays	R TB	52	199	54	12	0	2	72	31	27	13	0	28	3	0	4	3	1	.75	3	.271	.320	.362
1997 Chston-SC	A TB	135	494	116	31	2	11	184	55	70	53	3	120	4	0	9	12	1	.92	12	.235	.309	.372
1998 St. Pete	A+ TB	129	492	139	27	4	8	198	64	63	43	1	116	4	0	8	1	1	.50	14	.283	.340	.402
1999 Orlando	AA TB	129	480	121	24	1	18	201	67	74	42	2	89	4	0	3	0	0	—	16	.252	.316	.419
2000 Orlando	AA TB	132	503	140	27	2	9	198	45	58	40	1	88	5	0	3	1	3	.25	11	.278	.336	.394
5 Min. YEARS		577	2168	570	121	9	48	853	262	292	191	7	441	20	0	27	17	6	.74	56	.263	.325	.393

Tom Becker

Pitches: Right **Bats:** Right **Pos:** RP-39   **Ht:** 6'3" **Wt:** 205 **Born:** 1/13/75 **Age:** 26

Year Team	Lg Org	G	GS	CG	GF	IP	BFP	H	R	ER	HR	SH	SF	HB	TBB	IBB	SO	WP	Bk	W	L	Pct.	ShO	Sv	ERA
		HOW MUCH HE PITCHED						WHAT HE GAVE UP												THE RESULTS					
1994 Yankees	R NYY	7	7	0	0	31.2	147	26	24	10	0	1	0	0	23	0	29	5	0	1	3	.250	0	0	2.84
1995 Oneonta	A- NYY	15	15	0	0	77.2	353	83	55	46	0	4	4	2	40	0	65	12	2	6	6	.500	0	0	5.33
1996 Greensboro	A NYY	40	14	1	9	127	558	116	69	52	7	2	6	3	75	4	97	10	2	6	9	.400	0	0	3.69
1997 Tampa	A+ NYY	25	9	0	9	43	192	45	29	24	2	1	2	0	26	4	26	6	1	2	1	.667	0	0	5.02
1998 Cook County	IND —	23	0	0	20	31	115	13	3	0	0	1	0	0	7	1	38	1	0	5	0	1.000	0	12	0.00
Atlantic Ct	IND —	5	0	0	2	10	50	12	10	8	1	0	0	2	5	0	9	2	0	1	0	1.000	0	0	7.20
1999 Cook County	IND —	24	11	3	12	95.2	414	88	52	27	7	1	1	6	30	2	107	8	0	9	4	.692	0	4	2.54
2000 Lakeland	A+ Det	2	0	0	1	6	22	3	1	1	0	1	0	0	2	0	1	0	0	1	0	1.000	0	1	1.50
Jacksnville	AA Det	37	0	0	16	58.1	261	65	47	43	5	0	2	6	24	2	47	6	0	0	4	.000	0	0	6.63
7 Min. YEARS		178	47	4	69	480.1	2112	451	290	211	22	11	15	19	232	13	419	50	5	31	27	.534	0	17	3.95

Ryan Becks

Pitches: Left **Bats:** Left **Pos:** SP-18; RP-15   **Ht:** 6'3" **Wt:** 185 **Born:** 4/7/76 **Age:** 25

Year Team	Lg Org	G	GS	CG	GF	IP	BFP	H	R	ER	HR	SH	SF	HB	TBB	IBB	SO	WP	Bk	W	L	Pct.	ShO	Sv	ERA
		HOW MUCH HE PITCHED						WHAT HE GAVE UP												THE RESULTS					
1997 Vermont	A- Mon	15	15	0	0	78.2	368	92	61	51	4	4	2	7	33	0	57	12	1	2	8	.200	0	0	5.83
1998 Cape Fear	A Mon	28	22	1	1	122.1	549	140	88	72	13	7	4	10	55	0	72	12	1	11	6	.647	0	0	5.30
1999 Cape Fear	A Mon	34	6	0	11	93.2	408	96	52	40	10	2	2	6	32	1	62	5	0	6	6	.625	0	1	3.84
2000 Jupiter	A+ Mon	30	17	0	5	110.1	507	139	74	62	4	3	6	11	42	0	45	2	0	5	10	.333	0	0	5.06
Ottawa	AAA Mon	3	1	0	0	12		21	16	13	5	0	0	0	7	0	4	1	0	0	1	.000	0	0	9.75
4 Min. YEARS		110	61	2	17	417	1896	488	291	238	36	16	14	34	169	1	240	32	2	28	31	.475	0	1	5.14

Joe Beimel

Pitches: Left **Bats:** Left **Pos:** SP-28 **Ht:** 6'2" **Wt:** 201 **Born:** 4/19/77 **Age:** 24

		HOW MUCH HE PITCHED						WHAT HE GAVE UP											THE RESULTS					
Year Team	Lg Org	G	GS	CG	GF	IP	BFP	H	R	ER	HR	SH	SF	HB	TBB	IBB	SO	WP	Bk	W	L	Pct.	ShO	Sv	ERA
1998 Erie	A- Pit	17	6	0	3	47	220	56	39	33	6	3	1	5	22	0	37	3	1	1	4	.200	0	0	6.32
1999 Hickory	A Pit	29	22	0	3	130	570	146	81	64	12	4	5	12	43	0	102	10	2	5	11	.313	0	0	4.43
2000 Lynchburg	A+ Pit	18	18	2	0	120.2	515	111	49	45	6	7	6	8	44	1	82	2	0	10	6	.625	1	0	3.36
Altoona	AA Pit	10	10	1	0	62.2	279	72	38	29	8	0	2	6	21	0	28	1	3	1	6	.143	0	0	4.16
3 Min. YEARS		74	56	3	6	360.1	1584	385	207	171	32	14	14	31	130	1	249	16	6	17	27	.386	1	0	4.27

Andrew Beinbrink

Bats: Right **Throws:** Right **Pos:** 3B-128; DH-5 **Ht:** 6'3" **Wt:** 207 **Born:** 9/24/76 **Age:** 24

		BATTING														BASERUNNING				PERCENTAGES		
Year Team	Lg Org	G	AB	H	2B	3B	HR	TB	R	RBI	TBB	IBB	SO	HBP	SH	SF	SB	CS	SB%	GDP	Avg	OBP	SLG
1999 Hudson Val	A- TB	76	292	99	24	2	11	160	46	51	39	2	49	8	0	4	13	4	.76	4	.339	.426	.548
2000 St. Pete	A+ TB	130	475	141	28	0	7	190	70	58	43	3	70	8	2	6	3	4	.43	10	.297	.361	.400
Orlando	AA TB	3	11	5	0	0	1	8	2	3	1	0	1	0	0	0	0	0	—	1	.455	.500	.727
2 Min. YEARS		209	778	245	52	2	19	358	118	112	83	5	120	16	2	10	16	8	.67	15	.315	.388	.460

Jason Bell

Pitches: Right **Bats:** Right **Pos:** RP-29; SP-5 **Ht:** 6'3" **Wt:** 214 **Born:** 9/30/74 **Age:** 26

		HOW MUCH HE PITCHED						WHAT HE GAVE UP											THE RESULTS					
Year Team	Lg Org	G	GS	CG	GF	IP	BFP	H	R	ER	HR	SH	SF	HB	TBB	IBB	SO	WP	Bk	W	L	Pct.	ShO	Sv	ERA
1995 Fort Wayne	A Min	9	6	0	2	34.1	139	26	11	5	0	3	0	1	6	0	40	6	2	3	1	.750	0	0	1.31
1996 Fort Myers	A+ Min	13	13	0	0	90.1	350	61	20	17	1	4	2	6	22	0	83	3	0	6	3	.667	0	0	1.69
Hardware Cy	AA Min	16	16	2	0	94	410	93	54	46	13	5	2	5	38	1	94	6	1	2	6	.250	1	0	4.40
1997 New Britain	AA Min	28	28	3	0	164.2	700	163	71	62	19	3	2	5	64	0	142	13	2	11	9	.550	1	0	3.39
1998 New Britain	AA Min	29	29	2	0	169.2	694	148	90	88	21	3	2	5	61	1	166	4	2	8	11	.421	0	0	4.67
1999 Salt Lake	AAA Min	18	15	0	0	76.1	364	96	58	54	12	3	4	3	35	0	72	4	1	5	5	.500	0	0	6.37
New Britain	AA Min	7	7	0	0	47.1	198	46	21	18	4	2	1	2	11	0	34	0	1	3	3	.500	0	0	3.42
2000 Tennessee	AA Tor	12	2	0	3	35.2	151	30	19	14	2	6	4	2	10	1	32	0	0	4	3	.571	0	0	3.53
Syracuse	AAA Tor	22	3	0	7	41.2	175	41	25	23	3	3	4	1	16	1	28	2	0	3	4	.429	0	0	4.97
6 Min. YEARS		154	119	7	12	754	3181	704	369	327	75	32	21	30	263	4	691	38	9	45	45	.500	2	0	3.90

Mike Bell

Pitches: Left **Bats:** Left **Pos:** RP-5; SP-1 **Ht:** 6'1" **Wt:** 198 **Born:** 10/14/72 **Age:** 28

		HOW MUCH HE PITCHED						WHAT HE GAVE UP											THE RESULTS					
Year Team	Lg Org	G	GS	CG	GF	IP	BFP	H	R	ER	HR	SH	SF	HB	TBB	IBB	SO	WP	Bk	W	L	Pct.	ShO	Sv	ERA
1995 Vermont	A- Mon	7	0	0	4	16.2	59	7	5	1	0	1	0	1	5	2	12	0	0	0	0	—	0	1	0.54
Albany	A Mon	12	0	0	4	20.2	81	13	8	6	0	2	0	1	8	0	14	0	0	3	3	.500	0	0	2.61
1996 Wst Plm Bch	A+ Mon	13	0	0	5	15.1	82	27	19	15	1	2	0	1	11	1	11	1	0	0	1	.000	0	0	8.80
Delmarva	A Mon	40	0	0	15	59.2	232	39	13	9	1	6	0	3	18	0	59	1	1	6	1	.857	0	5	1.36
1997 Wst Plm Bch	A+ Mon	41	3	0	15	81.1	328	60	30	28	2	4	2	5	27	0	56	2	0	5	4	.556	0	4	3.10
1998 Jupiter	A+ Mon	5	0	0	2	7	37	16	8	4	1	0	1	0	2	0	5	2	0	0	1	.000	0	0	5.14
Frederick	A+ Bal	38	0	0	20	60.1	236	53	22	18	3	6	3	2	13	2	38	3	0	7	4	.636	0	7	2.69
1999 Bowie	AA Bal	41	13	0	13	131.1	575	134	80	67	13	4	3	12	49	1	79	3	1	7	7	.500	0	1	4.59
2000 Bowie	AA Bal	6	1	0	3	8.1	41	12	9	9	3	1	0	1	2	0	4	0	0	0	1	.000	0	1	9.72
6 Min. YEARS		203	17	0	73	400.2	1671	361	194	157	24	26	9	26	135	6	278	12	2	28	22	.560	0	19	3.53

Esteban Beltre

Bats: Right **Throws:** Right **Pos:** SS-75; 2B-32; 3B-26; PH-4; PR-2 **Ht:** 5'10" **Wt:** 180 **Born:** 12/26/67 **Age:** 33

		BATTING														BASERUNNING				PERCENTAGES		
Year Team	Lg Org	G	AB	H	2B	3B	HR	TB	R	RBI	TBB	IBB	SO	HBP	SH	SF	SB	CS	SB%	GDP	Avg	OBP	SLG
1984 Calgary	R+ Mon	18	20	4	0	0	0	4	1	2	2	0	8	0	0	0	1	0	1.00	1	.200	.273	.200
1985 Utica	A- Mon	72	241	48	6	2	0	58	19	22	18	0	58	3	8	1	8	7	.53	4	.199	.262	.241
1986 Wst Plm Bch	A+ Mon	97	285	69	11	1	1	85	24	20	16	2	59	0	4	1	4	2	.67	9	.242	.281	.298
1987 Jacksonville	AA Mon	142	491	104	15	4	4	139	55	34	40	4	98	3	10	4	9	8	.53	7	.212	.275	.283
1988 Jacksonville	AA Mon	35	113	17	2	0	0	19	5	6	3	0	28	0	0	0	1	0	1.00	1	.150	.172	.168
Wst Plm Bch	A+ Mon	69	226	63	5	6	0	80	23	15	11	0	38	1	11	1	4	0	1.00	6	.279	.314	.354
1989 Rockford	A Mon	104	375	80	15	3	2	107	42	33	33	1	83	0	5	1	9	3	.75	8	.213	.276	.285
1990 Indianapolis	AAA Mon	133	407	92	11	2	1	110	33	37	32	1	77	2	5	4	8	2	.80	9	.226	.283	.270
1991 Denver	AAA Mil	27	78	14	1	3	0	21	11	9	9	0	16	0	0	0	3	2	.60	5	.179	.264	.269
Vancouver	AAA CWS	88	347	94	11	3	0	111	48	30	23	0	61	0	7	1	8	7	.53	4	.271	.315	.320
1992 Vancouver	AAA CWS	40	161	43	5	2	0	52	17	16	8	1	27	1	5	1	4	4	.50	3	.267	.304	.323
1993 Nashville	AAA CWS	134	489	143	24	4	8	199	67	52	33	1	102	0	5	4	18	6	.75	13	.292	.337	.407
1996 Scranton-WB	AAA Phi	4	15	2	0	0	0	2	1	1	0	0	1	0	0	0	0	0	—	2	.133	.133	.133
Richmond	AAA Atl	10	28	7	3	0	0	10	3	0	1	0	2	0	0	0	0	0	—	0	.250	.276	.357
1998 Salt Lake	AAA Min	133	510	142	24	4	2	180	84	49	39	0	109	0	5	4	26	11	.70	7	.278	.327	.353
1999 Rochester	AAA Bal	92	314	83	19	3	1	111	45	23	23	1	64	1	4	1	5	3	.63	11	.264	.316	.354
Charlotte	AAA CWS	38	121	31	8	0	2	45	27	17	7	0	16	0	3	2	4	0	1.00	6	.256	.295	.372
2000 Tucson	AAA Ari	129	452	142	23	4	3	182	52	60	28	0	71	0	3	2	6	9	.40	12	.314	.353	.403
1991 Chicago	AL	8	6	1	0	0	0	1	0	1	0	1	1	0	0	0	1	0	1.00	0	.167	.286	.167
1992 Chicago	AL	49	110	21	2	0	1	26	21	10	3	0	18	0	2	1	1	0	1.00	3	.191	.211	.236
1994 Texas	AL	48	131	37	5	0	0	42	12	12	16	0	25	0	5	1	2	5	.29	5	.282	.358	.321
1995 Texas	AL	54	92	20	8	0	0	28	7	7	4	0	15	0	4	0	1	0	1.00	1	.217	.250	.304
1996 Boston	AL	27	31	8	0	0	0	8	6	6	4	0	14	0	1	1	1	0	1.00	1	.258	.299	.290
14 Min. YEARS		1365	4673	1178	183	41	24	1515	557	426	326	7	918	11	75	19	118	64	.65	106	.252	.301	.324
5 Maj. YEARS		186	401	95	17	0	1	115	46	35	28	0	73	0	11	3	5	5	.50	8	.237	.285	.287

Brian Benefield

Bats: Right **Throws:** Right **Pos:** 2B-24; OF-19; 3B-15; DH-9   **Ht:** 6'0" **Wt:** 181 **Born:** 8/12/76 **Age:** 24

					BATTING												BASERUNNING				PERCENTAGES		
Year Team	Lg Org	G	AB	H	2B	3B	HR	TB	R	RBI	TBB	IBB	SO	HBP	SH	SF	SB	CS	SB%	GDP	Avg	OBP	SLG
1997 Watertown	A- Cle	69	265	76	9	1	4	99	47	19	49	3	40	1	2	1	23	7	.77	3	.287	.399	.374
1998 Kinston	A+ Cle	71	259	57	9	2	5	85	44	34	31	1	50	4	4	2	8	4	.67	1	.220	.311	.328
1999 Columbus	A Cle	81	303	83	14	1	15	144	60	51	43	1	67	8	2	5	18	12	.60	4	.274	.373	.475
Akron	AA Cle	44	145	28	3	2	3	44	14	14	16	0	32	0	0	0	3	3	.50	1	.193	.273	.303
2000 Akron	AA Cle	1	2	0	0	0	0	0	0	0	1	0	2	0	0	0	0	0	—	0	.000	.333	.000
Kinston	A+ Cle	66	236	67	19	6	2	104	45	19	35	0	55	1	2	2	10	3	.77	9	.284	.376	.441
4 Min. YEARS		332	1210	311	54	12	29	476	210	137	175	5	246	14	10	10	62	29	.68	18	.257	.355	.393

Adam Benes

Pitches: Right **Bats:** Left **Pos:** RP-16; SP-10   **Ht:** 6'2" **Wt:** 195 **Born:** 3/12/73 **Age:** 28

		HOW MUCH HE PITCHED						WHAT HE GAVE UP										THE RESULTS						
Year Team	Lg Org	G	GS	CG	GF	IP	BFP	H	R	ER	HR	SH	SF	HB	TBB	IBB	SO	WP	Bk	W	L	Pct.	ShO	Sv	ERA
1995 New Jersey	A- StL	19	10	0	3	75	311	71	30	28	3	0	4	3	23	0	47	5	2	5	3	.625	0	0	3.36
1996 Peoria	A StL	43	0	0	15	65	278	58	31	27	4	2	0	2	28	0	64	2	1	2	2	.500	0	0	3.74
1997 Pr William	A+ StL	33	5	0	9	70.1	326	92	54	49	15	3	2	2	29	0	44	4	0	3	3	.500	0	0	6.27
1998 Pr William	A+ StL	10	0	0	1	13.1	58	12	6	2	1	0	0	0	4	0	9	0	0	1	0	1.000	0	0	1.35
Arkansas	AA StL	12	0	0	6	16.1	73	21	12	11	2	1	2	1	2	1	8	2	0	0	0	—	0	0	6.06
1999 Arkansas	AA StL	28	0	0	10	40.1	182	51	30	24	9	0	2	1	15	1	19	0	1	1	1	.500	0	0	5.36
2000 Arkansas	AA StL	26	10	0	4	83.1	355	93	43	40	8	5	5	1	20	5	55	3	0	2	5	.286	0	0	4.32
6 Min. YEARS		171	25	0	48	363.2	1583	398	206	181	42	11	15	10	121	7	246	16	4	14	14	.500	0	0	4.48

David Benham

Bats: Right **Throws:** Right **Pos:** C-44; DH-2   **Ht:** 6'2" **Wt:** 187 **Born:** 10/12/75 **Age:** 25

					BATTING												BASERUNNING				PERCENTAGES		
Year Team	Lg Org	G	AB	H	2B	3B	HR	TB	R	RBI	TBB	IBB	SO	HBP	SH	SF	SB	CS	SB%	GDP	Avg	OBP	SLG
1998 Red Sox	R Bos	6	22	8	3	0	1	14	3	3	2	0	1	1	0	0	0	0	—	0	.364	.440	.636
Lowell	A- Bos	41	131	36	12	0	2	54	17	6	7	0	23	3	1	0	1	0	1.00	4	.275	.326	.412
1999 Augusta	A Bos	3	9	0	0	0	0	0	0	0	0	0	7	0	0	0	0	0	—	0	.000	.000	.000
Sarasota	A+ Bos	33	105	25	5	0	3	39	10	11	5	0	18	3	0	1	0	0	—	3	.238	.289	.371
Potomac	A+ StL	9	26	4	1	0	0	5	2	1	1	0	7	2	1	0	0	0	—	2	.154	.241	.192
2000 Potomac	A+ StL	28	85	16	4	1	1	25	12	7	6	0	20	8	2	1	0	0	—	5	.188	.300	.294
Arkansas	AA StL	18	57	13	5	1	0	20	9	6	7	1	10	0	0	0	0	3	.00	5	.228	.313	.351
3 Min. YEARS		138	435	102	30	2	7	157	53	34	28	1	86	17	4	2	1	3	.25	14	.234	.305	.361

Jason Benham

Bats: Left **Throws:** Right **Pos:** 3B-16; 2B-10; PH-5; PR-5; SS-1; DH-1   **Ht:** 6'1" **Wt:** 185 **Born:** 10/12/75 **Age:** 25

					BATTING												BASERUNNING				PERCENTAGES		
Year Team	Lg Org	G	AB	H	2B	3B	HR	TB	R	RBI	TBB	IBB	SO	HBP	SH	SF	SB	CS	SB%	GDP	Avg	OBP	SLG
1998 Bluefield	R+ Bal	57	202	45	6	3	6	75	38	28	21	0	36	1	1	1	3	1	.75	2	.223	.298	.371
Frederick	A+ Bal	4	16	4	0	0	0	4	2	2	1	0	3	0	0	0	1	0	1.00	1	.250	.294	.250
1999 Frederick	A+ Bal	16	27	4	0	0	0	4	3	2	2	0	2	0	1	1	0	0	—	1	.148	.200	.148
Delmarva	A Bal	7	21	2	2	0	0	4	1	3	3	1	6	0	0	0	0	0	—	0	.095	.208	.190
2000 Frederick	A+ Bal	28	66	13	1	1	0	16	7	9	6	0	17	0	0	0	1	0	1.00	5	.197	.264	.242
Arkansas	AA StL	5	11	6	2	0	0	8	3	1	1	0	0	0	0	0	0	0	—	0	.545	.583	.727
3 Min. YEARS		117	343	74	11	4	6	111	54	45	34	1	64	1	2	2	5	1	.83	8	.216	.287	.324

Yamil Benitez

Bats: Right **Throws:** Right **Pos:** OF-17; DH-2   **Ht:** 6'2" **Wt:** 207 **Born:** 5/10/72 **Age:** 29

					BATTING												BASERUNNING				PERCENTAGES		
Year Team	Lg Org	G	AB	H	2B	3B	HR	TB	R	RBI	TBB	IBB	SO	HBP	SH	SF	SB	CS	SB%	GDP	Avg	OBP	SLG
1990 Expos	R Mon	22	83	19	1	0	1	23	6	5	8	0	18	0	0	0	0	0	—	1	.229	.297	.277
1991 Expos	R Mon	54	197	47	9	5	5	81	20	38	12	1	55	1	1	5	10	5	.67	3	.239	.279	.411
1992 Albany	A Mon	23	79	13	3	2	1	23	6	6	5	1	49	0	0	0	1	0	.00	1	.165	.214	.291
Jamestown	A- Mon	44	162	44	6	6	3	71	24	23	14	0	52	2	1	0	19	1	.95	5	.272	.337	.438
1993 Burlington	A Mon	111	411	112	21	5	15	188	70	61	29	1	99	1	3	6	18	7	.72	8	.273	.323	.421
1994 Harrisburg	AA Mon	126	475	123	18	4	17	200	58	91	36	2	134	2	1	4	18	15	.55	12	.259	.311	.421
1995 Ottawa	AAA Mon	127	474	123	24	6	18	213	66	69	44	3	128	2	2	2	14	6	.70	10	.259	.324	.449
1996 Ottawa	AAA Mon	114	439	122	20	2	23	215	56	81	28	5	120	1	0	6	11	4	.73	5	.278	.319	.490
1997 Omaha	AAA KC	92	329	97	14	1	21	176	61	71	24	1	82	1	0	4	12	3	.80	8	.295	.341	.535
1999 Louisville	AAA Mil	99	341	73	24	2	12	137	47	49	29	0	103	2	1	1	13	4	.76	7	.214	.279	.402
2000 Charlotte	AAA CWS	19	66	13	1	0	1	17	4	2	3	0	17	1	0	0	1	0	1.00	2	.197	.243	.258
1995 Montreal	NL	14	39	15	2	1	2	25	8	7	1	0	7	0	0	0	0	2	.00	1	.385	.400	.641
1996 Montreal	NL	11	12	2	0	0	0	2	0	2	0	0	4	0	0	0	0	0	—	0	.167	.167	.167
1997 Kansas City	AL	53	191	51	7	1	8	84	22	21	10	0	49	1	2	0	2	2	.50	2	.267	.307	.440
1998 Arizona	NL	91	206	41	7	1	9	77	17	30	14	1	46	4	0	1	2	2	.50	6	.199	.262	.420
10 Min. YEARS		831	3056	786	141	33	117	1344	418	496	232	14	857	15	12	25	116	47	.71	62	.257	.310	.440
4 Maj. YEARS		169	448	109	16	3	19	188	47	60	25	1	106	5	2	1	4	6	.40	9	.243	.290	.420

Joel Bennett

Pitches: Right **Bats:** Right **Pos:** RP-36; SP-6   **Ht:** 6'1" **Wt:** 171 **Born:** 1/31/70 **Age:** 31

		HOW MUCH HE PITCHED						WHAT HE GAVE UP										THE RESULTS						
Year Team	Lg Org	G	GS	CG	GF	IP	BFP	H	R	ER	HR	SH	SF	HB	TBB	IBB	SO	WP	Bk	W	L	Pct.	ShO	Sv	ERA
1991 Red Sox	R Bos	2	2	0	0	10	38	6	2	2	0	0	1	1	4	0	8	2	1	0	0	—	0	0	1.80
Elmira	A- Bos	13	12	1	0	81	325	60	29	22	3	3	1	6	30	0	75	7	0	5	3	.625	1	0	2.44
1992 Winter Havn	A+ Bos	26	26	4	0	161.2	690	161	86	76	7	7	5	7	55	2	154	7	3	7	11	.389	0	0	4.23

Year Team	Lg Org	G	GS	CG	GF	IP	BFP	H	R	ER	HR	SH	SF	HB	TBB	IBB	SO	WP	Bk	W	L	Pct.	ShO	Sv	ERA
		HOW MUCH HE PITCHED						WHAT HE GAVE UP												THE RESULTS					
1993 Lynchburg	A+ Bos	29	29	3	0	181	754	151	93	77	17	7	9	4	67	6	221	18	0	7	12	.368	1	0	3.83
1994 New Britain	AA Bos	23	23	1	0	130.2	560	119	65	59	9	2	2	4	56	0	130	10	0	11	7	.611	1	0	4.06
Pawtucket	AAA Bos	4	4	0	0	21	91	19	16	16	8	0	0	1	12	0	24	1	0	1	3	.250	0	0	6.86
1995 Pawtucket	AAA Bos	20	13	0	2	77	357	91	57	50	6	0	4	3	45	3	50	6	0	2	4	.333	0	0	5.84
1996 Trenton	AA Bos	3	0	0	1	4.1	18	3	4	4	2	0	0	0	2	0	8	0	0	1	0	1.000	0	0	8.31
Newburgh	IND —	9	9	2	0	57	211	18	8	5	2	0	1	2	16	0	82	3	0	6	0	1.000	2	0	0.79
Bowie	AA Bal	10	8	0	0	54.2	211	36	21	20	5	0	0	1	17	0	48	0	0	2	3	.400	0	0	3.29
1997 Bowie	AA Bal	44	10	0	12	113.1	461	89	45	40	12	6	3	4	40	6	146	2	1	6	8	.429	0	0	3.18
1998 Rochester	AA Bal	18	15	1	0	101.1	425	99	46	41	9	2	3	2	37	1	99	3	0	10	0	1.000	0	0	3.64
Scranton-WB	AAA Phi	8	7	0	0	47.2	215	51	29	28	6	0	1	1	25	1	35	0	0	1	2	.333	0	0	5.29
1999 Scranton-WB	AAA Phi	20	20	1	0	127	550	134	71	65	10	2	6	6	47	2	125	5	0	10	4	.714	1	0	4.61
2000 Trenton	AA Bos	23	6	1	10	64.1	272	60	35	32	4	4	1	1	32	0	54	3	0	4	3	.571	0	0	4.48
Pawtucket	AAA Bos	19	0	0	3	33.2	147	37	21	19	5	2	3	1	15	1	29	0	0	1	1	.500	0	0	5.08
1998 Baltimore	AL	2	0	0	2	2	11	2	1	1	0	0	0	0	3	0	0	0	0	0	0	—	0	0	4.50
1999 Philadelphia	NL	5	3	0	0	17	83	26	17	17	10	2	0	0	7	0	13	0	0	2	1	.667	0	0	9.00
10 Min. YEARS		271	184	14	28	1265.2	5325	1134	628	556	105	35	40	44	500	22	1288	67	5	74	61	.548	6	6	3.95
2 Maj. YEARS		7	3	0	2	19	94	28	18	18	10	2	0	0	10	0	13	0	0	2	1	.667	0	0	8.53

Shayne Bennett

Pitches: Right Bats: Right Pos: SP-15; RP-7   Ht: 6'5" Wt: 220 Born: 4/10/72 Age: 29

Year Team	Lg Org	G	GS	CG	GF	IP	BFP	H	R	ER	HR	SH	SF	HB	TBB	IBB	SO	WP	Bk	W	L	Pct.	ShO	Sv	ERA
		HOW MUCH HE PITCHED						WHAT HE GAVE UP												THE RESULTS					
1993 Red Sox	R Bos	2	1	0	1	7	25	2	1	1	0	0	0	0	1	0	4	1	0	0	0	—	0	1	1.29
Ft. Laud	A+ Bos	23	0	0	18	31.1	128	26	8	6	1	4	1	0	11	1	23	2	2	1	2	.333	0	6	1.72
1994 Sarasota	A+ Bos	15	8	0	4	48.1	216	46	31	24	1	2	1	3	27	0	28	1	1	1	6	.143	0	3	4.47
1995 Sarasota	A+ Bos	52	0	0	43	59.2	255	50	23	17	3	4	2	4	21	4	69	5	1	2	5	.286	0	24	2.56
Trenton	AA Bos	10	0	0	6	10.2	48	16	6	6	3	1	0		3	0	6	1	0	0	1	.000	0	3	5.06
1996 Harrisburg	AA Mon	53	0	0	27	92.2	393	83	32	26	6	3	3	5	35	2	89	2	2	8	8	.500	0	12	2.53
1997 Harrisburg	AA Mon	23	1	0	7	47	210	47	28	23	6	3	1	4	20	0	38	1	0	4	2	.667	0	2	4.40
Ottawa	AAA Mon	25	0	0	21	34.1	142	23	8	6	0	2	1	2	21	1	29	2	0	1	2	.333	0	14	1.57
1999 Ottawa	AAA Mon	38	8	0	17	89.1	397	96	53	50	12	5	4	4	37	3	70	5	1	3	9	.250	0	5	5.04
2000 Ottawa	AAA Mon	22	15	0	2	78.2	375	94	61	55	13	3	2	2	45	2	54	4	0	3	5	.375	0	0	6.29
1997 Montreal	NL	16	0	0	3	22.2	98	21	9	8	2	1	3	0	9	3	8	0	0	0	1	.000	0	0	3.18
1998 Montreal	NL	62	0	0	11	91.2	417	97	61	56	8	9	6	6	45	3	59	3	1	5	5	.500	0	1	5.50
1999 Montreal	NL	5	0	0	0	11.1	59	24	18	18	4	0	1	1	3	0	4	0	0	0	1	.000	0	0	14.29
7 Min. YEARS		263	33	0	146	499	2189	483	251	214	43	29	17	24	221	13	410	24	7	23	40	.365	0	73	3.86
3 Maj. YEARS		83	1	0	15	125.2	574	142	88	82	14	10	10	7	57	6	71	3	1	5	7	.417	0	1	5.87

Joaquin Benoit

Pitches: Right Bats: Right Pos: SP-16   Ht: 6'4" Wt: 205 Born: 7/26/78 Age: 22

Year Team	Lg Org	G	GS	CG	GF	IP	BFP	H	R	ER	HR	SH	SF	HB	TBB	IBB	SO	WP	Bk	W	L	Pct.	ShO	Sv	ERA
		HOW MUCH HE PITCHED						WHAT HE GAVE UP												THE RESULTS					
1997 Rangers	R Tex	10	10	1	0	44	177	40	14	10	1	0	1	1	11	0	38	1	0	3	3	.500	0	0	2.05
1998 Savannah	A Tex	15	15	0	0	80	339	79	41	34	8	3	1	3	18	0	68	3	1	4	3	.571	0	0	3.83
1999 Charlotte	A+ Tex	22	22	0	0	105	483	117	67	62	5	1	7	11	50	0	83	3	2	7	4	.636	0	0	5.31
2000 Tulsa	AA Tex	16	16	0	0	82.1	346	73	40	35	6	0	4	4	30	0	72	6	0	4	4	.500	0	0	3.83
4 Min. YEARS		63	63	2	0	311.1	1345	309	162	141	19	5	12	19	109	0	261	13	3	18	14	.563	0	0	4.08

Jake Benz

Pitches: Left Bats: Left Pos: RP-29   Ht: 5'9" Wt: 162 Born: 2/27/72 Age: 29

Year Team	Lg Org	G	GS	CG	GF	IP	BFP	H	R	ER	HR	SH	SF	HB	TBB	IBB	SO	WP	Bk	W	L	Pct.	ShO	Sv	ERA
		HOW MUCH HE PITCHED						WHAT HE GAVE UP												THE RESULTS					
1994 Vermont	A- Mon	28	0	0	12	46	188	24	11	8	1	1	2	4	19	3	36	1	0	4	1	.800	0	3	1.57
1995 Wst Plm Bch	A+ Mon	44	0	0	38	54	220	44	13	7	0	3	2	3	18	3	48	4	1	0	2	.000	0	22	1.17
1996 Harrisburg	AA Mon	34	0	0	20	37.2	181	42	30	25	7	3	2	2	27	3	25	4	0	1	4	.200	0	4	5.97
Wst Plm Bch	A+ Mon	17	0	0	9	20.1	93	19	10	5	0	4	0	0	11	1	14	7	0	2	4	.333	0	2	2.21
1997 Wst Plm Bch	A+ Mon	14	0	0	3	24	94	18	9	7	1	1	1	2	6	0	28	3	0	0	2	.000	0	0	2.63
Harrisburg	AA Mon	23	0	0	9	38.2	168	39	12	10	3	1	1	1	20	0	36	4	0	4	1	.800	0	2	2.33
1998 Harrisburg	AA Mon	16	0	0	7	33.1	133	19	5	4	2	1	1	1	11	3	31	0	0	3	1	.750	0	4	1.08
Ottawa	AAA Mon	25	3	0	4	49.1	230	63	34	32	8	3	1	2	24	2	40	3	0	1	5	.167	0	1	5.84
1999 Ottawa	AAA Mon	18	0	0	3	30.1	152	42	20	20	3	1	4	1	20	3	34	2	0	2	3	.400	0	1	5.93
Calgary	AAA Fla	2	0	0	0	4	18	3	1	0	0	0	0	0	3	0	4	0	0	1	0	1.000	0	0	0.00
Portland	AA Fla	23	0	0	11	33.1	152	33	19	16	6	0	2	0	23	0	24	3	1	1	0	1.000	0	0	4.32
2000 Portland	AA Fla	14	0	0	4	18.1	85	21	11	9	1	1	0	1	11	1	11	1	0	1	1	.500	0	0	4.42
Calgary	AAA Fla	15	0	0	4	25.1	116	21	16	15	2	0	1	0	20	1	24	0	0	1	0	—	0	0	5.33
7 Min. YEARS		273	3	0	134	414.2	1830	388	198	158	31	21	19	17	212	20	355	32	2	20	24	.455	0	39	3.43

Jeff Berblinger

Bats: Right Throws: Right Pos: 2B-1   Ht: 6'0" Wt: 190 Born: 11/19/70 Age: 30

Year Team	Lg Org	G	AB	H	2B	3B	HR	TB	R	RBI	TBB	IBB	SO	HBP	SH	SF	SB	CS	SB%	GDP	Avg	OBP	SLG
		BATTING															BASERUNNING				PERCENTAGES		
1993 Glens Falls	A- StL	38	138	43	9	0	2	58	26	21	11	0	14	3	1	3	9	4	.69	2	.312	.368	.420
St. Pete	A+ StL	19	70	13	1	0	0	14	7	5	5	0	10	1	2	0	3	1	.75	1	.186	.250	.200
1994 Savannah	A StL	132	479	142	27	7	8	207	86	67	52	0	85	25	6	5	24	5	.83	8	.296	.390	.432
1995 Arkansas	AA StL	87	332	106	15	4	5	144	66	29	48	1	40	9	1	2	16	16	.50	2	.319	.417	.434
1996 Arkansas	AA StL	134	500	144	32	7	11	223	78	53	52	0	66	8	3	7	23	10	.70	9	.288	.360	.446
1997 Louisville	AAA StL	133	513	135	19	7	11	201	63	58	55	1	98	6	1	5	24	12	.67	15	.263	.339	.392
1998 Tacoma	AAA Sea	109	390	93	19	2	6	134	48	38	22	1	59	8	4	0	11	7	.61	5	.238	.293	.344
1999 Somerset	IND —	102	397	130	26	2	11	193	81	39	34	1	54	7	0	2	47	11	.81	6	.327	.389	.486
2000 Omaha	AAA KC	1	3	2	0	0	0	4	1	0	0	0	1	0	0	0	0	0	—	0	.667	.750	1.333

		BATTING														BASERUNNING				PERCENTAGES		
Year Team	Lg Org	G	AB	H	2B	3B	HR	TB	R	RBI	TBB	IBB	SO	HBP	SH	SF	SB	CS	SB%	GDP	Avg	OBP	SLG
1997 St. Louis	NL	7	5	0	0	0	0	0	1	0	0	0	1	0	1	0	0	0	—	0	.000	.000	.000
8 Min. YEARS		755	2822	808	150	29	54	1178	456	310	279	4	426	68	18	24	157	66	.70	48	.286	.362	.417

Brandon Berger

Bats: Right **Throws:** Right **Pos:** OF-119; DH-10; PR-1   **Ht:** 5'11" **Wt:** 200 **Born:** 2/21/75 **Age:** 26

		BATTING														BASERUNNING				PERCENTAGES		
Year Team	Lg Org	G	AB	H	2B	3B	HR	TB	R	RBI	TBB	IBB	SO	HBP	SH	SF	SB	CS	SB%	GDP	Avg	OBP	SLG
1996 Spokane	A- KC	71	283	87	12	1	13	140	46	58	31	0	64	2	1	3	17	5	.77	7	.307	.376	.495
1997 Lansing	A KC	107	393	115	22	6	12	185	64	73	42	1	79	7	0	4	13	1	.93	8	.293	.368	.471
1998 Wilmington	A+ KC	110	338	75	18	3	8	123	53	50	53	1	94	5	7	5	13	3	.81	11	.222	.332	.364
1999 Wilmington	A+ KC	119	450	132	27	4	16	215	73	73	45	0	93	8	6	6	29	7	.81	3	.293	.363	.478
2000 Wichita	AA KC	27	86	14	2	0	3	25	9	8	7	0	27	2	1	1	6	1	.86	2	.163	.240	.291
Wilmington	A+ KC	102	379	108	18	4	15	179	63	71	40	2	71	17	4	3	12	4	.75	8	.285	.376	.472
5 Min. YEARS		536	1929	531	99	18	67	867	308	333	218	4	428	41	19	22	90	21	.81	39	.275	.357	.449

Harry Berrios

Bats: Right **Throws:** Right **Pos:** OF-71; DH-13; 3B-1; PH-1   **Ht:** 5'11" **Wt:** 205 **Born:** 12/2/71 **Age:** 29

		BATTING														BASERUNNING				PERCENTAGES		
Year Team	Lg Org	G	AB	H	2B	3B	HR	TB	R	RBI	TBB	IBB	SO	HBP	SH	SF	SB	CS	SB%	GDP	Avg	OBP	SLG
1993 Albany	A Bal	46	145	30	5	1	3	46	16	16	18	1	20	5	0	2	2	0	1.00	3	.207	.312	.317
1994 Albany	A Bal	42	162	54	12	2	6	88	42	35	18	1	23	9	0	1	14	0	1.00	4	.333	.426	.543
Frederick	A+ Bal	86	325	113	13	0	13	165	70	71	32	2	47	18	2	2	42	14	.75	6	.348	.432	.508
Bowie	AA Bal	1	4	1	1	0	0	2	1	0	0	0	1	0	0	0	0	0	—	0	.250	.250	.500
1995 Frederick	A+ Bal	71	240	50	5	2	10	89	33	28	32	3	66	4	0	1	10	6	.63	3	.208	.309	.371
Bowie	AA Bal	56	208	51	13	0	5	79	32	21	26	1	44	1	1	0	12	2	.86	6	.245	.332	.380
1996 Bowie	AA Bal	37	123	23	4	0	6	45	19	17	16	1	24	6	1	1	7	2	.78	3	.187	.308	.366
Frederick	A+ Bal	43	161	37	9	1	4	60	25	20	12	0	21	3	1	2	8	3	.73	5	.230	.292	.373
Kinston	A+ Cle	24	73	14	5	0	2	25	7	11	9	0	16	0	1	1	2	0	1.00	2	.192	.277	.342
1997 Sioux Falls	IND —	75	294	83	14	1	14	141	41	61	21	2	60	7	1	2	7	1	.88	6	.282	.343	.480
1998 Sioux Falls	IND —	25	94	30	8	0	5	53	20	16	14	0	19	4	0	1	2	0	1.00	5	.319	.425	.564
Thunder Bay	IND —	33	137	44	9	0	6	71	24	22	7	0	16	0	0	1	10	2	.83	6	.321	.352	.518
1999 Schaumburg	IND —	84	359	111	15	1	11	161	65	59	24	1	56	8	2	1	26	6	.81	8	.309	.365	.448
2000 Schaumburg	IND —	62	256	84	25	1	11	144	56	38	24	2	56	4	0	1	17	1	.94	5	.328	.393	.563
Tulsa	AA Tex	24	102	33	6	1	5	56	20	18	3	0	12	0	1	1	5	1	.83	3	.324	.340	.549
8 Min. YEARS		709	2683	758	144	10	101	1225	471	433	256	14	481	69	10	18	164	38	.81	65	.283	.358	.457

Mike Berry

Bats: Right **Throws:** Right **Pos:** 3B-89; 2B-7; DH-5; PH-1   **Ht:** 5'10" **Wt:** 185 **Born:** 8/12/70 **Age:** 30

		BATTING														BASERUNNING				PERCENTAGES		
Year Team	Lg Org	G	AB	H	2B	3B	HR	TB	R	RBI	TBB	IBB	SO	HBP	SH	SF	SB	CS	SB%	GDP	Avg	OBP	SLG
1993 Burlington	A Mon	31	92	22	2	0	1	27	15	6	20	0	22	0	3	0	0	1	.00	4	.239	.375	.293
1994 Burlington	A Mon	94	334	105	18	1	10	155	67	45	53	0	59	1	1	1	7	3	.70	7	.314	.409	.464
1995 Wst Plm Bch	A+ Mon	24	79	13	3	1	1	21	16	2	13	0	16	0	0	0	0	1	.00	1	.165	.283	.266
Visalia	A+ Mon	98	368	113	28	4	9	176	69	61	57	1	70	5	1	3	12	6	.67	9	.307	.404	.478
1996 Frederick	A+ Bal	3	8	1	0	0	1	4	2	1	4	0	2	0	0	0	0	0	—	1	.125	.417	.500
Bowie	AA Bal	2	7	1	0	0	0	1	1	2	0	0	4	0	0	0	0	0	—	0	.143	.125	.143
High Desert	A+ Bal	121	463	167	44	5	13	260	109	113	99	3	67	7	0	3	7	4	.64	9	.361	.477	.562
1997 Bowie	AA Bal	53	204	47	10	0	8	81	34	30	24	0	53	3	1	2	1	1	.50	6	.230	.318	.397
Rochester	AAA Bal	54	177	53	11	3	1	73	23	19	13	0	31	1	0	1	1	1	.50	4	.299	.349	.412
1998 Columbus	AAA NYY	25	87	25	6	0	1	34	7	9	10	0	14	0	0	4	0	0	—	2	.287	.347	.391
Norwich	AA NYY	107	399	117	35	2	14	198	50	63	53	1	58	3	0	5	8	2	.80	8	.293	.376	.496
1999 Carolina	AA Col	90	306	74	15	2	9	120	36	38	26	0	61	2	0	3	0	0	.00	11	.242	.303	.392
2000 Newark	IND —	66	248	72	17	2	4	105	29	37	27	1	48	1	2	3	5	4	.56	10	.290	.358	.423
San Antonio	AA LA	30	112	41	7	1	3	59	13	20	14	0	17	0	0	0	2	3	.40	4	.366	.437	.527
Albuquerque	AAA LA	1	2	0	0	0	0	0	0	0	0	0	1	0	0	0	0	0	—	0	.000	.000	.000
8 Min. YEARS		799	2886	851	196	21	75	1314	471	446	413	6	523	23	8	26	43	28	.61	76	.295	.384	.455

Mike Bertotti

Pitches: Left **Bats:** Left **Pos:** SP-15; RP-4   **Ht:** 6'1" **Wt:** 185 **Born:** 1/18/70 **Age:** 31

		HOW MUCH HE PITCHED						WHAT HE GAVE UP										THE RESULTS					
Year Team	Lg Org	G	GS	CG	GF	IP	BFP	H	R	ER	HR	SH	SF	HB	TBB	IBB	SO	WP	Bk	W	L	Pct.	ShO	Sv	ERA
1991 Utica	A- CWS	14	5	0	3	37.1	186	38	33	24	2	1	3	2	36	0	33	9	1	3	4	.429	0	0	5.79
1992 South Bend	A CWS	11	0	0	5	19.1	86	12	8	8	1	1	1	1	22	0	17	1	1	3	0	.000	0	1	3.72
Utica	A- CWS	17	1	0	5	33.1	164	36	28	23	2	0	1	2	31	0	23	7	1	2	2	.500	0	1	6.21
1993 Hickory	A CWS	9	9	2	0	59.2	248	42	19	14	2	4	0	1	29	1	77	2	3	3	3	.500	0	0	2.11
South Bend	A CWS	17	16	2	0	111	466	93	51	43	5	6	6	6	44	2	108	7	1	5	7	.417	2	0	3.49
1994 Pr William	A+ CWS	16	15	2	0	104.2	435	90	48	41	11	3	2	3	43	0	103	8	1	7	6	.538	1	0	3.53
Birmingham	AA CWS	10	10	1	0	68.1	273	55	25	22	1	2	3	0	21	1	44	5	0	4	3	.571	1	0	2.90
1995 Birmingham	AA CWS	12	12	1	0	63	279	60	38	35	4	0	4	2	36	0	53	8	0	2	7	.222	0	0	5.00
Nashville	AAA CWS	7	6	0	1	32	154	41	34	31	8	0	1	3	17	0	35	0	0	2	3	.400	0	0	8.72
1996 Nashville	AAA CWS	28	9	1	5	82.1	365	80	43	40	10	5	4	2	42	3	73	3	0	5	3	.625	0	1	4.37
1997 Nashville	AAA CWS	21	20	1	0	107.2	505	90	70	64	17	1	7	2	105	0	87	15	0	5	9	.357	0	0	5.35
1998 Calgary	AAA CWS	43	6	0	16	80.1	383	90	56	53	10	3	6	4	50	0	64	8	0	3	2	.600	0	3	5.94
1999 Tacoma	AAA Sea	3	3	0	0	7	43	6	8	8	0	1	0	0	17	0	6	1	0	0	2	.000	0	0	10.29
Midland	AA Oak	20	0	0	6	25.2	141	30	26	24	0	0	1	3	37	0	25	7	0	3	2	.400	0	1	8.42
Waterbury	IND —	7	7	0	0	35.2	159	39	25	24	5	0	3	1	17	0	40	3	0	0	1	.000	0	0	6.06
2000 Midland	IND —	12	12	5	0	81.1	324	82	27	18	3	5	1	2	35	0	86	6	0	5	7	.417	1	0	1.99
Columbus	AAA NYY	7	3	0	2	24	104	23	16	12	2	0	0	0	8	0	23	2	0	1	1	.500	0	0	4.50
1995 Chicago	AL	4	4	0	0	14.1	80	23	20	20	6	0	3	3	11	0	15	2	1	1	1	.500	0	0	12.56
1996 Chicago	AL	15	2	0	4	28	130	28	18	16	5	0	1	0	20	3	19	1	0	1	0	1.000	0	0	5.14

Year Team	Lg Org	HOW MUCH HE PITCHED						WHAT HE GAVE UP												THE RESULTS					
		G	GS	CG	GF	IP	BFP	H	R	ER	HR	SH	SF	HB	TBB	IBB	SO	WP	Bk	W	L	Pct.	ShO	Sv	ERA
1997 Chicago	AL	9	0	0	2	3.2	23	9	3	3	0	0	1	0	2	0	4	0	1	0	0	—	0	0	7.36
10 Min. YEARS		254	134	15	43	972.2	4315	879	555	484	85	31	42	32	590	7	897	92	7	49	66	.426	5	7	4.48
3 Maj. YEARS		28	6	0	6	46	233	60	41	39	11	0	5	3	33	3	38	6	2	3	1	.750	0	0	7.63

Derek Besco

Bats: Right **Throws:** Right **Pos:** OF-52; DH-23; PH-1; PR-1   **Ht:** 6'2" **Wt:** 200 **Born:** 1/21/76 **Age:** 25

Year Team	Lg Org	BATTING														BASERUNNING				PERCENTAGES		
		G	AB	H	2B	3B	HR	TB	R	RBI	TBB	IBB	SO	HBP	SH	SF	SB	CS	SB%	GDP	Avg	OBP	SLG
1998 Jamestown	A- Det	49	183	43	9	1	6	72	27	18	17	0	30	2	0	2	11	3	.79	6	.235	.304	.393
1999 Lakeland	A+ Det	122	456	131	28	4	9	194	70	66	37	4	88	3	1	3	10	7	.59	12	.287	.343	.425
2000 Lakeland	A+ Det	20	82	23	4	0	2	33	15	12	4	0	15	1	0	0	1	0	1.00	1	.280	.322	.402
Toledo	AAA Det	25	79	21	3	0	3	33	12	11	5	0	11	1	0	0	0	0	—	0	.266	.314	.418
Jacksnville	AA Det	32	105	21	5	0	4	38	10	10	10	0	14	1	2	0	3	0	1.00	2	.200	.276	.362
3 Min. YEARS		248	905	239	49	5	24	370	134	117	73	4	158	8	3	6	25	10	.71	22	.264	.323	.409

Todd Betts

Bats: Left **Throws:** Right **Pos:** 1B-57; 3B-53; DH-6; PH-5   **Ht:** 6'0" **Wt:** 185 **Born:** 6/24/73 **Age:** 28

Year Team	Lg Org	BATTING														BASERUNNING				PERCENTAGES		
		G	AB	H	2B	3B	HR	TB	R	RBI	TBB	IBB	SO	HBP	SH	SF	SB	CS	SB%	GDP	Avg	OBP	SLG
1993 Burlington	R+ Cle	56	168	39	9	0	7	69	40	27	32	2	26	3	0	1	6	1	.86	4	.232	.363	.411
1994 Watertown	A- Cle	65	227	74	18	2	10	126	49	53	54	2	29	4	1	2	3	2	.60	1	.326	.460	.555
1995 Kinston	A+ Cle	109	331	90	15	3	9	138	52	44	88	2	56	6	1	4	2	3	.40	5	.272	.429	.417
1996 Canton-Akrn	AA Cle	77	238	60	13	0	1	76	35	26	38	2	51	5	0	4	0	1	.00	6	.252	.361	.319
1997 Akron	AA Cle	128	439	108	25	1	20	195	65	69	73	8	97	4	1	5	1	3	.25	6	.246	.355	.444
1998 Akron	AA Cle	91	318	86	18	3	17	161	55	46	64	5	71	4	0	2	1	0	1.00	1	.270	.397	.506
Buffalo	AAA Cle	14	35	8	3	0	2	17	5	6	8	0	7	0	0	1	0	0	—	0	.229	.364	.486
1999 Akron	AA Cle	104	375	105	24	1	19	188	60	67	61	2	65	7	0	3	2	1	.67	3	.280	.388	.501
2000 Calgary	AAA Fla	1	1	0	0	0	0	0	0	0	0	0	0	0	0	0	0	0	—	0	.000	.000	.000
Portland	AA Fla	119	421	135	26	2	9	192	74	71	64	3	57	8	0	5	4	3	.57	6	.321	.416	.456
8 Min. YEARS		764	2553	705	151	12	94	1162	435	409	482	26	459	41	3	27	19	14	.58	38	.276	.396	.455

James Betzsold

Bats: Right **Throws:** Right **Pos:** OF-76; PH-10; DH-7; PR-2; 1B-1   **Ht:** 6'3" **Wt:** 210 **Born:** 8/7/72 **Age:** 28

Year Team	Lg Org	BATTING														BASERUNNING				PERCENTAGES		
		G	AB	H	2B	3B	HR	TB	R	RBI	TBB	IBB	SO	HBP	SH	SF	SB	CS	SB%	GDP	Avg	OBP	SLG
1994 Watertown	A- Cle	66	212	61	18	0	12	115	48	46	53	1	68	15	1	2	3	3	.50	2	.288	.457	.542
1995 Kinston	A+ Cle	126	455	122	22	2	25	223	77	71	55	3	137	10	0	5	4	1	.80	3	.268	.357	.490
1996 Canton-Akrn	AA Cle	84	268	64	11	5	3	94	35	35	30	1	74	6	1	1	4	1	.80	3	.239	.328	.351
1997 Akron	AA Cle	118	434	115	21	5	19	203	76	79	60	2	119	10	0	2	4	5	.44	12	.265	.366	.468
1998 Buffalo	AAA Cle	74	209	51	10	1	10	93	36	27	27	0	72	6	0	0	4	4	.50	3	.244	.347	.445
1999 Jackson	AA Hou	38	126	30	6	1	6	56	30	17	22	0	35	5	1	0	4	3	.57	2	.238	.373	.444
New Orleans	AAA Hou	63	198	43	15	0	7	79	29	27	14	0	64	3	0	2	3	2	.60	1	.217	.276	.399
2000 New Orleans	AAA Hou	93	314	89	17	1	8	132	47	49	29	1	101	4	0	1	16	7	.70	8	.283	.351	.420
7 Min. YEARS		662	2216	575	120	15	90	995	378	351	290	8	670	59	3	12	41	30	.58	35	.259	.359	.449

Bobby Bevel

Pitches: Left **Bats:** Left **Pos:** RP-46; SP-1   **Ht:** 5'10" **Wt:** 180 **Born:** 10/10/73 **Age:** 27

Year Team	Lg Org	HOW MUCH HE PITCHED						WHAT HE GAVE UP												THE RESULTS					
		G	GS	CG	GF	IP	BFP	H	R	ER	HR	SH	SF	HB	TBB	IBB	SO	WP	Bk	W	L	Pct.	ShO	Sv	ERA
1995 Portland	A- Col	25	0	0	8	28	128	24	13	11	0	3	2	1	18	4	25	5	0	2	3	.400	0	1	3.54
1996 Asheville	A Col	41	0	0	10	68	286	61	25	24	4	3	1	2	30	2	60	6	0	4	2	.667	0	3	3.18
1997 Salem	A+ Col	50	0	0	18	66	290	69	37	34	5	2	7	9	17	0	57	3	0	4	7	.364	0	3	4.64
1998 Salem	A+ Col	51	0	0	26	91.2	373	72	26	23	4	2	3	4	24	0	92	5	1	6	4	.600	0	3	2.26
1999 Carolina	AA Col	48	0	0	22	67	294	70	37	33	7	4	1	2	27	2	58	9	0	3	7	.300	0	7	4.43
2000 San Antonio	AA LA	47	1	0	19	78.1	365	86	52	49	8	8	0	6	44	5	75	7	0	4	5	.444	0	2	5.63
6 Min. YEARS		262	1	0	103	399	1736	382	190	174	28	22	14	24	160	13	367	35	1	23	28	.451	0	16	3.92

Jason Beverlin

Pitches: Right **Bats:** Left **Pos:** SP-27   **Ht:** 6'5" **Wt:** 220 **Born:** 11/27/73 **Age:** 27

Year Team	Lg Org	HOW MUCH HE PITCHED						WHAT HE GAVE UP												THE RESULTS					
		G	GS	CG	GF	IP	BFP	H	R	ER	HR	SH	SF	HB	TBB	IBB	SO	WP	Bk	W	L	Pct.	ShO	Sv	ERA
1994 W Michigan	A Oak	17	1	0	5	41	168	32	12	8	0	1	0	2	14	0	48	3	4	3	2	.600	0	1	1.76
1995 W Michigan	A Oak	22	14	0	1	89	392	76	51	40	4	3	3	8	40	0	84	5	5	3	9	.250	0	0	4.04
Greensboro	A NYY	7	7	1	0	51	198	49	15	15	1	0	0	0	6	0	31	4	0	2	4	.333	1	0	2.65
1996 Norwich	AA NYY	8	4	0	1	16	81	25	21	15	2	0	2	0	6	1	17	0	0	0	3	.000	0	0	8.44
Tampa	A+ NYY	25	1	0	6	46.1	194	43	22	18	5	1	1	1	17	2	38	4	1	2	0	1.000	0	1	3.50
1997 Norwich	AA NYY	25	0	0	8	41.2	203	50	38	36	10	0	0	6	24	0	42	3	0	1	0	1.000	0	0	7.78
Tampa	A+ NYY	7	6	0	0	41.1	167	37	26	22	4	2	2	4	13	1	24	6	0	1	3	.250	0	0	4.79
1998 Norwich	AA NYY	25	9	0	8	81	343	68	34	33	5	2	4	3	38	0	86	6	1	3	5	.375	0	1	3.67
Tampa	A+ NYY	7	5	0	0	32	142	37	23	20	2	0	4	1	16	2	15	2	1	1	3	.250	0	0	5.63
1999 Norwich	AA NYY	28	27	1	0	173.1	743	153	91	71	16	6	7	6	81	0	147	10	1	15	9	.625	0	0	3.69
2000 Columbus	AAA NYY	3	3	0	0	6.2	45	13	14	14	1	0	0	0	14	0	6	1	0	0	3	.000	0	0	18.90
Norwich	AA NYY	24	24	1	0	143.2	618	110	61	45	7	3	4	10	87	2	100	6	0	8	9	.471	0	0	2.82
7 Min. YEARS		198	101	3	29	763	3294	693	408	337	57	18	27	41	356	8	638	50	13	39	50	.438	1	3	3.98

Andy Bevins

Bats: Right **Throws:** Right **Pos:** OF-88; DH-22; PH-12; 1B-9; PR-1 **Ht:** 6'3" **Wt:** 215 **Born:** 10/10/75 **Age:** 25

Year Team	Lg Org	G	AB	H	2B	3B	HR	TB	R	RBI	TBB	IBB	SO	HBP	SH	SF	SB	CS	SB%	GDP	Avg	OBP	SLG
1997 New Jersey	A- StL	65	235	64	9	5	9	110	35	44	18	1	66	3	0	3	2	1	.67	3	.272	.328	.468
1998 Peoria	A StL	130	508	124	30	3	18	214	68	98	34	1	145	10	1	3	6	4	.60	10	.244	.303	.421
1999 Potomac	A+ StL	138	513	142	30	2	25	251	92	97	44	2	128	11	3	4	6	2	.75	11	.277	.344	.489
2000 Arkansas	AA StL	125	430	138	27	4	25	248	84	88	34	0	87	11	0	3	0	4	.00	11	.321	.383	.577
Memphis	AAA StL	5	22	4	2	0	0	6	1	3	1	0	3	0	0	0	0	0	—	1	.182	.217	.273
4 Min. YEARS		463	1708	472	98	14	77	829	280	330	131	4	429	35	4	13	14	11	.56	36	.276	.338	.485

Nick Bierbrodt

Pitches: Left **Bats:** Left **Pos:** SP-13; RP-2 **Ht:** 6'5" **Wt:** 185 **Born:** 5/16/78 **Age:** 23

Year Team	Lg Org	G	GS	CG	GF	IP	BFP	H	R	ER	HR	SH	SF	HB	TBB	IBB	SO	WP	Bk	W	L	Pct.	ShO	Sv	ERA
1996 Diamondbcks	R Ari	8	8	0	0	38	147	25	9	7	1	0	0	0	13	0	46	2	1	1	1	.500	0	0	1.66
Lethbridge	R+ Ari	3	3	0	0	18	72	12	4	1	0	0	1	1	5	0	23	1	0	2	0	1.000	0	0	0.50
1997 South Bend	A Ari	15	15	0	0	75.2	340	77	43	34	4	3	1	9	37	0	64	6	1	2	4	.333	0	0	4.04
1998 High Desert	A+ Ari	24	23	1	0	129.2	560	122	66	49	7	3	6	7	64	0	88	9	0	8	7	.533	0	0	3.40
1999 El Paso	AA Ari	14	14	2	0	76	341	78	45	39	3	2	1	8	37	0	55	5	0	5	6	.455	1	0	4.62
Tucson	AAA Ari	11	11	0	0	43.1	213	57	42	35	9	4	0	3	30	0	43	3	0	1	4	.200	0	0	7.27
2000 Tucson	AAA Ari	4	3	0	0	18.2	77	13	10	10	3	0	0	2	14	0	11	0	0	2	1	.667	0	0	4.82
Diamondbcks	R Ari	4	3	0	0	8	34	4	4	4	0	0	0	1	5	0	10	1	0	0	0	—	0	0	4.50
El Paso	AA Ari	7	7	0	0	35.1	166	37	30	28	1	2	1	3	24	0	36	5	0	1	3	.250	0	0	7.13
5 Min. YEARS		90	87	3	0	442.2	1950	425	253	207	28	14	10	34	229	0	376	32	1	22	26	.458	1	0	4.21

Kurt Bierek

Bats: Left **Throws:** Right **Pos:** 1B-64; OF-33; DH-28; PH-10; PR-1 **Ht:** 6'4" **Wt:** 220 **Born:** 9/13/72 **Age:** 28

Year Team	Lg Org	G	AB	H	2B	3B	HR	TB	R	RBI	TBB	IBB	SO	HBP	SH	SF	SB	CS	SB%	GDP	Avg	OBP	SLG
1993 Oneonta	A- NYY	70	274	64	6	6	5	97	36	37	19	2	49	3	1	1	4	4	.50	4	.234	.290	.354
1994 Greensboro	A NYY	133	467	118	24	6	14	196	78	73	69	2	101	8	2	3	8	1	.89	10	.253	.356	.420
1995 Tampa	A+ NYY	126	447	111	16	2	4	143	60	53	61	3	73	4	2	2	3	4	.43	11	.248	.342	.320
1996 Tampa	A+ NYY	88	320	97	14	2	11	148	48	55	41	3	40	6	0	3	6	3	.67	5	.303	.389	.463
1997 Norwich	AA NYY	133	473	128	32	2	18	218	77	78	56	2	89	7	0	2	4	4	.50	8	.271	.355	.461
1998 Columbus	AAA NYY	14	50	15	5	1	1	25	8	8	5	0	8	0	0	0	0	0	—	2	.300	.364	.500
Norwich	AA NYY	95	344	81	13	2	13	137	44	61	50	1	61	3	0	2	0	1	.00	8	.235	.336	.398
1999 Columbus	AAA NYY	135	532	149	42	4	23	268	84	95	48	1	99	6	1	7	5	3	.63	14	.280	.342	.504
2000 Indianapolis	AAA Mil	128	430	114	22	2	19	197	61	72	57	5	77	2	1	3	1	0	1.00	9	.265	.352	.458
8 Min. YEARS		922	3337	877	174	27	108	1429	496	532	406	19	597	39	7	23	31	20	.61	71	.263	.347	.428

Steve Bieser

Bats: Left **Throws:** Right **Pos:** OF-59; PH-29; C-4; 3B-3; 2B-2; PR-2; DH-1; P-1 **Ht:** 5'10" **Wt:** 180 **Born:** 8/4/67 **Age:** 33

Year Team	Lg Org	G	AB	H	2B	3B	HR	TB	R	RBI	TBB	IBB	SO	HBP	SH	SF	SB	CS	SB%	GDP	Avg	OBP	SLG
1989 Batavia	A- Phi	25	75	18	3	1	1	26	13	13	12	0	20	2	2	2	2	1	.67	1	.240	.352	.347
1990 Batavia	A- Phi	54	160	37	11	1	0	50	36	12	26	1	27	1	2	2	13	2	.87	3	.231	.339	.313
1991 Spartanburg	A Phi	60	168	41	6	0	0	47	25	13	31	0	35	3	4	3	17	4	.81	4	.244	.366	.280
1992 Clearwater	A+ Phi	73	203	58	6	5	0	74	33	10	39	3	28	9	8	0	8	8	.50	2	.286	.422	.365
Reading	AA Phi	33	139	38	5	4	0	51	20	8	6	0	25	4	4	0	8	3	.73	3	.273	.322	.367
1993 Reading	AA Phi	53	170	53	6	3	1	68	21	19	15	1	24	2	1	0	9	5	.64	2	.312	.374	.400
Scranton-WB	AAA Phi	26	83	21	4	0	0	25	3	4	2	0	14	1	1	0	3	0	1.00	0	.253	.279	.301
1994 Scranton-WB	AAA Phi	93	228	61	13	1	0	76	42	15	17	1	40	5	4	2	12	8	.60	2	.268	.329	.333
1995 Scranton-WB	AAA Phi	95	245	66	12	6	1	93	37	33	22	1	56	10	6	2	14	5	.74	5	.269	.351	.380
1996 Ottawa	AAA Mon	123	382	123	24	4	1	158	63	32	35	4	55	6	23	2	27	7	.79	6	.322	.386	.414
1997 Norfolk	AAA NYM	41	122	20	5	0	0	25	6	4	9	0	20	5	2	0	4	3	.57	1	.164	.250	.205
1998 Nashville	AAA Pit	82	206	53	11	4	1	75	30	24	33	1	30	10	4	6	13	2	.87	4	.257	.376	.364
1999 Nashville	AAA Pit	6	13	3	1	0	0	4	3	3	2	0	4	1	0	0	0	0	—	0	.231	.375	.308
Altoona	AA Pit	40	148	31	5	2	4	52	24	23	21	0	32	4	0	1	3	4	.43	2	.209	.322	.351
Memphis	AAA StL	58	180	56	13	2	4	85	25	16	16	0	30	3	5	0	8	0	1.00	3	.311	.377	.472
2000 Memphis	AAA StL	94	262	67	11	3	0	84	41	14	35	2	29	7	4	1	10	3	.77	2	.256	.357	.321
1997 New York	NL	47	69	17	3	0	0	20	16	4	7	1	20	4	0	1	2	3	.40	1	.246	.346	.290
1998 Pittsburgh	NL	13	11	3	1	0	0	4	2	1	2	0	2	0	0	0	0	0	—	1	.273	.385	.364
12 Min. YEARS		956	2784	746	136	36	13	993	422	243	321	14	469	73	70	21	151	55	.73	39	.268	.356	.357
2 Maj. YEARS		60	80	20	4	0	0	24	18	5	9	1	22	4	0	1	2	3	.40	1	.250	.351	.300

Larry Bigbie

Bats: Left **Throws:** Left **Pos:** OF-86 **Ht:** 6'4" **Wt:** 190 **Born:** 11/4/77 **Age:** 23

Year Team	Lg Org	G	AB	H	2B	3B	HR	TB	R	RBI	TBB	IBB	SO	HBP	SH	SF	SB	CS	SB%	GDP	Avg	OBP	SLG
1999 Bluefield	R+ Bal	8	30	8	0	0	0	8	3	4	3	0	8	1	0	1	1	3	.25	1	.267	.343	.267
Delmarva	A Bal	43	165	46	7	3	2	65	18	27	29	0	42	0	0	3	3	1	.75	4	.279	.381	.394
2000 Frederick	A+ Bal	55	201	59	11	0	2	76	33	28	23	2	34	0	1	4	7	3	.70	3	.294	.360	.378
Bowie	AA Bal	31	112	27	6	0	0	33	11	5	11	0	28	0	1	0	3	0	1.00	3	.241	.309	.295
2 Min. YEARS		137	508	140	24	3	4	182	65	64	66	2	112	1	2	8	14	7	.67	11	.276	.355	.358

Brent Billingsley

Pitches: Left **Bats:** Left **Pos:** SP-20 **Ht:** 6'2" **Wt:** 200 **Born:** 4/19/75 **Age:** 26

Year Team	Lg Org	G	GS	CG	GF	IP	BFP	H	R	ER	HR	SH	SF	HB	TBB	IBB	SO	WP	Bk	W	L	Pct.	ShO	Sv	ERA
1996 Utica	A- Fla	15	15	0	0	89.2	373	83	46	40	6	0	4	3	28	0	82	5	1	4	5	.444	0	0	4.01
1997 Kane County	A Fla	26	26	3	0	170.2	697	146	67	57	9	7	1	11	50	0	175	13	1	14	7	.667	1	0	3.01
1998 Portland	AA Fla	28	28	0	0	171	741	172	90	71	24	5	2	6	70	2	183	17	1	6	13	.316	0	0	3.74
1999 Calgary	AAA Fla	21	21	0	0	116.2	522	133	81	72	15	9	3	1	48	0	79	8	0	2	9	.182	0	0	5.55
2000 Ottawa	AAA Mon	20	20	0	0	103.1	464	118	73	65	14	4	2	3	46	0	76	7	0	8	9	.471	0	0	5.66
1999 Florida	NL	8	0	0	3	7.2	42	11	14	14	3	0	1	2	10	0	3	1	0	0	0	—	0	0	16.43
5 Min. YEARS		110	110	3	0	651.1	2797	652	357	305	68	25	12	24	242	2	595	50	3	34	43	.442	1	0	4.21

Darren Blakely

Bats: Both **Throws:** Right **Pos:** OF-111; DH-11 **Ht:** 6'0" **Wt:** 190 **Born:** 3/14/77 **Age:** 24

Year Team	Lg Org	G	AB	H	2B	3B	HR	TB	R	RBI	TBB	IBB	SO	HBP	SH	SF	SB	CS	SB%	GDP	Avg	OBP	SLG
1998 Boise	A- Ana	71	267	74	9	6	5	110	50	33	34	3	69	22	1	4	9	3	.75	2	.277	.398	.412
1999 Lk Elsinore	A+ Ana	124	510	128	38	10	12	222	88	63	36	1	159	20	1	4	23	13	.64	3	.251	.323	.435
2000 Erie	AA Ana	122	439	104	20	7	16	186	72	54	30	1	136	20	6	2	13	5	.72	11	.237	.314	.424
3 Min. YEARS		317	1216	306	67	23	33	518	210	150	100	5	364	62	8	10	45	21	.68	16	.252	.337	.426

Willie Bloomquist

Bats: Right **Throws:** Right **Pos:** 2B-103; SS-11; PR-1 **Ht:** 5'11" **Wt:** 180 **Born:** 11/27/77 **Age:** 23

Year Team	Lg Org	G	AB	H	2B	3B	HR	TB	R	RBI	TBB	IBB	SO	HBP	SH	SF	SB	CS	SB%	GDP	Avg	OBP	SLG
1999 Everett	A- Sea	42	178	51	10	3	2	73	35	27	22	0	25	1	0	1	17	5	.77	1	.287	.366	.410
2000 Lancaster	A+ Sea	64	256	97	19	6	2	134	63	51	37	2	27	0	1	1	22	12	.65	3	.379	.456	.523
Tacoma	AAA Sea	51	191	43	5	1	1	53	17	23	7	0	28	0	4	3	5	0	1.00	1	.225	.249	.277
2 Min. YEARS		157	625	191	34	10	5	260	115	101	66	2	80	1	5	5	44	17	.72	7	.306	.370	.416

Greg Blosser

Bats: Left **Throws:** Left **Pos:** OF-79; DH-18; PH-9 **Ht:** 6'3" **Wt:** 215 **Born:** 6/26/71 **Age:** 30

Year Team	Lg Org	G	AB	H	2B	3B	HR	TB	R	RBI	TBB	IBB	SO	HBP	SH	SF	SB	CS	SB%	GDP	Avg	OBP	SLG
1989 Red Sox	R Bos	40	146	42	7	3	2	61	17	20	25	1	19	1	0	2	3	0	1.00	7	.288	.391	.418
Winter Havn	A+ Bos	28	94	24	1	1	2	33	6	14	8	0	14	1	0	1	1	0	1.00	1	.255	.317	.351
1990 Lynchburg	A+ Bos	119	447	126	23	1	18	205	63	62	55	3	99	1	0	1	5	4	.56	13	.282	.361	.459
1991 New Britain	AA Bos	134	452	98	21	3	8	149	48	46	63	0	114	1	0	4	9	4	.69	16	.217	.312	.330
1992 New Britain	AA Bos	129	434	105	23	4	22	202	59	71	64	9	122	1	0	3	0	2	.00	4	.242	.339	.465
Pawtucket	AAA Bos	1	0	0	0	0	0	0	1	0	1	0	0	0	0	0	0	0	—	0	—	1.000	—
1993 Pawtucket	AAA Bos	130	478	109	22	2	23	204	66	66	58	5	139	2	1	4	3	3	.50	4	.228	.312	.427
1994 Pawtucket	AAA Bos	97	350	91	21	1	17	165	52	54	44	5	97	0	1	0	11	3	.79	9	.260	.342	.471
1995 Pawtucket	AAA Bos	17	50	10	0	0	1	13	5	4	5	0	13	0	0	1	0	0	—	0	.200	.268	.260
Trenton	AA Bos	49	179	44	13	0	11	90	25	34	13	0	42	0	1	3	3	2	.60	4	.246	.292	.503
1996 Rochester	AAA Bal	38	115	27	6	1	2	41	11	12	12	0	29	0	0	1	2	1	.67	3	.235	.307	.357
1997 St. Pete	A+ TB	52	189	59	9	2	12	108	40	32	35	5	42	0	0	0	7	9	.44	3	.312	.416	.571
Okla City	AAA TB	54	178	54	11	1	12	103	33	27	27	0	46	0	0	2	6	2	.75	2	.303	.391	.579
1998 Durham	AAA TB	115	371	94	23	0	25	192	78	72	73	3	114	2	1	6	10	5	.67	4	.253	.374	.518
2000 Fresno	AAA SF	18	44	7	3	0	0	10	4	8	7	1	9	0	0	1	2	0	1.00	1	.159	.269	.227
Somerset	IND —	85	271	82	17	1	20	161	54	54	38	2	64	2	0	3	6	3	.67	2	.303	.389	.594
1993 Boston	AL	17	28	2	1	0	0	3	1	1	2	0	7	0	0	0	1	0	1.00	0	.071	.133	.107
1994 Boston	AL	5	11	1	0	0	0	1	2	1	4	0	4	0	0	0	0	0	—	0	.091	.333	.091
11 Min. YEARS		1106	3798	972	200	20	175	1737	562	576	528	34	963	11	3	34	68	38	.64	76	.256	.346	.457
2 Maj. YEARS		22	39	3	1	0	0	4	3	2	6	0	11	0	0	0	1	0	1.00	0	.077	.200	.103

Jaime Bluma

Pitches: Right **Bats:** Right **Pos:** RP-30; SP-2 **Ht:** 5'11" **Wt:** 195 **Born:** 5/18/72 **Age:** 29

Year Team	Lg Org	G	GS	CG	GF	IP	BFP	H	R	ER	HR	SH	SF	HB	TBB	IBB	SO	WP	Bk	W	L	Pct.	ShO	Sv	ERA
1994 Eugene	A- KC	26	0	0	23	36.1	133	19	5	4	0	1	1	0	6	0	35	0	0	2	1	.667	0	12	0.99
Wilmington	A+ KC	7	0	0	7	9.2	34	7	2	1	0	0	0	0	0	0	5	0	0	4	0	1.000	0	2	0.93
1995 Wichita	AA KC	42	0	0	40	55.1	214	38	19	19	9	3	1	1	9	2	31	1	0	4	3	.571	0	22	3.09
Omaha	AAA KC	18	0	0	18	23.2	101	21	13	8	1	3	3	0	14	4	12	3	0	0	0	—	0	4	3.04
1996 Omaha	AAA KC	52	0	0	47	57.2	251	57	22	20	7	0	2	1	20	3	40	5	2	1	2	.333	0	25	3.12
1998 Omaha	AAA KC	14	0	0	9	14.1	67	19	13	10	4	0	1	0	7	2	8	0	0	0	1	.000	0	0	6.28
Wichita	AA KC	39	0	0	18	62	291	67	49	37	10	1	0	4	35	6	38	5	0	1	2	.333	0	0	5.37
1999 Wichita	AA KC	30	0	0	22	38.1	169	40	25	23	9	0	1	0	16	3	21	0	1	2	6	.250	0	0	5.40
Omaha	AAA KC	17	0	0	10	22.1	92	21	10	8	5	1	0	0	4	1	19	0	0	0	0	—	0	2	3.22
2000 Omaha	AAA KC	30	2	0	13	54	236	58	34	30	8	1	3	4	19	2	30	3	0	5	3	.625	0	1	5.00
Wichita	AA KC	8	0	0	2	2	12	3	4	4	0	0	0	0	0	0	2	0	0	0	0	—	0	0	18.00
1996 Kansas City	AL	17	0	0	10	20	82	18	9	8	2	2	1	2	4	1	14	1	0	0	0	—	0	5	3.60
6 Min. YEARS		277	2	0	201	375.2	1600	350	196	164	53	10	12	10	133	23	241	17	3	19	18	.514	0	76	3.93

Kurt Bogott

Pitches: Left **Bats:** Left **Pos:** RP-20 **Ht:** 6'4" **Wt:** 195 **Born:** 9/30/72 **Age:** 28

Year Team	Lg Org	G	GS	CG	GF	IP	BFP	H	R	ER	HR	SH	SF	HB	TBB	IBB	SO	WP	Bk	W	L	Pct.	ShO	Sv	ERA
1993 Red Sox	R Bos	13	2	0	0	15	57	10	3	3	1	0	0	2	4	0	20	3	0	0	1	.000	0	0	1.80
Utica	A- Bos	13	10	0	0	56.2	260	64	37	28	4	2	1	3	23	0	53	8	3	1	7	.125	0	0	4.45

Year Team	Lg Org	HOW MUCH HE PITCHED						WHAT HE GAVE UP												THE RESULTS					
		G	GS	CG	GF	IP	BFP	H	R	ER	HR	SH	SF	HB	TBB	IBB	SO	WP	Bk	W	L	Pct.	ShO	Sv	ERA
1994 Red Sox	R Bos	3	2	0	0	13.2	49	7	1	1	0	0	0	1	3	0	12	2	0	1	0	1.000	0	0	0.66
Lynchburg	A+ Bos	6	6	0	0	26.1	127	32	23	18	1	1	1	1	14	0	14	2	0	2	3	.400	0	0	6.15
1995 Sarasota	A+ Bos	41	9	0	15	88.2	388	89	44	30	3	4	1	4	41	0	62	8	3	6	4	.600	0	0	3.05
Trenton	AA Bos	2	0	0	2	3.1	13	3	1	1	1	0	0	0	1	0	2	0	0	0	1	.000	0	0	2.70
1996 Knoxville	AA Tor	33	0	0	9	54	256	64	34	32	2	0	2	5	29	2	56	12	1	2	2	.500	0	3	5.33
Dunedin	A+ Tor	19	0	0	8	30.1	133	22	16	6	2	0	0	3	20	1	41	8	0	1	1	.500	0	4	1.78
1997 Syracuse	AAA Tor	16	0	0	6	21.2	106	23	20	19	2	2	2	3	15	1	16	1	0	1	3	.250	0	1	7.89
Knoxville	AA Tor	35	1	0	14	64.2	284	66	32	28	10	1	3	6	25	2	77	6	1	2	1	.667	0	2	3.90
1998 Dunedin	A+ Tor	3	0	0	0	6.1	21	2	0	0	0	0	0	0	1	0	8	0	0	0	0		0	0	0.00
1999 Syracuse	AAA Tor	46	4	0	10	85.2	392	80	52	44	11	3	3	8	44	4	76	9	0	8	6	.571	0	1	4.62
2000 Syracuse	AAA Tor	20	0	0	6	24.2	109	25	12	11	4	2	1	4	12	1	17	2	0	1	0	1.000	0	1	4.01
8 Min. YEARS		240	34	0	70	491	2195	487	275	221	41	15	14	40	232	11	454	61	8	25	29	.463	0	11	4.05

Papo Bolivar

Bats: Right **Throws:** Right **Pos:** OF-112; PH-5; DH-3; PR-1 **Ht:** 5'9" **Wt:** 195 **Born:** 10/18/78 **Age:** 22

Year Team	Lg Org	BATTING																BASERUNNING				PERCENTAGES		
		G	AB	H	2B	3B	HR	TB	R	RBI	TBB	IBB	SO	HBP	SH	SF		SB	CS	SB%	GDP	Avg	OBP	SLG
1996 Twins	R Min	41	155	53	7	1	1	65	30	18	8	0	32	2	0	3		26	6	.81	2	.342	.375	.419
1997 Fort Wayne	A Min	91	324	85	12	6	7	130	30	42	11	0	82	3	2	3		18	9	.67	7	.262	.290	.401
1998 Fort Myers	A+ Min	126	489	129	15	2	5	163	59	45	29	1	104	1	3	1		14	11	.56	14	.264	.306	.333
1999 Fort Myers	A+ Min	114	433	132	21	3	3	168	54	37	27	1	56	4	3	1		8	9	.47	10	.305	.351	.388
2000 New Britain	AA Min	117	406	113	19	7	2	152	46	42	24	0	69	5	3	4		14	8	.64	14	.278	.323	.374
5 Min. YEARS		489	1807	512	74	19	18	678	219	184	99	2	343	15	11	12		80	43	.65	47	.283	.324	.375

Rod Bolton

Pitches: Right **Bats:** Right **Pos:** RP-17; SP-5 **Ht:** 6'2" **Wt:** 190 **Born:** 9/23/68 **Age:** 32

Year Team	Lg Org	HOW MUCH HE PITCHED						WHAT HE GAVE UP												THE RESULTS					
		G	GS	CG	GF	IP	BFP	H	R	ER	HR	SH	SF	HB	TBB	IBB	SO	WP	Bk	W	L	Pct.	ShO	Sv	ERA
1990 Utica	A- CWS	6	6	1	0	44	168	27	4	2	0	1	0	3	11	0	45	0	0	5	1	.833	1	0	0.41
South Bend	A CWS	7	7	3	0	51	196	34	14	11	0	1	1	1	12	1	50	1	1	5	1	.833	1	0	1.94
1991 Sarasota	A+ CWS	15	15	5	0	103.2	412	81	29	22	2	5	1	2	23	0	77	3	1	7	6	.538	2	0	1.91
Birmingham	AA CWS	12	12	3	0	89	360	73	26	16	3	0	2	8	21	1	57	3	0	8	4	.667	2	0	1.62
1992 Vancouver	AAA CWS	27	27	3	0	187.1	781	174	72	61	9	9	4	1	59	2	111	9	2	11	9	.550	2	0	2.93
1993 Nashville	AAA CWS	18	16	1	1	115.2	486	108	40	37	10	2	3	3	37	2	75	11	0	10	1	.909	0	1	2.88
1994 Nashville	AAA CWS	17	17	1	0	116	480	108	43	33	4	6	1	4	35	2	63	2	0	7	5	.583	0	0	2.56
1995 Nashville	AAA CWS	20	20	3	0	131.1	534	127	44	42	13	2	2	7	23	1	76	2	0	14	3	.824	1	0	2.88
1997 Indianapols	AAA Cin	28	27	1	0	169.2	730	185	96	81	21	6	4	3	47	0	108	16	2	9	8	.529	1	0	4.30
1998 Indianapols	AAA Cin	29	29	1	0	177	746	166	82	75	15	3	2	5	64	1	117	6	1	12	11	.522	1	0	3.81
1999 Scranton-WB	AAA Phi	24	24	4	0	153	655	161	76	65	10	5	1	1	52	3	85	6	0	11	10	.524	2	0	3.82
2000 Indianapols	AAA Mil	22	5	0	5	56.1	252	66	35	34	9	2	2	1	21	2	37	4	0	2	6	.250	0	3	5.43
1993 Chicago	AL	9	8	0	0	42.1	197	55	40	35	4	1	4	1	16	0	17	4	0	2	6	.250	0	0	7.44
1995 Chicago	AL	8	3	0	2	22	109	33	23	20	4	0	1	0	14	1	10	1	0	0	2	.000	0	0	8.18
10 Min. YEARS		225	205	26	6	1394	5800	1310	561	479	96	42	23	39	405	15	901	63	7	101	65	.608	13	3	3.09
2 Maj. YEARS		17	11	0	2	64.1	306	88	63	55	8	1	5	1	30	1	27	5	0	2	8	.200	0	0	7.69

Chris Booker

Pitches: Right **Bats:** Right **Pos:** RP-43 **Ht:** 6'3" **Wt:** 230 **Born:** 12/9/76 **Age:** 24

Year Team	Lg Org	HOW MUCH HE PITCHED						WHAT HE GAVE UP												THE RESULTS					
		G	GS	CG	GF	IP	BFP	H	R	ER	HR	SH	SF	HB	TBB	IBB	SO	WP	Bk	W	L	Pct.	ShO	Sv	ERA
1995 Cubs	R ChC	13	7	0	2	42.1	173	36	22	13	0	0	2	0	16	0	43	4	1	3	2	.600	0	1	2.76
1996 Daytona	A+ ChC	1	1	0	0	2.1	11	1	1	0	0	0	0	0	3	0	2	1	0	0	0		0	0	0.00
Williamsprt	A- ChC	14	14	0	0	61	292	57	51	36	2	0	6	3	51	1	52	7	2	4	6	.400	0	0	5.31
1997 Williamsprt	A- ChC	24	3	0	11	45.2	200	39	20	17	2	3	4	0	25	0	60	9	0	1	5	.167	0	1	3.35
1998 Rockford	A ChC	44	1	0	22	64.1	270	47	32	24	2	3	5	4	53	4	78	8	1	1	2	.333	0	4	3.36
1999 Daytona	A+ ChC	42	0	0	29	73	328	72	45	32	6	2	3	3	37	1	68	5	0	2	5	.286	0	6	3.95
2000 Daytona	A+ ChC	31	0	0	24	27.2	122	25	12	7	0	2	0	1	14	1	34	2	0	0	2	.000	0	10	2.28
West Tenn	AA ChC	12	0	0	3	14.2	65	10	8	6	1	0	0	0	12	0	21	0	0	1	0	1.000	0	0	3.68
6 Min. YEARS		181	26	0	91	331	1478	287	191	135	13	10	20	11	211	7	358	36	4	12	22	.353	0	22	3.67

Joe Borchard

Bats: Both **Throws:** Right **Pos:** OF-20; DH-7 **Ht:** 6'5" **Wt:** 220 **Born:** 11/25/78 **Age:** 22

Year Team	Lg Org	BATTING																BASERUNNING				PERCENTAGES		
		G	AB	H	2B	3B	HR	TB	R	RBI	TBB	IBB	SO	HBP	SH	SF		SB	CS	SB%	GDP	Avg	OBP	SLG
2000 White Sox	R CWS	7	29	12	4	0	0	16	3	8	4	0	4	0	0	0		0	0	—	0	.414	.485	.552
Winston-Sal	A+ CWS	14	52	15	3	0	2	24	7	7	6	0	9	2	0	1		0	0	—	0	.288	.377	.462
Birmingham	AA CWS	6	22	5	0	1	0	7	3	3	3	0	8	0	0	1		0	0	—	0	.227	.308	.318
1 Min. YEARS		27	103	32	7	1	2	47	13	18	13	0	21	2	0	2		0	0	—	1	.311	.392	.456

Pat Borders

Bats: Right **Throws:** Right **Pos:** C-81; DH-11; 1B-3; PH-2 **Ht:** 6'2" **Wt:** 200 **Born:** 5/14/63 **Age:** 38

Year Team	Lg Org	BATTING																BASERUNNING				PERCENTAGES		
		G	AB	H	2B	3B	HR	TB	R	RBI	TBB	IBB	SO	HBP	SH	SF		SB	CS	SB%	GDP	Avg	OBP	SLG
1982 Medcine Hat	A+ Tor	61	217	66	12	2	5	97	30	33	24	1	52	2	1	1		1	2	.33	—	.304	.377	.447
1983 Florence	A Tor	131	457	125	31	4	5	179	62	54	46	2	116	1	1	1		4	1	.80	—	.274	.341	.392
1984 Florence	A Tor	131	467	129	32	5	12	207	69	85	56	0	109	1	0	3		3	4	.43	6	.276	.353	.443
1985 Kinston	A+ Tor	127	460	120	16	1	10	168	43	60	45	1	116	1	0	2		6	5	.55	11	.261	.327	.365
1986 Florence	A Tor	16	40	15	7	0	0	22	8	9	2	0	9	0	0	0		0	0	—	0	.375	.405	.775
Knoxville	AA Tor	12	34	12	1	0	2	19	3	5	1	0	6	0	2	0		0	3	.00	2	.353	.371	.559
Kinston	A+ Tor	49	174	57	10	0	6	85	24	26	10	0	42	1	1			0	0	—	5	.328	.366	.489

Year Team	Lg Org	BATTING															BASERUNNING				PERCENTAGES		
		G	AB	H	2B	3B	HR	TB	R	RBI	TBB	IBB	SO	HBP	SH	SF	SB	CS	SB%	GDP	Avg	OBP	SLG
1987 Dunedin	A+ Tor	3	11	4	0	0	0	4	0	1	0	0	3	0	0	0	0	0	—	0	.364	.364	.364
Knoxville	AA Tor	94	349	102	14	1	11	151	44	51	20	1	56	2	0	3	2	5	.29	13	.292	.332	.433
1988 Syracuse	AAA Tor	35	120	29	8	0	3	46	11	14	16	0	22	0	0	2	0	0	—	1	.242	.326	.383
1999 Buffalo	AAA Cle	55	198	47	7	0	5	69	17	23	12	2	31	4	3	2	1	1	.00	5	.237	.290	.348
2000 Durham	AAA TB	96	348	95	16	0	12	147	44	55	20	2	66	1	0	4	7	2	.78	8	.273	.311	.422
1988 Toronto	AL	56	154	42	6	3	6	69	15	21	3	0	24	0	2	1	0	0	—	5	.273	.285	.448
1989 Toronto	AL	94	241	62	11	1	3	84	22	29	11	2	45	1	1	2	2	1	.67	7	.257	.290	.349
1990 Toronto	AL	125	346	99	24	2	15	172	36	49	18	2	57	0	1	3	0	1	.00	17	.286	.319	.497
1991 Toronto	AL	105	291	71	17	0	5	103	22	36	11	1	45	1	6	3	0	0	—	8	.244	.271	.354
1992 Toronto	AL	138	480	116	26	2	13	185	47	53	33	3	75	2	1	5	1	1	.50	11	.242	.290	.385
1993 Toronto	AL	138	488	124	30	0	9	181	38	55	20	2	66	2	7	3	2	2	.50	18	.254	.285	.371
1994 Toronto	AL	85	295	73	13	1	3	97	24	26	15	0	50	0	1	0	1	1	.50	7	.247	.284	.329
1995 Kansas City	AL	52	143	33	8	1	4	55	14	13	7	1	22	0	0	0	0	0	—	1	.231	.267	.385
Houston	NL	11	35	4	0	0	0	4	1	0	2	1	7	0	0	0	0	0	—	2	.114	.162	.114
1996 St. Louis	NL	26	69	22	3	0	0	25	3	4	1	0	14	0	1	0	0	1	.00	0	.319	.329	.362
California	AL	19	57	13	3	0	2	22	6	8	3	0	11	0	1	0	0	1	.00	1	.228	.267	.386
Chicago	AL	31	94	26	1	0	3	36	6	6	5	0	18	0	3	0	0	0	—	2	.277	.313	.383
1997 Cleveland	AL	55	159	47	7	1	4	68	17	15	9	0	27	2	0	0	0	2	.00	5	.296	.341	.428
1998 Cleveland	AL	54	160	38	6	0	0	44	12	6	10	0	40	2	2	1	0	2	.00	3	.238	.289	.275
1999 Cleveland	AL	6	20	6	0	1	0	8	2	3	0	0	3	0	0	0	0	0	—	0	.300	.300	.400
Toronto	AL	6	14	3	0	0	1	6	1	3	1	0	2	0	0	0	0	0	—	0	.214	.267	.429
9 Min. YEARS		810	2875	801	154	13	74	1203	355	416	252	9	628	12	6	18	23	23	.50	—	.279	.337	.418
12 Maj. YEARS		1001	3046	779	155	12	67	1159	266	327	149	12	506	10	26	18	6	13	.32	88	.256	.291	.380

Toby Borland

Pitches: Right Bats: Right Pos: RP-8; SP-1 **Ht: 6'6" Wt: 193 Born: 5/29/69 Age: 32**

Year Team	Lg Org	HOW MUCH HE PITCHED						WHAT HE GAVE UP										THE RESULTS					
		G	GS	CG	GF	IP	BFP	H	R	ER	HR	SH	SF	HB	TBB	IBB	SO	WP	Bk	W	L	Pct.	ShO	Sv	ERA
1988 Martinsvlle	R+ Phi	34	0	0	23	49	215	42	26	22	1	2	1	2	29	1	43	2	1	2	3	.400	0	12	4.04
1989 Spartanburg	A Phi	47	0	0	46	66.2	296	62	29	22	3	2	2	7	35	1	48	15	1	4	5	.444	0	9	2.97
1990 Clearwater	A+ Phi	44	0	0	23	59.2	257	44	21	15	1	7	1	3	35	4	44	6	1	1	2	.333	0	5	2.26
Reading	AA Phi	14	0	0	5	25	100	16	6	4	1	0	2	1	11	1	26	2	0	4	1	.800	0	0	1.44
1991 Reading	AA Phi	59	0	0	50	76.2	358	68	31	23	2	2	5	2	56	5	72	5	3	8	3	.727	0	24	2.70
1992 Scranton-WB	AAA Phi	27	0	0	6	27.1	131	25	23	22	2	3	1	2	26	3	25	4	0	0	1	.000	0	1	7.24
Reading	AA Phi	32	0	0	18	42	196	39	23	16	2	2	1	1	32	3	45	3	0	2	4	.333	0	5	3.43
1993 Scranton-WB	AAA Phi	26	0	0	15	29.2	136	31	20	19	4	4	0	1	20	3	26	2	1	2	4	.333	0	1	5.76
Reading	AA Phi	44	0	0	37	53.2	219	38	17	15	2	1	2	0	20	1	74	1	0	2	2	.500	0	13	2.52
1994 Scranton-WB	AAA Phi	27	1	0	15	53.2	214	36	12	10	2	1	3	1	21	7	61	2	1	4	1	.800	0	4	1.68
1995 Scranton-WB	AAA Phi	8	0	0	3	11.1	45	5	0	0	0	0	0	1	6	1	15	2	0	0	1	.000	0	1	0.00
1997 Pawtucket	AAA Bos	28	2	0	13	47.1	213	50	22	21	5	0	0	2	25	3	46	5	0	2	0	1.000	0	2	3.99
1998 Reading	AA Phi	8	0	0	8	9.1	51	18	12	10	4	1	0	0	5	0	13	1	0	1	3	.250	0	3	9.64
Scranton-WB	AAA Phi	13	0	0	8	12.2	52	14	8	8	1	0	1	1	3	0	15	1	0	0	2	.000	0	5	5.68
Charlotte	AAA Fla	19	0	0	6	36.2	158	33	12	11	3	0	1	1	21	1	26	4	1	3	0	1.000	0	0	2.70
1999 Edmonton	AAA Ana	21	0	0	10	27	136	31	24	21	5	1	3	3	23	2	34	2	0	2	1	.667	0	0	7.00
2000 Erie	AA Ana	9	1	0	5	12	57	12	8	6	0	0	4	1	7	0	12	4	0	1	3	.250	0	0	4.50
1994 Philadelphia	NL	24	0	0	7	34.1	144	31	10	9	1	1	0	4	14	3	26	4	0	1	0	1.000	0	1	2.36
1995 Philadelphia	NL	50	0	0	18	74	339	81	37	31	3	3	2	5	37	7	59	12	0	1	3	.250	0	6	3.77
1996 Philadelphia	NL	69	0	0	11	90.2	399	83	51	41	9	4	1	3	43	3	76	10	0	7	3	.700	0	0	4.07
1997 New York	NL	13	0	0	5	13.1	76	11	9	9	1	0	0	1	14	0	7	3	0	0	1	.000	0	1	6.08
Boston	AL	3	0	0	0	3.1	24	6	5	5	1	0	0	2	7	0	1	0	0	0	0	—	0	0	13.50
1998 Philadelphia	NL	6	0	0	3	9	39	8	5	5	1	1	0	0	5	0	2	1	0	0	0	—	0	0	5.00
12 Min. YEARS		460	4	0	291	639.2	2834	564	294	245	38	26	24	28	375	36	625	61	9	38	35	.521	0	87	3.45
5 Maj. YEARS		165	0	0	44	224.2	1010	220	117	100	16	9	3	15	120	13	178	31	0	9	7	.563	0	8	4.01

Shawn Boskie

Pitches: Right Bats: Right Pos: SP-13; RP-13 **Ht: 6'3" Wt: 210 Born: 3/28/67 Age: 34**

Year Team	Lg Org	HOW MUCH HE PITCHED						WHAT HE GAVE UP										THE RESULTS					
		G	GS	CG	GF	IP	BFP	H	R	ER	HR	SH	SF	HB	TBB	IBB	SO	WP	Bk	W	L	Pct.	ShO	Sv	ERA
1986 Wytheville	R+ ChC	14	12	1	0	54	268	42	41	32	4	0	1	7	57	1	40	15	0	4	4	.500	0	0	5.33
1987 Peoria	A ChC	26	25	1	0	149	657	149	91	72	12	4	5	7	56	2	100	7	5	9	11	.450	0	0	4.35
1988 Winston-Sal	A+ ChC	27	27	4	0	186	825	176	83	70	9	4	7	17	89	1	164	14	4	12	7	.632	2	0	3.39
1989 Charlotte	AA ChC	28	28	5	0	181	813	196	105	88	10	3	8	19	84	3	164	11	1	11	8	.579	0	0	4.38
1990 Iowa	AAA ChC	8	8	0	0	51	217	46	22	18	1	2	1	2	21	1	51	1	0	4	2	.667	0	0	3.18
1991 Iowa	AAA ChC	7	6	2	0	45.1	186	43	19	18	1	5	1	2	11	0	29	1	1	2	2	.500	0	0	3.57
1992 Iowa	AAA ChC	2	2	0	0	7.1	32	8	4	3	0	0	0	0	3	0	3	0	0	0	0	—	0	0	3.68
1993 Iowa	AAA ChC	11	11	1	0	71.2	300	70	35	34	4	2	1	7	21	0	35	1	0	6	1	.857	0	0	4.27
1995 Lk Elsinore	A+ Ana	3	3	0	0	11	53	15	7	5	1	0	0	0	4	0	8	0	0	0	0	—	0	0	4.09
Vancouver	AAA Ana	1	1	0	0	6	25	4	2	2	1	0	0	0	4	0	1	0	0	1	0	1.000	0	0	3.00
1998 Ottawa	AAA Mon	13	13	0	0	87	375	100	48	44	7	0	2	5	21	1	51	5	0	5	7	.417	0	0	4.55
1999 Albuquerque	AAA LA	15	15	0	0	86.1	401	111	66	56	14	3	4	4	37	2	62	5	0	4	8	.333	0	0	5.84
2000 Erie	AA Ana	6	6	0	0	28	133	38	22	20	3	3	3	2	10	0	21	1	0	0	2	.000	0	0	6.43
Edmonton	AAA Ana	14	2	0	2	40	180	51	22	19	4	0	2	2	16	0	22	5	0	3	2	.600	0	0	4.28
Tucson	AAA Ari	6	5	0	1	32	147	37	26	18	4	2	4	3	6	0	16	1	0	2	4	.333	0	0	5.06
1990 Chicago	NL	15	15	1	0	97.2	415	99	42	40	8	8	2	1	31	3	49	3	2	5	6	.455	0	0	3.69
1991 Chicago	NL	28	20	0	2	129	582	150	78	75	14	8	6	5	52	4	62	1	1	4	9	.308	0	0	5.23
1992 Chicago	NL	23	18	0	2	91.2	393	96	55	51	14	9	6	4	36	3	39	5	1	5	11	.313	0	0	5.01
1993 Chicago	NL	39	2	0	10	65.2	277	63	30	25	7	4	1	7	21	2	39	5	0	5	3	.625	0	0	3.43
1994 Chicago	NL	2	0	0	0	3.2	14	3	0	0	0	0	0	0	0	0	2	1	0	0	0	—	0	0	0.00
Philadelphia	NL	18	14	1	1	84.1	367	85	56	49	14	2	3	6	29	2	59	6	0	4	6	.400	0	0	5.23
Seattle	AL	2	1	0	0	2.2	13	4	2	2	1	0	0	1	1	0	0	0	0	0	1	.000	0	0	6.75
1995 California	AL	20	20	1	0	111.2	494	127	73	70	16	4	6	7	25	0	51	4	0	7	7	.500	0	0	5.64
1996 California	AL	37	28	1	1	189.1	860	226	126	112	40	6	4	13	67	7	133	10	0	12	11	.522	0	0	5.32
1997 Baltimore	AL	28	9	0	8	77	349	95	57	55	14	2	7	2	26	1	50	1	0	6	6	.500	0	1	6.43
1998 Montreal	NL	5	5	0	0	17.2	90	34	21	18	5	1	1	2	4	1	10	0	0	1	3	.250	0	0	9.17
12 Min. YEARS		181	164	15	3	1035.2	4612	1086	593	499	75	28	39	87	440	11	767	67	11	63	58	.521	2	0	4.34
9 Maj. YEARS		217	132	4	24	870.1	3854	982	540	497	133	44	36	44	292	24	494	36	4	49	63	.438	0	1	5.14

29

Heath Bost

Pitches: Right **Bats:** Right **Pos:** RP-19; SP-1 **Ht:** 6'3" **Wt:** 195 **Born:** 10/13/74 **Age:** 26

Year Team	Lg Org	G	GS	CG	GF	IP	BFP	H	R	ER	HR	SH	SF	HB	TBB	IBB	SO	WP	Bk	W	L	Pct.	ShO	Sv	ERA
1995 Portland	A- Col	10	0	0	1	16	63	15	6	6	1	0	0	0	0	0	25	1	0	1	0	1.000	0	0	3.38
Asheville	A Col	9	2	0	4	23.2	90	20	6	4	1	0	0	1	3	0	17	1	2	4	1	.800	0	0	1.52
1996 New Haven	AA Col	4	0	0	2	6	24	5	1	1	0	0	0	0	2	0	7	0	0	1	0	1.000	0	0	1.50
Asheville	A Col	41	0	0	29	76	293	45	13	11	3	6	0	1	19	5	102	2	0	5	2	.714	0	15	1.30
1997 Salem	A+ Col	13	0	0	10	15	57	9	4	4	1	1	0	0	2	0	9	0	0	1	0	1.000	0	3	2.40
Colo Sprngs	AAA Col	2	0	0	0	3	21	10	8	7	1	0	1	0	1	0	3	0	0	0	1	.000	0	0	21.00
New Haven	AA Col	38	0	0	32	43	180	44	18	17	3	0	0	0	10	1	45	5	0	2	2	.500	0	20	3.56
1998 New Haven	AA Col	41	0	0	14	46.1	193	43	20	17	2	5	0	4	11	0	48	3	1	4	2	.667	0	2	3.30
1999 Colo Sprngs	AAA Col	38	6	0	8	86.1	378	120	59	53	10	2	1	4	12	2	67	0	0	5	4	.556	0	0	5.53
2000 Salem	A+ Col	7	1	0	2	14.2	69	24	10	10	2	0	0	0	1	0	14	1	0	2	1	.667	0	0	6.14
Carolina	AA Col	6	0	0	1	9	33	6	2	1	1	0	0	0	2	0	10	0	0	1	0	1.000	0	0	1.00
Colo Sprngs	AAA Col	7	0	0	1	11	46	8	8	6	1	0	1	0	4	0	7	0	0	0	0	—	0	0	4.91
6 Min. YEARS		216	9	0	104	350	1447	349	155	137	26	14	3	10	67	8	354	13	3	26	13	.667	0	40	3.52

Steve Bourgeois

Pitches: Right **Bats:** Right **Pos:** SP-6; RP-3 **Ht:** 6'1" **Wt:** 220 **Born:** 8/4/74 **Age:** 26

Year Team	Lg Org	G	GS	CG	GF	IP	BFP	H	R	ER	HR	SH	SF	HB	TBB	IBB	SO	WP	Bk	W	L	Pct.	ShO	Sv	ERA
1993 Everett	A- SF	15	15	0	0	77	337	62	44	36	7	0	3	7	44	0	77	4	1	5	3	.625	0	0	4.21
1994 Clinton	A SF	20	20	0	0	106.1	464	97	57	43	16	4	2	7	54	0	88	11	0	8	5	.615	0	0	3.64
San Jose	A+ SF	7	7	0	0	36.2	167	40	22	22	4	1	1	1	22	0	27	5	0	4	0	1.000	0	0	5.40
1995 Shreveport	AA SF	22	22	2	0	145.1	604	140	50	46	8	4	5	4	53	1	91	11	1	12	3	.800	2	0	2.85
Phoenix	AAA SF	6	5	0	0	34.2	153	38	18	13	2	0	0	2	13	0	23	4	1	1	1	.500	0	0	3.38
1996 Phoenix	AAA SF	20	18	2	0	97	435	112	50	39	6	2	4	6	42	1	65	5	1	8	6	.571	1	0	3.62
1997 Colo Sprngs	AAA Col	33	18	2	5	121.2	571	154	96	81	18	2	3	5	66	3	86	7	0	9	7	.563	2	0	5.99
1998 Colo Sprngs	AAA Col	38	13	0	7	114.2	571	154	82	71	14	4	3	5	62	5	87	8	0	5	7	.417	0	1	5.57
2000 Colo Sprngs	AAA Col	9	6	0	1	44	194	40	30	25	6	1	0	2	21	0	39	5	0	2	3	.400	0	0	5.11
1996 San Francisco	NL	15	5	0	4	40	198	60	35	28	4	2	2	4	21	4	17	4	0	1	3	.250	0	0	6.30
7 Min. YEARS		170	124	6	13	777.1	3456	837	449	376	81	18	21	39	377	10	583	60	4	54	35	.607	5	1	4.35

Rafael Bournigal

Bats: Right **Throws:** Right **Pos:** SS-19 **Ht:** 5'11" **Wt:** 175 **Born:** 5/12/66 **Age:** 35

Year Team	Lg Org	G	AB	H	2B	3B	HR	TB	R	RBI	TBB	IBB	SO	HBP	SH	SF	SB	CS	SB%	GDP	Avg	OBP	SLG
1987 Great Falls	R+ LA	30	82	12	4	0	0	16	5	4	3	0	7	1	1	0	0	1	.00	1	.146	.186	.195
1988 Salem	A- LA	70	275	86	10	1	0	98	54	25	38	0	32	0	6	2	11	6	.65	5	.313	.394	.356
1989 Vero Beach	A+ LA	132	484	128	11	1	1	144	74	37	33	0	21	3	5	3	18	13	.58	19	.264	.314	.298
1990 San Antonio	AA LA	69	194	41	4	2	0	49	20	14	8	0	24	0	7	2	2	1	.67	9	.211	.240	.253
1991 Vero Beach	A+ LA	20	66	16	2	0	0	18	6	3	1	0	3	0	1	1	2	1	.67	1	.242	.250	.273
San Antonio	AA LA	16	65	21	2	0	0	23	6	9	2	0	7	0	1	1	2	3	.40	2	.323	.338	.354
Albuquerque	AAA LA	66	215	63	5	5	0	78	34	29	14	1	13	0	8	4	4	1	.80	3	.293	.330	.363
1992 Albuquerque	AAA LA	122	395	128	18	1	0	148	47	34	22	5	7	5	10	4	5	3	.63	17	.324	.364	.375
1993 Albuquerque	AAA LA	134	465	129	25	0	4	166	75	55	29	1	18	3	8	5	3	5	.38	11	.277	.321	.357
1994 Albuquerque	AAA LA	61	208	69	8	0	1	80	29	22	9	1	9	0	2	1	2	3	.40	7	.332	.358	.385
1995 Albuquerque	AAA LA	15	31	4	1	0	0	5	2	1	1	0	2	1	0	0	0	0	—	0	.129	.182	.161
Harrisburg	AA Mon	29	95	21	3	1	0	26	12	7	11	0	8	1	6	1	1	0	1.00	2	.221	.306	.274
Ottawa	AAA Mon	19	54	11	4	0	0	15	2	6	2	0	4	1	1	0	0	0	—	2	.204	.246	.278
1997 Modesto	A+ Oak	7	21	5	1	0	0	6	0	2	3	0	2	0	0	0	0	0	—	1	.238	.333	.286
1999 Oklahoma	AAA Tex	17	56	21	6	0	3	36	16	14	12	0	5	0	0	1	1	1	.50	1	.375	.478	.643
2000 Norfolk	AAA NYM	19	75	23	4	0	0	27	7	4	5	2	2	0	1	1	1	1	.50	3	.307	.350	.360
1992 Los Angeles	NL	10	20	3	1	0	0	4	1	0	1	0	2	1	0	0	0	0	—	0	.150	.227	.200
1993 Los Angeles	NL	8	18	9	1	0	0	10	0	3	0	0	2	0	0	0	0	0	—	0	.500	.500	.556
1994 Los Angeles	NL	40	116	26	3	1	0	31	2	11	9	1	5	2	5	0	0	0	—	4	.224	.291	.267
1996 Oakland	AL	88	252	61	14	2	0	79	33	18	16	0	19	1	8	0	4	3	.57	6	.242	.290	.313
1997 Oakland	AL	79	222	62	9	0	1	74	29	20	16	1	19	4	7	1	2	1	.67	11	.279	.339	.333
1998 Oakland	AL	85	209	47	11	0	1	61	23	19	10	1	11	2	6	2	6	1	.86	6	.225	.265	.292
1999 Seattle	AL	55	95	26	5	0	2	37	16	14	7	0	6	0	4	2	0	0	—	5	.274	.317	.389
12 Min. YEARS		826	2781	778	108	11	9	935	389	266	193	10	164	15	57	25	52	39	.57	84	.280	.327	.336
7 Maj. YEARS		365	932	234	44	3	4	296	104	85	59	3	64	10	30	4	12	5	.71	32	.251	.301	.318

Brent Bowers

Bats: Right **Throws:** Left **Pos:** OF-64; PH-2; DH-1 **Ht:** 6'4" **Wt:** 215 **Born:** 5/2/71 **Age:** 30

Year Team	Lg Org	G	AB	H	2B	3B	HR	TB	R	RBI	TBB	IBB	SO	HBP	SH	SF	SB	CS	SB%	GDP	Avg	OBP	SLG
1989 Medcine Hat	R+ Tor	54	207	46	2	2	0	52	16	13	19	0	55	0	0	1	6	2	.75	5	.222	.286	.251
1990 Medcine Hat	R+ Tor	60	212	58	7	3	3	80	30	27	31	0	35	1	1	0	19	8	.70	2	.274	.369	.377
1991 Myrtle Bch	A Tor	120	402	101	8	4	2	123	53	44	31	1	76	2	9	4	35	12	.74	11	.251	.305	.306
1992 Dunedin	A+ Tor	128	524	133	10	3	3	158	74	46	34	0	99	3	8	1	31	15	.67	4	.254	.302	.302
1993 Knoxville	AA Tor	141	577	143	23	4	5	189	63	43	21	1	121	3	13	0	36	19	.65	5	.248	.278	.328
1994 Knoxville	AA Tor	127	472	129	18	11	4	181	52	49	20	4	75	1	7	2	15	8	.65	8	.273	.303	.383
1995 Syracuse	AAA Tor	111	305	77	16	5	5	118	38	26	10	0	57	1	1	1	5	1	.83	3	.252	.278	.387
1996 Bowie	AA Bal	58	228	71	11	5	9	111	37	25	17	2	40	2	3	0	10	4	.71	1	.311	.364	.487
Rochester	AAA Bal	49	206	67	8	4	4	95	40	19	14	0	41	0	3	0	9	3	.75	1	.325	.368	.461
1997 Scranton-WB	AAA Phi	39	110	28	2	0	3	39	15	7	8	0	28	1	0	1	1	1	.50	1	.255	.308	.355
1998 Norfolk	AAA NYM	82	275	67	8	3	5	96	36	31	21	0	59	0	3	5	17	6	.74	6	.244	.292	.349
Knoxville	AA ChC	27	100	30	5	1	2	43	19	12	16	1	18	0	1	1	9	1	.90	3	.280	.374	.402
1999 West Tenn	AA ChC	35	100	16	4	0	2	26	10	9	11	1	16	1	1	1	4	0	1.00	2	.160	.248	.260
2000 Albany-Col	IND —	36	146	48	5	4	3	70	26	23	16	4	18	0	0	2	5	3	.63	2	.329	.390	.479
New Jersey	IND —	25	87	28	6	1	1	39	5	12	9	0	18	1	0	2	2	1	.67	3	.322	.384	.448
Chattanooga	AA Cin	6	21	2	0	0	1	5	5	5	5	0	4	0	0	0	1	0	1.00	1	.095	.269	.238

			BATTING														BASERUNNING				PERCENTAGES		
Year Team	Lg Org	G	AB	H	2B	3B	HR	TB	R	RBI	TBB	IBB	SO	HBP	SH	SF	SB	CS	SB%	GDP	Avg	OBP	SLG
1996 Baltimore	AL	21	39	12	2	0	0	14	6	3	0	0	7	0	0	0	0	0	—	1	.308	.308	.359
12 Min. YEARS		1098	3979	1044	133	46	52	1425	519	391	283	14	760	16	50	20	204	85	.71	57	.262	.312	.358

Cedrick Bowers

Pitches: Left **Bats:** Right **Pos:** SP-23; RP-1   **Ht:** 6'2" **Wt:** 215 **Born:** 2/10/78 **Age:** 23

			HOW MUCH HE PITCHED				WHAT HE GAVE UP										THE RESULTS					
Year Team	Lg Org	G	GS	CG	GF	IP	BFP	H	R	ER	HR	SH	SF	HB	TBB	IBB	SO	WP	Bk	W	L	Pct.	ShO	Sv	ERA
1996 Devil Rays	R TB	13	13	0	0	60.1	268	50	39	36	2	0	2	3	39	0	85	5	5	3	5	.375	0	0	5.37
1997 Chston-SC	A TB	28	28	0	0	157	657	119	74	56	11	4	3	3	78	0	164	15	1	8	10	.444	0	0	3.21
1998 St. Pete	A+ TB	28	26	0	1	150	655	144	89	73	14	6	4	1	80	1	156	6	2	5	9	.357	0	0	4.38
1999 Orlando	AA TB	27	27	1	0	125	567	125	94	83	18	3	5	4	76	0	138	12	1	6	9	.400	0	0	5.98
2000 Orlando	AA TB	20	19	1	0	106.2	443	85	45	33	8	4	2	3	44	0	92	3	1	5	8	.385	0	0	2.78
Durham	AAA TB	4	4	0	0	19.2	92	21	13	12	2	0	0	0	13	0	20	1	0	3	1	.750	0	0	5.49
5 Min. YEARS		120	117	2	1	618.2	2682	544	354	293	55	17	16	14	330	1	655	42	10	30	42	.417	0	0	4.26

Shane Bowers

Pitches: Right **Bats:** Right **Pos:** RP-19; SP-17   **Ht:** 6'5" **Wt:** 220 **Born:** 7/27/71 **Age:** 29

			HOW MUCH HE PITCHED				WHAT HE GAVE UP										THE RESULTS					
Year Team	Lg Org	G	GS	CG	GF	IP	BFP	H	R	ER	HR	SH	SF	HB	TBB	IBB	SO	WP	Bk	W	L	Pct.	ShO	Sv	ERA
1993 Elizabethtn	R+ Min	7	1	0	4	11.1	48	13	7	6	0	1	1	0	1	0	13	3	0	2	0	1.000	0	0	4.76
1994 Fort Wayne	A Min	27	11	1	9	81.2	333	76	32	30	3	5	1	6	18	1	72	8	0	4		.600	0	5	3.31
Fort Myers	A+ Min	13	0	0	5	17.2	85	28	7	7	1	0	0	0	4	0	19	2	0	0		—	0	0	3.57
1995 Fort Myers	A+ Min	23	23	1	0	145.2	580	119	43	35	6	2	4	12	32	1	103	6	1	13	5	.722	0	0	2.16
1996 Hardware Cy	AA Min	27	22	1	1	131	569	134	71	61	15	2	3	6	42	1	96	11	0	6	8	.429	0	0	4.19
1997 New Britain	AA Min	14	13	1	0	71.1	299	65	29	27	6	2	3	4	22	0	59	2	0	7	2	.778	1	0	3.41
Salt Lake	AAA Min	9	9	0	0	56.1	247	64	35	30	12	1	4	3	14	0	46	2	0	6	2	.750	0	0	4.79
1998 Salt Lake	AAA Min	33	16	2	2	110	498	137	76	72	18	1	1	1	40	0	101	6	0	9	7	.563	0	0	5.89
1999 Salt Lake	AAA Min	31	18	0	1	122	560	149	86	77	25	2	5	1	54	0	103	11	0	7	4	.636	0	0	5.68
2000 Scranton-WB	AAA Phi	36	17	3	4	137.1	588	129	73	71	19	3	1	2	37	1	99	4	1	8	7	.533	1	1	4.65
1997 Minnesota	AL	5	5	0	0	19	92	27	20	17	2	0	1	1	8	0	7	1	0	0	3	.000	0	0	8.05
8 Min. YEARS		220	130	10	26	884.1	3786	914	459	416	105	19	23	35	264	4	711	55	2	64	39	.621	2	6	4.23

Micah Bowie

Pitches: Left **Bats:** Left **Pos:** SP-27   **Ht:** 6'4" **Wt:** 210 **Born:** 11/10/74 **Age:** 26

			HOW MUCH HE PITCHED				WHAT HE GAVE UP										THE RESULTS					
Year Team	Lg Org	G	GS	CG	GF	IP	BFP	H	R	ER	HR	SH	SF	HB	TBB	IBB	SO	WP	Bk	W	L	Pct.	ShO	Sv	ERA
1994 Braves	R Atl	6	5	0	1	29.2	124	27	14	10	1	0	2	1	5	0	35	1	0	3	0	.000	0	0	3.03
Danville	R+ Atl	7	5	0	0	32.2	141	28	16	13	4	2	3	3	13	1	38	2	0	3	1	.750	0	0	3.58
1995 Macon	A Atl	5	5	0	0	27.2	104	9	8	7	1	0	0	3	11	0	36	1	0	4	1	.800	0	0	2.28
Durham	A+ Atl	23	23	1	0	130.1	561	119	65	52	8	13	3	8	61	3	91	4	3	4	11	.267	0	0	3.59
1996 Durham	A+ Atl	14	13	0	0	66.1	283	55	29	27	4	3	3	7	33	0	65	2	0	3	6	.333	0	0	3.66
1997 Durham	A+ Atl	9	6	0	0	39.1	167	29	16	16	2	0	2	0	27	0	44	2	0	2	2	.500	0	0	3.66
Greenville	AA Atl	8	7	0	0	43.2	193	34	19	17	3	1	2	3	26	1	41	2	0	3	2	.600	0	0	3.50
1998 Greenville	AA Atl	30	29	1	0	163	676	132	76	63	12	7	2	6	64	0	160	7	3	11	6	.647	0	0	3.48
1999 Richmond	AAA Atl	13	13	0	0	73	288	65	24	24	4	2	2	0	14	0	82	0	0	4	4	.500	0	0	2.96
2000 Iowa	AAA ChC	9	9	0	0	45.1	220	59	44	40	9	3	1	1	31	3	35	2	0	1	7	.125	0	0	7.94
West Tenn	AA ChC	18	18	1	0	117.1	481	91	47	45	6	7	1	3	48	1	106	1	0	7	6	.538	1	0	3.45
1999 Atlanta	NL	3	0	0	2	4	23	8	6	6	1	0	0	0	4	0	2	0	0	0	1	.000	0	0	13.50
Chicago	NL	11	11	0	0	47	242	73	54	52	8	3	3	2	30	2	39	4	2	2	6	.250	0	0	9.96
7 Min. YEARS		142	133	3	1	768.1	3238	648	355	314	54	41	21	35	333	9	733	26	6	42	49	.462	1	0	3.68

Brian Bowles

Pitches: Right **Bats:** Right **Pos:** RP-49   **Ht:** 6'5" **Wt:** 205 **Born:** 8/18/76 **Age:** 24

			HOW MUCH HE PITCHED				WHAT HE GAVE UP										THE RESULTS					
Year Team	Lg Org	G	GS	CG	GF	IP	BFP	H	R	ER	HR	SH	SF	HB	TBB	IBB	SO	WP	Bk	W	L	Pct.	ShO	Sv	ERA
1995 Blue Jays	R Tor	8	0	0	2	15	70	18	12	4	2	0	1	1	3	0	11	2	1	0	1	.000	0	0	2.40
1996 Medcine Hat	R+ Tor	24	0	0	7	39.2	193	53	35	28	5	1	3	5	21	1	29	9	0	2	2	.500	0	1	6.35
1997 Hagerstown	A Tor	4	0	0	1	10.1	49	14	10	8	2	0	1	1	5	0	9	1	0	1	0	1.000	0	0	6.97
Dunedin	A+ Tor	7	1	0	3	14.1	104	20	14	12	2	0	1	0	7	1	9	3	1	0	2	.000	0	0	7.53
St.Cathrnes	A- Tor	16	16	0	0	78.2	351	76	53	44	6	0	3	11	35	0	64	4	1	5	8	.385	0	0	5.03
1998 Dunedin	A+ Tor	9	2	1	0	27	126	32	13	10	2	1	1	1	16	0	17	1	1	1	2	.333	0	0	3.33
Hagerstown	A Tor	31	4	0	22	67.2	306	80	41	34	4	2	3	9	18	1	48	6	0	2	4	.333	0	0	4.52
1999 Hagerstown	A Tor	48	1	0	22	79.1	355	73	41	35	4	3	4	12	39	3	80	9	0	6	2	.750	0	3	3.97
2000 Tennessee	AA Tor	49	0	0	12	81.2	343	64	31	27	1	2	3	8	36	1	72	11	0	4	4	.500	0	0	2.98
6 Min. YEARS		196	24	1	56	413.2	1861	430	250	202	28	9	20	48	180	7	339	46	4	21	25	.457	0	4	4.39

Justin Bowles

Bats: Left **Throws:** Left **Pos:** OF-117; PH-6; DH-4; PR-3   **Ht:** 6'0" **Wt:** 185 **Born:** 8/20/73 **Age:** 27

			BATTING														BASERUNNING				PERCENTAGES		
Year Team	Lg Org	G	AB	H	2B	3B	HR	TB	R	RBI	TBB	IBB	SO	HBP	SH	SF	SB	CS	SB%	GDP	Avg	OBP	SLG
1996 Sou Oregon	A- Oak	56	214	61	20	1	11	116	44	45	31	2	53	1	0	0	8	3	.73	1	.285	.378	.542
Huntsville	AA Oak	3	12	4	0	0	0	4	1	2	0	0	5	1	0	0	0	0	—	0	.333	.385	.333
1997 Modesto	A+ Oak	107	394	129	39	9	7	207	66	51	56	2	85	5	5	5	6	3	.67	3	.327	.413	.525
1998 Huntsville	AA Oak	74	274	76	21	4	10	129	50	48	37	0	60	1	4	3	2	1	.67	11	.277	.362	.471
1999 Midland	AA Oak	131	489	140	27	8	20	243	73	73	44	1	122	2	3	4	10	7	.59	13	.286	.345	.497
2000 Midland	AA Oak	124	443	120	24	6	16	204	76	65	40	0	111	2	1	6	6	6	.50	11	.271	.330	.460
5 Min. YEARS		495	1826	530	131	25	64	903	307	284	208	5	436	12	13	18	32	20	.62	39	.290	.363	.495

Ryan Bradley

Pitches: Right **Bats:** Right **Pos:** RP-49   **Ht:** 6'4" **Wt:** 226 **Born:** 10/26/75 **Age:** 25

		HOW MUCH HE PITCHED						WHAT HE GAVE UP										THE RESULTS					
Year Team	Lg Org	G	GS	CG	GF	IP	BFP	H	R	ER	HR	SH	SF	HB	TBB	IBB	SO	WP	Bk	W	L	Pct.	ShO	Sv	ERA
1997 Oneonta	A- NYY	14	0	0	9	26.2	103	22	5	4	1	0	0	0	5	1	22	0	1	3	1	.750	0	1	1.35
1998 Tampa	A+ NYY	32	11	1	18	94.2	383	59	29	25	5	1	1	6	30	4	112	16	2	7	4	.636	1	7	2.38
Norwich	AA NYY	3	3	1	0	25	89	8	4	4	1	0	0	0	8	0	25	0	0	2	0	1.000	1	0	1.44
Columbus	AAA NYY	3	3	0	0	16	72	15	13	11	4	0	0	0	13	0	12	1	0	0	1	.000	0	0	6.19
1999 Columbus	AAA NYY	29	24	1	1	145	664	163	112	100	28	5	9	10	73	0	118	23	1	5	12	.294	0	0	6.21
2000 Columbus	AAA NYY	49	0	0	15	72.2	346	82	52	47	11	4	2	7	52	1	54	12	1	5	1	.833	0	0	5.82
1998 New York	AL	5	1	0	1	12.2	59	12	9	8	2	0	1	1	9	0	13	0	0	2	1	.667	0	0	5.68
4 Min. YEARS		130	41	3	43	380	1657	349	215	191	50	10	12	23	181	6	343	52	5	22	19	.537	2	8	4.52

J.D. Brammer

Pitches: Right **Bats:** Right **Pos:** RP-41   **Ht:** 6'4" **Wt:** 235 **Born:** 1/30/75 **Age:** 26

		HOW MUCH HE PITCHED						WHAT HE GAVE UP										THE RESULTS					
Year Team	Lg Org	G	GS	CG	GF	IP	BFP	H	R	ER	HR	SH	SF	HB	TBB	IBB	SO	WP	Bk	W	L	Pct.	ShO	Sv	ERA
1996 Watertown	A- Cle	17	0	0	5	38	173	27	22	15	0	0	3	3	28	1	49	8	5	5	0	1.000	0	1	3.55
1997 Columbus	A Cle	28	23	0	1	116.2	542	132	102	91	11	2	7	18	50	0	105	9	4	6	10	.375	0	1	7.02
1998 Kinston	A+ Cle	15	0	0	8	27	106	15	6	4	1	0	0	1	8	0	33	1	1	3	2	.600	0	2	1.33
Akron	AA Cle	11	0	0	4	20.2	95	21	12	12	3	0	1	1	10	1	23	4	2	1	0	1.000	0	3	5.23
1999 Akron	AA Cle	47	0	0	24	75.2	349	53	44	40	6	4	3	9	60	0	69	11	3	3	2	.600	0	8	4.76
2000 Akron	AA Cle	16	0	0	6	23.1	88	12	4	3	1	0	1	0	6	0	20	3	0	2	1	.667	0	1	1.16
Buffalo	AAA Cle	25	0	0	13	35.2	156	38	21	19	2	1	2	3	17	0	28	5	0	2	0	1.000	0	4	4.79
5 Min. YEARS		159	23	0	61	337	1509	298	211	184	24	7	17	35	179	2	327	41	15	22	15	.595	0	16	4.91

Brian Brantley

Pitches: Right **Bats:** Right **Pos:** RP-42   **Ht:** 6'4" **Wt:** 185 **Born:** 4/23/76 **Age:** 25

		HOW MUCH HE PITCHED						WHAT HE GAVE UP										THE RESULTS					
Year Team	Lg Org	G	GS	CG	GF	IP	BFP	H	R	ER	HR	SH	SF	HB	TBB	IBB	SO	WP	Bk	W	L	Pct.	ShO	Sv	ERA
1998 Portland	A- Col	10	10	0	0	49	218	43	27	22	1	2	2	7	26	0	39	7	0	3	4	.429	0	0	4.04
1999 Asheville	A Col	34	3	0	13	90.1	406	89	65	59	6	7	2	11	44	0	100	13	1	6	6	.500	0	3	5.88
2000 Carolina	AA Col	1	0	0	0	4	23	7	6	6	0	0	0	0	4	0	4	1	0	0	0	—	0	0	13.50
Salem	A+ Col	41	0	0	19	59	264	38	22	17	1	7	3	9	40	0	75	5	0	3	3	.500	0	4	2.59
3 Min. YEARS		86	13	0	32	202.1	911	177	120	104	8	16	7	27	114	0	218	26	1	12	13	.480	0	7	4.63

Bryan Braswell

Pitches: Left **Bats:** Left **Pos:** SP-10; RP-9   **Ht:** 6'1" **Wt:** 200 **Born:** 6/30/75 **Age:** 26

		HOW MUCH HE PITCHED						WHAT HE GAVE UP										THE RESULTS					
Year Team	Lg Org	G	GS	CG	GF	IP	BFP	H	R	ER	HR	SH	SF	HB	TBB	IBB	SO	WP	Bk	W	L	Pct.	ShO	Sv	ERA
1996 Auburn	A- Hou	15	14	0	1	73	325	70	40	35	2	1	2	11	29	2	77	9	1	4	8	.333	0	0	4.32
1997 Quad City	A Hou	19	19	1	0	116.1	495	107	70	49	10	0	4	2	32	0	118	2	5	6	6	.500	0	0	3.79
1998 Kissimmee	A+ Hou	27	26	2	0	159.2	698	176	92	70	22	3	3	4	48	0	118	7	2	11	9	.550	1	0	3.95
1999 Jackson	AA Hou	28	28	1	0	171.1	741	180	104	86	27	4	6	4	54	0	131	10	0	9	10	.474	0	0	4.52
2000 Round Rock	AA Hou	19	10	1	1	71.1	309	78	48	40	13	4	2	0	22	1	38	2	1	5	4	.556	0	0	5.05
5 Min. YEARS		108	97	5	2	591.2	2568	611	354	280	74	12	17	21	185	3	482	30	9	35	37	.486	1	0	4.26

Danny Bravo

Bats: Both **Throws:** Right **Pos:** 2B-46; OF-22; SS-19; 3B-6; 1B-2; PH-2; PR-2; DH-1   **Ht:** 5'11" **Wt:** 175 **Born:** 5/27/77 **Age:** 24

		BATTING													BASERUNNING				PERCENTAGES		
Year Team	Lg Org	G	AB	H	2B	3B	HR	TB	R	RBI	TBB	IBB	SO	HBP	SH	SF	SB	CS	SB%	GDP	Avg	OBP	SLG
1996 Wst Plm Bch	A+ Mon	48	137	27	2	2	0	33	15	12	14	0	30	1	3	0	3	4	.43	0	.197	.276	.241
Delmarva	A Mon	18	61	14	6	1	0	22	10	7	2	0	14	1	2	1	1	0	1.00	1	.230	.262	.361
1997 Wst Plm Bch	A+ Mon	15	37	6	1	1	0	9	3	0	2	0	5	0	0	0	0	0	—	0	.162	.205	.243
Cape Fear	A Mon	73	253	68	9	1	3	88	28	34	9	0	31	4	3	3	3	4	.43	4	.269	.301	.348
1998 Cape Fear	A Mon	101	343	95	12	4	4	127	48	44	32	2	65	8	14	1	7	10	.41	11	.277	.352	.370
Jupiter	A+ Mon	24	71	11	1	0	0	12	5	3	8	0	14	2	0	2	1	1	.50	1	.155	.253	.169
1999 Jupiter	A+ Mon	7	20	6	3	0	1	12	5	3	1	0	5	1	2	0	0	0	—	1	.300	.364	.600
Harrisburg	AA Mon	12	28	4	1	0	0	5	0	2	1	0	6	0	1	0	0	0	—	0	.143	.172	.179
Birmingham	AA CWS	76	270	76	12	1	2	96	49	38	41	1	39	2	3	3	6	5	.55	9	.281	.377	.356
2000 Birmingham	AA CWS	96	340	79	12	0	3	100	48	29	42	0	56	2	2	3	11	9	.55	5	.232	.318	.294
5 Min. YEARS		470	1560	386	59	10	13	504	211	172	152	3	265	21	30	13	32	33	.49	31	.247	.320	.323

Brent Brede

Bats: Left **Throws:** Left **Pos:** OF-68; PH-26; 1B-17; PR-1   **Ht:** 6'4" **Wt:** 208 **Born:** 9/13/71 **Age:** 29

		BATTING													BASERUNNING				PERCENTAGES		
Year Team	Lg Org	G	AB	H	2B	3B	HR	TB	R	RBI	TBB	IBB	SO	HBP	SH	SF	SB	CS	SB%	GDP	Avg	OBP	SLG
1990 Elizabethtn	R+ Min	46	143	35	5	0	0	40	39	14	30	0	29	0	0	1	14	0	1.00	0	.245	.374	.280
1991 Kenosha	A Min	53	156	30	3	2	0	37	12	10	16	0	31	0	5	3	4	5	.44	8	.192	.263	.237
Elizabethtn	R+ Min	68	253	61	13	0	3	83	24	36	30	2	48	1	2	4	13	4	.76	7	.241	.319	.328
1992 Kenosha	A Min	110	363	88	15	0	0	103	44	29	53	1	77	4	4	4	10	12	.45	8	.242	.343	.284
1993 Fort Myers	A+ Min	53	182	60	10	1	0	72	27	27	32	3	19	1	2	1	8	4	.67	6	.330	.433	.396
1994 Fort Myers	A+ Min	116	419	110	21	4	2	145	49	45	63	2	60	0	3	1	18	4	.82	7	.263	.358	.346
1995 Hardware Cy	AA Min	134	449	123	28	2	3	164	71	39	69	2	82	3	6	5	14	6	.70	13	.274	.371	.365
1996 Salt Lake	AAA Min	132	483	168	38	8	11	255	102	86	87	9	87	3	4	5	14	6	.70	4	.348	.446	.528
1997 Salt Lake	AAA Min	84	328	116	27	4	9	178	82	76	47	0	62	0	0	5	4	2	.67	6	.354	.432	.543
1998 Tucson	AAA Ari	29	96	30	8	1	2	46	16	16	21	0	20	0	0	1	2	1	.67	3	.313	.432	.479
2000 Nashville	AAA Pit	101	269	67	15	0	1	85	38	23	35	0	51	1	2	2	2	1	.67	8	.249	.336	.316
1996 Minnesota	AL	10	20	6	0	1	0	8	2	2	1	0	5	0	0	0	0	0	—	1	.300	.333	.400

			BATTING															BASERUNNING				PERCENTAGES		
Year Team	Lg Org	G	AB	H	2B	3B	HR	TB	R	RBI	TBB	IBB	SO	HBP	SH	SF		SB	CS	SB%	GDP	Avg	OBP	SLG
1997 Minnesota	AL	61	190	52	11	1	3	74	25	21	21	0	38	1	1	1		7	2	.78	1	.274	.347	.389
1998 Arizona	NL	98	212	48	9	3	2	69	23	17	24	2	43	2	0	0		1	0	1.00	6	.226	.311	.325
10 Min. YEARS		926	3141	888	183	22	31	1208	504	401	483	20	566	15	28	30		103	45	.70	74	.283	.378	.385
3 Maj. YEARS		169	422	106	20	5	5	151	50	40	46	2	86	3	1	1		8	2	.80	8	.251	.328	.358

Jason Brester

Pitches: Left **Bats:** Left **Pos:** SP-19; RP-6   **Ht:** 6'3" **Wt:** 190 **Born:** 12/7/76 **Age:** 24

		HOW MUCH HE PITCHED						WHAT HE GAVE UP											THE RESULTS				
Year Team	Lg Org	G	GS	CG	GF	IP	BFP	H	R	ER	HR	SH	SF	HB	TBB	IBB	SO	WP	Bk	W	L	Pct.	ShO	Sv	ERA
1995 Bellingham	A- SF	8	6	0	0	24	104	23	11	11	3	0	0	1	12	0	17	0	0	1	0	1.000	0	0	4.13
1996 Burlington	A SF	27	27	0	0	157	659	139	78	69	14	4	7	3	64	0	143	13	1	10	9	.526	0	0	3.96
1997 San Jose	A+ SF	26	26	0	0	142.1	625	164	80	67	4	4	3	3	52	0	172	10	7	9	9	.500	0	0	4.24
1998 Shreveport	AA SF	19	19	0	0	113	490	117	58	48	11	7	4	0	44	3	79	4	2	2	8	.200	0	0	3.82
New Haven	AA Col	5	4	0	0	22.2	97	22	7	4	0	1	0	1	7	0	15	3	1	1	0	1.000	0	0	1.59
1999 Carolina	AA Col	11	11	0	0	59.1	268	71	45	38	8	1	1	2	26	0	44	3	3	2	6	.250	0	0	5.76
Reading	AA Phi	16	16	3	0	105.1	436	105	48	44	8	4	6	2	26	1	87	6	2	7	5	.583	1	0	3.76
2000 Reading	AA Phi	25	19	0	2	116	539	107	65	55	7	7	6	12	89	2	74	7	3	11	6	.647	0	0	4.27
6 Min. YEARS		137	128	3	2	739.2	3218	748	392	336	55	28	27	24	320	6	631	46	19	44	43	.506	1	0	4.09

Billy Brewer

Pitches: Left **Bats:** Left **Pos:** RP-9   **Ht:** 6'1" **Wt:** 200 **Born:** 4/15/68 **Age:** 33

		HOW MUCH HE PITCHED						WHAT HE GAVE UP											THE RESULTS				
Year Team	Lg Org	G	GS	CG	GF	IP	BFP	H	R	ER	HR	SH	SF	HB	TBB	IBB	SO	WP	Bk	W	L	Pct.	ShO	Sv	ERA
1990 Jamestown	A- Mon	11	2	0	4	27.2	115	23	10	9	0	1	0	0	13	0	37	2	1	2	3	.400	0	1	2.93
1991 Rockford	A Mon	29	0	0	16	41	176	32	12	9	1	2	1	1	25	0	43	6	0	3	3	.500	0	5	1.98
1992 Wst Plm Bch	A Mon	28	0	0	20	36.1	144	27	10	7	0	1	0	2	14	1	37	2	0	2	2	.500	0	8	1.73
Harrisburg	AA Mon	20	0	0	4	23.1	114	25	15	13	1	0	1	1	18	1	18	5	0	2	0	1.000	0	0	5.01
1995 Springfield	A KC	1	0	0	1	2	9	2	1	0	0	0	0	0	1	0	2	0	0	0	0	—	0	1	0.00
Omaha	AAA KC	6	0	0	1	7	25	7	0	0	0	0	0	0	7	0	5	2	1	0	0	—	0	0	0.00
1996 Albuquerque	AAA LA	31	0	0	12	31.2	141	28	13	11	5	1	0	0	22	6	33	3	3	2	2	.500	0	2	3.13
Columbus	AAA NYY	13	4	0	6	25	122	27	21	20	4	0	2	2	19	0	27	3	0	2	0	.000	0	0	7.20
1997 Visalia	A+ Oak	2	0	0	0	3	15	1	1	0	0	0	1	0	4	0	5	0	0	0	0	—	0	0	0.00
Edmonton	AAA Oak	7	1	0	2	8	36	8	5	5	2	0	0	1	6	0	11	1	0	0	1	.000	0	1	5.63
Scranton-WB	AAA Phi	11	0	0	6	9	41	10	7	3	2	2	0	0	5	1	9	0	0	2	1	.667	0	1	3.00
1999 Scranton-WB	AAA Phi	33	5	0	10	69	293	59	32	29	5	1	6	5	28	0	57	9	0	6	1	.857	0	2	3.78
2000 Rochester	AAA Bal	9	0	0	4	11.1	54	13	5	5	3	0	0	0	7	0	3	0	0	2	0	.000	0	0	3.97
1993 Kansas City	AL	46	0	0	14	39	157	31	16	15	6	1	1	0	20	4	28	2	1	2	2	.500	0	0	3.46
1994 Kansas City	AL	50	0	0	17	38.2	157	28	11	11	4	2	2	2	16	1	25	3	0	4	1	.800	0	3	2.56
1995 Kansas City	AL	48	0	0	13	45.1	209	54	28	28	9	1	0	2	20	1	31	5	1	2	4	.333	0	0	5.56
1996 New York	AL	4	0	0	1	5.2	32	7	6	6	0	0	0	0	8	0	0	0	0	1	0	1.000	0	0	9.53
1997 Oakland	AL	3	0	0	1	2	12	4	3	3	1	0	1	0	2	0	1	0	0	0	0	—	0	0	13.50
Philadelphia	NL	25	0	0	4	22	93	15	8	8	2	0	2	0	11	0	16	1	0	1	2	.333	0	0	3.27
1998 Philadelphia	NL	2	0	0	0	0.1	6	3	4	4	0	0	0	0	2	0	0	0	0	0	0	.000	0	0	108.00
1999 Philadelphia	NL	25	0	0	8	25.2	118	30	20	20	4	1	1	0	14	1	28	1	0	1	1	.500	0	2	7.01
8 Min. YEARS		201	14	0	86	294.1	1285	256	132	111	23	8	11	12	169	9	287	33	6	19	16	.543	0	21	3.39
7 Maj. YEARS		203	0	0	58	178.2	784	172	96	95	25	5	7	4	93	7	137	12	2	11	11	.500	0	5	4.79

Donnie Bridges

Pitches: Right **Bats:** Right **Pos:** SP-30   **Ht:** 6'4" **Wt:** 220 **Born:** 12/10/78 **Age:** 22

		HOW MUCH HE PITCHED						WHAT HE GAVE UP											THE RESULTS				
Year Team	Lg Org	G	GS	CG	GF	IP	BFP	H	R	ER	HR	SH	SF	HB	TBB	IBB	SO	WP	Bk	W	L	Pct.	ShO	Sv	ERA
1997 Expos	R Mon	5	2	0	0	10	49	14	9	7	0	0	1	2	5	0	6	0	0	0	2	.000	0	0	6.30
1998 Vermont	A- Mon	13	13	0	0	68	311	71	42	37	2	2	2	8	37	0	43	8	0	5	6	.455	0	0	4.90
1999 Cape Fear	A Mon	8	8	1	0	47.1	189	37	12	12	2	2	0	5	17	0	44	5	0	6	1	.857	1	0	2.28
Jupiter	A+ Mon	18	18	1	0	99	429	116	53	45	5	3	8	2	36	0	63	7	0	4	6	.400	1	0	4.09
2000 Jupiter	A+ Mon	11	11	0	0	73.1	296	58	29	26	0	1	4	1	20	0	66	2	0	5	5	.500	0	0	3.19
Harrisburg	AA Mon	19	19	6	0	128	528	104	39	34	5	3	4	8	49	0	84	7	0	11	7	.611	4	0	2.39
4 Min. YEARS		74	71	8	0	425.2	1802	400	184	161	14	11	19	26	164	0	306	29	0	31	27	.534	6	0	3.40

Kary Bridges

Bats: Left **Throws:** Right **Pos:** 2B-54; PH-7; DH-2   **Ht:** 5'10" **Wt:** 170 **Born:** 10/27/72 **Age:** 28

		BATTING																BASERUNNING				PERCENTAGES		
Year Team	Lg Org	G	AB	H	2B	3B	HR	TB	R	RBI	TBB	IBB	SO	HBP	SH	SF		SB	CS	SB%	GDP	Avg	OBP	SLG
1993 Quad City	A Hou	65	263	74	9	0	3	92	37	24	31	1	18	2	1	3		15	10	.60	7	.281	.358	.350
1994 Quad City	A Hou	117	447	135	20	4	1	166	66	53	38	3	29	3	8	4		14	11	.56	9	.302	.358	.371
1995 Jackson	AA Hou	118	418	126	22	4	3	165	56	43	49	3	17	0	6	4		10	12	.45	12	.301	.372	.395
1996 Jackson	AA Hou	87	338	110	12	2	4	138	51	33	32	1	14	1	7	3		4	5	.44	11	.325	.382	.408
Tucson	AAA Hou	42	140	44	9	1	1	58	24	21	9	1	8	1	0	1		1	3	.25	3	.314	.355	.414
1997 New Orleans	AAA Hou	23	64	11	1	2	0	16	6	3	5	0	9	1	0	1		0	1	1.00	0	.172	.239	.250
Carolina	AA Pit	66	283	95	17	1	3	123	43	29	9	0	10	0	3	2		9	5	.64	7	.336	.354	.435
Calgary	AAA Pit	33	95	25	4	0	0	29	9	6	7	1	6	1	0	0		1	0	1.00	3	.263	.314	.305
1998 West Tenn	AA ChC	48	196	60	7	1	0	69	30	21	18	1	9	0	2	2		6	4	.60	4	.306	.363	.352
Iowa	AAA ChC	64	181	39	10	1	0	51	25	14	11	0	12	1	0	2		0	2	.00	4	.215	.262	.282
1999 Iowa	AAA ChC	10	25	3	0	0	0	3	1	0	1	0	5	0	0	0		0	0	—	0	.120	.154	.120
Oklahoma	AAA Tex	75	239	82	14	0	7	117	38	39	21	2	14	1	4	2		6	3	.67	8	.343	.394	.490
2000 Ottawa	AAA Mon	61	210	71	12	3	2	95	35	27	27	0	7	1	5	2		1	3	.77	9	.338	.413	.452
8 Min. YEARS		809	2899	875	137	19	24	1122	421	313	258	13	158	11	36	27		77	58	.57	77	.302	.358	.387

Stoney Briggs

Bats: Right **Throws:** Right **Pos:** OF-132; DH-2 **Ht:** 6'3" **Wt:** 215 **Born:** 12/26/71 **Age:** 29

Year Team	Lg Org	G	AB	H	2B	3B	HR	TB	R	RBI	TBB	IBB	SO	HBP	SH	SF	SB	CS	SB%	GDP	Avg	OBP	SLG
1991 Medcine Hat	R+ Tor	64	236	70	8	0	8	102	45	29	18	0	62	2	0	2	9	5	.64	2	.297	.349	.432
1992 Myrtle Bch	A Tor	136	514	123	18	5	11	184	75	41	43	0	156	8	6	2	33	14	.70	6	.239	.307	.358
1993 Waterloo	A SD	125	421	108	15	5	9	160	57	55	30	1	103	12	4	5	21	8	.72	3	.257	.321	.380
1994 Rancho Cuca	A+ SD	121	417	112	22	2	17	189	63	76	54	1	124	9	2	7	14	13	.52	7	.269	.359	.453
1995 Memphis	AA SD	118	385	95	14	7	8	147	60	46	40	5	133	10	1	3	17	8	.68	13	.247	.331	.382
1996 Memphis	AA SD	133	452	124	24	6	12	196	72	80	62	4	123	4	4	3	28	11	.72	18	.274	.365	.434
1997 Las Vegas	AAA SD	119	435	117	21	5	11	181	58	57	28	1	122	6	0	4	18	12	.60	10	.269	.319	.416
1998 Iowa	AAA ChC	2	4	1	0	0	0	1	1	1	0	0	0	0	0	0	0	0	—	0	.250	.250	.250
Newburgh	IND —	24	87	29	6	0	8	59	21	25	6	1	16	2	0	1	9	1	.90	2	.333	.385	.678
2000 Jacksnville	AA Det	134	496	126	39	2	17	220	65	65	60	1	145	6	2	4	17	6	.74	14	.254	.339	.444
9 Min. YEARS		976	3447	905	167	32	101	1439	517	475	341	14	984	59	19	31	166	78	.68	75	.263	.337	.417

Jim Brink

Pitches: Right **Bats:** Right **Pos:** RP-48 **Ht:** 6'0" **Wt:** 185 **Born:** 9/11/76 **Age:** 24

		HOW MUCH HE PITCHED						WHAT HE GAVE UP											THE RESULTS					
Year Team	Lg Org	G	GS	CG	GF	IP	BFP	H	R	ER	HR	SH	SF	HB	TBB	IBB	SO	WP	Bk	W	L	Pct.	ShO	Sv	ERA
1998 Sou Oregon	A- Oak	24	1	0	17	56.1	241	63	32	27	4	1	2	1	16	2	43	2	2	3	0	1.000	0	11	4.31
1999 Midland	AA Oak	5	0	0	2	8	35	10	7	7	4	0	0	1	1	0	4	0	0	1	1	.500	0	0	7.88
Modesto	A+ Oak	47	0	0	41	45.1	204	53	24	23	2	5	4	0	18	3	38	0	0	3	0	1.000	0	29	4.57
2000 Midland	AA Oak	6	0	0	3	9.1	44	13	8	8	2	0	1	0	5	1	5	1	0	0	0	—	0	0	7.71
Modesto	A+ Oak	42	0	0	33	47.1	209	49	21	18	2	3	2	2	17	5	41	3	0	3	2	.600	0	19	3.42
3 Min. YEARS		124	1	0	96	166.1	733	188	92	83	14	9	9	4	57	11	131	6	2	10	3	.769	0	59	4.49

Darryl Brinkley

Bats: Right **Throws:** Right **Pos:** OF-54; DH-8; PH-8 **Ht:** 5'11" **Wt:** 210 **Born:** 12/23/68 **Age:** 32

Year Team	Lg Org	G	AB	H	2B	3B	HR	TB	R	RBI	TBB	IBB	SO	HBP	SH	SF	SB	CS	SB%	GDP	Avg	OBP	SLG
1994 Winnipeg	IND —	72	294	86	18	3	8	134	48	44	21	0	31	6	3	1	32	13	.71	5	.293	.351	.456
1995 Winnipeg	IND —	30	131	44	2	1	4	60	22	19	8	1	13	3	1	2	6	4	.60	4	.336	.382	.458
1996 Rancho Cuca	A+ SD	65	259	94	28	2	9	153	52	59	23	2	37	2	0	6	18	10	.64	13	.363	.410	.591
Memphis	AA SD	60	203	60	9	0	9	96	36	29	22	2	33	3	1	1	13	5	.72	6	.296	.371	.473
1997 Mobile	AA SD	55	215	66	14	1	5	97	41	33	26	1	30	5	0	0	10	9	.53	6	.307	.394	.451
1998 Nashville	AAA Pit	114	372	132	23	3	9	188	57	51	27	2	53	13	0	1	5	5	.50	9	.355	.416	.505
1999 Nashville	AAA Pit	111	372	120	35	2	14	201	68	75	31	0	58	1	0	3	5	5	.50	11	.323	.373	.540
2000 Nashville	AAA Pit	38	113	34	5	1	2	47	19	16	13	1	27	1	0	1	3	3	.50	2	.301	.375	.416
Rochester	AAA Bal	31	120	43	5	1	0	50	16	20	9	1	14	1	0	2	6	0	1.00	7	.358	.402	.417
7 Min. YEARS		576	2079	679	139	14	60	1026	359	346	180	10	296	35	5	17	103	57	.64	59	.327	.387	.494

Juan Brito

Bats: Right **Throws:** Right **Pos:** C-64; DH-7; PH-2; PR-1 **Ht:** 5'11" **Wt:** 185 **Born:** 11/7/79 **Age:** 21

Year Team	Lg Org	G	AB	H	2B	3B	HR	TB	R	RBI	TBB	IBB	SO	HBP	SH	SF	SB	CS	SB%	GDP	Avg	OBP	SLG
1997 Royals	R KC	25	70	22	4	0	3	35	14	15	5	1	5	1	1	0	0	0	—	1	.314	.368	.500
1998 Lansing	A KC	63	212	52	7	0	0	59	16	22	17	0	41	2	1	2	2	2	.50	6	.245	.305	.278
1999 Wilmington	A+ KC	14	46	13	1	0	0	14	3	1	1	0	11	0	0	0	0	0	—	1	.283	.298	.304
Wichita	AA KC	4	11	1	0	0	0	1	0	0	2	0	3	0	0	0	0	0	—	2	.091	.231	.091
Chston-WV	A KC	61	208	50	6	0	0	56	14	19	11	0	37	1	3	0	1	2	.33	8	.240	.282	.269
Omaha	AAA KC	2	7	2	2	0	0	4	1	0	0	0	2	0	0	0	0	0	—	0	.286	.286	.571
2000 Wilmington	A+ KC	22	54	12	4	0	0	16	4	9	8	0	7	0	0	1	1	0	1.00	2	.222	.317	.296
Omaha	AAA KC	17	49	14	1	0	1	18	8	2	3	0	10	0	1	0	1	1	.50	0	.286	.327	.367
Wichita	AA KC	34	105	27	2	0	0	29	9	10	11	2	15	1	0	2	2	1	.67	4	.257	.328	.276
4 Min. YEARS		242	762	193	27	0	4	232	69	78	58	3	131	5	6	5	7	6	.54	24	.253	.308	.304

Tilson Brito

Bats: Right **Throws:** Right **Pos:** 2B-11; 3B-4 **Ht:** 6'0" **Wt:** 180 **Born:** 5/28/72 **Age:** 29

Year Team	Lg Org	G	AB	H	2B	3B	HR	TB	R	RBI	TBB	IBB	SO	HBP	SH	SF	SB	CS	SB%	GDP	Avg	OBP	SLG
1992 Blue Jays	R Tor	54	189	58	10	4	3	85	36	36	22	1	22	6	0	5	16	8	.67	5	.307	.387	.450
Knoxville	AA Tor	7	24	5	1	2	0	10	2	2	0	0	9	0	0	0	0	0	—	0	.208	.208	.417
1993 Dunedin	A+ Tor	126	465	125	21	3	6	170	80	44	59	0	60	1	10	3	27	16	.63	8	.269	.361	.366
1994 Knoxville	AA Tor	139	476	127	17	7	5	173	61	57	35	2	68	8	9	7	33	12	.73	7	.267	.323	.363
1995 Syracuse	AAA Tor	90	327	79	16	3	7	122	49	32	29	0	69	4	2	1	17	8	.68	6	.242	.310	.373
1996 Syracuse	AAA Tor	108	400	111	22	8	10	179	63	54	38	1	65	5	3	4	11	10	.52	8	.278	.345	.448
1997 Modesto	A+ Oak	4	9	3	1	0	1	7	3	2	3	0	1	2	0	0	0	0	—	0	.333	.538	.778
1998 Tacoma	AAA Sea	42	143	37	12	1	2	57	20	12	8	0	29	2	3	1	0	1	.00	4	.259	.305	.399
1999 Charlotte	AAA CWS	111	406	129	30	5	11	202	60	58	34	3	66	12	3	3	6	4	.60	5	.318	.385	.498
2000 Toledo	AAA Det	15	49	13	2	1	0	17	4	1	5	0	12	1	0	1	1	0	1.00	3	.265	.339	.347
1996 Toronto	AL	26	80	19	7	0	1	29	10	7	10	0	18	3	2	0	1	1	.50	0	.238	.344	.363
1997 Toronto	AL	49	126	28	3	0	3	40	9	8	9	0	28	2	0	2	1	0	1.00	2	.222	.281	.246
Oakland		17	46	13	2	1	2	23	8	6	1	0	10	0	1	0	0	0	—	0	.283	.298	.500
9 Min. YEARS		696	2488	687	132	34	45	1022	378	299	232	7	401	50	30	25	111	59	.65	46	.276	.347	.411
2 Maj. YEARS		92	252	60	12	1	3	83	27	21	20	0	56	5	4	2	2	1	.67	2	.238	.305	.329

Corey Brittan

Pitches: Right **Bats:** Right **Pos:** RP-55   **Ht:** 6'6" **Wt:** 209 **Born:** 2/23/75 **Age:** 26

Year Team	Lg Org	G	GS	CG	GF	IP	BFP	H	R	ER	HR	SH	SF	HB	TBB	IBB	SO	WP	Bk	W	L	Pct.	ShO	Sv	ERA
1996 Pittsfield	A- NYM	14	14	2	0	98	390	74	30	25	2	5	1	4	20	0	84	5	2	8	3	.727	0	0	2.30
1997 St. Lucie	A+ NYM	51	1	0	18	78	338	91	35	31	4	4	0	1	21	4	57	2	0	3	5	.375	0	3	3.58
1998 Binghamton	AA NYM	9	0	0	3	9.1	40	9	4	4	0	0	1	0	4	0	5	3	0	1	1	.500	0	1	3.86
St. Lucie	A+ NYM	34	0	0	17	67	290	74	35	29	1	2	2	2	14	0	40	5	1	4	2	.667	0	2	3.90
1999 Binghamton	AA NYM	54	0	0	27	90.2	375	84	36	28	6	3	2	1	23	0	60	3	2	2	4	.333	0	7	2.78
2000 Binghamton	AA NYM	55	0	0	27	74.1	305	67	28	19	2	2	1	2	28	1	48	2	0	7	1	.875	0	12	2.30
5 Min. YEARS		217	15	2	92	417.1	1738	399	168	136	15	16	7	10	110	5	294	20	5	25	16	.610	0	24	2.93

Troy Brohawn

Pitches: Left **Bats:** Left **Pos:** RP-10; SP-4   **Ht:** 6'1" **Wt:** 190 **Born:** 1/14/73 **Age:** 28

Year Team	Lg Org	G	GS	CG	GF	IP	BFP	H	R	ER	HR	SH	SF	HB	TBB	IBB	SO	WP	Bk	W	L	Pct.	ShO	Sv	ERA
1994 San Jose	A+ SF	4	4	0	0	16.2	80	27	15	13	2	1	0	2	5	0	13	1	0	0	2	.000	0	0	7.02
1995 San Jose	A+ SF	11	10	0	1	65.1	246	45	14	12	4	1	1	1	20	0	57	5	1	7	3	.700	0	0	1.65
1996 Shreveport	AA SF	28	28	0	0	156.2	668	163	99	80	30	7	3	6	49	0	82	8	3	9	10	.474	0	0	4.60
1997 Shreveport	AA SF	26	26	1	0	169	695	148	57	48	10	3	1	2	64	0	98	4	3	13	5	.722	1	0	2.56
1998 Fresno	AAA SF	30	19	0	4	121.2	528	144	75	71	18	1	5	3	36	1	87	8	0	10	8	.556	0	0	5.25
1999 Tucson	AAA Ari	3	2	0	0	13.2	67	22	8	5	1	3	0	0	3	0	12	0	0	1	0	1.000	0	0	3.29
2000 Diamondbcks	R Ari	3	3	0	0	4	16	5	1	0	0	0	0	0	1	0	6	0	0	0	0	—	0	0	0.00
Tucson	AAA Ari	11	1	0	2	16.2	71	18	7	7	5	1	2	1	5	0	16	0	1	0	0	—	0	0	3.78
7 Min. YEARS		116	93	1	7	563.2	2371	572	276	236	70	27	12	15	183	1	371	26	8	40	28	.588	1	0	3.77

Jacob Brooks

Pitches: Right **Bats:** Right **Pos:** RP-21; SP-12   **Ht:** 6'1" **Wt:** 175 **Born:** 3/23/78 **Age:** 23

Year Team	Lg Org	G	GS	CG	GF	IP	BFP	H	R	ER	HR	SH	SF	HB	TBB	IBB	SO	WP	Bk	W	L	Pct.	ShO	Sv	ERA
1998 Butte	R+ Ana	28	3	0	14	54.2	274	64	53	43	7	1	1	5	39	0	63	8	0	2	7	.222	0	4	7.08
1999 Lk Elsinore	A+ Ana	27	0	0	15	36.2	176	38	33	29	7	2	3	1	29	1	43	9	1	3	3	.500	0	4	7.12
2000 Lk Elsinore	A+ Ana	28	7	0	7	78.1	354	82	52	37	5	3	3	5	33	2	80	8	4	7	3	.700	0	4	4.25
Erie	AA Ana	5	5	0	0	24.1	110	25	13	11	2	0	0	1	10	0	11	2	1	2	1	.667	0	0	4.07
3 Min. YEARS		88	15	0	36	194	914	209	151	120	21	6	7	12	111	3	197	27	6	14	14	.500	0	8	5.57

Ben Broussard

Bats: Left **Throws:** Left **Pos:** OF-70; 1B-15; PH-2   **Ht:** 6'2" **Wt:** 220 **Born:** 9/24/76 **Age:** 24

Year Team	Lg Org	G	AB	H	2B	3B	HR	TB	R	RBI	TBB	IBB	SO	HBP	SH	SF	SB	CS	SB%	GDP	Avg	OBP	SLG
1999 Billings	R+ Cin	38	145	59	11	2	14	116	39	48	34	2	30	4	0	1	1	0	1.00	0	.407	.527	.800
Clinton	A Cin	5	20	11	4	1	2	23	8	6	3	0	4	0	0	0	0	0	—	1	.550	.609	1.150
Chattanooga	AA Cin	35	127	27	5	0	8	56	26	21	11	1	41	3	0	0	1	0	1.00	0	.213	.291	.441
2000 Chattanooga	AA Cin	87	286	73	8	4	14	131	64	51	72	3	78	6	0	2	15	2	.88	6	.255	.413	.458
2 Min. YEARS		165	578	170	28	7	38	326	137	126	120	6	153	13	0	3	17	2	.89	7	.294	.424	.564

Alvin Brown

Pitches: Right **Bats:** Right **Pos:** RP-7   **Ht:** 6'1" **Wt:** 200 **Born:** 9/2/70 **Age:** 30

Year Team	Lg Org	G	GS	CG	GF	IP	BFP	H	R	ER	HR	SH	SF	HB	TBB	IBB	SO	WP	Bk	W	L	Pct.	ShO	Sv	ERA
1993 Bristol	R+ Det	15	6	0	4	39	182	27	30	27	0	0	1	4	47	0	30	14	0	2	2	.500	0	1	6.23
1994 Lakeland	A+ Det	4	0	0	3	7	40	11	8	7	0	0	0	0	7	0	9	1	0	0	0	—	0	0	9.00
Fayettevlle	A Det	33	12	1	11	97.2	441	61	60	47	3	4	0	7	83	0	109	27	2	6	7	.462	1	0	4.33
1995 Lakeland	A+ Det	9	0	0	6	46.2	202	35	23	22	1	1	0	4	33	0	35	9	1	2	3	.400	0	0	4.24
1996 San Berndno	A+ LA	42	0	0	16	68.2	306	43	40	29	2	5	2	2	62	0	84	17	1	2	4	.333	0	2	3.80
1997 San Antonio	AA LA	16	16	2	0	96.1	406	83	48	40	2	3	2	5	33	0	67	9	2	6	5	.545	1	0	3.74
Albuquerque	AAA LA	12	11	1	0	61.2	291	74	50	42	9	4	2	1	35	0	43	6	1	4	6	.400	0	0	6.13
1999 Altoona	AA Pit	7	6	0	0	26.1	124	29	22	19	0	3	3	1	17	0	15	6	1	4	1	.800	0	0	6.49
Lafayette	IND —	1	0	0	1	6	23	3	2	2	0	0	1	2	1	0	5	1	0	0	0	—	0	0	3.00
Erie	AA Ana	6	0	0	4	6.2	39	9	6	5	0	0	0	2	7	0	6	3	0	0	1	.000	0	2	6.75
2000 Erie	AA Ana	7	0	0	3	7.1	44	12	9	8	0	0	0	1	9	0	3	2	0	0	0	—	0	0	9.82
7 Min. YEARS		152	62	4	42	463.1	2098	387	298	248	26	19	12	29	334	0	406	95	8	26	29	.473	3	5	4.82

Elliot Brown

Pitches: Right **Bats:** Both **Pos:** RP-46   **Ht:** 6'2" **Wt:** 191 **Born:** 6/7/75 **Age:** 26

Year Team	Lg Org	G	GS	CG	GF	IP	BFP	H	R	ER	HR	SH	SF	HB	TBB	IBB	SO	WP	Bk	W	L	Pct.	ShO	Sv	ERA
1997 Chston-SC	A TB	33	16	0	6	118.2	525	117	73	57	11	4	2	8	45	0	86	12	0	5	8	.385	0	3	4.32
1998 Chston-SC	A TB	40	15	0	5	107	475	123	72	59	10	1	5	10	40	0	59	8	1	2	7	.222	0	0	4.96
1999 Orlando	AA TB	10	1	0	5	18.2	89	25	18	16	2	0	1	0	12	0	12	3	0	0	2	.000	0	0	7.71
St. Pete	A+ TB	38	0	0	15	57.1	230	44	20	17	1	2	1	3	14	1	42	5	0	5	3	.625	0	3	2.67
2000 Orlando	AA TB	45	0	0	7	71.2	321	75	44	38	6	2	3	8	24	3	39	5	0	3	4	.429	0	1	4.77
Durham	AAA TB	1	0	0	1	1	6	1	1	1	0	0	0	0	2	0	0	1	0	0	1	.000	0	0	9.00
4 Min. YEARS		167	32	0	39	374.1	1646	385	228	188	30	9	12	29	137	4	238	34	1	15	25	.375	0	7	4.52

Jamie Brown

Pitches: Right **Bats:** Right **Pos:** SP-17   **Ht:** 6'2" **Wt:** 205 **Born:** 3/31/77 **Age:** 24

Year Team	Lg Org	G	GS	CG	GF	IP	BFP	H	R	ER	HR	SH	SF	HB	TBB	IBB	SO	WP	Bk	W	L	Pct.	ShO	Sv	ERA
1997 Watertown	A- Cle	13	13	1	0	73	303	66	35	25	6	1	2	4	15	0	57	1	1	10	2	.833	0	0	3.08
1998 Kinston	A+ Cle	27	27	2	0	172.2	717	162	91	73	12	10	3	11	44	1	148	4	2	11	9	.550	0	0	3.81
Akron	AA Cle	1	1	0	0	7	28	5	2	2	1	0	0	1	1	0	5	0	0	1	0	1.000	0	0	2.57
1999 Akron	AA Cle	23	23	1	0	138	586	140	72	70	11	7	10	13	39	1	98	2	3	5	9	.357	0	0	4.57
Buffalo	AAA Cle	1	0	0	0	5	23	8	4	3	0	1	0	0	1	0	2	0	0	1	0	1.000	0	0	5.40
2000 Akron	AA Cle	17	17	1	0	96.2	416	95	49	47	12	4	1	6	26	0	57	1	0	7	6	.538	0	0	4.38
4 Min. YEARS		82	81	5	0	492.1	2073	476	253	220	42	23	17	35	126	2	367	8	6	35	26	.574	0	0	4.02

Jason Brown

Bats: Right **Throws:** Right **Pos:** C-40; DH-25; PH-4; 1B-1   **Ht:** 6'2" **Wt:** 205 **Born:** 5/22/74 **Age:** 27

Year Team	Lg Org	G	AB	H	2B	3B	HR	TB	R	RBI	TBB	IBB	SO	HBP	SH	SF	SB	CS	SB%	GDP	Avg	OBP	SLG
1997 Yakima	A- LA	18	59	12	0	0	1	15	6	5	6	0	13	4	1	0	0	0	—	0	.203	.319	.254
San Berndno	A+ LA	30	102	26	10	0	0	36	15	13	3	0	26	4	3	2	0	3	.00	2	.255	.297	.353
1998 Vero Beach	A+ LA	85	267	61	13	0	4	86	23	27	26	1	60	4	3	1	0	0	—	9	.228	.305	.322
1999 San Berndno	A+ LA	68	234	51	11	2	6	84	28	28	23	1	64	7	3	0	1	2	.33	9	.218	.307	.359
2000 Orlando	AA TB	69	230	60	12	1	8	98	21	29	14	0	53	7	1	4	1	0	1.00	8	.261	.318	.426
4 Min. YEARS		270	892	210	46	3	19	319	93	102	72	2	216	26	11	7	2	5	.29	28	.235	.309	.358

Rich Brown

Bats: Left **Throws:** Left **Pos:** OF-83; DH-9; PH-1; PR-1   **Ht:** 6'1" **Wt:** 196 **Born:** 4/28/77 **Age:** 24

Year Team	Lg Org	G	AB	H	2B	3B	HR	TB	R	RBI	TBB	IBB	SO	HBP	SH	SF	SB	CS	SB%	GDP	Avg	OBP	SLG
1996 Yankees	R NYY	47	164	47	8	3	0	61	33	23	23	1	32	1	1	3	2	1	.67	2	.287	.372	.372
1997 Yankees	R NYY	10	30	11	3	0	0	14	7	3	5	0	6	0	1	0	1	0	—	2	.367	.444	.467
1998 Yankees	R NYY	6	14	6	0	0	2	12	6	2	1	0	3	1	0	0	2	0	1.00	0	.429	.500	.857
Tampa	A+ NYY	80	282	84	13	3	11	136	46	38	45	1	54	5	2	0	8	6	.57	3	.298	.404	.482
1999 Norwich	AA NYY	104	383	100	18	8	6	152	46	54	34	0	81	3	0	4	5	8	.38	6	.261	.323	.397
2000 Columbus	AAA NYY	10	37	8	2	0	0	10	1	2	1	0	7	0	0	0	0	0	—	1	.216	.237	.270
Norwich	AA NYY	82	319	76	15	3	4	109	52	30	25	0	34	1	1	0	15	7	.68	6	.238	.296	.342
5 Min. YEARS		339	1229	332	59	17	23	494	191	152	134	2	217	11	4	8	32	22	.59	20	.270	.345	.402

Tighe Brown

Pitches: Right **Bats:** Right **Pos:** RP-23; SP-7   **Ht:** 6'4" **Wt:** 195 **Born:** 9/10/76 **Age:** 24

Year Team	Lg Org	G	GS	CG	GF	IP	BFP	H	R	ER	HR	SH	SF	HB	TBB	IBB	SO	WP	Bk	W	L	Pct.	ShO	Sv	ERA
1995 White Sox	R CWS	3	0	0	1	7.2	28	3	1	1	0	1	0	0	2	0	12	1	0	0	0	—	0	0	1.17
1998 White Sox	R CWS	5	0	0	2	6.1	33	7	8	3	1	0	0	1	4	0	10	1	1	0	0	—	0	0	4.26
1999 Bristol	R+ CWS	7	0	0	4	9.2	52	18	12	11	1	1	1	0	5	1	11	0	0	1	2	.333	0	0	10.24
Burlington	A CWS	4	0	0	1	4.2	25	3	4	4	1	0	0	0	6	0	8	1	0	0	0	—	0	1	7.71
2000 Billings	R+ Cin	7	5	0	0	37.1	156	29	16	13	4	0	1	2	16	0	30	4	0	3	1	.750	0	0	3.13
Dayton	A Cin	21	2	0	4	39	189	55	39	34	4	2	3	3	20	0	25	4	0	2	2	.500	0	0	7.85
Chattanooga	AA Cin	2	0	0	1	5.2	22	3	0	0	0	0	0	1	2	0	4	0	0	0	0	—	0	0	0.00
4 Min. YEARS		49	7	0	13	110.1	505	118	80	66	11	3	6	7	55	1	100	11	1	6	5	.545	0	1	5.38

Vick Brown

Bats: Right **Throws:** Right **Pos:** 2B-68; PH-26; OF-5; PR-4   **Ht:** 6'1" **Wt:** 170 **Born:** 8/14/72 **Age:** 28

Year Team	Lg Org	G	AB	H	2B	3B	HR	TB	R	RBI	TBB	IBB	SO	HBP	SH	SF	SB	CS	SB%	GDP	Avg	OBP	SLG
1993 Yankees	R NYY	52	212	52	7	1	0	61	31	15	19	1	44	7	1	3	18	2	.90	1	.245	.324	.288
1994 Greensboro	A NYY	117	382	88	8	1	0	98	69	20	73	0	79	4	4	1	27	10	.73	4	.230	.359	.257
1995 Greensboro	A NYY	118	432	98	10	4	2	116	66	36	44	0	93	6	8	1	24	9	.73	11	.227	.306	.269
1996 Tampa	A+ NYY	35	89	18	3	0	0	21	17	7	14	0	22	2	2	0	2	0	1.00	3	.202	.324	.236
Greensboro	A NYY	25	91	29	6	0	1	38	8	9	11	0	23	1	0	0	9	2	.82	0	.319	.398	.418
1997 Tampa	A+ NYY	123	463	135	19	4	2	168	77	42	38	0	78	11	6	5	55	13	.81	6	.292	.356	.363
1998 Norwich	AA NYY	102	352	105	14	3	6	143	62	34	40	0	75	6	1	0	35	10	.78	7	.298	.374	.406
1999 Norwich	AA NYY	132	482	121	19	1	5	157	86	48	83	0	101	7	5	5	50	14	.78	15	.251	.366	.326
2000 Colo Sprngs	AAA Col	47	78	16	6	0	0	22	14	7	13	2	20	0	1	0	2	0	1.00	3	.205	.319	.282
El Paso	AA Ari	18	56	14	3	0	0	17	14	4	8	0	8	0	0	0	2	0	1.00	0	.250	.344	.304
Tucson	AAA Ari	33	102	25	3	2	1	35	16	7	12	0	15	1	1	0	6	3	.67	3	.245	.330	.343
8 Min. YEARS		802	2739	701	98	13	17	876	460	229	355	3	558	45	29	15	230	63	.78	53	.256	.349	.320

Mo Bruce

Bats: Right **Throws:** Right **Pos:** 3B-66; SS-54; DH-4; PH-2; OF-1; 1B-1   **Ht:** 5'10" **Wt:** 190 **Born:** 5/1/75 **Age:** 26

Year Team	Lg Org	G	AB	H	2B	3B	HR	TB	R	RBI	TBB	IBB	SO	HBP	SH	SF	SB	CS	SB%	GDP	Avg	OBP	SLG
1996 Kingsport	R+ NYM	11	38	7	0	1	0	9	5	4	0	0	7	1	0	1	2	1	.67	1	.184	.200	.237
Mets	R NYM	30	120	33	5	3	0	44	16	7	3	0	15	0	3	1	6	1	.86	1	.275	.290	.367
1997 Kingsport	R+ NYM	34	128	47	8	3	3	70	35	21	16	0	20	2	0	0	14	4	.78	1	.367	.445	.547
Pittsfield	A- NYM	29	115	40	7	3	4	65	26	14	11	0	23	2	0	1	12	2	.86	4	.348	.408	.565
1998 Capital Cty	A NYM	126	516	176	24	4	15	253	81	74	41	4	117	1	1	1	45	15	.75	5	.341	.390	.490
1999 Binghamton	AA NYM	133	500	135	25	4	9	195	80	76	61	2	134	4	5	5	33	11	.75	9	.270	.351	.390
2000 Binghamton	AA NYM	81	314	86	16	3	2	114	50	23	27	0	55	1	2	1	21	10	.68	8	.274	.332	.363
Norfolk	AAA NYM	43	151	35	5	1	2	48	24	10	10	1	46	2	0	1	8	3	.73	5	.232	.288	.318
5 Min. YEARS		487	1882	559	90	22	35	798	317	229	169	7	407	13	11	11	141	47	.75	34	.297	.357	.424

36

Cliff Brumbaugh

Bats: Right **Throws:** Right **Pos:** OF-73; 1B-47; 3B-19; PH-2; DH-1   **Ht:** 6'2" **Wt:** 205 **Born:** 4/21/74 **Age:** 27

Year Team	Lg Org	G	AB	H	2B	3B	HR	TB	R	RBI	TBB	IBB	SO	HBP	SH	SF	SB	CS	SB%	GDP	Avg	OBP	SLG
1995 Hudson Val	A- Tex	74	282	101	19	4	2	134	44	45	39	4	51	2	0	2	15	3	.83	11	.358	.437	.475
1996 Chston-SC	A Tex	132	458	111	23	7	6	166	70	45	72	2	103	1	1	2	20	7	.74	5	.242	.345	.362
1997 Charlotte	A+ Tex	139	522	136	27	4	15	216	78	70	47	2	99	6	0	4	13	11	.54	7	.261	.326	.414
1998 Tulsa	AA Tex	132	483	125	34	1	15	206	65	76	54	5	77	4	3	5	1	3	.25	12	.259	.335	.427
1999 Tulsa	AA Tex	135	513	144	35	3	25	260	94	89	71	1	88	2	0	4	18	4	.82	5	.281	.368	.507
Oklahoma	AAA Tex	4	12	3	0	0	0	3	1	1	0	0	2	0	0	0	0	0	—	0	.250	.250	.250
2000 Tulsa	AA Tex	7	27	6	1	0	2	13	5	3	9	0	10	0	0	0	1	0	1.00	2	.222	.417	.481
Oklahoma	AAA Tex	127	454	126	28	4	10	192	81	56	85	1	72	1	4	3	9	12	.43	13	.278	.390	.423
6 Min. YEARS		750	2751	752	167	23	75	1190	438	385	377	15	502	16	8	20	77	40	.66	55	.273	.362	.433

Jacob Brumfield

Bats: Right **Throws:** Right **Pos:** OF-73; DH-4; PH-3; PR-1   **Ht:** 6'0" **Wt:** 190 **Born:** 5/27/65 **Age:** 36

Year Team	Lg Org	G	AB	H	2B	3B	HR	TB	R	RBI	TBB	IBB	SO	HBP	SH	SF	SB	CS	SB%	GDP	Avg	OBP	SLG
1986 Fort Myers	A+ KC	12	41	13	3	1	1	21	3	5	2	0	11	0	0	0	1	0	1.00	0	.317	.349	.512
1987 Memphis	AA KC	9	39	13	3	2	1	23	7	6	3	0	8	0	1	0	2	1	.67	0	.333	.381	.590
Fort Myers	A+ KC	114	379	93	14	10	6	145	56	34	45	2	78	0	1	0	43	14	.75	12	.245	.325	.383
1988 Memphis	AA KC	128	433	98	15	5	6	141	70	28	52	0	104	1	8	5	47	7	.87	2	.226	.308	.326
1989 Memphis	AA KC	104	346	79	14	2	1	100	43	25	53	0	74	3	5	0	28	12	.70	1	.228	.336	.289
1990 Baseball Cy	A+ KC	109	372	125	24	3	0	155	66	40	60	6	44	2	2	2	47	10	.82	7	.336	.429	.417
Omaha	AAA KC	24	77	25	6	1	2	39	10	11	7	0	14	0	1	2	10	3	.77	2	.325	.372	.506
1991 Omaha	AAA KC	111	397	106	14	7	3	143	62	43	33	0	64	1	2	3	36	17	.68	9	.267	.323	.360
1992 Nashville	AAA Cin	56	208	59	10	3	5	90	32	19	26	0	35	2	3	0	22	11	.67	1	.284	.369	.433
1993 Indianaplos	AAA Cin	33	126	41	14	1	4	69	23	19	6	0	14	1	2	1	11	0	1.00	4	.325	.358	.548
1995 Carolina	AA Pit	3	12	5	0	1	1	11	2	2	1	0	2	0	0	0	0	2	.00	0	.417	.462	.917
1997 Dunedin	A+ Tor	6	25	4	0	0	0	4	3	2	2	0	6	0	0	0	1	1	.50	1	.160	.160	.160
1998 Charlotte	AAA Fla	95	227	38	13	0	3	60	24	25	34	4	41	4	1	2	7	1	.88	6	.167	.285	.264
2000 Syracuse	AAA Tor	11	43	10	3	1	1	18	5	4	2	0	7	0	0	1	1	0	1.00	2	.233	.267	.419
Birmingham	AA CWS	18	59	11	2	0	0	13	6	2	9	0	8	0	1	1	3	2	.60	0	.186	.294	.220
Charlotte	AAA CWS	51	180	39	13	0	2	58	25	16	17	0	24	1	0	1	4	1	.80	5	.217	.286	.322
1992 Cincinnati	NL	24	30	4	0	0	0	4	6	2	2	1	4	1	0	0	6	0	1.00	1	.133	.212	.133
1993 Cincinnati	NL	103	272	73	17	3	6	114	40	23	21	4	47	1	3	2	20	8	.71	1	.268	.321	.419
1994 Cincinnati	NL	68	122	38	10	2	4	64	36	11	15	0	18	0	2	0	6	3	.67	3	.311	.381	.525
1995 Pittsburgh	NL	116	402	109	23	2	4	148	64	26	37	0	71	5	0	1	22	12	.65	3	.271	.339	.368
1996 Pittsburgh	NL	29	80	20	9	0	2	35	11	8	5	1	17	0	0	1	3	1	.75	4	.250	.291	.438
Toronto	AL	90	308	79	19	2	12	138	52	52	24	1	58	4	1	3	12	3	.80	10	.256	.316	.448
1997 Toronto	AL	58	174	36	5	1	2	49	22	20	14	0	31	1	1	1	4	4	.50	4	.207	.268	.282
1999 Los Angeles	NL	18	17	5	0	1	0	7	4	1	0	0	5	0	0	0	0	0	—	0	.294	.294	.412
Toronto	AL	62	170	40	8	3	2	60	25	19	19	0	39	0	3	3	1	2	.33	2	.235	.307	.353
12 Min. YEARS		884	2964	759	148	36	37	1090	436	281	350	8	534	15	27	16	262	83	.76	51	.256	.336	.368
7 Maj. YEARS		568	1575	404	91	14	32	619	260	162	137	7	290	12	10	13	74	33	.69	27	.257	.318	.393

Sean Brummett

Pitches: Left **Bats:** Left **Pos:** RP-27; SP-14   **Ht:** 6'0" **Wt:** 200 **Born:** 1/10/78 **Age:** 23

Year Team	Lg Org	G	GS	CG	GF	IP	BFP	H	R	ER	HR	SH	SF	HB	TBB	IBB	SO	WP	Bk	W	L	Pct.	ShO	Sv	ERA
1999 Boise	A- Ana	17	3	0	2	32.1	148	41	25	24	3	1	0	1	12	1	26	1	0	1	2	.333	0	0	6.68
2000 Cedar Rapds	A Ana	32	5	1	17	72.1	290	58	16	8	0	5	0	3	23	3	53	4	1	7	4	.636	0	5	1.00
Erie	AA Ana	9	9	1	0	49	225	63	33	29	6	1	2	1	25	0	30	0	0	0	7	.000	0	0	5.33
2 Min. YEARS		58	17	2	19	153.2	663	162	74	61	9	7	2	5	60	4	109	5	1	8	13	.381	0	5	3.57

Will Brunson

Pitches: Left **Bats:** Left **Pos:** RP-18   **Ht:** 6'5" **Wt:** 185 **Born:** 3/20/70 **Age:** 31

Year Team	Lg Org	G	GS	CG	GF	IP	BFP	H	R	ER	HR	SH	SF	HB	TBB	IBB	SO	WP	Bk	W	L	Pct.	ShO	Sv	ERA
1992 Princeton	R+ Cin	13	13	0	0	72.2	313	68	34	29	6	4	2	3	28	0	48	2	0	5	5	.500	0	0	3.59
1993 Chston-WV	A Cin	37	15	0	4	123.2	545	119	69	54	10	4	4	11	50	1	103	7	2	5	6	.455	0	0	3.93
1994 Winston-Sal	A+ Cin	30	22	3	3	165	711	161	83	73	22	5	7	12	58	2	129	6	4	12	7	.632	0	0	3.98
1995 San Berndno	A+ LA	13	13	0	0	83.1	334	68	24	19	4	3	5	5	21	0	70	3	0	10	0	1.000	0	0	2.05
San Antonio	AA LA	14	14	0	0	80	356	105	46	44	4	3	1	4	22	0	44	5	1	4	5	.444	0	0	4.95
1996 San Antonio	AA LA	11	5	0	1	42	166	32	13	10	2	2	0	1	15	0	38	2	1	3	1	.750	0	0	2.14
Albuquerque	AAA LA	9	9	1	0	54.1	239	53	29	27	7	2	1	2	23	1	47	2	0	3	4	.429	0	0	4.47
1997 Albuquerque	AAA LA	27	0	0	9	26.1	125	39	19	19	3	1	1	1	10	1	25	0	0	1	1	.500	0	0	6.49
San Antonio	AA LA	17	11	2	4	72.2	299	68	30	28	8	7	1	6	13	0	71	2	0	5	5	.500	1	0	3.47
1998 Albuquerque	AAA LA	34	15	1	5	120	520	135	69	62	11	5	3	4	40	1	100	3	1	5	8	.385	0	2	4.65
1999 Toledo	AAA Det	38	1	0	15	47.2	201	45	28	24	5	3	0	2	17	1	41	2	1	3	1	.750	0	3	4.53
2000 Sacramento	AAA Oak	18	0	0	1	24.2	111	26	12	10	0	2	0	1	11	0	22	0	0	1	0	1.000	0	0	3.65
1998 Los Angeles	NL	2	0	0	1	2.1	11	3	3	3	0	0	0	0	2	0	1	0	0	0	1	.000	0	0	11.57
Detroit	AL	8	0	0	1	3	11	2	0	0	0	0	0	0	1	0	9	1	0	0	0	—	0	0	0.00
1999 Detroit	AL	17	0	0	1	12	58	18	9	8	3	2	0	0	6	1	1	0	0	1	0	1.000	0	0	6.00
9 Min. YEARS		261	118	7	46	912.1	3920	919	455	399	82	37	25	52	308	8	738	34	10	59	43	.578	1	5	3.94
2 Maj. YEARS		27	0	0	3	17.1	80	23	12	11	3	2	0	0	9	1	11	1	0	1	1	.500	0	0	5.71

Jim Buccheri

Bats: Right Throws: Right Pos: OF-71; DH-12; PH-2; PR-2   Ht: 5'11" Wt: 165 Born: 11/12/68 Age: 32

Year Team	Lg Org	G	AB	H	2B	3B	HR	TB	R	RBI	TBB	IBB	SO	HBP	SH	SF	SB	CS	SB%	GDP	Avg	OBP	SLG
1988 Sou Oregon	A- Oak	58	232	67	8	1	0	77	42	17	20	0	35	4	0	3	25	7	.78	7	.289	.351	.332
1989 Madison	A Oak	115	433	101	9	0	2	116	56	28	26	1	61	5	3	3	43	12	.78	5	.233	.283	.268
1990 Modesto	A+ Oak	36	125	35	4	1	0	41	27	7	25	0	16	2	2	0	15	9	.63	2	.280	.408	.328
Huntsville	AA Oak	84	278	58	2	1	0	62	39	22	40	0	38	3	7	1	14	6	.70	5	.209	.314	.223
1991 Huntsville	AA Oak	100	340	72	15	0	0	87	48	22	71	0	60	7	5	4	35	7	.83	5	.212	.355	.256
1992 Huntsville	AA Oak	20	60	9	2	1	1	16	8	5	9	0	18	0	1	1	5	3	.63	1	.150	.257	.267
Reno	A+ Oak	63	259	95	14	2	4	125	65	38	56	3	40	2	2	2	33	13	.72	5	.367	.480	.483
Tacoma	AAA Oak	46	127	38	6	3	0	50	24	13	27	1	25	2	0	0	10	5	.67	2	.299	.429	.394
1993 Modesto	A+ Oak	2	7	2	0	0	0	2	3	1	2	0	2	1	0	0	0	0	—	1	.286	.500	.286
Tacoma	AAA Oak	90	293	81	9	3	2	102	45	40	39	1	46	2	10	1	12	9	.57	6	.276	.364	.348
1994 Tacoma	AAA Oak	121	448	136	8	3	3	159	59	39	42	1	45	4	7	2	32	14	.70	8	.304	.367	.355
1995 Ottawa	AAA Mon	133	470	126	16	4	0	150	64	30	49	5	58	3	11	2	44	11	.80	7	.268	.340	.319
1996 Ottawa	AAA Mon	65	206	53	3	4	1	67	40	12	33	0	28	2	1	2	33	6	.85	1	.257	.362	.325
1997 St. Pete	A+ TB	58	204	50	9	0	0	59	29	13	27	0	20	1	3	3	25	7	.78	2	.245	.332	.289
1998 Durham	AAA TB	106	351	107	14	3	6	145	51	34	25	1	28	5	6	0	37	13	.74	11	.305	.360	.413
1999 Durham	AAA TB	6	8	1	1	0	0	2	2	2	2	0	0	0	1	1	2	0	1.00	1	.125	.273	.250
Orlando	AA TB	45	161	50	8	1	1	63	18	16	15	0	24	3	3	0	5	4	.56	2	.311	.380	.391
Binghamton	AA NYM	4	17	5	1	1	0	8	1	1	0	0	4	0	1	0	0	0	—	1	.294	.294	.471
Norfolk	AAA NYM	32	92	21	3	0	0	24	9	5	4	0	15	0	1	0	4	1	.80	4	.228	.260	.261
2000 Durham	AAA TB	84	316	81	10	1	4	105	37	26	27	0	53	4	3	1	18	4	.82	9	.256	.322	.332
13 Min. YEARS		1268	4427	1188	142	29	24	1460	667	371	539	13	616	50	67	26	392	131	.75	86	.268	.352	.330

Brandon Buckley

Bats: Right Throws: Right Pos: C-46; PH-1; PR-1   Ht: 6'2" Wt: 205 Born: 1/25/77 Age: 24

Year Team	Lg Org	G	AB	H	2B	3B	HR	TB	R	RBI	TBB	IBB	SO	HBP	SH	SF	SB	CS	SB%	GDP	Avg	OBP	SLG
1998 Auburn	A- Hou	26	76	17	4	0	0	21	5	9	12	0	13	0	1	0	0	1	.00	2	.224	.330	.276
1999 Kissimmee	A+ Hou	51	146	29	5	0	1	37	13	11	11	1	29	0	3	1	1	3	.25	4	.199	.253	.253
2000 Round Rock	AA Hou	1	5	2	1	0	0	3	1	1	0	0	0	0	0	0	0	0	—	0	.400	.400	.600
Kissimmee	A+ Hou	45	129	34	3	1	2	45	19	16	11	0	27	2	2	0	0	1	.00	3	.264	.331	.349
3 Min. YEARS		123	356	82	13	1	3	106	38	37	34	1	69	2	6	1	1	5	.17	9	.230	.300	.298

Mark Budzinski

Bats: Left Throws: Left Pos: OF-136   Ht: 6'2" Wt: 175 Born: 8/26/73 Age: 27

Year Team	Lg Org	G	AB	H	2B	3B	HR	TB	R	RBI	TBB	IBB	SO	HBP	SH	SF	SB	CS	SB%	GDP	Avg	OBP	SLG
1995 Watertown	A- Cle	70	253	64	12	8	3	101	50	25	52	1	49	8	3	2	15	5	.75	3	.253	.394	.399
1996 Columbus	A Cle	74	260	68	12	4	3	97	42	38	59	4	68	4	2	1	12	3	.80	5	.262	.404	.373
1997 Kinston	A+ Cle	68	241	69	13	3	7	109	43	39	48	1	61	1	2	0	6	4	.60	3	.286	.407	.452
1998 Akron	AA Cle	127	478	125	21	5	10	186	68	62	50	2	125	1	4	2	12	8	.60	9	.262	.331	.389
1999 Akron	AA Cle	86	297	84	17	6	6	131	58	46	48	0	63	5	2	0	9	4	.69	3	.283	.391	.441
Buffalo	AAA Cle	47	133	38	7	3	2	57	24	17	22	2	36	0	2	0	4	2	.67	3	.286	.387	.429
2000 Akron	AA Cle	18	71	17	2	0	1	22	7	5	6	1	20	1	1	0	3	2	.60	0	.239	.308	.310
Buffalo	AAA Cle	118	427	124	21	7	6	177	68	37	49	3	81	1	5	0	12	4	.75	2	.290	.365	.415
6 Min. YEARS		608	2160	589	105	36	38	880	360	269	334	14	503	21	21	5	73	32	.70	28	.273	.375	.407

Scott Bullett

Bats: Left Throws: Left Pos: OF-10; PH-1   Ht: 6'2" Wt: 225 Born: 12/25/68 Age: 32

Year Team	Lg Org	G	AB	H	2B	3B	HR	TB	R	RBI	TBB	IBB	SO	HBP	SH	SF	SB	CS	SB%	GDP	Avg	OBP	SLG
1988 Pirates	R Pit	21	61	11	1	0	0	12	6	8	7	1	9	0	1	1	2	5	.29	0	.180	.261	.197
1989 Pirates	R Pit	46	165	42	7	3	1	58	24	16	12	2	31	5	1	0	15	5	.75	2	.255	.324	.352
1990 Welland	A- Pit	74	256	77	11	4	3	105	46	33	13	2	50	2	1	0	30	6	.83	7	.301	.339	.410
1991 Augusta	A Pit	95	384	109	21	6	1	145	61	36	27	2	79	2	1	1	48	17	.74	1	.284	.333	.378
Salem	A+ Pit	39	156	52	7	5	2	75	22	15	8	1	29	0	0	0	15	7	.68	0	.333	.366	.481
1992 Carolina	AA Pit	132	518	140	20	5	8	194	59	45	28	5	98	10	2	7	29	21	.58	7	.270	.316	.375
Buffalo	AAA Pit	3	10	4	0	2	0	8	1	0	0	0	2	0	0	0	0	0	—	0	.400	.400	.800
1993 Buffalo	AAA Pit	110	408	117	13	6	1	145	62	30	39	0	67	1	8	0	28	17	.62	5	.287	.350	.355
1994 Iowa	AAA ChC	135	530	163	28	4	13	238	75	69	19	4	110	5	11	6	27	16	.63	5	.308	.334	.449
1996 Orlando	AA ChC	3	11	2	0	0	0	2	2	0	1	0	2	0	0	0	2	0	1.00	0	.182	.250	.182
1997 Rochester	AAA Bal	136	512	128	24	8	9	195	73	58	45	2	112	7	0	2	19	11	.63	17	.250	.318	.381
1999 Allentown	IND —	22	83	30	8	1	3	49	17	28	4	2	9	3	0	1	7	1	.88	1	.361	.407	.590
2000 Colo Spmgs	AAA Col	11	40	19	3	0	0	22	6	8	2	0	5	0	0	0	2	3	.40	1	.475	.500	.550
1991 Pittsburgh	NL	11	4	0	0	0	0	0	2	0	0	0	3	1	0	0	1	1	.50	0	.000	.000	.000
1993 Pittsburgh	NL	23	55	11	0	2	0	15	2	4	3	0	15	0	0	1	3	2	.60	1	.200	.237	.273
1995 Chicago	NL	104	150	41	5	7	3	69	19	22	12	2	30	1	1	0	8	3	.73	4	.273	.331	.460
1996 Chicago	NL	109	165	35	5	0	3	49	26	16	10	0	54	0	1	1	7	3	.70	2	.212	.256	.297
11 Min. YEARS		827	3134	894	143	44	41	1248	454	346	205	21	603	35	25	18	224	109	.67	46	.285	.334	.398
4 Maj. YEARS		247	374	87	10	9	6	133	49	42	25	2	102	2	2	2	19	9	.68	7	.233	.283	.356

Nate Bump

Pitches: Right Bats: Right Pos: SP-26   Ht: 6'2" Wt: 185 Born: 7/24/76 Age: 24

	HOW MUCH HE PITCHED						WHAT HE GAVE UP											THE RESULTS					
Year Team	Lg Org	G	GS	CG	GF	IP	BFP	H	R	ER	HR	SH	SF	HB	TBB	IBB	SO	WP	Bk	W	L	Pct.	ShO	Sv	ERA
1998 Salem-Keizr	A- SF	2	2	0	0	8	31	5	0	0	0	0	0	2	3	0	8	1	0	0	0	—	0	0	0.00
San Jose	A+ SF	11	11	0	0	61.2	240	37	13	12	2	1	1	2	24	0	61	2	0	6	1	.857	0	0	1.75

38

		HOW MUCH HE PITCHED						WHAT HE GAVE UP									THE RESULTS					
Year Team	Lg Org	G	GS	CG	GF	IP	BFP	H	R	ER	HR	SH	SF	HB	TBB	IBB	SO	WP	Bk	W	L	Pct.	ShO	Sv	ERA
1999 Shreveport	AA SF	17	17	1	0	92.1	394	85	40	34	9	6	0	5	32	0	59	2	0	4	10	.286	1	0	3.31
Portland	AA Fla	8	8	0	0	43	203	57	38	29	3	1	2	5	12	0	33	1	0	2	6	.250	0	0	6.07
2000 Portland	AA Fla	26	26	3	0	149.2	663	169	85	76	16	5	4	15	49	1	98	5	0	8	9	.471	1	0	4.57
3 Min. YEARS		64	64	4	0	354.2	1531	353	176	151	30	13	7	29	120	1	259	11	0	20	26	.435	2	0	3.83

Jamie Burke

Bats: Right **Throws:** Right **Pos:** 3B-56; C-19; 2B-1; DH-1; PH-1   **Ht:** 6'0" **Wt:** 195 **Born:** 9/24/71 **Age:** 29

		BATTING														BASERUNNING				PERCENTAGES		
Year Team	Lg Org	G	AB	H	2B	3B	HR	TB	R	RBI	TBB	IBB	SO	HBP	SH	SF	SB	CS	SB%	GDP	Avg	OBP	SLG
1993 Boise	A- Ana	66	226	68	11	1	1	84	32	30	39	3	28	5	2	2	2	3	.40	4	.301	.412	.372
1994 Cedar Rapds	A Ana	127	469	124	24	1	1	153	57	47	40	3	64	12	4	8	6	8	.43	15	.264	.333	.326
1995 Lk Elsinore	A+ Ana	106	365	100	15	6	2	133	47	56	32	1	53	9	11	4	6	4	.60	12	.274	.344	.364
1996 Midland	AA Ana	45	144	46	8	2	2	64	24	16	20	1	22	2	1	0	1	1	.50	1	.319	.410	.444
Vancouver	AAA Ana	41	156	39	5	0	1	47	12	14	7	0	18	1	1	2	2	1	.67	5	.250	.283	.301
1997 Midland	AA Ana	116	428	141	44	3	6	209	77	72	40	0	46	8	0	3	2	3	.40	12	.329	.395	.488
Vancouver	AAA Ana	8	27	8	1	0	0	9	4	3	3	0	2	1	0	0	0	0	—	0	.296	.387	.333
1998 Vancouver	AAA Ana	61	162	35	6	0	2	47	16	14	13	0	25	6	2	2	0	1	.00	7	.216	.295	.290
Midland	AA Ana	12	41	10	1	0	0	11	7	4	7	0	4	0	0	0	0	0	—	4	.244	.354	.268
1999 Edmonton	AAA Ana	46	149	50	9	0	3	68	29	16	23	0	18	3	2	0	1	0	.00	3	.336	.434	.456
2000 Edmonton	AAA Ana	75	263	63	12	0	0	75	25	17	19	2	42	5	2	2	1	1	.50	5	.240	.301	.285
8 Min. YEARS		703	2430	684	136	13	18	900	330	289	243	10	322	52	25	23	20	23	.47	68	.281	.356	.370

Lance Burkhart

Bats: Right **Throws:** Right **Pos:** C-68; 1B-21; DH-14; PH-9; OF-1   **Ht:** 5'9" **Wt:** 220 **Born:** 12/16/74 **Age:** 26

		BATTING														BASERUNNING				PERCENTAGES		
Year Team	Lg Org	G	AB	H	2B	3B	HR	TB	R	RBI	TBB	IBB	SO	HBP	SH	SF	SB	CS	SB%	GDP	Avg	OBP	SLG
1997 Vermont	A- Mon	38	143	24	6	1	0	32	15	12	17	0	40	1	0	0	3	3	.50	3	.168	.261	.224
1998 Vermont	A- Mon	16	44	13	4	1	0	19	13	5	13	0	13	1	1	1	0	0	—	0	.295	.458	.432
Cape Fear	A Mon	17	50	12	3	1	1	20	10	11	16	1	17	2	1	1	1	3	.25	0	.240	.435	.400
1999 Cape Fear	A Mon	2	6	1	1	0	0	2	2	0	2	0	4	0	0	0	0	0	—	0	.167	.375	.333
Ottawa	AAA Mon	2	8	1	0	0	0	1	1	0	0	0	5	0	0	0	0	0	—	0	.125	.125	.125
Jupiter	A+ Mon	45	131	28	8	0	5	51	19	21	13	1	35	2	0	2	1	1	.50	1	.214	.291	.389
2000 Beloit	A Mil	58	202	57	18	0	17	126	42	64	34	4	42	4	0	5	0	2	.00	5	.282	.388	.624
Huntsville	AA Mil	51	155	30	6	1	6	56	17	19	19	3	43	1	4	0	0	0	—	2	.194	.286	.361
4 Min. YEARS		229	739	166	46	4	29	307	119	132	114	9	199	11	6	9	5	9	.36	11	.225	.333	.415

Gary Burnham

Bats: Left **Throws:** Left **Pos:** 1B-73; DH-25; PH-15; PR-1   **Ht:** 5'11" **Wt:** 200 **Born:** 10/13/74 **Age:** 26

		BATTING														BASERUNNING				PERCENTAGES		
Year Team	Lg Org	G	AB	H	2B	3B	HR	TB	R	RBI	TBB	IBB	SO	HBP	SH	SF	SB	CS	SB%	GDP	Avg	OBP	SLG
1997 Batavia	A- Phi	73	289	94	22	4	5	139	44	45	30	0	47	5	1	2	3	1	.75	8	.325	.396	.481
1998 Clearwater	A+ Phi	139	513	152	33	10	8	229	93	70	63	8	76	14	0	7	10	4	.71	9	.296	.384	.446
1999 Reading	AA Phi	116	354	88	20	0	12	144	47	49	41	3	49	15	6	1	11	3	.79	16	.249	.350	.407
2000 Reading	AA Phi	111	355	95	28	0	13	162	53	61	40	2	47	14	0	2	0	1	.00	10	.268	.363	.456
4 Min. YEARS		439	1511	429	103	14	38	674	237	225	174	13	219	48	7	12	24	9	.73	43	.284	.373	.446

Kevin Burns

Bats: Left **Throws:** Left **Pos:** 1B-38; DH-29; PH-24; PR-1   **Ht:** 6'5" **Wt:** 220 **Born:** 9/9/75 **Age:** 25

		BATTING														BASERUNNING				PERCENTAGES		
Year Team	Lg Org	G	AB	H	2B	3B	HR	TB	R	RBI	TBB	IBB	SO	HBP	SH	SF	SB	CS	SB%	GDP	Avg	OBP	SLG
1995 Astros	R Hou	42	136	34	4	1	3	49	17	23	12	1	24	0	0	1	8	3	.73	5	.250	.309	.360
1996 Auburn	A- Hou	71	269	71	19	3	11	129	27	55	15	1	77	4	0	5	2	1	.67	1	.264	.307	.480
1997 Quad City	A Hou	131	477	129	28	1	20	219	72	86	53	8	114	6	0	4	1	2	.33	12	.270	.348	.459
1998 Kissimmee	A+ Hou	128	470	127	24	4	19	216	69	81	69	5	124	5	0	3	11	3	.79	8	.270	.367	.460
1999 Jackson	AA Hou	113	352	99	21	2	12	160	55	58	42	4	74	4	0	4	6	3	.67	2	.281	.361	.455
2000 New Orleans	AAA Hou	4	14	3	1	1	0	6	3	1	1	0	2	0	0	0	0	0	—	0	.214	.267	.429
Round Rock	AA Hou	87	255	81	17	2	8	126	48	46	28	5	58	3	0	3	1	2	.33	5	.318	.388	.494
6 Min. YEARS		576	1973	544	114	14	73	905	291	350	220	24	473	22	0	20	29	14	.67	33	.276	.352	.459

Adrian Burnside

Pitches: Left **Bats:** Right **Pos:** SP-17   **Ht:** 6'3" **Wt:** 168 **Born:** 3/15/77 **Age:** 24

		HOW MUCH HE PITCHED						WHAT HE GAVE UP									THE RESULTS					
Year Team	Lg Org	G	GS	CG	GF	IP	BFP	H	R	ER	HR	SH	SF	HB	TBB	IBB	SO	WP	Bk	W	L	Pct.	ShO	Sv	ERA
1996 Great Falls	R+ LA	14	5	0	1	41	204	44	35	31	3	0	2	6	38	0	33	6	0	1	3	.250	0	0	6.80
1997 Yakima	A- LA	15	13	0	0	65.2	314	67	53	36	9	1	3	5	49	1	66	4	4	6	3	.667	0	0	4.93
1998 San Berndno	A+ LA	21	12	0	2	78.1	381	97	79	68	6	5	6	8	48	0	65	8	0	1	10	.091	0	0	7.81
Yakima	A- LA	8	6	0	1	33.1	156	37	21	15	0	1	2	2	30	0	34	8	1	1	4	.200	0	0	4.05
1999 San Berndno	A+ LA	26	22	0	2	131.2	571	124	69	61	7	3	4	11	55	0	129	10	2	10	9	.526	0	0	4.17
2000 San Antonio	AA LA	17	17	0	0	93	400	73	40	30	6	7	4	7	55	3	82	3	0	6	5	.545	0	0	2.90
5 Min. YEARS		101	75	0	4	443	2026	432	297	241	31	17	21	39	275	4	409	39	7	25	34	.424	0	0	4.90

Andy Burress

Bats: Right **Throws:** Right **Pos:** OF-119; PH-7; C-1; DH-1; P-1   **Ht:** 6'0" **Wt:** 200 **Born:** 7/18/77 **Age:** 23

		BATTING														BASERUNNING				PERCENTAGES		
Year Team	Lg Org	G	AB	H	2B	3B	HR	TB	R	RBI	TBB	IBB	SO	HBP	SH	SF	SB	CS	SB%	GDP	Avg	OBP	SLG
1995 Billings	R+ Cin	35	103	27	9	2	2	46	17	18	6	0	16	3	0	1	0	2	.00	4	.262	.319	.447

(continued batting table - top)

Year Team	Lg Org	G	AB	H	2B	3B	HR	TB	R	RBI	TBB	IBB	SO	HBP	SH	SF	SB	CS	SB%	GDP	Avg	OBP	SLG
1996 Billings	R+ Cin	27	107	34	5	2	5	58	23	25	7	0	16	1	0	1	4	1	.80	3	.318	.362	.542
1997 Chston-WV	A Cin	38	87	18	0	0	2	24	12	14	4	0	26	0	0	2	1	0	1.00	3	.207	.237	.276
Billings	R+ Cin	27	102	31	7	0	5	53	13	18	6	0	20	0	0	0	1	1	.50	4	.304	.343	.520
1998 Burlington	A Cin	124	449	126	25	10	9	198	75	67	62	2	91	3	0	5	25	5	.83	12	.281	.368	.441
1999 Rockford	A Cin	72	270	82	24	2	4	122	45	32	17	1	45	2	1	3	17	6	.74	4	.304	.346	.452
Chattanooga	AA Cin	63	257	70	12	1	7	105	42	28	18	1	41	2	2	1	11	4	.73	6	.272	.324	.409
2000 Chattanooga	AA Cin	123	400	100	15	7	6	147	54	41	51	0	78	3	5	3	15	14	.52	7	.250	.337	.368
6 Min. YEARS		509	1775	488	97	24	40	753	281	243	171	4	333	14	8	16	74	33	.69	43	.275	.341	.424

Sean Burroughs

Bats: Left **Throws:** Right **Pos:** 3B-108   **Ht:** 6'2" **Wt:** 200 **Born:** 9/12/80 **Age:** 20

Year Team	Lg Org	G	AB	H	2B	3B	HR	TB	R	RBI	TBB	IBB	SO	HBP	SH	SF	SB	CS	SB%	GDP	Avg	OBP	SLG
1999 Fort Wayne	A SD	122	426	153	30	3	5	204	65	80	74	7	59	14	2	5	17	15	.53	10	.359	.464	.479
Rancho Cuca	A+ SD	6	23	10	3	0	1	16	3	5	3	0	3	1	0	0	0	1	.00	1	.435	.519	.696
2000 Mobile	AA SD	108	392	114	29	4	2	157	46	42	58	6	45	3	4	4	6	8	.43	10	.291	.383	.401
2 Min. YEARS		236	841	277	62	7	8	377	114	127	135	13	107	18	6	9	23	24	.49	21	.329	.429	.448

Terry Burrows

Pitches: Left **Bats:** Left **Pos:** SP-2   **Ht:** 6'1" **Wt:** 190 **Born:** 11/28/68 **Age:** 32

Year Team	Lg Org	G	GS	CG	GF	IP	BFP	H	R	ER	HR	SH	SF	HB	TBB	IBB	SO	WP	Bk	W	L	Pct.	ShO	Sv	ERA
1990 Butte	R+ Tex	14	11	1	1	62.2	275	56	35	28	1	3	1	0	35	0	64	6	2	3	6	.333	0	0	4.02
1991 Gastonia	A Tex	27	26	0	0	147.2	614	107	79	73	11	3	0	5	78	0	151	6	6	12	8	.600	0	0	4.45
1992 Charlotte	A+ Tex	14	14	0	0	80	327	71	22	18	2	2	1	4	25	1	66	5	4	4	2	.667	0	0	2.03
Tulsa	AA Tex	14	13	1	0	76	314	66	22	18	3	0	0	0	35	0	59	4	0	6	3	.667	0	0	2.13
Okla City	AAA Tex	1	1	0	0	8	30	3	1	1	1	0	0	0	5	0	0	0	0	1	0	1.000	0	0	1.13
1993 Okla City	AAA Tex	27	25	1	0	138	645	171	107	98	19	8	7	2	76	0	74	8	5	7	15	.318	0	0	6.39
1994 Okla City	AAA Tex	44	5	0	15	82.1	353	75	43	39	9	4	3	4	37	3	57	4	5	3	5	.375	0	1	4.26
1995 Okla City	AAA Tex	5	0	0	0	2.2	16	5	4	3	0	0	0	0	2	0	4	1	0	0	1	.000	0	0	10.13
1996 New Orleans	AAA Mil	18	0	0	0	28.2	108	19	9	8	1	0	1	0	8	0	17	1	1	1	0	1.000	0	6	2.51
Columbus	AAA NYY	23	0	0	5	22.2	102	24	16	15	1	1	1	2	11	0	20	1	0	1	0	1.000	0	0	5.96
1997 Las Vegas	AAA SD	31	1	0	10	33.2	160	44	24	24	3	1	1	1	19	3	26	1	1	1	5	.167	0	2	6.42
Edmonton	AAA Oak	13	0	0	3	27	127	35	18	17	2	1	2	0	15	2	24	2	0	2	2	.500	0	0	5.67
1998 Rochester	AAA Bal	29	15	1	3	132.1	531	104	49	43	8	1	7	2	42	0	112	2	1	9	6	.600	0	0	2.92
1999 Orioles	R Bal	2	2	0	0	5	17	0	1	0	0	0	0	1	1	0	4	0	1	0	0	.000	0	0	0.00
Rochester	AAA Bal	17	17	0	0	93	382	74	49	41	9	2	6	7	39	0	75	1	2	1	6	.143	0	0	3.97
2000 Sacramento	AAA Oak	2	1	0	0	13	51	8	2	2	1	0	1	0	4	1	7	0	0	0	1	.000	0	0	1.38
1994 Texas	AL	1	0	0	0	1	5	1	1	1	1	0	0	0	1	0	0	0	0	0	0		0	0	9.00
1995 Texas	AL	28	3	0	6	44.2	207	60	37	32	11	0	0	2	19	0	22	4	0	2	2	.500	0	1	6.45
1996 Milwaukee	AL	8	0	0	0	12.2	58	12	4	4	2	1	0	1	10	0	5	0	0	0	0		0	0	2.84
1997 San Diego	NL	13	0	0	4	10.1	52	12	13	12	1	1	0	1	8	1	8	0	0	2	2	.000	0	0	10.45
11 Min. YEARS		281	132	5	46	952.2	4052	862	481	428	71	26	30	29	432	10	760	42	28	53	60	.469	0	9	4.04
4 Maj. YEARS		50	3	0	14	68.2	322	85	55	49	15	2	0	4	38	1	35	4	0	4	4	.500	0	1	6.42

Darren Burton

Bats: Both **Throws:** Right **Pos:** OF-69; PH-6; PR-2; DH-1; P-1   **Ht:** 6'1" **Wt:** 185 **Born:** 9/16/72 **Age:** 28

Year Team	Lg Org	G	AB	H	2B	3B	HR	TB	R	RBI	TBB	IBB	SO	HBP	SH	SF	SB	CS	SB%	GDP	Avg	OBP	SLG
1990 Royals	R KC	15	58	12	0	1	0	14	10	2	4	0	17	0	1	2	6	0	1.00	0	.207	.250	.241
1991 Appleton	A KC	134	532	143	32	6	2	193	78	51	45	4	122	1	3	6	37	12	.76	18	.269	.324	.363
1992 Baseball Cy	A+ KC	123	431	106	15	6	4	145	54	36	49	7	93	6	4	3	16	14	.53	7	.246	.329	.336
1993 Wilmington	A+ KC	134	549	152	23	5	10	215	82	45	48	1	111	1	13	4	30	10	.75	7	.277	.334	.392
1994 Memphis	AA KC	97	373	95	12	3	3	122	55	37	35	4	53	1	4	5	10	6	.63	5	.255	.316	.327
1995 Omaha	AAA KC	2	5	0	0	0	0	0	0	0	0	0	1	0	0	0	0	0	—	0	.000	.000	.000
Wichita	AA KC	41	163	39	9	1	1	53	13	20	12	0	27	1	0	0	6	6	.50	2	.239	.295	.325
Orlando	AA ChC	62	222	68	16	2	4	100	40	21	27	2	42	0	0	0	7	4	.64	5	.306	.382	.450
1996 Omaha	AAA KC	129	463	125	28	5	15	208	75	67	59	6	89	6	9	4	7	7	.50	10	.270	.357	.450
1997 Scranton-WB	AAA Phi	70	253	63	16	3	8	109	34	39	19	1	40	3	1	4	3	0	1.00	6	.249	.305	.431
Reading	AA Phi	45	184	58	11	3	8	99	23	34	9	2	39	3	2	3	1	1	.50	1	.315	.352	.538
1998 Scranton-WB	AAA Phi	117	394	105	21	3	18	186	56	64	53	1	83	6	2	3	9	0	1.00	10	.266	.360	.472
1999 Scranton-WB	AAA Phi	118	409	107	30	3	13	182	61	63	44	2	96	5	3	4	2	2	.78	9	.262	.338	.445
2000 Scranton-WB	AAA Phi	14	29	7	4	0	0	11	0	1	7	2	8	0	1	0	2	0	1.00	2	.241	.389	.379
Altoona	AA Pit	63	229	75	8	2	5	102	44	33	23	0	42	5	3	3	1	0	1.00	3	.328	.396	.445
11 Min. YEARS		1164	4294	1155	225	43	91	1739	625	513	434	32	856	38	55	41	144	62	.70	85	.269	.338	.405

Mike Busby

Pitches: Right **Bats:** Right **Pos:** RP-24; SP-8   **Ht:** 6'4" **Wt:** 225 **Born:** 12/27/72 **Age:** 28

Year Team	Lg Org	G	GS	CG	GF	IP	BFP	H	R	ER	HR	SH	SF	HB	TBB	IBB	SO	WP	Bk	W	L	Pct.	ShO	Sv	ERA
1991 Cardinals	R StL	11	11	0	0	59	267	67	35	23	1	0	2	2	29	0	71	3	1	4	3	.571	0	0	3.51
1992 Savannah	A StL	28	28	1	0	149.2	665	145	96	61	11	7	17	7	67	0	84	16	1	4	13	.235	0	0	3.67
1993 Savannah	A StL	23	21	1	0	143.2	579	116	49	39	8	6	4	10	31	0	125	5	2	12	2	.857	1	0	2.44
1994 St. Pete	A+ StL	26	26	1	0	151.2	663	166	82	75	11	8	5	14	49	1	89	5	2	6	13	.316	0	0	4.45
1995 Arkansas	AA StL	20	20	1	0	134	565	125	63	49	8	3	3	6	35	1	95	5	0	7	6	.538	0	0	3.29
Louisville	AAA StL	6	6	1	0	38.1	154	28	18	14	2	2	2	3	11	0	26	2	0	2	2	.500	0	0	3.29
1996 Louisville	AAA StL	14	14	0	0	72	343	89	57	51	11	0	4	6	44	1	53	7	2	2	5	.286	0	0	6.38
1997 Louisville	AAA StL	15	14	1	0	93.2	395	95	49	48	12	0	1	7	30	1	65	0	0	4	8	.333	1	0	4.61
1998 Memphis	AAA StL	7	2	0	2	8	29	5	3	3	1	0	1	0	2	0	5	1	0	0	0		0	0	3.38
1999 Memphis	AAA StL	29	10	0	2	72.2	359	112	69	60	12	2	5	3	36	1	50	8	0	3	4	.429	0	0	7.43

40

		HOW MUCH HE PITCHED						WHAT HE GAVE UP											THE RESULTS					
Year Team	Lg Org	G	GS	CG	GF	IP	BFP	H	R	ER	HR	SH	SF	HB	TBB	IBB	SO	WP	Bk	W	L	Pct.	ShO	Sv	ERA
2000 Indianapolis	AAA Mil	19	2	0	6	27.1	165	49	42	35	5	2	5	5	25	3	14	5	0	2	1	.667	0	0	11.52
Salt Lake	AAA Min	7	0	0	1	9.1	52	16	7	7	2	0	0	0	9	0	8	2	0	0	0	—	0	0	6.75
Sioux City	IND —	6	6	0	0	44.1	192	43	21	20	4	2	2	5	15	0	44	2	0	2	1	.667	0	0	4.06
1996 St. Louis	NL	1	1	0	0	4	28	9	13	8	4	1	0	1	4	0	4	0	0	0	1	.000	0	0	18.00
1997 St. Louis	NL	3	3	0	0	14.1	67	24	14	14	2	1	1	0	4	0	6	0	0	0	2	.000	0	0	8.79
1998 St. Louis	NL	26	2	0	7	46	202	45	23	23	3	3	2	5	15	0	33	3	0	5	2	.714	0	0	4.50
1999 St. Louis	NL	15	0	0	3	17.2	86	21	15	14	2	0	2	2	14	0	7	1	0	0	1	.000	0	0	7.13
10 Min. YEARS		211	160	7	15	1003.2	4428	1056	591	485	88	29	38	78	383	8	729	69	8	48	58	.453	2	0	4.35
4 Maj. YEARS		45	6	0	10	82	383	99	65	59	11	5	3	8	37	0	50	4	0	5	6	.455	0	0	6.48

Darren Bush

Bats: Left **Throws:** Right **Pos:** DH-72; C-30; PH-9; OF-3 — **Ht:** 6'0" **Wt:** 200 **Born:** 1/18/74 **Age:** 27

		BATTING														BASERUNNING				PERCENTAGES		
Year Team	Lg Org	G	AB	H	2B	3B	HR	TB	R	RBI	TBB	IBB	SO	HBP	SH	SF	SB	CS	SB%	GDP	Avg	OBP	SLG
1996 Zanesville	IND —	66	211	56	8	1	3	75	33	21	27	6	32	3	3	1	22	7	.76	6	.265	.355	.355
1997 Springfield	IND —	75	278	80	15	3	7	122	47	45	40	2	39	1	0	1	2	7	.22	6	.288	.376	.439
1998 Springfield	IND —	76	304	101	22	5	16	181	63	66	44	2	41	1	1	5	1	4	.20	11	.332	.412	.595
1999 Rancho Cuca	A+ SD	77	238	67	9	1	8	102	35	36	36	1	51	1	2	0	7	4	.64	7	.282	.378	.429
2000 Rancho Cuca	A+ SD	108	340	94	23	1	6	137	50	60	54	2	57	2	3	3	1	3	.25	11	.276	.376	.403
Las Vegas	AAA SD	1	4	2	1	0	0	3	0	1	0	0	0	0	0	0	0	0	—	0	.500	.500	.750
5 Min. YEARS		403	1375	400	78	11	40	620	228	229	201	13	220	8	9	12	33	25	.57	41	.291	.382	.451

Brent Butler

Bats: Right **Throws:** Right **Pos:** 2B-100; SS-25; PH-4 — **Ht:** 6'0" **Wt:** 180 **Born:** 2/11/78 **Age:** 23

		BATTING														BASERUNNING				PERCENTAGES		
Year Team	Lg Org	G	AB	H	2B	3B	HR	TB	R	RBI	TBB	IBB	SO	HBP	SH	SF	SB	CS	SB%	GDP	Avg	OBP	SLG
1996 Johnson Cty	R+ StL	62	248	85	21	1	8	132	45	50	25	1	29	2	1	2	8	1	.89	11	.343	.404	.532
1997 Peoria	A StL	129	480	147	37	2	15	233	81	71	63	6	69	4	0	5	6	4	.60	9	.306	.388	.485
1998 Pr William	A+ StL	126	475	136	27	2	11	200	63	76	39	2	74	9	2	7	3	4	.43	12	.286	.347	.421
1999 Arkansas	AA StL	139	528	142	21	1	13	204	68	54	26	0	47	6	0	5	0	4	.00	15	.269	.308	.386
2000 Colo Sprngs	AAA Col	122	438	128	35	1	8	189	73	54	44	1	46	4	7	9	1	3	.25	15	.292	.356	.432
5 Min. YEARS		578	2169	638	141	7	55	958	330	305	197	10	265	25	10	28	18	16	.53	63	.294	.356	.442

Garrett Butler

Bats: Both **Throws:** Right **Pos:** OF-36; PR-4; DH-1 — **Ht:** 6'2" **Wt:** 170 **Born:** 5/20/76 **Age:** 25

		BATTING														BASERUNNING				PERCENTAGES		
Year Team	Lg Org	G	AB	H	2B	3B	HR	TB	R	RBI	TBB	IBB	SO	HBP	SH	SF	SB	CS	SB%	GDP	Avg	OBP	SLG
1994 Yankees	R NYY	52	152	32	3	1	0	37	22	12	22	0	55	4	4	1	9	6	.60	7	.211	.324	.243
1995 Yankees	R NYY	48	185	43	4	4	0	55	40	16	16	0	45	5	8	1	11	0	1.00	1	.232	.309	.297
1996 Oneonta	A- NYY	69	207	58	3	1	0	63	36	16	30	0	46	1	7	1	29	7	.81	2	.280	.372	.304
1997 Greensboro	A NYY	82	237	46	14	1	1	65	31	14	11	0	58	4	4	1	11	5	.69	4	.194	.241	.274
1998 Chston-SC	A TB	45	171	42	7	0	3	58	28	25	6	0	29	1	2	1	8	3	.73	4	.246	.274	.339
Hudson Val	A- TB	68	280	85	14	2	2	109	47	44	23	0	48	1	6	2	21	8	.72	1	.304	.356	.389
1999 St. Pete	A+ TB	94	329	82	14	3	2	108	36	31	17	0	61	2	5	1	16	6	.73	3	.249	.289	.328
2000 Orlando	AA TB	38	117	28	5	0	1	36	14	7	7	0	17	4	0	0	3	4	.43	5	.239	.305	.308
7 Min. YEARS		496	1678	416	64	12	9	531	254	165	132	0	359	22	36	8	108	39	.73	27	.248	.310	.316

Rich Butler

Bats: Left **Throws:** Right **Pos:** OF-49; DH-19; PH-2 — **Ht:** 6'1" **Wt:** 205 **Born:** 5/1/73 **Age:** 28

		BATTING														BASERUNNING				PERCENTAGES		
Year Team	Lg Org	G	AB	H	2B	3B	HR	TB	R	RBI	TBB	IBB	SO	HBP	SH	SF	SB	CS	SB%	GDP	Avg	OBP	SLG
1991 Blue Jays	R Tor	59	213	56	6	7	0	76	30	13	17	1	45	0	4	0	10	6	.63	0	.263	.317	.357
1992 Myrtle Bch	A Tor	130	441	100	14	1	2	122	43	43	37	1	90	7	6	0	11	15	.42	6	.227	.297	.277
1993 Dunedin	A+ Tor	110	444	136	19	8	11	204	68	65	48	10	64	3	1	4	11	13	.46	4	.306	.375	.459
Knoxville	AA Tor	6	21	2	0	1	0	4	3	0	3	0	5	0	0	0	0	0	—	0	.095	.208	.190
1994 Knoxville	AA Tor	53	192	56	7	4	3	80	29	22	19	1	31	2	1	1	7	4	.64	1	.292	.360	.417
Syracuse	AAA Tor	94	302	73	6	2	3	92	34	27	22	0	66	0	0	2	8	8	.50	6	.242	.292	.305
1995 Syracuse	AAA Tor	69	199	32	4	2	2	46	20	14	9	0	45	0	0	1	2	3	.40	5	.161	.196	.231
Knoxville	AA Tor	58	217	58	12	3	4	88	27	33	25	1	41	2	1	0	11	3	.79	5	.267	.348	.406
1996 Dunedin	A+ Tor	10	28	2	0	0	0	2	1	0	5	0	9	0	0	0	4	1	.80	1	.071	.212	.071
1997 Syracuse	AAA Tor	137	537	161	30	9	24	281	93	87	60	2	107	4	3	3	20	7	.74	11	.300	.373	.523
1998 Durham	AAA TB	38	145	43	8	0	8	75	28	35	22	3	24	2	0	0	6	2	.75	1	.297	.390	.517
1999 Durham	AAA TB	90	332	96	28	2	10	158	52	63	41	4	70	3	3	3	2	5	.29	4	.289	.369	.476
2000 Tacoma	AAA Sea	32	124	23	7	1	2	38	11	9	10	1	26	0	0	0	0	1	.00	3	.185	.246	.306
New Haven	AA Sea	26	103	25	3	1	5	45	16	23	6	0	22	0	0	2	1	0	1.00	1	.243	.304	.437
Oklahoma	AAA Tex	12	47	11	1	0	2	18	4	5	3	0	0	0	0	2	1	0	1.00	3	.234	.269	.383
1997 Toronto	AL	7	14	4	1	0	0	5	3	2	2	0	3	0	0	0	0	0	.00	0	.286	.375	.357
1998 Tampa Bay	AL	72	217	49	3	3	7	79	25	20	15	0	37	2	0	1	4	2	.67	4	.226	.278	.364
1999 Tampa Bay	AL	7	20	3	1	0	0	4	2	0	2	0	4	0	0	0	0	0	—	0	.150	.227	.200
10 Min. YEARS		924	3345	874	145	41	76	1329	459	439	329	24	653	25	24	20	95	68	.58	51	.261	.330	.397
3 Maj. YEARS		86	251	56	5	3	7	88	30	22	19	0	44	2	0	1	4	3	.57	4	.223	.280	.351

Mike Byas

Bats: Both **Throws:** Right **Pos:** OF-132; PH-3; DH-1 — **Ht:** 6'0" **Wt:** 170 **Born:** 4/21/76 **Age:** 25

		BATTING														BASERUNNING				PERCENTAGES		
Year Team	Lg Org	G	AB	H	2B	3B	HR	TB	R	RBI	TBB	IBB	SO	HBP	SH	SF	SB	CS	SB%	GDP	Avg	OBP	SLG
1997 Salem-Keizr	A- SF	71	290	80	9	1	0	91	68	16	48	0	44	2	1	0	51	9	.85	4	.276	.382	.314
1998 San Jose	A+ SF	135	521	131	10	2	1	148	87	36	81	1	98	0	2	5	30	22	.58	8	.251	.349	.284

		BATTING																BASERUNNING				PERCENTAGES		
Year Team	Lg Org	G	AB	H	2B	3B	HR	TB	R	RBI	TBB	IBB	SO	HBP	SH	SF	SB	CS	SB%	GDP	Avg	OBP	SLG
1999 Shreveport	AA SF	129	487	132	9	1	0	143	76	41	68	0	79	1	3	0	31	15	.67	7	.271	.362	.294
Fresno	AAA SF	5	22	8	2	0	0	10	4	2	5	1	4	0	0	0	2	1	.67	0	.364	.481	.455
2000 Fresno	AAA SF	135	516	136	10	1	2	154	84	34	78	0	89	1	5	2	36	18	.67	5	.264	.360	.298
4 Min. YEARS		475	1836	487	40	5	3	546	319	129	280	2	314	4	11	7	150	65	.70	24	.265	.362	.297

Mike Bynum

Pitches: Left **Bats:** Left **Pos:** SP-27   **Ht:** 6'4" **Wt:** 200 **Born:** 3/20/78 **Age:** 23

		HOW MUCH HE PITCHED						WHAT HE GAVE UP										THE RESULTS					
Year Team	Lg Org	G	GS	CG	GF	IP	BFP	H	R	ER	HR	SH	SF	HB	TBB	IBB	SO	WP	Bk	W	L	Pct.	ShO	Sv	ERA
1999 Idaho Falls	R+ SD	5	3	0	0	17	60	7	0	0	0	1	0	0	4	0	21	0	0	1	0	1.000	0	0	0.00
Rancho Cuca	A+ SD	7	7	0	0	38.1	159	35	17	14	1	1	1	2	8	0	44	2	2	3	1	.750	0	0	3.29
2000 Rancho Cuca	A+ SD	21	21	0	0	126	517	101	55	42	4	3	5	8	51	0	129	7	1	9	6	.600	0	0	3.00
Mobile	AA SD	6	6	0	0	34	144	31	12	11	2	1	2	2	16	0	27	1	1	3	1	.750	0	0	2.91
2 Min. YEARS		39	37	0	0	215.1	880	174	84	67	7	6	8	12	79	0	221	10	4	16	8	.667	0	0	2.80

Wilmy Caceres

Bats: Both **Throws:** Right **Pos:** SS-79; 2B-56; PH-1   **Ht:** 6'0" **Wt:** 165 **Born:** 10/2/78 **Age:** 22

		BATTING																BASERUNNING				PERCENTAGES		
Year Team	Lg Org	G	AB	H	2B	3B	HR	TB	R	RBI	TBB	IBB	SO	HBP	SH	SF	SB	CS	SB%	GDP	Avg	OBP	SLG
1997 Billings	R+ SD	15	38	10	2	0	0	12	10	9	2	0	3	1	0	0	1	1	.50	0	.263	.317	.316
1998 Chston-WV	A Cin	103	394	102	12	7	0	128	48	27	18	0	62	9	7	0	24	14	.63	9	.259	.306	.325
Burlington	A Cin	35	150	44	8	0	1	55	23	14	4	0	24	3	1	0	7	5	.58	3	.293	.325	.367
1999 Reds	R Cin	2	9	3	0	0	0	3	2	0	0	0	1	0	0	0	0	0	—	0	.333	.333	.333
Clinton	A Cin	117	476	124	18	5	1	155	77	30	30	1	65	2	2	2	52	22	.70	6	.261	.306	.326
2000 Chattanooga	AA Cin	130	534	143	23	4	2	180	69	33	37	3	71	4	5	5	36	19	.65	10	.268	.317	.337
4 Min. YEARS		402	1601	426	63	16	4	533	229	113	91	4	226	19	15	7	120	61	.66	28	.266	.312	.333

Tony Calabrese

Bats: Right **Throws:** Right **Pos:** SS-22; PR-11; DH-7; PH-6; 1B-4; 2B-2; OF-2; 3B-1   **Ht:** 6'4" **Wt:** 200 **Born:** 11/5/78 **Age:** 22

		BATTING																BASERUNNING				PERCENTAGES		
Year Team	Lg Org	G	AB	H	2B	3B	HR	TB	R	RBI	TBB	IBB	SO	HBP	SH	SF	SB	CS	SB%	GDP	Avg	OBP	SLG
2000 Norwich	AA NYY	1	1	0	0	0	0	0	0	0	0	0	1	0	0	0	0	0	—	0	.000	.000	.000
Staten Ilnd	A- NYY	43	74	23	1	1	0	26	16	8	15	0	12	0	0	1	2	1	.67	5	.311	.422	.351
1 Min. YEARS		44	75	23	1	1	0	26	16	8	15	0	13	0	0	1	2	1	.67	5	.307	.418	.347

Ian Calais

Bats: Right **Throws:** Right **Pos:** SS-22; PH-3; OF-2; PR-2   **Ht:** 6'1" **Wt:** 180 **Born:** 9/8/76 **Age:** 24

		BATTING																BASERUNNING				PERCENTAGES		
Year Team	Lg Org	G	AB	H	2B	3B	HR	TB	R	RBI	TBB	IBB	SO	HBP	SH	SF	SB	CS	SB%	GDP	Avg	OBP	SLG
1999 Jamestown	A- Atl	68	224	47	8	1	0	57	19	20	23	0	47	2	4	1	4	5	.44	6	.210	.288	.254
2000 Myrtle Bch	A+ Atl	5	13	1	0	0	0	1	3	1	1	0	4	1	0	0	1	1	.50	0	.077	.200	.077
Richmond	AAA Atl	8	15	5	2	0	0	7	4	2	11	0	4	0	0	0	0	2	.00	0	.333	.615	.467
Greenville	AA Atl	14	31	5	0	0	0	5	5	0	7	0	11	0	1	0	0	1	.00	0	.161	.316	.161
2 Min. YEARS		95	283	58	10	1	0	70	31	23	42	0	66	3	5	1	5	9	.36	6	.205	.313	.247

Kiko Calero

Pitches: Right **Bats:** Right **Pos:** SP-25; RP-3   **Ht:** 6'1" **Wt:** 170 **Born:** 1/9/75 **Age:** 26

		HOW MUCH HE PITCHED						WHAT HE GAVE UP										THE RESULTS					
Year Team	Lg Org	G	GS	CG	GF	IP	BFP	H	R	ER	HR	SH	SF	HB	TBB	IBB	SO	WP	Bk	W	L	Pct.	ShO	Sv	ERA
1996 Spokane	A- KC	17	11	0	0	75	318	77	34	21	5	0	6	3	18	0	61	2	2	4	2	.667	0	1	2.52
1997 Wichita	AA KC	23	22	2	0	127.2	541	120	78	63	15	4	6	4	44	0	100	2	2	11	9	.550	0	0	4.44
1998 Lansing	A KC	4	4	0	0	16.2	76	19	7	7	1	0	0	2	7	0	10	1	1	1	0	1.000	0	0	3.78
Wichita	AA KC	3	3	0	0	14	72	23	16	15	2	1	0	1	6	0	5	0	0	1	0	1.000	0	0	9.64
Wilmington	A+ KC	17	17	0	0	97.2	409	74	33	31	7	1	3	7	51	1	90	6	0	7	3	.700	0	0	2.86
1999 Wichita	AA KC	26	23	1	1	129.1	579	143	67	59	14	2	2	6	57	3	92	7	2	9	3	.750	1	0	4.11
2000 Wichita	AA KC	28	25	0	0	153.2	648	141	74	62	16	7	3	10	66	2	130	7	1	10	7	.588	0	0	3.63
5 Min. YEARS		118	105	3	4	614	2643	597	309	258	60	15	20	33	249	6	488	25	8	43	24	.642	1	2	3.78

Mickey Callaway

Pitches: Right **Bats:** Right **Pos:** SP-20; RP-6   **Ht:** 6'2" **Wt:** 190 **Born:** 5/13/75 **Age:** 26

		HOW MUCH HE PITCHED						WHAT HE GAVE UP										THE RESULTS					
Year Team	Lg Org	G	GS	CG	GF	IP	BFP	H	R	ER	HR	SH	SF	HB	TBB	IBB	SO	WP	Bk	W	L	Pct.	ShO	Sv	ERA
1996 Butte	R+ TB	16	11	0	1	63	274	70	37	26	5	0	3	3	25	0	57	7	0	6	2	.750	0	0	3.71
1997 St. Pete	A+ TB	28	28	3	0	170.2	696	162	74	61	9	2	3	5	39	0	109	7	7	11	7	.611	0	0	3.22
1998 Orlando	AA TB	18	17	0	0	89.2	407	103	56	44	8	1	1	4	44	0	57	7	2	5	6	.455	0	0	4.42
Durham	AAA TB	9	8	0	0	47.2	209	49	27	24	6	1	0	1	17	0	19	2	0	5	3	.625	0	0	4.53
1999 Orlando	AA TB	2	2	0	0	10	44	10	5	5	1	0	0	0	2	0	7	1	0	1	1	.500	0	0	4.50
Durham	AAA TB	15	15	0	0	81.1	350	86	45	38	5	0	3	8	28	0	56	6	1	7	1	.875	0	0	4.20
2000 Durham	AAA TB	26	20	0	2	117.1	542	151	88	69	11	1	7	2	50	2	64	2	2	11	6	.647	0	0	5.29
1999 Tampa Bay	AL	5	4	0	0	19.1	99	30	20	16	2	0	1	0	14	1	11	1	0	1	2	.333	0	0	7.45
5 Min. YEARS		114	101	3	3	579.2	2522	636	333	267	45	5	17	23	205	2	369	32	12	46	26	.639	0	0	4.15

Jeremy Callier

Pitches: Right Bats: Right Pos: RP-48; SP-2   Ht: 6'0" Wt: 195 Born: 11/18/75 Age: 25

Year Team	Lg Org	G	GS	CG	GF	IP	BFP	H	R	ER	HR	SH	SF	HB	TBB	IBB	SO	WP	Bk	W	L	Pct.	ShO	Sv	ERA
1998 Butte	R+ Ana	19	11	2	1	101.2	433	102	51	40	7	1	2	8	26	0	78	3	2	3	9	.250	0	0	3.54
1999 Erie	AA Ana	1	0	0	1	1	7	2	2	2	0	0	0	0	2	0	2	0	0	0	0	—	0	0	18.00
Lk Elsinore	A+ Ana	34	7	0	9	95.2	418	107	48	41	5	5	0	3	33	2	69	6	1	5	3	.625	0	2	3.86
2000 Erie	AA Ana	41	0	0	28	58	238	52	30	26	5	0	2	2	24	1	44	2	0	2	3	.400	0	11	4.03
Edmonton	AAA Ana	9	2	0	3	22.1	104	29	14	14	0	2	1	1	7	1	16	0	0	2	2	.500	0	0	5.64
3 Min. YEARS		104	20	2	42	278.2	1200	292	145	123	17	8	5	14	92	4	209	11	3	12	17	.414	0	13	3.97

Jason Camilli

Bats: Right Throws: Right Pos: 3B-63; SS-15; 2B-15; 1B-5; PH-3; OF-2; DH-1   Ht: 6'0" Wt: 190 Born: 10/18/75 Age: 25

Year Team	Lg Org	G	AB	H	2B	3B	HR	TB	R	RBI	TBB	IBB	SO	HBP	SH	SF	SB	CS	SB%	GDP	Avg	OBP	SLG
1994 Expos	R Mon	53	212	54	4	3	0	64	33	13	31	1	44	0	0	1	5	6	.45	4	.255	.348	.302
1995 Albany	A Mon	53	181	34	5	0	3	48	28	16	38	0	50	3	0	2	13	10	.57	0	.188	.335	.265
Vermont	A- Mon	63	243	59	10	2	1	76	37	21	30	1	52	2	3	2	17	10	.63	4	.243	.329	.313
1996 Delmarva	A Mon	119	426	95	13	2	3	121	53	36	63	1	89	5	9	2	26	17	.60	4	.223	.329	.284
1997 Cape Fear	A Mon	98	396	118	35	2	3	166	57	43	31	0	64	5	7	2	22	11	.67	7	.298	.355	.419
Wst Plm Bch	A+ Mon	15	47	6	3	0	0	9	1	1	2	0	12	0	1	0	0	1	.00	1	.128	.163	.191
1998 Jupiter	A+ Mon	89	314	81	15	1	2	104	45	33	35	2	55	2	1	1	9	10	.47	2	.258	.335	.331
Harrisburg	AA Mon	6	18	2	0	0	0	2	1	1	3	0	5	0	0	0	0	0	—	0	.111	.238	.111
1999 Ottawa	AAA Mon	35	102	27	6	0	0	33	12	8	11	0	19	0	0	0	4	1	.80	3	.265	.336	.324
Harrisburg	AA Mon	63	154	33	7	0	4	52	26	16	23	0	31	2	0	1	0	2	.00	3	.214	.322	.338
2000 Expos	R Mon	5	15	4	1	0	0	5	1	2	0	0	3	0	0	1	1	0	1.00	0	.267	.316	.333
Ottawa	AAA Mon	21	77	12	4	1	0	18	7	11	3	0	21	0	0	1	0	0	—	1	.156	.185	.234
Harrisburg	AA Mon	65	240	51	10	3	3	76	27	19	24	1	51	3	4	2	3	6	.33	2	.213	.290	.317
7 Min. YEARS		685	2425	576	113	14	19	774	328	220	296	6	496	22	26	16	100	74	.57	31	.238	.324	.319

Jared Camp

Pitches: Right Bats: Right Pos: RP-32   Ht: 6'2" Wt: 195 Born: 5/4/75 Age: 26

Year Team	Lg Org	G	GS	CG	GF	IP	BFP	H	R	ER	HR	SH	SF	HB	TBB	IBB	SO	WP	Bk	W	L	Pct.	ShO	Sv	ERA
1995 Helena	R+ Mil	8	8	0	0	34.1	166	44	39	33	1	1	3	3	20	0	26	6	2	1	4	.200	0	0	8.65
1996 Beloit	A Mil	11	11	0	0	53	251	56	42	32	4	3	9	2	39	0	47	10	1	3	5	.375	0	0	5.43
Watertown	A- Cle	15	15	1	0	95.2	380	68	29	18	2	1	1	7	30	0	99	6	0	10	2	.833	1	0	1.69
1997 Akron	AA Cle	12	12	1	0	64	293	79	49	44	13	4	1	1	26	1	39	4	0	2	8	.200	0	0	6.19
Kinston	A+ Cle	13	12	0	0	73.2	297	57	36	31	11	5	1	2	20	0	64	1	1	5	4	.556	0	0	3.79
1998 Akron	AA Cle	18	16	0	2	85.2	364	84	37	36	8	3	5	5	31	0	42	2	1	6	2	.750	0	0	3.78
1999 Kinston	A+ Cle	18	6	1	7	54.2	224	48	15	12	2	0	3	4	16	0	59	4	0	3	2	.600	0	4	1.98
Buffalo	AAA Cle	10	0	0	7	10.2	51	4	2	1	0	0	1	1	13	0	14	4	0	0	0	—	0	1	0.84
Akron	AA Cle	17	0	0	13	18	92	22	17	13	0	2	3	2	16	0	18	2	1	1	2	.333	0	7	6.50
2000 Akron	AA Cle	9	0	0	1	17.1	88	28	21	18	6	0	1	1	7	0	13	2	0	0	0	—	0	1	9.35
Buffalo	AAA Cle	3	0	0	2	4	20	5	2	1	0	1	0	1	2	0	0	1	0	0	0	—	0	1	2.25
Tulsa	AA Tex	7	0	0	3	10	48	10	6	0	1	1	0	1	7	0	4	2	0	0	0	—	0	0	0.00
Omaha	AAA KC	13	0	0	2	12.2	71	19	24	19	4	0	0	2	13	0	13	1	0	1	2	.333	0	0	13.50
6 Min. YEARS		154	80	3	37	533.2	2345	524	319	258	52	21	28	32	240	1	438	45	6	32	31	.508	1	14	4.35

Shawn Camp

Pitches: Right Bats: Right Pos: RP-59   Ht: 6'1" Wt: 200 Born: 11/18/75 Age: 25

Year Team	Lg Org	G	GS	CG	GF	IP	BFP	H	R	ER	HR	SH	SF	HB	TBB	IBB	SO	WP	Bk	W	L	Pct.	ShO	Sv	ERA
1997 Idaho Falls	R+ SD	30	0	0	24	32.2	150	41	24	20	3	1	1	2	14	0	41	4	0	2	1	.667	0	12	5.51
1998 Clinton	A SD	47	0	0	39	55	240	48	19	16	0	3	3	7	20	4	62	6	1	3	5	.375	0	13	2.62
1999 Rancho Cuca	A+ SD	53	0	0	28	66	285	68	37	29	4	4	4	1	25	3	78	7	1	1	5	.167	0	6	3.95
2000 Rancho Cuca	A+ SD	14	0	0	13	18.2	72	10	3	3	0	0	0	2	5	0	18	2	0	1	0	1.000	0	6	1.45
Mobile	AA SD	45	0	0	11	59.1	252	47	23	16	4	2	2	1	30	2	53	4	0	3	3	.500	0	1	2.43
4 Min. YEARS		189	0	0	115	231.2	999	214	104	84	11	10	10	13	94	9	252	23	2	10	14	.417	0	38	3.26

Carlos Campusano

Bats: Right Throws: Right Pos: SS-55; 3B-17; 2B-6; PH-6; DH-3; PR-2   Ht: 5'11" Wt: 160 Born: 9/2/75 Age: 25

Year Team	Lg Org	G	AB	H	2B	3B	HR	TB	R	RBI	TBB	IBB	SO	HBP	SH	SF	SB	CS	SB%	GDP	Avg	OBP	SLG
1995 Brewers	R Mil	54	173	43	4	1	1	52	25	15	14	1	27	5	1	1	7	3	.70	2	.249	.321	.301
1996 Beloit	A Mil	108	337	83	17	4	1	111	33	20	10	0	63	5	5	1	4	3	.57	7	.246	.278	.329
1997 Bakersfield	A+ SF	61	191	38	8	3	1	55	17	15	7	0	49	4	3	2	2	0	1.00	3	.199	.240	.288
1998 San Jose	A+ SF	34	98	18	1	2	0	23	11	7	5	0	29	3	1	1	0	0	—	3	.184	.243	.235
1999 San Jose	A+ SF	27	84	26	2	1	1	33	13	7	6	0	15	4	3	1	4	1	.80	1	.310	.359	.393
Shreveport	AA SF	15	39	6	0	2	1	13	5	6	3	0	10	0	0	0	1	0	1.00	1	.154	.214	.333
Bakersfield	A+ SF	14	51	18	2	0	1	23	7	4	1	0	13	2	0	0	2	2	.50	0	.353	.389	.451
Fresno	AAA SF	16	46	13	2	0	0	15	2	3	2	0	9	3	0	1	0	0	—	4	.283	.346	.326
2000 Shreveport	AA SF	11	25	5	1	0	0	6	5	1	0	0	9	0	0	0	0	0	—	0	.200	.200	.240
San Jose	A+ SF	1	3	1	0	0	0	1	0	0	0	0	0	0	0	0	0	0	—	0	.333	.333	.333
Fresno	AAA SF	2	3	0	0	0	0	0	0	0	0	0	1	0	0	0	0	0	—	0	.000	.000	.000
Bakersfield	A+ SF	68	246	62	10	4	1	83	33	26	11	0	47	7	7	1	13	3	.81	5	.252	.302	.337
6 Min. YEARS		411	1296	313	47	17	7	415	151	104	59	1	272	33	21	8	33	12	.73	30	.242	.290	.320

Robinson Cancel

Bats: Right **Throws:** Right **Pos:** DH-11; C-8; PH-2; 1B-1   **Ht:** 6'0" **Wt:** 195 **Born:** 5/4/76 **Age:** 25

								BATTING										BASERUNNING				PERCENTAGES		
Year Team	Lg Org	G	AB	H	2B	3B	HR	TB	R	RBI	TBB	IBB	SO	HBP	SH	SF	SB	CS	SB%	GDP	Avg	OBP	SLG
1994 Brewers	R Mil	29	70	12	0	0	0	12	6	8	9	1	19	2	0	2	0	2	.00	2	.171	.277	.171
1995 Helena	R+ Mil	46	154	37	9	0	0	46	18	24	9	0	20	2	1	2	8	3	.73	3	.240	.287	.299
1996 Beloit	A Mil	72	218	48	3	1	1	56	26	29	14	0	31	1	5	1	13	5	.72	7	.220	.269	.257
1997 Beloit	A Mil	17	50	15	3	0	0	18	9	4	7	0	9	3	0	0	0	2	.00	1	.300	.417	.360
Stockton	A+ Mil	64	211	59	11	0	1	73	25	16	13	0	40	2	7	1	9	3	.75	6	.280	.326	.346
1998 Stockton	A+ Mil	11	32	6	1	0	0	7	3	2	4	0	8	0	0	0	2	1	.67	1	.188	.278	.219
El Paso	AA Mil	58	158	51	10	0	1	64	17	30	22	1	32	0	4	1	2	2	.50	5	.323	.403	.405
1999 Huntsville	AA Mil	66	223	56	10	1	5	83	35	32	23	0	38	3	0	1	8	5	.62	10	.251	.328	.372
Louisville	AAA Mil	39	117	43	8	0	5	66	22	28	14	0	28	1	1	1	6	2	.75	6	.368	.436	.564
2000 Huntsville	AA Mil	22	71	19	3	0	1	25	11	12	11	0	16	0	0	1	5	1	.83	2	.268	.361	.352
1999 Milwaukee	NL	15	44	8	2	0	0	10	5	5	2	0	12	1	1	0	0	0	—	0	.182	.234	.227
7 Min. YEARS		424	1304	346	58	2	14	450	172	185	126	2	241	14	18	10	53	26	.67	43	.265	.334	.345

Casey Candaele

Bats: Both **Throws:** Right **Pos:** 2B-55; OF-32; 3B-17; DH-4; C-1; PH-1; PR-1   **Ht:** 5'9" **Wt:** 165 **Born:** 1/12/61 **Age:** 40

								BATTING										BASERUNNING				PERCENTAGES		
Year Team	Lg Org	G	AB	H	2B	3B	HR	TB	R	RBI	TBB	IBB	SO	HBP	SH	SF	SB	CS	SB%	GDP	Avg	OBP	SLG
1983 Wst Plm Bch	A+ Mon	127	511	156	26	9	0	200	77	45	51	2	44	2	8	1	22	17	.56	—	.305	.370	.391
Memphis	A Mon	5	19	4	1	0	0	5	4	1	1	0	3	0	0	0	1	0	1.00	—	.211	.250	.263
1984 Jacksnville	AA Mon	132	532	145	23	2	2	178	68	53	30	1	35	1	5	6	26	18	.59	13	.273	.309	.335
1985 Indianapols	AAA Mon	127	390	101	13	5	0	124	55	35	44	2	33	0	11	1	13	10	.57	15	.259	.333	.318
1986 Indianapols	AAA Mon	119	480	145	32	6	2	195	77	42	46	6	29	1	11	2	16	10	.62	8	.302	.363	.406
1988 Indianapols	AAA Mon	60	239	63	11	6	2	92	23	36	12	0	20	0	1	7	5	1	.83	5	.264	.291	.385
Tucson	AAA Hou	17	66	17	3	0	0	20	8	5	4	0	6	0	0	0	4	2	.67	5	.258	.300	.303
1989 Tucson	AAA Hou	68	206	45	6	1	0	53	22	17	20	4	37	0	4	1	6	3	.67	7	.218	.286	.257
1990 Tucson	AAA Hou	7	28	6	1	0	0	7	2	2	3	1	2	1	1	0	1	2	.33	1	.214	.313	.250
1993 Tucson	AAA Hou	6	27	8	1	0	0	9	4	4	3	1	2	0	0	0	1	2	.33	2	.296	.367	.333
1994 Indianapols	AAA Cin	131	511	144	31	7	4	201	66	52	32	4	65	0	3	4	8	6	.57	21	.282	.322	.393
1995 Albuquerque	AAA LA	12	27	7	0	0	0	7	2	2	4	0	4	0	1	0	1	0	1.00	1	.259	.344	.259
Buffalo	AAA Cle	97	364	90	10	7	4	126	50	38	22	1	42	2	4	7	9	2	.82	6	.247	.289	.346
1996 Buffalo	AAA Cle	94	392	122	22	2	6	166	66	37	27	2	35	1	3	3	3	5	.38	6	.311	.355	.423
1997 Buffalo	AAA Cle	79	311	71	21	0	7	113	39	38	31	2	43	1	4	4	1	6	.14	12	.228	.297	.363
1998 Nashville	AAA Pit	44	147	40	11	2	1	52	18	15	13	1	19	1	1	0	1	1	.50	3	.272	.335	.354
New Orleans	AAA Hou	66	221	64	11	2	1	82	36	25	18	2	34	0	0	2	2	0	1.00	12	.290	.340	.371
1999 New Orleans	AAA Hou	126	467	124	38	3	7	185	56	42	47	1	54	3	2	0	3	9	.25	7	.266	.337	.396
2000 Nashua	IND —	81	308	85	18	1	2	111	54	29	49	2	30	3	2	4	5	7	.42	5	.276	.376	.360
Calgary	AAA Fla	22	84	18	4	2	0	26	11	11	11	0	5	1	0	2	4	1	.80	3	.214	.306	.310
1986 Montreal	NL	30	104	24	4	1	0	30	9	6	5	0	15	0	0	1	3	5	.38	3	.231	.264	.288
1987 Montreal	NL	138	449	122	23	4	1	156	62	23	38	3	28	2	4	2	7	10	.41	5	.272	.330	.347
1988 Montreal	NL	36	116	20	5	1	0	27	9	4	10	1	11	0	0	2	1	0	1.00	7	.172	.238	.233
Houston	NL	21	31	5	3	0	0	8	2	1	1	0	6	0	1	0	0	1	.00	7	.161	.188	.258
1990 Houston	NL	130	262	75	8	6	3	104	30	22	31	5	42	1	4	0	7	5	.58	4	.286	.364	.397
1991 Houston	NL	151	461	121	20	7	4	167	44	50	40	7	49	0	0	1	9	3	.75	5	.262	.319	.362
1992 Houston	NL	135	320	68	12	1	1	85	19	18	24	3	36	3	7	6	7	1	.88	5	.213	.269	.266
1993 Houston	NL	75	121	29	8	0	1	40	18	7	10	0	14	0	0	0	2	3	.40	0	.240	.298	.331
1996 Cleveland	AL	24	44	11	2	0	1	16	8	4	1	0	9	0	0	0	0	0	—	0	.250	.267	.364
1997 Cleveland	AL	14	26	8	1	0	0	9	5	4	1	0	1	0	0	0	1	0	1.00	0	.308	.333	.346
15 Min. YEARS		1420	5330	1455	273	55	38	1952	738	529	468	32	542	17	61	45	131	103	.56	—	.273	.331	.366
9 Maj. YEARS		754	1934	483	86	20	11	642	206	139	161	19	211	6	19	12	37	28	.57	29	.250	.308	.332

Ben Candelaria

Bats: Left **Throws:** Right **Pos:** OF-79; PH-2   **Ht:** 5'11" **Wt:** 167 **Born:** 1/29/75 **Age:** 26

								BATTING										BASERUNNING				PERCENTAGES		
Year Team	Lg Org	G	AB	H	2B	3B	HR	TB	R	RBI	TBB	IBB	SO	HBP	SH	SF	SB	CS	SB%	GDP	Avg	OBP	SLG
1992 Blue Jays	R Tor	29	77	12	2	1	0	16	10	3	6	0	16	0	1	1	4	3	.57	0	.156	.214	.208
1993 Medcine Hat	R+ Tor	62	208	55	7	1	5	79	24	34	27	1	49	3	5	4	3	3	.50	3	.264	.351	.380
1994 Hagerstown	A Tor	3	13	3	0	0	0	6	2	3	0	0	4	0	0	0	0	0	—	0	.231	.231	.462
St.Cathrnes	A- Tor	71	250	66	15	1	2	89	36	37	35	1	55	1	3	1	8	4	.67	6	.264	.355	.356
1995 Dunedin	A+ Tor	125	471	122	21	5	5	168	66	49	53	1	98	0	3	5	11	4	.73	11	.259	.331	.357
1996 Knoxville	AA Tor	55	162	45	11	2	3	69	16	14	18	0	40	2	2	0	3	3	.50	7	.278	.357	.426
Dunedin	A+ Tor	39	125	25	5	0	1	33	13	6	12	0	25	0	1	0	1	4	.20	1	.200	.270	.264
1997 Knoxville	AA Tor	120	472	139	32	5	15	226	81	67	42	2	89	5	4	6	4	3	.57	9	.294	.354	.479
1998 Knoxville	AA Tor	36	156	52	8	3	10	96	33	31	9	0	31	1	1	1	0	3	.00	2	.333	.371	.615
Syracuse	AAA Tor	69	251	62	13	2	7	100	28	32	23	2	68	0	0	3	2	0	1.00	5	.247	.312	.398
1999 Jacksnville	AA Det	120	464	125	31	3	18	216	65	77	35	3	93	1	0	5	6	7	.46	13	.269	.319	.466
2000 St. Paul	IND —	60	223	66	12	0	6	96	31	35	27	3	24	4	1	0	8	2	.80	5	.296	.382	.430
Portland	AA Fla	20	66	17	3	0	2	26	8	15	7	1	16	1	0	0	0	0	—	0	.258	.329	.394
9 Min. YEARS		809	2938	789	160	23	75	1220	413	403	294	14	608	20	22	28	50	36	.58	62	.269	.336	.415

Jon Cannon

Pitches: Left **Bats:** Right **Pos:** RP-37; SP-2   **Ht:** 6'3" **Wt:** 200 **Born:** 1/1/75 **Age:** 26

		HOW MUCH HE PITCHED						WHAT HE GAVE UP												THE RESULTS					
Year Team	Lg Org	G	GS	CG	GF	IP	BFP	H	R	ER	HR	SH	SF	HB	TBB	IBB	SO	WP	Bk	W	L	Pct.	ShO	Sv	ERA
1996 Williamsprt	A- ChC	14	13	0	1	83.1	329	61	31	28	6	0	0	3	26	0	66	2	5	6	4	.600	0	0	3.02
1997 Rockford	A ChC	24	20	1	3	129.1	548	110	53	45	13	2	3	7	50	1	130	16	3	9	6	.600	0	0	3.13
Daytona	A+ ChC	2	2	0	0	13.2	55	7	2	2	1	2	1	0	10	1	13	0	0	1	0	1.000	0	0	1.32
1998 Daytona	A+ ChC	7	7	1	0	31.1	142	37	22	13	1	2	2	0	12	0	28	1	0	1	3	.000	0	0	3.73
1999 Daytona	A+ ChC	33	11	1	12	95.2	424	83	55	47	8	7	5	10	66	3	77	6	2	3	5	.375	0	0	4.42
2000 Daytona	A+ ChC	7	1	0	3	16.1	62	7	0	0	1	0	0	0	7	0	11	1	0	0	0	—	0	1	0.00
West Tenn	AA ChC	32	1	0	9	53	225	35	19	18	4	4	2	2	31	1	44	1	0	1	2	.333	0	1	3.06
5 Min. YEARS		119	55	3	28	422.2	1785	340	182	153	33	17	13	22	202	6	369	27	10	20	20	.500	0	2	3.26

Aaron Capista

Bats: Both **Throws:** Right **Pos:** SS-125; PH-3   **Ht:** 6'2" **Wt:** 189 **Born:** 5/31/79 **Age:** 22

					BATTING												BASERUNNING				PERCENTAGES		
Year Team	Lg Org	G	AB	H	2B	3B	HR	TB	R	RBI	TBB	IBB	SO	HBP	SH	SF	SB	CS	SB%	GDP	Avg	OBP	SLG
1997 Red Sox	R Bos	38	134	32	6	1	0	40	16	14	16	1	17	0	0	2	6	2	.75	3	.239	.316	.299
1998 Michigan	A Bos	127	471	123	25	5	5	173	58	68	23	0	47	6	2	6	5	3	.63	16	.261	.300	.367
1999 Sarasota	A+ Bos	130	518	137	18	3	5	176	64	47	45	2	60	3	8	4	25	10	.71	9	.264	.325	.340
2000 Trenton	AA Bos	126	434	103	20	3	2	135	52	36	37	0	68	4	2	2	9	4	.69	6	.237	.302	.311
4 Min. YEARS		421	1557	395	69	12	12	524	190	165	121	3	192	13	12	14	45	19	.70	34	.254	.310	.337

Carmine Cappuccio

Bats: Left **Throws:** Right **Pos:** OF-27; 1B-14; PH-11; DH-10   **Ht:** 6'3" **Wt:** 200 **Born:** 2/1/70 **Age:** 31

					BATTING												BASERUNNING				PERCENTAGES		
Year Team	Lg Org	G	AB	H	2B	3B	HR	TB	R	RBI	TBB	IBB	SO	HBP	SH	SF	SB	CS	SB%	GDP	Avg	OBP	SLG
1992 Utica	A- CWS	22	87	24	4	2	0	32	15	13	6	0	10	1	0	1	5	0	1.00	3	.276	.326	.368
South Bend	A CWS	49	182	53	9	2	0	66	23	19	21	1	21	1	1	1	2	3	.40	4	.291	.366	.363
1993 Sarasota	A+ CWS	24	90	17	2	2	1	26	9	12	4	1	10	0	0	0	3	0	1.00	1	.189	.223	.289
South Bend	A CWS	101	383	117	26	5	4	165	59	52	42	6	56	6	0	1	2	6	.25	11	.305	.382	.431
1994 Pr William	A+ CWS	101	401	117	30	1	12	185	71	60	25	1	53	9	2	4	8	4	.67	7	.292	.344	.461
1995 Birmingham	AA CWS	65	248	69	13	3	4	100	34	38	22	4	21	2	3	2	2	2	.50	10	.278	.339	.403
Nashville	AAA CWS	66	216	59	14	0	5	88	30	24	29	4	26	1	1	1	0	2	.00	6	.273	.360	.407
1996 Nashville	AAA CWS	120	407	111	22	3	10	169	55	61	25	7	48	6	3	2	1	3	.25	15	.273	.323	.415
1997 Nashville	AAA CWS	55	177	39	11	0	4	62	22	21	16	2	24	0	1	2	1	0	1.00	10	.220	.282	.350
1999 New Jersey	IND —	80	301	105	28	1	17	186	59	75	30	8	37	5	0	4	0	1	.00	9	.349	.412	.618
2000 Reading	AA Phi	60	187	43	5	1	10	80	23	36	10	0	22	1	1	3	0	1	.00	7	.230	.269	.428
8 Min. YEARS		743	2679	754	164	20	67	1159	400	411	230	34	328	32	12	21	24	22	.52	83	.281	.343	.433

Dan Carlson

Pitches: Right **Bats:** Right **Pos:** SP-3; RP-1   **Ht:** 6'0" **Wt:** 200 **Born:** 1/26/70 **Age:** 31

		HOW MUCH HE PITCHED						WHAT HE GAVE UP										THE RESULTS					
Year Team	Lg Org	G	GS	CG	GF	IP	BFP	H	R	ER	HR	SH	SF	HB	TBB	IBB	SO	WP	Bk	W	L	Pct.	ShO	Sv	ERA
1990 Everett	A- SF	17	11	0	3	62.1	279	60	42	37	5	1	4	1	33	1	77	9	5	2	6	.250	0	0	5.34
1991 Clinton	A SF	27	27	5	0	181.1	740	149	69	62	11	3	3	2	76	0	164	18	5	16	7	.696	3	0	3.08
1992 Shreveport	AA SF	27	27	4	0	186	765	166	85	66	11	5	3	1	60	3	157	4	0	15	9	.625	1	0	3.19
1993 Phoenix	AAA SF	13	12	0	0	70	320	79	54	51	12	2	1	5	32	1	48	4	0	5	6	.455	0	0	6.56
Shreveport	AA SF	15	15	2	0	100.1	397	86	30	25	9	4	4	0	26	3	81	5	0	7	4	.636	1	0	2.24
1994 Phoenix	AAA SF	31	22	0	2	151.1	665	173	90	78	21	3	9	1	55	1	117	10	0	13	6	.684	0	1	4.64
1995 Phoenix	AAA SF	23	22	2	1	132.2	582	138	67	63	11	7	7	3	66	0	93	6	1	9	5	.643	0	0	4.27
1996 Phoenix	AAA SF	33	15	2	3	146.2	604	135	61	56	18	5	5	2	46	0	123	3	0	13	6	.684	0	1	3.44
1997 Bakersfield	A+ SF	2	2	0	0	6	22	3	0	0	0	0	0	0	1	0	7	0	0	0	0	—	0	0	0.00
Phoenix	AAA SF	29	14	0	7	109	451	102	53	47	12	3	3	2	36	1	108	6	1	13	3	.813	0	3	3.88
1998 Durham	AAA TB	19	11	0	3	68	316	87	52	48	8	1	3	3	28	0	59	4	1	3	5	.375	0	0	6.35
1999 Tucson	AAA Ari	32	18	0	5	117.2	527	130	82	71	19	3	1	6	52	6	118	4	2	4	9	.308	0	0	5.43
2000 Tucson	AAA Ari	4	3	0	1	22	96	25	9	4	1	1	2	0	7	0	12	1	0	0	1	.000	0	0	1.64
1996 San Francisco	NL	5	0	0	3	10	46	13	6	3	2	0	2	0	2	0	4	0	0	1	0	1.000	0	0	2.70
1997 San Francisco	NL	6	0	0	2	15.1	72	20	14	13	5	0	1	0	8	1	14	0	0	0	0	—	0	0	7.63
1998 Tampa Bay	AL	10	0	0	1	17.2	86	25	15	15	3	2	1	3	8	0	16	0	0	0	0	—	0	0	7.64
1999 Arizona	NL	2	0	0	1	4	18	5	4	4	0	0	0	0	0	0	3	0	0	0	0	—	0	0	9.00
11 Min. YEARS		272	199	15	25	1353.1	5764	1333	684	608	142	38	43	26	518	16	1164	74	15	100	67	.599	5	5	4.04
4 Maj. YEARS		23	0	0	7	47	222	63	39	35	10	2	4	3	18	1	37	0	0	1	0	1.000	0	0	6.70

Rafael Carmona

Pitches: Right **Bats:** Left **Pos:** RP-3   **Ht:** 6'2" **Wt:** 185 **Born:** 10/2/72 **Age:** 28

		HOW MUCH HE PITCHED						WHAT HE GAVE UP										THE RESULTS					
Year Team	Lg Org	G	GS	CG	GF	IP	BFP	H	R	ER	HR	SH	SF	HB	TBB	IBB	SO	WP	Bk	W	L	Pct.	ShO	Sv	ERA
1993 Bellingham	A- Sea	23	0	0	9	35.2	159	33	19	15	1	5	1	1	14	1	30	4	0	2	3	.400	0	2	3.79
1994 Riverside	A+ Sea	50	0	0	48	67.1	264	48	22	21	3	1	4	0	19	0	63	3	0	8	2	.800	0	21	2.81
1995 Port City	AA Sea	15	0	0	15	15	59	11	5	3	0	1	1	1	3	0	17	2	0	1	0	1.000	0	4	1.80
Tacoma	AAA Sea	8	8	1	0	48	212	52	29	27	6	1	2	3	19	1	37	1	3	4	3	.571	1	0	5.06
1996 Tacoma	AAA Sea	4	1	0	2	6.1	29	5	1	1	1	0	0	0	5	0	9	0	1	0	0	—	0	0	1.42
1997 Tacoma	AAA Sea	32	5	0	19	59.1	262	52	31	25	7	2	1	2	35	2	56	3	2	2	5	.286	0	4	3.79
1998 Lancaster	A+ Sea	4	4	0	0	13	55	12	10	9	1	0	0	0	5	0	11	0	2	0	1	.000	0	0	6.23
Orlando	AA Sea	4	4	0	0	11.1	57	18	14	18	1	4	1	0	6	0	11	2	2	0	3	.000	0	0	14.29
1999 Tacoma	AAA Sea	27	0	0	9	43.1	185	39	18	17	6	1	0	1	20	0	38	2	0	1	3	.250	0	2	3.53
2000 Tacoma	AAA Sea	3	0	0	1	4	26	12	9	9	3	0	0	0	2	0	1	1	0	0	1	.000	0	0	20.25
1995 Seattle	AL	15	3	0	6	47.2	230	55	31	30	9	1	5	2	34	1	28	3	1	2	4	.333	0	1	5.66
1996 Seattle	AL	53	1	0	15	90.1	415	95	47	43	11	7	2	3	55	9	62	4	0	8	3	.727	0	1	4.28
1997 Seattle	AL	4	0	0	1	5.2	22	3	2	2	1	0	0	0	2	0	6	1	0	0	0	—	0	0	3.18
1999 Seattle	AL	9	0	0	3	11.1	57	18	11	10	3	2	2	0	9	1	10	1	0	1	0	1.000	0	0	7.94
8 Min. YEARS		170	22	1	103	303.1	1309	282	162	145	32	12	5	13	128	4	273	18	11	17	22	.436	1	33	4.30
4 Maj. YEARS		81	4	0	25	155	724	171	92	85	24	10	9	5	100	11	96	8	1	11	7	.611	0	2	4.94

Matt Carnes

Pitches: Right **Bats:** Right **Pos:** SP-23; RP-10   **Ht:** 6'3" **Wt:** 201 **Born:** 8/18/75 **Age:** 25

		HOW MUCH HE PITCHED						WHAT HE GAVE UP										THE RESULTS					
Year Team	Lg Org	G	GS	CG	GF	IP	BFP	H	R	ER	HR	SH	SF	HB	TBB	IBB	SO	WP	Bk	W	L	Pct.	ShO	Sv	ERA
1997 Elizabethtn	R+ Min	8	7	1	0	38	156	33	17	13	3	2	0	1	5	0	42	7	1	3	0	1.000	0	0	3.08
Fort Wayne	A Min	1	1	0	0	4	18	2	4	4	1	0	0	0	5	0	3	1	1	0	1	.000	0	0	9.00
1998 Fort Wayne	A Min	47	10	1	18	104	473	119	74	63	5	4	8	7	36	5	92	8	1	8	5	.615	0	5	5.45
1999 Fort Myers	A+ Min	52	1	0	20	81	343	74	48	33	4	8	7	2	26	0	67	6	1	4	4	.500	0	4	3.67
2000 Fort Myers	A+ Min	19	9	0	1	54.1	228	54	20	16	1	1	3	2	19	3	48	4	0	0	2	.000	0	0	2.65
New Britain	AA Min	14	14	0	0	88.2	392	99	59	51	7	1	6	4	37	1	63	4	0	1	8	.111	0	0	5.18
4 Min. YEARS		141	42	2	39	370	1610	381	222	180	21	20	24	15	128	9	315	30	4	16	20	.444	0	9	4.38

Dustin Carr

Bats: Right **Throws:** Right **Pos:** 2B-56; 3B-35; OF-11; DH-9; SS-4; 1B-1; PH-1; PR-1 **Ht:** 5'11" **Wt:** 192 **Born:** 6/7/75 **Age:** 26

Year Team	Lg Org	G	AB	H	2B	3B	HR	TB	R	RBI	TBB	IBB	SO	HBP	SH	SF	SB	CS	SB%	GDP	Avg	OBP	SLG
1997 Hudson Val	A- TB	74	281	81	12	2	5	112	46	47	42	2	42	2	0	3	4	2	.67	10	.288	.381	.399
1998 St. Pete	A+ TB	138	516	132	23	5	6	183	85	52	70	4	86	11	8	3	11	4	.73	9	.256	.355	.355
1999 Orlando	AA TB	125	461	139	22	3	6	185	76	63	70	0	62	4	8	3	7	2	.78	12	.302	.396	.401
2000 Orlando	AA TB	2	11	3	0	0	0	3	1	1	0	0	2	0	0	0	0	0	—	0	.273	.273	.273
Durham	AAA TB	111	365	80	14	2	3	107	38	36	49	0	61	3	7	3	9	2	.82	9	.219	.314	.293
4 Min. YEARS		450	1634	435	71	12	20	590	246	199	231	6	253	20	23	12	31	10	.76	40	.266	.362	.361

Jeremy Carr

Bats: Right **Throws:** Right **Pos:** OF-50; DH-2; PR-1 **Ht:** 5'9" **Wt:** 180 **Born:** 3/30/71 **Age:** 30

Year Team	Lg Org	G	AB	H	2B	3B	HR	TB	R	RBI	TBB	IBB	SO	HBP	SH	SF	SB	CS	SB%	GDP	Avg	OBP	SLG
1993 Eugene	A- KC	42	136	31	2	5	0	43	33	12	20	1	18	6	2	2	30	3	.91	4	.228	.348	.316
1994 Rockford	A KC	121	437	112	9	5	1	134	85	32	60	1	59	16	2	4	52	22	.70	8	.256	.364	.307
1995 Wilmington	A+ KC	5	13	3	1	0	0	4	1	0	1	0	3	0	0	0	0	1	.00	0	.231	.286	.308
Bakersfield	A+ KC	128	499	128	22	2	1	157	92	38	79	0	73	11	6	0	52	21	.71	9	.257	.370	.315
1996 Wichita	AA KC	129	453	118	23	2	6	163	68	40	47	1	64	12	3	3	41	9	.82	15	.260	.344	.360
1997 Wichita	AA KC	91	340	104	19	1	8	149	76	40	50	1	53	9	3	1	39	8	.83	4	.306	.408	.438
Omaha	AAA KC	35	120	32	3	2	2	45	17	9	15	0	17	3	1	0	12	3	.80	3	.267	.362	.375
1998 Omaha	AAA KC	49	178	52	14	3	5	87	40	23	19	1	31	1	2	2	19	5	.79	3	.292	.360	.489
1999 Omaha	AAA KC	73	275	72	12	1	4	98	47	25	42	1	58	5	9	0	15	8	.65	4	.262	.370	.356
2000 Omaha	AAA KC	53	190	46	9	1	1	60	20	15	17	0	33	5	4	0	18	9	.67	4	.242	.321	.316
8 Min. YEARS		726	2641	698	114	22	28	940	479	234	350	6	409	68	32	12	278	89	.76	54	.264	.363	.356

Dan Carrasco

Pitches: Right **Bats:** Right **Pos:** RP-44 **Ht:** 6'2" **Wt:** 191 **Born:** 4/12/77 **Age:** 24

Year Team	Lg Org	G	GS	CG	GF	IP	BFP	H	R	ER	HR	SH	SF	HB	TBB	IBB	SO	WP	Bk	W	L	Pct.	ShO	Sv	ERA
1998 Watertown	A- Cle	13	1	0	6	31.2	145	36	23	19	3	1	0	2	14	0	38	1	0	1	1	.500	0	2	5.40
1999 Williamsprt	A- Pit	18	4	0	6	51.2	212	43	20	17	2	1	3	3	23	0	49	7	4	4	2	.667	0	0	2.96
Lynchburg	A+ Pit	2	0	0	0	5.2	29	9	8	4	0	1	0	0	3	0	4	0	0	0	1	.000	0	0	6.35
2000 Hickory	A Pit	27	0	0	25	40.1	176	35	10	6	0	1	0	7	20	1	40	2	0	5	4	.556	0	6	1.34
Lynchburg	A+ Pit	8	0	0	6	10.1	45	8	5	4	1	1	0	0	8	0	10	1	0	1	0	1.000	0	2	3.48
Altoona	AA Pit	9	0	0	3	14	68	16	14	13	0	0	0	1	13	0	10	1	0	1	1	.500	0	0	8.36
3 Min. YEARS		77	5	0	46	153.2	675	147	80	63	6	5	3	13	81	1	151	12	4	12	9	.571	0	10	3.69

Troy Carrasco

Pitches: Left **Bats:** Both **Pos:** RP-8 **Ht:** 5'11" **Wt:** 172 **Born:** 1/27/75 **Age:** 26

Year Team	Lg Org	G	GS	CG	GF	IP	BFP	H	R	ER	HR	SH	SF	HB	TBB	IBB	SO	WP	Bk	W	L	Pct.	ShO	Sv	ERA
1993 Elizabethtn	R+ Min	14	10	0	3	70.1	292	46	32	25	2	5	1	3	39	3	75	6	2	2	4	.333	0	2	3.20
1994 Fort Wayne	A Min	28	28	2	0	160.2	685	159	88	73	14	5	1	4	60	0	146	9	0	10	10	.500	1	0	4.09
1995 Fort Myers	A+ Min	25	25	2	0	138	596	131	62	48	6	4	7	8	63	0	96	11	2	12	4	.750	0	0	3.13
1996 Hardware Cy	AA Min	34	17	1	8	110	504	113	74	62	9	5	2	6	66	1	69	15	1	6	9	.400	1	0	5.07
1997 Fort Myers	A+ Min	12	8	0	3	55.1	241	61	37	33	5	3	2	0	18	2	36	4	1	3	3	.500	0	0	5.37
New Britain	AA Min	31	3	0	16	65.1	305	69	53	36	11	4	2	2	44	4	46	4	1	4	4	.500	0	1	4.96
1998 Fort Myers	A+ Min	19	4	0	2	45.2	209	52	29	23	4	2	2	1	26	0	35	6	1	0	4	.000	0	0	4.53
2000 Orlando	AA TB	8	0	0	4	8.2	46	15	9	9	1	0	0	0	6	0	5	0	0	0	0	—	0	0	9.35
7 Min. YEARS		171	95	5	36	654	2878	646	384	309	52	28	17	28	322	10	508	55	8	37	38	.493	2	3	4.25

Jamey Carroll

Bats: Right **Throws:** Right **Pos:** 2B-66; 3B-58; SS-15; DH-2; PH-2; PR-1 **Ht:** 5'11" **Wt:** 170 **Born:** 2/18/75 **Age:** 26

Year Team	Lg Org	G	AB	H	2B	3B	HR	TB	R	RBI	TBB	IBB	SO	HBP	SH	SF	SB	CS	SB%	GDP	Avg	OBP	SLG
1996 Vermont	A- Mon	54	203	56	6	1	0	64	40	17	29	0	25	0	3	2	16	11	.59	1	.276	.363	.315
1997 Wst Plm Bch	A+ Mon	121	407	99	19	1	0	120	56	38	43	0	48	4	8	4	17	11	.61	6	.243	.319	.295
1998 Jupiter	A+ Mon	55	222	58	5	0	0	63	40	14	24	1	26	5	2	1	11	4	.73	2	.261	.345	.284
Harrisburg	AA Mon	75	261	66	11	3	0	83	43	20	41	0	29	5	5	0	11	5	.69	4	.253	.365	.318
1999 Harrisburg	AA Mon	141	561	164	34	5	5	223	78	63	48	2	58	5	4	4	21	10	.68	13	.292	.351	.398
2000 Harrisburg	AA Mon	45	169	49	5	3	0	60	23	18	12	0	13	0	1	1	8	2	.80	5	.290	.335	.355
Ottawa	AAA Mon	91	349	97	17	2	2	124	53	23	33	1	32	2	6	2	6	3	.67	9	.278	.342	.355
5 Min. YEARS		582	2172	589	97	15	7	737	333	193	230	4	231	21	30	14	90	46	.66	38	.271	.345	.339

Charley Carter

Bats: Right **Throws:** Right **Pos:** 1B-114; DH-16; PH-2 **Ht:** 6'2" **Wt:** 205 **Born:** 12/11/75 **Age:** 25

Year Team	Lg Org	G	AB	H	2B	3B	HR	TB	R	RBI	TBB	IBB	SO	HBP	SH	SF	SB	CS	SB%	GDP	Avg	OBP	SLG
1998 Auburn	A- Hou	61	218	72	24	1	8	122	32	42	22	1	35	1	1	4	1	1	.50	5	.330	.388	.560
1999 Kissimmee	A+ Hou	115	416	114	19	2	12	173	62	56	28	2	77	3	0	4	0	3	.00	7	.274	.322	.416
2000 Kissimmee	A+ Hou	106	398	110	32	0	10	172	51	66	21	0	64	1	0	8	2	1	.67	16	.276	.308	.432
Round Rock	AA Hou	24	90	24	7	0	3	40	12	21	6	0	15	0	0	0	0	0	—	0	.267	.309	.444
3 Min. YEARS		306	1122	320	82	3	33	507	157	185	77	3	191	5	1	17	3	5	.38	30	.285	.329	.452

Lance Carter

Pitches: Right **Bats:** Right **Pos:** RP-28; SP-6   **Ht:** 6'1" **Wt:** 190 **Born:** 12/18/74 **Age:** 26

Year Team	Lg Org	G	GS	CG	GF	IP	BFP	H	R	ER	HR	SH	SF	HB	TBB	IBB	SO	WP	Bk	W	L	Pct.	ShO	Sv	ERA
1994 Eugene	A- KC	8	7	0	1	26.1	118	28	17	16	2	1	3	1	15	0	23	4	3	1	0	1.000	0	0	5.47
Royals	R KC	5	5	0	0	31	110	19	1	1	1	1	0	0	3	0	36	1	0	3	0	1.000	0	0	0.29
1995 Springfield	A KC	27	24	1	0	137.2	584	151	77	61	14	2	4	8	22	0	118	11	1	9	5	.643	1	0	3.99
1996 Wilmington	A+ KC	16	12	0	3	65.1	292	81	50	46	8	1	0	2	17	2	49	3	0	3	6	.333	0	0	6.34
1998 Lansing	A KC	15	2	0	10	40.1	158	34	6	3	0	1	1	0	9	1	37	0	0	3	1	.750	0	2	0.67
Wilmington	A+ KC	28	1	0	11	52	217	50	21	19	5	5	3	4	14	1	61	4	0	1	4	.200	0	5	3.29
1999 Wichita	AA KC	44	0	0	33	69.2	282	49	10	6	1	1	1	2	27	5	77	3	0	5	2	.714	0	13	0.78
2000 Omaha	AAA KC	34	6	0	13	76.1	321	88	46	42	13	2	2	1	18	0	51	0	1	2	8	.200	0	5	4.95
1999 Kansas City	AL	6	0	0	3	5.1	21	3	3	3	2	0	0	0	3	0	3	0	0	0	1	.000	0	0	5.06
6 Min. YEARS		177	57	1	71	498.2	2082	500	228	194	44	14	14	18	125	10	452	26	5	27	26	.509	1	25	3.50

Joe Caruso

Bats: Right **Throws:** Right **Pos:** OF-67; 3B-23; 2B-14; DH-10; PH-4; SS-2; PR-1   **Ht:** 5'9" **Wt:** 190 **Born:** 12/30/74 **Age:** 26

Year Team	Lg Org	G	AB	H	2B	3B	HR	TB	R	RBI	TBB	IBB	SO	HBP	SH	SF	SB	CS	SB%	GDP	Avg	OBP	SLG
1997 Spokane	A- KC	57	194	58	12	3	5	91	48	36	29	1	30	6	8	0	10	4	.71	1	.299	.406	.469
1998 Lansing	A KC	120	417	112	23	7	9	176	73	60	60	1	61	13	1	5	24	9	.73	8	.269	.374	.422
1999 Wilmington	A+ KC	102	361	85	13	6	5	125	60	37	34	0	68	6	4	6	6	4	.60	7	.235	.313	.346
2000 Wichita	AA KC	108	400	125	26	1	13	192	69	66	34	3	45	16	5	5	10	5	.67	4	.313	.385	.480
4 Min. YEARS		387	1372	380	74	17	32	584	250	199	157	5	204	43	20	13	50	22	.69	20	.277	.366	.426

Mike Caruso

Bats: Left **Throws:** Right **Pos:** SS-66; 2B-23; PH-1   **Ht:** 6'1" **Wt:** 172 **Born:** 5/27/77 **Age:** 24

Year Team	Lg Org	G	AB	H	2B	3B	HR	TB	R	RBI	TBB	IBB	SO	HBP	SH	SF	SB	CS	SB%	GDP	Avg	OBP	SLG
1996 Bellingham	A- SF	73	312	91	13	1	2	112	48	24	16	2	23	2	3	6	24	10	.71	2	.292	.324	.359
1997 San Jose	A+ SF	108	441	147	24	11	2	199	76	50	38	3	19	6	4	3	11	16	.41	3	.333	.391	.451
Winston-Sal	A+ CWS	28	119	27	3	2	0	34	12	14	4	0	8	2	0	0	3	0	1.00	6	.227	.264	.286
2000 Charlotte	AAA CWS	29	309	76	11	5	0	97	38	26	22	0	23	3	8	2	5	7	.42	7	.246	.301	.314
1998 Chicago	AL	133	523	160	17	6	5	204	81	55	14	0	38	7	8	3	22	6	.79	8	.306	.331	.390
1999 Chicago	AL	136	529	132	11	4	2	157	60	35	20	0	36	3	11	1	12	14	.46	6	.250	.286	.297
3 Min. YEARS		297	1181	341	51	19	4	442	174	114	80	5	73	13	15	11	43	33	.57	12	.289	.338	.374
2 Maj. YEARS		269	1052	292	28	10	7	361	141	90	34	0	74	10	19	4	34	20	.63	14	.278	.305	.343

Jhonny Carvajal

Bats: Right **Throws:** Right **Pos:** SS-37; 2B-25; 3B-24; PH-6; DH-4; 1B-3; OF-1; PR-1   **Ht:** 5'10" **Wt:** 180 **Born:** 7/24/74 **Age:** 26

Year Team	Lg Org	G	AB	H	2B	3B	HR	TB	R	RBI	TBB	IBB	SO	HBP	SH	SF	SB	CS	SB%	GDP	Avg	OBP	SLG
1993 Princeton	R+ Cin	67	253	74	10	5	0	94	41	16	29	1	31	4	8	0	7	11	.39	3	.292	.374	.372
1994 Chston-WV	A Cin	67	198	45	6	0	0	51	27	13	19	0	25	2	2	3	12	3	.80	3	.227	.297	.258
Princeton	R+ Cin	53	218	59	10	4	2	83	35	29	14	2	38	5	5	3	31	11	.74	0	.271	.325	.381
1995 Chston-WV	A Cin	135	486	128	18	5	0	156	78	42	58	0	77	6	4	4	44	19	.70	4	.263	.347	.321
1996 Wst Plm Bch	A+ Mon	114	426	101	18	0	2	125	50	38	44	0	73	6	7	4	14	16	.47	9	.237	.315	.293
Harrisburg	AA Mon	16	60	18	3	2	0	25	7	4	5	0	10	1	1	0	1	1	.50	1	.300	.364	.417
1997 Harrisburg	AA Mon	116	378	98	12	1	1	115	36	31	27	3	66	4	4	3	10	7	.59	8	.259	.313	.304
1998 Harrisburg	AA Mon	112	338	88	12	4	0	108	37	21	34	5	69	6	8	3	4	6	.40	12	.260	.338	.320
1999 Ottawa	AAA Mon	106	355	82	20	4	0	110	28	34	21	2	67	5	3	6	7	3	.70	8	.231	.279	.310
2000 Ottawa	AAA Mon	11	26	5	0	1	0	7	3	5	0	3	0	0	0	1	0	1.00	0	.192	.323	.269	
Harrisburg	AA Mon	24	73	18	7	0	1	28	8	11	7	0	12	1	0	1	2	1	.67	3	.247	.317	.384
Tucson	AAA Ari	56	179	53	8	2	0	65	28	14	16	1	37	2	4	0	4	4	.50	5	.296	.360	.363
8 Min. YEARS		877	2990	769	124	28	6	967	378	253	279	14	508	42	46	25	137	82	.63	56	.257	.327	.323

Scott Cassidy

Pitches: Right **Bats:** Right **Pos:** SP-20; RP-2   **Ht:** 6'3" **Wt:** 175 **Born:** 10/3/75 **Age:** 25

Year Team	Lg Org	G	GS	CG	GF	IP	BFP	H	R	ER	HR	SH	SF	HB	TBB	IBB	SO	WP	Bk	W	L	Pct.	ShO	Sv	ERA
1998 Medcine Hat	R+ Tor	15	14	0	0	81.1	325	71	31	22	4	2	3	5	14	0	82	2	0	8	1	.889	0	0	2.43
1999 Hagerstown	A Tor	27	27	1	0	170.2	694	151	78	62	13	2	1	21	30	0	178	6	1	13	7	.650	0	0	3.27
2000 Dunedin	A+ Tor	14	13	1	1	88	342	53	15	13	4	3	2	3	34	2	89	4	0	9	3	.750	0	0	1.33
Tennessee	AA Tor	8	7	0	0	42.2	190	48	30	28	7	1	4	4	15	0	39	0	2	2	2	.500	0	0	5.91
3 Min. YEARS		64	61	2	1	382.2	1551	323	154	125	28	8	10	33	93	2	388	12	3	32	13	.711	0	0	2.94

Carlos Castillo

Pitches: Right **Bats:** Right **Pos:** RP-16; SP-15   **Ht:** 6'2" **Wt:** 250 **Born:** 4/21/75 **Age:** 26

Year Team	Lg Org	G	GS	CG	GF	IP	BFP	H	R	ER	HR	SH	SF	HB	TBB	IBB	SO	WP	Bk	W	L	Pct.	ShO	Sv	ERA
1994 White Sox	R CWS	12	12	0	0	59	250	53	20	17	4	2	2	2	10	0	57	3	4	4	3	.571	0	0	2.59
Hickory	A CWS	3	1	0	2	12	42	3	0	0	0	0	0	0	2	0	17	0	0	2	0	1.000	0	0	0.00
1995 Hickory	A CWS	14	12	2	2	79.2	343	85	42	33	11	1	3	3	18	0	67	3	6	5	6	.455	0	0	3.73
1996 South Bend	A CWS	20	19	5	1	133.1	557	131	74	60	12	3	9	5	20	0	128	6	9	9	9	.500	0	0	4.05
Pr William	A+ CWS	6	6	0	0	43.1	180	45	22	19	0	3	5	2	4	1	30	1	1	2	4	.333	0	0	3.95
1997 Nashville	AAA CWS	4	0	0	4	6	24	4	1	1	0	0	0	0	1	0	4	0	0	0	0	—	0	3	1.50
1998 Calgary	AAA CWS	2	2	0	0	9	40	12	8	8	4	0	0	0	4	0	4	0	0	1	0	.500	0	0	9.00
1999 Charlotte	AAA CWS	20	20	5	0	136.1	588	150	88	78	28	3	4	3	30	1	105	5	3	9	6	.600	0	0	5.15
2000 Calgary	AAA Fla	13	10	0	1	61.2	291	94	59	49	6	3	3	6	16	0	37	3	2	1	7	.125	0	1	7.15
Red Sox	R Bos	2	1	0	0	7.2	40	11	8	2	0	0	0	0	5	0	5	1	1	1	0	1.000	0	0	2.35
Pawtucket	AAA Bos	16	4	0	4	48.1	195	42	26	25	8	1	4	4	8	1	27	0	0	2	3	.400	0	0	4.66

Year Team	Lg Org	G	GS	CG	GF	IP	BFP	H	R	ER	HR	SH	SF	HB	TBB	IBB	SO	WP	Bk	W	L	Pct.	ShO	Sv	ERA
		\<HOW MUCH HE PITCHED\>						\<WHAT HE GAVE UP\>												\<THE RESULTS\>					
1997 Chicago	AL	37	2	0	14	66.1	295	68	35	33	9	0	4	1	33	3	43	3	0	2	1	.667	0	0	4.48
1998 Chicago	AL	54	2	0	11	100.1	431	94	61	57	17	2	7	5	35	1	64	4	3	6	4	.600	0	0	5.11
1999 Chicago	AL	18	2	0	6	41	178	45	26	26	10	0	0	0	14	1	23	0	2	2	2	.500	0	0	5.71
7 Min. YEARS		112	87	16	14	595.1	2534	630	348	292	74	18	27	25	126	3	481	25	24	36	39	.480	0	5	4.41
3 Maj. YEARS		109	6	0	31	207.2	904	207	122	116	36	2	11	6	82	5	130	7	5	10	7	.588	0	1	5.03

Nelson Castro

Bats: Both **Throws:** Right **Pos:** SS-119; PH-1 **Ht:** 5'10" **Wt:** 190 **Born:** 6/4/76 **Age:** 25

Year Team	Lg Org	G	AB	H	2B	3B	HR	TB	R	RBI	TBB	IBB	SO	HBP	SH	SF	SB	CS	SB%	GDP	Avg	OBP	SLG
		\<BATTING\>															\<BASERUNNING\>				\<PERCENTAGES\>		
1995 Angels	R Ana	55	190	37	1	2	0	42	34	22	27	0	50	4	4	1	15	7	.68	2	.195	.306	.221
1996 Boise	A- Ana	1	1	0	0	0	0	0	0	0	0	0	0	0	0	0	0	0	—	0	.000	.000	.000
Angels	R Ana	53	186	38	4	3	3	57	31	14	32	0	42	2	1	0	25	8	.76	3	.204	.327	.306
1997 Boise	A- Ana	69	293	86	16	1	7	125	74	37	38	1	53	4	1	1	26	6	.81	1	.294	.381	.427
1998 Lk Elsinore	A+ Ana	131	470	110	16	7	4	152	73	41	40	1	101	6	0	3	36	12	.75	5	.234	.301	.323
1999 Lk Elsinore	A+ Ana	125	444	111	16	12	1	154	68	50	36	1	75	3	5	4	53	19	.74	5	.250	.308	.347
2000 Bakersfield	A+ SF	53	218	62	14	3	5	97	38	41	20	0	40	0	4	6	27	8	.77	5	.284	.336	.445
Fresno	AAA SF	67	244	62	7	2	5	88	27	20	14	0	51	0	1	1	10	4	.71	7	.254	.293	.361
6 Min. YEARS		554	2046	506	74	30	25	715	345	225	207	3	412	19	16	16	192	64	.75	28	.247	.320	.349

Mike Cather

Pitches: Right **Bats:** Right **Pos:** RP-43 **Ht:** 6'2" **Wt:** 205 **Born:** 12/17/70 **Age:** 30

Year Team	Lg Org	G	GS	CG	GF	IP	BFP	H	R	ER	HR	SH	SF	HB	TBB	IBB	SO	WP	Bk	W	L	Pct.	ShO	Sv	ERA
		\<HOW MUCH HE PITCHED\>						\<WHAT HE GAVE UP\>												\<THE RESULTS\>					
1993 Rangers	R Tex	25	0	0	17	30.2	124	20	7	6	0	0	0	3	9	0	30	2	1	1	1	.500	0	4	1.76
1994 Charlotte	A+ Tex	44	0	0	37	60.1	270	56	33	26	2	3	2	3	40	3	53	1	0	8	6	.571	0	4	3.88
1995 Tulsa	AA Tex	18	0	0	12	21.2	90	20	11	8	0	4	1	1	7	5	15	0	0	0	2	.000	0	0	3.32
Winnipeg	IND —	27	0	0	24	31	123	18	6	5	1	2	0	0	12	3	35	2	0	4	2	.667	0	8	1.45
1996 Greenville	AA Atl	53	0	0	18	87.2	384	89	42	36	2	6	2	8	29	5	61	2	1	3	4	.429	0	5	3.70
1997 Greenville	AA Atl	22	0	0	2	37.1	153	37	18	18	2	1	2	6	7	1	29	0	0	5	2	.714	0	1	4.34
Richmond	AAA Atl	13	0	0	10	26	102	17	6	5	1	2	0	1	9	1	22	0	0	0	0	—	0	3	1.73
1998 Richmond	AAA Atl	11	0	0	2	15.1	72	22	12	10	1	2	0	0	6	0	10	2	0	0	1	.000	0	0	5.87
1999 Richmond	AAA Atl	45	0	0	20	67.2	308	71	57	51	4	8	5	1	34	2	60	5	3	2	7	.222	0	1	6.78
2000 Calgary	AAA Fla	43	0	0	28	63.1	280	66	34	28	6	4	3	3	27	2	62	0	0	4	5	.444	0	8	3.98
1997 Atlanta	NL	35	0	0	10	37.2	155	23	12	10	1	2	0	2	19	4	29	0	0	1	2	.333	0	0	2.39
1998 Atlanta	NL	36	0	0	11	41.1	173	39	21	18	7	4	2	2	12	1	33	0	0	2	2	.500	0	0	3.92
1999 Atlanta	NL	4	0	0	0	2.2	13	5	3	3	2	0	0	0	1	0	0	0	0	1	0	1.000	0	0	10.13
8 Min. YEARS		301	0	0	170	441	1906	416	226	193	19	32	15	26	180	22	377	14	5	27	30	.474	0	36	3.94
3 Maj. YEARS		75	0	0	21	81.2	341	67	36	31	10	6	2	4	32	5	62	0	0	5	6	.455	0	0	3.42

Blas Cedeno

Pitches: Right **Bats:** Right **Pos:** RP-36 **Ht:** 6'0" **Wt:** 165 **Born:** 11/15/72 **Age:** 28

Year Team	Lg Org	G	GS	CG	GF	IP	BFP	H	R	ER	HR	SH	SF	HB	TBB	IBB	SO	WP	Bk	W	L	Pct.	ShO	Sv	ERA
		\<HOW MUCH HE PITCHED\>						\<WHAT HE GAVE UP\>												\<THE RESULTS\>					
1991 Bristol	R+ Det	14	2	0	6	45	202	47	36	19	7	0	3	2	18	1	37	3	4	1	4	.200	0	0	3.80
1992 Bristol	R+ Det	13	13	3	0	80.2	335	64	21	18	2	3	1	5	41	0	77	6	0	8	2	.800	2	0	2.01
Fayettevlle	A Det	2	1	1	1	9	32	3	3	3	0	0	0	0	4	0	12	0	0	0	1	.000	0	1	3.00
1993 Fayettevlle	A Det	28	22	1	3	148.2	621	145	64	52	11	5	3	11	55	0	103	6	0	6	6	.500	1	0	3.15
1994 Lakeland	A+ Det	5	0	0	3	14	52	9	3	2	1	1	1	0	4	0	16	1	0	1	0	1.000	0	0	1.29
Trenton	AA Det	34	0	0	18	52.1	228	50	18	15	5	4	0	2	27	2	40	4	0	1	3	.250	0	3	2.58
1995 Jacksnville	AA Det	48	5	0	13	80.2	329	71	34	31	7	1	1	1	36	1	53	2	1	3	2	.600	0	4	3.46
1996 Lakeland	A+ Det	10	0	0	5	16.1	72	17	10	10	3	0	0	1	7	0	11	2	0	1	1	.500	0	5	5.51
Jacksnville	AA Det	26	2	0	8	46.2	219	63	34	28	7	2	3	3	26	0	30	3	0	0	0	—	0	1	5.40
1997 Rockford	A ChC	22	0	0	13	40.1	168	36	19	13	3	1	1	1	14	2	25	0	0	3	3	.500	0	2	2.90
1998 New Jersey	IND —	12	7	0	2	48.1	224	62	34	24	3	0	3	0	14	1	37	7	0	1	6	.143	0	1	4.47
1999 Clearwater	A+ Phi	34	0	0	8	57.2	243	63	33	27	5	2	4	1	17	1	42	4	0	4	5	.500	0	1	4.21
Reading	AA Phi	19	0	0	5	31.2	131	30	16	15	5	2	4	0	12	3	18	0	0	2	2	.500	0	0	4.26
2000 Reading	AA Phi	36	0	0	20	54.2	228	47	31	29	4	0	1	1	24	1	34	3	0	3	1	.750	0	7	4.77
10 Min. YEARS		303	52	5	105	726	3084	707	356	286	63	21	19	31	299	12	535	41	5	34	35	.493	3	13	3.55

Domingo Cedeno

Bats: Both **Throws:** Right **Pos:** 3B-2; PH-1 **Ht:** 6'0" **Wt:** 170 **Born:** 11/4/68 **Age:** 32

Year Team	Lg Org	G	AB	H	2B	3B	HR	TB	R	RBI	TBB	IBB	SO	HBP	SH	SF	SB	CS	SB%	GDP	Avg	OBP	SLG
		\<BATTING\>															\<BASERUNNING\>				\<PERCENTAGES\>		
1989 Myrtle Bch	A Tor	9	35	7	0	0	0	7	4	2	3	0	12	0	1	0	1	1	.50	0	.200	.263	.200
Dunedin	A+ Tor	9	28	6	0	1	0	8	3	1	3	0	10	0	0	0	0	1	.00	1	.214	.290	.286
Medcine Hat	R+ Tor	53	194	45	6	4	1	62	28	20	23	0	65	3	3	1	6	6	.50	0	.232	.322	.320
1990 Dunedin	A+ Tor	124	493	109	12	10	7	162	64	61	48	2	127	2	4	8	10	6	.63	4	.221	.289	.329
1991 Knoxville	AA Tor	100	336	75	7	6	1	97	39	26	29	1	78	1	12	1	11	6	.65	2	.223	.286	.289
1992 Knoxville	AA Tor	106	337	76	7	7	2	103	31	21	18	0	88	4	7	0	8	9	.47	6	.226	.273	.306
Syracuse	AAA Tor	18	57	11	4	0	0	15	4	5	3	0	14	0	2	0	0	0	—	1	.193	.233	.263
1993 Syracuse	AAA Tor	103	382	104	16	10	2	146	58	28	33	2	67	1	8	2	15	10	.60	6	.272	.330	.382
1994 Syracuse	AAA Tor	22	80	23	5	1	1	33	11	9	8	1	13	0	1	0	3	2	.60	1	.288	.352	.413
1997 Tulsa	AA Tex	2	9	4	1	0	0	5	0	0	0	0	3	0	0	0	0	0	—	0	.444	.444	.667
Okla City	AAA Tex	6	28	10	2	0	0	12	0	2	0	0	6	0	0	1	0	1	.00	0	.357	.357	.429
1999 Tacoma	AAA Sea	33	112	30	8	1	1	43	17	13	7	1	36	2	0	0	1	2	.33	0	.268	.322	.384
2000 Norfolk	AAA NYM	3	5	1	1	0	0	2	1	2	0	0	1	0	0	2	0	0	—	0	.200	.143	.400
1993 Toronto	AL	15	46	8	0	0	0	8	5	7	1	0	10	0	2	1	1	0	1.00	2	.174	.188	.174
1994 Toronto	AL	47	97	19	2	3	0	27	14	10	10	0	31	0	3	4	1	2	.33	1	.196	.261	.278
1995 Toronto	AL	51	161	38	6	1	4	58	18	14	10	0	35	2	1	0	2	1	.67	3	.236	.289	.360

Year Team	Lg Org	G	AB	H	2B	3B	HR	TB	R	RBI	TBB	IBB	SO	HBP	SH	SF	SB	CS	SB%	GDP	Avg	OBP	SLG
1996 Toronto	AL	77	282	79	10	2	2	99	44	17	15	0	60	2	7	1	5	3	.63	6	.280	.320	.351
Chicago	AL	12	19	3	2	0	0	5	2	3	0	0	4	0	1	2	1	0	1.00	1	.158	.143	.263
1997 Texas	AL	113	365	103	19	6	4	146	49	36	27	0	77	2	2	1	3	3	.50	5	.282	.334	.400
1998 Texas	AL	61	141	37	9	1	2	54	19	21	10	0	32	0	1	1	2	1	.67	4	.262	.309	.383
1999 Seattle	AL	21	42	9	2	0	2	17	4	8	5	0	9	1	0	0	1	1	.50	1	.214	.313	.405
Philadelphia	NL	32	66	10	4	0	1	17	5	5	5	0	22	0	1	0	0	1	.00	2	.152	.211	.258
9 Min. YEARS		588	2096	501	68	41	15	696	260	190	175	7	520	13	38	14	55	44	.56	23	.239	.300	.332
7 Maj. YEARS		429	1219	306	54	13	15	431	160	121	83	0	280	7	18	10	14	12	.54	25	.251	.300	.354

Jose Cepeda

Bats: Right **Throws:** Right **Pos:** PH-14; 2B-8; OF-7; DH-5; PR-1 **Ht:** 6'0" **Wt:** 185 **Born:** 8/1/74 **Age:** 26

Year Team	Lg Org	G	AB	H	2B	3B	HR	TB	R	RBI	TBB	IBB	SO	HBP	SH	SF	SB	CS	SB%	GDP	Avg	OBP	SLG
1995 Royals	R KC	54	187	65	6	4	0	79	32	21	15	0	5	2	1	4	2	2	.50	0	.348	.394	.422
1996 Lansing	A KC	135	558	161	29	3	3	205	87	81	38	0	44	11	9	8	10	3	.77	8	.289	.341	.367
1997 Wilmington	A+ KC	28	71	20	0	0	0	20	9	3	12	0	10	0	3	0	1	0	1.00	1	.282	.386	.282
Lansing	A KC	89	326	91	17	1	2	116	40	35	42	0	35	3	5	4	4	2	.67	10	.279	.363	.356
1998 Wilmington	A+ KC	115	391	110	20	5	1	143	46	38	36	3	55	11	10	5	19	3	.86	8	.281	.354	.366
1999 Wilmington	A+ KC	59	227	71	7	2	0	82	35	25	22	0	19	5	6	3	5	8	.38	9	.313	.381	.361
Myrtle Bch	A+ Atl	1	5	0	0	0	0	0	1	0	1	0	1	0	0	0	0	0	—	0	.000	.000	.000
Greenville	AA Atl	58	196	54	8	2	1	69	19	17	13	0	15	1	2	3	2	3	.40	7	.276	.319	.352
2000 Richmond	AAA Atl	4	15	3	0	0	0	3	2	1	0	0	2	0	0	0	0	0	—	0	.200	.200	.200
Greenville	AA Atl	30	67	19	0	1	0	21	4	3	6	0	10	0	0	0	0	0	—	0	.284	.338	.313
6 Min. YEARS		573	2043	594	87	18	7	738	275	223	185	3	196	33	36	28	43	21	.67	43	.291	.355	.361

Matt Ceriani

Bats: Right **Throws:** Right **Pos:** C-51; PH-3; DH-1; P-1 **Ht:** 6'2" **Wt:** 210 **Born:** 10/9/76 **Age:** 24

Year Team	Lg Org	G	AB	H	2B	3B	HR	TB	R	RBI	TBB	IBB	SO	HBP	SH	SF	SB	CS	SB%	GDP	Avg	OBP	SLG
1998 Evansville	IND —	23	59	12	5	0	1	20	8	11	9	0	11	2	2	0	0	1	.00	1	.203	.329	.339
Helena	R+ Mil	45	155	35	7	0	2	48	24	24	26	0	26	3	2	1	0	2	.00	8	.226	.346	.310
1999 Helena	R+ Mil	57	162	49	11	0	1	63	22	25	15	0	23	4	2	1	4	0	1.00	5	.302	.374	.389
2000 Huntsville	AA Mil	8	16	0	0	0	0	0	1	1	1	0	4	0	1	0	0	0	—	0	.000	.056	.000
Mudville	A+ Mil	48	150	39	8	1	2	55	14	16	15	0	27	0	5	0	2	3	.40	4	.260	.327	.367
3 Min. YEARS		181	542	135	31	1	6	186	69	77	66	0	91	9	13	3	6	6	.50	18	.249	.339	.343

Juan Cerros

Pitches: Right **Bats:** Right **Pos:** RP-48; SP-2 **Ht:** 6'1" **Wt:** 203 **Born:** 9/25/76 **Age:** 24

		HOW MUCH HE PITCHED						WHAT HE GAVE UP									THE RESULTS					
Year Team	Lg Org	G	GS	CG	GF	IP	BFP	H	R	ER	HR	SH	SF	HB	TBB	IBB	SO	WP	Bk	W	L	Pct.	ShO	Sv	ERA
1999 St. Lucie	A+ NYM	5	0	0	2	7.2	137	5	1	0	0	0	0	1	4	0	6	0	1	2	0	1.000	0	0	0.00
2000 Binghamton	AA NYM	50	2	0	23	74.2	327	71	33	29	8	0	3	4	30	1	52	6	0	10	4	.714	0	3	3.50
2 Min. YEARS		55	2	0	25	82.1	359	76	34	29	8	0	3	5	34	1	58	6	1	12	4	.750	0	3	3.17

Chris Cervantes

Pitches: Left **Bats:** Left **Pos:** SP-26; RP-1 **Ht:** 6'1" **Wt:** 165 **Born:** 2/4/79 **Age:** 22

		HOW MUCH HE PITCHED						WHAT HE GAVE UP									THE RESULTS					
Year Team	Lg Org	G	GS	CG	GF	IP	BFP	H	R	ER	HR	SH	SF	HB	TBB	IBB	SO	WP	Bk	W	L	Pct.	ShO	Sv	ERA
1998 South Bend	A Ari	21	0	0	10	33.2	137	29	8	5	0	3	2	1	6	1	37	4	0	2	2	.500	0	2	1.34
1999 South Bend	A Ari	38	10	0	14	115	490	109	49	40	9	5	1	4	34	0	89	10	1	8	5	.615	0	3	3.13
High Desert	A+ Ari	1	0	0	0	0.1	11	5	6	6	1	0	0	0	1	0	1	0	0	0	0	—	0	0	162.00
2000 South Bend	A Ari	11	11	0	0	59.1	247	62	29	20	3	0	3	2	11	0	54	2	0	5	4	.556	0	0	3.03
El Paso	AA Ari	16	15	0	0	95	411	108	50	46	13	5	1	7	21	0	72	3	2	7	5	.583	0	0	4.36
3 Min. YEARS		87	36	0	24	303.1	1292	313	142	117	26	13	7	14	73	1	253	19	3	22	16	.579	0	5	3.47

Dionys Cesar

Bats: Both **Throws:** Right **Pos:** OF-62; SS-34; 2B-16; 3B-7; PH-6; 1B-2; DH-2 **Ht:** 5'10" **Wt:** 155 **Born:** 9/27/76 **Age:** 24

Year Team	Lg Org	G	AB	H	2B	3B	HR	TB	R	RBI	TBB	IBB	SO	HBP	SH	SF	SB	CS	SB%	GDP	Avg	OBP	SLG
1995 Athletics	R Oak	48	171	55	11	4	2	80	41	21	23	0	29	2	3	2	17	10	.63	2	.322	.404	.468
1996 Modesto	A+ Oak	22	60	12	2	0	0	14	5	4	7	0	19	0	6	0	1	3	.25	0	.200	.284	.233
Sou Oregon	A- Oak	52	203	55	7	4	1	73	37	12	19	0	46	4	7	1	18	6	.75	3	.271	.344	.360
1997 Visalia	A+ Oak	97	285	68	16	2	1	91	60	11	43	1	79	1	6	0	10	12	.45	5	.239	.340	.319
1998 Visalia	A+ Oak	130	501	141	34	8	7	212	87	54	56	2	98	1	6	3	31	12	.72	6	.281	.353	.423
1999 Midland	AA Oak	35	105	20	4	3	3	39	15	15	18	0	28	1	1	1	1	4	.20	2	.190	.312	.371
Visalia	A+ Oak	77	320	103	21	5	7	155	59	62	41	3	51	3	2	5	21	11	.66	8	.322	.398	.484
2000 Visalia	A+ Oak	5	22	5	2	0	2	13	3	6	1	0	4	0	0	1	0	0	—	2	.227	.250	.591
Midland	AA Oak	111	433	120	21	2	4	157	62	37	38	0	65	0	4	3	13	10	.57	7	.277	.333	.363
6 Min. YEARS		577	2100	579	118	28	27	834	369	222	246	6	419	12	35	16	112	68	.62	31	.276	.353	.397

Dan Cey

Bats: Right **Throws:** Right **Pos:** 2B-4; DH-2; SS-1; 3B-1; PH-1; PR-1 **Ht:** 5'11" **Wt:** 168 **Born:** 11/8/75 **Age:** 25

Year Team	Lg Org	G	AB	H	2B	3B	HR	TB	R	RBI	TBB	IBB	SO	HBP	SH	SF	SB	CS	SB%	GDP	Avg	OBP	SLG
1996 Fort Wayne	A Min	27	85	22	4	0	0	26	8	6	8	0	11	0	0	0	2	1	.67	2	.259	.323	.306
1997 Fort Myers	A+ Min	127	521	148	34	5	7	213	84	60	34	1	85	5	3	4	23	9	.72	11	.284	.332	.409

Year Team	Lg Org	BATTING																BASERUNNING				PERCENTAGES		
		G	AB	H	2B	3B	HR	TB	R	RBI	TBB	IBB	SO	HBP	SH	SF	SB	CS	SB%	GDP	Avg	OBP	SLG
1998 New Britain	AA Min	136	569	143	28	2	8	199	82	50	40	0	95	3	3	1	23	7	.77	13	.251	.303	.350
1999 Salt Lake	AAA Min	117	403	119	18	3	11	176	63	56	32	1	66	7	2	3	10	2	.83	12	.295	.355	.437
2000 Salt Lake	AAA Min	8	27	5	1	0	0	6	1	4	0	0	5	0	0	0	2	0	1.00	1	.185	.185	.222
5 Min. YEARS		415	1605	437	85	10	26	620	238	176	114	2	262	15	8	8	60	19	.76	39	.272	.325	.386

Gustavo Chacin

Pitches: Left **Bats:** Left **Pos:** SP-23; RP-4   **Ht:** 5'11" **Wt:** 170 **Born:** 12/4/80 **Age:** 20

Year Team	Lg Org	HOW MUCH HE PITCHED						WHAT HE GAVE UP										THE RESULTS				
		G	GS	CG	GF	IP	BFP	H	R	ER	HR	SH	SF	HB	TBB	IBB	SO	WP	Bk	W	L	Pct.	ShO	Sv	ERA
1999 Medcine Hat	R+ Tor	15	9	0	2	64	280	68	33	22	6	4	4	7	23	0	50	4	3	4	3	.571	0	1	3.09
2000 Tennessee	AA Tor	2	2	0	0	5	31	10	7	7	1	0	0	1	6	0	5	0	1	0	2	.000	0	0	12.60
Dunedin	A+ Tor	25	21	0	1	127.2	584	138	69	57	14	1	2	3	64	0	77	9	0	9	5	.643	0	0	4.02
2 Min. YEARS		42	32	0	3	196.2	895	216	109	86	21	5	6	11	93	0	132	13	4	13	10	.565	0	1	3.94

Shawn Chacon

Pitches: Right **Bats:** Right **Pos:** SP-27   **Ht:** 6'3" **Wt:** 212 **Born:** 12/23/77 **Age:** 23

Year Team	Lg Org	HOW MUCH HE PITCHED						WHAT HE GAVE UP										THE RESULTS				
		G	GS	CG	GF	IP	BFP	H	R	ER	HR	SH	SF	HB	TBB	IBB	SO	WP	Bk	W	L	Pct.	ShO	Sv	ERA
1996 Rockies	R Col	11	11	1	0	56.1	241	46	17	10	1	0	2	4	15	0	64	3	2	1	2	.333	0	0	1.60
Portland	A- Col	4	4	0	0	19.2	92	24	18	15	2	0	0	1	9	0	17	5	0	0	2	.000	0	0	6.86
1997 Asheville	A Col	28	27	1	0	162	701	155	80	70	13	5	3	14	63	1	149	15	1	11	7	.611	0	0	3.89
1998 Salem	A+ Col	12	12	0	0	56	258	53	35	33	5	3	2	6	31	0	54	8	1	0	4	.000	0	0	5.30
1999 Salem	A+ Col	12	12	0	0	72	316	69	44	33	3	1	3	2	34	0	66	5	0	5	5	.500	0	0	4.13
2000 Carolina	AA Col	27	27	4	0	173.2	739	151	71	61	10	4	2	9	85	1	172	16	0	10	10	.500	3	0	3.16
5 Min. YEARS		94	93	6	0	539.2	2347	498	265	222	34	13	12	36	237	2	522	52	4	27	30	.474	3	0	3.70

Jim Chamblee

Bats: Right **Throws:** Right **Pos:** OF-121; PR-6; DH-2; PH-1   **Ht:** 6'4" **Wt:** 176 **Born:** 5/6/75 **Age:** 26

Year Team	Lg Org	BATTING																BASERUNNING				PERCENTAGES		
		G	AB	H	2B	3B	HR	TB	R	RBI	TBB	IBB	SO	HBP	SH	SF	SB	CS	SB%	GDP	Avg	OBP	SLG
1995 Utica	A- Bos	62	200	51	9	1	2	68	36	16	23	0	45	6	1	1	9	7	.56	5	.255	.348	.340
1996 Michigan	A Bos	100	303	66	15	2	1	88	31	39	16	0	75	7	4	4	2	2	.50	1	.218	.270	.290
1997 Michigan	A Bos	133	487	146	29	5	22	251	112	73	53	3	107	17	0	5	18	4	.82	8	.300	.384	.515
1998 Trenton	AA Bos	136	489	118	33	3	17	208	71	65	62	1	144	16	6	4	9	5	.64	2	.241	.343	.425
1999 Pawtucket	AAA Bos	127	464	127	21	3	24	226	84	88	43	2	126	13	4	3	5	3	.63	4	.274	.350	.487
2000 Pawtucket	AAA Bos	127	407	105	26	4	17	190	72	56	50	1	129	7	2	2	8	3	.73	4	.258	.348	.467
6 Min. YEARS		685	2350	613	133	18	83	1031	406	337	247	7	626	66	17	19	51	24	.68	24	.261	.345	.439

Carlos Chantres

Pitches: Right **Bats:** Right **Pos:** SP-22; RP-7   **Ht:** 6'3" **Wt:** 175 **Born:** 4/1/76 **Age:** 25

Year Team	Lg Org	HOW MUCH HE PITCHED						WHAT HE GAVE UP										THE RESULTS				
		G	GS	CG	GF	IP	BFP	H	R	ER	HR	SH	SF	HB	TBB	IBB	SO	WP	Bk	W	L	Pct.	ShO	Sv	ERA
1994 White Sox	R CWS	16	2	0	3	35	150	28	21	14	2	1	0	3	13	0	29	6	1	0	1	.000	0	1	3.60
1995 White Sox	R CWS	11	11	2	0	61.2	257	65	32	22	2	1	1	1	14	0	47	1	2	2	3	.400	0	0	3.21
1996 Hickory	A CWS	18	18	0	0	119.2	497	108	63	50	10	6	3	1	38	0	93	8	5	6	7	.462	0	0	3.76
South Bend	A CWS	10	9	1	0	65	274	61	31	26	3	1	2	2	19	0	41	3	1	4	5	.444	0	0	3.60
1997 Winston-Sal	A+ CWS	26	26	2	0	164.2	712	152	94	86	21	6	5	4	71	1	158	10	2	9	11	.450	0	0	4.70
1998 Birmingham	AA CWS	20	5	0	7	52.2	251	58	35	34	5	4	6	0	42	1	49	3	0	2	4	.333	0	1	5.81
Winston-Sal	A+ CWS	13	13	1	0	88.1	370	71	43	37	10	3	6	8	41	1	86	5	0	5	5	.500	1	0	3.77
1999 Birmingham	AA CWS	28	21	1	5	141.1	596	122	64	55	13	1	7	7	61	0	105	9	1	6	8	.429	0	2	3.50
2000 Charlotte	AAA CWS	29	22	0	2	142.2	601	136	59	56	12	4	4	8	54	2	85	8	2	10	4	.714	0	0	3.53
7 Min. YEARS		171	127	7	17	871	3708	801	442	380	78	29	34	34	353	4	693	53	14	44	48	.478	0	4	3.93

Jake Chapman

Pitches: Left **Bats:** Right **Pos:** RP-55; SP-1   **Ht:** 6'1" **Wt:** 175 **Born:** 1/11/74 **Age:** 27

Year Team	Lg Org	HOW MUCH HE PITCHED						WHAT HE GAVE UP										THE RESULTS				
		G	GS	CG	GF	IP	BFP	H	R	ER	HR	SH	SF	HB	TBB	IBB	SO	WP	Bk	W	L	Pct.	ShO	Sv	ERA
1996 Spokane	A- KC	19	7	0	3	68.1	274	44	19	18	2	2	2	6	20	1	71	3	1	7	1	.875	0	1	2.37
1997 Wilmington	A+ KC	27	26	0	0	154.1	673	163	83	66	7	3	5	5	59	5	122	4	0	8	9	.471	0	0	3.85
1998 Wilmington	A+ KC	27	26	1	0	162.1	665	158	72	59	4	6	3	6	37	1	113	5	2	13	9	.591	1	0	3.27
1999 Wichita	AA KC	52	0	0	13	69.2	316	87	38	34	3	5	0	3	29	6	53	4	0	3	0	1.000	0	3	4.39
2000 Ottawa	AAA Mon	7	1	0	0	8.2	40	9	2	2	0	0	0	0	5	0	8	0	0	1	0	1.000	0	0	2.08
Harrisburg	AA Mon	49	0	0	11	66.1	295	73	34	28	4	3	2	1	26	1	53	1	0	4	5	.444	0	1	3.80
5 Min. YEARS		181	60	1	27	529.2	2263	534	248	207	20	19	12	21	176	14	420	17	3	36	24	.600	1	5	3.52

Robinson Checo

Pitches: Right **Bats:** Left **Pos:** SP-15; RP-1   **Ht:** 6'1" **Wt:** 185 **Born:** 9/9/71 **Age:** 29

Year Team	Lg Org	HOW MUCH HE PITCHED						WHAT HE GAVE UP										THE RESULTS				
		G	GS	CG	GF	IP	BFP	H	R	ER	HR	SH	SF	HB	TBB	IBB	SO	WP	Bk	W	L	Pct.	ShO	Sv	ERA
1997 Sarasota	A+ Bos	11	11	0	0	56	250	54	37	33	9	3	5	1	27	0	63	4	5	1	4	.200	0	0	5.30
Trenton	AA Bos	1	1	0	0	7.2	29	6	3	2	0	1	0	1	1	0	9	0	0	1	0	1.000	0	0	2.35
Pawtucket	AAA Bos	9	9	2	0	55.1	220	41	22	21	8	1	0	0	16	0	56	3	0	4	2	.667	1	0	3.42
1998 Red Sox	R Bos	3	3	0	0	9	37	9	5	3	1	0	0	1	0	0	13	0	0	1	0	1.000	0	0	3.00
Sarasota	A+ Bos	1	1	0	0	2	10	3	2	2	0	0	0	0	1	0	4	0	0	0	1	.000	0	0	9.00
Pawtucket	AAA Bos	11	10	0	0	53.1	233	48	30	27	8	0	2	5	26	1	46	4	0	6	2	.750	0	0	4.56

Year Team	Lg Org	G	GS	CG	GF	IP	BFP	H	R	ER	HR	SH	SF	HB	TBB	IBB	SO	WP	Bk	W	L	Pct.	ShO	Sv	ERA
		HOW	**MUCH**	**HE**	**PITCHED**			**WHAT**	**HE**	**GAVE**	**UP**									**THE**	**RESULTS**				
1999 Toledo	AAA Det	2	1	0	0	5	19	2	0	0	0	0	0	1	1	0	6	0	0	0	0	—	0	0	0.00
San Berndno	A+ LA	2	2	0	0	5	23	5	6	6	2	0	0	0	3	0	6	1	0	0	0	—	0	0	10.80
Albuquerque	AAA LA	16	15	0	0	79	342	68	40	38	15	1	2	3	39	1	98	5	4	3	6	.333	0	0	4.33
2000 Albuquerque	AAA LA	16	15	1	0	86.2	358	78	36	35	11	2	1	3	33	0	85	2	1	8	3	.727	0	0	3.63
1997 Boston	AL	5	2	0	1	13.1	54	12	5	5	0	0	0	0	3	0	14	0	0	1	1	.500	0	0	3.38
1998 Boston	AL	2	2	0	0	7.2	34	11	8	8	3	0	0	0	5	0	5	1	0	0	2	.000	0	0	9.39
1999 Los Angeles	NL	9	2	0	1	15.2	85	24	20	18	5	0	0	0	13	1	11	2	0	0	2	.500	0	0	10.34
4 Min. YEARS		72	68	3	0	359	1521	314	181	167	55	7	11	14	147	2	386	19	10	24	18	.571	1	0	4.19
3 Maj. YEARS		16	6	0	2	36.2	173	47	33	31	8	0	0	0	21	1	30	3	0	3	5	.375	0	0	7.61

Chin-Feng Chen

Bats: Right **Throws:** Right **Pos:** OF-127; DH-6   **Ht:** 6'1" **Wt:** 189 **Born:** 10/28/77 **Age:** 23

Year Team	Lg Org	G	AB	H	2B	3B	HR	TB	R	RBI	TBB	IBB	SO	HBP	SH	SF	SB	CS	SB%	GDP	Avg	OBP	SLG
		BATTING															**BASERUNNING**				**PERCENTAGES**		
1999 San Berndno	A+ LA	131	510	161	22	10	31	296	98	123	75	6	129	5	0	7	31	7	.82	7	.316	.404	.580
2000 San Antonio	AA LA	133	516	143	27	3	6	194	66	67	61	3	131	3	1	3	23	15	.61	7	.277	.355	.376
2 Min. YEARS		264	1026	304	49	13	37	490	164	190	136	9	260	8	1	10	54	22	.71	14	.296	.380	.478

Virgil Chevalier

Bats: Right **Throws:** Right **Pos:** OF-85; 1B-8; C-4; DH-3; PR-1   **Ht:** 6'2" **Wt:** 240 **Born:** 10/31/73 **Age:** 27

Year Team	Lg Org	G	AB	H	2B	3B	HR	TB	R	RBI	TBB	IBB	SO	HBP	SH	SF	SB	CS	SB%	GDP	Avg	OBP	SLG
		BATTING															**BASERUNNING**				**PERCENTAGES**		
1995 Utica	A- Bos	64	250	77	12	2	7	114	34	46	11	0	35	3	0	3	15	6	.71	6	.308	.341	.456
Michigan	A Bos	2	6	4	1	0	0	5	2	0	1	0	0	0	0	0	1	0	1.00	0	.667	.714	.833
1996 Michigan	A Bos	126	483	120	31	3	8	181	61	62	33	1	69	1	1	5	11	4	.73	11	.248	.295	.375
1997 Sarasota	A+ Bos	94	289	60	13	1	6	93	31	37	19	0	43	3	2	3	8	7	.53	6	.208	.261	.322
1998 Sarasota	A+ Bos	81	327	107	22	4	8	161	59	59	27	3	59	1	1	6	13	4	.76	5	.327	.374	.492
Trenton	AA Bos	30	117	32	7	2	2	49	19	16	4	0	17	0	3	1	2	2	.50	2	.274	.295	.419
1999 Trenton	AA Bos	131	509	149	29	4	13	225	81	76	50	2	73	2	8	8	9	9	.50	11	.293	.353	.442
2000 Pawtucket	AAA Bos	8	24	3	0	0	0	3	1	0	1	0	0	0	0	0	0	0	—	1	.125	.160	.125
Trenton	AA Bos	89	346	107	25	1	7	155	58	67	34	1	35	2	0	8	3	2	.60	11	.309	.367	.448
6 Min. YEARS		625	2351	659	140	17	51	986	346	363	180	5	331	12	15	34	62	34	.65	53	.280	.330	.419

Paul Chiaffredo

Bats: Right **Throws:** Right **Pos:** C-32; 1B-7; DH-4; PH-1   **Ht:** 6'2" **Wt:** 195 **Born:** 5/30/76 **Age:** 25

Year Team	Lg Org	G	AB	H	2B	3B	HR	TB	R	RBI	TBB	IBB	SO	HBP	SH	SF	SB	CS	SB%	GDP	Avg	OBP	SLG
		BATTING															**BASERUNNING**				**PERCENTAGES**		
1997 St.Cathrnes	A- Tor	48	163	39	8	1	2	55	20	15	9	0	42	9	1	1	5	2	.71	1	.239	.313	.337
1998 Dunedin	A+ Tor	89	290	68	19	0	4	99	34	41	16	0	68	6	6	3	1	3	.25	8	.234	.286	.341
1999 Knoxville	AA Tor	11	39	3	1	0	1	7	3	3	0	0	10	2	2	0	0	0	—	2	.077	.122	.179
Dunedin	A+ Tor	88	261	66	22	2	3	101	39	21	17	0	44	12	4	4	1	4	.20	12	.253	.323	.387
2000 Hagerstown	A Tor	13	45	16	6	0	1	25	9	5	9	0	6	3	0	0	0	0	—	0	.356	.491	.556
Tennessee	AA Tor	18	63	7	1	0	0	8	6	2	5	0	16	1	0	0	0	1	.00	0	.111	.188	.127
Dunedin	A+ Tor	11	38	11	1	0	2	18	7	6	5	0	9	1	0	0	0	0	—	0	.289	.386	.474
4 Min. YEARS		278	899	210	58	3	13	313	118	93	61	0	195	34	13	8	7	10	.41	23	.234	.304	.348

Giuseppe Chiaramonte

Bats: Right **Throws:** Right **Pos:** C-111; DH-9; PH-2   **Ht:** 6'0" **Wt:** 200 **Born:** 2/19/76 **Age:** 25

Year Team	Lg Org	G	AB	H	2B	3B	HR	TB	R	RBI	TBB	IBB	SO	HBP	SH	SF	SB	CS	SB%	GDP	Avg	OBP	SLG
		BATTING															**BASERUNNING**				**PERCENTAGES**		
1997 San Jose	A+ SF	64	223	51	11	1	12	100	29	44	25	1	58	4	0	3	0	0	—	7	.229	.314	.448
1998 San Jose	A+ SF	129	502	137	33	3	22	242	87	87	47	4	139	4	0	12	5	2	.71	7	.273	.333	.482
1999 Shreveport	AA SF	114	400	98	20	2	19	179	54	74	40	1	88	6	0	5	4	2	.67	5	.245	.319	.448
2000 Fresno	AAA SF	122	443	113	30	6	24	227	70	79	47	1	81	3	1	3	2	1	.67	7	.255	.329	.512
4 Min. YEARS		429	1568	399	94	12	77	748	240	284	159	7	366	17	1	23	11	5	.69	26	.254	.325	.477

Jin Ho Cho

Pitches: Right **Bats:** Right **Pos:** SP-22; RP-4   **Ht:** 6'3" **Wt:** 220 **Born:** 8/16/75 **Age:** 25

Year Team	Lg Org	G	GS	CG	GF	IP	BFP	H	R	ER	HR	SH	SF	HB	TBB	IBB	SO	WP	Bk	W	L	Pct.	ShO	Sv	ERA
		HOW	**MUCH**	**HE**	**PITCHED**			**WHAT**	**HE**	**GAVE**	**UP**									**THE**	**RESULTS**				
1998 Sarasota	A+ Bos	5	5	0	0	32	132	33	14	11	1	0	4	0	5	0	30	2	0	3	1	.750	0	0	3.09
Trenton	AA Bos	13	13	1	0	74	299	59	21	18	4	3	4	3	19	2	62	0	0	5	2	.714	1	0	2.19
1999 Pawtucket	AAA Bos	17	17	4	0	109.2	447	99	46	42	12	2	3	4	29	1	80	1	0	9	3	.750	0	0	3.45
2000 Sarasota	A+ Bos	3	3	0	0	15	60	13	5	4	1	0	0	0	0	0	15	0	0	1	1	.500	0	0	2.40
Trenton	AA Bos	10	10	0	0	58.2	260	76	45	38	8	2	3	3	8	0	32	0	0	3	5	.375	0	0	5.83
Pawtucket	AAA Bos	13	9	1	2	71.2	298	77	37	37	7	3	2	0	13	3	37	0	0	4	3	.571	1	0	4.65
1998 Boston	AL	4	4	0	0	18.2	87	28	17	17	4	0	1	1	3	0	15	1	0	0	3	.000	0	0	8.20
1999 Boston	AL	9	7	0	1	39.1	171	45	26	25	7	1	3	2	8	0	16	0	0	2	3	.400	0	0	5.72
3 Min. YEARS		61	57	6	2	361	1496	357	168	150	35	10	16	10	74	6	256	3	0	25	15	.625	1	0	3.74
2 Maj. YEARS		13	11	0	1	58	258	73	43	42	11	1	4	3	11	0	31	1	0	2	6	.250	0	0	6.52

Hee Seop Choi

Bats: Left **Throws:** Left **Pos:** 1B-120; DH-11; PH-3   **Ht:** 6'5" **Wt:** 235 **Born:** 3/16/79 **Age:** 22

Year Team	Lg Org	G	AB	H	2B	3B	HR	TB	R	RBI	TBB	IBB	SO	HBP	SH	SF	SB	CS	SB%	GDP	Avg	OBP	SLG
		BATTING															**BASERUNNING**				**PERCENTAGES**		
1999 Lansing	A ChC	79	290	93	18	6	18	177	71	70	50	0	68	2	0	2	2	1	.67	8	.321	.422	.610

Year Team	Lg Org	BATTING														BASERUNNING				PERCENTAGES		
		G	AB	H	2B	3B	HR	TB	R	RBI	TBB	IBB	SO	HBP	SH	SF	SB	CS	SB%	GDP	Avg	OBP	SLG
2000 Daytona	A+ ChC	96	345	102	25	6	15	184	60	70	37	5	78	6	0	5	4	1	.80	7	.296	.369	.533
West Tenn	AA ChC	36	122	37	9	0	10	76	25	25	25	0	38	0	0	1	3	1	.75	5	.303	.419	.623
2 Min. YEARS		211	757	232	52	12	43	437	156	165	112	5	184	8	0	8	9	3	.75	20	.306	.398	.577

Ben Christensen

Pitches: Right **Bats:** Right **Pos:** SP-17   **Ht:** 6'4" **Wt:** 205 **Born:** 2/7/78 **Age:** 23

Year Team	Lg Org	HOW MUCH HE PITCHED						WHAT HE GAVE UP										THE RESULTS					
		G	GS	CG	GF	IP	BFP	H	R	ER	HR	SH	SF	HB	TBB	IBB	SO	WP	Bk	W	L	Pct.	ShO	Sv	ERA
1999 Cubs	R ChC	3	3	0	0	9	39	8	3	3	0	0	0	1	5	0	10	1	1	0	1	.000	0	0	3.00
Eugene	A- ChC	5	5	0	0	21.1	100	21	14	14	2	0	1	0	14	0	21	2	0	0	2	.000	0	0	5.91
Daytona	A+ ChC	4	4	0	0	22.2	106	25	16	16	4	1	1	3	11	0	18	1	1	1	3	.250	0	0	6.35
2000 Daytona	A+ ChC	10	10	1	0	64.1	253	43	18	15	6	0	0	3	15	0	63	2	0	4	2	.667	0	0	2.10
West Tenn	AA ChC	7	7	0	0	42.1	177	36	18	13	2	2	3	1	15	0	42	1	0	3	1	.750	0	0	2.76
2 Min. YEARS		29	29	1	0	159.2	675	133	69	61	14	3	5	8	60	0	154	7	2	8	9	.471	0	0	3.44

Tim Christman

Pitches: Left **Bats:** Left **Pos:** RP-8   **Ht:** 6'0" **Wt:** 195 **Born:** 3/31/75 **Age:** 26

Year Team	Lg Org	HOW MUCH HE PITCHED						WHAT HE GAVE UP										THE RESULTS					
		G	GS	CG	GF	IP	BFP	H	R	ER	HR	SH	SF	HB	TBB	IBB	SO	WP	Bk	W	L	Pct.	ShO	Sv	ERA
1996 Portland	A- Col	21	0	0	7	40	176	30	23	19	6	1	3	1	23	0	56	2	1	1	2	.333	0	2	4.28
1997 Asheville	A Col	29	0	0	11	63.1	263	55	32	24	8	5	3	3	18	1	87	7	4	7	3	.700	0	3	3.41
1999 Salem	A+ Col	38	0	0	7	48.1	188	38	18	13	0	1	2	2	12	0	64	1	0	1	2	.333	0	2	2.42
2000 Carolina	AA Col	8	0	0	3	10.2	48	6	3	3	0	0	0	2	7	0	13	0	0	0	0	—	0	0	2.53
4 Min. YEARS		96	0	0	28	162.1	675	129	76	59	14	7	8	8	60	1	220	10	5	9	7	.563	0	7	3.27

Alex Cintron

Bats: Both **Throws:** Right **Pos:** SS-124; PH-1   **Ht:** 6'2" **Wt:** 180 **Born:** 12/17/78 **Age:** 22

Year Team	Lg Org	BATTING															BASERUNNING				PERCENTAGES		
		G	AB	H	2B	3B	HR	TB	R	RBI	TBB	IBB	SO	HBP	SH	SF	SB	CS	SB%	GDP	Avg	OBP	SLG
1997 Diamondbcks	R Ari	43	152	30	6	1	0	38	23	20	21	0	32	2	3	1	1	4	.20	3	.197	.301	.250
Lethbridge	R+ Ari	1	3	1	0	0	0	1	0	0	0	0	1	0	1	0	0	0	—	0	.333	.333	.333
1998 Lethbridge	R+ Ari	67	258	68	11	4	3	96	41	34	20	0	32	2	3	2	8	4	.67	8	.264	.319	.372
1999 High Desert	A+ Ari	128	499	153	25	4	3	195	78	64	19	0	65	3	17	4	15	8	.65	14	.307	.333	.391
2000 El Paso	AA Ari	125	522	157	30	6	4	211	83	59	29	0	56	2	13	7	9	9	.50	22	.301	.336	.404
4 Min. YEARS		364	1434	409	72	15	10	541	225	177	89	0	186	9	37	14	33	25	.57	47	.285	.328	.377

Stubby Clapp

Bats: Left **Throws:** Right **Pos:** 2B-127; PH-2; 3B-1   **Ht:** 5'8" **Wt:** 175 **Born:** 2/24/73 **Age:** 28

Year Team	Lg Org	BATTING															BASERUNNING				PERCENTAGES		
		G	AB	H	2B	3B	HR	TB	R	RBI	TBB	IBB	SO	HBP	SH	SF	SB	CS	SB%	GDP	Avg	OBP	SLG
1996 Johnson Cty	R+ StL	29	94	21	3	2	1	31	25	15	26	0	15	1	1	1	9	2	.82	2	.223	.393	.330
1997 Pr William	A+ StL	78	267	85	21	6	4	130	51	46	52	2	41	6	4	4	9	4	.69	2	.318	.435	.487
1998 Arkansas	AA StL	139	514	143	30	9	12	227	113	57	86	3	100	8	8	6	18	10	.64	10	.278	.386	.442
1999 Memphis	AAA StL	110	393	102	26	2	14	174	72	62	53	4	96	3	4	4	7	7	.50	9	.260	.349	.443
2000 Memphis	AAA StL	129	505	138	28	8	1	185	89	52	80	0	88	5	6	4	10	5	.67	7	.273	.375	.366
5 Min. YEARS		485	1773	489	108	27	32	747	350	232	297	9	340	23	23	19	53	28	.65	30	.276	.383	.421

Chris Clark

Pitches: Right **Bats:** Right **Pos:** RP-24; SP-8   **Ht:** 6'1" **Wt:** 180 **Born:** 10/29/74 **Age:** 26

Year Team	Lg Org	HOW MUCH HE PITCHED						WHAT HE GAVE UP										THE RESULTS					
		G	GS	CG	GF	IP	BFP	H	R	ER	HR	SH	SF	HB	TBB	IBB	SO	WP	Bk	W	L	Pct.	ShO	Sv	ERA
1994 Padres	R SD	17	1	0	6	33.2	153	35	17	12	2	1	0	2	18	0	25	5	0	0	0	—	0	1	3.21
1995 Padres	R SD	13	12	1	0	73	313	52	30	17	1	1	1	7	38	0	82	5	0	5	5	.500	0	0	2.10
Idaho Falls	R+ SD	1	1	0	0	6	24	3	3	3	1	0	0	0	4	0	9	1	0	0	0	—	0	0	4.50
1996 Clinton	A SD	24	11	0	7	82	385	96	58	46	5	4	3	7	51	1	74	9	1	3	8	.273	0	1	5.05
1997 Clinton	A SD	32	11	0	5	89	395	89	50	41	5	0	0	3	46	0	91	15	0	5	5	.500	0	3	4.15
1998 Brevard Cty	A+ Fla	40	2	0	30	60.2	288	52	38	29	1	3	7	4	46	3	58	12	0	2	3	.400	0	9	4.30
1999 Portland	AA Fla	4	0	0	1	6	29	5	5	5	1	1	0	7	4	1	4	1	0	1	0	1.000	0	0	7.50
Brevard Cty	A+ Fla	28	12	0	10	86	395	93	60	53	5	3	6	6	48	1	48	12	0	3	8	.273	0	1	5.55
2000 Portland	AA Fla	32	8	0	2	86.2	381	83	42	37	5	3	3	2	48	0	54	6	0	7	3	.700	0	0	3.84
7 Min. YEARS		191	58	1	61	523	2363	508	303	243	26	16	20	31	306	5	445	66	1	26	32	.448	0	15	4.18

Doug Clark

Bats: Left **Throws:** Right **Pos:** OF-122; DH-8; PH-1   **Ht:** 6'2" **Wt:** 205 **Born:** 3/5/76 **Age:** 25

Year Team	Lg Org	BATTING															BASERUNNING				PERCENTAGES		
		G	AB	H	2B	3B	HR	TB	R	RBI	TBB	IBB	SO	HBP	SH	SF	SB	CS	SB%	GDP	Avg	OBP	SLG
1998 Salem-Keizr	A- SF	59	227	76	8	6	3	105	49	41	32	0	31	3	1	1	12	8	.60	1	.335	.422	.463
1999 Bakersfield	A+ SF	118	420	137	17	2	11	191	67	58	59	4	89	5	0	0	17	11	.61	5	.326	.415	.455
Shreveport	AA SF	15	50	11	3	0	1	17	6	6	4	0	9	0	0	0	0	0	—	2	.220	.278	.340
2000 Shreveport	AA SF	131	492	134	20	7	10	198	68	75	43	5	102	5	1	7	12	4	.75	13	.272	.333	.402
3 Min. YEARS		323	1189	358	48	15	25	511	190	180	138	9	231	13	2	8	41	23	.64	21	.301	.378	.430

Howie Clark

Bats: Left **Throws:** Right **Pos:** 2B-30; OF-19; DH-13; 3B-3; 1B-3; PH-2; P-1   **Ht:** 5'10" **Wt:** 195 **Born:** 2/13/74 **Age:** 27

Year Team	Lg Org	G	AB	H	2B	3B	HR	TB	R	RBI	TBB	IBB	SO	HBP	SH	SF	SB	CS	SB%	GDP	Avg	OBP	SLG
1992 Orioles	R Bal	43	138	33	7	1	0	42	12	6	12	2	21	2	1	0	1	2	.33	2	.239	.309	.304
1993 Albany	A Bal	7	17	4	0	0	0	4	2	1	0	0	3	0	0	0	1	0	1.00	1	.235	.235	.235
Bluefield	R+ Bal	58	180	53	10	1	3	74	29	30	26	2	34	4	1	4	2	2	.50	4	.294	.388	.411
1994 Frederick	A+ Bal	2	7	1	1	0	0	2	1	0	0	0	2	0	0	0	0	0	—	1	.143	.143	.286
Albany	A Bal	108	353	95	22	7	2	137	56	47	51	3	58	7	4	1	5	4	.56	7	.269	.371	.388
1995 High Desert	A+ Bal	100	329	85	20	2	5	124	50	40	32	0	51	4	3	3	12	6	.67	4	.258	.329	.377
1996 Bowie	AA Bal	127	449	122	29	3	4	169	55	52	59	1	54	2	10	7	2	8	.20	8	.272	.354	.376
1997 Bowie	AA Bal	105	314	90	16	0	9	133	39	37	32	2	38	1	1	3	2	2	.50	5	.287	.351	.424
1998 Rochester	AAA Bal	30	95	22	4	1	3	37	13	8	9	0	11	0	0	0	1	2	.33	2	.232	.298	.389
Bowie	AA Bal	88	276	79	16	0	9	122	37	45	29	2	42	3	0	1	1	1	.50	7	.286	.359	.442
1999 Bowie	AA Bal	39	126	37	6	0	2	49	17	12	10	0	12	3	0	0	2	0	1.00	1	.294	.360	.389
Rochester	AAA Bal	79	279	82	19	4	6	127	33	28	34	2	24	1	1	2	1	2	.33	8	.294	.370	.455
2000 Bowie	AA Bal	13	53	18	6	0	1	27	11	9	3	0	6	1	0	1	0	0	—	1	.340	.379	.509
Rochester	AAA Bal	54	189	54	10	0	3	73	25	21	26	0	14	1	1	1	3	1	.75	4	.286	.373	.386
9 Min. YEARS		853	2805	775	166	19	47	1120	380	336	323	14	370	29	22	23	33	30	.52	54	.276	.354	.399

Jermaine Clark

Bats: Left **Throws:** Right **Pos:** 2B-132; PH-2; PR-1   **Ht:** 5'10" **Wt:** 175 **Born:** 9/29/76 **Age:** 24

Year Team	Lg Org	G	AB	H	2B	3B	HR	TB	R	RBI	TBB	IBB	SO	HBP	SH	SF	SB	CS	SB%	GDP	Avg	OBP	SLG
1997 Everett	A- Sea	59	199	67	13	2	3	93	42	29	34	1	31	3	3	2	22	3	.88	1	.337	.437	.467
1998 Wisconsin	A Sea	123	448	145	24	13	6	213	81	55	57	4	64	2	4	1	40	14	.74	3	.324	.402	.475
1999 Lancaster	A+ Sea	126	502	158	27	8	6	219	112	61	58	2	80	2	8	3	33	15	.69	10	.315	.386	.436
2000 New Haven	AA Sea	133	447	131	23	9	2	178	80	44	87	3	69	14	18	3	38	8	.83	7	.293	.421	.398
4 Min. YEARS		441	1596	501	87	32	17	703	315	189	236	10	244	21	33	9	133	40	.77	21	.314	.407	.440

Kevin Clark

Bats: Right **Throws:** Right **Pos:** C-39; DH-22; 1B-14; PH-7; OF-2   **Ht:** 6'1" **Wt:** 200 **Born:** 4/30/73 **Age:** 28

Year Team	Lg Org	G	AB	H	2B	3B	HR	TB	R	RBI	TBB	IBB	SO	HBP	SH	SF	SB	CS	SB%	GDP	Avg	OBP	SLG
1993 Red Sox	R Bos	40	137	28	9	0	1	40	14	19	16	1	24	3	0	4	1	1	.50	5	.204	.294	.292
1994 Utica	A- Bos	57	185	47	12	0	2	65	31	12	19	1	50	6	0	1	2	3	.40	2	.254	.341	.351
1995 Sarasota	A+ Bos	84	293	66	11	0	4	89	23	31	21	0	63	2	1	0	2	5	.29	9	.225	.282	.304
1996 Michigan	A Bos	126	474	131	32	3	10	199	53	56	30	2	94	12	1	4	4	5	.44	11	.276	.333	.420
1997 Sarasota	A+ Bos	3	5	3	0	0	0	3	1	0	1	0	2	1	0	0	0	0	—	0	.600	.667	.600
Rio Grande	IND —	66	250	71	15	0	10	116	50	45	28	2	57	3	0	2	3	0	1.00	9	.284	.360	.464
High Desert	A+ Ari	13	47	11	4	0	1	18	4	3	3	0	13	0	1	0	0	0	—	0	.234	.280	.383
1998 High Desert	A+ Ari	127	498	132	24	5	20	226	72	98	36	0	121	6	0	5	1	0	1.00	16	.265	.319	.454
1999 El Paso	AA Ari	106	373	111	24	3	8	165	44	64	21	4	75	3	0	2	0	2	.00	14	.298	.338	.442
2000 El Paso	AA Ari	27	78	14	4	0	1	21	7	10	4	0	29	2	0	2	0	0	—	0	.179	.233	.269
Chico	IND —	52	206	54	15	0	9	42	38	15	0	0	47	5	0	0	0	1	.00	8	.262	.325	.451
8 Min. YEARS		701	2546	668	150	11	65	1035	340	377	193	10	575	43	3	22	13	17	.43	75	.262	.322	.407

Chris Clemons

Pitches: Right **Bats:** Right **Pos:** SP-19; RP-5   **Ht:** 6'4" **Wt:** 225 **Born:** 10/31/72 **Age:** 28

Year Team	Lg Org	G	GS	CG	GF	IP	BFP	H	R	ER	HR	SH	SF	HB	TBB	IBB	SO	WP	Bk	W	L	Pct.	ShO	Sv	ERA
1994 White Sox	R CWS	2	2	0	0	7	27	5	3	3	0	0	0	0	1	0	5	0	0	0	1	.000	0	0	3.86
Hickory	A CWS	12	12	0	0	69.1	290	74	37	34	5	4	2	5	18	0	42	6	0	4	2	.667	0	0	4.41
1995 Pr William	A+ CWS	27	27	1	0	137	606	136	78	72	18	4	4	11	64	2	92	2	0	7	12	.368	0	0	4.73
1996 Pr William	A+ CWS	6	6	0	0	36	150	36	16	9	6	0	2	4	8	0	26	1	0	1	4	.200	0	0	2.25
Birmingham	AA CWS	19	16	1	2	94.1	400	91	39	33	7	0	1	6	40	2	69	1	1	5	2	.714	0	0	3.15
1997 Nashville	AAA CWS	22	21	1	1	124.2	543	115	73	63	15	2	3	4	65	0	70	6	1	5	5	.500	1	0	4.55
1998 Tucson	AAA Ari	20	19	0	1	86.1	410	103	69	59	13	2	4	9	44	0	79	2	0	3	9	.250	0	0	6.15
1999 Tucson	AAA Ari	45	3	0	11	68.1	329	77	53	45	11	6	4	4	44	3	75	8	0	6	4	.600	0	1	5.93
2000 El Paso	AA Ari	2	2	0	0	7.2	40	19	13	13	0	0	0	2	3	0	5	0	0	0	2	.000	0	0	15.26
Buffalo	AAA Cle	12	8	0	1	59	264	68	34	29	8	4	3	6	24	1	39	4	0	6	3	.667	0	0	4.42
Akron	AA Cle	10	9	0	0	48.1	229	63	37	32	5	3	5	8	15	0	26	1	0	1	3	.250	0	0	5.96
1997 Chicago	AL	5	2	0	3	12.2	67	19	13	12	4	0	0	1	11	0	8	1	0	0	2	.000	0	0	8.53
7 Min. YEARS		177	125	3	16	738	3288	787	452	392	88	25	28	57	326	8	528	31	2	38	47	.447	1	1	4.78

Ambioris Cleto

Bats: Right **Throws:** Right **Pos:** SS-17; 2B-17; PR-2; DH-1   **Ht:** 5'10" **Wt:** 158 **Born:** 1/5/80 **Age:** 21

Year Team	Lg Org	G	AB	H	2B	3B	HR	TB	R	RBI	TBB	IBB	SO	HBP	SH	SF	SB	CS	SB%	GDP	Avg	OBP	SLG
1997 Pirates	R Pit	35	101	19	4	0	1	26	9	3	15	0	27	5	1	0	1	7	.13	1	.188	.322	.257
Erie	A- Pit	8	22	4	0	0	0	4	2	3	0	0	11	1	1	0	0	3	.00	2	.182	.308	.182
1998 Erie	A- Pit	49	167	32	4	0	0	36	26	10	17	0	49	5	2	0	4	2	.67	4	.192	.286	.216
1999 Hickory	A Pit	24	66	7	1	0	0	8	6	6	17	0	23	0	1	0	0	2	.00	1	.106	.289	.121
2000 Hickory	A Pit	5	12	3	0	0	0	3	4	0	2	0	5	2	1	0	1	1	.50	0	.250	.438	.250
Williamsprt	A Pit	24	78	8	1	0	0	9	4	5	9	0	16	0	0	0	5	0	1.00	3	.103	.195	.115
Lynchburg	A+ Pit	4	6	3	1	1	0	6	2	0	0	0	1	1	0	0	0	0	—	0	.500	.571	1.000
Nashville	AAA Pit	4	14	2	0	0	0	2	0	2	1	0	5	1	0	0	0	0	—	0	.143	.250	.143
4 Min. YEARS		153	466	78	11	1	1	94	51	28	64	0	137	15	6	0	11	15	.42	9	.167	.288	.202

Russ Cleveland

Bats: Right **Throws:** Right **Pos:** C-44; DH-13; PH-1 **Ht:** 6'3" **Wt:** 205 **Born:** 12/26/79 **Age:** 21

Year Team	Lg Org	G	AB	H	2B	3B	HR	TB	R	RBI	TBB	IBB	SO	HBP	SH	SF	SB	CS	SB%	GDP	Avg	OBP	SLG
1998 Tigers	R Det	31	79	17	3	0	0	20	5	4	11	0	27	3	0	0	1	4	.20	1	.215	.333	.253
1999 Tigers	R Det	37	132	41	5	0	0	46	13	13	5	0	33	2	0	3	2	2	.50	4	.311	.338	.348
2000 Jacksnville	AA Det	1	1	0	0	0	0	0	0	0	0	0	1	0	0	0	0	0	—	0	.000	.000	.000
Lakeland	A+ Det	10	33	6	0	0	0	6	4	2	1	0	9	0	1	1	0	1	.00	0	.182	.200	.182
Oneonta	A- Det	46	163	38	5	1	0	45	20	15	19	0	35	1	1	0	2	3	.40	4	.233	.317	.276
3 Min. YEARS		125	408	102	13	1	0	117	42	34	36	0	105	6	2	4	5	10	.33	9	.250	.317	.287

Pat Cline

Bats: Right **Throws:** Right **Pos:** C-42; DH-14; PH-8; OF-1; 1B-1 **Ht:** 6'4" **Wt:** 230 **Born:** 10/9/74 **Age:** 26

Year Team	Lg Org	G	AB	H	2B	3B	HR	TB	R	RBI	TBB	IBB	SO	HBP	SH	SF	SB	CS	SB%	GDP	Avg	OBP	SLG
1993 Huntington	R+ ChC	33	96	18	5	0	2	29	17	13	17	0	28	1	1	3	0	0	—	1	.188	.308	.302
1994 Cubs	R ChC	3	0	0	0	0	0	0	0	0	0	0	0	0	0	0	0	0	—	0	—	—	—
1995 Rockford	A ChC	112	390	106	27	0	13	172	65	77	58	3	93	11	0	5	6	1	.86	6	.272	.377	.441
1996 Daytona	A+ ChC	124	434	121	30	2	17	206	75	76	54	2	79	12	0	2	10	2	.83	6	.279	.373	.475
1997 Iowa	AAA ChC	27	95	21	2	0	3	32	6	10	10	1	24	0	0	1	0	1	.00	4	.221	.292	.337
Orlando	AA ChC	78	271	69	19	0	7	109	39	37	27	1	78	5	0	2	2	2	.50	7	.255	.331	.402
1998 Iowa	AAA ChC	122	424	119	22	2	13	184	52	60	36	4	59	9	1	5	2	3	.40	14	.281	.346	.434
1999 Iowa	AAA ChC	98	290	66	20	1	6	106	27	42	26	0	73	4	0	1	1	2	.33	8	.228	.299	.366
2000 Iowa	AAA ChC	3	3	1	0	0	0	1	0	0	0	0	2	0	0	0	0	0	—	0	.333	.333	.333
Indianapols	AAA Mil	11	37	8	2	0	1	13	3	6	2	0	5	0	0	0	0	0	—	0	.216	.256	.351
Huntsville	AA Mil	19	51	6	4	0	0	10	2	4	6	0	11	2	0	1	0	0	—	1	.118	.233	.196
Dayton	A Cin	32	112	32	9	0	5	56	15	16	23	2	18	3	0	1	0	0	—	5	.286	.417	.500
8 Min. YEARS		662	2203	567	140	5	67	918	301	341	259	13	470	47	2	21	21	11	.66	52	.257	.345	.417

Ken Cloude

Pitches: Right **Bats:** Right **Pos:** SP-14 **Ht:** 6'1" **Wt:** 200 **Born:** 1/9/75 **Age:** 26

Year Team	Lg Org	G	GS	CG	GF	IP	BFP	H	R	ER	HR	SH	SF	HB	TBB	IBB	SO	WP	Bk	W	L	Pct.	ShO	Sv	ERA
1994 Mariners	R Sea	12	7	0	2	52.1	209	36	22	12	1	2	2	6	19	0	61	9	0	3	4	.429	0	0	2.06
1995 Wisconsin	A Sea	25	25	4	0	161	677	137	64	58	8	1	7	8	63	4	140	10	1	9	8	.529	0	0	3.24
1996 Lancaster	A+ Sea	28	28	1	0	168.1	727	167	94	79	15	4	6	8	60	0	161	6	1	15	4	.789	0	0	4.22
1997 Memphis	AA Sea	22	22	3	0	132.2	567	131	62	57	15	1	2	11	48	2	124	7	0	11	7	.611	2	0	3.87
1998 Tacoma	AAA Sea	1	1	0	0	4	16	4	3	3	1	0	0	0	1	0	4	0	0	0	1	.000	0	0	6.75
1999 Tacoma	AAA Sea	6	6	2	0	38.2	149	19	11	10	3	1	1	2	15	0	33	3	0	5	1	.833	0	0	2.33
2000 Tacoma	AAA Sea	14	14	1	0	75.1	345	88	56	43	10	2	1	4	36	0	62	2	2	5	5	.500	0	0	5.14
1997 Seattle	AL	10	9	0	0	51	219	41	32	29	8	1	1	3	26	0	46	2	0	4	2	.667	0	0	5.12
1998 Seattle	AL	30	30	0	0	155.1	722	187	116	110	29	4	4	3	80	4	114	2	1	8	10	.444	0	0	6.37
1999 Seattle	AL	31	6	0	8	72.1	362	106	67	64	10	1	4	5	46	5	35	8	0	4	4	.500	0	1	7.96
7 Min. YEARS		108	103	11	2	632.1	2690	582	312	262	53	11	19	39	242	6	585	37	4	48	30	.615	2	0	3.73
3 Maj. YEARS		71	45	0	8	278.2	1303	334	215	203	47	6	9	11	152	9	195	12	1	16	16	.500	0	1	6.56

Tony Cogan

Pitches: Left **Bats:** Left **Pos:** SP-16; RP-15 **Ht:** 6'2" **Wt:** 195 **Born:** 12/21/76 **Age:** 24

Year Team	Lg Org	G	GS	CG	GF	IP	BFP	H	R	ER	HR	SH	SF	HB	TBB	IBB	SO	WP	Bk	W	L	Pct.	ShO	Sv	ERA
1999 Spokane	A- KC	27	0	0	11	39.2	160	26	10	6	0	6	1	2	14	2	37	3	1	1	3	.250	0	4	1.36
2000 Chston-WV	A KC	13	13	0	0	78.2	303	65	19	16	3	1	1	2	14	0	51	5	1	6	2	.750	0	0	1.83
Wilmington	A+ KC	16	3	0	6	39.1	168	39	22	19	1	1	1	0	18	0	31	3	4	2	4	.333	0	1	4.35
Wichita	AA KC	2	0	0	1	2.1	15	6	4	3	0	1	0	0	2	1	1	0	0	1	1	.500	0	0	11.57
2 Min. YEARS		58	16	0	18	160	646	136	55	44	4	9	3	7	48	3	120	11	6	10	10	.500	0	5	2.48

Brian Cole

Bats: Right **Throws:** Right **Pos:** OF-129; DH-6; PH-2 **Ht:** 5'9" **Wt:** 168 **Born:** 9/28/78 **Age:** 22

Year Team	Lg Org	G	AB	H	2B	3B	HR	TB	R	RBI	TBB	IBB	SO	HBP	SH	SF	SB	CS	SB%	GDP	Avg	OBP	SLG
1998 Kingsport	R+ NYM	56	230	69	13	8	5	113	36	35	7	1	23	0	1	3	15	8	.65	1	.300	.317	.491
Pittsfield	A- NYM	2	8	2	1	0	0	3	0	1	0	0	1	0	0	0	1	0	1.00	0	.250	.250	.375
1999 Capital Cty	A NYM	125	500	158	41	4	18	261	97	71	37	0	77	2	1	5	50	16	.76	8	.316	.362	.522
2000 St. Lucie	A+ NYM	91	375	117	26	5	15	198	73	61	29	3	51	1	0	8	54	11	.83	7	.312	.356	.528
Binghamton	AA NYM	46	176	49	9	2	4	74	31	25	13	0	28	1	3	3	15	4	.79	2	.278	.326	.420
3 Min. YEARS		320	1289	395	90	19	42	649	237	193	86	4	180	4	5	19	135	39	.78	18	.306	.347	.503

Eric Cole

Bats: Right **Throws:** Right **Pos:** OF-128; DH-3; PH-1 **Ht:** 6'0" **Wt:** 185 **Born:** 11/15/75 **Age:** 25

Year Team	Lg Org	G	AB	H	2B	3B	HR	TB	R	RBI	TBB	IBB	SO	HBP	SH	SF	SB	CS	SB%	GDP	Avg	OBP	SLG
1995 Astros	R Hou	39	122	33	3	1	0	38	17	12	7	0	21	2	3	0	7	5	.58	0	.270	.321	.311
1996 Auburn	A- Hou	46	151	26	4	0	1	33	9	10	6	0	46	3	1	4	3	1	.75	7	.172	.213	.219
1997 Auburn	A- Hou	71	222	61	20	3	8	111	29	34	19	1	46	5	2	3	4	4	.50	3	.275	.341	.500
1998 Quad City	A Hou	132	500	140	30	6	11	215	73	83	24	0	104	5	0	1	32	15	.68	7	.280	.319	.430
1999 Kissimmee	A+ Hou	120	460	122	27	5	13	198	62	67	39	3	120	7	1	4	23	13	.64	12	.265	.329	.430
Jackson	AA Hou	15	54	9	1	0	2	16	4	8	1	0	11	0	1	0	0	0	—	3	.167	.182	.296
2000 Round Rock	AA Hou	132	543	158	46	0	22	270	90	94	43	3	98	9	0	6	21	10	.68	12	.291	.349	.497
6 Min. YEARS		555	2052	549	131	15	57	881	284	308	139	7	446	31	7	18	90	48	.65	44	.268	.321	.429

Victor Cole

Pitches: Right **Bats:** Both **Pos:** SP-3; RP-2   **Ht:** 5'10" **Wt:** 160 **Born:** 1/23/68 **Age:** 33

Year Team	Lg Org	G	GS	CG	GF	IP	BFP	H	R	ER	HR	SH	SF	HB	TBB	IBB	SO	WP	Bk	W	L	Pct.	ShO	Sv	ERA
1988 Eugene	A- KC	15	0	0	13	23.2	94	16	6	4	0	0	0	2	8	0	39	3	0	1	0	1.000	0	9	1.52
Baseball Cy	A+ KC	10	5	0	2	35	149	27	9	8	0	1	1	1	21	0	29	2	0	5	0	1.000	0	1	2.06
1989 Memphis	AA KC	13	13	0	0	63.2	303	67	53	45	4	4	1	5	51	1	52	4	1	1	9	.100	0	0	6.36
Baseball Cy	A+ KC	9	9	0	0	42	186	43	23	18	2	1	1	1	22	0	30	2	1	3	1	.750	0	0	3.86
1990 Memphis	AA KC	46	6	0	15	107.2	479	91	61	52	6	4	1	3	70	2	102	2	2	3	8	.273	0	4	4.35
1991 Omaha	AAA KC	6	0	0	1	13	54	9	6	6	1	0	0	0	9	1	12	0	0	1	1	.500	0	0	4.15
Carolina	AA Pit	20	0	0	17	28.1	116	13	8	6	1	0	1	2	19	1	32	3	2	0	2	.000	0	12	1.91
Buffalo	AAA Pit	19	1	0	9	24	115	23	11	10	2	0	1	1	20	0	23	3	0	1	2	.333	0	0	3.75
1992 Buffalo	AAA Pit	19	19	3	0	115.2	498	102	46	40	8	3	3	4	61	0	69	8	0	11	6	.647	1	0	3.11
1993 Buffalo	AAA Pit	6	6	0	0	26.1	134	35	25	25	5	2	1	0	24	0	14	1	0	1	3	.250	0	0	8.54
Carolina	AA Pit	27	0	0	13	41	189	39	30	27	5	1	0	2	31	2	35	6	0	0	4	.000	0	8	5.93
New Orleans	AAA Mil	6	1	0	0	6	34	9	7	7	0	0	1	1	7	0	5	0	0	0	2	.000	0	0	10.50
1994 El Paso	AA Mil	8	0	0	2	8	50	18	17	16	0	0	0	1	9	1	3	0	1	0	1	.000	0	0	18.00
Memphis	AA KC	6	6	0	0	35.2	162	32	22	19	3	4	0	0	23	0	22	2	0	2	1	.667	0	0	4.79
1995 Las Vegas	AAA SD	4	4	0	0	19.2	86	19	17	14	4	1	1	0	10	0	12	1	1	0	2	.000	0	0	6.41
Salinas	IND —	4	4	0	0	22.2	104	25	16	9	0	2	2	0	13	0	22	2	0	1	1	.500	0	0	3.57
Memphis	AA SD	8	2	0	3	20	81	15	5	3	0	0	0	0	8	1	17	0	0	1	0	1.000	0	0	1.35
1996 Pine Bluff	IND —	8	0	0	2	23.1	89	16	2	2	0	1	0	2	4	0	27	2	0	3	0	1.000	0	0	0.77
Memphis	AA SD	8	1	0	4	15	65	11	3	2	0	0	0	1	8	0	13	0	0	1	0	1.000	0	1	1.20
1998 West Tenn	AA ChC	19	0	0	2	30	127	26	12	8	1	1	1	1	11	1	31	2	0	2	2	.500	0	0	2.40
Iowa	AAA ChC	38	2	0	6	67.1	296	77	35	28	4	3	1	1	25	0	69	7	1	2	2	.500	0	0	3.74
1999 Iowa	AAA ChC	19	2	0	2	40.1	188	41	24	21	3	0	0	3	23	1	33	5	2	2	1	.667	0	0	4.69
West Tenn	AA ChC	17	0	0	8	23	103	21	11	10	0	2	0	1	18	0	17	2	0	3	1	.750	0	0	3.91
2000 Memphis	AAA StL	5	3	0	1	18.2	74	13	6	6	0	0	0	0	8	1	16	0	0	1	0	1.000	0	0	2.89
1992 Pittsburgh	NL	8	4	0	2	23	104	23	14	14	1	1	1	0	14	0	12	1	0	0	2	.000	0	0	5.48
12 Min. YEARS		340	84	3	100	850	3776	788	455	386	55	26	21	32	503	12	724	57	12	45	49	.479	1	35	4.09

Michael Coleman

Bats: Right **Throws:** Right **Pos:** OF-18   **Ht:** 5'11" **Wt:** 215 **Born:** 8/16/75 **Age:** 25

				BATTING												BASERUNNING				PERCENTAGES		
Year Team	Lg Org	G	AB	H	2B	3B	HR	TB	R	RBI	TBB	IBB	SO	HBP	SH	SF	SB	CS	SB%	GDP	Avg	OBP	SLG
1994 Red Sox	R Bos	25	95	26	6	1	3	43	15	15	10	0	20	3	0	1	5	3	.63	3	.274	.358	.453
Utica	A- Bos	23	65	11	2	0	1	16	16	3	14	0	21	0	3	0	11	1	.92	0	.169	.316	.246
1995 Michigan	A Bos	112	422	113	16	4	11	166	70	61	40	1	93	6	6	3	29	5	.85	7	.268	.338	.393
1996 Sarasota	A+ Bos	110	407	100	20	5	1	133	54	36	38	1	86	8	7	3	24	5	.83	10	.246	.320	.327
1997 Trenton	AA Bos	102	385	116	17	8	14	191	56	58	41	1	89	5	9	4	20	7	.74	5	.301	.372	.496
Pawtucket	AAA Bos	28	113	36	9	2	7	70	27	19	12	0	27	2	0	1	4	2	.67	2	.319	.391	.619
1998 Pawtucket	AAA Bos	93	340	86	13	0	14	141	47	37	27	0	92	8	3	1	12	9	.57	4	.253	.322	.415
1999 Pawtucket	AAA Bos	115	467	125	29	2	30	248	95	74	51	1	128	3	4	4	14	6	.70	7	.268	.341	.531
2000 Pawtucket	AAA Bos	18	66	17	5	1	6	42	11	15	3	0	23	0	0	1	3	0	1.00	0	.258	.286	.636
1997 Boston	AL	8	24	4	1	0	0	5	2	2	0	0	11	0	1	0	1	0	1.00	0	.167	.167	.208
1999 Boston	AL	2	5	1	0	0	0	1	1	0	1	0	0	0	0	0	0	0	—	0	.200	.333	.200
7 Min. YEARS		626	2360	630	117	21	87	1050	391	318	236	4	579	35	32	18	122	38	.76	38	.267	.340	.445
2 Mai. YEARS		10	29	5	1	0	0	6	3	2	1	0	11	0	1	0	1	0	1.00	0	.172	.200	.207

Javier Colina

Bats: Right **Throws:** Right **Pos:** 3B-121; PH-6; 2B-4; DH-3   **Ht:** 6'1" **Wt:** 180 **Born:** 2/15/79 **Age:** 22

				BATTING												BASERUNNING				PERCENTAGES		
Year Team	Lg Org	G	AB	H	2B	3B	HR	TB	R	RBI	TBB	IBB	SO	HBP	SH	SF	SB	CS	SB%	GDP	Avg	OBP	SLG
1998 Rockies	R Col	44	169	54	6	2	6	82	28	39	18	0	30	3	1	4	9	4	.69	5	.320	.387	.485
1999 Asheville	A Col	124	516	156	37	3	6	217	70	81	26	0	101	6	2	6	12	11	.52	12	.302	.339	.421
2000 Carolina	AA Col	130	429	93	12	1	2	113	34	35	44	2	81	3	10	4	5	2	.71	8	.217	.292	.263
3 Min. YEARS		298	1114	303	55	6	14	412	132	155	88	2	212	12	13	14	26	17	.60	25	.272	.328	.370

Jesus Colome

Pitches: Right **Bats:** Right **Pos:** SP-23   **Ht:** 6'2" **Wt:** 170 **Born:** 6/2/80 **Age:** 21

			HOW MUCH HE PITCHED						WHAT HE GAVE UP								THE RESULTS					
Year Team	Lg Org	G	GS	CG	GF	IP	BFP	H	R	ER	HR	SH	SF	HB	TBB	IBB	SO	WP	Bk	W	L	Pct.	ShO	Sv	ERA
1998 Athletics	R Oak	12	11	0	0	56.2	229	47	27	20	1	0	6	2	16	0	62	5	3	2	5	.286	0	0	3.18
1999 Modesto	A+ Oak	31	22	0	2	128.2	564	125	63	48	6	1	6	9	60	2	127	13	2	8	4	.667	0	1	3.36
2000 Midland	AA Oak	20	20	0	0	110.1	478	99	62	44	10	4	4	5	50	0	95	6	1	9	4	.692	0	0	3.59
Orlando	AA TB	3	3	0	0	14.2	72	18	12	11	2	1	0	2	7	0	9	0	0	1	2	.333	0	0	6.75
3 Min. YEARS		66	56	0	2	310.1	1343	289	164	123	19	6	11	22	133	2	293	24	6	20	15	.571	0	1	3.57

Scott Comer

Pitches: Left **Bats:** Left **Pos:** SP-28   **Ht:** 6'5" **Wt:** 205 **Born:** 6/23/77 **Age:** 24

			HOW MUCH HE PITCHED						WHAT HE GAVE UP								THE RESULTS					
Year Team	Lg Org	G	GS	CG	GF	IP	BFP	H	R	ER	HR	SH	SF	HB	TBB	IBB	SO	WP	Bk	W	L	Pct.	ShO	Sv	ERA
1996 Mets	R NYM	13	8	0	3	50	200	40	16	12	1	1	1	1	3	0	40	1	3	2	2	.500	0	0	2.16
1997 Pittsfield	A- NYM	14	14	1	0	93.1	359	71	25	18	4	1	1	1	12	0	98	0	0	7	1	.875	0	0	1.74
1998 Kane County	A Fla	15	14	2	1	97.1	395	91	42	31	13	1	2	4	9	0	85	0	0	6	4	.600	0	0	2.87
1999 Brevard Cty	A+ Fla	19	19	3	0	130	502	120	38	34	3	3	4	3	5	0	85	0	1	9	4	.692	1	0	2.35
2000 Portland	AA Fla	25	25	1	0	130.1	598	180	113	93	28	3	5	2	32	1	60	2	0	4	10	.286	1	0	6.42
Brevard Cty	A+ Fla	3	3	0	0	16	73	24	13	9	2	1	1	1	1	0	14	0	0	0	1	.000	0	0	5.06
5 Min. YEARS		89	83	9	4	517	2127	526	247	197	51	10	13	12	62	1	382	3	4	28	22	.560	2	0	3.43

Clay Condrey

Pitches: Right **Bats:** Right **Pos:** RP-53   **Ht:** 6'3" **Wt:** 195 **Born:** 11/19/75 **Age:** 25

		HOW MUCH HE PITCHED					WHAT HE GAVE UP										THE RESULTS				
Year Team	Lg Org	G	GS	CG	GF	IP	BFP	H	R	ER	HR	SH	SF	HB	TBB	IBB	SO	WP	Bk	W	L	Pct.	ShO	Sv	ERA
1998 Padres	R SD	5	0	0	4	5.1	26	6	4	2	0	0	0	0	5	1	4	1	1	0	1	.000	0	0	3.38
Idaho Falls	R+ SD	18	0	0	17	24.2	111	31	12	7	2	1	1	1	4	0	19	3	0	2	1	.667	0	5	2.55
1999 Fort Wayne	A SD	42	0	0	39	47.2	202	40	24	20	5	0	2	0	19	4	47	4	1	2	3	.400	0	20	3.78
Rancho Cuca	A+ SD	6	0	0	1	7.1	29	4	3	3	1	0	0	0	3	0	9	0	0	0	0	—	0	0	3.68
2000 Rancho Cuca	A+ SD	18	0	0	9	20.2	85	18	9	8	1	1	0	2	7	0	21	2	1	1	1	.500	0	4	3.48
Mobile	AA SD	35	0	0	19	43.2	195	41	27	26	4	3	2	5	20	0	25	1	0	2	2	.500	0	6	5.36
3 Min. YEARS		124	0	0	89	149.1	648	140	79	66	13	5	5	8	58	5	125	11	3	7	8	.467	0	35	3.98

Kevin Connacher

Bats: Right **Throws:** Right **Pos:** 2B-94; DH-7; PH-3   **Ht:** 5'9" **Wt:** 175 **Born:** 4/6/75 **Age:** 26

		BATTING														BASERUNNING				PERCENTAGES		
Year Team	Lg Org	G	AB	H	2B	3B	HR	TB	R	RBI	TBB	IBB	SO	HBP	SH	SF	SB	CS	SB%	GDP	Avg	OBP	SLG
1997 Winston-Sal	A+ CWS	70	243	70	16	2	3	99	32	27	28	0	50	2	2	3	12	8	.60	2	.288	.362	.407
1998 Winston-Sal	A+ CWS	80	212	51	9	3	7	87	45	23	34	1	63	3	9	1	15	5	.75	1	.241	.352	.410
1999 Winston-Sal	A+ CWS	121	413	107	14	5	10	161	60	48	63	0	101	1	6	0	27	13	.68	7	.259	.358	.390
Birmingham	AA CWS	7	18	4	0	0	0	4	1	0	2	0	5	0	0	0	1	0	1.00	0	.222	.300	.222
2000 Birmingham	AA CWS	4	15	3	0	0	0	3	3	2	0	0	6	1	0	0	1	0	1.00	1	.200	.250	.200
Winston-Sal	A+ CWS	97	360	103	24	3	10	163	70	43	59	2	100	5	2	2	24	8	.75	4	.286	.392	.453
4 Min. YEARS		379	1261	338	63	13	30	517	211	143	186	3	325	12	19	6	80	34	.70	15	.268	.366	.410

Steve Connelly

Pitches: Right **Bats:** Right **Pos:** RP-43   **Ht:** 6'4" **Wt:** 210 **Born:** 4/27/74 **Age:** 27

		HOW MUCH HE PITCHED						WHAT HE GAVE UP										THE RESULTS				
Year Team	Lg Org	G	GS	CG	GF	IP	BFP	H	R	ER	HR	SH	SF	HB	TBB	IBB	SO	WP	Bk	W	L	Pct.	ShO	Sv	ERA
1995 Sou Oregon	A- Oak	17	0	0	10	28.1	133	29	17	12	1	3	2	4	14	4	19	6	0	2	4	.333	0	2	3.81
1996 Modesto	A+ Oak	52	0	0	42	64.2	283	58	33	27	5	1	1	5	32	1	65	5	2	4	7	.364	0	14	3.76
1997 Huntsville	AA Oak	43	0	0	22	69.2	297	74	33	29	3	2	1	4	20	2	49	5	0	3	3	.500	0	7	3.75
1998 Edmonton	AAA Oak	55	0	0	27	76	310	64	34	32	7	1	2	2	24	2	62	5	0	6	0	1.000	0	13	3.79
1999 Fresno	AAA SF	54	0	0	20	72	338	93	58	42	8	2	2	5	32	3	47	14	1	6	4	.600	0	2	5.25
2000 Fresno	AAA SF	43	0	0	36	59.2	254	63	33	29	9	3	1	2	20	0	44	1	0	8	6	.571	0	9	4.37
1998 Oakland	AL	3	0	0	1	4.2	28	10	1	1	0	0	1	0	4	0	1	0	0	0	0	—	0	0	1.93
6 Min. YEARS		264	0	0	157	370.1	1615	381	208	171	33	12	9	22	142	12	286	36	3	29	24	.547	0	47	4.16

Greg Connors

Bats: Right **Throws:** Right **Pos:** 1B-112; C-10; PR-3; OF-1; PH-1   **Ht:** 6'2" **Wt:** 185 **Born:** 8/22/74 **Age:** 26

		BATTING														BASERUNNING				PERCENTAGES		
Year Team	Lg Org	G	AB	H	2B	3B	HR	TB	R	RBI	TBB	IBB	SO	HBP	SH	SF	SB	CS	SB%	GDP	Avg	OBP	SLG
1997 Everett	A- Sea	54	230	67	18	1	6	105	41	43	16	0	44	3	0	4	6	2	.75	3	.291	.340	.457
Lancaster	A+ Sea	10	37	9	2	0	1	14	5	5	4	0	10	0	0	0	0	1	.00	1	.243	.317	.378
1998 Lancaster	A+ Sea	27	101	29	11	1	6	60	17	26	3	0	16	2	0	1	0	0	—	1	.287	.318	.594
Wisconsin	A Sea	94	364	103	31	3	12	176	45	57	22	0	95	1	0	5	8	8	.50	5	.283	.321	.484
1999 Lancaster	A+ Sea	117	448	120	20	7	16	202	72	84	40	2	91	6	1	5	10	7	.59	3	.268	.333	.451
2000 New Haven	AA Sea	123	452	126	29	3	9	188	64	58	47	2	83	7	2	5	0	1	.00	7	.279	.352	.416
4 Min. YEARS		425	1632	454	111	15	50	745	244	273	132	2	339	19	3	20	24	19	.56	19	.278	.336	.456

Patrick Coogan

Pitches: Right **Bats:** Right **Pos:** SP-26; RP-1   **Ht:** 6'3" **Wt:** 195 **Born:** 9/12/75 **Age:** 25

		HOW MUCH HE PITCHED						WHAT HE GAVE UP										THE RESULTS				
Year Team	Lg Org	G	GS	CG	GF	IP	BFP	H	R	ER	HR	SH	SF	HB	TBB	IBB	SO	WP	Bk	W	L	Pct.	ShO	Sv	ERA
1997 New Jersey	A- StL	10	10	0	0	56	231	56	27	23	4	1	0	3	14	0	37	0	2	2	5	.286	0	0	3.70
1998 Pr William	A+ StL	14	14	0	0	74.1	340	94	55	46	7	3	4	4	25	0	57	5	2	4	5	.444	0	0	5.57
1999 Potomac	A+ StL	19	19	2	0	101	457	112	73	65	14	4	5	7	43	0	67	5	0	4	7	.364	0	0	5.79
2000 Arkansas	AA StL	27	26	1	1	150	661	164	96	85	21	6	6	9	62	0	79	7	1	9	13	.409	0	0	5.10
4 Min. YEARS		70	69	3	1	381.1	1689	426	251	219	46	14	15	23	144	0	240	17	5	19	30	.388	0	0	5.17

Derrick Cook

Pitches: Right **Bats:** Right **Pos:** SP-20; RP-1   **Ht:** 6'2" **Wt:** 195 **Born:** 8/6/75 **Age:** 25

		HOW MUCH HE PITCHED						WHAT HE GAVE UP										THE RESULTS				
Year Team	Lg Org	G	GS	CG	GF	IP	BFP	H	R	ER	HR	SH	SF	HB	TBB	IBB	SO	WP	Bk	W	L	Pct.	ShO	Sv	ERA
1996 Rangers	R Tex	6	5	1	0	23	100	25	14	12	1	0	1	2	11	0	13	1	0	2	1	.667	0	0	4.70
1997 Pulaski	R+ Tex	6	6	0	0	33.2	141	32	15	14	1	0	1	2	12	0	32	4	0	2	2	.500	0	0	3.74
Charlotte	A+ Tex	8	8	2	0	58.2	243	54	21	15	5	0	1	2	15	0	35	4	0	5	2	.714	0	0	2.30
1998 Charlotte	A+ Tex	26	26	1	0	167.1	710	170	81	68	13	8	2	5	64	1	111	13	1	13	7	.650	1	0	3.66
1999 Tulsa	AA Tex	21	21	2	0	114.1	524	137	81	72	12	3	6	4	45	3	71	17	0	7	6	.538	0	0	5.67
2000 Tulsa	AA Tex	21	20	0	0	113.2	498	111	71	58	12	0	3	8	54	1	72	8	0	5	8	.385	0	0	4.59
5 Min. YEARS		88	86	6	0	510.2	2216	529	283	239	44	11	14	23	201	5	334	47	1	34	26	.567	2	0	4.21

Brent Cookson

Bats: Right **Throws:** Right **Pos:** OF-31; PH-3; DH-2   **Ht:** 6'1" **Wt:** 200 **Born:** 9/7/69 **Age:** 31

		BATTING														BASERUNNING				PERCENTAGES		
Year Team	Lg Org	G	AB	H	2B	3B	HR	TB	R	RBI	TBB	IBB	SO	HBP	SH	SF	SB	CS	SB%	GDP	Avg	OBP	SLG
1991 Sou Oregon	A- Oak	6	9	0	0	0	0	0	0	0	0	0	7	0	0	0	0	0	—	1	.000	.000	.000
Athletics	R Oak	1	1	0	0	0	0	0	0	0	0	0	1	0	0	0	0	0	—	0	.000	.000	.000

Year Team	Lg Org	BATTING G	AB	H	2B	3B	HR	TB	R	RBI	TBB	IBB	SO	HBP	SH	SF	BASERUNNING SB	CS	SB%	GDP	PERCENTAGES Avg	OBP	SLG
1992 Clinton	A SF	46	145	31	5	1	8	62	30	20	22	0	48	3	1	1	9	3	.75	4	.214	.327	.428
San Jose	A+ SF	68	255	74	8	4	12	126	44	49	25	0	69	3	0	2	9	5	.64	8	.290	.358	.494
1993 San Jose	A+ SF	67	234	60	10	1	17	123	43	50	43	1	73	3	2	5	14	6	.70	5	.256	.372	.526
1994 Shreveport	AA SF	62	207	67	21	3	11	127	32	41	18	2	57	1	2	2	4	1	.80	4	.324	.377	.614
Phoenix	AAA SF	14	43	12	0	1	1	17	7	6	5	0	14	1	0	0	1	0	—	1	.279	.367	.395
1995 Phoenix	AAA SF	68	210	63	9	3	15	123	38	46	25	2	36	1	1	2	3	3	.50	0	.300	.374	.586
Omaha	AAA KC	40	137	55	13	0	4	80	28	20	17	0	24	4	0	2	0	0	—	3	.401	.475	.584
1996 Pawtucket	AAA Bos	73	255	69	13	1	19	141	51	50	24	1	72	5	0	2	2	4	.33	9	.271	.343	.553
Rochester	AAA Bal	30	113	30	7	0	6	55	22	21	9	0	20	2	0	1	2	1	.67	5	.265	.328	.487
1998 Tucson	AAA Ari	36	100	36	12	0	6	66	24	19	18	0	26	2	0	1	0	0	—	1	.360	.463	.660
1999 Albuquerque	AAA LA	85	277	89	18	1	28	193	57	70	38	2	56	2	1	4	7	1	.88	5	.321	.402	.697
2000 Albuquerque	AAA LA	34	115	36	5	0	11	74	30	38	22	2	22	0	0	1	4	2	.67	4	.313	.420	.643
1995 Kansas City	AL	22	35	5	1	0	0	6	2	5	2	0	7	0	1	0	1	0	1.00	0	.143	.189	.171
1999 Los Angeles	NL	3	5	1	0	0	0	1	0	0	0	0	1	0	0	0	0	0	—	0	.200	.200	.200
9 Min. YEARS		630	2101	622	121	15	138	1187	406	430	266	10	525	27	7	23	54	27	.67	54	.296	.379	.565
2 Maj. YEARS		25	40	6	1	0	0	7	2	5	2	0	8	0	1	0	1	0	1.00	0	.150	.190	.175

Mike Coolbaugh

Bats: Right **Throws:** Right **Pos:** SS-54; 2B-28; OF-23; 3B-13; 1B-6; PH-2; DH-1; PR-1 **Ht:** 6'1" **Wt:** 185 **Born:** 6/5/72 **Age:** 29

Year Team	Lg Org	BATTING G	AB	H	2B	3B	HR	TB	R	RBI	TBB	IBB	SO	HBP	SH	SF	BASERUNNING SB	CS	SB%	GDP	PERCENTAGES Avg	OBP	SLG
1990 Medcine Hat	R+ Tor	58	211	40	9	0	2	55	21	16	13	0	47	1	1	2	3	2	.60	8	.190	.238	.261
1991 St.Cathrnes	A- Tor	71	255	58	13	2	3	84	28	26	17	0	40	3	4	4	4	5	.44	1	.227	.280	.329
1992 St.Cathrnes	A- Tor	15	49	14	1	1	0	17	3	2	3	0	12	0	2	0	0	2	.00	1	.286	.327	.347
1993 Hagerstown	A Tor	112	389	94	23	1	16	167	58	62	32	5	94	3	4	4	4	3	.57	9	.242	.301	.429
1994 Dunedin	A+ Tor	122	456	120	33	3	16	207	53	66	28	3	94	7	3	4	3	4	.43	14	.263	.313	.454
1995 Knoxville	AA Tor	142	500	120	32	2	9	183	71	56	37	3	110	11	4	3	7	11	.39	13	.240	.305	.366
1996 Charlotte	A+ Tex	124	449	129	33	4	15	215	76	75	42	4	80	8	0	3	8	10	.44	10	.287	.357	.479
Tulsa	AA Tex	7	23	8	3	0	2	17	6	9	2	0	3	2	0	0	1	0	1.00	0	.348	.444	.739
1997 Huntsville	AA Oak	139	559	172	37	2	30	303	100	132	52	3	105	7	2	8	8	3	.73	17	.308	.369	.542
1998 Colo Sprngs	AAA Col	108	386	107	35	2	16	194	62	75	32	0	93	1	2	4	0	3	.00	13	.277	.331	.503
1999 Columbus	AAA NYY	114	391	108	31	2	15	188	65	66	38	0	112	2	2	4	5	7	.42	5	.276	.340	.481
2000 Columbus	AAA NYY	117	387	105	28	0	23	202	63	61	67	2	96	3	3	3	6	3	.67	5	.271	.380	.522
11 Min. YEARS		1129	4055	1075	278	19	147	1832	606	646	363	20	886	48	27	39	49	53	.48	96	.265	.330	.452

Archie Corbin

Pitches: Right **Bats:** Right **Pos:** RP-40 **Ht:** 6'4" **Wt:** 230 **Born:** 12/30/67 **Age:** 33

Year Team	Lg Org	HOW MUCH HE PITCHED G	GS	CG	GF	IP	BFP	WHAT HE GAVE UP H	R	ER	HR	SH	SF	HB	TBB	IBB	SO	WP	Bk	THE RESULTS W	L	Pct.	ShO	Sv	ERA
1986 Kingsport	R+ NYM	18	1	0	9	30.1	149	31	23	16	3	0	1	0	28	0	30	8	1	1	1	.500	0	0	4.75
1987 Kingsport	R+ NYM	6	6	0	0	25.2	128	24	21	18	3	0	0	2	26	0	17	6	0	2	3	.400	0	0	6.31
1988 Kingsport	R+ NYM	11	10	4	0	69.1	277	47	23	12	5	2	0	3	17	0	47	1	1	7	2	.778	1	0	1.56
1989 Columbia	A NYM	27	23	4	3	153.2	664	149	86	77	16	4	4	5	72	0	130	2	0	9	9	.500	2	1	4.51
1990 St. Lucie	A+ NYM	20	18	3	2	118	494	97	47	39	2	4	3	7	59	0	105	10	0	7	8	.467	0	0	2.97
1991 Memphis	AA KC	28	25	1	0	156.1	692	139	90	81	7	4	6	8	90	1	166	13	0	8	8	.500	0	0	4.66
1992 Memphis	AA KC	27	20	2	1	112.1	503	115	64	59	7	3	1	1	73	0	100	11	0	7	8	.467	0	0	4.73
Harrisburg	AA Mon	1	1	0	0	3	11	2	0	0	0	0	0	0	1	0	3	0	0	0	0	—	0	0	0.00
1993 Harrisburg	AA Mon	42	2	0	21	73.1	314	43	31	30	0	1	5	2	59	1	91	5	1	5	3	.625	0	3	3.68
1994 Buffalo	AAA Pit	14	1	0	3	22.2	99	44	13	12	0	1	1	1	18	0	23	2	0	0	0	—	0	0	4.76
1995 Calgary	AAA Pit	47	1	0	13	61	309	76	63	58	6	0	5	3	55	0	54	7	0	1	5	.167	0	0	8.56
1996 Rochester	AAA Bal	20	5	0	10	43.2	197	44	25	23	5	1	1	1	25	0	47	4	0	0	2	.000	0	1	4.74
1997 Rochester	AAA Bal	43	1	0	22	69.2	314	47	32	31	5	2	3	1	62	0	66	10	0	4	3	.571	0	5	4.00
1998 Las Vegas	AAA SD	6	0	0	1	4.1	36	7	16	13	0	1	0	3	13	0	3	3	0	0	0	—	0	0	27.00
Charlotte	AAA Fla	34	0	0	12	48.2	212	55	15	14	2	1	2	0	46	1	55	7	0	2	2	.500	0	3	2.59
1999 Calgary	AAA Fla	12	0	0	7	13.1	61	13	11	10	3	0	1	0	10	0	16	3	0	0	1	.000	0	0	6.75
2000 Omaha	AAA KC	32	0	0	15	43.1	221	56	44	39	5	3	2	3	40	1	29	9	0	1	5	.167	0	6	8.10
Charlotte	AAA CWS	8	0	0	1	10.2	50	13	8	5	1	2	0	0	6	0	11	1	0	2	0	1.000	0	0	4.22
1991 Kansas City	AL	2	0	0	2	2.1	12	3	1	1	0	0	0	0	2	0	1	0	1	0	0	—	0	0	3.86
1996 Baltimore	AL	18	0	0	5	27.1	123	22	7	7	2	0	1	1	22	0	22	0	2	0	0	1.000	0	0	2.30
1999 Florida	NL	17	0	0	4	21	104	25	20	17	2	1	1	1	15	0	30	0	1	0	2	.000	0	0	7.29
15 Min. YEARS		396	114	14	121	1059.1	4731	942	612	537	70	27	36	40	700	4	993	102	3	56	60	.483	3	21	4.56
3 Maj. YEARS		37	0	0	11	50.2	239	50	28	25	4	1	2	2	39	0	51	0	4	2	1	.667	0	0	4.44

Bryan Corey

Pitches: Right **Bats:** Right **Pos:** RP-41; SP-6 **Ht:** 6'0" **Wt:** 170 **Born:** 10/21/73 **Age:** 27

Year Team	Lg Org	HOW MUCH HE PITCHED G	GS	CG	GF	IP	BFP	WHAT HE GAVE UP H	R	ER	HR	SH	SF	HB	TBB	IBB	SO	WP	Bk	THE RESULTS W	L	Pct.	ShO	Sv	ERA
1995 Jamestown	A- Det	29	0	0	28	28	116	21	14	12	2	0	1	1	12	1	41	4	0	2	2	.500	0	10	3.86
1996 Fayetteville	A Det	60	0	0	53	82	315	50	19	11	2	4	6	2	17	3	101	6	2	6	4	.600	0	34	1.21
1997 Jacksnville	AA Det	52	0	0	36	68	298	74	42	36	8	5	3	1	21	3	37	4	0	3	8	.273	0	9	4.76
1998 Tucson	AAA Ari	39	10	0	14	87.2	401	116	61	53	14	1	2	6	24	0	50	2	2	4	6	.400	0	2	5.44
1999 Toledo	AAA Det	48	0	0	17	69.1	303	63	27	22	6	4	1	2	34	4	36	2	1	5	2	.714	0	2	2.86
2000 Sacramento	AAA Oak	47	6	0	16	85	362	88	43	40	11	4	3	3	29	2	55	2	1	8	3	.727	0	2	4.24
1998 Arizona	NL	3	0	0	2	4	20	6	4	4	1	1	0	1	2	0	1	0	0	0	0	—	0	0	9.00
6 Min. YEARS		275	16	0	164	420	1795	412	206	174	43	18	16	15	137	13	320	20	6	28	25	.528	0	61	3.73

Mark Corey

Pitches: Right **Bats:** Right **Pos:** RP-21; SP-13 · **Ht:** 6'2" **Wt:** 220 **Born:** 11/16/74 **Age:** 26

Year Team	Lg Org	G	GS	CG	GF	IP	BFP	H	R	ER	HR	SH	SF	HB	TBB	IBB	SO	WP	Bk	W	L	Pct.	ShO	Sv	ERA
1995 Princeton	R+ Cin	4	3	0	0	14.2	61	12	7	6	1	0	0	0	6	0	8	0	0	1	1	.500	0	0	3.68
1997 Chston-WV	A Cin	26	26	1	0	136	602	169	87	69	7	8	5	4	42	3	97	14	0	8	13	.381	0	0	4.57
1998 Burlington	A Cin	20	20	6	0	140	577	125	55	38	9	3	3	6	36	0	109	10	1	12	6	.667	2	0	2.44
Indianapolis	AAA Cin	1	1	1	0	6	24	4	3	3	1	1	0	0	3	0	2	0	0	0	1	.000	0	0	4.50
Chattanooga	AA Cin	6	6	0	0	26.1	127	32	25	24	6	1	2	2	16	1	6	0	0	0	4	.000	0	0	8.20
1999 Binghamton	AA NYM	29	27	0	0	155	698	175	108	93	18	4	1	9	64	0	111	1	1	7	13	.350	0	0	5.40
2000 Binghamton	AA NYM	14	2	0	2	25.2	101	15	5	3	0	1	1	0	11	0	19	2	0	0	0	—	0	0	1.05
Norfolk	AAA NYM	20	11	0	2	63.2	303	80	52	48	11	2	3	8	29	1	43	4	0	3	7	.300	0	0	6.79
5 Min. YEARS		120	96	8	4	567.1	2493	612	342	284	53	20	15	29	207	5	395	31	2	31	45	.408	2	1	4.51

Michael Corey

Pitches: Right **Bats:** Right **Pos:** RP-52 · **Ht:** 6'2" **Wt:** 215 **Born:** 9/29/74 **Age:** 26

Year Team	Lg Org	G	GS	CG	GF	IP	BFP	H	R	ER	HR	SH	SF	HB	TBB	IBB	SO	WP	Bk	W	L	Pct.	ShO	Sv	ERA
1998 Eugene	A- Atl	20	0	0	13	32	133	28	8	6	1	2	2	2	9	2	27	2	0	1	0	1.000	0	7	1.69
Danville	A+ Atl	2	0	0	2	3	11	3	0	0	0	0	0	0	0	0	2	0	0	1	0	1.000	0	0	0.00
1999 Macon	A Atl	21	0	0	17	33.2	126	18	4	2	2	1	0	1	7	0	39	6	0	1	1	.500	0	7	0.53
Myrtle Bch	A+ Atl	22	0	0	17	32	139	32	19	17	4	3	0	0	11	0	31	1	0	2	1	.667	0	4	4.78
2000 Greenville	AA Atl	52	0	0	20	66	294	67	35	33	6	4	3	2	29	3	66	1	1	7	6	.538	0	2	4.50
3 Min. YEARS		117	0	0	69	166.2	703	148	66	58	13	10	5	5	56	5	165	10	1	12	8	.600	0	22	3.13

Nate Cornejo

Pitches: Right **Bats:** Right **Pos:** SP-28 · **Ht:** 6'5" **Wt:** 200 **Born:** 9/24/79 **Age:** 21

Year Team	Lg Org	G	GS	CG	GF	IP	BFP	H	R	ER	HR	SH	SF	HB	TBB	IBB	SO	WP	Bk	W	L	Pct.	ShO	Sv	ERA
1998 Tigers	R Det	5	0	0	2	14.1	58	12	2	2	0	0	0	1	2	0	9	1	0	1	0	1.000	0	1	1.26
1999 W Michigan	A Det	28	28	4	0	174.2	750	173	87	72	4	10	9	12	67	0	125	11	5	9	11	.450	1	0	3.71
2000 Lakeland	A+ Det	12	12	1	0	77	322	67	37	26	5	0	1	4	31	0	60	2	1	5	5	.500	0	0	3.04
Jacksnville	AA Det	16	16	0	0	91.2	389	91	52	47	6	3	3	4	43	1	60	1	1	5	7	.417	0	0	4.61
3 Min. YEARS		61	56	5	2	357.2	1519	343	178	147	15	13	13	21	143	1	254	15	7	20	23	.465	1	1	3.70

Brad Cornett

Pitches: Right **Bats:** Right **Pos:** SP-16; RP-8 · **Ht:** 6'3" **Wt:** 188 **Born:** 2/4/69 **Age:** 32

Year Team	Lg Org	G	GS	CG	GF	IP	BFP	H	R	ER	HR	SH	SF	HB	TBB	IBB	SO	WP	Bk	W	L	Pct.	ShO	Sv	ERA
1992 St.Cathrnes	A- Tor	25	0	0	13	60	241	54	30	24	6	1	0	3	10	0	64	5	0	4	1	.800	0	1	3.60
1993 Hagerstown	A Tor	31	21	3	7	172.1	711	164	77	46	6	5	5	5	31	2	161	6	1	10	8	.556	1	3	2.40
1994 Knoxville	AA Tor	7	7	1	0	37.1	151	34	18	10	2	1	0	1	6	0	26	3	0	2	3	.400	0	0	2.41
Syracuse	AAA Tor	3	3	0	0	19	85	18	8	3	0	0	1	0	9	1	12	0	0	1	2	.333	0	0	1.42
1995 Syracuse	AAA Tor	3	3	0	0	11	49	13	6	6	1	0	1	0	4	0	3	0	0	0	1	.000	0	0	4.91
1996 Dunedin	A+ Tor	4	0	0	2	7.1	41	15	7	7	1	0	0	1	3	0	5	1	1	0	1	.000	0	0	8.59
1998 Tucson	AAA Ari	6	6	0	0	26.1	127	44	35	23	6	1	2	0	6	0	12	1	0	1	2	.333	0	0	7.86
El Paso	AA Mil	3	3	0	0	15.2	75	22	16	9	4	1	0	0	5	0	10	3	0	1	2	.000	0	0	5.17
Louisville	AAA Mil	12	8	0	0	61.2	256	64	30	25	9	4	1	2	14	0	34	1	0	3	3	.500	0	0	3.65
1999 Lehigh Val	IND —	23	23	3	0	162.1	679	172	84	71	17	2	4	3	37	1	118	0	0	11	9	.550	0	0	3.94
2000 Lehigh Val	IND —	5	4	0	0	26.1	122	33	15	14	0	0	0	0	10	0	20	2	0	2	1	.667	0	0	4.78
Durham	AAA TB	19	12	0	3	88.2	383	100	46	42	7	1	2	2	24	1	72	1	1	4	5	.444	0	0	4.26
1994 Toronto	AL	9	4	0	0	31	141	40	25	23	1	4	2	3	11	2	22	2	0	1	3	.250	0	0	6.68
1995 Toronto	AL	5	0	0	2	5	25	9	6	5	1	0	0	1	3	0	4	1	0	0	0	—	0	0	9.00
8 Min. YEARS		141	90	7	25	688	2920	733	362	280	59	16	16	17	159	5	537	23	4	38	38	.500	1	4	3.66
2 Maj. YEARS		14	4	0	2	36	166	49	31	28	2	4	2	4	14	2	26	3	0	1	3	.250	0	0	7.00

Ronnie Corona

Pitches: Right **Bats:** Right **Pos:** RP-23; SP-1 · **Ht:** 6'0" **Wt:** 185 **Born:** 1/27/79 **Age:** 22

Year Team	Lg Org	G	GS	CG	GF	IP	BFP	H	R	ER	HR	SH	SF	HB	TBB	IBB	SO	WP	Bk	W	L	Pct.	ShO	Sv	ERA
2000 Elizabethtn	R+ Min	3	1	0	1	7.2	35	8	4	3	0	1	0	1	2	0	8	0	0	0	0	—	0	0	3.52
Quad City	A Min	18	0	0	14	23.2	99	17	8	7	1	1	1	3	8	2	36	2	1	2	1	.667	0	0	2.66
New Britain	AA Min	3	0	0	1	5.2	28	6	4	4	0	0	0	0	2	0	9	1	0	0	0	—	0	0	6.35
1 Min. YEARS		24	1	0	16	37	162	31	16	14	1	2	1	4	12	2	53	3	1	2	1	.667	0	0	3.41

Edwin Corps

Pitches: Right **Bats:** Right **Pos:** RP-22; SP-14 · **Ht:** 5'11" **Wt:** 190 **Born:** 11/3/72 **Age:** 28

Year Team	Lg Org	G	GS	CG	GF	IP	BFP	H	R	ER	HR	SH	SF	HB	TBB	IBB	SO	WP	Bk	W	L	Pct.	ShO	Sv	ERA
1994 San Jose	A+ SF	29	29	0	0	168.1	731	180	95	74	6	5	6	20	43	1	91	4	1	10	6	.625	0	0	3.96
1995 Shreveport	AA SF	27	27	4	0	165.2	712	195	80	71	16	2	6	8	41	2	53	4	2	13	6	.684	0	0	3.86
1996 Shreveport	AA SF	38	3	0	6	70.1	305	74	46	35	6	1	1	3	26	2	39	2	0	2	3	.400	0	1	4.48
1997 Phoenix	AAA SF	7	2	0	1	19	88	26	14	12	0	0	2	0	8	1	8	0	0	2	1	.667	0	0	5.68
Shreveport	AA SF	43	1	0	20	72.1	306	66	38	35	6	5	4	0	35	2	24	4	0	5	3	.625	0	6	4.35
1998 Shreveport	AA SF	46	5	0	11	92.1	396	94	47	40	13	5	4	2	32	4	42	8	0	2	5	.286	0	1	3.90
1999 Shreveport	AA SF	24	12	0	0	84.1	376	98	54	43	9	4	2	4	29	1	34	5	1	4	4	.500	0	0	4.59
Fresno	AAA SF	4	0	0	3	7	33	9	7	3	0	0	0	0	3	0	11	1	0	0	0	—	0	0	3.86
2000 Shreveport	AA SF	36	14	1	7	112.1	480	120	47	39	10	5	2	0	34	3	63	3	0	5	6	.455	0	0	3.12
7 Min. YEARS		254	93	3	53	791.2	3427	862	428	352	66	27	27	37	251	16	365	31	4	43	34	.558	0	8	4.00

Jim Corsi

Pitches: Right **Bats:** Right **Pos:** RP-35; SP-2   **Ht:** 6'1" **Wt:** 230 **Born:** 9/9/61 **Age:** 39

Year Team	Lg Org	G	GS	CG	GF	IP	BFP	H	R	ER	HR	SH	SF	HB	TBB	IBB	SO	WP	Bk	W	L	Pct.	ShO	Sv	ERA
1982 Oneonta	A- NYY	1	0	0	0	3.1	—	5	4	4	0	—	—	0	2	0	6	0	0	0	0	—	0	0	10.80
Paintsville	R+ NYY	8	4	0	1	31	—	32	11	10	0	—	—	0	13	0	20	0	1	0	2	.000	0	0	2.90
1983 Greensboro	A NYY	12	7	1	2	50.2	—	59	37	23	0	—	—	5	33	1	37	8	3	2	2	.500	0	1	4.09
Oneonta	A- NYY	11	10	2	1	59.1	—	76	38	28	1	—	—	1	21	0	47	2	1	3	6	.333	0	0	4.25
1985 Greensboro	A Bos	41	2	1	36	78.2	363	94	49	37	1	4	3	4	23	3	84	4	0	5	8	.385	0	9	4.23
1986 New Britain	AA Bos	29	0	0	19	51.1	220	52	13	13	2	6	0	1	20	5	38	2	0	2	3	.400	0	3	2.28
1987 Modesto	A+ Oak	19	0	0	10	30	121	23	16	12	1	1	0	1	10	1	45	4	0	3	1	.750	0	6	3.60
Huntsville	AA Oak	28	0	0	18	48	182	30	17	15	1	2	0	0	15	1	33	5	0	8	1	.889	0	4	2.81
1988 Tacoma	AAA Oak	50	0	0	45	59	247	60	25	18	2	4	1	1	23	10	48	5	2	2	5	.286	0	16	2.75
1989 Tacoma	AAA Oak	23	0	0	18	28.1	131	40	17	13	1	2	0	1	9	4	23	2	1	2	3	.400	0	8	4.13
1990 Tacoma	AAA Oak	5	0	0	2	6	26	9	2	1	0	0	0	0	1	0	3	2	0	0	0	—	0	0	1.50
1991 Tucson	AAA Hou	2	0	0	2	3	11	2	0	0	0	0	0	0	0	0	4	0	0	0	0	—	0	0	0.00
1992 Tacoma	AAA Oak	26	0	0	22	29.1	121	22	8	4	0	2	2	1	10	3	21	2	1	0	0	—	0	12	1.23
1993 High Desert	A+ Fla	3	3	0	0	9	38	11	3	3	1	0	0	0	2	0	6	0	0	0	1	.000	0	0	3.00
1994 Brevard Cty	A+ Fla	6	0	0	2	11	43	8	3	2	0	0	0	0	5	0	11	0	0	0	1	.000	0	0	1.64
Edmonton	AAA Fla	15	0	0	1	22	103	29	15	11	1	2	0	0	10	0	15	0	0	0	1	.000	0	0	4.50
1995 Edmonton	AAA Oak	3	0	0	3	10		0	0	0	0	0	0	0	1	0	2	0	0	0	0	—	0	3	0.00
1996 Modesto	A+ Oak	1	1	0	0	1	3	0	0	0	0	0	0	0	0	0	2	0	0	0	0	—	0	0	0.00
1997 Pawtucket	AAA Bos	2	0	0	1	2.1	10	2	0	0	0	0	0	0	1	0	3	0	0	0	1	.000	0	1	0.00
Red Sox	R Bos	3	2	0	0	4	14	2	1	0	0	0	0	0	0	0	6	0	0	1	0	1.000	0	0	0.00
1998 Pawtucket	AAA Bos	1	1	0	0	2	3	0	0	0	0	0	0	0	0	0	1	0	0	0	0	—	0	0	0.00
1999 Rochester	AAA Bal	10	0	0	8	10.1	46	12	4	4	0	0	0	0	3	0	7	0	0	0	0	—	0	2	3.48
2000 Tucson	AAA Ari	32	2	0	9	36.1	156	35	23	21	4	1	1	0	21	0	33	1	2	4	3	.571	0	2	5.20
Rochester	AAA Bal	5	0	0	3	4.1	23	7	7	7	1	0	0	0	3	0	6	1	0	0	1	—	0	1	14.54
1988 Oakland	AL	11	1	0	7	21.1	89	20	10	9	1	3	3	0	6	1	10	1	1	0	0	.000	0	1	3.80
1989 Oakland	AL	22	0	0	14	38.1	149	26	8	8	2	2	2	1	10	0	21	0	0	1	2	.333	0	1	1.88
1991 Houston	NL	47	0	0	15	77.2	322	76	37	32	6	3	2	0	23	5	53	1	1	0	5	.000	0	0	3.71
1992 Oakland	AL	32	0	0	16	44	185	44	12	7	4	2	4	2	18	2	19	0	0	4	2	.667	0	0	1.43
1993 Florida	NL	15	0	0	6	20.1	97	28	15	15	1	3	1	0	10	3	7	0	0	0	0	—	0	0	6.64
1995 Oakland	AL	38	0	0	7	45	187	31	14	11	2	5	1	2	26	1	26	0	0	2	4	.333	0	0	2.20
1996 Oakland	AL	56	0	0	19	73.2	312	71	33	33	6	9	3	3	34	4	43	1	0	6	0	1.000	0	3	4.03
1997 Boston	AL	52	0	0	14	57.2	251	56	26	22	1	3	3	4	21	7	40	2	0	5	3	.625	0	0	3.43
1998 Boston	AL	59	0	0	9	66	274	58	23	19	6	2	1	1	23	2	49	3	0	3	2	.600	0	2	2.59
1999 Boston	AL	23	0	0	5	24	113	25	15	14	4	3	1	2	19	3	14	0	0	1	2	.333	0	0	5.25
Baltimore	AL	15							4	4	2	1	0	0	13	0	8	0	0	1	0	.000	0	0	2.70
18 Min. YEARS		336	32	4	203	583.1	—	613	293	226	16	—	—	15	221	28	502	38	11	32	37	.464	0	68	3.49
10 Maj. YEARS		368	1	0	115	481.1	2032	450	197	174	33	38	18	13	191	28	290	8	2	22	24	.478	0	7	3.25

Chris Coste

Bats: Right **Throws:** Right **Pos:** DH-32; C-29; 1B-22; 3B-10; PH-7; PR-2; OF-1   **Ht:** 6'1" **Wt:** 205 **Born:** 2/4/73 **Age:** 28

Year Team	Lg Org	G	AB	H	2B	3B	HR	TB	R	RBI	TBB	IBB	SO	HBP	SH	SF	SB	CS	SB%	GDP	Avg	OBP	SLG
1996 Fargo-Mh	IND —	81	315	99	30	0	6	147	40	56	17	0	56	10	4	4	2	3	.40	6	.314	.333	.467
1997 Fargo-Mh	IND —	84	337	105	22	0	12	163	45	50	23	0	53	9	3	5	7	1	.88	10	.312	.367	.484
1998 Fargo-Mh	IND —	85	326	107	17	2	10	158	59	55	31	0	30	3	0	2	6	3	.67	14	.328	.390	.485
1999 Fargo-Mh	IND —	85	352	118	18	2	16	188	67	60	31	1	42	2	0	3	4	1	.80	17	.335	.389	.534
2000 Buffalo	AAA Cle	31	96	29	2	0	4	43	15	8	3	0	12	1	1	0	0	1	.00	4	.302	.330	.448
Akron	AA Cle	65	240	80	20	4	2	114	32	31	15	2	33	4	0	1	1	2	.33	7	.333	.381	.475
5 Min. YEARS		431	1666	538	109	8	50	813	258	260	120	3	226	27	5	11	20	11	.65	58	.323	.376	.488

Humberto Cota

Bats: Right **Throws:** Right **Pos:** C-90; DH-19; PH-2; 1B-1   **Ht:** 6'0" **Wt:** 175 **Born:** 2/7/79 **Age:** 22

Year Team	Lg Org	G	AB	H	2B	3B	HR	TB	R	RBI	TBB	IBB	SO	HBP	SH	SF	SB	CS	SB%	GDP	Avg	OBP	SLG
1997 Devil Rays	R TB	44	133	32	6	1	2	46	14	20	17	0	27	3	1	3	3	1	.75	1	.241	.333	.346
Hudson Val	A- Fla	3	9	2	0	0	0	2	0	2	0	0	1	0	0	0	0	0	—	0	.222	.222	.222
1998 Princeton	R+ TB	67	245	76	13	4	15	142	48	61	32	1	59	6	1	3	4	4	.50	3	.310	.390	.580
1999 Chston-SC	A TB	85	336	94	21	1	9	144	42	61	20	1	51	2	1	5	1	1	.50	9	.280	.320	.429
Hickory	A Pit	37	133	36	11	2	2	57	28	20	21	1	20	0	0	2	3	1	.75	0	.271	.365	.429
2000 Altoona	AA Pit	112	429	112	20	1	8	158	49	44	21	1	80	3	1	5	6	4	.60	8	.261	.297	.368
4 Min. YEARS		348	1285	352	71	9	36	549	181	208	111	4	238	14	4	18	17	11	.61	21	.274	.334	.427

Marino Cota

Pitches: Right **Bats:** Right **Pos:** SP-12; RP-10   **Ht:** 6'0" **Wt:** 182 **Born:** 11/25/76 **Age:** 24

Year Team	Lg Org	G	GS	CG	GF	IP	BFP	H	R	ER	HR	SH	SF	HB	TBB	IBB	SO	WP	Bk	W	L	Pct.	ShO	Sv	ERA
2000 Binghamton	AA NYM	22	12	1	2	74	326	74	37	32	9	3	1	7	27	1	57	2	2	6	3	.667	1	0	3.89

Joe Cotton

Pitches: Right **Bats:** Right **Pos:** RP-40; SP-2   **Ht:** 6'2" **Wt:** 185 **Born:** 3/25/75 **Age:** 26

Year Team	Lg Org	G	GS	CG	GF	IP	BFP	H	R	ER	HR	SH	SF	HB	TBB	IBB	SO	WP	Bk	W	L	Pct.	ShO	Sv	ERA
1996 Batavia	A- Phi	9	0	0	0	46.1	196	43	23	22	2	3	1	1	19	0	37	4	0	2	4	.333	0	0	4.27
1997 Batavia	A- Phi	15	15	0	0	96.1	402	90	38	32	10	2	2	7	29	0	74	6	0	7	4	.636	0	0	2.99
1998 Piedmont	A Phi	44	0	0	20	77.1	322	73	48	38	14	4	6	6	16	1	79	3	0	6	8	.429	0	5	4.42
1999 Clearwater	A+ Phi	38	3	0	5	69.1	263	41	17	15	5	1	3	1	15	2	43	1	0	5	3	.625	0	1	1.95
2000 Clearwater	A+ Phi	9	0	0	4	16	65	16	7	7	1	0	1	0	7	0	19	1	0	0	0	.000	0	0	3.94
Reading	AA Phi	33	0	0	18	72	273	48	17	16	0	0	2	1	19	1	51	0	0	4	1	.800	0	6	2.00
5 Min. YEARS		148	29	0	47	377.1	1521	311	150	130	37	11	14	16	100	4	298	14	0	24	21	.533	0	12	3.10

John Cotton

Bats: Left **Throws:** Right **Pos:** OF-61; PH-20; DH-14; 2B-12; 3B-2; 1B-2; C-1   **Ht:** 6'0" **Wt:** 190 **Born:** 10/30/70 **Age:** 30

		BATTING															BASERUNNING				PERCENTAGES		
Year Team	Lg Org	G	AB	H	2B	3B	HR	TB	R	RBI	TBB	IBB	SO	HBP	SH	SF	SB	CS	SB%	GDP	Avg	OBP	SLG
1989 Burlington	R+ Cle	64	227	47	5	1	2	60	36	22	22	0	56	3	4	1	20	3	.87	5	.207	.285	.264
1990 Watertown	A- Cle	73	286	60	9	4	2	83	53	27	40	3	71	2	2	1	24	7	.77	4	.210	.310	.290
1991 Columbus	A Cle	122	405	92	11	9	13	160	88	42	93	1	135	3	3	3	56	15	.79	6	.227	.373	.395
1992 Kinston	A+ Cle	103	360	72	7	3	11	118	67	39	48	1	106	2	1	2	23	7	.77	3	.200	.296	.328
1993 Kinston	A+ Cle	127	454	120	16	3	13	181	81	51	59	1	130	11	5	2	28	24	.54	3	.264	.361	.399
1994 Springfield	A SD	24	82	19	5	3	1	33	14	8	12	0	19	0	0	0	7	1	.88	0	.232	.330	.402
Wichita	AA SD	34	85	16	4	0	3	29	9	14	13	3	20	1	0	2	2	0	1.00	3	.188	.297	.341
Rancho Cuca	A+ SD	48	171	35	3	2	4	54	35	19	22	0	48	2	0	0	9	3	.75	3	.205	.303	.316
1995 Memphis	AA SD	121	407	103	19	8	12	174	60	47	38	0	101	4	6	4	15	6	.71	2	.253	.320	.428
1996 Toledo	AAA Det	50	171	32	7	1	4	53	14	19	7	0	64	2	2	0	4	4	.50	1	.187	.228	.310
Jacksnville	AA Det	63	217	52	7	4	13	106	34	39	19	2	66	2	0	1	15	3	.83	2	.240	.305	.488
1997 Birmingham	AA CWS	33	124	36	10	2	7	71	23	26	9	0	33	2	0	1	1	2	.33	3	.290	.346	.573
Nashville	AAA CWS	94	323	87	14	3	11	140	45	50	24	1	94	0	1	2	8	2	.80	7	.269	.318	.433
1998 Daytona	A+ ChC	12	48	14	4	0	3	27	8	11	3	0	8	1	0	0	0	3	—	3	.292	.346	.563
West Tenn	AA ChC	90	319	93	14	3	13	152	46	53	19	1	68	4	0	5	10	3	.77	3	.292	.334	.476
1999 Carolina	AA Col	42	163	46	9	0	10	85	27	21	10	1	48	1	0	0	0	1	.00	3	.282	.328	.521
Colo Sprngs	AAA Col	70	235	74	18	1	15	139	50	48	14	4	64	2	1	3	4	2	.67	6	.315	.354	.591
2000 Colo Sprngs	AAA Col	103	314	103	21	5	16	182	58	62	30	3	97	1	0	2	13	0	1.00	6	.328	.386	.580
12 Min. YEARS		1273	4391	1101	183	52	153	1847	748	598	482	21	1228	43	25	29	239	83	.74	63	.251	.329	.421

Darron Cox

Bats: Right **Throws:** Right **Pos:** C-58; PH-14; DH-8   **Ht:** 6'1" **Wt:** 205 **Born:** 11/21/67 **Age:** 33

		BATTING															BASERUNNING				PERCENTAGES		
Year Team	Lg Org	G	AB	H	2B	3B	HR	TB	R	RBI	TBB	IBB	SO	HBP	SH	SF	SB	CS	SB%	GDP	Avg	OBP	SLG
1989 Billings	R+ Cin	49	157	43	6	0	0	49	20	18	21	0	34	5	2	0	11	3	.79	1	.274	.377	.312
1990 Chston-WV	A Cin	103	367	93	11	3	1	113	53	44	40	2	75	7	4	3	14	3	.82	12	.253	.336	.308
1991 Cedar Rapds	A Cin	21	60	16	4	0	0	20	12	4	8	0	11	4	1	0	7	1	.88	2	.267	.389	.333
Chattanooga	AA Cin	13	38	7	1	0	0	8	2	3	2	0	9	0	1	1	0	0	—	1	.184	.220	.211
Chston-WV	A Cin	79	294	71	14	1	2	93	37	29	24	0	40	2	1	7	8	4	.67	7	.241	.297	.316
1992 Chattanooga	AA Cin	98	331	84	19	1	1	108	29	38	15	0	63	5	1	6	8	3	.73	7	.254	.291	.326
1993 Chattanooga	AA Cin	89	300	65	9	5	3	93	35	26	38	2	63	3	7	1	7	4	.64	7	.217	.310	.310
1994 Iowa	AAA ChC	99	301	80	15	1	3	106	35	26	28	4	47	4	3	0	5	2	.71	12	.266	.336	.352
1995 Orlando	AA ChC	33	102	29	5	0	4	46	8	15	8	0	16	1	2	2	3	3	.50	3	.284	.336	.451
Iowa	AAA ChC	33	94	22	6	0	1	31	7	14	8	0	21	2	2	4	0	0	—	0	.234	.296	.330
1996 Richmond	AAA Atl	55	168	40	9	0	3	58	19	20	5	0	22	3	2	2	1	0	1.00	5	.238	.270	.345
1997 Orlando	AA ChC	3	9	2	1	0	1	6	2	4	1	0	1	0	0	1	0	0	—	0	.222	.273	.667
1998 Durham	AAA TB	84	278	84	16	1	9	129	45	35	23	0	41	5	0	6	2	2	.50	6	.302	.366	.464
1999 Ottawa	AAA Mon	3	9	0	0	0	0	0	0	0	0	0	5	2	0	0	0	0	—	0	.000	.000	.000
2000 Colo Sprngs	AAA Col	78	244	78	14	0	3	101	37	46	27	2	34	4	2	7	3	3	.50	10	.320	.387	.414
1999 Montreal	NL	15	25	6	1	0	1	10	2	2	0	0	5	2	0	0	0	0	—	0	.240	.296	.400
12 Min. YEARS		840	2752	714	130	12	31	961	341	321	249	10	479	45	36	34	69	28	.71	74	.259	.327	.349

Ryan Cox

Pitches: Right **Bats:** Right **Pos:** SP-26; RP-1   **Ht:** 6'3" **Wt:** 195 **Born:** 12/25/76 **Age:** 24

		HOW MUCH HE PITCHED						WHAT HE GAVE UP												THE RESULTS					
Year Team	Lg Org	G	GS	CG	GF	IP	BFP	H	R	ER	HR	SH	SF	HB	TBB	IBB	SO	WP	Bk	W	L	Pct.	ShO	Sv	ERA
1999 Salem-Keizr	A- SF	8	8	0	0	34.1	139	39	13	12	1	2	1	1	10	0	20	0	2	2	1	.667	0	0	3.15
Bakersfield	A+ SF	7	7	0	0	33.1	151	46	22	18	6	1	0	4	3	0	30	2	1	1	4	.200	0	0	4.86
2000 San Jose	A+ SF	19	19	0	0	107.1	463	122	67	55	12	3	7	5	28	0	54	5	0	5	8	.385	0	0	4.61
Shreveport	AA SF	7	7	0	0	33.1	158	53	35	30	5	0	1	3	5	0	24	0	0	2	2	.500	0	0	8.10
Fresno	AAA SF	1	0	0	0	1.0	6	3	2	2	0	0	0	0	0	0	1	1	0	0	0	—	0	0	18.00
2 Min. YEARS		42	41	0	0	209.1	917	263	139	117	24	6	9	10	46	0	129	8	2	10	15	.400	0	0	5.03

Robbie Crabtree

Pitches: Right **Bats:** Right **Pos:** RP-63   **Ht:** 6'1" **Wt:** 175 **Born:** 11/25/72 **Age:** 28

		HOW MUCH HE PITCHED						WHAT HE GAVE UP												THE RESULTS					
Year Team	Lg Org	G	GS	CG	GF	IP	BFP	H	R	ER	HR	SH	SF	HB	TBB	IBB	SO	WP	Bk	W	L	Pct.	ShO	Sv	ERA
1996 Bellingham	A- SF	28	0	0	13	52	206	38	18	16	8	2	1	6	14	1	72	3	0	3	3	.500	0	4	2.77
1997 Bakersfield	A+ SF	45	9	1	9	112.1	506	124	77	64	10	1	0	5	59	1	116	12	1	7	7	.500	0	1	5.13
1998 San Jose	A+ SF	24	0	0	10	54.1	213	39	6	6	0	4	0	3	8	0	67	1	0	6	1	.857	0	2	0.99
Shreveport	AA SF	26	0	0	13	54	205	30	11	10	4	1	0	2	16	2	56	0	0	2	0	1.000	0	4	1.67
Fresno	AAA SF	3	1	0	2	4.2	26	8	7	6	1	0	0	1	2	0	10	0	0	0	0	—	0	0	11.57
1999 Fresno	AAA SF	22	1	0	11	34.1	150	37	23	20	2	0	0	0	10	1	40	3	0	1	4	.200	0	1	5.24
Shreveport	AA SF	36	0	0	14	63.1	255	50	21	18	2	0	1	0	18	2	65	3	0	4	2	.667	0	2	2.56
2000 Fresno	AAA SF	63	0	0	21	127.2	544	126	67	54	8	7	4	7	31	5	116	2	0	5	6	.455	0	8	3.81
5 Min. YEARS		247	11	1	93	502.2	2101	452	230	194	35	15	6	18	158	12	542	26	1	28	23	.549	0	22	3.47

Kevin Crafton

Pitches: Right **Bats:** Right **Pos:** RP-59   **Ht:** 6'1" **Wt:** 185 **Born:** 5/10/74 **Age:** 27

		HOW MUCH HE PITCHED						WHAT HE GAVE UP												THE RESULTS					
Year Team	Lg Org	G	GS	CG	GF	IP	BFP	H	R	ER	HR	SH	SF	HB	TBB	IBB	SO	WP	Bk	W	L	Pct.	ShO	Sv	ERA
1996 New Jersey	A- StL	23	0	0	10	29	132	28	8	8	1	3	1	1	6	2	43	2	0	2	3	.400	0	2	2.18
1997 Peoria	A StL	50	0	0	45	55	219	40	16	12	2	5	2	2	18	7	59	2	1	7	2	.778	0	29	1.96
1998 Arkansas	AA StL	46	0	0	13	55.2	227	52	23	20	8	3	2	0	7	0	44	2	0	5	1	.833	0	1	3.23
1999 Memphis	AAA StL	4	0	0	0	4.1	26	12	12	11	2	0	1	1	0	0	2	0	0	0	1	.000	0	0	22.85
Arkansas	AA StL	42	0	0	14	46.1	209	57	41	39	9	2	1	1	16	1	41	2	0	7	2	.778	0	2	7.58
2000 Memphis	AAA StL	2	0	0	1	2.2	12	4	2	2	0	0	0	0	1	0	2	0	0	0	0	—	0	0	6.75
Arkansas	AA StL	57	0	0	28	70.2	302	69	24	20	5	4	4	2	28	4	48	1	0	5	5	.643	0	4	2.55
5 Min. YEARS		224	0	0	111	267.2	1127	262	126	112	27	17	11	7	76	14	237	9	1	30	14	.682	0	38	3.77

Joe Crawford

Pitches: Left   **Bats:** Left   **Pos:** SP-15; RP-4   **Ht:** 6'3"   **Wt:** 225   **Born:** 5/2/70   **Age:** 31

		HOW MUCH HE PITCHED						WHAT HE GAVE UP											THE RESULTS				
Year Team	Lg Org	G	GS	CG	GF	IP	BFP	H	R	ER	HR	SH	SF	HB	TBB	IBB	SO	WP	Bk	W	L	Pct.	ShO	Sv	ERA
1991 Kingsport	R+ NYM	19	0	0	16	32.1	118	16	5	4	0	0	0	1	8	0	43	3	1	0	0	—	0	11	1.11
Columbia	A NYM	3	0	0	2	3	9	0	0	0	0	0	0	0	0	0	6	0	0	0	0	—	0	0	0.00
1992 St. Lucie	A+ NYM	25	1	0	16	43.2	174	29	18	10	1	1	3	0	15	3	32	1	3	3	3	.500	0	2	2.06
1993 St. Lucie	A+ NYM	34	0	0	19	37	156	38	15	15	0	2	0	2	14	5	24	0	0	3	3	.500	0	5	3.65
1994 St. Lucie	A+ NYM	33	0	0	15	42.2	155	22	8	7	1	1	2	2	9	2	31	1	0	1	1	.500	0	5	1.48
Binghamton	AA NYM	13	0	0	6	14.2	70	20	10	9	2	0	2	0	8	0	9	0	0	1	0	1.000	0	0	5.52
1995 Binghamton	AA NYM	42	1	0	15	60.2	239	48	17	15	4	3	7	5	17	4	43	3	1	7	2	.778	0	0	2.23
Norfolk	AAA NYM	8	0	0	1	18.2	70	9	5	4	0	1	0	0	4	0	13	0	0	1	1	.500	0	0	1.93
1996 Binghamton	AA NYM	7	7	1	0	49.2	190	34	10	8	4	2	0	0	9	1	34	1	2	5	1	.833	1	0	1.45
Norfolk	AAA NYM	20	16	2	2	96.2	403	98	45	37	10	3	1	4	20	1	68	0	1	6	5	.545	1	0	3.44
1997 Norfolk	AAA NYM	16	16	0	0	99.2	431	109	45	39	6	5	5	1	31	0	72	4	2	8	2	.800	0	0	3.52
2000 Indianapolis	AAA Mil	3	0	0	0	0.2	6	3	2	2	1	0	0	1	0	0	1	1	0	0	0	—	0	0	27.00
Bridgeport	IND —	16	16	2	0	97	420	106	52	42	7	4	0	3	25	0	57	0	1	9	1	.900	0	0	3.90
1997 New York	NL	19	2	0	9	46.1	182	36	18	17	7	2	0	0	13	1	25	0	1	4	3	.571	0	0	3.30
8 Min. YEARS		239	56	5	92	596.1	2441	532	232	192	36	22	20	19	160	16	433	16	10	44	19	.698	3	24	2.90

Ryan Creek

Pitches: Right   **Bats:** Right   **Pos:** SP-13; RP-9   **Ht:** 6'1"   **Wt:** 180   **Born:** 9/24/72   **Age:** 28

		HOW MUCH HE PITCHED						WHAT HE GAVE UP											THE RESULTS				
Year Team	Lg Org	G	GS	CG	GF	IP	BFP	H	R	ER	HR	SH	SF	HB	TBB	IBB	SO	WP	Bk	W	L	Pct.	ShO	Sv	ERA
1993 Astros	R Hou	12	11	2	1	69.1	291	53	22	18	0	1	5	4	30	0	62	6	0	7	3	.700	1	0	2.34
1994 Quad City	A Hou	21	15	0	3	74	356	86	62	41	6	3	5	14	41	2	66	9	3	3	5	.375	0	0	4.99
1995 Jackson	AA Hou	26	24	1	1	143.2	622	137	74	58	11	6	8	6	64	0	120	12	2	9	7	.563	1	0	3.63
1996 Jackson	AA Hou	27	26	1	1	142	674	139	95	83	9	3	7	11	121	0	119	14	1	7	15	.318	0	0	5.26
1997 Jackson	AA Hou	19	19	0	0	105	471	95	57	48	10	5	1	3	74	1	88	14	0	10	5	.667	0	0	4.11
1999 Kissimmee	A+ Hou	7	7	0	0	35.1	153	36	19	16	4	1	2	4	12	0	23	0	0	2	4	.333	0	0	4.08
Jackson	AA Hou	8	7	0	0	43.1	199	47	25	22	4	1	0	2	25	0	32	2	0	4	3	.571	0	0	4.57
New Orleans	AAA Hou	6	5	0	0	31.2	141	30	17	14	4	4	0	2	16	0	20	2	0	1	2	.333	0	0	3.98
2000 Calgary	AAA Fla	3	0	0	2	3.2	25	8	8	8	0	0	3	0	6	0	3	0	0	0	0	—	0	0	19.64
El Paso	AA Ari	2	1	0	0	5	19	2	0	0	0	0	0	1	2	0	5	0	0	0	0	—	0	0	0.00
Tucson	AAA Ari	4	0	0	0	7	39	12	12	12	1	0	1	0	6	1	4	0	0	0	1	.000	0	0	15.43
Jackson	IND —	13	12	2	0	82	363	92	42	28	1	1	2	7	31	0	66	9	0	5	5	.500	0	0	3.07
7 Min. YEARS		148	127	6	8	742	3353	737	433	348	50	25	34	54	428	4	608	68	6	48	50	.490	2	1	4.22

Cesar Crespo

Bats: Both   **Throws:** Right   **Pos:** OF-114; 2B-18; SS-3; PH-1; PR-1   **Ht:** 5'11"   **Wt:** 170   **Born:** 5/23/79   **Age:** 22

		BATTING														BASERUNNING				PERCENTAGES		
Year Team	Lg Org	G	AB	H	2B	3B	HR	TB	R	RBI	TBB	IBB	SO	HBP	SH	SF	SB	CS	SB%	GDP	Avg	OBP	SLG
1998 Capital Cty	A NYM	116	428	108	18	4	6	152	61	48	44	1	114	3	7	1	47	14	.77	6	.252	.326	.355
1999 Brevard Cty	A+ Fla	115	427	122	17	2	6	161	63	40	62	2	86	1	7	2	22	8	.73	4	.286	.376	.377
2000 Portland	AA Fla	134	482	124	21	6	9	184	96	60	77	3	118	2	8	5	41	15	.73	8	.257	.359	.382
3 Min. YEARS		365	1337	354	56	12	21	497	220	148	183	6	318	6	22	8	110	37	.75	18	.265	.354	.372

Brad Cresse

Bats: Right   **Throws:** Right   **Pos:** C-53; DH-7; PH-4   **Ht:** 6'2"   **Wt:** 210   **Born:** 7/31/78   **Age:** 22

		BATTING														BASERUNNING				PERCENTAGES		
Year Team	Lg Org	G	AB	H	2B	3B	HR	TB	R	RBI	TBB	IBB	SO	HBP	SH	SF	SB	CS	SB%	GDP	Avg	OBP	SLG
2000 High Desert	A+ Ari	48	173	56	7	0	17	114	35	56	17	1	50	7	0	2	0	0	—	3	.324	.402	.659
El Paso	AA Ari	15	42	11	1	0	1	15	9	10	6	0	12	3	0	1	0	0	—	1	.262	.385	.357
1 Min. YEARS		63	215	67	8	0	18	129	44	66	23	1	62	10	0	3	0	0	—	4	.312	.398	.600

Bobby Cripps

Bats: Left   **Throws:** Right   **Pos:** C-68; DH-14; OF-8; PH-2   **Ht:** 6'2"   **Wt:** 190   **Born:** 5/9/77   **Age:** 24

		BATTING														BASERUNNING				PERCENTAGES		
Year Team	Lg Org	G	AB	H	2B	3B	HR	TB	R	RBI	TBB	IBB	SO	HBP	SH	SF	SB	CS	SB%	GDP	Avg	OBP	SLG
1996 Great Falls	R+ LA	49	139	43	4	3	2	59	23	28	9	0	19	2	1	5	6	5	.55	5	.309	.348	.424
1997 Great Falls	R+ LA	47	145	45	6	5	4	73	19	25	7	1	26	3	1	2	4	4	.50	3	.310	.350	.503
St.Cathrnes	A- Tor	14	40	5	0	1	1	10	4	3	4	0	11	2	0	0	0	0	—	1	.125	.239	.250
1998 Hagerstown	A Tor	123	423	112	17	3	29	222	64	88	41	3	123	7	5	4	2	3	.40	7	.265	.337	.525
1999 Dunedin	A+ Tor	5	16	1	0	0	0	1	1	1	1	0	7	0	0	0	0	0	—	0	.063	.118	.063
St.Cathrnes	A- Tor	10	31	9	0	0	2	15	3	7	2	0	9	0	0	1	0	0	—	0	.290	.324	.484
Knoxville	AA Tor	25	87	15	6	0	2	27	13	9	6	0	37	2	0	1	0	0	—	0	.172	.240	.310
2000 Chattanooga	AA Cin	8	21	5	2	0	0	7	2	6	0	0	5	0	0	0	0	0	—	1	.238	.238	.333
Clinton	A Cin	83	301	69	9	0	14	120	31	47	18	3	62	1	0	6	2	0	1.00	5	.229	.270	.399
5 Min. YEARS		364	1203	304	44	12	54	534	160	214	88	7	299	17	7	19	14	12	.54	23	.253	.308	.444

Brandon Cromer

Bats: Left   **Throws:** Right   **Pos:** 3B-23; SS-21; PH-7   **Ht:** 6'2"   **Wt:** 175   **Born:** 1/25/74   **Age:** 27

		BATTING														BASERUNNING				PERCENTAGES		
Year Team	Lg Org	G	AB	H	2B	3B	HR	TB	R	RBI	TBB	IBB	SO	HBP	SH	SF	SB	CS	SB%	GDP	Avg	OBP	SLG
1992 Blue Jays	R Tor	49	180	51	12	3	1	72	26	21	14	0	26	5	2	2	7	8	.47	2	.283	.348	.400
1993 St.Cathrnes	A- Tor	75	278	64	9	2	5	92	29	20	21	2	64	1	3	1	2	4	.33	1	.230	.286	.331
1994 Hagerstown	A Tor	80	259	35	8	5	6	71	25	26	25	0	98	0	2	3	0	2	.00	4	.135	.209	.274
1995 Dunedin	A+ Tor	106	329	78	11	3	6	113	40	43	43	3	84	5	5	3	0	5	.00	6	.237	.332	.343
1996 Knoxville	AA Tor	98	318	88	15	8	7	140	56	32	60	3	84	2	2	3	3	6	.33	2	.277	.392	.440

61

Year Team	Lg Org	G	AB	H	2B	3B	HR	TB	R	RBI	TBB	IBB	SO	HBP	SH	SF	SB	CS	SB%	GDP	Avg	OBP	SLG
1997 Carolina	AA Pit	55	193	44	12	4	4	76	23	14	29	0	50	0	4	2	1	5	.17	0	.228	.326	.394
Calgary	AAA Pit	68	228	53	15	2	8	96	30	36	19	2	46	0	1	3	3	1	.75	5	.232	.288	.421
1998 Portland	AA Fla	122	391	87	13	5	15	155	51	47	43	0	89	0	1	4	3	2	.60	12	.223	.297	.396
1999 Louisville	AAA Mil	115	330	71	12	1	24	157	46	61	40	5	103	2	1	0	6	0	1.00	1	.215	.304	.476
2000 Huntsville	AA Mil	22	68	14	5	0	2	25	11	8	13	0	17	1	1	0	2	1	.67	0	.206	.341	.368
Indianapols	AAA Mil	23	71	15	3	2	1	25	7	6	7	2	14	0	0	0	1	0	1.00	3	.211	.282	.352
9 Min. YEARS		813	2645	600	115	35	79	1022	344	314	314	17	675	16	22	21	28	34	.45	36	.227	.310	.386

Jim Crowell

Pitches: Left Bats: Right Pos: RP-35 **Ht: 6'4" Wt: 230 Born: 5/14/74 Age: 27**

Year Team	Lg Org	G	GS	CG	GF	IP	BFP	H	R	ER	HR	SH	SF	HB	TBB	IBB	SO	WP	Bk	W	L	Pct.	ShO	Sv	ERA
1995 Watertown	A- Cle	12	9	0	0	56.2	241	50	22	18	1	0	2	1	27	1	48	2	1	5	2	.714	0	0	2.86
1996 Columbus	A Cle	28	28	3	0	165.1	710	163	89	76	16	9	5	9	69	0	104	12	0	7	10	.412	0	0	4.14
1997 Kinston	A+ Cle	17	17	0	0	114	461	96	41	30	4	3	2	8	26	0	94	3	0	9	4	.692	0	0	2.37
Akron	AA Cle	3	3	0	0	18	80	13	12	9	2	1	1	1	11	0	7	1	0	1	0	1.000	0	0	4.50
Chattanooga	AA Cin	3	3	0	0	19	75	19	6	6	2	1	1	0	5	0	14	0	0	2	1	.667	0	0	2.84
Indianapols	AAA Cin	3	3	1	0	19.2	85	19	7	6	1	0	2	0	8	0	6	1	0	1	1	.500	1	0	2.75
1998 Chattanooga	AA Cin	5	5	0	0	24.1	129	38	27	23	2	0	3	0	17	0	10	2	0	0	4	.000	0	0	8.51
Chston-WV	A Cin	5	5	0	0	15	83	28	23	22	1	0	2	2	9	0	9	1	0	0	4	.000	0	0	13.20
Indianapols	AAA Cin	1	1	0	0	4	19	7	3	3	0	0	0	0	0	0	2	0	0	0	0	—	0	0	6.75
1999 Chattanooga	AA Cin	27	27	0	0	148.1	690	173	98	84	12	5	6	4	85	0	80	3	0	10	5	.667	0	0	5.10
2000 Chattanooga	AA Cin	23	0	0	5	29	148	35	23	19	3	1	0	3	22	2	20	0	0	0	0	—	0	0	5.90
Arkansas	AA StL	12	0	0	6	15	68	16	10	9	1	1	0	1	8	1	10	0	1	1	1	.500	0	0	5.40
1997 Cincinnati	NL	2	1	0	1	6.1	36	12	7	7	2	2	0	0	5	0	3	0	0	0	1	.000	0	0	9.95
6 Min. YEARS		139	101	4	11	628.1	2789	657	361	305	45	21	24	29	287	4	404	25	1	36	32	.529	1	1	4.37

Chuck Crumpton

Pitches: Right Bats: Right Pos: RP-36; SP-11 **Ht: 6'4" Wt: 210 Born: 12/30/76 Age: 24**

Year Team	Lg Org	G	GS	CG	GF	IP	BFP	H	R	ER	HR	SH	SF	HB	TBB	IBB	SO	WP	Bk	W	L	Pct.	ShO	Sv	ERA
1999 Vermont	A- Mon	19	0	0	13	23.1	102	24	11	5	0	1	1	3	6	0	24	2	1	1	2	.333	0	5	1.93
Cape Fear	A Mon	13	0	0	13	19	74	15	3	1	0	0	0	1	3	0	15	0	0	2	1	.667	0	7	0.47
2000 Jupiter	A+ Mon	16	0	0	13	18.1	82	20	13	12	1	0	2	0	6	1	12	0	0	0	0	—	0	7	5.89
Harrisburg	AA Mon	31	11	0	7	77.2	340	90	43	37	7	0	1	5	23	0	34	7	0	3	2	.600	0	1	4.29
2 Min. YEARS		79	11	0	46	138.1	598	149	70	55	8	1	4	9	38	1	85	9	1	6	5	.545	0	20	3.58

Michael Cuddyer

Bats: Right Throws: Right Pos: 3B-138 **Ht: 6'2" Wt: 202 Born: 3/27/79 Age: 22**

Year Team	Lg Org	G	AB	H	2B	3B	HR	TB	R	RBI	TBB	IBB	SO	HBP	SH	SF	SB	CS	SB%	GDP	Avg	OBP	SLG
1998 Fort Wayne	A Min	129	497	137	37	7	12	224	82	81	61	3	107	10	0	4	16	7	.70	13	.276	.364	.451
1999 Fort Myers	A+ Min	130	466	139	24	4	16	219	87	82	76	0	91	10	2	6	14	4	.78	20	.298	.403	.470
2000 New Britain	AA Min	138	490	129	30	8	6	193	72	61	55	2	93	12	6	2	5	4	.56	16	.263	.351	.394
3 Min. YEARS		397	1453	405	91	19	34	636	241	224	192	5	291	32	8	12	35	15	.70	49	.279	.372	.438

Chris Cumberland

Pitches: Left Bats: Right Pos: RP-15; SP-6 **Ht: 6'1" Wt: 189 Born: 1/15/73 Age: 28**

Year Team	Lg Org	G	GS	CG	GF	IP	BFP	H	R	ER	HR	SH	SF	HB	TBB	IBB	SO	WP	Bk	W	L	Pct.	ShO	Sv	ERA
1993 Oneonta	A- NYY	15	15	0	0	89	393	109	43	33	2	1	5	0	28	0	62	6	2	4	4	.500	0	0	3.34
1994 Greensboro	A NYY	22	22	1	0	137.2	559	123	55	45	9	4	2	4	41	0	95	11	2	14	5	.737	1	0	2.94
1995 Yankees	R NYY	4	4	0	0	7	26	3	1	1	0	0	0	0	1	0	7	0	0	0	1	.000	0	0	1.29
Tampa	A+ NYY	5	5	0	0	24.2	104	28	10	5	1	1	0	1	5	0	10	1	0	1	2	.333	0	0	1.82
1996 Columbus	AAA NYY	12	12	1	0	58	272	86	45	42	9	4	1	4	23	0	35	0	0	2	7	.222	0	0	6.52
Norwich	AA NYY	16	16	2	0	95.2	427	112	73	56	13	2	5	4	37	2	44	4	0	5	7	.417	1	0	5.27
1997 Norwich	AA NYY	25	25	3	0	154.2	686	188	100	69	12	5	3	5	59	1	81	10	4	11	10	.524	1	0	4.02
New Britain	AA Min	1	1	0	0	5.2	22	5	2	2	0	0	0	0	2	0	2	0	0	1	0	1.000	0	0	3.18
1998 New Britain	AA Min	37	2	0	16	54.2	220	44	24	16	1	1	2	0	17	2	48	6	0	3	4	.429	0	1	2.63
Salt Lake	AAA Min	17	1	1	4	30.1	142	37	21	20	2	3	1	1	18	1	19	1	0	3	2	.600	0	1	5.93
1999 Trenton	AA Bos	14	0	0	6	21	84	12	1	1	0	1	1	0	13	1	18	1	0	2	0	1.000	0	1	0.43
Pawtucket	AAA Bos	36	1	0	16	62.2	266	53	33	31	4	2	3	2	30	0	35	4	0	4	3	.571	0	0	4.45
2000 Fresno	AAA SF	9	4	0	0	29	137	40	32	32	12	1	2	0	15	0	10	1	0	0	3	.000	0	0	9.93
Greenville	AA Atl	12	2	0	3	21.2	97	19	12	11	1	1	0	1	10	1	10	0	0	2	1	.667	0	0	4.57
8 Min. YEARS		225	110	8	39	791.2	3435	862	452	364	66	26	25	23	299	8	476	54	11	52	49	.515	3	4	4.14

Ryan Cummings

Pitches: Right Bats: Right Pos: SP-16; RP-10 **Ht: 6'0" Wt: 210 Born: 6/3/76 Age: 25**

Year Team	Lg Org	G	GS	CG	GF	IP	BFP	H	R	ER	HR	SH	SF	HB	TBB	IBB	SO	WP	Bk	W	L	Pct.	ShO	Sv	ERA
1997 Boise	A- Ana	14	13	0	0	70	297	73	38	24	3	2	1	7	10	0	79	4	2	6	2	.750	0	0	3.09
1998 Lk Elsinore	A+ Ana	1	1	0	0	5	23	5	3	3	0	0	0	2	3	0	4	1	0	0	1	.000	0	0	5.40
1999 Cedar Rapds	A Ana	19	19	3	0	121	511	104	69	59	14	4	10	6	35	0	97	18	2	5	8	.385	1	0	4.39
Lk Elsinore	A+ Ana	7	7	0	0	46.2	203	43	19	17	3	1	0	4	15	1	41	1	0	3	1	.750	0	0	3.28
Erie	AA Ana	3	3	0	0	17.2	81	18	12	10	3	0	1	3	10	0	7	0	0	1	1	.500	0	0	5.09
2000 Erie	AA Ana	26	16	0	5	99.2	465	122	80	69	14	2	10	8	45	1	53	6	2	4	9	.308	0	0	6.23
4 Min. YEARS		70	59	3	5	360	1580	365	221	182	37	7	14	32	118	2	281	30	6	19	22	.463	1	0	4.55

John Curl

Bats: Left **Throws:** Right **Pos:** OF-59; PH-29; 1B-15; DH-11; PR-2; P-1   **Ht:** 6'3" **Wt:** 205 **Born:** 11/10/72 **Age:** 28

Year Team	Lg Org	G	AB	H	2B	3B	HR	TB	R	RBI	TBB	IBB	SO	HBP	SH	SF	SB	CS	SB%	GDP	Avg	OBP	SLG
1995 Medcine Hat	R+ Tor	69	270	86	26	1	7	135	47	63	31	8	61	0	0	3	5	1	.83	11	.319	.385	.500
1996 Dunedin	A+ Tor	125	447	110	20	2	18	188	52	62	44	1	133	1	2	5	7	4	.64	6	.246	.312	.421
1997 Knoxville	AA Tor	10	29	6	1	0	0	7	0	1	3	0	6	0	0	0	0	0	—	0	.207	.281	.241
Dunedin	A+ Tor	74	231	59	14	0	15	118	36	48	24	4	53	0	0	1	3	2	.60	4	.255	.324	.511
1998 Mobile	AA SD	104	363	100	22	2	16	174	47	66	40	1	108	0	0	1	6	1	.86	4	.275	.347	.479
1999 Mobile	AA SD	133	474	135	30	3	22	237	79	76	77	3	137	1	0	8	9	5	.64	0	.285	.380	.500
2000 Las Vegas	AAA SD	111	292	85	25	4	5	133	43	53	35	1	80	0	0	4	2	1	.67	4	.291	.363	.455
6 Min. YEARS		626	2106	581	138	12	83	992	304	369	254	18	578	2	2	22	32	14	.70	29	.276	.351	.471

Mike Curry

Bats: Left **Throws:** Right **Pos:** OF-121; DH-1; PH-1   **Ht:** 5'10" **Wt:** 190 **Born:** 2/15/77 **Age:** 24

Year Team	Lg Org	G	AB	H	2B	3B	HR	TB	R	RBI	TBB	IBB	SO	HBP	SH	SF	SB	CS	SB%	GDP	Avg	OBP	SLG
1998 Spokane	A- KC	67	227	57	8	2	1	72	53	25	46	2	41	3	2	6	30	7	.81	1	.251	.376	.317
1999 Chston-WV	A KC	85	318	99	13	3	0	118	70	25	48	0	58	9	6	3	61	13	.82	4	.311	.413	.371
Wilmington	A+ KC	54	200	46	4	2	1	57	31	16	34	1	39	1	3	2	24	9	.73	2	.230	.342	.285
2000 Wichita	AA KC	123	461	133	18	6	4	175	104	52	94	2	99	5	4	2	52	16	.76	4	.289	.413	.380
3 Min. YEARS		329	1206	335	43	13	6	422	258	118	222	5	237	18	15	13	167	45	.79	11	.278	.394	.350

Chris Curtis

Pitches: Right **Bats:** Right **Pos:** SP-5   **Ht:** 6'2" **Wt:** 195 **Born:** 5/8/71 **Age:** 30

Year Team	Lg Org	G	GS	CG	GF	IP	BFP	H	R	ER	HR	SH	SF	HB	TBB	IBB	SO	WP	Bk	W	L	Pct.	ShO	Sv	ERA
1991 Butte	R+ Tex	6	3	0	2	12.2	69	27	23	14	1	0	0	1	4	0	7	0	3	0	2	.000	0	0	9.95
Rangers	R Tex	7	7	0	0	35	134	27	9	8	1	0	4	2	9	0	23	0	1	4	0	1.000	0	0	2.06
1992 Gastonia	A Tex	24	24	1	0	147	590	117	60	43	3	1	5	6	54	0	107	6	7	8	11	.421	1	0	2.63
1993 Charlotte	A+ Tex	27	26	1	0	151	637	159	76	67	6	4	2	8	51	0	55	4	5	8	8	.500	0	0	3.99
1994 Tulsa	AA Tex	25	23	3	1	142.2	639	173	102	85	17	4	7	7	57	5	62	9	7	3	13	.188	1	0	5.36
1995 Okla City	AAA Tex	51	0	0	22	77.1	358	81	53	43	5	6	3	5	39	3	40	2	0	3	5	.375	0	5	5.00
1996 Okla City	AAA Tex	41	2	0	13	75.2	344	91	50	43	6	4	2	3	34	3	38	10	1	2	5	.286	0	1	5.11
1997 Bowie	AA Bal	36	6	0	14	87	361	100	41	35	10	3	2	2	17	1	48	4	2	6	1	.857	0	2	3.62
1998 Rochester	AAA Bal	18	7	0	1	54	244	68	48	46	12	3	1	4	21	0	23	3	1	2	6	.250	0	0	7.67
Bowie	AA Bal	12	1	0	3	22	97	27	18	17	3	0	0	0	11	0	11	2	0	0	2	.000	0	0	6.95
St. Paul	IND —	3	2	0	0	10.2	58	13	10	9	1	0	0	1	8	0	7	3	0	2	1	.667	0	0	7.59
2000 El Paso	AA Ari	5	5	0	0	25	120	40	22	20	1	0	1	1	9	0	20	1	0	0	4	.000	0	0	7.20
9 Min. YEARS		255	106	5	56	840	3651	923	512	430	70	26	26	40	314	12	441	44	28	38	58	.396	2	8	4.61

Matt Curtis

Bats: Both **Throws:** Right **Pos:** C-28; 1B-17; 3B-13; OF-11; PH-11; DH-7   **Ht:** 6'0" **Wt:** 195 **Born:** 8/14/74 **Age:** 26

Year Team	Lg Org	G	AB	H	2B	3B	HR	TB	R	RBI	TBB	IBB	SO	HBP	SH	SF	SB	CS	SB%	GDP	Avg	OBP	SLG
1996 Boise	A- Ana	75	305	93	29	3	12	164	57	62	37	0	47	8	0	4	2	1	.67	7	.305	.390	.538
1997 Cedar Rapds	A Ana	34	113	28	8	1	4	50	21	18	17	0	16	2	0	2	0	0	—	3	.248	.351	.442
Lk Elsinore	A+ Ana	74	264	87	25	8	17	179	58	55	25	1	54	2	0	1	3	1	.75	2	.330	.390	.678
1998 Midland	AA Ana	113	431	113	19	5	10	172	53	65	33	1	72	1	3	5	2	2	.50	14	.262	.313	.399
1999 Lk Elsinore	A+ Ana	126	460	120	26	2	17	201	72	76	68	3	84	2	0	6	2	2	.50	8	.261	.354	.437
2000 Akron	AA Cle	1	4	0	0	0	0	0	0	0	0	0	0	0	0	0	0	0	—	0	.000	.000	.000
Kinston	A+ Cle	82	256	79	19	0	10	128	37	48	33	3	46	0	0	3	4	2	.67	5	.309	.384	.500
5 Min. YEARS		505	1833	520	126	19	70	894	298	324	213	8	319	15	3	21	13	8	.62	39	.284	.359	.488

Jack Cust

Bats: Left **Throws:** Right **Pos:** OF-127; DH-1; PH-1   **Ht:** 6'1" **Wt:** 205 **Born:** 1/16/79 **Age:** 22

Year Team	Lg Org	G	AB	H	2B	3B	HR	TB	R	RBI	TBB	IBB	SO	HBP	SH	SF	SB	CS	SB%	GDP	Avg	OBP	SLG
1997 Diamondbcks	R Ari	35	121	37	11	1	3	59	26	33	31	0	39	0	0	0	2	0	1.00	4	.306	.447	.488
1998 South Bend	A Ari	16	62	15	3	0	0	18	5	4	5	1	20	0	0	1	0	1	.00	0	.242	.294	.290
Lethbridge	R+ Ari	73	223	77	20	2	11	134	75	56	86	3	71	4	0	2	15	8	.65	3	.345	.530	.601
1999 High Desert	A+ Ari	125	455	152	42	3	32	296	107	112	96	2	145	2	0	3	1	4	.20	5	.334	.450	.651
2000 El Paso	AA Ari	129	447	131	32	6	20	235	100	75	117	12	150	2	0	2	12	9	.57	10	.293	.440	.526
4 Min. YEARS		378	1308	412	108	12	66	742	313	280	335	18	425	8	0	8	30	22	.58	22	.315	.455	.567

Derek Dace

Pitches: Left **Bats:** Left **Pos:** RP-58; SP-1   **Ht:** 6'7" **Wt:** 200 **Born:** 4/11/75 **Age:** 26

Year Team	Lg Org	G	GS	CG	GF	IP	BFP	H	R	ER	HR	SH	SF	HB	TBB	IBB	SO	WP	Bk	W	L	Pct.	ShO	Sv	ERA
1994 Astros	R Hou	11	11	1	0	59	245	55	26	22	2	5	2	1	21	0	52	2	3	2	3	.400	0	0	3.36
1995 Astros	R Hou	11	10	2	0	69.1	274	60	20	15	2	3	1	4	6	0	77	5	2	3	4	.429	1	0	1.95
Kissimmee	A+ Hou	1	1	0	0	2.2	17	4	5	5	0	0	1	0	5	0	1	0	0	0	1	.000	0	0	16.88
1996 Kissimmee	A+ Hou	12	0	0	3	18.1	73	19	6	6	0	0	0	0	7	0	11	1	0	0	0	—	0	1	2.95
Jackson	AA Hou	1	1	0	0	4	21	5	1	1	1	0	0	0	5	0	0	0	0	0	0	—	0	0	2.25
Auburn	A- Hou	15	15	0	0	97	400	89	41	35	7	2	1	2	35	2	87	1	0	9	4	.692	0	0	3.25
1997 Lakeland	A+ Det	2	0	0	1	2.1	9	2	1	1	0	0	0	0	1	0	0	0	0	0	0	—	0	0	3.86
W Michigan	A Det	10	2	0	3	25	100	23	2	2	0	1	0	1	4	0	24	0	0	1	0	1.000	0	2	0.72
Toledo	AAA Det	5	0	0	3	10	48	13	8	4	0	1	0	1	6	0	6	1	0	0	0	—	0	0	3.60
1998 Jacksnville	AA Det	40	0	0	15	67	277	51	32	31	8	0	2	2	29	2	48	2	0	5	3	.625	0	3	4.16

63

Year Team	Lg Org	G	GS	CG	GF	IP	BFP	H	R	ER	HR	SH	SF	HB	TBB	IBB	SO	WP	Bk	W	L	Pct.	ShO	Sv	ERA
						HOW MUCH HE PITCHED						**WHAT HE GAVE UP**										**THE RESULTS**			
1999 El Paso	AA Ari	40	0	0	14	52	232	58	33	30	4	2	2	3	23	2	34	0	0	2	2	.500	0	0	5.19
2000 El Paso	AA Ari	28	0	0	12	33.1	139	28	15	13	1	3	1	1	19	3	25	1	0	2	2	.500	0	0	3.51
Tucson	AAA Ari	31	1	0	11	35	155	37	17	16	2	2	0	0	15	1	21	1	0	2	0	1.000	0	1	4.11
7 Min. YEARS		207	41	3	63	475	1990	444	207	181	28	18	10	12	176	8	386	14	5	26	19	.578	1	7	3.43

Scott Daeley

Bats: Right **Throws:** Right **Pos:** OF-107; PH-2; PR-1 **Ht:** 5'10" **Wt:** 178 **Born:** 2/25/77 **Age:** 24

Year Team	Lg Org	G	AB	H	2B	3B	HR	TB	R	RBI	TBB	IBB	SO	HBP	SH	SF	SB	CS	SB%	GDP	Avg	OBP	SLG
					BATTING												**BASERUNNING**				**PERCENTAGES**		
1999 Salem-Keizr	A- SF	69	268	66	12	1	0	80	42	22	43	0	29	1	6	3	29	9	.76	3	.246	.349	.299
San Jose	A+ SF	2	9	2	0	0	0	2	1	0	0	0	2	0	0	0	1	0	1.00	0	.222	.222	.222
2000 San Jose	A+ SF	106	418	110	20	2	1	137	83	44	64	0	71	8	6	2	33	12	.73	7	.263	.370	.328
Shreveport	AA SF	3	2	0	0	0	0	0	1	0	0	0	0	0	0	0	1	0	1.00	0	.000	.000	.000
2 Min. YEARS		180	697	178	32	3	1	219	127	66	107	0	102	9	12	5	64	21	.75	10	.255	.359	.314

Corey Dagley

Pitches: Right **Bats:** Right **Pos:** SP-19 **Ht:** 6'2" **Wt:** 180 **Born:** 4/15/77 **Age:** 24

Year Team	Lg Org	G	GS	CG	GF	IP	BFP	H	R	ER	HR	SH	SF	HB	TBB	IBB	SO	WP	Bk	W	L	Pct.	ShO	Sv	ERA
						HOW MUCH HE PITCHED							**WHAT HE GAVE UP**										**THE RESULTS**			
1998 Batavia	A- Phi	18	5	0	2	50	210	53	31	27	3	1	1	3	11	0	37	1	0	1	5	.167	0	0	4.86
1999 Batavia	A- Phi	15	12	0	1	65.1	287	77	35	31	1	0	4	6	19	0	44	5	1	5	5	.500	0	0	4.27
2000 Reading	AA Phi	1	1	0	0	2.1	18	9	9	9	0	0	0	0	1	0	0	0	0	0	1	.000	0	0	34.71
Clearwater	A+ Phi	3	3	0	0	13.1	62	17	13	12	1	1	1	1	8	0	8	0	0	0	1	.000	0	0	8.10
Batavia	A- Phi	15	15	2	0	102.2	428	83	53	41	4	4	2	11	28	5	45	3	1	4	4	.500	1	0	3.59
3 Min. YEARS		52	36	2	3	233.2	1005	239	141	120	9	6	8	21	67	5	134	9	2	10	16	.385	1	0	4.62

Carl Dale

Pitches: Right **Bats:** Right **Pos:** RP-17 **Ht:** 6'2" **Wt:** 200 **Born:** 12/7/72 **Age:** 28

Year Team	Lg Org	G	GS	CG	GF	IP	BFP	H	R	ER	HR	SH	SF	HB	TBB	IBB	SO	WP	Bk	W	L	Pct.	ShO	Sv	ERA
						HOW MUCH HE PITCHED							**WHAT HE GAVE UP**										**THE RESULTS**			
1994 New Jersey	A- StL	15	15	0	0	73	333	79	44	37	2	3	2	3	38	0	75	10	0	2	7	.222	0	0	4.56
1995 Peoria	A StL	24	24	2	0	143.2	613	124	66	47	8	3	2	1	62	0	104	4	1	9	9	.500	1	0	2.94
1996 Modesto	A+ Oak	26	24	0	0	128.1	565	124	79	61	11	2	5	5	72	0	102	12	0	8	2	.800	0	0	4.28
1997 Huntsville	AA Oak	20	16	0	0	85.1	389	95	61	51	10	1	3	8	43	0	57	4	0	6	4	.600	0	0	5.38
1998 Huntsville	AA Oak	3	3	0	0	13.2	60	13	7	7	2	0	2	0	8	0	10	0	0	1	1	.500	0	0	4.61
Modesto	A+ Oak	3	3	0	0	19	74	15	6	5	1	0	0	3	2	0	14	0	0	1	2	.333	0	0	2.37
Edmonton	AAA Oak	11	11	1	0	64	276	64	31	29	12	1	2	6	26	0	41	3	0	5	3	.625	1	0	4.08
1999 Vancouver	AAA Oak	29	0	0	11	44	189	41	19	17	0	1	1	2	18	1	27	1	0	4	3	.571	0	4	3.48
Louisville	AAA Mil	7	0	0	2	11.2	48	8	6	6	2	0	1	0	5	0	8	0	0	0	1	.000	0	1	4.63
2000 Akron	AA Cle	4	0	0	1	6	31	10	6	6	0	0	0	1	3	0	7	0	0	0	0	—	0	0	9.00
Buffalo	AAA Cle	7	0	0	5	14	68	17	9	9	1	0	0	0	9	0	6	1	0	0	0	—	0	0	5.79
Trenton	AA Bos	6	0	0	1	8	41	7	6	6	1	1	1	0	10	0	5	1	0	0	0	—	0	0	6.75
1999 Milwaukee	NL	4	0	0	1	4	27	8	9	9	2	0	0	1	6	0	4	0	0	0	1	.000	0	0	20.25
7 Min. YEARS		155	96	3	22	610.2	2687	597	340	281	50	12	19	29	296	1	456	36	1	36	32	.529	2	5	4.14

Mark Dalesandro

Bats: Right **Throws:** Right **Pos:** C-38; PH-6; 1B-5; OF-4; 3B-3; PR-2; 2B-1; DH-1 **Ht:** 6'0" **Wt:** 195 **Born:** 5/14/68 **Age:** 33

Year Team	Lg Org	G	AB	H	2B	3B	HR	TB	R	RBI	TBB	IBB	SO	HBP	SH	SF	SB	CS	SB%	GDP	Avg	OBP	SLG
					BATTING												**BASERUNNING**				**PERCENTAGES**		
1990 Boise	A- Ana	55	223	75	10	2	6	107	35	44	19	2	42	1	0	1	6	1	.86	6	.336	.389	.480
1991 Quad City	A Ana	125	487	133	17	8	5	181	63	69	34	1	58	6	0	4	1	2	.33	10	.273	.326	.372
1992 Palm Spring	A+ Ana	126	492	146	30	3	7	203	72	92	33	6	50	5	0	6	6	2	.75	20	.297	.343	.413
1993 Palm Spring	A+ Ana	46	176	43	5	3	1	57	22	25	15	1	20	0	0	7	3	2	.60	9	.244	.293	.324
Midland	AA Ana	57	235	69	9	0	2	84	33	36	8	2	30	4	0	5	1	1	.50	9	.294	.321	.357
Vancouver	AAA Ana	26	107	32	8	1	2	48	16	15	6	1	13	1	0	1	1	0	1.00	6	.299	.339	.449
1994 Vancouver	AAA Ana	51	199	63	9	1	1	77	29	31	7	0	19	1	0	2	1	0	1.00	6	.317	.340	.387
1995 Vancouver	AAA Ana	34	123	41	13	1	1	59	16	18	6	0	12	1	0	1	2	0	1.00	2	.333	.366	.480
1996 Columbus	AAA NYY	78	255	72	29	4	2	115	34	38	17	0	31	5	0	2	2	0	1.00	9	.282	.337	.451
1997 Iowa	AAA ChC	115	405	106	14	0	8	144	48	48	33	3	51	2	0	5	0	0	—	15	.262	.317	.356
1998 Syracuse	AAA Tor	45	164	44	9	1	10	85	25	30	12	1	20	5	0	1	1	0	1.00	3	.268	.335	.518
1999 Syracuse	AAA Tor	20	71	16	2	0	0	18	3	5	1	0	7	2	0	2	1	0	1.00	1	.225	.250	.254
2000 Syracuse	AAA Tor	1	3	1	0	0	1	4	1	1	0	0	1	0	0	0	0	0	—	0	.333	.333	1.333
Indianapols	AAA Mil	37	95	17	1	0	1	21	10	7	3	0	10	4	3	1	0	0	—	5	.179	.233	.221
Iowa	AAA ChC	15	49	19	3	1	0	24	5	8	1	0	4	0	0	2	1	0	1.00	6	.388	.400	.490
1994 California	AL	19	25	5	1	0	1	9	5	2	2	0	4	0	0	0	0	0	—	0	.200	.259	.360
1995 California	AL	11	10	1	1	0	0	2	1	0	0	0	2	0	0	0	0	0	—	0	.100	.100	.200
1998 Toronto	AL	32	67	20	5	0	2	31	8	14	1	0	6	0	0	1	0	0	—	3	.299	.304	.463
1999 Toronto	AL	16	27	5	0	0	0	5	3	1	0	0	2	1	0	0	1	0	1.00	0	.185	.207	.185
11 Min. YEARS		831	3084	877	159	25	47	1227	412	467	195	17	368	37	3	38	25	8	.76	101	.284	.331	.398
4 Maj. YEARS		78	129	31	7	0	3	47	17	17	3	0	14	1	0	2	1	0	1.00	6	.240	.259	.364

Brian Dallimore

Bats: Right **Throws:** Right **Pos:** 3B-54; 2B-38; PH-14; DH-7; SS-5; OF-1; PR-1 **Ht:** 6'1" **Wt:** 185 **Born:** 11/15/73 **Age:** 27

Year Team	Lg Org	G	AB	H	2B	3B	HR	TB	R	RBI	TBB	IBB	SO	HBP	SH	SF	SB	CS	SB%	GDP	Avg	OBP	SLG
					BATTING												**BASERUNNING**				**PERCENTAGES**		
1996 Auburn	A- Hou	74	290	77	17	3	5	115	50	30	18	0	38	10	0	4	7	5	.58	5	.266	.326	.397
1997 Quad City	A Hou	130	492	128	23	3	6	175	80	48	38	0	76	20	6	5	24	8	.75	19	.260	.335	.356
Kissimmee	A+ Hou	1	3	0	0	0	0	0	0	0	0	0	2	0	0	0	0	0	—	0	.000	.000	.000

64

Year Team	Lg Org	G	AB	H	2B	3B	HR	TB	R	RBI	TBB	IBB	SO	HBP	SH	SF	SB	CS	SB%	GDP	Avg	OBP	SLG
		BATTING															BASERUNNING				PERCENTAGES		
1998 Kissimmee	A+ Hou	62	240	61	11	1	0	74	34	19	19	0	42	5	4	1	7	5	.58	6	.254	.321	.308
1999 Kissimmee	A+ Hou	19	74	20	2	0	0	22	12	3	4	0	10	3	1	1	2	1	.67	1	.270	.329	.297
Jackson	AA Hou	70	251	67	13	1	5	97	38	19	16	0	44	10	2	1	13	3	.81	12	.267	.335	.386
2000 Round Rock	AA Hou	5	11	2	1	0	1	6	1	3	1	0	3	0	0	0	0	0	—	0	.182	.250	.545
El Paso	AA Ari	107	356	99	16	1	4	129	50	53	25	3	55	6	3	5	17	3	.85	13	.278	.332	.362
5 Min. YEARS		468	1717	454	83	9	21	618	265	175	121	3	270	54	16	17	70	25	.74	56	.264	.329	.360

Craig da Luz

Bats: Right **Throws:** Right **Pos:** 2B-29; 3B-24; 1B-20; OF-18; SS-10; DH-7; PH-1; PR-1 **Ht:** 6'3" **Wt:** 195 **Born:** 2/4/75 **Age:** 26

Year Team	Lg Org	G	AB	H	2B	3B	HR	TB	R	RBI	TBB	IBB	SO	HBP	SH	SF	SB	CS	SB%	GDP	Avg	OBP	SLG
		BATTING															BASERUNNING				PERCENTAGES		
1998 Jamestown	A- Det	47	159	41	6	3	4	65	27	19	5	0	29	7	3	1	6	4	.60	6	.258	.308	.409
1999 W Michigan	A Det	87	314	83	14	5	3	116	36	49	20	0	46	3	2	4	3	1	.75	6	.264	.311	.369
2000 Lakeland	A+ Det	102	382	93	25	4	3	135	40	46	17	0	72	3	1	4	3	8	.27	13	.243	.278	.353
Jacksnville	AA Det	4	9	2	0	1	1	7	2	2	2	0	1	0	0	0	0	0	—	0	.222	.364	.778
3 Min. YEARS		240	864	219	45	13	11	323	105	116	44	0	148	13	6	9	12	13	.48	25	.253	.297	.374

Pat Daneker

Pitches: Right **Bats:** Right **Pos:** SP-27; RP-2 **Ht:** 6'3" **Wt:** 195 **Born:** 1/14/76 **Age:** 25

Year Team	Lg Org	G	GS	CG	GF	IP	BFP	H	R	ER	HR	SH	SF	HB	TBB	IBB	SO	WP	Bk	W	L	Pct.	ShO	Sv	ERA
		HOW MUCH HE PITCHED						WHAT HE GAVE UP												THE RESULTS					
1997 Bristol	R+ CWS	12	12	0	0	63.2	294	83	55	46	5	2	3	5	20	1	53	4	5	3	6	.333	0	0	6.50
1998 Hickory	A CWS	17	17	2	0	117	474	115	50	41	14	2	0	1	16	0	95	2	6	6	6	.500	0	0	3.15
Winston-Sal	A+ CWS	7	7	2	0	53	210	51	13	12	3	2	0	2	5	1	43	1	4	5	0	1.000	0	0	2.04
1999 Birmingham	AA CWS	16	16	3	0	109	451	106	46	39	6	2	2	2	30	1	71	4	2	6	8	.429	0	0	3.22
Charlotte	AAA CWS	9	9	1	0	49.1	230	64	36	36	10	1	2	3	16	0	36	4	0	4	4	.500	0	0	6.57
2000 Charlotte	AAA CWS	27	25	0	0	144	633	168	102	92	26	2	3	4	49	1	69	4	4	8	12	.400	0	0	5.75
Syracuse	AAA Tor	2	2	0	0	13.2	58	18	6	5	2	0	1	1	2	0	4	1	0	1	1	.500	0	0	3.29
1999 Chicago	AL	3	2	0	1	15	64	14	8	7	1	2	1	0	6	0	5	0	0	0	0	—	0	0	4.20
4 Min. YEARS		90	88	8	0	549.2	2350	605	308	271	66	11	11	18	138	4	371	20	21	33	37	.471	0	0	4.44

David Daniels

Pitches: Right **Bats:** Right **Pos:** RP-40 **Ht:** 6'2" **Wt:** 182 **Born:** 7/25/73 **Age:** 27

Year Team	Lg Org	G	GS	CG	GF	IP	BFP	H	R	ER	HR	SH	SF	HB	TBB	IBB	SO	WP	Bk	W	L	Pct.	ShO	Sv	ERA
		HOW MUCH HE PITCHED						WHAT HE GAVE UP												THE RESULTS					
1995 Johnstown	IND —	28	0	0	9	44	186	36	22	16	1	3	1	4	15	1	40	1	3	4	1	.800	0	3	3.27
1996 Augusta	A Pit	11	0	0	7	12.1	58	21	8	7	0	1	0	0	3	1	14	0	1	0	1	.000	0	3	5.11
Erie	A- Pit	31	0	0	19	36.1	150	33	12	11	3	3	1	4	5	3	45	0	0	1	3	.250	0	7	2.72
1997 Augusta	A Pit	44	0	0	39	55	231	51	22	16	0	1	0	1	13	3	51	0	1	6	3	.667	0	18	2.62
Lynchburg	A+ Pit	10	0	0	8	10	36	6	2	2	1	0	0	0	1	0	6	1	0	1	1	.500	0	4	1.80
1998 Lynchburg	A+ Pit	14	0	0	12	18.1	65	9	3	3	2	1	0	0	3	0	19	0	0	0	0	—	0	9	1.47
Carolina	AA Pit	35	0	0	32	39.1	163	34	15	13	0	1	3	2	16	1	37	2	2	4	3	.571	0	16	2.97
Nashville	AAA Pit	2	0	0	0	1	4	0	0	0	0	0	0	0	2	0	1	0	0	0	0	—	0	0	0.00
1999 Altoona	AA Pit	55	0	0	29	67.1	276	55	21	20	6	3	1	2	19	2	63	1	0	2	2	.500	0	8	2.67
2000 Mobile	AA SD	9	0	0	0	11.1	50	10	7	5	0	0	0	0	5	0	11	0	0	0	1	.000	0	0	3.97
Potomac	A+ StL	31	0	0	3	42.1	158	27	8	6	1	0	1	3	8	0	36	3	0	2	2	.500	0	0	1.28
6 Min. YEARS		270	0	0	158	337.1	1377	282	120	99	14	13	7	16	90	11	323	8	7	20	17	.541	0	68	2.64

John Daniels

Pitches: Right **Bats:** Both **Pos:** RP-41 **Ht:** 6'3" **Wt:** 182 **Born:** 2/7/74 **Age:** 27

Year Team	Lg Org	G	GS	CG	GF	IP	BFP	H	R	ER	HR	SH	SF	HB	TBB	IBB	SO	WP	Bk	W	L	Pct.	ShO	Sv	ERA
		HOW MUCH HE PITCHED						WHAT HE GAVE UP												THE RESULTS					
1993 Mariners	R Sea	13	8	0	0	53	222	46	30	20	0	1	4	5	13	0	50	8	2	3	4	.429	0	0	3.40
1994 Bellingham	A- Sea	20	2	0	3	41.1	196	49	22	17	4	2	2	4	21	0	42	3	2	2	2	.500	0	1	3.70
1995 Wisconsin	A Sea	39	0	0	19	74.1	315	63	28	22	5	0	2	6	22	2	60	2	0	4	5	.444	0	7	2.66
1996 Lancaster	A+ Sea	43	0	0	23	95.1	412	91	51	35	9	3	2	8	30	1	100	3	0	3	5	.375	0	8	3.30
1997 St. Pete	A+ TB	55	0	0	44	61.1	255	53	24	18	4	3	1	3	14	3	72	3	0	4	4	.500	0	29	2.64
1998 Durham	AAA TB	4	0	0	1	9.2	34	4	2	2	1	0	1	0	3	0	9	1	0	2	0	1.000	0	1	1.86
Orlando	AA TB	11	0	0	3	18.2	82	14	12	11	4	0	3	2	9	3	19	0	0	1	2	.333	0	0	5.30
St. Pete	A+ TB	34	0	0	33	40.2	170	31	12	8	3	3	1	4	11	1	46	4	1	4	2	.667	0	19	1.77
1999 Durham	AAA TB	21	0	0	8	35	154	37	19	19	2	1	1	4	9	0	25	2	0	2	0	1.000	0	0	4.89
Orlando	AA TB	38	0	0	30	52	208	33	14	11	2	1	3	4	15	3	40	3	1	3	2	.600	0	14	1.90
2000 Reading	AA Phi	41	0	0	22	84.1	346	78	35	34	10	3	0	2	23	1	75	2	0	7	5	.583	0	10	3.63
8 Min. YEARS		319	10	0	186	565.2	2394	499	249	197	44	17	20	42	170	14	538	31	6	35	31	.530	0	89	3.13

Tommy Darrell

Pitches: Right **Bats:** Right **Pos:** RP-43; SP-3 **Ht:** 6'6" **Wt:** 220 **Born:** 7/21/76 **Age:** 24

Year Team	Lg Org	G	GS	CG	GF	IP	BFP	H	R	ER	HR	SH	SF	HB	TBB	IBB	SO	WP	Bk	W	L	Pct.	ShO	Sv	ERA
		HOW MUCH HE PITCHED						WHAT HE GAVE UP												THE RESULTS					
1995 Angels	R Ana	18	5	0	7	63	254	51	18	12	1	1	3	4	14	0	49	3	1	4	3	.571	0	2	1.71
1996 Boise	A- Ana	15	15	1	0	101	433	114	56	39	11	2	2	4	13	2	76	2	0	8	1	.889	1	0	3.48
1997 Cedar Rapds	A Ana	27	26	5	0	191.2	810	212	108	86	18	7	0	6	40	1	106	7	2	12	10	.545	0	0	4.04
1998 Lk Elsinore	A+ Ana	21	16	0	2	97.2	465	120	76	62	7	2	2	11	44	3	56	14	4	4	11	.267	0	0	5.71
Cedar Rapds	A Ana	9	9	3	0	66.2	281	68	35	30	7	0	3	2	17	0	44	7	0	3	4	.429	0	0	4.05
1999 Sarasota	A+ Bos	30	12	1	6	101	455	118	75	56	8	5	7	5	30	5	67	11	0	4	10	.286	0	3	4.99
2000 Sarasota	A+ Bos	44	3	0	21	96.2	422	98	53	44	8	3	4	9	34	6	71	2	0	4	4	.500	0	5	4.10
Trenton	AA Bos	2	0	0	1	2	8	2	0	0	0	0	0	0	1	0	1	1	0	0	0	—	0	1	0.00
6 Min. YEARS		166	86	10	37	719.2	3128	783	421	329	60	20	21	41	193	17	470	47	7	39	43	.476	1	11	4.11

Bobby Darula

Bats: Left **Throws:** Right **Pos:** OF-57; DH-43; PH-5; 1B-1; PR-1 **Ht:** 5'10" **Wt:** 175 **Born:** 10/29/74 **Age:** 26

Year Team	Lg Org	G	AB	H	2B	3B	HR	TB	R	RBI	TBB	IBB	SO	HBP	SH	SF	SB	CS	SB%	GDP	Avg	OBP	SLG
1996 Ogden	R+ Mil	45	106	29	4	0	4	45	19	23	17	0	22	2	0	1	2	0	1.00	2	.274	.381	.425
1997 Ogden	R+ Mil	69	262	87	26	4	6	139	61	52	42	0	23	5	1	4	11	2	.85	5	.332	.428	.531
1998 Stockton	A+ Mil	18	45	13	4	1	1	22	10	8	8	1	6	1	1	0	2	0	1.00	1	.289	.407	.489
1999 Beloit	A Mil	120	438	133	24	8	4	185	63	75	62	4	57	7	1	4	19	5	.79	7	.304	.395	.422
2000 Huntsville	AA Mil	35	117	28	7	0	1	38	17	10	14	0	17	3	0	1	3	1	.75	1	.239	.333	.325
Beloit	A Mil	71	237	91	18	3	3	124	56	43	44	2	25	0	0	3	16	2	.89	2	.384	.491	.523
5 Min. YEARS		358	1205	381	83	16	19	553	226	211	187	7	150	27	3	13	53	10	.84	18	.316	.416	.459

David Darwin

Pitches: Left **Bats:** Left **Pos:** RP-19; SP-5 **Ht:** 6'0" **Wt:** 185 **Born:** 12/19/73 **Age:** 27

Year Team	Lg Org	G	GS	CG	GF	IP	BFP	H	R	ER	HR	SH	SF	HB	TBB	IBB	SO	WP	Bk	W	L	Pct.	ShO	Sv	ERA
1996 Fayettevlle	A Det	17	9	0	0	59	234	54	22	21	2	0	1	2	12	1	49	5	3	5	2	.714	0	0	3.20
1997 W Michigan	A Det	21	4	0	10	40.1	164	23	7	4	2	0	2	2	20	2	31	0	1	1	0	1.000	0	3	0.89
Lakeland	A+ Det	12	12	1	0	82.2	326	70	23	23	2	3	2	0	18	0	41	1	1	10	1	.909	0	0	2.50
1998 Toledo	AAA Det	1	1	1	0	7	25	4	1	1	1	0	0	1	0	0	5	0	0	1	0	1.000	0	0	1.29
Jacksnville	AA Det	24	23	2	1	139.2	612	152	94	83	22	3	2	6	52	0	76	2	2	12	6	.667	1	0	5.35
1999 Jacksnville	AA Det	28	28	3	0	187.1	813	194	95	74	19	1	6	11	58	1	100	2	0	14	12	.538	1	0	3.56
2000 Toledo	AAA Det	24	5	0	8	64.2	292	70	44	42	11	1	3	2	41	0	47	3	0	1	6	.143	0	0	5.85
5 Min. YEARS		127	82	7	19	580.2	2466	567	286	248	59	8	16	24	201	4	349	13	7	44	27	.620	2	3	3.84

Joe Davenport

Pitches: Right **Bats:** Right **Pos:** RP-59 **Ht:** 6'5" **Wt:** 225 **Born:** 3/24/76 **Age:** 25

Year Team	Lg Org	G	GS	CG	GF	IP	BFP	H	R	ER	HR	SH	SF	HB	TBB	IBB	SO	WP	Bk	W	L	Pct.	ShO	Sv	ERA
1994 Blue Jays	R Tor	7	1	0	2	11	48	12	5	4	0	0	1	0	7	0	2	1	1	0	0	—	0	0	3.27
1995 Hagerstown	A Tor	13	0	0	2	17.2	91	22	19	12	3	0	1	1	13	0	13	6	0	0	1	.000	0	0	6.11
Blue Jays	R Tor	15	10	1	1	55.2	267	67	47	35	2	3	2	3	30	0	29	9	3	2	3	.400	0	1	5.66
1996 St.Cathrnes	A- Tor	20	8	0	3	66.2	295	71	44	38	5	4	3	5	23	0	43	0	0	2	4	.333	0	0	5.13
1997 Hagerstown	A Tor	37	0	0	29	51.1	225	43	26	21	0	4	1	4	24	2	43	8	0	4	6	.400	0	10	3.68
1998 Winston-Sal	A+ CWS	20	0	0	15	26	106	25	9	4	0	0	1	2	4	0	26	3	0	2	0	1.000	0	2	1.38
Birmingham	AA CWS	26	0	0	15	38.2	202	54	36	31	2	1	4	2	30	0	22	5	0	3	2	.600	0	1	7.22
1999 Charlotte	AAA CWS	6	0	0	1	9	40	13	8	8	0	0	0	1	1	0	6	0	0	0	0	—	0	0	8.00
Birmingham	AA CWS	40	0	0	33	49.1	213	43	26	17	3	4	3	2	19	1	24	8	0	3	5	.375	0	10	3.10
2000 Charlotte	AAA CWS	59	0	0	33	70.2	314	74	41	36	6	7	4	11	27	2	42	7	1	1	4	.200	0	9	4.58
1999 Chicago	AL	3	0	0	2	1.2	7	1	0	0	0	0	0	0	2	0	0	0	0	0	0	—	0	0	0.00
7 Min. YEARS		243	19	1	134	396	1801	424	261	206	21	23	19	32	178	5	250	55	5	17	25	.405	0	33	4.68

Cleatus Davidson

Bats: Both **Throws:** Right **Pos:** SS-109; 2B-8; DH-2; PH-2; PR-1 **Ht:** 5'10" **Wt:** 180 **Born:** 11/1/76 **Age:** 24

Year Team	Lg Org	G	AB	H	2B	3B	HR	TB	R	RBI	TBB	IBB	SO	HBP	SH	SF	SB	CS	SB%	GDP	Avg	OBP	SLG
1994 Twins	R Min	24	85	15	1	0	0	16	8	5	9	0	19	0	1	1	3	1	.75	0	.176	.253	.188
1995 Twins	R Min	21	75	15	2	1	0	19	11	5	10	0	17	0	0	0	8	3	.73	0	.200	.294	.253
Elizabethtn	R+ Min	39	152	45	6	2	3	64	27	27	11	0	31	0	0	0	10	4	.71	2	.296	.355	.421
1996 Fort Wayne	A Min	59	203	36	8	3	0	50	20	30	23	0	45	0	1	2	2	3	.40	4	.177	.259	.246
Elizabethtn	R+ Min	65	248	71	10	6	6	111	53	31	39	2	45	2	3	1	17	6	.74	5	.286	.386	.448
1997 Fort Wayne	A Min	124	478	122	16	8	6	172	80	52	52	1	100	1	5	4	39	9	.81	7	.255	.327	.360
1998 Fort Myers	A+ Min	130	527	127	12	7	2	159	97	45	45	0	99	3	13	3	44	16	.73	6	.241	.303	.302
1999 New Britain	AA Min	127	491	120	16	10	2	162	88	40	53	1	110	3	10	6	40	14	.74	8	.244	.318	.330
2000 New Britain	AA Min	119	445	102	13	7	0	129	42	31	28	0	93	3	10	1	15	7	.68	6	.229	.279	.290
1999 Minnesota	AL	12	22	3	0	0	0	3	3	3	0	0	4	0	2	0	2	0	1.00	2	.136	.136	.136
7 Min. YEARS		708	2704	653	84	44	19	882	426	266	270	4	559	15	43	18	178	63	.74	38	.241	.312	.326

Allen Davis

Pitches: Left **Bats:** Left **Pos:** SP-26; RP-3 **Ht:** 6'4" **Wt:** 195 **Born:** 10/1/75 **Age:** 25

Year Team	Lg Org	G	GS	CG	GF	IP	BFP	H	R	ER	HR	SH	SF	HB	TBB	IBB	SO	WP	Bk	W	L	Pct.	ShO	Sv	ERA
1998 Yakima	A- LA	4	2	0	1	16	61	10	4	2	0	0	0	0	3	0	14	1	0	2	0	1.000	0	0	1.13
San Berndo	A+ LA	5	5	0	0	31	127	30	13	10	2	1	1	0	7	0	34	1	2	1	2	.333	0	0	2.90
San Antonio	AA LA	6	5	0	0	31.1	132	31	13	11	2	1	0	1	9	0	33	0	1	2	2	.500	0	0	3.16
1999 San Antonio	AA LA	29	20	1	3	130	574	140	83	61	13	5	4	4	46	1	87	4	0	7	10	.412	1	0	4.22
2000 San Antonio	AA LA	29	26	3	0	163	706	187	91	82	18	6	6	6	51	0	123	1	0	10	8	.556	1	0	4.53
3 Min. YEARS		73	58	4	4	371.1	1600	398	204	166	35	13	11	11	116	1	291	7	3	22	22	.500	2	0	4.02

Clint Davis

Pitches: Right **Bats:** Right **Pos:** RP-58; SP-2 **Ht:** 6'3" **Wt:** 205 **Born:** 9/26/69 **Age:** 31

Year Team	Lg Org	G	GS	CG	GF	IP	BFP	H	R	ER	HR	SH	SF	HB	TBB	IBB	SO	WP	Bk	W	L	Pct.	ShO	Sv	ERA
1991 Cardinals	R StL	21	0	0	9	26.2	130	35	23	17	0	3	3	1	12	0	25	1	2	3	3	.500	0	0	5.74
1992 Savannah	A StL	51	0	0	23	65	272	49	24	16	0	4	3	4	21	6	61	3	0	4	2	.667	0	1	2.22
1993 St. Pete	A+ StL	29	0	0	26	58	118	26	8	6	0	1	1	0	10	0	44	0	0	1	0	1.000	0	19	1.93
Arkansas	AA StL	28	0	0	10	37	143	22	10	8	1	2	1	3	10	3	37	0	0	2	0	1.000	0	0	1.95
1995 Louisville	AAA StL	4	0	0	0	3.2	19	6	5	5	1	0	0	0	2	1	4	0	1	0	0	—	0	0	12.27
Rio Grande	IND —	38	0	0	36	40	162	29	17	12	4	2	0	2	9	2	59	0	1	5	2	.600	0	21	2.70

Year Team	Lg Org	G	GS	CG	GF	IP	BFP	H	R	ER	HR	SH	SF	HB	TBB	IBB	SO	WP	Bk	W	L	Pct.	ShO	Sv	ERA
1996 Okla City	AAA Tex	8	0	0	1	13	60	14	5	5	1	1	0	3	6	0	16	0	0	0	0	—	0	0	3.46
Tulsa	AA Tex	32	0	0	24	48	186	31	11	10	3	4	1	3	12	1	40	1	0	3	3	.500	0	10	1.88
1997 Okla City	AAA Tex	40	1	0	11	70.1	309	55	28	25	4	0	3	5	46	9	53	1	0	6	1	.857	0	0	3.20
1999 High Desert	A+ Ari	2	0	0	1	2	9	0	1	1	0	2	0	0	2	0	3	1	0	1	0	1.000	0	0	4.50
Atlantic Ct	IND —	18	0	0	11	19	82	17	8	7	2	1	1	2	6	0	25	0	0	1	1	.500	0	7	3.32
2000 El Paso	AA Ari	11	0	0	7	10.1	43	6	2	1	0	1	0	0	6	0	16	0	0	0	1	.000	0	1	0.87
Tucson	AAA Ari	49	2	0	19	74.2	336	80	43	34	3	4	3	2	30	5	56	2	1	1	3	.250	0	3	4.10
8 Min. YEARS		331	3	0	178	437.2	1869	370	185	147	19	24	15	26	172	21	439	9	5	25	16	.610	0	63	3.02

Glenn Davis

Bats: Both **Throws:** Left **Pos:** 1B-72; OF-31; DH-7; PH-4   **Ht:** 6'1" **Wt:** 200 **Born:** 11/25/75 **Age:** 25

					BATTING												BASERUNNING				PERCENTAGES		
Year Team	Lg Org	G	AB	H	2B	3B	HR	TB	R	RBI	TBB	IBB	SO	HBP	SH	SF	SB	CS	SB%	GDP	Avg	OBP	SLG
1997 San Berndno	A+ LA	64	228	56	16	0	9	99	44	36	46	0	77	2	0	0	7	3	.70	3	.246	.377	.434
1998 Vero Beach	A+ LA	102	376	89	14	2	20	167	63	63	70	1	106	2	0	5	13	4	.76	7	.237	.355	.444
San Antonio	AA LA	20	69	20	0	0	6	40	14	15	10	0	22	0	0	0	2	0	1.00	2	.290	.380	.580
1999 San Antonio	AA LA	134	492	128	33	4	10	199	72	63	69	4	130	0	1	2	6	7	.46	12	.260	.350	.404
2000 San Antonio	AA LA	113	377	78	17	6	9	134	54	40	58	2	113	3	2	1	2	0	1.00	11	.207	.317	.355
4 Min. YEARS		433	1542	371	82	12	54	639	247	217	253	7	448	7	3	8	30	14	.68	35	.241	.349	.414

Jason Davis

Pitches: Left **Bats:** Left **Pos:** RP-46   **Ht:** 6'3" **Wt:** 195 **Born:** 8/15/74 **Age:** 26

		HOW MUCH HE PITCHED						WHAT HE GAVE UP												THE RESULTS					
Year Team	Lg Org	G	GS	CG	GF	IP	BFP	H	R	ER	HR	SH	SF	HB	TBB	IBB	SO	WP	Bk	W	L	Pct.	ShO	Sv	ERA
1996 Piedmont	A Phi	19	0	0	10	24.2	100	16	6	5	1	0	2	4	5	1	22	1	1	6	1	.857	0	2	1.82
1997 Piedmont	A Phi	17	0	0	7	29.1	102	10	3	2	1	2	0	0	6	0	34	0	0	1	0	1.000	0	1	0.61
Clearwater	A+ Phi	24	0	0	6	42.1	169	31	11	7	0	2	0	1	17	0	36	4	1	2	1	.667	0	2	1.49
1998 Reading	AA Phi	45	10	0	11	104.2	488	116	68	56	8	5	1	8	55	3	81	6	2	6	8	.429	0	1	4.82
1999 Shreveport	AA SF	52	0	0	38	64	249	42	9	9	1	3	0	1	22	1	54	2	2	5	1	.833	0	21	1.27
2000 Fresno	AAA SF	46	0	0	16	77.2	372	104	60	54	10	2	1	3	36	0	39	9	1	4	5	.444	0	0	6.26
5 Min. YEARS		203	10	0	88	342.2	1480	319	157	133	21	14	4	17	141	5	266	22	7	24	16	.600	0	27	3.49

Lance Davis

Pitches: Left **Bats:** Right **Pos:** SP-21; RP-9   **Ht:** 6'0" **Wt:** 160 **Born:** 9/1/76 **Age:** 24

		HOW MUCH HE PITCHED						WHAT HE GAVE UP												THE RESULTS					
Year Team	Lg Org	G	GS	CG	GF	IP	BFP	H	R	ER	HR	SH	SF	HB	TBB	IBB	SO	WP	Bk	W	L	Pct.	ShO	Sv	ERA
1995 Abilene	IND —	3	0	0	1	3.1	18	5	3	2	1	0	0	0	2	0	0	1	0	0	0	—	0	0	5.40
Princeton	R+ Cin	15	9	0	0	58	271	77	39	25	2	2	1	3	25	2	43	6	2	3	7	.300	0	0	3.88
1996 Chston-WV	A Cin	4	0	0	2	3.2	17	4	1	1	1	0	0	0	2	0	5	0	0	1	0	1.000	0	0	2.45
Billings	R+ Cin	16	5	0	0	45.2	232	59	41	34	5	1	2	1	33	0	43	5	2	2	3	.400	0	0	6.70
Princeton	R+ Cin	2	2	1	0	15	55	6	4	2	0	0	0	0	3	0	19	0	0	2	0	1.000	1	0	1.20
1997 Burlington	A Cin	30	13	0	8	97	452	121	78	71	6	4	3	1	55	0	51	8	3	4	6	.400	0	0	6.59
1998 Burlington	A Cin	25	4	0	5	54.1	216	35	17	12	3	5	0	2	29	4	38	6	0	4	2	.667	0	1	1.99
1999 Rockford	A Cin	22	20	1	0	127.1	550	135	62	54	9	5	2	4	49	1	95	2	0	7	5	.583	0	0	3.82
2000 Chattanooga	AA Cin	25	16	1	3	115.2	484	96	41	28	4	6	2	2	52	3	98	9	1	7	5	.583	1	0	2.18
Louisville	AAA Cin	5	5	0	0	32	136	32	19	12	4	0	4	1	8	1	14	0	0	1	0	1.000	0	0	3.38
6 Min. YEARS		147	74	3	20	552	2431	570	305	241	35	23	14	14	258	11	406	37	8	31	28	.525	2	0	3.93

Tommy Davis

Bats: Right **Throws:** Right **Pos:** 1B-70; C-33; OF-11; 3B-7; DH-6; PH-2   **Ht:** 6'1" **Wt:** 210 **Born:** 5/21/73 **Age:** 28

					BATTING												BASERUNNING				PERCENTAGES		
Year Team	Lg Org	G	AB	H	2B	3B	HR	TB	R	RBI	TBB	IBB	SO	HBP	SH	SF	SB	CS	SB%	GDP	Avg	OBP	SLG
1994 Albany	A Bal	61	216	59	10	1	5	86	35	35	18	0	52	2	0	3	2	4	.33	6	.273	.331	.398
1995 Frederick	A+ Bal	130	496	133	26	3	15	210	62	57	41	7	105	4	1	3	7	1	.88	14	.268	.327	.423
Bowie	AA Bal	9	32	10	3	0	3	22	5	10	1	0	9	1	0	0	0	0	—	1	.313	.353	.688
1996 Bowie	AA Bal	137	524	137	32	2	14	215	75	54	41	4	113	10	3	3	5	8	.38	16	.261	.325	.410
1997 Rochester	AAA Bal	119	438	133	22	2	15	204	74	62	43	2	90	2	3	1	6	1	.86	16	.304	.368	.466
1998 Bowie	AA Bal	37	132	37	11	0	1	51	12	15	13	2	27	0	0	1	0	0	—	1	.280	.356	.386
1999 Rochester	AAA Bal	110	413	106	18	0	11	157	49	56	24	2	65	0	2	4	1	4	.20	11	.257	.295	.380
2000 Rochester	AAA Bal	122	456	131	27	0	15	203	65	64	45	7	93	0	7	0	6	3	.67	17	.287	.356	.445
1999 Baltimore	AL	5	6	1	0	0	0	1	0	0	0	0	2	0	0	0	0	0	—	1	.167	.167	.167
7 Min. YEARS		725	2707	746	149	8	79	1148	377	353	226	19	554	29	9	21	23	19	.55	82	.276	.336	.424

Zach Day

Pitches: Right **Bats:** Right **Pos:** SP-28   **Ht:** 6'4" **Wt:** 185 **Born:** 6/15/78 **Age:** 23

		HOW MUCH HE PITCHED						WHAT HE GAVE UP												THE RESULTS					
Year Team	Lg Org	G	GS	CG	GF	IP	BFP	H	R	ER	HR	SH	SF	HB	TBB	IBB	SO	WP	Bk	W	L	Pct.	ShO	Sv	ERA
1996 Yankees	R NYY	7	5	0	1	33.2	139	41	26	21	3	0	0	4	3	0	23	0	0	5	2	.714	0	0	5.61
1997 Oneonta	A- NYY	14	14	0	0	92	402	82	26	22	2	4	1	2	23	0	92	3	0	7	2	.778	0	0	2.15
1998 Tampa	A+ NYY	18	17	0	0	100	479	142	89	61	5	3	2	6	32	4	69	5	0	5	8	.385	0	0	5.49
Greensboro	A NYY	7	6	1	0	36	155	35	22	11	1	2	1	3	6	0	37	4	0	1	2	.333	0	0	2.75
1999 Yankees	R NYY	5	4	0	0	16.2	74	20	10	7	1	0	0	1	4	0	17	0	0	1	1	.500	0	0	3.78
Greensboro	A NYY	2	2	0	0	8	42	14	11	2	0	0	1	1	1	0	4	0	0	0	1	.000	0	0	2.25
2000 Yankees	A NYY	13	13	1	0	85.1	343	72	29	18	6	0	0	1	31	0	101	11	1	9	3	.750	1	0	1.90
Tampa	A+ NYY	7	7	0	0	34.1	150	33	22	16	2	0	2	1	15	1	36	1	0	3	4	.333	0	0	4.19
Akron	AA Cle	8	8	0	0	46	192	38	20	18	1	4	0	3	21	0	43	4	0	2	2	.667	0	0	3.52
5 Min. YEARS		81	76	2	1	452	1946	477	255	176	21	11	8	21	136	5	422	28	1	34	25	.576	1	0	3.50

67

Aaron Dean

Pitches: Right **Bats:** Right **Pos:** SP-23   **Ht:** 6'4" **Wt:** 180 **Born:** 4/9/79 **Age:** 22

Year Team	Lg Org	G	GS	CG	GF	IP	BFP	H	R	ER	HR	SH	SF	HB	TBB	IBB	SO	WP	Bk	W	L	Pct.	ShO	Sv	ERA
1999 St.Cathrnes	A- Tor	17	8	0	6	61.2	243	50	18	16	3	1	1	5	13	1	68	7	2	4	0	1.000	0	1	2.34
2000 Hagerstown	A Tor	19	19	0	0	112.2	472	99	55	41	8	2	6	6	38	0	89	4	0	8	3	.727	0	0	3.28
Tennessee	AA Tor	1	1	1	0	6	28	5	1	1	1	0	0	1	5	0	4	2	0	0	1	.000	0	0	1.50
Dunedin	A+ Tor	3	3	0	0	15.1	77	22	15	11	1	0	1	1	7	0	13	3	0	1	0	1.000	0	0	6.46
2 Min. YEARS		40	31	1	6	195.2	820	176	89	69	13	3	8	13	63	1	174	16	2	13	4	.765	0	1	3.17

Tim DeCinces

Bats: Left **Throws:** Right **Pos:** C-47; PH-12; DH-9; 1B-4   **Ht:** 6'2" **Wt:** 195 **Born:** 4/26/74 **Age:** 27

Year Team	Lg Org	G	AB	H	2B	3B	HR	TB	R	RBI	TBB	IBB	SO	HBP	SH	SF	SB	CS	SB%	GDP	Avg	OBP	SLG
1996 Bluefield	R+ Bal	39	128	38	8	0	7	67	24	32	24	0	28	2	0	5	3	1	.75	5	.297	.403	.523
1997 Delmarva	A Bal	127	416	107	20	0	13	166	65	70	97	1	117	0	1	3	3	4	.43	10	.257	.395	.399
1998 Rochester	AAA Bal	7	21	2	1	0	0	3	1	0	2	0	6	0	0	0	0	0	—	0	.095	.174	.143
Frederick	A+ Bal	110	374	100	25	0	16	173	50	64	59	2	90	4	1	2	3	4	.43	8	.267	.371	.463
Bowie	AA Bal	5	18	6	1	0	1	10	5	4	1	0	5	0	0	0	0	0	—	0	.333	.368	.556
1999 Bowie	AA Bal	84	258	67	15	0	12	118	38	36	54	3	52	0	0	1	0	2	.00	7	.260	.387	.457
Rochester	AAA Bal	16	53	14	5	0	2	25	7	8	0	0	12	0	0	0	0	0	—	2	.264	.264	.472
2000 Mobile	AA SD	72	207	56	9	0	11	98	34	44	42	1	28	0	0	7	1	0	1.00	4	.271	.383	.473
5 Min. YEARS		460	1475	390	84	0	62	660	224	258	279	7	338	6	2	18	10	11	.48	36	.264	.380	.447

Steve Decker

Bats: Right **Throws:** Right **Pos:** 1B-38; DH-31; C-26; 3B-15   **Ht:** 6'3" **Wt:** 217 **Born:** 10/25/65 **Age:** 35

Year Team	Lg Org	G	AB	H	2B	3B	HR	TB	R	RBI	TBB	IBB	SO	HBP	SH	SF	SB	CS	SB%	GDP	Avg	OBP	SLG
1988 Everett	A- SF	13	42	22	2	0	2	30	11	13	7	0	5	1	0	3	0	0	—	4	.524	.566	.714
San Jose	A+ SF	47	175	56	9	0	4	77	31	34	21	1	21	1	1	0	0	2	.00	4	.320	.396	.440
1989 San Jose	A+ SF	64	225	65	12	0	3	86	27	46	44	3	36	0	0	5	8	5	.62	9	.289	.398	.382
Shreveport	AA SF	44	142	46	8	0	1	57	19	18	11	0	24	0	1	1	0	3	.00	5	.324	.370	.401
1990 Shreveport	AA SF	116	403	118	22	1	15	187	52	80	40	2	64	2	0	7	3	7	.30	11	.293	.354	.464
1991 Phoenix	AAA SF	31	111	28	6	0	3	53	20	14	13	0	29	1	0	0	0	0	—	9	.252	.336	.477
1992 Phoenix	AAA SF	125	450	127	22	2	8	177	50	74	47	2	64	3	0	9	2	4	.33	19	.282	.348	.393
1994 Edmonton	AAA Fla	73	259	101	23	0	11	157	38	48	27	1	24	2	1	5	0	1	.00	7	.390	.447	.606
1996 Colo Spmgs	AAA Col	7	25	10	1	0	0	11	4	3	4	1	3	1	0	0	0	0	—	0	.400	.500	.440
1997 Tacoma	AAA Sea	99	350	104	25	1	10	161	44	52	22	0	37	1	0	5	0	0	—	10	.297	.336	.460
1998 Nashville	AAA Pit	18	62	8	3	0	2	17	5	4	5	0	14	0	0	0	0	0	—	4	.129	.194	.274
Norfolk	AAA NYM	102	354	111	21	0	12	168	55	60	54	2	49	4	0	4	2	2	.00	13	.314	.406	.475
1999 Edmonton	AAA Ana	64	225	64	19	2	15	132	51	51	44	3	38	3	0	7	0	0	—	5	.284	.398	.587
2000 Edmonton	AAA Ana	48	162	49	11	1	8	86	29	35	40	4	22	0	0	1	0	0	—	5	.302	.444	.531
Sacramento	AAA Oak	62	243	66	12	0	4	90	22	43	34	1	40	0	0	4	1	2	.33	4	.272	.356	.370
1990 San Francisco	NL	15	54	16	2	0	3	27	5	8	1	0	10	0	1	0	0	0	—	1	.296	.309	.500
1991 San Francisco	NL	79	233	48	7	1	5	72	11	24	16	1	44	3	2	4	0	1	.00	7	.206	.262	.309
1992 San Francisco	NL	15	43	7	1	0	0	8	3	1	6	0	7	1	0	0	0	0	—	0	.163	.280	.186
1993 Florida	NL	8	15	0	0	0	0	0	0	1	3	0	3	0	0	1	0	0	—	2	.000	.158	.000
1995 Florida	NL	51	133	30	2	1	3	43	12	13	19	1	22	0	0	1	0	0	—	3	.226	.318	.323
1996 San Francisco	NL	57	122	28	1	0	1	32	16	12	15	4	26	0	3	2	1	0	1.00	0	.230	.309	.262
Colorado	NL	10	25	8	2	0	1	13	8	4	3	0	6	0	0	0	1	0	1.00	0	.320	.393	.520
1999 Anaheim	AL	28	63	15	6	0	0	21	5	5	13	0	9	1	1	1	0	0	—	4	.238	.372	.333
11 Min. YEARS		913	3228	975	195	8	101	1489	458	575	413	20	470	21	3	49	14	26	.35	105	.302	.380	.461
7 Maj. YEARS		263	688	152	21	2	13	216	60	72	76	6	124	5	8	10	2	1	.67	18	.221	.299	.314

Jim Dedrick

Pitches: Right **Bats:** Both **Pos:** RP-26; SP-4   **Ht:** 6'0" **Wt:** 185 **Born:** 4/4/68 **Age:** 33

Year Team	Lg Org	G	GS	CG	GF	IP	BFP	H	R	ER	HR	SH	SF	HB	TBB	IBB	SO	WP	Bk	W	L	Pct.	ShO	Sv	ERA
1990 Wausau	A Bal	3	1	0	1	10	41	6	4	3	0	0	0	0	4	0	8	0	3	0	1	.000	0	0	2.70
1991 Kane County	A Bal	16	15	0	0	88.1	380	84	38	29	2	1	2	5	38	1	71	5	2	4	5	.444	0	0	2.95
1992 Frederick	A+ Bal	38	5	1	19	108.2	454	94	41	37	5	5	0	5	42	4	86	4	3	8	4	.667	0	3	3.06
1993 Bowie	AA Bal	38	6	1	14	106.1	426	84	36	30	4	5	0	3	32	1	78	1	0	8	3	.727	1	3	2.54
Rochester	AAA Bal	1	1	0	0	7	27	6	2	2	2	0	0	0	0	0	3	0	0	1	0	1.000	0	0	2.57
1994 Rochester	AAA Bal	44	1	0	18	99	421	98	56	42	7	3	1	3	35	7	70	4	1	3	6	.333	0	1	3.82
1995 Bowie	AA Bal	10	10	0	0	60.1	267	59	24	20	7	2	2	5	25	2	48	5	1	4	2	.667	0	0	2.98
Rochester	AAA Bal	24	2	0	4	45.2	190	45	9	9	0	2	4	1	14	1	31	0	4	4	0	1.000	0	1	1.77
1996 Bowie	AA Bal	39	3	0	20	66.1	316	88	59	48	14	2	4	1	41	0	37	5	1	6	3	.667	0	4	6.51
Bowie	AA Bal	13	0	0	4	26.2	116	28	10	10	3	1	0	0	14	1	21	1	0	1	1	.500	0	1	3.38
1997 Harrisburg	AA Mon	15	0	0	7	19.1	78	18	8	6	1	1	0	0	8	0	17	0	1	2	1	.667	0	0	2.79
Ottawa	AAA Mon	8	0	0	2	14	68	15	12	11	2	1	0	0	13	0	14	0	0	0	1	.000	0	0	7.07
Tulsa	AA Tex	12	0	0	4	23	100	26	9	6	0	0	1	0	9	0	16	5	0	1	0	1.000	0	0	2.35
Okla City	AAA Tex	8	0	0	4	10.2	57	16	7	7	0	0	0	0	10	0	2	1	0	0	0	—	0	3	5.91
1998 Richmond	AAA Atl	26	0	0	17	37.1	160	36	24	22	4	0	2	0	15	3	27	2	0	2	3	.400	0	0	5.30
1999 Akron	AA Cle	2	0	0	1	3	13	4	3	3	2	0	0	0	0	0	0	0	0	1	0	1.000	0	0	9.00
Buffalo	AAA Cle	30	0	0	0	46.1	211	49	23	21	5	1	2	1	27	1	26	1	1	2	2	.500	0	0	4.08
2000 Akron	AA Cle	3	0	0	0	5	17	1	0	0	0	0	0	0	2	0	2	0	0	1	0	1.000	0	0	0.00
Buffalo	AAA Cle	12	1	0	6	15	82	26	16	14	4	1	2	0	10	2	7	2	1	0	0	—	0	1	6.52
Trenton	AA Bos	15	3	0	4	39.1	169	44	17	15	1	1	3	0	15	0	25	1	1	3	3	.500	0	0	3.43
1995 Baltimore	AL	6	0	0	1	7.2	35	8	2	2	1	0	2	1	6	0	3	0	0	0	0	—	0	0	2.35
11 Min. YEARS		357	48	3	127	835.2	3606	827	398	335	63	26	21	26	354	23	589	41	17	51	37	.580	1	17	3.61

Fernando de la Cruz

Pitches: Right **Bats:** Right **Pos:** RP-41   **Ht:** 6'0" **Wt:** 175 **Born:** 1/25/71 **Age:** 30

		HOW MUCH HE PITCHED						WHAT HE GAVE UP											THE RESULTS					
Year Team	Lg Org	G	GS	CG	GF	IP	BFP	H	R	ER	HR	SH	SF	HB	TBB	IBB	SO	WP	Bk	W	L	Pct.	ShO	Sv	ERA
1995 Boise	A- Ana	1	0	0	0	1.1	11	3	6	2	1	0	0	1	2	0	4	0	0	0	0	—	0	0	13.50
1996 Lk Elsinore	A+ Ana	5	0	0	3	7.1	40	8	12	7	2	0	0	1	10	0	3	2	1	0	0	—	0	0	8.59
Cedar Rapds	A Ana	6	6	0	0	27	139	35	25	24	1	1	3	7	21	0	18	4	3	0	5	.000	0	0	8.00
Boise	A- Ana	15	15	0	0	85.2	400	85	55	47	5	0	1	13	51	3	61	6	2	6	3	.667	0	0	4.94
1997 Cedar Rapds	A Ana	10	0	0	4	13.1	80	19	22	17	1	1	2	6	14	0	10	2	0	0	2	.000	0	1	11.48
Lk Elsinore	A+ Ana	8	6	0	1	37.2	165	36	22	19	3	1	2	2	17	0	26	1	2	2	2	.500	0	0	4.54
Midland	AA Ana	13	13	0	0	71.2	348	81	70	62	10	3	3	10	46	0	44	8	2	2	5	.286	0	0	7.79
1998 Midland	AA Ana	2	0	0	1	2	13	5	7	6	0	0	0	1	4	0	1	0	0	0	0	—	0	0	54.00
Red Sox	R Bos	1	0	0	1	2	10	4	3	3	0	0	0	0	0	0	2	0	0	0	0	—	0	4	13.50
Sarasota	A+ Bos	12	0	0	8	17.1	67	10	2	2	1	1	1	1	7	0	10	0	0	0	0	—	0	1	1.04
Trenton	AA Bos	3	0	0	2	3.2	15	3	0	0	0	0	0	0	1	0	3	1	0	0	0	—	0	1	0.00
2000 Trenton	AA Bos	41	0	0	15	65	310	80	49	46	4	3	5	4	37	2	42	10	1	3	5	.375	0	0	6.37
5 Min. YEARS		117	40	0	34	333	1598	369	273	235	28	10	17	46	210	5	224	34	11	13	22	.371	0	8	6.35

Francisco de la Cruz

Pitches: Right **Bats:** Right **Pos:** RP-7   **Ht:** 6'2" **Wt:** 175 **Born:** 7/9/73 **Age:** 27

		HOW MUCH HE PITCHED						WHAT HE GAVE UP											THE RESULTS					
Year Team	Lg Org	G	GS	CG	GF	IP	BFP	H	R	ER	HR	SH	SF	HB	TBB	IBB	SO	WP	Bk	W	L	Pct.	ShO	Sv	ERA
1997 Norwich	AA NYY	2	2	0	0	8.1	39	8	3	3	0	1	0	2	7	0	0	0	0	0	1	.000	0	0	3.24
Tampa	A+ NYY	8	8	0	0	36.2	174	39	30	28	5	3	2	1	29	1	22	2	0	0	2	.000	0	0	6.87
Greensboro	A NYY	13	13	1	0	84.2	359	71	41	31	6	2	2	4	36	1	75	3	2	5	4	.556	0	0	3.30
1998 Norwich	AA NYY	2	2	0	0	4.2	31	8	13	4	2	0	1	1	4	0	5	0	0	0	2	.000	0	0	7.71
Yankees	R NYY	3	3	0	0	13.2	61	11	9	5	1	0	0	0	8	1	18	1	0	1	1	.500	0	0	3.29
Greensboro	A NYY	5	3	0	1	20.1	83	15	9	9	3	0	1	1	10	1	18	0	0	2	1	.667	0	0	3.98
Tampa	A+ NYY	19	12	0	5	75.1	344	81	55	38	5	4	1	3	36	1	66	5	0	5	6	.455	0	0	4.54
1999 Norwich	AA NYY	29	19	1	4	133.1	603	141	89	68	10	2	5	2	73	0	91	11	3	6	5	.545	0	0	4.59
2000 Orlando	AA TB	7	0	0	3	9	44	12	9	7	2	0	0	0	3	0	6	1	0	0	0	—	0	0	7.00
4 Min. YEARS		88	62	2	13	386	1738	386	258	193	34	12	12	14	206	5	301	23	5	19	22	.463	0	0	4.50

Javier de la Hoya

Pitches: Right **Bats:** Right **Pos:** SP-16; RP-2   **Ht:** 6'2" **Wt:** 182 **Born:** 2/21/70 **Age:** 31

		HOW MUCH HE PITCHED						WHAT HE GAVE UP											THE RESULTS					
Year Team	Lg Org	G	GS	CG	GF	IP	BFP	H	R	ER	HR	SH	SF	HB	TBB	IBB	SO	WP	Bk	W	L	Pct.	ShO	Sv	ERA
1989 Dodgers	R LA	9	8	2	1	55.1	212	28	13	9	0	1	4	4	19	0	70	3	1	4	3	.571	1	0	1.46
1990 Vero Beach	A+ LA	4	4	0	0	21	100	14	14	13	0	1	1	1	20	2	22	0	0	1	2	.333	0	0	5.57
Bakersfield	A+ LA	9	7	0	0	39.1	190	50	30	26	5	0	1	1	24	0	37	6	0	4	1	.800	0	0	5.95
Yakima	A- LA	14	14	0	0	70.2	326	65	52	35	2	2	5	7	39	2	71	9	0	3	5	.375	0	0	4.46
1991 Bakersfield	A+ LA	27	11	1	7	98	425	92	47	40	6	2	3	1	44	1	102	3	3	6	4	.600	0	2	3.67
1992 Vero Beach	A+ LA	14	14	2	0	80	325	68	25	25	4	1	1	4	26	0	92	2	0	4	5	.444	2	0	2.81
San Antonio	AA LA	5	5	0	0	25.1	116	20	11	8	1	1	2	1	17	0	24	1	0	2	1	.667	0	0	2.84
1993 San Antonio	AA LA	21	21	1	0	125.1	537	122	61	51	14	4	3	8	42	0	107	2	1	8	10	.444	0	0	3.66
1994 Portland	AA Fla	22	11	1	5	73.2	328	81	56	53	11	2	1	2	29	4	60	3	0	0	7	.000	0	2	6.48
Brevard Cty	A+ Fla	9	7	0	1	50	201	39	17	14	2	1	2	2	13	1	45	1	0	4	3	.571	0	0	2.52
1995 Brevard Cty	A+ Fla	5	0	0	1	10.1	40	6	2	2	1	0	0	2	2	0	8	0	0	1	0	1.000	0	0	1.74
1996 Bend	IND —	2	2	0	0	5.1	25	9	4	4	1	0	1	0	1	0	2	0	0	0	0	—	0	0	6.75
1998 Bowie	AA Bal	6	4	1	1	30.2	126	32	13	13	4	0	0	2	7	1	33	0	0	4	1	.800	0	0	3.82
1999 Bowie	AA Bal	14	12	1	0	77.2	310	64	29	29	12	2	1	1	18	1	68	4	0	9	1	.900	0	0	3.36
Rochester	AAA Bal	14	14	0	0	81.1	356	88	49	46	14	1	3	7	26	0	58	5	2	4	3	.571	0	0	5.09
2000 Rochester	AAA Bal	18	16	0	0	92.1	398	85	55	44	12	1	2	8	32	0	65	2	1	7	6	.538	0	0	4.29
11 Min. YEARS		191	150	9	16	936.1	4015	863	478	412	89	19	27	52	358	12	864	41	8	61	52	.540	3	4	3.96

Jorge DeLeon

Bats: Right **Throws:** Right **Pos:** 2B-49; 3B-36; SS-15; DH-4; PR-1   **Ht:** 6'2" **Wt:** 164 **Born:** 9/26/74 **Age:** 26

		BATTING															BASERUNNING				PERCENTAGES		
Year Team	Lg Org	G	AB	H	2B	3B	HR	TB	R	RBI	TBB	IBB	SO	HBP	SH	SF	SB	CS	SB%	GDP	Avg	OBP	SLG
1997 Lowell	A- Bos	3	12	4	0	0	0	4	1	2	0	0	0	0	0	0	0	0	—	0	.333	.333	.333
Michigan	A Bos	20	59	16	3	0	0	19	10	4	0	0	19	0	1	3	2	0	1.00	3	.271	.258	.322
1998 Michigan	A Bos	50	185	49	8	1	2	65	23	19	15	0	19	0	3	2	4	0	1.00	4	.265	.317	.351
Trenton	AA Bos	29	86	25	7	0	0	32	11	10	5	0	3	0	5	0	2	1	.67	5	.291	.330	.372
1999 Sarasota	A+ Bos	66	219	60	11	2	1	78	33	18	24	0	33	0	5	0	3	2	.60	5	.274	.346	.356
2000 Sarasota	A+ Bos	10	40	11	4	1	0	17	3	4	0	0	7	0	0	0	1	0	1.00	1	.275	.341	.425
Trenton	AA Bos	88	339	104	16	1	2	128	47	38	24	1	51	5	2	0	1	8	.11	8	.307	.361	.378
Pawtucket	AAA Bos	5	16	2	1	0	0	3	0	0	4	0	4	0	0	0	0	0	—	1	.125	.125	.188
4 Min. YEARS		271	956	271	50	5	5	346	130	94	72	1	136	5	16	5	13	11	.54	27	.283	.335	.362

Ernie Delgado

Pitches: Right **Bats:** Right **Pos:** RP-43   **Ht:** 6'2" **Wt:** 190 **Born:** 7/21/75 **Age:** 25

		HOW MUCH HE PITCHED						WHAT HE GAVE UP											THE RESULTS					
Year Team	Lg Org	G	GS	CG	GF	IP	BFP	H	R	ER	HR	SH	SF	HB	TBB	IBB	SO	WP	Bk	W	L	Pct.	ShO	Sv	ERA
1993 Marlins	R Fla	11	11	0	0	61.1	261	61	27	21	0	0	2	4	19	0	46	5	2	4	3	.571	0	0	3.08
1994 Brevard Cty	A+ Fla	1	1	0	0	6	25	3	3	2	0	1	2	0	4	0	1	0	0	0	1	.000	0	0	3.00
Marlins	R Fla	4	2	0	2	16	71	15	10	6	0	0	0	0	5	0	18	1	0	1	1	.500	0	1	3.38
1995 Brevard Cty	A+ Fla	18	10	0	4	62.1	308	74	51	49	4	1	4	7	59	0	36	7	2	1	6	.143	0	0	7.07
1996 Hagerstown	A Tor	35	2	0	16	85.1	386	89	50	34	2	5	5	7	45	1	70	12	0	4	7	.364	0	2	3.59
1997 Hagerstown	A Tor	32	17	0	5	134.1	618	163	96	78	10	6	6	10	56	0	103	12	0	5	10	.333	0	1	5.23
1998 Dunedin	A+ Tor	44	9	2	13	118.2	532	119	57	48	6	5	1	6	59	4	97	6	2	7	10	.412	1	1	3.64

69

Year Team	Lg Org	G	GS	CG	GF	IP	BFP	H	R	ER	HR	SH	SF	HB	TBB	IBB	SO	WP	Bk	W	L	Pct.	ShO	Sv	ERA
		HOW MUCH HE PITCHED						**WHAT HE GAVE UP**												**THE RESULTS**					
1999 Knoxville	AA Tor	31	0	0	12	51.1	219	49	27	20	1	1	3	1	23	0	33	5	0	4	1	.800	0	0	3.51
Syracuse	AAA Tor	14	4	0	2	27.2	139	38	29	29	3	1	1	0	19	0	15	2	0	0	4	.000	0	0	9.43
2000 Kinston	A+ Cle	9	0	0	2	17	71	11	3	3	0	0	0	1	10	0	22	2	0	1	0	1.000	0	0	1.59
Akron	AA Cle	34	0	0	22	44.1	210	43	26	23	5	0	1	0	40	1	31	6	0	3	4	.429	0	6	4.67
8 Min. YEARS		233	56	2	78	624.1	2840	665	379	313	30	21	23	36	339	6	472	59	8	30	47	.390	1	11	4.51

Jason Dellaero

Bats: Both **Throws:** Right **Pos:** SS-122 **Ht:** 6'2" **Wt:** 195 **Born:** 12/17/76 **Age:** 24

Year Team	Lg Org	G	AB	H	2B	3B	HR	TB	R	RBI	TBB	IBB	SO	HBP	SH	SF	SB	CS	SB%	GDP	Avg	OBP	SLG
		BATTING															**BASERUNNING**				**PERCENTAGES**		
1997 White Sox	R CWS	5	15	3	2	0	0	5	1	1	1	0	2	0	0	1	0	0	—		.200	.235	.333
Hickory	A CWS	55	191	53	10	3	6	87	37	29	17	0	49	3	0	3	3	1	.75	6	.277	.341	.455
1998 Winston-Sal	A+ CWS	121	428	89	23	3	10	148	45	49	25	2	147	5	3	2	12	4	.75	5	.208	.259	.346
1999 Winston-Sal	A+ CWS	54	184	41	13	0	2	60	22	19	18	1	59	3	4	0	9	4	.69	2	.223	.302	.326
Birmingham	AA CWS	81	272	73	13	3	10	122	40	44	14	0	76	3	8	3	6	8	.43	5	.268	.308	.449
2000 Birmingham	AA CWS	122	438	81	18	1	7	122	36	42	20	0	142	6	7	2	9	6	.60	7	.185	.230	.279
1999 Chicago	AL	11	33	3	0	0	0	3	1	2	1	0	13	0	0	1	0	0	—	0	.091	.114	.091
4 Min. YEARS		438	1528	340	79	10	35	544	181	184	95	3	475	20	22	11	39	23	.63	26	.223	.275	.356

Pete Della Ratta

Pitches: Right **Bats:** Right **Pos:** RP-15 **Ht:** 6'4" **Wt:** 223 **Born:** 2/14/74 **Age:** 27

Year Team	Lg Org	G	GS	CG	GF	IP	BFP	H	R	ER	HR	SH	SF	HB	TBB	IBB	SO	WP	Bk	W	L	Pct.	ShO	Sv	ERA
		HOW MUCH HE PITCHED						**WHAT HE GAVE UP**												**THE RESULTS**					
1996 Sou Oregon	A- Oak	22	0	0	6	41.1	194	45	34	33	10	2	2	4	24	4	41	3	1	0	5	.000	0	2	7.19
1997 Modesto	A+ Oak	45	0	0	19	83.2	362	73	45	31	5	5	4	6	31	8	81	6	0	6	7	.462	0	3	3.33
1998 Huntsville	AA Oak	5	0	0	2	8	49	21	12	10	2	0	1	0	4	2	3	0	0	0	1	.000	0	0	11.25
Visalia	A+ Oak	36	0	0	28	59	249	43	24	16	5	3	1	1	25	6	73	4	0	5	1	.833	0	13	2.44
1999 Binghamton	AA NYM	41	3	0	9	82.2	329	75	22	20	4	2	3	3	13	1	68	2	0	1	4	.200	0	0	2.18
2000 Binghamton	AA NYM	13	0	0	5	17.1	79	18	16	13	3	1	0	0	8	0	8	1	0	1	2	.333	0	0	6.75
St. Lucie	A+ NYM	2	0	0	0	1.1	7	2	0	0	0	0	0	0	0	0	2	0	0	0	0	—	0	0	0.00
5 Min. YEARS		164	3	0	69	293.1	1269	277	153	123	29	13	11	14	105	21	276	16	1	13	20	.394	0	18	3.77

Eddy de los Santos

Bats: Right **Throws:** Right **Pos:** SS-126 **Ht:** 6'2" **Wt:** 171 **Born:** 2/24/78 **Age:** 23

Year Team	Lg Org	G	AB	H	2B	3B	HR	TB	R	RBI	TBB	IBB	SO	HBP	SH	SF	SB	CS	SB%	GDP	Avg	OBP	SLG
		BATTING															**BASERUNNING**				**PERCENTAGES**		
1996 Devil Rays	R TB	50	196	48	6	1	0	56	18	20	13	0	58	3	2	0	11	3	.79	4	.245	.302	.286
Butte	R+ TB	16	59	16	0	0	0	16	15	12	6	0	17	0	2	2	1	1	.50	1	.271	.328	.271
1997 Chston-SC	A TB	127	432	101	11	2	2	122	46	40	20	0	101	2	5	4	8	9	.47	3	.234	.269	.282
1998 St. Pete	A+ TB	111	393	94	11	1	0	107	33	32	17	1	64	3	5	3	6	4	.60	7	.239	.274	.272
Durham	AAA TB	4	11	3	2	0	0	5	2	2	0	0	6	1	0	0	0	0	—	0	.273	.333	.455
1999 Orlando	AA TB	128	448	123	24	4	3	164	53	49	29	0	69	2	5	7	3	2	.60	9	.275	.317	.366
2000 Orlando	AA TB	48	171	40	6	1	0	48	11	8	5	0	26	2	1	1	2	3	.40	2	.234	.263	.281
Durham	AAA TB	78	271	68	4	1	3	83	27	32	21	0	50	2	5	1	3	2	.60	5	.251	.308	.306
5 Min. YEARS		562	1981	493	64	10	8	601	205	195	111	1	391	15	25	18	34	24	.59	35	.249	.291	.303

Rich DeLucia

Pitches: Right **Bats:** Right **Pos:** SP-10 **Ht:** 6'0" **Wt:** 190 **Born:** 10/7/64 **Age:** 36

Year Team	Lg Org	G	GS	CG	GF	IP	BFP	H	R	ER	HR	SH	SF	HB	TBB	IBB	SO	WP	Bk	W	L	Pct.	ShO	Sv	ERA
		HOW MUCH HE PITCHED						**WHAT HE GAVE UP**												**THE RESULTS**					
1986 Bellingham	A- Sea	13	11	1	1	74	0	44	20	14	4	0	0	4	24	0	69	3	0	8	2	.800	1	0	1.70
1988 San Berndno	A+ Sea	22	22	0	0	127.2	541	110	57	44	4	2	6	7	59	3	118	6	2	7	8	.467	0	0	3.10
1989 Williamsprt	AA Sea	10	10	0	0	54.2	234	59	28	23	5	3	2	1	13	0	41	5	0	3	4	.429	0	0	3.79
1990 San Berndno	A+ Sea	5	5	1	0	30.2	116	19	9	7	4	1	0	4	3	0	35	1	0	4	1	.800	0	0	2.05
Williamsprt	AA Sea	18	18	2	0	115	447	92	30	27	7	3	3	2	30	2	76	1	0	6	6	.500	1	0	2.11
Calgary	AAA Sea	5	5	1	0	32.1	139	30	17	13	2	0	1	0	12	0	23	3	0	2	2	.500	0	0	3.62
1992 Calgary	AAA Sea	8	5	2	3	40.1	162	32	11	11	2	0	1	0	14	0	38	2	0	4	2	.667	0	1	2.45
1993 Calgary	AAA Sea	8	7	0	1	44	192	45	30	28	6	0	3	0	20	1	38	4	0	1	5	.167	0	1	5.73
1994 Indianapols	AAA Cin	36	0	0	31	43	172	22	12	11	2	3	0	1	24	1	52	1	0	5	1	.833	0	19	2.30
1996 San Jose	A+ SF	5	4	0	0	7.1	28	5	2	2	0	0	0	0	3	0	11	0	0	0	0	—	0	0	2.45
1999 Buffalo	AAA Cle	44	0	0	33	47.1	210	39	24	22	6	1	1	2	29	3	46	4	0	2	3	.400	0	19	4.18
2000 Sacramento	AAA Oak	10	10	0	0	50	212	50	27	22	7	0	1	0	18	0	34	3	0	3	1	.750	0	0	3.96
1990 Seattle	AL	5	5	1	0	36	144	30	9	8	2	2	0	0	9	0	20	0	0	1	2	.333	0	0	2.00
1991 Seattle	AL	32	31	0	0	182	779	176	107	103	31	5	14	4	78	4	98	10	0	12	13	.480	0	0	5.09
1992 Seattle	AL	30	11	0	6	83.2	382	100	55	51	13	2	2	2	35	1	66	1	0	3	6	.333	0	1	5.49
1993 Seattle	AL	30	1	0	11	42.2	195	46	24	22	5	1	1	1	23	3	48	4	0	3	6	.333	0	0	4.64
1994 Cincinnati	NL	8	0	0	2	10.2	47	9	6	5	4	0	0	0	5	0	15	1	0	0	0	—	0	0	4.22
1995 St. Louis	NL	56	1	0	18	82.1	342	63	38	31	9	5	2	3	36	2	76	5	0	8	7	.533	0	0	3.39
1996 San Francisco	NL	56	0	0	20	61.2	209	62	44	40	8	4	2	3	31	6	55	7	0	3	6	.333	0	0	5.84
1997 San Francisco	NL	3	0	0	0	1.2	12	6	3	2	0	0	0	0	0	0	2	1	0	0	0	—	0	0	10.80
Anaheim	AL	33	0	0	13	42.1	174	29	18	17	2	2	1	0	27	2	42	1	0	6	4	.600	0	3	3.61
1998 Anaheim	AL	61	0	0	18	71.2	314	56	36	34	10	5	7	3	46	5	73	8	1	2	6	.250	0	4	4.27
1999 Cleveland	AL	6	0	0	2	9.1	50	13	7	7	4	0	0	0	9	2	7	1	0	0	1	.000	0	0	6.75
10 Min. YEARS		184	97	7	69	666.1	2453	547	267	224	49	13	20	20	249	10	581	33	2	45	35	.563	3	40	3.03
10 Maj. YEARS		320	49	1	80	624	2718	590	347	320	91	26	30	17	299	25	502	39	1	38	51	.427	0	7	4.62

Chris Demetral

Bats: Left **Throws:** Right **Pos:** 2B-78; 3B-17; DH-8; SS-2; OF-2; PH-2   **Ht:** 5'11" **Wt:** 175 **Born:** 12/8/69 **Age:** 31

Year Team	Lg Org	G	AB	H	2B	3B	HR	TB	R	RBI	TBB	IBB	SO	HBP	SH	SF	SB	CS	SB%	GDP	Avg	OBP	SLG
1991 Yakima	A- LA	65	226	64	11	0	2	81	43	41	34	2	32	1	6	0	4	3	.57	2	.283	.379	.358
1992 Bakersfield	A+ LA	90	306	84	14	1	4	112	38	36	33	7	45	1	4	3	7	8	.47	3	.275	.344	.366
1993 Vero Beach	A+ LA	122	437	142	22	3	5	185	63	48	69	2	47	2	6	3	6	6	.50	9	.325	.417	.423
1994 San Antonio	AA LA	108	368	96	26	3	6	146	44	39	34	5	44	1	11	2	5	2	.71	8	.261	.323	.397
1995 Albuquerque	AAA LA	87	187	52	7	1	3	70	34	19	24	2	28	0	3	0	1	6	.14	7	.278	.360	.374
1996 San Berndno	A+ LA	11	32	9	3	0	1	15	5	4	6	1	5	0	0	0	0	3	.00	0	.281	.395	.469
Albuquerque	AAA LA	99	209	55	8	0	4	75	30	26	40	5	35	0	5	5	4	3	.57	6	.263	.374	.359
1997 Albuquerque	AAA LA	12	24	6	2	0	1	11	1	1	6	0	3	0	0	0	0	1	.00	1	.250	.400	.458
Vero Beach	A+ LA	86	278	77	13	3	12	132	52	45	48	0	40	2	2	4	5	2	.71	6	.277	.383	.475
1998 Tulsa	AA Tex	45	147	40	9	3	4	67	22	18	33	0	24	1	2	0	2	3	.40	4	.272	.409	.456
Oklahoma	AAA Tex	57	157	47	6	0	4	65	26	16	20	0	31	0	4	2	3	2	.60	1	.299	.374	.414
1999 Oklahoma	AAA Tex	65	183	48	7	1	4	69	29	18	28	0	35	0	7	1	1	2	.33	3	.262	.358	.377
2000 Oklahoma	AAA Tex	106	355	85	9	5	8	128	55	47	55	2	53	1	9	3	2	3	.40	5	.239	.341	.361
10 Min. YEARS		953	2909	805	137	20	58	1156	442	358	430	26	422	9	59	23	40	44	.48	55	.277	.369	.397

Chris Demouy

Pitches: Left **Bats:** Right **Pos:** RP-49; SP-1   **Ht:** 6'1" **Wt:** 205 **Born:** 11/11/75 **Age:** 25

Year Team	Lg Org	G	GS	CG	GF	IP	BFP	H	R	ER	HR	SH	SF	HB	TBB	IBB	SO	WP	Bk	W	L	Pct.	ShO	Sv	ERA
1998 Boise	A- Ana	20	0	0	17	23.1	96	11	5	4	0	3	1	1	11	0	29	2	2	5	1	.833	0	9	1.54
1999 Cedar Rapds	A Ana	46	0	0	28	48.2	212	39	18	13	3	7	3	1	28	2	51	8	0	2	1	.667	0	16	2.40
2000 Lk Elsinore	A+ Ana	40	1	0	17	59.1	264	62	21	15	0	1	2	3	26	0	44	3	0	7	2	.778	0	2	2.28
Edmonton	AAA Ana	1	0	0	0	3	11	1	1	1	0	0	0	0	1	0	0	0	0	0	0	—	0	0	3.00
Erie	AA Ana	9	0	0	8	17.2	83	22	12	10	2	1	2	0	7	1	11	0	0	0	1	.000	0	0	5.09
3 Min. YEARS		116	1	0	70	152	666	135	57	43	5	12	8	4	73	3	135	13	2	14	5	.737	0	27	2.55

Les Dennis

Bats: Right **Throws:** Right **Pos:** 3B-30; 2B-21; SS-13; PH-3; DH-1   **Ht:** 6'0" **Wt:** 175 **Born:** 6/3/73 **Age:** 28

Year Team	Lg Org	G	AB	H	2B	3B	HR	TB	R	RBI	TBB	IBB	SO	HBP	SH	SF	SB	CS	SB%	GDP	Avg	OBP	SLG
1995 Oneonta	A- NYY	48	148	39	6	2	1	52	24	13	14	0	40	3	0	2	5	2	.71	4	.264	.335	.351
1996 Greensboro	A NYY	33	75	19	3	0	1	25	15	9	11	0	27	1	2	0	1	2	.33	2	.253	.356	.333
Oneonta	A- NYY	72	276	67	3	2	0	74	36	43	33	1	76	1	5	6	20	9	.69	2	.243	.320	.268
1997 Norwich	AA NYY	10	30	10	1	0	0	11	4	2	5	0	11	0	2	0	1	1	.50	0	.333	.429	.367
Tampa	A+ NYY	85	177	46	4	0	0	50	24	17	16	0	36	1	6	1	1	6	.14	6	.260	.323	.282
1998 Tampa	A+ NYY	44	104	19	4	0	1	26	16	8	5	0	20	0	5	0	1	0	1.00	6	.183	.220	.250
Norwich	AA NYY	32	93	23	5	1	0	30	12	13	24	0	20	0	2	0	2	2	.50	5	.247	.402	.323
1999 Tampa	A+ NYY	23	89	27	3	1	0	32	20	7	15	0	20	0	1	1	0	1	.00	3	.303	.400	.360
Yankees	R NYY	3	8	2	0	0	0	2	2	0	1	0	0	0	0	0	1	0	1.00	0	.250	.333	.250
Norwich	AA NYY	53	176	44	10	0	0	54	27	14	27	0	50	3	2	1	0	2	.00	5	.250	.357	.307
2000 Augusta	A Bos	23	81	20	7	0	1	30	10	13	11	1	23	3	4	0	2	0	1.00	3	.247	.358	.370
Sarasota	A+ Bos	23	82	31	5	0	1	39	11	12	12	0	17	3	0	1	0	1	.00	1	.378	.469	.476
Trenton	AA Bos	20	60	12	0	0	1	15	8	3	7	0	15	0	1	0	0	1	.00	0	.200	.284	.250
6 Min. YEARS		469	1399	359	51	6	6	440	209	152	181	2	355	15	29	12	34	27	.56	36	.257	.345	.315

Darrell Dent

Bats: Left **Throws:** Left **Pos:** OF-111; PR-4; PH-3   **Ht:** 6'2" **Wt:** 175 **Born:** 5/26/77 **Age:** 24

Year Team	Lg Org	G	AB	H	2B	3B	HR	TB	R	RBI	TBB	IBB	SO	HBP	SH	SF	SB	CS	SB%	GDP	Avg	OBP	SLG
1995 Orioles	R Bal	36	125	35	7	3	0	48	24	6	21	0	22	2	0	1	6	2	.75	2	.280	.389	.384
1996 Bluefield	R+ Bal	59	193	43	6	2	0	53	40	14	28	1	49	0	1	4	30	9	.77	2	.223	.316	.275
1997 Delmarva	A Bal	128	441	103	17	4	1	131	69	37	63	2	110	4	7	6	60	15	.80	2	.234	.331	.297
1998 Frederick	A+ Bal	131	456	112	19	1	0	133	65	24	43	1	95	4	13	3	33	16	.67	4	.246	.314	.292
1999 Bowie	AA Bal	108	250	53	9	2	0	66	41	17	37	0	58	2	12	4	24	5	.83	4	.212	.314	.264
Rochester	AAA Bal	9	30	4	0	0	2	10	5	3	0	0	8	0	1	1	4	0	1.00	0	.133	.206	.333
2000 Bowie	AA Bal	115	362	94	11	1	0	107	52	25	56	0	63	2	7	2	20	11	.65	4	.260	.360	.296
6 Min. YEARS		586	1857	444	69	13	3	548	295	128	251	4	405	14	41	21	177	58	.75	18	.239	.331	.295

Doug Dent

Pitches: Right **Bats:** Right **Pos:** SP-23; RP-5   **Ht:** 6'8" **Wt:** 210 **Born:** 3/23/77 **Age:** 24

Year Team	Lg Org	G	GS	CG	GF	IP	BFP	H	R	ER	HR	SH	SF	HB	TBB	IBB	SO	WP	Bk	W	L	Pct.	ShO	Sv	ERA
1998 Braves	R Atl	4	4	0	0	14.2	61	14	11	7	1	0	2	2	4	0	16	1	2	0	2	.000	0	0	4.30
Danville	R+ Atl	9	9	1	0	47.1	212	57	28	19	4	2	3	3	19	0	29	1	1	5	3	.625	0	0	3.61
1999 Macon	A Atl	17	17	0	0	89	375	78	42	34	8	1	3	2	30	0	64	5	1	4	5	.444	0	0	3.44
Fort Wayne	A SD	8	8	0	0	48.2	201	43	23	19	2	0	1	1	17	0	32	4	1	4	1	.800	0	0	3.51
2000 Rancho Cuca	A+ SD	10	7	0	1	40.2	176	34	17	11	2	1	1	3	19	0	31	4	0	2	1	.667	0	0	2.43
Mobile	AA SD	18	16	0	0	82.2	392	97	65	54	8	3	5	11	44	0	47	10	1	4	9	.308	0	0	5.88
3 Min. YEARS		66	61	1	1	323	1417	323	186	144	25	7	13	22	133	0	219	25	6	19	21	.475	0	0	4.01

Joe DePastino

Bats: Right **Throws:** Right **Pos:** C-34; DH-7; 1B-3; PH-2   **Ht:** 6'2" **Wt:** 210 **Born:** 9/4/73 **Age:** 27

Year Team	Lg Org	G	AB	H	2B	3B	HR	TB	R	RBI	TBB	IBB	SO	HBP	SH	SF	SB	CS	SB%	GDP	Avg	OBP	SLG
1992 Red Sox	R Bos	40	157	41	6	1	1	52	13	16	7	1	25	3	0	2	1	1	.50	2	.261	.302	.331

Year Team	Lg Org	G	AB	H	2B	3B	HR	TB	R	RBI	TBB	IBB	SO	HBP	SH	SF	SB	CS	SB%	GDP	Avg	OBP	SLG
1993 Utica	A- Bos	62	221	56	9	1	2	73	28	32	16	0	51	4	1	5	3	2	.60	4	.253	.309	.330
1994 Utica	A- Bos	51	172	46	11	1	5	74	23	31	22	1	41	3	1	2	5	2	.71	1	.267	.357	.430
1995 Michigan	A Bos	98	325	90	20	4	10	148	47	53	30	1	70	8	0	5	3	3	.50	5	.277	.348	.455
1996 Sarasota	A+ Bos	97	344	90	16	2	6	128	35	44	29	1	71	3	0	4	2	3	.40	7	.262	.321	.372
1997 Trenton	AA Bos	79	276	70	14	1	17	137	51	55	32	0	63	7	0	1	1	2	.33	10	.254	.345	.496
1998 Red Sox	R Bos	6	17	5	1	1	1	11	2	1	5	0	3	0	0	0	0	0	—	0	.294	.455	.647
Pawtucket	AAA Bos	9	33	8	1	0	0	9	1	4	0	0	8	1	0	0	1	1	.50	0	.242	.265	.273
Trenton	AA Bos	73	275	81	16	0	10	127	34	43	28	5	51	1	0	2	3	0	1.00	6	.295	.359	.462
1999 Trenton	AA Bos	6	23	5	1	0	2	12	5	5	3	0	3	1	0	0	1	0	1.00	4	.217	.333	.522
Pawtucket	AAA Bos	77	257	65	13	0	13	117	35	52	27	0	40	1	0	2	1	1	.50	4	.253	.324	.455
2000 Rochester	AAA Bal	20	71	18	3	0	0	21	7	5	8	0	16	1	1	0	1	1	.50	1	.254	.338	.296
Bowie	AA Bal	19	65	14	6	0	2	26	11	9	6	0	13	0	0	0	0	0	—	4	.215	.282	.400
Round Rock	AA Hou	5	18	8	0	1	2	16	3	4	0	0	2	0	0	0	0	1	.00	0	.444	.444	.889
9 Min. YEARS		642	2254	597	117	12	71	951	295	354	213	9	457	33	3	23	22	17	.56	50	.265	.334	.422

Jeff DePippo

Bats: Right **Throws:** Right **Pos:** C-56; PR-1 **Ht:** 5'7" **Wt:** 170 **Born:** 4/29/76 **Age:** 25

Year Team	Lg Org	G	AB	H	2B	3B	HR	TB	R	RBI	TBB	IBB	SO	HBP	SH	SF	SB	CS	SB%	GDP	Avg	OBP	SLG
1998 Burlington	R+ Cle	39	115	24	6	0	1	33	16	9	10	0	33	6	0	1	0	2	.00	2	.209	.303	.287
1999 Kinston	A+ Cle	68	174	37	8	1	2	53	33	19	29	0	51	17	8	3	3	1	.75	1	.213	.372	.305
2000 Akron	AA Cle	57	172	39	6	1	3	56	20	19	13	0	60	6	7	2	2	1	.67	2	.227	.301	.326
3 Min. YEARS		164	461	100	20	2	6	142	69	47	52	0	144	29	15	6	5	4	.56	5	.217	.330	.308

Derrick DePriest

Pitches: Right **Bats:** Right **Pos:** RP-32 **Ht:** 6'8" **Wt:** 235 **Born:** 11/21/76 **Age:** 24

Year Team	Lg Org	G	GS	CG	GF	IP	BFP	H	R	ER	HR	SH	SF	HB	TBB	IBB	SO	WP	Bk	W	L	Pct.	ShO	Sv	ERA
2000 Cape Fear	A Mon	21	0	0	17	31	119	21	8	5	1	1	0	1	6	0	28	0	1	0	2	.000	0	8	1.45
Jupiter	A+ Mon	4	0	0	4	4	14	3	1	1	0	0	0	0	0	0	4	1	0	1	0	1.000	0	3	2.25
Harrisburg	AA Mon	7	0	0	2	9	42	8	6	6	0	0	0	0	6	0	3	0	0	0	0	—	0	0	6.00
1 Min. YEARS		32	0	0	23	44	175	32	15	12	1	1	0	1	12	0	35	1	1	1	2	.333	0	11	2.45

Tony DeRosso

Bats: Right **Throws:** Right **Pos:** 3B-69; 1B-37; DH-15; PH-1 **Ht:** 6'3" **Wt:** 226 **Born:** 11/7/75 **Age:** 25

Year Team	Lg Org	G	AB	H	2B	3B	HR	TB	R	RBI	TBB	IBB	SO	HBP	SH	SF	SB	CS	SB%	GDP	Avg	OBP	SLG
1994 Red Sox	R Bos	46	168	42	6	0	4	60	23	22	12	0	33	5	0	3	1	0	1.00	6	.250	.314	.357
1995 Michigan	A Bos	106	382	89	20	1	13	150	57	50	38	2	93	11	1	2	9	1	.90	5	.233	.319	.393
1996 Sarasota	A+ Bos	116	416	107	19	5	14	178	64	60	31	2	84	8	2	5	15	2	.88	10	.257	.317	.428
1997 Trenton	AA Bos	102	357	77	18	1	14	139	50	40	26	0	94	2	3	2	13	1	.93	5	.216	.271	.389
1998 Trenton	AA Bos	9	28	3	0	0	1	6	3	3	2	0	12	0	0	1	0	0	—	0	.107	.161	.214
Red Sox	R Bos	4	15	7	2	0	0	9	4	3	1	0	3	0	0	0	0	0	—	0	.467	.500	.600
Sarasota	A+ Bos	4	13	4	3	0	0	7	1	5	3	1	1	0	0	0	0	0	—	0	.308	.438	.538
1999 Red Sox	R Bos	5	18	5	3	0	1	11	3	7	2	0	2	0	0	1	1	0	1.00	1	.278	.333	.611
Augusta	A Bos	36	128	38	7	1	6	65	19	27	16	0	21	1	0	2	0	0	—	3	.297	.374	.508
2000 Trenton	AA Bos	120	449	126	28	4	20	222	77	85	45	1	91	0	1	1	0	0	1.00	14	.281	.351	.494
7 Min. YEARS		548	1974	498	106	12	73	847	301	302	176	6	434	32	6	18	38	6	.86	40	.252	.321	.429

Jim Deschaine

Bats: Right **Throws:** Right **Pos:** SS-111; DH-13; OF-9; PH-2; PR-1 **Ht:** 6'0" **Wt:** 200 **Born:** 9/18/77 **Age:** 23

Year Team	Lg Org	G	AB	H	2B	3B	HR	TB	R	RBI	TBB	IBB	SO	HBP	SH	SF	SB	CS	SB%	GDP	Avg	OBP	SLG
1999 Eugene	A- ChC	73	272	81	12	0	10	123	49	48	29	0	59	0	1	0	7	7	.50	8	.298	.365	.452
2000 Lansing	A ChC	130	478	140	33	4	16	229	81	73	69	2	91	6	2	6	19	9	.68	13	.293	.385	.479
Iowa	AAA ChC	4	8	2	0	0	2	8	3	5	2	0	1	0	0	0	0	0	—	0	.250	.400	1.000
2 Min. YEARS		207	758	223	45	4	28	360	133	126	100	2	151	6	3	6	26	16	.62	21	.294	.378	.475

Marc Deschenes

Pitches: Right **Bats:** Right **Pos:** RP-41 **Ht:** 6'0" **Wt:** 175 **Born:** 1/6/73 **Age:** 28

Year Team	Lg Org	G	GS	CG	GF	IP	BFP	H	R	ER	HR	SH	SF	HB	TBB	IBB	SO	WP	Bk	W	L	Pct.	ShO	Sv	ERA
1996 Columbus	A Cle	16	16	0	0	76.2	343	70	38	29	9	1	3	1	41	0	67	6	0	5	2	.714	0	0	3.40
1997 Columbus	A Cle	40	0	0	39	42.2	180	31	11	9	2	0	1	1	21	0	69	3	0	2	2	.500	0	19	1.90
Kinston	A+ Cle	20	0	0	19	22.1	79	9	2	2	2	0	0	0	4	0	39	1	0	2	0	1.000	0	10	0.81
1998 Kinston	A+ Cle	1	0	0	1	1	4	0	0	0	0	0	0	0	1	0	2	0	0	0	0	—	0	0	0.00
Akron	AA Cle	47	0	0	26	58.1	259	52	36	25	4	2	4	0	34	6	52	5	0	4	6	.400	0	5	3.86
1999 Akron	AA Cle	43	0	0	26	65.1	277	57	28	24	5	5	2	2	31	6	64	3	0	3	2	.600	0	3	3.31
2000 Akron	AA Cle	41	0	0	31	54.1	238	43	27	24	3	3	2	4	31	3	64	4	0	2	4	.333	0	2	3.98
5 Min. YEARS		208	16	0	142	320.2	1380	262	142	113	25	11	12	8	163	15	357	22	0	18	16	.529	0	39	3.17

John DeSilva

Pitches: Right **Bats:** Right **Pos:** SP-19; RP-10 **Ht:** 6'0" **Wt:** 195 **Born:** 9/30/67 **Age:** 33

Year Team	Lg Org	G	GS	CG	GF	IP	BFP	H	R	ER	HR	SH	SF	HB	TBB	IBB	SO	WP	Bk	W	L	Pct.	ShO	Sv	ERA
1989 Niagara Fal	A- Det	4	4	0	0	24	95	15	5	5	0	1	0	2	8	0	24	3	1	3	0	1.000	0	0	1.88
Fayetteville	A Det	9	9	1	0	52.2	215	40	23	16	4	1	2	0	21	0	54	2	3	2	2	.500	0	0	2.73

Year Team	Lg Org	G	GS	CG	GF	IP	BFP	H	R	ER	HR	SH	SF	HB	TBB	IBB	SO	WP	Bk	W	L	Pct.	ShO	Sv	ERA
1990 Lakeland	A+ Det	14	14	0	0	91	349	54	18	15	4	1	4	4	25	0	113	1	1	8	1	.889	0	0	1.48
London	AA Det	14	14	1	0	89	372	87	47	37	4	1	4	2	27	0	76	3	0	5	6	.455	1	0	3.74
1991 London	AA Det	11	11	2	0	73.2	294	51	24	23	4	2	2	0	24	0	80	1	0	5	4	.556	1	0	2.81
Toledo	AAA Det	11	11	1	0	58.2	254	62	33	30	10	0	1	1	21	0	56	1	0	5	4	.556	0	0	4.60
1992 Toledo	AAA Det	7	2	0	3	19	89	26	18	18	5	1	0	0	8	0	21	0	0	0	3	.000	0	0	8.53
London	AA Det	9	9	1	0	52.1	216	51	24	24	4	1	2	1	13	0	53	1	1	2	4	.333	1	0	4.13
1993 Toledo	AAA Det	25	24	1	0	161	675	145	73	66	13	2	5	0	60	2	136	3	1	7	10	.412	0	0	3.69
1994 Albuquerque	AAA LA	25	6	0	4	66.2	317	90	62	58	7	1	3	4	27	0	39	3	0	3	5	.375	0	1	7.83
San Antonio	AA LA	25	2	0	7	46	202	46	29	26	3	2	1	1	18	2	46	2	1	1	3	.250	0	2	5.09
1995 Rochester	AAA Bal	26	25	2	1	150.2	644	156	78	70	19	3	3	6	51	0	82	2	1	11	9	.550	0	0	4.18
1996 Palm Spring	IND —	1	1	0	0	5	18	1	2	2	1	0	0	0	2	0	7	0	0	1	0	1.000	0	0	3.60
Pawtucket	AAA Bos	16	16	0	0	84.2	373	99	55	49	12	2	1	0	27	0	68	1	0	4	3	.571	0	0	5.21
1998 New Jersey	IND —	11	11	4	0	80.2	315	53	17	14	4	5	0	3	24	2	90	8	0	8	1	.889	1	0	1.56
Ottawa	AAA Mon	7	7	0	0	48.1	191	42	15	14	5	1	2	2	12	0	25	1	1	4	2	.667	0	0	2.61
1999 Ottawa	AAA Mon	22	15	0	3	90.1	377	73	35	29	4	6	5	2	41	1	75	5	0	4	1	.800	0	0	2.89
2000 Calgary	AAA Fla	29	19	3	5	140.1	613	150	78	73	21	6	8	5	43	2	94	3	2	10	9	.526	0	0	4.68
1993 Detroit	AL	1	0	0	1	1	4	2	1	1	0	0	1	0	0	0	0	0	0	0	0	—	0	0	9.00
Los Angeles	NL	3	0	0	2	5.1	23	6	4	4	0	0	0	0	1	0	6	0	0	0	0	—	0	0	6.75
1995 Baltimore	AL	2	2	0	0	8.2	41	8	7	7	3	1	1	1	7	0	1	0	0	1	0	1.000	0	0	7.27
11 Min. YEARS		266	200	16	23	1334	5609	1241	636	569	124	36	41	33	452	9	1139	43	12	83	67	.553	4	5	3.84
2 Maj. YEARS		6	2	0	3	15	68	16	12	12	3	1	2	1	8	0	7	0	0	1	0	1.000	0	0	7.20

Jason Dewey

Bats: Right Throws: Right Pos: C-83; DH-9; PH-4   Ht: 6'1" Wt: 200 Born: 4/18/77 Age: 24

Year Team	Lg Org	G	AB	H	2B	3B	HR	TB	R	RBI	TBB	IBB	SO	HBP	SH	SF	SB	CS	SB%	GDP	Avg	OBP	SLG
1997 Boise	A- Ana	68	272	88	17	2	13	148	55	64	41	4	70	2	1	2	5	2	.71	2	.324	.413	.544
1998 Lk Elsinore	A+ Ana	111	391	115	30	3	15	196	64	66	66	0	118	0	0	2	8	8	.50	10	.294	.394	.501
1999 Erie	AA Ana	40	139	31	7	0	4	50	17	14	17	1	50	0	0	0	0	1	.00	2	.223	.308	.360
Lk Elsinore	A+ Ana	66	242	78	23	0	10	131	48	31	30	0	62	2	0	0	0	0	—	8	.322	.399	.541
2000 Carolina	AA Col	96	318	72	24	0	9	123	29	44	34	1	101	6	6	2	1	3	.25	9	.226	.311	.387
4 Min. YEARS		381	1362	384	101	5	51	648	213	219	188	6	401	10	7	8	14	14	.50	31	.282	.371	.476

Scott DeWitt

Pitches: Left Bats: Right Pos: RP-34   Ht: 6'4" Wt: 200 Born: 10/6/74 Age: 26

Year Team	Lg Org	G	GS	CG	GF	IP	BFP	H	R	ER	HR	SH	SF	HB	TBB	IBB	SO	WP	Bk	W	L	Pct.	ShO	Sv	ERA
1995 Marlins	R Fla	11	10	1	0	63.2	245	48	15	14	1	3	2	2	9	0	70	1	1	5	3	.625	0	0	1.98
Kane County	A Fla	1	1	0	0	3	10	0	0	0	0	0	0	1	1	0	2	0	0	0	0	—	0	0	0.00
1996 Kane County	A Fla	27	27	1	0	148.2	667	151	96	78	8	5	4	19	59	0	119	2	2	10	11	.476	1	0	4.72
1997 Brevard Cty	A+ Fla	25	24	0	1	132	585	145	80	61	13	6	3	8	51	0	121	3	1	4	10	.286	0	0	4.16
1998 Portland	AA Fla	50	3	0	13	59.2	278	61	35	30	7	2	3	4	36	0	64	4	1	4	4	.500	0	1	4.53
1999 Carolina	AA Col	45	0	0	15	66.2	309	84	34	29	2	3	2	4	21	1	65	6	1	2	4	.333	0	2	3.92
2000 Carolina	AA Col	34	0	0	12	51.1	224	44	22	18	5	2	2	7	19	1	36	4	0	5	2	.714	0	1	3.16
6 Min. YEARS		193	65	2	41	525	2318	533	282	230	36	21	16	45	196	2	477	20	6	29	32	.475	1	4	3.94

Alejandro Diaz

Bats: Right Throws: Right Pos: OF-122   Ht: 5'9" Wt: 190 Born: 7/9/78 Age: 22

Year Team	Lg Org	G	AB	H	2B	3B	HR	TB	R	RBI	TBB	IBB	SO	HBP	SH	SF	SB	CS	SB%	GDP	Avg	OBP	SLG
1999 Clinton	A Cin	55	221	63	14	3	6	101	39	41	12	1	35	2	0	4	28	11	.72	6	.285	.322	.457
Chattanooga	AA Cin	55	220	58	9	8	3	104	27	35	8	0	31	3	2	2	6	2	.75	3	.264	.296	.473
2000 Chattanooga	AA Cin	122	491	131	19	8	13	205	69	66	14	1	77	4	0	5	18	20	.47	5	.267	.290	.418
2 Min. YEARS		232	932	252	42	19	26	410	135	142	34	2	143	9	2	11	52	33	.61	14	.270	.299	.440

Edwin Diaz

Bats: Right Throws: Right Pos: 2B-25; 3B-23; SS-6; DH-1; PH-1   Ht: 5'11" Wt: 170 Born: 1/15/75 Age: 26

Year Team	Lg Org	G	AB	H	2B	3B	HR	TB	R	RBI	TBB	IBB	SO	HBP	SH	SF	SB	CS	SB%	GDP	Avg	OBP	SLG
1993 Rangers	R Tex	43	154	47	10	5	1	70	27	23	19	1	21	4	0	2	12	5	.71	4	.305	.391	.455
1994 Chston-SC	A Tex	122	413	109	22	7	11	178	52	60	22	0	107	8	8	9	11	14	.44	7	.264	.308	.431
1995 Charlotte	A+ Tex	115	450	128	26	5	8	188	48	56	33	0	94	7	3	2	8	13	.38	10	.284	.341	.418
1996 Tulsa	AA Tex	121	499	132	33	6	16	225	70	65	25	4	122	9	8	4	9	8	.47	9	.265	.309	.451
1997 Okla City	AAA Tex	20	73	8	3	1	1	16	6	4	2	0	27	2	1	1	1	1	.50	1	.110	.156	.219
Tulsa	AA Tex	105	440	121	31	1	15	199	65	46	33	0	102	8	2	5	6	9	.40	6	.275	.335	.452
1998 Tucson	AAA Ari	131	510	134	31	12	2	195	61	49	27	0	105	4	2	5	6	4	.60	9	.263	.302	.382
1999 Tucson	AAA Ari	107	415	129	24	1	11	188	72	50	17	3	77	7	3	4	6	7	.46	6	.311	.345	.453
2000 Oklahoma	AAA Tex	55	198	45	10	0	6	73	28	11	0		43	1	3	4	1	0	1.00	2	.227	.266	.369
1998 Arizona	NL	3	7	0	0	0	0	0	0	0	0	0	2	0	0	0	0	0	—	0	.000	.000	.000
1999 Arizona	NL	4	5	2	2	0	0	4	2	1	3	1	1	0	0	0	0	0	—	2	.400	.625	.800
8 Min. YEARS		819	3152	853	190	38	71	1332	428	381	189	8	698	50	30	32	62	64	.49	55	.271	.319	.423
2 Maj. YEARS		7	12	2	2	0	0	4	2	1	3	1	3	0	0	0	0	0	—	2	.167	.333	.333

Juan Diaz

Bats: Right Throws: Right Pos: 1B-61; DH-16   Ht: 6'2" Wt: 228 Born: 2/19/76 Age: 25

Year Team	Lg Org	G	AB	H	2B	3B	HR	TB	R	RBI	TBB	IBB	SO	HBP	SH	SF	SB	CS	SB%	GDP	Avg	OBP	SLG
1997 Savannah	A LA	127	460	106	24	2	25	209	63	83	48	2	155	4	1	4	2	2	.50	10	.230	.306	.454
Vero Beach	A+ LA	1	3	2	0	0	1	5	2	1	3	0	0	1	0	0	0	0	—	0	.667	.750	1.667

(continued)

Year Team	Lg Org	G	AB	H	2B	3B	HR	TB	R	RBI	TBB	IBB	SO	HBP	SH	SF	SB	CS	SB%	GDP	Avg	OBP	SLG
1998 Vero Beach	A+ LA	67	250	73	12	1	17	138	33	51	21	2	52	4	0	3	1	2	.33	4	.292	.353	.552
San Antonio	AA LA	56	188	50	13	0	13	102	26	30	15	1	45	2	0	0	1	0	—	4	.266	.327	.543
1999 San Antonio	AA LA	66	254	77	21	1	9	127	42	52	26	1	77	3	0	4	0	0	—	4	.303	.369	.500
2000 Sarasota	A+ Bos	14	51	14	2	1	4	30	7	12	4	0	15	1	0	1	0	0	—	1	.275	.333	.588
Trenton	AA Bos	50	198	62	14	1	17	129	36	53	10	0	56	0	0	2	0	0	—	6	.313	.343	.652
Pawtucket	AAA Bos	13	43	12	0	0	7	33	11	17	6	0	9	0	0	2	1	0	1.00	2	.279	.353	.767
4 Min. YEARS		394	1447	396	86	6	93	773	220	301	130	6	410	15	1	16	4	4	.50	31	.274	.336	.534

Maikell Diaz

Bats: Right **Throws:** Right **Pos:** 2B-39; SS-37; 3B-3; PR-2   **Ht:** 5'10" **Wt:** 158 **Born:** 9/29/78 **Age:** 22

Year Team	Lg Org	G	AB	H	2B	3B	HR	TB	R	RBI	TBB	IBB	SO	HBP	SH	SF	SB	CS	SB%	GDP	Avg	OBP	SLG
1997 Orioles	R Bal	46	137	35	5	2	1	47	19	15	20	0	30	0	3	1	18	2	.90	1	.255	.348	.343
Frederick	A+ Bal	7	15	0	0	0	0	0	2	0	3	0	3	0	1	0	1		.00	0	.000	.167	.000
1998 Delmarva	A Bal	59	169	41	7	4	3	65	26	24	20	0	40	4	6	1	4	2	.67	1	.243	.335	.385
Frederick	A+ Bal	13	47	10	0	0	0	10	3	4	1	0	10	0	1	0	1	1	.50	3	.213	.229	.213
Bluefield	R+ Bal	11	40	12	1	0	0	13	4	6	4	0	6	0	0	2	2	1	.67	0	.300	.348	.325
1999 Delmarva	A Bal	91	322	89	8	3	2	109	45	34	42	0	68	11	5	1	31	15	.67	9	.276	.378	.339
2000 Bowie	AA Bal	5	15	2	0	0	0	2	1	0	0	0	6	0	1	0	0	0	—	0	.133	.133	.133
Frederick	A+ Bal	74	240	62	7	2	0	73	31	22	31	1	58	3	7	1	9	7	.56	9	.258	.349	.304
4 Min. YEARS		306	985	251	28	11	6	319	131	105	121	1	221	18	24	6	65	29	.69	23	.255	.345	.324

R.A. Dickey

Pitches: Right **Bats:** Right **Pos:** SP-23; RP-7   **Ht:** 6'2" **Wt:** 205 **Born:** 10/29/74 **Age:** 26

Year Team	Lg Org	G	GS	CG	GF	IP	BFP	H	R	ER	HR	SH	SF	HB	TBB	IBB	SO	WP	Bk	W	L	Pct.	ShO	Sv	ERA
1997 Charlotte	A+ Tex	8	6	0	2	35	162	51	32	27	8	0	0	0	12	1	32	5	3	1	4	.200	0	0	6.94
1998 Charlotte	A+ Tex	57	0	0	54	60	260	58	31	22	9	4	1	0	23	3	53	3	2	1	5	.167	0	38	3.30
1999 Tulsa	AA Tex	35	11	0	21	95	419	105	60	48	13	1	4	2	40	1	59	9	0	6	7	.462	0	10	4.55
Oklahoma	AAA Tex	6	2	0	1	22.2	99	23	12	11	3	0	1	1	7	1	17	2	0	2	2	.500	0	0	4.37
2000 Oklahoma	AAA Tex	30	23	2	2	158.1	680	167	83	79	13	4	9	7	65	1	85	5	2	8	9	.471	0	1	4.49
4 Min. YEARS		136	42	2	80	371	1620	404	218	187	44	12	14	10	146	7	246	24	7	18	27	.400	0	49	4.54

Mark DiFelice

Pitches: Right **Bats:** Right **Pos:** SP-22; RP-1   **Ht:** 6'2" **Wt:** 190 **Born:** 8/23/76 **Age:** 24

Year Team	Lg Org	G	GS	CG	GF	IP	BFP	H	R	ER	HR	SH	SF	HB	TBB	IBB	SO	WP	Bk	W	L	Pct.	ShO	Sv	ERA
1998 Portland	A- Col	15	13	0	2	81.2	343	83	45	30	6	1	2	3	11	0	62	3	1	4	6	.400	0	0	3.31
1999 Salem	A+ Col	27	23	3	1	156.1	642	142	71	67	20	4	6	4	36	0	142	3	1	8	12	.400	0	0	3.86
2000 Carolina	AA Col	23	22	2	0	133	556	152	58	53	15	2	3	0	19	0	98	2	0	7	5	.583	0	0	3.59
3 Min. YEARS		65	58	5	3	371	1541	377	174	150	41	7	11	7	66	0	302	8	2	19	23	.452	0	0	3.64

Joe Dillon

Bats: Right **Throws:** Right **Pos:** 3B-95; DH-10; PH-3; PR-1   **Ht:** 6'2" **Wt:** 205 **Born:** 8/2/75 **Age:** 25

Year Team	Lg Org	G	AB	H	2B	3B	HR	TB	R	RBI	TBB	IBB	SO	HBP	SH	SF	SB	CS	SB%	GDP	Avg	OBP	SLG
1997 Spokane	A- KC	19	70	15	3	0	2	24	6	6	5	0	13	1	0	0	1	0	1.00	2	.214	.276	.343
1998 Lansing	A KC	73	268	70	17	2	15	136	37	43	36	1	57	0	4	0	2	2	.82	5	.261	.349	.507
1999 Wilmington	A+ KC	134	503	133	31	2	16	216	73	90	59	4	124	7	2	5	9	6	.60	12	.264	.347	.429
2000 Wichita	AA KC	62	220	70	16	2	10	120	35	43	39	1	38	7	2	5	0	0	—	6	.318	.428	.545
Omaha	AAA KC	45	149	42	11	2	1	60	19	11	17	0	26	2	0	0	1	0	1.00	6	.282	.363	.403
4 Min. YEARS		333	1210	330	78	8	44	556	170	193	156	6	258	17	8	10	20	8	.71	31	.273	.361	.460

Allen Dina

Bats: Right **Throws:** Right **Pos:** OF-113; DH-3; PH-3; PR-3   **Ht:** 5'10" **Wt:** 195 **Born:** 9/28/73 **Age:** 27

Year Team	Lg Org	G	AB	H	2B	3B	HR	TB	R	RBI	TBB	IBB	SO	HBP	SH	SF	SB	CS	SB%	GDP	Avg	OBP	SLG
1998 Pittsfield	A- NYM	68	278	83	16	5	5	124	47	39	24	0	34	1	1	4	18	5	.78	1	.299	.352	.446
Capital Cty	A NYM	2	8	3	2	0	0	5	1	3	0	0	1	0	0	0	0	0	—	0	.375	.375	.625
1999 St. Lucie	A+ NYM	85	343	118	16	4	12	178	65	47	25	0	54	6	4	3	34	10	.77	2	.344	.395	.519
Binghamton	AA NYM	49	192	44	10	3	0	60	25	15	9	0	46	1	0	2	9	3	.75	6	.229	.265	.313
2000 Binghamton	AA NYM	121	419	108	22	4	7	159	58	46	22	0	78	3	9	3	21	10	.68	7	.258	.310	.379
3 Min. YEARS		325	1240	356	66	16	24	526	196	150	80	0	213	11	14	12	82	28	.75	16	.287	.337	.424

Mike Diorio

Pitches: Right **Bats:** Right **Pos:** SP-3; RP-3   **Ht:** 6'2" **Wt:** 215 **Born:** 3/1/73 **Age:** 28

Year Team	Lg Org	G	GS	CG	GF	IP	BFP	H	R	ER	HR	SH	SF	HB	TBB	IBB	SO	WP	Bk	W	L	Pct.	ShO	Sv	ERA
1993 Auburn	A- Hou	15	15	0	0	79	356	98	57	45	6	2	2	3	27	0	57	6	0	3	7	.300	0	0	5.13
1994 Astros	R Hou	2	0	0	0	2.1	15	5	6	6	1	0	0	0	3	0	2	0	0	0	1	.000	0	0	23.14
Osceola	A+ Hou	13	7	0	0	44	191	48	24	14	4	1	2	0	11	0	27	2	0	3	2	.600	0	0	2.86
1995 Quad City	A Hou	33	11	0	4	91.2	391	82	39	33	6	4	0	4	36	1	81	13	2	6	4	.600	0	1	3.24
1997 Jackson	AA Hou	8	0	0	2	11.1	63	18	17	12	1	1	0	2	6	1	9	1	0	1	3	.250	0	0	9.53
Kissimmee	A+ Hou	36	0	0	30	39.1	161	33	15	13	1	1	0	1	10	1	30	1	1	3	2	.600	0	19	2.97
1998 Jackson	AA Hou	32	0	0	24	43	182	35	16	10	0	3	0	2	21	4	31	2	0	2	3	.400	0	11	2.09
New Orleans	AAA Hou	21	0	0	8	29.1	134	38	24	17	3	2	1	1	11	4	14	1	0	4	2	.667	0	2	5.22

Year Team	Lg Org	G	GS	CG	GF	IP	BFP	H	R	ER	HR	SH	SF	HB	TBB	IBB	SO	WP	Bk	W	L	Pct.	ShO	Sv	ERA
1999 New Orleans	AAA Hou	50	0	0	14	70.1	333	85	59	50	10	2	2	7	31	6	32	6	0	2	3	.400	0	1	6.40
2000 Nashville	AAA Pit	6	3	0	1	16.1	76	11	7	7	2	0	1	1	17	1	12	1	0	0	0	—	0	0	3.86
7 Min. YEARS		216	36	0	83	426.2	1902	453	264	207	34	16	9	21	173	18	295	33	5	24	27	.471	0	35	4.37

Glenn Dishman

Pitches: Left **Bats:** Right **Pos:** RP-41; SP-1 **Ht:** 6'1" **Wt:** 205 **Born:** 11/5/70 **Age:** 30

Year Team	Lg Org	G	GS	CG	GF	IP	BFP	H	R	ER	HR	SH	SF	HB	TBB	IBB	SO	WP	Bk	W	L	Pct.	ShO	Sv	ERA
1993 Spokane	A- SD	12	12	2	0	77.2	307	59	25	19	3	2	1	1	13	0	79	3	1	6	3	.667	2	0	2.20
Rancho Cuca	A+ SD	2	2	0	0	11.1	52	14	9	9	0	0	0	1	5	0	6	1	1	0	1	.000	0	0	7.15
1994 Wichita	AA SD	27	27	1	0	169.1	693	156	73	53	6	8	3	3	42	2	165	4	1	11	8	.579	0	0	2.82
Las Vegas	AAA SD	2	2	0	0	13	55	15	7	5	1	0	2	0	1	0	12	0	0	1	1	.500	0	0	3.46
1995 Las Vegas	AAA SD	14	14	3	0	106	430	91	37	30	12	4	1	0	20	2	64	3	1	6	3	.667	1	0	2.55
1996 Las Vegas	AAA SD	26	26	3	0	155	669	177	103	96	17	3	9	3	43	5	115	7	1	6	8	.429	1	0	5.57
1997 Toledo	AAA Det	21	18	1	2	114	467	112	53	49	12	3	3	2	32	0	77	4	1	7	6	.538	0	1	3.87
1999 Sonoma Cty	IND —	5	3	0	1	14.2	75	27	16	15	2	0	0	1	6	0	9	2	0	0	1	.000	0	0	9.20
2000 Huntsville	AA Mil	42	1	0	5	64.1	295	67	39	36	12	4	1	6	35	3	59	8	1	1	2	.333	0	5	5.04
1995 San Diego	NL	19	16	0	1	97	421	104	60	54	11	6	3	4	34	1	43	3	1	4	8	.333	0	0	5.01
1996 San Diego	NL	3	0	0	2	2.1	11	3	2	2	0	0	0	0	1	0	1	0	0	0	0	—	0	0	7.71
Philadelphia	NL	4	1	0	2	7	31	9	6	6	2	0	1	0	2	0	3	0	0	0	0	—	0	0	7.71
1997 Detroit	AL	7	4	0	1	29	125	30	18	17	4	1	2	2	8	0	20	0	0	1	2	.333	0	0	5.28
7 Min. YEARS		151	105	10	8	725.1	3043	718	362	312	65	24	20	17	197	12	586	32	7	38	33	.535	4	1	3.87
3 Maj. YEARS		33	21	0	6	135.1	588	146	86	79	17	7	6	6	45	1	66	4	1	5	10	.333	0	0	5.25

Rich Dishman

Pitches: Right **Bats:** Right **Pos:** SP-13; RP-3 **Ht:** 6'5" **Wt:** 220 **Born:** 4/26/75 **Age:** 26

Year Team	Lg Org	G	GS	CG	GF	IP	BFP	H	R	ER	HR	SH	SF	HB	TBB	IBB	SO	WP	Bk	W	L	Pct.	ShO	Sv	ERA
1997 Eugene	A- Atl	19	1	0	6	51	213	47	19	17	2	1	0	7	13	0	60	5	1	2	2	.500	0	3	3.00
1998 Macon	A Atl	18	0	0	6	39.1	170	38	22	17	2	3	0	0	17	1	44	2	1	1	1	.500	0	1	3.89
Danville	A+ Atl	20	11	0	6	77.1	308	54	20	16	1	3	1	3	28	0	85	3	0	3	2	.600	0	1	1.86
1999 Greenville	AA Atl	30	24	1	1	139.2	613	146	76	65	19	6	4	7	58	0	131	5	0	6	13	.316	0	1	4.19
2000 Braves	R Atl	5	5	0	0	10	48	18	8	7	1	0	1	0	0	0	12	3	0	0	1	.000	0	0	6.30
Richmond	AAA Atl	11	8	0	1	38	182	48	29	27	0	3	3	1	20	0	23	9	1	2	5	.286	0	0	6.39
4 Min. YEARS		103	49	1	20	355.1	1534	351	174	149	25	16	9	19	136	1	355	27	3	14	24	.368	0	5	3.77

Tim Dixon

Pitches: Left **Bats:** Left **Pos:** RP-36; SP-3 **Ht:** 6'2" **Wt:** 215 **Born:** 2/26/72 **Age:** 29

Year Team	Lg Org	G	GS	CG	GF	IP	BFP	H	R	ER	HR	SH	SF	HB	TBB	IBB	SO	WP	Bk	W	L	Pct.	ShO	Sv	ERA
1995 Vermont	A- Mon	18	9	0	2	69	287	58	20	14	0	3	0	8	16	0	58	5	7	7	2	.778	0	1	1.83
1996 Wst Plm Bch	A+ Mon	37	16	0	8	124	528	126	55	40	10	8	5	6	35	3	87	7	0	5	11	.313	0	2	2.90
1997 Ottawa	AAA Mon	5	0	0	1	9.1	45	12	10	10	2	1	1	0	5	1	8	2	0	1	1	.500	0	0	9.64
Harrisburg	AA Mon	37	2	0	6	69.1	296	66	34	26	6	4	3	4	24	2	75	4	0	5	2	.714	0	3	3.38
1998 Harrisburg	AA Mon	37	0	0	15	58	249	58	29	25	5	3	2	1	16	2	52	4	0	2	5	.286	0	2	3.88
Ottawa	AAA Mon	9	0	0	5	18.1	84	22	15	12	2	0	1	0	7	0	13	3	0	0	0	—	0	0	5.89
1999 Harrisburg	AA Mon	2	0	0	0	4.2	20	4	4	3	1	0	1	0	2	0	4	1	0	0	1	.000	0	0	5.79
Ottawa	AAA Mon	2	0	0	1	1.1	6	3	1	1	1	0	0	0	1	0	1	0	0	0	0	—	0	0	6.75
Pawtucket	AAA Bos	2	0	0	0	5	25	6	5	5	3	0	0	1	3	0	1	0	0	0	1	.000	0	0	9.00
Trenton	AA Bos	8	2	0	1	18.1	73	15	6	6	2	1	0	2	6	0	10	2	0	2	0	1.000	0	0	2.95
Huntsville	AA Mil	24	1	0	15	39.1	174	33	16	12	3	2	2	4	19	0	43	2	0	0	0	—	0	6	2.75
2000 Huntsville	AA Mil	35	0	0	10	41.2	189	41	31	26	6	2	5	6	17	1	38	7	0	2	4	.333	0	0	5.62
Winnipeg	IND —	4	3	0	1	13	68	24	16	15	4	0	0	0	6	0	10	1	0	1	2	.333	0	0	10.38
6 Min. YEARS		220	33	0	65	471.1	2044	468	242	195	45	24	20	32	156	9	403	38	7	25	29	.463	0	11	3.72

Robert Dodd

Pitches: Left **Bats:** Left **Pos:** RP-11; SP-5 **Ht:** 6'3" **Wt:** 195 **Born:** 3/14/73 **Age:** 28

Year Team	Lg Org	G	GS	CG	GF	IP	BFP	H	R	ER	HR	SH	SF	HB	TBB	IBB	SO	WP	Bk	W	L	Pct.	ShO	Sv	ERA
1994 Batavia	A- Phi	14	7	0	4	52	209	42	16	13	0	2	1	2	14	1	44	4	0	2	4	.333	0	1	2.25
1995 Clearwater	A+ Phi	26	26	0	0	151	636	144	64	53	4	3	6	1	58	0	110	3	7	8	7	.533	0	0	3.16
Reading	AA Phi	1	0	0	0	1.1	5	0	0	0	0	0	0	0	2	0	0	0	0	0	0	—	0	0	0.00
1996 Reading	AA Phi	18	5	0	4	43	185	41	21	17	4	4	3	3	24	2	35	0	0	2	3	.400	0	0	3.56
Scranton-WB	AAA Phi	8	2	0	2	20	101	32	21	18	4	0	0	1	9	0	12	1	0	0	0	—	0	0	8.10
1997 Reading	AA Phi	63	0	0	23	80.1	314	61	29	29	8	6	0	0	21	1	94	1	0	9	4	.692	0	8	3.25
1998 Scranton-WB	AAA Phi	42	0	0	16	41.2	177	37	15	15	4	2	1	1	19	2	41	0	0	4	1	.800	0	6	3.24
1999 Reading	AA Phi	42	0	0	18	80	335	78	38	34	8	2	2	3	23	1	79	1	2	10	2	.833	0	5	3.83
2000 Scranton-WB	AAA Phi	6	4	1	1	29.2	114	19	5	3	1	1	1	1	6	0	23	0	0	4	0	1.000	0	1	0.91
Scranton-WB	AAA Phi	16	5	0	4	33.2	166	44	24	22	4	2	1	1	25	1	15	2	0	0	2	.000	0	0	5.88
1998 Philadelphia	NL	4	0	0	3	5	25	7	6	4	1	0	2	1	1	0	4	1	1	1	0	1.000	0	0	7.20
7 Min. YEARS		236	49	1	70	532.2	2242	498	233	204	37	22	15	13	201	8	453	12	10	39	23	.629	0	21	3.45

Jeremy Dodson

Bats: Left **Throws:** Right **Pos:** OF-127; PH-5 **Ht:** 6'2" **Wt:** 200 **Born:** 5/3/77 **Age:** 24

Year Team	Lg Org	G	AB	H	2B	3B	HR	TB	R	RBI	TBB	IBB	SO	HBP	SH	SF	SB	CS	SB%	GDP	Avg	OBP	SLG
1998 Spokane	A- KC	69	268	90	19	5	9	146	56	59	25	2	59	6	0	5	8	4	.67	5	.336	.398	.545
1999 Wichita	AA KC	133	452	116	20	1	21	201	63	58	51	2	95	2	1	0	9	5	.64	12	.257	.335	.445

75

Year Team	Lg Org	G	AB	H	2B	3B	HR	TB	R	RBI	TBB	IBB	SO	HBP	SH	SF	SB	CS	SB%	GDP	Avg	OBP	SLG
2000 Wichita	AA KC	128	450	107	16	4	18	185	69	57	52	2	111	7	5	0	17	8	.68	7	.238	.326	.411
3 Min. YEARS		330	1170	313	55	10	48	532	188	174	128	6	265	15	6	5	34	17	.67	24	.268	.346	.455

Andy Dominique

Bats: Right **Throws:** Right **Pos:** C-60; 1B-39; PH-9; DH-4; 3B-2; PR-1   **Ht:** 6'0" **Wt:** 224 **Born:** 10/30/75 **Age:** 25

Year Team	Lg Org	G	AB	H	2B	3B	HR	TB	R	RBI	TBB	IBB	SO	HBP	SH	SF	SB	CS	SB%	GDP	Avg	OBP	SLG
1997 Batavia	A- Phi	72	277	77	17	0	14	136	52	48	26	0	60	10	0	5	4	1	.80	6	.278	.355	.491
1998 Piedmont	A Phi	133	514	145	38	0	24	255	82	102	61	4	97	12	0	4	0	2	.00	9	.282	.369	.496
1999 Clearwater	A+ Phi	130	487	124	29	5	14	205	77	92	69	4	84	10	3	8	3	3	.50	13	.255	.354	.421
2000 Reading	AA Phi	104	327	78	27	0	13	144	46	50	35	0	56	8	3	4	0	1	.00	9	.239	.324	.440
4 Min. YEARS		439	1605	424	111	5	65	740	257	292	191	8	297	40	6	21	7	7	.50	37	.264	.353	.461

Bo Donaldson

Pitches: Right **Bats:** Right **Pos:** RP-57   **Ht:** 6'0" **Wt:** 200 **Born:** 10/10/74 **Age:** 26

Year Team	Lg Org	G	GS	CG	GF	IP	BFP	H	R	ER	HR	SH	SF	HB	TBB	IBB	SO	WP	Bk	W	L	Pct.	ShO	Sv	ERA
1997 North	A- Ana	27	0	0	25	52	208	31	16	7	0	3	1	2	20	1	88	10	2	3	1	.750	0	15	1.21
1998 Lk Elsinore	A+ Ana	54	3	0	42	76.1	340	65	38	32	7	5	3	9	40	4	99	12	4	4	6	.400	0	20	3.77
1999 Rockford	A Cin	19	0	0	7	30	119	17	7	4	0	4	0	0	12	3	50	2	1	2	1	.667	0	1	1.20
Chattanooga	AA Cin	38	0	0	19	51.1	199	30	18	17	2	3	1	1	16	2	67	2	1	5	3	.625	0	6	2.98
2000 Chattanooga	AA Cin	57	0	0	46	61.2	284	50	31	25	7	4	1	4	48	6	78	6	2	1	4	.200	0	24	3.65
4 Min. YEARS		195	3	0	139	271.1	1150	193	104	85	16	19	6	16	136	16	382	32	10	15	15	.500	0	66	2.82

Brendan Donnelly

Pitches: Right **Bats:** Right **Pos:** RP-46   **Ht:** 6'3" **Wt:** 205 **Born:** 7/4/71 **Age:** 29

Year Team	Lg Org	G	GS	CG	GF	IP	BFP	H	R	ER	HR	SH	SF	HB	TBB	IBB	SO	WP	Bk	W	L	Pct.	ShO	Sv	ERA
1992 White Sox	R CWS	9	7	0	1	41.2	191	41	25	17	0	0	2	8	21	0	31	6	0	0	3	.000	0	1	3.67
1993 Geneva	A- ChC	21	3	0	7	43	198	39	34	30	4	1	1	6	29	0	29	7	3	4	0	1.000	0	1	6.28
1994 Ohio Valley	IND —	10	0	0	1	13.2	59	13	5	4	1	0	0	3	4	0	20	1	0	1	1	.500	0	0	2.63
1995 Chston-WV	A Cin	24	0	0	22	30.1	112	14	4	4	0	1	2	1	7	1	33	1	0	1	1	.500	0	1	1.19
Winston-Sal	A+ Cin	23	0	0	14	35.1	138	20	6	4	1	2	0	2	14	2	32	0	1	1	2	.333	0	12	1.02
Indianapols	AAA Cin	3	0	0	0	2.2	18	7	8	7	2	0	1	1	2	0	1	2	0	1	1	.500	0	0	23.63
1996 Chattanooga	AA Cin	22	0	0	10	29.1	133	27	21	18	4	0	1	1	17	2	22	1	0	1	2	.333	0	0	5.52
1997 Chattanooga	AA Cin	62	0	0	21	82.2	359	71	43	30	6	4	3	4	37	4	64	9	0	6	4	.600	0	6	3.27
1998 Chattanooga	AA Cin	38	0	0	35	45.1	203	43	16	15	4	1	1	3	24	5	47	8	0	2	5	.286	0	13	2.98
Indianapols	AAA Cin	19	1	0	6	37.1	157	29	16	11	3	1	0	3	16	3	39	2	0	4	1	.800	0	0	2.65
1999 Nashua	IND —	3	0	0	3	3	11	1	1	1	1	0	0	0	3	0	4	0	0	0	0	—	0	0	3.00
Durham	AAA TB	37	1	0	10	62	247	53	23	21	5	0	4	4	18	1	61	5	0	5	5	.500	0	2	3.05
Altoona	AA Pit	2	0	0	2	2.1	12	4	2	2	0	1	2	0	2	0	0	0	0	0	0	—	0	1	7.71
Syracuse	AAA Tor	5	0	0	2	9.1	39	8	4	3	1	2	0	0	4	1	9	1	0	0	1	.000	0	0	2.89
2000 Syracuse	AAA Tor	37	0	0	7	42.2	203	47	34	26	5	4	1	1	27	2	34	1	0	4	6	.400	0	0	5.48
Iowa	AAA ChC	9	0	0	3	16.2	83	25	19	14	3	0	1	2	6	1	14	2	0	0	3	.000	0	1	7.56
9 Min. YEARS		324	12	0	144	497.1	2163	442	261	207	40	17	19	39	231	22	440	46	4	30	35	.462	0	39	3.75

Randey Dorame

Pitches: Left **Bats:** Left **Pos:** SP-20   **Ht:** 6'2" **Wt:** 205 **Born:** 1/23/79 **Age:** 22

Year Team	Lg Org	G	GS	CG	GF	IP	BFP	H	R	ER	HR	SH	SF	HB	TBB	IBB	SO	WP	Bk	W	L	Pct.	ShO	Sv	ERA
1999 Vero Beach	A+ LA	3	2	0	0	11	48	15	9	7	2	0	0	0	1	0	5	0	0	0	2	.000	0	0	5.73
San Berndno	A+ LA	24	24	1	0	154.1	613	130	52	43	9	3	6	3	37	0	159	7	1	14	3	.824	1	0	2.51
2000 Vero Beach	A+ LA	9	9	0	0	57	226	50	15	14	3	3	2	2	13	0	49	2	0	7	1	.875	0	0	2.21
San Antonio	AA LA	9	9	0	0	58.1	238	53	29	25	5	3	3	1	18	0	28	2	1	3	4	.429	0	0	3.86
Carolina	AA Col	2	2	0	0	10.2	46	7	6	6	3	0	0	2	4	0	9	0	0	0	2	.000	0	0	5.06
2 Min. YEARS		47	46	3	0	291.1	1171	255	111	95	22	9	11	8	73	0	250	11	2	24	12	.667	1	0	2.93

David Doster

Bats: Right **Throws:** Right **Pos:** 3B-72; 2B-27; OF-18; PH-5; DH-4; PR-3   **Ht:** 5'10" **Wt:** 182 **Born:** 10/8/70 **Age:** 30

Year Team	Lg Org	G	AB	H	2B	3B	HR	TB	R	RBI	TBB	IBB	SO	HBP	SH	SF	SB	CS	SB%	GDP	Avg	OBP	SLG
1993 Spartanburg	A Phi	60	223	61	15	0	3	85	34	20	25	1	36	3	6	1	1	0	1.00	1	.274	.353	.381
Clearwater	A+ Phi	9	28	10	3	1	0	15	4	2	2	0	2	0	0	0	0	0	—	1	.357	.400	.536
1994 Clearwater	A+ Phi	131	480	135	42	4	13	224	76	74	54	3	71	11	3	8	12	7	.63	12	.281	.362	.467
1995 Reading	AA Phi	139	551	146	39	3	21	254	84	79	51	2	61	7	8	4	11	7	.61	11	.265	.333	.461
1996 Scranton-WB	AAA Phi	88	322	83	20	0	7	124	37	48	26	1	54	2	3	5	7	3	.70	8	.258	.313	.385
1997 Scranton-WB	AAA Phi	108	410	129	32	2	16	213	70	79	30	1	60	8	2	3	5	5	.50	9	.315	.370	.520
1998 Scranton-WB	AAA Phi	141	579	160	38	4	16	254	79	84	51	2	80	4	1	10	23	6	.79	14	.276	.334	.439
2000 Scranton-WB	AAA Phi	124	450	122	28	7	10	194	69	66	39	0	70	2	6	6	13	4	.76	16	.271	.328	.431
1996 Philadelphia	NL	39	105	28	8	0	1	39	14	9	8	7	0	21	0	1	0	0	0	—	1	.267	.313	.371
1999 Philadelphia	NL	99	97	19	2	0	3	30	9	10	12	1	23	0	2	1	1	0	1.00	2	.196	.282	.309
7 Min. YEARS		800	3043	846	217	21	86	1363	453	452	278	10	434	37	29	37	72	32	.69	76	.278	.342	.448
2 Maj. YEARS		138	202	47	10	0	4	69	23	18	19	1	44	0	3	1	1	0	1.00	3	.233	.297	.342

Jeb Dougherty

Bats: Right **Throws:** Right **Pos:** OF-73; DH-19; PH-3; PR-3   **Ht:** 6'0" **Wt:** 180 **Born:** 7/16/75 **Age:** 25

					BATTING													BASERUNNING				PERCENTAGES		
Year Team	Lg Org	G	AB	H	2B	3B	HR	TB	R	RBI	TBB	IBB	SO	HBP	SH	SF	SB	CS	SB%	GDP	Avg	OBP	SLG
1997 Boise	A- Ana	25	92	28	5	1	0	35	20	8	8	0	10	3	0	0	3	0	1.00	2	.304	.379	.380
Lk Elsinore	A+ Ana	12	26	6	0	0	0	6	2	1	1	0	5	0	0	0	3	2	.60	0	.231	.259	.231
1998 Cedar Rapds	A Ana	107	425	107	12	3	2	131	62	42	26	0	69	12	6	4	40	8	.83	5	.252	.310	.308
1999 Lk Elsinore	A+ Ana	115	381	99	13	4	7	141	66	45	54	0	68	10	4	3	35	13	.73	11	.260	.364	.370
2000 Erie	AA Ana	76	267	64	9	3	1	82	33	32	36	0	42	2	6	7	20	7	.74	2	.240	.327	.307
Lk Elsinore	A+ Ana	18	59	17	2	0	0	19	12	5	12	0	12	1	3	1	7	3	.70	0	.288	.411	.322
4 Min. YEARS		353	1250	321	41	11	10	414	195	133	137	0	206	28	19	15	108	33	.77	20	.257	.340	.331

Jim Dougherty

Pitches: Right **Bats:** Right **Pos:** RP-60   **Ht:** 6'1" **Wt:** 225 **Born:** 3/8/68 **Age:** 33

		HOW MUCH HE PITCHED						WHAT HE GAVE UP											THE RESULTS					
Year Team	Lg Org	G	GS	CG	GF	IP	BFP	H	R	ER	HR	SH	SF	HB	TBB	IBB	SO	WP	Bk	W	L	Pct.	ShO	Sv	ERA
1991 Asheville	A Hou	61	0	0	48	82	324	63	17	14	0	7	0	3	24	6	76	0	2	3	1	.750	0	27	1.54
1992 Osceola	A+ Hou	57	0	0	52	81	325	66	21	14	1	4	2	2	22	4	77	0	1	5	2	.714	0	31	1.56
1993 Jackson	AA Hou	52	0	0	50	53	207	39	15	11	3	0	0	1	21	0	55	0	0	2	2	.500	0	36	1.87
1994 Tucson	AAA Hou	55	0	0	48	59	276	70	32	27	9	1	1	2	30	6	49	4	0	5	4	.556	0	21	4.12
1995 Tucson	AAA Hou	8	0	0	3	11	46	11	4	4	1	0	0	0	5	0	12	0	1	1	0	1.000	0	1	3.27
1996 Tucson	AAA Hou	46	0	0	23	61.2	269	65	35	24	0	1	1	2	27	3	53	2	1	4	3	.571	0	1	3.50
1997 Norfolk	AAA NYM	49	0	0	24	62	259	45	11	10	3	4	2	2	43	3	59	4	0	10	1	.909	0	4	1.45
1998 Edmonton	AAA Oak	45	0	0	26	57.2	254	57	24	24	7	2	1	2	33	4	45	1	0	2	1	.667	0	6	3.75
1999 Nashville	AAA Pit	53	0	0	20	59.2	274	69	38	36	9	3	4	0	27	5	55	0	0	3	3	.500	0	10	5.43
2000 Memphis	AAA StL	60	0	0	24	81.1	342	76	33	30	5	6	4	5	29	5	82	3	2	3	7	.300	0	6	3.32
1995 Houston	NL	56	0	0	11	67.2	294	76	37	37	7	3	3	3	25	1	49	1	0	8	4	.667	0	1	4.92
1996 Houston	NL	12	0	0	2	13	64	14	14	13	2	1	1	1	11	1	6	0	0	0	2	.000	0	0	9.00
1998 Oakland	AL	9	0	0	4	12	59	17	11	11	2	1	0	1	7	0	3	0	0	0	1	.000	0	0	8.25
1999 Pittsburgh	NL	2	0	0	0	2	12	3	3	2	0	0	0	0	3	0	1	0	0	0	0	—	0	0	9.00
10 Min. YEARS		486	0	0	318	608.1	2576	561	190	194	38	28	15	19	261	36	563	14	7	38	24	.613	0	143	2.87
4 Mai. YEARS		79	0	0	17	94.2	429	110	65	63	11	5	4	5	46	2	59	1	0	8	8	.500	0	1	5.99

Tony Dougherty

Pitches: Right **Bats:** Right **Pos:** RP-33; SP-1   **Ht:** 6'2" **Wt:** 200 **Born:** 4/12/73 **Age:** 28

		HOW MUCH HE PITCHED						WHAT HE GAVE UP											THE RESULTS					
Year Team	Lg Org	G	GS	CG	GF	IP	BFP	H	R	ER	HR	SH	SF	HB	TBB	IBB	SO	WP	Bk	W	L	Pct.	ShO	Sv	ERA
1994 Watertown	A- Cle	26	0	0	13	40.2	178	33	20	13	0	3	0	4	19	2	37	3	2	6	1	.857	0	2	2.88
1995 Columbus	A Cle	27	10	0	3	87.2	405	85	61	46	5	2	4	5	50	4	78	4	1	4	4	.500	0	0	4.72
1996 Columbus	A Cle	19	1	0	8	49	202	30	16	16	3	2	2	4	22	0	44	4	1	3	1	.750	0	2	2.94
Canton-Akrn	AA Cle	3	0	0	0	5	26	3	5	5	1	0	0	0	8	1	6	0	0	0	0	—	0	0	9.00
Kinston	A+ Cle	18	0	0	15	33.1	135	29	6	6	2	3	0	1	11	2	32	3	1	3	1	.750	0	8	1.62
1997 Akron	AA Cle	28	0	0	26	39	163	31	11	11	2	1	2	1	19	1	31	0	0	2	0	1.000	0	2	2.54
Buffalo	AAA Cle	18	0	0	7	28.2	128	31	17	12	2	1	0	0	18	0	21	5	0	2	0	1.000	0	0	3.77
1998 Akron	AA Cle	43	0	0	25	76.1	328	68	29	26	5	7	1	2	36	3	60	4	0	6	5	.545	0	5	3.07
Buffalo	AAA Cle	1	0	0	0	3	15	4	4	1	0	0	0	0	2	0	1	0	0	0	0	—	0	0	3.00
1999 Buffalo	AAA Cle	16	1	0	4	24	112	28	17	15	3	0	3	1	15	2	8	1	1	0	2	.000	0	0	5.63
Altoona	AA Pit	9	0	0	3	15.2	80	29	19	13	3	0	1	1	7	1	6	0	0	0	1	.000	0	0	7.47
Sarasota	A+ Bos	4	0	0	2	3	13	3	1	1	1	0	0	1	1	0	2	0	0	0	0	—	0	0	3.00
Trenton	AA Bos	6	1	0	2	7.2	41	12	8	7	0	0	0	1	6	0	10	0	0	0	1	.000	0	1	8.22
2000 San Angelo	IND —	18	0	0	16	20	92	22	14	6	1	0	0	2	7	1	13	1	0	1	1	.500	0	9	2.70
Ottawa	AAA Mon	16	1	0	5	26.1	130	37	23	21	2	0	3	1	11	0	10	1	1	3	2	.600	0	0	7.18
7 Min. YEARS		252	14	0	129	459.1	2048	445	251	199	30	19	16	27	232	17	359	26	7	28	20	.583	0	37	3.90

Brian Doughty

Pitches: Right **Bats:** Right **Pos:** SP-22; RP-9   **Ht:** 6'5" **Wt:** 235 **Born:** 9/21/74 **Age:** 26

		HOW MUCH HE PITCHED						WHAT HE GAVE UP											THE RESULTS					
Year Team	Lg Org	G	GS	CG	GF	IP	BFP	H	R	ER	HR	SH	SF	HB	TBB	IBB	SO	WP	Bk	W	L	Pct.	ShO	Sv	ERA
1992 Bellingham	A- Sea	11	5	1	3	38.2	157	32	16	11	2	4	1	0	9	0	27	3	0	3	1	.750	0	0	2.56
1993 Bellingham	A- Sea	14	14	1	0	76	331	65	30	21	4	3	1	0	42	1	39	9	0	5	4	.556	0	0	2.49
1994 Appleton	A Sea	12	7	1	2	38.2	173	44	32	25	8	1	0	1	19	0	14	6	1	1	5	.167	0	0	5.82
Mariners	R Sea	7	6	0	0	37	154	36	15	11	0	0	1	4	4	0	27	1	0	1	3	.250	0	0	2.68
1995 Wisconsin	A Sea	32	3	0	12	84.1	360	83	50	37	4	4	3	6	26	3	54	5	0	5	7	.417	0	4	3.95
1996 Reno	IND —	18	18	4	0	132.2	575	143	71	63	12	6	2	8	44	0	73	8	0	11	3	.786	1	0	4.27
1997 Reno	IND —	19	19	3	0	130.2	596	180	93	68	7	5	5	3	30	0	83	1	1	11	3	.786	0	0	4.68
1998 Rancho Cuca	A+ SD	16	2	0	3	31.2	134	29	14	9	2	1	1	3	8	0	23	2	2	2	1	.667	0	0	2.56
Mobile	AA SD	17	0	0	2	38	189	62	33	23	3	1	2	2	8	0	19	1	0	0	0	—	0	0	5.45
1999 Mobile	AA SD	36	15	0	3	137.2	592	161	85	73	20	7	4	3	29	1	69	1	0	8	10	.444	0	1	4.77
2000 Mobile	AA SD	31	22	1	2	134	577	154	83	62	13	4	2	6	26	0	67	1	1	9	10	.474	1	0	4.16
9 Min. YEARS		213	111	11	27	879.1	3837	989	522	403	75	34	22	37	245	5	495	38	5	56	47	.544	3	6	4.12

Sean Douglass

Pitches: Right **Bats:** Right **Pos:** SP-27   **Ht:** 6'6" **Wt:** 200 **Born:** 4/28/79 **Age:** 22

		HOW MUCH HE PITCHED						WHAT HE GAVE UP											THE RESULTS					
Year Team	Lg Org	G	GS	CG	GF	IP	BFP	H	R	ER	HR	SH	SF	HB	TBB	IBB	SO	WP	Bk	W	L	Pct.	ShO	Sv	ERA
1997 Orioles	R Bal	9	1	0	5	17.2	80	20	14	12	2	4	0	2	9	0	10	1	0	1	3	.250	0	0	6.11
1998 Bluefield	R+ Bal	10	10	0	0	53	210	45	20	19	6	0	1	0	14	0	62	3	0	2	2	.500	0	0	3.23
1999 Frederick	A+ Bal	16	16	1	0	97.2	425	101	48	36	9	4	3	5	35	0	89	3	0	5	6	.455	0	0	3.32
2000 Bowie	AA Bal	27	27	1	0	160.2	687	155	79	72	17	3	2	5	55	1	118	5	0	9	8	.529	0	0	4.03
4 Min. YEARS		62	54	2	5	329	1402	321	161	139	34	11	6	12	113	1	279	12	0	17	19	.472	0	0	3.80

Matt Drews

Pitches: Right **Bats:** Right **Pos:** SP-1 **Ht:** 6'8" **Wt:** 230 **Born:** 8/29/74 **Age:** 26

Year Team	Lg Org	G	GS	CG	GF	IP	BFP	H	R	ER	HR	SH	SF	HB	TBB	IBB	SO	WP	Bk	W	L	Pct.	ShO	Sv	ERA
1994 Oneonta	A- NYY	14	14	1	0	90	369	76	31	21	1	1	2	8	19	0	69	3	0	7	6	.538	1	0	2.10
1995 Tampa	A+ NYY	28	28	3	0	182	748	142	73	46	5	5	5	17	58	0	140	8	2	15	7	.682	0	0	2.27
1996 Columbus	AAA NYY	7	7	0	0	20.1	113	18	27	19	4	1	5	7	27	0	7	8	0	0	4	.000	0	0	8.41
Tampa	A+ NYY	4	4	0	0	17.2	93	26	20	14	0	2	1	3	12	2	12	1	0	0	3	.000	0	0	7.13
Norwich	AA NYY	9	9	0	0	46	210	40	26	23	4	1	0	5	33	1	37	1	0	1	3	.250	0	0	4.50
Jacksnville	AA Det	6	6	1	0	31	138	26	18	15	3	0	0	4	19	0	40	2	1	0	4	.000	0	0	4.35
1997 Jacksnville	AA Det	24	24	4	0	144.1	652	160	109	88	23	1	6	16	50	0	85	3	0	8	11	.421	1	0	5.49
Toledo	AAA Det	3	3	0	0	15	72	14	11	11	2	2	0	0	14	1	7	2	0	0	2	.000	0	0	6.60
1998 Toledo	AAA Det	27	27	1	0	149.1	702	175	120	109	26	5	11	16	78	1	86	15	2	5	17	.227	0	0	6.57
1999 Toledo	AAA Det	28	22	0	3	136	668	171	136	125	21	1	10	14	91	2	70	16	2	2	14	.125	0	0	8.28
2000 Durham	AAA TB	1	1	0	0	0.2	8	0	4	4	0	0	0	2	4	0	1	3	0	0	0	—	0	0	54.00
7 Min. YEARS		151	145	10	3	832.1	3773	848	575	475	89	19	40	92	405	7	554	62	7	38	71	.349	2	0	5.14

Travis Driskill

Pitches: Right **Bats:** Right **Pos:** SP-28 **Ht:** 6'0" **Wt:** 185 **Born:** 8/1/71 **Age:** 29

Year Team	Lg Org	G	GS	CG	GF	IP	BFP	H	R	ER	HR	SH	SF	HB	TBB	IBB	SO	WP	Bk	W	L	Pct.	ShO	Sv	ERA
1993 Watertown	A- Cle	21	8	0	7	63	276	62	38	29	4	3	6	5	21	0	53	6	0	5	4	.556	0	3	4.14
1994 Columbus	A Cle	62	0	0	59	64.1	267	51	25	18	2	5	2	1	30	4	88	6	0	5	5	.500	0	35	2.52
1995 Canton-Akrn	AA Cle	33	0	0	22	46.1	200	46	24	24	3	1	1	1	19	1	39	0	1	3	4	.429	0	4	4.66
Kinston	A+ Cle	15	0	0	9	23	90	17	7	7	2	0	3	1	5	1	24	1	0	0	2	.000	0	0	2.74
1996 Canton-Akrn	AA Cle	29	24	4	0	172	732	169	89	69	8	6	6	3	63	0	148	10	2	13	7	.650	2	0	3.61
1997 Buffalo	AAA Cle	29	24	1	1	147	645	159	86	76	22	6	6	3	60	0	102	15	1	8	7	.533	0	0	4.65
1998 Akron	AA Cle	5	4	0	1	26.1	109	27	12	10	4	0	1	1	7	0	16	0	0	3	0	1.000	0	0	3.42
Buffalo	AAA Cle	1	1	0	0	6	28	9	6	6	0	0	0	0	1	0	5	0	0	0	0	—	0	0	9.00
1999 Buffalo	AAA Cle	31	18	0	3	132.1	561	146	78	71	21	5	5	6	32	2	90	4	1	9	8	.529	0	0	4.83
2000 New Orleans	AAA Hou	28	28	2	0	179.1	774	201	101	80	15	5	3	7	45	0	113	6	0	12	11	.522	1	0	4.01
8 Min. YEARS		254	107	7	102	859.2	3682	887	466	390	81	27	33	28	283	8	678	48	5	58	48	.547	3	42	4.08

Mike Drumright

Pitches: Right **Bats:** Left **Pos:** SP-22; RP-12 **Ht:** 6'4" **Wt:** 210 **Born:** 4/19/74 **Age:** 27

Year Team	Lg Org	G	GS	CG	GF	IP	BFP	H	R	ER	HR	SH	SF	HB	TBB	IBB	SO	WP	Bk	W	L	Pct.	ShO	Sv	ERA
1995 Lakeland	A+ Det	5	5	0	0	21	87	19	11	10	2	1	0	0	9	0	19	1	2	1	1	.500	0	0	4.29
Jacksnville	AA Det	5	5	0	0	31.2	137	30	13	13	4	0	0	2	15	1	34	1	5	0	1	.000	0	0	3.69
1996 Jacksnville	AA Det	18	18	1	0	99.2	418	80	51	44	11	1	3	3	48	0	109	10	6	6	4	.600	1	0	3.97
1997 Jacksnville	AA Det	5	5	0	0	28.2	112	16	7	5	0	1	1	3	13	0	24	2	0	1	1	.500	0	0	1.57
Toledo	AAA Det	23	23	0	0	133.1	612	134	78	75	22	8	8	4	91	1	115	5	4	5	10	.333	0	0	5.06
1998 Toledo	AAA Det	29	27	1	1	154	733	188	130	119	21	3	13	7	94	0	91	16	1	4	19	.174	0	0	6.95
1999 Toledo	AAA Det	21	21	1	0	120.2	535	116	88	80	17	2	7	7	59	2	76	8	0	6	10	.375	0	0	5.97
Calgary	AAA Fla	12	0	0	1	21	113	39	33	32	5	1	0	1	13	0	15	2	0	0	2	.000	0	0	13.71
2000 Calgary	AAA Fla	34	22	1	3	131.1	641	164	105	91	10	3	5	4	101	0	87	12	1	9	8	.529	0	0	6.24
6 Min. YEARS		152	126	4	5	741.1	3388	786	516	469	92	20	37	31	443	4	570	57	19	32	56	.364	1	0	5.69

Renney Duarte

Pitches: Right **Bats:** Right **Pos:** RP-29 **Ht:** 6'0" **Wt:** 220 **Born:** 11/7/78 **Age:** 22

Year Team	Lg Org	G	GS	CG	GF	IP	BFP	H	R	ER	HR	SH	SF	HB	TBB	IBB	SO	WP	Bk	W	L	Pct.	ShO	Sv	ERA
1996 Angels	R Ana	10	1	1	4	27.2	111	23	14	11	1	1	1	3	8	0	28	2	0	2	0	1.000	0	1	3.58
1997 Butte	R+ Ana	15	15	5	0	110.1	454	113	54	43	7	2	5	1	19	0	65	5	0	8	4	.667	0	0	3.51
1998 Cedar Rapids	A Ana	4	4	2	0	32	119	17	7	2	1	0	0	1	1	0	28	0	0	3	1	.750	0	0	0.56
Lk Elsinore	A+ Ana	32	14	3	11	127	567	148	84	70	14	5	5	5	48	4	74	8	1	6	7	.462	0	3	4.96
1999 Lk Elsinore	A+ Ana	3	3	0	0	14	71	22	13	10	2	0	0	1	8	1	6	0	1	0	1	.000	0	0	6.43
Cedar Rapids	A Ana	31	18	3	4	132.2	561	145	81	70	19	4	4	2	33	0	102	5	1	6	11	.353	2	1	4.75
2000 Lk Elsinore	A+ Ana	17	0	0	3	31	141	33	22	16	3	1	3	1	13	2	24	0	0	2	2	.500	0	0	4.65
Edmonton	AAA Ana	1	0	0	1	2	10	3	2	2	1	0	1	0	1	0	1	0	0	0	0	—	0	0	9.00
Erie	AA Ana	11	0	0	3	23.1	106	25	20	16	3	2	1	2	9	0	12	1	0	0	1	.000	0	1	6.17
5 Min. YEARS		124	55	14	26	500	2140	529	297	240	51	15	19	16	140	7	340	21	3	27	27	.500	2	6	4.32

Eric DuBose

Pitches: Left **Bats:** Left **Pos:** RP-23 **Ht:** 6'3" **Wt:** 215 **Born:** 5/15/76 **Age:** 25

Year Team	Lg Org	G	GS	CG	GF	IP	BFP	H	R	ER	HR	SH	SF	HB	TBB	IBB	SO	WP	Bk	W	L	Pct.	ShO	Sv	ERA
1997 Sou Oregon	A- Oak	10	1	0	0	10	39	5	0	0	0	0	0	0	6	0	15	0	0	1	0	1.000	0	0	0.00
Visalia	A+ Oak	10	9	0	0	38.1	194	43	37	30	4	2	0	5	28	0	39	6	3	1	3	.250	0	0	7.04
1998 Visalia	A+ Oak	17	10	0	4	72	307	56	34	27	5	1	2	5	35	0	85	8	2	6	1	.857	0	1	3.38
Huntsville	AA Oak	14	14	1	0	83.1	363	86	37	25	2	3	4	7	34	1	66	4	0	7	6	.538	1	0	2.70
1999 Midland	AA Oak	21	14	0	3	77	361	89	57	47	10	2	4	7	44	1	68	8	0	4	2	.667	0	1	5.49
2000 Visalia	A+ Oak	5	0	0	2	10.2	46	8	2	2	0	0	0	1	5	1	12	1	0	0	1	.000	0	1	1.69
Midland	AA Oak	18	0	0	1	28.1	131	25	16	13	1	0	0	3	18	2	20	2	0	5	1	.833	0	0	4.13
4 Min. YEARS		88	48	1	10	319.2	1441	312	183	144	22	8	10	28	170	5	305	29	5	24	14	.632	1	3	4.05

Justin Duchscherer

Pitches: Right **Bats:** Right **Pos:** SP-24   **Ht:** 6'3" **Wt:** 164 **Born:** 11/19/77 **Age:** 23

Year Team	Lg Org	G	GS	CG	GF	IP	BFP	H	R	ER	HR	SH	SF	HB	TBB	IBB	SO	WP	Bk	W	L	Pct.	ShO	Sv	ERA
1996 Red Sox	R Bos	13	8	0	2	54.2	232	52	26	19	0	3	3	3	14	0	45	4	6	0	2	.000	0	1	3.13
1997 Red Sox	R Bos	10	8	0	0	44.2	190	34	18	9	0	2	1	3	17	0	59	5	4	2	3	.400	0	0	1.81
Michigan	A Bos	4	4	0	0	24	109	26	17	15	1	0	1	0	10	0	19	0	0	1	1	.500	0	0	5.63
1998 Michigan	A Bos	30	26	0	2	142.2	627	166	87	76	9	7	3	13	47	3	106	7	1	7	12	.368	0	0	4.79
1999 Augusta	A Bos	6	6	0	0	41	150	21	1	1	0	0	0	0	8	0	39	1	0	4	0	1.000	0	0	0.22
Sarasota	A+ Bos	20	18	0	0	112.1	475	101	62	56	14	2	5	12	30	0	105	5	0	7	7	.500	0	0	4.49
2000 Trenton	AA Bos	24	24	2	0	143.1	593	134	59	54	7	3	5	6	35	1	126	6	1	7	9	.438	2	0	3.39
5 Min. YEARS		107	94	2	4	562.2	2376	534	270	230	31	17	18	40	161	4	499	28	12	28	34	.452	2	1	3.68

Brandon Duckworth

Pitches: Right **Bats:** Both **Pos:** SP-27   **Ht:** 6'2" **Wt:** 185 **Born:** 1/23/76 **Age:** 25

Year Team	Lg Org	G	GS	CG	GF	IP	BFP	H	R	ER	HR	SH	SF	HB	TBB	IBB	SO	WP	Bk	W	L	Pct.	ShO	Sv	ERA
1998 Piedmont	A Phi	21	21	5	0	147.2	577	116	58	46	10	1	5	7	24	0	119	8	2	9	8	.529	3	0	2.80
Clearwater	A+ Phi	9	9	1	0	53	235	64	25	22	2	2	1	1	22	0	46	4	0	6	2	.750	1	0	3.74
1999 Clearwater	A+ Phi	27	17	0	1	132	602	164	84	71	13	5	7	5	40	0	101	10	1	11	5	.688	0	1	4.84
2000 Reading	AA Phi	27	27	1	0	165	688	145	70	58	17	5	2	7	52	0	178	6	3	13	7	.650	0	0	3.16
3 Min. YEARS		84	74	7	1	497.2	2102	489	237	197	42	13	15	20	138	0	444	28	6	39	22	.639	4	1	3.56

Matt Duff

Pitches: Right **Bats:** Right **Pos:** RP-47   **Ht:** 6'1" **Wt:** 192 **Born:** 10/6/74 **Age:** 26

Year Team	Lg Org	G	GS	CG	GF	IP	BFP	H	R	ER	HR	SH	SF	HB	TBB	IBB	SO	WP	Bk	W	L	Pct.	ShO	Sv	ERA
1997 Springfield	IND —	14	12	2	1	79.2	334	70	33	24	3	2	6	3	27	1	76	3	0	7	4	.636	0	0	2.71
Augusta	A Pit	2	1	0	1	6	26	6	1	1	0	0	0	1	2	0	6	0	0	0	1	.000	0	0	1.50
1998 Augusta	A Pit	10	0	0	9	9	42	8	3	3	1	0	0	1	4	0	12	0	0	1	0	1.000	0	3	3.00
Lynchburg	A+ Pit	40	0	0	25	62.2	257	52	26	23	4	3	3	1	20	2	61	4	0	4	5	.444	0	10	3.30
1999 Lynchburg	A+ Pit	7	7	0	0	39	169	41	22	22	6	1	1	0	13	0	40	0	1	2	3	.400	0	0	5.08
Altoona	AA Pit	44	0	0	29	57.2	241	43	19	18	5	4	2	2	35	4	59	4	1	2	4	.333	0	12	2.81
2000 Altoona	AA Pit	47	0	0	22	55	253	50	31	24	1	4	2	1	36	9	61	2	1	0	4	.000	0	6	3.93
4 Min. YEARS		164	20	2	87	309	1322	270	135	115	20	14	14	9	137	16	315	13	3	16	21	.432	0	31	3.35

Courtney Duncan

Pitches: Right **Bats:** Left **Pos:** RP-61   **Ht:** 6'0" **Wt:** 185 **Born:** 10/9/74 **Age:** 26

Year Team	Lg Org	G	GS	CG	GF	IP	BFP	H	R	ER	HR	SH	SF	HB	TBB	IBB	SO	WP	Bk	W	L	Pct.	ShO	Sv	ERA
1996 Williamsprt	A- ChC	15	15	1	0	90.1	360	58	28	22	6	3	0	5	34	0	91	8	0	11	1	.917	0	0	2.19
1997 Daytona	A+ ChC	19	19	1	0	121.2	489	90	35	22	3	6	1	4	35	0	120	8	1	8	4	.667	0	0	1.63
Orlando	AA ChC	8	8	0	0	45	196	37	28	17	2	1	2	1	29	5	45	4	0	2	2	.500	0	0	3.40
1998 West Tenn	AA ChC	29	29	0	0	162.2	730	141	89	77	7	9	7	14	108	5	157	9	2	7	9	.438	0	0	4.26
1999 West Tenn	AA ChC	11	8	0	2	41.2	210	44	42	33	3	2	6	2	42	4	42	8	0	1	7	.125	0	0	7.13
Daytona	A+ ChC	13	11	1	0	65	300	70	60	40	6	3	2	4	34	1	48	5	0	4	5	.444	1	1	5.54
2000 West Tenn	AA ChC	61	0	0	41	73.1	307	57	32	25	2	4	3	0	33	2	72	3	0	5	4	.556	0	25	3.07
5 Min. YEARS		158	90	3	46	599.2	2592	497	314	236	29	28	21	34	315	17	575	45	3	38	32	.543	1	26	3.54

Geoff Duncan

Pitches: Right **Bats:** Right **Pos:** RP-26   **Ht:** 6'2" **Wt:** 185 **Born:** 4/1/75 **Age:** 26

Year Team	Lg Org	G	GS	CG	GF	IP	BFP	H	R	ER	HR	SH	SF	HB	TBB	IBB	SO	WP	Bk	W	L	Pct.	ShO	Sv	ERA
1996 Utica	A- Fla	24	1	0	8	40.1	191	46	23	17	3	0	1	4	19	5	52	5	3	2	5	.286	0	2	3.79
1997 Kane County	A Fla	44	2	0	13	86.1	375	85	46	39	7	7	2	5	30	5	96	4	0	7	2	.778	0	1	4.07
1998 Brevard Cty	A+ Fla	17	0	0	9	32	135	35	15	8	1	2	0	2	9	3	30	2	0	1	3	.250	0	2	2.25
Portland	AA Fla	42	0	0	29	57.1	242	39	21	18	2	1	1	6	31	5	74	5	1	9	2	.818	0	11	2.83
1999 Calgary	AAA Fla	5	0	0	2	9	39	4	4	4	0	0	0	2	10	0	5	1	0	1	0	1.000	0	1	4.00
Portland	AA Fla	43	0	0	22	66.1	276	59	24	21	8	1	0	2	26	2	59	3	1	2	3	.400	0	4	2.85
2000 Portland	AA Fla	2	0	0	1	1.1	6	1	0	0	0	0	0	1	0	0	1	0	0	0	0	—	0	0	0.00
Calgary	AAA Fla	24	0	0	13	27.1	132	35	26	26	7	2	1	1	15	2	30	5	0	2	0	1.000	0	0	8.56
5 Min. YEARS		201	3	0	97	320	1396	304	159	133	28	13	5	23	140	22	347	25	5	24	15	.615	0	22	3.74

Sean Duncan

Pitches: Left **Bats:** Left **Pos:** RP-46   **Ht:** 6'2" **Wt:** 195 **Born:** 6/9/73 **Age:** 28

Year Team	Lg Org	G	GS	CG	GF	IP	BFP	H	R	ER	HR	SH	SF	HB	TBB	IBB	SO	WP	Bk	W	L	Pct.	ShO	Sv	ERA
1994 White Sox	R CWS	16	0	0	10	24	94	18	5	4	1	1	0	0	6	1	21	3	0	0	1	.000	0	2	1.50
Hickory	A CWS	7	0	0	4	13	54	9	7	6	1	1	1	0	7	0	14	0	0	0	0	—	0	0	4.15
1995 White Sox	R CWS	3	0	0	1	6	25	5	3	0	0	0	0	0	1	0	6	1	0	0	0	—	0	1	0.00
South Bend	A CWS	12	0	0	7	11.1	44	8	2	1	0	0	0	0	3	0	8	0	0	0	0	—	0	0	0.79
1996 South Bend	A CWS	43	0	0	16	56	238	43	29	21	3	10	1	2	23	0	54	5	0	2	5	.286	0	3	3.38
Pr William	A+ CWS	6	0	0	6	15.2	75	17	11	10	3	1	0	0	9	1	13	2	0	0	0	—	0	1	5.74
1997 Winston-Sal	A+ CWS	6	0	0	2	9.1	53	16	12	9	4	0	1	0	7	0	9	1	0	0	1	.000	0	0	8.68
Quad City	A Hou	34	0	0	14	46.2	193	39	19	15	4	2	1	4	15	5	46	4	0	6	0	1.000	0	3	2.89
1998 Kissimmee	A+ Hou	23	0	0	10	32.2	144	29	13	12	1	1	2	4	17	0	20	0	0	2	0	1.000	0	1	3.31
Jackson	AA Hou	28	0	0	10	39.1	170	27	15	12	6	1	1	1	24	4	37	2	0	3	1	.750	0	1	2.75
1999 Charlotte	A+ Tex	45	0	0	25	80	360	71	38	28	4	4	6	2	52	5	65	9	2	7	6	.538	0	8	3.15
2000 Tulsa	AA Tex	46	0	0	23	79.2	368	69	56	41	10	3	2	3	60	2	57	8	0	3	5	.375	0	2	4.63
7 Min. YEARS		269	0	0	128	413.2	1818	351	210	159	37	26	17	16	221	16	350	35	2	23	19	.548	0	23	3.46

Todd Dunn

Bats: Right **Throws:** Right **Pos:** OF-35; DH-14; PH-14; PR-1   **Ht:** 6'5" **Wt:** 224 **Born:** 7/29/70 **Age:** 30

Year Team	Lg Org	G	AB	H	2B	3B	HR	TB	R	RBI	TBB	IBB	SO	HBP	SH	SF	SB	CS	SB%	GDP	Avg	OBP	SLG
1993 Helena	R+ Mil	43	150	46	11	2	10	91	33	42	22	1	52	6	1	2	5	2	.71	2	.307	.411	.607
1994 Beloit	A Mil	129	429	94	13	2	23	180	72	63	50	3	131	6	4	4	18	8	.69	6	.219	.307	.420
1995 Stockton	A+ Mil	67	249	73	20	2	7	118	44	40	19	2	67	2	1	1	14	3	.82	5	.293	.347	.474
1996 El Paso	AA Mil	98	359	122	24	5	19	213	72	78	45	1	84	2	2	4	13	4	.76	11	.340	.412	.593
1997 Tucson	AAA Mil	93	332	101	31	4	18	194	66	66	39	1	83	8	0	1	5	5	.50	11	.304	.389	.584
1998 Stockton	A+ Mil	3	13	2	1	0	0	3	2	0	0	0	4	0	0	0	0	0	—	1	.154	.154	.231
El Paso	AA Mil	75	294	92	28	3	13	165	60	57	27	1	63	6	0	3	7	2	.78	6	.313	.379	.561
Louisville	AAA Mil	10	34	13	3	0	1	19	5	1	0	0	10	2	0	0	0	2	.00	1	.382	.417	.559
1999 Louisville	AAA Mil	40	106	23	1	1	5	41	14	16	14	0	32	2	0	0	2	1	.67	2	.217	.320	.387
Rochester	AAA Bal	30	98	17	5	0	2	28	8	15	8	0	35	2	1	1	1	2	.33	9	.173	.248	.286
Altoona	AA Pit	8	30	5	2	0	0	7	0	2	2	0	10	0	0	0	0	1	.00	1	.167	.219	.233
2000 Norfolk	AAA NYM	62	172	37	10	0	7	68	20	19	12	0	67	3	0	0	4	2	.67	3	.215	.278	.395
1996 Milwaukee	AL	6	10	3	1	0	0	4	2	1	0	0	3	0	0	1	0	0	—	1	.300	.300	.400
1997 Milwaukee	AL	44	118	27	5	0	3	41	17	9	2	0	39	0	0	0	3	0	1.00	2	.229	.242	.347
8 Min. YEARS		658	2266	625	149	19	105	1127	396	399	238	9	638	39	9	16	69	32	.68	57	.276	.352	.497
2 Maj. YEARS		50	128	30	6	0	3	45	19	10	2	0	42	0	0	1	3	0	1.00	3	.234	.246	.352

William Duplissea

Bats: Right **Throws:** Right **Pos:** C-19; DH-3; PH-3; 3B-1; PR-1   **Ht:** 6'0" **Wt:** 200 **Born:** 9/27/77 **Age:** 23

Year Team	Lg Org	G	AB	H	2B	3B	HR	TB	R	RBI	TBB	IBB	SO	HBP	SH	SF	SB	CS	SB%	GDP	Avg	OBP	SLG
1999 Yakima	A- LA	13	33	5	2	0	1	10	5	4	5	0	7	3	0	1	2	1	.67	1	.152	.310	.303
2000 San Berndno	A+ LA	7	9	2	0	0	0	2	1	1	2	0	4	0	0	0	1	0	1.00	0	.222	.364	.222
Great Falls	R+ LA	5	13	2	0	0	0	2	1	1	2	0	3	0	0	1	0	0	—	0	.154	.250	.154
Albuquerque	AAA La	9	19	5	2	0	1	10	3	4	0	0	8	1	0	0	0	0	—	0	.263	.300	.526
Vero Beach	A+ LA	3	7	1	1	0	0	2	1	0	2	0	1	0	0	0	0	0	—	0	.143	.333	.286
2 Min. YEARS		37	81	15	5	0	2	26	11	10	11	0	23	4	0	2	3	1	.75	1	.185	.306	.321

Jayson Durocher

Pitches: Right **Bats:** Right **Pos:** RP-58   **Ht:** 6'3" **Wt:** 195 **Born:** 8/18/74 **Age:** 26

Year Team	Lg Org	G	GS	CG	GF	IP	BFP	H	R	ER	HR	SH	SF	HB	TBB	IBB	SO	WP	Bk	W	L	Pct.	ShO	Sv	ERA
1993 Expos	R Mon	7	7	3	0	39	150	32	23	15	0	0	3	13	0	21	3	1	2	3	.400	0	0	3.46
1994 Vermont	A- Mon	15	15	3	0	99	422	92	40	34	0	0	3	2	44	1	74	11	1	9	2	.818	1	0	3.09
1995 Albany	A Mon	24	22	1	1	122	526	105	67	53	5	4	11	5	56	1	88	11	1	3	7	.300	0	0	3.91
1996 Wst Plm Bch	A+ Mon	23	23	1	0	129.1	557	118	65	48	5	4	3	7	44	0	101	15	3	7	6	.538	1	0	3.34
1997 Wst Plm Bch	A+ Mon	25	17	0	2	87	385	84	58	37	6	3	3	4	39	0	71	10	2	6	4	.600	0	0	3.83
1998 Jupiter	A+ Mon	23	0	0	12	36.1	162	47	21	17	3	1	2	1	8	0	27	4	0	2	1	.667	0	5	4.21
Harrisburg	AA Mon	10	0	0	4	11.1	48	10	8	5	0	1	1	0	6	0	12	1	0	0	1	.000	0	1	3.97
1999 Harrisburg	AA Mon	29	1	0	11	51.2	224	44	29	20	5	2	2	6	25	1	36	3	1	1	3	.250	0	4	3.48
Ottawa	AAA Mon	17	0	0	6	35.2	146	17	12	6	2	3	1	1	20	2	22	3	0	1	3	.250	0	4	1.51
2000 Mobile	AA SD	27	0	0	23	30.1	132	26	7	7	4	2	1	3	12	1	43	3	0	1	1	.500	0	14	2.08
Las Vegas	AAA SD	31	0	0	18	40	187	44	25	22	2	2	3	25	3	38	6	0	3	5	.375	0	7	4.95
8 Min. YEARS		231	85	8	77	681.2	2939	619	355	264	32	24	29	35	292	9	533	70	9	35	36	.493	4	35	3.49

Radhames Dykhoff

Pitches: Left **Bats:** Left **Pos:** RP-48; SP-1   **Ht:** 6'0" **Wt:** 200 **Born:** 9/27/74 **Age:** 26

Year Team	Lg Org	G	GS	CG	GF	IP	BFP	H	R	ER	HR	SH	SF	HB	TBB	IBB	SO	WP	Bk	W	L	Pct.	ShO	Sv	ERA
1993 Orioles	R Bal	14	3	0	1	45	184	37	22	17	2	4	3	2	11	0	29	3	0	1	2	.333	0	1	3.40
1994 Orioles	R Bal	12	12	1	0	73	307	69	34	27	2	0	5	0	17	0	67	4	1	3	6	.333	0	0	3.33
1995 High Desert	A+ Bal	34	2	0	10	80.2	389	95	68	45	8	7	7	0	44	2	88	0	2	1	5	.167	0	3	5.02
1996 Frederick	A+ Bal	33	0	0	15	62	290	77	45	39	7	4	4	1	22	2	75	0	0	2	6	.250	0	3	5.66
1997 Bowie	AA Bal	7	0	0	4	8.2	43	10	9	8	2	0	0	0	7	0	7	0	0	0	0	—	0	0	8.31
Delmarva	A Bal	1	0	0	1	3	12	3	0	0	0	0	0	0	0	0	3	0	0	0	0	—	0	1	0.00
Frederick	A+ Bal	31	0	0	18	67	282	48	19	18	4	6	1	0	38	3	98	0	1	3	3	.500	0	5	2.42
1998 Bowie	AA Bal	38	8	0	9	93.2	411	83	51	49	10	2	3	4	52	1	98	3	0	3	7	.300	0	0	4.71
1999 Rochester	AAA Bal	47	0	0	6	82.1	341	69	42	36	11	3	2	3	31	0	57	1	0	2	0	1.000	0	1	3.94
2000 Norfolk	AAA NYM	32	0	0	11	38.1	176	40	23	21	5	1	3	1	21	3	43	3	0	2	3	.400	0	0	4.93
Binghamton	AA NYM	17	1	0	2	25.2	104	16	7	6	2	0	0	1	8	0	30	0	0	3	0	1.000	0	1	2.10
1998 Baltimore	AL	1	0	0	1	1	6	2	2	2	0	0	0	0	1	0	1	0	0	0	0	—	0	0	18.00
8 Min. YEARS		266	26	1	77	579.1	2539	547	320	266	53	26	28	12	251	11	595	14	4	20	32	.385	0	16	4.13

Derrin Ebert

Pitches: Left **Bats:** Right **Pos:** SP-23; RP-9   **Ht:** 6'3" **Wt:** 200 **Born:** 8/21/76 **Age:** 24

Year Team	Lg Org	G	GS	CG	GF	IP	BFP	H	R	ER	HR	SH	SF	HB	TBB	IBB	SO	WP	Bk	W	L	Pct.	ShO	Sv	ERA
1994 Braves	R Atl	10	7	1	2	43	176	40	18	14	4	0	0	1	8	0	25	1	3	1	3	.250	1	0	2.93
1995 Macon	A Atl	28	28	0	0	182	766	184	87	67	12	5	4	7	46	0	124	3	2	14	5	.737	0	0	3.31
1996 Durham	A+ Atl	27	27	2	0	166.1	711	189	102	74	13	8	9	4	37	1	99	5	0	12	9	.571	0	0	4.00
1997 Greenville	AA Atl	27	25	0	0	175.2	743	191	95	80	24	9	6	4	48	1	101	10	0	11	8	.579	2	0	4.10
1998 Richmond	AAA Atl	29	29	0	0	163.2	710	195	94	82	14	5	3	3	49	1	88	4	0	9	9	.500	0	0	4.51
1999 Richmond	AAA Atl	25	24	2	0	150.2	646	173	79	72	13	5	6	2	44	0	82	7	0	8	7	.533	1	0	4.30
2000 Richmond	AAA Atl	32	23	0	2	150.2	670	192	94	80	21	4	7	4	44	0	91	4	0	5	9	.357	0	0	4.78
1999 Atlanta	NL	5	0	0	0	8	35	9	5	5	2	0	0	0	5	1	4	0	0	0	1	.000	0	1	5.63
7 Min. YEARS		178	163	5	4	1032	4422	1164	569	469	101	36	35	25	276	3	610	34	5	60	50	.545	2	0	4.09

Kevin Eberwein

Bats: Right **Throws:** Right **Pos:** 1B-97; 3B-2; DH-1; PH-1   **Ht:** 6'4" **Wt:** 200 **Born:** 3/30/77 **Age:** 24

Year Team	Lg Org	G	AB	H	2B	3B	HR	TB	R	RBI	TBB	IBB	SO	HBP	SH	SF	SB	CS	SB%	GDP	Avg	OBP	SLG
1998 Clinton	A SD	65	247	73	20	3	10	129	42	38	26	0	66	6	2	2	4	2	.67	6	.296	.374	.522
1999 Mobile	AA SD	10	35	6	1	0	1	10	5	2	3	0	16	0	0	1	0	0	—	0	.171	.231	.286
Rancho Cuca	A+ SD	110	417	108	30	4	18	200	69	69	42	0	139	12	2	2	7	5	.58	7	.259	.342	.480
2000 Mobile	AA SD	100	372	98	16	2	18	172	57	71	45	3	77	2	0	4	2	2	.50	8	.263	.343	.462
3 Min. YEARS		285	1071	285	67	9	47	511	173	180	116	3	298	20	4	9	13	9	.59	21	.266	.346	.477

Alex Eckelman

Bats: Right **Throws:** Right **Pos:** 2B-36; 3B-29; OF-18; PH-7; DH-4; P-2; SS-1; PR-1   **Ht:** 5'11" **Wt:** 190 **Born:** 7/16/74 **Age:** 26

Year Team	Lg Org	G	AB	H	2B	3B	HR	TB	R	RBI	TBB	IBB	SO	HBP	SH	SF	SB	CS	SB%	GDP	Avg	OBP	SLG
1997 Johnson Cty	R+ StL	49	165	53	13	1	7	89	30	27	10	0	23	7	1	2	3	1	.75	3	.321	.380	.539
1998 Peoria	A StL	16	52	17	4	1	1	26	7	11	5	0	9	0	0	1	0	2	.00	0	.327	.386	.500
Pr William	A+ StL	38	89	26	1	1	2	35	15	9	9	0	14	0	1	1	2	2	.50	2	.292	.354	.393
1999 Potomac	A+ StL	52	161	31	5	2	4	52	20	14	13	0	39	5	1	0	3	3	.50	2	.193	.274	.323
Arkansas	AA StL	41	116	28	4	3	1	41	5	13	5	0	20	4	2	3	0	0	—	4	.241	.289	.353
2000 Memphis	AAA StL	6	16	6	0	0	0	6	2	1	0	0	1	0	0	0	0	0	—	0	.375	.375	.375
Arkansas	AA StL	85	280	87	16	3	4	121	42	33	24	1	27	8	7	3	4	1	.80	6	.311	.378	.432
4 Min. YEARS		287	879	248	43	11	19	370	121	108	66	1	133	24	12	9	12	9	.57	17	.282	.346	.421

David Eckstein

Bats: Right **Throws:** Right **Pos:** 2B-130; PH-4; SS-1   **Ht:** 5'8" **Wt:** 168 **Born:** 1/20/75 **Age:** 26

Year Team	Lg Org	G	AB	H	2B	3B	HR	TB	R	RBI	TBB	IBB	SO	HBP	SH	SF	SB	CS	SB%	GDP	Avg	OBP	SLG
1997 Lowell	A- Bos	68	249	75	11	4	4	106	43	39	33	1	29	12	8	1	21	5	.81	2	.301	.407	.426
1998 Sarasota	A+ Bos	135	503	154	29	4	3	200	99	58	87	3	51	22	1	2	45	16	.74	8	.306	.428	.398
1999 Trenton	AA Bos	131	483	151	22	5	6	201	109	52	89	0	48	25	13	5	32	13	.71	6	.313	.440	.416
2000 Pawtucket	AAA Bos	119	422	104	20	0	1	127	77	31	60	0	45	20	9	4	11	8	.58	8	.246	.364	.301
Edmonton	AAA Ana	15	52	18	8	0	3	35	17	8	9	0	1	5	0	0	5	3	.63	0	.346	.485	.673
4 Min. YEARS		468	1709	502	90	13	17	669	345	188	278	4	174	84	31	12	114	45	.72	24	.294	.415	.391

Geoff Edsell

Pitches: Right **Bats:** Right **Pos:** RP-15; SP-10   **Ht:** 6'2" **Wt:** 194 **Born:** 12/10/71 **Age:** 29

Year Team	Lg Org	G	GS	CG	GF	IP	BFP	H	R	ER	HR	SH	SF	HB	TBB	IBB	SO	WP	Bk	W	L	Pct.	ShO	Sv	ERA
1993 Boise	A- Ana	13	13	1	0	64	296	64	52	49	10	1	5	3	40	0	63	6	3	4	3	.571	0	0	6.89
1994 Cedar Rapids	A Ana	17	17	4	0	125.1	538	109	54	42	10	5	0	6	65	1	84	10	4	11	5	.688	1	0	3.02
Lk Elsinore	A+ Ana	9	7	0	1	40	174	38	21	18	3	0	0	2	24	1	26	3	2	2	2	.500	0	0	4.05
1995 Lk Elsinore	A+ Ana	23	22	1	0	139.2	600	127	81	57	11	7	3	7	67	0	134	6	1	8	12	.400	1	0	3.67
Midland	AA Ana	5	5	1	0	32	140	39	26	21	5	1	2	0	16	0	19	5	0	2	3	.400	0	0	5.91
1996 Midland	AA Ana	14	14	0	0	88	382	84	53	46	10	3	5	6	47	0	60	5	1	5	5	.500	0	0	4.70
Vancouver	AAA Ana	15	15	3	0	105	437	93	45	40	7	5	4	3	45	1	48	2	2	4	6	.400	2	0	3.43
1997 Vancouver	AAA Ana	30	29	6	1	183.1	826	196	121	105	11	5	6	12	96	1	95	8	0	14	11	.560	1	0	5.15
1998 Vancouver	AAA Ana	56	0	0	27	69	305	63	45	32	8	3	4	5	33	1	64	6	0	4	8	.333	0	4	4.17
1999 Erie	AA Ana	26	2	0	14	39	179	45	20	15	1	1	3	6	13	0	28	0	0	2	3	.400	0	2	3.46
Edmonton	AAA Ana	30	0	0	7	46.2	208	46	27	26	6	1	2	2	25	2	37	1	0	1	4	.200	0	0	5.01
2000 San Antonio	AA LA	25	10	0	4	83	365	84	50	41	9	1	1	5	33	2	74	3	0	5	5	.500	0	1	4.45
8 Min. YEARS		263	134	16	54	1015	4450	988	595	492	91	33	35	57	504	9	732	55	13	62	67	.481	5	7	4.36

Mike Edwards

Bats: Right **Throws:** Right **Pos:** 3B-131; DH-4; PH-1   **Ht:** 6'1" **Wt:** 185 **Born:** 11/24/76 **Age:** 24

Year Team	Lg Org	G	AB	H	2B	3B	HR	TB	R	RBI	TBB	IBB	SO	HBP	SH	SF	SB	CS	SB%	GDP	Avg	OBP	SLG
1995 Burlington	R+ Cle	43	130	22	2	0	0	24	20	5	17	0	35	2	0	0	5	2	.71	2	.169	.275	.185
1996 Burlington	R+ Cle	58	206	58	13	1	1	76	31	17	37	0	26	3	3	3	5	4	.56	4	.282	.394	.369
1997 Burlington	R+ Cle	60	236	68	16	2	4	100	50	41	38	1	53	1	0	2	10	5	.67	2	.288	.386	.424
1998 Columbus	A Cle	124	497	146	34	4	8	212	82	81	66	2	95	3	3	2	16	6	.73	13	.294	.379	.427
1999 Kinston	A+ Cle	133	456	132	25	4	16	213	76	89	93	6	117	9	4	9	8	3	.73	12	.289	.413	.467
2000 Akron	AA Cle	136	481	142	25	2	11	204	72	63	68	2	86	5	3	3	7	3	.70	9	.295	.386	.424
6 Min. YEARS		554	2006	568	115	13	40	829	331	296	319	11	412	23	9	19	51	23	.69	42	.283	.384	.413

Scott Eibey

Pitches: Left **Bats:** Left **Pos:** RP-41   **Ht:** 6'4" **Wt:** 208 **Born:** 1/19/74 **Age:** 27

Year Team	Lg Org	G	GS	CG	GF	IP	BFP	H	R	ER	HR	SH	SF	HB	TBB	IBB	SO	WP	Bk	W	L	Pct.	ShO	Sv	ERA
1995 Bluefield	R+ Bal	14	6	0	3	43.2	196	51	32	27	4	2	0	2	24	0	26	6	1	3	1	.750	0	0	5.56
1996 High Desert	A+ Bal	11	0	0	1	11.2	65	17	16	11	0	0	1	0	10	2	7	2	0	1	0	1.000	0	0	8.49
Bluefield	R+ Bal	24	0	0	10	45	187	30	19	14	3	0	3	3	17	0	59	4	1	5	1	.833	0	2	2.80
1997 Delmarva	A Bal	47	0	0	19	93.1	371	85	25	19	3	7	0	2	33	5	82	4	0	10	4	.714	0	7	1.83
1998 Bowie	AA Bal	24	0	0	8	36.1	159	40	20	17	5	0	1	0	14	0	29	1	1	1	1	.500	0	1	4.21
Frederick	A+ Bal	21	0	0	5	35	152	47	17	15	3	4	1	0	8	0	20	3	0	1	2	.333	0	1	3.86
1999 Frederick	A+ Bal	15	0	0	6	26	120	26	14	12	2	0	1	0	10	1	27	0	0	0	2	.000	0	0	3.72
Bowie	AA Bal	27	4	0	3	51.1	222	49	17	15	2	1	1	1	25	2	29	5	2	2	0	1.000	0	0	2.63
2000 Frederick	A+ Bal	4	0	0	3	6.2	30	9	4	3	0	1	0	0	1	1	5	1	0	1	0	1.000	0	0	4.05
Bowie	AA Bal	37	0	0	15	57	256	59	34	32	8	4	4	2	25	4	32	0	0	4	4	.500	0	1	5.05
6 Min. YEARS		224	10	0	73	409	1758	393	198	165	31	18	12	10	166	14	316	26	5	28	16	.636	0	12	3.63

Mark Eichhorn

Pitches: Right **Bats:** Right **Pos:** RP-22   **Ht:** 6'3" **Wt:** 200 **Born:** 11/21/60 **Age:** 40

Year Team	Lg Org	G	GS	CG	GF	IP	BFP	H	R	ER	HR	SH	SF	HB	TBB	IBB	SO	WP	Bk	W	L	Pct.	ShO	Sv	ERA
1979 Medcine Hat	R+ Tor	16	14	3	—	93	—	101	62	35	7	—	—	5	26	2	66	4	4	7	6	.538	1	0	3.39
1980 Kinston	A+ Tor	26	26	9	—	183	—	158	72	59	5	—	—	3	56	3	119	8	4	14	10	.583	2	0	2.90
1981 Knoxville	AA Tor	30	29	9	0	192	—	202	112	85	23	—	—	3	57	2	99	10	3	10	14	.417	1	0	3.98
1982 Syracuse	AAA Tor	27	27	6	0	156.2	—	158	92	79	18	—	—	7	71	5	83	8	3	10	11	.476	1	0	4.54
1983 Syracuse	AAA Tor	7	5	0	1	30.2	—	36	32	27	8	—	—	2	21	1	12	1	1	0	5	.000	0	0	7.92
Knoxville	AA Tor	21	20	3	1	120.2	—	124	65	58	17	—	—	1	47	0	54	4	0	6	12	.333	0	0	4.33
1984 Syracuse	AAA Tor	36	18	3	7	117.2	541	147	92	78	13	3	3	4	51	0	54	8	0	5	9	.357	1	0	5.97
1985 Knoxville	AA Tor	26	10	2	2	116.1	473	101	49	39	11	5	4	4	34	2	76	2	1	5	1	.833	1	0	3.02
Syracuse	AAA Tor	8	7	0	1	37.1	154	38	24	20	5	2	1	0	7	0	27	1	0	2	5	.286	0	0	4.82
1988 Syracuse	AAA Tor	18	1	0	8	38.1	162	35	9	5	0	0	2	4	15	5	34	0	0	4	4	.500	0	2	1.17
1989 Richmond	AAA Atl	25	0	0	24	41	152	29	6	6	0	2	2	2	6	0	33	0	0	1	0	1.000	0	19	1.32
1996 Lk Elsinore	A+ Ana	12	4	0	1	15.1	62	15	9	8	1	2	1	0	2	0	21	0	0	1	0	1.000	0	0	4.70
1998 Durham	AAA TB	53	0	0	45	58	239	59	27	25	7	9	2	4	11	2	44	0	0	5	3	.625	0	18	3.88
2000 Dunedin	A+ Tor	5	0	0	4	5.1	20	3	0	0	0	1	0	0	2	0	8	1	0	0	0	—	0	0	0.00
Syracuse	AAA Tor	17	0	0	4	16.1	57	5	2	2	2	0	0	0	2	0	17	0	0	1	0	1.000	0	0	1.10
1982 Toronto	AL	7	7	0	0	38	171	40	28	23	4	1	2	0	14	1	16	3	0	0	3	.000	0	0	5.45
1986 Toronto	AL	69	0	0	38	157	612	105	32	30	8	9	2	7	45	14	166	2	1	14	6	.700	0	10	1.72
1987 Toronto	AL	89	0	0	27	127.2	540	110	47	45	14	7	4	6	52	13	96	3	1	10	6	.625	0	4	3.17
1988 Toronto	AL	37	0	0	17	66.2	302	79	32	31	3	8	1	6	27	4	28	3	6	0	3	.000	0	1	4.19
1989 Atlanta	NL	45	0	0	13	68.1	286	70	36	33	6	7	4	1	19	8	49	0	1	5	5	.500	0	0	4.35
1990 California	AL	60	0	0	40	84.2	374	98	36	29	2	2	4	6	23	0	69	2	0	2	5	.286	0	13	3.08
1991 California	AL	70	0	0	23	81.2	311	63	21	18	2	5	3	2	13	1	49	0	0	3	3	.500	0	1	1.98
1992 California	AL	42	0	0	19	56.2	237	51	19	15	2	2	3	0	18	8	42	3	1	2	4	.333	0	2	2.38
Toronto	AL	23	0	0	7	31	135	35	15	15	1	1	2	2	7	0	19	6	0	2	0	1.000	0	0	4.35
1993 Toronto	AL	54	0	0	16	72.2	309	76	26	22	3	3	2	3	22	7	47	2	0	3	1	.750	0	0	2.72
1994 Baltimore	AL	43	0	0	20	71	290	62	19	17	1	4	4	5	19	4	35	1	0	6	5	.545	0	1	2.15
1996 California	AL	24	0	0	6	30.1	135	36	17	17	3	3	2	2	11	3	24	0	1	1	2	.333	0	0	5.04
12 Min. YEARS		327	161	35	98	1221.2	—	1211	653	526	117	—	—	39	406	22	747	47	16	71	80	.470	7	39	3.88
11 Maj. YEARS		563	7	0	226	885.2	3702	825	328	295	49	52	33	40	270	63	640	25	11	48	43	.527	0	32	3.00

Joey Eischen

Pitches: Left **Bats:** Left **Pos:** SP-19; RP-2   **Ht:** 6'1" **Wt:** 200 **Born:** 5/25/70 **Age:** 31

Year Team	Lg Org	G	GS	CG	GF	IP	BFP	H	R	ER	HR	SH	SF	HB	TBB	IBB	SO	WP	Bk	W	L	Pct.	ShO	Sv	ERA
1989 Butte	R+ Tex	12	12	0	0	52.2	248	50	45	31	4	1	0	6	38	0	57	13	11	3	7	.300	0	0	5.30
1990 Gastonia	A Tex	17	14	0	0	73.1	311	51	36	24	3	4	4	3	40	0	69	9	0	3	7	.300	0	0	2.70
1991 Charlotte	A+ Tex	18	18	1	0	108.1	467	99	59	40	5	6	3	4	55	1	80	8	1	4	10	.286	0	0	3.32
Wst Plm Bch	A+ Mon	8	8	1	0	38.1	177	34	27	22	3	3	1	2	24	0	26	3	0	4	2	.667	1	0	5.17
1992 Wst Plm Bch	A+ Mon	27	26	3	0	169.2	705	128	68	58	5	4	3	8	83	2	167	6	0	9	8	.529	2	0	3.08
1993 Harrisburg	AA Mon	20	20	0	0	119.1	533	122	62	48	11	3	6	4	60	0	110	9	1	14	4	.778	0	0	3.62
Ottawa	AAA Mon	6	6	0	0	40.2	166	34	18	16	3	1	2	0	15	0	29	1	0	2	2	.500	0	0	3.54
1994 Ottawa	AAA Mon	48	2	0	20	62	274	54	38	34	7	3	4	0	40	4	57	10	0	2	6	.250	0	4	4.94
1995 Ottawa	AAA Mon	11	0	0	3	15.2	61	9	4	3	0	1	0	0	8	1	13	0	0	2	1	.667	0	0	1.72
Albuquerque	AAA LA	13	0	0	6	16.1	59	8	0	0	0	1	0	1	3	0	14	1	0	3	0	1.000	0	2	0.00
1997 Indianapolis	AAA Cin	26	5	0	7	42.2	173	41	7	6	1	2	0	1	13	1	26	2	0	1	0	1.000	0	2	1.27
1998 Indianapolis	AAA Cin	61	0	0	18	73.1	326	73	42	37	9	7	3	4	29	3	60	7	0	2	5	.286	0	4	4.54
1999 Tucson	AAA Ari	27	1	0	8	41.2	209	63	47	42	7	1	1	1	26	3	36	6	0	1	3	.250	0	1	9.07
Adirondack	IND —	7	7	1	0	48	204	52	22	20	1	0	2	1	11	0	49	4	0	4	2	.667	0	0	3.75
2000 Buffalo	AAA Cle	1	0	0	0	0.2	6	4	3	3	0	0	0	0	2	0	1	0	0	0	0	—	0	0	40.50
Adirondack	IND —	10	10	0	0	65	269	55	25	13	2	2	1	0	24	0	57	3	0	7	1	.875	0	0	1.80
Ottawa	AAA Mon	10	9	0	1	59.1	254	55	31	24	8	4	2	6	22	0	34	2	2	0	4	.000	0	0	3.64
1994 Montreal	NL	1	0	0	0	0.2	7	4	4	4	0	0	0	0	1	0	1	0	0	0	0	—	0	0	54.00
1995 Los Angeles	NL	17	0	0	8	20.1	95	19	9	7	1	0	0	2	11	1	15	1	0	0	0	—	0	0	3.10
1996 Los Angeles	NL	28	0	0	11	43.1	198	48	25	23	4	3	1	4	20	4	36	1	0	1	0	1.000	0	0	4.78
Detroit	AL	24	0	0	3	25	110	27	11	9	3	0	1	0	14	3	15	3	0	1	1	.500	0	0	3.24
1997 Cincinnati	NL	1	0	0	0	1.1	7	2	1	1	0	0	0	0	1	0	2	1	0	0	0	—	0	0	6.75
11 Min. YEARS		322	138	6	63	1027	4442	932	534	419	66	41	32	41	491	15	884	84	15	61	62	.496	3	9	3.67
4 Maj. YEARS		71	0	0	22	90.2	417	100	51	44	8	3	2	7	46	8	69	6	0	1	2	.333	0	0	4.37

David Elder

Pitches: Right **Bats:** Right **Pos:** SP-21; RP-12   **Ht:** 6'0" **Wt:** 180 **Born:** 9/23/75 **Age:** 25

Year Team	Lg Org	G	GS	CG	GF	IP	BFP	H	R	ER	HR	SH	SF	HB	TBB	IBB	SO	WP	Bk	W	L	Pct.	ShO	Sv	ERA
1997 Pulaski	R+ Tex	20	0	0	17	32.1	127	18	8	7	2	0	0	0	12	0	57	4	0	2	2	.500	0	6	1.95
1999 Charlotte	A+ Tex	24	1	0	16	44.1	186	33	15	14	2	4	0	2	25	0	42	4	0	4	2	.667	0	4	2.84
Tulsa	AA Tex	3	0	0	1	6.2	32	8	7	6	0	0	0	0	6	1	7	0	0	1	0	1.000	0	0	8.10
2000 Tulsa	AA Tex	33	21	0	8	116.2	554	121	80	64	9	4	4	4	88	0	104	11	0	7	6	.538	0	3	4.94
3 Min. YEARS		80	22	0	42	200	899	180	110	91	13	8	4	6	131	1	210	19	0	14	10	.583	0	13	4.10

Mark Ellis

Bats: Right **Throws:** Right **Pos:** SS-128; 2B-10; DH-1; PH-1; PR-1   **Ht:** 5'11" **Wt:** 180 **Born:** 6/6/77 **Age:** 24

Year Team	Lg Org	G	AB	H	2B	3B	HR	TB	R	RBI	TBB	IBB	SO	HBP	SH	SF	SB	CS	SB%	GDP	Avg	OBP	SLG
1999 Spokane	A- KC	71	281	92	14	0	7	127	67	47	47	3	40	3	5	4	21	7	.75	1	.327	.424	.452
2000 Wilmington	A+ KC	132	484	146	27	4	6	199	83	62	78	0	72	7	4	3	25	7	.78	11	.302	.404	.411
Wichita	AA KC	7	22	7	1	0	0	8	4	4	5	0	5	0	0	0	1	0	1.00	0	.318	.444	.364
2 Min. YEARS		210	787	245	42	4	13	334	154	113	130	3	117	10	9	7	47	14	.77	12	.311	.412	.424

Robert Ellis

Pitches: Right **Bats:** Right **Pos:** RP-16   **Ht:** 6'5" **Wt:** 220 **Born:** 12/15/70 **Age:** 30

Year Team	Lg Org	G	GS	CG	GF	IP	BFP	H	R	ER	HR	SH	SF	HB	TBB	IBB	SO	WP	Bk	W	L	Pct.	ShO	Sv	ERA
1991 Utica	A- CWS	15	15	1	0	87.2	407	87	66	45	4	6	5	6	61	0	66	13	0	3	9	.250	1	0	4.62
1992 White Sox	R CWS	1	1	0	0	5	24	10	6	6	0	0	0	0	1	0	4	0	0	1	0	1.000	0	0	10.80
South Bend	A CWS	18	18	1	0	123	481	90	46	32	3	4	2	4	35	0	97	7	2	6	5	.545	1	0	2.34
1993 Sarasota	A+ CWS	15	15	8	0	104	414	81	37	29	3	4	3	3	31	1	79	6	1	7	8	.467	2	0	2.51
Birmingham	AA CWS	12	12	2	0	81.1	336	68	33	28	2	1	1	4	21	0	77	6	0	6	3	.667	1	0	3.10
1994 Nashville	AAA CWS	19	19	1	0	105	483	126	77	71	19	5	6	2	55	1	76	1	4	4	10	.286	0	0	6.09
1995 Nashville	AAA CWS	4	4	0	0	20.2	85	16	7	5	2	0	1	1	10	0	9	1	0	1	1	.500	0	0	2.18
1996 Nashville	AAA CWS	19	13	1	2	70.1	327	78	49	47	6	5	3	7	45	3	35	8	0	3	8	.273	0	0	6.01
Birmingham	AA CWS	2	2	0	0	7.1	35	6	9	9	1	0	1	1	8	0	8	1	0	0	1	.000	0	0	11.05
Vancouver	AAA Ana	7	7	1	0	44.1	186	30	19	16	2	2	2	0	28	0	29	5	0	2	3	.400	0	0	3.25
1997 Vancouver	AAA Ana	29	23	3	1	149	698	185	108	98	15	6	6	7	83	1	70	15	1	9	10	.474	0	0	5.92
1998 Louisville	AAA Mil	30	28	0	0	150.1	693	171	103	94	21	7	2	8	78	1	79	13	0	10	10	.500	0	0	5.63
1999 New Orleans	AAA Hou	27	27	1	0	155.2	690	176	106	94	20	5	6	5	51	1	105	11	2	7	12	.368	0	0	5.43
2000 Syracuse	AAA Tor	16	0	0	10	18	85	17	10	9	2	3	0	2	15	1	10	3	1	1	1	.500	0	2	4.50
1996 California	AL	3	0	0	3	5	19	0	0	0	0	0	0	0	4	0	5	1	0	0	0	—	0	0	0.00
10 Min. YEARS		214	184	19	13	1121.2	4944	1141	676	583	100	48	38	50	522	9	752	90	11	60	81	.426	5	2	4.68

Jason Ellison

Pitches: Right **Bats:** Right **Pos:** RP-10   **Ht:** 6'4" **Wt:** 188 **Born:** 7/24/75 **Age:** 25

Year Team	Lg Org	G	GS	CG	GF	IP	BFP	H	R	ER	HR	SH	SF	HB	TBB	IBB	SO	WP	Bk	W	L	Pct.	ShO	Sv	ERA
1996 Yankees	R NYY	21	3	0	17	36	151	24	8	5	0	1	0	3	15	0	42	2	1	3	2	.600	0	7	1.25
Oneonta	A- NYY	1	0	0	1	1	5	2	1	1	0	0	0	0	0	0	2	0	0	0	0	—	0	0	9.00
1997 Oneonta	A- NYY	11	0	0	3	20.2	82	19	6	4	0	0	1	0	4	0	19	2	0	0	1	.000	0	0	1.74
Greensboro	A NYY	9	0	0	4	13	60	16	10	7	1	0	0	1	3	0	11	1	0	1	0	1.000	0	1	4.85
1998 Greensboro	A NYY	54	0	0	49	65.1	279	56	30	23	5	5	0	2	27	3	71	6	0	4	6	.400	0	28	3.17
1999 Tampa	A+ NYY	49	0	0	42	54.1	226	42	15	13	0	4	2	4	19	1	56	0	0	0	2	.000	0	35	2.15
2000 Norwich	AA NYY	10	0	0	8	9.1	48	18	11	9	1	2	0	0	2	1	5	0	1	1	1	.500	0	4	8.68
5 Min. YEARS		155	3	0	124	199.2	851	177	81	62	7	12	3	10	70	5	206	11	2	9	12	.429	0	75	2.79

Jamie Emiliano

Pitches: Right **Bats:** Right **Pos:** RP-47   **Ht:** 5'10" **Wt:** 210 **Born:** 8/2/74 **Age:** 26

Year Team	Lg Org	G	GS	CG	GF	IP	BFP	H	R	ER	HR	SH	SF	HB	TBB	IBB	SO	WP	Bk	W	L	Pct.	ShO	Sv	ERA
1995 Portland	A- Col	28	0	0	22	38.2	165	31	18	15	0	2	1	4	16	2	41	5	0	4	1	.800	0	11	3.49
1996 Asheville	A Col	6	0	0	4	5.2	25	7	6	6	1	0	0	0	2	0	7	1	1	0	1	.500	0	1	9.53
1997 Asheville	A Col	18	0	0	12	20	96	24	15	13	1	0	0	0	12	0	20	3	0	1	0	1.000	0	0	5.85
1998 Salem	A+ Col	4	0	0	1	7.2	36	9	3	3	0	0	1	0	5	0	6	1	0	1	1	.500	0	0	3.52
Asheville	A Col	41	0	0	38	43.2	208	56	22	17	2	4	1	5	21	0	35	1	0	3	4	.429	0	18	3.50
1999 Salem	A+ Col	45	0	0	23	53.2	240	50	26	21	4	3	2	5	29	1	47	8	0	5	1	.833	0	7	3.52
2000 Carolina	AA Col	47	0	0	11	58	250	52	27	17	1	4	1	4	23	3	37	3	0	3	4	.429	0	2	2.64
6 Min. YEARS		189	0	0	111	227.1	1020	229	117	92	9	13	6	18	108	6	193	22	1	17	13	.567	0	39	3.64

Angelo Encarnacion

Bats: Right **Throws:** Right **Pos:** C-59; PR-1   **Ht:** 5'9" **Wt:** 190 **Born:** 4/18/73 **Age:** 28

Year Team	Lg Org	G	AB	H	2B	3B	HR	TB	R	RBI	TBB	IBB	SO	HBP	SH	SF	SB	CS	SB%	GDP	Avg	OBP	SLG
1991 Welland	A- Pit	50	181	46	3	2	0	53	21	15	5	0	27	1	0	0	4	3	.57	5	.254	.278	.293
1992 Augusta	A Pit	94	314	80	14	3	1	103	39	29	25	1	37	1	4	2	2	4	.33	5	.255	.310	.328
1993 Salem	A+ Pit	70	238	61	12	1	3	84	20	24	13	1	27	0	0	1	1	4	.20	5	.256	.294	.353
Buffalo	AAA Pit	3	9	3	0	0	0	3	1	2	0	0	0	0	0	0	0	0	—	0	.333	.333	.333
1994 Carolina	AA Pit	67	227	66	17	0	3	92	26	32	11	1	28	2	0	4	2	2	.50	4	.291	.324	.405
1995 Calgary	AAA Pit	21	80	20	3	0	1	26	8	6	1	1	12	0	0	0	1	0	1.00	2	.250	.259	.325
1996 Calgary	AAA Pit	75	263	84	18	0	4	114	38	31	10	2	19	3	0	2	6	2	.75	10	.319	.349	.433
1997 Las Vegas	AAA SD	79	253	62	12	1	8	85	27	23	15	1	32	1	1	0	1	5	.17	5	.245	.290	.336
1998 Vancouver	AAA Ana	8	25	6	2	0	0	8	3	2	0	0	2	0	0	0	0	1	.00	1	.240	.240	.320
Midland	AA Ana	39	93	20	1	0	2	27	9	7	8	0	11	1	2	0	0	0	—	2	.215	.284	.290
1999 Akron	AA Cle	34	127	27	7	0	1	37	9	21	6	0	19	0	1	1	1	1	.50	5	.213	.248	.291
West Tenn	AA ChC	30	101	26	6	1	1	37	11	10	4	0	12	1	0	0	2	0	1.00	1	.257	.292	.366
2000 Iowa	AAA ChC	10	24	6	1	0	0	7	2	1	1	0	3	0	0	0	0	0	—	0	.250	.280	.292
Newark	IND —	30	107	29	6	0	1	38	15	7	6	0	13	0	1	2	2	2	.50	4	.271	.310	.355
Pawtucket	AAA Bos	19	59	18	4	0	0	22	7	3	4	0	4	0	2	0	0	0	—	3	.305	.349	.373
1995 Pittsburgh	NL	58	159	36	7	2	2	53	18	10	13	5	28	0	3	0	1	1	.50	3	.226	.285	.333
1996 Pittsburgh	NL	7	22	7	2	0	0	9	3	1	0	0	5	0	0	0	0	0	—	0	.318	.318	.409
1997 Anaheim	AL	11	17	7	1	0	1	11	2	4	0	0	1	0	0	0	1	0	1.00	1	.412	.412	.647
10 Min. YEARS		618	2101	554	106	8	20	736	236	213	109	7	246	10	11	9	22	24	.48	56	.264	.302	.350
3 Maj. YEARS		76	198	50	10	2	3	73	23	15	13	5	34	0	3	0	3	1	.75	4	.253	.299	.369

Mario Encarnacion

Bats: Right **Throws:** Right **Pos:** OF-79; DH-7   **Ht:** 6'2" **Wt:** 205 **Born:** 9/24/77 **Age:** 23

Year Team	Lg Org	G	AB	H	2B	3B	HR	TB	R	RBI	TBB	IBB	SO	HBP	SH	SF	SB	CS	SB%	GDP	Avg	OBP	SLG
1996 W Michigan	A Oak	118	401	92	14	3	7	133	55	43	49	0	131	5	4	0	23	8	.74	12	.229	.321	.332
1997 Modesto	A+ Oak	111	364	108	17	9	18	197	70	78	42	1	121	6	0	1	14	11	.56	7	.297	.310	.541
1998 Huntsville	AA Oak	110	357	97	15	2	15	161	70	61	60	1	123	4	3	1	11	8	.58	9	.272	.382	.451
1999 Midland	AA Oak	94	353	109	21	4	18	192	69	71	47	4	86	1	0	2	9	9	.50	6	.309	.390	.544
Vancouver	AAA Oak	39	145	35	5	0	3	49	18	17	6	0	44	2	0	1	6	.56	7		.241	.277	.338

83

Year Team	Lg Org	G	AB	H	2B	3B	HR	TB	R	RBI	TBB	IBB	SO	HBP	SH	SF	SB	CS	SB%	GDP	Avg	OBP	SLG
2000 Modesto	A+ Oak	5	15	3	0	0	0	3	1	1	1	0	4	0	0	0	0	0	—	2	.200	.250	.200
Sacramento	AAA Oak	81	301	81	16	3	13	142	51	61	36	2	95	3	1	5	15	7	.68	8	.269	.348	.472
5 Min. YEARS		558	1936	525	88	21	74	877	334	332	241	8	604	21	8	11	77	47	.62	51	.271	.356	.453

Chad Epperson

Bats: Left **Throws:** Right **Pos:** C-77; OF-21; 1B-10; DH-7; PH-2; 3B-1; PR-1; P-1   **Ht:** 6'3" **Wt:** 215 **Born:** 3/26/72 **Age:** 29

Year Team	Lg Org	G	AB	H	2B	3B	HR	TB	R	RBI	TBB	IBB	SO	HBP	SH	SF	SB	CS	SB%	GDP	Avg	OBP	SLG
1992 Mets	R NYM	37	97	16	2	0	1	21	7	12	12	0	20	3	0	3	1	1	.50	2	.165	.270	.216
1993 Kingsport	R+ NYM	38	117	40	7	0	6	65	15	26	18	0	24	1	1	0	3	1	.75	4	.342	.434	.556
1994 St. Lucie	A+ NYM	50	148	32	7	0	2	45	15	10	16	2	42	0	1	2	1	2	.33	2	.216	.289	.304
1995 Binghamton	AA NYM	7	17	1	0	1	0	3	0	0	1	1	8	0	0	0	0	0	—	0	.059	.111	.176
St. Lucie	A+ NYM	42	121	23	7	1	1	35	7	14	17	2	32	0	1	2	1	0	1.00	7	.190	.286	.289
1996 Lafayette	IND —	56	217	73	15	4	10	126	46	49	29	1	44	0	1	3	9	3	.75	4	.336	.410	.581
1997 Sarasota	A+ Bos	107	367	100	25	1	8	151	45	48	32	3	95	1	1	1	13	8	.62	8	.272	.332	.411
Trenton	AA Bos	3	9	3	1	0	0	4	2	1	0	0	2	0	0	0	1	0	1.00	0	.333	.333	.444
1998 Trenton	AA Bos	109	383	97	27	2	15	173	53	57	38	2	129	6	3	4	2	8	.20	6	.253	.327	.452
1999 Sarasota	A+ Bos	26	99	24	1	1	3	36	9	14	3	0	18	0	0	0	2	1	.67	2	.242	.265	.364
Trenton	AA Bos	55	188	37	10	1	2	55	24	15	31	1	46	0	0	1	1	2	.33	10	.197	.311	.293
2000 Bowie	AA Bal	10	42	9	3	0	1	15	6	5	3	0	9	0	0	0	1	0	1.00	1	.214	.267	.357
Nashua	IND —	104	361	89	18	3	8	137	57	43	43	0	92	0	0	4	10	4	.71	5	.247	.324	.380
9 Min. YEARS		644	2166	544	123	14	57	866	286	294	243	12	561	11	8	19	46	30	.61	51	.251	.327	.400

Corey Erickson

Bats: Right **Throws:** Right **Pos:** 3B-68; 2B-60; DH-5; SS-1; PH-1   **Ht:** 5'11" **Wt:** 190 **Born:** 1/10/77 **Age:** 24

Year Team	Lg Org	G	AB	H	2B	3B	HR	TB	R	RBI	TBB	IBB	SO	HBP	SH	SF	SB	CS	SB%	GDP	Avg	OBP	SLG
1995 Mets	R NYM	53	178	50	6	1	7	79	38	35	37	3	40	4	0	5	10	3	.77	2	.281	.406	.444
Kingsport	R+ NYM	2	9	3	0	0	1	6	1	4	0	0	3	0	0	0	0	0	—	0	.333	.333	.667
1996 Capital Cty	A NYM	58	209	46	14	0	1	63	16	17	19	0	57	3	3	4	5	3	.63	2	.220	.289	.301
Pittsfield	A- NYM	73	258	68	19	1	11	122	49	49	43	2	71	4	0	4	6	3	.67	3	.264	.372	.473
1997 St. Lucie	A+ NYM	46	134	27	3	0	3	39	10	11	22	0	43	3	1	2	0	2	.00	1	.201	.323	.291
Capital Cty	A NYM	49	173	37	11	2	2	58	18	16	11	0	49	1	1	3	3	1	.75	2	.214	.261	.335
1998 St. Lucie	A+ NYM	100	346	78	23	4	6	127	49	33	16	0	88	9	0	1	5	2	.71	6	.225	.277	.367
1999 Capital Cty	A NYM	129	424	100	21	1	23	192	64	57	46	0	120	14	0	6	9	3	.75	4	.236	.327	.453
2000 Kinston	A+ Cle	120	422	113	27	0	22	206	66	72	51	3	109	11	0	5	9	2	.82	3	.268	.358	.488
Akron	AA Cle	7	28	6	2	0	3	17	4	9	2	0	11	0	0	0	0	0	—	0	.214	.267	.607
6 Min. YEARS		637	2181	528	126	9	79	909	315	303	247	8	591	49	5	30	47	19	.71	23	.242	.329	.417

Matt Erickson

Bats: Left **Throws:** Right **Pos:** SS-51; 3B-42; 2B-12; PH-1   **Ht:** 5'11" **Wt:** 190 **Born:** 7/30/75 **Age:** 25

Year Team	Lg Org	G	AB	H	2B	3B	HR	TB	R	RBI	TBB	IBB	SO	HBP	SH	SF	SB	CS	SB%	GDP	Avg	OBP	SLG
1997 Utica	A- Fla	69	238	78	10	0	5	103	44	44	48	3	36	11	2	4	9	3	.75	7	.328	.455	.433
1998 Kane County	A Fla	124	441	143	32	2	4	191	83	64	72	1	62	18	7	3	17	7	.71	8	.324	.436	.433
1999 Portland	AA Fla	107	361	97	20	2	0	121	38	35	51	0	65	3	5	5	2	3	.40	9	.269	.360	.335
2000 Portland	AA Fla	100	335	101	23	4	2	138	56	41	59	3	62	9	1	3	8	3	.73	9	.301	.416	.412
4 Min. YEARS		400	1375	419	85	8	11	553	221	184	230	7	225	41	15	15	36	16	.69	33	.305	.415	.402

Mark Ernster

Bats: Right **Throws:** Right **Pos:** SS-112; PH-5; 2B-1; 3B-1; DH-1   **Ht:** 6'0" **Wt:** 190 **Born:** 12/10/77 **Age:** 23

Year Team	Lg Org	G	AB	H	2B	3B	HR	TB	R	RBI	TBB	IBB	SO	HBP	SH	SF	SB	CS	SB%	GDP	Avg	OBP	SLG
1999 Ogden	R+ Mil	5	22	5	1	1	0	8	3	2	1	0	1	1	1	0	1	0	1.00	1	.227	.292	.364
2000 Mudville	A+ Mil	61	204	47	9	1	3	67	30	22	13	0	40	3	3	1	4	2	.67	8	.230	.285	.328
Huntsville	AA Mil	57	205	50	9	0	5	74	27	26	35	2	46	1	3	1	10	6	.63	6	.244	.355	.361
2 Min. YEARS		123	431	102	19	2	8	149	60	50	49	2	87	5	7	2	15	8	.65	15	.237	.320	.346

Jaime Escalante

Pitches: Right **Bats:** Both **Pos:** RP-33; SP-1   **Ht:** 6'2" **Wt:** 210 **Born:** 4/5/77 **Age:** 24

Year Team	Lg Org	G	GS	CG	GF	IP	BFP	H	R	ER	HR	SH	SF	HB	TBB	IBB	SO	WP	Bk	W	L	Pct.	ShO	Sv	ERA
1997 Orioles	R Bal	1	0	0	1	3		0	0	0	0	0	0	1	0	1	0	0	0	0	0	—	0	0	0.00
2000 Cedar Rapds	A Ana	25	0	0	16	40.2	171	24	14	11	1	1	2	3	23	2	41	2	0	0	1	.000	0	7	2.43
Erie	AA Ana	3	1	0	0	3	19	4	6	5	0	1	1	0	6	0	2	0	0	0	1	.000	0	0	15.00
Lk Elsinore	A+ Ana	6	0	0	4	8.2	37	6	2	2	1	0	0	0	4	0	18	0	0	1	1	.500	0	1	2.08
2 Min. YEARS		35	1	0	20	53.1	230	34	22	18	2	2	3	3	34	2	62	2	0	1	3	.250	0	8	3.04

Emiliano Escandon

Bats: Both **Throws:** Right **Pos:** 2B-60; DH-36; 3B-3; PR-3; PH-2   **Ht:** 5'10" **Wt:** 180 **Born:** 11/6/74 **Age:** 26

Year Team	Lg Org	G	AB	H	2B	3B	HR	TB	R	RBI	TBB	IBB	SO	HBP	SH	SF	SB	CS	SB%	GDP	Avg	OBP	SLG
1995 Spokane	A- KC	13	44	14	1	1	1	20	7	12	6	0	11	1	0	0	1	0	1.00	0	.318	.392	.455
1996 Lansing	A KC	107	372	101	18	5	4	141	50	52	46	3	47	3	6	2	8	5	.62	0	.272	.355	.379
1997 Wilmington	A+ KC	80	238	65	9	3	2	86	40	32	57	3	54	1	5	2	9	4	.69	3	.273	.413	.361
1998 Wilmington	A+ KC	116	353	92	23	1	5	132	50	58	74	5	64	3	1	5	5	9	.36	10	.261	.389	.374

Year Team	Lg Org	G	AB	H	2B	3B	HR	TB	R	RBI	TBB	IBB	SO	HBP	SH	SF	SB	CS	SB%	GDP	Avg	OBP	SLG
1999 Wichita	AA KC	120	340	88	18	5	7	137	59	57	73	3	46	4	4	7	5	7	.42	9	.259	.389	.403
2000 Omaha	AAA KC	103	302	69	12	0	7	102	35	32	50	0	58	2	7	6	4	0	1.00	6	.228	.336	.338
6 Min. YEARS		539	1649	429	81	15	26	618	241	243	306	14	280	14	23	22	32	25	.56	31	.260	.376	.375

Alex Escobar

Bats: Right **Throws:** Right **Pos:** OF-119; DH-2; PR-1 **Ht:** 6'1" **Wt:** 180 **Born:** 9/6/78 **Age:** 22

Year Team	Lg Org	G	AB	H	2B	3B	HR	TB	R	RBI	TBB	IBB	SO	HBP	SH	SF	SB	CS	SB%	GDP	Avg	OBP	SLG
1996 Mets	R NYM	24	75	27	4	0	0	31	15	10	4	0	9	3	0	1	7	1	.88	0	.360	.410	.413
1997 Kingsport	R+ NYM	10	36	7	3	0	0	10	6	3	3	1	8	0	0	1	1	0	1.00	3	.194	.250	.278
Mets	R NYM	26	73	18	4	1	1	27	12	11	10	0	17	1	0	1	0	0	—	0	.247	.341	.370
1998 Capital Cty	A NYM	112	416	129	23	5	27	243	90	91	54	1	133	5	5	3	49	7	.88	1	.310	.393	.584
1999 Mets	R NYM	2	8	3	2	0	0	5	1	1	1	0	2	0	0	0	0	0	—	0	.375	.444	.625
St. Lucie	A+ NYM	1	3	2	0	0	1	5	1	3	1	0	1	0	0	1	1	1	.50	0	.667	.600	1.667
2000 Binghamton	AA NYM	122	437	126	25	7	16	213	79	67	57	5	114	7	0	5	24	5	.83	8	.288	.375	.487
5 Min. YEARS		297	1048	312	61	13	45	534	204	186	130	7	284	16	5	12	82	14	.85	13	.298	.380	.510

Vaughn Eshelman

Pitches: Left **Bats:** Left **Pos:** SP-5 **Ht:** 6'3" **Wt:** 205 **Born:** 5/22/69 **Age:** 32

Year Team	Lg Org	G	GS	CG	GF	IP	BFP	H	R	ER	HR	SH	SF	HB	TBB	IBB	SO	WP	Bk	W	L	Pct.	ShO	Sv	ERA
1991 Bluefield	R+ Bal	3	3	0	0	14	59	10	4	1	1	0	1	0	9	0	15	1	0	1	0	1.000	0	0	0.64
Kane County	A Bal	11	11	2	0	77.2	319	57	23	20	3	1	3	3	35	0	90	2	2	5	3	.625	1	0	2.32
1993 Frederick	A+ Bal	24	24	2	0	143.1	608	128	70	62	10	4	3	7	59	0	122	7	1	7	10	.412	1	0	3.89
1994 Bowie	AA Bal	27	25	2	0	166.1	713	175	81	74	13	7	3	3	60	1	133	8	0	11	9	.550	2	0	4.00
1995 Trenton	AA Bos	2	2	0	0	7	25	3	1	0	0	0	0	1	0	0	7	0	0	1	0	.000	0	0	0.00
1996 Pawtucket	AAA Bos	7	7	1	0	43.2	190	40	21	21	6	3	0	3	19	1	28	1	0	1	2	.333	0	0	4.33
1997 Pawtucket	AAA Bos	14	13	0	0	66.2	281	63	38	36	4	7	4	5	22	0	57	3	0	3	4	.429	0	1	4.86
2000 Reds	R Cin	2	2	0	0	9.2	35	1	2	2	0	1	0	0	4	0	6	0	0	0	1	.000	0	0	1.86
Louisville	AAA Cin	1	1	0	0	4	21	7	7	4	0	0	1	0	3	0	2	0	0	0	1	.000	0	0	9.00
Dayton	A Cin	2	2	0	0	7	32	8	5	5	0	0	0	1	4	0	4	1	0	0	1	.000	0	0	6.43
1995 Boston	AL	23	14	0	4	81.2	356	86	47	44	3	0	3	1	36	0	41	4	0	6	3	.667	0	0	4.85
1996 Boston	AL	39	10	0	11	87.2	428	112	79	69	13	3	5	2	58	4	59	4	0	6	3	.667	0	0	7.08
1997 Boston	AL	21	6	0	6	42.2	198	58	32	30	3	1	2	2	17	5	18	2	0	3	3	.500	0	0	6.33
7 Min. YEARS		93	90	7	1	539.1	2283	492	252	225	37	25	13	23	215	2	464	23	3	28	32	.467	4	1	3.75
3 Maj. YEARS		83	30	0	11	212	982	256	158	143	19	4	10	5	111	9	118	10	0	15	9	.625	0	0	6.07

Josue Espada

Bats: Right **Throws:** Right **Pos:** 2B-49; SS-10; DH-3; PH-1; PR-1 **Ht:** 5'10" **Wt:** 175 **Born:** 8/30/75 **Age:** 25

Year Team	Lg Org	G	AB	H	2B	3B	HR	TB	R	RBI	TBB	IBB	SO	HBP	SH	SF	SB	CS	SB%	GDP	Avg	OBP	SLG
1996 Sou Oregon	A- Oak	15	54	12	1	0	1	16	7	5	5	0	10	1	1	0	0	0	—	1	.222	.300	.296
W Michigan	A Oak	23	74	20	2	0	0	22	9	4	13	0	11	2	0	0	3	1	.75	2	.270	.393	.297
1997 Visalia	A+ Oak	118	445	122	7	3	3	144	90	39	72	1	69	9	7	3	46	17	.73	6	.274	.384	.324
1998 Huntsville	AA Oak	51	161	41	7	1	1	53	29	22	27	0	15	4	5	1	7	4	.64	4	.255	.373	.329
1999 Midland	AA Oak	113	435	147	15	2	6	184	85	51	62	0	51	2	2	3	22	16	.58	5	.338	.420	.423
Vancouver	AAA Oak	6	26	8	1	0	0	9	2	0	3	0	4	0	0	0	1	2	.33	0	.308	.379	.346
2000 Sacramento	AAA Oak	40	145	34	7	0	0	41	21	10	27	0	23	1	3	0	7	2	.78	5	.234	.358	.283
Midland	AA Oak	23	98	26	7	0	0	33	17	7	12	0	12	2	0	0	2	2	.50	4	.265	.357	.337
5 Min. YEARS		389	1438	410	47	6	11	502	260	138	221	1	195	21	18	7	88	44	.67	27	.285	.386	.349

Rendy Espina

Pitches: Left **Bats:** Left **Pos:** RP-53 **Ht:** 6'0" **Wt:** 180 **Born:** 5/11/78 **Age:** 23

Year Team	Lg Org	G	GS	CG	GF	IP	BFP	H	R	ER	HR	SH	SF	HB	TBB	IBB	SO	WP	Bk	W	L	Pct.	ShO	Sv	ERA
1995 Twins	R Min	4	2	0	1	10	50	11	10	1	0	1	0	0	6	0	3	3	2	0	1	.000	0	0	0.90
1996 Twins	R Min	7	1	0	2	11.2	54	18	12	12	0	0	0	1	8	0	10	1	1	0	2	.000	0	0	9.26
1997 Twins	R Min	8	7	0	0	34.2	132	24	11	5	0	1	0	2	6	0	34	4	0	2	2	.500	0	0	1.30
Elizabethtn	R+ Min	6	3	0	1	17	86	25	21	15	2	0	0	3	9	0	15	3	1	0	3	.000	0	0	7.94
1999 Batavia	A- Phi	1	0	0	0	1	9	5	4	4	1	0	0	0	1	0	1	0	0	0	1	.000	0	0	36.00
Phillies	R Phi	2	0	0	2	1	4	1	0	0	0	0	0	0	0	0	1	0	0	1	0	1.000	0	0	0.00
Piedmont	A Phi	15	0	0	7	35	143	35	20	18	1	2	2	1	10	1	31	3	1	2	0	.000	0	3	4.63
2000 Tennessee	AA Tor	53	0	0	19	59.2	264	49	22	14	1	2	2	5	35	1	41	2	1	6	1	.857	0	3	2.11
5 Min. YEARS		96	13	0	32	170	742	168	100	69	5	6	4	12	75	2	136	16	6	9	12	.429	0	7	3.65

Juan Espinal

Bats: Right **Throws:** Right **Pos:** 3B-61; DH-34; 1B-12; SS-1 **Ht:** 5'11" **Wt:** 200 **Born:** 4/15/76 **Age:** 25

Year Team	Lg Org	G	AB	H	2B	3B	HR	TB	R	RBI	TBB	IBB	SO	HBP	SH	SF	SB	CS	SB%	GDP	Avg	OBP	SLG
1993 Padres	R SD	37	136	41	11	1	2	60	23	19	15	1	40	1	0	1	3	3	.50	2	.301	.373	.441
1994 Springfield	A SD	118	386	95	27	3	14	170	66	50	36	1	102	3	4	5	0	2	.00	2	.246	.312	.440
1995 Clinton	A SD	116	336	70	11	0	7	102	28	46	47	2	79	4	4	6	3	3	.50	8	.208	.307	.304
1996 Bakersfield	A+ SD	137	522	143	38	0	26	259	81	98	74	2	126	6	1	6	1	4	.20	11	.274	.367	.496
1997 Sarasota	A+ Bos	109	322	80	20	2	7	125	49	45	51	0	79	6	2	3	4	5	.44	2	.248	.359	.388
1998 Sarasota	A+ Bos	127	508	141	32	1	16	223	76	88	37	2	107	4	1	5	3	1	.75	20	.278	.330	.439
1999 Sarasota	A+ Bos	111	411	123	26	0	10	179	78	67	47	0	83	6	1	4	12	4	.75	9	.299	.376	.436
Trenton	AA Bos	17	65	12	1	0	2	19	11	7	5	0	19	1	0	2	0	1	.00	2	.185	.247	.292
2000 Trenton	AA Bos	15	54	16	4	1	3	31	13	9	6	0	13	0	0	0	2	0	.00	0	.296	.355	.574
Sarasota	A+ Bos	93	330	89	17	1	14	150	51	66	55	3	81	6	0	6	3	7	.30	8	.270	.378	.455
8 Min. YEARS		880	3070	810	187	9	101	1318	476	495	373	11	729	37	15	38	29	30	.49	64	.264	.347	.429

Johnny Estrada

Bats: Both **Throws:** Right **Pos:** C-86; DH-7; PH-6   **Ht:** 5'11" **Wt:** 209 **Born:** 6/27/76 **Age:** 25

Year Team	Lg Org	G	AB	H	2B	3B	HR	TB	R	RBI	TBB	IBB	SO	HBP	SH	SF	SB	CS	SB%	GDP	Avg	OBP	SLG
1997 Batavia	A- Phi	58	223	70	17	2	6	109	28	43	9	1	15	1	2	5	0	0	—	9	.314	.336	.489
1998 Piedmont	A Phi	77	303	94	14	2	7	133	33	44	6	1	19	5	0	3	0	1	.00	11	.310	.331	.439
Clearwater	A+ Phi	37	117	26	8	0	0	34	8	13	5	0	7	0	2	2	0	0	—	2	.222	.250	.291
1999 Clearwater	A+ Phi	98	346	96	15	0	9	138	35	52	14	3	26	2	6	8	1	0	1.00	12	.277	.303	.399
2000 Reading	AA Phi	95	356	105	18	0	12	159	42	42	10	2	20	4	2	0	1	0	1.00	8	.295	.322	.447
4 Min. YEARS		365	1345	391	72	4	34	573	146	194	44	7	87	12	12	18	2	1	.67	42	.291	.315	.426

Luis Estrella

Pitches: Right **Bats:** Right **Pos:** RP-24; SP-13   **Ht:** 6'1" **Wt:** 220 **Born:** 10/7/74 **Age:** 26

Year Team	Lg Org	G	GS	CG	GF	IP	BFP	H	R	ER	HR	SH	SF	HB	TBB	IBB	SO	WP	Bk	W	L	Pct.	ShO	Sv	ERA
1996 Bellingham	A- SF	23	0	0	6	55.1	213	35	13	11	3	1	0	0	22	1	52	6	0	4	0	1.000	0	1	1.79
1997 San Jose	A+ SF	42	0	0	15	77	332	84	39	29	3	1	0	2	25	3	59	7	6	5	5	.500	0	2	3.39
1998 San Jose	A+ SF	36	2	0	12	72	315	79	41	38	5	3	1	2	27	0	57	9	1	5	6	.455	0	2	4.75
1999 Fresno	AAA SF	8	0	0	7	11.2	63	23	16	16	4	1	1	0	7	0	5	1	0	0	1	.000	0	0	12.34
Shreveport	AA SF	40	5	0	15	92.1	375	77	33	31	2	2	1	2	33	1	75	7	1	6	4	.600	0	4	3.02
2000 Fresno	AAA SF	16	7	0	0	57	267	75	52	47	9	1	1	2	31	0	32	4	0	1	5	.167	0	0	7.42
Shreveport	AA SF	21	6	0	7	59	237	51	24	18	2	6	1	1	22	3	31	5	0	1	4	.200	0	1	2.75
5 Min. YEARS		186	20	0	62	424.1	1802	424	218	190	28	15	5	9	167	8	311	39	8	22	25	.468	0	10	4.03

Bart Evans

Pitches: Right **Bats:** Right **Pos:** SP-15; RP-9   **Ht:** 6'2" **Wt:** 210 **Born:** 12/30/70 **Age:** 30

Year Team	Lg Org	G	GS	CG	GF	IP	BFP	H	R	ER	HR	SH	SF	HB	TBB	IBB	SO	WP	Bk	W	L	Pct.	ShO	Sv	ERA
1992 Eugene	A- KC	13	1	0	4	26	126	17	20	18	1	1	2	4	31	0	39	14	0	1	1	.500	0	0	6.23
1993 Rockford	A KC	27	16	0	4	99	439	95	52	48	5	1	2	4	60	0	120	10	1	10	4	.714	0	0	4.36
1994 Wilmington	A+ KC	26	26	0	0	145	587	107	53	48	7	1	0	4	61	0	145	10	0	10	3	.769	0	0	2.98
1995 Wichita	AA KC	7	7	0	0	22.1	123	22	28	26	3	1	0	1	45	0	13	7	1	0	4	.000	0	0	10.48
Wilmington	A+ KC	16	6	0	4	46.2	215	30	21	15	0	0	1	5	44	0	47	7	0	4	1	.800	0	2	2.89
1996 Wichita	AA KC	9	7	0	0	24.1	146	31	38	32	7	3	2	6	36	0	16	12	0	1	2	.333	0	0	11.84
1997 Wilmington	A+ KC	16	2	0	8	20.2	101	22	18	15	1	0	2	3	15	0	22	3	0	0	1	.000	0	0	6.53
Wichita	AA KC	32	0	0	22	33.1	148	45	20	17	4	2	1	0	8	2	28	1	0	1	2	.333	0	6	4.59
1998 Omaha	AAA KC	49	0	0	40	57	236	50	18	16	4	2	0	2	22	2	54	3	0	3	1	.750	0	27	2.53
1999 Omaha	AAA KC	30	0	0	12	33.1	172	33	34	30	5	1	1	9	36	2	34	6	0	4	5	.444	0	2	8.10
2000 Toledo	AAA Det	24	15	1	2	83.1	398	81	63	58	12	2	1	2	69	0	72	5	0	5	4	.556	1	0	6.26
1998 Kansas City	AL	8	0	0	3	9	34	7	3	2	1	0	0	0	8	0	7	0	0	0	0	—	0	0	2.00
9 Min. YEARS		249	80	1	96	591	2691	533	365	323	49	14	12	40	427	6	590	78	3	39	28	.582	1	37	4.92

Dave Evans

Pitches: Right **Bats:** Right **Pos:** RP-38; SP-3   **Ht:** 6'3" **Wt:** 205 **Born:** 1/1/68 **Age:** 33

Year Team	Lg Org	G	GS	CG	GF	IP	BFP	H	R	ER	HR	SH	SF	HB	TBB	IBB	SO	WP	Bk	W	L	Pct.	ShO	Sv	ERA
1990 San Berndno	A+ Sea	26	26	4	0	155	673	135	83	72	9	4	7	7	74	0	143	10	0	14	9	.609	0	0	4.18
1991 Jacksnville	AA Sea	21	20	1	0	115.2	507	118	74	67	15	2	7	9	49	0	76	12	0	5	9	.357	0	0	5.21
1993 Appleton	A Sea	5	5	0	0	27.2	117	21	9	7	0	0	0	2	15	0	23	5	2	2	1	.667	0	0	2.28
Riverside	A+ Sea	8	8	1	0	41.2	187	41	22	21	5	1	1	5	23	0	42	2	0	3	2	.600	1	0	4.54
1994 Jacksnville	AA Sea	31	6	0	8	81.1	354	86	59	50	11	3	4	5	31	2	62	4	0	3	5	.375	0	2	5.53
1995 Jackson	AA Hou	49	0	0	37	67.2	278	50	29	25	2	5	3	4	28	6	54	0	1	2	9	.182	0	18	3.33
Tucson	AAA Hou	2	0	0	0	3	12	2	0	0	0	0	0	0	0	0	4	0	0	0	0	—	0	0	0.00
1996 Tucson	AAA Hou	43	15	0	12	111.2	511	120	77	65	8	8	3	12	47	3	80	11	0	6	12	.333	0	1	5.24
1998 Carolina	AA Pit	26	3	0	6	56.2	254	56	36	33	8	3	1	0	30	1	52	0	0	5	4	.556	0	0	5.24
Nashville	AAA Pit	7	1	0	4	11.2	67	19	12	11	2	2	0	3	8	1	8	4	0	0	2	.000	0	0	8.49
Bowie	AA Bal	14	0	0	6	18.1	84	17	9	4	1	1	1	5	6	0	26	2	0	1	1	.500	0	0	1.96
1999 Rochester	AAA Bal	60	0	0	32	70.2	309	70	48	42	11	5	2	5	27	2	65	9	1	2	11	.154	0	2	5.35
2000 Tucson	AAA Ari	41	3	0	15	74.2	343	82	47	41	11	4	2	0	41	2	60	8	0	6	4	.600	0	2	4.94
9 Min. YEARS		333	87	6	120	835.2	3696	817	505	438	83	38	31	57	380	17	695	75	7	49	69	.415	1	25	4.72

Keith Evans

Pitches: Right **Bats:** Right **Pos:** SP-8; RP-7   **Ht:** 6'5" **Wt:** 220 **Born:** 11/2/75 **Age:** 25

Year Team	Lg Org	G	GS	CG	GF	IP	BFP	H	R	ER	HR	SH	SF	HB	TBB	IBB	SO	WP	Bk	W	L	Pct.	ShO	Sv	ERA
1997 Cape Fear	A Mon	21	21	3	0	138	551	113	56	40	6	2	4	8	18	0	102	1	0	12	7	.632	1	0	2.61
Wst Plm Bch	A+ Mon	7	7	2	0	43.2	185	42	23	21	4	2	2	5	11	0	20	1	0	2	4	.333	2	0	4.33
1998 Jupiter	A+ Mon	8	8	1	0	50.1	194	45	18	16	1	0	1	3	5	0	25	1	0	5	2	.714	0	0	2.86
Harrisburg	AA Mon	20	20	1	0	124	520	133	59	49	13	6	2	8	30	2	76	2	0	8	9	.471	0	0	3.56
1999 Harrisburg	AA Mon	5	5	0	0	27	120	29	14	11	5	1	0	3	5	0	21	1	0	0	2	.000	0	0	3.67
Ottawa	AAA Mon	24	18	2	0	122	525	143	79	65	17	3	1	10	22	0	74	2	0	2	13	.133	0	0	4.80
2000 Ottawa	AAA Mon	15	8	0	1	52	240	64	29	23	3	3	2	4	20	0	22	3	0	2	4	.333	0	0	3.98
4 Min. YEARS		100	87	9	1	557	2335	569	278	225	49	17	12	43	111	2	340	11	0	31	41	.431	3	0	3.64

Lee Evans

Bats: Both **Throws:** Right **Pos:** C-89; 1B-22; DH-9; PH-3; PR-1   **Ht:** 6'1" **Wt:** 185 **Born:** 7/20/77 **Age:** 23

Year Team	Lg Org	G	AB	H	2B	3B	HR	TB	R	RBI	TBB	IBB	SO	HBP	SH	SF	SB	CS	SB%	GDP	Avg	OBP	SLG
1996 Pirates	R Pit	32	111	31	5	2	3	49	27	20	18	1	26	3	1	0	3	0	1.00	2	.279	.394	.441

(continued)

Year Team	Lg Org	G	AB	H	2B	3B	HR	TB	R	RBI	TBB	IBB	SO	HBP	SH	SF	SB	CS	SB%	GDP	Avg	OBP	SLG
1997 Augusta	A Pit	54	186	36	9	2	2	55	19	23	14	1	52	1	0	1	6	3	.67	5	.194	.252	.296
Erie	A- Pit	40	141	42	6	0	5	63	20	16	11	1	30	2	1	1	1	2	.33	3	.298	.355	.447
1998 Augusta	A Pit	98	337	75	19	1	5	111	43	43	28	0	90	3	0	4	6	3	.67	6	.223	.285	.329
1999 Lynchburg	A+ Pit	117	413	93	18	2	11	148	44	58	37	2	129	1	1	8	3	6	.33	4	.225	.292	.358
2000 Lynchburg	A+ Pit	90	305	79	15	3	9	127	45	37	43	0	88	2	2	2	16	1	.94	6	.259	.352	.416
Altoona	AA Pit	32	118	28	4	1	1	37	18	8	14	2	28	1	4	0	1	1	.50	3	.237	.323	.314
5 Min. YEARS		463	1611	384	76	11	36	590	216	205	165	7	443	17	10	16	36	16	.69	29	.238	.313	.366

Adam Everett

Bats: Right **Throws:** Right **Pos:** SS-124; PH-2 **Ht:** 6'0" **Wt:** 156 **Born:** 2/2/77 **Age:** 24

Year Team	Lg Org	G	AB	H	2B	3B	HR	TB	R	RBI	TBB	IBB	SO	HBP	SH	SF	SB	CS	SB%	GDP	Avg	OBP	SLG
1998 Lowell	A- Bos	21	71	21	6	2	0	31	11	9	11	0	13	3	1	1	2	1	.67	2	.296	.407	.437
1999 Trenton	AA Bos	98	338	89	11	0	10	130	56	44	41	0	64	10	4	4	21	5	.81	3	.263	.356	.385
2000 New Orleans	AAA Hou	126	453	111	25	2	5	155	82	37	75	0	100	11	4	4	13	4	.76	6	.245	.363	.342
3 Min. YEARS		245	862	221	42	4	15	316	149	90	127	0	177	24	14	9	36	10	.78	11	.256	.364	.367

Bill Everly

Pitches: Right **Bats:** Right **Pos:** RP-50 **Ht:** 6'1" **Wt:** 175 **Born:** 6/15/75 **Age:** 26

Year Team	Lg Org	G	GS	CG	GF	IP	BFP	H	R	ER	HR	SH	SF	HB	TBB	IBB	SO	WP	Bk	W	L	Pct.	ShO	Sv	ERA
1997 Yakima	A- LA	28	1	0	11	58	259	48	26	22	4	2	3	9	33	6	63	5	1	2	3	.400	0	3	3.41
1998 Vero Beach	A+ LA	49	4	0	30	106.1	464	108	65	54	12	6	5	9	31	2	59	2	2	7	6	.538	0	4	4.57
Albuquerque	AAA LA	2	0	0	0	2	13	6	6	6	2	0	0	0	1	0	1	0	0	0	1	.000	0	0	27.00
1999 San Berndno	A+ LA	60	0	0	57	63.1	272	66	26	24	6	4	0	3	21	3	51	3	0	7	4	.636	0	34	3.41
2000 San Antonio	AA LA	11	0	0	7	14.2	68	16	12	10	0	1	1	1	7	1	4	0	0	2	0	1.000	0	2	6.14
Vero Beach	A+ LA	39	0	0	29	61.2	260	57	23	23	2	2	4	8	24	2	20	2	0	1	5	.167	0	12	3.36
4 Min. YEARS		189	5	0	134	306	1336	301	158	139	26	15	13	30	117	14	198	12	3	19	19	.500	0	54	4.09

Bryan Eversgerd

Pitches: Left **Bats:** Right **Pos:** RP-48 **Ht:** 6'1" **Wt:** 190 **Born:** 2/11/69 **Age:** 32

Year Team	Lg Org	G	GS	CG	GF	IP	BFP	H	R	ER	HR	SH	SF	HB	TBB	IBB	SO	WP	Bk	W	L	Pct.	ShO	Sv	ERA
1989 Johnson Cty	R+ StL	16	1	0	5	29.2	127	30	16	12	1	2	6	0	12	1	19	2	0	2	3	.400	0	0	3.64
1990 Springfield	A StL	20	15	2	2	104.1	457	123	60	48	6	5	4	4	26	1	55	2	0	6	8	.429	0	0	4.14
1991 Savannah	A StL	72	0	0	22	93.1	390	71	43	36	7	2	0	3	34	4	98	11	0	1	5	.167	0	1	3.47
1992 St. Pete	A+ StL	57	1	0	13	74	305	65	25	22	0	9	4	2	25	4	57	1	1	3	2	.600	0	0	2.68
Arkansas	AA StL	6	0	0	2	5.1	25	7	4	4	0	1	0	0	2	1	4	0	0	0	1	.000	0	0	6.75
1993 Arkansas	AA StL	62	0	0	32	66	269	60	24	16	3	2	1	1	19	4	68	7	1	4	4	.500	0	2	2.18
1994 Louisville	AAA StL	12	0	0	2	12	54	11	7	6	0	1	2	1	8	0	8	1	1	1	1	.500	0	0	4.50
1995 Ottawa	AAA Mon	38	0	0	9	53	232	49	21	14	1	2	3	1	26	1	45	2	0	6	2	.750	0	2	2.38
1996 Trenton	AA Bos	4	0	0	2	7	31	6	2	2	0	1	0	1	4	1	2	0	0	1	0	1.000	0	0	2.57
Okla City	AAA Tex	38	5	0	14	65.2	266	57	21	20	3	2	1	4	14	0	60	3	0	3	3	.500	0	4	2.74
1997 Okla City	AAA Tex	26	7	0	5	76.1	339	91	48	36	12	4	2	2	24	2	43	5	1	1	3	.250	0	0	4.24
1998 Memphis	AAA StL	49	0	0	17	56.2	238	51	25	21	9	1	0	1	20	1	50	2	1	5	5	.286	0	0	3.34
1999 Memphis	AAA StL	59	0	0	27	66	269	56	26	21	4	0	4	0	15	0	46	0	0	6	6	.500	0	2	2.86
2000 Memphis	AAA StL	48	0	0	8	72	299	67	32	28	9	1	4	1	20	0	52	0	0	4	4	.500	0	0	3.50
1994 St. Louis	NL	40	1	0	8	67.2	283	75	36	34	8	5	2	2	20	1	47	3	1	2	3	.400	0	0	4.52
1995 Montreal	NL	25	0	0	5	21	95	22	13	12	2	1	2	1	9	2	8	1	0	0	0	—	0	0	5.14
1997 Texas	AL	3	0	0	1	1.1	12	5	3	3	0	0	1	0	3	0	2	0	0	0	2	.000	0	0	20.25
1998 St. Louis	NL	8	0	0	2	6	31	9	7	6	1	0	2	1	2	0	0	0	0	0	0	—	0	0	9.00
12 Min. YEARS		504	29	2	160	781.1	3301	744	354	286	60	37	26	23	249	20	607	36	5	40	47	.460	0	9	3.29
4 Maj. YEARS		76	1	0	16	96	421	111	59	55	11	6	6	4	34	3	61	4	1	2	5	.286	0	0	5.16

Ethan Faggett

Bats: Left **Throws:** Left **Pos:** OF-127; DH-2; PH-2; PR-2 **Ht:** 6'0" **Wt:** 190 **Born:** 8/21/74 **Age:** 26

Year Team	Lg Org	G	AB	H	2B	3B	HR	TB	R	RBI	TBB	IBB	SO	HBP	SH	SF	SB	CS	SB%	GDP	Avg	OBP	SLG
1992 Red Sox	R Bos	34	103	18	1	1	1	24	9	9	10	0	37	2	0	0	1	2	.33	1	.175	.261	.233
1993 Red Sox	R Bos	23	58	10	2	1	0	14	4	2	10	0	15	1	0	0	5	1	.83	0	.172	.300	.241
1994 Red Sox	R Bos	41	117	34	2	2	1	43	14	17	12	0	33	1	0	0	10	7	.59	2	.291	.366	.368
1995 Michigan	A Bos	115	399	97	11	7	8	146	56	47	37	3	112	4	3	2	23	7	.77	9	.243	.312	.366
1996 Sarasota	A+ Bos	110	408	112	12	8	4	152	48	35	35	0	118	6	7	1	24	10	.71	9	.275	.340	.373
1997 Sarasota	A+ Bos	114	410	120	19	9	3	166	56	46	43	4	87	7	4	4	23	12	.66	4	.293	.366	.405
Trenton	AA Bos	17	56	16	2	0	2	24	10	8	8	0	17	1	2	1	2	0	1.00	4	.286	.379	.429
1998 Sarasota	A+ Bos	62	233	65	12	1	4	91	42	25	25	1	55	3	7	3	13	5	.72	3	.279	.352	.391
Mobile	AA SD	54	162	40	7	1	3	53	22	25	16	1	40	3	3	2	7	1	.88	4	.247	.322	.327
1999 Mobile	AA SD	128	527	128	18	11	6	186	82	43	53	0	126	7	3	4	63	14	.82	4	.243	.320	.353
2000 Mobile	AA SD	97	370	89	20	4	2	123	55	23	42	0	84	6	2	1	12	15	.44	9	.241	.327	.332
Las Vegas	AAA SD	34	137	38	7	2	6	67	21	15	16	0	31	2	0	0	7	3	.70	4	.277	.361	.489
9 Min. YEARS		829	2980	767	108	47	40	1089	419	295	307	9	755	44	31	15	190	77	.71	49	.257	.334	.365

Chad Faircloth

Bats: Left **Throws:** Right **Pos:** OF-42; PH-13; PR-1; P-1 **Ht:** 6'0" **Wt:** 180 **Born:** 4/25/75 **Age:** 26

Year Team	Lg Org	G	AB	H	2B	3B	HR	TB	R	RBI	TBB	IBB	SO	HBP	SH	SF	SB	CS	SB%	GDP	Avg	OBP	SLG
1997 Salem-Keizr	A- SF	31	102	29	5	2	0	38	13	13	14	0	30	1	0	1	2	0	1.00	3	.284	.373	.373
Bakersfield	A+ SF	19	73	19	5	0	1	27	8	7	6	0	22	0	3	0	0	1	1.00	1	.260	.316	.370

Year Team	Lg Org	G	AB	H	2B	3B	HR	TB	R	RBI	TBB	IBB	SO	HBP	SH	SF	SB	CS	SB%	GDP	Avg	OBP	SLG
1998 Bakersfield	A+ SF	84	288	74	13	3	3	102	39	30	16	0	78	2	1	1	12	2	.86	5	.257	.300	.354
San Jose	A+ SF	18	63	13	3	1	0	18	5	2	1	0	12	0	0	0	1	1	.50	0	.206	.219	.286
1999 Fresno	AAA SF	1	1	0	0	0	0	0	0	0	0	0	0	0	0	0	0	0	—	0	.000	.000	.000
Shreveport	AA SF	23	37	8	2	0	0	10	4	3	2	0	14	0	0	0	0	0	—	2	.216	.256	.270
Bakersfield	A+ SF	51	145	38	12	1	0	52	14	16	14	1	35	0	1	2	5	4	.56	2	.262	.323	.359
2000 San Jose	A+ SF	31	80	17	2	0	2	25	12	8	3	0	22	2	1	0	2	1	.67	1	.213	.259	.313
Shreveport	AA SF	23	52	12	0	0	0	12	3	4	2	0	10	1	1	0	0	2	.00	1	.231	.273	.231
4 Min. YEARS		281	841	210	42	7	6	284	98	83	58	1	223	6	7	4	23	10	.70	15	.250	.301	.338

Alex Fajardo

Bats: Right **Throws:** Right **Pos:** OF-82; DH-14; PH-1 **Ht:** 6'0" **Wt:** 180 **Born:** 2/6/76 **Age:** 25

Year Team	Lg Org	G	AB	H	2B	3B	HR	TB	R	RBI	TBB	IBB	SO	HBP	SH	SF	SB	CS	SB%	GDP	Avg	OBP	SLG
1997 Batavia	A- Phi	52	200	54	7	4	2	75	35	29	7	1	34	3	3	1	9	2	.82	5	.270	.303	.375
1998 Piedmont	A Phi	115	457	128	24	1	5	169	83	46	44	1	88	1	12	4	38	4	.90	6	.280	.342	.370
1999 Piedmont	A Phi	118	444	108	16	6	6	154	66	43	52	0	91	6	10	3	44	10	.81	7	.243	.329	.347
2000 San Jose	A+ SF	93	331	93	9	3	0	108	47	39	54	0	67	3	4	4	23	6	.79	8	.281	.383	.326
Fresno	AAA SF	4	12	3	0	1	0	5	1	1	0	0	3	0	1	0	0	0	—	0	.250	.250	.417
4 Min. YEARS		382	1444	386	56	15	13	511	232	158	157	2	283	13	30	12	114	22	.84	26	.267	.342	.354

Steve Falteisek

Pitches: Right **Bats:** Right **Pos:** RP-4; SP-1 **Ht:** 6'2" **Wt:** 200 **Born:** 1/28/72 **Age:** 29

Year Team	Lg Org	G	GS	CG	GF	IP	BFP	H	R	ER	HR	SH	SF	HB	TBB	IBB	SO	WP	Bk	W	L	Pct.	ShO	Sv	ERA
1992 Jamestown	A- Mon	15	15	2	0	96	407	84	47	38	3	4	1	5	31	2	82	9	10	3	8	.273	0	0	3.56
1993 Burlington	A Mon	14	14	0	0	76.1	345	86	59	50	4	1		2	35	0	63	4	1	3	5	.375	0	0	5.90
1994 Wst Plm Bch	A+ Mon	27	24	1	0	159.2	658	144	72	45	3	0	6	3	49	0	91	11	4	9	4	.692	0	0	2.54
1995 Harrisburg	AA Mon	25	25	5	0	168	707	152	74	55	3	7	5	11	64	4	112	6	1	9	6	.600	0	0	2.95
Ottawa	AAA Mon	3	3	1	0	23	86	17	4	3	0	0	0	1	5	0	18	0	1	2	0	1.000	1	0	1.17
1996 Ottawa	AAA Mon	12	12	0	0	58	272	75	45	41	10	1	0	5	25	0	26	3	0	2	5	.286	0	0	6.36
Harrisburg	AA Mon	17	17	1	0	115.2	492	111	60	49	9	7	0	5	48	1	62	5	3	6	5	.545	0	0	3.81
1997 Ottawa	AAA Mon	22	22	1	0	125	555	135	67	55	10	7	7	5	54	1	56	12	1	6	9	.400	0	0	3.96
1998 Ottawa	AAA Mon	34	22	1	1	161.2	719	186	110	98	17	4	4	11	59	1	83	10	0	10	11	.476	0	0	5.46
1999 Louisville	AAA Mil	42	4	0	8	76.1	359	98	65	58	13	2	2	4	41	4	34	7	1	5	11	.313	0	0	6.84
2000 Calgary	AAA Fla	5	1	0	0	7.2	53	23	18	17	2	0	0	1	5	0	5	1	0	0	1	.000	0	0	19.96
1997 Montreal	NL	5	0	0	2	8	34	8	4	3	0	0	2	1	3	0	2	0	0	0	0	—	0	0	3.38
1999 Milwaukee	NL	10	0	0	3	12	52	18	10	10	3	0	1	0	3	0	5	0	0	0	0	—	0	0	7.50
9 Min. YEARS		216	159	12	9	1067.1	4653	1111	621	509	74	36	26	53	416	13	632	68	22	55	65	.458	1	0	4.29
2 Maj. YEARS		15	0	0	5	20	86	26	14	13	3	0	3	1	6	0	7	0	0	0	0	—	0	0	5.85

Cordell Farley

Bats: Right **Throws:** Right **Pos:** OF-76; PH-15; PR-10 **Ht:** 6'0" **Wt:** 185 **Born:** 3/29/73 **Age:** 28

Year Team	Lg Org	G	AB	H	2B	3B	HR	TB	R	RBI	TBB	IBB	SO	HBP	SH	SF	SB	CS	SB%	GDP	Avg	OBP	SLG
1996 Johnson Cty	R+ StL	15	63	18	4	3	0	28	17	9	4	0	20	1	0	0	2	2	.50	1	.286	.338	.444
Peoria	A StL	29	82	19	1	1	0	22	10	7	4	0	23	0	0	0	1	4	.20	3	.232	.267	.268
St. Pete	A+ StL	5	4	0	0	0	0	0	1	0	1	0	1	1	0	0	0	0	—	0	.000	.333	.000
1997 New Jersey	A- StL	6	19	7	0	0	0	7	6	1	2	0	6	1	0	0	1	0	1.00	0	.368	.455	.368
Pr William	A+ StL	61	211	55	9	3	3	79	34	32	15	1	46	1	3	1	24	7	.77	2	.261	.311	.374
1998 Pr William	A+ StL	134	546	159	28	11	11	242	92	59	27	1	145	7	4	0	50	17	.75	4	.291	.333	.443
1999 Arkansas	AA StL	122	421	109	16	8	8	165	43	41	19	0	97	2	5	3	24	16	.60	3	.259	.292	.392
2000 Arkansas	AA StL	96	249	57	7	1	7	87	37	24	22	0	76	3	5	1	17	8	.68	1	.229	.298	.349
5 Min. YEARS		468	1595	424	65	27	29	630	240	173	94	2	414	16	17	5	119	54	.69	14	.266	.312	.395

Jeff Farnsworth

Pitches: Right **Bats:** Right **Pos:** RP-31; SP-8 **Ht:** 6'2" **Wt:** 190 **Born:** 10/6/75 **Age:** 25

Year Team	Lg Org	G	GS	CG	GF	IP	BFP	H	R	ER	HR	SH	SF	HB	TBB	IBB	SO	WP	Bk	W	L	Pct.	ShO	Sv	ERA
1996 Everett	A- Sea	10	7	0	1	39.1	158	33	19	18	4	0	1	0	13	0	42	6	5	3	3	.500	0	0	4.12
1997 Lancaster	A+ Sea	5	5	0	0	20.2	93	24	20	16	2	1	1	3	8	0	18	2	0	1	1	.500	0	0	6.97
1999 Lancaster	A+ Sea	26	9	0	6	72	351	91	61	52	7	1	10	15	43	1	43	10	0	3	6	.333	0	3	6.50
2000 New Haven	AA Sea	39	8	0	6	101.1	414	91	40	39	6	2	2	9	25	1	70	3	1	9	3	.750	0	2	3.46
4 Min. YEARS		80	29	0	13	233.1	1016	239	140	125	19	4	14	27	89	2	173	21	6	16	13	.552	0	5	4.82

Pedro Feliciano

Pitches: Left **Bats:** Left **Pos:** RP-33; SP-2 **Ht:** 5'11" **Wt:** 165 **Born:** 8/25/76 **Age:** 24

Year Team	Lg Org	G	GS	CG	GF	IP	BFP	H	R	ER	HR	SH	SF	HB	TBB	IBB	SO	WP	Bk	W	L	Pct.	ShO	Sv	ERA
1995 Great Falls	R+ LA	6	0	0	3	6.2	43	12	12	11	0	0	0	0	7	1	9	4	2	0	0	—	0	0	13.50
1996 Great Falls	R+ LA	22	1	0	10	41	206	50	36	26	1	0	5	3	26	2	39	4	3	2	3	.400	0	0	5.71
1997 Savannah	A LA	36	9	1	8	105.2	437	90	45	31	11	3	3	1	39	0	94	6	4	3	7	.300	0	4	2.64
Vero Beach	A+ LA	1	0	0	0	2	7	3	1	1	0	0	0	0	0	0	0	1	0	0	0	—	0	0	4.50
1998 Vero Beach	A+ LA	22	10	0	8	68.1	300	68	44	35	8	0	1	2	30	1	51	2	0	2	5	.286	0	2	4.61
2000 Vero Beach	A+ LA	25	2	0	7	61.1	289	76	31	26	4	4	5	2	24	1	48	3	0	4	5	.444	0	2	3.82
San Antonio	AA LA	9	0	0	3	9.1	37	7	2	2	0	0	1	0	8	1	11	0	0	0	0	—	0	0	1.93
Albuquerque	AAA LA	1	0	0	1	1	9	3	3	2	0	0	0	0	1	0	2	0	0	0	0	—	0	0	18.00
5 Min. YEARS		122	22	1	40	295.1	1328	309	174	133	27	8	13	12	131	6	255	19	11	11	20	.355	0	11	4.05

Jeff Ferguson

Bats: Right **Throws:** Right **Pos:** 2B-27; 3B-14; DH-14; SS-13; OF-11; PH-7; PR-5   **Ht:** 5'10" **Wt:** 184 **Born:** 6/18/73 **Age:** 28

Year	Team	Lg Org	G	AB	H	2B	3B	HR	TB	R	RBI	TBB	IBB	SO	HBP	SH	SF	SB	CS	SB%	GDP	Avg	OBP	SLG
1994	Fort Wayne	A Min	22	89	23	7	1	1	35	15	6	11	0	18	1	0	0	4	1	.80	1	.258	.347	.393
1996	Hardware Cy	AA Min	89	284	81	16	2	5	116	46	20	37	2	67	3	0	1	5	4	.56	2	.285	.372	.408
1997	New Britain	AA Min	36	135	33	4	0	1	40	19	21	12	0	31	1	1	1	1	1	.50	2	.244	.309	.296
	Salt Lake	AAA Min	65	241	68	19	2	8	115	51	35	24	0	48	6	1	1	4	2	.67	5	.282	.360	.477
1998	Salt Lake	AAA Min	81	223	46	6	1	3	63	35	20	24	0	42	13	3	0	7	2	.78	7	.206	.319	.283
1999	Salt Lake	AAA Min	95	298	79	16	2	4	111	44	48	28	0	39	8	5	3	7	5	.58	12	.265	.341	.372
2000	Salt Lake	AAA Min	78	235	57	14	2	2	81	46	31	29	0	51	4	4	2	4	0	1.00	5	.243	.333	.345
6	Min. YEARS		466	1505	387	82	10	24	561	256	181	165	2	296	36	14	8	32	15	.68	34	.257	.343	.373

Alex Fernandez

Bats: Left **Throws:** Left **Pos:** OF-87; DH-10; PH-5; PR-2   **Ht:** 6'1" **Wt:** 205 **Born:** 5/15/81 **Age:** 20

Year	Team	Lg Org	G	AB	H	2B	3B	HR	TB	R	RBI	TBB	IBB	SO	HBP	SH	SF	SB	CS	SB%	GDP	Avg	OBP	SLG
1998	Mariners	R Sea	44	151	50	11	6	5	88	25	31	9	3	23	1	0	2	3	1	.75	3	.331	.368	.583
1999	Lancaster	A+ Sea	118	426	120	29	2	14	195	63	62	21	1	83	4	5	2	21	11	.66	13	.282	.320	.458
2000	New Haven	AA Sea	101	350	89	22	1	4	125	32	40	11	1	51	1	1	2	10	4	.71	9	.254	.277	.357
3	Min. YEARS		263	927	259	62	9	23	408	120	133	41	5	157	6	6	6	34	16	.68	25	.279	.312	.440

Jared Fernandez

Pitches: Right **Bats:** Right **Pos:** RP-22; SP-9   **Ht:** 6'2" **Wt:** 223 **Born:** 2/2/72 **Age:** 29

Year	Team	Lg Org	G	GS	CG	GF	IP	BFP	H	R	ER	HR	SH	SF	HB	TBB	IBB	SO	WP	Bk	W	L	Pct.	ShO	Sv	ERA
1994	Utica	A- Bos	21	1	0	15	30	144	43	18	12	4	0	0	8	8	2	24	0	1	1	1	.500	0	4	3.60
1995	Utica	A- Bos	5	5	1	0	38	148	30	11	8	2	0	1	1	9	1	23	1	0	3	2	.600	0	0	1.89
	Trenton	AA Bos	11	10	1	0	67	290	64	32	29	4	3	1	5	28	1	42	0	2	5	4	.556	0	0	3.90
1996	Trenton	AA Bos	30	29	3	0	179	798	185	115	101	19	5	9	10	83	5	94	10	0	9	9	.500	0	0	5.08
1997	Pawtucket	AAA Bos	11	11	0	0	60.2	281	76	45	39	7	2	2	5	28	1	33	4	0	0	3	.000	0	0	5.79
	Trenton	AA Bos	21	16	1	4	121.1	560	138	90	73	12	2	2	0	66	0	73	14	0	4	6	.400	0	0	5.41
1998	Trenton	AA Bos	36	7	0	10	118.1	527	132	80	69	8	8	3	3	51	3	70	15	1	3	7	.300	0	1	5.25
	Pawtucket	AAA Bos	5	2	0	2	24.2	107	26	16	13	5	0	2	3	7	0	15	4	0	1	1	.500	0	0	4.74
1999	Trenton	AA Bos	7	0	0	4	18.2	80	18	9	7	4	0	0	0	8	0	10	1	0	3	0	1.000	0	1	3.38
	Pawtucket	AAA Bos	27	20	3	2	163.1	687	172	88	77	20	7	5	5	39	0	76	3	1	12	9	.571	0	0	4.24
2000	Pawtucket	AAA Bos	31	9	2	17	113.1	464	103	51	38	10	4	4	5	36	0	65	11	1	10	4	.714	0	4	3.02
7	Min. YEARS		205	110	11	54	934.1	4086	987	555	466	95	31	29	37	363	13	523	65	4	51	46	.526	0	10	4.49

Jose Fernandez

Bats: Right **Throws:** Right **Pos:** 3B-123; PH-8; 1B-4; 2B-1; DH-1   **Ht:** 6'3" **Wt:** 220 **Born:** 11/2/74 **Age:** 26

Year	Team	Lg Org	G	AB	H	2B	3B	HR	TB	R	RBI	TBB	IBB	SO	HBP	SH	SF	SB	CS	SB%	GDP	Avg	OBP	SLG
1994	Expos	R Mon	44	168	39	8	0	5	62	27	23	13	0	33	2	0	1	11	1	.92	2	.232	.293	.369
1995	Vermont	A- Mon	66	270	74	6	7	4	106	38	41	13	2	51	1	1	2	29	4	.88	2	.274	.308	.393
1996	Delmarva	A Mon	126	421	115	23	6	12	186	72	70	50	5	76	7	0	3	23	13	.64	5	.273	.358	.442
1997	Wst Plm Bch	A+ Mon	97	350	108	21	3	9	162	49	58	37	3	76	7	0	0	22	14	.61	8	.309	.386	.463
	Harrisburg	AA Mon	29	96	22	3	1	4	39	10	11	11	0	28	1	0	0	2	0	1.00	4	.229	.315	.406
1998	Harrisburg	AA Mon	104	369	109	27	1	17	189	59	58	36	3	73	9	1	5	16	6	.73	8	.295	.368	.512
	Ottawa	AAA Mon	21	60	16	4	1	0	22	8	4	5	0	14	0	1	1	3	1	.75	2	.267	.318	.367
1999	Ottawa	AAA Mon	124	465	126	30	2	14	202	73	68	31	0	136	5	1	3	14	7	.67	11	.271	.321	.434
2000	Indianapols	AAA Mil	133	468	134	37	4	11	212	70	68	49	0	93	6	1	6	10	3	.77	11	.286	.357	.453
1999	Montreal	NL	8	24	5	2	0	0	7	0	1	1	0	7	0	0	0	0	0	—	1	.208	.240	.292
7	Min. YEARS		744	2667	743	159	25	76	1180	406	401	245	13	580	38	5	21	130	49	.73	48	.279	.345	.442

Sean Fesh

Pitches: Left **Bats:** Left **Pos:** RP-45   **Ht:** 6'2" **Wt:** 165 **Born:** 11/3/72 **Age:** 28

Year	Team	Lg Org	G	GS	CG	GF	IP	BFP	H	R	ER	HR	SH	SF	HB	TBB	IBB	SO	WP	Bk	W	L	Pct.	ShO	Sv	ERA
1991	Astros	R Hou	6	0	0	2	12.1	53	5	4	3	0	0	0	0	11	0	7	4	0	0	0	—	0	0	2.19
1992	Osceola	A+ Hou	3	0	0	2	5.1	24	5	3	1	0	0	0	0	1	0	5	3	0	1	0	1.000	0	0	1.69
	Astros	R Hou	18	0	0	12	36.1	142	25	7	7	0	3	0	4	8	0	35	4	0	1	0	1.000	0	0	1.73
1993	Asheville	A Hou	65	0	0	58	82.1	353	75	39	33	4	11	6	5	37	8	49	4	1	10	6	.625	0	20	3.61
1994	Osceola	A+ Hou	43	0	0	29	49.2	222	50	27	14	2	5	0	6	24	6	32	2	0	2	4	.333	0	11	2.54
	Jackson	AA Hou	20	1	0	5	25.2	122	34	17	12	2	2	1	0	11	0	19	2	0	1	2	.333	0	0	4.21
1995	Tucson	AAA Hou	10	0	0	1	13.1	52	11	2	2	0	0	0	0	3	0	7	0	0	1	0	1.000	0	0	1.35
	Las Vegas	AAA SD	30	0	0	11	38	185	53	21	14	2	4	0	3	16	5	18	1	1	2	1	.667	0	1	3.32
1996	Memphis	AA SD	7	0	0	2	8	36	7	5	5	2	0	0	0	7	1	5	0	0	1	1	.500	0	0	5.63
1997	Rancho Cuca	A+ SD	4	0	0	1	4.2	28	10	7	6	2	1	0	1	3	0	5	0	0	0	1	.000	0	0	11.57
	Binghamton	AA NYM	45	0	0	13	55.1	255	60	26	20	0	1	2	4	24	0	37	2	3	3	1	.750	0	4	3.25
1998	Scranton-WB	AAA Phi	8	0	0	1	6	25	3	2	2	0	0	0	0	4	1	4	0	0	0	0	—	0	0	3.00
	Reading	AA Phi	31	0	0	23	33	140	19	8	5	1	1	5	0	19	1	41	1	0	3	1	.750	0	4	1.36
1999	Scranton-WB	AAA Phi	45	0	0	16	53.1	235	50	29	26	5	4	1	0	31	5	38	0	4	4	3	.571	0	1	4.39
2000	Scranton-WB	AAA Phi	37	0	0	10	55	245	46	22	20	0	6	0	4	38	5	44	2	0	0	2	.000	0	2	3.27
	Colo Sprngs	AAA Col	8	0	0	1	7.1	39	11	7	7	0	0	1	1	5	0	4	0	0	0	0	—	0	0	8.59
10	Min. YEARS		380	1	0	187	485.2	2156	464	226	177	23	37	11	32	242	32	350	29	7	28	24	.538	0	54	3.28

Mike Figga

Bats: Right **Throws:** Right **Pos:** C-43; DH-15; 1B-5; PH-5; OF-4; PR-1   **Ht:** 6'0" **Wt:** 200 **Born:** 7/31/70 **Age:** 30

Year Team	Lg Org	G	AB	H	2B	3B	HR	TB	R	RBI	TBB	IBB	SO	HBP	SH	SF	SB	CS	SB%	GDP	Avg	OBP	SLG
1990 Yankees	R NYY	40	123	35	1	1	2	44	19	18	17	2	33	1	0	1	4	2	.67	2	.285	.373	.358
1991 Pr William	A+ NYY	55	174	34	6	0	3	49	15	17	19	0	51	0	2	1	2	1	.67	9	.195	.273	.282
1992 Pr William	A+ NYY	3	10	2	1	0	0	3	0	0	2	0	3	0	0	0	1	0	1.00	0	.200	.333	.300
Ft. Laud	A+ NYY	80	249	44	13	0	1	60	12	15	13	1	78	2	3	0	3	1	.75	7	.177	.223	.241
1993 San Berndno	A+ NYY	83	308	82	17	1	25	176	48	71	17	0	84	2	2	3	2	3	.40	7	.266	.306	.571
Albany-Col	AA NYY	6	22	5	0	0	0	5	3	2	2	0	9	0	0	0	1	0	1.00	0	.227	.292	.227
1994 Albany-Col	AA NYY	1	2	1	1	0	0	2	1	0	0	0	1	0	0	0	0	0	—	0	.500	.500	1.000
Tampa	A+ NYY	111	420	116	17	5	15	188	48	75	22	1	94	2	1	5	3	0	1.00	12	.276	.312	.448
1995 Norwich	AA NYY	109	399	108	22	4	13	177	59	61	43	3	90	1	2	6	1	0	1.00	10	.271	.339	.444
Columbus	AAA NYY	8	25	7	1	0	1	11	2	3	3	0	5	0	1	0	0	0	—	0	.280	.357	.440
1996 Columbus	AAA NYY	4	11	3	1	0	0	4	3	0	1	0	3	0	0	0	0	0	—	0	.273	.333	.364
1997 Columbus	AAA NYY	110	390	95	14	4	12	153	48	54	18	0	104	2	1	3	3	3	.50	9	.244	.278	.392
1998 Columbus	AAA NYY	123	461	129	30	3	26	243	57	95	35	4	109	2	0	1	2	2	.50	15	.280	.333	.527
2000 Trenton	AA Bos	8	27	5	0	0	1	8	1	2	2	0	8	0	0	0	0	0	—	0	.185	.241	.296
Pawtucket	AAA Bos	2	8	0	0	0	0	0	0	0	1	0	2	0	0	0	0	0	—	0	.000	.111	.000
San Antonio	AA LA	43	148	35	5	0	8	64	16	21	12	0	37	1	0	0	0	0	—	5	.236	.298	.432
Albuquerque	AAA LA	15	35	13	4	0	0	17	10	8	2	0	12	0	0	1	0	0	—	2	.371	.395	.486
1997 New York	AL	2	4	0	0	0	0	0	0	0	0	0	3	0	0	0	0	0	—	0	.000	.000	.000
1998 New York	AL	1	4	1	0	0	0	1	1	0	0	0	1	0	0	0	0	0	—	0	.250	.250	.250
1999 New York	AL	2	0	0	0	0	0	0	0	0	0	0	0	0	0	0	0	0	—	0	—	—	—
Baltimore	AL	41	86	19	4	0	1	26	12	5	2	0	27	0	2	1	0	2	.00	1	.221	.236	.302
10 Min. YEARS		801	2812	714	133	18	107	1204	342	442	209	11	723	13	12	21	22	12	.65	78	.254	.306	.428
3 Maj. YEARS		46	94	20	4	0	1	27	13	5	2	0	31	0	2	1	0	2	.00	1	.213	.227	.287

Eduardo Figueroa

Bats: Right **Throws:** Right **Pos:** OF-50; 1B-1; DH-1   **Ht:** 6'2" **Wt:** 164 **Born:** 6/4/82 **Age:** 19

Year Team	Lg Org	G	AB	H	2B	3B	HR	TB	R	RBI	TBB	IBB	SO	HBP	SH	SF	SB	CS	SB%	GDP	Avg	OBP	SLG
2000 Mariners	R Sea	48	179	54	8	3	7	89	47	33	21	1	37	6	3	3	7	1	.88	1	.302	.388	.497
Tacoma	AAA Sea	4	13	1	0	0	0	1	0	1	0	0	2	0	0	0	0	0	—	0	.077	.077	.077
1 Min. YEARS		52	192	55	8	3	7	90	47	34	21	1	39	6	3	3	7	1	.88	1	.286	.369	.469

Juan Figueroa

Pitches: Right **Bats:** Right **Pos:** SP-23; RP-3   **Ht:** 6'3" **Wt:** 150 **Born:** 6/24/79 **Age:** 22

Year Team	Lg Org	G	GS	CG	GF	IP	BFP	H	R	ER	HR	SH	SF	HB	TBB	IBB	SO	WP	Bk	W	L	Pct.	ShO	Sv	ERA
1997 White Sox	R CWS	11	10	0	0	64.1	274	66	31	24	4	0	3	7	14	0	43	1	0	1	4	.200	0	0	3.36
1998 Bristol	R+ CWS	13	13	2	0	80	353	87	58	45	14	2	3	4	22	0	102	4	1	5	5	.500	1	0	5.06
1999 Burlington	A CWS	17	16	2	0	115.1	491	100	51	40	8	0	6	5	44	0	139	4	1	8	4	.667	0	0	3.12
Winston-Sal	A+ CWS	10	10	1	0	56.1	252	67	47	33	2	3	2	2	19	0	50	3	0	2	5	.286	0	0	5.27
2000 Winston-Sal	A+ CWS	9	7	1	2	52	224	58	30	27	3	3	1	3	8	0	65	3	0	4	4	.500	0	0	4.67
Birmingham	AA CWS	10	9	0	0	55.2	241	57	25	21	4	1	3	6	24	0	42	3	1	2	3	.400	0	0	3.40
Bowie	AA Bal	7	7	0	0	39	183	46	24	24	3	2	2	2	21	2	42	3	0	2	2	.500	0	0	5.54
4 Min. YEARS		77	72	6	2	462.2	2018	481	266	214	38	11	20	29	152	2	483	21	3	24	27	.471	1	0	4.16

Luis Figueroa

Bats: Right **Throws:** Right **Pos:** 3B-115; DH-2   **Ht:** 6'0" **Wt:** 175 **Born:** 3/2/77 **Age:** 24

Year Team	Lg Org	G	AB	H	2B	3B	HR	TB	R	RBI	TBB	IBB	SO	HBP	SH	SF	SB	CS	SB%	GDP	Avg	OBP	SLG
1995 Mariners	R Sea	32	120	35	2	0	0	37	14	11	12	0	9	2	0	1	1	2	.33	4	.292	.363	.308
1996 Lancaster	A+ Sea	9	31	12	4	1	0	18	5	6	2	0	6	0	0	0	0	1	.00	0	.387	.424	.581
Everett	A- Sea	4	13	6	1	1	0	9	4	3	2	0	1	0	0	0	0	0	—	1	.462	.533	.692
Wisconsin	A Sea	36	137	40	9	0	2	55	18	19	6	0	14	3	1	2	1	1	.50	6	.292	.331	.401
1997 Wisconsin	A Sea	125	482	138	27	2	3	178	56	60	33	1	21	6	2	1	3	3	.50	18	.286	.339	.369
1998 Wisconsin	A Sea	96	306	89	18	0	1	110	41	48	42	5	18	8	0	1	7	1	.88	13	.291	.389	.359
1999 Lancaster	A+ Sea	39	146	52	8	1	4	74	21	20	18	2	8	2	0	2	2	2	.50	10	.356	.429	.507
Mariners	R Sea	3	10	5	1	0	0	6	2	1	0	0	0	0	0	0	0	0	—	1	.500	.500	.600
2000 New Haven	AA Sea	117	427	116	24	1	1	145	49	37	34	1	39	2	2	2	0	1	.00	14	.272	.327	.340
6 Min. YEARS		461	1672	493	94	6	11	632	210	205	149	9	116	23	5	9	14	11	.56	67	.295	.359	.378

Luis Figueroa

Bats: Both **Throws:** Right **Pos:** SS-105; PH-9; 2B-6; 3B-1; PR-1   **Ht:** 5'9" **Wt:** 144 **Born:** 2/16/74 **Age:** 27

Year Team	Lg Org	G	AB	H	2B	3B	HR	TB	R	RBI	TBB	IBB	SO	HBP	SH	SF	SB	CS	SB%	GDP	Avg	OBP	SLG
1997 Augusta	A Pit	71	248	56	8	0	0	64	38	21	35	0	29	1	9	2	22	6	.79	5	.226	.322	.258
Lynchburg	A+ Pit	26	89	25	5	0	0	30	12	2	7	0	6	0	0	0	1	2	.33	5	.281	.333	.337
1998 Carolina	AA Pit	117	350	87	9	3	0	102	54	24	71	3	46	2	10	2	6	5	.55	12	.249	.376	.291
1999 Altoona	AA Pit	131	418	110	15	5	3	144	61	50	52	0	44	3	16	3	9	9	.50	7	.263	.347	.344
2000 Altoona	AA Pit	94	342	97	10	4	1	118	45	28	37	1	32	2	10	1	14	5	.74	8	.284	.356	.345
Nashville	AAA Pit	23	64	16	1	0	3	26	6	8	1	0	8	0	0	0	2	1	.67	2	.250	.262	.406
4 Min. YEARS		462	1511	391	48	12	7	484	216	133	203	4	165	8	45	8	54	28	.66	36	.259	.348	.320

Bob File

Pitches: Right **Bats:** Right **Pos:** RP-56   **Ht:** 6'4" **Wt:** 215 **Born:** 1/28/77 **Age:** 24

Year Team	Lg Org	G	GS	CG	GF	IP	BFP	H	R	ER	HR	SH	SF	HB	TBB	IBB	SO	WP	Bk	W	L	Pct.	ShO	Sv	ERA
1998 Medcine Hat	R+ Tor	28	0	0	26	32	124	24	7	5	1	1	2	2	5	0	28	1	0	2	1	.667	0	16	1.41
1999 Dunedin	A+ Tor	47	0	0	42	53	203	30	13	10	2	3	0	4	14	0	48	1	1	4	1	.800	0	26	1.70
2000 Tennessee	AA Tor	36	0	0	32	34.2	153	29	20	12	1	2	1	2	13	0	40	0	1	4	3	.571	0	20	3.12
Syracuse	AAA Tor	20	0	0	11	19.1	69	14	2	2	1	0	0	1	2	0	10	0	0	2	0	1.000	0	8	0.93
3 Min. YEARS		131	0	0	111	139	549	97	42	29	5	6	3	9	34	0	126	2	2	12	5	.706	0	70	1.88

Mark Fischer

Bats: Right **Throws:** Right **Pos:** OF-52; DH-29; PH-5; PR-2   **Ht:** 6'1" **Wt:** 205 **Born:** 4/15/76 **Age:** 25

Year Team	Lg Org	G	AB	H	2B	3B	HR	TB	R	RBI	TBB	IBB	SO	HBP	SH	SF	SB	CS	SB%	GDP	Avg	OBP	SLG
1997 Lowell	A- Bos	48	179	59	15	1	5	91	25	25	15	0	38	3	0	1	13	2	.87	4	.330	.389	.508
1998 Red Sox	R Bos	7	26	5	0	0	2	11	5	5	4	1	8	0	1	0	2	0	1.00	5	.192	.300	.423
Michigan	A Bos	102	379	96	19	2	8	143	52	50	36	2	93	1	0	3	9	6	.60	5	.253	.317	.377
1999 Sarasota	A+ Bos	106	359	91	14	3	5	126	42	40	28	0	85	1	4	1	11	6	.65	11	.253	.308	.351
2000 Sarasota	A+ Bos	51	180	54	15	0	9	96	31	30	21	1	45	1	0	2	5	2	.71	1	.300	.373	.533
Trenton	AA Bos	34	108	22	6	1	1	33	15	15	12	0	39	1	0	4	1	1	.50	1	.204	.280	.306
4 Min. YEARS		348	1231	327	69	7	30	500	170	165	116	4	308	7	4	11	41	17	.71	22	.266	.330	.406

Steve Fish

Pitches: Right **Bats:** Right **Pos:** RP-17; SP-7   **Ht:** 6'1" **Wt:** 190 **Born:** 10/25/74 **Age:** 26

Year Team	Lg Org	G	GS	CG	GF	IP	BFP	H	R	ER	HR	SH	SF	HB	TBB	IBB	SO	WP	Bk	W	L	Pct.	ShO	Sv	ERA
1997 Boise	A- Ana	24	4	0	2	75	314	69	41	34	4	6	3	3	23	3	79	5	0	5	2	.714	0	4	4.08
1998 Cedar Rapds	A Ana	30	14	3	4	127.2	516	111	52	35	7	2	4	3	28	0	121	5	1	10	4	.714	1	0	2.47
1999 Lk Elsinore	A+ Ana	32	29	5	0	196.2	876	220	125	107	17	0	8	10	72	3	180	15	2	11	11	.500	2	0	4.90
2000 Erie	AA Ana	24	7	0	2	62	287	76	47	46	7	0	2	6	29	1	44	3	0	2	5	.286	0	0	6.68
4 Min. YEARS		110	54	8	8	461.1	1993	476	265	222	35	8	17	22	152	7	424	28	3	28	22	.560	3	0	4.33

Louis Fisher

Pitches: Right **Bats:** Right **Pos:** RP-4   **Ht:** 6'0" **Wt:** 200 **Born:** 10/14/76 **Age:** 24

Year Team	Lg Org	G	GS	CG	GF	IP	BFP	H	R	ER	HR	SH	SF	HB	TBB	IBB	SO	WP	Bk	W	L	Pct.	ShO	Sv	ERA
1995 Orioles	R Bal	9	7	2	0	39	167	27	23	8	0	0	3	0	24	0	29	4	2	4	3	.571	1	0	1.85
1996 Bluefield	R+ Bal	14	13	1	0	71.2	318	58	43	35	2	0	1	2	48	0	52	15	1	3	4	.429	1	0	4.40
1997 Williamsprt	A- ChC	11	9	0	0	40.1	188	41	27	21	2	0	0	2	32	0	31	8	0	1	3	.250	0	0	4.69
1998 Daytona	A+ ChC	49	1	0	14	65.2	283	50	40	34	4	5	6	5	38	2	54	11	0	3	4	.429	0	1	4.66
1999 Daytona	A+ ChC	40	0	0	21	69.2	321	63	59	43	5	3	1	2	50	2	64	13	0	3	8	.273	0	9	5.56
2000 West Tenn	AA ChC	4	0	0	0	6.2	31	7	6	5	2	0	1	0	5	0	5	0	0	1	0	1.000	0	0	6.75
6 Min. YEARS		127	30	3	35	293	1308	246	198	146	15	8	12	11	197	4	235	51	3	15	22	.405	2	10	4.48

Pete Fisher

Pitches: Right **Bats:** Right **Pos:** SP-26; RP-3   **Ht:** 6'3" **Wt:** 219 **Born:** 7/7/77 **Age:** 23

Year Team	Lg Org	G	GS	CG	GF	IP	BFP	H	R	ER	HR	SH	SF	HB	TBB	IBB	SO	WP	Bk	W	L	Pct.	ShO	Sv	ERA
1998 Elizabethtn	R+ Min	12	12	0	0	66.1	290	82	43	38	9	5	1	3	9	0	57	2	2	5	3	.625	0	0	5.16
1999 Fort Myers	A+ Min	25	24	0	0	146.2	639	171	74	61	10	3	6	9	38	0	91	14	3	5	10	.333	0	0	3.74
2000 New Britain	AA Min	15	12	0	2	60.2	286	89	55	45	4	1	3	5	14	0	36	2	1	2	5	.286	0	0	6.68
Fort Myers	A+ Min	14	14	2	0	88.2	370	75	34	31	9	3	0	7	37	0	67	2	0	8	3	.727	0	0	3.15
3 Min. YEARS		66	62	2	2	362.1	1585	417	206	175	32	12	10	24	98	0	251	20	6	20	21	.488	0	0	4.35

Brian Fitzgerald

Pitches: Left **Bats:** Left **Pos:** RP-42; SP-2   **Ht:** 5'11" **Wt:** 175 **Born:** 12/26/74 **Age:** 26

Year Team	Lg Org	G	GS	CG	GF	IP	BFP	H	R	ER	HR	SH	SF	HB	TBB	IBB	SO	WP	Bk	W	L	Pct.	ShO	Sv	ERA
1996 Everett	A- Sea	29	1	0	8	39	181	56	36	28	2	1	1	0	8	0	31	1	2	1	2	.333	0	1	6.46
1997 Wisconsin	A Sea	41	1	0	28	69.2	281	63	16	15	4	1	0	0	19	2	68	2	1	3	1	.750	0	10	1.94
1998 Lancaster	A+ Sea	41	0	0	18	70.2	315	79	39	33	5	2	1	2	24	2	48	1	0	1	2	.333	0	1	4.20
Orlando	AA Sea	2	0	0	1	4.1	18	5	1	1	0	0	0	0	1	0	4	0	0	0	0	—	0	1	2.08
1999 Lancaster	A+ Sea	6	6	0	0	34	153	50	35	27	3	0	2	0	4	0	23	1	0	1	3	.250	0	0	7.15
New Haven	AA Sea	29	1	0	13	54	228	58	24	23	2	2	2	1	18	0	37	0	0	2	2	.500	0	3	3.83
2000 New Haven	AA Sea	44	0	0	18	79	331	84	33	31	7	1	1	3	19	0	62	1	1	6	4	.600	0	4	3.53
5 Min. YEARS		184	10	0	86	350.2	1507	395	184	158	23	7	7	6	93	4	273	6	4	14	14	.500	0	20	4.06

Jason Fitzgerald

Bats: Left **Throws:** Left **Pos:** OF-121; DH-17; PH-2; PR-1   **Ht:** 6'1" **Wt:** 190 **Born:** 9/16/75 **Age:** 25

Year Team	Lg Org	G	AB	H	2B	3B	HR	TB	R	RBI	TBB	IBB	SO	HBP	SH	SF	SB	CS	SB%	GDP	Avg	OBP	SLG
1997 Watertown	A- Cle	34	112	22	8	0	1	33	11	13	17	0	31	0	1	2	2	0	1.00	4	.196	.298	.295
1998 Columbus	A Cle	132	490	134	28	3	16	216	60	80	38	1	117	4	1	9	21	6	.78	4	.273	.325	.441
1999 Kinston	A+ Cle	82	310	74	17	3	4	109	26	39	22	1	77	1	1	3	15	7	.68	5	.239	.289	.352
2000 Kinston	A+ Cle	82	318	80	16	3	4	114	42	44	29	2	55	2	1	4	21	4	.84	3	.252	.314	.358
Akron	AA Cle	56	208	58	8	4	4	86	27	30	23	1	38	1	1	2	7	6	.54	0	.279	.350	.413
4 Min. YEARS		386	1438	368	77	13	29	558	166	206	129	5	318	8	5	20	66	23	.74	13	.256	.317	.388

Jason Flach

Pitches: Right **Bats:** Right **Pos:** RP-19; SP-14   **Ht:** 6'0" **Wt:** 165 **Born:** 11/25/73 **Age:** 27

		HOW MUCH HE PITCHED						WHAT HE GAVE UP											THE RESULTS					
Year Team	Lg Org	G	GS	CG	GF	IP	BFP	H	R	ER	HR	SH	SF	HB	TBB	IBB	SO	WP	Bk	W	L	Pct.	ShO	Sv	ERA
1996 Eugene	A- Atl	27	0	0	14	59.2	238	45	18	15	2	3	1	1	17	1	68	2	0	4	1	.800	0	11	2.26
1997 Eugene	A- Atl	23	0	0	18	39.1	180	40	18	13	2	4	1	1	24	5	51	2	0	4	3	.571	0	5	2.97
1998 Danville	A+ Atl	37	11	0	7	106	453	110	43	37	5	6	4	6	31	4	108	6	0	5	5	.500	0	1	3.14
Greenville	AA Atl	1	0	0	0	1.1	7	3	0	0	0	0	0	0	0	0	4	0	0	0	0	—	0	0	0.00
1999 Myrtle Bch	A+ Atl	24	14	0	4	108.1	460	101	50	37	8	5	2	3	37	1	63	3	0	9	4	.692	0	2	3.07
Greenville	AA Atl	12	2	0	4	36.2	163	44	29	27	4	3	3	3	10	0	15	1	0	1	2	.333	0	1	6.63
2000 Greenville	AA Atl	28	13	0	3	95.2	399	95	47	46	12	6	3	3	30	2	64	4	0	4	6	.400	0	0	4.33
Richmond	AAA Atl	5	1	1	1	19.1	90	29	11	11	1	0	2	2	5	0	8	1	0	2	0	1.000	0	0	5.12
5 Min. YEARS		157	41	1	51	466.1	1990	467	216	186	34	27	16	19	154	13	381	19	0	29	21	.580	0	18	3.59

Tim Flaherty

Bats: Right **Throws:** Right **Pos:** 1B-83; DH-16; PH-11; OF-2; 3B-1   **Ht:** 6'4" **Wt:** 220 **Born:** 7/11/76 **Age:** 24

		BATTING														BASERUNNING				PERCENTAGES		
Year Team	Lg Org	G	AB	H	2B	3B	HR	TB	R	RBI	TBB	IBB	SO	HBP	SH	SF	SB	CS	SB%	GDP	Avg	OBP	SLG
1997 Salem-Keizr	A- SF	32	110	25	6	0	4	43	16	17	15	0	44	1	1	2	1	0	1.00	1	.227	.320	.391
1998 Bakersfield	A+ SF	124	478	112	27	0	24	211	72	90	41	1	171	7	0	5	0	0	—	6	.234	.301	.441
1999 San Jose	A+ SF	132	490	131	33	3	25	245	82	88	69	3	168	9	0	5	11	3	.79	5	.267	.365	.500
2000 Shreveport	AA SF	92	264	54	13	0	8	91	29	34	31	3	97	9	3	2	8	2	.80	5	.205	.307	.345
Bakersfield	A+ SF	18	62	16	2	0	5	33	17	15	14	0	20	1	0	2	2	0	1.00	2	.258	.392	.532
4 Min. YEARS		398	1404	338	81	3	66	623	216	244	170	7	500	27	4	16	22	5	.81	19	.241	.331	.444

Will Fleck

Pitches: Right **Bats:** Right **Pos:** RP-34   **Ht:** 6'0" **Wt:** 175 **Born:** 8/29/76 **Age:** 24

		HOW MUCH HE PITCHED						WHAT HE GAVE UP											THE RESULTS					
Year Team	Lg Org	G	GS	CG	GF	IP	BFP	H	R	ER	HR	SH	SF	HB	TBB	IBB	SO	WP	Bk	W	L	Pct.	ShO	Sv	ERA
1997 Danville	R+ Atl	23	0	0	18	35.1	158	36	17	14	2	1	1	1	17	3	56	3	1	2	3	.400	0	6	3.57
1998 Macon	A Atl	48	0	0	38	71.1	298	56	26	21	6	4	5	1	27	1	91	6	1	7	0	1.000	0	14	2.65
1999 Myrtle Bch	A+ Atl	40	0	0	17	75	342	67	56	54	14	5	1	3	52	3	72	9	0	10	10	.500	0	8	6.48
2000 Myrtle Bch	A+ Atl	1	0	0	1	2	8	1	2	2	1	0	0	0	1	0	2	0	0	0	0	—	0	0	9.00
Greenville	AA Atl	2	0	0	1	2	15	6	6	6	1	0	0	0	3	1	2	0	0	0	0	—	0	0	27.00
Allentown	IND —	31	0	0	28	34.1	149	27	13	13	3	2	1	3	19	4	48	5	0	2	2	.500	0	14	3.41
4 Min. YEARS		145	0	0	103	220	970	193	120	110	27	12	8	8	119	12	271	23	2	21	15	.583	0	34	4.50

Ryan Fleming

Bats: Left **Throws:** Left **Pos:** OF-123; PH-5; DH-3; PR-3   **Ht:** 5'11" **Wt:** 180 **Born:** 2/11/76 **Age:** 25

		BATTING														BASERUNNING				PERCENTAGES		
Year Team	Lg Org	G	AB	H	2B	3B	HR	TB	R	RBI	TBB	IBB	SO	HBP	SH	SF	SB	CS	SB%	GDP	Avg	OBP	SLG
1998 Medcine Hat	R+ Tor	70	255	78	20	1	2	106	64	41	37	0	29	4	2	4	17	3	.85	0	.306	.397	.416
1999 Dunedin	A+ Tor	51	123	28	7	1	0	37	17	9	10	1	19	4	3	1	4	3	.57	3	.228	.304	.301
Hagerstown	A Tor	61	227	76	9	2	4	101	34	35	23	1	26	0	2	4	7	6	.54	4	.335	.390	.445
2000 Syracuse	AAA Tor	3	11	2	0	0	0	2	1	1	0	0	0	0	0	0	0	0	—	0	.182	.182	.182
Dunedin	A+ Tor	90	309	94	18	1	4	126	42	32	28	1	38	1	6	5	6	8	.43	1	.304	.359	.408
Tennessee	AA Tor	37	105	18	4	0	2	28	16	9	20	0	17	1	3	0	2	1	.67	1	.171	.310	.267
3 Min. YEARS		312	1030	296	58	5	12	400	174	127	118	3	129	10	16	14	36	21	.63	9	.287	.362	.388

Huck Flener

Pitches: Left **Bats:** Both **Pos:** RP-15   **Ht:** 5'11" **Wt:** 180 **Born:** 2/25/69 **Age:** 32

		HOW MUCH HE PITCHED						WHAT HE GAVE UP											THE RESULTS					
Year Team	Lg Org	G	GS	CG	GF	IP	BFP	H	R	ER	HR	SH	SF	HB	TBB	IBB	SO	WP	Bk	W	L	Pct.	ShO	Sv	ERA
1990 St.Cathrnes	A- Tor	14	7	0	3	61.2	258	45	29	23	4	3	0	1	33	0	46	4	3	4	3	.571	0	1	3.36
1991 Myrtle Bch	A Tor	55	0	0	44	79.1	334	58	28	16	1	5	3	0	41	0	107	7	2	6	4	.600	0	13	1.82
1992 Dunedin	A+ Tor	41	8	0	19	112.1	451	70	35	28	4	5	2	7	50	2	93	2	1	7	3	.700	0	8	2.24
1993 Knoxville	AA Tor	38	16	2	10	136.1	556	130	56	50	9	6	4	3	39	1	114	9	8	13	6	.684	2	4	3.30
1994 Syracuse	AAA Tor	6	6	0	0	37	155	38	22	19	6	0	0	0	8	0	20	2	1	1	3	.000	0	0	4.62
1995 Syracuse	AAA Tor	30	23	1	3	134.2	572	131	70	59	20	1	6	6	41	2	83	2	2	6	11	.353	0	0	3.94
1996 Syracuse	AAA Tor	14	14	0	0	86.2	350	73	27	22	3	3	3	2	23	1	62	2	3	7	3	.700	0	0	2.28
1997 Syracuse	AAA Tor	20	20	1	0	124	524	126	71	57	14	3	3	2	43	1	58	6	2	6	6	.500	1	0	4.14
1998 Akron	AA Cle	12	10	3	1	73	289	57	18	15	2	2	0	3	22	0	51	5	3	3	3	.500	2	0	1.85
Buffalo	AAA Cle	14	8	0	3	60.2	278	73	52	45	12	3	1	0	26	1	35	2	0	7	3	.700	0	0	6.68
1999 Tacoma	AAA Sea	22	5	0	6	66	292	72	41	40	6	2	2	3	26	2	48	5	1	4	4	.500	0	1	5.45
2000 Mobile	AA SD	15	0	0	1	14	59	12	5	5	2	0	0	0	4	0	10	1	0	0	0	—	0	0	3.21
1993 Toronto	AL	6	0	0	1	6.2	30	7	3	3	0	0	0	0	4	1	2	1	0	0	0	—	0	0	4.05
1996 Toronto	AL	15	11	0	0	70.2	309	68	40	36	9	0	4	1	33	1	44	1	0	3	2	.600	0	0	4.58
1997 Toronto	AL	8	1	0	3	17.1	97	40	19	19	3	0	1	0	6	0	9	2	0	0	1	.000	0	0	9.87
11 Min. YEARS		281	117	7	90	985.2	4118	885	454	379	83	33	27	28	356	10	727	47	26	63	49	.563	5	27	3.46
3 Maj. YEARS		29	12	0	4	94.2	436	115	62	58	12	0	5	1	43	2	55	4	0	3	3	.500	0	0	5.51

Ignacio Flores

Pitches: Right **Bats:** Right **Pos:** RP-3; SP-2   **Ht:** 6'2" **Wt:** 180 **Born:** 5/8/75 **Age:** 26

		HOW MUCH HE PITCHED						WHAT HE GAVE UP											THE RESULTS					
Year Team	Lg Org	G	GS	CG	GF	IP	BFP	H	R	ER	HR	SH	SF	HB	TBB	IBB	SO	WP	Bk	W	L	Pct.	ShO	Sv	ERA
1995 Great Falls	R+ LA	16	12	0	1	68.2	301	66	42	36	3	0	1	4	38	0	76	4	2	6	4	.600	0	0	4.72
1997 San Antonio	AA LA	27	18	0	3	133	547	125	59	48	5	3	2	3	39	0	102	14	2	10	7	.588	0	1	3.25
1998 Albuquerque	AAA LA	17	17	0	0	88.2	415	113	72	70	16	0	3	1	48	1	63	10	0	4	10	.286	0	0	7.11
2000 San Antonio	AA LA	3	0	0	1	7	30	5	2	2	0	0	1	0	6	0	7	2	0	0	0	—	0	1	2.57
Albuquerque	AAA LA	2	2	0	0	8.1	43	10	9	7	1	0	0	0	9	0	5	0	0	0	2	.000	0	0	7.56
4 Min. YEARS		65	49	0	5	305.2	1336	319	184	163	25	3	7	8	140	1	253	30	4	20	23	.465	0	2	4.80

92

Javier Flores

Bats: Right Throws: Right Pos: C-60; SS-15; 1B-9; 2B-5; DH-2; PH-1   Ht: 6'0" Wt: 185 Born: 12/20/75 Age: 25

Year	Team	Lg Org	G	AB	H	2B	3B	HR	TB	R	RBI	TBB	IBB	SO	HBP	SH	SF	SB	CS	SB%	GDP	Avg	OBP	SLG
1997	Sou Oregon	A- Oak	45	160	53	11	3	1	73	25	25	17	0	22	9	1	3	2	1	.67	2	.331	.418	.456
1998	Visalia	A+ Oak	49	163	41	7	1	2	56	19	17	12	0	32	8	3	1	0	0	—	4	.252	.332	.344
1999	Visalia	A+ Oak	103	362	107	22	1	5	146	48	63	27	0	59	9	2	6	6	3	.67	8	.296	.354	.403
2000	Midland	AA Oak	12	33	8	4	0	0	12	3	4	5	0	5	0	1	0	0	0	—	0	.242	.342	.364
	Visalia	A+ Oak	77	257	66	9	1	4	89	35	41	33	1	34	4	1	4	2	3	.40	5	.257	.346	.346
4 Min. YEARS			286	975	275	53	6	12	376	130	150	94	1	152	30	8	14	10	7	.59	19	.282	.358	.386

Jose Flores

Bats: Right Throws: Right Pos: SS-71; 3B-24; 2B-7; DH-3; PH-2; PR-1   Ht: 5'11" Wt: 180 Born: 6/28/73 Age: 28

Year	Team	Lg Org	G	AB	H	2B	3B	HR	TB	R	RBI	TBB	IBB	SO	HBP	SH	SF	SB	CS	SB%	GDP	Avg	OBP	SLG
1994	Batavia	A- Phi	68	229	58	7	3	0	71	41	16	41	0	31	6	2	2	23	8	.74	3	.253	.378	.310
1995	Clearwater	A+ Phi	49	185	41	4	3	1	54	25	19	15	0	27	4	7	1	12	5	.71	4	.222	.293	.292
	Piedmont	A Phi	61	186	49	7	0	0	56	22	19	24	0	29	3	5	4	11	8	.58	6	.263	.350	.301
1996	Scranton-WB	AAA Phi	26	70	18	1	0	0	19	10	3	12	0	10	2	1	1	0	1	.00	2	.257	.376	.271
	Clearwater	A+ Phi	84	281	64	6	5	1	83	39	39	34	0	42	3	5	1	15	2	.88	6	.228	.317	.295
1997	Scranton-WB	AAA Phi	71	204	51	14	1	1	70	32	18	28	1	51	2	5	2	3	1	.75	2	.250	.343	.343
1998	Scranton-WB	AAA Phi	98	345	104	18	2	6	144	53	34	49	1	45	2	7	2	12	6	.67	7	.301	.389	.417
1999	Scranton-WB	AAA Phi	64	228	56	6	2	0	66	35	18	37	1	43	7	4	0	13	3	.81	1	.246	.368	.289
	Tacoma	AAA Sea	42	143	44	6	1	3	61	33	15	37	1	23	5	2	2	4	3	.57	2	.308	.460	.427
2000	New Haven	AA Sea	12	38	7	3	0	0	10	5	1	7	0	5	2	1	0	0	0	—	0	.184	.340	.263
	Tacoma	AAA Sea	91	328	93	14	4	3	124	53	30	53	0	44	5	1	3	19	7	.73	6	.284	.388	.378
7 Min. YEARS			666	2237	585	86	21	15	758	348	212	337	5	350	41	40	18	112	44	.72	39	.262	.366	.339

Randy Flores

Pitches: Left Bats: Left Pos: SP-24; RP-11   Ht: 6'0" Wt: 180 Born: 7/31/75 Age: 25

Year	Team	Lg Org	G	GS	CG	GF	IP	BFP	H	R	ER	HR	SH	SF	HB	TBB	IBB	SO	WP	Bk	W	L	Pct.	ShO	Sv	ERA
1997	Oneonta	A- NYY	13	13	2	0	74.2	308	64	32	27	3	0	1	4	23	1	70	5	1	4	4	.500	1	0	3.25
1998	Tampa	A+ NYY	5	5	0	0	23.2	115	28	23	17	2	2	2	1	16	2	15	0	4	1	2	.333	0	0	6.46
	Greensboro	A NYY	21	20	2	0	130.2	535	119	48	38	6	2	3	7	33	0	139	2	4	12	7	.632	1	0	2.62
1999	Norwich	AA NYY	4	4	0	0	25	120	32	20	18	0	2	0	1	11	1	19	1	1	0	1	.000	0	0	6.48
	Tampa	A+ NYY	21	20	1	1	135	555	118	56	43	4	4	4	7	38	0	99	5	0	11	4	.733	1	0	2.87
2000	Norwich	AA NYY	31	20	3	3	141	601	138	64	46	8	4	2	5	58	1	97	8	1	10	9	.526	0	1	2.94
	Columbus	AAA NYY	4	4	0	0	23.1	117	43	21	19	3	0	0	0	7	0	16	1	1	1	2	.333	0	0	7.33
4 Min. YEARS			99	86	8	4	553.1	2351	542	264	208	26	14	12	25	186	5	455	22	12	39	29	.574	3	1	3.38

Tim Florez

Bats: Right Throws: Right Pos: 2B-27; SS-11; PH-11; 3B-6; PR-4   Ht: 5'10" Wt: 170 Born: 7/23/69 Age: 31

Year	Team	Lg Org	G	AB	H	2B	3B	HR	TB	R	RBI	TBB	IBB	SO	HBP	SH	SF	SB	CS	SB%	GDP	Avg	OBP	SLG
1991	Everett	A- SF	59	193	48	8	4	0	64	33	25	12	1	33	1	2	1	7	1	.88	4	.249	.295	.332
1992	Clinton	A SF	81	292	68	12	2	2	90	39	25	30	2	53	3	0	2	20	5	.80	6	.233	.309	.308
	San Jose	A+ SF	38	131	32	6	1	1	43	15	17	4	0	21	0	4	4	3	3	.50	2	.244	.259	.328
1993	Shreveport	AA SF	106	318	81	17	2	1	105	33	26	16	4	43	2	3	2	3	5	.38	9	.255	.293	.330
1994	Phoenix	AAA SF	13	24	6	1	0	1	10	5	2	1	0	4	0	0	0	0	0	—	1	.250	.280	.417
	Shreveport	AA SF	61	158	34	10	0	1	47	21	13	21	3	34	1	2	1	0	3	.00	4	.215	.309	.297
1995	Shreveport	AA SF	100	295	79	11	2	9	121	37	46	26	1	49	4	3	3	4	3	.57	7	.268	.332	.410
1996	Shreveport	AA SF	18	66	18	1	0	2	25	9	8	7	1	11	1	0	0	2	0	1.00	0	.273	.351	.379
	Phoenix	AAA SF	113	366	106	31	3	4	155	42	39	34	4	56	10	0	3	0	5	.00	12	.290	.363	.423
1997	Phoenix	AAA SF	114	402	121	24	4	7	174	57	61	32	2	68	8	5	1	6	3	.67	5	.301	.363	.433
1998	Tucson	AAA Ari	77	227	64	5	1	3	80	31	23	18	1	49	3	0	5	4	2	.67	10	.282	.336	.352
1999	Somerset	IND —	9	23	6	0	0	1	9	3	5	3	0	3	0	1	0	0	0	—	1	.261	.346	.391
	Nashua	IND —	47	180	48	8	1	1	61	25	12	10	0	22	1	1	5	5	3	.63	9	.267	.307	.339
	Chattanooga	AA Cin	39	139	35	8	1	5	60	24	22	15	0	23	3	1	3	7	2	.78	6	.252	.331	.432
2000	Iowa	AAA ChC	14	42	11	4	0	0	15	4	3	3	0	10	0	0	0	1	0	0	0	.262	.304	.357
	Chattanooga	AA Cin	42	98	16	3	1	2	27	11	6	8	0	24	2	2	0	1	6	.14	1	.163	.241	.276
10 Min. YEARS			931	2954	773	149	22	40	1086	389	333	240	19	503	39	28	27	62	41	.60	77	.262	.323	.368

Pat Flury

Pitches: Right Bats: Right Pos: RP-52   Ht: 6'1" Wt: 220 Born: 3/14/73 Age: 28

Year	Team	Lg Org	G	GS	CG	GF	IP	BFP	H	R	ER	HR	SH	SF	HB	TBB	IBB	SO	WP	Bk	W	L	Pct.	ShO	Sv	ERA
1993	Eugene	A- KC	27	0	0	19	33	144	25	15	12	0	2	2	2	22	1	34	4	0	2	2	.500	0	7	3.27
1994	Rockford	A KC	34	0	0	18	55	254	61	27	24	3	2	2	5	33	2	41	3	2	1	3	.250	0	2	3.93
1995	Wilmington	A+ KC	15	0	0	6	22	89	18	6	6	2	0	1	1	9	1	14	1	1	1	0	1.000	0	1	2.45
	Springfield	A KC	34	0	0	19	54.1	246	65	32	26	5	4	1	1	24	0	35	2	0	2	6	.250	0	1	4.31
1996	Wilmington	A+ KC	45	0	0	19	84.1	339	66	22	18	2	2	1	0	29	4	67	9	0	7	2	.778	0	5	1.92
1997	Wichita	AA KC	42	0	0	19	48	215	47	26	19	4	2	3	4	18	3	47	1	0	8	3	.727	0	5	3.56
	Omaha	AAA KC	18	0	0	7	26.2	124	29	18	18	5	0	2	2	16	2	24	1	0	1	0	1.000	0	0	6.08
1998	Wichita	AA KC	8	0	0	2	11.2	59	14	11	7	0	1	0	3	7	0	13	1	0	1	1	.500	0	0	5.40
	Trenton	AA Bos	26	0	0	24	30.2	122	24	6	6	2	0	0	0	11	1	37	3	0	0	0	—	0	16	1.76
	Pawtucket	AAA Bos	17	0	0	5	22.1	100	23	15	14	3	1	0	0	16	0	22	4	0	0	0	—	0	5	5.64
1999	Chattanooga	AA Cin	43	0	0	21	53.1	221	36	20	17	5	3	0	0	31	0	69	4	1	1	1	.500	0	15	2.87
	Indianapolis	AAA Cin	23	0	0	6	23.1	115	27	18	18	4	0	1	1	20	0	20	6	0	1	1	.500	0	6	7.04
2000	Calgary	AAA Fla	12	0	0	4	19.1	100	28	18	17	5	2	0	1	14	0	15	6	0	1	0	1.000	0	1	7.91
	Ottawa	AAA Mon	40	0	0	25	57	232	40	10	9	0	2	2	3	26	1	46	2	1	4	3	.571	0	1	1.42
8 Min. YEARS			384	0	0	202	540.2	2360	503	244	211	37	25	11	23	276	15	484	47	5	30	22	.577	0	64	3.51

93

Josh Fogg

Pitches: Right **Bats:** Right **Pos:** SP-27   **Ht:** 6'2" **Wt:** 205 **Born:** 12/13/76 **Age:** 24

Year Team	Lg Org	G	GS	CG	GF	IP	BFP	H	R	ER	HR	SH	SF	HB	TBB	IBB	SO	WP	Bk	W	L	Pct.	ShO	Sv	ERA
1998 White Sox	R CWS	2	0	0	0	4	13	0	0	0	0	1	0	0	1	0	5	1	0	1	0	1.000	0	0	0.00
Hickory	A CWS	8	8	0	0	41.1	173	36	17	10	4	1	0	1	13	0	29	1	1	1	3	.250	0	0	2.18
Winston-Sal	A+ CWS	1	0	0	1	1	6	2	2	0	0	0	0	0	0	0	2	1	0	0	1	.000	0	0	0.00
1999 Winston-Sal	A+ CWS	17	17	1	0	103.1	441	93	44	34	3	1	1	11	33	0	109	2	0	10	5	.667	1	0	2.96
Birmingham	AA CWS	10	10	0	0	55	249	66	37	36	8	1	2	5	18	0	40	2	1	3	2	.600	0	0	5.89
2000 Birmingham	AA CWS	27	27	2	0	192.1	787	190	68	55	7	5	4	6	44	2	136	9	1	11	7	.611	0	0	2.57
3 Min. YEARS		65	62	3	1	397	1669	387	168	135	22	9	7	23	109	2	321	16	3	26	18	.591	1	0	3.06

Franklin Font

Bats: Right **Throws:** Right **Pos:** 2B-74; 3B-14; PH-12; OF-5; PR-2; SS-1   **Ht:** 5'10" **Wt:** 195 **Born:** 11/4/77 **Age:** 23

Year Team	Lg Org	G	AB	H	2B	3B	HR	TB	R	RBI	TBB	IBB	SO	HBP	SH	SF	SB	CS	SB%	GDP	Avg	OBP	SLG
1996 Cubs	R ChC	59	239	72	5	4	0	85	43	18	17	0	36	4	2	2	31	9	.78	0	.301	.355	.356
1997 Williamsprt	A- ChC	33	135	42	6	2	0	52	13	12	7	0	20	2	1	2	10	4	.71	2	.311	.349	.385
Orlando	AA ChC	10	20	6	0	0	0	6	3	2	2	0	1	0	0	0	0	1	.00	1	.300	.364	.300
Daytona	A+ ChC	19	59	13	2	1	0	17	8	2	4	0	13	0	1	0	2	1	.67	0	.220	.270	.288
1998 Rockford	A ChC	66	237	64	5	2	0	73	34	15	20	0	39	5	4	1	25	6	.81	5	.270	.338	.308
Daytona	A+ ChC	60	204	60	2	1	0	64	26	16	18	0	35	1	2	0	7	6	.54	3	.294	.354	.314
1999 Daytona	A+ ChC	87	315	93	7	4	2	114	48	33	21	0	38	2	8	3	14	6	.70	10	.295	.340	.362
West Tenn	AA ChC	25	96	33	2	1	0	40	14	17	8	1	14	1	1	1	4	4	.50	0	.344	.396	.417
2000 West Tenn	AA ChC	104	329	86	9	3	0	101	39	26	26	1	44	5	4	1	9	4	.69	6	.261	.324	.307
5 Min. YEARS		463	1634	469	38	18	3	552	228	141	123	2	240	20	23	10	102	41	.71	27	.287	.342	.338

Joe Foote

Pitches: Right **Bats:** Right **Pos:** SP-26   **Ht:** 6'2" **Wt:** 190 **Born:** 8/30/79 **Age:** 21

Year Team	Lg Org	G	GS	CG	GF	IP	BFP	H	R	ER	HR	SH	SF	HB	TBB	IBB	SO	WP	Bk	W	L	Pct.	ShO	Sv	ERA
1998 Twins	R Min	13	10	0	1	57.2	255	61	35	25	4	1	1	3	15	1	60	6	0	6	3	.667	0	0	3.90
1999 Quad City	A Min	44	18	1	7	135	582	131	72	59	6	4	4	5	44	2	111	9	1	7	5	.583	1	2	3.93
2000 Quad City	A Min	25	25	4	0	146	634	152	86	63	13	7	1	7	43	2	128	9	0	9	8	.529	1	0	3.88
New Britain	AA Min	1	1	0	0	5	26	7	7	7	2	0	0	1	4	0	3	0	0	0	1	.000	0	0	12.60
3 Min. YEARS		83	54	5	8	343.2	1497	351	200	154	25	12	6	16	106	5	302	24	1	22	17	.564	2	2	4.03

P.J. Forbes

Bats: Right **Throws:** Right **Pos:** OF-66; 3B-23; PH-11; DH-3; PR-2; SS-1; 2B-1   **Ht:** 5'10" **Wt:** 160 **Born:** 9/22/67 **Age:** 33

Year Team	Lg Org	G	AB	H	2B	3B	HR	TB	R	RBI	TBB	IBB	SO	HBP	SH	SF	SB	CS	SB%	GDP	Avg	OBP	SLG
1990 Boise	A- Ana	43	170	42	9	1	0	53	29	19	23	1	21	0	7	1	11	4	.73	5	.247	.335	.312
1991 Palm Spring	A+ Ana	94	349	93	14	2	2	117	45	26	36	1	44	4	12	0	18	8	.69	7	.266	.342	.335
1992 Quad City	A Ana	105	376	106	16	5	2	138	53	46	44	1	51	2	24	5	15	6	.71	4	.282	.356	.367
1993 Midland	AA Ana	126	498	159	23	2	15	231	90	64	26	1	50	4	14	2	6	8	.43	13	.319	.357	.464
Vancouver	AAA Ana	5	16	4	2	0	0	6	1	3	0	0	3	0	1	0	0	0	—	0	.250	.250	.375
1994 Angels	R Ana	2	6	0	0	0	0	0	1	0	0	0	1	0	0	0	0	0	—	0	.000	.000	.000
Vancouver	AAA Ana	90	318	91	21	2	1	119	39	40	22	0	42	2	7	5	4	2	.67	6	.286	.331	.374
1995 Vancouver	AAA Ana	109	369	101	22	3	1	132	47	52	21	0	46	2	7	10	4	6	.40	4	.274	.308	.358
1996 Vancouver	AAA Ana	117	409	112	24	2	0	140	58	46	42	3	44	5	10	4	4	3	.57	13	.274	.346	.342
1997 Rochester	AAA Bal	116	434	118	22	3	8	168	67	54	35	0	42	6	8	3	15	4	.79	11	.272	.333	.387
1998 Rochester	AAA Bal	116	460	135	37	3	6	196	74	52	36	1	54	5	8	3	10	2	.83	15	.293	.349	.426
1999 Oklahoma	AAA Tex	22	67	7	1	0	0	8	4	2	5	0	12	1	2	0	0	0	—	2	.104	.178	.119
Rochester	AAA Bal	88	349	92	16	1	0	110	49	19	26	0	40	3	11	2	5	0	1.00	10	.264	.318	.315
2000 Scranton-WB	AAA Phi	99	334	92	22	1	2	122	51	32	30	0	29	4	0	4	7	2	.78	10	.275	.339	.365
1998 Baltimore	AL	9	10	1	0	0	0	1	0	0	2	0	0	0	0	0	0	0	—	0	.100	.100	.100
11 Min. YEARS		1132	4155	1152	229	24	37	1540	608	455	346	8	479	38	111	39	99	45	.69	92	.277	.336	.371

Tom Fordham

Pitches: Left **Bats:** Left **Pos:** RP-45; SP-3   **Ht:** 6'2" **Wt:** 205 **Born:** 2/20/74 **Age:** 27

Year Team	Lg Org	G	GS	CG	GF	IP	BFP	H	R	ER	HR	SH	SF	HB	TBB	IBB	SO	WP	Bk	W	L	Pct.	ShO	Sv	ERA
1993 White Sox	R CWS	3	0	0	1	10	41	9	2	2	0	0	0	0	3	0	12	1	0	1	1	.500	0	0	1.80
Sarasota	A+ CWS	2	0	0	1	5	21	3	1	0	0	0	0	0	3	2	5	1	1	0	0	—	0	0	0.00
Hickory	A CWS	8	8	1	0	48.2	194	36	21	21	3	1	6	0	21	0	27	3	2	4	3	.571	0	0	3.88
1994 Hickory	A CWS	17	17	1	0	109	452	101	47	38	10	1	1	3	30	1	121	5	4	10	5	.667	1	0	3.14
South Bend	A CWS	11	11	1	0	74.2	315	82	46	36	4	4	3	0	14	0	48	4	0	4	4	.500	1	0	4.34
1995 Pr William	A+ CWS	13	13	1	0	84	340	66	20	19	7	2	1	2	35	2	78	1	0	9	0	1.000	1	0	2.04
Birmingham	AA CWS	14	14	2	0	82.2	348	79	35	31	9	2	2	0	28	2	61	3	0	6	3	.667	1	0	3.38
1996 Birmingham	AA CWS	6	6	0	0	37.1	147	26	13	11	4	0	2	0	14	1	37	2	0	2	1	.667	0	0	2.65
Nashville	AAA CWS	22	22	3	0	140.2	589	117	60	54	15	4	2	4	69	1	118	7	1	10	8	.556	2	0	3.45
1997 Nashville	AAA CWS	21	20	2	0	114	493	113	64	60	14	1	5	1	53	1	90	6	1	6	7	.462	0	0	4.74
1998 Calgary	AAA CWS	9	9	0	0	56.2	225	38	21	19	6	1	3	0	26	0	39	3	0	4	2	.667	0	0	3.02
1999 Charlotte	AAA CWS	29	21	0	2	112	538	144	101	91	25	2	4	3	66	0	101	10	0	4	7	.364	0	0	7.31
2000 Indianapols	AAA Mil	48	3	0	11	66	295	48	29	26	2	2	2	0	49	0	64	6	0	3	6	.333	0	0	3.55
1997 Chicago	AL	7	1	0	1	17.1	78	17	13	12	2	1	2	1	10	2	10	0	0	1	0	1.000	0	0	6.23
1998 Chicago	AL	29	5	0	5	48	228	51	36	36	7	1	1	1	42	0	23	1	0	1	3	.333	0	0	6.75
8 Min. YEARS		203	144	11	15	940.2	3998	862	460	408	99	20	31	13	411	10	801	52	9	63	47	.573	6	0	3.90
2 Maj. YEARS		36	6	0	6	65.1	306	68	49	48	9	2	3	2	52	2	33	1	0	1	3	.250	0	0	6.61

Jim Foster

Bats: Right **Throws:** Right **Pos:** C-50; DH-8; 1B-1; PH-1   **Ht:** 6'3" **Wt:** 220 **Born:** 8/18/71 **Age:** 29

Year Team	Lg Org	G	AB	H	2B	3B	HR	TB	R	RBI	TBB	IBB	SO	HBP	SH	SF	SB	CS	SB%	GDP	Avg	OBP	SLG
1993 Bluefield	R+ Bal	61	218	71	21	1	10	124	59	45	42	1	34	3	0	3	3	1	.75	4	.326	.436	.569
1994 Albany	A Bal	121	421	112	29	3	8	171	61	56	54	0	59	11	0	6	5	3	.63	13	.266	.360	.406
1995 Frederick	A+ Bal	128	429	112	27	3	6	163	44	56	51	5	63	8	0	5	2	3	.40	10	.261	.347	.380
1996 Frederick	A+ Bal	82	278	70	20	2	7	115	35	42	39	1	32	4	0	3	6	3	.67	7	.252	.349	.414
Bowie	AA Bal	9	33	10	0	1	2	18	7	9	7	0	6	0	0	1	0	0	—	0	.303	.415	.545
1997 Rochester	AAA Bal	3	9	5	2	0	0	7	4	4	3	0	0	0	0	0	0	1	.00	1	.556	.667	.778
Frederick	A+ Bal	61	200	70	12	1	16	132	48	65	45	7	28	7	0	3	8	0	1.00	5	.350	.478	.660
Bowie	AA Bal	63	211	58	12	0	7	91	36	41	36	0	31	1	1	2	1	1	.50	6	.275	.380	.431
1998 Bowie	AA Bal	66	221	53	17	0	5	85	24	33	31	1	38	5	0	0	1	1	.50	6	.240	.346	.385
Rochester	AAA Bal	43	153	36	9	0	5	60	22	26	18	1	22	2	0	1	3	1	.75	5	.235	.322	.392
1999 Rochester	AAA Bal	35	118	27	3	1	0	32	6	11	12	1	19	0	0	0	4	2	.67	2	.229	.300	.271
Tucson	AAA Ari	11	26	7	1	0	0	8	4	3	4	0	2	0	0	1	0	0	—	3	.269	.355	.308
Erie	AA Ana	4	16	4	1	0	1	8	2	3	2	0	0	0	0	0	0	0	—	1	.250	.333	.500
Edmonton	AAA Ana	24	88	26	10	0	2	42	13	15	4	0	13	0	0	1	1	0	1.00	0	.295	.323	.477
2000 Birmingham	AA CWS	10	35	9	1	0	0	10	1	3	1	0	3	0	0	0	0	0	—	0	.257	.278	.286
Charlotte	AAA CWS	49	152	41	7	0	2	54	13	14	15	0	16	2	1	1	0	1	.00	5	.270	.341	.355
8 Min. YEARS		770	2608	711	172	12	71	1120	379	426	364	17	366	43	4	27	34	17	.67	69	.273	.368	.429

Kevin Foster

Pitches: Right **Bats:** Right **Pos:** SP-20   **Ht:** 6'1" **Wt:** 175 **Born:** 1/13/69 **Age:** 32

Year Team	Lg Org	G	GS	CG	GF	IP	BFP	H	R	ER	HR	SH	SF	HB	TBB	IBB	SO	WP	Bk	W	L	Pct.	ShO	Sv	ERA
1990 Expos	R Mon	4	0	0	1	10.2	47	9	6	6	0	1	0	1	6	0	11	0	0	2	0	1.000	0	0	5.06
Gate City	R+ Mon	10	10	0	0	55	248	43	42	28	3	0	1	6	34	0	52	10	0	1	7	.125	0	0	4.58
1991 Sumter	A Mon	34	11	1	9	102	445	62	36	31	3	1	5	9	68	1	114	5	4	10	4	.714	1	1	2.74
1992 Wst Plm Bch	A+ Mon	16	11	0	2	69.1	279	45	19	15	4	0	2	3	31	1	66	1	1	7	2	.778	0	0	1.95
1993 Jacksnville	AA Sea	12	12	1	0	65.2	278	53	32	29	2	0	2	4	29	0	72	4	1	4	4	.500	1	0	3.97
Scranton-WB	AAA Phi	17	9	1	0	71	304	63	32	31	7	0	0	3	29	0	59	5	0	1	1	.500	0	0	3.93
1994 Reading	AA Phi	1	1	0	0	6	26	7	4	4	1	0	0	0	1	0	3	0	0	0	1	.000	0	0	6.00
Orlando	AA ChC	3	3	1	0	19	66	8	2	2	2	1	0	1	2	0	21	0	0	1	0	1.000	1	0	0.95
Iowa	AAA ChC	6	6	1	0	33.2	140	28	17	16	6	2	1	0	14	0	35	0	0	3	1	.750	0	0	4.28
1996 Iowa	AAA ChC	18	18	3	0	115	484	106	56	55	23	2	2	0	46	2	87	6	1	7	6	.538	1	0	4.30
1998 Daytona	A+ ChC	3	0	0	0	2.2	19	2	7	3	1	0	0	0	7	1	3	0	0	0	0	—	0	0	10.13
West Tenn	AA ChC	2	0	0	0	4	17	5	1	1	0	0	0	0	1	0	5	0	0	1	0	1.000	0	0	2.25
Iowa	AAA ChC	17	11	1	4	67	300	74	52	51	19	1	2	0	38	0	75	5	0	5	6	.455	1	0	6.85
2000 Trenton	AA Bos	11	11	1	0	62.1	261	49	30	29	0	0	1	2	30	0	52	1	0	4	3	.571	0	0	4.19
Pawtucket	AAA Bos	9	9	0	0	47	203	39	23	21	2	3	1	0	27	1	50	0	0	2	4	.333	0	0	4.02
1993 Philadelphia	NL	2	1	0	0	6.2	40	13	11	11	3	0	0	0	7	0	6	2	0	0	1	.000	0	0	14.85
1994 Chicago	NL	13	13	0	0	81	337	70	31	26	7	1	1	1	35	1	75	1	1	3	4	.429	0	0	2.89
1995 Chicago	NL	30	28	0	1	167.2	703	149	90	84	32	4	6	6	65	4	146	2	2	12	11	.522	0	0	4.51
1996 Chicago	NL	17	16	1	0	87	386	98	63	60	16	5	4	2	35	3	53	2	0	7	6	.538	0	0	6.21
1997 Chicago	NL	26	25	1	0	146.1	637	141	79	75	27	9	7	2	66	4	118	3	0	10	7	.588	0	0	4.61
1998 Chicago	NL	7	0	0	1	3.1	20	8	6	6	1	0	2	0	2	0	3	0	0	0	0	—	0	0	16.20
8 Min. YEARS		163	112	10	16	730.1	3117	593	359	322	73	11	17	29	363	6	705	37	7	48	39	.552	5	1	3.97
6 Maj. YEARS		91	83	2	2	492	2123	479	280	262	86	19	20	11	210	12	401	10	3	32	29	.525	0	0	4.79

Quincy Foster

Bats: Left **Throws:** Right **Pos:** OF-67; DH-2; PR-1   **Ht:** 6'2" **Wt:** 175 **Born:** 10/30/74 **Age:** 26

Year Team	Lg Org	G	AB	H	2B	3B	HR	TB	R	RBI	TBB	IBB	SO	HBP	SH	SF	SB	CS	SB%	GDP	Avg	OBP	SLG
1996 Utica	A- Fla	73	244	53	7	1	1	65	34	22	30	0	71	4	3	4	24	6	.80	3	.221	.313	.271
1997 Brevard Cty	A+ Fla	61	186	46	8	2	1	61	25	11	14	0	47	3	2	0	12	4	.75	0	.247	.310	.328
1998 Kane County	A Fla	134	545	138	14	10	0	172	90	37	51	4	114	8	8	4	73	19	.79	7	.253	.324	.316
1999 Brevard Cty	A+ Fla	134	568	167	13	6	3	201	78	54	36	1	96	8	2	2	56	23	.71	4	.294	.344	.354
2000 Marlins	R Fla	5	16	4	1	0	0	5	2	1	1	0	0	1	0	0	0	1	.00	0	.250	.333	.313
Portland	AA Fla	65	248	77	7	4	2	98	60	21	23	0	42	7	3	2	25	8	.76	2	.310	.382	.395
5 Min. YEARS		472	1803	485	50	23	7	602	289	146	155	5	370	31	18	12	190	61	.76	16	.269	.335	.334

Zach Frachiseur

Pitches: Right **Bats:** Right **Pos:** RP-37; SP-6   **Ht:** 6'0" **Wt:** 190 **Born:** 9/30/76 **Age:** 24

Year Team	Lg Org	G	GS	CG	GF	IP	BFP	H	R	ER	HR	SH	SF	HB	TBB	IBB	SO	WP	Bk	W	L	Pct.	ShO	Sv	ERA
1998 Eugene	A- Atl	23	1	0	7	58.1	271	74	45	33	3	4	2	1	21	1	74	2	7	5	4	.556	0	1	5.09
1999 Macon	A Atl	4	0	0	4	21	4	5	3	3	1	0	0	0	2	0	6	0	0	0	1	.000	0	0	6.75
Myrtle Bch	A+ Atl	37	5	0	9	98	397	75	34	30	5	2	4	2	31	1	93	5	0	7	3	.700	0	2	2.76
2000 Greenville	AA Atl	42	5	0	14	86.2	379	92	54	46	8	0	8	4	29	1	58	4	0	2	7	.222	0	2	4.78
Richmond	AAA Atl	1	1	0	0	5	27	12	8	8	1	0	1	0	1	0	0	0	0	0	1	.000	0	0	14.40
3 Min. YEARS		107	12	0	32	252	1095	258	144	120	18	6	15	7	84	3	231	11	7	14	16	.467	0	5	4.29

Aaron France

Pitches: Right **Bats:** Left **Pos:** SP-12; RP-10   **Ht:** 6'3" **Wt:** 188 **Born:** 4/17/74 **Age:** 27

Year Team	Lg Org	G	GS	CG	GF	IP	BFP	H	R	ER	HR	SH	SF	HB	TBB	IBB	SO	WP	Bk	W	L	Pct.	ShO	Sv	ERA
1994 Welland	A- Pit	7	5	0	1	24	98	22	12	6	1	0	1	4	6	0	16	1	1	0	2	.000	0	0	2.25
1995 Augusta	A Pit	18	15	0	0	94.2	388	80	29	26	4	3	3	5	26	0	77	6	2	6	6	.500	0	0	2.47
1996 Lynchburg	A+ Pit	13	13	0	0	60.1	286	79	53	43	6	1	0	3	32	1	40	8	3	0	8	.000	0	0	6.41
Augusta	A Pit	5	5	0	0	25	105	23	9	7	2	2	0	1	7	0	24	0	1	2	1	.667	0	0	2.52

Year Team	Lg Org	HOW MUCH HE PITCHED						WHAT HE GAVE UP												THE RESULTS					
		G	GS	CG	GF	IP	BFP	H	R	ER	HR	SH	SF	HB	TBB	IBB	SO	WP	Bk	W	L	Pct.	ShO	Sv	ERA
1997 Augusta	A Pit	26	17	1	2	107.1	458	98	48	42	5	0	2	8	44	0	89	6	3	7	4	.636	0	0	3.52
1998 Lynchburg	A+ Pit	26	20	0	2	129	529	99	51	39	9	3	1	12	45	0	110	7	0	6	5	.545	0	0	2.72
1999 Altoona	AA Pit	33	11	0	7	95.2	414	79	50	39	8	5	3	5	48	1	70	7	3	4	5	.444	0	0	3.67
2000 Altoona	AA Pit	22	12	0	0	81	355	83	41	31	4	0	5	1	27	1	57	6	0	5	2	.714	0	0	3.44
7 Min. YEARS		150	98	1	12	617	2633	563	293	233	39	14	15	38	235	3	483	41	13	30	33	.476	0	0	3.40

David Francia

Bats: Left   **Throws:** Left   **Pos:** OF-89; PH-16; PR-2; 1B-1; DH-1   **Ht:** 6'0"   **Wt:** 167   **Born:** 4/16/75   **Age:** 26

Year Team	Lg Org	BATTING															BASERUNNING				PERCENTAGES		
		G	AB	H	2B	3B	HR	TB	R	RBI	TBB	IBB	SO	HBP	SH	SF	SB	CS	SB%	GDP	Avg	OBP	SLG
1996 Batavia	A- Phi	69	280	81	14	5	4	117	45	29	8	0	25	6	2	2	16	6	.73	1	.289	.321	.418
1997 Piedmont	A Phi	112	424	127	24	7	9	192	72	65	25	2	61	19	4	8	39	12	.76	5	.300	.359	.453
Clearwater	A+ Phi	21	75	21	3	1	0	26	5	10	6	0	7	1	3	0	5	2	.71	1	.280	.341	.347
1998 Clearwater	A+ Phi	48	194	54	13	0	6	85	33	23	12	0	30	7	2	2	13	4	.76	4	.278	.340	.438
Reading	AA Phi	68	269	64	12	4	3	93	29	20	13	0	41	2	3	2	6	7	.46	3	.238	.276	.346
1999 Reading	AA Phi	107	339	92	22	5	4	136	41	43	21	3	57	13	6	1	13	4	.76	5	.271	.337	.401
2000 Reading	AA Phi	56	210	61	8	3	3	84	36	26	11	0	29	10	8	2	16	7	.70	2	.290	.352	.400
Scranton-WB	AAA Phi	48	117	34	9	0	2	49	16	15	18	1	17	2	2	0	7	4	.64	0	.291	.394	.419
5 Min. YEARS		529	1908	534	105	25	31	782	277	231	114	6	267	60	30	17	115	46	.71	21	.280	.337	.410

Mike Frank

Bats: Left   **Throws:** Left   **Pos:** OF-108; PH-7; PR-4; DH-1   **Ht:** 6'2"   **Wt:** 195   **Born:** 1/14/75   **Age:** 26

Year Team	Lg Org	BATTING															BASERUNNING				PERCENTAGES		
		G	AB	H	2B	3B	HR	TB	R	RBI	TBB	IBB	SO	HBP	SH	SF	SB	CS	SB%	GDP	Avg	OBP	SLG
1997 Billings	R+ Cin	69	266	100	22	6	10	164	62	62	35	5	24	2	0	3	18	8	.69	7	.376	.448	.617
1998 Indianapols	AAA Cin	22	88	30	4	0	0	34	8	13	7	0	9	0	0	0	1	0	1.00	1	.341	.389	.386
Chattanooga	AA Cin	58	231	75	12	4	12	131	43	43	19	1	28	1	0	3	5	2	.71	3	.325	.374	.567
1999 Indianapols	AAA Cin	121	433	128	36	7	9	205	73	62	36	2	55	8	2	3	10	6	.63	10	.296	.358	.473
2000 Chattanooga	AA Cin	8	30	8	1	2	0	13	6	5	1	0	1	0	0	0	0	0	—	0	.267	.290	.433
Louisville	AAA Cin	62	197	54	16	2	6	92	30	28	20	2	26	4	1	1	8	1	.89	5	.274	.351	.467
Columbus	AAA NYY	45	138	33	5	3	2	50	19	12	16	1	13	3	1	1	5	3	.63	5	.239	.329	.362
1998 Cincinnati	NL	28	89	20	6	0	0	26	14	7	7	0	12	0	1	1	0	0	—	3	.225	.278	.292
4 Min. YEARS		385	1383	428	96	24	39	689	241	225	134	11	156	18	4	11	47	20	.70	33	.309	.375	.498

Ryan Franklin

Pitches: Right   **Bats:** Right   **Pos:** SP-22; RP-9   **Ht:** 6'3"   **Wt:** 165   **Born:** 3/5/73   **Age:** 28

Year Team	Lg Org	HOW MUCH HE PITCHED						WHAT HE GAVE UP												THE RESULTS					
		G	GS	CG	GF	IP	BFP	H	R	ER	HR	SH	SF	HB	TBB	IBB	SO	WP	Bk	W	L	Pct.	ShO	Sv	ERA
1993 Bellingham	A- Sea	15	14	1	0	74	321	72	38	24	2	2	1	3	27	0	55	7	3	5	3	.625	1	0	2.92
1994 Appleton	A Sea	18	18	5	0	118	493	105	60	41	6	3	1	17	23	0	102	6	3	9	6	.600	1	0	3.13
Calgary	AAA Sea	1	1	0	0	5.2	28	9	6	5	2	0	0	0	1	0	2	0	0	0	0	—	0	0	7.94
Riverside	A+ Sea	8	8	1	0	61.2	261	61	26	21	5	1	3	4	8	0	35	0	1	4	2	.667	1	0	3.06
1995 Port City	AA Sea	31	20	1	2	146	627	153	84	70	13	11	3	12	43	4	102	6	2	6	10	.375	1	0	4.32
1996 Port City	AA Sea	28	27	2	0	182	764	186	99	81	23	6	3	16	37	0	127	4	2	6	12	.333	0	0	4.01
1997 Memphis	AA Sea	11	8	2	2	59.1	234	45	22	20	4	0	3	1	14	1	49	1	0	4	2	.667	2	0	3.03
Tacoma	AAA Sea	14	14	0	0	90.1	386	97	48	42	11	7	2	8	24	1	59	1	1	5	5	.500	0	0	4.18
1998 Tacoma	AAA Sea	34	16	1	10	127.2	561	148	75	64	18	4	8	10	32	2	90	0	0	5	6	.455	0	1	4.51
1999 Tacoma	AAA Sea	29	19	2	4	135.2	574	142	81	71	17	2	4	9	33	1	94	1	1	6	9	.400	1	2	4.71
2000 Tacoma	AAA Sea	31	22	4	2	164	665	147	85	71	28	3	3	12	35	1	142	2	0	11	5	.688	0	2	3.90
1999 Seattle	AL	6	0	0	2	11.1	51	10	6	6	2	0	0	1	8	1	6	0	0	0	0	—	0	0	4.76
8 Min. YEARS		220	167	19	20	1164.1	4914	1165	624	510	129	39	31	92	277	10	857	28	13	61	60	.504	7	3	3.94

Lance Franks

Pitches: Right   **Bats:** Right   **Pos:** RP-36; SP-7   **Ht:** 5'11"   **Wt:** 180   **Born:** 8/20/75   **Age:** 25

Year Team	Lg Org	HOW MUCH HE PITCHED						WHAT HE GAVE UP												THE RESULTS					
		G	GS	CG	GF	IP	BFP	H	R	ER	HR	SH	SF	HB	TBB	IBB	SO	WP	Bk	W	L	Pct.	ShO	Sv	ERA
1997 Johnson Cty	R+ StL	26	0	0	23	30.2	113	16	4	4	1	0	0	0	7	1	40	2	0	0	0	—	0	12	1.17
Pr William	A+ StL	2	0	0	0	4.1	16	3	1	1	1	0	0	0	1	0	4	0	0	1	0	1.000	0	0	2.08
1998 Peoria	A StL	58	0	0	23	75	295	57	23	19	4	4	3	3	20	4	68	5	0	4	6	.400	0	4	2.28
1999 Potomac	A+ StL	54	0	0	6	78.2	308	63	25	23	5	2	2	3	17	0	61	2	0	5	1	.833	0	2	2.63
2000 Arkansas	AA StL	43	7	0	5	89	396	90	59	51	16	5	3	6	44	3	56	3	1	6	4	.600	0	0	5.16
4 Min. YEARS		183	7	0	57	277.2	1128	229	112	98	27	11	8	9	89	9	229	12	1	16	11	.593	0	16	3.18

Dan Fraraccio

Bats: Right   **Throws:** Right   **Pos:** SS-35; 3B-21; OF-13; 2B-8; DH-5; 1B-3; PH-2; PR-2   **Ht:** 5'11"   **Wt:** 175   **Born:** 9/18/70   **Age:** 30

Year Team	Lg Org	BATTING															BASERUNNING				PERCENTAGES		
		G	AB	H	2B	3B	HR	TB	R	RBI	TBB	IBB	SO	HBP	SH	SF	SB	CS	SB%	GDP	Avg	OBP	SLG
1992 White Sox	R CWS	52	149	31	5	1	0	38	19	8	5	0	18	4	1	1	5	7	.42	1	.208	.252	.255
Sarasota	A+ CWS	1	3	1	0	0	0	1	0	0	0	0	0	0	0	0	0	0	—	0	.333	.333	.333
1993 Hickory	A CWS	41	147	31	9	1	1	45	13	15	6	0	21	3	0	1	2	2	.50	2	.211	.255	.306
South Bend	A CWS	49	135	37	10	0	0	47	23	21	6	0	29	3	1	1	0	1	.00	4	.274	.317	.348
1994 Pr William	A+ CWS	26	80	19	1	1	1	25	10	7	3	0	19	0	1	1	1	0	1.00	1	.238	.262	.313
White Sox	R CWS	3	2	1	0	0	0	1	0	0	1	0	1	0	0	0	0	0	—	0	.500	.667	.500
1995 Nashville	AAA CWS	10	28	7	0	0	0	7	2	3	1	0	6	0	0	1	0	1	.00	1	.250	.276	.250
Pr William	A+ CWS	24	74	17	5	0	2	28	11	6	8	0	12	0	1	0	0	0	—	5	.230	.305	.378
1996 Pr William	A+ CWS	44	149	41	9	0	0	50	16	20	12	0	20	1	2	0	1	0	1.00	5	.275	.333	.336
Thunder Bay	IND	36	132	39	11	2	1	60	19	17	10	0	23	0	1	3	0	0	—	1	.295	.338	.455
1997 St. Pete	A+ TB	129	463	137	34	3	1	180	67	63	53	0	50	14	5	6	7	7	.50	11	.296	.381	.389

Year Team	Lg Org	G	AB	H	2B	3B	HR	TB	R	RBI	TBB	IBB	SO	HBP	SH	SF	SB	CS	SB%	GDP	Avg	OBP	SLG
1998 Bridgeport	IND —	87	305	84	19	2	6	125	53	42	44	1	25	9	3	4	9	5	.64	7	.275	.378	.410
1999 Orlando	AA TB	82	254	73	19	3	7	119	48	28	25	1	43	2	2	4	1	4	.20	7	.287	.351	.469
Durham	AAA TB	15	30	8	3	0	1	14	5	4	4	0	4	1	0	0	2	0	1.00	1	.267	.371	.467
2000 Bridgeport	IND —	31	111	25	7	0	2	38	19	13	14	0	19	4	1	0	5	0	1.00	4	.225	.333	.342
Orlando	AA TB	9	28	3	0	0	1	6	2	1	1	0	5	0	0	0	0	0	—	1	.107	.138	.214
Durham	AAA TB	15	46	8	0	0	0	8	6	4	5	0	6	1	3	0	1	1	.50	2	.174	.269	.174
Quebec	IND —	11	22	5	1	0	0	6	3	1	4	0	5	2	1	0	1	0	1.00	1	.227	.393	.273
Las Vegas	AAA SD	20	63	12	3	0	1	18	6	12	5	0	19	2	0	1	2	0	1.00	0	.190	.268	.286
9 Min. YEARS		685	2221	579	136	13	25	816	322	265	207	2	326	46	23	22	39	27	.59	55	.261	.333	.367

Mike Freehill

Pitches: Right **Bats:** Right **Pos:** RP-42   **Ht:** 6'2" **Wt:** 175 **Born:** 6/2/71 **Age:** 30

Year Team	Lg Org	G	GS	CG	GF	IP	BFP	H	R	ER	HR	SH	SF	HB	TBB	IBB	SO	WP	Bk	W	L	Pct.	ShO	Sv	ERA
1994 Boise	A- Ana	28	0	0	19	45	179	37	20	16	2	4	0	1	10	5	38	2	1	3	6	.333	0	8	3.20
1995 Cedar Rapids	A Ana	54	0	0	49	55	234	54	25	16	4	3	0	7	12	5	47	10	1	4	5	.444	0	28	2.62
1996 Vancouver	AAA Ana	7	0	0	3	10	53	16	11	11	1	0	1	1	8	1	5	4	0	1	1	.500	0	0	9.90
Midland	AA Ana	47	0	0	45	50	224	49	25	19	4	3	1	1	21	1	48	10	2	7	6	.538	0	17	3.42
1997 Midland	AA Ana	35	0	0	28	37	177	46	33	29	4	3	4	3	20	0	32	8	2	0	7	.000	0	10	7.05
Lk Elsinore	A+ Ana	21	0	0	18	22.2	89	18	7	5	1	0	0	0	8	0	20	1	0	0	1	.000	0	1	1.99
1999 Cedar Rapids	A Ana	2	0	0	1	2.1	15	2	3	3	0	0	0	1	4	0	2	0	1	0	0	—	0	0	11.57
Charlotte	A+ Tex	17	0	0	16	17.2	79	15	11	7	1	1	0	2	9	0	18	5	0	2	2	.500	0	8	3.57
2000 Oklahoma	AAA Tex	16	0	0	7	24	122	32	16	15	3	0	0	2	20	1	17	2	0	2	2	.500	0	0	5.63
Tulsa	AA Tex	26	0	0	14	45.1	215	52	30	28	5	3	2	7	26	1	31	7	0	0	3	.000	0	1	5.56
6 Min. YEARS		253	0	0	200	309	1387	321	181	149	25	17	8	25	138	14	258	49	7	19	33	.365	0	80	4.34

Ryan Freel

Bats: Right **Throws:** Right **Pos:** OF-38; 2B-26; DH-20; 3B-12; SS-1; PR-1   **Ht:** 5'10" **Wt:** 175 **Born:** 3/8/76 **Age:** 25

Year Team	Lg Org	G	AB	H	2B	3B	HR	TB	R	RBI	TBB	IBB	SO	HBP	SH	SF	SB	CS	SB%	GDP	Avg	OBP	SLG
1995 St.Cathrnes	A- Tor	65	243	68	10	5	3	97	30	29	22	0	49	7	7	5	12	7	.63	3	.280	.350	.399
1996 Dunedin	A+ Tor	104	381	97	23	3	4	138	64	41	33	0	76	5	14	2	19	15	.56	4	.255	.321	.362
1997 Knoxville	AA Tor	33	94	19	1	1	0	22	18	4	19	0	13	2	1	0	5	3	.63	3	.202	.348	.234
Dunedin	A+ Tor	61	181	51	8	2	3	72	42	17	46	2	28	9	6	1	24	5	.83	3	.282	.447	.398
1998 Knoxville	AA Tor	66	252	72	17	3	4	107	47	36	33	1	32	1	3	4	18	9	.67	3	.286	.366	.425
Syracuse	AAA Tor	37	118	27	4	0	2	37	19	12	26	0	16	4	0	3	9	4	.69	3	.229	.377	.314
1999 Knoxville	AA Tor	11	46	13	5	1	1	23	9	9	8	0	4	0	0	1	4	2	.67	0	.283	.382	.500
Syracuse	AAA Tor	20	77	23	3	2	1	33	15	11	8	0	13	4	1	0	10	3	.77	3	.299	.393	.429
2000 Dunedin	A+ Tor	4	18	9	1	0	3	19	7	6	0	0	1	0	0	0	5	0	—	0	.500	.500	1.056
Tennessee	AA Tor	12	44	13	3	1	0	18	11	8	8	0	6	1	0	2	2	3	.40	3	.295	.400	.409
Syracuse	AAA Tor	80	283	81	14	5	10	135	62	30	35	1	44	9	4	2	30	7	.81	3	.286	.380	.477
6 Min. YEARS		493	1737	473	89	23	31	701	324	203	238	3	282	42	36	20	133	58	.70	28	.272	.370	.404

Kai Freeman

Pitches: Right **Bats:** Right **Pos:** RP-28; SP-2   **Ht:** 6'2" **Wt:** 182 **Born:** 3/11/77 **Age:** 24

Year Team	Lg Org	G	GS	CG	GF	IP	BFP	H	R	ER	HR	SH	SF	HB	TBB	IBB	SO	WP	Bk	W	L	Pct.	ShO	Sv	ERA
1998 White Sox	R CWS	1	0	0	0	2	8	1	1	1	0	1	0	1	0	2	1	0	0	0	0	—	0	0	4.50
Bristol	R+ CWS	11	9	1	0	57.2	252	56	28	21	1	2	0	4	21	0	44	5	3	6	2	.750	0	0	3.28
1999 Winston-Sal	A+ CWS	32	8	0	5	95.1	417	100	58	52	13	6	4	5	32	1	64	1	1	2	6	.250	0	1	4.91
2000 Birmingham	AA CWS	30	2	0	8	52.2	238	57	32	23	5	3	4	1	22	1	31	4	0	3	2	.600	0	0	3.93
3 Min. YEARS		74	19	1	13	207.2	915	214	119	97	19	11	9	10	76	2	141	11	4	11	10	.524	0	1	4.20

Alejandro Freire

Bats: Right **Throws:** Right **Pos:** DH-70; 1B-61; OF-7; PH-1   **Ht:** 6'2" **Wt:** 185 **Born:** 8/23/74 **Age:** 26

Year Team	Lg Org	G	AB	H	2B	3B	HR	TB	R	RBI	TBB	IBB	SO	HBP	SH	SF	SB	CS	SB%	GDP	Avg	OBP	SLG
1994 Astros	R Hou	29	83	25	4	0	1	32	8	13	5	0	17	3	2	2	5	1	.83	0	.301	.355	.386
1995 Quad City	A Hou	125	417	127	23	1	15	197	71	65	50	1	83	6	2	7	9	5	.64	9	.305	.381	.472
1996 Kissimmee	A+ Hou	115	384	98	24	1	12	160	40	42	24	1	66	7	1	2	11	7	.61	11	.255	.309	.417
1997 Lakeland	A+ Det	130	477	154	30	2	24	260	85	92	50	1	84	12	0	1	13	4	.76	10	.323	.396	.545
1998 Jacksnville	AA Det	129	494	136	30	0	16	214	79	78	33	1	83	17	1	9	3	1	.75	16	.275	.336	.433
1999 Lakeland	A+ Det	13	41	9	3	0	1	15	6	5	10	0	7	3	1	1	0	0	—	1	.220	.400	.366
Jacksnville	AA Det	66	243	72	20	0	10	122	45	43	23	0	44	6	0	4	2	0	1.00	8	.296	.366	.502
2000 Jacksnville	AA Det	135	471	129	16	0	25	220	73	77	69	1	111	16	0	6	2	4	.33	13	.274	.381	.467
7 Min. YEARS		742	2610	750	150	4	104	1220	407	415	264	5	495	70	7	38	45	22	.67	68	.287	.364	.467

Brian Fuentes

Pitches: Left **Bats:** Left **Pos:** SP-26   **Ht:** 6'4" **Wt:** 220 **Born:** 8/9/75 **Age:** 25

Year Team	Lg Org	G	GS	CG	GF	IP	BFP	H	R	ER	HR	SH	SF	HB	TBB	IBB	SO	WP	Bk	W	L	Pct.	ShO	Sv	ERA
1996 Everett	A- Sea	13	2	0	3	26.2	114	23	14	13	2	0	1	0	13	0	26	5	0	0	1	.000	0	0	4.39
1997 Wisconsin	A Sea	22	22	0	0	118.2	486	84	52	47	6	3	3	8	59	0	153	11	3	6	7	.462	0	0	3.56
1998 Lancaster	A+ Sea	24	22	0	1	118.2	541	121	73	55	8	1	6	9	81	0	137	14	2	7	7	.500	0	0	4.17
1999 New Haven	AA Sea	15	14	0	0	60	272	53	36	33	5	2	5	11	46	0	66	1	1	3	3	.500	0	0	4.95
2000 New Haven	AA Sea	26	26	1	0	139.2	610	127	80	70	7	4	7	13	70	0	152	14	0	7	12	.368	0	0	4.51
5 Min. YEARS		100	86	1	4	463.2	2023	408	255	218	28	10	22	41	269	0	534	45	6	23	30	.434	0	0	4.23

97

Javier Fuentes

Bats: Right **Throws:** Right **Pos:** 3B-46; 2B-30; 1B-8; PH-5; DH-4; SS-2; OF-1; PR-1   **Ht:** 6'1" **Wt:** 182 **Born:** 9/27/74 **Age:** 26

					BATTING												BASERUNNING				PERCENTAGES		
Year Team	Lg Org	G	AB	H	2B	3B	HR	TB	R	RBI	TBB	IBB	SO	HBP	SH	SF	SB	CS	SB%	GDP	Avg	OBP	SLG
1996 Lowell	A- Bos	46	157	45	6	1	2	59	21	21	21	0	23	2	0	0	2	1	.67	4	.287	.378	.376
1997 Michigan	A Bos	30	77	13	1	1	0	16	10	8	7	0	18	4	2	0	1	1	.50	2	.169	.273	.208
Sarasota	A+ Bos	47	147	42	6	2	2	58	16	22	12	0	19	1	2	0	4	6	.40	2	.286	.344	.395
1998 Sarasota	A+ Bos	82	251	69	14	1	4	97	45	29	38	1	38	7	1	0	5	2	.71	5	.275	.385	.386
1999 Augusta	A Bos	39	130	33	4	1	1	42	16	13	22	0	13	4	1	1	6	1	.86	0	.254	.376	.323
Sarasota	A+ Bos	64	176	51	4	0	0	55	28	13	33	0	17	6	3	3	6	1	.86	2	.290	.413	.313
2000 Sarasota	A+ Bos	4	10	3	1	0	0	4	2	3	1	0	1	0	1	0	0	0	—	0	.300	.364	.400
Trenton	AA Bos	2	6	1	0	0	0	1	0	1	0	0	1	0	0	0	0	1	.00	0	.167	.286	.167
El Paso	AA Ari	5	7	2	0	0	0	2	1	0	2	0	0	0	0	0	0	0	—	0	.286	.444	.286
South Bend	A Ari	80	278	80	9	1	3	100	38	33	32	0	24	7	6	4	7	2	.78	6	.288	.371	.360
5 Min. YEARS		399	1239	339	45	7	12	434	177	142	169	1	153	31	16	8	31	15	.67	21	.274	.372	.350

Jody Fuller

Pitches: Right **Bats:** Right **Pos:** SP-21; RP-8   **Ht:** 6'3" **Wt:** 225 **Born:** 9/12/76 **Age:** 24

		HOW MUCH HE PITCHED						WHAT HE GAVE UP										THE RESULTS					
Year Team	Lg Org	G	GS	CG	GF	IP	BFP	H	R	ER	HR	SH	SF	HB	TBB	IBB	SO	WP	Bk	W	L	Pct.	ShO	Sv	ERA
1998 Lethbridge	R+ Ari	18	7	0	5	54.2	225	45	26	24	5	2	0	2	24	0	41	3	0	5	1	.833	0	0	3.95
1999 South Bend	A Ari	36	11	0	10	116.1	524	133	68	58	6	1	7	4	43	0	83	7	0	7	4	.636	0	0	4.49
2000 Tucson	AAA Ari	1	0	0	0	5	18	3	2	2	1	0	0	0	0	0	4	0	0	1	0	1.000	0	0	3.60
South Bend	A Ari	20	20	1	0	123.2	516	116	58	43	8	4	6	6	37	3	76	9	0	9	6	.600	0	0	3.13
El Paso	AA Ari	8	1	0	3	22.1	89	24	12	12	1	0	3	1	5	0	10	1	0	0	0	—	0	0	4.84
3 Min. YEARS		83	39	1	18	322	1372	321	166	139	21	7	16	13	109	3	214	20	0	22	11	.667	0	0	3.89

Joe Funaro

Bats: Right **Throws:** Right **Pos:** SS-50; 2B-16; OF-7; 3B-4; PH-4   **Ht:** 5'9" **Wt:** 175 **Born:** 3/20/73 **Age:** 28

					BATTING												BASERUNNING				PERCENTAGES		
Year Team	Lg Org	G	AB	H	2B	3B	HR	TB	R	RBI	TBB	IBB	SO	HBP	SH	SF	SB	CS	SB%	GDP	Avg	OBP	SLG
1995 Elmira	A- Fla	56	189	50	10	3	2	72	24	16	17	1	21	0	1	2	5	2	.71	3	.265	.322	.381
1996 Kane County	A Fla	89	291	90	20	2	7	135	57	43	40	2	42	7	5	4	5	3	.63	5	.309	.401	.464
1997 Brevard Cty	A+ Fla	125	470	150	16	6	4	190	67	53	49	3	65	7	3	6	9	5	.64	8	.319	.384	.404
1998 Portland	AA Fla	95	340	97	10	4	5	130	54	28	32	1	44	3	2	2	6	4	.60	8	.285	.350	.382
1999 Portland	AA Fla	74	268	98	19	1	3	128	42	40	31	1	22	4	3	4	6	6	.50	6	.366	.433	.478
2000 Calgary	AAA Fla	49	142	40	1	1	0	43	22	11	23	3	13	5	3	1	0	2	.00	3	.282	.398	.303
Portland	AA Fla	26	68	17	2	0	0	19	7	5	17	0	12	5	2	1	1	0	1.00	3	.250	.429	.279
6 Min. YEARS		514	1768	542	78	17	21	717	273	196	209	11	219	31	19	20	35	24	.59	36	.307	.386	.406

Eddy Furniss

Bats: Left **Throws:** Left **Pos:** 1B-77; DH-27; PH-19; PR-1   **Ht:** 6'2" **Wt:** 225 **Born:** 9/18/75 **Age:** 25

					BATTING												BASERUNNING				PERCENTAGES		
Year Team	Lg Org	G	AB	H	2B	3B	HR	TB	R	RBI	TBB	IBB	SO	HBP	SH	SF	SB	CS	SB%	GDP	Avg	OBP	SLG
1998 Augusta	A Pit	24	86	40	7	0	9	74	32	31	24	1	20	0	0	2	1	1	.50	2	.465	.571	.860
Carolina	AA Pit	16	44	6	1	0	0	7	1	3	4	0	13	0	0	2	0	0	—	1	.136	.200	.159
Lynchburg	A+ Pit	31	109	21	7	0	2	34	7	11	17	0	38	1	0	1	1	0	1.00	1	.193	.305	.312
1999 Lynchburg	A+ Pit	128	444	116	33	1	23	220	96	87	94	5	113	6	0	5	5	4	.56	13	.261	.393	.495
2000 Altoona	AA Pit	121	348	83	16	1	11	134	50	52	68	3	82	3	1	5	4	4	.50	4	.239	.363	.385
3 Min. YEARS		320	1031	266	64	2	45	469	186	184	207	9	266	10	1	15	11	9	.55	21	.258	.382	.455

Bryon Gainey

Bats: Left **Throws:** Right **Pos:** 1B-86; DH-14; PH-7; PR-1   **Ht:** 6'5" **Wt:** 225 **Born:** 1/23/76 **Age:** 25

					BATTING												BASERUNNING				PERCENTAGES		
Year Team	Lg Org	G	AB	H	2B	3B	HR	TB	R	RBI	TBB	IBB	SO	HBP	SH	SF	SB	CS	SB%	GDP	Avg	OBP	SLG
1994 Mets	R NYM	47	179	41	8	1	5	66	26	28	17	0	54	3	1	5	0	1	.00	1	.229	.299	.369
Kingsport	R+ NYM	10	32	5	0	0	3	14	4	7	4	1	16	0	0	0	0	2	.00	0	.156	.250	.438
1995 Capital Cty	A NYM	124	448	109	20	5	14	181	49	64	30	1	157	9	0	2	1	3	.25	7	.243	.303	.404
1996 Capital Cty	A NYM	122	446	97	23	0	14	162	53	62	41	3	169	5	0	3	5	2	.71	13	.217	.289	.363
1997 St. Lucie	A+ NYM	117	405	97	22	0	13	158	33	51	18	2	133	6	0	3	0	2	.00	7	.240	.280	.390
1998 Mets	R NYM	8	28	3	0	0	1	6	2	1	0	0	11	0	0	0	0	0	—	0	.107	.107	.214
St. Lucie	A+ NYM	88	336	94	15	3	19	172	47	57	16	2	116	3	0	3	1	3	.25	8	.280	.316	.512
1999 Binghamton	AA NYM	137	502	119	28	6	25	234	68	78	40	2	184	6	0	5	1	2	.33	9	.237	.298	.466
2000 Binghamton	AA NYM	106	345	70	18	0	11	121	36	49	23	3	132	0	1	1	1	2	.33	9	.203	.252	.351
7 Min. YEARS		759	2721	635	134	15	105	1114	318	397	189	14	972	32	2	22	9	17	.35	54	.233	.289	.409

Steve Gajkowski

Pitches: Right **Bats:** Right **Pos:** RP-46   **Ht:** 6'3" **Wt:** 215 **Born:** 12/30/69 **Age:** 31

		HOW MUCH HE PITCHED						WHAT HE GAVE UP										THE RESULTS					
Year Team	Lg Org	G	GS	CG	GF	IP	BFP	H	R	ER	HR	SH	SF	HB	TBB	IBB	SO	WP	Bk	W	L	Pct.	ShO	Sv	ERA
1990 Burlington	R+ Cle	14	10	1	1	63.2	287	74	34	29	0	0	3	3	23	0	44	0	1	2	6	.250	0	0	4.10
1991 Columbus	A Cle	3	0	0	2	6	24	3	2	2	0	0	0	0	5	0	5	0	0	0	0	—	0	0	3.00
Watertown	A- Cle	20	4	0	7	48	221	41	36	28	0	1	2	6	32	1	34	7	2	3	3	.500	0	0	5.25
1992 Utica	A- CWS	29	0	0	26	47	184	33	14	7	1	0	2	1	10	1	38	6	0	3	2	.600	0	14	1.34
1993 Sarasota	A+ CWS	43	0	0	38	69.2	273	52	21	16	1	3	3	4	17	5	45	5	1	3	3	.500	0	15	2.07
Birmingham	AA CWS	1	0	0	0	2.1	8	0	0	0	0	0	0	0	2	0	0	0	0	0	0	—	0	0	0.00
1994 Birmingham	AA CWS	58	0	0	32	82.1	355	78	35	28	6	4	3	3	26	1	44	2	0	11	5	.688	0	8	3.06
1995 Nashville	AAA CWS	15	0	0	5	24.2	103	26	15	7	2	0	1	1	8	1	12	1	0	1	0	1.000	0	0	2.55
Birmingham	AA CWS	35	0	0	14	51.2	230	64	27	24	4	2	0	2	16	1	29	1	0	4	4	.500	0	2	4.18

Year Team	Lg Org	G	GS	CG	GF	IP	BFP	H	R	ER	HR	SH	SF	HB	TBB	IBB	SO	WP	Bk	W	L	Pct.	ShO	Sv	ERA
		HOW MUCH HE PITCHED						WHAT HE GAVE UP												THE RESULTS					
1996 Nashville	AAA CWS	49	8	0	17	107.1	472	113	61	47	11	4	5	5	41	5	47	6	0	5	6	.455	0	2	3.94
1997 Tacoma	AAA Sea	44	3	0	10	93	394	100	43	40	11	2	1	5	24	0	48	3	1	5	3	.625	0	2	3.87
1998 Tacoma	AAA Sea	53	0	0	44	73.2	299	60	23	21	3	2	2	2	20	3	61	0	0	3	3	.500	0	24	2.57
1999 Iowa	AAA ChC	58	0	0	31	79.2	334	79	36	33	8	5	0	0	25	0	64	4	0	5	8	.385	0	9	3.73
2000 Midland	AA Oak	10	0	0	7	16	68	13	11	8	2	0	2	0	6	1	18	0	0	1	1	.500	0	1	4.50
Sacramento	AAA Oak	36	0	0	14	61.2	260	73	32	28	8	2	1	1	11	0	41	1	0	3	3	.500	0	5	4.09
1998 Seattle	AL	9	0	0	3	8.2	42	14	8	7	3	0	0	2	4	0	3	0	0	0	0	—	0	0	7.27
11 Min. YEARS		468	25	1	248	826.2	3512	809	390	318	57	27	25	35	264	19	532	36	5	48	48	.500	0	82	3.46

Shawn Gallagher

Bats: Right **Throws:** Right **Pos:** DH-56; 1B-48; OF-10; PH-4; PR-2; 3B-1   **Ht:** 6'0" **Wt:** 205 **Born:** 11/8/76 **Age:** 24

Year Team	Lg Org	G	AB	H	2B	3B	HR	TB	R	RBI	TBB	IBB	SO	HBP	SH	SF	SB	CS	SB%	GDP	Avg	OBP	SLG
		BATTING															BASERUNNING				PERCENTAGES		
1995 Rangers	R Tex	58	210	71	13	3	7	111	34	40	19	0	44	1	0	3	17	4	.81	7	.338	.391	.529
Hudson Val	A- Tex	5	20	3	2	0	0	5	1	4	1	0	4	1	0	0	0	0	—	2	.150	.227	.250
1996 Chston-SC	A Tex	88	303	68	11	4	7	108	29	32	18	0	104	6	3	2	6	1	.86	6	.224	.280	.356
Hudson Val	A- Tex	44	176	48	10	2	4	74	15	29	7	0	48	2	0	1	8	5	.62	5	.273	.306	.420
1997 Charlotte	A+ Tex	27	99	14	4	0	0	18	7	8	5	0	35	1	0	1	0	0	—	0	.141	.189	.182
Pulaski	R+ Tex	50	199	64	13	3	15	128	41	52	10	0	49	4	0	4	2	0	1.00	1	.322	.359	.643
1998 Charlotte	A+ Tex	137	520	160	37	4	26	283	111	121	66	3	116	7	0	10	18	6	.75	4	.308	.386	.544
1999 Tulsa	AA Tex	112	452	128	30	3	18	218	61	78	26	2	84	4	0	2	1	0	1.00	3	.283	.326	.482
2000 Tulsa	AA Tex	29	113	32	8	0	5	55	22	24	12	0	30	1	0	2	0	0	—	3	.283	.352	.487
Oklahoma	AAA Tex	64	219	52	9	3	6	85	27	30	23	1	43	1	1	5	1	4	.20	6	.237	.306	.388
Harrisburg	AA Mon	21	68	13	3	0	0	16	7	5	7	0	14	4	0	1	3	1	.75	3	.191	.300	.235
6 Min. YEARS		635	2379	653	140	22	88	1101	355	423	194	6	571	32	4	31	56	21	.73	46	.274	.333	.463

Randy Galvez

Pitches: Right **Bats:** Right **Pos:** SP-12   **Ht:** 6'2" **Wt:** 167 **Born:** 7/26/78 **Age:** 22

Year Team	Lg Org	G	GS	CG	GF	IP	BFP	H	R	ER	HR	SH	SF	HB	TBB	IBB	SO	WP	Bk	W	L	Pct.	ShO	Sv	ERA
		HOW MUCH HE PITCHED						WHAT HE GAVE UP												THE RESULTS					
1997 Great Falls	R+ LA	16	1	0	5	29.2	128	29	14	12	0	1	3	10	0	29	1	0	3	1	.750	0	0	3.64
2000 San Antonio	AA LA	12	12	0	0	63.1	281	74	40	36	5	1	4	30	0	35	3	0	4	4	.500	0	0	5.12
2 Min. YEARS		28	13	0	5	93	409	103	54	48	5	1	2	7	40	0	64	4	0	7	5	.583	0	0	4.65

Gus Gandarillas

Pitches: Right **Bats:** Right **Pos:** RP-62; SP-1   **Ht:** 6'0" **Wt:** 190 **Born:** 7/19/71 **Age:** 29

Year Team	Lg Org	G	GS	CG	GF	IP	BFP	H	R	ER	HR	SH	SF	HB	TBB	IBB	SO	WP	Bk	W	L	Pct.	ShO	Sv	ERA
		HOW MUCH HE PITCHED						WHAT HE GAVE UP												THE RESULTS					
1992 Elizabethtn	R+ Min	29	0	0	29	36	148	24	14	12	1	0	0	3	10	2	34	4	1	1	2	.333	0	13	3.00
1993 Fort Wayne	A Min	52	0	0	48	66.1	295	66	37	24	8	5	5	1	22	2	59	4	0	5	5	.500	0	25	3.26
1994 Fort Myers	A+ Min	37	0	0	34	46.2	190	37	7	4	0	3	2	2	13	4	39	5	0	4	1	.800	0	20	0.77
Nashville	AA Min	28	0	0	20	37	156	34	13	13	1	2	1	4	10	0	29	6	0	2	2	.500	0	3	3.16
1995 Salt Lake	AAA Min	22	0	0	13	29.1	135	34	23	21	5	3	1	1	19	4	17	5	0	2	3	.400	0	6	6.44
Hardware Cy	AA Min	25	0	0	18	32.1	152	38	26	22	1	7	0	3	16	0	25	3	0	2	4	.333	0	7	6.12
1996 Twins	R Min	3	1	0	2	9	43	10	3	1	1	1	0	0	3	0	14	1	0	0	0	—	0	2	1.00
Fort Wayne	A+ Min	4	0	0	3	6	35	9	7	6	0	0	1	1	8	0	3	1	0	0	0	—	0	1	9.00
1997 New Britain	AA Min	17	7	1	2	61.1	253	67	34	32	6	0	2	3	15	0	29	5	0	2	4	.333	0	0	4.70
Salt Lake	AAA Min	11	2	0	2	22.2	93	22	8	8	1	0	1	0	6	1	13	1	0	1	0	1.000	0	2	3.18
1998 Salt Lake	AAA Min	53	1	0	24	70	322	88	47	41	4	1	2	0	24	5	42	9	0	4	5	.444	0	4	5.27
1999 New Britain	AA Min	18	0	0	5	32.1	155	38	32	31	3	2	1	2	21	2	26	5	0	1	3	.250	0	0	8.63
Salt Lake	AAA Min	42	0	0	8	61.1	279	73	37	31	8	0	2	2	20	4	47	7	1	2	2	.500	0	2	4.55
2000 Salt Lake	AAA Min	63	1	0	26	89.2	399	105	50	43	9	4	7	2	33	4	75	6	0	9	4	.692	0	7	4.32
9 Min. YEARS		404	12	1	234	600	2655	645	338	289	48	23	21	25	220	28	452	62	2	35	35	.500	0	94	4.34

Jamie Gann

Bats: Right **Throws:** Right **Pos:** OF-103; PH-10; PR-3; DH-2   **Ht:** 6'1" **Wt:** 197 **Born:** 5/1/75 **Age:** 26

Year Team	Lg Org	G	AB	H	2B	3B	HR	TB	R	RBI	TBB	IBB	SO	HBP	SH	SF	SB	CS	SB%	GDP	Avg	OBP	SLG
		BATTING															BASERUNNING				PERCENTAGES		
1996 Lethbridge	R+ Ari	49	129	37	10	1	2	55	19	22	10	0	42	2	0	1	3	3	.50	4	.287	.345	.426
1997 South Bend	A Ari	12	36	6	1	0	0	7	4	3	1	0	9	0	1	0	0	1	.00	0	.167	.189	.194
High Desert	A+ Ari	91	267	60	12	2	6	94	33	32	17	2	71	1	2	2	2	1	.67	6	.225	.272	.352
1998 Diamondbcks	R Ari	2	7	3	1	0	0	4	1	1	0	0	2	0	0	0	0	0	—	0	.429	.429	.571
High Desert	A+ Ari	59	217	48	8	3	6	80	25	25	8	0	59	5	0	1	9	4	.69	4	.221	.264	.369
1999 El Paso	AA Ari	109	443	116	24	6	9	179	69	56	32	0	141	8	3	2	7	11	.39	8	.262	.322	.404
2000 El Paso	AA Ari	42	153	31	5	0	4	48	19	10	6	0	35	2	0	0	4	2	.67	4	.203	.242	.314
Diamondbcks	R Ari	6	19	9	3	0	0	12	5	7	0	0	1	0	0	0	2	0	1.00	0	.474	.500	.632
Tucson	AAA Ari	65	208	52	12	2	5	83	35	33	3	0	44	4	1	3	3	1	.75	6	.250	.271	.399
5 Min. YEARS		435	1479	362	76	14	32	562	210	189	77	2	404	23	7	9	30	23	.57	32	.245	.291	.380

Eddy Garabito

Bats: Both **Throws:** Right **Pos:** 2B-107; SS-9; DH-7; 3B-3; PR-1   **Ht:** 5'8" **Wt:** 170 **Born:** 12/2/78 **Age:** 22

Year Team	Lg Org	G	AB	H	2B	3B	HR	TB	R	RBI	TBB	IBB	SO	HBP	SH	SF	SB	CS	SB%	GDP	Avg	OBP	SLG
		BATTING															BASERUNNING				PERCENTAGES		
1997 Delmarva	A Bal	2	4	0	0	0	0	0	0	0	0	0	0	0	0	0	0	0	—	0	.000	.000	.000
Bluefield	R+ Bal	61	231	70	12	3	5	103	47	44	21	0	30	3	2	7	26	9	.74	5	.303	.359	.446
1998 Delmarva	A Bal	135	481	119	20	8	9	182	81	66	44	3	93	5	4	12	25	15	.63	9	.247	.310	.378
Frederick	A+ Bal	4	19	4	1	0	0	7	4	2	1	0	5	0	0	0	0	1	.00	1	.211	.250	.368
1999 Frederick	A+ Bal	132	539	138	24	4	6	188	76	77	52	1	68	4	8	10	38	18	.68	7	.256	.321	.349

Year Team	Lg Org	G	AB	H	2B	3B	HR	TB	R	RBI	TBB	IBB	SO	HBP	SH	SF	SB	CS	SB%	GDP	Avg	OBP	SLG
						BATTING												BASERUNNING				PERCENTAGES		
2000 Rochester	AAA Bal	9	35	3	1	0	0	4	3	0	2	0	10	0	0	0	1	0	1.00	2	.086	.135	.114
Bowie	AA Bal	116	482	121	21	3	6	166	72	52	27	1	55	5	8	7	22	9	.71	7	.251	.294	.344
4 Min. YEARS		459	1791	455	79	19	26	650	283	241	147	5	261	17	22	36	112	52	.68	30	.254	.311	.363

Amaury Garcia

Bats: Right **Throws:** Right **Pos:** 2B-92; OF-27; DH-1; PH-1   **Ht:** 5'10" **Wt:** 160 **Born:** 5/20/75 **Age:** 26

Year Team	Lg Org	G	AB	H	2B	3B	HR	TB	R	RBI	TBB	IBB	SO	HBP	SH	SF	SB	CS	SB%	GDP	Avg	OBP	SLG
1994 Marlins	R Fla	58	208	65	9	3	0	80	46	25	33	0	49	2	1	2	10	3	.77	4	.313	.408	.385
1995 Kane County	A Fla	26	58	14	4	1	1	23	19	5	10	0	12	1	0	0	5	2	.71	1	.241	.429	.397
Elmira	A- Fla	62	231	63	7	3	0	76	40	17	34	2	50	4	3	0	41	12	.77	1	.273	.375	.329
1996 Kane County	A Fla	105	391	103	19	7	6	154	65	36	62	2	83	5	7	2	37	19	.66	8	.263	.370	.394
1997 Brevard Cty	A+ Fla	124	479	138	30	2	7	193	77	44	49	2	97	5	14	5	45	11	.80	4	.288	.358	.403
1998 Portland	AA Fla	137	544	147	19	6	13	217	79	62	45	0	126	2	14	1	23	15	.61	7	.270	.328	.399
1999 Calgary	AAA Fla	119	479	152	37	9	17	258	94	53	44	0	79	6	7	1	17	11	.61	9	.317	.381	.539
2000 Calgary	AAA Fla	120	479	140	26	3	13	211	83	47	41	0	79	4	7	3	35	15	.70	15	.292	.351	.441
1999 Florida	NL	10	24	6	0	1	2	14	6	2	3	0	11	0	0	0	0	0	—	0	.250	.333	.583
7 Min. YEARS		751	2869	822	151	34	57	1212	503	289	326	6	575	29	53	12	213	88	.71	49	.287	.364	.422

Apostol Garcia

Pitches: Right **Bats:** Right **Pos:** RP-14; SP-8   **Ht:** 6'0" **Wt:** 155 **Born:** 8/3/76 **Age:** 24

Year Team	Lg Org	G	GS	CG	GF	IP	BFP	H	R	ER	HR	SH	SF	HB	TBB	IBB	SO	WP	Bk	W	L	Pct.	ShO	Sv	ERA
1997 W Michigan	A Det	33	5	0	10	65.2	275	48	26	22	2	1	0	4	31	0	52	10	2	7	2	.778	0	1	3.02
1998 Lakeland	A+ Det	34	16	1	6	119.1	560	155	89	72	14	2	2	10	52	0	56	8	1	5	8	.385	0	1	5.43
1999 Jacksnville	AA Det	3	0	0	2	4.1	14	0	0	0	0	0	0	0	1	0	0	0	0	0	0	—	0	0	0.00
San Antonio	AA LA	32	11	0	8	101.2	455	110	57	38	5	5	4	7	45	3	50	7	2	7	5	.583	0	1	3.36
2000 San Antonio	AA LA	18	4	0	6	34.1	171	49	39	28	4	3	3	3	23	1	22	4	0	0	3	.000	0	0	7.34
San Berndno	A+ LA	4	4	0	0	20	86	24	10	9	1	0	1	0	6	0	17	4	0	1	2	.333	0	0	4.05
4 Min. YEARS		124	40	1	32	345.1	1561	386	221	169	26	11	10	24	158	4	197	33	5	20	20	.500	0	3	4.40

Carlos Garcia

Bats: Right **Throws:** Right **Pos:** 2B-44; 3B-27; SS-21; PR-4; PH-2   **Ht:** 6'1" **Wt:** 195 **Born:** 10/15/67 **Age:** 33

Year Team	Lg Org	G	AB	H	2B	3B	HR	TB	R	RBI	TBB	IBB	SO	HBP	SH	SF	SB	CS	SB%	GDP	Avg	OBP	SLG
1987 Macon	A Pit	110	373	95	14	3	3	124	44	38	23	2	80	6	2	2	20	10	.67	6	.255	.307	.332
1988 Augusta	A Pit	73	269	78	13	2	1	98	32	45	22	0	46	1	2	1	11	6	.65	5	.290	.345	.364
Salem	A+ Pit	62	236	65	9	3	1	83	21	28	10	0	32	1	0	3	8	2	.80	9	.275	.304	.352
1989 Salem	A+ Pit	81	304	86	12	4	7	127	45	49	18	0	51	4	1	5	19	6	.76	3	.283	.326	.418
Harrisburg	AA Pit	54	188	53	5	5	3	77	28	25	8	0	36	0	0	1	6	4	.60	4	.282	.310	.410
1990 Harrisburg	AA Pit	65	242	67	11	2	5	97	36	25	16	0	36	3	1	1	12	1	.92	6	.277	.328	.401
Buffalo	AAA Pit	63	197	52	10	0	5	77	23	18	16	2	40	2	1	2	7	4	.64	5	.264	.323	.391
1991 Buffalo	AAA Pit	127	463	123	21	6	7	177	62	60	33	5	78	7	6	3	30	7	.81	6	.266	.322	.382
1992 Buffalo	AAA Pit	113	426	129	28	9	13	214	73	70	24	2	64	4	4	5	21	7	.75	7	.303	.342	.502
1996 Calgary	AAA Pit	2	6	2	0	0	0	4	0	0	0	0	0	0	0	0	0	0	—	0	.333	.333	.667
1998 Vancouver	AAA Ana	44	161	41	6	0	3	56	18	15	8	1	22	2	0	1	2	5	.29	2	.255	.297	.348
1999 Las Vegas	AAA SD	78	274	77	19	0	3	105	36	28	17	1	61	0	0	0	5	0	1.00	10	.281	.330	.383
2000 Columbus	AAA NYY	93	280	76	17	1	2	101	35	39	27	0	53	0	4	2	7	6	.54	7	.271	.333	.361
1990 Pittsburgh	NL	4	4	2	0	0	0	2	1	0	0	0	2	0	0	0	0	0	—	0	.500	.500	.500
1991 Pittsburgh	NL	12	24	6	0	0	0	10	2	1	1	0	8	0	0	0	0	0	—	1	.250	.280	.417
1992 Pittsburgh	NL	22	39	8	1	0	0	9	4	4	0	0	9	0	1	2	0	0	—	1	.205	.195	.231
1993 Pittsburgh	NL	141	546	147	25	5	12	218	77	47	31	2	67	9	6	5	18	11	.62	9	.269	.316	.399
1994 Pittsburgh	NL	98	412	114	15	2	6	151	49	28	16	2	67	4	1	1	18	9	.67	6	.277	.309	.367
1995 Pittsburgh	NL	104	367	108	24	2	6	154	41	50	25	5	55	2	5	3	8	4	.67	4	.294	.340	.420
1996 Pittsburgh	NL	101	390	111	18	4	6	155	66	44	23	3	58	4	3	2	16	6	.73	3	.285	.329	.397
1997 Toronto	AL	103	350	77	18	2	3	108	29	23	15	0	60	2	10	4	11	3	.79	7	.220	.253	.309
1998 Anaheim	AL	19	35	5	1	0	0	6	4	0	3	0	11	1	1	0	2	0	1.00	4	.143	.231	.171
1999 San Diego	NL	6	11	2	0	0	0	2	1	0	1	0	3	0	0	0	0	0	—	2	.182	.250	.182
10 Min. YEARS		965	3419	944	165	36	53	1340	453	440	222	13	599	33	21	26	148	58	.72	70	.276	.324	.392
10 Maj. YEARS		610	2178	580	102	17	33	815	274	197	115	12	340	22	27	17	73	33	.69	33	.266	.307	.374

Freddy Garcia

Bats: Right **Throws:** Right **Pos:** DH-51; 3B-37; OF-15; PH-3   **Ht:** 6'2" **Wt:** 224 **Born:** 8/1/72 **Age:** 28

Year Team	Lg Org	G	AB	H	2B	3B	HR	TB	R	RBI	TBB	IBB	SO	HBP	SH	SF	SB	CS	SB%	GDP	Avg	OBP	SLG
1993 Medcine Hat	R+ Tor	72	264	63	8	2	11	108	47	42	31	1	71	2	1	4	4	5	.44	3	.239	.319	.409
1994 St.Cathrnes	A- Tor	73	260	74	10	2	13	127	46	40	33	1	57	2	1	3	1	3	.25	6	.285	.366	.488
1996 Lynchburg	A+ Pit	129	474	145	39	3	21	253	79	86	44	2	86	1	0	12	4	2	.67	10	.306	.358	.534
1997 Calgary	AAA Pit	35	121	29	6	0	5	50	21	17	9	3	20	1	0	2	0	0	—	6	.240	.293	.413
Carolina	AA Pit	73	282	82	17	4	19	164	47	57	18	2	56	6	0	1	0	1	.00	11	.291	.342	.582
1998 Nashville	AAA Pit	88	326	88	24	4	22	186	52	55	25	0	89	4	0	3	0	2	.00	12	.270	.327	.571
1999 Nashville	AAA Pit	4	9	0	0	0	0	0	0	0	1	0	3	0	0	0	0	0	—	1	.000	.100	.000
2000 Pawtucket	AAA Bos	105	386	101	27	2	24	204	52	74	27	0	82	4	0	3	0	3	.00	11	.262	.315	.530
1995 Pittsburgh	NL	42	57	8	1	0	0	11	5	1	8	0	17	0	1	0	0	1	.00	0	.140	.246	.193
1997 Pittsburgh	NL	20	40	6	1	0	3	16	4	5	2	0	17	0	0	0	0	0	—	0	.150	.190	.400
1998 Pittsburgh	NL	56	172	44	11	1	9	84	27	26	18	3	45	2	0	1	0	2	.00	3	.256	.332	.488
1999 Pittsburgh	NL	55	130	30	5	0	6	53	16	23	4	0	41	0	0	1	0	0	—	3	.231	.252	.408
Atlanta	NL	2	2	1	0	0	0	1	1	1	0	0	1	0	0	0	0	0	—	0	.500	.667	2.000
7 Min. YEARS		579	2121	582	131	17	115	1092	344	371	188	9	464	20	2	31	9	16	.36	61	.274	.335	.515
4 Maj. YEARS		175	401	89	18	2	19	168	53	56	33	3	121	2	1	2	0	3	.00	6	.222	.283	.419

Guillermo Garcia

Bats: Right **Throws:** Right **Pos:** C-51; 1B-29; PH-9; DH-7; SS-3; 3B-3; PR-2; 2B-1   **Ht:** 6'3" **Wt:** 215 **Born:** 4/4/72 **Age:** 29

Year	Team	Lg Org	G	AB	H	2B	3B	HR	TB	R	RBI	TBB	IBB	SO	HBP	SH	SF	SB	CS	SB%	GDP	Avg	OBP	SLG
1990	Mets	R NYM	42	136	25	1	2	0	30	9	6	7	1	34	1	2	1	1	1	.50	2	.184	.228	.221
1991	Kingsport	R+ NYM	15	33	8	1	1	0	11	9	2	4	0	4	0	0	0	0	0	—	1	.242	.324	.333
	Pittsfield	A- NYM	45	157	43	13	2	0	60	22	24	15	0	38	1	3	3	4	1	.80	5	.274	.335	.382
1992	Pittsfield	A- NYM	73	272	54	11	1	2	73	36	26	20	0	52	2	0	3	3	4	.43	5	.199	.256	.268
1993	Capital Cty	A NYM	119	429	124	28	2	3	165	64	72	49	1	60	10	1	3	10	8	.56	11	.289	.373	.385
1994	St. Lucie	A+ NYM	55	203	48	9	1	1	62	22	23	13	1	24	3	2	0	0	2	.00	6	.236	.292	.305
1995	Winston-Sal	A+ Cin	78	245	58	10	2	3	81	26	29	28	0	32	1	2	2	2	2	.50	7	.237	.315	.331
1996	Indianapols	AAA Cin	16	47	12	2	0	0	14	4	0	2	2	6	0	0	0	0	0	—	5	.255	.286	.298
	Chattanooga	AA Cin	60	203	64	12	0	6	94	25	36	12	2	32	1	2	1	3	3	.50	3	.315	.355	.463
1997	Chattanooga	AA Cin	20	74	21	1	1	4	36	11	19	8	0	13	0	0	1	0	0	—	1	.284	.349	.486
	Indianapols	AAA Cin	55	151	36	2	0	10	68	16	20	9	0	46	1	0	2	0	2	.00	9	.238	.282	.450
1998	Indianapols	AAA Cin	93	334	85	20	0	19	162	48	60	22	1	81	0	1	0	0	0	—	9	.254	.301	.485
1999	Chattanooga	AA Cin	10	42	13	3	3	1	25	11	7	2	0	6	1	0	0	0	0	—	3	.310	.356	.595
	Indianapols	AAA Cin	65	233	67	9	0	10	106	30	28	22	2	44	5	0	5	1	1	.50	12	.288	.355	.455
2000	Louisville	AAA StL	102	327	89	24	2	14	159	38	55	25	1	54	2	1	5	2	2	.50	9	.272	.323	.486
1998	Cincinnati	NL	12	36	7	2	0	2	15	3	4	2	0	13	0	0	0	0	0	—	2	.194	.237	.417
1999	Florida	NL	4	4	1	0	0	0	1	0	0	0	0	2	0	0	0	0	0	—	0	.250	.250	.250
11	Min. YEARS		848	2886	747	146	17	73	1146	371	407	238	11	526	28	14	26	26	28	.48	83	.259	.319	.397
2	Maj. YEARS		16	40	8	2	0	2	16	3	4	2	0	15	0	0	0	0	0	—	2	.200	.238	.400

Jose Garcia

Pitches: Right **Bats:** Right **Pos:** SP-18; RP-1   **Ht:** 6'3" **Wt:** 195 **Born:** 4/29/78 **Age:** 23

Year	Team	Lg Org	G	GS	CG	GF	IP	BFP	H	R	ER	HR	SH	SF	HB	TBB	IBB	SO	WP	Bk	W	L	Pct.	ShO	Sv	ERA
1996	Helena	R+ Mil	2	0	0	0	1.2	9	3	3	3	0	0	0	0	3	0	2	1	0	0	0	—	0	0	16.20
1997	Beloit	A Mil	27	26	2	0	155.1	682	145	89	69	9	7	3	5	70	1	126	12	4	6	11	.353	0	0	4.00
1998	Stockton	A+ Mil	28	28	1	0	169.1	749	147	89	69	12	3	9	10	91	1	167	16	0	11	12	.478	0	0	3.67
2000	Huntsville	AA Mil	19	18	0	0	103	463	107	52	43	8	3	4	5	54	0	78	6	0	4	8	.333	0	0	3.76
4	Min. YEARS		76	72	3	0	429.1	1903	400	233	184	29	13	16	20	218	2	373	35	4	21	31	.404	0	0	3.86

Luis Garcia

Bats: Right **Throws:** Right **Pos:** SS-94; 3B-9; PH-9; 2B-4; DH-1   **Ht:** 6'0" **Wt:** 175 **Born:** 5/20/75 **Age:** 26

Year	Team	Lg Org	G	AB	H	2B	3B	HR	TB	R	RBI	TBB	IBB	SO	HBP	SH	SF	SB	CS	SB%	GDP	Avg	OBP	SLG
1993	Bristol	R+ Det	24	57	12	1	0	1	16	7	7	3	0	11	0	1	0	3	1	.75	1	.211	.250	.281
1994	Jamestown	A- Det	67	239	47	8	2	1	62	21	19	8	0	48	1	6	3	6	9	.40	4	.197	.223	.259
1995	Lakeland	A+ Det	102	361	101	10	4	2	125	39	35	8	0	42	1	4	4	9	10	.47	6	.280	.294	.346
	Jacksnville	AA Det	17	47	13	0	0	0	13	6	5	1	0	8	1	0	0	2	1	.67	0	.277	.306	.277
1996	Jacksnville	AA Det	131	522	128	22	4	9	185	68	46	12	1	90	2	7	2	15	12	.56	9	.245	.264	.354
1997	Jacksnville	AA Det	126	456	122	19	1	5	158	55	48	10	0	59	3	6	6	3	2	.60	15	.268	.284	.346
1998	Toledo	AAA Det	114	407	105	19	4	3	141	37	31	8	0	59	1	3	3	3	2	.60	11	.258	.272	.346
1999	Toledo	AAA Det	89	308	82	19	1	3	112	30	34	5	0	41	1	3	5	3	3	.50	12	.266	.276	.364
2000	Memphis	AAA StL	112	386	112	17	3	11	168	53	44	13	0	65	5	4	2	5	5	.50	11	.290	.320	.435
1999	Detroit	AL	8	9	1	0	0	0	2	0	0	0	0	2	0	0	0	0	0	—	0	.111	.111	.222
8	Min. YEARS		782	2783	722	115	19	35	980	316	269	68	1	423	15	34	25	49	45	.52	69	.259	.278	.352

Neil Garcia

Bats: Both **Throws:** Right **Pos:** C-43; DH-9; PH-3; 1B-2; PR-2; 3B-1   **Ht:** 6'0" **Wt:** 206 **Born:** 4/6/73 **Age:** 28

Year	Team	Lg Org	G	AB	H	2B	3B	HR	TB	R	RBI	TBB	IBB	SO	HBP	SH	SF	SB	CS	SB%	GDP	Avg	OBP	SLG
1995	Fayetteville	A Det	88	251	58	12	1	7	93	46	33	59	0	49	10	2	4	3	6	.33	5	.231	.392	.371
1997	St. Pete	A+ TB	75	195	44	10	2	0	58	33	21	31	3	20	2	5	5	2	3	.40	7	.226	.330	.297
1998	St. Pete	A+ TB	92	328	105	20	0	6	143	45	52	40	4	40	2	1	2	3	4	.43	6	.320	.395	.436
1999	Orlando	AA TB	31	95	27	6	0	1	36	13	11	10	0	16	1	3	3	0	1	.00	2	.284	.349	.379
	Durham	AAA TB	12	33	3	1	0	1	7	1	2	2	0	8	0	0	1	1	0	1.00	1	.091	.139	.212
2000	Durham	AAA TB	24	85	17	4	0	0	21	8	6	8	0	15	1	0	1	1	1	.50	2	.200	.274	.247
	Orlando	AA TB	34	99	20	3	2	1	30	11	6	16	1	27	0	0	1	0	0	—	1	.202	.310	.303
5	Min. YEARS		356	1086	274	56	5	16	388	157	131	166	8	175	16	11	17	10	15	.40	24	.252	.355	.357

Osmani Garcia

Bats: Right **Throws:** Right **Pos:** 3B-83; SS-3; DH-1; PH-1; PR-1   **Ht:** 6'0" **Wt:** 210 **Born:** 9/6/74 **Age:** 26

Year	Team	Lg Org	G	AB	H	2B	3B	HR	TB	R	RBI	TBB	IBB	SO	HBP	SH	SF	SB	CS	SB%	GDP	Avg	OBP	SLG
2000	Charlotte	A+ Tex	44	170	57	12	1	6	89	26	34	5	0	14	1	4	2	1	2	.33	3	.335	.354	.524
	Oklahoma	AAA Tex	43	148	40	7	0	2	53	17	20	10	0	14	1	1	1	1	2	.33	2	.270	.319	.358
1	Min. YEARS		87	318	97	19	1	8	142	43	54	15	0	28	2	5	3	2	4	.33	5	.305	.337	.447

Lee Gardner

Pitches: Right **Bats:** Right **Pos:** RP-57   **Ht:** 6'0" **Wt:** 211 **Born:** 1/16/75 **Age:** 26

Year	Team	Lg Org	G	GS	CG	GF	IP	BFP	H	R	ER	HR	SH	SF	HB	TBB	IBB	SO	WP	Bk	W	L	Pct.	ShO	Sv	ERA
1998	St. Pete	A+ TB	3	0	0	1	4	15	3	0	0	0	0	0	0	1	0	2	0	0	0	0	—	0	0	0.00
	Chston-SC	A TB	28	0	0	13	35.2	154	38	18	16	3	2	0	1	4	0	55	1	0	0	3	.000	0	3	4.04
1999	Orlando	AA TB	1	0	0	0	2	9	3	2	2	0	0	0	0	1	0	1	0	0	0	0	—	0	0	9.00
	St. Pete	A+ TB	20	0	0	13	23	96	20	7	5	1	1	1	2	5	0	22	0	0	2	0	1.000	0	7	1.96

101

Year Team	Lg Org	G	GS	CG	GF	IP	BFP	H	R	ER	HR	SH	SF	HB	TBB	IBB	SO	WP	Bk	W	L	Pct.	ShO	Sv	ERA
		HOW MUCH HE PITCHED						WHAT HE GAVE UP												THE RESULTS					
2000 Orlando	AA TB	36	0	0	24	45	186	34	19	17	0	4	3	2	14	1	48	6	0	3	2	.600	0	12	3.40
Durham	AAA TB	21	0	0	9	18.2	75	12	7	7	1	1	0	0	9	1	8	1	0	1	0	1.000	0	5	3.38
3 Min. YEARS		109	0	0	60	128.1	535	110	53	47	5	8	4	5	34	2	136	8	0	6	5	.545	0	27	3.30

Hal Garrett

Pitches: Right **Bats:** Right **Pos:** RP-41; SP-7 **Ht:** 6'2" **Wt:** 175 **Born:** 4/27/75 **Age:** 26

Year Team	Lg Org	G	GS	CG	GF	IP	BFP	H	R	ER	HR	SH	SF	HB	TBB	IBB	SO	WP	Bk	W	L	Pct.	ShO	Sv	ERA
		HOW MUCH HE PITCHED						WHAT HE GAVE UP												THE RESULTS					
1993 Padres	R SD	14	14	0	0	72.1	317	64	40	26	3	0	1	5	31	2	83	6	0	6	5	.545	0	0	3.24
1994 Springfield	A SD	21	20	0	0	102.1	454	93	67	54	8	2	5	6	54	2	79	9	2	7	4	.636	0	0	4.75
1995 Clinton	A SD	11	11	1	0	58	268	58	43	36	4	5	2	4	34	3	41	5	0	3	8	.273	0	0	5.59
Rancho Cuca	A+ SD	23	1	0	5	42	196	40	21	13	2	2	5	2	25	0	43	7	1	0	4	.000	0	0	2.79
1996 Clinton	A SD	25	3	0	11	49.2	229	45	28	25	4	2	2	5	31	2	60	3	0	2	3	.400	0	1	4.53
Rancho Cuca	A+ SD	24	1	0	3	51	214	41	12	11	3	1	2	3	20	0	56	6	0	4	1	.800	0	0	1.94
1997 Carolina	AA Pit	6	0	0	2	13.1	64	19	14	13	6	1	0	0	6	1	7	2	0	1	2	.333	0	0	8.78
Lynchburg	A+ Pit	29	5	0	11	56	250	56	36	30	5	4	3	4	22	3	45	5	0	2	5	.286	0	5	4.82
Savannah	A LA	8	1	0	4	16	78	21	15	15	0	1	0	2	7	0	13	4	0	0	3	.000	0	0	8.44
1998 Vero Beach	A+ LA	20	20	1	0	112.1	506	111	75	62	11	1	3	7	57	0	86	10	0	6	6	.500	0	0	4.97
San Antonio	AA LA	11	2	0	6	22.1	95	21	9	9	1	0	0	0	13	0	13	2	0	2	1	.667	0	2	3.63
1999 San Antonio	AA LA	42	4	0	13	94.2	404	70	47	38	8	7	2	1	55	4	76	9	0	5	9	.357	0	2	3.61
Albuquerque	AAA LA	1	0	0	0	2.1	11	3	4	4	1	0	0	0	2	0	1	0	0	0	1	1.000	0	0	15.43
2000 Albuquerque	AAA LA	27	2	0	8	40	182	42	27	24	4	1	0	2	23	0	29	5	0	3	4	.429	0	1	5.40
San Antonio	AA LA	21	5	0	6	47.1	236	57	39	33	3	2	1	5	40	1	32	5	1	1	6	.143	0	0	6.27
8 Min. YEARS		283	89	2	69	779.2	3504	741	477	393	63	29	26	46	420	18	664	78	4	42	62	.404	0	11	4.54

Josh Garrett

Pitches: Right **Bats:** Right **Pos:** RP-16; SP-13 **Ht:** 6'4" **Wt:** 205 **Born:** 1/12/78 **Age:** 23

Year Team	Lg Org	G	GS	CG	GF	IP	BFP	H	R	ER	HR	SH	SF	HB	TBB	IBB	SO	WP	Bk	W	L	Pct.	ShO	Sv	ERA
		HOW MUCH HE PITCHED						WHAT HE GAVE UP												THE RESULTS					
1996 Red Sox	R Bos	7	5	0	0	27	108	22	8	5	0	2	0	5	5	0	17	0	0	1	1	.500	0	0	1.67
1997 Michigan	A Bos	22	22	2	0	138.2	619	164	94	74	13	7	4	13	35	0	64	23	3	8	10	.444	0	0	4.80
1998 Sarasota	A+ Bos	26	25	5	0	155.1	692	182	108	90	17	3	5	14	40	1	68	4	1	8	12	.400	2	0	5.21
1999 Sarasota	A+ Bos	26	26	0	0	149	682	189	87	76	9	1	6	17	50	2	95	7	0	8	10	.444	0	0	4.59
2000 Trenton	AA Bos	13	5	0	0	37.1	198	69	48	37	3	2	4	2	16	1	22	2	1	1	3	.250	0	0	8.92
Sarasota	A+ Bos	16	8	0	1	54	248	68	46	41	9	4	1	8	9	2	36	1	1	2	6	.250	0	0	6.83
5 Min. YEARS		110	91	7	1	561.1	2548	694	391	323	51	19	20	59	155	6	302	37	6	28	42	.400	2	0	5.18

Matt Garrick

Bats: Right **Throws:** Right **Pos:** C-98; PH-3; 3B-1; OF-1; PR-1 **Ht:** 6'0" **Wt:** 185 **Born:** 8/19/75 **Age:** 25

Year Team	Lg Org	G	AB	H	2B	3B	HR	TB	R	RBI	TBB	IBB	SO	HBP	SH	SF	SB	CS	SB%	GDP	Avg	OBP	SLG
		BATTING															BASERUNNING				PERCENTAGES		
1997 Boise	A- Ana	5	20	6	0	0	0	6	1	4	3	0	2	0	0	0	0	0	—	1	.300	.391	.300
Cedar Rapds	A Ana	28	95	21	6	1	0	29	11	14	12	0	23	2	1	0	1		1.00	7	.221	.321	.305
1998 Cedar Rapds	A Ana	61	212	52	13	0	4	77	27	25	29	0	55	1	2	0	5	1	.83	7	.245	.339	.363
1999 Potomac	A+ StL	70	216	36	10	1	3	57	17	17	32	0	57	0	3	1	1	5	.17	4	.167	.273	.264
2000 Arkansas	AA StL	101	325	76	17	0	4	105	33	35	36	3	71	2	1	1	1	2	.33	12	.234	.313	.323
4 Min. YEARS		265	868	191	46	2	11	274	89	95	112	3	208	5	7	2	8	8	.50	26	.220	.312	.316

Chris Garza

Pitches: Left **Bats:** Left **Pos:** RP-58 **Ht:** 5'11" **Wt:** 187 **Born:** 7/23/75 **Age:** 25

Year Team	Lg Org	G	GS	CG	GF	IP	BFP	H	R	ER	HR	SH	SF	HB	TBB	IBB	SO	WP	Bk	W	L	Pct.	ShO	Sv	ERA
		HOW MUCH HE PITCHED						WHAT HE GAVE UP												THE RESULTS					
1996 Elizabethtn	R+ Min	22	0	0	12	36.1	145	26	8	8	1	1	1	2	12	0	44	3	3	4	0	1.000	0	5	1.98
1997 Fort Wayne	A Min	60	0	0	32	95	385	67	28	21	2	3	2	3	38	1	90	11	0	5	2	.714	0	15	1.99
1998 Fort Myers	A+ Min	58	0	0	43	82	358	73	33	25	3	9	4	4	46	3	63	9	0	5	5	.500	0	14	2.74
1999 Fort Myers	A+ Min	21	1	0	10	40.1	169	36	16	14	1	1	1	3	18	0	30	3	1	1	2	.333	0	2	3.12
New Britain	AA Min	31	0	0	8	30.1	129	14	10	7	0	2	1	4	19	0	40	4	0	1	0	1.000	0	0	2.08
2000 New Britain	AA Min	39	0	0	10	43.2	195	34	21	17	1	2	2	2	26	2	52	1	0	2	4	.333	0	0	3.50
Salt Lake	AAA Min	19	0	0	11	20.2	101	28	19	14	1	2	1	0	13	1	19	2	0	1	1	.500	0	0	6.10
5 Min. YEARS		250	1	0	126	348.1	1482	278	135	106	11	20	12	18	172	7	338	33	4	19	14	.576	0	36	2.74

Matt Gawer

Pitches: Left **Bats:** Left **Pos:** RP-33 **Ht:** 6'4" **Wt:** 235 **Born:** 4/15/78 **Age:** 23

Year Team	Lg Org	G	GS	CG	GF	IP	BFP	H	R	ER	HR	SH	SF	HB	TBB	IBB	SO	WP	Bk	W	L	Pct.	ShO	Sv	ERA
		HOW MUCH HE PITCHED						WHAT HE GAVE UP												THE RESULTS					
1999 Jamestown	A- Atl	21	0	0	13	30	128	24	12	11	1	0	2	2	18	0	44	4	0	2	1	.667	0	6	3.30
2000 Richmond	AAA Atl	3	0	0	3	5	26	6	6	6	1	0	1	1	2	0	5	0	0	0	0	—	0	0	10.80
Macon	A Atl	30	0	0	14	51.1	211	36	20	17	2	4	1	2	20	1	59	2	0	5	1	.833	0	2	2.98
2 Min. YEARS		54	0	0	30	86.1	365	66	38	34	4	4	4	5	40	1	108	6	0	7	2	.778	0	7	3.54

Marty Gazarek

Bats: Right **Throws:** Right **Pos:** OF-56; DH-3; PH-3 **Ht:** 6'2" **Wt:** 205 **Born:** 6/1/73 **Age:** 28

Year Team	Lg Org	G	AB	H	2B	3B	HR	TB	R	RBI	TBB	IBB	SO	HBP	SH	SF	SB	CS	SB%	GDP	Avg	OBP	SLG
		BATTING															BASERUNNING				PERCENTAGES		
1994 Williamsprt	A- ChC	45	181	68	13	0	2	87	22	18	6	0	17	2	3	0	14	7	.67	2	.376	.402	.481
Peoria	A ChC	23	89	29	6	0	1	38	18	12	2	0	14	3	0	2	2	3	.40	4	.326	.354	.427

Year Team	Lg Org	G	AB	H	2B	3B	HR	TB	R	RBI	TBB	IBB	SO	HBP	SH	SF	SB	CS	SB%	GDP	Avg	OBP	SLG
1995 Rockford	A ChC	107	399	104	24	1	3	139	57	53	27	1	58	8	2	3	7	5	.58	8	.261	.318	.348
1996 Daytona	A+ ChC	129	472	131	31	4	11	203	68	77	28	0	52	12	0	5	15	13	.54	10	.278	.331	.430
1997 Orlando	AA ChC	76	290	96	23	0	10	149	55	52	20	2	31	5	0	2	10	3	.77	3	.331	.382	.514
1998 West Tenn	AA ChC	21	64	21	4	2	1	32	14	11	13	1	10	2	0	1	6	2	.75	3	.328	.450	.500
Iowa	AAA ChC	88	238	61	16	0	4	89	33	16	16	0	38	5	2	0	4	3	.57	5	.256	.317	.374
1999 Iowa	AAA ChC	40	128	41	12	0	5	68	13	16	5	1	13	1	0	1	0	1	.00	2	.320	.348	.531
West Tenn	AA ChC	35	128	38	9	1	6	67	16	27	4	1	7	3	0	1	2	5	.29	3	.297	.331	.523
2000 Greenville	AA Atl	61	202	58	10	0	7	89	27	28	18	0	32	8	0	2	5	3	.63	4	.287	.365	.441
7 Min. YEARS		625	2191	647	148	8	50	961	323	310	139	6	272	49	7	17	65	45	.59	44	.295	.348	.439

Geoff Geary

Pitches: Right Bats: Right Pos: SP-22   Ht: 6'0" Wt: 175 Born: 8/26/76 Age: 24

Year Team	Lg Org	G	GS	CG	GF	IP	BFP	H	R	ER	HR	SH	SF	HB	TBB	IBB	SO	WP	Bk	W	L	Pct.	ShO	Sv	ERA
1998 Batavia	A- Phi	16	15	1	1	95.1	368	78	20	17	6	3	0	0	14	0	101	3	0	9	1	.900	1	0	1.60
1999 Clearwater	A+ Phi	24	19	2	0	139	611	175	77	61	11	6	4	5	31	1	77	6	3	10	5	.667	0	0	3.95
2000 Reading	AA Phi	22	22	1	0	129.1	553	141	66	59	15	2	4	7	22	0	112	1	2	7	6	.538	0	0	4.11
3 Min. YEARS		62	56	4	1	363.2	1532	394	163	137	32	11	8	12	67	1	290	10	5	26	12	.684	1	0	3.39

Chris George

Pitches: Left Bats: Left Pos: SP-26   Ht: 6'1" Wt: 165 Born: 9/16/79 Age: 21

Year Team	Lg Org	G	GS	CG	GF	IP	BFP	H	R	ER	HR	SH	SF	HB	TBB	IBB	SO	WP	Bk	W	L	Pct.	ShO	Sv	ERA
1998 Royals	R KC	5	4	0	0	15.2	65	14	9	5	1	1	0	0	4	0	10	0	0	0	1	.000	0	0	2.87
1999 Wilmington	A+ KC	27	27	0	0	145	618	142	65	58	8	3	4	5	53	0	142	5	1	9	7	.563	0	0	3.60
2000 Wichita	AA KC	18	18	0	0	97.1	429	92	41	34	5	3	6	6	51	1	80	2	2	8	5	.615	0	0	3.14
Omaha	AAA KC	8	8	0	0	44.2	194	47	29	24	8	0	1	1	20	0	27	1	1	3	2	.600	0	0	4.84
3 Min. YEARS		58	57	0	0	302.2	1306	295	144	121	22	7	11	12	128	1	259	8	4	20	15	.571	0	0	3.60

Esteban German

Bats: Right Throws: Right Pos: 2B-130; PR-4; SS-2   Ht: 5'9" Wt: 165 Born: 12/26/78 Age: 22

Year Team	Lg Org	G	AB	H	2B	3B	HR	TB	R	RBI	TBB	IBB	SO	HBP	SH	SF	SB	CS	SB%	GDP	Avg	OBP	SLG
1998 Athletics	R Oak	55	202	62	3	10	2	91	52	28	33	0	43	4	2	1	40	8	.83	1	.307	.413	.450
1999 Modesto	A+ Oak	128	501	156	16	12	4	208	107	52	102	0	128	5	5	7	40	16	.71	3	.311	.428	.415
2000 Midland	AA Oak	24	75	16	1	0	1	20	13	6	18	0	21	2	2	0	5	3	.63	1	.213	.379	.267
Visalia	A+ Oak	109	428	113	14	10	2	153	82	35	61	0	86	5	4	2	78	8	.91	4	.264	.361	.357
3 Min. YEARS		316	1206	347	34	32	9	472	254	121	214	0	278	16	13	10	163	35	.82	9	.288	.399	.391

Jody Gerut

Bats: Left Throws: Left Pos: OF-90; DH-16; PH-6   Ht: 6'0" Wt: 190 Born: 9/18/77 Age: 23

Year Team	Lg Org	G	AB	H	2B	3B	HR	TB	R	RBI	TBB	IBB	SO	HBP	SH	SF	SB	CS	SB%	GDP	Avg	OBP	SLG
1999 Salem	A+ Col	133	499	144	33	11	11	232	80	63	61	4	65	3	1	3	25	12	.68	10	.289	.367	.465
2000 Carolina	AA Col	109	362	103	32	3	3	150	48	57	76	2	54	2	1	7	18	11	.62	9	.285	.405	.414
2 Min. YEARS		242	861	247	65	14	14	382	128	120	137	6	119	5	2	10	43	23	.65	19	.287	.384	.444

Jay Gibbons

Bats: Left Throws: Left Pos: 1B-101; DH-23; OF-12; PH-3   Ht: 6'0" Wt: 200 Born: 3/2/77 Age: 24

Year Team	Lg Org	G	AB	H	2B	3B	HR	TB	R	RBI	TBB	IBB	SO	HBP	SH	SF	SB	CS	SB%	GDP	Avg	OBP	SLG
1998 Medcine Hat	R+ Tor	73	290	115	29	1	19	203	66	98	37	1	25	3	0	9	2	1	.67	7	.397	.457	.700
1999 Hagerstown	A Tor	71	292	89	20	2	16	161	53	69	32	1	56	1	0	5	3	0	1.00	12	.305	.370	.551
Dunedin	A+ Tor	60	212	66	14	0	9	107	34	39	25	0	38	0	0	1	2	1	.67	4	.311	.382	.505
2000 Tennessee	AA Tor	132	474	152	38	1	19	249	85	75	61	5	67	10	0	7	3	1	.75	10	.321	.404	.525
3 Min. YEARS		336	1268	422	101	4	63	720	238	281	155	7	186	14	0	22	10	3	.77	33	.333	.405	.568

Kevin Gibbs

Bats: Both Throws: Right Pos: OF-21; DH-8; PR-1   Ht: 6'2" Wt: 185 Born: 4/3/74 Age: 27

Year Team	Lg Org	G	AB	H	2B	3B	HR	TB	R	RBI	TBB	IBB	SO	HBP	SH	SF	SB	CS	SB%	GDP	Avg	OBP	SLG
1995 Yakima	A- LA	52	182	57	6	4	1	74	36	18	36	1	46	5	2	3	38	5	.88	3	.313	.434	.407
Vero Beach	A+ LA	7	20	5	1	0	0	6	1	2	0	0	0	0	0	0	1	0	1.00	0	.250	.250	.300
San Berndno	A+ LA	5	13	3	1	0	0	4	1	0	0	0	2	0	0	0	1	0	1.00	0	.231	.231	.308
1996 Vero Beach	A+ LA	118	423	114	9	11	0	145	69	33	65	0	80	4	6	4	60	19	.76	6	.270	.369	.343
1997 San Antonio	AA LA	101	358	120	21	6	2	159	89	34	72	3	48	6	6	3	49	19	.72	2	.335	.451	.444
1998 Albuquerque	AAA LA	2	8	1	0	0	0	1	1	1	2	0	1	0	0	0	0	0	—	0	.125	.300	.125
1999 Albuquerque	AAA LA	11	21	6	3	0	0	9	4	1	4	0	6	1	1	0	2	2	.50	0	.286	.423	.429
2000 Albuquerque	AAA LA	2	6	0	0	0	0	0	0	0	0	0	2	0	0	0	0	0	—	0	.000	.000	.000
Vero Beach	A+ LA	3	8	4	0	0	1	7	3	3	2	0	0	0	0	0	2	1	.67	0	.500	.600	.875
San Berndno	A+ LA	13	53	19	3	2	1	29	13	13	11	0	9	0	0	1	10	3	.77	1	.358	.462	.547
San Antonio	AA LA	11	42	8	0	1	0	10	5	4	6	0	9	1	0	1	4	1	.80	1	.190	.300	.238
Carolina	AA Col	1	1	1	0	0	0	1	0	0	0	0	0	0	0	0	0	0	—	0	1.000	1.000	1.000
6 Min. YEARS		326	1135	338	44	24	5	445	222	109	198	4	203	17	15	12	167	50	.77	12	.298	.406	.392

David Gibralter

Bats: Right **Throws:** Right **Pos:** 1B-125; DH-9; PH-1   **Ht:** 6'3" **Wt:** 224 **Born:** 6/19/75 **Age:** 26

Year Team	Lg Org	G	AB	H	2B	3B	HR	TB	R	RBI	TBB	IBB	SO	HBP	SH	SF	SB	CS	SB%	GDP	Avg	OBP	SLG
1993 Red Sox	R Bos	48	177	48	14	0	3	71	23	27	11	1	34	6	1	2	1	1	.50	3	.271	.332	.401
1994 Sarasota	A+ Bos	51	184	35	5	1	4	54	20	18	6	1	41	1	0	0	1	2	.33	2	.190	.220	.293
Utica	A- Bos	62	222	57	11	0	5	83	31	32	14	2	40	5	1	2	3	1	.75	5	.257	.313	.374
1995 Michigan	A Bos	121	456	115	34	1	16	199	48	82	20	2	79	8	3	4	3	4	.43	7	.252	.293	.436
1996 Sarasota	A+ Bos	120	452	129	34	3	12	205	47	70	30	3	101	9	0	4	8	7	.53	9	.285	.339	.454
1997 Trenton	AA Bos	123	478	131	25	1	14	200	70	86	44	3	103	9	1	4	3	5	.38	10	.274	.344	.418
1998 Trenton	AA Bos	100	385	100	16	0	15	161	48	61	25	2	91	7	1	6	2	3	.40	5	.260	.312	.418
1999 Trenton	AA Bos	124	448	134	22	1	24	230	76	97	32	3	68	13	2	5	5	5	.50	13	.299	.359	.513
2000 Bowie	AA Bal	134	497	141	20	1	19	220	70	87	39	0	81	12	2	9	3	1	.75	18	.284	.345	.443
8 Min. YEARS		883	3299	890	181	8	112	1423	433	560	221	17	638	70	11	36	29	29	.50	72	.270	.326	.431

Steve Gibralter

Bats: Right **Throws:** Right **Pos:** OF-61; PH-3; DH-1   **Ht:** 6'0" **Wt:** 195 **Born:** 10/9/72 **Age:** 28

Year Team	Lg Org	G	AB	H	2B	3B	HR	TB	R	RBI	TBB	IBB	SO	HBP	SH	SF	SB	CS	SB%	GDP	Avg	OBP	SLG
1990 Reds	R Cin	52	174	45	11	3	4	74	26	27	23	1	30	3	3	1	8	2	.80	5	.259	.353	.425
1991 Chston-WV	A Cin	140	544	145	36	7	6	213	72	71	31	2	117	5	2	6	11	13	.46	14	.267	.309	.392
1992 Cedar Rapds	A Cin	137	529	162	32	3	19	257	92	99	51	4	99	12	1	3	12	9	.57	8	.306	.378	.486
1993 Chattanooga	AA Cin	132	477	113	25	3	11	177	65	47	20	2	108	7	3	4	7	12	.37	6	.237	.276	.371
1994 Chattanooga	AA Cin	133	460	124	28	3	14	200	71	63	47	0	114	9	4	5	10	8	.56	5	.270	.345	.435
1995 Indianapols	AAA Cin	79	263	83	19	3	18	162	49	63	25	3	70	4	1	2	0	2	.00	6	.316	.381	.616
1996 Indianapols	AAA Cin	126	447	114	29	2	11	180	58	54	26	6	114	2	1	3	2	3	.40	10	.255	.297	.403
1997 Chattanooga	AA Cin	30	97	25	9	0	2	40	20	12	13	1	22	2	1	3	0	0	—	6	.258	.348	.412
1998 Chattanooga	AA Cin	17	67	18	4	0	1	25	8	4	6	0	13	1	1	0	1	0	1.00	3	.269	.338	.373
Indianapols	AAA Cin	68	226	58	12	4	11	111	34	31	10	0	66	2	0	1	1	2	.33	3	.257	.293	.491
1999 Omaha	AAA KC	110	417	111	21	1	28	218	77	78	27	1	97	13	2	2	6	3	.67	9	.266	.329	.523
2000 Charlotte	AAA CWS	65	237	60	9	2	11	106	33	37	17	3	54	1	1	2	7	0	1.00	5	.253	.304	.447
1995 Cincinnati	NL	4	3	1	0	0	0	1	0	0	0	0	0	0	0	0	0	0	—	0	.333	.333	.333
1996 Cincinnati	NL	2	2	0	0	0	0	0	0	0	0	0	2	0	0	0	0	0	—	0	.000	.000	.000
11 Min. YEARS		1089	3938	1058	235	31	136	1763	605	586	296	23	904	61	20	32	65	54	.55	77	.269	.327	.448
2 Maj. YEARS		6	5	1	0	0	0	1	0	0	0	0	2	0	0	0	0	0	—	0	.200	.200	.200

Derrick Gibson

Bats: Right **Throws:** Right **Pos:** OF-94; PH-5; DH-1; PR-1   **Ht:** 6'2" **Wt:** 244 **Born:** 2/5/75 **Age:** 26

Year Team	Lg Org	G	AB	H	2B	3B	HR	TB	R	RBI	TBB	IBB	SO	HBP	SH	SF	SB	CS	SB%	GDP	Avg	OBP	SLG
1993 Rockies	R Col	34	119	18	2	2	0	24	13	10	5	0	55	3	0	1	3	0	1.00	1	.151	.203	.202
1994 Bend	A- Col	73	284	75	19	5	12	140	47	57	29	5	102	9	0	1	14	4	.78	4	.264	.350	.493
1995 Asheville	A Col	135	506	148	16	10	32	280	91	115	29	5	136	19	1	6	31	13	.70	10	.292	.350	.553
1996 New Haven	AA Col	122	449	115	21	4	15	189	58	62	31	1	125	8	1	4	3	12	.20	15	.256	.313	.421
1997 New Haven	AA Col	119	461	146	24	2	23	243	91	75	36	7	100	10	0	2	20	13	.61	8	.317	.377	.527
Colo Spngs	AAA Col	21	78	33	7	0	3	49	14	12	5	1	9	0	0	1	0	2	.00	1	.423	.458	.628
1998 Colo Spngs	AAA Col	126	497	145	20	3	14	213	84	81	35	2	110	3	0	2	14	6	.70	17	.292	.341	.429
1999 Colo Spngs	AAA Col	110	385	106	19	6	17	188	68	67	30	0	82	6	0	2	12	6	.67	5	.275	.336	.488
2000 Calgary	AAA Fla	100	340	95	12	2	10	141	43	43	18	2	84	9	1	2	13	7	.65	5	.279	.331	.415
1998 Colorado	NL	7	21	9	1	0	0	10	4	2	1	0	4	1	0	0	0	0	—	0	.429	.478	.476
1999 Colorado	NL	10	28	5	1	0	2	12	2	6	0	0	7	1	0	0	0	0	—	2	.179	.207	.429
8 Min. YEARS		840	3119	881	140	34	126	1467	509	522	218	23	803	67	3	20	110	63	.64	66	.282	.341	.470
2 Maj. YEARS		17	49	14	2	0	2	22	6	8	1	0	11	2	0	0	0	0	—	2	.286	.327	.449

David Gil

Pitches: Right **Bats:** Right **Pos:** SP-7; RP-3   **Ht:** 6'4" **Wt:** 215 **Born:** 10/1/78 **Age:** 22

Year Team	Lg Org	G	GS	CG	GF	IP	BFP	H	R	ER	HR	SH	SF	HB	TBB	IBB	SO	WP	Bk	W	L	Pct.	ShO	Sv	ERA
2000 Dayton	A Cin	4	4	0	0	26.2	109	20	13	8	1	2	0	1	11	0	15	1	0	1	1	.500	0	0	2.70
Chattanooga	AA Cin	6	3	0	1	25	105	15	7	6	1	0	0	8	13	0	25	3	0	2	0	1.000	0	1	2.16
1 Min. YEARS		10	7	0	1	51.2	214	35	20	14	2	2	0	9	24	0	40	4	0	3	1	.750	0	1	2.44

Geronimo Gil

Bats: Right **Throws:** Right **Pos:** C-91; OF-20; PH-4; 3B-3; 1B-3; DH-2   **Ht:** 6'2" **Wt:** 195 **Born:** 8/7/75 **Age:** 25

Year Team	Lg Org	G	AB	H	2B	3B	HR	TB	R	RBI	TBB	IBB	SO	HBP	SH	SF	SB	CS	SB%	GDP	Avg	OBP	SLG
1996 Savannah	A LA	79	276	67	13	1	7	103	29	38	8	3	69	5	1	3	0	2	.00	4	.243	.274	.373
1997 Vero Beach	A+ LA	66	213	53	13	1	6	86	30	24	15	0	41	4	1	0	3	0	1.00	5	.249	.310	.404
1998 San Antonio	AA LA	75	241	70	17	3	6	111	27	29	15	0	43	0	2	2	2	1	.67	8	.290	.329	.461
1999 San Antonio	AA LA	106	343	97	26	1	15	170	47	59	49	1	58	2	0	4	2	0	1.00	15	.283	.372	.496
2000 San Antonio	AA LA	100	352	100	19	1	11	154	42	58	33	3	65	6	1	5	3	2	.60	8	.284	.351	.438
Albuquerque	AAA LA	15	50	19	5	0	2	30	9	22	5	0	8	0	0	2	0	1	.00	1	.380	.421	.600
5 Min. YEARS		441	1475	406	93	7	47	654	184	230	125	7	284	17	5	16	10	6	.63	41	.275	.336	.443

Marcus Giles

Bats: Right **Throws:** Right **Pos:** 2B-125; PH-4; DH-3   **Ht:** 5'8" **Wt:** 180 **Born:** 5/18/78 **Age:** 23

Year Team	Lg Org	G	AB	H	2B	3B	HR	TB	R	RBI	TBB	IBB	SO	HBP	SH	SF	SB	CS	SB%	GDP	Avg	OBP	SLG
1997 Danville	R+ Atl	55	207	72	13	3	8	115	53	45	32	1	47	3	1	3	5	2	.71	4	.348	.437	.556

Year Team	Lg Org	G	AB	H	2B	3B	HR	TB	R	RBI	TBB	IBB	SO	HBP	SH	SF	SB	CS	SB%	GDP	Avg	OBP	SLG
1998 Macon	A Atl	135	505	166	38	3	37	321	111	108	85	4	103	10	0	3	12	5	.71	15	.329	.433	.636
1999 Myrtle Bch	A+ Atl	126	497	162	40	7	13	255	80	73	54	5	89	4	0	5	9	6	.60	9	.326	.393	.513
2000 Greenville	AA Atl	132	458	133	28	2	17	216	73	62	72	6	71	2	0	1	25	5	.83	11	.290	.388	.472
4 Min. YEARS		448	1667	533	119	15	75	907	317	288	243	15	310	19	1	12	51	18	.74	39	.320	.410	.544

Tim Giles

Bats: Left **Throws:** Right **Pos:** DH-71; 1B-43; PH-2; PR-1; P-1   **Ht:** 6'3" **Wt:** 215 **Born:** 9/12/75 **Age:** 25

Year Team	Lg Org	G	AB	H	2B	3B	HR	TB	R	RBI	TBB	IBB	SO	HBP	SH	SF	SB	CS	SB%	GDP	Avg	OBP	SLG
1996 Medcine Hat	R+ Tor	68	258	69	17	0	10	116	36	45	19	2	52	0	0	3	5	0	1.00	7	.267	.314	.450
1997 Hagerstown	A Tor	112	380	127	32	0	12	195	54	56	46	4	95	2	0	7	2	2	.50	8	.334	.402	.513
1998 Dunedin	A+ Tor	102	363	110	20	2	18	188	53	65	31	3	83	0	1	3	3	2	.60	4	.303	.355	.518
1999 Knoxville	AA Tor	133	505	157	24	2	18	239	76	114	56	5	93	6	1	10	2	2	.00	13	.311	.380	.473
2000 Tennessee	AA Tor	115	397	105	18	0	13	162	43	56	53	6	98	1	0	5	1	6	.14	11	.264	.349	.408
5 Min. YEARS		530	1903	568	111	4	71	900	262	336	205	20	421	9	2	28	11	12	.48	43	.298	.365	.473

Jason Gilfillan

Pitches: Right **Bats:** Right **Pos:** RP-43   **Ht:** 6'6" **Wt:** 215 **Born:** 8/31/76 **Age:** 24

Year Team	Lg Org	G	GS	CG	GF	IP	BFP	H	R	ER	HR	SH	SF	HB	TBB	IBB	SO	WP	Bk	W	L	Pct.	ShO	Sv	ERA
1997 Spokane	A- KC	16	0	0	5	16	82	16	13	9	0	1	0	1	16	1	22	3	0	2	1	.667	0	0	5.06
1998 Royals	R KC	7	6	0	0	9	42	10	8	8	1	0	0	1	4	0	6	1	0	1	1	.500	0	0	8.00
Spokane	A- KC	6	0	0	0	7.1	36	7	5	4	0	0	1	1	6	0	8	0	0	0	0	—	0	0	4.91
1999 Chston-WV	A KC	8	0	0	1	11.2	66	22	21	19	2	0	0	1	6	0	9	1	0	0	1	.000	0	0	14.66
Spokane	A- KC	25	0	0	7	34.2	161	31	23	22	6	3	4	6	22	0	37	3	1	4	1	.800	0	1	5.71
2000 Chston-WV	A KC	30	0	0	19	45	202	45	24	21	3	0	3	4	21	0	44	4	0	1	2	.333	0	7	4.20
Wilmington	A+ KC	12	0	0	3	15.1	74	13	6	3	0	0	0	1	13	1	20	2	0	3	1	.750	0	1	1.76
Omaha	AAA KC	1	0	0	1	1	4	0	0	0	0	0	0	0	1	0	2	0	0	0	0	—	0	0	0.00
4 Min. YEARS		105	6	0	36	140	667	144	100	86	12	4	8	15	89	2	148	14	1	11	7	.611	0	9	5.53

Eric Gillespie

Bats: Left **Throws:** Right **Pos:** 1B-32; 3B-17; DH-14; OF-6; PH-2; 2B-1   **Ht:** 5'10" **Wt:** 200 **Born:** 6/6/75 **Age:** 26

Year Team	Lg Org	G	AB	H	2B	3B	HR	TB	R	RBI	TBB	IBB	SO	HBP	SH	SF	SB	CS	SB%	GDP	Avg	OBP	SLG
1996 Boise	A- Ana	61	192	53	11	5	3	83	28	38	25	1	50	1	1	3	8	0	1.00	4	.276	.357	.432
1997 Cedar Rapds	A Ana	122	421	107	26	7	18	201	78	72	55	0	80	4	0	4	8	0	1.00	7	.254	.343	.477
1998 Lk Elsinore	A+ Ana	30	98	31	12	0	3	52	13	11	14	1	21	1	0	0	2	1	.67	1	.316	.407	.531
1999 Jacksnville	AA Det	118	474	145	28	6	19	242	80	88	53	2	89	2	0	5	12	2	.86	12	.306	.375	.511
2000 Toledo	AAA Det	69	239	62	17	0	8	103	25	39	19	0	49	0	0	2	0	2	.00	3	.259	.312	.431
5 Min. YEARS		400	1424	398	94	18	51	681	224	248	166	4	289	8	1	14	22	6	.79	27	.279	.355	.478

Isabel Giron

Pitches: Right **Bats:** Right **Pos:** RP-69   **Ht:** 6'2" **Wt:** 170 **Born:** 11/17/77 **Age:** 23

Year Team	Lg Org	G	GS	CG	GF	IP	BFP	H	R	ER	HR	SH	SF	HB	TBB	IBB	SO	WP	Bk	W	L	Pct.	ShO	Sv	ERA
1998 Hagerstown	A Tor	21	21	4	0	126.1	517	110	57	35	11	6	3	7	27	1	129	7	2	10	9	.526	3	0	2.49
Knoxville	AA Tor	6	5	0	0	35.1	145	29	15	15	5	0	1	0	13	1	35	3	0	1	1	.500	0	0	3.82
1999 Knoxville	AA Tor	17	16	0	0	95.2	423	97	59	52	12	3	6	7	39	0	81	1	1	7	5	.583	0	0	4.89
Mobile	AA SD	11	11	0	0	62.2	273	71	49	44	17	1	3	1	15	1	45	2	0	4	7	.364	0	0	6.32
2000 Mobile	AA SD	69	0	0	21	79	339	71	52	49	9	5	1	7	32	2	77	4	1	5	5	.500	0	5	5.58
3 Min. YEARS		124	53	4	21	399	1697	378	232	195	54	15	14	22	126	5	367	17	4	27	27	.500	3	5	4.40

Chris Gissell

Pitches: Right **Bats:** Right **Pos:** SP-16   **Ht:** 6'5" **Wt:** 200 **Born:** 1/4/78 **Age:** 23

Year Team	Lg Org	G	GS	CG	GF	IP	BFP	H	R	ER	HR	SH	SF	HB	TBB	IBB	SO	WP	Bk	W	L	Pct.	ShO	Sv	ERA
1996 Cubs	R ChC	11	10	0	0	61.1	246	54	23	16	1	0	1	4	8	0	64	1	3	4	2	.667	0	0	2.35
1997 Rockford	A ChC	26	24	3	1	143.2	646	155	89	71	7	5	4	11	62	1	105	11	3	6	11	.353	1	0	4.45
1998 Rockford	A ChC	5	5	0	0	33.2	138	27	8	3	0	1	1	1	15	0	23	1	0	3	0	1.000	0	0	0.80
Daytona	A+ ChC	22	21	1	0	136	597	149	80	63	12	3	5	11	38	1	123	7	0	7	6	.538	0	0	4.17
West Tenn	AA ChC	1	1	0	0	4	21	5	7	6	2	0	0	0	4	0	1	0	0	0	1	.000	0	0	13.50
1999 West Tenn	AA ChC	20	18	0	0	97.2	470	121	76	65	10	4	6	10	62	3	57	9	2	3	8	.273	0	0	5.99
2000 West Tenn	AA ChC	16	16	0	0	93	395	80	39	32	6	3	2	6	41	1	65	2	0	7	5	.583	0	0	3.10
5 Min. YEARS		101	95	4	1	569.1	2513	591	322	256	38	16	19	43	230	8	441	31	8	30	33	.476	1	0	4.05

Mike Glavine

Bats: Left **Throws:** Left **Pos:** 1B-108; OF-15; PH-10   **Ht:** 6'3" **Wt:** 210 **Born:** 1/24/73 **Age:** 28

Year Team	Lg Org	G	AB	H	2B	3B	HR	TB	R	RBI	TBB	IBB	SO	HBP	SH	SF	SB	CS	SB%	GDP	Avg	OBP	SLG
1995 Burlington	R+ Cle	46	155	38	10	0	11	81	28	28	22	0	37	1	0	2	1	0	1.00	0	.245	.339	.523
1996 Columbus	A Cle	38	119	33	5	0	6	56	17	16	28	2	33	1	0	2	0	0	—	2	.277	.416	.471
1997 Columbus	A Cle	114	397	95	16	0	28	195	62	75	80	1	127	3	0	1	0	0	.00	1	.239	.370	.491
1998 Kinston	A+ Cle	125	398	87	23	1	22	178	61	76	73	4	117	5	2	6	1	4	.20	4	.219	.342	.447
1999 Greenville	AA Atl	107	305	82	24	0	17	157	47	52	49	0	65	1	0	2	0	3	.00	3	.269	.370	.515
2000 Greenville	AA Atl	128	423	99	26	0	11	158	37	81	36	3	83	5	0	7	1	1	.50	7	.234	.297	.374
6 Min. YEARS		558	1797	434	104	1	95	825	252	328	288	10	462	16	2	19	3	9	.25	26	.242	.348	.459

Mike Glendenning

Bats: Right **Throws:** Right **Pos:** OF-61; DH-37; 1B-20; PH-10   **Ht:** 6'0" **Wt:** 225 **Born:** 8/26/76 **Age:** 24

		BATTING															BASERUNNING				PERCENTAGES		
Year Team	Lg Org	G	AB	H	2B	3B	HR	TB	R	RBI	TBB	IBB	SO	HBP	SH	SF	SB	CS	SB%	GDP	Avg	OBP	SLG
1996 Bellingham	A- SF	73	265	69	19	4	12	132	54	48	39	0	80	1	1	2	4	6	.40	6	.260	.355	.498
1997 Bakersfield	A+ SF	134	503	130	27	0	33	256	95	100	63	1	150	4	0	7	1	4	.20	15	.258	.341	.509
1998 Shreveport	AA SF	78	254	62	12	2	7	99	27	33	35	1	57	4	0	0	0	0	—	2	.244	.344	.390
San Jose	A+ SF	48	176	44	9	0	10	83	26	33	24	0	66	0	0	0	1	1	.50	5	.250	.340	.472
1999 San Jose	A+ SF	104	368	90	26	1	23	187	71	80	71	2	112	11	0	3	7	4	.64	10	.245	.380	.508
Shreveport	AA SF	32	106	28	6	0	5	49	14	19	12	0	30	1	0	1	1	1	.50	2	.264	.342	.462
2000 Fresno	AAA SF	40	139	27	7	0	6	52	17	18	13	0	41	1	0	2	0	1	.00	2	.194	.265	.374
Shreveport	AA SF	85	291	76	14	0	16	138	50	54	36	4	87	5	0	2	1	1	.50	5	.261	.350	.474
5 Min. YEARS		594	2102	526	120	7	112	996	354	385	293	8	623	27	1	18	15	18	.45	47	.250	.347	.474

Dave Glick

Pitches: Left **Bats:** Left **Pos:** RP-35   **Ht:** 6'1" **Wt:** 190 **Born:** 4/2/76 **Age:** 25

		HOW MUCH HE PITCHED						WHAT HE GAVE UP												THE RESULTS					
Year Team	Lg Org	G	GS	CG	GF	IP	BFP	H	R	ER	HR	SH	SF	HB	TBB	IBB	SO	WP	Bk	W	L	Pct.	ShO	Sv	ERA
1995 Brewers	R Mil	18	0	0	4	25.1	115	24	13	12	0	1	0	1	14	0	29	4	4	2	0	1.000	0	0	4.26
1996 Ogden	R+ Mil	24	0	0	4	34.1	165	31	16	13	3	2	1	4	21	3	41	3	0	3	1	.750	0	0	3.41
1997 Duluth-Sup	IND —	25	9	0	5	75	335	89	49	37	8	3	5	5	23	1	56	3	1	3	4	.429	0	0	4.44
1998 Duluth-Sup	IND —	21	20	1	0	119.2	553	149	85	69	10	1	4	9	44	1	76	6	1	7	10	.412	1	0	5.19
1999 Michigan	A Hou	10	0	0	3	16.1	66	7	2	1	0	0	0	3	5	1	20	2	0	1	0	1.000	0	1	0.55
Kissimmee	A+ Hou	32	0	0	10	44	206	47	29	23	1	2	2	4	22	2	41	3	0	0	3	.000	0	0	4.70
2000 Kissimmee	A+ Hou	3	0	0	2	4	17	4	2	2	0	0	0	0	1	0	4	1	0	0	0	—	0	0	4.50
Round Rock	AA Hou	32	0	0	18	33	163	40	23	20	2	3	0	4	27	0	21	2	0	2	2	.500	0	0	5.45
6 Min. YEARS		165	29	1	46	351.2	1620	391	218	177	24	12	12	30	157	8	288	24	6	18	20	.474	1	1	4.53

Gary Glover

Pitches: Right **Bats:** Right **Pos:** SP-27   **Ht:** 6'5" **Wt:** 205 **Born:** 12/3/76 **Age:** 24

		HOW MUCH HE PITCHED						WHAT HE GAVE UP												THE RESULTS					
Year Team	Lg Org	G	GS	CG	GF	IP	BFP	H	R	ER	HR	SH	SF	HB	TBB	IBB	SO	WP	Bk	W	L	Pct.	ShO	Sv	ERA
1994 Blue Jays	R Tor	2	0	0	0	1.1	13	4	8	7	1	0	0	1	4	0	2	1	1	0	0	—	0	0	47.25
1995 Blue Jays	R Tor	12	10	2	0	62.1	279	62	48	34	4	4	3	11	26	0	46	8	0	3	7	.300	0	0	4.91
1996 Medcine Hat	R+ Tor	15	15	2	0	83.2	410	119	94	72	14	2	4	6	29	1	54	8	1	3	12	.200	0	0	7.75
1997 Hagerstown	A Tor	28	28	3	0	173.2	751	165	94	72	9	3	5	10	58	1	155	20	4	6	17	.261	0	0	3.73
1998 Knoxville	AA Tor	8	8	0	0	37.1	183	41	36	28	2	1	3	3	28	0	14	2	0	0	5	.000	0	0	6.75
Dunedin	A+ Tor	19	18	0	0	109.1	484	117	66	52	8	1	6	7	36	0	88	11	1	7	6	.538	0	0	4.28
1999 Knoxville	AA Tor	13	13	1	0	86	346	70	39	34	5	2	1	4	27	0	77	4	0	8	2	.800	0	0	3.56
Syracuse	AAA Tor	14	14	0	0	76.1	347	93	50	44	10	0	3	4	35	0	57	3	1	4	6	.400	0	0	5.19
2000 Syracuse	AAA Tor	27	27	1	0	166.2	731	181	104	93	21	2	4	2	62	0	119	5	0	9	9	.500	0	0	5.02
1999 Toronto	AL	1	0	0	1	1	3	0	0	0	0	0	0	0	1	0	0	0	0	0	0	—	0	0	0.00
7 Min. YEARS		138	133	9	0	796.2	3544	852	539	436	74	15	29	44	305	2	612	62	8	40	64	.385	0	0	4.93

Geoff Goetz

Pitches: Left **Bats:** Left **Pos:** RP-44   **Ht:** 5'11" **Wt:** 163 **Born:** 4/3/79 **Age:** 22

		HOW MUCH HE PITCHED						WHAT HE GAVE UP												THE RESULTS					
Year Team	Lg Org	G	GS	CG	GF	IP	BFP	H	R	ER	HR	SH	SF	HB	TBB	IBB	SO	WP	Bk	W	L	Pct.	ShO	Sv	ERA
1997 Mets	R NYM	8	6	0	1	26.1	112	23	11	8	0	1	2	0	18	0	28	1	2	0	2	.000	0	1	2.73
1998 Capital Cty	A NYM	15	15	0	0	77.1	336	68	45	34	3	0	1	6	37	0	68	12	1	5	4	.556	0	0	3.96
Kane County	A Fla	9	9	0	0	42.2	189	44	22	22	4	1	1	2	24	1	36	5	0	1	4	.200	0	0	4.64
1999 Kane County	A Fla	16	12	0	0	50.2	223	52	28	24	4	0	4	6	24	0	43	7	0	5	3	.625	0	0	4.26
2000 Brevard Cty	A+ Fla	27	0	0	15	67	270	43	19	13	1	3	1	0	36	1	61	6	0	6	2	.750	0	5	1.75
Portland	AA Fla	17	0	0	7	22.2	105	27	15	15	3	4	0	1	11	0	21	1	0	1	2	.333	0	1	5.96
4 Min. YEARS		92	42	0	23	286.2	1235	257	140	116	15	9	9	15	150	2	257	32	3	18	17	.514	0	7	3.64

Lonnie Goldberg

Bats: Right **Throws:** Right **Pos:** 2B-73; DH-9; PR-1   **Ht:** 5'10" **Wt:** 170 **Born:** 8/1/70 **Age:** 30

		BATTING															BASERUNNING				PERCENTAGES		
Year Team	Lg Org	G	AB	H	2B	3B	HR	TB	R	RBI	TBB	IBB	SO	HBP	SH	SF	SB	CS	SB%	GDP	Avg	OBP	SLG
1993 Erie	A- Tex	72	283	72	11	1	1	88	39	37	32	0	40	1	3	3	22	10	.69	2	.254	.329	.311
1994 Chston-SC	A Tex	67	198	46	10	1	0	58	24	10	15	0	55	0	5	0	6	1	.86	2	.232	.286	.293
1995 Okla City	AAA Tex	10	30	7	3	0	1	13	2	5	2	0	4	0	0	0	1	0	1.00	1	.233	.281	.433
Chston-SC	A Tex	100	340	74	12	1	2	94	29	31	26	1	54	1	2	4	17	11	.61	3	.218	.272	.276
1996 Bangor	IND —	79	317	90	20	1	3	121	51	37	30	1	45	2	2	4	49	7	.88	2	.284	.346	.382
2000 Yuma	IND —	76	262	65	13	1	5	95	44	29	39	1	63	4	11	2	9	6	.60	2	.248	.352	.363
Colo Sprngs	AAA Col	7	25	8	2	0	1	13	5	6	2	0	5	0	0	1	0	0	—	0	.320	.357	.520
5 Min. YEARS		411	1455	362	71	5	13	482	194	155	146	3	266	8	23	14	104	35	.75	12	.249	.318	.331

Ramon Gomez

Bats: Right **Throws:** Right **Pos:** OF-107; PH-12; PR-2   **Ht:** 6'2" **Wt:** 175 **Born:** 10/6/75 **Age:** 25

		BATTING															BASERUNNING				PERCENTAGES		
Year Team	Lg Org	G	AB	H	2B	3B	HR	TB	R	RBI	TBB	IBB	SO	HBP	SH	SF	SB	CS	SB%	GDP	Avg	OBP	SLG
1995 Hickory	A CWS	76	231	53	6	0	0	59	26	9	18	0	64	2	3	0	17	9	.65	5	.229	.291	.255
White Sox	R CWS	30	103	27	3	0	1	33	16	6	12	0	22	3	0	0	12	4	.75	2	.262	.356	.320
1996 Hickory	A CWS	116	418	104	8	3	1	121	73	30	44	0	99	2	11	2	57	19	.75	5	.249	.322	.289
1997 Winston-Sal	A+ CWS	118	477	132	23	12	2	185	78	42	42	0	132	3	8	2	53	21	.72	9	.277	.338	.388
1998 Winston-Sal	A+ CWS	43	124	27	5	2	0	36	21	10	12	1	36	2	3	0	13	3	.81	1	.218	.297	.290
1999 Birmingham	AA CWS	99	274	78	10	5	0	98	47	26	31	1	81	2	6	1	26	10	.72	1	.285	.360	.358

Year Team	Lg Org	G	AB	H	2B	3B	HR	TB	R	RBI	TBB	IBB	SO	HBP	SH	SF	SB	CS	SB%	GDP	Avg	OBP	SLG
							BATTING										BASERUNNING			PERCENTAGES			
2000 High Desert	A+ Ari	41	130	40	3	4	2	57	21	9	11	0	30	1	1	0	10	4	.71	1	.308	.366	.438
El Paso	AA Ari	74	264	75	8	8	2	105	42	37	26	0	50	2	1	2	18	2	.90	2	.284	.350	.398
6 Min. YEARS		597	2021	536	66	34	8	694	324	169	196	2	514	17	33	7	206	72	.74	26	.265	.334	.343

Dicky Gonzalez

Pitches: Right **Bats:** Right **Pos:** SP-25; RP-1   **Ht:** 5'11" **Wt:** 170 **Born:** 12/21/78 **Age:** 22

Year Team	Lg Org	G	GS	CG	GF	IP	BFP	H	R	ER	HR	SH	SF	HB	TBB	IBB	SO	WP	Bk	W	L	Pct.	ShO	Sv	ERA
						HOW MUCH HE PITCHED					WHAT HE GAVE UP											THE RESULTS			
1996 Mets	R NYM	11	8	2	1	47.1	195	50	19	14	1	2	0	2	3	0	51	1	0	4	2	.667	1	0	2.66
Kingsport	R+ NYM	1	1	0	0	5	20	4	2	1	0	1	0	0	1	0	7	1	0	1	0	1.000	0	0	1.80
1997 Capital Cty	A NYM	10	7	1	2	47.1	204	50	28	26	8	2	1	1	15	0	49	2	0	1	4	.200	0	0	4.94
Kingsport	R+ NYM	12	12	1	0	66	282	70	38	32	7	4	2	4	10	0	76	0	0	3	6	.333	0	0	4.36
1998 St. Lucie	A+ NYM	8	8	0	0	46.2	193	46	22	16	8	1	0	1	13	0	23	1	0	2	1	.667	0	0	3.09
Capital Cty	A NYM	18	18	1	0	111.1	449	104	57	41	9	5	1	9	14	1	107	5	1	10	3	.769	0	0	3.31
1999 Norfolk	AAA NYM	1	1	0	0	6.2	23	5	2	2	0	0	0	0	1	0	3	0	0	0	1	.000	0	0	2.70
St. Lucie	A+ NYM	25	25	3	0	168.2	673	156	66	53	11	4	0	6	30	1	143	4	1	14	9	.609	0	0	2.83
2000 Binghamton	AA NYM	26	25	2	0	147.2	609	130	75	63	14	4	2	11	36	0	138	6	0	13	5	.722	1	0	3.84
5 Min. YEARS		112	105	10	3	646.2	2648	615	309	248	58	23	6	34	122	2	597	20	2	48	31	.608	2	0	3.45

Enrique Gonzalez

Pitches: Right **Bats:** Right **Pos:** RP-12   **Ht:** 5'10" **Wt:** 155 **Born:** 8/6/82 **Age:** 18

Year Team	Lg Org	G	GS	CG	GF	IP	BFP	H	R	ER	HR	SH	SF	HB	TBB	IBB	SO	WP	Bk	W	L	Pct.	ShO	Sv	ERA
						HOW MUCH HE PITCHED					WHAT HE GAVE UP											THE RESULTS			
2000 Diamondbcks	R Ari	11	0	0	8	17.2	80	16	13	3	0	0	0	1	12	0	17	3	0	1	0	1.000	0	1	1.53
Tucson	AAA Ari	1	0	0	0	4	12	1	0	0	0	0	0	0	1	0	1	0	0	1	0	1.000	0	0	0.00
1 Min. YEARS		12	0	0	8	21.2	92	17	13	3	0	0	0	1	13	0	18	3	0	2	0	1.000	0	1	1.25

Gabe Gonzalez

Pitches: Left **Bats:** Left **Pos:** RP-58   **Ht:** 6'1" **Wt:** 150 **Born:** 5/24/72 **Age:** 29

Year Team	Lg Org	G	GS	CG	GF	IP	BFP	H	R	ER	HR	SH	SF	HB	TBB	IBB	SO	WP	Bk	W	L	Pct.	ShO	Sv	ERA
						HOW MUCH HE PITCHED					WHAT HE GAVE UP											THE RESULTS			
1995 Kane County	A Fla	32	0	0	10	43.1	181	32	18	11	0	2	1	2	14	2	41	1	0	4	4	.500	0	1	2.28
1996 Charlotte	AAA Fla	2	0	0	1	3	15	4	1	1	0	0	0	0	2	0	3	0	0	0	0	—	0	0	3.00
Brevard Cty	A+ Fla	47	0	0	32	76.1	308	56	20	15	2	9	1	3	23	7	62	2	0	2	7	.222	0	9	1.77
1997 Portland	AA Fla	29	0	0	10	42.2	171	43	12	10	1	3	3	0	5	1	28	1	0	3	2	.600	0	3	2.11
Charlotte	AAA Fla	37	1	0	11	42.2	176	38	15	13	3	1	2	2	14	1	24	0	0	2	2	.500	0	3	2.74
1998 Charlotte	AAA Fla	57	4	0	13	87	412	101	67	53	8	8	7	1	53	5	41	2	1	3	9	.250	0	5	5.48
1999 Portland	AA Fla	26	0	0	11	38	161	38	19	15	2	4	1	3	8	1	34	2	0	2	4	.333	0	0	3.55
Calgary	AAA Fla	24	0	0	10	28	123	27	15	13	2	0	2	2	9	1	23	0	0	1	1	.500	0	4	4.18
2000 Ottawa	AAA Mon	14	0	0	5	25	130	34	21	19	3	0	2	1	20	0	11	2	0	1	2	.333	0	1	6.84
Harrisburg	AA Mon	44	0	0	8	44.2	188	46	24	19	4	2	3	0	12	1	25	0	1	2	0	1.000	0	3	3.83
1998 Florida	NL	3	0	0	1	1	5	1	1	1	0	0	0	1	0	0	0	0	0	0	0	—	0	0	9.00
6 Min. YEARS		312	5	0	111	430.2	1865	419	212	169	20	29	22	14	160	19	292	10	2	20	31	.392	0	19	3.53

Jimmy Gonzalez

Bats: Right **Throws:** Right **Pos:** C-55; DH-16; PH-4; 1B-1   **Ht:** 6'3" **Wt:** 235 **Born:** 3/8/73 **Age:** 28

Year Team	Lg Org	G	AB	H	2B	3B	HR	TB	R	RBI	TBB	IBB	SO	HBP	SH	SF	SB	CS	SB%	GDP	Avg	OBP	SLG
								BATTING										BASERUNNING			PERCENTAGES		
1991 Astros	R Hou	34	103	21	3	0	0	24	7	3	7	0	33	0	1	0	3	5	.38	1	.204	.255	.233
1992 Burlington	A Hou	91	301	53	13	0	4	78	32	21	34	0	119	1	0	1	0	3	.00	6	.176	.262	.259
1993 Quad City	A Hou	47	154	35	9	1	0	46	20	15	14	1	36	4	1	1	2	2	.50	4	.227	.306	.299
Asheville	A Hou	43	149	33	5	0	4	50	16	15	7	0	37	0	2	1	3	1	.75	3	.221	.255	.336
1994 Jackson	AA Hou	4	6	0	0	0	0	0	0	0	0	0	0	0	0	0	0	0	.000		.000	.000	.000
Osceola	A+ Hou	99	321	74	18	0	5	107	33	38	20	0	80	4	2	2	2	0	1.00	10	.231	.282	.333
1995 Quad City	A Hou	35	78	19	3	1	1	27	4	14	8	0	13	1	0	1	1	2	.33	2	.244	.318	.346
1996 Jackson	AA Hou	2	5	1	0	0	0	1	0	1	0	0	1	0	0	0	0	0	.200		.200	.333	.200
Kissimmee	A+ Hou	73	208	35	4	1	6	59	19	17	25	0	59	3	2	3	1	0	1.00	8	.168	.264	.284
1997 Kissimmee	A+ Hou	12	44	15	6	2	2	31	7	6	1	0	9	3	0	1	0	0	—	1	.341	.388	.705
Jackson	AA Hou	97	342	87	18	0	14	147	49	58	37	1	91	6	0	3	2	1	.67	7	.254	.338	.430
1998 Mobile	AA SD	26	85	25	8	0	6	51	14	17	13	0	22	0	1	2	0	0		1	.294	.388	.600
Las Vegas	AAA SD	51	160	38	9	0	5	62	22	21	15	1	44	1	1	2	1	0	1.00	1	.238	.303	.388
1999 Mobile	AA SD	21	68	18	3	0	2	27	15	8	7	1	16	0	0	1	0	0	—	0	.265	.354	.397
Las Vegas	AAA SD	40	112	33	9	1	3	53	10	19	14	1	29	0	0	3	1	0	—	2	.295	.364	.473
2000 Binghamton	AA NYM	73	234	65	13	1	8	104	32	30	21	0	52	5	0	1	1	2	.33	3	.278	.349	.444
10 Min. YEARS		748	2370	552	121	7	60	867	281	282	224	5	641	33	9	19	16	16	.50	50	.233	.306	.366

Lariel Gonzalez

Pitches: Right **Bats:** Right **Pos:** RP-52   **Ht:** 6'4" **Wt:** 228 **Born:** 5/25/76 **Age:** 25

Year Team	Lg Org	G	GS	CG	GF	IP	BFP	H	R	ER	HR	SH	SF	HB	TBB	IBB	SO	WP	Bk	W	L	Pct.	ShO	Sv	ERA
						HOW MUCH HE PITCHED					WHAT HE GAVE UP											THE RESULTS			
1995 Portland	A- Col	15	11	0	2	57.2	258	44	31	26	4	1	1	7	43	0	48	9	5	3	4	.429	0	0	4.06
1996 Asheville	A Col	35	0	0	24	45	208	37	21	18	2	0	0	1	37	0	53	4	2	1	1	.500	0	4	3.60
1997 Salem	A+ Col	44	0	0	25	57	237	42	19	16	3	2	2	3	23	1	79	4	0	5	0	1.000	0	8	2.53
1998 New Haven	AA Col	58	0	0	45	58	255	46	30	27	5	3	3	3	40	2	63	11	0	0	4	.000	0	22	4.19
1999 Colo Sprngs	AAA Col	11	0	0	4	13.1	66	18	16	15	2	1	1	0	12	2	9	1	0	1	0	1.000	0	0	10.13
Carolina	AA Col	30	0	0	24	34	167	39	27	20	4	3	6	4	22	0	41	0	0	2	1	.667	0	14	5.29
2000 Norfolk	AAA NYM	52	0	0	19	66.2	304	68	33	31	4	3	6	4	38	3	61	8	0	5	5	.500	0	5	4.19
1998 Colorado	NL	1	0	0	1	1	3	0	0	0	0	0	0	0	0	0	1	0	0	0	0	—	0	0	0.00
6 Min. YEARS		245	11	0	143	331.2	1495	294	177	153	24	14	14	19	215	8	354	45	7	16	16	.500	0	55	4.15

Manny Gonzalez

Bats: Both **Throws:** Right **Pos:** OF-82; DH-3; PH-1 | **Ht:** 6'2" **Wt:** 195 **Born:** 5/5/76 **Age:** 25

Year Team	Lg Org	G	AB	H	2B	3B	HR	TB	R	RBI	TBB	IBB	SO	HBP	SH	SF	SB	CS	SB%	GDP	Avg	OBP	SLG
						BATTING											BASERUNNING				PERCENTAGES		
1995 Great Falls	R+ LA	59	197	71	9	3	4	98	35	30	9	1	27	0	1	3	16	7	.70	2	.360	.383	.497
1996 San Berndno	A+ LA	43	168	51	7	3	0	64	29	21	12	0	32	0	2	0	10	8	.56	2	.304	.350	.381
Savannah	A LA	65	231	53	10	2	1	70	30	19	20	0	52	1	1	2	15	8	.65	3	.229	.291	.303
1997 Hickory	A CWS	116	469	129	21	2	11	187	70	54	28	1	78	1	7	5	31	12	.72	11	.275	.314	.399
1998 Birmingham	AA CWS	102	371	112	24	2	2	146	51	35	23	0	52	4	8	1	9	7	.56	11	.302	.348	.394
1999 Charlotte	AAA CWS	48	129	40	6	1	1	51	14	25	5	1	20	0	8	0	1	4	.20	1	.310	.336	.395
St. Paul	IND —	18	83	24	4	1	2	36	13	12	5	0	9	1	0	0	5	4	.56	1	.289	.337	.434
2000 Charlotte	AAA CWS	2	4	1	0	0	0	1	0	0	0	0	0	0	0	0	0	1	.00	0	.250	.250	.250
Solano	IND —	83	347	109	26	1	13	176	58	78	17	0	55	3	2	6	13	10	.57	8	.314	.346	.507
6 Min. YEARS		536	1999	590	107	15	34	829	300	274	119	3	325	10	29	17	100	61	.62	39	.295	.335	.415

Arnie Gooch

Pitches: Right **Bats:** Right **Pos:** SP-21 | **Ht:** 6'2" **Wt:** 195 **Born:** 11/12/76 **Age:** 24

Year Team	Lg Org	G	GS	CG	GF	IP	BFP	H	R	ER	HR	SH	SF	HB	TBB	IBB	SO	WP	Bk	W	L	Pct.	ShO	Sv	ERA
				HOW MUCH HE PITCHED						WHAT HE GAVE UP										THE RESULTS				
1994 Rockies	R Col	15	9	0	1	58	238	45	28	17	2	0	2	2	16	0	66	12	1	2	4	.333	0	0	2.64
1995 Asheville	A Col	21	21	1	0	128.2	541	111	51	42	8	3	3	4	57	0	117	13	0	5	8	.385	1	0	2.94
Capital Cty	A NYM	6	6	0	0	38.1	169	39	25	19	3	0	1	2	15	0	34	5	0	2	3	.400	0	0	4.46
1996 St. Lucie	A+ NYM	26	26	2	0	167.2	680	131	74	48	7	6	4	4	51	3	141	11	0	12	12	.500	2	0	2.58
1997 Binghamton	AA NYM	27	27	4	0	161	727	179	106	91	12	4	7	5	76	3	98	12	0	10	12	.455	1	0	5.09
1998 Binghamton	AA NYM	27	27	2	0	163.2	705	164	92	71	15	5	5	1	60	4	116	14	0	11	14	.440	1	0	3.90
1999 Reds	R Cin	2	2	0	0	8	32	5	2	1	0	0	0	1	1	0	6	0	0	1	1	.500	0	0	1.13
Clinton	A Cin	2	2	0	0	8	36	8	5	4	1	0	0	0	3	0	5	0	0	1	1	.500	0	0	4.50
2000 Chattanooga	AA Cin	21	21	1	0	135.2	583	133	78	62	13	4	1	8	55	4	80	16	0	9	7	.563	0	0	4.11
7 Min. YEARS		147	141	10	1	869	3711	815	461	355	61	22	23	27	334	14	663	83	1	53	62	.461	3	0	3.68

Steve Goodell

Bats: Right **Throws:** Right **Pos:** 1B-20; DH-19; 2B-18; SS-9; PH-9; 3B-8 | **Ht:** 6'3" **Wt:** 196 **Born:** 4/23/75 **Age:** 26

Year Team	Lg Org	G	AB	H	2B	3B	HR	TB	R	RBI	TBB	IBB	SO	HBP	SH	SF	SB	CS	SB%	GDP	Avg	OBP	SLG
						BATTING											BASERUNNING				PERCENTAGES		
1995 Elmira	A- Fla	69	253	64	14	4	7	107	42	30	36	0	50	14	1	2	4	5	.44	8	.253	.374	.423
Kane County	A Fla	2	7	2	0	0	0	2	0	1	2	0	2	0	0	0	0	0	—	0	.286	.444	.286
1996 Brevard Cty	A+ Fla	1	4	1	0	0	0	1	0	0	0	0	0	0	0	0	0	0	—	0	.250	.250	.250
Kane County	A Fla	86	282	79	17	2	9	127	34	39	30	2	68	13	2	5	1	1	.50	8	.280	.370	.450
1997 Brevard Cty	A+ Fla	117	381	103	18	2	11	158	48	61	60	0	67	14	6	7	1	1	.50	7	.270	.383	.415
1998 Portland	AA Fla	48	118	22	6	0	1	31	13	11	26	1	35	4	2	0	0	1	.00	3	.186	.351	.263
Danville	A+ Atl	54	198	59	14	2	5	92	21	20	17	1	42	6	4	3	3	4	.43	5	.298	.366	.465
Greenville	AA Atl	5	18	5	1	0	0	3	6	7	6	3	0	3	1	0	0	0	1	.278	.409	.833
1999 Greenville	AA Atl	102	338	101	25	2	15	175	69	58	55	2	61	12	0	3	8	6	.57	5	.299	.412	.518
2000 Atlantic Ct	IND —	4	10	2	0	0	1	5	2	1	0	0	2	0	0	0	0	0	—	0	.200	.200	.500
Carolina	AA Col	76	229	59	13	1	11	107	39	42	48	2	48	10	0	1	2	1	.67	7	.258	.406	.467
6 Min. YEARS		564	1838	497	108	13	63	800	275	269	277	8	378	74	15	21	19	19	.50	44	.270	.384	.446

Jason Gooding

Pitches: Left **Bats:** Right **Pos:** RP-23; SP-6 | **Ht:** 5'11" **Wt:** 190 **Born:** 7/29/74 **Age:** 26

Year Team	Lg Org	G	GS	CG	GF	IP	BFP	H	R	ER	HR	SH	SF	HB	TBB	IBB	SO	WP	Bk	W	L	Pct.	ShO	Sv	ERA
				HOW MUCH HE PITCHED						WHAT HE GAVE UP										THE RESULTS				
1997 Spokane	A- KC	11	11	0	0	55.2	220	44	16	14	2	0	0	3	11	0	58	3	0	4	0	1.000	0	0	2.26
Lansing	A KC	1	1	0	0	4.2	24	6	5	3	0	0	1	1	1	0	3	2	0	0	1	.000	0	0	5.79
1998 Wichita	AA KC	25	23	0	1	129.1	593	171	93	75	15	9	9	10	43	1	68	8	2	5	7	.417	0	0	5.22
1999 Omaha	AAA KC	1	1	0	0	6	26	8	4	4	1	0	1	0	1	0	2	0	0	0	1	.000	0	0	6.00
Wichita	AA KC	23	23	0	0	139	599	176	80	73	16	3	2	2	39	5	63	3	0	13	7	.650	0	0	4.73
2000 Wichita	AA KC	29	6	0	7	81	348	97	47	36	12	3	0	1	26	2	46	2	0	6	3	.667	0	2	4.00
4 Min. YEARS		90	65	0	8	415.2	1810	502	245	205	46	15	13	17	121	8	240	18	2	28	19	.596	0	2	4.44

Randy Goodrich

Pitches: Right **Bats:** Right **Pos:** RP-50; SP-1 | **Ht:** 6'4" **Wt:** 210 **Born:** 11/8/76 **Age:** 24

Year Team	Lg Org	G	GS	CG	GF	IP	BFP	H	R	ER	HR	SH	SF	HB	TBB	IBB	SO	WP	Bk	W	L	Pct.	ShO	Sv	ERA
				HOW MUCH HE PITCHED						WHAT HE GAVE UP										THE RESULTS				
1998 Salem-Keizr	A- SF	17	10	0	1	62.1	274	74	43	36	5	0	3	4	17	1	38	2	3	4	5	.444	0	0	5.20
1999 San Jose	A+ SF	38	18	0	4	136.2	623	174	95	73	6	5	6	11	34	0	82	6	3	8	8	.500	0	1	4.81
2000 Shreveport	AA SF	51	1	0	25	75	331	90	36	31	10	7	1	0	17	4	48	2	1	4	5	.444	0	12	3.72
3 Min. YEARS		106	29	0	30	274	1228	338	174	140	21	12	10	15	68	5	168	10	7	16	18	.471	0	13	4.60

Curtis Goodwin

Bats: Left **Throws:** Left **Pos:** OF-56; PH-2; DH-1; PR-1 | **Ht:** 5'11" **Wt:** 180 **Born:** 9/30/72 **Age:** 28

Year Team	Lg Org	G	AB	H	2B	3B	HR	TB	R	RBI	TBB	IBB	SO	HBP	SH	SF	SB	CS	SB%	GDP	Avg	OBP	SLG
						BATTING											BASERUNNING				PERCENTAGES		
1991 Orioles	R Bal	48	151	39	5	0	0	44	32	9	38	0	25	1	5	0	26	5	.84	3	.258	.411	.291
1992 Kane County	A Bal	134	542	153	7	5	1	173	85	42	38	0	106	2	14	0	52	18	.74	1	.282	.332	.319
1993 Frederick	A+ Bal	138	555	156	15	10	2	197	98	42	52	0	90	1	7	1	61	15	.80	8	.281	.343	.355
1994 Bowie	AA Bal	142	597	171	18	8	2	211	105	37	40	0	78	3	13	2	59	10	.86	7	.286	.333	.353
1995 Rochester	AAA Bal	36	140	37	3	3	0	46	24	7	12	0	15	1	3	0	17	3	.85	4	.264	.327	.329
1996 Indianapols	AAA Cin	91	337	88	19	4	2	121	57	30	54	2	67	1	5	0	40	12	.77	2	.261	.364	.359
1997 Indianapols	AAA Cin	30	116	32	4	1	1	41	14	7	15	0	20	0	1	0	11	8	.58	0	.276	.359	.353

Year Team	Lg Org	G	AB	H	2B	3B	HR	TB	R	RBI	TBB	IBB	SO	HBP	SH	SF	SB	CS	SB%	GDP	Avg	OBP	SLG
								BATTING										**BASERUNNING**				**PERCENTAGES**		
2000 Atlantic Ct	IND —	12	41	7	0	0	0	7	5	3	5	0	9	1	1	0	5	0	1.00	1	.171	.277	.171
Sonoma Cty	IND —	10	39	14	2	0	0	16	5	4	9	0	3	0	1	0	0	1	.00	0	.359	.479	.410
Solano	IND —	27	111	33	7	4	0	48	28	9	13	0	21	2	4	0	7	0	1.00	0	.297	.381	.432
Wichita	AA KC	11	38	10	1	0	0	11	8	2	6	0	5	0	0	0	2	1	.67	1	.263	.364	.289
1995 Baltimore	AL	87	289	76	11	3	1	96	40	24	15	0	53	2	7	3	22	4	.85	5	.263	.301	.332
1996 Cincinnati	NL	49	136	31	3	0	0	34	20	5	19	0	34	0	1	0	15	6	.71	1	.228	.323	.250
1997 Cincinnati	NL	85	265	67	11	0	1	81	27	12	24	0	53	1	6	1	22	13	.63	6	.253	.316	.306
1998 Colorado	NL	119	159	39	7	0	1	49	27	6	16	0	40	0	10	1	5	1	.83	3	.245	.313	.308
1999 Chicago	NL	89	157	38	6	1	0	46	15	9	13	1	38	0	4	1	2	4	.33	7	.242	.298	.293
Toronto	AL	2	8	0	0	0	0	0	0	0	0	0	3	0	0	0	0	0	.000	0	.000	.000	.000
8 Min. YEARS		679	2667	740	81	35	8	915	461	192	282	2	439	12	54	4	280	73	.79	27	.277	.349	.343
5 Maj. YEARS		431	1014	251	38	4	3	306	129	56	87	1	221	3	28	6	66	28	.70	22	.248	.307	.302

Keith Gordon

Bats: Right **Throws:** Right **Pos:** OF-101; PH-5; DH-2; PR-1 **Ht:** 6'2" **Wt:** 200 **Born:** 1/22/69 **Age:** 32

Year Team	Lg Org	G	AB	H	2B	3B	HR	TB	R	RBI	TBB	IBB	SO	HBP	SH	SF	SB	CS	SB%	GDP	Avg	OBP	SLG
								BATTING										**BASERUNNING**				**PERCENTAGES**		
1990 Billings	R+ Cin	49	154	36	5	1	1	46	21	14	24	1	49	3	2	1	6	4	.60	2	.234	.346	.299
1991 Chston-WV	A Cin	123	388	104	14	10	8	162	63	46	50	2	134	5	7	1	25	9	.74	5	.268	.358	.418
1992 Cedar Rapds	A Cin	114	375	94	19	3	12	155	59	63	43	2	135	3	1	4	21	10	.68	5	.251	.329	.413
1993 Chattanooga	AA Cin	116	419	122	26	3	14	196	69	59	19	0	132	4	0	2	13	17	.43	15	.291	.327	.468
1994 Indianapols	AAA Cin	18	58	12	1	0	1	16	3	4	4	0	25	0	1	0	0	0	—	1	.207	.258	.276
Chattanooga	AA Cin	82	254	71	16	2	8	115	46	38	21	0	74	1	0	2	11	7	.61	6	.280	.335	.453
1995 Indianapols	AAA Cin	89	265	70	14	1	6	104	36	38	15	0	94	0	1	0	3	4	.43	3	.264	.304	.392
1996 Rochester	AAA Bal	33	104	26	4	1	5	47	15	19	9	0	27	0	0	0	3	0	.00	3	.250	.310	.452
Bowie	AA Bal	82	306	80	13	2	5	112	38	28	22	0	80	1	1	0	13	11	.54	5	.261	.313	.366
1997 Chattanooga	AA Cin	4	12	2	0	0	1	5	2	2	3	0	7	0	0	0	1	1	.50	1	.167	.333	.417
1998 New Jersey	IND —	82	298	93	16	0	16	157	47	70	17	3	67	5	0	5	19	10	.66	6	.312	.354	.527
1999 Nashua	IND —	27	95	16	6	0	0	22	11	4	2	1	26	0	0	0	10	1	.91	4	.168	.186	.232
Atlantic Ct	IND —	56	216	66	17	1	8	109	32	29	10	0	45	1	0	0	19	9	.68	7	.306	.339	.505
2000 Atlantic Ct	IND —	83	330	112	18	3	16	184	63	59	13	0	47	1	2	1	16	6	.73	13	.339	.365	.558
New Haven	AA Sea	23	77	19	4	0	2	29	4	9	3	0	24	1	0	0	0	0	—	4	.247	.284	.377
1993 Cincinnati	NL	3	6	1	0	0	0	1	0	0	0	0	2	0	0	0	0	0	—	0	.167	.167	.167
11 Min. YEARS		981	3351	923	173	27	103	1459	509	482	255	9	966	25	15	16	157	92	.63	77	.275	.330	.435

Robb Gorr

Bats: Right **Throws:** Right **Pos:** 1B-63; DH-14; PH-10 **Ht:** 6'0" **Wt:** 195 **Born:** 9/14/76 **Age:** 24

Year Team	Lg Org	G	AB	H	2B	3B	HR	TB	R	RBI	TBB	IBB	SO	HBP	SH	SF	SB	CS	SB%	GDP	Avg	OBP	SLG
								BATTING										**BASERUNNING**				**PERCENTAGES**		
1998 Yakima	A- LA	66	254	67	9	2	5	95	43	35	15	2	33	1	2	4	2	1	.67	4	.264	.303	.374
1999 San Berndno	A+ LA	132	546	174	22	6	11	241	67	106	30	5	59	5	3	7	5	2	.71	14	.319	.355	.441
2000 San Antonio	AA LA	87	280	73	14	0	8	111	32	41	21	1	54	5	6	3	3	3	.50	8	.261	.320	.396
3 Min. YEARS		285	1080	314	45	8	24	447	142	182	66	8	146	11	11	14	10	6	.63	26	.291	.334	.414

John Grabow

Pitches: Left **Bats:** Left **Pos:** SP-24 **Ht:** 6'2" **Wt:** 189 **Born:** 11/4/78 **Age:** 22

Year Team	Lg Org	G	GS	CG	GF	IP	BFP	H	R	ER	HR	SH	SF	HB	TBB	IBB	SO	WP	Bk	W	L	Pct.	ShO	Sv	ERA
				HOW MUCH HE PITCHED							**WHAT HE GAVE UP**											**THE RESULTS**			
1997 Pirates	R Pit	11	8	0	0	45.1	204	57	32	23	0	1	2	0	14	0	28	3	0	2	7	.222	0	0	4.57
1998 Augusta	A Pit	17	16	0	0	71.2	329	84	59	46	7	1	5	3	34	0	67	9	0	6	3	.667	0	0	5.78
1999 Hickory	A Pit	26	26	0	0	156.1	654	152	82	66	16	3	3	5	32	0	164	8	0	9	10	.474	0	0	3.80
2000 Altoona	AA Pit	24	24	1	0	145.1	637	145	81	70	10	1	6	5	65	0	109	8	1	8	7	.533	0	0	4.33
4 Min. YEARS		78	74	1	0	418.2	1824	438	254	205	33	6	16	13	145	0	368	23	1	25	27	.481	0	0	4.41

Jason Grabowski

Bats: Left **Throws:** Right **Pos:** 3B-130; DH-5 **Ht:** 6'3" **Wt:** 200 **Born:** 5/24/76 **Age:** 25

Year Team	Lg Org	G	AB	H	2B	3B	HR	TB	R	RBI	TBB	IBB	SO	HBP	SH	SF	SB	CS	SB%	GDP	Avg	OBP	SLG
								BATTING										**BASERUNNING**				**PERCENTAGES**		
1997 Pulaski	R+ Tex	50	174	51	14	0	4	77	36	24	40	2	32	0	1	1	6	1	.86	2	.293	.423	.443
1998 Savannah	A Tex	104	352	95	13	6	14	162	63	52	57	0	93	1	0	1	16	9	.64	7	.270	.372	.460
1999 Charlotte	A+ Tex	123	434	136	31	6	12	215	68	87	65	3	66	5	1	2	13	10	.57	8	.313	.407	.495
Tulsa	AA Tex	2	6	1	0	0	0	1	0	2	1	2	0	0	0	0	0	—	0	.167	.375	.167
2000 Tulsa	AA Tex	135	493	135	33	5	19	235	93	90	88	2	106	4	0	7	8	7	.53	12	.274	.383	.477
4 Min. YEARS		414	1459	418	91	17	49	690	261	253	252	7	299	10	2	11	43	27	.61	29	.286	.393	.473

Mike Grace

Pitches: Right **Bats:** Right **Pos:** RP-31; SP-3 **Ht:** 6'4" **Wt:** 225 **Born:** 6/20/70 **Age:** 31

Year Team	Lg Org	G	GS	CG	GF	IP	BFP	H	R	ER	HR	SH	SF	HB	TBB	IBB	SO	WP	Bk	W	L	Pct.	ShO	Sv	ERA
				HOW MUCH HE PITCHED							**WHAT HE GAVE UP**											**THE RESULTS**			
1991 Batavia	A- Phi	6	6	0	0	32.1	123	20	9	5	3	2	0	1	14	1	36	1	2	1	2	.333	0	0	1.39
Spartanburg	A Phi	6	6	0	0	33.1	127	24	7	7	1	2	1	0	9	0	23	1	0	3	1	.750	0	0	1.89
1992 Spartanburg	A Phi	6	6	0	0	27.1	114	25	16	15	3	0	0	1	8	0	21	2	0	0	1	.000	0	0	4.94
1994 Spartanburg	A Phi	15	15	0	0	80.1	345	84	50	43	6	4	1	8	20	1	45	2	0	5	5	.500	0	0	4.82
1995 Reading	AA Phi	24	24	2	0	147.1	606	137	65	58	13	5	0	6	35	0	118	3	2	13	6	.684	0	0	3.54
Scranton-WB	AAA Phi	2	2	1	0	17	68	17	3	3	0	0	0	2	0	13	2	0	2	0	1.000	0	0	1.59
1997 Reading	AA Phi	4	4	0	0	20.1	93	28	17	13	4	1	0	0	6	0	10	1	0	1	3	.250	0	0	5.75
Scranton-WB	AAA Phi	12	12	4	0	75	331	84	43	38	9	0	3	5	27	1	55	1	0	5	6	.455	0	0	4.56
1998 Scranton-WB	AAA Phi	11	10	2	0	75	327	92	44	42	8	9	3	5	18	1	39	2	0	3	6	.333	0	0	5.04

Year Team	Lg Org	G	GS	CG	GF	IP	BFP	H	R	ER	HR	SH	SF	HB	TBB	IBB	SO	WP	Bk	W	L	Pct.	ShO	Sv	ERA
1999 Scranton-WB	AAA Phi	10	9	0	0	46.2	202	52	25	23	6	2	1	2	17	0	27	1	0	2	2	.500	0	0	4.44
2000 Rochester	AAA Bal	34	3	0	5	76.1	317	66	36	34	5	2	0	8	16	1	43	1	0	4	3	.571	0	1	4.01
1995 Philadelphia	NL	2	2	0	0	11.1	47	10	4	4	0	1	0	0	4	0	7	0	0	1	1	.500	0	0	3.18
1996 Philadelphia	NL	12	12	1	0	80	323	72	33	31	9	4	0	1	16	1	49	0	1	7	2	.778	1	0	3.49
1997 Philadelphia	NL	6	6	1	0	39	151	32	16	15	3	0	1	1	10	1	26	2	0	3	2	.600	1	0	3.46
1998 Philadelphia	NL	21	15	0	1	90.1	418	116	61	55	10	7	1	8	30	1	46	1	1	4	7	.364	0	0	5.48
1999 Philadelphia	NL	27	5	0	1	55	273	80	48	47	5	3	3	6	30	0	28	4	0	1	4	.200	0	0	7.69
8 Min. YEARS		130	97	9	5	631	2653	629	315	281	49	31	11	34	172	5	430	17	4	39	35	.527	0	1	4.01
5 Maj. YEARS		68	40	2	2	275.2	1212	310	162	152	27	15	5	16	90	3	156	7	2	16	16	.500	2	0	4.96

Jess Graham

Bats: Left **Throws:** Left **Pos:** OF-85; PH-4; DH-2; PR-1   **Ht:** 6'0" **Wt:** 180 **Born:** 10/12/75 **Age:** 25

			BATTING														BASERUNNING				PERCENTAGES		
Year Team	Lg Org	G	AB	H	2B	3B	HR	TB	R	RBI	TBB	IBB	SO	HBP	SH	SF	SB	CS	SB%	GDP	Avg	OBP	SLG
1997 Chillicothe	IND —	48	146	51	7	2	3	71	41	17	23	0	16	4	2	1	12	5	.71	4	.349	.448	.486
1998 Michigan	A Bos	113	414	108	22	5	8	164	73	61	50	1	96	12	2	2	10	4	.71	12	.261	.356	.396
1999 Sarasota	A+ Bos	129	462	124	33	5	7	188	66	65	49	3	77	19	6	2	5	4	.56	8	.268	.361	.407
2000 Sarasota	A+ Bos	13	42	7	1	0	1	11	4	2	6	0	7	1	0	1	2	1	.67	2	.167	.280	.262
Trenton	AA Bos	75	256	61	11	3	5	93	28	33	20	2	61	5	2	2	0	3	.00	8	.238	.304	.363
4 Min. YEARS		378	1320	351	74	15	24	527	212	178	148	6	257	41	12	8	29	17	.63	34	.266	.356	.399

Joe Grahe

Pitches: Right **Bats:** Right **Pos:** SP-6   **Ht:** 6'0" **Wt:** 208 **Born:** 8/14/67 **Age:** 33

Year Team	Lg Org	G	GS	CG	GF	IP	BFP	H	R	ER	HR	SH	SF	HB	TBB	IBB	SO	WP	Bk	W	L	Pct.	ShO	Sv	ERA
1990 Midland	AA Ana	18	18	1	0	119	513	145	75	68	10	2	2	4	34	1	58	10	1	7	5	.583	0	0	5.14
Edmonton	AAA Ana	5	5	2	0	40	159	35	10	6	4	0	0	0	11	0	21	0	0	3	0	1.000	0	0	1.35
1991 Edmonton	AAA Ana	14	14	3	0	94.1	428	121	55	42	3	4	2	3	30	0	55	6	0	9	3	.750	1	0	4.01
1992 Edmonton	AAA Ana	3	3	0	0	19.2	78	18	7	7	0	0	0	0	5	0	12	1	0	1	0	1.000	0	0	3.20
1993 Vancouver	AAA Ana	4	2	0	0	6	26	4	3	3	1	1	0	0	2	0	5	1	0	1	1	.500	0	0	4.50
1995 Colo Spmgs	AAA Col	2	2	1	0	11	41	7	4	4	1	1	1	0	3	0	4	0	0	1	1	.500	0	0	3.27
1997 Bangor	IND —	7	5	1	2	28.1	117	25	13	8	4	1	0	2	8	0	19	1	0	3	2	.600	1	2	2.54
1998 Nashua	IND —	10	10	3	0	66.1	262	49	23	18	5	2	3	2	21	4	43	1	0	4	3	.571	0	0	2.44
Columbus	AAA NYY	12	5	1	2	43.2	185	42	23	22	4	0	1	3	11	1	22	4	1	4	2	.667	0	0	4.53
1999 Reading	AA Phi	7	0	0	6	10	39	7	3	1	0	0	0	0	2	0	12	0	0	0	0	—	0	4	0.90
Scranton-WB	AAA Phi	23	4	0	18	36	157	38	15	12	3	1	2	1	15	1	25	3	0	3	1	.750	0	10	3.00
2000 Scranton-WB	AAA Phi	3	3	0	0	16	67	19	8	8	0	0	1	0	3	0	5	0	0	1	0	1.000	0	0	4.50
Phillies	R Phi	3	3	0	0	6	28	7	4	3	0	0	0	2	1	0	2	0	0	0	0	—	0	0	4.50
1990 California	AL	8	8	0	0	43.1	200	51	30	24	3	0	0	3	23	1	25	1	0	3	4	.429	0	0	4.98
1991 California	AL	18	10	1	2	73	330	84	43	39	2	1	1	3	33	0	40	2	0	3	7	.300	0	0	4.81
1992 California	AL	46	7	0	31	94.2	399	85	37	37	5	4	4	6	39	2	39	3	0	5	6	.455	0	21	3.52
1993 California	AL	45	0	0	32	56.2	247	54	22	18	5	2	3	2	25	4	31	3	0	4	1	.800	0	11	2.86
1994 California	AL	40	0	0	32	43.1	218	68	34	32	5	3	3	6	18	4	26	4	1	2	5	.286	0	13	6.65
1995 Colorado	NL	17	9	0	0	56.2	265	69	42	32	6	3	3	3	27	2	27	3	2	4	3	.571	0	0	5.08
1999 Philadelphia	NL	13	5	0	4	32.2	153	40	16	14	1	0	3	3	17	0	16	2	1	1	4	.200	0	0	3.86
9 Min. YEARS		111	74	12	28	496.1	2106	517	243	202	35	12	13	17	146	7	283	27	2	37	18	.673	2	16	3.66
7 Maj. YEARS		187	39	1	101	400.1	1812	451	223	196	27	13	17	26	182	13	204	18	4	22	30	.423	0	45	4.41

Alex Graman

Pitches: Left **Bats:** Left **Pos:** SP-29   **Ht:** 6'4" **Wt:** 200 **Born:** 11/17/77 **Age:** 23

Year Team	Lg Org	G	GS	CG	GF	IP	BFP	H	R	ER	HR	SH	SF	HB	TBB	IBB	SO	WP	Bk	W	L	Pct.	ShO	Sv	ERA
1999 Staten Ilnd	A- NYY	14	14	0	0	81.1	324	74	30	27	7	3	1	1	16	0	85	1	1	6	3	.667	0	0	2.99
2000 Tampa	A+ NYY	28	28	3	0	143	598	120	64	58	6	5	2	3	58	1	111	9	1	8	9	.471	1	0	3.65
Norwich	AA NYY	1	1	0	0	5.1	25	6	7	7	3	0	0	1	4	0	3	0	0	0	1	.000	0	0	11.81
2 Min. YEARS		43	43	3	0	229.2	947	200	101	92	16	8	3	5	78	1	199	10	2	14	13	.519	1	0	3.61

Jeff Granger

Pitches: Left **Bats:** Right **Pos:** RP-24; SP-10   **Ht:** 6'4" **Wt:** 200 **Born:** 12/16/71 **Age:** 29

Year Team	Lg Org	G	GS	CG	GF	IP	BFP	H	R	ER	HR	SH	SF	HB	TBB	IBB	SO	WP	Bk	W	L	Pct.	ShO	Sv	ERA
1993 Eugene	A- KC	8	7	0	0	36	146	28	17	12	2	1	0	1	10	1	56	1	0	3	3	.500	0	0	3.00
1994 Memphis	AA KC	25	25	0	0	139.2	615	155	72	60	8	3	3	0	61	0	112	14	3	7	7	.500	0	0	3.87
1995 Wichita	AA KC	18	18	0	0	95.2	439	122	76	63	9	3	4	1	40	0	81	10	0	4	7	.364	0	0	5.93
1996 Omaha	AAA KC	45	0	0	25	77	314	65	24	20	10	2	2	2	29	2	68	3	0	5	3	.625	0	4	2.34
1997 Calgary	AAA Pit	30	12	0	7	82.2	387	111	63	51	7	3	1	3	33	5	68	6	0	1	7	.125	0	0	5.55
1998 Oklahoma	AAA Tex	32	19	0	6	129	574	160	80	67	10	4	7	2	38	1	94	10	0	4	8	.333	0	1	4.67
1999 Louisville	AAA Mil	56	1	0	21	59	271	72	40	31	8	5	2	3	25	3	50	0	0	1	6	.143	0	3	4.73
2000 Albuquerque	AAA LA	2	0	0	0	1	11	7	7	7	0	0	0	3	1	0	1	0	0	0	1	.000	0	0	63.00
Long Island	IND —	6	5	0	1	28.2	138	35	21	15	0	1	3	2	18	0	22	2	0	2	1	.667	0	0	4.71
Richmond	AAA Atl	10	3	0	3	23.2	127	45	33	27	2	2	2	3	11	1	11	1	0	1	4	.200	0	0	10.27
Greenville	AA Atl	16	2	1	6	36	150	38	17	14	0	2	1	0	12	2	12	0	0	3	2	.600	0	1	3.50
1993 Kansas City	AL	1	0	0	0	1	8	3	3	3	0	0	0	0	2	0	1	0	0	0	0	—	0	0	27.00
1994 Kansas City	AL	3	0	0	0	9.1	47	13	8	7	2	0	1	0	6	0	3	0	0	0	1	.000	0	0	6.75
1996 Kansas City	AL	15	0	0	5	16.1	80	21	13	12	0	0	0	1	10	0	11	2	0	0	0	—	0	0	6.61
1997 Pittsburgh	NL	9	0	0	1	5	32	10	10	10	3	0	0	0	8	1	4	2	0	0	0	—	0	0	18.00
8 Min. YEARS		248	92	1	69	708.1	3172	838	450	367	56	26	25	17	268	15	575	47	3	31	49	.388	0	10	4.66
4 Maj. YEARS		27	0	0	6	31.2	167	47	34	32	8	0	2	2	26	1	19	4	0	0	1	.000	0	0	9.09

Bryan Graves

Bats: Right **Throws:** Right **Pos:** C-50; DH-9   **Ht:** 6'0" **Wt:** 220 **Born:** 10/8/74 **Age:** 26

Year Team	Lg Org	G	AB	H	2B	3B	HR	TB	R	RBI	TBB	IBB	SO	HBP	SH	SF	SB	CS	SB%	GDP	Avg	OBP	SLG
1995 Boise	A- Ana	32	53	11	2	0	1	16	9	5	17	0	12	0	0	0	0	0	—	0	.208	.400	.302
1996 Cedar Rapds	A Ana	83	228	51	5	2	4	72	27	27	46	0	59	5	1	3	4	2	.67	3	.224	.362	.316
1997 Cedar Rapds	A Ana	68	191	39	12	0	1	54	14	17	32	0	32	3	0	0	1	2	.33	4	.204	.327	.283
1998 Lk Elsinore	A+ Ana	8	20	4	1	0	0	5	1	1	1	0	7	0	0	0	0	0	—	0	.200	.238	.250
Midland	AA Ana	29	85	19	3	0	1	25	8	6	16	0	18	2	1	1	0	1	.00	5	.224	.356	.294
1999 Lk Elsinore	A+ Ana	15	38	9	2	0	0	11	3	6	7	0	13	0	0	1	0	0	—	1	.237	.348	.289
Edmonton	AAA Ana	2	5	2	1	0	0	3	2	1	1	0	2	1	0	0	0	0	—	0	.400	.571	.600
Erie	AA Ana	37	103	20	2	1	1	27	22	8	32	0	32	2	3	0	1	0	1.00	1	.194	.394	.262
2000 Erie	AA Ana	34	97	21	5	0	1	29	12	14	21	0	23	1	0	2	0	1	.00	5	.216	.355	.299
Edmonton	AAA Ana	25	63	15	3	0	0	18	8	13	13	0	18	0	0	3	0	1	.00	2	.238	.354	.286
6 Min. YEARS		333	883	191	36	3	9	260	106	98	186	0	216	14	5	10	6	7	.46	21	.216	.358	.294

Chad Green

Bats: Both **Throws:** Right **Pos:** OF-125; PH-2; PR-2   **Ht:** 5'10" **Wt:** 180 **Born:** 6/28/75 **Age:** 26

Year Team	Lg Org	G	AB	H	2B	3B	HR	TB	R	RBI	TBB	IBB	SO	HBP	SH	SF	SB	CS	SB%	GDP	Avg	OBP	SLG
1996 Ogden	R+ Mil	21	81	29	4	1	3	44	22	8	15	0	23	1	1	2	12	3	.80	0	.358	.455	.543
1997 Stockton	A+ Mil	127	513	128	26	14	2	188	78	43	37	2	138	2	11	4	37	16	.70	3	.250	.300	.366
1998 Stockton	A+ Mil	40	151	52	13	2	0	69	30	17	12	3	22	1	1	1	22	5	.81	2	.344	.394	.457
El Paso	AA Mil	7	6	0	0	0	0	0	0	0	1	0	3	0	0	0	0	0	—	0	.000	.143	.000
1999 Huntsville	AA Mil	116	422	104	22	3	10	162	56	46	46	2	109	2	2	3	28	13	.68	6	.246	.321	.384
2000 Indianapols	AAA Mil	43	123	25	8	2	3	46	18	10	10	0	36	1	2	1	6	2	.75	2	.203	.267	.374
Huntsville	AA Mil	85	317	74	22	2	3	109	44	27	29	1	85	1	1	3	19	6	.76	2	.233	.297	.344
5 Min. YEARS		439	1613	412	95	24	21	618	248	151	150	8	416	8	18	14	124	45	.73	15	.255	.319	.383

Steve Green

Pitches: Right **Bats:** Right **Pos:** SP-21   **Ht:** 6'2" **Wt:** 180 **Born:** 1/26/78 **Age:** 23

Year Team	Lg Org	G	GS	CG	GF	IP	BFP	H	R	ER	HR	SH	SF	HB	TBB	IBB	SO	WP	Bk	W	L	Pct.	ShO	Sv	ERA
1998 Cedar Rapds	A Ana	18	10	1	5	83.1	356	86	49	42	9	3	3	3	25	0	61	9	1	2	6	.250	0	0	4.54
1999 Lk Elsinore	A+ Ana	19	19	4	0	120.2	526	130	70	53	9	4	1	6	37	2	91	1	3	7	6	.538	4	0	3.95
Erie	AA Ana	6	6	1	0	40.2	176	34	25	15	4	1	2	2	19	0	32	1	0	3	1	.750	0	0	3.32
2000 Erie	AA Ana	13	13	0	0	79.1	330	71	34	30	7	2	0	3	34	0	66	1	0	7	4	.636	0	0	3.40
Edmonton	AAA Ana	8	8	0	0	42	208	55	35	34	4	1	0	2	27	1	24	1	2	0	4	.000	0	0	7.29
3 Min. YEARS		64	56	6	5	366	1596	376	213	174	33	11	6	16	142	3	274	13	6	19	21	.475	4	0	4.28

Tyler Green

Pitches: Right **Bats:** Right **Pos:** RP-7; SP-5   **Ht:** 6'5" **Wt:** 207 **Born:** 2/18/70 **Age:** 31

Year Team	Lg Org	G	GS	CG	GF	IP	BFP	H	R	ER	HR	SH	SF	HB	TBB	IBB	SO	WP	Bk	W	L	Pct.	ShO	Sv	ERA
1991 Batavia	A- Phi	3	3	0	0	15	58	7	2	2	0	0	0	2	6	0	19	2	0	1	0	1.000	0	0	1.20
Clearwater	A+ Phi	2	2	0	0	13	50	3	2	2	0	0	0	0	8	0	20	2	0	2	0	1.000	0	0	1.38
1992 Reading	AA Phi	12	12	0	0	62.1	249	46	16	13	2	4	1	1	20	0	67	5	0	6	3	.667	0	0	1.88
Scranton-WB	AAA Phi	2	2	0	0	10.1	50	7	7	7	1	0	0	1	12	0	15	0	1	0	1	.000	0	0	6.10
1993 Scranton-WB	AAA Phi	28	14	4	6	118.1	496	102	62	52	8	3	4	5	43	2	87	8	2	6	10	.375	0	0	3.95
1994 Scranton-WB	AAA Phi	27	26	4	0	162	725	179	110	100	25	4	4	12	77	3	95	14	1	7	16	.304	0	0	5.56
1997 Scranton-WB	AAA Phi	12	12	3	0	72.1	322	80	54	49	13	1	0	1	29	3	40	4	0	4	8	.333	0	0	6.10
1999 Scranton-WB	AAA Phi	19	7	1	4	50.1	248	78	47	43	8	1	3	4	24	1	31	3	0	4	6	.400	0	0	7.69
2000 Kinston	A+ Cle	1	1	0	0	5	23	7	4	2	0	0	0	1	1	0	1	1	0	0	1	.000	0	0	3.60
Buffalo	AAA Cle	11	4	0	3	29	144	42	28	27	2	0	2	1	20	2	11	3	0	2	2	.500	0	0	8.38
1993 Philadelphia	NL	3	2	0	1	7.1	41	16	9	6	1	0	0	0	5	0	7	2	0	0	0	—	0	0	7.36
1995 Philadelphia	NL	26	25	4	0	140.2	623	157	86	83	15	5	6	4	66	3	85	9	2	8	9	.471	2	0	5.31
1997 Philadelphia	NL	14	14	0	0	76.2	340	72	50	42	8	0	3	1	45	4	58	7	0	4	4	.500	0	0	4.93
1998 Philadelphia	NL	27	27	0	0	159.1	699	142	97	89	23	5	6	9	85	1	113	8	0	6	12	.333	0	0	5.03
7 Min. YEARS		117	83	12	13	537.2	2365	551	332	297	59	13	14	28	240	11	386	42	4	32	47	.405	0	0	4.97
4 Maj. YEARS		70	68	4	1	384	1703	387	242	220	47	10	15	14	201	8	263	26	2	18	25	.419	2	0	5.16

Rick Greene

Pitches: Right **Bats:** Right **Pos:** RP-54   **Ht:** 6'5" **Wt:** 200 **Born:** 1/2/71 **Age:** 30

Year Team	Lg Org	G	GS	CG	GF	IP	BFP	H	R	ER	HR	SH	SF	HB	TBB	IBB	SO	WP	Bk	W	L	Pct.	ShO	Sv	ERA
1993 Lakeland	A+ Det	26	0	0	11	40.2	184	57	28	28	1	6	0	1	16	1	32	5	2	2	3	.400	0	2	6.20
London	AA Det	23	0	0	11	29	135	31	22	21	1	3	3	1	20	3	19	3	2	2	2	.500	0	4	6.52
1994 Trenton	AA Det	20	0	0	14	19.1	92	17	17	17	0	3	2	0	21	2	5	2	0	1	1	.500	0	3	7.91
Lakeland	A+ Det	19	2	0	11	33.1	158	50	23	16	0	1	0	0	10	1	28	0	0	0	4	.000	0	4	4.32
1995 Jacksnville	AA Det	32	0	0	6	38.2	177	45	19	15	3	1	0	3	15	2	29	0	0	6	2	.750	0	0	3.49
1996 Jacksnville	AA Det	57	0	0	48	56	275	67	44	31	8	6	0	2	39	4	42	2	0	2	7	.222	0	30	4.98
1997 Toledo	AAA Det	57	0	0	14	70	289	49	29	22	4	7	2	5	32	3	51	8	0	6	8	.429	0	1	2.83
1998 Louisville	AAA Mil	58	0	0	44	66.2	302	73	31	26	6	2	1	3	33	7	44	2	0	6	6	.500	0	18	3.51
1999 Indianapols	AAA Cin	61	0	0	29	78	331	78	37	32	3	4	5	2	35	4	40	6	0	5	7	.417	0	4	3.69
2000 Salt Lake	AAA Min	22	0	0	9	26.1	125	30	21	17	2	1	0	3	19	3	15	1	1	2	2	.500	0	3	5.81
Louisville	AAA Cin	32	0	0	26	38.1	162	31	21	12	2	2	1	1	19	2	13	0	0	4	4	.500	0	7	2.82
1999 Cincinnati	NL	1	0	0	0	5.2	25	7	4	3	2	0	0	0	1	0	3	0	0	0	0	—	0	0	4.76
8 Min. YEARS		407	2	0	223	496.1	2230	528	292	237	30	36	15	21	259	32	318	35	5	36	46	.439	0	77	4.30

Ryan Greene

Pitches: Right **Bats:** Right **Pos:** RP-38   **Ht:** 6'4" **Wt:** 215 **Born:** 8/6/74 **Age:** 26

Year Team	Lg Org	G	GS	CG	GF	IP	BFP	H	R	ER	HR	SH	SF	HB	TBB	IBB	SO	WP	Bk	W	L	Pct.	ShO	Sv	ERA
1997 Eugene	A- Atl	15	15	0	0	84.1	381	96	52	43	2	2	4	6	30	1	72	10	6	3	7	.300	0	0	4.59
1998 Macon	A Atl	22	0	0	10	37.1	160	40	19	12	4	2	2	6	6	1	46	3	0	3	3	.500	0	2	2.89
1999 Myrtle Bch	A+ Atl	44	0	0	29	82	339	65	32	31	7	5	1	2	29	1	85	11	0	3	5	.375	0	16	3.40
2000 Greenville	AA Atl	24	0	0	9	32.1	140	29	10	10	3	1	2	0	18	0	25	3	0	1	0	1.000	0	0	2.78
Myrtle Bch	A+ Atl	14	0	0	8	22	94	16	16	11	3	1	1	0	10	0	23	2	0	2	2	.500	0	1	4.50
4 Min. YEARS		119	15	0	56	258	1114	246	129	107	19	11	10	8	93	3	251	29	6	12	17	.414	0	19	3.73

Kevin Gregg

Pitches: Right **Bats:** Right **Pos:** SP-27; RP-1   **Ht:** 6'6" **Wt:** 200 **Born:** 6/20/78 **Age:** 23

Year Team	Lg Org	G	GS	CG	GF	IP	BFP	H	R	ER	HR	SH	SF	HB	TBB	IBB	SO	WP	Bk	W	L	Pct.	ShO	Sv	ERA
1996 Athletics	R Oak	11	9	0	0	40.2	169	30	14	14	1	1	1	2	21	0	48	11	0	3	3	.500	0	0	3.10
1997 Visalia	A+ Atl	25	24	0	0	115.1	534	116	81	73	8	2	3	5	74	0	136	28	0	6	8	.429	0	0	5.70
1998 Modesto	A+ Atl	30	24	0	3	144	640	139	72	61	7	9	2	6	76	2	141	7	0	8	7	.533	0	1	3.81
1999 Visalia	A+ Atl	13	11	1	2	64	271	60	34	27	3	1	2	4	23	0	48	7	1	4	4	.500	1	1	3.80
Midland	AA Oak	16	16	2	0	91.1	380	75	45	38	7	0	3	6	31	1	66	6	0	4	7	.364	0	0	3.74
Vancouver	AAA Oak	1	1	0	0	5	21	6	2	2	0	0	0	0	2	0	4	2	0	1	0	1.000	0	0	3.60
2000 Midland	AA Oak	28	27	0	0	140.2	655	171	120	100	18	5	6	8	73	0	97	6	0	5	14	.263	0	0	6.40
5 Min. YEARS		124	112	3	5	601	2670	597	368	315	44	18	17	31	300	3	540	67	1	31	43	.419	1	2	4.72

Kevin Grijak

Bats: Left **Throws:** Right **Pos:** 1B-60; OF-37; PH-17; DH-9; PR-2; C-1   **Ht:** 6'2" **Wt:** 215 **Born:** 8/6/70 **Age:** 30

Year Team	Lg Org	G	AB	H	2B	3B	HR	TB	R	RBI	TBB	IBB	SO	HBP	SH	SF	SB	CS	SB%	GDP	Avg	OBP	SLG
1991 Idaho Falls	R+ Atl	52	202	68	9	1	10	109	33	58	16	1	15	1	2	4	4	1	.80	5	.337	.381	.540
1992 Pulaski	R+ Atl	10	31	11	3	0	0	14	1	6	6	0	0	0	0	0	2	2	.50	1	.355	.459	.452
Macon	A Atl	47	157	41	13	0	5	69	20	21	15	2	16	3	0	2	3	0	1.00	3	.261	.333	.439
1993 Macon	A Atl	120	389	115	26	5	7	172	50	58	37	4	37	6	2	12	9	5	.64	9	.296	.356	.442
1994 Durham	A+ Atl	22	68	25	3	0	11	61	18	22	12	4	6	3	0	1	1	1	.50	1	.368	.476	.897
Greenville	AA Atl	100	348	94	19	1	11	148	40	58	20	1	40	6	0	7	2	3	.40	11	.270	.315	.425
1995 Greenville	AA Atl	21	74	32	5	0	2	43	14	11	7	0	9	2	0	2	0	1	.00	0	.432	.482	.581
Richmond	AAA Atl	106	309	92	16	5	12	154	35	56	25	4	47	4	0	4	1	3	.25	10	.298	.354	.498
1996 Richmond	AAA Atl	13	30	11	3	0	1	17	3	8	5	0	7	1	0	0	1	0	.00	1	.367	.472	.567
1997 Greenville	AA Atl	72	240	60	12	1	13	113	35	48	18	2	35	5	1	3	0	1	.00	8	.250	.312	.471
1998 Carolina	AA Pit	46	146	51	8	0	9	86	29	33	18	2	15	4	0	3	1	0	1.00	4	.349	.427	.589
Nashville	AAA Pit	67	227	65	17	0	15	127	32	40	23	0	34	3	1	1	1	4	.20	4	.286	.358	.559
1999 Albuquerque	AAA LA	119	401	127	28	1	18	211	58	80	19	2	50	3	2	3	2	6	.25	4	.317	.350	.526
2000 Albuquerque	AAA LA	112	337	96	20	3	17	173	61	79	31	5	55	3	0	5	10	9	.53	8	.285	.346	.513
10 Min. YEARS		907	2959	888	182	17	131	1497	429	578	252	27	366	44	8	47	36	37	.49	73	.300	.359	.506

Kevin Gryboski

Pitches: Right **Bats:** Right **Pos:** RP-47   **Ht:** 6'5" **Wt:** 220 **Born:** 11/15/73 **Age:** 27

Year Team	Lg Org	G	GS	CG	GF	IP	BFP	H	R	ER	HR	SH	SF	HB	TBB	IBB	SO	WP	Bk	W	L	Pct.	ShO	Sv	ERA
1995 Everett	A- Sea	25	0	0	14	36	156	27	18	14	2	3	1	3	18	2	25	3	0	1	5	.167	0	2	3.50
1996 Wisconsin	A Sea	32	21	3	5	138.2	630	146	90	73	7	9	6	12	62	2	100	12	0	10	5	.667	0	1	4.74
1997 Lancaster	A+ Sea	21	15	0	4	67.1	332	113	82	74	13	2	8	1	26	0	41	7	0	0	7	.000	0	0	9.89
1998 Orlando	AA Sea	2	0	0	0	5	23	8	5	5	1	0	0	0	1	0	4	2	0	0	0	—	0	0	9.00
Lancaster	A+ Sea	37	3	0	17	85	351	75	35	25	4	1	2	4	31	1	73	3	0	5	5	.500	0	8	2.65
1999 New Haven	AA Sea	47	0	0	32	62.1	267	67	27	20	5	5	2	3	20	4	41	3	0	2	5	.286	0	10	2.89
2000 New Haven	AA Sea	16	0	0	14	18	78	15	5	5	0	1	0	1	8	1	20	4	0	1	1	.500	0	9	2.50
Tacoma	AAA Sea	31	0	0	18	41	181	45	23	22	3	2	0	0	23	4	35	7	0	2	2	.500	0	2	4.83
6 Min. YEARS		211	39	3	104	453.1	2018	496	285	238	35	23	19	24	189	14	339	41	0	21	30	.412	0	32	4.73

Creighton Gubanich

Bats: Right **Throws:** Right **Pos:** C-78; DH-17; PH-11; 1B-6   **Ht:** 6'3" **Wt:** 200 **Born:** 3/27/72 **Age:** 29

Year Team	Lg Org	G	AB	H	2B	3B	HR	TB	R	RBI	TBB	IBB	SO	HBP	SH	SF	SB	CS	SB%	GDP	Avg	OBP	SLG
1991 Sou Oregon	A- Oak	43	132	30	7	2	4	53	23	18	19	0	35	6	0	0	0	4	.00	2	.227	.350	.402
1992 Madison	A Oak	121	404	100	19	3	9	152	46	55	41	1	102	16	8	1	0	7	.00	8	.248	.340	.376
1993 Madison	A Oak	119	373	100	19	2	19	180	65	78	63	2	105	11	2	12	3	3	.50	7	.268	.379	.483
1994 Modesto	A+ Oak	108	375	88	20	3	15	159	53	55	54	0	102	7	5	2	5	4	.56	9	.235	.344	.424
1995 Huntsville	AA Oak	94	274	60	7	1	13	108	37	43	48	0	82	7	2	5	1	0	1.00	6	.219	.344	.394
1996 Huntsville	AA Oak	62	217	60	19	0	9	106	40	43	31	1	71	4	3	2	1	0	1.00	5	.276	.374	.488
Edmonton	AAA Oak	34	117	29	7	1	4	50	14	19	6	0	33	1	0	1	3	0	1.00	4	.248	.288	.427
1997 Edmonton	AAA Oak	43	145	48	13	0	7	82	23	34	14	0	42	2	1	1	0	2	.00	4	.331	.395	.566
Tucson	AAA Mil	24	85	29	5	0	5	49	13	17	1	0	19	1	0	0	1	0	1.00	3	.341	.356	.576
Colo Sprngs	AAA Col	14	47	9	1	0	3	19	4	6	4	0	18	0	0	0	1	0	—	2	.191	.255	.404
1998 Las Vegas	AAA SD	86	292	85	22	0	19	164	48	70	30	3	85	3	0	6	1	1	.50	4	.291	.356	.562
1999 Pawtucket	AAA Bos	27	92	26	3	0	5	44	12	10	6	0	23	0	0	1	0	0	—	4	.283	.323	.478
2000 Indianapols	AAA Mil	109	380	108	34	0	16	190	48	71	35	6	95	2	2	3	0	1	.00	11	.284	.345	.500
1999 Boston	AL	18	47	13	2	1	1	20	4	11	3	0	13	2	0	0	0	0	—	3	.277	.346	.426
10 Min. YEARS		884	2933	772	176	12	128	1356	426	519	352	13	812	60	23	34	15	22	.41	67	.263	.350	.462

Mark Guerra

Pitches: Right **Bats:** Right **Pos:** RP-37; SP-8   **Ht:** 6'2" **Wt:** 200 **Born:** 11/4/71 **Age:** 29

Year Team	Lg Org	G	GS	CG	GF	IP	BFP	H	R	ER	HR	SH	SF	HB	TBB	IBB	SO	WP	Bk	W	L	Pct.	ShO	Sv	ERA
1994 Pittsfield	A- NYM	14	14	2	0	94	392	105	47	36	4	4	5	4	21	1	62	2	2	7	6	.538	0	0	3.45
1995 St. Lucie	A+ NYM	23	23	4	0	160	644	148	55	47	5	4	4	4	33	1	110	2	3	9	9	.500	3	0	2.64
Binghamton	AA NYM	6	5	1	0	32.2	139	35	24	21	6	1	0	0	9	1	24	0	0	2	1	.667	0	0	5.79
1996 Binghamton	AA NYM	27	20	1	3	140.1	577	143	60	55	23	5	2	2	34	3	84	1	1	7	6	.538	0	0	3.53
1997 Binghamton	AA NYM	48	7	1	17	94.2	403	96	46	34	10	3	2	1	30	1	74	2	0	4	8	.333	0	7	3.23
1998 Norfolk	AAA NYM	18	0	0	8	30.2	142	40	24	22	6	2	3	1	14	1	19	0	0	2	1	.667	0	0	6.46
Binghamton	AA NYM	30	2	0	21	41.1	171	38	17	13	5	1	3	0	11	1	30	0	0	3	3	.500	0	12	2.83
1999 Norfolk	AAA NYM	63	2	0	11	89	391	90	45	29	5	3	2	0	39	8	70	2	0	8	3	.727	0	0	2.93
2000 Norfolk	AAA NYM	36	0	0	16	48.2	219	55	29	26	5	3	0	2	23	7	29	3	0	1	4	.200	0	1	4.81
New Orleans	AAA Hou	9	8	0	1	45	199	58	32	30	3	2	1	4	5	1	25	0	0	1	4	.200	0	0	6.00
7 Min. YEARS		274	81	9	77	776.1	3277	808	379	313	72	28	22	18	219	25	527	12	6	44	45	.494	3	20	3.63

Junior Guerrero

Pitches: Right **Bats:** Right **Pos:** SP-24; RP-4   **Ht:** 6'2" **Wt:** 175 **Born:** 8/21/79 **Age:** 21

Year Team	Lg Org	G	GS	CG	GF	IP	BFP	H	R	ER	HR	SH	SF	HB	TBB	IBB	SO	WP	Bk	W	L	Pct.	ShO	Sv	ERA
1998 Royals	R KC	13	6	0	3	61.1	257	57	24	22	2	4	2	2	19	0	58	5	1	4	4	.500	0	0	3.23
1999 Chston-WV	A KC	19	19	0	0	104.1	441	90	39	32	6	4	5	3	45	0	113	10	2	7	3	.700	0	0	2.76
Wilmington	A+ KC	9	9	0	0	51.1	206	30	10	8	2	1	1	0	26	0	68	4	0	4	2	.667	0	0	1.40
2000 Wichita	AA KC	28	24	0	2	131	603	153	93	83	25	1	6	3	69	2	79	8	3	4	10	.286	0	0	5.70
3 Min. YEARS		69	58	0	5	348	1507	330	166	145	35	10	14	8	159	2	318	27	6	19	19	.500	0	0	3.75

Matt Guerrier

Pitches: Right **Bats:** Right **Pos:** RP-53   **Ht:** 6'3" **Wt:** 190 **Born:** 8/2/78 **Age:** 22

Year Team	Lg Org	G	GS	CG	GF	IP	BFP	H	R	ER	HR	SH	SF	HB	TBB	IBB	SO	WP	Bk	W	L	Pct.	ShO	Sv	ERA
1999 Bristol	R+ CWS	21	0	0	19	25.2	109	18	9	3	1	0	2	1	14	2	37	1	1	5	0	1.000	0	10	1.05
Winston-Sal	A+ CWS	4	0	0	4	3.1	15	3	2	2	0	0	0	1	0	0	5	2	0	0	0	—	0	2	5.40
2000 Winston-Sal	A+ CWS	30	0	0	28	34.2	147	25	13	5	0	2	1	3	12	0	35	2	0	0	3	.000	0	19	1.30
Birmingham	AA CWS	23	0	0	19	23.1	95	17	9	7	1	0	0	1	12	1	19	3	0	3	1	.750	0	7	2.70
2 Min. YEARS		78	0	0	70	87	366	63	33	17	2	2	3	6	38	3	96	8	1	8	4	.667	0	38	1.76

Giomar Guevara

Bats: Both **Throws:** Right **Pos:** SS-73; 2B-35; PH-2; 3B-1   **Ht:** 5'8" **Wt:** 150 **Born:** 10/23/72 **Age:** 28

Year Team	Lg Org	G	AB	H	2B	3B	HR	TB	R	RBI	TBB	IBB	SO	HBP	SH	SF	SB	CS	SB%	GDP	Avg	OBP	SLG
1993 Bellingham	A- Sea	62	211	48	8	3	1	65	31	23	34	2	46	2	4	0	4	7	.36	3	.227	.340	.308
1994 Appleton	A Sea	110	385	116	23	3	8	169	57	46	42	1	77	2	5	1	9	16	.36	6	.301	.372	.439
Jacksnville	AA Sea	7	20	4	2	0	1	9	2	3	2	0	9	0	1	0	0	0	—	0	.200	.273	.450
1995 Riverside	A+ Sea	83	292	71	12	3	2	95	53	34	30	1	71	1	6	6	7	4	.64	4	.243	.310	.325
1996 Port City	AA Sea	119	414	110	18	2	2	138	60	41	54	1	102	4	9	4	21	7	.75	12	.266	.353	.333
1997 Tacoma	AAA Sea	54	176	43	5	1	2	56	29	13	5	0	39	1	5	0	3	7	.30	2	.244	.269	.318
Memphis	AA Sea	65	228	60	10	4	4	90	30	28	20	0	42	0	0	1	5	5	.50	3	.263	.321	.395
1998 Lancaster	A+ Sea	19	61	15	4	0	0	19	15	3	14	0	20	1	1	0	1	1	.50	1	.246	.395	.311
Orlando	AA Sea	14	45	15	5	1	0	22	13	6	8	0	11	0	1	0	0	0	—	3	.333	.434	.489
1999 Tacoma	AAA Sea	32	116	34	13	0	3	56	15	15	12	0	22	2	1	0	0	1	.00	3	.293	.369	.483
2000 Toledo	AAA Det	109	383	108	23	2	7	156	61	33	44	0	65	4	5	3	4	5	.44	10	.282	.359	.407
1997 Seattle	AL	5	4	0	0	0	0	0	0	0	0	0	2	0	0	0	1	0	1.00	0	.000	.000	.000
1998 Seattle	AL	11	13	3	2	0	0	5	4	0	4	0	4	1	0	0	0	0	—	1	.231	.444	.385
1999 Seattle	AL	10	12	3	2	0	0	5	2	2	0	0	2	0	0	0	0	1	.00	0	.250	.250	.417
8 Min. YEARS		674	2331	624	123	19	30	875	366	245	265	5	504	17	37	15	54	53	.50	47	.268	.345	.375
3 Maj. YEARS		26	29	6	4	0	0	4	6	2	4	0	8	1	0	0	1	1	.00	1	.207	.324	.345

Aaron Guiel

Bats: Left **Throws:** Right **Pos:** OF-70; DH-3   **Ht:** 5'10" **Wt:** 190 **Born:** 10/5/72 **Age:** 28

Year Team	Lg Org	G	AB	H	2B	3B	HR	TB	R	RBI	TBB	IBB	SO	HBP	SH	SF	SB	CS	SB%	GDP	Avg	OBP	SLG
1993 Boise	A- Ana	35	104	31	6	4	2	51	24	12	26	1	21	4	2	0	3	0	1.00	1	.298	.455	.490
1994 Cedar Rapds	A Ana	127	454	122	30	1	18	208	84	82	64	2	93	6	5	3	21	7	.75	7	.269	.364	.458
1995 Lk Elsinore	A+ Ana	113	409	110	25	7	7	170	73	58	69	0	96	7	4	4	7	6	.54	7	.269	.380	.416
1996 Midland	AA Ana	129	439	118	29	7	10	191	72	48	56	0	71	10	2	1	11	7	.61	6	.269	.364	.435
1997 Midland	AA Ana	116	419	138	37	4	22	255	91	85	59	3	94	18	2	3	14	10	.58	9	.329	.431	.609
Mobile	AA SD	8	26	10	2	0	1	15	9	9	5	0	4	1	0	0	1	0	1.00	0	.385	.500	.577
1998 Padres	R SD	8	16	8	3	1	1	16	8	6	5	1	5	3	0	0	1	1	.50	0	.500	.667	1.000
Las Vegas	AAA SD	60	183	57	15	4	5	95	33	31	28	2	51	4	1	2	5	1	.83	4	.311	.410	.519
1999 Las Vegas	AAA SD	84	257	63	25	2	12	128	46	39	44	3	86	5	0	3	5	4	.56	6	.245	.362	.498
2000 Omaha	AAA KC	73	258	74	15	2	13	132	47	40	35	0	54	8	0	0	6	0	1.00	3	.287	.389	.512
8 Min. YEARS		753	2565	731	187	35	91	1261	487	410	391	12	575	66	16	16	74	36	.67	43	.285	.391	.492

Jeff Guiel

Bats: Left **Throws:** Right **Pos:** DH-46; OF-35; 1B-24; 3B-14; PH-1   **Ht:** 5'11" **Wt:** 195 **Born:** 1/12/74 **Age:** 27

Year Team	Lg Org	G	AB	H	2B	3B	HR	TB	R	RBI	TBB	IBB	SO	HBP	SH	SF	SB	CS	SB%	GDP	Avg	OBP	SLG
1997 Cedar Rapds	A Ana	41	132	42	7	0	10	79	32	26	35	5	28	3	0	1	13	2	.87	6	.318	.465	.598
1998 Lk Elsinore	A+ Ana	101	315	85	24	7	16	171	64	60	83	5	87	8	0	3	19	9	.68	3	.270	.430	.543

Year Team	Lg Org	G	AB	H	2B	3B	HR	TB	R	RBI	TBB	IBB	SO	HBP	SH	SF	SB	CS	SB%	GDP	Avg	OBP	SLG
1999 Lk Elsinore	A+ Ana	15	58	19	4	2	3	36	12	12	11	0	18	0	0	0	2	1	.67	0	.328	.435	.621
Erie	AA Ana	57	175	46	10	3	6	80	34	24	33	0	33	2	1	3	3	3	.50	1	.263	.380	.457
2000 Erie	AA Ana	118	410	104	25	3	16	183	55	59	49	3	97	10	1	9	2	4	.33	8	.254	.341	.446
4 Min. YEARS		332	1090	296	70	15	51	549	197	181	211	13	263	23	2	17	39	19	.67	14	.272	.395	.504

Matt Guiliano

Bats: Right **Throws:** Right **Pos:** SS-79; 3B-34; 2B-5; PH-5; PR-3   **Ht:** 5'9" **Wt:** 180 **Born:** 10/7/72 **Age:** 28

Year Team	Lg Org	G	AB	H	2B	3B	HR	TB	R	RBI	TBB	IBB	SO	HBP	SH	SF	SB	CS	SB%	GDP	Avg	OBP	SLG
1994 Martinsvlle	R+ Phi	58	190	42	5	0	5	62	33	16	24	0	57	7	3	2	16	3	.84	4	.221	.327	.326
1995 Piedmont	A Phi	129	451	102	22	12	4	160	67	59	51	1	114	7	9	6	6	8	.43	7	.226	.311	.355
1996 Reading	AA Phi	74	220	44	9	3	0	59	19	19	25	1	59	3	3	1	0	0	—	4	.200	.289	.268
Clearwater	A+ Phi	55	166	37	8	2	1	52	12	14	6	0	46	6	6	3	2	3	.40	3	.223	.271	.313
1997 Reading	AA Phi	119	367	83	15	3	7	125	38	37	34	4	99	5	8	3	7	6	.54	8	.226	.299	.341
1998 Reading	AA Phi	126	439	99	15	2	12	154	47	44	45	4	102	4	6	1	2	4	.33	16	.226	.303	.351
1999 Scranton-WB	AAA Phi	71	216	41	15	0	2	62	20	24	17	0	61	2	5	2	3	2	.60	4	.190	.253	.287
2000 Huntsville	AA Mil	20	44	8	0	0	0	8	3	3	8	1	14	2	0	1	1	0	1.00	1	.182	.327	.182
Long Island	IND —	96	289	67	8	4	9	110	42	43	21	0	89	11	4	2	5	5	.50	3	.232	.307	.381
7 Min. YEARS		748	2382	523	97	26	40	792	281	259	231	11	641	47	44	20	42	31	.58	50	.220	.299	.332

Mike Gulan

Bats: Right **Throws:** Right **Pos:** 3B-53; OF-48; SS-12; PH-8; DH-7   **Ht:** 6'1" **Wt:** 190 **Born:** 12/18/70 **Age:** 30

Year Team	Lg Org	G	AB	H	2B	3B	HR	TB	R	RBI	TBB	IBB	SO	HBP	SH	SF	SB	CS	SB%	GDP	Avg	OBP	SLG
1992 Hamilton	A- StL	62	242	66	8	4	7	103	33	36	23	0	53	1	0	4	12	4	.75	7	.273	.333	.426
1993 Springfield	A StL	132	455	118	28	4	23	223	81	76	34	0	135	9	3	3	8	4	.67	4	.259	.321	.490
1994 St. Pete	A+ StL	120	466	113	30	2	8	171	39	56	26	2	108	2	0	6	2	8	.20	8	.242	.282	.367
1995 Arkansas	AA StL	64	242	76	16	3	12	134	47	48	11	1	52	6	0	1	4	2	.67	4	.314	.358	.554
Louisville	AAA StL	58	195	46	10	4	5	79	21	27	10	1	53	3	0	2	2	2	.50	6	.236	.281	.405
1996 Louisville	AAA StL	123	419	107	27	4	17	193	47	55	26	1	119	7	1	2	7	2	.78	10	.255	.308	.461
1997 Louisville	AAA StL	116	412	110	20	6	14	184	50	61	28	0	121	3	1	3	5	2	.71	12	.267	.316	.447
1998 Portland	AA Fla	46	160	49	16	2	5	84	24	23	10	0	40	1	0	1	3	2	.60	6	.306	.349	.525
1999 Calgary	AAA Fla	84	286	79	23	2	13	145	41	51	10	0	82	4	1	3	2	1	.67	9	.276	.307	.507
2000 Calgary	AAA Fla	119	426	135	40	2	17	230	66	74	27	1	94	8	0	2	5	1	.83	12	.317	.367	.540
1997 St. Louis	NL	5	9	0	0	0	0	0	2	1	1	0	5	0	0	0	0	0	—	0	.000	.100	.000
9 Min. YEARS		924	3303	899	218	33	121	1546	449	507	205	6	857	44	6	27	50	28	.64	78	.272	.321	.468

Lindsay Gulin

Pitches: Left **Bats:** Left **Pos:** SP-26; RP-2   **Ht:** 6'3" **Wt:** 175 **Born:** 11/22/76 **Age:** 24

Year Team	Lg Org	G	GS	CG	GF	IP	BFP	H	R	ER	HR	SH	SF	HB	TBB	IBB	SO	WP	Bk	W	L	Pct.	ShO	Sv	ERA
1995 Mets	R NYM	10	4	0	3	47.1	182	36	11	9	4	0	1	1	13	0	48	2	2	6	0	1.000	0	0	1.71
Pittsfield	A- NYM	1	1	0	0	7	29	4	4	3	1	1	0	0	3	0	3	1	1	1	0	1.000	0	0	3.86
1996 Capital Cty	A NYM	19	19	1	0	112.1	470	88	40	33	6	0	2	6	57	0	134	5	6	7	7	.500	0	0	2.64
1997 St. Lucie	A+ NYM	9	6	0	0	26.1	136	36	31	27	2	0	2	1	21	1	11	6	1	0	3	.000	0	0	9.23
Capital Cty	A NYM	17	15	1	2	99	421	77	37	32	2	2	2	5	60	0	118	9	1	8	1	.889	1	0	2.91
1998 St. Lucie	A+ NYM	6	4	0	0	27	106	16	9	7	2	2	0	1	11	1	19	1	0	1	1	.500	0	0	2.33
Lancaster	A+ Sea	9	3	0	3	24.2	118	32	17	16	3	0	0	1	15	0	18	1	2	2	2	.500	0	0	5.84
Wisconsin	A Sea	13	8	0	2	48.1	207	47	24	20	5	3	1	3	20	0	51	6	0	1	3	.250	0	1	3.72
1999 St. Paul	IND —	16	16	0	0	102	419	83	41	36	8	1	3	5	46	0	83	6	6	8	2	.800	0	0	3.18
Daytona	A+ ChC	3	1	0	0	13.2	53	7	0	0	1	0	0	0	7	0	19	0	0	2	0	1.000	0	0	0.00
2000 Daytona	A+ ChC	19	17	0	1	109.2	447	93	34	30	8	5	1	3	43	0	97	5	3	11	2	.846	1	0	2.46
West Tenn	AA ChC	9	9	1	0	52.1	237	49	33	29	4	1	3	4	30	0	54	4	2	5	2	.714	1	0	4.99
6 Min. YEARS		131	103	3	11	669.2	2825	568	281	242	45	16	15	30	326	2	655	46	24	52	23	.693	2	1	3.25

Shane Gunderson

Bats: Right **Throws:** Right **Pos:** DH-8; OF-7; PH-4; 1B-1; PR-1   **Ht:** 6'0" **Wt:** 216 **Born:** 10/16/73 **Age:** 27

Year Team	Lg Org	G	AB	H	2B	3B	HR	TB	R	RBI	TBB	IBB	SO	HBP	SH	SF	SB	CS	SB%	GDP	Avg	OBP	SLG
1995 Elizabethtn	R+ Min	37	139	43	11	2	7	79	32	30	20	0	24	2	0	1	4	0	1.00	3	.309	.401	.568
Fort Wayne	A Min	26	87	22	7	0	2	35	17	12	10	1	17	2	4	0	2	1	.67	0	.253	.343	.402
1996 Fort Myers	A+ Min	117	410	103	20	5	5	148	61	50	63	2	85	14	6	2	12	8	.60	5	.251	.368	.361
1997 New Britain	AA Min	33	117	30	7	3	2	49	17	10	19	0	31	1	4	0	7	2	.78	1	.256	.365	.419
Fort Wayne	A Min	13	45	12	1	0	0	13	3	7	3	0	33	0	1	1	1	1	.50	2	.267	.306	.289
Fort Myers	A+ Min	14	50	14	4	0	0	18	5	5	7	0	8	1	0	1	3	1	.75	2	.280	.379	.360
1998 New Britain	AA Min	23	62	10	0	0	3	19	8	14	12	0	11	2	1	1	0	0	—	2	.161	.312	.306
Fort Myers	A+ Min	42	149	40	12	2	5	71	25	20	23	1	42	3	4	1	3	2	.60	1	.268	.375	.477
1999 New Britain	AA Min	46	154	39	11	1	3	61	15	16	7	0	37	2	2	0	1	1	.50	6	.253	.294	.396
2000 New Britain	AA Min	19	50	14	4	0	1	21	9	3	2	0	8	2	0	0	0	0	—	0	.280	.333	.420
6 Min. YEARS		370	1263	327	77	13	28	514	192	167	166	4	266	29	22	6	33	16	.67	22	.259	.357	.407

Rick Guttormson

Pitches: Right **Bats:** Right **Pos:** SP-15; RP-2   **Ht:** 6'2" **Wt:** 185 **Born:** 1/11/77 **Age:** 24

Year Team	Lg Org	G	GS	CG	GF	IP	BFP	H	R	ER	HR	SH	SF	HB	TBB	IBB	SO	WP	Bk	W	L	Pct.	ShO	Sv	ERA
1997 Padres	R SD	5	0	0	4	11	55	17	11	6	3	0	1	0	4	0	19	0	0	1	1	.500	0	1	4.91
Idaho Falls	R+ SD	18	2	0	8	28	129	34	25	20	2	5	2	2	11	2	19	5	0	3	2	.600	0	3	6.43
1998 Clinton	A SD	30	25	0	4	159	673	155	66	46	9	1	4	12	41	1	141	7	1	10	7	.588	0	2	2.60

Year Team	Lg Org	G	GS	CG	GF	IP	BFP	H	R	ER	HR	SH	SF	HB	TBB	IBB	SO	WP	Bk	W	L	Pct.	ShO	Sv	ERA
1999 Rancho Cuca	A+ SD	28	28	1	0	174.1	714	165	83	72	15	4	1	9	36	0	125	6	2	14	8	.636	0	0	3.72
2000 Mobile	AA SD	17	15	0	0	81.1	361	88	44	36	9	4	2	5	35	0	36	1	2	4	4	.500	0	0	3.98
4 Min. YEARS		98	70	1	16	453.2	1932	459	229	180	38	14	10	28	127	3	340	19	5	32	22	.593	0	6	3.57

Brad Guy

Pitches: Right **Bats:** Right **Pos:** RP-53; SP-1 **Ht:** 6'2" **Wt:** 192 **Born:** 10/25/75 **Age:** 25

Year Team	Lg Org	G	GS	CG	GF	IP	BFP	H	R	ER	HR	SH	SF	HB	TBB	IBB	SO	WP	Bk	W	L	Pct.	ShO	Sv	ERA
1997 Erie	A- Pit	25	0	0	6	52.2	201	37	12	11	3	3	0	2	7	0	53	9	1	5	1	.833	0	1	1.88
1998 Augusta	A Pit	56	0	0	24	86.1	363	75	39	29	7	6	0	4	26	4	94	10	3	6	4	.600	0	4	3.02
1999 Lynchburg	A+ Pit	49	0	0	27	72.1	308	77	35	33	2	5	2	1	17	2	60	7	1	6	6	.500	0	10	4.11
2000 Altoona	AA Pit	54	1	0	27	81.2	354	82	35	32	3	2	1	1	25	1	37	6	0	4	6	.400	0	7	3.53
4 Min. YEARS		184	1	0	84	293	1226	271	121	105	15	16	3	8	75	7	244	32	5	21	17	.553	0	22	3.23

Edwards Guzman

Bats: Left **Throws:** Right **Pos:** 2B-33; C-30; 3B-14; DH-14; OF-12; PH-9; 1B-6 **Ht:** 5'10" **Wt:** 205 **Born:** 9/11/76 **Age:** 24

Year Team	Lg Org	G	AB	H	2B	3B	HR	TB	R	RBI	TBB	IBB	SO	HBP	SH	SF	SB	CS	SB%	GDP	Avg	OBP	SLG
1996 San Jose	A+ SF	106	367	99	19	5	1	131	41	40	39	4	60	5	6	5	3	5	.38	6	.270	.344	.357
1997 Shreveport	AA SF	118	380	108	15	4	3	140	52	42	33	4	57	1	5	3	3	1	.75	6	.284	.341	.368
1998 Fresno	AAA SF	102	325	99	17	0	9	143	50	48	24	4	47	3	3	1	1	0	1.00	4	.305	.357	.440
1999 Fresno	AAA SF	90	358	98	13	0	7	132	48	48	17	0	50	3	4	4	6	5	.55	11	.274	.309	.369
2000 Fresno	AAA SF	115	421	118	24	1	6	162	52	52	17	0	43	5	4	3	1	5	.17	17	.280	.314	.385
1999 San Francisco	NL	14	15	0	0	0	0	0	0	0	0	0	4	0	1	0	0	0	—	0	.000	.000	.000
5 Min. YEARS		531	1851	522	88	10	26	708	243	230	130	12	257	17	22	16	14	16	.47	44	.282	.332	.382

Juan Guzman

Pitches: Right **Bats:** Right **Pos:** SP-21 **Ht:** 6'2" **Wt:** 184 **Born:** 3/4/78 **Age:** 23

Year Team	Lg Org	G	GS	CG	GF	IP	BFP	H	R	ER	HR	SH	SF	HB	TBB	IBB	SO	WP	Bk	W	L	Pct.	ShO	Sv	ERA
1998 Bluefield	R+ Bal	15	0	0	9	25.1	106	22	12	4	1	0	0	1	7	0	26	1	1	1	2	.333	0	1	1.42
1999 Delmarva	A Bal	29	18	0	6	124.1	531	124	51	49	10	2	2	7	44	0	134	6	4	9	5	.643	0	3	3.55
2000 Frederick	A+ Bal	3	3	0	0	17.2	68	11	3	3	0	0	0	0	4	0	20	2	0	3	0	1.000	0	0	1.53
Bowie	AA Bal	18	18	1	0	97	449	114	59	50	5	4	2	3	46	3	57	2	2	5	9	.357	0	0	4.64
3 Min. YEARS		65	39	1	17	264.1	1154	271	125	106	16	6	4	11	101	3	237	11	7	18	16	.529	0	4	3.61

Leiby Guzman

Pitches: Right **Bats:** Right **Pos:** SP-20; RP-4 **Ht:** 6'5" **Wt:** 160 **Born:** 9/27/76 **Age:** 24

Year Team	Lg Org	G	GS	CG	GF	IP	BFP	H	R	ER	HR	SH	SF	HB	TBB	IBB	SO	WP	Bk	W	L	Pct.	ShO	Sv	ERA
1999 Rangers	R Tex	1	1	0	0	3	11	2	0	0	0	0	0	0	0	0	1	0	0	0	0	—	0	0	0.00
Charlotte	A+ Tex	19	18	0	1	93.1	420	114	67	61	16	0	5	9	40	0	45	5	0	5	6	.455	0	0	5.88
2000 Tulsa	AA Tex	24	20	0	2	115.1	544	143	86	73	15	1	4	8	58	1	84	4	0	7	9	.438	0	0	5.70
2 Min. YEARS		44	39	0	3	211.2	975	259	153	134	31	1	9	17	98	1	130	9	0	12	15	.444	0	0	5.70

Wilson Guzman

Pitches: Left **Bats:** Left **Pos:** SP-28 **Ht:** 5'9" **Wt:** 200 **Born:** 7/14/77 **Age:** 23

Year Team	Lg Org	G	GS	CG	GF	IP	BFP	H	R	ER	HR	SH	SF	HB	TBB	IBB	SO	WP	Bk	W	L	Pct.	ShO	Sv	ERA
1997 Pirates	R Pit	9	8	0	0	40.1	173	43	15	13	1	1	2	3	8	0	48	2	1	4	1	.800	0	0	2.90
Erie	A- Pit	5	5	0	0	26.2	112	26	20	15	4	2	1	1	6	0	25	0	0	1	2	.333	0	0	5.06
1998 Lynchburg	A+ Pit	3	0	0	3	2.2	17	4	4	4	1	1	0	0	5	1	2	0	0	0	1	.000	0	0	13.50
Augusta	A Pit	42	0	0	15	70	287	55	24	20	0	1	3	2	24	1	73	0	1	6	3	.667	0	4	2.57
1999 Lynchburg	A+ Pit	35	0	0	13	65.1	283	70	35	25	3	0	4	1	12	0	78	2	1	1	2	.333	0	2	3.44
2000 Lynchburg	A+ Pit	10	10	0	0	59.1	259	65	28	19	5	2	0	1	19	0	58	1	0	4	3	.571	0	0	2.88
Altoona	AA Pit	18	18	3	0	119.1	492	99	49	40	6	8	3	2	45	1	77	1	3	10	4	.714	1	0	3.02
4 Min. YEARS		122	41	3	31	383.2	1623	362	175	136	20	15	13	10	119	3	361	6	5	26	16	.619	1	6	3.19

Yamid Haad

Bats: Right **Throws:** Right **Pos:** C-66; DH-8; PH-6; 1B-3; OF-1 **Ht:** 6'2" **Wt:** 204 **Born:** 9/2/77 **Age:** 23

Year Team	Lg Org	G	AB	H	2B	3B	HR	TB	R	RBI	TBB	IBB	SO	HBP	SH	SF	SB	CS	SB%	GDP	Avg	OBP	SLG
1997 Erie	A- Pit	43	155	45	7	3	1	61	27	19	7	0	27	0	1	6	3	3	.50	5	.290	.310	.394
1998 Lynchburg	A+ Pit	88	299	76	8	2	5	103	32	34	13	0	54	3	4	1	1	7	.13	11	.254	.288	.344
1999 Lynchburg	A+ Pit	59	209	53	11	1	5	81	31	33	33	1	42	1	2	3	5	2	.71	8	.254	.354	.388
Altoona	AA Pit	43	137	25	3	0	6	46	20	10	19	0	32	0	1	1	7	2	.78	4	.182	.280	.336
2000 Altoona	AA Pit	59	183	36	7	0	4	55	24	13	18	0	44	0	1	1	1	1	.50	4	.197	.267	.301
Lynchburg	A+ Pit	25	91	23	8	0	3	40	14	9	11	0	16	0	0	4	2	0	1.00	4	.253	.330	.440
1999 Pittsburgh	NL	1	1	0	0	0	0	0	0	0	0	0	0	0	0	0	0	0	—	0	.000	.000	.000
4 Min. YEARS		317	1074	258	44	6	24	386	148	118	101	1	215	4	9	16	19	15	.56	36	.240	.304	.359

Chris Haas

Bats: Left **Throws:** Right **Pos:** 3B-68; 1B-29; PH-9; DH-3; OF-1   **Ht:** 6'2" **Wt:** 210 **Born:** 10/15/76 **Age:** 24

		BATTING																BASERUNNING				PERCENTAGES		
Year Team	Lg Org	G	AB	H	2B	3B	HR	TB	R	RBI	TBB	IBB	SO	HBP	SH	SF	SB	CS	SB%	GDP	Avg	OBP	SLG
1995 Johnson Cty	R+ StL	67	242	65	15	3	7	107	43	50	52	0	93	1	0	0	1	3	.25	8	.269	.400	.442
1996 Peoria	A StL	124	421	101	19	1	11	155	56	65	64	3	169	7	1	3	3	2	.60	4	.240	.347	.368
1997 Peoria	A StL	36	115	36	11	0	5	62	23	22	22	1	38	3	0	2	3	0	1.00	4	.313	.430	.539
Pr William	A+ StL	100	361	86	10	2	14	142	58	54	42	2	144	4	1	2	1	1	.50	7	.238	.323	.393
1998 Arkansas	AA StL	132	445	122	27	4	20	217	75	83	73	5	129	8	0	5	1	2	.33	5	.274	.382	.488
1999 Memphis	AAA StL	114	397	91	19	2	18	168	63	73	66	3	155	2	3	5	4	4	.50	4	.229	.338	.423
2000 Memphis	AAA StL	23	56	12	1	0	1	16	7	9	9	0	11	0	0	0	0	0	—	2	.214	.323	.286
Arkansas	AA StL	82	291	79	14	2	17	148	52	59	40	2	84	4	1	3	0	1	.00	11	.271	.364	.509
6 Min. YEARS		678	2328	592	116	14	93	1015	377	415	368	16	823	29	6	20	13	13	.50	45	.254	.360	.436

Steve Hacker

Bats: Right **Throws:** Right **Pos:** DH-9; PH-5; 1B-4   **Ht:** 6'5" **Wt:** 230 **Born:** 9/6/74 **Age:** 26

		BATTING																BASERUNNING				PERCENTAGES		
Year Team	Lg Org	G	AB	H	2B	3B	HR	TB	R	RBI	TBB	IBB	SO	HBP	SH	SF	SB	CS	SB%	GDP	Avg	OBP	SLG
1995 Eugene	A- Atl	16	57	12	3	0	2	21	4	9	1	0	13	2	0	1	0	0	—	1	.211	.246	.368
1996 Eugene	A- Atl	75	292	73	15	1	21	153	45	61	26	3	64	6	0	6	0	0	—	2	.250	.318	.524
1997 Macon	A Atl	117	460	149	35	1	33	285	80	119	34	7	91	5	0	9	1	0	1.00	5	.324	.370	.620
1998 Twins	R Min	6	24	5	0	0	1	8	5	3	2	0	2	0	0	0	0	0	—	0	.208	.269	.333
Fort Myers	A+ Min	62	251	62	11	0	11	106	29	38	17	0	40	2	0	2	0	1	.00	9	.247	.298	.422
1999 New Britain	AA Min	118	461	139	36	0	27	256	71	97	39	2	103	5	0	6	0	2	.00	13	.302	.358	.555
Salt Lake	AAA Min	8	20	3	0	0	2	9	2	3	5	1	7	1	0	0	0	1	.00	1	.150	.346	.450
2000 Salt Lake	AAA Min	17	48	10	1	0	0	11	3	2	3	0	12	0	0	0	0	0	—	1	.208	.255	.229
6 Min. YEARS		419	1613	453	101	2	97	849	239	332	127	13	332	21	0	24	1	4	.20	32	.281	.337	.526

Jeff Hafer

Pitches: Right **Bats:** Right **Pos:** RP-40   **Ht:** 6'1" **Wt:** 200 **Born:** 10/27/74 **Age:** 26

		HOW MUCH HE PITCHED						WHAT HE GAVE UP												THE RESULTS					
Year Team	Lg Org	G	GS	CG	GF	IP	BFP	H	R	ER	HR	SH	SF	HB	TBB	IBB	SO	WP	Bk	W	L	Pct.	ShO	Sv	ERA
1996 Kingsport	R+ NYM	24	0	0	14	33.2	137	29	9	8	1	1	0	1	8	1	43	7	0	0	2	.000	0	6	2.14
1997 Capital Cty	A NYM	37	2	0	18	69.1	284	59	29	23	2	3	1	2	21	3	74	10	1	6	5	.545	0	7	2.99
1998 Mets	R NYM	4	4	0	0	7.2	30	8	3	3	1	0	0	0	1	0	6	2	0	0	0	—	0	0	3.52
St. Lucie	A+ NYM	24	0	0	11	41.2	200	63	42	37	7	1	4	2	11	1	37	3	0	3	3	.500	0	1	7.99
1999 St. Lucie	A+ NYM	36	2	0	21	67	306	74	43	24	3	3	3	2	16	4	51	3	2	4	2	.667	0	5	3.22
Binghamton	AA NYM	7	0	0	1	14.1	54	12	5	5	2	0	0	0	0	0	9	1	0	0	2	.000	0	0	3.14
2000 St. Lucie	A+ NYM	11	0	0	9	16.1	69	14	8	7	0	1	0	1	4	0	12	0	0	1	1	.500	0	1	3.86
Binghamton	AA NYM	29	0	0	17	49	236	64	46	43	6	1	2	8	20	0	29	4	1	1	3	.250	0	2	7.90
5 Min. YEARS		172	8	0	91	299	1316	323	185	150	22	10	10	16	81	9	261	30	4	15	18	.455	0	22	4.52

Steve Hagins

Bats: Right **Throws:** Right **Pos:** C-52; DH-11; 1B-2   **Ht:** 6'1" **Wt:** 205 **Born:** 3/7/75 **Age:** 26

		BATTING																BASERUNNING				PERCENTAGES		
Year Team	Lg Org	G	AB	H	2B	3B	HR	TB	R	RBI	TBB	IBB	SO	HBP	SH	SF	SB	CS	SB%	GDP	Avg	OBP	SLG
1997 Butte	R+ Ana	64	268	94	20	1	17	167	59	56	17	2	53	10	1	1	13	3	.81	5	.351	.409	.623
1998 Lk Elsinore	A+ Ana	97	359	100	26	3	17	183	64	68	27	2	98	12	1	4	5	5	.50	10	.279	.346	.510
1999 Lk Elsinore	A+ Ana	40	141	37	14	1	4	65	21	22	5	0	39	5	0	1	2	1	.67	3	.262	.309	.461
2000 Erie	AA Ana	12	43	8	4	0	1	15	2	7	1	0	12	0	0	0	0	1	.00	0	.186	.205	.349
Winnipeg	IND —	14	48	11	3	0	0	14	3	6	1	0	12	0	0	1	2	0	1.00	1	.229	.240	.292
Sioux Falls	IND —	24	83	23	8	0	0	31	8	10	4	0	24	4	1	1	2	1	.33	0	.277	.337	.373
St. Paul	IND —	15	52	11	2	0	0	13	3	4	1	0	15	0	0	1	0	1	.00	0	.212	.222	.250
4 Min. YEARS		266	994	284	77	5	39	488	160	173	56	4	253	31	3	9	23	13	.64	19	.286	.340	.491

Talley Haines

Pitches: Right **Bats:** Right **Pos:** RP-50   **Ht:** 6'5" **Wt:** 194 **Born:** 11/16/76 **Age:** 24

		HOW MUCH HE PITCHED						WHAT HE GAVE UP												THE RESULTS					
Year Team	Lg Org	G	GS	CG	GF	IP	BFP	H	R	ER	HR	SH	SF	HB	TBB	IBB	SO	WP	Bk	W	L	Pct.	ShO	Sv	ERA
1998 Princeton	R+ TB	27	1	0	9	43.1	197	54	32	25	4	0	1	2	17	0	37	5	1	2	3	.400	0	2	5.19
1999 St. Pete	A+ TB	2	0	0	1	4.1	13	1	0	0	0	0	0	0	0	0	4	0	0	0	0	—	0	0	0.00
Chston-SC	A TB	47	0	0	34	61	248	51	33	22	2	2	0	3	12	4	68	5	1	3	2	.600	0	18	3.25
2000 St. Pete	A+ TB	16	0	0	10	22.2	94	22	10	7	1	0	0	0	2	1	22	0	0	2	1	.667	0	3	2.78
Durham	AAA TB	1	0	0	0	1	10	6	4	4	1	0	0	0	1	0	2	1	0	0	1	.000	0	0	27.00
Orlando	AA TB	33	0	0	21	54.1	222	36	18	9	2	6	2	1	21	5	47	3	0	3	3	.500	0	3	1.49
3 Min. YEARS		126	1	0	75	187	784	170	97	67	10	8	3	8	53	10	180	14	2	10	10	.500	0	26	3.22

Noah Hall

Bats: Right **Throws:** Right **Pos:** OF-119; DH-15; PH-1; PR-1   **Ht:** 5'11" **Wt:** 200 **Born:** 6/9/77 **Age:** 24

		BATTING																BASERUNNING				PERCENTAGES		
Year Team	Lg Org	G	AB	H	2B	3B	HR	TB	R	RBI	TBB	IBB	SO	HBP	SH	SF	SB	CS	SB%	GDP	Avg	OBP	SLG
1996 Expos	R Mon	41	134	32	5	3	0	46	24	18	19	2	22	5	1	2	6	2	.75	2	.239	.350	.343
1997 Wst Plm Bch	A+ Mon	1	1	0	0	0	0	0	0	0	0	0	1	0	0	0	0	0	—	0	.000	.000	.000
Vermont	A- Mon	73	266	73	12	8	2	107	43	45	45	2	48	3	0	0	22	5	.81	1	.274	.383	.402
1998 Cape Fear	A Mon	127	447	142	21	7	11	210	84	90	52	2	69	14	3	3	33	9	.79	16	.318	.403	.470
Jupiter	A+ Mon	8	8	2	0	0	0	2	2	0	3	0	1	1	0	0	1	1	.50	0	.250	.500	.250
1999 Jupiter	A+ Mon	119	398	94	10	3	8	134	57	49	49	1	60	8	6	7	32	11	.74	12	.236	.327	.337
2000 Jupiter	A+ Mon	90	310	89	8	2	3	110	64	40	57	1	36	8	1	2	26	11	.70	3	.287	.408	.355
Harrisburg	AA Mon	45	147	38	8	2	1	59	25	24	35	2	19	3	2	2	8	5	.62	3	.259	.406	.401
5 Min. YEARS		500	1711	470	64	25	28	668	299	266	260	10	256	42	13	18	128	44	.74	37	.275	.380	.390

Ryan Halla

Pitches: Right **Bats:** Both **Pos:** RP-43 　　　　**Ht:** 6'4" **Wt:** 248 **Born:** 10/3/73 **Age:** 27

Year Team	Lg Org	G	GS	CG	GF	IP	BFP	H	R	ER	HR	SH	SF	HB	TBB	IBB	SO	WP	Bk	W	L	Pct.	ShO	Sv	ERA
1997 Augusta	A Pit	32	0	0	22	46.1	176	26	10	9	2	2	1	2	10	1	51	3	0	1	1	.500	0	8	1.75
1998 Lynchburg	A+ Pit	40	0	0	13	56	238	51	27	23	5	3	2	2	22	1	51	1	1	5	4	.556	0	4	3.70
1999 Lynchburg	A+ Pit	46	0	0	29	54.1	246	60	34	31	5	5	4	2	20	1	56	7	0	2	7	.222	0	7	5.13
2000 Elmira	IND —	25	0	0	24	25.2	97	15	9	4	1	0	1	0	7	1	36	1	0	0	2	.000	0	20	1.40
Richmond	AAA Atl	18	0	0	10	16.2	80	19	11	8	1	0	0	0	12	3	19	2	0	1	1	.500	0	1	4.32
4 Min. YEARS		161	0	0	98	199	837	171	91	75	14	10	8	6	71	7	213	14	1	9	15	.375	0	40	3.39

Pat Hallmark

Bats: Right **Throws:** Right **Pos:** OF-89; DH-31; 1B-11; PH-5; PR-3; C-1 　　**Ht:** 6'0" **Wt:** 170 **Born:** 12/31/73 **Age:** 27

Year Team	Lg Org	G	AB	H	2B	3B	HR	TB	R	RBI	TBB	IBB	SO	HBP	SH	SF	SB	CS	SB%	GDP	Avg	OBP	SLG
1995 Spokane	A- KC	56	227	69	11	0	4	92	36	25	13	0	37	2	2	2	5	3	.63	5	.304	.344	.405
1996 Lansing	A KC	118	453	127	23	5	1	163	68	53	34	2	80	3	6	1	33	9	.79	3	.280	.334	.360
1997 Lansing	A KC	88	306	87	13	6	0	112	49	39	28	0	43	7	1	5	22	5	.81	8	.284	.353	.366
Wilmington	A+ KC	27	100	30	5	0	2	41	22	11	12	0	16	3	1	2	8	3	.73	0	.300	.385	.410
1998 Wilmington	A+ KC	103	364	99	19	1	5	135	59	35	46	0	71	5	6	5	33	19	.63	6	.272	.357	.371
1999 Wichita	AA KC	75	242	69	7	2	5	95	35	24	21	0	62	5	3	2	14	7	.67	3	.285	.352	.393
2000 Wichita	AA KC	132	479	156	26	3	10	218	80	79	52	6	74	20	5	6	41	14	.75	10	.326	.409	.455
6 Min. YEARS		599	2171	637	104	17	27	856	349	266	206	8	383	45	24	23	156	60	.72	35	.293	.363	.394

Jimmy Hamilton

Pitches: Left **Bats:** Left **Pos:** RP-53 　　　　　　**Ht:** 6'3" **Wt:** 190 **Born:** 8/1/75 **Age:** 25

Year Team	Lg Org	G	GS	CG	GF	IP	BFP	H	R	ER	HR	SH	SF	HB	TBB	IBB	SO	WP	Bk	W	L	Pct.	ShO	Sv	ERA
1996 Burlington	R+ Cle	10	10	0	0	45	193	45	22	20	7	1	2	0	16	0	50	8	0	1	3	.250	0	0	4.00
1997 Columbus	A Cle	22	22	0	0	123	547	123	68	61	10	3	2	0	66	0	137	11	0	5	7	.417	0	0	4.46
1998 Kinston	A+ Cle	44	0	0	15	75.1	305	61	25	23	5	8	3	4	21	5	83	4	0	4	6	.400	0	4	2.75
1999 Akron	AA Cle	25	0	0	10	31.1	134	19	14	13	1	1	1	1	24	2	27	4	0	0	2	.000	0	2	3.73
Buffalo	AAA Cle	26	0	0	4	24.1	122	24	22	14	3	1	3	1	27	0	25	1	0	1	2	.333	0	0	5.18
Rochester	AAA Bal	3	0	0	0	2	11	1	3	3	0	0	1	0	4	0	2	0	0	0	0	—	0	0	13.50
2000 Rochester	AAA Bal	2	0	0	2	1	4	0	1	0	0	0	0	0	1	0	1	0	0	0	0	—	0	0	0.00
Bowie	AA Bal	51	0	0	14	57.2	252	53	26	24	6	1	4	1	29	1	49	3	0	5	4	.556	0	4	3.75
5 Min. YEARS		183	32	0	45	359.2	1568	326	180	158	32	15	16	10	188	8	374	31	0	16	24	.400	0	10	3.95

Jon Hamilton

Bats: Left **Throws:** Left **Pos:** OF-129; DH-8; PH-1 　　　　**Ht:** 6'1" **Wt:** 195 **Born:** 10/23/77 **Age:** 23

Year Team	Lg Org	G	AB	H	2B	3B	HR	TB	R	RBI	TBB	IBB	SO	HBP	SH	SF	SB	CS	SB%	GDP	Avg	OBP	SLG
1997 Burlington	R+ Ari	66	235	57	8	3	4	89	50	20	51	3	69	5	1	2	25	5	.83	0	.243	.380	.360
1998 Columbus	A Cle	133	487	127	22	10	15	214	88	71	79	1	130	7	3	4	22	9	.71	4	.261	.369	.439
1999 Kinston	A+ Cle	131	473	132	29	5	13	210	74	65	61	1	114	1	5	4	9	4	.69	3	.279	.360	.444
2000 Akron	AA Cle	137	493	123	28	3	7	178	57	56	62	2	117	3	0	4	12	6	.67	8	.249	.335	.361
4 Min. YEARS		465	1700	442	90	21	39	691	269	212	253	7	430	16	9	14	68	24	.74	15	.260	.359	.406

Rob Hammock

Bats: Right **Throws:** Right **Pos:** C-64; DH-8; PH-8; 3B-3; OF-3; 1B-3; PR-1 　　**Ht:** 5'11" **Wt:** 190 **Born:** 5/13/77 **Age:** 24

Year Team	Lg Org	G	AB	H	2B	3B	HR	TB	R	RBI	TBB	IBB	SO	HBP	SH	SF	SB	CS	SB%	GDP	Avg	OBP	SLG
1998 Lethbridge	R+ Ari	62	227	65	14	2	10	113	46	56	28	1	34	2	0	2	5	4	.56	3	.286	.367	.498
1999 High Desert	A+ Ari	114	379	126	20	7	9	187	80	72	47	2	63	2	0	6	3	6	.33	9	.332	.403	.493
2000 High Desert	A+ Ari	40	136	48	15	1	3	74	25	23	27	1	24	1	0	3	3	3	.50	5	.353	.455	.544
El Paso	AA Ari	45	140	35	5	1	1	45	22	15	11	1	25	1	0	2	1	2	.33	1	.250	.305	.321
3 Min. YEARS		261	882	274	54	11	23	419	173	166	113	5	146	6	0	13	12	15	.44	17	.311	.388	.475

Jed Hansen

Bats: Right **Throws:** Right **Pos:** 2B-41; PH-9; SS-7; DH-4; PR-4; 3B-3; OF-3 　　**Ht:** 6'1" **Wt:** 195 **Born:** 8/19/72 **Age:** 28

Year Team	Lg Org	G	AB	H	2B	3B	HR	TB	R	RBI	TBB	IBB	SO	HBP	SH	SF	SB	CS	SB%	GDP	Avg	OBP	SLG
1994 Eugene	A- KC	66	235	57	8	2	3	78	26	17	24	2	56	8	2	1	6	4	.60	1	.243	.332	.332
1995 Springfield	A KC	122	414	107	27	7	9	175	86	50	78	0	73	7	6	1	44	10	.81	8	.258	.384	.423
1996 Wichita	AA KC	99	405	116	27	4	12	187	60	50	29	0	72	4	4	2	14	8	.64	6	.286	.339	.462
Omaha	AAA KC	29	99	23	4	0	3	36	14	9	12	0	22	3	1	1	2	0	1.00	1	.232	.330	.364
1997 Omaha	AAA KC	114	380	102	20	2	11	159	43	44	32	0	78	2	5	2	8	1	.89	9	.268	.327	.418
1998 Omaha	AAA KC	127	417	116	19	7	16	197	63	56	44	0	125	4	4	7	17	9	.65	7	.278	.347	.472
1999 Omaha	AAA KC	54	175	48	8	5	7	87	35	22	32	2	72	3	3	0	8	3	.73	2	.274	.395	.497
2000 Las Vegas	AAA SD	14	24	5	1	0	2	12	3	5	5	0	11	0	1	0	1	0	1.00	2	.208	.345	.500
Norfolk	AAA NYM	39	96	14	2	0	4	28	13	9	18	1	31	1	3	1	2	4	.33	2	.146	.284	.292
Louisville	AAA Cin	16	51	9	1	0	1	13	7	2	4	0	15	0	1	0	1	1	.50	2	.176	.236	.255
1997 Kansas City	AL	34	94	29	6	1	1	40	11	14	13	0	29	1	2	1	3	2	.60	2	.309	.394	.426
1998 Kansas City	AL	4	3	0	0	0	0	0	0	0	0	0	3	0	0	0	0	0	—	0	.000	.000	.000
1999 Kansas City	AL	49	79	16	1	0	3	26	16	5	10	0	32	0	4	1	1	0	1.00	0	.203	.289	.329
7 Min. YEARS		680	2296	597	117	27	68	972	350	264	278	5	555	32	30	15	103	40	.72	40	.260	.346	.423
3 Maj. YEARS		87	176	45	7	1	4	66	27	19	23	0	64	1	6	2	4	2	.67	2	.256	.342	.375

Mike Hardge

Bats: Right **Throws:** Right **Pos:** 2B-87; SS-3; OF-2; PH-2; 3B-1; DH-1 **Ht:** 5'11" **Wt:** 183 **Born:** 1/27/72 **Age:** 29

Year Team	Lg Org	BATTING																BASERUNNING				PERCENTAGES		
		G	AB	H	2B	3B	HR	TB	R	RBI	TBB	IBB	SO	HBP	SH	SF		SB	CS	SB%	GDP	Avg	OBP	SLG
1990 Expos	R Mon	53	176	39	5	0	1	47	33	13	15	0	43	2	0	2		5	2	.71	1	.222	.287	.267
1991 Expos	R Mon	60	237	60	17	3	3	92	44	30	23	0	41	2	0	4		20	7	.74	3	.253	.320	.388
1992 Rockford	A Mon	127	448	97	21	2	12	158	63	49	47	0	141	3	4	2		44	13	.77	7	.217	.294	.353
Wst Plm Bch	A+ Mon	4	15	5	1	0	0	6	3	0	2	0	5	0	0	0		2	0	1.00	0	.333	.412	.400
1993 Wst Plm Bch	A+ Mon	27	92	21	2	1	1	28	14	12	14	0	16	0	4	3		5	6	.45	1	.228	.321	.304
Harrisburg	AA Mon	99	386	94	14	10	6	146	70	35	37	0	97	3	3	1		27	8	.77	3	.244	.314	.378
1994 Harrisburg	AA Mon	121	453	101	10	2	6	133	60	42	56	0	109	0	8	1		30	18	.63	8	.223	.308	.294
1995 Pawtucket	AAA Bos	29	91	23	3	0	1	29	9	5	8	0	16	0	0	0		1	3	.25	2	.253	.313	.319
Trenton	AA Bos	40	127	31	4	1	0	37	18	12	11	0	26	0	1	2		3	4	.43	7	.244	.300	.291
1996 Lubbock	IND —	98	393	119	24	7	8	181	77	64	35	2	57	4	4	1		26	5	.84	5	.303	.365	.461
1997 Lubbock	IND —	87	361	122	27	4	8	181	75	54	26	0	43	3	3	4		22	11	.67	12	.338	.383	.501
1998 Arkansas	AA StL	106	355	104	24	2	8	156	60	66	43	2	78	3	1	5		8	8	.50	7	.293	.369	.439
1999 Arkansas	AA StL	54	141	32	3	1	5	52	15	11	25	1	43	4	0	0		3	3	.50	2	.227	.359	.369
2000 Norwich	AA NYY	24	83	20	7	1	0	29	9	6	9	0	26	0	0	0		2	3	.40	1	.241	.315	.349
Amarillo	IND —	69	301	99	28	2	10	161	70	58	32	0	47	3	1	0		27	3	.90	5	.329	.399	.535
11 Min. YEARS		998	3659	967	190	36	69	1436	620	457	383	5	788	27	29	25		225	94	.71	64	.264	.336	.392

Jason Hardtke

Bats: Both **Throws:** Right **Pos:** 2B-5; SS-1; 3B-1; PH-1 **Ht:** 5'10" **Wt:** 175 **Born:** 9/15/71 **Age:** 29

Year Team	Lg Org	BATTING																BASERUNNING				PERCENTAGES		
		G	AB	H	2B	3B	HR	TB	R	RBI	TBB	IBB	SO	HBP	SH	SF		SB	CS	SB%	GDP	Avg	OBP	SLG
1990 Burlington	R+ Cle	39	142	38	7	0	4	57	18	16	23	0	19	2	0	0		11	1	.92	3	.268	.377	.401
1991 Columbus	A Cle	139	534	155	26	8	12	233	104	81	75	5	48	7	6	6		22	4	.85	6	.290	.381	.436
1992 Kinston	A+ Cle	6	19	4	0	0	0	4	3	1	4	0	4	0	0	0		0	0	—	0	.211	.348	.211
Waterloo	A SD	110	411	125	27	4	8	184	75	47	38	3	33	5	1	5		9	7	.56	9	.304	.366	.448
High Desert	A+ SD	10	41	11	1	0	2	18	9	8	4	0	4	1	0	1		1	1	.50	1	.268	.340	.439
1993 Rancho Cuca	A+ SD	130	523	167	38	7	11	252	98	85	61	2	54	2	2	6		7	8	.47	12	.319	.389	.482
1994 Wichita	AA SD	75	255	60	15	1	5	92	26	29	21	1	44	0	2	4		1	2	.33	4	.235	.289	.361
Rancho Cuca	A+ SD	4	13	4	0	0	0	4	2	0	3	0	2	0	0	0		1	0	1.00	0	.308	.438	.308
1995 Norfolk	AAA NYM	4	7	2	1	0	0	3	1	0	2	0	0	0	0	0		1	1	.50	0	.286	.444	.429
Binghamton	AA NYM	121	455	130	42	4	4	192	65	52	66	1	58	4	2	9		6	8	.43	7	.286	.375	.422
1996 Binghamton	AA NYM	35	137	36	11	0	3	56	23	16	16	1	16	0	1	0		0	1	.00	3	.263	.340	.409
Norfolk	AAA NYM	71	257	77	17	2	9	125	49	35	29	1	29	0	4	2		4	6	.40	7	.300	.368	.486
1997 Norfolk	AAA NYM	97	388	107	23	3	11	169	46	45	40	1	54	0	4	1		3	6	.33	9	.276	.343	.436
Binghamton	AA NYM	6	26	10	2	0	1	15	3	4	2	0	2	0	0	0		0	0	—	0	.385	.429	.577
1998 Iowa	AAA ChC	91	333	96	20	1	11	151	67	53	35	1	46	4	1	2		7	7	.50	7	.288	.361	.453
1999 Indianapols	AAA Cin	101	416	137	37	2	12	214	74	61	35	1	43	2	1	4		7	4	.64	7	.329	.381	.514
2000 Colo Spngs	AAA Col	5	20	4	0	0	0	4	3	1	2	1	3	0	0	0		0	0	—	1	.200	.273	.200
1996 New York	NL	19	57	11	5	0	0	16	3	6	2	0	12	1	0	0		0	0	—	1	.193	.233	.281
1997 New York	NL	30	56	15	2	0	2	23	9	8	4	1	6	1	0	1		1	1	.50	3	.268	.323	.411
1998 Chicago	NL	18	21	5	0	0	0	5	2	2	2	0	6	0	0	0		0	0	—	0	.238	.304	.238
11 Min. YEARS		1044	3977	1163	267	32	93	1773	666	534	456	18	459	27	24	40		79	57	.58	73	.292	.366	.446
3 Maj. YEARS		67	134	31	7	0	2	44	14	16	8	1	24	2	0	1		1	1	.50	4	.231	.283	.328

Tim Harikkala

Pitches: Right **Bats:** Right **Pos:** RP-22; SP-14 **Ht:** 6'2" **Wt:** 185 **Born:** 7/15/71 **Age:** 29

Year Team	Lg Org	HOW MUCH HE PITCHED						WHAT HE GAVE UP											THE RESULTS					
		G	GS	CG	GF	IP	BFP	H	R	ER	HR	SH	SF	HB	TBB	IBB	SO	WP	Bk	W	L	Pct.	ShO	Sv	ERA
1992 Bellingham	A- Sea	15	2	0	2	33.1	145	37	15	10	2	3	2	0	16	0	18	1	2	2	0	1.000	0	1	2.70
1993 Bellingham	A- Sea	4	0	0	0	8	30	3	1	1	0	0	0	1	2	0	12	0	0	1	0	1.000	0	0	1.13
Appleton	A Sea	15	4	0	5	38.2	175	50	30	28	3	2	1	2	12	2	33	4	3	3	3	.500	0	0	6.52
1994 Appleton	A Sea	13	13	3	0	93.2	373	69	31	20	6	2	3	5	24	0	63	5	0	8	3	.727	0	0	1.92
Riverside	A+ Sea	4	4	0	0	29	108	16	6	2	1	0	1	0	10	0	30	1	0	4	0	1.000	0	0	0.62
Jacksnville	AA Sea	9	9	0	0	54.1	245	70	30	24	4	1	3	1	19	0	22	4	0	4	1	.800	0	0	3.98
1995 Tacoma	AAA Sea	25	24	4	0	146.1	638	151	78	69	13	3	4	2	55	3	73	7	0	5	12	.294	1	0	4.24
1996 Tacoma	AAA Sea	27	27	1	0	158.1	715	204	98	85	12	3	6	5	48	2	115	5	1	8	12	.400	1	0	4.83
1997 Tacoma	AAA Sea	21	21	0	0	113.1	538	160	93	81	11	3	5	4	50	2	86	7	0	6	8	.429	0	0	6.43
Memphis	AA Sea	5	5	1	0	33.2	146	39	18	14	3	0	1	3	4	0	26	1	0	3	1	.750	0	0	3.74
Tacoma	AAA Sea	15	15	3	0	103.1	429	112	56	52	9	5	2	7	14	0	55	0	0	5	7	.417	2	0	4.53
1998 Orlando	AA Sea	18	4	1	9	57	257	74	32	31	6	1	1	1	13	0	44	0	0	2	3	.400	1	1	4.89
1999 Pawtucket	AAA Bos	14	1	0	4	30	141	44	19	18	2	0	1	2	7	1	19	0	0	1	2	.333	0	0	5.40
2000 Huntsville	AA Mil	22	4	0	5	48.1	205	54	20	16	1	3	1	1	8	0	34	0	0	5	3	.625	0	0	2.98
Indianapols	AAA Mil	14	10	0	3	63.2	271	73	36	32	5	0	4	1	15	0	22	3	0	4	2	.667	0	0	4.52
1995 Seattle	AL	1	0	0	1	3.1	18	7	6	6	1	0	0	0	1	0	1	0	0	0	0	—	0	0	16.20
1996 Seattle	AL	1	1	0	0	4.1	20	4	6	6	1	1	0	1	2	0	1	0	0	0	1	.000	0	0	12.46
1999 Boston	AL	7	0	0	2	13	58	15	9	9	2	0	1	0	6	1	7	1	0	1	1	.500	0	0	6.23
9 Min. YEARS		221	143	13	28	1011	4416	1156	563	483	78	26	31	34	297	10	652	38	6	61	57	.517	5	3	4.30
3 Maj. YEARS		9	1	0	3	20.2	96	26	21	21	3	0	2	1	9	1	9	1	0	1	2	.333	0	0	9.15

Brett Haring

Pitches: Left **Bats:** Right **Pos:** SP-22; RP-6 **Ht:** 5'11" **Wt:** 180 **Born:** 2/7/75 **Age:** 26

Year Team	Lg Org	HOW MUCH HE PITCHED						WHAT HE GAVE UP											THE RESULTS					
		G	GS	CG	GF	IP	BFP	H	R	ER	HR	SH	SF	HB	TBB	IBB	SO	WP	Bk	W	L	Pct.	ShO	Sv	ERA
1997 Billings	R+ Cin	14	0	0	4	23.1	106	30	14	12	2	0	0	2	9	0	16	1	0	0	2	.000	0	0	4.63
1998 Chston-WV	A Cin	38	13	2	15	108.1	457	123	48	40	6	8	3	2	26	1	91	5	0	2	9	.182	0	4	3.32
1999 Rockford	A Cin	25	18	3	1	124	516	113	53	46	7	4	3	4	42	0	94	5	0	10	3	.769	3	1	3.34
Chattanooga	AA Cin	7	4	0	0	36.1	159	46	18	15	1	3	0	0	12	0	15	2	0	2	1	.667	0	0	3.72
2000 Chattanooga	AA Cin	23	17	0	1	106.2	491	133	73	61	5	7	5	7	53	2	69	4	0	6	7	.462	0	0	5.15
Dayton	A Cin	5	5	0	0	34.1	147	36	14	11	1	2	0	2	8	0	15	0	0	1	2	.333	0	0	2.88
4 Min. YEARS		112	57	5	21	433	1876	481	220	185	22	24	11	17	150	3	300	17	0	21	24	.467	3	5	3.85

Kip Harkrider

Bats: Left **Throws:** Right **Pos:** SS-49; 3B-24; PH-18; 2B-5; DH-5; 1B-1; PR-1   **Ht:** 5'11" **Wt:** 175 **Born:** 9/16/75 **Age:** 25

Year Team	Lg Org	G	AB	H	2B	3B	HR	TB	R	RBI	TBB	IBB	SO	HBP	SH	SF	SB	CS	SB%	GDP	Avg	OBP	SLG
1997 Savannah	A LA	18	71	13	0	0	0	13	8	4	2	0	6	0	1	1	0	0	—	0	.183	.203	.183
Vero Beach	A+ LA	33	103	29	5	0	0	34	18	14	5	0	13	1	2	0	2	1	.67	2	.282	.321	.330
1998 San Antonio	AA LA	103	343	82	18	4	3	117	37	40	30	2	57	2	12	2	8	4	.67	7	.239	.302	.341
2000 San Antonio	AA LA	97	286	66	9	1	4	89	29	35	18	1	39	2	9	1	1	0	1.00	10	.231	.280	.311
3 Min. YEARS		251	803	190	32	5	7	253	92	93	55	3	115	5	24	4	11	5	.69	19	.237	.288	.315

Brandon Harper

Bats: Right **Throws:** Right **Pos:** C-40; DH-5   **Ht:** 6'4" **Wt:** 200 **Born:** 4/29/76 **Age:** 25

Year Team	Lg Org	G	AB	H	2B	3B	HR	TB	R	RBI	TBB	IBB	SO	HBP	SH	SF	SB	CS	SB%	GDP	Avg	OBP	SLG
1997 Marlins	R Fla	2	6	0	0	0	0	0	0	1	0	0	1	0	0	0	0	0	—	1	.000	.000	.000
Utica	A- Fla	47	152	39	7	2	2	56	27	22	19	2	32	1	1	0	1	1	.50	9	.257	.339	.368
1998 Kane County	A Fla	113	412	95	22	2	4	133	34	50	42	3	64	4	1	5	1	3	.25	16	.231	.305	.323
1999 Brevard Cty	A+ Fla	81	280	75	9	0	4	96	35	40	30	2	31	3	4	3	1	1	.50	4	.268	.342	.343
2000 Marlins	R Fla	8	27	8	1	0	0	9	8	2	7	0	4	0	0	0	0	0	—	0	.296	.441	.333
Portland	AA Fla	37	125	26	3	0	5	44	15	17	12	0	23	1	0	0	0	0	—	4	.208	.283	.352
4 Min. YEARS		288	1002	243	42	4	15	338	119	132	110	7	155	9	5	10	3	5	.38	34	.243	.320	.337

Brian Harper

Bats: Right **Throws:** Right **Pos:** C-1   **Ht:** 6'2" **Wt:** 206 **Born:** 10/16/59 **Age:** 41

Year Team	Lg Org	G	AB	H	2B	3B	HR	TB	R	RBI	TBB	IBB	SO	HBP	SH	SF	SB	CS	SB%	GDP	Avg	OBP	SLG
1977 Idaho Falls	R+ Ana	52	186	60	9	3	1	78	28	33	13	—	31	1	3	7	4	1	.80	—	.323	.357	.419
1978 Quad City	A Ana	129	508	149	31	2	24	256	80	101	37	—	66	5	0	3	1	0	1.00	—	.293	.345	.504
1979 El Paso	AA Ana	132	531	167	37	3	14	252	85	90	50	2	47	2	3	9	10	2	.83	—	.315	.370	.475
1980 El Paso	AA Ana	105	400	114	23	3	12	179	61	66	38	—	46	5	1	2	3	2	.60	—	.285	.353	.448
1981 Salt Lk Cty	AAA Ana	134	549	192	45	9	28	339	99	122	39	2	33	2	0	9	0	2	.00	—	.350	.389	.617
1982 Portland	AAA Pit	101	395	112	29	8	17	208	71	73	25	2	29	8	1	6	3	2	.60	—	.284	.334	.527
1986 Nashville	AAA Det	95	317	83	11	1	11	129	41	45	26	1	27	2	1	5	3	8	.27	9	.262	.317	.407
1987 San Jose	A+ —	8	29	9	0	0	3	18	5	8	2	0	0	0	0	1	0	1	.00	0	.310	.344	.621
1988 Portland	AAA Min	46	170	60	10	1	13	111	34	42	14	3	7	3	0	4	2	0	1.00	6	.353	.403	.653
2000 Tacoma	AAA Sea	1	4	0	0	0	0	0	0	0	0	0	1	0	0	1	0	0	—	1	.000	.000	.000
1979 California	AL	1	2	0	0	0	0	0	0	0	0	0	1	0	0	0	0	0	—	0	.000	.000	.000
1981 California	AL	4	11	3	0	0	0	3	1	1	0	0	0	0	0	0	1	0	1.00	0	.273	.250	.273
1982 Pittsburgh	NL	20	29	8	1	0	2	15	4	4	1	1	4	0	1	0	0	0	—	0	.276	.300	.517
1983 Pittsburgh	NL	61	131	29	4	1	7	56	16	20	2	0	15	1	2	4	0	0	—	3	.221	.232	.427
1984 Pittsburgh	NL	46	112	29	4	0	2	39	4	11	5	0	11	2	1	1	0	0	—	4	.259	.300	.348
1985 St. Louis	NL	43	52	13	4	0	0	17	5	8	2	0	3	0	0	1	0	0	—	2	.250	.273	.327
1986 Detroit	AL	19	36	5	1	0	0	6	2	3	3	0	3	0	0	0	0	0	—	1	.139	.200	.167
1987 Oakland	AL	11	17	4	1	0	0	5	1	3	0	0	4	0	1	1	0	0	—	0	.235	.222	.294
1988 Minnesota	AL	60	166	49	11	1	3	71	15	20	10	1	12	3	2	1	0	3	.00	12	.295	.344	.428
1989 Minnesota	AL	126	385	125	24	0	8	173	43	57	13	3	16	6	4	4	2	4	.33	11	.325	.353	.449
1990 Minnesota	AL	134	479	141	42	3	6	207	61	54	19	2	27	7	0	4	2	6	.20	20	.294	.328	.432
1991 Minnesota	AL	123	441	137	28	1	10	197	54	69	14	3	22	6	2	6	1	2	.33	14	.311	.336	.447
1992 Minnesota	AL	140	502	154	25	0	9	206	58	73	26	7	22	7	1	10	0	1	.00	15	.307	.343	.410
1993 Minnesota	AL	147	530	161	26	1	12	225	52	73	29	9	29	9	0	5	1	3	.25	15	.304	.347	.425
1994 Milwaukee	AL	64	251	73	15	0	4	100	23	32	9	1	18	3	0	4	0	2	.00	8	.291	.318	.398
1995 Oakland	AL	2	7	0	0	0	0	0	0	0	0	0	1	0	0	0	0	0	—	0	.000	.000	.000
10 Min. YEARS		897	3412	1046	212	30	132	1714	545	642	272	—	310	32	13	58	27	20	.57	—	.307	.358	.502
16 Maj. YEARS		1001	3151	931	186	7	63	1320	339	428	133	27	188	44	15	43	8	17	.32	107	.295	.329	.419

Brian Harris

Bats: Both **Throws:** Right **Pos:** 2B-87; SS-23; PH-2; PR-2   **Ht:** 5'10" **Wt:** 171 **Born:** 4/28/75 **Age:** 26

Year Team	Lg Org	G	AB	H	2B	3B	HR	TB	R	RBI	TBB	IBB	SO	HBP	SH	SF	SB	CS	SB%	GDP	Avg	OBP	SLG
1997 Batavia	A- Phi	51	148	46	7	1	0	55	31	19	31	0	27	4	3	1	11	6	.65	1	.311	.440	.372
1998 Clearwater	A+ Phi	118	437	121	17	6	5	165	55	65	47	2	56	9	6	3	20	13	.61	13	.277	.353	.378
Reading	AA Phi	11	40	10	0	1	0	12	5	4	5	0	7	0	0	1	1	0	1.00	0	.250	.326	.300
1999 Reading	AA Phi	119	380	84	13	3	5	118	42	41	46	1	58	1	7	6	9	5	.64	10	.221	.303	.311
2000 Reading	AA Phi	110	351	94	22	3	10	152	46	41	38	0	48	4	10	4	12	5	.71	7	.268	.343	.433
4 Min. YEARS		409	1356	355	59	14	20	502	179	170	167	3	196	18	26	21	52	30	.63	31	.262	.346	.370

Jeff Harris

Pitches: Right **Bats:** Right **Pos:** RP-24   **Ht:** 6'0" **Wt:** 195 **Born:** 7/4/74 **Age:** 26

		HOW MUCH HE PITCHED						WHAT HE GAVE UP										THE RESULTS					
Year Team	Lg Org	G	GS	CG	GF	IP	BFP	H	R	ER	HR	SH	SF	HB	TBB	IBB	SO	WP	Bk	W	L	Pct.	ShO	Sv	ERA
1995 Elizabethtn	R+ Min	21	0	0	10	33	154	42	15	14	2	1	0	4	13	1	27	6	1	1	3	.250	0	0	3.82
1996 Fort Wayne	A Min	42	0	0	15	89.2	387	90	35	31	4	3	8	4	33	1	85	10	1	8	3	.727	0	3	3.11
1997 Fort Myers	A+ Min	24	0	0	6	42	164	30	11	10	4	3	1	0	15	2	32	1	0	2	4	.333	0	2	2.14
New Britain	AA Min	28	0	0	14	42.1	175	30	15	11	2	3	2	3	16	0	44	3	0	2	1	.667	0	3	2.34
1998 New Britain	AA Min	26	0	0	11	38	138	21	7	7	3	1	1	0	5	0	40	0	0	1	0	1.000	0	1	1.66
Salt Lake	AAA Min	25	0	0	18	32	148	38	24	21	4	3	0	0	19	4	24	3	0	0	1	.000	0	5	5.91
1999 Salt Lake	AAA Min	36	0	0	7	45.2	220	61	38	35	7	3	4	3	26	1	20	2	0	4	3	.571	0	2	6.90
New Britain	AA Min	20	0	0	6	24.1	106	21	5	4	0	3	3	2	14	2	12	1	0	3	1	.750	0	1	1.48
2000 New Britain	AA Min	24	0	0	12	28	129	35	17	15	5	2	2	3	10	0	28	2	0	2	0	1.000	0	4	4.82
6 Min. YEARS		246	0	0	99	375	1621	368	167	148	31	22	21	18	151	11	312	28	3	31	15	.674	0	15	3.55

Reggie Harris

Pitches: Right Bats: Right Pos: RP-38
Ht: 6'1" Wt: 217 Born: 8/12/68 Age: 32

			HOW MUCH HE PITCHED						WHAT HE GAVE UP											THE RESULTS				
Year Team	Lg Org	G	GS	CG	GF	IP	BFP	H	R	ER	HR	SH	SF	HB	TBB	IBB	SO	WP	Bk	W	L	Pct.	ShO	Sv	ERA
1987 Elmira	A- Bos	9	8	1	0	46.2	212	50	29	26	3	1	1	6	22	0	25	3	0	2	3	.400	1	0	5.01
1988 Lynchburg	A+ Bos	17	11	0	2	64	310	86	60	53	8	0	3	4	34	5	48	5	7	1	8	.111	0	0	7.45
Elmira	A- Bos	10	10	0	0	54.1	237	56	37	32	5	1	3	2	28	0	46	1	2	3	6	.333	0	0	5.30
1989 Winter Havn	A+ Bos	29	26	1	2	153.1	670	144	81	68	6	5	11	7	77	2	85	7	4	10	13	.435	0	0	3.99
1990 Huntsville	AA Oak	5	5	0	0	29.2	131	26	12	10	3	1	1	4	16	0	34	4	0	0	2	.000	0	0	3.03
1991 Tacoma	AAA Oak	16	15	0	0	83	380	83	55	46	11	0	4	3	58	0	72	5	0	5	4	.556	0	0	4.99
1992 Tacoma	AAA Oak	29	28	1	0	149.2	676	141	108	95	12	3	5	6	117	0	111	20	6	6	16	.273	0	0	5.71
1993 Jacksnville	AA Sea	9	8	0	1	37.2	167	33	24	20	4	1	1	3	22	0	30	3	2	1	4	.200	0	0	4.78
Calgary	AAA Sea	17	15	1	0	88.1	393	74	55	51	7	1	3	8	61	1	75	10	0	8	6	.571	0	0	5.20
1994 Calgary	AAA Sea	20	18	0	0	98.2	481	137	99	89	21	0	3	8	51	1	73	5	2	6	9	.400	0	0	8.12
1995 Omaha	AAA KC	2	0	0	0	7	12	5	4	4	1	0	0	0	1	0	2	1	0	0	1	.000	0	0	18.00
1996 Trenton	AA Bos	33	0	0	30	37	144	17	6	6	2	0	3	0	19	2	43	1	1	2	1	.667	0	17	1.46
1998 New Orleans	AAA Hou	51	0	0	41	52.2	221	38	27	26	7	2	0	0	28	3	53	2	0	2	3	.400	0	0	4.44
1999 Louisville	AAA Mil	41	0	0	37	40	182	43	21	21	7	0	2	3	20	1	45	5	0	3	4	.429	0	16	4.73
2000 Durham	AAA TB	4	0	0	2	5.2	28	8	4	4	1	0	0	0	3	0	8	1	0	0	0	—	0	0	6.35
Richmond	AAA Atl	5	0	0	1	6.2	39	14	9	9	3	1	0	1	4	0	4	0	0	0	1	.000	0	0	12.15
Indianapolis	AAA Mil	29	0	0	15	37	171	44	28	24	8	1	2	2	17	2	22	2	0	2	1	.667	0	0	5.84
1990 Oakland	AL	16	1	0	9	41.1	168	25	16	16	5	1	2	2	21	1	31	2	0	1	0	1.000	0	0	3.48
1991 Oakland	AL	2	0	0	1	3	15	5	4	4	0	0	1	0	3	1	2	2	0	0	0	—	0	0	12.00
1996 Boston	AL	4	0	0	1	4.1	24	7	6	6	2	0	0	1	5	0	4	0	0	0	0	—	0	0	12.46
1997 Philadelphia	NL	50	0	0	13	54.1	264	55	33	32	1	3	4	5	43	1	45	5	1	1	3	.250	0	0	5.30
1998 Houston	NL	6	0	0	2	6	26	6	4	4	1	0	1	0	2	0	2	0	0	0	0	—	0	0	6.00
1999 Milwaukee	NL	8	0	0	2	12	53	9	4	4	1	0	1	2	7	0	11	2	0	0	0	—	0	0	3.00
13 Min. YEARS		326	144	4	131	986.1	4454	999	659	584	109	17	42	57	578	17	776	75	24	51	82	.383	1	56	5.33
6 Maj. YEARS		86	1	0	28	121	550	106	67	66	10	4	9	10	81	3	95	11	1	2	3	.400	0	0	4.91

Adonis Harrison

Bats: Left Throws: Right Pos: 2B-81; SS-14; 3B-11; PR-6; DH-3; PH-1
Ht: 5'9" Wt: 165 Born: 9/28/76 Age: 24

					BATTING											BASERUNNING				PERCENTAGES		
Year Team	Lg Org	G	AB	H	2B	3B	HR	TB	R	RBI	TBB	IBB	SO	HBP	SH	SF	SB	CS	SB%	GDP	Avg	OBP	SLG
1995 Mariners	R Sea	45	155	45	7	5	1	65	31	14	37	0	37	3	0	4	7	9	.44	0	.290	.427	.419
1996 Lancaster	A+ Sea	16	40	14	4	0	0	18	7	5	8	0	13	0	0	0	4	1	.80	0	.350	.458	.450
Wisconsin	A Sea	54	196	52	15	2	1	74	29	24	19	0	36	1	1	0	5	3	.63	3	.265	.333	.378
1997 Wisconsin	A Sea	125	412	131	26	6	7	190	61	62	55	2	74	6	5	3	25	18	.58	11	.318	.403	.461
1998 Lancaster	A+ Sea	69	258	87	21	4	2	122	63	35	49	0	48	2	1	2	24	14	.63	4	.337	.444	.473
Orlando	AA Sea	58	191	44	6	2	3	63	35	21	30	0	30	3	1	1	6	4	.60	2	.230	.342	.330
1999 New Haven	AA Sea	120	449	122	16	0	2	144	54	45	38	0	75	6	1	4	22	17	.56	12	.272	.334	.321
2000 Orlando	AA TB	25	80	17	3	0	0	20	10	5	8	1	11	0	2	0	5	3	.63	3	.213	.284	.250
Long Island	IND —	87	316	97	9	3	0	112	56	31	35	1	25	2	4	1	35	14	.71	3	.307	.379	.354
6 Min. YEARS		599	2097	609	107	22	16	808	346	242	279	4	349	23	15	15	133	83	.62	38	.290	.377	.385

Tommy Harrison

Pitches: Right Bats: Right Pos: RP-8; SP-1
Ht: 6'2" Wt: 185 Born: 9/30/71 Age: 29

				HOW MUCH HE PITCHED						WHAT HE GAVE UP											THE RESULTS				
Year Team	Lg Org	G	GS	CG	GF	IP	BFP	H	R	ER	HR	SH	SF	HB	TBB	IBB	SO	WP	Bk	W	L	Pct.	ShO	Sv	ERA
1995 Durham	A+ Atl	7	6	0	0	37.2	145	22	5	4	1	0	0	1	13	1	25	0	0	3	1	.750	0	0	0.96
Greenville	AA Atl	14	14	1	0	88.1	370	87	50	43	9	7	1	2	27	3	57	5	0	6	4	.600	0	0	4.38
Richmond	AAA Atl	9	6	0	1	42	182	34	17	15	2	4	3	2	20	1	16	0	1	2	1	.667	0	1	3.21
1996 Richmond	AAA Atl	10	0	0	3	19	87	16	12	11	5	0	2	2	12	0	12	3	0	0	0	—	0	0	5.21
Greenville	AA Atl	20	16	0	3	99.1	421	88	55	52	11	2	6	3	34	0	82	7	1	8	4	.667	0	0	4.71
1997 Richmond	AAA Atl	22	22	1	0	122	519	118	64	57	21	2	4	5	40	2	92	3	0	9	7	.563	0	0	4.20
1998 Richmond	AAA Atl	2	2	0	0	10	41	9	5	5	0	0	0	0	3	0	11	0	0	2	0	1.000	0	0	4.50
1999 Greenville	AA Atl	16	12	0	1	63.1	311	75	59	52	11	2	3	7	43	1	42	5	2	3	7	.300	0	0	7.39
Richmond	AAA Atl	4	0	0	1	10	52	17	9	9	2	0	0	0	6	1	6	1	0	0	1	.000	0	0	8.10
2000 Richmond	AAA Atl	9	1	0	0	20.1	101	27	20	18	5	2	1	1	12	0	11	0	0	0	3	.000	0	0	7.97
6 Min. YEARS		113	79	2	8	512	2229	493	296	266	67	19	20	23	210	9	354	24	4	33	28	.541	0	1	4.68

Jason Hart

Bats: Right Throws: Right Pos: 1B-130; DH-9; PH-1
Ht: 6'3" Wt: 225 Born: 9/5/77 Age: 23

					BATTING											BASERUNNING				PERCENTAGES		
Year Team	Lg Org	G	AB	H	2B	3B	HR	TB	R	RBI	TBB	IBB	SO	HBP	SH	SF	SB	CS	SB%	GDP	Avg	OBP	SLG
1998 Sou Oregon	A- Oak	75	295	76	19	1	20	157	58	69	36	2	67	3	0	8	0	0	.00	9	.258	.336	.532
1999 Modesto	A+ Oak	135	550	168	48	2	19	277	96	123	56	1	105	4	0	7	2	5	.29	18	.305	.370	.504
2000 Midland	AA Oak	135	546	178	44	3	30	318	98	121	67	5	112	6	0	7	4	0	1.00	18	.326	.401	.582
Sacramento	AAA Oak	5	18	5	1	0	1	9	4	4	3	0	7	0	0	0	0	0	—	0	.278	.381	.500
3 Min. YEARS		350	1409	427	112	6	70	761	256	317	162	8	291	13	0	22	6	6	.50	45	.303	.375	.540

Len Hart

Pitches: Left Bats: Left Pos: RP-45
Ht: 5'11" Wt: 190 Born: 10/8/73 Age: 27

				HOW MUCH HE PITCHED						WHAT HE GAVE UP											THE RESULTS				
Year Team	Lg Org	G	GS	CG	GF	IP	BFP	H	R	ER	HR	SH	SF	HB	TBB	IBB	SO	WP	Bk	W	L	Pct.	ShO	Sv	ERA
1996 Williamsprt	A- ChC	28	0	0	13	31.1	129	15	6	5	0	2	0	0	24	1	26	1	0	2	3	.400	0	0	1.44
1997 Rockford	A ChC	27	0	0	5	47.1	194	30	11	11	0	1	0	2	28	1	55	5	0	2	1	.667	0	0	2.09
Daytona	A+ ChC	8	0	0	3	9.1	44	6	6	6	0	1	0	1	7	0	12	1	0	1	2	.333	0	0	5.79
1998 Daytona	A+ ChC	37	0	0	11	50.2	221	52	28	20	4	1	3	2	20	1	46	0	0	3	3	.500	0	2	3.55
1999 Rancho Cuca	A+ SD	33	0	0	12	43.1	166	19	5	4	1	0	0	1	18	0	54	3	0	2	1	.667	0	3	0.83
Mobile	AA SD	2	0	0	0	2.2	14	4	1	1	0	0	0	0	1	0	6	0	0	0	0	—	0	0	3.38

Year Team	Lg Org	G	GS	CG	GF	IP	BFP	H	R	ER	HR	SH	SF	HB	TBB	IBB	SO	WP	Bk	W	L	Pct.	ShO	Sv	ERA
2000 Rancho Cuca	A+ SD	13	0	0	2	15.2	61	13	4	3	0	3	0	0	4	1	12	1	0	0	0	—	0	0	1.72
Mobile	AA SD	32	0	0	14	39	168	37	17	17	2	1	1	0	20	1	29	3	0	1	1	.500	0	1	3.92
5 Min. YEARS		180	0	0	57	239.1	997	180	78	67	7	9	4	6	123	5	238	16	0	11	11	.500	0	8	2.52

Chad Harville

Pitches: Right **Bats:** Right **Pos:** RP-53 **Ht:** 5'9" **Wt:** 180 **Born:** 9/16/76 **Age:** 24

Year Team	Lg Org	G	GS	CG	GF	IP	BFP	H	R	ER	HR	SH	SF	HB	TBB	IBB	SO	WP	Bk	W	L	Pct.	ShO	Sv	ERA
1997 Sou Oregon	A- Oak	3	0	0	1	5	23	3	0	0	0	1	0	2	3	0	6	0	0	1	0	1.000	0	0	0.00
Visalia	A+ Oak	14	0	0	1	18.2	92	25	14	12	2	1	1	0	13	1	24	1	3	0	0	—	0	0	5.79
1998 Visalia	A+ Oak	24	7	0	12	69	294	59	25	23	0	0	2	5	31	0	76	6	2	4	3	.571	0	4	3.00
Huntsville	AA Oak	12	0	0	10	14.2	63	6	4	4	0	0	1	0	13	1	24	1	0	0	0	—	0	8	2.45
1999 Midland	AA Oak	17	0	0	16	22.1	90	13	6	5	1	0	1	1	9	0	35	2	0	2	0	1.000	0	7	2.01
Vancouver	AAA Oak	22	0	0	19	25.2	114	24	5	5	0	0	0	3	11	1	36	4	0	1	0	1.000	0	11	1.75
2000 Sacramento	AAA Oak	53	0	0	29	64	280	53	35	32	8	2	1	3	35	0	77	8	0	5	3	.625	0	9	4.50
1999 Oakland	AL	15	0	0	8	14.1	69	18	11	11	2	0	1	0	10	1	15	3	1	0	2	.000	0	0	6.91
4 Min. YEARS		145	7	0	88	219.1	956	183	89	81	11	4	6	14	115	3	278	22	5	13	6	.684	0	39	3.32

Derek Hasselhoff

Pitches: Right **Bats:** Right **Pos:** RP-45; SP-1 **Ht:** 6'2" **Wt:** 185 **Born:** 10/10/73 **Age:** 27

Year Team	Lg Org	G	GS	CG	GF	IP	BFP	H	R	ER	HR	SH	SF	HB	TBB	IBB	SO	WP	Bk	W	L	Pct.	ShO	Sv	ERA
1995 Bristol	R+ CWS	12	11	0	1	66.1	281	66	32	27	4	1	1	2	14	0	46	2	2	7	3	.700	0	0	3.66
1996 South Bend	A CWS	35	0	0	29	47.2	205	46	19	17	4	4	1	2	17	0	39	5	0	6	3	.667	0	10	3.21
Pr William	A+ CWS	5	0	0	4	10.1	49	14	7	6	1	0	0	0	6	2	9	0	0	0	1	.000	0	1	5.23
1997 Winston-Sal	A+ CWS	20	0	0	11	34.2	138	22	10	6	1	2	1	0	15	3	41	4	0	3	2	.600	0	3	1.56
Birmingham	AA CWS	18	0	0	10	33.2	141	35	10	9	3	0	1	1	11	0	22	1	0	5	2	.714	0	3	2.41
Nashville	AAA CWS	6	0	0	1	7.1	37	9	8	8	2	0	0	0	7	0	2	0	0	1	1	.500	0	0	9.82
1998 Calgary	AAA CWS	13	0	0	5	19	89	23	15	14	3	1	1	1	8	0	24	0	1	2	0	1.000	0	0	6.63
White Sox	R CWS	6	1	0	1	10	36	6	1	0	0	0	0	0	0	0	16	0	0	0	0	—	0	0	0.00
Winston-Sal	A+ CWS	1	0	0	0	2	9	3	0	0	0	0	0	0	0	0	3	0	0	0	0	—	0	0	0.00
1999 Charlotte	AAA CWS	49	0	0	18	71	311	83	46	38	7	1	0	0	25	1	65	3	0	6	0	1.000	0	4	4.82
2000 Charlotte	AAA CWS	46	1	0	23	65.2	281	62	32	27	6	2	2	2	23	2	51	1	0	7	4	.636	0	6	3.70
6 Min. YEARS		211	13	0	103	367.2	1577	369	180	152	31	11	7	8	126	8	318	16	3	37	16	.698	0	27	3.72

Chris Hatcher

Bats: Right **Throws:** Right **Pos:** OF-53; DH-38; 1B-20; PH-7 **Ht:** 6'3" **Wt:** 235 **Born:** 1/7/69 **Age:** 32

Year Team	Lg Org	G	AB	H	2B	3B	HR	TB	R	RBI	TBB	IBB	SO	HBP	SH	SF	SB	CS	SB%	GDP	Avg	OBP	SLG
1990 Auburn	A- Hou	72	259	64	10	0	9	101	37	45	27	3	86	5	0	5	8	2	.80	4	.247	.324	.390
1991 Burlington	A Hou	129	497	117	23	6	13	191	69	65	46	4	180	9	0	4	10	5	.67	6	.235	.309	.384
1992 Osceola	A+ Hou	97	367	103	19	6	17	185	49	68	20	1	97	5	0	5	11	0	1.00	6	.281	.322	.504
1993 Jackson	AA Hou	101	367	95	15	3	15	161	45	64	11	0	104	11	0	3	5	8	.38	8	.259	.298	.439
1994 Tucson	AAA Hou	108	349	104	28	4	12	176	55	73	19	0	90	4	0	6	5	1	.83	6	.298	.336	.504
1995 Jackson	AA Hou	11	39	12	1	0	1	16	5	3	4	0	6	1	0	1	0	2	.00	1	.308	.378	.410
Tucson	AAA Hou	94	290	83	19	2	14	148	59	50	42	2	107	4	1	2	7	3	.70	9	.286	.382	.510
1996 Jackson	AA Hou	41	156	48	9	1	13	98	29	36	9	2	39	4	0	1	2	1	.67	5	.308	.359	.628
Tucson	AAA Hou	95	348	105	21	4	18	188	53	61	14	1	87	5	0	5	10	8	.56	9	.302	.333	.540
1997 Wichita	AA KC	11	42	11	0	0	5	26	7	7	4	0	16	1	0	0	1	0	1.00	6	.262	.340	.619
Omaha	AAA KC	68	222	51	9	0	11	93	34	24	17	2	68	6	0	3	0	1	.00	4	.230	.298	.419
1998 Omaha	AAA KC	126	485	150	21	2	46	313	84	106	25	3	125	3	0	3	8	6	.57	9	.309	.345	.645
1999 Colo Sprngs	AAA Col	98	334	115	24	2	21	206	63	69	23	1	89	10	0	5	12	4	.75	12	.344	.398	.617
2000 Iowa	AAA ChC	86	288	80	15	1	24	169	46	71	26	1	64	10	0	2	4	4	.50	4	.278	.356	.587
Edmonton	AAA Ana	30	115	39	8	4	7	76	19	24	8	1	24	3	0	1	1	0	1.00	3	.339	.394	.661
1998 Kansas City	AL	8	15	1	0	0	0	1	0	1	1	0	7	0	0	0	0	0	—	0	.067	.125	.067
11 Min. YEARS		1167	4158	1177	222	35	226	2147	654	766	295	21	1182	81	1	46	84	45	.65	85	.283	.339	.516

Kevin Haverbusch

Bats: Right **Throws:** Right **Pos:** 3B-34; PH-6; DH-4; OF-1 **Ht:** 6'3" **Wt:** 199 **Born:** 6/16/76 **Age:** 25

Year Team	Lg Org	G	AB	H	2B	3B	HR	TB	R	RBI	TBB	IBB	SO	HBP	SH	SF	SB	CS	SB%	GDP	Avg	OBP	SLG
1997 Erie	A- Pit	67	241	75	15	2	10	124	37	55	13	1	37	4	2	4	4	4	.50	6	.311	.351	.515
1998 Lynchburg	A+ Pit	49	181	60	12	1	8	98	25	39	9	0	33	6	0	2	4	2	.67	5	.331	.379	.541
Carolina	AA Pit	46	168	63	10	0	3	82	28	29	13	1	20	3	0	0	1	3	.25	9	.375	.429	.488
1999 Altoona	AA Pit	93	332	95	22	2	14	163	57	61	12	0	60	19	1	9	6	3	.67	9	.286	.339	.491
2000 Altoona	AA Pit	43	140	39	3	1	5	59	23	21	11	0	15	2	0	0	2	2	.50	5	.279	.340	.421
4 Min. YEARS		298	1062	332	62	6	40	526	170	205	58	2	165	34	3	15	17	14	.55	28	.313	.363	.495

Al Hawkins

Pitches: Right **Bats:** Right **Pos:** SP-18 **Ht:** 6'1" **Wt:** 210 **Born:** 1/1/78 **Age:** 23

Year Team	Lg Org	G	GS	CG	GF	IP	BFP	H	R	ER	HR	SH	SF	HB	TBB	IBB	SO	WP	Bk	W	L	Pct.	ShO	Sv	ERA
1996 Ogden	R+ Mil	9	5	0	1	33.2	144	31	16	12	1	0	0	0	13	0	23	1	3	3	3	.500	0	0	3.21
1997 Beloit	A Mil	6	6	0	0	24.2	133	46	33	29	8	0	1	5	12	0	17	2	1	1	4	.200	0	0	10.58
Ogden	R+ Mil	14	14	0	0	81	394	113	74	53	8	0	2	4	24	0	47	5	0	2	8	.200	0	0	5.89
1998 Beloit	A Mil	15	14	1	0	88	382	94	52	35	4	7	2	7	20	0	64	3	1	6	3	.667	0	0	3.58
Stockton	A+ Mil	9	9	0	0	55.1	252	60	37	28	7	1	4	3	26	0	32	4	1	3	4	.429	0	0	4.55

Year Team	Lg Org	G	GS	CG	GF	IP	BFP	H	R	ER	HR	SH	SF	HB	TBB	IBB	SO	WP	Bk	W	L	Pct.	ShO	Sv	ERA
		HOW MUCH HE PITCHED						**WHAT HE GAVE UP**												**THE RESULTS**					
1999 Stockton	A+ Mil	4	4	0	0	25	105	26	12	10	2	1	0	1	6	0	11	2	0	3	0	1.000	0	0	3.60
Huntsville	AA Mil	19	19	0	0	99.2	447	126	71	59	10	1	6	10	29	2	56	14	1	8	9	.471	0	0	5.33
2000 Huntsville	AA Mil	18	18	0	0	97	414	88	49	40	12	7	2	3	43	1	66	7	0	7	7	.500	0	0	3.71
5 Min. YEARS		94	89	1	1	504.1	2271	584	344	266	52	17	17	33	173	2	316	38	7	33	38	.465	0	0	4.75

Heath Hayes

Bats: Right **Throws:** Right **Pos:** C-12; OF-3; PH-3; 1B-1; DH-1 **Ht:** 6'3" **Wt:** 195 **Born:** 2/29/72 **Age:** 29

Year Team	Lg Org	G	AB	H	2B	3B	HR	TB	R	RBI	TBB	IBB	SO	HBP	SH	SF	SB	CS	SB%	GDP	Avg	OBP	SLG
		BATTING															**BASERUNNING**				**PERCENTAGES**		
1994 Watertown	A- Cle	46	147	38	5	1	4	57	31	27	22	0	31	1	0	3	3	1	.75	4	.259	.353	.388
1995 Watertown	A- Cle	15	52	11	3	0	0	14	4	6	7	0	14	0	0	1	1	1	.50	1	.212	.300	.269
1996 Columbus	A Cle	104	348	81	14	0	22	161	51	57	36	0	106	6	0	5	2	1	.67	2	.233	.311	.463
1997 Kinston	A+ Cle	103	378	96	22	0	24	190	54	59	40	3	107	2	0	2	2	3	.40	7	.254	.327	.503
1998 Akron	AA Cle	91	329	68	14	1	11	117	36	46	24	1	95	2	2	3	2	3	.40	7	.207	.263	.356
1999 Akron	AA Cle	119	418	111	15	2	16	178	51	68	41	1	111	7	1	5	2	1	.67	8	.266	.338	.426
2000 Buffalo	AAA Cle	11	39	5	1	0	1	9	4	5	2	0	16	0	0	2	1	0	1.00	1	.128	.163	.231
Albuquerque	AAA LA	6	18	2	0	0	0	2	0	3	1	0	5	0	0	0	0	1	.00	0	.111	.158	.111
San Antonio	AA LA	3	5	2	1	0	0	3	1	2	1	1	1	0	0	1	0	0	—	0	.400	.429	.600
7 Min. YEARS		498	1734	414	75	4	78	731	232	273	174	6	486	18	3	22	13	11	.54	30	.239	.311	.422

Heath Haynes

Pitches: Right **Bats:** Right **Pos:** RP-6; SP-3 **Ht:** 6'0" **Wt:** 175 **Born:** 11/30/68 **Age:** 32

Year Team	Lg Org	G	GS	CG	GF	IP	BFP	H	R	ER	HR	SH	SF	HB	TBB	IBB	SO	WP	Bk	W	L	Pct.	ShO	Sv	ERA
		HOW MUCH HE PITCHED						**WHAT HE GAVE UP**												**THE RESULTS**					
1991 Jamestown	A- Mon	29	0	0	23	56.1	221	31	15	13	3	5	1	4	18	4	93	4	3	10	1	.909	0	11	2.08
1992 Rockford	A Mon	45	0	0	36	57	239	49	19	12	0	4	1	4	15	3	78	1	3	3	1	.750	0	15	1.89
Harrisburg	AA Mon	3	0	0	1	4.2	17	2	1	1	1	0	0	0	1	0	6	0	0	2	0	1.000	0	0	1.93
1993 Harrisburg	AA Mon	57	0	0	22	66	270	46	27	19	2	5	3	2	19	4	78	4	2	8	0	1.000	0	5	2.59
1994 Ottawa	AAA Mon	56	0	0	25	87	350	72	32	23	7	7	2	1	15	7	75	3	0	6	7	.462	0	4	2.38
1995 Edmonton	AAA Oak	12	0	0	1	18.2	87	21	14	13	1	0	3	0	11	3	13	2	0	2	0	1.000	0	0	6.27
1996 Lk Elsinore	A+ Ana	31	0	0	11	38.1	142	29	9	7	1	1	0	3	2	0	44	1	1	5	1	.833	0	2	1.64
1997 Trenton	AA Bos	14	0	0	3	26.2	116	26	8	7	2	1	0	2	8	3	26	0	1	1	1	.500	0	2	2.36
New Haven	AA Col	5	0	0	1	8	31	7	1	1	0	0	0	0	1	0	8	0	0	0	0	—	0	0	1.13
Portland	AA Fla	28	0	0	11	38	159	36	16	16	4	3	2	3	7	4	39	0	1	4	0	1.000	0	1	3.79
2000 Valley	IND —	7	3	1	2	36	135	25	13	12	3	2	1	0	4	0	37	1	0	5	1	.833	1	0	3.00
New Orleans	AAA Hou	2	0	0	1	2.2	17	6	7	7	1	0	0	1	3	2	3	0	0	0	0	—	0	0	23.63
1994 Montreal	NL	4	0	0	2	3.2	17	3	1	0	0	0	1	0	3	0	1	0	0	0	0	—	0	0	0.00
8 Min. YEARS		289	3	1	137	439.1	1784	350	162	131	25	28	13	20	104	30	500	16	11	46	12	.793	1	40	2.68

Nathan Haynes

Bats: Left **Throws:** Left **Pos:** OF-115; DH-3 **Ht:** 5'9" **Wt:** 170 **Born:** 9/7/79 **Age:** 21

Year Team	Lg Org	G	AB	H	2B	3B	HR	TB	R	RBI	TBB	IBB	SO	HBP	SH	SF	SB	CS	SB%	GDP	Avg	OBP	SLG
		BATTING															**BASERUNNING**				**PERCENTAGES**		
1997 Athletics	R Oak	17	54	15	1	0	0	16	8	6	7	0	9	2	1	0	5	1	.83	3	.278	.381	.296
Sou Oregon	A- Oak	24	82	23	1	1	0	26	18	9	26	0	21	2	0	1	19	3	.86	1	.280	.459	.317
1998 Modesto	A+ Oak	125	507	128	13	7	1	158	89	41	54	2	139	4	6	2	42	18	.70	10	.252	.328	.312
1999 Visalia	A+ Oak	35	145	45	7	1	1	57	28	14	17	0	27	3	2	1	12	10	.55	1	.310	.392	.393
Lk Elsinore	A+ Ana	26	110	36	5	5	1	54	19	15	12	0	19	1	0	1	10	5	.67	2	.327	.395	.491
Erie	AA Ana	5	19	3	1	0	0	4	3	0	5	0	5	1	0	0	0	0	—	2	.158	.360	.211
2000 Erie	AA Ana	118	457	116	16	4	6	158	56	43	33	0	107	9	8	2	37	20	.65	3	.254	.315	.346
4 Min. YEARS		350	1374	366	44	18	9	473	221	128	154	2	327	22	17	7	125	57	.69	22	.266	.348	.344

Andy Hazlett

Pitches: Left **Bats:** Left **Pos:** RP-41; SP-4 **Ht:** 6'3" **Wt:** 187 **Born:** 8/27/75 **Age:** 25

Year Team	Lg Org	G	GS	CG	GF	IP	BFP	H	R	ER	HR	SH	SF	HB	TBB	IBB	SO	WP	Bk	W	L	Pct.	ShO	Sv	ERA
		HOW MUCH HE PITCHED						**WHAT HE GAVE UP**												**THE RESULTS**					
1997 Lowell	A- Bos	19	3	0	12	50.1	206	44	16	9	1	0	1	0	7	0	66	0	0	5	0	1.000	0	4	1.61
Michigan	A Bos	2	2	0	0	12	50	15	7	7	2	0	0	0	1	0	12	0	0	1	0	1.000	0	0	5.25
1998 Sarasota	A+ Bos	30	22	4	1	160.2	662	154	76	57	4	2	7	3	25	2	135	3	1	11	7	.611	2	1	3.19
1999 Trenton	AA Bos	27	26	2	1	164.1	674	155	84	76	15	5	2	8	41	0	123	7	3	9	9	.500	1	1	4.16
2000 Pawtucket	AAA Bos	3	0	0	0	3	20	11	8	8	1	0	1	0	0	0	4	0	0	0	0	—	0	0	24.00
Trenton	AA Bos	42	4	0	18	92.1	389	85	43	34	9	5	1	5	23	4	84	1	0	6	6	.500	0	6	3.31
4 Min. YEARS		123	57	6	32	482.2	2001	464	234	191	32	12	12	16	97	6	424	11	4	32	22	.593	3	12	3.56

Shane Heams

Pitches: Right **Bats:** Right **Pos:** RP-45 **Ht:** 6'1" **Wt:** 175 **Born:** 9/29/75 **Age:** 25

Year Team	Lg Org	G	GS	CG	GF	IP	BFP	H	R	ER	HR	SH	SF	HB	TBB	IBB	SO	WP	Bk	W	L	Pct.	ShO	Sv	ERA
		HOW MUCH HE PITCHED						**WHAT HE GAVE UP**												**THE RESULTS**					
1996 Mariners	R Sea	9	0	0	0	15.1	64	10	7	5	0	0	0	1	6	0	12	3	1	1	1	.500	0	2	2.93
1997 Mariners	R Sea	21	0	0	14	37	168	30	20	7	2	3	0	5	22	0	42	7	0	6	2	.750	0	2	1.70
1998 Jamestown	A- Det	24	0	0	14	47.1	202	43	27	21	1	0	1	2	16	0	73	5	0	2	2	.500	0	6	3.99
1999 W Michigan	A Det	51	0	0	30	69	294	41	26	18	1	3	4	1	39	2	101	15	1	5	4	.556	0	10	2.35
2000 Jacksnville	AA Det	39	0	0	19	55.2	238	35	17	16	4	3	1	2	34	2	67	2	0	6	2	.750	0	5	2.59
Toledo	AAA Det	6	0	0	0	9.2	52	13	12	12	3	0	2	1	12	0	7	3	0	0	0	—	0	0	11.17
5 Min. YEARS		150	0	0	84	234	1018	172	109	79	11	9	8	12	129	4	302	35	2	20	11	.645	0	25	3.04

Mike Heathcott

Pitches: Right **Bats:** Right **Pos:** RP-38; SP-3   **Ht:** 6'4" **Wt:** 190 **Born:** 5/16/69 **Age:** 32

Year Team	Lg Org	G	GS	CG	GF	IP	BFP	H	R	ER	HR	SH	SF	HB	TBB	IBB	SO	WP	Bk	W	L	Pct.	ShO	Sv	ERA
1991 Utica	A- CWS	6	6	0	0	33	138	26	19	13	4	1	1	1	14	0	14	1	0	3	1	.750	0	0	3.55
1992 South Bend	A CWS	15	14	0	1	82	340	67	28	14	3	5	2	0	32	0	49	8	0	9	5	.643	0	0	1.54
1993 Sarasota	A+ CWS	26	26	6	0	179.1	739	174	90	72	5	12	10	4	62	7	83	16	1	11	10	.524	1	0	3.61
1994 Birmingham	AA CWS	17	17	0	0	98	449	126	71	63	11	1	6	2	44	4	44	9	0	3	7	.300	0	0	5.79
Pr William	A+ CWS	9	8	1	1	43	193	51	28	19	7	1	0	1	23	0	27	6	0	1	2	.333	0	0	3.98
1995 Pr William	A+ CWS	27	14	1	4	88.2	387	96	56	46	8	2	7	2	36	3	68	18	0	4	9	.308	0	3	4.67
1996 Birmingham	AA CWS	23	23	1	0	147.2	625	138	72	66	9	5	5	4	55	3	108	5	0	11	8	.579	0	0	4.02
1997 Nashville	AAA CWS	17	0	0	7	27	129	39	23	22	5	1	0	0	12	0	23	6	0	2	3	.400	0	0	7.33
Birmingham	AA CWS	30	1	0	12	59	247	50	20	12	2	3	0	1	25	0	47	3	0	3	1	.750	0	7	1.83
1998 Calgary	AAA CWS	39	13	1	10	109	483	113	65	61	12	2	4	5	51	2	77	8	0	9	6	.600	0	1	5.04
1999 Charlotte	AAA CWS	32	21	1	5	139.1	632	177	89	80	14	6	4	4	64	1	77	9	0	10	8	.556	0	0	5.17
2000 Iowa	AAA ChC	38	1	0	20	73.2	336	93	52	46	8	0	6	2	32	1	37	8	0	5	3	.625	0	2	5.62
Edmonton	AAA Ana	3	2	0	0	14.1	61	14	6	6	0	1	0	2	7	0	4	1	0	1	1	.500	0	0	3.77
1998 Chicago	AL	1	0	0	0	3	12	2	1	1	0	0	0	0	1	0	3	0	0	0	0	—	0	0	3.00
10 Min. YEARS		282	146	11	60	1094	4759	1164	619	520	88	40	45	28	457	21	658	98	1	72	64	.529	1	13	4.28

Jeff Heaverlo

Pitches: Right **Bats:** Right **Pos:** SP-29   **Ht:** 6'1" **Wt:** 215 **Born:** 1/13/78 **Age:** 23

Year Team	Lg Org	G	GS	CG	GF	IP	BFP	H	R	ER	HR	SH	SF	HB	TBB	IBB	SO	WP	Bk	W	L	Pct.	ShO	Sv	ERA
1999 Everett	A- Sea	3	0	0	1	8.2	35	5	5	2	1	1	0	1	2	0	9	1	0	1	0	1.000	0	0	2.08
Wisconsin	A Sea	3	3	1	0	17.2	75	15	6	5	1	0	1	0	7	0	24	0	1	1	0	1.000	0	0	2.55
2000 Tacoma	AAA Sea	2	2	0	0	13	54	14	7	7	2	0	1	0	6	0	4	1	0	0	1	.000	0	0	4.85
Lancaster	A+ Sea	27	27	0	0	155.2	685	170	84	73	18	4	5	6	52	0	159	9	2	14	6	.700	1	0	4.22
2 Min. YEARS		35	32	1	1	195	849	204	102	87	22	6	6	8	67	0	196	11	3	16	7	.696	1	0	4.02

Bryan Hebson

Pitches: Right **Bats:** Right **Pos:** SP-29   **Ht:** 6'6" **Wt:** 210 **Born:** 3/12/76 **Age:** 25

Year Team	Lg Org	G	GS	CG	GF	IP	BFP	H	R	ER	HR	SH	SF	HB	TBB	IBB	SO	WP	Bk	W	L	Pct.	ShO	Sv	ERA
1998 Expos	R Mon	4	4	0	0	17	64	10	1	1	0	0	0	0	7	0	16	2	0	2	0	1.000	0	0	0.53
Cape Fear	A Mon	16	16	0	0	72.2	323	71	42	38	8	1	4	11	29	0	57	1	0	4	5	.444	0	0	4.71
1999 Cape Fear	A Mon	6	6	0	0	33.1	142	22	13	10	2	1	1	3	17	0	34	2	0	1	0	1.000	0	0	2.67
Jupiter	A+ Mon	17	16	0	1	103.1	414	85	33	23	5	2	3	5	26	0	79	3	0	7	6	.538	0	0	2.00
2000 Harrisburg	AA Mon	29	29	3	0	171.1	753	175	102	87	23	7	2	14	66	2	90	3	0	7	15	.318	1	0	4.57
3 Min. YEARS		72	71	3	1	398	1696	363	191	159	38	11	10	33	145	2	276	11	0	20	27	.426	1	0	3.60

Bronson Heflin

Pitches: Right **Bats:** Right **Pos:** RP-30   **Ht:** 6'3" **Wt:** 200 **Born:** 8/29/71 **Age:** 29

Year Team	Lg Org	G	GS	CG	GF	IP	BFP	H	R	ER	HR	SH	SF	HB	TBB	IBB	SO	WP	Bk	W	L	Pct.	ShO	Sv	ERA
1994 Batavia	A- Phi	14	13	1	0	83	353	85	38	33	5	5	0	6	20	0	71	11	2	6	5	.545	0	0	3.58
1995 Clearwater	A+ Phi	57	0	0	44	61	256	52	25	20	3	6	1	0	21	5	84	4	0	2	3	.400	0	21	2.95
Reading	AA Phi	1	0	0	1	4	4	0	0	0	0	0	0	0	1	0	2	0	0	0	0	—	0	0	0.00
1996 Reading	AA Phi	25	0	0	12	29.1	139	37	20	17	3	2	0	2	15	2	27	2	0	2	2	.500	0	1	5.22
Scranton-WB	AAA Phi	30	0	0	27	38	140	25	11	11	4	0	3	1	3	1	23	1	0	4	0	1.000	0	12	2.61
1997 Scranton-WB	AAA Phi	35	0	0	27	43.1	185	29	17	11	3	2	1	0	25	2	36	2	0	1	1	.500	0	13	2.28
1998 Scranton-WB	AAA Phi	10	0	0	2	10	49	12	10	8	3	0	0	0	7	0	9	1	0	0	0	—	0	0	7.20
Arkansas	AA StL	2	0	0	1	1.1	8	1	1	1	0	0	1	0	4	0	0	0	0	0	1	.000	0	0	6.75
Memphis	AAA StL	2	0	0	0	2	8	2	2	2	1	0	1	0	0	0	1	0	0	0	0	—	0	0	9.00
1999 Madison	IND —	25	0	0	21	29.2	134	31	14	11	2	3	4	0	13	2	21	3	0	3	4	.429	0	8	3.34
2000 Madison	IND —	26	0	0	24	30	127	29	11	10	3	2	0	1	10	1	43	1	0	0	0	.000	0	17	3.00
Nashville	AAA Pit	4	0	0	2	4.2	15	1	0	0	0	0	0	0	0	0	3	0	0	0	0	—	0	0	0.00
1996 Philadelphia	NL	3	0	0	2	6.2	34	11	7	5	1	0	1	0	3	0	4	0	0	0	0	—	0	0	6.75
7 Min. YEARS		231	13	1	161	333.1	1418	304	149	124	27	20	11	10	119	13	320	25	2	18	20	.474	0	72	3.35

Chris Heintz

Bats: Right **Throws:** Right **Pos:** C-56; 1B-10; DH-6; PH-1   **Ht:** 6'1" **Wt:** 200 **Born:** 8/6/74 **Age:** 26

Year Team	Lg Org	G	AB	H	2B	3B	HR	TB	R	RBI	TBB	IBB	SO	HBP	SH	SF	SB	CS	SB%	GDP	Avg	OBP	SLG
1996 Bristol	R+ CWS	8	29	10	7	0	2	23	7	8	4	0	2	0	0	0	1	1	.50	0	.345	.424	.793
South Bend	A CWS	64	230	61	12	1	1	78	25	22	23	1	46	3	1	1	1	1	.50	3	.265	.339	.339
1997 Hickory	A CWS	107	388	110	28	1	2	146	57	54	28	0	57	9	2	5	1	3	.25	6	.284	.342	.376
1998 Winston-Sal	A+ CWS	130	508	147	21	4	8	200	66	79	31	0	87	5	3	9	10	8	.56	17	.289	.331	.394
1999 Winston-Sal	A+ CWS	118	417	122	33	2	7	180	55	60	40	1	72	4	3	2	6	3	.67	7	.293	.359	.432
2000 Birmingham	AA CWS	73	239	64	15	1	2	87	27	34	21	0	33	0	1	6	4	1	.80	2	.268	.320	.364
5 Min. YEARS			500	1811	514	116	9	22	714	237	257	147	2	297	21	10	23	17	.58	35	.284	.341	.394

Rick Heiserman

Pitches: Right **Bats:** Right **Pos:** RP-54; SP-1   **Ht:** 6'7" **Wt:** 225 **Born:** 2/22/73 **Age:** 28

Year Team	Lg Org	G	GS	CG	GF	IP	BFP	H	R	ER	HR	SH	SF	HB	TBB	IBB	SO	WP	Bk	W	L	Pct.	ShO	Sv	ERA
1994 Watertown	A- Cle	7	0	0	2	11.2	48	6	3	3	0	0	1	1	5	0	6	2	2	1	0	1.000	0	0	2.31
1995 Kinston	A+ Cle	19	19	1	0	113	470	97	55	47	13	3	4	9	42	1	86	6	1	9	3	.750	0	0	3.74
St. Pete	A+ StL	6	5	0	1	28	118	28	18	17	2	0	2	1	11	0	18	4	0	2	3	.400	0	0	5.46

123

Year Team	Lg Org	G	GS	CG	GF	IP	BFP	H	R	ER	HR	SH	SF	HB	TBB	IBB	SO	WP	Bk	W	L	Pct.	ShO	Sv	ERA
1996 St. Pete	A+ StL	26	26	1	0	155.1	663	168	68	56	8	6	3	9	41	0	104	4	0	10	8	.556	1	0	3.24
1997 Arkansas	AA StL	34	20	1	9	131.2	569	151	73	61	19	6	2	8	36	2	90	8	0	5	8	.385	1	4	4.17
Louisville	AAA StL	1	0	0	1	2	10	2	1	1	1	0	0	1	1	0	0	0	0	0	0	—	0	0	4.50
1998 Arkansas	AA StL	18	0	0	18	16.1	76	20	11	9	1	1	0	1	5	0	9	2	0	0	3	.000	0	0	4.96
Memphis	AAA StL	40	0	0	16	40.1	185	54	21	18	2	2	1	2	14	1	28	1	0	2	3	.400	0	6	4.02
1999 Memphis	AAA StL	52	0	0	38	61.2	266	67	37	35	7	1	1	4	21	1	57	6	0	2	3	.400	0	20	5.11
2000 Memphis	AAA StL	55	1	0	22	77	340	85	36	35	10	6	3	2	29	3	55	6	0	6	3	.667	0	6	4.09
1999 St. Louis	NL	3	0	0	0	4.1	24	8	4	4	2	0	0	0	4	0	4	2	0	0	0	—	0	0	8.31
7 Min. YEARS		258	71	3	107	637	2745	678	323	282	63	25	17	37	205	8	453	39	3	37	34	.521	2	45	3.98

Dan Held

Bats: Right Throws: Right Pos: 1B-67; DH-34; 3B-18; PH-5   Ht: 6'1" Wt: 215 Born: 10/7/70 Age: 30

		BATTING															BASERUNNING				PERCENTAGES		
Year Team	Lg Org	G	AB	H	2B	3B	HR	TB	R	RBI	TBB	IBB	SO	HBP	SH	SF	SB	CS	SB%	GDP	Avg	OBP	SLG
1993 Batavia	A- Phi	45	151	31	8	1	3	50	18	16	16	0	40	6	1	2	2	3	.40	3	.205	.303	.331
1994 Spartanburg	A Phi	130	484	123	32	1	18	211	69	69	52	2	119	9	1	11	2	0	1.00	11	.254	.331	.436
1995 Clearwater	A+ Phi	134	489	133	35	1	21	233	82	82	56	1	127	19	1	4	2	1	.67	13	.272	.366	.476
Reading	AA Phi	2	4	2	1	0	1	6	2	3	2	0	1	0	0	0	1	0	1.00	0	.500	.667	1.500
1996 Reading	AA Phi	136	497	121	17	5	26	226	77	92	60	4	141	22	0	6	3	8	.27	10	.243	.347	.455
Scranton-WB	AAA Phi	4	14	0	0	0	0	0	1	0	1	0	6	1	0	0	0	0	—	0	.000	.125	.000
1997 Reading	AA Phi	138	525	143	31	4	26	260	80	86	42	1	116	18	0	4	1	3	.25	14	.272	.345	.495
1998 Scranton-WB	AAA Phi	119	398	106	28	3	15	185	64	57	34	4	102	9	2	3	2	3	.40	9	.266	.336	.465
1999 Lehigh Val	IND —	87	340	94	25	0	25	194	72	62	40	1	62	10	0	1	7	3	.70	7	.276	.368	.571
2000 Norfolk	AAA NYM	3	7	2	1	0	0	3	1	0	1	0	2	0	0	0	0	0	—	0	.286	.375	.429
Binghamton	AA NYM	114	381	119	23	1	11	177	66	69	28	3	71	17	0	3	4	3	.57	9	.312	.382	.465
8 Min. YEARS		912	3290	874	201	16	146	1545	532	536	332	16	787	111	5	34	24	24	.50	76	.266	.350	.470

Bret Hemphill

Bats: Both Throws: Right Pos: C-90; DH-8; PH-3; 1B-1   Ht: 6'2" Wt: 215 Born: 12/17/71 Age: 29

		BATTING															BASERUNNING				PERCENTAGES		
Year Team	Lg Org	G	AB	H	2B	3B	HR	TB	R	RBI	TBB	IBB	SO	HBP	SH	SF	SB	CS	SB%	GDP	Avg	OBP	SLG
1994 Boise	A- Ana	71	252	74	16	1	3	101	44	36	40	2	53	1	1	6	1	1	.50	6	.294	.385	.401
1995 Lk Elsinore	A+ Ana	45	146	29	7	0	1	39	12	17	18	0	36	3	0	3	2	1	.67	4	.199	.294	.267
Cedar Rapds	A Ana	72	234	59	11	1	8	96	36	28	21	0	54	4	1	4	0	2	.00	7	.252	.319	.410
1996 Lk Elsinore	A+ Ana	108	399	105	21	3	17	183	64	64	52	1	93	4	6	1	4	3	.57	7	.263	.353	.459
1997 Midland	AA Ana	78	266	82	15	2	10	131	46	63	47	2	56	6	1	5	0	2	.00	6	.308	.417	.492
1998 Vancouver	AAA Ana	47	155	39	10	2	4	65	16	12	12	0	33	0	0	0	1	0	.00	6	.252	.305	.419
1999 Edmonton	AAA Ana	74	246	77	16	1	7	116	29	31	31	0	58	4	7	2	1	0	1.00	8	.313	.396	.472
2000 Edmonton	AAA Ana	41	147	41	10	1	6	71	22	21	21	0	28	0	0	0	0	0	—	2	.279	.369	.483
Erie	AA Ana	59	207	48	6	3	4	72	31	24	22	0	41	1	3	2	0	1	.00	4	.232	.306	.348
1999 Anaheim	AL	12	21	3	0	0	0	3	3	2	4	0	4	0	1	1	0	0	—	1	.143	.269	.143
7 Min. YEARS		595	2052	554	112	14	60	874	300	296	264	5	452	23	19	23	8	11	.42	48	.270	.356	.426

Rod Henderson

Pitches: Right Bats: Right Pos: SP-16; RP-11   Ht: 6'4" Wt: 195 Born: 3/11/71 Age: 30

Year Team	Lg Org	G	GS	CG	GF	IP	BFP	H	R	ER	HR	SH	SF	HB	TBB	IBB	SO	WP	Bk	W	L	Pct.	ShO	Sv	ERA
1992 Jamestown	A- Mon	1	1	0	0	3	13	2	3	2	0	0	0	0	5	0	2	0	0	0	0	—	0	0	6.00
1993 Wst Plm Bch	A+ Mon	22	22	1	0	143	580	110	50	46	3	4	5	6	44	0	127	8	6	12	7	.632	1	0	2.90
Harrisburg	AA Mon	5	5	0	0	29.2	125	20	10	6	1	0	1	0	15	0	25	2	1	5	0	1.000	0	0	1.82
1994 Harrisburg	AA Mon	2	2	0	0	12	44	5	2	2	1	0	0	0	4	0	16	0	0	2	0	1.000	0	0	1.50
Ottawa	AAA Mon	23	21	0	1	122.2	545	123	67	63	16	2	5	2	67	3	100	1	0	6	9	.400	0	1	4.62
1995 Harrisburg	AA Mon	12	12	0	0	56.1	240	51	28	27	4	0	1	5	18	0	53	1	0	3	6	.333	0	0	4.31
1996 Ottawa	AAA Mon	25	23	3	0	121.1	526	117	75	70	12	1	4	4	52	1	83	2	0	4	11	.267	1	0	5.19
1997 Ottawa	AAA Mon	26	20	2	3	123.2	542	136	72	68	18	4	2	6	49	3	103	6	0	5	9	.357	1	1	4.95
1998 Ottawa	AAA Mon	6	0	0	1	11	66	23	17	11	3	1	0	0	12	0	12	0	0	0	1	.000	0	0	9.00
El Paso	AA Mil	1	0	0	0	1.2	10	4	1	1	0	0	0	0	1	0	0	0	0	0	0	—	0	0	5.40
Louisville	AAA Mil	22	19	1	1	121.1	493	100	45	40	4	2	1	4	39	0	68	1	0	11	5	.688	0	0	2.97
1999 Louisville	AAA Mil	28	22	0	0	120.2	550	119	109	85	20	5	5	7	64	0	76	6	0	7	11	.389	0	0	6.34
2000 Binghamton	AA NYM	9	0	0	7	12.1	50	7	6	6	0	0	0	0	5	0	10	1	0	1	0	1.000	0	0	4.38
Long Island	IND —	14	12	1	1	78	303	48	20	19	3	0	4	3	28	0	66	4	0	9	1	.900	1	0	2.19
Tacoma	AAA Sea	4	4	0	0	16.1	77	19	11	11	1	0	0	1	14	0	12	0	0	2	1	.667	0	0	6.06
1994 Montreal	NL	3	2	0	0	6.2	37	9	9	7	1	3	0	0	7	0	3	0	0	0	1	.000	0	0	9.45
1998 Milwaukee	NL	2	0	0	0	3.2	17	5	4	4	2	0	0	0	7	0	4	0	0	0	0	—	0	0	9.82
9 Min. YEARS		200	163	8	15	973	4166	884	516	457	85	20	28	38	417	7	753	32	7	67	61	.523	4	2	4.23
2 Maj. YEARS		5	2	0	0	10.1	54	14	13	11	3	3	0	0	7	0	4	0	0	0	1	.000	0	0	9.58

Ryan Henderson

Pitches: Right Bats: Right Pos: RP-20; SP-1   Ht: 6'1" Wt: 190 Born: 9/30/69 Age: 31

Year Team	Lg Org	G	GS	CG	GF	IP	BFP	H	R	ER	HR	SH	SF	HB	TBB	IBB	SO	WP	Bk	W	L	Pct.	ShO	Sv	ERA
1992 Great Falls	R+ LA	11	11	1	0	55	228	37	22	13	0	3	0	2	25	0	54	5	6	5	1	.833	1	0	2.13
Bakersfield	A+ LA	3	3	0	0	16	72	17	10	9	1	0	0	0	9	1	15	0	3	0	2	.000	0	0	5.06
1993 Vero Beach	A+ LA	30	0	0	25	34	158	29	24	15	2	4	1	0	28	4	34	1	1	0	3	.000	0	10	3.97
San Antonio	AA LA	23	0	0	20	25	110	19	10	7	0	3	1	0	16	2	22	1	1	0	0	—	0	5	2.52
1994 Bakersfield	A+ LA	29	0	0	27	31.1	145	26	14	10	1	2	0	1	26	0	38	8	1	1	0	1.000	0	14	2.87
San Antonio	AA LA	11	1	0	0	21.2	105	25	18	17	2	0	1	1	18	1	15	3	1	1	2	.333	0	0	7.06
1995 Vero Beach	A+ LA	39	6	0	10	104.1	453	98	53	45	1	6	1	5	58	3	86	9	2	11	5	.688	0	2	3.88
1996 Albuquerque	AAA LA	3	0	0	0	5.2	31	5	9	5	0	0	0	1	5	0	9	0	0	0	0	—	0	0	7.94
San Antonio	AA LA	39	0	0	19	63.2	275	59	29	27	2	2	4	5	29	0	46	4	0	3	3	.500	0	6	3.82

124

Year Team	Lg Org	G	GS	CG	GF	IP	BFP	H	R	ER	HR	SH	SF	HB	TBB	IBB	SO	WP	Bk	W	L	Pct.	ShO	Sv	ERA
		HOW MUCH HE PITCHED						**WHAT HE GAVE UP**												**THE RESULTS**					
1997 Albuquerque	AAA LA	13	0	0	4	17.1	87	20	14	12	0	3	0	1	14	3	17	1	0	1	3	.250	0	0	6.23
Colo Spngs	AAA Col	6	1	0	2	13	67	20	18	18	3	0	0	1	9	1	12	0	0	1	1	.500	0	0	12.46
New Haven	AA Col	24	4	0	7	50.2	228	54	29	27	2	2	3	2	27	2	46	6	0	2	5	.286	0	0	4.80
1998 Binghamton	AA NYM	29	0	0	16	40.1	173	34	18	15	2	1	1	0	20	3	39	3	1	0	3	.000	0	4	3.35
Norfolk	AAA NYM	3	0	0	0	4	23	6	5	5	0	0	0	0	6	0	2	0	0	0	0	—	0	0	11.25
El Paso	AA Mil	20	0	0	11	22	105	22	14	9	0	0	0	3	13	2	20	2	0	2	0	1.000	0	5	3.68
1999 Huntsville	AAA Mil	12	0	0	10	14.1	59	12	2	1	0	1	0	0	6	1	13	2	0	2	0	1.000	0	6	0.63
Louisville	AAA Mil	21	0	0	7	35.1	168	35	32	25	2	0	1	3	25	3	34	7	0	1	0	1.000	0	0	6.37
Norfolk	AAA NYM	7	2	0	1	13.1	63	14	13	12	2	0	1	0	9	0	12	2	0	0	0	—	0	0	8.10
Binghamton	AA NYM	5	2	0	1	7.2	35	9	6	6	1	0	0	1	6	0	8	2	0	0	0	—	0	0	7.04
2000 Portland	AA Fla	10	1	0	4	17.1	89	22	16	10	1	1	1	3	12	1	19	3	0	2	3	.400	0	0	5.19
Calgary	AAA Fla	11	0	0	1	22.2	119	33	27	21	5	0	1	2	18	0	21	2	0	0	0	—	0	0	8.34
9 Min. YEARS		349	31	1	166	614.2	2793	596	383	309	27	28	15	32	380	27	560	65	18	31	36	.463	1	52	4.52

Scott Henderson

Pitches: Right **Bats:** Right **Pos:** RP-47   **Ht:** 6'3" **Wt:** 195 **Born:** 2/27/75 **Age:** 26

Year Team	Lg Org	G	GS	CG	GF	IP	BFP	H	R	ER	HR	SH	SF	HB	TBB	IBB	SO	WP	Bk	W	L	Pct.	ShO	Sv	ERA
		HOW MUCH HE PITCHED						**WHAT HE GAVE UP**												**THE RESULTS**					
1997 Utica	A- Fla	15	1	0	6	39.2	151	28	11	10	1	2	1	1	7	0	51	3	0	5	1	.833	0	4	2.27
1998 Kane County	A Fla	40	1	0	19	81.1	337	64	29	27	2	4	2	4	27	7	96	2	0	10	7	.588	0	4	2.99
1999 Portland	AA Fla	46	1	0	21	85	343	67	32	28	4	4	2	8	26	4	83	7	0	6	3	.667	0	7	2.96
2000 Calgary	AAA Fla	8	0	0	2	10.2	51	10	10	6	1	0	1	1	6	0	12	4	0	0	1	.000	0	0	5.06
Portland	AA Fla	39	0	0	20	63.1	266	47	23	22	5	1	1	1	25	0	73	6	1	7	2	.778	0	4	3.13
4 Min. YEARS		148	3	0	68	280	1148	216	105	93	13	11	7	15	91	11	315	22	1	28	14	.667	0	19	2.99

Mark Hendrickson

Pitches: Left **Bats:** Left **Pos:** SP-18   **Ht:** 6'9" **Wt:** 230 **Born:** 6/23/74 **Age:** 27

Year Team	Lg Org	G	GS	CG	GF	IP	BFP	H	R	ER	HR	SH	SF	HB	TBB	IBB	SO	WP	Bk	W	L	Pct.	ShO	Sv	ERA
		HOW MUCH HE PITCHED						**WHAT HE GAVE UP**												**THE RESULTS**					
1998 Dunedin	A+ Tor	16	5	0	1	49.1	207	44	16	13	2	2	2	0	26	1	38	2	0	4	3	.571	0	1	2.37
1999 Knoxville	AA Tor	12	11	0	0	55.2	254	73	46	41	4	2	0	2	21	0	39	2	1	2	7	.222	0	0	6.63
2000 Dunedin	A+ Tor	12	12	1	0	51.1	235	63	34	32	7	1	5	0	29	0	38	1	0	2	2	.500	0	0	5.61
Tennessee	AA Tor	6	6	0	0	39.2	161	32	17	16	5	1	0	0	12	0	29	4	0	3	1	.750	0	0	3.63
3 Min. YEARS		46	34	1	1	196	857	212	113	102	18	6	7	2	88	1	144	9	1	11	13	.458	0	1	4.68

Oscar Henriquez

Pitches: Right **Bats:** Right **Pos:** RP-16   **Ht:** 6'6" **Wt:** 220 **Born:** 1/28/74 **Age:** 27

Year Team	Lg Org	G	GS	CG	GF	IP	BFP	H	R	ER	HR	SH	SF	HB	TBB	IBB	SO	WP	Bk	W	L	Pct.	ShO	Sv	ERA
		HOW MUCH HE PITCHED						**WHAT HE GAVE UP**												**THE RESULTS**					
1993 Asheville	A Hou	27	26	2	0	150	679	154	95	74	12	6	5	10	70	2	117	7	3	9	10	.474	1	0	4.44
1995 Kissimmee	A+ Hou	20	0	0	7	44.2	207	40	29	25	2	2	2	6	30	0	36	3	0	3	4	.429	0	1	5.04
1996 Kissimmee	A+ Hou	37	0	0	33	34	162	28	18	15	0	1	1	3	29	2	40	4	0	0	0	.000	0	15	3.97
1997 New Orleans	AAA Hou	60	0	0	37	74	313	65	28	23	4	6	3	5	27	3	80	7	1	4	5	.444	0	12	2.80
1998 Charlotte	AAA Fla	26	0	0	19	31.2	134	29	12	9	3	0	1	2	12	0	37	4	0	1	0	1.000	0	11	2.56
1999 Norfolk	AAA NYM	53	0	0	41	54	254	54	31	24	8	4	3	3	38	4	65	8	1	3	4	.429	0	23	4.00
2000 Norfolk	AAA NYM	16	0	0	11	14	65	12	10	10	2	2	1	1	11	1	14	2	0	0	1	.000	0	4	6.43
1997 Houston	NL	4	0	0	1	4	17	2	2	2	0	1	0	1	3	0	3	0	0	0	1	.000	0	0	4.50
1998 Florida	NL	15	0	0	4	20	100	26	22	19	4	0	2	1	12	0	19	1	0	0	0	—	0	0	8.55
7 Min. YEARS		239	26	2	148	402.1	1814	382	223	180	31	21	16	30	217	12	389	35	5	20	28	.417	1	66	4.03
2 Maj. YEARS		19	0	0	5	24	117	28	24	21	4	1	2	2	15	0	22	1	0	0	1	.000	0	0	7.88

Drew Henson

Bats: Right **Throws:** Right **Pos:** 3B-69; DH-11   **Ht:** 6'5" **Wt:** 222 **Born:** 2/13/80 **Age:** 21

Year Team	Lg Org	G	AB	H	2B	3B	HR	TB	R	RBI	TBB	IBB	SO	HBP	SH	SF	SB	CS	SB%	GDP	Avg	OBP	SLG
		BATTING															**BASERUNNING**				**PERCENTAGES**		
1998 Yankees	R NYY	10	38	12	3	0	1	18	5	2	3	1	9	0	0	0	0	0	—	1	.316	.366	.474
1999 Tampa	A+ NYY	69	254	71	12	0	13	122	37	37	26	0	71	0	0	3	3	1	.75	6	.280	.345	.480
2000 Tampa	A+ NYY	5	21	7	2	0	1	12	4	1	1	0	7	0	0	0	0	1	.00	0	.333	.364	.571
Norwich	A+ NYY	59	223	64	9	2	7	98	39	39	20	1	75	1	0	1	0	5	.00	6	.287	.347	.439
Chattanooga	AA Cin	16	64	11	8	0	1	22	7	9	4	0	25	0	0	0	2	0	1.00	0	.172	.221	.344
3 Min. YEARS		159	600	165	34	2	23	272	92	88	54	2	187	2	0	4	5	7	.42	15	.275	.335	.453

Russ Herbert

Pitches: Right **Bats:** Right **Pos:** RP-35; SP-3   **Ht:** 6'3" **Wt:** 195 **Born:** 4/21/72 **Age:** 29

Year Team	Lg Org	G	GS	CG	GF	IP	BFP	H	R	ER	HR	SH	SF	HB	TBB	IBB	SO	WP	Bk	W	L	Pct.	ShO	Sv	ERA
		HOW MUCH HE PITCHED						**WHAT HE GAVE UP**												**THE RESULTS**					
1994 White Sox	R CWS	4	2	0	1	13	46	6	3	3	0	0	0	0	0	0	19	0	0	0	1	.000	0	0	2.08
Hickory	A CWS	8	7	0	1	36.2	154	33	14	14	3	1	0	2	15	0	34	1	2	2	1	.667	0	0	3.44
1995 Hickory	A CWS	18	18	1	0	114.2	474	83	48	34	9	3	3	8	46	0	115	5	2	8	3	.273	1	0	2.67
South Bend	A CWS	9	9	0	0	53.2	224	46	25	21	3	1	0	3	27	0	48	1	2	2	4	.333	0	0	3.52
1996 Pr William	A+ CWS	25	25	1	0	144	609	129	73	54	12	8	11	6	62	3	148	3	2	6	10	.375	0	0	3.38
1997 Birmingham	AA CWS	27	26	3	0	158.2	681	136	72	64	14	3	6	14	80	0	126	7	0	13	5	.722	1	0	3.63
1998 Calgary	AAA CWS	28	28	2	0	163.2	728	182	100	92	25	3	6	10	74	0	147	5	1	9	10	.474	0	0	5.06
1999 Reading	AA Phi	26	9	0	7	83.1	369	90	53	44	7	3	6	8	32	1	55	1	3	3	5	.375	0	3	4.75
2000 Round Rock	AA Hou	38	3	0	6	87.1	374	84	45	41	10	2	4	4	48	0	83	4	0	4	2	.667	0	2	4.23
7 Min. YEARS		183	127	7	15	855	3659	789	433	367	83	24	36	56	386	4	775	27	12	42	46	.477	2	5	3.86

Maximo Heredia

Pitches: Right **Bats:** Right **Pos:** RP-9   **Ht:** 6'0" **Wt:** 183 **Born:** 9/27/76 **Age:** 24

Year Team	Lg Org	G	GS	CG	GF	IP	BFP	H	R	ER	HR	SH	SF	HB	TBB	IBB	SO	WP	Bk	W	L	Pct.	ShO	Sv	ERA
1996 Orioles	R Bal	17	0	0	7	34.1	143	22	15	11	1	1	0	4	12	0	25	2	0	3	1	.750	0	4	2.88
1997 Delmarva	A Bal	37	6	0	13	114	441	97	29	27	4	3	3	0	20	0	73	2	0	10	5	.667	0	1	2.13
1998 Bowie	AA Bal	5	4	0	0	13	56	18	9	9	2	0	0	1	2	0	7	0	0	1	1	.500	0	0	6.23
Frederick	A+ Bal	29	3	0	8	64	279	71	44	35	8	5	3	2	19	3	36	3	0	1	3	.250	0	3	4.92
1999 Bowie	AA Bal	50	0	0	17	76.1	341	80	42	36	12	1	1	5	33	4	56	3	1	6	4	.600	0	0	4.24
2000 Bowie	AA Bal	9	0	0	4	15.2	72	19	6	4	2	1	0	0	6	0	12	1	0	0	2	.000	0	0	2.30
5 Min. YEARS		147	13	0	49	317.1	1332	307	145	122	29	11	7	12	92	7	209	11	1	21	16	.568	0	8	3.46

Adrian Hernandez

Pitches: Right **Bats:** Right **Pos:** SP-12   **Ht:** 6'1" **Wt:** 180 **Born:** 3/2/75 **Age:** 26

Year Team	Lg Org	G	GS	CG	GF	IP	BFP	H	R	ER	HR	SH	SF	HB	TBB	IBB	SO	WP	Bk	W	L	Pct.	ShO	Sv	ERA
2000 Tampa	A+ NYY	1	1	0	0	6.2	24	3	1	1	0	0	0	0	1	0	13	1	0	1	0	1.000	0	0	1.35
Norwich	AA NYY	6	6	1	0	35.2	159	34	17	16	1	0	1	3	18	0	44	2	2	5	1	.833	0	0	4.04
Columbus	AAA NYY	5	5	2	0	30.2	134	24	18	15	2	1	2	3	18	0	29	2	2	2	1	.667	1	0	4.40
1 Min. YEARS		12	12	3	0	73	317	61	36	32	3	1	3	6	37	0	86	5	4	8	2	.800	1	0	3.95

Fernando Hernandez

Pitches: Right **Bats:** Right **Pos:** RP-50; SP-1   **Ht:** 6'2" **Wt:** 185 **Born:** 6/16/71 **Age:** 30

Year Team	Lg Org	G	GS	CG	GF	IP	BFP	H	R	ER	HR	SH	SF	HB	TBB	IBB	SO	WP	Bk	W	L	Pct.	ShO	Sv	ERA
1990 Indians	R Cle	11	11	2	0	69.2	289	61	36	31	3	2	2	1	30	0	43	2	7	4	4	.500	0	0	4.00
1991 Burlington	R+ Cle	14	13	0	1	77	326	74	33	25	4	2	0	7	19	0	86	12	1	4	4	.500	0	0	2.92
1992 Columbus	A Cle	11	11	1	0	68.2	268	42	16	12	4	1	0	6	33	1	70	4	1	4	5	.444	1	0	1.57
Kinston	A+ Cle	8	8	1	0	41.2	177	36	23	21	2	3	3	1	22	0	32	3	0	1	3	.250	0	0	4.54
1993 Kinston	A+ Cle	8	8	0	0	51	200	34	15	10	1	2	1	2	18	0	53	1	0	2	3	.400	0	0	1.76
Canton-Akrn	AA Cle	2	2	0	0	7.2	40	14	11	10	1	0	1	0	5	0	6	0	0	0	1	.000	0	0	11.74
Rancho Cuca	A+ SD	17	17	1	0	99.2	441	90	54	46	8	3	4	2	67	0	121	4	1	7	5	.583	0	0	4.15
1994 Wichita	AA SD	23	23	1	0	131.1	595	124	82	70	12	8	9	10	77	6	95	8	0	7	9	.438	1	0	4.80
1995 Las Vegas	AAA SD	8	8	0	0	37.2	186	43	32	32	3	0	2	3	31	3	40	4	0	1	6	.143	0	0	7.65
Memphis	AA SD	12	12	0	0	66.1	303	72	46	38	4	0	0	3	42	1	74	8	1	4	6	.400	0	0	5.16
1996 Memphis	AA SD	27	27	0	0	147.1	655	128	83	76	8	3	8	8	85	4	161	11	1	11	10	.524	0	0	4.64
1997 Toledo	AAA Det	55	1	0	18	76.2	350	71	44	35	5	4	2	1	51	1	98	1	1	6	5	.545	0	0	4.11
1998 Tucson	AAA Ari	3	2	0	0	10	55	23	17	17	5	1	1	0	13	2	13	2	0	0	1	.000	0	0	15.30
1999 Tucson	AAA Ari	5	1	0	1	16	75	22	16	15	3	1	0	1	4	0	14	0	0	0	2	.000	0	0	8.44
2000 Round Rock	AA Hou	15	0	0	6	30	123	19	12	11	1	2	2	1	15	2	43	3	0	4	1	.800	0	2	3.30
New Orleans	AAA Hou	36	1	0	13	60.2	257	41	28	22	5	2	0	3	33	4	88	4	0	3	3	.500	0	3	3.26
1997 Detroit	AL	2	0	0	0	1.1	13	5	6	6	0	0	0	1	3	1	2	0	0	0	0	—	0	0	40.50
11 Min. YEARS		255	145	6	39	991.1	4340	894	548	471	69	34	35	50	533	22	1039	67	13	58	68	.460	2	9	4.28

Michel Hernandez

Bats: Right **Throws:** Right **Pos:** C-96   **Ht:** 6'0" **Wt:** 211 **Born:** 8/12/78 **Age:** 22

Year Team	Lg Org	G	AB	H	2B	3B	HR	TB	R	RBI	TBB	IBB	SO	HBP	SH	SF	SB	CS	SB%	GDP	Avg	OBP	SLG
1998 Oneonta	A- NYY	61	205	52	8	2	0	64	29	24	20	0	19	0	1	1	4	4	.50	10	.254	.319	.312
1999 Tampa	A+ NYY	82	281	69	10	1	2	87	26	23	18	0	49	3	3	2	2	2	.50	8	.246	.296	.310
2000 Norwich	AA NYY	21	66	14	2	0	0	16	7	4	4	0	13	0	2	1	1	0	1.00	1	.212	.254	.242
Tampa	A+ NYY	75	231	51	12	0	1	66	17	28	29	0	23	3	4	3	3	4	.43	4	.221	.312	.286
3 Min. YEARS		239	783	186	32	3	3	233	79	79	71	0	104	6	10	7	10	10	.50	23	.238	.303	.298

Junior Herndon

Pitches: Right **Bats:** Right **Pos:** SP-26   **Ht:** 6'1" **Wt:** 190 **Born:** 9/11/78 **Age:** 22

Year Team	Lg Org	G	GS	CG	GF	IP	BFP	H	R	ER	HR	SH	SF	HB	TBB	IBB	SO	WP	Bk	W	L	Pct.	ShO	Sv	ERA
1997 Padres	R SD	14	14	0	0	77.1	348	80	51	38	2	3	3	5	32	0	65	6	2	3	2	.600	0	0	4.42
Idaho Falls	R+ SD	1	1	0	0	5	20	5	0	0	0	0	0	0	1	0	3	0	0	0	0	—	0	0	0.00
1998 Clinton	A SD	21	21	3	0	132.1	543	119	59	44	3	4	5	8	34	0	101	2	0	10	8	.556	1	0	2.99
Rancho Cuca	A+ SD	6	6	0	0	39.2	165	37	18	15	5	2	2	2	13	0	29	1	0	3	2	.600	0	0	3.40
1999 Mobile	AA SD	26	26	2	0	163	706	172	96	85	24	9	1	8	52	3	87	10	0	10	9	.526	2	0	4.69
2000 Las Vegas	AAA SD	26	26	3	0	135	610	151	90	77	13	5	2	4	65	2	75	5	0	10	11	.476	0	0	5.13
4 Min. YEARS		94	94	8	0	552.1	2392	564	314	259	47	23	13	27	197	5	360	24	2	36	32	.529	3	0	4.22

Alex Herrera

Pitches: Left **Bats:** Left **Pos:** RP-39   **Ht:** 5'11" **Wt:** 175 **Born:** 11/5/79 **Age:** 21

Year Team	Lg Org	G	GS	CG	GF	IP	BFP	H	R	ER	HR	SH	SF	HB	TBB	IBB	SO	WP	Bk	W	L	Pct.	ShO	Sv	ERA
2000 Columbus	A Cle	20	0	0	2	42	186	41	25	16	1	3	3	3	21	1	41	2	1	4	3	.571	0	0	3.43
Kinston	A+ Cle	17	0	0	6	31	138	28	11	8	1	0	1	1	19	0	40	3	1	0	1	.000	0	1	2.32
Akron	AA Cle	2	0	0	1	1.1	6	2	1	0	0	1	0	0	1	0	1	0	0	0	0	—	0	0	0.00
1 Min. YEARS		39	0	0	9	74.1	330	71	37	24	2	4	4	4	41	1	82	5	2	4	4	.500	0	1	2.91

Jose Herrera

Bats: Left   **Throws:** Left   **Pos:** OF-124; DH-6; PH-2   **Ht:** 6'0"   **Wt:** 165   **Born:** 8/30/72   **Age:** 28

Year Team	Lg Org	G	AB	H	2B	3B	HR	TB	R	RBI	TBB	IBB	SO	HBP	SH	SF	SB	CS	SB%	GDP	Avg	OBP	SLG
1991 Medcine Hat	R+ Tor	40	143	35	5	1	1	45	21	11	6	1	38	3	1	0	6	7	.46	0	.245	.289	.315
St.Cathrnes	A- Tor	3	9	3	1	0	0	4	3	2	1	0	2	1	0	0	0	1	.00	0	.333	.455	.444
1992 Medcine Hat	R+ Tor	72	265	72	9	2	0	85	45	21	32	1	62	6	7	0	32	8	.80	4	.272	.363	.321
1993 Hagerstown	A Tor	95	388	123	22	5	5	170	60	42	26	1	63	7	5	4	36	20	.64	3	.317	.367	.438
Madison	A Oak	4	14	3	0	0	0	3	1	0	0	0	6	0	1	0	1	1	.50	0	.214	.214	.214
1994 Modesto	A+ Oak	103	370	106	20	3	11	165	59	56	38	3	76	10	5	6	21	12	.64	5	.286	.363	.446
1995 Huntsville	AA Oak	92	358	101	11	4	6	138	37	45	27	2	58	2	0	2	9	8	.53	8	.282	.334	.385
1996 Huntsville	AA Oak	23	84	24	4	0	1	31	18	7	14	1	15	0	0	2	3	2	.60	2	.286	.380	.369
1997 Edmonton	AAA Oak	122	421	125	21	2	4	162	64	41	42	2	64	1	7	2	7	5	.58	12	.297	.361	.385
1998 Syracuse	AAA Tor	118	473	129	21	6	12	198	72	40	32	1	60	1	6	4	27	12	.69	11	.273	.318	.419
1999 Rochester	AAA Bal	39	127	26	7	1	2	41	11	16	2	0	20	0	2	1	3	1	.75	4	.205	.215	.323
2000 Rochester	AAA Bal	132	552	163	35	7	4	224	79	54	37	1	73	4	3	3	12	8	.60	11	.295	.342	.406
1995 Oakland	AL	33	70	17	1	2	0	22	9	2	6	0	11	0	0	1	1	3	.25	1	.243	.299	.314
1996 Oakland	AL	108	320	86	15	1	6	121	44	30	20	1	59	3	3	0	8	2	.80	5	.269	.318	.378
10 Min. YEARS		843	3204	910	156	31	46	1266	470	335	257	13	537	35	37	24	157	85	.65	60	.284	.341	.395
2 Maj. YEARS		141	390	103	16	3	6	143	53	32	26	1	70	3	3	1	9	5	.64	6	.264	.314	.367

Mike Hessman

Bats: Right   **Throws:** Right   **Pos:** 3B-123; PH-5   **Ht:** 6'5"   **Wt:** 215   **Born:** 3/5/78   **Age:** 23

Year Team	Lg Org	G	AB	H	2B	3B	HR	TB	R	RBI	TBB	IBB	SO	HBP	SH	SF	SB	CS	SB%	GDP	Avg	OBP	SLG
1996 Braves	R Atl	53	190	41	10	1	1	56	13	15	12	1	41	4	4	0	1	1	.50	0	.216	.277	.295
1997 Macon	A Atl	122	459	108	25	0	21	196	69	74	41	0	167	6	0	2	0	2	.00	6	.235	.305	.427
1998 Danville	A+ Atl	118	445	89	21	0	20	170	47	63	30	0	172	6	0	2	3	3	.50	6	.200	.259	.382
1999 Myrtle Bch	A+ Atl	103	365	90	25	0	23	184	62	54	47	3	135	11	0	3	0	3	.00	3	.247	.347	.504
2000 Greenville	AA Atl	127	437	80	23	1	19	162	52	50	37	0	178	8	0	2	3	1	.75	9	.183	.258	.371
5 Min. YEARS		523	1896	408	104	2	84	768	243	256	167	4	693	35	4	9	7	10	.41	24	.215	.290	.405

Phil Hiatt

Bats: Right   **Throws:** Right   **Pos:** 1B-118; OF-9; 3B-7; PH-4; DH-3; P-1   **Ht:** 6'3"   **Wt:** 200   **Born:** 5/1/69   **Age:** 32

Year Team	Lg Org	G	AB	H	2B	3B	HR	TB	R	RBI	TBB	IBB	SO	HBP	SH	SF	SB	CS	SB%	GDP	Avg	OBP	SLG
1990 Eugene	A- KC	73	289	85	18	5	2	119	33	44	17	1	69	1	1	4	15	4	.79	1	.294	.331	.412
1991 Baseball Cy	A+ KC	81	315	94	21	6	5	142	41	33	22	4	70	3	1	2	28	14	.67	8	.298	.348	.451
Memphis	AA KC	56	206	47	7	1	6	74	29	33	9	1	63	3	0	6	6	1	.86	3	.228	.263	.359
1992 Memphis	AA KC	129	487	119	20	5	27	230	71	83	25	1	157	5	1	3	5	10	.33	11	.244	.287	.472
Omaha	AAA KC	5	14	3	0	0	2	9	3	4	2	0	3	0	0	0	1	0	1.00	0	.214	.313	.643
1993 Omaha	AAA KC	12	51	12	2	0	3	23	8	10	4	0	20	1	0	0	0	0	—	0	.235	.304	.451
1994 Omaha	AAA KC	6	22	4	1	0	1	8	2	2	0	0	4	1	0	0	1	0	1.00	2	.182	.217	.364
Memphis	AA KC	108	400	120	26	4	17	205	57	66	40	4	116	13	2	2	12	8	.60	4	.300	.380	.513
1995 Omaha	AAA KC	20	76	12	5	0	2	23	7	8	2	0	25	0	0	1	0	0	—	0	.158	.177	.303
1996 Toledo	AAA Det	142	555	145	27	3	42	304	99	119	50	3	180	2	0	4	17	6	.74	13	.261	.322	.548
1998 Buffalo	AAA Cle	119	453	112	19	0	31	224	81	74	41	1	146	4	2	3	4	1	.80	16	.247	.313	.494
1999 Indianapols	AAA Cin	78	311	74	11	0	18	139	46	54	30	0	103	2	0	3	0	0	—	3	.238	.306	.447
2000 Colo Sprngs	AAA Col	136	507	157	36	1	36	303	106	109	63	1	149	5	0	9	14	2	.88	9	.310	.385	.598
1993 Kansas City	AL	81	238	52	12	1	7	87	30	36	16	0	82	7	0	2	6	3	.67	8	.218	.285	.366
1995 Kansas City	AL	52	113	23	6	0	4	41	11	12	9	0	37	0	0	2	1	0	1.00	3	.204	.262	.363
1996 Detroit	AL	7	21	4	1	0	0	6	3	1	2	0	11	0	0	0	0	0	—	0	.190	.261	.286
10 Min. YEARS		965	3686	984	193	25	192	1803	583	639	305	16	1105	40	8	37	103	46	.69	75	.267	.327	.489
3 Maj. YEARS		140	372	79	18	2	11	134	44	49	27	0	130	7	2	2	7	3	.70	12	.212	.277	.360

Terrance Hill

Pitches: Left   **Bats:** Left   **Pos:** RP-52   **Ht:** 5'10"   **Wt:** 179   **Born:** 10/17/75   **Age:** 25

Year Team	Lg Org	G	GS	CG	GF	IP	BFP	H	R	ER	HR	SH	SF	HB	TBB	IBB	SO	WP	Bk	W	L	Pct.	ShO	Sv	ERA
1998 Lowell	A- Bos	19	7	0	6	63	282	60	28	14	2	0	2	2	33	3	61	6	0	0	4	.000	0	0	2.00
1999 Augusta	A Bos	53	0	0	15	92.1	383	77	30	28	6	5	3	3	25	2	95	11	0	3	6	.333	0	1	2.73
2000 Sarasota	A+ Bos	34	0	0	13	60.1	246	50	20	20	3	2	2	5	18	3	54	1	0	4	0	1.000	0	2	2.98
Trenton	AA Bos	18	0	0	9	24.2	112	25	15	12	1	1	0	3	13	3	28	2	0	2	3	.400	0	1	4.38
3 Min. YEARS		124	7	0	43	240.1	1023	212	93	74	12	8	7	13	89	11	238	20	0	9	13	.409	0	4	2.77

Shea Hillenbrand

Bats: Right   **Throws:** Right   **Pos:** 1B-65; 3B-35; DH-33; PH-2   **Ht:** 6'1"   **Wt:** 200   **Born:** 7/27/75   **Age:** 25

Year Team	Lg Org	G	AB	H	2B	3B	HR	TB	R	RBI	TBB	IBB	SO	HBP	SH	SF	SB	CS	SB%	GDP	Avg	OBP	SLG
1996 Lowell	A- Bos	72	279	88	18	2	1	116	33	38	18	1	32	8	0	2	4	3	.57	6	.315	.371	.416
1997 Michigan	A Bos	64	224	65	13	3	3	93	28	39	9	1	20	1	0	4	1	3	.25	2	.290	.315	.415
Sarasota	A+ Bos	57	220	65	12	0	2	83	25	28	7	1	29	2	1	2	9	8	.53	4	.295	.320	.377
1998 Michigan	A Bos	129	498	174	33	4	19	272	80	92	19	2	49	10	1	3	13	7	.65	11	.349	.383	.546
1999 Trenton	AA Bos	69	282	73	15	0	7	109	41	36	14	3	27	3	0	3	6	5	.55	6	.259	.298	.387
2000 Trenton	AA Bos	135	529	171	35	3	11	245	77	79	19	0	39	8	0	2	3	3	.50	15	.323	.355	.463
5 Min. YEARS		526	2032	636	126	12	44	918	284	312	86	8	196	32	2	16	36	29	.55	44	.313	.348	.452

127

Eric Hillman

Pitches: Left **Bats:** Left **Pos:** SP-1 **Ht:** 6'10" **Wt:** 225 **Born:** 4/27/66 **Age:** 35

Year Team	Lg Org	G	GS	CG	GF	IP	BFP	H	R	ER	HR	SH	SF	HB	TBB	IBB	SO	WP	Bk	W	L	Pct.	ShO	Sv	ERA
1987 Little Fall	A- NYM	13	13	2	0	79	346	84	44	37	4	2	5	3	30	2	80	8	1	6	4	.600	1	0	4.22
1988 Columbia	A NYM	17	13	0	4	73	320	54	45	32	2	2	2	6	43	0	60	5	3	1	6	.143	0	1	3.95
1989 Columbia	A NYM	9	7	0	2	33.2	151	28	17	7	1	1	2	4	21	0	33	1	0	2	1	.667	0	1	1.87
St. Lucie	A+ NYM	19	14	1	1	88.1	404	96	59	54	3	3	2	3	53	0	67	15	1	6	6	.500	0	0	5.50
1990 St. Lucie	A+ NYM	4	3	0	0	27	99	15	2	2	0	1	0	1	8	0	23	3	0	2	0	1.000	0	0	0.67
Jackson	AA NYM	15	15	0	0	89.1	386	93	42	39	2	1	1	4	30	1	61	7	2	6	5	.545	0	0	3.93
1991 Tidewater	AAA NYM	27	27	2	0	161.2	710	184	89	72	9	15	6	10	58	0	91	12	3	5	12	.294	0	0	4.01
1992 Tidewater	AAA NYM	34	9	0	7	91.1	380	93	39	37	6	2	4	2	27	1	49	6	2	9	2	.818	0	0	3.65
1993 Norfolk	AAA NYM	10	9	3	1	61	238	52	18	15	2	2	2	2	12	1	27	2	0	6	2	.750	1	0	2.21
1994 Norfolk	AAA NYM	16	16	6	0	106	421	103	39	34	12	3	2	3	19	0	55	5	0	10	1	.909	1	0	2.89
2000 Round Rock	AA Hou	1	1	0	0	5	20	3	0	0	0	0	0	0	2	0	4	0	0	1	0	1.000	0	0	0.00
1992 New York	NL	11	8	0	2	52.1	227	67	31	31	9	3	1	2	10	2	16	1	0	2	2	.500	0	0	5.33
1993 New York	NL	27	22	3	1	145	627	173	83	64	12	10	10	4	24	2	60	0	1	2	9	.182	1	0	3.97
1994 New York	NL	11	6	0	0	34.2	156	45	30	30	9	2	1	2	11	3	20	1	1	0	3	.000	0	0	7.79
9 Min. YEARS		165	127	14	15	815.1	3475	805	394	329	41	32	26	38	303	5	550	64	12	54	39	.581	3	2	3.63
3 Maj. YEARS		49	36	3	3	232	1010	285	144	125	30	15	12	8	45	7	96	2	2	4	14	.222	1	0	4.85

Eric Hinske

Bats: Left **Throws:** Right **Pos:** 3B-115; OF-6; 1B-6; PH-5; DH-2; PR-1 **Ht:** 6'2" **Wt:** 225 **Born:** 8/5/77 **Age:** 23

Year Team	Lg Org	G	AB	H	2B	3B	HR	TB	R	RBI	TBB	IBB	SO	HBP	SH	SF	SB	CS	SB%	GDP	Avg	OBP	SLG
1998 Williamsprt	A- ChC	68	248	74	20	0	9	121	46	57	35	3	61	2	0	4	19	3	.86	2	.298	.384	.488
Rockford	A ChC	6	20	9	4	0	1	16	8	4	5	0	6	0	0	1	1	0	1.00	0	.450	.538	.800
1999 Daytona	A+ ChC	130	445	132	28	6	19	229	76	79	62	7	90	5	1	5	16	10	.62	5	.297	.385	.515
Iowa	AAA ChC	4	15	4	0	1	1	9	3	2	1	0	4	0	0	0	0	0	—	0	.267	.313	.600
2000 West Tenn	AA ChC	131	436	113	21	9	20	212	76	73	78	3	133	3	0	3	14	5	.74	7	.259	.373	.486
3 Min. YEARS		339	1164	332	73	16	50	587	209	215	181	13	294	10	1	13	50	18	.74	14	.285	.382	.504

Kevin Hite

Pitches: Right **Bats:** Right **Pos:** RP-27 **Ht:** 6'1" **Wt:** 155 **Born:** 7/23/74 **Age:** 26

Year Team	Lg Org	G	GS	CG	GF	IP	BFP	H	R	ER	HR	SH	SF	HB	TBB	IBB	SO	WP	Bk	W	L	Pct.	ShO	Sv	ERA
1996 Padres	R SD	13	12	2	0	77	326	86	44	31	1	3	0	1	15	0	65	4	2	5	5	.500	1	0	3.62
1997 Clinton	A SD	38	4	1	17	87	354	86	38	32	6	0	4	1	11	0	85	2	1	5	5	.500	0	1	3.31
1998 Rancho Cuca	A+ SD	30	0	0	25	41.2	166	36	16	14	2	0	3	0	8	1	45	4	0	4	0	1.000	0	12	3.02
1999 Rancho Cuca	A+ SD	7	0	0	7	6.2	27	6	3	3	0	1	0	0	1	0	8	0	0	0	1	.000	0	4	4.05
Mobile	AA SD	51	0	0	39	58.1	256	71	30	28	6	1	4	3	17	4	52	2	1	2	4	.333	0	15	4.32
2000 Mobile	AA SD	27	0	0	7	37.1	162	38	19	16	6	2	2	1	14	2	33	0	0	0	1	.000	0	1	3.86
5 Min. YEARS		166	16	3	95	308	1291	323	150	124	21	7	13	6	66	7	288	12	4	16	16	.500	1	33	3.62

Wes Hoane

Pitches: Right **Bats:** Right **Pos:** RP-16 **Ht:** 6'4" **Wt:** 230 **Born:** 9/6/77 **Age:** 23

Year Team	Lg Org	G	GS	CG	GF	IP	BFP	H	R	ER	HR	SH	SF	HB	TBB	IBB	SO	WP	Bk	W	L	Pct.	ShO	Sv	ERA
2000 Mariners	R Sea	15	0	0	10	25.1	93	17	8	7	0	1	1	0	4	0	24	2	0	1	0	1.000	0	4	2.49
Tacoma	AAA Sea	1	0	0	1	1	7	3	2	2	0	0	0	0	1	0	2	0	0	0	0	—	0	0	18.00
1 Min. YEARS		16	0	0	11	26.1	100	20	10	9	0	1	1	0	5	0	26	2	0	1	0	1.000	0	4	3.08

Scott Hodges

Bats: Left **Throws:** Right **Pos:** 3B-111; DH-6; 1B-1; PH-1; PR-1 **Ht:** 6'0" **Wt:** 190 **Born:** 12/26/78 **Age:** 22

Year Team	Lg Org	G	AB	H	2B	3B	HR	TB	R	RBI	TBB	IBB	SO	HBP	SH	SF	SB	CS	SB%	GDP	Avg	OBP	SLG
1997 Expos	R Mon	57	198	47	13	2	2	70	27	23	24	1	48	2	1	3	2	2	.50	2	.237	.322	.354
1998 Vermont	A- Mon	67	266	74	13	3	3	102	35	35	11	1	59	1	2	4	8	1	.89	3	.278	.305	.383
1999 Cape Fear	A Mon	127	449	116	31	2	8	175	62	59	45	2	105	3	1	9	8	15	.35	11	.258	.324	.390
2000 Jupiter	A+ Mon	111	422	129	32	1	14	205	75	83	49	6	66	3	2	11	8	2	.80	8	.306	.373	.486
Harrisburg	AA Mon	6	17	3	0	0	1	6	2	5	2	2	4	0	0	2	1	0	1.00	0	.176	.238	.353
4 Min. YEARS		368	1352	369	89	8	28	558	201	205	131	12	282	9	6	29	27	20	.57	24	.273	.335	.413

Aaron Holbert

Bats: Right **Throws:** Right **Pos:** SS-68; 3B-26; 2B-9; DH-7; PR-4 **Ht:** 6'0" **Wt:** 160 **Born:** 1/9/73 **Age:** 28

Year Team	Lg Org	G	AB	H	2B	3B	HR	TB	R	RBI	TBB	IBB	SO	HBP	SH	SF	SB	CS	SB%	GDP	Avg	OBP	SLG
1990 Johnson Cty	R+ StL	54	176	30	4	1	1	39	27	18	24	1	33	3	1	1	3	5	.38	2	.170	.279	.222
1991 Springfield	A StL	59	215	48	5	1	1	58	22	24	15	0	26	6	1	2	5	8	.38	3	.223	.290	.270
1992 Savannah	A StL	119	438	117	17	4	1	145	53	34	40	0	57	8	6	3	62	25	.71	4	.267	.337	.331
1993 St. Pete	A+ StL	121	457	121	18	3	2	151	60	31	28	2	61	4	15	1	45	22	.67	5	.265	.312	.330
1994 Cardinals	R StL	5	12	2	0	0	0	2	3	0	2	0	2	0	0	0	2	0	1.00	0	.167	.286	.167
Arkansas	AA StL	59	233	69	10	6	2	97	41	19	14	0	25	2	4	1	9	7	.56	5	.296	.340	.416
1995 Louisville	AAA StL	112	401	103	16	4	9	154	57	40	20	1	60	1	5	3	14	6	.70	10	.257	.297	.384
1996 Louisville	AAA StL	112	436	115	16	6	4	155	54	32	21	0	61	2	5	4	20	14	.59	8	.264	.298	.356
1997 Louisville	AAA StL	93	314	80	14	3	4	112	32	32	15	1	56	2	3	4	9	5	.64	2	.255	.290	.357
1998 Orlando	AA Sea	68	251	72	13	5	3	104	46	34	22	0	41	5	4	1	10	14	.42	3	.287	.355	.414
Tacoma	AAA Sea	56	229	72	12	0	9	111	38	31	12	0	40	3	2	1	6	6	.50	3	.314	.355	.485
1999 Durham	AAA TB	100	347	108	18	4	12	170	77	56	25	0	56	6	8	5	14	5	.74	4	.311	.361	.490

128

Year Team	Lg Org	G	AB	H	2B	3B	HR	TB	R	RBI	TBB	IBB	SO	HBP	SH	SF	SB	CS	SB%	GDP	Avg	OBP	SLG
2000 Pawtucket	AAA Bos	80	294	74	13	2	3	100	38	23	15	0	54	4	1	0	8	6	.57	4	.252	.297	.340
Calgary	AAA Fla	29	104	29	5	1	4	48	18	18	10	0	12	1	0	0	3	4	.43	2	.279	.348	.462
1996 St. Louis	NL	1	3	0	0	0	0	0	0	0	0	0	0	0	0	0	0	0	—	0	.000	.000	.000
11 Min. YEARS		1067	3907	1040	161	40	55	1446	566	392	263	5	584	50	53	28	210	127	.62	63	.266	.319	.370

Damon Hollins

Bats: Right **Throws:** Left **Pos:** OF-82; PH-8; PR-3; DH-1   **Ht:** 5'11" **Wt:** 180 **Born:** 6/12/74 **Age:** 27

Year Team	Lg Org	G	AB	H	2B	3B	HR	TB	R	RBI	TBB	IBB	SO	HBP	SH	SF	SB	CS	SB%	GDP	Avg	OBP	SLG
1992 Braves	R Atl	49	179	41	12	1	1	58	35	15	30	0	22	2	2	0	15	2	.88	3	.229	.346	.324
1993 Danville	R+ Atl	62	240	77	15	2	7	117	37	51	19	0	30	1	0	3	10	2	.83	5	.321	.369	.488
1994 Durham	A+ Atl	131	485	131	28	0	23	228	76	88	45	0	115	4	2	3	12	7	.63	9	.270	.335	.470
1995 Greenville	AA Atl	129	466	115	26	2	18	199	64	77	44	6	120	4	1	6	6	6	.50	7	.247	.313	.427
1996 Richmond	AAA Atl	42	146	29	9	0	0	38	16	8	16	1	37	0	1	0	2	3	.40	2	.199	.278	.260
1997 Richmond	AAA Atl	134	498	132	31	3	20	229	73	63	45	4	84	3	6	1	7	2	.78	18	.265	.329	.460
1998 Richmond	AAA Atl	119	436	115	26	3	13	186	61	48	45	2	85	0	1	4	10	2	.83	16	.264	.330	.427
1999 Indianapols	AAA Cin	106	328	86	19	0	9	132	58	43	31	1	44	1	1	0	11	2	.85	13	.262	.328	.402
2000 Indianapols	AAA Mil	87	287	82	16	3	2	110	33	32	21	0	35	1	0	2	5	3	.63	5	.286	.334	.383
1998 Atlanta	NL	3	6	1	0	0	0	1	0	0	0	0	1	0	0	0	0	0	—	0	.167	.167	.167
Los Angeles	NL	5	9	2	0	0	0	2	1	2	0	0	2	0	0	0	1	0	1.00	0	.222	.222	.222
9 Min. YEARS		859	3065	808	182	14	93	1297	453	425	296	14	572	16	13	19	78	29	.73	78	.264	.330	.423

Dave Hollins

Bats: Both **Throws:** Right **Pos:** DH-19; 3B-14; 1B-3   **Ht:** 6'1" **Wt:** 232 **Born:** 5/25/66 **Age:** 35

Year Team	Lg Org	G	AB	H	2B	3B	HR	TB	R	RBI	TBB	IBB	SO	HBP	SH	SF	SB	CS	SB%	GDP	Avg	OBP	SLG
1987 Spokane	A- SD	75	278	86	14	4	2	114	52	44	53	7	36	2	3	4	20	5	.80	3	.309	.418	.410
1988 Riverside	A+ SD	139	516	157	32	1	9	218	90	92	82	2	67	1	0	9	13	11	.54	15	.304	.395	.422
1989 Wichita	AA SD	131	459	126	29	4	9	190	69	79	63	4	88	5	1	10	8	3	.73	4	.275	.361	.414
1991 Scranton-WB	AAA Phi	72	229	61	11	6	8	108	37	35	43	3	42	4	0	2	4	1	.80	7	.266	.388	.472
1994 Scranton-WB	AAA Phi	6	19	4	0	0	1	7	6	3	5	0	4	0	0	0	0	0	—	1	.211	.375	.368
1999 Syracuse	AAA Tor	4	15	3	1	0	0	4	2	1	1	0	5	1	0	0	0	0	—	0	.200	.294	.267
Charlotte	AAA CWS	63	199	63	18	0	8	105	49	33	33	2	37	13	0	4	5	1	.83	4	.317	.438	.528
2000 Durham	AAA TB	11	27	5	2	0	1	10	4	3	10	0	6	3	0	0	1	0	1.00	1	.185	.450	.370
Rochester	AAA Bal	20	70	19	2	0	0	21	8	8	9	0	12	1	1	1	1	0	1.00	0	.271	.358	.300
Buffalo	AAA Cle	5	13	1	1	0	0	2	0	2	2	0	6	0	0	0	0	0	—	1	.077	.200	.154
1990 Philadelphia	NL	72	114	21	0	0	5	36	14	15	10	3	28	1	0	0	0	0	—	2	.184	.252	.316
1991 Philadelphia	NL	56	151	45	10	2	6	77	18	21	17	1	26	3	0	1	1	1	.50	2	.298	.378	.510
1992 Philadelphia	NL	156	586	158	28	4	27	275	104	93	76	4	110	19	0	4	9	6	.60	8	.270	.369	.469
1993 Philadelphia	NL	143	543	148	30	4	18	240	104	93	85	5	109	5	0	7	2	3	.40	15	.273	.372	.442
1994 Philadelphia	NL	44	162	36	7	1	4	57	28	26	23	0	32	4	0	3	1	0	1.00	6	.222	.328	.352
1995 Philadelphia	NL	65	205	47	12	2	7	84	46	25	53	4	38	5	0	1	1	1	.50	4	.229	.393	.410
Boston	AL	5	13	2	0	0	0	2	2	1	4	0	7	0	0	0	0	0	—	0	.154	.353	.154
1996 Minnesota	AL	121	422	102	26	0	13	167	71	53	71	5	102	10	0	0	6	4	.60	9	.242	.364	.396
Seattle	AL	28	94	33	3	0	3	45	17	25	13	2	15	3	1	2	0	2	.00	2	.351	.438	.479
1997 Anaheim	AL	149	572	165	29	2	16	246	101	85	62	2	124	8	1	5	16	6	.73	12	.288	.363	.430
1998 Anaheim	AL	101	363	88	16	2	11	141	60	39	44	2	69	7	2	2	11	3	.79	5	.242	.334	.388
1999 Toronto	AL	27	99	22	5	0	2	33	12	6	5	0	22	0	0	0	0	0	—	2	.222	.260	.333
7 Min. YEARS		526	1825	525	110	15	38	779	317	300	301	18	303	30	5	30	52	21	.71	36	.288	.392	.427
10 Maj. YEARS		967	3324	867	166	17	112	1403	577	482	463	28	682	65	4	30	47	26	.64	66	.261	.359	.422

Heath Honeycutt

Bats: Right **Throws:** Right **Pos:** 3B-60; DH-4; PH-2; PR-1   **Ht:** 6'4" **Wt:** 210 **Born:** 7/30/76 **Age:** 24

Year Team	Lg Org	G	AB	H	2B	3B	HR	TB	R	RBI	TBB	IBB	SO	HBP	SH	SF	SB	CS	SB%	GDP	Avg	OBP	SLG
1998 Utica	A- Fla	68	245	59	8	2	7	92	40	33	25	2	67	6	0	0	11	2	.85	4	.241	.326	.376
1999 Brevard Cty	A+ Fla	103	376	107	18	8	5	156	58	50	25	1	78	9	0	3	6	1	.86	10	.285	.341	.415
2000 Portland	AA Fla	50	170	31	4	1	2	43	19	15	12	0	58	4	0	3	3	0	1.00	3	.182	.249	.253
Brevard Cty	A+ Fla	16	54	14	2	0	1	19	8	6	6	1	13	1	0	0	1	0	1.00	3	.259	.344	.352
3 Min. YEARS		237	845	211	32	11	15	310	125	101	68	4	216	20	0	6	21	3	.88	20	.250	.318	.367

Jay Hood

Bats: Right **Throws:** Right **Pos:** SS-97   **Ht:** 6'0" **Wt:** 185 **Born:** 3/8/77 **Age:** 24

Year Team	Lg Org	G	AB	H	2B	3B	HR	TB	R	RBI	TBB	IBB	SO	HBP	SH	SF	SB	CS	SB%	GDP	Avg	OBP	SLG
1998 Boise	A- Ana	41	132	26	6	0	3	41	20	19	23	0	22	5	0	2	1	1	.50	2	.197	.333	.311
1999 Lk Elsinore	A+ Ana	102	374	88	14	5	3	121	48	43	24	0	81	2	5	6	8	9	.47	7	.235	.281	.324
2000 Lk Elsinore	A+ Ana	26	103	19	3	0	0	22	9	9	4	0	25	2	1	1	1	2	.33	0	.184	.227	.214
Erie	AA Ana	71	240	51	16	0	4	79	25	29	16	0	50	2	1	0	3	0	1.00	6	.213	.267	.329
3 Min. YEARS		240	849	184	39	5	10	263	102	100	67	0	178	11	7	9	13	12	.52	15	.217	.280	.310

Dave Hooten

Pitches: Right **Bats:** Right **Pos:** RP-48; SP-2   **Ht:** 6'0" **Wt:** 182 **Born:** 5/8/75 **Age:** 26

		HOW MUCH HE PITCHED					WHAT HE GAVE UP										THE RESULTS					
Year Team	Lg Org	G	GS	CG	GF	IP	BFP	H	R	ER	HR	SH	SF	HB	TBB	IBB	SO	WP	Bk	W	L	Pct.	ShO	Sv	ERA
1996 Elizabethtn	R+ Min	6	0	0	5	8.1	37	6	4	4	0	0	2	1	5	0	15	0	2	1	0	1.000	0	1	4.32
Fort Wayne	A Min	21	0	0	14	37.1	155	30	11	10	0	2	4	2	13	1	39	1	1	4	1	.800	0	2	2.41
1997 Fort Wayne	A Min	28	27	2	0	165.2	675	134	57	48	5	4	2	9	54	0	138	4	6	11	8	.579	2	0	2.61

129

Year Team	Lg Org	G	GS	CG	GF	IP	BFP	H	R	ER	HR	SH	SF	HB	TBB	IBB	SO	WP	Bk	W	L	Pct.	ShO	Sv	ERA
		HOW MUCH HE PITCHED						**WHAT HE GAVE UP**												**THE RESULTS**					
1998 Fort Myers	A+ Min	28	28	0	0	158.1	714	185	94	79	7	0	10	11	57	0	136	4	0	9	11	.450	0	0	4.49
1999 New Britain	AA Min	52	5	0	17	103.2	450	94	55	41	10	3	6	1	49	2	89	3	0	6	6	.500	0	1	3.56
2000 New Britain	AA Min	37	2	0	8	61.1	264	59	38	36	6	1	4	4	26	1	64	1	0	4	3	.571	0	1	5.28
Salt Lake	AAA Min	13	0	0	4	27.2	112	26	14	12	7	0	0	0	10	0	15	0	0	1	2	.333	0	1	3.90
5 Min. YEARS		185	62	2	48	562.1	2407	534	273	230	35	10	28	28	214	4	496	15	9	36	31	.537	2	6	3.68

Paul Hoover

Bats: Right **Throws:** Right **Pos:** 3B-43; OF-28; C-24; SS-9; 1B-7; 2B-2; PH-1; PR-1   **Ht:** 6'1" **Wt:** 210 **Born:** 4/14/76 **Age:** 25

Year Team	Lg Org	G	AB	H	2B	3B	HR	TB	R	RBI	TBB	IBB	SO	HBP	SH	SF	SB	CS	SB%	GDP	Avg	OBP	SLG
		BATTING															**BASERUNNING**				**PERCENTAGES**		
1997 Princeton	R+ TB	66	251	76	16	4	4	112	55	37	20	0	37	6	3	4	7	4	.64	3	.303	.363	.446
1998 Chston-SC	A TB	40	124	36	10	1	3	57	24	19	22	1	29	5	0	0	2	1	.67	0	.290	.417	.460
Hudson Val	A- TB	73	269	76	20	1	4	110	51	37	39	3	44	11	0	6	26	3	.90	5	.283	.388	.409
1999 St. Pete	A+ TB	118	408	111	13	6	8	160	66	54	54	3	81	16	0	4	23	7	.77	13	.272	.376	.392
2000 Orlando	AA TB	106	360	90	20	4	3	127	54	44	67	2	66	13	1	5	9	8	.53	5	.250	.382	.353
Durham	AAA TB	4	10	3	0	0	0	3	0	0	0	0	5	1	0	0	1	0	1.00	0	.300	.364	.300
4 Min. YEARS		407	1422	392	79	16	22	569	250	191	202	9	262	52	4	19	68	23	.75	26	.276	.381	.400

Shane Hopper

Bats: Right **Throws:** Right **Pos:** 3B-62; OF-24; DH-23; 1B-8; PH-2   **Ht:** 6'1" **Wt:** 205 **Born:** 9/22/75 **Age:** 25

Year Team	Lg Org	G	AB	H	2B	3B	HR	TB	R	RBI	TBB	IBB	SO	HBP	SH	SF	SB	CS	SB%	GDP	Avg	OBP	SLG
		BATTING															**BASERUNNING**				**PERCENTAGES**		
1999 Johnstown	IND	83	328	122	27	3	8	179	65	83	34	1	66	4	0	7	12	1	.92	14	.372	.429	.546
2000 Las Vegas	AAA SD	5	21	8	3	0	0	11	3	5	0	0	5	0	0	0	0	0	—	0	.381	.381	.524
Rancho Cuca	A+ SD	108	447	135	28	7	11	210	77	58	28	1	110	5	1	3	15	11	.58	15	.302	.348	.470
2 Min. YEARS		196	796	265	58	10	19	400	145	146	62	2	181	9	1	10	27	12	.69	29	.333	.383	.503

Joe Horgan

Pitches: Left **Bats:** Left **Pos:** SP-27; RP-1   **Ht:** 6'1" **Wt:** 200 **Born:** 6/7/77 **Age:** 24

Year Team	Lg Org	G	GS	CG	GF	IP	BFP	H	R	ER	HR	SH	SF	HB	TBB	IBB	SO	WP	Bk	W	L	Pct.	ShO	Sv	ERA
		HOW MUCH HE PITCHED						**WHAT HE GAVE UP**												**THE RESULTS**					
1996 Burlington	R+ Cle	23	0	0	18	34.1	157	37	25	16	1	0	0	4	9	0	48	4	0	1	2	.333	0	7	4.19
1997 Watertown	A- Cle	15	4	0	2	38.1	179	48	31	26	4	2	2	1	18	1	31	4	1	0	1	.000	0	0	6.10
Kinston	A+ Cle	4	2	0	0	17.1	83	23	15	14	1	1	0	1	9	1	9	0	0	1	2	.333	0	0	7.27
1998 Columbus	A Cle	22	1	0	9	34	134	19	9	9	3	0	0	0	21	0	27	7	0	2	1	.667	0	0	2.38
1999 Bakersfield	A+ SF	25	19	1	1	117.1	520	129	76	68	18	2	2	10	43	0	101	5	2	6	10	.375	0	0	5.22
2000 San Jose	A+ SF	27	27	1	0	166.1	739	190	104	85	15	5	6	14	66	0	92	14	0	14	10	.583	0	0	4.60
Shreveport	AA SF	1	0	0	1	5.1	20	2	2	2	0	0	0	0	2	1	3	0	0	0	0	—	0	0	3.38
5 Min. YEARS		117	53	2	31	413	1832	448	262	220	42	10	10	30	168	2	311	34	3	24	26	.480	0	7	4.79

Jeff Horn

Bats: Right **Throws:** Right **Pos:** PH-5; C-4; 1B-2; DH-2   **Ht:** 6'1" **Wt:** 213 **Born:** 8/23/70 **Age:** 30

Year Team	Lg Org	G	AB	H	2B	3B	HR	TB	R	RBI	TBB	IBB	SO	HBP	SH	SF	SB	CS	SB%	GDP	Avg	OBP	SLG
		BATTING															**BASERUNNING**				**PERCENTAGES**		
1992 Elizabethtn	R+ Min	41	144	35	6	0	1	44	20	26	25	1	25	4	0	2	2	0	1.00	5	.243	.366	.306
1993 Fort Wayne	A Min	66	200	39	7	0	5	61	19	23	18	0	51	4	1	4	1	2	.33	4	.195	.270	.305
1994 Fort Myers	A+ Min	34	100	28	3	0	0	31	10	9	8	1	11	3	0	1	0	2	.00	6	.280	.348	.310
1995 Salt Lake	AAA Min	3	10	5	1	0	0	6	0	2	0	0	1	0	0	0	0	0	—	0	.500	.500	.600
Fort Myers	A+ Min	66	199	53	5	1	0	60	25	20	38	1	30	4	1	3	2	3	.40	4	.266	.389	.302
1996 Salt Lake	AAA Min	25	83	28	5	0	3	42	14	13	12	1	5	2	2	2	0	1	.00	4	.337	.424	.506
Hardware Cy	AA Min	12	45	12	2	0	0	14	4	3	6	1	7	0	0	0	0	1	.00	0	.267	.353	.311
1997 New Britain	AA Min	56	184	47	10	0	4	69	17	26	19	0	24	7	2	2	2	4	.33	7	.255	.344	.375
Salt Lake	AAA Min	23	78	26	6	0	1	35	16	13	11	0	22	1	0	0	0	0	—	0	.333	.422	.449
1998 Salt Lake	AAA Min	24	72	22	5	0	1	30	14	6	12	0	18	1	2	0	1	2	.33	0	.306	.412	.417
1999 Greenville	AA Atl	66	166	38	6	0	2	50	19	27	16	0	28	4	0	3	0	1	.00	4	.229	.301	.301
2000 Richmond	AAA Atl	13	32	6	3	0	1	12	2	5	3	0	11	1	1	0	0	0	—	0	.188	.278	.375
9 Min. YEARS		429	1313	339	59	1	18	454	160	173	168	5	233	31	9	17	8	16	.33	33	.258	.352	.346

Tyrone Horne

Bats: Left **Throws:** Right **Pos:** DH-50; OF-11; PH-4   **Ht:** 5'10" **Wt:** 185 **Born:** 11/2/70 **Age:** 30

Year Team	Lg Org	G	AB	H	2B	3B	HR	TB	R	RBI	TBB	IBB	SO	HBP	SH	SF	SB	CS	SB%	GDP	Avg	OBP	SLG
		BATTING															**BASERUNNING**				**PERCENTAGES**		
1989 Expos	R Mon	24	68	14	3	2	0	21	7	13	11	0	29	0	0	0	4	4	.50	0	.206	.316	.309
1990 Gate City	R+ Mon	56	202	57	11	2	1	75	26	13	24	1	62	2	2	2	23	8	.74	1	.282	.361	.371
Jamestown	A- Mon	7	23	7	2	1	0	11	1	5	4	0	5	0	0	0	3	0	1.00	1	.304	.407	.478
1991 Sumter	A Mon	118	428	114	20	3	10	170	69	49	42	1	133	2	1	4	23	12	.66	4	.266	.332	.397
1992 Rockford	A Mon	129	480	134	27	4	12	205	71	48	62	5	141	1	2	2	23	13	.64	1	.279	.361	.427
Harrisburg	AA Mon	1	1	1	0	0	0	1	0	0	0	0	0	0	0	0	0	0	—	0	1.000	1.000	1.000
1993 Wst Plm Bch	A+ Mon	82	288	85	19	2	10	138	43	44	40	1	72	0	1	3	11	10	.52	1	.295	.378	.479
Harrisburg	AA Mon	35	128	46	8	1	4	68	22	22	22	0	37	1	1	0	3	2	.60	3	.359	.457	.531
1994 Expos	R Mon	7	29	7	1	0	1	11	3	7	4	0	9	0	0	0	1	0	1.00	0	.241	.333	.379
Harrisburg	AA Mon	90	311	89	15	0	9	131	56	48	50	1	92	1	1	2	11	13	.46	7	.286	.385	.421
1995 Harrisburg	AA Mon	87	294	87	17	4	14	154	59	47	58	2	65	1	3	3	14	8	.64	3	.296	.410	.524
Norwich	AA NYY	46	166	47	16	1	2	71	23	22	26	1	36	0	0	3	4	2	.67	4	.283	.374	.428
1996 Edmonton	AAA Oak	67	204	47	7	2	4	70	28	16	32	1	53	1	0	2	5	3	.63	6	.230	.335	.343
Binghamton	AA NYM	43	125	34	10	0	3	53	17	19	15	4	39	1	0	0	3	0	1.00	4	.272	.355	.424
1997 Kane County	A Fla	133	468	143	24	2	21	234	89	91	104	18	88	3	0	1	18	7	.72	13	.306	.434	.500

Year Team	Lg Org	G	AB	H	2B	3B	HR	TB	R	RBI	TBB	IBB	SO	HBP	SH	SF	SB	CS	SB%	GDP	Avg	OBP	SLG
1998 Arkansas	AA StL	123	443	138	13	3	37	268	94	139	70	7	97	1	0	6	18	7	.72	8	.312	.402	.605
Memphis	AAA StL	3	11	4	1	0	0	5	1	1	1	0	4	0	0	0	0	0	—	0	.364	.417	.455
1999 Reading	AA Phi	80	262	70	13	2	5	102	37	37	43	1	64	0	0	2	13	8	.62	4	.267	.368	.389
2000 Aberdeen	IND —	33	121	42	9	0	3	60	24	22	19	0	20	0	0	1	1	1	.50	5	.347	.433	.496
Norwich	AA NYY	31	99	25	4	0	2	35	11	9	15	1	26	0	0	0	1	1	.50	3	.253	.351	.354
12 Min. YEARS		1195	4151	1191	220	29	138	1883	681	652	642	44	1072	14	11	31	179	99	.64	68	.287	.382	.454

Jim Horner

Bats: Right **Throws:** Right **Pos:** C-62; DH-2; PR-1   **Ht:** 6'0" **Wt:** 210 **Born:** 11/11/73 **Age:** 27

Year Team	Lg Org	G	AB	H	2B	3B	HR	TB	R	RBI	TBB	IBB	SO	HBP	SH	SF	SB	CS	SB%	GDP	Avg	OBP	SLG
1996 Everett	A- Sea	18	60	9	2	0	2	17	6	5	10	1	16	1	0	0	0	0	—	1	.150	.282	.283
1997 Wisconsin	A Sea	47	161	40	10	1	5	67	19	24	17	0	53	5	1	1	0	1	.00	4	.248	.337	.416
Lancaster	A+ Sea	45	163	42	6	0	9	75	26	27	16	0	48	2	0	1	2	0	1.00	4	.258	.330	.460
1998 Orlando	AA Sea	73	247	54	9	1	9	92	29	36	33	0	59	3	1	5	2	1	.67	5	.219	.313	.372
1999 New Haven	AA Sea	76	278	75	17	0	6	110	29	50	17	0	51	4	1	2	1	1	.50	10	.270	.319	.396
2000 New Haven	AA Sea	65	245	59	11	2	9	101	36	33	20	1	42	5	0	2	4	1	.80	7	.241	.309	.412
5 Min. YEARS		324	1154	279	55	4	40	462	145	175	113	2	269	20	3	11	9	4	.69	31	.242	.317	.400

Dwayne Hosey

Bats: Both **Throws:** Right **Pos:** OF-21; DH-20; PH-5   **Ht:** 5'10" **Wt:** 180 **Born:** 3/11/67 **Age:** 34

Year Team	Lg Org	G	AB	H	2B	3B	HR	TB	R	RBI	TBB	IBB	SO	HBP	SH	SF	SB	CS	SB%	GDP	Avg	OBP	SLG
1987 White Sox	R CWS	41	129	36	2	1	1	43	26	10	18	1	22	3	0	2	19	4	.83	1	.279	.375	.333
1988 South Bend	A CWS	95	311	71	11	0	2	88	53	24	28	2	55	5	4	2	36	15	.71	5	.228	.301	.283
Utica	A- CWS	3	7	1	0	0	0	1	0	0	2	0	1	0	0	0	1	0	1.00	0	.143	.333	.143
1989 Madison	A Oak	123	470	115	16	6	11	176	72	51	44	3	82	8	2	3	33	18	.65	9	.245	.319	.374
1990 Modesto	A+ Oak	113	453	133	21	5	16	212	77	61	50	5	70	8	8	2	30	23	.57	2	.294	.372	.468
1991 Huntsville	AA Oak	28	102	25	6	0	1	34	16	7	9	1	15	1	1	1	5	4	.56	1	.245	.310	.333
Stockton	A+ Mil	85	356	97	12	7	15	168	55	62	31	1	58	3	1	9	22	8	.73	4	.272	.328	.472
1992 Wichita	AA SD	125	427	108	23	5	9	168	56	40	40	3	70	10	1	7	16	11	.59	3	.253	.326	.393
1993 Wichita	AA SD	86	326	95	19	2	18	172	52	61	25	4	44	2	0	4	13	4	.76	4	.291	.342	.528
Las Vegas	AAA SD	32	110	29	4	4	3	50	21	12	11	1	17	4	0	0	7	4	.64	0	.264	.352	.455
1994 Omaha	AAA KC	112	406	135	23	8	27	255	95	80	61	10	85	8	0	6	27	12	.69	3	.333	.424	.628
1995 Omaha	AAA KC	75	271	80	21	4	12	145	59	50	29	2	45	1	1	2	15	6	.71	1	.295	.363	.535
1996 Pawtucket	AAA Bos	93	367	109	25	4	14	184	77	53	40	2	67	3	0	5	20	7	.74	3	.297	.366	.501
1999 Ottawa	AAA Mon	33	94	17	3	1	1	25	16	11	15	1	26	4	1	3	6	4	.60	1	.181	.310	.266
Winnipeg	IND —	58	206	68	18	2	6	108	47	46	41	1	27	2	0	4	6	8	.43	3	.330	.439	.524
2000 Edmonton	AAA Ana	46	150	35	5	2	6	62	25	19	20	2	25	1	2	2	7	1	.88	2	.233	.324	.413
1995 Boston	AL	24	68	23	8	1	3	42	20	7	8	0	16	0	1	0	6	0	1.00	1	.338	.408	.618
1996 Boston	AL	28	78	17	2	2	1	26	13	3	7	0	17	0	0	2	6	3	.67	0	.218	.282	.333
12 Min. YEARS		1148	4185	1154	209	51	142	1891	747	615	464	39	709	63	21	51	263	129	.67	42	.276	.353	.452
2 Maj. YEARS		52	146	40	10	3	4	68	33	10	15	0	33	0	3	0	12	3	.80	1	.274	.342	.466

Tom Howard

Pitches: Left **Bats:** Right **Pos:** RP-36; SP-4   **Ht:** 6'5" **Wt:** 230 **Born:** 7/29/75 **Age:** 25

		HOW MUCH HE PITCHED					WHAT HE GAVE UP										THE RESULTS				
Year Team	Lg Org	G	GS	CG	GF	IP	BFP	H	R	ER	HR	SH	SF	HB	TBB	IBB	SO	WP	Bk	W	L	Pct.	ShO	Sv	ERA
1993 Marlins	R Fla	8	6	1	0	34	151	35	16	12	0	0	2	0	20	0	31	5	0	2	4	.333	0	0	3.18
1994 Marlins	R Fla	11	4	0	2	32	157	28	22	21	0	1	0	2	34	0	37	8	0	1	2	.333	0	1	5.91
1995 Elmira	A- Fla	10	0	0	5	13.1	69	9	13	11	0	0	1	0	21	0	7	6	0	0	0	—	0	0	7.43
1998 Chston-SC	A TB	33	0	0	8	51.1	234	55	25	18	2	3	0	2	25	1	39	8	0	3	3	.500	0	0	3.16
1999 Quad City	A Min	15	1	0	4	29.1	118	26	6	5	1	0	4	0	4	0	22	2	0	2	1	.667	0	0	1.53
Fort Myers	A+ Min	22	0	0	14	42.2	194	43	28	24	3	1	3	2	25	0	22	4	0	1	2	.333	0	0	5.06
2000 Fort Myers	A+ Min	27	2	0	3	59	268	65	32	27	2	1	3	2	21	0	52	3	0	2	2	.500	0	2	4.12
New Britain	AA Min	13	2	0	4	24.2	114	32	12	10	1	0	1	1	13	0	8	1	0	0	1	.000	0	0	3.65
6 Min. YEARS		139	15	1	40	286.1	1305	293	154	128	9	6	9	9	163	1	218	37	0	11	15	.423	0	3	4.02

Ken Huckaby

Bats: Right **Throws:** Right **Pos:** C-61; 3B-5; DH-5; PH-4; OF-2; 1B-1; PR-1   **Ht:** 6'1" **Wt:** 205 **Born:** 1/27/71 **Age:** 30

Year Team	Lg Org	G	AB	H	2B	3B	HR	TB	R	RBI	TBB	IBB	SO	HBP	SH	SF	SB	CS	SB%	GDP	Avg	OBP	SLG
1991 Great Falls	R+ LA	57	213	55	16	0	3	80	39	37	17	0	38	4	1	3	3	2	.60	4	.258	.321	.376
1992 Vero Beach	A+ LA	73	261	63	9	0	0	72	14	21	7	0	42	1	2	2	1	1	.50	5	.241	.262	.276
1993 Vero Beach	A+ LA	79	281	75	14	1	4	103	22	41	11	1	35	2	3	2	2	1	.67	3	.267	.297	.367
San Antonio	AA LA	28	82	18	1	0	0	19	4	5	2	1	7	0	0	0	0	0	—	0	.220	.253	.232
1994 San Antonio	AA LA	11	41	11	1	0	1	15	3	9	1	1	1	0	0	0	1	0	1.00	1	.268	.286	.366
Bakersfield	A+ LA	77	270	81	18	1	2	107	29	30	10	0	37	2	2	2	3	2	.40	7	.300	.329	.396
1995 Albuquerque	AAA LA	89	278	90	16	2	1	113	30	40	12	1	26	4	3	1	3	1	.75	16	.324	.359	.406
1996 Albuquerque	AAA LA	103	286	79	16	2	3	108	37	41	17	1	35	0	6	3	0	0	—	10	.276	.320	.378
1997 Albuquerque	AAA LA	69	201	40	5	1	0	47	14	19	9	1	36	0	3	2	1	0	1.00	5	.199	.231	.234
1998 Tacoma	AAA Sea	16	49	11	2	0	0	13	4	1	5	0	6	0	0	0	0	0	—	3	.224	.296	.265
Columbus	AAA NYY	36	101	21	3	1	1	29	13	10	11	0	14	0	0	3	0	2	.00	3	.208	.286	.287
1999 Tucson	AAA Ari	107	355	100	20	1	2	135	44	42	13	2	33	2	4	5	0	0	—	11	.301	.325	.380
2000 Tucson	AAA Ari	76	243	67	11	1	4	92	13	33	10	2	30	2	0	3	2	2	.50	10	.276	.306	.379
10 Min. YEARS		821	2661	718	132	10	21	933	284	328	125	10	340	21	22	21	15	12	.56	77	.270	.306	.351

Joe Hudson

Pitches: Right **Bats:** Right **Pos:** RP-29

Ht: 6'1" **Wt:** 180 **Born:** 9/29/70 **Age:** 30

Year Team	Lg Org	G	GS	CG	GF	IP	BFP	H	R	ER	HR	SH	SF	HB	TBB	IBB	SO	WP	Bk	W	L	Pct.	ShO	Sv	ERA
1992 Elmira	A- Bos	19	7	0	6	72	320	76	46	35	2	3	0	2	33	0	38	4	2	3	3	.500	0	0	4.38
1993 Lynchburg	A+ Bos	49	1	0	30	84.1	372	97	49	38	1	2	2	2	38	2	62	10	2	8	6	.571	0	6	4.06
1994 Sarasota	A+ Bos	30	0	0	21	48.1	215	42	20	12	0	1	1	2	27	0	33	6	0	3	1	.750	0	7	2.23
New Britain	AA Bos	23	0	0	11	39	183	49	18	17	0	3	1	2	18	1	24	1	1	5	3	.625	0	7	3.92
1995 Trenton	AA Bos	22	0	0	17	31.2	133	20	8	6	0	1	0	1	17	3	24	2	1	0	1	.000	0	8	1.71
1996 Pawtucket	AAA Bos	25	0	0	15	33.1	151	29	19	13	0	0	1	1	21	0	18	4	0	1	1	.500	0	5	3.51
1997 Pawtucket	AAA Bos	29	0	0	17	32	148	25	22	8	1	2	2	3	23	3	14	3	0	2	1	.667	0	7	2.25
1998 Pawtucket	AAA Bos	46	0	0	26	47.2	222	57	32	24	3	2	2	0	23	3	32	4	0	2	2	.500	0	10	4.53
Louisville	AAA Mil	9	0	0	1	12.1	57	13	7	7	1	0	1	2	5	1	4	0	0	1	0	1.000	0	0	5.11
1999 Oklahoma	AAA Tex	5	0	0	3	9	42	15	6	5	1	0	1	0	4	0	4	1	0	1	1	.500	0	0	5.00
2000 Louisville	AAA Cin	29	0	0	19	31.1	152	34	20	17	2	1	0	2	21	2	21	1	0	1	2	.333	0	6	4.88
1995 Boston	AL	39	0	0	11	46	205	53	21	21	2	3	1	2	23	1	29	6	0	0	1	.000	0	1	4.11
1996 Boston	AL	36	0	0	16	45	214	57	35	27	4	1	2	0	32	4	19	0	0	3	5	.375	0	1	5.40
1997 Boston	AL	26	0	0	9	35.2	154	39	16	14	1	1	0	4	14	2	14	1	0	3	1	.750	0	0	3.53
1998 Milwaukee	NL	1	0	0	0	0.1	7	2	6	6	0	0	1	0	4	1	0	0	0	0	0	—	0	0	162.00
9 Min. YEARS		286	8	0	166	441	1995	457	247	182	11	15	11	17	230	15	274	36	6	27	21	.563	0	49	3.71
4 Maj. YEARS		102	0	0	36	127	580	151	78	68	7	5	4	6	73	8	62	7	0	6	7	.462	0	2	4.82

Orlando Hudson

Bats: Both **Throws:** Right **Pos:** 3B-121; 2B-17; SS-1

Ht: 6'0" **Wt:** 175 **Born:** 12/12/77 **Age:** 23

Year Team	Lg Org	G	AB	H	2B	3B	HR	TB	R	RBI	TBB	IBB	SO	HBP	SH	SF	SB	CS	SB%	GDP	Avg	OBP	SLG
1998 Medcine Hat	R+ Tor	65	242	71	18	1	8	115	50	42	22	0	36	7	0	2	6	5	.55	3	.293	.366	.475
1999 Hagerstown	A Tor	132	513	137	36	6	7	206	66	74	42	3	85	2	1	5	8	6	.57	10	.267	.322	.402
2000 Dunedin	A+ Tor	96	358	102	16	2	7	143	54	48	37	1	42	2	4	1	9	5	.64	15	.285	.354	.399
Tennessee	AA Tor	39	134	32	4	3	2	48	17	15	15	1	18	2	1	2	3	2	.60	3	.239	.320	.358
3 Min. YEARS		332	1247	342	74	12	24	512	187	179	116	5	181	13	6	10	26	18	.59	31	.274	.340	.411

B.J. Huff

Bats: Right **Throws:** Right **Pos:** OF-53; DH-10; PH-7; PR-4

Ht: 6'1" **Wt:** 189 **Born:** 8/1/75 **Age:** 25

Year Team	Lg Org	G	AB	H	2B	3B	HR	TB	R	RBI	TBB	IBB	SO	HBP	SH	SF	SB	CS	SB%	GDP	Avg	OBP	SLG
1996 Pittsfield	A- NYM	42	138	27	4	2	2	41	19	14	7	0	36	1	1	1	3	1	.75	2	.196	.238	.297
1997 Capital Cty	A NYM	99	363	92	20	5	7	143	49	41	19	1	78	4	1	2	11	3	.79	8	.253	.296	.394
1998 St. Lucie	A+ NYM	118	451	117	23	3	11	179	60	60	25	0	108	7	1	6	8	10	.44	14	.259	.305	.397
1999 Binghamton	AA NYM	57	205	51	9	1	7	83	26	32	19	1	46	1	0	2	9	2	.82	4	.249	.313	.405
2000 Binghamton	AA NYM	73	208	44	8	1	4	66	18	24	22	0	79	1	1	1	1	2	.33	3	.212	.289	.317
5 Min. YEARS		389	1365	331	64	12	31	512	172	171	92	2	347	14	4	12	32	18	.64	31	.242	.295	.375

Jake Huff

Bats: Right **Throws:** Right **Pos:** C-41; DH-20; OF-2; PH-2; PR-1

Ht: 6'3" **Wt:** 210 **Born:** 7/8/77 **Age:** 23

Year Team	Lg Org	G	AB	H	2B	3B	HR	TB	R	RBI	TBB	IBB	SO	HBP	SH	SF	SB	CS	SB%	GDP	Avg	OBP	SLG
1999 Idaho Falls	R+ SD	30	108	34	7	0	4	53	25	29	17	0	25	2	0	1	0	0	—	6	.315	.414	.491
2000 Fort Wayne	A SD	61	200	48	11	0	2	65	15	22	25	0	62	2	0	1	1	0	1.00	6	.240	.329	.325
Mobile	AA SD	4	8	2	0	0	0	2	0	0	0	0	0	0	0	0	0	0	—	0	.250	.250	.250
2 Min. YEARS		95	316	84	18	0	6	120	40	51	42	0	87	4	0	2	1	0	1.00	7	.266	.357	.380

Larry Huff

Bats: Right **Throws:** Right **Pos:** 3B-54; SS-19; DH-8; 2B-7; PR-4; OF-2; P-1

Ht: 6'0" **Wt:** 175 **Born:** 1/24/72 **Age:** 29

Year Team	Lg Org	G	AB	H	2B	3B	HR	TB	R	RBI	TBB	IBB	SO	HBP	SH	SF	SB	CS	SB%	GDP	Avg	OBP	SLG
1994 Martinsvlle	R+ Phi	39	143	36	2	1	1	43	24	7	29	0	20	6	1	0	17	4	.81	3	.252	.399	.301
Batavia	A- Phi	20	67	15	1	0	0	16	13	2	12	1	10	0	2	0	5	0	1.00	1	.224	.342	.239
1995 Piedmont	A Phi	130	481	131	26	4	1	168	86	51	74	5	64	10	7	4	26	8	.76	9	.272	.378	.349
1996 Clearwater	A+ Phi	128	483	132	17	5	0	159	73	37	60	1	65	6	10	4	37	11	.77	4	.273	.358	.329
1997 Reading	AA Phi	124	425	112	21	3	5	154	54	41	36	3	57	6	6	0	24	7	.77	10	.264	.330	.362
1998 Reading	AA Phi	40	136	46	7	2	7	78	26	25	19	0	15	5	1	1	10	2	.83	4	.338	.435	.574
1999 Reading	AA Phi	121	427	111	28	3	3	154	72	54	60	1	69	10	6	8	28	6	.82	11	.260	.358	.361
Scranton-WB	AAA Phi	9	17	4	2	0	0	6	4	1	5	0	2	1	0	0	0	0	—	0	.235	.435	.353
2000 Wichita	AA KC	83	290	87	14	1	3	112	48	43	51	0	48	3	7	3	13	8	.62	9	.300	.406	.386
7 Min. YEARS		694	2469	674	118	19	20	890	404	261	346	11	350	47	40	20	160	46	.78	51	.273	.370	.360

Royce Huffman

Bats: Right **Throws:** Right **Pos:** 3B-65; 2B-53; OF-9; DH-7

Ht: 6'0" **Wt:** 195 **Born:** 1/11/77 **Age:** 24

Year Team	Lg Org	G	AB	H	2B	3B	HR	TB	R	RBI	TBB	IBB	SO	HBP	SH	SF	SB	CS	SB%	GDP	Avg	OBP	SLG
1999 Martinsvlle	R+ Hou	53	196	58	16	7	2	94	39	36	31	0	29	4	0	4	18	2	.90	2	.296	.396	.480
2000 Kissimmee	A+ Hou	129	450	134	32	4	5	189	82	55	84	2	49	6	1	6	31	4	.89	12	.298	.410	.420
Round Rock	AA Hou	4	17	6	1	0	0	7	2	2	0	0	2	1	0	0	1	1	.50	1	.353	.389	.412
2 Min. YEARS		186	663	198	49	11	7	290	123	93	115	2	80	11	1	10	50	7	.88	15	.299	.406	.437

David Huggins

Pitches: Right **Bats:** Right **Pos:** RP-44   Ht: 6'5" **Wt:** 190 **Born:** 12/19/75 **Age:** 25

		HOW MUCH HE PITCHED						WHAT HE GAVE UP												THE RESULTS					
Year Team	Lg Org	G	GS	CG	GF	IP	BFP	H	R	ER	HR	SH	SF	HB	TBB	IBB	SO	WP	Bk	W	L	Pct.	ShO	Sv	ERA
1997 St.Cathrnes	A- Tor	27	2	0	18	35.2	159	33	18	13	1	0	2	4	15	1	42	1	2	0	3	.000	0	11	3.28
1998 Hagerstown	A Tor	12	0	0	11	14.2	77	16	15	13	0	2	1	3	14	0	13	3	0	0	2	.000	0	2	7.98
St.Cathrnes	A- Tor	15	15	0	0	84.2	373	85	46	39	4	0	3	6	35	0	67	2	1	7	5	.583	0	1	4.15
1999 Dunedin	A+ Tor	42	3	0	12	70	325	72	29	24	3	2	0	1	52	4	57	3	1	2	3	.400	0	1	3.09
2000 Tennessee	AA Tor	6	0	0	2	9.2	47	10	10	9	0	1	0	4	5	0	10	1	0	1	1	.500	0	1	8.38
Dayton	A Cin	38	0	0	28	38.2	186	24	21	16	1	3	2	7	39	1	46	10	0	2	5	.286	0	16	3.72
4 Min. YEARS		140	20	0	71	253.1	1167	240	139	114	9	8	8	25	160	6	235	20	4	12	19	.387	0	31	4.05

Bobby Hughes

Bats: Right **Throws:** Right **Pos:** C-66; PH-3   Ht: 6'4" **Wt:** 229 **Born:** 3/10/71 **Age:** 30

		BATTING														BASERUNNING				PERCENTAGES		
Year Team	Lg Org	G	AB	H	2B	3B	HR	TB	R	RBI	TBB	IBB	SO	HBP	SH	SF	SB	CS	SB%	GDP	Avg	OBP	SLG
1992 Helena	R+ Mil	11	40	7	1	1	0	10	5	6	4	0	14	2	0	0	0	0	—	0	.175	.283	.250
1993 Beloit	A Mil	98	321	89	11	3	17	157	42	56	23	0	77	6	5	0	1	3	.25	2	.277	.337	.489
1994 El Paso	AA Mil	12	36	10	4	1	0	16	3	12	5	0	7	1	0	2	0	1	.00	1	.278	.364	.444
Stockton	A+ Mil	95	322	81	24	3	11	144	54	53	33	0	83	9	1	2	2	1	.67	8	.252	.336	.447
1995 Stockton	A+ Mil	52	179	42	9	2	8	79	22	31	17	1	41	1	0	3	2	2	.50	10	.235	.300	.441
El Paso	AA Mil	51	173	46	12	0	7	79	11	27	12	1	30	2	0	2	0	2	.00	2	.266	.317	.457
1996 New Orleans	AAA Mil	37	125	25	5	0	4	42	11	15	4	0	31	3	0	0	1	1	.50	2	.200	.242	.336
El Paso	AA Mil	67	237	72	18	1	15	137	43	39	30	1	40	2	0	3	3	3	.50	5	.304	.382	.578
1997 Tucson	AAA Mil	89	290	90	29	2	7	144	43	51	24	1	46	9	0	4	0	0	—	9	.310	.376	.497
1999 Louisville	AAA Mil	10	32	6	2	0	1	11	5	2	2	0	7	1	0	0	0	0	—	0	.188	.257	.344
2000 Buffalo	AAA Cle	69	224	57	13	0	7	91	30	32	15	0	44	6	1	2	2	2	.50	3	.254	.316	.406
1998 Milwaukee	NL	85	218	50	7	2	9	88	28	29	16	1	54	1	1	1	1	2	.33	3	.229	.284	.404
1999 Milwaukee	NL	48	101	26	2	0	3	37	10	8	5	0	28	0	0	0	0	0	—	3	.257	.292	.366
8 Min. YEARS		591	1979	525	128	13	77	910	269	324	169	4	420	42	7	18	11	15	.42	44	.265	.333	.460
2 Maj. YEARS		133	319	76	9	2	12	125	38	37	21	1	82	1	1	1	1	2	.33	6	.238	.287	.392

Jason Huisman

Bats: Right **Throws:** Right **Pos:** 1B-45; 3B-41; 2B-33; DH-4; SS-1; OF-1   Ht: 6'3" **Wt:** 195 **Born:** 4/16/76 **Age:** 25

		BATTING														BASERUNNING				PERCENTAGES		
Year Team	Lg Org	G	AB	H	2B	3B	HR	TB	R	RBI	TBB	IBB	SO	HBP	SH	SF	SB	CS	SB%	GDP	Avg	OBP	SLG
1998 Boise	A- Ana	73	292	95	20	2	5	134	47	59	27	2	52	9	0	1	5	0	1.00	7	.325	.398	.459
1999 Lk Elsinore	A+ Ana	91	346	95	17	3	3	127	50	43	24	0	64	8	0	4	10	5	.67	8	.275	.332	.367
2000 Erie	AA Ana	120	441	121	23	4	3	161	52	42	40	1	75	9	3	1	14	4	.78	9	.274	.346	.365
3 Min. YEARS		284	1079	311	60	9	11	422	149	144	91	3	191	26	3	6	29	9	.76	24	.288	.356	.391

Rick Huisman

Pitches: Right **Bats:** Right **Pos:** RP-48   Ht: 6'3" **Wt:** 210 **Born:** 5/17/69 **Age:** 32

		HOW MUCH HE PITCHED						WHAT HE GAVE UP												THE RESULTS					
Year Team	Lg Org	G	GS	CG	GF	IP	BFP	H	R	ER	HR	SH	SF	HB	TBB	IBB	SO	WP	Bk	W	L	Pct.	ShO	Sv	ERA
1990 Everett	A- SF	1	0	0	0	2	10	3	1	1	0	0	0	0	2	0	2	1	0	0	0	—	0	0	4.50
Clinton	A SF	14	13	0	0	79	315	57	19	18	2	1	2	0	33	0	103	5	4	6	5	.545	0	0	2.05
1991 San Jose	A+ SF	26	26	7	0	182.1	720	126	45	37	5	11	3	3	73	1	216	13	3	16	4	.800	1	0	1.83
1992 Shreveport	AA SF	17	16	1	0	103.1	403	79	33	27	3	2	0	5	31	1	100	3	1	7	4	.636	1	0	2.35
Phoenix	AAA SF	9	8	0	0	56	230	45	16	15	3	1	1	1	24	0	44	1	0	3	2	.600	0	0	2.41
1993 San Jose	A+ SF	4	4	1	0	23.1	97	19	6	6	0	2	1	2	12	0	15	1	0	2	1	.667	0	0	2.31
Phoenix	AAA SF	14	14	0	0	72.1	333	78	54	48	5	1	1	1	45	0	59	8	4	3	4	.429	0	0	5.97
Tucson	AAA Hou	2	0	0	0	3.2	18	6	5	3	0	0	0	0	1	0	4	5	0	1	0	1.000	0	0	7.36
1994 Jackson	AA Hou	49	0	0	46	50.1	204	32	10	9	1	1	1	2	24	2	63	1	0	3	0	1.000	0	31	1.61
1995 Tucson	AAA Hou	42	0	0	28	54.2	246	58	33	27	1	0	3	1	28	3	47	3	1	6	1	.857	0	4	4.45
Omaha	AAA KC	5	0	0	3	5	19	3	1	1	1	0	0	0	4	0	13	0	0	0	0	—	0	1	1.80
1996 Omaha	AAA KC	27	4	0	6	57.1	243	54	32	31	9	0	1	2	24	0	50	0	1	2	4	.333	0	0	4.87
1997 Omaha	AAA KC	37	1	0	8	59.2	268	59	29	24	7	1	3	3	35	1	57	7	0	1	5	.167	0	2	3.62
1998 Fresno	AAA SF	44	0	0	17	72	309	65	43	43	18	0	2	1	34	2	80	4	0	2	6	.250	0	5	5.38
1999 New Orleans	AAA Hou	35	0	0	15	52.1	217	42	23	21	6	0	1	1	16	2	67	0	0	3	1	.750	0	3	3.61
2000 New Orleans	AAA Hou	48	0	0	27	54.1	217	36	26	21	5	1	2	0	20	1	64	5	0	3	5	.375	0	10	3.48
1995 Kansas City	AL	7	0	0	2	9.2	44	14	8	8	2	1	0	0	1	0	12	0	0	0	0	—	0	0	7.45
1996 Kansas City	AL	22	0	0	5	29.1	130	25	15	15	4	2	2	0	18	2	23	0	0	2	1	.667	0	1	4.60
11 Min. YEARS		374	86	9	150	927.2	3849	762	376	332	66	21	21	22	403	13	984	57	14	58	42	.580	5	53	3.22
2 Maj. YEARS		29	0	0	7	39	174	39	23	23	6	3	2	0	19	2	35	0	0	2	1	.667	0	1	5.31

Steve Huls

Bats: Right **Throws:** Right **Pos:** 2B-51; SS-26; PR-11; OF-7; 3B-6; 1B-6; PH-3; DH-1; P-1   Ht: 6'0" **Wt:** 178 **Born:** 10/11/74 **Age:** 26

		BATTING														BASERUNNING				PERCENTAGES		
Year Team	Lg Org	G	AB	H	2B	3B	HR	TB	R	RBI	TBB	IBB	SO	HBP	SH	SF	SB	CS	SB%	GDP	Avg	OBP	SLG
1996 Fort Wayne	A Min	60	201	43	3	1	1	51	21	11	12	1	53	1	6	2	2	2	.50	3	.214	.259	.254
1997 Fort Wayne	A Min	56	158	30	7	0	0	37	20	16	12	0	37	0	2	1	2	1	.67	2	.190	.246	.234
1998 Fort Myers	A+ Min	74	223	47	3	0	1	53	30	25	20	0	43	2	4	3	3	5	.38	7	.211	.278	.238
1999 New Britain	AA Min	56	152	33	1	0	0	34	13	10	23	0	32	3	3	1	4	2	.67	5	.217	.330	.224
Salt Lake	AAA Min	17	30	7	0	0	0	7	6	2	3	0	7	0	0	0	0	1	.00	2	.233	.303	.233
2000 New Britain	AA Min	102	249	51	4	2	0	59	24	15	32	0	51	3	3	1	4	2	.67	2	.205	.302	.237
5 Min. YEARS		365	1013	211	18	3	2	241	114	79	102	1	223	9	18	8	15	13	.54	21	.208	.284	.238

Jeff Hundley

Pitches: Left **Bats:** Left **Pos:** SP-25; RP-5   **Ht:** 6'2" **Wt:** 205 **Born:** 2/19/77 **Age:** 24

Year Team	Lg Org	G	GS	CG	GF	IP	BFP	H	R	ER	HR	SH	SF	HB	TBB	IBB	SO	WP	Bk	W	L	Pct.	ShO	Sv	ERA
1998 Boise	A- Ana	16	16	0	0	92.2	376	77	42	35	7	1	4	2	27	1	89	7	2	8	3	.727	0	0	3.40
1999 Cedar Rapds	A Ana	25	25	6	0	158	698	163	99	71	17	5	8	8	62	0	140	10	2	9	9	.500	1	0	4.04
2000 Edmonton	AAA Ana	2	1	0	0	9.1	47	14	12	12	0	0	3	2	4	0	2	2	0	0	2	.000	0	0	11.57
Erie	AA Ana	10	9	0	0	45	230	74	51	46	10	1	2	2	27	0	21	2	0	0	8	.000	0	0	9.20
Lk Elsinore	A+ Ana	18	15	0	1	97	403	85	48	30	3	5	2	2	36	1	69	6	0	5	5	.500	0	0	2.78
3 Min. YEARS		71	66	6	1	402	1754	413	252	194	37	12	19	16	156	2	321	27	4	22	27	.449	1	0	4.34

Scott Hunter

Bats: Right **Throws:** Right **Pos:** OF-93; DH-8; PR-3; PH-2   **Ht:** 6'1" **Wt:** 210 **Born:** 12/17/75 **Age:** 25

Year Team	Lg Org	G	AB	H	2B	3B	HR	TB	R	RBI	TBB	IBB	SO	HBP	SH	SF	SB	CS	SB%	GDP	Avg	OBP	SLG
1994 Great Falls	R+ LA	64	237	75	12	4	2	101	45	28	25	1	40	5	4	3	17	5	.77	1	.316	.389	.426
1995 San Berndno	A+ LA	113	379	108	19	3	11	166	68	59	36	1	83	6	4	1	27	8	.77	0	.285	.355	.438
Capital Cty	A NYM	12	40	10	0	0	0	10	2	1	2	0	13	1	1	1	2	1	.67	2	.250	.295	.250
1996 St. Lucie	A+ NYM	127	475	122	19	1	2	149	71	38	38	4	68	8	3	3	49	12	.80	6	.257	.321	.314
1997 Binghamton	AA NYM	80	289	74	12	2	10	120	45	31	25	1	52	4	1	4	24	9	.73	6	.256	.320	.415
1998 Norfolk	AAA NYM	7	21	3	0	0	0	3	2	3	3	0	5	2	1	0	1	2	.33	1	.143	.308	.143
Binghamton	AA NYM	130	487	153	25	3	14	226	80	65	47	2	75	7	1	8	39	15	.72	6	.314	.377	.464
1999 Norfolk	AAA NYM	50	180	41	4	0	8	69	20	23	8	0	42	3	1	2	6	6	.50	2	.228	.269	.383
Ottawa	AAA Mon	78	280	63	13	0	8	100	22	41	21	0	64	3	2	5	2	5	.29	1	.225	.282	.357
2000 Ottawa	AAA Mon	7	20	4	2	0	0	6	2	3	1	0	5	1	1	0	1	0	1.00	1	.200	.261	.300
Akron	AA Cle	94	347	79	16	3	5	116	35	33	14	0	61	8	3	5	11	6	.65	5	.228	.270	.334
Buffalo	AAA Cle	1	1	0	0	0	0	0	0	0	0	1	0	0	0	0	0	0	—	0	.000	.500	.000
7 Min. YEARS		763	2756	732	122	16	60	1066	392	325	221	9	509	48	22	33	179	69	.72	30	.266	.327	.387

Scott Huntsman

Pitches: Right **Bats:** Right **Pos:** RP-58; SP-1   **Ht:** 6'2" **Wt:** 236 **Born:** 10/28/72 **Age:** 28

Year Team	Lg Org	G	GS	CG	GF	IP	BFP	H	R	ER	HR	SH	SF	HB	TBB	IBB	SO	WP	Bk	W	L	Pct.	ShO	Sv	ERA
1994 Brewers	R Mil	4	0	0	4	3.2	12	1	0	0	0	0	0	0	0	0	3	0	0	0	0	—	0	1	0.00
Helena	R+ Mil	17	0	0	11	20	99	28	19	15	2	3	1	1	11	1	22	1	0	1	0	1.000	0	5	6.75
1995 Beloit	A Mil	43	0	0	14	49.2	229	42	17	15	3	2	1	5	34	2	49	5	0	4	3	.571	0	1	2.72
1996 Stockton	A+ Mil	43	0	0	29	48.1	213	37	21	15	3	0	3	2	27	0	56	2	0	4	3	.571	0	12	2.79
1997 El Paso	AA Mil	42	0	0	13	55	272	76	56	44	5	0	5	4	21	2	37	4	2	4	4	.500	0	3	7.20
1998 El Paso	AA Mil	52	0	0	12	74.1	353	106	71	69	12	1	4	4	31	2	49	5	1	4	3	.571	0	3	8.35
1999 Huntsville	AA Mil	47	0	0	20	69.1	300	72	33	28	8	2	3	3	25	3	31	1	0	1	4	.200	0	5	3.63
2000 Huntsville	AA Mil	59	1	0	26	71.2	315	81	45	37	6	1	3	6	19	2	43	4	0	4	4	.500	0	6	4.65
7 Min. YEARS		307	1	0	129	392	1793	443	262	223	39	9	19	25	168	12	290	22	3	22	21	.512	0	36	5.12

Brent Husted

Pitches: Right **Bats:** Right **Pos:** RP-52   **Ht:** 6'3" **Wt:** 198 **Born:** 3/30/76 **Age:** 25

Year Team	Lg Org	G	GS	CG	GF	IP	BFP	H	R	ER	HR	SH	SF	HB	TBB	IBB	SO	WP	Bk	W	L	Pct.	ShO	Sv	ERA
1997 Yakima	A- LA	10	6	0	1	29.2	145	45	32	23	0	0	0	1	11	3	22	2	0	1	5	.167	0	0	6.98
1998 San Berndno	A+ LA	49	0	0	20	85	360	77	41	34	6	4	2	2	24	4	68	6	0	3	6	.333	0	1	3.60
1999 Vero Beach	A+ LA	47	0	0	44	54	222	42	30	25	9	2	3	1	17	0	41	2	0	2	4	.333	0	27	4.17
2000 San Antonio	AA LA	52	0	0	26	70.1	300	64	37	32	7	5	3	4	22	2	48	0	0	4	9	.308	0	3	4.09
4 Min. YEARS		158	6	0	91	239	1027	228	140	114	22	11	8	8	74	9	179	10	0	10	24	.294	0	31	4.29

Norm Hutchins

Bats: Both **Throws:** Left **Pos:** OF-84; PH-5; DH-3   **Ht:** 5'11" **Wt:** 198 **Born:** 11/20/75 **Age:** 25

Year Team	Lg Org	G	AB	H	2B	3B	HR	TB	R	RBI	TBB	IBB	SO	HBP	SH	SF	SB	CS	SB%	GDP	Avg	OBP	SLG
1994 Angels	R Ana	43	136	26	4	1	0	32	8	7	3	0	44	1	1	1	5	2	.71	0	.191	.213	.235
1995 Angels	R Ana	14	59	16	1	1	0	19	9	7	4	0	10	1	2	1	8	4	.67	1	.271	.323	.322
Boise	A- Ana	45	176	44	6	2	2	60	34	11	15	0	44	2	4	1	10	6	.63	2	.250	.314	.341
1996 Cedar Rapds	A Ana	126	466	105	13	16	2	156	59	52	28	0	110	6	8	2	22	8	.73	5	.225	.277	.335
1997 Lk Elsinore	A+ Ana	132	564	163	31	12	15	263	82	69	23	4	147	6	5	6	39	17	.70	5	.289	.321	.466
1998 Midland	AA Ana	89	394	123	20	10	10	193	74	50	14	0	84	4	0	1	32	10	.76	8	.312	.341	.490
Vancouver	AAA Ana	7	29	6	0	0	1	9	4	3	2	0	9	1	0	1	1	2	.33	0	.207	.273	.310
1999 Edmonton	AAA Ana	126	521	130	27	6	7	190	80	51	40	1	127	8	4	4	25	17	.60	8	.250	.311	.365
2000 Colo Sprngs	AAA Col	15	44	10	1	2	1	18	8	4	2	0	15	1	1	1	2	1	.67	1	.227	.271	.409
Carolina	AA Col	77	281	68	13	4	4	101	31	29	21	0	69	6	3	2	19	6	.76	4	.242	.306	.359
7 Min. YEARS		674	2670	691	116	54	42	1041	389	283	152	5	659	36	28	20	163	73	.69	31	.259	.305	.390

Chad Hutchinson

Pitches: Right **Bats:** Right **Pos:** SP-15; RP-1   **Ht:** 6'5" **Wt:** 230 **Born:** 2/21/77 **Age:** 24

Year Team	Lg Org	G	GS	CG	GF	IP	BFP	H	R	ER	HR	SH	SF	HB	TBB	IBB	SO	WP	Bk	W	L	Pct.	ShO	Sv	ERA
1998 New Jersey	A- StL	3	3	0	0	15.1	67	15	7	6	0	0	0	2	4	0	20	0	0	0	1	.000	0	0	3.52
Pr William	A+ StL	5	5	0	0	29	118	20	12	9	4	1	0	1	11	0	31	0	2	1	0	1.000	0	0	2.79
1999 Arkansas	AA StL	25	25	0	0	141	624	127	79	74	12	8	5	4	85	0	150	20	3	7	11	.389	0	0	4.72
Memphis	AAA StL	2	2	0	0	12.1	48	4	3	3	2	0	0	0	8	0	16	0	0	2	0	1.000	0	0	2.19
2000 Memphis	AAA StL	5	4	0	0	8.1	63	10	24	24	1	2	3	3	27	0	9	3	0	0	1	.000	0	0	25.92
Arkansas	AA StL	11	11	1	0	48	206	40	21	18	1	0	1	2	27	0	54	2	0	2	3	.400	1	0	3.38
3 Min. YEARS		51	50	1	0	254	1126	216	146	134	20	11	9	12	162	0	280	25	5	13	16	.448	1	0	4.75

134

Mark Hutton

Pitches: Right **Bats:** Right **Pos:** RP-49   **Ht:** 6'8" **Wt:** 240 **Born:** 2/6/70 **Age:** 31

		HOW MUCH HE PITCHED						WHAT HE GAVE UP									THE RESULTS				
Year Team	Lg Org	G	GS	CG	GF	IP	BFP	H	R	ER	HR	SH	SF	HB	TBB	IBB	SO	WP	Bk	W	L	Pct.	ShO	Sv	ERA
1989 Oneonta	A- NYY	12	12	0	0	66.1	283	70	39	30	1	2	4	1	24	0	62	5	2	6	2	.750	0	0	4.07
1990 Greensboro	A NYY	21	19	0	1	81.1	394	77	78	57	2	2	3	7	62	0	72	14	1	1	10	.091	0	0	6.31
1991 Ft. Laud	A+ NYY	24	24	3	0	147	606	98	54	40	5	6	1	11	65	5	117	4	4	5	8	.385	0	0	2.45
Columbus	AAA NYY	1	1	0	0	6	24	3	2	1	0	0	0	0	5	0	5	0	0	1	0	1.000	0	0	1.50
1992 Albany-Col	AA NYY	25	25	1	0	165.1		146	75	66	6	2	3	11	66	1	128	2	1	13	7	.650	0	0	3.59
Columbus	AAA NYY	1	0	0	0	5	22	7	4	3	0	0	0	0	2	0	4	0	0	0	1	.000	0	0	5.40
1993 Columbus	AAA NYY	21	21	0	0	133	544	98	52	47	14	2	0	10	53	0	112	2	1	10	4	.714	0	0	3.18
1994 Columbus	AAA NYY	22	5	0	12	34.2	146	31	16	14	5	1	2	2	12	0	27	0	0	2	5	.286	0	3	3.63
1995 Columbus	AAA NYY	11	11	0	0	52.1	243	64	51	49	7	0	3	4	24	1	23	2	0	2	6	.250	0	0	8.43
1996 Tampa	A+ NYY	3	2	0	0	5	18	2	1	1	0	0	0	0	1	0	6	0	0	0	0	—	0	0	1.80
Columbus	AAA NYY	2	0	0	1	2	8	0	0	0	0	0	0	0	2	0	3	1	0	0	0	—	0	0	0.00
1998 Indianapolis	AAA Cin	16	16	0	0	83.1	370	91	50	41	7	3	4	5	37	0	47	4	0	4	6	.400	0	0	4.43
2000 Round Rock	AA Hou	3	0	0	1	4.2	24	6	4	4	1	0	1	1	3	0	4	0	0	0	0	—	0	0	7.71
New Orleans	AAA Hou	46	0	0	19	60	259	58	27	24	8	2	3	3	24	0	27	1	0	4	2	.667	0	3	3.60
1993 New York	AL	7	4	0	2	22	104	24	17	14	2	2	2	1	17	0	12	0	0	1	1	.500	0	0	5.73
1994 New York	AL	2	0	0	1	3.2	16	4	3	2	0	0	0	0	1	0	1	0	0	0	0	—	0	0	4.91
1996 New York	AL	12	2	0	5	30.1	140	32	19	17	3	0	2	1	18	1	25	0	0	2	0	.000	0	0	5.04
Florida	NL	13	9	0	0	56.1	234	47	23	23	6	0	1	3	18	0	31	2	0	5	1	.833	0	0	3.67
1997 Florida	NL	32	0	0	9	47.2	204	50	24	20	7	5	3	2	19	3	29	3	1	3	1	.750	0	0	3.78
Colorado	NL	8	1	0	0	12.2	68	22	10	10	3	2	1	4	7	0	10	0	0	0	1	.000	0	0	7.11
1998 Cincinnati	NL	10	2	0	2	17	87	24	14	14	2	0	0	1	17	0	3	1	0	0	0	—	0	0	7.41
10 Min. YEARS		208	136	4	34	846	3644	751	453	377	56	20	24	55	380	7	637	35	9	48	51	.485	0	6	4.01
5 Maj. YEARS		84	18	0	19	189.2	853	203	110	100	23	9	9	12	96	4	111	6	1	9	7	.563	0	0	4.75

Brandon Hyde

Bats: Right **Throws:** Right **Pos:** 1B-25; C-14; DH-13; PH-5   **Ht:** 6'3" **Wt:** 210 **Born:** 10/3/73 **Age:** 27

		BATTING														BASERUNNING				PERCENTAGES		
Year Team	Lg Org	G	AB	H	2B	3B	HR	TB	R	RBI	TBB	IBB	SO	HBP	SH	SF	SB	CS	SB%	GDP	Avg	OBP	SLG
1997 White Sox	R CWS	28	77	15	4	0	1	22	10	14	11	0	24	2	1	1	0	0	—	2	.195	.308	.286
1998 Bristol	R+ CWS	27	94	35	9	0	5	59	21	26	21	0	20	8	0	0	0	1	.00	3	.372	.520	.628
1999 Birmingham	AA CWS	7	18	5	3	0	0	8	4	2	3	0	4	0	0	0	0	1	.00	0	.278	.381	.444
Burlington	A CWS	65	210	60	15	0	6	93	33	40	33	0	60	6	1	3	1	1	.50	4	.286	.393	.443
2000 Charlotte	AAA CWS	9	23	3	1	0	1	7	2	4	2	0	9	0	1	2	0	0	—	1	.130	.185	.304
Winston-Sal	A+ CWS	47	136	25	6	0	1	34	15	15	21	0	42	4	0	3	1	2	.33	8	.184	.305	.250
4 Min. YEARS		183	558	143	38	0	14	223	85	101	91	0	159	20	3	9	2	5	.29	18	.256	.375	.400

Anthony Iapoce

Bats: Right **Throws:** Left **Pos:** OF-81; PH-13; PR-3; P-1   **Ht:** 5'10" **Wt:** 175 **Born:** 8/23/73 **Age:** 27

		BATTING														BASERUNNING				PERCENTAGES		
Year Team	Lg Org	G	AB	H	2B	3B	HR	TB	R	RBI	TBB	IBB	SO	HBP	SH	SF	SB	CS	SB%	GDP	Avg	OBP	SLG
1994 Brewers	R Mil	55	222	55	7	2	0	66	37	25	15	0	43	5	3	1	16	3	.84	1	.248	.309	.297
1995 Brewers	R Mil	3	3	1	0	0	0	1	2	0	1	0	1	0	0	0	1	0	1.00	0	.333	.500	.333
Helena	R+ Mil	39	146	44	7	0	0	51	43	13	28	0	24	2	2	2	19	3	.86	2	.301	.416	.349
1996 Beloit	A Mil	77	266	78	6	3	1	93	62	11	43	0	53	7	3	0	23	13	.64	4	.293	.405	.350
1997 Tucson	AAA Mil	7	21	7	4	0	0	11	5	3	1	0	4	0	0	0	0	0	—	1	.333	.364	.524
Stockton	A+ Mil	99	387	103	13	4	1	127	48	27	30	0	71	6	9	2	22	12	.65	3	.266	.327	.328
1998 El Paso	AA Mil	133	576	181	23	6	2	222	97	53	33	1	67	11	9	2	35	20	.64	4	.314	.362	.385
1999 Louisville	AAA Mil	26	83	14	2	0	0	16	6	0	7	1	30	0	1	0	6	3	.67	3	.169	.233	.193
Huntsville	AA Mil	50	133	35	7	0	0	42	17	5	12	0	25	1	0	0	2	2	.50	0	.263	.329	.316
2000 Indianapolis	AAA Mil	25	39	7	0	0	0	7	3	1	4	0	10	0	0	0	2	0	1.00	1	.179	.256	.179
Huntsville	AA Mil	72	247	55	7	0	0	62	24	20	23	1	57	3	3	3	16	4	.80	4	.223	.293	.251
7 Min. YEARS		586	2123	580	76	15	4	698	344	158	197	3	385	35	30	10	142	60	.70	23	.273	.343	.329

Mario Iglesias

Pitches: Right **Bats:** Both **Pos:** RP-43; SP-2   **Ht:** 6'3" **Wt:** 195 **Born:** 6/2/74 **Age:** 27

		HOW MUCH HE PITCHED						WHAT HE GAVE UP									THE RESULTS				
Year Team	Lg Org	G	GS	CG	GF	IP	BFP	H	R	ER	HR	SH	SF	HB	TBB	IBB	SO	WP	Bk	W	L	Pct.	ShO	Sv	ERA
1996 Bristol	R+ CWS	3	0	0	1	8.1	29	6	2	2	1	0	1	0	1	0	2	1	0	0	0	—	0	1	2.16
Hickory	A CWS	10	5	0	2	34.2	155	45	19	19	4	0	0	6	6	0	31	1	1	2	3	.400	0	0	4.93
1997 Hickory	A CWS	36	0	0	27	68.2	289	64	29	26	4	3	2	1	26	5	64	7	2	8	4	.667	0	10	3.41
1998 Winston-Sal	A+ CWS	35	0	0	18	78	305	51	24	20	5	4	2	4	19	0	90	3	0	13	1	.929	0	5	2.31
1999 Birmingham	AA CWS	23	2	0	9	50	216	51	29	26	8	2	1	2	21	1	29	0	0	5	3	.625	0	0	4.68
Bowie	AA Bal	14	2	0	3	26.1	123	22	6	3	0	1	6	2	16	2	27	0	0	1	4	.200	0	2	7.52
2000 Bowie	AA Bal	37	0	0	14	58.2	258	63	29	23	6	5	6	4	22	3	49	4	0	3	3	.500	0	2	3.53
Iowa	AAA ChC	8	2	0	3	20.1	105	31	30	25	5	0	1	0	11	2	15	4	0	1	1	.500	0	0	11.07
5 Min. YEARS		166	11	0	72	345	1480	339	185	163	39	17	13	18	122	13	307	23	3	33	19	.635	0	19	4.25

Mike Iglesias

Pitches: Right **Bats:** Right **Pos:** RP-12; SP-1   **Ht:** 6'5" **Wt:** 223 **Born:** 11/9/72 **Age:** 28

		HOW MUCH HE PITCHED						WHAT HE GAVE UP									THE RESULTS				
Year Team	Lg Org	G	GS	CG	GF	IP	BFP	H	R	ER	HR	SH	SF	HB	TBB	IBB	SO	WP	Bk	W	L	Pct.	ShO	Sv	ERA
1991 Dodgers	R LA	8	6	0	1	23	109	26	13	12	1	1	1	0	17	0	17	2	3	1	1	.500	0	0	4.70
1992 Great Falls	R+ LA	12	12	0	0	56	272	69	56	38	4	0	1	4	26	0	37	10	1	3	6	.333	0	0	6.11
1993 Bakersfield	A+ LA	6	3	0	0	19.1	93	26	16	12	2	1	0	1	10	0	10	3	1	1	2	.333	0	0	5.59
Yakima	A- LA	10	5	0	0	30.2	150	42	29	26	1	0	5	2	21	1	24	5	1	0	3	.000	0	0	7.63
1994 Vero Beach	A+ LA	19	14	1	3	89.2	376	87	46	42	9	2	4	1	29	2	50	4	1	3	6	.333	0	0	4.22
1995 Bakersfield	A+ LA	24	23	2	0	143.2	586	124	65	52	11	5	3	11	38	0	108	7	0	7	10	.412	0	0	3.26
San Berndno	A+ LA	4	3	0	0	15	74	26	14	11	4	0	0	2	12	0	12	1	0	0	2	.333	0	0	6.60

Year Team	Lg Org	G	GS	CG	GF	IP	BFP	H	R	ER	HR	SH	SF	HB	TBB	IBB	SO	WP	Bk	W	L	Pct.	ShO	Sv	ERA
1996 Vero Beach	A+ LA	31	16	0	14	104	463	112	68	59	9	1	4	5	37	1	101	6	1	5	8	.385	0	7	5.11
1997 San Antonio	AA LA	42	0	0	20	59.1	247	51	25	24	7	2	1	0	26	1	55	5	1	6	2	.750	0	8	3.64
1998 Albuquerque	AAA LA	39	9	0	6	95.2	419	112	43	39	9	4	4	2	29	2	57	2	0	7	1	.875	0	0	3.67
1999 Richmond	AAA Atl	3	0	0	0	4	22	6	7	7	0	0	0	0	4	1	7	0	0	0	2	.000	0	0	15.75
Greenville	AA Atl	4	4	0	0	14	66	19	11	11	2	0	1	0	6	0	5	1	1	0	3	.000	0	0	7.07
2000 Huntsville	AA Mil	13	1	0	7	32	141	37	24	24	5	1	2	0	8	1	21	0	0	0	2	.000	0	0	6.75
10 Min. YEARS		215	96	3	51	686.1	3018	737	417	357	61	17	26	28	255	9	504	48	10	34	48	.415	1	15	4.68

Brandon Inge

Bats: Both **Throws:** Right **Pos:** C-120; DH-11; PH-3; OF-1   **Ht:** 5'11" **Wt:** 185 **Born:** 5/19/77 **Age:** 24

Year Team	Lg Org	G	AB	H	2B	3B	HR	TB	R	RBI	TBB	IBB	SO	HBP	SH	SF	SB	CS	SB%	GDP	Avg	OBP	SLG
1998 Jamestown	A- Det	51	191	44	10	1	8	80	24	29	17	1	53	6	0	1	8	8	.50	4	.230	.312	.419
1999 W Michigan	A Det	100	352	86	25	2	9	142	54	46	39	0	87	3	2	6	15	3	.83	7	.244	.320	.403
2000 Jacksnville	AA Det	78	298	77	25	1	6	122	39	53	26	1	73	0	1	5	10	3	.77	10	.258	.313	.409
Toledo	AAA Det	55	190	42	9	3	5	72	24	20	15	0	51	1	1	1	2	1	.67	5	.221	.280	.379
3 Min. YEARS		284	1031	249	69	7	28	416	141	148	97	2	264	10	4	13	35	15	.70	26	.242	.309	.403

Jeff Inglin

Bats: Right **Throws:** Right **Pos:** OF-55; DH-55; PR-1   **Ht:** 5'11" **Wt:** 185 **Born:** 10/8/75 **Age:** 25

Year Team	Lg Org	G	AB	H	2B	3B	HR	TB	R	RBI	TBB	IBB	SO	HBP	SH	SF	SB	CS	SB%	GDP	Avg	OBP	SLG
1996 Bristol	R+ CWS	50	193	56	10	0	8	90	27	24	11	0	25	9	0	0	9	6	.60	8	.290	.357	.466
Hickory	A CWS	22	83	30	6	2	2	46	12	15	4	0	11	1	0	1	2	1	.67	3	.361	.393	.554
1997 Hickory	A CWS	135	536	179	34	6	16	273	100	102	49	4	87	4	0	9	31	8	.79	12	.334	.388	.509
1998 Birmingham	AA CWS	139	494	121	22	6	24	227	75	100	78	3	101	4	0	9	3	2	.60	12	.245	.347	.460
1999 Charlotte	AAA CWS	14	39	8	0	0	3	17	8	4	4	0	9	1	0	0	0	1	.00	0	.205	.295	.436
Birmingham	AA CWS	117	432	126	26	4	15	205	63	63	58	3	62	6	2	2	20	2	.91	13	.292	.382	.475
2000 Birmingham	AA CWS	65	244	71	12	3	5	104	43	40	34	0	43	4	2	4	5	2	.71	7	.291	.381	.426
Charlotte	AAA CWS	45	146	44	8	1	5	69	19	31	12	0	17	2	1	1	3	0	1.00	7	.301	.360	.473
5 Min. YEARS		587	2167	635	118	22	78	1031	347	383	250	10	355	31	5	26	73	22	.77	62	.293	.370	.476

Garey Ingram

Bats: Right **Throws:** Right **Pos:** OF-96; PH-5; PR-4; 2B-3; DH-2   **Ht:** 5'11" **Wt:** 195 **Born:** 7/25/70 **Age:** 30

Year Team	Lg Org	G	AB	H	2B	3B	HR	TB	R	RBI	TBB	IBB	SO	HBP	SH	SF	SB	CS	SB%	GDP	Avg	OBP	SLG
1990 Great Falls	R+ LA	56	198	68	12	8	2	102	43	21	22	0	37	3	0	1	10	6	.63	3	.343	.415	.515
1991 Bakersfield	A+ LA	118	445	132	16	4	9	183	75	61	52	4	70	14	5	6	30	13	.70	5	.297	.383	.411
San Antonio	AA LA	1	1	0	0	0	0	0	0	1	0	0	1	0	0	0	0	0	—	0	.000	.000	.000
1992 San Antonio	AA LA	65	198	57	9	5	2	82	34	17	28	2	43	12	2	1	11	6	.65	4	.288	.406	.414
1993 San Antonio	AA LA	84	305	82	14	5	6	124	43	33	31	0	50	5	2	2	19	6	.76	3	.269	.344	.407
1994 San Antonio	AA LA	99	345	89	24	3	8	143	68	28	43	3	61	9	2	0	19	5	.79	5	.258	.355	.414
Albuquerque	AAA LA	2	8	2	0	0	0	2	2	0	0	0	1	0	0	0	0	1	1.00	0	.250	.250	.250
1995 Albuquerque	AAA LA	63	232	57	11	4	1	79	28	30	21	1	40	3	0	3	10	4	.71	4	.246	.313	.341
1996 Albuquerque	AAA LA	6	10	1	0	0	0	1	1	0	1	0	2	0	0	0	0	0	—	1	.100	.182	.100
1997 San Antonio	AA LA	92	348	104	28	7	12	182	60	52	37	1	50	4	1	2	16	6	.73	5	.299	.371	.523
1998 Albuquerque	AAA LA	108	377	114	25	5	8	173	60	58	30	1	69	5	7	2	20	6	.77	7	.302	.360	.459
1999 Pawtucket	AAA Bos	85	296	73	15	3	9	121	49	39	17	0	52	3	7	2	11	2	.85	5	.247	.292	.409
2000 Pawtucket	AAA Bos	103	311	74	17	2	10	125	44	36	45	1	53	9	5	4	5	2	.71	9	.238	.347	.402
1994 Los Angeles	NL	26	78	22	1	0	3	32	10	8	7	3	22	0	1	0				3	.282	.341	.410
1995 Los Angeles	NL	44	55	11	2	0	0	13	5	3	9	0	8	0	2	0	3	0	1.00	0	.200	.313	.236
1997 Los Angeles	NL	12	9	4	0	0	0	4	2	1	1	0	3	0	0	0	1	0	1.00	0	.444	.500	.444
11 Min. YEARS		882	3074	853	171	46	67	1317	515	376	327	13	529	67	31	24	152	56	.73	52	.277	.357	.428
3 Maj. YEARS		82	142	37	3	0	3	49	17	12	17	3	33	0	3	0	4	0	1.00	3	.261	.340	.345

Eric Ireland

Pitches: Right **Bats:** Right **Pos:** SP-29   **Ht:** 6'1" **Wt:** 170 **Born:** 3/11/77 **Age:** 24

Year Team	Lg Org	G	GS	CG	GF	IP	BFP	H	R	ER	HR	SH	SF	HB	TBB	IBB	SO	WP	Bk	W	L	Pct.	ShO	Sv	ERA
1996 Astros	R Hou	12	11	0	0	53.2	235	54	33	28	1	3	1	3	23	1	43	13	1	3	4	.429	0	0	4.70
1997 Auburn	A- Hou	16	16	2	0	107	458	111	55	44	4	2	0	12	21	1	78	3	0	5	7	.417	0	0	3.70
1998 Quad City	A Hou	29	28	6	1	206	860	172	80	66	15	5	4	15	71	2	191	7	3	14	9	.609	2	0	2.88
1999 Jackson	AA Hou	3	3	0	0	14.2	64	19	9	7	1	1	0	0	2	1	15	2	0	1	0	1.000	0	0	4.30
Kissimmee	A+ Hou	24	24	5	0	170.1	684	145	59	39	12	7	1	8	30	1	133	13	2	10	7	.588	2	0	2.06
2000 Round Rock	AA Hou	29	29	2	0	179.2	754	171	84	68	14	7	4	5	64	0	123	12	0	11	9	.550	2	0	3.41
5 Min. YEARS		113	111	15	2	731.1	3055	672	320	252	47	25	10	43	211	6	583	50	6	43	37	.538	6	0	3.10

Hansel Izquierdo

Pitches: Right **Bats:** Right **Pos:** RP-14; SP-8   **Ht:** 6'2" **Wt:** 205 **Born:** 1/2/77 **Age:** 24

Year Team	Lg Org	G	GS	CG	GF	IP	BFP	H	R	ER	HR	SH	SF	HB	TBB	IBB	SO	WP	Bk	W	L	Pct.	ShO	Sv	ERA
1995 Marlins	R Fla	1	0	0	0	2	10	3	3	0	0	1	0	0	2	0	1	0	0	0	0		0	0	0.00
1996 Marlins	R Fla	12	0	0	10	13.1	52	7	4	4	0	0	0	3	5	0	17	3	1	0	1	.000	0	3	2.70
1997 White Sox	R CWS	5	0	0	2	10.1	45	9	4	4	0	1	0	0	8	0	15	1	0	0	0	—	0	0	3.48
Bristol	R+ CWS	9	2	0	2	23	104	25	14	11	5	0	0	4	8	0	24	0	1	2	2	.500	0	0	4.30
1998 Hickory	A CWS	28	27	2	1	175	771	159	104	85	14	6	2	22	76	0	186	15	1	9	11	.450	2	0	4.37
Winston-Sal	A+ CWS	1	0	0	1	2	7	1	0	0	0	0	0	0	1	0	2	0	0	0	0	—	0	0	0.00
1999 Winston-Sal	A+ CWS	18	13	0	4	82.2	371	76	46	38	5	5	2	8	46	1	72	13	1	3	5	.375	0	0	4.14

Year Team	Lg Org	G	GS	CG	GF	IP	BFP	H	R	ER	HR	SH	SF	HB	TBB	IBB	SO	WP	Bk	W	L	Pct.	ShO	Sv	ERA
2000 Birmingham	AA CWS	8	0	0	5	12	53	12	11	10	3	1	1	0	5		5	1	0	1	2	.333	0	1	7.50
Kinston	A+ Cle	10	5	0	2	41.1	178	39	29	22	4	2	2	5	13	0	34	1	0	1	3	.250	0	1	4.79
Sonoma Cty	IND —	4	3	0	0	13	72	16	14	14	0	1	1	3	17	1	10	2	0	0	1	.000	0	0	9.69
6 Min. YEARS		96	50	2	27	374.2	1663	347	229	188	30	17	8	45	181	3	365	37	4	16	25	.390	1	5	4.52

Cesar Izturis

Bats: Both **Throws:** Right **Pos:** SS-131; PR-1 **Ht:** 5'9" **Wt:** 175 **Born:** 2/10/80 **Age:** 21

Year Team	Lg Org	G	AB	H	2B	3B	HR	TB	R	RBI	TBB	IBB	SO	HBP	SH	SF	SB	CS	SB%	GDP	Avg	OBP	SLG
1997 St.Cathrnes	A- Tor	70	231	44	3	0	1	50	32	11	15	0	27	1	8	2	6	3	.67	3	.190	.241	.216
1998 Hagerstown	A Tor	130	413	108	13	1	1	126	56	38	20	0	43	2	9	2	20	9	.69	5	.262	.297	.305
1999 Dunedin	A+ Tor	131	536	165	28	12	3	226	77	77	22	4	58	6	17	9	32	16	.67	9	.308	.337	.422
2000 Syracuse	AAA Tor	132	435	95	16	5	0	121	54	27	20	0	44	1	13	2	21	11	.66	5	.218	.253	.278
4 Min. YEARS		463	1615	412	60	18	5	523	219	153	77	4	172	10	47	15	79	39	.67	22	.255	.291	.324

Gavin Jackson

Bats: Right **Throws:** Right **Pos:** SS-31; 2B-21 **Ht:** 5'10" **Wt:** 170 **Born:** 7/19/73 **Age:** 27

Year Team	Lg Org	G	AB	H	2B	3B	HR	TB	R	RBI	TBB	IBB	SO	HBP	SH	SF	SB	CS	SB%	GDP	Avg	OBP	SLG
1993 Red Sox	R Bos	42	160	50	7	2	0	61	29	11	14	0	18	11	2	0	11	5	.69	2	.313	.405	.381
1994 Sarasota	A+ Bos	108	321	77	6	1	0	85	46	27	33	0	40	7	12	0	9	10	.47	1	.240	.324	.265
1995 Sarasota	A+ Bos	100	342	91	19	1	0	112	61	36	40	3	43	6	8	4	11	12	.48	8	.266	.349	.327
1996 Trenton	AA Bos	6	20	5	2	0	0	7	2	3	2	0	3	0	0	1	0	1	.00	0	.250	.318	.350
Pawtucket	AAA Bos	15	44	11	2	0	0	13	5	1	3	0	8	0	1	0	0	1	.00	0	.250	.298	.295
Sarasota	A+ Bos	87	276	66	13	2	0	83	26	24	33	0	47	7	8	3	4	6	.40	6	.239	.332	.301
1997 Trenton	AA Bos	100	301	82	12	0	1	97	46	46	48	0	36	6	12	2	2	6	.25	11	.272	.381	.322
1998 Trenton	AA Bos	50	168	41	7	1	0	50	12	17	18	0	21	0	1	2	3	1	.75	5	.244	.314	.298
Pawtucket	AAA Bos	67	206	49	4	1	3	64	21	24	27	0	40	3	2	4	3	2	.60	5	.238	.329	.311
1999 Trenton	AA Bos	27	71	15	1	0	0	16	11	5	27	0	12	4	3	1	2	1	.67	1	.211	.374	.225
Pawtucket	AAA Bos	49	140	23	3	0	0	26	17	5	27	0	32	0	1	0	2	0	1.00	4	.164	.299	.186
2000 Pawtucket	AAA Bos	18	60	13	0	0	0	13	3	2	3	0	12	0	0	0	1	0	1.00	1	.217	.254	.217
Binghamton	AA NYM	33	98	22	0	1	0	24	13	9	22	0	21	1	1	2	1	2	.33	4	.224	.366	.245
8 Min. YEARS		702	2207	545	76	9	4	651	292	210	285	3	333	45	51	18	49	47	.51	48	.247	.342	.295

Ryan Jackson

Bats: Left **Throws:** Left **Pos:** 1B-137; DH-2; PH-2; PR-1; P-1 **Ht:** 6'3" **Wt:** 185 **Born:** 11/15/71 **Age:** 29

Year Team	Lg Org	G	AB	H	2B	3B	HR	TB	R	RBI	TBB	IBB	SO	HBP	SH	SF	SB	CS	SB%	GDP	Avg	OBP	SLG
1994 Elmira	A- Fla	72	276	80	18	1	6	118	46	41	22	1	40	1	0	6	4	3	.57	2	.290	.338	.428
1995 Kane County	A Fla	132	471	138	39	6	10	219	78	82	67	7	74	4	0	5	13	8	.62	9	.293	.382	.465
1996 Marlins	R Fla	7	25	9	0	0	0	9	5	5	1	0	3	1	0	0	2	0	1.00	0	.360	.407	.360
Brevard Cty	A+ Fla	6	26	8	2	0	1	13	4	4	1	0	7	0	0	0	1	0	1.00	0	.308	.333	.500
1997 Portland	AA Fla	134	491	153	28	4	26	267	87	98	51	2	85	3	1	0	2	5	.29	6	.312	.380	.544
1998 Charlotte	AAA Fla	13	50	19	4	0	2	29	5	11	4	0	14	0	0	0	2	0	1.00	1	.380	.426	.580
1999 Tacoma	AAA Sea	105	409	126	25	2	8	179	57	62	36	5	64	1	1	7	12	3	.80	9	.308	.360	.438
2000 Durham	AAA TB	139	502	156	38	2	18	252	69	85	50	4	112	0	2	8	6	4	.60	8	.311	.368	.502
1998 Florida	NL	111	260	65	15	1	5	97	26	31	20	0	73	1	2	1	1	1	.50	3	.250	.305	.373
1999 Seattle	AL	32	68	16	3	0	0	19	4	10	6	0	19	1	0	2	3	3	.50	2	.235	.299	.279
7 Min. YEARS		608	2250	689	154	15	71	1086	351	388	232	19	399	10	4	26	42	23	.65	35	.306	.370	.483
2 Maj. YEARS		143	328	81	18	1	5	116	30	41	26	0	92	2	2	3	4	4	.50	6	.247	.304	.354

Russell Jacob

Pitches: Right **Bats:** Right **Pos:** RP-6; SP-1 **Ht:** 6'6" **Wt:** 240 **Born:** 1/2/75 **Age:** 26

Year Team	Lg Org	G	GS	CG	GF	IP	BFP	H	R	ER	HR	SH	SF	HB	TBB	IBB	SO	WP	Bk	W	L	Pct.	ShO	Sv	ERA
1994 Mariners	R Sea	8	2	0	2	13.1	52	9	4	4	0	0	1	0	5	0	12	1	0	0	0	—	0	0	2.70
1995 Mariners	R Sea	12	11	0	1	56.1	248	47	29	18	0	0	1	3	31	0	54	6	2	6	2	.750	0	0	2.88
1996 Wisconsin	A Sea	24	10	0	4	68.1	310	67	48	40	2	2	3	2	53	0	63	13	2	4	4	.500	0	2	5.27
1997 Wisconsin	A Sea	21	9	0	2	77	339	62	41	38	7	3	4	3	58	1	76	14	1	4	2	.667	0	1	4.44
1998 High Desert	A+ Ari	31	7	0	4	67.1	310	78	42	33	2	2	1	2	26	0	64	7	0	3	2	.600	0	1	4.41
1999 El Paso	AA Ari	3	0	0	2	2.2	16	5	4	2	0	0	0	0	2	0	3	0	0	0	0	—	0	0	6.75
2000 El Paso	AA Ari	7	1	0	1	9.2	40	10	2	2	0	1	0	0	3	0	4	0	0	1	0	1.000	0	0	1.86
7 Min. YEARS		106	40	0	16	294.2	1318	278	170	137	12	8	10	10	178	1	276	41	5	18	10	.643	0	4	4.18

Ryan Jacobs

Pitches: Left **Bats:** Right **Pos:** RP-43; SP-1 **Ht:** 6'2" **Wt:** 215 **Born:** 2/3/74 **Age:** 27

Year Team	Lg Org	G	GS	CG	GF	IP	BFP	H	R	ER	HR	SH	SF	HB	TBB	IBB	SO	WP	Bk	W	L	Pct.	ShO	Sv	ERA
1992 Braves	R Atl	12	2	0	6	35	148	30	18	10	1	3	2	1	8	2	40	2	0	1	3	.250	0	1	2.57
1993 Danville	R+ Atl	10	10	0	0	42.2	188	35	24	19	5	1	2	1	25	0	32	6	0	4	3	.571	0	0	4.01
1994 Macon	A Atl	27	18	1	2	121.2	532	105	54	39	9	4	2	6	62	2	81	6	1	8	7	.533	1	1	2.88
1995 Durham	A+ Atl	29	25	1	3	148.2	640	145	72	58	12	6	5	3	57	3	99	10	0	11	6	.647	0	0	3.51
1996 Greenville	AA Atl	21	21	0	0	99.2	468	127	83	74	19	3	4	4	57	1	64	8	0	3	9	.250	0	0	6.68
1997 Greenville	AA Atl	28	6	0	3	68.2	328	84	61	55	8	4	1	1	43	1	52	6	0	1	8	.111	0	0	7.21
1998 Richmond	AAA Atl	2	0	0	0	4.1	28	9	9	9	1	0	0	0	1	0	0	1	0	0	0	—	0	0	18.69
Greenville	AA Atl	35	15	0	7	101	478	104	63	60	14	3	8	2	72	3	74	12	1	6	9	.400	0	0	5.35
1999 Carolina	AA Col	28	21	1	2	114	535	120	76	67	10	6	4	8	68	1	89	5	0	6	12	.333	0	0	5.29
2000 Mudville	A+ Mil	26	1	0	4	36	175	41	35	30	4	2	1	0	29	0	31	6	2	2	3	.400	0	0	7.50
Huntsville	AA Mil	18	0	0	8	29	134	32	18	14	5	1	1	3	16	0	23	2	0	1	0	.000	0	1	4.34
9 Min. YEARS		236	119	3	35	800.2	3654	832	523	435	88	30	34	25	443	13	586	64	6	42	61	.408	1	4	4.89

Bucky Jacobsen

Bats: Right **Throws:** Right **Pos:** 1B-77; PH-4; DH-1   **Ht:** 6'4" **Wt:** 220 **Born:** 8/30/75 **Age:** 25

Year Team	Lg Org	G	AB	H	2B	3B	HR	TB	R	RBI	TBB	IBB	SO	HBP	SH	SF	SB	CS	SB%	GDP	Avg	OBP	SLG
1997 Ogden	R+ Mil	67	238	78	17	2	8	123	57	52	41	0	44	3	0	4	6	6	.50	4	.328	.427	.517
1998 Beloit	A Mil	135	499	146	31	1	27	260	96	100	83	3	133	8	0	4	5	2	.71	10	.293	.399	.521
1999 Huntsville	AA Mil	47	150	29	6	1	3	46	20	19	20	0	32	3	0	5	4	1	.80	4	.193	.292	.307
Stockton	A+ Mil	46	156	39	8	0	5	62	22	22	21	1	40	4	0	1	3	3	.50	4	.250	.352	.397
2000 Huntsville	AA Mil	81	268	74	14	0	18	142	44	50	51	2	69	4	0	4	4	2	.67	8	.276	.394	.530
4 Min. YEARS		376	1311	366	76	4	61	633	239	243	216	6	318	22	0	18	22	14	.61	30	.279	.385	.483

Delvin James

Pitches: Right **Bats:** Right **Pos:** SP-28   **Ht:** 6'4" **Wt:** 222 **Born:** 1/3/78 **Age:** 23

Year Team	Lg Org	G	GS	CG	GF	IP	BFP	H	R	ER	HR	SH	SF	HB	TBB	IBB	SO	WP	Bk	W	L	Pct.	ShO	Sv	ERA
1996 Devil Rays	R TB	11	11	1	0	47.2	236	64	52	47	0	1	3	11	21	0	40	11	2	2	8	.200	0	0	8.87
1997 Princeton	R+ TB	20	5	0	2	58.1	276	71	57	32	11	1	2	4	24	1	46	4	2	4	4	.500	0	0	4.94
1998 St. Pete	A+ TB	1	0	0	0	1.2	7	2	2	2	0	0	0	1	0	0	0	0	0	0	0	—	0	0	10.80
Chston-SC	A TB	7	0	0	2	8.1	40	12	5	5	0	0	0	2	2	0	8	0	0	2	0	1.000	0	0	5.40
Hudson Val	A- TB	15	15	0	0	81.2	345	71	39	27	2	1	1	5	32	0	64	6	0	7	4	.636	0	0	2.98
1999 Chston-SC	A TB	25	25	1	0	158.1	654	142	76	64	13	9	4	8	33	1	106	8	1	8	8	.500	0	0	3.64
St. Pete	A+ TB	3	2	0	1	17	71	18	6	6	0	0	0	3	4	0	6	1	0	3	0	1.000	0	0	3.18
2000 St. Pete	A+ TB	22	22	3	0	137.1	576	142	74	65	10	2	2	7	27	2	74	5	0	7	9	.438	1	0	4.26
Orlando	AA TB	6	6	1	0	37	153	31	15	12	3	0	3	3	7	0	26	1	0	1	3	.250	0	0	2.92
5 Min. YEARS		110	86	6	5	547.1	2358	553	326	260	39	14	17	43	150	4	370	36	5	34	36	.486	1	0	4.28

Kenny James

Bats: Both **Throws:** Right **Pos:** OF-136; PH-2; PR-1   **Ht:** 6'0" **Wt:** 198 **Born:** 10/9/76 **Age:** 24

Year Team	Lg Org	G	AB	H	2B	3B	HR	TB	R	RBI	TBB	IBB	SO	HBP	SH	SF	SB	CS	SB%	GDP	Avg	OBP	SLG
1995 Expos	R Mon	43	156	33	1	0	0	34	20	3	20	0	43	3	0	0	11	8	.58	1	.212	.313	.218
1996 Expos	R Mon	44	165	35	5	2	0	44	24	12	15	1	33	3	2	0	4	3	.57	0	.212	.290	.267
1997 Vermont	A- Mon	71	301	70	4	5	2	90	61	23	13	1	52	11	2	1	37	4	.90	0	.233	.288	.299
1998 Cape Fear	A Mon	114	451	114	10	3	2	136	73	32	21	0	68	11	12	1	41	6	.87	6	.253	.302	.302
1999 Harrisburg	AA Mon	29	102	26	4	2	0	34	8	6	1	0	19	1	5	0	7	3	.70	1	.255	.269	.333
Jupiter	A+ Mon	99	372	88	9	1	2	105	68	32	31	2	57	6	8	1	37	7	.84	8	.237	.305	.282
2000 Harrisburg	AA Mon	91	321	77	12	4	2	103	47	32	42	0	54	4	4	2	31	5	.86	7	.240	.333	.321
Ottawa	AAA Mon	48	180	44	7	3	1	60	26	11	9	0	28	3	5	0	9	0	1.00	3	.244	.292	.333
6 Min. YEARS		539	2048	487	52	20	9	606	327	151	152	4	354	42	38	5	177	36	.83	26	.238	.303	.296

Marty Janzen

Pitches: Right **Bats:** Right **Pos:** SP-7; RP-7   **Ht:** 6'3" **Wt:** 197 **Born:** 5/31/73 **Age:** 28

Year Team	Lg Org	G	GS	CG	GF	IP	BFP	H	R	ER	HR	SH	SF	HB	TBB	IBB	SO	WP	Bk	W	L	Pct.	ShO	Sv	ERA
1992 Yankees	R NYY	12	11	0	0	68.2	277	55	21	18	0	3	2	5	15	0	73	3	3	7	2	.778	0	0	2.36
Greensboro	A NYY	2	0	0	2	5	20	5	2	2	0	0	0	0	1	0	5	2	0	0	0	—	0	1	3.60
1993 Yankees	R NYY	5	5	0	0	22.1	93	20	5	3	0	0	0	1	3	0	19	0	0	1	0	1.000	0	0	1.21
1994 Greensboro	A NYY	17	17	0	0	104	431	98	57	45	8	0	0	2	25	1	92	2	2	3	7	.300	0	0	3.89
1995 Tampa	A+ NYY	18	18	1	0	113.2	461	102	38	33	4	1	2	4	30	0	104	3	4	10	3	.769	0	0	2.61
Norwich	AA NYY	3	3	0	0	20	85	17	11	11	2	0	0	2	7	0	16	2	0	1	2	.333	0	0	4.95
Knoxville	AA Tor	7	7	2	0	48	188	35	14	14	2	0	2	1	14	0	44	1	1	5	1	.833	1	0	2.63
1996 Syracuse	AAA Tor	10	10	0	0	55.2	257	74	54	48	12	1	4	2	24	2	34	2	0	3	4	.429	0	0	7.76
1997 Syracuse	AAA Tor	22	9	0	6	65	304	76	58	52	12	3	3	3	36	0	56	8	0	0	5	.000	0	1	7.20
1998 Columbus	AAA NYY	16	12	1	0	68.2	318	78	48	44	8	0	3	1	38	0	54	6	0	5	6	.455	0	0	5.77
Yankees	R NYY	1	1	0	0	3	10	1	0	0	0	0	0	0	0	0	5	0	0	0	0	—	0	0	0.00
Norwich	AA NYY	11	7	1	2	34.2	168	42	28	15	3	2	3	2	19	1	38	2	0	1	7	.125	0	0	3.89
1999 Indianapolis	AAA Cin	9	1	0	3	16.2	73	16	9	9	0	1	1	2	8	2	8	1	0	1	1	.500	0	0	4.86
Chattanooga	AA Cin	30	4	0	7	54.2	246	54	32	30	6	4	1	7	29	4	41	5	0	1	3	.250	0	0	4.94
2000 Tucson	AAA Ari	10	3	0	2	25.2	123	30	16	16	9	1	0	3	14	1	15	0	0	1	0	1.000	0	1	5.61
Nashua	IND —	4	4	0	0	25	96	16	3	3	0	0	0	0	6	0	30	1	1	3	0	1.000	0	0	1.08
1996 Toronto	AL	15	11	0	3	73.2	344	95	65	60	16	1	3	2	38	3	47	7	0	4	6	.400	0	0	7.33
1997 Toronto	AL	12	0	0	6	25	105	23	11	10	4	0	0	0	13	0	17	0	0	2	1	.667	0	0	3.60
9 Min. YEARS		177	112	5	22	730.2	3150	719	396	343	66	16	21	37	269	11	634	38	11	41	42	.494	1	3	4.22
2 Maj. YEARS		27	11	0	9	98.2	449	118	76	70	20	1	3	2	51	3	64	7	0	6	7	.462	0	0	6.39

Domingo Jean

Pitches: Right **Bats:** Right **Pos:** RP-62   **Ht:** 6'2" **Wt:** 175 **Born:** 1/9/69 **Age:** 32

Year Team	Lg Org	G	GS	CG	GF	IP	BFP	H	R	ER	HR	SH	SF	HB	TBB	IBB	SO	WP	Bk	W	L	Pct.	ShO	Sv	ERA
1990 White Sox	R CWS	13	13	1	0	78.2	312	55	32	20	1	0	1	6	16	0	65	10	2	7	2	.286	0	0	2.29
1991 South Bend	A CWS	25	25	2	0	158	680	121	75	58	7	3	7	10	65	0	141	17	5	12	8	.600	0	0	3.30
1992 Ft. Laud	A+ NYY	23	23	5	0	158.2	637	118	57	46	3	7	6	6	49	1	172	4	1	6	11	.353	1	0	2.61
Albany-Col	AA NYY	1	1	0	0	4	17	3	2	1	0	0	0	0	3	0	1	0	0	0	0	—	0	0	2.25
1993 Albany-Col	AA NYY	11	11	1	0	61	257	42	24	17	1	1	5	3	33	0	41	4	0	5	3	.625	0	0	2.51
Columbus	AAA NYY	7	7	0	0	44.2	180	40	15	14	2	0	2	2	13	1	39	3	0	2	2	.500	0	0	2.82
Pr William	A+ NYY	1	0	0	0	1.2	6	1	0	0	0	0	0	0	0	0	1	0	0	0	0	—	0	0	0.00
1994 Tucson	AAA Hou	6	3	0	1	19	88	20	13	12	3	0	1	2	11	1	16	0	0	0	2	.000	0	0	5.68
1995 Tucson	AAA Hou	3	3	0	0	13.2	62	15	10	10	1	0	0	0	7	0	14	3	0	0	2	.000	0	0	6.59
Okla City	AAA Tex	24	13	1	9	88	418	102	70	60	12	4	2	1	61	1	72	14	3	3	8	.273	0	1	6.14
Indianapols	AAA Cin	2	0	0	0	2	7	1	0	0	0	1	0	0	2	0	0	0	0	1	0	1.000	0	0	0.00
1996 Indianapols	AAA Cin	7	0	0	2	9.1	49	13	11	9	2	0	0	1	8	1	5	0	0	1	1	.500	0	0	8.68
Chattanooga	AA Cin	39	0	0	37	39.2	169	34	19	18	1	3	0	0	17	2	33	5	0	2	3	.400	0	31	4.08

Year Team	Lg Org	G	GS	CG	GF	IP	BFP	H	R	ER	HR	SH	SF	HB	TBB	IBB	SO	WP	Bk	W	L	Pct.	ShO	Sv	ERA
1997 Chattanooga	AA Cin	10	0	0	4	12	69	17	20	13	2	0	1	2	15	1	9	1	0	1	1	.500	0	1	9.75
1998 New Haven	A Col	12	5	0	4	27	131	30	21	21	1	2	0	1	19	0	17	3	1	2	2	.500	0	1	7.00
Colo Spngs	AAA Col	36	0	0	12	47.2	226	64	33	29	5	1	7	3	25	1	38	6	0	3	2	.600	0	0	5.48
1999 Bridgeport	IND —	42	0	0	19	48	227	55	43	36	8	0	3	6	25	0	38	7	0	2	1	.667	0	4	6.75
2000 Norwich	AA NYY	62	0	0	46	86.1	357	63	30	30	8	4	1	5	39	5	73	12	3	9	4	.692	0	28	3.13
1993 New York	AL	10	6	0	1	40.1	176	37	20	20	7	0	1	0	19	1	20	1	0	1	1	.500	0	0	4.46
11 Min. YEARS		324	104	11	134	899.1	3892	794	475	394	57	26	33	48	406	14	781	88	15	53	52	.505	1	66	3.94

Doug Jennings

Bats: Left **Throws:** Left **Pos:** OF-57; 1B-47; DH-14; PH-1 **Ht:** 5'10" **Wt:** 175 **Born:** 9/30/64 **Age:** 36

Year Team	Lg Org	G	AB	H	2B	3B	HR	TB	R	RBI	TBB	IBB	SO	HBP	SH	SF	SB	CS	SB%	GDP	Avg	OBP	SLG
1984 Salem	A- Ana	52	173	45	7	1	1	57	29	17	40	1	45	3	1	4	12	12	.50	2	.260	.400	.329
1985 Quad City	A Ana	95	319	81	17	7	5	127	50	54	62	1	76	5	2	6	10	8	.56	7	.254	.398	.398
1986 Palm Spring	A+ Ana	129	429	136	31	9	17	236	95	89	117	7	103	10	2	8	7	11	.39	6	.317	.466	.550
1987 Midland	AA Ana	126	464	157	33	1	30	282	106	104	94	11	136	13	2	4	7	3	.70	8	.338	.459	.608
1988 Tacoma	AAA Oak	16	49	16	1	0	0	17	12	9	18	1	13	2	2	0	5	1	.83	1	.327	.522	.347
1989 Tacoma	AAA Oak	137	497	136	35	5	11	214	99	64	93	7	95	16	2	8	10	12	.45	8	.274	.399	.431
1990 Tacoma	AAA Oak	60	208	72	19	1	6	111	32	30	31	4	36	2	1	3	4	2	.67	1	.346	.430	.534
1991 Tacoma	AAA Oak	95	332	89	17	2	3	119	43	44	47	1	65	11	1	9	5	1	.83	6	.268	.368	.358
1992 Rochester	AAA Bal	119	396	109	23	5	14	184	70	76	68	5	80	9	0	4	11	4	.73	10	.275	.390	.465
1993 Iowa	AAA ChC	65	228	67	20	1	7	110	38	37	29	2	64	4	0	2	3	4	.43	5	.294	.380	.482
1994 Indianapolis	AAA Cin	130	436	129	34	4	23	240	77	92	72	5	105	12	1	5	6	4	.60	4	.296	.406	.550
1999 Newark	IND —	84	293	77	16	0	17	144	46	51	33	0	76	9	0	1	1	1	.50	4	.263	.354	.491
2000 Omaha	AAA KC	33	124	40	12	1	6	72	23	18	13	0	21	2	0	0	2	3	.40	2	.323	.396	.581
Long Island	IND —	84	273	90	22	4	14	158	65	64	68	8	42	15	0	11	13	7	.65	2	.330	.471	.579
1988 Oakland	AL	71	101	21	6	0	1	30	9	15	21	1	28	2	1	3	0	1	.00	1	.208	.346	.297
1989 Oakland	AL	4	4	0	0	0	0	0	0	0	0	0	2	0	0	0	0	0	—	0	.000	.000	.000
1990 Oakland	AL	64	156	30	7	2	2	47	19	14	17	0	48	2	2	3	0	3	.00	1	.192	.275	.301
1991 Oakland	AL	8	9	1	0	0	0	1	0	0	2	0	2	0	0	0	0	1	.00	1	.111	.273	.111
1993 Chicago	NL	42	52	13	3	1	2	24	8	3	3	0	10	2	0	0	0	0			.250	.316	.462
13 Min. YEARS		1225	4221	1244	287	39	154	2071	785	749	785	53	957	113	14	65	96	73	.57	66	.295	.413	.491
5 Maj. YEARS		189	322	65	16	3	5	102	36	37	43	1	90	6	3	6	0	5	.00	3	.202	.302	.317

Jason Jennings

Pitches: Right **Bats:** Left **Pos:** SP-28 **Ht:** 6'2" **Wt:** 230 **Born:** 7/17/78 **Age:** 22

Year Team	Lg Org	G	GS	CG	GF	IP	BFP	H	R	ER	HR	SH	SF	HB	TBB	IBB	SO	WP	Bk	W	L	Pct.	ShO	Sv	ERA
1999 Portland	A- Col	2	2	0	0	9	33	5	1	1	0	0	0	0	2	0	11	0	0	1	0	1.000	0	0	1.00
Asheville	A Col	12	12	0	0	58.1	242	55	27	24	3	3	2	6	8	0	69	4	0	2	2	.500	0	0	3.70
2000 Salem	A+ Col	22	22	3	0	150.1	632	136	66	58	6	3	5	2	42	0	133	8	1	7	10	.412	1	0	3.47
Carolina	AA Col	6	6	0	0	36.2	149	32	19	14	4	1	0	0	11	0	33	1	0	1	3	.250	0	0	3.44
2 Min. YEARS		42	42	3	0	254.1	1056	228	113	97	13	7	7	8	63	0	246	13	1	11	15	.423	1	0	3.43

Robin Jennings

Bats: Left **Throws:** Left **Pos:** OF-98; DH-16; 1B-10; PH-3; PR-2; P-1 **Ht:** 6'2" **Wt:** 210 **Born:** 4/11/72 **Age:** 29

Year Team	Lg Org	G	AB	H	2B	3B	HR	TB	R	RBI	TBB	IBB	SO	HBP	SH	SF	SB	CS	SB%	GDP	Avg	OBP	SLG
1992 Geneva	A- ChC	72	275	82	12	2	7	119	39	47	20	5	43	2	0	0	10	3	.77	7	.298	.350	.433
1993 Peoria	A ChC	132	474	146	29	5	3	194	65	65	46	2	73	4	5	3	11	11	.50	9	.308	.372	.409
1994 Daytona	A+ ChC	128	476	133	24	5	8	191	54	60	45	5	54	4	4	4	2	10	.17	13	.279	.344	.401
1995 Orlando	AA ChC	132	490	145	27	7	17	237	71	79	44	5	61	4	0	5	7	14	.33	11	.296	.355	.484
1996 Iowa	AAA ChC	86	331	94	15	6	18	175	53	56	32	1	53	1	0	3	2	0	1.00	6	.284	.346	.529
1997 Iowa	AAA ChC	126	464	128	25	5	20	223	67	71	56	5	73	0	0	2	5	3	.63	5	.276	.359	.481
1998 West Tenn	AA ChC	2	6	0	0	0	0	0	0	0	0	0	2	0	0	0	0	0	—	0	.000	.000	.000
Iowa	AAA ChC	81	298	74	23	2	16	149	57	62	33	1	49	6	1	0	4	4	.50	9	.248	.335	.500
1999 West Tenn	AA ChC	13	53	17	3	0	1	35	11	17	5	0	7	1	0	2	1	0	1.00	3	.321	.377	.660
Iowa	AAA ChC	67	259	80	20	5	9	137	47	43	25	0	34	1	0	0	6	4	.60	7	.309	.372	.529
2000 Salt Lake	AAA Min	91	345	107	33	6	11	185	70	61	35	1	45	3	4	8	2	1	.67	4	.310	.371	.536
Louisville	AAA Cin	32	122	46	14	1	5	77	18	27	9	3	15	2	3	0	2	0	.00	3	.377	.419	.631
1996 Chicago	NL	31	58	13	5	0	0	18	7	4	3	0	9	1	0	0	1	0	1.00	0	.224	.274	.310
1997 Chicago	NL	9	18	3	1	0	0	4	1	2	0	0	2	0	0	1	0	0	—	0	.167	.158	.222
1999 Chicago	NL	5	5	1	0	0	0	1	0	0	0	0	2	0	0	0	0	0	—	0	.200	.200	.200
9 Min. YEARS		962	3593	1052	225	44	119	1722	552	588	350	28	509	33	16	30	52	53	.50	78	.293	.358	.479
3 Maj. YEARS		45	81	17	6	0	0	23	8	6	3	0	13	1	0	1	1	0	1.00	1	.210	.244	.284

Justin Jensen

Pitches: Left **Bats:** Left **Pos:** RP-21; SP-10 **Ht:** 6'3" **Wt:** 210 **Born:** 12/19/73 **Age:** 27

Year Team	Lg Org	G	GS	CG	GF	IP	BFP	H	R	ER	HR	SH	SF	HB	TBB	IBB	SO	WP	Bk	W	L	Pct.	ShO	Sv	ERA
1994 Bristol	R+ Det	11	9	0	0	44	190	39	28	20	2	3	1	1	25	0	39	5	1	2	4	.333	0	0	4.09
1995 Jamestown	A- Det	14	14	0	0	74.1	332	73	53	40	7	0	5	4	41	0	63	9	3	2	8	.200	0	0	4.84
1996 Fayetteville	A Det	26	26	2	0	153	646	127	78	55	8	4	4	13	58	0	148	11	1	7	11	.389	0	0	3.24
1997 Lakeland	A+ Det	25	25	1	0	143.1	624	143	78	66	10	1	4	8	68	0	112	9	0	7	10	.412	0	0	4.14
1998 Lakeland	A+ Det	30	13	0	7	104.2	477	106	57	47	6	6	7	4	62	0	86	12	0	5	7	.417	0	1	4.04
1999 Somerset	IND —	24	23	2	0	156.1	644	120	55	48	13	3	2	7	77	1	111	8	2	12	5	.706	0	0	2.76
2000 Trenton	AA Bos	10	0	0	7	14.1	64	13	12	12	3	1	1	1	8	0	6	2	0	1	1	.500	0	0	7.53
Sarasota	A+ Bos	12	1	0	5	16	79	24	12	12	2	1	1	0	15	0	10	0	0	1	1	.500	0	0	6.75
Somerset	IND —	9	9	0	0	47.1	210	47	25	23	7	3	0	1	22	1	44	3	0	3	1	.750	0	0	4.37
7 Min. YEARS		161	120	5	19	753.1	3266	692	398	323	59	22	29	35	366	2	624	59	7	40	48	.455	0	2	3.86

Ryan Jensen

Pitches: Right **Bats:** Right **Pos:** SP-26 **Ht:** 6'0" **Wt:** 205 **Born:** 9/17/75 **Age:** 25

Year Team	Lg Org	G	GS	CG	GF	IP	BFP	H	R	ER	HR	SH	SF	HB	TBB	IBB	SO	WP	Bk	W	L	Pct.	ShO	Sv	ERA
						HOW MUCH HE PITCHED						**WHAT HE GAVE UP**										**THE RESULTS**			
1996 Bellingham	A- SF	13	11	0	0	47	208	35	30	26	4	1	0	1	38	0	31	7	0	2	4	.333	0	0	4.98
1997 Bakersfield	A+ SF	1	1	0	0	1.1	7	3	2	2	1	0	1	0	0	0	2	0	0	0	0	—	0	0	13.50
Salem-Keizr	A- SF	16	16	0	0	80.1	353	87	55	46	10	2	2	4	32	0	67	2	1	7	3	.700	0	0	5.15
1998 Bakersfield	A+ SF	29	27	0	1	168.1	726	162	89	63	14	6	1	8	61	3	164	10	2	11	12	.478	0	0	3.37
Fresno	AAA SF	2	1	0	0	5.2	25	4	5	3	2	0	1	0	4	0	6	0	0	0	0	—	0	0	4.76
1999 Fresno	AAA SF	27	27	0	0	156.1	688	160	96	89	17	6	6	6	68	1	150	13	0	11	10	.524	0	0	5.12
2000 Fresno	AAA SF	26	26	1	0	135.1	628	167	106	87	18	4	9	4	63	0	114	3	1	5	8	.385	0	0	5.79
5 Min. YEARS		114	109	1	1	594.1	2635	618	383	316	66	19	20	23	266	4	534	35	4	36	37	.493	0	0	4.79

Tristan Jerue

Pitches: Right **Bats:** Right **Pos:** RP-10; SP-4 **Ht:** 6'1" **Wt:** 185 **Born:** 12/12/75 **Age:** 25

Year Team	Lg Org	G	GS	CG	GF	IP	BFP	H	R	ER	HR	SH	SF	HB	TBB	IBB	SO	WP	Bk	W	L	Pct.	ShO	Sv	ERA
						HOW MUCH HE PITCHED						**WHAT HE GAVE UP**										**THE RESULTS**			
1997 New Jersey	A- StL	13	13	0	0	71.2	310	73	35	28	3	2	5	5	21	0	55	4	1	5	4	.556	0	0	3.52
1998 Peoria	A StL	20	20	1	0	131.2	544	107	48	37	7	4	3	10	48	0	100	4	1	12	4	.750	0	0	2.53
Pr William	A+ StL	7	7	0	0	42.2	167	31	13	10	0	2	1	2	11	0	34	2	1	3	3	.500	0	0	2.11
1999 Potomac	A+ StL	4	3	0	0	14.2	72	18	12	12	0	1	1	1	8	0	9	2	0	0	1	.000	0	0	7.36
2000 Arkansas	AA StL	4	4	0	0	10.2	60	14	13	10	2	6	1	1	16	0	5	1	0	0	2	.000	0	0	8.44
Potomac	A+ StL	10	0	0	0	10	49	12	7	6	1	1	0	1	8	0	12	3	0	1	1	.500	0	0	5.40
4 Min. YEARS		58	47	1	0	281.1	1197	255	128	103	13	15	11	20	112	0	215	16	3	21	15	.583	0	0	3.30

Joe Jester

Bats: Right **Throws:** Right **Pos:** 2B-111; DH-6; PH-2 **Ht:** 5'10" **Wt:** 180 **Born:** 7/17/78 **Age:** 22

Year Team	Lg Org	G	AB	H	2B	3B	HR	TB	R	RBI	TBB	IBB	SO	HBP	SH	SF	SB	CS	SB%	GDP	Avg	OBP	SLG
						BATTING											**BASERUNNING**				**PERCENTAGES**		
1999 Salem-Keizr	A- SF	72	263	79	19	1	8	124	67	40	50	3	57	7	7	2	13	6	.68	2	.300	.422	.471
2000 San Jose	A+ SF	114	429	113	13	4	8	158	94	46	69	0	75	17	3	6	24	8	.75	7	.263	.382	.368
Fresno	AAA SF	4	15	3	1	0	0	4	1	0	2	0	4	0	0	0	0	0	—	1	.200	.294	.267
2 Min. YEARS		190	707	195	33	5	16	286	162	86	121	3	136	24	10	8	37	14	.73	10	.276	.395	.405

D'Angelo Jimenez

Bats: Both **Throws:** Right **Pos:** 2B-21; SS-11; 3B-3; DH-2; PH-1 **Ht:** 6'0" **Wt:** 194 **Born:** 12/21/77 **Age:** 23

Year Team	Lg Org	G	AB	H	2B	3B	HR	TB	R	RBI	TBB	IBB	SO	HBP	SH	SF	SB	CS	SB%	GDP	Avg	OBP	SLG
						BATTING											**BASERUNNING**				**PERCENTAGES**		
1995 Yankees	R NYY	57	214	60	14	8	2	96	41	28	23	1	31	1	3	4	6	3	.67	4	.280	.347	.449
1996 Greensboro	A NYY	138	537	131	25	5	6	184	68	48	56	2	113	3	4	3	15	17	.47	7	.244	.317	.343
1997 Columbus	AAA NYY	2	7	1	0	0	0	1	1	1	0	0	1	0	0	1	0	0	—	1	.143	.125	.143
Tampa	A+ NYY	94	352	99	14	6	6	143	52	48	50	4	50	2	3	6	8	14	.36	3	.281	.368	.406
1998 Norwich	AA NYY	40	152	41	6	2	2	57	21	21	25	1	26	2	2	1	5	5	.50	3	.270	.378	.375
Columbus	AAA NYY	91	344	88	19	4	8	139	55	51	46	0	67	1	1	5	6	6	.50	7	.256	.341	.404
1999 Columbus	AAA NYY	126	526	172	32	5	15	259	97	88	59	1	75	1	6	6	26	14	.65	8	.327	.392	.492
2000 Yankees	R NYY	4	10	1	0	0	0	1	2	0	5	0	1	0	0	0	0	0	—	0	.100	.400	.100
Tampa	A+ NYY	12	41	8	1	1	1	14	8	2	8	1	7	0	0	1	0	0	—	1	.195	.320	.341
Columbus	AAA NYY	21	73	17	3	1	1	25	11	5	7	1	12	1	0	0	2	0	1.00	0	.233	.309	.342
1999 New York	AL	7	20	8	2	0	0	10	3	4	3	0	4	0	0	0	0	0	—	0	.400	.478	.500
6 Min. YEARS		585	2256	618	114	32	41	919	356	292	279	11	383	11	19	27	68	59	.54	36	.274	.353	.407

Jason Jimenez

Pitches: Left **Bats:** Right **Pos:** RP-47; SP-2 **Ht:** 6'2" **Wt:** 210 **Born:** 1/10/76 **Age:** 25

Year Team	Lg Org	G	GS	CG	GF	IP	BFP	H	R	ER	HR	SH	SF	HB	TBB	IBB	SO	WP	Bk	W	L	Pct.	ShO	Sv	ERA
						HOW MUCH HE PITCHED						**WHAT HE GAVE UP**										**THE RESULTS**			
1997 Hudson Val	A- TB	19	0	0	5	31.2	121	16	5	1	1	0	0	2	10	0	31	0	1	3	0	1.000	0	0	0.28
1998 St. Pete	A+ TB	13	0	0	8	19	97	24	20	18	3	0	2	3	10	2	15	3	1	0	2	.000	0	0	8.53
Hudson Val	A- TB	29	0	0	6	39.1	154	20	13	7	1	3	0	5	13	1	55	2	1	5	2	.714	0	4	1.60
1999 St. Pete	A+ TB	41	1	0	19	56.2	229	46	23	15	2	2	0	3	21	2	47	2	0	4	4	.500	0	5	2.38
2000 Durham	AAA TB	19	1	0	7	31.2	147	33	17	17	4	0	0	1	25	0	28	1	0	1	1	.500	0	0	4.83
Orlando	AA TB	30	1	0	8	46.1	185	29	13	10	4	0	1	2	12	0	53	3	0	5	1	.833	0	0	1.94
4 Min. YEARS		151	3	0	53	224.2	933	168	91	68	15	5	3	16	91	5	229	11	3	18	10	.643	0	9	2.72

Brett Jodie

Pitches: Right **Bats:** Right **Pos:** SP-21; RP-7 **Ht:** 6'4" **Wt:** 208 **Born:** 3/25/77 **Age:** 24

Year Team	Lg Org	G	GS	CG	GF	IP	BFP	H	R	ER	HR	SH	SF	HB	TBB	IBB	SO	WP	Bk	W	L	Pct.	ShO	Sv	ERA
						HOW MUCH HE PITCHED						**WHAT HE GAVE UP**										**THE RESULTS**			
1998 Oneonta	A- NYY	15	15	1	0	94	381	87	40	27	7	1	3	0	21	0	73	3	1	7	6	.538	1	0	2.59
1999 Greensboro	A NYY	25	20	2	3	120.1	497	125	59	51	10	0	1	1	18	0	106	9	0	9	6	.600	0	1	3.81
2000 Tampa	A+ NYY	25	18	3	2	143.2	582	134	53	41	4	5	3	3	29	5	122	5	1	11	4	.733	1	0	2.57
Norwich	AA NYY	3	3	1	0	20	77	16	8	7	3	0	1	0	5	0	9	0	0	2	1	.667	1	0	3.15
3 Min. YEARS		68	56	7	5	378	1537	362	160	126	24	6	8	4	73	5	310	17	2	29	17	.630	3	1	3.00

Keith Johns

Bats: Right **Throws:** Right **Pos:** 2B-73; 3B-20; PH-16; SS-15; OF-6; PR-2; 1B-1   **Ht:** 6'1" **Wt:** 175 **Born:** 7/19/71 **Age:** 29

					BATTING										BASERUNNING				PERCENTAGES		
Year Team	Lg Org	G	AB	H	2B	3B	HR	TB	R	RBI	TBB	IBB	SO	HBP	SH	SF	SB	CS	SB%	GDP	Avg	OBP	SLG
1992 Hamilton	A- StL	70	275	78	11	1	1	94	36	28	27	0	42	1	1	3	15	10	.60	5	.284	.346	.342
1993 Springfield	A StL	132	467	121	24	1	2	153	74	40	70	0	68	4	9	5	40	20	.67	8	.259	.357	.328
1994 St. Pete	A+ StL	122	464	106	20	2	3	135	52	47	37	1	49	2	12	4	18	9	.67	7	.228	.286	.291
1995 Arkansas	AA StL	111	396	111	13	2	2	134	69	28	55	0	53	2	11	2	14	7	.67	11	.280	.369	.338
Louisville	AAA StL	5	10	0	0	0	0	0	0	0	0	0	2	0	0	0	0	0	—	0	.000	.000	.000
1996 Arkansas	AA StL	127	447	110	17	1	1	132	52	40	47	0	61	4	7	1	8	9	.47	17	.246	.323	.295
1997 Tucson	AAA Mil	112	333	88	21	3	5	130	45	36	43	0	61	2	6	2	4	2	.67	7	.264	.350	.390
Rochester	AAA Bal	1	1	0	0	0	0	0	0	0	0	0	0	1	0	0	0	0	—	0	.000	.500	.000
1998 Pawtucket	AAA Bos	96	329	75	12	1	8	113	31	38	28	0	82	4	1	5	6	.25	10	.228	.292	.343		
1999 Edmonton	AAA Ana	81	236	49	9	2	3	71	32	26	26	0	38	2	1	2	2	0	1.00	6	.208	.289	.301
2000 Iowa	AAA ChC	115	353	86	24	0	2	116	50	26	33	1	75	2	1	3	3	4	.43	3	.244	.309	.329
1998 Boston	AL	2	0	0	0	0	0	0	0	0	1	0	0	0	0	0	0	0	—	0	—	1.000	—
9 Min. YEARS		972	3311	824	151	11	27	1078	441	309	366	2	531	24	49	27	106	67	.61	76	.249	.326	.326

Adam Johnson

Bats: Left **Throws:** Left **Pos:** DH-61; OF-35; 1B-9; PH-2; PR-1   **Ht:** 6'0" **Wt:** 185 **Born:** 7/18/75 **Age:** 25

					BATTING										BASERUNNING				PERCENTAGES		
Year Team	Lg Org	G	AB	H	2B	3B	HR	TB	R	RBI	TBB	IBB	SO	HBP	SH	SF	SB	CS	SB%	GDP	Avg	OBP	SLG
1996 Eugene	A- Atl	76	318	100	22	9	7	161	58	56	19	3	32	4	1	2	4	1	.80	4	.314	.359	.506
1997 Durham	A+ Atl	133	502	141	39	3	26	264	80	92	50	9	94	4	0	16	18	8	.69	10	.281	.341	.526
1998 Greenville	AA Atl	121	411	104	21	3	19	188	67	77	42	6	71	4	0	7	7	7	.50	10	.253	.323	.457
1999 Richmond	AAA Atl	14	42	14	2	0	1	19	7	6	2	0	5	1	1	0	1	1	.50	3	.333	.378	.452
Greenville	AA Atl	104	394	114	27	2	14	187	50	72	31	1	74	4	0	5	1	6	.14	11	.289	.343	.475
2000 Birmingham	AA CWS	105	379	88	21	2	11	146	42	60	42	2	74	2	0	3	3	5	.38	10	.232	.310	.385
5 Min. YEARS		553	2046	561	132	19	78	965	304	363	186	21	350	19	2	33	34	28	.55	45	.274	.335	.472

Barry Johnson

Pitches: Right **Bats:** Right **Pos:** RP-55; SP-1   **Ht:** 6'4" **Wt:** 200 **Born:** 8/21/69 **Age:** 31

		HOW MUCH HE PITCHED						WHAT HE GAVE UP										THE RESULTS					
Year Team	Lg Org	G	GS	CG	GF	IP	BFP	H	R	ER	HR	SH	SF	HB	TBB	IBB	SO	WP	Bk	W	L	Pct.	ShO	Sv	ERA
1991 Expos	R Mon	7	1	0	3	12.2	55	10	9	5	0	0	0	4	6	0	10	2	0	0	2	.000	0	0	3.55
1992 South Bend	A CWS	16	16	5	0	109.1	463	111	56	46	5	1	5	6	23	0	74	8	1	7	5	.583	1	0	3.79
1993 Sarasota	A+ CWS	18	1	0	7	54.1	205	33	5	4	1	5	2	2	8	0	40	1	1	5	0	1.000	0	1	0.66
Birmingham	AA CWS	13	1	0	8	21.2	97	27	11	8	2	1	1	0	6	0	16	2	1	2	0	1.000	0	1	3.32
1994 Birmingham	AA CWS	51	4	0	12	97.2	427	100	51	35	7	8	3	2	30	3	67	2	0	6	2	.750	0	1	3.23
1995 Birmingham	AA CWS	47	0	0	10	78	308	64	21	16	1	2	1	2	15	1	53	2	1	7	4	.636	0	1	1.85
1996 Birmingham	AA CWS	9	0	0	7	10.2	35	2	0	0	1	0	0	1	0	0	15	0	0	0	0	—	0	4	0.00
Nashville	AAA CWS	38	8	0	8	103	430	93	38	32	11	2	3	1	39	3	68	4	0	7	2	.778	0	0	2.80
1997 Nashville	AAA CWS	14	0	0	5	25.1	108	24	10	10	1	1	1	0	11	1	10	3	0	4	1	.800	0	2	3.55
Calgary	AAA Pit	34	1	0	12	56.2	247	55	30	26	7	1	3	1	23	2	51	3	0	5	2	.714	0	1	4.13
1998 Oklahoma	AAA Tex	31	7	1	10	77.1	343	96	66	57	13	2	1	3	21	0	54	3	0	2	8	.200	0	1	6.63
Tucson	AAA Ari	5	1	0	0	11.2	56	16	12	9	2	0	0	1	5	1	10	1	0	0	1	.000	0	0	6.94
Norwich	AA NYY	7	0	0	3	12	53	13	6	5	1	1	1	0	5	0	12	1	0	1	0	1.000	0	0	3.75
1999 Scranton-WB	AAA Phi	31	18	1	5	136.1	602	157	83	76	12	1	5	1	49	2	88	7	0	6	10	.375	1	0	5.02
2000 Scranton-WB	AAA Phi	56	1	0	22	81	339	66	25	24	6	3	2	4	30	4	57	1	0	7	4	.636	0	3	2.67
10 Min. YEARS		377	59	7	112	887.2	3768	867	423	353	69	29	28	27	272	17	625	40	4	59	41	.590	2	14	3.58

Craig Johnson

Pitches: Right **Bats:** Right **Pos:** SP-15; RP-5   **Ht:** 6'3" **Wt:** 200 **Born:** 11/8/75 **Age:** 25

		HOW MUCH HE PITCHED						WHAT HE GAVE UP										THE RESULTS					
Year Team	Lg Org	G	GS	CG	GF	IP	BFP	H	R	ER	HR	SH	SF	HB	TBB	IBB	SO	WP	Bk	W	L	Pct.	ShO	Sv	ERA
1997 Jamestown	A- Det	14	14	3	0	83.1	349	88	59	41	4	1	6	6	10	0	66	1	2	3	10	.231	0	0	4.43
1998 Toledo	AAA Det	1	1	0	0	5	22	6	4	3	1	0	0	0	1	0	1	0	0	1	0	1.000	0	0	5.40
W Michigan	A Det	26	26	3	0	164.2	658	146	66	51	14	2	4	9	22	0	116	4	1	14	6	.700	2	0	2.79
1999 Lakeland	A+ Det	26	25	0	1	144	638	176	93	82	20	6	7	6	31	0	98	2	0	11	11	.500	0	0	5.13
2000 Toledo	AAA Det	1	1	0	0	5	22	6	5	4	1	0	0	0	2	0	2	0	0	0	0	—	0	0	7.20
Lakeland	A+ Det	19	14	1	2	86	357	85	51	40	9	0	3	5	16	0	60	4	1	3	6	.333	1	0	4.19
4 Min. YEARS		87	81	7	3	488	2046	507	278	221	49	9	20	26	82	0	343	11	5	32	33	.492	3	0	4.08

Gary Johnson

Bats: Left **Throws:** Left **Pos:** OF-137; DH-3; PH-1   **Ht:** 6'3" **Wt:** 210 **Born:** 10/29/75 **Age:** 25

					BATTING										BASERUNNING				PERCENTAGES		
Year Team	Lg Org	G	AB	H	2B	3B	HR	TB	R	RBI	TBB	IBB	SO	HBP	SH	SF	SB	CS	SB%	GDP	Avg	OBP	SLG
1999 Boise	A- Ana	71	264	83	17	1	2	108	56	48	34	3	44	2	0	3	6	2	.75	6	.314	.393	.409
2000 Lk Elsinore	A+ Ana	70	266	90	20	2	13	153	56	62	41	1	59	4	0	5	13	6	.68	6	.338	.427	.575
Erie	AA Ana	71	258	74	10	4	10	122	44	56	35	0	63	3	0	1	4	4	.50	4	.287	.377	.473
2 Min. YEARS		212	788	247	47	7	25	383	156	166	110	4	166	9	0	9	23	12	.66	16	.313	.400	.486

James Johnson

Pitches: Left **Bats:** Both **Pos:** SP-21; RP-6   **Ht:** 6'1" **Wt:** 175 **Born:** 8/7/76 **Age:** 24

		HOW MUCH HE PITCHED						WHAT HE GAVE UP										THE RESULTS					
Year Team	Lg Org	G	GS	CG	GF	IP	BFP	H	R	ER	HR	SH	SF	HB	TBB	IBB	SO	WP	Bk	W	L	Pct.	ShO	Sv	ERA
1998 Ogden	R+ Mil	13	13	0	0	68.1	305	75	51	37	10	0	2	0	27	0	77	11	1	5	6	.455	0	0	4.87
1999 Stockton	A+ Mil	29	23	1	1	129.1	568	146	83	68	13	6	5	2	47	1	135	23	1	5	6	.455	1	0	4.73
2000 Mudville	A+ Mil	11	11	0	0	58.2	241	45	25	20	1	1	2	0	20	0	66	4	0	3	5	.375	0	0	3.07
Huntsville	AA Mil	16	10	0	1	68	299	74	42	35	9	2	1	0	22	0	74	11	0	4	3	.571	0	0	4.63
3 Min. YEARS		69	57	1	2	324.1	1413	340	201	160	33	9	10	2	116	1	352	49	2	17	20	.459	1	0	4.44

141

Nick Johnson

Bats: Left **Throws:** Left **Pos:** 1B **Ht:** 6'3" **Wt:** 195 **Born:** 9/19/78 **Age:** 22

Year Team	Lg Org	G	AB	H	2B	3B	HR	TB	R	RBI	TBB	IBB	SO	HBP	SH	SF	SB	CS	SB%	GDP	Avg	OBP	SLG
1996 Yankees	R NYY	47	157	45	11	1	2	64	31	33	30	0	35	9	0	3	0	0	.00	5	.287	.422	.408
1997 Greensboro	A NYY	127	433	118	23	1	16	191	77	75	76	1	99	18	0	6	16	3	.84	5	.273	.398	.441
1998 Tampa	A+ NYY	92	303	96	14	1	17	163	69	58	68	3	76	19	0	3	1	4	.20	5	.317	.466	.538
1999 Norwich	AA NYY	132	420	145	33	5	14	230	114	87	123	6	88	37	0	1	8	6	.57	9	.345	.525	.548
2000	NYY	DNP—Hand Injury																					
4 Min. YEARS		398	1313	404	81	8	49	648	291	253	297	10	298	83	0	13	25	13	.66	24	.308	.460	.494

Rontrez Johnson

Bats: Right **Throws:** Right **Pos:** OF-133; PH-1; PR-1 **Ht:** 5'10" **Wt:** 165 **Born:** 12/8/76 **Age:** 24

Year Team	Lg Org	G	AB	H	2B	3B	HR	TB	R	RBI	TBB	IBB	SO	HBP	SH	SF	SB	CS	SB%	GDP	Avg	OBP	SLG
1995 Red Sox	R Bos	52	193	49	4	2	0	57	37	11	30	0	30	1	3	1	25	5	.83	1	.254	.356	.295
1996 Red Sox	R Bos	28	85	25	6	0	0	31	20	9	17	0	11	0	1	0	6	2	.75	2	.294	.412	.365
Lowell	A- Bos	35	135	30	4	0	4	46	27	12	21	1	30	0	0	2	7	3	.70	2	.222	.323	.341
1997 Michigan	A Bos	118	411	99	10	6	5	136	87	40	65	0	96	9	6	3	29	12	.71	2	.241	.355	.331
1998 Michigan	A Bos	85	306	83	15	5	5	123	65	32	66	0	46	4	1	5	24	8	.75	4	.271	.402	.402
1999 Sarasota	A+ Bos	132	494	148	30	4	8	210	97	59	74	0	63	8	8	7	18	15	.55	7	.300	.395	.425
2000 Trenton	AA Bos	134	524	141	21	2	6	184	83	53	55	1	73	6	3	4	30	19	.61	12	.269	.343	.351
6 Min. YEARS		584	2148	575	90	19	28	787	416	216	328	2	349	28	22	22	139	64	.68	30	.268	.369	.366

Doug Johnston

Pitches: Right **Bats:** Right **Pos:** SP-18; RP-14 **Ht:** 6'5" **Wt:** 180 **Born:** 3/16/78 **Age:** 23

Year Team	Lg Org	G	GS	CG	GF	IP	BFP	H	R	ER	HR	SH	SF	HB	TBB	IBB	SO	WP	Bk	W	L	Pct.	ShO	Sv	ERA
1997 Helena	R+ Mil	13	13	0	0	74.1	172	64	39	36	5	1	1	6	34	0	66	5	0	6	2	.750	0	0	4.36
1998 Beloit	A Mil	14	14	2	0	91	379	77	30	25	6	1	0	7	28	1	71	3	1	8	2	.800	1	0	2.47
Stockton	A+ Mil	9	9	1	0	60.1	240	47	20	18	3	0	1	5	26	0	54	1	2	5	1	.833	0	0	2.69
1999 Huntsville	AA Mil	21	21	1	0	118.2	516	128	72	66	17	5	3	9	43	3	80	5	1	7	11	.389	0	0	5.01
2000 Huntsville	AA Mil	2	2	0	0	6.1	35	10	11	10	2	1	1	0	6	0	5	3	0	0	1	.000	0	0	14.21
West Tenn	AA ChC	30	16	0	3	116.2	499	106	52	50	6	9	2	6	51	3	82	7	0	4	4	.500	0	1	3.86
4 Min. YEARS		89	75	4	3	467.1	1987	432	224	205	39	17	8	33	188	7	358	24	4	30	21	.588	1	1	3.95

Greg Jones

Pitches: Right **Bats:** Right **Pos:** RP-52 **Ht:** 6'2" **Wt:** 190 **Born:** 11/15/76 **Age:** 24

Year Team	Lg Org	G	GS	CG	GF	IP	BFP	H	R	ER	HR	SH	SF	HB	TBB	IBB	SO	WP	Bk	W	L	Pct.	ShO	Sv	ERA
1997 Boise	A- Ana	21	4	0	4	37.1	172	35	19	15	1	2	4	3	19	1	39	5	1	2	2	.500	0	2	3.62
1998 Boise	A- Ana	22	0	0	3	34.2	152	37	22	19	3	2	1	3	13	0	28	3	0	0	2	.000	0	1	4.93
1999 Cedar Rapds	A Ana	34	0	0	29	40	165	37	18	17	5	2	0	0	13	2	41	5	0	2	4	.333	0	13	3.83
2000 Lk Elsinore	A+ Ana	16	0	0	12	17.2	81	19	9	8	0	2	1	1	10	3	12	3	0	0	0	—	0	3	4.08
Erie	AA Ana	11	0	0	8	15	66	19	9	9	1	0	0	0	4	0	7	0	0	0	2	.000	0	3	5.40
Edmonton	AAA Ana	25	0	0	13	42.1	217	57	42	36	5	1	3	4	33	1	21	6	0	2	2	.500	0	1	7.65
4 Min. YEARS		129	4	0	69	187	853	204	119	104	15	9	9	11	92	7	148	22	1	6	12	.333	0	22	5.01

Jaime Jones

Bats: Left **Throws:** Left **Pos:** OF-46; PH-4 **Ht:** 6'3" **Wt:** 190 **Born:** 8/2/76 **Age:** 24

Year Team	Lg Org	G	AB	H	2B	3B	HR	TB	R	RBI	TBB	IBB	SO	HBP	SH	SF	SB	CS	SB%	GDP	Avg	OBP	SLG
1995 Marlins	R Fla	5	18	4	0	0	0	4	2	3	5	1	4	0	0	0	0	0	—	0	.222	.391	.222
Elmira	A- Fla	31	116	33	6	2	4	55	21	11	9	0	30	0	0	0	5	4	.56	2	.284	.336	.474
1996 Kane County	A Fla	62	237	59	17	1	8	102	29	45	19	0	74	0	0	5	7	2	.78	6	.249	.299	.430
1997 Brevard Cty	A+ Fla	95	373	101	27	4	10	166	63	60	44	2	86	1	0	4	6	1	.86	7	.271	.346	.445
1998 Portland	AA Fla	123	438	123	27	0	10	180	58	63	55	3	118	3	0	3	4	1	.80	11	.281	.363	.411
1999 Calgary	AAA Fla	41	138	34	6	0	0	40	12	7	10	1	30	0	0	0	1	3	.25	5	.246	.297	.290
Portland	AA Fla	73	244	62	16	0	7	99	39	31	47	1	81	0	0	2	2	0	1.00	3	.254	.376	.406
2000 Portland	AA Fla	50	185	42	6	2	6	70	25	30	13	0	47	3	0	2	0	4	.00	2	.227	.286	.378
6 Min. YEARS		480	1749	458	105	9	45	716	249	250	202	8	470	9	0	16	25	15	.63	36	.262	.339	.409

Jay Jones

Bats: Left **Throws:** Right **Pos:** C-24; DH-9; 1B-2; PH-2; PR-1 **Ht:** 6'0" **Wt:** 195 **Born:** 10/24/74 **Age:** 26

Year Team	Lg Org	G	AB	H	2B	3B	HR	TB	R	RBI	TBB	IBB	SO	HBP	SH	SF	SB	CS	SB%	GDP	Avg	OBP	SLG
1996 Utica	A- Fla	37	116	33	6	0	0	39	9	9	6	0	17	0	2	1	0	1	.00	5	.284	.317	.336
1997 Kane County	A Fla	64	210	62	6	0	4	80	20	31	8	1	29	3	1	0	0	2	.00	7	.295	.330	.381
1998 Brevard Cty	A+ Fla	74	262	58	8	0	3	75	15	25	13	3	34	1	2	3	1	3	.25	11	.221	.258	.286
1999 Asheville	A Col	43	148	44	8	0	4	64	22	20	8	0	16	2	0	0	2	0	1.00	1	.297	.342	.432
Salem	A+ Col	18	60	9	3	0	0	12	4	8	4	0	9	1	0	2	0	0	—	0	.150	.209	.200
2000 Carolina	AA Col	1	0	0	0	0	0	0	0	0	0	0	0	0	0	0	0	0	—	0	—	—	—
Salem	A+ Col	36	126	36	10	1	2	54	15	24	9	0	13	0	1	2	1	0	1.00	3	.286	.328	.429
5 Min. YEARS		273	922	242	41	1	13	324	85	117	48	4	118	7	6	8	4	6	.40	27	.262	.302	.351

Jeremy Jones

Bats: Right **Throws:** Right **Pos:** C-73; DH-4; PH-4; PR-2; 1B-1 · **Ht:** 6'3" **Wt:** 195 **Born:** 8/12/77 **Age:** 23

Year Team	Lg Org	G	AB	H	2B	3B	HR	TB	R	RBI	TBB	IBB	SO	HBP	SH	SF	SB	CS	SB%	GDP	Avg	OBP	SLG
1998 Pulaski	R+ Tex	26	101	28	3	1	3	42	11	14	10	0	18	0	0	1	0	0	—	5	.277	.339	.416
1999 Charlotte	A+ Tex	11	31	6	1	0	1	10	4	4	4	0	10	0	0	0	1	0	1.00	1	.194	.286	.323
Savannah	A Tex	43	133	32	6	2	0	42	18	16	15	0	27	1	2	3	0	1	.00	6	.241	.316	.316
2000 Charlotte	A+ Tex	50	155	45	11	2	2	66	17	24	17	1	24	4	0	1	1	1	.50	4	.290	.373	.426
Tulsa	AA Tex	30	97	28	6	1	2	42	18	13	13	0	19	0	3	2	0	2	.00	2	.289	.366	.433
3 Min. YEARS		160	517	139	27	6	8	202	68	71	59	1	98	5	5	7	2	4	.33	14	.269	.345	.391

Ryan Jones

Bats: Right **Throws:** Right **Pos:** 1B-69; DH-49; PH-1 · **Ht:** 6'2" **Wt:** 225 **Born:** 11/5/74 **Age:** 26

Year Team	Lg Org	G	AB	H	2B	3B	HR	TB	R	RBI	TBB	IBB	SO	HBP	SH	SF	SB	CS	SB%	GDP	Avg	OBP	SLG
1993 Medcine Hat	R+ Tor	47	171	42	5	0	3	56	20	27	12	0	46	3	0	1	1	1	.50	9	.246	.305	.327
1994 Hagerstown	A Tor	115	402	96	29	0	18	179	60	72	45	0	124	6	0	5	1	0	1.00	6	.239	.321	.445
1995 Dunedin	A+ Tor	127	478	119	28	0	18	201	65	78	41	3	92	7	0	5	1	1	.50	7	.249	.315	.421
1996 Knoxville	AA Tor	134	506	137	26	3	20	229	70	97	60	6	88	6	0	6	2	2	.50	6	.271	.351	.453
1997 Syracuse	AAA Tor	41	123	17	5	1	3	33	8	16	15	0	28	3	0	4	0	2	.00	2	.138	.241	.268
Knoxville	AA Tor	86	328	84	19	3	12	145	41	51	27	1	63	3	0	4	0	1	.00	5	.256	.315	.442
1998 Knoxville	AA Tor	109	408	102	21	0	11	156	50	51	44	0	79	5	0	3	4	4	.50	6	.250	.328	.382
1999 Jacksnville	AA Det	125	487	123	21	3	19	207	66	73	50	0	115	3	0	3	1	1	.50	7	.253	.324	.425
2000 Akron	AA Cle	56	209	54	13	2	9	98	30	38	21	1	40	4	0	5	0	1	.00	7	.258	.331	.469
Winnipeg	IND —	63	247	64	13	1	13	118	40	47	30	0	43	5	0	4	3	2	.60	5	.259	.346	.478
8 Min. YEARS		903	3359	838	180	13	126	1422	450	550	345	11	718	45	0	40	13	15	.46	60	.249	.324	.423

Ricardo Jordan

Pitches: Left **Bats:** Left **Pos:** RP-56; SP-2 · **Ht:** 6'0" **Wt:** 160 **Born:** 6/27/70 **Age:** 31

Year Team	Lg Org	G	GS	CG	GF	IP	BFP	H	R	ER	HR	SH	SF	HB	TBB	IBB	SO	WP	Bk	W	L	Pct.	ShO	Sv	ERA
1990 Dunedin	A+ Tor	13	2	0	4	22.2	103	15	9	6	0	1	1	1	19	3	16	1	5	0	2	.000	0	1	2.38
1991 Myrtle Bch	A Tor	29	23	3	3	144.2	606	100	58	44	3	3	4	6	79	0	152	3	5	9	8	.529	1	1	2.74
1992 Dunedin	A+ Tor	45	0	0	32	47	208	44	26	20	3	3	0	2	28	3	49	7	2	0	5	.000	0	15	3.83
1993 Dunedin	A+ Tor	15	0	0	3	24.2	104	20	13	12	0	1	0	1	15	1	24	3	0	2	0	1.000	0	1	4.38
Knoxville	AA Tor	25	0	0	8	36.2	158	33	17	10	2	5	1	0	18	1	35	0	0	1	4	.200	0	2	2.45
1994 Knoxville	AA Tor	53	0	0	40	64.1	273	54	25	19	2	4	2	4	23	2	70	4	0	4	3	.571	0	17	2.66
1995 Syracuse	AAA Tor	13	0	0	5	12.1	59	15	9	9	1	0	0	1	7	1	17	2	0	0	0	—	0	0	6.57
1996 Scranton-WB	AAA Phi	32	0	0	15	39.1	180	40	30	23	5	3	0	1	22	1	40	2	0	3	3	.500	0	1	5.26
1997 Norfolk	AAA NYM	34	0	0	10	29	128	20	11	9	1	0	1	2	24	2	34	1	0	0	1	.000	0	1	2.79
1998 Indianapolis	AAA Cin	37	6	0	6	69.2	309	70	39	27	8	2	3	2	33	2	52	1	0	2	4	.333	0	2	3.49
Columbus	AAA NYY	5	5	0	0	26	119	28	15	14	4	0	1	1	17	0	22	0	0	2	0	1.000	0	0	4.85
1999 Albuquerque	AAA LA	37	0	0	10	30	142	33	26	24	5	0	3	4	21	1	35	0	0	4	1	.800	0	2	7.20
Somerset	IND —	18	0	0	4	32.2	137	29	19	14	4	3	0	0	13	0	29	2	0	2	3	.400	0	1	3.86
2000 Indianapols	AAA Mil	4	0	0	2	5	19	7	1	1	1	0	0	0	1	0	3	0	0	0	0	—	0	0	1.80
Richmond	AAA Atl	39	0	0	21	42.2	186	40	27	25	4	2	4	4	18	1	35	2	0	3	2	.600	0	4	5.27
Somerset	IND —	15	2	0	7	38.2	165	31	22	17	4	1	3	6	16	0	27	4	0	2	2	.500	0	3	3.96
1995 Toronto	AL	15	0	0	3	15	76	18	11	11	3	0	2	2	13	1	10	1	0	1	0	1.000	0	1	6.60
1996 Philadelphia	NL	26	0	0	2	25	103	18	6	5	0	1	1	0	12	0	17	1	0	2	2	.500	0	0	1.80
1997 New York	NL	22	0	0	4	27	123	31	17	16	1	2	2	2	15	2	19	0	0	1	2	.333	0	0	5.33
1998 Cincinnati	NL	6	0	0	0	3.1	11	4	9	9	2	0	1	0	7	0	1	0	0	1	0	1.000	0	0	24.30
11 Min. YEARS		414	38	3	170	665.1	2896	579	347	274	47	28	23	35	354	18	640	32	12	34	38	.472	1	48	3.71
4 Maj. YEARS		69	0	0	9	70.1	323	71	43	41	6	3	6	4	47	3	47	2	0	5	4	.556	0	1	5.25

Kevin Joseph

Pitches: Right **Bats:** Right **Pos:** SP-16; RP-11 · **Ht:** 6'4" **Wt:** 200 **Born:** 8/1/76 **Age:** 24

Year Team	Lg Org	G	GS	CG	GF	IP	BFP	H	R	ER	HR	SH	SF	HB	TBB	IBB	SO	WP	Bk	W	L	Pct.	ShO	Sv	ERA
1997 Salem-Keizr	A- SF	17	6	0	0	45	208	44	35	27	4	1	2	2	26	0	45	10	3	3	5	.375	0	1	5.40
1998 Bakersfield	A+ SF	6	6	0	0	21	120	35	26	19	3	1	1	2	20	0	17	7	0	0	4	.000	0	0	8.14
Salem-Keizr	A- SF	23	0	0	0	43.1	194	36	25	21	3	1	3	5	27	0	37	8	1	1	1	.500	0	0	4.36
1999 San Jose	A+ SF	20	0	0	9	30.2	122	17	9	8	1	3	0	0	13	0	30	2	1	1	2	.333	0	2	2.35
Shreveport	AA SF	7	0	0	3	12.2	52	8	4	2	0	1	0	1	5	0	16	0	0	0	2	.000	0	1	1.42
2000 Shreveport	AA SF	27	16	0	8	102.2	454	116	60	59	8	5	7	5	48	1	71	4	0	3	11	.214	0	0	5.17
4 Min. YEARS		100	28	0	25	255.1	1150	256	159	136	19	12	13	15	139	1	216	31	5	8	25	.242	0	4	4.79

Josh Kalinowski

Pitches: Left **Bats:** Left **Pos:** SP-6 · **Ht:** 6'2" **Wt:** 190 **Born:** 12/12/76 **Age:** 24

Year Team	Lg Org	G	GS	CG	GF	IP	BFP	H	R	ER	HR	SH	SF	HB	TBB	IBB	SO	WP	Bk	W	L	Pct.	ShO	Sv	ERA
1997 Portland	A- Col	6	6	0	0	18.2	78	15	6	5	0	0	0	0	10	0	27	3	0	1	0	.000	0	0	2.41
1998 Asheville	A Col	28	28	3	0	172.1	743	159	93	75	15	7	4	8	65	0	215	17	3	12	10	.545	1	0	3.92
1999 Salem	A+ Col	27	27	1	0	162.1	659	119	47	38	3	4	2	6	71	0	176	11	1	11	6	.647	0	0	2.11
2000 Carolina	AA Col	6	6	0	0	26	119	30	22	18	0	1	1	1	12	0	27	2	1	0	4	.250	0	0	6.23
4 Min. YEARS		67	67	4	0	379.1	1599	323	168	136	18	12	7	15	158	0	445	33	5	24	20	.545	1	0	3.23

Jason Karnuth

Pitches: Right **Bats:** Right **Pos:** SP-21; RP-3 **Ht:** 6'2" **Wt:** 190 **Born:** 5/15/76 **Age:** 25

Year Team	Lg Org	G	GS	CG	GF	IP	BFP	H	R	ER	HR	SH	SF	HB	TBB	IBB	SO	WP	Bk	W	L	Pct.	ShO	Sv	ERA
1997 New Jersey	A- StL	7	7	0	0	38.2	158	33	8	8	0	1	1	2	9	0	23	2	0	4	1	.800	0	0	1.86
Peoria	A StL	4	4	0	0	23	102	29	19	17	1	1	1	1	7	1	12	2	1	0	3	.000	0	0	6.65
1998 Pr William	A+ StL	16	15	2	1	108	411	86	26	20	3	6	0	7	14	0	53	4	0	8	1	.889	2	0	1.67
1999 Arkansas	AA StL	26	26	2	0	160.1	696	175	105	93	16	5	7	11	55	0	71	2	0	7	11	.389	0	0	5.22
2000 Arkansas	AA StL	8	8	1	0	50.1	220	59	30	21	3	1	2	1	14	0	31	5	1	2	3	.400	0	0	3.75
Memphis	AAA StL	16	13	0	1	78	341	89	47	35	7	4	2	5	27	0	28	3	0	5	4	.556	0	0	4.04
4 Min. YEARS		77	73	5	2	458.1	1928	471	235	194	30	18	13	27	126	1	218	18	2	26	23	.531	2	0	3.81

Brad Kaufman

Pitches: Right **Bats:** Right **Pos:** RP-45; SP-1 **Ht:** 6'2" **Wt:** 210 **Born:** 4/26/72 **Age:** 29

Year Team	Lg Org	G	GS	CG	GF	IP	BFP	H	R	ER	HR	SH	SF	HB	TBB	IBB	SO	WP	Bk	W	L	Pct.	ShO	Sv	ERA
1993 Spokane	A- SD	25	8	1	11	53.2	264	56	56	41	8	0	3	3	41	2	48	4	2	5	4	.556	0	4	6.88
1994 Springfield	A SD	31	20	3	4	145.1	602	124	62	54	9	5	3	4	63	6	122	14	1	10	9	.526	0	3	3.34
1995 Memphis	AA SD	27	27	0	0	148.1	676	142	112	95	17	6	5	14	90	4	119	10	0	11	10	.524	0	0	5.76
1996 Memphis	AA SD	29	29	3	0	178.1	768	161	84	72	18	8	4	4	83	4	163	8	0	12	10	.545	1	0	3.63
1997 Las Vegas	AAA SD	6	6	0	0	32.1	151	40	37	29	9	0	1	1	15	0	19	1	0	0	5	.000	0	0	8.07
Mobile	AA SD	22	22	1	0	125.1	585	138	97	86	10	9	11	5	66	0	103	3	0	5	13	.278	0	0	6.18
1998 Mobile	AA SD	5	5	0	0	24.1	96	18	3	3	0	2	0	2	8	0	21	1	0	1	0	1.000	0	0	1.11
Las Vegas	AAA SD	23	22	0	0	118.1	559	148	90	84	12	2	3	6	65	0	83	8	0	9	9	.500	0	0	6.39
Columbus	AAA NYY	3	3	0	0	15	72	17	15	12	3	1	0	0	12	0	13	0	0	1	2	.333	0	0	7.20
1999 Norwich	AA NYY	40	5	0	9	83	361	76	45	38	6	2	3	2	38	5	81	7	0	3	2	.600	0	1	4.12
2000 New Orleans	AAA Hou	40	1	0	16	60	297	74	51	38	5	3	5	4	44	3	53	5	0	1	6	.143	0	2	5.70
Round Rock	AA Hou	6	0	0	0	11	49	13	7	5	3	1	0	1	5	0	7	0	0	0	3	.000	0	0	4.09
8 Min. YEARS		257	148	8	41	995	4480	1007	659	557	100	39	38	46	530	24	832	61	3	58	73	.443	1	7	5.04

Justin Kaye

Pitches: Right **Bats:** Right **Pos:** RP-50 **Ht:** 6'4" **Wt:** 185 **Born:** 6/9/76 **Age:** 25

Year Team	Lg Org	G	GS	CG	GF	IP	BFP	H	R	ER	HR	SH	SF	HB	TBB	IBB	SO	WP	Bk	W	L	Pct.	ShO	Sv	ERA
1995 Mariners	R Sea	12	0	0	4	19.1	111	33	28	23	1	0	2	1	19	0	13	4	0	0	1	.000	0	0	10.71
1996 Mariners	R Sea	20	0	0	12	32.1	156	34	23	13	4	0	1	5	19	1	36	7	2	1	0	1.000	0	3	3.62
1997 Wisconsin	A Sea	28	26	0	2	127	618	129	113	103	13	6	5	16	104	0	115	21	6	8	12	.400	0	0	7.30
1998 Wisconsin	A Sea	28	0	0	23	47.1	196	25	11	9	2	6	0	2	30	4	79	6	0	6	2	.750	0	9	1.71
Lancaster	A+ Sea	16	0	0	7	30.1	139	37	24	23	4	2	1	0	13	2	34	9	0	1	2	.333	0	0	6.82
1999 Lancaster	A+ Sea	53	0	0	46	61	289	68	42	39	4	2	3	5	40	1	66	6	0	3	5	.375	0	14	5.75
2000 New Haven	AA Sea	50	0	0	23	84.1	368	80	32	25	3	3	3	5	36	4	109	4	3	2	5	.286	0	8	2.67
6 Min. YEARS		207	26	0	117	401.2	1877	406	273	235	31	19	15	34	261	12	452	57	11	21	27	.438	0	34	5.27

Greg Keagle

Pitches: Right **Bats:** Right **Pos:** SP-16; RP-2 **Ht:** 6'2" **Wt:** 195 **Born:** 6/28/71 **Age:** 30

Year Team	Lg Org	G	GS	CG	GF	IP	BFP	H	R	ER	HR	SH	SF	HB	TBB	IBB	SO	WP	Bk	W	L	Pct.	ShO	Sv	ERA
1993 Spokane	A- SD	15	15	1	0	83	368	80	37	30	2	4	4	7	40	2	77	4	4	3	3	.500	0	0	3.25
1994 Rancho Cuca	A+ SD	14	14	1	0	92	377	62	23	21	2	1	3	5	41	1	91	1	0	11	1	.917	1	0	2.05
Wichita	AA SD	13	13	0	0	70.1	321	84	53	49	5	5	2	2	32	1	57	3	1	3	9	.250	0	0	6.27
1995 Memphis	AA SD	15	15	1	0	81	365	82	52	46	11	1	3	6	41	2	82	8	3	4	9	.308	0	0	5.11
Rancho Cuca	A+ SD	2	2	0	0	14	59	14	9	7	1	0	1	2	2	0	11	1	0	0	0	—	0	0	4.50
Las Vegas	AAA SD	14	13	0	1	75.2	351	76	47	36	3	6	5	6	42	2	49	2	0	7	6	.538	0	0	4.28
1996 Toledo	AAA Det	6	6	0	0	27	135	42	32	30	7	1	2	4	11	0	24	0	1	2	3	.400	0	0	10.00
1997 Toledo	AAA Det	23	23	3	0	151.1	645	136	68	64	8	4	2	10	61	0	140	4	1	11	7	.611	1	0	3.81
1998 Toledo	AAA Det	15	14	0	1	81.2	365	94	48	42	12	1	2	6	32	0	61	1	2	5	3	.625	0	0	4.63
1999 Lakeland	A+ Det	6	6	0	0	36	153	35	19	18	5	2	2	4	13	0	26	1	3	1	3	.250	0	0	4.50
Jacksnville	AA Det	9	9	1	0	53.2	238	58	22	17	4	0	1	1	22	0	28	1	2	4	2	.667	0	0	2.85
Toledo	AAA Det	7	7	0	0	32.1	158	50	29	26	3	1	2	4	13	0	19	1	1	1	4	.200	0	0	7.16
2000 Edmonton	AAA Ana	1	0	0	0	3	16	5	5	5	1	0	0	0	2	0	2	1	0	0	0	—	0	0	15.00
Elmira	IND —	17	16	4	0	106.2	448	95	44	36	5	5	2	6	39	0	81	6	1	8	4	.667	3	0	3.04
1996 Detroit	AL	26	6	0	5	87.2	435	104	76	72	13	2	7	9	68	5	70	2	0	3	6	.333	0	0	7.39
1997 Detroit	AL	11	10	0	0	45.1	214	58	33	33	9	2	1	5	18	0	33	1	0	3	5	.375	0	0	6.55
1998 Detroit	AL	9	7	0	0	38.2	180	46	26	24	7	0	0	4	20	0	25	2	0	0	5	.000	0	0	5.59
8 Min. YEARS		157	153	11	2	908	3999	913	488	427	69	31	31	63	391	8	748	34	19	60	54	.526	5	0	4.23
3 Maj. YEARS		46	23	0	5	171.2	829	208	135	129	27	4	8	18	106	5	128	5	0	6	16	.273	0	0	6.76

Brian Keck

Bats: Right **Throws:** Right **Pos:** SS-19; 3B-16; 1B-16; 2B-12; PH-3; OF-1; DH-1 **Ht:** 6'3" **Wt:** 185 **Born:** 1/15/74 **Age:** 27

Year Team	Lg Org	G	AB	H	2B	3B	HR	TB	R	RBI	TBB	IBB	SO	HBP	SH	SF	SB	CS	SB%	GDP	Avg	OBP	SLG
1996 Portland	A- Col	43	156	41	1	2	0	46	29	20	22	0	23	1	3	1	7	2	.78	1	.263	.356	.295
1997 Asheville	A Col	37	124	29	3	0	0	32	8	8	9	0	22	0	7	0	5	2	.71	5	.234	.286	.258
Salem	A+ Col	48	121	34	4	0	0	38	22	11	11	1	21	3	5	2	17	3	.85	5	.281	.350	.314
1998 Salem	A+ Col	85	263	72	8	3	1	89	30	24	24	0	39	1	1	2	10	11	.48	3	.274	.334	.338
1999 Salem	A+ Col	103	347	84	10	3	3	109	54	30	37	1	53	1	14	5	14	2	.88	9	.242	.313	.314
Carolina	AA Col	5	15	3	0	1	0	5	0	2	4	0	3	0	0	0	2	1	.67	1	.200	.368	.333
2000 Carolina	AA Col	63	203	53	10	1	3	74	22	28	18	1	44	3	6	3	9	5	.64	6	.261	.326	.365
5 Min. YEARS		384	1229	316	36	10	7	393	165	123	125	3	205	9	46	13	64	26	.71	33	.257	.327	.320

144

Rusty Keith

Bats: Right Throws: Right Pos: OF-106; DH-20   Ht: 6'0" Wt: 209 Born: 9/18/77 Age: 23

				BATTING													BASERUNNING				PERCENTAGES		
Year Team	Lg Org	G	AB	H	2B	3B	HR	TB	R	RBI	TBB	IBB	SO	HBP	SH	SF	SB	CS	SB%	GDP	Avg	OBP	SLG
1998 Athletics	R Oak	48	179	57	18	4	3	92	37	39	20	0	21	2	1	6	6	3	.67	4	.318	.382	.514
1999 Visalia	A+ Oak	124	448	140	28	3	10	204	87	62	82	1	59	7	3	4	10	8	.56	13	.313	.423	.455
2000 Sacramento	AAA Oak	4	16	8	4	0	2	18	5	6	2	0	2	0	0	0	0	0	—	0	.500	.556	1.125
Modesto	A+ Oak	104	389	123	22	1	8	171	84	61	82	1	72	3	4	3	10	3	.77	11	.316	.436	.440
Midland	AA Oak	18	61	12	2	0	1	17	8	6	9	0	11	1	0	0	0	0	—	2	.197	.310	.279
3 Min. YEARS		298	1093	340	74	8	24	502	221	174	195	2	165	13	8	13	26	14	.65	30	.311	.417	.459

Kris Keller

Pitches: Right Bats: Right Pos: RP-62   Ht: 6'2" Wt: 225 Born: 3/1/78 Age: 23

		HOW MUCH HE PITCHED						WHAT HE GAVE UP										THE RESULTS					
Year Team	Lg Org	G	GS	CG	GF	IP	BFP	H	R	ER	HR	SH	SF	HB	TBB	IBB	SO	WP	Bk	W	L	Pct.	ShO	Sv	ERA
1996 Tigers	R Det	8	6	0	0	34	143	23	16	9	0	1	2	0	21	0	23	1	1	1	1	.500	0	0	2.38
1997 Jamestown	A- Det	16	0	0	10	27	143	37	33	26	3	1	3	3	20	0	18	5	2	0	2	.000	0	0	8.67
1998 Jamestown	A- Det	27	0	0	24	33	141	29	12	12	3	1	2	1	16	0	41	3	0	1	3	.250	0	8	3.27
1999 W Michigan	A Det	49	0	0	28	77	324	63	28	25	6	4	3	3	36	1	87	11	2	5	3	.625	0	8	2.92
2000 Jacksnville	AA Det	62	0	0	58	68	299	58	24	22	0	1	5	0	44	3	60	9	0	2	3	.400	0	26	2.91
5 Min. YEARS		162	6	0	120	239	1050	210	109	94	12	8	15	7	137	4	229	35	5	9	12	.429	0	42	3.54

Rich Kelley

Pitches: Left Bats: Left Pos: RP-45; SP-6   Ht: 6'3" Wt: 210 Born: 5/27/70 Age: 31

		HOW MUCH HE PITCHED						WHAT HE GAVE UP										THE RESULTS					
Year Team	Lg Org	G	GS	CG	GF	IP	BFP	H	R	ER	HR	SH	SF	HB	TBB	IBB	SO	WP	Bk	W	L	Pct.	ShO	Sv	ERA
1991 Niagara Fal	A- Det	15	13	0	1	81.1	341	76	38	30	7	0	2	1	33	1	78	4	0	4	8	.333	0	0	3.32
1992 Fayettevlle	A Det	28	26	2	0	162.2	664	140	62	51	15	2	4	6	63	0	117	12	9	13	5	.722	0	0	2.82
1993 Lakeland	A+ Det	26	9	0	10	85.2	350	78	31	29	2	2	2	4	31	1	45	5	4	4	5	.444	0	2	3.05
London	AA Det	7	0	0	5	5	25	7	5	5	1	0	0	0	5	0	3	3	1	0	0	—	0	0	9.00
1994 Lakeland	A+ Det	13	0	0	10	38	156	32	15	10	2	2	5	0	15	1	23	0	0	4	2	.667	0	1	2.37
Trenton	AA Det	16	4	0	2	42.1	178	46	28	27	8	1	1	0	20	0	29	3	1	1	2	.333	0	0	5.74
1995 Jacksnville	AA Det	7	0	0	1	6	24	9	3	3	1	1	1	0	0	0	2	0	1	1	0	1.000	0	0	4.50
1998 Rochester	AAA Bal	15	3	0	4	38	156	34	28	23	6	0	1	1	17	0	24	2	1	1	3	.250	0	1	5.45
Bowie	AA Bal	18	13	0	1	85	355	80	38	35	12	1	3	2	34	2	56	2	2	8	2	.800	0	0	3.71
1999 Huntsville	AA Mil	25	0	0	12	28.1	123	30	19	18	3	2	0	3	8	0	26	1	1	1	3	.250	0	3	5.72
2000 Erie	AA Ana	44	4	1	18	97.1	428	120	58	48	12	3	8	3	32	1	72	3	3	5	6	.455	0	2	4.44
Edmonton	AAA Ana	7	2	0	3	20.1	100	29	17	15	4	0	1	1	10	0	12	0	1	0	0	—	0	0	6.64
8 Min. YEARS		221	74	3	62	690	2900	681	342	294	73	14	28	21	268	6	487	35	24	42	37	.532	0	9	3.83

Ryan Kellner

Bats: Right Throws: Right Pos: C-76; DH-1   Ht: 6'2" Wt: 205 Born: 12/9/77 Age: 23

				BATTING													BASERUNNING				PERCENTAGES		
Year Team	Lg Org	G	AB	H	2B	3B	HR	TB	R	RBI	TBB	IBB	SO	HBP	SH	SF	SB	CS	SB%	GDP	Avg	OBP	SLG
1998 Yakima	A- LA	19	55	15	1	1	1	21	6	5	1	0	22	2	0	0	0	0	—	1	.273	.310	.382
1999 Vero Beach	A+ LA	54	179	37	1	1	2	46	21	14	10	0	51	2	3	0	1	1	.50	5	.207	.257	.257
2000 Vero Beach	A+ LA	62	221	58	13	0	3	80	23	24	18	1	44	3	1	4	0	4	.00	7	.262	.321	.362
San Antonio	AA LA	15	44	4	0	0	0	4	4	1	4	0	14	0	0	0	0	0	—	1	.091	.167	.091
3 Min. YEARS		150	499	114	15	2	6	151	54	44	33	1	131	7	4	4	1	5	.17	14	.228	.284	.303

Robbie Kent

Bats: Right Throws: Right Pos: PH-14; 1B-9; DH-6   Ht: 5'10" Wt: 185 Born: 1/8/74 Age: 27

				BATTING													BASERUNNING				PERCENTAGES		
Year Team	Lg Org	G	AB	H	2B	3B	HR	TB	R	RBI	TBB	IBB	SO	HBP	SH	SF	SB	CS	SB%	GDP	Avg	OBP	SLG
1996 Idaho Falls	R+ SD	47	181	56	14	0	2	76	40	25	21	0	28	4	1	1	4	1	.80	5	.309	.391	.420
1997 Rancho Cuca	A+ SD	81	295	73	18	0	4	103	35	32	22	0	65	4	3	4	0	2	.00	4	.247	.305	.349
1998 Rancho Cuca	A+ SD	116	457	123	22	3	7	172	65	59	33	0	81	7	8	5	2	1	.67	15	.269	.325	.376
1999 Mobile	AA SD	109	336	91	17	3	8	138	48	56	44	3	71	2	2	3	2	0	1.00	8	.271	.355	.411
2000 Mobile	AA SD	29	61	5	1	0	0	6	6	4	7	0	10	2	0	1	0	0	—	3	.082	.197	.098
5 Min. YEARS		382	1330	348	72	6	21	495	194	176	127	3	255	19	14	14	8	4	.67	35	.262	.332	.372

Jason Kershner

Pitches: Left Bats: Left Pos: SP-21; RP-8   Ht: 6'2" Wt: 165 Born: 12/19/76 Age: 24

		HOW MUCH HE PITCHED						WHAT HE GAVE UP										THE RESULTS					
Year Team	Lg Org	G	GS	CG	GF	IP	BFP	H	R	ER	HR	SH	SF	HB	TBB	IBB	SO	WP	Bk	W	L	Pct.	ShO	Sv	ERA
1995 Martinsvlle	R+ Phi	13	13	0	0	63	278	67	42	36	10	0	2	3	29	0	64	6	0	4	2	.667	0	0	5.14
1996 Piedmont	A Phi	28	28	2	0	168	703	154	81	70	12	5	4	3	59	0	156	12	1	11	9	.550	1	0	3.75
1997 Clearwater	A+ Phi	22	16	0	3	99.1	417	113	49	43	9	2	4	2	21	0	51	2	0	5	10	.333	0	1	3.90
1998 Clearwater	A+ Phi	41	8	0	11	94.1	405	108	57	42	8	1	3	6	25	0	65	8	0	3	3	.500	0	3	4.01
1999 Reading	AA Phi	57	2	0	30	92.2	412	99	67	59	14	3	6	5	40	3	86	5	0	4	4	.500	0	8	5.73
2000 Clearwater	A+ Phi	2	2	0	0	14	52	7	1	1	0	0	0	0	5	0	15	0	0	1	0	1.000	0	0	0.64
Reading	AA Phi	27	19	0	3	119	501	125	49	48	15	6	1	5	25	0	80	3	0	9	2	.818	0	1	3.63
6 Min. YEARS		190	88	2	47	650.1	2768	673	346	299	69	17	20	28	204	3	517	36	1	37	30	.552	1	13	4.14

Kyle Kessel

Pitches: Left **Bats:** Right **Pos:** SP-25; RP-1   **Ht:** 6'0" **Wt:** 160 **Born:** 6/2/76 **Age:** 25

		HOW MUCH HE PITCHED						WHAT HE GAVE UP										THE RESULTS					
Year Team	Lg Org	G	GS	CG	GF	IP	BFP	H	R	ER	HR	SF	HB	TBB	IBB	SO	WP	Bk	W	L	Pct.	ShO	Sv	ERA
1995 Mets	R NYM	7	7	0	0	40	160	29	12	8	1	1	2	11	0	47	3	0	3	0	1.000	0	0	1.80
Kingsport	R+ NYM	5	5	0	0	30	134	33	11	6	1	0	4	10	1	23	0	0	4	0	1.000	0	0	1.80
1996 Pittsfield	A- NYM	13	13	0	0	79.2	332	80	44	42	6	0	4	19	0	67	4	2	2	6	.250	0	0	4.74
1997 Capital Cty	A NYM	27	27	5	0	168.2	685	131	63	51	8	9	5	9	53	3	151	8	0	11	11	.500	1	0	2.72
1998 Mets	R NYM	4	4	0	0	14	53	5	4	1	1	1	0	1	5	0	19	0	0	1	1	.500	0	0	0.64
St. Lucie	A+ NYM	16	16	0	0	89.1	394	101	58	51	11	2	1	7	27	0	61	3	1	2	7	.222	0	0	5.14
1999 Mets	R NYM	3	3	0	0	8	29	5	4	3	0	0	0	1	2	0	11	1	0	0	1	.000	0	0	3.38
St. Lucie	A+ NYM	8	8	0	0	35	157	35	22	18	4	2	1	1	16	0	24	0	0	1	2	.333	0	0	4.63
2000 Kissimmee	A+ Hou	12	12	0	0	75	315	74	37	28	3	3	0	2	24	1	56	1	0	4	5	.444	0	0	3.36
Round Rock	AA Hou	14	13	0	0	72	320	68	45	39	12	4	1	4	48	1	43	0	0	6	5	.545	0	0	4.88
6 Min. YEARS		109	108	5	0	611.2	2579	561	300	247	47	22	10	35	215	6	502	20	3	34	38	.472	1	0	3.63

Bobby Kielty

Bats: Both **Throws:** Right **Pos:** OF-136; DH-2; PH-1   **Ht:** 6'1" **Wt:** 215 **Born:** 8/5/76 **Age:** 24

		BATTING															BASERUNNING				PERCENTAGES		
Year Team	Lg Org	G	AB	H	2B	3B	HR	TB	R	RBI	TBB	IBB	SO	HBP	SH	SF	SB	CS	SB%	GDP	Avg	OBP	SLG
1999 Quad City	A Min	69	245	72	13	1	13	126	52	43	43	1	56	3	2	3	12	3	.80	7	.294	.401	.514
2000 New Britain	AA Min	129	451	118	30	3	14	196	79	65	98	4	109	5	0	4	6	4	.60	16	.262	.396	.435
Salt Lake	AAA Min	9	33	8	4	0	0	12	8	2	7	0	10	0	0	0	0	0	—	0	.242	.375	.364
2 Min. YEARS		207	729	198	47	4	27	334	139	110	148	5	175	8	2	7	18	7	.72	23	.272	.397	.458

Skip Kiil

Bats: Right **Throws:** Right **Pos:** OF-94; DH-4; PH-2   **Ht:** 6'0" **Wt:** 172 **Born:** 4/10/74 **Age:** 27

		BATTING															BASERUNNING				PERCENTAGES		
Year Team	Lg Org	G	AB	H	2B	3B	HR	TB	R	RBI	TBB	IBB	SO	HBP	SH	SF	SB	CS	SB%	GDP	Avg	OBP	SLG
1997 Piedmont	A Phi	82	261	59	15	3	7	101	48	34	35	0	74	13	3	3	13	2	.87	0	.226	.343	.387
1998 Clearwater	A+ Phi	116	397	109	31	3	14	188	90	70	70	3	109	5	6	4	23	6	.79	4	.275	.387	.474
1999 Clearwater	A+ Phi	86	305	91	15	8	14	164	74	55	70	0	101	7	5	3	24	5	.83	2	.298	.436	.538
2000 Reading	AA Phi	58	182	37	10	0	6	65	24	19	40	0	60	3	4	2	5	3	.63	2	.203	.352	.357
Clearwater	A+ Phi	40	148	40	13	0	4	65	25	25	23	0	46	4	1	1	7	2	.78	1	.270	.381	.439
4 Min. YEARS		382	1293	336	84	14	45	583	261	203	238	3	390	32	19	13	72	18	.80	9	.260	.385	.451

Joe Kilburg

Bats: Left **Throws:** Right **Pos:** 2B-24; OF-16; 3B-9; DH-6; 1B-3; SS-1; PH-1; PR-1   **Ht:** 5'11" **Wt:** 180 **Born:** 12/20/75 **Age:** 25

		BATTING															BASERUNNING				PERCENTAGES		
Year Team	Lg Org	G	AB	H	2B	3B	HR	TB	R	RBI	TBB	IBB	SO	HBP	SH	SF	SB	CS	SB%	GDP	Avg	OBP	SLG
1997 Burlington	R+ Cle	52	182	61	8	7	3	92	59	30	39	0	46	7	3	2	29	5	.85	1	.335	.465	.505
Kinston	A+ Cle	9	30	7	2	0	1	12	5	5	5	0	6	0	0	0	1	0	1.00	0	.233	.343	.400
1998 Columbus	A Cle	121	446	112	19	4	7	160	81	44	67	0	93	4	11	0	24	10	.71	8	.251	.354	.359
1999 Akron	AA Cle	42	137	41	8	1	3	60	34	17	29	1	19	4	3	0	3	3	.50	1	.299	.435	.438
Akron	AA Cle	42	144	39	8	0	1	50	20	14	23	1	28	5	1	0	1	2	.33	3	.271	.390	.347
2000 Akron	AA Cle	1	2	0	0	0	0	0	0	0	0	0	1	0	0	0	0	0	—	0	.000	.000	.000
Kinston	A+ Cle	25	86	18	4	1	0	24	12	7	11	0	23	5	0	1	2	3	.40	4	.209	.330	.279
Dayton	A Cin	20	80	15	0	1	0	17	14	4	8	0	13	4	1	0	5	2	.71	2	.188	.293	.213
Clinton	A Cin	12	35	14	2	0	0	16	9	3	14	0	6	2	0	0	6	0	1.00	1	.400	.588	.457
4 Min. YEARS		324	1142	307	51	14	15	431	234	124	196	2	235	31	19	3	71	25	.74	20	.269	.389	.377

Sun-Woo Kim

Pitches: Right **Bats:** Right **Pos:** SP-25; RP-1   **Ht:** 6'2" **Wt:** 180 **Born:** 9/4/77 **Age:** 23

		HOW MUCH HE PITCHED						WHAT HE GAVE UP										THE RESULTS					
Year Team	Lg Org	G	GS	CG	GF	IP	BFP	H	R	ER	HR	SH	SF	HB	TBB	IBB	SO	WP	Bk	W	L	Pct.	ShO	Sv	ERA
1998 Sarasota	A+ Bos	26	24	5	0	153	655	159	88	82	18	2	8	2	40	1	132	11	0	12	8	.600	0	0	4.82
1999 Trenton	AA Bos	26	26	1	0	149	641	160	86	81	16	2	5	9	44	2	130	4	0	9	8	.529	1	0	4.89
2000 Pawtucket	AAA Bos	26	25	0	0	134.1	603	170	98	90	17	2	4	5	42	1	116	5	0	11	7	.611	0	0	6.03
3 Min. YEARS		78	75	6	0	436.1	1899	489	272	253	51	6	17	16	126	4	378	20	0	32	23	.582	1	0	5.22

Andy Kimball

Pitches: Right **Bats:** Right **Pos:** RP-45   **Ht:** 6'0" **Wt:** 190 **Born:** 8/23/75 **Age:** 25

		HOW MUCH HE PITCHED						WHAT HE GAVE UP										THE RESULTS					
Year Team	Lg Org	G	GS	CG	GF	IP	BFP	H	R	ER	HR	SH	SF	HB	TBB	IBB	SO	WP	Bk	W	L	Pct.	ShO	Sv	ERA
1997 Sou Oregon	A- Oak	13	7	0	0	54.2	230	37	29	22	4	1	1	3	17	0	75	8	2	3	2	.600	0	0	3.62
1998 Modesto	A+ Oak	42	8	0	24	97.1	440	113	62	48	7	3	8	6	29	5	96	6	2	5	6	.455	0	12	4.44
1999 Midland	AA Oak	47	0	0	15	89.1	412	112	64	54	14	2	4	2	40	4	87	13	4	9	5	.643	0	2	5.44
2000 Midland	AA Oak	29	0	0	11	47.1	223	60	42	39	9	1	1	6	20	0	38	2	0	3	4	.429	0	2	7.42
Modesto	A+ Oak	16	0	0	9	32.2	140	31	22	10	1	0	2	1	13	3	29	5	0	1	6	.143	0	0	2.76
4 Min. YEARS		147	15	0	59	321.1	1445	353	219	173	35	7	16	18	119	12	325	34	8	21	23	.477	0	16	4.85

Brad King

Bats: Right **Throws:** Right **Pos:** C-39; PH-3; PR-1; P-1   **Ht:** 6'2" **Wt:** 205 **Born:** 12/3/74 **Age:** 26

		BATTING															BASERUNNING				PERCENTAGES		
Year Team	Lg Org	G	AB	H	2B	3B	HR	TB	R	RBI	TBB	IBB	SO	HBP	SH	SF	SB	CS	SB%	GDP	Avg	OBP	SLG
1996 Williamsprt	A- ChC	23	70	12	2	1	0	16	7	8	4	0	20	4	0	1	0	1	.00	0	.171	.253	.229
1997 Rockford	A ChC	68	204	51	14	1	7	88	31	29	19	2	35	8	2	4	4	4	.50	5	.250	.332	.431

Year Team	Lg Org	G	AB	H	2B	3B	HR	TB	R	RBI	TBB	IBB	SO	HBP	SH	SF	SB	CS	SB%	GDP	Avg	OBP	SLG
					BATTING												BASERUNNING				PERCENTAGES		
1998 Daytona	A+ ChC	84	276	81	17	0	1	101	49	37	30	0	37	7	2	2	5	6	.45	11	.293	.375	.366
1999 West Tenn	AA ChC	92	232	53	10	0	0	63	29	25	38	5	34	9	2	6	2	1	.67	7	.228	.351	.272
2000 Chattanooga	AA Cin	41	108	27	5	0	2	38	18	11	18	1	26	3	0	3	3	3	.50	2	.250	.364	.352
5 Min. YEARS		308	890	224	48	2	10	306	134	110	109	8	152	31	6	16	14	15	.48	25	.252	.348	.344

Brett King

Bats: Right **Throws:** Right **Pos:** 2B-44; SS-28; 3B-11; PH-7; PR-5; OF-1   **Ht:** 6'1" **Wt:** 190 **Born:** 7/20/72 **Age:** 28

Year Team	Lg Org	G	AB	H	2B	3B	HR	TB	R	RBI	TBB	IBB	SO	HBP	SH	SF	SB	CS	SB%	GDP	Avg	OBP	SLG
					BATTING												BASERUNNING				PERCENTAGES		
1993 Everett	A- SF	69	243	55	10	0	2	71	43	24	40	2	63	5	9	0	26	11	.70	2	.226	.347	.292
1994 San Jose	A+ SF	48	188	47	8	2	1	62	24	11	19	1	62	4	1	0	6	8	.43	0	.250	.332	.330
Clinton	A SF	68	261	57	13	2	5	89	45	30	23	1	86	2	3	2	12	3	.80	2	.218	.285	.341
1995 San Jose	A+ SF	107	394	108	29	4	3	154	61	41	41	1	86	5	5	6	28	8	.78	8	.274	.345	.391
1996 Shreveport	AA SF	127	459	107	23	4	7	159	61	48	49	0	116	6	17	1	19	9	.68	5	.233	.315	.346
1997 Shreveport	AA SF	79	193	42	6	1	6	68	28	20	30	1	55	1	1	1	4	5	.44	3	.218	.324	.352
1998 Shreveport	AA SF	85	257	44	9	2	3	66	29	19	27	1	64	3	2	2	4	2	.67	4	.171	.256	.257
1999 West Tenn	AA ChC	54	142	31	6	0	3	46	27	13	39	1	49	4	2	2	7	6	.54	0	.218	.396	.324
Iowa	AAA ChC	32	112	22	6	0	4	40	16	10	17	0	27	1	2	1	6	1	.86	2	.196	.305	.357
2000 West Tenn	AA ChC	48	126	18	4	2	2	32	12	14	28	1	41	3	1	0	3	2	.60	2	.143	.312	.254
Iowa	AAA ChC	11	35	6	3	0	0	9	1	0	5	1	8	0	0	0	0	2	.00	0	.171	.275	.257
Edmonton	AAA Ana	11	35	6	0	0	2	12	4	5	1	0	16	1	3	0	0	0	.00	1	.171	.216	.343
Erie	AA Ana	9	26	5	1	0	0	6	0	3	1	0	11	1	0	0	0	1	.00	0	.192	.250	.231
8 Min. YEARS		755	2471	548	118	17	38	814	351	238	320	10	684	36	46	15	115	58	.66	29	.222	.318	.329

Cesar King

Bats: Right **Throws:** Right **Pos:** C-51; PH-3; DH-2   **Ht:** 6'0" **Wt:** 215 **Born:** 2/28/78 **Age:** 23

Year Team	Lg Org	G	AB	H	2B	3B	HR	TB	R	RBI	TBB	IBB	SO	HBP	SH	SF	SB	CS	SB%	GDP	Avg	OBP	SLG
					BATTING												BASERUNNING				PERCENTAGES		
1996 Chston-SC	A Tex	84	276	69	10	1	7	102	35	28	21	0	58	1	0	2	8	5	.62	5	.250	.303	.370
1997 Charlotte	A+ Tex	91	307	91	14	4	6	131	51	37	35	0	58	1	3	4	8	6	.57	5	.296	.366	.427
Tulsa	AA Tex	14	45	16	1	0	1	20	6	8	5	0	3	0	0	0	1	0	.00	2	.356	.420	.444
1998 Tulsa	AA Tex	90	316	70	16	2	3	99	40	39	30	2	68	2	3	6	1	1	.50	10	.222	.288	.313
1999 Tulsa	AA Tex	95	321	73	19	2	11	129	41	45	32	1	70	2	3	1	2	1	.67	7	.227	.301	.402
2000 Oklahoma	AAA Tex	13	42	6	2	1	0	10	3	7	4	0	10	1	0	0	0	1	.00	1	.143	.234	.238
Scranton-WB	AAA Phi	43	129	30	7	0	2	43	13	19	8	0	25	2	1	2	0	0	—	4	.233	.284	.333
5 Min. YEARS		430	1436	355	69	10	30	534	189	183	135	3	292	9	10	15	19	15	.56	34	.247	.313	.372

Brendan Kingman

Bats: Right **Throws:** Right **Pos:** 1B-10; DH-9; 3B-2; C-1   **Ht:** 6'1" **Wt:** 235 **Born:** 5/22/73 **Age:** 28

Year Team	Lg Org	G	AB	H	2B	3B	HR	TB	R	RBI	TBB	IBB	SO	HBP	SH	SF	SB	CS	SB%	GDP	Avg	OBP	SLG
					BATTING												BASERUNNING				PERCENTAGES		
1992 Marlins	R Fla	42	121	28	2	1	0	32	8	13	22	0	29	2	2	0	2	2	.50	5	.231	.347	.264
1993 Marlins	R Fla	57	203	51	14	1	2	73	34	37	25	0	36	2	0	4	0	0	—	5	.251	.333	.360
1994 Kane County	A Fla	93	334	81	15	3	8	131	41	38	24	0	67	4	4	0	2	3	.40	4	.243	.301	.332
1995 Brevard Cty	A+ Fla	95	348	88	19	4	8	139	37	47	31	3	45	1	0	4	1	0	1.00	21	.253	.313	.399
1998 Lancaster	A+ Sea	112	456	155	30	3	16	239	91	78	40	6	55	6	1	4	6	7	.46	20	.340	.397	.524
1999 New Haven	AA Sea	130	509	142	20	0	10	192	58	56	26	2	71	5	1	4	0	0	—	18	.279	.318	.377
2000 New Haven	AA Sea	11	39	11	3	0	0	14	3	5	0	0	4	2	0	0	0	0	—	2	.282	.317	.359
Catskill	IND —	11	42	10	1	0	0	11	5	4	2	0	7	0	0	0	0	0	—	2	.238	.273	.262
7 Min. YEARS		551	2052	566	104	12	39	811	277	278	170	11	314	22	8	16	11	12	.48	77	.276	.335	.395

Jarrod Kingrey

Pitches: Right **Bats:** Right **Pos:** RP-53   **Ht:** 6'1" **Wt:** 205 **Born:** 8/23/76 **Age:** 24

Year Team	Lg Org	G	GS	CG	GF	IP	BFP	H	R	ER	HR	SH	SF	HB	TBB	IBB	SO	WP	Bk	W	L	Pct.	ShO	Sv	ERA
		HOW MUCH HE PITCHED						WHAT HE GAVE UP												THE RESULTS					
1998 St.Cathrnes	A- Tor	25	0	0	24	37.2	148	21	7	2	1	1	0	0	17	0	58	5	1	0	0	—	0	16	0.48
Hagerstown	A Tor	1	0	0	0	2.1	10	3	2	1	0	1	0	0	0	0	3	0	0	0	1	.000	0	0	3.86
1999 Hagerstown	A Tor	56	0	0	48	61	259	49	24	21	5	1	0	6	26	0	69	0	4	3	2	.600	0	27	3.10
2000 Dunedin	A+ Tor	37	0	0	34	39.1	177	33	20	13	2	2	2	3	23	1	35	5	1	4	2	.667	0	23	2.97
Tennessee	AA Tor	16	0	0	15	17	76	11	6	4	0	2	1	1	15	2	16	1	0	2	0	1.000	0	7	2.12
3 Min. YEARS		135	0	0	121	157.1	670	117	59	41	8	7	3	10	81	3	181	11	6	9	5	.643	0	73	2.35

Scott Kirby

Bats: Right **Throws:** Right **Pos:** OF-82; 3B-21; PH-10; DH-5; PR-2   **Ht:** 6'2" **Wt:** 190 **Born:** 7/18/77 **Age:** 23

Year Team	Lg Org	G	AB	H	2B	3B	HR	TB	R	RBI	TBB	IBB	SO	HBP	SH	SF	SB	CS	SB%	GDP	Avg	OBP	SLG
					BATTING												BASERUNNING				PERCENTAGES		
1996 Helena	R+ Mil	47	145	29	4	0	4	45	26	21	19	0	42	4	1	2	0	3	.00	4	.200	.306	.310
1997 Helena	R+ Mil	68	248	65	10	1	11	110	65	47	53	0	65	7	0	4	8	6	.57	5	.262	.401	.444
1998 Beloit	A Mil	107	359	73	19	2	8	120	51	40	47	0	109	6	5	1	5	4	.56	7	.203	.305	.334
1999 Beloit	A Mil	68	247	75	14	1	17	142	54	47	47	0	59	3	0	3	3	1	.75	5	.304	.417	.575
Stockton	A+ Mil	60	202	58	15	3	10	109	35	36	25	2	59	7	0	4	3	3	.50	7	.287	.378	.540
2000 Huntsville	AA Mil	118	344	75	11	1	12	124	54	45	66	2	112	12	2	1	7	5	.58	4	.218	.362	.360
5 Min. YEARS		468	1545	375	73	8	62	650	285	236	257	4	446	39	8	15	26	22	.54	32	.243	.362	.421

Wayne Kirby

Bats: Left **Throws:** Right **Pos:** OF-103; DH-25; PH-1   **Ht:** 5'10" **Wt:** 185 **Born:** 1/22/64 **Age:** 37

					BATTING											BASERUNNING				PERCENTAGES		
Year Team	Lg Org	G	AB	H	2B	3B	HR	TB	R	RBI	TBB	IBB	SO	HBP	SH	SF	SB	CS	SB%	GDP	Avg	OBP	SLG
1983 Dodgers	R LA	60	216	63	7	1	0	72	43	13	34	0	19	1	4	1	23	8	.74	—	.292	.389	.333
1984 Vero Beach	A+ LA	76	224	61	6	3	0	73	39	21	21	2	30	6	5	2	11	9	.55	3	.272	.348	.326
Great Falls	R+ LA	20	84	26	2	2	1	35	19	11	12	2	9	0	1	1	19	3	.86	2	.310	.392	.417
Bakersfield	A+ LA	23	84	23	3	0	0	26	14	10	4	0	5	0	2	1	8	3	.73	0	.274	.303	.310
1985 Vero Beach	A+ LA	122	437	123	9	3	0	138	70	28	41	1	41	3	4	3	31	14	.69	3	.281	.345	.316
1986 Vero Beach	A+ LA	114	387	101	9	4	2	124	60	31	37	3	30	1	2	2	28	17	.62	5	.261	.326	.320
1987 San Antonio	AA LA	24	80	19	1	2	1	27	7	9	4	0	7	0	3	0	6	4	.60	0	.238	.274	.338
Bakersfield	A+ LA	105	416	112	14	3	0	132	77	34	49	1	41	3	5	2	56	21	.73	3	.269	.349	.317
1988 Bakersfield	A+ LA	12	47	13	0	1	0	15	12	4	11	0	4	0	0	0	9	2	.82	0	.277	.414	.319
San Antonio	AA LA	100	334	80	9	2	0	93	50	21	21	2	42	3	10	1	26	10	.72	5	.240	.290	.278
1989 San Antonio	AA LA	44	140	30	3	1	0	35	14	7	18	0	17	1	2	1	11	6	.65	4	.214	.306	.250
Albuquerque	AAA LA	78	310	106	18	8	0	140	62	30	26	1	27	1	5	1	29	14	.67	2	.342	.393	.452
1990 Albuquerque	AAA LA	119	342	95	14	5	0	119	56	30	28	1	36	3	4	3	29	7	.81	2	.278	.335	.348
1991 Colo Spmgs	AAA Cle	118	385	113	14	4	1	138	66	39	34	2	36	2	5	3	29	14	.67	3	.294	.351	.358
1992 Colo Spmgs	AAA Cle	123	470	162	18	16	11	245	101	74	36	4	28	2	4	2	51	20	.72	7	.345	.392	.521
1993 Charlotte	AAA Cle	17	76	22	6	2	3	41	10	7	3	0	10	0	0	0	4	2	.67	1	.289	.316	.539
1997 Albuquerque	AAA LA	68	269	90	16	5	10	146	57	43	26	0	33	1	1	2	18	5	.78	5	.335	.393	.543
1998 Memphis	AAA StL	58	227	64	15	3	5	100	36	32	15	1	33	0	2	0	10	2	.83	2	.282	.326	.441
Norfolk	AAA NYM	42	162	50	8	3	5	79	32	23	21	1	18	2	1	0	11	5	.69	1	.309	.395	.488
1999 Las Vegas	AAA SD	66	160	48	7	3	10	91	29	31	28	0	36	0	1	1	2	4	.33	1	.300	.402	.569
2000 Rochester	AAA Bal	129	507	144	24	11	6	208	76	60	46	5	61	1	1	2	10	4	.71	12	.284	.344	.410
1991 Cleveland	AL	21	43	9	2	0	0	11	4	5	2	0	6	0	1	1	1	2	.33	2	.209	.239	.256
1992 Cleveland	AL	21	18	3	1	0	1	7	9	1	3	0	2	0	0	0	0	3	.00	1	.167	.286	.389
1993 Cleveland	AL	131	458	123	19	5	6	170	71	60	37	2	58	3	7	6	17	5	.77	8	.269	.323	.371
1994 Cleveland	AL	78	191	56	6	0	5	77	33	23	13	0	30	1	2	0	11	4	.73	1	.293	.341	.403
1995 Cleveland	AL	101	188	39	10	2	1	56	29	14	13	0	32	1	1	2	10	3	.77	4	.207	.260	.298
1996 Cleveland	AL	27	16	4	1	0	0	5	3	1	2	0	2	0	0	0	0	1	.00	1	.250	.333	.313
Los Angeles	NL	65	188	51	10	1	1	66	23	11	17	1	17	1	1	1	4	2	.67	3	.271	.333	.351
1997 Los Angeles	NL	46	65	11	2	0	0	13	6	4	10	0	12	0	0	0	0	0	—	1	.169	.280	.200
1998 New York	NL	26	31	6	0	1	0	8	5	0	9	0	9	0	1	0	1	1	.50	1	.194	.219	.258
15 Min. YEARS		1518	5357	1545	203	82	55	2077	930	558	515	26	563	30	62	28	421	174	.71	—	.288	.352	.388
8 Maj. YEARS		516	1198	302	51	9	14	413	183	119	98	3	168	6	13	10	44	21	.68	21	.252	.309	.345

Rick Kirsten

Pitches: Right **Bats:** Right **Pos:** SP-20; RP-4   **Ht:** 6'0" **Wt:** 165 **Born:** 7/23/78 **Age:** 22

		HOW MUCH HE PITCHED						WHAT HE GAVE UP												THE RESULTS				
Year Team	Lg Org	G	GS	CG	GF	IP	BFP	H	R	ER	HR	SH	SF	HB	TBB	IBB	SO	WP	Bk	W	L	Pct.	ShO	Sv	ERA
1999 Tigers	R Det	11	4	0	4	25.2	112	18	15	15	2	3	2	2	17	0	27	1	0	1	1	.500	0	0	5.26
Lakeland	A+ Det	2	2	1	0	16.2	60	7	1	1	0	0	0	0	6	0	8	1	0	2	0	1.000	1	0	0.54
2000 W Michigan	A Det	6	6	0	0	39.1	163	36	10	8	1	1	0	3	5	0	25	2	0	4	1	.800	0	0	1.83
Lakeland	A+ Det	14	13	2	0	87.1	364	80	42	32	8	4	4	11	23	0	45	3	1	5	4	.556	0	0	3.30
Jacksnville	AA Det	4	1	0	2	9.1	37	9	6	6	4	0	1	1	3	0	5	0	0	1	1	.500	0	0	5.79
2 Min. YEARS		37	26	3	6	178.1	736	150	74	62	15	8	7	17	57	0	110	7	1	13	7	.650	1	0	3.13

Josh Klimek

Bats: Left **Throws:** Right **Pos:** OF-49; 3B-48; PH-10; DH-6   **Ht:** 6'1" **Wt:** 175 **Born:** 2/2/74 **Age:** 27

					BATTING											BASERUNNING				PERCENTAGES		
Year Team	Lg Org	G	AB	H	2B	3B	HR	TB	R	RBI	TBB	IBB	SO	HBP	SH	SF	SB	CS	SB%	GDP	Avg	OBP	SLG
1996 Helena	R+ Mil	67	253	75	17	0	6	110	56	51	42	5	39	0	0	3	5	1	.83	4	.296	.393	.435
1997 Beloit	A Mil	121	443	118	31	3	12	191	62	66	39	1	56	5	2	6	4	8	.33	8	.266	.329	.431
1998 Stockton	A+ Mil	124	440	125	27	6	9	191	61	56	36	7	60	4	1	6	4	2	.67	6	.284	.340	.434
1999 Huntsville	AA Mil	123	431	103	28	0	14	173	46	71	33	6	78	4	2	8	3	2	.60	5	.239	.294	.401
2000 Huntsville	AA Mil	108	378	106	22	0	14	170	53	62	29	0	71	5	0	6	3	4	.43	4	.280	.335	.450
5 Min. YEARS		543	1945	527	125	9	55	835	278	306	179	19	304	18	5	29	19	17	.53	27	.271	.333	.429

Brandon Knight

Pitches: Right **Bats:** Left **Pos:** SP-28   **Ht:** 6'0" **Wt:** 170 **Born:** 10/1/75 **Age:** 25

		HOW MUCH HE PITCHED						WHAT HE GAVE UP												THE RESULTS				
Year Team	Lg Org	G	GS	CG	GF	IP	BFP	H	R	ER	HR	SH	SF	HB	TBB	IBB	SO	WP	Bk	W	L	Pct.	ShO	Sv	ERA
1995 Rangers	R Tex	3	2	0	0	12	54	12	7	7	0	0	1	0	6	0	11	2	0	2	1	.667	0	0	5.25
Chston-SC	A Tex	9	9	0	0	54.2	218	37	22	19	5	0	4	0	21	0	52	4	1	4	2	.667	0	0	3.13
1996 Hudson Val	A- Tex	9	9	0	0	53	236	59	29	26	1	2	1	1	21	0	52	2	1	2	2	.500	0	0	4.42
Charlotte	A+ Tex	19	17	2	0	102	463	118	65	58	9	4	7	2	45	0	74	6	0	4	10	.286	0	0	5.12
1997 Charlotte	A+ Tex	14	12	3	1	92.2	380	82	33	23	9	3	2	1	22	0	91	0	2	7	4	.636	1	0	2.23
Tulsa	AA Tex	14	14	2	0	90	383	83	52	45	12	0	4	2	35	0	84	9	4	6	4	.600	1	0	4.50
1998 Tulsa	AA Tex	14	14	0	0	86.1	379	94	54	49	11	1	3	0	37	0	87	12	0	6	6	.500	0	0	5.11
Oklahoma	AAA Tex	16	12	0	0	64.2	315	100	75	70	16	0	2	1	29	0	52	9	1	0	7	.000	0	0	9.74
1999 Oklahoma	AAA Tex	27	26	5	0	163	706	173	96	89	23	1	3	10	47	2	97	9	3	9	8	.529	2	0	4.91
2000 Columbus	AAA NYY	28	28	8	0	184.2	783	172	105	91	21	5	7	3	61	3	138	10	3	10	12	.455	1	0	4.44
6 Min. YEARS		153	143	20	1	903	3917	930	538	477	107	16	34	20	324	5	738	63	15	50	56	.472	3	0	4.75

Brian Knoll

Pitches: Right **Bats:** Right **Pos:** SP-20; RP-11   **Ht:** 6'3" **Wt:** 200 **Born:** 8/4/73 **Age:** 27

		HOW MUCH HE PITCHED						WHAT HE GAVE UP												THE RESULTS				
Year Team	Lg Org	G	GS	CG	GF	IP	BFP	H	R	ER	HR	SH	SF	HB	TBB	IBB	SO	WP	Bk	W	L	Pct.	ShO	Sv	ERA
1995 Bellingham	A- SF	22	2	0	5	57	232	44	22	13	1	4	1	3	17	0	35	2	1	5	2	.714	0	0	2.05
1996 Burlington	A SF	52	0	0	16	79	342	76	43	32	5	6	2	4	34	2	56	4	0	3	8	.273	0	1	3.65

Year Team	Lg Org	G	GS	CG	GF	IP	BFP	H	R	ER	HR	SH	SF	HB	TBB	IBB	SO	WP	Bk	W	L	Pct.	ShO	Sv	ERA
		HOW MUCH HE PITCHED						**WHAT HE GAVE UP**												**THE RESULTS**					
1997 Bakersfield	A+ SF	49	0	0	23	68	323	88	50	43	6	3	1	2	35	3	56	10	0	3	6	.333	0	2	5.69
1998 San Jose	A+ SF	42	6	1	15	114.2	490	135	47	44	4	3	3	5	21	0	109	5	0	7	7	.500	1	3	3.45
1999 Shreveport	AA SF	33	17	1	6	128.1	530	117	54	50	15	5	4	11	34	0	91	6	0	9	7	.563	1	1	3.51
2000 Shreveport	AA SF	21	10	1	5	79.2	346	80	34	30	8	4	7	4	26	2	62	0	0	7	5	.583	0	3	3.39
Fresno	AAA SF	10	10	0	0	62	277	76	46	43	13	5	4	5	19	0	36	1	0	3	4	.429	0	0	6.24
6 Min. YEARS		229	45	3	70	588.2	2540	616	296	255	52	30	22	34	186	7	445	28	1	37	39	.487	2	10	3.90

Eric Knott

Pitches: Left **Bats:** Left **Pos:** SP-7; RP-4   **Ht:** 6'0" **Wt:** 188 **Born:** 9/23/74 **Age:** 26

Year Team	Lg Org	G	GS	CG	GF	IP	BFP	H	R	ER	HR	SH	SF	HB	TBB	IBB	SO	WP	Bk	W	L	Pct.	ShO	Sv	ERA
		HOW MUCH HE PITCHED						**WHAT HE GAVE UP**												**THE RESULTS**					
1997 Lethbridge	R+ Ari	21	3	0	7	47	195	41	21	15	4	2	1	0	9	1	62	2	0	0	4	.000	0	3	2.87
1998 High Desert	A+ Ari	28	22	1	3	143.1	616	175	84	72	16	3	4	1	28	1	96	3	3	12	7	.632	0	0	4.52
1999 El Paso	AA Ari	27	27	3	0	161.1	711	198	95	82	11	4	5	5	42	0	83	3	2	7	11	.389	0	0	4.57
2000 Tucson	AAA Ari	11	7	0	1	39.2	180	59	30	28	6	2	3	1	8	0	21	0	0	3	2	.600	0	0	6.35
4 Min. YEARS		87	59	4	11	391.1	1702	473	230	197	37	11	13	7	87	2	262	8	5	22	24	.478	0	3	4.53

Gary Knotts

Pitches: Right **Bats:** Right **Pos:** SP-27   **Ht:** 6'4" **Wt:** 200 **Born:** 2/12/77 **Age:** 24

Year Team	Lg Org	G	GS	CG	GF	IP	BFP	H	R	ER	HR	SH	SF	HB	TBB	IBB	SO	WP	Bk	W	L	Pct.	ShO	Sv	ERA
		HOW MUCH HE PITCHED						**WHAT HE GAVE UP**												**THE RESULTS**					
1996 Marlins	R Fla	12	9	1	2	57.1	227	35	16	13	0	2	2	6	17	0	46	5	0	4	2	.667	1	0	2.04
1997 Kane County	A Fla	7	7	0	0	20	113	33	34	29	2	2	0	3	17	0	19	8	1	1	5	.167	0	0	13.05
Utica	A- Fla	12	12	1	0	69.2	304	70	34	28	3	1	2	8	27	1	65	3	0	3	5	.375	0	0	3.62
1998 Kane County	A Fla	27	27	3	0	158.1	686	144	84	68	11	4	6	11	66	1	148	7	0	8	8	.500	0	0	3.87
1999 Brevard Cty	A+ Fla	16	16	3	0	94	402	101	52	48	7	1	3	8	29	0	65	1	0	9	6	.600	2	0	4.60
Portland	AA Fla	12	12	1	0	81.2	358	79	39	34	12	4	3	8	33	0	63	4	0	6	3	.667	1	0	3.75
2000 Portland	AA Fla	27	27	2	0	156.1	687	161	102	81	15	3	5	7	63	1	113	8	0	9	8	.529	0	0	4.66
5 Min. YEARS		113	110	11	2	637.1	2777	623	361	301	50	17	21	51	252	3	519	36	1	40	37	.519	4	0	4.25

Jason Knupfer

Bats: Right **Throws:** Right **Pos:** 2B-42; 1B-28; 3B-16; PH-7; SS-3   **Ht:** 6'0" **Wt:** 185 **Born:** 9/21/74 **Age:** 26

Year Team	Lg Org	G	AB	H	2B	3B	HR	TB	R	RBI	TBB	IBB	SO	HBP	SH	SF	SB	CS	SB%	GDP	Avg	OBP	SLG
		BATTING															**BASERUNNING**				**PERCENTAGES**		
1996 Batavia	A- Phi	66	218	61	5	1	1	71	32	24	25	0	43	4	3	2	5	5	.50	4	.280	.361	.326
1997 Clearwater	A+ Phi	108	365	94	15	0	1	112	56	40	49	1	70	4	7	5	5	6	.45	7	.258	.348	.307
1998 Reading	AA Phi	63	193	42	7	2	0	53	27	15	27	1	46	3	4	4	2	1	.67	7	.218	.317	.275
1999 Clearwater	A+ Phi	15	45	13	2	0	0	15	13	3	12	0	5	0	3	0	1	0	1.00	0	.289	.439	.333
2000 Reading	AA Phi	84	279	75	14	1	4	103	53	24	39	1	46	0	11	3	6	6	.50	4	.269	.355	.369
5 Min. YEARS		336	1100	285	43	4	6	354	181	106	152	3	210	11	28	14	19	18	.51	22	.259	.351	.322

Toby Kominek

Bats: Right **Throws:** Right **Pos:** OF-75; 1B-47; PH-10; DH-3   **Ht:** 6'1" **Wt:** 200 **Born:** 6/13/73 **Age:** 28

Year Team	Lg Org	G	AB	H	2B	3B	HR	TB	R	RBI	TBB	IBB	SO	HBP	SH	SF	SB	CS	SB%	GDP	Avg	OBP	SLG
		BATTING															**BASERUNNING**				**PERCENTAGES**		
1995 Helena	R+ Mil	13	48	16	1	1	3	28	7	18	3	0	9	1	0	1	2	1	.67	0	.333	.377	.583
Beloit	A Mil	55	187	52	14	2	5	91	38	30	18	1	56	10	0	2	12	2	.86	1	.278	.369	.487
1996 Stockton	A+ Mil	100	358	106	17	7	7	158	76	47	49	1	97	8	4	3	10	7	.59	7	.296	.390	.441
1997 Stockton	A+ Mil	128	476	143	28	7	15	230	83	72	50	3	107	24	1	2	22	14	.61	8	.300	.393	.483
1998 El Paso	AA Mil	135	496	150	33	4	17	242	114	83	73	4	120	22	0	4	21	16	.57	5	.302	.412	.488
1999 Huntsville	AA Mil	128	456	106	20	3	12	168	56	59	52	2	118	18	1	3	7	10	.41	9	.232	.333	.368
2000 Huntsville	AA Mil	130	427	111	18	6	10	171	56	68	62	0	104	14	2	5	16	7	.70	8	.260	.368	.400
6 Min. YEARS		689	2448	684	131	30	71	1088	430	377	307	11	611	97	8	20	90	57	.61	38	.279	.379	.444

Mike Koplove

Pitches: Right **Bats:** Right **Pos:** RP-55   **Ht:** 6'0" **Wt:** 160 **Born:** 8/30/76 **Age:** 24

Year Team	Lg Org	G	GS	CG	GF	IP	BFP	H	R	ER	HR	SH	SF	HB	TBB	IBB	SO	WP	Bk	W	L	Pct.	ShO	Sv	ERA
		HOW MUCH HE PITCHED						**WHAT HE GAVE UP**												**THE RESULTS**					
1998 Diamondbcks	R Ari	2	0	0	0	4	19	4	4	4	0	0	0	1	2	0	5	0	0	0	0	—	0	0	9.00
Lethbridge	R+ Ari	12	1	0	4	28	114	23	12	11	2	0	1	4	3	0	22	0	0	1	2	.333	0	2	3.54
1999 South Bend	A Ari	45	0	0	19	84	351	70	23	19	5	3	0	11	29	0	98	4	0	5	2	.714	0	7	2.04
2000 High Desert	A+ Ari	20	0	0	19	25.1	100	14	4	4	0	3	0	1	10	0	31	2	0	2	0	1.000	0	6	1.42
El Paso	AA Ari	35	0	0	16	46.1	197	38	28	20	2	0	2	7	19	1	47	1	1	4	3	.571	0	6	3.88
3 Min. YEARS		114	1	0	58	187.2	781	149	71	58	9	6	3	24	63	1	203	7	1	12	7	.632	0	23	2.78

Scott Krause

Bats: Right **Throws:** Right **Pos:** OF-60; PH-16; DH-5   **Ht:** 6'1" **Wt:** 187 **Born:** 8/16/73 **Age:** 27

Year Team	Lg Org	G	AB	H	2B	3B	HR	TB	R	RBI	TBB	IBB	SO	HBP	SH	SF	SB	CS	SB%	GDP	Avg	OBP	SLG
		BATTING															**BASERUNNING**				**PERCENTAGES**		
1994 Helena	R+ Mil	63	252	90	18	3	4	126	51	52	18	2	49	9	1	2	13	6	.68	2	.357	.416	.500
1995 Beloit	A Mil	134	481	119	30	4	13	196	83	76	50	5	126	12	3	7	24	10	.71	7	.247	.329	.407
1996 El Paso	AA Mil	24	85	27	5	2	3	45	16	11	2	0	19	1	1	0	2	0	1.00	1	.318	.341	.529
Stockton	A+ Mil	108	427	128	22	4	19	215	82	83	32	0	101	16	1	3	25	6	.81	9	.300	.368	.504
1997 El Paso	AA Mil	125	474	171	33	11	16	274	97	88	20	3	108	7	4	7	13	4	.76	7	.361	.390	.578
1998 Louisville	AAA Mil	117	390	114	25	4	26	221	71	82	46	3	104	15	3	1	11	4	.73	16	.292	.387	.567
1999 Louisville	AAA Mil	133	499	138	26	7	15	223	57	89	33	2	104	13	7	8	10	6	.63	13	.277	.333	.447

			BATTING															BASERUNNING				PERCENTAGES		
Year Team	Lg Org	G	AB	H	2B	3B	HR	TB	R	RBI	TBB	IBB	SO	HBP	SH	SF	SB	CS	SB%	GDP	Avg	OBP	SLG
2000 Indianaplos	AAA Mil	67	208	56	15	0	7	92	29	33	15	1	57	5	1	1	1	0	1.00	2	.269	.332	.442
Huntsville	AA Mil	11	28	9	3	0	0	12	2	5	0	0	8	0	0	0	0	0	—	1	.321	.321	.429
7 Min. YEARS		782	2844	852	177	33	103	1404	488	519	216	16	676	78	21	29	99	36	.73	58	.300	.362	.494

Jack Krawczyk

Pitches: Right **Bats:** Right **Pos:** RP-50　　　　　　　　　　　　　　　**Ht:** 6'4" **Wt:** 195 **Born:** 8/12/75 **Age:** 25

		HOW MUCH HE PITCHED						WHAT HE GAVE UP										THE RESULTS					
Year Team	Lg Org	G	GS	CG	GF	IP	BFP	H	R	ER	HR	SH	SF	HB	TBB	IBB	SO	WP	Bk	W	L	Pct.	ShO	Sv	ERA
1998 Helena	R+ Mil	7	0	0	7	8.1	41	10	7	4	1	0	1	0	3	1	11	0	0	0	1	.000	0	0	4.32
Beloit	A Mil	19	3	0	5	40.1	165	37	23	21	3	2	0	1	11	1	42	0	0	3	1	.750	0	0	4.69
1999 Beloit	A Mil	6	0	0	6	6.1	24	5	0	0	0	0	0	0	1	0	11	0	0	0	0	—	0	3	0.00
Stockton	A+ Mil	41	1	0	13	77	331	87	48	40	8	5	3	1	19	2	74	3	0	5	4	.556	0	2	4.68
2000 Huntsville	AA Mil	1	0	0	1	4	16	4	2	2	1	0	0	1	0	0	2	0	0	0	0	—	0	0	4.50
Mudville	A+ Mil	49	0	0	42	86	321	62	14	14	2	5	1	1	9	1	80	1	0	7	1	.875	0	15	1.47
3 Min. YEARS		123	4	0	73	222	898	205	94	81	15	12	5	3	44	5	220	4	0	15	7	.682	0	20	3.28

Mike Kremblas

Bats: Right **Throws:** Right **Pos:** C-38; DH-6; PR-5; OF-3; 3B-2; PH-2; 2B-1; 1B-1　　　　**Ht:** 6'0" **Wt:** 180 **Born:** 10/1/75 **Age:** 25

		BATTING																BASERUNNING				PERCENTAGES		
Year Team	Lg Org	G	AB	H	2B	3B	HR	TB	R	RBI	TBB	IBB	SO	HBP	SH	SF	SB	CS	SB%	GDP	Avg	OBP	SLG
1998 Medcine Hat	R+ Tor	59	184	54	15	0	4	81	40	36	40	1	30	9	1	2	5	4	.56	4	.293	.438	.440
1999 Hagerstown	A Tor	58	165	34	7	0	0	41	22	7	15	0	28	14	1	1	2	0	1.00	5	.206	.323	.248
2000 Dunedin	A+ Tor	25	64	18	2	1	0	22	15	10	16	0	7	6	0	1	1	0	1.00	1	.281	.460	.344
Tennessee	AA Tor	30	69	19	4	0	1	26	16	6	9	0	14	10	5	2	1	1	.50	2	.275	.422	.377
3 Min. YEARS		172	482	125	28	1	5	170	93	59	80	1	79	39	7	6	9	5	.64	12	.259	.402	.353

Rick Krivda

Pitches: Left **Bats:** Right **Pos:** SP-26　　　　　　　　　　　　　　**Ht:** 6'1" **Wt:** 185 **Born:** 1/19/70 **Age:** 31

		HOW MUCH HE PITCHED						WHAT HE GAVE UP										THE RESULTS					
Year Team	Lg Org	G	GS	CG	GF	IP	BFP	H	R	ER	HR	SH	SF	HB	TBB	IBB	SO	WP	Bk	W	L	Pct.	ShO	Sv	ERA
1991 Bluefield	R+ Bal	15	8	0	2	67	265	48	20	14	0	2	1	0	24	0	79	1	4	7	1	.875	0	1	1.88
1992 Kane County	A Bal	18	18	2	0	121.2	502	108	53	41	6	0	3	1	41	0	124	5	1	12	5	.706	0	0	3.03
Frederick	A+ Bal	9	9	1	0	57.1	236	51	23	19	7	0	1	1	15	0	64	1	1	5	1	.833	1	0	2.98
1993 Bowie	AA Bal	22	22	0	0	125.2	522	114	46	43	10	2	1	2	50	0	108	1	2	7	5	.583	0	0	3.08
Rochester	AAA Bal	5	5	0	0	33.1	133	20	7	7	2	1	0	1	16	0	23	1	0	3	0	1.000	0	0	1.89
1994 Rochester	AAA Bal	28	26	3	2	163	688	149	75	64	12	1	6	4	73	4	122	9	1	9	10	.474	2	0	3.53
1995 Rochester	AAA Bal	16	16	1	0	101.2	409	96	44	36	11	6	4	2	32	0	74	3	3	6	5	.545	0	0	3.19
1996 Rochester	AAA Bal	8	8	0	0	44	191	51	24	21	6	0	1	1	15	0	34	2	2	3	1	.750	0	0	4.30
1997 Rochester	AAA Bal	22	21	6	0	146	589	122	61	55	13	0	2	5	34	0	128	2	2	14	2	.875	3	0	3.39
1999 Omaha	AAA KC	21	18	0	0	115.1	541	154	94	73	17	2	3	5	41	0	70	3	3	6	8	.429	0	0	5.70
2000 Rochester	AAA Bal	26	26	0	0	152.2	645	142	75	53	15	3	8	3	61	0	99	5	0	11	9	.550	0	0	3.12
1995 Baltimore	AL	13	13	1	0	75.1	319	76	40	38	9	0	4	4	25	1	53	2	2	2	7	.222	0	0	4.54
1996 Baltimore	AL	22	11	0	4	81.2	359	89	48	45	14	2	2	1	39	2	54	3	1	3	5	.375	0	0	4.96
1997 Baltimore	AL	10	10	0	0	50	225	67	36	35	7	1	2	0	18	1	29	0	2	4	2	.667	0	0	6.30
1998 Cleveland	AL	11	1	0	5	25	112	24	10	9	2	0	0	0	16	1	10	1	1	2	0	1.000	0	0	3.24
Cincinnati	NL	16	1	0	1	26.1	138	41	34	33	7	3	1	3	19	1	19	1	1	0	2	.000	0	0	11.28
9 Min. YEARS		190	177	13	4	1127.2	4741	1055	522	426	99	17	29	25	402	4	925	33	19	83	47	.638	6	1	3.40
4 Maj. YEARS		72	36	1	10	258.1	1153	297	168	160	39	6	9	8	117	6	165	7	7	11	16	.407	0	0	5.57

Marc Kroon

Pitches: Right **Bats:** Right **Pos:** RP-3; SP-1　　　　　　　　　　　　**Ht:** 6'2" **Wt:** 195 **Born:** 4/2/73 **Age:** 28

		HOW MUCH HE PITCHED						WHAT HE GAVE UP										THE RESULTS					
Year Team	Lg Org	G	GS	CG	GF	IP	BFP	H	R	ER	HR	SH	SF	HB	TBB	IBB	SO	WP	Bk	W	L	Pct.	ShO	Sv	ERA
1991 Mets	R NYM	12	10	1	2	47.2	208	39	33	24	1	0	1	4	22	0	39	10	5	2	3	.400	0	0	4.53
1992 Kingsport	R+ NYM	12	12	0	0	68	307	52	41	31	3	0	3	1	57	0	60	13	2	3	5	.375	0	0	4.10
1993 Capital Cty	A NYM	29	19	0	8	124.1	542	123	65	48	6	1	8	5	70	0	122	10	2	2	11	.154	0	2	3.47
1994 Rancho Cuca	A+ SD	26	26	0	0	143.1	655	143	86	77	14	4	9	11	81	1	153	9	3	11	6	.647	0	0	4.83
1995 Memphis	AA SD	22	19	0	2	115.1	497	90	49	45	12	2	2	6	61	1	123	16	1	7	5	.583	0	2	3.51
1996 Memphis	AA SD	44	0	0	43	46.2	208	33	19	15	4	1	4	3	28	1	56	6	1	2	4	.333	0	22	2.89
1997 Las Vegas	AAA SD	46	0	0	33	41.2	175	34	22	21	5	2	2	3	22	0	53	6	0	1	3	.250	0	15	4.54
1998 Indianapolis	AAA Cin	39	0	0	9	46.1	219	39	29	29	6	1	2	5	47	0	36	14	0	3	2	.600	0	1	5.63
1999 Mariners	R Sea	4	4	0	0	7	27	5	3	3	2	0	0	0	0	0	12	0	0	0	0	—	0	0	3.86
Tacoma	AAA Sea	13	5	0	1	35.1	161	31	24	24	5	0	1	4	21	0	38	1	1	3	2	.600	0	0	6.11
2000 Albuquerque	AAA LA	4	1	0	2	3.2	23	6	4	3	0	0	0	0	7	0	1	0	0	0	1	.000	0	1	7.36
1995 San Diego	NL	2	0	0	1	1.2	7	1	2	2	0	0	0	0	2	0	2	0	0	0	1	.000	0	0	10.80
1997 San Diego	NL	12	0	0	2	11.1	56	14	9	9	2	0	0	1	5	0	12	1	0	0	1	.000	0	0	7.15
1998 San Diego	NL	2	0	0	2	2.1	8	2	0	0	0	0	0	0	1	0	2	0	0	0	0	—	0	0	0.00
Cincinnati	NL	4	0	0	2	5	30	7	8	8	0	0	0	1	8	0	4	2	0	0	0	—	0	0	13.50
10 Min. YEARS		251	96	1	100	679.1	3022	595	375	320	58	11	32	42	416	3	693	85	15	34	42	.447	0	43	4.24
3 Maj. YEARS		20	0	0	7	20.2	101	22	19	19	2	0	0	2	16	0	20	3	0	0	2	.000	0	0	8.27

Jeff Kubenka

Pitches: Left **Bats:** Right **Pos:** RP-16; SP-5　　　　　　　　　　　　**Ht:** 6'1" **Wt:** 191 **Born:** 8/24/74 **Age:** 26

		HOW MUCH HE PITCHED						WHAT HE GAVE UP										THE RESULTS					
Year Team	Lg Org	G	GS	CG	GF	IP	BFP	H	R	ER	HR	SH	SF	HB	TBB	IBB	SO	WP	Bk	W	L	Pct.	ShO	Sv	ERA
1996 Yakima	A- LA	28	0	0	24	32.1	127	20	11	9	2	0	0	0	10	1	61	4	1	5	1	.833	0	14	2.51
1997 San Berndno	A+ LA	34	0	0	32	39	152	24	4	4	1	4	2	1	11	1	62	3	0	5	1	.833	0	19	0.92
Albuquerque	AAA LA	8	0	0	6	7.1	37	11	9	7	2	0	0	0	2	0	10	3	0	0	2	.000	0	2	8.59
San Antonio	AA LA	19	0	0	17	25.2	93	10	2	2	1	0	0	0	6	0	38	1	0	3	0	1.000	0	4	0.70

Year Team	Lg Org	G	GS	CG	GF	IP	BFP	H	R	ER	HR	SH	SF	HB	TBB	IBB	SO	WP	Bk	W	L	Pct.	ShO	Sv	ERA
1998 San Antonio	AA LA	9	0	0	6	9	47	10	11	7	2	0	1	1	7	0	10	3	1	0	0	—	0	0	7.00
Albuquerque	AAA LA	28	0	0	22	40.1	163	32	11	11	1	1	3	0	12	2	40	1	0	2	5	.286	0	9	2.45
1999 Albuquerque	AAA LA	51	0	0	27	67	283	60	30	22	6	3	2	4	22	3	63	4	0	4	4	.500	0	11	2.96
2000 Tucson	AAA Ari	4	0	0	1	9.1	42	10	7	7	1	0	0	1	6	1	6	0	0	0	2	.000	0	0	6.75
Sacramento	AAA Oak	17	5	0	6	48.1	223	57	41	35	8	2	2	2	23	0	33	3	0	1	0	.667	0	1	6.52
1998 Los Angeles	NL	6	0	0	2	9.1	40	4	1	1	0	2	1	0	8	0	10	1	0	1	0	1.000	0	0	0.96
1999 Los Angeles	NL	6	0	0	2	7.2	42	13	12	10	1	2	1	0	4	0	2	0	0	1	0	.000	0	0	11.74
5 Min. YEARS		198	5	0	141	278.1	1167	234	126	104	24	10	11	9	99	8	323	22	2	21	16	.568	0	60	3.36
2 Maj. YEARS		12	0	0	4	17	82	17	13	11	1	4	2	0	12	0	12	1	0	1	1	.500	0	0	5.82

Tim Kubinski

Pitches: Left **Bats:** Left **Pos:** RP-40; SP-1 **Ht:** 6'4" **Wt:** 205 **Born:** 1/20/72 **Age:** 29

Year Team	Lg Org	G	GS	CG	GF	IP	BFP	H	R	ER	HR	SH	SF	HB	TBB	IBB	SO	WP	Bk	W	L	Pct.	ShO	Sv	ERA
1993 Athletics	R Oak	1	1	0	0	3	13	5	2	2	1	0	0	0	0	0	3	0	0	0	1	.000	0	0	6.00
Sou Oregon	A- Oak	12	12	1	0	70	294	67	36	22	4	2	2	6	18	0	51	2	2	5	5	.500	0	0	2.83
1994 W Michigan	A Oak	30	23	1	4	158.2	677	168	82	64	8	13	4	7	36	0	126	8	10	14	6	.700	0	0	3.63
1995 Edmonton	AAA Oak	6	5	0	0	32	136	34	18	17	4	0	0	4	10	0	12	0	4	1	2	.333	0	0	4.78
Modesto	A+ Oak	25	17	0	4	109	485	126	73	60	12	6	5	8	24	0	83	10	1	6	10	.375	0	2	4.95
1996 Huntsville	AA Oak	43	3	0	15	102	418	84	41	27	7	4	3	3	36	6	78	8	3	8	7	.533	0	3	2.38
Edmonton	AAA Oak	1	0	0	1	1	4	1	0	0	0	0	0	0	1	0	0	0	0	0	0	—	0	0	0.00
1997 Edmonton	AAA Oak	47	0	0	17	76	315	64	39	38	8	6	1	1	34	4	53	7	2	4	4	.500	0	7	4.50
1998 Edmonton	AAA Oak	57	1	0	23	75.1	321	77	40	38	8	2	3	3	22	3	54	3	1	6	5	.545	0	2	4.54
1999 Vancouver	AAA Oak	46	1	0	17	73.1	314	70	30	28	2	6	2	2	27	3	56	5	2	5	3	.625	0	5	3.44
2000 Sacramento	AAA Oak	41	1	0	14	67.2	309	84	52	45	10	3	3	0	22	3	51	4	1	6	5	.545	0	1	5.99
1997 Oakland	AL	11	0	0	3	12.2	56	12	9	8	2	0	2	1	6	1	10	0	0	0	0	—	0	0	5.68
1999 Oakland	AL	14	0	0	4	12.1	57	14	8	8	3	0	1	1	5	1	7	0	0	0	0	—	0	0	5.84
8 Min. YEARS		309	64	2	95	768	3286	780	413	341	64	42	23	34	230	19	567	47	26	55	48	.534	0	21	4.00
2 Maj. YEARS		25	0	0	7	25	113	26	17	16	5	0	3	2	11	2	17	0	0	0	0	—	0	0	5.76

Mike Kusiewicz

Pitches: Left **Bats:** Right **Pos:** SP-26; RP-1 **Ht:** 6'2" **Wt:** 185 **Born:** 11/1/76 **Age:** 24

Year Team	Lg Org	G	GS	CG	GF	IP	BFP	H	R	ER	HR	SH	SF	HB	TBB	IBB	SO	WP	Bk	W	L	Pct.	ShO	Sv	ERA
1995 Salem	A+ Col	1	1	0	0	6	26	7	1	1	0	0	0	2	0	0	7	0	1	0	0	—	0	0	1.50
Asheville	A Col	21	21	0	0	122.1	484	92	40	28	6	2	0	6	34	0	103	9	1	8	4	.667	0	0	2.06
1996 Salem	A+ Col	5	3	0	2	23	100	19	15	13	2	1	1	1	12	0	18	2	0	0	1	.000	0	1	5.09
New Haven	AA Col	14	14	0	0	76.1	326	83	38	28	4	2	3	2	27	2	64	0	1	2	4	.333	0	0	3.30
1997 New Haven	AA Col	10	4	0	0	28.1	138	41	28	20	2	2	2	2	10	1	11	1	0	2	4	.333	0	0	6.35
Salem	A+ Col	19	18	1	0	117.2	480	99	44	33	5	4	5	9	32	0	107	7	1	8	6	.571	1	0	2.52
1998 New Haven	AA Col	27	26	2	0	178.2	740	161	59	46	4	12	6	16	35	0	151	9	1	14	7	.667	0	0	2.32
1999 Rockies	R Col	6	6	0	0	24.2	112	26	16	15	0	1	1	2	9	0	27	1	1	3	1	.250	0	0	5.47
2000 Tennessee	AA Tor	27	26	1	1	156	684	149	83	63	14	8	4	9	59	1	115	10	0	7	9	.438	0	0	3.63
6 Min. YEARS		130	119	4	3	733	3090	677	324	247	37	32	22	53	218	4	603	39	6	42	38	.525	1	1	3.03

John Lackey

Pitches: Right **Bats:** Right **Pos:** SP-28 **Ht:** 6'5" **Wt:** 200 **Born:** 10/23/78 **Age:** 22

Year Team	Lg Org	G	GS	CG	GF	IP	BFP	H	R	ER	HR	SH	SF	HB	TBB	IBB	SO	WP	Bk	W	L	Pct.	ShO	Sv	ERA
1999 Boise	A- Ana	15	15	1	0	81.1	372	81	59	45	7	5	2	8	50	1	77	14	1	6	2	.750	0	0	4.98
2000 Cedar Rapds	A Ana	5	5	0	0	30.1	115	20	7	7	1	0	0	2	5	0	21	4	0	3	2	.600	0	0	2.08
Lk Elsinore	A+ Ana	15	15	2	0	100.2	433	94	56	38	9	0	5	9	42	0	74	12	3	6	6	.500	1	0	3.40
Erie	AA Ana	8	8	2	0	57.1	234	58	23	21	6	1	0	1	9	0	43	0	0	6	1	.857	0	0	3.30
2 Min. YEARS		43	43	5	0	269.2	1154	253	145	111	23	6	7	20	106	1	215	30	4	21	11	.656	1	0	3.70

Steve Lackey

Bats: Right **Throws:** Right **Pos:** SS-125; 2B-5; PH-4 **Ht:** 5'11" **Wt:** 159 **Born:** 9/25/74 **Age:** 26

Year Team	Lg Org	G	AB	H	2B	3B	HR	TB	R	RBI	TBB	IBB	SO	HBP	SH	SF	SB	CS	SB%	GDP	Avg	OBP	SLG
1992 Mets	R NYM	12	47	9	1	0	0	10	6	3	3	0	7	1	1	0	0	1	.00	0	.191	.255	.213
Kingsport	R+ NYM	38	148	26	2	0	0	28	16	10	17	0	22	3	0	1	3	4	.43	5	.176	.274	.189
1993 Kingsport	R+ NYM	53	172	25	4	0	0	29	14	9	14	0	30	0	1	1	3	4	.43	4	.145	.209	.169
1994 Pittsfield	A- NYM	3	4	1	0	0	0	1	1	0	2	0	0	0	2	0	0	0	—	0	.250	.500	.250
Kingsport	R+ NYM	56	187	37	6	1	0	45	22	7	24	1	31	3	3	0	2	2	.50	3	.198	.299	.241
1995 Pittsfield	A- NYM	21	75	18	5	0	0	23	7	6	2	0	16	1	1	1	1	0	1.00	1	.240	.266	.307
Capital Cty	A NYM	67	178	34	8	0	1	45	21	11	11	1	42	2	5	3	9	2	.82	2	.191	.242	.253
1996 Fayettevlle	A Det	82	310	67	13	0	4	92	38	43	28	0	58	3	5	5	24	6	.80	5	.216	.283	.297
Visalia	A+ Det	46	184	49	11	1	4	74	27	29	16	0	44	1	2	2	7	1	.88	7	.266	.325	.402
1997 Jacksnville	AA Det	5	13	1	0	0	0	1	1	0	1	0	1	0	1	0	0	1	1.00	0	.077	.077	.077
Lakeland	A+ Det	71	247	55	14	0	0	69	24	22	10	0	58	1	6	2	5	4	.56	3	.223	.254	.279
1998 Jacksnville	AA Det	12	34	11	1	0	0	12	6	3	5	0	5	0	0	0	0	2	—	2	.324	.410	.353
Lakeland	A+ Det	102	415	118	14	3	3	147	68	39	31	0	73	4	9	5	19	7	.73	4	.284	.336	.354
1999 Myrtle Bch	A+ Atl	53	216	59	10	2	0	73	24	16	15	0	33	4	1	2	13	4	.76	1	.273	.329	.338
Greenville	AA Atl	80	315	92	18	4	3	128	50	38	21	0	55	0	6	3	9	8	.53	7	.292	.333	.406
2000 Greenville	AA Atl	129	489	114	9	0	3	132	61	33	39	0	95	3	10	2	24	8	.75	15	.233	.293	.270
9 Min. YEARS		830	3034	716	116	10	19	909	386	279	238	2	570	26	53	26	120	51	.70	60	.236	.295	.300

Shawn Lagana

Bats: Right **Throws:** Right **Pos:** 2B-37; SS-20; 3B-20; PR-2; PH-1　　　　**Ht:** 6'2" **Wt:** 175 **Born:** 4/28/81 **Age:** 20

		BATTING															BASERUNNING				PERCENTAGES		
Year Team	Lg Org	G	AB	H	2B	3B	HR	TB	R	RBI	TBB	IBB	SO	HBP	SH	SF	SB	CS	SB%	GDP	Avg	OBP	SLG
1999 Diamondbcks	R Ari	39	159	41	8	1	0	51	28	21	10	0	33	1	0	3	5	3	.63	5	.258	.301	.321
2000 Tucson	AAA Ari	2	0	0	0	0	0	0	0	0	0	0	0	0	0	0	0	0	—	0	—	—	—
Missoula	R+ Ari	68	226	65	12	2	2	87	40	20	33	0	33	2	1	0	10	1	.91	3	.288	.383	.385
2 Min. YEARS		109	385	106	20	3	2	138	68	41	43	0	66	3	1	3	15	4	.79	8	.275	.350	.358

Denny Lail

Pitches: Right **Bats:** Right **Pos:** SP-22; RP-5　　　　**Ht:** 6'1" **Wt:** 172 **Born:** 9/10/74 **Age:** 26

		HOW MUCH HE PITCHED						WHAT HE GAVE UP												THE RESULTS					
Year Team	Lg Org	G	GS	CG	GF	IP	BFP	H	R	ER	HR	SH	SF	HB	TBB	IBB	SO	WP	Bk	W	L	Pct.	ShO	Sv	ERA
1995 Oneonta	A- NYY	13	13	0	0	68	309	66	38	30	2	1	4	5	31	0	59	1	0	5	6	.455	0	0	3.97
1996 Greensboro	A NYY	11	0	0	1	23	100	19	16	12	2	0	0	2	11	1	24	4	0	1	0	1.000	0	0	4.70
Tampa	A+ NYY	31	0	0	8	35.1	152	37	11	10	0	1	0	1	14	2	21	2	0	4	0	1.000	0	1	2.55
1997 Tampa	A+ NYY	44	1	0	13	62.1	267	67	38	27	2	1	5	0	23	7	40	4	0	3	5	.375	0	1	3.90
1998 Norwich	AA NYY	8	0	0	0	10	49	15	6	6	1	0	0	0	7	2	9	0	0	0	0	—	0	0	5.40
Tampa	A+ NYY	31	0	0	13	48.2	211	44	24	22	3	1	2	1	25	0	46	4	1	4	0	1.000	0	1	4.07
1999 Tampa	A+ NYY	22	4	0	6	60.2	237	45	17	14	2	0	1	1	16	0	53	1	0	1	3	.250	0	2	2.08
Norwich	AA NYY	6	6	0	0	41.1	156	24	12	8	1	1	0	0	11	0	29	1	1	5	0	1.000	0	0	1.74
2000 Columbus	AAA NYY	27	22	0	3	147.1	625	149	83	76	23	2	4	1	52	1	114	4	4	7	7	.500	0	0	4.64
6 Min. YEARS		193	46	0	44	496.2	2106	466	245	205	37	7	16	11	190	13	395	21	6	30	21	.588	0	5	3.71

Tim Laker

Bats: Right **Throws:** Right **Pos:** C-67; 1B-31; DH-18; PH-5; 3B-4　　　　**Ht:** 6'3" **Wt:** 225 **Born:** 11/27/69 **Age:** 31

		BATTING															BASERUNNING				PERCENTAGES		
Year Team	Lg Org	G	AB	H	2B	3B	HR	TB	R	RBI	TBB	IBB	SO	HBP	SH	SF	SB	CS	SB%	GDP	Avg	OBP	SLG
1988 Jamestown	A- Mon	47	152	34	9	0	0	43	14	17	8	0	30	0	2	1	2	1	.67	4	.224	.261	.283
1989 Rockford	A Mon	14	48	11	1	1	0	14	4	4	3	0	6	0	0	0	1	0	1.00	1	.229	.275	.292
Jamestown	A- Mon	58	216	48	9	1	2	65	25	24	16	1	40	2	0	3	8	4	.67	4	.222	.278	.301
1990 Rockford	A Mon	120	425	94	18	3	7	139	46	57	32	1	83	1	1	8	7	2	.78	9	.221	.273	.327
Wst Plm Bch	A+ Mon	2	3	0	0	0	0	0	0	0	0	0	1	0	0	0	0	0	—	0	.000	.000	.000
1991 Wst Plm Bch	A+ Mon	100	333	77	15	2	5	111	36	33	22	0	52	2	0	4	10	1	.91	9	.231	.280	.333
Harrisburg	AA Mon	11	35	10	1	0	1	14	4	5	2	0	5	1	0	0	1	0	1.00	1	.286	.342	.400
1992 Harrisburg	AA Mon	117	409	99	19	3	15	169	55	68	39	2	89	5	0	5	3	1	.75	10	.242	.312	.413
1993 Ottawa	AAA Mon	56	204	47	10	2	4	69	26	23	21	0	41	1	0	1	3	2	.60	10	.230	.304	.338
1994 Ottawa	AAA Mon	118	424	131	32	2	12	203	68	71	47	2	96	3	2	1	11	6	.65	10	.309	.381	.479
1997 Rochester	AAA Bal	79	290	75	11	1	11	121	45	37	34	1	49	5	0	4	1	2	.33	4	.259	.342	.417
1998 Durham	AAA TB	40	134	32	7	0	11	72	36	26	28	1	32	1	0	1	1	1	.50	4	.239	.372	.537
Nashville	AAA Pit	44	152	54	16	1	11	105	30	34	21	0	26	3	0	1	1	0	1.00	6	.355	.441	.691
1999 Nashville	AAA Pit	112	405	109	29	3	12	180	48	65	29	2	68	4	0	3	3	0	1.00	11	.269	.322	.444
2000 Nashville	AAA Pit	121	421	104	28	4	19	197	70	75	54	1	73	1	0	8	5	0	1.00	9	.247	.329	.468
1992 Montreal	NL	28	46	10	3	0	0	13	8	4	2	0	14	0	0	0	1	1	.50	1	.217	.250	.283
1993 Montreal	NL	43	86	17	2	1	0	21	3	7	2	0	16	1	3	1	2	0	1.00	4	.198	.222	.244
1995 Montreal	NL	64	141	33	8	1	3	52	17	20	14	4	38	1	1	1	0	1	.00	5	.234	.306	.369
1997 Baltimore	AL	7	14	0	0	0	0	0	0	1	2	0	9	0	1	1	0	0	—	0	.000	.118	.000
1998 Tampa Bay	AL	3	5	1	0	0	0	1	1	0	1	0	1	0	0	0	0	0	—	1	.200	.333	.200
1999 Pittsburgh	NL	14	24	9	1	0	1	13	2	2	1	0	3	0	0	0	0	0	—	1	.375	.385	.542
Pittsburgh	NL	6	9	3	0	0	0	3	0	0	0	0	2	0	0	0	0	0	—	0	.333	.333	.333
11 Min. YEARS		1039	3651	925	205	21	110	1502	507	539	356	11	691	29	5	40	56	21	.73	91	.253	.321	.411
6 Maj. YEARS		165	325	73	14	2	4	103	31	34	22	4	83	2	5	4	3	3	.50	9	.225	.275	.317

Jason Lakman

Pitches: Right **Bats:** Right **Pos:** RP-42; SP-2　　　　**Ht:** 6'4" **Wt:** 220 **Born:** 10/17/76 **Age:** 24

		HOW MUCH HE PITCHED						WHAT HE GAVE UP												THE RESULTS					
Year Team	Lg Org	G	GS	CG	GF	IP	BFP	H	R	ER	HR	SH	SF	HB	TBB	IBB	SO	WP	Bk	W	L	Pct.	ShO	Sv	ERA
1995 White Sox	R CWS	9	5	0	1	41.1	181	44	17	15	2	0	3	1	12	0	23	2	2	3	0	1.000	0	0	3.27
1996 Hickory	A CWS	13	13	0	0	63.2	302	66	55	48	7	0	1	4	43	0	43	7	3	0	6	.000	0	0	6.79
Bristol	R+ CWS	13	13	1	0	66.2	312	70	48	42	5	0	3	6	38	0	64	13	1	4	4	.500	0	0	5.67
1997 Hickory	A CWS	27	27	3	0	154.2	667	139	82	67	11	5	1	4	70	0	168	24	1	10	9	.526	0	0	3.90
1998 Winston-Sal	A+ CWS	13	13	1	0	86	363	62	37	36	0	2	2	17	30	0	98	3	0	3	2	.600	0	0	3.77
Birmingham	AA CWS	15	15	0	0	72.1	352	89	70	64	15	1	3	4	40	0	79	6	2	0	10	.000	0	0	7.97
1999 Birmingham	AA CWS	3	3	0	2	3	22	3	5	5	0	0	4	2	9	0	3	5	0	0	0	—	0	0	15.00
Winston-Sal	A+ CWS	20	20	2	0	119.2	531	108	69	58	4	3	4	8	55	1	110	14	0	9	8	.529	0	0	4.36
2000 Birmingham	AA CWS	27	2	0	12	45.2	225	49	25	21	2	0	2	3	30	0	44	7	0	2	2	.500	0	1	4.14
Bowie	AA Bal	17	0	0	5	22.1	102	18	17	14	5	5	0	0	15	2	24	3	0	1	3	.250	0	0	5.64
6 Min. YEARS		157	108	7	20	675.1	3042	648	425	370	51	16	18	57	342	3	656	84	9	32	44	.421	0	1	4.93

Justin Lamber

Pitches: Left **Bats:** Right **Pos:** RP-43　　　　**Ht:** 6'0" **Wt:** 210 **Born:** 5/22/76 **Age:** 25

		HOW MUCH HE PITCHED						WHAT HE GAVE UP												THE RESULTS					
Year Team	Lg Org	G	GS	CG	GF	IP	BFP	H	R	ER	HR	SH	SF	HB	TBB	IBB	SO	WP	Bk	W	L	Pct.	ShO	Sv	ERA
1997 Spokane	A- KC	25	0	0	12	27.1	126	24	14	13	1	0	1	1	20	0	40	10	0	1	1	.500	0	4	4.28
1998 Wilmington	A+ KC	32	0	0	16	53.1	228	43	21	20	3	1	2	1	29	3	68	6	0	2	2	.500	0	2	3.38
1999 Wilmington	A+ KC	39	2	0	18	68.2	304	68	29	28	2	1	0	2	33	2	67	8	0	5	3	.625	0	6	3.67
2000 Wichita	AA KC	43	0	0	19	68.2	327	85	54	50	8	5	2	2	58	10	43	6	1	5	3	.625	0	2	6.55
4 Min. YEARS		139	2	0	65	218	985	220	118	111	14	7	5	6	140	15	218	30	1	13	9	.591	0	14	4.58

Jeremy Lambert

Pitches: Right **Bats:** Right **Pos:** RP-52; SP-3   **Ht:** 6'1" **Wt:** 195 **Born:** 1/10/79 **Age:** 22

Year Team	Lg Org	G	GS	CG	GF	IP	BFP	H	R	ER	HR	SH	SF	HB	TBB	IBB	SO	WP	Bk	W	L	Pct.	ShO	Sv	ERA
1997 Johnson Cty	R+ StL	27	0	0	4	32.1	181	46	42	33	3	1	1	5	37	1	29	6	0	1	1	.500	0	1	9.19
1998 Johnson Cty	R+ StL	13	11	0	0	64	294	73	44	35	7	1	2	6	37	0	30	4	1	4	4	.500	0	0	4.92
1999 Peoria	A StL	21	0	0	1	34.1	175	48	36	34	5	0	2	2	27	0	27	3	0	2	1	.667	0	0	8.91
2000 Potomac	A+ StL	16	3	0	2	28.2	121	30	17	14	1	1	1	1	7	0	28	1	0	0	0	—	0	0	4.40
Arkansas	AA StL	39	0	0	5	47	207	41	27	20	1	2	1	1	28	7	63	0	0	0	2	.000	0	3	3.83
4 Min. YEARS		116	14	0	12	206.1	978	238	166	136	17	5	7	15	136	8	177	14	1	7	8	.467	0	4	5.93

Dan Lampley

Pitches: Right **Bats:** Right **Pos:** SP-16; RP-14   **Ht:** 6'5" **Wt:** 225 **Born:** 11/1/75 **Age:** 25

Year Team	Lg Org	G	GS	CG	GF	IP	BFP	H	R	ER	HR	SH	SF	HB	TBB	IBB	SO	WP	Bk	W	L	Pct.	ShO	Sv	ERA
1998 Red Sox	R Bos	1	0	0	0	3.1	12	1	0	0	0	0	0	0	0	0	3	1	0	1	0	1.000	0	0	0.00
Lowell	A- Bos	13	11	0	2	64	275	51	25	17	4	0	2	9	22	0	95	7	2	7	2	.778	0	0	2.39
1999 Sarasota	A+ Bos	25	25	2	0	140.1	623	152	85	71	13	1	5	18	54	1	126	7	0	10	8	.556	1	0	4.55
2000 Trenton	AA Bos	3	0	0	0	7.1	38	12	10	7	0	1	0	0	2	0	12	1	0	1	1	.500	0	0	8.59
Sarasota	A+ Bos	27	16	2	5	121	527	133	59	45	8	2	4	6	36	2	107	7	0	6	7	.462	0	2	3.35
3 Min. YEARS		69	52	4	7	336	1475	349	179	140	25	4	11	33	114	3	343	23	2	25	18	.581	1	2	3.75

Jacques Landry

Bats: Right **Throws:** Right **Pos:** 3B-122; DH-4; PH-1   **Ht:** 6'3" **Wt:** 205 **Born:** 8/15/73 **Age:** 27

Year Team	Lg Org	G	AB	H	2B	3B	HR	TB	R	RBI	TBB	IBB	SO	HBP	SH	SF	SB	CS	SB%	GDP	Avg	OBP	SLG
1996 Lakeland	A+ Det	11	35	3	1	0	0	4	2	2	3	0	15	0	0	1	0	0	—	0	.086	.154	.114
Fayettevlle	A Det	31	101	19	4	0	1	26	10	3	5	0	36	1	0	1	1	0	1.00	2	.188	.234	.257
1997 W Michigan	A Det	103	369	101	18	5	16	177	51	52	21	1	99	8	0	5	15	3	.83	2	.274	.323	.480
1998 Lakeland	A+ Det	105	397	100	17	2	11	154	51	51	26	1	105	4	4	2	8	6	.57	4	.252	.303	.388
1999 Modesto	A+ Oak	133	508	158	46	6	27	297	92	111	47	2	128	10	3	12	18	4	.82	5	.311	.373	.585
2000 Midland	AA Oak	127	470	120	32	3	18	212	83	80	47	2	143	10	0	5	9	5	.64	5	.255	.333	.451
5 Min. YEARS		510	1880	501	118	16	73	870	289	299	149	6	526	33	7	25	51	18	.74	23	.266	.327	.463

Ryan Lane

Bats: Right **Throws:** Right **Pos:** OF-54; DH-54; 1B-5; 3B-4; P-1   **Ht:** 6'1" **Wt:** 185 **Born:** 7/6/74 **Age:** 26

Year Team	Lg Org	G	AB	H	2B	3B	HR	TB	R	RBI	TBB	IBB	SO	HBP	SH	SF	SB	CS	SB%	GDP	Avg	OBP	SLG
1993 Twins	R Min	43	138	20	3	2	0	27	15	5	15	0	38	2	3	1	3	1	.75	2	.145	.237	.196
1994 Elizabethtn	R+ Min	59	202	48	13	0	3	70	32	18	26	0	47	2	3	2	4	3	.57	4	.238	.328	.347
1995 Fort Wayne	A Min	115	432	115	37	1	6	172	69	56	65	0	92	7	6	4	17	9	.65	4	.266	.368	.398
1996 Fort Myers	A+ Min	106	404	110	20	7	9	171	74	62	60	0	96	6	6	9	21	9	.70	2	.272	.367	.423
Hardware Cy	A Min	33	117	26	5	1	2	39	13	12	8	0	29	0	2	1	3	4	.43	1	.222	.270	.333
1997 New Britain	AA Min	128	444	115	26	2	5	160	63	56	43	0	79	1	8	7	18	7	.72	5	.259	.321	.360
1998 Twins	R Min	18	65	19	5	1	2	32	9	10	4	0	13	0	1	0	2	1	.67	1	.292	.333	.492
1999 New Britain	AA Min	17	49	14	0	1	3	25	6	6	7	1	10	2	0	0	2	2	.50	1	.286	.397	.510
Tulsa	AA Tex	77	264	72	23	5	9	132	38	48	26	0	47	1	0	4	5	2	.71	9	.273	.336	.500
2000 Tulsa	AA Tex	117	425	137	29	2	16	218	75	79	69	4	94	3	0	5	15	7	.68	5	.322	.416	.513
8 Min. YEARS		713	2540	676	161	22	55	1046	394	352	323	5	545	24	29	33	90	45	.67	39	.266	.350	.412

Otoniel Lanfranco

Pitches: Right **Bats:** Right **Pos:** SP-18; RP-15   **Ht:** 6'0" **Wt:** 160 **Born:** 7/17/76 **Age:** 24

Year Team	Lg Org	G	GS	CG	GF	IP	BFP	H	R	ER	HR	SH	SF	HB	TBB	IBB	SO	WP	Bk	W	L	Pct.	ShO	Sv	ERA
1997 Johnson Cty	R+ StL	14	14	0	0	68.1	319	85	60	58	14	1	1	6	31	0	69	1	0	2	8	.200	0	0	7.64
1998 New Jersey	A- StL	5	5	0	0	29	116	14	5	4	0	2	1	3	13	0	35	1	1	1	0	1.000	0	0	1.24
Peoria	A StL	11	11	0	0	72.2	296	67	25	21	4	1	1	1	22	0	51	1	0	7	1	.875	0	0	2.60
1999 Potomac	A+ StL	21	21	0	0	115.1	475	105	59	55	13	4	3	9	35	0	83	4	1	8	6	.571	0	0	4.29
2000 Arkansas	AA StL	33	18	0	4	119.2	527	123	75	67	17	3	5	6	52	0	70	3	1	9	6	.600	0	0	5.04
4 Min. YEARS		84	69	0	4	405	1733	394	224	205	48	11	11	25	153	0	308	10	3	27	21	.563	0	0	4.56

Selwyn Langaigne

Bats: Left **Throws:** Left **Pos:** OF-85; PR-11; 1B-7; PH-4; DH-2   **Ht:** 6'0" **Wt:** 185 **Born:** 3/22/76 **Age:** 25

Year Team	Lg Org	G	AB	H	2B	3B	HR	TB	R	RBI	TBB	IBB	SO	HBP	SH	SF	SB	CS	SB%	GDP	Avg	OBP	SLG
1996 Medcine Hat	R+ Tor	32	100	26	4	1	2	38	19	11	17	0	20	1	2	0	8	2	.80	4	.260	.373	.380
Hagerstown	A Tor	4	14	2	0	0	0	2	1	1	1	0	5	0	0	0	2	0	1.00	0	.143	.200	.143
Dunedin	A+ Tor	31	117	26	2	3	0	34	16	4	9	0	30	2	4	0	1	3	.25	5	.222	.289	.291
1997 Dunedin	A+ Tor	42	90	17	3	0	1	23	9	7	10	0	26	0	4	0	4	1	.80	4	.189	.270	.256
St.Cathrnes	A- Tor	74	266	85	15	4	1	111	50	39	48	1	46	2	0	3	19	9	.68	5	.320	.423	.417
1998 Dunedin	A+ Tor	128	475	124	7	0	0	131	52	38	37	0	73	2	7	2	21	17	.55	12	.261	.316	.276
1999 Knoxville	AA Tor	40	123	30	4	1	0	36	18	10	10	0	25	0	2	0	3	4	.43	10	.244	.301	.293
Dunedin	A+ Tor	62	201	59	9	1	2	76	35	25	16	0	29	0	3	3	5	5	.50	2	.294	.341	.378
2000 Dunedin	A+ Tor	5	10	6	1	0	0	7	2	1	1	1	2	0	0	0	0	0	—	1	.600	.636	.700
Tennessee	AA Tor	76	213	52	4	1	0	58	26	22	21	1	43	1	2	1	1	5	.17	7	.244	.314	.272
Syracuse	AAA Tor	16	46	11	5	0	0	16	3	0	1	0	8	0	1	0	0	1	.00	1	.239	.255	.348
5 Min. YEARS		510	1655	438	54	11	6	532	231	158	171	3	307	8	25	9	64	47	.58	50	.265	.335	.321

Derrick Lankford

Bats: Left Throws: Right Pos: OF-65; 1B-14; DH-13; PH-4; P-2; PR-1   Ht: 6'2" Wt: 228 Born: 9/21/74 Age: 26

Year Team	Lg Org	G	AB	H	2B	3B	HR	TB	R	RBI	TBB	IBB	SO	HBP	SH	SF	SB	CS	SB%	GDP	Avg	OBP	SLG
1997 Erie	A- Pit	58	195	60	11	3	10	107	36	55	33	4	57	1	0	2	2	0	1.00	1	.308	.407	.549
1998 Augusta	A Pit	127	457	127	25	4	22	226	72	89	59	5	119	5	0	7	8	5	.62	11	.278	.362	.495
1999 Lynchburg	A+ Pit	123	456	133	28	8	20	237	80	88	52	1	124	7	0	6	4	0	1.00	7	.292	.369	.520
2000 Altoona	AA Pit	96	314	92	16	2	10	142	41	40	47	3	60	0	0	3	4	1	.80	7	.293	.382	.452
4 Min. YEARS		404	1422	412	80	17	62	712	229	272	191	13	360	13	0	18	18	6	.75	26	.290	.375	.501

Frank Lankford

Pitches: Right Bats: Right Pos: RP-22; SP-8   Ht: 6'2" Wt: 190 Born: 3/26/71 Age: 30

Year Team	Lg Org	G	GS	CG	GF	IP	BFP	H	R	ER	HR	SH	SF	HB	TBB	IBB	SO	WP	Bk	W	L	Pct.	ShO	Sv	ERA
1993 Oneonta	A- NYY	16	7	0	1	64.2	276	60	41	24	3	3	2	1	22	0	61	5	0	4	5	.444	0	0	3.34
1994 Greensboro	A NYY	54	0	0	27	82.1	352	79	37	27	3	6	1	1	18	3	74	7	1	7	6	.538	0	7	2.95
1995 Tampa	A+ NYY	55	0	0	36	73	305	64	29	21	0	7	0	2	22	6	58	1	0	4	6	.400	0	15	2.59
1996 Norwich	AA NYY	61	0	0	25	88	392	82	42	26	4	9	1	2	40	6	61	3	0	7	8	.467	0	4	2.66
1997 Norwich	AA NYY	11	11	2	0	68.1	277	58	28	22	3	1	1	2	15	1	39	1	1	4	2	.667	0	0	2.90
Columbus	AAA NYY	15	13	1	2	93.2	374	84	33	28	2	3	1	2	22	1	40	1	0	7	4	.636	1	0	2.69
1998 Columbus	AAA NYY	15	15	3	0	94	413	110	60	53	12	3	0	1	32	0	58	3	0	5	9	.357	0	0	5.07
1999 Yankees	R NYY	1	1	0	0	2	8	2	1	1	0	0	0	0	1	0	2	1	0	0	0	—	0	0	4.50
2000 Modesto	A+ Oak	1	1	0	0	2	6	0	0	0	0	0	0	0	0	0	2	0	0	0	0	—	0	0	0.00
Sacramento	AAA Oak	29	7	0	4	67	284	68	32	28	4	1	2	3	25	1	33	3	1	1	5	.167	0	0	3.76
1998 Los Angeles	NL	12	0	0	9	19.2	89	23	13	13	2	0	0	2	7	0	7	1	0	0	2	.000	0	1	5.95
8 Min. YEARS		258	55	6	95	635	2687	607	303	230	31	33	8	14	197	18	428	25	3	39	45	.464	1	26	3.26

Mick LaPlante

Pitches: Right Bats: Right Pos: SP-11; RP-6   Ht: 6'2" Wt: 180 Born: 12/9/69 Age: 31

Year Team	Lg Org	G	GS	CG	GF	IP	BFP	H	R	ER	HR	SH	SF	HB	TBB	IBB	SO	WP	Bk	W	L	Pct.	ShO	Sv	ERA
1992 Welland	A- Pit	11	11	1	0	69	282	54	34	24	1	3	1	5	13	1	75	8	2	1	5	.167	1	0	3.13
Augusta	A Pit	3	3	0	0	18.1	77	20	7	7	1	1	1	0	6	0	7	1	0	1	1	.500	0	0	3.44
1993 Augusta	A Pit	14	14	0	0	83.1	351	89	37	32	5	3	0	3	10	1	80	4	0	5	5	.500	0	0	3.46
Salem	A+ Pit	11	11	0	0	65.1	278	71	35	25	6	1	3	0	19	0	44	10	1	3	2	.600	0	0	3.44
1994 Carolina	AA Pit	28	26	3	0	163	705	180	110	89	20	6	8	6	41	1	110	5	0	7	12	.368	0	0	4.91
1995 Pirates	R Pit	2	0	0	2	3	12	1	0	0	0	0	0	0	0	0	4	0	0	0	0	—	0	1	0.00
Lynchburg	A+ Pit	5	2	0	0	15.1	73	21	14	14	4	0	1	1	3	0	13	2	0	1	1	.500	0	0	8.22
1996 Madison	IND —	19	17	6	1	129.1	548	134	62	52	7	3	3	4	41	4	82	6	3	10	7	.588	0	0	3.62
1998 Madison	IND —	17	16	2	0	118.2	500	124	63	58	19	5	3	3	29	1	88	1	0	8	7	.533	0	0	4.40
1999 Quebec	IND —	20	18	3	1	131	512	108	38	30	7	8	3	3	23	2	143	4	0	11	2	.846	1	0	2.06
2000 Ottawa	AAA Mon	3	0	0	2	4	19	4	4	4	1	0	0	0	3	0	2	0	0	0	0	—	0	0	9.00
Quebec	IND —	5	5	0	0	29	116	25	11	10	5	2	1	1	5	0	29	1	0	2	2	.500	0	0	3.10
Greenville	AA Atl	1	1	0	0	7	28	4	1	1	0	0	1	0	2	0	6	0	1	1	0	1.000	0	0	1.29
Richmond	AAA Atl	8	5	0	0	30.1	136	40	24	22	6	1	1	1	9	0	17	1	0	0	3	.000	0	0	6.53
8 Min. YEARS		147	129	15	6	866.2	3637	875	440	368	82	33	26	27	204	10	700	43	7	50	47	.515	2	1	3.82

Nelson Lara

Pitches: Right Bats: Right Pos: RP-28   Ht: 6'4" Wt: 185 Born: 7/15/78 Age: 22

Year Team	Lg Org	G	GS	CG	GF	IP	BFP	H	R	ER	HR	SH	SF	HB	TBB	IBB	SO	WP	Bk	W	L	Pct.	ShO	Sv	ERA
1995 Marlins	R Fla	11	0	0	4	21.2	101	21	13	9	1	0	1	2	11	1	9	2	1	1	1	.500	0	1	3.74
1996 Marlins	R Fla	7	0	0	0	9.2	54	6	11	6	0	2	1	3	12	2	3	4	1	1	2	.333	0	0	5.59
1997 Kane County	A Fla	29	0	0	18	38.1	169	37	20	17	1	3	3	1	14	0	43	3	1	1	2	.333	0	3	3.99
1998 Brevard Cty	A+ Fla	19	4	0	5	28.2	149	27	36	30	2	0	4	7	33	0	32	8	0	2	5	.286	0	0	9.42
Kane County	A Fla	10	4	0	2	29.1	141	29	23	20	1	1	2	7	23	0	21	4	1	2	2	.500	0	0	6.14
1999 Kane County	A Fla	46	0	0	34	52	257	50	38	35	5	3	3	7	47	1	45	8	0	3	2	.600	0	10	6.06
2000 Portland	AA Fla	21	0	0	8	30.2	165	35	31	28	5	1	1	7	32	0	38	3	2	1	1	.500	0	1	8.22
Brevard Cty	A+ Fla	7	0	0	1	10.2	57	12	11	11	0	1	1	4	10	0	6	2	0	0	0	—	0	0	9.28
6 Min. YEARS		150	8	0	73	221	1093	217	183	156	15	11	16	38	182	4	197	34	6	11	15	.423	0	15	6.35

Stephen Larkin

Bats: Left Throws: Left Pos: OF-36; PH-19; PR-7; DH-4; 1B-1   Ht: 6'0" Wt: 190 Born: 7/24/73 Age: 27

Year Team	Lg Org	G	AB	H	2B	3B	HR	TB	R	RBI	TBB	IBB	SO	HBP	SH	SF	SB	CS	SB%	GDP	Avg	OBP	SLG
1994 Hudson Val	A- Tex	66	237	47	10	1	2	65	26	22	30	1	47	1	0	3	10	5	.67	3	.198	.288	.274
1995 Chston-SC	A Tex	113	369	94	19	1	5	130	50	45	54	2	80	1	3	5	18	10	.64	7	.255	.347	.352
Winston-Sal	A+ Cin	13	50	11	1	0	0	12	2	4	3	1	12	0	0	1	2	2	.50	0	.220	.259	.240
1996 Winston-Sal	A+ Cin	39	117	21	2	0	3	32	13	6	14	2	25	0	1	1	6	1	.86	6	.179	.265	.274
Chston-WV	A Cin	58	203	55	7	2	5	81	30	33	35	4	40	4	1	1	5	4	.56	2	.271	.387	.399
1997 Chston-WV	A Cin	129	464	129	23	10	13	211	88	79	52	1	83	5	0	5	28	9	.76	6	.278	.354	.455
1998 Chattanooga	AA Cin	80	267	61	22	1	3	94	33	31	23	0	52	1	1	4	3	4	.43	7	.228	.288	.352
1999 Chattanooga	AA Cin	104	264	79	16	2	4	111	34	42	31	3	44	0	3	6	7	3	.70	3	.299	.365	.420
2000 Chattanooga	AA Cin	64	150	33	5	3	1	47	15	17	14	1	30	1	0	0	4	5	.44	0	.220	.291	.313
1998 Cincinnati	NL	1	3	1	0	0	0	1	0	0	0	0	1	0	0	0	0	0	—	0	.333	.333	.333
7 Min. YEARS		666	2121	530	105	20	36	783	291	279	256	12	413	13	9	26	83	43	.66	34	.250	.331	.369

Brandon Larson

Bats: Right **Throws:** Right **Pos:** 3B-124; PH-3; DH-1   **Ht:** 6'0" **Wt:** 210 **Born:** 5/24/76 **Age:** 25

Year Team	Lg Org	G	AB	H	2B	3B	HR	TB	R	RBI	TBB	IBB	SO	HBP	SH	SF	SB	CS	SB%	GDP	Avg	OBP	SLG
1997 Chattanooga	AA Cin	11	41	11	5	1	0	18	4	6	1	0	10	0	0	1	0	0	—	1	.268	.279	.439
1998 Burlington	A Cin	18	68	15	3	0	2	24	5	9	4	0	16	0	0	0	2	1	.67	1	.221	.264	.353
1999 Rockford	A Cin	69	250	75	18	1	13	134	38	52	25	1	67	3	0	3	12	2	.86	7	.300	.367	.536
Chattanooga	AA Cin	43	172	49	10	0	12	95	28	42	10	1	51	3	0	2	4	5	.44	3	.285	.332	.552
2000 Louisville	AAA Cin	17	63	18	7	1	2	33	11	4	4	0	16	0	0	0	0	0	—	1	.286	.328	.524
Chattanooga	AA Cin	111	427	116	26	0	20	202	61	64	31	5	122	8	0	3	15	5	.75	5	.272	.330	.473
4 Min. YEARS		269	1021	284	69	3	49	506	147	177	75	7	282	14	0	9	33	13	.72	21	.278	.333	.496

Chris Latham

Bats: Both **Throws:** Right **Pos:** OF-117; PH-14; PR-5   **Ht:** 6'0" **Wt:** 205 **Born:** 5/26/73 **Age:** 28

Year Team	Lg Org	G	AB	H	2B	3B	HR	TB	R	RBI	TBB	IBB	SO	HBP	SH	SF	SB	CS	SB%	GDP	Avg	OBP	SLG
1991 Dodgers	R LA	43	109	26	2	1	0	30	17	11	16	0	45	0	0	1	14	4	.78	0	.239	.333	.275
1992 Great Falls	R+ LA	17	37	12	2	0	0	14	8	3	8	0	8	0	0	0	1	1	.50	0	.324	.444	.378
Dodgers	R LA	14	48	11	2	0	0	13	4	2	5	1	17	0	1	1	2	3	.40	0	.229	.296	.271
1993 Yakima	A- LA	54	192	50	2	6	4	76	46	17	39	0	53	1	0	0	24	9	.73	2	.260	.388	.396
Bakersfield	A+ LA	6	27	5	1	0	0	6	1	3	4	0	5	0	0	0	2	2	.50	2	.185	.290	.222
1994 Bakersfield	A+ LA	52	191	41	5	2	2	56	29	15	28	1	49	2	4	0	28	7	.80	2	.215	.321	.293
Yakima	A- LA	71	288	98	19	8	5	148	69	32	55	7	66	2	3	0	33	20	.62	1	.340	.449	.514
1995 Vero Beach	A+ LA	71	259	74	13	4	6	113	53	39	56	4	54	2	2	3	42	11	.79	2	.286	.413	.436
San Antonio	AA LA	58	214	64	14	5	9	115	38	37	33	0	59	2	1	1	11	11	.50	2	.299	.396	.537
Albuquerque	AAA LA	5	18	3	0	1	0	5	2	3	1	0	4	0	1	0	1	0	1.00	0	.167	.200	.278
1996 Salt Lake	AAA Min	115	376	103	16	6	9	158	59	50	36	1	91	2	4	3	26	9	.74	5	.274	.338	.420
1997 Salt Lake	AAA Min	118	492	152	22	5	8	208	78	58	58	0	110	4	4	1	21	19	.53	8	.309	.386	.423
1998 Salt Lake	AAA Min	97	377	122	21	4	11	184	81	51	56	4	99	1	4	0	29	5	.85	5	.324	.412	.488
1999 Salt Lake	AAA Min	94	382	123	24	8	15	208	93	51	54	2	95	1	4	2	18	13	.58	5	.322	.405	.545
2000 Colo Sprngs	AAA Col	126	339	83	16	6	7	132	76	49	71	3	105	2	3	6	29	7	.81	6	.245	.373	.389
1997 Minnesota	AL	15	22	4	1	0	0	5	4	1	0	0	8	0	0	0	0	0	—	0	.182	.182	.227
1998 Minnesota	AL	34	94	15	1	0	1	19	14	5	13	0	36	0	1	0	4	2	.67	0	.160	.262	.202
1999 Minnesota	AL	14	22	2	0	0	0	2	1	3	0	0	13	0	0	2	0	0	—	0	.091	.083	.091
10 Min. YEARS		941	3349	967	159	56	76	1466	654	421	520	23	860	19	30	19	281	121	.70	42	.289	.385	.438
3 Maj. YEARS		63	138	21	2	0	1	26	19	9	13	0	57	0	1	2	4	2	.67	0	.152	.222	.188

Brian Lawrence

Pitches: Right **Bats:** Right **Pos:** SP-29   **Ht:** 6'0" **Wt:** 195 **Born:** 5/14/76 **Age:** 25

Year Team	Lg Org	G	GS	CG	GF	IP	BFP	H	R	ER	HR	SH	SF	HB	TBB	IBB	SO	WP	Bk	W	L	Pct.	ShO	Sv	ERA
1998 Idaho Falls	R+ SD	4	4	2	0	22	92	22	7	6	1	0	1	2	5	0	21	0	0	3	0	1.000	1	0	2.45
Clinton	A SD	12	12	2	0	80.1	323	67	34	25	5	2	1	4	13	0	79	0	0	5	3	.625	0	0	2.80
1999 Rancho Cuca	A+ SD	27	27	4	0	175.1	723	178	72	66	6	7	5	10	30	1	166	7	5	12	8	.600	3	0	3.39
2000 Mobile	AA SD	21	21	0	0	126.2	496	99	40	34	6	1	0	10	28	0	119	1	0	7	6	.538	0	0	2.42
Las Vegas	AAA SD	8	8	0	0	46.2	193	48	13	10	6	0	0	4	7	0	46	0	0	4	0	1.000	0	0	1.93
3 Min. YEARS		72	72	8	0	451	1827	414	166	141	24	10	7	30	83	1	431	8	5	31	17	.646	4	0	2.81

Clint Lawrence

Pitches: Left **Bats:** Left **Pos:** RP-33; SP-1   **Ht:** 6'4" **Wt:** 200 **Born:** 10/19/76 **Age:** 24

Year Team	Lg Org	G	GS	CG	GF	IP	BFP	H	R	ER	HR	SH	SF	HB	TBB	IBB	SO	WP	Bk	W	L	Pct.	ShO	Sv	ERA
1995 Blue Jays	R Tor	12	9	0	3	45.1	202	40	33	23	1	0	1	1	26	0	40	9	1	1	5	.167	0	0	4.57
1996 St.Cathrnes	A- Tor	9	8	2	0	57.2	230	53	18	16	1	1	2	1	11	0	25	5	0	4	1	.800	1	0	2.50
Hagerstown	A Tor	6	6	0	0	36.1	144	26	12	8	2	1	2	0	10	0	27	1	0	3	1	.750	0	0	1.98
1997 Hagerstown	A Tor	27	27	1	0	170.1	718	179	76	67	8	4	4	6	40	0	149	3	1	13	10	.565	1	0	3.54
1998 Knoxville	AA Tor	7	7	0	0	25	131	31	24	19	4	0	0	0	23	2	16	2	1	1	2	.333	0	0	6.84
Dunedin	A+ Tor	20	12	1	4	84.1	391	107	54	46	6	1	0	5	41	0	55	12	0	6	3	.667	1	1	4.91
1999 Dunedin	A+ Tor	15	3	0	7	23.2	115	29	23	20	5	1	0	0	20	0	16	3	0	1	2	.333	0	0	7.61
2000 Tennessee	AA Tor	34	1	0	18	54.1	268	63	33	32	7	3	2	1	43	2	31	6	0	3	3	.500	0	0	5.30
6 Min. YEARS		130	73	4	32	497	2199	528	273	231	34	11	11	14	214	4	359	41	3	32	27	.542	3	2	4.18

Joe Lawrence

Bats: Right **Throws:** Right **Pos:** C-97; DH-43   **Ht:** 6'2" **Wt:** 200 **Born:** 2/13/77 **Age:** 24

Year Team	Lg Org	G	AB	H	2B	3B	HR	TB	R	RBI	TBB	IBB	SO	HBP	SH	SF	SB	CS	SB%	GDP	Avg	OBP	SLG
1996 St.Cathrnes	A- Tor	29	98	22	7	2	0	33	23	11	14	1	17	2	1	3	1	1	.50	1	.224	.325	.337
1997 Hagerstown	A Tor	116	446	102	24	1	8	152	63	38	49	0	107	5	3	2	10	12	.45	3	.229	.311	.341
1998 Dunedin	A+ Tor	125	454	140	31	6	11	216	102	44	105	2	88	4	5	1	15	12	.56	11	.308	.441	.476
1999 Knoxville	AA Tor	70	250	66	16	2	7	107	52	24	56	0	48	3	0	2	7	6	.54	10	.264	.402	.428
2000 Dunedin	A+ Tor	101	375	113	32	1	13	186	69	67	69	6	74	5	0	3	21	7	.75	9	.301	.414	.496
Tennessee	AA Tor	39	133	35	9	0	0	44	22	9	30	0	27	3	1	1	7	1	.88	2	.263	.407	.331
5 Min. YEARS		480	1756	478	119	12	39	738	331	193	323	9	361	22	10	12	61	39	.61	36	.272	.389	.420

Jalal Leach

Bats: Left **Throws:** Left **Pos:** OF-96; PH-16; DH-5   **Ht:** 6'2" **Wt:** 200 **Born:** 3/14/69 **Age:** 32

Year Team	Lg Org	G	AB	H	2B	3B	HR	TB	R	RBI	TBB	IBB	SO	HBP	SH	SF	SB	CS	SB%	GDP	Avg	OBP	SLG
1990 Oneonta	A- NYY	69	257	74	7	1	2	89	41	18	37	3	52	0	4	0	33	13	.72	1	.288	.378	.346

155

Year Team	Lg Org	G	AB	H	2B	3B	HR	TB	R	RBI	TBB	IBB	SO	HBP	SH	SF	SB	CS	SB%	GDP	Avg	OBP	SLG
1991 Ft. Laud	A+ NYY	122	468	119	13	9	2	156	48	42	44	3	122	0	3	3	28	12	.70	5	.254	.317	.333
1992 Pr William	A+ NYY	128	462	122	22	7	5	173	61	65	47	2	114	0	3	5	18	9	.67	8	.264	.329	.374
1993 Albany-Col	AA NYY	125	457	129	19	9	14	208	64	79	47	3	113	1	0	4	16	12	.57	5	.282	.348	.455
1994 Columbus	AAA NYY	132	444	116	18	9	6	170	56	56	39	3	106	1	3	4	14	12	.54	8	.261	.320	.383
1995 Columbus	AAA NYY	88	272	66	12	5	6	106	37	31	22	1	60	2	1	4	11	4	.73	5	.243	.300	.390
1996 Harrisburg	AA Mon	83	268	88	22	3	6	134	38	48	21	4	55	0	2	4	3	7	.30	6	.328	.372	.500
Ottawa	AAA Mon	37	101	32	4	0	3	45	12	9	8	1	17	0	0	0	0	0	—	1	.317	.367	.446
1997 Tacoma	AAA Sea	115	415	128	26	3	9	187	56	55	32	2	74	1	2	3	6	6	.50	11	.308	.357	.451
1998 Shreveport	AA SF	72	253	87	17	2	10	138	43	45	36	3	35	0	0	5	10	2	.83	6	.344	.418	.545
Fresno	AAA SF	35	130	46	8	2	9	85	23	26	8	1	26	0	0	1	3	2	.60	1	.354	.388	.654
1999 Fresno	AAA SF	116	371	109	19	5	15	183	58	75	27	2	67	0	2	4	8	7	.53	8	.294	.338	.493
2000 Scranton-WB	AAA Phi	65	180	48	9	2	4	73	24	21	19	3	34	0	1	1	4	5	.44	6	.267	.335	.406
Fresno	AAA SF	51	198	75	16	5	12	137	34	45	18	1	28	0	0	0	8	3	.73	2	.379	.431	.692
11 Min. YEARS		1238	4276	1239	212	62	103	1884	595	615	405	32	903	5	21	38	162	94	.63	73	.290	.349	.441

Nick Leach

Bats: Left **Throws:** Right **Pos:** 1B-86; DH-16; PH-12; 3B-1; PR-1   **Ht:** 6'1" **Wt:** 190 **Born:** 12/7/77 **Age:** 23

Year Team	Lg Org	G	AB	H	2B	3B	HR	TB	R	RBI	TBB	IBB	SO	HBP	SH	SF	SB	CS	SB%	GDP	Avg	OBP	SLG
1996 Great Falls	R+ LA	58	199	50	8	1	9	87	42	25	36	2	33	3	0	0	2	4	.33	3	.251	.374	.437
1997 Savannah	A LA	37	131	35	6	0	0	41	14	13	14	0	23	4	0	0	1	2	.33	2	.267	.356	.313
Yakima	A- LA	54	192	60	18	1	7	101	33	47	32	4	37	6	0	1	5	0	1.00	4	.313	.424	.526
San Berndno	A+ LA	16	60	22	6	1	4	42	11	12	5	0	11	2	0	0	0	1	.00	1	.367	.433	.700
1998 San Berndno	A+ LA	131	469	110	30	2	6	162	49	48	44	4	96	5	2	1	6	11	.35	6	.235	.306	.345
1999 Vero Beach	A+ LA	128	449	127	21	0	20	208	58	74	62	3	73	6	0	3	10	5	.67	6	.283	.375	.463
2000 Norwich	AA NYY	113	354	98	23	1	7	144	44	49	56	3	79	3	2	1	5	3	.63	6	.277	.379	.407
5 Min. YEARS		537	1854	502	112	6	53	785	251	268	249	16	352	29	4	6	29	26	.53	28	.271	.365	.423

Juan LeBron

Bats: Right **Throws:** Right **Pos:** OF-81; DH-15   **Ht:** 6'4" **Wt:** 195 **Born:** 6/7/77 **Age:** 24

Year Team	Lg Org	G	AB	H	2B	3B	HR	TB	R	RBI	TBB	IBB	SO	HBP	SH	SF	SB	CS	SB%	GDP	Avg	OBP	SLG
1995 Royals	R KC	47	147	26	5	2	2	41	17	13	10	0	38	2	0	4	0	3	.00	6	.177	.233	.279
1996 Royals	R KC	58	215	62	9	2	3	84	19	30	6	0	34	2	0	0	1	2	.33	9	.288	.314	.391
1997 Lansing	A KC	35	113	24	7	0	3	40	12	20	0	0	32	1	0	2	0	0	—	6	.212	.216	.354
Spokane	A- KC	69	288	88	27	1	7	138	49	45	17	2	74	2	0	1	8	4	.67	5	.306	.347	.479
1998 Lansing	A KC	121	442	111	26	9	17	206	70	84	57	5	129	8	1	5	18	11	.62	11	.251	.344	.466
2000 Binghamton	AA NYM	72	238	54	17	0	6	89	26	25	16	0	82	3	0	2	2	4	.33	3	.227	.282	.374
St. Lucie	A+ NYM	24	90	18	2	0	2	26	6	8	6	0	25	1	0	1	0	0	—	3	.200	.255	.289
5 Min. YEARS		426	1533	383	93	14	40	624	199	225	112	7	414	19	1	15	29	24	.55	41	.250	.306	.407

A.J. Leday

Bats: Right **Throws:** Right **Pos:** OF-109; PH-8; DH-2   **Ht:** 6'3" **Wt:** 210 **Born:** 2/17/73 **Age:** 28

Year Team	Lg Org	G	AB	H	2B	3B	HR	TB	R	RBI	TBB	IBB	SO	HBP	SH	SF	SB	CS	SB%	GDP	Avg	OBP	SLG
1995 Lethbridge	R+ —	61	229	68	10	3	2	90	30	41	18	2	33	6	1	2	6	8	.43	9	.297	.361	.393
1996 Chston-WV	A Cin	9	26	6	1	0	1	10	3	5	6	0	9	1	0	0	1	2	.33	0	.231	.394	.385
Duluth-Sup	IND —	80	315	103	29	2	20	196	59	65	28	0	60	3	0	5	6	1	.86	6	.327	.382	.622
1997 Kingsport	R+ NYM	15	45	15	3	0	3	27	10	9	9	0	17	0	0	1	1	1	.50	1	.333	.444	.600
Duluth-Sup	IND —	83	333	100	19	5	7	150	63	57	24	1	54	14	1	3	12	5	.71	8	.300	.369	.450
1998 Rancho Cuca	A+ SD	134	539	166	33	5	24	281	94	94	28	2	98	6	2	5	15	10	.60	15	.308	.346	.521
1999 Jackson	AA Hou	63	187	45	7	0	4	64	21	16	9	0	38	8	1	2	4	2	.67	3	.241	.301	.342
Mobile	AA SD	44	136	33	7	0	4	52	12	18	6	0	35	2	0	0	1	3	.25	4	.243	.285	.382
2000 Mobile	AA SD	117	407	115	20	2	12	175	45	70	26	1	84	14	0	4	4	2	.67	9	.283	.344	.430
6 Min. YEARS		606	2217	651	129	17	77	1045	337	375	154	6	428	54	5	21	50	34	.60	53	.294	.351	.471

Corey Lee

Pitches: Left **Bats:** Left **Pos:** SP-21; RP-5   **Ht:** 6'2" **Wt:** 185 **Born:** 12/26/74 **Age:** 26

Year Team	Lg Org	G	GS	CG	GF	IP	BFP	H	R	ER	HR	SH	SF	HB	TBB	IBB	SO	WP	Bk	W	L	Pct.	ShO	Sv	ERA
1996 Hudson Val	A- TB	9	9	0	0	54.2	226	42	24	20	1	2	3	1	21	1	59	1	2	1	4	.200	0	0	3.29
1997 Charlotte	A+ Tex	23	23	6	0	160.2	654	132	66	62	9	5	3	2	60	0	147	7	0	15	5	.750	2	0	3.47
1998 Tulsa	AA Tex	26	25	1	0	143.2	625	105	81	72	16	3	5	5	102	1	132	12	1	10	9	.526	0	0	4.51
1999 Tulsa	AA Tex	22	22	0	0	127.2	549	132	76	63	11	1	1	4	44	0	121	3	1	8	5	.615	0	0	4.44
Oklahoma	AAA Tex	4	4	0	0	26.2	105	21	6	6	2	0	0	0	8	0	25	2	0	3	0	1.000	0	0	2.03
2000 Oklahoma	AAA Tex	26	21	0	0	112	569	163	128	109	15	3	3	2	87	1	84	3	2	2	12	.143	0	0	8.76
1999 Texas	AL	1	0	0	1	1	6	2	3	3	1	0	0	0	1	0	0	1	0	0	1	.000	0	0	27.00
5 Min. YEARS		110	104	7	0	625.1	2728	595	381	332	54	14	15	19	322	3	568	28	6	39	35	.527	2	0	4.78

Derek Lee

Pitches: Left **Bats:** Left **Pos:** SP-22; RP-9   **Ht:** 6'4" **Wt:** 185 **Born:** 8/20/74 **Age:** 26

Year Team	Lg Org	G	GS	CG	GF	IP	BFP	H	R	ER	HR	SH	SF	HB	TBB	IBB	SO	WP	Bk	W	L	Pct.	ShO	Sv	ERA
1997 Ogden	R+ Mil	14	13	0	0	74.1	325	89	49	32	3	2	6	3	20	0	71	8	1	4	4	.500	0	0	3.87
1998 Stockton	A+ Mil	30	18	1	2	136	583	134	70	63	9	4	5	8	48	1	141	8	0	5	9	.357	1	1	4.17
1999 Huntsville	AA Mil	26	21	4	0	140	604	143	70	60	16	6	2	8	51	4	77	5	1	8	8	.500	2	0	3.86
2000 Indianapols	AAA Mil	3	2	0	0	13.1	62	16	7	7	2	0	1	0	6	0	9	0	0	2	0	1.000	0	0	4.73
Huntsville	AA Mil	28	20	1	2	131.1	544	121	48	37	6	2	5	6	41	0	87	6	2	11	3	.786	1	0	2.54
4 Min. YEARS		101	74	6	4	495	2118	503	244	199	36	14	19	22	166	5	385	27	4	30	24	.556	4	1	3.62

Garrett Lee

Pitches: Right **Bats:** Right **Pos:** RP-24; SP-7   **Ht:** 6'5" **Wt:** 210 **Born:** 8/17/76 **Age:** 24

Year Team	Lg Org	G	GS	CG	GF	IP	BFP	H	R	ER	HR	SH	SF	HB	TBB	IBB	SO	WP	Bk	W	L	Pct.	ShO	Sv	ERA
1996 Braves	R Atl	13	3	0	2	39	152	32	12	12	2	2	0	4	3	0	36	4	2	1	2	.333	0	1	2.77
1997 Danville	R+ Atl	14	14	1	0	84	360	87	57	46	8	3	2	7	17	1	72	3	1	5	5	.500	1	0	4.93
1998 Eugene	A- Atl	9	9	0	0	47	216	56	41	33	7	1	2	7	11	1	47	1	2	2	3	.400	0	0	6.32
1999 Jamestown	A- Atl	13	13	1	0	77.1	323	79	39	35	8	1	5	6	16	0	47	0	2	4	3	.571	0	0	4.07
Myrtle Bch	A+ Atl	3	3	0	0	17.2	77	21	12	10	1	1	0	0	3	0	12	0	0	1	1	.500	0	0	5.09
2000 Myrtle Bch	A+ Atl	29	6	0	5	79.2	322	61	19	18	2	3	1	7	21	0	60	2	1	7	3	.700	0	1	2.03
Richmond	AAA Atl	2	1	0	0	7	30	6	2	2	0	0	0	3	3	0	3	0	0	0	0	—	0	0	2.57
5 Min. YEARS		83	49	2	7	351.2	1480	342	182	156	28	11	10	34	74	2	277	10	8	20	17	.541	1	2	3.99

Jonathan Lee

Pitches: Right **Bats:** Right **Pos:** RP-17   **Ht:** 6'5" **Wt:** 215 **Born:** 7/24/78 **Age:** 22

Year Team	Lg Org	G	GS	CG	GF	IP	BFP	H	R	ER	HR	SH	SF	HB	TBB	IBB	SO	WP	Bk	W	L	Pct.	ShO	Sv	ERA
2000 Diamondbcks	R Ari	9	0	0	2	24.1	106	30	15	9	0	1	0	3	8	1	19	4	1	0	1	.000	0	0	3.33
Tucson	AAA Ari	1	0	0	0	2.2	11	1	0	0	0	0	0	2	0	0	1	0	0	1	0	1.000	0	0	0.00
South Bend	A Ari	7	0	0	4	7	35	9	5	5	1	2	1	0	4	0	4	2	0	0	0	—	0	2	6.43
1 Min. YEARS		17	0	0	6	34	152	40	20	14	1	3	1	3	12	1	24	6	1	1	1	.500	0	3	3.71

Randy Leek

Pitches: Left **Bats:** Left **Pos:** SP-27; RP-1   **Ht:** 6'0" **Wt:** 175 **Born:** 4/18/77 **Age:** 24

Year Team	Lg Org	G	GS	CG	GF	IP	BFP	H	R	ER	HR	SH	SF	HB	TBB	IBB	SO	WP	Bk	W	L	Pct.	ShO	Sv	ERA
1999 Oneonta	A- Det	21	3	1	4	63.1	249	58	16	11	0	1	1	2	9	1	66	2	0	6	3	.667	0	1	1.56
2000 Lakeland	A+ Det	20	20	2	0	126.2	520	122	60	48	9	1	6	5	25	1	97	3	0	3	6	.333	0	0	3.41
Toledo	AAA Det	1	1	0	0	4.2	22	6	5	5	1	0	0	0	3	0	1	0	0	0	0	—	0	0	9.64
Jacksnville	AA Det	7	6	0	0	31	146	43	29	27	6	1	1	2	8	0	21	0	0	2	2	.500	0	0	7.84
2 Min. YEARS		49	30	3	4	225.2	937	229	110	91	16	3	8	9	45	2	185	5	0	11	11	.500	0	1	3.63

Brandon Leese

Pitches: Right **Bats:** Right **Pos:** SP-25; RP-2   **Ht:** 6'4" **Wt:** 205 **Born:** 10/8/75 **Age:** 25

Year Team	Lg Org	G	GS	CG	GF	IP	BFP	H	R	ER	HR	SH	SF	HB	TBB	IBB	SO	WP	Bk	W	L	Pct.	ShO	Sv	ERA
1996 Bellingham	A- SF	16	15	0	0	80.1	341	59	39	29	6	0	2	5	37	0	90	8	0	5	6	.455	0	0	3.25
1997 San Jose	A+ SF	19	19	0	0	112	475	99	44	38	11	1	0	4	46	2	99	15	0	7	5	.583	0	0	3.05
Kane County	A Fla	7	6	0	0	42.1	171	27	18	18	0	1	2	3	18	0	32	3	1	3	1	.750	0	0	3.83
1998 Brevard Cty	A+ Fla	8	8	0	0	47.1	209	63	36	30	3	1	1	2	7	0	30	2	0	1	5	.167	0	0	5.70
Portland	AA Fla	20	20	0	0	126.1	544	137	70	58	16	11	1	5	37	1	94	2	0	4	7	.364	0	0	4.13
1999 Portland	AA Fla	20	11	0	2	81.2	370	110	66	52	8	2	0	7	20	0	52	2	2	4	4	.500	0	0	5.73
2000 Portland	AA Fla	27	25	6	1	173.2	728	179	82	67	18	8	5	7	47	1	96	6	1	12	9	.571	1	1	3.47
5 Min. YEARS		117	104	6	3	663.2	2838	674	355	292	62	24	11	33	212	4	493	38	4	36	37	.493	1	1	3.96

Justin Lehr

Pitches: Right **Bats:** Right **Pos:** SP-26; RP-4   **Ht:** 6'1" **Wt:** 200 **Born:** 8/3/77 **Age:** 23

Year Team	Lg Org	G	GS	CG	GF	IP	BFP	H	R	ER	HR	SH	SF	HB	TBB	IBB	SO	WP	Bk	W	L	Pct.	ShO	Sv	ERA
1999 Sou Oregon	A- Oak	14	4	0	7	42.1	207	62	36	28	3	5	1	2	17	3	40	9	0	2	6	.250	0	0	5.95
2000 Sacramento	AAA Oak	1	1	0	0	4	21	7	5	5	1	0	0	0	3	0	3	0	0	0	0	—	0	0	11.25
Modesto	A+ Oak	29	25	0	1	175	709	161	71	62	10	8	4	5	46	1	138	15	5	13	6	.684	0	0	3.19
2 Min. YEARS		44	30	0	8	221.1	937	230	112	95	14	13	5	7	66	4	181	24	5	15	12	.556	0	0	3.86

Chris Lemonis

Bats: Left **Throws:** Right **Pos:** 2B-45; DH-23; 1B-14; PH-3; SS-1; P-1   **Ht:** 5'11" **Wt:** 185 **Born:** 8/21/73 **Age:** 27

Year Team	Lg Org	G	AB	H	2B	3B	HR	TB	R	RBI	TBB	IBB	SO	HBP	SH	SF	SB	CS	SB%	GDP	Avg	OBP	SLG
1995 Jamestown	A- Det	57	191	45	7	2	0	56	19	21	18	0	32	2	3	1	5	1	.83	4	.236	.307	.293
1996 Visalia	A+ Det	126	482	134	27	3	14	209	69	82	35	6	99	6	2	4	12	5	.71	12	.278	.332	.434
1997 W Michigan	A Det	48	158	48	10	1	3	69	27	30	9	1	31	1	0	0	2	5	.29	3	.304	.345	.437
1998 Lakeland	A+ Det	93	327	92	17	1	3	120	45	48	27	3	46	2	0	3	1	1	.50	10	.281	.337	.367
1999 Jacksnville	AA Det	75	265	75	16	1	5	108	35	38	19	0	45	6	0	0	1	2	.33	6	.283	.345	.408
2000 Toledo	AAA Det	84	288	62	21	3	8	98	30	23	17	2	53	1	1	0	1	1	.50	10	.215	.261	.340
6 Min. YEARS		483	1711	456	98	11	28	660	225	242	125	7	306	18	6	8	22	15	.59	45	.267	.322	.386

Patrick Lennon

Bats: Right **Throws:** Right **Pos:** DH-75; OF-22; 1B-16; PH-6   **Ht:** 6'2" **Wt:** 200 **Born:** 4/27/68 **Age:** 33

Year Team	Lg Org	G	AB	H	2B	3B	HR	TB	R	RBI	TBB	IBB	SO	HBP	SH	SF	SB	CS	SB%	GDP	Avg	OBP	SLG
1986 Bellingham	A- Sea	51	169	41	5	2	3	59	35	27	36	0	50	0	1	1	8	6	.57	3	.243	.374	.349
1987 Wausau	A Sea	98	319	80	21	3	7	128	54	34	46	1	82	1	1	2	25	8	.76	10	.251	.345	.401
1988 Vermont	AA Sea	95	321	83	9	3	9	125	44	40	21	1	87	3	3	4	15	6	.71	9	.259	.307	.389
1989 Williamsprt	AA Sea	66	248	65	14	2	3	92	32	31	23	2	53	0	0	5	7	4	.64	9	.262	.319	.371
1990 San Berndno	A+ Sea	44	163	47	6	2	8	81	29	30	15	1	51	0	0	1	6	0	1.00	4	.288	.346	.497
Williamsprt	AA Sea	49	167	49	6	4	5	78	24	22	10	0	37	2	0	3	10	4	.71	2	.293	.335	.467
1991 Calgary	AAA Sea	112	416	137	29	5	15	221	75	74	46	4	68	1	1	1	12	5	.71	9	.329	.400	.531

157

Year Team	Lg Org	G	AB	H	2B	3B	HR	TB	R	RBI	TBB	IBB	SO	HBP	SH	SF	SB	CS	SB%	GDP	Avg	OBP	SLG
1992 Calgary	AAA Sea	13	48	17	3	0	1	23	8	9	6	0	10	0	0	0	4	1	.80	1	.354	.426	.479
1993 Canton-Akrn	AA Cle	45	152	39	7	1	4	60	24	22	30	1	45	1	0	2	4	2	.67	4	.257	.378	.395
1994 New Britain	AA Bos	114	429	140	30	5	17	231	80	67	48	1	96	5	0	1	13	9	.59	10	.326	.400	.538
1995 Pawtucket	AAA Bos	40	128	35	6	2	3	54	20	20	16	0	42	1	0	1	6	4	.60	6	.273	.356	.422
Trenton	AA Bos	27	98	39	7	0	1	49	19	8	14	0	22	1	0	0	7	2	.78	3	.398	.478	.500
Salt Lake	AAA Min	34	115	46	15	0	6	79	26	29	12	2	29	1	0	1	2	1	.67	1	.400	.457	.687
1996 Edmonton	AAA Oak	68	251	82	16	2	12	138	37	42	28	2	82	2	0	0	3	3	.50	9	.327	.399	.550
1997 Edmonton	AAA Oak	39	134	46	7	0	9	80	28	35	22	4	34	2	0	2	0	0	—	5	.343	.438	.597
Modesto	A+ Oak	5	16	3	1	0	1	7	3	4	3	1	5	0	0	0	0	0	—	0	.188	.316	.438
1998 Syracuse	AAA Tor	126	438	127	22	4	27	238	87	95	87	3	121	2	0	2	12	4	.75	21	.290	.408	.543
1999 Syracuse	AAA Tor	37	134	45	5	0	9	77	26	33	22	0	40	1	0	1	3	3	.50	2	.336	.430	.575
Toledo	AAA Det	74	280	74	16	1	21	155	49	50	33	0	66	2	0	1	1	2	.33	10	.264	.345	.554
2000 Ottawa	AAA Mon	118	418	122	21	2	14	189	69	63	52	1	110	5	0	3	0	6	.00	12	.292	.374	.452
1991 Seattle	AL	9	8	1	1	0	0	2	2	1	3	0	1	0	0	0	0	0	—	0	.125	.364	.250
1992 Seattle	AL	1	2	0	0	0	0	0	0	0	0	0	0	0	0	0	0	0	—	0	.000	.000	.000
1996 Kansas City	AL	14	30	7	3	0	0	10	5	1	7	0	10	0	0	0	0	0	—	0	.233	.378	.333
1997 Oakland	AL	56	116	34	6	1	1	45	14	14	15	0	35	0	0	0	0	1	.00	3	.293	.374	.388
1998 Toronto	AL	2	4	2	2	0	0	4	1	0	0	0	1	0	0	0	0	0	—	0	.500	.500	1.000
1999 Toronto	AL	9	29	6	2	0	1	11	3	6	2	0	12	1	0	0	0	0	—	0	.207	.281	.379
15 Min. YEARS		1255	4444	1317	246	38	175	2164	769	735	570	24	1130	33	6	31	138	70	.66	130	.296	.378	.487
6 Maj. YEARS		91	189	50	14	1	2	72	25	22	27	0	59	1	0	0	0	1	.00	3	.265	.359	.381

Carlos Leon

Bats: Both **Throws:** Right **Pos:** 2B-102; SS-1; PH-1 **Ht:** 5'10" **Wt:** 169 **Born:** 8/31/79 **Age:** 21

Year Team	Lg Org	G	AB	H	2B	3B	HR	TB	R	RBI	TBB	IBB	SO	HBP	SH	SF	SB	CS	SB%	GDP	Avg	OBP	SLG
1997 Red Sox	R Bos	44	126	31	5	3	0	42	18	15	14	0	25	1	3	0	10	3	.77	4	.246	.326	.333
1998 Michigan	A Bos	107	372	93	7	3	3	115	59	37	50	0	81	11	10	3	10	10	.50	4	.250	.353	.309
1999 Sarasota	A+ Bos	47	154	24	1	1	0	27	16	14	12	0	16	3	5	0	9	1	.90	3	.156	.231	.175
Augusta	A Bos	60	210	49	7	0	1	59	34	19	23	0	42	10	0	1	13	4	.76	2	.233	.336	.281
2000 Sarasota	A+ Bos	88	302	93	14	4	1	118	61	31	37	2	24	6	4	3	12	10	.55	14	.308	.391	.391
Trenton	AA Bos	15	49	10	4	0	0	14	4	4	5	0	13	1	2	0	1	2	.33	1	.204	.291	.286
4 Min. YEARS		361	1213	300	38	11	5	375	192	120	141	2	201	32	24	7	55	30	.65	28	.247	.340	.309

Danilo Leon

Pitches: Right **Bats:** Right **Pos:** SP-3 **Ht:** 6'1" **Wt:** 175 **Born:** 4/3/67 **Age:** 34

Year Team	Lg Org	G	GS	CG	GF	IP	BFP	H	R	ER	HR	SH	SF	HB	TBB	IBB	SO	WP	Bk	W	L	Pct.	ShO	Sv	ERA
1986 Expos	R Mon	15	1	0	8	29.1	—	32	18	14	1	—	—	3	13	0	21	2	0	1	2	.333	0	2	4.30
1987 Jamestown	A- Mon	3	0	0	1	1.2	—	4	3	3	0	—	—	2	1	0	3	0	0	0	0	—	0	0	16.20
1988 Wst Plm Bch	A+ Mon	6	0	0	1	14	—	12	6	5	1	—	—	2	5	0	15	0	2	0	0	—	0	0	3.21
Jamestown	A- Mon	15	15	7	0	116	—	75	29	15	3	—	—	7	48	1	100	7	3	10	3	.769	4	0	1.16
1989 Jacksnville	AA Mon	18	18	1	0	95.1	—	85	62	49	2	—	—	9	55	0	64	10	5	7	4	.636	0	0	4.63
1992 Charlotte	A+ Tex	4	0	0	3	9.1	35	5	2	2	0	0	0	1	2	0	7	0	2	0	0	—	0	0	1.93
Tulsa	AA Tex	12	0	0	4	30	113	15	4	2	0	1	1	1	8	1	34	3	1	5	0	1.000	0	1	0.60
Okla City	AAA Tex	3	0	0	1	4.2	19	2	0	0	0	0	0	0	3	0	4	0	0	1	0	1.000	0	0	0.00
1993 Okla City	AAA Tex	13	1	0	5	31	156	28	21	19	3	4	3	8	26	4	33	6	2	2	2	.500	0	0	5.52
2000 Nashville	AAA Pit	3	3	0	0	15.2	69	11	8	7	1	0	0	1	12	1	9	0	0	2	0	.333	0	0	4.02
1992 Texas	AL	15	0	0	3	18.1	84	18	14	12	5	0	0	3	10	0	15	0	0	1	1	.500	0	0	5.89
7 Min. YEARS		92	38	8	20	347	—	269	153	116	11	—	—	34	173	7	290	28	15	27	13	.675	4	3	3.01

Donny Leon

Bats: Both **Throws:** Right **Pos:** 3B-58; DH-28; PH-1 **Ht:** 6'2" **Wt:** 185 **Born:** 5/7/76 **Age:** 25

Year Team	Lg Org	G	AB	H	2B	3B	HR	TB	R	RBI	TBB	IBB	SO	HBP	SH	SF	SB	CS	SB%	GDP	Avg	OBP	SLG
1995 Yankees	R NYY	16	41	7	1	0	0	8	3	5	3	0	14	0	0	0	0	1	.00	0	.171	.227	.195
1996 Yankees	R NYY	53	191	69	14	4	6	109	30	46	9	2	30	4	1	4	1	2	.33	2	.361	.394	.571
1997 Greensboro	A NYY	137	516	131	32	1	12	201	45	74	15	2	106	5	2	7	6	4	.60	13	.254	.278	.390
1998 Tampa	A+ NYY	100	385	112	24	1	10	168	54	59	23	1	64	7	1	2	0	0	—	9	.291	.341	.436
1999 Norwich	AA NYY	118	457	138	34	2	21	239	69	100	34	2	102	3	1	7	0	0	—	10	.302	.349	.523
2000 Columbus	AAA NYY	59	204	51	10	1	9	90	30	26	20	0	49	2	2	2	3	3	.50	6	.250	.320	.441
Yankees	R NYY	5	18	3	0	0	2	9	3	4	0	0	6	1	0	2	0	0	—	1	.167	.190	.500
Tampa	A+ NYY	23	79	17	6	0	1	26	5	14	6	2	23	1	0	1	0	0	—	1	.215	.276	.329
6 Min. YEARS		511	1891	528	121	9	61	850	239	328	110	9	394	23	7	25	10	10	.50	41	.279	.323	.449

Jose Leon

Bats: Right **Throws:** Right **Pos:** 3B-64; 1B-22; DH-13; PH-8; OF-4; PR-2 **Ht:** 6'0" **Wt:** 175 **Born:** 12/8/76 **Age:** 24

Year Team	Lg Org	G	AB	H	2B	3B	HR	TB	R	RBI	TBB	IBB	SO	HBP	SH	SF	SB	CS	SB%	GDP	Avg	OBP	SLG
1994 Cardinals	R StL	46	161	37	3	2	0	44	16	17	11	0	51	3	1	4	1	4	.20	4	.230	.285	.273
1995 Savannah	A StL	41	133	22	4	1	0	28	15	11	10	1	46	1	0	0	0	1	.00	6	.165	.229	.211
1996 Johnson Cty	R+ StL	59	222	55	9	3	10	100	29	36	17	0	92	2	2	1	5	3	.63	1	.248	.306	.450
New Jersey	A- StL	7	28	8	3	1	1	16	4	3	0	0	7	0	0	0	0	0	—	0	.286	.333	.571
1997 Peoria	A StL	118	399	92	21	2	20	177	50	54	32	1	122	9	2	2	6	5	.55	10	.231	.301	.444
1998 Pr William	A+ StL	124	436	127	31	3	21	227	77	74	53	4	137	9	2	4	5	3	.63	6	.291	.376	.521
1999 Arkansas	AA StL	112	335	78	17	0	18	149	37	54	25	0	114	6	1	1	3	3	.50	5	.233	.297	.445
2000 Arkansas	AA StL	90	297	80	16	3	14	144	41	41	16	0	66	5	0	2	2	1	.67	7	.269	.318	.485
Bowie	AA Bal	18	68	17	1	0	1	21	7	6	4	0	13	2	0	0	5	2	.71	2	.250	.311	.309
7 Min. YEARS		615	2079	516	105	15	85	906	276	296	168	6	648	39	11	12	27	22	.55	41	.248	.315	.436

158

John LeRoy

Pitches: Right **Bats:** Right **Pos:** SP-11; RP-7 **Ht:** 6'3" **Wt:** 175 **Born:** 4/19/75 **Age:** 26

		HOW MUCH HE PITCHED						WHAT HE GAVE UP										THE RESULTS				
Year Team	Lg Org	G	GS	CG	GF	IP	BFP	H	R	ER	HR	SH	SF	HB	TBB	IBB	SO	WP	Bk	W	L	Pct.	ShO	Sv	ERA
1993 Braves	R Atl	10	2	0	4	26.1	107	21	9	6	1	1	1	0	8	1	32	2	0	2	2	.500	0	1	2.05
1994 Macon	A Atl	10	9	0	0	40.1	173	36	21	20	4	2	1	0	20	0	44	1	5	3	3	.500	0	0	4.46
1995 Durham	A+ Atl	24	22	1	0	125.2	545	128	82	76	17	2	5	5	57	1	77	5	1	6	9	.400	0	0	5.44
1996 Durham	A+ Atl	19	19	0	0	110.2	463	91	47	43	6	4	5	2	52	0	94	10	2	7	4	.636	0	0	3.50
Greenville	AA Atl	8	8	0	0	45.1	193	43	18	15	5	2	2	2	18	1	38	4	1	1	1	.500	0	0	2.98
1997 Greenville	AA Atl	29	14	0	9	98.1	444	105	59	55	20	1	2	5	43	1	84	15	1	5	5	.500	0	1	5.03
1998 Durham	AAA TB	4	0	0	1	4	27	11	12	12	1	0	0	0	5	0	1	0	1	0	1	.000	0	0	27.00
St. Pete	A+ TB	11	0	0	3	17.2	75	18	9	9	1	3	0	2	6	0	17	0	0	1	1	.500	0	0	4.58
Orlando	AA TB	12	0	0	3	22.1	97	22	17	16	5	0	0	0	10	0	12	1	0	1	0	1.000	0	0	6.45
1999 Orlando	AA TB	4	0	0	2	6	30	7	3	3	2	0	0	0	5	0	5	0	0	0	0	—	0	0	4.50
2000 New Jersey	IND —	12	11	1	0	70	289	50	28	26	2	1	3	5	30	2	57	10	1	2	4	.333	0	0	3.34
Chattanooga	AA Cin	6	0	0	2	11	48	9	7	7	3	0	1	0	6	0	9	1	0	1	0	1.000	0	0	5.73
1997 Atlanta	NL	1	0	0	0	2	10	1	0	0	0	0	0	0	3	1	3	0	1	1	0	1.000	0	0	0.00
8 Min. YEARS		149	85	2	24	577.2	2491	541	312	288	67	16	20	21	260	6	470	49	12	29	30	.492	0	2	4.49

Jesse Levis

Bats: Left **Throws:** Right **Pos:** C-51; DH-2 **Ht:** 5'9" **Wt:** 200 **Born:** 4/14/68 **Age:** 33

		BATTING														BASERUNNING				PERCENTAGES		
Year Team	Lg Org	G	AB	H	2B	3B	HR	TB	R	RBI	TBB	IBB	SO	HBP	SH	SF	SB	CS	SB%	GDP	Avg	OBP	SLG
1989 Colo Sprngs	AAA Cle	1	1	0	0	0	0	0	0	0	0	0	0	0	0	0	0	0	—	1	.000	.000	.000
Burlington	R+ Cle	27	93	32	4	0	4	48	11	16	10	3	7	2	0	1	1	0	1.00	3	.344	.415	.516
Kinston	A+ Cle	27	87	26	6	0	2	38	11	11	12	0	15	2	0	0	1	0	1.00	3	.299	.396	.437
1990 Kinston	A+ Cle	107	382	113	18	3	7	158	63	64	64	1	42	5	1	6	4	1	.80	5	.296	.398	.414
1991 Canton-Akrn	AA Cle	115	382	101	17	3	6	142	31	45	40	5	36	0	4	2	2	5	.29	11	.264	.333	.372
1992 Colo Sprngs	AAA Cle	87	253	92	20	1	6	132	39	44	37	0	25	1	3	2	1	3	.25	9	.364	.444	.522
1993 Charlotte	AAA Cle	47	129	32	6	1	2	46	10	20	15	1	12	1	1	1	0	2	.00	7	.248	.327	.357
1994 Charlotte	AAA Cle	111	375	107	20	0	10	157	55	59	55	6	39	1	4	6	2	0	1.00	14	.285	.374	.419
1995 Buffalo	AAA Cle	66	196	61	16	0	4	89	26	20	32	0	11	2	1	0	0	0	—	7	.311	.413	.454
1999 Orlando	AA TB	13	48	19	7	0	1	29	6	11	6	0	4	0	1	0	0	0	—	0	.396	.455	.604
Durham	AAA TB	27	94	31	5	0	1	39	20	8	15	1	9	2	0	1	0	0	.00	4	.330	.429	.415
2000 Buffalo	AAA Cle	53	168	48	8	0	3	65	17	21	17	0	12	1	2	1	0	0	—	5	.286	.353	.387
1992 Cleveland	AL	28	43	12	4	0	1	19	2	3	0	0	5	0	0	0	0	0	—	1	.279	.279	.442
1993 Cleveland	AL	31	63	11	2	0	0	13	7	4	2	0	10	0	1	1	0	0	—	0	.175	.197	.206
1994 Cleveland	AL	1	1	1	0	0	0	1	0	0	0	0	0	0	0	0	0	0	—	0	1.000	1.000	1.000
1995 Cleveland	AL	12	18	6	2	0	0	8	1	3	1	0	1	0	0	2	0	0	—	1	.333	.333	.444
1996 Milwaukee	AL	104	233	55	6	1	1	66	27	21	38	0	15	2	1	0	1	0	—	6	.236	.348	.283
1997 Milwaukee	AL	99	200	57	7	0	1	67	19	19	24	0	17	1	5	2	1	1	1.00	4	.285	.361	.335
1998 Milwaukee	NL	22	37	13	0	0	0	13	4	4	7	2	6	2	1	1	1	0	1.00	3	.351	.468	.351
1999 Cleveland	AL	10	26	4	0	0	0	4	0	3	1	0	6	1	0	0	0	0	—	2	.154	.214	.154
9 Min. YEARS		681	2208	662	127	8	46	943	289	319	303	17	212	17	12	21	11	14	.44	70	.300	.385	.427
8 Maj. YEARS		307	621	159	21	1	3	191	60	57	73	2	59	6	10	6	2	0	1.00	17	.256	.337	.308

Derrick Lewis

Pitches: Right **Bats:** Right **Pos:** SP-27 **Ht:** 6'5" **Wt:** 215 **Born:** 5/7/76 **Age:** 25

		HOW MUCH HE PITCHED						WHAT HE GAVE UP										THE RESULTS				
Year Team	Lg Org	G	GS	CG	GF	IP	BFP	H	R	ER	HR	SH	SF	HB	TBB	IBB	SO	WP	Bk	W	L	Pct.	ShO	Sv	ERA
1997 Danville	R+ Atl	16	9	0	2	49.2	241	59	48	35	5	1	1	2	31	0	46	8	0	2	4	.333	0	0	6.34
1998 Macon	A Atl	23	23	0	0	113.1	502	108	64	48	7	1	4	8	55	0	100	15	2	5	6	.455	0	0	3.81
1999 Myrtle Bch	A+ Atl	24	23	0	0	131	551	100	44	35	9	1	3	3	81	0	102	6	1	8	4	.667	0	0	2.40
2000 Greenville	AA Atl	27	27	1	0	163.2	706	146	70	60	5	4	4	6	83	2	143	10	0	7	9	.438	1	0	3.30
4 Min. YEARS		90	82	1	2	457.2	2000	413	226	178	26	7	12	19	250	2	391	39	3	22	23	.489	1	0	3.50

Marc Lewis

Bats: Right **Throws:** Right **Pos:** OF-37; DH-22; PH-6; PR-1; P-1 **Ht:** 6'2" **Wt:** 185 **Born:** 5/20/75 **Age:** 26

		BATTING														BASERUNNING				PERCENTAGES		
Year Team	Lg Org	G	AB	H	2B	3B	HR	TB	R	RBI	TBB	IBB	SO	HBP	SH	SF	SB	CS	SB%	GDP	Avg	OBP	SLG
1994 Red Sox	R Bos	50	197	64	13	2	3	90	32	32	10	0	19	1	2	4	16	3	.84	4	.325	.354	.457
Lynchburg	A+ Bos	8	32	6	1	0	1	10	3	5	3	0	4	0	0	0	0	2	.00	0	.188	.257	.313
1995 Michigan	A Bos	36	92	14	2	1	1	21	14	5	9	0	16	0	2	0	10	3	.77	1	.152	.228	.228
Utica	A- Bos	69	272	82	15	5	5	122	47	39	17	0	32	0	2	3	24	9	.73	6	.301	.339	.449
1996 Macon	A Atl	66	241	76	14	3	5	111	36	28	21	1	31	1	1	6	25	8	.76	5	.315	.364	.461
Durham	A+ Atl	68	262	78	12	2	6	112	43	26	24	2	37	2	3	1	25	9	.74	5	.298	.360	.427
1997 Greenville	AA Atl	135	512	140	17	3	17	214	64	67	25	3	84	8	4	2	21	14	.60	9	.273	.316	.418
1998 Salt Lake	AAA Min	119	444	130	31	1	14	205	61	68	23	0	64	1	3	2	10	11	.48	15	.293	.328	.462
1999 New Britain	AA Min	101	384	100	27	0	9	154	38	52	38	1	79	4	0	2	6	4	.60	12	.260	.332	.401
2000 Trenton	AA Bos	63	207	58	14	3	5	93	26	30	10	0	44	1	1	1	4	2	.67	3	.280	.315	.449
7 Min. YEARS		715	2643	748	146	20	66	1132	364	352	180	7	410	18	18	21	141	65	.68	61	.283	.331	.428

Richie Lewis

Pitches: Right **Bats:** Right **Pos:** SP-11 **Ht:** 5'10" **Wt:** 175 **Born:** 1/25/66 **Age:** 35

		HOW MUCH HE PITCHED						WHAT HE GAVE UP										THE RESULTS				
Year Team	Lg Org	G	GS	CG	GF	IP	BFP	H	R	ER	HR	SH	SF	HB	TBB	IBB	SO	WP	Bk	W	L	Pct.	ShO	Sv	ERA
1987 Indianapls	AAA Mon	2	0	0	2	3.2	19	6	4	4	2	0	0	0	2	0	3	0	0	0	0	—	0	0	9.82
1988 Jacksnville	AA Mon	12	12	1	0	61.1	275	37	32	23	2	0	3	3	56	0	60	7	4	5	3	.625	0	0	3.38
1989 Jacksnville	AA Mon	17	17	0	0	94.1	414	80	37	27	2	7	1	2	55	0	105	8	2	5	4	.556	0	0	2.58
1990 Wst Plm Bch	A+ Mon	10	0	0	6	15	68	12	8	5	0	1	0	0	11	0	14	1	0	0	1	.000	0	2	3.00
Jacksnville	AA Mon	11	0	0	8	14.1	54	7	2	2	0	1	0	1	5	0	14	3	0	0	0	—	0	5	1.26

159

		HOW MUCH HE PITCHED				WHAT HE GAVE UP							THE RESULTS					
Year Team	Lg Org	G	GS	CG	GF	IP	BFP	H	R	ER	HR	SH	SF	HB	TBB	IBB	SO	WP	Bk	W	L	Pct.	ShO	Sv	ERA
1991 Harrisburg	AA Mon	34	6	0	16	74.2	318	67	33	31	2	3	2	2	40	1	82	5	2	6	5	.545	0	5	3.74
Indianapolis	AAA Mon	5	4	0	0	27.2	131	35	12	11	1	0	1	0	20	1	22	1	0	1	0	1.000	0	0	3.58
Rochester	AAA Bal	2	2	0	0	16	62	13	5	5	1	0	0	0	7	0	18	1	0	1	0	1.000	0	0	2.81
1992 Rochester	AAA Bal	24	23	6	1	159.1	668	136	63	58	15	1	4	3	61	2	154	13	2	10	9	.526	1	0	3.28
1995 Charlotte	AAA Fla	17	8	1	4	59	243	50	22	21	5	2	4	0	20	0	45	4	2	5	2	.714	0	0	3.20
1996 Toledo	AAA Det	2	0	0	0	4	13	1	1	1	1	0	0	0	1	0	4	0	0	0	0	—	0	0	2.25
1997 Edmonton	AAA Oak	11	1	0	4	20	96	24	13	13	2	1	1	1	14	1	25	3	0	1	1	.500	0	1	5.85
Indianapols	AAA Cin	27	0	0	17	29.2	120	22	7	5	0	1	2	2	7	2	33	3	0	0	1	.000	0	9	1.52
1998 Rochester	AAA Bal	21	21	2	0	124	526	107	77	69	17	1	3	7	42	0	131	10	0	5	7	.417	0	0	5.01
1999 Norfolk	AAA NYM	20	20	3	0	122.2	542	128	82	69	19	6	2	5	49	7	101	4	2	7	8	.467	1	0	5.06
2000 Norfolk	AAA NYM	9	9	0	0	53.1	221	49	20	19	0	3	0	2	17	1	40	2	0	3	4	.429	0	0	3.21
Buffalo	AAA Cle	2	2	0	0	8	32	8	4	4	2	0	0	0	3	0	5	0	0	1	0	1.000	0	0	4.50
1992 Baltimore	AL	2	2	0	0	6.2	40	13	8	8	1	0	1	0	7	0	4	0	0	1	1	.500	0	0	10.80
1993 Florida	NL	57	0	0	14	77.1	341	68	37	28	7	8	4	1	43	6	65	9	1	6	3	.667	0	0	3.26
1994 Florida	NL	45	0	0	9	54	261	62	44	34	7	3	1	1	38	9	45	10	1	1	4	.200	0	0	5.67
1995 Florida	NL	21	1	0	6	36	152	30	15	15	9	2	0	1	15	5	32	1	2	0	1	.000	0	0	3.75
1996 Detroit	AL	72	0	0	19	90.1	412	78	45	42	9	5	10	4	65	9	78	14	2	4	6	.400	0	2	4.18
1997 Oakland	AL	14	0	0	5	18.2	94	24	21	20	7	1	1	1	15	0	12	2	0	2	0	1.000	0	0	9.64
Cincinnati	NL	4	0	0	0	5.2	25	4	5	4	3	2	0	0	3	0	4	0	0	0	0	—	0	0	6.35
1998 Baltimore	AL	2	1	0	0	4.2	25	8	8	8	2	1	0	0	5	0	4	1	0	0	0	—	0	0	15.43
12 Min. YEARS		226	125	13	58	887	3802	782	422	367	71	26	24	27	410	15	856	66	14	50	45	.526	2	22	3.72
7 Maj. YEARS		217	4	0	53	293.1	1350	287	183	159	45	21	18	8	191	29	244	37	6	14	15	.483	0	2	4.88

Kevin Lidle

Bats: Right **Throws:** Right **Pos:** C-48; P-1   **Ht:** 5'11" **Wt:** 170 **Born:** 3/22/72 **Age:** 29

		BATTING															BASERUNNING				PERCENTAGES		
Year Team	Lg Org	G	AB	H	2B	3B	HR	TB	R	RBI	TBB	IBB	SO	HBP	SH	SF	SB	CS	SB%	GDP	Avg	OBP	SLG
1992 Niagara Fal	A- Det	58	140	34	6	2	1	47	21	18	8	0	42	1	6	3	3	2	.60	1	.243	.283	.336
1993 Fayettevlle	A Det	58	197	42	14	1	5	73	29	25	34	0	42	1	0	1	2	0	1.00	0	.213	.330	.371
1994 Lakeland	A+ Det	56	187	49	13	2	6	84	26	30	19	0	46	4	1	1	1	1	.50	2	.262	.341	.449
1995 Jacksnville	AA Det	36	80	13	7	0	1	23	12	5	1	0	31	0	1	0	1	0	1.00	1	.163	.173	.288
Fayettevlle	A Det	36	113	16	4	1	4	34	15	13	16	0	44	1	3	2	1	1	.00	1	.142	.250	.301
1996 Lakeland	A+ Det	97	320	69	18	1	8	113	37	41	30	0	90	3	0	1	1	1	.50	4	.216	.288	.353
Jacksnville	AA Det	4	8	2	0	0	1	5	2	2	1	0	2	0	0	0	1	0	1.00	0	.250	.333	.625
1997 Jacksnville	AA Det	59	186	28	7	0	1	38	18	16	17	0	77	2	3	2	0	0	—	4	.151	.227	.204
1998 Salem	A+ Col	31	59	7	4	0	2	17	6	7	3	0	14	0	0	0	0	0	—	2	.119	.161	.288
New Haven	AA Col	11	35	5	2	0	2	13	5	5	3	0	13	0	1	0	0	0	—	0	.143	.211	.371
Colo Sprngs	AAA Col	5	15	4	1	1	0	7	2	1	1	0	8	1	0	0	0	0	—	0	.267	.353	.467
1999 Mobile	AA SD	63	180	40	8	0	6	66	23	26	30	2	40	5	2	2	1	3	.25	4	.222	.346	.367
Las Vegas	AAA SD	10	29	8	3	0	2	17	5	5	3	0	8	0	0	1	0	0	—	2	.276	.333	.586
2000 Somerset	IND —	20	60	10	2	1	0	14	3	8	5	0	20	2	1	1	0	0	—	1	.167	.250	.233
Erie	AA Ana	29	82	18	2	0	0	20	11	3	10	1	14	1	2	0	1	2	.33	0	.220	.319	.244
9 Min. YEARS		573	1691	345	91	9	39	571	215	205	181	4	491	22	18	14	13	11	.54	22	.204	.287	.338

David Lindstrom

Bats: Right **Throws:** Right **Pos:** C-46; OF-12; DH-12; PH-9; 3B-5; 2B-2; 1B-2   **Ht:** 5'10" **Wt:** 185 **Born:** 8/6/74 **Age:** 26

		BATTING															BASERUNNING				PERCENTAGES		
Year Team	Lg Org	G	AB	H	2B	3B	HR	TB	R	RBI	TBB	IBB	SO	HBP	SH	SF	SB	CS	SB%	GDP	Avg	OBP	SLG
1996 Jamestown	A- Det	52	165	41	10	0	5	66	19	13	10	0	29	2	5	0	1	0	1.00	3	.248	.299	.400
1997 Lakeland	A+ Det	76	213	44	8	0	3	61	25	14	24	0	25	3	5	2	1	0	1.00	9	.207	.293	.286
1998 Toledo	AAA Det	1	3	0	0	0	0	0	0	0	0	0	1	0	0	0	0	0	—	0	.000	.000	.000
Lakeland	A+ Det	103	337	83	20	2	5	122	52	42	50	1	46	11	3	7	0	3	.00	8	.246	.356	.362
1999 Jacksnville	AA Det	66	214	58	17	1	7	98	30	35	24	0	35	6	1	5	1	3	.25	9	.271	.353	.458
2000 Toledo	AAA Det	12	36	10	0	0	2	16	6	5	2	0	3	1	1	0	0	0	—	3	.278	.333	.444
Jacksnville	AA Det	68	222	52	11	0	7	84	26	36	19	0	17	4	0	3	1	0	1.00	6	.234	.302	.378
5 Min. YEARS		378	1190	288	66	3	29	447	158	146	129	1	156	27	15	17	4	6	.40	38	.242	.326	.376

Doug Linton

Pitches: Right **Bats:** Right **Pos:** SP-28   **Ht:** 6'1" **Wt:** 190 **Born:** 2/9/65 **Age:** 36

		HOW MUCH HE PITCHED						WHAT HE GAVE UP												THE RESULTS					
Year Team	Lg Org	G	GS	CG	GF	IP	BFP	H	R	ER	HR	SH	SF	HB	TBB	IBB	SO	WP	Bk	W	L	Pct.	ShO	Sv	ERA
1987 Myrtle Bch	A Tor	20	19	2	1	122	480	94	34	21	9	0	2	2	25	0	155	8	1	14	2	.875	0	1	1.55
Knoxville	AA Tor	1	1	0	0	3	15	5	3	3	0	0	0	1	1	0	1	0	0	0	0	—	0	0	9.00
1988 Dunedin	A+ Tor	12	0	0	6	27.2	111	19	5	5	0	1	1	0	9	1	28	2	2	2	1	.667	0	2	1.63
1989 Dunedin	A+ Tor	9	1	0	5	27.1	117	27	12	9	1	0	1	0	9	0	35	1	0	1	2	.333	0	2	2.96
Knoxville	AA Tor	14	13	3	0	90	355	68	28	26	2	3	1	2	23	2	93	6	1	5	4	.556	2	0	2.60
1990 Syracuse	AAA Tor	26	26	8	0	177.1	753	174	77	67	14	2	10	8	67	3	113	4	1	10	10	.500	3	0	3.40
1991 Syracuse	AAA Tor	30	26	3	1	161.2	710	181	108	90	21	6	10	10	56	2	93	5	0	10	12	.455	1	0	5.01
1992 Syracuse	AAA Tor	25	25	7	0	170.2	741	176	83	71	17	5	4	7	70	3	126	12	1	12	10	.545	1	0	3.74
1993 Syracuse	AAA Tor	13	7	0	4	47.1	206	48	29	28	11	2	1	3	14	3	42	2	0	2	6	.250	0	0	5.32
1994 Norfolk	AAA NYM	3	3	0	0	18	66	11	6	4	1	0	0	1	1	0	15	0	0	2	1	.667	0	0	2.00
1995 Omaha	AAA KC	18	18	2	0	108.1	472	129	60	53	9	5	3	7	24	2	85	3	1	7	7	.500	1	0	4.40
1996 Omaha	AAA KC	4	4	0	0	22.2	99	26	13	12	1	0	1	2	7	0	14	2	0	1	1	.500	0	0	4.76
1998 Salt Lake	AAA Min	18	14	0	2	79.2	348	106	57	53	19	1	3	1	14	1	60	5	2	4	4	.500	0	0	5.99
1999 Rochester	AAA Bal	18	18	1	0	118.1	510	120	58	48	13	3	4	10	27	1	97	3	0	7	5	.583	0	0	3.65
2000 Colo Sprngs	AAA Col	28	28	6	0	174	753	189	109	104	15	11	10	12	42	2	136	7	2	10	13	.435	3	0	5.38
1992 Toronto	AL	8	3	0	2	24	116	31	23	23	5	1	2	0	17	0	16	2	0	1	3	.250	0	0	8.63
1993 Toronto	AL	4	1	0	0	11	55	11	8	8	0	0	2	1	9	0	4	0	0	0	0	—	0	0	6.55
California	AL	19	4	0	6	25.2	123	35	22	22	8	0	1	0	14	1	19	2	0	2	0	1.000	0	0	7.71
1994 New York	NL	32	3	0	8	50.1	241	74	27	25	4	3	1	0	20	3	29	2	0	6	2	.750	0	0	4.47
1995 Kansas City	AL	7	2	0	0	22.1	104	22	21	18	4	0	0	2	10	1	13	0	0	0	1	.000	0	0	7.25
1996 Kansas City	AL	21	18	0	0	104	452	111	65	58	13	6	4	8	26	1	87	1	0	7	9	.438	0	0	5.02
1999 Baltimore	AL	14	4	0	0	59	264	69	41	39	14	4	0	2	25	1	31	4	0	1	4	.200	0	0	5.95
13 Min. YEARS		239	203	32	19	1348	5736	1373	682	594	133	39	51	66	389	20	1093	60	12	87	78	.527	11	7	3.97
6 Maj. YEARS		105	35	0	16	296.1	1349	353	207	193	48	14	8	13	121	7	199	13	1	17	20	.459	0	0	5.86

Jim Lira

Pitches: Right **Bats:** Right **Pos:** RP-44   **Ht:** 6'1" **Wt:** 160 **Born:** 5/19/77 **Age:** 24

Year Team	Lg Org	G	GS	CG	GF	IP	BFP	H	R	ER	HR	SH	SF	HB	TBB	IBB	SO	WP	Bk	W	L	Pct.	ShO	Sv	ERA
1998 Princeton	R+ TB	29	0	0	22	36	161	36	18	15	3	2	1	1	19	2	51	3	0	4	1	.800	0	14	3.75
1999 St. Pete	A+ TB	36	0	0	13	44.1	191	45	18	15	1	2	2	2	17	1	25	4	0	4	1	.800	0	0	3.05
2000 St. Pete	A+ TB	42	0	0	22	52.1	214	47	15	13	2	1	2	1	15	0	39	2	0	2	4	.333	0	2	2.24
Orlando	AA TB	2	0	0	0	3	17	4	4	4	1	0	0	0	3	0	4	0	0	0	0	—	0	0	12.00
3 Min. YEARS		109	0	0	57	135.2	583	132	55	47	7	5	5	4	54	3	119	9	0	10	6	.625	0	16	3.12

Joe Lisio

Pitches: Right **Bats:** Right **Pos:** RP-44   **Ht:** 6'2" **Wt:** 205 **Born:** 8/5/73 **Age:** 27

Year Team	Lg Org	G	GS	CG	GF	IP	BFP	H	R	ER	HR	SH	SF	HB	TBB	IBB	SO	WP	Bk	W	L	Pct.	ShO	Sv	ERA
1994 Kingsport	R+ NYM	21	0	0	19	23.1	100	22	9	7	3	0	0	1	7	0	22	1	0	2	3	.400	0	9	2.70
1995 Pittsfield	A- NYM	28	0	0	23	33.1	141	27	8	6	0	2	5	1	14	1	24	2	0	2	2	.500	0	12	1.62
1996 Capital Cty	A NYM	40	0	0	37	44.1	186	40	16	10	0	3	2	1	15	1	42	3	0	2	5	.286	0	18	2.03
1997 St. Lucie	A+ NYM	48	0	0	44	47.1	209	48	27	24	4	4	0	4	19	5	42	3	2	2	6	.250	0	16	4.56
1998 High Desert	A+ Ari	11	0	0	3	15.1	79	19	11	10	1	1	0	2	11	1	17	1	0	1	2	.333	0	0	5.87
Tulsa	AA Tex	9	0	0	3	13.1	67	21	13	12	1	0	1	0	8	0	13	0	0	0	0	—	0	0	8.10
Norwich	AA NYY	1	0	0	1	1	5	1	0	0	0	1	0	0	1	0	1	0	0	1	0	1.000	0	0	0.00
Tampa	A+ NYY	31	0	0	28	32.2	135	19	13	9	2	4	0	3	16	2	43	2	0	2	3	.400	0	15	2.48
1999 Norwich	AA NYY	59	0	0	56	56.2	245	58	27	26	4	2	1	1	27	1	49	2	0	2	6	.250	0	33	4.13
2000 Norwich	AA NYY	42	0	0	14	50.2	240	55	30	28	4	2	3	2	33	4	42	0	0	1	3	.250	0	2	4.97
Columbus	AAA NYY	2	0	0	2	3	16	1	2	2	0	0	2	1	5	0	1	0	0	0	0	—	0	0	6.00
7 Min. YEARS		292	0	0	229	321	1423	311	156	134	19	20	14	17	156	15	296	14	4	15	30	.333	0	105	3.76

Mark Little

Bats: Right **Throws:** Right **Pos:** OF-104; PH-2; PR-2   **Ht:** 6'0" **Wt:** 195 **Born:** 7/11/72 **Age:** 28

Year Team	Lg Org	G	AB	H	2B	3B	HR	TB	R	RBI	TBB	IBB	SO	HBP	SH	SF	SB	CS	SB%	GDP	Avg	OBP	SLG
1994 Hudson Val	A- Tex	54	208	61	15	5	3	95	33	27	22	1	38	1	0	4	14	5	.74	4	.293	.357	.457
1995 Charlotte	A+ Tex	115	438	112	31	8	9	186	75	50	51	1	108	14	2	2	20	14	.59	4	.256	.350	.425
1996 Tulsa	AA Tex	101	409	119	24	2	13	186	69	50	48	0	88	10	5	3	22	10	.69	5	.291	.377	.455
1997 Okla City	AAA Tex	121	415	109	23	4	15	185	72	45	39	1	100	8	8	0	21	9	.70	5	.263	.338	.446
1998 Oklahoma	AAA Tex	69	274	81	20	4	8	133	58	46	16	0	60	10	0	5	9	6	.60	4	.296	.351	.485
Memphis	AAA StL	19	63	17	3	3	0	26	9	6	6	1	10	2	0	2	0	3	.00	0	.270	.342	.413
1999 Memphis	AAA StL	51	196	58	11	5	3	88	40	22	10	1	48	6	1	1	12	5	.71	3	.296	.347	.449
2000 Memphis	AAA StL	107	424	120	29	7	15	208	70	64	51	1	98	11	1	2	22	11	.67	2	.283	.373	.491
1998 St. Louis	NL	7	12	1	0	0	0	1	0	0	2	0	5	0	1	0	1	0	1.00	0	.083	.214	.083
7 Min. YEARS		637	2427	677	156	38	66	1107	426	310	243	6	550	62	17	19	120	63	.66	30	.279	.357	.456

Scott Livingstone

Bats: Left **Throws:** Right **Pos:** DH-13; 1B-7; 3B-4; PH-1   **Ht:** 6'0" **Wt:** 190 **Born:** 7/15/65 **Age:** 35

Year Team	Lg Org	G	AB	H	2B	3B	HR	TB	R	RBI	TBB	IBB	SO	HBP	SH	SF	SB	CS	SB%	GDP	Avg	OBP	SLG
1988 Lakeland	A+ Det	53	180	51	8	1	2	67	28	25	11	3	25	3	2	2	1	1	.50	3	.283	.332	.372
1989 London	AA Det	124	452	98	18	1	14	160	46	71	52	4	67	2	0	6	1	1	.50	4	.217	.297	.354
1990 Toledo	AAA Det	103	345	94	19	0	6	131	44	36	21	0	40	1	0	1	1	5	.17	7	.272	.315	.380
1991 Toledo	AAA Det	92	331	100	13	3	3	128	48	62	40	3	52	2	3	6	2	1	.67	9	.302	.375	.387
1997 Rancho Cuca	A+ SD	3	8	2	0	0	0	2	2	0	3	0	0	0	0	0	1	0	1.00	0	.250	.455	.250
Louisville	AAA StL	9	25	9	1	0	0	10	4	2	2	0	3	0	1	1	0	0	—	0	.360	.393	.400
1999 Albuquerque	AAA LA	28	78	16	1	0	1	20	11	4	9	1	12	0	0	0	2	1	.67	1	.205	.287	.256
Rochester	AAA Bal	14	43	16	4	0	0	20	5	7	7	2	4	0	0	1	1	0	1.00	5	.372	.451	.465
Norfolk	AAA NYM	36	114	34	7	0	1	44	10	20	7	0	9	0	1	1	2	0	1.00	6	.298	.336	.386
2000 Oklahoma	AAA Tex	25	92	28	5	0	1	36	16	9	10	1	12	0	0	0	0	0	—	7	.304	.373	.391
1991 Detroit	AL	44	127	37	5	0	2	48	19	11	10	0	25	0	1	1	2	1	.67	0	.291	.341	.378
1992 Detroit	AL	117	354	100	21	0	4	133	43	46	21	1	36	0	3	4	1	3	.25	4	.282	.319	.376
1993 Detroit	AL	98	304	89	10	2	2	109	39	39	19	1	32	0	1	6	1	3	.25	4	.293	.328	.359
1994 Detroit	AL	15	23	5	1	0	0	6	0	1	1	0	4	0	0	0	0	0	—	0	.217	.250	.261
San Diego	NL	57	180	49	12	1	2	69	11	10	6	0	22	0	0	1	2	2	.50	5	.272	.294	.383
1995 San Diego	NL	99	196	66	15	0	5	96	26	32	15	1	22	0	0	0	2	1	.67	3	.337	.380	.490
1996 San Diego	NL	102	172	51	4	1	2	63	20	20	9	0	22	0	0	0	0	1	.00	6	.297	.331	.366
1997 San Diego	NL	23	26	4	1	0	0	5	1	3	2	0	1	0	0	0	0	0	—	0	.154	.214	.192
St. Louis	NL	42	41	7	1	0	0	8	3	3	1	0	10	0	0	2	1	0	1.00	1	.171	.182	.195
1998 Montreal	NL	76	110	23	6	0	0	29	1	12	5	2	15	0	0	3	1	1	.50	2	.209	.237	.264
7 Min. YEARS		487	1668	448	76	5	28	618	214	236	162	14	224	8	7	18	10	10	.50	42	.269	.333	.371
8 Maj. YEARS		673	1533	431	76	4	17	566	163	177	89	5	189	0	5	19	10	12	.45	29	.281	.317	.369

Mike Lockwood

Bats: Left **Throws:** Left **Pos:** OF-131; DH-6; PH-1; PR-1   **Ht:** 6'0" **Wt:** 190 **Born:** 12/27/76 **Age:** 24

Year Team	Lg Org	G	AB	H	2B	3B	HR	TB	R	RBI	TBB	IBB	SO	HBP	SH	SF	SB	CS	SB%	GDP	Avg	OBP	SLG
1999 Sou Oregon	A- Oak	69	255	92	18	5	7	141	48	51	39	1	49	8	0	6	6	5	.55	5	.361	.451	.553
2000 Modesto	A+ Oak	47	159	50	12	0	6	80	42	35	46	6	25	4	3	7	9	1	.90	3	.314	.463	.503
Sacramento	AAA Oak	36	126	32	3	0	1	38	14	13	17	1	14	1	2	3	0	2	.00	1	.254	.340	.302
Midland	AA Oak	56	236	73	16	1	4	103	45	31	21	0	33	6	2	2	1	1	.50	4	.309	.377	.436
2 Min. YEARS		208	776	247	49	6	18	362	149	130	123	8	121	19	7	18	16	9	.64	13	.318	.416	.466

161

Carlton Loewer

Pitches: Right **Bats:** Right **Pos:** SP-2   **Ht:** 6'6" **Wt:** 211 **Born:** 9/24/73 **Age:** 27

Year Team	Lg Org	HOW MUCH HE PITCHED						WHAT HE GAVE UP												THE RESULTS					
		G	GS	CG	GF	IP	BFP	H	R	ER	HR	SH	SF	HB	TBB	IBB	SO	WP	Bk	W	L	Pct.	ShO	Sv	ERA
1995 Clearwater	A+ Phi	20	20	1	0	114.2	502	124	59	42	6	3	5	5	36	0	83	7	3	7	5	.583	0	0	3.30
Reading	AA Phi	8	8	0	0	50	212	42	17	12	3	1	0	1	31	0	35	4	0	4	1	.800	0	0	2.16
1996 Reading	AA Phi	27	27	3	0	171	753	191	115	100	24	7	3	8	57	3	119	9	1	7	10	.412	1	0	5.26
1997 Scranton-WB	AAA Phi	29	29	4	0	184	797	198	120	94	20	8	4	7	50	6	152	3	0	5	13	.278	0	0	4.60
1998 Scranton-WB	AAA Phi	12	12	5	0	94	385	89	34	30	5	5	2	5	22	0	69	3	0	7	3	.700	2	0	2.87
1999 Phillies	R Phi	1	1	0	0	2	8	2	0	0	0	0	0	0	0	0	2	1	0	0	0	—	0	0	0.00
Clearwater	A+ Phi	3	3	0	0	7	31	10	6	6	0	0	0	0	1	0	5	2	0	0	2	.000	0	0	7.71
2000 Las Vegas	AAA SD	1	1	0	0	4.2	27	3	0	0	0	0	0	0	0	0	4	0	0	0	0	—	0	0	0.00
Rancho Cuca	A+ SD	1	1	0	0	7	27	7	3	2	2	0	0	0	0	0	4	0	0	0	0	—	0	0	2.57
1998 Philadelphia	NL	21	21	1	0	122.2	549	154	86	83	18	5	8	3	39	1	58	4	0	7	8	.467	0	0	6.09
1999 Philadelphia	NL	20	13	2	2	89.2	385	100	54	51	9	5	6	0	26	0	48	3	0	2	6	.250	1	0	5.12
6 Min. YEARS		102	102	13	0	634.1	2732	666	354	286	60	24	14	26	197	9	473	29	4	30	34	.469	3	0	4.06
2 Maj. YEARS		41	34	3	2	212.1	934	254	140	134	27	10	14	3	65	1	106	7	0	9	14	.391	1	0	5.68

Kyle Logan

Bats: Left **Throws:** Right **Pos:** OF-111; PH-20; PR-2   **Ht:** 6'0" **Wt:** 196 **Born:** 7/11/75 **Age:** 25

Year Team	Lg Org	BATTING															BASERUNNING				PERCENTAGES		
		G	AB	H	2B	3B	HR	TB	R	RBI	TBB	IBB	SO	HBP	SH	SF	SB	CS	SB%	GDP	Avg	OBP	SLG
1997 Auburn	A- Hou	71	260	76	16	4	0	100	27	29	20	3	60	1	0	0	5	10	.33	3	.292	.345	.385
1998 Quad City	A Hou	110	352	93	22	2	4	131	50	49	36	3	50	2	2	5	22	13	.63	4	.264	.332	.372
1999 Kissimmee	A+ Hou	113	399	116	33	7	7	184	57	62	33	4	62	3	1	3	16	5	.76	5	.291	.347	.461
2000 Round Rock	AA Hou	109	343	75	17	0	6	110	44	31	35	2	63	4	1	5	13	5	.72	4	.219	.295	.321
Kissimmee	A+ Hou	17	51	14	1	2	0	19	8	4	13	2	6	2	0	2	7	0	1.00	1	.275	.426	.373
4 Min. YEARS		420	1405	374	89	15	17	544	186	175	137	14	241	12	4	15	63	33	.66	16	.266	.333	.387

Kyle Lohse

Pitches: Right **Bats:** Right **Pos:** SP-28   **Ht:** 6'2" **Wt:** 190 **Born:** 10/4/78 **Age:** 22

Year Team	Lg Org	HOW MUCH HE PITCHED						WHAT HE GAVE UP												THE RESULTS					
		G	GS	CG	GF	IP	BFP	H	R	ER	HR	SH	SF	HB	TBB	IBB	SO	WP	Bk	W	L	Pct.	ShO	Sv	ERA
1997 Cubs	R ChC	12	11	0	0	47.2	210	46	22	16	0	1	1	1	22	0	49	3	0	2	2	.500	0	0	3.02
1998 Rockford	A ChC	28	26	3	1	170.2	712	158	76	61	8	8	5	11	45	1	121	13	1	13	8	.619	1	0	3.22
1999 Daytona	A+ ChC	9	9	1	0	53	217	48	21	17	4	2	1	0	16	0	41	1	0	5	3	.625	1	0	2.89
Fort Myers	A+ Min	7	7	0	0	41.2	180	47	28	24	5	2	4	4	9	0	33	1	0	2	3	.400	0	0	5.18
New Britain	AA Min	11	11	1	0	70.1	311	87	49	46	9	3	4	5	23	0	41	2	0	3	4	.429	0	0	5.89
2000 New Britain	AA Min	28	28	0	0	167	744	196	123	112	23	5	6	3	55	0	124	6	0	3	18	.143	0	0	6.04
4 Min. YEARS		95	92	5	1	550.1	2374	582	319	276	49	21	21	24	170	1	409	26	1	28	38	.424	2	0	4.51

Steve Lomasney

Bats: Right **Throws:** Right **Pos:** C-66; DH-6   **Ht:** 6'0" **Wt:** 195 **Born:** 8/29/77 **Age:** 23

Year Team	Lg Org	BATTING															BASERUNNING				PERCENTAGES		
		G	AB	H	2B	3B	HR	TB	R	RBI	TBB	IBB	SO	HBP	SH	SF	SB	CS	SB%	GDP	Avg	OBP	SLG
1995 Red Sox	R Bos	29	92	15	6	0	0	21	10	7	8	1	16	5	1	0	2	1	.67	0	.163	.267	.228
1996 Lowell	A- Bos	59	173	24	10	0	4	46	26	21	42	0	63	2	0	0	2	0	1.00	2	.139	.313	.266
1997 Michigan	A Bos	102	324	89	27	3	12	158	50	51	32	0	98	9	3	3	3	4	.43	8	.275	.353	.488
1998 Sarasota	A+ Bos	122	443	106	22	1	22	196	74	63	59	3	145	16	1	2	13	4	.76	7	.239	.348	.442
1999 Sarasota	A+ Bos	55	189	51	10	0	8	85	35	28	26	0	57	8	0	0	5	2	.71	2	.270	.381	.450
Trenton	AA Bos	47	151	37	6	0	12	79	24	31	31	2	44	9	1	1	7	5	.58	5	.245	.401	.523
2000 Trenton	AA Bos	66	233	57	16	1	8	99	30	27	24	0	81	12	1	2	4	6	.40	8	.245	.343	.425
Red Sox	R Bos	6	15	4	2	0	0	6	2	1	4	0	6	0	0	0	0	1	.00	0	.267	.421	.400
1999 Boston	AL	1	2	0	0	0	0	0	0	0	0	0	2	0	0	0	0	0	—	0	.000	.000	.000
6 Min. YEARS		486	1620	383	99	5	66	690	251	229	226	6	510	61	7	8	36	23	.61	32	.236	.350	.426

Garrett Long

Bats: Right **Throws:** Right **Pos:** OF-26; 1B-10; PH-4; DH-3   **Ht:** 6'3" **Wt:** 207 **Born:** 10/5/76 **Age:** 24

Year Team	Lg Org	BATTING															BASERUNNING				PERCENTAGES		
		G	AB	H	2B	3B	HR	TB	R	RBI	TBB	IBB	SO	HBP	SH	SF	SB	CS	SB%	GDP	Avg	OBP	SLG
1995 Pirates	R Pit	20	63	22	2	1	1	29	13	8	17	0	10	0	0	0	0	1	.00	3	.349	.488	.460
Erie	A- Pit	29	108	30	4	0	2	40	17	16	15	0	25	1	0	2	2	2	.50	6	.278	.365	.370
1996 Erie	A- Pit	20	70	20	2	1	0	24	5	7	9	0	17	1	1	1	1	2	.33	3	.286	.370	.343
1997 Augusta	A Pit	83	280	84	10	2	7	119	50	41	61	2	78	1	0	1	5	2	.71	3	.300	.426	.425
Lynchburg	A+ Pit	9	29	6	3	0	1	12	1	5	3	0	10	0	0	0	0	0	—	3	.207	.281	.414
1998 Lynchburg	A+ Pit	91	309	87	29	1	7	139	46	43	49	2	83	3	0	3	7	2	.78	8	.282	.382	.450
Carolina	AA Pit	28	98	29	3	0	0	32	14	8	11	1	27	1	0	0	1	0	1.00	6	.296	.373	.327
1999 Altoona	AA Pit	109	355	87	12	4	18	161	56	63	63	1	100	7	4	2	6	6	.50	7	.245	.368	.454
2000 Altoona	AA Pit	42	122	28	8	0	4	48	18	18	17	0	33	2	0	1	0	1	.00	6	.230	.331	.393
6 Min. YEARS		431	1434	393	73	9	40	604	225	202	245	6	383	16	5	10	22	16	.58	45	.274	.384	.421

Ryan Long

Bats: Right **Throws:** Right **Pos:** OF-88; DH-21; PH-2; 1B-1   **Ht:** 6'2" **Wt:** 215 **Born:** 2/3/73 **Age:** 28

Year Team	Lg Org	BATTING															BASERUNNING				PERCENTAGES		
		G	AB	H	2B	3B	HR	TB	R	RBI	TBB	IBB	SO	HBP	SH	SF	SB	CS	SB%	GDP	Avg	OBP	SLG
1991 Royals	R KC	48	177	54	2	2	0	60	17	20	10	0	20	2	0	1	5	4	.56	3	.305	.347	.339
1992 Eugene	A- KC	54	183	42	5	2	0	51	19	18	3	0	33	4	2	1	7	5	.58	4	.230	.257	.279
1993 Rockford	A KC	107	396	115	27	6	8	178	46	68	16	3	76	18	2	5	16	6	.73	6	.290	.343	.449
1994 Wilmington	A+ KC	123	494	130	25	5	11	198	69	68	16	0	72	8	3	3	7	3	.70	4	.263	.296	.401

Year Team	Lg Org	G	AB	H	2B	3B	HR	TB	R	RBI	TBB	IBB	SO	HBP	SH	SF	SB	CS	SB%	GDP	Avg	OBP	SLG
1995 Wichita	AA KC	102	342	79	26	0	5	120	36	34	10	1	48	5	1	0	4	4	.50	9	.231	.263	.351
1996 Wichita	AA KC	122	442	125	29	1	20	216	64	78	17	0	71	5	1	2	6	5	.55	9	.283	.315	.489
1997 Omaha	AAA KC	113	411	109	26	0	19	192	48	56	18	2	98	7	3	3	2	4	.33	14	.265	.305	.467
1998 Omaha	AAA KC	18	59	12	2	0	4	26	6	8	8	0	13	2	0	0	0	0	—	0	.203	.319	.441
Wichita	AA KC	67	248	63	14	1	7	100	32	29	17	1	51	3	1	1	2	2	.50	10	.254	.309	.403
1999 Orlando	AA TB	8	30	7	1	0	0	8	2	4	1	0	3	0	0	0	0	0	—	3	.233	.258	.267
Newark	IND —	67	205	44	10	2	6	76	24	21	22	0	38	2	0	1	1	1	.50	5	.215	.296	.371
Lehigh Val	IND —	33	121	34	9	0	4	55	15	23	7	0	28	1	0	0	2	0	—	3	.281	.321	.455
2000 Winston-Sal	A+ CWS	19	71	20	1	1	10	53	15	18	9	1	17	2	0	2	0	1	.00	0	.282	.369	.746
Birmingham	AA CWS	89	315	76	14	0	10	120	37	39	23	0	86	10	2	0	1	0	1.00	9	.241	.313	.381
Charlotte	AAA CWS	3	9	0	0	0	0	0	0	0	0	0	6	0	0	0	0	0	—	0	.000	.000	.000
1997 Kansas City	AL	6	9	2	0	0	0	2	2	2	0	0	3	1	0	0	0	0	—	0	.222	.300	.222
10 Min. YEARS		973	3503	910	191	20	104	1453	430	484	177	8	660	69	15	21	51	35	.59	79	.260	.307	.415

Alex Lontayo

Pitches: Left **Bats:** Left **Pos:** RP-35; SP-5 **Ht:** 6'1" **Wt:** 195 **Born:** 12/12/75 **Age:** 25

Year Team	Lg Org	G	GS	CG	GF	IP	BFP	H	R	ER	HR	SH	SF	HB	TBB	IBB	SO	WP	Bk	W	L	Pct.	ShO	Sv	ERA
1999 Augusta	A Bos	40	0	0	14	58.2	255	55	31	28	7	1	2	4	26	0	80	3	1	2	0	1.000	0	0	4.30
2000 Lk Elsinore	A+ Ana	6	3	0	1	21.2	95	21	14	8	0	1	1	0	12	0	19	0	0	2	0	1.000	0	1	3.32
Erie	AA Ana	34	2	0	11	57	249	55	39	33	7	3	6	3	27	1	37	2	1	1	4	.200	0	2	5.21
2 Min. YEARS		80	5	0	26	137.1	599	131	84	69	14	5	9	7	65	1	136	5	2	5	4	.556	0	3	4.52

Brian Looney

Pitches: Left **Bats:** Left **Pos:** RP-9; SP-2 **Ht:** 5'10" **Wt:** 180 **Born:** 9/26/69 **Age:** 31

Year Team	Lg Org	G	GS	CG	GF	IP	BFP	H	R	ER	HR	SH	SF	HB	TBB	IBB	SO	WP	Bk	W	L	Pct.	ShO	Sv	ERA
1991 Jamestown	A- Mon	11	11	2	0	62.1	246	42	12	8	0	2	2	0	28	0	64	6	0	7	1	.875	1	0	1.16
1992 Rockford	A Mon	17	0	0	5	31.1	141	28	13	11	0	2	0	1	23	0	34	1	0	3	1	.750	0	0	3.16
Albany	A Mon	11	11	1	0	67.1	265	51	22	16	1	1	3	0	30	0	56	4	0	3	2	.600	1	0	2.14
1993 Wst Plm Bch	A+ Mon	18	16	0	1	106	451	108	48	37	2	7	3	5	29	0	109	2	1	4	6	.400	0	0	3.14
Harrisburg	AA Mon	8	8	1	0	56.2	221	36	15	15	2	1	1	1	17	1	76	0	0	3	2	.600	1	0	2.38
1994 Ottawa	AAA Mon	27	16	0	2	124.2	565	134	71	60	10	3	6	3	67	4	90	2	0	7	7	.500	0	0	4.33
1995 Pawtucket	AAA Bos	18	18	1	0	100.2	438	106	44	39	9	2	0	3	33	0	78	7	2	4	7	.364	0	0	3.49
1996 Pawtucket	AAA Bos	27	9	1	7	82.1	357	78	55	44	14	0	2	4	27	2	78	3	0	5	6	.455	1	1	4.81
1997 Salt Lake	AAA Min	17	0	0	6	24.2	103	20	7	6	4	1	0	0	10	2	21	2	0	0	2	.000	0	1	2.19
1998 Columbus	AAA NYY	41	10	0	7	92.2	424	97	52	46	13	3	5	1	52	2	63	3	0	4	4	.500	0	0	4.47
1999 Toledo	AAA Det	47	1	0	11	55	255	51	38	38	7	5	4	2	44	0	52	7	0	3	0	1.000	0	0	6.22
Scranton-WB	AAA Phi	3	3	0	0	16	74	19	9	7	3	0	0	1	6	0	12	1	1	1	0	1.000	0	0	3.94
2000 Buffalo	AAA Cle	8	0	0	3	12.2	63	15	13	12	1	1	2	2	8	1	8	0	0	1	0	1.000	0	0	8.53
Calgary	AAA Fla	3	2	0	1	9	39	11	7	7	1	1	0	2	2	0	6	0	0	0	2	.000	0	0	7.00
1993 Montreal	NL	3	1	0	1	6	28	8	2	2	0	0	0	0	2	0	7	0	0	0	0	—	0	0	3.00
1994 Montreal	NL	1	0	0	0	2	11	4	5	5	1	0	0	1	0	0	2	0	0	0	0	—	0	0	22.50
1995 Boston	AL	3	1	0	0	4.2	29	12	9	9	1	1	2	0	4	1	2	0	0	0	1	.000	0	0	17.36
10 Min. YEARS		256	105	6	43	841.1	3642	796	406	346	67	29	29	23	376	12	747	38	4	45	40	.529	4	4	3.70
3 Maj. YEARS		7	2	0	1	12.2	68	24	16	16	2	1	2	1	6	1	11	0	1	0	1	.000	0	0	11.37

Felipe Lopez

Bats: Both **Throws:** Right **Pos:** SS-127; PH-3 **Ht:** 6'1" **Wt:** 175 **Born:** 5/12/80 **Age:** 21

Year Team	Lg Org	G	AB	H	2B	3B	HR	TB	R	RBI	TBB	IBB	SO	HBP	SH	SF	SB	CS	SB%	GDP	Avg	OBP	SLG
1998 St.Cathrnes	A- Tor	19	83	31	5	2	1	43	14	11	3	0	14	0	0	0	4	2	.67	0	.373	.395	.518
Dunedin	A+ Tor	4	13	5	0	1	1	10	3	1	0	0	3	0	0	0	0	0	—	1	.385	.385	.769
1999 Hagerstown	A Tor	134	537	149	27	4	14	226	87	80	61	0	157	3	0	6	21	14	.60	7	.277	.351	.421
2000 Tennessee	AA Tor	127	463	119	18	4	9	172	52	41	31	0	110	1	8	3	12	11	.52	6	.257	.303	.371
3 Min. YEARS		284	1096	304	50	11	25	451	156	133	95	0	284	4	8	9	37	27	.58	15	.277	.335	.411

Johan Lopez

Pitches: Right **Bats:** Right **Pos:** RP-29 **Ht:** 6'2" **Wt:** 210 **Born:** 4/4/75 **Age:** 26

Year Team	Lg Org	G	GS	CG	GF	IP	BFP	H	R	ER	HR	SH	SF	HB	TBB	IBB	SO	WP	Bk	W	L	Pct.	ShO	Sv	ERA
1992 Astros	R Hou	17	0	0	4	34	160	42	28	17	1	0	3		13	0	19	7	4	1	1	.500	0	0	4.50
1994 Auburn	A- Hou	14	14	2	0	76.2	339	86	49	41	4	2	4	4	24	0	74	7	3	7	5	.583	1	0	4.81
1995 Kissimmee	A+ Hou	18	12	0	3	69	283	55	30	20	3	1	2	3	25	0	67	5	3	5	5	.500	0	1	2.61
1996 Kissimmee	A+ Hou	19	19	2	0	98.1	434	114	50	41	5	0	5	1	35	1	70	9	3	3	10	.231	1	0	3.75
1997 Jackson	AA Hou	35	19	0	5	133.2	586	131	79	65	18	7	2	6	57	3	109	11	4	6	8	.429	0	1	4.38
1998 New Orleans	AAA Hou	45	6	0	7	80.1	357	84	52	50	11	6	1	2	18	1	77	3	0	7	2	.778	0	0	5.60
1999 Binghamton	AA NYM	2	0	0	1	2	11	3	3	3	0	1	0	0	3	0	1	0	0	0	0	—	0	0	13.50
Norfolk	AAA NYM	33	8	0	6	102	438	98	49	47	13	6	0	2	44	6	84	10	1	3	5	.375	0	0	4.15
2000 Oklahoma	AAA Tex	29	0	0	16	56.1	230	44	28	26	6	0	3	2	20	2	42	3	0	6	2	.750	0	5	4.15
8 Min. YEARS		212	78	4	42	652.1	2838	657	368	310	61	24	17	23	249	13	543	55	18	38	38	.500	2	8	4.28

Luis Lopez

Bats: Right **Throws:** Right **Pos:** 3B-54; DH-46; 1B-31; PH-1 **Ht:** 6'0" **Wt:** 205 **Born:** 10/5/73 **Age:** 27

Year Team	Lg Org	G	AB	H	2B	3B	HR	TB	R	RBI	TBB	IBB	SO	HBP	SH	SF	SB	CS	SB%	GDP	Avg	OBP	SLG
1995 Ogden	R+ —	46	182	65	15	0	7	101	36	39	16	0	20	2	3	2	1	1	.50	5	.357	.411	.555
1996 St.Cathrnes	A- Tor	74	260	74	17	2	7	116	36	40	27	1	31	7	4	3	2	3	.40	4	.285	.364	.446

Year Team	Lg Org	G	AB	H	2B	3B	HR	TB	R	RBI	TBB	IBB	SO	HBP	SH	SF	SB	CS	SB%	GDP	Avg	OBP	SLG
1997 Hagerstown	A Tor	136	503	180	47	4	11	268	96	99	60	4	45	8	0	6	5	8	.38	14	.358	.430	.533
1998 Syracuse	AAA Tor	11	41	9	0	0	1	12	6	3	6	0	6	0	0	1	0	0	—	2	.220	.313	.293
Knoxville	AA Tor	119	450	141	27	1	15	215	70	85	58	3	55	3	0	8	0	2	.00	18	.313	.389	.478
1999 Syracuse	AAA Tor	136	531	171	35	2	4	222	76	69	40	2	58	1	2	8	1	0	1.00	22	.322	.366	.418
2000 Syracuse	AAA Tor	130	491	161	27	1	7	211	64	79	48	1	33	2	0	8	3	1	.75	10	.328	.384	.430
6 Min. YEARS		652	2458	801	168	10	52	1145	384	414	255	11	248	23	9	36	12	15	.44	75	.326	.389	.466

Mickey Lopez

Bats: Both **Throws:** Right **Pos:** 2B-97; SS-14; PH-10; 3B-1; DH-1; PR-1   **Ht:** 5'10" **Wt:** 165 **Born:** 11/17/73 **Age:** 27

Year Team	Lg Org	G	AB	H	2B	3B	HR	TB	R	RBI	TBB	IBB	SO	HBP	SH	SF	SB	CS	SB%	GDP	Avg	OBP	SLG
1995 Helena	R+ Mil	57	225	73	19	2	1	99	66	41	38	3	20	5	2	4	12	8	.60	1	.324	.426	.440
1996 Beloit	A Mil	61	236	64	10	2	0	78	35	14	28	0	36	1	10	0	12	8	.60	8	.271	.351	.331
Stockton	A+ Mil	64	217	61	10	1	0	73	30	25	23	0	36	4	9	1	6	4	.60	0	.281	.359	.336
1997 El Paso	AA Mil	134	483	145	21	10	3	195	79	58	48	2	60	5	9	5	20	10	.67	10	.300	.366	.404
1998 El Paso	AA Mil	120	459	127	24	9	2	175	81	64	46	1	61	2	4	5	12	10	.55	11	.277	.342	.381
Louisville	AAA Mil	3	4	1	0	0	0	1	1	0	2	1	0	0	0	0	0	0	—	0	.250	.500	.250
1999 Huntsville	AA Mil	83	315	94	16	5	5	135	58	40	46	2	46	5	3	4	31	4	.89	9	.298	.392	.429
Louisville	AAA Mil	49	181	58	17	2	5	94	43	31	37	0	25	2	2	1	11	7	.61	1	.320	.439	.519
2000 Indianapolis	AAA Mil	67	208	54	14	1	2	76	38	22	37	0	26	4	1	4	14	7	.67	5	.260	.375	.365
Huntsville	AA Mil	53	212	71	22	4	4	113	42	26	30	0	32	0	6	1	16	7	.70	5	.335	.416	.533
6 Min. YEARS		691	2540	748	153	36	22	1039	473	321	335	9	342	28	46	25	134	65	.67	50	.294	.379	.409

Pedro Lopez

Bats: Right **Throws:** Right **Pos:** PH-6; C-2   **Ht:** 6'1" **Wt:** 200 **Born:** 3/29/69 **Age:** 32

Year Team	Lg Org	G	AB	H	2B	3B	HR	TB	R	RBI	TBB	IBB	SO	HBP	SH	SF	SB	CS	SB%	GDP	Avg	OBP	SLG
1988 Padres	R SD	42	156	44	4	6	1	63	18	22	10	0	24	0	0	0	9	4	.69	2	.282	.325	.404
1989 Waterloo	A SD	97	319	61	13	1	2	82	32	26	25	1	61	4	6	1	4	4	.50	12	.191	.258	.257
1990 Chston-SC	A SD	32	101	20	2	0	0	22	9	5	7	0	18	4	0	2	0	1	.00	2	.198	.272	.218
1991 Waterloo	A SD	102	342	97	13	1	8	136	49	57	47	5	66	2	2	4	3	3	.50	4	.284	.370	.398
1992 Wichita	AA SD	96	319	78	8	4	6	112	35	48	13	0	68	7	2	6	4	3	.57	7	.245	.284	.351
1993 Rancho Cuca	A+ SD	37	103	26	10	0	1	39	25	9	24	1	19	2	0	0	0	1	.00	3	.252	.403	.379
1994 Wichita	AA SD	42	131	33	7	0	1	43	15	12	15	0	16	3	1	2	0	2	.00	2	.252	.338	.328
Rancho Cuca	A+ SD	7	20	5	2	0	0	7	1	1	1	0	2	0	0	0	0	0	—	1	.250	.286	.350
Las Vegas	AAA SD	17	47	10	2	0	1	15	3	4	1	0	7	0	1	1	0	0	—	1	.213	.224	.319
1995 El Paso	AA Mil	84	218	68	15	2	4	99	32	28	18	1	45	4	3	0	0	3	.00	8	.312	.375	.454
New Orleans	AAA Mil	3	8	0	0	0	0	0	0	0	0	0	3	0	0	0	0	0	—	0	.000	.000	.000
1996 El Paso	AA Mil	46	144	44	10	1	2	62	22	20	17	1	24	0	3	2	2	2	.50	2	.306	.374	.431
New Orleans	AAA Mil	34	87	19	4	0	0	23	7	3	13	1	22	0	0	0	0	1	.00	5	.218	.320	.264
1997 Kissimmee	A+ Hou	25	69	14	4	1	0	20	7	8	4	0	11	0	0	1	0	1	.00	1	.203	.243	.290
Jackson	AA Hou	27	88	26	5	0	2	37	9	13	4	0	16	1	0	0	0	1	.00	1	.295	.333	.420
1998 Jackson	AA Hou	60	178	51	14	0	9	92	29	28	17	0	27	8	1	1	2	0	1.00	6	.287	.373	.517
1999 New Orleans	AAA Hou	19	60	16	4	0	2	26	11	11	7	1	8	0	2	0	0	0	—	0	.267	.343	.433
Jackson	AA Hou	81	255	47	11	0	6	76	20	28	12	0	52	2	4	2	1	1	.50	2	.184	.225	.298
2000 New Orleans	AAA Hou	8	9	2	0	0	0	2	2	1	1	0	0	0	0	0	0	0	—	0	.222	.300	.222
13 Min. YEARS		909	2796	690	135	16	49	1004	338	338	258	13	513	38	26	22	28	26	.52	65	.247	.317	.359

Pee Wee Lopez

Bats: Right **Throws:** Right **Pos:** C-63; PH-5; OF-1; DH-1   **Ht:** 6'0" **Wt:** 195 **Born:** 10/22/76 **Age:** 24

Year Team	Lg Org	G	AB	H	2B	3B	HR	TB	R	RBI	TBB	IBB	SO	HBP	SH	SF	SB	CS	SB%	GDP	Avg	OBP	SLG
1996 Kingsport	R+ NYM	65	250	79	22	4	7	130	53	56	31	1	25	4	0	2	0	1	.00	4	.316	.397	.520
Pittsfield	A- NYM	5	14	6	0	1	0	8	2	3	1	0	1	0	0	0	0	0	—	1	.429	.467	.571
1997 St. Lucie	A+ NYM	113	375	93	19	0	3	121	40	30	39	3	56	0	1	1	3	2	.60	10	.248	.318	.323
1998 Mariners	R Sea	5	15	5	2	0	0	7	1	2	1	0	2	0	0	0	0	0	—	1	.333	.375	.467
Wisconsin	A Sea	35	121	27	5	1	1	37	11	12	9	0	18	1	0	0	0	0	—	0	.223	.282	.306
1999 New Haven	AA Sea	8	32	6	1	0	0	7	1	1	0	0	5	0	0	0	0	0	—	1	.188	.188	.219
Lancaster	A+ Sea	72	247	71	10	3	5	102	37	28	15	0	36	5	2	1	5	4	.56	11	.287	.340	.413
2000 West Tenn	AA ChC	69	227	59	12	1	1	76	19	26	14	1	33	1	2	1	0	1	.00	13	.260	.305	.335
5 Min. YEARS		372	1281	346	71	10	17	488	164	160	110	5	176	11	5	5	8	8	.50	44	.270	.332	.381

Mike Lopez-Cao

Bats: Left **Throws:** Right **Pos:** C-39; DH-18; PH-7; 2B-1; 1B-1   **Ht:** 5'6" **Wt:** 180 **Born:** 8/14/75 **Age:** 25

Year Team	Lg Org	G	AB	H	2B	3B	HR	TB	R	RBI	TBB	IBB	SO	HBP	SH	SF	SB	CS	SB%	GDP	Avg	OBP	SLG
1997 Hudson Val	A- TB	14	44	13	3	0	1	19	6	7	3	0	10	0	0	1	2	0	1.00	2	.295	.333	.432
Princeton	R+ TB	17	53	12	0	1	1	17	7	7	5	0	8	0	0	1	0	0	—	0	.226	.288	.321
1998 Chston-SC	A TB	14	24	6	0	0	0	6	2	4	4	0	4	1	0	1	2	0	1.00	0	.250	.367	.250
1999 Delmarva	A Bal	2	6	1	0	0	1	4	2	3	1	0	0	0	0	0	0	0	—	0	.167	.250	.667
Frederick	A+ Bal	29	88	21	4	0	2	31	12	11	9	0	16	0	1	1	1	0	1.00	1	.239	.306	.352
Bowie	AA Bal	16	47	12	1	0	2	19	5	7	2	0	8	0	0	1	0	0	—	1	.255	.286	.404
2000 Frederick	A+ Bal	49	117	23	8	0	7	52	15	24	14	0	23	5	1	2	0	1	.00	5	.197	.304	.444
Bowie	AA Bal	17	49	11	3	0	0	14	7	4	4	0	7	1	0	0	0	0	—	1	.224	.296	.286
4 Min. YEARS		158	428	99	19	1	14	162	56	67	42	0	76	7	2	7	5	1	.83	10	.231	.306	.379

Luis Lorenzana

Bats: Right **Throws:** Right **Pos:** 3B-35; SS-29; 2B-15; PH-7; PR-2; 1B-1; P-1 **Ht:** 6'2" **Wt:** 193 **Born:** 11/9/78 **Age:** 22

Year Team	Lg Org	G	AB	H	2B	3B	HR	TB	R	RBI	TBB	IBB	SO	HBP	SH	SF	SB	CS	SB%	GDP	Avg	OBP	SLG
1996 Pirates	R Pit	18	53	8	1	0	0	9	4	5	12	0	8	1	1	1	0	1	.00	1	.151	.313	.170
Erie	A- Pit	44	128	25	8	1	0	35	19	12	16	0	26	3	4	3	1	4	.20	4	.195	.293	.273
1997 Augusta	A Pit	92	288	68	11	1	0	81	36	20	31	0	66	2	4	1	4	5	.44	5	.236	.314	.281
1998 Lynchburg	A+ Pit	95	283	67	7	2	2	84	27	24	35	1	62	5	9	2	2	2	.50	8	.237	.329	.297
1999 Lynchburg	A+ Pit	49	156	40	7	0	2	53	15	14	11	0	37	4	0	1	2	3	.40	5	.256	.320	.340
Altoona	AA Pit	34	74	16	2	1	2	26	9	8	14	0	17	4	1	3	0	0	—	2	.216	.358	.351
2000 Altoona	AA Pit	24	51	8	2	0	0	10	7	2	4	0	15	0	2	0	0	0	—	0	.157	.218	.196
Lynchburg	A+ Pit	58	170	39	3	4	1	53	22	9	20	0	35	2	9	1	3	3	.50	2	.229	.316	.312
5 Min. YEARS		414	1203	271	41	9	7	351	139	94	143	1	266	21	30	12	12	18	.40	27	.225	.315	.292

Chris Lotterhos

Bats: Right **Throws:** Right **Pos:** 2B-18; SS-14; PH-3; DH-1; PR-1 **Ht:** 5'10" **Wt:** 165 **Born:** 4/26/77 **Age:** 24

Year Team	Lg Org	G	AB	H	2B	3B	HR	TB	R	RBI	TBB	IBB	SO	HBP	SH	SF	SB	CS	SB%	GDP	Avg	OBP	SLG
1999 Mahoning Vy	A- Cle	41	124	26	7	2	1	40	21	9	23	0	33	2	0	1	5	6	.45	2	.210	.340	.323
2000 Mahoning Vy	A- Cle	5	16	3	1	0	0	4	2	1	3	0	6	1	0	0	0	0	—	0	.188	.350	.250
South Bend	A Ari	3	9	1	1	0	0	2	0	0	0	0	3	0	1	0	0	0	—	0	.111	.111	.222
Richmond	IND —	17	55	12	3	1	0	17	4	9	10	1	21	0	2	1	2	2	.50	1	.218	.333	.309
Louisville	AAA Cin	3	12	5	0	0	1	8	3	2	1	0	1	0	0	0	0	0	—	0	.417	.462	.667
2 Min. YEARS		69	216	47	12	3	2	71	30	21	37	1	64	3	3	2	7	8	.47	3	.218	.337	.329

Shane Loux

Pitches: Right **Bats:** Right **Pos:** SP-27 **Ht:** 6'2" **Wt:** 205 **Born:** 8/31/79 **Age:** 21

Year Team	Lg Org	G	GS	CG	GF	IP	BFP	H	R	ER	HR	SH	SF	HB	TBB	IBB	SO	WP	Bk	W	L	Pct.	ShO	Sv	ERA
1997 Tigers	R Det	10	9	1	0	43	158	19	7	4	0	0	0	1	10	0	33	2	1	4	1	.800	1	0	0.84
1998 W Michigan	A Det	28	28	2	0	157	698	184	96	81	13	2	4	8	52	0	88	12	2	7	13	.350	1	0	4.64
1999 W Michigan	A Det	8	8	0	0	47.1	215	55	39	33	5	1	2	8	16	1	43	4	0	1	3	.250	0	0	6.27
Lakeland	A+ Det	17	17	0	0	91	412	92	48	41	8	2	5	10	47	0	52	7	1	6	5	.545	0	0	4.05
2000 Lakeland	A+ Det	1	1	0	0	5	19	2	1	1	0	1	0	0	3	0	6	0	0	0	1	.000	0	0	1.80
Jacksnville	AA Det	26	26	2	0	157.2	670	150	78	67	12	3	7	14	55	0	130	7	0	12	9	.571	0	0	3.82
4 Min. YEARS		90	89	5	0	501	2172	502	269	227	38	9	18	41	183	1	352	32	4	30	32	.484	2	0	4.08

Benny Lowe

Pitches: Left **Bats:** Left **Pos:** RP-37 **Ht:** 5'10" **Wt:** 185 **Born:** 6/13/74 **Age:** 27

Year Team	Lg Org	G	GS	CG	GF	IP	BFP	H	R	ER	HR	SH	SF	HB	TBB	IBB	SO	WP	Bk	W	L	Pct.	ShO	Sv	ERA
1994 Blue Jays	R Tor	22	1	0	5	22.1	104	20	16	11	0	4	0	2	14	1	27	1	1	2	1	.667	0	1	4.43
1995 St.Cathrnes	A- Tor	15	15	0	0	78.2	358	89	43	38	3	3	3	9	40	0	61	10	1	4	5	.444	0	0	4.35
1996 Hagerstown	A Tor	46	1	0	34	65.2	289	40	24	17	2	2	1	7	52	0	89	2	0	2	3	.400	0	9	2.33
1997 Knoxville	AA Tor	18	0	0	8	26	124	33	21	16	6	1	1	4	14	1	29	2	2	3	1	.750	0	0	5.54
Dunedin	A+ Tor	13	0	0	13	14.2	57	7	3	3	0	0	1	1	3	0	19	1	0	2	1	.667	0	5	1.84
Hagerstown	A Tor	2	0	0	2	2	10	3	3	0	0	0	0	0	0	0	4	0	0	0	0	—	0	0	0.00
1998 Dunedin	A+ Tor	9	0	0	2	9.1	46	8	5	2	0	1	1	2	6	0	13	1	0	0	0	—	0	0	1.93
1999 Knoxville	AA Tor	58	0	0	19	68.1	309	68	44	39	8	6	4	3	40	0	70	7	0	4	6	.400	0	3	5.14
2000 Lakeland	A+ Det	20	0	0	19	19	78	11	6	5	1	1	0	0	10	0	17	0	0	0	2	.000	0	11	2.37
Jacksnville	AA Det	17	0	0	4	23.1	117	28	21	21	3	2	0	1	17	1	25	5	0	0	0	—	0	0	8.10
7 Min. YEARS		220	17	0	106	329.1	1492	307	186	152	23	20	11	27	196	3	354	29	4	17	19	.472	0	29	4.15

Brian Loyd

Bats: Right **Throws:** Right **Pos:** C-56; DH-18; PH-8; 1B-1 **Ht:** 6'2" **Wt:** 210 **Born:** 12/3/73 **Age:** 27

Year Team	Lg Org	G	AB	H	2B	3B	HR	TB	R	RBI	TBB	IBB	SO	HBP	SH	SF	SB	CS	SB%	GDP	Avg	OBP	SLG
1996 Clinton	A SD	10	37	11	2	0	0	13	3	2	0	0	6	2	0	0	0	0	—	0	.297	.333	.351
1997 Clinton	A SD	73	259	71	10	0	2	87	35	33	25	2	41	8	4	5	6	4	.60	12	.274	.350	.336
1998 Rancho Cuca	A+ SD	87	318	97	19	1	4	130	55	35	42	1	45	10	2	1	1	4	.20	8	.305	.401	.409
Dunedin	A+ Tor	16	49	10	0	0	1	13	8	5	5	0	10	1	1	2	1	0	1.00	3	.204	.281	.265
1999 Knoxville	AA Tor	104	364	102	18	1	11	155	53	65	46	3	57	4	4	6	9	2	.82	11	.280	.362	.426
2000 Tennessee	AA Tor	58	194	58	10	1	1	73	21	23	29	1	22	2	0	2	7	3	.70	6	.299	.392	.376
Syracuse	AAA Tor	22	52	7	0	0	1	10	2	4	3	0	9	1	0	1	0	2	.00	2	.135	.193	.192
5 Min. YEARS		370	1273	356	59	3	20	481	177	167	150	7	190	28	11	18	24	15	.62	42	.280	.364	.378

Matt Lubozynski

Pitches: Left **Bats:** Right **Pos:** RP-12; SP-11 **Ht:** 6'3" **Wt:** 180 **Born:** 11/9/76 **Age:** 24

Year Team	Lg Org	G	GS	CG	GF	IP	BFP	H	R	ER	HR	SH	SF	HB	TBB	IBB	SO	WP	Bk	W	L	Pct.	ShO	Sv	ERA
1998 Boise	A- Ana	9	0	0	2	27.2	103	17	5	5	1	1	1	0	7	0	21	2	0	2	1	.667	0	1	1.63
Cedar Rapds	A Ana	19	0	0	6	21.1	80	17	10	6	6	0	0	1	5	0	12	0	0	2	0	1.000	0	1	2.53
1999 Lk Elsinore	A+ Ana	30	0	0	15	39	164	35	12	10	1	2	0	0	17	2	18	4	1	1	1	.500	0	3	2.31
Edmonton	AAA Ana	1	0	0	1	2	8	1	0	0	0	0	0	0	1	0	1	0	0	0	0	—	0	0	0.00
2000 Erie	AA Ana	23	11	2	5	83	356	88	47	41	9	2	3	0	26	0	66	6	2	1	8	.111	0	0	4.45
3 Min. YEARS		82	11	2	29	173	711	158	74	62	17	5	4	1	56	2	118	12	3	6	10	.375	0	5	3.23

165

Lou Lucca

Bats: Right **Throws:** Right **Pos:** 3B-117; 1B-3; 2B-2; PH-2; SS-1; DH-1　　**Ht:** 5'11" **Wt:** 210 **Born:** 10/13/70 **Age:** 30

Year Team	Lg Org	G	AB	H	2B	3B	HR	TB	R	RBI	TBB	IBB	SO	HBP	SH	SF	SB	CS	SB%	GDP	Avg	OBP	SLG
1992 Erie	A- Fla	76	263	74	16	1	13	131	51	44	33	0	40	5	0	2	6	3	.67	8	.281	.370	.498
1993 Kane County	A Fla	127	419	116	25	2	6	163	52	53	60	0	58	9	2	7	4	10	.29	9	.277	.374	.389
1994 Brevard Cty	A+ Fla	130	441	125	29	1	8	180	62	76	72	2	73	4	0	6	3	7	.30	18	.283	.384	.408
1995 Portland	AA Fla	112	388	107	28	1	9	164	57	64	59	5	77	5	0	2	4	4	.50	18	.276	.377	.423
1996 Charlotte	AAA Fla	87	273	71	14	1	7	108	26	35	11	0	62	4	0	3	0	3	.00	11	.260	.296	.396
1997 Charlotte	AAA Fla	96	292	83	22	1	18	161	40	51	22	4	56	2	0	3	5	4	.56	7	.284	.335	.551
1998 Charlotte	AAA Fla	112	397	115	32	0	11	180	47	51	13	2	75	5	0	2	2	6	.25	10	.290	.319	.453
1999 Scranton-WB	AAA Phi	136	533	143	33	2	12	216	61	70	22	0	94	9	0	5	4	6	.40	15	.268	.306	.405
2000 Memphis	AAA StL	122	462	131	31	2	14	208	70	70	32	3	61	9	2	3	7	4	.64	10	.284	.340	.450
9 Min. YEARS		998	3468	965	230	11	98	1511	466	514	324	16	596	52	4	33	35	47	.43	106	.278	.346	.436

Brian Luderer

Bats: Right **Throws:** Right **Pos:** C-54; DH-18; PH-4　　**Ht:** 5'11" **Wt:** 195 **Born:** 8/19/78 **Age:** 22

Year Team	Lg Org	G	AB	H	2B	3B	HR	TB	R	RBI	TBB	IBB	SO	HBP	SH	SF	SB	CS	SB%	GDP	Avg	OBP	SLG
1996 Athletics	R Oak	6	13	4	0	0	0	4	1	2	0	0	1	0	1	0	0	0	—	0	.308	.308	.308
1997 Athletics	R Oak	39	123	33	4	0	3	46	21	26	17	0	12	6	1	1	3	4	.43	6	.268	.381	.374
1998 Modesto	A+ Oak	19	45	6	2	2	0	12	3	3	4	0	6	0	2	0	0	0	—	0	.133	.204	.267
Sou Oregon	A- Oak	10	37	11	2	1	2	21	9	7	2	0	7	0	0	0	0	0	—	0	.297	.333	.568
Huntsville	AA Oak	17	38	11	1	1	0	14	4	5	3	0	7	1	1	0	0	0	—	1	.289	.357	.368
1999 Vancouver	AAA Oak	10	28	9	1	0	0	10	6	4	4	0	2	1	0	0	0	0	—	0	.321	.424	.357
Modesto	A+ Oak	55	182	52	13	2	1	72	22	22	16	1	25	2	2	2	3	3	.50	5	.286	.347	.396
2000 Modesto	A+ Oak	40	136	41	2	0	4	55	22	23	22	0	22	3	2	1	1	1	.50	4	.301	.407	.404
Midland	AA Oak	33	108	34	6	0	4	52	18	16	15	0	11	0	0	0	1	0	.00	4	.315	.389	.481
5 Min. YEARS		229	710	201	31	6	14	286	106	108	83	1	93	13	9	7	7	9	.44	20	.283	.365	.403

Eric Ludwick

Pitches: Right **Bats:** Right **Pos:** SP-11; RP-1　　**Ht:** 6'5" **Wt:** 210 **Born:** 12/14/71 **Age:** 29

Year Team	Lg Org	G	GS	CG	GF	IP	BFP	H	R	ER	HR	SH	SF	HB	TBB	IBB	SO	WP	Bk	W	L	Pct.	ShO	Sv	ERA
1993 Pittsfield	A- NYM	10	10	1	0	51	219	51	27	18	0	3	1	0	18	0	40	4	2	4	4	.500	0	0	3.18
1994 St. Lucie	A+ NYM	27	27	3	0	150.1	671	162	102	76	6	1	12	6	77	1	77	3	5	7	13	.350	0	0	4.55
1995 Binghamton	AA NYM	23	22	3	0	143.1	590	108	52	47	9	4	6	2	68	1	131	6	0	12	5	.706	2	0	2.95
Norfolk	AAA NYM	4	3	0	0	20	88	22	15	13	3	0	0	1	7	0	9	1	1	1	1	.500	0	0	5.85
1996 Louisville	AAA StL	11	11	0	0	60.1	253	55	24	19	4	2	1	1	24	2	73	2	0	3	4	.429	0	0	2.83
1997 Louisville	AAA StL	24	11	1	12	80	325	67	31	26	7	1	1	4	26	0	85	4	0	6	8	.429	0	4	2.93
Edmonton	AAA Oak	6	3	0	0	19	84	22	7	7	1	1	1	1	4	0	20	2	0	1	1	.500	0	0	3.32
1998 Charlotte	AAA Fla	8	8	0	0	26.2	118	25	17	11	1	1	0	1	13	0	26	3	0	1	3	.250	0	0	3.71
1999 Calgary	AAA Fla	48	0	0	44	58.1	270	65	33	25	5	3	1	2	36	4	61	1	0	11	6	.647	0	14	3.86
2000 Indianapols	AAA Mil	12	11	0	0	64.1	276	55	26	20	3	5	1	3	32	1	52	4	0	6	3	.667	0	0	2.80
1996 St. Louis	NL	6	1	0	2	10	45	11	11	10	4	0	1	1	3	0	12	0	0	0	0	.000	0	0	9.00
1997 St. Louis	NL	5	0	0	3	6.2	36	12	7	7	1	0	0	0	6	0	7	0	0	0	1	.000	0	0	9.45
Oakland	AL	6	5	0	0	24	116	32	24	22	7	2	0	1	16	1	14	0	0	1	4	.200	0	0	8.25
1998 Florida	NL	13	6	0	0	32.2	159	46	31	27	7	2	2	0	17	1	27	2	0	1	4	.200	0	0	7.44
1999 Toronto	AL	1	0	0	0	1	8	3	3	3	0	0	0	0	2	0	0	0	0	0	0	—	0	0	27.00
8 Min. YEARS		173	106	8	56	673.1	2894	632	334	262	39	21	25	21	305	9	574	30	7	52	48	.520	2	18	3.50
4 Maj. YEARS		31	12	0	5	74.1	364	104	76	69	19	4	3	2	44	2	60	2	0	2	10	.167	0	0	8.35

Mark Lukasiewicz

Pitches: Left **Bats:** Left **Pos:** RP-45　　**Ht:** 6'5" **Wt:** 230 **Born:** 3/8/73 **Age:** 28

Year Team	Lg Org	G	GS	CG	GF	IP	BFP	H	R	ER	HR	SH	SF	HB	TBB	IBB	SO	WP	Bk	W	L	Pct.	ShO	Sv	ERA
1994 Hagerstown	A Tor	29	17	0	5	98	449	108	70	52	8	6	4	7	51	0	84	8	0	3	6	.333	0	0	4.78
1995 Dunedin	A+ Tor	31	13	0	11	88.1	383	80	62	55	13	1	2	4	42	0	71	7	0	3	6	.333	0	1	5.60
1996 Dunedin	A+ Tor	23	0	0	5	31.1	144	28	20	16	1	1	1	4	22	1	31	1	0	2	1	.667	0	1	4.60
Bakersfield	A+ Tor	7	0	0	3	12.2	66	17	14	13	2	1	0	1	11	0	9	1	0	0	2	.000	0	0	9.24
Hagerstown	A Tor	9	1	0	4	15.2	63	8	5	4	0	0	0	1	7	0	20	1	0	2	0	1.000	0	0	2.30
1997 Knoxville	AA Tor	27	0	0	8	37	149	26	17	15	1	1	1	1	14	1	43	4	0	2	0	1.000	0	7	3.65
Syracuse	AAA Tor	30	0	0	9	31.1	146	37	22	18	7	1	2	2	13	1	31	1	0	2	3	.400	0	0	5.17
1998 Dunedin	A+ Tor	9	0	0	1	10.2	42	7	2	1	0	0	1	0	4	0	8	0	0	1	1	.500	0	0	0.84
Knoxville	AA Tor	5	0	0	2	9.1	33	6	2	2	0	0	0	0	1	0	16	0	0	0	0	—	0	1	1.93
Syracuse	AAA Tor	22	4	0	3	47.2	201	38	18	18	8	0	0	3	24	1	30	3	0	2	2	.500	0	1	3.40
1999 Syracuse	AAA Tor	37	9	1	6	97.2	431	109	59	58	20	1	2	0	40	1	77	5	1	4	4	.500	0	3	5.34
2000 Tennessee	AA Tor	3	0	0	1	4.2	22	4	3	3	1	0	0	0	4	0	6	0	0	0	0	—	0	0	5.79
Syracuse	AAA Tor	42	0	0	12	41.1	176	34	17	16	7	2	0	2	25	1	52	3	0	2	1	.667	0	0	3.48
7 Min. YEARS		274	44	1	70	525.2	2305	502	311	271	69	14	13	26	258	6	478	34	1	23	26	.469	0	14	4.64

Spike Lundberg

Pitches: Right **Bats:** Both **Pos:** RP-27; SP-13　　**Ht:** 6'1" **Wt:** 185 **Born:** 5/4/77 **Age:** 24

Year Team	Lg Org	G	GS	CG	GF	IP	BFP	H	R	ER	HR	SH	SF	HB	TBB	IBB	SO	WP	Bk	W	L	Pct.	ShO	Sv	ERA
1997 Rangers	R Tex	14	1	0	11	32.1	115	13	4	3	1	0	1	0	11	0	32	0	1	1	1	.500	0	5	0.84
1998 Savannah	A Tex	50	0	0	43	87.2	396	105	69	54	9	7	2	7	27	1	70	5	1	6	9	.400	0	14	5.54
1999 Charlotte	A+ Tex	30	21	4	1	156	656	162	63	49	4	2	6	9	44	1	81	4	4	14	7	.667	1	0	2.83
2000 Tulsa	AA Tex	40	13	0	16	150.2	637	148	61	51	9	5	5	8	54	4	102	5	1	14	7	.667	0	4	3.05
4 Min. YEARS		134	35	4	71	426.2	1804	428	197	157	23	14	14	24	136	6	285	14	7	35	24	.593	1	23	3.31

Manny Lutz

Bats: Left Throws: Right Pos: DH-24; 1B-21; OF-16; 3B-6; PH-6; 2B-2; P-1   Ht: 6'2" Wt: 230 Born: 6/14/76 Age: 25

Year Team	Lg Org	G	AB	H	2B	3B	HR	TB	R	RBI	TBB	IBB	SO	HBP	SH	SF	SB	CS	SB%	GDP	Avg	OBP	SLG
1995 White Sox	R CWS	46	160	45	10	3	3	70	23	31	19	2	42	2	0	2	0	0	—	3	.281	.361	.438
1996 Hickory	A CWS	44	143	34	2	0	1	39	10	12	9	2	46	3	1	3	0	1	.00	3	.238	.291	.273
Bristol	R+ CWS	55	202	51	12	1	6	83	26	23	17	3	53	2	2	1	5	1	.83	3	.252	.315	.411
1997 Bristol	R+ CWS	65	249	81	11	3	13	137	50	61	19	0	71	4	0	3	6	3	.67	3	.325	.378	.550
1998 Bristol	R+ CWS	65	279	85	21	0	17	157	52	58	14	2	56	4	1	0	2	1	.67	7	.305	.347	.563
1999 Lakeland	A+ Det	46	177	51	15	0	3	75	19	23	9	0	45	1	0	1	0	2	.00	6	.288	.324	.424
2000 W Michigan	A Det	12	44	14	2	0	1	19	8	7	6	2	9	1	0	0	0	0	—	2	.318	.412	.432
Lakeland	A+ Det	59	205	53	16	0	4	81	19	34	11	2	58	3	0	0	1	5	.17	3	.259	.306	.395
Jacksnville	AA Det	1	3	1	1	0	0	2	1	3	0	0	0	0	0	0	0	0	—	0	.333	.333	.667
6 Min. YEARS		393	1462	415	90	7	48	663	208	252	104	13	380	20	4	10	14	13	.52	30	.284	.338	.453

Scott Lydy

Bats: Right Throws: Right Pos: OF-103; DH-9; PR-3; 3B-2; PH-2   Ht: 6'5" Wt: 195 Born: 10/26/68 Age: 32

Year Team	Lg Org	G	AB	H	2B	3B	HR	TB	R	RBI	TBB	IBB	SO	HBP	SH	SF	SB	CS	SB%	GDP	Avg	OBP	SLG
1990 Madison	A Oak	54	174	33	6	2	4	55	33	19	25	1	62	1	0	2	7	5	.58	1	.190	.292	.316
Athletics	R Oak	18	50	17	6	0	2	29	8	11	10	0	14	0	0	0	0	0	—	1	.340	.450	.580
1991 Madison	A Oak	127	464	120	26	2	12	186	64	69	66	5	109	5	0	4	24	9	.73	10	.259	.354	.401
1992 Reno	A+ Oak	33	124	49	13	2	2	72	29	27	26	2	30	0	0	0	9	4	.69	1	.395	.500	.581
Huntsville	AA Oak	109	387	118	20	3	9	171	64	67	67	5	95	4	0	4	16	5	.76	1	.305	.409	.442
1993 Tacoma	AAA Oak	95	341	100	22	6	9	161	70	41	50	3	87	1	2	3	12	4	.75	8	.293	.382	.472
1994 Tacoma	AAA Oak	135	508	160	37	3	17	254	98	73	58	1	108	6	1	6	22	6	.79	14	.315	.388	.500
1995 Edmonton	AAA Oak	104	400	116	29	7	16	207	78	65	33	3	66	6	3	5	15	4	.79	11	.290	.349	.518
1998 Rochester	AAA Bal	20	66	9	5	0	1	17	3	8	4	0	15	1	0	1	1	0	1.00	5	.136	.194	.258
Winnipeg	IND —	3	10	1	1	0	0	2	1	2	1	0	7	1	0	0	0	0	—	0	.100	.250	.200
1999 Charlotte	AAA CWS	19	66	14	2	0	2	22	11	3	15	0	15	0	0	2	1	0	1.00	2	.212	.289	.333
Birmingham	AA CWS	111	400	106	25	1	20	193	74	65	67	3	61	3	1	1	18	3	.86	5	.265	.374	.483
2000 Charlotte	AAA CWS	116	368	100	15	4	14	165	66	45	69	3	70	8	0	3	15	2	.88	9	.272	.395	.448
1993 Oakland	AL	41	102	23	5	0	2	34	11	7	8	0	39	1	0	0	2	0	1.00	1	.225	.288	.333
9 Min. YEARS		944	3358	943	207	30	108	1534	599	503	484	26	739	36	7	31	140	42	.77	68	.281	.374	.457

Jim Lynch

Pitches: Right Bats: Right Pos: SP-20   Ht: 6'1" Wt: 200 Born: 12/12/75 Age: 25

Year Team	Lg Org	G	GS	CG	GF	IP	BFP	H	R	ER	HR	SH	SF	HB	TBB	IBB	SO	WP	Bk	W	L	Pct.	ShO	Sv	ERA
1994 Astros	R Hou	20	2	0	11	42.1	177	29	20	10	0	1	1	6	20	0	35	3	1	5	2	.714	0	5	2.13
1995 Astros	R Hou	17	1	0	12	34.2	148	14	12	6	1	0	0	4	26	0	49	10	2	2	1	.667	0	3	1.56
1996 Quad City	A Hou	31	1	0	15	60.2	276	51	28	27	3	1	0	4	50	0	51	7	1	1	1	.500	0	1	4.01
1997 Quad City	A Hou	37	0	0	14	58.1	280	44	37	30	4	1	1	10	46	4	68	5	2	3	3	.500	0	1	4.63
1998 Quad City	A Hou	20	17	0	1	101	438	80	47	38	4	2	4	13	58	1	97	9	2	8	6	.571	0	0	3.39
Kissimmee	A+ Hou	9	9	1	0	55	227	36	22	18	4	0	5	6	28	0	40	2	2	5	2	.714	1	0	2.95
1999 Kissimmee	A+ Hou	28	21	3	2	129.2	588	131	82	71	14	4	5	10	61	2	99	12	0	3	14	.176	0	0	4.93
2000 Fresno	AAA SF	2	2	0	0	10	46	9	7	7	2	0	0	1	7	0	6	1	0	1	0	1.000	0	0	6.30
Bakersfield	A+ SF	18	18	0	0	100.1	422	74	36	32	3	1	4	1	56	0	109	8	1	6	4	.600	0	0	2.87
7 Min. YEARS		182	71	4	55	592	2602	468	291	239	35	10	20	51	352	7	554	57	11	34	33	.507	1	11	3.63

Curt Lyons

Pitches: Right Bats: Right Pos: SP-17; RP-1   Ht: 6'5" Wt: 240 Born: 10/17/74 Age: 26

Year Team	Lg Org	G	GS	CG	GF	IP	BFP	H	R	ER	HR	SH	SF	HB	TBB	IBB	SO	WP	Bk	W	L	Pct.	ShO	Sv	ERA
1992 Princeton	R+ Cin	11	11	0	0	55.1	240	61	36	17	2	1	2	4	17	0	33	6	1	5	3	.625	0	0	2.77
1993 Billings	R+ Cin	15	12	2	0	84	353	89	35	28	3	2	2	3	20	0	64	10	0	7	3	.700	0	0	3.00
1994 Chston-WV	A Cin	12	11	0	0	65.1	276	64	30	28	2	1	1	8	22	0	55	12	0	3	6	.333	0	0	3.86
Princeton	R+ Cin	4	4	0	0	27.1	104	16	9	6	0	1	0	2	2	0	28	2	0	1	1	.500	0	0	1.98
1995 Winston-Sal	A+ Cin	26	26	0	0	160.1	672	139	66	53	10	6	2	15	67	3	122	9	3	9	9	.500	0	0	2.98
1996 Chattanooga	AA Cin	24	24	1	0	141.2	577	113	48	38	8	4	1	10	52	0	176	6	0	13	4	.765	0	0	2.41
1997 Iowa	AAA ChC	8	8	0	0	29.2	145	35	23	21	4	0	0	4	21	0	26	2	0	0	2	.000	0	0	6.37
Orlando	AA ChC	2	2	0	0	6	26	6	5	5	0	0	1	2	2	0	8	1	0	0	0	—	0	0	7.50
1998 Chattanooga	AA Cin	3	3	0	0	7	35	6	7	7	0	0	0	1	8	0	10	0	0	0	1	.000	0	0	9.00
1999 Yankees	R NYY	1	0	0	0	2	9	1	0	0	1	0	0	0	2	0	0	0	0	0	0	—	0	0	0.00
2000 Atlantic Ct	IND —	11	10	0	1	58.2	250	41	21	19	4	0	0	5	40	0	75	2	0	2	4	.333	0	0	2.91
Akron	AA Cle	3	3	0	0	15	68	15	9	9	1	0	0	2	8	0	20	1	0	2	1	.667	0	0	5.40
Yuma	IND —	4	4	0	0	19	71	8	7	5	1	0	2	1	0	0	23	1	0	1	0	1.000	0	0	2.37
1996 Cincinnati	NL	3	3	0	0	16	70	17	8	8	1	0	0	1	7	0	14	0	0	1	0	1.000	0	0	4.50
9 Min. YEARS		124	118	3	1	671.1	2826	594	296	236	41	13	9	57	266	3	643	52	4	43	34	.558	0	0	3.16

Mike MacDougal

Pitches: Right Bats: Both Pos: SP-27; RP-1   Ht: 6'4" Wt: 195 Born: 3/5/77 Age: 24

Year Team	Lg Org	G	GS	CG	GF	IP	BFP	H	R	ER	HR	SH	SF	HB	TBB	IBB	SO	WP	Bk	W	L	Pct.	ShO	Sv	ERA
1999 Spokane	A- KC	11	11	0	0	46.1	196	43	25	23	3	1	1	6	17	0	57	8	1	2	2	.500	0	0	4.47
2000 Wilmington	A+ KC	26	25	0	1	144.2	620	115	79	63	5	5	1	14	76	0	129	21	4	9	7	.563	0	1	3.92
Wichita	AA KC	2	2	0	0	11.2	54	16	10	10	0	0	1	1	7	0	9	1	0	0	1	.000	0	0	7.71
2 Min. YEARS		39	38	0	1	202.2	870	174	114	96	8	6	3	21	100	0	195	30	5	11	10	.524	0	1	4.26

Anderson Machado

Bats: Both **Throws:** Right **Pos:** SS-120   **Ht:** 5'11" **Wt:** 165 **Born:** 1/25/81 **Age:** 20

Year Team	Lg Org	G	AB	H	2B	3B	HR	TB	R	RBI	TBB	IBB	SO	HBP	SH	SF	SB	CS	SB%	GDP	Avg	OBP	SLG
1999 Clearwater	A+ Phi	1	2	0	0	0	0	0	0	0	0	0	1	0	0	0	0	0	—	0	.000	.000	.000
Phillies	R Phi	43	143	37	6	3	2	55	26	12	15	1	38	2	7	1	6	3	.67	5	.259	.335	.385
Piedmont	A Phi	20	60	14	4	2	0	22	7	7	7	0	20	1	1	0	2	1	.67	0	.233	.324	.367
2000 Clearwater	A+ Phi	117	417	102	19	7	1	138	55	35	54	0	103	0	5	2	32	18	.64	7	.245	.330	.331
Reading	AA Phi	3	11	4	1	0	1	8	2	2	0	0	4	0	0	0	0	0	—	0	.364	.364	.727
2 Min. YEARS		184	633	157	30	12	4	223	90	56	76	1	166	3	13	3	40	22	.65	12	.248	.330	.352

Richard Mackiewitz

Bats: Left **Throws:** Left **Pos:** 1B-78; PH-1   **Ht:** 6'2" **Wt:** 217 **Born:** 6/6/76 **Age:** 25

Year Team	Lg Org	G	AB	H	2B	3B	HR	TB	R	RBI	TBB	IBB	SO	HBP	SH	SF	SB	CS	SB%	GDP	Avg	OBP	SLG
1998 Ogden	R+ Mil	65	251	74	15	1	2	97	45	45	27	0	37	6	2	3	3	2	.60	4	.295	.373	.386
1999 Erie	A Mil	102	355	93	19	1	8	138	44	57	28	2	57	3	2	3	1	0	1.00	9	.262	.319	.389
2000 Albany-Col	IND —	69	259	71	23	0	4	106	30	24	22	3	52	1	2	1	1	0	1.00	8	.274	.332	.409
Carolina	AA Col	10	30	8	1	0	0	9	2	1	3	0	5	1	0	0	0	0	—	1	.267	.353	.300
3 Min. YEARS		246	895	246	58	2	14	350	121	131	80	5	151	11	6	7	5	2	.71	22	.275	.339	.391

Rob Mackowiak

Bats: Left **Throws:** Right **Pos:** 2B-71; OF-39; 3B-23; SS-2; DH-2; PH-1; PR-1   **Ht:** 5'10" **Wt:** 166 **Born:** 6/20/76 **Age:** 25

Year Team	Lg Org	G	AB	H	2B	3B	HR	TB	R	RBI	TBB	IBB	SO	HBP	SH	SF	SB	CS	SB%	GDP	Avg	OBP	SLG
1996 Pirates	R Pit	27	86	23	6	1	0	31	8	14	13	1	11	1	0	1	3	1	.75	3	.267	.366	.360
1997 Erie	A- Pit	61	203	58	14	2	1	79	26	25	21	0	47	7	3	1	1	7	.13	5	.286	.371	.389
1998 Augusta	A Pit	25	70	17	4	0	1	24	16	8	13	0	19	1	1	0	4	2	.67	2	.243	.369	.343
Lynchburg	A+ Pit	86	292	80	24	6	3	125	30	31	17	0	65	4	4	2	6	3	.67	4	.274	.321	.428
1999 Lynchburg	A+ Pit	74	263	80	7	4	7	116	51	30	18	0	57	6	4	0	9	4	.69	5	.304	.362	.441
Altoona	AA Pit	53	195	51	15	3	3	81	21	27	8	1	34	7	2	4	0	2	.00	6	.262	.308	.415
2000 Altoona	AA Pit	134	526	156	33	4	13	236	82	87	22	0	96	9	4	7	18	5	.78	8	.297	.332	.449
5 Min. YEARS		460	1635	465	103	20	28	692	234	222	112	2	329	35	18	15	41	24	.63	33	.284	.341	.423

Scott MacRae

Pitches: Right **Bats:** Right **Pos:** RP-55   **Ht:** 6'3" **Wt:** 205 **Born:** 8/13/74 **Age:** 26

		HOW MUCH HE PITCHED						WHAT HE GAVE UP											THE RESULTS					
Year Team	Lg Org	G	GS	CG	GF	IP	BFP	H	R	ER	HR	SH	SF	HB	TBB	IBB	SO	WP	Bk	W	L	Pct.	ShO	Sv	ERA
1995 Billings	R+ Cin	18	0	0	4	27	135	32	24	17	0	0	5	3	20	4	9	2	1	0	1	.000	0	1	5.67
1996 Chston-WV	A Cin	29	20	1	2	123.2	530	118	61	46	3	4	3	7	53	0	82	8	0	8	7	.533	0	0	3.35
1997 Burlington	A Cin	27	26	4	0	160.1	694	159	76	68	9	7	4	4	57	0	89	18	1	11	4	.733	1	0	3.82
1998 Chattanooga	AA Cin	49	5	0	6	113.2	492	105	70	56	5	3	2	3	56	2	67	10	0	9	4	.692	0	0	4.43
1999 Chattanooga	AA Cin	39	17	0	2	128.1	555	139	76	63	18	3	2	5	49	1	81	6	0	8	7	.533	0	0	4.42
2000 Chattanooga	AA Cin	55	0	0	17	77.2	339	75	32	31	4	8	1	5	40	9	61	4	0	4	1	.800	0	1	3.59
6 Min. YEARS		217	68	5	31	630.2	2745	628	339	281	39	25	17	32	275	16	389	48	2	40	24	.625	1	2	4.01

Bob Macrory

Bats: Right **Throws:** Right **Pos:** 2B-58; OF-1   **Ht:** 6'1" **Wt:** 165 **Born:** 2/18/75 **Age:** 26

Year Team	Lg Org	G	AB	H	2B	3B	HR	TB	R	RBI	TBB	IBB	SO	HBP	SH	SF	SB	CS	SB%	GDP	Avg	OBP	SLG
1997 New Jersey	A- StL	67	248	76	9	2	1	92	52	26	18	0	27	2	3	2	23	3	.88	3	.306	.356	.371
1998 Peoria	A StL	123	488	141	13	3	1	163	86	63	47	1	70	7	16	3	40	15	.73	10	.289	.358	.334
1999 Potomac	A+ StL	114	434	101	15	2	2	126	52	29	24	0	70	5	5	1	27	10	.73	8	.233	.280	.290
2000 Arkansas	AA StL	9	38	8	0	0	0	8	3	2	3	0	5	0	0	0	1	0	1.00	1	.211	.268	.211
Potomac	A+ StL	49	170	41	7	1	0	50	23	14	12	0	26	2	4	2	3	4	.43	10	.241	.296	.294
4 Min. YEARS		362	1378	367	44	8	4	439	216	134	104	1	198	16	28	8	94	32	.75	32	.266	.323	.319

Garry Maddox Jr.

Bats: Left **Throws:** Right **Pos:** OF-91; DH-6; PH-3; PR-2   **Ht:** 6'3" **Wt:** 180 **Born:** 10/24/74 **Age:** 26

Year Team	Lg Org	G	AB	H	2B	3B	HR	TB	R	RBI	TBB	IBB	SO	HBP	SH	SF	SB	CS	SB%	GDP	Avg	OBP	SLG
1997 High Desert	A+ Ari	101	409	125	22	12	7	192	89	44	52	2	94	0	3	0	25	8	.76	8	.306	.384	.469
1998 High Desert	A+ Ari	2	8	5	2	0	1	10	3	4	1	0	1	0	0	1	1	0	1.00	0	.625	.600	1.250
Jackson	AA Hou	25	94	33	3	2	3	49	20	14	5	0	20	0	0	0	3	2	.60	0	.351	.384	.521
Tucson	AAA Ari	81	269	71	13	4	4	104	36	18	15	0	57	3	0	1	4	3	.57	6	.264	.309	.387
1999 El Paso	AA Ari	127	492	145	35	9	15	243	80	75	31	2	106	8	1	4	22	5	.81	5	.295	.344	.494
2000 Trenton	AA Bos	100	363	100	13	3	4	131	58	40	36	0	87	2	2	2	7	5	.58	2	.275	.342	.361
4 Min. YEARS		436	1635	479	88	30	34	729	286	195	140	4	365	13	6	8	62	23	.73	21	.293	.352	.446

Kats Maeda

Pitches: Right **Bats:** Right **Pos:** RP-38; SP-2   **Ht:** 6'2" **Wt:** 215 **Born:** 6/23/71 **Age:** 30

		HOW MUCH HE PITCHED						WHAT HE GAVE UP											THE RESULTS					
Year Team	Lg Org	G	GS	CG	GF	IP	BFP	H	R	ER	HR	SH	SF	HB	TBB	IBB	SO	WP	Bk	W	L	Pct.	ShO	Sv	ERA
1996 Yankees	R NYY	2	2	1	0	9	35	4	3	3	1	0	1	1	2	0	7	0	0	1	1	.500	1	0	3.00
Tampa	A+ NYY	2	2	0	0	10.2	50	11	5	5	0	1	0	2	6	0	8	0	0	0	0		0	0	4.22
Norwich	AA NYY	9	9	1	0	53.1	221	49	25	24	4	1	2	1	21	0	30	4	0	3	2	.600	1	0	4.05
1997 Norwich	AA NYY	25	21	1	2	124.1	545	117	75	63	14	4	2	8	62	1	76	11	2	8	10	.444	1	0	4.56

168

Year Team	Lg Org		HOW MUCH HE PITCHED					WHAT HE GAVE UP												THE RESULTS					
		G	GS	CG	GF	IP	BFP	H	R	ER	HR	SH	SF	HB	TBB	IBB	SO	WP	Bk	W	L	Pct.	ShO	Sv	ERA
1998 Columbus	AAA NYY	13	0	0	9	14.1	62	13	5	4	1	1	0	0	8	1	16	2	0	0	1	.000	0	0	2.51
Norwich	AA NYY	28	0	0	10	37.1	186	44	36	32	4	1	0	0	31	2	27	5	0	1	3	.250	0	1	7.71
1999 Norwich	AA NYY	25	7	1	11	76.2	345	82	41	37	7	0	5	3	40	0	48	10	0	3	2	.600	0	1	4.34
2000 Norwich	AA NYY	39	2	0	19	50.2	235	44	31	27	1	2	3	3	44	1	54	7	0	2	2	.500	0	0	4.80
Columbus	AAA NYY	1	0	0	0	2	9	3	2	2	0	0	0	0	0	1	0	0	0	0	0	—	0	0	9.00
5 Min. YEARS		144	43	4	51	378.1	1688	367	223	197	34	10	14	18	214	5	267	39	2	18	21	.462	3	2	4.69

Ricky Magdaleno

Bats: Right Throws: Right Pos: SS-44; 1B-21; 2B-12; PH-10; 3B-8; OF-4; DH-2; C-1   Ht: 6'0" Wt: 185 Born: 7/6/74 Age: 26

Year Team	Lg Org		BATTING														BASERUNNING				PERCENTAGES		
		G	AB	H	2B	3B	HR	TB	R	RBI	TBB	IBB	SO	HBP	SH	SF	SB	CS	SB%	GDP	Avg	OBP	SLG
1993 Chston-WV	A Cin	131	447	107	15	4	3	139	49	25	37	0	103	1	6	1	8	8	.50	15	.239	.298	.311
1994 Winston-Sal	A+ Cin	127	437	114	22	2	13	179	52	49	49	1	80	0	2	4	7	9	.44	9	.261	.333	.410
1995 Chattanooga	AA Cin	11	40	7	2	0	1	12	2	2	4	0	13	0	0	0	0	0	—	3	.175	.250	.300
Winston-Sal	A+ Cin	91	309	69	13	1	7	105	30	40	15	0	69	2	3	3	3	1	.75	4	.223	.261	.340
Indianapolis	AAA Cin	4	8	1	0	0	1	4	1	1	0	0	3	0	1	0	0	0	—	0	.125	.125	.500
1996 Chattanooga	AA Cin	132	424	94	21	1	17	168	60	63	64	4	135	1	5	4	2	7	.22	8	.222	.323	.396
1997 Chattanooga	AA Cin	61	187	49	13	1	8	88	33	34	42	1	51	1	1	1	1	1	.50	11	.262	.398	.471
Indianapolis	AAA Cin	56	155	32	11	0	4	55	20	14	16	0	48	0	1	2	0	1	.00	4	.206	.277	.355
1998 Richmond	AAA Atl	73	249	73	11	1	5	101	32	29	23	1	63	0	1	2	1	3	.25	3	.293	.350	.406
1999 Charlotte	AAA CWS	27	81	19	5	1	0	26	7	7	7	1	20	0	2	1	0	1	.00	0	.235	.292	.321
Lancaster	A+ Sea	23	89	31	4	2	1	42	12	14	11	0	12	1	0	2	2	1	.67	1	.348	.417	.472
New Haven	AA Sea	68	258	70	13	1	1	88	30	24	21	0	45	1	2	2	1	3	.25	6	.271	.326	.341
2000 Tacoma	AAA Sea	18	54	7	1	0	1	11	7	5	11	0	14	0	1	0	0	0	—	1	.130	.277	.204
Sonoma Cty	IND —	25	92	30	3	0	3	42	21	12	22	0	18	0	1	0	3	5	.38	2	.326	.456	.457
Mobile	AA SD	57	144	29	7	1	2	44	14	12	31	0	23	0	3	0	1	1	.50	3	.201	.343	.306
8 Min. YEARS		904	2974	732	141	15	67	1104	370	331	353	8	697	7	29	22	29	41	.41	70	.246	.325	.371

Chris Magruder

Bats: Both Throws: Right Pos: OF-132; PH-3; DH-1   Ht: 5'11" Wt: 200 Born: 4/26/77 Age: 24

Year Team	Lg Org		BATTING														BASERUNNING				PERCENTAGES		
		G	AB	H	2B	3B	HR	TB	R	RBI	TBB	IBB	SO	HBP	SH	SF	SB	CS	SB%	GDP	Avg	OBP	SLG
1998 Bakersfield	A+ SF	22	92	28	7	0	1	38	21	4	13	1	16	0	0	0	3	0	1.00	2	.304	.390	.413
Salem-Keizr	A- SF	47	177	59	8	5	3	86	43	18	37	1	21	8	2	2	14	7	.67	2	.333	.464	.486
1999 Shreveport	AA SF	133	476	122	21	4	6	169	78	60	69	4	85	8	2	3	17	12	.59	15	.256	.358	.355
2000 Shreveport	AA SF	134	496	140	33	3	4	191	85	39	67	2	75	8	6	3	18	10	.64	11	.282	.375	.385
3 Min. YEARS		336	1241	349	69	12	14	484	227	121	186	8	197	24	10	8	52	29	.64	30	.281	.383	.390

Alan Mahaffey

Pitches: Left Bats: Left Pos: RP-19; SP-15   Ht: 6'1" Wt: 199 Born: 2/2/74 Age: 27

Year Team	Lg Org		HOW MUCH HE PITCHED						WHAT HE GAVE UP												THE RESULTS					
		G	GS	CG	GF	IP	BFP	H	R	ER	HR	SH	SF	HB	TBB	IBB	SO	WP	Bk	W	L	Pct.	ShO	Sv	ERA
1995 Elizabethtn	R+ Min	13	12	1	0	70	308	66	42	27	4	6	2	3	21	0	73	4	8	5	6	.455	0	0	3.47
1996 Fort Wayne	A Min	30	19	2	1	126.1	545	139	84	68	13	8	4	2	35	1	75	4	7	7	10	.412	0	0	4.84
1997 Fort Myers	A+ Min	38	0	0	11	48.1	200	46	27	22	2	3	2	1	8	0	55	1	0	1	2	.333	0	1	4.10
New Britain	AA Min	13	1	0	5	22.2	98	19	11	9	2	1	3	0	10	0	29	4	0	1	2	.333	0	1	3.57
1998 New Britain	AA Min	34	1	0	13	52.1	236	62	27	26	6	3	1	0	17	1	61	0	0	2	3	.400	0	0	4.47
1999 Salt Lake	AAA Min	7	5	0	0	21.1	106	28	17	13	1	1	0	1	15	1	11	1	1	1	2	.333	0	0	5.48
New Britain	AA Min	33	12	1	7	98.1	435	109	47	45	15	3	5	6	34	0	89	3	8	8	6	.571	0	1	4.12
2000 Salt Lake	AAA Min	34	15	0	5	102	449	118	62	60	16	2	4	3	40	0	74	2	3	7	3	.700	0	2	5.29
6 Min. YEARS		202	65	4	42	541.1	2377	587	317	270	59	27	23	17	180	3	467	19	21	32	34	.485	0	5	4.49

T.J. Maier

Bats: Right Throws: Right Pos: 2B-91; SS-9; DH-4; PH-4; PR-3   Ht: 6'0" Wt: 180 Born: 2/24/75 Age: 26

Year Team	Lg Org		BATTING														BASERUNNING				PERCENTAGES		
		G	AB	H	2B	3B	HR	TB	R	RBI	TBB	IBB	SO	HBP	SH	SF	SB	CS	SB%	GDP	Avg	OBP	SLG
1997 New Jersey	A- StL	50	155	33	9	1	2	50	19	22	20	0	30	2	1	1	6	2	.75	2	.213	.309	.323
1998 Peoria	A StL	84	271	73	14	1	2	95	47	28	45	0	52	6	4	1	6	5	.55	5	.269	.384	.351
1999 Potomac	A+ StL	102	353	93	15	0	2	114	53	38	55	0	61	3	0	4	12	7	.63	6	.263	.364	.323
2000 Arkansas	AA StL	110	364	107	16	3	6	147	59	42	49	1	42	6	1	2	13	7	.65	7	.294	.385	.404
4 Min. YEARS		346	1143	306	54	5	12	406	178	130	169	1	185	17	6	8	37	21	.64	20	.268	.368	.355

Jaime Malave

Bats: Right Throws: Right Pos: C-38; DH-24; PH-15; 1B-6; 3B-1   Ht: 6'0" Wt: 196 Born: 3/22/75 Age: 26

Year Team	Lg Org		BATTING														BASERUNNING				PERCENTAGES		
		G	AB	H	2B	3B	HR	TB	R	RBI	TBB	IBB	SO	HBP	SH	SF	SB	CS	SB%	GDP	Avg	OBP	SLG
1995 Yakima	A- LA	44	137	37	13	2	1	57	12	15	6	0	41	1	1	2	1	1	.50	1	.270	.301	.416
1996 Savannah	A LA	6	16	4	0	0	0	4	2	5	0	0	3	0	0	0	0	0	—	1	.250	.278	.250
Yakima	A- LA	40	108	22	6	0	5	43	14	16	6	0	33	0	1	0	0	0	—	2	.204	.246	.398
1997 Savannah	A LA	58	206	52	11	1	9	92	23	32	4	0	54	1	1	1	2	1	.67	2	.252	.269	.447
San Berndno	A+ LA	1	4	1	0	0	0	1	0	0	0	0	0	0	0	0	0	0	—	0	.250	.250	.250
1998 Vero Beach	A+ LA	28	89	24	6	1	4	44	12	9	10	0	16	0	0	0	1	0	1.00	1	.270	.343	.494
San Antonio	AA LA	28	55	14	5	0	1	22	3	4	6	1	10	0	2	0	0	0	—	2	.255	.328	.400
1999 Waterbury	IND —	19	72	19	2	0	3	30	12	9	10	0	17	1	0	0	0	0	—	1	.264	.361	.417
Jupiter	A+ Mon	3	10	4	2	0	0	6	2	2	2	0	1	0	0	0	0	0	—	1	.400	.462	.600
Ottawa	AAA Mon	3	8	2	0	0	0	2	0	1	0	0	4	0	0	0	0	0	—	0	.250	.333	.250
Harrisburg	AA Mon	12	18	4	0	0	3	13	4	4	0	0	6	0	0	0	0	0	—	0	.222	.222	.722
2000 Ottawa	AAA Mon	1	3	2	0	0	0	2	0	0	0	0	0	0	0	0	0	0	—	0	.667	.667	.667
Harrisburg	AA Mon	77	192	49	13	0	13	101	26	36	17	1	63	3	0	3	0	0	—	2	.255	.321	.526
6 Min. YEARS		320	918	234	58	4	39	417	112	132	64	2	246	6	6	8	4	2	.67	13	.255	.306	.454

Carlos Maldonado

Bats: Right Throws: Right Pos: C-116; PH-2   Ht: 6'2" Wt: 185 Born: 1/3/79 Age: 22

Year Team	Lg Org	G	AB	H	2B	3B	HR	TB	R	RBI	TBB	IBB	SO	HBP	SH	SF	SB	CS	SB%	GDP	Avg	OBP	SLG
1996 Mariners	R Sea	29	100	22	0	0	2	28	10	18	6	0	10	1	1	4	0	1	.00	7	.220	.261	.280
1997 Wisconsin	A Sea	97	316	60	8	2	0	72	15	25	17	1	33	3	8	3	2	3	.40	8	.190	.236	.228
1998 Wisconsin	A Sea	7	23	4	0	0	0	4	4	1	2	0	1	0	0	0	0	0	—	1	.174	.240	.174
Tacoma	AAA Sea	3	9	0	0	0	0	0	0	0	0	0	1	0	0	0	0	0	—	0	.000	.000	.000
Everett	A- Sea	42	150	43	10	0	5	68	19	24	10	0	17	2	0	2	1	0	1.00	5	.287	.335	.453
1999 Wisconsin	A Sea	92	302	93	13	0	0	106	35	33	43	1	32	0	2	2	4	6	.40	10	.308	.392	.351
2000 Round Rock	AA Hou	116	423	114	24	2	5	157	46	52	35	3	71	5	5	6	5	4	.56	15	.270	.328	.371
5 Min. YEARS		386	1323	336	55	4	12	435	129	153	113	5	165	11	16	17	12	14	.46	46	.254	.314	.329

Will Malerich

Pitches: Left Bats: Left Pos: RP-39; SP-1   Ht: 5'10" Wt: 180 Born: 10/25/75 Age: 25

Year Team	Lg Org	G	GS	CG	GF	IP	BFP	H	R	ER	HR	SH	SF	HB	TBB	IBB	SO	WP	Bk	W	L	Pct.	ShO	Sv	ERA
1997 Salem-Keizr	A- SF	21	0	0	5	26.2	116	26	14	9	1	2	1	3	21	1	43	4	0	2	1	.667	0	0	3.04
1998 Bakersfield	A+ SF	26	0	0	5	42	184	36	22	22	3	2	1	7	25	1	35	4	0	1	1	.500	0	1	4.71
San Jose	A+ SF	20	0	0	10	32.1	140	28	14	8	1	2	2	4	14	1	24	0	0	2	2	.500	0	2	2.23
1999 San Jose	A+ SF	45	0	0	14	72.2	338	95	43	36	5	3	2	4	38	1	59	3	0	5	4	.556	0	1	4.46
2000 Shreveport	AA SF	4	0	0	3	4.2	30	12	9	9	2	0	0	1	3	0	4	0	0	0	1	.000	0	0	17.36
Bakersfield	A+ SF	36	1	0	8	56.2	258	64	33	25	4	1	1	4	31	0	49	2	1	2	1	.667	0	0	3.97
4 Min. YEARS		152	1	0	45	235	1080	261	135	109	17	10	6	23	132	4	214	13	1	12	10	.545	0	4	4.17

Bryan Malko

Pitches: Right Bats: Right Pos: RP-34; SP-3   Ht: 6'3" Wt: 215 Born: 1/23/77 Age: 24

Year Team	Lg Org	G	GS	CG	GF	IP	BFP	H	R	ER	HR	SH	SF	HB	TBB	IBB	SO	WP	Bk	W	L	Pct.	ShO	Sv	ERA
1995 Twins	R Min	10	4	0	3	33	142	23	14	10	1	3	1	4	23	0	29	5	0	1	2	.333	0	1	2.73
1996 Elizabethtn	R+ Min	12	12	1	0	66.2	288	73	36	34	5	1	3	4	27	0	54	5	0	5	3	.625	0	0	4.59
1997 Fort Wayne	A Min	14	13	0	1	64.1	271	68	29	27	2	1	4	2	22	0	59	3	1	4	4	.500	0	0	3.78
1998 Fort Wayne	A Min	22	11	0	1	74.2	324	72	38	33	1	3	1	2	30	0	53	6	0	8	3	.727	0	0	3.98
Fort Myers	A+ Min	7	0	0	3	13	67	19	14	10	0	1	0	1	9	0	5	3	0	0	1	.000	0	2	6.92
1999 Fort Myers	A+ Min	30	18	2	4	110.1	492	120	60	55	8	2	3	9	48	0	102	5	0	7	9	.438	1	1	4.49
2000 Fort Myers	A+ Min	19	0	0	13	27	106	16	10	8	0	0	1	1	12	1	26	0	0	2	1	.667	0	2	2.67
New Britain	AA Min	18	3	0	5	36	151	34	14	13	5	0	1	1	14	0	28	5	0	3	2	.600	0	1	3.25
6 Min. YEARS		132	61	3	30	425	1841	425	215	190	22	11	14	24	185	1	356	32	1	30	25	.545	1	7	4.02

Marty Malloy

Bats: Left Throws: Right Pos: 2B-34; SS-2; DH-2; PH-1   Ht: 5'10" Wt: 165 Born: 7/6/72 Age: 28

Year Team	Lg Org	G	AB	H	2B	3B	HR	TB	R	RBI	TBB	IBB	SO	HBP	SH	SF	SB	CS	SB%	GDP	Avg	OBP	SLG
1992 Idaho Falls	R+ Atl	62	251	79	18	1	2	105	45	28	11	0	43	2	0	1	8	4	.67	2	.315	.347	.418
1993 Macon	A Atl	109	376	110	19	3	2	141	55	36	39	3	70	2	3	3	24	8	.75	4	.293	.360	.375
1994 Durham	A+ Atl	118	428	113	22	1	6	155	53	35	52	2	69	2	2	3	18	12	.60	9	.264	.344	.362
1995 Greenville	AA Atl	124	461	128	20	3	10	184	73	59	39	1	58	0	7	8	11	12	.48	6	.278	.329	.399
1996 Richmond	AAA Atl	18	64	13	2	1	0	17	7	8	5	1	7	0	2	1	3	0	1.00	1	.203	.257	.266
Greenville	AA Atl	111	429	134	27	2	4	177	82	36	54	6	50	4	6	2	11	10	.52	11	.312	.393	.413
1997 Richmond	AAA Atl	108	414	118	19	5	2	153	66	25	41	1	61	1	5	0	17	7	.71	6	.285	.351	.370
1998 Richmond	AAA Atl	124	483	140	25	3	7	192	75	54	51	2	65	5	5	4	20	7	.74	12	.290	.361	.398
1999 Richmond	AAA Atl	114	407	119	23	1	7	165	58	36	53	2	52	2	4	3	19	15	.56	2	.292	.374	.405
2000 Tigers	R Det	2	1	1	0	0	0	1	0	1	2	0	0	0	0	0	0	0	—	0	1.000	1.000	1.000
Lakeland	A+ Det	7	26	6	1	0	1	10	4	4	1	0	1	1	0	0	1	0	1.00	0	.231	.286	.385
Toledo	AAA Det	30	115	27	8	0	4	47	16	16	7	0	18	0	1	1	0	0	—	0	.235	.276	.409
1998 Atlanta	NL	11	28	5	1	0	1	9	3	1	2	0	2	0	0	0	0	0	—	0	.179	.233	.321
9 Min. YEARS		927	3455	988	184	20	45	1347	534	338	355	18	494	19	35	26	132	75	.64	53	.286	.353	.390

Sean Maloney

Pitches: Right Bats: Right Pos: RP-43   Ht: 6'7" Wt: 210 Born: 5/25/71 Age: 30

Year Team	Lg Org	G	GS	CG	GF	IP	BFP	H	R	ER	HR	SH	SF	HB	TBB	IBB	SO	WP	Bk	W	L	Pct.	ShO	Sv	ERA
1993 Helena	R+ Mil	17	3	1	10	47.2	209	55	31	23	2	3	2	2	11	1	35	3	0	2	2	.500	0	0	4.34
1994 Beloit	A Mil	51	0	0	41	59	272	73	42	36	3	2	5	4	10	5	53	6	1	2	6	.250	0	22	5.49
1995 El Paso	AA Mil	43	0	0	27	64.2	292	69	41	30	4	4	4	3	28	9	54	5	0	7	5	.583	0	15	4.18
1996 El Paso	AA Mil	51	0	0	49	56.2	230	49	11	9	1	2	1	1	12	1	57	6	1	3	2	.600	0	38	1.43
1997 Tucson	AAA Mil	15	0	0	10	18.2	82	24	10	10	3	5	0	0	3	3	21	1	0	0	2	.000	0	4	4.82
1998 Albuquerque	AAA LA	26	0	0	23	35	150	38	21	18	6	1	0	1	8	1	38	4	0	3	2	.600	0	9	4.63
1999 Orioles	R Bal	1	0	0	0	2	7	1	0	0	0	0	0	0	1	0	3	0	0	0	0	—	0	0	0.00
Frederick	A+ Bal	15	0	0	8	25.1	109	21	10	4	2	0	1	1	10	1	22	0	0	1	0	1.000	0	1	1.42
Bowie	AA Bal	4	0	0	1	10.2	46	10	4	4	1	0	0	0	3	0	17	1	0	0	0	—	0	2	3.38
2000 Bowie	AA Bal	6	0	0	5	6.1	23	3	1	1	0	0	0	0	1	0	9	0	0	0	0	—	0	5	1.42
Rochester	AAA Bal	37	0	0	26	44.1	187	37	24	23	4	3	1	2	17	1	43	3	2	2	5	.286	0	6	4.67
1997 Milwaukee	AL	3	0	0	2	7	29	7	4	4	1	0	2	2	2	0	5	2	0	0	0	—	0	0	5.14
1998 Los Angeles	NL	11	0	0	2	12.2	57	13	7	7	2	1	0	2	5	0	11	1	0	0	1	.000	0	0	4.97
8 Min. YEARS		266	3	1	200	370.1	1607	380	195	158	26	20	14	14	104	22	352	29	4	20	24	.455	0	102	3.84
2 Maj. YEARS		14	0	0	4	19.2	86	20	11	11	3	1	2	4	7	0	16	3	0	0	1	.000	0	0	5.03

170

Dwight Maness

Bats: Right **Throws:** Right **Pos:** OF-108; PH-6; PR-4; DH-2   **Ht:** 6'3" **Wt:** 188 **Born:** 4/3/74 **Age:** 27

Year Team	Lg Org	G	AB	H	2B	3B	HR	TB	R	RBI	TBB	IBB	SO	HBP	SH	SF	SB	CS	SB%	GDP	Avg	OBP	SLG
1992 Dodgers	R LA	44	139	35	6	3	0	47	24	12	14	0	36	8	3	3	18	9	.67	1	.252	.348	.338
1993 Vero Beach	A+ LA	118	409	106	21	4	6	153	57	42	32	0	105	15	8	7	22	13	.63	3	.259	.330	.374
1994 San Antonio	AA LA	57	215	47	5	5	5	77	32	20	25	0	54	6	2	0	15	16	.48	1	.219	.317	.358
Bakersfield	A+ LA	74	248	62	13	1	3	86	38	26	29	3	67	11	5	5	21	9	.70	1	.250	.348	.347
1995 San Antonio	AA LA	57	179	40	2	3	5	63	29	24	20	0	44	5	5	2	4	6	.40	3	.223	.316	.352
Vero Beach	A+ LA	43	143	33	3	0	3	45	16	23	11	0	29	6	2	5	13	5	.72	2	.231	.303	.315
St. Lucie	A+ NYM	14	44	9	4	0	0	13	4	5	7	0	6	0	1	0	1	2	.33	0	.205	.314	.295
1996 Binghamton	AA NYM	130	399	97	14	7	6	143	65	47	52	2	80	8	7	5	25	8	.76	2	.243	.338	.358
1997 St. Lucie	A+ NYM	45	179	53	9	2	3	75	29	19	12	0	29	3	0	0	12	6	.67	1	.296	.351	.419
Binghamton	AA NYM	74	259	49	13	3	5	83	33	31	24	1	73	5	4	2	4	4	.50	2	.189	.269	.320
1998 Binghamton	AA NYM	27	93	22	3	0	3	34	15	10	14	0	28	2	1	0	3	5	.38	4	.237	.349	.366
Norfolk	AAA NYM	6	10	1	0	0	0	1	1	0	0	0	4	0	0	0	2	0	1.00	0	.100	.100	.100
Trenton	AA Bos	85	313	77	12	5	11	132	48	32	37	0	80	8	8	3	15	6	.71	4	.246	.338	.422
1999 Somerset	IND —	75	282	75	17	2	12	132	48	42	27	1	49	7	0	2	21	9	.70	4	.266	.343	.468
New Haven	AA Sea	27	87	21	2	1	5	40	11	12	11	0	18	1	0	0	9	5	.64	3	.241	.333	.460
2000 New Haven	AA Sea	114	407	93	20	5	12	159	54	52	29	1	98	8	3	6	19	11	.64	3	.229	.289	.391
9 Min. YEARS		990	3406	820	144	41	79	1283	504	397	344	8	800	93	49	40	194	108	.64	31	.241	.324	.377

Nick Maness

Pitches: Right **Bats:** Right **Pos:** SP-26; RP-2   **Ht:** 6'4" **Wt:** 210 **Born:** 10/17/78 **Age:** 22

Year Team	Lg Org	G	GS	CG	GF	IP	BFP	H	R	ER	HR	SH	SF	HB	TBB	IBB	SO	WP	Bk	W	L	Pct.	ShO	Sv	ERA
1997 Mets	R NYM	11	6	0	2	44.2	205	52	25	15	3	1	1	1	20	0	54	2	2	3	2	.600	0	0	3.02
1998 Kingsport	R+ NYM	13	13	0	0	64.1	289	68	41	32	7	2	5	1	30	0	76	7	1	5	3	.625	0	0	4.48
1999 Capital Cty	A NYM	23	22	0	0	107.1	469	92	74	59	8	3	5	6	57	0	99	20	2	5	6	.455	0	0	4.95
2000 Binghamton	AA NYM	2	1	0	0	9.1	38	8	2	2	1	0	0	0	4	0	3	0	1	1	0	1.000	0	0	1.93
St. Lucie	A+ NYM	26	25	0	1	145.1	602	116	58	52	14	5	4	5	68	1	124	3	5	11	7	.611	0	0	3.22
4 Min. YEARS		75	67	0	3	371	1603	336	200	160	33	11	15	13	179	1	356	32	11	25	18	.581	0	0	3.88

Jim Manias

Pitches: Left **Bats:** Left **Pos:** SP-21; RP-11   **Ht:** 6'4" **Wt:** 190 **Born:** 10/21/74 **Age:** 26

Year Team	Lg Org	G	GS	CG	GF	IP	BFP	H	R	ER	HR	SH	SF	HB	TBB	IBB	SO	WP	Bk	W	L	Pct.	ShO	Sv	ERA
1996 Butte	R+ TB	16	13	0	1	72	336	98	64	42	8	2	5	3	22	0	55	5	1	5	4	.556	0	0	5.25
1997 St. Pete	A+ TB	28	28	2	0	171.1	710	163	84	72	16	3	4	11	40	0	119	6	0	13	5	.722	2	0	3.78
1998 St. Pete	A+ TB	30	21	0	3	137	618	167	99	85	27	3	11	9	37	0	79	7	0	6	13	.316	0	0	5.58
1999 Chattanooga	AA Cin	1	0	0	0	0.2	2	0	0	0	0	0	0	0	0	0	0	0	0	0	0	—	0	0	0.00
Rockford	A Cin	30	10	4	1	90.2	391	84	46	37	5	1	1	2	36	2	103	5	0	9	7	.563	1	0	3.67
2000 Dayton	A Cin	17	16	6	0	120.1	496	112	53	43	11	0	4	2	25	0	109	5	0	6	6	.500	1	0	3.22
Chattanooga	AA Cin	15	5	1	3	45.2	200	41	23	21	6	2	1	0	23	6	45	3	0	1	4	.200	0	0	4.14
5 Min. YEARS		137	93	13	8	637.2	2753	665	369	300	73	11	26	27	183	8	510	31	1	40	39	.506	4	0	4.23

David Manning

Pitches: Right **Bats:** Right **Pos:** SP-11; RP-8   **Ht:** 6'3" **Wt:** 215 **Born:** 8/14/72 **Age:** 28

Year Team	Lg Org	G	GS	CG	GF	IP	BFP	H	R	ER	HR	SH	SF	HB	TBB	IBB	SO	WP	Bk	W	L	Pct.	ShO	Sv	ERA
1992 Butte	R+ Tex	8	7	0	0	25.1	143	50	41	31	4	1	0	3	15	0	13	6	5	0	4	.000	0	0	11.01
Rangers	R Tex	5	3	0	0	16.1	75	22	13	11	0	1	0	1	4	0	9	1	0	1	1	.500	0	0	6.06
1993 Chston-SC	A Tex	37	10	0	8	116	495	112	54	39	3	5	5	7	39	4	83	11	3	6	7	.462	0	2	3.03
1994 Charlotte	A+ Tex	20	20	0	0	97	438	119	69	60	5	4	3	6	39	0	46	8	2	4	11	.267	0	0	5.57
1995 Charlotte	A+ Tex	26	20	0	2	128.2	545	127	56	50	7	3	3	3	46	0	66	0	0	9	5	.643	0	0	3.50
1996 Okla City	AAA Tex	1	1	0	0	5	21	6	3	3	0	0	1	0	2	0	1	0	0	0	0	—	0	0	5.40
Tulsa	AA Tex	39	5	0	13	91	394	89	36	33	5	3	5	2	45	6	48	5	0	3	0	.545	0	3	3.26
1997 Tulsa	AA Tex	13	12	1	1	75.2	324	77	46	41	8	2	3	0	27	0	55	5	0	4	7	.364	0	0	4.88
Okla City	AAA Tex	5	5	0	0	28.2	130	33	17	14	6	0	0	2	9	0	15	1	0	1	3	.250	0	0	4.40
Charlotte	A+ Tex	1	1	0	0	6	26	4	1	1	1	0	0	0	4	0	0	0	0	0	0	—	0	0	1.50
1998 Tulsa	AA Tex	6	0	0	1	13	61	13	7	7	2	0	1	1	11	0	15	2	0	2	0	1.000	0	0	4.85
Rangers	R Tex	3	3	0	0	5	22	6	3	3	0	1	1	0	1	0	2	1	0	0	0	—	0	0	5.40
Charlotte	A+ Tex	7	0	0	2	8.1	36	4	4	0	1	0	0	0	6	0	11	0	0	0	0	—	0	0	0.00
Oklahoma	AAA Tex	6	0	0	4	9	36	11	1	1	1	0	0	0	9	0	9	0	0	0	1	—	0	1	1.00
1999 Iowa	AAA ChC	7	0	0	2	9.2	44	9	6	5	2	0	3	0	8	0	7	0	0	0	0	—	0	0	4.66
West Tenn	AA ChC	23	18	6	0	123.1	518	113	59	54	7	5	4	3	51	1	78	7	0	8	5	.615	2	0	3.94
2000 Iowa	AAA ChC	19	11	0	2	66.2	304	82	52	47	11	2	1	3	25	1	40	3	0	2	5	.286	0	0	6.35
9 Min. YEARS		226	116	8	35	824.2	3612	877	468	400	63	27	30	30	332	12	502	50	16	43	53	.448	2	6	4.37

Nate Manning

Bats: Right **Throws:** Right **Pos:** 1B-43; OF-27; DH-14; 3B-7; PH-3; PR-1   **Ht:** 6'2" **Wt:** 215 **Born:** 12/20/73 **Age:** 27

Year Team	Lg Org	G	AB	H	2B	3B	HR	TB	R	RBI	TBB	IBB	SO	HBP	SH	SF	SB	CS	SB%	GDP	Avg	OBP	SLG
1996 Williamsprt	A- ChC	62	240	76	14	1	4	104	28	32	14	2	62	2	0	1	4	0	1.00	3	.317	.357	.433
1997 Daytona	A+ ChC	120	454	111	29	0	7	161	51	54	14	0	93	6	0	6	5	4	.56	12	.244	.273	.355
1998 West Tenn	AA ChC	16	57	11	1	0	0	12	5	6	2	0	14	1	0	0	0	0	.00	2	.193	.233	.211
Daytona	A+ ChC	108	427	115	23	1	16	188	61	71	26	5	89	10	2	4	4	2	.33	13	.269	.323	.440
1999 West Tenn	AA ChC	13	27	6	2	0	0	8	0	5	2	0	11	0	0	0	1	0	1.00	0	.222	.323	.296
Daytona	A+ ChC	110	393	99	23	3	11	161	48	57	33	1	83	7	2	4	2	2	.50	10	.252	.318	.410
2000 West Tenn	AA ChC	2	5	1	0	0	0	1	1	0	0	0	0	0	0	0	0	0	—	0	.200	.200	.200
New Britain	AA Min	18	51	14	0	0	0	19	6	8	5	0	11	1	0	0	0	0	—	1	.275	.351	.373
Fort Myers	A+ Min	66	245	53	13	1	2	74	28	23	17	1	52	3	0	0	0	0	—	9	.216	.275	.302
5 Min. YEARS		515	1899	486	110	6	40	728	230	254	113	9	413	32	4	16	14	12	.54	50	.256	.306	.383

Julio Manon

Pitches: Right   Bats: Right   Pos: RP-14; SP-4   Ht: 6'1"   Wt: 183   Born: 7/10/73   Age: 27

Year Team	Lg Org	G	GS	CG	GF	IP	BFP	H	R	ER	HR	SH	SF	HB	TBB	IBB	SO	WP	Bk	W	L	Pct.	ShO	Sv	ERA
1993 Cardinals	R StL	15	4	0	1	33.1	151	44	21	19	2	0	3	0	12	0	22	5	4	2	3	.400	0	0	5.13
1994 Johnson Cty	R+ StL	5	0	0	2	8.2	43	11	8	8	2	0	0	0	5	0	7	0	0	1	2	.333	0	0	8.31
Cardinals	R StL	14	0	0	4	16	69	20	9	9	0	0	0	0	1	0	18	1	2	1	0	1.000	0	1	5.06
1995 River City	R+ StL	16	8	2	3	74	319	75	34	30	4	0	3	2	30	2	77	10	0	3	4	.429	0	1	3.65
1997 Chston-SC	A TB	27	9	0	4	88.2	392	95	53	44	8	5	3	3	22	1	98	7	0	3	5	.375	0	1	4.47
1998 Orlando	AA TB	13	0	0	5	20.2	96	22	19	14	3	0	1	0	9	0	22	3	0	0	2	.000	0	0	6.10
St. Pete	A+ TB	38	0	0	14	55.2	219	41	25	23	7	0	0	2	19	1	73	4	1	5	5	.500	0	1	3.72
1999 Orlando	AA TB	30	5	0	8	67	303	80	43	38	9	0	1	2	23	0	53	3	0	3	3	.500	0	0	5.10
St. Paul	IND —	4	3	0	0	20.1	85	18	9	5	0	0	1	0	7	0	21	1	0	1	1	.500	0	0	2.21
2000 Expos	R Mon	4	0	0	1	10.1	36	4	1	1	0	2	0	1	2	0	10	0	0	2	0	1.000	0	0	0.87
Harrisburg	AA Mon	14	4	0	4	31.1	136	32	19	18	7	1	2	2	8	0	25	1	0	2	1	.667	0	1	5.17
7 Min. YEARS		180	33	2	46	426	1849	442	241	209	42	8	14	12	138	4	426	35	7	22	27	.449	0	4	4.42

Tim Manwiller

Pitches: Right   Bats: Right   Pos: SP-24; RP-6   Ht: 6'2"   Wt: 205   Born: 9/5/74   Age: 26

Year Team	Lg Org	G	GS	CG	GF	IP	BFP	H	R	ER	HR	SH	SF	HB	TBB	IBB	SO	WP	Bk	W	L	Pct.	ShO	Sv	ERA
1997 Sou Oregon	A- Oak	12	3	0	5	29	115	19	8	6	0	2	1	0	10	0	30	1	2	2	0	1.000	0	2	1.86
Modesto	A+ Oak	7	0	0	2	20.2	85	21	8	7	1	2	3	0	7	2	18	1	1	1	1	.500	0	0	3.05
1998 Modesto	A+ Oak	30	21	1	2	156.1	650	150	69	55	8	1	5	3	46	1	129	3	2	13	6	.684	0	1	3.17
Edmonton	AAA Oak	2	0	0	1	11	39	8	1	1	0	0	1	0	2	0	10	0	0	1	0	1.000	0	0	0.82
1999 Midland	AA Oak	17	13	0	1	84.2	366	95	43	33	6	4	2	4	24	2	58	3	0	6	2	.750	0	0	3.51
Vancouver	AAA Oak	11	11	0	0	54.1	247	72	42	39	9	2	4	4	14	0	30	1	0	4	2	.667	0	0	6.46
2000 Sacramento	AAA Oak	5	5	0	0	26.1	124	34	23	19	6	1	2	0	12	0	22	0	1	1	2	.333	0	0	6.49
Midland	AA Oak	25	19	0	1	114.1	495	122	65	56	16	5	3	7	36	0	80	3	0	4	5	.444	0	0	4.41
4 Min. YEARS		109	72	1	10	496.2	2121	521	259	216	46	17	21	18	151	5	377	12	6	32	18	.640	0	3	3.91

Roberto Manzueta

Pitches: Right   Bats: Left   Pos: RP-27; SP-4   Ht: 6'1"   Wt: 197   Born: 12/28/78   Age: 22

Year Team	Lg Org	G	GS	CG	GF	IP	BFP	H	R	ER	HR	SH	SF	HB	TBB	IBB	SO	WP	Bk	W	L	Pct.	ShO	Sv	ERA
1999 High Desert	A+ Ari	40	0	0	19	66.2	294	63	29	26	4	1	2	8	31	2	59	8	0	2	2	.500	0	2	3.51
2000 Altoona	AA Pit	8	0	0	0	21.1	104	26	16	12	0	1	0	0	13	0	14	2	0	0	1	.000	0	0	5.06
Lynchburg	A+ Pit	23	2	0	9	42.2	194	49	28	23	3	2	1	1	13	0	38	6	0	0	4	.000	0	0	4.85
2 Min. YEARS		71	4	0	28	130.2	592	138	73	61	7	3	4	9	57	2	111	16	0	2	7	.222	0	2	4.20

T.R. Marcinczyk

Bats: Right   Throws: Right   Pos: DH-44; 1B-35; PH-5; OF-2   Ht: 6'3"   Wt: 195   Born: 10/11/73   Age: 27

Year Team	Lg Org	G	AB	H	2B	3B	HR	TB	R	RBI	TBB	IBB	SO	HBP	SH	SF	SB	CS	SB%	GDP	Avg	OBP	SLG
1996 Sou Oregon	A- Oak	63	216	48	13	2	7	86	29	38	22	0	57	5	5	4	3	3	.50	3	.222	.304	.398
1997 Modesto	A+ Oak	133	463	128	41	2	23	242	89	91	71	5	107	11	1	6	4	4	.50	7	.276	.381	.523
1998 Huntsville	AA Oak	131	501	135	25	2	26	242	90	88	51	3	127	9	0	7	2	6	.25	15	.269	.343	.483
1999 Midland	AA Oak	127	477	133	39	1	23	243	87	111	62	2	109	12	0	7	2	0	1.00	12	.279	.371	.509
2000 Sacramento	AAA Oak	11	39	9	1	0	1	13	4	3	4	0	7	1	0	0				0	.231	.318	.333
Modesto	A+ Oak	10	40	13	5	0	1	21	9	11	3	0	6	1	0	0	1	0	1.00	1	.325	.386	.525
Fort Myers	A+ Min	4	16	3	0	0	0	3	1	1	0	0	3	1	0	0	0	0		2	.188	.222	.188
New Britain	AA Min	60	191	43	9	0	7	73	21	23	27	1	53	2	0	0	1	2	.33	6	.225	.327	.382
5 Min. YEARS		539	1943	512	133	7	88	923	330	366	240	11	469	42	6	25	13	15	.46	46	.264	.353	.475

Mike Maroth

Pitches: Left   Bats: Left   Pos: SP-26; RP-1   Ht: 6'0"   Wt: 180   Born: 8/17/77   Age: 23

Year Team	Lg Org	G	GS	CG	GF	IP	BFP	H	R	ER	HR	SH	SF	HB	TBB	IBB	SO	WP	Bk	W	L	Pct.	ShO	Sv	ERA
1998 Red Sox	R Bos	4	2	0	1	12.2	49	9	3	0	0	0	0	0	2	0	14	0	0	1	1	.500	0	0	0.00
Lowell	A- Bos	6	6	0	0	31	127	22	13	10	1	0	1	3	13	0	34	3	0	2	3	.400	0	0	2.90
1999 Sarasota	A+ Bos	20	19	0	0	111.1	497	124	65	50	3	6	4	10	35	1	64	11	2	11	6	.647	0	0	4.04
Lakeland	A+ Det	3	3	0	0	16.2	71	18	7	6	1	1	0	0	7	0	11	2	0	2	1	.667	0	0	3.24
Jacksnville	AA Det	4	4	0	0	20.2	96	27	15	11	2	1	1	0	7	0	10	1	0	2	1	.333	0	0	4.79
2000 Jacksnville	AA Det	27	26	2	0	164.1	689	176	79	72	14	9	9	3	58	0	85	6	1	9	14	.391	1	0	3.94
3 Min. YEARS		64	60	2	1	356.2	1529	376	182	149	21	17	15	16	122	1	218	23	3	26	27	.491	1	0	3.76

Robert Marquez

Pitches: Right   Bats: Right   Pos: RP-53   Ht: 6'0"   Wt: 190   Born: 4/21/73   Age: 28

Year Team	Lg Org	G	GS	CG	GF	IP	BFP	H	R	ER	HR	SH	SF	HB	TBB	IBB	SO	WP	Bk	W	L	Pct.	ShO	Sv	ERA
1995 Vermont	A- Mon	29	0	0	29	32	122	15	5	3	0	1	1	0	11	0	32	1	0	1	1	.500	0	21	0.84
1996 Wst Plm Bch	A+ Mon	11	0	0	7	11	54	14	10	9	0	0	0	4	5	0	8	0	0	1	0		0	6	7.36
Delmarva	A Mon	29	0	0	14	46.2	210	44	23	19	4	2	5	3	22	0	49	5	0	1	2	.333	0	1	3.66
1997 Cape Fear	A Mon	12	0	0	5	18.1	81	15	6	6	0	0	0	1	12	0	18	0	2	0	0		0	2	2.95
Wst Plm Bch	A+ Mon	21	0	0	13	28	117	28	12	8	3	1	0	0	3	0	22	0	0	1	1	.500	0	0	2.57
1998 Jupiter	A+ Mon	39	0	0	14	51.1	234	60	28	22	4	4	0	7	16	0	46	0	0	5	4	.556	0	6	3.86
Harrisburg	AA Mon	7	0	0	3	6	22	4	2	2	0	0	0	0	2	0	5	0	0	0	0		0	0	3.00
1999 Jupiter	A+ Mon	13	0	0	9	15.2	60	5	2	0	0	1	0	0	6	0	15	0	1	3	0	1.000	0	3	0.00
Harrisburg	AA Mon	18	0	0	11	25.2	116	31	15	13	1	3	1	2	8	1	22	0	0	2	2	.500	0	1	4.56
Ottawa	AAA Mon	18	0	0	7	27.2	131	33	19	15	1	1	1	1	14	2	15	0	0	1	1	.500	0	1	4.88
2000 Ottawa	AAA Mon	53	0	0	15	96	435	116	61	54	8	5	5	11	34	1	63	6	0	4	5	.500	0	3	5.06
6 Min. YEARS		247	0	0	127	358.1	1582	365	183	151	26	17	12	31	133	4	296	13	4	19	16	.543	0	48	3.79

Lee Marshall

Pitches: Right **Bats:** Right **Pos:** RP-59   **Ht:** 6'5" **Wt:** 204 **Born:** 9/25/76 **Age:** 24

		HOW MUCH HE PITCHED						WHAT HE GAVE UP										THE RESULTS					
Year Team	Lg Org	G	GS	CG	GF	IP	BFP	H	R	ER	HR	SH	SF	HB	TBB	IBB	SO	WP	Bk	W	L	Pct.	ShO	Sv	ERA
1995 Twins	R Min	6	1	0	0	11	57	16	10	6	1	1	1	2	8	0	7	2	0	0	1	.000	0	0	4.91
1996 Twins	R Min	12	12	3	0	70	283	59	31	18	0	1	1	2	18	2	39	2	1	4	4	.500	1	0	2.31
1997 Elizabethtn	R+ Min	14	14	1	0	84	369	93	56	36	6	4	1	5	16	0	41	2	0	5	3	.625	0	0	3.86
1998 Fort Wayne	A Min	46	12	0	9	104	481	133	74	60	5	1	2	5	33	1	71	9	2	8	5	.615	0	1	5.19
1999 Fort Myers	A+ Min	28	0	0	18	36.2	144	32	10	6	1	4	3	0	5	0	25	1	0	2	2	.500	0	5	1.47
2000 New Britain	AA Min	59	0	0	43	69.1	308	82	35	31	4	8	2	2	27	2	52	5	0	5	4	.556	0	8	4.02
6 Min. YEARS		165	39	4	70	375	1642	415	216	157	17	19	10	16	107	5	235	21	3	24	19	.558	1	14	3.77

Damaso Marte

Pitches: Left **Bats:** Left **Pos:** RP-4; SP-2   **Ht:** 6'0" **Wt:** 170 **Born:** 2/14/75 **Age:** 26

		HOW MUCH HE PITCHED						WHAT HE GAVE UP										THE RESULTS					
Year Team	Lg Org	G	GS	CG	GF	IP	BFP	H	R	ER	HR	SH	SF	HB	TBB	IBB	SO	WP	Bk	W	L	Pct.	ShO	Sv	ERA
1995 Everett	A- Sea	11	5	0	1	36.2	141	25	11	9	2	1	1	1	10	0	39	3	0	2	2	.500	0	0	2.21
1996 Wisconsin	A Sea	26	26	2	0	142.1	626	134	82	71	8	1	3	6	75	5	115	4	3	8	6	.571	1	0	4.49
1997 Lancaster	A+ Sea	25	25	2	0	139.1	609	144	75	64	15	4	4	8	62	1	127	8	4	8	8	.500	1	0	4.13
1998 Orlando	AA Sea	22	20	0	0	121.1	541	136	82	71	14	2	6	2	47	0	99	6	2	7	6	.538	0	0	5.27
1999 Tacoma	AAA Sea	31	11	0	4	73.2	335	79	43	42	13	1	1	2	40	1	59	1	2	3	3	.500	0	0	5.13
2000 Mariners	R Sea	2	2	0	0	5	17	1	0	0	0	0	0	1	0	0	6	0	0	0	0	—	0	0	0.00
New Haven	AA Sea	4	0	0	2	5.2	23	6	1	1	1	0	0	0	2	0	4	0	1	0	0	—	0	0	1.59
1999 Seattle	AL	5	0	0	2	8.2	47	16	9	9	3	0	0	0	6	0	3	0	0	0	1	.000	0	0	9.35
6 Min. YEARS		121	89	4	7	524	2292	525	294	258	53	9	15	20	236	7	449	22	12	28	25	.528	2	0	4.43

Chandler Martin

Pitches: Right **Bats:** Right **Pos:** SP-14   **Ht:** 6'1" **Wt:** 180 **Born:** 10/23/73 **Age:** 27

		HOW MUCH HE PITCHED						WHAT HE GAVE UP										THE RESULTS					
Year Team	Lg Org	G	GS	CG	GF	IP	BFP	H	R	ER	HR	SH	SF	HB	TBB	IBB	SO	WP	Bk	W	L	Pct.	ShO	Sv	ERA
1995 Portland	A- Col	7	7	0	0	38	153	20	10	7	0	2	0	2	21	0	34	3	3	4	1	.800	0	0	1.66
Asheville	A Col	8	8	0	0	49.1	216	48	23	21	0	2	0	3	27	0	32	6	1	4	3	.571	0	0	3.83
1996 New Haven	AA Col	1	1	0	0	5	22	6	4	4	2	0	1	1	3	0	4	0	0	1	0	1.000	0	0	7.20
Asheville	A Col	14	14	0	0	86	347	65	26	21	2	1	0	3	31	0	73	11	0	9	0	1.000	0	0	2.20
Salem	A+ Col	13	13	1	0	69	333	80	56	45	5	0	2	5	53	1	59	12	0	2	8	.200	1	0	5.87
1997 Salem	A+ Col	16	5	0	8	45.1	205	46	25	20	1	1	0	3	25	0	30	7	0	1	5	.167	0	1	3.97
1998 Salem	A+ Col	24	24	7	0	160	641	136	54	44	9	5	1	4	43	0	104	14	0	12	7	.632	0	0	2.48
1999 Carolina	AA Col	27	27	2	0	164.1	707	153	82	69	14	6	4	14	63	0	130	11	6	13	8	.619	0	0	3.78
2000 Portland	A- Col	3	3	0	0	16	67	15	5	5	0	0	0	2	1	0	14	0	0	3	0	1.000	0	0	2.81
Salem	A+ Col	7	7	1	0	45.2	184	41	18	18	1	2	1	1	12	0	25	1	0	5	1	.833	0	0	3.55
Carolina	AA Col	4	4	1	0	23	105	27	10	10	1	1	1	1	11	0	10	1	0	0	3	.000	0	0	3.91
6 Min. YEARS		124	113	12	8	701.2	2980	637	313	264	35	20	10	39	290	1	515	66	10	54	36	.600	2	1	3.39

Jeff Martin

Pitches: Right **Bats:** Right **Pos:** RP-44; SP-1   **Ht:** 6'0" **Wt:** 207 **Born:** 1/25/74 **Age:** 27

		HOW MUCH HE PITCHED						WHAT HE GAVE UP										THE RESULTS					
Year Team	Lg Org	G	GS	CG	GF	IP	BFP	H	R	ER	HR	SH	SF	HB	TBB	IBB	SO	WP	Bk	W	L	Pct.	ShO	Sv	ERA
1995 Royals	R KC	11	10	1	0	55	216	35	12	9	1	0	2	7	11	0	53	2	3	3	1	.750	1	0	1.47
1996 Wilmington	A+ KC	5	5	0	0	20.1	87	24	11	11	3	1	0	0	5	0	12	0	0	0	1	.000	0	0	4.87
1997 Lynchburg	A+ Pit	24	21	0	1	115.1	527	139	86	74	8	3	2	6	48	1	101	9	2	8	10	.444	1	0	5.77
1998 Lynchburg	A+ Pit	2	2	0	0	6	30	7	6	6	0	0	0	1	5	0	5	0	0	0	0	—	0	0	9.00
Pirates	R Pit	1	0	0	0	1	7	4	2	0	0	0	0	0	0	0	5	0	0	0	0	—	0	0	0.00
1999 Hickory	A Pit	13	0	0	3	24	97	19	6	5	1	1	0	3	8	1	23	1	0	0	2	.000	0	0	1.88
Lynchburg	A+ Pit	10	3	0	2	30.2	143	34	27	19	2	0	1	1	13	1	27	3	0	2	1	.667	0	0	5.58
2000 Altoona	AA Pit	17	0	0	9	21.1	109	28	16	11	2	0	3	6	15	0	16	1	0	0	2	.000	0	0	4.64
Lynchburg	A+ Pit	28	1	0	8	43	183	36	27	22	5	1	0	2	20	1	33	4	0	2	2	.500	0	0	4.60
6 Min. YEARS		111	42	1	23	316.2	1399	325	193	157	22	6	8	26	125	4	270	20	5	15	19	.441	1	0	4.46

Norberto Martin

Bats: Right **Throws:** Right **Pos:** 2B-54; OF-33; 3B-18; SS-15; PH-11; PR-4   **Ht:** 5'10" **Wt:** 164 **Born:** 12/10/66 **Age:** 34

		BATTING															BASERUNNING				PERCENTAGES		
Year Team	Lg Org	G	AB	H	2B	3B	HR	TB	R	RBI	TBB	IBB	SO	HBP	SH	SF	SB	CS	SB%	GDP	Avg	OBP	SLG
1984 White Sox	R CWS	56	205	56	8	2	1	71	36	30	21	0	31	4	1	4	18	5	.78	3	.273	.346	.346
1985 Appleton	A CWS	30	96	19	2	0	0	21	15	5	9	0	23	0	3	0	2	2	.50	1	.198	.267	.219
Niagara Fal	A- CWS	60	217	55	9	0	1	67	22	13	7	0	41	1	5	0	6	4	.60	2	.253	.280	.309
1986 Appleton	A CWS	9	33	10	2	0	0	12	4	2	2	0	5	0	0	0	1	0	1.00	1	.303	.343	.364
1987 Chston-WV	A CWS	68	250	78	14	1	5	109	44	35	17	1	40	4	4	3	14	4	.78	1	.312	.361	.436
Peninsula	A+ CWS	41	162	42	6	1	1	53	21	18	18	0	19	1	0	4	11	6	.65	3	.259	.330	.327
1988 Tampa	A+ CWS	101	360	93	10	4	2	117	44	33	17	0	49	3	7	3	24	5	.83	13	.258	.295	.325
1990 Vancouver	AAA CWS	130	508	135	20	4	3	172	77	45	27	0	63	5	8	6	10	7	.59	14	.266	.306	.339
1991 Vancouver	AAA CWS	93	338	94	9	0	0	103	39	20	21	0	38	3	10	2	11	7	.61	14	.278	.324	.305
1992 Vancouver	AAA CWS	135	497	143	12	7	0	169	72	29	29	1	44	2	14	2	29	12	.71	11	.288	.328	.340
1993 Nashville	AAA CWS	137	580	179	21	6	9	239	87	74	26	0	59	2	12	6	31	5	.86	17	.309	.337	.412
1994 Nashville	AAA CWS	43	172	44	8	0	2	58	26	12	10	2	14	1	3	2	6	4	.60	4	.256	.297	.337
1996 Nashville	AAA CWS	17	68	14	3	0	2	23	9	8	4	0	10	1	1	1	1	0	1.00	1	.206	.257	.338
1999 Syracuse	AAA Tor	81	319	94	11	2	5	124	45	34	12	0	33	2	3	3	14	1	.93	9	.295	.322	.389
2000 Indianapols	AAA Mil	117	406	114	26	3	1	149	51	41	22	0	38	3	11	3	10	3	.77	13	.281	.320	.367
1993 Chicago	AL	8	14	5	0	0	0	5	3	2	1	0	0	0	0	0	0	0	—	0	.357	.400	.357
1994 Chicago	AL	45	131	36	7	1	1	48	19	16	9	0	16	0	2	0	4	2	.67	2	.275	.317	.366
1995 Chicago	AL	72	160	43	7	4	2	64	17	17	3	0	25	1	2	3	5	0	1.00	5	.269	.281	.400
1996 Chicago	AL	70	140	49	7	0	1	59	30	14	7	0	17	0	4	1	10	2	.83	4	.350	.374	.421

Year Team	Lg Org	G	AB	H	2B	3B	HR	TB	R	RBI	TBB	IBB	SO	HBP	SH	SF	SB	CS	SB%	GDP	Avg	OBP	SLG
1997 Chicago	AL	71	213	64	7	1	2	79	24	27	6	0	31	0	0	0	1	4	.20	2	.300	.320	.371
1998 Anaheim	AL	79	195	42	2	0	1	47	20	13	6	0	29	0	3	2	3	1	.75	9	.215	.236	.241
1999 Toronto	AL	9	27	6	2	0	0	8	3	0	4	0	4	2	0	0	0	0	—	0	.222	.364	.296
13 Min. YEARS		1118	4211	1170	161	30	32	1487	592	399	242	4	507	32	82	38	186	67	.74	109	.278	.319	.353
7 Maj. YEARS		354	880	245	32	6	7	310	116	89	35	0	123	3	12	8	23	9	.72	24	.278	.306	.352

Chris Martine

Bats: Right **Throws:** Right **Pos:** C-5 **Ht:** 6'2" **Wt:** 190 **Born:** 7/10/75 **Age:** 25

Year Team	Lg Org	G	AB	H	2B	3B	HR	TB	R	RBI	TBB	IBB	SO	HBP	SH	SF	SB	CS	SB%	GDP	Avg	OBP	SLG
1997 New Jersey	A- StL	47	142	30	5	0	0	35	22	12	22	0	37	2	0	3	0	0	—	3	.211	.320	.246
1998 Pr William	A+ StL	96	279	52	13	0	2	71	29	25	38	0	77	4	5	3	2	6	.25	4	.186	.290	.254
1999 Potomac	A+ StL	42	136	28	7	2	1	42	11	14	16	0	42	2	3	2	1	2	.33	3	.206	.295	.309
Arkansas	AA StL	18	40	6	1	0	0	7	3	1	2	0	12	4	2	0	0	0	—	1	.150	.261	.175
2000 Arkansas	AA StL	5	16	1	0	0	0	1	1	0	0	0	6	0	0	0	0	0	—	0	.063	.063	.063
4 Min. YEARS		208	613	117	26	2	3	156	66	52	78	0	174	12	10	8	3	8	.27	11	.191	.291	.254

Jason Martines

Pitches: Right **Bats:** Left **Pos:** RP-55 **Ht:** 6'2" **Wt:** 190 **Born:** 1/21/76 **Age:** 25

		HOW MUCH HE PITCHED						WHAT HE GAVE UP											THE RESULTS					
Year Team	Lg Org	G	GS	CG	GF	IP	BFP	H	R	ER	HR	SH	SF	HB	TBB	IBB	SO	WP	Bk	W	L	Pct.	ShO	Sv	ERA
1997 Lethbridge	R+ Ari	22	0	0	6	43	180	45	15	15	4	1	1	2	11	0	34	1	0	3	3	.500	0	0	3.14
1998 Tucson	AAA Ari	1	0	0	0	1.1	6	0	0	0	0	0	0	0	2	0	2	0	0	0	0	—	0	0	0.00
High Desert	A+ Ari	5	0	0	1	10.2	50	16	10	9	3	1	2	0	3	0	7	1	0	0	1	.000	0	0	7.59
South Bend	A Ari	21	0	0	16	33.1	148	33	16	13	1	0	1	1	15	0	31	4	1	0	2	.000	0	0	3.51
1999 High Desert	A+ Ari	43	0	0	37	71.2	306	68	33	18	5	2	1	2	28	4	73	1	1	9	7	.563	0	9	2.26
2000 El Paso	AA Ari	55	0	0	20	86.1	356	72	32	27	3	2	6	4	27	3	77	0	0	9	1	.900	0	2	2.81
4 Min. YEARS		147	0	0	80	246.1	1046	234	106	82	16	6	11	9	86	7	224	7	2	21	14	.600	0	11	3.00

Belvani Martinez

Bats: Right **Throws:** Right **Pos:** 2B-106; SS-7; DH-2; PH-2; PR-2 **Ht:** 5'11" **Wt:** 172 **Born:** 12/14/78 **Age:** 22

Year Team	Lg Org	G	AB	H	2B	3B	HR	TB	R	RBI	TBB	IBB	SO	HBP	SH	SF	SB	CS	SB%	GDP	Avg	OBP	SLG
1997 Diamondbcks	R Ari	30	134	43	11	2	0	58	25	11	3	0	18	3	2	2	7	2	.78	3	.321	.345	.433
Lethbridge	R+ Ari	25	90	31	4	1	6	55	21	13	5	0	13	4	1	1	4	1	.80	2	.344	.400	.611
1998 South Bend	A Ari	18	80	20	2	0	0	22	11	6	3	0	22	2	0	0	5	1	.83	3	.250	.294	.275
Lethbridge	R+ Ari	63	256	78	11	3	5	110	56	25	12	0	30	4	2	3	30	10	.75	5	.305	.342	.430
1999 High Desert	A+ Ari	109	477	159	23	9	8	224	84	55	18	1	69	9	3	4	35	30	.54	7	.333	.366	.470
2000 Carolina	AA Col	115	406	101	18	4	3	136	50	36	11	2	63	5	6	0	25	10	.71	11	.249	.277	.335
4 Min. YEARS		360	1443	432	69	19	22	605	247	146	52	3	215	27	14	10	106	54	.66	33	.299	.334	.419

Eddy Martinez

Bats: Right **Throws:** Right **Pos:** SS-88; 2B-4; 3B-2 **Ht:** 6'2" **Wt:** 173 **Born:** 10/23/77 **Age:** 23

Year Team	Lg Org	G	AB	H	2B	3B	HR	TB	R	RBI	TBB	IBB	SO	HBP	SH	SF	SB	CS	SB%	GDP	Avg	OBP	SLG
1995 Bluefield	R+ Bal	57	185	57	11	3	1	77	42	35	23	0	42	5	1	1	5	5	.50	1	.308	.397	.416
1996 Frederick	A+ Bal	74	244	54	4	0	2	64	21	25	21	0	48	2	1	1	13	8	.62	5	.221	.287	.262
Bluefield	R+ Bal	37	122	27	3	0	1	33	18	15	13	0	29	2	3	0	15	5	.75	1	.221	.307	.270
1997 Bowie	AA Bal	16	45	7	3	0	0	10	3	1	6	0	12	0	3	0	2	0	1.00	0	.156	.255	.222
Frederick	A+ Bal	54	174	42	6	0	1	51	14	14	19	0	43	2	3	2	6	7	.46	9	.241	.320	.293
Rochester	AAA Bal	12	27	2	1	0	0	3	0	3	1	0	8	0	1	0	0	0	—	0	.074	.107	.111
1998 Delmarva	A Bal	113	361	95	16	1	2	119	46	39	33	0	66	2	13	3	21	7	.75	9	.263	.326	.330
Bowie	AA Bal	5	14	4	0	0	0	4	1	1	1	0	3	0	1	0	0	0	—	0	.286	.333	.286
1999 Frederick	A+ Bal	127	416	121	21	1	2	150	68	55	52	1	99	13	5	5	8	4	.67	6	.291	.383	.361
2000 Rochester	AAA Bal	13	36	8	2	0	0	10	7	1	5	0	7	0	0	0	1	0	1.00	1	.222	.317	.278
Frederick	A+ Bal	40	152	46	10	1	0	58	23	15	24	0	34	2	5	0	7	6	.54	6	.303	.404	.382
Bowie	AA Bal	41	127	32	2	2	1	41	17	20	17	1	21	5	3	1	0	0	—	2	.252	.360	.323
6 Min. YEARS		589	1903	495	79	8	10	620	260	224	215	2	412	33	39	13	78	42	.65	40	.260	.343	.326

Gabby Martinez

Bats: Right **Throws:** Right **Pos:** SS-79; 2B-13; PH-5; PR-3; 3B-1 **Ht:** 6'2" **Wt:** 170 **Born:** 1/7/74 **Age:** 27

Year Team	Lg Org	G	AB	H	2B	3B	HR	TB	R	RBI	TBB	IBB	SO	HBP	SH	SF	SB	CS	SB%	GDP	Avg	OBP	SLG
1992 Brewers	R Mil	48	165	43	7	2	0	54	29	24	12	0	19	3	2	2	7	5	.58	3	.261	.319	.327
1993 Beloit	A Mil	94	285	69	14	5	0	93	40	24	14	0	52	1	15	4	22	10	.69	2	.242	.276	.326
1994 Stockton	A+ Mil	112	364	90	18	3	0	114	37	32	17	1	66	4	4	4	19	11	.63	8	.247	.285	.313
1995 Stockton	A+ Mil	64	213	55	13	3	1	77	25	20	10	0	25	2	9	3	13	6	.68	6	.258	.294	.362
El Paso	AA Mil	44	133	37	3	2	0	44	13	11	2	0	22	2	3	1	5	1	.83	2	.278	.297	.331
1996 El Paso	AA Mil	91	338	85	11	8	0	112	44	37	18	1	57	2	13	4	8	9	.47	3	.251	.290	.331
1997 Yankees	R NYY	2	5	2	0	0	1	5	3	2	1	0	0	0	0	0	2	0	1.00	0	.400	.500	1.000
Norwich	AA NYY	77	312	100	12	5	6	140	49	54	11	0	44	5	10	3	21	6	.78	5	.321	.350	.449
1998 Columbus	AAA NYY	36	131	31	3	1	0	36	17	8	4	0	22	1	2	1	5	3	.63	6	.237	.263	.275
Tampa	A+ NYY	44	166	53	8	1	5	78	26	24	5	2	20	3	1	0	21	6	.78	5	.319	.351	.470
1999 Charlotte	AAA CWS	16	49	14	1	0	4	27	8	5	5	0	6	0	3	0	3	3	.50	2	.286	.352	.551
2000 Long Island	IND —	10	42	11	3	0	1	17	7	6	2	0	6	1	1	0	9	0	1.00	0	.262	.311	.405
West Tenn	AA ChC	13	42	9	1	0	2	16	5	5	3	1	6	0	2	0	5	2	.71	1	.214	.267	.381
Iowa	AAA ChC	25	65	11	1	0	1	15	6	5	1	0	9	1	1	0	2	1	.67	1	.169	.194	.231
Binghamton	AA NYM	48	165	41	4	3	2	57	22	12	11	0	22	0	6	0	8	8	.50	8	.248	.295	.345
9 Min. YEARS		724	2475	651	99	33	23	885	331	269	116	5	376	25	72	22	150	71	.68	55	.263	.300	.358

Greg Martinez

Bats: Both **Throws:** Right **Pos:** OF-34; PR-3; DH-2; PH-1   **Ht:** 5'10" **Wt:** 168 **Born:** 1/27/72 **Age:** 29

Year Team	Lg Org	G	AB	H	2B	3B	HR	TB	R	RBI	TBB	IBB	SO	HBP	SH	SF	SB	CS	SB%	GDP	Avg	OBP	SLG
1993 Brewers	R Mil	5	19	12	0	0	0	12	6	3	4	0	0	1	0	0	7	1	.88	0	.632	.708	.632
Helena	R+ Mil	52	183	53	4	2	0	61	45	19	30	0	26	6	3	5	30	6	.83	0	.290	.397	.333
1994 Beloit	A Mil	81	224	62	8	1	0	72	39	20	25	1	32	3	6	1	27	11	.71	4	.277	.356	.321
1995 Stockton	A+ Mil	114	410	113	8	2	0	125	80	43	69	1	64	2	10	1	55	9	.86	7	.276	.382	.305
1996 Stockton	A+ Mil	73	286	82	5	1	0	89	51	26	29	0	34	0	8	2	30	9	.77	3	.287	.350	.311
El Paso	AA Mil	41	166	52	2	2	1	61	27	21	13	0	19	3	6	1	14	4	.78	4	.313	.372	.367
1997 El Paso	AA Mil	95	381	111	10	10	1	144	75	29	32	0	55	3	9	2	39	7	.85	5	.291	.349	.378
Tucson	AAA Mil	3	12	5	2	0	0	7	2	3	0	0	1	0	0	0	0	0	—	0	.417	.417	.583
1998 Louisville	AAA Mil	115	376	98	4	11	4	136	65	25	51	0	80	0	10	0	43	7	.86	3	.261	.349	.362
1999 Huntsville	AA Mil	25	98	27	3	2	0	34	18	6	12	1	13	0	1	0	8	2	.80	2	.276	.355	.347
Louisville	AAA Mil	107	419	111	13	4	4	144	79	29	53	0	50	4	5	1	48	7	.87	10	.265	.352	.344
2000 Athletics	R Oak	6	22	5	0	0	0	5	4	2	4	0	5	1	0	0	2	0	1.00	0	.227	.370	.227
Modesto	A+ Oak	3	11	4	0	0	0	4	1	0	2	0	0	1	0	0	1	1	.50	0	.364	.500	.364
Midland	AA Oak	28	81	22	1	1	0	25	13	7	12	0	14	0	2	0	10	1	.91	2	.272	.366	.309
1998 Milwaukee	NL	13	3	0	0	0	0	0	2	0	1	0	2	0	0	0	2	0	1.00	0	.000	.250	.000
8 Min. YEARS		748	2688	757	60	36	10	919	505	233	336	3	393	24	60	13	314	65	.83	41	.282	.365	.342

Jesus Martinez

Pitches: Left **Bats:** Left **Pos:** RP-11; SP-4   **Ht:** 6'2" **Wt:** 145 **Born:** 3/13/74 **Age:** 27

Year Team	Lg Org	G	GS	CG	GF	IP	BFP	H	R	ER	HR	SH	SF	HB	TBB	IBB	SO	WP	Bk	W	L	Pct.	ShO	Sv	ERA
1992 Great Falls	R+ LA	6	6	0	0	18.1	112	36	30	27	4	0	0	2	21	0	23	9	0	0	3	.000	0	0	13.25
Dodgers	R LA	7	7	1	0	41	174	38	19	15	1	2	0	1	11	0	39	5	0	1	4	.200	0	0	3.29
1993 Bakersfield	A+ LA	30	21	0	2	145.2	653	144	95	67	12	5	11	5	75	0	108	6	5	4	13	.235	0	0	4.14
1994 San Antonio	AA LA	1	1	0	0	4	14	3	2	2	0	0	0	0	2	0	3	0	0	0	1	.000	0	0	4.50
Vero Beach	A+ LA	18	18	1	0	87.2	386	91	65	61	7	2	3	6	43	0	69	3	0	7	9	.438	1	0	6.26
1995 San Antonio	AA LA	24	24	1	0	139.2	603	129	64	55	6	7	4	7	71	0	83	16	4	6	9	.400	0	0	3.54
Albuquerque	AAA LA	2	0	0	1	4	20	4	2	2	0	1	1	1	4	2	5	0	0	1	1	.500	0	0	4.50
1996 San Antonio	AA LA	27	27	0	0	161.2	706	157	90	79	7	5	7	5	92	0	124	20	0	10	13	.435	0	0	4.40
1997 Albuquerque	AAA LA	26	12	0	6	84	404	112	64	58	8	3	1	1	52	0	80	15	1	7	1	.875	0	0	6.21
1998 Indianapolis	AAA Cin	22	18	0	0	93.1	425	119	78	71	10	4	4	5	42	0	39	7	3	7	6	.538	0	0	6.85
1999 Sarasota	A+ Bos	16	2	0	8	32.2	151	36	20	19	2	2	6	3	17	1	20	5	0	1	2	.333	0	0	5.23
2000 Akron	AA Cle	7	0	0	1	14.2	68	17	8	6	2	0	0	1	10	0	5	1	0	1	0	1.000	0	0	3.68
Kinston	A+ Cle	2	0	0	2	4	17	3	0	0	0	0	0	0	3	0	3	0	0	0	0	—	0	0	0.00
Binghamton	AA NYM	6	4	0	0	20	90	20	11	10	1	0	2	2	12	0	16	2	1	1	0	.500	0	0	4.50
9 Min. YEARS		194	140	3	20	850.2	3823	909	548	472	60	31	39	39	455	0	617	89	14	45	64	.413	1	0	4.99

Jose Martinez

Pitches: Right **Bats:** Right **Pos:** SP-23; RP-6   **Ht:** 6'0" **Wt:** 165 **Born:** 2/4/75 **Age:** 26

Year Team	Lg Org	G	GS	CG	GF	IP	BFP	H	R	ER	HR	SH	SF	HB	TBB	IBB	SO	WP	Bk	W	L	Pct.	ShO	Sv	ERA
1996 Chston-SC	A Tex	11	1	0	3	21	105	34	24	23	7	0	1	2	7	1	17	6	2	1	2	.333	0	0	9.86
Hudson Val	A- Tex	16	5	0	4	54.2	233	56	35	23	3	3	2	0	11	0	38	6	3	2	3	.400	0	0	3.79
1997 Charlotte	A+ Tex	26	0	0	13	57.2	229	52	25	24	6	3	0	0	13	0	48	4	1	3	1	.750	0	2	3.75
1998 Tulsa	AA Tex	7	7	0	0	34.1	160	46	34	29	6	1	2	2	14	0	21	3	2	2	2	.500	0	0	7.60
Charlotte	A+ Tex	19	19	2	0	123.2	521	120	55	38	12	3	3	5	28	3	86	5	3	7	5	.583	0	0	2.77
1999 Tulsa	AA Tex	33	9	0	10	98	441	112	69	59	16	2	6	2	36	0	70	2	1	4	4	.500	0	3	5.42
2000 Tulsa	AA Tex	18	13	1	1	103.1	431	97	44	36	7	6	2	0	21	0	79	10	0	5	6	.455	1	0	3.14
Oklahoma	AAA Tex	11	10	0	0	53	248	77	49	43	10	2	2	4	14	0	23	6	0	2	5	.286	0	0	7.30
5 Min. YEARS		141	64	3	31	545.2	2368	594	335	275	67	20	18	15	144	4	382	42	12	26	28	.481	1	5	4.54

Louis Martinez

Bats: Right **Throws:** Right **Pos:** 2B-27; SS-24; 3B-9; PH-2; PR-2   **Ht:** 6'0" **Wt:** 175 **Born:** 11/1/76 **Age:** 24

Year Team	Lg Org	G	AB	H	2B	3B	HR	TB	R	RBI	TBB	IBB	SO	HBP	SH	SF	SB	CS	SB%	GDP	Avg	OBP	SLG
1999 Braves	R Atl	23	87	28	4	1	0	34	8	14	8	0	13	1	2	0	0	2	.00	1	.322	.385	.391
Myrtle Bch	A+ Atl	5	15	2	1	0	0	3	1	0	1	0	2	0	0	0	0	0	—	0	.133	.188	.200
2000 Macon	A Atl	33	114	25	3	0	0	28	16	4	11	0	10	2	2	0	4	1	.80	2	.219	.299	.246
Richmond	AAA Atl	28	71	12	3	1	0	17	3	2	2	1	12	0	3	1	2	0	1.00	0	.169	.189	.239
2 Min. YEARS		89	287	67	11	2	0	82	28	20	22	1	37	3	7	1	6	3	.67	3	.233	.294	.286

Manny Martinez

Bats: Right **Throws:** Right **Pos:** OF-116; PH-9; PR-6   **Ht:** 6'0" **Wt:** 180 **Born:** 10/3/70 **Age:** 30

Year Team	Lg Org	G	AB	H	2B	3B	HR	TB	R	RBI	TBB	IBB	SO	HBP	SH	SF	SB	CS	SB%	GDP	Avg	OBP	SLG
1990 Sou Oregon	A- Oak	66	244	60	5	0	2	71	35	17	16	0	59	5	1	0	6	4	.60	5	.246	.306	.291
1991 Modesto	A+ Oak	125	502	136	32	3	3	183	73	55	34	2	80	7	7	3	26	19	.58	7	.271	.324	.365
1992 Modesto	A+ Oak	121	495	125	23	1	9	177	70	45	39	3	75	4	12	5	17	13	.57	7	.253	.309	.358
1993 San Berndno	A+ Oak	109	459	148	26	3	11	213	88	52	41	2	60	5	6	4	28	21	.57	10	.322	.381	.464
Tacoma	AAA Oak	20	59	18	2	0	1	23	9	6	4	0	12	0	1	0	2	3	.40	2	.305	.349	.390
1994 Tacoma	AAA Oak	137	536	137	25	5	4	199	76	60	28	3	72	10	9	5	18	10	.64	14	.256	.302	.371
1995 Iowa	AAA ChC	122	397	115	17	8	8	172	63	49	20	0	64	3	7	2	11	8	.58	3	.290	.327	.433
1996 Tacoma	AAA Sea	66	277	87	15	1	4	116	54	24	23	1	41	2	3	5	14	10	.58	6	.314	.367	.419
Scranton-WB	AAA Phi	17	67	14	1	1	0	17	3	5	4	0	17	1	0	0	3	0	1.00	0	.209	.264	.254
1997 Calgary	AAA Pit	109	420	139	34	1	16	223	78	66	33	4	80	0	2	1	17	9	.65	3	.331	.379	.531
1998 Nashville	AAA Pit	22	75	18	5	0	1	26	12	6	7	0	20	0	0	1	5	3	.63	1	.240	.305	.347
2000 Calgary	AAA Fla	126	380	101	19	1	9	149	57	54	31	0	58	1	3	9	20	6	.77	4	.266	.316	.392

175

Year Team	Lg Org	G	AB	H	2B	3B	HR	TB	R	RBI	TBB	IBB	SO	HBP	SH	SF	SB	CS	SB%	GDP	Avg	OBP	SLG
1996 Seattle	AL	9	17	4	2	1	0	8	3	3	3	0	5	0	0	0	2	1	1.00	1	.235	.350	.471
Philadelphia	NL	13	36	8	0	2	0	12	2	0	1	0	11	1	1	0	2	1	.67	1	.222	.263	.333
1998 Pittsburgh	NL	73	180	45	11	2	6	78	21	24	9	0	44	2	3	2	0	3	.00	3	.250	.290	.433
1999 Montreal	NL	137	331	81	12	7	2	113	48	26	17	0	51	0	6	3	19	6	.76	4	.245	.279	.341
10 Min. YEARS		1040	3911	1098	204	24	73	1569	623	439	280	15	638	38	51	32	167	106	.61	62	.281	.332	.401
3 Maj. YEARS		232	564	138	25	12	8	211	74	53	30	0	111	3	10	5	23	10	.70	9	.245	.284	.374

Pablo Martinez

Bats: Both **Throws:** Right **Pos:** SS-51; 2B-25; PH-14; OF-4; PR-3; 3B-1   **Ht:** 5'10" **Wt:** 155 **Born:** 6/29/69 **Age:** 32

Year Team	Lg Org	G	AB	H	2B	3B	HR	TB	R	RBI	TBB	IBB	SO	HBP	SH	SF	SB	CS	SB%	GDP	Avg	OBP	SLG
1989 Spokane	A- SD	2	8	2	0	0	0	2	3	0	0	0	0	0	0	0	1	0	1.00	1	.250	.250	.250
Padres	R SD	45	178	42	3	1	0	47	31	12	22	1	25	2	0	0	29	4	.88	1	.236	.327	.264
Chston-SC	A SD	31	80	14	2	0	0	16	13	4	11	0	21	0	3	1	0	1	.00	2	.175	.272	.200
1990 Chston-SC	A SD	136	453	100	12	6	0	124	51	33	41	0	104	4	7	2	16	10	.62	6	.221	.290	.274
1991 Chston-SC	A SD	121	442	118	17	6	3	156	62	36	42	1	64	0	6	2	39	19	.67	8	.267	.329	.353
1992 High Desert	A+ SD	126	427	102	8	4	0	118	60	39	50	0	74	1	2	4	19	14	.58	16	.239	.317	.276
1993 Wichita	AA SD	45	130	36	5	1	2	49	19	14	11	1	24	1	1	1	8	5	.62	2	.277	.336	.377
Las Vegas	AAA SD	76	251	58	4	1	2	70	24	20	18	3	46	3	10	2	8	2	.80	5	.231	.288	.279
1994 Norfolk	AAA NYM	34	80	12	1	0	0	13	8	5	4	0	22	0	3	0	1	1	.50	0	.150	.190	.163
Binghamton	AA NYM	13	48	9	2	2	0	15	3	4	5	0	12	0	2	0	0	1	.00	3	.188	.264	.313
St. Lucie	A+ NYM	49	177	42	5	0	1	50	19	10	13	0	29	0	3	1	7	7	.50	4	.237	.288	.282
1995 Greenville	AA Atl	120	462	118	22	4	5	163	70	29	37	0	89	2	8	1	12	12	.50	7	.255	.313	.353
Richmond	AAA Atl	14	48	11	0	2	0	15	5	4	2	0	7	0	0	1	1	1	.50	3	.229	.260	.313
1996 Greenville	AA Atl	9	37	12	2	2	1	21	7	11	2	0	6	0	1	1	3	0	1.00	1	.324	.350	.568
Richmond	AAA Atl	77	263	71	12	3	1	92	29	18	12	0	58	1	11	1	14	7	.67	3	.270	.303	.350
1997 Richmond	AAA Atl	96	296	76	14	1	4	104	32	20	26	0	77	0	8	2	9	11	.45	3	.257	.315	.351
1998 Louisville	AAA Mil	63	186	44	4	1	2	56	22	9	18	3	31	1	2	2	6	3	.67	5	.237	.304	.301
Allentown	IND —	10	34	9	4	0	0	13	6	2	4	0	4	0	0	0	4	1	.80	1	.265	.342	.382
Richmond	AAA Atl	15	36	10	1	0	0	11	3	3	2	0	10	0	0	0	1	2	.33	0	.278	.316	.306
1999 Greenville	AA Atl	57	228	54	9	3	1	72	28	19	20	0	41	0	2	3	6	8	.43	6	.237	.295	.316
Richmond	AAA Atl	63	186	36	7	3	1	52	18	18	25	1	42	3	7	1	13	3	.81	1	.194	.298	.280
2000 Richmond	AAA Atl	41	128	27	5	1	0	34	7	12	13	0	23	0	5	1	8	1	.89	4	.211	.282	.266
Memphis	AAA StL	52	151	33	5	0	1	41	16	15	10	0	42	1	4	2	6	2	.75	8	.219	.268	.272
1996 Atlanta	NL	4	2	1	0	0	0	1	1	0	0	0	0	0	1	0	0	1	.00	0	.500	.500	.500
12 Min. YEARS		1295	4329	1036	144	41	24	1334	536	337	388	10	851	19	85	27	211	115	.65	90	.239	.303	.308

Eric Martins

Bats: Right **Throws:** Right **Pos:** 3B-27; 2B-25; OF-15; DH-9; PR-2; PH-1   **Ht:** 5'9" **Wt:** 170 **Born:** 11/19/72 **Age:** 28

Year Team	Lg Org	G	AB	H	2B	3B	HR	TB	R	RBI	TBB	IBB	SO	HBP	SH	SF	SB	CS	SB%	GDP	Avg	OBP	SLG
1994 Sou Oregon	A- Oak	56	236	78	16	3	4	112	47	34	23	1	36	5	2	0	17	10	.63	4	.331	.402	.475
W Michigan	A Oak	18	71	22	4	1	0	28	11	7	5	0	12	0	1	2	1	2	.33	2	.310	.346	.394
1995 Modesto	A+ Oak	106	407	118	17	5	1	148	71	54	62	0	74	4	18	4	7	8	.47	8	.290	.386	.364
1996 Huntsville	AA Oak	111	388	99	23	2	1	129	61	34	47	0	77	5	8	1	7	7	.50	6	.255	.342	.332
1997 Huntsville	AA Oak	61	205	53	10	3	3	78	33	31	23	0	31	2	3	2	2	1	.67	9	.259	.336	.380
Edmonton	AAA Oak	27	82	23	7	1	1	35	17	8	11	0	19	1	2	0	0	0	—	3	.280	.372	.427
1998 Huntsville	AA Oak	70	234	71	15	1	3	97	45	24	34	1	32	6	10	1	6	4	.60	8	.303	.404	.415
Edmonton	AAA Oak	39	129	36	8	0	3	53	14	16	9	1	22	0	0	1	1	0	1.00	2	.279	.324	.411
1999 Vancouver	AAA Oak	97	301	72	15	5	3	106	39	33	31	2	47	4	3	2	2	1	.67	8	.239	.317	.352
2000 Sacramento	AAA Oak	76	261	66	10	1	2	84	35	25	37	0	32	0	2	1	1	5	.17	11	.253	.344	.322
7 Min. YEARS		661	2314	638	125	22	21	870	373	262	282	5	382	27	49	14	44	38	.54	61	.276	.359	.376

Raul Marval

Bats: Right **Throws:** Right **Pos:** 2B-49; 3B-28; SS-20; PH-11; PR-3; 1B-2; P-1   **Ht:** 6'0" **Wt:** 170 **Born:** 12/13/75 **Age:** 25

Year Team	Lg Org	G	AB	H	2B	3B	HR	TB	R	RBI	TBB	IBB	SO	HBP	SH	SF	SB	CS	SB%	GDP	Avg	OBP	SLG
1993 Giants	R SF	19	47	11	2	0	0	13	8	3	3	0	4	0	0	1	3	1	.75	2	.234	.275	.277
1994 Everett	A- SF	29	99	21	5	0	1	29	9	12	4	0	22	1	1	3	4	4	.50	3	.212	.243	.293
Clinton	A SF	81	273	60	9	3	0	75	27	28	16	0	75	2	4	6	4	5	.44	5	.220	.263	.275
1995 San Jose	A+ SF	10	36	10	0	0	0	10	1	3	1	0	5	0	2	0	1	1	.50	0	.278	.297	.278
Burlington	A SF	88	296	79	8	2	1	94	42	19	10	0	32	6	3	1	4	6	.40	9	.267	.304	.318
1996 Burlington	A SF	44	159	32	10	0	0	42	13	9	6	0	12	3	4	2	3	1	.75	7	.201	.241	.264
San Jose	A+ SF	39	137	32	6	0	0	38	19	19	9	0	13	1	4	1	0	0	—	3	.234	.284	.277
1997 Bakersfield	A+ SF	115	437	112	15	3	2	139	41	42	11	0	66	2	6	3	8	6	.57	8	.256	.276	.318
1998 Shreveport	AA SF	96	296	70	6	1	1	81	14	21	13	0	35	1	4	3	2	2	.50	9	.236	.268	.274
1999 Shreveport	AA SF	2	4	1	0	0	0	1	0	0	0	0	1	0	0	0	1	0	1.00	0	.250	.250	.250
Fresno	AAA SF	97	280	84	15	1	7	122	42	46	16	1	48	3	9	5	2	3	.40	4	.300	.339	.436
2000 Fresno	AAA SF	50	159	33	5	0	2	44	15	12	10	0	23	0	6	0	4	5	.44	4	.208	.254	.277
Shreveport	AA SF	53	150	32	6	1	0	40	9	15	5	0	14	2	4	1	1	1	.50	9	.213	.246	.267
8 Min. YEARS		723	2373	577	81	11	16	728	240	229	108	1	350	21	47	26	36	36	.50	63	.243	.279	.307

Damon Mashore

Bats: Right **Throws:** Right **Pos:** OF-34; PH-4; DH-1   **Ht:** 5'11" **Wt:** 209 **Born:** 10/31/69 **Age:** 31

Year Team	Lg Org	G	AB	H	2B	3B	HR	TB	R	RBI	TBB	IBB	SO	HBP	SH	SF	SB	CS	SB%	GDP	Avg	OBP	SLG
1991 Sou Oregon	A- Oak	73	264	72	17	6	6	119	48	31	34	1	94	2	2	3	15	5	.75	6	.273	.356	.451
1992 Modesto	A+ Oak	124	471	133	22	3	18	215	91	64	73	3	136	6	5	1	29	17	.63	6	.282	.385	.456
1993 Huntsville	AA Oak	70	253	59	7	2	3	79	35	20	25	0	64	4	1	2	18	4	.82	5	.233	.310	.312
1994 Athletics	R Oak	11	34	14	2	0	0	16	6	6	4	0	3	1	0	1	1	1	.50	3	.412	.475	.471
Huntsville	AA Oak	59	210	47	11	2	3	71	24	21	13	1	53	0	1	3	6	1	.86	3	.224	.265	.338

176

Year Team	Lg Org	G	AB	H	2B	3B	HR	TB	R	RBI	TBB	IBB	SO	HBP	SH	SF	SB	CS	SB%	GDP	Avg	OBP	SLG
1995 Edmonton	AAA Oak	117	337	101	19	5	1	133	50	37	42	0	77	5	3	3	17	5	.77	9	.300	.382	.395
1996 Edmonton	AAA Oak	50	183	49	9	1	8	84	32	29	19	0	48	5	2	2	6	2	.75	3	.268	.349	.459
1998 Vancouver	AAA Ana	42	143	39	7	0	2	52	19	15	18	0	28	1	2	0	1	1	.50	2	.273	.358	.364
1999 Fresno	AAA SF	110	347	91	20	1	20	173	62	69	38	0	98	4	4	2	7	3	.70	15	.262	.340	.499
2000 Tucson	AAA Ari	23	66	12	2	1	0	16	10	3	14	0	11	1	0	0	2	1	.67	3	.182	.333	.242
Yuma	IND —	16	63	27	10	0	1	40	17	15	8	1	13	1	0	0	6	1	.86	1	.429	.500	.635
1996 Oakland	AL	50	105	28	7	1	3	46	20	12	16	0	31	1	1	1	4	0	1.00	2	.267	.366	.438
1997 Oakland	AL	92	279	69	10	2	3	92	55	18	50	1	82	5	7	1	5	4	.56	5	.247	.370	.330
1998 Anaheim	AL	43	98	23	6	0	2	35	13	11	9	0	22	3	1	0	1	0	1.00	3	.235	.318	.357
9 Min. YEARS		695	2371	644	126	21	62	998	394	310	288	6	625	30	20	17	108	41	.72	56	.272	.356	.421
3 Maj. YEARS		185	482	120	23	3	8	173	88	41	75	1	135	9	9	2	10	4	.71	10	.249	.359	.359

Justin Mashore

Bats: Right **Throws:** Right **Pos:** OF-71; 3B-6; PH-4; SS-3; 2B-1; DH-1; PR-1 **Ht:** 5'9" **Wt:** 190 **Born:** 2/14/72 **Age:** 29

Year Team	Lg Org	G	AB	H	2B	3B	HR	TB	R	RBI	TBB	IBB	SO	HBP	SH	SF	SB	CS	SB%	GDP	Avg	OBP	SLG
1991 Bristol	R+ Det	58	177	36	3	0	3	48	29	11	28	1	65	0	2	0	17	6	.74	1	.203	.312	.271
1992 Fayettevlle	A Det	120	401	96	18	3	4	132	54	43	36	2	117	3	9	1	31	8	.79	3	.239	.306	.329
1993 Lakeland	A+ Det	118	442	113	11	4	3	141	64	30	37	4	92	6	16	5	26	13	.67	9	.256	.318	.319
1994 Trenton	AA Det	131	450	100	13	5	7	144	63	45	36	0	120	3	8	3	31	7	.82	9	.222	.283	.320
1995 Toledo	AAA Det	72	223	49	4	3	4	71	32	21	14	1	62	3	9	2	12	9	.57	1	.220	.273	.318
Jacksnville	AA Det	40	148	36	8	2	4	60	26	15	6	0	41	3	3	0	5	1	.83	2	.243	.287	.405
1996 Jacksnville	AA Det	120	453	129	27	8	7	193	67	50	33	1	97	4	7	2	17	13	.57	10	.285	.337	.426
1997 Mobile	AA SD	90	281	67	10	5	11	120	53	41	32	2	70	5	3	3	11	8	.58	8	.238	.324	.427
1998 Chico	IND —	87	369	107	18	5	14	177	88	69	31	3	91	5	4	2	45	15	.75	6	.290	.351	.480
1999 Trenton	AA Bos	5	16	6	2	2	0	12	3	5	1	1	4	0	0	0	1	0	1.00		.375	.412	.750
Sarasota	A+ Bos	17	49	8	3	0	2	17	6	4	5	0	13	0	1	0	1	0	1.00		.163	.241	.347
St. Lucie	A+ NYM	28	104	22	4	2	1	33	13	10	7	1	25	2	0	1	1	4	.20	3	.212	.272	.317
Binghamton	AA NYM	13	42	9	2	0	1	14	4	3	0	0	13	1	1	0	1	0	1.00	2	.214	.233	.333
2000 Yuma	IND —	66	269	91	19	6	8	146	61	47	30	2	55	4	3	3	13	4	.76	5	.338	.408	.543
Carolina	AA Col	17	43	10	1	1	1	16	4	4	4	1	8	2	0	0	2	1	.67	2	.233	.327	.372
10 Min. YEARS		982	3467	879	143	46	70	1324	567	398	300	19	873	41	66	22	214	89	.71	62	.254	.319	.382

Steve Matcuk

Pitches: Right **Bats:** Right **Pos:** RP-19; SP-8 **Ht:** 6'2" **Wt:** 185 **Born:** 4/8/76 **Age:** 25

Year Team	Lg Org	G	GS	CG	GF	IP	BFP	H	R	ER	HR	SH	SF	HB	TBB	IBB	SO	WP	Bk	W	L	Pct.	ShO	Sv	ERA
1996 Portland	A- Col	10	10	0	0	56.2	238	52	31	27	11	1	2	4	15	0	49	1	1	5	3	.625	0	0	4.29
1997 Asheville	A Col	28	27	3	1	159.2	674	157	86	79	15	2	5	10	55	1	100	2	1	5	12	.294	0	1	4.45
1998 Asheville	A Col	13	7	0	3	48.2	223	60	32	25	7	2	0	3	22	0	32	4	0	1	3	.250	0	1	4.62
Salem	A+ Col	18	15	1	1	99.1	420	107	59	52	12	4	4	12	18	0	69	4	0	3	11	.214	0	0	4.71
1999 Salem	A+ Col	26	26	1	0	152.2	672	157	100	86	10	8	1	20	64	0	103	6	0	8	11	.421	0	0	5.07
2000 Carolina	AA Col	5	1	0	1	18	90	25	14	14	1	0	4	4	10	0	6	2	0	1	0	1.000	0	0	7.00
Salem	A+ Col	22	7	0	0	60.2	287	72	48	45	5	3	1	5	33	0	42	4	0	4	3	.571	0	5	6.68
5 Min. YEARS		122	93	5	15	595.2	2604	630	370	328	61	20	17	58	217	1	401	23	2	27	43	.386	0	7	4.96

Henry Mateo

Bats: Both **Throws:** Right **Pos:** 2B-132; DH-5; PH-3 **Ht:** 5'11" **Wt:** 180 **Born:** 10/14/76 **Age:** 24

Year Team	Lg Org	G	AB	H	2B	3B	HR	TB	R	RBI	TBB	IBB	SO	HBP	SH	SF	SB	CS	SB%	GDP	Avg	OBP	SLG
1995 Expos	R Mon	38	122	18	0	0	0	18	11	6	14	0	47	5	5	1	2	7	.22	2	.148	.261	.148
1996 Expos	R Mon	14	44	11	3	0	0	14	8	3	5	0	11	3	2	0	5	1	.83	0	.250	.365	.318
1997 Vermont	A- Mon	67	228	56	9	3	1	74	32	31	30	1	44	7	3	2	21	11	.66	4	.246	.348	.325
1998 Cape Fear	A Mon	114	416	115	20	5	4	157	72	41	40	2	111	13	15	4	22	16	.58	5	.276	.355	.377
Jupiter	A+ Mon	12	43	12	3	1	0	17	11	6	2	0	6	2	1	1	3	0	1.00	0	.279	.333	.395
1999 Jupiter	A+ Mon	118	447	116	27	7	4	169	69	58	44	3	112	10	17	6	32	16	.67	4	.260	.335	.378
2000 Harrisburg	AA Mon	140	530	152	25	11	5	214	91	63	58	0	97	6	4	2	48	16	.75	4	.287	.362	.404
6 Min. YEARS		503	1830	480	87	27	14	663	294	208	193	6	428	46	47	16	133	67	.67	19	.262	.345	.362

Terry Mathews

Pitches: Right **Bats:** Left **Pos:** RP-7 **Ht:** 6'2" **Wt:** 225 **Born:** 10/5/64 **Age:** 36

Year Team	Lg Org	G	GS	CG	GF	IP	BFP	H	R	ER	HR	SH	SF	HB	TBB	IBB	SO	WP	Bk	W	L	Pct.	ShO	Sv	ERA
1987 Gastonia	A Tex	34	1	0	13	48.1	234	53	35	30	5	4	5	2	32	4	46	7	1	3	3	.500	0	0	5.59
1988 Charlotte	A+ Tex	27	26	2	0	163.2	672	141	68	51	6	3	3	4	49	2	94	11	3	13	6	.684	1	0	2.80
1989 Tulsa	AA Tex	10	10	1	0	45.1	211	53	40	31	3	2	6	2	24	1	32	6	3	2	5	.286	0	0	6.15
Charlotte	A+ Tex	10	10	0	0	59.1	241	55	28	24	2	1	3	2	17	0	30	2	0	4	2	.667	0	0	3.64
1990 Tulsa	AA Tex	14	14	4	0	86.1	375	88	50	41	1	1	6	2	36	2	48	9	0	5	7	.417	2	0	4.27
Okla City	AAA Tex	12	11	1	0	70.2	307	81	39	29	4	3	4	3	15	0	36	2	0	2	7	.222	1	0	3.69
1991 Okla City	AAA Tex	18	13	1	2	95.1	410	98	39	37	2	3	3	2	34	3	63	4	1	5	6	.455	0	1	3.49
1992 Okla City	AAA Tex	9	2	0	3	16.2	73	17	8	8	1	0	0	1	7	0	13	2	0	1	1	.500	0	1	4.32
1993 Jackson	AA Hou	17	17	0	0	103	449	116	53	42	11	3	1	3	29	2	74	1	0	6	5	.545	0	0	3.67
Tucson	AAA Hou	16	4	0	4	33	152	40	14	13	1	2	0	3	11	1	34	1	0	5	0	1.000	0	2	3.55
1994 Edmonton	AAA Fla	13	12	3	0	84	358	88	43	40	4	1	4	3	22	1	46	3	0	4	4	.500	0	0	4.29
1995 Charlotte	AAA Fla	2	0	0	0	3.2	15	5	2	2	0	0	0	0	0	0	5	0	0	0	0	—	0	0	4.91
1998 Bowie	AA Bal	1	1	0	0	3	12	3	2	2	1	0	0	0	1	0	2	0	0	0	0	—	0	0	6.00
Rochester	AAA Bal	1	0	0	0	3	15	4	1	1	0	0	0	0	0	0	2	0	0	0	1	.000	0	0	3.00
Edmonton	AAA Oak	13	8	0	0	43.1	186	47	22	22	9	1	0	3	11	0	33	2	0	2	2	.500	0	0	4.57
1999 Royals	R KC	1	0	0	0	2	6	0	0	0	0	0	0	0	0	0	2	0	0	0	0	—	0	0	0.00
Wichita	AA KC	1	0	0	0	2	8	2	1	1	0	0	0	0	2	0	2	0	0	0	0	—	0	0	4.50
Omaha	AAA KC	7	0	0	2	16.1	60	11	4	3	0	0	0	0	5	0	11	2	0	1	0	1.000	0	0	1.65

Year Team	Lg Org	G	GS	CG	GF	IP	BFP	H	R	ER	HR	SH	SF	HB	TBB	IBB	SO	WP	Bk	W	L	Pct.	ShO	Sv	ERA
2000 Oklahoma	AAA Tex	7	0	0	3	11.1	53	13	10	8	1	1	1	0	5	1	10	2	0	0	1	.000	0	1	6.35
1991 Texas	AL	34	2	0	8	57.1	236	54	24	23	5	2	0	1	18	3	51	5	0	4	0	1.000	0	1	3.61
1992 Texas	AL	40	0	0	11	42.1	199	48	29	28	4	1	3	1	31	3	26	2	1	2	4	.333	0	0	5.95
1994 Florida	NL	24	2	0	5	43	179	45	16	16	4	1	0	1	9	1	21	1	0	2	1	.667	0	0	3.35
1995 Florida	NL	57	0	0	14	82.2	332	70	32	31	9	5	1	1	27	4	72	3	0	4	4	.500	0	3	3.38
1996 Florida	NL	57	0	0	19	55	247	59	33	30	7	2	1	1	27	5	49	0	0	2	4	.333	0	4	4.91
Baltimore	AL	14	0	0	5	18.2	79	20	7	7	3	1	0	0	7	0	13	0	0	2	2	.500	0	0	3.38
1997 Baltimore	AL	57	0	0	19	63.1	285	63	35	31	8	9	4	0	36	2	39	3	0	4	4	.500	0	1	4.41
1998 Baltimore	AL	17	0	0	2	20.1	90	26	15	14	6	5	1	0	8	3	10	0	0	0	1	.000	0	0	6.20
1999 Kansas City	AL	24	1	0	7	39	175	44	21	19	4	0	4	2	17	1	19	0	0	2	1	.667	0	1	4.38
12 Min. YEARS		213	131	12	26	890.1	3837	915	461	385	52	25	36	30	300	17	585	54	8	53	50	.515	4	6	3.89
8 Maj. YEARS		324	5	0	90	421.2	1822	429	212	199	50	26	14	7	180	22	300	14	1	22	21	.512	0	10	4.25

Jared Mathis

Bats: Right **Throws:** Right **Pos:** OF-35; 3B-29; 2B-23; SS-14; PH-8; C-5; 1B-1; PR-1; P-1   **Ht:** 5'10" **Wt:** 180 **Born:** 8/8/75 **Age:** 25

Year Team	Lg Org	G	AB	H	2B	3B	HR	TB	R	RBI	TBB	IBB	SO	HBP	SH	SF	SB	CS	SB%	GDP	Avg	OBP	SLG
1997 Lafayette	IND —	10	41	12	0	0	1	15	4	1	2	0	3	0	1	0	1	2	.33	1	.293	.326	.366
Lubbock	IND —	36	133	39	7	0	0	46	24	20	26	1	16	1	1	3	1	0	1.00	1	.293	.405	.346
Ogden	R+ Mil	54	197	55	14	0	0	69	30	29	6	0	20	4	4	1	7	3	.70	3	.279	.313	.350
1998 Beloit	A Mil	24	90	24	5	0	0	29	12	3	1	0	8	1	4	0	0	1	.00	4	.267	.283	.322
Stockton	A+ Mil	69	204	59	6	0	0	65	24	17	3	0	17	4	8	3	8	0	1.00	3	.289	.308	.319
1999 Stockton	A+ Mil	23	61	14	1	0	0	15	7	10	2	0	3	2	0	1	1	3	.25	3	.230	.273	.246
Huntsville	AA Mil	74	218	49	5	1	2	62	23	24	8	0	32	1	9	1	2	3	.40	2	.225	.254	.284
2000 Huntsville	AA Mil	101	351	91	23	1	2	122	49	21	12	1	49	13	9	1	5	9	.36	6	.259	.308	.348
4 Min. YEARS		391	1295	343	61	2	5	423	173	125	60	2	148	26	36	10	25	21	.54	21	.265	.308	.327

Francisco Matos

Bats: Right **Throws:** Right **Pos:** 2B-36; 3B-26; SS-13; DH-10; 1B-7; PH-5; PR-1; P-1   **Ht:** 6'1" **Wt:** 160 **Born:** 7/23/69 **Age:** 31

Year Team	Lg Org	G	AB	H	2B	3B	HR	TB	R	RBI	TBB	IBB	SO	HBP	SH	SF	SB	CS	SB%	GDP	Avg	OBP	SLG
1989 Modesto	A+ Oak	65	200	41	5	1	1	51	14	23	12	0	41	0	0	1	6	5	.55	5	.205	.249	.255
1990 Modesto	A+ Oak	83	321	88	12	1	1	105	46	20	15	0	65	5	7	2	26	5	.84	5	.274	.315	.327
Huntsville	AA Oak	45	180	41	3	3	0	50	18	12	9	1	18	1	2	1	7	4	.64	3	.228	.267	.278
1991 Huntsville	AA Oak	55	191	37	1	2	0	42	18	19	17	1	28	2	5	0	12	2	.86	8	.194	.267	.220
Modesto	A+ Oak	50	189	53	4	0	1	60	32	22	30	1	24	1	4	1	19	8	.70	5	.280	.380	.317
1992 Huntsville	AA Oak	44	150	33	5	1	1	43	11	14	11	0	27	2	1	1	4	4	.50	4	.220	.280	.287
1993 Huntsville	AA Oak	123	461	127	12	3	1	148	69	32	22	1	54	4	4	3	16	6	.73	6	.275	.312	.321
1994 Tacoma	AAA Oak	86	336	103	10	1	0	115	40	30	14	0	32	0	4	1	16	9	.64	13	.307	.331	.342
1995 Calgary	AAA Pit	100	341	110	11	6	3	142	36	40	5	0	25	2	3	1	9	2	.82	11	.323	.335	.416
1996 Ottawa	AAA Mon	100	307	73	15	3	2	100	30	23	16	0	35	3	3	2	4	5	.44	14	.238	.280	.326
1997 Rochester	AAA Bal	101	389	126	17	4	4	163	51	51	9	0	42	4	9	3	8	2	.80	15	.324	.343	.419
1998 Durham	AAA TB	32	114	27	2	3	0	35	13	14	1	0	15	1	2	1	2	1	.67	4	.237	.248	.307
Columbus	AAA NYY	76	293	99	18	2	2	127	42	33	20	0	26	2	0	1	3	2	.60	13	.338	.383	.433
1999 Tacoma	AAA Sea	100	393	122	24	3	3	161	43	33	18	0	41	2	5	5	4	6	.40	10	.310	.340	.410
2000 Rochester	AAA Bal	91	333	93	19	3	1	121	37	24	13	1	34	1	4	1	7	3	.70	15	.279	.309	.363
1994 Oakland	AL	14	28	7	1	0	0	8	1	2	1	0	2	0	0	1	1	0	1.00	1	.250	.267	.286
12 Min. YEARS		1151	4198	1173	158	36	20	1463	500	390	212	5	507	30	53	26	143	64	.69	128	.279	.317	.348

Josue Matos

Pitches: Right **Bats:** Right **Pos:** SP-28   **Ht:** 6'4" **Wt:** 190 **Born:** 3/15/78 **Age:** 23

Year Team	Lg Org	G	GS	CG	GF	IP	BFP	H	R	ER	HR	SH	SF	HB	TBB	IBB	SO	WP	Bk	W	L	Pct.	ShO	Sv	ERA
1997 Mariners	R Sea	14	1	0	5	45.1	190	48	27	21	4	1	1	0	6	0	50	3	4	1	0	1.000	0	1	4.17
Everett	A- Sea	2	0	0	1	4.1	20	5	2	1	0	0	0	0	2	0	6	1	1	0	0	—	0	0	2.08
1998 Mariners	R Sea	17	2	0	6	41	164	29	14	10	2	1	0	2	11	0	51	3	2	3	0	1.000	0	0	2.20
1999 Wisconsin	A Sea	25	22	2	0	138	596	143	78	71	19	1	5	4	42	1	136	4	2	9	9	.500	1	0	4.63
2000 Lancaster	A+ Sea	14	14	0	0	88.2	358	78	29	26	8	2	0	3	22	1	93	3	4	3	3	.500	0	0	2.64
New Haven	AA Sea	14	14	1	0	84.1	349	77	36	34	11	2	2	6	23	0	60	1	1	4	5	.444	0	0	3.63
4 Min. YEARS		86	53	3	12	401.2	1677	380	186	163	44	7	8	15	106	2	396	15	18	20	17	.541	1	1	3.65

Julius Matos

Bats: Right **Throws:** Right **Pos:** SS-128; 2B-5; DH-1; PH-1   **Ht:** 5'11" **Wt:** 175 **Born:** 12/12/74 **Age:** 26

Year Team	Lg Org	G	AB	H	2B	3B	HR	TB	R	RBI	TBB	IBB	SO	HBP	SH	SF	SB	CS	SB%	GDP	Avg	OBP	SLG
1994 Watertown	A- Cle	43	138	34	2	2	0	40	13	18	13	0	33	0	0	2	3	2	.60	6	.246	.307	.290
1995 Columbus	A Cle	52	155	38	7	3	0	51	16	13	11	1	21	3	1	0	2	2	.50	8	.245	.308	.329
1996 Thunder Bay	IND —	82	295	81	13	0	3	103	33	32	14	0	48	2	5	1	8	7	.53	9	.275	.311	.349
1997 Sioux City	IND —	83	353	94	12	3	6	130	64	44	20	0	38	4	1	2	8	7	.53	4	.266	.311	.368
1998 High Desert	A+ Ari	111	439	132	27	4	4	179	70	60	23	0	40	2	7	8	19	13	.59	9	.301	.333	.408
1999 El Paso	AA Ari	120	425	119	17	5	5	161	54	41	13	1	37	1	4	3	5	2	.71	10	.280	.301	.379
2000 Mobile	AA SD	135	546	144	30	0	5	189	61	35	31	0	57	2	7	0	11	9	.55	13	.264	.306	.346
7 Min. YEARS		626	2351	642	108	17	23	853	311	243	125	1	274	14	25	16	56	42	.57	59	.273	.312	.363

Pascual Matos

Bats: Right **Throws:** Right **Pos:** C-85; PH-5; DH-4   **Ht:** 6'2" **Wt:** 160 **Born:** 12/23/74 **Age:** 26

Year Team	Lg Org	G	AB	H	2B	3B	HR	TB	R	RBI	TBB	IBB	SO	HBP	SH	SF	SB	CS	SB%	GDP	Avg	OBP	SLG
1992 Braves	R Atl	13	33	5	1	0	0	6	3	0	10	0	12	0	0	0	0	1	.00	1	.152	.349	.182
1993 Braves	R Atl	36	119	27	5	1	0	34	12	15	3	0	32	2	1	1	3	1	.75	1	.227	.256	.286
1994 Macon	A Atl	11	29	5	2	0	0	7	1	2	0	0	10	1	0	0	1	0	1.00	0	.172	.200	.241
Idaho Falls	R+ Atl	43	157	40	7	1	7	70	22	29	2	0	39	0	1	2	7	2	.78	1	.255	.261	.446
1995 Macon	A Atl	72	238	44	11	1	5	72	23	26	11	0	86	1	0	0	2	2	.50	4	.185	.224	.303
1996 Durham	A+ Atl	67	219	49	9	3	6	82	24	28	7	0	70	3	0	1	6	0	1.00	0	.224	.257	.374
1997 Durham	A+ Atl	117	430	104	18	3	18	182	51	50	14	3	122	2	0	1	4	5	.44	12	.242	.268	.423
1998 Greenville	AA Atl	98	338	84	16	1	12	138	40	58	14	2	102	4	3	2	4	1	.80	6	.249	.285	.408
1999 Richmond	AAA Atl	66	224	47	7	0	3	63	17	21	6	0	47	1	3	2	3	1	.75	6	.210	.232	.281
2000 Richmond	AAA Atl	70	230	55	9	2	4	80	21	21	8	0	65	3	3	0	1	1	.50	5	.239	.274	.348
Greenville	AA Atl	24	84	14	7	0	0	21	7	5	5	0	26	1	0	1	1	0	1.00	5	.167	.220	.250
1999 Atlanta	NL	6	8	1	0	0	0	1	0	2	0	0	1	0	0	0	0	0	—	1	.125	.125	.125
9 Min. YEARS		617	2101	474	92	12	55	755	221	255	80	5	611	18	11	10	32	14	.70	49	.226	.259	.359

David Matranga

Bats: Right **Throws:** Right **Pos:** SS-115; PH-5   **Ht:** 6'0" **Wt:** 196 **Born:** 1/8/77 **Age:** 24

Year Team	Lg Org	G	AB	H	2B	3B	HR	TB	R	RBI	TBB	IBB	SO	HBP	SH	SF	SB	CS	SB%	GDP	Avg	OBP	SLG
1998 Auburn	A- Hou	40	144	44	13	1	4	71	34	24	25	1	38	5	1	1	16	3	.84	0	.306	.423	.493
1999 Kissimmee	A+ Hou	124	472	109	20	4	6	155	70	48	68	0	118	12	9	2	17	10	.63	3	.231	.341	.328
2000 Round Rock	AA Hou	120	373	87	14	3	6	125	50	44	48	0	99	17	2	1	5	5	.50	1	.233	.346	.335
3 Min. YEARS		284	989	240	47	8	16	351	154	116	141	1	255	34	12	4	38	18	.68	4	.243	.355	.355

Troy Mattes

Pitches: Right **Bats:** Right **Pos:** SP-28   **Ht:** 6'7" **Wt:** 230 **Born:** 8/26/75 **Age:** 25

Year Team	Lg Org	G	GS	CG	GF	IP	BFP	H	R	ER	HR	SH	SF	HB	TBB	IBB	SO	WP	Bk	W	L	Pct.	ShO	Sv	ERA
1994 Expos	R Mon	12	11	1	0	55.2	221	35	25	21	2	0	0	3	21	0	51	7	0	3	2	.600	1	0	3.40
1995 Albany	A Mon	4	4	0	0	19.2	90	21	12	11	0	2	0	0	12	1	15	1	1	0	2	.000	0	0	5.03
Vermont	A- Mon	10	10	0	0	46	209	51	34	19	3	5	4	5	25	0	23	7	0	3	4	.429	0	0	3.72
Expos	R Mon	2	2	0	0	12	43	7	0	0	0	0	0	0	3	0	8	0	0	2	0	1.000	0	0	0.00
1996 Delmarva	A Mon	27	27	5	0	173.1	714	142	77	55	14	6	4	14	50	0	151	17	1	10	9	.526	3	0	2.86
1997 Wst Plm Bch	A+ Mon	20	16	2	3	102	441	123	61	56	8	3	5	5	20	0	61	11	1	6	9	.400	2	1	4.94
1998 Jupiter	A+ Mon	17	10	0	2	73.1	307	73	33	25	4	2	1	3	19	0	42	2	1	7	6	.538	0	0	3.07
1999 Jupiter	A+ Mon	5	5	0	0	24.1	103	27	11	10	2	1	1	3	7	0	12	0	0	3	0	1.000	0	0	3.70
Harrisburg	AA Mon	20	19	0	0	97.1	433	114	67	58	12	8	4	7	38	0	58	3	0	5	8	.385	0	0	5.36
2000 Harrisburg	AA Mon	28	28	4	0	174.1	729	170	91	81	20	5	3	4	56	1	109	6	0	11	9	.550	0	0	4.18
7 Min. YEARS		145	132	12	5	778	3290	763	411	336	65	32	22	44	251	2	530	54	4	50	49	.505	6	1	3.89

Rob Mattson

Pitches: Right **Bats:** Left **Pos:** SP-23; RP-1   **Ht:** 6'1" **Wt:** 190 **Born:** 11/18/66 **Age:** 34

Year Team	Lg Org	G	GS	CG	GF	IP	BFP	H	R	ER	HR	SH	SF	HB	TBB	IBB	SO	WP	Bk	W	L	Pct.	ShO	Sv	ERA
1991 Macon	A Atl	23	7	3	4	76.2	312	61	29	24	1	1	4	4	17	1	51	5	1	5	2	.714	1	0	2.82
Durham	A+ Atl	8	8	2	1	45.2	190	48	23	22	2	2	1	0	9	1	32	3	2	1	4	.200	0	0	4.34
1992 Beloit	A Mil	8	1	0	2	17.1	76	15	8	8	1	1	1	0	7	1	16	0	2	1	0	1.000	0	0	4.15
1995 Memphis	AA SD	30	28	11	1	201.2	862	199	109	92	20	7	15	20	73	2	139	4	4	12	13	.480	3	0	4.11
1996 Memphis	AA SD	27	27	3	0	164.1	708	172	87	79	19	2	4	7	54	2	88	5	2	13	8	.619	1	0	4.33
2000 Nashville	AAA Pit	17	17	0	0	98	437	103	67	61	13	7	1	9	48	0	66	4	1	6	8	.429	0	0	5.60
Altoona	AA Pit	7	6	0	0	37	179	48	33	26	4	2	2	5	16	1	19	0	0	1	1	.500	0	0	6.32
5 Min. YEARS		121	94	19	8	640.2	2764	646	356	312	60	22	28	45	224	8	411	21	12	39	36	.520	5	1	4.38

Brian Matz

Pitches: Left **Bats:** Left **Pos:** RP-28; SP-13   **Ht:** 6'1" **Wt:** 195 **Born:** 9/23/74 **Age:** 26

Year Team	Lg Org	G	GS	CG	GF	IP	BFP	H	R	ER	HR	SH	SF	HB	TBB	IBB	SO	WP	Bk	W	L	Pct.	ShO	Sv	ERA
1996 Vermont	A- Mon	14	9	0	3	55.1	224	41	20	16	3	1	0	2	18	0	53	2	0	5	3	.625	0	0	2.60
1997 Cape Fear	A Mon	44	5	0	12	96.1	424	102	54	47	9	5	6	8	41	0	64	13	1	4	6	.400	1	0	4.39
1998 Cape Fear	A Mon	17	16	0	0	98.2	391	75	35	31	5	4	1	3	28	0	63	11	0	3	5	.375	0	0	2.83
Jupiter	A+ Mon	15	6	0	4	41.2	196	54	31	28	3	1	0	2	19	0	29	2	0	2	4	.333	0	2	6.05
1999 Jupiter	A+ Mon	41	1	0	17	91.1	375	77	30	24	3	7	0	6	31	1	46	4	1	5	2	.714	0	7	2.36
2000 Harrisburg	AA Mon	41	13	0	15	94	409	95	62	48	10	3	4	4	34	0	57	2	1	7	6	.538	0	2	4.60
5 Min. YEARS		172	50	1	51	477.1	2019	444	232	194	33	21	11	25	171	1	312	34	3	25	24	.510	1	11	3.66

Mike Maurer

Pitches: Right **Bats:** Right **Pos:** RP-36; SP-1   **Ht:** 6'2" **Wt:** 185 **Born:** 7/4/72 **Age:** 28

Year Team	Lg Org	G	GS	CG	GF	IP	BFP	H	R	ER	HR	SH	SF	HB	TBB	IBB	SO	WP	Bk	W	L	Pct.	ShO	Sv	ERA
1994 Sou Oregon	A- Oak	17	8	0	5	63.1	285	68	42	25	2	4	4	5	20	1	67	7	3	2	6	.250	0	3	3.55
1995 Huntsville	AA Oak	17	0	0	14	20.2	100	34	18	15	2	1	0	5	5	2	19	2	0	0	0	.000	0	6	6.53
Modesto	A+ Oak	39	0	0	37	40.1	157	27	9	8	3	2	2	0	9	0	44	2	0	2	2	.500	0	18	1.79
1996 Huntsville	AA Oak	52	0	0	41	64.2	298	67	31	27	3	3	2	3	35	9	46	5	0	4	6	.400	0	8	3.76
1997 Huntsville	AA Oak	52	5	0	34	84.2	371	86	48	36	10	5	4	2	31	3	61	5	1	8	7	.533	0	2	3.83
1999 Athletics	R Oak	7	0	0	6	7.1	26	4	1	1	1	0	0	0	1	0	8	0	0	0	0	—	0	2	1.23
Modesto	A+ Oak	15	0	0	3	17	81	23	6	5	0	0	0	0	6	0	15	3	0	1	0	1.000	0	0	2.65

Year Team	Lg Org	G	GS	CG	GF	IP	BFP	H	R	ER	HR	SH	SF	HB	TBB	IBB	SO	WP	Bk	W	L	Pct.	ShO	Sv	ERA
2000 Midland	AA Oak	12	0	0	4	14.1	70	16	11	10	1	0	0	0	12	1	17	1	0	0	0	—	0	2	6.28
Athletics	R Oak	11	1	0	8	10.1	38	5	5	4	1	0	0	0	1	0	5	1	1	1	0	1.000	0	0	3.48
Visalia	A+ Oak	14	0	0	4	20.2	84	15	9	8	2	3	0	0	8	1	21	1	1	2	1	.667	0	0	3.48
6 Min. YEARS		236	14	0	146	343.1	1510	345	182	139	24	19	13	13	127	17	303	27	6	20	24	.455	0	43	3.64

Derrick May

Bats: Left **Throws:** Right **Pos:** DH-41; OF-14; PH-1   **Ht:** 6'4" **Wt:** 235 **Born:** 7/14/68 **Age:** 32

		BATTING																	BASERUNNING				PERCENTAGES		
Year Team	Lg Org	G	AB	H	2B	3B	HR	TB	R	RBI	TBB	IBB	SO	HBP	SH	SF		SB	CS	SB%	GDP		Avg	OBP	SLG
1986 Wytheville	R+ ChC	54	178	57	6	1	0	65	25	23	16	1	15	2	0	1		17	4	.81	3		.320	.381	.365
1987 Peoria	A ChC	128	439	131	19	8	9	193	60	52	42	4	106	1	0	5		5	7	.42	5		.298	.357	.440
1988 Winston-Sal	A+ ChC	130	485	148	29	9	8	219	76	65	37	4	82	5	0	5		13	8	.62	3		.305	.357	.452
1989 Charlotte	AA ChC	136	491	145	26	5	9	208	72	70	33	4	76	5	1	0		19	7	.73	8		.295	.346	.424
1990 Iowa	AAA ChC	119	459	136	27	1	8	189	55	69	23	4	50	0	1	6		5	6	.45	11		.296	.326	.412
1991 Iowa	AAA ChC	82	310	92	18	4	3	127	47	49	19	4	38	4	1	3		7	9	.44	9		.297	.342	.410
1992 Iowa	AAA ChC	8	30	11	4	1	2	23	6	8	3	0	3	0	0	0		0	0	—	1		.367	.424	.767
1998 Ottawa	AAA Bal	21	69	26	6	0	6	50	16	21	13	0	7	1	0	0		0	1	.00	0		.377	.482	.725
1999 Rochester	AAA Bal	71	295	82	19	3	5	122	39	43	22	1	28	1	0	2		4	2	.67	10		.278	.328	.414
2000 Rochester	AAA Bal	56	213	60	16	0	5	91	27	34	28	2	25	0	0	3		2	2	.50	6		.282	.361	.427
1990 Chicago	NL	17	61	15	3	0	1	21	8	11	2	0	7	0	0	0		1	0	1.00	1		.246	.270	.344
1991 Chicago	NL	15	22	5	2	0	1	10	4	3	2	0	1	0	0	0		0	0	—	1		.227	.280	.455
1992 Chicago	NL	124	351	96	11	0	8	131	33	45	14	4	40	3	2	1		5	3	.63	10		.274	.306	.373
1993 Chicago	NL	128	465	137	25	2	10	196	62	77	31	6	41	1	0	6		10	3	.77	15		.295	.336	.422
1994 Chicago	NL	100	345	98	19	2	8	145	43	51	30	4	34	0	1	2		3	2	.60	11		.284	.340	.420
1995 Milwaukee	AL	32	113	28	3	1	1	36	15	9	5	0	18	1	0	0		1	0	1.00	1		.248	.286	.319
Houston	NL	78	206	62	15	1	8	103	29	41	19	0	24	1	0	3		5	0	1.00	4		.301	.358	.500
1996 Houston	NL	109	259	65	12	3	5	98	24	33	30	8	33	2	0	3		2	2	.50	3		.251	.330	.378
1997 Philadelphia	NL	83	149	34	5	1	1	44	8	13	8	3	26	0	0	1		4	1	.80	4		.228	.266	.295
1998 Montreal	NL	85	180	43	8	0	5	66	13	15	11	1	24	0	0	1		0	0	—	5		.239	.281	.367
1999 Baltimore	AL	26	49	13	0	0	4	25	5	12	4	0	6	0	0	1		0	0	—	1		.265	.315	.510
10 Min. YEARS		805	2969	888	170	32	55	1287	423	434	236	24	430	19	3	25		72	46	.61	56		.299	.352	.433
10 Maj. YEARS		797	2200	596	103	10	52	875	244	310	156	26	254	8	3	19		30	12	.71	57		.271	.319	.398

Blake Mayo

Pitches: Right **Bats:** Right **Pos:** RP-21; SP-17   **Ht:** 6'2" **Wt:** 210 **Born:** 12/18/72 **Age:** 28

Year Team	Lg Org	G	GS	CG	GF	IP	BFP	H	R	ER	HR	SH	SF	HB	TBB	IBB	SO	WP	Bk	W	L	Pct.	ShO	Sv	ERA
1996 Yakima	A- LA	20	6	0	8	67.1	256	44	15	9	1	0	1	0	12	0	68	5	1	5	2	.714	0	1	1.20
1997 San Berndno	A+ LA	20	0	0	5	29.2	141	36	18	17	0	1	1	1	17	2	29	6	0	1	1	.500	0	5	5.16
1998 Vero Beach	A+ LA	32	7	0	21	82.2	356	70	35	27	7	8	2	1	48	4	53	4	0	4	7	.364	0	5	2.94
San Antonio	AA LA	13	0	0	5	18.1	73	13	3	3	0	0	0	0	6	0	15	3	1	2	1	.667	0	1	1.47
1999 San Antonio	AA LA	41	0	0	17	51	192	63	40	33	5	2	2	2	20	2	31	2	0	2	2	.500	0	3	5.82
El Paso	AA Ari	15	1	0	1	25	127	41	16	15	0	1	0	1	13	1	18	6	0	1	1	.500	0	1	5.40
2000 El Paso	AA Ari	38	17	0	1	136.1	617	157	73	62	5	8	4	8	57	1	120	11	0	8	3	.727	0	0	4.09
5 Min. YEARS		179	31	0	58	410.1	1800	424	200	166	18	20	10	13	173	10	334	37	2	23	17	.575	0	11	3.64

Josh McAffee

Bats: Right **Throws:** Right **Pos:** C-26; DH-7; PH-3   **Ht:** 6'0" **Wt:** 209 **Born:** 11/4/77 **Age:** 23

		BATTING																	BASERUNNING				PERCENTAGES		
Year Team	Lg Org	G	AB	H	2B	3B	HR	TB	R	RBI	TBB	IBB	SO	HBP	SH	SF		SB	CS	SB%	GDP		Avg	OBP	SLG
1996 Diamondbcks	R Ari	39	102	15	5	0	0	20	13	7	18	0	39	6	0	2		1	1	.50	1		.147	.305	.196
1997 South Bend	A Ari	50	168	33	9	1	4	56	16	17	12	0	67	6	0	0		0	1	.00	5		.196	.274	.333
Lethbridge	R+ Ari	36	101	20	5	2	4	41	26	18	13	0	32	5	2	1		0	1	.00	3		.198	.317	.406
1998 Tucson	AAA Ari	1	1	0	0	0	0	0	0	0	0	0	0	0	0	0		0	0	—	1		.000	.000	.000
High Desert	A+ Ari	4	9	2	1	0	0	3	3	2	2	0	5	0	0	0		0	0	—	0		.222	.462	.333
Lethbridge	R+ Ari	17	56	10	1	0	2	17	9	5	7	0	23	2	0	0		0	0	—	1		.179	.292	.304
South Bend	A Ari	21	66	6	1	0	2	13	3	4	7	0	31	1	0	0		0	0	—	0		.091	.189	.197
1999 South Bend	A Ari	68	232	57	16	0	5	88	32	24	35	0	76	5	0	2		0	1	.00	3		.246	.354	.379
2000 High Desert	A+ Ari	5	12	2	2	0	0	4	0	4	1	0	2	0	0	0		0	0	—	0		.167	.231	.333
Kissimmee	A+ Hou	26	84	13	1	0	3	23	10	15	5	0	33	0	0	0		1	0	1.00	0		.155	.245	.274
Tulsa	AA Tex	4	8	2	2	0	0	4	1	0	1	0	3	0	1	0		0	1	.00	0		.250	.333	.500
5 Min. YEARS		271	839	160	43	3	20	269	113	96	101	0	311	32	3	5		2	5	.29	17		.191	.300	.321

Jeff McAvoy

Pitches: Right **Bats:** Right **Pos:** RP-28   **Ht:** 6'2" **Wt:** 215 **Born:** 3/15/77 **Age:** 24

Year Team	Lg Org	G	GS	CG	GF	IP	BFP	H	R	ER	HR	SH	SF	HB	TBB	IBB	SO	WP	Bk	W	L	Pct.	ShO	Sv	ERA
2000 Cape Fear	A Mon	22	0	0	8	38.2	170	46	20	19	2	3	3	1	9	0	25	3	0	1	2	.333	0	2	4.42
Ottawa	AAA Mon	6	0	0	2	7.2	26	3	0	0	0	1	0	2	2	0	4	0	0	1	0	1.000	0	0	0.00
1 Min. YEARS		28	0	0	10	46.1	196	49	20	19	2	3	4	1	11	0	29	3	0	2	2	.500	0	2	3.69

Chris McBride

Pitches: Right **Bats:** Left **Pos:** RP-18; SP-4   **Ht:** 6'5" **Wt:** 210 **Born:** 10/13/73 **Age:** 27

Year Team	Lg Org	G	GS	CG	GF	IP	BFP	H	R	ER	HR	SH	SF	HB	TBB	IBB	SO	WP	Bk	W	L	Pct.	ShO	Sv	ERA
1994 St.Cathrnes	A- Tor	13	13	1	0	69.2	302	81	39	33	4	1	1	4	12	0	30	5	0	4	4	.500	0	0	4.26
1995 Hagerstown	A Tor	19	19	2	0	107	461	121	61	51	4	5	3	5	27	1	52	3	1	5	10	.333	0	0	4.29
1996 St.Cathrnes	A- Tor	6	6	1	0	43	169	37	14	12	2	0	4	4	7	0	28	2	0	3	1	.750	0	0	2.51
Hagerstown	A Tor	8	8	3	0	58.2	222	42	13	11	4	0	2	4	9	0	34	0	0	5	2	.714	2	0	1.69

Year Team	Lg Org	G	GS	CG	GF	IP	BFP	H	R	ER	HR	SH	SF	HB	TBB	IBB	SO	WP	Bk	W	L	Pct.	ShO	Sv	ERA
1997 Dunedin	A+ Tor	10	4	0	1	31	153	44	25	21	4	0	0	3	17	0	25	5	0	3	0	1.000	0	0	6.10
Knoxville	AA Tor	10	10	0	0	60.2	256	61	30	25	5	2	1	3	14	0	33	3	1	4	4	.500	0	0	3.71
1998 Knoxville	AA Tor	35	21	1	5	155.1	681	185	102	76	18	4	11	6	37	1	90	1	0	10	5	.667	0	2	4.40
2000 Tennessee	AA Tor	22	4	0	9	60.1	240	51	18	16	5	2	4	2	9	0	37	5	0	2	2	.500	0	1	2.39
6 Min. YEARS		123	85	8	15	585.2	2484	622	302	245	46	14	20	33	132	2	329	24	2	36	28	.563	2	3	3.76

Greg McCarthy

Pitches: Left **Bats:** Left **Pos:** RP-40 **Ht:** 6'2" **Wt:** 215 **Born:** 10/30/68 **Age:** 32

Year Team	Lg Org	G	GS	CG	GF	IP	BFP	H	R	ER	HR	SH	SF	HB	TBB	IBB	SO	WP	Bk	W	L	Pct.	ShO	Sv	ERA
1987 Utica	A- Bal	20	0	0	13	29.2	130	14	9	3	0	2	1	2	23	2	40	1	2	4	1	.800	0	3	0.91
1988 Spartanburg	A Phi	34	1	0	20	64.2	297	52	36	29	3	3	3	10	52	0	65	8	3	4	2	.667	0	4	4.04
1989 Spartanburg	A Phi	24	15	2	4	112	499	90	58	52	3	3	5	9	80	0	115	8	2	5	8	.385	1	0	4.18
1990 Clearwater	A+ Phi	42	1	0	19	59.2	265	47	32	22	4	2	4	1	38	1	67	5	2	1	3	.250	0	5	3.32
1992 Kinston	A+ Cle	23	0	0	21	27.1	105	14	0	0	0	1	0	5	9	0	37	8	0	3	0	1.000	0	12	0.00
1993 Kinston	A+ Cle	9	0	0	6	10.2	51	8	4	2	0	0	0	0	13	0	14	2	0	0	0	—	0	2	1.69
Canton-Akrn	AA Cle	33	0	0	19	34.1	156	28	18	18	1	0	3	2	37	2	39	5	0	2	3	.400	0	6	4.72
1994 Canton-Akrn	AA Cle	22	0	0	19	32	133	19	12	8	0	0	0	1	23	2	39	2	0	2	3	.400	0	9	2.25
Charlotte	AAA Cle	18	0	0	11	23.1	118	17	22	18	1	1	2	6	28	1	21	5	0	1	0	1.000	0	1	6.94
1995 Birmingham	AA CWS	38	0	0	13	44.2	195	37	28	25	4	4	2	2	29	3	48	3	1	3	3	.500	0	5	5.04
1996 Tacoma	AAA Sea	39	0	0	14	68.1	317	58	31	25	2	3	1	5	53	2	90	11	4	4	2	.667	0	3	3.29
1997 Tacoma	AAA Sea	22	0	0	10	22	103	21	8	8	3	1	0	2	16	2	34	1	0	2	1	.667	0	3	3.27
1998 Tacoma	AAA Sea	19	0	0	6	19.1	95	15	14	9	2	1	1	2	22	0	24	4	0	1	2	.333	0	1	4.19
1999 Tacoma	AAA Sea	18	0	0	6	22	94	18	6	5	0	0	1	2	13	1	14	3	0	0	1	.000	0	2	2.05
Columbus	AAA NYY	29	0	0	17	35	150	24	19	15	4	0	2	1	19	0	21	3	0	2	1	.667	0	1	3.86
2000 Calgary	AAA Fla	40	0	0	10	38.1	198	43	38	31	3	8	1	3	30	0	30	1	0	4	3	.571	0	1	7.28
1996 Seattle	AL	10	0	0	1	9.2	45	8	2	2	0	1	1	4	10	0	7	0	0	0	0	—	0	0	1.86
1997 Seattle	AL	37	0	0	4	29.2	130	26	21	18	4	0	0	1	16	0	34	4	0	1	1	.500	0	0	5.46
1998 Seattle	AL	29	0	0	5	23.1	106	18	13	13	6	2	0	3	17	2	25	1	0	1	2	.333	0	0	5.01
13 Min. YEARS		430	17	2	208	643.1	2906	505	335	270	30	29	24	58	485	16	698	70	12	38	33	.535	1	52	3.78
3 Maj. YEARS		76	0	0	10	62.2	281	52	36	33	10	3	1	8	37	2	66	5	0	2	3	.400	0	0	4.74

Scott McClain

Bats: Right **Throws:** Right **Pos:** 3B-120; DH-2; PH-2; PR-1 **Ht:** 6'4" **Wt:** 220 **Born:** 5/19/72 **Age:** 29

Year Team	Lg Org	G	AB	H	2B	3B	HR	TB	R	RBI	TBB	IBB	SO	HBP	SH	SF	SB	CS	SB%	GDP	Avg	OBP	SLG
1990 Bluefield	R+ Bal	40	107	21	2	0	4	35	20	15	22	0	35	2	0	4	2	3	.40	1	.196	.333	.327
1991 Kane County	A Bal	25	81	18	0	0	0	18	9	4	17	0	25	0	1	0	1	1	.50	4	.222	.357	.222
Bluefield	R+ Bal	41	149	39	5	0	0	44	16	24	14	0	39	3	0	1	5	3	.63	3	.262	.335	.295
1992 Kane County	A Bal	96	316	84	12	2	3	109	43	30	48	1	62	6	6	1	7	4	.64	5	.266	.372	.345
1993 Frederick	A+ Bal	133	427	111	22	2	9	164	65	54	70	0	88	6	3	2	10	6	.63	8	.260	.370	.384
1994 Bowie	AA Bal	133	427	103	29	1	11	167	71	58	72	2	89	1	2	7	6	3	.67	14	.241	.347	.391
1995 Rochester	AAA Bal	61	199	50	9	0	8	85	32	22	23	0	34	1	1	0	2	1	.00	5	.251	.329	.427
Bowie	AA Bal	70	259	72	14	1	13	127	41	61	25	1	44	3	0	4	2	1	.67	13	.278	.344	.490
1996 Rochester	AAA Bal	131	463	130	23	4	17	212	76	69	61	1	109	1	0	7	8	6	.57	6	.281	.361	.458
1997 Norfolk	AAA NYM	127	429	120	29	2	21	216	71	64	64	5	93	2	1	8	1	3	.25	8	.280	.370	.503
1998 Durham	AAA TB	126	472	141	35	0	34	278	91	109	66	5	113	2	1	3	6	2	.75	9	.299	.385	.589
1999 Durham	AAA TB	137	533	134	33	1	28	253	106	104	73	1	156	3	0	6	4	2	.67	11	.251	.341	.475
2000 Colo Sprngs	AAA Col	123	438	121	25	3	25	227	76	87	62	2	89	6	0	6	8	9	.47	11	.276	.369	.518
1998 Tampa Bay	AL	9	20	2	0	0	0	2	2	0	2	0	6	1	0	0	0	0	—	0	.100	.217	.100
11 Min. YEARS		1243	4300	1144	238	17	173	1935	717	701	617	18	976	36	15	51	60	44	.58	98	.266	.359	.450

Matt McClellan

Pitches: Right **Bats:** Right **Pos:** SP-27; RP-1 **Ht:** 6'7" **Wt:** 210 **Born:** 8/13/76 **Age:** 24

Year Team	Lg Org	G	GS	CG	GF	IP	BFP	H	R	ER	HR	SH	SF	HB	TBB	IBB	SO	WP	Bk	W	L	Pct.	ShO	Sv	ERA
1997 Medcine Hat	R+ Tor	14	6	0	1	39	192	50	36	30	7	0	3	3	24	0	43	2	0	2	5	.286	0	0	6.92
1998 Hagerstown	A Tor	25	25	1	0	139.2	589	109	65	48	8	5	4	14	58	3	126	6	5	8	7	.533	0	0	3.09
1999 Dunedin	A+ Tor	26	25	1	0	147.1	612	114	69	62	15	1	5	10	61	0	146	6	3	13	5	.722	0	0	3.79
2000 Tennessee	AA Tor	28	27	0	0	168.2	743	174	100	90	16	2	4	11	69	1	140	11	3	6	12	.333	0	0	4.80
4 Min. YEARS		93	83	2	1	494.2	2136	447	270	230	46	8	16	38	212	4	455	25	11	29	29	.500	0	0	4.18

Matt McClendon

Pitches: Right **Bats:** Right **Pos:** SP-27; RP-1 **Ht:** 6'6" **Wt:** 220 **Born:** 10/13/77 **Age:** 23

Year Team	Lg Org	G	GS	CG	GF	IP	BFP	H	R	ER	HR	SH	SF	HB	TBB	IBB	SO	WP	Bk	W	L	Pct.	ShO	Sv	ERA
1999 Jamestown	A- Atl	7	7	0	0	23	94	18	11	10	2	0	0	1	11	0	24	2	0	1	1	.500	0	0	3.91
2000 Myrtle Bch	A+ Atl	6	6	0	0	39.2	147	24	7	7	1	1	0	0	8	0	43	1	0	3	1	.750	0	0	1.59
Greenville	AA Atl	22	21	1	1	131	561	124	59	55	6	4	8	5	54	0	90	12	0	7	6	.538	1	0	3.78
2 Min. YEARS		35	34	1	1	193.2	802	166	77	72	9	5	8	6	73	0	157	15	0	11	8	.579	1	0	3.35

Travis McClendon

Bats: Right **Throws:** Right **Pos:** C-44; PH-2; OF-1; DH-1 **Ht:** 5'11" **Wt:** 185 **Born:** 10/22/72 **Age:** 28

Year Team	Lg Org	G	AB	H	2B	3B	HR	TB	R	RBI	TBB	IBB	SO	HBP	SH	SF	SB	CS	SB%	GDP	Avg	OBP	SLG
1995 New Jersey	A- StL	50	161	46	9	1	1	60	25	18	10	1	25	5	1	1	6	3	.67	5	.286	.345	.373
1996 Peoria	A StL	60	155	30	8	0	0	38	23	23	17	1	27	4	4	1	1	4	.20	5	.194	.288	.245
1997 Peoria	A StL	6	14	3	0	0	0	3	1	2	3	0	4	0	0	0	0	0	—	0	.214	.353	.214

Year Team	Lg Org	BATTING G	AB	H	2B	3B	HR	TB	R	RBI	TBB	IBB	SO	HBP	SH	SF	BASERUNNING SB	CS	SB%	GDP	PERCENTAGES Avg	OBP	SLG
1998 Elmira	IND —	60	180	50	8	1	2	66	25	21	20	2	33	4	4	2	14	1	.93	3	.278	.359	.367
1999 Zion	IND —	71	276	100	17	4	3	134	59	36	21	0	29	5	2	1	23	4	.85	6	.362	.416	.486
2000 Tacoma	AAA Sea	1	1	0	0	0	0	0	0	0	0	0	0	0	0	0	0	0	—	0	.000	.000	.000
New Haven	AA Sea	3	13	2	0	0	0	2	1	0	0	0	1	0	0	0	0	0	—	0	.154	.154	.154
Lancaster	A+ Sea	43	136	34	5	0	0	39	17	20	18	0	23	4	3	2	7	3	.70	3	.250	.350	.287
6 Min. YEARS		294	936	265	47	6	6	342	151	120	89	4	142	22	14	7	51	15	.77	22	.283	.357	.365

Brian McClure

Bats: Left **Throws:** Right **Pos:** OF-51; 2B-22; PH-12; DH-8; 1B-6; SS-4; 3B-2; P-1 **Ht:** 6'0" **Wt:** 195 **Born:** 1/15/74 **Age:** 27

Year Team	Lg Org	BATTING G	AB	H	2B	3B	HR	TB	R	RBI	TBB	IBB	SO	HBP	SH	SF	BASERUNNING SB	CS	SB%	GDP	PERCENTAGES Avg	OBP	SLG
1996 Idaho Falls	R+ SD	72	308	99	18	6	6	147	62	45	38	0	63	3	0	4	10	2	.83	6	.321	.397	.477
1997 Clinton	A SD	118	416	115	18	11	4	167	75	55	90	4	64	1	3	6	12	11	.52	7	.276	.402	.401
1998 Rancho Cuca	A+ SD	129	492	130	25	11	9	204	89	57	66	2	98	7	5	4	4	3	.57	8	.264	.357	.415
1999 Rancho Cuca	A+ SD	36	116	26	5	1	2	39	26	15	26	0	22	1	3	2	4	1	.80	1	.224	.366	.336
Mobile	AA SD	51	169	35	10	3	1	54	17	27	17	1	34	2	1	2	0	0	—	4	.207	.284	.320
2000 Toledo	AAA Det	16	48	15	2	1	0	19	7	3	9	0	8	0	0	0	1	0	1.00	0	.313	.421	.396
Jacksnville	AA Det	81	246	70	17	0	1	90	33	18	40	0	46	0	1	1	2	1	.67	4	.285	.383	.366
5 Min. YEARS		503	1795	490	95	33	23	720	309	220	286	7	335	14	13	19	33	18	.65	30	.273	.374	.401

Sam McConnell

Pitches: Left **Bats:** Left **Pos:** SP-21; RP-7 **Ht:** 6'1" **Wt:** 213 **Born:** 12/31/75 **Age:** 25

Year Team	Lg Org	HOW MUCH HE PITCHED G	GS	CG	GF	IP	BFP	WHAT HE GAVE UP H	R	ER	HR	SH	SF	HB	TBB	IBB	SO	WP	Bk	THE RESULTS W	L	Pct.	ShO	Sv	ERA
1997 Erie	A- Pit	17	10	0	0	58.2	261	56	38	33	7	1	3	3	24	0	45	6	0	2	2	.500	0	0	5.06
1998 Augusta	A Pit	8	8	1	0	45	183	36	22	16	2	1	1	1	13	1	35	1	1	4	3	.571	0	0	3.20
Lynchburg	A+ Pit	19	19	3	0	121	483	118	48	39	4	2	1	1	20	0	80	2	0	8	5	.615	1	0	2.90
Carolina	AA Pit	2	1	0	0	12	53	15	7	6	2	1	1	0	3	0	5	0	0	0	1	.000	0	0	4.50
1999 Lynchburg	A+ Pit	15	15	4	0	101.2	402	84	41	36	8	3	5	5	27	1	70	6	0	7	3	.700	2	0	3.19
Altoona	AA Pit	13	12	1	0	62.1	299	82	52	46	7	6	3	4	33	1	40	5	1	1	7	.125	0	0	6.64
2000 Altoona	AA Pit	20	13	3	0	106	422	83	24	19	3	2	2	2	26	0	61	1	1	9	2	.818	1	0	1.61
Nashville	AAA Pit	8	8	0	0	49	216	58	36	35	8	1	2	4	16	0	22	1	0	2	4	.200	0	0	6.43
4 Min. YEARS		102	86	12	0	555.2	2319	532	268	230	41	17	17	20	162	3	358	22	3	32	27	.542	4	0	3.73

Scott McCrary

Pitches: Right **Bats:** Right **Pos:** RP-28 **Ht:** 6'4" **Wt:** 207 **Born:** 1/8/74 **Age:** 27

Year Team	Lg Org	HOW MUCH HE PITCHED G	GS	CG	GF	IP	BFP	WHAT HE GAVE UP H	R	ER	HR	SH	SF	HB	TBB	IBB	SO	WP	Bk	THE RESULTS W	L	Pct.	ShO	Sv	ERA
1997 Mets	R NYM	5	0	0	4	9	36	5	3	0	0	0	0	1	2	0	15	2	1	1	0	1.000	0	2	0.00
Capital Cty	A NYM	13	0	0	5	28	104	20	4	3	1	1	1	0	5	1	24	2	0	3	2	.600	0	0	0.96
1998 Binghamton	AA NYM	1	1	0	0	6	21	1	0	0	0	0	0	0	1	0	8	0	0	1	0	1.000	0	0	0.00
St. Lucie	A+ NYM	37	4	0	14	92.1	373	78	40	30	9	3	2	2	18	2	75	7	1	8	4	.667	0	6	2.92
1999 Binghamton	AA NYM	17	6	0	3	53.2	247	72	34	29	8	4	4	1	21	0	29	1	0	1	5	.167	0	0	4.86
2000 Binghamton	AA NYM	5	0	0	1	11	53	15	10	10	1	0	2	0	8	0	11	1	0	0	0	—	0	1	8.18
St. Lucie	A+ NYM	23	0	0	10	40	172	39	20	18	3	3	1	0	12	1	34	1	0	2	3	.400	0	2	4.05
4 Min. YEARS		101	11	0	37	240	1006	230	111	90	22	11	10	5	67	4	196	14	2	16	14	.533	0	11	3.38

Paul McCurtain

Pitches: Right **Bats:** Right **Pos:** RP-42; SP-2 **Ht:** 6'1" **Wt:** 190 **Born:** 2/5/76 **Age:** 25

Year Team	Lg Org	HOW MUCH HE PITCHED G	GS	CG	GF	IP	BFP	WHAT HE GAVE UP H	R	ER	HR	SH	SF	HB	TBB	IBB	SO	WP	Bk	THE RESULTS W	L	Pct.	ShO	Sv	ERA
1998 Portland	AA Fla	1	0	0	0	1.2	8	0	1	1	0	1	0	0	2	0	2	1	0	0	0	—	0	0	5.40
Utica	A Fla	17	2	0	5	39	173	35	25	19	1	5	0	3	19	2	33	7	0	0	1	.000	0	1	4.38
1999 Brevard Cty	A+ Fla	40	0	0	32	57.2	261	59	32	22	1	0	1	2	25	0	49	2	1	3	2	.600	0	12	3.43
2000 Brevard Cty	A+ Fla	3	0	0	0	6	24	6	2	2	0	0	0	0	2	1	8	1	0	0	0	—	0	0	3.00
Portland	AA Fla	41	2	0	16	85.1	382	98	46	39	9	4	3	5	34	2	56	1	0	6	1	.857	0	2	4.11
3 Min. YEARS		102	4	0	53	189.2	848	198	106	83	11	10	4	10	82	5	148	12	1	9	4	.692	0	15	3.94

Mike McCutcheon

Pitches: Left **Bats:** Left **Pos:** RP-30; SP-10 **Ht:** 5'11" **Wt:** 158 **Born:** 7/5/77 **Age:** 23

Year Team	Lg Org	HOW MUCH HE PITCHED G	GS	CG	GF	IP	BFP	WHAT HE GAVE UP H	R	ER	HR	SH	SF	HB	TBB	IBB	SO	WP	Bk	THE RESULTS W	L	Pct.	ShO	Sv	ERA
1996 Diamondbcks	R Ari	14	0	0	11	18.1	70	9	3	1	0	1	0	2	7	0	18	1	0	0	1	.000	0	2	0.49
1997 South Bend	A Ari	31	17	0	6	105.2	464	104	55	40	5	3	5	5	49	1	67	9	2	7	5	.583	0	1	3.41
1998 South Bend	A Ari	13	6	0	4	49.1	214	53	30	20	2	2	1	0	22	0	32	8	2	3	3	.500	0	0	3.65
Lethbridge	R+ Ari	17	10	0	0	64.2	291	66	45	39	4	2	1	3	34	0	40	6	3	5	3	.625	0	0	5.43
1999 El Paso	AA Ari	3	1	0	0	8.2	41	7	8	6	1	0	1	0	9	0	8	1	0	1	1	.500	0	0	6.23
South Bend	A Ari	28	8	0	6	87.2	384	87	48	39	5	2	2	1	36	0	74	3	1	6	2	.750	0	0	4.00
2000 South Bend	A Ari	10	10	1	0	57.2	251	62	34	25	1	3	1	4	20	1	37	3	0	2	6	.250	0	0	3.90
El Paso	AA Ari	30	0	0	13	40.2	173	40	21	18	2	1	0	2	13	0	32	6	0	4	1	.800	0	0	3.98
5 Min. YEARS		146	52	1	40	432.2	1888	428	244	188	20	15	10	17	190	2	308	37	8	28	22	.560	0	3	3.91

Darnell McDonald

Bats: Right **Throws:** Right **Pos:** OF-104; DH-12   **Ht:** 5'11" **Wt:** 201 **Born:** 11/17/78 **Age:** 22

Year Team	Lg Org	G	AB	H	2B	3B	HR	TB	R	RBI	TBB	IBB	SO	HBP	SH	SF	SB	CS	SB%	GDP	Avg	OBP	SLG
1998 Delmarva	A Bal	134	528	138	24	5	6	190	87	44	33	0	117	5	4	5	35	11	.76	5	.261	.308	.360
Frederick	A+ Bal	4	18	4	2	0	1	9	3	2	3	0	6	0	0	0	2	0	1.00	1	.222	.333	.500
1999 Frederick	A+ Bal	130	507	135	23	5	6	186	81	73	61	0	92	5	7	7	26	9	.74	13	.266	.347	.367
2000 Bowie	AA Bal	116	459	111	13	5	6	152	59	43	29	0	87	4	6	4	11	4	.73	7	.242	.290	.331
3 Min. YEARS		384	1512	388	62	15	19	537	230	162	126	0	302	14	17	16	74	24	.76	26	.257	.317	.355

Donzell McDonald

Bats: Both **Throws:** Right **Pos:** OF-67; DH-1   **Ht:** 5'11" **Wt:** 180 **Born:** 2/20/75 **Age:** 26

Year Team	Lg Org	G	AB	H	2B	3B	HR	TB	R	RBI	TBB	IBB	SO	HBP	SH	SF	SB	CS	SB%	GDP	Avg	OBP	SLG
1995 Yankees	R NYY	28	110	26	5	1	0	33	23	9	16	0	24	2	0	1	11	2	.85	1	.236	.341	.300
1996 Oneonta	A- NYY	74	282	78	8	10	2	112	57	30	43	0	62	2	3	2	54	4	.93	1	.277	.374	.397
1997 Tampa	A+ NYY	77	297	88	23	8	3	136	69	23	48	0	75	4	1	1	39	18	.68	3	.296	.400	.458
1998 Norwich	AA NYY	134	495	125	20	7	6	177	80	36	55	1	127	4	7	4	35	22	.61	7	.253	.330	.358
Tampa	A+ NYY	5	18	6	1	2	0	11	6	2	2	0	7	1	1	0	2	0	1.00	1	.333	.429	.611
1999 Norwich	AA NYY	137	533	145	19	10	4	196	95	33	90	0	110	6	11	1	54	20	.73	5	.272	.383	.368
2000 Columbus	AAA NYY	24	77	19	4	4	1	34	17	6	23	0	11	2	2	0	12	0	1.00	0	.247	.431	.442
Norwich	AA NYY	44	170	41	7	2	2	58	23	10	35	1	36	0	0	0	13	7	.65	1	.241	.371	.341
6 Min. YEARS		523	1982	528	87	44	18	757	370	149	312	2	452	21	25	9	220	73	.75	18	.266	.370	.382

Mike McDougal

Pitches: Right **Bats:** Left **Pos:** RP-14   **Ht:** 6'4" **Wt:** 215 **Born:** 3/22/75 **Age:** 26

		HOW MUCH HE PITCHED						WHAT HE GAVE UP										THE RESULTS					
Year Team	Lg Org	G	GS	CG	GF	IP	BFP	H	R	ER	HR	SH	SF	HB	TBB	IBB	SO	WP	Bk	W	L	Pct.	ShO	Sv	ERA
1995 Johnson Cty	R StL	1	0	0	0	1		0	0	0	0	0	0	0	1	0	0	0	0	0	0	—	0	0	0.00
1996 New Jersey	A- StL	14	0	0	4	20.1	87	20	17	16	4	1	1	1	4	0	25	1	0	1	1	.500	0	0	7.08
1997 New Jersey	A- StL	13	11	2	0	68.2	272	62	24	19	1	3	0	2	9	0	63	1	0	4	4	.500	2	0	2.49
1998 Pr William	A+ StL	17	2	0	3	32	132	38	11	10	4	1	0	1	2	0	28	1	0	3	0	1.000	0	0	2.81
Arkansas	AA StL	24	0	0	8	31	143	45	21	17	7	0	2	2	5	1	16	1	0	2	3	.400	0	1	4.94
1999 Delmarva	A Bal	1	0	0	0	2	9	3	0	0	0	0	0	0	0	0	3	0	0	1	0	1.000	0	0	0.00
Bowie	AA Bal	48	0	0	22	61.1	285	70	34	29	10	7	0	4	31	6	47	2	0	5	7	.417	0	8	4.26
2000 Rochester	AAA Bal	14	0	0	4	30	128	34	21	15	5	0	0	0	6	0	25	1	0	1	2	.333	0	0	4.50
6 Min. YEARS		132	13	2	41	245.1	1057	272	128	106	31	12	3	10	58	7	207	7	0	17	17	.500	2	9	3.89

Sean McGowan

Bats: Right **Throws:** Right **Pos:** 1B-118; DH-14   **Ht:** 6'6" **Wt:** 240 **Born:** 5/15/77 **Age:** 24

Year Team	Lg Org	G	AB	H	2B	3B	HR	TB	R	RBI	TBB	IBB	SO	HBP	SH	SF	SB	CS	SB%	GDP	Avg	OBP	SLG
1999 Salem-Keizr	A- SF	63	257	86	12	1	15	145	40	62	20	4	56	1	0	0	3	1	.75	6	.335	.385	.564
San Jose	A+ SF	2	8	3	1	0	0	4	1	1	0	0	3	0	0	0	0	1	.00	0	.375	.375	.500
2000 San Jose	A+ SF	114	456	149	32	2	12	221	58	106	43	1	71	6	0	3	4	3	.57	12	.327	.390	.485
Shreveport	AA SF	18	69	24	4	0	0	28	5	12	1	0	8	0	0	0	0	0	—	2	.348	.357	.406
2 Min. YEARS		197	790	262	49	3	27	398	104	181	64	5	138	7	0	3	7	5	.58	20	.332	.385	.504

Cody McKay

Bats: Left **Throws:** Right **Pos:** C-92; DH-24; 3B-10; 1B-7; PH-1   **Ht:** 6'0" **Wt:** 207 **Born:** 1/11/74 **Age:** 27

Year Team	Lg Org	G	AB	H	2B	3B	HR	TB	R	RBI	TBB	IBB	SO	HBP	SH	SF	SB	CS	SB%	GDP	Avg	OBP	SLG
1996 Sou Oregon	A- Oak	69	254	68	13	0	3	90	33	30	25	0	42	6	1	3	0	5	.00	7	.268	.344	.354
1997 Modesto	A+ Oak	125	390	97	20	1	7	140	47	50	46	2	69	16	3	4	4	2	.67	9	.249	.349	.359
1998 Huntsville	AA Oak	9	21	6	0	0	1	9	5	1	6	0	5	2	0	0	0	0	—	0	.286	.483	.429
Edmonton	AAA Oak	19	57	13	3	0	0	16	6	5	7	0	5	3	2	0	1	0	1.00	0	.228	.343	.281
Modesto	A+ Oak	107	402	114	25	1	6	159	59	58	40	1	62	17	3	3	2	4	.33	12	.284	.370	.396
1999 Midland	AA Oak	94	333	98	21	1	6	139	59	43	38	5	40	8	1	5	1	2	.33	11	.294	.375	.417
2000 Midland	AA Oak	115	427	136	35	2	5	190	70	89	67	6	54	10	0	10	1	5	.17	15	.319	.414	.445
Sacramento	AAA Oak	16	58	13	4	0	1	20	8	7	5	1	14	1	0	0	0	0	—	2	.224	.297	.345
5 Min. YEARS		554	1942	545	121	5	29	763	287	283	234	15	291	63	10	25	9	18	.33	56	.281	.372	.393

Walt McKeel

Bats: Right **Throws:** Right **Pos:** C-57; PH-6; DH-5; 1B-4   **Ht:** 6'0" **Wt:** 200 **Born:** 1/17/72 **Age:** 29

Year Team	Lg Org	G	AB	H	2B	3B	HR	TB	R	RBI	TBB	IBB	SO	HBP	SH	SF	SB	CS	SB%	GDP	Avg	OBP	SLG
1990 Red Sox	R Bos	13	44	11	3	0	0	14	2	6	3	0	8	0	0	1	0	2	.00	2	.250	.292	.318
1991 Red Sox	R Bos	35	113	15	0	1	2	23	10	12	17	0	20	1	0	4	0	0	—	5	.133	.244	.204
1992 Lynchburg	A+ Bos	96	288	64	11	0	12	111	33	33	22	0	77	3	5	1	2	1	.67	3	.222	.283	.385
1993 Lynchburg	A+ Bos	80	247	59	17	2	5	95	28	32	26	0	40	3	6	3	0	1	.00	6	.239	.315	.385
1994 Sarasota	A+ Bos	37	137	38	8	1	2	54	15	15	8	1	19	1	0	1	1	0	1.00	1	.277	.322	.394
New Britain	AA Bos	50	164	30	6	1	1	41	10	17	7	1	35	3	1	2	0	0	—	5	.183	.227	.250
1995 Trenton	AA Bos	29	84	20	3	1	2	31	11	11	8	0	15	0	0	2	1	1	.67	1	.238	.298	.369
Sarasota	A+ Bos	62	198	66	14	0	8	104	26	35	25	0	28	3	0	5	6	3	.67	4	.333	.407	.525
1996 Trenton	AA Bos	128	464	140	19	1	16	209	86	78	60	3	52	7	5	7	2	4	.33	13	.302	.385	.450
1997 Pawtucket	AAA Bos	66	237	60	15	0	6	93	34	30	34	3	39	1	1	2	0	1	.00	8	.253	.347	.392
Trenton	AA Bos	7	25	4	2	0	0	6	0	4	1	0	2	0	1	0	0	0	—	1	.160	.192	.240
1998 Red Sox	R Bos	13	36	9	2	0	1	14	1	4	4	0	8	0	0	1	0	0	—	1	.250	.317	.389
Pawtucket	AAA Bos	48	170	49	4	0	4	73	26	26	21	0	27	1	0	2	1	2	.33	8	.288	.370	.429

BATTING																	BASERUNNING				PERCENTAGES		
Year Team	Lg Org	G	AB	H	2B	3B	HR	TB	R	RBI	TBB	IBB	SO	HBP	SH	SF	SB	CS	SB%	GDP	Avg	OBP	SLG
1999 Toledo	AAA Det	67	215	52	9	1	7	84	21	37	26	0	32	4	1	2	2	2	.50	6	.242	.332	.391
Sonoma Cty	IND —	2	9	4	0	0	1	7	1	1	0	0	3	0	0	0	0	0	—	0	.444	.444	.778
2000 Carolina	AA Col	72	227	51	15	0	8	90	29	26	31	0	45	8	2	2	3	3	.50	7	.225	.336	.396
1996 Boston	AL	1	0	0	0	0	0	0	0	0	0	0	0	0	0	0	0	0	—	0			
1997 Boston	AL	5	3	0	0	0	0	0	0	0	0	0	1	0	0	0	0	0	—	0	.000	.000	.000
11 Min. YEARS		805	2658	672	134	9	75	1049	333	367	293	8	450	35	22	32	19	20	.49	70	.253	.331	.395
2 Maj. YEARS		6	3	0	0	0	0	0	0	0	0	0	1	0	0	0	0	0	—	0	.000	.000	.000

Dan McKinley

Bats: Left **Throws:** Right **Pos:** OF-137; DH-7; PH-1 **Ht:** 6'0" **Wt:** 180 **Born:** 5/15/76 **Age:** 25

BATTING																	BASERUNNING				PERCENTAGES		
Year Team	Lg Org	G	AB	H	2B	3B	HR	TB	R	RBI	TBB	IBB	SO	HBP	SH	SF	SB	CS	SB%	GDP	Avg	OBP	SLG
1998 Shreveport	AA SF	33	112	20	3	3	0	29	16	11	11	1	30	3	0	1	2	3	.40	3	.179	.268	.259
Bakersfield	A+ SF	94	379	114	16	4	6	156	58	44	30	2	84	10	4	2	19	6	.76	8	.301	.366	.412
1999 San Jose	A+ SF	15	53	12	2	1	1	19	7	3	7	1	13	1	1	0	2	0	1.00	1	.226	.328	.358
Akron	AA Cle	111	463	119	20	6	3	160	70	37	24	0	87	4	8	3	3	5	.38	8	.257	.298	.346
2000 Kinston	A+ Cle	13	62	20	5	0	0	25	8	7	2	0	11	1	1	0	4	1	.80	1	.323	.354	.403
Harrisburg	AA Mon	131	517	145	20	14	4	205	66	57	25	1	75	9	8	3	23	7	.77	3	.280	.323	.397
3 Min. YEARS		397	1586	430	66	28	14	594	225	159	99	5	300	28	22	9	53	22	.71	24	.271	.323	.375

Marty McLeary

Pitches: Right **Bats:** Right **Pos:** RP-35; SP-8 **Ht:** 6'5" **Wt:** 220 **Born:** 10/26/74 **Age:** 26

HOW MUCH HE PITCHED						WHAT HE GAVE UP												THE RESULTS					
Year Team	Lg Org	G	GS	CG	GF	IP	BFP	H	R	ER	HR	SH	SF	HB	TBB	IBB	SO	WP	Bk	W	L	Pct.	ShO	Sv	ERA
1997 Lowell	A- Bos	13	13	0	0	62.1	275	53	38	26	2	3	3	5	36	1	43	6	2	3	6	.333	0	0	3.75
1998 Michigan	A Bos	37	7	0	11	88.2	396	99	58	41	4	1	3	5	35	2	54	5	1	5	7	.417	0	0	4.16
1999 Sarasota	A+ Bos	8	0	0	0	12.2	73	29	20	17	1	2	1	1	7	0	11	2	0	1	0	1.000	0	0	12.08
Augusta	A Bos	35	9	0	16	80.2	338	73	34	28	8	3	2	4	25	1	90	5	2	5	6	.455	0	3	3.12
2000 Trenton	AA Bos	43	8	0	22	96.2	449	114	66	49	5	2	6	2	53	3	53	8	1	2	9	.182	0	5	4.56
4 Min. YEARS		136	37	0	49	341	1531	368	216	161	20	11	15	17	156	7	251	26	6	16	28	.364	0	8	4.25

Mike McMullen

Pitches: Right **Bats:** Right **Pos:** RP-36 **Ht:** 6'6" **Wt:** 230 **Born:** 10/13/73 **Age:** 27

HOW MUCH HE PITCHED						WHAT HE GAVE UP												THE RESULTS					
Year Team	Lg Org	G	GS	CG	GF	IP	BFP	H	R	ER	HR	SH	SF	HB	TBB	IBB	SO	WP	Bk	W	L	Pct.	ShO	Sv	ERA
1993 Giants	R SF	14	14	0	0	64	306	70	60	45	1	3	2	5	53	0	44	12	0	1	6	.143	0	0	6.33
1994 Clinton	A SF	14	1	0	5	24.1	122	34	25	17	5	1	1	4	14	0	22	4	2	1	3	.250	0	0	6.29
Giants	R SF	10	9	0	0	49	205	47	21	18	2	2	3	3	15	1	40	3	0	3	3	.500	0	0	3.31
1995 Burlington	A SF	29	11	2	6	83.2	410	98	76	51	5	2	4	9	54	3	53	9	2	4	10	.286	0	0	5.49
1996 Burlington	A SF	38	0	0	7	56.1	241	47	22	18	3	4	2	5	28	0	33	5	0	0	2	.000	0	0	2.88
1997 San Jose	A+ SF	56	0	0	23	91	377	85	37	27	1	9	4	5	33	3	71	6	0	6	4	.600	0	7	2.67
1998 Shreveport	AA SF	52	0	0	37	67.2	296	47	23	16	1	5	1	6	41	9	76	5	0	6	4	.600	0	9	2.13
Fresno	AAA SF	2	0	0	0	3.1	14	2	2	2	0	0	0	0	2	0	2	0	0	1	0	1.000	0	0	5.40
1999 Fresno	AAA SF	41	0	0	13	66	290	52	36	32	5	1	1	10	41	2	56	4	1	2	2	.500	0	0	4.36
2000 Fresno	AAA SF	36	0	0	12	50.1	246	37	35	27	2	3	5	12	52	1	41	12	1	4	2	.667	0	1	4.83
8 Min. YEARS		292	35	2	103	555.2	2507	519	337	253	24	30	23	56	333	19	438	60	7	28	36	.438	0	17	4.10

Sean McNally

Bats: Right **Throws:** Right **Pos:** 3B-93; DH-9; 1B-4; PH-4; SS-3 **Ht:** 6'4" **Wt:** 210 **Born:** 12/14/72 **Age:** 28

BATTING																	BASERUNNING				PERCENTAGES		
Year Team	Lg Org	G	AB	H	2B	3B	HR	TB	R	RBI	TBB	IBB	SO	HBP	SH	SF	SB	CS	SB%	GDP	Avg	OBP	SLG
1994 Eugene	A- KC	74	278	69	16	2	3	98	44	30	24	1	66	4	2	2	4	7	.36	5	.248	.315	.353
1995 Springfield	A KC	132	479	130	28	8	12	210	60	79	35	6	119	8	0	6	6	3	.67	10	.271	.328	.438
1996 Wilmington	A+ KC	126	428	118	27	1	8	171	49	63	57	2	83	5	1	8	3	3	.50	8	.276	.361	.400
1997 Wichita	AA KC	18	53	13	4	0	0	17	9	2	11	0	12	0	0	0	1	2	.33	2	.245	.375	.321
Wilmington	A+ KC	95	323	86	22	2	17	163	51	68	40	4	98	2	3	1	2	1	.67	6	.266	.350	.505
1998 Wichita	AA KC	98	319	84	21	3	6	129	43	44	39	0	86	1	2	5	2	4	.33	9	.263	.341	.404
1999 Wichita	AA KC	129	440	124	24	2	36	260	97	109	93	2	132	6	1	3	7	3	.70	12	.282	.411	.591
2000 Calgary	AAA Fla	112	374	98	22	4	12	164	58	41	42	0	104	5	3	3	2	4	.33	12	.262	.342	.439
7 Min. YEARS		784	2694	722	164	22	94	1212	411	436	341	15	700	31	12	28	27	27	.50	64	.268	.354	.450

Rusty McNamara

Bats: Right **Throws:** Right **Pos:** 3B-52; 2B-27; OF-25; DH-25; PH-6 **Ht:** 5'9" **Wt:** 190 **Born:** 1/23/75 **Age:** 26

BATTING																	BASERUNNING				PERCENTAGES		
Year Team	Lg Org	G	AB	H	2B	3B	HR	TB	R	RBI	TBB	IBB	SO	HBP	SH	SF	SB	CS	SB%	GDP	Avg	OBP	SLG
1997 Batavia	A- Phi	72	295	92	17	0	6	127	55	54	15	0	33	10	0	6	3	3	.50	4	.312	.359	.431
1998 Clearwater	A+ Phi	134	529	154	36	1	9	219	78	94	23	1	44	14	3	9	14	7	.67	20	.291	.332	.414
1999 Clearwater	A+ Phi	69	274	88	12	2	3	113	40	43	29	1	22	9	2	2	5	3	.63	8	.321	.401	.412
Reading	AA Phi	50	177	44	9	1	5	70	26	20	17	0	22	4	4	0	0	2	.00	2	.249	.328	.395
2000 Reading	AA Phi	125	466	137	24	6	14	215	79	76	43	1	41	18	1	6	3	3	.50	10	.294	.371	.461
4 Min. YEARS		450	1741	515	98	10	37	744	278	287	127	3	162	55	10	23	25	18	.58	48	.296	.358	.427

Josh McNatt

Pitches: Left **Bats:** Both **Pos:** RP-17   **Ht:** 6'4" **Wt:** 205 **Born:** 7/23/77 **Age:** 23

Year Team	Lg Org	G	GS	CG	GF	IP	BFP	H	R	ER	HR	SH	SF	HB	TBB	IBB	SO	WP	Bk	W	L	Pct.	ShO	Sv	ERA
1996 Orioles	R Bal	12	8	0	2	53.2	206	36	15	13	1	1	2	0	12	0	42	1	0	3	2	.600	0	0	2.18
Bluefield	R+ Bal	2	1	0	0	6.1	33	10	6	6	1	0	0	0	6	0	7	1	0	0	1	.000	0	0	8.53
1997 Delmarva	A Bal	28	11	0	2	96.2	425	97	48	39	4	2	6	1	45	1	73	4	0	6	2	.750	0	1	3.63
1998 Frederick	A+ Bal	27	26	3	0	157.1	661	141	78	55	10	8	4	5	70	2	118	17	3	11	8	.579	1	0	3.15
1999 Orioles	R Bal	1	0	0	0	2	7	1	0	0	0	0	0	0	0	0	2	0	0	1	0	1.000	0	0	0.00
Frederick	A+ Bal	19	6	0	3	45	219	41	36	30	5	2	5	3	44	2	29	12	0	2	3	.400	0	0	6.00
Bowie	AA Bal	2	1	0	0	7	32	8	5	4	0	1	0	0	6	0	1	2	0	0	1	.000	0	0	5.14
2000 Orioles	R Bal	9	0	0	2	14.2	78	19	19	14	1	0	0	0	17	0	10	3	0	0	0	—	0	0	8.59
Delmarva	A Bal	7	0	0	0	10	49	15	9	9	1	1	0	0	7	1	2	1	0	0	1	.000	0	0	8.10
Bowie	AA Bal	1	0	0	1	0.1	1	0	0	0	0	0	0	0	0	0	0	0	0	0	0	—	0	0	0.00
5 Min. YEARS		108	53	3	10	393	1711	368	216	170	23	15	17	10	207	6	284	41	3	23	18	.561	1	1	3.89

Aaron McNeal

Bats: Right **Throws:** Right **Pos:** 1B-91; PH-6; DH-2   **Ht:** 6'3" **Wt:** 230 **Born:** 4/28/78 **Age:** 23

Year Team	Lg Org	G	AB	H	2B	3B	HR	TB	R	RBI	TBB	IBB	SO	HBP	SH	SF	SB	CS	SB%	GDP	Avg	OBP	SLG
1996 Astros	R Hou	55	200	50	10	2	2	70	22	31	13	1	52	4	0	2	0	2	.00	5	.250	.306	.350
1997 Auburn	A- Hou	12	40	10	3	0	0	13	5	3	4	0	10	0	0	0	1	0	1.00	1	.250	.318	.325
Astros	R Hou	46	164	48	12	0	3	69	22	26	11	0	28	0	0	2	0	5	.00	4	.293	.333	.421
1998 Quad City	A Hou	112	370	105	15	1	14	164	54	61	31	2	112	5	1	0	3	3	.50	12	.284	.347	.443
1999 Michigan	A Hou	133	536	166	29	3	38	315	95	131	40	4	121	2	0	3	7	1	.88	13	.310	.358	.588
2000 Round Rock	AA Hou	97	361	112	20	2	11	169	40	69	24	3	91	1	1	3	0	4	.00	11	.310	.352	.468
5 Min. YEARS		455	1671	491	89	8	68	800	238	321	123	10	414	12	2	10	11	15	.42	46	.294	.345	.479

Brian McNichol

Pitches: Left **Bats:** Left **Pos:** RP-30; SP-13   **Ht:** 6'5" **Wt:** 225 **Born:** 5/20/74 **Age:** 27

Year Team	Lg Org	G	GS	CG	GF	IP	BFP	H	R	ER	HR	SH	SF	HB	TBB	IBB	SO	WP	Bk	W	L	Pct.	ShO	Sv	ERA
1995 Williamsprt	A- ChC	9	9	0	0	49.2	215	57	28	17	1	1	1	2	8	0	35	1	1	3	1	.750	0	0	3.08
1996 Daytona	A+ ChC	8	7	0	0	34.2	162	39	24	18	4	0	1	0	14	0	22	1	0	1	2	.333	0	0	4.67
Cubs	R ChC	1	1	0	0	3.1	16	4	2	0	0	0	0	0	0	0	2	0	0	0	0	—	0	0	0.00
1997 Daytona	A+ ChC	6	6	0	0	39	161	32	14	10	1	1	2	3	10	1	40	1	0	2	2	.500	0	0	2.31
Orlando	AA ChC	22	22	0	0	119.1	544	153	89	77	18	3	7	2	42	6	97	9	0	7	10	.412	0	0	5.81
1998 West Tenn	AA ChC	28	26	4	0	179	753	170	88	74	14	5	6	7	62	5	168	9	1	12	9	.571	1	0	3.72
Iowa	AAA ChC	1	1	0	0	7	31	12	6	6	0	0	1	0	1	0	5	0	0	0	0	—	0	0	7.71
1999 Iowa	AAA ChC	28	28	2	0	161.1	720	194	108	100	21	7	2	7	55	0	120	6	0	10	11	.476	1	0	5.58
2000 Iowa	AAA ChC	43	13	0	14	115	519	131	81	75	20	2	6	4	52	1	105	2	1	3	8	.273	0	1	5.87
1999 Chicago	NL	4	2	0	1	10.2	54	15	8	8	4	0	1	1	7	0	12	0	0	0	2	.000	0	0	6.75
6 Min. YEARS		146	113	6	14	708.1	3121	792	440	377	81	19	25	25	244	13	594	29	3	38	43	.469	2	1	4.79

Tydus Meadows

Bats: Right **Throws:** Right **Pos:** OF-112; PH-10; DH-5   **Ht:** 6'2" **Wt:** 215 **Born:** 9/5/77 **Age:** 23

Year Team	Lg Org	G	AB	H	2B	3B	HR	TB	R	RBI	TBB	IBB	SO	HBP	SH	SF	SB	CS	SB%	GDP	Avg	OBP	SLG
1998 Cubs	R ChC	27	98	36	8	4	3	61	25	26	17	1	17	2	0	0	6	5	.55	1	.367	.470	.622
Rockford	A ChC	35	134	39	5	0	7	65	35	24	15	1	32	4	0	1	6	1	.86	1	.291	.377	.485
1999 Lansing	A ChC	126	449	135	32	6	17	230	80	74	66	2	85	11	0	4	18	10	.64	13	.301	.400	.512
2000 Daytona	A+ ChC	46	167	52	11	2	6	85	30	24	17	0	36	4	1	2	11	4	.73	1	.311	.384	.509
West Tenn	AA ChC	80	249	65	14	4	5	102	33	32	20	0	72	4	2	5	4	2	.67	2	.261	.320	.410
3 Min. YEARS		314	1097	327	70	16	38	543	203	180	135	4	242	25	3	12	45	22	.67	18	.298	.384	.495

Rafael Medina

Pitches: Right **Bats:** Right **Pos:** RP-31; SP-2   **Ht:** 6'3" **Wt:** 240 **Born:** 2/15/75 **Age:** 26

Year Team	Lg Org	G	GS	CG	GF	IP	BFP	H	R	ER	HR	SH	SF	HB	TBB	IBB	SO	WP	Bk	W	L	Pct.	ShO	Sv	ERA
1993 Yankees	R NYY	5	5	0	0	27.1	107	16	6	2	0	1	1	1	12	0	21	1	1	2	0	1.000	0	0	0.66
1994 Oneonta	A- NYY	14	14	1	0	73.1	319	67	54	38	7	2	1	1	35	0	59	7	3	3	7	.300	0	0	4.66
1995 Greensboro	A NYY	19	19	1	0	98.2	418	86	48	44	8	0	5	6	38	0	108	6	3	4	4	.500	0	0	4.01
Tampa	A+ NYY	6	6	0	0	30.1	131	29	12	8	0	0	1	0	12	0	25	0	2	2	2	.500	0	0	2.37
1996 Norwich	AA NYY	19	19	1	0	103	446	78	48	35	7	5	1	6	55	2	112	11	4	5	8	.385	0	0	3.06
1997 Rancho Cuca	A+ SD	3	3	0	0	18	68	13	4	4	1	1	0	0	5	0	14	1	0	2	0	1.000	0	0	2.00
Las Vegas	AAA SD	13	13	0	0	66.2	321	90	60	56	12	1	1	2	39	1	50	8	2	4	5	.444	0	0	7.56
1998 Charlotte	AAA Fla	11	9	3	1	57.2	245	53	27	25	8	0	2	2	26	1	41	4	1	4	2	.667	1	0	3.90
1999 Calgary	AAA Fla	25	0	0	9	35	153	29	15	13	1	1	0	2	21	0	34	3	0	1	2	.333	0	1	3.34
2000 Syracuse	AAA Tor	33	2	0	16	54.2	235	37	18	17	2	0	2	3	35	1	33	4	0	3	1	.750	0	1	2.80
1998 Florida	NL	12	12	0	0	67.1	327	76	50	45	8	5	4	3	52	3	49	5	0	2	6	.250	0	0	6.01
1999 Florida	NL	20	0	0	4	23.1	110	20	15	15	3	1	0	1	20	2	16	2	1	1	1	.500	0	0	5.79
8 Min. YEARS		148	90	6	26	564.2	2443	498	292	242	46	11	17	24	278	5	497	45	16	30	31	.492	1	2	3.86
2 Maj. YEARS		32	12	0	4	90.2	437	96	65	60	11	6	4	4	72	5	65	7	1	3	7	.300	0	0	5.96

Ryan Medrano

Bats: Right **Throws:** Right **Pos:** 3B-32; 2B-19; SS-13; PH-10; DH-7; OF-4; PR-2   **Ht:** 5'11" **Wt:** 190 **Born:** 3/27/74 **Age:** 27

Year Team	Lg Org	G	AB	H	2B	3B	HR	TB	R	RBI	TBB	IBB	SO	HBP	SH	SF	SB	CS	SB%	GDP	Avg	OBP	SLG
1998 Chston-WV	A Cin	115	361	82	19	0	7	122	54	30	50	0	73	6	1	0	6	2	.75	9	.227	.331	.338

Year Team	Lg Org	G	AB	H	2B	3B	HR	TB	R	RBI	TBB	IBB	SO	HBP	SH	SF	SB	CS	SB%	GDP	Avg	OBP	SLG
1999 Nashua	IND —	103	309	90	21	4	11	152	58	47	69	1	74	4	12	2	1	2	.33	3	.291	.424	.492
2000 New Haven	AA Sea	77	216	52	9	0	2	67	25	26	39	0	45	2	2	3	2	1	.67	8	.241	.358	.310
3 Min. YEARS		295	886	224	49	4	20	341	137	103	158	1	192	12	15	5	9	5	.64	20	.253	.371	.385

Steve Medrano

Bats: Both **Throws:** Right **Pos:** SS-61; PH-2   **Ht:** 6'0" **Wt:** 150 **Born:** 10/8/77 **Age:** 23

Year Team	Lg Org	G	AB	H	2B	3B	HR	TB	R	RBI	TBB	IBB	SO	HBP	SH	SF	SB	CS	SB%	GDP	Avg	OBP	SLG
1996 Royals	R KC	46	154	42	10	0	1	55	24	11	19	2	21	2	3	0	3	1	.75	4	.273	.360	.357
1997 Lansing	A KC	97	321	71	7	5	0	88	35	29	34	0	39	3	3	3	10	5	.67	8	.221	.299	.274
1998 Lansing	A KC	106	340	88	14	5	0	112	45	29	34	0	39	4	13	2	15	3	.83	6	.259	.332	.329
1999 Wilmington	A+ KC	98	362	91	4	3	0	101	41	24	30	1	66	1	8	1	12	10	.55	5	.251	.310	.279
2000 Chston-WV	A KC	44	163	35	3	0	0	38	30	9	24	0	28	1	4	1	5	1	.83	6	.215	.317	.233
Wilmington	A+ KC	3	13	2	0	0	0	2	1	0	0	0	0	0	1	0	0	0	—	0	.154	.154	.154
Wichita	AA KC	16	49	11	0	0	0	11	5	4	2	0	9	0	1	1	0	2	.00	1	.224	.250	.224
5 Min. YEARS		410	1402	340	38	13	1	407	181	106	143	5	202	11	33	8	45	22	.67	28	.243	.316	.290

Tony Medrano

Bats: Right **Throws:** Right **Pos:** SS-36; OF-35; 2B-22; 3B-22; 1B-20; PH-1   **Ht:** 5'10" **Wt:** 175 **Born:** 12/8/74 **Age:** 26

Year Team	Lg Org	G	AB	H	2B	3B	HR	TB	R	RBI	TBB	IBB	SO	HBP	SH	SF	SB	CS	SB%	GDP	Avg	OBP	SLG
1993 Blue Jays	R Tor	39	158	42	9	0	0	51	20	9	10	0	9	3	0	0	6	2	.75	1	.266	.322	.323
1994 Blue Jays	R Tor	6	22	8	4	0	1	15	2	5	1	0	0	0	0	0	0	0	—	2	.364	.391	.682
Dunedin	A+ Tor	60	199	47	6	4	4	73	20	21	12	0	26	3	3	1	3	3	.50	4	.236	.288	.367
1995 Wichita	AA KC	1	5	0	0	0	0	0	0	0	0	0	3	0	0	0	0	0	—	0	.000	.000	.000
Wilmington	A+ KC	123	460	131	20	6	3	172	69	43	34	2	42	5	15	4	11	6	.65	10	.285	.338	.374
1996 Wichita	AA KC	125	474	130	26	1	8	182	59	55	18	0	36	2	7	2	10	8	.56	8	.274	.302	.384
1997 Wichita	AA KC	108	349	86	9	1	4	109	45	42	26	1	32	1	9	4	8	2	.80	10	.246	.297	.312
Omaha	AAA KC	17	59	12	0	0	4	24	10	9	4	1	5	0	0	3	0	1	.00	1	.203	.242	.407
1998 Wichita	AA KC	95	301	92	14	2	10	140	48	46	28	0	36	9	8	3	3	3	.50	7	.306	.378	.465
1999 Wichita	AA KC	73	257	87	15	1	5	119	45	32	21	0	23	4	5	6	4	2	.67	3	.339	.389	.463
Omaha	AAA KC	33	112	35	6	1	2	49	14	23	10	0	15	1	3	2	0	1	.00	3	.313	.368	.438
2000 Omaha	AAA KC	128	485	129	23	1	8	178	65	55	33	0	45	3	7	4	18	8	.69	14	.266	.314	.367
8 Min. YEARS		808	2881	799	132	17	49	1112	397	340	197	4	272	31	57	29	63	36	.64	63	.277	.327	.386

Mike Meggers

Bats: Right **Throws:** Right **Pos:** OF-40; 1B-33; DH-28; PH-3; 3B-1   **Ht:** 6'2" **Wt:** 200 **Born:** 7/6/70 **Age:** 30

Year Team	Lg Org	G	AB	H	2B	3B	HR	TB	R	RBI	TBB	IBB	SO	HBP	SH	SF	SB	CS	SB%	GDP	Avg	OBP	SLG
1992 Billings	R+ Cin	73	257	69	16	3	12	127	47	48	48	1	72	3	1	2	10	7	.59	4	.268	.387	.494
1993 Chston-WV	A Cin	116	388	80	14	2	12	134	43	49	33	1	118	3	2	5	3	5	.38	2	.206	.270	.345
1994 Winston-Sal	A+ Cin	114	418	95	25	2	25	199	62	80	31	0	139	1	0	7	6	2	.75	8	.227	.278	.476
1995 Winston-Sal	A+ Cin	76	272	67	18	1	20	147	45	54	32	5	69	1	0	4	7	3	.70	5	.246	.324	.540
1996 Chattanooga	AA Cin	38	111	22	6	0	5	43	13	18	16	0	33	1	0	2	1	2	.33	1	.198	.300	.387
Madison	IND —	57	215	64	15	1	14	123	40	39	25	0	70	1	2	1	0	0	—	4	.298	.372	.572
1997 Winnipeg	IND —	40	172	50	10	0	16	108	38	57	17	0	54	4	0	2	5	0	1.00	4	.291	.364	.628
Duluth-Sup	IND —	41	166	53	7	1	16	110	39	42	16	1	48	1	0	2	3	1	.75	1	.319	.378	.663
1998 Duluth-Sup	IND —	24	82	30	9	1	12	77	20	34	22	3	26	2	0	2	0	1	.00	0	.366	.500	.939
1999 Binghamton	AA NYM	18	56	9	4	0	1	16	6	6	7	1	29	0	0	0	0	0	—	0	.161	.254	.286
2000 Newark	IND —	54	229	64	16	0	9	107	34	36	13	0	53	0	0	5	0	2	.00	4	.279	.312	.467
Carolina	AA Col	47	157	28	7	0	7	56	12	19	13	1	51	1	1	1	0	0	—	2	.178	.244	.357
9 Min. YEARS		698	2523	631	147	11	149	1247	399	482	273	13	762	18	6	33	35	23	.60	35	.250	.324	.494

Dan Meier

Bats: Left **Throws:** Left **Pos:** 1B-51; DH-30; PH-12; OF-3   **Ht:** 6'0" **Wt:** 202 **Born:** 8/13/77 **Age:** 23

Year Team	Lg Org	G	AB	H	2B	3B	HR	TB	R	RBI	TBB	IBB	SO	HBP	SH	SF	SB	CS	SB%	GDP	Avg	OBP	SLG
1998 South Bend	A Ari	22	56	10	3	0	0	13	7	5	11	0	20	0	0	0	0	0	—	1	.179	.313	.232
Tucson	AAA Ari	10	29	6	3	0	0	9	5	2	1	0	9	0	0	1	0	0	—	1	.207	.226	.310
Diamondbcks	R Ari	12	35	12	3	0	1	18	10	5	11	0	8	0	0	1	1	0	1.00	0	.343	.489	.514
1999 High Desert	A+ Ari	129	418	112	25	4	24	217	85	89	70	3	138	9	1	1	0	0	—	6	.268	.384	.519
2000 El Paso	AA Ari	25	62	12	1	1	2	21	8	7	3	0	25	0	0	1	0	0	.00	3	.194	.227	.339
High Desert	A+ Ari	11	30	8	1	0	2	15	6	4	7	0	8	0	0	1	0	0	—	1	.267	.395	.500
Lynchburg	A+ Pit	57	202	62	12	2	14	120	45	43	29	1	46	7	0	1	2	2	.50	5	.307	.410	.594
3 Min. YEARS		266	832	222	48	7	43	413	166	155	132	4	254	16	1	6	3	3	.50	17	.267	.375	.496

Alex Melconian

Bats: Right **Throws:** Right **Pos:** C-33; OF-30; PH-10; PR-7   **Ht:** 5'10" **Wt:** 190 **Born:** 3/18/75 **Age:** 26

Year Team	Lg Org	G	AB	H	2B	3B	HR	TB	R	RBI	TBB	IBB	SO	HBP	SH	SF	SB	CS	SB%	GDP	Avg	OBP	SLG
1997 Utica	A- Fla	62	215	60	6	2	2	76	37	22	18	0	48	15	4	1	6	6	.50	5	.279	.373	.353
Kane County	A Fla	3	10	1	0	0	0	1	0	0	1	0	2	1	0	0	0	0	—	1	.100	.250	.100
1998 Kane County	A Fla	132	453	103	10	1	6	133	61	53	50	1	135	28	10	8	21	3	.88	12	.227	.336	.294
1999 Brevard Cty	A+ Fla	58	205	54	6	1	4	74	26	20	24	0	48	9	4	1	11	9	.55	9	.263	.364	.361
2000 Brevard Cty	A+ Fla	3	6	1	0	0	1	4	2	5	2	0	0	0	0	1	1	0	1.00	0	.167	.333	.667
Calgary	AAA Fla	10	21	6	2	0	0	8	5	2	2	0	7	0	1	1	1	0	1.00	0	.286	.348	.381
Portland	AA Fla	61	146	26	7	0	4	45	15	30	9	0	58	6	1	1	0	1	.00	2	.178	.253	.308
4 Min. YEARS		329	1056	251	31	4	17	341	146	132	106	1	298	59	20	12	40	19	.68	29	.238	.337	.323

186

Dave Meliah

Bats: Left **Throws:** Right **Pos:** 3B-66; 2B-34; OF-6; 1B-5; DH-5; PH-2; PR-1   **Ht:** 6'3" **Wt:** 185 **Born:** 3/11/77 **Age:** 24

Year Team	Lg Org	G	AB	H	2B	3B	HR	TB	R	RBI	TBB	IBB	SO	HBP	SH	SF	SB	CS	SB%	GDP	Avg	OBP	SLG
1998 Pulaski	R+ Tex	48	183	48	8	0	5	71	21	28	13	1	26	2	1	3	5	3	.63	0	.262	.313	.388
1999 Savannah	A Tex	93	358	106	21	3	8	157	53	49	16	0	80	3	0	2	3	6	.33	8	.296	.330	.439
2000 Tulsa	AA Tex	10	36	9	1	2	0	14	2	5	1	1	7	0	0	0	0	0	—	0	.250	.263	.389
Charlotte	A+ Tex	104	407	118	24	7	6	174	65	50	16	2	53	3	3	5	2	2	.50	7	.290	.318	.428
3 Min. YEARS		255	984	281	54	12	19	416	141	132	46	4	166	8	4	11	10	11	.48	15	.286	.319	.423

Jackson Melian

Bats: Right **Throws:** Right **Pos:** OF-80; PH-4; DH-1; PR-1   **Ht:** 6'2" **Wt:** 190 **Born:** 1/7/80 **Age:** 21

Year Team	Lg Org	G	AB	H	2B	3B	HR	TB	R	RBI	TBB	IBB	SO	HBP	SH	SF	SB	CS	SB%	GDP	Avg	OBP	SLG
1997 Yankees	R NYY	57	213	56	11	2	3	80	32	36	20	0	52	0	0	2	9	1	.90	8	.263	.323	.376
1998 Greensboro	A NYY	135	467	119	18	2	8	165	66	45	41	0	120	7	1	4	15	12	.56	12	.255	.322	.353
1999 Tampa	A+ NYY	128	467	132	17	13	6	193	65	61	49	1	98	10	1	8	11	8	.58	8	.283	.358	.413
2000 Norwich	AA NYY	81	290	73	8	4	9	116	34	38	18	1	69	3	2	3	17	1	.94	6	.252	.299	.400
Chattanooga	AA Cin	2	6	1	0	0	0	1	0	0	0	0	0	0	0	0	0	0	—	0	.167	.167	.167
4 Min. YEARS		403	1443	381	54	21	26	555	197	180	128	2	339	20	4	17	52	22	.70	34	.264	.329	.385

Carlos Mendez

Bats: Right **Throws:** Right **Pos:** C-32; 1B-32; DH-21; OF-18; PH-2; 3B-1; P-1   **Ht:** 6'0" **Wt:** 210 **Born:** 6/18/74 **Age:** 27

Year Team	Lg Org	G	AB	H	2B	3B	HR	TB	R	RBI	TBB	IBB	SO	HBP	SH	SF	SB	CS	SB%	GDP	Avg	OBP	SLG
1992 Royals	R KC	49	200	61	16	1	3	88	34	33	8	2	13	2	0	3	2	1	.67	2	.305	.333	.440
1993 Royals	R KC	50	163	51	10	0	4	73	18	27	4	1	15	2	0	4	6	1	.86	2	.313	.329	.448
1994 Rockford	A KC	104	363	129	26	2	5	174	45	51	13	2	50	5	4	4	0	2	.00	11	.355	.382	.479
1995 Wilmington	A+ KC	107	396	108	19	2	7	152	46	61	18	1	36	0	1	5	0	4	.00	17	.273	.301	.384
1996 Wilmington	A+ KC	109	406	119	25	3	4	162	40	59	22	4	39	3	3	7	3	1	.75	6	.293	.329	.399
1997 Wichita	AA KC	129	507	165	32	1	12	235	72	90	19	2	43	1	0	8	4	7	.36	19	.325	.346	.464
1998 Omaha	AAA KC	50	173	47	13	0	2	66	23	18	10	0	24	1	0	2	3	0	1.00	4	.272	.312	.382
Wichita	AA KC	52	207	66	14	0	9	107	37	39	7	1	20	0	1	5	4	1	.80	7	.319	.333	.517
1999 Omaha	AAA KC	84	293	82	25	0	10	137	38	37	6	0	32	0	3	4	4	3	.57	8	.280	.291	.468
2000 Toledo	AAA Det	100	374	108	21	0	19	186	49	72	12	0	37	3	0	7	0	0	—	11	.289	.311	.497
9 Min. YEARS		834	3082	936	201	9	75	1380	402	487	119	13	309	17	12	48	26	20	.57	90	.304	.328	.448

Paul Menhart

Pitches: Right **Bats:** Right **Pos:** RP-32   **Ht:** 6'2" **Wt:** 190 **Born:** 3/25/69 **Age:** 32

Year Team	Lg Org	G	GS	CG	GF	IP	BFP	H	R	ER	HR	SH	SF	HB	TBB	IBB	SO	WP	Bk	W	L	Pct.	ShO	Sv	ERA
1990 St.Cathrnes	A- Tor	8	8	0	0	40	180	34	27	18	2	1	5	5	19	0	38	6	2	0	5	.000	0	0	4.05
Myrtle Bch	A	5	4	1	1	30.2	113	18	5	2	1	1	0	0	5	0	18	1	0	3	0	1.000	0	0	0.59
1991 Dunedin	A+ Tor	20	20	3	0	128.1	521	114	42	38	3	2	2	3	34	0	114	4	1	10	6	.625	0	0	2.66
1992 Knoxville	AA Tor	28	28	2	0	177.2	735	181	85	76	14	2	6	11	38	0	104	12	1	10	11	.476	1	0	3.85
1993 Syracuse	AAA Tor	25	25	4	0	151	646	143	74	61	16	4	3	7	67	4	108	8	1	9	10	.474	0	0	3.64
1995 Syracuse	AAA Tor	10	10	0	0	51.1	234	62	42	36	5	2	3	0	25	0	30	3	1	2	4	.333	0	0	6.31
1996 Tacoma	AAA Sea	6	6	0	0	26	142	53	33	32	4	0	3	1	16	0	12	3	0	0	3	.000	0	0	11.08
1997 Tacoma	AAA Sea	15	10	0	0	61.1	285	76	46	42	11	2	1	4	34	1	51	4	1	4	7	.364	0	1	6.16
Las Vegas	AAA SD	11	11	1	0	66.1	294	78	46	44	7	7	3	2	21	1	44	2	1	0	7	.000	0	0	5.97
1998 Las Vegas	AAA SD	49	2	0	16	64	310	79	45	38	10	4	3	5	39	6	50	3	2	7	6	.538	0	4	5.34
1999 Edmonton	AAA Ana	9	9	0	0	42.1	190	58	34	32	10	1	0	1	14	1	21	0	0	3	3	.500	0	0	6.80
Buffalo	AAA Cle	7	0	0	0	13	60	18	7	7	0	0	0	1	4	0	10	2	0	2	1	.667	0	0	4.85
Calgary	AAA Fla	8	8	0	0	38.2	185	48	26	21	0	3	0	1	23	0	30	2	0	2	2	.500	0	0	4.89
2000 Solano	IND —	18	0	0	7	22	89	18	10	9	0	3	0	0	7	1	20	2	0	2	2	.500	0	3	3.68
Colo Spngs	AAA Col	14	0	0	4	20.1	104	29	19	13	3	1	0	1	12	0	20	3	0	2	1	.667	0	1	5.75
1995 Toronto	AL	21	9	1	6	78.2	350	72	49	43	9	3	4	6	47	4	50	6	0	1	4	.200	0	0	4.92
1996 Seattle	AL	11	6	0	4	42	196	55	36	34	9	1	0	2	25	0	18	1	0	2	2	.500	0	0	7.29
1997 San Diego	NL	9	8	0	0	44	180	42	23	23	6	2	1	0	13	0	22	4	0	2	3	.400	0	0	4.70
10 Min. YEARS		233	141	11	30	933	4088	1009	541	469	86	30	28	41	358	14	668	55	10	56	68	.452	1	9	4.52
3 Maj. YEARS		41	23	1	10	164.2	726	169	108	100	24	6	5	8	85	4	90	11	0	5	9	.357	0	0	5.47

Todd Mensik

Bats: Left **Throws:** Left **Pos:** DH-66; OF-38; 1B-15; PH-7   **Ht:** 6'2" **Wt:** 195 **Born:** 2/27/75 **Age:** 26

Year Team	Lg Org	G	AB	H	2B	3B	HR	TB	R	RBI	TBB	IBB	SO	HBP	SH	SF	SB	CS	SB%	GDP	Avg	OBP	SLG
1996 Sou Oregon	A- Oak	59	192	46	8	0	0	54	21	14	19	2	39	2	0	4	2	0	1.00	6	.240	.309	.281
1997 Visalia	A+ Oak	15	45	9	1	0	1	13	3	6	6	0	11	1	0	1	0	0	—	2	.200	.302	.289
1998 Modesto	A+ Oak	111	379	104	26	2	14	176	56	59	63	2	103	2	2	1	1	4	.20	2	.274	.380	.464
1999 Visalia	A+ Oak	134	505	147	29	4	29	271	93	123	79	11	114	9	0	3	5	1	.83	8	.291	.394	.537
2000 Midland	AA Oak	124	414	109	24	2	23	206	56	84	72	6	114	5	0	0	0	0	—	11	.263	.375	.498
5 Min. YEARS		443	1535	415	88	8	67	720	229	286	239	21	381	19	4	14	8	5	.62	29	.270	.372	.469

Jorge Meran

Bats: Right **Throws:** Right **Pos:** C-63; DH-3; SS-1   **Ht:** 6'1" **Wt:** 168 **Born:** 6/18/77 **Age:** 24

Year Team	Lg Org	G	AB	H	2B	3B	HR	TB	R	RBI	TBB	IBB	SO	HBP	SH	SF	SB	CS	SB%	GDP	Avg	OBP	SLG
1998 Lakeland	A+ Det	7	20	4	3	0	0	7	0	1	0	0	7	0	0	0	0	0	—	0	.200	.200	.350
Jamestown	A- Det	30	110	30	7	1	4	51	13	20	15	2	24	2	0	0	3	1	.75	3	.273	.370	.464

					BATTING													BASERUNNING				PERCENTAGES		
Year Team	Lg Org	G	AB	H	2B	3B	HR	TB	R	RBI	TBB	IBB	SO	HBP	SH	SF	SB	CS	SB%	GDP	Avg	OBP	SLG
1999 W Michigan	A Det	44	152	30	9	4	2	53	18	23	7	0	38	1	1	2	1	3	.25	1	.197	.235	.349
2000 Jacksnville	AA Det	4	13	2	0	0	0	2	2	0	0	0	1	1	0	0	0	0	—	0	.154	.214	.154
Lakeland	A+ Det	63	224	60	10	3	7	97	22	19	10	0	45	0	0	0	2	3	.40	2	.268	.299	.433
3 Min. YEARS		148	519	126	29	8	13	210	55	63	32	2	115	4	1	2	6	7	.46	6	.243	.291	.405

Orlando Merced

Bats: Left **Throws:** Right **Pos:** OF-12; 3B-4; 1B-1; DH-1; PH-1   **Ht:** 6'1" **Wt:** 195 **Born:** 11/2/66 **Age:** 34

					BATTING													BASERUNNING				PERCENTAGES		
Year Team	Lg Org	G	AB	H	2B	3B	HR	TB	R	RBI	TBB	IBB	SO	HBP	SH	SF	SB	CS	SB%	GDP	Avg	OBP	SLG
1985 Pirates	R Pit	40	136	31	6	0	1	40	16	13	9	0	9	1	0	0	3	1	.75	3	.228	.281	.294
1986 Macon	A Pit	65	173	34	4	1	2	46	20	24	12	0	38	1	0	2	5	3	.63	3	.197	.250	.266
Watertown	A- Pit	27	89	16	0	1	3	27	12	9	14	2	21	2	0	1	6	2	.75	2	.180	.302	.303
1987 Macon	A Pit	4	4	0	0	0	0	0	1	0	1	0	3	0	0	0	0	0	—	0	.000	.000	.000
Watertown	A- Pit	4	12	5	0	1	0	7	4	3	1	0	1	1	0	0	1	0	1.00	0	.417	.500	.583
1988 Augusta	A Pit	37	136	36	6	3	1	51	19	17	7	1	20	2	0	1	2	0	1.00	2	.265	.308	.375
Salem	A+ Pit	80	298	87	12	7	7	134	47	42	27	1	64	1	1	5	13	3	.81	7	.292	.347	.450
1989 Harrisburg	AA Pit	95	341	82	16	4	6	124	43	48	32	6	65	2	1	4	13	3	.81	6	.240	.306	.364
Buffalo	AAA Pit	35	129	44	5	3	1	58	18	16	7	1	26	0	2	1	0	1	.00	2	.341	.372	.450
1990 Buffalo	AAA Pit	101	378	99	12	6	9	150	52	55	46	3	63	0	1	0	14	5	.74	8	.262	.341	.397
1991 Buffalo	AAA Pit	3	12	2	0	0	0	2	1	0	1	0	4	0	0	0	1	1	.50	0	.167	.231	.167
2000 New Orleans	AAA Hou	17	67	18	4	0	1	25	8	14	2	0	4	0	0	0	0	1	.00	2	.269	.290	.373
1990 Pittsburgh	NL	25	24	5	1	0	0	6	3	0	1	0	9	0	0	0	0	0	—	1	.208	.240	.250
1991 Pittsburgh	NL	120	411	113	17	2	10	164	83	50	64	4	81	1	1	1	8	4	.67	6	.275	.373	.399
1992 Pittsburgh	NL	134	405	100	28	5	6	156	50	60	52	8	63	2	1	5	5	4	.56	6	.247	.332	.385
1993 Pittsburgh	NL	137	447	140	26	4	8	198	68	70	77	10	64	1	0	2	3	3	.50	9	.313	.414	.443
1994 Pittsburgh	NL	108	386	105	21	3	9	159	48	51	42	5	58	1	0	4	4	1	.80	17	.272	.343	.412
1995 Pittsburgh	NL	132	487	146	29	4	15	228	75	83	52	9	74	1	0	5	7	2	.78	9	.300	.365	.468
1996 Pittsburgh	NL	120	453	130	24	1	17	207	69	80	51	5	74	0	0	3	8	4	.67	9	.287	.357	.457
1997 Toronto	AL	98	368	98	23	2	9	152	45	40	47	1	62	3	0	2	7	3	.70	6	.266	.352	.413
1998 Minnesota	AL	63	204	59	12	0	5	86	22	33	17	3	29	1	0	1	1	4	.20	4	.289	.345	.422
Boston	AL	9	9	0	0	0	0	0	0	2	2	0	3	0	0	0	0	0	—	0	.000	.167	.000
Chicago	NL	12	10	3	0	0	1	6	2	5	1	0	2	0	0	1	0	0	—	1	.300	.333	.600
1999 Montreal	NL	93	194	52	12	1	8	90	25	26	26	0	27	0	0	1	2	1	.67	5	.268	.353	.464
8 Min. YEARS		508	1775	454	65	26	31	664	241	241	159	14	318	10	5	15	58	20	.74	35	.256	.318	.374
10 Maj. YEARS		1051	3398	951	193	22	88	1452	490	500	432	45	546	10	2	24	45	26	.63	74	.280	.361	.427

Henry Mercedes

Bats: Right **Throws:** Right **Pos:** C-4; PH-1   **Ht:** 6'1" **Wt:** 210 **Born:** 7/23/69 **Age:** 31

					BATTING													BASERUNNING				PERCENTAGES		
Year Team	Lg Org	G	AB	H	2B	3B	HR	TB	R	RBI	TBB	IBB	SO	HBP	SH	SF	SB	CS	SB%	GDP	Avg	OBP	SLG
1988 Athletics	R Oak	2	5	2	0	0	0	2	1	0	0	0	0	0	0	0	0	0	—	0	.400	.400	.400
1989 Madison	A Oak	51	152	32	3	0	2	41	11	13	22	1	46	1	3	0	0	0	—	1	.211	.314	.270
Modesto	A+ Oak	16	37	3	0	0	1	6	6	3	7	0	22	0	0	0	0	0	—	0	.081	.227	.162
Sou Oregon	A- Oak	22	61	10	0	1	0	12	6	1	10	0	24	1	0	0	0	2	.00	0	.164	.292	.197
1990 Tacoma	AAA Oak	12	31	6	1	0	0	7	3	2	3	0	7	0	2	0	0	1	.00	0	.194	.265	.226
Madison	A Oak	90	282	64	13	2	3	90	29	38	30	0	100	1	6	2	6	0	1.00	5	.227	.302	.319
1991 Modesto	A+ Oak	116	388	100	17	3	4	135	55	61	68	1	110	2	3	3	5	8	.38	6	.258	.369	.348
1992 Tacoma	AAA Oak	85	246	57	9	2	0	70	36	20	26	0	60	0	4	0	1	3	.25	8	.232	.305	.285
1993 Tacoma	AAA Oak	85	256	61	13	1	4	88	37	32	31	2	53	1	3	7	1	2	.33	8	.238	.315	.344
1994 Tacoma	AAA Oak	66	205	39	5	1	1	49	16	17	13	0	60	0	5	3	1	2	.33	4	.190	.235	.239
1995 Omaha	AAA KC	86	275	59	12	0	11	104	37	37	22	0	90	3	6	1	2	0	1.00	7	.215	.279	.378
1996 Omaha	AAA KC	72	223	48	9	1	8	83	28	35	28	0	60	0	6	2	0	0	—	2	.215	.300	.372
1997 Okla City	AAA Tex	16	57	14	3	0	1	20	6	4	9	0	12	0	0	0	0	0	—	3	.246	.348	.351
1998 Fresno	AAA SF	27	88	19	5	2	2	34	17	11	15	0	28	1	3	0	0	0	—	0	.216	.337	.386
Indianapls	AAA Cin	8	16	2	0	0	0	2	1	1	1	0	5	0	0	0	0	0	—	1	.125	.176	.125
1999 Omaha	AAA KC	69	193	47	8	0	6	73	27	32	27	0	63	2	3	1	4	1	.80	2	.244	.341	.378
2000 Memphis	AAA StL	5	12	4	0	1	1	9	4	3	2	0	6	0	1	0	0	0	—	0	.333	.429	.750
1992 Oakland	AL	9	5	4	0	1	0	6	1	1	0	0	1	0	0	0	0	0	—	0	.800	.800	1.200
1993 Oakland	AL	20	47	10	2	0	0	12	5	3	2	0	15	1	0	0	1	1	.50	0	.213	.260	.255
1995 Kansas City	AL	23	43	11	2	0	0	13	7	9	8	0	13	1	1	2	0	0	—	0	.256	.370	.302
1996 Kansas City	AL	4	4	1	0	0	0	1	1	0	0	0	1	0	0	0	0	0	—	1	.250	.250	.250
1997 Texas	AL	23	47	10	4	0	0	14	4	4	6	0	25	0	3	0	0	0	—	0	.213	.302	.298
13 Min. YEARS		828	2527	567	98	14	44	825	320	310	314	4	746	12	45	19	20	19	.51	61	.224	.311	.326
5 Maj. YEARS		79	146	36	8	1	0	46	18	17	16	0	55	2	4	2	1	1	.50	0	.247	.325	.315

Phil Merrell

Pitches: Right **Bats:** Right **Pos:** RP-12; SP-11   **Ht:** 6'4" **Wt:** 215 **Born:** 3/11/78 **Age:** 23

		HOW MUCH HE PITCHED						WHAT HE GAVE UP										THE RESULTS					
Year Team	Lg Org	G	GS	CG	GF	IP	BFP	H	R	ER	HR	SH	SF	HB	TBB	IBB	SO	WP	Bk	W	L	Pct.	ShO	Sv	ERA
1996 Billings	R+ Cin	14	13	1	1	69	339	83	63	54	11	4	5	5	48	0	54	11	2	4	7	.364	0	0	7.04
1997 Billings	R+ Cin	14	14	0	1	72.2	313	72	51	35	6	3	1	2	27	1	62	2	0	2	6	.250	0	0	4.33
1998 Chston-WV	A Cin	26	25	4	0	149.1	656	169	91	77	11	8	4	9	43	0	117	14	1	5	15	.250	0	0	4.64
1999 Clinton	A Cin	16	16	3	0	102.1	402	75	32	25	3	3	1	5	31	0	87	10	0	8	3	.727	3	0	2.20
Indianapols	AAA Cin	3	3	0	0	11	59	21	21	18	4	0	1	1	4	0	6	3	1	0	3	.000	0	0	14.73
Chattanooga	AA Cin	7	7	0	0	35.1	166	47	32	26	3	3	2	2	14	1	15	6	0	2	2	.500	0	0	6.62
2000 Chattanooga	AA Cin	7	7	0	0	32.1	150	34	26	23	3	3	2	3	24	0	25	3	0	1	4	.200	0	0	6.40
Reds	R Cin	3	3	0	0	12.1	58	11	9	4	1	0	0	2	4	0	17	0	0	2	0	.000	0	0	2.92
Dayton	A Cin	13	1	0	3	16.2	89	19	17	13	2	1	0	5	20	0	14	7	0	0	1	.000	0	1	7.02
5 Min. YEARS		103	89	8	4	501	2232	531	342	275	44	22	15	34	215	2	397	56	4	22	43	.338	3	2	4.94

Joey Messman

Pitches: Right **Bats:** Right **Pos:** RP-38   **Ht:** 6'2" **Wt:** 175 **Born:** 7/29/75 **Age:** 25

Year Team	Lg Org	G	GS	CG	GF	IP	BFP	H	R	ER	HR	SH	SF	HB	TBB	IBB	SO	WP	Bk	W	L	Pct.	ShO	Sv	ERA
1997 Auburn	A- Hou	25	0	0	10	28	132	26	13	10	1	3	0	6	21	3	31	8	0	1	2	.333	0	1	3.21
1998 Quad City	A Hou	63	0	0	16	87.2	359	70	36	30	2	2	3	4	33	4	74	9	0	6	3	.667	0	5	3.08
1999 Kissimmee	A+ Hou	45	0	0	40	59.1	251	38	20	16	6	4	0	4	35	2	47	6	2	3	4	.429	0	15	2.43
San Jose	A+ SF	2	0	0	2	1.2	13	6	5	5	0	0	0	0	3	0	0	3	0	0	0	—	0	0	27.00
2000 Shreveport	AA SF	38	0	0	11	60.2	248	51	27	23	7	2	4	0	23	2	46	8	1	5	2	.714	0	1	3.41
4 Min. YEARS		173	0	0	79	237.1	1003	191	101	84	16	11	7	14	115	11	198	34	3	15	11	.577	0	22	3.19

Jake Messner

Bats: Left **Throws:** Left **Pos:** DH-72; OF-33; PH-26   **Ht:** 6'1" **Wt:** 205 **Born:** 5/18/77 **Age:** 24

Year Team	Lg Org	G	AB	H	2B	3B	HR	TB	R	RBI	TBB	IBB	SO	HBP	SH	SF	SB	CS	SB%	GDP	Avg	OBP	SLG
1995 Burlington	R+ Cle	46	144	32	2	4	0	42	17	9	14	0	40	1	0	1	8	5	.62	0	.222	.294	.292
1996 Burlington	R+ Cle	47	164	41	7	1	3	59	20	20	11	0	41	1	0	2	6	3	.67	0	.250	.298	.360
1997 Burlington	R+ Cle	49	179	45	10	0	9	82	28	26	8	1	47	1	0	3	7	3	.70	3	.251	.283	.458
1998 Columbus	A Cle	25	78	13	2	0	3	24	9	13	5	0	21	0	0	2	3	1	.75	0	.167	.212	.308
1999 Salem-Keizr	A- SF	8	19	5	0	0	1	8	4	5	5	0	4	0	0	0	0	0	—	0	.263	.417	.421
Bakersfield	A+ SF	55	172	50	11	6	7	94	33	35	16	1	45	1	0	2	2	2	.50	1	.291	.351	.547
2000 Bakersfield	A+ SF	98	311	98	18	2	16	168	56	59	32	2	67	3	0	2	7	5	.58	3	.315	.382	.540
Shreveport	AA SF	22	58	20	6	0	3	35	7	9	9	0	14	0	0	0	2	1	.67	2	.345	.433	.603
6 Min. YEARS		350	1125	304	56	13	42	512	174	176	100	4	279	7	0	12	35	20	.64	9	.270	.330	.455

Rod Metzler

Bats: Both **Throws:** Right **Pos:** 2B-109; PH-5; OF-1; DH-1   **Ht:** 5'11" **Wt:** 185 **Born:** 11/19/74 **Age:** 26

Year Team	Lg Org	G	AB	H	2B	3B	HR	TB	R	RBI	TBB	IBB	SO	HBP	SH	SF	SB	CS	SB%	GDP	Avg	OBP	SLG
1997 Spokane	A- KC	62	224	51	5	5	3	75	37	31	18	0	48	1	5	2	9	2	.82	1	.228	.286	.335
1998 Lansing	A KC	88	323	81	17	4	2	112	45	34	36	0	77	3	4	0	17	6	.74	2	.251	.331	.347
1999 Chston-WV	A KC	130	462	122	23	7	7	180	64	60	48	0	98	9	5	1	29	14	.67	7	.264	.344	.390
Wichita	AA KC	3	10	5	2	0	2	13	5	4	0	0	3	1	1	0	0	0	—	0	.500	.545	1.300
2000 Wichita	AA KC	111	361	96	15	3	5	132	50	44	28	4	74	5	5	1	7	8	.47	4	.266	.327	.366
4 Min. YEARS		394	1380	355	62	19	19	512	201	173	130	4	300	19	20	4	62	30	.67	14	.257	.329	.371

Jake Meyer

Pitches: Right **Bats:** Right **Pos:** RP-23; SP-3   **Ht:** 6'1" **Wt:** 195 **Born:** 1/7/75 **Age:** 26

Year Team	Lg Org	G	GS	CG	GF	IP	BFP	H	R	ER	HR	SH	SF	HB	TBB	IBB	SO	WP	Bk	W	L	Pct.	ShO	Sv	ERA
1997 Bristol	R+ CWS	17	0	0	15	20	84	15	7	5	3	1	0	0	7	0	25	4	0	1	1	.500	0	5	2.25
1998 Hickory	A CWS	35	0	0	24	56	244	58	30	20	5	2	1	0	22	1	47	7	1	0	6	.000	0	11	3.21
Winston-Sal	A+ CWS	11	0	0	10	12.1	51	12	6	4	1	0	0	0	3	2	13	2	0	0	1	.000	0	2	2.92
1999 Rockford	A Cin	33	0	0	31	46	197	40	16	13	1	4	0	3	18	4	51	2	0	3	2	.600	0	16	2.54
Chattanooga	AA Cin	20	0	0	10	22.2	102	24	17	15	1	0	1	0	14	0	16	4	0	2	2	.500	0	0	5.96
2000 New Haven	AA Sea	15	0	0	10	19.2	81	17	5	5	0	0	0	1	8	0	20	4	0	1	0	1.000	0	2	2.29
Mariners	R Sea	3	3	0	0	4	19	4	2	2	0	0	0	0	3	0	6	0	0	0	0	—	0	0	4.50
Tacoma	AAA Sea	8	0	0	4	12.2	52	9	5	5	2	1	0	0	5	1	14	3	0	0	1	.000	0	0	3.55
4 Min. YEARS		142	3	0	104	193.1	830	179	88	69	13	8	2	4	80	8	192	26	1	7	13	.350	0	36	3.21

Mike Meyers

Pitches: Right **Bats:** Right **Pos:** SP-21; RP-1   **Ht:** 6'2" **Wt:** 210 **Born:** 10/18/77 **Age:** 23

Year Team	Lg Org	G	GS	CG	GF	IP	BFP	H	R	ER	HR	SH	SF	HB	TBB	IBB	SO	WP	Bk	W	L	Pct.	ShO	Sv	ERA
1997 Cubs	R ChC	12	2	0	4	38.1	166	34	15	6	2	1	1	2	13	0	45	0	0	3	1	.750	0	3	1.41
Williamsprt	A- ChC	1	1	0	0	4	15	3	0	0	1	0	0	0	1	0	2	0	0	0	0	—	0	0	0.00
1998 Rockford	A ChC	17	16	0	0	85.2	363	75	37	32	3	2	0	3	32	2	86	5	1	7	5	.583	0	0	3.36
1999 Daytona	A+ ChC	19	17	2	2	107.1	436	68	30	23	9	2	3	9	40	0	122	4	0	10	3	.769	0	0	1.93
West Tenn	AA ChC	5	5	0	0	33	128	21	5	4	1	1	1	0	10	1	51	1	0	4	0	1.000	0	0	1.09
2000 West Tenn	AA ChC	9	9	3	0	59	242	41	18	16	4	5	2	4	26	0	51	2	0	5	2	.714	1	0	2.44
Iowa	AAA ChC	13	12	0	0	59.1	278	74	51	48	9	2	5	6	30	2	44	2	1	2	6	.250	0	0	7.28
4 Min. YEARS		76	62	5	6	386.2	1628	316	156	129	28	14	12	24	152	5	401	14	2	31	17	.646	1	3	3.00

Bart Miadich

Pitches: Right **Bats:** Right **Pos:** RP-38   **Ht:** 6'4" **Wt:** 205 **Born:** 2/3/76 **Age:** 25

Year Team	Lg Org	G	GS	CG	GF	IP	BFP	H	R	ER	HR	SH	SF	HB	TBB	IBB	SO	WP	Bk	W	L	Pct.	ShO	Sv	ERA
1998 Sarasota	A+ Bos	22	0	0	15	48.2	199	40	20	17	1	3	0	1	15	4	64	2	1	3	2	.600	0	7	3.14
Trenton	AA Bos	22	8	0	4	54.1	253	66	39	36	4	1	2	5	26	1	33	2	0	1	6	.143	0	1	5.96
1999 El Paso	AA Ari	12	0	0	2	20	104	37	22	18	3	1	1	2	7	1	16	0	0	0	2	.000	0	1	8.10
High Desert	A+ Ari	21	16	0	1	98	448	125	71	59	9	2	4	12	40	0	85	1	1	3	8	.273	0	0	5.42
2000 Erie	AA Ana	28	0	0	17	40.1	171	27	16	15	2	1	2	4	21	0	38	4	0	3	1	.750	0	2	3.35
Edmonton	AAA Ana	10	0	0	3	21.2	101	25	14	11	3	1	0	0	9	0	20	2	0	2	1	.667	0	1	4.57
3 Min. YEARS		115	24	0	42	283	1276	320	182	156	22	9	9	24	118	6	256	12	2	12	20	.375	0	12	4.96

Jason Michaels

Bats: Right Throws: Right Pos: OF-111; PH-3; DH-2   Ht: 6'0" Wt: 204 Born: 5/4/76 Age: 25

					BATTING													BASERUNNING				PERCENTAGES		
Year Team	Lg Org	G	AB	H	2B	3B	HR	TB	R	RBI	TBB	IBB	SO	HBP	SH	SF		SB	CS	SB%	GDP	Avg	OBP	SLG
1998 Batavia	A- Phi	67	235	63	14	3	11	116	45	49	40	3	69	4	0	2		4	2	.67	5	.268	.381	.494
1999 Clearwater	A+ Phi	122	451	138	31	6	14	223	91	65	68	2	103	3	1	6		10	7	.59	7	.306	.396	.494
2000 Reading	AA Phi	113	437	129	30	4	10	197	71	74	28	1	87	3	3	7		7	4	.64	9	.295	.337	.451
3 Min. YEARS		302	1123	330	75	13	35	536	207	188	136	6	259	10	4	15		21	13	.62	21	.294	.371	.477

Chris Michalak

Pitches: Left Bats: Left Pos: SP-21; RP-8   Ht: 6'2" Wt: 195 Born: 1/4/71 Age: 30

		HOW MUCH HE PITCHED						WHAT HE GAVE UP											THE RESULTS					
Year Team	Lg Org	G	GS	CG	GF	IP	BFP	H	R	ER	HR	SH	SF	HB	TBB	IBB	SO	WP	Bk	W	L	Pct.	ShO	Sv	ERA
1993 Sou Oregon	A- Oak	16	15	0	0	79	346	77	41	25	2	2	5	6	36	0	57	4	3	7	3	.700	0	0	2.85
1994 W Michigan	A Oak	15	10	0	2	67	291	66	32	29	3	4	2	8	28	0	38	2	3	5	3	.625	0	0	3.90
Modesto	A+ Oak	17	10	1	3	77.1	310	67	28	25	1	3	2	3	20	1	46	4	3	5	3	.625	0	2	2.91
1995 Huntsville	AA Oak	7	0	0	4	5.2	32	10	7	7	1	1	0	1	5	0	4	2	0	1	1	.500	0	1	11.12
Modesto	A+ Oak	44	0	0	16	65.1	266	56	26	19	3	4	3	4	27	1	49	2	1	3	2	.600	0	2	2.62
1996 Modesto	A+ Oak	21	0	0	13	38.2	173	37	21	13	4	0	2	2	17	0	39	0	2	2	2	.500	0	4	3.03
Huntsville	AA Oak	21	0	0	4	23.1	123	32	29	20	2	1	1	1	26	4	15	4	0	4	0	1.000	0	0	7.71
1997 High Desert	A+ Ari	49	0	0	17	85	362	76	36	25	4	3	0	9	31	1	74	6	1	3	7	.300	0	4	2.65
1998 Tulsa	AA Ari	10	0	0	3	19.2	73	10	4	4	2	2	0	2	2	0	15	0	2	1	2	.333	0	0	1.83
Tucson	AAA Ari	29	9	0	6	73.1	326	91	47	41	11	2	5	4	29	3	50	4	3	3	8	.273	0	0	5.03
1999 Edmonton	AAA Ana	24	0	0	7	28.1	125	28	20	18	3	0	2	1	14	0	25	1	0	1	0	1.000	0	0	5.72
Tucson	AAA Ari	21	6	0	7	64	275	64	30	26	6	2	2	6	26	2	41	1	1	5	0	1.000	0	3	3.66
2000 Durham	AAA TB	6	0	0	1	6.1	26	6	4	4	1	0	0	0	1	0	7	1	0	0	0	—	0	0	5.68
Albuquerque	AAA LA	23	21	1	0	133	587	166	72	63	18	6	4	4	55	0	83	4	3	11	3	.786	0	0	4.26
1998 Arizona	NL	5	0	0	2	5.1	29	9	7	7	1	0	1	0	4	0	5	0	0	0	0	—	0	0	11.81
8 Min. YEARS		303	71	2	83	766	3315	786	397	319	73	29	29	51	317	12	543	35	22	51	34	.600	0	16	3.75

Jason Middlebrook

Pitches: Right Bats: Right Pos: SP-25   Ht: 6'3" Wt: 215 Born: 6/26/75 Age: 26

		HOW MUCH HE PITCHED						WHAT HE GAVE UP											THE RESULTS					
Year Team	Lg Org	G	GS	CG	GF	IP	BFP	H	R	ER	HR	SH	SF	HB	TBB	IBB	SO	WP	Bk	W	L	Pct.	ShO	Sv	ERA
1997 Rancho Cuca	A+ SD	6	6	0	0	22.1	105	29	15	10	1	1	3	0	12	1	18	2	1	0	2	.000	0	0	4.03
Clinton	A SD	14	14	2	0	81.1	353	76	46	36	4	3	1	1	39	0	86	6	5	6	4	.600	1	0	3.98
1998 Rancho Cuca	A+ SD	28	28	0	0	150	665	162	99	82	10	1	9	4	63	0	132	17	4	10	12	.455	0	0	4.92
1999 Padres	R SD	1	1	0	0	5	25	9	5	4	0	0	0	0	1	0	3	0	0	1	0	1.000	0	0	7.20
Mobile	AA SD	13	13	0	0	63.2	302	78	59	57	9	1	5	8	30	1	38	5	0	4	6	.400	0	0	8.06
2000 Las Vegas	AAA SD	1	1	0	0	0.1	9	8	8	8	1	0	1	0	0	0	0	0	0	0	1	.000	0	0	216.00
Mobile	AA SD	24	24	0	0	120	533	133	89	82	15	5	4	4	52	0	75	3	0	5	13	.278	0	0	6.15
4 Min. YEARS		87	87	2	0	442.2	1992	495	321	279	40	11	23	17	197	2	352	33	10	26	38	.406	1	0	5.67

Adam Milburn

Pitches: Left Bats: Right Pos: RP-17   Ht: 6'1" Wt: 195 Born: 4/27/74 Age: 27

		HOW MUCH HE PITCHED						WHAT HE GAVE UP											THE RESULTS					
Year Team	Lg Org	G	GS	CG	GF	IP	BFP	H	R	ER	HR	SH	SF	HB	TBB	IBB	SO	WP	Bk	W	L	Pct.	ShO	Sv	ERA
1996 Eugene	A- Atl	24	0	0	16	42.1	176	28	17	14	1	2	3	1	21	4	33	4	1	3	1	.750	0	7	2.98
1997 Macon	A Atl	46	0	0	18	70	301	71	29	26	6	2	1	3	23	2	51	2	0	4	1	.800	0	4	3.34
1998 Danville	A Atl	45	0	0	16	53.1	248	62	32	24	5	3	4	1	27	8	33	3	0	0	2	.000	0	2	4.05
1999 Myrtle Bch	A+ Atl	39	0	0	32	45	195	53	27	21	5	4	6	1	14	6	27	0	0	2	4	.333	0	15	4.20
Greenville	AA Atl	14	0	0	9	19	85	23	10	10	2	0	0	1	7	1	10	1	1	1	0	1.000	0	0	4.74
2000 Greenville	AA Atl	12	0	0	1	11	49	13	8	8	2	1	1	1	5	1	5	0	0	1	1	.500	0	0	6.55
Yuma	IND —	5	0	0	1	3	19	3	6	5	1	0	0	0	7	0	2	1	0	1	1	.500	0	0	15.00
5 Min. YEARS		185	0	0	93	243.2	1073	253	129	108	22	12	15	8	104	22	161	11	2	12	10	.545	0	28	3.99

Benji Miller

Pitches: Right Bats: Right Pos: RP-58   Ht: 6'2" Wt: 180 Born: 5/2/76 Age: 25

		HOW MUCH HE PITCHED						WHAT HE GAVE UP											THE RESULTS					
Year Team	Lg Org	G	GS	CG	GF	IP	BFP	H	R	ER	HR	SH	SF	HB	TBB	IBB	SO	WP	Bk	W	L	Pct.	ShO	Sv	ERA
1998 Salem-Keizr	A- SF	30	0	0	27	44	180	33	13	11	1	0	0	0	20	0	51	4	0	4	3	.571	0	17	2.25
1999 San Jose	A+ SF	47	0	0	38	59.2	248	53	26	20	3	2	4	1	17	0	61	6	2	3	2	.600	0	20	3.02
2000 Shreveport	AA SF	58	0	0	29	86	372	81	44	32	10	6	2	2	37	7	71	3	3	4	9	.308	0	4	3.35
3 Min. YEARS		135	0	0	94	189.2	800	167	83	63	14	8	6	3	74	7	183	13	5	11	14	.440	0	41	2.99

Corky Miller

Bats: Right Throws: Right Pos: C-103   Ht: 6'1" Wt: 215 Born: 3/18/76 Age: 25

					BATTING													BASERUNNING				PERCENTAGES		
Year Team	Lg Org	G	AB	H	2B	3B	HR	TB	R	RBI	TBB	IBB	SO	HBP	SH	SF		SB	CS	SB%	GDP	Avg	OBP	SLG
1998 Billings	R+ Cin	45	129	35	8	0	5	58	28	24	24	0	24	21	2	2		1	4	.20	2	.271	.455	.450
1999 Rockford	A Cin	66	195	56	10	1	10	98	43	40	33	1	42	20	1	1		3	6	.33	5	.287	.438	.503
Chattanooga	AA Cin	33	104	23	10	0	4	45	20	16	11	0	30	11	0	1		0	0	—	3	.221	.354	.433
2000 Chattanooga	AA Cin	103	317	74	18	0	9	119	40	44	41	1	51	30	1	1		5	8	.38	12	.233	.373	.375
3 Min. YEARS		247	745	188	46	1	28	320	131	124	109	2	147	82	4	5		9	18	.33	22	.252	.403	.430

190

David Miller

Bats: Left **Throws:** Left **Pos:** 1B-48; OF-42; PH-7; DH-4 **Ht:** 6'3" **Wt:** 185 **Born:** 12/9/73 **Age:** 27

					BATTING														BASERUNNING				PERCENTAGES		
Year Team	Lg Org	G	AB	H	2B	3B	HR	TB	R	RBI	TBB	IBB	SO	HBP	SH	SF		SB	CS	SB%	GDP	Avg	OBP	SLG
1996 Kinston	A+ Cle	129	488	124	23	1	7	170	71	54	38	4	94	0	2	5		14	7	.67	7	.254	.305	.348
1997 Akron	AA Cle	134	509	153	27	9	4	210	84	61	48	2	77	2	6	4		22	11	.67	5	.301	.361	.413
1998 Buffalo	AAA Cle	115	415	111	19	2	9	161	56	54	61	3	72	2	4	3		6	8	.43	10	.267	.362	.388
1999 Buffalo	AAA Cle	101	325	78	21	3	2	111	37	37	33	2	57	0	1	1		12	5	.71	8	.240	.309	.342
2000 Akron	AA Cle	56	198	48	16	1	6	84	28	31	29	0	26	0	1	1		6	1	.86	5	.242	.338	.424
Buffalo	AAA Cle	9	31	6	2	0	3	17	5	6	0	0	6	0	0	0		0	0	—	0	.194	.194	.548
Greenville	AA Atl	31	92	22	8	0	1	33	8	11	8	0	18	0	0	0		3	0	1.00	2	.239	.300	.359
5 Min. YEARS		575	2058	542	116	16	32	786	289	254	217	11	350	4	14	14		63	32	.66	37	.263	.333	.382

Ernie Miller

Pitches: Left **Bats:** Left **Pos:** RP-10; SP-6 **Ht:** 6'5" **Wt:** 195 **Born:** 7/19/75 **Age:** 25

		HOW MUCH HE PITCHED						WHAT HE GAVE UP												THE RESULTS					
Year Team	Lg Org	G	GS	CG	GF	IP	BFP	H	R	ER	HR	SH	SF	HB	TBB	IBB	SO	WP	Bk		W	L	Pct.	ShO	Sv	ERA
1997 Butte	R+ Ana	20	2	0	7	39.1	204	53	41	35	1	0	2	2	26	0	39	12	0		1	4	.200	0	1	8.01
1998 Cedar Rapds	A Ana	8	8	0	0	43.1	188	49	24	18	3	3	0	1	9	0	25	2	0		3	2	.600	0	0	3.74
2000 Cedar Rapds	A Ana	15	5	1	5	54	240	63	33	28	4	4	1	1	19	0	26	3	0		5	.286	0	1	4.67
Edmonton	AAA Ana	1	1	0	0	3.1	12	1	1	1	0	0	0	0	1	0	0	0	0		0	0	—	0	0	2.70
3 Min. YEARS		44	16	1	12	140	644	166	99	82	8	7	3	4	55	0	90	17	0		6	11	.353	0	2	5.27

Greg Miller

Pitches: Left **Bats:** Left **Pos:** SP-24; RP-2 **Ht:** 6'5" **Wt:** 215 **Born:** 9/30/79 **Age:** 21

		HOW MUCH HE PITCHED						WHAT HE GAVE UP												THE RESULTS					
Year Team	Lg Org	G	GS	CG	GF	IP	BFP	H	R	ER	HR	SH	SF	HB	TBB	IBB	SO	WP	Bk		W	L	Pct.	ShO	Sv	ERA
1997 Red Sox	R Bos	4	4	0	0	9.2	40	8	6	4	0	0	0	6	0	6	0	2		0	2	.000	0	0	3.72
1998 Red Sox	R Bos	11	7	0	0	43.1	187	33	18	12	2	2	2	4	18	0	47	3	2		6	0	1.000	0	0	2.49
1999 Augusta	A Bos	25	25	1	0	136.2	558	109	54	47	8	1	0	5	56	0	146	4	3		10	6	.625	0	0	3.10
2000 Kissimmee	A+ Hou	24	24	1	0	146	604	131	63	60	13	4	5	2	46	1	109	5	2		10	8	.556	0	0	3.70
Round Rock	AA Hou	2	0	0	0	2.1	0	0	0	0	0	0	0	0	1	0	2	0	0		0	0	—	0	0	0.00
4 Min. YEARS		66	60	2	0	338	1397	281	141	123	23	7	7	11	127	1	310	12	9		26	16	.619	0	0	3.28

Justin Miller

Pitches: Right **Bats:** Right **Pos:** SP-27 **Ht:** 6'2" **Wt:** 195 **Born:** 8/27/77 **Age:** 23

		HOW MUCH HE PITCHED						WHAT HE GAVE UP												THE RESULTS					
Year Team	Lg Org	G	GS	CG	GF	IP	BFP	H	R	ER	HR	SH	SF	HB	TBB	IBB	SO	WP	Bk		W	L	Pct.	ShO	Sv	ERA
1997 Portland	A- Col	14	11	0	1	67.1	288	68	26	16	3	2	2	4	20	0	54	6	0		4	2	.667	0	0	2.14
1998 Asheville	A Col	27	27	3	0	163.1	705	177	89	67	14	4	3	15	40	0	142	5	0		13	8	.619	1	0	3.69
1999 Salem	A+ Col	8	8	0	0	37	159	35	18	17	3	0	0	5	11	0	35	5	0		1	2	.333	0	0	4.14
2000 Midland	AA Oak	18	18	0	0	87	371	74	49	44	8	2	0	6	41	1	82	9	1		5	4	.556	0	0	4.55
Sacramento	AAA Oak	9	9	0	0	54.2	217	42	18	15	3	0	1	3	13	0	34	2	0		4	1	.800	0	0	2.47
4 Min. YEARS		76	73	3	1	409.1	1740	396	200	159	31	8	6	33	125	1	347	27	1		27	17	.614	1	0	3.50

Matt Miller

Pitches: Left **Bats:** Left **Pos:** SP-20 **Ht:** 6'3" **Wt:** 175 **Born:** 8/2/74 **Age:** 26

		HOW MUCH HE PITCHED						WHAT HE GAVE UP												THE RESULTS					
Year Team	Lg Org	G	GS	CG	GF	IP	BFP	H	R	ER	HR	SH	SF	HB	TBB	IBB	SO	WP	Bk		W	L	Pct.	ShO	Sv	ERA
1996 Jamestown	A- Det	6	6	0	0	25.1	115	33	16	13	0	1	0	3	13	0	21	6	2		1	3	.250	0	0	4.62
1998 W Michigan	A Det	14	14	3	0	95	366	59	20	16	1	5	0	4	26	0	102	4	1		7	4	.636	1	0	1.52
Jacksnville	AA Det	13	13	0	0	61.1	297	70	49	48	6	0	2	2	50	1	49	3	1		3	7	.300	0	0	7.04
1999 Lakeland	A+ Det	19	19	1	0	108.1	473	108	58	50	9	5	2	2	45	0	82	0	1		4	9	.308	0	0	4.15
Jacksnville	AA Det	7	7	0	0	40.2	176	43	23	20	3	3	1	2	12	0	25	0	0		4	1	.800	0	0	4.43
2000 Jacksnville	AA Det	20	20	1	0	121.2	513	126	50	43	10	4	3	5	32	1	99	4	0		8	5	.615	0	0	3.18
4 Min. YEARS		79	79	5	0	452.1	1940	439	216	190	29	18	8	18	178	2	378	17	5		27	29	.482	1	0	3.78

Matt Miller

Pitches: Right **Bats:** Right **Pos:** RP-43 **Ht:** 6'3" **Wt:** 215 **Born:** 11/23/71 **Age:** 29

		HOW MUCH HE PITCHED						WHAT HE GAVE UP												THE RESULTS					
Year Team	Lg Org	G	GS	CG	GF	IP	BFP	H	R	ER	HR	SH	SF	HB	TBB	IBB	SO	WP	Bk		W	L	Pct.	ShO	Sv	ERA
1996 Greenville	IND —	19	6	0	5	69.2	331	77	51	47	2	1	3	8	50	0	54	3	2		5	2	.714	0	1	6.07
1997 Greenville	IND —	15	15	5	0	107.1	433	76	34	27	0	3	2	4	49	0	129	10	1		12	3	.800	3	0	2.26
1998 Greenville	IND —	8	8	4	0	53.2	228	46	26	17	1	6	2	1	19	1	49	2	0		1	7	.125	0	0	2.85
Savannah	A Tex	17	0	0	10	35.1	137	25	9	9	0	2	0	2	10	0	46	2	0		3	1	.750	0	3	2.29
1999 Charlotte	A+ Tex	22	0	0	20	29.2	132	27	12	10	0	0	1	1	13	1	39	2	0		1	2	.333	0	8	3.03
Tulsa	AA Tex	34	0	0	25	56	235	42	24	21	2	4	5	1	28	2	83	5	0		6	4	.600	0	7	3.38
2000 Rangers	R Tex	1	0	0	0	2	9	2	1	1	0	0	0	1	0	0	4	0	0		0	0	—	0	0	4.50
Tulsa	AA Tex	3	0	0	0	3.2	22	7	7	6	0	0	1	0	4	0	4	1	0		0	0	—	0	0	14.73
Oklahoma	AAA Tex	39	0	0	25	60.1	276	61	29	24	6	4	4	3	34	4	69	4	0		3	3	.500	0	4	3.58
5 Min. YEARS		158	29	9	85	417.2	1803	363	193	162	11	20	18	21	207	8	477	29	3		31	22	.585	3	23	3.49

Orlando Miller

Bats: Right **Throws:** Right **Pos:** SS-15; 2B-2; 1B-2; 3B-1; DH-1; PH-1 **Ht:** 6'3" **Wt:** 205 **Born:** 1/13/69 **Age:** 32

					BATTING														BASERUNNING				PERCENTAGES		
Year Team	Lg Org	G	AB	H	2B	3B	HR	TB	R	RBI	TBB	IBB	SO	HBP	SH	SF		SB	CS	SB%	GDP	Avg	OBP	SLG
1988 Ft. Laud	A+ NYY	3	11	3	0	0	0	3	0	1	0	0	1	0	0	0		0	0	—	1	.273	.273	.273
Yankees	R NYY	14	44	8	1	0	0	9	5	5	3	1	10	0	0	0		1	0	1.00	1	.182	.234	.205

Year Team	Lg Org	G	AB	H	2B	3B	HR	TB	R	RBI	TBB	IBB	SO	HBP	SH	SF	SB	CS	SB%	GDP	Avg	OBP	SLG
								BATTING									**BASERUNNING**				**PERCENTAGES**		
1989 Oneonta	A- NYY	58	213	62	5	2	1	74	29	25	6	0	38	3	3	1	8	2	.80	3	.291	.318	.347
1990 Asheville	A Hou	121	438	137	29	6	4	190	60	62	25	2	52	10	2	4	12	5	.71	12	.313	.361	.434
1991 Jackson	AA Hou	23	70	13	6	0	1	22	5	5	5	1	13	2	2	0	0	0	—	2	.186	.260	.314
Osceola	A+ Hou	74	272	81	11	2	0	96	27	36	13	0	30	8	2	3	1	3	.25	5	.298	.345	.353
1992 Jackson	AA Hou	115	379	100	26	5	5	151	51	53	16	0	75	4	2	4	7	5	.58	5	.264	.298	.398
Tucson	AAA Hou	10	37	9	0	0	2	15	4	8	1	0	2	0	0	1	0	0	—	1	.243	.256	.405
1993 Tucson	AAA Hou	122	471	143	29	16	16	252	86	89	20	0	95	7	1	4	2	4	.33	12	.304	.339	.535
1994 Tucson	AAA Hou	93	338	87	16	6	10	145	54	55	16	1	77	6	3	7	3	3	.50	8	.257	.297	.429
1997 Lakeland	A+ Det	5	21	4	1	1	0	7	1	0	1	0	4	0	0	0	0	0	—	1	.190	.227	.333
Jacksnville	A+ Det	3	11	4	1	0	1	8	2	3	1	0	1	1	0	0	0	0	—	0	.364	.462	.727
Toledo	AAA Det	8	30	8	1	0	1	12	3	5	2	0	5	0	0	0	2	1	.67	1	.267	.313	.400
1998 Omaha	AAA KC	39	114	28	10	0	2	44	16	15	15	1	32	1	0	2	1	0	1.00	5	.246	.333	.386
Rochester	AAA Bal	37	143	42	4	1	5	63	21	25	9	0	31	5	0	0	3	1	.75	1	.294	.357	.441
New Orleans	AAA Hou	29	98	29	6	2	0	39	15	9	10	0	25	1	0	1	1	0	1.00	2	.296	.364	.398
1999 Buffalo	AAA Cle	68	233	60	17	0	7	98	27	33	12	1	52	5	1	0	5	0	1.00	6	.258	.308	.421
2000 San Antonio	AA LA	14	53	15	4	0	3	28	6	8	0	0	12	4	0	0	0	0	—	2	.283	.333	.528
Albuquerque	AAA LA	7	25	7	2	0	1	12	2	4	3	1	3	0	0	0	0	1	.00	1	.280	.357	.480
1994 Houston	NL	16	40	13	0	1	2	21	3	9	2	2	12	2	0	0	1	0	1.00	0	.325	.386	.525
1995 Houston	NL	92	324	85	20	1	5	122	36	36	22	8	71	5	4	0	3	4	.43	7	.262	.319	.377
1996 Houston	NL	139	468	120	26	2	15	195	43	58	14	4	116	10	1	3	3	7	.30	14	.256	.291	.417
1997 Detroit	AL	50	111	26	7	1	2	41	13	10	5	0	24	4	1	1	1	0	1.00	1	.234	.289	.369
11 Min. YEARS		843	3001	840	169	41	59	1268	414	441	158	8	558	57	16	27	46	25	.65	68	.280	.325	.423
4 Maj. YEARS		297	943	244	53	5	24	379	95	113	43	14	223	21	6	4	8	11	.42	22	.259	.305	.402

Ryan Miller

Bats: Right **Throws:** Right **Pos:** 2B-77; PH-32; DH-10; SS-1; 3B-1   **Ht:** 6'0" **Wt:** 175 **Born:** 10/22/72 **Age:** 28

Year Team	Lg Org	G	AB	H	2B	3B	HR	TB	R	RBI	TBB	IBB	SO	HBP	SH	SF	SB	CS	SB%	GDP	Avg	OBP	SLG
								BATTING									**BASERUNNING**				**PERCENTAGES**		
1994 Pittsfield	A- NYM	68	277	71	11	1	1	87	37	23	16	1	37	4	3	2	3	3	.50	0	.256	.304	.314
1995 St. Lucie	A+ NYM	89	279	68	10	3	2	90	32	23	13	0	42	7	8	2	5	3	.63	7	.244	.292	.323
Binghamton	AA NYM	9	19	1	0	0	0	1	3	0	2	0	4	0	1	0	1	0	1.00	0	.053	.143	.053
1996 St. Lucie	A+ NYM	86	310	79	8	3	2	99	32	23	22	1	51	3	13	1	8	5	.62	5	.255	.310	.319
1997 St. Lucie	A+ NYM	61	193	49	12	1	2	69	27	28	11	0	38	1	2	2	5	5	.50	3	.254	.295	.358
Kissimmee	A+ Hou	13	34	9	0	0	0	9	5	1	5	0	3	0	2	1	1	0	1.00	1	.265	.359	.265
Jackson	AA Hou	20	55	11	0	2	1	18	6	8	5	0	10	0	1	1	1	0	1.00	1	.200	.262	.327
1998 New Orleans	AAA Hou	8	17	5	1	0	0	6	4	3	1	0	3	1	0	0	1	0	1.00	0	.294	.368	.353
Jackson	AA Hou	102	293	90	20	0	3	119	36	26	9	0	43	9	3	4	6	4	.60	10	.307	.343	.406
1999 Jackson	AA Hou	27	75	11	0	1	0	13	5	4	2	0	11	2	0	0	5	0	1.00	4	.147	.190	.173
New Orleans	AAA Hou	64	174	48	8	0	1	59	19	25	5	0	29	1	0	1	0	2	.00	3	.276	.298	.339
2000 New Orleans	AAA Hou	111	299	75	18	1	3	104	31	35	18	1	58	10	3	5	1	5	.17	7	.251	.310	.348
7 Min. YEARS		658	2025	517	88	12	15	674	237	199	109	3	329	38	36	18	37	27	.58	40	.255	.303	.333

Ralph Milliard

Bats: Right **Throws:** Right **Pos:** SS-52; 2B-46; 3B-13; PH-4; PR-2; DH-1   **Ht:** 5'11" **Wt:** 175 **Born:** 12/30/73 **Age:** 27

Year Team	Lg Org	G	AB	H	2B	3B	HR	TB	R	RBI	TBB	IBB	SO	HBP	SH	SF	SB	CS	SB%	GDP	Avg	OBP	SLG
								BATTING									**BASERUNNING**				**PERCENTAGES**		
1993 Marlins	R Fla	53	192	45	15	0	0	60	35	25	30	0	17	6	0	1	11	5	.69	8	.234	.354	.313
1994 Kane County	A Fla	133	515	153	34	2	8	215	97	67	68	2	63	9	4	7	10	10	.50	6	.297	.384	.417
1995 Portland	AA Fla	128	464	124	22	3	11	185	104	40	85	3	83	14	13	4	22	10	.69	5	.267	.393	.399
1996 Charlotte	AAA Fla	69	250	69	15	2	6	106	47	26	38	0	43	5	1	1	8	4	.67	5	.276	.381	.424
Portland	AA Fla	6	20	4	0	1	0	6	2	2	1	0	5	0	0	0	1	0	1.00	0	.200	.238	.300
1997 Charlotte	AAA Fla	33	132	35	5	1	4	54	19	14	9	0	21	3	4	0	5	3	.63	1	.265	.326	.409
Portland	AA Fla	19	69	19	1	2	0	24	13	5	7	0	8	1	3	0	3	2	.60	2	.275	.351	.348
1998 Norfolk	AAA NYM	127	417	108	24	4	15	185	73	52	79	0	59	8	5	2	17	6	.74	4	.259	.385	.444
1999 Chattanooga	AA Cin	32	102	30	3	1	4	47	19	23	20	1	13	3	1	2	2	3	.40	1	.294	.417	.461
2000 Las Vegas	AAA SD	108	371	104	26	3	5	151	61	40	63	2	63	5	7	2	18	9	.67	7	.280	.390	.407
1996 Florida	NL	24	62	10	2	0	0	12	7	1	14	1	16	0	0	1	2	0	1.00	1	.161	.312	.194
1997 Florida	NL	8	30	6	0	0	0	6	2	2	3	0	3	2	1	0	1	1	.50	2	.200	.314	.200
1998 New York	NL	10	1	0	0	0	0	0	3	0	0	0	1	0	0	0	0	0	—	0	.000	.000	.000
8 Min. YEARS		708	2532	691	145	19	53	1033	470	298	400	8	375	54	38	19	97	52	.65	39	.273	.381	.408
3 Maj. YEARS		42	93	16	2	0	0	18	12	3	17	1	20	2	1	1	3	1	.75	3	.172	.310	.194

Ryan Mills

Pitches: Left **Bats:** Right **Pos:** SP-28   **Ht:** 6'5" **Wt:** 205 **Born:** 7/21/77 **Age:** 23

Year Team	Lg Org	G	GS	CG	GF	IP	BFP	H	R	ER	HR	SH	SF	HB	TBB	IBB	SO	WP	Bk	W	L	Pct.	ShO	Sv	ERA
								WHAT HE GAVE UP													**THE RESULTS**				
1998 Fort Myers	A+ Min	2	2	0	0	5	20	2	3	1	0	0	0	0	1	0	3	3	0	0	0	—	0	0	1.80
1999 Fort Myers	A+ Min	27	21	0	3	95.1	499	121	107	94	6	0	6	16	87	1	70	20	0	3	10	.231	0	0	8.87
2000 Quad City	A Min	20	20	0	0	119.2	518	101	54	47	5	7	3	15	64	0	110	9	0	3	6	.333	0	0	3.53
New Britain	AA Min	8	8	0	0	32	185	47	49	33	6	1	2	6	34	0	21	3	0	0	7	.000	0	0	9.28
3 Min. YEARS		57	51	0	3	252	1222	271	213	175	17	8	11	37	186	1	204	35	0	6	23	.207	0	0	6.25

Steve Mintz

Pitches: Right **Bats:** Left **Pos:** RP-30; SP-2   **Ht:** 5'11" **Wt:** 195 **Born:** 11/24/68 **Age:** 32

Year Team	Lg Org	G	GS	CG	GF	IP	BFP	H	R	ER	HR	SH	SF	HB	TBB	IBB	SO	WP	Bk	W	L	Pct.	ShO	Sv	ERA
								WHAT HE GAVE UP													**THE RESULTS**				
1990 Yakima	A- LA	20	0	0	12	26	113	21	9	7	1	3	1	1	16	1	38	2	1	2	3	.400	0	3	2.42
1991 Bakersfield	A+ LA	28	11	0	6	92	419	85	56	44	2	5	4	4	58	1	101	9	1	6	6	.500	0	3	4.30
1992 Vero Beach	A+ LA	43	2	0	21	77.2	323	66	29	27	7	5	3	3	30	2	66	7	3	3	6	.333	0	6	3.13
1993 New Britain	AA Bos	43	1	0	20	69.1	287	52	22	16	3	5	1	2	30	5	51	7	0	2	4	.333	0	7	2.08

192

Year Team	Lg Org	G	GS	CG	GF	IP	BFP	H	R	ER	HR	SH	SF	HB	TBB	IBB	SO	WP	Bk	W	L	Pct.	ShO	Sv	ERA
1994 Phoenix	AAA SF	24	0	0	13	36	161	40	24	22	8	1	3	1	13	3	27	3	0	0	1	.000	0	3	5.50
Shreveport	AA SF	30	0	0	12	65.1	261	45	29	16	5	2	1	2	22	1	42	8	0	10	2	.833	0	0	2.20
1995 Phoenix	AAA SF	31	0	0	19	49	205	42	16	13	4	3	0	2	21	4	36	4	0	5	2	.714	0	7	2.39
1996 Phoenix	AAA SF	59	0	0	45	57	256	63	39	34	6	1	3	2	25	3	35	5	2	3	5	.375	0	27	5.37
1997 Las Vegas	AAA SD	27	0	0	16	34.2	171	50	31	31	7	1	2	2	17	3	28	2	0	5	2	.714	0	5	8.05
1998 Nashville	AAA Pit	56	0	0	18	72.2	334	85	48	44	7	4	4	3	32	2	45	3	0	4	4	.500	0	1	5.45
1999 Erie	AA Ana	26	0	0	14	32.1	135	26	12	8	3	1	1	2	12	0	33	0	0	1	1	.500	0	9	2.23
Edmonton	AAA Ana	31	0	0	27	30.2	127	31	11	8	2	0	1	2	6	0	17	2	0	4	3	.571	0	9	2.35
2000 Edmonton	AAA Ana	32	2	0	19	41.2	210	60	42	35	4	4	3	0	28	1	24	3	0	4	4	.500	0	2	7.56
1995 San Francisco	NL	14	0	0	3	19.1	96	26	16	16	4	2	1	2	12	3	7	0	0	1	2	.333	0	0	7.45
1999 Anaheim	AL	3	0	0	2	5	23	8	2	2	1	0	0	0	2	0	2	0	0	0	0	—	0	0	3.60
11 Min. YEARS		450	16	0	242	684.1	3002	666	368	305	59	35	27	26	310	26	543	55	7	49	43	.533	0	82	4.01
2 Maj. YEARS		17	0	0	5	24.1	119	34	18	18	5	2	1	2	14	3	9	0	0	1	2	.333	0	0	6.66

Marc Mirizzi

Bats: Both **Throws:** Right **Pos:** 2B-56; SS-21; 3B-11; DH-6; 1B-5; PR-3; PH-1; P-1   **Ht:** 6'1" **Wt:** 190 **Born:** 6/17/75 **Age:** 26

		BATTING															BASERUNNING				PERCENTAGES		
Year Team	Lg Org	G	AB	H	2B	3B	HR	TB	R	RBI	TBB	IBB	SO	HBP	SH	SF	SB	CS	SB%	GDP	Avg	OBP	SLG
1997 Oneonta	A- NYY	74	245	64	5	1	1	74	40	33	38	0	36	3	3	3	12	7	.63	4	.261	.363	.302
1998 Greensboro	A NYY	103	373	104	29	1	11	168	57	44	31	1	85	5	1	2	4	5	.44	10	.279	.341	.450
1999 Greensboro	A NYY	9	34	9	0	1	1	14	5	3	5	0	9	1	0	0	0	0	—	1	.265	.375	.412
Norwich	AA NYY	15	47	5	0	0	1	8	6	6	5	0	13	1	0	3	0	0	—	1	.106	.196	.170
Tampa	A+ NYY	90	330	79	16	3	6	119	40	30	37	1	87	5	4	2	1	0	1.00	3	.239	.324	.361
2000 Norwich	AA NYY	93	318	76	16	0	6	110	40	29	40	2	73	2	2	1	5	4	.56	13	.239	.327	.346
4 Min. YEARS		384	1347	337	66	6	26	493	188	145	156	4	303	17	10	11	22	16	.58	37	.250	.333	.366

Dean Mitchell

Pitches: Right **Bats:** Right **Pos:** RP-45   **Ht:** 5'11" **Wt:** 175 **Born:** 3/19/74 **Age:** 27

		HOW MUCH HE PITCHED						WHAT HE GAVE UP												THE RESULTS				
Year Team	Lg Org	G	GS	CG	GF	IP	BFP	H	R	ER	HR	SH	SF	HB	TBB	IBB	SO	WP	Bk	W	L	Pct.	ShO	Sv	ERA
1996 Yakima	A- LA	15	5	0	3	52.1	233	53	25	20	4	1	5	0	25	1	61	3	1	2	2	.500	0	2	3.44
1997 Savannah	A LA	52	7	1	38	122	499	110	50	39	6	5	3	1	25	1	118	2	1	11	5	.688	0	16	2.88
San Berndno	A+ LA	1	0	0	1	1	4	0	0	0	0	0	0	0	0	1	0	0	0	0	0	—	0	0	0.00
1998 San Antonio	AA LA	46	3	0	29	79	331	74	31	29	8	5	1	3	22	2	76	4	0	2	5	.286	0	14	3.30
1999 Albuquerque	AAA LA	31	0	0	15	47.2	232	61	41	39	9	1	3	1	28	2	42	6	0	2	1	.667	0	0	7.36
San Antonio	AA LA	10	7	0	2	31.2	144	36	20	11	2	2	2	0	14	0	28	3	0	1	2	.333	0	3	3.13
2000 Oklahoma	AAA Tex	45	0	0	18	59	272	69	43	39	5	2	4	2	32	3	39	6	0	3	4	.429	0	3	5.95
5 Min. YEARS		200	22	1	106	392.2	1715	403	210	177	34	14	18	7	147	9	365	24	2	21	19	.525	0	35	4.06

Derek Mitchell

Bats: Right **Throws:** Right **Pos:** SS-115; PR-4   **Ht:** 6'2" **Wt:** 170 **Born:** 3/9/75 **Age:** 26

		BATTING															BASERUNNING				PERCENTAGES		
Year Team	Lg Org	G	AB	H	2B	3B	HR	TB	R	RBI	TBB	IBB	SO	HBP	SH	SF	SB	CS	SB%	GDP	Avg	OBP	SLG
1996 Jamestown	A- Det	56	184	45	10	2	2	65	25	25	18	0	38	2	7	2	7	4	.64	1	.245	.316	.353
1997 W Michigan	A Det	110	353	70	14	2	1	91	47	31	50	1	91	5	8	3	11	8	.58	5	.198	.304	.258
1998 Jacksnville	AA Det	128	421	93	21	2	2	124	58	54	68	1	94	6	4	8	6	3	.67	9	.221	.332	.295
1999 Jacksnville	AA Det	124	422	102	17	1	7	142	56	49	53	0	117	2	4	5	4	2	.67	3	.242	.326	.336
2000 Jacksnville	AA Det	116	330	65	14	0	1	82	38	27	54	0	76	0	7	1	3	3	.50	4	.197	.309	.248
5 Min. YEARS		534	1710	375	76	7	13	504	224	186	243	2	416	15	30	19	31	20	.61	22	.219	.319	.295

Mike Mitchell

Bats: Left **Throws:** Right **Pos:** 1B-81; DH-10; PH-7   **Ht:** 6'3" **Wt:** 205 **Born:** 4/5/73 **Age:** 28

		BATTING															BASERUNNING				PERCENTAGES		
Year Team	Lg Org	G	AB	H	2B	3B	HR	TB	R	RBI	TBB	IBB	SO	HBP	SH	SF	SB	CS	SB%	GDP	Avg	OBP	SLG
1994 Oneonta	A- NYY	28	104	31	6	0	2	43	13	12	10	0	9	1	0	1	0	0	—	2	.298	.362	.413
Greensboro	A NYY	39	133	35	5	1	3	51	15	19	14	1	19	1	0	1	0	1	.00	1	.263	.336	.383
Albany-Col	AA NYY	8	24	8	2	0	0	10	3	2	4	1	5	0	0	0	0	0	—	1	.333	.429	.417
1995 Tampa	A+ NYY	102	368	98	16	1	8	140	40	61	29	1	52	2	1	6	1	0	1.00	10	.266	.319	.380
1997 Rancho Cuca	A+ SD	109	440	154	36	1	17	243	78	106	35	0	83	6	0	5	2	0	1.00	7	.350	.401	.552
1998 Mobile	AA SD	134	509	162	32	2	15	243	72	97	61	1	95	1	0	3	0	0	—	7	.318	.390	.477
1999 Las Vegas	AAA SD	27	87	21	5	0	1	29	7	11	12	0	20	0	0	1	0	0	—	3	.241	.330	.333
2000 Tucson	AAA Ari	84	279	86	25	2	4	127	50	40	40	2	41	2	3	2	2	2	.50	7	.308	.396	.455
Arkansas	AA StL	13	46	14	5	0	0	19	3	4	4	0	8	0	0	0	0	1	.00	1	.304	.360	.413
6 Min. YEARS		544	1990	609	132	7	50	905	281	352	209	6	332	13	4	19	5	4	.56	43	.306	.372	.455

Scott Mitchell

Pitches: Right **Bats:** Right **Pos:** RP-15; SP-13   **Ht:** 6'0" **Wt:** 180 **Born:** 3/19/73 **Age:** 28

		HOW MUCH HE PITCHED						WHAT HE GAVE UP												THE RESULTS				
Year Team	Lg Org	G	GS	CG	GF	IP	BFP	H	R	ER	HR	SH	SF	HB	TBB	IBB	SO	WP	Bk	W	L	Pct.	ShO	Sv	ERA
1995 Vermont	A- Mon	18	1	0	5	40.1	171	35	18	10	1	2	2	4	15	0	30	2	4	3	1	.750	0	1	2.23
1996 Delmarva	A Mon	33	5	1	10	76.2	320	69	29	20	7	3	1	5	24	1	76	3	3	5	6	.455	0	1	2.35
1997 Wst Plm Bch	A+ Mon	39	3	0	15	73.2	291	61	21	21	4	3	1	3	18	0	56	4	0	5	3	.625	0	3	2.57
Harrisburg	AA Mon	9	0	0	0	17.1	67	17	7	7	3	1	0	1	3	0	13	1	0	1	0	1.000	0	0	3.63
1998 Harrisburg	AA Mon	32	17	2	5	135	558	136	58	57	13	3	6	6	37	1	81	0	0	9	3	.750	1	2	3.80
1999 Harrisburg	AA Mon	3	3	1	0	19	74	16	9	9	5	0	1	0	3	0	10	1	1	2	0	1.000	0	0	4.26
Ottawa	AAA Mon	18	9	0	1	62.1	282	78	43	39	11	1	3	3	25	0	28	0	1	4	4	.500	0	0	5.63
2000 Ottawa	AAA Mon	28	13	0	0	89.1	397	109	63	60	13	4	5	5	28	2	52	5	1	4	5	.545	0	0	6.04
6 Min. YEARS		175	54	4	36	513.2	2160	515	248	223	57	18	18	27	153	4	346	16	10	35	22	.614	1	7	3.91

Greg Mix

Pitches: Right **Bats:** Right **Pos:** RP-38   **Ht:** 6'4" **Wt:** 225 **Born:** 8/21/71 **Age:** 29

Year Team	Lg Org	G	GS	CG	GF	IP	BFP	H	R	ER	HR	SH	SF	HB	TBB	IBB	SO	WP	Bk	W	L	Pct.	ShO	Sv	ERA
1993 Elmira	A- Fla	17	1	0	8	45.1	205	51	26	21	4	0	1	4	17	0	38	0	0	3	3	.500	0	4	4.17
1994 Brevard Cty	A+ Fla	44	0	0	22	78	314	65	29	27	2	4	4	2	20	2	51	1	0	6	2	.750	0	4	3.12
1995 Brevard Cty	A+ Fla	5	4	1	0	29.2	119	27	13	13	1	0	0	3	10	0	17	1	1	3	1	.750	0	0	3.94
Portland	AA Fla	24	13	0	1	92.1	401	98	51	48	9	2	4	4	25	5	56	3	0	6	4	.600	0	0	4.68
1996 Charlotte	AAA Fla	4	4	0	0	18.1	87	27	15	14	4	2	0	2	7	1	9	1	0	1	3	.250	0	0	6.87
Portland	AA Fla	25	5	0	8	65.2	296	80	40	33	8	4	5	5	19	5	57	6	2	3	0	1.000	0	1	4.52
1997 Portland	AA Fla	30	13	0	4	102.2	461	121	70	54	16	7	5	8	32	0	74	5	0	7	7	.500	0	0	4.73
1998 Greenville	AA Atl	22	0	0	9	25	119	32	19	14	2	0	3	0	11	0	18	3	0	1	1	.500	0	2	5.04
Richmond	AAA Atl	28	2	0	13	64.2	268	52	24	21	8	1	2	4	19	0	59	1	0	2	4	.333	0	2	2.92
1999 Pawtucket	AAA Bos	46	4	0	13	85.1	388	89	45	35	9	3	5	4	40	0	79	9	1	4	4	.500	0	1	3.69
2000 Indianapols	AAA Mil	38	0	0	10	54.1	240	57	33	28	8	4	6	2	18	2	42	7	0	3	2	.600	0	0	4.64
8 Min. YEARS		283	46	1	88	661.1	2898	699	365	308	71	27	35	38	218	15	500	41	4	39	31	.557	0	14	4.19

Kevin Mobley

Pitches: Right **Bats:** Right **Pos:** RP-38; SP-5   **Ht:** 6'7" **Wt:** 245 **Born:** 1/26/75 **Age:** 26

Year Team	Lg Org	G	GS	CG	GF	IP	BFP	H	R	ER	HR	SH	SF	HB	TBB	IBB	SO	WP	Bk	W	L	Pct.	ShO	Sv	ERA
1997 Jamestown	A- Det	18	0	0	9	25.2	115	27	10	9	1	4	2	1	11	1	24	0	0	2	1	.667	0	0	3.16
1998 Lakeland	A+ Det	34	8	1	10	79.1	345	80	44	42	9	0	3	5	36	2	58	4	0	4	3	.571	1	2	4.76
1999 Lakeland	A+ Det	46	5	0	12	96.2	414	107	48	41	11	5	8	3	26	1	73	5	0	7	4	.636	0	2	3.82
2000 Jacksnville	AA Det	43	5	1	8	90	368	62	31	27	5	0	4	3	42	2	72	7	0	6	0	1.000	1	0	2.70
4 Min. YEARS		141	18	2	39	291.2	1242	276	133	119	26	9	17	12	115	6	227	16	0	19	8	.704	2	4	3.67

Izzy Molina

Bats: Right **Throws:** Right **Pos:** C-59; DH-30; PH-2; PR-1   **Ht:** 6'1" **Wt:** 224 **Born:** 6/3/71 **Age:** 30

Year Team	Lg Org	G	AB	H	2B	3B	HR	TB	R	RBI	TBB	IBB	SO	HBP	SH	SF	SB	CS	SB%	GDP	Avg	OBP	SLG
1990 Athletics	R Oak	38	122	43	12	2	0	59	19	18	9	1	21	2	1	3	5	0	1.00	5	.352	.397	.484
1991 Madison	A Oak	95	316	89	16	1	3	116	35	45	15	1	40	6	1	4	6	4	.60	9	.282	.323	.367
1992 Reno	A+ Oak	116	436	113	17	2	10	164	71	75	39	0	57	7	7	6	8	7	.53	20	.259	.326	.376
Tacoma	AAA Oak	10	36	7	0	1	0	9	3	5	2	0	6	0	0	0	1	0	1.00	1	.194	.237	.250
1993 Modesto	A+ Oak	125	444	116	26	5	6	170	61	69	44	0	85	3	4	11	2	8	.20	11	.261	.325	.383
1994 Huntsville	AA Oak	116	388	84	17	2	8	129	31	50	16	0	47	5	7	7	5	1	.83	10	.216	.252	.332
1995 Edmonton	AAA Oak	2	6	1	0	0	0	1	0	0	0	0	2	0	0	0	0	0	—	0	.167	.167	.167
Huntsville	AA Oak	83	301	78	16	1	8	120	38	26	26	0	62	8	0	2	3	4	.43	6	.259	.332	.399
1996 Edmonton	AAA Oak	98	342	90	12	3	12	144	45	56	25	4	55	3	5	2	2	5	.29	9	.263	.317	.421
1997 Edmonton	AAA Oak	61	218	57	11	3	6	92	33	34	12	0	27	0	1	0	2	0	1.00	9	.261	.300	.422
1998 Edmonton	AAA Oak	86	303	73	15	2	8	116	29	38	17	0	60	4	1	3	3	0	1.00	16	.241	.287	.383
1999 Columbus	AAA NYY	97	338	83	16	1	4	113	44	51	18	0	47	1	2	6	4	2	.67	9	.246	.281	.334
2000 Omaha	AAA KC	90	311	73	9	1	10	114	39	36	14	0	55	2	0	5	5	4	.56	6	.235	.268	.367
1996 Oakland	AL	14	25	5	2	0	0	7	0	1	1	0	3	0	0	0	0	0	—	0	.200	.231	.280
1997 Oakland	AL	48	111	22	3	1	3	36	6	7	3	0	17	0	1	0	0	0	—	1	.198	.219	.324
1998 Oakland	AL	2	2	1	0	0	0	1	1	0	0	0	0	0	0	0	0	0	—	0	.500	.500	.500
11 Min. YEARS		1017	3561	907	167	24	75	1347	448	503	237	6	564	41	29	49	46	35	.57	101	.255	.305	.378
3 Maj. YEARS		68	138	28	5	1	3	44	7	8	4	0	20	0	1	0	0	0	—	1	.203	.225	.319

Jose Molina

Bats: Right **Throws:** Right **Pos:** C-73; PH-2; 1B-1; DH-1   **Ht:** 6'1" **Wt:** 215 **Born:** 6/3/75 **Age:** 26

Year Team	Lg Org	G	AB	H	2B	3B	HR	TB	R	RBI	TBB	IBB	SO	HBP	SH	SF	SB	CS	SB%	GDP	Avg	OBP	SLG
1993 Cubs	R ChC	33	78	17	2	0	0	19	5	4	12	0	12	0	4	0	3	2	.60	2	.218	.322	.244
Daytona	A+ ChC	3	7	1	0	0	0	1	0	1	2	0	0	0	0	0	0	1	.00	0	.143	.333	.143
1994 Peoria	A ChC	78	253	58	13	1	1	76	31	33	24	1	61	4	5	4	4	3	.57	5	.229	.302	.300
1995 Daytona	A+ ChC	82	233	55	9	1	1	69	27	19	29	0	53	7	2	2	1	0	1.00	5	.236	.336	.296
1996 Rockford	A ChC	96	305	69	10	1	2	87	35	27	36	0	71	3	7	4	2	4	.33	8	.226	.310	.285
1997 Iowa	AAA ChC	1	3	1	0	0	0	1	0	0	1	0	1	0	0	0	0	0	—	0	.333	.500	.333
Daytona	A+ ChC	55	179	45	9	1	0	56	17	23	14	0	25	1	5	2	4	0	1.00	6	.251	.306	.313
Orlando	AA ChC	37	99	17	3	0	1	23	10	15	12	5	28	2	1	3	0	1	.00	4	.172	.267	.232
1998 West Tenn	AA ChC	109	320	71	10	1	2	89	33	28	32	1	74	3	10	3	1	5	.17	10	.222	.296	.278
1999 West Tenn	AA ChC	14	35	6	3	0	0	9	2	5	2	0	14	0	1	1	0	0	—	1	.171	.211	.257
Iowa	AAA ChC	74	240	63	11	1	4	88	24	26	20	5	54	4	2	2	0	1	.00	3	.263	.327	.367
2000 Iowa	AAA ChC	76	248	58	9	0	1	70	22	17	23	1	61	0	1	3	1	4	.20	6	.234	.296	.282
1999 Chicago	NL	10	19	5	1	0	0	6	3	1	2	1	4	0	0	0	0	0	—	0	.263	.333	.316
8 Min. YEARS		658	2000	461	79	6	12	588	206	198	207	13	454	24	38	24	16	21	.43	52	.231	.307	.294

Shane Monahan

Bats: Left **Throws:** Right **Pos:** OF-66; PH-11; DH-8; 3B-2   **Ht:** 6'0" **Wt:** 195 **Born:** 8/12/74 **Age:** 26

Year Team	Lg Org	G	AB	H	2B	3B	HR	TB	R	RBI	TBB	IBB	SO	HBP	SH	SF	SB	CS	SB%	GDP	Avg	OBP	SLG
1995 Wisconsin	A Sea	59	233	66	9	6	1	90	34	32	11	0	40	2	7	3	9	2	.82	4	.283	.317	.386
1996 Lancaster	A+ Sea	132	585	164	31	12	14	261	107	97	30	2	124	4	3	8	19	5	.79	8	.280	.316	.446
1997 Memphis	AA Sea	107	401	121	24	6	12	193	52	76	30	2	100	2	1	2	14	7	.67	4	.302	.352	.481
Tacoma	AAA Sea	21	85	25	4	0	2	35	15	12	5	0	21	1	2	0	5	1	.83	1	.294	.341	.412
1998 Tacoma	AAA Sea	69	277	69	8	5	4	99	32	33	19	3	47	0	4	2	6	4	.60	3	.249	.295	.357
1999 Tacoma	AAA Sea	108	399	102	21	2	7	148	51	32	19	2	81	3	1	2	9	3	.75	4	.256	.293	.371

Year Team	Lg Org	G	AB	H	2B	3B	HR	TB	R	RBI	TBB	IBB	SO	HBP	SH	SF	SB	CS	SB%	GDP	Avg	OBP	SLG
2000 Tacoma	AAA Sea	8	27	8	1	1	1	14	3	8	1	0	4	1	0	1	1	1	.50	0	.296	.333	.519
Las Vegas	AAA SD	13	39	7	2	0	0	9	5	5	5	0	6	0	1	0	0	2	.00	0	.179	.273	.231
Chattanooga	AA Cin	25	80	20	8	0	4	40	10	16	7	0	18	1	0	1	3	0	1.00	1	.250	.315	.500
Louisville	AAA Cin	18	62	20	3	2	3	36	12	11	3	0	12	1	1	0	2	0	1.00	0	.323	.364	.581
Colo Sprngs	AAA Col	21	66	15	3	1	1	23	8	13	6	0	10	1	1	1	1	3	.25	0	.227	.297	.348
1998 Seattle	AL	62	211	51	8	1	4	73	17	28	8	0	53	0	4	0	1	2	.33	0	.242	.269	.346
1999 Seattle	AL	16	15	2	0	0	0	2	3	0	0	0	6	0	0	0	0	0	—	0	.133	.133	.133
6 Min. YEARS		581	2254	617	114	35	49	948	329	335	136	9	463	16	21	20	69	28	.71	25	.274	.317	.421
2 Maj. YEARS		78	226	53	8	1	4	75	20	28	8	0	59	0	4	0	1	2	.33	0	.235	.261	.332

Craig Monroe

Bats: Right **Throws:** Right **Pos:** OF-119; DH-1   **Ht:** 6'1" **Wt:** 195 **Born:** 2/27/77 **Age:** 24

Year Team	Lg Org	G	AB	H	2B	3B	HR	TB	R	RBI	TBB	IBB	SO	HBP	SH	SF	SB	CS	SB%	GDP	Avg	OBP	SLG
1995 Rangers	R Tex	54	193	48	6	2	0	58	22	33	18	0	25	2	1	2	13	2	.87	1	.249	.316	.301
1996 Chston-SC	A Tex	49	153	23	11	1	0	36	11	9	18	0	48	3	0	0	2	2	.50	3	.150	.253	.235
Hudson Val	A- Tex	67	268	74	16	6	5	117	53	29	23	0	63	2	0	2	21	7	.75	4	.276	.336	.437
1997 Charlotte	A+ Tex	92	328	77	23	1	7	123	54	41	44	1	80	0	0	6	24	1	.96	5	.235	.320	.375
1998 Charlotte	A+ Tex	132	472	114	26	7	17	205	73	76	66	0	102	3	0	7	50	13	.79	15	.242	.334	.434
1999 Charlotte	A+ Tex	130	480	125	21	1	17	199	77	81	42	2	102	4	3	7	40	16	.71	8	.260	.321	.415
Oklahoma	AAA Tex	6	16	4	1	0	0	5	2	1	1	0	4	0	1	0	0	0	—	0	.250	.294	.313
2000 Tulsa	AA Tex	120	464	131	34	5	20	235	89	89	64	4	91	2	1	8	12	13	.48	12	.282	.366	.506
6 Min. YEARS		650	2374	596	138	23	66	978	381	359	276	7	515	16	6	32	162	54	.75	48	.251	.329	.412

Ivan Montane

Pitches: Right **Bats:** Right **Pos:** RP-42   **Ht:** 6'2" **Wt:** 195 **Born:** 6/3/73 **Age:** 28

		HOW MUCH HE PITCHED						WHAT HE GAVE UP									THE RESULTS					
Year Team	Lg Org	G	GS	CG	GF	IP	BFP	H	R	ER	HR	SH	SF	HB	TBB	IBB	SO	WP	Bk	W	L	Pct.	ShO	Sv	ERA
1992 Mariners	R Sea	13	11	0	1	46	224	44	39	29	0	0	0	3	41	0	48	18	4	1	3	.250	0	0	5.67
1993 Bellingham	A- Sea	15	15	1	0	73.1	305	55	36	32	7	2	1	3	37	0	53	9	3	5	4	.556	0	0	3.93
1994 Appleton	A Sea	29	26	1	0	159	680	132	79	68	13	4	6	12	82	0	155	19	2	8	9	.471	1	0	3.85
1995 Riverside	A+ Sea	24	16	0	6	92.2	442	101	67	58	3	3	6	10	71	0	79	19	0	5	5	.500	0	0	5.63
1996 Lancaster	A+ Sea	11	11	0	0	59.1	273	57	37	24	2	5	3	2	43	0	54	9	0	2	2	.500	0	0	3.64
Port City	AA Sea	18	18	0	0	100.1	461	96	67	57	6	1	2	9	75	0	81	16	2	3	8	.273	0	0	5.11
1997 Memphis	AA Sea	22	12	0	6	71.2	347	83	70	60	16	1	5	6	51	0	63	11	0	0	8	.000	0	0	7.53
Lancaster	A+ Sea	6	6	0	0	32.1	150	40	25	19	2	1	2	2	13	1	34	8	1	1	2	.333	0	0	5.29
1998 Orlando	AA Sea	2	0	0	0	2.1	12	3	3	3	0	0	0	0	5	0	0	0	0	0	0	—	0	0	11.57
1999 Wisconsin	A Sea	10	0	0	9	12.2	49	5	1	1	0	0	0	0	5	0	18	2	0	0	0	—	0	3	0.71
New Haven	AA Sea	41	0	0	25	54.2	219	38	16	15	2	3	0	2	22	2	70	5	0	4	2	.667	0	10	2.47
2000 New Haven	AA Sea	26	0	0	15	38.2	189	50	36	32	3	1	0	4	22	1	39	6	1	2	5	.286	0	0	7.45
Tacoma	AAA Sea	16	0	0	5	24.1	124	29	18	16	2	0	2	3	23	0	24	1	0	0	2	.000	0	0	5.92
9 Min. YEARS		233	115	2	67	767.1	3475	733	494	414	56	21	27	56	487	4	718	123	13	31	50	.383	1	13	4.86

Ricardo Montas

Bats: Right **Throws:** Right **Pos:** 1B-86; 3B-6; 2B-5; SS-3; DH-3; PH-2; PR-2   **Ht:** 6'1" **Wt:** 170 **Born:** 3/9/77 **Age:** 24

Year Team	Lg Org	G	AB	H	2B	3B	HR	TB	R	RBI	TBB	IBB	SO	HBP	SH	SF	SB	CS	SB%	GDP	Avg	OBP	SLG
1995 Royals	R KC	22	28	2	0	0	1	5	2	3	3	0	6	1	0	0	0	0	—	1	.071	.188	.179
1996 Lansing	A KC	8	24	7	0	0	0	7	1	0	2	0	4	0	0	0	0	0	—	0	.292	.346	.292
Royals	R KC	50	182	48	6	1	2	62	25	22	20	2	31	3	2	1	5	1	.83	7	.264	.345	.341
1997 Lansing	A- KC	4	10	3	0	0	0	3	0	1	0	0	2	0	0	1	0	0	—	0	.300	.273	.300
Spokane	A- KC	66	217	65	5	3	2	82	42	20	35	1	39	2	2	2	5	3	.63	5	.300	.398	.378
1998 Lansing	A KC	51	140	32	4	1	1	41	21	14	22	2	28	1	1	0	4	2	.67	4	.229	.337	.293
Spokane	A- KC	63	211	64	10	0	1	77	45	27	30	1	28	1	4	4	10	1	.91	10	.303	.386	.365
1999 Wilmington	A+ KC	98	349	86	15	0	2	107	46	31	47	0	60	3	5	2	4	2	.67	4	.246	.339	.307
2000 Wichita	AA KC	11	37	8	2	0	0	10	5	3	0	0	5	0	0	0	0	0	—	1	.216	.216	.270
Wilmington	A+ KC	93	314	87	17	0	0	104	43	36	42	0	49	5	2	4	6	1	.86	9	.277	.367	.331
6 Min. YEARS		466	1512	402	59	5	9	498	230	157	201	6	252	16	16	14	34	10	.77	44	.266	.355	.329

Matt Montgomery

Pitches: Right **Bats:** Right **Pos:** RP-44; SP-4   **Ht:** 6'4" **Wt:** 210 **Born:** 5/13/76 **Age:** 25

		HOW MUCH HE PITCHED						WHAT HE GAVE UP									THE RESULTS					
Year Team	Lg Org	G	GS	CG	GF	IP	BFP	H	R	ER	HR	SH	SF	HB	TBB	IBB	SO	WP	Bk	W	L	Pct.	ShO	Sv	ERA
1997 Yakima	A- LA	11	9	0	0	55.1	229	48	23	15	3	2	0	1	17	0	38	2	2	2	2	.500	0	0	2.44
Great Falls	R+ LA	4	4	0	0	23	92	24	11	10	1	0	0	0	3	0	6	1	0	1	1	.500	0	0	3.91
1998 San Berndno	A+ LA	63	0	0	58	79	331	69	31	28	6	4	3	1	27	4	81	5	1	4	6	.400	0	26	3.19
Albuquerque	AAA LA	3	0	0	3	3	11	0	0	0	0	1	0	1	2	0	3	0	0	0	0	—	0	2	0.00
1999 San Antonio	AA LA	58	0	0	56	55.1	254	65	35	16	1	3	2	3	17	2	39	5	1	5	6	.455	0	26	2.60
2000 Albuquerque	AAA LA	7	0	0	1	10	51	15	8	8	3	0	0	0	7	0	6	2	0	1	0	1.000	0	0	7.20
San Antonio	AA LA	41	4	0	19	89	402	98	55	39	5	8	5	5	37	0	82	5	0	5	5	.500	0	5	3.94
4 Min. YEARS		187	17	0	137	314.2	1370	319	163	116	19	18	10	11	110	6	255	20	4	18	20	.474	0	59	3.32

Ray Montgomery

Bats: Right **Throws:** Right **Pos:** OF-64; PH-8; PR-1   **Ht:** 6'3" **Wt:** 225 **Born:** 8/8/70 **Age:** 30

Year Team	Lg Org	G	AB	H	2B	3B	HR	TB	R	RBI	TBB	IBB	SO	HBP	SH	SF	SB	CS	SB%	GDP	Avg	OBP	SLG
1990 Auburn	A- Hou	61	193	45	8	1	0	55	19	13	23	1	32	1	4	1	11	5	.69	5	.233	.317	.285
1991 Burlington	A Hou	120	433	109	24	3	3	148	60	57	37	1	66	8	11	2	17	14	.55	10	.252	.321	.342

Year Team	Lg Org	G	AB	H	2B	3B	HR	TB	R	RBI	TBB	IBB	SO	HBP	SH	SF	SB	CS	SB%	GDP	Avg	OBP	SLG
1992 Jackson	AA Hou	51	148	31	4	1	1	40	13	10	7	2	27	0	1	1	4	1	.80	5	.209	.244	.270
1993 Tucson	AAA Hou	15	50	17	3	1	2	28	9	6	5	0	7	1	1	0	1	2	.33	1	.340	.411	.560
Jackson	AA Hou	100	338	95	16	3	10	147	50	59	36	1	54	6	1	6	12	6	.67	7	.281	.355	.435
1994 Tucson	AAA Hou	103	332	85	19	6	7	137	51	51	35	6	54	2	2	3	5	3	.63	9	.256	.328	.413
1995 Jackson	AA Hou	35	127	38	8	1	10	78	24	24	13	2	13	5	0	1	6	3	.67	3	.299	.384	.614
Tucson	AAA Hou	88	291	88	19	0	11	140	48	68	24	1	58	2	1	8	5	3	.63	3	.302	.351	.481
1996 Jackson	AA Hou	100	360	110	20	0	22	196	70	75	59	7	54	3	0	1	7	1	.88	12	.306	.407	.544
1997 New Orleans	AAA Hou	20	73	21	5	0	6	44	17	13	11	0	15	0	0	0	1	1	.50	2	.288	.381	.603
1998 New Orleans	AAA Hou	75	272	79	18	1	9	126	42	45	26	0	48	3	0	4	4	2	.67	8	.290	.354	.463
1999 Nashville	AAA Pit	90	272	90	23	2	16	165	57	52	24	0	49	5	1	5	5	3	.63	5	.331	.389	.607
2000 Nashville	AAA Pit	71	228	59	10	1	7	92	36	29	19	1	38	7	0	0	3	5	.38	8	.259	.335	.404
1996 Houston	NL	12	14	3	1	0	1	7	4	4	1	0	5	0	0	0	0	0	—	0	.214	.267	.500
1997 Houston	NL	29	68	16	4	1	0	22	8	4	5	0	18	0	0	3	0	0	—	0	.235	.276	.324
1998 Houston	NL	6	5	2	0	0	0	2	2	0	0	0	0	0	0	0	0	0	—	2	.400	.400	.400
11 Min. YEARS		929	3117	867	177	20	104	1396	496	502	319	22	515	43	22	32	81	49	.62	78	.278	.350	.448
3 Maj. YEARS		47	87	21	5	1	1	31	14	8	6	0	23	0	0	3	0	0	—	2	.241	.281	.356

Samuel Montilla

Bats: Right **Throws:** Right **Pos:** C-43; DH-2; PH-2; 1B-1   **Ht:** 5'11" **Wt:** 170 **Born:** 2/7/82 **Age:** 19

Year Team	Lg Org	G	AB	H	2B	3B	HR	TB	R	RBI	TBB	IBB	SO	HBP	SH	SF	SB	CS	SB%	GDP	Avg	OBP	SLG
2000 Diamondbcks	R Ari	45	125	34	8	0	3	51	23	18	9	0	23	1	0	1	6	1	.86	2	.272	.324	.408
Tucson	AAA Ari	2	2	1	0	0	0	1	0	1	0	0	0	0	0	0	0	0	—	0	.500	.500	.500
1 Min. YEARS		47	127	35	8	0	3	52	23	19	9	0	23	1	0	1	6	1	.86	2	.276	.326	.409

Saul Montoya

Pitches: Right **Bats:** Right **Pos:** SP-11; RP-5   **Ht:** 6'2" **Wt:** 210 **Born:** 12/17/80 **Age:** 20

Year Team	Lg Org	G	GS	CG	GF	IP	BFP	H	R	ER	HR	SH	SF	HB	TBB	IBB	SO	WP	Bk	W	L	Pct.	ShO	Sv	ERA
1999 Diamondbcks	R Ari	17	0	0	4	29	132	33	14	13	3	0	1	1	11	0	39	5	1	2	1	.667	0	1	4.03
2000 South Bend	A Ari	2	1	0	0	7	28	4	2	2	0	0	0	0	5	0	3	0	0	0	0	—	0	0	2.57
Tucson	AAA Ari	3	1	0	0	7.1	29	6	2	2	1	0	0	0	2	0	8	0	0	0	0	—	0	0	2.45
Diamondbcks	R Ari	3	1	0	0	11.1	61	15	13	12	0	0	0	2	8	0	5	1	4	1	2	.333	0	0	9.53
Missoula	R+ Ari	8	8	0	0	49.1	197	36	15	13	0	3	0	2	16	0	39	2	1	2	2	.500	0	0	2.37
2 Min. YEARS		33	11	0	4	104	447	94	46	42	4	3	1	5	42	0	94	8	6	5	5	.500	0	1	3.63

Eric Moody

Pitches: Pitches: Right **Bats:** Right **Pos:** RP-37; SP-2   **Ht:** 6'6" **Wt:** 185 **Born:** 1/6/71 **Age:** 30

Year Team	Lg Org	G	GS	CG	GF	IP	BFP	H	R	ER	HR	SH	SF	HB	TBB	IBB	SO	WP	Bk	W	L	Pct.	ShO	Sv	ERA
1993 Erie	A- Tex	17	7	0	4	54	229	54	30	23	3	0	1	2	13	1	33	3	1	3	3	.500	0	0	3.83
1994 Hudson Val	A- Tex	15	12	1	1	89	355	82	32	28	2	2	3	2	18	1	68	3	4	7	3	.700	0	0	2.83
1995 Charlotte	A+ Tex	13	13	2	0	88.1	353	84	30	27	2	3	1	5	13	0	57	0	0	5	5	.500	2	0	2.75
1996 Tulsa	AA Tex	44	5	0	29	95.2	395	92	40	38	4	1	3	1	23	2	80	4	0	8	4	.667	0	16	3.57
1997 Okla City	AAA Tex	35	10	1	10	112	469	114	49	43	13	5	1	4	21	1	72	1	0	5	6	.455	1	1	3.46
1998 Oklahoma	AAA Tex	45	6	0	29	101.1	436	112	51	38	9	2	4	6	23	4	73	4	1	6	6	.500	0	12	3.38
1999 Charlotte	A+ Tex	1	1	0	0	2	9	2	2	2	0	0	1	0	0	0	1	0	0	0	0	—	0	0	9.00
Oklahoma	AAA Tex	39	1	0	20	73.2	309	78	33	28	5	3	3	4	13	3	31	3	0	7	4	.636	0	4	3.42
2000 Las Vegas	AAA SD	4	1	0	0	7.1	34	12	4	4	1	0	0	0	0	0	4	0	0	1	0	1.000	0	0	4.91
Calgary	AAA Fla	35	1	0	12	50.1	226	75	37	35	12	1	0	1	8	1	26	0	0	1	3	.250	0	2	6.26
1997 Texas	AL	10	1	0	3	19	82	26	10	9	4	0	1	0	2	0	12	0	0	0	1	.000	0	0	4.26
8 Min. YEARS		248	57	4	105	673.2	2815	705	308	266	51	17	17	25	132	13	445	18	6	42	35	.545	3	35	3.55

Brian Moon

Bats: Both **Throws:** Right **Pos:** C-100; PH-7; 1B-1   **Ht:** 6'0" **Wt:** 190 **Born:** 7/15/77 **Age:** 23

Year Team	Lg Org	G	AB	H	2B	3B	HR	TB	R	RBI	TBB	IBB	SO	HBP	SH	SF	SB	CS	SB%	GDP	Avg	OBP	SLG
1997 Helena	R+ Mil	49	170	48	5	0	0	53	15	22	8	0	23	5	4	2	2	1	.67	4	.282	.330	.312
1998 Beloit	A Mil	118	438	112	20	1	1	137	62	54	46	4	62	23	9	7	0	1	.00	9	.256	.352	.313
1999 Stockton	A+ Mil	116	385	102	14	2	2	126	52	30	37	4	40	7	2	4	6	6	.50	9	.265	.337	.327
2000 Huntsville	AA Mil	106	312	57	13	1	1	75	34	33	45	5	49	10	3	4	2	4	.33	9	.183	.302	.240
4 Min. YEARS		389	1305	319	52	4	4	391	163	139	136	13	174	45	18	17	10	12	.45	31	.244	.333	.300

Brandon Moore

Bats: Right **Throws:** Right **Pos:** 2B-50; 3B-43; PR-6; PH-3; SS-1; OF-1   **Ht:** 5'11" **Wt:** 175 **Born:** 8/23/72 **Age:** 28

Year Team	Lg Org	G	AB	H	2B	3B	HR	TB	R	RBI	TBB	IBB	SO	HBP	SH	SF	SB	CS	SB%	GDP	Avg	OBP	SLG
1994 White Sox	R CWS	4	10	1	0	0	0	1	1	0	1	0	1	0	0	0	0	0	—	0	.100	.182	.100
Hickory	A CWS	60	230	57	5	2	1	69	43	26	33	1	28	1	7	3	10	6	.63	7	.248	.341	.300
1995 South Bend	A CWS	132	510	131	9	3	0	146	75	37	48	1	49	3	7	5	34	8	.81	15	.257	.322	.286
1996 Pr William	A+ CWS	125	439	106	13	2	1	126	56	41	82	1	70	3	2	3	9	11	.45	14	.241	.362	.287
1997 Birmingham	AA CWS	125	414	106	15	1	1	126	58	47	45	0	48	1	21	4	4	7	.36	14	.256	.328	.304
1998 Calgary	AAA CWS	86	244	51	4	1	2	63	37	19	20	1	30	2	3	1	5	3	.63	11	.209	.273	.258
1999 Birmingham	AA CWS	36	119	23	3	2	0	30	11	13	17	0	20	2	1	1	2	1	.67	9	.193	.292	.252
Charlotte	AAA CWS	90	299	85	21	2	1	113	44	41	21	1	41	2	13	4	3	2	.60	6	.284	.331	.378
2000 Charlotte	AAA CWS	96	300	71	10	2	0	85	34	22	39	0	33	0	8	0	3	4	.43	10	.237	.324	.283
7 Min. YEARS		754	2565	631	80	15	6	759	359	246	306	5	320	12	63	21	72	43	.63	78	.246	.327	.296

Mike Moore

Bats: Right **Throws:** Right **Pos:** OF-63; PH-11; DH-7   **Ht:** 6'4" **Wt:** 225 **Born:** 3/7/71 **Age:** 30

					BATTING											BASERUNNING				PERCENTAGES		
Year Team	Lg Org	G	AB	H	2B	3B	HR	TB	R	RBI	TBB	IBB	SO	HBP	SH	SF	SB	CS	SB%	GDP	Avg	OBP	SLG
1992 Yakima	A- LA	18	58	12	1	0	2	19	12	6	9	1	25	0	0	0	3	2	.60	1	.207	.313	.328
1993 Bakersfield	A+ LA	100	403	116	25	1	13	182	61	58	29	0	103	3	0	4	23	10	.70	6	.288	.337	.452
1994 San Antonio	AA LA	72	254	57	12	1	5	86	32	32	22	0	75	6	0	1	11	7	.61	2	.224	.300	.339
Bakersfield	A+ LA	21	81	24	5	0	2	35	17	8	13	1	21	0	0	0	2	0	1.00	3	.296	.394	.432
1995 Vero Beach	A+ LA	7	22	6	1	0	0	7	3	1	6	0	8	0	0	0	0	1	.00	1	.273	.429	.318
1996 San Antonio	AA LA	64	200	48	10	4	2	72	21	21	17	0	64	2	0	1	8	4	.67	4	.240	.305	.360
1997 Binghamton	AA NYM	50	130	39	11	1	2	58	19	13	18	1	47	1	0	1	7	3	.70	2	.300	.387	.446
Norfolk	AAA NYM	34	83	20	4	0	2	30	10	6	9	0	33	0	0	0	1	0	1.00	3	.241	.315	.361
1998 Lancaster	A+ LA	19	63	13	3	1	3	27	12	11	5	0	27	1	0	2	0	1	.00	0	.206	.268	.429
Missn Viejo	IND —	35	133	30	7	1	6	57	26	16	15	0	41	3	0	0	8	0	1.00	1	.226	.314	.429
Nashua	IND —	35	132	33	10	0	8	67	25	19	17	0	48	1	0	0	4	0	1.00	2	.250	.340	.508
1999 Nashua	IND —	105	390	110	22	1	26	212	65	82	44	2	110	3	1	1	6	2	.75	3	.282	.358	.544
2000 Huntsville	AA Mil	26	76	14	2	1	2	24	5	8	5	0	37	1	0	0	0	1	.00	1	.184	.244	.316
Greenville	AA Atl	29	104	23	3	1	7	49	12	14	6	0	50	2	0	0	1	0	1.00	2	.221	.277	.471
Richmond	AAA Atl	24	63	11	5	0	2	22	10	5	6	0	28	1	0	0	0	0	—	2	.175	.257	.349
9 Min. YEARS		639	2192	556	121	12	82	947	330	300	221	5	717	24	1	12	74	31	.70	33	.254	.327	.432

Steve Morales

Bats: Both **Throws:** Right **Pos:** C-34; DH-10; PH-5   **Ht:** 5'10" **Wt:** 195 **Born:** 5/4/78 **Age:** 23

					BATTING											BASERUNNING				PERCENTAGES		
Year Team	Lg Org	G	AB	H	2B	3B	HR	TB	R	RBI	TBB	IBB	SO	HBP	SH	SF	SB	CS	SB%	GDP	Avg	OBP	SLG
1997 Marlins	R Fla	20	62	13	1	0	2	20	7	13	6	0	10	1	0	2	1	1	.50	3	.210	.282	.323
1998 Portland	AA Fla	3	10	3	0	0	0	3	0	3	0	0	2	0	0	0	0	0	—	1	.300	.300	.300
Utica	A- Fla	26	85	21	2	0	3	32	14	14	5	0	18	0	0	2	2	1	.67	2	.247	.283	.376
1999 Kane County	A Fla	28	96	26	5	0	2	37	12	11	4	0	16	1	2	0	0	0	—	2	.271	.307	.385
2000 Kane County	A Fla	42	114	25	3	0	4	40	9	19	11	0	24	3	2	1	0	0	—	2	.219	.302	.351
Calgary	AAA Fla	3	3	0	0	0	0	0	0	0	0	0	0	0	0	0	0	0	—	1	.000	.000	.000
4 Min. YEARS		122	370	88	11	0	11	132	42	60	26	0	70	5	4	5	3	2	.60	11	.238	.293	.357

Juan Moreno

Pitches: Left **Bats:** Left **Pos:** RP-5; SP-1   **Ht:** 6'1" **Wt:** 205 **Born:** 2/28/75 **Age:** 26

		HOW MUCH HE PITCHED						WHAT HE GAVE UP										THE RESULTS					
Year Team	Lg Org	G	GS	CG	GF	IP	BFP	H	R	ER	HR	SH	SF	HB	TBB	IBB	SO	WP	Bk	W	L	Pct.	ShO	Sv	ERA
1995 Athletics	R Oak	20	0	0	8	44.2	181	36	16	6	1	1	1	0	20	0	49	2	5	6	2	.750	0	0	1.21
1996 W Michigan	A Oak	38	11	0	5	107	475	98	60	52	6	6	6	2	69	5	97	6	2	4	6	.400	0	0	4.37
1999 Tulsa	AA Tex	42	0	0	27	62.2	255	33	20	16	5	2	3	3	32	2	83	6	0	4	3	.571	0	3	2.30
2000 Charlotte	A+ Tex	1	1	0	0	2	7	0	0	0	0	0	0	0	1	0	0	0	0	0	0	—	0	0	0.00
Tulsa	AA Tex	5	0	0	3	6.2	30	6	4	4	0	0	1	0	5	0	12	1	0	0	0	—	0	1	5.40
4 Min. YEARS		106	12	0	43	223	948	173	94	78	12	9	11	5	127	7	241	15	7	14	11	.560	0	4	3.15

Juan Moreno

Bats: Right **Throws:** Right **Pos:** OF-87; DH-7; PR-6; PH-4   **Ht:** 6'2" **Wt:** 185 **Born:** 3/19/76 **Age:** 25

					BATTING											BASERUNNING				PERCENTAGES		
Year Team	Lg Org	G	AB	H	2B	3B	HR	TB	R	RBI	TBB	IBB	SO	HBP	SH	SF	SB	CS	SB%	GDP	Avg	OBP	SLG
1996 Mets	R NYM	16	53	14	4	1	0	20	7	7	4	0	11	1	0	0	2	0	1.00	2	.264	.328	.377
1997 Pittsfield	A- NYM	71	287	83	17	4	2	114	35	41	12	2	60	0	0	1	19	6	.76	6	.289	.317	.397
1998 Capital Cty	A NYM	113	435	124	22	1	10	178	69	51	36	0	98	3	0	2	31	8	.79	4	.285	.342	.409
1999 St. Lucie	A+ NYM	120	424	127	18	5	4	167	64	47	51	0	70	2	7	4	28	11	.72	10	.300	.374	.394
2000 Binghamton	AA NYM	32	90	18	4	0	0	22	6	8	7	0	18	0	3	1	3	2	.60	1	.200	.255	.244
St. Lucie	A+ NYM	68	243	68	7	3	2	87	42	31	27	0	38	1	5	3	37	8	.82	1	.280	.350	.358
5 Min. YEARS		420	1532	434	72	14	18	588	223	185	137	2	295	7	15	11	120	35	.77	24	.283	.343	.384

Julio Moreno

Pitches: Right **Bats:** Right **Pos:** RP-18   **Ht:** 6'1" **Wt:** 180 **Born:** 10/23/75 **Age:** 25

		HOW MUCH HE PITCHED						WHAT HE GAVE UP										THE RESULTS					
Year Team	Lg Org	G	GS	CG	GF	IP	BFP	H	R	ER	HR	SH	SF	HB	TBB	IBB	SO	WP	Bk	W	L	Pct.	ShO	Sv	ERA
1994 Orioles	R Bal	4	2	0	0	8.1	41	14	14	11	2	0	2	0	1	0	6	0	0	0	2	.000	0	0	11.88
1995 Orioles	R Bal	5	5	1	0	34	131	17	9	6	0	1	2	1	7	0	29	1	1	3	2	.600	1	0	1.59
Bluefield	R+ Bal	9	8	0	1	49.1	214	61	31	23	3	1	3	0	12	0	36	3	1	4	3	.571	0	0	4.20
1996 Frederick	A+ Bal	28	26	0	1	162	682	167	80	63	14	8	0	9	38	0	147	8	1	9	10	.474	0	0	3.50
1997 Bowie	AA Bal	27	25	1	0	138.2	596	141	76	59	20	2	3	6	64	4	106	6	3	9	6	.600	0	0	3.83
1999 Orioles	R Bal	4	2	0	0	10	39	8	4	2	1	0	1	0	5	0	6	0	0	1	0	1.000	0	0	1.80
Bowie	AA Bal	10	10	0	0	44.1	202	46	29	26	9	1	2	1	27	0	25	4	0	2	2	.500	0	0	5.28
2000 Orioles	R Bal	3	0	0	0	6	27	6	3	0	0	0	0	0	3	0	6	0	0	0	0	—	0	0	0.00
Frederick	A+ Bal	2	0	0	0	4	15	2	2	2	2	0	0	0	1	0	1	0	0	0	0	—	0	0	4.50
Bowie	AA Bal	13	0	0	4	31	144	43	21	19	6	0	2	1	10	1	14	3	0	1	1	.500	0	0	5.52
6 Min. YEARS		105	78	2	6	487.2	2091	505	269	211	57	13	15	18	164	5	375	26	6	29	26	.527	1	0	3.89

Ramon Moreta

Bats: Right **Throws:** Right **Pos:** OF-121; PH-5   **Ht:** 5'11" **Wt:** 185 **Born:** 9/5/75 **Age:** 25

					BATTING											BASERUNNING				PERCENTAGES		
Year Team	Lg Org	G	AB	H	2B	3B	HR	TB	R	RBI	TBB	IBB	SO	HBP	SH	SF	SB	CS	SB%	GDP	Avg	OBP	SLG
1997 Great Falls	R+ LA	68	265	89	6	2	1	102	45	20	18	0	38	1	6	0	29	17	.63	5	.336	.380	.385
1998 San Berndno	A LA	134	536	138	19	7	1	174	67	24	44	1	109	2	11	0	46	23	.67	4	.257	.316	.325
Albuquerque	AAA LA	8	27	10	1	2	0	15	5	3	1	0	9	0	0	1	2	2	.50	0	.370	.379	.556

197

Year Team	Lg Org	G	AB	H	2B	3B	HR	TB	R	RBI	TBB	IBB	SO	HBP	SH	SF	SB	CS	SB%	GDP	Avg	OBP	SLG
								BATTING											**BASERUNNING**			**PERCENTAGES**	
1999 San Antonio	AA LA	117	397	121	13	3	2	146	56	42	18	0	66	0	11	2	26	16	.62	12	.305	.333	.368
2000 San Antonio	AA LA	126	468	112	16	2	11	165	61	31	37	1	86	5	7	2	26	20	.57	8	.239	.301	.353
4 Min. YEARS		453	1693	470	55	16	15	602	234	120	118	2	308	8	35	5	129	78	.62	33	.278	.327	.356

Russ Morgan

Pitches: Left **Bats:** Right **Pos:** RP-13 **Ht:** 6'1" **Wt:** 205 **Born:** 11/20/77 **Age:** 23

Year Team	Lg Org	G	GS	CG	GF	IP	BFP	H	R	ER	HR	SH	SF	HB	TBB	IBB	SO	WP	Bk	W	L	Pct.	ShO	Sv	ERA
				HOW MUCH HE PITCHED						**WHAT HE GAVE UP**											**THE RESULTS**			
2000 Mariners	R Sea	12	0	0	8	20	81	17	10	6	2	1	0	1	3	0	29	0	0	1	0	1.000	0	1	2.70
Tacoma	AAA Sea	1	0	0	0	1.1	8	3	5	5	1	0	0	0	2	0	1	1	1	0	0	—	0	0	33.75
1 Min. YEARS		13	0	0	8	21.1	89	20	15	11	3	1	0	1	5	0	30	1	1	1	0	1.000	0	1	4.64

Scott Morgan

Bats: Right **Throws:** Right **Pos:** OF-94; DH-5; PH-2; 1B-1 **Ht:** 6'7" **Wt:** 230 **Born:** 7/19/73 **Age:** 27

Year Team	Lg Org	G	AB	H	2B	3B	HR	TB	R	RBI	TBB	IBB	SO	HBP	SH	SF	SB	CS	SB%	GDP	Avg	OBP	SLG
								BATTING											**BASERUNNING**			**PERCENTAGES**	
1995 Watertown	A- Cle	66	244	64	18	0	2	88	42	33	26	0	63	8	0	4	6	5	.55	11	.262	.348	.361
1996 Columbus	A Cle	87	305	95	25	1	22	188	62	80	46	0	70	11	0	4	9	5	.64	5	.311	.415	.616
1997 Kinston	A+ Cle	95	368	116	32	3	23	223	86	67	47	3	87	5	0	4	4	2	.67	8	.315	.396	.606
Akron	AA Cle	21	69	12	3	0	2	21	11	6	8	0	20	1	0	1	1	0	1.00	6	.174	.266	.304
1998 Akron	AA Cle	119	456	134	31	4	25	248	95	89	56	1	124	8	0	4	4	5	.44	9	.294	.378	.544
1999 Akron	AA Cle	88	344	97	26	2	26	205	72	70	38	5	96	2	0	1	6	1	.86	4	.282	.356	.596
Buffalo	AAA Cle	48	171	44	9	0	8	77	32	31	18	0	38	3	0	3	2	3	.40	2	.257	.333	.450
2000 Buffalo	AAA Cle	11	33	12	3	0	0	15	5	4	7	0	7	1	0	1	1	0	1.00	1	.364	.476	.455
Edmonton	AAA Ana	90	320	79	25	2	9	135	53	54	32	1	74	0	0	2	8	3	.73	5	.247	.319	.422
6 Min. YEARS		625	2310	653	172	12	117	1200	458	434	278	10	579	42	0	24	41	24	.63	45	.283	.367	.519

Mike Moriarty

Bats: Right **Throws:** Right **Pos:** SS-126; PH-2; DH-1; PR-1 **Ht:** 6'0" **Wt:** 190 **Born:** 3/8/74 **Age:** 27

Year Team	Lg Org	G	AB	H	2B	3B	HR	TB	R	RBI	TBB	IBB	SO	HBP	SH	SF	SB	CS	SB%	GDP	Avg	OBP	SLG
								BATTING											**BASERUNNING**			**PERCENTAGES**	
1995 Fort Wayne	A Min	62	203	46	6	3	4	70	26	26	27	1	44	2	2	3	8	0	1.00	1	.227	.319	.345
1996 Fort Myers	A+ Min	133	428	107	18	2	3	138	76	39	59	0	67	8	5	4	14	15	.48	2	.250	.349	.322
1997 New Britain	AA Min	135	421	93	22	5	6	143	60	48	53	1	68	3	10	5	12	5	.71	10	.221	.309	.340
1998 New Britain	AA Min	38	112	32	8	0	4	52	22	15	17	0	16	3	3	1	0	4	.00	1	.286	.391	.464
Salt Lake	AAA Min	64	161	36	8	2	3	57	21	19	22	0	39	1	2	1	2	1	.67	1	.224	.319	.354
1999 Salt Lake	AAA Min	128	380	98	21	7	4	145	63	51	56	1	62	6	11	5	6	4	.60	9	.258	.358	.382
2000 Salt Lake	AAA Min	127	390	97	23	4	13	167	73	55	63	0	58	5	9	4	1	2	.33	9	.249	.357	.428
6 Min. YEARS		687	2095	509	106	23	37	772	341	253	297	3	354	28	42	23	43	31	.58	33	.243	.341	.368

Cesar Morillo

Bats: Both **Throws:** Right **Pos:** SS-37; PH-29; 2B-20; DH-16; OF-6; 3B-4; 1B-1 **Ht:** 5'11" **Wt:** 180 **Born:** 7/21/73 **Age:** 27

Year Team	Lg Org	G	AB	H	2B	3B	HR	TB	R	RBI	TBB	IBB	SO	HBP	SH	SF	SB	CS	SB%	GDP	Avg	OBP	SLG
								BATTING											**BASERUNNING**			**PERCENTAGES**	
1990 Royals	R KC	55	185	50	6	2	1	63	21	17	22	0	45	2	3	0	7	4	.64	4	.270	.354	.341
1991 Baseball Cy	A+ KC	62	226	39	8	0	0	47	11	13	13	0	68	2	7	2	6	5	.55	4	.173	.222	.208
Appleton	A KC	63	236	59	9	3	1	77	35	17	38	0	54	1	1	1	9	8	.53	2	.250	.355	.326
1992 Baseball Cy	A+ KC	35	102	17	5	1	0	24	8	7	10	0	23	1	3	1	1	0	1.00	7	.167	.246	.235
Eugene	A- KC	51	180	44	9	1	1	58	28	17	21	0	40	1	3	0	6	4	.60	1	.244	.327	.322
1993 Rockford	A KC	101	327	85	13	3	3	113	47	36	30	3	65	3	5	2	4	1	.80	6	.260	.326	.346
1994 Wilmington	A+ KC	16	55	9	1	0	0	10	3	4	5	1	17	1	0	1	1	0	1.00	1	.164	.242	.182
Rockford	A KC	70	242	68	11	2	2	89	23	25	15	2	35	2	1	2	4	3	.57	6	.281	.326	.368
1995 Bakersfield	A+ KC	108	371	113	25	1	1	143	41	37	31	2	71	4	5	1	4	12	.25	6	.305	.364	.385
1996 Wichita	AA KC	45	119	28	3	1	2	39	8	7	7	0	18	0	5	0	3	0	1.00	3	.235	.278	.328
1997 Tulsa	AA Tex	84	288	76	18	1	1	99	38	23	28	2	53	0	4	1	0	4	.00	3	.264	.328	.344
1998 Bakersfield	A+ SF	14	38	7	0	0	0	7	3	6	3	0	10	0	1	1	0	0	—	1	.184	.238	.184
Shreveport	AA SF	10	18	2	0	0	0	2	1	2	1	0	3	0	0	0	0	0	—	0	.111	.158	.111
Newark	IND —	11	36	10	1	0	0	11	5	4	1	0	3	1	1	1	1	2	.33	1	.278	.308	.306
Nashua	IND —	28	98	28	3	2	1	38	16	18	9	0	15	1	1	0	9	3	.75	3	.286	.352	.388
Atlantic Ct	IND —	31	123	43	10	0	1	56	16	13	8	0	20	0	3	0	7	2	.78	2	.350	.389	.455
1999 Newark	IND —	91	338	99	21	2	6	142	60	42	24	0	55	1	8	1	19	6	.76	9	.293	.341	.420
2000 El Paso	AA Ari	10	21	4	1	0	0	5	0	1	0	0	6	0	0	0	0	0	—	0	.190	.190	.238
Round Rock	AA Hou	88	281	83	15	0	3	107	43	37	25	4	56	5	0	2	9	7	.56	5	.295	.361	.381
11 Min. YEARS		973	3284	864	159	19	23	1130	407	326	291	14	657	25	51	16	90	61	.60	62	.263	.326	.344

Bobby Morris

Bats: Left **Throws:** Right **Pos:** 2B-40; PH-27; DH-16; 3B-5; PR-2; SS-1 **Ht:** 6'0" **Wt:** 175 **Born:** 11/22/72 **Age:** 28

Year Team	Lg Org	G	AB	H	2B	3B	HR	TB	R	RBI	TBB	IBB	SO	HBP	SH	SF	SB	CS	SB%	GDP	Avg	OBP	SLG
								BATTING											**BASERUNNING**			**PERCENTAGES**	
1993 Huntington	R+ ChC	50	170	49	8	3	1	66	29	24	24	0	29	1	2	3	6	7	.46	2	.288	.374	.388
1994 Peoria	A ChC	101	362	128	33	1	7	184	61	64	53	4	63	7	10	2	7	7	.50	10	.354	.443	.508
1995 Daytona	A+ ChC	95	344	106	18	2	2	134	44	55	38	6	46	8	2	5	22	8	.73	5	.308	.385	.390
1996 Orlando	AA ChC	131	465	122	29	3	8	181	72	62	65	4	73	6	0	4	12	14	.46	12	.262	.355	.389
1997 Orlando	AA ChC	4	16	5	1	0	0	6	3	1	2	0	4	0	0	0	0	0	—	0	.313	.389	.375
Kinston	A+ Cle	10	32	5	1	0	2	12	6	10	4	0	6	2	0	1	0	0	—	1	.156	.282	.375
Akron	AA Cle	42	119	30	9	1	1	44	17	15	22	0	21	2	2	1	0	2	.00	3	.252	.375	.370
1998 Kinston	A+ Cle	25	65	17	2	1	1	24	11	14	6	0	12	3	3	1	2	1	.67	1	.262	.347	.415
1999 Tulsa	AA Tex	6	21	7	2	0	0	9	0	2	4	0	1	1	0	0	1	0	—	1	.333	.462	.429
2000 Chattanooga	AA Cin	87	245	67	14	1	5	98	34	35	32	0	42	2	1	1	6	2	.75	9	.273	.358	.400
8 Min. YEARS		551	1839	536	117	12	28	761	277	282	250	14	296	32	20	24	56	41	.58	45	.291	.381	.414

Jeremy Morris

Bats: Right **Throws:** Right **Pos:** OF-10; PH-6; DH-4; 1B-3; PR-1 **Ht:** 6'3" **Wt:** 225 **Born:** 10/7/74 **Age:** 26

Year Team	Lg Org	G	AB	H	2B	3B	HR	TB	R	RBI	TBB	IBB	SO	HBP	SH	SF	SB	CS	SB%	GDP	Avg	OBP	SLG
1997 Oneonta	A- NYY	68	239	67	19	1	2	94	44	28	29	0	47	5	0	3	10	3	.77	0	.280	.366	.393
1998 Tampa	A+ NYY	124	445	134	25	1	13	200	69	72	48	1	96	1	2	6	11	3	.79	8	.301	.366	.449
1999 Yankees	R NYY	5	15	6	0	0	2	12	7	7	6	0	5	1	0	0	0	0	—	1	.400	.591	.800
Norwich	AA NYY	111	392	97	16	1	9	142	50	52	31	0	91	2	2	2	8	2	.80	7	.247	.304	.362
2000 Norwich	AA NYY	17	44	10	3	0	1	16	7	5	6	1	12	0	0	0	0	0	1.00	1	.227	.320	.364
Columbus	AAA NYY	4	7	2	1	0	0	3	0	0	0	0	2	0	0	0	0	0	—	1	.286	.286	.429
4 Min. YEARS		329	1142	316	64	3	27	467	177	164	120	2	253	9	4	11	30	8	.79	18	.277	.347	.409

Robbie Morrison

Pitches: Right **Bats:** Right **Pos:** RP-33; SP-1 **Ht:** 6'0" **Wt:** 215 **Born:** 12/7/76 **Age:** 24

Year Team	Lg Org	G	GS	CG	GF	IP	BFP	H	R	ER	HR	SH	SF	HB	TBB	IBB	SO	WP	Bk	W	L	Pct.	ShO	Sv	ERA
1998 Spokane	A- KC	26	0	0	22	25.1	111	15	8	6	2	2	1	1	18	2	33	1	0	3	0	1.000	0	13	2.13
1999 Wilmington	A+ KC	28	0	0	22	43.2	173	31	13	11	2	2	1	4	13	1	47	0	1	2	5	.286	0	6	2.27
Wichita	AA KC	15	0	0	11	22.1	97	26	7	5	0	0	0	1	7	1	21	3	0	2	0	1.000	0	5	2.01
2000 Wichita	AA KC	34	1	0	18	61.1	263	58	30	23	6	2	0	0	29	3	49	5	0	3	3	.500	0	5	3.38
3 Min. YEARS		103	1	0	73	152.2	644	130	58	45	10	6	2	6	67	7	150	9	1	10	8	.556	0	29	2.65

Paul Morse

Pitches: Right **Bats:** Right **Pos:** SP-25; RP-2 **Ht:** 6'2" **Wt:** 185 **Born:** 2/27/73 **Age:** 28

Year Team	Lg Org	G	GS	CG	GF	IP	BFP	H	R	ER	HR	SH	SF	HB	TBB	IBB	SO	WP	Bk	W	L	Pct.	ShO	Sv	ERA
1994 Elizabethtn	R+ Min	7	0	0	5	7.1	35	8	7	6	2	0	0	0	3	0	8	0	0	0	0	—	0	0	7.36
Fort Wayne	A Min	16	0	0	11	20.1	97	27	15	13	2	1	0	2	10	0	17	0	0	0	3	.000	0	3	5.75
1995 Fort Myers	A+ Min	35	0	0	29	61.1	247	57	30	26	3	1	4	3	12	0	56	4	1	3	1	.750	0	15	3.82
1996 Fort Myers	A+ Min	13	0	0	12	14	50	8	4	4	1	0	0	0	5	0	10	0	0	1	0	1.000	0	9	2.57
Hardware Cy	A+ Min	35	1	0	23	55.2	249	55	36	33	5	4	4	1	26	2	48	4	1	6	4	.600	0	1	5.34
1997 New Britain	AA Min	37	17	0	9	111.1	508	124	91	74	16	4	2	6	70	2	75	11	0	3	11	.214	0	1	5.98
1998 San Berndno	A+ LA	30	26	0	2	153.2	696	160	110	90	13	6	9	6	77	0	116	17	2	7	14	.333	0	0	5.27
Albuquerque	AAA LA	2	2	0	0	15	59	15	5	5	1	0	1	3	6	0	11	0	0	1	1	.500	0	0	3.00
1999 Edmonton	AAA Ana	10	9	0	1	49.1	232	64	44	39	10	1	1	1	34	0	30	6	1	1	5	.167	0	0	7.11
Erie	AA Ana	15	14	2	0	97.1	419	83	46	36	9	5	1	5	54	0	52	10	1	8	6	.571	0	0	3.33
2000 Erie	AA Ana	14	14	2	0	80.1	368	80	48	39	4	4	3	3	58	0	46	11	0	3	8	.273	1	0	4.37
Edmonton	AAA Ana	13	11	0	0	73.2	334	73	47	39	9	0	6	1	44	0	31	7	0	6	5	.545	0	0	4.76
7 Min. YEARS		227	94	4	92	739.1	3294	747	481	404	75	27	33	37	399	4	500	70	6	39	58	.402	1	32	4.92

Mark Mortimer

Bats: Right **Throws:** Right **Pos:** C-45; DH-22; 1B-16; PH-8; OF-1 **Ht:** 6'1" **Wt:** 215 **Born:** 9/15/75 **Age:** 25

Year Team	Lg Org	G	AB	H	2B	3B	HR	TB	R	RBI	TBB	IBB	SO	HBP	SH	SF	SB	CS	SB%	GDP	Avg	OBP	SLG
1997 Danville	R+ Atl	5	13	1	0	0	0	1	1	3	4	0	1	0	1	1	0	0	—	1	.077	.278	.077
Eugene	A- Atl	53	174	53	7	2	2	70	25	21	16	0	24	2	0	2	1	1	.50	3	.305	.366	.402
1998 Macon	A Atl	28	94	28	7	0	5	50	21	26	18	0	11	2	0	0	1	0	1.00	2	.298	.421	.532
Danville	A+ Atl	98	338	80	11	2	6	113	32	33	41	4	53	5	0	2	0	4	.00	12	.237	.326	.334
1999 Greenville	AA Atl	11	30	7	1	0	0	8	4	5	3	0	7	0	0	1	0	0	—	0	.233	.294	.267
Myrtle Bch	A+ Atl	73	250	69	13	0	3	91	29	31	28	0	48	5	3	4	1	0	1.00	6	.276	.355	.364
2000 Greenville	AA Atl	41	118	21	3	0	4	36	14	12	12	0	15	1	1	0	0	0	—	5	.178	.260	.305
Myrtle Bch	A+ Atl	41	135	36	4	1	1	45	17	14	22	0	26	2	1	0	0	1	.00	5	.267	.377	.333
Richmond	AAA Atl	4	10	2	0	0	0	2	1	1	1	0	1	0	0	0	0	0	—	0	.200	.333	.200
4 Min. YEARS		354	1162	297	46	5	21	416	144	146	145	4	186	18	6	10	3	6	.33	31	.256	.345	.358

Ryan Moskau

Pitches: Left **Bats:** Right **Pos:** SP-25; RP-1 **Ht:** 6'3" **Wt:** 210 **Born:** 8/22/77 **Age:** 23

Year Team	Lg Org	G	GS	CG	GF	IP	BFP	H	R	ER	HR	SH	SF	HB	TBB	IBB	SO	WP	Bk	W	L	Pct.	ShO	Sv	ERA
1998 Yakima	A- LA	9	6	0	3	36.2	156	22	11	5	3	2	0	3	13	0	42	0	1	3	0	1.000	0	2	1.23
San Berndno	A+ LA	6	6	1	0	39	163	37	18	15	2	1	0	4	16	1	31	1	1	3	3	.500	0	0	3.46
1999 Vero Beach	A+ LA	17	17	0	0	104	443	99	54	48	8	3	4	7	40	0	68	6	4	5	5	.500	0	0	4.15
Brevard Cty	A+ Fla	9	9	2	0	63.2	261	50	22	19	4	4	0	1	21	0	49	0	0	4	3	.571	0	0	2.69
2000 Portland	AA Fla	16	16	2	0	84.2	377	96	58	52	9	8	2	3	38	0	53	3	0	3	8	.273	0	0	5.53
Brevard Cty	A+ Fla	10	9	1	0	52.2	245	74	40	38	6	0	2	2	15	0	43	1	0	2	5	.286	0	0	6.49
3 Min. YEARS		67	63	6	3	380.2	1645	378	203	177	32	18	8	20	143	1	277	11	6	20	24	.455	1	2	4.18

Julio Mosquera

Bats: Right **Throws:** Right **Pos:** C-59; PH-3; PR-3; DH-2; 1B-1 **Ht:** 6'0" **Wt:** 190 **Born:** 1/29/72 **Age:** 29

Year Team	Lg Org	G	AB	H	2B	3B	HR	TB	R	RBI	TBB	IBB	SO	HBP	SH	SF	SB	CS	SB%	GDP	Avg	OBP	SLG
1993 Blue Jays	R Tor	35	108	28	3	2	0	35	9	15	8	0	16	1	2	1	3	2	.60	3	.259	.314	.324
1994 Medcine Hat	R+ Tor	59	229	78	17	1	2	103	33	44	18	3	35	3	0	2	3	3	.50	4	.341	.393	.450
1995 Hagerstown	A Tor	108	406	118	22	5	3	159	64	46	29	2	53	13	3	5	5	5	.50	13	.291	.353	.392
1996 Knoxville	AA Tor	92	318	73	17	0	2	96	36	31	29	1	55	4	0	3	1	1	.55	16	.230	.301	.302
Syracuse	AAA Tor	23	72	18	1	0	0	19	6	5	1	0	14	1	0	0	0	0	—	1	.250	.316	.264
1997 Syracuse	AAA Tor	10	35	8	1	0	0	9	5	1	2	0	5	0	0	1	0	0	—	0	.229	.289	.257
Knoxville	AA Tor	87	309	90	23	1	5	130	47	50	22	0	56	5	2	3	3	4	.43	10	.291	.345	.421
1998 Syracuse	AAA Tor	28	94	20	6	0	2	32	10	4	5	0	12	4	1	1	0	1	1.00	2	.213	.279	.340
Knoxville	AA Tor	12	43	12	1	0	0	13	6	4	5	0	7	0	1	0	0	0	—	3	.279	.333	.302

Year Team	Lg Org	G	AB	H	2B	3B	HR	TB	R	RBI	TBB	IBB	SO	HBP	SH	SF	SB	CS	SB%	GDP	Avg	OBP	SLG
1999 Orlando	AA TB	80	259	79	13	1	4	106	36	37	15	2	40	3	1	4	1	0	1.00	14	.305	.345	.409
2000 Columbus	AAA NYY	35	101	24	6	2	1	37	17	14	8	0	20	6	1	1	6	0	1.00	3	.238	.328	.366
Norwich	AA NYY	29	74	17	3	2	0	24	9	3	8	0	12	1	2	1	2	2	.50	2	.230	.310	.324
1996 Toronto	AL	8	22	5	2	0	0	7	2	2	0	0	3	1	0	0	0	1	.00	0	.227	.261	.318
1997 Toronto	AL	3	8	2	1	0	0	3	0	0	0	0	2	0	0	0	0	0	—	0	.250	.250	.375
8 Min. YEARS		598	2048	565	113	14	19	763	276	258	154	8	325	42	15	20	30	21	.59	70	.276	.336	.373
2 Maj. YEARS		11	30	7	3	0	0	10	2	2	0	0	5	1	0	0	0	1	.00	0	.233	.258	.333

Damian Moss

Pitches: Left **Bats:** Right **Pos:** SP-28; RP-1 **Ht:** 6'0" **Wt:** 187 **Born:** 11/24/76 **Age:** 24

Year Team	Lg Org	G	GS	CG	GF	IP	BFP	H	R	ER	HR	SH	SF	HB	TBB	IBB	SO	WP	Bk	W	L	Pct.	ShO	Sv	ERA
1994 Danville	R+ Atl	12	12	1	0	60.1	265	30	28	24	1	1	0	14	55	0	77	12	3	2	5	.286	1	0	3.58
1995 Macon	A Atl	27	27	0	0	149.1	653	134	73	59	13	0	2	12	70	0	177	14	5	9	10	.474	0	0	3.56
1996 Durham	A+ Atl	14	14	0	0	84	333	52	25	21	9	3	3	2	40	0	89	7	2	9	1	.900	0	0	2.25
Greenville	AA Atl	11	10	0	0	58	262	57	41	32	5	0	3	3	35	0	48	12	0	2	5	.286	0	0	4.97
1997 Greenville	AA Atl	21	19	1	0	112.2	498	111	73	67	13	1	8	9	58	0	116	14	2	6	8	.429	0	0	5.35
1999 Macon	A Atl	12	12	0	0	41.2	172	33	20	20	8	1	0	4	15	0	49	2	1	0	3	.000	0	0	4.32
Greenville	AA Atl	7	7	0	0	32.2	171	50	33	31	6	0	3	2	21	0	22	8	0	1	3	.250	0	0	8.54
2000 Richmond	AAA Atl	29	28	0	0	160.2	710	130	67	56	14	8	5	6	106	0	123	10	2	9	6	.600	0	0	3.14
6 Min. YEARS		133	129	2	0	699.1	3064	597	360	310	69	14	24	52	400	0	701	79	15	38	41	.481	1	0	3.99

Tony Mota

Bats: Both **Throws:** Right **Pos:** OF-94; PH-9; DH-1 **Ht:** 6'1" **Wt:** 170 **Born:** 10/31/77 **Age:** 23

Year Team	Lg Org	G	AB	H	2B	3B	HR	TB	R	RBI	TBB	IBB	SO	HBP	SH	SF	SB	CS	SB%	GDP	Avg	OBP	SLG
1996 Yakima	A- LA	60	225	62	11	3	3	88	29	29	13	0	37	1	3	1	13	7	.65	0	.276	.317	.391
1997 San Berndno	A+ LA	111	420	101	14	13	4	153	53	49	30	2	97	4	6	2	11	8	.58	9	.240	.296	.364
1998 Vero Beach	A+ LA	61	254	81	18	5	7	130	45	35	18	3	27	2	0	0	13	8	.62	6	.319	.369	.512
San Antonio	AA LA	59	222	54	10	6	2	82	20	22	12	1	36	0	2	3	16	8	.67	6	.243	.278	.369
1999 San Antonio	AA LA	98	345	112	31	2	15	192	65	75	41	6	56	0	4	2	13	5	.72	14	.325	.394	.557
2000 Albuquerque	AAA LA	102	372	100	11	4	6	137	57	47	28	2	61	0	0	2	8	6	.57	9	.269	.318	.368
5 Min. YEARS		491	1838	510	95	33	37	782	269	257	142	14	314	7	15	10	74	42	.64	44	.277	.330	.425

Tony Mounce

Pitches: Left **Bats:** Left **Pos:** RP-28; SP-4 **Ht:** 6'2" **Wt:** 175 **Born:** 2/8/75 **Age:** 26

Year Team	Lg Org	G	GS	CG	GF	IP	BFP	H	R	ER	HR	SH	SF	HB	TBB	IBB	SO	WP	Bk	W	L	Pct.	ShO	Sv	ERA
1994 Astros	R Hou	11	11	0	0	59.2	246	56	24	18	1	2	1	1	18	0	72	2	2	4	2	.667	0	0	2.72
1995 Quad City	A Hou	25	25	3	0	159	649	118	55	43	6	6	6	3	57	2	143	6	2	16	8	.667	1	0	2.43
1996 Kissimmee	A+ Hou	25	25	4	0	155.2	675	139	65	39	7	6	3	10	68	1	102	7	0	9	9	.500	2	0	2.25
1997 New Orleans	AAA Hou	1	1	0	0	4.2	21	2	1	1	1	0	0	0	6	0	6	0	0	0	0	—	0	0	1.93
Jackson	AA Hou	25	25	1	0	145	645	165	91	81	18	6	5	2	66	3	116	7	0	8	9	.471	0	0	5.03
1998 Jackson	AA Hou	32	17	1	3	109.2	498	128	73	62	14	3	5	2	48	0	82	5	0	6	6	.500	0	0	5.09
Kissimmee	A+ Hou	5	5	0	0	26	122	35	22	20	2	2	0	2	13	1	15	1	0	1	2	.333	0	0	6.92
1999 New Orleans	AAA Hou	14	0	0	2	11	55	10	3	3	0	0	1	0	13	0	10	2	0	0	1	.000	0	0	2.45
Jackson	AA Hou	31	6	0	11	68.1	300	64	33	28	6	1	1	2	30	0	80	5	0	5	2	.714	0	0	3.69
2000 Oklahoma	AAA Tex	32	4	0	6	62	287	74	49	39	4	2	6	1	30	1	48	4	0	1	4	.200	0	1	5.66
7 Min. YEARS		201	119	9	22	801	3498	791	416	334	59	28	28	23	349	8	674	39	4	50	43	.538	3	1	3.75

Sean Mulligan

Bats: Right **Throws:** Right **Pos:** C-97; DH-5; PH-4; 3B-1 **Ht:** 6'2" **Wt:** 210 **Born:** 4/25/70 **Age:** 31

Year Team	Lg Org	G	AB	H	2B	3B	HR	TB	R	RBI	TBB	IBB	SO	HBP	SH	SF	SB	CS	SB%	GDP	Avg	OBP	SLG
1991 Chston-SC	A SD	60	215	56	9	3	4	83	24	30	17	0	56	6	1	1	4	1	.80	5	.260	.331	.386
1992 High Desert	A+ SD	35	118	19	4	0	4	35	14	14	11	1	38	3	0	1	0	0	—	3	.161	.248	.297
Waterloo	A SD	79	278	70	13	1	5	100	24	43	20	0	62	5	2	4	1	0	1.00	8	.252	.309	.360
1993 Rancho Cuca	A+ SD	79	268	75	10	3	6	109	29	36	34	0	33	3	0	4	1	3	.25	16	.280	.362	.407
1994 Rancho Cuca	A+ SD	66	243	74	18	1	9	121	45	49	24	1	39	5	1	8	1	0	1.00	4	.305	.368	.498
Wichita	AA SD	56	208	73	14	0	1	90	29	30	11	2	25	5	0	3	2	3	.40	9	.351	.392	.433
1995 Las Vegas	AAA SD	101	339	93	20	1	7	136	34	43	27	2	61	8	1	3	0	0	—	7	.274	.340	.401
1996 Las Vegas	AAA SD	102	358	103	24	3	19	190	55	75	30	4	68	7	0	2	1	2	.33	8	.288	.353	.531
1997 Akron	AA Cle	2	7	3	1	0	0	4	1	1	1	0	0	0	0	0	0	0	—	0	.429	.500	.571
1998 St. Paul	IND —	3	12	2	0	0	0	2	1	2	0	0	5	1	0	0	0	0	—	1	.167	.231	.167
1999 Duluth-Sup	IND —	52	200	50	10	0	5	75	23	25	14	2	21	4	0	0	1	0	1.00	5	.250	.312	.375
Bridgeport	IND —	18	62	11	3	0	1	17	7	6	5	0	20	2	0	1	0	0	—	1	.177	.257	.274
2000 Ottawa	AAA Mon	15	50	11	4	0	0	15	3	3	0	0	7	1	0	1	0	0	—	0	.220	.231	.300
Bridgeport	IND —	90	305	101	26	0	13	166	46	75	28	1	36	9	5	4	0	0	.00	8	.331	.399	.544
1996 San Diego	NL	2	1	0	0	0	0	0	0	0	0	0	0	0	0	0	0	0	—	0	.000	.000	.000
10 Min. YEARS		758	2663	741	156	12	74	1143	335	432	222	13	471	59	10	32	11	10	.52	79	.278	.343	.429

Rob Mummau

Bats: Right **Throws:** Right **Pos:** 3B-24; DH-11; 2B-10; C-4; PR-4; SS-3; OF-3; PH-2 **Ht:** 5'11" **Wt:** 185 **Born:** 8/21/71 **Age:** 29

Year Team	Lg Org	G	AB	H	2B	3B	HR	TB	R	RBI	TBB	IBB	SO	HBP	SH	SF	SB	CS	SB%	GDP	Avg	OBP	SLG
1993 St.Cathrnes	A- Tor	75	257	62	9	3	3	86	35	21	23	1	44	5	2	0	7	12	.37	3	.241	.316	.335
1994 Dunedin	A+ Tor	21	50	11	1	0	0	12	5	6	4	0	15	0	1	0	0	0	.00	0	.220	.278	.240
Hagerstown	A Tor	46	169	50	10	2	1	67	20	24	10	0	32	2	0	3	2	1	.50	4	.296	.337	.396

BATTING / BASERUNNING / PERCENTAGES

Year Team	Lg Org	G	AB	H	2B	3B	HR	TB	R	RBI	TBB	IBB	SO	HBP	SH	SF	SB	CS	SB%	GDP	Avg	OBP	SLG
1995 Hagerstown	A Tor	107	366	94	17	3	5	132	63	42	42	1	74	14	6	3	6	1	.86	7	.257	.353	.361
1996 Dunedin	A+ Tor	36	106	22	3	0	0	25	10	10	12	0	22	0	7	0	2	4	.33	2	.208	.288	.236
Syracuse	AAA Tor	4	3	0	0	0	0	0	0	1	0	0	0	1	0	0	0	0	—	0	.000	.000	.000
Knoxville	AA Tor	47	154	43	11	0	2	60	23	22	15	1	25	3	3	2	1	4	.20	6	.279	.351	.390
1997 Syracuse	AAA Tor	103	333	85	17	2	8	130	47	40	35	3	60	7	5	2	2	3	.40	3	.255	.337	.390
1998 Knoxville	AA Tor	39	141	41	5	2	3	59	28	28	11	0	24	2	3	3	4	1	.80	3	.291	.344	.418
Syracuse	AAA Tor	3	7	3	1	0	0	4	0	2	0	0	1	0	0	0	0	0	—	0	.429	.429	.571
1999 Syracuse	AAA Tor	123	433	105	29	3	5	155	52	58	28	1	61	6	6	7	2	1	.67	7	.242	.293	.358
2000 Syracuse	AAA Tor	54	155	25	5	1	0	32	13	8	13	1	28	0	2	1	0	0	—	6	.161	.225	.206
8 Min. YEARS		658	2174	541	108	16	27	762	297	261	193	8	387	39	35	21	26	30	.46	41	.249	.319	.351

Billy Munoz

Bats: Left **Throws:** Left **Pos:** 1B-119; DH-14; PH-5 **Ht:** 6'2" **Wt:** 220 **Born:** 6/30/75 **Age:** 26

Year Team	Lg Org	G	AB	H	2B	3B	HR	TB	R	RBI	TBB	IBB	SO	HBP	SH	SF	SB	CS	SB%	GDP	Avg	OBP	SLG
1998 Columbus	A Cle	120	417	111	24	1	12	173	61	60	48	2	104	1	0	1	3	2	.60	6	.266	.370	.415
1999 Kinston	A+ Cle	106	378	96	25	1	9	150	46	55	48	2	108	1	1	1	3	2	.60	9	.254	.339	.397
2000 Kinston	A+ Cle	63	213	67	13	1	11	115	28	39	21	0	46	3	0	3	0	1	.00	5	.315	.379	.540
Akron	AA Cle	74	281	77	15	4	14	142	41	48	29	2	66	4	1	1	1	0	1.00	3	.274	.349	.505
3 Min. YEARS		363	1289	351	77	7	46	580	176	202	166	6	324	9	2	6	7	5	.58	23	.272	.358	.450

Bobby Munoz

Pitches: Right **Bats:** Right **Pos:** SP-15; RP-6 **Ht:** 6'8" **Wt:** 260 **Born:** 3/3/68 **Age:** 33

Year Team	Lg Org	G	GS	CG	GF	IP	BFP	H	R	ER	HR	SH	SF	HB	TBB	IBB	SO	WP	Bk	W	L	Pct.	ShO	Sv	ERA
1989 Yankees	R NYY	2	2	0	0	10.1	41	5	4	4	0	0	0	0	4	0	13	1	1	1	1	.500	0	0	3.48
Ft. Laud	A+ NYY	3	3	0	0	13.1	58	16	8	7	2	0	0	0	7	0	2	0	1	1	2	.333	0	0	4.73
1990 Greensboro	A NYY	25	24	0	0	132.2	581	134	70	55	4	2	2	5	58	1	100	4	6	5	12	.294	0	0	3.73
1991 Ft. Laud	A+ NYY	19	19	4	0	108	443	91	45	28	4	2	4	4	40	0	53	6	2	5	8	.385	2	0	2.33
Columbus	AAA NYY	1	1	0	0	3	17	8	8	8	0	0	0	0	3	0	2	0	0	0	1	.000	0	0	24.00
1992 Albany-Col	AA NYY	22	22	0	0	112.1	491	96	55	41	2	2	4	4	70	0	66	8	0	7	5	.583	0	0	3.28
1993 Columbus	AAA NYY	22	1	0	18	31.1	124	24	6	5	0	1	0	0	8	0	16	1	0	3	1	.750	0	10	1.44
1994 Scranton-WB	AAA Phi	6	5	0	0	34	138	27	9	8	2	0	1	0	14	1	24	3	0	2	3	.400	0	0	2.12
1995 Reading	AA Phi	4	4	0	0	15	74	28	19	18	4	0	0	0	3	0	9	1	0	0	4	.000	0	0	10.80
Scranton-WB	AAA Phi	2	2	1	0	16	57	8	2	1	0	0	0	2	3	1	10	1	0	1	0	1.000	1	0	0.56
1996 Clearwater	A+ Phi	2	2	0	1	14	58	15	4	3	0	1	0	0	2	0	7	0	0	1	1	.500	0	0	1.93
Scranton-WB	AAA Phi	8	8	0	0	50.2	207	50	24	22	6	1	1	0	7	0	34	2	0	4	2	.667	0	0	3.91
Reading	AA Phi	4	4	0	0	27.2	113	24	13	9	3	1	0	1	8	0	29	2	1	1	0	.000	0	0	2.93
1997 Las Vegas	AAA SD	17	1	0	6	22.2	108	30	26	25	2	0	2	0	11	0	13	1	0	0	2	.000	0	0	9.93
Albuquerque	AAA LA	18	0	0	6	31	145	43	17	15	2	0	1	0	15	3	20	1	0	0	3	.000	0	0	4.35
1998 Rochester	AAA Bal	44	0	0	34	59.1	228	40	9	7	5	1	1	5	13	0	46	4	0	3	1	.750	0	19	1.06
1999 Durham	AAA TB	39	3	0	11	55.1	251	55	35	27	5	2	3	1	31	1	50	7	0	3	3	.500	0	5	4.39
2000 Louisville	AAA Cin	21	15	1	0	84.2	379	77	55	45	6	2	3	3	56	0	64	7	0	6	8	.429	0	1	4.78
1993 New York	AL	38	0	0	12	45.2	208	48	27	27	1	1	3	0	26	5	33	2	0	3	3	.500	0	0	5.32
1994 Philadelphia	NL	21	14	1	1	104.1	447	101	40	31	8	5	5	1	35	0	59	5	1	7	5	.583	0	1	2.67
1995 Philadelphia	NL	3	3	0	0	15.2	70	15	13	10	2	0	2	3	9	0	6	0	0	0	2	.000	0	0	5.74
1996 Philadelphia	NL	6	6	0	0	25.1	123	42	28	22	5	2	1	1	7	1	8	0	0	0	3	.000	0	0	7.82
1997 Philadelphia	NL	8	7	0	1	33.1	161	47	35	33	4	2	3	2	15	1	20	3	1	1	5	.167	0	0	8.91
1998 Baltimore	AL	9	1	0	5	12	72	18	13	13	4	1	3	1	6	0	6	0	0	1	0	—	0	0	9.75
12 Min. YEARS		259	116	6	81	821.1	3517	771	409	328	47	15	22	25	353	7	557	49	11	42	58	.420	3	35	3.59
6 Maj. YEARS		85	31	1	19	236.1	1067	271	156	136	24	11	17	8	98	7	132	10	3	11	18	.379	0	1	5.18

Juan Munoz

Bats: Left **Throws:** Left **Pos:** 1B-50; OF-41; PH-13; DH-1; P-1 **Ht:** 5'9" **Wt:** 170 **Born:** 3/27/74 **Age:** 27

Year Team	Lg Org	G	AB	H	2B	3B	HR	TB	R	RBI	TBB	IBB	SO	HBP	SH	SF	SB	CS	SB%	GDP	Avg	OBP	SLG
1995 Johnson Cty	R+ StL	57	190	66	12	1	7	101	43	31	27	0	17	0	0	2	13	2	.87	1	.347	.425	.532
1996 Peoria	A StL	31	111	38	9	0	0	47	19	19	14	0	14	1	0	3	4	1	.80	2	.342	.411	.423
St. Pete	A+ StL	90	330	80	12	3	1	101	41	46	38	0	35	1	3	3	6	5	.55	8	.242	.320	.306
1997 Pr William	A+ StL	66	256	80	16	7	4	122	41	48	19	3	25	0	0	4	3	1	.75	5	.313	.355	.477
Arkansas	AA StL	58	215	60	9	2	6	91	28	31	16	0	26	1	2	1	6	10	.38	2	.279	.330	.423
1998 Arkansas	AA StL	28	119	32	9	0	0	41	16	18	3	0	15	0	0	3	0	0	—	4	.269	.280	.345
Memphis	AAA StL	117	399	107	17	5	4	146	54	44	29	5	58	0	5	2	9	4	.69	9	.268	.316	.366
1999 Arkansas	AA StL	2	3	2	0	0	0	2	1	0	0	0	1	0	0	0	0	0	—	0	.667	.667	.667
2000 Arkansas	AA StL	68	247	85	14	1	5	116	41	31	16	0	16	1	1	1	5	2	.71	7	.344	.385	.470
Memphis	AAA StL	32	79	17	7	0	0	24	6	7	2	0	10	0	0	1	2	1	.67	2	.215	.232	.304
6 Min. YEARS		549	1949	567	105	19	27	791	290	275	164	8	216	4	11	20	48	26	.65	40	.291	.344	.406

Mike Murphy

Bats: Right **Throws:** Right **Pos:** OF-80; DH-11; PR-4; 1B-3; PH-1 **Ht:** 6'2" **Wt:** 185 **Born:** 1/23/72 **Age:** 29

Year Team	Lg Org	G	AB	H	2B	3B	HR	TB	R	RBI	TBB	IBB	SO	HBP	SH	SF	SB	CS	SB%	GDP	Avg	OBP	SLG
1990 Martinsvlle	R+ Phi	9	31	3	0	0	0	3	4	1	7	0	17	0	0	0	1	2	.33	1	.097	.263	.097
1991 Martinsvlle	R+ Phi	44	156	34	3	0	0	37	15	7	11	1	40	1	2	0	9	2	.82	5	.218	.274	.237
1992 Batavia	A- Phi	63	228	58	6	2	2	74	32	27	21	0	48	4	3	0	15	8	.65	6	.254	.328	.325
1993 Spartanburg	A Phi	133	509	147	29	6	3	197	70	60	35	1	91	9	9	2	33	14	.70	15	.289	.344	.387
1994 Dunedin	A+ Tor	125	469	129	11	4	1	151	57	34	55	3	106	9	4	3	31	10	.76	9	.275	.360	.322
1995 Canton-Akrn	AA Cle	10	23	1	0	0	0	1	0	0	4	0	3	0	0	0	0	0	1.00	0	.043	.185	.043
Kinston	A+ Cle	67	177	41	6	0	1	50	26	15	15	1	30	3	1	1	13	4	.76	2	.232	.301	.282
1996 Charlotte	A+ Tex	87	358	119	20	7	7	174	73	52	32	1	94	3	3	0	22	9	.71	5	.332	.392	.486
Tulsa	AA Tex	34	121	28	7	2	4	51	22	16	21	0	29	3	1	1	1	0	1.00	2	.231	.356	.421

			BATTING													BASERUNNING				PERCENTAGES		
Year Team	Lg Org	G	AB	H	2B	3B	HR	TB	R	RBI	TBB	IBB	SO	HBP	SH	SF	SB	CS	SB%	GDP	Avg	OBP	SLG
1997 Tulsa	AA Tex	46	156	40	10	1	4	64	30	19	35	0	45	4	0	0	6	3	.67	3	.256	.405	.410
Okla City	AAA Tex	73	243	80	13	5	5	118	37	25	38	1	66	4	4	2	14	5	.74	1	.329	.425	.486
1998 Charlotte	A+ Tex	3	7	2	1	0	0	3	4	1	3	0	1	0	0	0	1	0	1.00	0	.286	.500	.429
Tulsa	AA Tex	58	196	49	8	2	4	73	26	22	27	1	56	2	0	2	6	2	.75	8	.250	.344	.372
Oklahoma	AAA Tex	24	74	16	1	0	0	17	10	5	6	0	23	0	1	0	3	1	.75	1	.216	.275	.230
Rochester	AAA Bal	8	29	11	0	0	1	14	3	2	3	0	7	0	0	0	1	1	.50	0	.379	.438	.483
1999 Rochester	AAA Bal	70	217	49	6	3	1	64	35	21	34	0	63	1	3	3	7	3	.70	6	.226	.329	.295
Tacoma	AAA Sea	38	129	38	7	3	2	57	22	22	13	0	36	2	1	3	10	4	.71	2	.295	.361	.442
2000 Tacoma	AAA Sea	97	360	102	18	4	6	146	54	38	32	0	86	3	1	1	10	3	.77	4	.283	.346	.406
11 Min. YEARS		989	3483	947	146	39	41	1294	523	367	392	9	841	48	33	18	183	72	.72	70	.272	.352	.372

Nate Murphy

Bats: Left Throws: Left Pos: OF-114; DH-3; PH-2   Ht: 6'0" Wt: 195 Born: 4/15/75 Age: 26

			BATTING													BASERUNNING				PERCENTAGES		
Year Team	Lg Org	G	AB	H	2B	3B	HR	TB	R	RBI	TBB	IBB	SO	HBP	SH	SF	SB	CS	SB%	GDP	Avg	OBP	SLG
1996 Boise	A- Ana	67	266	76	18	1	7	117	58	41	41	1	63	1	0	1	12	4	.75	4	.286	.382	.440
1997 Cedar Rapds	A Ana	51	149	33	4	2	0	41	21	13	19	1	43	1	0	1	4	2	.67	2	.221	.312	.275
1998 Lk Elsinore	A+ Ana	40	120	20	2	0	5	37	15	10	9	1	46	0	1	0	5	2	.71	2	.167	.225	.308
1999 Lk Elsinore	A+ Ana	28	107	38	8	1	5	63	21	20	11	1	27	2	0	1	9	4	.69	0	.355	.421	.589
Erie	AA Ana	104	359	96	17	8	14	171	48	56	54	3	85	3	4	2	6	5	.55	7	.267	.366	.476
2000 Edmonton	AAA Ana	119	393	101	17	6	8	154	60	38	52	3	91	2	3	2	6	4	.60	11	.257	.345	.392
5 Min. YEARS		409	1394	364	66	18	39	583	223	178	186	10	355	9	8	7	42	21	.67	26	.261	.350	.418

Glenn Murray

Bats: Right Throws: Right Pos: OF-115; DH-8; PH-1   Ht: 6'2" Wt: 225 Born: 11/23/70 Age: 30

			BATTING													BASERUNNING				PERCENTAGES		
Year Team	Lg Org	G	AB	H	2B	3B	HR	TB	R	RBI	TBB	IBB	SO	HBP	SH	SF	SB	CS	SB%	GDP	Avg	OBP	SLG
1989 Expos	R Mon	27	87	15	6	2	0	25	10	7	6	0	30	2	0	1	8	1	.89	1	.172	.240	.287
Jamestown	A- Mon	3	10	3	1	0	0	4	1	1	1	0	1	0	0	0	0	0	—	0	.300	.364	.400
1990 Jamestown	A- Mon	53	165	37	8	4	1	56	20	14	21	0	43	3	0	0	11	3	.79	3	.224	.323	.339
1991 Rockford	A Mon	124	479	113	16	14	5	172	73	60	77	3	137	2	0	8	22	19	.54	8	.236	.339	.359
1992 Wst Plm Bch	A+ Mon	119	414	96	14	5	13	159	79	41	75	3	150	4	2	1	26	11	.70	4	.232	.354	.384
1993 Harrisburg	AA Mon	127	475	120	21	4	26	227	82	96	56	1	111	8	0	2	16	7	.70	3	.253	.340	.478
1994 Pawtucket	AAA Bos	130	465	104	17	1	25	198	74	64	55	4	134	4	0	2	9	3	.75	10	.224	.310	.426
1995 Pawtucket	AAA Bos	104	336	82	15	0	25	172	66	66	34	1	109	11	1	5	5	6	.45	4	.244	.329	.512
1996 Scranton-WB	AAA Phi	41	142	52	10	2	7	87	31	22	22	0	29	1	0	1	7	0	1.00	1	.366	.452	.613
1997 Indianapols	AAA Cin	7	12	2	1	0	0	3	1	0	2	0	3	0	0	0	0	0	—	0	.167	.286	.250
Chattanooga	AA Cin	94	329	93	16	2	26	191	66	73	56	2	91	4	0	6	7	5	.58	5	.283	.387	.581
1998 Indianapols	AAA Cin	42	126	25	6	0	4	43	20	16	13	0	47	0	0	0	1	2	.33	0	.198	.273	.341
Chattanooga	AA Cin	60	217	54	16	1	8	96	35	31	42	0	67	3	0	3	3	3	.50	1	.249	.374	.442
1999 Nashua	IND —	118	434	118	16	4	29	229	82	102	68	4	119	7	0	9	22	2	.92	6	.272	.373	.528
2000 Arkansas	AA StL	10	37	9	1	1	3	21	9	5	3	0	8	2	0	0	0	0	—	0	.243	.333	.568
Nashua	IND —	114	410	118	23	2	28	229	89	94	67	5	99	2	0	7	21	4	.84	3	.288	.385	.559
1996 Philadelphia	NL	38	97	19	3	0	2	28	8	6	7	0	36	0	0	0	1	1	.50	0	.196	.250	.289
12 Min. YEARS		1173	4138	1041	187	42	200	1912	738	692	598	23	1178	53	3	45	158	66	.71	51	.252	.350	.462

Heath Murray

Pitches: Left Bats: Left Pos: SP-24; RP-5   Ht: 6'4" Wt: 215 Born: 4/19/73 Age: 28

		HOW MUCH HE PITCHED						WHAT HE GAVE UP										THE RESULTS						
Year Team	Lg Org	G	GS	CG	GF	IP	BFP	H	R	ER	HR	SH	SF	HB	TBB	IBB	SO	WP	Bk	W	L	Pct.	ShO	Sv	ERA
1994 Spokane	A- SD	15	15	2	0	99.1	408	101	46	32	6	6	2	5	18	0	78	4	3	5	6	.455	1	0	2.90
1995 Rancho Cuca	A+ SD	14	14	4	0	92.1	381	80	37	32	5	3	2	4	38	1	81	6	3	9	4	.692	2	0	3.12
Memphis	AA SD	14	14	0	0	77.1	363	83	36	29	1	3	3	4	42	1	71	7	1	5	4	.556	0	0	3.38
1996 Memphis	AA SD	27	27	1	0	174	728	154	83	62	13	4	3	6	60	2	156	7	3	13	9	.591	1	0	3.21
1997 Las Vegas	AAA SD	19	19	2	0	109	493	142	72	66	10	1	2	5	41	1	99	8	1	6	8	.429	1	0	5.45
1998 Las Vegas	AAA SD	27	27	3	0	162.1	726	191	103	90	13	9	5	8	62	3	121	6	3	9	11	.450	0	0	4.99
1999 Las Vegas	AAA SD	15	15	1	0	82.1	366	99	45	39	5	1	3	2	32	0	65	4	0	5	4	.556	1	0	4.26
2000 Albuquerque	AAA LA	29	24	3	0	156	703	184	96	82	8	4	7	8	66	5	110	7	1	7	10	.412	1	0	4.73
1997 San Diego	NL	17	3	0	1	33.1	162	50	25	25	3	3	1	4	21	3	16	1	1	1	2	.333	0	0	6.75
1999 San Diego	NL	22	8	0	1	50	234	60	33	32	7	3	2	1	26	4	25	1	1	0	4	.000	0	0	5.76
7 Min. YEARS		160	155	16	0	952.2	4168	1034	518	432	61	31	27	42	359	13	781	49	15	59	56	.513	7	0	4.08
2 Maj. YEARS		39	11	0	2	83.1	396	110	58	57	10	6	3	5	47	7	41	2	2	1	6	.143	0	0	6.16

Adrian Myers

Bats: Right Throws: Right Pos: OF-84; DH-5; PH-3; PR-2   Ht: 5'10" Wt: 175 Born: 5/10/75 Age: 26

			BATTING													BASERUNNING				PERCENTAGES		
Year Team	Lg Org	G	AB	H	2B	3B	HR	TB	R	RBI	TBB	IBB	SO	HBP	SH	SF	SB	CS	SB%	GDP	Avg	OBP	SLG
1996 Hudson Val	A- Tex	54	142	24	5	4	1	40	22	15	17	0	44	8	0	2	19	2	.90	2	.169	.290	.282
1997 Charlotte	A+ Tex	90	287	71	7	4	0	86	40	21	36	0	73	3	1	1	18	15	.55	5	.247	.336	.300
1998 Charlotte	A+ Tex	122	454	122	20	7	6	174	84	64	55	1	98	3	7	9	51	23	.69	11	.269	.345	.383
1999 Tulsa	AA Tex	99	357	84	12	4	1	107	60	28	44	0	63	3	1	1	33	7	.83	14	.235	.323	.300
2000 New Haven	AA Sea	92	334	95	19	3	2	126	60	34	59	1	69	2	0	1	8	10	.44	5	.284	.394	.377
5 Min. YEARS		457	1574	396	63	22	10	533	266	162	211	2	347	19	9	14	129	57	.69	37	.252	.344	.339

Rod Myers

Bats: Left   **Throws:** Left   **Pos:** OF-27; DH-3

Ht: 6'1"   **Wt:** 190   **Born:** 1/14/73   **Age:** 28

Year Team	Lg Org	G	AB	H	2B	3B	HR	TB	R	RBI	TBB	IBB	SO	HBP	SH	SF	SB	CS	SB%	GDP	Avg	OBP	SLG
1991 Royals	R KC	44	133	37	2	3	1	48	14	18	6	1	27	5	0	1	12	2	.86	1	.278	.331	.361
Baseball Cy	A+ KC	4	11	2	0	0	0	2	1	0	0	0	5	0	0	0	1	1	.50	1	.182	.182	.182
1992 Appleton	A KC	71	218	48	10	2	4	74	31	30	39	1	67	2	4	4	25	6	.81	3	.220	.338	.339
1993 Rockford	A KC	129	474	123	24	5	9	184	69	68	58	6	117	5	6	4	49	16	.75	7	.259	.344	.388
1994 Wilmington	A+ KC	126	457	120	20	4	12	184	76	65	67	3	93	6	12	1	31	11	.74	4	.263	.363	.403
1995 Wichita	AA KC	131	499	153	22	6	7	208	71	62	34	3	77	4	8	3	29	16	.64	7	.307	.354	.417
1996 Omaha	AAA KC	112	411	120	27	1	16	197	68	54	49	6	106	9	9	3	37	8	.82	6	.292	.377	.479
1997 Wichita	AA KC	4	16	5	2	0	0	7	3	3	3	0	3	0	0	0	0	1	.00	0	.313	.421	.438
Omaha	AAA KC	38	142	36	10	0	2	52	21	10	15	0	37	0	4	1	6	4	.60	0	.254	.323	.366
1998 Wichita	AA KC	41	143	32	11	0	4	55	19	21	30	1	31	0	3	2	8	1	.89	0	.224	.354	.385
Omaha	AAA KC	30	101	22	4	1	0	28	15	10	12	0	25	0	1	2	4	4	.50	3	.218	.296	.277
1999 San Antonio	AA LA	46	147	37	11	0	2	54	21	16	18	0	35	1	3	2	2	2	.50	2	.252	.333	.367
2000 Winston-Sal	A+ CWS	17	59	15	0	0	0	15	11	3	8	0	10	3	1	0	3	1	.75	0	.254	.371	.254
Charlotte	AAA CWS	13	59	14	4	0	1	21	7	3	6	0	11	0	0	0	1	2	.33	0	.237	.308	.356
1996 Kansas City	AL	22	63	18	7	0	1	28	9	11	7	0	16	0	0	0	3	2	.60	1	.286	.357	.444
1997 Kansas City	AL	31	101	26	7	0	2	39	14	9	17	0	22	1	2	0	4	0	1.00	2	.257	.370	.386
10 Min. YEARS		806	2870	764	147	22	58	1129	427	363	345	21	644	35	51	23	208	75	.73	34	.266	.350	.393
2 Maj. YEARS		53	164	44	14	0	3	67	23	20	24	0	38	1	2	0	7	2	.78	3	.268	.365	.409

Dan Naulty

Pitches: Right   **Bats:** Right   **Pos:** RP-11; SP-10

Ht: 6'6"   **Wt:** 224   **Born:** 1/6/70   **Age:** 31

Year Team	Lg Org	G	GS	CG	GF	IP	BFP	H	R	ER	HR	SH	SF	HB	TBB	IBB	SO	WP	Bk	W	L	Pct.	ShO	Sv	ERA
1992 Kenosha	A Min	6	2	0	1	18	83	22	12	11	3	1	0	1	7	0	14	1	1	0	1	.000	0	0	5.50
1993 Fort Myers	A+ Min	7	6	0	0	30	148	41	22	19	4	1	1	6	14	1	20	3	0	0	3	.000	0	0	5.70
Fort Wayne	A Min	18	18	3	0	116	478	101	45	42	5	3	1	2	48	0	96	7	5	6	8	.429	2	0	3.26
1994 Fort Myers	A+ Min	16	15	1	1	88.1	380	78	35	29	6	1	5	3	32	2	83	5	0	8	4	.667	0	0	2.95
Nashville	AA Min	9	9	0	0	47.1	208	48	32	31	4	2	5	1	22	1	29	3	0	0	7	.000	0	0	5.89
1995 Salt Lake	AAA Min	42	8	0	19	90.1	393	92	55	52	10	2	1	2	47	2	76	6	0	2	6	.250	0	4	5.18
1997 Twins	R Min	2	2	0	0	4	15	2	1	1	0	0	1	0	3	0	3	0	0	0	0	—	0	0	2.25
Salt Lake	AAA Min	6	0	0	2	6.1	34	11	10	8	4	1	0	0	2	0	5	0	0	0	1	.000	0	0	11.37
1998 Salt Lake	AAA Min	5	0	0	2	5.1	24	8	4	4	0	0	0	2	2	0	5	0	0	1	0	1.000	0	0	6.75
1999 Columbus	AAA NYY	7	0	0	2	10.1	48	14	6	5	1	0	2	0	4	0	5	1	0	2	1	.667	0	0	4.35
2000 Omaha	AAA KC	4	0	0	0	1.2	19	5	9	9	1	0	0	1	8	0	1	1	0	0	0	—	0	0	48.60
Atlantic Ct	IND —	17	10	0	3	50.1	235	55	35	31	6	2	2	6	26	1	33	3	0	2	4	.333	0	2	5.54
1996 Minnesota	AL	49	0	0	15	57	245	43	26	24	5	2	0	0	35	3	56	2	0	3	2	.600	0	4	3.79
1997 Minnesota	AL	29	0	0	8	30.2	128	29	20	20	8	0	4	0	10	0	23	0	0	1	1	.500	0	1	5.87
1998 Minnesota	AL	19	0	0	9	23.2	104	25	16	13	3	0	1	0	10	1	15	0	0	2	0	.000	0	0	4.94
1999 New York	AL	33	0	0	20	49.1	206	40	24	24	8	1	1	4	22	0	25	2	0	1	0	1.000	0	0	4.38
8 Min. YEARS		139	70	4	30	468	2065	477	266	242	44	13	18	22	215	7	369	32	6	21	35	.375	2	6	4.65
4 Maj. YEARS		130	0	0	52	160.2	683	137	86	81	24	3	6	4	77	4	119	7	0	5	5	.500	0	5	4.54

Jason Navarro

Pitches: Left   **Bats:** Left   **Pos:** RP-56

Ht: 6'4"   **Wt:** 225   **Born:** 7/5/75   **Age:** 25

Year Team	Lg Org	G	GS	CG	GF	IP	BFP	H	R	ER	HR	SH	SF	HB	TBB	IBB	SO	WP	Bk	W	L	Pct.	ShO	Sv	ERA
1997 New Jersey	A- StL	10	10	1	0	44.2	211	60	40	34	4	0	1	1	22	0	41	7	3	1	6	.143	0	0	6.85
1998 Pr William	A+ StL	30	24	0	3	136.1	600	143	79	66	12	1	8	5	66	1	105	9	1	6	7	.462	0	0	4.36
1999 Potomac	A+ StL	39	14	0	3	111.1	508	134	82	75	12	3	6	6	49	0	66	7	1	5	13	.278	0	0	6.06
2000 Potomac	A+ StL	23	0	0	8	27.2	114	22	11	10	3	1	2	4	10	2	24	0	0	1	2	.333	0	0	3.25
Arkansas	AA StL	33	0	0	8	34.2	154	36	25	22	2	1	3	5	18	2	35	2	0	2	2	.500	0	2	5.71
4 Min. YEARS		135	48	1	22	354.2	1587	395	237	207	33	6	20	20	165	5	271	25	5	15	30	.333	0	2	5.25

Scott Navarro

Pitches: Left   **Bats:** Left   **Pos:** RP-16; SP-10

Ht: 6'1"   **Wt:** 185   **Born:** 11/13/74   **Age:** 26

Year Team	Lg Org	G	GS	CG	GF	IP	BFP	H	R	ER	HR	SH	SF	HB	TBB	IBB	SO	WP	Bk	W	L	Pct.	ShO	Sv	ERA
1997 Chico	IND —	21	20	1	0	119.1	525	137	67	53	3	6	5	7	36	0	84	7	0	8	8	.500	1	0	4.00
1998 Chico	IND —	19	19	2	0	121.1	509	119	57	45	8	3	4	8	40	1	66	7	1	10	4	.714	2	0	3.34
1999 Kissimmee	A+ Hou	37	11	1	5	112.2	452	108	39	36	4	5	5	3	17	3	86	7	2	8	3	.727	1	0	2.88
2000 Round Rock	AA Hou	22	7	0	5	64.2	293	76	49	38	9	2	1	2	23	0	30	0	1	4	4	.500	0	0	5.29
Kissimmee	A+ Hou	4	3	1	1	25	106	23	12	9	1	0	2	1	6	0	20	1	0	2	2	.500	0	0	3.24
4 Min. YEARS		103	60	5	11	443	1885	463	224	181	25	16	15	16	122	4	286	22	4	32	21	.604	4	0	3.68

Ntema Ndungidi

Bats: Left   **Throws:** Right   **Pos:** OF-128; DH-3; PR-1

Ht: 6'2"   **Wt:** 199   **Born:** 3/15/79   **Age:** 22

Year Team	Lg Org	G	AB	H	2B	3B	HR	TB	R	RBI	TBB	IBB	SO	HBP	SH	SF	SB	CS	SB%	GDP	Avg	OBP	SLG
1997 Orioles	R Bal	18	54	10	2	1	2	20	10	7	12	0	15	1	0	0	4	0	1.00	1	.185	.343	.370
1998 Bluefield	R+ Bal	59	210	62	10	5	7	103	26	35	35	2	52	1	0	0	6	5	.55	3	.295	.398	.490
Frederick	A+ Bal	1	2	0	0	0	0	0	0	0	0	0	1	0	0	0	0	0	—	0	.000	.000	.000
1999 Delmarva	A Bal	64	217	42	8	2	0	54	33	24	49	2	54	3	1	1	18	2	.90	7	.194	.348	.249
Frederick	A+ Bal	60	192	51	10	3	0	67	40	18	39	0	43	3	1	1	4	2	.67	6	.266	.396	.349
2000 Frederick	A+ Bal	90	313	89	16	4	10	143	53	59	60	2	83	3	3	5	16	5	.76	4	.284	.399	.457
Bowie	AA Bal	41	136	32	6	0	3	47	17	14	25	0	33	3	0	0	2	2	.50	5	.235	.366	.346
4 Min. YEARS		333	1124	286	52	15	22	434	179	157	220	6	281	14	5	7	50	16	.76	26	.254	.381	.386

Mike Neill

Bats: Left   **Throws:** Left   **Pos:** OF-77; DH-33; PH-2   **Ht:** 6'2"   **Wt:** 200   **Born:** 4/27/70   **Age:** 31

Year Team	Lg Org	G	AB	H	2B	3B	HR	TB	R	RBI	TBB	IBB	SO	HBP	SH	SF	SB	CS	SB%	GDP	Avg	OBP	SLG
1991 Sou Oregon	A- Oak	63	240	84	14	0	5	113	42	42	35	3	54	0	4	1	9	3	.75	1	.350	.431	.471
1992 Reno	A+ Oak	130	473	159	26	7	5	214	101	76	81	2	96	5	6	2	23	11	.68	15	.336	.437	.452
Huntsville	AA Oak	5	16	5	0	0	0	5	4	2	2	0	7	0	1	1	1	0	1.00	0	.313	.368	.313
1993 Huntsville	AA Oak	54	179	44	8	0	1	55	30	15	34	0	45	1	0	1	3	4	.43	4	.246	.367	.307
Modesto	A+ Oak	17	62	12	3	0	0	15	4	4	12	0	12	0	1	0	0	1	.00	0	.194	.324	.242
1994 Tacoma	AAA Oak	7	22	5	1	0	0	6	1	2	3	0	7	0	0	0	0	0	—	2	.227	.320	.273
Modesto	A+ Oak	47	165	48	4	1	2	60	22	18	26	1	50	1	2	1	1	1	.50	4	.291	.389	.364
1995 Modesto	A+ Oak	71	257	71	17	1	6	108	39	36	34	2	65	2	5	1	4	4	.50	6	.276	.364	.420
Huntsville	AA Oak	33	107	32	6	1	2	46	11	16	12	1	29	0	0	1	1	0	1.00	1	.299	.367	.430
1996 Edmonton	AAA Oak	6	20	3	1	0	1	7	4	4	2	0	3	0	1	0	0	0	—	0	.150	.227	.350
Modesto	A+ Oak	114	446	150	20	6	19	239	101	78	68	4	123	4	2	2	28	7	.80	3	.339	.430	.541
1997 Edmonton	AAA Oak	7	21	4	0	0	0	4	3	3	7	0	7	0	2	0	1	1	.50	1	.190	.393	.190
Huntsville	AA Oak	122	486	165	30	2	14	241	129	80	72	0	113	4	3	3	16	7	.70	8	.340	.427	.496
1998 Edmonton	AAA Oak	99	371	112	18	4	10	168	72	48	65	0	91	2	6	1	6	5	.55	12	.302	.408	.453
Huntsville	AA Oak	12	35	9	5	0	0	14	1	2	4	1	13	0	1	0	0	0	—	0	.257	.333	.400
1999 Vancouver	AAA Oak	96	365	108	23	2	10	165	61	61	57	3	97	2	2	4	10	5	.67	11	.296	.390	.452
2000 Tacoma	AAA Sea	112	397	123	38	1	11	196	69	63	75	6	105	6	4	1	9	4	.69	10	.310	.423	.494
1998 Oakland	AL	6	15	4	1	0	0	5	2	0	2	0	4	0	0	0	0	0	—	0	.267	.353	.333
10 Min. YEARS		995	3658	1134	214	25	86	1656	694	550	589	23	917	27	42	22	112	53	.68	78	.310	.407	.453

Bry Nelson

Bats: Both   **Throws:** Right   **Pos:** 3B-51; OF-14; DH-5; 2B-1; 1B-1; PH-1   **Ht:** 5'10"   **Wt:** 205   **Born:** 1/27/74   **Age:** 27

Year Team	Lg Org	G	AB	H	2B	3B	HR	TB	R	RBI	TBB	IBB	SO	HBP	SH	SF	SB	CS	SB%	GDP	Avg	OBP	SLG
1994 Quad City	A Hou	45	156	38	6	0	1	47	20	6	11	0	15	0	0	0	3	5	.38	3	.244	.293	.301
Auburn	A- Hou	65	261	84	16	7	6	132	53	35	11	0	13	1	3	1	2	1	.67	9	.322	.350	.506
1995 Kissimmee	A+ Hou	105	395	129	34	5	3	182	47	52	20	0	37	1	1	6	14	10	.58	8	.327	.355	.461
Quad City	A Hou	6	26	1	1	0	0	2	1	2	0	0	3	0	0	0	0	0	—	2	.038	.038	.077
1996 Kissimmee	A+ Hou	89	345	87	21	6	3	129	38	52	19	3	27	1	1	4	8	2	.80	13	.252	.290	.374
1997 Orlando	AA ChC	110	382	110	33	2	8	171	51	58	45	4	43	1	1	6	5	7	.42	15	.288	.359	.448
1998 West Tenn	AA ChC	32	102	29	6	2	2	45	10	18	12	2	12	0	0	1	4	2	.67	5	.284	.357	.441
1999 West Tenn	AA ChC	129	471	126	24	5	16	208	66	78	42	4	52	2	1	4	10	7	.59	13	.268	.328	.442
2000 Tucson	AAA Ari	69	261	81	21	0	5	117	34	31	16	0	20	0	0	2	4	2	.67	8	.310	.348	.448
7 Min. YEARS		650	2399	685	162	27	44	1033	320	332	176	13	222	6	7	24	50	36	.58	76	.286	.333	.431

Yuji Nerei

Bats: Left   **Throws:** Left   **Pos:** OF-54; DH-13; 1B-10; PH-5; PR-1   **Ht:** 5'10"   **Wt:** 200   **Born:** 9/9/77   **Age:** 23

Year Team	Lg Org	G	AB	H	2B	3B	HR	TB	R	RBI	TBB	IBB	SO	HBP	SH	SF	SB	CS	SB%	GDP	Avg	OBP	SLG
2000 Cape Fear	A Mon	14	34	10	4	1	3	25	8	8	9	0	8	2	0	0	0	0	—	0	.294	.477	.735
Harrisburg	AA Mon	12	24	6	1	0	0	7	5	1	7	0	7	0	0	1	1	1	.50	0	.250	.455	.292
Ottawa	AAA Mon	55	162	40	10	1	2	58	18	16	27	3	35	1	0	3	0	0	—	5	.247	.352	.358
1 Min. YEARS		81	220	56	15	2	5	90	31	25	43	3	50	5	0	3	1	1	.50	5	.255	.384	.409

Scott Neuberger

Bats: Right   **Throws:** Right   **Pos:** OF-117; DH-1   **Ht:** 6'3"   **Wt:** 208   **Born:** 8/14/77   **Age:** 23

Year Team	Lg Org	G	AB	H	2B	3B	HR	TB	R	RBI	TBB	IBB	SO	HBP	SH	SF	SB	CS	SB%	GDP	Avg	OBP	SLG
1997 Princeton	R+ TB	67	254	70	11	2	9	112	46	53	30	0	59	2	0	3	7	1	.88	5	.276	.353	.441
1998 Chston-SC	A TB	132	475	115	18	1	4	147	53	58	41	2	134	3	3	4	5	7	.42	16	.242	.304	.309
1999 St. Pete	A+ TB	127	442	115	14	3	10	165	55	63	24	0	104	8	1	6	1	2	.33	12	.260	.306	.373
2000 Orlando	AA TB	118	418	91	15	1	8	132	36	40	31	0	75	10	8	2	4	5	.44	8	.218	.286	.316
4 Min. YEARS		444	1589	391	58	7	31	556	190	214	126	2	372	23	12	15	17	15	.53	41	.246	.308	.350

Nick Neugebauer

Pitches: Right   **Bats:** Right   **Pos:** SP-28   **Ht:** 6'3"   **Wt:** 225   **Born:** 7/15/80   **Age:** 20

Year Team	Lg Org	G	GS	CG	GF	IP	BFP	H	R	ER	HR	SH	SF	HB	TBB	IBB	SO	WP	Bk	W	L	Pct.	ShO	Sv	ERA
1999 Beloit	A Mil	18	18	0	0	80.2	372	50	41	35	4	2	3	4	80	0	125	10	2	7	5	.583	0	0	3.90
2000 Mudville	A+ Mil	18	18	0	0	77.1	349	43	40	36	0	0	2	4	87	0	117	10	1	4	4	.500	0	0	4.19
Huntsville	AA Mil	10	10	0	0	50.2	229	35	28	21	2	0	0	3	47	0	57	1	0	1	3	.250	0	0	3.73
2 Min. YEARS		46	46	0	0	208.2	950	128	109	92	6	2	5	13	214	0	299	21	3	12	12	.500	0	0	3.97

Tom Nevers

Bats: Right   **Throws:** Right   **Pos:** SS-41; PH-16; 2B-9; 3B-8; OF-2; 1B-2   **Ht:** 6'1"   **Wt:** 190   **Born:** 9/13/71   **Age:** 29

Year Team	Lg Org	G	AB	H	2B	3B	HR	TB	R	RBI	TBB	IBB	SO	HBP	SH	SF	SB	CS	SB%	GDP	Avg	OBP	SLG
1990 Astros	R Hou	50	185	44	10	5	2	70	23	32	27	0	38	3	0	3	3	3	.81	3	.238	.339	.378
1991 Asheville	A Hou	129	441	111	26	2	16	189	59	71	53	0	124	3	3	5	10	12	.45	11	.252	.333	.429
1992 Osceola	A+ Hou	125	455	114	24	6	8	174	49	55	22	1	124	3	2	1	6	2	.75	10	.251	.289	.382
1993 Jackson	AA Hou	55	184	50	8	2	1	65	21	10	16	2	36	2	1	1	7	2	.78	5	.272	.335	.353
1994 Jackson	AA Hou	125	449	120	25	2	8	173	54	62	31	2	101	4	1	7	10	5	.67	8	.267	.316	.385
1995 Jackson	AA Hou	83	298	72	7	3	8	109	36	35	24	2	58	2	2	2	5	2	.71	10	.242	.301	.366
Stockton	A+ Mil	4	14	4	0	0	0	4	2	3	0	0	6	2	0	0	1	0	1.00	0	.286	.375	.286
El Paso	AA Mil	35	118	30	5	1	1	40	19	12	11	0	21	0	1	1	2	1	.67	6	.254	.333	.339

Year Team	Lg Org	G	AB	H	2B	3B	HR	TB	R	RBI	TBB	IBB	SO	HBP	SH	SF	SB	CS	SB%	GDP	Avg	OBP	SLG
1996 Hardware Cy	AA Min	127	459	121	27	7	7	183	65	44	46	1	87	3	2	3	3	10	.23	18	.264	.333	.399
1997 Louisville	AAA StL	71	227	53	9	0	8	86	22	27	12	0	48	2	2	2	1	3	.25	12	.233	.276	.379
1998 Vancouver	AAA Ana	30	89	18	0	0	1	21	7	4	5	0	18	0	0	1	1	0	1.00	3	.202	.242	.236
Chattanooga	AA Cin	58	221	48	9	4	7	86	30	31	17	3	53	2	4	1	1	0	1.00	6	.217	.278	.389
1999 Chattanooga	AA Cin	111	380	112	23	2	17	190	61	65	15	0	74	2	2	2	3	5	.38	14	.295	.323	.500
2000 Louisville	AAA Cin	76	221	52	9	0	5	76	28	22	20	1	59	3	0	2	2	2	.50	7	.235	.305	.344
11 Min. YEARS		1079	3741	949	182	34	89	1466	476	473	299	12	847	34	16	30	65	47	.58	113	.254	.312	.392

Eric Newman

Pitches: Right **Bats:** Right **Pos:** RP-22; SP-8   **Ht:** 6'4" **Wt:** 205 **Born:** 8/27/72 **Age:** 28

Year Team	Lg Org	G	GS	CG	GF	IP	BFP	H	R	ER	HR	SH	SF	HB	TBB	IBB	SO	WP	Bk	W	L	Pct.	ShO	Sv	ERA
1995 Clinton	A SD	11	10	1	0	42.1	212	52	41	36	5	1	2	2	38	2	31	3	3	1	7	.125	0	0	7.65
Idaho Falls	R+ SD	15	14	0	0	81.2	365	91	49	40	3	5	4	7	35	0	65	3	1	8	4	.667	0	0	4.41
1996 Clinton	A SD	34	14	0	6	113.1	501	101	71	54	9	3	7	7	67	0	108	13	1	5	7	.417	0	1	4.29
1997 Rancho Cuca	A+ SD	35	15	0	3	123.2	542	104	64	57	12	1	3	7	73	1	141	12	0	13	6	.684	0	0	4.15
1998 Mobile	AA SD	27	25	1	0	140	632	152	100	87	14	5	9	6	71	1	120	17	0	9	12	.429	1	0	5.59
1999 West Tenn	AA ChC	58	0	0	15	84.1	359	61	37	30	5	5	2	5	49	6	90	8	0	5	3	.625	0	8	3.20
2000 Iowa	AAA ChC	30	8	0	10	79	350	74	54	48	12	6	3	1	52	4	68	5	0	3	5	.375	0	0	5.47
6 Min. YEARS		210	86	2	34	664.1	2961	635	416	352	60	26	30	35	385	14	623	61	5	44	44	.500	1	9	4.77

Doug Newstrom

Bats: Left **Throws:** Right **Pos:** 3B-41; PH-20; OF-17; 1B-14; 2B-6; DH-5; C-3; PR-2; P-2   **Ht:** 6'1" **Wt:** 195 **Born:** 9/18/71 **Age:** 29

Year Team	Lg Org	G	AB	H	2B	3B	HR	TB	R	RBI	TBB	IBB	SO	HBP	SH	SF	SB	CS	SB%	GDP	Avg	OBP	SLG
1993 Yakima	A- LA	75	279	83	16	2	2	109	51	36	53	4	44	1	1	3	11	1	.92	7	.297	.408	.391
1994 Vero Beach	A+ LA	119	405	117	22	5	2	155	47	46	59	3	51	2	0	5	4	5	.44	5	.289	.378	.383
1995 San Berndno	A+ LA	97	316	92	22	1	6	134	53	58	40	0	58	2	6	3	19	9	.68	5	.291	.371	.424
1996 High Desert	A+ LA	122	403	126	30	3	11	195	84	75	72	0	62	0	2	6	15	8	.65	9	.313	.412	.484
1997 New Haven	AA Col	95	244	65	10	1	1	80	29	43	39	1	32	1	2	4	9	5	.64	8	.266	.365	.328
1998 New Haven	AA Col	102	331	94	21	1	5	132	38	24	41	4	53	0	3	2	7	5	.58	7	.284	.361	.399
1999 Birmingham	AA CWS	82	253	72	11	1	3	94	30	23	29	2	42	0	0	2	3	4	.43	8	.285	.356	.372
2000 Tucson	AAA Ari	57	143	42	7	0	1	52	16	20	16	1	25	0	2	3	2	1	.67	5	.294	.358	.364
El Paso	AA Ari	40	109	23	9	0	0	32	9	6	9	0	24	0	0	1	4	1	.80	3	.211	.269	.294
8 Min. YEARS		789	2483	714	148	14	31	983	357	331	358	15	391	6	16	29	74	39	.65	59	.288	.375	.396

Ruben Niebla

Pitches: Left **Bats:** Left **Pos:** RP-35; SP-7   **Ht:** 5'10" **Wt:** 175 **Born:** 12/19/71 **Age:** 29

Year Team	Lg Org	G	GS	CG	GF	IP	BFP	H	R	ER	HR	SH	SF	HB	TBB	IBB	SO	WP	Bk	W	L	Pct.	ShO	Sv	ERA
1995 Laredo	IND —	2	1	0	1	9	37	11	3	3	1	0	0	0	1	0	10	1	0	1	0	1.000	0	0	3.00
Corp.Chrsti	IND —	13	0	0	2	17	84	24	13	10	2	0	1	0	11	0	16	1	0	0	0	—	0	0	5.29
1996 Palm Spring	IND —	24	18	2	2	140.2	608	166	74	61	10	3	4	10	38	0	68	3	3	8	9	.471	0	0	3.90
1997 Tri-City	IND —	20	15	1	1	112	463	108	45	38	8	4	4	3	36	1	76	0	2	8	6	.571	0	0	3.05
1998 Jupiter	A+ Mon	13	0	0	3	22.2	90	15	8	3	1	0	1	1	5	0	22	1	0	0	1	.000	0	0	1.19
Harrisburg	AA Mon	24	1	0	3	43	178	45	23	22	5	1	6	1	6	0	30	4	0	0	2	.000	0	1	4.60
Ottawa	AAA Mon	6	0	0	3	12.1	58	20	12	7	4	0	0	0	4	0	7	0	0	0	1	.000	0	0	5.11
1999 Harrisburg	AA Mon	29	0	0	12	30.2	142	31	22	19	2	0	2	1	22	0	23	2	1	2	0	1.000	0	0	5.58
Reno	A+ LA	3	3	0	0	18.2	83	21	19	14	5	3	1	0	5	0	15	0	0	0	1	.000	0	0	6.75
San Berndno	A+ LA	3	0	0	1	5.2	25	9	3	3	1	0	0	0	1	0	6	0	0	0	0	—	0	0	4.76
Vero Beach	A+ LA	1	0	0	0	2	7	0	0	0	0	0	0	0	0	0	4	0	0	0	0	—	0	0	0.00
San Antonio	AA LA	12	0	0	4	14.1	65	19	7	6	2	0	0	0	5	1	12	0	0	2	1	.667	0	0	3.77
2000 San Antonio	AA LA	10	0	0	5	15	59	13	5	4	2	0	0	0	4	0	10	0	0	1	0	1.000	0	0	2.40
Albuquerque	AAA LA	24	0	0	11	32.2	151	42	25	25	3	2	2	3	15	0	25	1	3	0	2	.000	0	1	6.89
Chico	IND —	8	7	0	1	42.2	189	39	25	20	2	3	2	3	22	1	37	3	0	4	3	.571	0	0	4.22
6 Min. YEARS		192	45	3	49	518.1	2239	564	284	235	46	17	23	22	175	3	361	16	9	26	27	.491	0	3	4.08

Brad Niedermaier

Pitches: Right **Bats:** Right **Pos:** RP-12   **Ht:** 6'2" **Wt:** 209 **Born:** 2/9/73 **Age:** 28

Year Team	Lg Org	G	GS	CG	GF	IP	BFP	H	R	ER	HR	SH	SF	HB	TBB	IBB	SO	WP	Bk	W	L	Pct.	ShO	Sv	ERA
1995 Elizabethtn	R+ Min	7	7	0	0	40.2	171	33	14	10	1	0	1	0	17	0	47	9	0	2	1	1.000	0	0	2.21
1996 Fort Wayne	A Min	32	3	0	14	69.1	295	64	39	25	3	3	4	0	29	2	72	11	0	6	4	.600	0	2	3.25
1997 Fort Myers	A+ Min	32	0	0	29	36.2	154	27	15	6	2	2	4	0	12	2	47	4	0	2	3	.400	0	17	1.47
Salt Lake	AAA Min	16	0	0	5	26	118	29	22	17	7	2	0	0	13	2	20	1	0	2	1	.667	0	0	5.88
1998 Fort Myers	A+ Min	25	0	0	13	40	202	59	39	35	3	2	0	1	21	1	44	13	0	4	2	.667	0	3	7.88
New Britain	AA Min	8	1	0	2	9	45	14	5	5	1	0	0	0	4	0	8	1	0	0	0	—	0	0	5.00
1999 New Britain	AA Min	41	0	0	23	49.2	222	50	29	24	6	2	1	1	27	0	47	7	0	2	2	.500	0	9	4.35
2000 Tampa	A+ NYY	5	0	0	0	7	33	11	5	4	1	1	1	1	2	1	5	0	0	1	0	1.000	0	0	5.14
Colo Sprngs	AAA Col	7	0	0	6	8.2	43	15	6	6	1	0	0	0	5	0	6	2	0	0	0	—	0	0	6.23
6 Min. YEARS		173	11	0	92	287	1286	302	174	132	25	12	11	3	130	8	296	48	0	19	12	.613	0	31	4.14

Wilbert Nieves

Bats: Right **Throws:** Right **Pos:** C-84; PH-9; 1B-4; 2B-2; DH-2   **Ht:** 5'11" **Wt:** 190 **Born:** 9/25/77 **Age:** 23

Year Team	Lg Org	G	AB	H	2B	3B	HR	TB	R	RBI	TBB	IBB	SO	HBP	SH	SF	SB	CS	SB%	GDP	Avg	OBP	SLG
1996 Padres	R SD	43	113	39	5	0	2	50	23	22	13	0	19	0	2	0	3	4	.43	1	.345	.413	.442
1997 Clinton	A SD	18	55	12	1	1	1	18	6	7	6	0	10	0	1	1	2	1	.67	0	.218	.290	.327
Padres	R SD	8	27	8	2	0	0	10	2	2	5	0	5	0	1	0	1	0	1.00	0	.296	.406	.370

205

Year Team	Lg Org	G	AB	H	2B	3B	HR	TB	R	RBI	TBB	IBB	SO	HBP	SH	SF	SB	CS	SB%	GDP	Avg	OBP	SLG
1998 Clinton	A SD	115	380	97	22	0	3	128	47	55	47	4	69	7	4	6	7	9	.44	16	.255	.343	.337
1999 Rancho Cuca	A+ SD	120	427	140	26	2	7	191	58	61	40	1	54	5	1	4	2	7	.22	12	.328	.389	.447
2000 Rancho Cuca	A+ SD	31	101	26	5	0	0	31	16	9	15	0	17	0	2	1	2	0	1.00	3	.257	.350	.307
Las Vegas	AAA SD	1	1	0	0	0	0	0	0	0	0	0	0	0	0	0	0	0	—	0	.000	.000	.000
Mobile	AA SD	68	214	57	4	0	4	73	18	30	16	4	22	1	2	1	1	1	.50	9	.266	.319	.341
5 Min. YEARS		404	1318	379	65	3	17	501	170	186	142	9	196	13	13	13	18	22	.45	41	.288	.359	.380

Drew Niles

Bats: Both **Throws:** Right **Pos:** SS-72; 2B-6; PH-4; 3B-3; OF-2; PR-1 **Ht:** 6'1" **Wt:** 175 **Born:** 3/17/77 **Age:** 24

Year Team	Lg Org	G	AB	H	2B	3B	HR	TB	R	RBI	TBB	IBB	SO	HBP	SH	SF	SB	CS	SB%	GDP	Avg	OBP	SLG
1998 Kane County	A Fla	26	87	24	4	0	0	28	12	9	12	1	20	0	0	4	2	1	.67	1	.276	.350	.322
Charlotte	AAA Fla	16	49	13	1	0	1	17	5	5	6	0	12	1	0	0	0	1	.00	1	.265	.351	.347
1999 Brevard Cty	A+ Fla	40	117	20	1	1	1	26	12	12	15	0	30	1	0	2	0	0	—	2	.171	.267	.222
Utica	A- Fla	18	66	15	3	0	0	18	4	7	9	0	15	0	2	0	0	3	.00	1	.227	.320	.273
Portland	AA Fla	46	135	31	3	0	0	34	12	9	21	0	34	0	3	2	0	2	.00	7	.230	.329	.252
2000 Kane County	A Fla	14	40	7	0	2	0	11	4	5	4	0	9	0	1	2	1	1	.50	1	.175	.239	.275
Portland	AA Fla	39	124	30	3	1	0	35	14	10	9	0	21	1	1	0	2	0	1.00	3	.242	.299	.282
Brevard Cty	A+ Fla	32	94	22	2	1	0	26	9	5	13	0	22	0	3	1	2	1	.67	3	.234	.324	.277
3 Min. YEARS		231	712	162	17	5	2	195	72	62	89	1	163	3	10	12	7	9	.44	19	.228	.311	.274

Randy Niles

Pitches: Right **Bats:** Right **Pos:** RP-37; SP-1 **Ht:** 6'2" **Wt:** 200 **Born:** 8/28/75 **Age:** 25

Year Team	Lg Org	G	GS	CG	GF	IP	BFP	H	R	ER	HR	SH	SF	HB	TBB	IBB	SO	WP	Bk	W	L	Pct.	ShO	Sv	ERA
1997 Sou Oregon	A- Oak	7	4	0	0	22.2	98	14	12	5	0	1	1	4	12	0	15	4	5	0	1	.000	0	0	1.99
Modesto	A+ Oak	7	5	0	0	34.2	148	32	13	10	3	1	0	6	9	0	20	0	0	4	0	1.000	0	0	2.60
1998 Visalia	A+ Oak	31	22	0	2	148.1	648	144	92	67	12	11	4	11	54	3	103	9	5	6	12	.333	0	0	4.07
1999 Modesto	A+ Oak	8	4	0	3	34.1	144	39	13	12	2	1	0	3	8	1	35	4	0	3	0	1.000	0	2	3.15
Midland	AA Oak	23	14	0	2	88	435	126	78	56	7	2	5	1	47	0	46	6	0	4	6	.400	0	0	5.73
2000 Midland	AA Oak	38	1	0	11	76.1	346	87	52	45	6	0	3	5	35	1	45	7	0	5	0	1.000	0	1	5.31
4 Min. YEARS		114	50	0	18	404.1	1819	442	260	195	30	16	13	30	165	5	264	30	10	22	19	.537	0	3	4.34

Elvin Nina

Pitches: Right **Bats:** Right **Pos:** SP-12; RP-3 **Ht:** 6'0" **Wt:** 185 **Born:** 11/25/75 **Age:** 25

Year Team	Lg Org	G	GS	CG	GF	IP	BFP	H	R	ER	HR	SH	SF	HB	TBB	IBB	SO	WP	Bk	W	L	Pct.	ShO	Sv	ERA
1997 Sou Oregon	A- Oak	18	2	0	8	31	150	36	24	18	4	0	0	2	18	1	26	2	2	1	3	.250	0	1	5.23
1998 Visalia	A+ Oak	30	21	1	5	130.1	583	135	77	65	9	2	6	5	62	1	131	13	2	8	8	.500	1	0	4.49
Edmonton	AAA Oak	1	0	0	0	0.1	4	1	0	0	0	1	0	0	2	1	0	1	0	0	0	—	0	0	0.00
1999 Modesto	A+ Oak	17	12	0	0	73.1	319	59	31	17	2	3	0	6	41	1	74	5	0	5	2	.714	0	0	2.09
Midland	AA Oak	7	4	0	2	30	140	36	21	16	0	0	1	2	18	0	18	2	0	3	2	.600	0	0	4.80
Erie	AA Ana	4	4	0	0	24.1	103	20	12	11	2	1	1	0	15	0	19	1	0	3	0	1.000	0	0	4.07
2000 Erie	AA Ana	12	10	2	0	57.1	243	51	31	27	3	4	1	3	24	0	30	2	0	2	4	.333	0	0	4.24
Edmonton	AAA Ana	3	2	0	0	9.1	44	11	6	3	0	0	0	0	6	0	3	0	1	0	0	—	0	0	2.89
4 Min. YEARS		92	55	3	15	356	1586	349	202	157	20	11	10	18	186	4	301	26	5	22	19	.537	1	1	3.97

Ray Noriega

Pitches: Left **Bats:** Right **Pos:** RP-45 **Ht:** 5'10" **Wt:** 170 **Born:** 3/28/74 **Age:** 27

Year Team	Lg Org	G	GS	CG	GF	IP	BFP	H	R	ER	HR	SH	SF	HB	TBB	IBB	SO	WP	Bk	W	L	Pct.	ShO	Sv	ERA
1996 Sou Oregon	A- Oak	17	14	0	0	61	263	61	28	24	3	2	0	2	22	0	50	4	0	4	4	.500	0	0	3.54
1997 Modesto	A+ Oak	28	28	0	0	156	698	161	101	70	17	8	2	4	69	1	119	10	3	5	8	.385	0	0	4.04
1998 Visalia	A+ Oak	36	6	0	10	71.1	328	91	55	49	8	2	4	2	24	1	77	6	0	3	5	.375	0	2	6.18
1999 Visalia	A+ Oak	60	0	0	34	69.1	308	67	36	31	6	4	4	2	32	2	62	6	0	5	3	.625	0	11	4.02
2000 Oakland	A+ Oak	24	0	0	18	26.1	114	22	8	3	0	2	1	0	15	2	20	5	0	0	3	.000	0	12	1.03
Midland	AA Oak	21	0	0	7	26.2	113	21	13	11	1	1	2	2	11	0	17	0	1	3	0	1.000	0	0	3.71
5 Min. YEARS		186	48	0	69	410.2	1824	423	241	188	35	19	13	12	173	6	345	31	4	20	23	.465	0	26	4.12

Les Norman

Bats: Right **Throws:** Right **Pos:** OF-95; DH-12; 1B-1; PR-1 **Ht:** 6'1" **Wt:** 185 **Born:** 2/25/69 **Age:** 32

Year Team	Lg Org	G	AB	H	2B	3B	HR	TB	R	RBI	TBB	IBB	SO	HBP	SH	SF	SB	CS	SB%	GDP	Avg	OBP	SLG
1991 Eugene	A- KC	30	102	25	4	1	2	37	14	18	9	0	18	1	2	1	2	1	.67	4	.245	.310	.363
1992 Appleton	A KC	59	218	82	17	1	4	113	38	47	22	0	18	1	2	3	8	6	.57	5	.376	.430	.518
Memphis	AA KC	72	271	74	14	5	3	107	32	20	22	0	37	2	1	1	4	4	.50	2	.273	.331	.395
1993 Memphis	AA KC	133	484	141	32	5	17	234	78	81	50	3	88	14	7	2	11	9	.55	8	.291	.373	.483
1994 Omaha	AAA KC	13	38	7	3	0	1	13	4	4	6	0	11	1	1	0	1	0	1.00	2	.184	.311	.342
Memphis	AA KC	106	383	101	19	4	13	167	53	55	36	1	44	7	3	4	7	7	.50	0	.264	.336	.436
1995 Omaha	AAA KC	83	313	89	19	3	9	141	46	33	18	2	48	4	3	2	5	3	.63	3	.284	.329	.450
1996 Omaha	AAA KC	24	77	20	6	0	1	29	8	13	6	0	8	1	0	1	0	1	.00	2	.260	.318	.377
1997 Buffalo	AAA Cle	118	428	111	20	1	17	184	71	56	43	2	80	8	6	4	7	6	.54	5	.259	.335	.430
1998 Oklahoma	AAA Tex	100	380	116	32	2	10	182	64	51	17	0	79	9	5	3	6	2	.75	8	.305	.347	.479
1999 Omaha	AAA KC	89	333	91	20	2	13	154	53	40	14	0	45	5	3	5	7	3	.70	6	.273	.308	.462
2000 Omaha	AAA KC	109	411	106	22	4	11	169	63	30	44	2	62	7	2	6	7	4	.64	5	.258	.315	.411
1995 Kansas City	AL	24	40	9	0	1	0	11	6	4	6	0	6	1	0	1	1	1	.50	0	.225	.326	.275
1996 Kansas City	AL	54	49	6	0	0	0	6	9	0	6	0	14	1	0	0	0	1	.00	0	.122	.232	.122
10 Min. YEARS		936	3438	963	208	28	101	1530	514	481	273	12	538	60	35	30	64	47	.58	50	.280	.341	.445
2 Maj. YEARS		78	89	15	0	1	0	17	15	4	12	0	20	1	0	1	1	2	.33	0	.169	.275	.191

Ben Norris

Pitches: Left **Bats:** Left **Pos:** SP-17; RP-2   **Ht:** 6'3" **Wt:** 185 **Born:** 12/6/77 **Age:** 23

		HOW MUCH HE PITCHED					WHAT HE GAVE UP												THE RESULTS					
Year Team	Lg Org	G	GS	CG	GF	IP	BFP	H	R	ER	HR	SH	SF	HB	TBB	IBB	SO	WP	Bk	W	L	Pct.	ShO	Sv	ERA
1996 Diamondbcks	R Ari	8	7	0	0	31.1	133	33	21	16	3	3	0	4	4	0	37	2	0	2	2	.500	0	0	4.60
Lethbridge	R+ Ari	3	3	0	0	11.1	54	14	9	8	0	0	2	0	5	0	12	2	1	0	0	—	0	0	6.35
1997 South Bend	A Ari	14	13	0	0	60.1	291	69	44	27	7	2	2	6	31	0	40	2	1	1	8	.111	0	0	4.03
Lethbridge	R+ Ari	14	14	0	0	83.1	373	93	61	45	6	1	3	8	23	0	54	4	0	7	3	.700	0	0	4.86
1998 South Bend	A Ari	15	15	0	0	89.1	389	98	44	33	6	1	5	10	27	0	53	7	0	1	5	.167	0	0	3.32
High Desert	A+ Ari	9	6	0	2	40.2	180	48	27	25	7	2	0	0	18	0	17	1	0	2	2	.500	0	1	5.53
1999 High Desert	A+ Ari	8	8	0	0	40.2	181	39	27	20	4	0	3	4	24	0	45	0	0	2	2	.500	0	0	4.43
El Paso	AA Ari	20	20	0	0	119	535	132	61	55	13	3	2	8	53	0	87	6	2	10	6	.625	0	0	4.16
2000 Tucson	AAA Ari	12	10	0	0	55.1	275	88	56	49	7	5	2	2	29	1	28	2	1	2	6	.250	0	0	7.97
El Paso	AA Ari	7	7	1	0	45	192	41	14	11	1	2	0	3	18	1	24	1	0	4	1	.800	0	0	2.20
5 Min. YEARS		110	103	1	2	576.1	2603	655	364	289	54	19	19	45	232	2	397	27	5	31	35	.470	0	1	4.51

Dax Norris

Bats: Right **Throws:** Right **Pos:** C-64; DH-42; 1B-30; PH-2   **Ht:** 5'10" **Wt:** 190 **Born:** 1/14/73 **Age:** 28

		BATTING														BASERUNNING				PERCENTAGES		
Year Team	Lg Org	G	AB	H	2B	3B	HR	TB	R	RBI	TBB	IBB	SO	HBP	SH	SF	SB	CS	SB%	GDP	Avg	OBP	SLG
1996 Eugene	A- Atl	60	232	67	17	0	7	105	31	37	18	0	32	3	3	1	2	0	1.00	4	.289	.346	.453
1997 Greenville	AA Atl	2	9	3	0	0	1	6	3	3	0	0	1	0	0	0	0	0	—	0	.333	.333	.667
Durham	A+ Atl	95	338	80	19	0	7	120	29	45	32	1	49	4	0	3	2	5	.29	10	.237	.308	.355
1998 Danville	A+ Atl	28	92	30	12	1	3	53	9	21	7	1	15	2	0	3	1	2	.33	1	.326	.375	.576
Greenville	AA Atl	64	199	46	15	0	6	79	30	26	15	0	43	4	1	1	1	2	.33	7	.231	.297	.397
1999 Greenville	AA Atl	120	403	112	27	0	15	184	59	66	41	2	59	7	0	4	2	1	.67	10	.278	.352	.457
2000 Greenville	AA Atl	132	484	122	27	0	13	188	56	72	50	5	74	8	0	5	1	1	.50	12	.252	.329	.388
5 Min. YEARS		501	1757	460	117	1	52	735	217	270	163	9	273	28	4	17	9	11	.45	44	.262	.331	.418

Chris Norton

Bats: Right **Throws:** Right **Pos:** 1B-42; DH-38; C-9; PH-8; OF-2   **Ht:** 6'2" **Wt:** 215 **Born:** 9/21/70 **Age:** 30

		BATTING														BASERUNNING				PERCENTAGES		
Year Team	Lg Org	G	AB	H	2B	3B	HR	TB	R	RBI	TBB	IBB	SO	HBP	SH	SF	SB	CS	SB%	GDP	Avg	OBP	SLG
1992 Watertown	A- Cle	1	4	0	0	0	0	0	1	0	0	0	2	0	0	0	0	0	—	0	.000	.000	.000
Burlington	R+ Cle	4	12	3	0	0	0	3	2	2	1	0	4	0	0	1	0	0	—	0	.250	.286	.250
Jamestown	A- Mon	60	207	42	4	1	4	60	15	27	15	0	64	0	0	2	3	0	1.00	3	.203	.261	.290
1993 Cardinals	R StL	27	83	19	5	3	0	30	10	11	11	1	23	1	0	0	0	0	—	2	.229	.326	.361
1994 Savannah	A StL	126	439	116	11	2	26	209	75	82	73	4	144	4	3	2	6	4	.60	11	.264	.373	.476
1995 Arkansas	AA StL	10	25	6	2	0	0	8	6	6	11	2	5	0	0	1	0	0	—	0	.240	.459	.320
Lubbock	IND —	97	327	95	16	3	21	180	61	61	75	7	87	1	0	2	6	2	.75	5	.291	.422	.550
1996 Lubbock	IND —	51	187	71	13	1	15	131	39	54	27	3	27	4	0	2	6	0	1.00	7	.380	.464	.701
Norwich	AA NYY	47	172	48	12	1	7	83	24	28	15	0	43	1	0	0	3	2	.60	3	.279	.340	.483
1997 Lk Elsinore	A+ Ana	37	138	38	7	2	11	82	34	35	22	1	41	2	0	1	0	1	.00	2	.275	.380	.594
Midland	AA Ana	58	200	53	8	1	16	111	40	47	35	0	57	0	0	2	2	1	.67	8	.265	.371	.555
Vancouver	AAA Ana	1	5	1	0	0	1	4	1	1	0	0	2	0	0	0	0	0	—	0	.200	.200	.800
1998 Midland	AA Ana	17	60	19	1	0	4	32	10	12	9	0	23	1	0	0	0	0	—	1	.317	.414	.533
Vancouver	AAA Ana	43	148	31	11	0	5	57	14	17	18	0	46	1	0	1	0	0	—	0	.209	.298	.385
Portland	AA Fla	22	68	24	4	1	6	48	12	19	12	0	17	0	0	0	0	0	—	1	.353	.450	.706
1999 Portland	AA Fla	120	406	118	25	0	38	257	74	97	71	2	124	1	0	1	1	2	.33	15	.291	.397	.633
2000 Sacramento	AAA Oak	13	45	11	0	0	2	17	7	9	8	0	10	1	0	1	0	0	—	0	.244	.364	.378
Midland	AA Oak	20	69	15	6	1	0	23	10	11	12	1	17	1	0	1	0	0	—	3	.217	.337	.333
Brevard Cty	A+ Fla	2	7	3	1	0	0	4	1	1	0	0	2	0	0	0	0	0	—	1	.429	.429	.571
Portland	AA Fla	61	206	57	8	0	10	95	39	43	31	0	55	2	0	4	1	0	1.00	5	.277	.370	.461
9 Min. YEARS		817	2808	770	134	16	166	1434	475	563	446	21	793	22	3	21	28	12	.70	70	.274	.375	.511

Jason Norton

Pitches: Right **Bats:** Right **Pos:** RP-35; SP-6   **Ht:** 6'3" **Wt:** 205 **Born:** 4/9/76 **Age:** 25

		HOW MUCH HE PITCHED						WHAT HE GAVE UP												THE RESULTS					
Year Team	Lg Org	G	GS	CG	GF	IP	BFP	H	R	ER	HR	SH	SF	HB	TBB	IBB	SO	WP	Bk	W	L	Pct.	ShO	Sv	ERA
1998 Red Sox	R Bos	3	0	0	3	6	20	2	1	1	1	0	0	0	1	0	9	1	0	1	1	.500	0	0	1.50
Lowell	A- Bos	6	4	0	0	25.1	105	22	17	13	1	0	0	1	7	0	33	1	3	1	1	.500	0	0	4.62
Michigan	A Bos	7	7	0	0	42	173	34	14	9	1	1	1	1	12	2	36	3	0	3	1	.750	0	0	1.93
1999 Augusta	A Bos	30	17	2	5	136	544	106	50	35	11	1	2	4	28	1	150	7	0	9	6	.600	1	0	2.32
2000 Sarasota	A+ Bos	40	5	0	12	91	405	102	53	39	6	4	2	3	29	3	89	4	2	7	7	.500	0	1	3.86
Trenton	AA Bos	1	1	0	0	7	26	3	0	0	0	0	0	0	3	0	10	1	0	1	0	1.000	0	0	0.00
3 Min. YEARS		87	34	2	20	307.1	1273	269	135	97	20	6	5	9	80	6	327	17	5	22	16	.579	1	1	2.84

Abraham Nunez

Bats: Both **Throws:** Right **Pos:** DH-88; PH-12; OF-6   **Ht:** 6'2" **Wt:** 186 **Born:** 2/5/80 **Age:** 21

		BATTING														BASERUNNING				PERCENTAGES		
Year Team	Lg Org	G	AB	H	2B	3B	HR	TB	R	RBI	TBB	IBB	SO	HBP	SH	SF	SB	CS	SB%	GDP	Avg	OBP	SLG
1997 Diamondbcks	R Ari	54	213	65	17	4	0	90	52	21	26	0	40	2	2	1	3	3	.50	4	.305	.384	.423
Lethbridge	R+ Ari	2	6	1	0	0	0	1	2	1	1	0	0	0	0	0	0	0	—	0	.167	.286	.167
1998 South Bend	A Ari	110	364	93	14	2	9	138	44	47	67	4	81	3	3	5	12	14	.46	4	.255	.371	.379
1999 High Desert	A+ Ari	130	488	133	29	6	22	240	106	93	86	2	122	2	1	8	40	13	.75	10	.273	.378	.492
2000 Brevard Cty	A+ Fla	31	103	20	4	0	1	27	17	9	28	1	34	2	0	1	11	3	.79	3	.194	.376	.262
Portland	AA Fla	74	221	61	17	3	6	102	39	42	44	1	64	0	0	3	8	6	.57	3	.276	.392	.462
4 Min. YEARS		401	1395	373	81	15	38	598	260	213	252	8	341	9	6	17	74	39	.65	24	.267	.379	.429

Argelis Nunez

Bats: Right **Throws:** Right **Pos:** OF-45; DH-6; PH-4; PR-2   **Ht:** 6'1" **Wt:** 170 **Born:** 10/25/81 **Age:** 19

					BATTING											BASERUNNING				PERCENTAGES		
Year Team	Lg Org	G	AB	H	2B	3B	HR	TB	R	RBI	TBB	IBB	SO	HBP	SH	SF	SB	CS	SB%	GDP	Avg	OBP	SLG
2000 Tucson	AAA Ari	4	3	1	0	0	0	1	0	2	0	0	2	0	0	1	0	0	—	0	.333	.250	.333
Diamondbcks	R Ari	23	73	25	6	1	3	42	15	15	5	0	20	2	1	0	2	2	.50	0	.342	.400	.575
South Bend	A Ari	24	77	10	0	3	1	19	4	9	4	0	26	0	4	0	0	2	.00	2	.130	.173	.247
1 Min. YEARS		51	153	36	6	4	4	62	19	26	9	0	48	2	5	1	2	4	.33	2	.235	.285	.405

Jorge Nunez

Bats: Right **Throws:** Right **Pos:** SS-128; PR-1   **Ht:** 5'10" **Wt:** 158 **Born:** 3/3/78 **Age:** 23

					BATTING											BASERUNNING				PERCENTAGES		
Year Team	Lg Org	G	AB	H	2B	3B	HR	TB	R	RBI	TBB	IBB	SO	HBP	SH	SF	SB	CS	SB%	GDP	Avg	OBP	SLG
1998 Hagerstown	A Tor	4	16	4	0	0	0	4	0	1	0	0	1	0	0	0	1	0	1.00	0	.250	.250	.250
Medcine Hat	R+ Tor	74	317	101	9	11	6	150	74	52	28	0	45	1	1	0	31	2	.94	3	.319	.376	.473
1999 Hagerstown	A Tor	133	564	151	28	11	14	243	116	61	40	1	103	2	1	2	51	8	.86	8	.268	.317	.431
2000 Vero Beach	A+ LA	128	534	154	17	8	4	199	86	39	38	0	104	2	5	2	54	22	.71	5	.288	.337	.373
Albuquerque	AAA LA	1	3	0	0	0	0	0	0	0	0	0	0	0	0	0	0	0	—	0	.000	.000	.000
3 Min. YEARS		340	1434	410	54	30	24	596	276	153	106	1	253	5	7	4	137	32	.81	16	.286	.336	.416

Maximo Nunez

Pitches: Right **Bats:** Right **Pos:** RP-37; SP-2   **Ht:** 6'5" **Wt:** 165 **Born:** 1/15/73 **Age:** 28

		HOW MUCH HE PITCHED						WHAT HE GAVE UP										THE RESULTS					
Year Team	Lg Org	G	GS	CG	GF	IP	BFP	H	R	ER	HR	SH	SF	HB	TBB	IBB	SO	WP	Bk	W	L	Pct.	ShO	Sv	ERA
1994 Blue Jays	R Tor	20	0	0	15	24.2	119	32	23	11	0	1	1	1	10	0	17	2	2	1	5	.167	0	2	4.01
1995 Hagerstown	A Tor	22	0	0	11	37.1	172	40	29	23	4	3	2	3	20	0	21	8	0	1	1	.500	0	0	5.54
St.Cathmes	A- Tor	7	0	0	4	7.2	42	11	10	8	1	2	0	1	7	0	6	1	0	1	0	1.000	0	0	9.39
1996 Hickory	A CWS	31	24	3	3	152.1	660	173	93	79	12	3	9	7	45	0	105	5	3	5	16	.238	1	0	4.67
1997 Winston-Sal	A+ CWS	28	0	0	19	52	210	35	15	10	5	3	2	1	21	1	53	2	0	0	2	.000	0	8	1.73
Birmingham	AA CWS	14	0	0	3	17.2	85	19	18	15	1	0	1	1	13	0	14	3	2	0	0	—	0	0	7.64
1998 Orlando	AA TB	6	0	0	5	11.2	43	5	1	1	0	1	1	0	4	1	14	2	0	2	0	1.000	0	2	0.77
Durham	AAA TB	58	0	0	32	63	292	67	39	35	9	5	1	5	40	7	53	5	1	3	6	.333	0	5	5.00
1999 Durham	AAA TB	21	0	0	9	31.2	147	25	20	19	2	1	0	5	28	0	31	6	0	1	0	1.000	0	2	5.40
Orlando	AA TB	26	0	0	18	26	121	23	11	10	2	1	1	3	17	0	19	0	0	0	2	.000	0	9	3.46
2000 Albuquerque	AAA LA	1	0	0	0	2	12	1	1	1	0	0	1	1	5	0	0	1	0	0	0	—	0	0	4.50
San Antonio	AA LA	38	2	0	10	65	319	79	57	48	7	2	5	8	43	1	59	7	0	2	6	.250	0	1	6.65
7 Min. YEARS		272	26	3	129	491	2222	510	317	260	44	22	24	36	253	10	392	42	8	16	38	.296	1	29	4.77

Mark Nussbeck

Pitches: Right **Bats:** Left **Pos:** SP-25   **Ht:** 6'4" **Wt:** 180 **Born:** 5/25/74 **Age:** 27

		HOW MUCH HE PITCHED						WHAT HE GAVE UP										THE RESULTS					
Year Team	Lg Org	G	GS	CG	GF	IP	BFP	H	R	ER	HR	SH	SF	HB	TBB	IBB	SO	WP	Bk	W	L	Pct.	ShO	Sv	ERA
1996 New Jersey	A- StL	16	14	0	1	79.2	325	72	31	26	4	2	2	4	16	0	74	3	3	6	3	.667	0	0	2.94
1997 Peoria	A StL	27	27	2	0	151.1	683	181	92	77	14	4	8	3	56	3	132	6	4	8	12	.400	2	0	4.58
1998 Pr William	A+ StL	14	13	0	0	86	349	75	40	34	10	2	1	1	16	0	65	0	0	3	6	.333	0	0	3.56
Arkansas	AA StL	10	8	0	0	42.1	192	44	30	24	7	2	2	1	18	1	21	2	0	4	2	.667	0	0	5.10
1999 Arkansas	AA StL	2	2	0	0	11.2	54	12	8	8	1	0	0	0	9	0	11	2	0	1	0	1.000	0	0	6.17
Memphis	AAA StL	36	16	0	6	101.2	481	145	100	93	23	7	4	3	37	1	82	5	1	6	10	.375	0	0	8.23
2000 Memphis	AAA StL	21	21	1	0	125	536	127	69	55	11	4	1	2	44	0	76	3	2	9	4	.692	1	0	3.96
Rochester	AAA Bal	4	4	0	0	18.2	79	21	8	8	2	0	0	0	4	0	13	0	0	1	2	.333	0	0	3.86
5 Min. YEARS		130	105	3	7	616.1	2699	677	378	325	72	21	18	14	200	5	474	21	10	37	40	.481	3	0	4.75

Javier Ochoa

Bats: Right **Throws:** Right **Pos:** C-39; DH-1; PH-1   **Ht:** 6'1" **Wt:** 170 **Born:** 1/8/79 **Age:** 22

					BATTING											BASERUNNING				PERCENTAGES		
Year Team	Lg Org	G	AB	H	2B	3B	HR	TB	R	RBI	TBB	IBB	SO	HBP	SH	SF	SB	CS	SB%	GDP	Avg	OBP	SLG
1997 Astros	R Hou	30	81	16	2	1	0	20	7	14	7	0	13	2	1	0	1	1	.50	1	.198	.278	.247
1998 Quad City	A Hou	5	7	0	0	0	0	0	1	0	1	0	2	0	0	0	0	0	—	0	.000	.125	.000
Astros	R Hou	34	85	18	2	1	0	22	7	6	14	0	15	6	2	1	1	2	.33	0	.212	.358	.259
1999 Auburn	A- Hou	15	47	13	2	1	0	17	5	11	3	0	7	0	0	2	0	1	.00	1	.277	.308	.362
2000 Pittsfield	A- NYM	5	17	1	0	0	0	1	0	0	0	0	2	1	0	0	0	0	—	1	.059	.111	.059
Capital Cty	A NYM	35	126	35	9	0	2	50	13	13	4	0	21	2	0	0	2	0	.00	1	.278	.311	.397
Norfolk	AAA NYM	1	1	0	0	0	0	0	0	0	0	0	0	0	0	0	0	0	—	0	.000	.000	.000
4 Min. YEARS		125	364	83	15	3	2	110	33	44	29	0	60	11	3	3	2	6	.25	5	.228	.302	.302

Pablo Ochoa

Pitches: Right **Bats:** Right **Pos:** SP-26   **Ht:** 6'0" **Wt:** 185 **Born:** 10/21/75 **Age:** 25

		HOW MUCH HE PITCHED						WHAT HE GAVE UP										THE RESULTS					
Year Team	Lg Org	G	GS	CG	GF	IP	BFP	H	R	ER	HR	SH	SF	HB	TBB	IBB	SO	WP	Bk	W	L	Pct.	ShO	Sv	ERA
1999 Capital Cty	A NYM	3	0	0	2	5.2	19	2	0	0	0	0	0	0	1	0	4	0	0	0	0	—	0	1	0.00
2000 Binghamton	AA NYM	26	26	1	0	146.2	659	171	94	85	10	6	9	4	75	0	106	8	1	9	12	.429	1	0	5.22
2 Min. YEARS		29	26	1	2	152.1	678	173	94	85	10	6	9	4	76	0	110	8	1	9	12	.429	1	1	5.02

Chad Ogea

Pitches: Right **Bats:** Right **Pos:** SP-5   **Ht:** 6'2" **Wt:** 220 **Born:** 11/9/70 **Age:** 30

Year Team	Lg Org	G	GS	CG	GF	IP	BFP	H	R	ER	HR	SH	SF	HB	TBB	IBB	SO	WP	Bk	W	L	Pct.	ShO	Sv	ERA
1992 Kinston	A+ Cle	21	21	5	0	139.1	573	135	61	54	6	6	4	5	29	0	123	7	4	13	3	.813	2	0	3.49
Canton-Akrn	AA Cle	7	7	1	0	49	195	38	12	12	2	1	0	4	12	0	40	3	0	6	1	.857	1	0	2.20
1993 Charlotte	AAA Cle	29	29	2	0	181.2	751	169	91	77	26	4	3	2	54	0	135	6	4	13	8	.619	0	0	3.81
1994 Charlotte	AAA Cle	24	23	6	1	163.2	658	146	80	70	21	4	8	4	34	0	113	3	1	9	10	.474	0	1	3.85
1995 Buffalo	AAA Cle	4	4	0	0	17.2	79	16	12	9	1	0	0	2	8	0	11	0	0	1	1	.000	0	0	4.58
1996 Buffalo	AAA Cle	5	5	0	0	25.2	108	27	15	15	4	0	0	1	6	0	20	0	0	0	1	.000	0	0	5.26
1997 Buffalo	AAA Cle	4	4	0	0	21	88	24	10	10	2	0	0	0	6	0	11	0	0	1	1	.500	0	0	4.29
1998 Buffalo	AAA Cle	9	9	1	0	42.1	178	42	19	17	2	1	1	4	5	0	34	1	0	2	1	.667	0	0	3.61
2000 Akron	AA Cle	4	4	0	0	25.1	111	26	17	13	4	1	2	3	5	0	16	0	0	2	1	.667	0	0	4.62
Buffalo	AAA Cle	1	1	0	0	1.1	13	8	6	6	2	0	0	0	1	0	0	0	0	0	0	—	0	0	40.50
1994 Cleveland	AL	4	1	0	0	16.1	80	21	11	11	2	0	0	1	10	2	11	0	0	0	1	.000	0	0	6.06
1995 Cleveland	AL	20	14	1	3	106.1	442	95	38	36	11	0	5	1	29	0	57	3	1	8	3	.727	0	0	3.05
1996 Cleveland	AL	29	21	1	2	146.2	620	151	82	78	22	3	3	5	42	3	101	2	0	10	6	.625	1	0	4.79
1997 Cleveland	AL	21	21	1	0	126.1	552	139	79	70	13	3	5	5	47	4	80	4	2	8	9	.471	0	0	4.99
1998 Cleveland	AL	19	9	0	1	69	307	74	44	43	9	1	3	7	25	1	43	0	0	5	4	.556	0	0	5.61
1999 Philadelphia	NL	36	28	0	3	168	746	192	110	105	36	10	4	4	61	1	77	5	2	6	12	.333	0	0	5.63
8 Min. YEARS		108	107	15	1	667	2754	631	323	283	70	17	18	25	160	0	503	20	9	46	27	.630	3	1	3.82
6 Maj. YEARS		129	94	3	9	632.2	2747	672	364	343	93	17	20	23	214	11	369	14	5	37	35	.514	1	0	4.88

Kirt Ojala

Pitches: Left **Bats:** Left **Pos:** RP-7   **Ht:** 6'2" **Wt:** 215 **Born:** 12/24/68 **Age:** 32

Year Team	Lg Org	G	GS	CG	GF	IP	BFP	H	R	ER	HR	SH	SF	HB	TBB	IBB	SO	WP	Bk	W	L	Pct.	ShO	Sv	ERA
1990 Oneonta	A- NYY	14	14	1	0	79	353	75	28	19	2	5	2	3	43	0	87	1	2	7	2	.778	0	0	2.16
1991 Pr William	A+ NYY	25	23	1	0	156.2	636	120	52	44	5	3	4	4	61	1	112	3	1	7	7	.533	0	0	2.53
1992 Albany-Col	AA NYY	24	23	2	0	151.2	642	130	71	61	10	3	7	0	80	0	116	10	0	12	8	.600	1	0	3.62
1993 Albany-Col	AA NYY	1	1	0	0	6.1	26	5	0	0	0	0	0	0	2	0	6	0	0	1	0	1.000	0	0	0.00
Columbus	AAA NYY	31	20	0	3	126	575	145	85	77	13	4	5	3	71	2	83	13	1	8	9	.471	0	0	5.50
1994 Columbus	AAA NYY	25	23	1	0	148	638	157	78	63	12	4	2	4	46	1	81	10	1	11	7	.611	1	0	3.83
1995 Columbus	AAA NYY	32	20	0	5	145.2	619	138	74	64	15	6	2	3	54	3	107	7	1	8	7	.533	0	1	3.95
1996 Indianapols	AAA Cin	22	21	3	0	133.2	569	143	67	56	15	2	6	6	31	0	92	3	0	7	7	.500	0	0	3.77
1997 Charlotte	AAA Fla	25	24	0	1	149	627	148	74	58	13	4	1	3	55	2	119	4	0	8	7	.533	0	0	3.50
1999 Calgary	AAA Fla	16	14	1	0	78.2	381	110	70	63	12	4	5	2	44	0	54	6	0	3	8	.273	0	0	7.21
2000 Trenton	AA Bos	7	0	0	4	11	43	7	3	3	2	0	1	0	3	0	6	0	0	0	0	—	0	1	2.45
1997 Florida	NL	7	5	0	1	28.2	130	28	10	10	4	0	1	0	18	0	19	0	0	1	2	.333	0	0	3.14
1998 Florida	NL	41	13	1	4	125	554	128	71	59	14	10	2	4	59	4	75	6	0	2	7	.222	0	0	4.25
1999 Florida	NL	8	1	0	2	10.2	56	21	17	17	1	0	2	0	6	0	5	0	0	0	1	.000	0	0	14.34
10 Min. YEARS		222	183	9	13	1185.2	5109	1178	602	508	99	33	35	28	490	9	863	59	6	73	62	.541	2	2	3.86
3 Maj. YEARS		56	19	1	7	164.1	740	177	98	86	19	10	5	4	83	4	99	6	0	3	10	.231	0	0	4.71

Brian Oliver

Bats: Right **Throws:** Right **Pos:** SS-10; 2B-7   **Ht:** 5'10" **Wt:** 170 **Born:** 11/7/76 **Age:** 24

Year Team	Lg Org	G	AB	H	2B	3B	HR	TB	R	RBI	TBB	IBB	SO	HBP	SH	SF	SB	CS	SB%	GDP	Avg	OBP	SLG
1998 Boise	A- Ana	17	54	14	3	1	0	19	6	5	8	0	6	1	3	0	0	1	.00	3	.259	.365	.352
1999 Cedar Rapids	A Ana	66	252	69	16	1	6	105	43	29	26	0	30	6	4	4	12	1	.92	3	.274	.351	.417
2000 Erie	AA Ana	17	59	12	0	0	0	12	3	3	4	0	9	4	2	0	2	1	.67	0	.203	.299	.203
3 Min. YEARS		100	365	95	19	2	6	136	52	37	38	0	45	11	9	4	14	3	.82	6	.260	.344	.373

Miguel Olivo

Bats: Right **Throws:** Right **Pos:** C-64; DH-12; PH-2; PR-1   **Ht:** 6'0" **Wt:** 180 **Born:** 7/15/78 **Age:** 22

Year Team	Lg Org	G	AB	H	2B	3B	HR	TB	R	RBI	TBB	IBB	SO	HBP	SH	SF	SB	CS	SB%	GDP	Avg	OBP	SLG
1998 Athletics	R Oak	46	164	51	11	3	2	74	30	23	8	0	43	4	0	1	2	2	.50	5	.311	.356	.451
1999 Modesto	A+ Oak	73	243	74	13	6	9	126	46	42	21	1	60	2	1	1	4	5	.44	6	.305	.363	.519
2000 Midland	AA Oak	19	59	14	2	0	1	19	8	9	5	0	15	0	1	0	0	0	—	3	.237	.297	.322
Modesto	A+ Oak	58	227	64	11	5	5	100	40	35	16	0	53	2	0	2	5	2	.71	8	.282	.332	.441
3 Min. YEARS		196	693	203	37	14	17	319	124	109	50	1	171	8	2	4	11	9	.55	22	.293	.346	.460

Kevin Olore

Pitches: Right **Bats:** Left **Pos:** RP-41   **Ht:** 6'2" **Wt:** 200 **Born:** 9/21/78 **Age:** 22

Year Team	Lg Org	G	GS	CG	GF	IP	BFP	H	R	ER	HR	SH	SF	HB	TBB	IBB	SO	WP	Bk	W	L	Pct.	ShO	Sv	ERA
1999 Everett	A- Sea	46	0	0	12	31.1	141	31	14	14	0	0	0	2	21	1	31	4	2	0	0	—	0	2	4.88
2000 Wisconsin	A Sea	12	0	0	4	20	101	25	16	16	1	1	1	4	14	1	17	1	0	1	3	.250	0	0	7.20
New Haven	AA Sea	3	0	0	2	4.1	21	7	5	4	1	0	0	0	2	0	2	0	0	0	0	—	0	0	8.31
Everett	A- Sea	26	0	0	7	55	246	50	28	18	5	2	1	3	28	2	64	5	0	1	3	.250	0	2	2.95
2 Min. YEARS		63	0	0	25	110.2	509	113	70	55	12	3	2	9	65	4	114	10	2	2	6	.250	0	4	4.47

Kevin Olsen

Pitches: Right **Bats:** Right **Pos:** SP-27   **Ht:** 6'2" **Wt:** 200 **Born:** 7/26/76 **Age:** 24

Year Team	Lg Org	G	GS	CG	GF	IP	BFP	H	R	ER	HR	SH	SF	HB	TBB	IBB	SO	WP	Bk	W	L	Pct.	ShO	Sv	ERA
1998 Utica	A- Fla	21	4	0	8	45	181	37	21	13	3	1	0	1	10	1	56	1	1	4	3	.571	0	2	2.60

Year Team	Lg Org	G	GS	CG	GF	IP	BFP	H	R	ER	HR	SH	SF	HB	TBB	IBB	SO	WP	Bk	W	L	Pct.	ShO	Sv	ERA
1999 Brevard Cty	A+ Fla	11	11	0	0	57	253	70	37	32	8	1	1	1	13	0	45	3	0	2	5	.286	0	0	5.05
Kane County	A Fla	10	9	0	0	61.1	257	65	25	23	3	0	3	2	16	0	52	2	0	5	2	.714	1	0	3.38
2000 Brevard Cty	A+ Fla	18	18	1	0	110	436	93	40	35	2	2	4	6	25	2	77	4	0	4	8	.333	0	0	2.86
Portland	AA Fla	9	9	0	0	54	234	54	30	29	8	1	0	2	21	0	47	3	0	3	4	.429	0	0	4.83
3 Min. YEARS		69	51	1	8	327.1	1361	319	153	132	24	5	8	12	85	3	277	13	1	18	22	.450	0	2	3.63

Mike Oquist

Pitches: Right **Bats:** Right **Pos:** SP-28; RP-1   **Ht:** 6'2" **Wt:** 190 **Born:** 5/30/68 **Age:** 33

Year Team	Lg Org	G	GS	CG	GF	IP	BFP	H	R	ER	HR	SH	SF	HB	TBB	IBB	SO	WP	Bk	W	L	Pct.	ShO	Sv	ERA
1989 Erie	A- Bal	15	15	1	0	97.2	402	86	43	39	7	2	1	3	25	0	109	1	1	7	4	.636	1	0	3.59
1990 Frederick	A+ Bal	25	25	3	0	166.1	678	134	64	52	11	6	6	4	48	3	170	9	1	9	8	.529	1	0	2.81
1991 Hagerstown	AA Bal	27	26	1	1	166.1	717	168	82	75	15	4	7	0	62	4	136	7	1	10	9	.526	0	0	4.06
1992 Rochester	AAA Bal	26	24	5	0	153.1	665	164	80	70	17	5	4	5	45	1	111	6	1	10	12	.455	0	0	4.11
1993 Rochester	AAA Bal	28	21	2	1	149.1	617	144	62	58	20	5	1	2	41	1	128	5	1	9	8	.529	1	0	3.50
1994 Rochester	AAA Bal	13	8	0	4	50.2	213	54	23	21	5	0	1	1	15	0	36	3	1	3	2	.600	0	3	3.73
1995 Rochester	AAA Bal	7	0	0	3	12	56	17	8	7	0	0	0	0	5	1	11	0	0	0	0	—	0	2	5.25
1996 Las Vegas	AAA SD	27	20	2	4	140.1	586	136	55	45	12	6	6	3	44	2	110	4	0	9	4	.692	0	1	2.89
1997 Edmonton	AAA Oak	9	9	1	0	52.2	225	57	23	19	3	2	1	0	16	0	37	0	0	6	1	.857	0	0	3.25
Modesto	A+ Oak	2	2	0	0	3.2	17	5	2	2	1	0	0	0	1	0	5	0	0	0	0	—	0	0	4.91
1999 Vancouver	AAA Oak	1	1	0	0	6	22	2	0	0	0	0	0	0	1	0	2	1	0	1	0	1.000	0	0	0.00
2000 Toledo	AAA Det	29	28	3	0	161	723	214	106	93	18	4	7	8	43	1	97	8	0	7	15	.318	1	0	5.20
1993 Baltimore	AL	5	0	0	2	11.2	50	12	5	5	0	0	0	0	4	1	8	0	0	0	0	—	0	0	3.86
1994 Baltimore	AL	15	9	0	3	58.1	278	75	41	40	7	3	4	6	30	4	39	3	0	3	3	.500	0	0	6.17
1995 Baltimore	AL	27	0	0	2	54	255	51	27	25	6	1	4	2	41	3	27	2	0	2	1	.667	0	0	4.17
1996 San Diego	NL	8	0	0	3	7.2	30	6	2	2	0	0	0	0	4	2	4	1	0	0	0	—	0	0	2.35
1997 Oakland	AL	19	17	1	0	107.2	473	111	62	60	15	3	3	6	43	3	72	2	0	4	6	.400	0	0	5.02
1998 Oakland	AL	31	29	0	2	175	777	210	125	121	27	5	6	5	57	1	112	4	0	7	11	.389	0	0	6.22
1999 Oakland	AL	28	24	0	1	140.2	629	158	86	84	18	3	1	2	64	5	89	2	0	9	10	.474	0	0	5.37
11 Min. YEARS		209	179	18	13	1159.1	4921	1181	548	481	109	34	34	26	346	13	952	44	6	71	63	.530	4	6	3.73
7 Maj. YEARS		133	79	1	13	555	2492	623	348	337	73	15	18	21	243	19	351	14	0	25	31	.446	0	0	5.46

Kevin Orie

Bats: Right **Throws:** Right **Pos:** 3B-95   **Ht:** 6'4" **Wt:** 215 **Born:** 9/1/72 **Age:** 28

Year Team	Lg Org	G	AB	H	2B	3B	HR	TB	R	RBI	TBB	IBB	SO	HBP	SH	SF	SB	CS	SB%	GDP	Avg	OBP	SLG
1993 Peoria	A ChC	65	238	64	17	1	7	104	28	45	24	1	51	10	2	2	3	5	.38	7	.269	.351	.437
1994 Daytona	A+ ChC	6	17	7	3	1	1	15	4	5	8	1	4	1	0	0	0	1	.00	0	.412	.615	.882
1995 Daytona	A+ ChC	119	409	100	17	4	9	152	54	51	42	2	71	15	0	6	5	4	.56	11	.244	.333	.372
1996 Orlando	AA ChC	82	296	93	25	0	8	142	42	58	48	3	52	0	0	6	2	0	1.00	5	.314	.403	.480
Iowa	AAA ChC	14	48	10	1	0	2	17	5	6	6	1	10	0	0	0	0	0	—	1	.208	.296	.354
1997 Orlando	AA ChC	3	13	5	2	0	2	13	3	6	2	1	1	0	0	0	0	0	—	0	.385	.467	1.000
Iowa	AAA ChC	9	32	12	4	0	1	19	7	8	5	0	5	0	0	0	0	0	—	0	.375	.459	.594
1998 Iowa	AAA ChC	24	92	34	8	0	9	69	27	24	12	1	15	2	0	0	1	0	1.00	3	.370	.453	.750
1999 Calgary	AAA Fla	23	72	23	9	0	3	41	10	8	13	0	7	1	0	0	0	0	—	0	.319	.430	.569
2000 Omaha	AAA KC	54	175	49	11	2	5	79	30	23	28	0	24	5	0	2	3	3	.50	8	.280	.390	.451
Columbus	AAA NYY	41	149	43	13	0	4	68	19	19	12	0	28	3	0	1	0	1	1.00	4	.289	.354	.456
1997 Chicago	NL	114	364	100	23	5	8	157	40	44	39	3	57	5	3	4	2	2	.50	13	.275	.350	.431
1998 Chicago	NL	64	204	37	14	0	2	57	24	21	18	0	35	3	1	4	1	1	.50	4	.181	.253	.279
Florida	NL	48	175	46	8	1	6	74	23	17	14	2	24	5	1	0	1	0	1.00	4	.263	.335	.423
1999 Florida	NL	77	240	61	16	0	6	95	26	29	22	1	43	3	0	2	1	0	1.00	8	.254	.322	.396
8 Min. YEARS		440	1541	440	110	8	51	719	229	253	197	10	268	37	2	16	15	13	.54	42	.286	.376	.467
3 Maj. YEARS		303	983	244	61	6	22	383	113	111	93	6	159	16	5	10	5	3	.63	29	.248	.320	.390

Eddie Oropesa

Pitches: Left **Bats:** Left **Pos:** RP-57; SP-2   **Ht:** 6'3" **Wt:** 215 **Born:** 11/23/71 **Age:** 29

Year Team	Lg Org	G	GS	CG	GF	IP	BFP	H	R	ER	HR	SH	SF	HB	TBB	IBB	SO	WP	Bk	W	L	Pct.	ShO	Sv	ERA
1994 Vero Beach	A+ LA	19	10	1	3	72	285	54	24	17	2	3	2	4	25	2	67	2	0	4	3	.571	1	0	2.13
1995 San Antonio	AA LA	16	0	0	7	17.1	87	22	8	6	2	1	2	3	12	1	16	0	1	1	1	.500	0	1	3.12
Vero Beach	A+ LA	19	1	0	7	28.1	120	25	12	12	0	1	2	3	10	0	23	4	2	3	1	.750	0	1	3.81
San Berndno	A+ LA	1	0	0	1	1	3	0	0	0	0	0	0	0	0	0	0	0	0	0	0	—	0	1	0.00
1996 San Berndno	A+ LA	33	19	0	2	156.1	669	133	74	58	8	1	3	6	77	1	133	8	4	11	6	.647	0	1	3.34
1997 Shreveport	AA SF	43	9	1	12	124	531	122	58	54	7	7	4	4	64	0	65	6	6	7	7	.500	0	0	3.92
1998 Shreveport	AA SF	32	20	2	3	143	623	143	71	60	6	7	5	7	67	3	104	15	2	7	11	.389	0	0	3.78
1999 Bakersfield	A+ SF	2	1	0	0	10	41	13	5	4	2	0	0	0	1	0	10	2	0	2	0	1.000	0	0	3.60
Fresno	AAA SF	21	18	1	0	102	460	113	69	55	15	3	1	3	49	0	61	13	4	6	5	.545	0	0	4.85
2000 Shreveport	AA SF	59	2	0	23	76.1	341	70	38	26	6	3	1	3	40	6	76	3	2	2	4	.333	0	4	3.07
7 Min. YEARS		245	80	5	58	730.1	3160	695	359	292	48	26	20	33	345	13	555	53	21	43	38	.531	1	8	3.60

Bill Ortega

Bats: Right **Throws:** Right **Pos:** OF-84; PH-2   **Ht:** 6'4" **Wt:** 205 **Born:** 7/24/75 **Age:** 25

Year Team	Lg Org	G	AB	H	2B	3B	HR	TB	R	RBI	TBB	IBB	SO	HBP	SH	SF	SB	CS	SB%	GDP	Avg	OBP	SLG
1997 Pr William	A+ StL	73	249	57	14	0	0	71	23	15	21	1	42	0	1	0	1	2	.33	10	.229	.289	.285
1998 Peoria	A StL	105	398	110	23	2	2	143	60	39	0	0	69	5	3	2	4	8	.33	14	.276	.347	.359
1999 Potomac	A+ StL	110	421	129	27	4	9	191	66	74	38	2	69	4	6	3	7	7	.50	17	.306	.367	.454
Arkansas	AA StL	20	69	26	9	0	2	41	10	10	10	0	9	0	1	0	0	0	—	4	.377	.456	.594
2000 Arkansas	AA StL	86	332	108	18	5	12	172	51	62	28	4	42	4	0	4	1	5	.17	10	.325	.380	.518
4 Min. YEARS		394	1469	430	91	11	25	618	207	221	136	7	231	13	11	9	13	22	.37	55	.293	.356	.421

Luis Ortiz

Bats: Right **Throws:** Right **Pos:** 3B-32; 1B-30; DH-23; PH-15; PR-2 **Ht:** 6'0" **Wt:** 195 **Born:** 5/25/70 **Age:** 31

Year Team	Lg Org	G	AB	H	2B	3B	HR	TB	R	RBI	TBB	IBB	SO	HBP	SH	SF	SB	CS	SB%	GDP	Avg	OBP	SLG
1991 Red Sox	R Bos	42	153	51	11	2	4	78	21	29	7	0	9	2	1	1	2	1	.67	1	.333	.368	.510
1992 Lynchburg	A+ Bos	94	355	103	27	1	10	162	43	61	22	3	55	2	0	5	4	2	.67	8	.290	.331	.456
1993 Pawtucket	AAA Bos	102	402	118	28	1	18	202	45	81	13	3	74	2	0	4	1	1	.50	10	.294	.316	.502
1994 Pawtucket	AAA Bos	81	317	99	15	3	6	138	47	36	29	5	29	0	0	0	1	4	.20	9	.312	.370	.435
1995 Okla City	AAA Tex	47	170	52	10	5	2	78	19	20	8	2	20	0	1	3	1	1	.50	7	.306	.331	.459
1996 Okla City	AAA Tex	124	501	159	25	0	14	226	70	73	22	2	36	4	0	6	0	5	.00	17	.317	.347	.451
1997 Okla City	AAA Tex	22	82	25	5	0	1	33	9	11	5	0	7	0	0	3	1	1	.50	2	.305	.333	.402
1998 Omaha	AAA KC	44	138	42	13	0	5	70	27	22	10	1	11	0	0	2	0	2	.00	6	.304	.351	.507
1999 Louisville	AAA Mil	96	304	80	11	0	11	124	36	33	23	0	41	0	0	4	0	2	.00	8	.263	.311	.408
2000 Diamondbcks	R Ari	1	3	3	1	0	0	4	3	2	1	0	0	0	0	0	0	0	—	0	1.000	1.000	1.333
Tucson	AAA Ari	92	308	93	26	3	10	155	50	65	16	0	17	4	3	6	0	0	—	17	.302	.338	.503
1993 Boston	AL	9	12	3	0	0	0	3	0	1	0	0	2	0	0	0	0	0	—	0	.250	.250	.250
1994 Boston	AL	7	18	3	2	0	0	5	3	6	1	0	5	0	0	1	0	0	—	0	.167	.182	.278
1995 Texas	AL	41	108	25	5	2	1	37	10	18	6	0	18	0	0	1	0	1	.00	7	.231	.270	.343
1996 Texas	AL	3	7	2	0	0	0	7	1	1	1	0	0	1	0	0	0	0	—	0	.286	.286	1.000
10 Min. YEARS		745	2733	825	172	15	81	1270	370	433	156	16	299	14	5	32	10	19	.34	85	.302	.339	.465
4 Maj. YEARS		60	145	33	7	3	2	52	14	26	7	0	26	0	1	4	0	1	.00	7	.228	.256	.359

Nicky Ortiz

Bats: Right **Throws:** Right **Pos:** SS-108; 2B-11; 3B-1; OF-1; DH-1; PH-1 **Ht:** 6'0" **Wt:** 160 **Born:** 7/9/73 **Age:** 27

Year Team	Lg Org	G	AB	H	2B	3B	HR	TB	R	RBI	TBB	IBB	SO	HBP	SH	SF	SB	CS	SB%	GDP	Avg	OBP	SLG
1991 Red Sox	R Bos	35	100	26	3	1	0	31	16	13	22	4	24	4	1	0	1	2	.33	1	.260	.413	.310
1992 Red Sox	R Bos	50	163	43	9	3	0	58	25	15	28	0	36	0	2	1	3	2	.60	4	.264	.370	.356
Elmira	A- Bos	9	28	5	3	0	0	8	2	1	5	0	13	0	0	0	0	0	—	0	.179	.303	.286
1993 Ft. Laud	A+ Bos	36	112	23	9	1	1	37	9	14	9	0	39	0	4	0	2	1	.67	4	.205	.264	.330
Utica	A- Bos	63	197	53	14	1	2	75	31	26	19	0	56	6	1	2	4	1	.80	3	.269	.348	.381
1994 Sarasota	A+ Bos	81	283	76	18	3	2	106	34	40	21	1	57	3	6	3	7	2	.78	11	.269	.323	.375
1995 Sarasota	A+ Bos	91	304	75	20	1	5	112	38	38	27	0	68	4	1	1	6	4	.60	3	.247	.315	.368
1996 Michigan	A Bos	73	242	73	14	4	2	101	37	25	20	1	44	5	1	1	1	1	.50	7	.302	.366	.417
Trenton	AA Bos	38	130	29	4	0	3	42	20	13	13	2	28	0	1	0	2	2	.50	3	.223	.294	.323
1997 Trenton	AA Bos	87	288	81	17	2	8	126	47	53	27	1	55	5	6	5	3	2	.60	3	.281	.348	.438
1998 Ottawa	AAA Mon	12	32	3	1	0	0	4	1	0	6	0	10	0	1	0	0	0	—	0	.094	.237	.125
Harrisburg	AA Mon	56	163	44	11	2	6	77	18	24	18	0	37	2	7	2	2	3	.40	7	.270	.346	.472
Trenton	AA Bos	39	131	30	6	0	1	39	17	9	14	0	27	1	3	0	0	0	—	3	.229	.308	.298
1999 Buffalo	AAA Cle	22	51	13	4	0	0	17	7	1	3	0	10	0	0	0	0	0	—	2	.255	.296	.333
Akron	AA Cle	55	195	52	15	2	2	77	24	13	17	0	40	4	0	3	1	2	.33	5	.267	.333	.395
San Antonio	AA LA	14	40	7	1	0	0	8	4	2	3	0	7	0	0	0	0	0	—	2	.175	.233	.200
2000 Wichita	AA KC	111	381	112	19	2	10	165	59	62	52	1	66	1	9	2	14	6	.70	13	.294	.378	.433
Norwich	AA NYY	11	37	6	0	0	0	6	4	1	7	0	8	1	0	0	0	0	—	0	.162	.311	.162
10 Min. YEARS		883	2877	751	168	22	42	1089	393	350	311	6	625	36	43	20	46	28	.62	75	.261	.338	.379

Garret Osilka

Bats: Right **Throws:** Right **Pos:** 3B-29; 2B-24; PH-7; SS-6; 1B-6; DH-6; PR-3; OF-1 **Ht:** 6'1" **Wt:** 195 **Born:** 9/14/77 **Age:** 23

Year Team	Lg Org	G	AB	H	2B	3B	HR	TB	R	RBI	TBB	IBB	SO	HBP	SH	SF	SB	CS	SB%	GDP	Avg	OBP	SLG
1996 Helena	R+ Mil	53	165	35	2	1	2	45	34	19	25	0	33	4	5	0	6	6	.50	1	.212	.330	.273
1997 Ogden	R+ Mil	64	231	59	9	2	0	72	41	19	32	1	50	6	5	0	10	4	.71	0	.255	.361	.312
1998 Beloit	A Mil	127	492	128	26	3	7	181	74	32	65	1	118	10	18	5	18	11	.62	3	.260	.355	.368
1999 Stockton	A+ Mil	100	278	71	11	1	4	96	43	28	24	0	60	7	5	2	7	9	.44	2	.255	.328	.345
2000 Harrisburg	AA Mon	20	43	7	0	1	0	9	3	6	2	0	16	1	2	1	2	0	1.00	1	.163	.213	.209
Jupiter	A+ Mon	57	186	42	8	0	1	53	21	23	20	0	41	10	4	0	8	5	.62	7	.226	.333	.285
5 Min. YEARS		421	1395	342	56	8	14	456	216	127	168	2	318	38	39	8	51	35	.59	14	.245	.341	.327

Gavin Osteen

Pitches: Left **Bats:** Right **Pos:** RP-19; SP-8 **Ht:** 6'0" **Wt:** 195 **Born:** 11/27/69 **Age:** 31

		HOW MUCH HE PITCHED						WHAT HE GAVE UP												THE RESULTS				
Year Team	Lg Org	G	GS	CG	GF	IP	BFP	H	R	ER	HR	SH	SF	HB	TBB	IBB	SO	WP	Bk	W	L	Pct.	ShO	Sv	ERA
1989 Sou Oregon	A- Oak	16	6	3	0	46.1	211	44	24	18	3	4	1	3	29	0	42	9	0	2	2	.500	0	0	3.50
1990 Madison	A Oak	27	27	1	0	154	659	126	69	53	6	5	6	3	80	0	120	10	4	10	10	.500	1	0	3.10
1991 Huntsville	AA Oak	28	28	2	0	173	742	176	82	68	4	6	9	4	65	2	105	4	2	13	9	.591	1	0	3.54
1992 Tacoma	AAA Oak	4	4	0	0	14.1	77	21	18	16	4	2	3	2	13	0	7	1	1	0	2	.000	0	0	10.05
Huntsville	AA Oak	16	16	1	0	102.1	425	106	45	41	9	5	5	1	27	0	56	2	2	5	5	.500	0	0	3.61
1993 Huntsville	AA Oak	11	11	2	0	70.1	288	56	21	18	1	1	1	2	25	1	46	2	0	7	3	.700	0	0	2.30
Tacoma	AAA Oak	16	15	0	0	83.1	356	89	51	47	4	4	5	1	31	1	46	0	1	7	7	.500	0	0	5.08
1994 Tacoma	AAA Oak	24	24	2	0	138.1	618	169	95	81	17	3	12	4	39	0	71	0	0	8	9	.471	1	0	5.27
1995 Athletics	R Oak	1	1	0	0	2	7	1	0	0	0	0	0	0	1	0	1	0	0	0	0	—	0	0	0.00
1997 Bowie	AA Bal	18	2	0	2	30.2	119	20	7	7	1	0	0	0	11	0	22	2	0	1	1	.500	0	0	2.05
1998 Rochester	AAA Bal	44	0	0	18	72.2	310	74	37	32	10	1	2	3	25	0	46	4	2	1	2	.333	0	2	3.96
1999 Albuquerque	AAA LA	34	12	0	10	103.2	464	127	64	59	10	2	1	6	33	4	65	3	0	6	8	.429	0	2	5.12
2000 Altoona	AA Pit	1	0	0	0	1.2	9	1	0	0	0	0	0	0	4	0	0	0	0	0	0	—	0	0	0.00
Nashville	AAA Pit	14	0	0	7	11.1	50	11	8	7	2	0	0	1	4	0	7	1	0	4	1	.800	0	0	5.56
Bridgeport	IND —	12	8	0	0	50	216	42	22	17	4	1	1	3	17	0	37	1	0	6	2	.750	0	0	3.06
11 Min. YEARS		266	154	8	40	1054	4551	1063	543	464	75	34	46	34	401	8	673	39	12	70	61	.534	3	4	3.96

Jimmy Osting

Pitches: Left **Bats:** Right **Pos:** SP-27; RP-1   **Ht:** 6'5" **Wt:** 190 **Born:** 4/7/77 **Age:** 24

Year Team	Lg Org	G	GS	CG	GF	IP	BFP	H	R	ER	HR	SH	SF	HB	TBB	IBB	SO	WP	Bk	W	L	Pct.	ShO	Sv	ERA
1995 Danville	R+ Atl	11	10	0	0	39	190	46	34	31	1	0	1	0	25	0	43	12	0	2	7	.222	0	0	7.15
1996 Eugene	A- Atl	5	5	0	0	24.1	99	14	11	7	1	0	0	0	13	0	35	1	0	2	1	.667	0	0	2.59
1997 Macon	A Atl	15	15	0	0	57.2	251	54	28	21	3	1	0	2	29	0	62	5	0	2	3	.400	0	0	3.28
1999 Macon	A Atl	27	22	0	5	147	581	130	52	47	13	2	1	5	30	0	131	2	0	14	4	.778	0	2	2.88
2000 Myrtle Bch	A+ Atl	4	4	0	0	23	94	25	8	8	0	0	1	0	5	0	17	0	0	2	2	.500	0	0	3.13
Richmond	AAA Atl	3	3	0	0	9.1	52	15	12	12	2	1	1	0	11	1	2	1	0	0	2	.000	0	0	11.57
Greenville	AA Atl	11	11	0	0	71.1	302	67	30	21	6	2	1	0	29	1	52	1	0	2	6	.250	0	0	2.65
Reading	AA Phi	10	9	1	0	56.2	245	53	17	15	1	6	2	4	26	2	31	2	0	4	2	.667	1	0	2.38
5 Min. YEARS		86	79	1	5	428.1	1814	404	192	162	27	12	7	11	168	4	373	24	0	28	27	.509	1	2	3.40

Roy Oswalt

Pitches: Right **Bats:** Right **Pos:** SP-26; RP-1   **Ht:** 6'0" **Wt:** 170 **Born:** 8/29/77 **Age:** 23

Year Team	Lg Org	G	GS	CG	GF	IP	BFP	H	R	ER	HR	SH	SF	HB	TBB	IBB	SO	WP	Bk	W	L	Pct.	ShO	Sv	ERA
1997 Astros	R Hou	5	5	0	0	28.1	117	25	7	2	2	0	0	0	7	0	28	0	0	1	1	.500	0	0	0.64
Auburn	A- Hou	9	9	1	0	51.2	220	50	29	26	1	0	1	6	15	1	44	3	1	2	4	.333	1	0	4.53
1998 Astros	R Hou	4	4	0	0	16	62	10	6	4	2	1	1	3	1	0	27	0	1	1	1	.500	0	0	2.25
Auburn	A- Hou	11	11	0	0	70.1	289	49	24	17	3	1	2	3	31	0	67	2	1	4	5	.444	0	0	2.18
1999 Michigan	A Hou	22	22	2	0	151.1	643	144	78	75	8	2	5	7	54	0	143	8	4	13	4	.765	0	0	4.46
2000 Kissimmee	A+ Hou	9	9	0	0	45.1	191	52	15	15	1	1	1	1	11	0	47	0	1	4	3	.571	0	0	2.98
Round Rock	AA Hou	19	18	2	0	129.2	521	106	37	28	5	4	2	3	22	1	141	4	1	11	4	.733	2	0	1.94
4 Min. YEARS		78	77	5	0	492.2	2043	436	196	167	22	9	12	23	141	2	497	17	9	36	22	.621	3	0	3.05

Willis Otanez

Bats: Right **Throws:** Right **Pos:** 3B-40; 1B-9; DH-3; PH-1   **Ht:** 6'1" **Wt:** 215 **Born:** 4/19/73 **Age:** 28

Year Team	Lg Org	G	AB	H	2B	3B	HR	TB	R	RBI	TBB	IBB	SO	HBP	SH	SF	SB	CS	SB%	GDP	Avg	OBP	SLG
1991 Great Falls	R+ LA	58	222	64	9	2	6	95	38	39	19	0	34	2	1	4	3	3	.50	7	.288	.344	.428
1992 Vero Beach	A+ LA	117	390	86	18	0	3	113	27	27	24	0	60	4	5	3	2	4	.33	10	.221	.271	.290
1993 Bakersfield	A+ LA	95	325	85	11	2	10	130	34	39	29	1	63	2	4	2	1	4	.20	9	.262	.324	.400
1994 Vero Beach	A+ LA	131	476	132	27	1	19	218	77	72	53	2	98	4	0	7	4	2	.67	10	.277	.350	.458
1995 Vero Beach	A+ LA	92	354	92	24	0	10	146	39	53	28	3	59	2	0	5	1	1	.50	15	.260	.314	.412
San Antonio	AA LA	27	100	24	4	1	1	33	8	7	6	0	25	0	0	1	0	1	.00	3	.240	.278	.330
1996 Bowie	AA Bal	138	506	134	27	2	24	237	60	75	45	2	97	1	2	5	3	7	.30	17	.265	.323	.468
1997 Orioles	R Bal	8	25	8	2	0	2	16	5	3	2	0	4	1	0	0	0	0	—	1	.320	.393	.640
Bowie	AA Bal	19	78	26	9	0	3	44	13	13	9	0	19	0	0	1	0	1	.00	3	.333	.398	.564
Rochester	AAA Bal	49	168	35	9	0	5	59	20	25	15	0	35	0	0	3	0	0	—	8	.208	.269	.351
1998 Rochester	AAA Bal	124	481	137	24	2	27	246	87	100	41	6	104	6	1	8	1	0	1.00	8	.285	.343	.511
2000 Tennessee	AA Tor	27	103	33	5	0	5	53	13	19	10	1	16	1	0	1	0	0	—	2	.320	.383	.515
Syracuse	AAA Tor	22	76	13	3	0	2	22	6	14	6	0	15	0	0	1	0	0	—	4	.171	.229	.289
1998 Baltimore	AL	3	5	1	0	0	0	1	0	0	0	0	2	0	0	0	0	0	—	0	.200	.200	.200
1999 Baltimore	AL	29	80	17	3	0	2	26	7	11	6	0	16	1	1	1	0	0	—	3	.213	.273	.325
Toronto	AL	42	127	32	8	0	5	55	21	13	9	0	30	1	0	0	0	0	—	3	.252	.307	.433
9 Min. YEARS		907	3304	869	172	10	117	1412	427	486	287	15	629	23	13	42	15	23	.39	97	.263	.322	.427
2 Maj. YEARS		74	212	50	11	0	7	82	28	24	15	0	48	2	1	1	0	0	—	6	.236	.291	.387

William Otero

Bats: Right **Throws:** Right **Pos:** 2B-70; DH-19; 3B-11; PH-5; PR-2; SS-1   **Ht:** 5'11" **Wt:** 175 **Born:** 9/30/74 **Age:** 26

Year Team	Lg Org	G	AB	H	2B	3B	HR	TB	R	RBI	TBB	IBB	SO	HBP	SH	SF	SB	CS	SB%	GDP	Avg	OBP	SLG
1997 Salem-Keizr	A- SF	46	147	35	9	3	0	50	22	12	17	1	32	4	0	1	2	1	.67	4	.238	.331	.340
1998 Bakersfield	A+ SF	69	245	72	14	0	3	95	33	36	35	1	50	2	7	3	8	0	1.00	4	.294	.382	.388
1999 San Jose	A+ SF	96	402	134	28	3	10	198	81	56	37	0	67	2	1	1	20	4	.83	5	.333	.391	.493
2000 Shreveport	AA SF	46	145	30	7	0	2	43	14	20	20	2	30	3	4	2	0	2	.00	2	.207	.312	.297
San Jose	A+ SF	59	209	44	8	1	3	63	22	22	21	0	53	1	3	3	6	2	.75	7	.211	.282	.301
4 Min. YEARS		316	1148	315	66	7	18	449	172	146	130	4	232	12	15	10	36	9	.80	22	.274	.352	.391

Paul Ottavinia

Bats: Left **Throws:** Left **Pos:** OF-82; 1B-43; DH-11; PH-1; PR-1   **Ht:** 6'1" **Wt:** 190 **Born:** 4/22/73 **Age:** 28

Year Team	Lg Org	G	AB	H	2B	3B	HR	TB	R	RBI	TBB	IBB	SO	HBP	SH	SF	SB	CS	SB%	GDP	Avg	OBP	SLG
1994 Burlington	A Mon	49	187	38	8	0	2	52	17	21	7	0	28	0	0	2	5	1	.83	2	.203	.230	.278
1995 Wst Plm Bch	A+ Mon	112	395	93	20	2	1	120	35	37	34	2	44	2	5	2	13	6	.68	10	.235	.298	.304
1996 Expos	R Mon	3	10	4	0	0	0	4	1	1	2	0	1	0	0	0	0	0	—	0	.400	.500	.400
Wst Plm Bch	A+ Mon	45	141	30	2	1	1	37	15	10	12	0	20	0	3	1	2	1	.67	2	.213	.273	.262
1997 Fargo-Mh	IND —	42	168	56	16	3	0	78	45	22	16	0	16	2	0	0	12	4	.75	2	.333	.398	.464
1998 Fargo-Mh	IND —	10	44	18	4	3	1	31	11	19	1	0	6	0	0	0	1	1	.50	2	.409	.422	.705
Tampa	A+ NYY	57	174	44	13	3	5	78	25	28	14	2	20	0	0	5	2	0	1.00	3	.253	.301	.448
1999 Norwich	AA NYY	59	191	55	11	3	7	93	26	31	14	1	40	1	0	1	5	3	.63	5	.288	.338	.487
2000 Norwich	AA NYY	127	477	144	27	8	8	211	80	58	56	7	50	10	0	5	15	5	.75	10	.302	.383	.442
7 Min. YEARS		504	1787	482	101	23	25	704	255	227	156	12	225	15	8	16	55	21	.72	34	.270	.331	.394

Lyle Overbay

Bats: Left Throws: Left Pos: 1B-126; DH-8   Ht: 6'2" Wt: 215 Born: 1/28/77 Age: 24

Year Team	Lg Org	G	AB	H	2B	3B	HR	TB	R	RBI	TBB	IBB	SO	HBP	SH	SF	SB	CS	SB%	GDP	Avg	OBP	SLG
1999 Missoula	R+ Ari	75	306	105	25	7	12	180	66	101	40	2	53	2	0	4	10	3	.77	14	.343	.418	.588
2000 South Bend	A Ari	71	259	86	19	3	6	129	47	47	27	0	36	2	0	2	9	2	.82	2	.332	.397	.498
El Paso	AA Ari	62	244	86	16	2	8	130	43	49	28	0	39	2	0	2	3	2	.60	6	.352	.420	.533
2 Min. YEARS		208	809	277	60	12	26	439	156	197	95	2	128	6	0	8	22	7	.76	22	.342	.412	.543

Ryan Owens

Bats: Right Throws: Right Pos: 3B-108; 2B-16; DH-4; 1B-3; SS-2; PH-2; PR-1   Ht: 6'2" Wt: 200 Born: 3/18/78 Age: 23

Year Team	Lg Org	G	AB	H	2B	3B	HR	TB	R	RBI	TBB	IBB	SO	HBP	SH	SF	SB	CS	SB%	GDP	Avg	OBP	SLG
1999 El Paso	AA Ari	31	113	36	5	1	1	46	11	18	8	0	36	2	0	1	1	2	.33	1	.319	.371	.407
High Desert	A+ Ari	26	103	41	7	3	4	66	19	28	9	0	30	1	1	1	1	2	.33	0	.398	.447	.641
2000 El Paso	AA Ari	60	208	45	7	4	5	75	30	24	21	1	60	2	1	0	5	4	.56	3	.216	.294	.361
South Bend	A Ari	71	270	67	20	0	9	114	52	43	47	1	76	4	1	0	15	4	.79	6	.248	.368	.422
2 Min. YEARS		188	694	189	39	8	19	301	112	113	85	2	202	9	3	2	22	12	.65	10	.272	.358	.434

Todd Ozias

Pitches: Right Bats: Right Pos: RP-48   Ht: 6'1" Wt: 185 Born: 8/13/76 Age: 24

Year Team	Lg Org	G	GS	CG	GF	IP	BFP	H	R	ER	HR	SH	SF	HB	TBB	IBB	SO	WP	Bk	W	L	Pct.	ShO	Sv	ERA
1998 Salem-Keizr	A- SF	27	0	0	15	45.2	184	38	23	20	6	5	1	2	12	1	51	6	0	3	4	.429	0	2	3.94
1999 Bakersfield	A+ SF	52	0	0	49	56.1	235	47	21	16	6	0	2	1	25	1	67	6	0	5	5	.500	0	26	2.56
2000 San Jose	A+ SF	47	0	0	44	52	227	49	28	20	4	2	3	1	17	0	61	7	0	2	1	.667	0	21	3.46
Shreveport	AA SF	1	0	0	0	2	12	5	2	2	1	0	0	0	1	0	1	0	0	0	0	—	0	0	9.00
3 Min. YEARS		127	0	0	108	156	658	139	74	58	17	7	6	4	55	2	180	19	0	10	10	.500	0	49	3.35

Delvis Pacheco

Pitches: Right Bats: Right Pos: RP-26; SP-10   Ht: 6'2" Wt: 180 Born: 6/25/78 Age: 23

Year Team	Lg Org	G	GS	CG	GF	IP	BFP	H	R	ER	HR	SH	SF	HB	TBB	IBB	SO	WP	Bk	W	L	Pct.	ShO	Sv	ERA
1995 Braves	R Atl	13	13	0	0	60	260	47	26	17	1	0	1	3	38	0	52	5	2	1	8	.111	0	0	2.55
1996 Danville	R+ Atl	13	12	0	0	64.2	271	56	28	19	1	1	1	2	21	0	60	5	0	8	1	.889	0	0	2.64
1997 Macon	A Atl	35	4	0	7	80	335	77	39	36	8	1	2	3	23	0	74	1	0	1	3	.250	0	2	4.05
1998 Macon	A Atl	18	10	0	3	63.1	272	67	39	35	12	1	2	6	14	0	42	5	1	7	4	.636	0	0	4.97
1999 Myrtle Bch	A+ Atl	40	3	0	16	99.1	429	87	47	38	9	5	2	6	42	3	87	7	0	6	5	.545	0	2	3.44
2000 Richmond	AAA Atl	25	0	0	6	58.2	238	61	32	31	6	3	4	2	18	2	44	2	0	1	2	.333	0	0	4.76
Greenville	AA Atl	11	10	0	0	58.2	245	55	22	20	9	0	0	1	23	0	51	2	0	6	2	.750	0	0	3.07
6 Min. YEARS		155	52	0	32	484.2	2050	450	233	196	46	11	12	23	179	5	410	27	3	30	25	.545	0	4	3.64

John Pachot

Bats: Right Throws: Right Pos: C-92; DH-4; 1B-3; PH-3   Ht: 6'2" Wt: 168 Born: 11/11/74 Age: 26

Year Team	Lg Org	G	AB	H	2B	3B	HR	TB	R	RBI	TBB	IBB	SO	HBP	SH	SF	SB	CS	SB%	GDP	Avg	OBP	SLG
1993 Expos	R Mon	35	121	37	4	1	0	43	13	16	2	0	7	0	4	2	0	1	.00	0	.306	.312	.355
1994 Burlington	A Mon	100	351	89	17	0	1	109	37	26	13	1	46	3	5	4	1	2	.33	12	.254	.283	.311
1995 Wst Plm Bch	A+ Mon	67	227	57	10	0	0	67	17	23	12	0	38	2	3	1	1	2	.33	4	.251	.293	.295
1996 Expos	R Mon	8	30	9	1	1	0	12	3	3	1	0	0	1	1	0	0	0	—	0	.300	.344	.400
Wst Plm Bch	A+ Mon	44	163	31	9	0	0	40	8	19	2	0	19	0	1	0	0	1	.00	1	.190	.200	.245
1997 Harrisburg	AA Mon	94	323	90	23	3	7	140	40	50	22	0	42	3	2	5	6	6	.50	10	.279	.326	.433
1998 Ottawa	AAA Mon	100	344	78	18	1	2	104	33	39	15	1	45	3	3	3	2	2	.50	13	.227	.263	.302
1999 Ottawa	AAA Mon	17	56	12	4	0	0	16	7	6	6	1	9	0	1	1	0	0	—	2	.214	.286	.286
Tucson	AAA Ari	35	102	27	4	0	1	34	10	11	3	0	10	0	0	1	1	0	1.00	5	.265	.286	.333
2000 El Paso	AA Ari	5	14	2	1	0	0	3	1	1	0	0	1	0	0	0	0	0	—	1	.143	.143	.214
Portland	AA Fla	97	323	94	19	0	3	122	35	57	22	0	41	2	5	4	0	4	.00	6	.291	.336	.378
8 Min. YEARS		602	2054	526	110	6	14	690	204	251	98	3	258	14	25	20	11	18	.38	54	.256	.292	.336

Juan Padilla

Pitches: Right Bats: Right Pos: RP-55   Ht: 6'0" Wt: 188 Born: 2/17/77 Age: 24

Year Team	Lg Org	G	GS	CG	GF	IP	BFP	H	R	ER	HR	SH	SF	HB	TBB	IBB	SO	WP	Bk	W	L	Pct.	ShO	Sv	ERA
1998 Twins	R Min	17	0	0	14	25.2	100	19	4	4	1	1	0	2	1	0	27	1	0	1	1	.500	0	10	1.40
1999 Quad City	A Min	12	0	0	4	15	69	18	8	4	0	0	1	0	6	2	16	4	1	0	2	.000	0	2	2.40
New Britain	AA Min	11	0	0	3	19	92	31	15	14	3	2	1	1	7	0	12	2	0	1	1	.500	0	2	6.63
Fort Myers	A+ Min	22	0	0	11	33.2	146	32	14	13	1	3	2	1	17	2	28	3	0	2	2	.500	0	0	3.48
2000 Quad City	A Min	32	0	0	27	33	133	24	7	7	0	3	0	1	9	2	40	1	0	2	2	.500	0	16	1.91
New Britain	AA Min	23	0	0	6	33.2	144	35	15	14	1	1	0	2	11	0	24	0	0	0	1	.000	0	0	3.74
3 Min. YEARS		117	0	0	65	160	684	159	63	56	6	10	4	7	51	6	147	11	1	6	9	.400	0	28	3.15

Roy Padilla

Pitches: Left Bats: Left Pos: RP-30   Ht: 6'5" Wt: 227 Born: 8/4/75 Age: 25

Year Team	Lg Org	G	GS	CG	GF	IP	BFP	H	R	ER	HR	SH	SF	HB	TBB	IBB	SO	WP	Bk	W	L	Pct.	ShO	Sv	ERA
1993 Red Sox	R Bos	13	1	0	3	30.2	130	25	10	8	0	0	2		17	0	18	5	0	0	1	.000	0	0	2.35
1994 Red Sox	R Bos	15	12	0	1	72.1	325	68	39	24	0	0	2	6	34	0	52	9	2	6	1	.857	0	1	2.99

Year Team	Lg Org	HOW MUCH HE PITCHED					WHAT HE GAVE UP								THE RESULTS					
		G	GS	CG	GF	IP	BFP	H	R	ER	HR	SH	SF	HB	TBB	IBB	SO	WP	Bk	W	L	Pct.	ShO	Sv	ERA
1995 Michigan	A Bos	4	1	0	2	8.1	46	10	9	6	0	0	1	3	7	0	7	2	0	0	1	.000	0	0	6.48
Butte	R+ Bos	15	14	0	0	70	340	80	60	46	1	2	4	7	54	0	49	11	0	2	7	.222	0	0	5.91
1999 Columbus	A Cle	30	0	0	11	59.2	263	53	27	20	3	0	2	10	27	0	56	9	0	2	2	.500	0	3	3.02
Kinston	A+ Cle	8	0	0	2	13	57	9	6	6	1	0	0	2	10	0	7	0	0	0	0	—	0	1	4.15
2000 Kinston	A+ Cle	14	0	0	4	23.2	110	14	21	13	0	0	1	4	21	0	32	4	0	1	1	.500	0	0	4.94
Akron	AA Cle	16	0	0	0	23.1	117	20	16	11	0	0	1	3	25	0	18	3	0	0	1	.000	0	0	4.24
5 Min. YEARS		115	28	0	23	301	1388	279	188	134	5	2	11	37	195	0	239	43	2	11	14	.440	0	5	4.01

Geraldo Padua

Pitches: Right **Bats:** Right **Pos:** SP-23; RP-3 **Ht:** 6'2" **Wt:** 165 **Born:** 2/9/77 **Age:** 24

Year Team	Lg Org	HOW MUCH HE PITCHED					WHAT HE GAVE UP								THE RESULTS					
		G	GS	CG	GF	IP	BFP	H	R	ER	HR	SH	SF	HB	TBB	IBB	SO	WP	Bk	W	L	Pct.	ShO	Sv	ERA
1997 Yankees	R NYY	11	8	1	1	61.2	237	46	24	20	5	2	0	1	8	0	36	5	1	8	0	1.000	1	0	2.92
1998 Oneonta	A- NYY	15	14	1	0	86	362	79	40	30	3	1	2	3	29	0	75	2	1	8	0	1.000	0	0	3.14
1999 Greensboro	A NYY	21	21	1	0	139.2	569	120	53	44	12	0	1	2	35	0	155	13	1	9	4	.692	1	0	2.84
Rancho Cuca	A+ SD	7	7	0	0	40.2	174	43	21	21	4	0	0	0	18	0	41	6	0	3	3	.500	0	0	4.65
2000 Altoona	AA Pit	9	9	0	0	41.1	202	59	42	32	3	3	1	2	20	0	31	3	0	1	6	.143	0	0	6.97
Lynchburg	A+ Pit	17	14	0	0	92	396	102	57	43	11	5	2	1	22	0	57	7	0	4	9	.308	0	0	4.21
4 Min. YEARS		80	73	2	3	461.1	1940	449	237	190	38	11	6	9	132	0	395	36	3	33	22	.600	2	0	3.71

Javier Pamus

Pitches: Right **Bats:** Right **Pos:** RP-35 **Ht:** 6'1" **Wt:** 195 **Born:** 2/11/75 **Age:** 26

Year Team	Lg Org	HOW MUCH HE PITCHED					WHAT HE GAVE UP								THE RESULTS					
		G	GS	CG	GF	IP	BFP	H	R	ER	HR	SH	SF	HB	TBB	IBB	SO	WP	Bk	W	L	Pct.	ShO	Sv	ERA
1998 Lansing	A KC	7	1	0	2	9	47	15	14	13	0	0	0	0	6	0	8	1	0	0	2	.000	0	0	13.00
Spokane	A- KC	12	4	0	0	36.1	169	40	30	21	2	1	1	3	16	1	33	3	1	2	1	.667	0	0	5.20
1999 Chston-WV	A KC	44	0	0	17	90.1	398	87	37	28	1	5	0	5	34	2	81	3	0	3	3	.500	0	4	2.79
2000 Wilmington	A+ KC	32	0	0	9	43.1	207	56	35	28	0	2	2	2	18	3	19	4	0	2	3	.400	0	0	5.82
Wichita	AA KC	3	0	0	1	5	19	5	1	1	0	0	0	0	1	0	1	0	0	0	0	—	0	0	1.80
3 Min. YEARS		98	5	0	29	184	840	203	117	91	3	8	3	10	75	6	142	11	1	7	9	.438	0	4	4.45

Christian Parker

Pitches: Right **Bats:** Right **Pos:** SP-28 **Ht:** 6'1" **Wt:** 200 **Born:** 7/3/75 **Age:** 25

Year Team	Lg Org	HOW MUCH HE PITCHED					WHAT HE GAVE UP								THE RESULTS					
		G	GS	CG	GF	IP	BFP	H	R	ER	HR	SH	SF	HB	TBB	IBB	SO	WP	Bk	W	L	Pct.	ShO	Sv	ERA
1996 Vermont	A- Mon	14	14	2	0	80	322	63	26	22	1	2	1	4	22	0	61	8	3	7	1	.875	1	0	2.48
1997 Cape Fear	A Mon	25	25	0	0	153	640	146	72	53	5	9	6	7	49	0	106	9	2	11	10	.524	0	0	3.12
Wst Plm Bch	A+ Mon	3	3	0	0	19	81	22	7	7	0	0	0	0	5	0	10	2	0	0	1	.000	0	0	3.32
1998 Harrisburg	AA Mon	36	16	0	8	126.2	550	124	66	49	9	6	2	10	47	3	73	8	0	6	6	.500	0	5	3.48
1999 Ottawa	AAA Mon	7	0	0	2	10.2	49	10	9	9	0	1	1	2	7	0	5	0	0	0	1	.000	0	0	7.59
Harrisburg	AA Mon	36	6	0	16	88.2	386	86	39	36	11	5	0	15	37	2	45	10	2	8	5	.615	0	3	3.65
2000 Norwich	AA NYY	28	28	4	0	204	860	196	86	71	8	11	6	9	58	5	147	8	5	14	6	.700	0	0	3.13
5 Min. YEARS		149	92	6	26	682	2888	647	305	247	34	34	16	47	225	10	447	45	12	46	30	.605	1	8	3.26

Chad Paronto

Pitches: Right **Bats:** Right **Pos:** SP-14; RP-6 **Ht:** 6'5" **Wt:** 255 **Born:** 7/28/75 **Age:** 25

Year Team	Lg Org	HOW MUCH HE PITCHED					WHAT HE GAVE UP								THE RESULTS					
		G	GS	CG	GF	IP	BFP	H	R	ER	HR	SH	SF	HB	TBB	IBB	SO	WP	Bk	W	L	Pct.	ShO	Sv	ERA
1996 Frederick	A+ Bal	8	1	0	2	15	63	11	9	8	0	2	0	0	8	0	6	2	0	0	1	.000	0	0	4.80
Bluefield	R+ Bal	9	2	0	1	21.1	82	16	4	4	0	0	0	0	5	0	24	0	1	1	1	.500	0	1	1.69
1997 Delmarva	A Bal	28	23	0	2	127.1	569	133	95	67	9	5	5	1	56	1	93	6	0	6	9	.400	0	0	4.74
1998 Frederick	A+ Bal	18	18	0	0	103.2	451	116	44	36	4	3	2	3	39	0	87	8	0	7	6	.538	0	0	3.13
Bowie	AA Bal	8	7	0	1	35.2	165	38	30	23	1	0	1	3	23	0	28	4	0	1	3	.250	0	1	5.80
1999 Bowie	AA Bal	15	9	0	0	41	209	59	39	37	3	1	1	4	32	1	27	3	0	0	4	.000	0	0	8.12
Frederick	A+ Bal	13	13	1	0	72.1	323	81	46	38	7	2	1	5	26	1	55	2	0	3	5	.375	0	0	4.73
2000 Bowie	AA Bal	8	8	1	0	47	183	29	19	15	2	1	2	2	16	0	31	0	0	4	2	.667	0	0	2.87
Rochester	AAA Bal	12	6	0	2	36	162	40	26	23	5	2	3	1	15	0	18	2	0	1	1	.500	0	0	5.75
5 Min. YEARS		119	87	2	8	499.1	2207	523	312	251	31	14	15	19	220	3	369	27	1	23	32	.418	0	2	4.52

Bronswell Patrick

Pitches: Right **Bats:** Right **Pos:** SP-23; RP-4 **Ht:** 6'1" **Wt:** 237 **Born:** 9/16/70 **Age:** 30

Year Team	Lg Org	HOW MUCH HE PITCHED					WHAT HE GAVE UP								THE RESULTS					
		G	GS	CG	GF	IP	BFP	H	R	ER	HR	SH	SF	HB	TBB	IBB	SO	WP	Bk	W	L	Pct.	ShO	Sv	ERA
1988 Athletics	R Oak	14	13	2	0	96.1	390	99	37	32	7	1	2	2	16	1	64	1	2	8	3	.727	0	0	2.99
1989 Madison	A Oak	12	10	0	1	54.1	238	62	29	22	3	2	0	0	14	0	32	3	2	2	5	.286	0	0	3.64
1990 Modesto	A+ Oak	14	14	0	0	74.2	340	92	58	43	10	3	1	4	32	0	37	5	1	3	7	.300	0	0	5.18
Madison	A Oak	13	12	3	0	80	337	88	44	32	6	5	4	1	19	0	40	3	0	3	7	.300	0	0	3.60
1991 Modesto	A+ Oak	28	26	3	1	169.2	716	158	77	61	9	4	4	1	60	4	95	7	0	12	12	.500	1	0	3.24
1992 Huntsville	AA Oak	29	29	3	0	179.1	758	187	84	75	20	1	3	4	46	0	98	3	0	13	7	.650	0	0	3.76
1993 Tacoma	AAA Oak	35	13	1	12	104.2	496	156	87	82	12	3	12	4	42	3	56	3	0	3	8	.273	0	1	7.05
1994 Huntsville	AA Oak	7	3	0	1	27.2	120	31	11	9	2	1	0	2	10	0	16	1	1	2	0	1.000	0	1	2.93
Tacoma	AAA Oak	30	0	0	9	47.1	208	50	31	25	5	3	1	0	20	2	38	2	0	1	5	.500	0	2	4.75
1995 Tucson	AAA Hou	43	4	0	10	81.2	352	91	42	38	3	2	3	1	21	1	62	4	0	5	1	.833	0	1	4.19
1996 Tucson	AAA Hou	33	15	0	2	118	521	137	59	46	7	1	14	0	33	4	82	1	0	7	3	.700	0	1	3.51
1997 New Orleans	AAA Hou	30	12	1	10	100.2	426	108	45	36	10	6	2	0	30	4	88	5	0	6	5	.545	1	0	3.22
1998 Louisville	AAA Mil	6	6	0	0	37.2	167	43	21	18	6	0	1	1	9	0	25	3	0	3	1	.750	0	0	4.30
1999 Fresno	AAA SF	28	28	1	0	164	719	194	116	89	33	5	5	3	42	0	142	6	1	14	11	.560	0	0	4.88
2000 Calgary	AAA Fla	27	23	0	1	128.1	595	174	114	101	18	8	4	3	42	0	72	1	0	5	12	.294	0	0	7.08

Year Team	Lg Org	G	GS	CG	GF	IP	BFP	H	R	ER	HR	SH	SF	HB	TBB	IBB	SO	WP	Bk	W	L	Pct.	ShO	Sv	ERA
1998 Milwaukee	NL	32	3	0	8	78.2	334	83	43	41	9	4	3	0	29	1	49	2	0	4	1	.800	0	0	4.69
1999 San Francisco	NL	6	0	0	2	5.1	28	9	7	6	1	0	1	0	3	0	6	0	0	0	1	1.000	0	0	10.13
13 Min. YEARS		349	208	14	47	1464.1	6383	1670	855	709	151	45	56	26	436	19	950	44	7	87	83	.512	2	6	4.36
2 Maj. YEARS		38	3	0	10	84	362	92	50	47	10	4	4	0	32	1	55	2	0	5	1	.833	0	1	5.04

Jarrod Patterson

Bats: Left **Throws:** Right **Pos:** 3B-92; PH-16; DH-2; C-1; 1B-1 **Ht:** 6'1" **Wt:** 195 **Born:** 9/7/73 **Age:** 27

Year Team	Lg Org	G	AB	H	2B	3B	HR	TB	R	RBI	TBB	IBB	SO	HBP	SH	SF	SB	CS	SB%	GDP	Avg	OBP	SLG
1993 Mets	R NYM	46	166	40	9	1	2	57	27	25	24	1	28	0	1	4	1	3	.25	5	.241	.330	.343
1994 Kingsport	R+ NYM	36	112	29	5	2	5	53	12	18	12	2	39	1	0	0	2	0	1.00	1	.259	.336	.473
Pittsfield	A- NYM	29	106	19	6	1	1	30	8	15	10	0	34	0	0	2	0	1	.00	1	.179	.246	.283
1995 Kingsport	R+ NYM	64	240	67	17	3	13	129	45	57	28	2	50	0	0	3	3	1	.75	2	.279	.351	.538
1996 St. Lucie	A+ NYM	17	61	11	2	0	1	16	6	6	3	0	19	1	0	1	1	0	1.00	0	.180	.227	.262
Capital Cty	A NYM	70	213	49	9	1	3	69	26	37	33	3	65	2	0	4	1	1	.50	3	.230	.333	.324
1997 Regina	IND —	65	240	87	24	2	7	136	52	50	38	2	47	2	2	1	7	3	.70	1	.363	.452	.567
1998 High Desert	A+ Ari	131	492	165	34	9	18	271	89	102	66	4	97	2	0	3	9	2	.82	8	.335	.414	.551
1999 El Paso	AA Ari	67	249	95	27	3	8	152	63	51	51	6	45	1	0	3	3	2	.60	3	.382	.484	.610
Tucson	AAA Ari	75	274	92	25	3	11	156	46	47	36	0	37	3	0	3	4	1	.80	3	.336	.415	.569
2000 Altoona	AA Pit	11	36	5	1	0	0	6	1	4	3	0	11	1	0	1	0	0	—	1	.139	.220	.167
Nashville	AAA Pit	70	198	55	10	0	5	80	25	30	13	0	40	2	2	2	0	2	.00	2	.278	.326	.404
Ottawa	AAA Mon	25	92	25	6	1	0	33	9	16	4	0	13	0	0	0	1	0	1.00	4	.272	.302	.359
8 Min. YEARS		706	2479	739	175	26	74	1188	409	458	321	20	525	15	5	27	32	16	.67	40	.298	.378	.479

John Patterson

Pitches: Right **Bats:** Right **Pos:** SP-2; RP-1 **Ht:** 6'5" **Wt:** 183 **Born:** 1/30/78 **Age:** 23

Year Team	Lg Org	G	GS	CG	GF	IP	BFP	H	R	ER	HR	SH	SF	HB	TBB	IBB	SO	WP	Bk	W	L	Pct.	ShO	Sv	ERA
1997 South Bend	A Ari	18	18	0	0	78	327	63	32	28	3	1	2	5	34	0	95	8	0	1	9	.100	0	0	3.23
1998 High Desert	A+ Ari	25	25	0	0	127	519	102	54	40	12	0	3	4	42	0	148	5	0	8	7	.533	0	0	2.83
1999 El Paso	AA Ari	18	18	2	0	100	429	98	61	53	16	3	1	0	42	0	117	3	0	8	6	.571	0	0	4.77
Tucson	AAA Ari	7	6	0	0	30.2	148	43	26	24	3	0	0	0	18	0	29	0	0	1	5	.167	0	0	7.04
2000 Tucson	AAA Ari	3	2	0	0	15	76	21	14	13	1	1	1	0	9	0	10	2	0	0	2	.000	0	0	7.80
4 Min. YEARS		71	69	2	0	350.2	1499	327	187	158	35	5	7	9	145	0	399	18	0	18	29	.383	0	0	4.06

Jeff Patzke

Bats: Both **Throws:** Right **Pos:** SS-41; 3B-24; 2B-9; PR-2; PH-1 **Ht:** 6'0" **Wt:** 190 **Born:** 11/19/73 **Age:** 27

Year Team	Lg Org	G	AB	H	2B	3B	HR	TB	R	RBI	TBB	IBB	SO	HBP	SH	SF	SB	CS	SB%	GDP	Avg	OBP	SLG
1992 Blue Jays	R Tor	6	21	2	0	0	0	2	3	1	3	0	2	0	0	0	0	1	.00	0	.095	.208	.095
Medcine Hat	R+ Tor	59	193	42	4	0	2	52	19	17	17	0	42	0	3	0	3	1	.75	4	.218	.281	.269
1993 Medcine Hat	R+ Tor	71	273	80	11	2	1	98	45	22	34	1	31	2	3	1	5	7	.42	5	.293	.374	.359
1994 Hagerstown	A Tor	80	271	55	10	1	4	79	43	22	36	1	57	3	2	3	7	3	.70	3	.203	.300	.292
1995 Dunedin	A+ Tor	129	470	124	32	6	11	201	68	75	85	8	81	2	1	2	5	3	.63	10	.264	.377	.428
1996 Knoxville	AA Tor	124	429	130	31	4	4	181	70	66	80	6	103	6	0	2	6	5	.55	2	.303	.418	.422
1997 Syracuse	AAA Tor	96	316	90	25	2	2	125	38	29	51	3	66	1	3	2	0	3	.00	4	.285	.384	.396
1998 Dunedin	A+ Tor	20	62	18	0	0	0	18	10	4	9	0	18	0	0	0	0	1	.00	0	.290	.380	.290
Nashville	AAA Pit	104	361	108	16	0	7	145	48	48	48	0	74	9	2	1	5	6	.45	6	.299	.394	.402
1999 Altoona	AA Pit	53	198	59	12	1	2	79	31	25	33	1	45	2	0	2	4	2	.67	4	.298	.400	.399
Nashville	AAA Pit	59	173	38	5	1	2	51	20	14	32	1	29	2	1	2	2	3	.40	2	.220	.344	.295
2000 Akron	AA Cle	7	19	6	0	0	0	6	8	2	11	0	5	0	0	0	1	1	.50	1	.316	.567	.316
Buffalo	AAA Cle	69	210	52	14	2	2	76	35	18	34	0	57	1	3	2	4	1	.80	4	.248	.352	.362
9 Min. YEARS		877	2996	804	160	19	37	1113	438	343	473	21	610	28	18	17	42	37	.53	45	.268	.371	.371

Dave Pavlas

Pitches: Right **Bats:** Right **Pos:** RP-45 **Ht:** 6'7" **Wt:** 205 **Born:** 8/12/62 **Age:** 38

Year Team	Lg Org	G	GS	CG	GF	IP	BFP	H	R	ER	HR	SH	SF	HB	TBB	IBB	SO	WP	Bk	W	L	Pct.	ShO	Sv	ERA
1985 Peoria	A ChC	17	15	3	2	110	452	90	40	32	7	3	1	3	32	0	86	6	1	8	3	.727	1	1	2.62
1986 Winston-Sal	A+ ChC	28	26	5	0	173.1	739	172	91	74	8	6	4	6	57	2	143	11	1	14	6	.700	2	0	3.84
1987 Pittsfield	AA ChC	7	7	0	0	45	199	49	25	19	6	0	3	3	17	0	27	1	1	6	1	.857	0	0	3.80
Tulsa	AA Tex	13	12	0	0	59.2	280	79	51	51	9	1	0	3	27	0	46	7	0	1	6	.143	0	0	7.69
1988 Tulsa	AA Tex	26	5	1	9	77.1	299	52	26	17	3	6	2	5	18	1	69	4	6	5	2	.714	0	2	1.98
Okla City	AAA Tex	13	8	0	2	52.1	237	59	29	26	1	1	2	3	28	0	40	2	1	3	1	.750	0	0	4.47
1989 Okla City	AAA Tex	29	21	4	4	143.2	652	175	89	75	7	6	7	7	67	4	94	8	1	2	14	.125	0	0	4.70
1990 Iowa	AAA ChC	53	3	0	22	99.1	421	84	38	36	4	4	3	10	48	6	96	8	1	8	3	.727	0	8	3.26
1991 Iowa	AAA ChC	61	0	0	19	97.1	418	92	49	43	5	10	5	5	43	9	54	13	0	5	6	.455	0	7	3.98
1992 Iowa	AAA ChC	12	4	0	6	37.1	166	43	20	14	5	2	0	1	8	0	34	0	0	3	3	.500	0	0	3.38
1995 Columbus	AAA NYY	48	0	0	32	58.2	233	43	19	17	2	4	1	1	20	2	51	4	0	3	3	.500	0	18	2.61
1996 Columbus	AAA NYY	57	0	0	46	77	306	64	20	17	5	1	0	1	13	1	65	3	0	8	2	.800	0	26	1.99
1997 Columbus	AAA NYY	26	0	0	25	25.1	116	33	14	13	3	2	1	1	4	2	34	0	0	1	3	.250	0	12	4.62
1998 Tucson	AAA Ari	9	0	0	2	8.1	46	15	11	8	3	0	1	1	5	1	8	0	0	2	0	.000	0	1	8.64
Edmonton	AAA Oak	26	3	0	10	58	239	51	23	20	4	0	3	1	12	1	41	2	0	2	2	.500	0	1	3.10
1999 Columbus	AAA NYY	38	2	0	13	62.1	256	69	32	28	5	0	3	2	9	1	49	1	0	4	2	.667	0	1	4.04
2000 Nashville	AAA Pit	45	0	0	17	71.2	311	71	36	28	8	7	3	4	23	3	61	2	0	4	2	.667	0	5	3.39
1990 Chicago	NL	13	0	0	3	21.1	93	23	7	5	2	0	2	0	6	2	12	3	0	2	0	1.000	0	0	2.11
1991 Chicago	NL	1	0	0	1	1	5	3	2	2	1	1	0	0	0	0	0	0	0	0	0	—	0	0	18.00
1995 New York	AL	4	0	0	1	5.2	24	8	2	2	0	0	0	0	0	0	3	0	0	0	0	—	0	0	3.18
1996 New York	AL	16	0	0	8	23	97	23	7	6	0	4	0	1	7	2	14	3	0	0	0	—	0	0	2.35
14 Min. YEARS		508	106	13	226	1256.2	5370	1241	613	517	85	53	39	55	431	33	998	72	12	77	61	.558	3	82	3.70
4 Maj. YEARS		34	0	0	13	51	219	57	18	15	3	3	2	1	13	4	33	6	0	2	0	1.000	0	0	2.65

Rich Paz

Bats: Right **Throws:** Right **Pos:** 2B-93; 3B-11; SS-9; DH-7 **Ht:** 5'8" **Wt:** 172 **Born:** 7/30/77 **Age:** 23

Year Team	Lg Org	G	AB	H	2B	3B	HR	TB	R	RBI	TBB	IBB	SO	HBP	SH	SF	SB	CS	SB%	GDP	Avg	OBP	SLG
1996 High Desert	A+ Bal	7	17	3	1	0	0	4	2	0	1	0	4	0	2	0	0	0	—	1	.176	.222	.235
Bluefield	R+ Bal	50	170	50	7	0	1	60	42	21	42	0	24	3	1	4	9	4	.69	1	.294	.434	.353
1997 Delmarva	A Bal	111	389	94	14	4	2	122	60	48	38	1	60	5	15	4	15	5	.75	8	.242	.314	.314
1998 Delmarva	A Bal	98	325	104	10	4	5	137	55	56	75	2	42	8	2	5	22	7	.76	6	.320	.453	.422
Frederick	A+ Bal	40	143	35	10	0	3	54	31	8	21	0	22	4	3	0	6	3	.67	3	.245	.357	.378
1999 Frederick	A+ Bal	54	163	41	9	0	0	50	27	18	47	0	27	2	3	5	15	6	.71	2	.252	.415	.307
Bowie	AA Bal	79	273	78	12	2	2	100	39	20	51	0	35	6	8	2	11	3	.79	4	.286	.407	.366
2000 Frederick	A+ Bal	79	268	82	13	0	4	107	53	45	71	0	47	3	6	6	15	8	.65	5	.306	.448	.399
Bowie	AA Bal	40	137	39	9	3	1	57	18	17	27	0	28	2	4	1	3	2	.60	0	.285	.407	.416
5 Min. YEARS		558	1885	526	85	13	18	691	327	233	373	3	289	33	44	27	96	38	.72	30	.279	.402	.367

Josh Pearce

Pitches: Right **Bats:** Right **Pos:** SP-27 **Ht:** 6'3" **Wt:** 215 **Born:** 8/20/77 **Age:** 23

| | | HOW MUCH HE PITCHED | | | | | | WHAT HE GAVE UP | | | | | | | | | | | | THE RESULTS | | | | | |
Year Team	Lg Org	G	GS	CG	GF	IP	BFP	H	R	ER	HR	SH	SF	HB	TBB	IBB	SO	WP	Bk	W	L	Pct.	ShO	Sv	ERA
1999 New Jersey	A- StL	14	14	1	0	77.2	336	78	45	43	8	2	6	5	20	0	78	14	1	3	7	.300	1	0	4.98
2000 Potomac	A+ StL	10	10	1	0	62.2	259	70	25	24	5	0	1	1	10	0	42	0	0	5	3	.625	0	0	3.45
Arkansas	AA StL	17	17	0	0	97.1	441	117	68	59	13	6	2	6	35	2	63	5	1	5	6	.455	0	0	5.46
2 Min. YEARS		41	41	2	0	237.2	1036	265	138	126	26	8	9	12	65	2	183	19	2	13	16	.448	1	0	4.77

J.J. Pearsall

Pitches: Left **Bats:** Left **Pos:** RP-50 **Ht:** 6'2" **Wt:** 202 **Born:** 9/9/73 **Age:** 27

| | | HOW MUCH HE PITCHED | | | | | | WHAT HE GAVE UP | | | | | | | | | | | | THE RESULTS | | | | | |
Year Team	Lg Org	G	GS	CG	GF	IP	BFP	H	R	ER	HR	SH	SF	HB	TBB	IBB	SO	WP	Bk	W	L	Pct.	ShO	Sv	ERA
1995 San Berndno	A+ LA	6	0	0	2	10.2	54	15	10	10	3	3	0	0	7	0	5	1	0	0	1	.000	0	0	8.44
Yakima	A- LA	20	1	0	8	38.2	167	39	18	14	1	1	2	2	14	0	26	5	0	2	3	.400	0	1	3.26
1996 Savannah	A LA	45	2	0	13	87.2	394	76	48	32	6	3	2	7	46	3	88	8	3	6	5	.545	0	3	3.29
1997 San Berndno	A+ LA	31	28	0	1	160.2	696	145	91	81	12	4	4	8	93	0	112	9	2	14	11	.560	0	0	4.54
1998 San Antonio	AA LA	46	4	0	11	72	320	71	38	35	8	0	2	2	37	2	63	5	0	6	5	.545	0	4	4.38
Albuquerque	AAA LA	8	0	0	4	13	62	16	10	9	1	1	1	1	8	0	8	1	1	1	1	.500	0	1	6.23
1999 San Antonio	AA LA	10	0	0	3	16	75	14	11	8	1	0	1	1	8	0	13	0	0	0	0	—	0	0	4.50
Chattanooga	AA Cin	32	0	0	7	39.2	184	40	31	26	5	0	1	0	28	3	36	2	0	3	1	.750	0	0	5.90
2000 Chattanooga	AA Cin	22	0	0	10	18.1	88	18	16	14	5	1	1	0	15	2	23	1	1	4	1	.800	0	1	6.87
Tulsa	AA Tex	28	0	0	10	43.1	197	40	22	16	3	4	0	6	20	1	37	1	0	4	1	1.000	0	3	3.32
6 Min. YEARS		248	35	0	69	500	2237	474	295	245	45	17	14	28	276	11	411	33	6	40	28	.588	0	9	4.41

Eddie Pearson

Bats: Both **Throws:** Right **Pos:** 1B-45; DH-16; PH-13 **Ht:** 6'3" **Wt:** 225 **Born:** 1/31/74 **Age:** 27

Year Team	Lg Org	G	AB	H	2B	3B	HR	TB	R	RBI	TBB	IBB	SO	HBP	SH	SF	SB	CS	SB%	GDP	Avg	OBP	SLG
1992 White Sox	R CWS	28	102	24	5	0	0	29	10	12	9	1	17	2	0	1	1	3	.25	3	.235	.307	.284
1993 Hickory	A CWS	87	343	83	15	3	4	116	37	40	20	0	59	1	5	1	5	1	.83	8	.242	.285	.338
South Bend	A CWS	48	190	62	16	0	1	81	23	26	13	2	29	1	0	3	0	1	.00	1	.326	.367	.426
1994 Pr William	A+ CWS	130	502	139	28	3	12	209	58	80	45	1	80	3	0	0	0	0	—	11	.277	.338	.416
1995 White Sox	R CWS	6	20	6	2	0	1	11	7	6	3	0	2	0	0	0	0	0	—	0	.300	.391	.550
Birmingham	AA CWS	50	201	45	13	0	2	64	20	25	7	0	36	1	0	2	1	0	1.00	9	.224	.251	.318
1996 Birmingham	AA CWS	85	323	72	20	0	8	116	38	40	31	3	57	2	0	3	2	2	.50	6	.223	.292	.359
1997 Birmingham	AA CWS	95	382	125	33	1	5	175	59	59	23	1	50	2	0	3	1	1	.50	13	.327	.366	.458
Nashville	AAA CWS	41	148	33	4	0	4	49	17	16	6	1	23	0	1	1	1	1	.50	3	.223	.252	.331
1998 Calgary	AAA CWS	99	354	103	21	1	7	147	32	53	22	5	63	1	0	5	1	2	.33	13	.291	.330	.415
2000 Arkansas	AA StL	74	257	77	15	0	10	122	28	38	22	6	34	1	0	0	0	0	—	12	.300	.355	.475
8 Min. YEARS		743	2822	769	172	8	54	1119	329	395	201	20	450	14	6	24	12	11	.52	79	.273	.321	.397

Jay Pecci

Bats: Both **Throws:** Right **Pos:** 2B-117; SS-12; PH-3; PR-3 **Ht:** 5'11" **Wt:** 185 **Born:** 9/26/76 **Age:** 24

Year Team	Lg Org	G	AB	H	2B	3B	HR	TB	R	RBI	TBB	IBB	SO	HBP	SH	SF	SB	CS	SB%	GDP	Avg	OBP	SLG
1998 Sou Oregon	A- Oak	39	130	38	2	0	0	40	21	14	22	0	22	4	1	1	3	4	.43	0	.292	.408	.308
Modesto	A+ Oak	21	73	23	2	1	1	30	9	6	4	0	11	1	2	0	2	1	.67	1	.315	.359	.411
1999 Visalia	A+ Oak	119	377	95	14	2	1	116	60	43	42	0	56	10	7	1	12	7	.63	9	.252	.342	.308
2000 Visalia	A+ Oak	26	102	38	9	0	3	56	21	23	15	2	12	2	0	1	6	4	.60	3	.373	.458	.549
Midland	AA Oak	102	353	87	15	3	2	114	52	36	44	1	50	15	4	5	5	7	.42	13	.246	.350	.323
3 Min. YEARS		307	1035	281	42	6	7	356	163	122	127	3	151	32	14	8	28	23	.55	26	.271	.366	.344

Mike Peeples

Bats: Right **Throws:** Right **Pos:** OF-52; 3B-41; 2B-31; PH-3; DH-2; PR-1 **Ht:** 6'0" **Wt:** 175 **Born:** 9/3/76 **Age:** 24

Year Team	Lg Org	G	AB	H	2B	3B	HR	TB	R	RBI	TBB	IBB	SO	HBP	SH	SF	SB	CS	SB%	GDP	Avg	OBP	SLG
1994 Blue Jays	R Tor	47	172	40	5	3	0	51	22	11	13	1	25	4	3	2	17	5	.77	0	.233	.298	.297
1995 Medcine Hat	R+ Tor	72	285	89	14	4	3	120	55	50	35	1	46	5	2	3	27	5	.84	14	.312	.393	.421
1996 Hagerstown	A Tor	74	268	63	15	1	3	89	30	31	37	0	55	3	4	3	15	5	.75	5	.235	.331	.332
1997 Dunedin	A+ Tor	129	477	122	29	2	2	161	73	42	54	1	83	3	9	7	26	16	.62	8	.256	.331	.338
1998 Knoxville	AA Tor	113	395	99	16	3	7	142	58	42	36	0	62	2	17	3	20	10	.67	5	.251	.314	.359
1999 Dunedin	A+ Tor	132	541	156	34	6	20	262	100	68	49	1	80	7	5	5	20	11	.65	7	.288	.352	.484
2000 Tennessee	AA Tor	123	475	133	26	4	18	221	70	73	46	1	71	7	9	4	11	8	.58	14	.280	.350	.465
7 Min. YEARS		690	2613	702	139	23	53	1046	408	317	270	5	422	31	49	27	136	60	.69	53	.269	.341	.400

Alex Pelaez

Bats: Right **Throws:** Right **Pos:** 3B-97; 2B-13; 1B-11; DH-4; PH-4; PR-1 **Ht:** 5'9" **Wt:** 190 **Born:** 4/6/76 **Age:** 25

Year Team	Lg Org	G	AB	H	2B	3B	HR	TB	R	RBI	TBB	IBB	SO	HBP	SH	SF	SB	CS	SB%	GDP	Avg	OBP	SLG
1998 Idaho Falls	R+ SD	63	262	89	17	1	8	132	52	51	29	0	32	1	0	2	3	1	.75	10	.340	.405	.504
1999 Las Vegas	AAA SD	5	13	4	0	0	0	4	1	0	0	0	2	0	0	0	0	0	—	1	.308	.308	.308
Rancho Cuca	A+ SD	117	443	132	21	4	4	173	62	54	35	3	53	1	1	2	7	3	.70	24	.298	.349	.391
2000 Rancho Cuca	A+ SD	62	235	66	20	0	2	92	29	28	23	0	27	0	0	4	2	2	.50	11	.281	.340	.391
Las Vegas	AAA SD	34	108	27	3	0	1	33	13	15	4	1	20	1	5	1	0	0	—	2	.250	.281	.306
Mobile	AA SD	28	90	24	3	0	2	33	8	11	10	0	15	0	0	1	0	0	—	5	.267	.337	.367
3 Min. YEARS		309	1151	342	64	5	17	467	165	159	101	4	149	3	6	10	12	6	.67	53	.297	.353	.406

Kit Pellow

Bats: Right **Throws:** Right **Pos:** 1B-116; DH-1; PR-1 **Ht:** 6'1" **Wt:** 205 **Born:** 8/28/73 **Age:** 27

Year Team	Lg Org	G	AB	H	2B	3B	HR	TB	R	RBI	TBB	IBB	SO	HBP	SH	SF	SB	CS	SB%	GDP	Avg	OBP	SLG
1996 Spokane	A- KC	71	279	80	18	2	18	156	48	66	20	0	52	8	1	7	8	3	.73	5	.287	.344	.559
1997 Lansing	A KC	65	256	76	17	2	11	130	39	52	24	1	74	6	0	4	2	0	1.00	5	.297	.366	.508
Wichita	AA KC	68	241	60	12	1	10	104	40	41	21	1	72	2	2	3	5	2	.71	5	.249	.311	.432
1998 Wichita	AA KC	103	374	100	24	3	29	217	70	73	27	2	107	6	1	3	4	3	.57	2	.267	.324	.580
Omaha	AAA KC	14	54	10	3	0	2	19	8	6	2	0	19	0	0	2	2	0	1.00	1	.185	.207	.352
1999 Omaha	AAA KC	131	475	136	28	4	35	277	88	99	20	3	117	18	1	7	6	5	.55	11	.286	.335	.583
2000 Omaha	AAA KC	117	421	105	17	3	22	194	61	75	38	1	89	16	1	5	6	4	.60	5	.249	.331	.461
5 Min. YEARS		569	2100	567	119	15	127	1097	354	412	152	8	530	56	6	31	33	17	.66	34	.270	.331	.522

Angel Pena

Bats: Right **Throws:** Right **Pos:** C-64; 1B-18; PH-5; DH-3; 3B-1 **Ht:** 5'10" **Wt:** 228 **Born:** 2/16/75 **Age:** 26

Year Team	Lg Org	G	AB	H	2B	3B	HR	TB	R	RBI	TBB	IBB	SO	HBP	SH	SF	SB	CS	SB%	GDP	Avg	OBP	SLG
1995 Great Falls	R+ LA	49	138	40	11	1	4	65	24	15	21	2	32	3	0	3	2	1	.67	5	.290	.388	.471
1996 Savannah	A LA	36	127	26	4	0	6	48	13	16	7	1	37	0	1	0	1	1	.50	1	.205	.246	.378
1997 San Berndno	A+ LA	86	322	89	22	4	16	167	53	64	32	4	84	2	0	2	3	5	.38	9	.276	.344	.519
1998 San Antonio	AA LA	126	483	162	32	2	22	264	81	105	48	3	80	6	3	2	9	5	.64	7	.335	.401	.547
1999 Albuquerque	AAA LA	34	127	37	10	1	1	52	15	24	10	0	24	0	0	2	3	2	.60	1	.291	.343	.409
2000 Albuquerque	AAA LA	87	315	97	12	3	17	166	52	61	28	0	75	0	1	2	3	1	.75	4	.308	.362	.527
1998 Los Angeles	NL	6	13	3	0	0	0	3	1	0	0	0	6	0	0	0	0	0	—	0	.231	.231	.231
1999 Los Angeles	NL	43	120	25	6	0	4	43	14	21	12	0	24	0	1	2	0	1	.00	6	.208	.276	.358
6 Min. YEARS		418	1512	451	91	11	66	762	238	285	146	10	332	11	5	9	21	15	.58	27	.298	.362	.504
2 Maj. YEARS		49	133	28	6	0	4	46	15	21	12	0	30	0	1	2	0	1	.00	6	.211	.272	.346

Carlos Pena

Bats: Left **Throws:** Left **Pos:** 1B-136; DH-2 **Ht:** 6'2" **Wt:** 210 **Born:** 5/17/78 **Age:** 23

Year Team	Lg Org	G	AB	H	2B	3B	HR	TB	R	RBI	TBB	IBB	SO	HBP	SH	SF	SB	CS	SB%	GDP	Avg	OBP	SLG
1998 Rangers	R Tex	2	5	2	0	0	0	2	1	0	3	0	1	0	0	0	1	1	.50	0	.400	.625	.400
Savannah	A Tex	30	117	38	14	0	6	70	22	20	8	0	26	4	0	1	3	2	.60	0	.325	.385	.598
Charlotte	A+ Tex	7	22	6	1	0	0	7	1	3	2	0	8	1	0	0	0	1	.00	0	.273	.360	.318
1999 Charlotte	A+ Tex	136	501	128	31	8	18	229	85	103	74	2	135	16	0	6	2	5	.29	7	.255	.365	.457
2000 Tulsa	AA Tex	138	529	158	36	4	28	282	117	105	101	10	108	9	1	8	12	0	1.00	7	.299	.414	.533
3 Min. YEARS		313	1174	332	82	10	52	590	226	231	188	12	278	30	1	15	18	9	.67	14	.283	.391	.503

Tyrone Pendergrass

Bats: Both **Throws:** Right **Pos:** OF-111; PH-3; DH-1; PR-1 **Ht:** 6'1" **Wt:** 180 **Born:** 7/31/76 **Age:** 24

Year Team	Lg Org	G	AB	H	2B	3B	HR	TB	R	RBI	TBB	IBB	SO	HBP	SH	SF	SB	CS	SB%	GDP	Avg	OBP	SLG
1995 Braves	R Atl	52	188	34	4	0	1	41	19	7	15	0	51	1	0	0	28	4	.67	5	.181	.245	.218
1996 Danville	R+ Atl	54	220	68	8	7	3	99	50	23	24	0	39	4	2	2	40	6	.87	4	.309	.384	.450
Macon	A Atl	12	45	12	1	1	1	18	8	3	4	0	12	1	0	0	5	3	.63	0	.267	.340	.400
1997 Macon	A Atl	127	489	127	16	5	6	171	81	37	60	0	101	4	3	3	70	15	.82	5	.260	.344	.350
1998 Danville	A+ Atl	132	518	143	23	10	4	198	74	35	40	0	91	7	5	1	39	18	.68	7	.276	.339	.382
Greenville	AA Atl	5	16	2	0	0	0	2	3	0	2	0	4	0	0	0	1	0	1.00	0	.125	.222	.125
1999 Greenville	AA Atl	100	344	90	12	3	6	126	60	31	37	0	61	2	5	3	19	14	.58	3	.262	.334	.366
2000 Richmond	AAA Atl	115	407	84	14	3	0	104	47	32	47	1	83	4	5	3	13	7	.65	6	.206	.289	.256
6 Min. YEARS		597	2227	560	78	29	21	759	342	168	232	1	442	23	25	12	195	67	.74	30	.251	.327	.341

Mike Penney

Pitches: Right **Bats:** Right **Pos:** RP-37; SP-13 **Ht:** 6'1" **Wt:** 190 **Born:** 3/29/77 **Age:** 24

Year Team	Lg Org	G	GS	CG	GF	IP	BFP	H	R	ER	HR	SH	SF	HB	TBB	IBB	SO	WP	Bk	W	L	Pct.	ShO	Sv	ERA
1998 Helena	R+ Mil	10	10	0	0	46.1	217	63	44	38	8	1	4	2	20	0	36	4	1	1	5	.167	0	0	7.38
1999 Beloit	A Mil	27	27	4	0	170	740	171	94	80	16	2	3	7	70	2	109	11	2	9	12	.429	2	0	4.24
2000 Mudville	A+ Mil	13	13	0	0	66.2	287	63	31	24	3	2	4	6	28	0	45	6	0	2	4	.333	0	0	3.24
Huntsville	AA Mil	20	0	0	11	20.1	83	19	7	6	0	0	0	1	6	0	22	4	0	1	0	.000	0	7	2.66
Indianapols	AAA Mil	17	0	0	10	18.1	80	16	9	7	2	2	0	0	10	1	13	1	0	1	1	.500	0	1	3.44
3 Min. YEARS		87	50	4	21	321.2	1407	332	188	155	29	7	11	16	134	3	225	26	3	13	23	.361	2	8	4.34

Danny Peoples

Bats: Right **Throws:** Right **Pos:** 1B-112; DH-12; PH-1   **Ht:** 6'1" **Wt:** 225 **Born:** 1/20/75 **Age:** 26

Year Team	Lg Org	G	AB	H	2B	3B	HR	TB	R	RBI	TBB	IBB	SO	HBP	SH	SF	SB	CS	SB%	GDP	Avg	OBP	SLG
1996 Watertown	A- Cle	35	117	28	7	0	3	44	20	26	28	2	36	2	0	1	3	1	.75	2	.239	.392	.376
1997 Kinston	A+ Cle	121	409	102	21	1	34	227	82	84	84	4	145	6	0	6	8	1	.89	6	.249	.380	.555
1998 Akron	AA Cle	60	222	62	19	0	8	105	30	32	29	1	61	1	0	2	1	1	.50	7	.279	.362	.473
1999 Akron	AA Cle	127	494	124	23	3	21	216	75	78	55	1	142	4	0	2	2	1	.67	9	.251	.330	.437
2000 Buffalo	AAA Cle	124	420	109	19	2	21	195	68	74	63	1	122	4	0	4	2	4	.33	8	.260	.358	.464
5 Min. YEARS		467	1662	425	89	6	87	787	275	294	259	9	506	17	0	15	16	8	.67	32	.256	.359	.474

Dario Perez

Pitches: Right **Bats:** Right **Pos:** RP-37; SP-6   **Ht:** 6'1" **Wt:** 150 **Born:** 6/27/70 **Age:** 31

		HOW MUCH HE PITCHED						WHAT HE GAVE UP										THE RESULTS					
Year Team	Lg Org	G	GS	CG	GF	IP	BFP	H	R	ER	HR	SH	SF	HB	TBB	IBB	SO	WP	Bk	W	L	Pct.	ShO	Sv	ERA
1990 Royals	R KC	10	10	0	0	50.2	206	43	20	11	0	1	1	1	11	0	37	4	3	2	4	.333	0	0	1.95
1991 Appleton	A KC	34	9	0	6	100	418	86	45	36	7	0	5	4	41	0	73	10	5	7	5	.583	0	0	3.24
Memphis	AA KC	3	2	0	1	12.2	57	15	12	12	5	0	0	0	5	0	12	2	0	1	0	1.000	0	0	8.53
1992 Baseball Cy	A+ KC	28	16	2	4	118	495	107	46	40	7	0	6	9	36	0	82	8	4	8	4	.667	1	0	3.05
1993 Wilmington	A+ KC	33	3	0	13	68.2	294	77	41	31	8	5	1	4	14	0	56	4	1	3	9	.250	0	1	4.06
1994 Wilmington	A+ KC	31	4	0	12	61	259	63	38	36	9	0	2	2	15	2	56	3	0	3	3	.500	0	2	5.31
1999 Calgary	AAA Fla	28	21	0	2	132	563	150	94	84	22	7	3	7	31	0	66	3	0	7	13	.350	0	0	5.73
2000 Trenton	AA Bos	29	6	0	10	74.2	330	82	42	31	9	0	1	3	16	1	67	2	2	4	3	.571	0	1	3.74
Pawtucket	AAA Bos	14	0	0	6	33	135	28	14	12	2	0	0	2	12	3	27	1	0	5	1	.833	0	0	3.27
7 Min. YEARS		210	71	2	54	650.2	2757	651	352	293	69	13	19	32	181	6	476	37	15	39	43	.476	1	4	4.05

Jhonny Perez

Bats: Right **Throws:** Right **Pos:** OF-64; PH-12; 2B-10; SS-6; DH-3; PR-2   **Ht:** 5'10" **Wt:** 180 **Born:** 10/23/76 **Age:** 24

Year Team	Lg Org	G	AB	H	2B	3B	HR	TB	R	RBI	TBB	IBB	SO	HBP	SH	SF	SB	CS	SB%	GDP	Avg	OBP	SLG
1994 Astros	R Hou	36	144	46	12	2	1	65	37	27	15	1	16	1	1	1	18	3	.86	4	.319	.385	.451
1995 Kissimmee	A+ Hou	65	214	58	12	0	4	82	34	31	22	1	37	7	0	0	23	7	.77	5	.271	.358	.383
1996 Kissimmee	A+ Hou	90	322	87	20	2	12	147	54	49	26	1	70	2	3	0	16	16	.50	3	.270	.329	.457
1997 Kissimmee	A+ Hou	69	273	72	16	5	3	107	40	22	12	0	38	1	2	3	8	6	.57	5	.264	.294	.392
Jackson	AA Hou	48	154	39	7	0	3	55	16	17	12	0	26	1	1	0	4	3	.57	2	.253	.311	.357
1998 Jackson	AA Hou	130	439	125	20	0	10	175	65	39	45	4	72	1	6	0	22	11	.67	9	.285	.353	.399
1999 Jackson	AA Hou	76	276	69	16	4	4	105	37	25	19	0	44	1	6	2	7	8	.47	5	.250	.299	.380
2000 Kissimmee	A+ Hou	13	51	18	1	0	0	19	6	4	5	0	8	0	1	0	5	2	.71	1	.353	.411	.373
Round Rock	AA Hou	79	273	81	9	1	7	113	44	31	17	0	40	1	5	0	14	4	.78	6	.297	.340	.414
7 Min. YEARS		606	2146	595	113	14	44	868	323	245	173	7	351	15	25	6	117	60	.66	43	.277	.335	.404

Josue Perez

Bats: Both **Throws:** Right **Pos:** OF-98; DH-3; PR-2   **Ht:** 6'0" **Wt:** 180 **Born:** 8/12/77 **Age:** 23

Year Team	Lg Org	G	AB	H	2B	3B	HR	TB	R	RBI	TBB	IBB	SO	HBP	SH	SF	SB	CS	SB%	GDP	Avg	OBP	SLG
1999 Vero Beach	A+ LA	62	201	56	14	1	2	78	24	22	21	0	29	2	1	2	14	11	.56	5	.279	.350	.388
Clearwater	A+ Phi	23	93	23	2	0	0	25	15	6	7	0	17	1	0	2	6	1	.86	3	.247	.301	.269
2000 Clearwater	A+ Phi	70	279	83	9	8	3	117	41	32	28	2	48	6	3	3	18	14	.56	2	.297	.370	.419
Reading	AA Phi	32	96	23	5	1	1	33	10	8	9	0	19	0	1	1	2	5	.29	1	.240	.302	.344
2 Min. YEARS		187	669	185	30	10	6	253	90	68	65	2	113	9	5	8	40	31	.56	11	.277	.345	.378

Nestor Perez

Bats: Right **Throws:** Right **Pos:** SS-122   **Ht:** 5'10" **Wt:** 168 **Born:** 11/24/76 **Age:** 24

Year Team	Lg Org	G	AB	H	2B	3B	HR	TB	R	RBI	TBB	IBB	SO	HBP	SH	SF	SB	CS	SB%	GDP	Avg	OBP	SLG
1998 Chston-SC	A TB	62	211	37	4	0	0	41	20	22	13	0	36	0	9	3	3	4	.43	6	.175	.220	.194
Princeton	R+ TB	66	244	63	7	0	0	70	41	25	33	1	29	3	17	3	13	8	.62	2	.258	.350	.287
1999 St. Pete	A+ TB	111	364	96	8	1	0	106	33	23	10	0	53	2	14	1	4	5	.44	8	.264	.286	.291
2000 St. Pete	A+ TB	47	193	48	8	0	0	56	16	13	9	0	21	0	6	0	3	2	.60	4	.249	.282	.290
Orlando	AA TB	75	240	49	4	0	0	53	15	14	14	0	40	2	13	0	0	3	.00	5	.204	.254	.221
3 Min. YEARS		361	1252	293	31	1	0	326	125	97	79	1	179	7	59	7	23	22	.51	25	.234	.282	.260

Robert Perez

Bats: Right **Throws:** Right **Pos:** OF-134; DH-2; PH-1   **Ht:** 6'3" **Wt:** 195 **Born:** 6/4/69 **Age:** 32

Year Team	Lg Org	G	AB	H	2B	3B	HR	TB	R	RBI	TBB	IBB	SO	HBP	SH	SF	SB	CS	SB%	GDP	Avg	OBP	SLG
1990 St.Cathrnes	A- Tor	52	207	54	10	2	5	83	20	25	8	1	34	2	0	0	7	5	.58	7	.261	.295	.401
Myrtle Bch	A Tor	21	72	21	2	0	1	26	8	10	3	0	9	2	0	1	2	1	.67	3	.292	.333	.361
1991 Dunedin	A+ Tor	127	480	145	28	6	4	197	50	50	22	3	72	5	7	2	8	8	.50	19	.302	.338	.410
Syracuse	AAA Tor	4	20	4	1	0	0	5	2	1	0	0	2	0	0	0	0	0	—	0	.200	.200	.250
1992 Knoxville	AA Tor	139	526	137	25	5	9	199	59	59	13	0	87	2	3	7	11	10	.52	10	.260	.277	.378
1993 Syracuse	AAA Tor	138	524	154	26	10	12	236	72	64	24	4	65	4	5	1	13	15	.46	19	.294	.329	.450
1994 Syracuse	AAA Tor	128	510	155	28	3	10	219	63	65	27	7	76	2	4	8	7	3	.36	21	.304	.336	.429
1995 Syracuse	AAA Tor	122	502	172	38	6	9	249	70	67	13	4	60	2	1	4	7	5	.58	17	.343	.359	.496
2000 Tennessee	AA Tor	136	547	157	33	1	19	249	66	92	26	3	82	6	2	3	8	7	.53	12	.287	.325	.455
1994 Toronto	AL	4	8	1	0	0	0	1	0	0	0	0	1	0	0	0	0	0	—	1	.125	.125	.125
1995 Toronto	AL	17	48	9	2	0	1	14	2	3	0	0	5	0	0	0	0	0	—	1	.188	.188	.292
1996 Toronto	AL	86	202	66	10	0	2	82	30	21	8	0	17	1	4	1	3	0	1.00	6	.327	.354	.406
1997 Toronto	AL	37	78	15	4	1	2	27	4	6	0	0	16	0	0	0	0	0	—	2	.192	.192	.346

218

Year Team	Lg Org	G	AB	H	2B	3B	HR	TB	R	RBI	TBB	IBB	SO	HBP	SH	SF	SB	CS	SB%	GDP	Avg	OBP	SLG
1998 Seattle	AL	17	35	6	1	0	2	13	3	6	0	0	5	0	0	0	0	0	—	1	.171	.171	.371
Montreal	NL	52	106	25	1	0	1	29	9	8	2	0	23	1	0	1	0	0	—	4	.236	.255	.274
7 Min. YEARS		867	3388	999	191	33	69	1463	410	433	136	19	487	25	22	26	60	58	.51	108	.295	.324	.432
5 Maj. YEARS		213	477	122	18	1	8	166	48	44	10	0	67	2	4	2	3	0	1.00	15	.256	.273	.348

Dan Perkins

Pitches: Right **Bats:** Right **Pos:** SP-22; RP-11   **Ht:** 6'2" **Wt:** 193 **Born:** 3/15/75 **Age:** 26

Year Team	Lg Org	G	GS	CG	GF	IP	BFP	H	R	ER	HR	SH	SF	HB	TBB	IBB	SO	WP	Bk	W	L	Pct.	ShO	Sv	ERA
1993 Elizabethtn	R+ Min	10	10	0	0	45	210	46	33	25	3	1	1	5	25	0	30	5	1	3	3	.500	0	0	5.00
1994 Fort Wayne	A Min	12	12	0	0	50.2	229	61	38	35	3	3	1	4	22	1	34	4	1	1	8	.111	0	0	6.22
Elizabethtn	R+ Min	10	9	1	0	54	223	51	31	22	2	2	1	7	14	0	34	9	1	0	2	.000	0	0	3.67
1995 Fort Wayne	A Min	29	22	0	2	121.1	562	133	86	74	3	3	4	13	69	1	89	22	2	7	12	.368	0	0	5.49
1996 Fort Myers	A+ Min	39	13	3	10	136.2	557	125	52	45	5	4	6	11	37	1	111	9	1	13	7	.650	1	2	2.96
1997 New Britain	AA Min	24	24	2	0	144.2	644	158	94	79	17	8	2	11	53	1	114	10	0	7	10	.412	0	0	4.91
1998 New Britain	AA Min	20	19	1	0	117.2	508	140	64	52	8	3	3	3	31	1	79	6	0	13	5	.722	1	0	3.98
Salt Lake	AAA Min	7	7	1	0	46.2	205	48	30	25	8	0	2	2	20	1	33	2	0	5	0	1.000	0	0	4.82
1999 Salt Lake	AAA Min	3	2	0	0	12.2	57	11	6	6	3	0	0	2	4	0	7	3	0	0	0	—	0	0	4.26
2000 Salt Lake	AAA Min	33	22	0	3	141	667	207	131	115	26	1	7	5	51	0	97	6	3	9	10	.474	0	1	7.34
1999 Minnesota	AL	29	12	0	7	86.2	413	117	69	63	14	2	4	5	43	0	44	6	2	1	7	.125	0	0	6.54
8 Min. YEARS		187	140	8	15	870.1	3862	980	565	478	78	25	27	63	326	6	628	76	9	58	57	.504	2	3	4.94

Brandon Pernell

Bats: Right **Throws:** Right **Pos:** OF-114; PH-6; PR-5   **Ht:** 6'2" **Wt:** 195 **Born:** 4/11/77 **Age:** 24

Year Team	Lg Org	G	AB	H	2B	3B	HR	TB	R	RBI	TBB	IBB	SO	HBP	SH	SF	SB	CS	SB%	GDP	Avg	OBP	SLG
1995 Padres	R SD	48	174	43	11	1	2	62	22	29	16	0	54	1	2	3	8	2	.80	2	.247	.309	.356
1996 Padres	R SD	53	174	58	9	10	1	90	38	33	18	0	30	0	1	2	14	4	.78	1	.333	.392	.517
1997 Clinton	A SD	95	340	96	26	3	12	164	63	41	44	1	77	5	2	1	15	5	.75	5	.282	.372	.482
1998 Rancho Cuca	A+ SD	44	125	25	8	4	2	47	18	7	11	0	39	2	2	0	1	2	.33	0	.200	.275	.376
1999 Rancho Cuca	A+ SD	133	529	148	30	7	21	255	96	84	50	1	156	8	5	6	33	14	.70	14	.280	.347	.482
2000 West Tenn	AA ChC	61	196	39	14	2	2	63	20	26	18	2	67	3	0	4	7	1	.88	1	.199	.271	.321
Daytona	A+ ChC	59	210	54	6	3	7	87	34	35	16	0	44	2	1	6	20	5	.80	5	.257	.308	.414
6 Min. YEARS		493	1748	463	104	30	47	768	291	255	173	4	467	21	13	22	98	33	.75	28	.265	.335	.439

Mark Persails

Pitches: Right **Bats:** Right **Pos:** RP-48; SP-2   **Ht:** 6'3" **Wt:** 190 **Born:** 10/25/75 **Age:** 25

Year Team	Lg Org	G	GS	CG	GF	IP	BFP	H	R	ER	HR	SH	SF	HB	TBB	IBB	SO	WP	Bk	W	L	Pct.	ShO	Sv	ERA
1995 Tigers	R Det	11	10	0	0	51	237	50	37	25	4	5	3	4	25	0	30	8	1	1	4	.200	0	0	4.41
1996 Jamestown	A- Det	13	13	0	0	63.2	275	53	35	30	6	1	0	6	29	0	37	6	0	1	4	.200	0	0	4.24
1997 Jamestown	A- Det	15	14	2	1	84.2	384	103	64	54	5	1	3	3	33	1	56	13	0	3	7	.300	0	0	5.74
1998 W Michigan	A Det	39	5	0	15	92.1	372	75	33	29	7	7	1	3	29	0	64	4	0	11	5	.688	0	2	2.83
1999 Kissimmee	A+ Hou	10	0	0	2	20.1	92	26	9	5	1	0	0	1	4	0	15	3	0	1	1	.500	0	0	2.21
Jackson	AA Hou	12	0	0	2	19.2	82	15	5	3	1	1	0	0	10	0	20	2	0	1	0	1.000	0	1	1.37
2000 Round Rock	AA Hou	50	0	0	16	78.1	375	101	64	55	10	7	3	4	41	4	63	8	0	3	2	.600	0	3	6.32
6 Min. YEARS		150	42	2	36	410	1817	423	247	201	34	22	10	21	171	5	285	44	1	21	23	.477	0	5	4.41

Tommy Peterman

Bats: Left **Throws:** Left **Pos:** 1B-83; DH-22; OF-11; PH-9   **Ht:** 6'0" **Wt:** 228 **Born:** 5/21/75 **Age:** 26

Year Team	Lg Org	G	AB	H	2B	3B	HR	TB	R	RBI	TBB	IBB	SO	HBP	SH	SF	SB	CS	SB%	GDP	Avg	OBP	SLG
1996 Elizabethtn	R+ Min	3	10	3	0	0	1	6	5	4	5	0	1	0	0	0	0	0	—	0	.300	.533	.600
Fort Wayne	A Min	58	176	45	11	0	3	65	17	28	10	3	30	2	0	3	0	1	.00	1	.256	.298	.369
1997 Fort Wayne	A Min	113	417	122	22	0	7	165	46	57	28	4	69	1	1	5	0	4	.00	5	.293	.335	.396
1998 Fort Myers	A+ Min	135	519	162	36	2	20	262	71	110	63	13	86	4	1	6	2	0	1.00	11	.312	.387	.505
1999 New Britain	AA Min	140	538	141	28	0	20	229	68	84	61	5	84	3	0	4	1	2	.33	10	.262	.338	.426
2000 New Britain	AA Min	118	394	107	18	1	9	154	54	43	34	2	54	3	1	2	2	1	.67	13	.272	.333	.391
5 Min. YEARS		567	2054	580	115	3	60	881	261	326	201	27	324	13	3	20	5	8	.38	44	.282	.347	.429

Chris Petersen

Bats: Right **Throws:** Right **Pos:** 2B-50; SS-33; PH-8; 3B-3; P-1   **Ht:** 5'11" **Wt:** 175 **Born:** 11/6/70 **Age:** 30

Year Team	Lg Org	G	AB	H	2B	3B	HR	TB	R	RBI	TBB	IBB	SO	HBP	SH	SF	SB	CS	SB%	GDP	Avg	OBP	SLG
1992 Geneva	A- ChC	71	244	55	8	0	1	66	36	23	32	0	69	4	9	2	11	7	.61	4	.225	.323	.270
1993 Daytona	A+ ChC	130	473	101	10	0	0	111	66	28	58	0	105	9	17	1	19	11	.63	10	.214	.311	.235
1994 Orlando	AA ChC	117	376	85	12	3	1	106	34	26	37	0	89	2	16	1	8	11	.42	7	.226	.298	.282
1995 Orlando	AA ChC	125	382	81	10	3	4	109	48	36	45	3	97	4	5	3	7	3	.70	14	.212	.300	.285
1996 Orlando	AA ChC	47	152	45	3	4	2	62	21	12	18	0	31	5	0	1	3	5	.38	5	.296	.386	.408
Iowa	AAA ChC	63	194	48	6	3	0	60	12	23	12	1	46	1	2	1	1	2	.33	5	.247	.293	.340
1997 Iowa	AAA ChC	119	391	94	16	2	3	123	49	33	32	4	89	6	4	3	1	6	.14	15	.240	.306	.315
1998 Iowa	AAA ChC	118	389	91	16	2	8	135	54	41	21	3	100	7	5	2	2	4	.33	12	.234	.284	.347
1999 Colo Spmgs	AAA Col	107	370	96	21	1	6	137	56	34	29	1	85	7	3	2	4	0	1.00	12	.259	.324	.370
2000 Iowa	AAA ChC	9	18	1	0	0	2	1	2	1	0	0	5	0	0	0	0	0	—	1	.056	.150	.111
Richmond	AAA Atl	79	252	57	10	0	0	67	12	21	14	0	42	2	6	1	2	4	.33	4	.226	.271	.266
1999 Colorado	NL	7	13	2	0	0	0	2	1	2	2	0	3	0	0	0	0	0	—	0	.154	.267	.154
9 Min. YEARS		985	3241	754	113	18	27	984	389	277	300	12	758	47	67	17	58	53	.52	88	.233	.305	.304

Kyle Peterson

Pitches: Right Bats: Left Pos: SP-4   Ht: 6'3" Wt: 215 Born: 4/9/76 Age: 25

		HOW MUCH HE PITCHED					WHAT HE GAVE UP												THE RESULTS					
Year Team	Lg Org	G	GS	CG	GF	IP	BFP	H	R	ER	HR	SH	SF	HB	TBB	IBB	SO	WP	Bk	W	L	Pct.	ShO	Sv	ERA
1997 Ogden	R+ Mil	3	3	0	0	10.1	40	5	2	1	1	0	0	1	4	0	11	0	0	0	0	—	0	0	0.87
1998 Stockton	A+ Mil	17	17	0	0	96.1	430	99	54	38	4	6	1	8	33	0	109	5	5	4	7	.364	0	0	3.55
El Paso	AA Mil	7	7	1	0	43	187	41	24	21	2	2	2	1	16	0	33	1	0	3	2	.600	0	0	4.40
Louisville	AAA Mil	1	1	0	0	5.2	27	8	5	5	0	0	0	0	2	0	4	0	0	1	0	1.000	0	0	7.94
1999 Louisville	AAA Mil	18	18	1	0	109	466	90	52	43	13	3	3	6	42	1	95	5	2	7	6	.538	1	0	3.55
2000 Beloit	A Mil	3	3	0	0	15	58	10	4	3	2	0	1	1	4	0	17	0	0	1	1	.500	0	0	1.80
Huntsville	AA Mil	1	1	0	0	4.2	25	6	7	4	1	1	0	0	4	0	1	0	0	0	1	.000	0	0	7.71
1999 Milwaukee	NL	17	12	0	2	77	341	87	46	39	3	4	3	4	25	2	34	1	0	4	7	.364	0	0	4.56
4 Min. YEARS		50	50	2	0	284	1233	259	148	115	23	12	7	17	105	1	270	12	7	16	17	.485	1	0	3.64

Adam Pettyjohn

Pitches: Left Bats: Right Pos: SP-15   Ht: 6'3" Wt: 190 Born: 6/11/77 Age: 24

		HOW MUCH HE PITCHED					WHAT HE GAVE UP												THE RESULTS					
Year Team	Lg Org	G	GS	CG	GF	IP	BFP	H	R	ER	HR	SH	SF	HB	TBB	IBB	SO	WP	Bk	W	L	Pct.	ShO	Sv	ERA
1998 Jamestown	A- Det	4	4	0	0	22	93	21	10	7	0	1	2	2	4	0	24	1	1	2	2	.500	0	0	2.86
W Michigan	A Det	8	8	1	0	50.1	210	46	15	11	3	3	0	4	9	0	64	1	0	4	2	.667	1	0	1.97
1999 Lakeland	A+ Det	9	9	2	0	59.2	255	62	35	25	2	2	0	1	11	0	51	2	0	3	4	.429	0	0	3.77
Jacksnville	AA Det	20	20	0	0	126.2	548	134	75	66	13	3	5	8	35	0	92	4	0	9	5	.643	0	0	4.69
2000 Jacksnville	AA Det	8	8	0	0	50.1	203	43	20	19	4	1	0	4	12	0	45	2	0	2	2	.500	0	0	3.40
Toledo	AAA Det	7	7	0	0	39	182	45	34	29	5	2	3	2	22	0	23	1	0	0	4	.000	0	0	6.69
3 Min. YEARS		56	56	3	0	348	1491	351	189	157	27	12	10	21	93	0	299	11	1	20	19	.513	1	0	4.06

Tommy Phelps

Pitches: Left Bats: Left Pos: RP-27; SP-11   Ht: 6'3" Wt: 192 Born: 3/4/74 Age: 27

		HOW MUCH HE PITCHED					WHAT HE GAVE UP												THE RESULTS					
Year Team	Lg Org	G	GS	CG	GF	IP	BFP	H	R	ER	HR	SH	SF	HB	TBB	IBB	SO	WP	Bk	W	L	Pct.	ShO	Sv	ERA
1993 Burlington	A Mon	8	8	0	0	41	173	36	18	17	4	1	1	1	13	0	33	2	0	2	4	.333	0	0	3.73
Jamestown	A- Mon	16	15	1	0	92.1	416	102	62	47	4	4	3	5	37	1	74	7	1	3	8	.273	0	0	4.58
1994 Burlington	A Mon	23	23	1	0	118.1	534	143	91	73	9	7	7	5	48	1	82	7	0	8	8	.500	1	0	5.55
1995 Wst Plm Bch	A+ Mon	2	2	0	0	5	33	10	10	9	0	0	0	0	11	0	5	2	0	0	2	.000	0	0	16.20
Albany	A Mon	24	24	1	0	135.1	597	142	76	50	6	0	4	5	45	0	119	5	1	10	9	.526	0	0	3.33
1996 Wst Plm Bch	A+ Mon	18	18	1	0	112	468	105	42	36	5	4	1	2	35	0	71	8	0	10	2	.833	1	0	2.89
Harrisburg	AA Mon	8	8	2	0	47.1	195	43	16	13	3	2	0	1	19	2	23	0	0	2	2	.500	2	0	2.47
1997 Harrisburg	AA Mon	18	18	0	0	101.1	462	115	68	53	14	8	5	5	39	1	86	3	1	10	6	.625	0	0	4.71
1998 Jupiter	A+ Mon	7	7	0	0	41	181	42	21	20	3	0	2	2	15	0	21	1	0	2	2	.500	0	0	4.39
Harrisburg	AA Mon	12	10	0	0	59.2	247	57	29	24	5	4	3	0	26	0	26	2	0	5	4	.556	0	0	3.62
1999 Harrisburg	AA Mon	13	13	1	0	64.2	306	76	53	41	13	3	6	7	26	0	36	2	0	3	6	.333	0	0	5.71
2000 Jacksnville	AA Det	38	11	0	7	102	435	111	59	56	17	1	0	7	26	2	62	1	0	6	6	.500	0	0	4.94
8 Min. YEARS		187	157	7	7	920	4047	982	545	439	83	34	32	40	340	7	638	40	3	61	59	.508	4	0	4.29

Travis Phelps

Pitches: Right Bats: Right Pos: SP-27   Ht: 6'2" Wt: 165 Born: 7/25/77 Age: 23

		HOW MUCH HE PITCHED					WHAT HE GAVE UP												THE RESULTS					
Year Team	Lg Org	G	GS	CG	GF	IP	BFP	H	R	ER	HR	SH	SF	HB	TBB	IBB	SO	WP	Bk	W	L	Pct.	ShO	Sv	ERA
1997 Princeton	R+ TB	14	13	1	0	62.2	279	73	42	34	4	3	1	2	23	0	60	4	1	4	3	.571	0	0	4.88
1998 Chston-SC	A TB	18	18	0	0	91	401	100	54	49	4	1	1	3	35	0	96	7	3	5	8	.385	0	0	4.85
1999 St. Pete	A+ TB	24	23	1	0	133.2	574	148	70	63	6	4	4	11	39	0	101	2	0	10	8	.556	1	0	4.24
2000 Orlando	AA TB	21	21	2	0	108	448	85	44	36	5	1	1	13	46	0	106	5	0	7	8	.467	0	0	3.00
Durham	AAA TB	6	6	0	0	29.2	131	29	17	16	6	2	0	0	16	0	21	0	0	3	1	.750	0	0	4.85
4 Min. YEARS		83	81	4	0	425	1833	435	227	198	25	11	7	29	159	0	384	18	4	29	28	.509	1	0	4.19

Andy Phillips

Bats: Right Throws: Right Pos: 3B-132; DH-2   Ht: 6'0" Wt: 205 Born: 4/6/77 Age: 24

		BATTING										BASERUNNING										PERCENTAGES		
Year Team	Lg Org	G	AB	H	2B	3B	HR	TB	R	RBI	TBB	IBB	SO	HBP	SH	SF	SB	CS	SB%	GDP	Avg	OBP	SLG
1999 Staten IInd	A- NYY	64	233	75	11	7	7	121	35	48	37	1	40	3	0	3	3	3	.50	4	.322	.417	.519
2000 Tampa	A+ NYY	127	478	137	33	2	13	213	66	58	46	0	98	2	0	8	2	1	1.00	9	.287	.346	.446
Norwich	AA NYY	7	28	7	2	1	0	11	5	3	3	0	11	0	1	0	1	0	1.00	1	.250	.323	.393
2 Min. YEARS		198	739	219	46	10	20	345	106	109	86	1	149	5	1	11	6	3	.67	14	.296	.369	.467

J.R. Phillips

Bats: Left Throws: Left Pos: 1B-71; OF-47; DH-15; PH-4   Ht: 6'1" Wt: 205 Born: 4/29/70 Age: 31

		BATTING										BASERUNNING										PERCENTAGES		
Year Team	Lg Org	G	AB	H	2B	3B	HR	TB	R	RBI	TBB	IBB	SO	HBP	SH	SF	SB	CS	SB%	GDP	Avg	OBP	SLG
1988 Bend	A- Ana	56	210	40	8	0	4	60	24	23	21	1	70	1	1	3	3	1	.75	5	.190	.264	.286
1989 Quad City	A Ana	125	442	85	29	1	8	140	41	50	49	2	146	4	4	4	3	3	.50	5	.192	.277	.317
1990 Palm Spring	A+ Ana	46	162	32	4	1	1	41	14	15	10	1	58	0	1	1	3	3	.50	7	.198	.247	.253
Boise	A- Ana	68	238	46	6	0	10	82	30	34	19	0	78	0	1	2	1	1	.50	4	.193	.251	.345
1991 Palm Spring	A+ Ana	130	471	117	22	2	20	203	64	70	57	4	144	3	1	2	15	13	.54	8	.248	.332	.431
1992 Midland	AA Ana	127	497	118	32	4	14	200	58	77	32	4	165	2	1	4	5	3	.63	9	.237	.284	.402
1993 Phoenix	AAA SF	134	506	133	35	2	27	253	80	94	53	9	127	6	0	6	7	5	.58	2	.263	.336	.500
1994 Phoenix	AAA SF	95	360	108	28	5	27	227	69	79	45	4	96	4	0	7	4	5	.44	4	.300	.382	.631
1996 Scranton-WB	AAA Phi	53	200	57	14	2	13	114	33	42	19	0	53	1	0	2	2	2	.50	9	.285	.347	.570
1997 New Orleans	AAA Hou	104	411	119	28	0	21	210	59	71	39	3	112	0	0	0	0	1	.00	11	.290	.348	.511
1998 New Orleans	AAA Hou	56	225	68	18	0	21	149	51	60	21	2	65	1	0	2	1	1	.50	4	.302	.361	.662
1999 Colo Sprngs	AAA Col	124	479	149	22	0	41	294	87	100	54	6	143	1	0	3	4	3	.57	13	.311	.380	.614

Year Team	Lg Org	G	AB	H	2B	3B	HR	TB	R	RBI	TBB	IBB	SO	HBP	SH	SF	SB	CS	SB%	GDP	Avg	OBP	SLG
2000 Charlotte	AAA CWS	59	210	46	9	0	10	85	22	35	18	1	65	1	0	2	3	0	1.00	6	.219	.281	.405
New Orleans	AAA Hou	73	269	72	8	0	14	122	35	52	28	4	77	4	0	3	1	0	1.00	4	.268	.342	.454
1993 San Francisco	NL	11	16	5	1	1	1	11	1	4	0	0	5	0	0	0	0	0	—	0	.313	.313	.688
1994 San Francisco	NL	15	38	5	0	0	1	8	1	3	1	0	13	0	0	1	1	0	1.00	1	.132	.150	.211
1995 San Francisco	NL	92	231	45	9	0	9	81	27	28	19	2	69	0	2	0	1	1	.50	3	.195	.256	.351
1996 San Francisco	NL	15	25	5	0	0	2	11	3	5	1	0	13	0	0	0	0	0	—	0	.200	.231	.440
Philadelphia	NL	35	79	12	5	0	5	32	9	10	10	1	38	1	0	0	0	0	—	1	.152	.256	.405
1997 Houston	NL	13	15	2	0	0	1	5	2	4	0	0	7	0	0	1	0	0	—	0	.133	.125	.333
1998 Houston	NL	36	58	11	0	0	2	17	4	9	7	1	22	0	0	0	0	0	—	1	.190	.277	.293
1999 Colorado	NL	25	39	9	4	0	2	19	5	4	0	0	13	1	0	0	0	0	—	0	.231	.250	.487
12 Min. YEARS		1250	4680	1190	263	17	231	2180	667	802	465	41	1399	29	9	40	52	39	.57	91	.254	.323	.466
7 Maj. YEARS		242	501	94	19	1	23	184	52	67	38	4	180	2	2	2	2	1	.67	6	.188	.247	.367

Jason Phillips

Pitches: Right **Bats:** Right **Pos:** SP-6 **Ht:** 6'6" **Wt:** 225 **Born:** 3/22/74 **Age:** 27

Year Team	Lg Org	G	GS	CG	GF	IP	BFP	H	R	ER	HR	SH	SF	HB	TBB	IBB	SO	WP	Bk	W	L	Pct.	ShO	Sv	ERA
1992 Pirates	R Pit	4	4	0	0	17	88	21	21	16	0	1	1	0	13	0	10	4	4	1	2	.333	0	0	8.47
1993 Welland	A- Pit	14	14	0	0	71.1	323	60	44	28	2	1	2	9	36	0	66	15	4	4	6	.400	0	0	3.53
1994 Augusta	A Pit	23	23	1	0	108.1	531	118	97	81	4	3	4	12	88	1	108	21	3	6	12	.333	0	0	6.73
1995 Augusta	A Pit	30	6	0	3	80	354	76	46	32	2	2	2	0	53	1	65	10	0	4	3	.571	0	0	3.60
1996 Augusta	A Pit	14	14	1	0	89.2	366	79	35	24	3	2	3	6	29	1	75	9	1	5	4	.556	1	0	2.41
Lynchburg	A+ Pit	13	13	1	0	73.2	343	82	47	37	3	2	2	5	35	0	63	6	1	5	6	.455	1	0	4.52
1997 Lynchburg	A+ Pit	23	23	2	0	138.2	577	129	66	58	10	4	2	6	35	0	140	9	1	11	6	.647	1	0	3.76
Carolina	AA Pit	4	4	2	0	31	127	21	8	8	1	1	2	4	9	0	22	2	0	1	2	.333	1	0	2.32
1998 Carolina	AA Pit	25	25	1	0	151	663	161	89	79	14	8	1	9	52	3	114	10	3	7	13	.350	1	0	4.71
Nashville	AAA Pit	5	5	0	0	31.1	136	38	10	9	3	3	0	1	12	0	21	3	0	2	0	1.000	0	0	2.59
1999 Nashville	AAA Pit	1	1	0	0	3	19	6	5	5	0	0	0	0	5	1	5	1	0	0	0	—	0	0	15.00
2000 Nashville	AAA Pit	6	6	0	0	30.2	138	30	20	16	4	2	0	3	18	0	18	0	0	2	4	.333	0	0	4.70
1999 Pittsburgh	NL	6	0	0	0	7	37	11	9	9	2	2	1	0	6	1	7	2	0	0	0	—	0	0	11.57
9 Min. YEARS		162	138	8	3	825.2	3665	821	489	393	46	29	19	55	385	7	707	90	17	48	58	.453	5	0	4.28

Jason Phillips

Bats: Right **Throws:** Right **Pos:** C-99; DH-8; PH-2 **Ht:** 6'1" **Wt:** 177 **Born:** 9/27/76 **Age:** 24

Year Team	Lg Org	G	AB	H	2B	3B	HR	TB	R	RBI	TBB	IBB	SO	HBP	SH	SF	SB	CS	SB%	GDP	Avg	OBP	SLG
1997 Pittsfield	A- NYM	48	155	32	9	0	2	47	15	17	13	0	24	4	1	2	4	0	1.00	1	.206	.282	.303
1998 St. Lucie	A+ NYM	8	28	13	2	0	0	15	4	2	2	0	1	0	1	0	0	0	—	1	.464	.500	.536
Capital Cty	A NYM	69	251	68	15	1	5	100	36	37	23	1	35	5	1	1	5	2	.71	3	.271	.343	.398
1999 Binghamton	AA NYM	39	141	32	5	0	7	58	13	23	13	0	20	3	2	1	0	0	—	4	.227	.304	.411
St. Lucie	A+ NYM	81	283	73	12	1	9	114	36	48	23	0	28	8	0	4	0	1	.00	10	.258	.327	.403
2000 St. Lucie	A+ NYM	80	297	82	21	0	6	121	53	41	23	2	19	8	1	1	1	1	.50	12	.276	.343	.407
Binghamton	AA NYM	27	98	38	4	0	0	42	16	13	7	0	9	2	0	1	0	0	—	3	.388	.435	.429
4 Min. YEARS		352	1253	338	68	2	29	497	173	181	104	3	136	30	6	10	10	4	.71	35	.270	.338	.397

Paul Phillips

Bats: Right **Throws:** Right **Pos:** C-72; DH-8; PH-3; OF-1; PR-1 **Ht:** 5'11" **Wt:** 180 **Born:** 4/15/77 **Age:** 24

Year Team	Lg Org	G	AB	H	2B	3B	HR	TB	R	RBI	TBB	IBB	SO	HBP	SH	SF	SB	CS	SB%	GDP	Avg	OBP	SLG
1998 Spokane	A- KC	59	234	72	12	2	4	100	55	25	18	0	19	4	0	1	12	1	.92	2	.308	.366	.427
Wilmington	A+ KC	2	5	2	0	0	0	2	0	2	0	0	1	0	0	1	0	0	—	0	.400	.333	.400
1999 Wichita	AA KC	108	393	105	20	2	3	138	58	56	26	0	38	2	3	3	8	9	.47	8	.267	.314	.351
2000 Wichita	AA KC	82	291	85	11	5	4	118	49	30	21	1	22	1	1	4	4	5	.44	11	.292	.338	.405
3 Min. YEARS		251	923	264	43	9	11	358	162	113	65	1	80	7	4	9	24	15	.62	21	.286	.335	.388

Wynter Phoenix

Bats: Left **Throws:** Left **Pos:** OF-108; PH-9; DH-7; PR-1 **Ht:** 6'2" **Wt:** 208 **Born:** 12/7/74 **Age:** 26

Year Team	Lg Org	G	AB	H	2B	3B	HR	TB	R	RBI	TBB	IBB	SO	HBP	SH	SF	SB	CS	SB%	GDP	Avg	OBP	SLG
1997 Yakima	A- LA	56	186	47	14	2	3	74	29	17	23	2	36	3	5	1	11	4	.73	1	.253	.343	.398
1998 San Berndno	A+ LA	110	318	79	16	3	7	122	38	47	35	2	67	3	3	2	20	11	.65	2	.248	.327	.384
1999 Vero Beach	A+ LA	62	202	70	10	2	5	99	43	31	42	4	30	8	1	1	6	5	.55	1	.347	.474	.490
San Antonio	AA LA	60	169	42	6	1	5	65	22	22	21	1	41	2	4	2	1	2	.33	3	.249	.335	.385
2000 Portland	AA Fla	121	385	99	23	6	10	164	69	62	61	3	95	7	2	1	10	7	.59	6	.257	.367	.426
4 Min. YEARS		409	1260	337	69	14	30	524	201	179	182	12	269	23	15	8	48	29	.62	13	.267	.368	.416

Calvin Pickering

Bats: Left **Throws:** Left **Pos:** 1B-56; DH-2; PH-2 **Ht:** 6'5" **Wt:** 275 **Born:** 9/29/76 **Age:** 24

Year Team	Lg Org	G	AB	H	2B	3B	HR	TB	R	RBI	TBB	IBB	SO	HBP	SH	SF	SB	CS	SB%	GDP	Avg	OBP	SLG
1995 Orioles	R Bal	15	60	30	10	0	1	43	8	22	2	0	6	0	0	1	0	0	—	3	.500	.508	.717
1996 Bluefield	R+ Bal	60	200	65	14	1	18	135	45	66	28	2	64	2	0	1	8	2	.80	4	.325	.411	.675
1997 Delmarva	A Bal	122	444	138	31	1	25	246	88	79	53	2	139	9	0	1	6	3	.67	14	.311	.394	.554
1998 Bowie	AA Bal	139	488	151	28	2	31	276	93	114	98	16	119	11	0	2	4	6	.40	20	.309	.434	.566
1999 Rochester	AAA Bal	103	372	106	20	0	16	174	63	63	60	6	99	11	0	4	1	3	.25	10	.285	.396	.468
2000 Rochester	AAA Bal	60	197	43	10	0	6	71	20	30	36	2	70	1	0	2	2	5	.29	5	.218	.339	.360
1998 Baltimore	AL	9	21	5	0	0	2	11	4	3	3	0	4	0	0	0	1	0	1.00	2	.238	.333	.524
1999 Baltimore	AL	23	40	5	1	0	1	9	4	5	11	0	16	0	0	0	0	0	—	1	.125	.314	.225
6 Min. YEARS		499	1761	533	113	4	97	945	317	374	277	30	497	34	0	11	21	16	.57	55	.303	.405	.537
2 Maj. YEARS		32	61	10	1	0	3	20	8	8	14	0	20	0	0	0	1	0	1.00	3	.164	.320	.328

Kevin Pickford

Pitches: Left   **Bats:** Left   **Pos:** SP-10; RP-10   **Ht:** 6'4"   **Wt:** 200   **Born:** 3/12/75   **Age:** 26

Year Team	Lg Org	G	GS	CG	GF	IP	BFP	H	R	ER	HR	SH	SF	HB	TBB	IBB	SO	WP	Bk	W	L	Pct.	ShO	Sv	ERA
1993 Pirates	R Pit	9	7	0	1	34.1	151	24	19	13	1	1	2	3	20	0	28	0	2	0	4	.000	0	0	3.41
1994 Augusta	A Pit	2	2	0	0	8.2	37	9	6	4	1	0	0	0	5	0	7	1	0	0	1	.000	0	0	4.15
Welland	A- Pit	15	15	1	0	84.2	377	86	52	46	7	1	6	5	36	0	52	2	2	5	8	.385	1	0	4.89
1995 Lynchburg	A+ Pit	4	4	0	0	27.1	110	31	15	15	5	0	1	0	0	0	15	2	1	0	3	.000	0	0	4.94
Augusta	A Pit	16	16	0	0	85.2	354	85	28	19	5	2	1	5	16	1	59	2	0	7	3	.700	0	0	2.00
1996 Lynchburg	A+ Pit	28	28	4	0	172.1	749	195	99	78	15	7	6	11	25	0	100	4	1	11	11	.500	1	0	4.07
1997 Carolina	AA Pit	21	1	0	7	29.1	152	48	29	24	3	1	1	3	15	3	24	0	0	1	2	.333	0	1	7.36
Lynchburg	A+ Pit	14	10	0	1	73.1	296	72	31	29	3	4	1	2	11	0	50	2	0	3	4	.429	0	1	3.56
1998 Carolina	AA Pit	13	8	1	2	57.2	228	48	26	25	7	1	0	3	15	1	43	2	0	5	1	.833	0	0	3.90
Nashville	AAA Pit	13	12	0	0	80	336	84	33	31	7	4	2	0	20	2	59	4	0	6	1	.857	0	0	3.49
2000 Altoona	AA Pit	10	4	0	1	21.2	115	38	29	24	2	3	3	2	14	0	9	1	1	0	5	.000	0	0	9.97
Lynchburg	A+ Pit	10	6	0	1	30.2	153	42	30	21	3	1	2	8	14	0	13	1	0	1	2	.333	0	0	6.16
7 Min. YEARS		155	113	6	13	705.2	3058	762	397	329	59	25	25	42	191	7	459	21	7	39	45	.464	2	2	4.20

Jeff Pickler

Bats: Left   **Throws:** Right   **Pos:** 2B-119; PH-7; PR-3   **Ht:** 5'10"   **Wt:** 180   **Born:** 1/6/76   **Age:** 25

Year Team	Lg Org	G	AB	H	2B	3B	HR	TB	R	RBI	TBB	IBB	SO	HBP	SH	SF	SB	CS	SB%	GDP	Avg	OBP	SLG
1998 Ogden	R+ Mil	71	280	102	22	0	4	136	55	49	39	0	25	2	4	2	20	8	.71	4	.364	.443	.486
1999 Stockton	A+ Mil	80	311	105	14	3	1	128	40	42	23	2	29	0	1	1	7	6	.54	6	.338	.382	.412
Huntsville	AA Mil	51	183	51	8	1	1	64	20	23	15	0	25	0	2	2	9	4	.69	11	.279	.330	.350
2000 Huntsville	AA Mil	71	254	77	11	0	0	88	34	26	30	0	28	1	4	2	15	12	.56	7	.303	.376	.346
Indianapolis	AAA Mil	56	189	58	6	1	1	69	34	20	24	0	27	1	1	0	14	3	.82	6	.307	.388	.365
3 Min. YEARS		329	1217	393	61	5	7	485	183	160	131	2	134	4	12	7	65	33	.66	34	.323	.389	.399

Tony Pierce

Pitches: Right   **Bats:** Right   **Pos:** SP-15; RP-5   **Ht:** 6'0"   **Wt:** 170   **Born:** 6/21/76   **Age:** 25

Year Team	Lg Org	G	GS	CG	GF	IP	BFP	H	R	ER	HR	SH	SF	HB	TBB	IBB	SO	WP	Bk	W	L	Pct.	ShO	Sv	ERA
1999 Jamestown	A- Atl	17	0	0	14	26.2	107	14	9	8	0	0	1	2	12	0	44	1	0	0	1	.000	0	8	2.70
Macon	A Atl	8	0	0	3	15	63	11	3	3	1	0	1	0	7	0	23	4	0	0	0	—	0	0	1.80
2000 Macon	A Atl	1	1	0	0	5	22	7	4	4	2	0	0	0	0	0	4	0	0	0	1	.000	0	0	7.20
Greenville	AA Atl	1	0	0	0	2	8	0	0	0	0	0	0	0	1	0	2	0	0	0	0	—	0	0	0.00
Myrtle Bch	A+ Atl	18	14	0	1	72.1	316	64	35	33	8	1	1	3	44	0	63	5	1	2	5	.286	0	0	4.11
2 Min. YEARS		45	15	0	18	121	516	96	51	48	11	1	3	5	64	0	136	10	1	2	7	.222	0	8	3.57

Chris Piersoll

Pitches: Right   **Bats:** Right   **Pos:** RP-47   **Ht:** 6'4"   **Wt:** 195   **Born:** 9/25/77   **Age:** 23

Year Team	Lg Org	G	GS	CG	GF	IP	BFP	H	R	ER	HR	SH	SF	HB	TBB	IBB	SO	WP	Bk	W	L	Pct.	ShO	Sv	ERA
1997 Cubs	R ChC	14	0	0	3	31.2	130	21	11	8	0	0	0	2	9	0	35	2	4	4	0	1.000	0	2	2.27
1998 Rockford	A ChC	27	4	1	11	59.2	251	52	28	26	8	1	0	4	20	0	55	3	0	2	0	1.000	0	2	3.92
1999 Daytona	A+ ChC	33	0	0	20	67.2	296	68	30	28	7	1	0	7	24	2	74	9	0	7	3	.700	0	5	3.72
West Tenn	AA ChC	8	1	0	4	14.1	57	12	1	1	0	1	0	0	3	0	14	2	0	0	0	—	0	1	0.63
2000 West Tenn	AA ChC	47	0	0	16	60.2	258	51	17	14	4	4	1	2	28	1	54	5	3	3	3	.500	0	2	2.08
4 Min. YEARS		129	5	1	54	234	992	204	87	77	19	7	1	15	84	3	232	21	7	16	6	.727	0	12	2.96

Anthony Pigott

Bats: Right   **Throws:** Right   **Pos:** OF-103; PR-5; DH-1; PH-1   **Ht:** 6'1"   **Wt:** 194   **Born:** 6/13/76   **Age:** 25

Year Team	Lg Org	G	AB	H	2B	3B	HR	TB	R	RBI	TBB	IBB	SO	HBP	SH	SF	SB	CS	SB%	GDP	Avg	OBP	SLG
1997 Hudson Val	A- TB	1	4	0	0	0	0	0	0	1	0	0	1	0	0	0	0	0	—	0	.000	.000	.000
Princeton	R+ TB	46	151	35	4	1	0	41	20	14	8	0	34	1	1	1	2	1	.67	3	.232	.273	.272
1998 Hudson Val	A- TB	9	16	4	1	0	0	5	3	3	1	0	2	0	0	0	1	0	1.00	1	.250	.294	.313
Chston-SC	A TB	29	100	17	3	1	2	28	9	11	2	0	26	0	0	1	0	1	.00	4	.170	.184	.280
1999 St. Pete	A+ TB	105	339	91	9	4	2	114	41	33	11	0	84	4	3	1	16	8	.67	5	.268	.299	.336
Orlando	AA TB	4	8	2	1	0	0	3	0	0	0	0	2	0	0	0	0	0	—	0	.250	.250	.375
2000 Orlando	AA TB	43	125	30	5	0	0	35	13	9	6	0	29	0	3	0	2	3	.40	4	.240	.275	.280
St. Pete	A+ TB	62	243	65	12	1	2	85	36	17	6	0	50	1	1	0	11	5	.69	2	.267	.288	.350
4 Min. YEARS		299	986	244	35	7	6	311	122	88	34	0	228	6	8	3	32	18	.64	19	.247	.276	.315

Rafael Pina

Pitches: Right   **Bats:** Right   **Pos:** SP-20; RP-6   **Ht:** 6'1"   **Wt:** 170   **Born:** 8/16/71   **Age:** 29

Year Team	Lg Org	G	GS	CG	GF	IP	BFP	H	R	ER	HR	SH	SF	HB	TBB	IBB	SO	WP	Bk	W	L	Pct.	ShO	Sv	ERA
1991 Elizabethtn	R+ Min	16	13	3	1	89.1	394	79	42	25	1	3	2	5	44	0	64	8	10	4	5	.444	1	0	2.52
1992 Elizabethtn	R+ Min	11	11	1	0	66	292	68	39	27	2	3	0	2	22	0	43	7	1	6	2	.750	0	0	3.68
1999 Rochester	AAA Bal	48	10	0	18	111.1	488	113	60	54	15	1	3	2	48	2	88	7	1	8	10	.444	0	5	4.37
2000 Rochester	AAA Bal	14	9	0	1	56.2	247	64	44	37	9	3	1	4	19	1	34	3	0	0	6	.000	0	0	5.88
El Paso	AA Ari	12	11	0	0	71	318	82	40	31	6	3	1	4	21	0	65	3	1	3	3	.500	0	0	3.93
4 Min. YEARS		101	53	4	20	394.1	1739	406	225	174	33	13	7	17	154	3	294	28	13	21	26	.447	1	5	3.97

Juan Piniella

Bats: Right **Throws:** Right **Pos:** OF-124; DH-1; PH-1   **Ht:** 5'10" **Wt:** 160 **Born:** 3/13/78 **Age:** 23

Year Team	Lg Org	G	AB	H	2B	3B	HR	TB	R	RBI	TBB	IBB	SO	HBP	SH	SF	SB	CS	SB%	GDP	Avg	OBP	SLG
1996 Rangers	R Tex	55	223	53	6	2	0	63	38	18	15	0	54	5	4	2	19	5	.79	1	.238	.298	.283
1997 Pulaski	R+ Tex	33	126	34	4	3	1	47	20	17	8	0	22	0	3	2	9	4	.69	1	.270	.309	.373
1998 Savannah	A Tex	72	255	87	13	6	3	121	51	39	30	0	48	4	7	2	28	11	.72	0	.341	.416	.475
Charlotte	A+ Tex	61	222	68	8	3	2	88	37	23	25	0	38	1	1	0	23	6	.79	0	.306	.373	.396
1999 Tulsa	AA Tex	124	458	121	23	2	9	175	69	46	61	0	120	7	1	8	15	6	.71	6	.264	.354	.382
2000 Tulsa	AA Tex	126	447	110	17	1	5	144	68	40	67	0	105	4	12	1	24	8	.75	5	.246	.349	.322
5 Min. YEARS		471	1731	473	71	17	20	638	283	183	206	0	387	21	28	15	118	40	.75	13	.273	.355	.369

Rene Pinto

Bats: Right **Throws:** Right **Pos:** C-52   **Ht:** 6'0" **Wt:** 185 **Born:** 7/17/77 **Age:** 23

Year Team	Lg Org	G	AB	H	2B	3B	HR	TB	R	RBI	TBB	IBB	SO	HBP	SH	SF	SB	CS	SB%	GDP	Avg	OBP	SLG
1994 Yankees	R NYY	40	134	38	8	3	1	55	15	18	10	0	26	3	0	3	0	3	.00	5	.284	.340	.410
1995 Yankees	R NYY	15	49	9	0	1	0	11	2	4	7	0	11	1	0	1	0	0	—	3	.184	.293	.224
1996 Greensboro	A NYY	52	165	34	9	1	1	48	13	14	5	0	41	2	2	0	2	1	.67	5	.206	.238	.291
Oneonta	A- NYY	53	199	41	1	2	2	52	15	20	13	0	54	3	3	3	1	1	.50	4	.206	.261	.261
1997 Greensboro	A NYY	35	105	30	9	1	2	47	20	10	3	0	34	1	0	2	0	0	—	5	.286	.306	.448
Oneonta	A- NYY	52	187	54	8	2	4	78	31	29	11	1	37	5	1	4	1	3	.25	5	.289	.338	.417
1998 Greensboro	A NYY	109	365	83	25	1	0	110	31	40	32	0	87	8	2	1	2	5	.29	11	.227	.303	.301
1999 Greensboro	A NYY	19	58	15	1	1	2	24	9	6	5	0	13	1	0	0	0	1	.00	2	.259	.328	.414
Tampa	A+ NYY	22	70	16	5	2	1	28	9	6	3	0	19	1	1	0	0	0	—	3	.229	.267	.400
2000 Tampa	A+ NYY	24	73	10	4	0	2	20	4	7	4	0	24	2	0	0	0	0	—	1	.137	.203	.274
Norwich	AA NYY	28	77	18	2	0	4	32	10	13	3	0	24	2	2	2	0	1	.00	1	.234	.274	.416
7 Min. YEARS		449	1482	348	72	14	19	505	159	167	96	1	370	29	11	17	6	15	.29	41	.235	.291	.341

Joey Pipes

Pitches: Right **Bats:** Right **Pos:** SP-19   **Ht:** 6'4" **Wt:** 220 **Born:** 11/9/73 **Age:** 27

Year Team	Lg Org	G	GS	CG	GF	IP	BFP	H	R	ER	HR	SH	SF	HB	TBB	IBB	SO	WP	Bk	W	L	Pct.	ShO	Sv	ERA
1998 Astros	R Hou	4	0	0	3	7.1	26	5	1	1	0	0	0	0	2	0	7	0	1	0	0	—	0	0	1.23
Kissimmee	A+ Hou	9	0	0	8	26.1	131	35	17	12	2	4	1	2	13	3	17	3	0	2	1	.667	0	4	4.10
1999 River City	IND —	11	10	5	1	68.2	305	71	45	34	3	4	3	6	19	1	54	5	0	4	6	.400	0	1	4.46
Cedar Rapds	A Ana	7	6	1	1	42.2	184	45	24	14	1	1	1	4	11	0	23	2	1	4	1	.800	0	0	2.95
Lk Elsinore	A+ Ana	2	2	1	0	16	64	16	3	3	1	1	0	0	4	0	19	0	1	1	0	1.000	0	0	1.69
2000 Erie	AA Ana	2	2	0	0	6.1	36	10	10	8	1	1	0	0	6	0	3	0	0	0	2	.000	0	0	11.37
River City	IND —	17	17	3	0	119.1	516	123	55	42	5	6	0	8	39	1	111	2	0	9	3	.750	1	0	3.17
3 Min. YEARS		63	37	10	13	286.2	1262	305	155	114	13	17	5	20	94	5	234	12	3	20	13	.606	1	2	3.58

Marc Pisciotta

Pitches: Right **Bats:** Right **Pos:** RP-19   **Ht:** 6'5" **Wt:** 220 **Born:** 8/7/70 **Age:** 30

Year Team	Lg Org	G	GS	CG	GF	IP	BFP	H	R	ER	HR	SH	SF	HB	TBB	IBB	SO	WP	Bk	W	L	Pct.	ShO	Sv	ERA
1991 Welland	A- Pit	24	0	0	21	34	143	16	4	1	0	2	1	3	20	1	47	7	1	1	1	.500	0	8	0.26
1992 Augusta	A Pit	20	12	1	5	79.1	372	91	51	40	4	5	1	10	43	2	54	12	2	4	5	.444	0	1	4.54
1993 Augusta	A Pit	34	0	0	28	43.2	188	31	18	13	0	5	0	5	17	1	49	5	0	5	2	.714	0	12	2.68
Salem	A+ Pit	20	0	0	18	18.1	88	23	13	6	0	1	1	0	13	0	13	2	0	0	0	—	0	12	2.95
1994 Carolina	AA Pit	26	0	0	17	25.2	127	32	21	16	2	6	2	3	15	2	21	1	1	3	4	.429	0	5	5.61
Salem	A+ Pit	31	0	0	30	29.1	134	24	14	5	1	2	1	3	13	1	23	4	0	1	4	.200	0	19	1.53
1995 Carolina	AA Pit	56	0	0	27	69.1	313	60	37	32	2	7	3	6	45	8	57	4	0	6	4	.600	0	9	4.15
1996 Calgary	AAA Pit	57	0	0	27	65.2	308	71	38	30	3	1	2	2	46	8	46	7	0	2	7	.222	0	1	4.11
1997 Iowa	AAA ChC	42	0	0	38	45.2	194	29	12	12	2	4	0	2	23	3	48	6	0	6	2	.750	0	22	2.36
1998 Iowa	AAA ChC	28	0	0	24	30.2	140	34	24	22	4	3	1	2	16	1	29	4	0	3	5	.375	0	4	6.46
1999 Richmond	AAA Atl	23	0	0	3	35.2	153	34	25	24	3	2	3	0	17	3	27	3	0	3	2	.600	0	0	6.06
Omaha	AAA KC	10	0	0	5	13.2	67	18	18	17	3	0	2	1	11	1	8	2	0	0	1	.000	0	0	11.20
2000 Buffalo	AAA Cle	19	0	0	7	27.1	135	31	23	17	2	1	3	0	22	1	22	6	1	2	2	.500	0	0	5.60
1997 Chicago	NL	24	0	0	7	28.1	119	20	10	10	1	1	1	1	16	0	21	2	0	3	1	.750	0	0	3.18
1998 Chicago	NL	43	0	0	12	44	206	44	21	20	4	1	1	2	32	3	31	6	0	1	2	.333	0	0	4.09
1999 Kansas City	AL	8	0	0	3	8.1	42	9	8	8	1	0	0	0	10	0	3	1	1	0	0	—	0	0	8.64
10 Min. YEARS		390	12	1	250	518.1	2362	494	298	235	26	39	20	37	301	32	444	63	5	36	39	.480	0	97	4.08
3 Maj. YEARS		75	0	0	22	80.2	367	73	39	38	6	2	2	3	58	3	55	9	1	4	5	.444	0	0	4.24

Erik Plantenberg

Pitches: Left **Bats:** Both **Pos:** RP-32; SP-8   **Ht:** 6'1" **Wt:** 187 **Born:** 10/30/68 **Age:** 32

Year Team	Lg Org	G	GS	CG	GF	IP	BFP	H	R	ER	HR	SH	SF	HB	TBB	IBB	SO	WP	Bk	W	L	Pct.	ShO	Sv	ERA
1990 Elmira	A- Bos	16	5	0	4	40.1	186	44	26	18	2	6	1	0	19	0	36	4	1	2	3	.400	0	1	4.02
1991 Lynchburg	A+ Bos	20	20	0	0	103	461	116	59	43	3	4	2	4	51	1	73	8	0	11	5	.688	0	0	3.76
1992 Lynchburg	A+ Bos	21	12	0	4	81.2	384	112	69	47	7	2	4	5	36	0	62	6	0	2	3	.400	0	0	5.18
1993 Jacksnville	AA Sea	34	0	0	13	44.2	182	38	11	10	0	1	1	0	14	1	49	1	0	2	1	.667	0	1	2.01
1994 Jacksnville	AA Sea	14	0	0	7	20.1	85	19	6	3	0	1	1	0	8	2	23	0	0	0	1	.000	0	4	1.33
Calgary	AAA Sea	19	19	1	0	101.2	480	122	82	66	10	2	3	2	62	1	69	14	0	6	7	.462	1	0	5.84
1995 Las Vegas	AAA SD	2	0	0	0	0.1	5	3	3	3	0	0	0	0	1	0	1	0	0	0	0	—	0	0	81.00
Memphis	AA SD	20	0	0	9	21.2	80	19	4	4	2	1	2	1	1	0	16	1	0	2	0	1.000	0	2	1.66
1996 Canton-Akrn	AA Cle	19	0	0	7	21	84	17	7	7	3	1	0	0	6	2	26	2	0	0	0	—	0	0	3.00
Buffalo	AAA Cle	17	1	0	7	33.2	148	35	16	14	2	0	1	0	14	0	28	3	0	2	2	.500	0	1	3.74
1997 Scranton-WB	AAA Phi	18	0	0	14	14.1	72	22	12	12	1	1	1	0	9	2	12	1	0	0	2	.000	0	0	7.53
1998 Fresno	AAA SF	53	1	0	17	77.1	356	78	45	38	6	6	3	6	43	4	67	10	2	4	5	.444	0	4	4.42

Year Team	Lg Org	G	GS	CG	GF	IP	BFP	H	R	ER	HR	SH	SF	HB	TBB	IBB	SO	WP	Bk	W	L	Pct.	ShO	Sv	ERA
1999 Durham	AAA TB	23	7	0	5	58.1	270	75	43	39	19	1	0	1	28	0	51	3	1	5	4	.556	0	0	6.02
Rochester	AAA Bal	17	0	0	7	22.1	101	25	16	14	1	0	0	0	13	0	21	5	0	2	1	.667	0	0	5.64
2000 New Orleans	AAA Hou	24	0	0	7	23	98	17	11	10	3	0	2	0	17	1	15	3	0	2	0	1.000	0	1	3.91
Calgary	AAA Fla	6	0	0	0	3.2	24	6	9	9	2	0	0	0	8	0	3	1	0	0	0	—	0	0	22.09
Winnipeg	IND —	4	2	0	0	10.2	60	23	15	14	3	2	0	0	5	0	10	4	0	0	2	.000	0	0	11.81
Waterbury	IND —	6	6	0	0	35	162	34	21	14	1	1	1	4	22	0	24	2	0	2	2	.500	0	0	3.60
1993 Seattle	AL	20	0	0	4	9.2	53	11	7	7	0	1	0	1	12	1	3	1	0	0	0	—	0	1	6.52
1994 Seattle	AL	6	0	0	2	7	31	4	0	0	0	0	0	1	7	0	1	0	0	0	0	—	0	0	0.00
1997 Philadelphia	NL	35	0	0	9	25.2	113	25	14	14	1	1	1	1	12	0	12	2	0	0	0	—	0	0	4.91
11 Min. YEARS		333	73	1	97	713	3240	809	455	365	65	29	19	23	353	14	587	65	4	42	38	.525	1	11	4.61
3 Maj. YEARS		61	0	0	15	42.1	197	40	21	21	1	2	1	3	31	1	16	3	0	0	0	—	0	1	4.46

Eric Plunk

Pitches: Right **Bats:** Right **Pos:** RP-7   **Ht:** 6'6" **Wt:** 220 **Born:** 9/3/63 **Age:** 37

Year Team	Lg Org	G	GS	CG	GF	IP	BFP	H	R	ER	HR	SH	SF	HB	TBB	IBB	SO	WP	Bk	W	L	Pct.	ShO	Sv	ERA
1981 Gcyankees	R NYY	11	11	1	0	54	—	56	29	23	1	—	—	2	20	1	47	2	3	3	4	.429	0	0	3.83
1982 Paintsville	A+ NYY	12	8	4	2	64	—	63	35	33	2	—	—	3	30	0	59	9	1	6	3	.667	0	0	4.64
1983 Ft. Lauderd	A+ NYY	20	20	5	0	125	—	115	55	38	1	—	—	3	63	4	109	6	0	8	10	.444	4	0	2.74
1984 Ft. Laud	A+ NYY	28	28	7	0	176.1	791	153	85	56	5	5	8	6	123	1	152	17	7	12	12	.500	1	0	2.86
1985 Huntsville	AA Oak	13	13	2	0	79.1	347	61	36	30	9	1	3	2	56	0	68	4	1	8	2	.800	1	0	3.40
Tacoma	AAA Oak	11	10	0	0	53	0	51	41	34	3	0	0	2	50	3	43	4	3	0	5	.000	0	0	5.77
1986 Tacoma	AAA Oak	6	6	0	0	32.2	147	25	18	17	4	2	3	0	33	0	31	3	2	2	3	.400	0	0	4.68
1987 Tacoma	AAA Oak	24	0	0	19	34.2	140	21	8	6	1	1	0	0	17	2	56	6	0	1	1	.500	0	9	1.56
1992 Canton-Akrn	AA Cle	9	0	0	3	15.2	63	11	4	3	0	2	0	1	5	0	19	2	2	1	2	.333	0	1	1.72
2000 West Tenn	AA ChC	7	0	0	2	9	41	5	3	2	1	0	0	1	6	0	9	0	0	2	0	1.000	0	1	2.00
1986 Oakland	AL	26	15	0	2	120.1	537	91	75	71	14	2	3	5	102	2	98	9	6	4	7	.364	0	0	5.31
1987 Oakland	AL	32	11	0	11	95	432	91	53	50	8	3	5	2	62	3	90	5	2	4	6	.400	0	2	4.74
1988 Oakland	AL	49	0	0	22	78	331	62	27	26	6	3	2	1	39	4	79	4	7	7	2	.778	0	5	3.00
1989 Oakland	AL	23	0	0	12	28.2	113	17	7	7	1	1	0	1	12	0	24	4	0	1	1	.500	0	1	2.20
New York	AL	27	7	0	5	75.2	332	65	36	31	9	2	4	0	52	2	61	6	3	7	5	.583	0	0	3.69
1990 New York	AL	47	0	0	16	72.2	310	58	27	22	6	7	0	2	43	4	67	4	2	6	3	.667	0	0	2.72
1991 New York	AL	43	8	0	6	111.2	521	128	69	59	18	6	4	1	62	1	103	6	2	2	5	.286	0	0	4.76
1992 Cleveland	AL	58	0	0	20	71.2	309	61	31	29	5	3	2	0	38	2	50	5	0	9	6	.600	0	4	3.64
1993 Cleveland	AL	70	0	0	40	71	306	61	29	22	5	4	2	0	30	4	77	6	0	4	5	.444	0	15	2.79
1994 Cleveland	AL	41	0	0	18	71	306	61	25	20	3	2	1	2	37	5	73	7	0	7	2	.778	0	3	2.54
1995 Cleveland	AL	56	0	0	22	64	263	48	19	19	5	2	4	2	27	2	71	3	0	6	2	.750	0	2	2.67
1996 Cleveland	AL	56	0	0	12	77.2	318	56	21	21	6	1	4	3	34	2	85	4	1	3	2	.600	0	2	2.43
1997 Cleveland	AL	55	0	0	22	65.2	293	62	37	34	12	1	2	1	36	7	66	6	0	4	5	.444	0	0	4.66
1998 Cleveland	AL	37	0	0	6	41	178	44	23	22	6	3	2	4	15	1	38	0	0	3	1	.750	0	0	4.83
Milwaukee	NL	26	0	0	7	31.2	143	33	14	13	3	1	2	3	15	1	36	1	0	1	2	.333	0	1	3.69
1999 Milwaukee	NL	68	0	0	13	75.1	338	71	44	42	15	5	2	5	43	5	63	5	1	4	4	.500	0	0	5.02
9 Min. YEARS		141	96	19	26	643.2	—	561	314	242	27	—	—	20	403	11	593	53	19	43	42	.506	6	10	3.38
14 Maj. YEARS		714	41	0	234	1151	5030	1009	537	488	122	46	37	32	647	45	1081	75	24	72	58	.554	0	35	3.82

Scott Podsednik

Bats: Left **Throws:** Left **Pos:** OF-42; DH-7; PH-1   **Ht:** 6'0" **Wt:** 170 **Born:** 3/18/76 **Age:** 25

Year Team	Lg Org	G	AB	H	2B	3B	HR	TB	R	RBI	TBB	IBB	SO	HBP	SH	SF	SB	CS	SB%	GDP	Avg	OBP	SLG
1994 Rangers	R Tex	60	211	48	7	1	1	60	34	17	41	0	34	3	2	3	18	5	.78	1	.227	.357	.284
1995 Hudson Val	A- Tex	65	252	67	3	0	0	70	42	20	35	3	31	1	1	2	20	6	.77	9	.266	.355	.278
1996 Brevard Cty	A+ Fla	108	383	100	9	2	0	113	39	30	45	0	65	3	7	0	20	10	.67	8	.261	.343	.295
1997 Kane County	A Fla	135	531	147	23	4	3	187	80	49	60	2	72	3	14	3	28	11	.72	5	.277	.352	.352
1998 Tulsa	AA Tex	17	75	18	4	1	0	24	9	4	6	0	11	0	0	0	5	2	.71	3	.240	.296	.320
Charlotte	A+ Tex	81	302	86	12	4	4	118	55	39	44	0	32	0	4	6	26	8	.76	2	.285	.369	.391
1999 Rangers	R Tex	5	17	7	2	0	0	9	6	5	2	0	3	0	0	0	1	0	1.00	1	.412	.474	.529
Tulsa	AA Tex	37	116	18	4	0	0	22	10	1	5	0	13	0	2	0	6	2	.75	3	.155	.190	.190
2000 Tulsa	AA Tex	49	169	42	7	2	2	59	20	13	30	1	33	1	1	2	19	4	.83	4	.249	.361	.349
7 Min. YEARS		557	2056	533	71	14	10	662	295	178	268	6	294	11	31	16	143	48	.75	36	.259	.345	.322

Ryan Poe

Pitches: Right **Bats:** Right **Pos:** RP-35; SP-7   **Ht:** 6'2" **Wt:** 220 **Born:** 9/3/77 **Age:** 23

Year Team	Lg Org	G	GS	CG	GF	IP	BFP	H	R	ER	HR	SH	SF	HB	TBB	IBB	SO	WP	Bk	W	L	Pct.	ShO	Sv	ERA
1998 Helena	R+ Mil	14	5	0	2	46.1	202	52	30	24	3	1	1	3	15	0	43	1	1	3	3	.500	0	1	4.66
1999 Beloit	A Mil	33	5	0	28	96	398	94	46	38	9	1	2	3	16	3	108	5	1	6	10	.375	0	9	3.56
2000 Mudville	A+ Mil	33	7	0	21	82.2	323	56	19	18	5	1	3	3	21	1	98	2	1	7	5	.583	0	9	1.96
Huntsville	AA Mil	9	0	0	8	21.1	94	18	8	8	1	2	1	2	9	2	20	1	0	1	3	.250	0	3	3.38
3 Min. YEARS		105	17	0	59	246.1	1017	220	103	88	18	5	7	11	61	6	269	9	3	17	21	.447	0	22	3.22

Chad Poeck

Pitches: Right **Bats:** Right **Pos:** RP-45; SP-1   **Ht:** 6'2" **Wt:** 190 **Born:** 10/18/72 **Age:** 28

Year Team	Lg Org	G	GS	CG	GF	IP	BFP	H	R	ER	HR	SH	SF	HB	TBB	IBB	SO	WP	Bk	W	L	Pct.	ShO	Sv	ERA
1996 Thunder Bay	IND —	19	12	1	3	87	377	78	37	31	7	1	4	1	48	3	56	10	1	5	8	.385	0	1	3.21
1997 Sioux Falls	IND —	16	13	0	0	77	342	84	44	44	11	1	1	7	33	2	70	8	2	1	4	.200	0	0	5.14
1998 Thunder Bay	IND —	17	11	1	2	70	286	45	31	27	6	0	2	3	38	2	78	3	1	4	4	.500	1	0	3.47
1999 Schaumburg	IND —	20	1	0	14	31.2	188	21	11	10	1	2	1	1	11	0	34	0	0	3	4	.429	0	3	2.84
Charlotte	A+ Tex	9	0	0	3	15	59	10	3	2	0	4	0	0	6	0	12	2	0	0	0	—	0	1	1.20
2000 Tulsa	AA Tex	46	1	0	29	79	349	87	46	37	6	3	9	3	34	0	65	4	0	2	3	.400	0	10	4.22
5 Min. YEARS		127	38	2	51	359.2	1541	325	176	151	31	9	17	15	170	7	315	27	4	15	23	.395	1	15	3.78

Corey Pointer

Bats: Right **Throws:** Right **Pos:** OF-14; PH-5; PR-1   **Ht:** 6'2" **Wt:** 208 **Born:** 9/2/75 **Age:** 25

Year Team	Lg Org	G	AB	H	2B	3B	HR	TB	R	RBI	TBB	IBB	SO	HBP	SH	SF	SB	CS	SB%	GDP	Avg	OBP	SLG
1994 Braves	R Atl	27	77	11	4	0	1	18	8	4	8	0	31	2	0	0	2	1	.67	2	.143	.241	.234
1995 Danville	R+ Atl	46	158	44	5	3	8	79	33	27	19	1	60	5	0	2	8	4	.67	1	.278	.370	.500
1996 Macon	A Atl	8	25	6	1	0	1	10	4	2	0	0	9	1	0	0	2	1	.67	0	.240	.269	.400
Eugene	A- Atl	65	233	57	12	3	14	117	46	39	35	4	88	5	0	5	10	2	.83	3	.245	.349	.502
Erie	A- Pit	5	21	4	1	0	0	5	1	2	0	0	9	1	0	0	0	0	—	1	.190	.227	.238
1997 Augusta	A Pit	84	248	47	9	0	7	77	38	26	26	0	116	9	3	3	23	3	.88	1	.190	.287	.310
Erie	A- Pit	18	43	5	0	0	2	11	5	7	3	0	22	4	0	1	3	1	.75	0	.116	.235	.256
1998 Lynchburg	A+ Pit	118	375	84	25	3	18	169	70	46	53	2	177	17	1	0	12	10	.55	2	.224	.346	.451
1999 Lynchburg	A+ Pit	108	327	59	18	1	15	124	55	44	44	0	147	14	2	2	13	12	.52	3	.180	.302	.379
2000 Altoona	AA Pit	19	39	6	1	1	0	9	6	4	7	0	18	0	1	3	0	0	—	1	.154	.265	.231
7 Min. YEARS		498	1546	323	76	11	66	619	266	201	195	7	677	58	7	16	73	34	.68	14	.209	.317	.400

Enohel Polanco

Bats: Right **Throws:** Right **Pos:** SS-65; 3B-17; PH-5; 2B-2; DH-1   **Ht:** 5'11" **Wt:** 165 **Born:** 8/11/75 **Age:** 25

Year Team	Lg Org	G	AB	H	2B	3B	HR	TB	R	RBI	TBB	IBB	SO	HBP	SH	SF	SB	CS	SB%	GDP	Avg	OBP	SLG
1995 Kingsport	R+ NYM	62	205	47	5	2	2	62	28	21	18	0	60	2	3	3	7	6	.54	5	.229	.294	.302
1996 Capital Cty	A NYM	92	299	65	12	1	1	82	34	24	18	0	78	5	9	1	6	3	.67	5	.217	.272	.274
1997 St. Lucie	A+ NYM	43	131	33	9	1	0	44	20	12	10	0	33	1	4	1	2	5	.29	4	.252	.308	.336
Binghamton	AA NYM	82	263	79	13	4	3	109	34	32	17	2	59	5	5	0	7	5	.58	3	.300	.354	.414
1998 Binghamton	AA NYM	26	79	19	4	0	0	23	10	5	7	2	27	0	1	0	1	1	.50	1	.241	.302	.291
St. Lucie	A+ NYM	75	239	63	8	1	2	79	35	19	11	0	38	5	5	2	6	2	.75	2	.264	.307	.331
1999 West Tenn	AA ChC	116	354	85	21	5	3	125	44	30	20	2	89	4	5	3	12	8	.60	9	.240	.286	.353
2000 Portland	AA Fla	4	15	2	0	1	0	4	1	1	0	0	7	0	0	0	0	1	.00	0	.133	.133	.267
Calgary	AAA Fla	9	20	2	0	0	0	2	1	1	1	0	7	0	0	1	1	0	1.00	0	.100	.136	.100
Duluth-Sup	IND —	36	117	28	6	0	0	34	14	9	3	0	28	0	1	0	4	1	.80	5	.239	.258	.291
Sioux Falls	IND —	24	110	31	6	1	0	39	11	4	4	0	18	1	2	0	3	3	.50	0	.282	.313	.355
Buffalo	AAA Cle	6	20	4	0	1	1	9	2	5	0	0	6	0	0	0	0	1	.00	0	.200	.200	.450
Akron	AA Cle	4	13	1	0	0	0	1	1	0	1	0	2	2	0	0	1	0	1.00	0	.077	.250	.077
Kinston	A+ Cle	3	11	0	0	0	0	0	1	0	1	0	5	0	0	1	1	0	—	1	.000	.000	.000
6 Min. YEARS		582	1876	459	84	17	12	613	236	163	110	6	457	25	35	11	50	36	.58	33	.245	.294	.327

Trey Poland

Pitches: Left **Bats:** Left **Pos:** RP-16; SP-14   **Ht:** 6'1" **Wt:** 190 **Born:** 4/3/75 **Age:** 26

		HOW MUCH HE PITCHED						WHAT HE GAVE UP										THE RESULTS					
Year Team	Lg Org	G	GS	CG	GF	IP	BFP	H	R	ER	HR	SH	SF	HB	TBB	IBB	SO	WP	Bk	W	L	Pct.	ShO	Sv	ERA
1997 Pulaski	R+ Tex	13	13	3	0	85.1	333	57	29	19	9	2	0	3	18	0	106	4	3	7	3	.700	2	0	2.00
1998 Charlotte	A+ Tex	26	25	1	0	148.2	645	150	82	64	15	4	4	4	60	0	138	7	2	8	5	.615	0	0	3.87
1999 Charlotte	A+ Tex	5	5	1	0	32.1	120	16	4	3	1	0	1	0	9	0	28	0	0	2	2	.500	1	0	0.84
Tulsa	AA Tex	21	21	2	0	118.2	546	139	74	65	11	3	3	5	56	0	80	9	2	5	8	.385	1	0	4.93
2000 Tulsa	AA Tex	30	14	0	4	98.2	449	115	85	73	12	1	7	2	46	0	67	9	0	6	8	.429	0	0	6.66
4 Min. YEARS		95	78	7	4	483.2	2093	477	274	224	48	8	15	14	189	0	419	29	7	28	26	.519	4	0	4.17

Joe Pomierski

Bats: Left **Throws:** Right **Pos:** DH-75; OF-55; PH-4; 1B-1   **Ht:** 6'2" **Wt:** 208 **Born:** 4/15/74 **Age:** 27

Year Team	Lg Org	G	AB	H	2B	3B	HR	TB	R	RBI	TBB	IBB	SO	HBP	SH	SF	SB	CS	SB%	GDP	Avg	OBP	SLG
1992 Mariners	R Sea	32	103	24	4	1	0	30	19	13	14	0	26	2	2	0	2	1	.67	0	.233	.336	.291
1993 Mariners	R Sea	48	173	39	8	4	2	61	19	29	19	0	39	2	1	3	4	1	.80	2	.225	.305	.353
1994 Bellingham	A- Sea	55	152	27	4	0	4	43	20	25	16	2	46	1	1	3	2	3	.40	2	.178	.256	.283
1995 Everett	A- Sea	59	217	48	15	3	11	102	31	38	26	0	58	4	0	0	4	2	.67	4	.221	.316	.470
1996 Hudson Val	A- TB	74	285	74	25	3	8	129	45	54	35	1	91	4	0	6	2	4	.33	6	.260	.342	.453
1997 St. Pete	A+ TB	119	422	112	25	5	11	180	64	49	43	4	78	4	2	3	4	3	.57	5	.265	.337	.427
1998 St. Pete	A+ TB	112	390	92	28	1	12	158	47	67	40	1	90	0	2	5	3	1	.75	9	.236	.303	.405
1999 Orlando	AA TB	62	188	49	10	3	9	92	31	33	22	0	44	5	2	2	1	1	.50	2	.261	.350	.489
2000 Orlando	AA TB	131	459	108	25	3	16	187	60	65	70	2	137	4	1	8	0	3	.00	6	.235	.336	.407
9 Min. YEARS		692	2389	573	144	23	73	982	336	373	285	10	609	26	11	30	22	19	.54	34	.240	.324	.411

Colin Porter

Bats: Left **Throws:** Left **Pos:** OF-121; PH-3   **Ht:** 6'2" **Wt:** 200 **Born:** 11/23/75 **Age:** 25

Year Team	Lg Org	G	AB	H	2B	3B	HR	TB	R	RBI	TBB	IBB	SO	HBP	SH	SF	SB	CS	SB%	GDP	Avg	OBP	SLG
1998 Auburn	A- Hou	67	240	68	18	4	4	106	40	30	19	0	61	5	2	1	14	11	.56	3	.283	.347	.442
1999 Michigan	A Hou	127	453	132	28	9	18	232	91	68	53	2	123	7	3	8	23	13	.64	4	.291	.369	.512
2000 Round Rock	AA Hou	124	435	119	25	5	14	196	76	57	56	4	130	6	0	1	17	9	.65	6	.274	.363	.451
3 Min. YEARS		318	1128	319	71	18	36	534	207	155	128	6	314	18	5	10	54	33	.62	13	.283	.362	.473

Mike Porzio

Pitches: Left **Bats:** Left **Pos:** SP-24; RP-2   **Ht:** 6'3" **Wt:** 190 **Born:** 8/20/72 **Age:** 28

		HOW MUCH HE PITCHED						WHAT HE GAVE UP										THE RESULTS					
Year Team	Lg Org	G	GS	CG	GF	IP	BFP	H	R	ER	HR	SH	SF	HB	TBB	IBB	SO	WP	Bk	W	L	Pct.	ShO	Sv	ERA
1993 Cubs	R ChC	10	8	0	2	42.1	200	42	26	18	1	3	2	3	30	0	30	1	2	1	3	.250	0	0	3.83
1994 Cubs	R ChC	7	0	0	6	13.2	64	19	10	9	0	0	0	1	6	0	5	0	0	0	3	.000	0	1	5.93
1995 Mobile	IND —	16	2	0	4	28.1	131	32	19	17	2	4	1	3	13	2	15	2	0	0	3	.000	0	0	5.40
Ogden	R+ —	8	8	2	0	48	220	66	39	34	4	0	3	2	15	0	26	6	0	4	3	.571	0	0	6.38

Year Team	Lg Org	G	GS	CG	GF	IP	BFP	H	R	ER	HR	SH	SF	HB	TBB	IBB	SO	WP	Bk	W	L	Pct.	ShO	Sv	ERA
1996 Tennessee	IND —	15	15	3	0	98.2	428	94	55	40	9	2	4	9	30	1	54	4	0	7	4	.636	0	0	3.65
1997 Sioux City	IND —	27	5	1	6	61.1	284	75	32	29	6	0	3	5	27	1	63	2	0	2	2	.500	1	0	4.26
1998 Danville	A+ Atl	26	11	1	8	97	384	74	34	27	7	5	3	1	30	5	95	1	0	3	2	.600	0	2	2.51
Salem	A+ Col	7	7	0	0	42.1	173	40	20	13	6	1	0	2	12	0	46	1	0	2	3	.400	0	0	2.76
1999 Colo Sprngs	AAA Col	35	0	0	6	42.2	198	44	16	16	5	3	0	3	30	4	33	4	1	5	1	.833	0	0	3.38
2000 Colo Sprngs	AAA Col	6	6	0	0	26	133	39	30	29	7	3	2	0	20	0	26	0	1	0	3	.000	0	0	10.04
Carolina	AA Col	20	18	1	2	121.1	502	111	53	46	11	5	4	5	31	0	90	5	0	7	4	.636	1	0	3.41
1999 Colorado	NL	16	0	0	3	14.2	75	21	14	14	1	0		1	10	0	10	0	0	0	0	—	0	0	8.59
8 Min. YEARS		177	80	8	34	621.2	2717	636	334	278	58	26	22	34	244	13	483	26	4	31	31	.500	2	3	4.02

Dave Post

Bats: Right **Throws:** Right **Pos:** 3B-34; SS-33; OF-29; PH-9; 2B-8; 1B-8; DH-4; P-4   **Ht:** 5'11" **Wt:** 170 **Born:** 9/3/73 **Age:** 27

Year Team	Lg Org	G	AB	H	2B	3B	HR	TB	R	RBI	TBB	IBB	SO	HBP	SH	SF	SB	CS	SB%	GDP	Avg	OBP	SLG
1992 Great Falls	R+ LA	41	138	40	8	0	1	51	23	25	23	0	16	4	3	2	10	5	.67	4	.290	.401	.370
1993 Yakima	A- LA	60	210	53	8	1	1	66	34	22	35	1	27	4	3	3	7	4	.64	3	.252	.365	.314
1994 Bakersfield	A+ LA	31	106	25	5	1	0	32	16	9	13	0	9	3	0	0	6	4	.60	2	.236	.336	.302
Yakima	A- LA	70	263	77	14	1	1	96	46	27	56	3	42	5	1	5	18	5	.78	3	.293	.419	.365
1995 Vero Beach	A+ LA	52	114	27	2	1	0	31	16	11	23	0	11	2	3	1	3	0	1.00	5	.237	.371	.272
1996 Expos	R Mon	8	25	2	0	0	1	5	3	1	4	1	6	0	1	0	1	0	1.00	0	.080	.207	.200
Wst Plm Bch	A+ Mon	79	258	72	15	6	5	114	42	35	37	1	32	5	5	4	8	4	.67	6	.279	.375	.442
1997 Harrisburg	AA Mon	48	156	41	10	0	3	60	26	18	24	0	24	5	3	1	5	1	.83	1	.263	.376	.385
1998 Harrisburg	AA Mon	19	58	20	3	1	1	28	9	9	7	0	3	1	0	0	1	1	.50	0	.345	.424	.483
Ottawa	AAA Mon	93	330	99	23	2	6	144	59	35	28	1	50	6	1	0	7	7	.50	5	.300	.365	.436
1999 Harrisburg	AA Mon	5	21	8	1	0	1	12	5	3	1	0	2	0	1	0	0	0	—	0	.381	.409	.571
Ottawa	AAA Mon	108	375	97	17	2	10	148	49	36	34	3	56	8	2	3	12	8	.60	9	.259	.331	.395
2000 Ottawa	AAA Mon	115	362	92	22	5	4	136	45	43	56	2	44	7	4	1	8	3	.73	10	.254	.364	.376
Buffalo	AAA Cle	5	16	5	0	0	0	5	1	0	5	0	2	0	0	0	0	0	—	0	.313	.476	.313
9 Min. YEARS		734	2432	658	128	20	34	928	374	274	346	12	324	50	27	20	86	42	.67	48	.271	.370	.381

Alonzo Powell

Bats: Right **Throws:** Right **Pos:** OF-42; DH-33; PH-9; 1B-3   **Ht:** 6'2" **Wt:** 190 **Born:** 12/12/64 **Age:** 36

Year Team	Lg Org	G	AB	H	2B	3B	HR	TB	R	RBI	TBB	IBB	SO	HBP	SH	SF	SB	CS	SB%	GDP	Avg	OBP	SLG
1983 Clinton	A SF	36	113	22	5	1	0	29	14	9	15	1	27	0	0	1	2	1	.67	—	.195	.287	.257
Great Falls	R+ SF	51	149	33	2	2	1	42	13	16	12	1	34	1	2	0	10	4	.71	—	.221	.284	.282
1984 Everett	A- SF	6	17	3	1	0	1	7	2	4	1	0	3	0	0	2	0	0	—	—	.176	.200	.412
Clinton	A SF	47	149	37	3	2	1	47	22	10	19	0	31	0	0	2	0	0	—	3	.248	.333	.315
1985 San Jose	A+ SF	136	473	122	27	6	9	188	79	62	71	0	118	3	3	6	34	11	.76	11	.258	.354	.397
1986 Wst Plm Bch	A+ Mon	23	76	25	7	1	4	46	20	18	22	0	16	0	0	1	5	1	.83	2	.329	.475	.605
Jacksnville	AA Mon	105	402	121	21	5	15	197	67	80	49	3	78	4	2	3	15	11	.58	10	.301	.380	.490
1987 Indianapols	AAA Mon	90	331	99	14	10	19	190	64	74	32	1	68	1	3	3	12	8	.60	7	.299	.360	.574
1988 Indianapols	AAA Mon	88	282	74	18	3	4	110	31	39	28	0	72	0	2	3	10	8	.56	7	.262	.326	.390
1989 Wst Plm Bch	A+ Mon	12	41	13	4	3	1	26	7	8	7	2	3	0	0	1	1	1	.50	1	.317	.408	.634
Indianapols	AAA Mon	121	423	98	26	5	13	173	50	59	38	2	106	2	1	3	9	6	.60	6	.232	.296	.409
1990 Portland	AAA Min	107	376	121	25	3	8	176	56	62	40	1	79	4	0	3	23	11	.68	9	.322	.390	.468
1991 Calgary	AAA Sea	53	192	72	18	7	7	125	45	43	31	2	33	0	0	5	2	6	.25	3	.375	.442	.651
1992 Calgary	AAA Sea	10	35	12	1	1	1	18	7	7	5	0	10	1	0	0	0	1	.00	2	.343	.439	.514
1998 Syracuse	AAA Tor	15	48	11	1	0	3	21	8	9	7	0	12	1	0	0	0	0	.00	2	.229	.339	.438
1999 Columbus	AAA NYY	130	470	148	23	1	24	245	97	90	82	3	110	2	0	6	1	3	.25	14	.315	.414	.521
2000 Colo Sprngs	AAA Col	21	58	15	7	0	1	25	9	4	10	0	12	0	0	1	0	0	—	1	.259	.368	.431
Columbus	AAA NYY	64	239	63	10	0	8	97	34	27	20	1	48	2	0	1	1	2	.33	3	.264	.324	.406
13 Min. YEARS		1115	3874	1089	213	50	120	1762	625	621	489	17	860	21	15	38	125	75	.63	—	.281	.362	.455
1987 Montreal	NL	14	41	8	3	0	0	11	3	4	5	0	17	0	0	0	0	0	—	0	.195	.283	.268
1991 Seattle	AL	57	111	24	6	1	3	41	16	12	11	0	24	1	0	2	0	2	.00	1	.216	.288	.369
2 Maj. YEARS		71	152	32	9	1	3	52	19	16	16	0	41	1	0	2	0	2	.00	1	.211	.287	.342

Corey Powell

Bats: Right **Throws:** Right **Pos:** OF-2; PH-1   **Ht:** 6'3" **Wt:** 210 **Born:** 9/3/70 **Age:** 30

Year Team	Lg Org	G	AB	H	2B	3B	HR	TB	R	RBI	TBB	IBB	SO	HBP	SH	SF	SB	CS	SB%	GDP	Avg	OBP	SLG
1990 Expos	R Mon	33	83	15	3	0	1	21	6	10	3	0	21	2	0	0	0	1	.00	2	.181	.227	.253
1993 Burlington	A Mon	115	433	121	18	5	13	188	55	62	29	3	97	3	1	3	2	1	.67	10	.279	.327	.434
1994 Osceola	A+ Hou	132	480	116	22	2	5	157	46	60	28	1	88	7	0	6	4	4	.50	25	.242	.290	.327
1995 Duluth-Sup	IND —	65	253	87	18	1	7	128	36	40	19	1	36	4	2	1	1	2	.33	6	.344	.397	.506
1996 Madison	IND —	84	335	102	19	1	17	174	66	63	20	4	70	2	2	1	3	3	.50	6	.304	.346	.519
2000 Pawtucket	AAA Bos	3	9	1	0	0	0	1	0	1	0	0	5	0	0	0	0	0	—	0	.111	.111	.111
6 Min. YEARS		432	1593	442	80	9	43	669	209	236	99	9	317	18	5	11	10	11	.48	49	.277	.325	.420

Dante Powell

Bats: Right **Throws:** Right **Pos:** OF-72; PH-18; DH-3   **Ht:** 6'2" **Wt:** 185 **Born:** 8/25/73 **Age:** 27

Year Team	Lg Org	G	AB	H	2B	3B	HR	TB	R	RBI	TBB	IBB	SO	HBP	SH	SF	SB	CS	SB%	GDP	Avg	OBP	SLG
1994 Everett	A- SF	41	165	51	15	1	5	83	31	25	19	1	47	4	0	2	27	1	.96	0	.309	.389	.503
San Jose	A+ SF	1	4	2	0	1	0	4	0	0	0	0	1	0	0	0	0	0	—	0	.500	.500	1.000
1995 San Jose	A+ SF	135	505	125	23	8	10	194	74	70	46	2	131	3	1	4	43	12	.78	8	.248	.312	.384
1996 Shreveport	AA SF	135	508	142	27	2	21	236	92	78	72	4	92	3	1	2	43	23	.65	6	.280	.371	.465
Phoenix	AAA SF	2	8	2	0	0	0	2	0	0	0	0	3	0	0	0	1	0	1.00	0	.250	.400	.500
1997 Phoenix	AAA SF	108	452	109	24	4	11	174	91	42	52	1	105	3	0	3	34	10	.77	9	.241	.323	.385
1998 Fresno	AAA SF	134	448	103	17	3	14	168	83	52	71	1	138	14	3	4	41	9	.82	6	.230	.350	.375

Year Team	Lg Org	G	AB	H	2B	3B	HR	TB	R	RBI	TBB	IBB	SO	HBP	SH	SF	SB	CS	SB%	GDP	Avg	OBP	SLG
1999 Tucson	AAA Ari	51	187	62	14	2	7	101	29	30	14	0	38	1	3	0	22	6	.79	0	.332	.381	.540
2000 San Antonio	AA LA	17	64	17	4	0	1	24	12	6	12	0	16	0	0	0	10	3	.77	2	.266	.382	.375
Albuquerque	AAA LA	65	181	40	7	1	6	67	36	21	21	0	51	3	2	1	13	4	.76	4	.221	.311	.370
1997 San Francisco	NL	27	39	12	1	0	1	16	8	3	4	0	11	0	1	0	1	1	.50	0	.308	.372	.410
1998 San Francisco	NL	8	4	2	0	0	1	5	2	1	3	0	0	0	0	0	0	0	—	0	.500	.714	1.250
1999 Arizona	NL	22	25	4	3	0	0	7	4	1	2	0	6	0	1	0	2	1	.67	0	.160	.222	.280
7 Min. YEARS		689	2522	653	131	23	75	1055	448	324	309	9	622	31	13	13	233	69	.77	36	.259	.345	.418
3 Maj. YEARS		57	68	18	4	0	2	28	14	5	9	0	17	0	2	0	3	2	.60	0	.265	.351	.412

John Powers

Bats: Left **Throws:** Right **Pos:** 2B-57; PH-19; DH-16; PR-2   **Ht:** 5'9" **Wt:** 165 **Born:** 6/2/74 **Age:** 27

Year Team	Lg Org	G	AB	H	2B	3B	HR	TB	R	RBI	TBB	IBB	SO	HBP	SH	SF	SB	CS	SB%	GDP	Avg	OBP	SLG
1996 Clinton	A SD	64	237	61	8	4	1	80	29	21	34	0	38	4	3	3	1	4	.20	5	.257	.356	.338
1997 Mobile	AA SD	14	48	12	0	0	1	15	8	8	9	0	9	2	0	2	2	0	1.00	1	.250	.367	.313
Rancho Cuca	A+ SD	107	402	102	28	5	10	170	77	44	63	0	90	11	5	3	7	8	.47	9	.254	.367	.423
1998 Mobile	AA SD	127	476	144	27	4	12	215	92	52	76	1	76	8	4	2	9	6	.60	8	.303	.406	.452
2000 Mobile	AA SD	93	305	80	23	1	3	114	61	22	50	0	56	6	1	2	6	3	.67	2	.262	.375	.374
4 Min. YEARS		405	1468	399	86	14	27	594	267	147	231	1	269	31	13	12	25	21	.54	25	.272	.379	.405

Andy Pratt

Pitches: Left **Bats:** Left **Pos:** SP-27   **Ht:** 5'11" **Wt:** 160 **Born:** 8/27/79 **Age:** 21

Year Team	Lg Org	G	GS	CG	GF	IP	BFP	H	R	ER	HR	SH	SF	HB	TBB	IBB	SO	WP	Bk	W	L	Pct.	ShO	Sv	ERA
1998 Rangers	R Tex	12	8	0	1	56	225	49	25	24	4	1	3	1	14	0	49	0	1	4	3	.571	0	0	3.86
1999 Savannah	A Tex	13	13	1	0	71.2	299	66	30	23	4	4	2	4	16	0	100	4	0	4	4	.500	1	0	2.89
2000 Charlotte	A+ Tex	16	16	2	0	92.2	365	68	37	28	8	1	2	1	26	0	95	1	2	7	4	.636	1	0	2.72
Tulsa	AA Tex	11	11	0	0	52.1	255	66	48	42	7	0	2	2	33	0	42	5	1	1	6	.143	0	0	7.22
3 Min. YEARS		52	48	3	1	272.2	1144	249	140	117	23	6	9	8	89	0	286	10	4	16	17	.485	2	0	3.86

Scott Pratt

Bats: Left **Throws:** Right **Pos:** 2B-131; PH-2; SS-1   **Ht:** 5'10" **Wt:** 185 **Born:** 2/4/77 **Age:** 24

Year Team	Lg Org	G	AB	H	2B	3B	HR	TB	R	RBI	TBB	IBB	SO	HBP	SH	SF	SB	CS	SB%	GDP	Avg	OBP	SLG
1998 Watertown	A- Cle	47	174	61	12	3	2	85	37	14	34	1	26	5	1	1	15	10	.60	4	.351	.467	.489
1999 Kinston	A+ Cle	133	486	120	27	6	9	186	86	54	77	3	95	6	1	3	47	11	.81	6	.247	.355	.383
2000 Akron	AA Cle	129	500	118	18	6	7	169	67	51	39	1	98	1	7	3	22	12	.65	7	.236	.291	.338
Buffalo	AAA Cle	4	12	1	0	0	0	1	0	1	0	0	4	0	0	1	0	0	—	1	.083	.077	.083
3 Min. YEARS		313	1172	300	57	15	18	441	190	120	150	5	223	12	9	8	84	33	.72	18	.256	.344	.376

Ryan Price

Pitches: Right **Bats:** Right **Pos:** SP-24; RP-2   **Ht:** 6'3" **Wt:** 190 **Born:** 1/31/78 **Age:** 23

Year Team	Lg Org	G	GS	CG	GF	IP	BFP	H	R	ER	HR	SH	SF	HB	TBB	IBB	SO	WP	Bk	W	L	Pct.	ShO	Sv	ERA
1997 Rockies	R Col	14	14	0	0	77	338	69	49	30	2	1	2	5	28	0	98	10	4	2	7	.222	0	0	3.51
1998 Asheville	A Col	27	26	5	1	168.1	717	178	93	77	23	4	5	8	41	0	145	11	3	10	7	.588	0	0	4.12
1999 Salem	A+ Col	28	27	1	0	171.2	762	198	102	94	13	6	5	8	57	0	143	22	0	10	12	.455	0	0	4.93
2000 Carolina	AA Col	20	18	0	1	86	415	86	69	59	5	3	3	8	76	2	67	25	0	6	7	.462	0	0	6.17
Salem	A+ Col	6	6	0	0	30	159	27	26	20	1	2	1	5	37	0	32	13	0	1	3	.250	0	0	6.00
4 Min. YEARS		95	91	6	2	533	2391	558	339	280	44	16	16	34	239	2	485	81	7	29	36	.446	0	0	4.73

Matt Priess

Bats: Right **Throws:** Right **Pos:** C-43; PH-8; DH-2; 1B-1   **Ht:** 6'2" **Wt:** 190 **Born:** 11/24/74 **Age:** 26

Year Team	Lg Org	G	AB	H	2B	3B	HR	TB	R	RBI	TBB	IBB	SO	HBP	SH	SF	SB	CS	SB%	GDP	Avg	OBP	SLG
1997 Salem-Keizr	A- SF	46	172	47	8	2	3	68	22	31	12	0	30	1	0	3	0	0	.00	3	.273	.319	.395
1998 Shreveport	AA SF	2	1	0	0	0	0	0	0	0	1	0	0	0	0	0	0	0	—	0	.000	.500	.000
Bakersfield	A+ SF	52	188	54	11	0	4	77	23	19	19	0	30	4	1	2	0	0	—	11	.287	.362	.410
1999 San Jose	A+ SF	86	293	67	11	2	1	85	35	28	38	1	38	2	4	4	1	2	.33	11	.229	.318	.290
Shreveport	AA SF	5	12	2	0	0	1	5	1	1	1	0	3	0	0	0	0	0	—	0	.167	.231	.417
2000 Shreveport	AA SF	52	143	35	6	0	5	56	16	18	15	0	26	0	1	0	1	1	.50	5	.245	.316	.392
4 Min. YEARS		243	809	205	36	4	14	291	97	97	86	1	127	7	6	9	2	4	.33	30	.253	.327	.360

Eddie Priest

Pitches: Left **Bats:** Right **Pos:** SP-27   **Ht:** 6'1" **Wt:** 200 **Born:** 4/8/74 **Age:** 27

Year Team	Lg Org	G	GS	CG	GF	IP	BFP	H	R	ER	HR	SH	SF	HB	TBB	IBB	SO	WP	Bk	W	L	Pct.	ShO	Sv	ERA
1994 Billings	R+ Cin	13	13	2	0	85	333	74	31	24	4	3	0	1	14	0	82	2	1	7	4	.636	0	0	2.54
1995 Winston-Sal	A+ Cin	12	12	1	0	67	275	60	32	27	7	2	2	0	22	0	60	2	0	5	5	.500	1	0	3.63
1996 Winston-Sal	A+ Cin	4	4	0	0	12.1	48	5	2	1	1	0	0	0	6	0	9	1	0	1	0	1.000	0	0	0.73
1997 Chston-WV	A Cin	14	14	0	0	77	321	79	38	31	6	2	3	2	10	0	70	5	0	5	3	.625	0	0	3.62
Chattanooga	AA Cin	14	14	1	0	91.2	379	101	39	35	7	2	2	0	17	1	63	3	1	4	6	.400	0	0	3.44
1998 Chattanooga	AA Cin	4	4	0	0	26	105	16	5	5	1	1	0	0	10	1	29	1	0	1	2	.333	0	0	1.73
Indianapols	AAA Cin	6	6	0	0	34	147	36	19	18	6	2	0	1	7	0	21	2	0	4	1	.800	0	0	4.76
Buffalo	AAA Cle	16	16	0	0	88	390	103	56	48	10	2	1	2	28	2	44	2	0	3	5	.375	0	0	4.91

227

HOW MUCH HE PITCHED			WHAT HE GAVE UP			THE RESULTS		
Year Team	Lg Org	G GS CG GF	IP BFP	H R ER HR SH SF HB	TBB IBB SO WP Bk	W L Pct.	ShO	Sv ERA
1999 Indianapols	AAA Cin	18 12 0 0	69 303	86 41 41 10 3 2	20 1 35 3 1	6 5 .545	0	2 5.35
Chattanooga	AA Cin	12 12 0 0	77 337	99 42 34 6 3 1	14 0 60 1 2	4 3 .571	0	2 3.97
2000 Chattanooga	AA Cin	27 27 3 0	180 770	182 78 56 5 10 5 8	59 1 149 11 0	11 7 .611	1	0 2.80
1998 Cincinnati	NL	2 2 0 0	6 29	12 8 7 2 0 1 0	1 0 1 0	0 0 1 .000	0	0 10.50
7 Min. YEARS		140 134 7 2	807 3408	840 384 320 62 28 17 19	207 5 622 33 5	51 41 .554	2	2 3.57

Alejandro Prieto

Bats: Right **Throws:** Right **Pos:** SS-54; 2B-47; 3B-21; PR-4; OF-1; PH-1   **Ht:** 5'11" **Wt:** 175 **Born:** 6/19/76 **Age:** 25

BATTING														BASERUNNING			PERCENTAGES		
Year Team	Lg Org	G	AB	H	2B	3B	HR	TB	R	RBI	TBB	IBB	SO	HBP	SH	SF	SB CS SB% GDP	Avg OBP SLG	
1993 Royals	R KC	45	114	28	3	0	0	31	14	6	9	1	13	0	4	0	4 2 .67 1	.246 .301 .272	
1994 Royals	R KC	18	60	18	5	0	2	29	15	17	2	1	5	4	0	1	1 0 1.00 0	.300 .358 .483	
1995 Springfield	A KC	124	431	108	9	3	2	129	61	44	40	1	69	6	12	2	11 7 .61 10	.251 .322 .299	
1996 Wilmington	A+ KC	119	447	127	19	6	1	161	65	40	31	0	66	3	8	5	26 15 .63 7	.284 .331 .360	
1997 Wilmington	A+ KC	129	437	94	13	3	3	122	52	38	41	1	59	2	11	6	20 8 .71 6	.215 .282 .279	
1998 Wichita	AA KC	113	384	101	18	7	2	139	61	35	31	0	54	2	8	0	4 8 .33 13	.263 .321 .362	
1999 Wichita	AA KC	114	360	106	23	4	6	155	56	41	35	1	47	1	13	3	12 6 .67 10	.294 .356 .431	
2000 Omaha	AAA KC	118	384	101	19	0	7	141	54	37	26	0	40	6	8	2	14 6 .70 12	.263 .318 .367	
8 Min. YEARS		780	2617	683	109	23	23	907	378	258	215	5	353	24	64	19	92 52 .64 59	.261 .321 .347	

Chris Prieto

Bats: Left **Throws:** Left **Pos:** OF-75; PH-14; PR-2   **Ht:** 5'11" **Wt:** 180 **Born:** 8/24/72 **Age:** 28

BATTING														BASERUNNING			PERCENTAGES		
Year Team	Lg Org	G	AB	H	2B	3B	HR	TB	R	RBI	TBB	IBB	SO	HBP	SH	SF	SB CS SB% GDP	Avg OBP SLG	
1993 Spokane	A- SD	73	280	81	17	5	1	111	64	28	47	0	30	5	0	3	36 3 .92 4	.289 .397 .396	
1994 Rancho Cuca	A+ SD	102	353	87	10	3	1	106	64	29	52	1	49	5	6	4	29 11 .73 3	.246 .348 .300	
1995 Rancho Cuca	A+ SD	114	366	100	12	6	2	130	80	35	64	2	55	5	8	5	39 14 .74 10	.273 .384 .355	
1996 Rancho Cuca	A+ SD	55	217	52	11	2	2	73	36	23	39	1	36	0	1	0	23 8 .74 2	.240 .355 .336	
Las Vegas	AAA SD	5	7	0	0	0	0	0	1	0	0	0	0	0	0	0	0 0 — 0	.000 .000 .000	
Memphis	AA SD	7	12	4	0	1	0	6	1	0	1	0	2	0	0	0	2 0 1.00 0	.333 .385 .500	
1997 Rancho Cuca	A+ SD	22	82	23	4	0	4	39	21	12	19	1	16	0	3	0	4 3 .57 0	.280 .416 .476	
Mobile	AA SD	109	388	124	22	9	2	170	80	58	59	0	55	10	1	5	26 6 .81 2	.320 .418 .438	
1998 Las Vegas	AAA SD	92	352	107	18	6	2	143	65	35	40	1	48	1	1	0	20 11 .65 4	.304 .377 .406	
1999 Las Vegas	AAA SD	108	348	84	14	6	6	128	66	29	46	0	51	6	2	2	21 6 .78 2	.241 .338 .368	
2000 Albuquerque	AAA LA	85	248	69	13	3	0	112	53	31	50	1	42	4	3	1	25 5 .83 3	.278 .406 .452	
8 Min. YEARS		772	2653	731	121	41	28	1018	531	280	417	7	384	36	25	20	225 67 .77 30	.276 .379 .384	

Rick Prieto

Bats: Both **Throws:** Right **Pos:** OF-118   **Ht:** 5'10" **Wt:** 175 **Born:** 8/24/72 **Age:** 28

BATTING														BASERUNNING			PERCENTAGES		
Year Team	Lg Org	G	AB	H	2B	3B	HR	TB	R	RBI	TBB	IBB	SO	HBP	SH	SF	SB CS SB% GDP	Avg OBP SLG	
1993 Watertown	A- Cle	68	219	64	15	4	4	99	53	40	39	2	61	8	1	1	11 1 .92 3	.292 .416 .452	
1994 Columbus	A Cle	124	378	81	14	8	8	135	67	39	65	3	87	15	4	0	21 10 .68 6	.214 .352 .357	
1995 Kinston	A+ Cle	26	88	17	2	1	1	24	12	10	13	0	20	0	1	0	3 1 .75 2	.193 .297 .273	
Bakersfield	A+ Cle	74	248	55	12	2	2	77	34	22	29	0	46	3	6	0	15 2 .88 1	.222 .311 .310	
Columbus	A Cle	4	18	4	0	0	1	7	1	2	0	0	4	0	0	0	0 0 — 0	.222 .222 .389	
1996 Salinas	IND —	88	364	123	27	10	5	185	83	49	38	1	42	7	0	1	30 1 .97 6	.338 .410 .508	
1997 Salinas	IND —	22	98	35	6	2	1	48	14	10	5	0	12	2	0	1	15 0 1.00 1	.357 .396 .490	
Rancho Cuca	A+ SD	68	281	82	12	3	5	115	47	31	44	0	45	6	2	0	11 6 .65 0	.292 .399 .409	
1998 Las Vegas	AAA SD	32	79	21	6	1	0	29	15	8	12	0	22	2	0	1	4 2 .67 0	.266 .372 .367	
Mobile	AA SD	72	218	52	9	2	4	77	30	25	21	1	49	3	0	0	9 2 .82 0	.239 .314 .353	
1999 Mobile	AA SD	118	359	103	14	4	6	143	61	43	57	0	55	5	5	1	28 5 .85 6	.287 .391 .398	
2000 Birmingham	AA CWS	118	432	110	15	3	1	134	65	40	86	1	59	2	14	3	30 5 .86 7	.255 .379 .310	
8 Min. YEARS		814	2782	747	132	40	38	1073	482	319	409	8	502	53	33	8	177 35 .83 32	.269 .372 .386	

Bret Prinz

Pitches: Right **Bats:** Right **Pos:** RP-59   **Ht:** 6'3" **Wt:** 200 **Born:** 6/15/77 **Age:** 24

HOW MUCH HE PITCHED			WHAT HE GAVE UP			THE RESULTS		
Year Team	Lg Org	G GS CG GF	IP BFP	H R ER HR SH SF HB	TBB IBB SO WP Bk	W L Pct.	ShO	Sv ERA
1998 Diamondbcks	R Ari	4 0 0 4	5.1 24	7 3 2 0 0 0 1	0 0 3 0 0	0 0 —	—	0 3.38
Lethbridge	R+ Ari	11 10 0 0	46.2 204	49 26 16 2 1 0 3	13 0 30 8 0	4 2 .667	0	0 3.09
1999 South Bend	A Ari	30 23 0 3	138.2 594	129 82 69 16 5 7 8	52 0 98 10 4	6 10 .375	0	0 4.48
2000 South Bend	A Ari	6 0 0 5	7.1 26	2 2 0 0 0 0 0	1 0 10 1 0	1 0 1.000	0	1 0.00
El Paso	AA Ari	53 0 0 42	60.2 265	71 24 24 6 1 1 5	16 3 69 3 0	9 1 .900	0	26 3.56
3 Min. YEARS		104 33 0 54	258.2 1113	258 137 111 24 7 8 18	82 3 210 22 4	20 13 .606	0	27 3.86

Alan Probst

Bats: Right **Throws:** Right **Pos:** C-34; PH-2   **Ht:** 6'4" **Wt:** 215 **Born:** 10/24/70 **Age:** 30

BATTING														BASERUNNING			PERCENTAGES		
Year Team	Lg Org	G	AB	H	2B	3B	HR	TB	R	RBI	TBB	IBB	SO	HBP	SH	SF	SB CS SB% GDP	Avg OBP SLG	
1992 Auburn	A- Hou	66	224	53	14	1	5	84	24	34	23	1	48	3	1	2	1 0 1.00 5	.237 .313 .375	
1993 Asheville	A Hou	40	124	32	4	0	5	51	14	21	12	0	34	0	0	1	0 2 .00 5	.258 .321 .411	
Quad City	A Hou	49	176	48	9	2	3	70	18	28	16	1	48	3	0	3	2 0 1.00 1	.273 .338 .398	
1994 Quad City	A Hou	113	375	87	14	1	9	130	50	41	37	3	98	2	3	3	2 5 .29 8	.232 .302 .347	
1995 Quad City	A Hou	52	151	39	12	1	7	74	23	27	13	0	28	1	1	1	2 0 1.00 6	.258 .319 .490	
Jackson	AA Hou	28	89	21	5	0	1	29	11	8	7	0	25	1	0	2	0 0 — 3	.236 .293 .326	
1996 Tucson	AAA Hou	2	7	2	1	0	0	3	0	1	1	0	3	0	0	0	0 0 — 0	.286 .375 .429	
Jackson	AA Hou	63	180	44	9	1	7	76	20	33	16	1	43	2	2	2	1 0 1.00 4	.244 .310 .422	

Year Team	Lg Org	G	AB	H	2B	3B	HR	TB	R	RBI	TBB	IBB	SO	HBP	SH	SF	SB	CS	SB%	GDP	Avg	OBP	SLG
1997 Jackson	AA Hou	8	24	8	2	0	1	13	2	7	3	0	7	0	0	0	0	0	—	0	.333	.407	.542
New Orleans	AAA Hou	46	112	25	6	0	2	37	8	10	9	0	27	0	1	2	0	0	—	4	.223	.276	.330
1998 Knoxville	AA Tor	79	261	68	22	0	10	120	53	44	35	0	81	2	1	3	2	1	.67	7	.261	.349	.460
Syracuse	AAA Tor	12	33	11	1	0	1	15	2	4	2	0	6	0	0	0	0	0	—	2	.333	.371	.455
1999 Syracuse	AAA Tor	23	59	13	2	0	1	18	6	5	4	0	18	0	0	1	0	0	—	1	.220	.266	.305
Knoxville	AA Tor	21	66	14	3	0	1	20	5	7	5	0	23	0	1	2	0	0	—	3	.212	.260	.303
2000 Norfolk	AAA NYM	36	104	28	5	0	2	39	11	13	10	0	38	0	1	0	0	0	—	1	.269	.333	.375
9 Min. YEARS		638	1985	493	109	6	55	779	247	283	193	6	527	14	11	22	10	8	.56	44	.248	.316	.392

Tim Pugh

Pitches: Right Bats: Right Pos: SP-20; RP-2   Ht: 6'6" Wt: 225 Born: 1/26/67 Age: 34

Year Team	Lg Org	G	GS	CG	GF	IP	BFP	H	R	ER	HR	SH	SF	HB	TBB	IBB	SO	WP	Bk	W	L	Pct.	ShO	Sv	ERA
1989 Billings	R+ Cin	13	13	2	0	77.2	333	81	44	34	4	6	2	5	25	0	72	4	6	2	6	.250	0	0	3.94
1990 Chston-WV	A Cin	27	27	8	0	177.1	733	142	58	37	5	5	3	7	56	0	154	10	0	15	6	.714	2	0	1.88
1991 Chattanooga	AA Cin	5	5	0	0	38.1	143	20	7	7	2	1	1	4	11	0	24	0	0	3	1	.750	0	0	1.64
Nashville	AAA Cin	23	23	3	0	148.2	612	130	68	63	9	3	6	10	56	2	89	9	1	7	11	.389	1	0	3.81
1992 Nashville	AAA Cin	27	27	3	0	169.2	725	165	75	67	10	6	5	8	65	3	117	4	0	12	9	.571	2	0	3.55
1994 Indianapolis	AAA Cin	9	7	1	0	45	201	50	26	23	7	4	0	3	15	0	21	1	0	2	3	.400	1	0	4.60
1995 Indianapolis	AAA Cin	6	6	1	0	42.1	184	42	24	22	4	1	4	5	14	1	20	1	0	2	4	.333	1	0	4.68
1996 Indianapolis	AAA Cin	4	4	1	0	25.2	102	19	7	7	1	0	0	2	4	0	18	1	0	2	1	.667	1	0	2.45
1997 Toledo	AAA Det	19	17	0	1	109	460	115	60	52	18	2	3	5	28	0	97	4	0	3	5	.375	0	0	4.29
1998 St. Paul	IND —	12	11	0	0	48.1	219	60	39	30	7	1	2	4	13	1	32	0	1	4	4	.500	0	0	5.59
2000 Somerset	IND —	4	4	0	0	22	94	25	11	11	2	0	1	1	2	0	21	2	0	2	1	.667	0	0	4.50
Richmond	AAA Atl	18	16	0	0	88.2	407	117	55	51	10	1	2	7	26	1	69	3	0	6	4	.600	0	0	5.18
1992 Cincinnati	NL	7	7	0	0	45.1	187	47	15	13	2	2	1	1	13	3	18	0	0	4	2	.667	0	0	2.58
1993 Cincinnati	NL	31	27	3	3	164.1	722	200	102	96	19	6	5	7	59	1	94	3	2	10	15	.400	1	0	5.26
1994 Cincinnati	NL	10	9	1	0	47.2	227	60	37	32	5	2	5	3	26	0	24	4	0	3	3	.500	0	0	6.04
1995 Cincinnati	NL	28	12	0	4	98.1	413	100	46	42	13	2	2	1	32	2	38	3	1	6	5	.545	0	0	3.84
1996 Cincinnati	NL	10	0	0	0	15.2	83	24	20	20	3	2	1	1	11	2	9	1	0	1	1	.500	0	0	11.49
Kansas City	AL	19	1	0	0	36.1	164	42	24	22	9	0	1	2	12	1	27	2	0	0	1	.000	0	0	5.45
1997 Detroit	AL	2	2	0	0	9	37	6	5	5	0	0	0	0	5	0	4	0	0	1	1	.500	0	0	5.00
10 Min. YEARS		167	160	19	1	992.2	4213	966	474	404	79	30	29	61	315	8	734	39	8	60	55	.522	8	0	3.66
6 Maj. YEARS		107	58	4	15	416.2	1849	479	249	230	51	14	15	15	158	9	214	13	3	25	28	.472	1	0	4.97

Rob Pugmire

Pitches: Right Bats: Right Pos: SP-9   Ht: 6'3" Wt: 205 Born: 9/5/78 Age: 22

Year Team	Lg Org	G	GS	CG	GF	IP	BFP	H	R	ER	HR	SH	SF	HB	TBB	IBB	SO	WP	Bk	W	L	Pct.	ShO	Sv	ERA
1997 Burlington	R+ Cle	14	14	0	0	66.2	302	72	42	29	4	3	4	9	29	0	62	7	2	1	2	.333	0	0	3.92
1999 Columbus	A Cle	10	10	0	0	57.2	229	43	20	17	4	1	1	2	14	0	71	1	1	6	1	.857	0	0	2.65
Kinston	A+ Cle	16	16	0	0	96	396	85	44	39	8	4	1	8	25	0	89	3	0	7	1	.875	0	0	3.66
2000 Akron	AA Cle	4	4	0	0	16.1	77	22	11	10	0	0	0	3	6	0	14	1	0	1	1	.500	0	0	5.51
Mahoning Vy	A- Cle	5	5	0	0	12.2	62	16	10	6	0	0	1	0	8	0	10	1	0	0	1	.000	0	0	4.26
3 Min. YEARS		49	49	0	0	249.1	1066	238	127	101	16	8	7	17	82	0	246	13	3	15	6	.714	0	0	3.65

Denis Pujals

Pitches: Right Bats: Right Pos: RP-21; SP-5   Ht: 6'3" Wt: 220 Born: 2/5/73 Age: 28

Year Team	Lg Org	G	GS	CG	GF	IP	BFP	H	R	ER	HR	SH	SF	HB	TBB	IBB	SO	WP	Bk	W	L	Pct.	ShO	Sv	ERA
1996 Butte	R+ TB	15	15	0	0	87.1	392	110	65	49	9	1	0	5	19	0	82	6	3	2	7	.222	0	0	5.05
1997 St. Pete	A+ TB	24	24	2	0	140.1	588	156	74	69	14	6	8	8	27	1	69	1	0	9	4	.692	1	0	4.43
1998 St. Pete	A+ TB	42	0	0	0	77.2	308	73	30	23	1	2	1	2	22	2	46	2	0	5	2	.714	0	1	2.85
1999 Orlando	AA TB	42	0	0	9	72.1	316	82	35	31	6	2	6	6	19	3	39	6	0	5	3	.625	0	0	3.86
2000 Durham	AAA TB	20	3	0	6	48	215	59	32	28	4	1	1	4	19	1	18	0	1	4	2	.667	0	0	5.25
Orlando	AA TB	6	2	0	0	19	75	14	6	5	1	0	1	2	4	0	7	1	0	1	2	.333	0	0	2.37
5 Min. YEARS		149	44	2	24	439.2	1894	494	242	205	35	12	17	24	110	7	261	16	4	26	20	.565	1	1	4.20

Albert Pujols

Bats: Right Throws: Right Pos: 3B-127; PH-3; OF-2; DH-2; PR-1   Ht: 6'3" Wt: 210 Born: 1/16/80 Age: 21

Year Team	Lg Org	G	AB	H	2B	3B	HR	TB	R	RBI	TBB	IBB	SO	HBP	SH	SF	SB	CS	SB%	GDP	Avg	OBP	SLG
2000 Peoria	A StL	109	395	128	32	6	17	223	62	84	38	7	37	5	0	2	2	4	.33	10	.324	.389	.565
Potomac	A+ StL	21	81	23	8	1	2	39	11	10	7	0	8	0	1	0	1	1	.50	3	.284	.341	.481
Memphis	AAA StL	3	14	3	1	0	0	4	1	2	1	0	2	0	0	0	1	0	1.00	0	.214	.267	.286
1 Min. YEARS		133	490	154	41	7	19	266	74	96	46	7	47	5	1	2	4	5	.44	13	.314	.378	.543

Harvey Pulliam

Bats: Right Throws: Right Pos: OF-13; PH-7; DH-3   Ht: 6'0" Wt: 205 Born: 10/20/67 Age: 33

Year Team	Lg Org	G	AB	H	2B	3B	HR	TB	R	RBI	TBB	IBB	SO	HBP	SH	SF	SB	CS	SB%	GDP	Avg	OBP	SLG
1986 Royals	R KC	48	168	35	3	0	4	50	14	23	8	1	33	3	2	3	3	2	.60	9	.208	.253	.298
1987 Appleton	A KC	110	395	109	20	1	9	158	54	55	26	0	79	3	1	3	21	7	.75	10	.276	.323	.400
1988 Baseball Cy	A+ KC	132	457	111	19	4	4	150	56	42	34	3	87	5	2	3	21	11	.66	13	.243	.301	.328
1989 Omaha	AAA KC	7	22	4	1	0	0	6	3	2	3	0	6	0	0	0	0	0	—	0	.182	.280	.273
Memphis	AA KC	116	417	121	28	8	10	195	67	67	44	4	65	5	0	3	5	5	.50	12	.290	.362	.468
1990 Omaha	AAA KC	123	436	117	18	5	16	193	72	72	49	0	82	3	2	4	9	3	.75	14	.268	.343	.443
1991 Omaha	AAA KC	104	346	89	18	2	6	129	35	39	31	0	62	1	1	3	2	4	.33	4	.257	.318	.373

Year Team	Lg Org	G	AB	H	2B	3B	HR	TB	R	RBI	TBB	IBB	SO	HBP	SH	SF	SB	CS	SB%	GDP	Avg	OBP	SLG
								BATTING										**BASERUNNING**				**PERCENTAGES**		
1992 Omaha	AAA KC	100	359	97	12	2	16	161	55	60	32	1	53	6	1	3	4	2	.67	15	.270	.338	.448
1993 Omaha	AAA KC	54	208	55	10	0	5	80	28	26	17	1	36	1	0	0	1	0	1.00	6	.264	.323	.385
1994 Las Vegas	AAA SD	95	314	72	10	0	20	142	48	53	21	0	65	4	0	2	0	1	.00	5	.229	.284	.452
1995 Colo Sprngs	AAA Col	115	407	133	30	6	25	250	90	91	49	10	59	3	0	6	6	2	.75	11	.327	.398	.614
1996 Colo Sprngs	AAA Col	79	283	78	13	1	10	123	46	58	32	4	49	3	0	4	2	3	.40	12	.276	.351	.435
1997 Colo Sprngs	AAA Col	40	137	55	10	2	12	105	44	43	21	3	19	4	0	0	1	0	1.00	1	.401	.494	.766
2000 Richmond	AAA Atl	21	59	16	5	0	2	27	7	4	6	0	9	2	0	0	0	0	—	1	.271	.358	.458
1991 Kansas City	AL	18	33	9	1	0	3	19	4	4	3	1	9	0	1	0	0	0	—	1	.273	.333	.576
1992 Kansas City	AL	4	5	1	1	0	0	2	2	0	1	0	3	0	0	0	0	0	—	0	.200	.333	.400
1993 Kansas City	AL	27	62	16	5	0	1	24	7	6	2	0	14	1	0	0	0	0	—	3	.258	.292	.387
1995 Colorado	NL	5	5	2	1	0	1	6	1	3	0	0	2	0	0	0	0	0	—	1	.400	.400	1.200
1996 Colorado	NL	10	15	2	0	0	0	2	2	0	2	0	6	0	0	0	0	0	—	1	.133	.235	.133
1997 Colorado	NL	59	67	19	3	0	3	31	15	9	5	0	15	0	0	0	1	0	.00	2	.284	.333	.463
13 Min. YEARS		1144	4008	1092	198	31	139	1769	619	635	373	27	704	43	9	34	75	40	.65	113	.272	.338	.441
6 Maj. YEARS		123	187	49	11	0	8	84	31	22	13	1	49	1	1	0	1	0	.00	7	.262	.313	.449

Ken Pumphrey

Pitches: Right **Bats:** Right **Pos:** SP-25; RP-1   **Ht:** 6'6" **Wt:** 208 **Born:** 9/10/76 **Age:** 24

Year Team	Lg Org	G	GS	CG	GF	IP	BFP	H	R	ER	HR	SH	SF	HB	TBB	IBB	SO	WP	Bk	W	L	Pct.	ShO	Sv	ERA
			HOW MUCH HE PITCHED							**WHAT HE GAVE UP**										**THE RESULTS**				
1994 Mets	R NYM	10	8	0	0	57.1	244	51	27	23	6	1	4	3	16	0	42	6	3	1	3	.250	0	0	3.61
1995 Kingsport	R+ NYM	12	12	0	0	65.1	283	50	32	28	3	3	0	6	42	0	76	7	0	7	3	.700	0	0	3.86
1996 Pittsfield	A- NYM	14	14	1	0	87	373	68	41	31	1	1	2	4	41	0	61	10	2	7	2	.778	1	0	3.21
1997 Capital Cty	A NYM	27	27	3	0	165.2	708	137	70	57	11	7	3	20	72	0	133	11	1	12	6	.667	2	0	3.10
1998 St. Lucie	A+ NYM	25	25	1	0	142.1	606	126	66	50	7	2	6	7	57	0	99	9	1	10	6	.625	0	0	3.16
Binghamton	AA NYM	3	2	0	0	8	36	10	4	4	0	0	0	0	3	0	6	0	0	1	0	1.000	0	0	4.50
1999 Binghamton	AA NYM	25	23	0	1	131.1	617	146	95	70	10	4	4	15	71	0	84	5	0	6	9	.400	0	0	4.80
2000 New Britain	AA Min	12	12	1	0	63.1	289	68	54	50	7	1	1	8	31	0	39	3	0	0	9	.000	0	0	7.11
Fort Myers	A+ Min	14	13	1	0	83.1	343	68	32	28	1	1	3	6	35	0	58	3	0	4	6	.400	0	0	3.02
7 Min. YEARS		142	136	7	1	803.2	3499	724	421	341	46	20	23	69	368	0	598	54	7	48	44	.522	3	0	3.82

Nick Punto

Bats: Both **Throws:** Right **Pos:** SS-120; PH-2   **Ht:** 5'9" **Wt:** 170 **Born:** 11/8/77 **Age:** 23

Year Team	Lg Org	G	AB	H	2B	3B	HR	TB	R	RBI	TBB	IBB	SO	HBP	SH	SF	SB	CS	SB%	GDP	Avg	OBP	SLG
								BATTING										**BASERUNNING**				**PERCENTAGES**		
1998 Batavia	A- Phi	72	279	69	9	4	1	89	51	20	42	0	48	1	0	1	19	7	.73	4	.247	.347	.319
1999 Clearwater	A+ Phi	106	400	122	18	6	1	155	65	48	67	3	53	3	3	5	16	7	.70	13	.305	.404	.388
2000 Reading	AA Phi	121	456	116	15	4	5	154	77	47	69	0	71	2	14	6	33	10	.77	5	.254	.351	.338
3 Min. YEARS		299	1135	307	42	14	7	398	193	115	178	3	172	6	17	12	68	24	.74	22	.270	.369	.351

Rob Purvis

Pitches: Right **Bats:** Right **Pos:** SP-28   **Ht:** 6'2" **Wt:** 200 **Born:** 8/11/77 **Age:** 23

Year Team	Lg Org	G	GS	CG	GF	IP	BFP	H	R	ER	HR	SH	SF	HB	TBB	IBB	SO	WP	Bk	W	L	Pct.	ShO	Sv	ERA
			HOW MUCH HE PITCHED							**WHAT HE GAVE UP**										**THE RESULTS**				
1999 White Sox	R CWS	4	0	0	3	9	48	12	10	4	0	0	0	0	6	0	7	1	4	0	1	.000	0	2	4.00
Burlington	A CWS	6	0	0	3	11.1	50	10	5	3	1	0	0	1	4	0	8	0	1	0	0	—	0	1	2.38
2000 Winston-Sal	A+ CWS	27	27	2	0	167.2	727	139	81	63	6	2	2	11	87	0	114	22	0	11	10	.524	0	0	3.38
Birmingham	AA CWS	1	1	0	0	4	24	6	8	2	1	0	1	0	3	0	3	0	0	0	1	.000	0	0	4.50
2 Min. YEARS		38	28	2	6	192	849	167	104	72	8	2	3	12	100	0	132	23	5	11	12	.478	0	3	3.38

Ed Quezada

Pitches: Right **Bats:** Right **Pos:** RP-21   **Ht:** 6'2" **Wt:** 150 **Born:** 1/15/75 **Age:** 26

Year Team	Lg Org	G	GS	CG	GF	IP	BFP	H	R	ER	HR	SH	SF	HB	TBB	IBB	SO	WP	Bk	W	L	Pct.	ShO	Sv	ERA
			HOW MUCH HE PITCHED							**WHAT HE GAVE UP**										**THE RESULTS**				
1995 Expos	R Mon	12	10	0	2	52.1	221	52	36	29	2	1	1	5	10	0	36	10	1	0	7	.000	0	0	4.99
1996 Vermont	A- Mon	14	14	2	0	92.2	378	82	32	24	3	3	1	4	20	0	79	7	0	6	5	.545	0	0	2.33
1997 Cape Fear	A Mon	30	19	0	5	141.1	589	143	73	67	12	1	1	11	31	0	87	4	0	8	6	.571	0	2	4.27
1998 Cape Fear	A Mon	30	19	2	1	138.1	592	136	72	63	12	5	9	12	51	0	82	5	1	8	8	.500	1	0	4.10
1999 Harrisburg	AA Mon	3	0	0	2	5	18	2	1	1	0	1	0	0	1	0	4	0	0	0	0	—	0	0	1.80
Jupiter	A+ Mon	34	1	0	14	63.2	273	64	34	31	4	1	1	7	17	0	25	6	1	2	6	.250	0	4	4.38
2000 Harrisburg	AA Mon	4	0	0	0	5.1	31	10	5	5	1	0	1	0	5	0	0	0	0	0	0	—	0	0	8.44
Jupiter	A+ Mon	17	0	0	5	25.1	110	24	17	11	4	1	3	3	8	1	7	2	0	2	2	.500	0	1	3.91
6 Min. YEARS		144	63	4	29	524	2212	513	270	231	39	12	17	45	143	1	320	34	3	26	34	.433	1	3	3.97

Rob Radlosky

Pitches: Right **Bats:** Right **Pos:** SP-16; RP-3   **Ht:** 6'2" **Wt:** 204 **Born:** 1/7/74 **Age:** 27

Year Team	Lg Org	G	GS	CG	GF	IP	BFP	H	R	ER	HR	SH	SF	HB	TBB	IBB	SO	WP	Bk	W	L	Pct.	ShO	Sv	ERA
			HOW MUCH HE PITCHED							**WHAT HE GAVE UP**										**THE RESULTS**				
1994 Twins	R Min	11	11	0	0	56.1	234	54	28	21	1	0	3	3	19	0	52	4	7	3	4	.429	0	0	3.36
1995 Fort Wayne	A Min	30	18	1	5	120.2	522	111	64	54	11	7	5	11	55	2	102	5	2	11	8	.579	0	0	4.03
1996 Fort Myers	A+ Min	28	16	1	5	104	467	116	70	63	11	2	3	9	46	0	80	10	0	4	6	.400	1	1	5.45
1997 Fort Myers	A+ Min	23	22	3	1	128.1	510	87	42	37	10	5	4	5	37	0	109	2	0	9	5	.643	1	0	2.59
1998 New Britain	AA Min	27	19	0	0	132	552	127	61	59	16	6	2	6	38	0	117	7	0	10	3	.769	0	0	4.02
1999 Salt Lake	AAA Min	22	20	1	1	101.1	440	98	49	44	12	2	4	6	38	1	68	2	0	8	4	.667	0	0	3.91
2000 New Britain	AA Min	6	6	1	0	31.2	140	35	21	18	4	1	3	5	6	0	26	0	0	1	2	.333	0	0	5.12
Salt Lake	AAA Min	5	2	0	0	19	81	18	10	9	3	0	0	2	7	0	19	1	1	0	0	—	0	0	4.26
Trenton	AA Bos	8	8	0	0	36	162	46	22	21	1	1	1	0	6	0	30	0	0	2	2	.333	0	0	5.25
1999 Minnesota	AL	7	0	0	2	8.2	45	15	12	12	7	0	0	1	4	0	3	1	0	0	1	.000	0	0	12.46
7 Min. YEARS		160	122	7	12	729.1	3108	692	367	326	69	24	25	50	252	3	603	31	10	47	34	.580	2	1	4.02

Ryan Radmanovich

Bats: Left Throws: Right Pos: OF-107; PH-14; PR-2   Ht: 6'2" Wt: 200 Born: 8/9/71 Age: 29

Year Team	Lg Org	G	AB	H	2B	3B	HR	TB	R	RBI	TBB	IBB	SO	HBP	SH	SF	SB	CS	SB%	GDP	Avg	OBP	SLG
1993 Fort Wayne	A Min	62	204	59	7	5	8	100	36	38	30	2	60	7	2	2	8	2	.80	4	.289	.395	.490
1994 Fort Myers	A+ Min	26	85	16	4	0	2	26	11	9	7	0	19	2	0	0	3	1	.75	0	.188	.266	.306
Fort Wayne	A Min	101	383	105	20	6	19	194	64	69	45	3	98	3	1	1	19	14	.58	7	.274	.354	.507
1995 Fort Myers	A+ Min	12	41	13	2	0	0	15	3	5	2	0	8	1	0	0	0	0	—	0	.317	.364	.366
1996 Hardware Cy	AA Min	125	453	127	31	2	25	237	77	86	49	6	122	3	3	2	4	11	.27	12	.280	.353	.523
1997 Salt Lake	AAA Min	133	485	128	25	4	28	245	92	78	67	7	138	4	1	5	11	4	.73	4	.264	.355	.505
1998 Tacoma	AAA Sea	110	397	119	33	2	15	201	73	65	46	3	83	1	5	7	2	4	.33	6	.300	.368	.506
1999 Tacoma	AAA Sea	109	420	120	24	3	17	201	69	80	53	5	83	4	3	6	10	4	.71	8	.286	.366	.479
2000 Las Vegas	AAA SD	120	399	109	31	3	11	179	74	59	60	3	84	0	0	5	4	3	.57	9	.273	.364	.449
1998 Seattle	AL	25	69	15	4	0	2	25	5	10	4	1	25	0	2	0	1	1	.50	0	.217	.260	.362
8 Min. YEARS		798	2867	796	177	25	125	1398	499	489	359	29	695	25	15	28	61	43	.59	50	.278	.360	.488

Aaron Rakers

Pitches: Right Bats: Right Pos: RP-50   Ht: 6'3" Wt: 205 Born: 1/22/77 Age: 24

Year Team	Lg Org	G	GS	CG	GF	IP	BFP	H	R	ER	HR	SH	SF	HB	TBB	IBB	SO	WP	Bk	W	L	Pct.	ShO	Sv	ERA
1999 Bluefield	R+ Bal	3	0	0	1	7	28	5	2	2	1	0	0	0	3	0	12	0	0	0	0	—	0	0	2.57
Delmarva	A Bal	18	0	0	16	25.1	97	9	6	4	0	0	1	0	13	0	38	1	1	4	1	.800	0	8	1.42
2000 Frederick	A+ Bal	26	0	0	19	40.2	157	23	8	7	2	0	2	2	12	1	57	1	0	1	1	.500	0	8	1.55
Bowie	AA Bal	24	0	0	18	29	118	20	11	9	5	1	3	1	10	0	21	0	0	3	2	.600	0	8	2.79
2 Min. YEARS		71	0	0	54	102	400	57	27	22	8	1	6	3	38	1	128	2	1	8	4	.667	0	24	1.94

Matt Raleigh

Bats: Right Throws: Right Pos: 1B-11; PH-10; DH-3   Ht: 5'11" Wt: 235 Born: 7/18/70 Age: 30

Year Team	Lg Org	G	AB	H	2B	3B	HR	TB	R	RBI	TBB	IBB	SO	HBP	SH	SF	SB	CS	SB%	GDP	Avg	OBP	SLG
1992 Jamestown	A- Mon	77	261	57	14	2	11	108	41	44	45	2	101	0	0	2	14	2	.88	3	.218	.331	.414
1993 Jamestown	A- Mon	77	263	62	17	0	15	124	51	42	39	0	99	1	0	4	5	2	.71	3	.236	.332	.471
1994 Burlington	A Mon	114	398	109	18	2	34	233	78	83	75	3	138	5	0	3	6	2	.75	8	.274	.393	.585
1995 Wst Plm Bch	A+ Mon	66	179	37	11	0	2	54	29	18	54	1	64	6	1	3	4	2	.67	4	.207	.401	.302
1996 Frederick	A+ Bal	21	57	13	0	1	1	18	8	8	12	0	22	2	0	2	3	0	1.00	0	.228	.370	.316
High Desert	A+ Bal	27	84	24	6	0	7	51	17	13	14	0	33	0	0	1	2	0	1.00	0	.286	.384	.607
Bowie	AA Bal	4	8	2	1	0	0	3	0	2	1	0	3	0	0	0	0	0	—	0	.250	.333	.375
1997 Binghamton	AA NYM	122	398	78	15	0	37	204	71	74	79	6	169	1	0	1	0	2	.00	7	.196	.330	.513
1998 Norfolk	AAA NYM	4	4	0	0	0	0	0	0	0	0	0	0	0	0	0	0	0	—	0	.000	.000	.000
Binghamton	AA NYM	47	140	28	6	0	6	52	22	28	29	0	60	1	0	2	1	4	.20	1	.200	.337	.371
1999 Lehigh Val	IND —	60	215	56	11	0	16	115	38	45	44	1	79	0	0	0	3	0	1.00	0	.260	.382	.535
Carolina	AA Col	48	115	24	8	0	4	44	13	12	23	1	60	1	1	0	0	0	—	2	.209	.345	.383
2000 Calgary	AAA Fla	6	6	2	1	0	0	3	1	1	2	0	2	0	0	0	0	0	—	0	.333	.500	.500
Portland	AA Fla	18	50	10	1	0	2	17	8	6	7	0	24	1	0	0	0	0	—	0	.200	.310	.340
9 Min. YEARS		689	2178	502	109	5	135	1026	377	376	424	14	857	18	2	21	38	14	.73	31	.230	.357	.471

Dan Ramirez

Bats: Right Throws: Right Pos: OF-102; PH-6; DH-2; PR-2   Ht: 6'1" Wt: 185 Born: 2/22/74 Age: 27

Year Team	Lg Org	G	AB	H	2B	3B	HR	TB	R	RBI	TBB	IBB	SO	HBP	SH	SF	SB	CS	SB%	GDP	Avg	OBP	SLG
1994 Mets	R NYM	44	176	50	10	2	0	64	26	29	11	0	23	3	0	0	7	5	.58	4	.284	.337	.364
1995 Kingsport	R+ NYM	62	226	56	6	2	2	72	30	32	15	1	44	1	9	0	21	10	.68	5	.248	.298	.319
1996 Capital Cty	A NYM	47	143	33	5	0	1	41	20	13	11	0	30	1	6	0	6	4	.60	2	.231	.290	.287
Pittsfield	A- NYM	70	260	73	5	5	1	91	28	22	14	0	45	4	4	2	24	9	.73	3	.281	.325	.350
1997 Capital Cty	A NYM	130	478	146	24	4	1	181	82	47	44	0	104	4	3	3	51	25	.67	4	.305	.367	.379
1998 St. Lucie	A+ NYM	123	469	127	17	2	5	163	65	50	32	0	93	3	10	6	27	19	.59	7	.271	.318	.348
1999 Birmingham	AA CWS	32	127	25	5	0	0	30	16	10	3	0	31	1	0	1	6	4	.60	0	.197	.220	.236
Winston-Sal	A+ CWS	85	360	96	4	3	1	109	56	19	29	0	58	2	2	1	44	17	.72	7	.267	.324	.303
Charlotte	AAA CWS	6	14	2	1	0	0	3	2	1	0	0	3	1	1	1	1	0	1.00	1	.143	.235	.214
2000 Carolina	AA Col	110	382	98	8	2	2	116	40	39	14	1	89	3	11	4	17	13	.57	4	.257	.285	.304
7 Min. YEARS		709	2635	706	85	20	13	870	365	258	174	2	520	23	46	18	204	106	.66	39	.268	.317	.330

Erasmo Ramirez

Pitches: Left Bats: Left Pos: RP-37; SP-2   Ht: 6'0" Wt: 180 Born: 4/29/76 Age: 25

Year Team	Lg Org	G	GS	CG	GF	IP	BFP	H	R	ER	HR	SH	SF	HB	TBB	IBB	SO	WP	Bk	W	L	Pct.	ShO	Sv	ERA
1998 Bakersfield	A+ SF	14	0	0	9	21.1	80	10	8	8	0	2	0	2	6	0	17	1	3	1	1	.500	0	3	3.38
Salem-Keizr	A- SF	9	2	0	0	19.1	81	19	11	8	3	1	0	1	2	0	23	0	0	0	1	.000	0	0	3.72
1999 San Jose	A+ SF	31	0	0	12	57.1	219	42	18	17	2	2	4	1	8	0	52	2	0	2	0	1.000	0	5	2.67
2000 Shreveport	AA SF	39	2	0	13	58.2	269	80	45	42	7	6	4	3	21	5	46	0	0	0	5	.000	0	1	6.44
3 Min. YEARS		93	4	0	34	156.2	649	151	82	75	12	11	8	7	37	5	138	3	3	3	7	.300	0	9	4.31

Jose Ramirez

Pitches: Left Bats: Left Pos: RP-19   Ht: 6'1" Wt: 170 Born: 9/1/75 Age: 25

Year Team	Lg Org	G	GS	CG	GF	IP	BFP	H	R	ER	HR	SH	SF	HB	TBB	IBB	SO	WP	Bk	W	L	Pct.	ShO	Sv	ERA
1996 Fayettevlle	A Det	15	1	0	5	26	126	35	15	12	2	1	0	1	14	1	30	3	0	1	1	.500	0	0	4.15
Tigers	R Det	13	11	0	2	59.2	280	69	49	26	0	4	1	3	23	0	47	7	5	2	7	.222	0	0	3.92
1997 Jamestown	A- Det	15	15	1	0	94.2	398	84	49	41	4	4	4	4	38	0	75	5	2	3	4	.429	0	0	3.90

Year Team	Lg Org	G	GS	CG	GF	IP	BFP	H	R	ER	HR	SH	SF	HB	TBB	IBB	SO	WP	Bk	W	L	Pct.	ShO	Sv	ERA
1998 Tigers	R Det	2	0	0	0	7	30	7	3	3	1	0	0	0	4	0	8	0	0	1	0	1.000	0	0	3.86
Jamestown	A- Det	1	0	0	0	4	15	4	0	0	0	0	0	0	1	0	5	1	0	1	0	1.000	0	0	0.00
W Michigan	A Det	22	10	1	4	72.1	315	69	49	40	5	2	3	2	31	1	60	7	0	4	5	.444	0	0	4.98
1999 Lakeland	A+ Det	29	6	0	7	84.2	370	79	53	47	9	1	2	2	46	2	62	5	1	5	5	.500	0	0	5.00
Toledo	AAA Det	1	1	0	0	5	23	3	1	1	0	0	0	1	4	1	3	0	0	0	0	—	0	0	1.80
2000 Jacksnville	AA Det	19	0	0	3	25	117	33	18	16	4	1	4	1	10	0	11	7	1	2	2	.500	0	0	5.76
5 Min. YEARS		117	44	2	21	378.1	1674	383	237	186	25	13	14	14	171	5	301	35	9	19	24	.442	0	0	4.42

Julio Ramirez

Bats: Right **Throws:** Right **Pos:** OF-90; PH-4   **Ht:** 5'11" **Wt:** 170 **Born:** 8/10/77 **Age:** 23

Year Team	Lg Org	G	AB	H	2B	3B	HR	TB	R	RBI	TBB	IBB	SO	HBP	SH	SF	SB	CS	SB%	GDP	Avg	OBP	SLG
1995 Marlins	R Fla	48	204	58	9	4	2	81	35	13	13	0	42	1	1	0	17	6	.74	2	.284	.330	.397
1996 Brevard Cty	A+ Fla	17	61	15	0	1	0	17	11	2	4	0	18	0	0	1	2	3	.40	1	.246	.288	.279
Marlins	R Fla	42	171	49	5	3	0	60	33	15	14	0	34	3	1	0	25	8	.76	0	.287	.351	.351
1997 Kane County	A Fla	99	376	96	18	7	14	170	70	53	37	1	122	5	14	2	41	6	.87	1	.255	.329	.452
1998 Brevard Cty	A+ Fla	135	559	156	20	12	13	239	90	58	45	2	147	4	3	2	71	27	.72	3	.279	.336	.428
1999 Portland	AA Fla	138	568	148	30	10	13	237	87	64	39	1	150	2	5	5	64	14	.82	5	.261	.308	.417
2000 Calgary	AAA Fla	94	350	93	18	3	7	138	45	52	21	1	86	3	2	4	20	14	.59	5	.266	.310	.394
1999 Florida	NL	15	21	3	1	0	0	4	3	2	1	0	6	0	0	0	1	0	.00	0	.143	.182	.190
6 Min. YEARS		573	2289	615	100	40	49	942	371	257	173	5	599	18	26	14	240	78	.75	17	.269	.323	.412

Omar Ramirez

Bats: Right **Throws:** Right **Pos:** OF-125; PH-9   **Ht:** 5'9" **Wt:** 170 **Born:** 11/2/70 **Age:** 30

Year Team	Lg Org	G	AB	H	2B	3B	HR	TB	R	RBI	TBB	IBB	SO	HBP	SH	SF	SB	CS	SB%	GDP	Avg	OBP	SLG
1990 Indians	R Cle	18	58	10	0	0	0	10	6	2	11	0	11	0	0	0	2	4	.33	2	.172	.304	.172
1991 Watertown	A- Cle	56	210	56	17	0	2	79	30	17	30	0	30	1	3	1	12	2	.86	2	.267	.360	.376
1992 Kinston	A+ Cle	110	411	123	20	5	13	192	73	49	38	1	53	3	8	2	19	12	.61	5	.299	.361	.467
1993 Canton-Akrn	AA Cle	125	516	162	24	6	7	219	116	53	53	2	49	5	4	1	24	6	.80	9	.314	.383	.424
1994 Charlotte	AAA Cle	134	419	97	20	2	8	145	66	45	54	0	43	1	2	3	15	7	.68	11	.232	.319	.346
1995 Canton-Akrn	AA Cle	10	34	11	0	0	0	11	6	3	3	0	3	0	1	0	0	0	—	0	.324	.378	.324
1996 Kinston	A+ Cle	2	5	2	0	0	1	5	1	3	1	0	0	0	0	0	0	0	—	1	.400	.500	1.000
1998 Rio Grande	IND —	71	284	96	18	4	12	158	66	58	37	1	24	3	1	2	26	3	.90	10	.338	.417	.556
1999 New Orleans	AAA Hou	110	379	96	15	2	6	133	56	51	30	2	49	2	2	2	8	3	.73	13	.253	.310	.351
2000 New Orleans	AAA Hou	133	469	150	24	2	2	184	73	53	69	1	36	6	5	4	19	13	.59	23	.320	.411	.392
10 Min. YEARS		769	2785	803	138	21	51	1136	493	334	326	7	298	21	26	15	125	50	.71	76	.288	.365	.408

Kelly Ramos

Bats: Both **Throws:** Right **Pos:** C-61; DH-14; 1B-5; PH-1   **Ht:** 6'0" **Wt:** 168 **Born:** 10/15/76 **Age:** 24

Year Team	Lg Org	G	AB	H	2B	3B	HR	TB	R	RBI	TBB	IBB	SO	HBP	SH	SF	SB	CS	SB%	GDP	Avg	OBP	SLG
1996 Mets	R NYM	20	59	11	0	1	0	13	3	7	3	0	10	0	1	0	0	2	.00	2	.186	.226	.220
1997 Kingsport	R+ NYM	50	170	38	3	1	7	64	25	32	17	3	33	1	4	0	2	3	.40	5	.224	.298	.376
1998 Pittsfield	A- NYM	63	215	64	10	6	3	95	31	34	13	1	36	1	0	4	0	1	.00	6	.298	.335	.442
1999 St. Lucie	A+ NYM	24	80	15	3	1	2	26	6	11	8	1	16	1	0	4	0	0	—	4	.188	.253	.325
Capital Cty	A NYM	82	262	67	14	0	10	111	31	34	9	0	52	10	2	1	4	2	.67	5	.256	.305	.424
2000 Trenton	AA Bos	8	25	5	1	0	0	6	2	0	2	0	8	0	1	0	0	0	—	0	.200	.259	.240
Augusta	A Bos	73	260	65	17	1	7	105	27	37	24	1	54	6	1	0	1	2	.33	9	.250	.328	.404
5 Min. YEARS		320	1071	265	48	10	29	420	125	155	76	6	209	18	13	8	7	10	.41	31	.247	.306	.392

Mario Ramos

Pitches: Left **Bats:** Left **Pos:** SP-28; RP-2   **Ht:** 5'11" **Wt:** 165 **Born:** 10/19/77 **Age:** 23

Year Team	Lg Org	G	GS	CG	GF	IP	BFP	H	R	ER	HR	SH	SF	HB	TBB	IBB	SO	WP	Bk	W	L	Pct.	ShO	Sv	ERA
2000 Modesto	A+ Oak	26	24	1	1	152	624	131	63	49	6	9	3	3	50	4	134	3	1	12	5	.706	1	0	2.90
Midland	AA Oak	4	4	0	0	27.1	107	24	6	4	0	1	1	0	6	0	19	0	0	2	0	1.000	0	0	1.32
1 Min. YEARS		30	28	1	1	179.1	731	155	69	53	6	10	4	3	56	4	153	3	1	14	5	.737	1	0	2.66

Scott Randall

Pitches: Right **Bats:** Right **Pos:** SP-24; RP-6   **Ht:** 6'3" **Wt:** 190 **Born:** 10/29/75 **Age:** 25

Year Team	Lg Org	G	GS	CG	GF	IP	BFP	H	R	ER	HR	SH	SF	HB	TBB	IBB	SO	WP	Bk	W	L	Pct.	ShO	Sv	ERA
1995 Portland	A- Col	15	15	1	0	95	391	76	35	21	2	2	2	8	28	1	78	7	2	7	3	.700	0	0	1.99
1996 Asheville	A Col	24	24	1	0	154.1	615	121	53	47	11	5	1	7	50	3	136	4	0	14	4	.778	1	0	2.74
1997 Salem	A+ Col	27	26	2	1	176	763	167	93	75	8	8	6	11	66	3	128	14	0	9	10	.474	1	0	3.84
1998 New Haven	AA Col	29	29	7	0	202	863	210	102	86	14	9	10	9	62	1	135	10	1	10	14	.417	2	0	3.83
1999 Colo Sprngs	AAA Col	9	9	0	0	42	205	62	41	37	5	3	1	1	22	1	25	5	1	1	4	.200	0	0	7.93
Carolina	AA Col	16	16	3	0	99.2	432	101	52	38	6	3	5	8	34	2	102	3	0	5	8	.385	1	0	3.43
2000 Salt Lake	AAA Min	14	14	0	0	75.2	344	105	52	46	9	1	1	1	22	0	54	5	0	5	3	.625	0	0	5.47
Oklahoma	AAA Tex	16	10	0	2	74.2	339	96	49	45	8	3	6	4	33	1	35	2	0	2	3	.400	0	0	5.42
6 Min. YEARS		150	143	14	3	919.1	3952	938	477	395	63	34	32	49	317	12	693	50	4	53	49	.520	5	0	3.87

Jaisen Randolph

Bats: Both **Throws:** Right **Pos:** OF-123; PH-3   **Ht:** 6'0" **Wt:** 180 **Born:** 1/19/79 **Age:** 22

		BATTING															BASERUNNING				PERCENTAGES		
Year Team	Lg Org	G	AB	H	2B	3B	HR	TB	R	RBI	TBB	IBB	SO	HBP	SH	SF	SB	CS	SB%	GDP	Avg	OBP	SLG
1997 Cubs	R ChC	53	218	58	1	4	0	67	42	26	26	0	45	5	0	2	24	5	.83	3	.266	.355	.307
1998 Rockford	A ChC	128	491	142	18	9	1	181	78	33	40	2	113	5	9	2	32	21	.60	4	.289	.348	.369
1999 Daytona	A+ ChC	130	511	139	16	5	2	171	70	37	43	1	86	8	4	0	25	26	.49	4	.272	.338	.335
2000 West Tenn	AA ChC	126	490	119	15	5	1	147	76	31	56	2	96	2	3	3	46	20	.70	3	.243	.321	.300
4 Min. YEARS		437	1710	458	50	23	4	566	266	127	165	5	340	20	16	7	127	72	.64	14	.268	.338	.331

Steve Randolph

Pitches: Left **Bats:** Left **Pos:** SP-3; RP-2   **Ht:** 6'3" **Wt:** 185 **Born:** 5/1/74 **Age:** 27

		HOW MUCH HE PITCHED						WHAT HE GAVE UP												THE RESULTS				
Year Team	Lg Org	G	GS	CG	GF	IP	BFP	H	R	ER	HR	SH	SF	HB	TBB	IBB	SO	WP	Bk	W	L	Pct.	ShO	Sv	ERA
1995 Yankees	R NYY	8	3	0	1	24.1	94	11	7	6	1	0	0	1	16	0	34	3	1	4	0	1.000	0	0	2.22
Oneonta	A- NYY	6	6	0	0	21.2	109	19	22	18	0	0	2	1	23	0	31	5	0	0	3	.000	0	0	7.48
1996 Greensboro	A NYY	32	17	0	7	100.1	451	64	46	42	8	4	5	5	96	1	111	13	3	4	7	.364	0	0	3.77
1997 Tampa	A+ NYY	34	13	1	6	95.1	417	74	55	41	8	7	3	3	63	5	108	4	1	4	7	.364	0	1	3.87
1998 High Desert	A+ Ari	17	17	0	0	85.1	357	71	44	34	6	3	2	3	42	0	104	0	0	4	4	.500	0	0	3.59
Tucson	AAA Ari	17	1	0	3	22.2	99	16	11	8	1	0	2	0	19	2	23	3	0	1	3	.250	0	0	3.18
1999 El Paso	AA Ari	8	8	0	0	44.1	186	39	14	13	1	2	0	1	23	0	38	1	1	2	2	.500	0	0	2.64
Diamondbcks	R Ari	2	2	0	0	6	25	5	3	3	0	0	0	0	2	0	7	0	0	0	0	—	0	0	4.50
El Paso	AA Ari	11	10	1	0	41.2	204	47	37	32	7	1	2	2	32	1	26	1	0	0	7	.000	0	0	6.91
2000 Tucson	AAA Ari	5	3	0	1	13.1	69	11	13	13	3	1	1	0	19	0	6	0	0	0	0	—	0	0	8.78
6 Min. YEARS		140	80	2	18	455	2011	357	252	210	35	18	17	16	335	9	488	30	6	19	33	.365	0	1	4.15

Julio Rangel

Pitches: Right **Bats:** Right **Pos:** RP-17; SP-12   **Ht:** 6'3" **Wt:** 160 **Born:** 9/28/75 **Age:** 25

		HOW MUCH HE PITCHED						WHAT HE GAVE UP												THE RESULTS				
Year Team	Lg Org	G	GS	CG	GF	IP	BFP	H	R	ER	HR	SH	SF	HB	TBB	IBB	SO	WP	Bk	W	L	Pct.	ShO	Sv	ERA
1994 Yankees	R NYY	5	0	0	2	7.1	34	7	6	2	0	0	0	1	1	0	9	1	0	0	0	—	0	0	2.45
1995 Yankees	R NYY	14	0	0	5	28.2	123	20	18	14	2	1	0	4	16	1	30	2	0	1	3	.250	0	0	4.40
1996 Oneonta	A- NYY	15	14	0	1	85	355	64	35	28	2	3	4	5	36	0	79	4	1	7	2	.778	0	0	2.96
1997 Greensboro	A NYY	26	26	4	0	163.2	681	147	80	65	17	7	5	6	49	0	122	9	5	12	9	.571	1	0	3.57
1998 Yankees	R NYY	3	3	0	0	13.2	63	18	8	8	2	1	0	2	7	0	19	1	2	1	0	1.000	0	0	5.27
Tampa	A+ NYY	10	7	0	2	43.2	208	47	30	25	5	1	2	1	30	2	31	3	1	2	3	.400	0	0	5.15
1999 Tampa	A+ NYY	12	9	0	1	55.1	225	48	23	18	1	1	2	2	17	1	36	4	0	3	3	.500	0	1	2.93
2000 Tampa	A+ NYY	12	10	0	1	63.1	266	48	24	20	1	2	2	0	26	0	67	1	1	7	1	.875	0	0	2.84
Norwich	AA NYY	17	2	0	7	38	177	48	34	23	2	1	2	2	20	0	24	1	0	0	3	.000	0	0	5.45
7 Min. YEARS		114	71	4	19	498.2	2132	458	252	203	32	17	15	26	202	4	417	27	11	33	24	.579	1	3	3.66

Cody Ransom

Bats: Right **Throws:** Right **Pos:** SS-128; PR-2   **Ht:** 6'2" **Wt:** 190 **Born:** 2/17/76 **Age:** 25

		BATTING															BASERUNNING				PERCENTAGES		
Year Team	Lg Org	G	AB	H	2B	3B	HR	TB	R	RBI	TBB	IBB	SO	HBP	SH	SF	SB	CS	SB%	GDP	Avg	OBP	SLG
1998 Salem-Keizr	A- SF	71	236	55	12	7	6	99	52	27	43	1	56	2	3	4	19	6	.76	4	.233	.351	.419
1999 Bakersfield	A+ SF	99	356	98	12	6	11	155	69	47	54	0	108	8	1	1	15	8	.65	2	.275	.382	.435
Shreveport	AA SF	14	41	5	0	0	2	11	6	4	4	0	22	1	1	2	0	0			.122	.208	.268
2000 Shreveport	AA SF	130	459	92	21	2	7	138	58	47	40	1	141	0	3	3	9	3	.75	9	.200	.263	.301
3 Min. YEARS		314	1092	250	45	15	26	403	185	125	141	2	327	11	8	10	43	17	.72	15	.229	.321	.369

Fred Rath

Pitches: Right **Bats:** Right **Pos:** RP-21; SP-16   **Ht:** 6'3" **Wt:** 220 **Born:** 1/5/73 **Age:** 28

		HOW MUCH HE PITCHED						WHAT HE GAVE UP												THE RESULTS				
Year Team	Lg Org	G	GS	CG	GF	IP	BFP	H	R	ER	HR	SH	SF	HB	TBB	IBB	SO	WP	Bk	W	L	Pct.	ShO	Sv	ERA
1995 Elizabethtn	R+ Min	27	0	0	25	33.1	134	20	8	5	2	2	0	1	11	1	50	3	0	1	1	.500	0	12	1.35
1996 Fort Wayne	A Min	32	0	0	29	41.2	163	26	12	7	1	0	2	0	10	0	63	3	0	1	2	.333	0	14	1.51
Fort Myers	A+ Min	22	0	0	16	29	123	25	10	9	1	1	0	2	10	0	29	3	0	2	5	.286	0	4	2.79
1997 Fort Myers	A+ Min	17	0	0	11	22	87	18	4	4	2	1	0	0	3	1	22	1	0	4	0	1.000	0	2	1.64
New Britain	AA Min	33	0	0	23	50.1	200	43	17	15	1	1	3	1	13	0	33	3	0	3	3	.500	0	12	2.68
Salt Lake	AAA Min	10	0	0	9	11	46	11	2	2	1	0	0	0	2	0	11	0	0	0	1	.000	0	3	1.64
1998 Salt Lake	AAA Min	27	0	0	22	31.2	133	35	16	16	4	1	0	2	8	0	15	3	0	1	2	.333	0	8	4.55
Colo Sprngs	AAA Col	23	0	0	14	28.1	132	37	17	16	2	1	2	2	15	1	20	4	0	5	1	.833	0	2	5.08
1999 Salt Lake	AAA Min	56	0	0	18	82.2	350	88	41	36	5	5	6	3	24	0	36	6	0	7	5	.583	0	4	3.92
2000 Salt Lake	AAA Min	12	0	0	1	18	80	21	12	6	1	0	0	1	5	0	14	1	0	2	1	.667	0	0	3.00
Memphis	AAA StL	18	9	0	2	63	274	72	40	36	9	4	1	2	24	0	33	2	0	2	3	.400	0	0	5.14
Nashville	AAA Pit	7	7	0	0	43.1	193	42	31	24	8	2	1	2	23	1	15	2	0	3	4	.429	0	0	4.98
1998 Colorado	NL	2	0	0	1	5.1	23	6	1	1	0	0	1	0	2	0	0	0	0	0	0	—	0	0	1.69
6 Min. YEARS		284	16	0	170	454.1	1915	438	210	176	41	16	15	19	148	4	341	31	0	31	28	.525	0	62	3.49

Gary Rath

Pitches: Left **Bats:** Left **Pos:** RP-24; SP-17   **Ht:** 6'2" **Wt:** 186 **Born:** 1/10/73 **Age:** 28

		HOW MUCH HE PITCHED						WHAT HE GAVE UP												THE RESULTS				
Year Team	Lg Org	G	GS	CG	GF	IP	BFP	H	R	ER	HR	SH	SF	HB	TBB	IBB	SO	WP	Bk	W	L	Pct.	ShO	Sv	ERA
1994 Vero Beach	A+ LA	13	11	0	0	62.2	261	55	26	19	3	3	3	2	23	0	50	4	0	5	6	.455	0	2	2.73
1995 San Antonio	AA LA	18	18	3	0	117	483	96	42	36	6	3	2	4	48	4	81	4	2	13	3	.813	1	0	2.77
Albuquerque	AAA LA	8	8	0	0	39	178	46	31	22	4	1	1	2	20	0	23	2	0	3	5	.375	0	0	5.08
1996 Albuquerque	AAA LA	30	30	0	0	180.1	784	177	97	84	13	9	4	3	89	8	125	8	0	10	11	.476	0	0	4.19
1997 Albuquerque	AAA LA	24	24	0	0	132.1	615	177	107	89	17	7	4	4	49	1	100	7	0	7	11	.389	0	0	6.05

Year Team	Lg Org	HOW MUCH HE PITCHED								WHAT HE GAVE UP									THE RESULTS					
		G	GS	CG	GF	IP	BFP	H	R	ER	HR	SH	SF	HB	TBB	IBB	SO	WP	Bk	W	L	Pct.	ShO	Sv	ERA
1998 Albuquerque	AAA LA	28	24	1	3	157.1	687	184	91	79	17	5	1	4	52	1	119	2	0	9	7	.563	0	1	4.52
1999 Salt Lake	AAA Min	20	18	1	1	99.1	454	129	76	62	12	7	7	1	27	1	67	7	0	3	8	.273	0	0	5.62
2000 Trenton	AA Bos	9	0	0	1	11	53	13	11	9	1	0	1	1	6	0	9	1	0	0	1	.000	0	0	7.36
Tucson	AAA Ari	11	1	0	5	9.1	52	16	12	11	2	1	1	0	10	2	8	1	0	0	0	—	0	0	10.61
Long Island	IND —	21	16	1	1	90.1	407	97	60	48	10	4	4	4	43	1	78	9	1	4	4	.500	1	0	4.78
1998 Los Angeles	NL	3	0	0	1	3.1	15	3	4	4	1	1	0	0	2	0	4	0	0	0	0	—	0	0	10.80
1999 Minnesota	AL	5	1	0	1	4.2	25	6	6	6	1	0	0	0	5	0	1	2	1	0	1	.000	0	0	11.57
7 Min. YEARS		182	150	7	11	898.2	3974	990	553	459	85	40	28	25	367	14	660	45	3	54	56	.491	3	1	4.60
2 Maj. YEARS		8	1	0	2	8	40	9	10	10	2	1	0	0	7	0	5	2	1	0	1	.000	0	0	11.25

Jon Rauch

Pitches: Right **Bats:** Right **Pos:** SP-26 **Ht:** 6'10" **Wt:** 230 **Born:** 9/27/78 **Age:** 22

Year Team	Lg Org	HOW MUCH HE PITCHED						WHAT HE GAVE UP										THE RESULTS					
		G	GS	CG	GF	IP	BFP	H	R	ER	HR	SH	SF	HB	TBB	IBB	SO	WP	Bk	W	L	Pct.	ShO	Sv	ERA
1999 Bristol	R+ CWS	14	9	0	3	56.2	264	65	44	28	4	1	2	3	16	1	66	6	2	4	4	.500	0	2	4.45
Winston-Sal	A+ CWS	1	1	0	0	6	26	4	3	2	1	0	0	0	3	0	7	1	0	0	0		0	0	3.00
2000 Winston-Sal	A+ CWS	18	18	1	0	110	456	102	45	35	10	4	3	5	33	0	124	4	1	11	3	.786	0	0	2.86
Birmingham	AA CWS	8	8	2	0	56	220	36	18	14	4	1	0	2	16	0	63	2	0	5	1	.833	2	0	2.25
2 Min. YEARS		41	36	3	3	228.2	966	207	114	79	19	6	5	10	68	1	260	13	3	20	8	.714	2	2	3.11

Luis Raven

Bats: Right **Throws:** Right **Pos:** OF-67; DH-31; 1B-14; PH-6 **Ht:** 6'4" **Wt:** 230 **Born:** 11/19/68 **Age:** 32

Year Team	Lg Org	BATTING															BASERUNNING				PERCENTAGES		
		G	AB	H	2B	3B	HR	TB	R	RBI	TBB	IBB	SO	HBP	SH	SF	SB	CS	SB%	GDP	Avg	OBP	SLG
1989 Angels	R Ana	43	145	30	6	2	1	43	15	20	8	0	43	1	0	3	3	0	1.00	3	.207	.248	.297
1991 Boise	A- Ana	38	84	23	2	0	2	31	13	13	9	0	19	1	0	0	1	1	.50	4	.274	.351	.369
1992 Palm Spring	A+ Ana	107	378	109	16	2	9	156	59	55	24	2	81	2	0	4	18	7	.72	5	.288	.331	.413
1993 Midland	AA Ana	43	167	43	12	1	2	63	21	30	5	1	45	1	1	0	4	2	.67	4	.257	.283	.377
Palm Spring	A+ Ana	85	343	95	20	2	7	140	38	52	22	0	84	3	1	2	15	11	.58	6	.277	.324	.408
1994 Midland	AA Ana	47	191	58	8	5	18	130	41	57	5	2	51	3	0	3	7	0	1.00	9	.304	.327	.681
Vancouver	AAA Ana	85	328	100	13	4	13	160	66	59	22	1	88	2	0	8	7	0	1.00	6	.305	.344	.488
1995 Lk Elsinore	A+ Ana	6	24	10	2	1	2	20	5	6	5	0	7	1	0	0	1	0	1.00	0	.417	.533	.833
Vancouver	AAA Ana	37	135	33	11	1	5	61	18	26	15	0	35	0	0	1	3	1	.75	5	.244	.318	.452
Midland	AA Ana	21	86	23	2	1	5	42	9	15	4	0	30	1	0	1	1	1	.50	2	.267	.304	.488
1996 Canton-Akrn	AA Cle	74	268	81	17	0	21	161	57	64	38	6	73	1	0	2	0	0		6	.302	.388	.601
1997 Birmingham	AA CWS	117	456	153	30	3	30	279	88	112	46	7	126	5	0	7	4	3	.57	5	.336	.397	.612
1999 Charlotte	AAA CWS	139	532	150	32	4	33	289	97	125	50	0	127	3	1	6	5	0	1.00	19	.282	.343	.543
2000 Calgary	AAA Fla	115	420	115	23	2	24	214	68	81	34	2	98	3	0	6	3	1	.75	0	.274	.328	.510
10 Min. YEARS		957	3557	1023	194	28	172	1789	595	715	287	21	907	27	4	43	69	28	.71	87	.288	.342	.503

Ken Ray

Pitches: Right **Bats:** Right **Pos:** RP-7 **Ht:** 6'2" **Wt:** 200 **Born:** 11/27/74 **Age:** 26

Year Team	Lg Org	HOW MUCH HE PITCHED						WHAT HE GAVE UP										THE RESULTS					
		G	GS	CG	GF	IP	BFP	H	R	ER	HR	SH	SF	HB	TBB	IBB	SO	WP	Bk	W	L	Pct.	ShO	Sv	ERA
1993 Royals	R KC	13	7	0	3	47.1	204	44	21	12	1	1	3	0	17	0	45	6	0	2	3	.400	0	0	2.28
1994 Rockford	A KC	27	18	0	6	128.2	516	94	34	26	5	4	1	0	56	2	128	18	2	10	4	.714	0	3	1.82
1995 Wilmington	A+ KC	13	13	1	0	77	320	74	32	23	3	3	3	1	22	2	63	17	2	6	4	.600	0	0	2.69
Wichita	AA KC	14	14	0	0	75.1	342	83	55	50	7	1	0	1	46	0	53	8	1	4	5	.444	0	0	5.97
1996 Wichita	AA KC	22	22	1	0	120.2	553	131	94	82	17	5	6	1	57	1	79	15	1	4	12	.250	0	0	6.12
1997 Omaha	AAA KC	25	21	2	1	113	516	131	86	80	21	2	5	4	63	2	96	8	1	5	12	.294	0	0	6.37
1998 Wichita	AA KC	24	21	0	0	117.2	530	149	79	68	7	5	5	3	47	2	71	1	0	10	5	.667	0	0	5.20
1999 Wichita	AA KC	14	0	0	13	21.1	90	23	12	12	2	1	0	1	10	0	18	1	1	0	0		0	7	5.06
Omaha	AAA KC	27	0	0	23	43.1	184	41	27	25	9	1	2	1	12	1	36	3	0	1	0	1.000	0	8	5.19
2000 Fresno	AAA SF	7	0	0	1	9.2	49	13	10	8	4	1	1	0	8	0	8	2	0	0	0		0	0	7.45
1999 Kansas City	AL	13	0	0	4	11.1	57	23	12	11	2	0	0	1	6	0	0	0	0	1	0	1.000	0	0	8.74
8 Min. YEARS		186	116	4	47	754	3304	803	450	386	76	24	26	12	338	10	597	79	8	42	45	.483	0	18	4.61

Kenny Rayborn

Pitches: Right **Bats:** Right **Pos:** RP-26; SP-8 **Ht:** 6'4" **Wt:** 210 **Born:** 11/22/74 **Age:** 26

Year Team	Lg Org	HOW MUCH HE PITCHED						WHAT HE GAVE UP										THE RESULTS					
		G	GS	CG	GF	IP	BFP	H	R	ER	HR	SH	SF	HB	TBB	IBB	SO	WP	Bk	W	L	Pct.	ShO	Sv	ERA
1997 Lowell	A- Bos	11	7	0	1	46	197	39	18	14	0	1	2	5	15	0	35	8	0	2	2	.500	0	1	2.74
1998 Michigan	A Bos	17	8	0	5	49.1	217	62	27	25	5	1	3	1	13	0	34	8	0	4	2	.667	0	0	4.56
1999 Greenville	IND —	18	18	2	0	115	532	140	86	62	5	7	4	10	43	0	80	9	0	6	9	.400	0	0	4.85
2000 Lancaster	A+ Sea	21	1	0	3	55.2	228	47	24	18	2	0	4	1	19	3	43	4	0	5	1	.833	0	1	2.91
New Haven	AA Sea	13	7	0	3	46.1	207	54	25	25	1	2	1	5	19	0	26	1	0	4	3	.571	0	0	4.86
4 Min. YEARS		80	41	2	12	312.1	1381	342	180	144	13	11	14	23	109	3	218	30	0	21	17	.553	0	2	4.15

Tim Redding

Pitches: Right **Bats:** Right **Pos:** SP-29 **Ht:** 6'0" **Wt:** 180 **Born:** 2/12/78 **Age:** 23

Year Team	Lg Org	HOW MUCH HE PITCHED						WHAT HE GAVE UP										THE RESULTS					
		G	GS	CG	GF	IP	BFP	H	R	ER	HR	SH	SF	HB	TBB	IBB	SO	WP	Bk	W	L	Pct.	ShO	Sv	ERA
1998 Auburn	A- Hou	16	15	0	1	73.2	323	49	44	37	2	2	3	7	50	0	98	10	4	7	3	.700	0	1	4.52
1999 Michigan	A Hou	43	11	0	24	105	470	84	69	58	4	6	3	5	76	1	141	19	2	8	6	.571	0	14	4.97
2000 Kissimmee	A+ Hou	24	24	0	0	154.2	649	125	62	46	5	4	6	9	57	1	170	13	0	12	5	.706	0	0	2.68
Round Rock	AA Hou	5	5	0	0	26	111	14	12	10	4	2	1	2	22	0	22	4	0	2	0	1.000	0	0	3.46
3 Min. YEARS		88	55	0	25	359.1	1553	272	187	151	15	14	16	20	205	2	431	46	6	29	14	.674	0	15	3.78

Josh Reding

Bats: Right **Throws:** Right **Pos:** SS-136; PH-1　　　　　**Ht:** 6'2" **Wt:** 175 **Born:** 3/7/77 **Age:** 24

		BATTING														BASERUNNING				PERCENTAGES		
Year Team	Lg Org	G	AB	H	2B	3B	HR	TB	R	RBI	TBB	IBB	SO	HBP	SH	SF	SB	CS	SB%	GDP	Avg	OBP	SLG
1997 Expos	R Mon	56	196	50	11	1	2	69	34	19	22	0	31	4	2	2	14	3	.82	3	.255	.339	.352
Vermont	A- Mon	8	24	4	2	1	0	8	2	0	3	0	11	0	0	0	0	0	—	0	.167	.259	.333
1998 Expos	R Mon	2	8	3	1	0	0	4	2	0	0	0	3	0	0	0	1	1	.50	1	.375	.375	.500
Cape Fear	A Mon	73	253	59	6	0	1	68	32	21	22	1	71	4	9	0	13	4	.76	8	.233	.305	.269
Jupiter	A+ Mon	4	12	3	1	0	0	4	2	2	0	0	3	0	0	0	0	0	.00	0	.250	.250	.333
1999 Jupiter	A+ Mon	121	415	109	10	2	2	129	54	31	22	0	73	1	12	6	30	9	.77	6	.263	.297	.311
2000 Harrisburg	AA Mon	137	457	100	11	5	2	127	58	48	58	0	110	10	9	4	25	6	.81	10	.219	.318	.278
4 Min. YEARS		401	1365	328	42	9	7	409	184	121	127	1	302	19	32	12	83	24	.78	28	.240	.311	.300

Brandon Reed

Pitches: Right **Bats:** Right **Pos:** RP-41; SP-4　　　　　**Ht:** 6'4" **Wt:** 195 **Born:** 12/18/74 **Age:** 26

		HOW MUCH HE PITCHED						WHAT HE GAVE UP											THE RESULTS					
Year Team	Lg Org	G	GS	CG	GF	IP	BFP	H	R	ER	HR	SH	SF	HB	TBB	IBB	SO	WP	Bk	W	L	Pct.	ShO	Sv	ERA
1994 Bristol	R+ Det	13	13	0	0	78	337	82	41	31	3	1	3	9	10	0	68	4	0	3	5	.375	0	0	3.58
1995 Fayetteville	A Det	55	0	0	53	64.2	252	40	11	7	1	1	0	3	18	1	78	8	0	3	0	1.000	0	41	0.97
1996 Tigers	R Det	1	1	0	0	2	6	0	0	0	0	0	0	1	0	0	2	0	0	0	0	—	0	0	0.00
Jacksnville	AA Det	7	3	0	1	26	94	18	6	6	1	0	1	1	3	0	18	0	0	1	0	1.000	0	1	2.08
1997 Jacksnville	AA Det	27	27	2	0	176	754	190	100	89	25	6	10	8	54	0	90	9	0	11	9	.550	0	0	4.55
1998 Toledo	AAA Det	39	17	0	6	117.1	540	159	84	78	17	4	4	5	46	1	70	2	0	5	7	.417	0	0	5.98
1999 Toledo	AAA Det	44	6	1	21	91.1	401	101	53	42	6	1	7	5	26	3	59	1	0	8	5	.615	0	3	4.14
2000 Toledo	AAA Det	45	4	0	26	73.1	330	80	52	49	13	2	3	2	36	4	56	3	2	7	6	.538	0	6	6.01
7 Min. YEARS		231	71	3	107	628.2	2714	670	347	302	66	15	28	34	193	9	441	27	2	38	32	.543	0	51	4.32

Nate Reese

Bats: Right **Throws:** Right **Pos:** C-23; DH-5　　　　　**Ht:** 5'11" **Wt:** 215 **Born:** 10/17/74 **Age:** 26

		BATTING														BASERUNNING				PERCENTAGES		
Year Team	Lg Org	G	AB	H	2B	3B	HR	TB	R	RBI	TBB	IBB	SO	HBP	SH	SF	SB	CS	SB%	GDP	Avg	OBP	SLG
1997 Marlins	R Fla	11	29	7	1	0	0	8	3	3	3	0	9	1	0	0	0	1	.00	1	.241	.333	.276
Utica	A- Fla	13	44	9	2	0	0	11	5	5	2	0	14	0	0	1	0	0	—	1	.205	.234	.250
1998 Brevard Cty	A+ Fla	11	40	7	2	0	2	15	3	7	3	0	9	0	1	0	0	0	—	2	.175	.233	.375
Kane County	A Fla	13	40	10	1	0	1	14	3	7	5	0	12	2	0	0	0	0	—	2	.250	.362	.350
Charlotte	AAA Fla	3	8	3	0	0	1	6	1	1	1	0	3	0	0	0	0	0	—	0	.375	.444	.750
1999 Portland	AA Fla	3	3	0	0	0	0	0	0	0	0	0	1	0	0	0	0	0	—	0	.000	.000	.000
Brevard Cty	A+ Fla	70	237	63	12	0	7	96	25	38	18	0	44	2	2	5	0	0	—	7	.266	.317	.405
Calgary	AAA Fla	9	20	5	1	0	0	6	4	2	1	0	5	0	0	0	0	0	—	1	.250	.286	.300
2000 Portland	AA Fla	3	8	2	0	0	0	2	0	3	0	0	3	0	1	0	0	0	—	0	.250	.250	.250
Brevard Cty	A+ Fla	9	29	6	2	0	0	8	3	2	2	0	6	0	0	0	0	0	—	0	.207	.258	.276
Myrtle Bch	A+ Atl	6	18	2	1	0	0	3	1	1	2	0	2	0	0	0	0	0	—	0	.111	.200	.167
Quebec	IND —	10	30	7	0	0	0	7	4	4	8	1	5	1	0	0	0	0	—	2	.233	.410	.233
4 Min. YEARS		161	506	121	22	0	11	176	52	73	45	1	113	6	4	6	0	1	.00	16	.239	.306	.348

Maximo Regalado

Pitches: Right **Bats:** Right **Pos:** RP-56　　　　　**Ht:** 6'2" **Wt:** 165 **Born:** 11/18/76 **Age:** 24

		HOW MUCH HE PITCHED						WHAT HE GAVE UP											THE RESULTS					
Year Team	Lg Org	G	GS	CG	GF	IP	BFP	H	R	ER	HR	SH	SF	HB	TBB	IBB	SO	WP	Bk	W	L	Pct.	ShO	Sv	ERA
1997 Great Falls	R+ LA	9	6	0	0	36.2	158	27	12	8	0	1	1	2	21	0	24	1	0	2	1	.667	0	0	1.96
1998 Vero Beach	A+ LA	4	4	0	0	16	78	17	15	12	3	0	0	1	13	0	14	1	0	2	0	.000	0	0	6.75
Great Falls	R+ LA	3	0	0	2	5.2	21	2	0	0	0	0	0	1	3	0	7	1	0	0	0	—	0	0	0.00
San Berndno	A+ LA	14	3	0	1	47.1	212	45	30	22	4	0	1	3	24	0	42	4	0	3	3	.500	0	0	4.18
1999 Vero Beach	A+ LA	20	19	1	0	90	429	110	65	58	16	5	3	12	49	0	58	7	0	2	12	.143	0	0	5.80
2000 Vero Beach	A+ LA	30	0	0	29	30.2	114	15	4	3	0	0	0	1	8	1	45	2	0	0	0	—	0	21	0.88
San Antonio	AA LA	26	0	0	22	23.1	103	22	8	8	1	0	0	0	15	0	27	2	0	1	2	.333	0	9	3.09
4 Min. YEARS		106	32	1	54	249.2	1115	238	134	111	24	6	5	20	133	1	217	18	0	8	20	.286	0	30	4.00

Chris Reinike

Pitches: Right **Bats:** Right **Pos:** RP-19　　　　　**Ht:** 6'0" **Wt:** 195 **Born:** 11/16/76 **Age:** 24

		HOW MUCH HE PITCHED						WHAT HE GAVE UP											THE RESULTS					
Year Team	Lg Org	G	GS	CG	GF	IP	BFP	H	R	ER	HR	SH	SF	HB	TBB	IBB	SO	WP	Bk	W	L	Pct.	ShO	Sv	ERA
1998 Watertown	A- Cle	15	15	0	0	89.2	367	64	21	19	1	0	2	8	33	1	92	2	0	10	2	.833	0	0	1.91
1999 Columbus	A Cle	11	11	0	0	48	222	55	28	23	3	0	1	4	21	0	41	1	1	3	4	.429	0	0	4.31
2000 Columbus	A Cle	7	0	0	1	12	49	6	2	2	0	0	0	2	4	0	19	2	0	0	0	—	0	0	1.50
Kinston	A+ Cle	11	0	0	3	20.2	83	13	7	5	0	1	1	2	8	0	25	2	0	0	1	.000	0	0	2.18
Akron	AA Cle	1	0	0	0	2	8	1	1	1	0	0	0	0	2	0	3	0	0	0	0	—	0	0	4.50
3 Min. YEARS		45	26	0	4	172.1	729	139	59	50	4	1	4	16	68	1	180	7	1	13	7	.650	0	0	2.61

Nataniel Reinoso

Bats: Left **Throws:** Left **Pos:** OF-93; DH-16; PH-1　　　　　**Ht:** 6'0" **Wt:** 192 **Born:** 12/12/74 **Age:** 26

		BATTING														BASERUNNING				PERCENTAGES		
Year Team	Lg Org	G	AB	H	2B	3B	HR	TB	R	RBI	TBB	IBB	SO	HBP	SH	SF	SB	CS	SB%	GDP	Avg	OBP	SLG
2000 Greenville	AA Atl	24	80	14	3	0	1	20	6	7	2	0	16	0	1	1	0	2	.00	3	.175	.193	.250
Myrtle Bch	A+ Atl	85	297	68	17	1	4	99	27	37	9	1	66	1	2	5	0	3	.00	6	.229	.250	.333
1 Min. YEARS		109	377	82	20	1	5	119	33	44	11	1	82	1	3	6	0	5	.00	9	.218	.238	.316

235

Brian Reith

Pitches: Right **Bats:** Right **Pos:** SP-28   **Ht:** 6'5" **Wt:** 190 **Born:** 2/28/78 **Age:** 23

Year Team	Lg Org	G	GS	CG	GF	IP	BFP	H	R	ER	HR	SH	SF	HB	TBB	IBB	SO	WP	Bk	W	L	Pct.	ShO	Sv	ERA
1996 Yankees	R NYY	10	4	0	1	32.2	143	31	16	15	1	2	2	1	16	0	21	3	0	2	3	.400	0	0	4.13
1997 Yankees	R NYY	12	11	1	0	63	270	70	28	20	1	2	2	3	14	0	40	8	0	4	2	.667	0	0	2.86
1998 Greensboro	A NYY	20	20	3	0	118.1	475	86	42	30	7	2	0	3	32	0	116	1	0	6	7	.462	1	0	2.28
1999 Tampa	A+ NYY	26	23	0	0	139.2	616	174	87	73	12	7	4	4	35	1	101	4	0	9	9	.500	0	0	4.70
2000 Tampa	A+ NYY	18	18	1	0	119.2	487	101	39	29	4	2	3	5	33	0	100	6	1	9	4	.692	1	0	2.18
Dayton	A Cin	5	5	0	0	34.1	139	33	12	11	2	0	0	0	8	0	30	2	0	2	1	.667	0	0	2.88
Chattanooga	AA Cin	5	5	0	0	30	128	31	14	13	3	2	2	1	11	0	29	2	0	1	3	.250	0	0	3.90
5 Min. YEARS		96	86	5	1	537.2	2258	526	238	191	30	17	13	17	149	1	437	26	1	33	29	.532	2	0	3.20

Chris Reitsma

Pitches: Right **Bats:** Right **Pos:** SP-25   **Ht:** 6'5" **Wt:** 214 **Born:** 12/31/77 **Age:** 23

Year Team	Lg Org	G	GS	CG	GF	IP	BFP	H	R	ER	HR	SH	SF	HB	TBB	IBB	SO	WP	Bk	W	L	Pct.	ShO	Sv	ERA
1996 Red Sox	R Bos	7	6	0	0	26.2	109	24	7	4	0	1	0	2	1	0	32	3	0	3	1	.750	0	0	1.35
1997 Michigan	A Bos	9	9	0	0	49.2	217	57	23	16	4	0	2	2	13	0	41	3	0	4	1	.800	0	0	2.90
1998 Sarasota	A+ Bos	8	8	0	0	12.2	55	12	6	4	0	0	1	0	5	0	9	0	0	0	0	—	0	0	2.84
1999 Sarasota	A+ Bos	19	19	0	0	96.1	440	116	71	60	11	1	4	10	31	1	79	7	3	4	10	.286	0	0	5.61
2000 Sarasota	A+ Bos	11	11	0	0	64	267	57	29	26	3	4	1	5	17	0	47	0	0	3	4	.429	0	0	3.66
Trenton	AA Bos	14	14	1	0	90.2	361	78	28	26	7	1	1	2	21	1	58	1	0	7	2	.778	0	0	2.58
5 Min. YEARS		68	67	1	0	340	1449	344	164	136	25	7	9	21	88	2	266	14	3	21	18	.538	0	0	3.60

Todd Revenig

Pitches: Right **Bats:** Right **Pos:** RP-18; SP-13   **Ht:** 6'1" **Wt:** 185 **Born:** 6/28/69 **Age:** 32

Year Team	Lg Org	G	GS	CG	GF	IP	BFP	H	R	ER	HR	SH	SF	HB	TBB	IBB	SO	WP	Bk	W	L	Pct.	ShO	Sv	ERA
1990 Sou Oregon	A- Oak	24	0	0	14	44.2	176	33	13	4	2	4	1	0	9	2	46	1	2	3	2	.600	0	6	0.81
1991 Madison	A Oak	26	0	0	22	28.2	109	13	6	3	1	3	0	0	10	2	27	1	1	1	0	1.000	0	13	0.94
Huntsville	AA Oak	12	0	0	6	18.1	68	11	3	2	1	0	1	2	4	0	10	0	0	1	2	.333	0	4	0.98
1992 Huntsville	AA Oak	53	0	0	48	63.2	233	33	14	12	8	2	2	0	11	0	49	1	0	1	1	.500	0	33	1.70
1994 Athletics	R Oak	4	4	0	0	7.2	33	7	4	3	1	1	0	0	2	0	6	0	0	0	0	—	0	0	3.52
1995 Edmonton	AAA Oak	45	0	0	30	54.1	230	53	32	26	5	3	3	2	15	1	28	2	0	4	5	.444	0	10	4.31
1996 Rochester	AAA Bal	3	0	0	0	6	25	8	5	5	2	0	0	0	0	0	4	0	0	2	0	1.000	0	0	7.50
Bowie	AA Bal	38	0	0	29	61.2	238	42	18	18	6	0	2	2	18	0	39	2	0	3	4	.429	0	7	2.63
2000 El Paso	AA Ari	12	11	0	0	60.1	276	90	50	42	7	3	3	6	14	0	50	0	0	2	4	.333	0	0	6.27
Diamondbcks	R Ari	2	2	0	0	9	2	0	0	0	0	0	0	0	0	0	1	0	0	0	0	—	0	0	0.00
Tucson	AAA Ari	17	0	0	9	26.1	110	29	8	8	1	1	0	0	4	0	28	1	0	2	1	.667	0	0	2.73
1992 Oakland	AL	2	0	0	2	2	7	2	0	0	0	0	0	0	0	0	1	0	0	0	0	—	0	0	0.00
7 Min. YEARS		236	17	0	158	373.2	1507	321	153	123	34	17	12	12	87	5	288	9	3	19	19	.500	0	71	2.96

Jackie Rexrode

Bats: Left **Throws:** Right **Pos:** 2B-90   **Ht:** 5'11" **Wt:** 175 **Born:** 9/16/78 **Age:** 22

Year Team	Lg Org	G	AB	H	2B	3B	HR	TB	R	RBI	TBB	IBB	SO	HBP	SH	SF	SB	CS	SB%	GDP	Avg	OBP	SLG
1996 Diamondbcks	R Ari	48	140	46	2	0	1	51	28	17	44	0	27	0	0	4	8	5	.62	1	.329	.479	.364
1997 South Bend	A Ari	92	330	93	10	5	2	119	60	27	55	0	47	2	5	3	15	5	.75	3	.282	.385	.361
Lethbridge	R+ Ari	26	89	30	2	2	1	39	29	14	29	0	17	1	2	1	7	3	.70	0	.337	.500	.438
1998 South Bend	A Ari	50	175	51	7	2	0	62	33	7	45	1	31	1	3	1	22	3	.88	1	.291	.437	.354
High Desert	A+ Ari	53	208	71	5	4	1	87	51	23	46	0	42	0	0	3	19	1	.95	2	.341	.455	.418
1999 Birmingham	AA Ari	70	213	57	7	5	0	74	34	25	28	0	30	0	5	4	14	4	.78	1	.268	.347	.347
El Paso	AA Ari	37	144	46	7	2	2	63	30	11	29	0	16	0	2	1	7	3	.70	0	.319	.431	.438
2000 Birmingham	AA CWS	90	337	97	10	3	0	113	60	14	68	1	39	2	3	2	19	11	.63	3	.288	.408	.335
5 Min. YEARS		466	1636	491	50	23	7	608	325	138	344	2	249	6	20	19	111	35	.76	11	.300	.419	.372

Eddy Reyes

Pitches: Right **Bats:** Right **Pos:** RP-50   **Ht:** 6'4" **Wt:** 203 **Born:** 4/24/76 **Age:** 25

Year Team	Lg Org	G	GS	CG	GF	IP	BFP	H	R	ER	HR	SH	SF	HB	TBB	IBB	SO	WP	Bk	W	L	Pct.	ShO	Sv	ERA
1997 Hudson Val	A- TB	31	0	0	29	32.2	144	24	12	10	1	2	0	4	18	0	29	0	5	0	2	.000	0	14	2.76
1998 Chston-SC	A TB	56	0	0	52	61.2	255	60	23	15	2	2	1	3	12	1	49	6	0	4	6	.400	0	24	2.19
1999 St. Pete	A+ TB	37	0	0	33	38.1	172	31	13	8	0	4	1	6	23	1	30	0	0	0	2	.000	0	25	1.88
Orlando	AA TB	18	0	0	11	28.2	133	31	16	13	3	1	1	6	11	2	25	2	3	1	3	.250	0	2	4.08
2000 Orlando	AA TB	50	0	0	35	59.1	280	52	32	26	5	1	1	11	48	0	44	3	0	2	5	.286	0	14	3.94
4 Min. YEARS		192	0	0	160	220.2	984	198	96	72	11	10	4	30	112	4	177	11	8	7	18	.280	0	79	2.94

Brian Richardson

Bats: Right **Throws:** Right **Pos:** 3B-87; OF-29; PH-10; DH-3; 2B-2; 1B-2   **Ht:** 6'2" **Wt:** 210 **Born:** 8/31/75 **Age:** 25

Year Team	Lg Org	G	AB	H	2B	3B	HR	TB	R	RBI	TBB	IBB	SO	HBP	SH	SF	SB	CS	SB%	GDP	Avg	OBP	SLG
1992 Dodgers	R LA	37	122	26	6	2	0	36	8	15	11	0	27	0	0	2	3	0	1.00	2	.213	.274	.295
1993 Great Falls	R+ LA	54	178	40	11	0	0	51	16	13	14	1	47	3	1	2	1	2	.33	7	.225	.289	.287
1994 Vero Beach	A+ LA	19	52	12	0	1	0	14	3	3	4	0	15	0	0	2	3	0	1.00	2	.231	.276	.269
Yakima	A- LA	70	266	62	15	0	5	92	35	44	35	1	82	1	0	0	12	4	.75	3	.233	.325	.346
1995 San Berndno	A+ LA	127	462	131	18	1	12	187	68	58	35	2	122	7	6	3	17	16	.52	11	.284	.341	.405
1996 San Antonio	AA LA	19	62	20	1	1	0	23	10	7	2	0	10	2	0	0	0	2	.00	3	.323	.364	.371
Albuquerque	AAA LA	105	355	87	17	2	9	135	52	43	32	6	89	3	4	4	4	1	.80	5	.245	.310	.380

Year Team	Lg Org	BATTING															BASERUNNING				PERCENTAGES		
		G	AB	H	2B	3B	HR	TB	R	RBI	TBB	IBB	SO	HBP	SH	SF	SB	CS	SB%	GDP	Avg	OBP	SLG
1997 San Antonio	AA LA	133	484	144	23	13	13	232	73	90	42	0	97	8	2	5	3	6	.33	12	.298	.360	.479
1998 Albuquerque	AAA LA	11	41	6	0	0	1	9	5	5	3	0	10	0	0	0	0	0	—	1	.146	.205	.220
New Haven	AA Col	6	20	2	0	0	0	2	1	2	1	0	4	0	0	0	1	0	1.00		.100	.143	.100
1999 Salt Lake	AAA Min	130	451	125	23	4	18	210	77	73	54	0	104	6	2	8	0	0	—	10	.277	.356	.466
2000 Salt Lake	AAA Min	42	155	39	7	1	0	48	20	17	6	0	35	1	0	1	2	0	1.00	3	.252	.282	.310
New Orleans	AAA Hou	77	249	65	9	5	3	93	33	35	20	0	62	3	3	4	1	0	1.00	8	.261	.319	.373
9 Min. YEARS		830	2897	759	130	30	61	1132	401	405	259	10	704	34	18	31	47	31	.60	66	.262	.327	.391

Chad Ricketts

Pitches: Right **Bats:** Right **Pos:** RP-54   **Ht:** 6'5" **Wt:** 225 **Born:** 2/12/75 **Age:** 26

Year Team	Lg Org	HOW MUCH HE PITCHED						WHAT HE GAVE UP												THE RESULTS					
		G	GS	CG	GF	IP	BFP	H	R	ER	HR	SH	SF	HB	TBB	IBB	SO	WP	Bk	W	L	Pct.	ShO	Sv	ERA
1995 Cubs	R ChC	2	2	0	0	1	1	1	0	0	0	0	1	1	0	5		0	0	1	0	1.000	0	0	0.00
Williamsprt	A- ChC	12	12	0	0	68.2	312	89	46	32	4	0	3	8	16	0	37	1	3	4	5	.444	0	0	4.19
1996 Rockford	A ChC	37	9	0	17	87.2	389	89	60	49	8	5	2	7	29	2	70	5	1	3	8	.273	0	4	5.03
1997 Rockford	A ChC	16	0	0	10	29	116	19	9	8	1	1	1	1	11	2	32	1	0	4	0	1.000	0	3	2.48
Daytona	A+ ChC	20	0	0	17	20.1	82	13	4	1	0	0	0	1	6	0	18	1	0	3	1	.750	0	8	0.44
Orlando	AA ChC	2	0	0	0	2	15	7	4	4	0	0	0	0	2	0	3	0	0	0	0	—	0	0	18.00
1998 Daytona	A+ ChC	47	0	0	41	49	204	41	15	10	0	3	0	3	11	1	59	2	0	2	1	.667	0	19	1.84
West Tenn	AA ChC	13	0	0	11	15.1	65	19	7	6	0	1	1	1	4	2	13	1	0	0	2	.000	0	4	3.52
1999 West Tenn	AA ChC	57	0	0	26	67	275	55	25	23	8	3	1	2	21	4	80	1	0	6	4	.600	0	8	3.09
2000 Albuquerque	AAA LA	54	0	0	27	67.2	294	59	35	26	7	5	2	5	36	2	75	3	0	6	2	.750	0	7	3.46
6 Min. YEARS		260	23	0	149	415.2	1784	392	206	159	28	17	10	29	137	13	392	15	4	29	23	.558	0	55	3.44

Jim Rickon

Bats: Right **Throws:** Right **Pos:** C-25; PH-3; 1B-2; 3B-1; OF-1; DH-1   **Ht:** 6'4" **Wt:** 225 **Born:** 6/1/76 **Age:** 25

Year Team	Lg Org	BATTING															BASERUNNING				PERCENTAGES		
		G	AB	H	2B	3B	HR	TB	R	RBI	TBB	IBB	SO	HBP	SH	SF	SB	CS	SB%	GDP	Avg	OBP	SLG
1999 Burlington	R+ Cle	31	96	29	5	0	4	46	16	17	19	0	25	1	0	0	2	1	.67	2	.302	.422	.479
Mahoning Vy	A- Cle	8	25	5	0	0	1	8	3	4	2	0	7	0	1	0	0	0	—	2	.200	.259	.320
2000 Columbus	A Cle	17	40	8	2	1	0	12	3	1	5	0	17	0	0	0	0	0	—	0	.200	.289	.300
Mahoning Vy	A- Cle	3	10	3	0	0	0	3	0	3	2	0	2	0	0	0	0	0	—	0	.300	.417	.300
Akron	AA Cle	3	4	2	1	0	0	3	1	0	0	0	0	0	0	0	0	0	—	0	.500	.500	.750
Kinston	A+ Cle	8	26	10	3	0	1	16	6	2	1	0	6	2	0	0	0	0	—	1	.385	.448	.615
2 Min. YEARS		70	201	57	11	1	6	88	29	27	29	0	57	3	1	0	2	1	.67	6	.284	.382	.438

Adam Riggs

Bats: Right **Throws:** Right **Pos:** 3B-76; 2B-33; PH-26; DH-5; OF-4; PR-2   **Ht:** 6'0" **Wt:** 190 **Born:** 10/4/72 **Age:** 28

Year Team	Lg Org	BATTING															BASERUNNING				PERCENTAGES		
		G	AB	H	2B	3B	HR	TB	R	RBI	TBB	IBB	SO	HBP	SH	SF	SB	CS	SB%	GDP	Avg	OBP	SLG
1994 Great Falls	R+ LA	62	234	73	20	3	5	114	55	44	31	1	38	4	2	2	19	8	.70	2	.312	.399	.487
Yakima	A- LA	4	7	2	1	0	0	3	1	0	0	0	1	0	0	0	0	0	—	0	.286	.286	.429
1995 San Berndno	A+ LA	134	542	196	39	6	24	317	111	106	59	1	93	10	7	4	31	10	.76	9	.362	.431	.585
1996 San Antonio	AA LA	134	506	143	31	6	14	228	68	66	37	1	82	9	5	5	16	6	.73	13	.283	.339	.451
1997 Albuquerque	AAA LA	57	227	69	8	3	13	122	59	28	29	1	39	3	0	0	12	2	.86	2	.304	.390	.537
1998 Albuquerque	AAA LA	44	170	63	13	3	4	94	30	25	21	1	29	3	1	1	12	6	.67	1	.371	.446	.553
1999 Albuquerque	AAA LA	133	513	150	29	7	13	232	87	81	54	0	114	10	2	5	25	17	.60	8	.292	.368	.452
2000 Albuquerque	AAA LA	124	348	109	24	4	12	177	71	57	35	0	67	2	6	3	11	7	.61	11	.313	.376	.509
1997 Los Angeles	NL	9	20	4	1	0	0	5	3	1	4	1	3	0	0	0	1	0	1.00	0	.200	.333	.250
7 Min. YEARS		692	2547	805	165	31	85	1287	482	407	266	5	463	41	23	20	126	56	.69	46	.316	.387	.505

Eric Riggs

Bats: Both **Throws:** Right **Pos:** SS-81; 2B-36; PH-4   **Ht:** 6'2" **Wt:** 190 **Born:** 8/19/76 **Age:** 24

Year Team	Lg Org	BATTING															BASERUNNING				PERCENTAGES		
		G	AB	H	2B	3B	HR	TB	R	RBI	TBB	IBB	SO	HBP	SH	SF	SB	CS	SB%	GDP	Avg	OBP	SLG
1998 Vero Beach	A+ LA	61	230	57	12	3	3	84	30	17	23	0	46	0	3	1	3	4	.43	1	.248	.315	.365
1999 San Berndno	A+ LA	130	523	144	18	10	16	230	105	69	70	2	92	6	7	5	27	11	.71	6	.275	.364	.440
2000 San Antonio	AA LA	117	421	94	19	4	7	142	56	39	54	2	85	2	15	2	18	6	.75	8	.223	.313	.337
3 Min. YEARS		308	1174	295	49	17	26	456	191	125	147	4	223	8	25	8	48	21	.70	15	.251	.337	.388

Randy Rigsby

Bats: Left **Throws:** Left **Pos:** OF-62; PH-6; 1B-5; DH-4   **Ht:** 6'0" **Wt:** 190 **Born:** 8/7/76 **Age:** 24

Year Team	Lg Org	BATTING															BASERUNNING				PERCENTAGES		
		G	AB	H	2B	3B	HR	TB	R	RBI	TBB	IBB	SO	HBP	SH	SF	SB	CS	SB%	GDP	Avg	OBP	SLG
1998 Utica	A- Fla	54	179	54	12	2	1	73	26	16	21	3	42	2	0	0	3	4	.43	3	.302	.381	.408
Charlotte	AAA Fla	14	14	3	0	0	0	3	1	0	1	0	4	0	0	0	0	0	—	0	.214	.267	.214
1999 Brevard Cty	A+ Fla	106	362	95	16	6	2	129	41	37	34	2	76	6	3	3	6	3	.67	6	.262	.333	.356
2000 Portland	AA Fla	4	9	2	0	0	0	2	1	1	0	0	3	0	2	0	0	0	—	0	.222	.222	.222
Brevard Cty	A+ Fla	71	247	67	16	5	4	105	40	29	23	0	41	1	1	3	15	1	.94	3	.271	.332	.425
3 Min. YEARS		239	811	221	44	13	7	312	109	83	79	5	166	9	6	6	24	8	.75	12	.273	.341	.385

Matt Riley

Pitches: Left **Bats:** Left **Pos:** SP-16; RP-5   **Ht:** 6'1" **Wt:** 201 **Born:** 8/2/79 **Age:** 21

Year Team	Lg Org	HOW MUCH HE PITCHED						WHAT HE GAVE UP												THE RESULTS					
		G	GS	CG	GF	IP	BFP	H	R	ER	HR	SH	SF	HB	TBB	IBB	SO	WP	Bk	W	L	Pct.	ShO	Sv	ERA
1998 Delmarva	A Bal	16	14	0	0	83	324	42	19	11	0	2	1	0	44	0	136	9	3	5	4	.556	0	0	1.19

Year Team	Lg Org	G	GS	CG	GF	IP	BFP	H	R	ER	HR	SH	SF	HB	TBB	IBB	SO	WP	Bk	W	L	Pct.	ShO	Sv	ERA
						HOW MUCH HE PITCHED					WHAT HE GAVE UP												THE RESULTS		
1999 Frederick	A+ Bal	8	8	0	0	51.2	200	34	19	15	5	3	0	1	14	0	58	1	1	3	2	.600	0	0	2.61
Bowie	AA Bal	20	20	3	0	125.2	520	113	53	45	13	2	3	5	42	0	131	10	4	10	6	.625	0	0	3.22
2000 Rochester	AAA Bal	2	2	0	0	7	41	15	12	11	3	0	0	1	4	0	8	2	0	0	2	.000	0	0	14.14
Bowie	AA Bal	19	14	2	2	74	333	74	56	50	9	0	0	2	49	0	66	7	0	5	7	.417	0	1	6.08
1999 Baltimore	AL	3	3	0	0	11	59	17	9	9	4	0	1	0	13	0	6	0	2	0	0	—	0	0	7.36
3 Min. YEARS		65	58	5	2	341.1	1418	278	159	132	30	7	4	9	153	0	399	29	8	23	21	.523	0	1	3.48

Mike Riley

Pitches: Left Bats: Left Pos: SP-24   Ht: 6'1" Wt: 162 Born: 1/2/75 Age: 26

Year Team	Lg Org	G	GS	CG	GF	IP	BFP	H	R	ER	HR	SH	SF	HB	TBB	IBB	SO	WP	Bk	W	L	Pct.	ShO	Sv	ERA
1996 Bellingham	A- SF	17	3	0	2	36.2	181	38	26	17	3	1	1	2	29	0	38	5	2	1	3	.250	0	0	4.17
1997 Bakersfield	A+ SF	6	4	0	0	20.1	94	25	20	19	4	0	1	0	8	0	17	0	0	1	2	.333	0	0	8.41
Salem-Keizr	A- SF	15	15	1	0	88.1	375	76	39	34	9	2	2	4	28	0	96	6	1	9	2	.818	0	0	3.46
1998 Bakersfield	A+ SF	40	15	2	7	128	555	130	73	64	8	3	3	3	58	1	110	9	1	6	12	.333	0	2	4.50
1999 Shreveport	AA SF	30	13	1	4	111	456	80	35	26	6	2	2	1	53	0	107	2	1	8	3	.727	1	1	2.11
2000 Fresno	AAA SF	24	24	0	0	128	578	141	92	84	21	5	3	4	54	0	114	6	0	6	8	.429	0	0	5.91
5 Min. YEARS		132	74	4	13	512.1	2239	490	285	244	51	13	12	14	230	1	482	28	5	31	30	.508	1	3	4.29

Juan Rincon

Pitches: Right Bats: Right Pos: SP-28   Ht: 5'11" Wt: 187 Born: 1/23/79 Age: 22

Year Team	Lg Org	G	GS	CG	GF	IP	BFP	H	R	ER	HR	SH	SF	HB	TBB	IBB	SO	WP	Bk	W	L	Pct.	ShO	Sv	ERA
1997 Twins	R Min	11	10	1	1	58	245	55	21	19	0	2	3	4	24	0	46	7	1	3	3	.500	0	0	2.95
Elizabethtn	R+ Min	2	1	0	0	9.1	41	11	4	4	0	0	0	3	3	0	7	2	0	0	1	.000	0	0	3.86
1998 Fort Wayne	A Min	37	13	0	17	96.1	427	84	51	41	6	5	1	5	54	1	74	12	0	6	4	.600	0	6	3.83
1999 Quad City	A Min	28	28	0	0	163.1	683	146	67	53	8	1	3	2	66	3	153	11	0	14	8	.636	0	0	2.92
2000 Fort Myers	A+ Min	13	13	0	0	76.1	309	67	26	18	3	1	0	4	23	2	55	10	0	5	3	.625	0	0	2.12
New Britain	AA Min	15	15	2	0	89	399	96	55	46	9	0	1	4	39	0	79	9	1	3	9	.250	0	0	4.65
4 Min. YEARS		106	80	3	18	492.1	2104	459	224	181	26	9	7	16	209	6	414	51	2	31	28	.525	0	6	3.31

Brian Rios

Bats: Right Throws: Right Pos: SS-36; 3B-30; 2B-21; 1B-10; PH-5; DH-3; PR-2   Ht: 6'3" Wt: 190 Born: 7/25/74 Age: 26

Year Team	Lg Org	G	AB	H	2B	3B	HR	TB	R	RBI	TBB	IBB	SO	HBP	SH	SF	SB	CS	SB%	GDP	Avg	OBP	SLG
1996 Jamestown	A- Det	36	102	31	2	6	1	44	19	17	19	0	15	0	0	1	4	1	.80	3	.304	.410	.431
1997 Jamestown	A- Det	45	167	44	6	1	4	64	23	23	14	0	22	4	0	2	3	0	1.00	6	.263	.332	.383
1998 W Michigan	A Det	100	343	91	18	1	3	120	44	46	23	2	60	3	3	5	5	4	.56	6	.265	.315	.350
1999 Lakeland	A+ Det	119	430	121	27	7	6	180	60	44	24	1	47	5	0	6	7	3	.70	13	.281	.323	.419
2000 Jacksnville	AA Det	95	315	82	23	3	5	126	42	36	29	0	59	8	3	4	1	1	.50	3	.260	.334	.400
5 Min. YEARS		395	1357	369	80	14	19	534	188	166	109	3	203	20	6	16	20	9	.69	31	.272	.332	.394

David Riske

Pitches: Right Bats: Right Pos: RP-4; SP-1   Ht: 6'2" Wt: 180 Born: 10/23/76 Age: 24

Year Team	Lg Org	G	GS	CG	GF	IP	BFP	H	R	ER	HR	SH	SF	HB	TBB	IBB	SO	WP	Bk	W	L	Pct.	ShO	Sv	ERA
1997 Kinston	A+ Cle	39	0	0	23	72	299	58	22	18	3	6	1	2	33	4	90	0	0	4	4	.500	0	2	2.25
1998 Kinston	A+ Cle	53	0	0	50	54	218	48	15	14	4	2	1	1	15	0	67	1	0	1	1	.500	0	33	2.33
Akron	AA Cle	2	0	0	1	3	11	1	0	0	0	0	0	0	1	0	5	0	0	0	0	—	0	1	0.00
1999 Akron	AA Cle	23	0	0	22	23.2	90	5	6	5	1	0	2	0	13	0	33	1	0	0	0	—	0	12	1.90
Buffalo	AAA Cle	23	0	0	19	27.2	101	14	3	2	0	1	0	0	7	0	22	0	0	3	0	1.000	0	6	0.65
2000 Buffalo	AAA Cle	2	0	0	3	3	13	2	1	1	0	0	0	0	2	0	2	2	0	0	0	—	0	0	3.00
Akron	AA Cle	3	1	0	1	4	15	2	0	0	0	0	0	1	0	0	4	0	0	0	0	—	0	1	0.00
1999 Cleveland	AL	12	0	0	3	14	68	20	15	13	2	1	1	0	6	0	16	0	0	1	1	.500	0	0	8.36
4 Min. YEARS		145	1	0	116	187.1	747	130	47	40	8	9	4	4	71	4	223	4	0	8	5	.615	0	55	1.92

Juan Rivera

Bats: Right Throws: Right Pos: OF-130; DH-2; PH-2; 1B-1   Ht: 6'2" Wt: 170 Born: 7/3/78 Age: 22

Year Team	Lg Org	G	AB	H	2B	3B	HR	TB	R	RBI	TBB	IBB	SO	HBP	SH	SF	SB	CS	SB%	GDP	Avg	OBP	SLG
1998 Yankees	R NYY	57	210	70	9	1	12	117	43	45	26	2	27	1	0	1	8	5	.62	10	.333	.408	.557
Oneonta	A- NYY	6	18	5	0	0	1	8	2	3	1	0	4	0	0	0	1	1	.50	1	.278	.316	.444
1999 Yankees	R NYY	5	18	6	0	0	1	9	7	4	4	0	1	0	0	0	0	0	—	1	.333	.455	.500
Tampa	A+ NYY	109	426	112	20	2	14	178	50	77	26	3	67	5	0	8	5	4	.56	13	.263	.308	.418
2000 Norwich	AA NYY	17	62	14	5	0	2	25	9	12	6	0	15	0	0	0	0	0	—	1	.226	.294	.403
Tampa	A+ NYY	115	409	113	26	1	14	183	62	69	33	1	56	6	0	5	11	7	.61	9	.276	.336	.447
3 Min. YEARS		309	1143	320	60	4	44	520	173	210	96	6	170	12	0	14	25	17	.60	35	.280	.338	.455

Mike Rivera

Bats: Right Throws: Right Pos: C-91; DH-11; 1B-5; PH-2   Ht: 6'0" Wt: 190 Born: 9/8/76 Age: 24

Year Team	Lg Org	G	AB	H	2B	3B	HR	TB	R	RBI	TBB	IBB	SO	HBP	SH	SF	SB	CS	SB%	GDP	Avg	OBP	SLG
1996 Springfield	IND —	3	1	0	0	0	0	0	0	0	0	0	0	0	0	0	0	0	—	0	.000	.000	.000
1997 Tigers	R Det	47	154	44	9	2	10	87	34	36	18	2	25	3	0	2	0	0	—	2	.286	.367	.565
1998 W Michigan	A Det	108	403	111	34	3	9	178	40	67	15	2	68	2	1	5	0	2	.00	8	.275	.301	.442
1999 Jacksnville	AA Det	7	23	4	1	0	2	11	3	6	2	0	5	0	0	0	0	0	—	0	.174	.240	.478
Lakeland	A+ Det	104	370	103	20	2	14	169	44	72	20	0	59	3	0	8	1	1	.50	10	.278	.314	.457

Year Team	Lg Org	G	AB	H	2B	3B	HR	TB	R	RBI	TBB	IBB	SO	HBP	SH	SF	SB	CS	SB%	GDP	Avg	OBP	SLG
2000 Lakeland	A+ Det	64	243	71	19	4	11	131	30	53	16	3	45	1	0	2	2	0	1.00	8	.292	.336	.539
Toledo	AAA Det	4	13	3	3	0	0	6	0	1	0	0	2	0	0	0	0	0	—	4	.231	.231	.462
Jacksnville	AA Det	39	150	29	8	1	2	45	10	9	7	0	30	0	0	1	0	0	—	4	.193	.228	.300
5 Min. YEARS		376	1357	365	94	12	48	627	161	244	78	5	234	9	1	18	3	3	.50	32	.269	.309	.462

Roberto Rivera

Bats: Both **Throws:** Right **Pos:** OF-99; DH-16; PH-2; PR-2; 1B-1   **Ht:** 6'2" **Wt:** 180 **Born:** 11/25/76 **Age:** 24

Year Team	Lg Org	G	AB	H	2B	3B	HR	TB	R	RBI	TBB	IBB	SO	HBP	SH	SF	SB	CS	SB%	GDP	Avg	OBP	SLG
1995 Orioles	R Bal	42	150	44	7	3	3	66	21	26	10	0	38	2	0	2	6	3	.67	5	.293	.341	.440
1996 Orioles	R Bal	4	8	5	1	1	0	8	7	2	3	0	1	0	0	1	3	0	1.00	0	.625	.667	1.000
Bluefield	R+ Bal	46	158	34	8	0	5	57	20	26	10	0	54	0	0	0	14	4	.78	3	.215	.262	.361
1997 Delmarva	A Bal	17	59	9	0	1	2	17	6	5	1	0	20	0	0	0	1	2	.33	1	.153	.167	.288
Frederick	A+ Bal	16	53	12	1	0	1	16	8	8	3	0	16	1	0	0	1	1	.50	0	.226	.281	.302
Bluefield	R+ Bal	50	192	61	20	2	3	94	28	27	13	1	43	1	2	1	6	6	.50	3	.318	.362	.490
1998 Frederick	A+ Bal	3	6	2	0	0	1	5	1	1	1	1	1	0	0	0	0	0	—	0	.333	.429	.833
Delmarva	A Bal	110	390	93	21	5	7	145	55	50	25	1	99	4	3	5	17	4	.81	5	.238	.288	.372
1999 Frederick	A+ Bal	118	460	126	21	4	12	191	70	53	39	0	89	3	0	3	18	9	.67	4	.274	.333	.415
Bowie	AA Bal	9	36	8	0	0	0	8	0	1	1	0	9	0	0	0	2	0	1.00	1	.222	.243	.222
2000 Bowie	AA Bal	80	272	61	13	3	4	92	31	34	31	1	62	1	1	4	10	2	.83	10	.224	.302	.338
Frederick	A+ Bal	36	116	29	5	3	1	43	14	18	12	3	30	2	1	2	4	0	1.00	0	.250	.326	.371
6 Min. YEARS		531	1900	484	97	22	39	742	261	251	149	7	462	14	7	18	82	31	.73	31	.255	.311	.391

Saul Rivera

Pitches: Right **Bats:** Right **Pos:** RP-51   **Ht:** 5'11" **Wt:** 155 **Born:** 12/7/77 **Age:** 23

		HOW MUCH HE PITCHED						WHAT HE GAVE UP									THE RESULTS					
Year Team	Lg Org	G	GS	CG	GF	IP	BFP	H	R	ER	HR	SH	SF	HB	TBB	IBB	SO	WP	Bk	W	L	Pct.	ShO	Sv	ERA
1998 Elizabethtn	R+ Min	23	0	0	21	36	147	19	10	9	4	2	0	0	19	2	65	1	0	3	3	.500	0	7	2.25
1999 Quad City	A Min	60	0	0	54	69.2	283	42	12	11	0	2	0	0	36	5	102	2	0	4	1	.800	0	23	1.42
2000 New Britain	AA Min	22	0	0	7	37	163	28	16	16	0	2	1	2	22	0	47	8	0	1	0	1.000	0	0	3.89
Fort Myers	A+ Min	29	0	0	22	37.2	166	34	15	15	0	2	0	0	19	3	45	6	1	8	1	.889	0	5	3.58
3 Min. YEARS		134	0	0	104	180.1	759	123	53	51	4	8	1	2	96	10	259	17	1	16	5	.762	0	35	2.55

Scott Rivette

Pitches: Right **Bats:** Both **Pos:** RP-21   **Ht:** 6'2" **Wt:** 200 **Born:** 2/8/74 **Age:** 27

		HOW MUCH HE PITCHED						WHAT HE GAVE UP									THE RESULTS					
Year Team	Lg Org	G	GS	CG	GF	IP	BFP	H	R	ER	HR	SH	SF	HB	TBB	IBB	SO	WP	Bk	W	L	Pct.	ShO	Sv	ERA
1995 Sou Oregon	A- Oak	9	1	0	3	19	83	16	5	2	0	1	1	1	11	2	22	1	0	2	0	1.000	0	2	0.95
W Michigan	A Oak	8	0	0	4	15.1	65	12	5	5	0	0	2	0	7	0	15	1	0	1	0	1.000	0	2	2.93
1996 W Michigan	A Oak	32	29	0	1	153.1	667	145	80	60	7	2	3	12	51	0	142	9	2	8	9	.471	0	1	3.52
1997 Modesto	A+ Oak	20	20	3	0	126	533	147	65	50	12	3	2	7	31	1	96	8	1	9	9	.500	0	0	3.57
Huntsville	AA Oak	7	6	0	0	39	180	52	29	29	3	2	3	0	19	0	33	3	1	3	1	.750	0	0	6.69
1998 Huntsville	AA Oak	35	0	0	9	68.1	309	75	46	35	7	0	4	5	32	0	53	5	0	6	4	.600	0	2	4.61
Knoxville	AA Tor	7	0	0	2	9.1	44	7	4	4	0	1	2	0	7	1	4	1	0	0	1	.000	0	0	3.86
1999 Knoxville	AA Tor	56	0	0	33	78	341	85	40	33	2	1	3	5	29	4	74	7	2	4	7	.364	0	10	3.81
2000 Tacoma	AAA Sea	3	0	0	1	3.1	17	5	3	3	0	0	0	0	3	0	4	2	0	0	0	—	0	0	8.10
New Haven	AA Sea	2	0	0	1	2	12	6	3	3	0	0	1	0	1	0	0	0	0	0	0	—	0	0	13.50
Sonoma Cty	IND —	16	0	0	16	18	75	16	5	5	1	1	0	1	5	0	15	3	0	0	2	.000	0	5	2.50
6 Min. YEARS		195	56	3	70	531.2	2326	566	285	229	32	11	21	31	196	8	458	40	6	33	33	.500	0	22	3.88

Todd Rizzo

Pitches: Left **Bats:** Right **Pos:** RP-61   **Ht:** 6'2" **Wt:** 220 **Born:** 5/24/71 **Age:** 30

		HOW MUCH HE PITCHED						WHAT HE GAVE UP									THE RESULTS					
Year Team	Lg Org	G	GS	CG	GF	IP	BFP	H	R	ER	HR	SH	SF	HB	TBB	IBB	SO	WP	Bk	W	L	Pct.	ShO	Sv	ERA
1992 Yakima	A- LA	15	0	0	8	26	121	21	13	13	3	0	1	2	24	0	26	6	0	2	0	1.000	0	4	4.50
Dodgers	R LA	3	1	0	1	7	31	4	4	3	0	0	1	8	0	7	0	0	1	0	.000	0	0	3.86
1995 Pr William	A+ CWS	36	0	0	10	68	307	68	30	21	2	2	1	3	39	8	59	13	0	3	5	.375	0	1	2.78
1996 Birmingham	AA CWS	46	0	0	19	68.2	300	61	28	21	0	3	2	1	40	7	48	7	0	4	4	.500	0	10	2.75
1997 Nashville	AAA CWS	54	0	0	23	70.2	318	63	39	28	6	3	1	3	33	3	60	9	0	4	5	.444	0	6	3.57
1998 Calgary	AAA CWS	50	0	0	19	72	358	102	62	54	6	3	3	3	39	3	58	10	1	7	3	.700	0	4	6.75
1999 Charlotte	AAA CWS	50	0	0	16	71	308	68	37	32	5	6	5	2	31	2	46	6	0	4	5	.444	0	8	4.06
2000 Salt Lake	AAA Min	61	0	0	14	71.2	315	76	31	27	1	4	1	1	27	1	43	4	0	6	4	.600	0	1	3.39
1998 Chicago	AL	9	0	0	1	6.2	38	12	12	10	0	0	1	0	6	0	3	2	0	0	0	—	0	0	13.50
1999 Chicago	AL	3	0	0	2	1.1	12	4	2	1	0	1	0	0	3	1	2	0	0	0	2	.000	0	0	6.75
7 Min. YEARS		318	1	0	110	455	2058	463	244	199	23	20	14	15	241	24	347	55	1	30	27	.526	0	30	3.94
2 Maj. YEARS		12	0	0	3	8	50	16	14	11	0	1	1	0	9	1	5	2	0	0	2	.000	0	0	12.38

Joe Roa

Pitches: Right **Bats:** Right **Pos:** SP-14; RP-5   **Ht:** 6'1" **Wt:** 194 **Born:** 10/11/71 **Age:** 29

		HOW MUCH HE PITCHED						WHAT HE GAVE UP									THE RESULTS					
Year Team	Lg Org	G	GS	CG	GF	IP	BFP	H	R	ER	HR	SH	SF	HB	TBB	IBB	SO	WP	Bk	W	L	Pct.	ShO	Sv	ERA
1989 Braves	R Atl	13	4	0	4	37.1	156	40	18	12	2	0	1	0	10	1	21	3	0	2	2	.500	0	0	2.89
1990 Pulaski	R+ Atl	14	11	3	1	75.2	313	55	29	25	3	2	1	2	26	0	49	2	2	4	2	.667	1	0	2.97
1991 Macon	A Atl	30	18	4	2	141	556	106	46	33	6	0	3	5	33	4	96	3	0	13	3	.813	2	1	2.11
1992 St. Lucie	A+ NYM	26	24	2	0	156.1	647	176	80	63	9	6	6	6	15	1	61	0	1	9	7	.563	1	0	3.63
1993 Binghamton	AA NYM	32	23	2	0	167.1	693	190	80	72	9	2	4	10	24	0	73	3	2	12	7	.632	1	0	3.87
1994 Binghamton	AA NYM	3	3	0	0	20	72	18	6	4	0	2	2	1	0	11	1	2	1	.667	0	0	1.80
Norfolk	AAA NYM	25	25	5	0	167.2	703	184	82	65	16	3	12	4	34	1	74	4	0	8	8	.500	1	0	3.49

239

		HOW MUCH HE PITCHED						WHAT HE GAVE UP												THE RESULTS					
Year Team	Lg Org	G	GS	CG	GF	IP	BFP	H	R	ER	HR	SH	SF	HB	TBB	IBB	SO	WP	Bk	W	L	Pct.	ShO	Sv	ERA
1995 Buffalo	AAA Cle	25	24	3	1	164.2	678	168	71	64	9	2	5	7	28	1	93	1	2	17	3	.850	0	0	3.50
1996 Buffalo	AAA Cle	26	24	5	0	165.1	676	161	66	60	19	5	3	6	36	0	82	6	1	11	8	.579	0	0	3.27
1997 Phoenix	AAA SF	6	5	0	0	36	158	43	21	19	4	1	0	1	11	0	16	0	0	3	1	.750	0	0	4.75
1998 Fresno	AAA SF	27	27	2	0	162	702	192	102	93	26	9	2	4	32	0	97	3	2	12	9	.571	1	0	5.17
2000 Akron	AA Cle	19	14	1	2	103	439	91	48	39	7	5	2	7	38	0	59	3	0	6	5	.545	0	0	3.41
1995 Cleveland	AL	1	1	0	0	6	28	9	4	4	1	1	0	0	2	0	0	0	0	0	1	.000	0	0	6.00
1996 Cleveland	AL	1	0	0	0	1.2	17	4	2	2	0	0	0	0	3	0	0	0	0	0	0	—	0	0	10.80
1997 San Francisco	NL	28	3	0	4	65.2	289	86	40	38	8	5	4	2	20	5	34	0	1	2	5	.286	0	0	5.21
11 Min. YEARS		246	202	27	10	1396.1	5803	1424	649	549	110	37	41	53	288	8	732	29	12	99	56	.639	6	1	3.54
3 Maj. YEARS		30	4	0	4	73.1	328	99	46	44	9	6	4	2	25	5	34	0	1	2	6	.250	0	0	5.40

Jason Roach

Pitches: Right **Bats:** Right **Pos:** SP-15   **Ht:** 6'4" **Wt:** 199 **Born:** 4/20/76 **Age:** 25

		HOW MUCH HE PITCHED						WHAT HE GAVE UP												THE RESULTS					
Year Team	Lg Org	G	GS	CG	GF	IP	BFP	H	R	ER	HR	SH	SF	HB	TBB	IBB	SO	WP	Bk	W	L	Pct.	ShO	Sv	ERA
1998 Capital Cty	A NYM	1	0	0	0	1	5	1	0	0	0	0	0	0	1	0	1	0	0	0	0	—	0	0	0.00
1999 St. Lucie	A+ NYM	2	0	0	1	2	7	1	0	0	0	0	0	0	0	0	3	0	0	0	0	—	0	0	0.00
2000 Pittsfield	A- NYM	5	5	0	0	26.2	108	18	11	7	0	0	0	2	7	0	26	0	1	1	1	.500	0	0	2.36
Binghamton	AA NYM	1	1	0	0	5	24	7	3	2	0	1	0	0	3	0	3	0	0	0	0	—	0	0	3.60
St. Lucie	A+ NYM	9	9	0	0	48.2	191	42	15	14	2	1	2	0	12	0	22	1	0	5	3	.625	0	0	2.59
3 Min. YEARS		18	15	0	2	83.1	335	69	29	23	2	2	2	2	23	0	55	1	1	6	4	.600	0	0	2.48

Jake Robbins

Pitches: Right **Bats:** Right **Pos:** RP-45; SP-4   **Ht:** 6'5" **Wt:** 190 **Born:** 5/23/76 **Age:** 25

		HOW MUCH HE PITCHED						WHAT HE GAVE UP												THE RESULTS					
Year Team	Lg Org	G	GS	CG	GF	IP	BFP	H	R	ER	HR	SH	SF	HB	TBB	IBB	SO	WP	Bk	W	L	Pct.	ShO	Sv	ERA
1994 Yankees	R NYY	8	3	0	0	23	102	21	16	13	2	1	3	1	15	0	14	2	1	0	2	.000	0	0	5.09
1995 Yankees	R NYY	14	3	0	3	37.1	159	32	26	23	2	2	1	1	18	1	17	4	0	2	3	.400	0	0	5.54
Oneonta	A- NYY	1	0	0	1	1	3	0	0	0	0	0	0	0	0	0	1	0	0	0	0	—	0	0	0.00
1996 Greensboro	A NYY	18	12	0	2	74	349	80	59	53	5	4	5	7	49	0	50	10	4	1	8	.111	0	0	6.45
Oneonta	A- NYY	11	11	0	0	66	298	64	42	33	3	5	1	2	35	1	47	6	1	3	4	.429	0	0	4.50
1997 Greensboro	A NYY	20	19	0	0	101.1	462	114	81	65	6	2	3	0	55	1	72	7	0	6	4	.600	0	0	5.77
Tampa	A+ NYY	3	3	0	0	16	73	18	14	9	2	0	2	0	10	1	5	2	0	1	1	.500	0	0	5.06
1998 Tampa	A+ NYY	26	25	2	0	152.1	674	167	83	65	5	5	6	1	72	2	87	4	1	11	6	.647	2	0	3.84
1999 Norwich	AA NYY	20	19	2	0	111	508	118	80	67	7	4	8	3	60	3	63	2	2	3	12	.200	1	0	5.43
Tampa	A+ NYY	7	7	0	0	41.2	187	44	30	22	3	1	2	2	19	2	31	5	0	3	3	.500	0	0	4.75
2000 Columbus	AAA NYY	1	0	0	1	1	7	3	1	1	0	0	0	0	1	0	0	0	0	0	0	—	0	0	9.00
Norwich	AA NYY	48	4	0	13	71.1	326	68	45	22	4	2	3	6	40	1	53	5	0	3	5	.375	0	0	2.78
7 Min. YEARS		177	106	4	20	696	3148	729	477	373	39	26	34	25	374	12	440	47	9	33	48	.407	3	0	4.82

J.P. Roberge

Bats: Right **Throws:** Right **Pos:** DH-27; 2B-21; 3B-13; PH-8; 1B-6; PR-2; OF-1   **Ht:** 6'0" **Wt:** 177 **Born:** 9/12/72 **Age:** 28

		BATTING														BASERUNNING				PERCENTAGES		
Year Team	Lg Org	G	AB	H	2B	3B	HR	TB	R	RBI	TBB	IBB	SO	HBP	SH	SF	SB	CS	SB%	GDP	Avg	OBP	SLG
1994 Great Falls	R+ LA	63	256	82	17	1	1	104	55	42	20	0	22	5	2	5	24	4	.86	7	.320	.374	.406
Yakima	A- LA	4	8	3	1	0	0	4	1	0	0	0	3	1	0	0	0	1	.00	0	.375	.444	.500
1995 Vero Beach	A+ LA	3	9	0	0	0	0	0	1	0	0	0	2	0	0	0	0	0	—	0	.000	.000	.000
San Berndno	A+ LA	116	450	129	22	1	17	204	92	59	34	0	62	8	2	3	31	8	.79	9	.287	.345	.453
1996 San Berndno	A+ LA	12	44	16	3	1	1	24	8	6	3	0	9	2	0	1	1	2	.33	0	.364	.420	.545
San Antonio	AA LA	62	232	68	14	2	6	104	28	27	14	1	39	2	2	2	9	3	.75	5	.293	.336	.448
Albuquerque	AAA LA	53	156	50	6	1	4	70	17	17	14	1	28	1	3	0	3	0	1.00	1	.321	.380	.449
1997 San Antonio	AA LA	134	516	166	26	4	17	251	94	105	39	3	70	7	2	5	18	9	.67	13	.322	.374	.486
1998 Albuquerque	AAA LA	136	475	144	30	1	10	206	83	67	31	1	64	5	2	5	22	6	.79	17	.303	.349	.434
1999 Omaha	AAA KC	116	437	137	31	3	13	213	77	66	26	0	59	5	5	0	16	5	.76	15	.314	.359	.487
2000 Columbus	AAA NYY	29	77	9	3	0	1	15	7	6	5	0	10	1	1	0	0	0	—	0	.117	.181	.195
Omaha	AAA KC	6	23	9	4	0	1	16	5	1	1	0	3	0	0	0	0	0	—	0	.391	.417	.696
Wichita	AA KC	36	124	30	6	0	1	39	20	13	10	1	17	1	0	1	1	1	.50	3	.242	.304	.315
7 Min. YEARS		770	2807	843	163	14	72	1250	488	409	197	7	388	38	19	21	125	39	.76	71	.300	.352	.445

Kevin Roberson

Bats: Both **Throws:** Right **Pos:** OF-28; DH-5; PH-3; PR-1   **Ht:** 6'4" **Wt:** 210 **Born:** 1/29/68 **Age:** 33

		BATTING														BASERUNNING				PERCENTAGES		
Year Team	Lg Org	G	AB	H	2B	3B	HR	TB	R	RBI	TBB	IBB	SO	HBP	SH	SF	SB	CS	SB%	GDP	Avg	OBP	SLG
1988 Wytheville	R+ ChC	63	225	47	12	2	3	72	39	29	40	0	86	3	0	2	3	2	.60	0	.209	.333	.320
1989 Chston-WV	A ChC	126	429	109	19	1	13	169	49	57	70	4	149	5	2	3	3	6	.33	7	.254	.363	.394
1990 Winston-Sal	A+ ChC	85	313	84	23	3	5	128	49	45	25	0	70	3	1	2	7	3	.70	6	.268	.327	.409
Charlotte	AA ChC	31	119	29	6	2	5	54	14	16	8	0	23	0	1	2	2	0	1.00	1	.244	.287	.454
1991 Charlotte	AA ChC	136	507	130	23	2	19	214	77	67	39	1	125	9	0	5	17	3	.85	10	.256	.318	.422
1992 Iowa	AAA ChC	51	197	60	15	4	6	101	25	34	5	1	46	2	1	1	0	0	—	4	.305	.327	.513
1993 Iowa	AAA ChC	67	263	80	20	1	16	150	48	50	19	3	66	4	0	3	3	2	.60	0	.304	.356	.570
1994 Iowa	AAA ChC	19	67	21	8	0	3	38	9	17	4	1	19	3	0	3	0	1	.00	0	.313	.364	.567
1995 Tacoma	AAA Sea	42	157	37	6	1	6	63	17	17	19	1	51	2	0	2	1	1	.50	4	.236	.322	.401
1996 Norfolk	AAA NYM	70	215	57	13	3	7	97	26	33	14	2	65	7	1	2	0	1	.00	4	.265	.328	.451
1997 Phoenix	AAA SF	109	349	100	19	5	14	171	60	67	37	2	98	11	0	2	9	5	.64	6	.287	.371	.490
1998 Calgary	AAA CWS	119	431	117	36	4	27	234	84	97	37	1	128	11	1	7	5	1	.83	5	.271	.340	.543
2000 Salt Lake	AAA Min	36	120	30	7	1	6	57	22	26	17	0	38	2	0	3	0	0	—	3	.250	.321	.475
1993 Chicago	NL	62	180	34	4	1	9	67	23	27	12	0	48	3	0	2	0	1	.00	2	.189	.251	.372
1994 Chicago	NL	44	55	12	4	0	4	28	8	9	2	0	14	2	0	0	0	0	—	6	.218	.271	.509
1995 Chicago	NL	32	38	7	1	0	4	20	5	6	6	0	14	1	0	0	0	1	.00	1	.184	.311	.526
1996 New York	NL	27	36	8	1	0	3	18	8	8	7	0	17	1	0	2	0	0	—	6	.222	.348	.500
12 Min. YEARS		954	3392	901	207	25	130	1548	519	555	329	16	964	62	7	37	50	25	.67	56	.266	.338	.456
4 Maj. YEARS		165	309	61	10	1	20	133	44	51	27	0	93	7	0	2	0	2	.00	6	.197	.275	.430

Mark Roberts

Pitches: Right **Bats:** Right **Pos:** SP-18; RP-13 **Ht:** 6'2" **Wt:** 205 **Born:** 9/29/75 **Age:** 25

Year Team	Lg Org	G	GS	CG	GF	IP	BFP	H	R	ER	HR	SH	SF	HB	TBB	IBB	SO	WP	Bk	W	L	Pct.	ShO	Sv	ERA
1996 Hickory	A CWS	13	13	0	0	72	298	70	42	39	12	3	2	3	19	0	62	4	3	4	6	.400	0	0	4.88
1997 Hickory	A CWS	4	4	0	0	22	96	23	12	9	3	1	1	0	9	0	14	1	0	0	2	.000	0	0	3.68
Winston-Sal	A+ CWS	14	14	3	0	91.1	379	78	48	41	10	1	3	3	45	0	64	4	0	5	9	.357	0	0	4.04
1998 Winston-Sal	A+ CWS	27	25	2	0	165.1	706	165	88	72	15	6	8	10	50	1	142	6	0	9	9	.500	1	0	3.92
1999 Birmingham	AA CWS	33	17	0	7	124.1	525	108	64	47	11	3	7	3	41	0	84	3	0	5	8	.385	0	2	3.40
2000 Birmingham	AA CWS	17	8	0	7	60	256	65	27	25	4	1	1	1	17	1	46	1	0	6	3	.667	0	3	3.75
Charlotte	AAA CWS	14	10	1	1	64.1	262	58	16	15	7	1	3	3	20	1	38	2	1	7	2	.778	0	0	2.10
5 Min. YEARS		122	91	6	15	599.1	2522	567	297	248	62	16	25	23	201	3	450	21	4	36	39	.480	1	5	3.72

Willis Roberts

Pitches: Right **Bats:** Right **Pos:** SP-25; RP-5 **Ht:** 6'3" **Wt:** 175 **Born:** 6/19/75 **Age:** 26

Year Team	Lg Org	G	GS	CG	GF	IP	BFP	H	R	ER	HR	SH	SF	HB	TBB	IBB	SO	WP	Bk	W	L	Pct.	ShO	Sv	ERA
1993 Bristol	R+ Det	10	2	0	2	26	116	24	16	4	0	2	0	1	11	0	23	2	0	2	3	.400	0	1	1.38
1994 Bristol	R+ Det	4	4	0	0	20.2	81	9	9	9	1	0	1	2	8	0	17	2	0	1	2	.333	0	0	3.92
1995 Fayetteville	A Det	17	15	0	0	80	339	72	33	24	2	1	2	6	40	0	52	15	3	6	3	.667	0	0	2.70
1996 Lakeland	A+ Det	23	22	2	0	149.1	636	133	60	48	5	8	9	6	69	0	105	13	3	9	7	.563	0	0	2.89
1997 Jacksnville	AA Det	26	26	2	0	149	685	181	120	104	18	6	7	6	64	0	86	6	6	6	15	.286	0	0	6.28
1998 Jacksnville	AA Det	12	2	0	5	24.2	105	21	10	6	0	2	0	3	10	1	15	1	0	3	1	.750	0	2	2.19
Toledo	AAA Det	39	0	0	16	54.2	248	63	33	28	4	3	1	2	28	2	40	4	1	3	3	.500	0	2	4.61
1999 Toledo	AAA Det	31	12	2	9	92	433	112	68	64	10	3	3	3	59	3	52	5	4	5	8	.385	0	0	6.26
2000 Chattanooga	AA Cin	5	5	0	0	32.1	137	33	12	11	0	3	1	2	13	1	28	0	0	4	0	1.000	0	0	3.06
Louisville	AAA Cin	25	20	2	1	124	550	138	80	78	19	5	4	6	55	0	66	3	1	7	8	.467	1	0	5.66
1999 Detroit	AL	1	0	0	0	1.1	8	3	4	2	0	0	1	0	1	0	0	0	0	0	0	—	0	0	13.50
8 Min. YEARS		192	108	8	33	752.2	3330	786	441	376	59	33	28	40	357	7	484	51	18	46	50	.479	1	3	4.50

Jeriome Robertson

Pitches: Left **Bats:** Left **Pos:** SP-24; RP-1 **Ht:** 6'1" **Wt:** 190 **Born:** 3/30/77 **Age:** 24

Year Team	Lg Org	G	GS	CG	GF	IP	BFP	H	R	ER	HR	SH	SF	HB	TBB	IBB	SO	WP	Bk	W	L	Pct.	ShO	Sv	ERA
1996 Astros	R Hou	13	13	1	0	78.1	304	51	20	15	2	3	0	4	15	0	98	6	2	5	3	.625	1	0	1.72
Kissimmee	A+ Hou	1	1	0	0	7	27	4	4	2	0	0	0	0	1	0	2	0	0	0	0	—	0	0	2.57
1997 Quad City	A Hou	26	25	2	1	146	647	151	86	66	12	1	4	8	56	1	135	5	3	11	8	.579	1	1	4.07
1998 Kissimmee	A+ Hou	28	28	2	0	175	740	185	83	72	13	3	5	7	53	3	131	5	0	10	10	.500	0	0	3.70
1999 Jackson	AA Hou	28	28	1	0	191	791	184	81	65	22	6	4	4	45	2	133	5	7	15	7	.682	0	0	3.06
2000 Kissimmee	A+ Hou	5	5	1	0	29	121	28	19	15	1	1	0	2	5	0	13	0	0	2	1	.667	1	0	4.66
Round Rock	AA Hou	11	10	0	1	61	265	62	36	28	8	3	1	2	18	1	30	4	1	2	2	.500	0	0	4.13
New Orleans	AAA Hou	9	9	0	0	49.2	228	64	42	39	10	2	2	3	23	1	27	1	0	1	7	.125	0	0	7.07
5 Min. YEARS		121	119	7	2	737	3123	729	371	302	68	19	16	34	216	8	569	26	19	46	38	.548	3	1	3.69

Mike Robertson

Bats: Left **Throws:** Left **Pos:** 1B-105; PH-12; OF-7; DH-6 **Ht:** 6'0" **Wt:** 189 **Born:** 10/9/70 **Age:** 30

Year Team	Lg Org	G	AB	H	2B	3B	HR	TB	R	RBI	TBB	IBB	SO	HBP	SH	SF	SB	CS	SB%	GDP	Avg	OBP	SLG
1991 Utica	A- CWS	13	54	9	2	1	0	13	6	8	5	0	10	0	0	0	2	1	.67	0	.167	.237	.241
South Bend	A CWS	54	210	69	16	2	1	92	30	26	18	3	24	3	3	3	7	6	.54	5	.329	.385	.438
1992 Sarasota	A+ CWS	106	395	99	21	3	10	156	50	59	50	3	55	7	1	5	5	7	.42	8	.251	.343	.395
Birmingham	AA CWS	27	90	17	8	1	1	30	6	9	10	1	19	0	1	1	0	1	.00	2	.189	.267	.333
1993 Birmingham	AA CWS	138	511	138	31	3	11	208	73	73	59	4	97	3	0	8	10	5	.67	10	.270	.344	.407
1994 Birmingham	AA CWS	53	196	62	20	2	3	95	32	30	31	4	34	2	0	2	6	3	.67	5	.316	.411	.485
Nashville	AAA CWS	67	213	48	8	1	8	82	21	21	15	4	27	3	0	0	0	3	.00	4	.225	.286	.385
1995 Nashville	AAA CWS	139	499	124	17	4	19	206	55	52	50	7	72	11	3	2	2	4	.33	8	.248	.329	.413
1996 Nashville	AAA CWS	54	450	116	16	4	21	203	64	74	38	4	83	5	9	2	1	2	.33	10	.258	.321	.451
1997 Scranton-WB	AAA Phi	121	416	124	17	3	12	183	61	72	58	4	67	4	1	6	0	2	.00	9	.298	.384	.440
1998 Tucson	AAA Pit	111	411	112	14	3	13	171	49	70	33	1	56	7	0	3	1	0	1.00	15	.273	.335	.416
1999 Altoona	AA Pit	46	175	49	12	0	9	88	31	28	24	2	26	1	3	0	0	3	.00	1	.280	.370	.503
Nashville	AAA Pit	74	220	68	16	1	9	113	34	31	10	1	32	3	1	3	2	1	.67	5	.309	.343	.514
2000 New Orleans	AAA Hou	121	401	97	23	5	9	157	57	49	45	8	56	6	1	2	1	3	.25	13	.242	.326	.392
1996 Chicago	AL	6	7	1	1	0	0	2	0	0	0	0	1	0	0	0	0	0	—	0	.143	.143	.286
1997 Philadelphia	NL	22	38	8	2	1	0	12	3	4	0	0	6	3	0	0	1	0	1.00	0	.211	.286	.316
1998 Arizona	NL	11	13	2	0	0	0	2	0	0	0	0	2	0	0	0	0	0	—	0	.154	.154	.154
10 Min. YEARS		1208	4241	1132	221	33	126	1797	569	602	446	46	658	55	23	35	37	41	.47	95	.267	.342	.424
3 Maj. YEARS		39	58	11	3	1	0	16	3	4	0	0	9	6	0	0	1	0	1.00	0	.190	.230	.276

Kerry Robinson

Bats: Left **Throws:** Left **Pos:** OF-114; PH-3; PR-3; DH-1 **Ht:** 6'0" **Wt:** 175 **Born:** 10/3/73 **Age:** 27

Year Team	Lg Org	G	AB	H	2B	3B	HR	TB	R	RBI	TBB	IBB	SO	HBP	SH	SF	SB	CS	SB%	GDP	Avg	OBP	SLG
1995 Johnson Cty	R+ StL	60	250	74	12	8	1	105	44	26	16	1	30	0	3	2	14	10	.58	3	.296	.336	.420
1996 Peoria	A StL	123	440	158	17	14	2	209	98	47	51	5	51	3	4	8	50	26	.66	2	.359	.424	.475
1997 Arkansas	AA StL	136	523	168	16	3	2	196	80	62	54	1	64	2	5	2	40	23	.63	7	.321	.386	.375
Louisville	AAA StL	2	9	1	0	0	0	1	0	0	0	0	1	0	0	0	0	0	—	0	.111	.111	.111
1998 Orlando	AA TB	72	309	83	7	5	2	106	45	26	27	0	28	0	4	2	28	9	.76	6	.269	.325	.343
Durham	AAA TB	58	242	73	7	4	1	91	28	20	23	0	30	0	2	1	18	11	.62	1	.302	.361	.376
1999 Tacoma	AAA Sea	79	335	108	16	9	0	142	53	34	14	0	44	0	3	2	30	7	.81	4	.322	.348	.424
Indianapols	AAA Cin	34	129	34	3	2	1	44	24	14	4	0	12	1	4	3	14	4	.78	2	.264	.285	.341
2000 Columbus	AAA NYY	119	437	139	17	9	0	174	71	32	41	0	40	2	10	1	37	18	.67	5	.318	.378	.398

		BATTING																BASERUNNING				PERCENTAGES		
Year Team	Lg Org	G	AB	H	2B	3B	HR	TB	R	RBI	TBB	IBB	SO	HBP	SH	SF	SB	CS	SB%	GDP	Avg	OBP	SLG
1998 Tampa Bay	AL	2	3	0	0	0	0	0	0	0	0	0	1	0	0	0	0	0	—	0	.000	.000	.000
1999 Cincinnati	NL	9	1	0	0	0	0	0	4	0	0	0	1	0	0	0	0	1	.00	0	.000	.000	.000
6 Min. YEARS		683	2674	838	95	54	9	1068	443	269	230	7	300	8	35	21	231	108	.68	30	.313	.367	.399
2 Maj. YEARS		11	4	0	0	0	0	0	4	0	0	0	2	0	0	0	0	1	.00	0	.000	.000	.000

Bobby Rodgers

Pitches: Right **Bats:** Right **Pos:** RP-48　　　　**Ht:** 6'3" **Wt:** 225 **Born:** 7/22/74 **Age:** 26

		HOW MUCH HE PITCHED						WHAT HE GAVE UP											THE RESULTS						
Year Team	Lg Org	G	GS	CG	GF	IP	BFP	H	R	ER	HR	SH	SF	HB	TBB	IBB	SO	WP	Bk	W	L	Pct.	ShO	Sv	ERA
1996 Lowell	A- Bos	14	14	2	0	90	363	60	33	19	3	2	2	3	31	0	108	9	2	7	4	.636	1	0	1.90
1997 Kane County	A Fla	27	27	2	0	165.2	699	154	81	71	9	6	4	14	61	0	138	7	1	8	10	.444	0	0	3.86
1998 Brevard Cty	A+ Fla	7	7	0	0	35.1	143	34	17	16	2	2	1	1	7	0	35	1	0	1	1	.500	0	0	4.08
Portland	AA Fla	14	14	2	0	82	339	68	37	34	8	5	3	3	28	0	72	2	1	6	5	.545	1	0	3.73
1999 Portland	AA Fla	26	22	0	1	122.2	576	147	85	74	13	4	3	6	70	0	109	8	0	5	10	.333	0	0	5.43
2000 Portland	AA Fla	48	0	0	46	55.1	234	38	23	20	3	4	1	2	31	2	58	3	0	3	5	.375	0	22	3.25
5 Min. YEARS		136	84	6	47	551	2354	501	276	234	38	23	14	29	228	2	520	30	4	30	35	.462	2	22	3.82

John Rodriguez

Bats: Left **Throws:** Left **Pos:** OF-101; 1B-9; PH-7; DH-6　　　　**Ht:** 6'0" **Wt:** 185 **Born:** 1/20/78 **Age:** 23

		BATTING																BASERUNNING				PERCENTAGES		
Year Team	Lg Org	G	AB	H	2B	3B	HR	TB	R	RBI	TBB	IBB	SO	HBP	SH	SF	SB	CS	SB%	GDP	Avg	OBP	SLG
1997 Yankees	R NYY	45	153	47	10	2	3	70	21	23	30	1	31	0	0	3	7	0	1.00	3	.307	.414	.458
1998 Greensboro	A NYY	119	408	103	18	4	10	159	64	49	64	1	93	4	0	3	14	3	.82	7	.252	.357	.390
1999 Yankees	R NYY	3	7	2	0	1	0	4	1	1	3	0	0	0	0	0	0	0	—	0	.286	.500	.571
Tampa	A+ NYY	71	269	82	14	3	8	126	37	43	41	7	52	3	1	3	2	5	.29	5	.305	.399	.468
2000 Norwich	AA NYY	17	56	11	4	0	1	18	4	10	8	0	22	1	0	0	0	0	—	1	.196	.308	.321
Tampa	A+ NYY	105	362	97	14	2	16	163	59	44	40	5	81	8	1	0	3	2	.60	6	.268	.354	.450
4 Min. YEARS		360	1255	342	60	12	38	540	196	170	186	14	279	16	2	9	26	10	.72	22	.273	.371	.430

Juan Rodriguez

Bats: Both **Throws:** Left **Pos:** 1B-65; OF-23; DH-7; PH-7; PR-2　　　　**Ht:** 5'10" **Wt:** 180 **Born:** 12/16/74 **Age:** 26

		BATTING																BASERUNNING				PERCENTAGES		
Year Team	Lg Org	G	AB	H	2B	3B	HR	TB	R	RBI	TBB	IBB	SO	HBP	SH	SF	SB	CS	SB%	GDP	Avg	OBP	SLG
1995 Angels	R Ana	54	215	64	8	8	1	91	27	31	7	0	49	3	1	2	4	7	.36	1	.298	.326	.423
1996 Cedar Rapds	A Ana	8	25	6	0	1	0	8	3	3	1	0	6	0	0	0	2	1	.67	1	.240	.269	.320
Boise	A- Ana	52	192	57	9	0	2	72	24	28	12	3	52	0	1	4	3	3	.50	5	.297	.332	.375
1997 Cedar Rapds	A Ana	111	416	117	18	8	12	187	66	55	43	0	106	1	18	3	11	12	.48	4	.281	.348	.450
1998 Lk Elsinore	A+ Ana	62	194	42	7	1	3	60	23	20	24	0	58	2	2	2	4	3	.57	1	.216	.306	.309
1999 Lk Elsinore	A+ Ana	86	315	95	12	6	6	137	54	50	32	0	70	2	4	1	7	5	.58	5	.302	.369	.435
2000 Lk Elsinore	A+ Ana	30	92	26	6	1	1	37	14	14	10	0	11	0	4	1	0	3	.00	0	.283	.350	.402
Erie	AA Ana	68	238	58	10	1	1	73	24	14	20	0	66	1	2	0	0	1	.00	1	.244	.305	.307
6 Min. YEARS		471	1687	465	70	26	26	665	235	215	149	3	418	9	32	13	31	35	.47	18	.276	.335	.394

Liu Rodriguez

Bats: Both **Throws:** Right **Pos:** 2B-79; SS-50; PH-2　　　　**Ht:** 5'9" **Wt:** 170 **Born:** 11/5/76 **Age:** 24

		BATTING																BASERUNNING				PERCENTAGES		
Year Team	Lg Org	G	AB	H	2B	3B	HR	TB	R	RBI	TBB	IBB	SO	HBP	SH	SF	SB	CS	SB%	GDP	Avg	OBP	SLG
1995 White Sox	R CWS	36	119	27	6	1	1	38	18	11	23	0	19	0	2	0	4	2	.67	2	.227	.352	.319
1996 Hickory	A CWS	122	430	107	18	0	0	125	57	30	60	2	77	9	8	2	15	14	.52	3	.249	.351	.291
1997 Hickory	A CWS	129	450	130	21	6	1	166	72	62	65	0	56	5	10	7	12	13	.48	13	.289	.380	.369
1998 Winston-Sal	A+ CWS	112	420	117	27	3	2	156	62	43	45	0	40	9	10	7	15	10	.60	13	.279	.356	.371
1999 Birmingham	AA CWS	64	244	71	11	1	3	93	42	37	22	0	35	3	8	3	5	3	.63	2	.291	.353	.381
2000 Charlotte	AAA CWS	126	396	108	20	3	4	146	44	46	54	1	39	7	16	5	3	7	.30	10	.273	.366	.369
1999 Chicago	AL	39	93	22	2	2	1	31	8	12	12	0	11	3	3	0	0	0	—	5	.237	.343	.333
6 Min. YEARS		589	2059	560	103	14	11	724	295	229	269	3	266	33	54	24	54	49	.52	43	.272	.361	.352

Luis Rodriguez

Bats: Right **Throws:** Right **Pos:** C-89; DH-11; OF-6; PH-2; PR-1　　　　**Ht:** 5'11" **Wt:** 185 **Born:** 1/3/74 **Age:** 27

		BATTING																BASERUNNING				PERCENTAGES		
Year Team	Lg Org	G	AB	H	2B	3B	HR	TB	R	RBI	TBB	IBB	SO	HBP	SH	SF	SB	CS	SB%	GDP	Avg	OBP	SLG
1995 St.Cathrnes	A- Tor	66	257	71	16	2	1	94	22	20	10	1	49	1	2	1	2	4	.33	7	.276	.305	.366
1996 Hagerstown	A Tor	79	256	53	8	1	1	66	19	25	24	0	58	1	5	1	6	4	.60	3	.207	.277	.258
1997 Syracuse	AAA Tor	3	2	0	0	0	0	0	0	0	0	0	2	0	0	0	0	0	—	0	.000	.000	.000
Hagerstown	A Tor	27	94	25	6	0	2	37	13	14	2	0	20	1	3	2	3	0	1.00	2	.266	.283	.394
Knoxville	AA Tor	24	78	21	3	1	0	26	6	6	3	0	20	1	0	0	0	1	.00	1	.269	.305	.333
1998 Syracuse	AAA Tor	5	15	2	0	0	0	2	1	2	0	0	6	0	1	1	0	0	—	0	.133	.125	.133
Dunedin	A+ Tor	67	196	57	15	0	4	84	34	41	10	0	39	2	5	4	11	2	.85	9	.291	.325	.429
Knoxville	AA Tor	8	17	7	0	1	0	9	6	1	7	0	5	0	1	0	1	0	1.00	1	.412	.583	.529
1999 Pawtucket	AAA Bos	2	3	0	0	0	0	0	0	0	1	0	0	0	0	0	0	0	—	0	.000	.000	.000
Sarasota	A+ Bos	31	114	33	8	0	3	50	19	14	8	0	17	1	1	2	5	1	.83	2	.289	.336	.439
Trenton	AA Bos	32	114	31	7	0	4	50	10	14	3	0	25	1	0	0	2	1	.67	4	.272	.297	.439
2000 Sarasota	A+ Bos	53	190	45	10	4	3	72	26	34	17	2	36	3	0	2	10	4	.71	6	.237	.307	.379
Pawtucket	AAA Bos	28	83	16	4	0	1	23	7	3	3	0	30	0	1	0	1	1	.50	1	.193	.221	.277
Trenton	AA Bos	27	93	26	1	0	6	45	14	14	7	0	23	1	0	0	2	0	1.00	6	.280	.333	.484
6 Min. YEARS		452	1512	387	78	9	25	558	177	188	94	3	331	12	18	14	43	18	.70	36	.256	.302	.369

Nerio Rodriguez

Pitches: Right **Bats:** Right **Pos:** SP-20; RP-11   **Ht:** 6'1" **Wt:** 205 **Born:** 3/22/73 **Age:** 28

		HOW MUCH HE PITCHED						WHAT HE GAVE UP										THE RESULTS					
Year Team	Lg Org	G	GS	CG	GF	IP	BFP	H	R	ER	HR	SH	SF	HB	TBB	IBB	SO	WP	Bk	W	L	Pct.	ShO	Sv	ERA
1995 High Desert	A+ Bal	7	0	0	3	10	44	8	2	2	0	0	0	0	7	0	10	0	0	0	0	—	0	0	1.80
1996 Frederick	A+ Bal	24	17	1	7	111.1	462	83	42	28	10	5	0	4	40	0	114	6	1	8	7	.533	0	2	2.26
Rochester	AAA Bal	2	2	0	0	15	58	10	3	3	0	0	0	0	2	0	6	2	0	1	0	1.000	0	0	1.80
1997 Rochester	AAA Bal	27	27	1	0	168.1	688	124	82	73	23	6	0	8	62	0	160	4	3	11	10	.524	1	0	3.90
1998 Rochester	AAA Bal	5	5	0	0	24.2	108	24	16	15	6	1	1	1	10	0	19	0	1	1	4	.200	0	0	5.47
Bowie	AA Bal	2	2	0	0	4	18	6	2	2	0	0	0	0	0	0	7	0	0	0	1	.000	0	0	4.50
1999 Syracuse	AAA Tor	27	27	1	0	162.2	688	161	84	82	17	3	5	7	53	0	137	5	2	10	8	.556	1	0	4.54
2000 Pawtucket	AAA Bos	12	1	0	2	24.2	118	38	28	26	9	0	1	0	9	0	23	3	0	0	1	.000	0	0	9.49
Trenton	AA Bos	19	19	1	0	109.1	466	115	64	58	9	4	5	3	34	0	93	3	0	7	7	.500	0	0	4.77
1996 Baltimore	AL	8	1	0	2	16.2	77	18	11	8	2	0	1	1	7	0	12	0	0	0	1	.000	0	0	4.32
1997 Baltimore	AL	6	2	0	1	22	98	21	15	12	2	1	4	1	8	0	11	1	0	2	1	.667	0	0	4.91
1998 Baltimore	AL	6	4	0	0	19	89	25	17	17	0	0	2	0	9	0	8	1	0	1	3	.250	0	0	8.05
Toronto	AL	7	0	0	3	8.1	44	10	9	9	1	0	0	1	8	0	3	0	0	1	0	1.000	0	0	9.72
1999 Toronto	AL	2	0	0	1	2	10	2	3	3	2	0	0	0	2	0	2	0	0	0	1	.000	0	0	13.50
6 Min. YEARS		125	100	4	12	630	2650	569	323	289	74	19	12	23	217	0	569	23	7	38	38	.500	2	2	4.13
4 Maj. YEARS		29	7	0	7	68	318	76	55	49	7	1	7	3	34	0	36	2	0	4	6	.400	0	0	6.49

Sammy Rodriguez

Bats: Right **Throws:** Right **Pos:** C-35; PH-7; DH-4   **Ht:** 5'9" **Wt:** 196 **Born:** 8/20/75 **Age:** 25

		BATTING															BASERUNNING				PERCENTAGES		
Year Team	Lg Org	G	AB	H	2B	3B	HR	TB	R	RBI	TBB	IBB	SO	HBP	SH	SF	SB	CS	SB%	GDP	Avg	OBP	SLG
1995 Mets	R NYM	6	18	5	0	0	0	5	1	1	2	0	4	0	0	0	0	1	.00	0	.278	.350	.278
Butte	R+ NYM	17	57	14	1	0	1	18	7	6	4	0	13	0	0	0	2	1	.67	0	.246	.295	.316
1996 Pittsfield	A- NYM	32	93	18	3	0	1	24	8	10	11	0	25	1	0	1	1	0	1.00	3	.194	.283	.258
1997 Pittsfield	A- NYM	36	110	27	6	2	5	52	15	20	21	1	33	2	1	2	2	1	.67	1	.245	.370	.473
1998 Binghamton	AA NYM	3	8	1	0	0	0	1	2	1	1	0	0	0	0	0	0	0	—	0	.125	.222	.125
St. Lucie	A+ NYM	53	152	39	9	1	2	56	20	24	20	0	36	2	4	2	3	1	.75	1	.257	.347	.368
1999 Norfolk	AAA NYM	5	9	2	0	0	2	8	2	4	3	0	2	0	0	0	0	0	—	0	.222	.417	.889
Binghamton	AA NYM	69	203	46	10	0	3	65	15	24	21	0	49	3	2	0	2	2	.50	2	.227	.308	.320
2000 Norfolk	AAA NYM	26	64	12	1	0	0	13	4	3	5	0	11	1	0	0	0	4	.00	3	.188	.257	.203
Binghamton	AA NYM	2	8	2	2	0	0	4	1	3	0	0	1	0	0	0	0	0	—	0	.250	.250	.500
St. Lucie	A+ NYM	17	53	14	2	0	1	19	11	5	8	1	9	4	0	1	0	0	—	2	.264	.394	.358
6 Min. YEARS		266	775	180	34	3	15	265	86	101	96	2	183	13	7	6	10	10	.50	12	.232	.325	.342

Victor Rodriguez

Bats: Right **Throws:** Right **Pos:** SS-124; 2B-6; DH-1   **Ht:** 6'1" **Wt:** 190 **Born:** 10/25/76 **Age:** 24

		BATTING															BASERUNNING				PERCENTAGES		
Year Team	Lg Org	G	AB	H	2B	3B	HR	TB	R	RBI	TBB	IBB	SO	HBP	SH	SF	SB	CS	SB%	GDP	Avg	OBP	SLG
1994 Marlins	R Fla	24	96	31	2	0	0	33	13	17	7	0	7	0	0	3	2	0	1.00	3	.323	.358	.344
1995 Kane County	A Fla	127	472	111	9	1	0	122	65	43	40	0	47	2	16	4	18	6	.75	17	.235	.295	.258
1996 Brevard Cty	A+ Fla	114	438	120	14	4	0	142	54	26	32	0	42	2	8	3	20	7	.74	13	.274	.324	.324
1997 Portland	AA Fla	113	401	111	18	4	3	146	63	38	30	0	43	0	10	3	13	7	.65	15	.277	.325	.364
1998 Portland	AA Fla	66	222	63	9	1	4	86	28	19	18	0	26	5	4	0	5	4	.56	7	.284	.351	.387
1999 Portland	AA Fla	38	97	20	3	1	1	28	13	12	10	0	9	2	3	1	0	1	.00	3	.206	.291	.289
2000 Kinston	A+ Cle	96	382	125	31	2	4	172	59	42	37	1	48	5	7	1	24	9	.73	7	.327	.393	.450
Akron	AA Cle	35	132	32	7	0	2	45	20	14	9	0	14	2	1	1	1	2	.33	2	.242	.299	.341
7 Min. YEARS		613	2240	613	93	13	14	774	315	211	183	1	236	18	49	16	83	36	.70	67	.274	.331	.346

Wilfredo Rodriguez

Pitches: Left **Bats:** Left **Pos:** SP-20   **Ht:** 6'3" **Wt:** 180 **Born:** 3/20/79 **Age:** 22

		HOW MUCH HE PITCHED						WHAT HE GAVE UP										THE RESULTS					
Year Team	Lg Org	G	GS	CG	GF	IP	BFP	H	R	ER	HR	SH	SF	HB	TBB	IBB	SO	WP	Bk	W	L	Pct.	ShO	Sv	ERA
1997 Astros	R Hou	12	12	1	0	68	279	54	30	23	1	1	1	2	32	0	71	6	4	8	2	.800	1	0	3.04
1998 Quad City	A Hou	28	27	1	0	165	667	122	70	56	7	6	3	9	62	1	170	8	9	11	5	.688	0	0	3.05
1999 Kissimmee	A+ Hou	25	24	0	1	153.1	624	108	55	49	8	2	5	13	62	0	148	5	1	15	7	.682	0	0	2.88
2000 Kissimmee	A+ Hou	9	9	1	0	53	234	43	29	28	5	1	4	6	30	0	52	4	1	3	5	.375	0	0	4.75
Round Rock	AA Hou	11	11	0	0	57.2	275	54	42	37	10	4	6	1	52	0	55	2	0	2	4	.333	0	0	5.77
4 Min. YEARS		85	83	3	1	497	2079	381	226	193	31	14	19	31	238	1	496	25	15	39	23	.629	1	0	3.49

Brian Rogers

Pitches: Right **Bats:** Right **Pos:** SP-27   **Ht:** 6'6" **Wt:** 200 **Born:** 2/13/77 **Age:** 24

		HOW MUCH HE PITCHED						WHAT HE GAVE UP										THE RESULTS					
Year Team	Lg Org	G	GS	CG	GF	IP	BFP	H	R	ER	HR	SH	SF	HB	TBB	IBB	SO	WP	Bk	W	L	Pct.	ShO	Sv	ERA
1998 Oneonta	A- NYY	6	6	0	0	35	135	23	9	9	3	1	1	1	10	0	34	2	1	2	2	.500	0	0	2.31
Tampa	A+ NYY	3	3	0	0	15	70	12	7	7	1	0	0	0	14	0	13	0	1	0	0	—	0	0	4.20
Greensboro	A NYY	3	3	0	0	16	71	18	15	14	6	0	1	1	6	0	19	3	0	2	1	.667	0	0	7.88
1999 Tampa	A+ NYY	25	23	1	0	134	577	141	62	57	13	2	1	2	43	1	129	7	0	8	10	.444	1	0	3.83
2000 Norwich	AA NYY	27	27	1	0	164.1	717	155	90	72	10	5	7	10	70	0	132	14	2	11	6	.647	0	0	3.94
3 Min. YEARS		64	62	2	0	364.1	1570	349	183	159	33	8	10	14	143	1	327	26	4	23	19	.548	1	0	3.93

Ed Rogers

Bats: Right **Throws:** Right **Pos:** SS-93; 2B-1   **Ht:** 6'1" **Wt:** 150 **Born:** 8/10/81 **Age:** 19

		BATTING															BASERUNNING				PERCENTAGES		
Year Team	Lg Org	G	AB	H	2B	3B	HR	TB	R	RBI	TBB	IBB	SO	HBP	SH	SF	SB	CS	SB%	GDP	Avg	OBP	SLG
1999 Orioles	R Bal	53	177	51	5	1	1	61	34	19	23	0	22	4	4	2	20	3	.87	2	.288	.379	.345

Year Team	Lg Org	G	AB	H	2B	3B	HR	TB	R	RBI	TBB	IBB	SO	HBP	SH	SF	SB	CS	SB%	GDP	Avg	OBP	SLG
2000 Delmarva	A Bal	80	332	91	14	5	5	130	46	42	22	0	63	0	10	3	27	6	.82	3	.274	.317	.392
Bowie	AA Bal	13	49	14	3	0	1	20	4	8	3	0	15	0	0	1	1	1	.50	0	.286	.321	.408
2 Min. YEARS		146	558	156	22	6	7	211	84	69	48	0	100	4	14	6	48	10	.83	5	.280	.338	.378

Mel Rojas

Pitches: Right **Bats:** Right **Pos:** SP-4; RP-4   **Ht:** 5'11" **Wt:** 212 **Born:** 12/10/66 **Age:** 34

		HOW MUCH HE PITCHED						WHAT HE GAVE UP										THE RESULTS					
Year Team	Lg Org	G	GS	CG	GF	IP	BFP	H	R	ER	HR	SH	SF	HB	TBB	IBB	SO	WP	Bk	W	L	Pct.	ShO	Sv	ERA
1986 Expos	R Mon	13	12	1	1	55.1	261	63	39	30	0	3	3	2	37	0	34	4	0	4	5	.444	0	0	4.88
1987 Burlington	A Mon	25	25	4	0	158.2	686	146	84	67	10	4	6	3	67	1	100	8	0	8	9	.471	1	0	3.80
1988 Rockford	A Mon	12	12	3	0	73.1	302	52	30	20	3	3	1	2	29	0	72	3	2	6	4	.600	0	0	2.45
Wst Plm Bch	A+ Mon	2	2	0	0	5	19	4	2	2	1	0	0	0	1	0	4	0	0	1	0	1.000	0	0	3.60
1989 Jacksnville	AA Mon	34	12	1	17	112	447	62	39	31	1	7	4	5	57	0	104	8	1	10	7	.588	1	5	2.49
1990 Indianapols	AAA Mon	17	17	0	0	97.2	412	84	42	34	9	5	2	1	47	3	64	3	1	2	4	.333	0	0	3.13
1991 Indianapols	AAA Mon	14	10	0	2	52.2	221	50	29	24	4	5	1	1	14	1	55	2	1	4	2	.667	0	1	4.10
1992 Indianapols	AAA Mon	4	0	0	1	8.1	37	10	5	5	0	0	0	0	3	0	7	1	0	2	1	.667	0	0	5.40
1999 Ottawa	AAA Mon	12	0	0	6	21	99	25	13	12	3	0	0	1	12	0	16	3	0	0	1	.000	0	2	5.14
2000 Sarasota	A+ Bos	5	4	0	0	7	30	10	6	6	1	0	0	0	2	0	5	1	0	0	1	.000	0	0	7.71
Pawtucket	AAA Bos	3	0	0	2	3	13	1	1	1	0	0	0	0	3	1	2	0	0	0	0	—	0	0	3.00
1990 Montreal	NL	23	0	0	5	40	173	34	17	16	5	2	0	2	24	4	26	2	0	3	1	.750	0	1	3.60
1991 Montreal	NL	37	0	0	13	48	200	42	21	20	4	0	2	1	13	1	37	3	0	3	3	.500	0	6	3.75
1992 Montreal	NL	68	0	0	26	100.2	399	71	17	16	2	4	2	2	34	8	70	2	0	7	1	.875	0	10	1.43
1993 Montreal	NL	66	0	0	25	88.1	378	80	39	29	6	8	6	4	30	3	48	5	0	5	8	.385	0	10	2.95
1994 Montreal	NL	58	0	0	27	84	341	71	35	31	11	2	1	4	21	0	84	3	0	3	2	.600	0	16	3.32
1995 Montreal	NL	59	0	0	48	67.2	302	69	32	31	2	2	1	7	29	4	61	6	0	1	4	.200	0	30	4.12
1996 Montreal	NL	74	0	0	64	81	326	56	30	29	5	2	4	2	28	3	92	3	0	7	4	.636	0	36	3.22
1997 Chicago	NL	54	0	0	38	59	259	54	30	29	11	2	1	5	30	1	61	2	0	0	4	.000	0	13	4.42
New York	NL	23	0	0	12	26.1	111	24	17	15	4	0	1	2	6	1	32	1	0	0	2	.000	0	2	5.13
1998 New York	NL	50	0	0	19	58	262	68	39	39	9	4	2	3	30	5	41	2	0	5	2	.714	0	2	6.05
1999 Los Angeles	NL	5	0	0	2	5	23	5	7	7	3	0	0	0	3	1	3	0	0	0	0	—	0	0	12.60
Detroit	AL	5	0	0	2	6.1	39	12	16	16	3	0	1	3	4	0	6	0	0	0	0	—	0	0	22.74
Montreal	NL	3	0	0	1	2.2	17	5	5	5	0	0	1	2	2	0	1	1	0	0	0	—	0	0	16.88
9 Min. YEARS		141	94	9	29	594	2527	507	290	232	32	27	17	15	272	6	463	33	5	37	34	.521	2	8	3.52
10 Maj. YEARS		525	0	0	282	667	2830	591	305	283	65	26	22	37	254	31	562	30	0	34	31	.523	0	126	3.82

Jason Romano

Bats: Right **Throws:** Right **Pos:** 2B-125; DH-6   **Ht:** 6'0" **Wt:** 185 **Born:** 6/24/79 **Age:** 22

		BATTING															BASERUNNING				PERCENTAGES		
Year Team	Lg Org	G	AB	H	2B	3B	HR	TB	R	RBI	TBB	IBB	SO	HBP	SH	SF	SB	CS	SB%	GDP	Avg	OBP	SLG
1997 Rangers	R Tex	34	109	28	5	3	2	45	27	11	13	0	19	3	1	1	13	4	.76	1	.257	.349	.413
1998 Savannah	A Tex	134	524	142	19	4	7	190	72	52	46	1	94	8	5	5	40	17	.70	6	.271	.336	.363
Charlotte	A+ Tex	7	24	5	1	0	0	6	3	1	2	0	2	0	1	1	1	2	.33	0	.208	.259	.250
1999 Charlotte	A+ Tex	120	459	143	27	14	13	237	84	71	39	2	72	13	4	7	34	16	.68	4	.312	.376	.516
2000 Tulsa	AA Tex	131	535	145	35	2	8	208	87	70	56	0	84	6	16	7	25	10	.71	13	.271	.343	.389
4 Min. YEARS		426	1651	463	87	23	30	686	273	205	156	3	271	30	27	21	113	49	.70	24	.280	.349	.415

Mike Romano

Pitches: Right **Bats:** Both **Pos:** SP-26   **Ht:** 6'2" **Wt:** 195 **Born:** 3/3/72 **Age:** 29

		HOW MUCH HE PITCHED						WHAT HE GAVE UP										THE RESULTS					
Year Team	Lg Org	G	GS	CG	GF	IP	BFP	H	R	ER	HR	SH	SF	HB	TBB	IBB	SO	WP	Bk	W	L	Pct.	ShO	Sv	ERA
1993 Medcine Hat	R+ Tor	9	8	0	0	41	175	34	20	12	1	0	0	7	11	0	28	3	0	4	1	.800	0	0	2.63
1994 Hagerstown	A Tor	18	18	2	0	108.1	453	91	47	37	10	2	3	9	40	0	90	5	2	10	2	.833	1	0	3.07
1995 Dunedin	A+ Tor	28	26	1	1	150.1	654	141	79	69	15	4	3	11	75	0	102	5	3	11	7	.611	1	0	4.13
1996 Knoxville	AA Tor	34	21	0	5	130	600	148	98	72	17	5	8	5	72	1	92	5	2	9	9	.500	0	1	4.98
1997 Syracuse	AAA Tor	40	12	0	9	108	487	100	56	51	10	1	3	6	74	2	83	7	0	2	4	.333	0	0	4.25
1998 Syracuse	AAA Tor	27	13	1	7	117.1	516	131	66	54	13	0	2	4	53	3	69	6	0	8	6	.571	0	1	4.14
1999 Syracuse	AAA Tor	29	28	2	0	174.1	760	160	90	80	21	4	4	8	84	2	104	8	1	12	8	.600	0	0	4.13
2000 Syracuse	AAA Tor	10	10	2	0	63.2	259	53	23	23	7	0	1	2	26	0	34	1	0	6	3	.667	1	0	3.25
Salt Lake	AAA Min	16	16	1	0	95.1	435	122	71	65	11	3	2	8	30	0	54	6	1	7	6	.538	0	0	6.14
1999 Toronto	AL	3	0	0	1	5.1	28	8	8	7	1	0	1	0	5	0	3	1	0	0	0	—	0	0	11.81
8 Min. YEARS		211	152	9	22	988.1	4335	980	550	463	105	19	26	60	465	8	656	46	9	69	46	.600	2	2	4.22

Mandy Romero

Bats: Both **Throws:** Right **Pos:** C-78; DH-5   **Ht:** 5'11" **Wt:** 196 **Born:** 10/29/67 **Age:** 33

		BATTING															BASERUNNING				PERCENTAGES		
Year Team	Lg Org	G	AB	H	2B	3B	HR	TB	R	RBI	TBB	IBB	SO	HBP	SH	SF	SB	CS	SB%	GDP	Avg	OBP	SLG
1988 Princeton	R+ Pit	30	71	22	6	0	2	34	7	11	13	0	15	1	0	0	1	0	1.00	0	.310	.424	.479
1989 Augusta	A Pit	121	388	87	26	3	4	131	58	55	67	4	74	6	3	6	8	5	.62	10	.224	.343	.338
1990 Salem	A+ Pit	124	460	134	31	3	17	222	62	90	55	3	68	5	2	4	0	2	.00	10	.291	.370	.483
1991 Carolina	AA Pit	98	323	70	12	0	3	91	28	31	45	4	53	1	2	2	1	2	.33	7	.217	.313	.282
1992 Carolina	AA Pit	80	269	58	16	0	3	83	28	27	29	0	39	1	1	1	0	3	.00	10	.216	.292	.309
1993 Buffalo	AAA Pit	42	136	31	6	1	2	45	11	14	6	1	12	0	1	1	1	0	1.00	5	.228	.259	.331
1994 Buffalo	AAA Pit	7	23	3	0	0	0	3	3	1	2	0	1	0	1	0	0	0	—	2	.130	.200	.130
1995 Wichita	AA KC	121	440	133	32	1	21	230	73	82	69	10	60	5	0	1	1	3	.25	15	.302	.402	.523
1996 Memphis	AA SD	88	297	80	15	0	10	125	40	46	41	2	52	1	1	2	3	1	.75	15	.269	.358	.421
1997 Mobile	AA SD	61	222	71	22	0	13	132	50	52	38	3	31	2	0	1	0	1	.00	4	.320	.422	.595
Las Vegas	AAA SD	33	91	28	4	1	3	43	19	13	11	1	19	1	0	1	0	0	—	4	.308	.385	.473
1998 Las Vegas	AAA SD	40	131	38	8	0	8	70	25	22	20	1	25	1	1	0	0	1	.00	9	.290	.388	.534
Pawtucket	AAA Bos	45	139	46	5	0	8	75	20	27	24	6	15	0	2	4	0	0	—	1	.331	.419	.540

Year Team	Lg Org	G	AB	H	2B	3B	HR	TB	R	RBI	TBB	IBB	SO	HBP	SH	SF	SB	CS	SB%	GDP	Avg	OBP	SLG
1999 Pawtucket	AAA Bos	46	143	31	7	0	3	47	8	22	13	0	26	0	2	1	0	0	—	6	.217	.280	.329
Norfolk	AAA NYM	28	97	25	6	0	1	34	7	9	9	0	18	1	1	1	0	0	—	5	.258	.324	.351
2000 Buffalo	AAA Cle	4	17	7	2	0	0	9	1	4	0	0	2	0	0	0	0	0	—	0	.412	.412	.529
Akron	AA Cle	79	280	87	19	2	12	146	55	46	43	3	34	2	1	4	1	1	.50	6	.311	.401	.521
1997 San Diego	NL	21	48	10	0	0	2	16	7	4	2	0	18	0	0	0	1	0	1.00	1	.208	.240	.333
1998 San Diego	NL	6	9	0	0	0	0	0	1	0	1	0	3	0	0	0	0	0	—	0	.000	.100	.000
Boston	AL	12	13	3	1	0	0	4	2	1	3	0	3	0	0	0	0	0	—	1	.231	.375	.308
13 Min. YEARS		1047	3527	951	217	11	110	1520	495	552	485	38	544	27	18	30	16	19	.46	111	.270	.360	.431
2 Maj. YEARS		39	70	13	1	0	2	20	10	5	6	0	24	0	0	0	1	0	1.00	2	.186	.250	.286

Marc Ronan

Bats: Left **Throws:** Right **Pos:** C-34; 1B-5; PH-2   **Ht:** 6'2" **Wt:** 190 **Born:** 9/19/69 **Age:** 31

Year Team	Lg Org	G	AB	H	2B	3B	HR	TB	R	RBI	TBB	IBB	SO	HBP	SH	SF	SB	CS	SB%	GDP	Avg	OBP	SLG
1990 Hamilton	A- StL	56	167	38	6	0	1	47	14	15	15	0	37	1	0	3	1	2	.33	3	.228	.290	.281
1991 Savannah	A StL	108	343	81	10	1	0	93	41	45	37	1	54	4	3	1	11	2	.85	13	.236	.317	.271
1992 Springfield	A StL	110	376	81	19	2	6	122	45	48	23	2	58	1	0	4	4	5	.44	11	.215	.260	.324
1993 St. Pete	A+ StL	25	87	27	5	0	0	32	13	6	6	0	10	0	3	2	0	0	—	1	.310	.347	.368
Arkansas	AAA StL	96	281	60	16	1	7	99	33	34	26	2	47	2	3	3	1	3	.25	4	.214	.282	.352
1994 Louisville	AAA StL	84	269	64	11	2	2	85	32	21	12	2	43	2	2	2	3	1	.75	9	.238	.274	.316
1995 Louisville	AAA StL	78	225	48	8	0	0	56	15	8	14	2	42	0	2	0	4	3	.57	10	.213	.259	.249
1996 Charlotte	AAA Fla	79	220	67	10	0	4	89	23	20	16	2	37	2	0	2	3	4	.43	4	.305	.354	.405
1997 Columbus	AAA NYY	55	156	43	12	0	1	58	16	19	27	3	24	1	0	3	1	3	.25	9	.276	.386	.372
1998 New Orleans	AAA Hou	51	123	30	5	0	1	38	7	10	17	2	25	1	0	0	0	0	—	3	.244	.340	.309
1999 Scranton-WB	AAA Phi	38	115	19	5	0	2	30	14	10	8	1	28	1	0	1	1	2	.33	4	.165	.224	.261
2000 Arkansas	AA StL	40	116	24	4	0	0	28	8	9	9	1	22	1	1	1	0	0	—	2	.207	.268	.241
1993 St. Louis	NL	6	12	1	0	0	0	1	0	0	0	0	5	0	0	0	0	0	—	0	.083	.083	.083
11 Min. YEARS		820	2478	582	111	6	24	777	261	245	210	18	427	16	14	19	29	25	.54	73	.235	.297	.314

Derek Root

Pitches: Left **Bats:** Left **Pos:** RP-34; SP-4   **Ht:** 6'5" **Wt:** 215 **Born:** 5/26/75 **Age:** 26

		HOW MUCH HE PITCHED						WHAT HE GAVE UP												THE RESULTS					
Year Team	Lg Org	G	GS	CG	GF	IP	BFP	H	R	ER	HR	SH	SF	HB	TBB	IBB	SO	WP	Bk	W	L	Pct.	ShO	Sv	ERA
1995 Kissimmee	A+ Hou	5	0	0	1	6	29	10	3	3	0	0	0	0	2	0	3	0	0	0	0	—	0	0	4.50
Auburn	A- Hou	17	3	0	5	38.1	165	28	14	14	0	2	1	2	24	0	37	4	1	2	0	1.000	0	1	3.29
1996 Quad City	A Hou	40	2	0	22	63	272	55	25	21	1	4	4	4	26	4	47	6	0	5	3	.625	0	7	3.00
1997 Kissimmee	A+ Hou	26	22	2	0	129	555	131	76	60	10	4	7	7	42	1	68	7	5	4	14	.222	0	0	4.19
1998 Kissimmee	A+ Hou	29	9	2	13	80.1	323	69	28	21	3	2	1	4	20	2	79	4	1	5	4	.556	2	4	2.35
Jackson	AA Hou	7	6	0	0	44	192	46	24	19	4	1	1	1	17	1	31	1	0	4	1	.800	0	0	3.89
New Orleans	AAA Hou	1	1	0	0	6.1	24	3	2	2	1	0	0	0	3	0	4	1	0	1	0	1.000	0	0	2.84
1999 Jackson	AA Hou	28	26	0	0	156.2	711	167	103	81	17	5	3	11	79	2	129	14	2	7	16	.304	0	0	4.65
2000 Las Vegas	AAA SD	9	2	0	2	14	71	18	15	14	1	0	1	1	10	1	7	2	0	0	0	—	0	0	9.00
Mobile	AA SD	15	2	0	3	22.1	96	15	9	9	1	0	0	0	18	0	13	0	0	4	0	1.000	0	2	3.63
St. Lucie	A+ NYM	5	0	0	2	7.1	33	10	3	3	0	0	0	1	2	0	9	1	0	0	0	—	0	0	3.68
Binghamton	AA NYM	9	0	0	1	12.2	61	13	13	11	0	2	0	1	11	1	7	0	0	0	1	.000	0	0	7.82
6 Min. YEARS		191	73	4	49	580	2532	565	315	258	38	20	18	32	254	12	434	40	9	32	39	.451	2	14	4.00

Juan Rosario

Pitches: Right **Bats:** Right **Pos:** RP-28   **Ht:** 6'4" **Wt:** 219 **Born:** 11/17/75 **Age:** 25

		HOW MUCH HE PITCHED						WHAT HE GAVE UP												THE RESULTS					
Year Team	Lg Org	G	GS	CG	GF	IP	BFP	H	R	ER	HR	SH	SF	HB	TBB	IBB	SO	WP	Bk	W	L	Pct.	ShO	Sv	ERA
1993 Great Falls	R+ LA	2	2	0	0	5.1	37	11	13	13	3	0	0	5	6	0	4	0	0	0	1	.000	0	0	21.94
1995 Marlins	R Fla	1	0	0	0	1.1	10	4	2	2	0	0	0	0	1	0	3	1	0	0	0	—	0	0	13.50
1996 Devil Rays	R TB	3	0	0	1	3	16	0	3	0	0	0	1	1	3	0	3	2	1	0	0	—	0	0	0.00
1998 Hudson Val	A- TB	22	2	0	4	34.2	161	39	33	29	2	1	2	6	20	0	27	7	1	1	4	.200	0	1	7.53
1999 St. Pete	A+ TB	15	15	0	0	94.1	391	80	34	28	2	5	3	11	25	0	37	2	1	5	3	.625	0	0	2.67
2000 Orlando	AA TB	28	0	0	12	44.2	202	43	26	19	4	3	1	10	18	0	21	4	1	1	3	.250	0	6	3.83
6 Min. YEARS		71	19	0	17	183.1	817	177	111	91	11	9	7	33	73	0	95	16	4	7	11	.389	0	7	4.47

Mel Rosario

Bats: Both **Throws:** Right **Pos:** C-78; DH-2; PH-2; 1B-1   **Ht:** 6'0" **Wt:** 200 **Born:** 5/25/73 **Age:** 28

Year Team	Lg Org	G	AB	H	2B	3B	HR	TB	R	RBI	TBB	IBB	SO	HBP	SH	SF	SB	CS	SB%	GDP	Avg	OBP	SLG
1992 Spokane	A- SD	66	237	54	13	1	10	99	38	40	20	2	62	4	0	4	5	3	.63	6	.228	.294	.418
1993 Waterloo	A SD	32	105	22	6	2	5	47	15	15	7	1	37	2	0	0	5	2	.71	0	.210	.272	.448
Spokane	A- SD	41	140	32	5	0	4	49	17	19	8	2	36	0	0	0	2	1	.67	1	.229	.270	.350
1995 South Bend	A CWS	118	450	123	30	6	15	210	58	57	30	7	109	4	1	3	1	8	.11	4	.273	.322	.467
1996 Rancho Cuca	A+ SD	10	33	9	3	0	3	21	7	10	3	0	8	0	0	0	1	0	1.00	0	.273	.333	.636
High Desert	A+ Bal	42	163	52	9	1	10	93	35	34	21	0	45	9	0	0	4	0	1.00	3	.319	.425	.571
Bowie	AA Bal	47	162	34	10	0	2	50	14	17	6	1	43	5	1	2	3	2	.60	4	.210	.257	.309
Rochester	AAA Bal	3	2	0	0	0	0	0	0	0	0	0	0	0	0	0	0	0	—	0	.000	.000	.000
1997 Bowie	AA Bal	123	430	113	26	1	12	177	68	60	27	2	106	9	1	4	4	7	.36	5	.263	.317	.412
1998 Rochester	AAA Bal	34	113	28	4	0	3	41	10	10	6	0	24	1	0	1	5	2	.71	1	.248	.289	.363
Bowie	AA Bal	39	130	35	5	4	5	63	22	25	9	1	31	3	1	2	2	1	.67	3	.269	.326	.485
1999 Altoona	AA Pit	26	87	21	9	0	1	33	11	11	6	0	15	0	0	1	0	0	—	6	.241	.287	.379
Oklahoma	AAA Tex	7	26	5	1	0	0	6	3	0	0	0	8	0	0	0	1	0	1.00	1	.192	.192	.231
Tulsa	AA Tex	28	96	20	3	0	8	47	12	19	3	0	28	1	1	1	1	0	1.00	1	.208	.238	.490
2000 Birmingham	AA CWS	83	289	75	23	3	6	122	34	42	21	1	63	5	2	2	2	2	.50	3	.260	.319	.422
1997 Baltimore	AL	4	3	0	0	0	0	0	0	0	0	0	1	0	0	0	0	0	—	0	.000	.000	.000
8 Min. YEARS		699	2463	623	147	18	84	1058	343	362	167	16	616	43	7	20	36	28	.56	33	.253	.309	.430

Omar Rosario

Bats: Left **Throws:** Left **Pos:** OF-97; DH-10; 1B-3; PH-2   **Ht:** 6'1" **Wt:** 185 **Born:** 1/14/78 **Age:** 23

Year Team	Lg Org	G	AB	H	2B	3B	HR	TB	R	RBI	TBB	IBB	SO	HBP	SH	SF	SB	CS	SB%	GDP	Avg	OBP	SLG
1997 Athletics	R Oak	56	216	52	9	3	0	67	48	28	38	0	51	7	1	3	40	3	.93	1	.241	.367	.310
1998 Visalia	A+ Oak	82	212	47	8	1	1	60	33	24	33	0	68	4	5	2	18	4	.82	2	.222	.335	.283
Sou Oregon	A- Oak	29	101	26	4	0	3	39	18	13	15	0	26	2	1	0	5	2	.71	0	.257	.364	.386
1999 Modesto	A+ Oak	116	419	125	23	6	5	175	82	57	70	1	94	6	4	4	19	12	.61	4	.298	.403	.418
2000 Sacramento	AAA Oak	8	27	8	1	0	0	9	4	1	2	0	5	1	0	0	0	0	—	0	.296	.367	.333
Visalia	A+ Oak	102	333	84	16	2	4	116	56	39	73	2	76	4	2	2	24	14	.63	5	.252	.391	.348
4 Min. YEARS		393	1308	342	61	12	13	466	241	162	231	3	320	24	13	11	106	35	.75	12	.261	.379	.356

Mike Rose

Bats: Both **Throws:** Right **Pos:** C-96; DH-11; PH-11; OF-3   **Ht:** 6'1" **Wt:** 185 **Born:** 8/25/76 **Age:** 24

Year Team	Lg Org	G	AB	H	2B	3B	HR	TB	R	RBI	TBB	IBB	SO	HBP	SH	SF	SB	CS	SB%	GDP	Avg	OBP	SLG
1995 Astros	R Hou	35	89	23	2	1	1	30	13	9	11	0	18	3	0	0	2	1	.67	1	.258	.359	.337
1996 Kissimmee	A+ Hou	2	1	0	0	0	0	0	0	0	0	0	1	0	0	0	0	0	—	0	.000	.000	.000
Auburn	A- Hou	61	180	45	5	1	2	58	20	11	30	0	41	1	4	0	9	3	.75	5	.250	.360	.322
1997 Quad City	A Hou	79	234	60	6	1	3	77	22	27	28	0	62	4	8	3	3	1	.75	1	.256	.342	.329
1998 Kissimmee	A+ Hou	18	62	14	4	0	3	27	9	9	8	0	14	0	1	0	1	0	1.00	1	.226	.314	.435
Quad City	A Hou	88	267	81	13	2	7	119	48	40	52	3	56	1	3	1	10	8	.56	5	.303	.417	.446
1999 Jackson	AA Hou	15	45	11	0	0	3	20	8	8	13	1	10	0	1	0	0	2	.00	1	.244	.414	.444
Kissimmee	A+ Hou	95	303	84	16	2	11	137	61	32	59	0	64	3	0	2	12	6	.67	7	.277	.398	.452
2000 El Paso	AA Ari	117	352	100	22	1	10	154	58	62	68	2	70	1	1	4	8	11	.42	16	.284	.398	.438
6 Min. YEARS		510	1533	418	68	8	40	622	239	198	269	6	336	13	18	10	45	32	.58	38	.273	.384	.406

Ted Rose

Pitches: Right **Bats:** Left **Pos:** RP-54   **Ht:** 6'2" **Wt:** 185 **Born:** 8/23/73 **Age:** 27

Year Team	Lg Org	G	GS	CG	GF	IP	BFP	H	R	ER	HR	SH	SF	HB	TBB	IBB	SO	WP	Bk	W	L	Pct.	ShO	Sv	ERA
1996 Princeton	R+ Cin	11	11	1	0	59.1	262	70	44	41	9	2	3	3	21	0	53	9	2	3	5	.375	1	0	6.22
1997 Chston-WV	A Cin	38	13	2	9	129.1	525	108	44	36	7	9	3	6	27	0	132	3	2	11	6	.647	2	4	2.51
1998 Chattanooga	AA Cin	29	29	1	0	168.1	745	191	97	86	12	1	6	6	66	3	108	6	4	11	10	.524	0	0	4.60
1999 Reds	R Cin	1	0	0	1	2	11	4	2	2	0	0	0	0	1	0	3	0	0	0	0	—	0	0	9.00
Chattanooga	AA Cin	13	0	0	4	17	75	17	8	8	2	0	1	2	9	1	23	0	0	2	0	1.000	0	2	4.24
2000 Chattanooga	AA Cin	31	0	0	17	41	154	24	8	5	1	1	3	0	9	2	51	1	2	4	2	.667	0	8	1.10
Louisville	AAA Cin	23	0	0	6	38	158	36	23	21	5	1	2	1	13	0	33	1	0	2	2	.500	0	2	4.97
5 Min. YEARS		146	53	4	37	455	1930	450	226	199	36	14	18	18	146	6	403	20	10	33	25	.569	3	16	3.94

Pete Rose Jr.

Bats: Left **Throws:** Right **Pos:** 3B-85; 1B-10; PH-9; DH-8; OF-3; PR-1   **Ht:** 6'1" **Wt:** 180 **Born:** 11/16/69 **Age:** 31

Year Team	Lg Org	G	AB	H	2B	3B	HR	TB	R	RBI	TBB	IBB	SO	HBP	SH	SF	SB	CS	SB%	GDP	Avg	OBP	SLG
1989 Frederick	A+ Bal	24	67	12	3	0	0	15	3	7	0	0	15	1	0	0	1	1	.50	1	.179	.191	.224
Erie	A- Bal	58	228	63	13	5	2	92	30	26	12	1	34	1	2	0	1	2	.33	3	.276	.315	.404
1990 Frederick	A+ Bal	97	323	75	14	2	1	96	32	41	26	0	33	1	7	5	0	3	.00	6	.232	.287	.297
1991 Sarasota	A+ CWS	99	323	70	12	2	0	86	31	35	36	3	35	2	8	3	5	6	.45	3	.217	.297	.266
1992 Columbus	A Cle	131	510	129	24	6	9	192	67	54	48	2	53	6	8	3	4	3	.57	9	.253	.323	.376
1993 Kinston	A+ Cle	74	284	62	10	1	7	95	33	30	25	0	34	2	6	1	1	3	.25	5	.218	.285	.335
1994 Hickory	A CWS	32	114	25	4	1	0	31	14	12	13	2	18	2	3	2	0	0	—	3	.219	.305	.272
White Sox	R CWS	2	4	2	0	0	0	2	1	1	0	0	0	0	0	0	0	0	—	0	.500	.500	.500
Pr William	A+ CWS	45	146	41	3	1	4	58	18	22	18	0	15	0	2	3	0	1	.00	2	.281	.353	.397
1995 Birmingham	AA CWS	5	13	5	1	0	0	6	1	2	3	0	3	0	0	0	0	0	—	0	.385	.500	.462
South Bend	A CWS	116	423	117	24	6	4	165	56	65	54	0	45	5	2	7	2	0	1.00	6	.277	.360	.390
1996 Birmingham	AA CWS	108	399	97	13	1	3	121	40	44	32	1	54	2	5	3	1	3	.25	9	.243	.300	.303
1997 Indianapols	AAA Cin	12	40	9	2	0	0	11	2	1	2	0	11	0	0	0	0	0	—	1	.225	.262	.275
Chattanooga	AA Cin	112	445	137	31	0	25	243	75	98	34	1	63	3	1	3	0	1	.00	9	.308	.359	.546
1998 Indianapols	AAA Cin	43	133	37	7	1	3	55	19	13	8	0	10	2	0	1	1	0	1.00	2	.278	.326	.414
Nashville	AAA Pit	28	72	15	1	0	1	19	8	12	3	0	13	0	1	1	0	0	—	3	.208	.237	.264
New Jersey	IND —	12	33	14	4	1	1	23	2	8	3	0	4	0	0	0	0	0	—	2	.424	.472	.697
1999 New Jersey	IND —	81	303	91	27	1	15	165	70	53	42	7	29	5	0	7	7	0	1.00	6	.300	.387	.545
2000 Reading	AA Phi	109	356	88	22	1	8	136	56	56	56	4	47	2	1	3	8	2	.80	6	.247	.350	.382
1997 Cincinnati	NL	11	14	2	0	0	0	2	2	0	2	0	9	0	0	0	0	0	—	0	.143	.250	.143
12 Min. YEARS		1188	4216	1089	215	29	83	1611	558	580	415	21	516	34	46	42	31	25	.55	72	.258	.327	.382

John Rosengren

Pitches: Left **Bats:** Left **Pos:** RP-26   **Ht:** 6'4" **Wt:** 190 **Born:** 8/10/72 **Age:** 28

Year Team	Lg Org	G	GS	CG	GF	IP	BFP	H	R	ER	HR	SH	SF	HB	TBB	IBB	SO	WP	Bk	W	L	Pct.	ShO	Sv	ERA
1992 Bristol	R+ Det	14	3	0	3	23	113	16	21	20	2	0	5	3	30	0	28	6	2	0	1	.000	0	0	7.83
1993 Niagara Fal	A- Det	15	15	0	0	82	333	52	32	22	3	1	4	6	38	0	91	6	1	7	3	.700	0	0	2.41
1994 Lakeland	A+ Det	22	22	4	0	135.2	569	113	51	38	4	2	4	7	56	0	101	3	2	9	6	.600	3	0	2.52
Trenton	AA Det	3	3	0	0	17.1	79	21	15	14	2	1	1	0	11	0	7	0	1	0	2	.000	0	0	7.27
1995 Jacksnville	AA Det	14	13	0	0	67.2	308	73	39	34	7	2	2	5	40	0	59	12	2	2	7	.222	0	0	4.52
Lakeland	A+ Det	13	8	0	1	56.1	253	46	33	25	6	2	2	7	36	0	35	2	0	3	3	.500	0	0	3.99
1996 Jacksnville	AA Det	60	0	0	15	56.1	249	48	36	28	2	3	2	3	37	3	47	4	0	5	1	.833	0	1	4.55
1997 Toledo	AAA Det	54	0	0	16	56.1	266	44	29	25	1	1	3	7	49	1	53	7	1	1	3	.250	0	2	3.99
2000 Altoona	AA Pit	22	0	0	10	21.1	100	17	17	17	1	2	0	1	21	1	24	1	1	2	1	.667	0	3	7.17
Nashville	AAA Pit	4	0	0	0	2.2	14	2	2	2	0	0	0	1	4	0	4	1	0	0	1	.000	0	0	6.75
7 Min. YEARS		221	64	4	45	517.2	2284	430	275	225	35	13	22	37	322	5	449	42	10	29	30	.492	3	6	3.91

Terry Rosenkranz

Pitches: Left **Bats:** Left **Pos:** RP-17 **Ht:** 6'4" **Wt:** 205 **Born:** 11/5/70 **Age:** 30

Year Team	Lg Org	HOW MUCH HE PITCHED						WHAT HE GAVE UP													THE RESULTS					
		G	GS	CG	GF	IP	BFP	H	R	ER	HR	SH	SF	HB	TBB	IBB	SO	WP	Bk	W	L	Pct.	ShO	Sv	ERA
1992 Butte	R+ Tex	14	0	0	8	26.2	127	34	22	17	4	1	3	1	12	0	23	2	1	0	0	—	0	0	5.74
1993 Rangers	R Tex	8	0	0	1	10.1	52	16	12	11	2	0	3	0	4	0	6	0	0	0	0	—	0	0	9.58
1994 Thunder Bay	IND —	11	3	1	3	41	196	54	30	25	3	3	2	1	22	0	16	3	0	0	2	.000	0	0	5.49
1995 Beloit	A Mil	4	0	0	2	8	30	2	2	0	0	0	0	0	2	0	4	0	0	0	0	—	0	0	0.00
Stockton	A+ Mil	35	1	0	14	49.1	234	44	34	34	4	5	4	1	49	2	43	4	0	1	2	.333	0	0	6.20
1996 Green Bay	IND —	17	16	8	1	115.2	540	132	85	73	12	4	6	3	65	1	104	7	0	8	6	.571	0	0	5.68
1997 Saskatoon	IND —	14	12	1	0	73	342	85	58	48	5	4	2	3	47	0	53	1	0	4	5	.444	0	0	5.92
1998 Bridgeport	IND —	39	0	0	6	58.2	237	31	17	14	3	1	2	1	27	0	61	3	0	8	2	.800	0	1	2.15
1999 Bridgeport	IND —	14	0	0	2	19.1	82	14	4	3	1	0	0	1	10	0	22	2	0	1	0	1.000	0	0	1.40
Bowie	AA Bal	26	0	0	9	43	186	36	20	19	5	3	3	0	26	0	36	4	0	3	1	.750	0	0	3.98
2000 Bowie	AA Bal	10	0	0	1	16	70	16	13	10	3	1	0	0	8	2	16	1	0	1	0	1.000	0	0	5.63
Bridgeport	IND —	7	0	0	2	9.1	41	7	4	2	1	0	2	0	8	0	8	0	0	2	0	1.000	0	1	1.93
9 Min. YEARS		199	32	10	51	470.1	2137	471	301	256	43	22	27	11	280	5	392	27	1	27	19	.587	0	2	4.90

David Ross

Bats: Right **Throws:** Right **Pos:** C-64; DH-9; PH-3 **Ht:** 6'2" **Wt:** 205 **Born:** 3/19/77 **Age:** 24

Year Team	Lg Org	BATTING															BASERUNNING				PERCENTAGES		
		G	AB	H	2B	3B	HR	TB	R	RBI	TBB	IBB	SO	HBP	SH	SF	SB	CS	SB%	GDP	Avg	OBP	SLG
1998 Yakima	A- LA	59	191	59	14	1	6	93	31	25	34	0	49	1	2	2	2	2	.50	5	.309	.412	.487
1999 Vero Beach	A+ LA	114	375	85	19	1	7	127	47	39	46	1	111	7	1	6	5	10	.33	10	.227	.318	.339
2000 San Antonio	AA LA	24	67	14	2	1	3	27	11	12	9	1	17	1	1	1	1	0	1.00	0	.209	.308	.403
San Berndno	A+ LA	51	191	49	11	1	7	83	27	21	17	1	43	1	3	1	3	2	.60	3	.257	.319	.435
3 Min. YEARS		248	824	207	46	4	23	330	116	97	106	3	220	10	7	10	11	14	.44	18	.251	.340	.400

Jason Ross

Bats: Right **Throws:** Right **Pos:** OF-69; PH-2; PR-2; DH-1 **Ht:** 6'4" **Wt:** 215 **Born:** 6/10/74 **Age:** 27

Year Team	Lg Org	BATTING															BASERUNNING				PERCENTAGES		
		G	AB	H	2B	3B	HR	TB	R	RBI	TBB	IBB	SO	HBP	SH	SF	SB	CS	SB%	GDP	Avg	OBP	SLG
1996 Danville	R+ Atl	43	149	40	8	1	3	59	26	20	11	0	42	4	0	0	6	3	.67	2	.268	.335	.396
Macon	A Atl	5	19	3	0	0	1	6	2	3	2	0	7	0	0	0	1	0	1.00	0	.158	.238	.316
1997 Macon	A Atl	112	430	111	20	5	9	168	70	59	37	0	121	9	2	3	16	7	.70	7	.258	.328	.391
1998 Danville	A+ Atl	115	378	80	14	3	6	118	36	34	15	0	107	3	2	2	11	5	.69	5	.212	.246	.312
1999 Myrtle Bch	A+ Atl	133	482	129	23	13	12	214	80	64	43	2	136	8	1	2	31	5	.86	11	.268	.336	.444
2000 Greenville	AA Atl	73	251	63	16	0	12	115	32	26	22	3	91	3	0	0	13	5	.72	7	.251	.319	.458
5 Min. YEARS		481	1709	426	81	22	43	680	246	206	130	5	504	27	3	7	78	25	.76	32	.249	.311	.398

Mike Rossiter

Pitches: Right **Bats:** Right **Pos:** RP-48 **Ht:** 6'6" **Wt:** 230 **Born:** 6/20/73 **Age:** 28

Year Team	Lg Org	HOW MUCH HE PITCHED						WHAT HE GAVE UP													THE RESULTS					
		G	GS	CG	GF	IP	BFP	H	R	ER	HR	SH	SF	HB	TBB	IBB	SO	WP	Bk	W	L	Pct.	ShO	Sv	ERA
1991 Athletics	R Oak	10	9	0	0	38.1	179	43	24	17	3	1	0	2	22	0	35	6	0	3	4	.429	0	0	3.99
1992 Madison	A Oak	27	27	2	0	154.2	651	135	83	68	17	2	5	4	68	1	135	4	3	8	14	.364	0	0	3.96
1993 Modesto	A+ Oak	20	17	2	0	112	491	120	62	54	14	4	1	1	45	0	96	5	0	8	6	.571	0	0	4.34
1994 Athletics	R Oak	2	0	0	0	3.2	20	8	6	2	0	1	0	0	0	0	3	1	0	0	1	.000	0	0	4.91
1995 Modesto	A+ Oak	18	7	0	3	68.2	290	68	33	32	5	2	2	2	19	0	70	1	1	7	2	.778	0	0	4.19
1996 Huntsville	AA Oak	27	25	2	1	145	636	167	92	78	15	2	10	7	44	4	116	5	0	8	9	.471	1	0	4.84
1997 Stockton	A+ Mil	34	8	0	9	86	368	83	31	26	6	2	2	15	27	0	79	3	0	8	1	.889	0	0	2.72
El Paso	AA Mil	8	0	0	4	20.2	87	22	6	6	0	1	1	1	8	0	11	1	0	2	0	1.000	0	0	2.61
1998 Mobile	AA SD	22	0	0	3	45.1	185	34	10	9	2	1	1	1	11	0	46	1	0	2	0	1.000	0	0	1.79
Las Vegas	AAA SD	31	0	0	13	41	185	44	20	20	2	1	2	7	17	3	34	0	0	2	2	.500	0	0	4.39
1999 Colo Sprngs	AAA Col	24	0	0	5	37	166	37	16	16	3	2	2	5	20	0	31	3	0	2	0	1.000	0	0	3.89
Rockies	R Col	1	0	0	0	2	6	0	0	0	0	0	0	0	0	0	5	0	0	0	0	—	0	0	0.00
Carolina	AA Col	16	0	0	8	21.2	80	11	5	5	0	1	0	1	9	0	24	2	0	1	0	.000	0	0	2.08
2000 Huntsville	AA Mil	48	0	0	38	45.1	217	47	32	31	7	2	2	9	31	1	41	2	0	0	5	.000	0	22	6.15
10 Min. YEARS		288	93	6	84	821.1	3561	819	420	364	74	22	27	55	321	9	726	34	4	49	45	.521	1	26	3.99

Aaron Rowand

Bats: Right **Throws:** Right **Pos:** OF-138; DH-1 **Ht:** 6'1" **Wt:** 200 **Born:** 8/29/77 **Age:** 23

Year Team	Lg Org	BATTING															BASERUNNING				PERCENTAGES		
		G	AB	H	2B	3B	HR	TB	R	RBI	TBB	IBB	SO	HBP	SH	SF	SB	CS	SB%	GDP	Avg	OBP	SLG
1998 Hickory	A CWS	61	222	76	13	3	5	110	42	32	21	0	36	6	5	2	7	3	.70	5	.342	.410	.495
1999 Winston-Sal	A+ CWS	133	512	143	37	3	24	258	96	88	33	2	94	13	2	5	15	10	.60	13	.279	.336	.504
2000 Birmingham	AA CWS	139	532	137	26	5	20	233	80	98	38	4	117	14	4	4	22	7	.76	12	.258	.321	.438
3 Min. YEARS		333	1266	356	76	11	49	601	218	218	92	6	247	33	11	11	44	20	.69	30	.281	.343	.475

Aaron Royster

Bats: Right **Throws:** Right **Pos:** OF-34; PH-8; PR-1 **Ht:** 6'1" **Wt:** 215 **Born:** 11/30/72 **Age:** 28

Year Team	Lg Org	BATTING															BASERUNNING				PERCENTAGES		
		G	AB	H	2B	3B	HR	TB	R	RBI	TBB	IBB	SO	HBP	SH	SF	SB	CS	SB%	GDP	Avg	OBP	SLG
1994 Martinsvlle	R+ Phi	54	168	46	11	2	7	82	31	39	28	1	47	2	0	1	7	4	.64	2	.274	.382	.488
1995 Piedmont	A Phi	126	489	129	23	3	8	182	73	58	39	1	106	7	0	4	22	9	.71	16	.264	.325	.372
1996 Clearwater	A+ Phi	72	289	81	10	2	11	128	35	60	23	0	56	3	3	2	4	3	.57	7	.280	.338	.443
Reading	AA Phi	65	230	59	11	0	4	82	42	20	30	2	56	5	3	1	4	5	.44	3	.257	.353	.357
1997 Reading	AA Phi	112	412	106	18	5	15	179	59	62	53	0	104	1	0	2	2	3	.40	12	.257	.342	.434
1998 Reading	AA Phi	112	430	110	27	4	7	166	67	55	57	1	117	2	0	0	3	1	.75	13	.256	.346	.386

Year Team	Lg Org	G	AB	H	2B	3B	HR	TB	R	RBI	TBB	IBB	SO	HBP	SH	SF	SB	CS	SB%	GDP	Avg	OBP	SLG
1999 Clearwater	A+ Phi	11	41	13	2	2	0	19	6	5	3	0	10	0	0	0	1	0	1.00	3	.317	.364	.463
Reading	AA Phi	91	310	90	17	2	8	135	53	48	48	2	90	3	2	3	11	5	.69	3	.290	.387	.435
2000 Scranton-WB	AAA Phi	14	29	4	1	0	0	5	3	2	1	0	14	0	0	2	1	0	1.00	1	.138	.156	.172
Reading	AA Phi	27	102	36	8	0	5	59	19	15	14	0	27	1	0		3	0	1.00	2	.353	.432	.578
7 Min. YEARS		684	2500	674	128	20	65	1037	388	364	296	8	627	24	8	16	58	30	.66	62	.270	.350	.415

Matt Ruebel

Pitches: Left Bats: Left Pos: RP-14; SP-4   Ht: 6'2" Wt: 180 Born: 10/16/69 Age: 31

Year Team	Lg Org	G	GS	CG	GF	IP	BFP	H	R	ER	HR	SH	SF	HB	TBB	IBB	SO	WP	Bk	W	L	Pct.	ShO	Sv	ERA
1991 Welland	A- Pit	6	6	0	0	27.2	113	16	9	6	3	0	1	4	11	0	27	2	3	1	1	.500	0	0	1.95
Augusta	A Pit	8	8	2	0	47	202	43	26	20	2	1	0	2	25	0	35	3	0	3	4	.429	1	0	3.83
1992 Augusta	A Pit	12	10	1	1	64.2	268	53	26	20	1	3	0	5	19	0	65	2	1	5	2	.714	0	0	2.78
Salem	A+ Pit	13	13	1	0	78.1	344	77	49	41	13	6	5	3	43	0	46	6	1	1	6	.143	0	0	4.71
1993 Salem	A+ Pit	19	1	0	4	33.1	168	34	31	22	6	3	0	3	32	3	29	8	2	1	4	.200	0	0	5.94
Augusta	A Pit	23	7	1	6	63.1	276	51	28	17	2	1	3	5	34	4	50	1	0	5	5	.500	1	0	2.42
1994 Carolina	AA Pit	6	3	0	0	16.1	78	28	15	12	3	1	1	1	3	0	14	0	0	1	1	.500	0	0	6.61
Salem	A+ Pit	21	13	0	0	86.1	374	87	49	33	9	2	3	7	27	0	72	4	1	6	6	.500	0	0	3.44
1995 Carolina	AA Pit	27	27	4	0	169.1	699	150	68	52	7	4	7	7	45	1	136	7	1	13	5	.722	3	0	2.76
1996 Calgary	AAA Pit	13	13	1	0	76.1	338	89	43	39	8	4	3	3	28	2	48	0	0	5	3	.625	0	0	4.60
1998 Durham	AAA TB	24	23	1	0	129	569	141	73	68	17	0	3	5	45	1	87	2	0	9	6	.600	1	0	4.74
1999 Tucson	AAA Ari	6	2	0	0	27	120	32	26	21	6	0	2	1	10	0	19	2	0	1	3	.250	0	0	7.00
Binghamton	AA NYM	6	5	0	0	26.1	114	24	13	8	2	0	0	1	8	0	25	1	0	2	0	1.000	0	0	2.73
Norfolk	AAA NYM	7	7	0	0	40	174	40	20	20	6	0	2	3	17	0	23	0	0	3	0	1.000	0	0	4.50
2000 Jupiter	A+ Mon	4	0	0	1	10	34	7	1	1	0	1	0	0	0	0	10	1	0	0	0	—	0	0	0.90
Ottawa	AAA Mon	7	4	0	1	23.1	115	37	22	18	3	1	2	3	11	0	5	1	0	0	2	.000	0	0	6.94
Zion	IND —	7	0	0	3	10.1	52	13	8	8	2	0	0	3	3	0	7	1	0	1	2	.333	0	0	6.97
1996 Pittsburgh	NL	26	7	0	3	58.2	265	64	38	30	7	0	3	6	25	0	22	2	0	1	1	.500	0	1	4.60
1997 Pittsburgh	NL	44	0	0	9	62.2	296	77	50	44	8	3	5	5	27	3	50	4	0	3	2	.600	0	0	6.32
1998 Tampa Bay	AL	7	1	0	0	8.2	39	11	7	6	3	0	0	0	4	0	6	0	0	0	2	.000	0	0	6.23
9 Min. YEARS		209	142	11	16	928.2	4038	922	507	406	90	27	32	56	361	11	698	41	9	57	50	.533	6	0	3.93
3 Maj. YEARS		77	8	0	13	130	600	152	95	80	18	3	8	11	56	3	78	6	0	4	5	.444	0	1	5.54

Toby Rumfield

Bats: Right Throws: Right Pos: 1B-63; C-32; DH-28; PH-12; PR-1   Ht: 6'3" Wt: 190 Born: 9/4/72 Age: 28

Year Team	Lg Org	G	AB	H	2B	3B	HR	TB	R	RBI	TBB	IBB	SO	HBP	SH	SF	SB	CS	SB%	GDP	Avg	OBP	SLG
1991 Princeton	R+ Cin	59	226	62	13	3	3	90	22	30	9	0	43	5	2	3	1	7	.13	6	.274	.313	.398
1992 Billings	R+ Cin	66	253	68	15	3	4	101	34	50	7	0	34	4	0	4	5	2	.71	4	.269	.295	.399
1993 Chston-WV	A Cin	97	333	75	20	1	5	112	36	50	6	1	74	3	0	4	6	4	.60	7	.225	.284	.336
1994 Winston-Sal	A+ Cin	123	462	115	11	4	29	221	79	88	48	1	107	2	0	7	2	3	.40	9	.249	.318	.478
1995 Chattanooga	AA Cin	92	273	72	12	1	8	110	32	53	26	2	47	3	3	5	0	3	.00	14	.264	.329	.403
1996 Chattanooga	AA Cin	113	364	102	25	1	9	156	49	53	37	1	51	6	3	6	2	1	.67	12	.280	.351	.429
1997 Chattanooga	AA Cin	101	331	95	22	1	5	134	35	38	18	3	32	2	4	2	0	1	.00	12	.287	.326	.405
1998 Greenville	AA Atl	125	462	134	32	0	10	196	61	66	43	1	67	3	1	8	9	4	.69	17	.290	.349	.424
1999 Richmond	AAA Atl	111	383	105	23	1	15	175	57	62	31	1	57	6	2	2	1	2	.33	13	.274	.336	.457
2000 Richmond	AAA Atl	127	430	116	18	0	19	191	61	70	32	1	59	4	3	3	4	7	.36	9	.270	.324	.444
10 Min. YEARS		1014	3517	944	191	15	107	1486	466	560	277	11	571	38	18	44	30	34	.47	103	.268	.325	.423

Tony Runion

Pitches: Right Bats: Right Pos: RP-19   Ht: 6'3" Wt: 229 Born: 12/6/71 Age: 29

Year Team	Lg Org	G	GS	CG	GF	IP	BFP	H	R	ER	HR	SH	SF	HB	TBB	IBB	SO	WP	Bk	W	L	Pct.	ShO	Sv	ERA
1993 Watertown	A- Cle	4	1	0	0	8	38	7	9	6	0	1	1	0	9	0	8	4	1	0	1	.000	0	0	6.75
Burlington	R+ Cle	3	2	0	0	12	47	10	4	4	1	1	0	0	6	0	6	2	0	0	0	—	0	0	3.00
1994 Columbus	A Cle	35	8	1	7	119	486	89	40	33	5	4	0	11	39	3	140	10	0	8	6	.571	0	2	2.50
1995 Kinston	A+ Cle	28	24	0	2	143	599	131	70	65	9	2	6	13	57	0	84	10	0	7	11	.389	0	0	4.09
1996 Kinston	A+ Cle	6	1	0	0	14	71	16	10	9	0	1	0	3	14	0	11	3	0	1	1	.500	0	0	5.79
Bakersfield	A+ Cle	7	6	1	0	35.2	197	61	56	45	5	2	2	3	27	0	20	9	0	0	6	.000	0	0	11.36
1997 Fargo-Mh	IND —	11	0	0	3	21.1	90	25	9	9	2	2	1	0	5	1	22	0	0	1	1	.500	0	1	3.80
Sioux Falls	IND —	26	0	0	15	33.2	151	36	16	15	3	4	0	2	12	0	26	1	0	7	2	.778	0	2	4.01
1998 Lynchburg	A+ Pit	36	0	0	15	57	239	49	21	19	5	4	1	6	20	2	72	7	0	5	8	.385	0	4	3.00
Carolina	AA Pit	7	0	0	6	9.1	47	11	7	5	0	1	0	0	7	1	11	1	1	1	2	.333	0	4	4.82
1999 Altoona	AA Pit	31	0	0	8	42.2	184	52	23	17	3	2	3	1	9	0	39	4	1	1	4	.200	0	2	3.59
2000 Mobile	AA SD	19	0	0	1	28	120	15	8	5	1	4	0	5	18	0	27	1	0	1	1	.500	0	1	1.61
8 Min. YEARS		213	42	2	59	523.2	2269	502	273	232	34	28	14	44	223	7	466	52	3	32	43	.427	0	11	3.99

Brian Rupp

Bats: Right Throws: Right Pos: 3B-1   Ht: 6'5" Wt: 185 Born: 9/20/71 Age: 29

Year Team	Lg Org	G	AB	H	2B	3B	HR	TB	R	RBI	TBB	IBB	SO	HBP	SH	SF	SB	CS	SB%	GDP	Avg	OBP	SLG
1992 Cardinals	R StL	56	207	80	20	1	0	102	34	40	21	5	16	1	0	7	10	7	.59	3	.386	.432	.493
1993 Savannah	A StL	122	472	151	31	7	4	208	80	81	48	2	70	3	1	5	3	2	.60	11	.320	.383	.441
1994 St. Pete	A+ StL	129	438	115	19	4	2	148	40	34	61	1	77	0	5	0	9	3	.75	20	.263	.353	.338
1995 St. Pete	A+ StL	90	325	90	12	2	0	106	30	23	27	1	43	1	4	0	0	0	—	14	.277	.334	.326
Arkansas	AA StL	23	77	25	3	0	0	28	10	6	6	0	12	0	1	1	1	0	1.00	3	.325	.373	.364
1996 Arkansas	AA StL	114	353	107	17	2	4	140	46	41	33	4	44	0	5	4	5	6	.45	14	.303	.359	.397
1997 Arkansas	AA StL	36	122	36	9	0	1	48	18	15	13	0	16	3	2	1	0	0	—	2	.295	.374	.393
Louisville	AAA StL	59	189	52	7	2	0	63	17	16	19	1	36	0	1	1	1	1	.50	5	.275	.340	.333
1998 Memphis	AAA StL	112	209	49	10	1	0	61	26	24	29	0	32	0	3	0	5	5	.50	11	.234	.328	.292
2000 Arkansas	AA StL	1	1	0	0	0	0	0	0	0	0	0	0	0	0	0	0	0	—	0	.000	.000	.000
8 Min. YEARS		742	2393	705	128	19	11	904	301	280	257	14	346	8	22	18	33	28	.54	83	.295	.362	.378

Brian Rust

Bats: Right **Throws:** Right **Pos:** 3B-37; DH-32; OF-26; 1B-23; 2B-6; PH-2; PR-1; P-1   **Ht:** 6'2" **Wt:** 205 **Born:** 8/1/74 **Age:** 26

Year Team	Lg Org	G	AB	H	2B	3B	HR	TB	R	RBI	TBB	IBB	SO	HBP	SH	SF	SB	CS	SB%	GDP	Avg	OBP	SLG
1995 Eugene	A- Atl	53	157	32	7	1	4	53	18	19	7	0	43	2	2	2	2	1	.67	2	.204	.244	.338
1996 Macon	A Atl	7	9	1	0	0	0	1	2	2	2	0	2	0	0	0	0	0	—	0	.111	.273	.111
Eugene	A- Atl	71	275	79	24	3	10	139	52	43	20	2	74	3	0	0	4	2	.67	4	.287	.342	.505
1997 Durham	A+ Atl	122	430	111	29	2	12	180	67	71	43	0	104	3	1	5	10	4	.71	8	.258	.326	.419
1998 Greenville	AA Atl	95	265	68	19	1	9	116	43	39	35	2	93	4	1	2	10	1	.91	5	.257	.350	.438
1999 Delmarva	A Bal	21	77	20	9	1	1	34	11	16	6	1	27	0	0	3	0	0	—	5	.260	.302	.442
Frederick	A+ Bal	9	27	4	1	0	0	5	7	1	5	0	7	2	0	0	0	0	—	0	.148	.324	.185
Bowie	AA Bal	52	149	46	11	0	4	69	24	21	17	0	29	3	2	3	2	0	1.00	3	.309	.384	.463
Rochester	AAA Bal	1	3	0	0	0	0	0	0	0	1	0	0	0	0	1	0	0	—	0	.000	.000	.000
2000 Frederick	A+ Bal	70	252	73	22	1	12	133	53	46	45	1	50	7	0	1	15	4	.79	5	.290	.410	.528
Rochester	AAA Bal	14	43	6	3	0	0	9	2	5	3	0	17	1	0	1	0	0	—	2	.140	.208	.209
Bowie	AA Bal	30	103	34	14	0	5	63	16	24	13	1	21	1	0	2	5	2	.71	2	.330	.403	.612
6 Min. YEARS		545	1790	474	139	9	57	802	295	288	196	7	467	26	7	20	48	14	.77	36	.265	.343	.448

Mark Rutherford

Pitches: Right **Bats:** Right **Pos:** SP-16; RP-15   **Ht:** 6'2" **Wt:** 211 **Born:** 11/9/74 **Age:** 26

Year Team	Lg Org	G	GS	CG	GF	IP	BFP	H	R	ER	HR	SH	SF	HB	TBB	IBB	SO	WP	Bk	W	L	Pct.	ShO	Sv	ERA
1997 Batavia	A- Phi	3	2	0	0	12	47	10	5	1	0	0	1	0	3	0	11	3	0	2	1	.667	0	0	0.75
Piedmont	A Phi	9	9	0	0	58.1	225	42	17	16	4	2	0	1	9	0	47	3	0	1	4	.200	0	0	2.47
1998 Clearwater	A+ Phi	18	18	0	0	119	452	94	40	35	11	3	3	5	20	0	71	3	1	8	5	.615	0	0	2.65
1999 Clearwater	A+ Phi	9	9	0	0	46	228	64	57	47	6	2	6	2	25	3	23	1	0	0	4	.000	0	0	9.20
Reading	AA Phi	4	4	0	0	18.1	72	11	3	2	1	0	0	0	9	0	10	1	0	1	0	1.000	0	0	0.98
2000 Scranton-WB	AA Phi	2	2	0	0	10	40	11	5	4	1	1	0	0	2	0	5	0	0	1	1	.500	0	0	3.60
Reading	AA Phi	29	14	0	6	114	493	121	65	55	13	8	5	3	34	3	62	1	1	7	9	.438	0	3	4.34
4 Min. YEARS		74	58	0	6	377.2	1557	353	192	160	36	16	15	11	102	6	229	12	3	20	24	.455	0	3	3.81

Ken Ryan

Pitches: Right **Bats:** Right **Pos:** RP-44   **Ht:** 6'3" **Wt:** 225 **Born:** 10/24/68 **Age:** 32

Year Team	Lg Org	G	GS	CG	GF	IP	BFP	H	R	ER	HR	SH	SF	HB	TBB	IBB	SO	WP	Bk	W	L	Pct.	ShO	Sv	ERA
1986 Elmira	A- Bos	13	1	0	10	21.2	103	20	14	14	0	2	1	4	21	2	22	1	0	1	2	.500	0	0	5.82
1987 Greensboro	A Bos	28	19	2	8	121.1	554	139	88	74	10	1	7	3	63	8	75	10	3	3	12	.200	0	0	5.49
1988 Lynchburg	A+ Bos	19	14	0	2	71.1	344	79	51	49	4	2	1	3	45	5	49	5	3	2	7	.222	0	0	6.18
1989 Winter Havn	A+ Bos	24	22	3	1	137	586	114	58	48	5	4	4	7	81	0	78	8	4	8	8	.500	0	0	3.15
1990 Lynchburg	A+ Bos	28	28	3	0	161.1	735	182	104	92	10	6	5	6	82	0	109	19	1	6	14	.300	1	0	5.13
1991 Winter Havn	A+ Bos	21	1	0	11	52.2	213	40	15	12	1	0	2	0	19	0	53	3	1	1	3	.250	0	1	2.05
New Britain	AA Bos	14	0	0	6	26	116	23	7	5	2	4	0	1	12	1	26	2	0	1	2	.333	0	1	1.73
Pawtucket	AAA Bos	9	0	0	4	18.1	80	15	11	10	2	2	2	1	11	1	14	2	0	1	0	1.000	0	1	4.91
1992 New Britain	AA Bos	44	0	0	42	50.2	220	44	17	11	0	0	2	1	24	2	51	4	0	1	4	.200	0	22	1.95
Pawtucket	AAA Bos	9	0	0	9	8.2	36	6	2	2	1	0	0	0	4	0	6	0	0	2	0	1.000	0	7	2.08
1993 Pawtucket	AAA Bos	18	0	0	15	25.1	112	18	9	7	1	3	1	2	17	4	22	2	1	0	2	.000	0	8	2.49
1994 Sarasota	A+ Bos	8	0	0	8	7.1	30	6	3	3	0	0	0	0	2	0	11	2	0	0	0	—	0	1	3.68
1995 Trenton	AA Bos	11	0	0	7	17	79	23	13	11	1	1	0	0	5	0	16	0	0	0	2	.000	0	2	5.82
Pawtucket	AAA Bos	9	0	0	5	10	42	12	7	7	1	0	1	0	4	0	6	1	0	0	1	.000	0	0	6.30
1997 Reading	AA Phi	2	2	0	0	2	7	1	0	0	0	0	0	0	1	0	0	0	0	0	0	—	0	0	0.00
Scranton-WB	AAA Phi	3	0	0	1	4	18	5	2	2	0	0	0	0	3	0	3	0	0	1	0	1.000	0	1	4.50
1998 Clearwater	A+ Phi	4	4	0	0	9	34	5	3	3	0	0	0	1	3	0	10	1	0	0	0	—	0	0	3.00
Scranton-WB	AAA Phi	6	0	0	3	8	34	7	0	0	0	0	0	1	3	0	9	0	0	1	0	1.000	0	1	0.00
1999 Scranton-WB	AAA Phi	31	0	0	18	41.1	197	54	30	26	2	3	3	0	19	2	33	1	0	2	2	.500	0	6	5.66
Nashville	AAA Pit	6	0	0	2	7	35	7	3	3	1	0	1	0	8	1	9	1	0	1	1	.500	0	0	3.86
2000 Nashville	IND	40	0	0	35	40.1	174	38	25	22	7	0	0	1	14	1	47	2	0	3	2	.600	0	24	4.91
Columbus	AAA NYY	4	0	0	3	3.2	22	8	7	7	1	0	0	0	3	0	3	1	0	0	0	—	0	0	17.18
1992 Boston	AL	7	0	0	6	7	30	4	5	5	2	1	1	0	5	0	5	0	0	0	0	—	0	0	6.43
1993 Boston	AL	47	0	0	26	50	223	43	23	20	2	4	4	3	29	5	49	3	0	7	2	.778	0	1	3.60
1994 Boston	AL	42	0	0	26	48	202	46	14	13	1	4	0	1	17	3	32	2	0	2	3	.400	0	13	2.44
1995 Boston	AL	28	0	0	20	32.1	153	34	20	18	4	1	0	1	24	6	34	1	0	0	4	.000	0	7	4.96
1996 Philadelphia	NL	62	0	0	26	89	370	71	32	24	4	5	0	1	45	8	70	4	3	3	5	.375	0	8	2.43
1997 Philadelphia	NL	22	0	0	10	20.2	108	31	23	22	5	1	2	2	13	1	10	0	0	1	0	1.000	0	0	9.58
1998 Philadelphia	NL	17	0	0	6	22.2	108	21	12	11	1	2	2	1	20	1	16	4	0	0	1	.000	0	0	4.37
1999 Philadelphia	NL	15	0	0	5	15.2	71	16	11	11	2	0	0	0	11	2	9	1	0	1	2	.333	0	0	6.32
14 Min. YEARS		351	91	8	190	844	3771	846	469	408	49	29	28	31	444	27	652	65	13	35	62	.361	0	75	4.35
8 Maj. YEARS		240	0	0	125	285.2	1265	266	140	124	21	18	9	9	164	26	225	15	3	14	17	.467	0	30	3.91

Matt Ryan

Pitches: Right **Bats:** Right **Pos:** RP-46   **Ht:** 6'5" **Wt:** 190 **Born:** 3/20/72 **Age:** 29

Year Team	Lg Org	G	GS	CG	GF	IP	BFP	H	R	ER	HR	SH	SF	HB	TBB	IBB	SO	WP	Bk	W	L	Pct.	ShO	Sv	ERA
1993 Pirates	R Pit	9	0	0	5	19.1	81	17	8	5	0	1	0	1	9	0	20	0	0	1	1	.500	0	2	2.33
Welland	A- Pit	16	0	0	12	17.1	84	11	10	3	0	0	1	1	12	1	25	5	0	0	0	—	0	5	1.56
1994 Augusta	A Pit	34	0	0	31	41	174	33	14	6	0	1	0	4	7	1	49	0	0	2	1	.667	0	13	1.32
Salem	A+ Pit	25	0	0	16	28.1	122	27	12	6	0	3	0	2	8	1	13	2	0	2	2	.500	0	7	1.91
1995 Calgary	AAA Pit	5	0	0	4	4.2	20	5	1	1	0	0	0	1	1	1	2	0	0	0	0	—	0	1	1.93
Carolina	AA Pit	44	0	0	38	46	188	33	10	8	4	2	2	2	19	2	23	3	0	2	1	.667	0	26	1.57
1996 Calgary	AAA Pit	51	0	0	44	52.2	259	70	39	31	4	3	1	6	28	2	35	6	0	2	6	.250	0	20	5.30
1997 Carolina	AA Pit	48	0	0	39	52.2	229	32	18	13	4	2	4	12	21	4	43	9	0	4	3	.571	0	14	2.22
1998 Nashville	AAA Pit	51	6	0	10	86.1	384	85	50	40	2	5	1	6	36	6	41	17	1	4	3	.571	0	4	4.17
1999 Nashville	AAA Pit	48	6	0	20	79.1	357	87	48	39	7	1	2	6	35	1	52	2	0	6	5	.545	0	8	4.42
2000 Rochester	AAA Bal	46	0	0	14	63	289	55	34	25	5	7	2	6	43	1	35	5	0	3	6	.333	0	2	3.57
8 Min. YEARS		377	12	0	233	490.2	2185	455	244	177	20	29	8	47	219	28	338	49	1	26	29	.473	0	101	3.25

Mike Ryan

Bats: Left Throws: Right Pos: OF-112; 2B-19; PH-3; DH-1 Ht: 5'10" Wt: 175 Born: 7/6/77 Age: 23

Year Team	Lg Org	G	AB	H	2B	3B	HR	TB	R	RBI	TBB	IBB	SO	HBP	SH	SF	SB	CS	SB%	GDP	Avg	OBP	SLG
1996 Twins	R Min	43	157	31	8	2	0	43	12	13	13	1	20	1	1	2	3	0	1.00	3	.197	.260	.274
1997 Elizabethtn	R+ Min	62	220	66	10	0	3	85	44	29	38	3	39	3	1	4	2	2	.50	8	.300	.404	.386
1998 Fort Wayne	A Min	113	412	131	24	6	9	194	69	71	44	2	92	2	3	5	7	3	.70	8	.318	.382	.471
1999 Fort Myers	A+ Min	131	507	139	26	5	8	199	85	71	63	2	60	5	4	6	3	4	.43	11	.274	.356	.393
2000 New Britain	AA Min	122	481	133	23	8	11	205	64	69	34	1	79	2	3	6	4	3	.57	13	.277	.323	.426
Salt Lake	AAA Min	3	9	2	0	0	0	2	1	2	3	0	2	0	0	0	0	0	—	1	.222	.417	.222
5 Min. YEARS		474	1786	502	91	21	31	728	275	255	195	9	292	13	12	23	19	12	.61	44	.281	.352	.408

C.C. Sabathia

Pitches: Left Bats: Left Pos: SP-27 Ht: 6'7" Wt: 235 Born: 7/21/80 Age: 20

Year Team	Lg Org	G	GS	CG	GF	IP	BFP	H	R	ER	HR	SH	SF	HB	TBB	IBB	SO	WP	Bk	W	L	Pct.	ShO	Sv	ERA
1998 Burlington	R+ Cle	5	5	0	0	18	83	20	14	9	1	0	1	1	8	0	35	1	1	1	0	1.000	0	0	4.50
1999 Mahoning Vy	A- Cle	6	6	0	0	19.2	77	9	5	4	0	0	2	0	12	0	27	0	0	0	0	—	0	0	1.83
Columbus	A Cle	3	3	0	0	16.2	64	8	2	2	1	1	0	1	5	0	20	1	0	2	0	1.000	0	0	1.08
Kinston	A+ Cle	7	7	0	0	32	143	30	22	19	3	3	3	1	19	0	29	6	0	3	3	.500	0	0	5.34
2000 Kinston	A+ Cle	10	10	2	0	56	232	48	23	22	4	0	1	2	24	0	69	2	1	3	2	.600	0	0	3.54
Akron	AA Cle	17	17	0	0	90.1	394	75	41	36	6	2	1	7	48	0	90	2	1	3	7	.300	0	0	3.59
3 Min. YEARS		48	48	2	0	232.2	993	190	107	92	15	6	8	12	116	0	270	12	3	12	12	.500	2	0	3.56

Erik Sabel

Pitches: Right Bats: Right Pos: SP-15; RP-14 Ht: 6'2" Wt: 185 Born: 10/14/74 Age: 26

Year Team	Lg Org	G	GS	CG	GF	IP	BFP	H	R	ER	HR	SH	SF	HB	TBB	IBB	SO	WP	Bk	W	L	Pct.	ShO	Sv	ERA
1996 Lethbridge	R+ Ari	20	3	0	5	42	184	43	23	13	3	1	1	3	7	0	41	4	0	1	4	.200	0	1	2.79
1997 High Desert	A+ Ari	31	22	0	4	143.2	646	174	101	85	21	10	6	10	40	0	86	6	0	11	11	.500	0	1	5.32
1998 High Desert	A+ Ari	14	0	0	9	22.2	100	25	8	8	2	1	0	0	4	3	18	0	0	0	1	.000	0	4	3.18
Tucson	AAA Ari	7	0	0	1	10.1	53	17	10	10	0	2	1	1	5	1	7	1	0	1	0	1.000	0	0	8.71
Tulsa	AA Tex	24	2	0	7	56.1	226	46	24	20	6	0	0	2	13	1	33	6	0	7	0	1.000	0	2	3.20
1999 El Paso	AA Ari	8	1	0	4	10	49	16	9	7	1	0	0	1	4	0	7	0	0	1	0	1.000	0	1	6.30
Tucson	AAA Ari	22	9	0	8	72.2	306	79	36	27	4	5	1	1	24	4	38	3	0	5	2	.714	0	3	3.34
2000 Tucson	AAA Ari	29	15	0	5	98.1	473	149	90	79	16	4	8	5	31	4	61	4	0	4	11	.267	0	1	7.23
1999 Arizona	NL	7	0	0	1	9.2	48	12	7	7	1	0	0	2	6	2	6	1	0	0	0	—	0	0	6.52
5 Min. YEARS		155	52	0	43	456	2037	549	301	249	53	23	17	23	128	13	291	24	0	29	30	.492	0	12	4.91

Bret Saberhagen

Pitches: Right Bats: Right Pos: SP-7 Ht: 6'1" Wt: 200 Born: 4/11/64 Age: 37

Year Team	Lg Org	G	GS	CG	GF	IP	BFP	H	R	ER	HR	SH	SF	HB	TBB	IBB	SO	WP	Bk	W	L	Pct.	ShO	Sv	ERA
1983 Fort Myers	A KC	16	16	3	0	109.2	—	98	34	28	4	—	—	0	19	0	82	4	2	10	5	.667	1	0	2.30
Jacksnville	AA KC	11	11	2	0	77.1	—	66	31	25	7	—	—	1	29	2	48	2	1	6	2	.750	1	0	2.91
1997 Lowell	A- Bos	1	1	0	0	3	10	1	0	0	0	0	0	0	0	0	2	0	0	0	0	—	0	0	0.00
Trenton	AA Bos	2	2	0	0	8	27	2	0	0	0	0	0	1	1	0	9	0	0	0	0	—	0	0	0.00
Pawtucket	AAA Bos	2	2	0	0	11	45	11	4	4	1	0	0	1	1	0	9	0	0	0	1	.000	0	0	3.27
1999 Trenton	AA Bos	1	1	0	0	6	19	2	0	0	0	0	0	0	0	0	5	0	0	1	0	1.000	0	0	0.00
2000 Sarasota	A+ Bos	1	1	0	0	1	8	5	3	3	0	0	0	0	0	0	2	0	0	0	1	.000	0	0	27.00
Lowell	A- Bos	1	1	0	0	3	10	1	0	0	0	0	0	0	0	0	5	0	0	0	0	—	0	0	0.00
Trenton	AA Bos	1	1	0	0	3	13	1	2	2	1	0	0	3	1	0	3	0	0	0	0	—	0	0	6.00
Pawtucket	AAA Bos	4	4	0	0	13	54	14	8	8	2	1	1	0	4	0	9	0	0	0	0	—	0	0	5.54
1984 Kansas City	AL	38	18	2	9	157.2	634	138	71	61	13	8	5	2	36	4	73	7	1	10	11	.476	1	1	3.48
1985 Kansas City	AL	32	32	10	0	235.1	931	211	79	75	19	9	7	1	38	1	158	1	3	20	6	.769	1	0	2.87
1986 Kansas City	AL	30	25	4	4	156	652	165	77	72	15	3	3	2	29	1	112	1	1	7	12	.368	2	0	4.15
1987 Kansas City	AL	33	33	15	0	257	1048	246	99	96	27	8	5	6	53	2	163	6	1	18	10	.643	4	0	3.36
1988 Kansas City	AL	35	35	9	0	260.2	1089	271	122	110	18	8	10	4	59	5	171	9	0	14	16	.467	0	0	3.80
1989 Kansas City	AL	36	35	12	0	262.1	1021	209	74	63	13	9	6	2	43	6	193	8	1	23	6	.793	4	0	2.16
1990 Kansas City	AL	20	20	5	0	135	561	146	52	49	9	4	4	1	28	1	87	1	0	5	9	.357	0	0	3.27
1991 Kansas City	AL	28	28	7	0	196.1	789	165	76	67	12	8	3	9	45	5	136	8	1	13	8	.619	2	0	3.07
1992 New York	NL	17	15	1	0	97.2	397	84	39	38	6	3	3	4	27	1	81	1	2	3	5	.375	1	0	3.50
1993 New York	NL	19	19	4	0	139.1	556	131	55	51	11	6	6	3	17	4	93	2	2	7	7	.500	1	0	3.29
1994 New York	NL	24	24	4	0	177.1	696	169	58	54	13	9	5	4	13	0	143	0	0	14	4	.778	0	0	2.74
1995 New York	NL	16	16	3	0	110	452	105	45	41	13	3	5	5	20	2	71	2	0	5	5	.500	0	0	3.35
Colorado	NL	9	9	0	0	43	206	60	33	30	8	2	0	5	13	1	29	1	0	2	1	.667	0	0	6.28
1997 Boston	AL	6	6	0	0	26	120	30	20	19	5	1	3	2	10	0	14	1	0	0	1	.000	0	0	6.58
1998 Boston	AL	31	31	0	0	175	725	181	82	77	22	2	3	6	29	1	100	4	0	15	8	.652	0	0	3.96
1999 Boston	AL	22	22	0	0	119	480	122	43	39	11	4	2	2	11	0	81	1	0	10	6	.625	0	0	2.95
4 Min. YEARS		40	40	5	0	235	—	201	82	70	15	—	—	6	55	2	174	6	3	17	9	.654	2	0	2.68
15 Maj. YEARS		396	368	76	13	2547.2	10357	2433	1025	942	215	89	68	58	471	34	1705	53	12	166	115	.591	16	1	3.33

Brent Sachs

Bats: Right Throws: Right Pos: DH-32; 2B-28; 3B-21; SS-17; OF-9; 1B-4; PH-3; PR-2; P-1 Ht: 6'1" Wt: 185 Born: 9/11/74 Age: 26

Year Team	Lg Org	G	AB	H	2B	3B	HR	TB	R	RBI	TBB	IBB	SO	HBP	SH	SF	SB	CS	SB%	GDP	Avg	OBP	SLG
1997 Canton	IND —	67	287	84	13	3	5	118	49	50	17	2	51	6	2	3	28	6	.82	6	.293	.342	.411
1998 Madison	IND —	70	232	61	13	3	2	86	32	24	22	2	55	8	5	2	13	9	.59	7	.263	.345	.371
1999 Winnipeg	IND —	78	290	81	10	9	6	127	56	44	31	3	53	4	2	5	21	3	.88	7	.279	.352	.438
2000 Lansing	A ChC	15	60	16	4	0	0	20	10	7	6	0	10	0	0	1	6	2	.75	2	.267	.328	.333
West Tenn	AA ChC	11	16	2	1	0	0	3	2	1	0	0	3	0	0	1	1	0	1.00	0	.125	.167	.188
Daytona	A+ ChC	82	298	90	19	1	3	120	44	42	26	1	56	5	3	3	14	10	.58	5	.302	.364	.403
4 Min. YEARS		323	1183	334	60	16	16	474	193	168	103	8	228	23	12	15	83	30	.73	27	.282	.347	.401

250

Marc Sagmoen

Bats: Left **Throws:** Left **Pos:** OF-112; PH-12; PR-1   **Ht:** 5'11" **Wt:** 185 **Born:** 4/16/71 **Age:** 30

Year Team	Lg Org	G	AB	H	2B	3B	HR	TB	R	RBI	TBB	IBB	SO	HBP	SH	SF	SB	CS	SB%	GDP	Avg	OBP	SLG
1993 Erie	A- Tex	6	23	7	1	1	0	10	6	2	3	0	7	1	0	1	0	0	—	0	.304	.393	.435
Chston-SC	A Tex	63	234	69	13	4	6	108	44	34	23	0	39	3	3	3	16	4	.80	2	.295	.361	.462
1994 Charlotte	A+ Tex	122	475	139	25	10	3	193	74	47	37	2	56	3	1	3	15	10	.60	15	.293	.346	.406
1995 Okla City	AAA Tex	56	188	42	11	3	3	68	20	25	16	0	31	2	1	4	5	2	.71	2	.223	.286	.362
Tulsa	AA Tex	63	242	56	8	5	6	92	36	22	23	0	23	4	1	2	5	4	.56	2	.231	.306	.380
1996 Tulsa	AA Tex	96	387	109	21	6	10	172	58	62	33	4	58	2	0	7	5	8	.38	7	.282	.336	.444
Okla City	AAA Tex	32	116	34	6	0	5	55	16	16	4	0	20	1	0	1	1	0	1.00	0	.293	.320	.474
1997 Okla City	AAA Tex	111	418	110	32	6	5	169	47	44	26	4	95	1	1	2	4	3	.57	10	.263	.306	.404
1998 Oklahoma	AAA Tex	113	403	108	26	6	14	188	61	65	35	0	86	4	3	3	6	2	.75	7	.268	.330	.467
1999 Oklahoma	AAA Tex	83	268	73	11	3	13	129	42	43	24	3	58	0	1	1	3	2	.60	7	.272	.331	.481
2000 New Orleans	AAA Hou	122	414	111	15	7	12	176	65	43	40	1	82	1	4	4	20	5	.80	3	.268	.331	.425
1997 Texas	AL	21	43	6	2	0	1	11	2	4	2	0	13	0	0	1	0	0	—	1	.140	.174	.256
8 Min. YEARS		867	3168	858	169	51	77	1360	469	403	264	14	555	22	15	31	80	40	.67	55	.271	.328	.429

Mike Saipe

Pitches: Right **Bats:** Right **Pos:** SP-17; RP-8   **Ht:** 6'1" **Wt:** 188 **Born:** 9/10/73 **Age:** 27

		HOW MUCH HE PITCHED						WHAT HE GAVE UP										THE RESULTS					
Year Team	Lg Org	G	GS	CG	GF	IP	BFP	H	R	ER	HR	SH	SF	HB	TBB	IBB	SO	WP	Bk	W	L	Pct.	ShO	Sv	ERA
1994 Bend	A- Col	16	16	0	0	84.1	363	73	52	39	7	3	4	7	34	0	74	6	2	3	7	.300	0	0	4.16
1995 Salem	A+ Col	21	9	0	7	85.1	347	68	35	33	7	1	1	2	32	4	90	9	1	4	5	.444	0	3	3.48
1996 New Haven	AA Col	32	19	1	5	138	562	114	53	47	12	4	3	4	42	6	126	4	4	10	7	.588	1	3	3.07
1997 New Haven	AA Col	19	19	4	0	136.2	550	127	57	47	18	3	1	5	29	2	123	4	1	8	5	.615	2	0	3.10
Colo Sprngs	AAA Col	10	10	1	0	60.1	278	74	42	37	10	1	0	4	24	3	40	2	3	4	3	.571	0	0	5.52
1998 Colo Sprngs	AAA Col	24	24	2	0	139.2	632	167	96	80	19	3	5	8	51	1	124	4	2	5	11	.313	0	0	5.16
1999 Colo Sprngs	AAA Col	11	11	0	0	54	232	62	36	29	11	0	4	1	20	0	39	3	0	1	5	.167	0	0	4.83
2000 Carolina	AA Col	4	4	1	0	26.1	118	29	17	16	2	3	0	1	12	1	13	1	0	1	3	.250	0	0	5.47
Colo Sprngs	AAA Col	15	8	0	1	54.1	270	94	67	58	18	3	5	4	16	0	37	1	0	4	5	.444	0	0	9.61
Las Vegas	AAA SD	2	2	0	0	7.1	39	13	11	11	4	0	0	0	6	0	4	0	0	0	0	—	0	0	13.50
Edmonton	AAA Ana	4	3	0	1	18.2	90	26	15	15	2	0	1	0	10	0	14	0	0	0	1	.000	0	1	7.23
1998 Colorado	NL	2	2	0	0	10	54	22	12	12	5	1	0	2	5	0	2	0	0	0	1	.000	0	0	10.80
7 Min. YEARS		158	125	9	14	805	3481	847	481	412	110	21	24	36	276	17	684	34	13	40	52	.435	3	7	4.61

Rich Saitta

Bats: Right **Throws:** Right **Pos:** 2B-59; OF-32; PH-10; SS-8; DH-2; PR-1   **Ht:** 5'10" **Wt:** 170 **Born:** 7/28/75 **Age:** 25

Year Team	Lg Org	G	AB	H	2B	3B	HR	TB	R	RBI	TBB	IBB	SO	HBP	SH	SF	SB	CS	SB%	GDP	Avg	OBP	SLG
1996 Yakima	A- LA	44	165	41	5	0	1	49	17	17	11	0	34	2	2	1	7	5	.58	5	.248	.302	.297
1997 Yakima	A- LA	44	183	57	13	2	1	77	37	15	14	0	27	2	1	1	6	2	.75	0	.311	.365	.421
Great Falls	R+ LA	16	58	14	3	0	0	17	4	4	2	0	9	0	0	0	0	1	.00	0	.241	.267	.293
1998 San Berndno	A+ LA	121	446	132	17	7	5	178	62	51	52	1	92	3	4	3	23	17	.58	6	.296	.370	.399
Albuquerque	AAA LA	5	16	1	0	0	0	1	1	0	0	0	5	0	0	0	0	0	—	0	.063	.063	.063
1999 San Antonio	AA LA	91	254	74	11	4	2	99	25	34	8	0	43	1	1	2	7	4	.64	3	.291	.313	.390
2000 San Antonio	AA LA	106	351	88	14	4	3	119	48	36	26	2	65	7	3	4	9	2	.82	10	.251	.312	.339
5 Min. YEARS		427	1473	407	63	17	12	540	194	157	113	4	275	15	11	12	52	31	.63	24	.276	.332	.367

Jim Sak

Pitches: Right **Bats:** Right **Pos:** RP-15   **Ht:** 6'1" **Wt:** 195 **Born:** 8/18/73 **Age:** 27

		HOW MUCH HE PITCHED						WHAT HE GAVE UP										THE RESULTS					
Year Team	Lg Org	G	GS	CG	GF	IP	BFP	H	R	ER	HR	SH	SF	HB	TBB	IBB	SO	WP	Bk	W	L	Pct.	ShO	Sv	ERA
1995 Idaho Falls	R+ SD	13	0	0	3	32.2	123	15	9	6	1	1	0	0	12	1	55	1	1	3	1	.750	0	1	1.65
Clinton	A SD	7	7	3	0	50	200	42	12	11	2	1	2	0	14	0	37	0	3	6	1	.857	0	0	1.98
1996 Rancho Cuca	A+ SD	4	4	0	0	15.2	78	21	13	11	2	1	0	2	12	0	14	0	0	0	3	.000	0	0	6.32
Clinton	A SD	21	7	0	6	65.2	291	46	31	26	2	4	2	4	45	1	72	4	0	3	4	.429	0	0	3.56
1997 Rancho Cuca	A+ SD	57	3	0	50	70.2	286	42	28	23	5	1	3	5	30	2	113	4	1	6	3	.667	0	27	2.93
1998 Mobile	AA SD	45	0	0	43	49	212	33	29	28	3	0	2	1	36	3	56	5	0	2	5	.286	0	16	5.14
1999 Mobile	AA SD	18	0	0	5	26.2	106	15	11	5	1	0	2	0	15	0	37	1	0	4	1	.800	0	2	1.69
Las Vegas	AAA SD	23	0	0	17	27.2	121	22	11	11	5	0	1	3	17	0	32	2	0	2	2	.500	0	6	3.58
2000 Nashville	AAA Pit	6	0	0	0	3.1	35	6	19	19	2	1	0	2	18	0	4	4	0	0	0	—	0	0	51.30
Pirates	R Pit	2	0	0	0	3	11	2	1	1	0	0	0	0	1	0	6	3	0	0	0	—	0	0	0.00
Altoona	AA Pit	7	0	0	3	5	32	2	4	6	1	0	0	2	13	0	5	0	0	0	1	.000	0	0	10.80
6 Min. YEARS		203	21	3	127	349.1	1495	244	172	146	24	9	12	19	214	7	430	26	5	26	21	.553	0	52	3.76

Oscar Salazar

Bats: Right **Throws:** Right **Pos:** SS-100; OF-9; 3B-6; PH-4; DH-2   **Ht:** 6'0" **Wt:** 155 **Born:** 6/27/78 **Age:** 23

Year Team	Lg Org	G	AB	H	2B	3B	HR	TB	R	RBI	TBB	IBB	SO	HBP	SH	SF	SB	CS	SB%	GDP	Avg	OBP	SLG
1998 Athletics	R Oak	26	102	33	7	5	2	56	29	18	12	0	15	1	0	0	4	1	.80	1	.324	.400	.549
Sou Oregon	A- Oak	28	101	32	4	1	5	53	19	28	16	0	22	0	1	3	5	2	.71	0	.317	.400	.525
1999 Modesto	A+ Oak	130	525	155	26	18	18	271	100	105	39	1	106	1	0	9	14	6	.70	10	.295	.340	.516
2000 Midland	AA Oak	111	427	128	27	1	13	196	70	57	39	2	71	2	2	3	4	4	.50	9	.300	.359	.459
Sacramento	AAA Oak	4	13	2	1	0	0	3	0	1	1	0	1	0	0	0	1	0	1.00	2	.154	.214	.231
3 Min. YEARS		299	1168	350	65	25	38	579	218	209	107	1	215	4	3	15	28	13	.68	22	.300	.356	.496

Roger Salkeld

Pitches: Right **Bats:** Right **Pos:** RP-3   **Ht:** 6'5" **Wt:** 215 **Born:** 3/6/71 **Age:** 30

Year Team	Lg Org	G	GS	CG	GF	IP	BFP	H	R	ER	HR	SH	SF	HB	TBB	IBB	SO	WP	Bk	W	L	Pct.	ShO	Sv	ERA
1989 Bellingham	A- Sea	8	6	0	1	42	168	27	17	6	0	0	1	4	10	0	55	3	3	2	2	.500	0	0	1.29
1990 San Berndno	A+ Sea	25	25	2	0	153.1	677	140	77	58	3	7	1	3	83	0	167	9	2	11	5	.688	0	0	3.40
1991 Jacksnville	AA Sea	23	23	5	0	153.2	634	131	56	52	9	5	5	10	55	1	159	12	2	8	8	.500	0	0	3.05
Calgary	AAA Sea	4	4	0	0	19.1	90	18	16	11	2	1	0	4	13	0	21	1	0	2	1	.667	0	0	5.12
1993 Jacksnville	AA Sea	14	14	0	0	77	334	71	39	28	8	3	5	5	29	1	56	2	1	4	3	.571	0	0	3.27
1994 Calgary	AAA Sea	13	13	0	0	67.1	315	74	54	46	11	0	5	4	39	2	54	5	0	3	7	.300	0	0	6.15
1995 Tacoma	AAA Sea	4	3	0	1	15	59	8	4	3	0	0	0	0	7	0	11	0	0	1	0	1.000	0	1	1.80
Indianapols	AAA Cin	20	20	1	0	119.1	497	96	60	56	13	3	4	2	57	1	86	3	0	12	2	.857	0	0	4.22
1997 Indianapols	AAA Cin	36	11	0	7	88	421	91	75	66	16	2	2	5	60	2	88	6	0	4	8	.333	0	1	6.75
1998 New Orleans	AAA Hou	37	11	0	9	82.1	391	82	57	53	8	4	6	3	64	1	79	9	0	3	6	.333	0	2	5.79
1999 Calgary	AAA Fla	27	2	0	10	35	159	37	21	18	5	0	3	2	20	1	32	4	0	1	1	.500	0	1	4.63
2000 Akron	AA Cle	3	0	0	1	4	16	2	0	0	1	0	0	0	3	0	4	0	0	0	0	—	0	0	0.00
1993 Seattle	AL	3	2	0	0	14.1	62	13	4	4	0	0	1	0	4	0	13	0	0	0	0	—	0	0	2.51
1994 Seattle	AL	13	13	0	0	59	291	76	47	47	7	0	3	1	45	1	46	2	0	2	5	.286	0	0	7.17
1996 Cincinnati	NL	29	19	1	2	116	509	114	69	67	18	10	3	6	54	2	82	7	1	8	5	.615	1	0	5.20
10 Min. YEARS		214	132	8	29	856.1	3761	777	476	397	75	26	32	42	440	9	812	54	8	51	43	.543	0	5	4.17
3 Maj. YEARS		45	34	1	2	189.1	861	203	120	118	25	10	6	8	103	3	141	9	1	10	10	.500	1	0	5.61

Cody Salter

Pitches: Right **Bats:** Right **Pos:** RP-18   **Ht:** 6'4" **Wt:** 200 **Born:** 10/8/75 **Age:** 25

Year Team	Lg Org	G	GS	CG	GF	IP	BFP	H	R	ER	HR	SH	SF	HB	TBB	IBB	SO	WP	Bk	W	L	Pct.	ShO	Sv	ERA
1998 Butte	R+ Ana	9	5	3	2	48.2	209	48	21	19	3	0	0	3	10	0	31	0	0	4	2	.667	0	0	3.51
1999 Lk Elsinore	A+ Ana	7	2	0	0	22	98	27	12	12	0	0	0	2	8	1	9	3	1	1	0	1.000	0	0	4.91
Erie	AA Ana	27	3	0	8	52.2	238	65	29	24	2	2	1	4	14	0	16	3	1	6	2	.750	0	0	4.10
2000 Erie	AA Ana	18	0	0	4	29	131	40	20	19	4	0	1	1	6	0	10	0	0	0	2	.000	0	0	5.90
3 Min. YEARS		61	10	3	14	152.1	676	180	82	74	9	2	2	10	38	1	66	6	2	11	6	.647	0	0	4.37

Jeremy Salyers

Pitches: Right **Bats:** Right **Pos:** RP-24; SP-11   **Ht:** 6'3" **Wt:** 205 **Born:** 1/31/76 **Age:** 25

Year Team	Lg Org	G	GS	CG	GF	IP	BFP	H	R	ER	HR	SH	SF	HB	TBB	IBB	SO	WP	Bk	W	L	Pct.	ShO	Sv	ERA
1996 Expos	R Mon	11	9	2	1	57	246	47	36	27	4	3	1	8	26	0	30	1	0	1	4	.200	0	1	4.26
1997 Vermont	A- Mon	16	14	0	0	77.1	346	87	53	43	4	3	6	5	31	0	32	6	2	3	4	.429	0	0	5.00
1998 Cape Fear	A Mon	42	2	0	18	71.2	310	70	41	30	8	5	1	8	23	0	32	8	2	4	4	.500	0	3	3.77
1999 Cape Fear	A Mon	22	7	0	6	63	257	62	22	16	3	3	2	3	18	0	37	2	0	2	3	.400	0	1	2.29
Ottawa	AAA Mon	1	1	0	0	6	24	6	2	1	0	1	0	0	2	0	2	1	0	0	0	—	0	0	1.50
Harrisburg	AA Mon	12	1	0	8	25.2	105	20	9	8	1	1	0	2	11	0	9	1	0	1	0	1.000	0	0	2.81
2000 Ottawa	AAA Mon	1	1	0	0	5	24	5	5	5	0	0	1	0	5	0	1	1	0	0	1	.000	0	0	9.00
Jupiter	A+ Mon	14	6	0	3	41	201	55	35	25	0	2	3	1	23	0	22	1	0	3	4	.429	0	0	5.49
Harrisburg	AA Mon	20	4	0	3	33.1	166	44	27	22	3	2	1	4	19	0	20	3	0	1	3	.250	0	0	5.94
5 Min. YEARS		139	45	2	39	380	1679	396	230	177	23	20	15	31	158	0	185	24	4	15	23	.395	0	5	4.19

Jerry Salzano

Bats: Right **Throws:** Right **Pos:** OF-24   **Ht:** 6'0" **Wt:** 175 **Born:** 10/27/74 **Age:** 26

Year Team	Lg Org	G	AB	H	2B	3B	HR	TB	R	RBI	TBB	IBB	SO	HBP	SH	SF	SB	CS	SB%	GDP	Avg	OBP	SLG
1992 Brewers	R Mil	51	177	43	5	0	0	48	18	20	23	0	31	4	2	3	1	3	.25	4	.243	.338	.271
1993 Helena	R+ Mil	66	227	59	12	2	1	78	30	18	25	0	39	3	4	2	6	3	.67	2	.260	.339	.344
1994 Beloit	A Mil	19	57	10	2	0	0	12	10	1	7	0	12	4	0	0	1	3	.25	2	.175	.309	.211
Williamsprt	A- ChC	75	283	80	15	3	2	107	33	37	15	0	44	8	1	2	5	5	.50	4	.283	.334	.378
1995 Williamsprt	A- ChC	62	218	65	13	2	0	82	28	23	22	0	28	4	0	1	4	3	.57	6	.298	.371	.376
Rockford	A ChC	6	21	6	1	1	0	9	0	2	1	0	1	0	0	0	0	1	.00	1	.286	.318	.429
1996 Lakeland	A+ Det	123	426	113	28	4	6	167	52	60	38	0	66	9	2	4	6	7	.46	10	.265	.335	.392
1997 Lakeland	A+ Det	40	135	30	4	1	2	42	20	8	22	2	27	2	1	0	1	1	.50	1	.222	.340	.311
Durham	A+ Atl	68	226	63	20	0	1	86	29	24	26	2	42	12	2	1	6	4	.60	10	.279	.381	.381
1998 Greenville	AA Atl	101	324	98	19	3	7	144	48	49	46	1	67	8	2	2	14	8	.64	8	.302	.400	.444
1999 Indianapols	AAA Cin	7	11	1	0	0	0	1	0	2	0	0	6	0	0	0	0	0	—	0	.091	.083	.091
Chattanooga	AA Cin	72	263	86	19	1	4	119	44	38	39	1	38	5	2	4	14	10	.58	5	.327	.418	.452
2000 Greenville	AA Atl	24	83	13	4	0	2	23	7	11	8	0	17	3	1	1	5	0	1.00	0	.157	.253	.277
9 Min. YEARS		714	2451	667	142	17	25	918	319	293	272	6	418	62	16	21	63	48	.57	53	.272	.357	.375

Nelson Samboy

Bats: Right **Throws:** Right **Pos:** 2B-58; OF-11; DH-5; PH-3   **Ht:** 5'10" **Wt:** 165 **Born:** 9/4/76 **Age:** 24

Year Team	Lg Org	G	AB	H	2B	3B	HR	TB	R	RBI	TBB	IBB	SO	HBP	SH	SF	SB	CS	SB%	GDP	Avg	OBP	SLG
1995 Astros	R Hou	55	192	60	12	2	1	79	39	22	26	0	19	3	4	1	21	8	.72	4	.313	.401	.411
1996 Kissimmee	A+ Hou	105	372	94	20	2	0	118	43	21	20	1	61	1	3	1	17	7	.71	7	.253	.292	.317
1997 Kissimmee	A+ Hou	48	190	60	9	2	1	76	20	13	7	0	34	2	2	0	9	6	.60	5	.316	.347	.400
Astros	R Hou	2	5	2	0	0	0	2	1	1	1	0	0	0	0	0	0	0	—	0	.400	.500	.400
Quad City	A Hou	14	51	18	3	0	0	21	2	8	2	0	8	0	0	0	1	1	.50	0	.353	.377	.412
1998 Kissimmee	A+ Hou	124	527	150	31	4	3	198	73	45	37	0	71	1	0	3	40	15	.73	10	.285	.331	.376
1999 Jackson	AA Hou	45	170	51	9	0	0	60	20	14	11	0	14	0	1	1	6	5	.55	1	.300	.341	.353
2000 Round Rock	AA Hou	13	47	13	3	0	1	19	11	3	3	0	9	0	0	1	2	3	.40	1	.277	.314	.404
Waterbury	IND —	64	248	81	16	1	2	105	41	26	22	1	30	4	3	1	16	8	.67	7	.327	.389	.423
6 Min. YEARS		470	1802	529	103	11	8	678	250	153	129	2	246	11	14	8	112	53	.68	35	.294	.343	.376

Benj Sampson

Pitches: Left **Bats:** Right **Pos:** SP-13; RP-5   Ht: 6'2" **Wt:** 210 **Born:** 4/27/75 **Age:** 26

Year Team	Lg Org	G	GS	CG	GF	IP	BFP	H	R	ER	HR	SH	SF	HB	TBB	IBB	SO	WP	Bk	W	L	Pct.	ShO	Sv	ERA
1993 Elizabethtn	R+ Min	11	6	0	2	42.1	171	33	12	9	1	2	0	1	15	1	34	5	0	4	1	.800	0	1	1.91
1994 Fort Wayne	A Min	25	25	0	0	139.2	617	149	72	59	10	7	5	5	60	0	111	5	4	6	9	.400	0	0	3.80
1995 Fort Myers	A+ Min	28	27	3	1	160	664	148	71	62	11	8	8	4	52	0	95	5	0	11	9	.550	2	0	3.49
1996 Fort Myers	A+ Min	11	11	2	0	70	282	55	28	27	5	1	2	1	26	0	65	1	0	7	1	.875	0	0	3.47
Hardware Cy	AA Min	16	16	1	0	75.1	353	108	54	48	8	0	2	2	25	0	51	2	1	5	7	.417	0	0	5.73
1997 New Britain	AA Min	25	20	0	1	118	498	112	56	55	12	2	5	1	49	1	92	4	2	10	6	.625	0	0	4.19
1998 Salt Lake	AAA Min	28	28	0	0	161	726	198	99	92	24	4	6	2	52	0	132	8	4	10	7	.588	0	0	5.14
1999 Salt Lake	AAA Min	3	3	0	0	15.2	72	25	16	14	3	0	2	1	1	0	7	1	0	1	1	.500	0	0	8.04
2000 Salt Lake	AAA Min	18	13	0	0	70.1	342	114	67	64	15	2	3	3	22	3	47	4	1	5	3	.625	0	0	8.19
1998 Minnesota	AL	5	2	0	1	17.1	67	10	3	3	0	0	2	1	6	0	16	2	0	1	0	1.000	0	0	1.56
1999 Minnesota	AL	30	4	0	2	71	345	107	65	64	17	1	5	0	34	3	56	2	2	3	2	.600	0	0	8.11
8 Min. YEARS		165	149	6	4	852.1	3725	942	475	430	89	26	33	20	302	5	634	35	12	59	44	.573	2	1	4.54
2 Maj. YEARS		35	6	0	3	88.1	412	117	68	67	17	1	7	1	40	3	72	4	2	4	2	.667	0	0	6.83

Alex Sanchez

Bats: Left **Throws:** Left **Pos:** OF-127   Ht: 5'10" **Wt:** 180 **Born:** 8/26/76 **Age:** 24

					BATTING											BASERUNNING				PERCENTAGES		
Year Team	Lg Org	G	AB	H	2B	3B	HR	TB	R	RBI	TBB	IBB	SO	HBP	SH	SF	SB	CS	SB%	GDP	Avg	OBP	SLG
1996 Devil Rays	R TB	56	227	64	7	6	1	86	36	22	10	0	35	6	1	1	20	12	.63	2	.282	.328	.379
1997 Chston-SC	A TB	131	537	155	15	6	0	182	73	34	37	2	72	3	12	4	92	40	.70	7	.289	.336	.339
1998 St. Pete	A+ TB	128	545	180	17	9	1	218	77	50	31	1	70	1	4	12	66	33	.67	5	.330	.360	.400
1999 Orlando	AA TB	i21	500	127	12	4	2	153	68	29	26	1	88	0	10	2	48	27	.64	8	.254	.290	.306
Durham	AAA TB	3	10	2	1	0	0	3	2	0	1	0	0	0	0	0	0	0	—	0	.200	.273	.300
2000 Orlando	AA TB	20	86	25	2	1	0	29	12	4	1	0	13	1	1	0	2	6	.25	1	.291	.307	.337
Durham	AAA TB	107	446	130	18	3	2	160	76	33	30	1	66	5	3	2	52	20	.72	6	.291	.342	.359
5 Min. YEARS		566	2351	683	72	29	6	831	344	172	136	5	344	16	31	21	280	138	.67	29	.291	.331	.353

Martin Sanchez

Pitches: Right **Bats:** Right **Pos:** SP-19; RP-9   Ht: 6'2" **Wt:** 180 **Born:** 1/19/77 **Age:** 24

Year Team	Lg Org	G	GS	CG	GF	IP	BFP	H	R	ER	HR	SH	SF	HB	TBB	IBB	SO	WP	Bk	W	L	Pct.	ShO	Sv	ERA
1996 Macon	A Atl	31	13	0	6	106.2	483	109	60	47	8	3	4	9	53	1	92	13	0	5	5	.500	0	1	3.97
1997 Kane County	A Fla	51	0	0	44	54	237	40	31	27	2	4	0	5	32	2	57	11	0	3	5	.375	0	22	4.50
1998 High Desert	A+ Ari	35	0	0	32	44.1	189	36	16	15	7	3	1	3	21	1	35	7	1	3	0	1.000	0	11	3.05
South Bend	A Ari	9	0	0	8	11.1	53	14	11	11	3	1	0	0	3	0	14	2	0	1	0	1.000	0	2	8.74
1999 El Paso	AA Ari	42	9	0	21	97	434	95	57	42	10	4	4	6	41	1	73	7	0	4	4	.500	0	6	3.90
2000 El Paso	AA Ari	28	19	0	3	110.2	484	112	70	61	15	0	6	3	42	0	88	4	1	7	6	.538	0	1	4.96
5 Min. YEARS		196	41	0	114	424	1880	406	245	203	45	15	15	26	192	5	359	44	2	23	20	.535	0	43	4.31

Victor Sanchez

Bats: Right **Throws:** Right **Pos:** DH-19; PH-19; 1B-14; OF-8; 3B-5; PR-1   Ht: 5'10" **Wt:** 215 **Born:** 12/20/71 **Age:** 29

					BATTING											BASERUNNING				PERCENTAGES		
Year Team	Lg Org	G	AB	H	2B	3B	HR	TB	R	RBI	TBB	IBB	SO	HBP	SH	SF	SB	CS	SB%	GDP	Avg	OBP	SLG
1994 Auburn	A- Hou	58	219	63	15	0	3	87	33	35	13	1	40	4	0	1	0	1	.00	7	.288	.338	.397
1995 Quad City	A Hou	13	34	8	0	0	0	8	3	1	6	0	10	0	0	0	1	0	1.00	2	.235	.350	.235
Kissimmee	A+ Hou	78	272	73	11	0	7	105	34	38	23	1	69	8	1	4	6	3	.67	2	.268	.339	.386
1996 Jackson	AA Hou	86	210	46	9	0	13	94	30	34	15	0	58	4	0	0	4	1	.80	7	.219	.284	.448
1997 Jackson	AA Hou	69	175	37	4	0	8	65	22	35	23	1	42	2	1	1	1	2	.33	5	.211	.308	.371
1998 Jackson	AA Hou	117	439	121	29	1	23	221	65	80	21	1	100	4	1	4	4	3	.57	12	.276	.312	.503
1999 Jackson	AA Hou	125	407	102	18	0	17	171	61	68	40	3	93	7	0	3	11	9	.55	17	.251	.326	.420
2000 New Orleans	AAA Hou	9	11	0	0	0	0	0	0	0	0	0	7	0	0	0	1	0	1.00	0	.000	.000	.000
Solano	IND —	14	56	21	7	0	2	34	8	13	6	0	8	2	0	0	1	1	.50	0	.375	.453	.607
Tucson	AAA Ari	6	8	2	1	0	0	3	1	1	1	0	3	0	0	0	0	0	—	0	.250	.300	.375
El Paso	AA Ari	31	96	27	2	1	1	34	12	17	6	1	21	2	0	0	2	2	.50	5	.281	.337	.354
7 Min. YEARS		606	1927	500	96	2	74	822	269	322	154	8	451	33	4	14	31	22	.58	63	.259	.323	.427

Wellington Sanchez

Bats: Right **Throws:** Right **Pos:** SS-68; PH-15; 3B-2; DH-2; PR-1   Ht: 6'0" **Wt:** 162 **Born:** 5/27/77 **Age:** 24

					BATTING											BASERUNNING				PERCENTAGES		
Year Team	Lg Org	G	AB	H	2B	3B	HR	TB	R	RBI	TBB	IBB	SO	HBP	SH	SF	SB	CS	SB%	GDP	Avg	OBP	SLG
1997 Helena	R+ Mil	61	236	64	13	0	2	83	46	20	14	0	47	1	3	0	10	7	.59	3	.271	.315	.352
1998 Beloit	A Mil	39	137	34	5	2	0	43	23	15	19	2	24	1	5	0	3	2	.60	4	.248	.344	.314
1999 Beloit	A Mil	71	261	68	14	3	0	88	35	23	25	0	58	4	4	0	9	3	.75	5	.261	.334	.337
2000 Huntsville	AA Mil	85	244	63	9	2	1	79	26	28	34	0	47	1	5	0	1	6	.14	5	.258	.354	.324
4 Min. YEARS		256	878	229	41	7	3	293	130	86	92	2	176	8	17	0	23	18	.56	17	.261	.336	.334

Yuri Sanchez

Bats: Left **Throws:** Right **Pos:** SS-47; 2B-21; 3B-3; PH-3; DH-1   Ht: 6'1" **Wt:** 165 **Born:** 11/11/73 **Age:** 27

					BATTING											BASERUNNING				PERCENTAGES		
Year Team	Lg Org	G	AB	H	2B	3B	HR	TB	R	RBI	TBB	IBB	SO	HBP	SH	SF	SB	CS	SB%	GDP	Avg	OBP	SLG
1992 Bristol	R+ Det	36	102	18	2	2	0	24	11	5	21	0	41	0	1	0	5	3	.63	1	.176	.317	.235
1993 Fayettevlle	A Det	111	340	69	7	6	0	88	53	30	73	0	125	2	7	3	20	9	.69	3	.203	.344	.259
1994 Lakeland	A+ Det	89	254	59	5	5	1	77	41	19	39	0	75	4	5	1	21	8	.72	6	.232	.342	.303
Trenton	AA Det	28	78	16	2	2	0	22	7	2	11	0	25	0	4	1	4	1	.80	1	.205	.303	.282
1995 Jacksnville	AA Det	121	342	73	8	7	6	113	52	28	38	0	116	1	15	0	15	6	.71	3	.213	.294	.330

Year Team	Lg Org	G	AB	H	2B	3B	HR	TB	R	RBI	TBB	IBB	SO	HBP	SH	SF	SB	CS	SB%	GDP	Avg	OBP	SLG
								BATTING										BASERUNNING				PERCENTAGES		
1996 Visalia	A+ Det	18	59	14	1	0	3	24	9	6	7	0	19	0	3	0	1	1	.50	0	.237	.318	.407
Winston-Sal	A+ Cin	100	353	76	15	3	5	112	48	39	43	0	103	0	10	3	9	6	.60	10	.215	.298	.317
Indianapols	AAA Cin	1	4	0	0	0	0	0	0	0	0	0	2	0	0	0	0	0	—	0	.000	.000	.000
1997 Burlington	A Cin	101	364	93	12	12	13	168	66	48	35	0	116	0	2	1	7	3	.70	9	.255	.320	.462
1998 Binghamton	AA NYM	93	316	82	14	7	3	119	47	26	35	1	95	4	11	0	11	7	.61	4	.259	.341	.377
1999 Binghamton	AA NYM	116	381	88	10	1	5	115	43	30	37	3	135	2	5	4	6	5	.55	3	.231	.300	.302
2000 Aberdeen	IND —	26	92	24	5	1	3	40	12	19	4	0	23	1	1	0	2	0	1.00	2	.261	.299	.435
Akron	AA Cle	4	9	1	0	0	0	1	1	0	0	0	3	0	0	0	0	0	—	0	.111	.111	.111
High Desert	A+ Ari	42	138	30	5	0	6	53	18	16	14	0	42	0	4	1	1	3	.25	2	.217	.288	.384
9 Min. YEARS		886	2832	643	86	46	45	956	408	266	357	4	920	14	66	13	102	52	.66	43	.227	.315	.338

Jared Sandberg

Bats: Right **Throws:** Right **Pos:** 3B-63; DH-7   **Ht:** 6'3" **Wt:** 212 **Born:** 3/2/78 **Age:** 23

Year Team	Lg Org	G	AB	H	2B	3B	HR	TB	R	RBI	TBB	IBB	SO	HBP	SH	SF	SB	CS	SB%	GDP	Avg	OBP	SLG
1996 Devil Rays	R TB	22	77	13	2	1	0	17	6	7	9	0	26	0	3	0	1	0	1.00	1	.169	.256	.221
1997 St. Pete	A+ TB	2	3	1	0	0	0	1	1	2	2	0	2	0	0	0	0	0	—	0	.333	.600	.333
Princeton	R+ TB	67	268	81	15	5	17	157	61	68	42	5	94	2	0	0	12	3	.80	4	.302	.401	.586
1998 Chston-SC	A TB	56	191	35	11	0	3	55	31	25	27	0	76	3	0	1	4	0	1.00	6	.183	.293	.288
Hudson Val	A- TB	73	271	78	15	2	12	133	49	54	42	1	76	5	0	4	13	3	.81	6	.288	.388	.491
1999 St. Pete	A+ TB	136	504	139	24	1	22	231	73	96	51	0	133	9	1	5	8	2	.80	12	.276	.350	.458
2000 Orlando	AA TB	67	244	63	15	1	5	95	30	35	33	0	55	2	0	3	5	3	.63	6	.258	.348	.389
Durham	AAA TB	3	15	6	3	0	2	15	2	7	0	0	6	0	0	1	0	0	—	1	.400	.400	1.000
5 Min. YEARS		426	1573	416	85	10	61	704	253	294	206	6	468	21	4	13	43	11	.80	36	.264	.355	.448

Deion Sanders

Bats: Left **Throws:** Left **Pos:** OF-25   **Ht:** 6'1" **Wt:** 196 **Born:** 8/9/67 **Age:** 33

Year Team	Lg Org	G	AB	H	2B	3B	HR	TB	R	RBI	TBB	IBB	SO	HBP	SH	SF	SB	CS	SB%	GDP	Avg	OBP	SLG
1988 Yankees	R NYY	17	75	21	4	2	0	29	7	6	2	0	10	1	0	1	11	2	.85	1	.280	.304	.387
Ft. Laud	A+ NYY	6	21	9	2	0	0	11	5	2	1	0	3	0	1	0	2	0	1.00	1	.429	.455	.524
Columbus	AAA NYY	5	20	3	1	0	0	4	3	0	1	0	4	2	1	0	1	1	.50	1	.150	.261	.200
1989 Albany-Col	AA NYY	33	119	34	2	2	1	43	28	6	11	1	20	7	1	0	17	5	.77	1	.286	.380	.361
Columbus	AAA NYY	70	259	72	12	7	5	113	38	30	22	1	48	1	4	3	16	7	.70	8	.278	.333	.436
1990 Columbus	AAA NYY	22	84	27	7	1	2	42	21	10	17	0	15	2	1	1	9	1	.90	1	.321	.442	.500
1991 Richmond	AAA Atl	29	130	34	6	3	5	61	20	16	10	0	28	0	0	1	12	4	.75	2	.262	.312	.469
1995 Chattanooga	AA Cin	2	7	4	0	0	1	7	1	2	0	0	1	0	0	0	1	0	1.00	0	.571	.571	1.000
2000 Louisville	AAA Cin	25	105	21	1	1	3	33	13	7	14	0	9	0	1	1	10	4	.71	2	.200	.292	.314
1989 New York	AL	14	47	11	2	0	2	19	7	7	3	1	8	0	0	0	1	0	1.00	0	.234	.280	.404
1990 New York	AL	57	133	21	2	2	3	36	24	9	13	0	27	1	1	1	8	2	.80	2	.158	.236	.271
1991 Atlanta	NL	54	110	21	1	2	4	38	16	13	12	0	23	0	0	0	11	3	.79	1	.191	.270	.345
1992 Atlanta	NL	97	303	92	6	14	8	150	54	28	18	0	52	2	1	1	26	9	.74	5	.304	.346	.495
1993 Atlanta	NL	95	272	75	18	6	6	123	42	28	16	3	42	3	1	2	19	7	.73	3	.276	.321	.452
1994 Atlanta	NL	46	191	55	10	4	4	77	32	21	16	1	28	1	1	2	19	7	.73	4	.288	.343	.403
Cincinnati	NL	46	184	51	7	4	0	66	26	7	16	0	35	2	1	0	19	9	.68	1	.277	.342	.359
1995 Cincinnati	NL	33	129	31	2	3	1	42	19	10	9	0	18	2	2	2	16	3	.84	0	.240	.296	.326
San Francisco	NL	52	214	61	9	5	5	95	29	18	18	0	42	2	1	0	8	6	.57	1	.285	.346	.444
1997 Cincinnati	NL	115	465	127	13	7	5	169	53	23	34	2	67	6	2	2	56	13	.81	4	.273	.329	.363
6 Min. YEARS		209	820	225	35	16	17	343	136	79	78	2	138	13	9	7	79	24	.77	17	.274	.344	.418
8 Maj. YEARS		609	2048	545	70	43	38	815	302	164	155	7	342	19	10	10	183	59	.76	21	.266	.322	.398

Frankie Sanders

Pitches: Right **Bats:** Right **Pos:** SP-12; RP-12   **Ht:** 5'11" **Wt:** 165 **Born:** 8/27/75 **Age:** 25

Year Team	Lg Org	G	GS	CG	GF	IP	BFP	H	R	ER	HR	SH	SF	HB	TBB	IBB	SO	WP	Bk	W	L	Pct.	ShO	Sv	ERA
1995 Burlington	R+ Cle	12	12	3	0	70	292	48	31	23	2	1	0	3	32	0	80	2	1	3	5	.375	0	0	2.96
Columbus	A Cle	2	0	0	1	9	39	9	3	3	0	1	0	1	4	0	9	1	0	1	1	.500	0	0	3.00
1996 Columbus	A Cle	22	22	0	0	121.1	508	103	52	34	8	3	2	6	37	1	109	13	4	9	3	.750	0	0	2.52
1997 Kinston	A+ Cle	25	25	2	0	146.1	611	130	72	66	10	6	2	2	66	1	127	8	0	11	5	.688	0	0	4.06
1998 Akron	AA Cle	29	29	2	0	186.1	781	175	82	72	15	8	6	11	71	0	108	6	0	11	8	.579	1	0	3.48
1999 Buffalo	AAA Cle	1	1	0	0	5	25	6	5	5	0	0	0		4	0	3	0	0	0	1	.000	0	0	9.00
Akron	AA Cle	33	13	0	6	120.2	546	139	72	65	12	6	7	6	51	2	72	9	0	6	6	.500	0	2	4.85
2000 Buffalo	AAA Cle	5	3	0	0	17.1	86	26	16	16	3	0	2	0	8	0	7	0	0	0	3	.000	0	0	8.31
Akron	AA Cle	19	9	0	3	69.1	312	77	47	40	9	5	3	6	29	2	50	2	0	5	5	.500	0	1	5.19
6 Min. YEARS		148	114	7	10	745.1	3200	713	380	324	61	30	20	37	302	6	565	41	5	46	37	.554	1	3	3.91

Scott Sanders

Pitches: Right **Bats:** Right **Pos:** SP-22; RP-7   **Ht:** 6'4" **Wt:** 220 **Born:** 3/25/69 **Age:** 32

Year Team	Lg Org	G	GS	CG	GF	IP	BFP	H	R	ER	HR	SH	SF	HB	TBB	IBB	SO	WP	Bk	W	L	Pct.	ShO	Sv	ERA
1990 Spokane	A- SD	3	3	0	0	19	70	12	3	2	0	1	0	1	5	0	21	0	1	2	1	.667	0	0	0.95
Waterloo	A SD	7	7	0	0	37	166	43	21	20	2	2	2	1	21	0	28	0	2	2	2	.500	0	0	4.86
1991 Waterloo	A SD	4	4	0	0	26.1	102	17	2	2	0	1	0	1	6	0	18	0	0	3	0	1.000	0	0	0.68
High Desert	A+ SD	21	21	4	0	132.2	569	114	72	54	7	4	2	7	72	2	93	8	2	9	6	.600	2	0	3.66
1992 Wichita	AA SD	14	14	0	0	87.2	377	85	35	34	7	5	4	3	37	2	95	4	0	7	5	.583	0	0	3.49
Las Vegas	AAA SD	14	12	1	1	72	340	97	49	44	7	3	1	3	31	1	51	6	0	3	6	.333	1	0	5.50
1993 Las Vegas	AAA SD	24	24	4	0	152.1	687	170	101	84	19	13	4	6	62	2	161	8	1	5	10	.333	0	0	4.96
1995 Las Vegas	AAA SD	1	1	0	0	3	14	3	0	0	0	0	0	0	2	0	2	0	0	0	0	—	0	0	0.00
1998 Las Vegas	AAA SD	15	3	0	6	36.2	151	34	14	14	2	3	0	1	12	3	43	0	0	1	2	.333	0	3	3.44

Year Team	Lg Org	HOW MUCH HE PITCHED G GS CG GF	IP BFP	WHAT HE GAVE UP H R ER HR SH SF HB	TBB IBB SO WP Bk	THE RESULTS W L Pct. ShO Sv ERA
2000 Buffalo	AAA Cle	7 7 0 0	42.1 178	35 20 17 5 0 1 1	16 0 38 1 0	3 1 .750 0 0 3.61
Edmonton	AAA Ana	6 2 0 1	22.2 101	25 15 14 3 0 0 0	12 0 18 2 0	0 2 .000 0 0 5.56
Calgary	AAA Fla	6 6 1 0	31.1 149	45 25 25 2 2 1 0	15 0 30 1 0	2 3 .400 0 0 7.18
Sacramento	AAA Oak	10 7 0 0	49.2 220	63 36 36 9 2 4 1	13 0 38 2 0	4 3 .571 0 0 6.52
1993 San Diego	NL	9 9 0 0	52.1 231	54 32 24 4 1 2 1	23 1 37 0 1	3 3 .500 0 0 4.13
1994 San Diego	NL	23 20 0 2	111 485	103 63 59 10 6 5 5	48 4 109 10 1	4 8 .333 0 1 4.78
1995 San Diego	NL	17 15 1 0	90 383	79 46 43 14 2 2 2	31 4 88 6 1	5 5 .500 0 0 4.30
1996 San Diego	NL	46 16 0 6	144 594	117 58 54 10 7 7 2	48 5 157 7 0	9 5 .643 0 0 3.38
1997 Seattle	AL	33 6 0 15	65.1 309	73 48 47 16 2 5 3	38 5 62 4 0	3 6 .333 0 2 6.47
Detroit	AL	14 14 1 0	74.1 317	79 44 44 14 1 5 1	24 1 58 4 0	3 8 .273 1 0 5.33
1998 Detroit	AL	3 2 0 1	9.2 57	24 19 19 1 0 0 0	6 2 6 1 0	0 2 .000 0 0 17.69
San Diego	NL	23 0 0 7	30.2 131	33 20 14 5 4 0 0	5 1 26 1 0	3 1 .750 0 0 4.11
1999 Chicago	NL	67 6 0 16	104.1 469	112 69 64 19 8 3 0	53 8 89 5 1	4 7 .364 0 2 5.52
7 Min. YEARS		132 111 10 8	712.2 3124	743 393 346 63 35 20 27	303 10 636 32 6	41 41 .500 3 3 4.37
7 Maj. YEARS		235 88 2 47	681.2 2976	674 399 368 93 31 29 14	276 31 632 38 4	34 45 .430 1 5 4.86

Tracy Sanders

Bats: Left   **Throws:** Right   **Pos:** 1B-37; DH-25; OF-8; PH-4   **Ht:** 6'1"   **Wt:** 210   **Born:** 7/26/69   **Age:** 31

Year Team	Lg Org	BATTING G AB H 2B 3B HR TB R RBI TBB IBB SO HBP SH SF	BASERUNNING SB CS SB% GDP	PERCENTAGES Avg OBP SLG
1990 Burlington	R+ Cle	51 178 50 12 1 10 94 38 34 33 0 36 2 0 1	10 3 .77 2	.281 .397 .528
Kinston	A+ Cle	10 32 14 3 3 0 23 6 9 7 0 6 0 0 0	1 1 .50 0	.438 .538 .719
1991 Kinston	A+ Cle	118 421 112 20 8 18 202 80 63 83 4 95 6 2 2	8 5 .62 9	.266 .393 .480
1992 Canton-Akrn	AA Cle	114 381 92 11 3 21 172 66 87 77 3 113 3 4 3	3 6 .33 8	.241 .371 .451
1993 Canton-Akrn	AA Cle	42 136 29 6 2 5 54 20 20 31 1 30 1 0 1	4 1 .80 1	.213 .361 .397
Wichita	AA SD	77 266 86 13 4 13 146 44 47 34 1 67 2 0 1	6 5 .55 2	.323 .403 .549
1994 Binghamton	AA NYM	101 275 66 20 4 8 118 44 37 60 1 88 3 0 5	8 6 .57 1	.240 .376 .429
1995 Binghamton	AA NYM	10 32 9 3 0 2 18 6 8 5 0 11 0 0 0	1 0 1.00 0	.281 .378 .563
Norfolk	AAA NYM	64 110 25 6 0 4 43 21 14 34 0 34 4 0 0	3 1 .75 2	.227 .426 .391
1996 Tulsa	AA Tex	52 168 39 10 0 7 70 31 20 33 2 49 2 0 0	2 1 .67 3	.232 .365 .417
Tri-City	IND —	35 123 30 6 0 9 63 25 24 29 1 38 2 0 2	5 3 .63 0	.244 .396 .512
1997 Carolina	AA Pit	116 376 102 13 1 21 190 77 78 74 0 88 6 1 3	7 6 .54 2	.271 .397 .505
1998 Carolina	AA Pit	113 342 80 18 2 22 168 69 70 97 2 86 5 0 7	3 4 .43 6	.234 .404 .491
2000 Lynchburg	A+ Pit	43 144 40 9 0 10 79 25 26 23 1 47 3 0 2	1 0 1.00 1	.278 .384 .549
Altoona	AA Pit	26 76 14 4 0 4 30 11 12 12 1 29 1 0 0	0 0 — 0	.184 .303 .395
Nashville	AAA Pit	4 7 1 0 0 0 1 0 1 0 0 4 0 0 0	0 0 — 0	.143 .143 .143
10 Min. YEARS		976 3067 789 164 28 154 1471 563 550 632 17 821 40 7 25	62 42 .60 37	.257 .388 .480

Danny Sandoval

Bats: Right   **Throws:** Right   **Pos:** SS-78; 2B-27; 3B-17; DH-10; PH-3   **Ht:** 5'11"   **Wt:** 180   **Born:** 4/7/79   **Age:** 22

Year Team	Lg Org	BATTING G AB H 2B 3B HR TB R RBI TBB IBB SO HBP SH SF	BASERUNNING SB CS SB% GDP	PERCENTAGES Avg OBP SLG
1998 Hickory	A CWS	126 430 99 12 2 0 115 43 30 29 0 88 5 14 2	13 15 .46 10	.230 .285 .267
1999 Burlington	A CWS	76 255 58 5 1 3 74 34 37 17 0 39 0 6 2	8 5 .62 7	.227 .274 .290
2000 Burlington	A CWS	75 269 87 9 3 0 102 34 34 18 1 22 2 8 1	37 18 .67 6	.323 .369 .379
Winston-Sal	A+ CWS	52 199 53 11 2 2 74 29 17 18 1 21 1 7 0	11 7 .61 7	.266 .330 .372
Charlotte	AAA CWS	2 8 1 0 0 0 1 0 1 1 0 1 0 0 0	0 0 — 0	.125 .222 .125
3 Min. YEARS		331 1161 298 37 8 5 366 140 119 83 2 171 8 35 5	69 45 .61 30	.257 .309 .315

Scott Sandusky

Bats: Right   **Throws:** Right   **Pos:** C-86; PH-4; DH-3; 1B-1   **Ht:** 6'0"   **Wt:** 195   **Born:** 3/6/76   **Age:** 25

Year Team	Lg Org	BATTING G AB H 2B 3B HR TB R RBI TBB IBB SO HBP SH SF	BASERUNNING SB CS SB% GDP	PERCENTAGES Avg OBP SLG
1998 Cape Fear	A Mon	189 54 5 0 1 62 16 19 11 0 54 0 5 0	3 1 .75 3	.286 .325 .328
1999 Jupiter	A+ Mon	108 354 90 9 1 1 104 31 22 20 0 72 8 7 0	4 5 .44 6	.254 .309 .294
2000 Jupiter	A+ Mon	43 140 36 4 1 2 48 18 25 8 0 29 1 4 2	0 1 .00 0	.257 .298 .343
Harrisburg	AA Mon	47 127 16 3 0 0 19 11 11 7 0 33 1 1 1	3 1 .75 2	.126 .176 .150
3 Min. YEARS		251 810 196 21 2 4 233 76 77 46 0 188 10 17 3	10 8 .56 11	.242 .290 .288

Osmany Santana

Bats: Left   **Throws:** Left   **Pos:** OF-81; DH-14   **Ht:** 5'11"   **Wt:** 185   **Born:** 8/9/76   **Age:** 24

Year Team	Lg Org	BATTING G AB H 2B 3B HR TB R RBI TBB IBB SO HBP SH SF	BASERUNNING SB CS SB% GDP	PERCENTAGES Avg OBP SLG
1998 Watertown	A- Cle	19 78 22 4 3 2 38 17 13 11 0 8 0 0 0	3 2 .60 2	.282 .371 .487
1999 Columbus	A Cle	38 133 43 6 0 0 49 23 17 10 1 21 1 1 1	15 6 .71 0	.323 .372 .368
Kinston	A+ Cle	43 145 35 8 0 3 52 16 20 8 0 26 1 1 0	7 0 1.00 2	.241 .286 .359
2000 Kinston	A+ Cle	44 190 62 12 2 0 78 27 14 15 0 27 0 2 1	13 4 .76 2	.326 .374 .411
Akron	AA Cle	51 191 54 6 0 1 63 16 23 11 0 23 1 5 0	14 1 .93 3	.283 .325 .330
3 Min. YEARS		195 737 216 36 5 6 280 99 87 55 1 105 3 9 2	52 13 .80 9	.293 .344 .380

Pedro Santana

Bats: Right   **Throws:** Right   **Pos:** 2B-112; PR-1   **Ht:** 5'11"   **Wt:** 160   **Born:** 9/21/76   **Age:** 24

Year Team	Lg Org	BATTING G AB H 2B 3B HR TB R RBI TBB IBB SO HBP SH SF	BASERUNNING SB CS SB% GDP	PERCENTAGES Avg OBP SLG
1996 Astros	R Hou	56 207 56 6 5 1 75 40 20 21 1 44 4 2 0	33 4 .89 3	.271 .349 .362
1997 W Michigan	A Det	74 287 75 10 6 3 106 36 28 14 0 55 6 3 0	20 3 .87 8	.261 .309 .369
1998 W Michigan	A Det	118 438 115 21 7 4 162 79 45 28 0 93 9 4 5	64 7 .90 4	.263 .317 .370
1999 Jacksnville	AA Det	120 512 143 35 6 5 205 89 49 34 0 98 3 8 5	34 9 .79 8	.279 .325 .400
2000 Jacksnville	AA Det	112 448 126 20 4 6 172 61 53 38 1 83 3 4 4	40 8 .83 2	.281 .339 .384
5 Min. YEARS		480 1892 515 92 28 19 720 305 195 135 2 373 25 21 14	191 31 .86 25	.272 .327 .381

Angel Santos

Bats: Both **Throws:** Right **Pos:** 2B-80   **Ht:** 5'11" **Wt:** 178 **Born:** 8/14/79 **Age:** 21

				BATTING												BASERUNNING				PERCENTAGES		
Year Team	Lg Org	G	AB	H	2B	3B	HR	TB	R	RBI	TBB	IBB	SO	HBP	SH	SF	SB	CS	SB%	GDP	Avg	OBP	SLG
1997 Red Sox	R Bos	17	60	11	1	0	0	12	8	7	7	0	11	0	1	2	8	3	.73	0	.183	.261	.200
1998 Red Sox	R Bos	23	77	27	5	1	0	34	14	13	13	0	10	0	1	2	7	3	.70	1	.351	.435	.442
Lowell	A- Bos	28	102	25	4	1	1	34	19	12	9	0	12	0	2	2	2	1	.67	4	.245	.306	.333
1999 Augusta	A Bos	130	466	126	30	2	15	205	83	55	62	4	88	5	2	3	25	10	.71	12	.270	.360	.440
2000 Trenton	AA Bos	80	275	71	17	2	3	101	32	32	32	0	60	2	1	4	18	8	.69	7	.258	.335	.367
4 Min. YEARS		278	980	260	57	6	19	386	156	119	123	4	181	7	7	11	60	25	.71	24	.265	.348	.394

Sneideer Santos

Bats: Left **Throws:** Right **Pos:** OF-24; DH-18; PH-5   **Ht:** 6'2" **Wt:** 192 **Born:** 9/29/79 **Age:** 21

				BATTING												BASERUNNING				PERCENTAGES		
Year Team	Lg Org	G	AB	H	2B	3B	HR	TB	R	RBI	TBB	IBB	SO	HBP	SH	SF	SB	CS	SB%	GDP	Avg	OBP	SLG
2000 Tucson	AAA Ari	1	1	0	0	0	0	0	0	0	0	0	0	0	0	0	0	0	—	1	.000	.000	.000
Diamondbcks	R Ari	43	152	52	6	6	2	76	28	23	10	0	32	3	0	2	4	3	.57	3	.342	.389	.500
1 Min. YEARS		44	153	52	6	6	2	76	28	23	10	0	32	3	0	2	4	3	.57	4	.340	.387	.497

Victor Santos

Pitches: Right **Bats:** Right **Pos:** SP-4   **Ht:** 6'3" **Wt:** 175 **Born:** 10/2/76 **Age:** 24

		HOW MUCH HE PITCHED						WHAT HE GAVE UP											THE RESULTS					
Year Team	Lg Org	G	GS	CG	GF	IP	BFP	H	R	ER	HR	SH	SF	HB	TBB	IBB	SO	WP	Bk	W	L	Pct.	ShO	Sv	ERA
1996 Tigers	R Det	9	9	0	0	50	199	44	12	11	1	3	1	7	13	0	39	3	0	3	2	.600	0	0	1.98
Lakeland	A+ Det	5	4	0	0	28.1	114	19	11	7	2	2	1	4	9	0	25	2	0	2	2	.500	0	0	2.22
1997 Lakeland	A+ Det	26	26	4	0	145	623	136	74	52	10	4	6	6	59	1	108	12	1	10	5	.667	2	0	3.23
1998 Toledo	AAA Det	5	3	0	1	14.2	80	24	22	18	5	0	0	1	10	0	12	0	0	1	2	.333	0	0	11.05
Lakeland	A+ Det	16	15	0	1	100.1	408	88	38	28	9	5	2	3	24	1	74	3	0	5	2	.714	0	1	2.51
Jacksnville	AA Det	6	6	0	0	36.2	159	40	20	17	2	1	3	1	15	1	37	1	0	4	2	.667	0	0	4.17
1999 Jacksnville	AA Det	28	28	2	0	173	722	150	86	67	16	1	5	7	58	2	146	3	0	12	6	.667	1	0	3.49
2000 Tigers	R Det	1	1	0	0	3	13	2	1	0	0	0	0	0	2	0	5	0	0	0	0	—	0	0	0.00
Lakeland	A+ Det	1	1	0	0	5	20	5	0	0	0	0	0	0	1	0	4	0	0	1	0	1.000	0	0	0.00
Toledo	AAA Det	2	2	0	0	6.1	33	7	8	8	4	2	0	0	6	0	2	0	0	0	1	.000	0	0	11.37
5 Min. YEARS		99	95	6	2	562.1	2371	515	272	208	49	13	18	29	197	5	452	24	1	38	22	.633	3	1	3.33

Damian Sapp

Bats: Right **Throws:** Right **Pos:** C-61; DH-20; 1B-4; OF-1; PR-1   **Ht:** 6'3" **Wt:** 243 **Born:** 5/20/76 **Age:** 25

				BATTING												BASERUNNING				PERCENTAGES		
Year Team	Lg Org	G	AB	H	2B	3B	HR	TB	R	RBI	TBB	IBB	SO	HBP	SH	SF	SB	CS	SB%	GDP	Avg	OBP	SLG
1994 Red Sox	R Bos	19	50	9	2	0	1	14	3	3	9	0	16	3	0	0	1	0	1.00	1	.180	.339	.280
1995 Utica	A- Bos	37	111	22	5	1	1	32	9	14	14	0	34	5	2	1	0	2	.00	2	.198	.313	.288
1996 Michigan	A Bos	90	335	108	21	4	18	191	55	52	38	1	88	4	0	3	3	2	.60	5	.322	.395	.570
1998 Sarasota	A+ Bos	35	127	31	9	0	7	61	18	23	15	0	38	2	0	3	1	0	1.00	3	.244	.327	.480
Trenton	AA Bos	28	91	22	5	0	5	42	9	10	9	0	35	3	0	0	0	0	—	4	.242	.330	.462
1999 Sarasota	A+ Bos	86	289	57	11	1	13	109	38	48	44	0	102	12	0	2	0	0	—	8	.197	.326	.377
2000 Sarasota	A+ Bos	11	39	13	4	0	3	26	9	14	6	0	14	1	0	0	0	0	—	0	.333	.435	.667
Pawtucket	AAA Bos	5	12	3	0	0	1	6	3	1	2	0	6	0	0	0	0	0	—	0	.250	.357	.500
Trenton	AA Bos	69	222	48	10	0	6	76	27	26	32	0	76	5	0	1	0	0	—	2	.216	.327	.342
6 Min. YEARS		380	1276	313	67	6	55	557	181	191	169	2	409	35	2	10	5	4	.56	23	.245	.347	.437

Rob Sasser

Bats: Right **Throws:** Right **Pos:** 3B-112; 1B-17; SS-5; OF-4; 2B-1; PH-1; PR-1   **Ht:** 6'3" **Wt:** 205 **Born:** 3/9/75 **Age:** 26

				BATTING												BASERUNNING				PERCENTAGES		
Year Team	Lg Org	G	AB	H	2B	3B	HR	TB	R	RBI	TBB	IBB	SO	HBP	SH	SF	SB	CS	SB%	GDP	Avg	OBP	SLG
1993 Braves	R Atl	33	113	27	4	0	0	31	19	7	6	0	25	4	0	2	2	1	.67	1	.239	.296	.274
1994 Idaho Falls	R+ Atl	58	219	50	9	6	2	77	32	26	19	3	58	1	0	1	13	1	.93	3	.228	.292	.352
1995 Danville	R+ Atl	12	47	15	2	1	0	19	8	7	4	1	7	0	0	1	5	1	.83	1	.319	.365	.404
Eugene	A- Atl	57	216	58	9	1	9	96	40	32	23	1	51	3	0	2	14	4	.78	2	.269	.344	.444
1996 Macon	A Atl	135	465	122	35	3	8	187	64	64	65	4	108	5	3	6	38	8	.83	4	.262	.355	.402
1997 Cedar Rapds	A Ana	134	497	135	26	5	17	222	103	77	69	6	92	8	0	3	37	13	.74	11	.272	.367	.447
1998 Charlotte	A+ Tex	4	13	4	2	0	0	6	1	3	3	0	5	0	0	0	1	0	1.00	1	.308	.438	.462
Tulsa	AA Tex	111	417	117	25	2	8	170	57	57	60	0	98	3	1	4	18	12	.60	11	.281	.372	.408
1999 Tulsa	AA Tex	5	19	5	2	0	0	7	3	0	2	0	2	0	0	0	0	0	—	0	.263	.300	.368
Jacksnville	AA Det	117	424	120	38	1	7	181	60	61	57	1	101	0	0	2	9	5	.64	7	.283	.370	.427
2000 Toledo	AAA Det	137	487	131	29	2	25	237	77	63	52	1	106	2	0	3	7	5	.58	9	.269	.340	.487
1998 Texas	AL	1	1	0	0	0	0	0	0	0	0	0	0	0	0	0	0	0	—	0	.000	.000	.000
8 Min. YEARS		803	2917	784	181	20	76	1233	464	402	359	17	653	29	4	25	144	50	.74	48	.269	.352	.423

Chris Saunders

Bats: Right **Throws:** Right **Pos:** 1B-37; DH-20; 3B-16; PH-16; 2B-2   **Ht:** 6'1" **Wt:** 203 **Born:** 7/19/70 **Age:** 30

				BATTING												BASERUNNING				PERCENTAGES		
Year Team	Lg Org	G	AB	H	2B	3B	HR	TB	R	RBI	TBB	IBB	SO	HBP	SH	SF	SB	CS	SB%	GDP	Avg	OBP	SLG
1992 Pittsfield	A- NYM	72	254	64	11	2	2	85	34	32	34	0	50	1	1	5	5	2	.71	5	.252	.337	.335
1993 St. Lucie	A+ NYM	123	456	115	14	4	4	149	45	64	40	4	89	1	1	4	6	7	.46	10	.252	.311	.327
1994 Binghamton	AA NYM	132	499	134	29	0	10	193	68	70	43	0	96	4	2	7	6	6	.50	12	.269	.327	.387
1995 Norfolk	AAA NYM	16	56	13	3	1	3	27	9	7	9	0	15	0	0	0	1	1	.50	1	.232	.338	.482
Binghamton	AA NYM	122	441	114	22	5	8	170	58	66	45	1	98	5	5	7	3	6	.33	7	.259	.329	.385
1996 Binghamton	AA NYM	141	510	152	28	3	17	236	82	105	73	3	88	8	2	11	5	4	.56	11	.298	.387	.463
1997 Binghamton	AA NYM	30	111	36	13	0	3	58	16	22	12	1	20	2	0	1	3	1	.75	2	.324	.388	.523
Norfolk	AAA NYM	68	173	43	9	0	0	52	24	24	37	2	37	0	2	1	2	2	.50	6	.249	.385	.301

Year Team	Lg Org	G	AB	H	2B	3B	HR	TB	R	RBI	TBB	IBB	SO	HBP	SH	SF	SB	CS	SB%	GDP	Avg	OBP	SLG
1998 Ottawa	AAA Mon	131	478	131	26	2	9	188	58	58	46	1	98	7	0	5	1	1	.50	10	.274	.343	.393
1999 Chattanooga	AA Cin	58	216	68	13	1	7	104	31	35	34	1	42	0	0	5	0	1	.00	6	.315	.400	.481
2000 Chattanooga	AA Cin	61	200	70	15	1	9	114	30	37	28	1	53	3	0	2	1	6	.14	2	.350	.433	.570
Louisville	AAA Cin	26	69	12	1	1	0	15	6	2	3	0	12	2	1	1	0	0	—	2	.174	.227	.217
9 Min. YEARS		980	3463	952	183	20	72	1391	461	522	404	14	698	35	14	52	33	37	.47	74	.275	.352	.402

Jamie Saylor

Bats: Left **Throws:** Right **Pos:** 2B-66; PH-16; SS-15; 3B-15; OF-12; 1B-1   **Ht:** 5'11" **Wt:** 185 **Born:** 9/11/74 **Age:** 26

Year Team	Lg Org	G	AB	H	2B	3B	HR	TB	R	RBI	TBB	IBB	SO	HBP	SH	SF	SB	CS	SB%	GDP	Avg	OBP	SLG
1993 Astros	R Hou	51	162	38	5	2	0	47	29	14	23	0	28	0	1	0	5	3	.63	1	.235	.330	.290
1994 Quad City	A Hou	92	321	84	16	2	2	110	57	22	28	2	65	7	7	1	14	5	.74	0	.262	.333	.343
1995 Kissimmee	A+ Hou	89	289	66	4	1	2	78	38	19	22	1	58	6	0	2	13	6	.68	5	.228	.295	.270
1996 Kissimmee	A+ Hou	59	181	37	3	3	1	49	17	6	10	0	43	0	3	2	8	6	.57	3	.204	.244	.271
Quad City	A Hou	23	58	7	1	0	0	8	8	5	3	0	13	2	2	2	4	2	.67	0	.121	.185	.138
1997 Quad City	A Hou	20	61	15	5	0	0	20	10	2	11	1	16	0	2	0	3	2	.60	3	.246	.361	.328
New Orleans	AAA Hou	2	0	0	0	0	0	0	0	0	0	0	0	0	0	0	0	0	—	0	—	—	—
Jackson	AA Hou	63	205	52	12	3	5	85	23	21	18	1	43	3	3	0	3	2	.60	1	.254	.323	.415
1998 New Orleans	AAA Hou	4	11	4	0	1	1	9	3	3	0	0	0	0	0	0	0	0	—	0	.364	.364	.818
Jackson	AA Hou	122	462	135	21	6	17	219	80	66	39	1	91	5	7	3	15	10	.60	4	.292	.352	.474
1999 New Orleans	AAA Hou	113	330	74	14	5	4	110	38	36	34	1	83	3	2	4	8	10	.44	6	.224	.299	.333
2000 New Orleans	AAA Hou	25	60	14	5	0	0	19	3	7	8	0	17	1	1	1	1	2	.33	2	.233	.329	.317
El Paso	AA Ari	90	286	61	12	10	1	96	50	28	44	2	71	6	2	2	14	2	.88	3	.213	.328	.336
8 Min. YEARS		753	2426	587	98	33	33	850	356	229	240	9	528	33	30	17	88	50	.64	28	.242	.317	.350

Jon Schaeffer

Bats: Right **Throws:** Right **Pos:** 1B-50; C-27; DH-16; PH-4; 3B-1; OF-1   **Ht:** 6'1" **Wt:** 197 **Born:** 1/20/76 **Age:** 25

Year Team	Lg Org	G	AB	H	2B	3B	HR	TB	R	RBI	TBB	IBB	SO	HBP	SH	SF	SB	CS	SB%	GDP	Avg	OBP	SLG
1997 Elizabethtn	R+ Min	48	165	55	13	0	6	86	35	34	33	3	32	4	0	2	0	1	.00	5	.333	.451	.521
New Britain	AA Min	10	29	6	2	0	0	8	1	4	2	0	7	0	0	1	1	1	.50	1	.207	.258	.276
1998 Fort Wayne	A Min	122	414	117	31	5	10	188	77	63	55	2	117	23	3	5	3	5	.38	15	.283	.392	.454
1999 Quad City	A Min	116	390	113	33	4	17	205	97	65	92	1	69	20	2	5	2	3	.40	12	.290	.444	.526
2000 Fort Myers	A+ Min	20	76	21	5	0	0	26	12	7	16	0	17	1	0	0	2	2	.50	1	.276	.409	.342
New Britain	AA Min	8	21	3	1	0	0	4	0	2	2	0	2	0	0	2	0	0	—	0	.143	.200	.190
Modesto	A+ Oak	52	191	50	10	2	4	76	33	32	28	0	34	2	1	2	2	3	.40	7	.262	.359	.398
Midland	AA Oak	14	37	8	2	0	1	13	5	8	5	0	6	0	0	2	0	0	—	1	.216	.295	.351
4 Min. YEARS		390	1323	373	97	11	38	606	260	215	233	6	284	50	6	18	10	15	.40	42	.282	.404	.458

Gene Schall

Bats: Right **Throws:** Right **Pos:** DH-68; 1B-36; OF-14; PH-6   **Ht:** 6'3" **Wt:** 201 **Born:** 6/5/70 **Age:** 31

Year Team	Lg Org	G	AB	H	2B	3B	HR	TB	R	RBI	TBB	IBB	SO	HBP	SH	SF	SB	CS	SB%	GDP	Avg	OBP	SLG
1991 Batavia	A- Phi	13	44	15	1	0	2	22	5	8	3	2	16	0	0	0	0	1	.00	1	.341	.383	.500
1992 Spartanburg	A Phi	77	276	74	13	1	8	113	44	41	29	0	52	3	2	2	3	2	.60	8	.268	.342	.409
Clearwater	A+ Phi	40	133	33	4	2	4	53	16	19	14	0	29	4	1	3	1	2	.33	2	.248	.331	.398
1993 Reading	AA Phi	82	285	93	12	4	15	158	51	60	24	0	56	10	0	3	2	1	.67	15	.326	.394	.554
Scranton-WB	AAA Phi	40	139	33	6	1	4	53	16	16	19	1	38	7	1	1	4	2	.67	2	.237	.355	.381
1994 Scranton-WB	AAA Phi	127	463	132	35	4	16	223	54	89	50	5	86	6	0	6	9	1	.90	11	.285	.358	.482
1995 Scranton-WB	AAA Phi	92	320	100	25	4	12	169	52	63	49	2	54	10	0	4	3	3	.50	14	.313	.415	.528
1996 Scranton-WB	AAA Phi	104	371	107	16	5	17	184	66	67	48	2	92	9	0	5	1	0	1.00	9	.288	.379	.496
1997 Nashville	AAA CWS	33	112	22	0	1	5	39	11	17	11	0	32	1	1	0	1	1	.50	1	.196	.274	.348
1998 Richmond	AAA Atl	100	340	102	22	0	22	190	60	73	37	3	80	9	0	6	1	3	.25	5	.300	.378	.559
1999 Richmond	AAA Atl	100	355	104	25	1	12	167	49	53	35	1	84	8	1	3	0	1	.00	7	.293	.367	.470
2000 Scranton-WB	AAA Phi	124	430	123	25	1	21	213	72	80	49	1	94	18	0	3	0	5	.00	21	.286	.380	.495
1995 Philadelphia	NL	24	65	15	2	0	0	17	2	5	6	1	16	1	0	0	0	0	—	1	.231	.306	.262
1996 Philadelphia	NL	28	66	18	5	1	2	31	7	10	12	0	15	1	0	0	0	0	—	2	.273	.392	.470
10 Min. YEARS		932	3268	938	184	24	138	1584	496	586	368	17	713	85	6	36	25	22	.53	96	.287	.370	.485
2 Maj. YEARS		52	131	33	7	1	2	48	9	15	18	1	31	2	0	0	0	0	—	3	.252	.351	.366

Jim Scharrer

Bats: Right **Throws:** Right **Pos:** 1B-17; DH-17; PH-2   **Ht:** 6'4" **Wt:** 220 **Born:** 11/5/76 **Age:** 24

Year Team	Lg Org	G	AB	H	2B	3B	HR	TB	R	RBI	TBB	IBB	SO	HBP	SH	SF	SB	CS	SB%	GDP	Avg	OBP	SLG
1995 Braves	R Atl	48	172	31	4	0	2	41	10	22	13	0	43	1	0	0	1	3	.25	3	.180	.242	.238
1996 Danville	R+ Atl	62	242	55	17	2	3	85	31	32	22	0	74	1	1	5	3	4	.43	3	.227	.289	.351
1997 Macon	A Atl	121	444	109	19	2	20	192	67	57	37	1	136	2	0	1	0	3	.00	1	.245	.306	.432
1998 Danville	A+ Atl	115	409	79	23	0	6	120	28	31	17	1	118	1	0	3	1	5	.17	9	.193	.226	.293
1999 Myrtle Bch	A+ Atl	119	466	121	18	0	7	160	52	54	30	4	120	3	3	4	0	1	.00	9	.260	.306	.343
2000 Lk Elsinore	A+ Ana	24	90	21	3	0	0	24	10	10	9	0	31	0	0	1	1	0	1.00	2	.233	.300	.267
Erie	AA Ana	11	29	5	0	0	0	5	1	1	2	0	12	0	0	0	1	0	1.00	1	.172	.226	.172
6 Min. YEARS		500	1852	421	84	4	38	627	199	207	130	6	534	8	4	14	7	16	.30	25	.227	.279	.339

Aaron Scheffer

Pitches: Right **Bats:** Left **Pos:** RP-50   **Ht:** 6'2" **Wt:** 165 **Born:** 10/15/75 **Age:** 25

Year Team	Lg Org	G	GS	CG	GF	IP	BFP	H	R	ER	HR	SH	SF	HB	TBB	IBB	SO	WP	Bk	W	L	Pct.	ShO	Sv	ERA
1994 Bellingham	A- Sea	2	0	0	0	3	16	4	4	2	0	0	1	0	3	0	5	0	0	0	0	—	0	0	6.00

Year Team	Lg Org	G	GS	CG	GF	IP	BFP	H	R	ER	HR	SH	SF	HB	TBB	IBB	SO	WP	Bk	W	L	Pct.	ShO	Sv	ERA
Mariners	R Sea	24	0	0	20	32.1	127	18	11	7	1	1	1	2	10	0	26	4	1	2	2	.500	0	6	1.95
1995 Wisconsin	A Sea	9	0	0	6	13.2	65	17	14	10	2	1	0	0	5	1	8	2	0	0	1	.000	0	0	6.59
Everett	A- Sea	24	0	0	9	43.1	185	44	23	18	4	1	0	2	16	1	38	2	1	2	5	.286	0	1	3.74
1996 Wisconsin	A Sea	45	1	0	28	67.2	292	55	35	28	5	2	2	3	34	4	89	16	5	8	1	.889	0	14	3.72
1997 Lancaster	A+ Sea	37	3	0	9	92.2	410	93	58	56	17	4	3	7	42	1	103	10	0	11	3	.786	0	4	5.44
1998 Lancaster	A+ Sea	25	0	0	19	43	189	46	19	15	0	2	1	1	12	3	65	5	0	2	2	.500	0	10	3.14
Orlando	AA Sea	19	0	0	11	32.2	132	23	8	8	3	2	0	0	13	0	33	1	1	1	0	1.000	0	5	2.20
1999 New Haven	AA Sea	10	0	0	4	17	79	19	9	7	3	1	0	1	8	0	24	1	0	2	0	1.000	0	0	3.71
Tacoma	AAA Sea	35	1	0	16	59.2	248	47	25	19	6	3	0	4	23	2	62	3	0	2	3	.400	0	9	2.87
2000 New Haven	AA Sea	29	0	0	22	38.2	173	33	15	15	4	5	3	4	19	5	53	5	0	2	2	.500	0	14	3.49
Tacoma	AAA Sea	21	0	0	6	32	141	26	22	18	5	6	5	1	15	1	21	2	0	1	6	.143	0	0	5.06
1999 Seattle	AL	4	0	0	3	4.2	24	6	5	1	0	0	3	1	3	0	4	0	0	0	0	—	0	0	1.93
7 Min. YEARS		280	5	0	150	475.2	2057	425	243	203	50	28	16	25	200	18	527	51	8	33	25	.569	0	63	3.84

John Scheschuk

Bats: Left **Throws:** Left **Pos:** 1B-133   **Ht:** 6'2" **Wt:** 208 **Born:** 2/2/77 **Age:** 24

Year Team	Lg Org	G	AB	H	2B	3B	HR	TB	R	RBI	TBB	IBB	SO	HBP	SH	SF	SB	CS	SB%	GDP	Avg	OBP	SLG
1999 Fort Wayne	A SD	66	242	61	14	0	3	84	35	36	43	4	34	2	1	6	3	1	.75	4	.252	.362	.347
2000 Las Vegas	AAA SD	2	7	3	1	0	0	4	2	1	1	0	0	0	0	0	0	0	—	0	.429	.500	.571
Fort Wayne	A SD	131	461	129	25	0	8	178	72	85	80	5	51	6	0	5	6	1	.86	13	.280	.389	.386
2 Min. YEARS		199	710	193	40	0	11	266	109	122	124	9	85	8	1	11	9	2	.82	17	.272	.381	.375

Tony Schifano

Bats: Right **Throws:** Right **Pos:** 3B-41; 2B-21; SS-18; OF-10; PR-2; 1B-1; PH-1   **Ht:** 6'1" **Wt:** 195 **Born:** 11/11/74 **Age:** 26

Year Team	Lg Org	G	AB	H	2B	3B	HR	TB	R	RBI	TBB	IBB	SO	HBP	SH	SF	SB	CS	SB%	GDP	Avg	OBP	SLG
1997 Brevard Cty	A+ Fla	1	1	0	0	0	0	0	0	0	0	0	1	0	0	0	0	0	—	0	.000	.000	.000
Utica	A- Fla	48	153	40	7	0	1	50	26	14	11	0	28	2	8	1	5	5	.50	3	.261	.317	.327
1998 Brevard Cty	A+ Fla	91	304	71	3	4	1	85	28	14	14	0	46	6	4	0	8	1	.89	9	.234	.281	.280
1999 Brevard Cty	A+ Fla	45	141	35	3	1	2	46	21	15	12	0	36	2	3	2	2	2	.50	1	.248	.312	.326
Portland	AA Fla	29	67	16	1	1	0	19	9	6	5	0	9	1	1	0	0	0	—	3	.239	.301	.284
Knoxville	AA Tor	27	92	25	4	1	0	31	12	15	3	0	15	1	1	1	5	3	.63	3	.272	.299	.337
2000 Tennessee	AA Tor	87	275	64	11	0	1	78	24	24	19	2	53	7	8	2	6	4	.60	4	.233	.297	.284
4 Min. YEARS		328	1033	251	29	7	5	309	120	88	64	2	188	19	25	6	26	15	.63	23	.243	.298	.299

Brian Schmack

Pitches: Right **Bats:** Right **Pos:** RP-51   **Ht:** 6'2" **Wt:** 195 **Born:** 12/7/73 **Age:** 27

Year Team	Lg Org	G	GS	CG	GF	IP	BFP	H	R	ER	HR	SH	SF	HB	TBB	IBB	SO	WP	Bk	W	L	Pct.	ShO	Sv	ERA
1995 Newark	IND —	7	4	0	2	30.1	135	40	21	18	3	5	0	2	10	0	16	1	0	2	1	.667	0	0	5.34
1996 Hickory	A CWS	43	0	0	25	62.1	264	61	24	16	4	9	0	4	16	5	56	3	1	6	4	.600	0	5	2.31
1997 Winston-Sal	A+ CWS	42	0	0	18	75.1	325	65	32	23	0	5	3	2	36	4	71	6	1	2	5	.286	0	6	2.75
1998 Winston-Sal	A+ CWS	42	0	0	34	61.1	256	48	23	15	3	5	0	9	17	0	52	2	1	5	5	.500	0	10	2.20
1999 Birmingham	AA CWS	43	0	0	26	63	270	60	31	24	3	2	1	8	18	0	56	6	0	4	4	.500	0	6	3.43
2000 Charlotte	AAA CWS	51	0	0	13	90.2	379	82	32	28	10	4	1	1	29	5	84	4	0	11	7	.611	0	1	2.78
6 Min. YEARS		228	4	0	118	383	1629	356	163	124	23	30	5	26	126	14	335	22	3	30	26	.536	0	28	2.91

Bryan Schmidt

Bats: Right **Throws:** Right **Pos:** 3B-18; 2B-16; PH-6; 1B-3; PR-3; DH-2; OF-1; P-1   **Ht:** 6'2" **Wt:** 180 **Born:** 6/28/75 **Age:** 26

Year Team	Lg Org	G	AB	H	2B	3B	HR	TB	R	RBI	TBB	IBB	SO	HBP	SH	SF	SB	CS	SB%	GDP	Avg	OBP	SLG
1998 Padres	R SD	47	194	56	12	0	0	68	29	22	19	2	28	4	1	4	6	3	.67	3	.289	.357	.351
Idaho Falls	R+ SD	4	14	5	0	0	0	5	5	2	1	0	1	1	0	1	4	0	1.00	0	.357	.412	.357
1999 Mobile	AA SD	17	32	6	1	0	0	7	7	3	5	0	8	0	0	0	0	0	—	1	.188	.297	.219
Fort Wayne	A SD	67	227	54	7	1	0	63	23	13	20	0	49	5	6	1	2	4	.33	3	.238	.312	.278
2000 Mobile	AA SD	13	29	6	1	0	0	7	1	3	1	0	5	1	1	0	0	1	.00	3	.207	.258	.241
Rancho Cuca	A+ SD	32	98	14	2	0	0	16	4	3	8	0	19	0	0	0	0	0	—	6	.143	.208	.163
3 Min. YEARS		180	594	141	23	1	0	166	69	46	54	2	110	11	8	6	12	8	.60	21	.237	.310	.279

Brian Scott

Pitches: Right **Bats:** Right **Pos:** SP-19; RP-11   **Ht:** 6'3" **Wt:** 190 **Born:** 4/29/76 **Age:** 25

Year Team	Lg Org	G	GS	CG	GF	IP	BFP	H	R	ER	HR	SH	SF	HB	TBB	IBB	SO	WP	Bk	W	L	Pct.	ShO	Sv	ERA
1997 Hickory	A CWS	13	13	1	0	83.1	321	57	26	20	4	4	0	1	23	0	69	2	3	6	3	.667	0	0	2.16
1998 Winston-Sal	A+ CWS	19	19	0	0	100.1	462	116	70	55	9	5	4	9	43	0	76	2	3	6	6	.500	0	0	4.93
Hickory	A CWS	6	6	0	0	38.2	164	33	16	12	3	3	1	1	11	0	38	2	1	4	2	.667	0	0	2.79
1999 Winston-Sal	A+ CWS	25	25	1	0	147.2	637	135	75	56	7	7	3	5	60	3	132	17	0	8	8	.500	0	0	3.41
2000 El Paso	AA Ari	16	14	0	1	61.2	303	73	55	46	6	4	0	6	46	0	43	15	0	3	8	.273	0	0	6.71
High Desert	A+ Ari	14	5	0	2	43	202	46	38	34	6	2	0	7	31	0	20	5	1	2	4	.333	0	0	7.12
4 Min. YEARS		93	82	2	3	474.2	2089	460	280	223	35	25	8	29	214	3	378	43	8	29	31	.483	0	0	4.23

Darryl Scott

Pitches: Right Bats: Right Pos: RP-39 Ht: 6'1" Wt: 185 Born: 8/6/68 Age: 32

		HOW MUCH HE PITCHED						WHAT HE GAVE UP												THE RESULTS					
Year Team	Lg Org	G	GS	CG	GF	IP	BFP	H	R	ER	HR	SH	SF	HB	TBB	IBB	SO	WP	Bk	W	L	Pct.	ShO	Sv	ERA
1990 Boise	A- Ana	27	0	0	11	53.2	221	40	11	8	3	0	1	0	19	1	57	5	0	2	1	.667	0	5	1.34
1991 Quad City	A Ana	47	0	0	36	75.1	285	35	18	13	2	2	0	1	26	4	123	9	1	4	3	.571	0	19	1.55
1992 Midland	AA Ana	27	0	0	22	29.2	126	20	9	6	0	2	2	2	14	1	35	4	0	1	1	.500	0	1	1.82
Edmonton	AAA Ana	31	0	0	17	36.1	164	41	21	21	1	0	3	0	21	1	48	4	2	0	2	.000	0	6	5.20
1993 Vancouver	AAA Ana	46	0	0	33	51.2	206	35	12	12	4	2	1	1	19	2	57	3	0	7	1	.875	0	15	2.09
1995 Colo Spngs	AAA Col	59	1	0	27	95.2	429	113	63	50	7	4	7	3	41	7	77	7	0	4	10	.286	0	4	4.70
1996 Buffalo	AAA Cle	50	1	0	30	81	323	61	29	26	11	4	2	0	24	4	73	2	0	3	5	.375	0	2	2.89
1997 Buffalo	AAA Cle	48	0	0	35	65.2	272	52	24	21	10	4	1	0	28	2	29	4	0	5	6	.455	0	12	2.88
1998 Ottawa	AAA Mon	8	0	0	2	11.2	53	12	6	4	1	1	1	0	5	0	7	0	0	0	1	.000	0	2	3.09
Reading	AA Phi	8	0	0	5	11	43	7	4	4	2	1	0	0	2	0	13	1	0	0	1	.000	0	1	3.27
Scranton-WB	AAA Phi	33	0	0	23	39.1	172	37	24	22	8	1	2	1	15	1	37	3	0	4	5	.444	0	10	5.03
1999 Scranton-WB	AAA Phi	57	4	0	30	105.2	456	100	53	48	11	4	2	2	47	4	91	7	0	7	6	.538	0	10	4.09
2000 Colo Spngs	AAA Col	2	0	0	1	3	13	5	2	2	0	0	0	0	0	0	2	1	0	1	0	1.000	0	0	6.00
Tucson	AAA Ari	14	0	0	5	20.2	104	31	28	24	6	0	0	0	12	1	21	2	0	1	2	.333	0	0	10.45
Clearwater	A+ Phi	4	0	0	3	7	29	4	1	1	0	0	0	1	4	1	5	3	0	0	1	.000	0	0	1.29
Reading	AA Phi	19	0	0	10	28.2	113	20	9	9	2	1	0	0	10	1	31	6	0	1	0	1.000	0	0	2.83
1993 California	AL	16	0	0	2	20	90	19	13	13	1	2	2	1	11	1	13	2	0	1	2	.333	0	0	5.85
10 Min. YEARS		480	6	0	290	716	3009	613	314	271	68	26	23	11	287	30	706	61	3	40	45	.471	0	104	3.41

Tim Scott

Pitches: Right Bats: Right Pos: RP-39 Ht: 6'2" Wt: 205 Born: 11/16/66 Age: 34

		HOW MUCH HE PITCHED						WHAT HE GAVE UP												THE RESULTS					
Year Team	Lg Org	G	GS	CG	GF	IP	BFP	H	R	ER	HR	SH	SF	HB	TBB	IBB	SO	WP	Bk	W	L	Pct.	ShO	Sv	ERA
1984 Great Falls	R+ LA	13	13	3	0	78	0	90	54	38	4	0	0	2	38	1	44	5	2	5	4	.556	2	0	4.38
1985 Bakersfield	A+ LA	12	10	2	1	63.2	0	84	46	41	4	0	0	1	28	0	31	2	4	3	4	.429	0	0	5.80
1986 Vero Beach	A+ LA	20	13	3	2	95.1	418	113	44	36	2	4	9	2	34	2	37	5	5	5	4	.556	1	0	3.40
1987 San Antonio	AA LA	2	2	0	0	5.1	33	14	10	10	2	0	1	0	2	0	6	1	0	0	1	.000	0	0	16.88
Bakersfield	A+ LA	7	5	1	1	32.1	137	33	19	16	2	0	1	1	10	1	29	2	0	2	3	.400	0	0	4.45
1988 Bakersfield	A+ LA	36	2	0	25	64.1	272	52	34	26	3	4	4	2	26	5	59	2	0	4	7	.364	0	7	3.64
1989 San Antonio	AA LA	48	0	0	28	88	308	71	30	28	3	5	3	0	36	5	64	1	4	4	2	.667	0	4	3.71
1990 Albuquerque	AAA LA	17	0	0	8	15	73	14	9	7	1	0	0	0	14	2	15	0	0	2	1	.667	0	3	4.20
San Antonio	AA LA	30	0	0	20	47.1	186	35	17	15	5	0	1	1	14	0	52	0	0	3	3	.500	0	7	2.85
1991 Las Vegas	AAA SD	41	11	0	9	111	497	133	78	64	8	5	2	1	39	4	74	1	0	8	8	.500	0	1	5.19
1992 Las Vegas	AAA SD	24	0	0	23	28	106	20	8	7	1	1	1	3	9	2	28	2	0	1	2	.333	0	15	2.25
1997 Colo Spngs	AAA Col	12	0	0	9	14.2	52	7	2	2	1	1	1	0	3	0	18	1	1	0	0	—	0	0	1.23
1998 San Berndno	A+ LA	2	2	0	0	4	15	4	2	2	1	0	0	0	1	0	2	0	0	0	1	.000	0	0	4.50
1999 Sacramento	IND —	17	0	0	17	17	65	11	3	3	1	2	0	0	3	0	23	0	0	1	1	.500	0	1	1.59
Nashville	AAA Pit	19	0	0	7	23	105	29	14	13	3	0	0	2	7	1	21	0	1	3	.250	0	0	5.09
2000 Solano	IND —	23	0	0	21	27	104	19	6	5	2	1	2	0	5	0	35	1	0	0	0	—	0	8	1.67
Louisville	AAA Cin	16	0	0	2	26	113	26	13	8	1	2	0	1	9	0	25	0	0	0	1	.000	0	0	2.77
1991 San Diego	NL	2	0	0	0	2		2	2	1	0	0	0	0	0	0	0	0		0	0	—	0	0	9.00
1992 San Diego	NL	34	0	0	16	37.2	173	39	24	22	4	4	1	1	21	6	30	0	1	4	1	.800	0	0	5.26
1993 San Diego	NL	24	0	0	2	37.2	169	38	13	10	1	2	2	4	15	0	30	1	1	2	0	1.000	0	1	2.39
Montreal	NL	32	0	0	16	34	148	31	15	14	1	3	0	0	19	2	35	1	0	5	2	.714	0	1	3.71
1994 Montreal	NL	40	0	0	8	53.1	223	51	17	16	0	0	0	2	18	3	37	1	1	5	2	.714	0	1	2.70
1995 Montreal	NL	62	0	0	15	63.1	268	52	30	28	4	1	6	1	23	2	57	4	0	2	0	1.000	0	2	3.98
1996 Montreal	NL	45	0	0	14	46.1	198	41	18	16	3	1	2	2	21	2	37	1	0	3	5	.375	0	1	3.11
San Francisco	NL	20	0	0	2	19.2	90	24	18	18	5	3	1	1	9	0	10	2	0	2	2	.500	0	0	8.24
1997 San Diego	NL	14	0	0	2	18.1	87	25	17	16	2	0	1	3	5	0	14	0	0	1	1	.500	0	0	7.85
Colorado	NL	3	0	0	0	2.2	14	5	3	3	0	1	0	0	2	0	2	0	0	0	0	—	0	0	10.13
13 Min. YEARS		339	58	9	173	720	2484	755	393	321	44	25	24	15	272	25	563	23	16	39	45	.464	3	53	4.01
7 Maj. YEARS		276	0	0	75	314	1375	308	157	144	24	16	8	19	133	15	253	10	3	24	13	.649	0	5	4.13

Marcos Scutaro

Bats: Right Throws: Right Pos: 2B-111; SS-20; PR-1 Ht: 5'10" Wt: 170 Born: 10/30/75 Age: 25

		BATTING																BASERUNNING				PERCENTAGES		
Year Team	Lg Org	G	AB	H	2B	3B	HR	TB	R	RBI	TBB	IBB	SO	HBP	SH	SF	SB	CS	SB%	GDP	Avg	OBP	SLG
1996 Columbus	A Cle	85	315	79	12	3	10	127	66	45	38	0	86	4	4	5	6	3	.67	6	.251	.334	.403
1997 Buffalo	AAA Cle	21	57	15	3	0	1	21	8	6	6	0	8	0	1	1	0	0	.00	4	.263	.328	.368
Kinston	A+ Cle	97	378	103	17	6	10	162	58	59	35	0	72	9	2	3	23	7	.77	3	.272	.346	.429
1998 Buffalo	AAA Cle	8	26	6	3	0	0	9	3	4	0	0	2	0	1	0	0	0	—	0	.231	.231	.346
Akron	AA Cle	124	462	146	27	6	11	218	68	62	47	0	71	10	4	6	33	16	.67	8	.316	.387	.472
1999 Buffalo	AAA Cle	129	462	126	24	2	8	178	76	51	61	2	69	6	6	4	21	6	.78	5	.273	.362	.385
2000 Buffalo	AAA Cle	124	425	117	20	5	5	162	67	54	61	0	53	9	7	7	9	6	.60	8	.275	.373	.381
Indianapolis	AAA Mil	4	13	7	1	1	1	13	5	3	1	0	2	0	0	0	1	0	1.00	1	.538	.571	1.000
5 Min. YEARS		592	2138	599	107	23	46	890	351	284	249	2	363	38	25	26	93	39	.70	35	.280	.361	.416

Scott Seabol

Bats: Right Throws: Right Pos: 3B-81; DH-27; OF-15; 1B-14; 2B-2; PH-2 Ht: 6'4" Wt: 200 Born: 5/17/75 Age: 26

		BATTING																BASERUNNING				PERCENTAGES		
Year Team	Lg Org	G	AB	H	2B	3B	HR	TB	R	RBI	TBB	IBB	SO	HBP	SH	SF	SB	CS	SB%	GDP	Avg	OBP	SLG
1996 Oneonta	A- NYY	43	142	30	9	1	3	50	16	10	15	0	30	6	2	0	2	3	.40	1	.211	.313	.352
1997 Greensboro	A NYY	48	136	36	12	2	2	58	11	15	9	0	26	4	0	2	3	1	.75	1	.265	.325	.426
1998 Greensboro	A NYY	71	210	60	11	0	7	92	24	33	13	2	40	3	1	2	2	2	.50	4	.286	.333	.438
1999 Greensboro	A NYY	138	543	171	55	6	15	283	86	89	45	1	91	9	0	11	6	5	.55	9	.315	.370	.521
2000 Norwich	AA NYY	132	493	146	45	2	20	255	82	78	42	1	108	4	1	3	2	4	.33	11	.296	.355	.517
5 Min. YEARS		432	1524	443	132	11	47	738	219	225	124	4	295	26	4	17	15	15	.50	26	.291	.351	.484

Todd Sears

Bats: Left **Throws:** Right **Pos:** 1B-118; DH-9; PH-2 **Ht:** 6'1" **Wt:** 186 **Born:** 10/23/75 **Age:** 25

Year Team	Lg Org	G	AB	H	2B	3B	HR	TB	R	RBI	TBB	IBB	SO	HBP	SH	SF	SB	CS	SB%	GDP	Avg	OBP	SLG
1997 Portland	A- Col	55	200	54	13	1	2	75	37	29	41	7	49	0	1	1	2	0	1.00	4	.270	.393	.375
1998 Asheville	A Col	130	459	133	26	2	11	196	71	82	72	1	89	5	1	6	10	4	.71	9	.290	.387	.427
1999 Salem	A+ Col	109	385	108	21	0	14	171	58	59	58	1	99	4	0	1	11	2	.85	9	.281	.379	.444
2000 Carolina	AA Col	86	299	90	21	0	12	147	54	72	72	11	76	2	0	5	12	3	.80	7	.301	.434	.492
New Britain	AA Min	40	140	44	8	1	3	63	15	15	18	1	40	1	0	0	1	0	1.00	5	.314	.396	.450
Salt Lake	AAA Min	3	11	4	1	0	1	8	2	4	1	0	2	0	0	0	0	0	—	1	.364	.417	.727
4 Min. YEARS		423	1494	433	90	4	43	660	237	261	262	21	355	12	2	13	36	9	.80	35	.290	.397	.442

Bobby Seay

Pitches: Left **Bats:** Left **Pos:** SP-24 **Ht:** 6'2" **Wt:** 221 **Born:** 6/20/78 **Age:** 23

Year Team	Lg Org	G	GS	CG	GF	IP	BFP	H	R	ER	HR	SH	SF	HB	TBB	IBB	SO	WP	Bk	W	L	Pct.	ShO	Sv	ERA
1997 Chston-SC	A TB	13	13	0	0	61.1	269	56	35	31	2	2	2	3	37	0	64	6	0	3	4	.429	0	0	4.55
1998 Chston-SC	A TB	15	15	0	0	69	289	59	40	33	10	3	2	5	29	0	74	7	2	1	7	.125	0	0	4.30
1999 Orlando	A+ TB	12	11	0	1	57	238	56	25	19	0	2	2	4	23	0	45	2	0	2	6	.250	0	0	3.00
Orlando	AA TB	6	6	0	0	17	85	22	15	15	2	0	1	0	15	0	16	4	2	1	2	.333	0	0	7.94
2000 Orlando	AA TB	24	24	0	0	132.1	568	132	64	57	13	4	5	8	53	1	106	4	0	8	7	.533	0	0	3.88
4 Min. YEARS		70	69	0	1	336.2	1449	325	179	155	27	11	12	20	157	1	305	23	4	15	26	.366	0	0	4.14

Ronni Seberino

Pitches: Left **Bats:** Left **Pos:** RP-48; SP-1 **Ht:** 6'1" **Wt:** 199 **Born:** 5/27/79 **Age:** 22

Year Team	Lg Org	G	GS	CG	GF	IP	BFP	H	R	ER	HR	SH	SF	HB	TBB	IBB	SO	WP	Bk	W	L	Pct.	ShO	Sv	ERA
1996 Devil Rays	R TB	18	6	0	8	52	215	50	22	20	2	2	2	2	15	0	49	10	1	4	2	.667	0	1	3.46
1997 Princeton	R+ TB	14	14	0	0	65.1	292	71	39	23	3	0	1	1	28	0	57	6	2	4	4	.500	0	0	3.17
1998 Hudson Val	A- TB	22	5	0	1	52	223	47	29	24	2	1	5	2	24	0	61	12	2	3	2	.600	0	0	4.15
1999 Chston-SC	A TB	50	0	0	11	74.2	315	57	29	22	5	0	4	1	38	3	73	10	1	6	2	.750	0	0	2.65
2000 St. Pete	A+ TB	33	1	0	13	39.1	166	30	17	12	0	0	4	0	20	1	33	2	0	6	0	1.000	0	4	2.75
Orlando	AA TB	4	0	0	1	8.2	36	6	2	2	0	2	2	0	6	0	6	3	0	0	0	—	0	0	2.08
Durham	AAA TB	12	0	0	4	17	74	6	9	4	3	1	0	1	14	0	14	4	0	1	0	1.000	0	1	2.12
5 Min. YEARS		153	26	0	38	309	1321	267	147	107	15	6	18	7	145	4	293	47	6	24	10	.706	0	6	3.12

Jason Secoda

Pitches: Right **Bats:** Right **Pos:** RP-21; SP-11 **Ht:** 6'1" **Wt:** 195 **Born:** 9/2/74 **Age:** 26

Year Team	Lg Org	G	GS	CG	GF	IP	BFP	H	R	ER	HR	SH	SF	HB	TBB	IBB	SO	WP	Bk	W	L	Pct.	ShO	Sv	ERA
1995 Bristol	R+ CWS	13	12	0	0	65.2	307	78	57	39	3	1	3	1	33	0	63	8	1	2	8	.200	0	0	5.35
1996 South Bend	A CWS	32	22	0	0	133.2	605	132	84	59	9	2	3	3	75	0	94	18	1	6	12	.333	0	1	3.97
1997 Winston-Sal	A+ CWS	29	15	1	5	119.2	525	118	67	55	11	3	5	4	57	1	85	16	1	7	4	.636	0	2	4.14
1998 Winston-Sal	A+ CWS	6	0	0	4	11.1	43	8	2	2	0	1	0	0	2	1	8	1	0	2	0	1.000	0	0	1.59
Birmingham	AA CWS	39	0	0	20	65.1	307	78	50	46	6	2	4	2	39	2	45	7	1	2	3	.400	0	1	6.34
1999 Birmingham	AA CWS	22	17	1	0	115	477	100	49	44	7	2	4	8	39	0	94	8	1	8	7	.533	1	0	3.44
Charlotte	AAA CWS	7	7	3	0	44.1	201	54	35	26	10	0	1	3	10	0	33	4	0	2	5	.286	0	0	5.28
2000 Charlotte	AAA CWS	32	11	0	4	100.1	461	122	76	67	20	4	1	3	49	3	75	8	1	2	7	.222	0	0	6.01
6 Min. YEARS		180	84	5	39	655.1	2926	690	408	338	66	15	21	24	304	7	497	70	6	31	46	.403	1	4	4.64

Joe Secoda

Bats: Right **Throws:** Right **Pos:** OF-26; PH-16; DH-9; PR-3; 2B-1; P-1 **Ht:** 6'1" **Wt:** 190 **Born:** 11/19/77 **Age:** 23

Year Team	Lg Org	G	AB	H	2B	3B	HR	TB	R	RBI	TBB	IBB	SO	HBP	SH	SF	SB	CS	SB%	GDP	Avg	OBP	SLG
1997 Johnson Cty	R+ StL	52	187	47	5	0	3	61	21	16	17	0	56	3	1	1	4	3	.57	3	.251	.322	.326
1998 Peoria	A StL	10	24	1	0	0	0	1	2	0	0	0	15	0	0	0	0	0	—	2	.042	.042	.042
New Jersey	A- StL	53	159	36	4	0	0	40	13	14	10	0	59	3	2	2	7	4	.64	1	.226	.282	.252
1999 Peoria	A StL	116	400	101	14	2	2	125	61	30	62	0	97	9	6	1	15	9	.63	2	.253	.364	.313
2000 Peoria	A StL	36	89	25	1	1	0	28	9	11	14	0	29	0	1	0	2	3	.40	0	.281	.379	.315
Arkansas	AA StL	17	30	6	1	0	0	7	4	2	0	0	11	2	0	2	0	0	—	2	.200	.235	.233
4 Min. YEARS		284	889	216	25	3	5	262	110	73	103	0	267	17	10	6	28	19	.60	10	.243	.331	.295

Reed Secrist

Bats: Left **Throws:** Right **Pos:** C-44; OF-12; 1B-7; DH-6; PH-5; PR-1 **Ht:** 6'1" **Wt:** 205 **Born:** 5/7/70 **Age:** 31

Year Team	Lg Org	G	AB	H	2B	3B	HR	TB	R	RBI	TBB	IBB	SO	HBP	SH	SF	SB	CS	SB%	GDP	Avg	OBP	SLG
1992 Welland	A- Pit	42	117	25	6	0	1	34	16	13	19	0	36	2	2	1	4	3	.57	2	.214	.331	.291
1993 Augusta	A Pit	90	266	71	16	3	6	111	38	47	27	1	43	1	2	4	4	1	.80	10	.267	.332	.417
1994 Salem	A+ Pit	80	221	54	12	0	10	96	29	35	22	0	58	1	2	1	2	2	.50	4	.244	.314	.434
1995 Lynchburg	A+ Pit	112	380	107	18	3	19	188	60	75	54	7	88	3	1	4	3	4	.43	6	.282	.372	.495
1996 Calgary	AAA Pit	128	420	129	30	4	17	210	68	66	52	11	105	4	3	5	2	4	.33	8	.307	.385	.500
1997 Calgary	AAA Pit	40	121	32	7	3	5	60	19	18	14	0	32	0	1	0	1	0	1.00	1	.264	.341	.496
1998 Memphis	AAA StL	75	214	46	10	0	6	74	34	29	31	1	57	1	0	3	1	2	.33	3	.215	.313	.346
Knoxville	AA Tor	15	50	12	4	1	2	24	9	8	4	1	14	0	0	0	0	0	—	2	.240	.296	.480
1999 Altoona	AA Pit	36	95	16	5	0	0	21	13	9	11	1	23	1	1	1	0	0	—	6	.168	.273	.221
Nashville	AAA Pit	46	102	27	8	1	2	43	12	15	8	1	22	2	1	1	1	1	.50	3	.265	.327	.422
2000 Tulsa	AA Tex	42	133	43	10	1	3	64	19	20	13	2	28	4	0	1	3	0	1.00	0	.323	.397	.481
Oklahoma	AAA Tex	31	104	25	2	1	4	41	13	14	13	0	24	1	1	1	1	1	.50	2	.240	.331	.394
9 Min. YEARS		737	2223	587	128	13	75	966	326	350	270	25	530	20	14	21	20	18	.53	46	.264	.346	.435

Shawn Sedlacek

Pitches: Right **Bats:** Right **Pos:** RP-19; SP-16 **Ht:** 6'4" **Wt:** 200 **Born:** 6/29/77 **Age:** 24

Year Team	Lg Org	G	GS	CG	GF	IP	BFP	H	R	ER	HR	SH	SF	HB	TBB	IBB	SO	WP	Bk	W	L	Pct.	ShO	Sv	ERA
1998 Spokane	A- KC	16	13	0	0	86	371	89	43	33	2	1	4	6	18	0	62	4	5	9	2	.818	0	0	3.45
1999 Wilmington	A+ KC	17	17	1	0	92	411	111	61	54	7	3	6		26	0	69	4	0	4	6	.400	0	0	5.28
2000 Wichita	AA KC	35	16	1	11	140.1	612	153	69	57	10	5	2	12	43	4	81	8	2	15	6	.714	0	3	3.66
3 Min. YEARS		68	46	2	11	318.1	1394	353	173	144	19	12	9	24	87	4	212	16	7	28	14	.667	0	3	4.07

Ryan Seifert

Pitches: Right **Bats:** Right **Pos:** RP-23; SP-9 **Ht:** 6'5" **Wt:** 215 **Born:** 8/14/75 **Age:** 25

Year Team	Lg Org	G	GS	CG	GF	IP	BFP	H	R	ER	HR	SH	SF	HB	TBB	IBB	SO	WP	Bk	W	L	Pct.	ShO	Sv	ERA
1997 Portland	A- Col	16	15	0	0	74.1	337	89	49	40	8		4	4	31	0	52	3	0	1	7	.125	0	0	4.84
1998 Asheville	A Col	36	0	0	19	87.1	363	66	44	40	8	12	4	6	37	0	90	1	0	7	6	.538	0	5	4.12
1999 Colo Sprngs	AAA Col	1	1	0	0	4	18	4	2	2	1	0	0	0	2	0	2	0	0	0	0	—	0	0	4.50
Salem	A+ Col	24	0	0	5	46.1	196	40	24	18	0	2	2	3	21	0	51	0	0	3	5	.375	0	0	3.50
2000 Carolina	AA Col	32	9	0	8	97.2	422	97	49	44	6	1	6	4	37	1	95	3	0	3	6	.333	0	0	4.05
4 Min. YEARS		109	25	0	32	309.2	1336	296	168	144	23	15	16	17	128	1	290	7	0	14	24	.368	0	5	4.19

Brad Seitzer

Bats: Right **Throws:** Right **Pos:** 3B-46; DH-27; 1B-8; PH-1 **Ht:** 6'2" **Wt:** 195 **Born:** 2/2/70 **Age:** 31

Year Team	Lg Org	G	AB	H	2B	3B	HR	TB	R	RBI	TBB	IBB	SO	HBP	SH	SF	SB	CS	SB%	GDP	Avg	OBP	SLG
1991 Bluefield	R+ Bal	12	45	13	2	0	3	24	5	5	5	0	10	0	0	0	1	1	.50	1	.289	.360	.533
Kane County	A Bal	58	197	55	11	1	2	74	34	28	36	3	36	1	1	1	1	0	1.00	3	.279	.391	.376
1992 Frederick	A+ Bal	129	459	114	21	3	14	183	59	61	38	2	111	7	4	3	2	4	.33	9	.248	.314	.399
1993 Frederick	A+ Bal	130	439	111	24	3	10	171	44	68	58	1	95	5	3	9	3	3	.50	6	.253	.341	.390
1994 Beloit	A Mil	102	343	86	13	0	11	132	45	53	58	1	78	3	6	4	2	2	.50	7	.251	.360	.385
1995 Stockton	A+ Mil	127	428	132	28	3	6	184	66	56	72	2	68	3	2	2	7	4	.64	10	.308	.410	.430
1996 El Paso	AA Mil	115	433	138	31	1	17	222	78	87	51	0	67	7	2	5	6	4	.60	9	.319	.395	.513
1997 Tucson	AAA Mil	62	234	74	13	3	9	120	50	42	22	0	33	3	0	4	0	1	.00	9	.316	.376	.513
Ottawa	AAA Mon	18	56	14	1	0	1	18	4	7	8	0	11	1	0	0	1	2	.33	3	.250	.354	.321
Omaha	AAA KC	21	63	12	3	0	0	15	4	4	5	0	10	0	0	1	0	0	—	4	.190	.246	.238
Memphis	AA Sea	17	70	23	8	1	2	39	14	13	6	0	13	1	0	1	1	0	1.00	4	.329	.385	.557
1998 Tacoma	AAA Sea	129	474	142	35	1	14	221	74	68	68	5	65	9	2	6	4	3	.57	13	.300	.393	.466
1999 Tacoma	AAA Sea	130	474	136	34	1	9	199	80	66	89	2	86	1	2	8	1	2	.33	14	.287	.395	.420
2000 Charlotte	AAA CWS	80	263	77	20	0	11	130	42	42	46	1	47	0	0	5	4	0	1.00	12	.293	.393	.494
10 Min. YEARS		1130	3978	1127	244	17	109	1732	599	600	562	17	730	41	27	48	29	27	.52	104	.283	.374	.435

Jason Sekany

Pitches: Right **Bats:** Right **Pos:** SP-16; RP-11 **Ht:** 6'4" **Wt:** 214 **Born:** 7/20/75 **Age:** 25

Year Team	Lg Org	G	GS	CG	GF	IP	BFP	H	R	ER	HR	SH	SF	HB	TBB	IBB	SO	WP	Bk	W	L	Pct.	ShO	Sv	ERA
1996 Red Sox	R Bos	5	2	0	2	11.2	50	14	3	3	1	0	0	1	3	0	16	2	0	0	0	—	0	1	2.31
1997 Michigan	A Bos	16	16	3	0	106	448	92	55	48	5	2	4	4	41	1	103	14	0	5	6	.455	0	0	4.08
Sarasota	A+ Bos	10	9	0	1	64.2	290	56	43	40	8	2	2	2	41	0	32	3	2	4	4	.500	0	0	5.57
1998 Trenton	AA Bos	28	28	1	0	148.2	643	151	101	86	21	4	5	5	57	0	113	14	0	10	10	.500	0	0	5.21
1999 Pawtucket	AAA Bos	1	1	0	0	5.2	27	7	4	3	2	0	0	0	4	0	1	0	0	0	1	.000	0	0	4.76
Trenton	AA Bos	27	22	3	1	161.1	674	143	65	60	8	3	4	6	64	0	116	10	1	14	4	.778	2	0	3.35
2000 Pawtucket	AAA Bos	17	7	1	2	52.2	229	59	34	32	8	0	5	2	16	2	29	4	0	3	3	.500	0	0	5.47
Chattanooga	AA Cin	10	9	0	1	43.1	200	49	36	34	8	3	1	1	28	1	28	5	0	1	6	.143	0	0	7.06
5 Min. YEARS		114	94	8	7	594	2561	571	341	306	61	14	21	21	254	4	438	52	3	37	34	.521	2	1	4.64

Chip Sell

Bats: Left **Throws:** Right **Pos:** OF-102; PH-6; DH-3; PR-2 **Ht:** 6'2" **Wt:** 205 **Born:** 6/19/71 **Age:** 30

Year Team	Lg Org	G	AB	H	2B	3B	HR	TB	R	RBI	TBB	IBB	SO	HBP	SH	SF	SB	CS	SB%	GDP	Avg	OBP	SLG
1994 Yakima	A- LA	54	172	52	12	3	3	79	29	21	16	1	37	0	1	0	12	3	.80	6	.302	.362	.459
1995 Vero Beach	A+ LA	80	222	60	6	1	1	71	21	23	18	0	33	4	2	2	1	3	.25	5	.270	.333	.320
1996 San Berndno	A+ LA	95	321	90	12	0	1	105	47	23	27	2	68	5	3	1	13	5	.72	6	.280	.345	.327
1997 Vero Beach	A+ LA	111	342	97	21	7	7	153	50	46	29	2	67	4	2	3	25	8	.76	4	.284	.344	.447
1998 Albuquerque	AAA LA	37	136	43	2	2	0	49	22	10	11	0	23	0	1	1	9	6	.60	1	.316	.365	.360
San Antonio	AA LA	64	218	55	12	6	3	88	36	37	22	1	40	3	3	4	6	0	1.00	5	.252	.324	.404
1999 El Paso	AA Ari	92	329	101	16	1	8	143	50	35	20	0	66	3	0	4	19	6	.76	5	.307	.348	.435
Tucson	AAA Ari	30	84	30	5	2	1	42	12	18	3	0	14	3	2	0	4	3	.57	2	.357	.400	.500
2000 Tucson	AAA Ari	112	405	132	23	7	4	181	65	54	28	2	71	8	5	5	8	6	.57	1	.326	.379	.447
7 Min. YEARS		675	2229	660	109	29	28	911	332	267	174	8	419	30	19	17	97	40	.71	36	.296	.353	.409

Tom Sergio

Bats: Left **Throws:** Right **Pos:** OF-50; DH-5; P-1 **Ht:** 5'9" **Wt:** 175 **Born:** 6/27/75 **Age:** 26

Year Team	Lg Org	G	AB	H	2B	3B	HR	TB	R	RBI	TBB	IBB	SO	HBP	SH	SF	SB	CS	SB%	GDP	Avg	OBP	SLG
1997 Pulaski	R+ Tex	58	226	74	14	4	9	123	57	40	38	0	42	4	1	1	25	6	.81	1	.327	.431	.544
1998 Tulsa	AA Tex	11	39	10	1	1	0	13	7	0	4	0	1	0	0	0	0	0	—	0	.256	.326	.333
Charlotte	A+ Tex	112	453	133	30	7	5	192	90	39	46	1	59	10	4	4	33	10	.77	6	.294	.368	.424
1999 Tulsa	AA Tex	128	512	149	38	6	10	229	88	72	58	3	59	5	5	4	19	5	.79	6	.291	.366	.447
2000 Oklahoma	AAA Tex	18	59	16	5	3	0	27	13	4	9	0	11	0	0	1	1	0	1.00	1	.271	.317	.458
Tulsa	AA Tex	37	141	36	8	0	1	47	20	19	21	0	14	3	1	1	7	0	1.00	1	.255	.361	.333
4 Min. YEARS		364	1430	418	96	21	25	631	275	174	171	4	186	22	11	10	85	21	.80	15	.292	.374	.441

Jim Serrano

Pitches: Right **Bats:** Right **Pos:** RP-55   **Ht:** 5'8" **Wt:** 165 **Born:** 5/9/76 **Age:** 25

Year Team	Lg Org	G	GS	CG	GF	IP	BFP	H	R	ER	HR	SH	SF	HB	TBB	IBB	SO	WP	Bk	W	L	Pct.	ShO	Sv	ERA
1998 Vermont	A- Mon	7	0	0	7	7.2	28	3	1	1	0	0	0	0	1	0	12	1	0	0	0	—	0	5	1.17
Cape Fear	A Mon	15	0	0	8	24.2	116	22	11	10	2	1	2	1	15	0	29	5	0	2	0	1.000	0	3	3.65
1999 Jupiter	A+ Mon	44	1	0	24	93	365	59	25	22	4	2	5	7	27	4	118	8	0	8	5	.615	0	8	2.13
2000 Harrisburg	AA Mon	55	0	0	34	75	335	64	39	35	6	6	5	7	43	2	80	6	0	4	5	.444	0	16	4.20
3 Min. YEARS		121	1	0	73	200.1	844	148	76	68	12	9	12	15	86	6	239	20	0	14	10	.583	0	32	3.05

Wascar Serrano

Pitches: Right **Bats:** Right **Pos:** SP-24   **Ht:** 6'2" **Wt:** 178 **Born:** 6/2/78 **Age:** 23

Year Team	Lg Org	G	GS	CG	GF	IP	BFP	H	R	ER	HR	SH	SF	HB	TBB	IBB	SO	WP	Bk	W	L	Pct.	ShO	Sv	ERA
1997 Idaho Falls	R+ SD	2	2	0	0	8.1	43	13	12	11	2	0	0	1	4	0	13	0	0	0	1	.000	0	0	11.88
Padres	R SD	12	11	0	1	70.2	301	60	43	25	4	0	4	4	22	0	75	8	3	6	3	.667	0	1	3.18
Clinton	A SD	1	1	1	0	6	24	6	5	4	0	0	0	0	2	1	2	1	0	0	1	.000	0	0	6.00
1998 Clinton	A SD	26	26	0	0	156.2	663	150	74	56	6	6	4	6	54	1	143	7	0	9	7	.563	0	0	3.22
1999 Rancho Cuca	A+ SD	21	21	1	0	132.1	537	110	58	49	10	1	5	1	43	0	129	8	5	9	8	.529	1	0	3.33
Mobile	AA SD	7	7	0	0	42.1	196	48	27	26	5	1	3	6	17	1	29	1	1	2	3	.400	0	0	5.53
2000 Las Vegas	AAA SD	4	4	0	0	13.1	75	24	23	21	5	0	0	2	10	0	19	4	1	0	1	.000	0	0	14.18
Mobile	AA SD	20	20	1	0	112.1	471	93	42	35	11	6	1	4	42	0	112	9	0	9	4	.692	0	0	2.80
4 Min. YEARS		93	92	3	1	542	2310	504	284	227	43	14	17	24	194	3	522	38	10	35	28	.556	1	1	3.77

Doug Sessions

Pitches: Right **Bats:** Right **Pos:** RP-56   **Ht:** 6'1" **Wt:** 192 **Born:** 9/28/76 **Age:** 24

Year Team	Lg Org	G	GS	CG	GF	IP	BFP	H	R	ER	HR	SH	SF	HB	TBB	IBB	SO	WP	Bk	W	L	Pct.	ShO	Sv	ERA
1998 Auburn	A- Hou	26	0	0	24	31.1	125	22	10	8	2	2	1	0	10	0	41	0	1	1	0	1.000	0	14	2.30
1999 Michigan	A Hou	12	0	0	12	13	44	6	1	1	1	1	0	1	1	0	18	0	0	0	0	—	0	5	0.69
Kissimmee	A+ Hou	35	0	0	27	45.2	183	35	11	10	1	1	0	1	14	1	55	2	0	3	0	1.000	0	13	1.97
2000 Round Rock	AA Hou	56	0	0	34	82.1	351	78	35	31	7	5	2	1	37	4	80	1	0	6	4	.600	0	10	3.39
3 Min. YEARS		129	0	0	97	172.1	703	141	57	50	11	9	3	3	62	5	194	3	1	10	4	.714	0	42	2.61

Jeff Sexton

Pitches: Right **Bats:** Right **Pos:** RP-27; SP-9   **Ht:** 6'2" **Wt:** 190 **Born:** 10/4/71 **Age:** 29

Year Team	Lg Org	G	GS	CG	GF	IP	BFP	H	R	ER	HR	SH	SF	HB	TBB	IBB	SO	WP	Bk	W	L	Pct.	ShO	Sv	ERA
1993 Watertown	A- Cle	17	1	1	9	33.2	145	35	15	10	1	1	0	1	10	3	30	3	0	1	1	.500	1	2	2.67
1994 Watertown	A- Cle	10	0	0	5	23	95	19	3	1	0	1	0	0	7	2	16	3	1	1	0	1.000	0	3	0.39
Columbus	A Cle	14	2	0	6	30	121	17	13	12	2	1	0	3	9	2	35	1	0	1	0	1.000	0	1	3.60
1995 Columbus	A Cle	14	13	2	0	82.1	318	66	27	20	2	1	1	3	16	0	71	1	0	6	2	.750	2	0	2.19
Kinston	A+ Cle	8	8	2	0	57	226	52	17	16	3	0	0	2	7	0	41	6	1	5	1	.833	1	0	2.53
1996 Canton-Akrn	AA Cle	9	0	0	0	49.1	210	45	29	28	6	2	0	2	23	1	34	1	0	2	4	.333	0	0	5.11
1997 Akron	AA Cle	16	3	0	5	47.1	215	55	27	25	4	4	4	5	15	1	38	1	2	2	0	1.000	0	1	4.75
Buffalo	AAA Cle	15	0	0	11	23.2	100	17	14	14	3	1	0	0	12	0	15	2	0	2	1	.667	0	5	5.32
1998 Akron	AA Cle	27	0	0	19	57.1	232	41	12	10	2	2	0	3	19	3	49	2	0	4	2	.667	0	11	1.57
Buffalo	AAA Cle	21	0	0	5	24.1	111	25	16	11	1	2	3	1	15	1	15	3	2	0	0	—	0	1	4.07
1999 Akron	AA Cle	15	0	0	11	20	89	24	10	8	1	2	5	1	9	0	16	1	0	1	0	1.000	0	2	3.60
Buffalo	AAA Cle	23	1	0	11	29	149	47	24	21	3	1	2	1	14	3	22	3	0	0	1	.000	0	0	6.52
2000 Carolina	AA Col	17	9	0	5	67.1	306	78	41	38	3	4	1	2	31	0	58	4	0	5	4	.556	0	1	5.08
Newark	IND —	19	0	0	11	20.2	95	23	16	15	4	0	0	0	11	0	20	3	0	1	1	.500	0	0	6.53
8 Min. YEARS		225	46	5	98	565	2412	544	264	229	35	22	16	24	198	16	460	34	6	31	17	.646	4	22	3.65

Jon Shave

Bats: Right **Throws:** Right **Pos:** 2B-42; 1B-36; 3B-26; SS-20; DH-6; OF-1; PH-1; PR-1   **Ht:** 6'0" **Wt:** 185 **Born:** 11/4/67 **Age:** 33

Year Team	Lg Org	G	AB	H	2B	3B	HR	TB	R	RBI	TBB	IBB	SO	HBP	SH	SF	SB	CS	SB%	GDP	Avg	OBP	SLG
1990 Butte	R+ Tex	64	250	88	9	3	2	109	41	42	25	0	27	3	2	4	21	7	.75	8	.352	.411	.436
1991 Gastonia	A Tex	55	213	62	11	0	2	79	29	24	20	0	26	1	3	0	11	9	.55	3	.291	.355	.371
Charlotte	A+ Tex	56	189	43	4	1	1	52	17	20	18	1	30	5	2	4	7	7	.50	3	.228	.306	.275
1992 Tulsa	AA Tex	118	453	130	23	5	2	169	57	36	37	1	59	4	7	5	6	7	.46	10	.287	.343	.373
1993 Okla City	AAA Tex	100	399	105	17	3	4	140	58	41	20	0	60	2	9	1	4	3	.57	12	.263	.301	.351
1994 Okla City	AAA Tex	95	332	73	15	2	1	95	29	31	14	1	61	5	12	5	6	2	.75	6	.220	.258	.286
1995 Okla City	AAA Tex	32	83	17	1	0	0	18	10	5	7	0	28	1	1	0	1	0	1.00	1	.205	.275	.217
1996 Okla City	AAA Tex	116	414	110	20	2	7	155	54	41	41	0	97	10	4	4	8	6	.57	7	.266	.343	.374
1997 Salt Lake	AAA Min	103	393	130	27	3	7	184	75	60	39	0	62	6	1	8	6	6	.50	9	.329	.391	.466
1998 Salt Lake	AAA Min	90	317	107	20	1	4	141	63	41	34	1	46	13	5	1	8	9	.47	7	.338	.422	.445
2000 Oklahoma	AAA Tex	131	510	148	21	5	10	209	85	54	40	3	65	17	3	3	12	5	.71	16	.290	.360	.410
1993 Texas	AL	17	47	15	2	0	0	17	3	7	0	0	8	0	3	2	1	3	.25	0	.319	.306	.362
1998 Minnesota	AL	19	40	10	3	0	1	16	7	5	3	0	10	0	0	0	1	2	.33	0	.250	.302	.400
1999 Texas	AL	43	73	21	4	0	0	25	10	9	5	0	17	2	3	0	1	0	1.00	0	.288	.330	.342
10 Min. YEARS		960	3555	1013	168	25	40	1351	518	395	295	7	561	67	49	35	90	61	.60	82	.285	.348	.380
3 Maj. YEARS		79	160	46	9	0	1	58	20	21	8	0	35	2	6	2	3	5	.38	0	.288	.326	.363

Tom Shearn

Pitches: Right **Bats:** Right **Pos:** SP-23; RP-2   **Ht:** 6'4" **Wt:** 200 **Born:** 8/28/77 **Age:** 23

Year Team	Lg Org	G	GS	CG	GF	IP	BFP	H	R	ER	HR	SH	SF	HB	TBB	IBB	SO	WP	Bk	W	L	Pct.	ShO	Sv	ERA
1996 Astros	R Hou	17	3	0	3	41.2	162	34	13	8	2	1	2	2	10	0	43	3	1	5	2	.714	0	0	1.73
1997 Auburn	A- Hou	14	14	2	0	82.1	349	79	42	32	4	1	4	9	26	3	59	7	1	4	6	.400	2	0	3.50
1998 Quad City	A Hou	21	21	2	0	120	487	88	38	30	8	4	0	6	52	1	93	3	0	7	7	.500	1	0	2.25
1999 Kissimmee	A+ Hou	24	24	0	0	145.1	624	144	75	63	11	5	5	4	53	2	107	15	1	10	6	.625	0	0	3.90
2000 Round Rock	AA Hou	25	23	0	0	136.1	602	134	79	71	14	4	5	8	67	1	102	7	0	9	6	.600	0	0	4.69
5 Min. YEARS		101	85	4	3	525.2	2224	479	247	204	39	15	16	29	208	7	404	35	3	35	27	.565	3	0	3.49

Ben Sheets

Pitches: Right **Bats:** Right **Pos:** SP-26; RP-1   **Ht:** 6'1" **Wt:** 195 **Born:** 7/18/78 **Age:** 22

Year Team	Lg Org	G	GS	CG	GF	IP	BFP	H	R	ER	HR	SH	SF	HB	TBB	IBB	SO	WP	Bk	W	L	Pct.	ShO	Sv	ERA
1999 Ogden	R+ Mil	2	2	0	0	8	33	8	5	5	2	0	0	1	2	0	12	0	0	0	1	.000	0	0	5.63
Stockton	A+ Mil	5	5	0	0	27.2	115	23	11	11	1	0	1	1	14	0	28	1	0	1	0	1.000	0	0	3.58
2000 Huntsville	AA Mil	13	13	0	0	72	288	55	17	15	4	1	4	2	25	0	60	2	0	5	3	.625	0	0	1.88
Indianapolis	AAA Mil	14	13	1	0	81.2	346	77	31	26	4	1	3	4	31	0	59	3	1	3	5	.375	0	0	2.87
2 Min. YEARS		34	33	1	0	189.1	782	163	64	57	11	2	8	8	72	0	159	6	1	9	9	.500	0	0	2.71

Chris Sheff

Bats: Right **Throws:** Right **Pos:** OF-92; PH-17; DH-7; PR-4   **Ht:** 6'3" **Wt:** 215 **Born:** 2/4/71 **Age:** 30

Year Team	Lg Org	G	AB	H	2B	3B	HR	TB	R	RBI	TBB	IBB	SO	HBP	SH	SF	SB	CS	SB%	GDP	Avg	OBP	SLG
1992 Erie	A- Fla	57	193	46	8	2	3	67	29	16	32	1	47	1	1	1	15	2	.88	8	.238	.348	.347
1993 Kane County	A Fla	129	456	124	22	5	5	171	79	50	58	2	100	2	3	5	33	10	.77	11	.272	.353	.375
1994 Brevard Cty	A+ Fla	32	118	44	8	3	1	61	21	19	17	0	23	0	0	1	7	2	.78	2	.373	.449	.517
Portland	AA Fla	106	395	101	19	1	5	137	50	30	31	0	76	0	3	2	18	4	.82	13	.256	.308	.347
1995 Portland	AA Fla	131	471	130	25	7	12	205	85	91	72	6	84	5	1	8	23	6	.79	10	.276	.372	.435
1996 Portland	AA Fla	27	105	31	12	2	2	53	16	17	13	3	23	0	0	0	3	2	.60	3	.295	.373	.505
Charlotte	AAA Fla	92	284	75	15	1	12	128	41	49	21	1	55	0	0	1	7	1	.88	10	.264	.314	.451
1997 Charlotte	AAA Fla	120	322	82	23	1	11	140	54	43	43	1	76	1	2	3	16	4	.80	5	.255	.341	.435
1998 Edmonton	AAA Oak	120	402	120	24	4	10	182	74	55	67	0	82	5	0	1	17	5	.77	13	.299	.404	.453
1999 Vancouver	AAA Oak	118	421	121	24	1	15	192	62	70	45	1	87	1	3	3	9	6	.60	15	.287	.355	.456
2000 Norfolk	AAA NYM	114	340	88	18	1	7	129	46	43	45	1	73	6	0	0	9	4	.69	10	.259	.355	.379
9 Min. YEARS		1046	3507	962	198	28	83	1465	557	483	444	16	726	21	13	25	157	46	.77	100	.274	.357	.418

Kevin Sheredy

Pitches: Right **Bats:** Right **Pos:** RP-50; SP-1   **Ht:** 6'4" **Wt:** 210 **Born:** 1/3/75 **Age:** 26

Year Team	Lg Org	G	GS	CG	GF	IP	BFP	H	R	ER	HR	SH	SF	HB	TBB	IBB	SO	WP	Bk	W	L	Pct.	ShO	Sv	ERA
1996 New Jersey	A- StL	8	5	0	0	23	100	21	15	11	2	2	1	1	13	0	13	1	0	0	1	.000	0	0	4.30
1998 Peoria	A StL	13	13	0	0	68	304	75	38	30	6	6	4	4	24	0	39	13	0	4	4	.500	0	0	3.97
1999 Potomac	A+ StL	41	12	0	12	104	462	100	58	46	6	3	6	6	53	1	69	13	0	5	5	.500	0	0	3.98
2000 Arkansas	AA StL	21	0	0	4	26.2	154	42	45	42	7	1	1	6	29	0	12	5	2	0	2	.000	0	0	14.18
Potomac	A+ StL	30	1	0	15	40.1	193	46	25	23	2	1	2	5	26	1	24	2	0	2	5	.286	0	4	5.13
4 Min. YEARS		113	31	0	31	262	1213	284	181	152	23	13	14	22	145	2	157	34	2	11	17	.393	0	4	5.22

Brian Sherlock

Bats: Right **Throws:** Right **Pos:** 3B-37; DH-19; 1B-12; 2B-9; OF-8; PH-5; PR-1; P-1   **Ht:** 5'10" **Wt:** 188 **Born:** 6/29/76 **Age:** 25

Year Team	Lg Org	G	AB	H	2B	3B	HR	TB	R	RBI	TBB	IBB	SO	HBP	SH	SF	SB	CS	SB%	GDP	Avg	OBP	SLG
1999 Medcine Hat	R+ Tor	73	265	77	16	0	6	111	43	50	46	0	49	3	2	2	17	5	.77	3	.291	.399	.419
2000 Cape Fear	A Mon	42	130	37	9	0	1	49	25	15	33	0	27	0	0	0	10	3	.77	2	.285	.429	.377
Harrisburg	AA Mon	44	129	31	5	0	1	39	14	8	15	1	28	2	0	0	0	2	.00	4	.240	.329	.302
2 Min. YEARS		159	524	145	30	0	8	199	82	73	94	1	104	5	2	2	27	10	.73	9	.277	.390	.380

Scot Shields

Pitches: Right **Bats:** Right **Pos:** SP-27   **Ht:** 6'1" **Wt:** 175 **Born:** 7/22/75 **Age:** 25

Year Team	Lg Org	G	GS	CG	GF	IP	BFP	H	R	ER	HR	SH	SF	HB	TBB	IBB	SO	WP	Bk	W	L	Pct.	ShO	Sv	ERA
1997 Boise	A- Ana	30	0	0	13	52	225	45	20	17	1	3	2	3	24	4	61	9	1	7	2	.778	0	2	2.94
1998 Cedar Rapds	A Ana	58	0	0	38	74	311	62	33	30	5	5	2	8	29	0	81	9	1	6	5	.545	0	7	3.65
1999 Lk Elsinore	A+ Ana	24	9	2	6	107.1	443	91	37	30	1	4	4	5	39	4	113	6	1	10	3	.769	1	1	2.52
Erie	AA Ana	10	10	1	0	74.2	300	57	26	24	10	4	0	6	26	0	81	2	0	4	4	.500	1	0	2.89
2000 Edmonton	AAA Ana	27	27	4	0	163	734	158	114	98	16	1	6	14	82	0	156	7	0	7	13	.350	1	0	5.41
4 Min. YEARS		149	46	7	57	471	2013	413	230	199	33	17	14	36	200	8	492	33	3	34	27	.557	3	10	3.80

Rick Short

Bats: Right **Throws:** Right **Pos:** DH-48; 3B-34; 2B-23; OF-17; 1B-16; PR-1   **Ht:** 6'0" **Wt:** 195 **Born:** 12/6/72 **Age:** 28

Year Team	Lg Org	G	AB	H	2B	3B	HR	TB	R	RBI	TBB	IBB	SO	HBP	SH	SF	SB	CS	SB%	GDP	Avg	OBP	SLG
1994 Bluefield	R+ Bal	64	229	69	8	0	4	89	39	35	22	1	23	2	0	2	4	6	.40	3	.301	.365	.389
1995 Frederick	A+ Bal	5	13	1	0	0	0	1	1	2	1	0	2	0	0	0	1	0	1.00	0	.077	.143	.077
Bluefield	R+ Bal	11	39	11	2	0	2	19	9	12	2	0	1	0	1	0	2	1	.67	2	.282	.326	.487
High Desert	A+ Bal	29	98	41	3	0	4	56	14	12	10	0	5	2	0	0	1	2	.33	2	.418	.482	.571

Year Team	Lg Org	BATTING															BASERUNNING				PERCENTAGES		
		G	AB	H	2B	3B	HR	TB	R	RBI	TBB	IBB	SO	HBP	SH	SF	SB	CS	SB%	GDP	Avg	OBP	SLG
1996 Frederick	A+ Bal	126	474	148	33	0	3	190	68	54	29	2	44	5	5	4	12	7	.63	14	.312	.355	.401
1997 Frederick	A+ Bal	126	480	153	29	1	10	214	73	72	38	2	44	12	7	1	10	7	.59	20	.319	.382	.446
1998 Frederick	A+ Bal	59	221	68	14	0	6	100	36	28	18	1	29	8	1	3	3	2	.60	12	.308	.376	.452
Bowie	AA Bal	34	87	20	4	0	2	30	12	18	13	0	18	0	1	4	0	0	—	2	.230	.317	.345
Rochester	AAA Bal	13	34	6	1	0	1	10	3	4	4	0	4	1	0	1	0	0	—	0	.176	.275	.294
1999 Bowie	AA Bal	112	392	123	19	0	16	190	60	62	43	2	48	9	0	5	6	0	1.00	9	.314	.390	.485
2000 Rochester	AAA Bal	13	37	9	1	0	1	13	3	3	4	0	4	2	0	0	0	0	—	0	.243	.349	.351
Bowie	AA Bal	116	447	148	39	1	9	216	63	82	44	2	54	8	0	8	3	3	.50	14	.331	.394	.483
7 Min. YEARS		708	2551	797	153	2	58	1128	381	384	228	10	276	50	14	29	42	28	.60	78	.312	.376	.442

Brian Shouse

Pitches: Left **Bats:** Left **Pos:** RP-47　　　　　　　　　　　　　　　　　　**Ht:** 5'11" **Wt:** 180 **Born:** 9/26/68 **Age:** 32

Year Team	Lg Org	HOW MUCH HE PITCHED						WHAT HE GAVE UP										THE RESULTS					
		G	GS	CG	GF	IP	BFP	H	R	ER	HR	SH	SF	HB	TBB	IBB	SO	WP	Bk	W	L	Pct.	ShO	Sv	ERA
1990 Welland	A- Pit	17	1	0	7	39.2	177	50	27	23	2	3	2	3	7	0	39	1	2	4	3	.571	0	2	5.22
1991 Augusta	A Pit	26	0	0	25	31	124	22	13	11	1	1	1	3	9	1	32	5	0	2	3	.400	0	3	3.19
Salem	A+ Pit	17	0	0	9	33.2	147	35	12	11	2	2	0	0	15	2	25	1	0	2	1	.667	0	3	2.94
1992 Carolina	AA Pit	59	0	0	33	77.1	323	71	31	21	3	8	2	2	28	4	79	4	1	5	6	.455	0	4	2.44
1993 Buffalo	AAA Pit	48	0	0	14	51.2	218	54	24	22	7	0	3	2	17	2	25	1	0	1	0	1.000	0	2	3.83
1994 Buffalo	AAA Pit	43	0	0	20	52	212	44	22	21	6	4	2	1	15	4	31	0	0	3	4	.429	0	3	3.63
1995 Calgary	AAA Pit	8	8	1	0	39.1	185	62	35	27	2	1	1	1	7	0	17	3	0	4	4	.500	0	0	6.18
Carolina	AA Pit	21	20	0	0	114.2	480	126	64	57	14	5	3	4	19	2	76	1	1	7	6	.538	0	0	4.47
1996 Calgary	AAA Pit	12	1	0	2	12.2	65	22	15	15	4	0	1	0	4	1	12	1	0	1	0	1.000	0	0	10.66
Rochester	AAA Bal	32	0	0	10	50	217	53	27	25	6	2	2	1	16	1	45	5	0	1	2	.333	0	2	4.50
1997 Rochester	AAA Bal	54	0	0	29	71.1	282	48	21	18	6	5	1	3	21	4	81	2	0	6	2	.750	0	9	2.27
1998 Pawtucket	AAA Bos	22	1	0	15	31	121	21	11	10	7	1	1	0	7	0	25	0	0	2	0	1.000	0	6	2.90
1999 Tucson	AAA Ari	30	0	0	8	44.2	213	63	35	31	4	6	2	1	18	3	32	2	0	3	4	.429	0	0	6.25
Rochester	AAA Bal	43	0	0	14	57.2	244	63	20	18	4	0	2	2	14	1	52	2	0	4	4	.500	0	2	2.81
1993 Pittsburgh	NL	6	0	0	1	4	22	7	4	4	1	0	1	0	2	0	3	1	0	0	0	—	0	0	9.00
1998 Boston	AL	7	0	0	4	8	36	9	5	5	2	0	0	0	4	0	5	0	0	0	1	.000	0	0	5.63
11 Min. YEARS		436	31	1	186	710	3024	740	362	315	70	38	23	23	199	25	572	28	4	45	40	.529	0	38	3.99
2 Maj. YEARS		13	0	0	5	12	58	16	9	9	3	0	1	0	6	0	8	1	0	0	1	.000	0	0	6.75

Allen Shrum

Bats: Right **Throws:** Right **Pos:** C-55; DH-11; PH-3; PR-1　　　　　　　　**Ht:** 6'3" **Wt:** 215 **Born:** 5/13/76 **Age:** 25

Year Team	Lg Org	BATTING															BASERUNNING				PERCENTAGES		
		G	AB	H	2B	3B	HR	TB	R	RBI	TBB	IBB	SO	HBP	SH	SF	SB	CS	SB%	GDP	Avg	OBP	SLG
1998 Twins	R Min	42	127	42	10	0	10	82	17	25	13	1	27	3	0	0	3	2	.60	2	.331	.406	.646
Fort Wayne	A Min	5	16	1	0	0	0	1	0	0	0	0	7	0	0	0	0	0	—	0	.063	.063	.063
1999 Quad City	A Min	68	191	45	12	0	1	60	14	22	16	0	52	3	1	2	0	0	—	8	.236	.302	.314
2000 Fort Myers	A+ Min	25	73	20	4	0	0	24	12	10	8	0	17	1	0	0	0	0	—	2	.274	.354	.329
New Britain	AA Min	41	127	28	5	0	2	39	13	20	9	0	32	0	0	1	0	0	—	8	.220	.270	.307
3 Min. YEARS		181	534	136	31	0	13	206	56	77	46	1	135	7	1	3	3	2	.60	20	.255	.320	.386

Anthony Shumaker

Pitches: Left **Bats:** Left **Pos:** SP-23; RP-9　　　　　　　　　　　　　　**Ht:** 6'5" **Wt:** 219 **Born:** 5/14/73 **Age:** 28

Year Team	Lg Org	HOW MUCH HE PITCHED						WHAT HE GAVE UP										THE RESULTS					
		G	GS	CG	GF	IP	BFP	H	R	ER	HR	SH	SF	HB	TBB	IBB	SO	WP	Bk	W	L	Pct.	ShO	Sv	ERA
1995 Martinsville	R+ Phi	6	4	0	0	28	120	31	16	14	1	2	0	1	8	0	26	3	0	1	3	.250	0	0	4.50
Batavia	A- Phi	9	4	1	0	39	157	38	10	7	0	0	0	0	4	0	31	2	0	2	2	.500	1	0	1.62
1996 Piedmont	A Phi	20	0	0	13	32.2	120	16	7	5	2	0	0	0	10	1	51	3	0	3	0	1.000	0	4	1.38
Clearwater	A+ Phi	31	0	0	13	29.1	137	42	18	18	1	3	0	0	12	5	25	1	0	5	3	.625	0	3	5.52
1997 Clearwater	A+ Phi	61	0	0	28	72	295	64	22	17	1	2	0	2	17	1	77	5	0	4	5	.556	0	9	2.13
1998 Reading	AA Phi	38	21	1	9	166.2	689	152	75	62	20	9	7	4	44	2	129	3	0	7	10	.412	1	2	3.35
1999 Reading	AA Phi	10	10	1	0	60.2	249	48	17	12	3	3	2	2	17	1	60	1	1	4	3	.571	0	0	1.78
Scranton-WB	AAA Phi	14	14	1	0	89.2	403	119	60	57	15	3	6	2	32	2	49	2	0	3	5	.375	0	0	5.72
2000 Scranton-WB	AAA Phi	1	1	0	0	4	20	6	4	4	0	0	2	0	3	0	1	0	0	0	1	.000	0	0	9.00
Norfolk	AAA NYM	21	17	1	1	101	451	121	58	56	12	6	5	6	35	2	55	5	1	4	5	.444	0	0	4.99
Rochester	AAA Bal	10	5	0	1	33	151	41	27	25	5	1	1	1	13	0	26	0	0	3	2	.600	0	0	6.82
1999 Philadelphia	NL	8	4	0	2	22.2	105	23	17	15	3	2	0	1	14	0	17	1	1	0	3	.000	0	0	5.96
6 Min. YEARS		221	76	5	65	656	2792	678	314	277	60	29	23	18	195	14	530	25	2	37	38	.493	2	18	3.80

Jacob Shumate

Pitches: Right **Bats:** Right **Pos:** RP-47　　　　　　　　　　　　　　　　**Ht:** 6'2" **Wt:** 190 **Born:** 1/22/76 **Age:** 25

Year Team	Lg Org	HOW MUCH HE PITCHED						WHAT HE GAVE UP										THE RESULTS					
		G	GS	CG	GF	IP	BFP	H	R	ER	HR	SH	SF	HB	TBB	IBB	SO	WP	Bk	W	L	Pct.	ShO	Sv	ERA
1994 Danville	R+ Atl	12	7	0	1	31.2	175	30	34	29	0	1	5	8	52	0	29	15	0	0	4	.000	0	0	8.24
1995 Macon	A Atl	17	14	0	0	56	296	38	56	45	7	1	3	9	87	0	57	19	2	0	8	.000	0	0	7.23
Danville	R+ Atl	7	2	0	2	13.1	80	6	21	16	1	0	2	2	32	0	16	14	0	1	2	.333	0	0	10.80
1996 Macon	A Atl	1	1	0	0	3	16	5	5	4	0	0	1	0	2	0	2	1	0	0	0	—	0	0	12.00
1997 Eugene	A- Atl	19	0	0	7	20.2	126	19	32	25	1	0	0	2	43	0	23	7	0	0	2	.000	0	0	10.89
1998 Macon	A Atl	44	0	0	10	50.2	280	44	54	38	2	3	3	13	75	0	65	39	1	5	4	.556	0	0	6.75
Greenville	AA Atl	2	0	0	0	2.1	13	3	4	4	0	0	0	0	4	0	1	1	0	1	0	1.000	0	0	15.43
1999 Myrtle Bch	A+ Atl	20	0	0	6	22.2	116	15	19	18	0	3	1	1	33	0	31	8	0	3	3	.500	0	0	7.15
Greenville	AA Atl	14	12	0	1	57	270	43	30	30	6	1	3	5	61	1	48	9	1	4	3	.429	0	4	4.74
2000 Greenville	AA Atl	47	0	0	39	45.2	208	32	23	21	3	1	0	2	41	0	41	10	0	2	1	.667	0	18	4.14
7 Min. YEARS		183	36	0	66	303	1580	235	278	230	23	9	18	42	430	1	313	123	4	14	29	.326	0	18	6.83

264

Joe Siddall

Bats: Left **Throws:** Right **Pos:** C-21; PH-3   **Ht:** 6'1" **Wt:** 200 **Born:** 10/25/67 **Age:** 33

Year Team	Lg Org	G	AB	H	2B	3B	HR	TB	R	RBI	TBB	IBB	SO	HBP	SH	SF	SB	CS	SB%	GDP	Avg	OBP	SLG
1988 Jamestown	A- Mon	53	178	38	5	3	1	52	18	16	14	1	29	1	4	2	5	4	.56	3	.213	.272	.292
1989 Rockford	A Mon	98	313	74	15	2	4	105	36	38	26	2	56	6	5	4	8	5	.62	3	.236	.304	.335
1990 Wst Plm Bch	A+ Mon	106	348	78	12	1	0	92	29	32	20	0	55	1	10	2	6	7	.46	7	.224	.267	.264
1991 Harrisburg	AA Mon	76	235	54	6	1	1	65	28	23	23	2	53	1	2	3	8	3	.73	7	.230	.298	.277
1992 Harrisburg	AA Mon	95	288	68	12	0	2	86	26	27	29	1	55	3	1	3	4	4	.50	7	.236	.310	.299
1993 Ottawa	AAA Mon	48	136	29	6	0	1	38	14	16	19	5	33	0	3	2	2	2	.50	6	.213	.306	.279
1994 Ottawa	AAA Mon	38	110	19	2	1	3	32	9	13	10	2	21	2	7	2	1	1	.50	3	.173	.250	.291
1995 Ottawa	AAA Mon	83	248	53	14	2	1	74	26	23	23	0	42	4	2	0	3	3	.50	6	.214	.291	.298
1996 Charlotte	AAA Fla	65	189	53	13	1	3	77	22	20	11	1	36	3	2	0	1	2	.33	2	.280	.330	.407
1997 Ottawa	AAA Mon	57	164	45	12	1	1	62	18	16	21	3	42	1	0	0	1	2	.33	2	.274	.360	.378
1998 Toledo	AAA Det	43	129	31	5	0	4	48	16	16	11	0	42	2	2	0	2	1	.67	2	.240	.310	.372
1999 Toledo	AAA Det	84	244	47	15	0	8	86	29	33	34	0	74	2	4	1	4	1	.80	6	.193	.295	.352
2000 Pawtucket	AAA Bos	23	77	18	4	0	3	31	7	14	8	0	16	0	0	0	0	0	—	3	.234	.302	.403
1993 Montreal	NL	19	20	2	1	0	0	3	0	1	1	1	5	0	0	0	0	0	—	0	.100	.143	.150
1995 Montreal	NL	7	10	3	0	0	0	3	4	1	3	0	3	1	0	0	0	0	—	0	.300	.500	.300
1996 Florida	NL	18	47	7	1	0	0	8	0	3	2	0	8	0	0	0	0	0	—	1	.149	.184	.170
1998 Detroit	AL	29	65	12	3	0	1	18	3	6	7	0	25	0	2	0	0	0	—	0	.185	.264	.277
13 Min. YEARS		869	2659	607	121	12	32	848	278	287	249	17	554	26	42	20	45	35	.56	57	.228	.299	.319
4 Maj. YEARS		73	142	24	5	0	1	32	7	11	13	1	41	1	2	0	0	0	—	1	.169	.244	.225

Wilson Sido

Pitches: Right **Bats:** Right **Pos:** SP-20; RP-11   **Ht:** 6'2" **Wt:** 178 **Born:** 6/18/76 **Age:** 25

Year Team	Lg Org	G	GS	CG	GF	IP	BFP	H	R	ER	HR	SH	SF	HB	TBB	IBB	SO	WP	Bk	W	L	Pct.	ShO	Sv	ERA
1998 Columbus	A Cle	4	4	0	0	24.2	101	17	7	7	1	0	0	3	8	1	27	0	1	2	0	1.000	0	0	2.55
1999 Kinston	A+ Cle	9	7	0	0	36.1	163	33	26	24	4	1	1	5	22	1	22	6	0	1	2	.333	0	0	5.94
Columbus	A Cle	13	12	0	0	49	232	63	43	40	5	2	2	3	23	0	51	4	3	3	7	.300	0	0	7.35
2000 Akron	AA Cle	1	1	1	0	7	25	4	2	1	0	0	0	2	0	0	6	0	0	1	0	1.000	0	0	1.29
Buffalo	AAA Cle	1	0	0	1	2	9	2	1	1	0	0	0	0	2	0	0	0	0	0	0	—	0	0	4.50
Kinston	A+ Cle	29	19	1	3	126.1	550	131	58	52	9	8	1	7	51	2	105	4	0	11	6	.647	1	0	3.70
3 Min. YEARS		57	43	2	4	245.1	1080	250	137	125	20	11	4	20	106	4	211	14	4	18	15	.545	1	0	4.59

Jerry Simmons

Bats: Right **Throws:** Right **Pos:** OF-71; DH-12; PR-11; PH-2   **Ht:** 6'0" **Wt:** 195 **Born:** 6/4/76 **Age:** 25

Year Team	Lg Org	G	AB	H	2B	3B	HR	TB	R	RBI	TBB	IBB	SO	HBP	SH	SF	SB	CS	SB%	GDP	Avg	OBP	SLG
1998 Eugene	A- Atl	73	284	78	14	3	11	131	48	40	25	3	65	11	0	2	26	11	.70	5	.275	.354	.461
1999 Jamestown	A- Atl	62	232	50	9	5	4	81	37	27	20	0	46	5	0	0	19	6	.76	3	.216	.292	.349
2000 Myrtle Bch	A+ Atl	12	34	6	1	0	0	7	3	1	2	0	8	0	0	0	0	1	.00	0	.176	.222	.206
Greenville	AA Atl	3	9	4	1	0	0	5	0	1	1	0	2	0	0	0	1	1	.50	0	.444	.500	.556
Macon	A Atl	77	252	75	15	4	8	122	31	41	20	1	42	3	0	0	16	9	.64	7	.298	.356	.484
3 Min. YEARS		227	811	213	40	12	23	346	119	110	68	4	163	19	0	2	62	28	.69	14	.263	.333	.427

Ben Simon

Pitches: Right **Bats:** Right **Pos:** SP-20; RP-13   **Ht:** 6'1" **Wt:** 185 **Born:** 11/12/74 **Age:** 26

Year Team	Lg Org	G	GS	CG	GF	IP	BFP	H	R	ER	HR	SH	SF	HB	TBB	IBB	SO	WP	Bk	W	L	Pct.	ShO	Sv	ERA
1996 Yakima	A- LA	15	10	0	1	66.1	275	59	34	27	5	3	5	3	21	2	62	0	1	2	6	.250	0	1	3.66
1997 Savannah	A LA	18	17	2	1	93.1	398	84	35	32	2	6	4	7	27	0	93	3	0	7	5	.583	1	0	3.09
1998 Vero Beach	A+ LA	7	5	0	1	18.2	81	22	14	14	1	0	0	0	7	0	16	2	0	1	2	.333	0	0	6.75
1999 Vero Beach	A+ LA	38	5	0	12	88.2	382	79	44	34	5	4	2	10	29	2	89	7	1	7	4	.636	0	2	3.45
2000 Vero Beach	A+ LA	4	4	0	0	23.2	97	23	12	10	4	1	1	3	5	0	16	0	1	1	0	1.000	0	0	3.80
San Antonio	AA LA	29	16	0	5	108.1	460	102	58	54	15	5	2	8	44	2	91	4	1	8	8	.500	0	2	4.49
5 Min. YEARS		111	57	2	20	399	1693	369	197	171	32	19	14	31	133	6	367	16	4	26	25	.510	1	5	3.86

Randall Simon

Bats: Left **Throws:** Left **Pos:** 1B-88; DH-19; PH-8; OF-3   **Ht:** 6'0" **Wt:** 180 **Born:** 5/26/75 **Age:** 26

Year Team	Lg Org	G	AB	H	2B	3B	HR	TB	R	RBI	TBB	IBB	SO	HBP	SH	SF	SB	CS	SB%	GDP	Avg	OBP	SLG
1993 Danville	R+ Atl	61	232	59	17	1	3	87	28	31	10	2	34	2	0	1	1	1	.50	4	.254	.289	.375
1994 Macon	A Atl	106	358	105	23	1	10	160	45	54	6	2	56	1	1	2	7	6	.54	7	.293	.305	.447
1995 Durham	A+ Atl	122	420	111	18	1	18	185	56	79	36	14	63	5	0	5	6	5	.55	15	.264	.326	.440
1996 Greenville	AA Atl	134	498	139	26	2	18	223	74	77	37	7	61	4	0	4	4	9	.31	13	.279	.331	.448
1997 Richmond	AAA Atl	133	519	160	45	1	14	249	62	102	17	2	76	4	1	1	1	6	.14	18	.308	.335	.480
1998 Richmond	AAA Atl	126	484	124	20	1	13	185	52	70	24	3	62	2	0	4	4	4	.50	22	.256	.292	.382
1999 Richmond	AAA Atl	15	59	16	4	0	1	23	7	8	3	2	10	0	0	1	0	1	.00	0	.271	.302	.390
2000 Calgary	AAA Fla	22	68	20	3	0	1	26	5	11	0	0	3	0	0	0	0	0	—	1	.294	.290	.382
Columbus	AAA NYY	94	364	97	20	4	17	176	52	74	35	5	42	0	0	7	6	5	.55	17	.266	.325	.484
1997 Atlanta	NL	13	14	6	1	0	0	7	2	1	1	0	2	0	0	0	0	0	—	0	.429	.467	.500
1998 Atlanta	NL	7	16	3	0	0	0	3	2	4	0	0	1	0	0	1	0	0	—	0	.188	.176	.188
1999 Atlanta	NL	90	218	69	16	0	5	100	26	25	17	6	25	1	0	1	2	2	.50	10	.317	.367	.459
8 Min. YEARS		813	3002	831	176	11	95	1314	381	506	168	37	407	18	2	27	29	37	.44	97	.277	.316	.438
3 Maj. YEARS		110	248	78	17	0	5	110	30	30	18	6	28	1	0	2	2	2	.50	11	.315	.361	.444

Mitch Simons

Bats: Right **Throws:** Right **Pos:** 2B-74; 3B-20; OF-10; PH-7; DH-6; PR-1 **Ht:** 5'9" **Wt:** 172 **Born:** 12/13/68 **Age:** 32

		BATTING															BASERUNNING				PERCENTAGES		
Year Team	Lg Org	G	AB	H	2B	3B	HR	TB	R	RBI	TBB	IBB	SO	HBP	SH	SF	SB	CS	SB%	GDP	Avg	OBP	SLG
1991 Jamestown	A- Mon	41	153	47	12	0	1	62	38	16	39	1	20	0	2	2	23	5	.82	1	.307	.443	.405
Wst Plm Bch	A+ Mon	15	50	9	2	1	0	13	3	4	5	0	8	0	0	0	1	0	1.00	0	.180	.255	.260
1992 Albany	A Mon	130	481	136	26	5	1	175	57	61	60	0	47	7	2	10	34	12	.74	6	.283	.364	.364
1993 Wst Plm Bch	A+ Mon	45	156	40	4	1	1	49	24	13	19	0	9	3	1	2	14	8	.64	3	.256	.344	.314
Harrisburg	AA Mon	29	77	18	1	0	1	21	5	5	7	0	14	0	2	1	2	0	1.00	1	.234	.294	.273
1994 Nashville	AA Min	102	391	124	26	0	3	159	46	48	39	0	38	6	3	5	30	9	.77	6	.317	.383	.407
1995 Salt Lake	AAA Min	130	480	156	34	4	3	207	87	46	47	2	45	10	4	2	32	16	.67	9	.325	.395	.431
1996 Salt Lake	AAA Min	129	512	135	27	8	5	193	76	59	43	3	59	8	3	4	35	11	.76	7	.264	.328	.377
1997 Salt Lake	AAA Min	115	462	138	34	10	5	207	87	59	47	4	48	5	9	5	26	5	.84	7	.299	.366	.448
1998 Rochester	AAA Bal	59	190	41	8	2	1	56	21	16	20	0	16	1	1	1	7	2	.78	4	.216	.292	.295
Tacoma	AAA Sea	47	180	42	6	2	2	58	27	21	15	0	23	4	2	1	10	1	.91	5	.233	.305	.322
1999 Charlotte	AAA CWS	119	474	137	32	1	7	192	85	52	45	0	67	11	6	2	22	6	.79	10	.289	.363	.405
2000 Norfolk	AAA NYM	113	409	109	22	4	0	139	52	48	37	1	55	4	7	2	16	13	.55	11	.267	.332	.340
10 Min. YEARS		1074	4015	1132	234	39	29	1531	608	448	423	11	449	59	42	37	252	88	.74	70	.282	.356	.381

Steve Sinclair

Pitches: Left **Bats:** Left **Pos:** RP-45 **Ht:** 6'2" **Wt:** 190 **Born:** 8/2/71 **Age:** 29

		HOW MUCH HE PITCHED						WHAT HE GAVE UP												THE RESULTS					
Year Team	Lg Org	G	GS	CG	GF	IP	BFP	H	R	ER	HR	SH	SF	HB	TBB	IBB	SO	WP	Bk	W	L	Pct.	ShO	Sv	ERA
1991 Medcine Hat	R+ Tor	12	0	0	8	14.2	76	17	15	11	1	1	0	3	11	0	14	0	0	0	1	.000	0	0	6.75
1992 Blue Jays	R Tor	5	4	0	0	23	92	23	10	7	2	0	0	0	5	0	18	1	0	1	2	.333	0	0	2.74
Medcine Hat	R+ Tor	9	7	0	1	43	189	54	25	22	2	2	3	1	12	0	28	3	0	2	3	.400	0	0	4.60
1993 Medcine Hat	R+ Tor	15	12	0	0	78.1	335	87	41	29	5	2	2	1	16	0	45	5	1	5	2	.714	0	0	3.33
1994 Hagerstown	A Tor	38	1	0	16	105	458	127	53	44	9	4	5	2	25	0	75	3	0	9	2	.818	0	3	3.77
1995 Dunedin	A+ Tor	46	0	0	18	73	297	69	26	21	4	1	1	3	17	1	52	2	3	5	3	.625	0	2	2.59
1996 Dunedin	A+ Tor	3	0	0	1	2.2	12	4	2	1	1	0	0	0	0	0	1	0	0	0	1	.000	0	0	3.38
1997 Dunedin	A+ Tor	43	0	0	20	68.1	296	63	36	22	4	4	1	2	26	3	66	4	1	2	5	.286	0	3	2.90
Syracuse	AAA Tor	6	0	0	1	9	40	11	6	6	0	0	0	0	3	0	9	0	0	0	0	—	0	0	6.00
1998 Syracuse	AAA Tor	43	1	0	16	49.2	204	37	15	12	2	1	2	1	23	2	45	0	0	3	1	.750	0	3	2.17
1999 Syracuse	AAA Tor	34	0	0	30	39.1	156	24	11	9	3	0	0	4	12	1	31	1	0	2	2	.500	0	18	2.06
Tacoma	AAA Sea	2	0	0	0	2	9	2	1	1	0	0	0	0	1	0	1	1	0	1	0	1.000	0	0	4.50
2000 Tacoma	AAA Sea	45	0	0	8	58	265	68	36	29	8	3	2	1	27	5	45	3	1	4	3	.571	0	4	4.50
1998 Toronto	AL	24	0	0	3	15	61	13	7	6	0	0	0	0	5	0	8	0	0	0	2	.000	0	0	3.60
1999 Toronto	AL	3	0	0	1	5.2	28	7	8	8	4	0	0	1	4	0	3	0	0	0	0	—	0	0	12.71
Seattle	AL	18	0	0	5	13.2	67	15	8	6	1	0	0	1	10	2	15	0	0	0	1	.000	0	0	3.95
10 Min. YEARS		301	25	0	119	566	2429	586	277	214	39	18	16	18	178	12	430	23	6	34	25	.576	0	32	3.40
2 Maj. YEARS		45	0	0	9	34.1	156	35	23	20	5	0	0	2	19	2	26	0	0	0	3	.000	0	0	5.24

Shaun Skrehot

Bats: Right **Throws:** Right **Pos:** SS-27; 2B-23; 3B-23; OF-22; PH-7; PR-5; DH-2 **Ht:** 5'9" **Wt:** 172 **Born:** 12/5/75 **Age:** 25

		BATTING															BASERUNNING				PERCENTAGES		
Year Team	Lg Org	G	AB	H	2B	3B	HR	TB	R	RBI	TBB	IBB	SO	HBP	SH	SF	SB	CS	SB%	GDP	Avg	OBP	SLG
1998 Erie	A- Pit	63	269	67	10	0	2	83	33	18	7	0	43	4	1	3	10	1	.91	3	.249	.276	.309
1999 Hickory	A Pit	115	461	108	17	5	1	138	53	37	16	0	72	5	7	4	12	8	.60	8	.234	.265	.299
2000 Lynchburg	A+ Pit	42	129	30	3	2	0	37	9	7	9	0	22	1	4	2	5	3	.63	2	.233	.284	.287
Altoona	AA Pit	57	158	36	4	1	0	42	14	9	16	0	32	3	1	0	7	2	.78	4	.228	.311	.266
3 Min. YEARS		277	1017	241	34	8	3	300	109	71	48	0	169	13	13	9	34	14	.71	17	.237	.278	.295

Aaron Sledd

Bats: Left **Throws:** Left **Pos:** OF-64; 1B-10; DH-10 **Ht:** 5'11" **Wt:** 200 **Born:** 12/27/75 **Age:** 25

		BATTING															BASERUNNING				PERCENTAGES		
Year Team	Lg Org	G	AB	H	2B	3B	HR	TB	R	RBI	TBB	IBB	SO	HBP	SH	SF	SB	CS	SB%	GDP	Avg	OBP	SLG
1998 Tupelo	IND —	6	17	2	1	0	0	3	2	2	1	0	5	0	0	0	0	0	—	0	.118	.167	.176
1999 Richmond	IND —	74	261	79	24	2	8	131	66	44	42	1	68	3	1	0	2	1	.67	2	.303	.405	.502
2000 Richmond	IND —	78	271	83	17	2	13	143	54	58	60	1	72	9	1	4	5	2	.71	5	.306	.442	.528
Louisville	AAA Cin	3	14	3	1	0	0	4	1	2	2	1	4	1	0	0	0	0	—	1	.214	.353	.286
3 Min. YEARS		161	563	167	43	4	21	281	123	106	105	3	149	13	2	4	7	3	.70	8	.297	.416	.499

Aaron Small

Pitches: Right **Bats:** Right **Pos:** SP-18; RP-18 **Ht:** 6'5" **Wt:** 235 **Born:** 11/23/71 **Age:** 29

		HOW MUCH HE PITCHED						WHAT HE GAVE UP												THE RESULTS					
Year Team	Lg Org	G	GS	CG	GF	IP	BFP	H	R	ER	HR	SH	SF	HB	TBB	IBB	SO	WP	Bk	W	L	Pct.	ShO	Sv	ERA
1989 Medcine Hat	R+ Tor	15	14	0	0	70.2	326	80	55	46	2	3	2	3	31	1	40	9	5	1	7	.125	0	0	5.86
1990 Myrtle Bch	A Tor	27	27	1	0	147.2	643	150	72	46	6	2	7	4	56	2	96	16	5	9	9	.500	0	0	2.80
1991 Dunedin	A+ Tor	24	23	1	0	148.1	595	129	51	45	5	5	5	5	42	1	92	7	0	8	7	.533	0	0	2.73
1992 Knoxville	AA Tor	27	24	2	0	135	610	152	94	79	13	2	4	6	61	0	79	14	0	5	12	.294	1	0	5.27
1993 Knoxville	AA Tor	48	9	0	32	93	408	99	44	35	5	3	0	2	40	4	44	8	0	4	4	.500	0	16	3.39
1994 Syracuse	AAA Tor	13	0	0	0	24.1	99	19	8	6	2	2	0	1	9	2	15	2	0	3	2	.600	0	0	2.22
Knoxville	AA Tor	29	11	1	13	96.1	405	92	37	32	4	3	5	3	38	0	75	5	1	5	5	.500	1	5	2.99
1995 Syracuse	AAA Tor	1	0	0	0	1.2	9	3	1	1	1	0	0	0	1	0	2	0	0	0	0	—	0	0	5.40
Charlotte	AAA Fla	33	0	0	17	40.2	170	36	15	13	2	0	1	2	10	1	31	0	0	2	1	.667	0	10	2.88
1996 Edmonton	AAA Oak	25	19	1	4	119.2	492	111	65	57	9	2	2	5	28	0	83	9	0	8	6	.571	1	1	4.29
1997 Edmonton	AAA Oak	1	1	0	0	5	16	7	1	0	0	0	0	0	0	0	4	0	0	1	0	1.000	0	0	0.00
1999 Louisville	AAA Mil	11	0	0	3	21	111	38	23	22	3	1	0	0	15	1	11	0	0	1	0	.500	0	0	9.43
Durham	AAA TB	21	18	0	0	99.1	444	118	81	70	16	1	8	3	32	2	52	4	0	4	6	.400	0	0	6.34
2000 Colo Sprngs	AAA Col	36	18	0	2	131.2	596	152	92	82	14	1	6	13	43	0	85	3	0	11	6	.647	0	0	5.61

Year Team	Lg Org	G	GS	CG	GF	IP	BFP	H	R	ER	HR	SH	SF	HB	TBB	IBB	SO	WP	Bk	W	L	Pct.	ShO	Sv	ERA
1994 Toronto	AL	1	0	0	1	2	13	5	2	2	1	0	1	0	2	0	0	0	0	0	0	—	0	0	9.00
1995 Florida	NL	7	0	0	1	6.1	32	7	2	1	1	0	0	0	6	0	5	0	0	1	0	1.000	0	0	1.42
1996 Oakland	AL	12	3	0	4	28.2	144	37	28	26	3	0	1	1	22	1	17	2	0	1	3	.250	0	0	8.16
1997 Oakland	AL	71	0	0	22	96.2	425	109	50	46	6	5	6	3	40	6	57	4	0	9	5	.643	0	4	4.28
1998 Oakland	AL	24	0	0	4	36	174	51	34	29	3	3	1	3	14	3	19	4	0	1	1	.500	0	0	7.25
Arizona	NL	23	0	0	9	31.2	130	32	14	13	5	2	0	1	8	1	14	0	0	3	1	.750	0	0	3.69
11 Min. YEARS		311	164	6	77	1134.1	4924	1180	633	534	82	25	40	47	406	14	709	84	11	62	66	.484	3	32	4.24
5 Maj. YEARS		138	3	0	41	201.1	918	241	130	117	19	10	9	8	92	11	112	10	0	15	10	.600	0	4	5.23

Mark Small

Pitches: Right **Bats:** Right **Pos:** RP-12   **Ht:** 6'3" **Wt:** 205 **Born:** 11/12/67 **Age:** 33

Year Team	Lg Org	G	GS	CG	GF	IP	BFP	H	R	ER	HR	SH	SF	HB	TBB	IBB	SO	WP	Bk	W	L	Pct.	ShO	Sv	ERA
1989 Auburn	A- Hou	10	3	0	4	19.2	87	17	13	11	3	0	1	0	11	0	23	3	0	0	1	.000	0	2	5.03
1990 Asheville	A Hou	34	0	0	16	52	252	54	36	24	2	4	3	4	37	5	34	9	0	3	4	.429	0	6	4.15
1991 Osceola	A+ Hou	26	0	0	10	44.2	172	30	10	8	2	1	0	1	19	1	44	2	0	3	0	1.000	0	1	1.61
1992 Osceola	A+ Hou	22	20	1	2	105	435	97	56	45	8	3	3	0	38	0	69	5	1	5	9	.357	0	0	3.86
1993 Jackson	AA Hou	51	0	0	18	84.2	361	71	34	30	8	8	3	3	41	6	64	8	2	7	2	.778	0	4	3.19
1994 Jackson	AA Hou	16	0	0	9	21	97	22	16	9	1	1	2	1	10	2	14	4	0	3	1	.750	0	3	3.86
Tucson	AAA Hou	41	0	0	12	70	321	88	48	41	9	3	3	2	34	2	30	13	0	8	5	.615	0	4	5.27
1995 Tucson	AAA Hou	51	0	0	40	66	285	74	32	30	5	1	2	1	19	2	51	8	0	3	3	.500	0	19	4.09
1996 Tucson	AAA Hou	32	0	0	20	39	166	32	17	9	3	3	0	0	18	4	36	4	1	3	3	.500	0	7	2.08
1997 New Orleans	AAA Hou	7	0	0	4	9.1	43	11	9	6	1	0	1	0	3	1	7	1	0	1	1	.500	0	0	5.79
Jackson	AA Hou	37	0	0	25	43	196	46	20	15	1	4	1	1	19	2	40	0	1	3	4	.429	0	9	3.14
1998 Oklahoma	AAA Tex	15	6	0	4	47	206	53	30	24	4	1	3	4	13	1	42	8	0	4	4	.500	0	0	4.60
1999 Ottawa	AAA Mon	42	0	0	10	66.2	309	85	50	41	9	4	0	1	32	0	43	6	0	4	5	.444	0	2	5.54
2000 Ottawa	AAA Mon	12	0	0	3	21	94	24	16	14	2	0	1	0	10	0	21	0	0	0	2	.000	0	1	6.00
1996 Houston	NL	16	0	0	4	24.1	122	33	23	16	1	1	0	1	13	3	16	1	1	0	1	.000	0	0	5.92
12 Min. YEARS		396	29	1	178	689	3024	704	387	307	58	33	23	19	304	26	518	71	5	47	44	.516	0	55	4.01

J.D. Smart

Pitches: Right **Bats:** Right **Pos:** RP-4   **Ht:** 6'2" **Wt:** 180 **Born:** 11/12/73 **Age:** 27

Year Team	Lg Org	G	GS	CG	GF	IP	BFP	H	R	ER	HR	SH	SF	HB	TBB	IBB	SO	WP	Bk	W	L	Pct.	ShO	Sv	ERA
1995 Expos	R Mon	2	2	0	0	10.2	43	10	2	2	0	0	1	2	1	0	6	0	0	2	0	1.000	0	0	1.69
Vermont	A- Mon	5	5	0	0	27.2	118	29	9	7	1	1	3	3	7	0	21	0	0	0	1	.000	0	0	2.28
1996 Delmarva	A Mon	25	25	3	0	156.2	655	155	75	59	14	2	7	10	31	0	109	8	0	9	8	.529	2	0	3.39
1997 Wst Plm Bch	A+ Mon	17	13	1	1	102	422	105	45	37	10	2	3	2	21	0	65	3	0	5	4	.556	0	1	3.26
Harrisburg	AA Mon	12	12	0	0	70.2	308	75	34	29	7	6	3	3	24	0	43	3	0	6	3	.667	0	0	3.69
1998 Cape Fear	A Mon	3	1	0	0	11	39	7	3	3	1	0	0	0	0	0	12	1	0	3	0	1.000	0	0	2.45
Harrisburg	AA Mon	14	11	2	2	77	311	67	23	21	2	3	1	3	18	0	47	3	1	3	5	.375	0	1	2.45
Ottawa	AAA Mon	6	6	0	0	35	149	34	22	19	3	2	2	2	11	0	16	0	0	2	3	.400	0	0	4.89
1999 Ottawa	AAA Mon	6	4	0	0	20.2	90	22	7	6	2	0	0	1	6	0	9	1	1	0	1	.000	0	0	2.61
2000 Ottawa	AAA Mon	4	0	0	2	6.2	34	15	8	8	2	0	0	2	2	0	3	0	0	0	1	.000	0	1	10.80
1999 Montreal	NL	29	0	0	6	52	223	56	30	29	4	2	1	0	17	0	21	0	0	0	1	.000	0	0	5.02
6 Min. YEARS		94	79	6	5	518	2169	519	228	191	42	16	20	26	120	0	331	19	2	30	26	.536	2	3	3.32

Bud Smith

Pitches: Left **Bats:** Left **Pos:** SP-26; RP-1   **Ht:** 6'0" **Wt:** 170 **Born:** 10/23/79 **Age:** 21

Year Team	Lg Org	G	GS	CG	GF	IP	BFP	H	R	ER	HR	SH	SF	HB	TBB	IBB	SO	WP	Bk	W	L	Pct.	ShO	Sv	ERA
1998 Johnson Cty	R+ StL	14	14	0	0	64.1	305	85	47	37	9	2	3	2	34	1	65	2	0	3	3	.500	0	0	5.18
1999 Peoria	A StL	9	9	0	0	54	219	53	20	17	4	1	3	2	16	0	59	2	1	4	1	.800	0	0	2.83
Potomac	A+ StL	18	18	0	0	103.1	433	91	47	34	2	3	2	9	32	0	93	4	0	4	9	.308	0	0	2.96
2000 Arkansas	AA StL	18	18	3	0	108.2	439	93	32	28	5	2	3	4	27	1	102	5	0	12	1	.923	3	0	2.32
Memphis	AAA StL	9	8	0	0	54.1	213	40	24	13	4	2	1	1	15	0	34	0	0	5	1	.833	0	0	2.15
3 Min. YEARS		68	67	3	0	384.2	1609	362	170	129	24	10	12	18	124	2	353	13	1	28	15	.651	3	0	3.02

Cam Smith

Pitches: Right **Bats:** Right **Pos:** RP-45; SP-1   **Ht:** 6'3" **Wt:** 190 **Born:** 9/20/73 **Age:** 27

Year Team	Lg Org	G	GS	CG	GF	IP	BFP	H	R	ER	HR	SH	SF	HB	TBB	IBB	SO	WP	Bk	W	L	Pct.	ShO	Sv	ERA
1993 Bristol	R+ Det	9	7	1	0	37.2	162	25	22	15	5	0	0	6	22	0	33	2	3	3	1	.750	0	0	3.58
Niagara Fal	A- Det	2	2	0	0	5	31	12	11	10	0	0	2	0	6	0	6	0	0	0	0	—	0	0	18.00
1994 Fayetteville	A Det	26	26	1	0	133.2	619	133	100	90	10	6	5	18	86	0	128	17	1	5	13	.278	0	0	6.06
1995 Fayetteville	A Det	29	29	2	0	149	652	110	75	63	6	3	3	18	87	0	166	21	1	13	8	.619	2	0	3.81
1996 Lakeland	A+ Det	22	21	0	1	113.2	500	93	64	58	10	1	5	7	71	0	114	8	0	5	8	.385	0	0	4.59
1997 Mobile	AA SD	26	15	0	4	79.1	390	85	70	62	5	1	1	3	73	0	88	14	0	3	5	.375	0	1	7.03
1998 Lancaster	A+ Sea	8	0	0	3	18	81	11	7	5	1	0	0	3	13	0	32	4	0	1	1	.500	0	2	2.50
Orlando	AA Sea	23	1	0	8	39	186	32	27	20	6	3	3	6	32	0	49	9	0	1	3	.250	0	0	4.62
1999 New Haven	AA Sea	41	0	0	10	55	267	42	39	31	3	1	5	9	61	0	59	20	0	1	4	.200	0	0	5.07
2000 San Antonio	AA LA	7	1	0	3	15.1	74	13	13	13	0	0	2	2	15	0	16	3	0	0	0	—	0	1	7.63
Albuquerque	AAA LA	39	0	0	12	61	297	61	43	29	3	5	6	12	48	0	56	5	0	7	3	.700	0	3	4.28
8 Min. YEARS		232	102	4	41	706.2	3259	617	471	396	49	20	32	84	514	0	741	105	5	39	46	.459	2	7	5.04

Casey Smith

Bats: Right **Throws:** Right **Pos:** C-73; DH-2 **Ht:** 6'3" **Wt:** 200 **Born:** 5/7/77 **Age:** 24

		BATTING																BASERUNNING				PERCENTAGES		
Year Team	Lg Org	G	AB	H	2B	3B	HR	TB	R	RBI	TBB	IBB	SO	HBP	SH	SF	SB	CS	SB%	GDP	Avg	OBP	SLG
1997 Burlington	R+ Cle	19	77	27	2	0	2	35	8	9	3	0	22	2	0	1	1	0	1.00	0	.351	.386	.455
Columbus	A Cle	13	36	12	0	0	1	15	6	3	8	0	15	1	0	0	0	0	—	0	.333	.467	.417
1998 Watertown	A- Cle	67	226	42	6	1	3	59	22	23	15	0	65	4	0	3	4	0	1.00	5	.186	.246	.261
1999 Columbus	A Cle	47	153	36	6	0	1	45	21	13	28	0	48	7	1	1	0	2	.00	1	.235	.376	.294
Kinston	A+ Cle	39	129	21	6	0	2	33	15	15	14	0	48	3	0	0	1	0	.00	2	.163	.260	.256
2000 Kinston	A+ Cle	69	230	52	14	0	3	75	27	21	28	0	60	5	2	1	3	0	1.00	10	.226	.322	.326
Akron	AA Cle	6	23	4	2	1	0	8	3	4	1	0	3	0	1	0	0	0	—	0	.174	.208	.348
4 Min. YEARS		260	874	194	36	2	12	270	102	88	97	0	261	22	4	6	8	3	.73	18	.222	.313	.309

Danny Smith

Pitches: Left **Bats:** Left **Pos:** RP-54; SP-1 **Ht:** 6'5" **Wt:** 205 **Born:** 4/20/69 **Age:** 32

		HOW MUCH HE PITCHED						WHAT HE GAVE UP												THE RESULTS					
Year Team	Lg Org	G	GS	CG	GF	IP	BFP	H	R	ER	HR	SH	SF	HB	TBB	IBB	SO	WP	Bk	W	L	Pct.	ShO	Sv	ERA
1990 Butte	R+ Tex	5	5	0	0	24.2	102	23	10	10	3	2	0	2	6	0	27	3	1	2	0	1.000	0	0	3.65
Tulsa	AA Tex	7	7	0	0	38.1	151	27	16	16	2	0	3	0	16	0	32	0	0	3	2	.600	0	0	3.76
1991 Okla City	AAA Tex	28	27	3	1	151.2	713	195	114	93	10	6	8	4	75	1	85	5	5	4	17	.190	0	0	5.52
1992 Tulsa	AA Tex	24	23	4	0	146.1	571	110	48	41	4	9	3	6	34	0	122	3	3	11	7	.611	3	0	2.52
1993 Charlotte	A+ Tex	1	1	0	0	7	24	3	0	0	0	0	0	0	0	0	5	1	0	1	0	1.000	0	0	0.00
Okla City	AAA Tex	3	3	0	0	15.1	66	16	11	8	2	1	1	1	5	0	12	0	0	1	2	.333	0	0	4.70
1994 Charlotte	A+ Tex	2	0	0	0	3.2	13	2	0	0	0	0	1	1	0	2	3	0	0	0	0	—	0	0	0.00
Okla City	AAA Tex	10	2	0	3	25.1	110	27	9	8	2	0	2	2	9	0	15	0	0	2	1	.667	0	2	2.84
1996 Okla City	AAA Tex	5	5	0	0	15	78	27	19	15	4	0	1	1	7	0	12	1	0	0	2	.000	0	0	9.00
Charlotte	A+ Tex	5	5	0	0	23	92	21	7	7	1	0	0	0	8	0	16	1	1	0	1	.000	0	0	2.74
1997 Tulsa	AA Tex	9	9	0	0	50.1	227	53	27	24	6	3	3	1	21	0	29	0	0	2	3	.400	0	0	4.29
Okla City	AAA Tex	5	5	0	0	29.2	128	25	18	12	3	0	2	0	15	0	27	1	0	1	1	.500	0	0	3.64
1998 St. Paul	IND —	19	18	3	0	112	488	119	64	57	9	3	2	9	55	1	107	1	2	8	9	.471	0	0	4.58
1999 West Tenn	AA ChC	56	0	0	21	74.2	321	70	38	35	9	4	4	1	31	0	78	2	0	5	3	.625	0	2	4.22
2000 Greenville	AA Atl	2	0	0	1	1.2	10	2	1	1	0	1	0	0	3	0	1	0	0	0	0	—	0	0	5.40
Richmond	AAA Atl	53	1	0	22	76.1	325	83	32	29	2	4	2	0	24	3	58	3	1	4	3	.571	0	0	3.42
1992 Texas	AL	4	2	0	1	14.1	67	18	8	8	1	2	1	0	8	1	5	0	0	0	3	.000	0	0	5.02
1994 Texas	AL	13	0	0	2	14.2	76	18	11	7	2	0	0	0	12	0	9	2	0	1	2	.333	0	0	4.30
10 Min. YEARS		257	134	13	48	924.1	3993	957	502	437	68	36	37	32	353	5	696	24	14	51	68	.429	4	4	4.25
2 Maj. YEARS		17	2	0	3	29	143	36	19	15	3	2	1	0	20	1	14	2	0	1	5	.167	0	0	4.66

Demond Smith

Bats: Both **Throws:** Right **Pos:** OF-115; DH-1; PH-1 **Ht:** 5'11" **Wt:** 170 **Born:** 11/6/72 **Age:** 28

		BATTING																BASERUNNING				PERCENTAGES		
Year Team	Lg Org	G	AB	H	2B	3B	HR	TB	R	RBI	TBB	IBB	SO	HBP	SH	SF	SB	CS	SB%	GDP	Avg	OBP	SLG
1990 Mets	R NYM	46	153	40	9	2	1	56	19	7	20	0	34	0	1	2	16	10	.62	2	.261	.343	.366
1991 Kingsport	R+ NYM	35	116	29	3	4	1	43	28	12	12	0	25	6	0	1	16	7	.70	0	.250	.348	.371
1992 Pittsfield	A- NYM	66	233	58	10	4	1	79	39	24	23	0	42	7	1	3	21	15	.58	0	.249	.331	.339
1993 Capital Cty	A NYM	1	2	0	0	0	0	0	0	0	1	0	0	0	0	0	2	0	1.00	0	.000	.333	.000
1994 Lk Elsinore	A+ Ana	12	26	3	0	1	0	5	1	1	4	0	8	0	1	0	0	4	.00	1	.115	.233	.192
Boise	A- Ana	71	279	78	9	7	5	116	60	45	43	2	57	2	7	4	26	9	.74	3	.280	.375	.416
1995 Cedar Rapds	A Ana	79	317	108	25	7	7	168	64	41	32	2	61	6	5	1	37	12	.76	3	.341	.410	.530
Lk Elsinore	A+ Ana	34	148	52	8	2	7	85	32	26	11	0	36	2	0	1	14	3	.82	1	.351	.401	.574
W Michigan	A Oak	8	32	10	1	1	2	19	6	3	2	1	8	1	1	0	3	2	.60	0	.313	.371	.594
1996 Huntsville	AA Oak	123	447	116	17	14	9	188	75	62	55	1	89	11	8	5	30	15	.67	6	.260	.351	.421
Edmonton	AAA Oak	2	3	1	0	0	0	1	0	0	0	0	2	0	0	0	0	0	—	0	.333	.333	.333
1997 Edmonton	AAA Oak	42	151	33	3	4	5	59	22	22	23	0	31	3	1	4	10	3	.77	3	.219	.326	.391
Huntsville	AA Oak	87	323	90	20	6	8	146	79	39	65	0	76	4	3	2	31	9	.78	3	.279	.404	.452
1998 Calgary	AAA CWS	5	17	1	0	0	0	1	0	0	1	0	6	0	0	0	0	0	—	0	.059	.111	.059
Birmingham	AA CWS	84	321	99	23	7	5	151	75	30	48	1	67	6	4	4	25	14	.64	2	.308	.404	.470
1999 Greenville	AA Atl	132	416	127	20	7	9	188	70	59	55	1	72	7	8	5	31	13	.70	5	.305	.391	.452
2000 Greenville	AA Atl	117	431	118	33	7	13	204	78	48	67	0	93	6	5	3	30	14	.68	5	.274	.377	.473
11 Min. YEARS		944	3415	963	181	73	73	1509	648	419	462	8	707	61	45	35	292	130	.69	31	.282	.374	.442

Hut Smith

Pitches: Right **Bats:** Right **Pos:** RP-27; SP-17 **Ht:** 6'3" **Wt:** 195 **Born:** 6/8/73 **Age:** 28

		HOW MUCH HE PITCHED						WHAT HE GAVE UP												THE RESULTS					
Year Team	Lg Org	G	GS	CG	GF	IP	BFP	H	R	ER	HR	SH	SF	HB	TBB	IBB	SO	WP	Bk	W	L	Pct.	ShO	Sv	ERA
1992 Orioles	R Bal	11	10	2	1	60	241	37	20	13	0	1	3	7	18	0	54	8	3	4	3	.571	2	0	1.95
1993 Orioles	R Bal	3	0	0	2	4	13	0	0	0	0	0	0	0	1	0	5	0	0	0	0	—	0	1	0.00
1994 Albany	A Bal	29	12	2	10	121	516	127	67	51	13	2	1	11	32	0	96	7	1	8	9	.471	0	0	3.79
1995 Frederick	A+ Bal	20	2	0	7	32	162	39	23	23	4	2	1	4	31	1	28	7	1	3	2	.600	0	2	6.47
High Desert	A+ Bal	11	9	0	1	46.1	216	58	54	47	10	2	5	8	15	0	38	4	1	3	4	.429	0	0	9.13
1996 High Desert	A+ Bal	10	7	1	0	50.1	216	59	34	30	7	1	1	3	16	0	34	6	3	3	4	.429	0	0	5.36
1997 Frederick	A+ Bal	16	11	0	1	79	323	63	42	34	7	2	2	3	27	0	77	3	1	4	1	.800	0	1	3.87
Bowie	AA Bal	14	13	0	1	81	347	90	45	38	14	4	2	7	22	1	46	2	0	5	4	.556	0	0	4.22
1998 Bowie	AA Bal	6	5	0	1	30	129	32	23	23	5	0	2	5	6	0	12	2	1	0	3	.000	0	0	6.90
Reading	AA Phi	22	8	0	1	62.2	289	84	43	37	8	4	3	2	20	2	27	3	2	2	6	.250	0	2	5.31
1999 Madison	IND —	7	6	0	0	44	195	58	29	26	8	0	1	2	8	0	19	3	0	3	1	.750	0	0	5.32
Allentown	IND —	5	5	0	0	28.2	129	38	19	15	3	1	0	1	11	0	21	0	0	2	4	.667	0	0	4.71
2000 Catskill	IND —	14	13	3	1	83.1	359	85	44	34	6	5	2	3	33	0	68	6	0	5	7	.417	0	0	3.67
Quebec	IND —	8	4	0	3	28	126	34	19	19	7	3	2	3	9	1	22	0	0	2	1	.667	0	0	6.11
Altoona	AA Pit	22	0	0	19	27.1	106	14	6	3	0	2	1	1	8	2	23	0	0	3	4	.429	0	12	0.99
9 Min. YEARS		198	105	8	54	777.2	3367	818	468	393	86	30	29	59	257	7	570	51	13	47	50	.485	3	19	4.55

Jason Smith

Bats: Left **Throws:** Right **Pos:** SS-117; PH-2   **Ht:** 6'3" **Wt:** 190 **Born:** 7/24/77 **Age:** 23

					BATTING													BASERUNNING				PERCENTAGES		
Year Team	Lg Org	G	AB	H	2B	3B	HR	TB	R	RBI	TBB	IBB	SO	HBP	SH	SF		SB	CS	SB%	GDP	Avg	OBP	SLG
1997 Williamsprt	A- ChC	51	205	59	5	2	0	68	25	11	10	0	44	0	0	0		9	2	.82	0	.288	.321	.332
Rockford	A ChC	9	33	6	0	1	0	8	4	3	2	0	11	0	0	0		1	0	1.00	1	.182	.229	.242
1998 Rockford	A ChC	126	464	111	15	9	7	165	67	60	31	1	122	1	6	4		23	6	.79	2	.239	.286	.356
1999 Daytona	A+ ChC	39	142	37	5	2	5	61	22	26	12	3	29	3	0	1		9	3	.75	2	.261	.329	.430
2000 West Tenn	AA ChC	119	481	114	22	7	12	186	55	61	22	3	130	2	2	1		16	10	.62	7	.237	.273	.387
4 Min. YEARS		344	1325	327	47	21	24	488	173	161	77	7	336	6	8	6		58	21	.73	12	.247	.290	.368

Jeff Smith

Bats: Left **Throws:** Right **Pos:** C-32; DH-26; PH-5; 1B-3   **Ht:** 6'3" **Wt:** 216 **Born:** 6/17/74 **Age:** 27

					BATTING													BASERUNNING				PERCENTAGES		
Year Team	Lg Org	G	AB	H	2B	3B	HR	TB	R	RBI	TBB	IBB	SO	HBP	SH	SF		SB	CS	SB%	GDP	Avg	OBP	SLG
1996 Fort Wayne	A Min	63	208	49	6	0	2	61	20	26	22	0	32	0	1	2		2	1	.67	4	.236	.306	.293
1997 Fort Myers	A+ Min	49	121	34	5	0	4	51	17	26	12	0	18	0	0	6		0	2	.00	4	.281	.331	.421
New Britain	A Min	5	18	4	1	0	0	5	1	3	2	0	4	0	0	0		0	0	—	0	.222	.300	.278
Salt Lake	AAA Min	7	12	3	2	0	0	5	2	2	1	0	3	0	0	0		0	0	—	1	.250	.308	.417
1998 Fort Myers	A+ Min	6	23	8	2	0	0	10	4	1	1	0	2	1	0	0		1	0	1.00	1	.348	.400	.435
Salt Lake	AAA Min	23	67	17	3	0	0	20	9	2	4	0	13	0	2	0		0	0	—	3	.254	.296	.299
New Britain	AA Min	27	84	23	11	0	1	37	11	12	5	2	21	1	1	2		0	0	—	3	.274	.315	.440
1999 New Britain	AA Min	79	265	67	13	0	6	98	25	31	23	0	40	3	3	4		1	0	1.00	4	.253	.315	.370
Salt Lake	AAA Min	5	18	7	3	0	1	13	5	3	0	0	1	0	0	0		0	0	—	0	.389	.389	.722
2000 New Britain	AA Min	37	140	54	13	1	5	84	23	30	7	0	17	0	0	1		1	1	.50	2	.386	.415	.600
Salt Lake	AAA Min	25	84	24	4	0	2	34	10	9	2	1	20	1	0	0		1	0	1.00	1	.286	.310	.405
5 Min. YEARS		326	1040	290	63	1	21	418	127	145	79	3	171	6	7	14		6	4	.60	22	.279	.329	.402

Rod Smith

Bats: Both **Throws:** Right **Pos:** 2B-108; PR-5; PH-2   **Ht:** 6'0" **Wt:** 185 **Born:** 9/2/75 **Age:** 25

					BATTING													BASERUNNING				PERCENTAGES		
Year Team	Lg Org	G	AB	H	2B	3B	HR	TB	R	RBI	TBB	IBB	SO	HBP	SH	SF		SB	CS	SB%	GDP	Avg	OBP	SLG
1994 Yankees	R NYY	56	196	56	7	4	1	74	41	18	41	1	51	1	2	0		20	4	.83	2	.286	.412	.378
Greensboro	A NYY	7	20	1	0	0	0	1	2	0	3	0	7	0	0	0		1	0	1.00	0	.050	.174	.050
1995 Greensboro	A NYY	62	235	57	5	6	0	74	31	9	34	1	41	2	2	0		17	12	.59	4	.243	.343	.315
Oneonta	A- NYY	49	187	44	8	3	0	58	34	10	30	0	49	2	0	1		24	7	.77	1	.235	.345	.310
1996 Greensboro	A NYY	132	481	102	15	8	4	145	71	32	64	0	128	7	10	0		57	13	.81	5	.212	.313	.301
1997 Greensboro	A NYY	137	528	131	25	6	13	207	96	50	69	0	148	5	2	1		54	20	.73	5	.248	.340	.392
1998 Tampa	A+ NYY	86	327	80	15	2	6	117	57	35	39	1	70	5	6	2		40	14	.74	5	.245	.332	.358
1999 Tampa	A+ NYY	126	507	134	33	8	6	201	92	45	69	0	102	11	3	1		38	18	.68	1	.264	.364	.396
Norwich	AA NYY	1	5	3	0	0	0	3	1	1	0	0	1	0	0	0		2	0	1.00	0	.600	.600	.600
2000 Norwich	AA NYY	18	35	6	3	0	0	9	5	1	8	0	9	0	0	0		1	2	.33	0	.171	.326	.257
St. Pete	A+ TB	36	142	41	14	2	1	62	27	10	21	0	37	0	1	0		18	5	.78	2	.289	.380	.437
Orlando	AA TB	60	206	50	8	0	0	58	21	12	28	0	45	2	4	4		12	9	.57	1	.243	.333	.282
7 Min. YEARS		770	2869	705	133	39	31	1009	478	223	406	3	688	35	30	9		284	104	.73	26	.246	.345	.352

Roy Smith

Pitches: Right **Bats:** Right **Pos:** RP-49   **Ht:** 6'6" **Wt:** 235 **Born:** 5/18/76 **Age:** 25

			HOW MUCH HE PITCHED				WHAT HE GAVE UP											THE RESULTS					
Year Team	Lg Org	G	GS	CG	GF	IP	BFP	H	R	ER	HR	SH	SF	HB	TBB	IBB	SO	WP	Bk	W	L	Pct.	ShO	Sv	ERA
1994 Mariners	R Sea	11	5	0	1	45	164	30	9	8	2	1	1	1	4	0	35	2	0	3	1	.750	0	0	1.60
1995 Wisconsin	A Sea	27	27	1	0	149	669	179	100	89	9	5	2	3	54	2	109	10	2	7	14	.333	0	0	5.38
1996 Wisconsin	A Sea	27	27	0	0	146	679	164	113	83	9	6	4	8	73	3	99	11	2	6	13	.316	0	0	5.12
1997 Memphis	AA Sea	4	0	0	3	4.1	20	6	5	5	0	0	1	0	1	0	6	1	0	0	0	—	0	0	10.38
Wisconsin	A Sea	18	11	0	4	66	304	81	50	41	3	1	2	2	31	0	38	14	2	3	4	.429	0	0	5.59
1998 St. Paul	IND —	18	18	1	0	105.2	467	119	75	59	10	3	3	1	36	0	74	6	0	6	7	.462	1	0	5.03
1999 St. Paul	IND —	8	7	0	0	42	182	38	18	15	3	1	0	1	23	0	43	1	0	4	2	.667	1	0	3.21
2000 Kinston	A+ Cle	21	0	0	9	45	183	35	15	14	0	0	1	3	21	1	45	3	0	2	2	.500	0	2	2.80
Akron	AA Cle	28	0	0	15	55	217	36	14	12	0	4	0	1	22	2	50	6	0	5	1	.833	0	6	1.96
7 Min. YEARS		162	95	3	32	658	2885	688	399	326	36	21	14	20	265	8	499	54	6	36	44	.450	2	8	4.46

Travis Smith

Pitches: Right **Bats:** Right **Pos:** SP-27; RP-3   **Ht:** 5'10" **Wt:** 165 **Born:** 11/7/72 **Age:** 28

			HOW MUCH HE PITCHED				WHAT HE GAVE UP											THE RESULTS					
Year Team	Lg Org	G	GS	CG	GF	IP	BFP	H	R	ER	HR	SH	SF	HB	TBB	IBB	SO	WP	Bk	W	L	Pct.	ShO	Sv	ERA
1995 Helena	R+ Mil	20	7	0	11	56	224	41	16	15	4	0	0	7	19	0	63	4	2	4	2	.667	0	5	2.41
1996 Stockton	A+ Mil	14	6	0	3	58.2	241	56	17	12	4	1	0	4	21	0	48	2	0	6	1	.857	0	1	1.84
El Paso	AA Mil	17	17	3	0	107.2	478	119	56	50	6	4	5	6	39	0	68	2	0	7	4	.636	1	0	4.18
1997 El Paso	AA Mil	28	28	5	0	184.1	805	210	106	85	12	7	5	7	58	2	107	7	3	16	3	.842	1	0	4.15
1998 Louisville	AAA Mil	12	11	0	0	67.2	296	77	44	40	9	3	4	2	25	1	36	3	0	4	6	.400	0	0	5.32
1999 Ogden	R+ Mil	1	1	0	0	1	5	0	1	0	0	0	0	1	0	0	3	0	0	0	0	—	0	0	0.00
Stockton	A+ Mil	3	3	0	0	7.1	35	6	5	5	1	1	0	1	9	0	8	0	0	0	2	.000	0	0	6.14
Huntsville	AA Mil	7	7	0	0	38.1	171	40	27	25	3	2	2	0	18	0	23	6	1	3	2	.600	0	0	5.87
2000 Indianapols	AAA Mil	3	3	0	0	10.2	58	19	18	15	6	1	1	2	9	1	5	0	0	1	1	.500	0	0	12.66
Huntsville	AA Mil	27	24	1	1	154.1	631	141	77	64	13	4	2	5	37	0	113	3	0	12	7	.632	1	0	3.73
1998 Milwaukee	NL	1	0	0	0	2	7	1	0	0	0	0	0	0	0	0	1	0	0	0	0	—	0	0	0.00
6 Min. YEARS		132	107	9	15	686	2944	712	368	311	58	23	19	34	229	4	474	27	11	53	28	.654	3	6	4.08

269

Stewart Smothers

Bats: Right **Throws:** Right **Pos:** OF-69; PR-4; PH-1   **Ht:** 5'10" **Wt:** 180 **Born:** 4/29/76 **Age:** 25

Year Team	Lg Org	G	AB	H	2B	3B	HR	TB	R	RBI	TBB	IBB	SO	HBP	SH	SF	SB	CS	SB%	GDP	Avg	OBP	SLG
1997 Eugene	A- Atl	59	233	64	11	6	2	93	31	27	21	0	57	1	3	0	12	4	.75	5	.275	.337	.399
1998 Macon	A Atl	139	506	103	17	3	9	153	61	60	46	1	145	5	7	8	17	12	.59	9	.204	.273	.302
1999 Myrtle Bch	A+ Atl	56	185	28	8	3	1	45	19	14	15	1	71	0	0	5	2	2	.50	3	.151	.210	.243
Macon	A Atl	63	219	62	12	0	7	95	32	39	16	0	61	0	2	5	2	3	.40	2	.283	.325	.434
2000 Myrtle Bch	A+ Atl	11	24	7	1	0	1	11	3	3	0	0	9	1	0	0	0	0	—	0	.292	.320	.458
Richmond	AAA Atl	5	18	1	0	0	0	1	3	0	1	0	9	0	0	0	0	0	—	0	.056	.105	.056
Greenville	AA Atl	57	158	35	6	2	4	57	28	11	31	1	51	0	2	1	7	0	1.00	7	.222	.347	.361
4 Min. YEARS		390	1343	300	55	14	24	455	177	154	130	3	403	7	14	19	40	21	.66	26	.223	.292	.339

John Sneed

Pitches: Right **Bats:** Left **Pos:** SP-27   **Ht:** 6'6" **Wt:** 250 **Born:** 6/30/76 **Age:** 25

Year Team	Lg Org	G	GS	CG	GF	IP	BFP	H	R	ER	HR	SH	SF	HB	TBB	IBB	SO	WP	Bk	W	L	Pct.	ShO	Sv	ERA
1997 Medcine Hat	R+ Tor	15	10	2	1	69.2	275	42	19	10	5	2	1	7	20	0	79	2	0	6	1	.857	0	0	1.29
1998 Hagerstown	A Tor	27	27	2	0	161.2	660	123	59	46	9	4	0	11	58	0	210	5	2	16	2	.889	1	0	2.56
1999 Dunedin	A+ Tor	21	20	0	0	125.1	511	107	53	48	10	3	4	6	36	1	143	5	0	11	2	.846	0	0	3.45
Knoxville	AA Tor	6	6	0	0	28.1	131	33	17	16	2	1	1	2	21	0	28	1	0	3	1	.750	0	0	5.08
2000 Tennessee	AA Tor	21	21	0	0	121	548	124	81	61	9	4	7	10	56	0	100	5	0	5	9	.357	0	0	4.54
Reading	AA Phi	6	6	0	0	25.2	126	31	28	25	5	4	2	2	19	0	24	0	0	1	3	.250	0	0	8.77
4 Min. YEARS		96	90	4	1	531.2	2251	460	257	206	40	18	15	38	210	1	584	18	2	42	18	.700	1	0	3.49

Clay Snellgrove

Bats: Right **Throws:** Right **Pos:** 2B-104; SS-7; 3B-3; PH-3; DH-2; PR-2; 1B-1; P-1   **Ht:** 6'0" **Wt:** 180 **Born:** 11/22/74 **Age:** 26

Year Team	Lg Org	G	AB	H	2B	3B	HR	TB	R	RBI	TBB	IBB	SO	HBP	SH	SF	SB	CS	SB%	GDP	Avg	OBP	SLG
1997 Idaho Falls	R+ SD	66	281	97	19	7	2	136	52	48	18	2	39	3	2	6	3	2	.60	7	.345	.383	.484
1998 Clinton	A SD	104	368	88	14	2	2	112	42	30	27	0	32	6	4	1	11	9	.55	7	.239	.301	.304
1999 Las Vegas	AAA SD	1	3	2	2	0	0	4	1	0	0	0	0	0	0	0	0	0	—	0	.667	.667	1.333
Rancho Cuca	A+ SD	116	426	125	20	2	3	158	62	43	19	0	42	7	4	5	8	7	.53	14	.293	.330	.371
2000 Mobile	AA SD	12	35	7	2	0	0	9	1	3	2	0	3	2	0	0	0	1	.00	5	.200	.282	.257
Rancho Cuca	A+ SD	104	388	107	18	2	1	132	33	44	35	2	36	3	1	5	9	7	.56	7	.276	.336	.340
4 Min. YEARS		403	1501	426	75	13	8	551	191	168	101	4	152	21	11	17	31	26	.54	35	.284	.334	.367

Chris Snopek

Bats: Right **Throws:** Right **Pos:** SS-48; 2B-24; 3B-16; 1B-11; DH-11; PR-2; PH-1   **Ht:** 6'1" **Wt:** 185 **Born:** 9/20/70 **Age:** 30

Year Team	Lg Org	G	AB	H	2B	3B	HR	TB	R	RBI	TBB	IBB	SO	HBP	SH	SF	SB	CS	SB%	GDP	Avg	OBP	SLG
1992 Utica	A- CWS	73	245	69	15	1	2	92	49	29	52	4	44	2	1	4	14	4	.78	4	.282	.406	.376
1993 South Bend	A CWS	22	72	28	8	1	5	53	20	18	15	0	13	3	0	2	1	1	.50	1	.389	.500	.736
Sarasota	A+ CWS	107	371	91	21	4	10	150	61	50	65	2	67	1	3	6	3	2	.60	2	.245	.354	.404
1994 Birmingham	AA CWS	106	365	96	25	3	6	145	58	54	58	3	49	5	3	5	9	4	.69	7	.263	.367	.397
1995 Nashville	AAA CWS	113	393	127	23	4	12	194	56	55	50	1	72	4	6	3	2	5	.29	5	.323	.402	.494
1996 Nashville	AAA CWS	40	153	38	8	0	2	52	18	12	21	1	24	1	1	0	2	2	.50	5	.248	.343	.340
1997 Nashville	AAA CWS	20	73	17	4	0	3	30	8	8	7	0	13	0	0	0	0	0	—	4	.233	.300	.411
1999 Pawtucket	AAA Bos	24	81	20	7	0	3	36	10	10	5	0	15	0	1	0	2	0	1.00	2	.247	.291	.444
Indianapolis	AAA Cin	103	381	107	24	3	9	164	66	64	42	0	51	4	2	5	17	6	.74	10	.281	.354	.430
2000 Tacoma	AAA Sea	104	393	118	24	2	13	185	76	48	44	2	40	4	2	1	12	6	.67	5	.300	.372	.471
1995 Chicago	AL	22	68	22	4	0	1	29	12	7	9	0	12	0	0	0	1	0	1.00	2	.324	.403	.426
1996 Chicago	AL	46	104	27	6	1	6	53	18	18	6	0	16	1	1	1	0	1	.00	5	.260	.304	.510
1997 Chicago	AL	86	298	65	15	0	5	95	27	35	18	0	51	1	4	3	3	2	.60	4	.218	.263	.319
1998 Chicago	AL	53	125	26	2	0	1	31	17	4	14	0	24	1	0	1	3	0	1.00	4	.208	.291	.248
Boston	AL	8	12	2	0	0	0	2	2	2	2	0	5	0	0	0	0	0	—	0	.167	.286	.167
8 Min. YEARS		712	2527	711	159	18	65	1101	422	348	359	13	388	24	19	30	62	30	.67	40	.281	.372	.436
4 Maj. YEARS		215	607	142	27	1	13	210	76	66	49	0	108	3	5	4	7	3	.70	15	.234	.293	.346

Bert Snow

Pitches: Right **Bats:** Right **Pos:** RP-62   **Ht:** 6'1" **Wt:** 190 **Born:** 3/23/77 **Age:** 24

Year Team	Lg Org	G	GS	CG	GF	IP	BFP	H	R	ER	HR	SH	SF	HB	TBB	IBB	SO	WP	Bk	W	L	Pct.	ShO	Sv	ERA
1998 Sou Oregon	A- Oak	11	8	0	1	44.2	215	52	38	28	2	5	3	6	18	1	35	5	1	1	3	.250	0	0	5.64
Modesto	A+ Oak	2	2	0	0	8.2	46	12	8	3	1	0	0	1	6	0	12	1	0	1	1	.500	0	0	3.12
1999 Visalia	A+ Oak	31	3	0	14	64.2	298	55	43	37	4	4	4	4	40	3	90	10	1	3	2	.600	0	5	5.15
Midland	AA Oak	21	0	0	21	21	84	14	4	4	3	0	0	0	9	3	32	1	0	1	1	.500	0	13	1.71
Vancouver	AAA Oak	2	0	0	0	2.1	11	3	1	1	0	1	0	0	3	0	3	0	0	1	0	1.000	0	0	3.86
2000 Sacramento	AAA Oak	3	0	0	0	2	10	1	1	1	0	0	0	0	3	0	3	0	0	0	0	—	0	0	4.50
Midland	AA Oak	59	0	0	53	67.2	297	58	33	27	6	4	4	2	36	6	98	12	0	1	7	.125	0	27	3.59
3 Min. YEARS		129	13	0	89	211	961	195	128	101	16	14	11	13	113	13	273	29	2	8	14	.364	0	45	4.31

Casey Snow

Bats: Both **Throws:** Right **Pos:** C-5   **Ht:** 5'10" **Wt:** 185 **Born:** 12/8/74 **Age:** 26

Year Team	Lg Org	G	AB	H	2B	3B	HR	TB	R	RBI	TBB	IBB	SO	HBP	SH	SF	SB	CS	SB%	GDP	Avg	OBP	SLG
1996 Great Falls	R+ LA	43	130	35	6	0	2	47	19	23	13	0	33	5	0	3	1	4	.20	0	.269	.351	.362
1997 San Berndno	A+ LA	43	132	26	5	3	1	40	10	10	4	0	35	2	1	0	2	3	.40	1	.197	.232	.303
Great Falls	R+ LA	17	53	17	3	0	2	26	5	9	8	1	10	1	3	0	2	0	1.00	5	.321	.419	.491

		BATTING														BASERUNNING				PERCENTAGES		
Year Team	Lg Org	G	AB	H	2B	3B	HR	TB	R	RBI	TBB	IBB	SO	HBP	SH	SF	SB	CS	SB%	GDP	Avg	OBP	SLG
1998 San Berndno	A+ LA	99	335	94	24	2	4	134	44	42	34	6	75	4	3	3	5	6	.45	2	.281	.351	.400
Albuquerque	AAA LA	7	20	4	2	0	0	6	2	2	4	0	7	1	0	1	0	0	—	0	.200	.346	.300
1999 San Antonio	AA LA	61	170	43	8	2	4	67	21	16	13	1	45	2	2	3	0	0	—	4	.253	.309	.394
2000 Akron	AA Cle	5	15	3	0	0	1	6	3	2	2	0	3	0	0	0	0	0	—	1	.200	.294	.400
5 Min. YEARS		275	855	222	48	7	14	326	104	104	78	8	208	15	9	10	10	13	.43	8	.260	.329	.381

Chris Snusz

Bats: Right **Throws:** Right **Pos:** C-54; PH-4; 1B-3; DH-3; P-2; OF-1   **Ht:** 6'0" **Wt:** 190 **Born:** 11/8/72 **Age:** 28

		BATTING														BASERUNNING				PERCENTAGES		
Year Team	Lg Org	G	AB	H	2B	3B	HR	TB	R	RBI	TBB	IBB	SO	HBP	SH	SF	SB	CS	SB%	GDP	Avg	OBP	SLG
1995 Batavia	A- Phi	21	66	15	1	0	1	19	9	5	6	0	6	0	0	0	1	1	.50	4	.227	.292	.288
1996 Batavia	A- Phi	13	31	5	0	0	0	5	6	0	6	0	4	0	1	0	0	0	—	0	.161	.297	.161
Piedmont	A Phi	4	11	1	0	0	0	1	2	0	2	0	1	0	0	0	0	0	.00	0	.091	.231	.091
1997 Clearwater	A+ Phi	36	105	21	7	0	0	28	12	3	2	0	22	0	3	0	0	0	—	3	.200	.215	.267
1998 Scranton-WB	AAA Phi	3	9	1	1	0	0	2	0	0	0	0	2	0	0	0	0	0	—	1	.111	.111	.222
Clearwater	A+ Phi	19	56	11	1	0	0	12	6	6	1	0	9	1	1	1	0	0	—	0	.196	.220	.214
Reading	AA Phi	12	28	9	2	0	0	11	6	1	3	0	6	0	0	0	0	0	—	0	.321	.387	.393
1999 Chattanooga	AA Cin	2	6	3	1	0	0	4	0	2	1	0	0	0	0	0	0	0	—	0	.500	.571	.667
Clinton	A Cin	4	21	4	1	1	0	7	2	3	1	0	8	0	0	0	0	0	—	0	.190	.227	.333
Rockford	A Cin	19	53	9	1	0	1	13	6	2	3	0	13	1	1	0	1	0	1.00	1	.170	.228	.245
Harrisburg	AA Mon	5	13	4	1	0	0	5	2	3	1	0	3	0	0	0	0	0	—	1	.308	.357	.385
Ottawa	AAA Mon	21	63	18	3	0	3	30	6	9	1	0	18	0	1	0	0	0	—	2	.286	.297	.476
2000 Ottawa	AAA Mon	63	195	41	8	2	5	68	24	25	7	1	58	1	1	0	0	0	—	7	.210	.241	.349
6 Min. YEARS		222	657	142	27	3	10	205	81	59	34	1	150	3	8	1	2	2	.50	19	.216	.258	.312

Bill Snyder

Pitches: T = Pitches: Right **Bats:** Right **Pos:** RP-47   **Ht:** 6'0" **Wt:** 190 **Born:** 1/29/75 **Age:** 26

		HOW MUCH HE PITCHED						WHAT HE GAVE UP											THE RESULTS					
Year Team	Lg Org	G	GS	CG	GF	IP	BFP	H	R	ER	HR	SH	SF	HB	TBB	IBB	SO	WP	Bk	W	L	Pct.	ShO	Sv	ERA
1997 Jamestown	A- Det	25	0	0	25	29	126	19	8	7	1	2	0	2	20	2	42	1	1	3	1	.250	0	9	2.17
1998 W Michigan	A Det	42	0	0	20	59.1	236	40	17	12	2	1	4	3	18	2	84	1	0	3	1	.750	0	4	1.82
1999 Lakeland	A+ Det	47	0	0	42	51.2	197	34	13	11	0	4	2	1	18	0	39	0	0	4	1	.800	0	16	1.92
Jacksnville	AA Det	14	0	0	8	18	80	16	6	5	0	1	0	3	5	1	17	0	0	1	0	1.000	0	2	2.50
2000 Toledo	AAA Det	18	0	0	5	22.2	119	28	26	26	5	1	4	2	24	0	10	1	0	0	0	—	0	0	10.32
Jacksnville	AA Det	29	0	0	13	40	177	33	16	16	4	2	2	2	23	2	38	1	1	1	2	.333	0	0	3.60
4 Min. YEARS		175	0	0	113	220.2	935	170	86	77	12	11	9	13	108	7	230	4	2	10	7	.588	0	31	3.14

Matt Snyder

Pitches: Right **Bats:** Right **Pos:** RP-20; SP-13   **Ht:** 5'11" **Wt:** 201 **Born:** 7/7/74 **Age:** 26

		HOW MUCH HE PITCHED						WHAT HE GAVE UP											THE RESULTS					
Year Team	Lg Org	G	GS	CG	GF	IP	BFP	H	R	ER	HR	SH	SF	HB	TBB	IBB	SO	WP	Bk	W	L	Pct.	ShO	Sv	ERA
1995 Bluefield	R+ Bal	17	0	0	15	34.2	150	35	9	4	1	0	0	3	13	0	46	1	0	0	0	—	0	8	1.04
1996 High Desert	A+ Bal	58	0	0	49	72	317	60	34	30	6	5	2	1	38	2	93	9	1	6	2	.750	0	20	3.75
1997 Bowie	AA Bal	67	0	0	45	80	366	89	48	37	11	8	4	4	42	5	68	10	0	7	5	.583	0	19	4.16
1998 Rochester	AAA Bal	12	0	0	5	19.2	77	17	9	8	3	0	0	1	6	0	13	0	0	2	1	.667	0	0	3.66
Bowie	AA Bal	22	20	4	0	120	510	127	66	58	14	1	3	4	30	0	116	0	1	9	6	.600	1	0	4.35
1999 Rochester	AAA Bal	48	3	0	15	84.2	380	95	60	49	14	3	4	4	30	4	59	6	0	6	6	.500	0	1	5.21
2000 Bowie	AA Bal	23	12	0	3	90	385	84	50	39	9	4	6	5	38	1	77	1	0	2	7	.222	0	1	3.90
Rochester	AAA Bal	10	1	0	2	23	97	23	13	13	7	0	1	0	8	0	18	0	0	1	0	1.000	0	1	5.09
6 Min. YEARS		257	36	4	134	524	2282	530	289	238	65	21	20	22	205	12	490	33	4	33	27	.550	1	50	4.09

Scott Sobkowiak

Pitches: Right **Bats:** Right **Pos:** SP-4   **Ht:** 6'5" **Wt:** 230 **Born:** 10/26/77 **Age:** 23

		HOW MUCH HE PITCHED						WHAT HE GAVE UP											THE RESULTS					
Year Team	Lg Org	G	GS	CG	GF	IP	BFP	H	R	ER	HR	SH	SF	HB	TBB	IBB	SO	WP	Bk	W	L	Pct.	ShO	Sv	ERA
1998 Eugene	A- Atl	8	8	0	0	40.2	163	25	12	7	1	0	1	3	13	0	55	4	0	3	2	.600	0	0	1.55
1999 Myrtle Bch	A+ Atl	27	26	0	1	139.1	572	100	50	44	10	3	2	2	63	1	161	12	1	9	4	.692	0	0	2.84
2000 Greenville	AA Atl	4	4	0	0	23.1	107	26	16	12	2	0	2	2	15	0	27	0	0	2	1	.667	0	0	4.63
3 Min. YEARS		39	38	0	1	203.1	842	151	78	63	13	3	5	7	91	1	243	16	1	14	7	.667	0	0	2.79

Steve Soderstrom

Pitches: Right **Bats:** Right **Pos:** SP-22; RP-9   **Ht:** 6'3" **Wt:** 205 **Born:** 4/3/72 **Age:** 29

		HOW MUCH HE PITCHED						WHAT HE GAVE UP											THE RESULTS					
Year Team	Lg Org	G	GS	CG	GF	IP	BFP	H	R	ER	HR	SH	SF	HB	TBB	IBB	SO	WP	Bk	W	L	Pct.	ShO	Sv	ERA
1994 San Jose	A+ SF	8	8	0	0	40.2	179	34	20	19	2	2	1	4	26	0	40	4	1	2	3	.400	0	0	4.20
1995 Shreveport	AA SF	22	22	0	0	116	508	106	53	44	6	5	2	10	51	0	91	12	2	9	5	.643	0	0	3.41
1996 Phoenix	AAA SF	29	29	0	0	171.1	728	178	94	84	13	8	4	7	58	1	80	9	5	7	8	.467	0	0	4.41
1997 Phoenix	AAA SF	31	15	0	8	105.2	498	141	81	76	12	2	2	6	52	1	78	10	1	4	8	.333	0	0	6.47
1998 Fresno	AAA SF	25	23	2	1	137.2	580	133	71	62	20	2	3	7	39	0	96	4	0	11	4	.733	0	1	4.05
1999 Fresno	AAA SF	22	13	0	3	71.2	355	90	64	54	16	4	4	8	35	0	58	8	0	2	8	.200	0	0	6.78
2000 Louisville	AAA Cin	31	22	0	2	137.1	601	160	84	75	8	6	8	1	49	4	67	3	4	9	11	.450	0	0	4.92
1996 San Francisco	NL	3	3	0	0	13.2	63	16	11	8	1	0	2	2	6	0	9	0	0	2	0	1.000	0	0	5.27
7 Min. YEARS		168	132	2	14	780.1	3449	842	467	414	77	29	24	43	310	6	510	50	13	44	47	.484	0	2	4.77

Clint Sodowsky

Pitches: Right **Bats:** Left **Pos:** RP-42　　　　　　**Ht:** 6'4" **Wt:** 195 **Born:** 7/13/72 **Age:** 28

Year Team	Lg Org	HOW MUCH HE PITCHED						WHAT HE GAVE UP												THE RESULTS					
		G	GS	CG	GF	IP	BFP	H	R	ER	HR	SH	SF	HB	TBB	IBB	SO	WP	Bk	W	L	Pct.	ShO	Sv	ERA
1991 Bristol	R+ Det	14	8	0	3	55	253	49	34	23	3	2	1	2	34	0	44	8	4	0	5	.000	0	0	3.76
1992 Bristol	R+ Det	15	6	0	2	56	243	46	35	22	3	1	2	4	29	0	48	6	1	2	2	.500	0	0	3.54
1993 Fayetteville	A Det	27	27	1	0	155.2	676	177	101	88	11	2	6	6	51	0	80	4	5	14	10	.583	0	0	5.09
1994 Lakeland	A+ Det	19	18	1	1	110.1	466	111	58	47	5	2	2	6	34	0	73	12	0	6	3	.667	1	0	3.83
1995 Jacksnville	AA Det	19	19	5	0	123.2	497	102	46	35	4	2	2	5	50	1	77	3	0	5	5	.500	3	0	2.55
Toledo	AAA Det	9	9	1	0	60	247	47	21	19	5	2	0	3	30	1	32	1	0	5	1	.833	0	0	2.85
1996 Toledo	AAA Det	19	19	1	0	118.2	525	128	67	52	8	8	3	6	51	0	59	3	2	6	8	.429	0	0	3.94
1997 Calgary	AAA Pit	8	0	0	1	13.2	64	19	10	10	1	0	0	0	6	0	9	1	0	0	1	.000	0	1	6.59
1998 Tucson	AAA Ari	2	2	0	0	9.1	42	11	4	4	0	0	0	0	3	0	7	0	1	0	1	.000	0	0	3.86
1999 Memphis	AAA StL	19	13	2	3	80.1	350	85	55	43	14	4	1	4	32	0	52	6	2	4	5	.444	1	3	4.82
2000 Akron	AA Cle	23	0	0	9	45.1	211	59	35	27	3	4	4	2	12	2	39	2	0	2	1	.667	0	3	5.36
Tulsa	AA Tex	6	0	0	3	9.1	41	6	6	5	0	1	0	0	6	0	8	0	1	0	0	—	0	0	4.82
Oklahoma	AAA Tex	13	0	0	7	21.2	88	23	7	7	2	0	0	2	4	0	13	3	0	2	1	.667	0	2	2.91
1995 Detroit	AL	6	6	0	0	23.1	112	24	15	13	4	1	0	0	18	0	14	1	1	2	2	.500	0	0	5.01
1996 Detroit	AL	7	7	0	0	24.1	132	40	34	32	5	1	0	3	20	0	9	3	0	1	3	.250	0	0	11.84
1997 Pittsburgh	NL	45	0	0	8	52	236	49	22	21	6	1	2	2	34	7	51	6	0	2	2	.500	0	0	3.63
1998 Arizona	NL	45	6	0	10	77.2	357	86	56	49	5	5	2	7	39	5	42	4	2	3	6	.333	0	0	5.68
1999 St. Louis	NL	3	1	0	0	6.1	39	15	11	11	1	0	0	0	6	0	2	0	0	0	1	.000	0	0	15.63
10 Min. YEARS		193	121	11	29	859	3703	863	479	382	59	28	21	40	342	4	541	49	16	46	43	.517	5	9	4.00
5 Maj. YEARS		106	20	0	18	183.2	876	214	138	126	21	8	4	12	117	12	118	14	3	8	14	.364	0	0	6.17

Danny Solano

Bats: Right **Throws:** Right **Pos:** SS-83; 2B-14; DH-5; 3B-3; PH-3; PR-2　　　**Ht:** 5'9" **Wt:** 155 **Born:** 12/3/78 **Age:** 22

Year Team	Lg Org	BATTING															BASERUNNING				PERCENTAGES		
		G	AB	H	2B	3B	HR	TB	R	RBI	TBB	IBB	SO	HBP	SH	SF	SB	CS	SB%	GDP	Avg	OBP	SLG
1998 Charlotte	A+ Tex	84	262	68	15	0	1	86	46	30	42	0	54	2	9	4	9	6	.60	2	.260	.361	.328
1999 Oklahoma	AAA Tex	3	6	0	0	0	0	0	0	1	0	0	4	0	0	1	0	0	—	0	.000	.000	.000
Charlotte	A+ Tex	116	421	114	18	4	7	161	64	44	74	0	74	6	12	0	21	13	.62	3	.271	.387	.382
2000 Tulsa	AA Tex	109	359	90	13	3	7	130	36	33	40	0	66	6	10	2	10	6	.63	11	.251	.334	.362
3 Min. YEARS		312	1048	272	46	7	15	377	146	108	156	0	198	14	31	7	40	25	.62	16	.260	.361	.360

Steve Soliz

Bats: Right **Throws:** Right **Pos:** C-72; DH-5; PH-1　　　**Ht:** 5'10" **Wt:** 180 **Born:** 1/27/71 **Age:** 30

Year Team	Lg Org	BATTING															BASERUNNING				PERCENTAGES		
		G	AB	H	2B	3B	HR	TB	R	RBI	TBB	IBB	SO	HBP	SH	SF	SB	CS	SB%	GDP	Avg	OBP	SLG
1993 Watertown	A- Cle	56	209	62	12	0	0	74	30	35	15	0	41	1	2	3	2	0	1.00	3	.297	.342	.354
1994 Kinston	A+ Cle	51	163	43	7	1	3	61	26	19	16	0	32	1	2	1	3	0	1.00	0	.264	.331	.374
Canton-Akrn	AA Cle	18	54	10	1	0	0	11	4	0	2	0	9	1	1	0	0	0	—	4	.185	.228	.204
1995 Bakersfield	A+ LA	44	159	39	5	0	1	47	9	11	15	0	34	2	0	0	2	1	.67	6	.245	.318	.296
Canton-Akrn	AA Cle	32	81	14	3	0	2	23	9	7	13	0	16	0	1	1	0	0	—	3	.173	.284	.284
1996 Canton-Akrn	AA Cle	46	143	37	4	2	2	51	18	15	11	0	28	2	0	2	1	2	.33	1	.259	.316	.357
1997 Buffalo	AAA Cle	62	151	29	5	0	1	37	12	13	10	0	40	0	5	3	0	1	.00	2	.192	.238	.245
1998 Buffalo	AAA Cle	39	112	25	6	0	0	31	14	9	11	0	23	3	1	1	1	1	.50	6	.223	.307	.277
1999 Akron	AA Cle	7	23	3	0	0	0	3	1	3	1	0	4	0	0	0	0	0	—	1	.130	.167	.130
Buffalo	AAA Cle	40	112	29	6	0	2	41	15	14	6	0	24	2	0	1	0	0	—	1	.259	.306	.366
2000 Mobile	AA SD	44	137	28	5	0	2	39	14	10	17	0	30	0	1	0	0	1	.00	4	.204	.292	.285
Las Vegas	AAA SD	34	119	26	8	0	0	34	16	8	14	1	22	2	1	1	0	0	—	3	.218	.309	.286
8 Min. YEARS		473	1463	345	62	3	13	452	168	144	131	1	303	14	16	13	9	6	.60	34	.236	.302	.309

Gabe Sollecito

Pitches: Right **Bats:** Both **Pos:** RP-7　　　**Ht:** 6'1" **Wt:** 190 **Born:** 3/3/72 **Age:** 29

Year Team	Lg Org	HOW MUCH HE PITCHED						WHAT HE GAVE UP												THE RESULTS					
		G	GS	CG	GF	IP	BFP	H	R	ER	HR	SH	SF	HB	TBB	IBB	SO	WP	Bk	W	L	Pct.	ShO	Sv	ERA
1993 Niagara Fal	A- Det	23	0	0	21	26.2	111	18	4	1	0	2	0	3	10	1	23	3	1	2	1	.667	0	14	0.34
1994 Fayettevlle	A Det	46	0	0	45	57	238	47	21	18	1	2	2	10	15	2	52	1	0	4	3	.571	0	18	2.84
1996 Salinas	IND —	1	0	0	0	0.2	1	0	0	0	0	0	0	0	0	0	0	0	0	0	0	—	0	0	0.00
1997 Sioux Falls	IND —	13	0	0	8	13	65	19	12	11	0	0	0	1	8	2	9	1	0	0	4	.000	0	1	7.62
Salinas	IND —	24	0	0	19	32.1	132	23	6	5	1	0	2	2	9	2	37	2	0	4	1	.800	0	5	1.39
1998 Charlotte	A+ Tex	37	0	0	18	60	251	54	13	6	1	1	3	6	14	2	50	0	0	5	2	.714	0	2	0.90
Tulsa	AA Tex	5	0	0	3	9.1	39	5	3	2	0	0	0	3	4	0	10	2	0	1	0	1.000	0	2	1.93
1999 Tulsa	AA Tex	53	0	0	23	96.1	400	85	28	26	6	3	3	8	29	1	80	3	1	5	4	.556	0	11	2.43
2000 Oklahoma	AAA Tex	7	0	0	1	9.1	46	12	8	8	2	0	1	0	6	0	10	0	0	0	0	—	0	0	7.71
7 Min. YEARS		209	0	0	138	304.2	1283	263	95	77	11	8	11	31	95	10	271	12	2	21	15	.583	0	51	2.27

Scott Sollmann

Bats: Left **Throws:** Left **Pos:** OF-108; PR-7; DH-3; PH-1　　　**Ht:** 5'10" **Wt:** 167 **Born:** 5/2/75 **Age:** 26

Year Team	Lg Org	BATTING															BASERUNNING				PERCENTAGES		
		G	AB	H	2B	3B	HR	TB	R	RBI	TBB	IBB	SO	HBP	SH	SF	SB	CS	SB%	GDP	Avg	OBP	SLG
1996 Jamestown	A- Det	67	253	71	5	5	0	86	49	19	34	1	47	7	6	2	35	14	.71	2	.281	.378	.340
1997 W Michigan	A Det	121	460	144	13	4	0	165	89	33	79	5	81	11	8	3	40	14	.74	1	.313	.423	.359
1998 Jacksnville	AA Det	10	26	2	0	0	0	2	4	1	7	0	4	1	2	0	1	1	.50	0	.077	.294	.077
Lakeland	A+ Det	104	401	101	11	4	2	126	81	35	62	0	52	3	7	3	59	17	.78	1	.252	.354	.314
1999 Stockton	A+ Mil	77	249	87	10	5	0	107	61	33	52	3	38	1	1	1	32	14	.70	1	.349	.462	.430
Huntsville	AA Mil	55	191	60	4	5	0	77	34	9	34	0	31	3	0	0	17	8	.68	3	.314	.425	.403
2000 Tennessee	AA Tor	114	385	91	16	5	0	117	66	27	53	1	58	8	6	3	19	10	.66	6	.236	.339	.304
5 Min. YEARS		538	1965	556	59	28	3	680	384	157	321	10	311	34	30	12	203	78	.72	14	.283	.391	.346

Shawn Sonnier

Pitches: Right **Bats:** Right **Pos:** RP-48   **Ht:** 6'5" **Wt:** 210 **Born:** 7/5/76 **Age:** 24

		HOW MUCH HE PITCHED						WHAT HE GAVE UP										THE RESULTS					
Year Team	Lg Org	G	GS	CG	GF	IP	BFP	H	R	ER	HR	SH	SF	HB	TBB	IBB	SO	WP	Bk	W	L	Pct.	ShO	Sv	ERA
1998 Spokane	A- KC	7	0	0	3	6.2	27	7	1	1	0	0	0	0	1	0	10	1	0	0	0	—	0	1	1.35
1999 Wilmington	A+ KC	44	0	0	38	59.1	237	46	20	19	1	2	0	1	19	2	73	2	0	1	2	.333	0	13	2.88
2000 Wichita	AA KC	48	0	0	42	64	260	41	22	16	6	0	0	3	26	3	90	4	0	0	3	.000	0	21	2.25
3 Min. YEARS		99	0	0	83	130	524	94	43	36	7	2	0	4	46	5	173	7	0	1	5	.167	0	35	2.49

Zach Sorensen

Bats: Both **Throws:** Right **Pos:** SS-108; PH-1   **Ht:** 6'0" **Wt:** 190 **Born:** 1/3/77 **Age:** 24

		BATTING													BASERUNNING				PERCENTAGES		
Year Team	Lg Org	G	AB	H	2B	3B	HR	TB	R	RBI	TBB	IBB	SO	HBP	SH	SF	SB	CS	SB%	GDP	Avg	OBP	SLG
1998 Watertown	A- Cle	53	200	60	7	8	4	95	38	26	35	0	35	0	2	0	14	4	.78	2	.300	.404	.475
1999 Kinston	A+ Cle	130	508	121	16	5	7	172	79	59	62	1	126	2	8	2	24	12	.67	6	.238	.322	.339
2000 Akron	AA Cle	96	382	99	17	4	6	142	62	38	42	0	62	2	4	3	16	6	.73	8	.259	.333	.372
Buffalo	AAA Cle	12	38	10	1	1	0	13	5	2	3	0	9	0	0	1	1	0	1.00	2	.263	.310	.342
3 Min. YEARS		291	1128	290	41	20	17	422	184	125	142	1	232	4	14	6	55	22	.71	18	.257	.341	.374

Jose Soriano

Bats: Right **Throws:** Right **Pos:** OF-9; DH-3; PR-2   **Ht:** 6'1" **Wt:** 190 **Born:** 4/20/74 **Age:** 27

		BATTING													BASERUNNING				PERCENTAGES		
Year Team	Lg Org	G	AB	H	2B	3B	HR	TB	R	RBI	TBB	IBB	SO	HBP	SH	SF	SB	CS	SB%	GDP	Avg	OBP	SLG
1993 Athletics	R Oak	48	181	48	7	5	3	74	30	31	12	1	51	0	1	2	8	3	.73	2	.265	.308	.409
1994 Sou Oregon	A- Oak	60	176	38	8	2	3	59	34	23	11	0	48	3	4	4	12	5	.71	3	.216	.268	.335
1995 W Michigan	A Oak	123	413	88	12	2	6	122	64	43	33	3	103	8	15	5	35	12	.74	7	.213	.281	.295
1996 W Michigan	A Oak	126	434	107	20	3	4	145	57	44	31	1	86	5	2	4	20	11	.65	15	.247	.302	.334
1997 Modesto	A+ Oak	124	360	82	13	3	5	116	51	44	37	0	95	5	6	7	28	11	.72	5	.228	.303	.322
1998 Visalia	A+ Oak	86	290	87	13	5	5	125	55	28	35	1	49	3	2	3	26	17	.60	2	.300	.378	.431
1999 Augusta	A Bos	38	148	51	7	5	5	83	28	28	10	0	37	2	0	3	12	5	.71	5	.345	.387	.561
Trenton	AA Bos	61	166	42	9	1	2	59	38	20	12	1	31	2	1	1	15	6	.71	3	.253	.309	.355
2000 Trenton	AA Bos	12	31	6	1	0	0	7	3	2	1	0	5	0	0	0	0	0	—	0	.194	.212	.226
8 Min. YEARS		678	2199	549	90	26	33	790	360	263	182	7	505	28	31	30	156	70	.69	42	.250	.311	.359

Paul Sorrento

Bats: Left **Throws:** Right **Pos:** 1B-33; DH-6; PH-1   **Ht:** 6'2" **Wt:** 210 **Born:** 11/17/65 **Age:** 35

		BATTING													BASERUNNING				PERCENTAGES		
Year Team	Lg Org	G	AB	H	2B	3B	HR	TB	R	RBI	TBB	IBB	SO	HBP	SH	SF	SB	CS	SB%	GDP	Avg	OBP	SLG
1986 Quad City	A Ana	53	177	63	11	2	6	96	33	34	24	0	40	2	0	1	0	0	—	4	.356	.436	.542
Palm Spring	A+ Ana	16	62	15	3	0	1	21	5	7	4	1	15	0	0	0	0	1	.00	3	.242	.288	.339
1987 Palm Spring	A+ Ana	114	370	83	14	2	8	125	66	45	78	7	95	3	0	3	1	2	.33	9	.224	.361	.338
1988 Palm Spring	A+ Ana	133	465	133	30	6	14	217	91	99	110	5	101	2	0	5	3	4	.43	10	.286	.421	.467
1989 Orlando	AA Min	140	509	130	35	2	27	250	81	112	84	7	119	7	0	4	1	1	.50	7	.255	.366	.491
1990 Portland	AAA Min	102	354	107	27	1	19	193	59	72	64	2	95	1	0	5	3	0	1.00	5	.302	.406	.545
1991 Portland	AAA Min	113	409	126	30	2	13	199	59	79	62	5	65	8	0	6	1	0	1.00	15	.308	.404	.487
2000 Sacramento	AAA Oak	40	139	38	9	1	6	67	25	32	33	0	34	0	0	1	1	0	1.00	2	.273	.406	.482
1989 Minnesota	AL	14	21	5	0	0	0	5	2	1	5	1	4	0	0	1	0	0	—	0	.238	.370	.238
1990 Minnesota	AL	41	121	25	4	1	5	46	11	13	12	0	31	1	0	1	1	1	.50	3	.207	.281	.380
1991 Minnesota	AL	26	47	12	2	0	4	26	6	13	4	2	11	0	0	0	0	0	—	3	.255	.314	.553
1992 Cleveland	AL	140	458	123	24	1	18	203	52	60	51	7	89	1	1	3	0	3	.00	13	.269	.341	.443
1993 Cleveland	AL	148	463	119	26	1	18	201	75	65	58	11	121	2	0	4	3	1	.75	10	.257	.340	.434
1994 Cleveland	AL	95	322	90	14	0	14	146	43	62	34	6	68	0	1	3	0	1	.00	7	.280	.345	.453
1995 Cleveland	AL	104	323	76	14	0	25	165	50	79	51	6	71	0	0	4	1	1	.50	10	.235	.336	.511
1996 Seattle	AL	143	471	136	32	1	23	239	67	93	57	10	103	7	2	5	0	2	.00	10	.289	.370	.507
1997 Seattle	AL	146	457	123	19	0	31	235	68	80	51	9	112	3	0	2	0	2	.00	15	.269	.345	.514
1998 Tampa Bay	AL	137	435	98	27	0	17	176	40	57	54	1	133	0	0	3	2	3	.40	8	.225	.313	.405
1999 Tampa Bay	AL	99	294	69	14	1	11	118	40	42	49	1	101	0	1	1	1	1	.50	4	.235	.351	.401
7 Min. YEARS		711	2485	695	159	16	94	1168	419	480	459	27	564	23	0	27	10	8	.56	58	.280	.393	.470
11 Maj. YEARS		1093	3412	876	176	5	166	1560	454	565	426	54	844	21	4	27	8	15	.35	81	.257	.340	.457

Juan Sosa

Bats: Right **Throws:** Right **Pos:** SS-116; OF-3; PH-2; PR-2   **Ht:** 6'1" **Wt:** 175 **Born:** 8/19/75 **Age:** 25

		BATTING													BASERUNNING				PERCENTAGES		
Year Team	Lg Org	G	AB	H	2B	3B	HR	TB	R	RBI	TBB	IBB	SO	HBP	SH	SF	SB	CS	SB%	GDP	Avg	OBP	SLG
1995 Vero Beach	A+ LA	8	27	6	1	1	1	12	2	6	0	0	4	0	0	0	2	0	.00	0	.222	.222	.444
Yakima	A- LA	61	217	51	10	4	3	78	26	16	15	2	39	1	4	0	8	1	.89	4	.235	.285	.359
1996 Savannah	A LA	112	370	94	21	2	7	140	58	38	30	2	64	1	4	1	14	12	.54	9	.254	.311	.378
1997 Vero Beach	A+ LA	92	250	55	5	2	5	79	32	29	14	0	39	2	3	3	20	8	.71	6	.220	.264	.316
1998 Salem	A+ Col	133	529	147	20	12	8	215	88	47	43	1	83	4	7	4	64	16	.80	12	.278	.334	.406
1999 Carolina	AA Col	125	490	135	22	5	7	188	70	42	31	0	65	2	5	6	38	15	.72	12	.276	.318	.384
Colo Sprngs	AAA Col	6	28	11	1	1	1	17	3	5	0	0	1	0	0	0	1	0	1.00	2	.393	.393	.607
2000 Colo Sprngs	AAA Col	118	449	123	25	9	9	193	67	69	31	1	54	3	9	2	23	10	.70	16	.274	.324	.430
1999 Colorado	NL	11	9	2	0	0	0	2	3	0	2	0	2	0	0	0	0	0	—	0	.222	.364	.222
6 Min. YEARS		655	2360	622	105	36	41	922	346	252	164	6	349	13	32	18	168	64	.72	61	.264	.313	.391

Dorian Speed

Bats: Right **Throws:** Right **Pos:** OF-7; DH-1; PR-1   **Ht:** 6'3" **Wt:** 205 **Born:** 3/1/74 **Age:** 27

Year Team	Lg Org	G	AB	H	2B	3B	HR	TB	R	RBI	TBB	IBB	SO	HBP	SH	SF	SB	CS	SB%	GDP	Avg	OBP	SLG
1995 Williamsprt	A- ChC	60	204	44	8	3	2	64	30	23	28	0	56	1	1	3	18	5	.78	3	.216	.309	.314
1997 Rockford	A ChC	44	157	39	7	1	1	51	27	18	18	0	45	4	3	1	18	4	.82	5	.248	.339	.325
1998 Daytona	A+ ChC	85	250	67	11	5	6	106	43	34	20	0	56	2	3	1	13	5	.72	2	.268	.326	.424
1999 West Tenn	AA ChC	121	415	111	21	8	14	190	70	57	27	0	106	8	2	1	22	11	.67	6	.267	.324	.458
2000 Tennessee	AA Tor	8	27	2	0	0	0	2	0	0	0	0	11	0	0	0	2	1	.67	0	.074	.074	.074
5 Min. YEARS		318	1053	263	47	17	23	413	172	132	93	0	274	15	9	6	73	26	.74	16	.250	.318	.392

Tim Spehr

Bats: Right **Throws:** Right **Pos:** C-77; PH-1   **Ht:** 6'2" **Wt:** 200 **Born:** 7/2/66 **Age:** 34

Year Team	Lg Org	G	AB	H	2B	3B	HR	TB	R	RBI	TBB	IBB	SO	HBP	SH	SF	SB	CS	SB%	GDP	Avg	OBP	SLG
1988 Appleton	A KC	31	110	29	3	0	5	47	15	22	10	0	28	4	0	2	3	0	1.00	1	.264	.341	.427
1989 Baseball Cy	A+ KC	18	64	16	5	0	1	24	8	7	5	0	17	0	2	0	1	0	1.00	1	.250	.304	.375
Memphis	AA KC	61	216	42	9	0	8	75	22	23	16	0	59	2	1	1	1	3	.25	2	.194	.255	.347
1990 Omaha	AAA KC	102	307	69	10	2	6	101	42	34	41	0	88	10	6	2	5	5	.50	4	.225	.333	.329
1991 Omaha	AAA KC	72	215	59	14	2	6	95	27	26	25	1	48	4	3	3	3	2	.60	0	.274	.356	.442
1992 Omaha	AAA KC	109	336	85	22	0	15	152	48	42	61	0	89	11	4	1	4	2	.67	5	.253	.384	.452
1993 Ottawa	AAA Mon	46	141	28	6	1	4	48	15	13	14	1	35	6	0	1	2	1	.67	0	.199	.296	.340
1997 Richmond	AAA Atl	36	120	23	5	0	3	37	13	14	12	0	37	1	0	2	0	0	—	1	.192	.267	.308
1998 St. Lucie	A+ NYM	14	38	7	2	0	1	12	7	6	9	0	16	3	0	1	0	0	—	0	.184	.373	.316
Norfolk	AAA NYM	1	1	1	0	0	0	1	0	0	0	0	0	0	0	0	0	0	—	0	1.000	1.000	1.000
2000 Pawtucket	AAA Bos	77	227	34	7	1	5	58	25	25	36	0	85	4	3	3	0	1	.00	3	.150	.274	.256
1991 Kansas City	AL	37	74	14	5	0	3	28	7	14	9	0	18	1	3	1	1	0	1.00	0	.189	.282	.378
1993 Montreal	NL	53	87	20	6	0	2	32	14	10	6	1	20	1	3	2	2	0	1.00	0	.230	.281	.368
1994 Montreal	NL	52	36	9	3	1	0	14	8	5	4	0	11	0	1	0	2	0	1.00	0	.250	.325	.389
1995 Montreal	NL	41	35	9	5	0	1	17	4	3	6	0	7	0	3	0	0	0	—	0	.257	.366	.486
1996 Montreal	NL	63	44	4	1	0	1	8	4	3	3	0	15	1	1	0	1	0	1.00	1	.091	.167	.182
1997 Kansas City	AL	17	35	6	0	0	1	9	3	2	2	0	12	1	0	0	0	0	—	0	.171	.237	.257
Atlanta	NL	8	14	3	1	0	1	7	2	4	0	0	4	0	0	0	1	0	1.00	0	.214	.214	.500
1998 New York	NL	21	51	7	1	0	0	8	3	3	7	1	16	2	0	0	1	0	1.00	1	.137	.267	.157
Kansas City	AL	11	25	6	2	0	1	11	5	2	8	0	3	2	1	0	0	0	—	1	.240	.457	.440
1999 Kansas City	AL	60	155	32	7	0	9	66	26	26	22	0	47	6	2	2	1	0	1.00	0	.206	.324	.426
9 Min. YEARS		567	1775	393	83	6	54	650	222	212	229	2	502	45	19	16	19	14	.58	21	.221	.323	.366
8 Maj. YEARS		363	556	110	31	1	19	200	76	72	67	2	153	14	14	5	9	0	1.00	6	.198	.298	.360

Mike Spiegel

Pitches: Left **Bats:** Left **Pos:** SP-12; RP-2   **Ht:** 6'5" **Wt:** 200 **Born:** 11/24/75 **Age:** 25

Year Team	Lg Org	G	GS	CG	GF	IP	BFP	H	R	ER	HR	SH	SF	HB	TBB	IBB	SO	WP	Bk	W	L	Pct.	ShO	Sv	ERA
1996 Burlington	R+ Cle	14	0	0	6	21.2	97	19	12	9	0	1	0	2	12	0	14	1	0	1	0	1.000	0	0	3.74
1997 Columbus	A Cle	2	2	0	0	10	39	6	4	4	1	0	0	1	5	0	6	0	0	0	0	—	0	0	3.60
1998 Watertown	A- Cle	1	1	0	0	6	25	2	1	0	0	0	0	0	5	0	7	0	1	1	0	1.000	0	0	0.00
Columbus	A Cle	13	13	0	0	65.1	297	75	53	45	7	2	1	6	34	0	61	6	2	5	6	.455	0	0	6.20
1999 Columbus	A Cle	7	7	0	0	35	145	27	13	11	4	1	0	1	14	0	38	2	2	2	0	1.000	0	0	2.83
Kinston	A+ Cle	18	18	0	0	96	405	69	46	33	8	6	4	7	51	0	103	11	0	5	3	.625	0	0	3.09
2000 Akron	AA Cle	9	7	0	1	36.2	182	48	32	29	6	0	3	2	24	1	18	2	0	1	3	.250	0	0	7.12
Kinston	A+ Cle	5	5	0	0	27	117	23	12	11	4	1	1	3	11	0	23	3	1	3	2	.600	0	0	3.67
5 Min. YEARS		69	53	0	7	297.2	1307	269	173	142	30	11	9	24	156	1	270	25	6	18	14	.563	0	0	4.29

Corey Spiers

Pitches: Left **Bats:** Left **Pos:** SP-18; RP-11   **Ht:** 6'0" **Wt:** 204 **Born:** 6/19/75 **Age:** 26

Year Team	Lg Org	G	GS	CG	GF	IP	BFP	H	R	ER	HR	SH	SF	HB	TBB	IBB	SO	WP	Bk	W	L	Pct.	ShO	Sv	ERA
1996 Elizabethtn	R+ Min	17	8	0	2	59.1	289	69	45	22	3	0	3	2	26	0	67	9	1	6	5	.545	0	0	3.34
Fort Wayne	A Min	2	1	0	1	4	23	6	3	3	0	0	0	0	5	0	2	0	0	0	1	.000	0	0	6.75
1997 Fort Wayne	A Min	24	23	0	0	120.1	530	154	83	65	5	4	5	2	33	0	94	12	1	5	9	.357	0	0	4.86
1998 Fort Wayne	A Min	5	5	0	0	27	103	15	7	2	0	0	0	0	13	0	20	0	0	2	0	1.000	0	0	0.67
Fort Myers	A+ Min	24	24	1	0	151.1	650	172	70	56	7	2	5	6	38	0	98	7	1	9	8	.529	0	0	3.33
1999 New Britain	AA Min	8	8	1	0	46.2	182	50	21	18	3	0	3	1	12	0	21	3	0	5	2	.714	1	0	3.47
2000 New Britain	AA Min	17	9	0	0	62	294	94	53	43	6	3	2	2	18	0	28	4	0	4	5	.444	0	0	6.24
Savannah	A Tex	12	9	2	0	65.2	255	51	19	17	3	2	3	2	10	0	54	3	0	4	3	.571	0	0	2.33
5 Min. YEARS		109	87	4	4	536.1	2336	611	301	226	27	11	21	15	155	0	384	38	3	35	33	.515	1	0	3.79

Ryan Spille

Pitches: Left **Bats:** Left **Pos:** SP-23; RP-1   **Ht:** 6'3" **Wt:** 180 **Born:** 11/11/76 **Age:** 24

Year Team	Lg Org	G	GS	CG	GF	IP	BFP	H	R	ER	HR	SH	SF	HB	TBB	IBB	SO	WP	Bk	W	L	Pct.	ShO	Sv	ERA
1999 St.Cathrnes	A- Tor	1	1	0	0	5	17	2	0	0	0	0	0	1	0	0	5	0	1	1	0	1.000	0	0	0.00
Hagerstown	A Tor	14	11	0	0	69.2	263	49	20	17	3	3	1	4	15	0	49	1	1	7	1	.875	0	0	2.20
2000 Dunedin	A+ Tor	20	19	1	0	109.2	451	107	55	52	9	2	4	5	35	1	82	4	0	10	6	.625	0	0	4.27
Tennessee	AA Tor	4	4	0	0	23.2	99	23	11	11	1	2	2	0	10	0	8	0	0	1	1	.500	0	0	4.18
2 Min. YEARS		39	35	1	0	208	830	181	86	80	13	7	7	10	60	1	144	5	2	19	8	.704	0	0	3.46

Junior Spivey

Bats: Right **Throws:** Right **Pos:** 2B-26; SS-6; 3B-1; PH-1 **Ht:** 6'0" **Wt:** 185 **Born:** 1/28/75 **Age:** 26

Year Team	Lg Org	G	AB	H	2B	3B	HR	TB	R	RBI	TBB	IBB	SO	HBP	SH	SF	SB	CS	SB%	GDP	Avg	OBP	SLG
1996 Diamondbcks	R Ari	20	69	23	0	0	0	23	13	3	12	0	16	4	1	1	11	2	.85	0	.333	.453	.333
Lethbridge	R+ Ari	31	107	36	3	4	2	53	30	25	23	0	24	3	1	2	8	3	.73	2	.336	.459	.495
1997 High Desert	A+ Ari	136	491	134	24	6	6	188	88	53	69	2	115	11	2	3	14	9	.61	9	.273	.373	.383
1998 High Desert	A+ Ari	79	285	80	14	5	5	119	64	35	64	0	61	3	0	1	34	12	.74	4	.281	.416	.418
Tulsa	AA Ari	34	119	37	10	1	3	58	26	16	28	1	25	3	1	1	8	4	.67	1	.311	.450	.487
1999 El Paso	AA Ari	44	164	48	10	4	3	75	40	19	36	0	27	2	1	1	14	10	.58	5	.293	.424	.457
2000 Tucson	AAA Ari	28	117	33	8	4	3	58	21	16	11	0	17	0	1	1	3	1	.75	4	.282	.341	.496
El Paso	AA Ari	6	19	8	5	0	1	16	5	2	0	0	5	1	0	0	0	0	—	1	.421	.421	.842
5 Min. YEARS		378	1371	399	74	24	23	590	287	169	243	3	290	26	8	10	92	41	.69	26	.291	.405	.430

Scott Stahoviak

Bats: Left **Throws:** Right **Pos:** OF-8; 3B-3; 1B-3; PH-3 **Ht:** 6'5" **Wt:** 220 **Born:** 3/6/70 **Age:** 31

Year Team	Lg Org	G	AB	H	2B	3B	HR	TB	R	RBI	TBB	IBB	SO	HBP	SH	SF	SB	CS	SB%	GDP	Avg	OBP	SLG
1991 Visalia	A+ Min	43	158	44	9	1	1	58	29	25	22	2	28	3	2	0	9	3	.75	3	.278	.377	.367
1992 Visalia	A+ Min	110	409	126	26	3	5	173	62	68	82	2	66	3	0	2	17	6	.74	6	.308	.425	.423
1993 Nashville	AA Min	93	331	90	25	1	12	153	40	56	56	2	95	1	1	4	10	2	.83	5	.272	.375	.462
1994 Salt Lake	AAA Min	123	437	139	41	6	13	231	96	94	70	5	90	5	0	6	6	8	.43	12	.318	.413	.529
1995 Salt Lake	AAA Min	9	33	10	1	0	0	11	6	5	6	0	3	0	0	0	2	0	1.00	0	.303	.410	.333
1997 Salt Lake	AAA Min	8	28	6	0	0	2	12	5	10	5	0	8	1	0	0	0	0	—	1	.214	.353	.429
1998 Salt Lake	AAA Min	111	399	126	33	6	18	225	71	82	45	4	94	1	0	7	5	2	.71	9	.316	.381	.564
1999 Iowa	AAA ChC	83	274	65	16	1	14	125	51	44	44	2	88	1	2	3	4	1	.80	3	.237	.342	.456
2000 Iowa	AAA ChC	15	36	10	4	0	1	17	3	13	11	2	2	0	0	1	0	1	1.00	1	.278	.438	.472
1993 Minnesota	AL	20	57	11	4	0	0	15	1	1	3	0	22	0	0	0	0	2	.00	2	.193	.233	.263
1995 Minnesota	AL	94	263	70	19	0	3	98	28	23	30	1	61	1	0	2	5	1	.83	3	.266	.341	.373
1996 Minnesota	AL	130	405	115	30	3	13	190	72	61	59	7	114	2	1	2	3	3	.50	9	.284	.376	.469
1997 Minnesota	AL	91	275	63	17	0	10	110	33	33	24	1	73	6	0	4	5	2	.71	7	.229	.301	.400
1998 Minnesota	AL	9	19	2	0	0	1	5	1	1	0	0	7	0	0	0	0	0	—	0	.105	.105	.263
9 Min. YEARS		595	2105	616	155	18	66	1005	363	397	341	19	474	15	5	23	54	22	.71	40	.293	.391	.477
5 Maj. YEARS		344	1019	261	70	3	27	418	135	119	116	9	277	9	1	8	13	8	.62	21	.256	.335	.410

Jason Standridge

Pitches: Right **Bats:** Right **Pos:** SP-27 **Ht:** 6'4" **Wt:** 217 **Born:** 11/9/78 **Age:** 22

Year Team	Lg Org	G	GS	CG	GF	IP	BFP	H	R	ER	HR	SH	SF	HB	TBB	IBB	SO	WP	Bk	W	L	Pct.	ShO	Sv	ERA
1997 Devil Rays	R TB	13	13	0	0	57.2	246	56	30	23	3	2	5	2	13	1	55	2	2	0	6	.000	0	0	3.59
1998 Princeton	R+ TB	12	12	0	0	63	298	82	61	49	4	2	4	3	28	0	47	9	0	4	4	.500	0	0	7.00
1999 Chston-SC	A TB	18	18	3	0	116	455	80	35	26	5	5	5	7	31	0	84	9	2	9	1	.900	3	0	2.02
St. Pete	A+ TB	8	8	0	0	48.1	208	49	21	21	0	1	0	4	20	0	26	6	1	4	4	.500	0	0	3.91
2000 St. Pete	A+ TB	10	10	1	0	56	243	45	28	21	4	0	1	1	31	0	41	6	0	2	4	.333	0	0	3.38
Orlando	AA TB	17	17	2	0	97	416	85	46	39	4	2	2	11	43	0	55	4	0	6	8	.429	0	0	3.62
4 Min. YEARS		78	78	6	0	438	1866	397	221	179	20	12	17	28	166	1	308	36	5	25	27	.481	3	0	3.68

Jason Stanford

Pitches: Left **Bats:** Left **Pos:** SP-26 **Ht:** 6'2" **Wt:** 200 **Born:** 1/23/77 **Age:** 24

Year Team	Lg Org	G	GS	CG	GF	IP	BFP	H	R	ER	HR	SH	SF	HB	TBB	IBB	SO	WP	Bk	W	L	Pct.	ShO	Sv	ERA
2000 Columbus	A Cle	14	14	0	0	79	335	82	32	24	3	1	3	2	20	0	72	3	0	7	4	.636	0	0	2.73
Kinston	A+ Cle	11	11	1	0	70	294	68	22	20	2	1	2	2	17	0	58	0	0	4	3	.571	0	0	2.57
Akron	AA Cle	1	1	0	0	5.2	23	5	1	1	0	0	0	1	1	0	5	0	0	1	0	1.000	0	0	1.59
1 Min. YEARS		26	26	1	0	154.2	652	155	55	45	5	2	5	5	38	0	135	3	0	12	7	.632	0	0	2.62

Andy Stankiewicz

Bats: Right **Throws:** Right **Pos:** 2B-19; 3B-2; PR-2; SS-1 **Ht:** 5'9" **Wt:** 165 **Born:** 8/10/64 **Age:** 36

Year Team	Lg Org	G	AB	H	2B	3B	HR	TB	R	RBI	TBB	IBB	SO	HBP	SH	SF	SB	CS	SB%	GDP	Avg	OBP	SLG
1986 Oneonta	A- NYY	59	216	64	8	3	0	78	51	17	38	0	41	5	4	4	14	3	.82	2	.296	.407	.361
1987 Ft. Laud	A+ NYY	119	456	140	18	7	2	178	80	47	62	1	84	4	7	1	26	13	.67	9	.307	.394	.390
1988 Albany-Col	AA NYY	109	414	111	20	2	1	138	63	33	39	0	53	9	9	2	15	10	.60	6	.268	.343	.333
Columbus	AAA NYY	29	114	25	0	0	0	25	4	4	6	0	25	0	1	0	2	0	1.00	4	.219	.258	.219
1989 Albany-Col	AA NYY	133	498	133	26	2	4	175	74	49	57	2	59	8	3	11	41	9	.82	8	.267	.345	.351
1990 Columbus	AAA NYY	135	446	102	14	4	1	127	68	48	71	1	63	10	7	4	25	8	.76	11	.229	.345	.285
1991 Columbus	AAA NYY	125	372	101	12	4	1	124	47	41	29	0	45	8	8	5	29	16	.64	9	.272	.333	.333
1993 Columbus	AAA NYY	90	331	80	12	5	0	102	45	32	29	0	46	3	4	3	12	8	.60	5	.242	.306	.308
1994 Jackson	AA Hou	5	12	5	0	0	0	5	1	3	0	0	0	0	0	0	0	0	—	1	.417	.385	.417
1995 Tucson	AAA Hou	25	87	24	4	0	1	31	16	15	14	0	14	0	2	1	3	1	.75	3	.276	.373	.356
1998 Diamondbcks	R Ari	3	10	3	0	0	0	3	2	3	0	0	0	0	0	0	0	0	—	0	.300	.300	.300
Tucson	AAA Ari	5	20	6	0	0	0	6	1	2	0	0	1	0	0	0	0	0	—	1	.300	.333	.300
1999 Columbus	AAA NYY	50	163	45	8	3	1	62	34	20	23	0	27	3	4	1	6	1	.86	3	.276	.374	.380
2000 Yankees	R NYY	1	3	0	0	0	0	0	0	0	2	0	1	0	0	0	0	0	—	0	.000	.400	.000
Columbus	AAA NYY	23	64	15	2	1	0	19	13	5	6	0	21	2	0	0	1	0	1.00	1	.234	.319	.297
1992 New York	AL	116	400	107	22	2	2	139	52	25	38	0	42	5	7	1	9	5	.64	13	.268	.338	.348
1993 New York	AL	16	9	0	0	0	0	0	5	0	1	0	1	0	0	0	0	0	—	0	.000	.100	.000
1994 Houston	NL	37	54	14	3	0	1	20	10	5	12	0	12	1	2	0	1	1	.50	2	.259	.403	.370
1995 Houston	NL	43	52	6	1	0	0	7	6	7	12	2	19	0	1	4	2	1	.67	1	.115	.281	.135
1996 Montreal	NL	64	77	22	5	1	0	29	12	9	6	1	12	1	0	0	1	0	1.00	5	.286	.356	.377
1997 Montreal	NL	76	107	24	9	0	1	36	11	5	4	0	22	0	1	1	1	1	.50	1	.224	.250	.336
1998 Arizona	NL	77	145	30	5	0	0	35	9	8	7	0	33	2	0	1	0	1	1.00	3	.207	.252	.241
12 Min. YEARS		911	3206	854	124	31	11	1073	499	319	376	4	473	53	49	33	173	70	.71	63	.266	.350	.335
7 Maj. YEARS		429	844	203	45	3	4	266	105	59	80	3	141	11	18	4	17	9	.65	21	.241	.313	.315

Denny Stark

Pitches: Right **Bats:** Right **Pos:** SP-8 **Ht:** 6'2" **Wt:** 210 **Born:** 10/27/74 **Age:** 26

Year Team	Lg Org	G	GS	CG	GF	IP	BFP	H	R	ER	HR	SH	SF	HB	TBB	IBB	SO	WP	Bk	W	L	Pct.	ShO	Sv	ERA
1996 Everett	A- Sea	12	4	0	4	30.1	133	25	19	15	2	3	1	1	17	0	49	5	1	1	3	.250	0	0	4.45
1997 Wisconsin	A Sea	16	15	1	0	91.1	361	52	27	20	3	4	1	2	33	0	105	5	1	6	3	.667	0	0	1.97
Lancaster	A+ Sea	3	3	0	0	16.2	71	13	7	6	1	1	0	2	10	0	17	0	0	1	1	.500	0	0	3.24
1998 Lancaster	A+ Sea	5	5	0	0	21	100	18	12	10	1	1	0	1	17	0	21	0	0	1	2	.333	0	0	4.29
Mariners	R Sea	3	1	0	0	8.1	36	9	2	2	0	0	0	0	2	0	13	0	0	0	0	—	0	0	2.16
1999 New Haven	AA Sea	26	26	2	0	147.1	646	151	82	72	14	6	2	13	62	0	103	7	1	9	11	.450	1	0	4.40
2000 New Haven	AA Sea	8	8	1	0	49.1	194	31	13	12	1	2	1	3	17	0	42	2	0	4	3	.571	0	0	2.19
1999 Seattle	AL	5	0	0	2	6.1	31	10	8	7	0	0	0	0	4	0	4	0	0	0	0	—	0	0	9.95
5 Min. YEARS		73	62	4	4	364.1	1541	299	162	137	22	17	5	22	158	0	350	19	3	22	23	.489	1	0	3.38

T.J. Staton

Bats: Left **Throws:** Left **Pos:** OF-42; PH-5 **Ht:** 6'3" **Wt:** 210 **Born:** 2/17/75 **Age:** 26

Year Team	Lg Org	G	AB	H	2B	3B	HR	TB	R	RBI	TBB	IBB	SO	HBP	SH	SF	SB	CS	SB%	GDP	Avg	OBP	SLG
1993 Pirates	R Pit	32	115	41	9	2	1	57	23	18	8	0	14	0	0	0	10	2	.83	0	.357	.398	.496
1994 Welland	A- Pit	12	45	8	3	0	0	11	4	4	0	0	7	0	0	0	5	0	1.00	1	.178	.178	.244
Pirates	R Pit	11	39	10	3	0	1	16	3	5	1	0	8	1	0	0	0	0	—	0	.256	.293	.410
Augusta	A Pit	37	125	27	6	1	0	35	9	5	10	0	38	0	1	1	6	1	.86	5	.216	.272	.280
1995 Augusta	A Pit	112	391	114	21	5	5	160	43	53	27	5	97	2	0	1	27	13	.68	6	.292	.340	.409
1996 Carolina	AA Pit	112	386	119	24	3	15	194	72	57	58	1	99	6	0	4	17	7	.71	4	.308	.403	.503
1997 Calgary	AAA Pit	65	199	47	14	0	2	67	30	22	22	0	51	2	1	1	3	3	.50	6	.236	.317	.337
Carolina	AA Pit	58	207	60	11	2	6	93	33	33	12	1	60	5	3	2	8	4	.67	3	.290	.341	.449
1998 Carolina	AA Pit	63	223	67	17	1	7	107	37	48	25	1	52	3	0	1	6	4	.60	5	.300	.375	.480
Nashville	AAA Pit	62	186	45	8	0	6	71	28	21	15	0	55	3	0	1	5	4	.56	3	.242	.307	.382
1999 Ottawa	AAA Mon	14	42	8	3	1	0	13	5	5	10	0	11	0	0	1	2	0	1.00	1	.190	.340	.310
2000 Ottawa	AAA Mon	47	146	35	5	0	3	49	14	16	23	3	35	1	0	0	2	2	.50	2	.240	.347	.336
8 Min. YEARS		625	2104	581	124	15	46	873	301	287	211	11	527	23	5	13	91	40	.69	36	.276	.347	.415

Kennie Steenstra

Pitches: Right **Bats:** Right **Pos:** SP-20; RP-14 **Ht:** 6'5" **Wt:** 215 **Born:** 10/13/70 **Age:** 30

Year Team	Lg Org	G	GS	CG	GF	IP	BFP	H	R	ER	HR	SH	SF	HB	TBB	IBB	SO	WP	Bk	W	L	Pct.	ShO	Sv	ERA
1992 Geneva	A- ChC	3	3	1	0	20	76	11	4	2	0	0	0	0	3	0	12	0	1	3	0	1.000	0	0	0.90
Peoria	A ChC	12	12	4	0	89.2	364	79	29	21	5	2	1	3	21	1	68	4	3	6	3	.667	2	0	2.11
1993 Daytona	A+ ChC	13	13	1	0	81.1	317	64	26	23	2	3	2	8	12	1	57	2	1	5	3	.625	1	0	2.55
Iowa	AAA ChC	1	1	0	0	6.2	32	9	5	5	2	0	0	0	4	0	6	0	0	1	0	1.000	0	0	6.75
Orlando	AA ChC	14	14	2	0	100.1	427	103	47	40	4	4	2	9	25	0	60	5	2	8	3	.727	2	0	3.59
1994 Iowa	AAA ChC	3	3	0	0	13	68	24	21	19	2	0	2	2	4	0	10	0	0	1	2	.333	0	0	13.15
Orlando	AA ChC	23	23	2	0	158.1	654	146	55	46	12	9	3	9	39	4	83	4	1	9	7	.563	1	0	2.61
1995 Iowa	AAA ChC	29	26	6	1	171.1	722	174	85	74	15	6	6	8	48	3	96	6	0	9	12	.429	2	0	3.89
1996 Iowa	AAA ChC	26	26	1	0	158	686	170	96	88	24	5	9	9	47	4	101	2	0	8	12	.400	0	0	5.01
1997 Iowa	AAA ChC	25	25	4	0	160.2	663	161	85	70	15	4	9	0	41	4	111	7	0	5	10	.333	0	0	3.92
1998 Iowa	AAA ChC	25	24	1	0	148	639	171	84	72	16	6	3	1	36	1	104	0	0	11	5	.688	1	0	4.38
1999 Tacoma	AAA Sea	13	10	0	1	51.2	231	60	40	32	5	1	7	3	15	0	24	1	0	1	4	.200	0	0	5.57
Greenville	AA Atl	8	0	0	1	19	80	25	8	8	1	0	1	0	1	0	12	2	0	2	1	.667	0	0	3.79
2000 Memphis	AAA StL	10	1	0	3	25.2	115	28	11	11	1	0	0	2	12	0	13	0	0	1	0	1.000	0	0	3.86
Tucson	AAA Ari	24	19	1	2	130.1	574	159	68	58	15	10	4	4	41	0	62	0	0	8	5	.615	0	0	4.01
1998 Chicago	NL	4	0	0	1	3.1	18	7	4	4	2	0	0	0	1	0	4	0	0	0	0	—	0	0	10.80
9 Min. YEARS		229	200	23	8	1334	5648	1384	664	569	119	50	49	58	349	18	819	33	8	78	67	.538	9	2	3.84

Mike Stefanski

Bats: Right **Throws:** Right **Pos:** C-25; PH-5; 1B-1; DH-1 **Ht:** 6'2" **Wt:** 202 **Born:** 9/12/69 **Age:** 31

Year Team	Lg Org	G	AB	H	2B	3B	HR	TB	R	RBI	TBB	IBB	SO	HBP	SH	SF	SB	CS	SB%	GDP	Avg	OBP	SLG
1991 Brewers	R Mil	56	206	76	5	5	0	91	43	43	22	0	22	5	0	6	3	2	.60	4	.369	.431	.442
1992 Beloit	A Mil	116	385	105	12	0	4	129	66	45	55	1	81	4	3	3	9	4	.69	11	.273	.367	.335
1993 Stockton	A+ Mil	97	345	111	22	2	10	167	58	57	49	2	45	5	1	2	6	1	.86	15	.322	.411	.484
1994 El Paso	AA Mil	95	312	82	7	6	8	125	59	56	32	0	80	0	2	5	4	3	.57	5	.263	.327	.401
1995 El Paso	AA Mil	6	27	11	3	0	1	17	5	6	0	0	3	0	0	0	1	0	1.00	0	.407	.407	.630
New Orleans	AAA Mil	78	228	56	10	2	2	76	30	24	14	0	28	1	5	5	2	0	1.00	8	.246	.286	.333
1996 Louisville	AAA StL	53	126	26	7	1	2	41	11	9	11	1	11	1	1	2	1	2	.33	4	.206	.271	.325
1997 Arkansas	AA StL	1	4	1	0	1	0	3	1	0	0	0	0	0	0	0	0	0	—	1	.250	.250	.750
Louisville	AAA StL	57	197	60	10	0	6	88	26	22	12	0	20	1	2	1	0	1	.00	6	.305	.346	.447
1998 Memphis	AAA StL	95	298	79	19	1	6	118	34	44	23	4	42	4	5	2	1	2	.33	11	.265	.324	.396
1999 Memphis	AAA StL	64	201	60	12	0	4	84	27	22	17	0	28	4	1	2	3	0	1.00	8	.299	.362	.418
2000 Louisville	AAA Cin	32	96	22	7	0	2	35	12	10	4	1	17	3	0	0	0	0	—	3	.229	.282	.365
10 Min. YEARS		750	2425	689	114	18	45	974	372	338	239	9	377	28	20	28	30	15	.67	76	.284	.351	.402

Dernell Stenson

Bats: Left **Throws:** Left **Pos:** 1B-67; OF-21; DH-10; PH-1 **Ht:** 6'1" **Wt:** 230 **Born:** 6/17/78 **Age:** 23

Year Team	Lg Org	G	AB	H	2B	3B	HR	TB	R	RBI	TBB	IBB	SO	HBP	SH	SF	SB	CS	SB%	GDP	Avg	OBP	SLG
1996 Red Sox	R Bos	32	97	21	3	1	2	32	16	15	16	0	26	7	0	5	4	3	.57	0	.216	.358	.330
1997 Michigan	A Bos	131	471	137	35	2	15	221	79	80	72	6	105	19	0	8	6	4	.60	10	.291	.400	.469
1998 Trenton	AA Bos	138	505	130	21	1	24	225	90	71	84	3	135	14	1	4	5	3	.63	6	.257	.376	.446
1999 Red Sox	R Bos	6	23	5	0	0	2	11	2	7	3	0	5	0	0	0	0	0	—	0	.217	.308	.478
Pawtucket	AAA Bos	121	440	119	28	2	18	205	64	82	55	5	119	6	2	5	2	1	.67	7	.270	.356	.466
2000 Pawtucket	AAA Bos	98	380	102	14	0	23	185	59	71	45	6	99	4	0	2	0	0	—	8	.268	.349	.487
5 Min. YEARS		526	1916	514	101	6	84	879	310	326	275	20	489	50	3	24	17	11	.61	31	.268	.370	.459

Brent Stentz

Pitches: Right **Bats:** Right **Pos:** RP-66 **Ht:** 6'5" **Wt:** 225 **Born:** 7/24/75 **Age:** 25

Year Team	Lg Org	G	GS	CG	GF	IP	BFP	H	R	ER	HR	SH	SF	HB	TBB	IBB	SO	WP	Bk	W	L	Pct.	ShO	Sv	ERA
1995 Tigers	R Det	24	0	0	24	26.2	107	21	7	7	1	1	1	1	12	2	28	4	1	2	1	.667	0	16	2.36
Lakeland	A+ Det	2	0	0	1	2	6	0	0	0	0	0	0	0	0	0	4	0	0	0	0	—	0	0	0.00
1996 Fayettevlle	A Det	45	8	0	7	98	413	91	51	38	4	4	1	6	27	1	92	5	2	7	8	.467	0	2	3.49
1997 Fort Myers	A+ Min	49	1	0	30	69.1	285	53	20	19	4	2	3	2	24	3	70	5	2	7	2	.778	0	17	2.47
1998 New Britain	AA Min	57	0	0	53	59	244	44	13	13	3	2	1	1	28	2	65	1	0	1	2	.333	0	43	1.98
1999 Salt Lake	AAA Min	23	0	0	15	25.2	139	43	34	32	6	2	2	0	21	1	23	3	1	0	3	.000	0	3	11.22
New Britain	AA Min	32	0	0	28	31.1	125	23	13	13	3	0	0	0	12	2	44	0	0	0	1	.000	0	9	3.73
2000 New Britain	AA Min	24	0	0	18	25	110	32	14	12	2	0	1	0	5	0	27	2	0	1	2	.333	0	7	4.32
Salt Lake	AAA Min	42	0	0	35	46.2	183	31	14	10	6	1	1	0	13	1	47	1	1	4	2	.667	0	13	1.93
6 Min. YEARS		298	9	0	211	383.2	1612	338	166	144	29	12	10	10	142	12	400	21	7	22	21	.512	0	110	3.38

Brian Stephenson

Pitches: Right **Bats:** Right **Pos:** SP-3; RP-1 **Ht:** 6'3" **Wt:** 210 **Born:** 7/17/73 **Age:** 27

Year Team	Lg Org	G	GS	CG	GF	IP	BFP	H	R	ER	HR	SH	SF	HB	TBB	IBB	SO	WP	Bk	W	L	Pct.	ShO	Sv	ERA
1994 Williamsprt	A- ChC	5	5	0	0	19	80	17	9	9	2	0	2	4	4	0	13	1	1	0	2	.000	0	0	4.26
Peoria	A ChC	6	6	2	0	42.1	180	41	18	15	3	3	0	6	6	1	29	1	0	3	1	.750	0	0	3.19
1995 Daytona	A+ ChC	26	26	0	0	150	640	145	79	66	7	6	3	7	58	2	109	14	2	10	9	.526	0	0	3.96
1996 Orlando	AA ChC	32	20	0	3	128.2	574	130	82	67	13	4	9	5	61	3	106	10	1	5	13	.278	0	1	4.69
1997 Orlando	AA ChC	6	0	0	2	9.1	42	10	10	10	4	0	1	0	5	0	9	4	0	0	2	.000	0	0	9.64
1999 Cubs	R ChC	1	0	0	0	2	6	1	0	0	0	0	0	0	0	0	0	0	0	0	0	—	0	0	0.00
Eugene	A- ChC	2	2	0	0	4	22	4	5	2	0	0	0	1	4	0	4	0	0	0	1	.000	0	0	4.50
2000 San Antonio	AA LA	4	3	0	0	16.1	73	19	11	9	1	0	4	0	8	0	14	1	0	1	0	1.000	0	0	4.96
6 Min. YEARS		82	62	2	5	371.2	1617	367	214	178	30	13	19	23	146	6	286	31	4	19	28	.404	0	1	4.31

Kris Stevens

Pitches: Left **Bats:** Right **Pos:** SP-7 **Ht:** 6'2" **Wt:** 188 **Born:** 9/19/77 **Age:** 23

Year Team	Lg Org	G	GS	CG	GF	IP	BFP	H	R	ER	HR	SH	SF	HB	TBB	IBB	SO	WP	Bk	W	L	Pct.	ShO	Sv	ERA
1996 Martinsvlle	R+ Phi	10	10	0	0	47	194	54	23	19	2	3	1	1	10	0	41	2	1	1	4	.200	0	0	3.64
Batavia	A- Phi	3	3	0	0	13.1	61	16	12	12	2	1	0	0	6	0	11	0	0	1	1	.500	0	0	8.10
1997 Piedmont	A Phi	14	14	3	0	89.1	361	66	30	22	2	1	1	3	31	0	72	4	0	6	4	.600	3	0	2.22
Clearwater	A+ Phi	13	13	0	0	71	319	80	42	36	4	3	4	3	30	0	53	3	0	6	3	.667	0	0	4.56
1998 Clearwater	A+ Phi	5	5	0	0	29	113	20	6	5	0	0	4	0	7	0	14	4	0	2	2	.500	0	0	1.55
Reading	AA Phi	25	24	1	0	146.2	658	163	99	94	9	10	4	3	70	0	113	6	2	8	11	.421	1	0	5.77
2000 Reading	AA Phi	7	7	0	0	40.1	173	44	22	21	3	1	0	0	12	0	20	1	0	5	2	.714	0	0	4.69
4 Min. YEARS		77	76	4	0	436.2	1879	443	234	209	22	19	10	10	166	0	324	20	3	29	27	.518	4	0	4.31

Tony Stevens

Bats: Both **Throws:** Right **Pos:** SS-123; OF-4 **Ht:** 5'9" **Wt:** 153 **Born:** 9/18/78 **Age:** 22

Year Team	Lg Org	G	AB	H	2B	3B	HR	TB	R	RBI	TBB	IBB	SO	HBP	SH	SF	SB	CS	SB%	GDP	Avg	OBP	SLG
1997 Twins	R Min	47	170	41	3	0	1	47	23	17	9	0	21	2	1	2	9	2	.82	8	.241	.284	.276
1998 Twins	R Min	52	187	48	7	1	3	66	30	12	11	0	19	2	1	1	3	7	.30	1	.257	.303	.353
Fort Myers	A+ Min	7	7	2	0	0	0	2	0	1	0	0	0	0	0	0	0	0	—	0	.286	.286	.286
2000 Quad City	A Min	116	443	103	15	2	0	122	53	30	34	0	61	9	13	4	14	11	.56	4	.233	.298	.275
New Britain	AA Min	11	46	12	2	0	0	14	1	4	1	0	9	1	1	1	0	1	.00	2	.261	.286	.304
3 Min. YEARS		229	853	206	27	3	4	251	107	64	55	0	110	14	16	8	26	21	.55	15	.242	.296	.294

Rod Stevenson

Pitches: Right **Bats:** Right **Pos:** RP-51 **Ht:** 6'2" **Wt:** 220 **Born:** 3/21/74 **Age:** 27

Year Team	Lg Org	G	GS	CG	GF	IP	BFP	H	R	ER	HR	SH	SF	HB	TBB	IBB	SO	WP	Bk	W	L	Pct.	ShO	Sv	ERA
1996 Vermont	A- Mon	22	0	0	5	31.2	133	24	11	10	1	1	0	1	13	0	46	2	2	5	2	.714	0	1	2.84
1997 Cape Fear	A Mon	16	0	0	15	17	66	7	3	1	0	0	0	0	6	1	20	1	0	1	1	.500	0	5	0.53
Wst Plm Bch	A+ Mon	26	0	0	12	35.1	158	31	13	7	2	2	1	1	16	0	39	0	0	3	3	.500	0	2	1.78
Harrisburg	AA Mon	4	0	0	2	7	33	9	5	3	1	0	0	0	5	1	6	1	0	0	0	—	0	0	3.86
1998 Jupiter	A+ Mon	19	0	0	14	23.2	91	13	7	7	2	1	1	0	6	0	21	1	0	0	1	.000	0	10	2.66
Harrisburg	AA Mon	37	0	0	23	39.1	168	32	19	19	3	2	2	2	18	5	47	1	0	5	0	1.000	0	8	4.35
1999 Ottawa	AAA Mon	17	0	0	11	18.1	76	15	9	8	4	0	3	2	7	0	12	1	0	2	1	.667	0	2	3.93
Harrisburg	AA Mon	37	0	0	25	51.1	224	54	32	25	8	2	5	1	21	1	34	5	0	2	9	.182	0	4	4.38
2000 Ottawa	AAA Mon	10	0	0	3	17	76	31	25	22	6	0	2	1	7	0	8	3	1	0	0	—	0	0	15.23
Harrisburg	AA Mon	41	0	0	14	53.2	238	63	26	23	3	2	3	3	15	0	38	0	0	4	1	.800	0	0	3.86
5 Min. YEARS		229	0	0	123	290.1	1263	279	150	125	30	10	17	11	114	8	271	15	3	22	18	.550	0	32	3.87

Paul Stewart

Pitches: Right **Bats:** Right **Pos:** SP-20; RP-7 **Ht:** 6'5" **Wt:** 200 **Born:** 10/21/78 **Age:** 22

Year Team	Lg Org	G	GS	CG	GF	IP	BFP	H	R	ER	HR	SH	SF	HB	TBB	IBB	SO	WP	Bk	W	L	Pct.	ShO	Sv	ERA
1996 Ogden	R+ Mil	12	9	1	0	43.2	211	47	49	38	11	0	4	4	26	0	39	6	1	1	4	.200	0	0	7.83
1997 Ogden	R+ Mil	15	15	1	0	81.1	370	88	59	48	13	1	3	6	30	0	82	3	2	5	6	.455	1	0	5.31
1998 Beloit	A Mil	26	25	1	0	143.1	633	164	99	78	22	1	4	9	45	1	114	8	0	8	10	.444	0	0	4.90
1999 Stockton	A+ Mil	27	25	5	0	170.1	733	171	90	75	18	6	9	4	61	0	117	7	1	10	11	.476	1	0	3.96
2000 Huntsville	AA Mil	10	10	0	0	47	224	75	36	32	5	2	0	2	22	0	30	5	1	1	7	.125	0	0	6.13
Mudville	A+ Mil	17	10	0	3	59.1	263	56	32	29	6	1	0	2	31	0	61	3	1	2	4	.333	0	0	4.40
5 Min. YEARS		107	94	7	4	545	2434	601	365	300	75	11	20	27	215	1	443	32	6	27	42	.391	2	0	4.95

Scott Stewart

Pitches: Left Bats: Right Pos: RP-52; SP-1   Ht: 6'2" Wt: 223 Born: 8/14/75 Age: 25

Year Team	Lg Org	G	GS	CG	GF	IP	BFP	H	R	ER	HR	SH	SF	HB	TBB	IBB	SO	WP	Bk	W	L	Pct.	ShO	Sv	ERA
1994 Rangers	R Tex	14	8	0	3	54.1	221	47	22	17	1	1	0	2	12	0	62	7	9	4	1	.800	0	1	2.82
1995 Chston-SC	A Tex	11	11	1	0	75.2	302	76	38	31	6	1	4	1	14	1	47	3	5	1	7	.125	0	0	3.69
Twins	R Min	3	1	0	0	5.2	29	7	4	4	0	0	0	1	4	0	9	0	1	0	0	—	0	0	6.35
1996 St. Paul	IND —	19	18	0	0	86.1	417	121	70	56	13	5	3	1	42	2	54	14	1	6	8	.429	0	0	5.84
1997 St. Lucie	A+ NYM	22	18	4	1	123.1	496	114	62	55	8	3	7	4	18	1	64	4	7	5	10	.333	0	0	4.01
1998 Norfolk	AAA NYM	9	9	0	0	51.2	235	60	43	38	12	3	2	1	22	0	32	0	0	0	6	.000	0	0	6.62
Binghamton	AA NYM	24	13	0	3	90	382	91	44	37	12	4	2	1	29	2	65	2	4	8	5	.615	0	2	3.70
1999 Binghamton	AA NYM	1	1	0	0	5	18	3	0	0	0	0	0	0	0	0	5	0	0	1	0	1.000	0	0	0.00
Norfolk	AAA NYM	35	14	0	3	99.2	442	109	55	49	9	5	2	2	36	1	85	5	3	6	4	.600	0	0	4.42
2000 Norfolk	AAA NYM	53	1	0	18	72	313	80	32	28	3	5	2	3	18	2	57	8	0	3	5	.375	0	5	3.50
7 Min. YEARS		191	94	5	28	663.2	2855	708	370	315	64	27	22	15	195	9	480	43	30	34	46	.425	0	8	4.27

Ricky Stone

Pitches: Right Bats: Right Pos: RP-41; SP-7   Ht: 6'1" Wt: 168 Born: 2/28/75 Age: 26

Year Team	Lg Org	G	GS	CG	GF	IP	BFP	H	R	ER	HR	SH	SF	HB	TBB	IBB	SO	WP	Bk	W	L	Pct.	ShO	Sv	ERA
1994 Great Falls	R+ LA	13	7	0	4	50.2	232	55	40	25	5	0	1	2	24	0	48	9	0	2	2	.500	0	2	4.44
1995 San Berndno	A+ LA	12	12	0	0	58	273	79	50	42	7	6	3	2	25	0	31	5	0	3	5	.375	0	0	6.52
Yakima	A- LA	16	6	0	7	48	213	54	31	28	5	2	2	2	20	0	28	4	1	4	4	.500	0	2	5.25
1996 Savannah	A LA	5	5	0	0	31.2	130	34	15	14	2	2	1	0	9	0	31	5	0	2	1	.667	0	0	3.98
Vero Beach	A+ LA	21	21	1	0	112.2	488	115	58	48	9	4	3	3	46	0	74	10	0	8	6	.571	0	0	3.83
1997 San Antonio	AA LA	25	5	0	10	52.2	245	63	33	32	4	4	1	3	30	0	46	3	0	0	3	.000	0	3	5.47
San Antonio	A+ LA	8	8	0	0	53.2	206	40	22	20	4	2	1	2	10	0	40	2	0	3	3	.500	0	0	3.35
1998 San Antonio	AA LA	13	13	1	0	82	336	76	40	35	7	5	1	1	26	0	69	6	0	7	2	.778	1	0	3.84
Albuquerque	AAA LA	18	16	0	0	105.1	465	120	69	63	13	2	1	3	41	0	85	9	1	5	5	.500	0	0	5.38
1999 Albuquerque	AAA LA	27	27	2	0	167	764	205	123	102	23	8	7	8	71	4	132	11	1	6	10	.375	0	0	5.50
2000 Albuquerque	AAA LA	48	7	0	22	120.1	535	146	79	66	9	7	6	7	42	3	75	10	0	9	5	.643	0	5	4.94
7 Min. YEARS		206	127	4	43	882	3887	987	560	475	88	42	27	33	344	7	659	74	3	49	46	.516	1	12	4.85

Mike Stoner

Bats: Right Throws: Right Pos: DH-58; 1B-37; OF-11; PH-8   Ht: 6'0" Wt: 200 Born: 5/23/73 Age: 28

Year Team	Lg Org	G	AB	H	2B	3B	HR	TB	R	RBI	TBB	IBB	SO	HBP	SH	SF	SB	CS	SB%	GDP	Avg	OBP	SLG
1996 Lethbridge	R+ Ari	24	78	25	1	2	1	33	13	13	12	0	13	2	1	2	1	0	1.00	1	.321	.415	.423
Bakersfield	A+ Ari	36	147	43	6	1	6	69	25	22	8	0	18	0	0	1	1	1	.50	4	.293	.327	.469
1997 High Desert	A+ Ari	136	567	203	44	5	33	356	115	142	36	4	91	3	1	11	6	4	.60	17	.358	.392	.628
1998 Tucson	AAA Ari	106	394	123	22	3	5	166	46	49	27	4	52	4	0	3	3	0	1.00	10	.312	.360	.421
1999 Tucson	AAA Ari	14	21	9	1	0	0	10	2	6	2	0	3	0	0	1	0	0	—	0	.429	.458	.476
El Paso	AA Ari	1	0	0	0	0	0	0	1	0	1	0	0	0	0	0	0	0	—	0	—	1.000	—
Erie	AA Ana	14	62	21	4	0	3	34	10	15	2	1	8	0	0	0	0	1	.00	0	.339	.359	.548
Edmonton	AAA Ana	22	81	28	5	1	3	44	12	12	4	0	11	0	0	0	0	1	.00	2	.346	.376	.543
2000 Edmonton	AAA Ana	85	329	90	11	2	13	144	48	44	16	0	42	4	0	2	1	2	.33	9	.274	.313	.438
Iowa	AAA ChC	26	85	29	6	0	2	41	16	17	6	1	6	0	0	0	0	0	—	2	.341	.418	.482
5 Min. YEARS		464	1764	571	100	14	66	897	288	320	114	10	244	19	2	21	12	9	.57	45	.324	.367	.509

Jim Stoops

Pitches: Right Bats: Right Pos: RP-36   Ht: 6'2" Wt: 180 Born: 6/30/72 Age: 29

Year Team	Lg Org	G	GS	CG	GF	IP	BFP	H	R	ER	HR	SH	SF	HB	TBB	IBB	SO	WP	Bk	W	L	Pct.	ShO	Sv	ERA
1995 Bellingham	A- SF	24	0	0	14	42	178	32	23	16	1	2	1	5	17	0	58	2	0	6	5	.545	0	4	3.43
1996 Burlington	A SF	46	0	0	18	60.2	262	43	24	17	2	4	1	6	40	4	69	6	1	3	3	.500	0	2	2.52
1997 San Jose	A+ SF	50	0	0	16	91.2	401	92	56	53	3	2	3	7	45	2	114	7	1	2	5	.286	0	4	5.20
1998 San Jose	A+ SF	45	0	0	43	55.1	222	28	7	6	0	0	0	3	25	0	96	1	0	2	1	.667	0	31	0.98
Salem	A+ Col	3	0	0	1	4.1	16	2	0	0	0	1	0	0	1	0	8	0	0	0	0	—	0	0	0.00
Colo Sprngs	AAA Col	11	0	0	6	14.2	58	6	2	2	0	0	2	1	8	0	17	0	0	1	0	1.000	0	1	1.23
1999 Colo Sprngs	AAA Col	55	5	0	22	88.2	400	93	54	51	11	6	6	4	56	2	57	7	0	3	7	.300	0	3	5.18
2000 Colo Sprngs	AAA Col	3	0	0	0	3.2	23	6	2	1	0	0	0	0	6	0	4	2	0	0	0	—	0	0	2.45
Carolina	AA Col	33	0	0	15	52.1	222	37	20	16	3	4	4	5	33	2	47	4	0	5	3	.625	0	2	2.75
1998 Colorado	NL	3	0	0	0	4	17	5	1	1	1	0	0	1	3	0	0	0	0	1	0	1.000	0	0	2.25
6 Min. YEARS		270	5	0	135	413.1	1782	339	192	162	20	19	17	31	231	10	470	29	2	22	24	.478	0	50	3.53

DaRond Stovall

Bats: Both Throws: Left Pos: OF-62; DH-15; PH-4   Ht: 6'1" Wt: 185 Born: 1/3/73 Age: 28

Year Team	Lg Org	G	AB	H	2B	3B	HR	TB	R	RBI	TBB	IBB	SO	HBP	SH	SF	SB	CS	SB%	GDP	Avg	OBP	SLG
1991 Johnson Cty	R+ StL	48	134	19	2	2	0	25	16	5	23	1	63	0	0	0	8	3	.73	1	.142	.268	.187
1992 Savannah	A StL	135	450	92	13	7	7	140	51	40	63	0	138	0	1	1	20	14	.59	13	.204	.302	.311
1993 Springfield	A StL	135	460	118	19	4	20	205	73	81	53	2	143	0	2	1	18	12	.60	5	.257	.333	.446
1994 St. Pete	A+ StL	134	507	113	20	6	15	190	68	69	62	4	154	0	2	5	24	8	.75	10	.223	.305	.375
1995 Wst Plm Bch	A+ Mon	121	461	107	22	2	4	145	52	51	44	2	117	0	2	3	18	12	.60	4	.232	.297	.315
1996 Expos	R Mon	9	34	15	3	2	0	22	7	3	6	0	6	0	0	0	3	0	1.00	0	.441	.486	.647
Wst Plm Bch	A+ Mon	8	31	14	4	0	1	21	8	8	6	0	7	0	0	0	2	2	.50	1	.452	.541	.677
Harrisburg	AA Mon	74	262	60	7	1	10	99	38	36	32	1	86	2	4	0	10	5	.67	5	.221	.307	.364
1997 Harrisburg	AA Mon	45	169	48	4	1	9	81	29	39	23	1	30	0	0	3	4	0	1.00	3	.284	.364	.479
Ottawa	AAA Mon	98	342	83	23	2	4	122	40	48	31	3	114	0	2	3	10	13	.43	6	.243	.306	.357
1998 Ottawa	AAA Mon	44	150	34	7	1	8	67	15	22	11	1	51	0	0	1	6	2	.75	6	.227	.320	.447

Year Team	Lg Org	G	AB	H	2B	3B	HR	TB	R	RBI	TBB	IBB	SO	HBP	SH	SF	SB	CS	SB%	GDP	Avg	OBP	SLG
1999 Calgary	AAA Fla	37	106	20	3	3	3	38	10	13	11	1	44	0	1	1	0	0	—	0	.189	.263	.358
San Antonio	AA LA	12	49	18	3	0	4	33	9	11	7	0	10	0	0	0	1	1	.50	0	.367	.446	.673
Albuquerque	AAA LA	46	160	35	12	0	7	68	30	21	22	0	65	0	0	3	8	4	.67	2	.219	.308	.425
2000 Edmonton	AAA Ana	79	252	66	7	7	9	114	35	32	35	0	76	1	2	0	10	4	.71	4	.262	.354	.452
1998 Montreal	NL	62	78	16	2	1	2	26	11	6	6	0	29	0	0	0	1	0	1.00	1	.205	.262	.333
10 Min. YEARS		1025	3577	842	149	38	101	1370	479	483	436	16	1104	5	18	22	142	80	.64	60	.235	.318	.383

Chris Stowers

Bats: Left **Throws:** Left **Pos:** OF-43; PH-7   **Ht:** 6'3" **Wt:** 195 **Born:** 8/18/74 **Age:** 26

Year Team	Lg Org	G	AB	H	2B	3B	HR	TB	R	RBI	TBB	IBB	SO	HBP	SH	SF	SB	CS	SB%	GDP	Avg	OBP	SLG
1996 Vermont	A- Mon	72	282	90	21	9	7	150	58	44	21	6	37	2	0	0	16	5	.76	4	.319	.370	.532
1997 Wst Plm Bch	A+ Mon	111	414	113	15	5	4	150	56	30	30	5	77	7	2	2	19	14	.58	0	.273	.331	.362
Harrisburg	AA Mon	19	59	17	4	2	0	25	9	5	5	2	11	0	1	0	3	1	.75	1	.288	.344	.424
1998 Harrisburg	AA Mon	134	510	137	31	5	17	229	86	66	42	2	109	8	3	3	24	7	.77	7	.269	.332	.449
1999 Ottawa	AAA Mon	118	431	102	17	4	5	142	60	37	39	2	92	4	3	2	28	9	.76	10	.237	.305	.329
2000 Ottawa	AAA Mon	49	135	26	2	0	1	31	10	13	13	1	27	1	1	1	4	0	1.00	4	.193	.267	.230
1999 Montreal	NL	4	2	0	0	0	0	0	0	0	0	0	0	0	0	0	0	0	—	0	.000	.000	.000
5 Min. YEARS		503	1831	485	90	25	34	727	279	195	150	18	353	22	10	8	94	36	.72	26	.265	.327	.397

Doug Strange

Bats: Both **Throws:** Right **Pos:** DH-11; 1B-5; 3B-1; OF-1   **Ht:** 6'1" **Wt:** 188 **Born:** 4/13/64 **Age:** 37

Year Team	Lg Org	G	AB	H	2B	3B	HR	TB	R	RBI	TBB	IBB	SO	HBP	SH	SF	SB	CS	SB%	GDP	Avg	OBP	SLG
1985 Bristol	R+ Det	65	226	69	16	1	6	105	43	45	22	1	30	3	4	3	6	0	1.00	6	.305	.370	.465
1986 Lakeland	A+ Det	126	466	119	29	4	2	162	59	63	65	5	59	2	7	6	18	6	.75	18	.255	.345	.348
1987 Glens Falls	AA Det	115	431	130	31	1	13	202	63	70	31	3	53	3	0	5	5	11	.31	17	.302	.349	.469
Toledo	AAA Det	16	45	11	2	0	1	16	7	5	4	0	7	0	1	1	3	2	.60	1	.244	.300	.356
1988 Toledo	AAA Det	82	278	56	8	2	6	86	23	19	8	0	38	2	2	2	9	7	.56	8	.201	.228	.309
Glens Falls	AA Det	57	218	61	11	1	1	77	32	36	16	2	28	0	1	8	11	1	.92	5	.280	.318	.353
1989 Toledo	AAA Det	83	304	75	15	2	8	118	38	42	34	2	49	2	2	2	8	3	.73	11	.247	.325	.388
1990 Tucson	AAA Hou	37	98	22	3	0	0	25	7	7	8	0	23	0	0	0	0	0	—	4	.224	.283	.255
Iowa	AAA ChC	82	269	82	17	1	5	116	31	35	28	2	42	1	3	1	6	3	.67	8	.305	.371	.431
1991 Iowa	AAA ChC	131	509	149	35	5	8	218	76	56	49	9	75	1	7	7	10	5	.67	12	.293	.352	.428
1992 Iowa	AAA ChC	55	212	65	16	1	4	95	32	26	9	0	32	1	1	4	3	3	.50	4	.307	.332	.448
1997 Ottawa	AAA Mon	2	7	3	1	0	0	4	3	0	1	0	1	0	0	0	0	0	—	0	.429	.500	.571
1998 Carolina	AA Pit	4	14	5	0	0	0	5	4	0	2	0	1	0	0	0	0	0	—	0	.357	.438	.357
1999 Nashville	AAA Pit	5	13	1	1	0	0	2	2	0	0	0	2	1	0	0	0	0	—	1	.077	.143	.154
2000 Greenville	AA Atl	18	58	12	3	0	0	15	4	5	5	0	12	2	0	1	0	1	.00	0	.207	.288	.259
1989 Detroit	AL	64	196	42	4	1	1	51	16	14	17	0	36	1	1	3	3	3	.50	6	.214	.280	.260
1991 Chicago	NL	3	9	4	1	0	0	5	0	1	0	0	1	1	0	1	1	0	1.00	0	.444	.455	.556
1992 Chicago	NL	52	94	15	1	0	1	19	7	5	10	2	15	0	2	0	1	0	1.00	1	.160	.240	.202
1993 Texas	AL	145	484	124	29	0	7	174	58	60	43	3	69	3	8	4	6	4	.60	12	.256	.318	.360
1994 Texas	AL	73	226	48	12	1	5	77	26	26	15	0	38	3	4	2	1	3	.25	6	.212	.268	.341
1995 Seattle	AL	74	155	42	9	2	2	61	19	21	10	0	25	2	1	0	0	3	.00	3	.271	.323	.394
1996 Seattle	AL	88	183	43	7	1	3	61	19	23	14	0	31	1	0	2	1	0	1.00	3	.235	.290	.333
1997 Montreal	NL	118	327	84	16	2	12	140	40	47	36	9	76	2	5	2	0	2	.00	4	.257	.332	.428
1998 Pittsburgh	NL	90	185	32	8	0	0	40	9	14	10	1	39	1	3	2	1	0	1.00	5	.173	.217	.216
12 Min. YEARS		878	3148	860	188	18	54	1246	424	409	282	24	452	18	30	40	79	42	.65	97	.273	.333	.396
9 Maj. YEARS		707	1859	434	87	7	31	628	194	211	155	15	330	14	26	13	14	15	.48	41	.233	.295	.338

Pat Strange

Pitches: Right **Bats:** Right **Pos:** SP-23; RP-6   **Ht:** 6'5" **Wt:** 243 **Born:** 8/23/80 **Age:** 20

Year Team	Lg Org	G	GS	CG	GF	IP	BFP	H	R	ER	HR	SH	SF	HB	TBB	IBB	SO	WP	Bk	W	L	Pct.	ShO	Sv	ERA
1998 Mets	R NYM	4	4	0	0	19	79	18	3	3	0	0	0	0	7	0	19	0	0	1	1	.500	0	0	1.42
1999 Capital Cty	A NYM	28	21	2	1	154	627	138	57	45	4	4	3	10	29	1	113	7	0	12	5	.706	0	1	2.63
2000 St. Lucie	A+ NYM	19	13	2	1	88	374	78	48	35	4	2	5	9	32	0	77	9	1	10	1	.909	0	0	3.58
Binghamton	AA NYM	10	10	0	0	55.1	252	62	30	28	2	3	2	1	30	0	36	3	0	4	3	.571	0	0	4.55
3 Min. YEARS		61	48	4	2	316.1	1332	296	138	111	10	9	10	21	98	1	245	19	1	27	10	.730	0	1	3.16

Mark Strittmatter

Bats: Right **Throws:** Right **Pos:** C-24; PH-3; DH-1   **Ht:** 6'1" **Wt:** 210 **Born:** 4/4/69 **Age:** 32

Year Team	Lg Org	G	AB	H	2B	3B	HR	TB	R	RBI	TBB	IBB	SO	HBP	SH	SF	SB	CS	SB%	GDP	Avg	OBP	SLG
1992 Bend	A- Col	35	101	26	6	0	2	38	17	13	12	0	28	3	0	0	0	4	.00	2	.257	.353	.376
1993 Central Val	A+ Col	59	179	47	8	0	2	61	21	15	31	0	29	2	2	3	3	0	1.00	8	.263	.372	.341
Colo Sprngs	AAA Col	5	10	2	1	0	0	3	1	2	0	0	2	1	0	0	0	0	—	2	.200	.273	.300
1994 New Haven	AA Col	73	215	49	8	0	2	63	20	26	33	1	39	9	3	4	1	2	.33	7	.228	.349	.293
1995 Colo Sprngs	AAA Col	5	17	5	2	0	0	7	1	3	0	0	6	0	0	0	0	0	—	0	.294	.294	.412
New Haven	AA Col	90	288	70	12	1	7	105	44	42	44	1	51	6	1	2	1	0	1.00	3	.243	.359	.365
1996 Colo Sprngs	AAA Col	58	159	37	8	1	2	53	21	18	17	3	30	7	1	0	2	1	.67	5	.233	.333	.333
1997 Colo Sprngs	AAA Col	45	114	28	8	0	2	42	16	12	11	3	21	5	4	1	0	1	.00	4	.246	.336	.368
1998 Colo Sprngs	AAA Col	87	255	71	15	3	6	110	32	38	30	1	48	12	2	2	0	0	—	6	.278	.378	.431
1999 Colo Sprngs	AAA Col	71	195	42	10	1	4	66	16	31	20	0	45	9	1	4	0	0	—	9	.215	.311	.338
2000 Colo Sprngs	AAA Col	13	27	8	0	0	0	8	3	3	9	0	9	1	1	0	0	0	—	0	.296	.375	.296
Las Vegas	AAA SD	15	40	9	2	0	0	11	1	4	3	0	11	1	0	0	0	0	—	0	.225	.295	.275
1998 Colorado	NL	4	4	0	0	0	0	0	0	0	0	0	3	0	0	0	0	0	—	0	.000	.000	.000
9 Min. YEARS		556	1600	394	80	6	27	567	193	207	207	9	316	56	15	17	7	8	.47	41	.246	.349	.354

Tim Sturdy

Pitches: Right **Bats:** Right **Pos:** SP-22; RP-2   **Ht:** 6'2" **Wt:** 179 **Born:** 10/8/78 **Age:** 22

			HOW MUCH HE PITCHED						WHAT HE GAVE UP									THE RESULTS					
Year Team	Lg Org	G	GS	CG	GF	IP	BFP	H	R	ER	HR	SH	SF	HB	TBB	IBB	SO	WP	Bk	W	L	Pct.	ShO	Sv	ERA
1997 Twins	R Min	9	2	1	3	24	88	12	4	2	0	0	0	0	6	0	14	0	2	1	1	.500	1	0	0.75
1998 Elizabethtn	R+ Min	12	12	0	0	69.2	302	65	38	31	4	1	2	6	27	0	46	8	1	5	1	.833	0	0	4.00
1999 Quad City	A Min	13	13	0	0	60.1	282	85	48	42	4	3	0	5	16	0	39	2	1	2	7	.222	0	0	6.27
Elizabethtn	R+ Min	12	12	0	0	73.1	311	71	33	27	2	3	1	4	17	0	64	9	1	6	1	.857	0	0	3.31
2000 Quad City	A Min	23	21	2	0	133.2	552	121	61	44	6	1	1	8	39	3	73	11	2	9	7	.563	1	0	2.96
New Britain	AA Min	1	1	0	0	7	31	7	5	4	0	1	0	1	1	0	5	0	0	0	1	.000	0	0	5.14
4 Min. YEARS		70	61	3	3	368	1566	361	189	150	16	9	4	24	106	3	241	30	7	23	18	.561	2	0	3.67

Felipe Suarez

Pitches: Right **Bats:** Right **Pos:** RP-52   **Ht:** 6'2" **Wt:** 185 **Born:** 3/12/76 **Age:** 25

			HOW MUCH HE PITCHED						WHAT HE GAVE UP									THE RESULTS					
Year Team	Lg Org	G	GS	CG	GF	IP	BFP	H	R	ER	HR	SH	SF	HB	TBB	IBB	SO	WP	Bk	W	L	Pct.	ShO	Sv	ERA
1998 Huntington	IND —	7	7	0	0	42.2	185	39	25	21	3	1	2	4	15	0	40	2	0	2	2	.500	0	0	4.43
1999 Boise	A- Ana	5	5	0	0	29.2	135	32	26	20	2	1	1	4	11	0	33	2	0	1	2	.333	0	0	6.07
2000 Lk Elsinore	A+ Ana	31	0	0	17	57.1	248	51	24	14	3	2	5	1	18	3	40	1	1	5	5	.500	0	5	2.20
Edmonton	AAA Ana	1	0	0	1	1	5	2	2	2	0	0	1	0	0	0	0	1	0	0	0	—	0	0	18.00
Erie	AA Ana	20	0	0	10	37	161	46	22	20	5	1	5	1	7	0	23	2	1	2	0	1.000	0	1	4.86
3 Min. YEARS		64	12	0	27	167.2	734	170	99	77	13	5	14	10	51	3	136	8	2	10	9	.526	0	6	4.13

Joe Sulentor

Bats: Both **Throws:** Right **Pos:** C-20; 1B-15; DH-15; PH-4   **Ht:** 6'4" **Wt:** 220 **Born:** 12/5/76 **Age:** 24

			BATTING													BASERUNNING				PERCENTAGES		
Year Team	Lg Org	G	AB	H	2B	3B	HR	TB	R	RBI	TBB	IBB	SO	HBP	SH	SF	SB	CS	SB%	GDP	Avg	OBP	SLG
2000 Fort Myers	A+ Min	46	128	31	5	1	0	38	5	12	12	1	31	0	2	0	1	1	.50	8	.242	.307	.297
New Britain	AA Min	4	13	3	0	0	0	3	0	2	0	0	1	0	0	0	0	0	—	0	.231	.231	.231
1 Min. YEARS		50	141	34	5	1	0	41	5	14	12	1	32	0	2	0	1	1	.50	8	.241	.301	.291

Brendan Sullivan

Pitches: Right **Bats:** Right **Pos:** RP-40; SP-5   **Ht:** 6'3" **Wt:** 190 **Born:** 12/15/74 **Age:** 26

			HOW MUCH HE PITCHED						WHAT HE GAVE UP									THE RESULTS					
Year Team	Lg Org	G	GS	CG	GF	IP	BFP	H	R	ER	HR	SH	SF	HB	TBB	IBB	SO	WP	Bk	W	L	Pct.	ShO	Sv	ERA
1996 Idaho Falls	R+ SD	33	0	0	15	43	190	41	25	25	6	1	0	1	27	0	41	1	0	2	1	.667	0	5	5.23
1997 Clinton	A SD	47	0	0	35	62.1	283	55	33	27	1	4	3	7	34	2	54	2	0	7	5	.583	0	6	3.90
1998 Rancho Cuca	A+ SD	35	0	0	31	41.2	168	23	7	5	0	1	0	4	19	2	37	1	0	3	2	.600	0	8	1.08
Mobile	AA SD	35	0	0	29	39	153	28	8	8	1	1	1	3	16	1	24	2	0	1	2	.333	0	13	1.85
1999 Las Vegas	AAA SD	45	0	0	14	66.1	332	88	60	56	6	3	5	12	38	3	50	2	0	2	4	.333	0	0	7.60
2000 Las Vegas	AAA SD	45	5	0	10	82.2	390	101	60	57	9	8	1	6	47	1	52	2	0	2	5	.286	0	0	6.21
5 Min. YEARS		240	5	0	134	335	1516	336	193	178	23	18	10	33	181	9	258	10	0	17	19	.472	0	32	4.78

John Summers

Bats: Both **Throws:** Right **Pos:** DH-60; 1B-41; PH-17; 3B-8; PR-1   **Ht:** 6'0" **Wt:** 195 **Born:** 11/16/76 **Age:** 24

			BATTING													BASERUNNING				PERCENTAGES		
Year Team	Lg Org	G	AB	H	2B	3B	HR	TB	R	RBI	TBB	IBB	SO	HBP	SH	SF	SB	CS	SB%	GDP	Avg	OBP	SLG
1998 Salem-Keizr	A- SF	56	211	64	13	2	1	84	33	38	24	1	48	3	1	1	5	0	1.00	6	.303	.381	.398
1999 Bakersfield	A+ SF	114	403	119	19	2	7	163	50	51	40	0	65	5	0	1	2	5	.29	4	.295	.365	.404
2000 San Jose	A+ SF	66	249	70	12	1	1	87	24	32	23	2	44	5	0	3	2	7	.22	6	.281	.350	.349
Shreveport	AA SF	54	151	39	8	1	1	52	15	10	7	0	31	2	1	1	0	1	.00	2	.258	.298	.344
Fresno	AAA SF	6	13	4	0	0	0	4	0	4	0	0	4	0	0	0	0	0	—	1	.308	.308	.308
3 Min. YEARS		296	1027	296	52	6	10	390	122	132	94	3	192	15	2	6	9	13	.41	19	.288	.355	.380

Brian Sweeney

Pitches: Right **Bats:** Right **Pos:** RP-13; SP-8   **Ht:** 6'2" **Wt:** 185 **Born:** 6/13/74 **Age:** 27

			HOW MUCH HE PITCHED						WHAT HE GAVE UP									THE RESULTS					
Year Team	Lg Org	G	GS	CG	GF	IP	BFP	H	R	ER	HR	SH	SF	HB	TBB	IBB	SO	WP	Bk	W	L	Pct.	ShO	Sv	ERA
1997 Lancaster	A+ Sea	40	0	0	13	85.1	358	83	39	36	11	2	4	2	21	1	73	8	0	6	3	.667	0	1	3.80
1998 Lancaster	A+ Sea	17	4	0	3	52	211	41	26	21	6	0	1	1	21	1	48	2	1	6	0	1.000	0	0	3.63
1999 Lancaster	A+ Sea	5	0	0	1	9.1	44	14	7	7	4	0	0	0	3	0	14	1	0	0	0	—	0	0	6.75
Tacoma	AAA Sea	5	1	0	2	16	75	26	17	12	5	2	0	0	2	0	10	1	0	0	2	.000	0	0	6.75
New Haven	AA Sea	23	18	0	3	111.1	478	125	65	58	18	1	3	4	31	1	83	4	0	4	6	.400	0	1	4.69
2000 Tacoma	AAA Sea	2	1	0	0	6	26	9	4	4	2	0	0	0	1	0	1	1	0	0	1	.000	0	0	6.00
New Haven	AA Sea	19	7	0	5	47.2	207	49	20	18	3	1	2	2	19	0	27	5	0	4	3	.571	0	1	3.40
4 Min. YEARS		111	31	0	27	327.2	1399	347	178	156	49	6	10	9	98	3	256	22	1	20	15	.571	0	3	4.28

Jamie Sykes

Bats: Right **Throws:** Right **Pos:** OF-117; PH-10; DH-5; PR-2   **Ht:** 5'11" **Wt:** 190 **Born:** 1/14/75 **Age:** 26

			BATTING													BASERUNNING				PERCENTAGES		
Year Team	Lg Org	G	AB	H	2B	3B	HR	TB	R	RBI	TBB	IBB	SO	HBP	SH	SF	SB	CS	SB%	GDP	Avg	OBP	SLG
1997 Lethbridge	R+ Ari	58	223	68	8	6	4	100	45	37	25	0	40	3	1	0	9	2	.82	5	.305	.382	.448
1998 High Desert	A+ Ari	36	125	21	5	2	3	39	13	16	19	0	33	0	0	1	5	2	.71	1	.168	.276	.312
South Bend	A Ari	26	93	19	2	3	2	33	12	10	16	0	20	2	0	0	5	0	1.00	0	.204	.333	.355
1999 South Bend	A Ari	127	479	137	34	10	15	236	75	83	53	1	111	4	1	4	17	8	.68	9	.286	.359	.493
2000 El Paso	AA Ari	48	154	31	5	2	3	49	16	21	19	1	45	0	0	3	6	3	.67	1	.201	.284	.318
High Desert	A+ Ari	83	303	87	15	6	16	162	64	57	45	0	80	1	0	2	11	6	.65	3	.287	.379	.535
4 Min. YEARS		378	1377	363	69	29	43	619	225	224	177	2	329	10	2	10	53	21	.72	20	.264	.349	.450

Jeff Tabaka

Pitches: Left **Bats:** Right **Pos:** RP-31 **Ht:** 6'2" **Wt:** 201 **Born:** 1/17/64 **Age:** 37

		HOW MUCH HE PITCHED					WHAT HE GAVE UP										THE RESULTS				
Year Team	Lg Org	G	GS	CG	GF	IP	BFP	H	R	ER	HR	SH	SF	HB	TBB	IBB	SO	WP	Bk	W	L	Pct.	ShO	Sv	ERA
1986 Jamestown	A- Mon	13	9	0	3	52.1	238	51	31	25	5	3	1	4	34	1	57	5	0	2	4	.333	0	0	4.30
1987 Wst Plm Bch	A+ Mon	28	15	0	8	95	421	90	46	44	3	2	6	3	58	3	71	6	0	8	6	.571	0	5	4.17
1988 Wst Plm Bch	A+ Mon	16	16	2	0	95	387	71	38	18	0	4	6	1	34	1	52	8	1	7	5	.583	2	0	1.71
Jacksnville	AA Mon	2	2	0	0	11	48	14	8	8	1	0	1	0	5	0	7	0	0	1	0	1.000	0	0	6.55
1989 Scranton-WB	AAA Phi	6	6	0	0	31.1	148	32	26	22	2	2	3	2	23	0	15	1	1	0	4	.000	0	0	6.32
Reading	AA Phi	21	17	6	1	100.2	461	109	59	52	8	3	3	4	54	3	80	9	0	8	7	.533	1	0	4.65
1990 Clearwater	A+ Phi	8	5	0	1	35.2	163	38	17	12	1	2	1	0	18	0	22	2	1	5	2	.714	0	0	3.03
1991 Reading	AA Phi	21	20	1	0	108.1	495	117	65	61	8	3	10	4	78	2	68	11	0	4	8	.333	1	0	5.07
Stockton	A+ Mil	4	4	0	0	17.1	82	19	11	10	1	1	0	0	16	0	19	2	0	0	2	.000	0	0	5.19
1992 El Paso	AA Mil	50	0	0	23	82	332	67	23	23	1	3	7	4	38	1	75	5	0	9	5	.643	0	10	2.52
1993 New Orleans	AAA Mil	53	0	0	22	58.1	254	50	26	21	3	1	4	3	30	2	63	7	1	6	6	.500	0	1	3.24
1994 Buffalo	AAA Pit	9	0	0	5	5.1	23	3	2	2	0	0	0	0	4	0	4	0	0	1	0	1.000	0	1	3.38
1995 Las Vegas	AAA SD	19	0	0	12	22.2	95	16	6	5	0	2	1	1	14	3	27	2	0	0	0	.000	0	6	1.99
1996 Tucson	AAA Hou	41	0	0	16	43	186	40	16	14	2	4	1	1	21	5	51	2	0	6	2	.750	0	4	2.93
1997 Indianapolis	AAA Cin	58	0	0	23	57.2	228	44	19	17	5	1	2	1	19	3	68	8	0	3	2	.600	0	3	2.65
1998 Nashville	AAA Pit	4	0	0	2	4.2	24	9	4	4	0	0	2	1	0	0	4	0	0	1	0	1.000	0	0	7.71
2000 Carolina	AA Col	9	0	0	4	9.1	36	7	2	2	0	1	0	0	1	0	7	1	0	0	0	—	0	0	1.93
Colo Spmgs	AAA Col	22	0	0	8	22.1	109	30	19	19	3	0	3	1	9	0	26	4	0	0	0	.000	0	0	7.66
1994 Pittsburgh	NL	5	0	0	2	4	24	4	8	8	1	0	0	0	8	0	2	0	0	0	0	—	0	0	18.00
San Diego	NL	34	0	0	8	37	157	28	21	16	0	3	1	0	19	3	30	1	0	3	1	.750	0	1	3.89
1995 San Diego	NL	10	0	0	3	6.1	32	10	5	5	1	0	0	0	5	1	6	1	0	0	0	—	0	0	7.11
Houston	NL	24	0	0	3	24.1	96	17	6	6	1	0	0	0	12	0	19	0	0	1	0	1.000	0	0	2.22
1996 Houston	NL	18	0	0	5	20.1	105	28	18	15	5	1	0	3	14	0	18	3	0	0	2	.000	0	1	6.64
1997 Cincinnati	NL	3	0	0	1	2	10	1	1	1	1	0	0	2	1	0	1	0	0	0	0	—	0	0	4.50
1998 Pittsburgh	NL	37	0	0	9	50.2	212	37	19	17	6	2	2	5	22	4	40	1	0	2	2	.500	0	0	3.02
14 Min. YEARS		384	94	9	128	852	3730	807	418	359	43	35	51	27	456	24	716	73	4	60	57	.513	4	30	3.79
5 Maj. YEARS		131	0	0	31	144.2	636	125	78	68	15	6	3	10	81	8	116	6	0	6	5	.545	0	2	4.23

Jeff Taglienti

Pitches: Right **Bats:** Right **Pos:** RP-48 **Ht:** 6'0" **Wt:** 210 **Born:** 11/13/75 **Age:** 25

		HOW MUCH HE PITCHED					WHAT HE GAVE UP										THE RESULTS				
Year Team	Lg Org	G	GS	CG	GF	IP	BFP	H	R	ER	HR	SH	SF	HB	TBB	IBB	SO	WP	Bk	W	L	Pct.	ShO	Sv	ERA
1997 Lowell	A- Bos	17	4	0	11	36.2	150	30	22	20	2	0	0	0	13	0	34	3	2	3	4	.429	0	6	4.91
1998 Michigan	A Bos	57	0	0	49	76.1	303	54	19	16	0	3	2	3	17	2	111	3	0	4	2	.667	0	30	1.89
1999 Sarasota	A+ Bos	14	0	0	5	30	128	26	12	10	1	2	2	2	12	1	27	4	0	1	1	.500	0	3	3.00
Trenton	AA Bos	10	0	0	4	19.1	72	9	6	6	2	1	1	0	5	0	17	0	0	0	0	—	0	2	2.79
2000 Trenton	AA Bos	38	0	0	31	51	216	59	26	21	3	3	0	0	7	0	33	2	0	3	1	.750	0	10	3.71
Carolina	AA Col	10	0	0	9	12.1	51	9	4	2	1	1	0	0	3	0	7	0	0	1	1	.500	0	0	1.46
4 Min. YEARS		146	4	0	109	225.2	920	187	89	75	9	10	5	5	57	3	229	12	2	12	9	.571	0	51	2.99

John Tamargo

Bats: Both **Throws:** Right **Pos:** 2B-64; SS-29; PH-7; DH-4; C-2; PR-1 **Ht:** 5'9" **Wt:** 165 **Born:** 5/3/75 **Age:** 26

		BATTING															BASERUNNING				PERCENTAGES		
Year Team	Lg Org	G	AB	H	2B	3B	HR	TB	R	RBI	TBB	IBB	SO	HBP	SH	SF	SB	CS	SB%	GDP	Avg	OBP	SLG
1996 Pittsfield	A- NYM	55	184	41	5	3	0	52	26	19	35	0	34	2	1	3	5	3	.63	5	.223	.348	.283
1997 Capital Cty	A NYM	113	393	98	17	2	1	122	44	47	45	2	72	2	5	1	13	7	.65	9	.249	.329	.310
1998 St. Lucie	A+ NYM	105	347	84	24	1	0	110	40	33	41	2	60	3	9	2	14	7	.67	3	.242	.326	.317
Norfolk	AAA NYM	3	8	0	0	0	0	0	0	0	1	0	3	0	0	0	0	0	—	0	.000	.111	.000
1999 Binghamton	AA NYM	112	363	78	13	3	4	109	27	37	40	1	55	4	5	3	7	5	.58	8	.215	.298	.300
2000 Norfolk	AAA NYM	4	11	2	1	0	0	3	2	0	2	0	1	1	0	0	0	1	.00	1	.182	.357	.273
Binghamton	AA NYM	96	291	75	18	1	1	98	47	29	43	0	47	2	8	0	5	6	.45	10	.258	.357	.337
5 Min. YEARS		488	1597	378	78	10	6	494	186	165	207	5	272	14	28	9	44	29	.60	36	.237	.328	.309

Ramon Tatis

Pitches: Left **Bats:** Left **Pos:** RP-4; SP-3 **Ht:** 6'3" **Wt:** 205 **Born:** 5/2/73 **Age:** 28

		HOW MUCH HE PITCHED					WHAT HE GAVE UP										THE RESULTS				
Year Team	Lg Org	G	GS	CG	GF	IP	BFP	H	R	ER	HR	SH	SF	HB	TBB	IBB	SO	WP	Bk	W	L	Pct.	ShO	Sv	ERA
1992 Mets	R NYM	11	1	0	4	36	184	56	40	34	2	0	1	4	15	0	25	7	1	1	3	.250	0	0	8.50
1993 Kingsport	R+ NYM	13	3	0	5	42.2	204	51	42	29	1	3	1	5	23	0	25	4	0	0	2	.000	0	1	6.12
1994 Kingsport	R+ NYM	13	4	0	8	40.2	187	35	25	15	2	2	1	2	31	0	36	5	2	1	3	.250	0	0	3.32
1995 Pittsfield	A- NYM	13	13	1	0	79.1	341	88	40	32	2	1	1	3	27	0	69	8	3	4	5	.444	1	0	3.63
Capital City	A NYM	18	2	0	9	32	141	34	27	20	1	2	1	1	14	0	27	5	0	2	3	.400	0	0	5.63
1996 St. Lucie	A+ NYM	46	1	0	20	74.1	325	71	35	28	4	7	2	2	38	8	46	14	1	4	2	.667	0	6	3.39
1998 Durham	AAA TB	19	9	0	4	61.1	267	66	29	25	5	1	2	3	24	2	44	4	1	1	3	.250	0	0	3.67
1999 Durham	AAA TB	28	28	0	0	155.1	692	178	100	95	19	2	4	4	74	0	97	9	9	12	8	.600	0	0	5.50
2000 Columbus	AAA NYY	7	3	0	1	22.2	115	31	30	27	2	1	3	0	18	1	15	1	1	0	1	.000	0	0	10.72
1997 Chicago	NL	56	0	0	12	55.2	255	66	36	33	13	6	3	3	29	6	33	4	2	1	1	.500	0	0	5.34
1998 Tampa Bay	AL	22	0	0	7	11.2	72	23	19	18	2	0	1	0	16	1	5	1	1	0	0	—	0	0	13.89
8 Min. YEARS		168	68	1	47	544.1	2456	610	368	305	38	19	16	24	264	11	384	57	18	25	30	.455	1	9	5.04
2 Maj. YEARS		78	0	0	19	67.1	327	89	55	51	15	6	4	3	45	7	38	5	3	1	1	.500	0	0	6.82

Jimmy Tatum

Bats: Right **Throws:** Right **Pos:** OF-24; DH-4; C-1; PH-1 **Ht:** 6'2" **Wt:** 205 **Born:** 10/9/67 **Age:** 33

		BATTING															BASERUNNING				PERCENTAGES		
Year Team	Lg Org	G	AB	H	2B	3B	HR	TB	R	RBI	TBB	IBB	SO	HBP	SH	SF	SB	CS	SB%	GDP	Avg	OBP	SLG
1985 Spokane	A- SD	74	281	64	9	1	1	78	21	32	20	0	60	5	4	1	0	1	.00	7	.228	.290	.278
1986 Chston-SC	A SD	120	431	112	19	2	10	165	55	62	41	2	83	4	4	5	2	4	.33	11	.260	.324	.383

Year Team	Lg Org	G	AB	H	2B	3B	HR	TB	R	RBI	TBB	IBB	SO	HBP	SH	SF	SB	CS	SB%	GDP	Avg	OBP	SLG
1987 Chston-SC	A SD	128	468	131	22	2	9	184	52	72	46	2	65	8	4	9	8	5	.62	16	.280	.348	.393
1988 Wichita	AA SD	118	402	105	26	1	8	157	38	54	30	2	73	1	5	3	2	3	.40	5	.261	.318	.391
1990 Canton-Akrn	AA Cle	30	106	19	6	0	2	31	6	11	6	1	19	1	0	2	1	0	1.00	2	.179	.226	.292
Stockton	A+ Mil	70	260	68	16	0	12	120	41	59	13	0	49	8	0	4	4	5	.44	1	.262	.312	.462
1991 El Paso	AA Mil	130	493	158	27	8	18	255	99	128	63	5	79	15	2	20	5	7	.42	21	.320	.399	.517
1992 Denver	AAA Mil	130	492	162	36	3	19	261	74	101	40	3	87	9	4	11	8	9	.47	11	.329	.382	.530
1993 Colo Sprngs	AAA Col	13	45	10	2	0	2	18	5	7	2	0	9	1	0	0	1	0	1.00	3	.222	.271	.400
1994 Colo Sprngs	AAA Col	121	439	154	43	1	21	262	76	97	44	4	84	5	1	10	2	2	.50	6	.351	.408	.597
1995 Colo Sprngs	AAA Col	27	93	30	7	0	6	55	17	18	6	0	21	1	0	2	1	0	1.00	2	.323	.363	.591
1996 Pawtucket	AAA Bos	19	66	18	2	0	5	35	11	16	7	0	12	1	0	0	2	0	1.00	3	.273	.351	.530
Las Vegas	AAA SD	64	233	80	20	1	12	138	40	56	23	6	53	3	0	1	4	0	1.00	9	.343	.408	.592
1997 Las Vegas	AAA SD	44	161	51	12	1	9	92	21	25	8	0	39	1	0	2	1	2	.33	1	.317	.349	.571
1999 Colo Sprngs	AAA Col	109	396	124	23	1	14	191	57	64	33	0	85	3	1	8	1	2	.33	14	.313	.364	.482
2000 Fresno	AAA SF	30	100	19	5	0	3	33	10	12	12	0	17	1	0	1	1	0	1.00	1	.190	.281	.330
1992 Milwaukee	AL	5	8	1	0	0	0	1	0	0	1	0	2	0	0	0	0	0	—	0	.125	.222	.125
1993 Colorado	NL	92	98	20	5	0	1	28	7	12	5	0	27	1	0	2	0	0	—	0	.204	.245	.286
1995 Colorado	NL	34	34	8	1	1	0	11	4	4	1	0	7	0	0	0	0	0	—	1	.235	.257	.324
1996 Boston	AL	2	8	1	0	0	0	1	1	0	0	0	2	0	0	0	0	0	—	0	.125	.125	.125
San Diego	NL	5	3	0	0	0	0	0	0	0	0	0	1	0	0	0	0	0	—	0	.000	.000	.000
1998 New York	NL	35	50	9	1	2	2	20	4	13	3	0	19	0	0	4	0	0	—	0	.180	.211	.400
14 Min. YEARS		1227	4466	1305	275	21	151	2075	623	814	394	25	835	69	26	79	41	42	.49	120	.292	.353	.465
5 Maj. YEARS		173	201	39	7	3	3	61	16	29	10	0	58	1	0	6	0	0	—	1	.194	.229	.303

Luis Taveras

Bats: Right **Throws:** Right **Pos:** C-81; DH-1   **Ht:** 5'10" **Wt:** 165 **Born:** 8/1/77 **Age:** 23

Year Team	Lg Org	G	AB	H	2B	3B	HR	TB	R	RBI	TBB	IBB	SO	HBP	SH	SF	SB	CS	SB%	GDP	Avg	OBP	SLG
1997 Rangers	R Tex	37	83	20	3	0	1	26	10	10	9	1	21	0	0	1	1	0	1.00	2	.241	.312	.313
1998 Charlotte	A+ Tex	76	246	40	4	2	3	57	21	24	14	0	70	0	2	4	4	6	.40	5	.163	.205	.232
1999 Charlotte	A+ Tex	95	308	81	18	4	6	125	36	46	30	0	69	3	3	4	10	4	.71	6	.263	.330	.406
2000 Tulsa	AA Tex	82	285	66	14	3	5	101	44	37	34	0	73	2	2	6	3	2	.60	8	.232	.312	.354
4 Min. YEARS		290	922	207	39	9	15	309	111	117	87	1	233	5	7	15	18	12	.60	21	.225	.291	.335

Kerry Taylor

Pitches: Right **Bats:** Right **Pos:** SP-17; RP-16   **Ht:** 6'3" **Wt:** 200 **Born:** 1/25/71 **Age:** 30

		HOW MUCH HE PITCHED						WHAT HE GAVE UP										THE RESULTS					
Year Team	Lg Org	G	GS	CG	GF	IP	BFP	H	R	ER	HR	SH	SF	HB	TBB	IBB	SO	WP	Bk	W	L	Pct.	ShO	Sv	ERA
1989 Elizabethtn	R+ Min	9	8	0	0	36	157	26	11	6	1	3	1	2	22	0	24	1	0	3	0	1.000	0	0	1.50
1990 Twins	R Min	14	13	1	1	63	275	57	37	25	2	0	4	4	33	0	59	5	4	3	1	.750	2	0	3.57
1991 Kenosha	A Min	26	26	2	0	132	586	121	74	56	4	2	5	10	84	1	84	11	1	7	11	.389	1	0	3.82
1992 Kenosha	A Min	27	27	2	0	170.1	733	150	71	52	3	6	2	10	68	0	158	11	1	10	9	.526	1	0	2.75
1994 Las Vegas	AAA SD	27	27	1	0	156	719	175	105	96	15	2	7	10	81	2	142	14	0	9	9	.500	0	0	5.54
1995 Las Vegas	AAA SD	8	8	0	0	37	174	44	21	18	3	4	0	2	21	1	21	0	0	2	2	.500	0	0	4.38
1997 Mobile	AA SD	5	5	0	0	26	117	27	14	14	4	0	0	1	13	0	30	2	0	2	1	.667	0	0	4.85
Las Vegas	AAA SD	22	22	3	0	144	628	150	84	69	15	8	8	11	55	3	103	4	0	7	9	.438	0	0	4.31
1998 Toledo	AAA Det	26	17	1	3	112.1	528	140	84	72	18	3	2	8	59	0	93	4	0	8	10	.444	0	0	5.77
1999 Atlantic Ct	IND —	13	11	0	0	67.2	290	72	40	36	7	3	3	6	23	0	49	0	0	4	2	.667	0	0	4.79
2000 Syracuse	AAA Tor	33	17	4	2	135.2	578	119	57	50	16	8	2	5	61	2	83	2	0	9	8	.529	2	0	3.32
1993 San Diego	NL	36	7	0	9	68.1	326	72	53	49	5	10	3	4	49	0	45	4	0	0	5	.000	0	0	6.45
1994 San Diego	NL	1	1	0	0	4.1	24	9	4	4	1	0	0	1	1	0	3	0	0	0	0	—	0	0	8.31
10 Min. YEARS		210	181	14	6	1080	4785	1081	598	494	88	39	34	69	520	9	846	54	6	64	62	.508	5	0	4.12
2 Maj. YEARS		37	8	0	9	72.2	350	81	57	53	6	10	3	5	50	0	48	4	0	0	5	.000	0	0	6.56

Nate Tebbs

Bats: Both **Throws:** Right **Pos:** 2B-52; SS-34; 3B-8; OF-7; PH-6; DH-3; P-3   **Ht:** 5'10" **Wt:** 170 **Born:** 12/14/72 **Age:** 28

Year Team	Lg Org	G	AB	H	2B	3B	HR	TB	R	RBI	TBB	IBB	SO	HBP	SH	SF	SB	CS	SB%	GDP	Avg	OBP	SLG
1993 Red Sox	R Bos	43	146	38	4	1	0	44	21	4	15	1	16	0	7	0	7	1	.88	1	.260	.329	.301
1994 Utica	A- Bos	70	219	44	5	0	0	49	18	23	11	0	34	1	4	1	9	4	.69	1	.201	.241	.224
1995 Sarasota	A+ Bos	118	440	128	15	4	2	157	58	52	39	0	80	3	4	1	25	15	.63	7	.291	.352	.357
1996 Sarasota	A+ Bos	116	420	105	11	2	1	123	44	34	24	1	68	3	10	1	17	4	.81	7	.250	.295	.293
1997 Sarasota	A+ Bos	111	375	98	14	3	5	133	52	39	27	3	65	0	2	3	15	9	.63	9	.261	.309	.355
Trenton	AA Bos	5	16	5	0	0	0	5	2	0	2	0	1	0	0	0	1	0	1.00	0	.313	.389	.313
1998 Trenton	AA Bos	104	394	101	21	2	2	132	44	31	36	0	63	3	3	1	14	13	.52	10	.256	.323	.335
Pawtucket	AAA Bos	17	57	16	2	0	0	18	7	4	3	0	13	0	2	0	5	2	.71	0	.281	.317	.316
1999 Pawtucket	AAA Bos	4	5	3	1	0	0	4	1	1	2	0	1	0	0	0	0	0	1.00	0	.600	.750	.800
Trenton	AA Bos	107	365	99	14	1	4	127	49	35	29	1	67	5	11	7	21	10	.68	7	.271	.328	.348
2000 Rochester	AAA Bal	4	9	3	0	0	0	3	1	1	2	0	1	0	0	0	0	0	—	2	.333	.455	.333
Mobile	AA SD	37	136	39	6	2	3	58	16	10	7	1	29	1	2	1	3	3	.50	1	.287	.324	.426
Las Vegas	AAA SD	38	133	34	4	0	2	44	18	21	7	0	24	0	1	4	4	0	1.00	6	.256	.285	.331
Arkansas	AA StL	29	116	29	7	0	0	36	13	14	8	0	20	0	1	0	2	4	.33	2	.250	.298	.310
8 Min. YEARS		803	2831	742	104	15	19	933	344	269	212	7	482	17	47	19	122	67	.65	51	.262	.315	.330

Fausto Tejero

Bats: Right **Throws:** Right **Pos:** C-32; PH-3; P-1   **Ht:** 6'2" **Wt:** 205 **Born:** 10/26/68 **Age:** 32

Year Team	Lg Org	G	AB	H	2B	3B	HR	TB	R	RBI	TBB	IBB	SO	HBP	SH	SF	SB	CS	SB%	GDP	Avg	OBP	SLG
1990 Boise	A- Ana	39	74	16	2	0	0	18	14	7	23	1	23	2	3	3	1	0	1.00	0	.216	.402	.243
1991 Quad City	A Ana	83	244	42	7	0	1	52	16	18	14	0	52	4	3	1	0	1	.00	5	.172	.228	.213

Year Team	Lg Org	G	AB	H	2B	3B	HR	TB	R	RBI	TBB	IBB	SO	HBP	SH	SF	SB	CS	SB%	GDP	Avg	OBP	SLG
1992 Edmonton	AAA Ana	8	17	4	1	0	0	5	0	0	4	0	2	1	2	0	0	2	.00	0	.235	.409	.294
Midland	AA Ana	84	266	50	11	0	2	67	21	30	11	0	63	4	5	3	1	2	.33	6	.188	.229	.252
1993 Palm Spring	A+ Ana	7	20	6	2	0	0	8	2	1	2	0	1	0	1	0	0	1	.00	0	.300	.364	.400
Vancouver	AAA Ana	20	59	9	0	0	0	9	2	2	4	1	12	1	2	1	1	1	.50	0	.153	.215	.153
Midland	AA Ana	26	69	9	1	1	1	15	3	7	8	0	17	2	1	1	0	0	—	3	.130	.238	.217
1994 Midland	AA Ana	50	150	32	3	0	5	50	17	24	15	0	31	1	1	2	2	2	.50	6	.213	.286	.333
Vancouver	AAA Ana	16	45	9	2	0	0	11	6	6	4	0	9	0	2	1	1	1	.50	1	.200	.260	.244
1995 Lk Elsinore	A+ Ana	8	21	5	1	0	0	6	5	3	5	0	6	0	0	1	1	0	1.00	1	.238	.370	.286
Vancouver	AAA Ana	37	96	25	3	0	0	28	10	8	10	1	22	0	1	0	1	0	1.00	0	.260	.330	.292
Midland	AA Ana	16	53	12	3	0	1	18	7	11	1	0	13	1	0	1	0	1	.00	1	.226	.250	.340
1996 Vancouver	AAA Ana	54	155	31	4	1	1	40	21	12	22	0	41	1	6	0	0	1	.00	6	.200	.303	.258
1997 Richmond	AAA Atl	76	225	52	11	0	6	81	31	28	23	2	41	4	2	2	0	1	.00	6	.231	.311	.360
1998 Richmond	AAA Atl	77	223	50	14	0	4	76	19	26	21	2	48	3	1	2	1	2	.33	6	.224	.297	.341
1999 Edmonton	AAA Ana	5	17	5	0	0	1	8	3	2	3	0	3	0	0	0	0	0	—	0	.294	.400	.471
Erie	AA Ana	62	211	45	9	0	3	63	19	18	13	0	38	3	4	0	0	2	.00	7	.213	.269	.299
2000 Scranton-WB	AAA Phi	36	87	10	3	1	0	15	3	9	5	0	20	0	2	3	0	0	—	3	.115	.158	.172
11 Min. YEARS		704	2032	412	77	3	25	570	199	212	188	7	442	27	36	21	10	17	.37	51	.203	.276	.281

Mike Terhune

Bats: Both **Throws:** Right **Pos:** OF-26; 3B-22; 2B-16; PH-14; SS-11; 1B-9; PR-5   **Ht:** 6'1" **Wt:** 185 **Born:** 10/14/75 **Age:** 25

Year Team	Lg Org	G	AB	H	2B	3B	HR	TB	R	RBI	TBB	IBB	SO	HBP	SH	SF	SB	CS	SB%	GDP	Avg	OBP	SLG
1996 Danville	R+ Atl	56	214	60	9	5	2	85	32	27	23	0	26	2	2	7	6	3	.67	6	.280	.346	.397
1997 Eugene	A- Atl	14	61	13	1	0	0	14	4	3	4	1	6	0	2	0	0	0	—	2	.213	.262	.230
Macon	A Atl	92	328	74	11	4	1	96	33	28	25	0	45	5	6	2	8	3	.73	4	.226	.289	.293
1998 Danville	A+ Atl	107	368	81	9	0	3	99	44	26	17	0	67	4	6	2	8	5	.62	13	.220	.261	.269
1999 Myrtle Bch	A+ Atl	92	312	70	10	3	1	89	24	26	27	0	51	0	6	1	3	2	.60	11	.224	.285	.285
2000 Greenville	AA Atl	82	186	42	10	1	1	57	31	15	17	0	32	1	8	5	1	4	.20	5	.226	.287	.306
5 Min. YEARS		443	1469	340	50	13	8	440	168	125	113	1	227	12	30	17	26	17	.60	41	.231	.289	.300

Nate Teut

Pitches: Left **Bats:** Right **Pos:** SP-21; RP-6   **Ht:** 6'7" **Wt:** 205 **Born:** 3/11/76 **Age:** 25

Year Team	Lg Org	G	GS	CG	GF	IP	BFP	H	R	ER	HR	SH	SF	HB	TBB	IBB	SO	WP	Bk	W	L	Pct.	ShO	Sv	ERA
1997 Williamsprt	A- ChC	9	9	0	0	49	203	55	23	14	0	1	2	0	6	1	37	2	1	3	4	.429	0	0	2.57
Rockford	A ChC	2	2	0	0	10.2	52	18	12	12	1	0	0	1	2	0	6	0	0	0	1	.000	0	0	10.13
1998 Rockford	A ChC	16	16	1	0	103.1	434	99	49	38	9	1	3	6	23	0	67	3	1	8	5	.615	0	0	3.31
Daytona	A+ ChC	11	11	1	0	65.2	302	88	48	40	7	0	3	3	19	0	54	1	1	5	3	.625	0	0	5.48
1999 Daytona	A+ ChC	26	26	1	0	132.2	613	180	113	94	16	3	3	9	41	0	91	13	1	5	12	.294	0	0	6.38
2000 West Tenn	AA ChC	27	21	1	2	138.1	583	133	53	47	13	4	2	10	44	0	106	4	0	11	6	.647	1	0	3.06
4 Min. YEARS		91	85	4	2	499.2	2187	573	298	245	46	9	16	29	135	1	361	27	4	32	31	.508	1	0	4.41

Marcus Thames

Bats: Right **Throws:** Right **Pos:** OF-111; DH-19; PH-3   **Ht:** 6'2" **Wt:** 205 **Born:** 3/6/77 **Age:** 24

Year Team	Lg Org	G	AB	H	2B	3B	HR	TB	R	RBI	TBB	IBB	SO	HBP	SH	SF	SB	CS	SB%	GDP	Avg	OBP	SLG
1997 Yankees	R NYY	57	195	67	17	4	7	113	51	36	16	0	26	3	1	4	6	4	.60	3	.344	.394	.579
Greensboro	A NYY	4	16	5	1	0	0	6	2	2	0	0	3	0	0	0	1	0	1.00	0	.313	.313	.375
1998 Tampa	A+ NYY	122	457	130	18	3	11	187	62	59	24	1	78	8	1	5	13	6	.68	5	.284	.328	.409
1999 Norwich	AA NYY	51	182	41	6	2	4	63	25	26	22	0	40	3	1	2	0	1	.00	2	.225	.316	.346
Tampa	A+ NYY	69	266	65	12	4	11	118	47	38	33	1	58	3	1	2	3	0	1.00	1	.244	.332	.444
2000 Norwich	AA NYY	131	474	114	30	2	15	193	72	79	50	1	89	4	0	8	1	5	.17	13	.241	.313	.407
4 Min. YEARS		434	1590	422	84	15	48	680	259	240	145	3	294	21	4	21	24	16	.60	24	.265	.331	.428

Nick Theodorou

B: Both **T:** Right **Pos:** OF-87; PH-16; 3B-11; C-3; 2B-3; SS-1; 1B-1; DH-1; PR-1; P-1   **Ht:** 5'11" **Wt:** 182 **Born:** 6/7/75 **Age:** 26

Year Team	Lg Org	G	AB	H	2B	3B	HR	TB	R	RBI	TBB	IBB	SO	HBP	SH	SF	SB	CS	SB%	GDP	Avg	OBP	SLG
1998 Yakima	A- LA	46	133	37	12	0	0	49	24	11	26	0	26	0	1	0	7	5	.58	1	.278	.396	.368
1999 San Berndno	A+ LA	104	355	110	11	4	0	129	57	44	72	3	62	7	5	1	14	14	.50	7	.310	.434	.363
2000 San Antonio	AA LA	113	266	64	14	3	1	87	29	25	49	3	39	1	2	3	3	3	.50	9	.241	.357	.327
3 Min. YEARS		263	754	211	37	7	1	265	110	80	147	6	127	8	8	4	24	22	.52	17	.280	.401	.351

E.J. t'Hoen

Bats: Right **Throws:** Right **Pos:** SS-50; 3B-47; 2B-8; PH-3; DH-1   **Ht:** 6'2" **Wt:** 185 **Born:** 11/8/75 **Age:** 25

Year Team	Lg Org	G	AB	H	2B	3B	HR	TB	R	RBI	TBB	IBB	SO	HBP	SH	SF	SB	CS	SB%	GDP	Avg	OBP	SLG
1996 Boise	A- Ana	18	60	12	1	0	2	19	6	4	4	0	17	1	1	0	0	0	—	2	.200	.262	.317
1997 Cedar Rapds	A Ana	123	384	78	19	3	3	112	41	46	31	0	114	7	7	3	2	3	.40	7	.203	.273	.292
1998 Cedar Rapds	A Ana	130	441	96	22	1	18	174	57	55	50	2	129	7	3	2	10	5	.67	6	.218	.306	.395
1999 Edmonton	AAA Ana	9	29	4	0	0	0	4	2	0	2	0	7	0	1	0	0	0	—	0	.138	.194	.138
Erie	AA Ana	56	187	38	12	1	2	58	18	21	13	0	52	3	5	1	6	2	.75	4	.203	.265	.310
2000 Erie	AA Ana	62	198	43	13	0	6	74	24	24	24	0	54	3	2	3	6	1	.86	4	.217	.307	.374
Edmonton	AAA Ana	39	120	25	6	0	3	40	13	10	8	0	36	1	1	0	1	1	.50	1	.208	.264	.333
5 Min. YEARS		437	1419	296	73	5	34	481	161	162	132	2	409	22	20	9	25	12	.68	23	.209	.284	.339

Brad Thomas

Pitches: Left Bats: Left Pos: SP-25; RP-1
Ht: 6'3" Wt: 204 Born: 10/22/77 Age: 23

Year Team	Lg Org	G	GS	CG	GF	IP	BFP	H	R	ER	HR	SH	SF	HB	TBB	IBB	SO	WP	Bk	W	L	Pct.	ShO	Sv	ERA
1996 Great Falls	R+ LA	11	5	0	3	35.2	163	48	27	25	2	1	1	0	11	0	28	5	4	3	2	.600	0	0	6.31
1997 Elizabethtn	R+ Min	14	13	0	0	70.1	307	78	43	35	5	3	0	3	21	0	53	8	2	3	4	.429	0	0	4.48
1998 Fort Wayne	A Min	27	26	1	1	152.1	650	146	68	50	9	4	5	8	45	1	125	11	3	11	8	.579	0	0	2.95
1999 Fort Myers	A+ Min	27	27	1	0	152.2	666	182	99	81	11	4	3	6	46	0	108	8	1	8	11	.421	1	0	4.78
2000 Fort Myers	A+ Min	12	12	0	0	65	279	62	33	12	3	1	0	3	16	0	57	3	0	6	2	.750	0	0	1.66
New Britain	AA Min	14	13	1	0	75.1	346	80	47	34	3	3	4	4	46	1	66	9	2	6	6	.500	1	0	4.06
5 Min. YEARS		105	96	3	4	551.1	2411	596	317	237	33	16	13	24	185	2	437	44	12	37	33	.529	2	0	3.87

Evan Thomas

Pitches: Right Bats: Right Pos: SP-27; RP-2
Ht: 5'10" Wt: 171 Born: 6/14/74 Age: 27

Year Team	Lg Org	G	GS	CG	GF	IP	BFP	H	R	ER	HR	SH	SF	HB	TBB	IBB	SO	WP	Bk	W	L	Pct.	ShO	Sv	ERA
1996 Batavia	A- Phi	13	13	0	0	81	321	60	29	25	3	1	3	5	23	0	75	6	0	10	2	.833	0	0	2.78
1997 Clearwater	A+ Phi	13	12	2	0	84.2	340	68	30	23	7	1	1	3	23	0	89	3	2	5	5	.500	0	0	2.44
Reading	AA Phi	15	15	0	0	83	377	98	51	38	10	5	2	7	32	1	83	3	2	3	6	.333	0	0	4.12
1998 Scranton-WB	AAA Phi	2	2	0	0	9	42	9	8	8	1	0	1	0	6	0	5	0	0	0	1	.000	0	0	8.00
Reading	AA Phi	24	24	3	0	158.1	676	180	66	59	12	3	5	4	44	2	134	3	1	8	5	.615	3	0	3.35
1999 Reading	AA Phi	36	15	1	8	127.1	545	123	53	46	7	3	7	5	50	2	127	2	0	9	5	.643	0	3	3.25
2000 Scranton-WB	AAA Phi	29	27	3	1	171	720	163	70	67	17	4	0	6	50	1	127	7	0	13	10	.565	2	0	3.53
5 Min. YEARS		132	108	9	9	714.1	3021	701	307	266	57	17	19	30	228	6	640	24	5	48	34	.585	5	3	3.35

Gary Thomas

Bats: Right Throws: Right Pos: OF-73; PR-5; PH-2
Ht: 5'7" Wt: 175 Born: 9/6/79 Age: 21

Year Team	Lg Org	G	AB	H	2B	3B	HR	TB	R	RBI	TBB	IBB	SO	HBP	SH	SF	SB	CS	SB%	GDP	Avg	OBP	SLG
1997 Athletics	R Oak	28	92	21	2	2	1	30	17	7	9	0	25	3	1	0	6	2	.75	2	.228	.317	.326
1998 Sou Oregon	A- Oak	61	207	42	8	1	0	52	30	21	31	0	42	4	2	2	11	2	.85	5	.203	.316	.251
1999 Modesto	A+ Oak	99	344	111	14	4	7	154	69	38	33	1	45	9	8	4	23	6	.79	7	.323	.392	.448
2000 Midland	AA Oak	74	190	47	7	0	1	57	28	26	24	0	30	9	4	0	5	5	.50	6	.247	.359	.300
4 Min. YEARS		262	833	221	31	7	9	293	144	92	97	1	142	25	15	6	45	15	.75	20	.265	.357	.352

Juan Thomas

Bats: Right Throws: Right Pos: DH-100; 1B-27
Ht: 6'4" Wt: 265 Born: 4/17/72 Age: 29

Year Team	Lg Org	G	AB	H	2B	3B	HR	TB	R	RBI	TBB	IBB	SO	HBP	SH	SF	SB	CS	SB%	GDP	Avg	OBP	SLG
1992 White Sox	R CWS	55	189	42	6	1	6	68	30	29	18	0	76	3	0	2	8	1	.89	4	.222	.297	.360
1993 White Sox	R CWS	20	59	18	3	2	1	28	12	9	12	0	12	1	0	0	5	4	.56	1	.305	.431	.475
Hickory	A CWS	90	328	75	14	6	12	137	51	46	35	1	124	7	1	3	2	4	.33	7	.229	.314	.418
1994 South Bend	A CWS	119	446	112	20	6	18	198	57	79	27	2	143	9	0	5	3	4	.43	13	.251	.304	.444
1995 Pr William	A+ CWS	132	464	109	20	4	26	215	64	69	40	4	156	8	1	2	4	5	.44	16	.235	.305	.463
1996 Pr William	A+ CWS	134	495	148	28	6	20	248	88	71	54	3	129	5	0	2	9	3	.75	15	.299	.372	.501
1997 Winston-Sal	A+ CWS	45	164	43	7	0	13	89	28	28	17	0	61	1	0	0	1	1	.50	5	.262	.335	.543
Birmingham	AA CWS	80	311	94	16	2	10	144	50	55	23	1	92	4	0	4	1	2	.33	4	.302	.354	.463
1998 Atlantic Ct	IND —	99	395	100	18	0	33	217	64	103	35	2	119	1	0	5	6	3	.67	6	.253	.312	.549
1999 Atlantic Ct	IND —	41	154	48	12	0	10	90	30	35	14	1	50	1	0	5	2	1	.67	3	.312	.362	.584
New Haven	AA Sea	71	267	65	13	0	16	126	47	51	14	1	92	6	0	1	0	0	—	6	.243	.295	.472
2000 New Haven	AA Sea	127	495	136	28	3	27	251	66	100	44	2	128	9	0	3	5	0	1.00	16	.275	.343	.507
9 Min. YEARS		1013	3767	990	185	30	192	1811	587	675	333	17	1182	55	2	32	46	28	.62	96	.263	.329	.481

Eric Thompson

Pitches: Right Bats: Right Pos: SP-22; RP-9
Ht: 6'2" Wt: 195 Born: 9/7/77 Age: 23

Year Team	Lg Org	G	GS	CG	GF	IP	BFP	H	R	ER	HR	SH	SF	HB	TBB	IBB	SO	WP	Bk	W	L	Pct.	ShO	Sv	ERA
1998 Sou Oregon	A- Oak	13	12	0	0	56.2	252	60	34	28	7	2	0	3	25	0	51	2	5	5	2	.714	0	0	4.45
1999 Visalia	A+ Oak	31	20	0	5	126.2	595	150	91	79	9	2	6	11	56	0	110	10	1	9	6	.600	0	1	5.61
2000 Visalia	A+ Oak	13	7	0	4	56	228	49	31	31	5	0	0	2	18	0	61	0	0	4	3	.571	0	1	4.98
Midland	AA Oak	18	15	0	1	101.1	425	107	52	44	5	2	1	0	23	0	79	0	1	6	6	.500	0	1	3.91
3 Min. YEARS		75	54	0	10	340.2	1500	366	208	182	26	6	7	16	122	2	301	12	7	24	17	.585	0	3	4.81

Justin Thompson

Pitches: Left Bats: Left Pos: SP-3
Ht: 6'4" Wt: 215 Born: 3/8/73 Age: 28

Year Team	Lg Org	G	GS	CG	GF	IP	BFP	H	R	ER	HR	SH	SF	HB	TBB	IBB	SO	WP	Bk	W	L	Pct.	ShO	Sv	ERA
1991 Bristol	R+ Det	10	10	0	0	50	217	45	29	20	4	0	1	2	24	1	60	7	6	2	5	.286	0	0	3.60
1992 Fayetteville	A Det	20	19	0	1	95	390	79	32	23	6	0	4	1	40	0	88	7	3	4	4	.500	0	0	2.18
1993 Lakeland	A+ Det	11	11	0	0	55.2	241	65	25	22	1	3	0	1	16	0	46	3	1	4	4	.500	0	0	3.56
London	AA Det	14	14	1	0	83.2	376	96	51	38	9	0	4	2	37	0	72	4	1	3	6	.333	0	0	4.09
1995 Lakeland	A+ Det	6	6	0	0	24	107	30	13	13	1	0	2	2	8	0	20	0	0	2	1	.667	0	0	4.88
Jacksnville	AA Det	18	18	3	0	123	502	110	55	51	7	4	2	3	38	2	98	3	0	6	7	.462	0	0	3.73
1996 Fayetteville	A Det	1	1	0	0	3	10	1	1	1	0	0	0	0	0	0	5	0	0	0	0	—	0	0	3.00
Visalia	A+ Det	1	1	0	0	3	13	2	0	0	0	0	0	0	2	0	7	1	0	0	0	—	0	0	0.00
Toledo	AAA Det	13	13	3	0	84.1	338	74	36	32	2	1	2	1	26	0	69	2	0	6	3	.667	1	0	3.42
2000 Charlotte	A+ Tex	1	1	0	0	4.1	17	3	1	1	0	0	0	0	3	0	2	0	0	0	0	—	0	0	2.08
Tulsa	AA Tex	1	1	0	0	5.2	25	8	3	3	1	0	0	0	4	0	4	0	0	1	0	1.000	0	0	4.76
Oklahoma	AAA Tex	1	1	0	0	5.2	30	10	8	7	0	0	1	0	4	0	1	1	0	0	0	—	0	0	11.12

Year Team	Lg Org	HOW MUCH HE PITCHED						WHAT HE GAVE UP												THE RESULTS					
		G	GS	CG	GF	IP	BFP	H	R	ER	HR	SH	SF	HB	TBB	IBB	SO	WP	Bk	W	L	Pct.	ShO	Sv	ERA
1996 Detroit	AL	11	11	0	0	59	267	62	35	30	7	0	2	2	31	2	44	1	0	1	6	.143	0	0	4.58
1997 Detroit	AL	32	32	4	0	223.1	891	188	82	75	20	5	10	2	66	1	151	4	0	15	11	.577	0	0	3.02
1998 Detroit	AL	34	34	5	0	222	946	227	114	100	20	10	6	2	79	4	149	4	0	11	15	.423	0	0	4.05
1999 Detroit	AL	24	24	0	0	142.2	626	152	85	81	24	1	7	4	59	1	83	2	0	9	11	.450	0	0	5.11
6 Min. YEARS		97	96	7	1	537.1	2266	523	254	211	31	8	16	12	199	3	475	28	11	28	30	.483	1	0	3.53
4 Maj. YEARS		101	101	9	0	647	2730	629	316	286	71	16	25	10	235	8	427	11	0	36	43	.456	0	0	3.98

Travis Thompson

Pitches: Right **Bats:** Right **Pos:** RP-50 **Ht:** 6'3" **Wt:** 189 **Born:** 1/10/75 **Age:** 26

Year Team	Lg Org	HOW MUCH HE PITCHED						WHAT HE GAVE UP												THE RESULTS					
		G	GS	CG	GF	IP	BFP	H	R	ER	HR	SH	SF	HB	TBB	IBB	SO	WP	Bk	W	L	Pct.	ShO	Sv	ERA
1996 Portland	A- Col	9	0	0	2	16.2	73	21	11	11	0	2	0	0	6	0	8	1	1	0	2	.000	0	0	5.94
Rockies	R Col	9	3	0	3	30	128	34	12	11	1	1	0	0	5	0	25	0	1	4	1	.800	0	0	3.30
1997 Portland	A- Col	18	11	0	2	74	328	88	51	37	6	2	6	6	16	0	51	2	0	5	5	.500	0	0	4.50
1998 Asheville	A Col	26	24	0	0	147.1	619	155	71	53	11	1	4	6	36	0	113	6	1	6	7	.462	0	0	3.24
1999 Salem	A+ Col	56	0	0	52	62	267	54	19	12	1	7	1	2	24	4	53	5	0	3	3	.500	0	27	1.74
2000 Carolina	AA Col	50	0	0	41	58.1	278	70	44	41	8	3	2	7	30	0	43	4	0	3	7	.300	0	17	6.33
5 Min. YEARS		168	38	0	100	388.1	1693	422	208	165	27	16	9	21	117	4	293	18	3	21	25	.457	0	44	3.82

Travis Thompson

Pitches: Right **Bats:** Right **Pos:** SP-25; RP-2 **Ht:** 6'5" **Wt:** 215 **Born:** 7/3/77 **Age:** 23

Year Team	Lg Org	HOW MUCH HE PITCHED						WHAT HE GAVE UP												THE RESULTS					
		G	GS	CG	GF	IP	BFP	H	R	ER	HR	SH	SF	HB	TBB	IBB	SO	WP	Bk	W	L	Pct.	ShO	Sv	ERA
1999 Billings	R+ Cin	8	0	0	3	20.2	72	14	1	0	0	1	0	0	3	0	27	4	0	1	0	1.000	0	0	0.00
2000 Clinton	A Cin	6	6	1	0	40.2	153	21	8	8	3	1	0	0	13	0	42	2	0	5	1	.833	1	0	1.77
Chattanooga	AA Cin	2	2	0	0	11.2	51	12	6	6	0	0	0	0	8	0	6	0	0	1	1	.500	0	0	4.63
Dayton	A Cin	19	17	4	0	136.1	574	133	52	42	6	4	1	5	39	0	115	4	1	11	4	.733	1	0	2.77
2 Min. YEARS		35	25	5	3	209.1	850	180	67	56	9	6	1	6	63	0	190	10	1	18	6	.750	2	0	2.41

Todd Thorn

Pitches: Left **Bats:** Left **Pos:** SP-18; RP-13 **Ht:** 6'2" **Wt:** 175 **Born:** 11/4/76 **Age:** 24

Year Team	Lg Org	HOW MUCH HE PITCHED						WHAT HE GAVE UP												THE RESULTS					
		G	GS	CG	GF	IP	BFP	H	R	ER	HR	SH	SF	HB	TBB	IBB	SO	WP	Bk	W	L	Pct.	ShO	Sv	ERA
1995 Royals	R KC	11	10	0	0	47.1	201	43	23	17	1	1	1	6	14	0	58	4	1	4	2	.667	0	0	3.23
1996 Lansing	A KC	27	27	2	0	170.2	695	161	70	59	13	6	4	5	34	0	107	8	0	11	5	.688	0	0	3.11
1997 Wilmington	A+ KC	27	21	1	4	132.2	584	163	89	76	14	3	6	7	30	3	71	7	5	6	10	.375	0	0	5.16
1998 Wilmington	A+ KC	26	24	4	0	149.1	604	128	60	52	12	7	9	7	28	2	103	5	3	9	8	.529	2	0	3.13
1999 Wilmington	A+ KC	34	13	0	6	126.2	559	143	85	79	14	4	4	9	44	1	89	6	2	8	5	.615	0	2	5.61
2000 High Desert	A+ Ari	8	8	0	0	42.1	199	64	39	34	5	1	0	3	15	0	24	2	1	0	5	.000	0	0	7.23
El Paso	AA Ari	23	10	0	4	87.2	410	113	63	49	4	6	3	10	32	1	65	5	0	3	8	.273	0	2	5.03
6 Min. YEARS		156	113	7	14	756.2	3252	815	429	366	63	28	27	47	197	7	517	37	12	41	43	.488	2	4	4.35

Jake Thrower

Bats: Both **Throws:** Right **Pos:** 2B-28; SS-5; 3B-1; PH-1; PR-1 **Ht:** 5'11" **Wt:** 180 **Born:** 11/19/75 **Age:** 25

Year Team	Lg Org	BATTING															BASERUNNING				PERCENTAGES		
		G	AB	H	2B	3B	HR	TB	R	RBI	TBB	IBB	SO	HBP	SH	SF	SB	CS	SB%	GDP	Avg	OBP	SLG
1997 Idaho Falls	R+ SD	35	141	48	10	4	3	75	37	28	31	2	16	4	0	1	10	1	.91	2	.340	.469	.532
Clinton	A SD	19	63	16	3	0	0	19	8	12	13	0	15	2	1	0	1	3	.25	0	.254	.397	.302
1998 Clinton	A SD	43	145	42	11	1	5	70	25	27	22	0	22	4	0	0	11	3	.79	5	.290	.398	.483
Rancho Cuca	A+ SD	37	127	34	7	0	1	44	24	10	19	0	19	1	0	1	4	1	.80	2	.268	.362	.346
1999 Mobile	AA SD	40	149	36	9	2	3	58	15	26	21	1	26	1	0	1	3	3	.50	2	.242	.337	.389
Las Vegas	AAA SD	72	267	77	17	4	4	114	40	30	27	2	56	2	3	2	4	4	.50	6	.288	.356	.427
2000 Las Vegas	AAA SD	4	16	5	0	0	0	5	4	2	2	0	2	0	0	0	0	0	—	0	.313	.389	.313
Mobile	AA SD	31	115	32	6	0	1	41	16	11	14	1	22	1	2	2	3	0	1.00	1	.278	.356	.357
4 Min. YEARS		281	1023	290	63	11	17	426	169	146	149	6	178	15	6	8	36	15	.71	18	.283	.380	.416

Corey Thurman

Pitches: Right **Bats:** Right **Pos:** SP-28 **Ht:** 6'1" **Wt:** 215 **Born:** 11/5/78 **Age:** 22

Year Team	Lg Org	HOW MUCH HE PITCHED						WHAT HE GAVE UP												THE RESULTS					
		G	GS	CG	GF	IP	BFP	H	R	ER	HR	SH	SF	HB	TBB	IBB	SO	WP	Bk	W	L	Pct.	ShO	Sv	ERA
1996 Royals	R KC	11	11	0	0	47.1	221	53	32	32	2	0	2	3	28	0	52	8	1	1	6	.143	0	0	6.08
1997 Royals	R KC	8	8	1	0	34	149	28	12	9	1	1	0	2	22	0	42	1	0	2	1	.667	0	0	2.38
Spokane	A- KC	5	5	0	0	22.2	106	23	19	13	2	0	2	2	13	0	24	2	1	1	2	.333	0	0	5.16
1998 Spokane	A- KC	12	11	0	0	60	278	72	35	27	3	1	3	5	31	0	49	6	0	3	3	.500	0	0	4.05
Lansing	A KC	14	11	0	2	62.1	261	47	31	25	6	0	1	4	30	0	61	10	0	5	6	.455	0	0	3.61
1999 Wilmington	A+ KC	27	27	0	0	149.1	667	160	89	81	14	4	5	9	64	0	131	11	1	8	11	.421	0	0	4.88
2000 Wilmington	A+ KC	19	19	1	0	115.2	468	97	33	29	6	1	5	4	46	0	96	7	0	10	5	.667	0	0	2.26
Wichita	AA KC	9	9	0	0	50.1	222	46	34	27	10	2	1	3	24	0	47	4	1	4	5	.444	0	0	4.83
5 Min. YEARS		105	101	2	2	541.2	2372	526	285	243	41	9	19	32	258	0	502	49	4	34	39	.466	0	0	4.04

Jerrey Thurston

Bats: Right **Throws:** Right **Pos:** C-31; PH-7; DH-1 **Ht:** 6'4" **Wt:** 200 **Born:** 4/17/72 **Age:** 29

Year Team	Lg Org	BATTING															BASERUNNING				PERCENTAGES		
		G	AB	H	2B	3B	HR	TB	R	RBI	TBB	IBB	SO	HBP	SH	SF	SB	CS	SB%	GDP	Avg	OBP	SLG
1990 Padres	R SD	42	144	33	6	1	0	41	22	16	14	0	37	0	2	0	4	1	.80	1	.229	.297	.285
1991 Chston-SC	A SD	42	137	14	2	0	0	16	5	4	9	0	50	0	1	1	1	1	.50	3	.102	.156	.117
Spokane	A- SD	60	201	43	9	0	1	55	26	20	20	1	61	2	2	2	2	2	.50	2	.214	.289	.274

			BATTING														BASERUNNING				PERCENTAGES		
Year Team	Lg Org	G	AB	H	2B	3B	HR	TB	R	RBI	TBB	IBB	SO	HBP	SH	SF	SB	CS	SB%	GDP	Avg	OBP	SLG
1992 Waterloo	A SD	96	263	37	7	0	0	44	20	14	12	0	73	2	6	2	1	0	1.00	4	.141	.183	.167
1993 Wichita	AA SD	78	197	48	10	0	2	64	22	22	14	0	62	6	3	0	2	0	1.00	3	.244	.313	.325
1994 Wichita	AA SD	77	238	51	10	2	4	77	30	28	19	1	73	8	2	1	1	4	.20	8	.214	.293	.324
1995 Las Vegas	AAA SD	5	20	4	1	0	0	5	2	0	0	0	5	1	0	0	0	0	—	0	.200	.238	.250
Rancho Cuca	A+ SD	76	200	44	9	0	1	56	24	13	21	0	64	7	4	3	1	0	1.00	0	.220	.312	.280
1996 Orlando	AA ChC	67	177	37	6	1	3	54	16	23	14	0	57	0	3	0	0	0	—	5	.209	.267	.305
1997 Lk Elsinore	A+ Ana	2	6	3	1	0	0	4	1	1	0	0	2	0	0	0	0	0	—	0	.500	.500	.667
Vancouver	AAA Ana	65	195	46	3	1	4	63	17	19	8	0	59	4	8	2	3	2	.60	2	.236	.278	.323
1998 Midland	AA Ana	29	95	30	4	0	2	40	20	22	8	0	24	2	0	1	0	0	—	2	.316	.377	.421
Vancouver	AAA Ana	9	25	4	1	0	0	5	0	1	3	0	8	0	0	0	0	0	—	0	.160	.250	.200
Ottawa	AAA Mon	13	30	1	0	0	0	1	2	0	4	0	15	0	0	0	0	0	—	0	.033	.147	.033
1999 New Orleans	AAA Hou	21	59	13	0	0	0	13	7	4	4	0	15	2	1	0	0	1	.00	3	.220	.292	.220
2000 Round Rock	AA Hou	24	77	19	2	1	1	26	4	7	1	0	19	1	1	0	0	1	.00	2	.247	.266	.338
New Orleans	AAA Hou	13	30	5	2	0	0	7	3	0	0	0	10	0	0	0	0	0	—	0	.167	.167	.233
11 Min. YEARS		719	2094	432	73	6	18	571	221	194	151	2	634	35	33	12	15	12	.56	38	.206	.270	.273

Brian Tokarse

Pitches: Right **Bats:** Right **Pos:** RP-34   **Ht:** 6'3" **Wt:** 200 **Born:** 2/28/75 **Age:** 26

		HOW MUCH HE PITCHED						WHAT HE GAVE UP										THE RESULTS					
Year Team	Lg Org	G	GS	CG	GF	IP	BFP	H	R	ER	HR	SH	SF	HB	TBB	IBB	SO	WP	Bk	W	L	Pct.	ShO	Sv	ERA
1997 Butte	R+ Ana	8	7	0	0	36.2	162	44	33	28	3	1	4	2	8	0	34	2	0	2	4	.333	0	0	6.87
1998 Lk Elsinore	A+ Ana	22	22	2	0	125.1	553	150	93	80	7	1	2	9	42	0	97	6	4	9	9	.500	0	0	5.74
Hickory	A CWS	2	2	0	0	3.2	17	3	3	3	1	0	0	2	3	0	3	1	0	0	1	.000	0	0	7.36
1999 Winston-Sal	A+ CWS	40	0	0	37	46.2	201	37	15	12	2	4	1	3	22	3	55	2	0	5	4	.556	0	14	2.31
Birmingham	AA CWS	6	0	0	0	10.2	46	12	7	6	1	1	0	0	3	0	11	1	0	0	1	.000	0	0	5.06
2000 Birmingham	AA CWS	34	0	0	15	41.2	188	40	26	26	5	5	1	3	28	3	52	7	1	6	3	.667	0	1	5.62
4 Min. YEARS		112	31	2	52	264.2	1167	286	177	155	19	12	8	19	106	6	252	19	5	22	22	.500	0	15	5.27

Juan Tolentino

Bats: Right **Throws:** Right **Pos:** OF-120; PH-2   **Ht:** 6'0" **Wt:** 165 **Born:** 3/12/76 **Age:** 25

			BATTING														BASERUNNING				PERCENTAGES		
Year Team	Lg Org	G	AB	H	2B	3B	HR	TB	R	RBI	TBB	IBB	SO	HBP	SH	SF	SB	CS	SB%	GDP	Avg	OBP	SLG
1996 Angels	R Ana	49	170	48	9	6	2	75	30	14	11	0	33	1	0	0	21	2	.91	4	.282	.330	.441
1997 Butte	R+ Ana	61	213	64	16	4	10	118	44	53	24	0	53	2	0	4	21	2	.91	2	.300	.370	.554
1998 Cedar Rapds	A Ana	133	495	129	27	6	11	201	82	57	51	1	135	6	3	2	49	25	.66	6	.261	.336	.406
1999 Erie	AA Ana	136	489	123	19	5	9	179	61	61	47	0	116	2	8	2	47	14	.77	7	.252	.319	.366
2000 Edmonton	AAA Ana	122	432	106	30	3	11	175	58	58	37	0	106	3	3	4	16	14	.53	5	.245	.307	.405
5 Min. YEARS		501	1799	470	101	24	43	748	275	243	170	1	443	14	14	12	154	57	.73	25	.261	.328	.416

Andy Tomberlin

Bats: Left **Throws:** Left **Pos:** DH-6; OF-5; PH-1   **Ht:** 5'11" **Wt:** 185 **Born:** 11/7/66 **Age:** 34

			BATTING														BASERUNNING				PERCENTAGES		
Year Team	Lg Org	G	AB	H	2B	3B	HR	TB	R	RBI	TBB	IBB	SO	HBP	SH	SF	SB	CS	SB%	GDP	Avg	OBP	SLG
1986 Sumter	A Atl	13	1	0	0	0	0	0	0	0	1	0	1	0	0	0	0	0	—	0	.000	.500	.000
Pulaski	R+ Atl	3	4	1	0	0	0	1	2	0	2	0	1	0	0	0	0	0	—	0	.250	.500	.250
1987 Pulaski	R+ Atl	14	7	2	0	0	0	2	1	1	0	0	0	0	0	0	0	0	—	0	.286	.286	.286
1988 Burlington	A Atl	43	134	46	7	3	3	68	24	18	22	2	33	2	1	1	7	4	.64	0	.343	.440	.507
Durham	A+ Atl	83	256	77	16	3	6	117	43	35	49	3	42	1	2	1	16	8	.67	2	.301	.414	.457
1989 Durham	A+ Atl	119	363	102	13	2	16	167	63	61	54	7	82	5	3	1	35	12	.74	4	.281	.381	.460
1990 Greenville	AA Atl	60	196	61	9	1	4	84	31	25	20	0	35	5	4	1	9	4	.69	1	.311	.387	.429
Richmond	AAA Atl	80	283	86	19	3	4	123	36	31	39	7	43	1	4	2	11	4	.73	7	.304	.388	.435
1991 Richmond	AAA Atl	93	329	77	13	2	2	100	47	24	41	3	85	8	9	1	10	6	.63	6	.234	.332	.304
1992 Richmond	AAA Atl	118	406	110	16	5	9	163	69	47	41	1	102	8	10	2	12	12	.50	2	.271	.348	.401
1993 Buffalo	AAA Pit	68	221	63	11	6	12	122	41	45	18	3	48	4	1	2	3	0	1.00	5	.285	.347	.552
1994 Pawtucket	AAA Bos	54	189	63	12	2	13	118	38	39	22	1	60	3	1	2	11	1	.92	1	.333	.407	.624
1995 Edmonton	AAA Oak	14	52	13	3	0	2	22	9	7	5	0	15	1	1	0	0	0	—	1	.250	.328	.423
1996 Edmonton	AAA Oak	17	60	17	2	1	0	21	12	5	8	0	15	2	0	0	1	0	1.00	0	.283	.386	.350
Norfolk	AAA NYM	38	129	42	6	1	8	74	17	18	8	1	29	2	3	0	1	3	.25	2	.326	.374	.574
1997 Mets	R NYM	7	22	7	0	0	2	13	6	7	3	0	7	0	0	0	1	0	1.00	1	.318	.400	.591
St. Lucie	A+ NYM	1	3	0	0	0	0	0	0	1	1	0	2	0	0	0	0	0	—	0	.000	.250	.000
1998 Toledo	AAA Det	14	47	16	2	1	2	26	13	4	8	0	15	4	0	0	1	1	.50	0	.340	.475	.553
Richmond	AAA Atl	39	104	27	3	0	4	42	12	15	15	1	29	7	0	1	1	1	.50	3	.260	.386	.404
1999 St. Lucie	A+ NYM	9	29	11	1	0	1	15	4	4	4	0	8	2	0	0	2	0	1.00	0	.379	.486	.517
Norfolk	AAA NYM	97	303	94	21	1	16	165	60	61	40	5	74	7	0	2	2	1	.67	4	.310	.401	.545
2000 Buffalo	AAA Cle	11	30	10	2	2	0	16	4	6	8	1	6	2	1	0	0	0	—	0	.333	.500	.533
1993 Pittsburgh	NL	27	42	12	0	1	1	17	4	7	5	2	14	1	0	0	0	0	—	0	.286	.333	.405
1994 Boston	AL	18	36	7	0	1	1	12	1	1	6	0	12	0	0	0	1	0	1.00	0	.194	.310	.333
1995 Oakland	AL	46	85	18	0	0	4	30	15	10	5	0	22	0	0	2	4	1	.80	3	.212	.256	.353
1996 New York	NL	63	66	17	4	0	3	30	12	10	9	0	27	1	0	0	0	0	—	0	.258	.355	.455
1997 New York	NL	6	7	2	0	0	0	2	0	0	1	0	3	0	0	0	0	0	—	0	.286	.375	.286
1998 Detroit	AL	32	69	15	0	0	2	23	8	12	3	1	25	3	0	0	1	0	1.00	3	.217	.280	.333
15 Min. YEARS		995	3168	925	156	33	104	1459	532	454	409	35	732	64	39	16	123	57	.68	39	.292	.382	.461
6 Maj. YEARS		192	305	71	6	2	11	114	40	38	26	1	103	5	2	2	6	1	.86	5	.233	.304	.374

Goefrey Tomlinson

Bats: Left **Throws:** Left **Pos:** OF-28; PR-1   **Ht:** 6'1" **Wt:** 190 **Born:** 8/19/76 **Age:** 24

			BATTING														BASERUNNING				PERCENTAGES		
Year Team	Lg Org	G	AB	H	2B	3B	HR	TB	R	RBI	TBB	IBB	SO	HBP	SH	SF	SB	CS	SB%	GDP	Avg	OBP	SLG
1997 Spokane	A- KC	58	210	71	16	0	4	99	49	28	32	0	20	8	4	2	19	1	.95	1	.338	.440	.471
1998 Lansing	A KC	68	274	78	16	7	7	129	55	39	39	2	34	5	0	0	21	6	.78	4	.285	.384	.471
Wilmington	A+ KC	38	136	38	8	1	0	48	15	16	14	2	26	0	2	0	2	2	.50	3	.279	.347	.353

			BATTING															BASERUNNING				PERCENTAGES		
Year Team	Lg Org	G	AB	H	2B	3B	HR	TB	R	RBI	TBB	IBB	SO	HBP	SH	SF	SB	CS	SB%	GDP	Avg	OBP	SLG
1999 Wichita	AA KC	128	479	134	31	4	4	185	100	46	72	4	82	4	8	5	24	19	.56	5	.280	.375	.386
2000 Omaha	AAA KC	29	98	28	3	2	0	35	12	9	17	0	11	1	1	4	5	5	.50	2	.286	.383	.357
4 Min. YEARS		321	1197	349	74	14	15	496	231	138	174	8	173	18	15	11	71	33	.68	15	.292	.386	.414

Mike Tonis

Bats: Right **Throws:** Right **Pos:** C-28; DH-1; PH-1 **Ht:** 6'3" **Wt:** 215 **Born:** 2/9/79 **Age:** 22

			BATTING															BASERUNNING				PERCENTAGES		
Year Team	Lg Org	G	AB	H	2B	3B	HR	TB	R	RBI	TBB	IBB	SO	HBP	SH	SF	SB	CS	SB%	GDP	Avg	OBP	SLG
2000 Chston-WV	A KC	28	100	20	8	0	0	28	10	17	9	1	22	1	1	2	1	0	1.00	1	.200	.268	.280
Omaha	AAA KC	2	8	4	0	0	0	4	1	3	0	0	3	0	0	0	0	0	—	0	.500	.500	.500
1 Min. YEARS		30	108	24	8	0	0	32	11	20	9	1	25	1	1	2	1	0	1.00	1	.222	.283	.296

Tony Torcato

Bats: Left **Throws:** Right **Pos:** 3B-107; DH-13; PH-1 **Ht:** 6'1" **Wt:** 195 **Born:** 10/25/79 **Age:** 21

			BATTING															BASERUNNING				PERCENTAGES		
Year Team	Lg Org	G	AB	H	2B	3B	HR	TB	R	RBI	TBB	IBB	SO	HBP	SH	SF	SB	CS	SB%	GDP	Avg	OBP	SLG
1998 Salem-Keizr	A- SF	59	220	64	15	2	3	92	31	43	14	0	38	3	0	6	4	2	.67	0	.291	.333	.418
1999 Bakersfield	A+ SF	110	422	123	25	0	4	160	50	58	30	3	67	3	1	7	2	1	.67	6	.291	.338	.379
2000 San Jose	A+ SF	119	490	159	37	2	7	221	77	88	41	8	62	6	0	7	19	4	.83	2	.324	.379	.451
Shreveport	AA SF	2	8	4	0	0	0	4	1	2	0	0	1	0	0	0	0	0	—	0	.500	.500	.500
3 Min. YEARS		290	1140	350	77	4	14	477	159	191	85	11	168	12	1	20	25	7	.78	8	.307	.356	.418

Yorvit Torrealba

Bats: Right **Throws:** Right **Pos:** C-106; PH-2 **Ht:** 5'11" **Wt:** 190 **Born:** 7/19/78 **Age:** 22

			BATTING															BASERUNNING				PERCENTAGES		
Year Team	Lg Org	G	AB	H	2B	3B	HR	TB	R	RBI	TBB	IBB	SO	HBP	SH	SF	SB	CS	SB%	GDP	Avg	OBP	SLG
1995 Bellingham	A- SF	26	71	11	3	0	0	14	2	8	2	0	14	1	0	1	0	1	.00	1	.155	.187	.197
1996 San Jose	A+ SF	2	5	0	0	0	0	0	0	0	1	0	1	0	0	0	0	0	—	0	.000	.167	.000
Burlington	A SF	1	4	0	0	0	0	0	0	0	0	0	1	0	0	0	0	0	—	0	.000	.000	.000
Bellingham	A- SF	48	150	40	4	0	1	47	23	10	9	0	27	0	4	2	4	1	.80	7	.267	.304	.313
1997 Bakersfield	A+ SF	119	446	122	15	3	4	155	52	40	31	0	58	5	1	3	4	2	.67	8	.274	.326	.348
1998 San Jose	A+ SF	21	70	20	2	0	0	22	10	10	1	0	6	0	2	1	2	2	.50	2	.286	.292	.314
Shreveport	AA SF	59	196	46	7	0	0	53	18	13	18	3	30	4	3	1	0	5	.00	3	.235	.311	.270
Fresno	AAA SF	4	11	2	1	0	0	3	1	1	1	1	4	0	0	0	0	0	—	0	.182	.250	.273
1999 Fresno	AAA SF	17	63	16	2	0	2	24	9	10	4	0	11	2	0	0	0	1	.00	2	.254	.319	.381
Shreveport	AA SF	65	217	53	10	1	4	77	25	19	9	0	34	2	2	2	0	2	.00	6	.244	.278	.355
San Jose	A+ SF	19	73	23	3	0	2	32	10	14	6	0	15	1	0	1	0	0	—	2	.315	.370	.438
2000 Shreveport	AA SF	108	398	114	21	1	4	149	50	32	34	2	55	6	0	2	2	3	.40	17	.286	.350	.374
6 Min. YEARS		489	1704	447	68	5	17	576	200	157	116	6	256	21	22	13	12	17	.41	49	.262	.315	.338

Andres Torres

Bats: Both **Throws:** Right **Pos:** OF-118; DH-4; PR-1 **Ht:** 5'10" **Wt:** 175 **Born:** 1/26/78 **Age:** 23

			BATTING															BASERUNNING				PERCENTAGES		
Year Team	Lg Org	G	AB	H	2B	3B	HR	TB	R	RBI	TBB	IBB	SO	HBP	SH	SF	SB	CS	SB%	GDP	Avg	OBP	SLG
1998 Jamestown	A- Det	48	192	45	2	6	1	62	28	21	25	0	50	1	1	2	13	2	.87	0	.234	.323	.323
1999 W Michigan	A Det	117	407	96	20	5	2	132	72	34	92	1	116	10	9	5	39	18	.68	2	.236	.385	.324
2000 Lakeland	A Det	108	398	118	11	11	3	160	82	33	63	2	82	5	10	0	65	16	.80	10	.296	.399	.402
Jacksnville	AA Det	14	54	8	0	0	0	8	3	0	5	0	14	0	0	0	2	0	1.00	0	.148	.220	.148
3 Min. YEARS		287	1051	267	33	22	6	362	185	88	185	3	262	16	20	7	119	36	.77	14	.254	.372	.344

Gabby Torres

Bats: Right **Throws:** Right **Pos:** C-80; DH-10; PH-4; 1B-1 **Ht:** 5'10" **Wt:** 189 **Born:** 3/20/78 **Age:** 23

			BATTING															BASERUNNING				PERCENTAGES		
Year Team	Lg Org	G	AB	H	2B	3B	HR	TB	R	RBI	TBB	IBB	SO	HBP	SH	SF	SB	CS	SB%	GDP	Avg	OBP	SLG
1996 Twins	R Min	22	66	23	4	1	1	32	9	5	7	0	10	1	0	0	1	3	.25	3	.348	.419	.485
1997 Twins	R Min	45	152	39	5	1	0	46	17	16	19	0	21	6	3	2	18	3	.86	7	.257	.358	.303
1998 Elizabethtn	R+ Min	46	161	40	7	0	4	59	19	25	19	0	23	4	1	1	1	2	.33	10	.248	.341	.366
1999 Elizabethtn	R+ Min	7	24	6	1	0	1	10	5	3	4	0	1	1	1	0	1	1	.50	3	.250	.379	.417
Fort Myers	A+ Min	22	68	15	3	0	1	21	7	6	3	0	8	2	1	1	0	0	—	5	.221	.277	.309
2000 Salt Lake	AAA Min	1	1	0	0	0	0	0	0	0	0	0	0	0	0	0	0	0	—	0	.000	.000	.000
Quad City	A Min	71	268	73	14	0	6	105	36	33	19	0	39	7	3	1	1	1	.50	8	.272	.336	.392
Fort Myers	A+ Min	20	46	9	3	0	0	12	5	3	6	0	5	1	0	0	0	0	—	3	.196	.296	.261
5 Min. YEARS		234	786	205	37	2	13	285	98	91	77	0	107	22	9	6	22	10	.69	39	.261	.341	.363

Melqui Torres

Pitches: Right **Bats:** Right **Pos:** SP-23; RP-5 **Ht:** 6'1" **Wt:** 165 **Born:** 5/27/77 **Age:** 24

		HOW MUCH HE PITCHED						WHAT HE GAVE UP											THE RESULTS						
Year Team	Lg Org	G	GS	CG	GF	IP	BFP	H	R	ER	HR	SH	SF	HB	TBB	IBB	SO	WP	Bk	W	L	Pct.	ShO	Sv	ERA
1997 Mariners	R Sea	13	10	0	2	54.2	266	60	63	40	1	0	0	11	38	0	42	9	1	2	6	.250	0	1	6.59
1998 Everett	A- Sea	16	15	0	1	72.2	356	92	72	49	4	5	8	6	40	0	41	7	1	3	10	.231	0	1	6.07
1999 Wisconsin	A Sea	27	27	3	0	171.2	736	185	99	86	9	3	14	10	45	0	129	12	6	13	9	.591	2	0	4.51
2000 Wisconsin	A Sea	9	4	0	1	33.2	154	35	33	15	2	0	2	2	13	1	28	0	0	2	3	.400	0	0	4.01
Lancaster	A+ Sea	18	18	0	0	102.2	448	119	60	50	7	3	3	4	29	0	79	4	2	8	4	.667	0	0	4.38
Tacoma	AAA Sea	1	1	0	0	5.1	22	7	3	3	0	0	0	0	1	0	0	1	0	1	0	1.000	0	0	5.06
4 Min. YEARS		84	75	3	4	440.2	1982	498	320	243	24	12	27	33	166	1	321	34	13	29	32	.475	2	2	4.96

Dave Toth

Bats: Right **Throws:** Right **Pos:** C-40; 1B-3; OF-2; PH-2; PR-1   **Ht:** 6'2" **Wt:** 208 **Born:** 12/8/69 **Age:** 31

Year Team	Lg Org	G	AB	H	2B	3B	HR	TB	R	RBI	TBB	IBB	SO	HBP	SH	SF	SB	CS	SB%	GDP	Avg	OBP	SLG
1990 Pulaski	R+ Atl	26	82	22	0	0	0	22	9	10	11	0	12	1	1	2	2	0	1.00	0	.268	.354	.268
1991 Idaho Falls	R+ Atl	47	160	34	3	0	4	49	27	22	18	1	21	4	1	2	1	0	1.00	6	.213	.304	.306
1992 Macon	A Atl	87	310	80	15	2	3	108	32	41	21	0	44	4	0	2	3	3	.50	6	.258	.312	.348
1993 Macon	A Atl	104	353	87	22	0	4	121	38	40	28	1	53	7	5	3	6	5	.55	11	.246	.312	.343
1994 Durham	A+ Atl	72	165	40	11	0	2	57	23	20	19	0	28	1	1	1	1	0	1.00	4	.242	.323	.345
1995 Richmond	AAA Atl	7	13	3	0	0	0	3	1	1	1	0	2	0	0	0	0	1	.00	1	.231	.286	.231
Durham	A+ Atl	85	257	63	6	0	6	87	20	26	25	1	42	6	0	1	3	3	.50	6	.245	.325	.339
1996 Greenville	AA Atl	120	376	100	31	1	10	163	63	55	58	0	61	11	1	4	2	3	.40	4	.266	.376	.434
1997 Richmond	AAA Atl	14	46	9	3	0	0	12	6	5	4	0	8	0	0	0	0	0	—	3	.196	.260	.261
Greenville	AA Atl	58	184	45	9	0	7	75	23	24	25	0	35	4	0	0	2	2	.50	7	.245	.347	.408
1998 Calgary	AAA CWS	72	246	57	12	0	6	87	31	30	24	0	44	3	4	4	3	2	.60	11	.232	.303	.354
1999 Charlotte	AAA CWS	79	261	64	14	0	6	96	36	33	24	0	38	3	1	0	1	2	.33	6	.245	.316	.368
2000 Charlotte	AAA CWS	46	131	29	6	0	2	41	15	23	17	0	14	1	3	3	0	0	—	2	.221	.309	.313
11 Min. YEARS		817	2584	633	132	3	50	921	324	330	275	3	402	45	17	22	24	21	.53	67	.245	.326	.356

Josh Towers

Pitches: Right **Bats:** Right **Pos:** SP-24   **Ht:** 6'1" **Wt:** 165 **Born:** 2/26/77 **Age:** 24

Year Team	Lg Org	G	GS	CG	GF	IP	BFP	H	R	ER	HR	SH	SF	HB	TBB	IBB	SO	WP	Bk	W	L	Pct.	ShO	Sv	ERA
1996 Bluefield	R+ Bal	14	9	0	1	55	234	63	35	32	7	1	1	1	5	0	61	4	1	4	1	.800	0	0	5.24
1997 Delmarva	A Bal	9	1	0	5	18.1	73	18	8	7	1	1	1	0	2	0	16	0	0	0	1	—	0	1	3.44
Frederick	A+ Bal	25	3	0	8	53.2	252	74	36	29	4	1	1	3	18	0	64	2	1	6	2	.750	0	1	4.86
1998 Frederick	A+ Bal	25	20	3	3	145.1	583	137	58	54	11	6	3	11	9	0	122	5	2	8	7	.533	0	1	3.34
Bowie	AA Bal	5	2	0	1	18	80	20	9	7	1	0	0	2	4	0	7	1	0	2	1	.667	0	0	3.50
1999 Bowie	AA Bal	29	28	5	1	189	786	204	86	79	26	12	4	5	26	1	106	5	3	12	7	.632	2	0	3.76
2000 Rochester	AAA Bal	24	24	5	0	148	618	157	63	57	17	2	4	8	21	0	102	1	1	8	6	.571	1	0	3.47
5 Min. YEARS		131	87	13	19	627.1	2626	673	295	265	69	22	14	30	85	1	478	18	8	40	24	.625	3	3	3.80

Francisco Trejo

Pitches: Left **Bats:** Left **Pos:** SP-15; RP-2   **Ht:** 6'0" **Wt:** 154 **Born:** 3/6/80 **Age:** 21

Year Team	Lg Org	G	GS	CG	GF	IP	BFP	H	R	ER	HR	SH	SF	HB	TBB	IBB	SO	WP	Bk	W	L	Pct.	ShO	Sv	ERA
1998 Diamondbcks	R Ari	13	6	0	1	40.2	193	45	37	29	0	2	4	4	27	0	48	9	0	2	5	.286	0	0	6.42
1999 High Desert	A+ Ari	3	0	0	2	6.2	32	5	6	5	1	0	1	7	0	6	3	0	0	0	—	0	0	6.75
Diamondbcks	R Ari	17	0	0	6	28.1	131	28	18	10	0	2	1	19	0	30	10	1	0	2	.000	0	1	3.18
2000 El Paso	AA Ari	2	1	0	0	5	21	2	1	1	1	0	0	0	5	0	4	0	0	0	0	—	0	0	1.80
Missoula	R+ Ari	10	10	0	0	46.1	209	53	29	21	2	2	0	2	17	0	48	3	0	3	3	.500	0	0	4.08
South Bend	A Ari	5	4	0	0	27.1	114	24	14	9	3	1	1	2	11	1	16	1	0	1	2	.333	0	0	2.96
3 Min. YEARS		50	21	0	9	154.1	700	157	106	75	7	7	5	10	86	1	152	26	1	6	12	.333	0	1	4.37

Chris Tremie

Bats: Right **Throws:** Right **Pos:** C-37; DH-6; PH-6; 3B-4; 1B-4; P-2; PR-1   **Ht:** 6'0" **Wt:** 215 **Born:** 10/17/69 **Age:** 31

Year Team	Lg Org	G	AB	H	2B	3B	HR	TB	R	RBI	TBB	IBB	SO	HBP	SH	SF	SB	CS	SB%	GDP	Avg	OBP	SLG
1992 Utica	A- CWS	6	16	1	0	0	0	1	1	0	0	0	5	0	0	0	0	0	—	0	.063	.063	.063
1993 White Sox	R CWS	2	4	0	0	0	0	0	0	0	0	0	0	0	0	0	0	0	—	0	.000	.000	.000
Sarasota	A+ CWS	14	37	6	1	0	0	7	2	5	2	0	4	3	0	0	0	0	—	1	.162	.262	.189
Hickory	A CWS	49	155	29	6	1	1	40	7	17	9	0	26	4	1	0	0	0	—	5	.187	.250	.258
1994 Birmingham	AA CWS	92	302	68	13	0	2	87	32	29	17	0	44	6	3	2	4	1	.80	3	.225	.278	.288
1995 Nashville	AAA CWS	67	190	38	4	0	2	48	13	16	13	0	37	2	4	0	0	0	—	6	.200	.259	.253
1996 Nashville	AAA CWS	70	215	47	10	1	0	59	17	26	18	0	48	2	6	3	2	0	1.00	6	.219	.282	.274
1997 Reading	AA Phi	97	295	60	11	1	2	79	20	31	36	0	61	5	5	5	0	5	.00	7	.203	.296	.268
1998 Oklahoma	AAA Tex	78	247	55	10	0	0	65	35	12	24	0	47	5	4	1	1	1	.50	12	.223	.303	.263
1999 Nashville	AAA Pit	47	121	30	7	0	3	46	20	16	14	0	29	2	3	2	4	0	1.00	4	.248	.331	.380
2000 Newark	IND —	11	33	6	0	0	0	6	4	6	8	0	8	1	0	1	0	0	—	0	.182	.349	.182
Atlantic Ct	IND —	2	7	2	0	0	1	5	1	1	0	0	0	1	0	1	0	0	—	0	.286	.286	.714
Calgary	AAA Fla	46	120	32	7	1	2	47	16	17	15	0	24	0	1	0	0	1	.00	4	.267	.348	.392
1995 Chicago	AL	10	24	4	0	0	0	4	0	0	1	0	2	0	1	0	0	0	—	0	.167	.200	.167
1998 Texas	AL	2	3	1	1	0	0	2	2	0	1	0	1	0	0	0	0	0	—	0	.333	.500	.667
1999 Pittsburgh	NL	9	14	1	0	0	0	1	0	0	0	0	7	0	1	0	0	0	—	0	.071	.188	.071
9 Min. YEARS		581	1742	374	69	4	13	490	168	176	156	1	334	30	27	14	11	8	.58	48	.215	.288	.281
3 Maj. YEARS		21	41	6	1	0	0	7	3	1	4	0	7	0	1	0	0	0	—	0	.146	.222	.171

John Tsoukalas

Bats: Left **Throws:** Right **Pos:** 3B-59; PH-18; 1B-12; DH-1   **Ht:** 6'1" **Wt:** 190 **Born:** 8/24/70 **Age:** 30

Year Team	Lg Org	G	AB	H	2B	3B	HR	TB	R	RBI	TBB	IBB	SO	HBP	SH	SF	SB	CS	SB%	GDP	Avg	OBP	SLG
1991 Medcine Hat	R+ Tor	64	242	69	11	0	2	86	35	39	24	0	21	5	1	0	4	2	.67	7	.285	.362	.355
1992 Myrtle Bch	A Tor	91	265	61	8	0	5	84	23	28	18	0	43	7	3	2	0	1	.00	5	.230	.295	.317
1995 Thunder Bay	IND —	80	290	85	13	0	3	107	34	38	35	2	38	1	2	4	4	4	.50	6	.293	.367	.369
1996 Thunder Bay	IND —	49	175	48	11	0	1	62	14	21	16	2	35	1	0	0	0	0	—	6	.274	.339	.354
Madison	IND —	18	70	24	7	0	1	34	15	12	6	1	8	0	1	2	1	0	1.00	0	.343	.385	.486
1997 Sioux Falls	IND —	81	300	90	19	0	2	115	44	34	38	1	40	1	0	4	6	4	.60	8	.300	.383	.383
1998 St. Paul	IND —	82	310	81	15	0	1	99	46	34	34	1	55	1	2	3	3	3	.50	6	.261	.334	.319
1999 San Jose	A+ SF	64	208	67	15	1	9	111	36	41	25	2	42	1	0	0	0	1	.00	3	.322	.397	.534
2000 Shreveport	AA SF	31	60	13	3	0	1	19	8	11	4	0	11	1	0	1	0	0	—	2	.217	.273	.317
Tri-City	IND —	57	211	54	9	0	1	66	27	17	24	0	30	3	1	1	5	2	.29	6	.256	.339	.313
8 Min. YEARS		617	2131	592	111	1	26	783	282	276	224	10	323	23	10	16	19	22	.46	45	.278	.350	.367

Pete Tucci

Bats: Right **Throws:** Right **Pos:** OF-128; PH-5; 1B-1 **Ht:** 6'2" **Wt:** 210 **Born:** 10/8/75 **Age:** 25

Year Team	Lg Org	G	AB	H	2B	3B	HR	TB	R	RBI	TBB	IBB	SO	HBP	SH	SF	SB	CS	SB%	GDP	Avg	OBP	SLG
1996 St.Cathrnes	A- Tor	54	205	52	8	7	7	95	28	33	23	1	58	1	2	3	5	3	.63	1	.254	.328	.463
1997 Hagerstown	A Tor	127	466	123	28	5	10	191	60	75	35	1	95	5	1	6	9	5	.64	9	.264	.318	.410
1998 Dunedin	A+ Tor	92	356	117	30	3	23	222	72	76	29	0	97	5	2	2	8	5	.62	6	.329	.385	.624
Knoxville	AA Tor	38	141	41	7	4	7	77	25	36	13	0	29	2	0	2	3	2	.60	2	.291	.354	.546
1999 Mobile	AA SD	83	312	78	15	0	11	126	45	35	26	3	83	4	0	1	11	6	.65	7	.250	.315	.404
2000 Mobile	AA SD	133	476	103	35	3	17	195	63	73	39	0	147	5	0	8	18	4	.82	4	.216	.278	.410
5 Min. YEARS		527	1956	514	123	22	75	906	293	328	165	5	509	22	5	22	54	25	.68	29	.263	.324	.463

Jason Turman

Pitches: Right **Bats:** Right **Pos:** RP-32; SP-7 **Ht:** 6'10" **Wt:** 210 **Born:** 11/10/75 **Age:** 25

Year Team	Lg Org	G	GS	CG	GF	IP	BFP	H	R	ER	HR	SH	SF	HB	TBB	IBB	SO	WP	Bk	W	L	Pct.	ShO	Sv	ERA
1997 Cape Fear	A Mon	19	15	1	1	88.1	374	84	45	41	4	1	1	6	35	0	72	8	0	5	7	.417	0	1	4.18
1998 Cape Fear	A Mon	21	20	0	1	111	490	126	69	57	11	1	4	9	30	0	76	8	0	8	5	.615	0	1	4.62
Jupiter	A+ Mon	8	6	1	0	35.1	149	37	20	13	1	2	3	1	12	0	15	3	0	3	2	.600	0	0	3.31
1999 Lancaster	A+ Sea	31	12	1	9	97	436	116	66	56	12	1	2	6	35	1	78	14	0	4	10	.286	0	1	5.20
2000 New Haven	AA Sea	39	7	0	11	100.2	429	102	53	49	7	3	2	4	34	1	94	8	0	3	4	.429	0	3	4.38
4 Min. YEARS		118	60	3	22	432.1	1878	465	253	216	35	8	12	26	146	2	335	41	0	23	28	.451	0	5	4.50

Dave Tuttle

Pitches: Right **Bats:** Right **Pos:** RP-28; SP-13 **Ht:** 6'3" **Wt:** 190 **Born:** 9/29/69 **Age:** 31

Year Team	Lg Org	G	GS	CG	GF	IP	BFP	H	R	ER	HR	SH	SF	HB	TBB	IBB	SO	WP	Bk	W	L	Pct.	ShO	Sv	ERA
1992 Chston-WV	A Cin	17	16	0	0	97.1	416	87	46	42	5	0	6	1	53	1	93	4	0	3	5	.375	0	0	3.88
1993 Chston-WV	A Cin	13	13	0	0	81.1	343	66	37	32	3	1	1	3	36	1	74	6	1	8	3	.727	0	0	3.54
Winston-Sal	A+ Cin	15	15	2	0	86.1	388	98	61	53	8	3	2	1	39	0	58	6	0	7	7	.500	1	0	5.53
1994 Chattanooga	AA Cin	14	14	0	0	84	377	82	60	42	8	4	2	7	48	5	54	10	0	2	9	.182	0	0	4.50
Winston-Sal	A+ Cin	13	13	2	0	76.2	315	58	26	18	8	0	0	3	27	0	64	2	0	5	2	.714	0	0	2.11
1995 Chattanooga	AA Cin	8	7	0	1	34.2	165	40	29	27	6	2	1	1	21	0	20	4	0	1	6	.143	0	0	7.01
Winston-Sal	A+ Cin	10	10	2	0	62.1	248	49	28	22	5	0	2	3	19	0	54	3	0	3	3	.500	1	0	3.18
Lakeland	A+ Det	6	4	1	1	31	132	31	11	10	1	0	3	2	12	0	28	1	0	1	4	.200	0	0	2.90
1996 Visalia	A+ Det	55	0	0	52	70.1	308	71	39	29	3	3	1	3	33	5	56	1	0	7	9	.438	0	21	3.71
1997 High Desert	A+ Ari	50	0	0	42	63	262	54	22	17	4	3	0		23	3	57	5	0	4	3	.571	0	19	2.43
1998 Tulsa	AA Ari	36	2	0	13	73.2	316	73	30	22	4	0	2	5	29	0	47	2	0	1	2	.333	0	4	2.69
Tucson	AAA Ari	10	3	0	3	26.1	125	32	20	20	2	2	1	2	16	1	8	0	0	1	2	.333	0	0	6.84
1999 Tucson	AAA Ari	35	9	0	11	84.1	385	100	62	61	8	3	6	4	48	2	55	4	1	2	5	.286	0	0	6.51
2000 El Paso	AA Ari	21	0	0	5	36.1	152	30	15	10	1	0	0	0	19	0	31	0	0	0	0	—	0	1	2.48
Tucson	AAA Ari	20	13	0	1	80.2	355	85	52	43	7	1	5	3	36	1	62	2	1	3	4	.429	0	0	4.80
9 Min. YEARS		323	119	7	129	988.1	4287	956	538	448	73	22	35	38	459	19	761	50	3	48	64	.429	2	45	4.08

Brad Tyler

Bats: Left **Throws:** Right **Pos:** OF-99; DH-8; PH-8; 3B-1 **Ht:** 6'2" **Wt:** 180 **Born:** 3/3/69 **Age:** 32

Year Team	Lg Org	G	AB	H	2B	3B	HR	TB	R	RBI	TBB	IBB	SO	HBP	SH	SF	SB	CS	SB%	GDP	Avg	OBP	SLG
1990 Wausau	A Bal	56	187	44	4	3	2	60	31	24	44	2	45	2	1	2	11	4	.73	2	.235	.383	.321
1991 Kane County	A Bal	60	199	54	10	3	3	79	35	29	44	1	25	1	1	2	5	3	.63	0	.271	.402	.397
Frederick	A+ Bal	56	187	48	6	0	4	66	26	26	33	3	33	2	1	1	3	2	.60	2	.257	.372	.353
1992 Frederick	A+ Bal	54	185	47	11	2	3	71	34	22	43	2	34	2	1	4	9	3	.75	2	.254	.393	.384
Hagerstown	AA Bal	83	256	57	9	1	2	74	41	21	34	2	45	2	1	0	23	5	.82	5	.223	.318	.289
1993 Bowie	AA Bal	129	437	103	23	17	10	190	85	44	84	2	89	1	1	3	24	11	.69	2	.236	.358	.435
1994 Rochester	AAA Bal	101	314	82	15	8	7	134	38	43	38	2	69	2	1	0	7	4	.64	4	.261	.345	.427
1995 Rochester	AAA Bal	114	361	93	17	3	17	167	60	52	71	4	63	4	0	5	10	5	.67	3	.258	.381	.463
1996 Rochester	AAA Bal	118	382	103	18	10	13	180	68	52	67	2	95	5	1	3	19	7	.73	2	.270	.383	.471
1997 Richmond	AAA Atl	129	383	101	15	10	18	190	69	77	55	2	110	3	3	7	13	6	.68	4	.264	.355	.496
1998 Edmonton	AAA Oak	131	430	115	24	4	18	201	68	75	62	1	107	0	0	6	10	1	.91	1	.267	.355	.467
1999 Richmond	AAA Atl	122	413	118	20	2	21	205	73	79	69	1	99	4	2	2	18	3	.86	4	.286	.391	.496
2000 Indianapolis	AAA Mil	113	371	92	16	3	8	138	59	49	67	9	63	1	1	5	13	3	.81	4	.248	.360	.372
11 Min. YEARS		1266	4105	1057	188	66	126	1755	687	593	711	33	877	29	14	40	165	57	.74	33	.257	.368	.428

Josh Tyler

Bats: Right **Throws:** Right **Pos:** OF-31; 2B-20; PH-12; C-8; 3B-4; 1B-3; DH-3; PR-3; P-2 **Ht:** 6'1" **Wt:** 185 **Born:** 9/6/73 **Age:** 27

Year Team	Lg Org	G	AB	H	2B	3B	HR	TB	R	RBI	TBB	IBB	SO	HBP	SH	SF	SB	CS	SB%	GDP	Avg	OBP	SLG
1994 Brewers	R Mil	54	193	52	4	3	0	62	35	24	30	0	34	6	0	4	8	4	.67	6	.269	.378	.321
1995 Beloit	A Mil	77	186	44	5	0	2	55	24	27	36	0	40	2	7	3	3	6	.33	4	.237	.361	.296
1996 Stockton	A+ Mil	75	273	88	14	2	2	112	42	33	25	0	35	11	7	2	4	8	.33	6	.322	.399	.410
1997 Stockton	A+ Mil	114	416	129	28	4	4	177	63	46	20	0	54	10	5	3	21	7	.75	7	.310	.354	.425
1998 San Jose	A+ SF	50	194	48	10	2	1	65	24	21	10	0	29	0	3	2	7	8	.47	8	.247	.282	.335
Shreveport	AA SF	14	39	8	0	0	0	8	5	3	1	1	4	1	0	1	0	0	—	1	.205	.238	.205
Fresno	AAA SF	3	3	0	0	0	0	0	0	0	1	0	1	0	0	0	0	0	—	0	.000	.250	.000
Bakersfield	A+ SF	22	220	59	14	1	6	93	27	43	11	0	32	3	3	2	12	2	.86	2	.268	.309	.423
1999 Shreveport	AA SF	105	331	87	17	0	3	113	41	39	30	1	53	4	3	2	14	5	.74	10	.263	.330	.341
2000 Fresno	AAA SF	78	212	58	10	1	0	70	24	11	24	0	29	5	1	1	12	4	.75	11	.274	.360	.330
7 Min. YEARS		623	2067	573	102	13	18	755	285	247	188	2	311	42	29	20	81	44	.65	55	.277	.347	.365

Dave Ullery

Bats: Left   **Throws:** Right   **Pos:** C-42; DH-17; PH-4; OF-1; 1B-1   **Ht:** 6'3"   **Wt:** 225   **Born:** 12/16/74   **Age:** 26

Year Team	Lg Org	G	AB	H	2B	3B	HR	TB	R	RBI	TBB	IBB	SO	HBP	SH	SF	SB	CS	SB%	GDP	Avg	OBP	SLG
1997 Anderson	IND —	6	16	5	2	0	0	7	5	2	4	0	4	0	0	0	0	0	—	1	.313	.450	.438
Spokane	A- KC	12	23	5	0	0	1	8	1	4	5	1	5	1	0	0	0	0	—	1	.217	.379	.348
Lansing	A KC	18	44	7	1	2	1	15	5	10	13	0	16	1	0	1	0	0	—	2	.159	.356	.341
1998 Wilmington	A+ KC	74	202	39	5	0	3	53	16	22	21	2	66	2	10	5	1	1	.50	5	.193	.270	.262
1999 Wilmington	A+ KC	60	199	46	18	0	2	70	20	27	18	1	70	2	0	4	0	0	—	3	.231	.296	.352
2000 Wichita	AA KC	62	202	58	9	0	5	82	22	42	15	1	47	1	2	7	1	2	.33	6	.287	.329	.406
4 Min. YEARS		232	686	160	35	2	12	235	69	107	76	5	208	7	12	17	2	3	.40	18	.233	.309	.343

Enmanuel Ulloa

Pitches: Right   **Bats:** Right   **Pos:** SP-28   **Ht:** 6'2"   **Wt:** 170   **Born:** 11/26/78   **Age:** 22

	HOW MUCH HE PITCHED						WHAT HE GAVE UP										THE RESULTS					
Year Team	Lg Org	G	GS	CG	GF	IP	BFP	H	R	ER	HR	SH	SF	HB	TBB	IBB	SO	WP	Bk	W	L	Pct.	ShO	Sv	ERA
1998 Mariners	R Sea	19	0	0	14	41	144	21	6	4	1	1	0	0	1	0	61	0	2	4	0	1.000	0	7	0.88
Wisconsin	A Sea	3	0	0	0	5	20	4	1	1	0	1	1	0	1	0	5	0	0	0	0	—	0	0	1.80
1999 Wisconsin	A Sea	35	10	0	17	88	384	90	50	45	9	1	0	1	36	2	98	8	6	7	3	.700	0	5	4.60
2000 Lancaster	A+ Sea	27	27	0	0	155.2	642	134	90	75	20	1	4	4	55	1	145	4	2	9	5	.643	0	0	4.34
Tacoma	AAA Sea	1	1	0	0	5	21	2	3	3	0	0	0	0	4	0	4	0	0	0	1	.000	0	0	5.40
3 Min. YEARS		85	38	0	31	294.2	1211	251	150	128	30	4	5	5	97	3	313	12	10	20	9	.690	0	12	3.91

Derick Urquhart

Bats: Left   **Throws:** Left   **Pos:** OF-46; DH-10; PH-2   **Ht:** 5'8"   **Wt:** 175   **Born:** 12/20/75   **Age:** 25

Year Team	Lg Org	G	AB	H	2B	3B	HR	TB	R	RBI	TBB	IBB	SO	HBP	SH	SF	SB	CS	SB%	GDP	Avg	OBP	SLG
1998 Vermont	A- Mon	76	243	60	15	2	0	79	32	26	31	0	43	1	4	1	13	7	.65	2	.247	.333	.325
1999 Jupiter	A+ Mon	23	44	8	1	0	0	9	5	5	7	0	7	0	0	0	2	0	1.00	0	.182	.294	.205
Cape Fear	A Mon	54	169	52	4	4	3	73	31	18	26	1	19	1	2	0	6	8	.43	1	.308	.403	.432
2000 Erie	AA Ana	57	189	45	8	2	4	69	30	21	34	0	23	0	2	2	4	4	.50	2	.238	.351	.365
3 Min. YEARS		210	645	165	28	8	7	230	98	70	98	1	92	2	8	3	25	19	.57	5	.256	.354	.357

Carlos Urquiola

Bats: Left   **Throws:** Right   **Pos:** OF-71; DH-24; PH-14   **Ht:** 5'8"   **Wt:** 150   **Born:** 4/22/80   **Age:** 21

Year Team	Lg Org	G	AB	H	2B	3B	HR	TB	R	RBI	TBB	IBB	SO	HBP	SH	SF	SB	CS	SB%	GDP	Avg	OBP	SLG
1997 Diamondbcks	R Ari	2	2	0	0	0	0	0	1	0	0	0	1	0	1	0	1	0	1.00	0	.000	.000	.000
1998 Diamondbcks	R Ari	9	34	21	3	4	0	32	14	10	5	0	5	3	0	0	13	1	.93	0	.618	.690	.941
South Bend	A Ari	39	166	53	8	4	0	69	28	16	10	0	15	1	0	2	10	8	.56	1	.319	.358	.416
1999 South Bend	A Ari	93	384	139	13	3	0	158	66	35	22	0	32	5	1	3	20	14	.59	2	.362	.401	.411
2000 High Desert	A+ Ari	40	165	60	6	2	0	70	34	12	15	0	16	3	1	1	24	5	.83	1	.364	.424	.424
El Paso	AA Ari	68	225	68	8	1	0	78	33	18	20	1	17	3	5	1	13	8	.62	2	.302	.365	.347
4 Min. YEARS		251	976	341	38	14	0	407	176	91	72	1	86	15	8	7	81	36	.69	6	.349	.400	.417

Brant Ust

Bats: Right   **Throws:** Right   **Pos:** 3B-111; SS-5; PH-1   **Ht:** 6'2"   **Wt:** 200   **Born:** 7/17/78   **Age:** 22

Year Team	Lg Org	G	AB	H	2B	3B	HR	TB	R	RBI	TBB	IBB	SO	HBP	SH	SF	SB	CS	SB%	GDP	Avg	OBP	SLG
1999 Oneonta	A- Det	58	226	59	12	3	5	92	23	34	16	2	54	4	1	3	3	4	.43	3	.261	.317	.407
2000 Jacksnville	AA Det	111	383	83	15	4	4	118	37	28	33	2	95	9	7	1	2	4	.33	12	.217	.293	.308
2 Min. YEARS		169	609	142	27	7	9	210	60	62	49	4	149	13	8	4	5	8	.38	15	.233	.302	.345

Rob Vael

Pitches: Right   **Bats:** Right   **Pos:** RP-32   **Ht:** 6'3"   **Wt:** 200   **Born:** 1/8/76   **Age:** 25

	HOW MUCH HE PITCHED						WHAT HE GAVE UP										THE RESULTS					
Year Team	Lg Org	G	GS	CG	GF	IP	BFP	H	R	ER	HR	SH	SF	HB	TBB	IBB	SO	WP	Bk	W	L	Pct.	ShO	Sv	ERA
1997 Watertown	A- Cle	12	12	1	0	62.1	279	63	38	32	5	6	3	0	30	2	47	4	1	1	4	.200	0	0	4.62
1998 Columbus	A Cle	9	9	0	0	42	206	65	51	48	10	2	3	1	21	0	35	5	0	0	6	.000	0	0	10.29
Watertown	A- Cle	12	9	0	1	54.2	228	56	25	25	7	0	1	3	16	0	52	5	0	4	3	.571	0	0	4.12
1999 Columbus	A Cle	42	7	0	16	92.2	422	89	59	50	14	3	2	5	53	1	91	12	1	5	4	.556	0	0	4.86
2000 Harrisburg	AA Mon	6	0	0	3	6	31	10	8	8	0	0	0	2	2	0	3	1	0	0	0	—	0	0	12.00
Jupiter	A+ Mon	26	0	0	8	44.2	195	51	27	24	3	2	1	6	11	1	25	7	0	2	1	.667	0	1	4.84
4 Min. YEARS		107	37	1	28	302.1	1361	334	208	187	39	13	10	17	133	4	253	34	2	12	18	.400	0	1	5.57

Vic Valencia

Bats: Right   **Throws:** Right   **Pos:** C-97; PH-2; 1B-1; DH-1   **Ht:** 6'2"   **Wt:** 185   **Born:** 5/13/77   **Age:** 24

Year Team	Lg Org	G	AB	H	2B	3B	HR	TB	R	RBI	TBB	IBB	SO	HBP	SH	SF	SB	CS	SB%	GDP	Avg	OBP	SLG
1995 Yankees	R NYY	25	58	14	1	0	1	18	5	8	6	0	22	0	0	0	0	0	—	1	.241	.310	.310
1996 Oneonta	A- NYY	72	261	51	8	0	3	68	30	25	21	0	86	0	3	3	3	0	1.00	4	.195	.253	.261
1997 Greensboro	A NYY	107	353	78	12	1	13	131	42	43	43	0	116	7	2	1	2	1	.67	6	.221	.317	.371
1998 Tampa	A+ NYY	122	411	92	18	1	16	160	53	43	26	2	139	3	5	4	0	1	.00	4	.224	.273	.389
1999 Norwich	AA NYY	119	396	88	18	0	22	172	57	72	45	0	142	5	4	3	0	0	—	4	.222	.307	.434
2000 Columbus	AAA NYY	15	48	12	1	0	4	25	6	9	2	0	19	0	0	0	0	0	—	1	.250	.280	.521
Norwich	AA NYY	84	256	51	12	0	8	87	23	36	40	2	74	2	6	1	1	1	.50	5	.199	.311	.340
6 Min. YEARS		544	1783	386	70	2	67	661	216	236	183	4	598	17	20	12	6	3	.67	25	.216	.294	.371

Eric Valent

Bats: Left **Throws:** Left **Pos:** OF-122; DH-3; PH-3   **Ht:** 6'0" **Wt:** 191 **Born:** 4/4/77 **Age:** 24

Year Team	Lg Org	G	AB	H	2B	3B	HR	TB	R	RBI	TBB	IBB	SO	HBP	SH	SF	SB	CS	SB%	GDP	Avg	OBP	SLG
1998 Piedmont	A Phi	22	89	38	12	0	8	74	24	28	14	2	19	0	0	1	0	0	—	0	.427	.500	.831
Clearwater	A+ Phi	34	125	33	8	1	5	58	24	25	16	0	29	3	0	1	1	2	.33	4	.264	.359	.464
1999 Clearwater	A+ Phi	134	520	150	31	9	20	259	91	106	58	5	110	5	1	10	5	3	.63	10	.288	.359	.498
2000 Reading	AA Phi	128	469	121	22	5	22	219	81	90	70	1	89	5	0	6	2	3	.40	7	.258	.356	.467
3 Min. YEARS		318	1203	342	73	15	55	610	220	249	158	8	247	13	1	18	8	8	.50	21	.284	.369	.507

Javier Valentin

Bats: Both **Throws:** Right **Pos:** C-24; DH-11; PH-5   **Ht:** 5'10" **Wt:** 192 **Born:** 9/19/75 **Age:** 25

Year Team	Lg Org	G	AB	H	2B	3B	HR	TB	R	RBI	TBB	IBB	SO	HBP	SH	SF	SB	CS	SB%	GDP	Avg	OBP	SLG
1993 Twins	R Min	32	103	27	6	1	1	38	18	19	14	0	19	1	0	4	0	2	.00	1	.262	.344	.369
Elizabethtn	R+ Min	9	24	5	1	0	0	6	3	3	4	0	2	1	0	0	0	0	—	0	.208	.345	.250
1994 Elizabethtn	R+ Min	54	210	44	5	0	9	76	23	27	15	0	44	2	0	5	0	1	.00	9	.210	.263	.362
1995 Fort Wayne	A Min	112	383	123	26	5	19	216	59	65	47	7	75	2	1	0	0	5	.00	7	.321	.398	.564
1996 Fort Myers	A+ Min	87	338	89	26	1	7	138	34	54	32	4	65	4	0	5	1	0	1.00	5	.263	.330	.408
Hardware Cy	AA Min	48	165	39	8	0	3	56	22	14	16	1	35	1	3	0	0	3	.00	2	.236	.308	.339
1997 New Britain	AA Min	102	370	90	17	0	8	131	41	50	30	1	61	1	2	6	2	3	.40	5	.243	.297	.354
2000 Salt Lake	AAA Min	39	140	50	16	2	7	91	25	35	9	0	27	1	0	1	1	0	1.00	1	.357	.397	.650
1997 Minnesota	AL	4	7	2	0	0	0	2	1	0	0	0	3	0	0	0	0	0	—	0	.286	.286	.286
1998 Minnesota	AL	55	162	32	7	1	3	50	11	18	11	1	30	0	3	1	0	0	—	7	.198	.247	.309
1999 Minnesota	AL	78	218	54	12	1	5	83	22	28	22	0	39	1	1	5	0	0	—	2	.248	.313	.381
6 Min. YEARS		483	1733	467	105	9	54	752	225	267	167	13	328	13	6	21	4	14	.22	30	.269	.335	.434
3 Maj. YEARS		137	387	88	19	2	8	135	34	46	33	1	72	1	4	6	0	0	—	9	.227	.286	.349

Claudio Vargas

Pitches: Right **Bats:** Right **Pos:** SP-25; RP-2   **Ht:** 6'3" **Wt:** 210 **Born:** 5/19/79 **Age:** 22

| | | HOW MUCH HE PITCHED | | | | | | WHAT HE GAVE UP | | | | | | | | | | | THE RESULTS | | | | |
Year Team	Lg Org	G	GS	CG	GF	IP	BFP	H	R	ER	HR	SH	SF	HB	TBB	IBB	SO	WP	Bk	W	L	Pct.	ShO	Sv	ERA
1998 Brevard Cty	A+ Fla	2	2	0	0	9.2	46	15	5	5	1	1	0	0	4	0	9	0	0	0	1	.000	0	0	4.66
Marlins	R Fla	5	4	0	0	28.2	117	24	15	13	1	0	1	3	7	0	27	2	0	0	4	.000	0	0	4.08
1999 Kane County	A Fla	19	19	1	0	99.2	426	97	47	43	8	2	3	0	41	0	88	2	2	5	5	.500	0	0	3.88
2000 Brevard Cty	A+ Fla	24	23	0	0	145.1	596	126	64	53	10	4	2	7	44	3	143	3	0	10	5	.667	0	0	3.28
Portland	AA Fla	3	2	0	0	15	68	16	9	6	1	1	2	1	6	0	13	0	0	1	1	.500	0	0	3.60
3 Min. YEARS		53	50	1	0	298.1	1253	278	140	120	21	8	8	11	102	3	280	7	2	16	16	.500	0	0	3.62

Martin Vargas

Pitches: Right **Bats:** Right **Pos:** RP-53   **Ht:** 6'0" **Wt:** 155 **Born:** 2/22/78 **Age:** 23

| | | HOW MUCH HE PITCHED | | | | | | WHAT HE GAVE UP | | | | | | | | | | | THE RESULTS | | | | |
Year Team	Lg Org	G	GS	CG	GF	IP	BFP	H	R	ER	HR	SH	SF	HB	TBB	IBB	SO	WP	Bk	W	L	Pct.	ShO	Sv	ERA
1998 Columbus	A Cle	7	7	0	0	29.2	153	42	36	33	7	0	2	3	24	0	25	7	0	1	4	.200	0	0	10.01
Burlington	R+ Cle	13	13	1	0	73.2	324	78	49	39	5	1	0	4	35	0	64	7	3	3	7	.300	0	0	4.76
1999 Columbus	A Cle	15	12	0	0	67.1	311	80	46	37	5	1	2	6	20	0	51	5	0	6	3	.667	0	0	4.95
Kinston	A+ Cle	20	0	0	6	42.1	179	31	16	13	3	5	3	3	20	1	44	2	0	6	1	.857	0	2	2.76
2000 Akron	AA Cle	53	0	0	26	81.1	374	96	52	49	4	6	3	6	30	3	58	10	0	10	8	.556	0	7	5.42
3 Min. YEARS		108	32	1	32	294.1	1341	327	199	171	24	13	10	22	129	4	242	31	3	26	23	.531	0	9	5.23

Geraldo Vasquez

Bats: Right **Throws:** Right **Pos:** 3B-24; SS-23; 2B-6; DH-5; PH-5; PR-4   **Ht:** 5'11" **Wt:** 145 **Born:** 11/5/79 **Age:** 21

Year Team	Lg Org	G	AB	H	2B	3B	HR	TB	R	RBI	TBB	IBB	SO	HBP	SH	SF	SB	CS	SB%	GDP	Avg	OBP	SLG
1998 Johnson Cty	R+ StL	31	62	9	2	3	0	17	11	5	12	0	21	0	0	1	5	1	.83	1	.145	.280	.274
1999 Johnson Cty	R+ StL	49	167	38	6	0	5	59	28	25	13	0	43	5	5	0	7	5	.58	4	.228	.303	.353
2000 Arkansas	AA StL	3	3	0	0	0	0	0	0	0	0	0	2	0	0	0	0	0	—	0	.000	.000	.000
New Jersey	A- StL	57	188	36	3	5	0	49	26	13	20	0	50	0	2	0	15	4	.79	4	.191	.269	.261
3 Min. YEARS		140	420	83	11	8	5	125	65	43	45	0	116	5	7	1	27	10	.73	9	.198	.282	.298

Leo Vasquez

Pitches: Left **Bats:** Left **Pos:** RP-35; SP-1   **Ht:** 6'4" **Wt:** 196 **Born:** 7/1/73 **Age:** 27

| | | HOW MUCH HE PITCHED | | | | | | WHAT HE GAVE UP | | | | | | | | | | | THE RESULTS | | | | |
Year Team	Lg Org	G	GS	CG	GF	IP	BFP	H	R	ER	HR	SH	SF	HB	TBB	IBB	SO	WP	Bk	W	L	Pct.	ShO	Sv	ERA
1996 Aberdeen	IND —	19	16	2	1	105.1	429	79	39	26	7	2	0	1	39	0	106	4	0	11	2	.846	2	0	2.22
1997 Binghamton	AA NYM	1	1	0	0	5.1	26	7	6	6	3	1	2	0	2	0	2	0	0	0	1	.000	0	0	10.13
Capital Cty	A NYM	22	8	0	8	56	250	63	37	32	4	1	2	3	22	1	49	7	1	4	5	.444	0	1	5.14
1998 Binghamton	AA NYM	14	2	0	2	29.1	140	28	16	15	1	2	1	2	25	0	28	3	0	1	1	.500	0	1	4.60
St. Lucie	A+ NYM	24	6	0	10	69	264	44	20	17	3	3	4	3	24	0	46	5	0	3	2	.600	0	4	2.22
1999 Binghamton	AA NYM	27	0	0	7	42.1	190	39	18	18	4	0	1	2	26	0	43	2	1	1	2	.333	0	1	3.83
Midland	AA Oak	13	0	0	5	23.1	103	18	11	8	2	1	1	2	13	1	24	1	1	3	1	.750	0	1	3.09
Vancouver	AAA Oak	1	0	0	0	1.2	8	2	1	1	0	0	0	0	0	0	0	0	0	0	0	—	0	0	5.40
2000 Midland	AA Oak	36	1	0	13	53	239	48	21	16	3	1	0	5	33	4	59	7	0	6	5	.545	0	4	2.72
5 Min. YEARS		157	34	2	46	385.1	1649	328	169	139	27	11	11	18	188	6	357	29	3	29	19	.604	2	12	3.25

Mike Vavrek

Pitches: Left Bats: Left Pos: RP-1   Ht: 6'2" Wt: 185 Born: 4/23/74 Age: 27

Year Team	Lg Org	G	GS	CG	GF	IP	BFP	H	R	ER	HR	SH	SF	HB	TBB	IBB	SO	WP	Bk	W	L	Pct.	ShO	Sv	ERA
1995 Portland	A- Col	3	3	0	0	14	52	8	0	0	0	0	0	0	3	0	14	0	0	0	0	—	0	0	0.00
Asheville	A Col	12	12	1	0	76.2	322	64	24	17	3	0	1	5	25	0	54	4	5	5	4	.556	0	0	2.00
1996 Salem	A+ Col	26	25	2	0	149.2	658	167	92	81	15	6	8	5	59	0	103	10	0	10	8	.556	1	0	4.87
1997 Salem	A+ Col	10	9	0	0	62.2	255	55	21	15	3	1	4	3	18	0	48	3	0	2	2	.500	0	0	2.15
New Haven	AA Col	17	17	2	0	122.2	491	94	38	35	7	8	4	1	34	0	101	4	0	12	3	.800	0	0	2.57
1998 Colo Sprngs	AAA Col	10	9	0	1	44.2	227	62	50	41	8	3	4	1	34	0	41	5	0	2	6	.250	0	0	8.26
New Haven	AA Col	19	19	0	0	114.2	530	142	83	70	24	3	4	4	49	0	70	11	0	5	12	.294	0	0	5.49
1999 Carolina	AA Col	10	9	0	0	46.1	230	71	42	38	11	3	1	0	19	0	41	8	0	1	5	.167	0	0	7.38
Salem	A+ Col	10	5	0	3	48.2	191	32	10	10	2	1	1	2	13	0	38	1	0	3	1	.750	0	0	1.85
2000 Carolina	AA Col	1	0	0	0	2.2	17	8	5	5	1	0	1	0	3	0	0	0	0	0	0	—	0	0	16.88
6 Min. YEARS		118	108	5	4	682.2	2973	703	365	312	74	25	28	21	257	0	510	46	5	40	41	.494	1	0	4.11

Roberto Vaz

Bats: Left Throws: Left Pos: OF-93; DH-18; PR-3; 1B-1; PH-1   Ht: 5'9" Wt: 195 Born: 3/15/75 Age: 26

Year Team	Lg Org	G	AB	H	2B	3B	HR	TB	R	RBI	TBB	IBB	SO	HBP	SH	SF	SB	CS	SB%	GDP	Avg	OBP	SLG
1997 Sou Oregon	A- Oak	22	78	25	6	0	3	40	11	15	7	1	4	1	0	1	5	3	.63	6	.321	.379	.513
Visalia	A+ Oak	19	73	26	5	0	3	40	9	13	8	0	10	0	2	0	2	5	.29	4	.356	.420	.548
1998 Huntsville	AA Oak	131	457	135	18	5	8	187	54	62	56	4	63	3	4	10	23	16	.59	14	.295	.369	.409
1999 Midland	AA Oak	10	32	13	3	0	1	19	4	12	8	0	5	0	1	2	0	1	.00	1	.406	.500	.594
Vancouver	AAA Oak	109	367	97	18	4	7	144	54	38	51	3	72	2	5	2	7	5	.58	8	.264	.355	.392
2000 Sacramento	AAA Oak	114	426	123	22	3	10	181	56	72	49	10	72	2	1	4	20	6	.77	9	.289	.362	.425
4 Min. YEARS		405	1433	419	72	12	32	611	188	212	179	18	226	8	13	19	57	36	.61	42	.292	.370	.426

Ramon Vazquez

Bats: Left Throws: Right Pos: SS-123; PR-1   Ht: 5'11" Wt: 170 Born: 8/21/76 Age: 24

Year Team	Lg Org	G	AB	H	2B	3B	HR	TB	R	RBI	TBB	IBB	SO	HBP	SH	SF	SB	CS	SB%	GDP	Avg	OBP	SLG
1995 Mariners	R Sea	39	141	29	3	1	0	34	20	11	19	0	27	2	0	1	4	3	.57	2	.206	.309	.241
1996 Everett	A- Sea	33	126	35	5	2	1	47	25	18	26	0	26	1	2	5	7	2	.78	3	.278	.392	.373
Tacoma	AAA Sea	18	49	11	2	1	0	15	7	4	4	0	12	1	0	0	0	0	—	0	.224	.296	.306
Wisconsin	A Sea	3	10	3	1	0	0	4	1	1	2	0	2	0	0	0	0	0	—	1	.300	.417	.400
1997 Wisconsin	A Sea	131	479	129	25	5	8	188	79	49	78	2	93	3	4	3	16	10	.62	8	.269	.373	.392
1998 Lancaster	A+ Sea	121	468	129	26	4	2	169	77	72	81	5	66	2	4	1	15	11	.58	6	.276	.384	.361
1999 New Haven	AA Sea	127	438	113	27	3	5	161	58	45	62	4	77	5	6	3	8	1	.89	11	.258	.354	.368
2000 New Haven	AA Sea	124	405	116	25	4	8	173	58	59	52	4	76	2	8	4	1	6	.14	6	.286	.367	.427
6 Min. YEARS		596	2116	565	114	20	24	791	325	259	324	15	379	16	24	16	51	33	.61	39	.267	.366	.374

Dario Veras

Pitches: Right Bats: Right Pos: RP-21   Ht: 6'1" Wt: 155 Born: 3/13/73 Age: 28

Year Team	Lg Org	G	GS	CG	GF	IP	BFP	H	R	ER	HR	SH	SF	HB	TBB	IBB	SO	WP	Bk	W	L	Pct.	ShO	Sv	ERA
1993 Bakersfield	A+ LA	7	0	0	1	13.1	61	13	11	11	1	0	0	1	8	2	11	0	0	1	0	1.000	0	0	7.43
Vero Beach	A+ LA	24	0	0	8	54.2	229	59	23	17	2	3	1	1	14	5	31	3	0	2	2	.500	0	2	2.80
1994 Rancho Cuca	A+ SD	59	0	0	13	79	332	66	28	18	7	7	0	6	25	9	56	2	0	9	2	.818	0	3	2.05
1995 Memphis	AA SD	58	0	0	22	82.2	360	81	38	35	8	3	1	7	27	11	70	5	1	7	3	.700	0	1	3.81
1996 Memphis	AA SD	29	0	0	8	42.2	172	38	14	11	4	1	2	1	9	2	47	2	1	3	1	.750	0	1	2.32
Las Vegas	AAA SD	19	1	0	9	40.1	165	41	17	13	1	3	1	0	6	2	30	2	0	2	2	.500	0	0	2.90
1997 Mobile	AA SD	5	2	0	2	5	25	8	5	5	1	0	0	0	3	0	5	0	0	0	0	—	0	0	9.00
Rancho Cuca	A+ SD	2	0	0	1	3	13	3	3	2	1	1	0	0	1	0	3	1	0	0	0	—	0	1	6.00
Las Vegas	AAA SD	12	0	0	5	14.1	59	14	8	8	1	0	0	0	6	0	13	3	0	0	2	.000	0	2	5.02
1998 Las Vegas	AAA SD	31	0	0	27	35.2	153	36	15	15	5	0	0	2	11	0	29	4	0	2	1	.667	0	9	3.79
Pawtucket	AAA Bos	23	0	0	21	29	124	30	12	12	4	1	1	0	11	3	27	0	0	0	7	.000	0	7	3.72
1999 Royals	R KC	3	2	0	0	4	15	3	0	0	0	0	0	0	0	0	3	0	0	0	0	—	0	0	0.00
Omaha	AAA KC	12	0	0	3	20.2	81	19	10	10	5	1	0	1	3	0	17	0	0	1	2	.333	0	0	4.35
2000 Kinston	A+ Cle	17	0	0	10	34.1	134	27	13	13	5	2	0	5	4	0	29	0	0	1	0	1.000	0	3	3.41
Akron	AA Cle	4	0	0	1	4.2	23	7	8	8	1	0	0	1	1	0	6	0	0	0	0	—	0	1	15.43
1996 San Diego	NL	23	0	0	6	29	117	24	10	9	3	1	1	1	10	4	23	1	0	3	1	.750	0	2	2.79
1997 San Diego	NL	23	0	0	7	24.2	114	28	14	14	6	1	0	2	12	3	21	0	0	2	1	.667	0	1	5.11
1998 Boston	AL	7	0	0	4	8	43	12	9	9	0	0	0	1	7	0	2	2	0	0	1	.000	0	0	10.13
8 Min. YEARS		305	5	0	131	463.1	1946	445	205	178	46	22	7	24	129	34	377	22	2	36	15	.706	0	31	3.46
3 Maj. YEARS		53	0	0	17	61.2	274	64	37	32	8	1	1	4	29	7	46	3	0	5	3	.625	0	0	4.67

Jason Verdugo

Pitches: Right Bats: Right Pos: RP-9; SP-7   Ht: 6'2" Wt: 195 Born: 3/28/75 Age: 26

Year Team	Lg Org	G	GS	CG	GF	IP	BFP	H	R	ER	HR	SH	SF	HB	TBB	IBB	SO	WP	Bk	W	L	Pct.	ShO	Sv	ERA
1997 Salem-Keizr	A- SF	16	14	0	0	78.1	347	85	48	42	7	5	1	6	25	1	82	1	1	4	4	.333	0	0	4.83
1998 Bakersfield	A+ SF	28	1	0	17	80.1	329	79	35	29	4	1	3	2	15	0	59	0	0	6	6	.500	0	3	3.25
San Jose	A+ SF	1	1	0	1	5	20	2	0	0	0	0	0	0	0	0	1	0	0	0	0	—	0	0	0.00
Shreveport	AA SF	9	1	0	2	19.1	81	17	9	8	4	1	1	0	6	2	27	0	0	1	2	.333	0	1	3.72
1999 Shreveport	AA SF	40	0	0	22	62.2	261	58	34	21	7	4	4	1	12	0	46	4	2	2	3	.400	0	8	3.02
Fresno	AAA SF	9	2	0	2	20.1	89	19	14	11	5	0	0	0	9	0	29	1	0	1	0	1.000	0	0	4.87
2000 Fresno	AAA SF	11	7	0	0	30.1	144	44	32	29	10	1	0	0	11	0	20	1	1	0	5	.000	0	0	8.60
Shreveport	AA SF	5	0	0	3	5.2	28	8	6	2	0	0	0	0	2	0	4	0	0	0	0	—	0	0	3.18
4 Min. YEARS		119	35	0	47	298	1284	312	178	142	37	12	10	9	80	3	268	7	4	14	25	.359	0	12	4.29

Jeff Verplancke

Pitches: Right **Bats:** Right **Pos:** SP-25; RP-2   **Ht:** 6'3" **Wt:** 200 **Born:** 11/18/77 **Age:** 23

Year Team	Lg Org	G	GS	CG	GF	IP	BFP	H	R	ER	HR	SH	SF	HB	TBB	IBB	SO	WP	Bk	W	L	Pct.	ShO	Sv	ERA
2000 San Jose	A+ SF	26	25	1	0	139.2	642	159	111	91	12	5	6	11	67	1	129	7	4	6	14	.300	0	0	5.86
Fresno	AAA SF	1	0	0	0	5	20	3	1	1	0	0	0	0	2	0	6	0	0	0	0	—	0	0	1.80
1 Min. YEARS		27	25	1	0	144.2	662	162	112	92	12	5	6	11	69	1	135	7	4	6	14	.300	0	0	5.72

Gilbert Vidal

Bats: Right **Throws:** Right **Pos:** C-44; DH-4; PH-4; OF-3   **Ht:** 5'11" **Wt:** 188 **Born:** 4/21/75 **Age:** 26

Year Team	Lg Org	G	AB	H	2B	3B	HR	TB	R	RBI	TBB	IBB	SO	HBP	SH	SF	SB	CS	SB%	GDP	Avg	OBP	SLG
1995 Rockies	R Col	39	136	39	11	1	1	55	19	20	23	0	20	1	0	3	3	3	.50	9	.287	.387	.404
1996 Portland	A- Col	32	106	24	8	1	1	37	16	11	18	2	20	0	0	2	0	1	.00	3	.226	.333	.349
1997 Salem	A+ Col	80	226	54	21	0	6	93	20	30	19	1	54	0	2	5	1	2	.33	4	.239	.292	.412
1998 Asheville	A Col	76	275	82	21	0	7	124	42	42	25	0	63	2	0	2	3	1	.75	9	.298	.359	.451
1999 Salem	A+ Col	13	46	9	3	0	1	15	6	6	7	1	12	1	1	0	1	0	1.00	4	.196	.315	.326
Carolina	AA Col	45	129	31	8	0	2	45	10	12	8	0	30	1	3	1	0	0	—	0	.240	.288	.349
2000 Carolina	AA Col	9	14	1	0	0	0	1	1	0	2	0	5	0	0	0	0	0	—	0	.071	.188	.071
Rio Grande	IND —	46	163	38	11	0	4	61	25	25	18	0	27	0	2	0	2	1	.67	2	.233	.309	.374
6 Min. YEARS		340	1095	278	83	2	22	431	139	146	120	4	231	5	8	13	10	8	.56	33	.254	.327	.394

Scott Vieira

Bats: Right **Throws:** Right **Pos:** 1B-47; OF-31; DH-14; PH-10   **Ht:** 5'11" **Wt:** 185 **Born:** 8/17/73 **Age:** 27

Year Team	Lg Org	G	AB	H	2B	3B	HR	TB	R	RBI	TBB	IBB	SO	HBP	SH	SF	SB	CS	SB%	GDP	Avg	OBP	SLG
1995 Williamsprt	A- ChC	61	214	68	8	2	6	98	35	46	25	1	37	9	0	4	3	1	.75	3	.318	.405	.458
1996 Rockford	A ChC	134	442	143	30	4	6	205	81	81	84	7	89	26	2	9	9	8	.53	6	.324	.451	.464
1997 Daytona	A+ ChC	134	476	131	27	3	18	218	84	80	70	1	125	17	1	7	9	7	.56	5	.275	.382	.458
1998 Cubs	R ChC	4	12	6	1	0	1	10	2	4	2	0	0	0	0	0	0	0	—	0	.500	.571	.833
Daytona	A+ ChC	15	54	20	6	0	1	29	11	13	9	0	12	3	0	1	3	0	1.00	1	.370	.478	.537
1999 West Tenn	AA ChC	126	455	133	44	4	10	215	63	58	53	4	126	12	0	3	10	6	.63	4	.292	.379	.473
2000 Iowa	AAA ChC	2	3	0	0	0	0	0	0	0	0	0	2	0	0	0	0	0	—	1	.000	.000	.000
West Tenn	AA ChC	97	322	71	16	2	7	112	44	34	44	1	112	8	0	3	1	3	.25	8	.220	.326	.348
6 Min. YEARS		573	1978	572	132	15	51	887	320	316	287	14	503	75	3	27	35	25	.58	28	.289	.395	.448

Carlos Villalobos

Bats: Right **Throws:** Right **Pos:** OF-15; DH-14; 3B-13; PH-2; 2B-1; PR-1   **Ht:** 6'0" **Wt:** 170 **Born:** 4/5/74 **Age:** 27

Year Team	Lg Org	G	AB	H	2B	3B	HR	TB	R	RBI	TBB	IBB	SO	HBP	SH	SF	SB	CS	SB%	GDP	Avg	OBP	SLG
1994 Mariners	R Sea	51	175	51	6	2	4	73	17	29	11	1	34	2	2	2	6	0	1.00	8	.291	.337	.417
1995 Wisconsin	A Sea	110	389	101	16	4	9	152	64	53	35	1	76	3	4	5	16	4	.80	3	.260	.322	.391
1996 Lancaster	A+ Sea	111	415	121	21	5	5	167	69	63	50	0	89	4	2	3	9	4	.69	9	.292	.371	.402
1997 Lancaster	A+ Sea	86	296	101	22	2	11	160	71	53	60	0	42	7	2	0	4	6	.40	7	.341	.463	.541
Lakeland	A+ Det	39	147	37	5	0	1	45	19	15	11	0	25	2	1	0	0	1	.00	3	.252	.313	.306
1998 Jacksnville	AA Det	128	497	159	34	2	18	251	96	80	55	2	85	3	0	6	8	0	1.00	16	.320	.387	.505
1999 New Orleans	AAA Hou	133	499	141	33	1	9	203	82	50	54	0	100	2	5	4	11	3	.79	11	.283	.352	.407
2000 Tigers	R Det	2	7	3	0	0	0	3	1	0	0	0	1	0	0	0	0	0	—	0	.429	.429	.429
Lakeland	A+ Det	25	85	20	4	0	1	27	10	7	11	1	15	0	0	1	0	0	—	3	.235	.320	.318
Toledo	AAA Det	18	48	6	0	1	0	8	2	4	9	0	12	0	0	2	0	0	—	1	.125	.263	.167
7 Min. YEARS		703	2558	740	141	17	58	1089	431	354	296	5	479	23	18	21	54	18	.75	62	.289	.365	.426

Mike Villano

Pitches: Right **Bats:** Right **Pos:** RP-44; SP-1   **Ht:** 6'0" **Wt:** 200 **Born:** 8/10/71 **Age:** 29

Year Team	Lg Org	G	GS	CG	GF	IP	BFP	H	R	ER	HR	SH	SF	HB	TBB	IBB	SO	WP	Bk	W	L	Pct.	ShO	Sv	ERA
1995 Burlington	A SF	16	0	0	7	25.1	120	20	12	8	1	2	1	4	21	0	29	5	0	3	1	.750	0	1	2.84
San Jose	A+ SF	21	0	0	16	32.2	137	27	7	6	2	0	1	0	11	0	42	3	0	0	1	.000	0	1	1.65
1996 San Jose	A+ SF	39	2	0	21	88	341	48	12	7	2	1	1	0	33	4	133	7	1	7	1	.875	0	8	0.72
Shreveport	AA SF	2	0	0	0	12	47	6	4	4	0	0	0	0	8	0	7	0	0	2	0	1.000	0	0	3.00
1997 Shreveport	AA SF	30	0	0	15	34.1	158	41	25	24	5	2	0	2	20	2	26	4	1	3	1	.750	0	2	6.29
Phoenix	AAA SF	13	11	0	1	71.1	309	75	36	33	7	3	2	2	27	1	41	2	0	5	3	.625	0	0	4.16
1998 Charlotte	AAA Fla	13	10	0	1	59.2	277	82	55	51	14	1	4	3	18	0	47	3	2	3	5	.375	0	0	7.69
1999 Calgary	AAA Fla	36	1	0	11	58	273	87	43	40	18	1	0	5	17	0	48	7	1	1	5	.167	0	2	6.21
Norfolk	AAA NYM	2	0	0	2	2	10	3	1	1	0	0	0	0	2	0	1	0	0	0	0	—	0	0	4.50
2000 Nashville	AAA Pit	45	1	0	11	75.2	338	77	64	54	13	3	2	3	43	3	56	6	2	5	3	.625	0	16	6.42
6 Min. YEARS		217	27	0	85	459	2010	466	259	228	62	13	11	20	200	10	430	37	7	29	20	.592	0	16	4.47

Oscar Villarreal

Pitches: Right **Bats:** Left **Pos:** RP-16; SP-9   **Ht:** 6'0" **Wt:** 177 **Born:** 11/22/81 **Age:** 19

Year Team	Lg Org	G	GS	CG	GF	IP	BFP	H	R	ER	HR	SH	SF	HB	TBB	IBB	SO	WP	Bk	W	L	Pct.	ShO	Sv	ERA
1999 Diamondbcks	R Ari	14	11	0	1	64.1	286	64	39	27	1	2	3	10	25	0	51	6	4	1	5	.167	0	0	3.78
2000 Tucson	AAA Ari	2	0	0	0	4.1	19	6	1	1	0	0	0	0	2	0	4	0	0	1	0	1.000	0	0	2.08
South Bend	A Ari	13	5	0	5	32.2	155	37	19	16	0	0	0	3	17	3	30	2	1	1	3	.250	0	0	4.41
Diamondbcks	R Ari	1	0	0	0	1	5	2	1	1	0	0	0	0	0	0	1	0	0	0	0	—	0	0	9.00
High Desert	A+ Ari	9	4	0	0	24.2	117	24	20	10	4	4	1	3	14	0	18	2	0	0	2	.000	0	0	3.65
2 Min. YEARS		39	20	0	6	127	582	133	80	55	5	6	4	16	58	3	104	10	5	3	10	.231	0	0	3.90

Miguel Villilo

Bats: Both **Throws:** Right **Pos:** 3B-38; DH-10; PH-2; PR-1 **Ht:** 6'1" **Wt:** 180 **Born:** 10/10/81 **Age:** 19

					BATTING											BASERUNNING				PERCENTAGES		
Year Team	Lg Org	G	AB	H	2B	3B	HR	TB	R	RBI	TBB	IBB	SO	HBP	SH	SF	SB	CS	SB%	GDP	Avg	OBP	SLG
2000 Mariners	R Sea	44	167	58	14	3	3	87	30	37	23	1	37	1	0	1	2	0	1.00	2	.347	.427	.521
Tacoma	AAA Sea	4	16	2	1	0	1	6	2	1	0	0	3	0	0	0	0	0	—	1	.125	.125	.375
1 Min. YEARS		48	183	60	15	3	4	93	32	38	23	1	40	1	0	1	2	0	1.00	3	.328	.404	.508

Julio Vinas

Bats: Right **Throws:** Right **Pos:** OF-24; DH-17; 1B-7; PH-2 **Ht:** 6'1" **Wt:** 205 **Born:** 2/14/73 **Age:** 28

					BATTING											BASERUNNING				PERCENTAGES		
Year Team	Lg Org	G	AB	H	2B	3B	HR	TB	R	RBI	TBB	IBB	SO	HBP	SH	SF	SB	CS	SB%	GDP	Avg	OBP	SLG
1991 White Sox	R CWS	50	187	42	9	0	3	60	21	29	19	0	40	2	0	2	2	3	.40	5	.225	.300	.321
1992 South Bend	A CWS	33	94	16	3	0	0	19	7	10	9	0	17	1	0	2	1	3	.25	1	.170	.245	.202
Utica	A- CWS	47	151	37	6	4	0	51	22	24	11	0	29	2	1	5	1	2	.33	2	.245	.296	.338
1993 South Bend	A CWS	55	188	60	15	1	9	104	24	37	12	1	29	1	2	2	1	1	.50	2	.319	.360	.553
Sarasota	A+ CWS	18	65	16	2	1	1	23	5	7	5	0	13	0	0	0	0	0	—	2	.246	.300	.354
1994 South Bend	A CWS	121	466	118	31	1	9	178	68	75	43	4	75	4	6	6	0	2	.00	9	.253	.318	.382
1995 Birmingham	AA CWS	102	372	100	16	2	6	138	47	61	37	1	80	5	0	7	3	3	.50	5	.269	.337	.371
1996 Nashville	AAA CWS	104	338	80	18	2	11	135	48	52	36	2	63	2	0	4	1	4	.20	8	.237	.311	.399
1997 Nashville	AAA CWS	91	314	73	12	2	11	122	39	41	25	2	72	2	3	5	4	4	.50	6	.232	.289	.389
1998 Rochester	AAA Bal	62	199	70	15	4	6	111	26	40	12	0	30	1	1	2	2	1	.67	3	.352	.388	.558
1999 Rochester	AAA Bal	126	484	151	32	2	20	247	67	83	25	1	73	1	0	7	4	3	.57	13	.312	.342	.510
2000 Akron	AA Cle	20	63	16	3	1	1	24	12	8	11	0	10	3	0	1	0	0	—	2	.254	.385	.381
Pawtucket	AAA Bos	29	107	27	5	0	4	44	14	16	9	1	20	1	0	0	1	0	1.00	1	.252	.316	.411
10 Min. YEARS		858	3028	806	167	20	81	1256	400	483	254	12	551	25	13	43	20	26	.43	61	.266	.324	.415

Ken Vining

Pitches: Left **Bats:** Left **Pos:** RP-43 **Ht:** 6'0" **Wt:** 180 **Born:** 12/5/74 **Age:** 26

		HOW MUCH HE PITCHED						WHAT HE GAVE UP										THE RESULTS					
Year Team	Lg Org	G	GS	CG	GF	IP	BFP	H	R	ER	HR	SH	SF	HB	TBB	IBB	SO	WP	Bk	W	L	Pct.	ShO	Sv	ERA
1996 Bellingham	A- SF	12	11	0	0	60.1	238	45	16	14	4	1	0	1	23	0	69	5	0	4	2	.667	0	0	2.09
1997 San Jose	A+ SF	23	23	1	0	136.2	592	140	77	64	9	1	6	5	60	0	142	3	1	9	6	.600	1	0	4.21
Winston-Sal	A+ CWS	5	5	0	0	34.2	153	36	17	11	2	3	0	0	11	0	38	2	0	2	2	.500	0	0	2.86
1998 Birmingham	AA CWS	29	28	1	0	172.2	793	187	103	78	8	5	5	4	91	1	133	16	0	10	12	.455	0	0	4.07
1999 Birmingham	AA CWS	3	3	0	0	11.2	62	20	16	12	1	0	1	1	9	0	8	0	1	0	2	.000	0	0	9.26
2000 Birmingham	AA CWS	43	0	0	13	46.1	188	36	26	21	2	1	1	3	18	4	41	4	0	1	5	.167	0	1	4.08
5 Min. YEARS		115	70	2	13	462.1	2026	464	255	200	26	11	13	14	212	5	431	30	2	26	29	.473	1	1	3.89

Jack Voigt

Bats: Right **Throws:** Right **Pos:** 1B-35; OF-19; DH-4; PH-3 **Ht:** 6'1" **Wt:** 178 **Born:** 5/17/66 **Age:** 35

					BATTING											BASERUNNING				PERCENTAGES		
Year Team	Lg Org	G	AB	H	2B	3B	HR	TB	R	RBI	TBB	IBB	SO	HBP	SH	SF	SB	CS	SB%	GDP	Avg	OBP	SLG
1987 Newark	A- Bal	63	219	70	10	1	11	115	41	52	33	0	45	0	1	1	1	3	.25	3	.320	.407	.525
Hagerstown	A+ Bal	2	9	1	0	0	0	1	0	1	1	0	4	0	0	0	0	0	—	0	.111	.200	.111
1988 Hagerstown	A+ Bal	115	367	83	18	2	12	141	62	42	66	2	92	6	3	2	5	2	.71	7	.226	.351	.384
1989 Frederick	A+ Bal	127	406	107	26	5	10	173	61	77	62	4	106	4	2	5	17	2	.89	5	.264	.363	.426
1990 Hagerstown	AA Bal	126	418	106	26	2	12	172	55	70	59	1	97	5	6	11	5	3	.63	7	.254	.345	.411
1991 Hagerstown	AA Bal	29	90	22	3	0	0	25	15	6	15	1	19	2	1	0	6	0	1.00	1	.244	.364	.278
Rochester	AAA Bal	83	267	72	11	4	6	109	46	35	40	2	53	1	5	2	9	1	.90	8	.270	.365	.408
1992 Rochester	AAA Bal	129	443	126	23	4	16	205	74	64	58	3	102	4	3	0	9	2	.82	10	.284	.372	.463
1993 Rochester	AAA Bal	18	61	22	6	1	3	39	16	11	9	0	14	0	0	0	1	0	1.00	1	.361	.443	.639
1994 Bowie	AA Bal	41	154	48	9	1	6	77	26	35	26	1	26	2	0	2	5	5	.50	2	.312	.413	.500
1995 Tulsa	AA Tex	4	16	3	0	0	1	6	1	3	2	0	5	0	0	0	1	0	1.00	0	.188	.278	.375
1996 Charlotte	A+ Tex	7	27	11	3	0	1	17	7	8	3	0	3	1	0	0	0	0	—	0	.407	.484	.630
Okla City	AAA Tex	127	445	132	26	1	21	223	77	80	76	4	103	1	2	6	5	5	.50	11	.297	.396	.501
1997 Tucson	AAA Mil	66	235	64	20	0	5	99	36	40	43	1	57	1	0	2	4	3	.57	4	.272	.384	.421
1998 Edmonton	AAA Oak	18	68	22	6	0	4	40	10	11	8	0	15	0	0	1	1	2	.33	0	.324	.395	.588
Oklahoma	AAA Tex	20	70	24	6	0	2	36	10	11	14	0	19	1	0	1	0	1	.00	1	.343	.453	.514
1999 Fresno	AAA SF	23	67	13	4	1	1	22	12	5	17	0	21	1	0	1	1	0	1.00	1	.194	.360	.328
Schaumburg	IND —	42	138	42	10	1	7	75	33	27	42	0	27	5	0	0	0	3	.00	5	.304	.481	.543
2000 Schaumburg	IND —	45	165	47	12	0	1	62	29	17	31	1	27	3	0	2	5	1	.83	4	.285	.403	.376
Oklahoma	AAA Tex	13	34	6	0	0	0	6	9	4	5	0	8	0	0	0	0	2	—	2	.176	.268	.176
1992 Baltimore	AL	1	0	0	0	0	0	0	0	0	0	0	0	0	0	0	0	0	—	0	—	—	—
1993 Baltimore	AL	64	152	45	11	1	6	76	32	23	25	0	33	0	0	1	1	0	1.00	3	.296	.395	.500
1994 Baltimore	AL	59	141	34	5	0	3	48	15	20	18	1	25	1	1	2	0	0	—	0	.241	.327	.340
1995 Baltimore	AL	3	1	1	0	0	0	1	1	0	0	0	0	0	0	0	0	0	—	0	1.000	1.000	1.000
Texas	AL	33	62	10	3	0	2	19	8	8	10	0	14	0	0	2	0	0	—	2	.161	.274	.306
1996 Texas	AL	5	9	1	0	0	0	1	1	0	0	0	2	0	0	0	0	0	—	0	.111	.111	.111
1997 Milwaukee	AL	72	151	37	9	2	8	74	20	22	19	2	36	1	2	1	1	2	.33	5	.245	.331	.490
1998 Oakland	AL	57	72	10	4	0	1	17	7	10	6	0	19	0	1	0	5	1	.83	3	.139	.205	.236
14 Min. YEARS		1098	3699	1021	219	23	119	1643	620	599	610	20	843	37	23	37	74	34	.69	74	.276	.381	.444
7 Maj. YEARS		294	588	138	32	3	20	236	84	83	78	3	129	2	4	4	7	3	.70	11	.235	.324	.401

Terrell Wade

Pitches: Left **Bats:** Left **Pos:** RP-27; SP-3 **Ht:** 6'3" **Wt:** 250 **Born:** 1/25/73 **Age:** 28

		HOW MUCH HE PITCHED						WHAT HE GAVE UP										THE RESULTS					
Year Team	Lg Org	G	GS	CG	GF	IP	BFP	H	R	ER	HR	SH	SF	HB	TBB	IBB	SO	WP	Bk	W	L	Pct.	ShO	Sv	ERA
1991 Braves	R Atl	10	2	0	0	23	112	29	17	16	0	1	2	0	15	0	22	3	2	2	0	1.000	0	0	6.26
1992 Idaho Falls	R+ Atl	13	11	0	0	50.1	257	59	46	36	5	4	5	2	42	0	54	5	0	1	4	.200	0	0	6.44

294

Year Team	Lg Org	G	GS	CG	GF	IP	BFP	H	R	ER	HR	SH	SF	HB	TBB	IBB	SO	WP	Bk	W	L	Pct.	ShO	Sv	ERA
						HOW MUCH HE PITCHED					**WHAT HE GAVE UP**												**THE RESULTS**			
1993 Macon	A Atl	14	14	0	0	83.1	336	57	16	16	1	0	1	1	36	0	121	11	0	8	2	.800	0	0	1.73
Durham	A+ Atl	5	5	0	0	33	137	26	13	12	3	0	1	0	18	0	47	0	1	2	1	.667	0	0	3.27
Greenville	AA Atl	8	8	1	0	42	179	32	16	15	6	1	0	1	29	0	40	2	0	2	1	.667	1	0	3.21
1994 Greenville	AA Atl	21	21	0	0	105.2	444	87	49	45	7	3	2	0	58	0	105	8	0	9	3	.750	0	0	3.83
Richmond	AAA Atl	4	4	0	0	24	103	23	9	7	1	0	1	0	15	0	26	1	0	2	2	.500	0	0	2.63
1995 Richmond	AAA Atl	24	23	1	0	142	600	137	76	72	10	3	5	1	63	1	124	5	1	10	9	.526	0	0	4.56
1997 Greenville	AA Atl	8	6	0	0	12.2	60	15	10	7	3	0	0	0	8	0	14	1	0	0	2	.000	0	0	4.97
1998 St. Pete	A+ TB	3	3	0	0	15	66	12	8	6	2	0	1	1	7	0	16	1	0	0	1	.000	0	0	3.60
Durham	AAA TB	4	4	0	0	19.2	92	21	12	10	1	0	0	1	12	1	14	0	0	1	1	.500	0	0	4.58
1999 Durham	AAA TB	34	19	0	4	98.2	501	140	112	104	21	1	8	2	80	0	61	5	0	1	7	.125	0	0	9.49
2000 Louisville	AAA Cin	2	2	0	0	6.2	39	11	9	9	0	0	0	1	8	0	7	1	0	0	2	.000	0	0	12.15
Chattanooga	AA Cin	28	1	0	10	39.2	172	34	23	18	3	2	4	1	23	1	42	2	0	0	5	.000	0	0	4.08
1995 Atlanta	NL	3	0	0	0	4	18	3	2	2	1	0	0	0	4	0	3	1	0	0	1	.000	0	0	4.50
1996 Atlanta	NL	44	8	0	13	69.2	305	67	23	23	9	5	1	1	47	6	79	2	0	5	0	1.000	0	1	2.97
1997 Atlanta	NL	12	9	0	1	42	197	60	31	25	6	2	5	2	16	1	35	1	0	2	3	.400	0	0	5.36
1998 Tampa Bay	AL	2	2	0	0	10.2	46	14	6	6	3	0	0	0	2	0	8	1	0	1	1	.500	0	0	5.06
9 Min. YEARS		178	123	2	14	695.2	3098	683	416	373	63	15	29	12	414	3	693	45	4	38	40	.487	1	0	4.83
4 Maj. YEARS		61	19	0	14	126.1	566	134	67	56	19	7	6	3	69	7	125	5	0	8	5	.615	0	1	3.99

Travis Wade

Pitches: Right **Bats:** Right **Pos:** RP-61　　**Ht:** 6'3" **Wt:** 220 **Born:** 7/8/75 **Age:** 25

Year Team	Lg Org	G	GS	CG	GF	IP	BFP	H	R	ER	HR	SH	SF	HB	TBB	IBB	SO	WP	Bk	W	L	Pct.	ShO	Sv	ERA
						HOW MUCH HE PITCHED					**WHAT HE GAVE UP**												**THE RESULTS**			
1997 Kalamazoo	IND —	2	1	0	0	2.1	20	7	10	8	2	0	0	2	4	0	0	0	0	0	2	.000	0	0	30.86
1998 Rio Grande	IND —	20	0	0	10	21.2	116	33	27	27	3	0	2	4	18	1	16	4	1	1	3	.250	0	4	11.22
Lubbock	IND —	11	0	0	11	15	69	18	11	11	1	0	2	1	7	0	10	3	1	0	0	—	0	3	6.60
1999 Kissimmee	A+ Hou	1	0	0	1	1	4	1	0	0	0	0	0	0	0	0	2	0	0	0	0	—	0	0	0.00
Auburn	A- Hou	26	0	0	23	37.2	150	25	10	10	0	3	0	2	13	0	53	0	1	1	1	.500	0	11	2.39
Michigan	A Hou	10	0	0	5	14	78	22	18	15	2	0	0	2	11	1	9	1	0	0	0	—	0	2	9.64
2000 Kissimmee	A+ Hou	38	0	0	33	48.2	187	36	9	4	2	1	0	1	10	2	51	1	1	4	1	.800	0	18	0.74
Round Rock	AA Hou	23	0	0	17	31.2	135	33	18	15	2	0	3	5	7	0	26	1	0	2	1	.667	0	6	4.26
4 Min. YEARS		131	1	0	100	172	759	175	103	90	12	4	7	17	70	4	167	10	3	8	8	.500	0	44	4.71

Denny Wagner

Pitches: Right **Bats:** Right **Pos:** SP-29　　**Ht:** 6'0" **Wt:** 205 **Born:** 11/8/76 **Age:** 24

Year Team	Lg Org	G	GS	CG	GF	IP	BFP	H	R	ER	HR	SH	SF	HB	TBB	IBB	SO	WP	Bk	W	L	Pct.	ShO	Sv	ERA
						HOW MUCH HE PITCHED					**WHAT HE GAVE UP**												**THE RESULTS**			
1997 Sou Oregon	A- Oak	10	4	0	1	14	86	29	27	24	3	0	0	1	14	0	11	8	1	1	1	.500	0	0	15.43
1998 Athletics	R Oak	3	1	0	0	7	28	4	4	3	0	0	1	1	3	0	11	1	0	2	1	.667	0	0	3.86
Sou Oregon	A- Oak	2	2	0	0	4	26	11	9	8	0	0	0	0	3	0	5	1	0	0	1	.000	0	0	18.00
1999 Modesto	A+ Oak	27	15	0	5	113.2	502	116	57	45	7	0	3	10	42	2	99	7	3	7	4	.636	0	3	3.56
Midland	AA Oak	5	5	0	0	27.2	127	28	22	13	1	0	2	2	14	1	12	3	0	1	2	.333	0	0	4.23
2000 Midland	AA Oak	29	29	1	0	180	793	209	106	91	13	4	4	10	63	2	109	11	0	7	9	.438	0	0	4.55
4 Min. YEARS		76	56	1	6	346.1	1562	397	225	184	24	4	10	24	139	5	247	31	4	18	18	.500	0	3	4.78

Chris Wakeland

Bats: Left **Throws:** Left **Pos:** OF-130; DH-8; PR-3　　**Ht:** 6'0" **Wt:** 185 **Born:** 6/15/74 **Age:** 27

Year Team	Lg Org	G	AB	H	2B	3B	HR	TB	R	RBI	TBB	IBB	SO	HBP	SH	SF	SB	CS	SB%	GDP	Avg	OBP	SLG
						BATTING												**BASERUNNING**			**PERCENTAGES**		
1996 Jamestown	A- Det	70	220	68	14	5	10	122	38	49	43	0	83	4	1	3	8	3	.73	1	.309	.426	.555
1997 W Michigan	A Det	111	414	118	38	2	7	181	64	75	43	5	120	4	0	7	20	6	.77	3	.285	.353	.437
1998 Lakeland	A+ Det	131	487	147	26	5	18	237	82	89	66	4	111	5	4	5	19	13	.59	4	.302	.387	.487
1999 Tigers	R Det	4	14	1	0	0	0	1	2	1	0	0	4	0	0	0	0	0	—	0	.071	.071	.071
Lakeland	A+ Det	4	17	7	1	0	0	8	3	7	0	0	0	0	0	0	1	0	1.00	0	.412	.412	.471
Jacksnville	AA Det	55	212	68	16	3	13	129	42	36	35	1	53	4	0	2	6	5	.55	2	.321	.423	.608
2000 Toledo	AAA Det	141	492	133	25	2	28	246	65	76	60	6	148	4	0	5	4	5	.44	8	.270	.351	.500
5 Min. YEARS		516	1856	542	120	17	76	924	296	333	247	16	519	21	5	22	58	32	.64	18	.292	.377	.498

Jamie Walker

Pitches: Left **Bats:** Left **Pos:** SP-15; RP-9　　**Ht:** 6'2" **Wt:** 190 **Born:** 7/1/71 **Age:** 29

Year Team	Lg Org	G	GS	CG	GF	IP	BFP	H	R	ER	HR	SH	SF	HB	TBB	IBB	SO	WP	Bk	W	L	Pct.	ShO	Sv	ERA
						HOW MUCH HE PITCHED					**WHAT HE GAVE UP**												**THE RESULTS**			
1992 Auburn	A- Hou	15	14	0	0	83.1	341	75	35	29	4	4	1	6	21	0	67	4	1	4	6	.400	0	0	3.13
1993 Quad City	A Hou	25	24	1	1	131.2	585	140	92	75	12	10	5	6	48	1	121	12	0	3	11	.214	1	0	5.13
1994 Quad City	A Hou	32	18	0	4	125	569	133	80	58	10	14	3	16	42	2	104	5	1	8	10	.444	0	1	4.18
1995 Jackson	AA Hou	50	0	0	19	58	250	59	29	29	6	3	2	2	24	5	38	4	1	4	2	.667	0	2	4.50
1996 Jackson	AA Hou	45	7	0	13	101	424	94	34	28	7	3	1	8	35	2	79	2	0	5	1	.833	0	2	2.50
1997 Wichita	AA KC	5	0	0	0	6.2	32	6	8	7	1	1	1	2	5	0	6	0	0	0	0	—	0	0	9.45
1998 Omaha	AAA KC	7	7	0	0	46.2	198	57	15	14	3	2	1	2	11	1	21	1	0	5	1	.833	0	0	2.70
1999 Royals	R KC	2	2	0	0	8	35	10	3	3	1	0	0	0	0	0	9	1	0	1	0	1.000	0	0	3.38
Omaha	AAA KC	4	4	0	0	17.1	79	22	12	9	1	1	2	2	4	0	11	0	0	1	0	.000	0	0	4.67
2000 Omaha	AAA KC	24	15	0	3	101.2	446	138	65	59	25	2	1	7	25	1	52	0	0	3	10	.231	0	0	5.22
1997 Kansas City	AL	50	0	0	15	43	197	46	28	26	6	2	3	3	20	3	24	2	0	3	3	.500	0	0	5.44
1998 Kansas City	AL	6	2	0	0	17.1	86	30	20	19	5	1	1	2	3	0	15	0	0	1	1	.000	0	0	9.87
9 Min. YEARS		209	91	1	40	679.1	2959	734	373	311	70	40	17	51	215	12	508	29	3	33	43	.434	1	5	4.12
2 Maj. YEARS		56	2	0	17	60.1	283	76	48	45	11	3	3	5	23	3	39	2	0	4	4	.429	0	0	6.71

Ron Walker

Bats: Right **Throws:** Right **Pos:** 1B-48; PH-22; DH-15; 3B-14   **Ht:** 6'2" **Wt:** 215 **Born:** 12/29/75 **Age:** 25

Year Team	Lg Org	G	AB	H	2B	3B	HR	TB	R	RBI	TBB	IBB	SO	HBP	SH	SF	SB	CS	SB%	GDP	Avg	OBP	SLG
1997 Williamsprt	A- ChC	54	189	66	10	1	9	105	30	39	17	7	48	5	0	2	0	1	.00	6	.349	.413	.556
Rockford	A ChC	4	15	5	0	0	1	8	1	5	3	0	2	0	0	0	0	0	—	0	.333	.444	.533
1998 Daytona	A+ ChC	100	357	102	20	1	24	196	57	78	46	1	80	7	0	0	5	2	.71	11	.286	.378	.549
1999 West Tenn	AA ChC	105	302	66	20	1	9	115	42	42	39	2	86	7	0	5	2	0	1.00	6	.219	.317	.381
2000 West Tenn	AA ChC	68	173	40	4	0	3	53	14	13	22	0	52	2	0	1	0	0	—	5	.231	.323	.306
Daytona	A+ ChC	30	111	32	7	0	4	51	19	23	16	1	17	1	0	1	0	4	.00	1	.288	.380	.459
4 Min. YEARS		361	1147	311	61	3	50	528	163	200	143	11	285	22	0	9	7	7	.50	29	.271	.360	.460

Tyler Walker

Pitches: Right **Bats:** Right **Pos:** SP-27   **Ht:** 6'3" **Wt:** 225 **Born:** 5/15/76 **Age:** 25

Year Team	Lg Org	G	GS	CG	GF	IP	BFP	H	R	ER	HR	SH	SF	HB	TBB	IBB	SO	WP	Bk	W	L	Pct.	ShO	Sv	ERA
1997 Mets	R NYM	5	0	0	5	9	37	8	1	0	1	0	0	0	2	1	9	0	0	0	0	—	0	3	1.00
Pittsfield	A- NYM	1	0	0	0	0.2	6	2	2	1	1	0	0	0	1	0	1	1	0	0	0	—	0	0	13.50
1998 Capital Cty	A NYM	34	13	0	3	115.2	503	122	63	53	9	3	4	3	38	0	110	8	1	5	5	.500	0	1	4.12
1999 St. Lucie	A+ NYM	13	13	2	0	79.2	329	64	31	26	6	3	2	3	29	2	64	4	1	6	5	.545	0	0	2.94
Binghamton	AA NYM	13	13	0	0	68	306	78	49	47	11	3	2	2	32	0	59	4	3	6	4	.600	0	0	6.22
2000 Binghamton	AA NYM	22	22	0	0	121	495	82	43	37	3	2	4	2	55	1	111	9	1	7	6	.538	0	0	2.75
Norfolk	AAA NYM	5	5	0	0	26.1	111	29	7	7	0	2	0	0	9	0	17	1	0	1	3	.250	0	0	2.39
4 Min. YEARS		93	66	2	8	420.1	1787	385	196	172	30	14	12	10	166	4	371	27	6	25	23	.521	0	4	3.68

Dave Walling

Pitches: Right **Bats:** Right **Pos:** SP-23   **Ht:** 6'6" **Wt:** 200 **Born:** 11/12/78 **Age:** 22

Year Team	Lg Org	G	GS	CG	GF	IP	BFP	H	R	ER	HR	SH	SF	HB	TBB	IBB	SO	WP	Bk	W	L	Pct.	ShO	Sv	ERA
1999 Staten Ilnd	A- NYY	14	14	0	0	80.1	331	76	31	28	3	1	2	2	18	1	82	1	3	8	2	.800	0	0	3.14
2000 Tampa	A+ NYY	9	9	0	0	58.2	237	48	17	13	1	1	2	4	12	0	45	2	0	7	2	.778	0	0	1.99
Norwich	AA NYY	14	14	2	0	85.1	378	101	54	50	10	3	3	6	26	0	70	2	5	3	9	.250	0	0	5.27
2 Min. YEARS		37	37	4	0	224.1	946	225	102	91	14	5	7	12	56	1	197	5	8	18	13	.581	0	0	3.65

Doug Walls

Pitches: Right **Bats:** Left **Pos:** SP-25; RP-4   **Ht:** 6'2" **Wt:** 204 **Born:** 3/21/74 **Age:** 27

Year Team	Lg Org	G	GS	CG	GF	IP	BFP	H	R	ER	HR	SH	SF	HB	TBB	IBB	SO	WP	Bk	W	L	Pct.	ShO	Sv	ERA
1993 Rockies	R Col	10	10	0	0	47.1	218	51	40	24	2	0	1	2	26	0	50	11	2	2	7	.222	0	0	4.56
1994 Asheville	A Col	21	21	1	0	106.1	470	81	68	59	6	3	7	8	71	1	111	16	5	6	10	.375	0	0	4.99
1995 Salem	A+ Col	15	15	0	0	79.2	344	61	39	34	10	1	3	3	49	1	79	5	2	5	5	.500	0	0	3.84
1996 Salem	A+ Col	5	3	0	1	14	70	17	12	11	3	0	0	0	10	0	17	3	0	0	1	—	0	1	7.07
1997 Portland	A- Col	5	5	0	0	22	92	19	3	3	0	0	0	1	10	0	23	1	0	1	0	1.000	0	0	1.23
Asheville	A Col	10	9	0	1	51.2	227	50	23	17	4	0	1	2	22	0	62	2	1	4	2	.667	0	0	2.96
1998 Salem	A+ Col	27	26	2	1	159	677	145	91	79	10	11	5	9	63	0	169	7	2	6	13	.316	0	0	4.47
1999 Carolina	AA Col	26	26	2	0	150.1	642	159	74	61	14	10	4	4	44	0	140	6	1	10	9	.526	0	0	3.65
2000 Jacksnville	AA Det	11	11	0	0	52.2	254	66	54	45	8	2	2	1	34	0	38	6	1	3	7	.300	0	0	7.69
Toledo	AAA Det	18	14	1	3	85.1	375	88	60	49	10	3	5	3	42	1	61	3	1	3	7	.300	0	0	5.17
8 Min. YEARS		148	140	6	6	768.1	3369	737	464	382	67	30	28	33	371	3	750	60	15	40	60	.400	1	1	4.47

Chris Walther

Bats: Right **Throws:** Right **Pos:** 3B-53; 1B-15; DH-3; PH-1; PR-1   **Ht:** 6'2" **Wt:** 200 **Born:** 8/28/76 **Age:** 24

Year Team	Lg Org	G	AB	H	2B	3B	HR	TB	R	RBI	TBB	IBB	SO	HBP	SH	SF	SB	CS	SB%	GDP	Avg	OBP	SLG
1995 Brewers	R Mil	50	174	45	3	2	0	52	28	19	10	0	9	1	1	0	3	4	.57	5	.259	.303	.299
1996 Ogden	R+ Mil	63	239	84	16	4	6	126	47	54	14	0	21	1	3	2	3	2	.60	7	.351	.387	.527
1997 Beloit	A Mil	113	437	131	25	4	0	164	55	38	28	0	41	5	3	1	5	7	.42	16	.300	.348	.375
1998 Stockton	A+ Mil	115	419	117	20	4	3	154	52	50	21	2	41	8	6	2	2	2	.50	7	.279	.324	.375
1999 Lk Elsinore	A+ Ana	100	380	112	26	2	3	151	48	60	27	3	31	0	1	6	3	3	.50	15	.295	.337	.397
Erie	AA Ana	9	31	11	2	1	1	18	5	6	4	0	4	0	0	0	0	0	—	3	.355	.429	.581
2000 Erie	AA Ana	71	251	64	10	1	1	79	20	19	19	0	25	1	1	1	0	3	.00	5	.255	.309	.315
6 Min. YEARS		521	1931	564	102	18	14	744	255	246	123	5	172	16	15	12	17	20	.46	58	.292	.338	.385

Jeremy Ward

Pitches: Right **Bats:** Right **Pos:** RP-5; SP-2   **Ht:** 6'3" **Wt:** 220 **Born:** 2/24/78 **Age:** 23

Year Team	Lg Org	G	GS	CG	GF	IP	BFP	H	R	ER	HR	SH	SF	HB	TBB	IBB	SO	WP	Bk	W	L	Pct.	ShO	Sv	ERA
1999 High Desert	A+ Ari	4	4	0	0	8.2	35	5	2	2	0	0	0	1	3	0	12	0	4	0	0	—	0	0	2.08
El Paso	AA Ari	19	0	0	17	25.2	101	18	7	7	1	0	1	0	9	1	26	1	0	1	1	.500	0	7	2.45
Tucson	AAA Ari	1	0	0	0	1.2	8	2	0	0	0	0	0	0	2	0	1	1	0	0	0	—	0	0	0.00
2000 Diamondbcks	R Ari	2	2	0	0	2	6	0	0	0	0	0	0	0	0	0	2	0	0	0	0	—	0	0	0.00
Tucson	AAA Ari	5	0	0	2	3.1	17	3	2	2	0	0	1	0	5	0	1	0	0	0	1	.000	0	0	5.40
2 Min. YEARS		31	6	0	19	41.1	167	28	11	11	1	0	1	2	19	1	42	2	4	1	2	.333	0	7	2.40

Jeremy Ware

Bats: Right **Throws:** Right **Pos:** OF-115; PH-6; DH-4 **Ht:** 6'0" **Wt:** 200 **Born:** 10/23/75 **Age:** 25

Year Team	Lg Org	G	AB	H	2B	3B	HR	TB	R	RBI	TBB	IBB	SO	HBP	SH	SF	SB	CS	SB%	GDP	Avg	OBP	SLG
1995 Expos	R Mon	38	116	28	4	2	2	42	18	15	18	0	28	3	0	1	5	4	.56	2	.241	.355	.362
1996 Expos	R Mon	15	44	16	3	3	0	25	10	17	9	0	4	0	2	0	6	1	.86	0	.364	.472	.568
Vermont	A- Mon	32	94	18	2	0	0	20	12	6	15	0	25	0	1	0	5	3	.63	1	.191	.303	.213
1997 Cape Fear	A Mon	138	529	139	32	5	16	229	84	77	43	2	114	6	0	6	32	7	.82	8	.263	.322	.433
1998 Jupiter	A+ Mon	127	492	121	35	3	10	192	51	64	23	1	102	7	4	7	21	5	.81	16	.246	.285	.390
1999 Jupiter	A+ Mon	7	25	8	2	0	2	16	5	11	2	0	5	0	0	0	3	0	1.00	0	.320	.370	.640
Harrisburg	AA Mon	111	381	100	23	2	9	154	57	56	41	2	79	2	2	5	12	5	.71	19	.262	.333	.404
2000 Harrisburg	AA Mon	123	442	123	23	2	10	180	62	63	39	2	87	2	0	5	12	11	.52	10	.278	.336	.407
6 Min. YEARS		591	2123	553	124	17	49	858	299	309	190	7	444	20	9	24	96	36	.73	56	.260	.324	.404

Rico Washington

Bats: Left **Throws:** Right **Pos:** 3B-73; 2B-61; PH-2 **Ht:** 5'10" **Wt:** 182 **Born:** 5/30/78 **Age:** 23

Year Team	Lg Org	G	AB	H	2B	3B	HR	TB	R	RBI	TBB	IBB	SO	HBP	SH	SF	SB	CS	SB%	GDP	Avg	OBP	SLG
1997 Pirates	R Pit	28	98	24	6	0	1	33	12	11	4	1	13	4	0	1	1	0	1.00	2	.245	.299	.337
1998 Pirates	R Pit	1	3	0	0	0	0	0	0	0	0	0	2	0	0	0	0	0	—	0	.000	.000	.000
Erie	A- Pit	51	197	65	14	2	6	101	31	31	17	2	33	7	0	0	1	2	.33	4	.330	.403	.513
Augusta	A Pit	12	50	15	2	1	2	25	12	12	7	0	9	2	0	1	2	0	1.00	0	.300	.400	.500
1999 Hickory	A Pit	76	287	102	15	1	13	158	70	50	48	7	45	8	0	6	5	1	.83	4	.355	.453	.551
Lynchburg	A+ Pit	57	205	58	7	0	7	86	31	32	30	0	45	4	1	2	4	1	.80	8	.283	.382	.420
2000 Altoona	AA Pit	135	503	130	22	7	8	190	74	59	55	1	74	5	9	4	4	9	.31	11	.258	.335	.378
4 Min. YEARS		360	1343	394	66	11	37	593	230	195	161	11	221	30	10	14	17	13	.57	29	.293	.378	.442

Derek Wathan

Bats: Both **Throws:** Right **Pos:** SS-131; DH-2; 3B-1 **Ht:** 6'3" **Wt:** 190 **Born:** 12/13/76 **Age:** 24

Year Team	Lg Org	G	AB	H	2B	3B	HR	TB	R	RBI	TBB	IBB	SO	HBP	SH	SF	SB	CS	SB%	GDP	Avg	OBP	SLG
1998 Utica	A- Fla	60	224	60	8	2	0	72	32	23	21	0	35	3	5	0	10	9	.53	6	.268	.339	.321
1999 Kane County	A Fla	125	469	119	18	4	1	148	71	49	53	2	54	5	10	3	33	12	.73	13	.254	.334	.316
2000 Brevard Cty	A+ Fla	91	364	94	18	6	6	142	53	49	45	4	54	2	5	2	19	11	.63	6	.258	.341	.390
Portland	AA Fla	41	141	31	3	2	0	38	13	17	13	0	20	1	0	2	3	1	.75	1	.220	.287	.270
3 Min. YEARS		317	1198	304	47	14	7	400	169	138	132	6	163	11	20	7	65	33	.66	26	.254	.332	.334

Dusty Wathan

Bats: Right **Throws:** Right **Pos:** C-57; 1B-5; 3B-3; PH-2; DH-1 **Ht:** 6'4" **Wt:** 215 **Born:** 8/22/73 **Age:** 27

Year Team	Lg Org	G	AB	H	2B	3B	HR	TB	R	RBI	TBB	IBB	SO	HBP	SH	SF	SB	CS	SB%	GDP	Avg	OBP	SLG
1994 Mariners	R Sea	35	86	18	2	0	1	23	14	7	11	0	13	3	0	0	0	0	—	0	.209	.320	.267
1995 Wisconsin	A Sea	5	11	1	0	0	0	1	1	3	1	0	3	1	0	0	0	0	—	0	.091	.167	.364
Everett	A- Sea	53	181	49	9	1	6	78	32	25	17	0	26	7	1	0	2	1	.67	4	.271	.356	.431
1996 Lancaster	A+ Sea	74	246	64	10	1	8	100	41	40	26	0	65	6	3	1	1	1	.50	5	.260	.344	.407
1997 Lancaster	A+ Sea	56	202	60	17	0	4	89	27	35	21	0	51	7	1	1	1	1	.50	7	.297	.381	.441
Memphis	AA Sea	49	149	40	4	1	4	58	20	19	19	0	28	5	0	1	1	1	.50	4	.268	.368	.389
1998 Tacoma	AAA Sea	19	51	15	1	1	0	18	6	8	6	0	10	2	2	0	0	0	—	4	.294	.390	.353
Orlando	AA Sea	69	234	60	10	0	2	76	32	21	28	2	39	15	2	2	3	1	.75	8	.256	.369	.325
1999 New Haven	AA Sea	96	333	93	16	2	4	125	37	37	24	1	60	12	4	1	4	1	.80	11	.279	.349	.375
2000 Tacoma	AAA Sea	64	203	66	12	0	3	87	25	29	15	1	28	12	4	1	0	2	.00	4	.325	.403	.429
7 Min. YEARS		520	1696	466	81	6	33	658	235	224	167	4	323	70	17	7	11	8	.58	47	.275	.362	.388

Pat Watkins

Bats: Right **Throws:** Right **Pos:** OF-107; DH-2; PH-2; 3B-1 **Ht:** 6'2" **Wt:** 195 **Born:** 9/2/72 **Age:** 28

Year Team	Lg Org	G	AB	H	2B	3B	HR	TB	R	RBI	TBB	IBB	SO	HBP	SH	SF	SB	CS	SB%	GDP	Avg	OBP	SLG
1993 Billings	R+ Cin	66	235	63	10	3	6	97	46	30	22	0	44	2	1	1	15	4	.79	4	.268	.335	.413
1994 Winston-Sal	A+ Cin	132	524	152	24	5	27	267	107	83	62	3	84	7	1	6	31	13	.70	8	.290	.369	.510
1995 Winston-Sal	A+ Cin	27	107	22	3	1	4	39	14	13	10	0	24	0	1	2	1	0	1.00	6	.206	.269	.364
Chattanooga	AA Cin	105	358	104	26	2	12	170	57	57	33	4	53	3	0	4	5	5	.50	7	.291	.352	.475
1996 Chattanooga	AA Cin	127	492	136	31	2	8	195	63	59	30	0	64	7	2	4	15	11	.58	17	.276	.325	.396
1997 Chattanooga	AA Cin	46	177	62	15	1	7	100	35	30	15	1	16	2	0	1	9	3	.75	3	.350	.405	.565
Indianapols	AAA Cin	84	325	91	14	7	9	146	46	34	24	2	55	1	3	1	13	9	.59	10	.280	.330	.449
1998 Indianapols	AAA Cin	44	188	71	12	1	3	94	37	24	15	0	26	1	1	1	8	3	.73	5	.378	.424	.500
1999 Colo Spnngs	AAA Col	12	30	10	1	0	0	11	4	2	2	0	6	0	0	0	0	0	—	0	.333	.364	.367
Carolina	AA Col	88	312	93	27	1	3	131	38	40	24	0	49	6	1	3	6	5	.55	3	.298	.357	.420
2000 Chattanooga	AA Cin	33	120	35	4	0	1	42	16	16	9	0	21	0	1	2	4	2	.67	3	.292	.336	.350
Toledo	AAA Det	77	304	76	12	0	8	112	50	36	19	0	28	2	3	2	4	8	.33	13	.250	.297	.368
1997 Cincinnati	NL	17	29	6	2	0	0	8	2	0	0	0	5	0	1	0	1	0	1.00	1	.207	.207	.276
1998 Cincinnati	NL	83	147	39	8	1	2	55	11	15	8	0	26	1	2	4	1	3	.25	3	.265	.300	.374
1999 Colorado	NL	16	19	1	0	0	0	1	2	0	2	0	5	0	0	0	0	0	—	1	.053	.143	.053
8 Min. YEARS		841	3172	915	179	23	88	1404	513	425	265	10	470	31	14	28	109	59	.65	78	.288	.346	.443
3 Maj. YEARS		116	195	46	10	1	2	64	15	15	10	0	36	1	4	4	2	3	.40	5	.236	.271	.328

Scott Watkins

Pitches: Left **Bats:** Left **Pos:** RP-36; SP-7   **Ht:** 6'3" **Wt:** 180 **Born:** 5/15/70 **Age:** 31

Year Team	Lg Org	G	GS	CG	GF	IP	BFP	H	R	ER	HR	SH	SF	HB	TBB	IBB	SO	WP	Bk	W	L	Pct.	ShO	Sv	ERA
1992 Kenosha	A Min	27	0	0	11	46.1	196	43	21	19	4	2	1	3	14	0	58	1	0	2	5	.286	0	1	3.69
1993 Fort Wayne	A Min	15	0	0	8	30.1	124	26	13	11	0	1	2	1	9	0	31	0	1	2	0	1.000	0	1	3.26
Fort Myers	A+ Min	20	0	0	10	27.2	125	27	14	9	0	2	0	0	12	0	41	2	1	2	2	.500	0	3	2.93
Nashville	AA Min	13	0	0	3	16.2	75	19	15	11	2	0	1	1	7	0	17	2	1	0	1	.000	0	0	5.94
1994 Nashville	AA Min	11	0	0	8	13.2	60	13	9	7	1	1	2	0	4	0	11	1	0	1	0	1.000	0	3	4.61
Salt Lake	AAA Min	46	0	0	26	57.1	269	73	46	43	10	4	5	1	28	5	47	1	1	2	6	.250	0	3	6.75
1995 Salt Lake	AAA Min	45	0	0	33	54.2	217	45	18	17	4	1	3	1	13	1	57	1	0	4	2	.667	0	20	2.80
1996 Salt Lake	AAA Min	47	0	0	29	50.1	244	60	46	43	6	5	3	2	34	5	43	3	1	4	6	.400	0	1	7.69
1997 Omaha	AAA KC	9	0	0	4	15.1	72	19	13	11	4	0	1	0	6	0	15	2	1	0	0	—	0	0	6.46
New Haven	AA Col	13	0	0	8	15.1	58	9	6	6	1	1	1	1	3	0	8	3	0	2	0	1.000	0	1	3.52
1998 Tulsa	AA Tex	10	1	0	4	21	80	14	5	5	1	0	0	2	2	0	25	1	0	1	0	1.000	0	1	2.14
Oklahoma	AAA Tex	38	0	0	22	49.2	214	44	19	18	6	2	1	3	22	1	50	5	0	6	1	.857	0	2	3.26
1999 Iowa	AAA ChC	47	3	0	10	63	287	71	47	43	11	3	3	2	33	1	54	7	0	1	2	.333	0	0	6.14
2000 Colo Sprngs	AAA Col	43	7	0	7	81	364	93	51	39	6	3	4	3	43	1	42	6	2	3	1	.750	0	1	4.33
1995 Minnesota	AL	27	0	0	7	21.2	94	22	14	13	2	1	3	0	11	1	11	0	0	0	0	—	0	0	5.40
9 Min. YEARS		384	11	0	183	542.1	2385	556	323	282	56	25	27	18	230	14	499	35	8	30	26	.536	0	36	4.68

Alan Webb

Pitches: Left **Bats:** Left **Pos:** SP-21; RP-5   **Ht:** 5'10" **Wt:** 165 **Born:** 9/26/79 **Age:** 21

Year Team	Lg Org	G	GS	CG	GF	IP	BFP	H	R	ER	HR	SH	SF	HB	TBB	IBB	SO	WP	Bk	W	L	Pct.	ShO	Sv	ERA
1997 Tigers	R Det	9	8	0	0	33.2	139	27	17	14	3	1	0	2	11	0	46	4	4	3	1	.750	0	0	3.74
1998 W Michigan	A Det	27	27	3	0	172	690	110	69	56	9	4	0	18	58	1	202	10	1	10	7	.588	2	0	2.93
1999 Jacksnville	AA Det	26	22	0	1	140	605	140	88	77	17	1	3	8	64	0	88	4	3	9	9	.500	0	0	4.95
2000 Tulsa	AA Tex	10	6	0	3	25.1	131	35	33	33	9	0	2	1	24	0	17	4	0	0	4	.000	0	0	11.72
Charlotte	A+ Tex	16	15	1	0	83.1	360	83	36	30	3	4	3	9	39	0	40	14	2	5	4	.556	1	0	3.24
4 Min. YEARS		88	78	4	4	454.1	1925	395	243	210	41	10	8	38	196	1	393	36	10	27	25	.519	3	0	4.16

Jake Weber

Bats: Left **Throws:** Right **Pos:** OF-122; DH-3; PH-3; PR-1   **Ht:** 5'11" **Wt:** 188 **Born:** 4/22/76 **Age:** 25

Year Team	Lg Org	G	AB	H	2B	3B	HR	TB	R	RBI	TBB	IBB	SO	HBP	SH	SF	SB	CS	SB%	GDP	Avg	OBP	SLG
1998 Everett	A- Sea	75	275	93	20	2	11	150	75	52	67	3	42	5	2	3	14	7	.67	3	.338	.471	.545
1999 New Haven	AA Sea	136	489	125	22	2	11	184	64	59	66	2	73	3	1	2	5	7	.42	7	.256	.346	.376
2000 New Haven	AA Sea	129	473	121	21	7	5	171	71	56	60	2	56	2	4	4	11	4	.73	9	.256	.340	.362
3 Min. YEARS		340	1237	339	63	11	27	505	210	167	193	7	171	10	5	9	30	18	.63	19	.274	.374	.408

Neil Weber

Pitches: Left **Bats:** Left **Pos:** RP-43; SP-3   **Ht:** 6'5" **Wt:** 215 **Born:** 12/6/72 **Age:** 28

Year Team	Lg Org	G	GS	CG	GF	IP	BFP	H	R	ER	HR	SH	SF	HB	TBB	IBB	SO	WP	Bk	W	L	Pct.	ShO	Sv	ERA
1993 Jamestown	A- Mon	16	16	2	0	94.1	398	84	46	29	3	0	4	4	36	0	80	3	3	6	5	.545	1	0	2.77
1994 Wst Plm Bch	A+ Mon	25	24	1	0	135	566	113	58	48	8	4	4	4	62	0	134	7	5	9	7	.563	0	0	3.20
1995 Harrisburg	AA Mon	28	28	0	0	152.2	696	157	98	85	16	11	7	8	90	1	119	7	1	6	11	.353	0	0	5.01
1996 Harrisburg	AA Mon	18	18	1	0	107	440	90	37	36	8	3	3	5	44	0	74	5	0	7	4	.636	0	0	3.03
1997 Ottawa	AAA Mon	9	9	0	0	39.2	204	46	46	35	7	2	1	2	40	0	27	2	0	2	5	.286	0	0	7.94
Harrisburg	AA Mon	18	18	1	0	112.2	477	93	56	48	17	6	1	8	51	1	121	6	0	7	6	.538	1	0	3.83
1998 Tucson	AAA Ari	46	11	1	6	112.2	508	116	82	64	17	5	3	4	55	0	79	12	1	5	9	.357	0	1	5.11
1999 Tucson	AAA Ari	9	0	0	3	12.2	65	23	16	15	2	0	0	1	4	1	16	0	0	1	1	.500	0	0	10.66
San Antonio	AA LA	12	11	0	0	55	253	62	39	32	3	2	3	6	24	0	31	4	0	4	2	.667	0	0	5.24
Albuquerque	AAA LA	9	0	0	4	16.2	87	30	19	19	6	2	1	1	9	0	14	3	0	0	1	.000	0	0	10.26
2000 Louisville	AAA Cin	2	0	0	0	3.2	18	6	3	3	0	0	0	0	2	0	4	0	0	0	0	—	0	0	7.36
Rochester	AAA Bal	1	1	0	0	4	19	3	2	1	0	0	0	1	2	0	3	0	0	0	0	—	0	0	2.25
Bowie	AA Bal	43	2	0	20	57.1	267	68	38	30	2	4	2	1	25	0	51	3	0	0	2	.000	0	3	4.71
1998 Arizona	NL	4	0	0	0	2.1	15	5	3	3	0	0	0	0	3	0	4	0	0	0	0	—	0	0	11.57
8 Min. YEARS		236	138	6	33	903.1	3998	891	540	445	89	39	29	45	444	3	753	52	10	47	53	.470	2	4	4.43

Clint Weibl

Pitches: Right **Bats:** Right **Pos:** SP-27; RP-2   **Ht:** 6'3" **Wt:** 180 **Born:** 3/17/75 **Age:** 26

Year Team	Lg Org	G	GS	CG	GF	IP	BFP	H	R	ER	HR	SH	SF	HB	TBB	IBB	SO	WP	Bk	W	L	Pct.	ShO	Sv	ERA
1996 Johnson Cty	R+ StL	7	7	0	0	44	172	27	12	10	1	0	0	1	12	0	51	0	0	4	1	.800	0	0	2.05
Peoria	A StL	5	5	0	0	29.2	122	27	16	16	2	0	1	2	7	0	21	0	0	1	2	.333	0	0	4.85
1997 Pr William	A+ StL	29	29	0	0	163	718	185	90	84	18	5	2	9	62	2	135	3	1	12	11	.522	0	0	4.64
1998 Memphis	AAA StL	1	1	0	0	5.2	24	6	5	4	0	0	0	0	2	0	2	0	0	1	0	1.000	0	0	6.35
Arkansas	AA StL	25	23	0	0	139	616	161	86	83	22	4	9	5	53	2	85	3	0	12	10	.545	0	0	5.37
1999 Arkansas	AA StL	28	17	1	2	110	483	121	59	57	11	3	0	3	49	1	75	4	1	4	9	.308	0	0	4.66
Memphis	AAA StL	5	0	0	0	8.1	36	10	9	5	2	1	1	0	2	0	8	0	0	1	0	1.000	0	0	5.40
2000 Arkansas	AA StL	10	9	0	0	57	243	57	35	30	10	0	2	1	19	0	51	1	0	3	3	.500	0	0	4.74
Memphis	AAA StL	19	18	2	0	120.2	481	98	45	38	11	1	2	6	37	0	92	1	1	9	4	.692	2	0	2.83
5 Min. YEARS		129	109	3	3	677.1	2895	692	357	327	77	14	17	27	243	5	520	14	3	46	41	.529	2	0	4.34

Chris Weidert

Pitches: Right **Bats:** Right **Pos:** RP-29; SP-1   **Ht:** 6'3" **Wt:** 215 **Born:** 4/3/74 **Age:** 27

Year Team	Lg Org	G	GS	CG	GF	IP	BFP	H	R	ER	HR	SH	SF	HB	TBB	IBB	SO	WP	Bk	W	L	Pct.	ShO	Sv	ERA
1994 Expos	R Mon	12	12	0	0	63.2	259	43	25	20	3	0	3	3	24	0	53	3	1	5	3	.625	0	0	2.83
1995 Albany	A Mon	3	3	0	0	10.1	55	16	14	9	3	0	1	0	5	0	17	0	0	1	2	.333	0	0	7.84
Vermont	A- Mon	15	15	1	0	95.1	378	67	31	19	4	0	2	4	21	0	52	8	0	11	1	.917	1	0	1.79
1996 Expos	R Mon	2	1	0	1	5	17	2	1	1	1	0	0	0	0	0	2	0	0	0	0	—	0	0	1.80
Wst Plm Bch	A+ Mon	20	20	1	0	106	462	106	54	40	4	3	3	7	37	1	64	4	1	3	8	.273	0	0	3.40
1997 Wst Plm Bch	A+ Mon	4	0	0	0	6	26	5	1	0	0	0	1	0	3	0	7	0	0	0	1	.000	0	0	0.00
1998 New Jersey	IND —	13	12	0	1	67	294	82	37	26	3	5	0	2	18	2	45	6	0	5	3	.625	0	0	3.49
1999 Kinston	A+ Cle	27	2	0	13	52.1	223	49	15	15	2	5	2	1	22	5	42	3	0	4	3	.571	0	0	2.58
2000 Bowie	AA Bal	2	0	0	0	4.1	17	3	1	1	0	0	0	0	1	0	5	0	0	0	0	—	0	0	2.08
Frederick	A+ Bal	24	0	0	5	47.2	220	60	37	28	8	2	3	2	16	3	28	3	1	3	2	.600	0	0	5.29
Kinston	A+ Cle	4	1	0	1	8	31	6	2	2	1	0	1	0	2	0	10	1	0	1	0	1.000	0	0	2.25
7 Min. YEARS		126	66	2	21	465.2	1982	439	218	161	29	15	16	19	149	11	325	28	3	33	23	.589	1	0	3.11

Matt Weimer

Pitches: Right **Bats:** Right **Pos:** RP-49   **Ht:** 6'2" **Wt:** 190 **Born:** 11/21/74 **Age:** 26

Year Team	Lg Org	G	GS	CG	GF	IP	BFP	H	R	ER	HR	SH	SF	HB	TBB	IBB	SO	WP	Bk	W	L	Pct.	ShO	Sv	ERA
1997 St.Cathrnes	A- Tor	23	0	0	15	35.1	132	35	21	14	1	1	2	3	4	0	22	3	0	2	2	.500	0	0	3.57
1998 Hagerstown	A Tor	48	0	0	29	72.2	308	62	31	23	3	2	2	8	26	2	59	5	0	7	6	.538	0	8	2.85
1999 Dunedin	A+ Tor	46	0	0	26	65.1	273	60	23	21	5	2	1	5	20	3	37	3	0	6	3	.667	0	6	2.89
2000 Tennessee	AA Tor	49	0	0	20	62.2	273	68	36	32	6	2	3	4	22	5	31	5	0	4	3	.571	0	2	4.60
4 Min. YEARS		166	0	0	90	236	1004	225	111	90	15	7	8	20	72	10	149	16	0	19	14	.576	0	16	3.43

Matt Wells

Pitches: Right **Bats:** Right **Pos:** RP-20   **Ht:** 6'2" **Wt:** 210 **Born:** 1/2/75 **Age:** 26

Year Team	Lg Org	G	GS	CG	GF	IP	BFP	H	R	ER	HR	SH	SF	HB	TBB	IBB	SO	WP	Bk	W	L	Pct.	ShO	Sv	ERA
1996 Bellingham	A- SF	12	11	0	0	44.2	220	57	38	35	9	1	2	2	30	0	41	0	0	2	4	.333	0	0	7.05
1997 Bakersfield	A+ SF	29	25	0	0	143.2	654	154	87	71	10	6	7	6	81	2	109	8	0	8	12	.400	0	0	4.45
1998 Bakersfield	A+ SF	40	6	0	15	104	472	107	63	52	9	4	7	8	46	3	70	3	3	3	8	.273	0	5	4.50
1999 San Jose	A+ SF	57	0	0	24	90.2	400	73	41	37	4	4	8	1	65	0	100	6	0	8	5	.615	0	7	3.67
2000 San Jose	A+ SF	16	0	0	2	25	116	24	15	12	1	0	0	1	19	1	25	1	0	1	1	.000	0	0	4.32
Shreveport	AA SF	4	0	0	0	7	42	11	11	6	0	0	0	1	9	3	6	0	0	1	0	1.000	0	0	7.71
5 Min. YEARS		158	42	0	43	415	1904	426	255	213	33	15	24	19	250	9	351	18	3	22	30	.423	0	12	4.62

Eric Welsh

Bats: Left **Throws:** Left **Pos:** 1B-55; DH-22; PH-11; OF-8   **Ht:** 6'3" **Wt:** 200 **Born:** 9/17/76 **Age:** 24

			BATTING												BASERUNNING				PERCENTAGES		
Year Team	Lg Org	G	AB	H	2B	3B	HR	TB	R	RBI	TBB	IBB	SO	HBP	SH	SF	SB	CS	SB%	GDP	Avg	OBP	SLG
1997 Billings	R+ Cin	67	244	77	13	2	11	127	41	54	38	2	0	3	2	4	.33	3	.315	.360	.508
1998 Burlington	A Cin	135	525	136	33	3	7	196	49	68	27	1	112	9	1	3	7	6	.54	5	.259	.305	.373
1999 Rockford	A Cin	101	368	103	23	0	16	174	52	64	23	3	57	1	0	2	3	2	.60	9	.280	.322	.473
2000 Dayton	A Cin	41	142	40	11	0	13	90	29	35	17	1	35	3	0	1	0	0	—	2	.282	.368	.634
Chattanooga	AA Cin	53	171	48	12	0	5	75	23	29	15	0	44	2	1	2	5	5	.50	2	.281	.342	.439
4 Min. YEARS		397	1466	409	92	5	52	667	194	250	100	6	286	17	2	11	17	17	.50	21	.279	.330	.455

Jayson Werth

Bats: Right **Throws:** Right **Pos:** C-98; DH-11; PR-2; OF-1   **Ht:** 6'5" **Wt:** 190 **Born:** 5/20/79 **Age:** 22

			BATTING												BASERUNNING				PERCENTAGES		
Year Team	Lg Org	G	AB	H	2B	3B	HR	TB	R	RBI	TBB	IBB	SO	HBP	SH	SF	SB	CS	SB%	GDP	Avg	OBP	SLG
1997 Orioles	R Bal	32	88	26	6	0	1	35	16	8	22	0	22	0	0	1	7	1	.88	0	.295	.432	.398
1998 Delmarva	A Bal	120	408	108	20	3	8	158	71	53	50	0	92	15	1	2	21	6	.78	14	.265	.364	.387
Bowie	AA Bal	5	19	3	2	0	0	5	2	1	2	0	6	0	0	0	1	0	1.00	0	.158	.238	.263
1999 Frederick	A+ Bal	66	236	72	10	1	3	93	41	30	37	2	37	3	1	2	16	3	.84	4	.305	.403	.394
Bowie	AA Bal	35	121	33	5	1	1	43	18	11	17	0	26	2	1	3	7	1	.88	1	.273	.364	.355
2000 Frederick	A+ Bal	24	83	23	3	0	2	32	16	18	10	1	15	0	1	2	5	1	.83	3	.277	.347	.386
Bowie	AA Bal	85	276	63	16	2	5	98	47	26	54	1	50	4	4	1	9	3	.75	10	.228	.361	.355
4 Min. YEARS		367	1231	328	62	7	20	464	211	147	192	4	248	24	8	11	66	15	.81	32	.266	.373	.377

Barry Wesson

Bats: Right **Throws:** Right **Pos:** OF-115; PH-6; 1B-1; PR-1   **Ht:** 6'2" **Wt:** 195 **Born:** 4/6/77 **Age:** 24

			BATTING												BASERUNNING				PERCENTAGES		
Year Team	Lg Org	G	AB	H	2B	3B	HR	TB	R	RBI	TBB	IBB	SO	HBP	SH	SF	SB	CS	SB%	GDP	Avg	OBP	SLG
1995 Astros	R Hou	45	138	26	2	2	2	38	14	18	19	0	40	1	1	1	4	0	1.00	2	.188	.289	.275
Jackson	AA Hou	4	3	2	0	1	0	4	2	1	0	0	0	0	0	0	0	0	—	0	.667	.667	1.333
1996 Auburn	A- Hou	55	176	28	7	0	0	35	11	12	12	1	46	1	1	3	5	3	.63	5	.159	.214	.199
1997 Auburn	A- Hou	58	208	54	7	3	3	76	24	26	10	0	45	1	1	1	8	4	.67	1	.260	.295	.365
1998 Quad City	A Hou	138	493	124	21	2	7	170	71	43	32	1	90	5	2	0	22	12	.65	10	.252	.304	.345
1999 Kissimmee	A+ Hou	115	352	76	15	1	4	105	32	34	26	0	84	4	2	2	8	7	.53	3	.216	.276	.298
2000 Kissimmee	A+ Hou	81	308	84	21	3	5	126	50	35	33	0	66	2	4	1	24	5	.83	2	.273	.346	.409
Round Rock	AA Hou	39	110	26	1	2	2	37	12	15	10	0	32	0	0	2	6	2	.75	2	.236	.295	.336
6 Min. YEARS		535	1788	420	74	14	23	591	216	184	142	2	403	14	11	10	77	33	.70	25	.235	.295	.331

Allan Westfall

Pitches: Right **Bats:** Right **Pos:** SP-18; RP-1 **Ht:** 5'11" **Wt:** 195 **Born:** 5/15/75 **Age:** 26

Year Team	Lg Org	G	GS	CG	GF	IP	BFP	H	R	ER	HR	SH	SF	HB	TBB	IBB	SO	WP	Bk	W	L	Pct.	ShO	Sv	ERA
1997 Lancaster	A+ Sea	15	0	0	8	19	88	23	17	13	4	1	0	2	8	0	14	1	0	0	3	.000	0	3	6.16
Wisconsin	A Sea	18	0	0	10	32.1	142	26	14	13	2	0	2	1	20	2	41	4	0	0	2	.000	0	3	3.62
1998 Lancaster	A+ Sea	37	0	0	27	52	229	39	21	18	1	6	1	6	28	2	55	5	1	4	3	.571	0	5	3.12
Orlando	AA Sea	8	0	0	2	17	87	19	13	13	3	0	0	3	16	0	13	0	0	2	1	.667	0	0	6.88
2000 Mariners	R Sea	1	1	0	0	3	12	2	0	0	0	0	0	0	0	0	5	0	0	0	0	—	0	0	0.00
New Haven	AA Sea	18	17	0	0	88.2	370	80	31	26	2	3	2	5	28	0	64	4	2	7	5	.583	0	0	2.64
3 Min. YEARS		97	18	0	47	212	928	189	96	83	12	10	5	17	100	4	192	14	3	13	14	.481	0	11	3.52

Marty Weymouth

Pitches: Right **Bats:** Right **Pos:** RP-37; SP-1 **Ht:** 6'2" **Wt:** 180 **Born:** 8/6/77 **Age:** 23

Year Team	Lg Org	G	GS	CG	GF	IP	BFP	H	R	ER	HR	SH	SF	HB	TBB	IBB	SO	WP	Bk	W	L	Pct.	ShO	Sv	ERA
1995 Mariners	R Sea	9	4	0	1	31.2	144	37	23	14	2	1	1	2	10	0	26	3	1	2	3	.400	0	0	3.98
1996 Everett	A- Sea	10	10	0	0	41	185	46	28	22	3	0	2	0	16	0	35	9	0	2	3	.400	0	0	4.83
1997 Wisconsin	A Sea	23	19	0	0	110.1	484	116	75	62	14	2	3	3	33	1	83	5	2	5	7	.417	0	0	5.06
1998 Hickory	A CWS	31	14	0	10	112	499	125	74	54	7	3	5	7	32	0	99	9	0	4	5	.444	0	3	4.34
1999 Winston-Sal	A+ CWS	41	0	0	16	57.1	257	62	35	30	1	3	1	1	21	3	42	3	1	5	6	.455	0	2	4.71
2000 Valley	IND —	1	1	0	0	3.2	18	1	3	3	0	0	1	1	5	0	2	2	0	1	0	1.000	0	0	7.36
Birmingham	AA CWS	37	0	0	23	44.1	194	47	26	18	3	6	3	3	15	3	33	2	0	0	5	.000	0	13	3.65
6 Min. YEARS		152	48	0	50	400.1	1781	434	264	203	30	15	16	17	132	7	320	33	4	18	30	.375	0	18	4.56

Chad Whitaker

Bats: Left **Throws:** Right **Pos:** OF-93; DH-11 **Ht:** 6'2" **Wt:** 190 **Born:** 9/16/76 **Age:** 24

Year Team	Lg Org	G	AB	H	2B	3B	HR	TB	R	RBI	TBB	IBB	SO	HBP	SH	SF	SB	CS	SB%	GDP	Avg	OBP	SLG
1996 Columbus	A Cle	66	234	55	10	1	12	103	32	29	25	1	80	1	0	1	2	2	.50	4	.235	.310	.440
1997 Columbus	A Cle	109	432	118	25	2	12	183	48	72	23	3	144	5	0	2	3	0	1.00	6	.273	.316	.424
1998 Kinston	A+ Cle	127	455	98	25	0	10	153	46	48	34	1	148	1	0	0	16	10	.62	6	.215	.271	.336
1999 Kinston	A+ Cle	76	280	67	14	0	9	108	34	36	21	1	62	1	0	2	2	3	.40	14	.239	.293	.386
Akron	AA Cle	41	149	48	12	2	5	79	18	38	15	0	40	0	0	2	0	1	.00	3	.322	.380	.530
2000 Akron	AA Cle	104	367	86	11	3	7	124	44	50	40	0	96	1	1	4	3	4	.43	5	.234	.308	.338
5 Min. YEARS		523	1917	472	97	8	55	750	222	273	158	6	570	9	1	11	26	20	.57	38	.246	.305	.391

Matt White

Pitches: Right **Bats:** Right **Pos:** SP-26 **Ht:** 6'5" **Wt:** 230 **Born:** 8/13/78 **Age:** 22

Year Team	Lg Org	G	GS	CG	GF	IP	BFP	H	R	ER	HR	SH	SF	HB	TBB	IBB	SO	WP	Bk	W	L	Pct.	ShO	Sv	ERA
1997 Hudson Val	A- TB	15	15	0	0	84	369	78	44	38	3	3	4	11	29	0	82	11	1	4	6	.400	0	0	4.07
1998 Chston-SC	A TB	12	12	0	0	75.1	316	72	41	32	1	3	2	5	21	0	59	10	1	4	3	.571	0	0	3.82
St. Pete	A+ TB	17	17	1	0	95.2	433	107	70	59	10	2	5	6	41	0	64	12	0	4	8	.333	0	0	5.55
1999 St. Pete	A+ TB	21	20	2	0	113	498	125	75	65	6	2	6	8	33	0	92	10	1	9	7	.563	0	0	5.18
2000 Orlando	AA TB	20	20	2	0	120	505	94	56	50	10	2	5	15	58	0	98	7	1	7	6	.538	0	0	3.75
Durham	AAA TB	6	6	0	0	35	153	36	14	11	1	0	0	3	16	1	28	3	0	3	2	.600	0	0	2.83
4 Min. YEARS		91	90	5	0	523	2274	512	300	255	31	12	20	48	198	1	423	53	4	31	32	.492	0	0	4.39

Walt White

Bats: Right **Throws:** Right **Pos:** 2B-64; PH-8; SS-5; 3B-3; PR-2 **Ht:** 6'0" **Wt:** 195 **Born:** 12/12/71 **Age:** 29

Year Team	Lg Org	G	AB	H	2B	3B	HR	TB	R	RBI	TBB	IBB	SO	HBP	SH	SF	SB	CS	SB%	GDP	Avg	OBP	SLG
1994 Elmira	A- Fla	70	215	57	7	0	0	64	41	19	27	0	45	4	2	1	0	2	.00	4	.265	.356	.298
1995 Kane County	A Fla	63	207	59	18	2	1	84	30	23	32	0	52	3	5	3	3	2	.60	3	.285	.384	.406
1996 Kane County	A Fla	95	308	54	15	3	1	78	26	24	35	0	90	4	5	1	1	4	.20	3	.175	.267	.253
1997 Brevard Cty	A+ Fla	54	163	33	8	0	1	44	18	15	14	1	41	1	0	0	0	0	—	4	.202	.268	.270
1998 Brevard Cty	A+ Fla	13	39	6	0	0	0	6	6	4	7	0	9	0	1	0	0	2	.00	2	.154	.283	.154
Portland	AA Fla	70	203	55	9	2	6	86	23	25	16	0	53	4	2	2	1	1	.50	5	.271	.333	.424
1999 El Paso	AA Ari	13	50	6	3	0	0	9	4	1	2	0	13	0	0	0	0	0	—	1	.120	.154	.180
Tucson	AAA Ari	54	153	31	8	1	3	50	18	13	14	1	39	0	1	1	0	0	—	6	.203	.268	.327
2000 Tucson	AAA Ari	23	55	15	4	0	1	22	4	10	5	1	10	0	2	0	1	0	1.00	1	.273	.333	.400
El Paso	AA Ari	53	158	45	9	1	1	59	20	19	15	1	37	3	4	1	3	2	.60	3	.285	.356	.373
7 Min. YEARS		508	1551	361	81	9	14	502	190	153	167	4	389	19	21	10	9	13	.41	32	.233	.313	.324

Braxton Whitehead

Bats: Right **Throws:** Right **Pos:** C-80; DH-5; 1B-3; PH-3; 3B-1 **Ht:** 6'2" **Wt:** 215 **Born:** 10/20/75 **Age:** 25

Year Team	Lg Org	G	AB	H	2B	3B	HR	TB	R	RBI	TBB	IBB	SO	HBP	SH	SF	SB	CS	SB%	GDP	Avg	OBP	SLG
1997 Burlington	A Cin	36	123	23	6	0	0	29	11	13	9	0	27	1	1	1	2	2	.50	5	.187	.246	.236
1998 Chston-WV	A Cin	116	408	101	24	0	4	137	33	48	32	1	79	6	0	5	6	5	.55	4	.248	.308	.336
1999 Clinton	A Cin	82	272	81	19	0	3	109	41	38	30	1	42	5	0	1	0	0	—	7	.298	.377	.401
2000 Chattanooga	AA Cin	5	19	7	2	0	1	12	5	5	2	0	6	0	0	0	0	0	—	0	.368	.429	.632
Dayton	A Cin	83	287	88	23	1	6	131	37	48	26	2	56	5	0	5	1	0	1.00	10	.307	.368	.456
4 Min. YEARS		322	1109	300	74	1	14	418	127	152	99	4	210	17	1	12	9	7	.56	26	.271	.336	.377

Shad Whiteley

Pitches: Right **Bats:** Right **Pos:** RP-40; SP-1 **Ht:** 6'6" **Wt:** 220 **Born:** 3/19/75 **Age:** 26

Year Team	Lg Org	G	GS	CG	GF	IP	BFP	H	R	ER	HR	SH	SF	HB	TBB	IBB	SO	WP	Bk	W	L	Pct.	ShO	Sv	ERA
1998 Oneonta	A- NYY	14	14	1	0	81	335	53	30	22	0	3	1	5	39	0	85	6	5	8	2	.800	0	0	2.44
1999 Greensboro	A NYY	15	8	0	1	55.1	276	67	52	47	7	1	0	6	42	0	62	5	4	1	9	.100	0	0	7.64
Staten Ilnd	A- NYY	12	12	0	0	61.2	279	69	39	34	1	1	3	2	26	0	71	9	0	3	4	.429	0	0	4.96
2000 Norwich	AA NYY	8	0	0	6	14	71	14	11	11	2	0	0	2	15	1	6	3	0	0	0	—	0	0	7.07
Tampa	A+ NYY	33	1	0	11	57	245	42	21	13	1	4	1	3	30	2	62	3	0	2	0	1.000	0	1	2.05
3 Min. YEARS		82	35	1	18	269	1206	245	153	127	11	9	5	18	152	3	286	23	9	14	15	.483	0	1	4.25

Curtis Whitley

Pitches: Left **Bats:** Left **Pos:** RP-28; SP-1 **Ht:** 6'4" **Wt:** 240 **Born:** 1/9/74 **Age:** 27

Year Team	Lg Org	G	GS	CG	GF	IP	BFP	H	R	ER	HR	SH	SF	HB	TBB	IBB	SO	WP	Bk	W	L	Pct.	ShO	Sv	ERA
1997 White Sox	R CWS	3	0	0	1	4.1	21	7	4	3	0	0	0	0	2	0	6	0	0	1	1	.500	0	0	6.23
Hickory	A CWS	9	0	0	6	12.1	58	11	7	5	1	0	0	1	5	0	8	2	0	1	0	1.000	0	0	3.65
1998 Hickory	A CWS	22	17	1	1	112.1	498	111	70	52	7	6	5	3	58	0	87	7	0	4	8	.333	1	1	4.17
Winston-Sal	A+ CWS	10	0	0	1	14.1	61	11	2	1	0	0	0	1	6	0	21	1	0	0	1	.000	0	0	0.63
1999 Winston-Sal	A+ CWS	9	0	0	3	8	34	9	4	4	3	0	1	0	4	0	8	0	0	0	0	—	0	2	4.50
Birmingham	AA CWS	36	0	0	14	50.1	228	58	31	28	4	1	1	0	25	0	24	5	0	4	2	.667	0	1	5.01
2000 Birmingham	AA CWS	29	1	0	11	31.1	144	37	21	20	2	1	1	2	19	2	19	3	0	1	1	.500	0	0	5.74
4 Min. YEARS		118	18	1	37	233	1044	244	139	113	17	8	8	7	119	2	173	18	0	10	14	.417	1	4	4.36

Brian Whitlock

Bats: Right **Throws:** Right **Pos:** SS-25; 3B-8; 2B-7; PR-7; OF-5; PH-5; DH-2; P-2; C-1 **Ht:** 6'1" **Wt:** 180 **Born:** 9/16/74 **Age:** 26

Year Team	Lg Org	G	AB	H	2B	3B	HR	TB	R	RBI	TBB	IBB	SO	HBP	SH	SF	SB	CS	SB%	GDP	Avg	OBP	SLG
1996 Watertown	A- Cle	47	152	33	5	2	3	51	23	14	23	0	49	3	2	1	2	0	1.00	5	.217	.330	.336
1997 Columbus	A Cle	92	327	86	14	7	11	147	56	41	28	0	92	6	6	2	5	4	.56	5	.263	.331	.450
1998 Akron	AA Cle	9	26	2	1	0	0	3	1	2	1	0	11	0	0	1	0	0	—	0	.077	.107	.115
Kinston	A+ Cle	73	198	42	9	3	5	72	24	30	24	0	74	2	5	0	4	1	.80	7	.212	.304	.364
1999 Kinston	A+ Cle	13	32	8	1	0	0	9	3	3	1	0	10	1	0	0	0	2	.00	0	.250	.286	.281
2000 Kinston	A+ Cle	24	68	12	2	0	1	17	5	4	5	0	25	0	0	0	2	0	1.00	0	.176	.233	.250
Akron	AA Cle	33	68	10	2	0	1	15	9	6	8	0	33	0	1	1	1	1	.50	1	.147	.234	.221
5 Min. YEARS		291	871	193	34	12	21	314	121	100	90	0	294	12	14	6	14	8	.64	13	.222	.301	.361

Darrell Whitmore

Bats: Left **Throws:** Right **Pos:** OF-53; PH-24; DH-14 **Ht:** 6'1" **Wt:** 210 **Born:** 11/18/68 **Age:** 32

Year Team	Lg Org	G	AB	H	2B	3B	HR	TB	R	RBI	TBB	IBB	SO	HBP	SH	SF	SB	CS	SB%	GDP	Avg	OBP	SLG
1990 Burlington	R+ Cle	30	112	27	3	2	0	34	18	13	9	0	30	2	0	1	9	5	.64	0	.241	.306	.304
1991 Watertown	A- Cle	6	19	7	2	1	0	11	2	3	3	0	2	0	0	0	0	0	—	0	.368	.455	.579
1992 Kinston	A+ Cle	121	443	124	22	2	10	180	71	52	56	5	92	5	0	5	17	9	.65	8	.280	.363	.406
1993 Edmonton	AAA Fla	73	273	97	24	2	9	152	52	62	22	0	53	0	0	3	11	8	.58	12	.355	.399	.557
1994 Edmonton	AAA Fla	115	421	119	24	5	20	213	72	61	41	3	76	2	0	3	14	3	.82	12	.283	.347	.506
1996 Charlotte	AAA Fla	55	204	62	13	0	11	108	27	36	7	2	43	1	0	2	5	5	.29	2	.304	.327	.529
1997 Syracuse	AAA Tor	58	195	50	15	0	4	77	23	21	24	3	54	1	0	2	7	4	.64	4	.256	.338	.395
Carolina	AA Pit	2	9	3	2	0	0	5	1	2	0	0	2	0	0	0	0	0	—	0	.333	.333	.556
1998 Nashville	AAA Pit	105	311	96	19	1	21	180	58	50	36	1	87	6	0	2	3	4	.43	3	.309	.389	.579
1999 Indianapols	AAA Cin	83	238	67	17	1	10	116	39	42	24	2	64	3	0	3	2	1	.67	8	.282	.351	.487
2000 Memphis	AAA StL	89	256	72	14	2	10	120	36	34	13	0	64	1	0	2	4	2	.67	3	.281	.316	.469
1993 Florida	NL	76	250	51	8	2	4	75	24	19	10	0	72	5	2	0	4	2	.67	8	.204	.249	.300
1994 Florida	NL	9	22	5	1	0	0	6	1	0	3	0	5	0	0	0	0	1	.00	0	.227	.320	.273
1995 Florida	NL	27	58	11	2	0	1	16	6	2	5	0	15	0	0	1	1	0	1.00	1	.190	.250	.276
10 Min. YEARS		737	2481	724	155	16	95	1196	399	376	235	16	567	21	0	23	69	41	.63	54	.292	.355	.482
3 Maj. YEARS		112	330	67	11	2	5	97	31	21	18	0	92	5	3	1	4	3	.57	9	.203	.254	.294

Ty Wigginton

Bats: Right **Throws:** Right **Pos:** 2B-68; 3B-53; PH-2; DH-1 **Ht:** 6'0" **Wt:** 200 **Born:** 10/11/77 **Age:** 23

Year Team	Lg Org	G	AB	H	2B	3B	HR	TB	R	RBI	TBB	IBB	SO	HBP	SH	SF	SB	CS	SB%	GDP	Avg	OBP	SLG
1998 Pittsfield	A- NYM	70	272	65	14	4	8	111	39	29	16	0	72	1	1	0	11	2	.85	4	.239	.284	.408
1999 St. Lucie	A+ NYM	123	456	133	23	5	21	229	69	73	56	4	92	4	2	7	9	12	.43	5	.292	.373	.502
2000 Binghamton	AA NYM	122	453	129	27	3	20	222	64	77	24	0	107	2	1	2	5	5	.50	4	.285	.319	.490
3 Min. YEARS		315	1181	327	64	12	49	562	172	179	96	4	261	7	6	9	25	19	.57	13	.277	.333	.476

Luke Wilcox

Bats: Left **Throws:** Right **Pos:** OF-119; DH-5 **Ht:** 6'4" **Wt:** 225 **Born:** 11/15/73 **Age:** 27

Year Team	Lg Org	G	AB	H	2B	3B	HR	TB	R	RBI	TBB	IBB	SO	HBP	SH	SF	SB	CS	SB%	GDP	Avg	OBP	SLG
1995 Oneonta	A- NYY	59	223	73	16	7	1	106	25	28	20	3	28	1	0	1	9	3	.75	0	.327	.382	.475
1996 Tampa	A+ NYY	119	470	133	32	5	11	208	72	76	40	1	71	3	4	6	14	10	.58	14	.283	.339	.443
1997 Tampa	A+ NYY	12	40	12	4	0	0	16	7	4	7	2	6	1	0	1	1	1	.50	0	.300	.408	.400
Norwich	AA NYY	74	300	83	13	1	6	116	45	34	18	1	36	3	1	1	13	3	.81	6	.277	.323	.387
1998 Norwich	AA TB	88	331	95	23	3	17	175	57	69	39	5	54	5	0	6	2	3	.40	6	.287	.365	.529
Durham	AAA TB	43	151	34	11	0	2	51	17	16	16	0	27	1	0	1	0	0	—	6	.225	.302	.338
1999 Orlando	AA TB	90	333	90	24	1	20	176	60	64	35	0	54	3	0	4	3	2	.60	9	.270	.341	.529
Durham	AAA TB	39	134	44	12	5	9	93	32	34	22	4	18	1	1	0	3	0	.25	2	.328	.427	.694

Year Team	Lg Org	G	AB	H	2B	3B	HR	TB	R	RBI	TBB	IBB	SO	HBP	SH	SF	SB	CS	SB%	GDP	Avg	OBP	SLG
2000 Columbus	AAA NYY	106	343	75	13	2	13	131	48	49	38	1	58	2	0	7	6	2	.75	7	.219	.295	.382
Norwich	AA NYY	18	70	19	7	0	2	32	10	18	10	1	10	0	0	2	2	2	.50	1	.271	.354	.457
6 Min. YEARS		648	2395	658	155	24	81	1104	373	393	245	18	362	20	6	30	51	29	.64	55	.275	.343	.461

Brad Wilkerson

Bats: Left **Throws:** Left **Pos:** OF-119; 1B-6; DH-5; PH-1   **Ht:** 6'0" **Wt:** 200 **Born:** 6/1/77 **Age:** 24

Year Team	Lg Org	G	AB	H	2B	3B	HR	TB	R	RBI	TBB	IBB	SO	HBP	SH	SF	SB	CS	SB%	GDP	Avg	OBP	SLG
1999 Harrisburg	AA Mon	138	422	99	21	3	8	150	66	49	88	3	100	7	1	5	3	5	.38	3	.235	.372	.355
2000 Harrisburg	AA Mon	66	229	77	36	2	6	135	53	44	42	1	38	4	1	3	8	4	.67	4	.336	.442	.590
Ottawa	AAA Mon	63	212	53	11	1	12	102	40	35	45	1	60	3	0	1	5	4	.56	0	.250	.387	.481
2 Min. YEARS		267	863	229	68	6	26	387	159	128	175	5	198	14	2	9	16	13	.55	7	.265	.394	.448

Jason Williams

Bats: Right **Throws:** Right **Pos:** 2B-113; PH-8; DH-2   **Ht:** 5'8" **Wt:** 185 **Born:** 12/18/73 **Age:** 27

Year Team	Lg Org	G	AB	H	2B	3B	HR	TB	R	RBI	TBB	IBB	SO	HBP	SH	SF	SB	CS	SB%	GDP	Avg	OBP	SLG
1997 Burlington	A Cin	68	256	83	17	1	7	123	49	41	21	0	40	5	6	3	9	6	.60	6	.324	.382	.480
Chattanooga	AA Cin	69	271	84	21	1	5	122	38	28	18	0	35	0	1	3	5	5	.50	7	.310	.349	.450
1998 Indianapolis	AAA Cin	119	406	108	25	1	2	141	60	45	70	2	63	6	5	7	5	2	.71	10	.266	.376	.347
1999 Chattanooga	AA Cin	87	332	106	27	2	7	158	65	45	46	2	40	6	1	4	3	4	.43	9	.319	.407	.476
Indianapolis	AAA Cin	40	160	61	18	2	2	89	30	19	14	1	25	5	1	1	4	1	.80	4	.381	.444	.556
2000 Louisville	AAA Cin	121	391	102	16	0	4	130	50	33	44	2	48	9	5	3	2	2	.50	15	.261	.347	.332
4 Min. YEARS		504	1816	544	124	7	27	763	292	211	213	7	251	31	19	21	28	20	.58	51	.300	.379	.420

Keith Williams

Bats: Right **Throws:** Right **Pos:** OF-79; PH-12; DH-6; PR-1   **Ht:** 6'0" **Wt:** 190 **Born:** 4/21/72 **Age:** 29

Year Team	Lg Org	G	AB	H	2B	3B	HR	TB	R	RBI	TBB	IBB	SO	HBP	SH	SF	SB	CS	SB%	GDP	Avg	OBP	SLG
1993 Everett	A- SF	75	288	87	21	5	12	154	57	49	48	4	73	3	2	0	21	7	.75	5	.302	.407	.535
1994 San Jose	A+ SF	128	504	151	30	8	21	260	91	97	60	2	102	4	0	8	4	3	.57	8	.300	.373	.516
1995 Shreveport	AA SF	75	275	84	20	1	9	133	39	55	23	3	39	0	0	1	5	3	.63	5	.305	.351	.484
Phoenix	AAA SF	24	83	25	4	1	2	37	7	14	5	0	11	1	4	2	0	0	—	4	.301	.341	.446
1996 Phoenix	AAA SF	108	398	109	25	3	13	179	63	63	52	4	96	0	1	5	2	2	.50	9	.274	.354	.450
1997 Phoenix	AAA SF	3	5	1	0	0	0	1	0	0	0	0	2	0	0	0	0	0	—	0	.200	.200	.200
Shreveport	AA SF	131	493	158	37	7	22	275	83	106	46	3	94	3	0	7	3	0	1.00	12	.320	.377	.558
1998 Fresno	AAA SF	113	353	103	23	2	19	187	47	68	18	1	74	2	1	4	0	1	.00	4	.292	.326	.530
1999 Fresno	AAA SF	89	294	83	23	3	11	145	46	50	34	1	50	2	2	3	4	2	.67	8	.282	.357	.493
2000 Fresno	AAA SF	60	184	40	5	1	5	62	29	23	22	1	52	0	0	1	1	1	.50	2	.217	.313	.337
Altoona	AA Pit	36	121	31	5	0	3	45	14	17	16	1	29	0	0	1	3	1	.75	6	.256	.341	.372
1996 San Francisco	NL	9	20	5	0	0	0	5	0	0	0	0	6	0	0	0	0	0	—	0	.250	.250	.250
8 Min. YEARS		842	2998	872	193	31	117	1478	476	542	324	20	622	19	10	38	43	20	.68	63	.291	.360	.493

Shad Williams

Pitches: Right **Bats:** Right **Pos:** RP-17; SP-5   **Ht:** 6'0" **Wt:** 198 **Born:** 3/10/71 **Age:** 30

Year Team	Lg Org	G	GS	CG	GF	IP	BFP	H	R	ER	HR	SH	SF	HB	TBB	IBB	SO	WP	Bk	W	L	Pct.	ShO	Sv	ERA
1992 Quad City	A Ana	27	26	7	0	179.1	748	161	81	65	14	6	6	7	55	0	152	9	1	13	11	.542	0	0	3.26
1993 Midland	AA Ana	27	27	2	0	175.2	758	192	100	92	16	6	6	3	65	1	91	9	1	7	10	.412	0	0	4.71
1994 Midland	AA Ana	5	5	1	0	32.1	112	13	4	4	1	0	0	1	4	0	29	2	0	3	0	1.000	1	0	1.11
Vancouver	AAA Ana	16	16	1	0	86	386	100	61	44	14	3	2	3	30	0	42	6	0	4	6	.400	1	0	4.60
1995 Vancouver	AAA Ana	25	25	3	0	149.2	627	142	65	56	16	3	3	4	48	2	114	7	1	9	7	.563	1	0	3.37
1996 Vancouver	AAA Ana	15	13	1	1	75	321	73	36	33	8	4	0	2	28	0	57	2	0	6	2	.750	1	0	3.96
1997 Vancouver	AAA Ana	40	10	0	7	99	424	98	52	42	13	0	4	5	41	2	52	5	0	6	2	.750	0	0	3.82
1998 Columbus	AAA NYY	5	1	0	0	12	66	24	19	17	1	0	1	1	8	0	10	0	0	0	1	.000	0	0	12.75
Norwich	AA NYY	9	8	0	0	42	188	55	22	20	4	2	0	2	11	0	18	2	0	4	2	.667	0	0	4.29
Vancouver	AAA Ana	14	10	1	1	68	281	80	30	24	9	2	0	1	18	0	29	2	1	1	4	.200	0	0	3.18
1999 Scranton-WB	AAA Phi	2	2	0	0	5	33	17	11	11	0	0	2	1	3	0	2	0	0	0	2	.000	0	0	19.80
Reading	AA Phi	16	2	0	5	31.2	133	30	17	11	3	3	2	1	10	0	19	1	0	2	2	.500	0	2	3.13
Edmonton	AAA Ana	16	11	1	1	75	303	73	36	31	9	1	3	1	19	0	35	2	0	5	3	.625	0	0	3.72
2000 Edmonton	AAA Ana	22	5	0	5	54	247	67	41	33	5	1	1	2	23	0	34	1	0	1	5	.167	0	1	5.50
1996 California	AL	13	2	0	3	28.1	150	42	34	28	7	3	1	2	21	4	26	2	0	0	2	.000	0	0	8.89
1997 Anaheim	AL	1	0	0	1	1	5	1	0	0	0	0	0	0	1	0	0	0	0	0	0	—	0	0	0.00
9 Min. YEARS		239	161	17	20	1084.2	4627	1110	575	483	113	31	30	33	363	5	684	48	4	61	57	.517	4	3	4.01
2 Maj. YEARS		14	2	0	4	29.1	155	43	34	28	7	3	1	2	22	4	26	2	0	0	2	.000	0	0	8.59

Todd Williams

Pitches: Right **Bats:** Right **Pos:** RP-50   **Ht:** 6'3" **Wt:** 210 **Born:** 2/13/71 **Age:** 30

Year Team	Lg Org	G	GS	CG	GF	IP	BFP	H	R	ER	HR	SH	SF	HB	TBB	IBB	SO	WP	Bk	W	L	Pct.	ShO	Sv	ERA
1991 Great Falls	R+ LA	28	0	0	14	53	232	50	26	16	1	0	1	1	24	1	59	4	1	5	2	.714	0	8	2.72
1992 Bakersfield	A+ LA	13	0	0	13	15.2	64	11	4	4	1	1	0	0	7	1	11	0	0	0	0	—	0	9	2.30
San Antonio	AA LA	39	0	0	34	44	196	47	17	16	0	4	1	4	23	6	35	3	0	7	4	.636	0	13	3.27
1993 Albuquerque	AAA LA	65	0	0	50	70.1	321	87	44	39	2	0	1	1	31	6	56	6	0	5	5	.500	0	21	4.99
1994 Albuquerque	AAA LA	59	0	0	36	72.1	427	78	29	25	5	1	3	6	17	3	30	6	1	4	2	.667	0	13	3.11
1995 Albuquerque	AAA LA	25	0	0	5	45.1	203	59	21	17	4	1	1	1	15	4	23	1	0	4	1	.800	0	0	3.38
1996 Edmonton	AAA Oak	35	10	0	7	91.2	427	125	71	56	4	2	5	3	37	3	33	3	0	5	3	.625	0	0	5.50
1997 Chattanooga	AA Cin	48	0	0	44	55.2	231	38	16	13	1	0	0	2	25	2	45	4	0	3	3	.500	0	31	2.10
Indianapolis	AAA Cin	12	0	0	5	12.2	54	11	4	3	0	1	0	1	6	1	11	2	0	2	0	1.000	0	2	2.13

Year Team	Lg Org	G	GS	CG	GF	IP	BFP	H	R	ER	HR	SH	SF	HB	TBB	IBB	SO	WP	Bk	W	L	Pct.	ShO	Sv	ERA
1998 Indianapols	AAA Cin	53	0	0	45	58.1	243	54	19	15	0	2	2	3	24	2	35	5	1	0	3	.000	0	26	2.31
1999 Indianapols	AAA Cin	38	0	0	33	42.1	174	38	24	24	3	2	2	5	13	0	35	0	1	1	3	.250	0	24	5.10
Tacoma	AAA Sea	1	0	0	1	1.2	5	1	0	0	0	0	0	0	0	0	0	0	0	0	0	—	0	1	0.00
2000 Tacoma	AAA Sea	50	0	0	46	51.1	213	51	20	17	2	3	2	0	18	1	26	0	0	2	3	.400	0	32	2.98
1995 Los Angeles	NL	16	0	0	5	19.1	83	19	11	11	3	3	1	0	7	2	8	0	0	2	2	.500	0	0	5.12
1998 Cincinnati	NL	6	0	0	2	9.1	50	15	8	8	1	0	0	0	6	4	0	0	0	0	1	.000	0	0	7.71
1999 Seattle	AL	13	0	0	7	9.2	47	11	5	5	1	1	0	1	7	0	7	0	0	0	0	—	0	0	4.66
10 Min. YEARS		466	10	0	333	614.1	2662	650	295	245	23	17	17	24	240	30	399	43	5	38	29	.567	0	180	3.59
3 Maj. YEARS		35	0	0	14	38.1	180	45	24	24	5	4	1	1	20	2	19	0	0	2	3	.400	0	0	5.63

Dave Willis

Bats: Right **Throws:** Right **Pos:** 1B-82; PH-8; DH-2; P-1   **Ht:** 6'5" **Wt:** 240 **Born:** 7/18/74 **Age:** 26

Year Team	Lg Org	G	AB	H	2B	3B	HR	TB	R	RBI	TBB	IBB	SO	HBP	SH	SF	SB	CS	SB%	GDP	Avg	OBP	SLG
1997 Spokane	A- KC	65	252	72	15	3	5	108	36	36	11	1	54	5	3	1	5	2	.71	3	.286	.327	.429
1998 Lansing	A KC	97	374	105	30	5	9	172	56	50	17	0	69	2	0	4	9	2	.82	8	.281	.312	.460
1999 Wilmington	A+ KC	116	441	115	26	1	16	191	58	72	20	0	84	7	0	7	4	4	.50	10	.261	.299	.433
2000 Wichita	AA KC	87	302	66	17	2	7	108	37	37	24	1	55	5	3	4	8	7	.53	10	.219	.284	.358
4 Min. YEARS		365	1369	358	88	11	37	579	187	195	72	2	262	19	6	16	26	15	.63	31	.262	.304	.423

Craig Wilson

Bats: Right **Throws:** Right **Pos:** C-71; 1B-30; PH-14; DH-12   **Ht:** 6'2" **Wt:** 217 **Born:** 11/30/76 **Age:** 24

Year Team	Lg Org	G	AB	H	2B	3B	HR	TB	R	RBI	TBB	IBB	SO	HBP	SH	SF	SB	CS	SB%	GDP	Avg	OBP	SLG
1995 Medcine Hat	R+ Tor	49	184	52	14	1	7	89	33	35	24	1	41	3	0	4	8	2	.80	1	.283	.367	.484
1996 Hagerstown	A Tor	131	495	129	27	5	11	199	66	70	32	1	120	10	0	4	17	11	.61	12	.261	.316	.402
1997 Lynchburg	A+ Pit	117	401	106	26	1	19	191	54	69	39	6	98	15	1	2	6	5	.55	3	.264	.350	.476
1998 Lynchburg	A+ Pit	61	219	59	12	2	12	111	26	45	22	1	53	5	0	1	2	1	.67	3	.269	.348	.507
Carolina	AA Pit	45	148	49	11	0	5	75	20	21	14	0	32	4	0	2	4	1	.80	2	.331	.399	.507
1999 Altoona	AA Pit	111	362	97	21	3	20	184	57	69	40	0	104	19	1	4	1	3	.25	8	.268	.367	.508
2000 Nashville	AAA Pit	124	396	112	24	2	33	239	83	86	44	2	121	25	0	7	1	2	.33	7	.283	.383	.604
6 Min. YEARS		638	2205	604	135	14	107	1088	339	395	215	11	569	81	2	24	39	25	.61	36	.274	.356	.493

Desi Wilson

Bats: Left **Throws:** Left **Pos:** OF-61; DH-38; 1B-26; PH-3   **Ht:** 6'7" **Wt:** 230 **Born:** 5/9/69 **Age:** 32

Year Team	Lg Org	G	AB	H	2B	3B	HR	TB	R	RBI	TBB	IBB	SO	HBP	SH	SF	SB	CS	SB%	GDP	Avg	OBP	SLG
1991 Rangers	R Tex	8	25	4	2	0	0	6	1	7	3	0	2	0	0	1	0	0	—	0	.160	.241	.240
1992 Butte	R+ Tex	72	253	81	9	4	5	113	45	42	31	1	45	1	0	0	13	11	.54	1	.320	.396	.447
1993 Charlotte	A+ Tex	131	511	156	21	7	3	200	83	70	50	4	90	7	0	2	29	11	.73	18	.305	.374	.391
1994 Tulsa	AA Tex	129	493	142	27	0	6	187	69	55	40	5	115	2	0	1	16	14	.53	14	.288	.343	.379
1995 Shreveport	AA SF	122	482	138	27	3	5	186	77	72	40	2	68	1	0	7	11	9	.55	18	.286	.338	.386
1996 Phoenix	AAA SF	113	407	138	26	7	5	193	56	59	18	3	80	3	0	3	15	4	.79	9	.339	.369	.474
1997 Phoenix	AAA SF	121	451	155	27	6	7	215	76	53	44	5	73	4	0	3	16	3	.84	11	.344	.404	.477
1999 Tucson	AAA Ari	130	452	146	27	7	6	205	65	62	34	2	76	2	0	3	2	3	.40	18	.323	.371	.454
2000 Charlotte	AAA CWS	124	439	118	23	1	3	152	58	55	51	2	79	4	0	2	17	4	.81	11	.269	.349	.346
1996 San Francisco	NL	41	118	32	2	0	2	40	10	12	12	2	27	0	0	0	3	2	.00	2	.271	.338	.339
9 Min. YEARS		950	3513	1078	189	35	40	1457	509	475	311	24	628	24	0	22	119	59	.67	100	.307	.365	.415

Jack Wilson

Bats: Right **Throws:** Right **Pos:** SS-134   **Ht:** 6'0" **Wt:** 170 **Born:** 12/29/77 **Age:** 23

Year Team	Lg Org	G	AB	H	2B	3B	HR	TB	R	RBI	TBB	IBB	SO	HBP	SH	SF	SB	CS	SB%	GDP	Avg	OBP	SLG
1998 Johnson Cty	R+ StL	61	241	90	18	4	4	128	50	29	18	0	30	3	1	0	22	6	.79	4	.373	.424	.531
1999 Peoria	A StL	64	251	86	22	4	3	125	47	28	15	0	23	2	3	0	11	5	.69	2	.343	.384	.498
Potomac	A+ StL	64	257	76	10	1	2	94	44	18	19	1	31	1	3	1	7	4	.64	2	.296	.345	.366
2000 Potomac	A+ StL	13	47	13	0	1	2	21	7	7	5	0	10	0	1	1	2	3	.40	1	.277	.340	.447
Arkansas	AA StL	88	343	101	20	8	6	155	65	34	36	0	59	5	5	2	2	3	.40	5	.294	.368	.452
Altoona	AA Pit	33	139	35	7	2	1	49	17	16	14	1	17	2	2	1	1	3	.25	3	.252	.325	.353
3 Min. YEARS		323	1278	401	77	20	18	572	230	132	107	2	170	13	15	6	45	24	.65	17	.314	.371	.448

Jeff Wilson

Pitches: Left **Bats:** Right **Pos:** SP-21; RP-9   **Ht:** 6'2" **Wt:** 180 **Born:** 5/30/76 **Age:** 25

Year Team	Lg Org	G	GS	CG	GF	IP	BFP	H	R	ER	HR	SH	SF	HB	TBB	IBB	SO	WP	Bk	W	L	Pct.	ShO	Sv	ERA
1997 Lethbridge	R+ Ari	22	0	0	9	36.1	157	35	22	18	4	2	1	0	12	0	49	5	0	1	1	.500	0	0	4.46
1998 High Desert	A+ Ari	12	0	0	4	20.2	96	28	14	12	1	1	0	0	8	0	18	0	0	2	0	1.000	0	0	5.23
South Bend	A Ari	12	4	0	6	38.2	163	34	17	11	0	2	1	1	13	2	30	6	1	1	5	.167	0	0	2.56
1999 High Desert	A+ Ari	32	17	0	2	110.0	494	106	66	53	12	2	4	3	67	2	122	8	2	7	4	.636	0	1	4.31
2000 Bowie	AA Bal	19	18	2	0	111	464	101	51	41	6	2	3	3	38	0	79	3	0	6	7	.462	0	0	3.32
Rochester	AAA Bal	11	3	0	1	35	157	26	16	15	1	0	3	2	29	0	25	1	1	2	2	.500	0	0	3.86
4 Min. YEARS		108	42	2	22	352.1	1531	330	186	150	24	9	12	9	167	4	323	23	4	19	19	.500	0	1	3.83

Tom Wilson

Bats: Right **Throws:** Right **Pos:** C-81; DH-13; OF-6; 1B-5; PH-5   **Ht:** 6'3" **Wt:** 210 **Born:** 12/19/70 **Age:** 30

Year Team	Lg Org	G	AB	H	2B	3B	HR	TB	R	RBI	TBB	IBB	SO	HBP	SH	SF	SB	CS	SB%	GDP	Avg	OBP	SLG
1991 Oneonta	A- NYY	70	243	59	12	2	4	87	38	42	34	2	71	3	0	5	4	4	.50	6	.243	.337	.358
1992 Greensboro	A NYY	117	395	83	22	0	6	123	50	48	68	0	128	3	1	8	2	1	.67	8	.210	.325	.311
1993 Greensboro	A NYY	120	394	98	20	1	10	150	55	63	91	0	112	4	3	8	2	5	.29	5	.249	.388	.381
1994 Albany-Col	AA NYY	123	408	100	20	1	7	143	54	42	58	2	100	6	4	4	4	6	.40	6	.245	.345	.350
1995 Columbus	AAA NYY	22	62	16	3	1	0	21	11	9	9	0	10	0	2	0	0	0	—	0	.258	.352	.339
Tampa	A+ NYY	17	48	8	0	0	0	8	3	2	11	0	13	0	1	1	1	0	1.00	0	.167	.317	.167
Norwich	AA NYY	28	84	12	4	0	0	16	6	4	17	0	22	0	0	0	0	0	—	3	.143	.287	.190
1996 Columbus	AAA NYY	1	1	0	0	0	0	0	0	0	1	0	0	0	0	0	0	0	—	0	.000	.500	.000
Buffalo	AAA Cle	72	208	56	14	2	9	101	28	30	35	0	66	6	1	0	0	1	.00	4	.269	.390	.486
1997 Columbus	AAA NYY	1	3	0	0	0	0	0	0	0	1	0	0	0	0	0	0	0	—	0	.000	.250	.000
Norwich	AA NYY	124	419	124	21	4	21	216	88	80	86	0	126	4	0	5	1	4	.20	8	.296	.416	.516
1998 Tucson	AAA Ari	111	370	112	17	3	12	171	59	54	41	3	81	7	0	3	3	1	.75	10	.303	.380	.462
1999 Orlando	AA TB	30	104	30	2	0	7	53	12	23	18	0	34	3	0	1	0	0	—	2	.288	.405	.510
Durham	AAA TB	67	215	60	19	0	16	127	41	44	49	1	59	0	0	1	1	0	2	.00	9	.279	.411	.591
2000 Columbus	AAA NYY	104	330	91	20	0	20	171	63	71	73	1	114	3	0	1	2	2	.50	9	.276	.410	.518
10 Min. YEARS		1007	3284	849	174	14	112	1387	508	512	580	9	936	39	13	37	19	26	.42	70	.259	.374	.422

Larry Wimberly

Pitches: Left **Bats:** Left **Pos:** RP-22; SP-12   **Ht:** 6'0" **Wt:** 190 **Born:** 8/22/75 **Age:** 25

Year Team	Lg Org	G	GS	CG	GF	IP	BFP	H	R	ER	HR	SH	SF	HB	TBB	IBB	SO	WP	Bk	W	L	Pct.	ShO	Sv	ERA
1994 Martinsvlle	R+ Phi	13	13	0	0	69.2	281	55	24	20	6	2	2	3	25	0	67	5	1	3	2	.600	0	0	2.58
1995 Piedmont	A Phi	24	24	0	0	135	542	99	48	40	9	1	3	9	44	0	139	8	4	10	3	.769	0	0	2.67
1996 Sarasota	A+ Bos	6	6	0	0	30	142	38	26	23	2	1	2	2	16	1	16	1	0	2	4	.333	0	0	6.90
Michigan	A Bos	14	14	2	0	66.1	272	58	27	21	5	1	3	4	24	1	41	1	2	3	4	.429	1	0	2.85
1997 Red Sox	R Bos	1	0	0	0	3	10	2	1	1	0	0	0	1	0	0	1	0	0	1	0	1.000	0	0	3.00
Michigan	A Bos	13	4	0	4	31.1	138	34	25	24	4	0	0	2	9	0	27	3	0	1	3	.250	0	0	6.89
1998 Clearwater	A+ Phi	14	10	0	1	72	293	77	30	29	4	0	4	3	12	0	66	0	0	7	2	.778	0	0	3.63
1999 Hickory	A Pit	17	5	0	3	47.2	182	32	8	8	2	2	1	1	11	3	57	3	0	3	1	.750	0	0	1.51
Lynchburg	A+ Pit	11	10	0	0	55.1	257	77	40	31	5	2	0	5	13	0	41	2	1	5	3	.625	0	0	5.04
2000 Altoona	AA Pit	10	2	0	0	21	104	29	22	16	4	0	1	2	11	0	25	2	0	4	1	.800	0	0	6.86
Lynchburg	A+ Pit	24	10	0	6	96	370	82	23	20	9	4	1	3	16	0	90	3	0	12	2	.857	0	0	1.88
7 Min. YEARS		147	98	2	18	627.1	2591	583	274	233	50	13	17	35	181	5	570	28	8	51	25	.671	1	1	3.34

Joe Winkelsas

Pitches: Right **Bats:** Right **Pos:** RP-4   **Ht:** 6'3" **Wt:** 188 **Born:** 9/14/73 **Age:** 27

Year Team	Lg Org	G	GS	CG	GF	IP	BFP	H	R	ER	HR	SH	SF	HB	TBB	IBB	SO	WP	Bk	W	L	Pct.	ShO	Sv	ERA
1996 Danville	R+ Atl	8	0	0	6	11.1	54	11	10	9	0	0	0	4	4	0	9	2	0	1	1	.500	0	2	7.15
1997 Macon	A Atl	38	0	0	15	62.2	242	44	17	14	1	3	0	4	13	0	45	4	2	3	2	.600	0	5	2.01
Durham	A+ Atl	13	0	0	8	19	93	24	18	15	0	5	2	4	11	1	17	1	0	1	4	.200	0	1	7.11
1998 Danville	A+ Atl	50	0	0	36	69	298	66	26	17	3	7	0	3	24	8	53	0	0	6	9	.400	0	22	2.22
Greenville	AA Atl	4	0	0	0	4.1	20	3	2	2	0	0	0	0	4	0	3	0	0	0	0	—	0	0	4.15
1999 Greenville	AA Atl	55	0	0	40	62.1	280	71	32	26	5	2	0	2	30	6	38	3	1	4	4	.500	0	12	3.75
2000 Richmond	AAA Atl	4	0	0	1	5	33	12	9	8	1	2	0	1	6	1	5	2	1	0	1	.000	0	0	14.40
1999 Atlanta	NL	1	0	0	0	0.1	6	4	2	2	0	1	0	1	1	1	0	0	0	0	0	—	0	0	54.00
5 Min. YEARS		172	0	0	106	233.2	1020	231	114	91	10	19	2	18	91	17	166	10	3	15	21	.417	0	42	3.50

Kevin Witt

Bats: Left **Throws:** Right **Pos:** 1B-109; DH-21; OF-6; PH-1; PR-1   **Ht:** 6'4" **Wt:** 200 **Born:** 1/5/76 **Age:** 25

Year Team	Lg Org	G	AB	H	2B	3B	HR	TB	R	RBI	TBB	IBB	SO	HBP	SH	SF	SB	CS	SB%	GDP	Avg	OBP	SLG
1994 Medcine Hat	R+ Tor	60	243	62	10	4	7	101	37	36	15	0	52	1	1	1	4	1	.80	3	.255	.300	.416
1995 Hagerstown	A Tor	119	479	111	35	1	14	190	58	50	28	2	148	4	3	0	1	5	.17	5	.232	.280	.397
1996 Dunedin	A+ Tor	124	446	121	18	6	13	190	63	70	39	3	96	6	2	5	9	4	.69	9	.271	.335	.426
1997 Knoxville	AA Tor	127	501	145	27	4	30	270	76	91	44	7	109	3	1	2	1	0	1.00	13	.289	.349	.539
1998 Syracuse	AAA Tor	126	455	124	20	3	23	219	71	67	53	6	124	7	1	5	3	3	.50	5	.273	.354	.481
1999 Syracuse	AAA Tor	114	421	117	24	3	24	219	72	74	64	10	109	3	2	2	0	0	—	11	.278	.376	.520
2000 Syracuse	AAA Tor	135	489	121	24	5	26	233	58	72	45	6	132	4	1	0	1	1	.50	9	.247	.316	.476
1998 Toronto	AL	5	7	1	0	0	0	1	0	0	0	0	3	0	0	0	0	0	—	0	.143	.143	.143
1999 Toronto	AL	15	34	7	1	0	1	11	3	5	2	0	9	0	1	0	0	0	—	0	.206	.250	.324
7 Min. YEARS		805	3034	801	158	26	137	1422	435	457	288	34	770	28	11	15	19	14	.58	55	.264	.332	.469
2 Maj. YEARS		20	41	8	1	0	1	12	3	5	2	0	12	0	1	0	0	0	—	0	.195	.233	.293

Steve Wojciechowski

Pitches: Left **Bats:** Left **Pos:** RP-19; SP-14   **Ht:** 6'2" **Wt:** 195 **Born:** 7/29/70 **Age:** 30

Year Team	Lg Org	G	GS	CG	GF	IP	BFP	H	R	ER	HR	SH	SF	HB	TBB	IBB	SO	WP	Bk	W	L	Pct.	ShO	Sv	ERA
1991 Sou Oregon	A- Oak	16	11	0	1	67	311	74	45	28	4	4	2	1	29	2	50	6	1	2	5	.286	0	0	3.76
1992 Modesto	A+ Oak	14	14	0	0	66.1	282	60	32	26	2	2	3	1	27	0	53	6	2	6	3	.667	0	0	3.53
1993 Modesto	A+ Oak	14	14	1	0	84.2	341	64	29	24	3	3	2	0	36	0	52	1	1	8	2	.800	1	0	2.55
Huntsville	AA Oak	13	13	1	0	67.2	310	91	50	40	6	1	5	2	30	1	52	5	1	4	6	.400	1	0	5.32
1994 Huntsville	AA Oak	27	26	1	1	177	716	148	72	61	7	7	3	0	62	1	114	10	2	10	5	.667	0	0	3.10
1995 Edmonton	AAA Oak	14	12	2	1	78	320	75	37	32	5	1	4	1	21	0	39	4	2	3	3	.667	1	0	3.69
1996 Edmonton	AAA Oak	11	11	1	0	60.1	257	56	32	25	3	2	2	2	21	1	46	4	0	4	3	.571	0	0	3.73
1997 Edmonton	AAA Oak	26	7	0	3	65.2	268	68	33	28	6	1	1	2	23	1	49	2	1	8	2	.800	0	1	3.84
1998 Twins	R Min	2	0	0	0	3.2	13	2	0	0	0	0	0	0	0	0	7	0	0	0	0	—	0	0	0.00
Salt Lake	AAA Min	9	1	0	1	11	52	13	10	8	0	0	1	0	7	0	6	1	0	0	2	.000	0	0	6.55

		HOW MUCH HE PITCHED				WHAT HE GAVE UP						THE RESULTS				
Year Team	Lg Org	G GS CG GF	IP	BFP	H R ER	HR SH SF HB	TBB IBB	SO WP	Bk	W L	Pct.	ShO	Sv	ERA
1999 Sonoma Cty	IND —	10 10 0 0	63.1	271	61 42 31	6 4 1 2	25 0	55 3	0	6 3	.667	0	0	4.41
2000 Fresno	AAA SF	13 8 0 4	44	213	66 38 33	5 2 1 0	23 0	37 3	0	0 4	.000	0	0	6.75
Calgary	AAA Fla	20 6 0 3	47.1	219	64 36 30	10 1 2 0	16 1	27 2	0	2 2	.500	0	1	5.70
1995 Oakland	AL	14 7 0 3	48.2	219	51 28 28	7 1 2 1	28 1	13 0	0	2 3	.400	0	0	5.18
1996 Oakland	AL	16 15 0 0	79.2	356	97 57 50	10 1 2 2	28 0	30 3	1	5 5	.500	0	0	5.65
1997 Oakland	AL	2 2 0 0	10.1	46	17 9 9	2 1 0 0	1 0	5 0	0	0 2	.000	0	0	7.84
10 Min. YEARS		189 133 6 14	836	3591	842 456 366	57 28 27 11	320 7	587 46	10	56 40	.583	4	2	3.94
3 Maj. YEARS		32 24 0 3	138.2	621	165 94 87	19 3 4 3	57 1	48 3	1	7 10	.412	0	0	5.65

Bryan Wolff

Pitches: Right **Bats:** Right **Pos:** SP-18; RP-2   **Ht:** 6'1" **Wt:** 195 **Born:** 3/16/72 **Age:** 29

		HOW MUCH HE PITCHED				WHAT HE GAVE UP						THE RESULTS				
Year Team	Lg Org	G GS CG GF	IP	BFP	H R ER	HR SH SF HB	TBB IBB	SO WP	Bk	W L	Pct.	ShO	Sv	ERA
1993 Spokane	A- SD	25 8 0 7	57	269	52 50 35	4 4 1 5	44 0	48 10	2	3 9	.250	0	1	5.53
1994 Springfield	A SD	60 0 0 47	63.2	298	46 43 38	3 7 1 0	58 4	99 11	4	3 8	.273	0	24	5.37
1995 Rancho Cuca	A+ SD	54 0 0 43	57	262	39 23 21	4 4 3 3	54 0	77 15	0	2 7	.222	0	18	3.32
1996 Wilmington	A+ KC	42 0 0 28	62.1	280	49 35 25	2 3 1 3	38 1	56 6	0	1 2	.333	0	4	3.61
1997 Wichita	AA KC	12 0 0 8	9.2	50	18 7 7	2 1 1 1	5 1	8 1	0	1 1	.500	0	1	6.52
Rancho Cuca	A+ SD	9 2 0 3	33.1	125	19 6 6	2 0 1 0	3 0	39 2	1	3 0	1.000	0	1	1.62
Mobile	AA SD	20 0 0 5	30	141	34 18 16	6 0 0 3	19 1	37 4	1	1 2	.333	0	0	4.80
1998 Las Vegas	AAA SD	9 0 0 5	10.2	50	14 8 8	5 2 1 0	5 0	8 0	0	0 0	—	0	1	6.75
Mobile	AA SD	33 14 3 7	133.2	527	90 40 34	7 5 2 4	43 2	134 4	1	9 3	.750	2	0	2.29
1999 Las Vegas	AAA SD	28 27 2 0	177.2	770	199 99 92	22 10 6 8	57 0	151 8	1	8 12	.400	0	0	4.66
2000 New Orleans	AAA Hou	11 11 1 0	62	268	63 38 34	6 3 1 3	26 0	46 4	1	2 3	.400	1	0	4.94
Salt Lake	AAA Min	9 7 0 1	51.2	227	53 33 32	8 1 3 1	19 0	43 4	0	4 1	.800	0	0	5.57
8 Min. YEARS		312 69 6 154	748.2	3267	676 400 348	71 40 20 31	374 9	746 69	11	37 48	.435	3	50	4.18

Jason Wood

Bats: Right **Throws:** Right **Pos:** 3B-36; SS-33; 2B-18; PH-6; 1B-2; DH-2   **Ht:** 6'1" **Wt:** 200 **Born:** 12/16/69 **Age:** 31

		BATTING															BASERUNNING				PERCENTAGES		
Year Team	Lg Org	G	AB	H	2B	3B	HR	TB	R	RBI	TBB	IBB	SO	HBP	SH	SF	SB	CS	SB%	GDP	Avg	OBP	SLG
1991 Sou Oregon	A- Oak	44	142	44	3	4	3	64	30	23	28	0	30	2	2	3	5	2	.71	0	.310	.423	.451
1992 Modesto	A+ Oak	128	454	105	28	3	6	157	66	49	40	1	106	4	3	5	5	4	.56	15	.231	.296	.346
1993 Huntsville	AA Oak	103	370	85	21	2	3	119	44	36	33	0	97	2	9	3	2	4	.33	7	.230	.294	.322
1994 Huntsville	AA Oak	134	468	128	29	2	6	179	54	84	44	1	83	6	5	15	3	6	.33	9	.274	.336	.382
1995 Edmonton	AAA Oak	127	421	99	20	5	2	135	49	50	29	3	72	3	4	6	1	4	.20	13	.235	.282	.321
1996 Huntsville	AA Oak	133	491	128	21	1	20	211	77	84	72	2	87	5	2	11	2	5	.29	14	.261	.354	.430
Edmonton	AAA Oak	3	12	0	0	0	0	0	0	0	5	0	6	0	0	0	0	1	.00	0	.000	.294	.000
1997 Edmonton	AAA Oak	130	505	162	35	7	19	268	83	87	45	0	74	8	2	4	2	4	.33	21	.321	.383	.531
1998 Edmonton	AAA Oak	80	307	86	20	0	18	160	52	73	37	1	71	2	0	6	1	1	.50	5	.280	.355	.521
Toledo	AAA Det	46	169	47	9	0	7	77	24	29	16	1	30	1	0	1	0	0	—	5	.278	.342	.456
1999 Lakeland	A+ Det	5	17	4	0	0	0	4	0	1	4	1	2	1	0	0	0	1	.00	0	.235	.409	.235
Toledo	AAA Det	48	185	53	11	0	6	82	34	24	22	0	43	1	0	2	0	2	.00	6	.286	.362	.443
2000 Nashville	AAA Pit	88	316	75	18	0	7	114	40	45	28	0	84	1	2	4	2	2	.50	7	.237	.298	.361
1998 Oakland	AL	3	1	0	0	0	0	0	1	0	0	0	1	0	0	0	0	0	—	0	.000	.000	.000
Detroit	AL	10	23	8	2	0	1	13	5	1	3	0	4	0	0	0	0	1	.00	0	.348	.423	.565
1999 Detroit	AL	27	44	7	1	0	1	11	5	8	2	0	13	0	1	0	0	0	—	0	.159	.196	.250
10 Min. YEARS		1069	3857	1016	215	24	97	1570	553	585	405	10	785	36	31	66	23	36	.39	102	.263	.334	.407
2 Maj. YEARS		40	68	15	3	0	2	24	11	9	5	0	18	0	1	0	0	1	.00	0	.221	.274	.353

Stanton Wood

Pitches: Right **Bats:** Right **Pos:** SP-17; RP-5   **Ht:** 6'2" **Wt:** 185 **Born:** 12/5/76 **Age:** 24

		HOW MUCH HE PITCHED				WHAT HE GAVE UP						THE RESULTS				
Year Team	Lg Org	G GS CG GF	IP	BFP	H R ER	HR SH SF HB	TBB IBB	SO WP	Bk	W L	Pct.	ShO	Sv	ERA
1997 Yankees	R NYY	17 0 0 14	25.2	99	18 7 7	3 0 1 0	7 0	21 1	0	2 0	1.000	0	8	2.45
1998 Oneonta	A- NYY	7 0 0 1	13.1	49	7 3 0	1 0 1 0	3 0	14 1	0	0 0	—	0	1	0.00
Greensboro	A NYY	31 2 0 14	64.2	269	57 29 28	13 2 1 0	20 3	67 1	0	5 2	.714	0	1	3.90
1999 Tampa	A+ NYY	50 0 0 19	81.2	355	89 43 34	2 3 2 2	23 3	66 4	0	4 1	.800	0	0	3.75
2000 Norwich	AA NYY	1 0 0 1	2	8	2 1 1	0 0 0 0	0 0	2 0	0	0 0	—	0	0	4.50
Solano	IND —	21 17 2 1	107.1	491	137 87 75	19 2 2 9	37 0	77 5	3	8 6	.571	0	0	6.29
4 Min. YEARS		127 19 2 50	294.2	1271	310 170 145	38 7 7 11	90 6	247 12	3	19 9	.679	0	10	4.43

Hank Woodman

Pitches: Right **Bats:** Both **Pos:** RP-38; SP-4   **Ht:** 6'1" **Wt:** 185 **Born:** 11/16/72 **Age:** 28

		HOW MUCH HE PITCHED				WHAT HE GAVE UP						THE RESULTS				
Year Team	Lg Org	G GS CG GF	IP	BFP	H R ER	HR SH SF HB	TBB IBB	SO WP	Bk	W L	Pct.	ShO	Sv	ERA
1993 Twins	R Min	13 0 0 8	26.1	117	14 7 4	0 2 0 2	23 0	19 3	0	0 1	.000	0	0	1.37
1998 Springfield	IND —	12 11 1 0	69.2	317	71 56 38	8 2 4 4	41 1	64 6	0	5 5	.500	0	0	4.91
1999 Richmond	IND —	5 5 1 0	38.1	161	34 12 7	0 1 0 1	18 0	37 0	0	1 3	.250	0	0	1.64
Charlotte	A+ Tex	6 6 2 0	30.2	137	33 19 14	1 0 2 1	14 0	19 1	0	2 2	.500	0	0	4.11
Tulsa	AA Tex	6 6 0 0	29.2	133	27 24 18	4 0 0 1	19 0	25 0	0	0 4	.000	0	0	5.46
2000 Tulsa	AA Tex	42 4 0 20	91.1	439	130 69 58	12 3 6 5	40 1	60 4	0	5 6	.455	0	8	5.72
4 Min. YEARS		84 32 4 28	286	1304	309 187 139	25 8 12 12	155 2	224 14	0	13 21	.382	0	8	4.37

Ken Woods

Bats: Right **Throws:** Right **Pos:** OF-128; PH-6 **Ht:** 5'10" **Wt:** 175 **Born:** 8/2/70 **Age:** 30

Year Team	Lg Org	G	AB	H	2B	3B	HR	TB	R	RBI	TBB	IBB	SO	HBP	SH	SF	SB	CS	SB%	GDP	Avg	OBP	SLG
1992 Everett	A- SF	64	257	65	9	1	0	76	50	31	35	1	46	7	1	0	20	17	.54	2	.253	.358	.296
1993 Clinton	A SF	108	320	90	10	1	4	114	56	44	41	1	55	4	7	2	30	5	.86	13	.281	.368	.356
1994 San Jose	A+ SF	90	336	100	18	3	6	142	58	49	45	0	43	4	3	3	15	7	.68	9	.298	.384	.423
1995 Shreveport	AA SF	89	209	53	11	0	3	73	30	23	23	2	29	1	2	1	4	5	.44	4	.254	.329	.349
1996 Shreveport	AA SF	83	287	80	17	1	1	102	36	29	29	0	35	4	4	6	14	10	.58	11	.279	.347	.355
Phoenix	AAA SF	56	208	58	12	1	2	78	32	13	19	0	29	1	0	3	3	4	.43	6	.279	.338	.375
1997 Phoenix	AAA SF	1	1	1	0	0	0	1	0	1	0	0	0	0	0	0	0	0	—	0	1.000	1.000	1.000
Shreveport	AA SF	104	293	88	14	2	2	112	41	32	28	0	40	3	4	3	6	4	.60	6	.300	.364	.382
1998 Shreveport	AA SF	94	335	103	20	2	4	139	44	33	28	1	31	2	1	3	8	9	.47	8	.307	.361	.415
Fresno	AAA SF	23	44	16	5	0	0	21	9	5	2	1	8	1	1	0	0	0	—	1	.364	.404	.477
1999 Fresno	AAA SF	124	469	152	23	4	6	201	77	73	33	0	45	3	2	9	19	4	.83	8	.324	.366	.429
2000 Scranton-WB	AAA Phi	133	512	155	28	6	2	201	89	35	39	0	47	5	8	1	20	7	.74	7	.303	.357	.393
9 Min. YEARS		969	3271	961	167	21	30	1260	522	368	322	6	408	35	32	31	139	72	.66	75	.294	.360	.385

Jay Woolf

Bats: Right **Throws:** Right **Pos:** SS-49; OF-15; 3B-9; PH-4; PR-3; DH-2 **Ht:** 6'1" **Wt:** 170 **Born:** 6/6/77 **Age:** 24

Year Team	Lg Org	G	AB	H	2B	3B	HR	TB	R	RBI	TBB	IBB	SO	HBP	SH	SF	SB	CS	SB%	GDP	Avg	OBP	SLG
1995 Johnson Cty	R+ StL	31	111	31	7	1	0	40	16	14	8	0	21	1	1	3	6	3	.67	0	.279	.325	.360
1996 Peoria	A StL	108	362	93	12	8	1	124	68	27	57	1	87	2	3	1	28	12	.70	3	.257	.360	.343
1997 Pr William	A+ StL	70	251	62	11	3	6	97	59	18	55	1	75	5	1	1	26	5	.84	0	.247	.391	.386
1998 Arkansas	AA StL	76	294	78	22	5	4	122	63	16	34	0	84	9	2	1	28	5	.85	2	.265	.358	.415
1999 Arkansas	AA StL	86	320	87	18	4	8	137	46	15	28	0	86	8	6	1	11	3	.79	5	.272	.345	.428
2000 Memphis	AAA StL	32	103	25	5	1	0	32	21	6	19	0	23	2	0	0	5	3	.63	1	.243	.371	.311
Arkansas	AA StL	45	165	39	8	2	3	60	22	13	16	3	40	4	1	0	7	8	.47	2	.236	.319	.364
6 Min. YEARS		448	1606	415	83	24	22	612	295	109	217	5	416	31	14	7	111	39	.74	11	.258	.356	.381

Greg Wooten

Pitches: Right **Bats:** Right **Pos:** SP-26 **Ht:** 6'7" **Wt:** 210 **Born:** 3/30/74 **Age:** 27

Year Team	Lg Org	G	GS	CG	GF	IP	BFP	H	R	ER	HR	SH	SF	HB	TBB	IBB	SO	WP	Bk	W	L	Pct.	ShO	Sv	ERA
1996 Wisconsin	A Sea	13	13	3	0	83.2	336	58	27	23	3	1	2	5	29	0	68	4	1	7	1	.875	1	0	2.47
Lancaster	A+ Sea	14	14	1	0	97	408	101	47	41	7	1	2	3	25	1	71	9	0	8	4	.667	0	0	3.80
1997 Memphis	AA Sea	26	26	0	0	155	681	166	91	77	14	5	5	6	59	1	98	12	0	11	10	.524	0	0	4.47
1998 Lancaster	A+ Sea	6	6	0	0	31.1	144	43	26	25	5	0	2	1	12	0	22	2	0	2	2	.500	0	0	7.18
1999 Lancaster	A+ Sea	17	17	3	0	114.1	489	123	62	55	13	2	3	6	30	1	72	5	0	10	4	.714	0	0	4.33
2000 New Haven	AA Sea	26	26	6	0	179.1	702	166	50	46	9	2	3	7	15	1	115	5	0	17	3	.850	4	0	2.31
5 Min. YEARS		102	102	13	0	660.2	2760	657	303	267	51	11	17	28	170	4	446	37	1	55	24	.696	5	0	3.64

Corey Wright

Bats: Left **Throws:** Left **Pos:** OF-115; PH-1 **Ht:** 5'11" **Wt:** 165 **Born:** 11/26/79 **Age:** 21

Year Team	Lg Org	G	AB	H	2B	3B	HR	TB	R	RBI	TBB	IBB	SO	HBP	SH	SF	SB	CS	SB%	GDP	Avg	OBP	SLG
1997 Rangers	R Tex	43	145	36	2	3	0	44	19	11	22	0	25	1	3	0	14	11	.56	1	.248	.351	.303
1998 Rangers	R Tex	11	44	12	2	1	0	16	6	3	7	0	11	0	0	0	3	2	.60	0	.273	.373	.364
Pulaski	R+ Tex	39	133	37	4	3	3	56	41	26	45	0	23	1	0	2	14	4	.78	2	.278	.459	.421
1999 Savannah	A Tex	95	316	83	15	5	1	111	61	23	64	1	73	5	1	1	13	13	.50	2	.263	.394	.351
2000 Tulsa	AA Tex	17	69	13	0	0	0	13	6	3	5	0	20	1	1	0	1	1	.50	1	.188	.253	.188
Charlotte	A+ Tex	99	370	94	17	5	0	121	76	24	79	4	81	10	3	2	31	11	.74	6	.254	.397	.327
4 Min. YEARS		304	1077	275	40	17	4	361	209	90	222	5	233	18	8	5	76	42	.64	12	.255	.390	.335

Danny Wright

Pitches: Right **Bats:** Right **Pos:** SP-28 **Ht:** 6'5" **Wt:** 225 **Born:** 12/14/77 **Age:** 23

Year Team	Lg Org	G	GS	CG	GF	IP	BFP	H	R	ER	HR	SH	SF	HB	TBB	IBB	SO	WP	Bk	W	L	Pct.	ShO	Sv	ERA
1999 Bristol	R+ CWS	10	0	0	3	18	79	14	8	2	1	0	0	1	9	1	18	3	0	2	0	1.000	0	1	1.00
Burlington	A CWS	2	0	0	0	6	26	5	4	4	1	0	0	1	3	0	3	0	0	0	0	—	0	0	6.00
2000 Winston-Sal	A+ CWS	21	21	1	0	132.1	577	135	64	55	4	4	5	10	50	0	106	18	2	9	8	.529	0	0	3.74
Birmingham	AA CWS	7	7	0	0	43.1	175	28	15	12	3	0	0	1	24	0	31	3	0	2	4	.333	0	0	2.49
2 Min. YEARS		40	28	1	3	199.2	857	182	91	73	9	4	5	13	86	1	158	24	2	13	12	.520	0	1	3.29

Ron Wright

Bats: Right **Throws:** Right **Pos:** 1B-70; DH-15; PH-13; PR-1 **Ht:** 6'1" **Wt:** 230 **Born:** 1/21/76 **Age:** 25

Year Team	Lg Org	G	AB	H	2B	3B	HR	TB	R	RBI	TBB	IBB	SO	HBP	SH	SF	SB	CS	SB%	GDP	Avg	OBP	SLG
1994 Braves	R Atl	45	169	29	9	0	1	41	10	16	10	0	21	0	0	0	1	0	1.00	6	.172	.218	.243
1995 Macon	A Atl	135	527	143	23	1	32	264	93	104	62	1	118	2	0	3	2	0	1.00	11	.271	.348	.501
1996 Durham	A+ Atl	66	240	66	15	2	20	145	47	62	37	2	71	0	0	7	1	0	1.00	5	.275	.363	.604
Greenville	AA Atl	63	232	59	11	1	16	120	39	52	38	5	73	2	0	4	1	0	1.00	4	.254	.360	.517
Carolina	AA Pit	4	14	2	0	0	0	2	1	0	2	0	7	0	0	0	0	1	.00	0	.143	.250	.143
1997 Calgary	AAA Pit	91	336	102	31	0	16	181	50	63	24	2	81	2	0	6	0	2	.00	4	.304	.348	.539
1998 Nashville	AAA Pit	17	56	12	3	0	0	15	6	9	9	0	18	1	0	1	0	0	—	2	.214	.328	.268
Pirates	R Pit	3	10	6	0	0	2	12	4	5	2	0	0	0	0	0	0	0	—	0	.600	.615	1.200
1999 Altoona	AA Pit	24	80	17	6	0	0	23	2	4	9	0	27	1	0	1	0	0	—	1	.213	.300	.288
2000 Louisville	AAA Cin	18	60	12	5	0	2	23	10	13	8	0	18	0	0	0	0	0	—	2	.200	.294	.383
Chattanooga	AA Cin	79	237	63	18	0	12	117	36	50	37	0	70	2	0	2	2	2	.50	3	.266	.367	.494
7 Min. YEARS		545	1961	511	121	4	101	943	298	378	238	10	504	10	0	23	7	5	.58	32	.261	.340	.481

L.J. Yankosky

Pitches: Right Bats: Right Pos: SP-24; RP-2   Ht: 6'2" Wt: 208 Born: 2/1/75 Age: 26

Year Team	Lg Org	G	GS	CG	GF	IP	BFP	H	R	ER	HR	SH	SF	HB	TBB	IBB	SO	WP	Bk	W	L	Pct.	ShO	Sv	ERA
1998 Macon	A Atl	20	2	0	11	47	192	33	22	15	3	2	0	1	18	1	37	2	0	4	1	.800	0	4	2.87
1999 Greenville	AA Atl	20	20	1	0	108.1	489	122	70	51	5	1	4	3	43	3	62	3	1	5	8	.385	0	0	4.24
2000 Greenville	AA Atl	26	24	1	0	140.2	589	139	57	54	7	5	3	11	42	1	100	4	0	10	8	.556	1	0	3.45
3 Min. YEARS		66	46	2	11	296	1270	294	149	120	15	8	7	15	103	5	199	9	1	19	17	.528	1	4	3.65

Tyler Yates

Pitches: Right Bats: Right Pos: RP-52   Ht: 6'4" Wt: 225 Born: 8/7/77 Age: 23

Year Team	Lg Org	G	GS	CG	GF	IP	BFP	H	R	ER	HR	SH	SF	HB	TBB	IBB	SO	WP	Bk	W	L	Pct.	ShO	Sv	ERA
1998 Athletics	R Oak	15	0	0	8	32.2	107	28	12	10	0	0	0	1	14	0	20	1	2	0	0	—	0	2	3.91
Sou Oregon	A- Oak	2	0	0	1	2.1	9	2	0	0	0	0	0	0	0	0	1	0	0	0	0	—	0	0	0.00
1999 Visalia	A+ Oak	47	1	0	19	82.1	382	98	64	50	12	3	2	4	35	3	74	12	0	2	5	.286	0	4	5.47
2000 Modesto	A+ Oak	30	0	0	5	56.2	237	50	23	18	2	1	1	1	23	4	61	8	0	4	2	.667	0	1	2.86
Midland	AA Oak	22	0	0	8	26.1	121	28	20	18	2	2	2	0	15	3	24	2	0	1	1	.500	0	0	6.15
3 Min. YEARS		116	1	0	41	190.2	856	206	119	96	16	6	5	6	87	10	180	23	2	7	8	.467	0	8	4.53

Jay Yennaco

Pitches: Right Bats: Right Pos: RP-60   Ht: 6'4" Wt: 238 Born: 11/17/75 Age: 25

Year Team	Lg Org	G	GS	CG	GF	IP	BFP	H	R	ER	HR	SH	SF	HB	TBB	IBB	SO	WP	Bk	W	L	Pct.	ShO	Sv	ERA
1996 Michigan	A Bos	28	28	4	0	169.2	763	195	112	87	13	2	7	6	68	0	117	20	1	10	10	.500	1	0	4.61
1997 Sarasota	A+ Bos	7	7	2	0	44.1	170	30	12	11	3	1	0	1	19	1	41	2	1	4	0	1.000	1	0	2.23
Trenton	AA Bos	21	21	0	0	122.1	557	146	89	86	8	3	10	8	54	0	73	5	0	5	11	.313	0	0	6.33
1998 Trenton	AA Bos	9	9	0	0	53.2	217	50	30	29	8	1	3	2	19	1	23	3	0	3	3	.500	0	0	4.86
Pawtucket	AAA Bos	11	11	1	0	60.1	266	77	43	39	6	1	1	0	16	1	34	5	0	3	2	.600	0	0	5.82
Syracuse	AAA Tor	7	6	1	0	38.2	174	55	27	23	4	1	1	3	10	2	27	0	0	0	3	.000	0	0	5.35
1999 Syracuse	AAA Tor	15	15	0	0	80	373	107	68	61	11	2	2	1	42	1	45	2	0	2	6	.250	0	0	6.86
Dunedin	A+ Tor	3	2	0	0	11	44	10	2	1	0	1	0	2	0	0	11	0	0	1	0	1.000	0	0	0.82
Knoxville	AA Tor	8	8	1	0	43.2	193	52	34	32	9	2	0	0	17	0	30	0	0	3	4	.429	0	0	6.60
2000 West Tenn	AA ChC	60	0	0	30	70.2	292	53	25	21	5	2	4	1	31	1	79	3	0	5	4	.556	0	10	2.67
5 Min. YEARS		169	107	9	30	694.1	3058	775	442	390	67	16	28	24	276	7	480	40	2	37	43	.463	2	10	5.06

Nate Yeskie

Pitches: Right Bats: Right Pos: RP-21; SP-7   Ht: 6'3" Wt: 201 Born: 8/13/74 Age: 26

Year Team	Lg Org	G	GS	CG	GF	IP	BFP	H	R	ER	HR	SH	SF	HB	TBB	IBB	SO	WP	Bk	W	L	Pct.	ShO	Sv	ERA
1996 Elizabethtn	R+ Min	7	6	0	0	32.2	141	38	27	19	3	0	0	0	8	0	28	2	0	3	3	.500	0	0	5.23
1997 Fort Wayne	A Min	27	27	2	0	165.1	718	190	99	89	12	3	3	5	41	1	111	7	3	11	7	.611	0	0	4.84
1998 Fort Myers	A+ Min	14	11	1	2	62.2	273	74	27	23	4	2	0	5	16	0	39	3	0	4	2	.667	0	0	3.30
New Britain	AA Min	1	1	0	0	1.2	10	4	3	3	0	0	0	0	2	0	1	0	0	0	0	—	0	0	16.20
1999 New Britain	AA Min	25	23	0	2	129.2	574	157	83	76	15	3	3	3	47	0	102	3	0	5	11	.313	0	0	5.28
2000 New Britain	AA Min	21	1	0	3	45	214	62	35	29	4	1	0	2	20	1	34	6	0	4	1	.800	0	0	5.80
Zion	IND —	7	6	0	0	39.2	181	44	20	19	2	1	0	3	21	1	33	0	0	3	2	.600	0	0	4.31
5 Min. YEARS		102	75	3	7	476.2	2111	569	294	258	40	10	6	18	155	3	348	21	3	30	26	.536	0	0	4.87

Jeff Yoder

Pitches: Right Bats: Left Pos: SP-5; RP-3   Ht: 6'2" Wt: 210 Born: 2/16/76 Age: 25

Year Team	Lg Org	G	GS	CG	GF	IP	BFP	H	R	ER	HR	SH	SF	HB	TBB	IBB	SO	WP	Bk	W	L	Pct.	ShO	Sv	ERA
1996 Rockford	A ChC	25	24	2	0	154.1	640	139	70	59	10	2	4	10	48	1	124	12	5	12	5	.706	0	0	3.44
1998 Daytona	A+ ChC	26	24	1	1	143	645	158	97	80	16	3	6	6	47	0	128	10	2	7	9	.438	0	0	5.03
1999 Daytona	A+ ChC	5	0	0	2	10.2	44	8	2	1	0	1	0	1	5	0	11	0	0	0	0	—	0	1	0.84
West Tenn	AA ChC	29	22	0	1	134.1	574	115	54	46	10	2	6	5	70	5	109	5	1	10	5	.667	0	0	3.08
2000 West Tenn	AA ChC	8	5	0	1	31.1	141	27	16	15	2	2		1	22	0	22	2	0	0	3	.000	0	0	4.31
4 Min. YEARS		93	75	3	5	473.2	2044	447	239	201	38	9	18	22	192	6	394	29	8	29	22	.569	0	1	3.82

Ernie Young

Bats: Right Throws: Right Pos: OF-112; DH-8; PH-6   Ht: 6'1" Wt: 234 Born: 7/8/69 Age: 31

Year Team	Lg Org	G	AB	H	2B	3B	HR	TB	R	RBI	TBB	IBB	SO	HBP	SH	SF	SB	CS	SB%	GDP	Avg	OBP	SLG
1990 Sou Oregon	A- Oak	50	168	47	6	2	6	75	34	23	28	2	53	3	0	2	4	4	.50	2	.280	.388	.446
1991 Madison	A Oak	114	362	92	19	2	15	160	75	71	58	0	115	9	9	6	20	9	.69	4	.254	.366	.442
1992 Modesto	A+ Oak	74	253	63	12	4	11	116	55	33	47	1	74	6	2	1	11	3	.79	5	.249	.378	.458
1993 Modesto	A+ Oak	85	301	92	18	6	23	191	83	71	72	0	92	4	0	3	23	7	.77	2	.306	.442	.635
Huntsville	AA Oak	45	120	25	5	0	5	45	26	15	24	0	36	2	2	0	8	5	.62	1	.208	.345	.375
1994 Tacoma	AAA Oak	29	102	29	4	0	6	51	19	16	13	0	27	2	0	2	0	5	.00	3	.284	.370	.500
Huntsville	AA Oak	72	257	89	19	4	14	158	45	55	37	2	45	2	2	4	5	6	.45	5	.346	.427	.615
1995 Edmonton	AAA Oak	95	347	96	21	4	15	170	70	72	49	1	73	3	1	7	2	2	.50	5	.277	.365	.490
1997 Edmonton	AAA Oak	54	165	63	10	0	9	100	39	45	37	1	46	6	1	2	5	2	.71	7	.323	.442	.513
1998 Omaha	AAA KC	79	297	97	13	1	22	178	58	55	29	2	68	5	0	1	6	4	.60	8	.327	.395	.599
1999 Tucson	AAA Ari	126	453	133	25	1	30	250	78	95	57	1	129	5	0	6	4	1	.80	9	.294	.374	.552
2000 Memphis	AAA StL	124	453	119	16	0	35	240	76	98	66	6	117	4	0	4	11	1	.92	17	.263	.359	.530
1994 Oakland	AL	11	30	2	1	0	0	3	2	3	1	0	8	0	0	0	0	0	—	1	.067	.097	.100
1995 Oakland	AL	26	50	10	3	0	2	19	9	5	8	0	12	0	0	0	0	0	—	1	.200	.310	.380
1996 Oakland	AL	141	462	112	19	4	19	196	72	64	52	1	118	7	3	4	7	5	.58	13	.242	.326	.424

Year Team	Lg Org	G	AB	H	2B	3B	HR	TB	R	RBI	TBB	IBB	SO	HBP	SH	SF	SB	CS	SB%	GDP	Avg	OBP	SLG
1997 Oakland	AL	71	175	39	7	0	5	61	22	15	19	0	57	2	2	2	1	3	.25	6	.223	.303	.349
1998 Kansas City	AL	25	53	10	3	0	1	16	2	3	2	0	9	1	0	0	2	1	.67	3	.189	.232	.302
1999 Arizona	NL	6	11	2	0	0	0	2	1	0	3	0	2	1	0	0	0	0	—	0	.182	.400	.182
10 Min. YEARS		947	3308	945	168	24	191	1734	658	649	517	16	875	51	17	40	99	49	.67	69	.286	.386	.524
6 Maj. YEARS		280	781	175	33	4	27	297	108	90	85	1	206	11	5	6	10	9	.53	24	.224	.307	.380

Travis Young

Bats: Right **Throws:** Right **Pos:** 2B-103; SS-2; 3B-2; DH-2; PH-2; 1B-1; PR-1 **Ht:** 6'1" **Wt:** 185 **Born:** 9/8/74 **Age:** 26

Year Team	Lg Org	G	AB	H	2B	3B	HR	TB	R	RBI	TBB	IBB	SO	HBP	SH	SF	SB	CS	SB%	GDP	Avg	OBP	SLG
1997 Salem-Keizr	A- SF	76	320	107	11	6	1	133	80	34	30	0	50	5	1	3	40	8	.83	3	.334	.397	.416
1998 San Jose	A+ SF	133	517	126	21	2	4	163	79	63	61	2	101	8	11	6	27	12	.69	14	.244	.329	.315
1999 Fresno	AAA SF	26	92	23	1	1	2	32	15	11	9	1	23	3	1	1	3	2	.60	1	.250	.333	.348
Shreveport	AA SF	108	416	110	28	2	5	157	68	38	33	0	75	8	7	2	16	11	.59	11	.264	.329	.377
2000 Fresno	AAA SF	13	32	5	0	0	0	5	2	0	3	0	8	0	2	0	0	0	—	1	.156	.229	.156
Shreveport	AA SF	97	334	83	14	4	6	123	41	31	25	0	65	7	2	4	14	7	.67	8	.249	.311	.368
4 Min. YEARS		453	1711	454	75	15	18	613	285	177	161	3	322	31	24	16	100	40	.71	38	.265	.337	.358

Mark Zamarripa

Pitches: Right **Bats:** Right **Pos:** RP-9; SP-8 **Ht:** 6'0" **Wt:** 175 **Born:** 7/28/74 **Age:** 26

	HOW MUCH HE PITCHED						WHAT HE GAVE UP									THE RESULTS				
Year Team	Lg Org	G	GS	CG	GF	IP	BFP	H	R	ER	HR	SH	SF	HB	TBB	IBB	SO	WP	Bk	W	L	Pct.	ShO	Sv	ERA
1995 Newark	IND —	7	2	0	1	20	98	24	22	17	0	1	0	1	13	0	16	2	1	2	1	.667	0	0	7.65
1996 Jamestown	A- Det	29	0	0	22	48.2	187	25	13	11	4	3	0	2	14	0	61	4	0	4	2	.667	0	4	2.03
1997 W Michigan	A Det	20	0	0	9	29.2	128	13	17	7	0	2	1	2	18	2	41	3	4	3	1	.750	0	2	2.12
Lakeland	A+ Det	11	0	0	8	12.1	59	16	12	11	0	0	0	0	11	0	9	1	0	2	1	.667	0	1	8.03
Tigers	R Det	4	0	0	1	8.1	35	6	6	6	2	0	0	0	6	0	11	2	1	0	0	—	0	1	6.48
1998 W Michigan	A Det	35	1	0	12	72.2	299	59	19	18	3	6	3	3	34	2	88	2	3	6	2	.750	0	1	2.23
1999 Columbus	A Cle	15	0	0	7	28.2	120	26	13	11	3	0	2	2	12	1	31	2	0	4	0	1.000	0	1	3.45
Schaumburg	IND —	5	5	1	0	39.1	161	26	9	8	2	2	0	2	26	1	25	3	0	2	0	1.000	0	0	1.83
Carolina	AA Col	5	4	0	0	20.1	93	20	11	10	0	0	0	2	14	0	12	1	2	2	1	.667	0	0	4.43
2000 High Desert	A+ Ari	5	4	0	1	21.2	85	13	7	7	0	1	2	1	13	0	23	1	2	1	1	.500	0	0	2.91
El Paso	AA Ari	12	4	0	2	39.1	179	40	30	19	6	2	1	5	25	1	22	1	3	1	3	.250	0	0	4.35
6 Min. YEARS		148	20	1	63	341	1444	268	159	125	20	16	10	19	186	7	339	22	14	27	12	.692	0	10	3.30

Carlos Zambrano

Pitches: Right **Bats:** Left **Pos:** RP-34; SP-9 **Ht:** 6'4" **Wt:** 220 **Born:** 6/1/81 **Age:** 20

	HOW MUCH HE PITCHED						WHAT HE GAVE UP									THE RESULTS				
Year Team	Lg Org	G	GS	CG	GF	IP	BFP	H	R	ER	HR	SH	SF	HB	TBB	IBB	SO	WP	Bk	W	L	Pct.	ShO	Sv	ERA
1998 Cubs	R ChC	14	2	0	4	40	177	39	17	14	0	0	0	0	25	3	36	3	1	0	1	.000	0	0	3.15
1999 Lansing	A ChC	27	24	2	2	153.1	663	150	87	71	9	5	4	10	62	1	98	10	2	13	7	.650	1	0	4.17
2000 West Tenn	AA ChC	9	9	0	0	60.1	241	39	14	9	2	1	0	3	21	0	43	4	0	3	1	.750	0	0	1.34
Iowa	AAA ChC	34	0	0	17	56.2	259	54	30	25	3	5	4	2	40	2	46	3	0	2	5	.286	0	6	3.97
3 Min. YEARS		84	35	2	23	310.1	1340	282	148	119	14	11	8	15	148	6	223	20	3	18	14	.563	1	7	3.45

Victor Zambrano

Pitches: Right **Bats:** Right **Pos:** RP-53 **Ht:** 6'0" **Wt:** 190 **Born:** 8/6/74 **Age:** 26

	HOW MUCH HE PITCHED						WHAT HE GAVE UP									THE RESULTS				
Year Team	Lg Org	G	GS	CG	GF	IP	BFP	H	R	ER	HR	SH	SF	HB	TBB	IBB	SO	WP	Bk	W	L	Pct.	ShO	Sv	ERA
1996 Devil Rays	R TB	1	0	0	0	3.1	16	4	4	3	0	0	0	0	0	0	6	0	0	0	0	—	0	0	8.10
1997 Devil Rays	R TB	2	0	0	0	3	10	1	0	0	0	0	0	0	0	0	2	0	0	0	0	—	0	0	0.00
Princeton	R+ TB	20	0	0	6	29.2	126	18	13	6	1	0	0	4	9	1	36	2	1	0	2	.000	0	0	1.82
1998 Chston-SC	A TB	48	2	0	15	77.1	330	72	32	29	5	5	0	12	20	1	89	7	1	6	4	.600	0	0	3.38
1999 St. Pete	A+ TB	7	0	0	1	9	43	10	6	4	1	0	1	1	5	0	15	1	0	0	2	.000	0	0	4.00
Orlando	AA TB	40	4	0	12	82.1	379	92	55	42	5	1	2	9	38	2	81	6	1	7	2	.778	0	1	4.59
2000 Durham	AAA TB	53	0	0	27	62.2	290	72	38	35	9	4	0	4	29	2	55	6	0	0	6	.000	0	8	5.03
5 Min. YEARS		171	6	0	61	267.1	1194	269	148	119	21	10	3	30	101	6	284	22	3	13	16	.448	0	9	4.01

Junior Zamora

Bats: Right **Throws:** Right **Pos:** 3B-36; SS-3; PH-1; PR-1 **Ht:** 6'2" **Wt:** 193 **Born:** 5/3/76 **Age:** 25

Year Team	Lg Org	G	AB	H	2B	3B	HR	TB	R	RBI	TBB	IBB	SO	HBP	SH	SF	SB	CS	SB%	GDP	Avg	OBP	SLG
1995 Mets	R NYM	20	56	13	2	2	0	19	9	4	5	0	10	1	1	1	0	0	—	2	.232	.302	.339
1996 Kingsport	R+ NYM	60	227	55	13	0	7	89	37	41	11	0	59	7	0	3	2	1	.67	3	.242	.294	.392
Capital Cty	A NYM	1	4	0	0	0	0	0	0	0	0	0	3	0	0	0	0	0	—	0	.000	.000	.000
1997 Capital Cty	A NYM	36	124	31	5	0	8	60	16	19	10	0	29	0	0	0	0	1	.00	2	.250	.306	.484
1998 Mets	R NYM	2	5	1	0	1	0	3	1	2	1	0	0	0	0	0	0	0	—	1	.200	.333	.600
St. Lucie	A+ NYM	99	368	105	17	4	10	160	58	53	25	1	60	5	0	0	4	3	.57	9	.285	.339	.435
1999 Binghamton	AA NYM	67	255	61	17	0	10	108	28	33	12	1	62	3	0	2	2	1	.67	13	.239	.279	.424
2000 Binghamton	AA NYM	40	130	21	3	0	4	36	14	11	9	0	29	2	0	0	3	1	.75	4	.162	.227	.277
6 Min. YEARS		325	1169	287	57	7	39	475	163	163	73	2	252	18	1	6	11	7	.61	34	.246	.299	.406

308

Pete Zamora

Pitches: Left **Bats:** Left **Pos:** RP-36; SP-7   **Ht:** 6'3" **Wt:** 185 **Born:** 8/13/75 **Age:** 25

Year Team	Lg Org	G	GS	CG	GF	IP	BFP	H	R	ER	HR	SH	SF	HB	TBB	IBB	SO	WP	Bk	W	L	Pct.	ShO	Sv	ERA
1997 Great Falls	R+ LA	13	10	1	2	69.2	289	59	27	20	3	1	1	3	30	0	73	3	1	2	5	.286	0	2	2.58
1998 San Berndno	A+ LA	25	5	0	15	81.2	321	43	21	19	1	5	1	4	33	0	77	3	2	4	1	.800	0	6	2.09
San Antonio	AA LA	12	12	0	0	66.2	299	71	52	33	6	4	3	1	27	0	47	1	1	3	8	.273	0	0	4.46
1999 San Antonio	AA LA	35	0	0	8	63.2	292	79	48	43	5	3	5	4	30	2	41	4	1	2	1	.667	0	3	6.08
2000 Reading	AA Phi	43	7	1	13	101.1	455	105	50	46	6	3	1	7	45	3	94	5	0	2	3	.400	1	6	4.09
4 Min. YEARS		128	34	2	38	383	1656	357	198	161	21	16	11	19	165	5	332	16	5	13	18	.419	1	17	3.78

Dave Zancanaro

Pitches: Left **Bats:** Left **Pos:** SP-20; RP-5   **Ht:** 6'1" **Wt:** 190 **Born:** 1/8/69 **Age:** 32

Year Team	Lg Org	G	GS	CG	GF	IP	BFP	H	R	ER	HR	SH	SF	HB	TBB	IBB	SO	WP	Bk	W	L	Pct.	ShO	Sv	ERA
1990 Sou Oregon	A- Oak	10	8	0	0	44.1	188	44	22	19	2	1	0	1	13	0	42	3	4	3	0	1.000	0	0	3.86
Modesto	A+ Oak	4	2	0	0	13	64	13	9	9	1	0	0	0	14	0	7	0	0	1	2	.333	0	0	6.23
1991 Huntsville	AA Oak	29	28	0	1	165	727	151	87	62	7	3	4	6	92	0	104	8	4	5	10	.333	0	0	3.38
1992 Tacoma	AAA Oak	23	19	0	0	105.2	486	108	61	50	3	5	7	2	75	0	47	7	2	2	11	.154	0	0	4.26
1995 W Michigan	A Oak	16	16	0	0	32.2	132	19	8	8	1	2	0	3	15	0	42	1	2	0	2	.000	0	0	2.20
1996 Modesto	A+ Oak	20	3	0	6	77.1	331	61	38	29	9	4	2	3	37	0	66	5	1	7	3	.700	0	3	3.38
Huntsville	AA Oak	10	10	0	0	43.1	206	54	32	27	4	0	1	2	26	1	36	3	0	3	3	.500	0	0	5.61
1997 Las Vegas	AAA SD	3	3	0	0	13.1	77	27	24	23	3	0	0	2	8	0	9	0	0	0	3	.000	0	0	15.53
Mobile	AA SD	27	19	3	3	133.2	581	140	69	66	15	5	3	4	57	0	66	10	1	10	8	.556	0	1	4.44
1998 Norwich	AA NYY	16	13	0	2	69	300	80	42	36	9	2	1	3	23	0	49	3	0	3	4	.429	0	0	4.70
1999 Norwich	AA NYY	15	11	1	1	79	327	64	25	20	4	5	1	2	32	1	61	2	0	6	1	.857	0	0	2.28
Columbus	AAA NYY	13	13	1	0	77.2	336	85	40	36	11	0	1	0	28	0	45	1	2	7	2	.778	0	0	4.17
2000 Iowa	AAA ChC	25	20	0	2	115.1	517	131	80	67	19	3	0	6	54	2	67	5	2	4	10	.286	0	0	5.23
9 Min. YEARS		211	165	5	15	969.1	4272	977	537	452	88	30	20	34	474	4	641	48	18	51	59	.464	0	4	4.20

Ryan Zeber

Bats: Right **Throws:** Right **Pos:** C-11; 3B-1; DH-1   **Ht:** 6'2" **Wt:** 190 **Born:** 5/24/78 **Age:** 23

Year Team	Lg Org	G	AB	H	2B	3B	HR	TB	R	RBI	TBB	IBB	SO	HBP	SH	SF	SB	CS	SB%	GDP	Avg	OBP	SLG
1997 Medcine Hat	R+ Tor	43	101	20	2	0	1	25	11	7	12	0	26	0	0	0	1	2	.33	2	.198	.283	.248
1998 Medcine Hat	R+ Tor	14	39	8	1	0	0	9	4	9	3	0	8	1	0	1	0	2	.00	2	.205	.273	.231
1999 Clinton	A Cin	2	2	0	0	0	0	0	0	0	1	0	0	0	0	0	0	0	—	0	.000	.333	.000
Reds	R Cin	3	6	1	0	0	0	1	1	0	0	0	0	0	0	0	0	0	—	0	.167	.167	.167
Rockford	A Cin	39	106	27	6	1	0	35	11	10	7	1	21	3	0	1	1	5	.17	3	.255	.316	.330
2000 Erie	AA Ana	1	4	1	0	0	0	1	0	1	0	0	0	0	0	0	0	0	—	0	.250	.250	.250
Lk Elsinore	A+ Ana	10	29	6	1	2	0	11	0	2	0	0	3	1	1	0	0	0	—	0	.207	.233	.379
Edmonton	AAA Ana	2	4	1	0	0	0	1	1	0	0	0	1	0	0	0	0	0	—	0	.250	.250	.250
4 Min. YEARS		114	291	64	10	3	1	83	28	29	24	1	59	5	1	2	2	9	.18	7	.220	.289	.285

Scott Zech

Bats: Right **Throws:** Right **Pos:** 3B-29; PH-27; 1B-22; OF-7; DH-7; 2B-5; PR-4; SS-3   **Ht:** 5'11" **Wt:** 175 **Born:** 6/6/74 **Age:** 27

Year Team	Lg Org	G	AB	H	2B	3B	HR	TB	R	RBI	TBB	IBB	SO	HBP	SH	SF	SB	CS	SB%	GDP	Avg	OBP	SLG
1997 Vermont	A- Mon	63	204	54	11	0	1	68	31	20	27	1	36	7	5	6	17	7	.71	4	.265	.361	.333
1998 Cape Fear	A Mon	102	304	87	20	2	3	120	53	45	43	0	48	13	9	4	13	8	.62	3	.286	.393	.395
1999 Cape Fear	A Mon	3	10	3	0	0	0	3	1	1	3	0	1	0	0	0	1	0	1.00	0	.300	.462	.300
Harrisburg	AA Mon	22	72	20	4	1	1	29	8	10	4	0	13	0	2	2	3	2	.60	0	.278	.308	.403
Jupiter	A+ Mon	68	203	57	13	0	1	73	28	18	29	0	30	5	10	3	15	5	.75	1	.281	.379	.360
2000 Jupiter	A+ Mon	2	3	0	0	0	0	0	1	0	2	0	0	0	0	0	0	0	—	0	.000	.400	.000
Harrisburg	AA Mon	87	178	35	5	1	0	42	28	18	37	1	31	3	6	1	6	3	.67	5	.197	.342	.236
4 Min. YEARS		347	974	256	53	4	6	335	150	112	145	2	159	28	32	16	55	25	.69	13	.263	.369	.344

Jordan Zimmerman

Pitches: Left **Bats:** Right **Pos:** RP-18; SP-10   **Ht:** 6'0" **Wt:** 200 **Born:** 4/28/75 **Age:** 26

Year Team	Lg Org	G	GS	CG	GF	IP	BFP	H	R	ER	HR	SH	SF	HB	TBB	IBB	SO	WP	Bk	W	L	Pct.	ShO	Sv	ERA
1997 Everett	A- Sea	11	9	0	1	39	177	37	27	18	2	0	3	3	23	0	54	1	2	2	3	.400	0	0	4.15
Wisconsin	A Sea	3	3	0	0	17	75	18	11	11	0	0	0	0	10	0	18	2	0	0	1	.000	0	0	5.82
1998 Mariners	R Sea	5	3	0	1	12	55	14	6	4	1	0	0	2	7	0	11	0	0	0	1	.000	0	0	3.00
Lancaster	A+ Sea	3	3	0	0	16.2	74	21	9	9	2	0	0	0	8	0	8	1	0	0	1	.000	0	0	4.86
1999 Everett	A- Sea	1	1	0	0	0.2	15	3	2	2	0	0	0	0	1	0	1	1	0	0	0	—	0	0	27.00
Tacoma	AAA Sea	9	0	0	2	7	35	13	4	4	1	0	0	0	4	1	4	1	0	0	0	—	0	0	5.14
New Haven	AA Sea	22	0	0	8	33.1	149	26	8	4	0	0	1	2	19	0	33	1	1	1	4	.200	0	2	1.08
2000 Mariners	R Sea	10	10	0	0	12	46	7	3	0	0	0	0	1	3	0	14	0	0	0	0	—	0	0	0.00
Lancaster	A+ Sea	3	0	0	1	3.1	13	0	0	0	0	1	0	0	2	0	2	0	0	0	0	—	0	0	0.00
Tacoma	AAA Sea	15	0	0	2	23	108	27	20	17	3	0	0	1	11	1	23	1	0	0	1	.000	0	0	6.65
1999 Seattle	AL	12	0	0	2	8	41	14	8	7	0	0	0	1	4	0	3	1	0	0	0	—	0	0	7.88
4 Min. YEARS		82	28	0	15	164	737	166	90	69	9	0	5	9	87	2	168	8	3	3	11	.214	0	2	3.79

Alan Zinter

Bats: Both **Throws:** Right **Pos:** 1B-47; C-19; PH-18; DH-15; OF-11; 3B-3   **Ht:** 6'2" **Wt:** 200 **Born:** 5/19/68 **Age:** 33

Year Team	Lg Org	G	AB	H	2B	3B	HR	TB	R	RBI	TBB	IBB	SO	HBP	SH	SF	SB	CS	SB%	GDP	Avg	OBP	SLG
1989 Pittsfield	A- NYM	12	41	15	2	1	2	25	11	12	12	0	4	0	0	1	0	1	.00	0	.366	.500	.610
St. Lucie	A+ NYM	48	159	38	10	0	3	57	17	32	18	2	31	1	1	5	0	1	.00	5	.239	.311	.358

Year Team	Lg Org	G	AB	H	2B	3B	HR	TB	R	RBI	TBB	IBB	SO	HBP	SH	SF	SB	CS	SB%	GDP	Avg	OBP	SLG
1990 St. Lucie	A+ NYM	98	333	97	19	6	7	149	63	63	54	1	70	1	0	6	8	1	.89	10	.291	.386	.447
Jackson	AA NYM	6	20	4	1	0	0	5	2	1	3	0	11	0	0	0	1	0	1.00	1	.200	.304	.250
1991 Williamsprt	AA NYM	124	422	93	13	6	9	145	44	54	59	1	106	3	2	2	3	3	.50	10	.220	.319	.344
1992 Binghamton	AA NYM	128	431	96	13	5	16	167	63	50	70	5	117	4	0	0	0	0	—	7	.223	.337	.387
1993 Binghamton	AA NYM	134	432	113	24	4	24	217	68	87	90	7	105	1	0	5	1	0	1.00	4	.262	.386	.502
1994 Toledo	AAA Det	134	471	112	29	5	21	214	66	58	69	4	185	7	0	0	13	5	.72	3	.238	.344	.454
1995 Toledo	AAA Det	101	334	74	15	4	13	136	42	48	36	1	102	2	2	5	4	1	.80	5	.222	.297	.407
1996 Pawtucket	AAA Bos	108	357	96	19	5	26	203	78	69	58	2	123	4	0	5	5	1	.83	3	.269	.373	.569
1997 Tacoma	AAA Sea	110	404	116	19	4	20	203	69	70	64	9	113	3	1	1	3	1	.75	7	.287	.388	.502
1998 Iowa	AAA ChC	129	419	130	23	1	23	224	82	81	75	1	116	3	0	3	3	5	.38	10	.310	.416	.535
1999 Iowa	AAA ChC	14	51	13	2	0	3	24	7	8	5	0	13	0	0	0	0	0	—	0	.255	.321	.471
2000 Iowa	AAA ChC	90	233	53	12	2	14	111	27	35	39	2	78	2	0	3	0	0	—	3	.227	.339	.476
Tucson	AAA Ari	11	36	13	5	1	1	23	9	5	8	1	8	0	0	0	0	0	—	1	.361	.477	.639
12 Min. YEARS		1247	4143	1063	206	44	182	1903	648	673	660	36	1182	31	6	36	41	19	.68	69	.257	.360	.459

Jon Zuber

Bats: Left **Throws:** Left **Pos:** 1B-58; DH-24; OF-4; PH-1   **Ht:** 6'0" **Wt:** 185 **Born:** 12/10/69 **Age:** 31

Year Team	Lg Org	G	AB	H	2B	3B	HR	TB	R	RBI	TBB	IBB	SO	HBP	SH	SF	SB	CS	SB%	GDP	Avg	OBP	SLG
1992 Batavia	A- Phi	22	88	30	6	3	1	45	14	21	9	1	11	1	0	1	1	1	.50	1	.341	.404	.511
Spartanburg	A Phi	54	206	59	13	1	3	83	24	36	33	1	31	1	0	1	3	1	.75	6	.286	.386	.403
1993 Clearwater	A+ Phi	129	494	152	37	5	5	214	70	69	49	5	47	0	3	4	6	6	.50	15	.308	.367	.433
1994 Reading	AA Phi	138	498	146	29	5	9	212	81	70	71	4	71	1	1	5	2	4	.33	11	.293	.379	.426
1995 Scranton-WB	AAA Phi	119	418	120	19	5	3	158	53	50	49	2	68	0	1	2	1	2	.33	12	.287	.360	.378
1996 Scranton-WB	AAA Phi	118	412	128	22	5	4	172	62	59	58	3	50	1	2	4	4	2	.67	15	.311	.394	.417
1997 Scranton-WB	AAA Phi	126	435	137	37	2	6	196	85	64	79	0	53	3	1	3	3	4	.43	11	.315	.421	.451
1998 Scranton-WB	AAA Phi	80	280	91	23	4	4	134	47	56	45	7	34	2	1	6	0	0	—	8	.325	.414	.479
1999 Scranton-WB	AAA Phi	111	387	114	24	2	6	160	69	54	86	6	48	1	0	4	7	1	.88	9	.295	.421	.413
2000 Columbus	AAA NYY	87	294	86	15	0	1	104	36	39	52	7	28	4	3	2	9	2	.82	8	.293	.403	.354
1996 Philadelphia	NL	30	91	23	4	0	1	30	7	10	6	1	11	0	1	1	1	0	1.00	3	.253	.296	.330
1998 Philadelphia	NL	38	45	11	3	1	2	22	6	6	6	0	9	1	0	0	0	0	—	1	.244	.346	.489
9 Min. YEARS		984	3512	1063	225	32	42	1478	541	518	531	36	441	14	12	32	36	23	.61	96	.303	.393	.421
2 Maj. YEARS		68	136	34	7	1	3	52	13	16	12	1	20	1	1	1	1	0	1.00	4	.250	.313	.382

Tony Zuniga

Bats: Right **Throws:** Right **Pos:** 3B-116; PH-8; 2B-4   **Ht:** 6'0" **Wt:** 185 **Born:** 1/13/75 **Age:** 26

Year Team	Lg Org	G	AB	H	2B	3B	HR	TB	R	RBI	TBB	IBB	SO	HBP	SH	SF	SB	CS	SB%	GDP	Avg	OBP	SLG
1996 Bellingham	A- SF	69	264	79	11	1	2	98	36	35	34	2	47	0	4	2	0	5	.00	2	.299	.377	.371
1997 San Jose	A+ SF	97	289	53	10	0	1	66	24	32	33	0	48	11	6	2	3	3	.50	11	.183	.290	.228
1998 San Jose	A+ SF	113	397	97	20	4	8	149	52	59	39	0	64	5	0	3	1	2	.33	7	.244	.318	.375
1999 San Jose	A+ SF	136	533	144	33	3	10	213	82	66	65	0	89	13	3	4	9	4	.69	8	.270	.361	.400
2000 Shreveport	AA SF	125	407	106	24	0	17	181	54	62	49	2	50	3	3	4	3	4	.43	12	.260	.341	.445
5 Min. YEARS		540	1890	479	98	8	38	707	248	254	220	4	298	32	16	15	16	18	.47	40	.253	.339	.374

Mike Zywica

Bats: Right **Throws:** Right **Pos:** OF-128; DH-2; PH-1; PR-1   **Ht:** 6'4" **Wt:** 190 **Born:** 9/14/74 **Age:** 26

Year Team	Lg Org	G	AB	H	2B	3B	HR	TB	R	RBI	TBB	IBB	SO	HBP	SH	SF	SB	CS	SB%	GDP	Avg	OBP	SLG
1996 Rangers	R Tex	33	110	30	7	1	3	48	18	22	14	1	24	8	0	0	3	0	1.00	1	.273	.394	.436
Chston-SC	A Tex	20	67	9	1	1	2	18	5	4	7	0	13	1	0	0	3	1	.75	2	.134	.227	.269
1997 Charlotte	A+ Tex	126	462	119	25	5	12	190	75	64	50	0	116	12	0	6	19	19	.50	10	.258	.342	.411
1998 Charlotte	A+ Tex	68	252	96	21	3	11	156	67	49	34	2	40	6	0	4	16	5	.76	4	.381	.459	.619
Tulsa	AA Tex	58	214	60	15	4	5	98	40	45	19	0	56	5	0	4	7	3	.70	3	.280	.347	.458
1999 Oklahoma	AAA Tex	135	495	131	31	3	9	195	80	79	33	0	119	7	1	7	4	1	.80	13	.265	.315	.394
2000 Tulsa	AA Tex	5	19	8	1	0	1	12	7	8	2	0	2	1	0	0	0	0	—	0	.421	.500	.632
Oklahoma	AAA Tex	126	420	110	25	4	9	170	57	58	46	0	123	5	3	4	8	7	.53	6	.262	.339	.405
5 Min. YEARS		571	2039	563	126	21	52	887	349	329	205	3	493	45	4	25	60	36	.63	39	.276	.351	.435

2000 Class-A and Rookie Statistics

Any player who appeared in Class-A or Rookie ball without reaching Double-A or Triple-A has his 2000 statistics in this section. Class-A (A+, A, A-) and Rookie (R+, R) have subclassifications to distinguish the level of competition. Ages are as of June 30, 2001. A complete list of statistical abbreviations can be found in the introduction to the Career Register section on page 2.

The handedness and position of each player is provided. An asterisk (*) identifies a lefthanded-hitting player or lefthanded pitcher. A player who switch-hits is noted with a pound sign (#).

A number of players in this section will be well-known prospects a year from now. In fact, Atlanta's Rafael Furcal went from these pages a year ago to major league starter last summer. Two lefthanded hurlers, San Diego's Kevin Walker and Mark Buehrle of the White Sox, also appeared in this section last year. Both rose from Class-A obscurity to make significant contributions to their clubs' bullpens. Players who are listed in the pages that follow and may emerge as top-flight prospects in 2001 include Cincinnati's Austin Kearns, Juan Cruz of the Cubs, Seattle's Antonio Perez and Olympic standout Jon Rauch of the White Sox.

Very few players reach Double-A or higher in their first pro season, so nearly all future major leaguers will be found in this section before reaching the majors. There are plenty of gems hidden away in these pages.

2000 Batting — Class-A and Rookie Leagues

BATTING																					BASERUNNING				PERCENTAGES		
Player	Pos	Team	Org	Lg	A	G	AB	H	2B	3B	HR	TB	R	RBI	TBB	IBB	SO	HBP	SH	SF	SB	CS	SB%	GDP	Avg	OBP	SLG
Aaron, Oginga	2b	St. Pete	TB	A+	21	1	1	0	0	0	0	0	0	0	0	0	0	0	0	0	0	0	.00	0	.000	.000	.000
		Princeton	TB	R+	21	42	144	34	2	1	0	38	23	6	13	0	33	3	2	0	5	5	.50	2	.236	.313	.264
Abad, Juan	c	Expos	Mon	R	20	29	101	15	1	0	0	16	9	4	3	0	32	2	0	0	1	0	1.00	4	.149	.189	.158
Abate, Mike	of	Lancaster	Sea	A+	22	24	69	16	3	0	2	25	14	12	9	0	21	3	0	0	5	2	.71	2	.232	.346	.362
		Mariners	Sea	R	22	7	24	4	0	0	1	7	3	3	9	0	11	1	0	0	0	0	.00	1	.167	.412	.292
		Wisconsin	Sea	A	22	24	91	26	4	0	0	30	9	8	5	0	22	0	2	2	1	2	.33	3	.286	.316	.330
Abercrombie, R.	of	Great Falls	LA	R+	20	54	220	60	7	1	2	75	40	29	22	0	66	8	3	0	32	8	.80	1	.273	.360	.341
Abreu, Cesar	1b	Reds	Cin	R	22	13	39	5	1	0	0	6	4	2	5	0	11	1	0	0	0	1	.00	1	.128	.244	.154
Abreu, Dave#	2b	St. Lucie	NYM	A+	22	8	30	10	0	0	0	10	3	3	4	1	6	0	1	0	3	2	.60	0	.333	.412	.333
		Capital Cty	NYM	A	22	78	285	82	14	3	1	105	40	35	26	1	51	4	8	0	29	12	.71	6	.288	.356	.368
Abreu, Nielsen	2b	Phillies	Phi	R	20	24	66	16	2	0	0	18	6	4	3	0	7	1	2	0	5	2	.71	5	.242	.286	.273
		Batavia	Phi	A-	20	6	8	1	0	0	0	1	2	1	0	0	1	0	0	0	0	0	.00	0	.125	.125	.125
Abruzzo, Jared#	c	Butte	Ana	R+	19	62	208	53	11	0	8	88	46	45	61	1	58	2	0	3	1	0	1.00	3	.255	.423	.423
Acevas, Jon	c	Winston-Sal	CWS	A+	23	76	259	55	17	2	3	85	41	17	20	2	65	5	1	2	3	1	.75	9	.212	.280	.328
Acevedo, Anthony*	of	Martinsvlle	Hou	R+	23	56	200	59	20	3	5	100	33	43	31	0	41	3	0	4	7	3	.70	4	.295	.391	.500
Acevedo, Carlos	of	Piedmont	Phi	A	20	37	106	24	3	1	0	29	10	8	12	0	23	0	2	1	5	2	.71	3	.226	.303	.274
		Batavia	Phi	A-	20	63	230	59	5	1	1	69	28	22	18	1	47	3	2	1	13	3	.81	1	.257	.317	.300
Acevedo, Inocencio	2b	Savannah	Tex	A	22	57	177	40	6	1	1	51	25	13	9	0	37	5	6	2	17	7	.71	2	.226	.280	.288
Acevedo, Juan#	of	Reds	Cin	R	19	49	172	31	5	2	2	46	23	13	20	1	71	3	0	0	8	6	.57	2	.180	.277	.267
Acevedo, Luis	2b	Dayton	Cin	A	23	20	60	14	2	0	0	16	4	3	6	0	15	1	0	0	1	1	.50	1	.233	.313	.267
		Clinton	Cin	A	23	6	13	1	0	0	0	1	2	1	1	0	6	1	0	1	1	0	1.00	0	.077	.188	.077
Acosta, Emilio	c	Johnson Cty	StL	R+	21	36	119	29	6	0	0	35	22	13	13	0	19	1	1	2	6	2	.75	4	.244	.319	.294
Acosta, Johe	of	Pirates	Pit	R	19	31	107	17	1	0	0	18	7	8	7	0	28	1	1	1	1	0	1.00	1	.159	.216	.168
Acuna, Ron	of	Capital Cty	NYM	A	22	13	39	7	2	0	0	9	1	0	1	0	17	0	0	0	3	1	.75	0	.179	.200	.231
		Pittsfield	NYM	A-	22	72	287	88	11	0	2	105	52	35	10	0	55	3	4	2	31	10	.76	3	.307	.334	.366
Adams, John	of	Rancho Cuca	SD	A+	24	110	395	91	12	2	13	146	47	57	17	2	103	3	0	2	14	5	.74	23	.230	.266	.370
Agar, Cory	c-dh	Twins	Min	R	20	48	157	47	17	0	2	70	27	30	29	1	20	3	0	2	0	3	.00	7	.299	.414	.446
Aguila, Chris	of	Brevard Cty	Fla	A+	22	136	518	125	27	3	9	185	68	56	37	1	105	1	3	3	8	8	.50	11	.241	.292	.357
Ahlers, Steve	2b	Cedar Rapds	Ana	A	22	15	54	11	3	0	0	14	3	3	9	0	12	0	2	1	2	3	.40	2	.204	.313	.259
Ahumada, Alex	ss	Sarasota	Bos	A+	22	125	457	121	18	3	6	163	55	47	16	0	80	8	1	3	9	7	.56	8	.265	.300	.357
Alamo, Efrain	of	Chston-SC	TB	A	24	10	34	5	1	0	1	9	2	6	0	0	15	1	0	1	0	0	.00	0	.147	.167	.265
Albertson, Justin	of	Johnson Cty	StL	R+	21	33	94	21	4	1	2	33	22	13	15	0	37	1	1	1	13	0	1.00	3	.223	.333	.351
Aldridge, Cory*	of	Myrtle Bch	Atl	A+	22	109	401	100	18	5	15	173	51	64	33	2	118	1	0	9	10	5	.67	0	.249	.302	.431
Alexander, Kevin	ss-2b	Salem-Keizr	SF	A-	20	24	66	12	1	0	0	13	6	4	17	0	9	1	1	0	0	2	.00	1	.182	.357	.197
		Giants	SF	R	20	14	43	18	1	0	1	22	8	8	9	0	5	0	2	0	4	1	.80	3	.419	.519	.512
		San Jose	SF	A+	20	2	6	1	0	0	0	1	0	0	1	0	1	0	0	0	0	1	.00	1	.167	.286	.167
Alexander, L.	of	Phillies	Phi	R	20	53	193	46	5	0	2	57	28	12	26	0	32	1	1	1	15	5	.75	4	.238	.330	.295
Alfano, Jeff	c	Mudville	Mil	A+	24	22	69	16	4	1	1	25	9	10	5	0	18	1	0	0	1	0	1.00	3	.232	.293	.362
Alfaro, Jason	ss	Kissimmee	Hou	A+	23	117	460	115	20	1	7	158	58	41	25	1	63	1	5	5	2	6	.25	15	.250	.287	.343
Alfieri, Frank	3b	Beloit	Mil	A	24	21	70	12	1	1	1	18	8	5	4	1	17	2	0	1	0	1	.00	3	.171	.234	.257
Alfonzo, Eliezer	c	Peoria	StL	A	22	49	175	54	16	0	5	85	28	21	6	0	35	6	1	2	2	0	1.00	6	.309	.349	.486
		Beloit	Mil	A	22	60	221	59	10	0	5	84	22	27	8	0	58	3	0	2	2	2	.50	6	.267	.299	.380
Aliendo, Humberto	of	Pirates	Pit	R	20	54	203	55	15	1	6	90	33	38	17	0	41	1	0	1	6	3	.67	8	.271	.329	.443
Allegra, Matt	of	Athletics	Oak	R	19	42	141	38	7	3	0	51	26	13	25	0	44	3	3	3	15	2	.88	1	.270	.384	.362
Alley, Chip#	c	Frederick	Bal	A+	24	35	98	24	3	0	2	33	15	12	18	0	20	1	2	1	0	0	.00	4	.245	.364	.337
		Orioles	Bal	R	24	6	15	5	2	0	0	7	3	3	4	1	4	1	0	1	0	1	.00	0	.333	.476	.467
		Delmarva	Bal	A	24	15	44	12	2	0	0	14	10	0	15	1	5	2	0	0	1	0	1.00	1	.273	.475	.318
Alvarado, Oscar	c	Auburn	Hou	A-	21	8	19	2	0	0	0	2	0	1	0	0	5	0	0	0	0	0	.00	0	.105	.105	.105
		Martinsvlle	Hou	R+	21	25	71	12	1	1	1	18	6	2	5	0	19	2	0	0	3	1	.75	2	.169	.244	.254
Alvarez, Aaron	c	Marlins	Fla	R	21	31	97	25	5	2	1	37	15	9	13	0	25	4	2	0	2	0	1.00	2	.258	.368	.381
Alvarez, Henrry	c	Chston-WV	KC	A	21	10	30	6	2	0	1	11	2	2	2	0	9	0	0	0	0	0	.00	1	.200	.250	.367
		Spokane	KC	A-	21	21	60	11	3	0	0	14	10	4	3	0	29	3	1	0	0	0	.00	1	.183	.258	.233
Alvarez, Jimmy#	2b	Quad City	Min	A	21	43	134	30	7	2	4	53	14	21	19	1	38	2	3	0	3	1	.75	0	.224	.329	.396
		Hagerstown	Tor	A	21	50	155	36	5	1	3	52	19	15	25	0	44	2	1	0	12	5	.71	0	.232	.346	.335
Alvarez, Nicholas	of	Yakima	LA	A-	24	61	217	65	14	2	10	113	39	36	24	0	31	5	5	3	20	5	.80	4	.300	.378	.521
Alvarez, Tony	of	Hickory	Pit	A	22	118	442	126	25	4	15	204	75	77	39	2	93	15	0	8	52	21	.71	8	.285	.357	.462
Alviso, Jerome#	1b	Salem	Col	A+	25	95	321	87	11	3	1	107	39	44	17	0	46	6	7	7	11	9	.55	8	.271	.313	.333
Amador, Chris	2b	White Sox	CWS	R	18	53	212	64	10	3	0	80	48	31	30	0	46	6	1	0	40	13	.75	6	.302	.403	.377
Amador, Jerry	of	W Michigan	Det	A	21	96	331	79	11	0	5	105	38	45	38	2	69	5	1	3	2	2	.50	5	.239	.324	.317
Ambres, Chip	of	Kane County	Fla	A	21	84	320	74	16	3	7	117	46	28	52	0	72	3	3	2	26	8	.76	3	.231	.342	.366
Ambrosini, D.*	of	Expos	Mon	R	20	27	86	26	3	2	0	33	10	8	9	0	16	0	2	1	1	0	1.00	6	.302	.365	.384
Amezaga, Alfredo	2b	Lk Elsinore	Ana	A+	23	108	420	117	13	4	4	150	90	44	63	0	70	4	5	5	73	21	.78	4	.279	.374	.357
Anderson, Bryan	ss	Billings	Cin	R+	22	58	218	56	4	3	3	75	51	24	42	0	38	5	4	0	7	2	.78	5	.257	.389	.344
Anderson, Dennis#	c	Kane County	Fla	A	23	29	81	18	3	1	0	23	7	9	9	0	17	6	0	2	0	0	.00	2	.222	.337	.284
		Brevard Cty	Fla	A+	23	23	56	11	2	0	0	13	6	3	9	0	16	4	1	0	0	1	.00	0	.196	.348	.232
Anderson, Jon#	ss	Augusta	Bos	A	24	87	287	69	9	0	0	78	40	35	46	0	39	2	11	4	12	11	.52	11	.240	.345	.272
Anderson, Melvin	3b-of	Phillies	Phi	R	21	36	120	22	6	0	2	34	7	16	12	0	25	2	1	1	0	2	.00	5	.183	.267	.283
Anderson, Nat*	1b	Tigers	Det	R	19	30	92	18	0	0	0	18	5	8	19	0	28	4	0	1	0	1	.00	2	.196	.353	.196
Anderson, Syketo*	of	Cubs	ChC	R	22	40	150	58	8	4	1	77	44	21	8	1	14	4	3	0	12	7	.63	1	.387	.432	.513
Andrianoff, J.	ss	Martinsvlle	Hou	R+	20	33	95	14	5	0	0	19	6	5	7	0	43	4	1	2	2	2	.50	1	.147	.231	.200
Angel, Tony	2b	Martinsvlle	Hou	R+	22	46	154	36	9	3	2	57	21	20	14	0	28	2	0	1	7	2	.78	3	.234	.304	.370
Angell, Rick	of	Savannah	Tex	A	24	123	418	100	11	8	5	142	46	44	29	0	79	7	10	3	28	9	.76	5	.239	.298	.340
Ansman, Craig	c	Missoula	Ari	R+	23	28	67	19	5	0	0	24	7	7	12	0	21	2	0	2	0	0	.00	1	.284	.398	.358
Anthony, Jake*	1b	W Michigan	Det	A	24	111	377	88	14	0	2	108	36	48	32	0	105	15	4	2	5	4	.56	10	.233	.317	.286
Aracena, Sandy	c	Yakima	LA	A-	20	27	92	20	5	0	0	25	7	12	6	0	20	0	2	1	6	1	.86	5	.217	.263	.272
		Great Falls	LA	R+	20	5	19	6	1	0	0	7	1	3	1	0	1	0	0	0	1	0	1.00	1	.316	.350	.368
Araujo, Danilo	2b	Peoria	StL	A	24	62	183	41	6	2	0	51	22	9	16	0	36	3	3	1	5	3	.63	4	.224	.296	.279

2000 Batting — Class-A and Rookie Leagues

BATTING																					BASERUNNING				PERCENTAGES		
Player	Pos	Team	Org	Lg	A	G	AB	H	2B	3B	HR	TB	R	RBI	TBB	IBB	SO	HBP	SH	SF	SB	CS	SB%	GDP	Avg	OBP	SLG
Arko, Tommy	c	Orioles	Bal	R	18	37	127	26	6	2	1	39	12	11	18	0	42	2	2	4	0	0	.00	6	.205	.305	.307
Arroyo, Abner*	of	Idaho Falls	SD	R+	21	25	109	43	11	0	3	63	26	28	3	0	13	0	0	2	2	2	.50	4	.394	.404	.578
		Fort Wayne	SD	A	21	36	131	29	7	0	2	42	14	11	10	0	28	0	1	1	4	3	.57	3	.221	.275	.321
Asadoorian, Rick	of	Red Sox	Bos	R	20	54	197	52	9	3	5	82	43	31	26	1	56	6	0	3	22	2	.92	2	.264	.362	.416
Asche, Kirk	of	Visalia	Oak	A+	23	118	421	104	30	4	18	196	65	63	66	3	128	4	1	2	17	8	.68	4	.247	.353	.466
Atkins, Garrett	1b	Portland	Col	A-	21	69	251	76	12	0	7	109	34	47	45	1	48	2	0	1	2	0	1.00	3	.303	.411	.434
Auterson, Jeff	of	Vero Beach	LA	A+	23	108	344	82	16	2	9	129	61	45	34	0	109	22	2	2	17	4	.81	7	.238	.343	.375
Autry, Brian	1b-dh	Cape Fear	Mon	A	25	25	81	21	5	1	3	37	7	13	4	1	21	2	0	1	1	0	1.00	4	.259	.307	.457
		Jupiter	Mon	A+	25	23	72	12	2	0	1	17	5	7	3	0	27	3	0	1	0	0	.00	1	.167	.228	.236
Avila, Rob	c	Batavia	Phi	A-	22	44	139	33	7	0	3	49	14	21	10	0	23	5	1	3	2	0	1.00	2	.237	.306	.353
Ayala, Abraham	c-dh	Martinsvlle	Hou	R+	20	38	130	38	6	0	1	47	19	11	10	0	8	3	1	0	4	3	.57	4	.292	.357	.362
Ayala, Elio	2b-3b	Ogden	Mil	R+	22	59	237	80	16	3	3	111	57	21	25	0	18	5	2	2	14	4	.78	4	.338	.409	.468
Ayala, Odanis	of	Royals	KC	R	20	37	101	27	2	3	0	35	20	9	27	0	20	5	1	2	4	1	.80	2	.267	.437	.347
Aybar, Willy#	3b	Great Falls	LA	R+	18	70	266	70	15	1	4	99	39	49	36	2	45	0	6	2	5	5	.50	3	.263	.349	.372
Baderdeen, Kevin	3b	Billings	Cin	R+	24	19	80	21	3	1	1	29	9	13	5	0	19	1	0	0	0	1	.00	4	.263	.314	.363
		Dayton	Cin	A	24	47	159	41	11	0	4	64	26	20	12	0	50	1	4	1	0	0	.00	4	.258	.312	.403
Baetzel, Mike#	2b	Bristol	CWS	R+	21	16	12	2	0	0	0	2	7	3	1	0	5	0	0	1	0	1	.00	0	.167	.214	.167
Baez, Manuel	of	Pulaski	Tex	R+	22	56	180	48	8	2	0	60	35	22	43	0	37	2	3	1	13	6	.68	3	.267	.412	.333
Bailey, Jeff	dh	Brevard Cty	Fla	A+	22	125	458	113	19	3	14	180	56	66	50	2	116	7	1	4	3	3	.50	9	.247	.328	.393
Bailey, Travis	1b-dh	Peoria	StL	A	24	118	418	103	21	5	9	161	64	58	58	4	154	4	3	4	10	7	.59	4	.246	.341	.385
Baker, Casey	2b	Yankees	NYY	R	20	33	64	10	3	0	0	13	9	5	8	0	20	6	1	1	4	1	.80	0	.156	.304	.203
Baker, Derek*	1b	Charlotte	Tex	A+	25	127	449	132	28	3	11	199	50	81	67	3	67	9	0	1	1	2	.33	8	.294	.395	.443
Baker, Jacob	of	Chston-WV	KC	A	25	88	295	60	12	3	3	87	26	26	37	0	99	0	0	3	3	2	.60	10	.203	.290	.295
Baldelli, Rocco	of	Princeton	TB	R+	19	60	232	50	9	2	3	72	33	25	12	0	56	5	2	0	11	3	.79	3	.216	.269	.310
Baldiris, Aaron	1b-3b	Kingsport	NYM	R+	18	32	105	23	3	1	2	34	14	20	7	0	20	1	0	4	2	1	.67	4	.219	.265	.324
Ballard, Ryan	dh	St. Pete	TB	A+	25	14	39	6	2	0	0	8	2	1	5	0	18	0	1	0	0	0	.00	1	.154	.250	.205
Banks, Almonzo	of	Butte	Ana	R+	20	20	19	4	1	0	0	5	6	1	2	0	10	0	0	0	0	0	.00	1	.211	.286	.263
Banks, Gary	of-dh	Cubs	ChC	R	19	31	110	30	3	2	1	40	19	11	6	0	35	3	3	0	3	2	.60	1	.273	.328	.364
Barbier, Blair	1b	Eugene	ChC	A-	23	67	234	69	13	1	4	96	28	34	29	2	37	8	0	7	4	1	.80	1	.295	.381	.410
Barmes, Clint	ss	Portland	Col	A-	22	45	181	51	6	4	2	71	37	16	18	0	28	5	0	1	12	9	.57	1	.282	.361	.392
		Asheville	Col	A	22	19	81	14	4	0	0	18	11	4	10	0	13	1	2	1	4	1	.80	3	.173	.269	.222
Barnette, Jason*	of	Batavia	Phi	A-	24	62	213	67	5	3	1	81	31	25	21	0	55	3	3	0	28	3	.90	3	.315	.384	.380
Barningham, Steve*	of	Charlotte	Tex	A+	26	102	351	96	15	8	3	136	68	30	41	3	52	10	6	2	16	7	.70	8	.274	.364	.387
Barnowski, Bryan	c-dh	Red Sox	Bos	R	20	50	166	50	9	0	13	98	40	33	23	0	46	4	0	1	1	0	1.00	2	.301	.397	.590
		Lowell	Bos	A-	20	5	16	3	1	0	0	4	1	1	1	0	4	0	0	0	0	0	.00	0	.188	.235	.250
Barns, B.J.*	of	Lynchburg	Pit	A+	23	120	398	97	20	1	8	143	46	48	44	2	95	9	2	5	8	5	.62	8	.244	.329	.359
Barr, Clint	c	Tampa	NYY	A+	24	13	20	3	1	0	0	4	0	1	2	0	8	0	0	0	0	0	.00	0	.150	.227	.200
Barrera, Reinaldo#	3b	Diamondbcks	Ari	R	18	37	138	45	5	6	0	62	30	27	8	0	16	3	1	2	5	2	.71	0	.326	.371	.449
Barrow, Corey	of	Billings	Cin	R+	21	45	163	38	3	4	2	55	29	21	15	0	43	5	1	1	5	4	.56	1	.233	.315	.337
Barski, Chris*	c-dh	Lk Elsinore	Ana	A+	23	19	66	10	4	0	0	14	6	4	6	0	18	0	1	0	0	1	.00	2	.152	.222	.212
		Cedar Rapds	Ana	A	23	36	123	30	5	0	1	38	13	9	19	0	32	0	0	0	0	1	.00	4	.244	.345	.309
Bartee, Khareta	of	Royals	KC	R	23	45	140	31	5	0	0	36	10	7	10	0	33	4	2	0	9	1	.90	2	.221	.292	.257
Basabe, Jesus	of	Modesto	Oak	A+	24	125	445	115	35	3	12	192	64	85	61	0	142	23	3	6	9	10	.47	9	.258	.372	.431
Basak, Chris	ss	Pittsfield	NYM	A-	23	63	249	87	18	4	0	113	46	15	26	2	36	3	3	0	32	12	.73	1	.349	.417	.454
		St. Lucie	NYM	A+	23	4	17	7	1	0	0	8	2	3	4	0	2	0	0	0	3	1	.75	1	.412	.524	.471
Bass, Chris	3b	Pirates	Pit	R	19	47	163	48	11	3	2	71	32	26	23	0	28	7	0	0	10	0	1.00	0	.294	.404	.436
Bass, Kevin#	of	Lansing	ChC	A	22	108	358	72	17	1	13	130	41	47	39	4	120	3	2	1	1	3	.25	8	.201	.284	.363
Bastardo, Angel	c	Mahoning Vy	Cle	A-	22	51	182	32	11	1	2	51	20	25	10	0	47	4	3	0	2	1	.67	6	.176	.235	.280
Batista, Angel*	of	Chston-SC	TB	A	21	44	137	28	7	2	2	45	28	8	12	0	38	0	3	0	8	2	.80	0	.204	.268	.328
Batista, Carlos	1b	Columbus	Cle	A	21	54	202	45	9	0	3	63	20	17	18	0	52	4	0	1	2	2	.50	2	.223	.298	.312
		Burlington	Cle	R+	21	32	110	26	4	1	1	35	8	14	7	0	33	1	1	0	1	4	.20	2	.236	.288	.318
Batson, Tom	3b	Clearwater	Phi	A+	24	40	147	36	9	0	1	48	16	16	16	1	28	2	0	1	0	2	.00	4	.245	.325	.327
		Piedmont	Phi	A	24	52	191	55	15	1	3	81	26	35	18	0	27	2	1	3	7	4	.64	6	.288	.350	.424
Bautista, Augusto	ss	Reds	Cin	R	19	21	65	13	4	0	0	17	8	2	3	0	21	2	0	0	0	0	.00	0	.200	.257	.262
Bay, Jason	dh-of	Vermont	Mon	A-	22	35	135	41	5	0	2	52	17	12	11	0	25	1	0	1	17	4	.81	2	.304	.358	.385
Bazzani, Matt	dh	Bakersfield	SF	A+	27	13	23	3	1	0	0	4	2	4	2	0	9	0	0	2	0	0	.00	1	.130	.185	.174
Beatriz, Ramy*	of	Mudville	Mil	A+	22	7	20	5	0	0	0	5	1	2	4	0	3	0	0	0	2	0	1.00	0	.250	.375	.250
Beattie, Andy#	ss	Dayton	Cin	A	23	20	57	13	2	0	2	21	15	7	5	0	14	0	2	0	1	3	.25	2	.228	.290	.368
		Clinton	Cin	A	23	101	398	124	30	4	4	174	65	52	44	5	58	1	7	5	18	7	.72	5	.312	.377	.437
Becker, Jeff	3b	Mahoning Vy	Cle	A-	24	71	264	57	12	4	7	98	52	30	36	1	56	20	2	2	1	1	.50	5	.216	.351	.371
Belcher, Jason*	c-dh	Helena	Mil	R+	19	46	162	54	18	2	4	88	30	36	20	1	25	1	1	3	3	1	.75	3	.333	.403	.543
Bell, Derek#	1b	Salem-Keizr	SF	A-	23	66	204	50	12	3	3	77	30	37	37	0	39	4	0	6	4	1	.80	2	.245	.363	.377
Bell, Josh	2b	Kingsport	NYM	R+	21	27	62	13	5	0	0	18	9	5	9	0	27	3	4	0	0	2	.00	0	.210	.338	.290
Bell, Paul	3b	Helena	Mil	R+	21	39	140	32	3	0	0	35	14	4	6	0	24	3	0	0	3	3	.50	2	.229	.275	.250
Bell, Ricky	3b	Vero Beach	LA	A+	22	127	481	122	18	0	5	155	59	45	37	2	75	3	1	6	7	3	.70	13	.254	.307	.322
Belliard, Francisco#	2b	High Desert	Ari	A+	21	111	368	83	14	4	3	114	46	39	24	0	96	7	2	3	7	9	.44	7	.226	.284	.310
Benjamin, Al	of	Rancho Cuca	SD	A+	23	137	552	154	30	8	9	227	71	81	24	1	89	5	1	5	16	16	.50	14	.279	.312	.411
Bennett, Ryan	c-dh	St. Lucie	NYM	A+	26	53	166	46	7	1	0	55	20	15	20	0	35	1	3	0	0	1	.00	4	.277	.358	.331
Bera, Roberto	of	Orioles	Bal	R	19	43	159	37	9	1	1	51	18	21	2	1	27	3	2	1	3	1	.75	5	.233	.255	.321
Berger, Matt	1b	Winston-Sal	CWS	A+	26	128	430	98	32	2	14	176	65	65	77	0	106	5	1	6	3	4	.43	10	.228	.347	.409
Bergolla, William	2b-3b	Reds	Cin	R	18	8	22	4	0	0	0	4	2	0	4	0	2	0	0	0	3	1	.75	0	.182	.308	.182
Bernard, Dagoberto	ss	Portland	Col	A-	21	54	179	36	11	1	0	49	16	10	3	0	42	3	5	1	5	4	.56	2	.201	.226	.274
Bernard, Miguel	c	Braves	Atl	R	20	42	137	33	5	0	1	41	20	10	9	0	18	3	0	0	0	0	.00	5	.241	.302	.299
Bernhardt, J.	1b	Dunedin	Tor	A+	20	3	4	1	1	0	0	2	0	3	1	0	1	0	0	0	0	0	.00	0	.250	.400	.500
		Hagerstown	Tor	A	20	2	8	1	1	0	0	2	1	0	0	0	3	0	0	0	0	0	.00	0	.125	.125	.250
		Queens	Tor	A-	20	17	59	8	2	0	0	10	1	3	4	0	10	0	0	0	0	0	.00	5	.136	.190	.169
Berroa, Angel	ss	Visalia	Oak	A+	21	129	429	119	25	6	10	186	61	63	30	1	70	10	2	3	11	9	.55	10	.277	.337	.434

2000 Batting — Class-A and Rookie Leagues

BATTING																					BASERUNNING				PERCENTAGES		
Player	Pos	Team	Org	Lg	A	G	AB	H	2B	3B	HR	TB	R	RBI	TBB	IBB	SO	HBP	SH	SF	SB	CS	SB%	GDP	Avg	OBP	SLG
Berroa, Cristian#	ss	Rancho Cuca	SD	A+	22	130	488	132	19	4	4	171	76	50	28	0	62	17	4	5	30	16	.65	25	.270	.329	.350
Bessa, Laumin	of	Braves	Atl	R	18	27	92	27	8	1	1	40	17	11	6	0	22	4	1	0	4	0	1.00	1	.293	.363	.435
Betancourt, Tony#	ss	Quad City	Min	A	24	14	18	1	0	1	0	3	1	3	1	0	8	0	0	1	0	0	.00	0	.056	.100	.167
		Expos	Mon	R	24	24	73	14	0	1	0	16	8	2	7	0	12	0	0	0	1	2	.33	1	.192	.263	.219
Betemit, Wilson#	ss	Jamestown	Atl	A-	20	69	269	89	15	2	5	123	54	37	30	2	37	1	3	5	3	4	.43	4	.331	.393	.457
Betts, DeWayne	of	Vancouver	Oak	A-	21	6	16	1	0	0	0	1	2	1	3	0	10	0	0	0	1	0	1.00	0	.063	.211	.063
Beverly, Shomari	of	Piedmont	Phi	A	23	80	309	67	14	1	2	89	30	20	21	0	108	0	2	3	19	9	.68	1	.217	.264	.288
Bikowski, Scott*	of	Cedar Rapds	Ana	A	24	117	422	104	14	3	8	148	53	55	61	2	79	7	4	3	6	9	.40	6	.246	.349	.351
Bird, T.J.*	of	Rockies	Col	R	22	45	171	49	8	6	4	81	38	38	21	0	27	5	1	1	3	2	.60	4	.287	.379	.474
Birkett, Matthew	of	Tigers	Det	R	19	42	114	20	1	0	0	21	16	11	8	0	42	5	1	0	5	2	.71	3	.175	.260	.184
Bitter, Jarrod	c-dh	Idaho Falls	SD	R+	22	11	40	17	7	1	0	26	12	12	9	0	6	2	0	2	0	0	.00	1	.425	.528	.650
		Fort Wayne	SD	A	22	33	113	26	10	0	2	42	10	17	10	0	27	6	0	3	1	1	.50	2	.230	.318	.372
Blackburn, John	c	Medcine Hat	Tor	R+	18	18	57	11	3	1	1	19	5	8	10	0	9	0	1	1	0	0	.00	0	.193	.309	.333
Blalock, Hank*	3b	Savannah	Tex	A	20	139	512	153	32	2	10	219	66	77	62	3	53	5	0	11	31	8	.79	14	.299	.373	.428
Blanco, Tony	3b	Red Sox	Bos	R	19	52	190	73	13	1	13	127	32	50	18	2	38	4	0	3	6	4	.60	3	.384	.442	.668
		Lowell	Bos	A-	19	9	28	4	1	0	0	5	1	0	2	0	12	1	0	0	1	0	1.00	0	.143	.226	.179
Blasi, Blake#	2b	Eugene	ChC	A-	22	72	276	65	12	1	3	88	52	28	44	0	50	6	6	1	27	7	.79	2	.236	.352	.319
Bledsoe, Hunter	dh	Vero Beach	LA	A+	25	116	447	143	25	2	7	193	61	75	36	2	49	6	0	7	17	4	.81	14	.320	.373	.432
Blocker, Kevin	3b-2b	Portland	Col	A-	22	20	85	21	3	1	0	26	11	14	6	0	12	1	0	0	5	1	.83	1	.247	.304	.306
Blum, Greg	c	Vermont	Mon	A-	22	42	146	35	7	0	2	48	22	17	17	1	34	10	1	1	9	3	.75	1	.240	.356	.329
Bly, Derrick	1b	Daytona	ChC	A+	26	83	294	72	10	5	6	110	30	31	17	0	75	4	5	2	2	4	.33	3	.245	.293	.374
Bocaranda, Nestor	c	Tigers	Det	R	22	43	149	37	7	0	2	50	22	33	5	0	30	5	0	6	4	2	.67	2	.248	.285	.336
Boitel, Rafael#	of	Elizabethtn	Min	R+	20	55	224	59	7	2	2	76	43	27	25	1	47	1	2	0	16	6	.73	1	.263	.340	.339
Bone, Blake*	3b	Everett	Sea	A-	22	68	241	68	16	2	8	112	50	43	47	5	55	2	1	2	7	6	.54	3	.282	.401	.465
Bonifay, Josh	2b	Hickory	Pit	A	22	106	377	106	17	2	14	169	62	62	48	3	104	3	2	3	11	5	.69	6	.281	.364	.448
Bonner, Adam*	of	Hudson Val	TB	A-	20	59	191	45	11	0	3	65	27	23	34	0	56	5	1	4	12	4	.75	1	.236	.359	.340
Bookout, Casey*	1b	Dayton	Cin	A	24	83	298	81	19	1	9	129	37	55	33	3	57	5	0	2	0	0	.00	8	.272	.352	.433
Boone, Matt	3b	Lakeland	Det	A+	21	119	441	110	21	3	6	155	47	48	35	2	112	1	1	0	5	6	.45	12	.249	.306	.351
Bordenick, Ryan	c	Beloit	Mil	A	25	87	300	65	18	1	7	106	30	39	42	1	82	5	7	2	4	1	.80	7	.217	.321	.353
Borges, Luis*	2b	Royals	KC	R	18	43	144	33	3	1	0	38	12	14	12	1	11	0	2	2	1	3	.25	4	.229	.285	.264
Borjas, Henry#	2b	Sarasota	Bos	A+	22	1	3	0	0	0	0	0	0	0	0	0	0	0	0	0	0	0	.00	0	.000	.000	.000
		Red Sox	Bos	R	22	15	45	14	2	0	1	19	7	9	7	0	3	1	0	1	2	0	1.00	1	.311	.407	.422
		Lowell	Bos	A-	22	35	122	30	3	0	0	33	10	10	9	0	17	0	3	0	2	2	.50	2	.246	.298	.270
Borrego, Ramon#	2b	Fort Myers	Min	A+	23	79	265	59	6	1	0	67	29	20	28	0	37	5	3	1	8	2	.80	6	.223	.308	.253
Boscan, Jean	c	Macon	Atl	A	21	93	302	62	12	0	9	101	31	35	42	1	74	5	2	1	1	1	.50	6	.205	.311	.334
Bost, Tom*	of	Columbus	Cle	A	25	54	208	60	14	5	8	108	30	42	11	1	36	3	0	2	18	1	.95	4	.288	.330	.519
		Kinston	Cle	A+	25	10	31	7	1	1	0	10	3	1	1	0	8	1	1	0	0	1	.00	1	.226	.273	.323
Botts, Jason#	1b	Rangers	Tex	R	20	48	163	52	12	0	6	82	36	34	26	4	29	10	0	1	4	1	.80	5	.319	.440	.503
Bourgeois, Jason#	2b	Rangers	Tex	R	19	24	88	21	4	0	0	25	18	6	14	0	15	2	2	0	9	2	.82	0	.239	.356	.284
Bowen, Rob#	c	Elizabethtn	Min	R+	20	21	73	21	3	0	4	36	17	19	11	0	18	0	0	0	0	0	.00	0	.288	.381	.493
Bowers, Jason	ss	Potomac	StL	A+	23	91	342	93	16	6	1	124	53	35	48	0	72	6	3	0	10	5	.67	5	.272	.371	.363
Bowser, Matt*	of	Vancouver	Oak	A-	22	68	237	54	11	2	4	81	29	39	32	6	61	4	0	1	1	1	.50	7	.228	.328	.342
Boyd, Shaun	of	Johnson Cty	StL	R+	19	43	152	40	9	0	2	55	15	15	10	1	22	2	1	1	6	5	.55	1	.263	.315	.362
Boyer, Bret	2b	Jupiter	Mon	A+	20	8	23	9	1	1	0	12	1	5	1	0	1	0	0	1	0	2	.00	1	.391	.400	.522
		Cape Fear	Mon	A	20	55	191	42	5	1	1	52	25	13	11	0	38	1	2	1	15	4	.79	2	.220	.265	.272
Bozanich, Sam	2b	Staten Ilnd	NYY	A-	22	71	239	63	11	1	3	85	40	25	50	0	30	5	4	3	15	4	.79	8	.264	.397	.356
Brack, Josh	3b	Athletics	Oak	R	24	47	165	49	12	5	1	74	44	29	52	0	48	4	0	1	6	2	.75	2	.297	.473	.448
Brandes, Landon	3b	New Jersey	StL	A-	22	52	184	43	12	0	0	55	11	14	8	0	53	6	4	3	11	2	.85	3	.234	.284	.299
Brazeal, Spencer	c	Greensboro	NYY	A	24	14	35	7	3	0	0	10	8	4	9	0	10	4	0	0	0	0	.00	1	.200	.417	.286
Brazell, Craig*	1b	Capital Cty	NYM	A	21	112	406	98	28	0	8	150	35	57	15	1	82	9	1	8	3	3	.50	6	.241	.279	.369
Brazoban, Yhency	of	Greensboro	NYY	A	20	12	48	9	3	0	0	12	6	8	3	0	15	0	0	1	1	0	1.00	0	.188	.231	.250
		Yankees	NYY	R	20	54	201	61	14	4	5	98	36	28	11	0	28	4	0	2	2	3	.40	7	.303	.349	.488
Brett, Jason	2b	Capital Cty	NYM	A	24	80	190	52	7	1	1	64	31	20	29	1	52	4	4	2	14	7	.67	3	.274	.378	.337
Brewer, Anthony	of	Marlins	Fla	R	18	47	181	39	9	3	3	63	35	18	25	0	54	5	0	1	13	1	.93	1	.215	.325	.348
Brewer, Jace	ss	Chston-SC	TB	A	22	37	137	30	7	2	0	41	10	15	6	0	28	1	0	3	3	0	1.00	1	.219	.252	.299
Brignac, Junior	of	Myrtle Bch	Atl	A+	23	128	475	100	17	3	7	144	58	42	43	1	145	8	9	1	27	8	.77	5	.211	.287	.303
Brisson, Dustin*	1b	Lowell	Bos	A-	23	65	238	58	7	2	6	87	25	39	29	0	63	3	0	5	1	2	.33	0	.244	.327	.366
Brito, Obispo	c	Mudville	Mil	A+	23	55	201	43	10	1	4	67	23	28	5	1	42	3	0	0	4	3	.57	3	.214	.244	.333
Bronowicz, Scott*	c	Myrtle Bch	Atl	A+	25	11	36	8	0	0	0	8	5	2	1	0	8	1	0	0	0	0	.00	0	.222	.263	.222
		Braves	Atl	R	25	4	8	0	0	0	0	0	1	0	2	0	2	0	0	0	0	0	.00	0	.000	.200	.000
		Macon	Atl	A	25	11	32	8	0	1	0	10	3	2	2	0	7	0	1	0	0	0	.00	1	.250	.294	.313
Brooks, Jeff	3b	High Desert	Ari	A+	21	127	506	124	29	4	9	188	62	78	25	0	117	7	0	4	8	4	.67	11	.245	.288	.372
Brosseau, Rick*	ss	Queens	Tor	A-	22	15	55	9	0	3	0	15	9	2	4	0	15	0	1	0	2	0	1.00	0	.164	.220	.273
Brown, Andy*	of	Greensboro	NYY	A	21	122	463	119	31	1	19	209	56	63	35	2	182	8	0	0	4	5	.44	3	.257	.320	.451
Brown, Billy	of	Tampa	NYY	A+	25	109	361	89	20	2	2	119	41	26	35	0	90	10	2	1	12	8	.60	5	.247	.329	.330
Brown, Larry*	of-dh	Mariners	Sea	R	20	35	121	40	6	0	2	52	24	15	14	0	30	8	0	1	1	2	.33	2	.331	.431	.430
Brown, Matt	3b	Expos	Mon	R	20	43	152	32	3	0	2	41	14	14	20	0	46	0	0	0	3	1	.75	1	.211	.302	.270
Brown, Tonayne	of	Sarasota	Bos	A+	23	127	507	138	16	5	2	170	83	40	33	1	79	9	11	2	33	13	.72	3	.272	.327	.335
Bruntlett, Eric	ss	Martinsvlle	Hou	R+	23	50	172	47	11	4	1	69	40	21	30	0	22	11	1	0	14	1	.93	2	.273	.413	.401
Bryan, Jason	of	Charlotte	Tex	A+	19	2	3	0	0	0	0	0	0	0	1	0	2	0	0	0	0	0	.00	0	.000	.250	.000
		Rangers	Tex	R	19	54	181	45	14	1	4	73	35	35	45	2	49	8	0	3	3	2	.60	5	.249	.414	.403
Bryant, Matt	3b	Clearwater	Phi	A+	26	67	221	57	8	2	0	69	27	30	34	0	31	3	1	2	2	2	.50	10	.258	.362	.312
Bubela, Brent*	c	Savannah	Tex	A	25	28	75	13	4	1	1	22	8	4	7	0	22	3	0	1	1	2	.33	2	.173	.267	.293
Bubela, Jaime*	of	Everett	Sea	A-	23	30	113	26	1	3	1	36	11	13	14	1	25	3	1	0	13	3	.81	0	.230	.331	.319
		Lancaster	Sea	A+	23	9	29	4	1	0	0	5	6	2	5	0	12	1	1	0	4	0	1.00	1	.138	.286	.172
Buck, John	c	Michigan	Hou	A	20	109	390	110	33	0	10	173	57	71	55	6	81	5	0	5	2	4	.33	8	.282	.374	.444
Buelna, Lorenzo	of	Butte	Ana	R+	20	59	202	53	10	3	3	78	44	25	14	0	31	6	3	3	17	6	.74	7	.262	.324	.386

2000 Batting — Class-A and Rookie Leagues

BATTING																					BASERUNNING				PERCENTAGES		
Player	Pos	Team	Org	Lg	A	G	AB	H	2B	3B	HR	TB	R	RBI	TBB	IBB	SO	HBP	SH	SF	SB	CS	SB%	GDP	Avg	OBP	SLG
Bullard, Kevin	c	Diamondbcks	Ari	R	22	3	7	2	1	0	0	3	2	2	2	0	2	0	0	0	0	0	.00	0	.286	.444	.429
Bultmann, Kurt	2b	Hickory	Pit	A	24	47	145	30	7	0	1	40	20	9	18	0	25	2	1	0	2	1	.67	6	.207	.303	.276
Bundy, Ryan	of	Dunedin	Tor	A+	23	2	5	0	0	0	0	0	1	0	0	0	2	0	0	0	0	0	.00	0	.000	.000	.000
		Hagerstown	Tor	A	23	25	87	20	6	0	2	32	10	13	11	0	31	0	1	0	2	2	.50	1	.230	.316	.368
Burford, Kevin*	of	Salem	Col	A+	23	127	465	136	40	4	16	232	73	80	58	2	79	10	0	4	11	4	.73	6	.292	.380	.499
Burnett, Mark*	2b	Clinton	Cin	A	24	131	489	147	33	3	7	207	92	65	81	2	73	4	2	4	24	13	.65	5	.301	.401	.423
Burns, Kevan*	of	Missoula	Ari	R+	24	4	15	8	0	2	0	12	6	4	3	0	1	0	0	0	3	1	.75	0	.533	.611	.800
		South Bend	Ari	A	24	110	401	107	16	6	4	147	62	53	45	2	65	1	2	6	26	6	.81	8	.267	.338	.367
Burns, Pat#	dh	St. Lucie	NYM	A+	23	109	386	115	21	2	4	152	53	61	49	5	109	5	0	4	3	1	.75	8	.298	.381	.394
Burrows, Angelo*	of	Danville	Atl	R+	20	44	171	47	6	2	0	57	28	20	11	1	20	2	2	1	8	3	.73	3	.275	.324	.333
Bush, Brian	of	Clearwater	Phi	A+	24	65	215	48	7	1	1	60	27	21	10	0	62	7	0	1	7	2	.78	2	.223	.279	.279
Buttler, Vic*	of	Pirates	Pit	R	20	4	15	2	0	0	0	2	1	1	1	0	0	0	0	0	0	1	.00	0	.133	.188	.133
		Williamsprt	Pit	A-	20	36	131	39	3	2	1	49	22	17	15	0	13	3	1	0	9	0	1.00	1	.298	.383	.374
Bynum, Freddie*	ss	Vancouver	Oak	A-	21	72	281	72	10	1	1	87	52	26	31	0	58	5	3	0	22	12	.65	3	.256	.341	.310
Byrd, Marlon	of	Piedmont	Phi	A	23	133	515	159	29	13	17	265	104	93	51	0	110	10	1	5	41	5	.89	7	.309	.379	.515
Cabrera, Jose	ss	Marlins	Fla	R	18	57	219	57	10	2	2	77	38	22	23	0	46	6	0	2	1	0	1.00	7	.260	.344	.352
		Utica	Fla	A-	18	8	32	8	2	0	0	10	3	6	2	0	6	0	0	0	0	0	.00	0	.250	.294	.313
Cabrera, Leonel	2b	Giants	SF	R	20	39	112	33	6	2	0	43	14	9	5	0	17	0	3	3	6	3	.67	1	.295	.317	.384
Cabrera, Ray	of	Delmarva	Bal	A	22	122	437	122	17	4	3	156	51	56	12	0	66	13	1	4	10	4	.71	15	.279	.315	.357
Cabrera, Yoelmis	of-2b	Pirates	Pit	R	20	40	141	38	6	3	2	56	32	19	18	0	23	1	0	2	12	3	.80	1	.270	.352	.397
Cadena, Alejandro	c-dh	Mariners	Sea	R	21	35	123	37	9	0	5	61	27	34	15	1	12	6	1	3	0	2	.00	2	.301	.395	.496
Cadiente, Brett*	of	Savannah	Tex	A	24	129	499	154	15	9	6	205	83	50	51	1	112	1	7	8	31	15	.67	6	.309	.369	.411
Caiazzo, Nick	1b	Mudville	Mil	A+	26	101	356	90	16	0	6	124	43	48	41	2	73	7	0	7	5	5	.50	2	.253	.336	.348
Calderon, Henry	3b	Wilmington	KC	A+	23	122	419	110	11	4	4	141	52	45	19	0	76	8	10	4	14	6	.70	14	.263	.304	.337
Calitri, Mike	1b	Billings	Cin	R+	23	7	24	13	2	1	1	20	11	11	8	0	5	1	0	0	1	0	1.00	0	.542	.667	.833
Callahan, Dave*	1b	Kane County	Fla	A	21	131	455	120	29	2	7	174	55	60	64	4	110	5	1	3	17	5	.77	14	.264	.359	.382
Callen, Tommy	2b	Medcine Hat	Tor	R+	23	50	182	47	4	1	2	59	44	25	39	0	39	12	4	0	5	3	.63	3	.258	.421	.324
Calloway, Ron*	of	Jupiter	Mon	A+	24	135	530	147	24	6	6	201	78	65	55	3	89	4	1	6	34	14	.71	13	.277	.346	.379
Calzado, Napolean	3b	Delmarva	Bal	A	21	131	503	140	20	6	7	193	81	83	31	0	68	11	4	8	29	12	.71	11	.278	.329	.384
Camacho, Juan#	3b	Yankees	NYY	R	20	46	162	49	10	2	4	75	21	27	19	1	24	2	1	1	1	0	1.00	5	.302	.380	.463
Cameron, Antoine*	of	Cubs	ChC	R	21	53	190	62	20	3	7	109	34	48	19	1	39	0	0	7	1	2	.33	2	.326	.375	.574
Cameron, Troy#	3b	Myrtle Bch	Atl	A+	22	123	401	85	23	3	15	159	53	51	59	0	131	8	0	2	0	2	.00	6	.212	.323	.397
Camilo, Juan*	of	Lakeland	Det	A+	23	114	373	92	13	2	12	145	49	45	46	5	142	2	2	3	4	9	.31	4	.247	.330	.389
Campana, Wandel	2b-ss	Clinton	Cin	A	21	39	103	16	2	0	1	21	8	9	2	0	18	2	5	1	5	5	.50	1	.155	.185	.204
		Billings	Cin	R+	21	66	248	69	6	3	2	87	42	34	10	0	28	6	4	2	22	9	.71	7	.278	.320	.351
Campbell, Sean*	c	Rancho Cuca	SD	A+	24	50	163	34	8	2	2	52	19	22	13	2	46	2	0	4	3	2	.60	2	.209	.269	.319
Campo, Michael*	of	Butte	Ana	R+	24	48	176	63	13	3	5	97	44	37	26	0	17	8	1	0	4	2	.67	4	.358	.462	.551
Campos, Julio	ss	Phillies	Phi	R	23	54	203	63	9	2	1	79	37	16	11	0	17	0	7	3	22	3	.88	3	.310	.341	.389
		Batavia	Phi	A-	23	3	12	3	0	0	0	3	1	0	0	0	5	0	0	0	1	0	1.00	1	.250	.250	.250
Campos, Tiago	of	Reds	Cin	R	20	30	101	20	4	2	0	28	6	7	5	0	26	1	0	1	10	4	.71	2	.198	.241	.277
Canales, Joel	of	Mexico	—	R	23	27	86	13	3	0	1	19	8	12	15	0	12	1	1	3	0	0	.00	2	.151	.276	.221
Cancio, Antonio	1b-dh	Phillies	Phi	R	19	18	69	16	2	1	1	23	8	9	5	0	19	2	0	0	0	0	.00	3	.232	.303	.333
Candela, Frank	of	Beloit	Mil	A	22	67	241	66	7	1	0	75	43	19	17	0	28	7	8	1	28	7	.80	6	.274	.338	.311
Candelaria, Scott	ss	Ogden	Mil	R+	22	66	281	81	16	1	7	120	41	42	9	2	39	5	3	3	4	2	.67	4	.288	.319	.427
Candelaria, Tito*	c	Yankees	NYY	R	23	7	18	1	0	0	0	1	0	1	3	0	4	0	0	0	0	0	.00	0	.056	.190	.056
		Staten Ilnd	NYY	A-	23	4	3	0	0	0	0	0	0	0	0	0	1	0	0	0	0	0	.00	0	.000	.000	.000
Candelario, Luis	of	Hudson Val	TB	A-	19	68	248	51	7	1	3	69	29	17	20	0	85	2	0	0	4	3	.57	4	.206	.270	.278
Cantu, Jorge	ss	Chston-SC	TB	A	19	46	186	55	13	2	2	78	25	24	11	1	39	3	1	1	3	2	.60	3	.296	.343	.419
		St. Pete	TB	A+	19	36	130	38	5	2	1	50	18	14	3	0	13	1	3	0	4	2	.67	3	.292	.313	.385
Caperton, Freddy	c	Pulaski	Tex	R+	21	9	24	7	4	1	0	13	7	4	2	0	7	2	0	0	0	0	.00	1	.292	.393	.542
Cappola, Tony*	3b	Boise	Ana	A-	22	16	33	7	2	0	0	9	4	4	3	0	7	0	1	0	0	0	.00	0	.212	.278	.273
Caraballo, Carlos	of	Red Sox	Bos	R	21	34	59	15	2	1	1	22	10	2	4	0	18	3	0	0	2	2	.50	0	.254	.333	.373
Caradonna, Brett*	of-dh	Winston-Sal	CWS	A+	22	103	365	76	20	2	2	106	39	32	29	2	70	2	1	0	3	1	.75	11	.208	.270	.290
Caraway, Brandon#	of	Batavia	Phi	A-	23	53	206	45	6	1	0	53	24	19	19	0	40	1	1	4	16	5	.76	2	.218	.283	.257
Cardona, Raynier#	dh-c	Kingsport	NYM	R+	20	5	12	3	0	0	0	3	1	2	5	0	5	1	0	0	1	0	1.00	1	.250	.500	.250
Caridi, Tony#	1b	Red Sox	Bos	R	21	18	39	3	0	0	0	3	7	2	12	0	10	0	0	1	1	0	1.00	1	.077	.288	.077
Carreno, Jose	c	Cape Fear	Mon	A	23	18	58	19	2	0	0	21	3	8	10	0	4	1	0	3	0	0	.00	1	.328	.417	.362
		Jupiter	Mon	A+	23	38	125	32	3	0	0	35	6	3	10	0	18	2	3	0	0	1	.00	2	.256	.321	.280
Carrera, Franklin	of	Padres	SD	R	18	20	44	10	2	1	0	14	4	4	2	0	15	0	1	0	0	0	.00	1	.227	.261	.318
Carrillo, Robert	1b-dh	Auburn	Hou	A-	22	42	141	21	5	0	1	29	9	8	1	0	47	2	0	1	1	0	1.00	4	.149	.166	.206
Carroll, Mark	c	Everett	Sea	A-	22	40	128	28	6	0	2	40	14	14	24	2	38	2	0	1	0	1	.00	1	.219	.348	.313
Carter, Bryan*	of	Salem-Keizr	SF	A-	23	63	226	60	8	2	3	81	24	28	20	0	37	3	2	0	13	3	.81	3	.265	.333	.358
Carter, Shannon*	of	Hagerstown	Tor	A	22	123	443	121	15	7	0	150	74	39	45	0	129	11	1	0	33	6	.85	5	.273	.355	.339
Carvajal, Ramon#	ss-2b	Peoria	StL	A	20	92	361	85	20	8	2	127	55	23	31	0	79	3	13	2	20	6	.77	3	.235	.300	.352
Cash, Condor	of	Eugene	ChC	A-	21	55	178	42	10	2	3	65	21	17	13	0	41	4	2	2	7	3	.70	4	.236	.299	.365
Cash, Kevin	c	Hagerstown	Tor	A	23	59	196	48	10	1	10	90	28	27	22	1	54	1	1	1	5	3	.63	7	.245	.323	.459
Casillas, Uriel	2b	Clearwater	Phi	A+	25	48	140	43	7	1	1	55	17	14	32	0	17	3	2	1	0	3	.00	3	.307	.443	.393
Casper, Brett	of	Bakersfield	SF	A+	25	128	436	106	27	3	15	184	85	70	97	1	146	13	2	3	22	4	.85	8	.243	.393	.422
Castaneda, Cesar	1b	Savannah	Tex	A	24	40	98	19	5	0	2	30	6	12	5	1	34	3	0	0	0	0	.00	2	.194	.255	.306
Castaneda, Jose	c	Pittsfield	NYM	A-	23	24	84	17	1	0	0	18	6	9	5	0	9	1	1	0	2	0	1.00	5	.202	.256	.214
		Capital Cty	NYM	A	23	14	43	5	0	0	0	5	5	0	7	0	8	0	0	0	0	0	.00	2	.116	.240	.116
Castellanos, Jose	of	Danville	Atl	R+	20	31	85	18	3	1	2	29	12	8	9	0	26	2	1	2	8	3	.73	2	.212	.296	.341
Castillo, Carlos#	2b-ss	St. Lucie	NYM	A+	20	3	7	2	1	0	0	3	1	0	1	0	1	0	1	0	1	0	1.00	1	.286	.375	.429
		Pittsfield	NYM	A-	20	15	52	14	2	0	0	16	6	2	3	0	11	1	1	1	5	0	1.00	0	.269	.316	.308
		Capital Cty	NYM	A	20	31	106	23	4	0	0	27	7	6	4	0	26	1	2	0	2	2	.50	0	.217	.252	.255
Castillo, David#	of	Idaho Falls	SD	R+	20	53	190	52	8	3	1	69	51	17	38	0	56	0	1	1	8	5	.62	6	.274	.393	.363
Castillo, Jose	ss	Hickory	Pit	A	20	125	529	158	32	8	16	254	95	72	29	0	107	10	7	2	16	12	.57	10	.299	.346	.480

2000 Batting — Class-A and Rookie Leagues

BATTING																					BASERUNNING				PERCENTAGES		
Player	Pos	Team	Org	Lg	A	G	AB	H	2B	3B	HR	TB	R	RBI	TBB	IBB	SO	HBP	SH	SF	SB	CS	SB%	GDP	Avg	OBP	SLG
Castillo, Ruben	ss	Wisconsin	Sea	A	20	123	416	89	14	4	2	117	57	46	29	0	101	2	8	4	21	6	.78	3	.214	.266	.281
Castillo, Victor	ss	Greensboro	NYY	A	20	82	282	63	7	0	0	70	37	28	39	0	73	5	4	2	8	4	.67	4	.223	.326	.248
Castro, Bernabel#	dh	Yankees	NYY	R	19	9	34	15	4	1	0	21	7	6	6	0	4	0	0	0	3	1	.75	1	.441	.525	.618
Castro, Javier	of	Royals	KC	R	19	44	140	32	2	1	0	36	18	8	8	0	40	3	3	0	5	2	.71	4	.229	.285	.257
Castro, Juan	of	Cubs	ChC	R	20	22	56	6	1	1	1	12	11	5	3	0	19	2	3	0	1	0	1.00	0	.107	.180	.214
Castro, Julio	3b	White Sox	CWS	R	20	47	161	46	9	3	0	61	34	36	25	1	35	5	1	6	20	2	.91	1	.286	.386	.379
Castro, Martires	of	Cape Fear	Mon	A	24	131	456	116	18	3	4	152	58	69	31	2	104	3	2	7	17	13	.57	11	.254	.302	.333
Castro, Ramon#	ss	Myrtle Bch	Atl	A+	21	108	385	97	20	3	5	138	52	44	44	0	76	12	3	1	13	5	.72	4	.252	.346	.358
Castro, Renato	of	Idaho Falls	SD	R+	21	41	155	45	7	1	3	63	20	33	10	1	32	2	0	3	0	4	.00	6	.290	.335	.406
Castro, Vince	of	Hickory	Pit	A	21	16	42	11	0	0	0	11	3	4	2	0	13	2	1	1	2	1	.67	0	.262	.319	.262
Catalanotte, Greg#	of	Asheville	Col	A	24	122	454	120	30	2	20	214	59	75	61	4	149	3	0	2	2	5	.29	10	.264	.354	.471
Cates, Gary	ss	Delmarva	Bal	A	19	107	311	78	18	2	1	103	40	30	18	0	48	4	12	2	11	8	.58	3	.251	.299	.331
Caudill, Clarke	of	Lowell	Bos	A-	24	30	89	18	2	0	0	20	8	6	12	0	26	2	0	0	0	2	.00	1	.202	.311	.225
Cavin, Jonathan*	of	White Sox	CWS	R	21	48	156	45	9	3	0	60	36	26	38	3	25	2	0	0	7	3	.70	1	.288	.434	.385
Cedano, Francisco	c	Johnson Cty	StL	R+	20	12	27	5	1	0	0	6	3	1	0	0	13	0	0	0	1	0	1.00	0	.185	.185	.222
Cedeno, Damaso#	ss-3b	Reds	Cin	R	18	48	167	45	5	1	0	52	15	19	11	0	27	1	1	0	1	5	.17	3	.269	.318	.311
Centeno, Edwin#	of	Bluefield	Bal	R+	23	37	93	21	2	1	1	28	26	12	21	0	36	5	1	0	10	0	1.00	1	.226	.395	.301
Centeno, Irwin	2b	Chston-SC	TB	A	20	30	111	30	5	1	0	37	16	13	12	0	19	4	2	2	7	3	.70	2	.270	.357	.333
		Hudson Val	TB	A-	20	65	232	58	12	0	0	70	37	18	36	0	50	5	5	2	26	8	.76	5	.250	.360	.302
Cepeda, Ali	of	San Jose	SF	A+	24	19	34	4	0	0	0	4	4	3	9	0	14	0	0	0	1	0	1.00	0	.118	.302	.118
Cepicky, Matt*	of	Jupiter	Mon	A+	23	131	536	160	32	7	5	221	61	88	24	4	64	2	1	5	32	13	.71	9	.299	.328	.412
Cerda, Jose	c	Giants	SF	R	24	8	23	8	2	0	0	10	3	6	2	0	3	1	0	0	1	2	.33	0	.348	.423	.435
		Salem-Keizr	SF	A-	24	17	56	13	3	0	1	19	8	5	6	0	15	0	0	0	1	0	1.00	0	.232	.306	.339
Cervenak, Mike	ss-3b	Greensboro	NYY	A	24	38	155	51	4	5	3	74	19	20	7	0	21	4	3	1	3	4	.43	1	.329	.371	.477
Chapman, Scott	c	Kissimmee	Hou	A+	23	107	373	95	26	1	8	147	51	59	50	1	85	3	0	6	0	1	.00	9	.255	.343	.394
Chapman, Travis	3b	Phillies	Phi	R	23	9	32	6	3	1	0	11	3	5	4	0	4	2	0	1	0	1	.00	0	.188	.308	.344
		Batavia	Phi	A-	23	49	174	55	10	2	1	72	23	28	12	0	24	7	2	2	0	1	.00	1	.316	.379	.414
Chauncey, Clinton	c	Yankees	NYY	R	20	10	23	6	0	0	0	6	1	5	3	0	5	0	0	2	0	0	.00	0	.261	.321	.261
Chaves, Brandon#	ss	Williamsprt	Pit	A-	21	55	169	26	4	0	0	30	14	11	18	0	37	9	3	2	0	7	.00	1	.154	.268	.178
Chavez, Angel	ss	Giants	SF	R	19	7	29	8	0	1	1	13	2	7	1	0	5	0	1	0	1	1	.50	2	.276	.300	.448
Chavez, Endy*	of	St. Lucie	NYM	A+	23	111	433	129	20	2	1	156	84	43	47	4	48	0	7	3	38	16	.70	3	.298	.364	.360
Chiarini, Mario	3b	Mariners	Sea	R	20	24	67	21	3	0	0	24	15	8	3	0	16	5	1	3	2	0	1.00	0	.313	.372	.358
Chilsom, Marques	of	Diamondbcks	Ari	R	19	53	199	35	12	1	0	49	25	19	23	0	63	3	2	2	5	6	.45	4	.176	.269	.246
Chilsom, Tawan	2b	Diamondbcks	Ari	R	20	26	38	5	0	0	0	5	2	2	8	0	13	0	1	1	5	1	.83	0	.132	.277	.132
Chirinos, Germain	of	Modesto	Oak	A+	22	21	67	15	1	3	1	25	11	8	10	0	21	0	1	2	4	0	1.00	2	.224	.316	.373
		Vancouver	Oak	A-	22	21	63	11	2	1	0	15	7	3	7	0	22	3	0	0	0	0	.00	1	.175	.288	.238
Chourio, Jorjanis	of	Pirates	Pit	R	20	51	182	53	13	2	0	70	37	23	21	0	46	2	2	3	23	5	.82	3	.291	.365	.385
		Williamsprt	Pit	A-	20	11	42	10	3	0	0	13	4	2	0	0	15	0	0	0	1	0	1.00	0	.238	.238	.310
Christensen, Mike	3b	Lk Elsinore	Ana	A+	25	129	523	141	30	2	14	217	66	95	26	1	101	3	2	5	3	3	.50	14	.270	.305	.415
Christianson, Ryan	c	Wisconsin	Sea	A	20	119	418	104	20	0	13	163	60	59	50	1	98	4	0	10	1	6	.14	10	.249	.328	.390
Church, Ryan*	of	Mahoning Vy	Cle	A-	22	73	272	81	16	5	10	137	51	65	38	3	49	8	0	3	11	4	.73	4	.298	.396	.504
Chwan, Brian*	c	Chston-SC	TB	A	24	20	52	15	2	0	0	17	7	7	3	0	12	2	0	1	0	0	.00	1	.288	.345	.327
Ciarrachi, Kevin	c	Williamsprt	Pit	A-	23	22	71	14	1	0	0	15	4	1	6	0	13	0	0	0	0	1	.00	3	.197	.260	.211
Ciraco, Darren	dh	White Sox	CWS	R	20	33	105	34	7	0	2	47	21	18	8	0	25	0	0	0	1	2	.33	2	.324	.372	.448
Cirone, Joe	of	Vancouver	Oak	A-	23	57	189	40	14	0	3	63	25	18	18	1	72	6	2	0	2	1	.67	6	.212	.300	.333
Clark, Chivas*	of	Queens	Tor	A-	22	15	41	9	1	1	0	12	9	5	17	0	9	0	2	1	2	1	.67	0	.220	.441	.293
		Hagerstown	Tor	A	22	37	113	18	6	0	0	24	15	10	15	1	27	1	2	0	1	2	.33	0	.159	.264	.212
Clark, Daryl*	3b	Ogden	Mil	R+	21	64	218	74	12	4	15	139	54	64	67	3	53	2	1	2	5	4	.56	1	.339	.495	.638
Clark, Greg	c	Peoria	StL	A	24	35	108	23	0	0	3	32	8	11	19	0	25	0	1	0	1	0	1.00	0	.213	.331	.296
Clark, Jeremy	dh	Lowell	Bos	A-	22	18	58	8	3	0	1	14	4	3	7	0	27	0	1	0	0	0	.00	3	.138	.231	.241
Clark, Tommy	of	Danville	Atl	R+	21	36	123	27	12	0	4	51	21	20	11	0	39	2	2	0	3	1	.75	0	.220	.294	.415
Clarke, Jason#	3b	Daytona	ChC	A+	25	13	42	7	2	0	1	12	8	4	2	0	8	0	0	0	2	0	1.00	0	.167	.205	.286
Clay, Mike	3b	Chston-WV	KC	A	24	71	228	54	8	1	3	73	17	18	18	0	33	8	1	4	1	1	.50	5	.237	.310	.320
Clements, Jason#	of	Vancouver	Oak	A-	23	23	67	16	1	0	1	20	8	4	7	0	23	0	2	0	2	4	.33	1	.239	.311	.299
		Modesto	Oak	A+	23	24	84	21	2	2	1	30	13	11	12	0	19	2	1	1	3	2	.60	1	.250	.354	.357
Clifton, Rodney	of	Modesto	Oak	A+	24	12	28	4	2	0	0	6	4	2	4	0	11	0	0	0	2	0	1.00	0	.143	.250	.214
Cline, Shawn	c-dh	Twins	Min	R	19	2	7	0	0	0	0	0	0	0	0	0	2	0	0	0	0	0	.00	2	.000	.000	.000
Close, James	of	Brevard Cty	Fla	A+	23	2	5	1	0	0	0	1	0	0	0	0	1	0	0	0	0	0	.00	0	.200	.200	.200
		Utica	Fla	A-	23	46	175	45	9	1	5	71	34	20	23	0	54	3	0	2	15	5	.75	3	.257	.350	.406
		Kane County	Fla	A	23	7	21	10	0	2	0	14	4	5	1	0	5	0	0	1	1	0	1.00	1	.476	.478	.667
Closser, J.D.#	c	South Bend	Ari	A	21	101	331	74	19	1	8	119	54	37	60	4	61	3	1	1	6	2	.75	7	.224	.347	.360
Coats, Buck*	of-1b	Cubs	ChC	R	19	30	98	29	6	3	0	41	20	14	12	2	24	4	0	0	7	1	.88	1	.296	.395	.418
Cochrane, Mark	dh-c	Burlington	CWS	A	21	6	16	3	2	0	0	5	2	0	3	0	7	0	0	0	0	0	.00	1	.188	.316	.313
		Bristol	CWS	R+	21	28	89	22	2	0	1	27	9	11	8	0	15	1	0	1	0	1	.00	2	.247	.313	.303
Colameco, Joe*	of	Yankees	NYY	R	25	11	27	3	1	0	0	4	1	4	6	0	6	0	1	0	1	0	1.00	0	.111	.273	.148
Coleman, Alph	of	Danville	Atl	R+	22	47	179	54	10	7	2	84	25	22	4	0	19	1	2	2	12	3	.80	7	.302	.317	.469
Colina, Alvin	c	Rockies	Col	R	19	35	122	43	7	1	4	64	25	28	9	0	26	6	0	2	2	3	.40	2	.352	.417	.525
Collazo, Julio	ss	Piedmont	Phi	A	20	89	293	61	6	1	1	72	40	21	35	0	76	5	6	6	11	5	.69	5	.208	.298	.246
Collins, Kevin*	1b	Cubs	ChC	R	20	36	127	31	5	1	4	50	18	18	14	0	35	2	1	1	0	2	.00	3	.244	.326	.394
Collins, Mike	2b	San Berndno	LA	A+	24	103	342	100	12	0	0	112	50	36	44	0	45	1	6	8	11	6	.65	6	.292	.367	.327
Colmenter, Jesus#	2b	Burlington	Cle	R+	19	42	152	41	8	0	2	55	20	22	8	0	21	1	3	0	3	1	.75	4	.270	.311	.362
Colon, Roberto	3b	Tigers	Det	R	21	15	38	9	2	0	1	14	4	5	8	0	10	0	0	1	0	0	.00	1	.237	.362	.368
Compton, Jack	of	Martinsvlle	Hou	R+	24	6	17	2	1	0	0	3	2	1	2	0	4	1	0	0	2	0	1.00	0	.118	.250	.176
Contrera, Albino*	of	Butte	Ana	R+	21	39	131	39	7	2	4	62	24	27	13	0	18	0	1	5	4	2	.67	3	.298	.349	.473
Contreras, Erick#	ss	Danville	Atl	R+	21	13	37	15	3	0	0	18	10	5	4	0	4	0	1	0	3	3	.50	0	.405	.463	.486
		Macon	Atl	A	21	18	39	10	2	0	0	12	9	2	11	0	9	1	0	0	1	1	.50	1	.256	.431	.308
Contreras, Sergio*	1b	Butte	Ana	R+	21	45	173	69	10	8	3	104	44	28	19	1	25	5	2	2	8	4	.67	2	.399	.467	.601

2000 Batting — Class-A and Rookie Leagues

BATTING																					BASERUNNING				PERCENTAGES		
Player	Pos	Team	Org	Lg	A	G	AB	H	2B	3B	HR	TB	R	RBI	TBB	IBB	SO	HBP	SH	SF	SB	CS	SB%	GDP	Avg	OBP	SLG
Conway, Dan	c	Portland	Col	A-	21	45	139	22	5	0	0	27	13	12	15	1	40	2	2	2	1	1	.50	5	.158	.247	.194
Conyer, Darryl*	of-dh	Diamondbcks	Ari	R	21	7	22	7	1	1	0	10	3	2	1	0	8	0	1	0	1	0	1.00	0	.318	.348	.455
		Missoula	Ari	R+	21	17	57	13	3	1	1	21	7	14	11	1	25	0	0	2	2	0	1.00	2	.228	.343	.368
Cook, Jon	of	Fort Wayne	SD	A	24	24	69	15	2	0	0	17	6	5	10	0	21	1	3	0	12	3	.80	0	.217	.325	.246
Cook, Josh	3b	Salem-Keizr	SF	A-	23	34	130	25	7	0	0	32	14	14	6	0	19	1	1	0	0	2	.00	3	.192	.234	.246
		San Jose	SF	A+	23	15	50	12	0	0	2	18	9	2	7	0	13	1	0	0	0	1	.00	0	.240	.345	.360
Cooper, Matt	1b	Red Sox	Bos	R	20	26	74	20	5	0	1	28	10	6	16	1	18	4	0	0	0	1	.00	2	.270	.426	.378
Cooper, Sam#	ss	Eugene	ChC	A-	23	14	27	4	0	0	0	4	4	1	5	0	2	2	1	0	0	0	.00	0	.148	.324	.148
		Daytona	ChC	A+	23	10	27	6	1	1	0	9	4	4	0	0	4	0	1	1	0	0	.00	0	.222	.214	.333
Copeland, Brandon	of	St. Lucie	NYM	A+	24	35	102	25	4	0	2	35	18	13	11	1	17	3	1	1	4	4	.50	2	.245	.333	.343
		Potomac	StL	A+	24	42	112	20	3	3	2	35	13	15	18	0	39	5	2	1	2	4	.33	2	.179	.316	.313
Cordido, Julio	3b	Bakersfield	SF	A+	20	130	460	116	17	3	10	169	70	64	46	0	99	7	5	6	13	12	.52	3	.252	.326	.367
Cordova, Ben*	of	Chston-WV	KC	A	21	26	86	17	4	1	0	23	11	7	13	0	24	0	2	0	1	0	1.00	2	.198	.303	.267
		Spokane	KC	A-	21	67	242	57	20	1	5	94	43	34	41	3	54	0	1	2	6	2	.75	6	.236	.344	.388
Cordova, Ricardo#	2b	Great Falls	LA	R+	19	41	133	42	3	0	0	45	29	14	20	0	25	1	5	1	9	1	.90	6	.316	.406	.338
Corporan, Elvis#	3b	Greensboro	NYY	A	21	63	255	63	10	1	4	87	37	31	28	0	66	0	1	0	10	2	.83	7	.247	.322	.341
		Staten Ilnd	NYY	A-	21	73	281	73	14	2	8	115	37	36	23	2	61	3	1	5	7	2	.78	8	.260	.317	.409
Corporan, Roberto#	2b	Diamondbcks	Ari	R	18	38	91	18	4	2	1	29	21	16	33	0	35	2	2	2	5	6	.45	1	.198	.414	.319
Cortes, Jorge*	of	Williamsprt	Pit	A-	20	51	173	35	11	0	4	58	18	22	20	1	48	2	0	2	0	2	.00	5	.202	.289	.335
Cosby, Rob#	3b	Hagerstown	Tor	A	20	77	291	69	9	0	4	90	31	29	16	0	37	0	0	2	2	3	.40	7	.237	.275	.309
		Queens	Tor	A-	20	42	163	44	8	0	0	52	15	22	14	1	22	0	0	1	4	2	.67	3	.270	.326	.319
Cosentino, Tony	c	Fort Wayne	SD	A	22	80	276	72	19	1	3	102	25	38	32	0	50	5	0	2	1	0	1.00	13	.261	.346	.370
Cosme, Caonabo	ss	Modesto	Oak	A+	22	133	548	132	33	2	2	175	73	53	56	0	163	2	12	3	44	15	.75	9	.241	.312	.319
Cotten, Jeremy	1b	Hickory	Pit	A	20	59	210	60	18	1	9	107	39	32	20	0	55	3	0	0	0	2	.00	1	.286	.356	.510
		Williamsprt	Pit	A-	20	2	5	0	0	0	0	0	0	0	1	0	2	0	0	0	0	0	.00	0	.000	.167	.000
Cotto, Luis	ss	Royals	KC	R	19	46	133	24	2	0	0	26	17	6	23	0	25	4	3	1	5	1	.83	0	.180	.317	.195
Coulie, Jason	of	Boise	Ana	A-	23	62	242	64	16	2	10	114	34	39	21	0	66	5	2	1	8	6	.57	5	.264	.335	.471
Covington, Kevin	of	Yakima	LA	A-	23	48	141	35	12	1	2	55	17	13	10	0	29	0	3	0	2	1	.67	0	.248	.298	.390
Cowan, Justin	of-c	Spokane	KC	A-	23	48	189	59	12	0	3	80	24	31	18	0	32	2	2	5	3	2	.60	4	.312	.369	.423
Coyne, Tony	2b	Kingsport	NYM	R+	22	13	40	9	3	0	1	15	6	3	4	0	10	1	1	0	2	1	.67	0	.225	.311	.375
		Pittsfield	NYM	A-	22	21	72	15	3	0	0	18	5	4	2	0	21	2	1	0	2	4	.33	1	.208	.250	.250
Craig, Beau#	c	Vancouver	Oak	A-	22	24	77	19	8	0	0	27	6	11	5	0	19	0	1	1	0	0	.00	2	.247	.289	.351
Crawford, Carl*	of	Chston-SC	TB	A	19	135	564	170	21	11	6	231	99	57	32	1	102	3	9	1	55	9	.86	1	.301	.342	.410
Crespo, Manny	2b	Everett	Sea	A-	22	46	162	42	6	0	3	57	28	25	19	1	53	4	1	1	2	2	.50	4	.259	.349	.352
Cridland, Mark*	of	Mudville	Mil	A+	26	131	503	131	25	6	21	231	78	66	49	4	101	9	1	3	20	9	.69	11	.260	.335	.459
Crisp, Covelli#	of	New Jersey	StL	A-	21	36	134	32	5	0	0	37	18	14	11	0	22	1	5	0	25	3	.89	1	.239	.301	.276
		Peoria	StL	A	21	27	98	27	9	0	0	36	14	7	16	0	15	0	4	0	7	3	.70	1	.276	.377	.367
Crocker, Nick*	of	Jamestown	Atl	A-	23	2	8	1	0	0	0	1	2	0	1	0	4	0	0	0	0	0	.00	0	.125	.222	.125
		Macon	Atl	A	23	58	221	51	12	0	8	87	24	38	14	0	61	3	1	3	7	4	.64	1	.231	.282	.394
Crosby, Bubba*	of	Vero Beach	LA	A+	24	73	274	73	13	8	8	126	50	51	31	3	41	7	3	1	27	10	.73	9	.266	.355	.460
		San Berndno	LA	A+	24	3	12	3	0	0	0	3	2	2	0	0	4	0	0	0	1	0	1.00	1	.250	.250	.250
Crozier, Eric*	of	Mahoning Vy	Cle	A-	22	52	179	38	9	0	4	59	31	24	30	0	61	0	1	1	4	2	.67	3	.212	.324	.330
Cruz, Alex	ss	Pirates	Pit	R	20	45	166	35	5	1	1	45	20	12	8	0	26	3	2	0	5	0	1.00	2	.211	.260	.271
Cruz, Edgar	c	Columbus	Cle	A	22	90	320	58	13	1	11	106	44	38	21	1	81	8	3	6	0	0	.00	8	.181	.245	.331
Cruz, Enrique	ss-3b	Capital Cty	NYM	A	19	49	157	29	12	0	1	44	19	12	25	1	44	1	1	1	1	3	.25	1	.185	.299	.280
		Kingsport	NYM	R+	19	63	223	56	14	0	9	97	35	39	26	1	56	3	4	2	19	7	.73	3	.251	.335	.435
Cruz, Israel	ss-2b	Mariners	Sea	R	21	47	176	56	9	1	1	70	33	34	6	0	18	0	2	2	6	3	.67	3	.318	.337	.398
		Lancaster	Sea	A+	21	1	4	0	0	0	0	0	0	1	0	0	1	0	0	0	0	0	.00	0	.000	.000	.000
Cruz, Orlando	dh	Rangers	Tex	R	19	9	24	4	1	1	0	7	5	1	5	0	9	0	2	0	0	0	.00	0	.167	.310	.292
Cuevas, Alvin	c	Royals	KC	R	20	21	52	6	0	1	0	8	5	4	8	0	18	0	1	0	0	0	.00	3	.115	.233	.154
Culwell, Nate#	c	Billings	Cin	R+	22	47	173	52	7	0	3	68	31	29	20	0	37	5	0	2	3	1	.75	3	.301	.385	.393
Cunningham, Marco	of	Spokane	KC	A-	23	75	282	78	16	4	2	108	58	42	54	1	51	10	9	1	31	7	.82	4	.277	.409	.383
Curry, Chris	c	Daytona	ChC	A+	23	20	59	9	0	0	0	9	5	3	4	0	17	1	1	0	0	0	.00	4	.153	.219	.153
		Lansing	ChC	A	23	48	131	27	3	1	6	50	17	23	12	0	41	1	0	1	0	0	.00	0	.206	.276	.382
Curry, Jesse*	of	Fort Wayne	SD	A	22	23	74	14	7	0	3	30	14	15	11	0	20	1	0	1	3	0	1.00	1	.189	.299	.405
Dacey, Ryan	ss	Yakima	LA	A-	23	55	155	50	11	0	1	64	27	16	27	0	32	8	5	1	3	3	.50	2	.323	.445	.413
Daedelow, Craig	2b	Frederick	Bal	A+	25	62	145	29	6	0	0	35	24	9	26	0	26	2	4	2	4	1	.80	3	.200	.326	.241
Daigle, Leo	1b	Lakeland	Det	A+	21	113	398	94	20	2	7	139	26	52	27	2	108	5	1	8	1	2	.33	12	.236	.288	.349
Dalton, David	ss	Myrtle Bch	Atl	A+	25	82	275	67	12	1	6	99	36	21	38	0	77	10	3	0	9	5	.64	3	.244	.356	.360
Danbert, John*	3b	Everett	Sea	A-	22	49	177	42	10	0	1	55	21	33	24	1	39	0	1	1	4	3	.57	4	.237	.327	.311
Daniels, Claiborne	of	Padres	SD	R	19	33	77	9	3	1	0	14	10	8	2	0	36	2	1	2	3	0	1.00	1	.117	.157	.182
Darr, Ryan	dh-3b	Potomac	StL	A+	23	88	280	68	17	0	2	91	43	26	43	0	90	4	3	2	7	1	.88	4	.243	.350	.325
Davenport, Ron*	1b	Medcine Hat	Tor	R+	19	59	229	79	16	2	4	111	37	46	21	0	28	3	0	2	5	2	.71	7	.345	.404	.485
Davis, Daniel*	of	Tigers	Det	R	20	46	141	26	4	0	2	36	13	16	22	2	56	5	0	1	4	2	.67	1	.184	.314	.255
Davis, J.J.	of	Lynchburg	Pit	A+	22	130	485	118	36	1	20	216	77	80	52	2	171	4	0	4	9	4	.69	11	.243	.319	.445
Davis, James	2b	Butte	Ana	R+	22	41	130	35	3	1	0	40	21	13	30	0	22	6	3	0	3	1	.75	2	.269	.428	.308
Davis, Monty	2b	Visalia	Oak	A+	23	11	23	11	2	0	0	13	7	5	8	1	1	2	1	0	1	2	.33	0	.478	.636	.565
Davis, Morrin	of	Medcine Hat	Tor	R+	18	40	162	36	6	2	5	61	17	16	11	0	59	1	0	0	2	1	.67	3	.222	.276	.377
Davis, Ryan*	of-1b	Giants	SF	R	22	50	154	41	5	1	0	48	24	24	32	0	35	3	2	6	8	4	.67	3	.266	.390	.312
		San Jose	SF	A+	22	2	5	2	0	0	0	2	0	1	1	0	0	0	0	0	0	0	.00	0	.400	.500	.400
Davison, Ashanti	of	Helena	Mil	R+	22	10	41	9	3	0	0	12	3	2	0	0	10	2	1	0	1	2	.33	0	.220	.256	.293
Day, Nick	of	Idaho Falls	SD	R+	23	9	36	16	1	1	2	25	13	7	6	1	3	2	0	0	3	1	.75	0	.444	.545	.694
		Fort Wayne	SD	A	23	29	97	22	7	0	3	38	12	11	6	0	22	1	0	2	0	0	.00	5	.227	.274	.392
Dean, Mike	dh	Giants	SF	R	23	46	131	39	5	2	0	48	19	21	22	0	40	2	2	4	8	10	.44	1	.298	.396	.366
Deardorff, Jeff	3b	Mudville	Mil	A+	22	111	421	103	20	7	10	167	48	54	32	2	120	1	0	6	7	10	.41	9	.245	.296	.397
De Aza, Modesto	of	Kissimmee	Hou	A+	22	4	1	0	0	0	0	0	1	0	0	0	1	0	0	0	0	0	.00	0	.000	.000	.000
		Michigan	Hou	A	22	25	77	17	2	3	0	25	8	6	2	0	24	2	1	1	11	1	.92	1	.221	.256	.325

2000 Batting — Class-A and Rookie Leagues

BATTING																					BASERUNNING				PERCENTAGES		
Player	Pos	Team	Org	Lg	A	G	AB	H	2B	3B	HR	TB	R	RBI	TBB	IBB	SO	HBP	SH	SF	SB	CS	SB%	GDP	Avg	OBP	SLG
		Auburn	Hou	A-	22	16	54	15	1	1	0	18	11	3	6	0	14	5	1	0	15	4	.79	0	.278	.400	.333
DeCaster, Yurendell	3b	Chston-SC	TB	A	21	69	242	58	21	0	7	100	34	28	16	0	89	6	2	4	4	1	.80	2	.240	.299	.413
Deck, Billy*	1b	Potomac	StL	A+	24	99	290	64	13	0	6	95	36	30	42	0	79	12	3	3	3	3	.50	6	.221	.340	.328
Declet, Miguel	3b	Vancouver	Oak	A-	21	55	178	40	9	0	1	52	20	19	14	0	60	2	2	3	3	0	1.00	1	.225	.284	.292
Decola, Dan	dh-c	Elizabethtn	Min	R+	21	35	136	46	10	1	3	67	27	28	7	0	24	9	1	1	0	0	.00	6	.338	.405	.493
Dees, Charlie	of	Delmarva	Bal	A	23	13	20	3	0	2	0	7	3	1	1	0	12	0	0	1	0	0	.00	1	.150	.182	.350
		Bluefield	Bal	R+	23	2	7	1	1	0	0	2	0	1	0	0	4	0	0	0	0	0	.00	0	.143	.143	.286
		Pulaski	Tex	R+	23	51	184	56	9	4	13	112	40	47	25	0	62	2	1	3	9	1	.90	2	.304	.388	.609
DeGroote, Casey*	dh	Staten Ilnd	NYY	A-	21	34	69	11	1	0	1	15	4	4	3	0	36	0	1	1	0	0	.00	0	.159	.192	.217
Dehner, Matt	3b	Clinton	Cin	A	24	108	325	76	18	1	3	105	48	26	23	0	80	13	4	2	15	8	.65	11	.234	.309	.323
Deitrick, Jeremy	c	Piedmont	Phi	A	24	54	159	45	8	0	3	62	21	18	10	0	34	1	1	2	2	1	.67	5	.283	.326	.390
de la Cruz, Eric	of	Beloit	Mil	A	22	68	190	52	10	0	2	68	25	17	14	0	26	3	6	1	2	5	.29	6	.274	.332	.358
de la Cruz, Jose	c	Modesto	Oak	A+	23	59	164	29	7	0	1	39	17	20	30	1	47	1	1	2	1	5	.17	5	.177	.305	.238
de la Cruz, Miguel	3b	Pirates	Pit	R	21	16	49	12	1	0	1	16	7	5	4	0	9	0	0	0	3	1	.75	0	.245	.302	.327
de la Cruz, Ruddi	ss-2b	Capital Cty	NYM	A	21	55	164	34	6	2	2	50	20	12	10	0	43	2	3	0	15	1	.94	2	.207	.261	.305
Delanves, Orlando	2b	Diamondbcks	Ari	R	20	47	130	33	3	0	0	36	19	8	15	0	24	1	3	1	10	4	.71	1	.254	.333	.277
de la Paz, Camilo	2b-3b	Helena	Mil	R+	21	40	122	23	9	0	1	35	15	16	16	0	33	1	1	2	5	2	.71	2	.189	.284	.287
Delgado, Ariel*	of	Lk Elsinore	Ana	A+	24	48	153	38	8	0	2	52	17	16	10	0	22	4	0	1	0	4	.00	3	.248	.310	.340
Delgado, Chris	1b	Asheville	Col	A	23	18	59	8	1	0	1	12	4	3	7	0	25	0	0	1	1	1	.50	2	.136	.224	.203
		Portland	Col	A-	23	3	13	5	0	0	0	5	2	2	0	0	2	1	0	0	0	0	.00	0	.385	.429	.385
Delgado, Dario	1b	Batavia	Phi	A-	21	63	216	52	8	2	7	85	37	40	29	0	44	4	0	5	0	0	.00	6	.241	.335	.394
Delgado, Jorge	c	Missoula	Ari	R+	20	43	138	43	6	0	5	64	26	29	28	0	17	12	0	3	5	1	.83	5	.312	.459	.464
		Diamondbcks	Ari	R	20	8	29	9	2	1	0	13	7	6	5	0	4	0	0	0	0	1	.00	0	.310	.412	.448
de los Santos, H.	2b	Augusta	Bos	A	21	7	16	3	0	0	0	3	1	2	0	0	3	0	0	1	1	0	1.00	0	.188	.176	.188
		Red Sox	Bos	R	21	46	149	44	7	2	1	58	28	11	5	0	13	2	0	0	19	2	.90	5	.295	.327	.389
de los Santos, N.#	dh-c	Helena	Mil	R+	22	47	169	51	12	4	2	77	27	31	17	0	32	2	2	3	9	4	.69	1	.302	.366	.456
		Mudville	Mil	A+	22	14	51	13	2	1	2	23	5	8	3	0	8	0	0	0	0	1	.00	0	.255	.296	.451
de los Santos, S.	ss	Johnson Cty	StL	R+	20	15	43	14	4	0	0	18	6	9	3	0	10	0	1	0	4	2	.67	0	.326	.370	.419
del Rosario, E.#	2b	Bluefield	Bal	R+	19	54	185	46	6	1	0	54	23	15	27	1	23	3	4	2	11	1	.92	8	.249	.350	.292
DeMarco, Matt*	3b	Marlins	Fla	R	21	1	3	0	0	0	0	0	0	0	1	0	1	0	0	0	0	0	.00	2	.000	.250	.000
		Kane County	Fla	A	21	29	92	21	8	1	1	34	12	16	9	0	15	1	0	0	1	0	1.00	2	.228	.304	.370
Dement, Dan	ss	Princeton	TB	R+	23	60	206	62	9	4	7	100	48	39	31	0	48	3	1	1	7	1	.88	5	.301	.398	.485
DePaula, Luis	ss	Princeton	TB	R+	18	30	116	34	8	0	0	42	9	10	7	1	26	0	1	2	1	3	.25	5	.293	.328	.362
DeRenne, Keoni	ss	Jamestown	Atl	A-	22	20	66	20	6	0	1	29	19	9	11	0	5	2	0	1	6	1	.86	3	.303	.413	.439
		Macon	Atl	A	22	38	145	38	9	1	1	52	13	11	11	0	20	2	0	2	3	3	.50	1	.262	.319	.359
Deschenes, Pat*	3b	Capital Cty	NYM	A	23	125	441	114	27	3	4	159	53	57	53	2	90	9	1	4	4	1	.80	7	.259	.347	.361
Detienne, Dave	2b	Great Falls	LA	R+	21	64	241	58	10	2	6	90	41	34	22	1	60	4	2	2	18	5	.78	3	.241	.312	.373
Devanez, Noel	of	Kingsport	NYM	R+	19	58	197	60	14	2	9	105	33	35	14	0	46	5	3	0	8	8	.50	3	.305	.366	.533
Devine, Rich*	of	Spokane	KC	A-	23	24	57	16	1	0	0	17	15	8	11	0	11	2	0	0	12	2	.86	0	.281	.414	.298
Devore, Doug*	of	South Bend	Ari	A	23	127	452	132	27	4	15	212	64	60	47	5	101	2	2	4	9	6	.60	9	.292	.358	.469
Diaz, Aneuris	3b	Johnson Cty	StL	R+	20	53	179	48	11	1	5	76	27	25	10	1	65	3	2	1	4	4	.50	3	.268	.316	.425
Diaz, Angel	c	Lk Elsinore	Ana	A+	24	45	133	47	11	1	3	69	24	18	19	0	29	4	1	2	7	3	.70	4	.353	.443	.519
Diaz, Jose	c	Great Falls	LA	R+	21	57	210	46	9	1	7	78	29	31	18	0	52	4	3	1	2	2	.50	4	.219	.292	.371
Diaz, Matt	of	St. Pete	TB	A+	23	106	392	106	21	3	6	151	37	53	11	0	54	11	1	5	2	3	.40	21	.270	.305	.385
Diaz, Miguel	of	Potomac	StL	A+	23	105	312	78	23	2	0	105	35	32	14	0	47	5	4	3	5	3	.63	8	.250	.290	.337
Diaz, Olan	2b	Rangers	Tex	R	26	3	9	3	0	0	0	3	1	0	1	0	2	1	0	0	1	0	1.00	0	.333	.455	.333
		Charlotte	Tex	A+	26	51	179	49	2	4	0	59	27	13	27	0	26	4	1	2	4	5	.44	1	.274	.377	.330
Dillard, Thomas	c	Elizabethtn	Min	R+	24	31	84	18	1	0	0	19	18	5	12	0	16	3	2	0	7	1	.88	1	.214	.333	.226
Dion, Nathanael	of	Princeton	TB	R+	19	50	155	27	4	1	1	36	18	6	14	0	51	2	0	2	1	1	.50	3	.174	.249	.232
D'Jesus, Francisco	c	Giants	SF	R	20	50	164	39	3	2	0	46	11	19	4	0	19	1	2	2	3	3	.50	6	.238	.257	.280
		Salem-Keizr	SF	A-	20	1	3	1	1	0	0	2	0	1	0	0	1	0	0	0	0	0	.00	0	.333	.333	.667
Docen, Jose#	2b	Cape Fear	Mon	A	21	34	116	32	3	0	0	35	19	15	14	0	18	3	5	1	6	5	.55	4	.276	.366	.302
		Vermont	Mon	A-	21	59	229	67	16	2	0	87	44	30	34	0	33	4	2	1	27	7	.79	6	.293	.392	.380
Dogero, Matt	dh-c	Johnson Cty	StL	R+	20	22	65	14	2	0	3	25	7	7	9	0	22	4	0	0	0	1	.00	0	.215	.346	.385
Dohrman, Bruce*	of-dh	Twins	Min	R	20	5	15	2	0	0	0	2	3	3	3	0	2	0	0	1	0	0	.00	1	.133	.263	.133
Dolton, Odis	of	Reds	Cin	R	21	35	114	23	5	1	0	30	9	8	8	0	44	3	1	0	4	4	.50	1	.202	.272	.263
Domero, William	3b-of	Tigers	Det	R	21	43	154	46	6	5	3	71	28	28	14	1	33	5	0	1	5	2	.71	4	.299	.374	.461
		W Michigan	Det	A	21	8	33	11	3	0	1	17	5	9	3	0	10	0	0	0	2	0	1.00	1	.333	.389	.515
Dominguez, Luis	3b	Michigan	Hou	A	21	84	247	51	5	2	1	63	44	26	48	1	48	3	1	5	8	2	.80	12	.206	.337	.255
Donato, Gregorio	dh-2b	Jamestown	Atl	A-	20	67	266	82	12	5	8	128	56	40	13	0	56	0	1	4	12	3	.80	5	.308	.336	.481
Donovan, Todd	of	Fort Wayne	SD	A	22	53	204	58	12	4	0	78	39	23	25	0	45	4	0	2	18	9	.67	1	.284	.370	.382
Dorman, John	ss	St. Lucie	NYM	A+	27	35	96	18	1	1	1	24	13	4	13	0	25	3	1	0	5	1	.83	3	.188	.304	.250
Dorner, Dwight*	c	Princeton	TB	R+	23	35	89	25	3	1	0	30	12	14	18	0	18	2	2	1	2	3	.40	7	.281	.409	.337
Dorsey, Ryan	2b-3b	Pirates	Pit	R	19	38	120	29	11	1	4	54	14	28	13	0	46	1	1	3	1	1	.50	2	.242	.314	.450
Doudt, Anthony	c	Cedar Rapds	Ana	A	24	34	104	27	2	0	2	35	8	11	11	0	32	3	0	1	0	1	.00	2	.260	.345	.337
Dougherty, Andy	c	Burlington	Cle	R+	24	6	13	1	0	0	0	1	0	0	2	0	3	0	1	0	0	0	.00	0	.077	.200	.077
Douglas, Harley*	of	Pittsfield	NYM	A-	23	20	43	7	1	0	0	8	3	2	5	1	13	3	2	1	2	2	.50	0	.163	.288	.186
		Kingsport	NYM	R+	23	16	47	13	2	1	0	17	6	4	3	0	11	0	2	1	6	1	.86	0	.277	.314	.362
Doumit, Ryan#	c	Williamsprt	Pit	A-	20	66	246	77	15	5	2	108	25	40	23	1	33	4	0	7	2	2	.50	7	.313	.371	.439
Downing, Brad*	dh	Boise	Ana	A-	25	75	285	96	17	0	7	134	52	46	41	4	57	5	0	2	1	1	.50	3	.337	.426	.470
Downing, Phillip*	of	Vermont	Mon	A-	22	61	218	53	9	8	1	81	38	24	48	1	62	4	0	2	15	3	.83	2	.243	.386	.372
Driggers, Richard	of	Phillies	Phi	R	19	36	118	31	3	0	0	34	14	8	5	0	26	1	2	0	7	3	.70	1	.263	.298	.288
Drobiak, Jayson*	3b	W Michigan	Det	A	22	94	313	70	17	0	5	102	38	43	35	2	88	2	0	4	5	1	.83	2	.224	.302	.326
Duarte, Justin	c	Batavia	Phi	A-	24	24	73	15	2	0	2	23	9	12	9	0	17	1	0	0	0	0	.00	1	.205	.301	.315
Duck, Kevin*	1b	Asheville	Col	A	23	39	125	21	5	0	0	26	7	5	12	0	39	2	1	0	1	1	.50	5	.168	.252	.208
Duenas, Manuel	2b	Idaho Falls	SD	R+	21	46	174	50	11	2	3	74	24	20	19	0	58	0	0	1	2	0	1.00	8	.287	.356	.425
Dunaway, Jason	2b	Rancho Cuca	SD	A+	24	55	156	38	3	1	0	43	25	10	17	0	39	4	3	2	9	5	.64	3	.244	.330	.276

2000 Batting — Class-A and Rookie Leagues

BATTING																					BASERUNNING				PERCENTAGES		
Player	Pos	Team	Org	Lg	A	G	AB	H	2B	3B	HR	TB	R	RBI	TBB	IBB	SO	HBP	SH	SF	SB	CS	SB%	GDP	Avg	OBP	SLG
Duncan, Carlos	of	Clearwater	Phi	A+	24	107	390	103	25	3	8	158	49	47	26	0	113	9	3	3	13	9	.59	3	.264	.322	.405
Duncan, Chris*	1b	Peoria	StL	A	20	122	450	115	34	0	8	173	52	57	36	1	111	6	1	1	1	2	.33	11	.256	.318	.384
Duncan, Jeff*	of	Pittsfield	NYM	A-	22	53	186	45	3	5	2	64	39	13	34	0	46	4	4	0	20	3	.87	1	.242	.371	.344
Duncheon, Ryan*	1b	Boise	Ana	A-	23	19	23	5	3	0	0	8	2	3	3	0	9	0	0	0	0	0	.00	0	.217	.308	.348
Dunn, Adam*	of	Dayton	Cin	A	21	122	420	118	29	1	16	197	101	79	100	4	101	12	0	6	24	5	.83	10	.281	.428	.469
Dunn, Casey	c-dh	Wilmington	KC	A+	24	62	205	58	11	0	1	72	18	28	12	0	35	5	3	3	1	0	1.00	9	.283	.333	.351
Duran, Deudis#	2b-3b	Phillies	Phi	R	19	34	121	34	7	0	2	47	19	11	10	0	18	3	3	0	6	2	.75	1	.281	.351	.388
Duran, Francisco	2b	Cedar Rapds	Ana	A	22	115	405	91	17	1	1	113	58	39	45	1	97	4	7	5	12	10	.55	7	.225	.305	.279
Durand, Jose	c	Royals	KC	R	20	37	99	15	5	0	0	20	8	3	18	1	29	1	0	1	1	1	.50	4	.152	.286	.202
Durango, Ariel#	2b	Wisconsin	Sea	A	22	117	447	117	19	2	6	158	80	59	29	1	110	9	7	3	49	17	.74	5	.262	.318	.353
Durham, Chad	of	Burlington	CWS	A	23	132	517	142	15	6	1	172	80	33	46	2	85	2	4	6	58	18	.76	5	.275	.333	.333
Durham, Miles*	dh	Tigers	Det	R	22	3	14	4	2	0	0	6	1	0	0	0	4	0	0	0	1	0	1.00	0	.286	.286	.429
Dusan, Joe*	dh-1b	Dunedin	Tor	A+	23	77	197	39	7	0	5	61	30	19	24	0	55	1	2	4	1	1	.50	6	.198	.283	.310
Dwyer, Mike*	1b	Sarasota	Bos	A+	23	110	383	80	20	4	6	126	36	43	25	3	103	0	1	2	2	5	.29	8	.209	.256	.329
Dyt, Darren*	dh	Potomac	StL	A+	25	24	71	13	3	1	0	18	5	3	3	0	27	0	0	0	1	0	1.00	2	.183	.216	.254
Dzurilla, Mike	2b	Lansing	ChC	A	23	67	263	64	10	1	4	88	32	33	25	1	33	2	1	5	6	4	.60	3	.243	.308	.335
Easterday, Matt	2b	Utica	Fla	A-	22	60	220	56	14	1	3	81	36	26	22	0	45	6	1	6	8	4	.67	6	.255	.331	.368
Eddlemon, Kelly	3b	Princeton	TB	R+	22	65	239	70	21	0	10	121	44	42	19	0	47	4	0	5	7	3	.70	2	.293	.348	.506
Edwards, Dytarious*	2b	Clinton	Cin	A	24	12	22	4	0	0	0	4	4	0	2	0	4	0	0	0	1	1	.50	1	.182	.250	.182
Edwards, John	of	Quad City	Min	A	23	92	323	78	15	2	7	118	46	32	18	1	90	3	1	2	8	4	.67	9	.241	.286	.365
Egly, John#	1b	Missoula	Ari	R+	21	59	205	52	8	2	9	91	43	30	29	0	65	3	0	1	9	5	.64	3	.254	.353	.444
		South Bend	Ari	A	21	9	31	7	1	0	0	8	0	5	5	0	11	0	0	0	0	1	.00	1	.226	.333	.258
Eiguren, Chaz	1b	Reds	Cin	R	24	1	2	1	0	0	0	1	3	0	3	0	0	0	0	0	0	0	.00	1	.500	.800	.500
Elder, Rick*	1b	Delmarva	Bal	A	21	14	48	4	1	0	1	8	4	6	9	0	18	0	0	1	0	2	.00	0	.083	.224	.167
Eldridge, Rashad#	of	Burlington	Cle	R+	19	48	173	30	5	0	1	38	11	12	12	0	42	3	0	0	1	3	.25	6	.173	.239	.220
Ellis, Alvyn	1b	Athletics	Oak	R	21	48	169	50	10	1	4	74	31	28	26	1	46	3	2	0	1	2	.33	4	.296	.399	.438
Ellis, Ryan	2b	Vermont	Mon	A-	22	34	101	20	4	0	0	24	14	8	7	0	25	6	1	2	5	1	.83	1	.198	.284	.238
Ellison, Jason	of	Salem-Keizr	SF	A-	23	74	300	90	15	2	0	109	67	28	29	1	45	7	4	1	13	7	.65	1	.300	.374	.363
Elwood, Brad	c	Tampa	NYY	A+	25	42	122	23	2	0	0	25	9	9	10	0	31	0	0	1	0	0	.00	6	.189	.248	.205
		Greensboro	NYY	A	25	11	39	12	0	1	0	14	9	2	7	0	4	0	0	0	0	1	.00	2	.308	.413	.359
Elzy, Steve	c	Capital Cty	NYM	A	23	57	182	41	9	0	2	56	22	12	17	0	28	1	0	1	2	0	1.00	5	.225	.294	.308
Emmerick, Josh	c	Expos	Mon	R	20	34	112	25	0	0	0	25	13	7	10	0	19	4	0	0	4	2	.67	7	.223	.310	.223
Encarnacion, A.	of	Utica	Fla	A-	21	60	193	41	4	2	0	49	21	15	8	0	38	2	1	2	15	6	.71	2	.212	.249	.254
Encarnacion, B.	2b	Lk Elsinore	Ana	A+	23	76	266	60	9	0	0	69	24	33	11	0	40	3	7	0	5	4	.56	6	.226	.264	.259
Encarnacion, E.*	3b	Rangers	Tex	R	19	51	177	55	6	3	0	67	31	36	21	1	27	1	3	3	3	1	.75	7	.311	.381	.379
Encarnacion, Julio	of	White Sox	CWS	R	19	48	168	51	16	3	0	73	24	25	6	0	46	1	0	1	4	5	.44	2	.304	.330	.435
Encarnacion, S.	3b	Idaho Falls	SD	R+	21	47	158	44	8	3	1	61	24	27	11	0	34	0	0	0	7	3	.70	5	.278	.325	.386
Epstein, Jake	1b	Butte	Ana	R+	23	39	143	48	14	1	5	79	16	33	13	0	32	4	0	2	1	0	1.00	5	.336	.401	.552
Ernst, Michael	c	Burlington	Cle	R+	22	6	16	3	1	0	1	7	2	3	2	0	4	0	0	0	0	0	.00	0	.188	.278	.438
Escalera, Jose	of	Great Falls	LA	R+	20	55	221	58	6	5	3	83	29	43	12	0	25	5	1	4	7	5	.58	4	.262	.310	.376
Escalona, Felix	2b-ss	Michigan	Hou	A	22	64	251	65	14	1	6	99	42	35	22	1	49	4	3	2	7	0	1.00	4	.259	.326	.394
		Kissimmee	Hou	A+	22	42	143	36	5	1	0	43	19	8	9	0	21	6	3	1	5	3	.63	3	.252	.321	.301
Escobar, Gustavo	2b	New Jersey	StL	A-	21	12	37	6	0	1	0	8	6	3	3	0	7	0	1	0	3	2	.60	2	.162	.225	.216
		Peoria	StL	A	21	43	128	23	3	2	0	30	12	10	15	1	29	0	4	2	3	3	.50	4	.180	.262	.234
Escobar, Luis*	c	Royals	KC	R	18	20	43	5	2	0	0	7	9	2	10	0	10	1	1	0	0	0	.00	0	.116	.296	.163
Espino, Jose	of	New Jersey	StL	A-	21	58	181	34	8	0	1	45	13	15	8	2	56	6	4	5	5	10	.33	4	.188	.240	.249
Espinoza, Andres	of	Cape Fear	Mon	A	22	38	99	18	1	0	2	25	13	11	16	0	28	0	2	0	6	1	.86	3	.182	.296	.253
Esposito, Brian	c	Lowell	Bos	A-	22	42	154	37	9	1	3	57	15	20	11	0	31	1	1	2	0	1	.00	2	.240	.292	.370
Esprit, Jermaine#	of	Burlington	Cle	R+	21	28	85	16	0	0	0	16	13	3	8	0	31	2	0	0	11	2	.85	0	.188	.274	.188
Espy, Nate	1b	Piedmont	Phi	A	23	130	452	141	32	2	21	240	88	87	101	7	105	4	0	4	7	0	1.00	12	.312	.439	.531
Esquerra, Marques#	dh	Columbus	Cle	A	25	48	162	46	6	1	2	60	22	16	11	0	18	3	3	0	6	3	.67	5	.284	.341	.370
		Kinston	Cle	A+	25	29	77	19	1	0	0	20	6	9	6	1	12	1	2	0	0	1	.00	1	.247	.310	.260
Essery, Fred	c	Rockies	Col	R	23	19	39	13	3	0	0	16	9	9	4	0	3	1	1	0	0	0	.00	1	.333	.409	.410
Essian, Jim#	of	Cubs	ChC	R	22	1	1	0	0	0	0	0	0	0	0	0	1	0	0	0	0	0	.00	0	.000	.000	.000
Estevez, Jose	of-dh	Kingsport	NYM	R+	21	2	4	1	0	0	0	1	0	0	2	0	2	0	0	0	0	1	.00	0	.250	.500	.250
Estrella, Gorky	3b	Wisconsin	Sea	A	24	104	342	68	14	1	10	114	52	48	64	2	109	9	3	4	4	6	.40	6	.199	.337	.333
Evans, Austin*	of	Pulaski	Tex	R+	23	66	254	67	8	2	1	82	48	29	52	1	29	1	2	2	23	7	.77	1	.264	.388	.323
Evans, Mitch	c	Yankees	NYY	R	20	16	43	8	1	0	0	9	3	1	5	0	4	1	0	1	0	1	.00	0	.186	.280	.209
Everett, Robert	c	Twins	Min	R	19	21	40	9	0	0	0	9	5	5	4	0	12	0	2	0	0	0	.00	0	.225	.295	.225
Ewan, Bry	c	Macon	Atl	A	22	29	81	14	1	0	2	21	9	14	10	0	32	1	1	0	0	0	.00	2	.173	.272	.259
Ewing, Byron	1b	Kinston	Cle	A+	24	98	314	52	11	1	3	74	38	22	44	0	102	7	2	0	16	5	.76	7	.166	.282	.236
Fagan, Shawn	3b	Queens	Tor	A-	23	25	90	26	6	1	2	40	17	13	12	1	22	3	0	1	0	1	.00	3	.289	.387	.444
		Hagerstown	Tor	A	23	45	172	48	8	1	2	64	20	23	18	0	28	1	0	0	5	1	.83	2	.279	.351	.372
Faison, Vince*	of	Fort Wayne	SD	A	20	117	457	100	20	2	12	160	65	39	26	0	159	5	2	2	21	4	.84	5	.219	.267	.350
Falcon, Omar	c	Padres	SD	R	18	40	120	33	9	2	4	58	23	25	22	0	43	4	0	1	1	1	.50	2	.275	.401	.483
Farnsworth, Troy	1b	Potomac	StL	A+	25	137	512	123	24	3	23	222	67	113	44	1	133	11	0	11	7	2	.78	7	.240	.308	.434
Farris, Brant	3b	Royals	KC	R	23	45	133	29	5	0	0	34	13	14	21	0	19	4	5	1	0	1	.00	6	.218	.340	.256
Fatheree, Danny	dh-c	Michigan	Hou	A	22	46	132	35	4	0	3	48	18	17	19	0	18	1	1	1	1	1	.50	5	.265	.359	.364
Fatur, Brian	ss	Johnson Cty	StL	R+	22	60	223	52	2	0	6	72	38	30	16	0	37	11	3	3	10	9	.53	5	.233	.312	.323
Fears, Chris#	of	Royals	KC	R	23	44	144	30	2	0	0	32	19	10	14	0	22	2	2	1	13	4	.76	1	.208	.286	.222
Feliciano, Jesus*	of	San Berndno	LA	A+	22	114	405	117	13	3	0	136	56	43	32	0	41	1	8	3	31	11	.74	8	.289	.340	.336
Felix, Hersy	c	Spokane	KC	A-	23	50	131	18	6	0	2	30	17	10	11	0	39	4	1	0	0	0	.00	5	.137	.226	.229
Felker, Jeff*	1b	Eugene	ChC	A-	23	27	66	12	7	0	0	19	3	5	1	0	14	1	0	0	0	1	.00	3	.182	.206	.288
Fennell, Jason#	dh	Winston-Sal	CWS	A+	23	17	50	9	2	0	0	11	7	4	10	0	12	0	4	0	1	2	.33	1	.180	.317	.220
		Burlington	CWS	A	23	79	249	59	13	1	4	86	26	36	32	0	42	5	3	2	3	2	.60	3	.237	.333	.345
Fenster, Darren	2b-ss	Spokane	KC	A-	22	60	182	43	5	1	1	53	30	23	32	0	34	1	4	3	4	2	.67	3	.236	.349	.291
Fera, Aaron	of	Hagerstown	Tor	A	23	50	166	40	11	0	4	63	22	32	20	0	53	6	0	2	5	0	1.00	1	.241	.340	.380

2000 Batting — Class-A and Rookie Leagues

BATTING																					BASERUNNING				PERCENTAGES		
Player	Pos	Team	Org	Lg	A	G	AB	H	2B	3B	HR	TB	R	RBI	TBB	IBB	SO	HBP	SH	SF	SB	CS	SB%	GDP	Avg	OBP	SLG
		Queens	Tor	A-	23	10	36	6	1	0	2	13	3	7	1	0	9	0	0	2	0	0	.00	0	.167	.179	.361
Fernandez, A.	c	Yankees	NYY	R	20	46	115	36	7	0	3	52	20	23	30	0	31	8	0	2	2	0	1.00	1	.313	.477	.452
		Staten Ilnd	NYY	A-	20	4	6	2	0	0	0	2	1	0	1	0	2	0	1	0	0	0	.00	0	.333	.429	.333
Fernandez, M.#	of	Kane County	Fla	A	22	25	70	12	3	0	0	15	8	6	10	0	15	2	1	1	3	3	.50	2	.171	.289	.214
		Utica	Fla	A-	22	47	167	41	3	3	0	50	22	9	13	0	28	4	2	0	11	7	.61	1	.246	.315	.299
Ferrand, Francisco*	of	Kane County	Fla	A	21	77	267	67	7	6	12	122	38	42	24	1	45	1	2	2	1	4	.20	1	.251	.313	.457
Figgins, Chone#	2b	Salem	Col	A+	23	134	522	145	26	14	3	208	92	48	67	0	107	1	6	5	37	19	.66	7	.278	.358	.398
Figueroa, Carlos*	2b	Rockies	Col	R	20	24	88	30	4	4	0	42	21	12	16	0	12	1	1	1	4	1	.80	0	.341	.443	.477
		Portland	Col	A-	20	28	108	27	5	0	1	35	11	6	12	1	14	0	0	1	3	2	.60	0	.250	.322	.324
Figueroa, Eduardo*	1b	Mudville	Mil	A+	24	85	289	74	8	0	6	100	42	36	45	1	75	9	0	3	0	3	.00	5	.256	.370	.346
		Beloit	Mil	A	24	21	65	12	2	0	2	20	6	4	13	0	29	0	0	0	1	1	.50	1	.185	.321	.308
Figueroa, Franky	1b	Frederick	Bal	A+	24	126	490	125	23	0	17	199	58	87	22	3	109	6	1	7	1	3	.25	15	.255	.291	.406
Filson, Greg*	3b	Lowell	Bos	A-	23	54	185	46	6	1	1	57	20	25	29	1	48	1	1	1	2	2	.50	1	.249	.352	.308
Finnerty, Francis#	1b-dh	Burlington	Cle	R+	20	55	213	61	8	1	7	92	23	35	10	0	31	3	0	2	2	0	1.00	4	.286	.325	.432
		Mahoning Vy	Cle	A-	20	3	10	3	0	0	1	6	2	3	0	0	1	0	0	1	0	0	.00	1	.300	.273	.600
Fiore, Curt	1b	Macon	Atl	A	23	108	360	102	17	1	8	145	64	47	42	0	56	14	2	2	8	1	.89	11	.283	.378	.403
Firlit, Dan	ss	New Jersey	StL	A-	22	54	173	33	4	1	1	42	14	12	11	0	57	3	1	2	10	4	.71	2	.191	.249	.243
Flanagan, Kevin	c	Staten Ilnd	NYY	A-	24	5	3	0	0	0	0	0	0	0	0	0	2	0	0	0	0	0	.00	0	.000	.000	.000
Flannigan, Tim	3b	Pittsfield	NYM	A-	22	58	199	40	7	3	0	53	20	22	31	1	60	1	2	2	2	1	.67	2	.201	.309	.266
Flores, Ralph	ss-3b	Bristol	CWS	R+	21	39	147	40	7	5	0	57	18	24	12	0	9	1	1	0	6	1	.86	4	.272	.331	.388
		Burlington	CWS	A	21	84	298	73	13	2	2	96	33	34	29	2	33	3	3	1	14	7	.67	6	.245	.317	.322
Floyd, Daniel	of	Mariners	Sea	R	18	43	190	61	14	1	2	83	32	34	11	1	18	2	2	4	3	1	.75	3	.321	.357	.437
Floyd, Mike	of	New Jersey	StL	A-	23	45	145	21	6	2	0	31	16	9	14	0	61	1	2	0	5	3	.63	0	.145	.225	.214
Folsom, Kenneth	of	Burlington	Cle	R+	20	51	176	40	8	0	4	60	11	16	10	0	62	3	0	0	3	0	1.00	3	.227	.280	.341
Forbes, Matt	of	Modesto	Oak	A+	23	52	178	44	6	1	0	52	23	17	20	0	52	1	4	1	9	3	.75	2	.247	.325	.292
Forbes, Michael*	3b	Jamestown	Atl	A-	21	61	196	63	13	3	5	97	29	43	36	1	43	3	2	4	2	0	1.00	5	.321	.427	.495
Ford, Lew	of	Augusta	Bos	A	24	126	514	162	35	11	9	246	122	74	52	3	83	12	3	2	52	4	.93	12	.315	.390	.479
Ford, Will*	of	Mudville	Mil	A+	24	13	45	13	1	0	2	20	7	8	3	1	13	1	0	0	2	0	1.00	1	.289	.347	.444
		Beloit	Mil	A	24	62	202	42	12	2	2	64	30	17	24	0	59	1	3	0	1	1	.50	3	.208	.295	.317
Forelli, Anthony	3b	Helena	Mil	R+	24	18	63	16	1	0	4	29	9	11	5	0	20	1	0	0	2	0	1.00	1	.254	.319	.460
Foreman, Julius*	of	South Bend	Ari	A	22	50	139	40	0	3	0	46	22	10	30	0	29	0	0	0	14	6	.70	1	.288	.414	.331
Foster, Brian	c	Ogden	Mil	R+	19	45	134	29	7	0	2	42	27	15	17	0	29	5	4	2	2	2	.50	4	.216	.323	.313
Foster, Gregg	of	Phillies	Phi	R	22	50	178	50	7	2	2	67	36	31	13	0	24	6	0	4	8	0	1.00	1	.281	.343	.376
Fowler, David	of	Greensboro	NYY	A	21	26	96	18	5	1	5	40	12	11	5	0	43	1	0	0	0	0	.00	0	.188	.235	.417
		Staten Ilnd	NYY	A-	21	49	138	35	6	0	2	47	25	15	12	0	51	5	4	2	6	5	.55	0	.254	.331	.341
Fox, Jason#	of	Mudville	Mil	A+	24	130	493	123	17	2	2	150	58	43	52	1	92	3	10	5	53	17	.76	4	.249	.322	.304
Francia, Juan#	2b	Tigers	Det	R	19	53	194	52	5	3	0	63	34	14	19	0	43	1	5	0	23	4	.85	0	.268	.336	.325
		Lakeland	Det	A+	19	11	40	9	2	0	0	11	3	0	7	0	9	0	2	0	5	2	.71	0	.225	.340	.275
Francisco, Ruben*	of	Orioles	Bal	R	20	46	151	31	4	2	2	45	32	17	14	0	22	2	7	2	7	2	.78	4	.205	.278	.298
Franco, Esterlin	2b	Martinsvlle	Hou	R+	20	43	154	39	9	2	1	55	17	14	10	0	22	2	0	0	8	5	.62	5	.253	.307	.357
Franco, Iker	c-dh	St. Pete	TB	A+	20	1	4	0	0	0	0	0	0	0	0	0	2	0	0	0	0	0	.00	0	.000	.000	.000
		Hudson Val	TB	A-	20	22	73	19	5	0	2	30	11	15	5	0	18	2	0	1	1	1	.50	1	.260	.321	.411
Franco, Raul	3b	Brevard Cty	Fla	A+	25	85	315	75	13	1	0	90	25	29	22	0	29	4	3	3	10	7	.59	4	.238	.294	.286
Frank, Nick	3b	Beloit	Mil	A	25	79	244	57	9	1	1	71	30	22	40	1	48	7	7	0	3	1	.75	1	.234	.357	.291
Frazier, Carlos	of	Giants	SF	R	22	40	82	11	0	1	0	13	5	4	5	0	22	0	2	1	5	6	.45	0	.134	.182	.159
Frazier, Charlie	of	Marlins	Fla	R	20	48	172	50	10	2	2	70	23	23	19	0	46	2	0	0	6	1	.86	2	.291	.368	.407
		Utica	Fla	A-	20	7	26	3	0	0	0	3	3	2	3	0	11	0	0	0	2	0	1.00	0	.115	.207	.115
Freeman, Choo	of	Salem	Col	A+	21	127	429	114	18	7	5	161	73	54	37	0	104	4	1	5	16	8	.67	7	.266	.326	.375
Freeman, Corey	ss	Lancaster	Sea	A+	21	27	112	24	6	1	0	32	19	7	8	0	23	2	0	1	5	6	.45	2	.214	.276	.286
		Everett	Sea	A-	21	65	216	47	12	2	0	63	32	11	24	0	64	0	6	3	12	6	.67	3	.218	.292	.292
Freeman, Miguel	of	Expos	Mon	R	21	49	183	45	11	4	4	76	18	21	13	0	58	3	1	0	0	1	.00	3	.246	.307	.415
Freeman, T.#	2b	Tigers	Det	R	26	1	3	1	1	0	0	2	0	1	1	0	0	0	0	0	0	0	.00	0	.333	.500	.667
		Lakeland	Det	A+	26	50	167	44	3	3	0	53	32	12	20	0	26	7	3	0	12	5	.71	1	.263	.366	.317
Freitas, Jeremy*	of-dh	Chston-WV	KC	A	26	59	187	45	9	5	9	91	27	31	34	0	47	1	1	3	1	0	1.00	4	.241	.356	.487
French, Ron	c	Rancho Cuca	SD	A+	23	12	16	2	0	0	0	2	1	1	1	0	5	2	0	1	0	0	.00	1	.125	.250	.125
Frese, Nate	ss	Daytona	ChC	A+	23	117	425	126	24	5	7	181	70	52	64	0	84	6	8	4	10	6	.63	9	.296	.393	.426
Friar, Roddy	c	New Jersey	StL	A-	25	30	91	15	1	0	1	19	6	8	9	0	33	0	0	0	1	1	.50	1	.165	.240	.209
Frick, Matt	c	Kane County	Fla	A	25	100	327	86	12	2	10	132	48	59	37	2	67	8	0	4	4	4	.50	12	.263	.348	.404
Fuentes, Omar	c	Greensboro	NYY	A	21	69	250	62	16	0	5	93	30	39	17	0	49	6	1	3	2	0	1.00	2	.248	.308	.372
Fukuhara, Pete	of	Daytona	ChC	A+	25	96	323	74	25	0	2	105	43	18	31	1	54	5	3	3	2	9	.18	8	.229	.304	.325
Fulse, Sheldon#	of	Lancaster	Sea	A+	19	17	62	17	4	3	0	27	11	7	8	0	18	1	2	0	0	1	.00	0	.274	.366	.435
		Wisconsin	Sea	A	19	64	216	55	8	0	2	69	45	22	38	2	58	5	3	3	30	7	.81	1	.255	.374	.319
Furmaniak, J.J.	ss	Idaho Falls	SD	R+	21	62	245	84	18	2	5	121	72	38	44	1	48	5	0	4	10	3	.77	8	.343	.446	.494
Gajewski, Matt#	3b	Pulaski	Tex	R+	23	38	118	29	6	0	3	44	26	18	31	0	24	4	0	1	8	0	1.00	5	.246	.416	.373
Galante, Matt	2b	New Jersey	StL	A-	22	54	165	37	4	0	0	41	12	14	26	0	24	2	3	1	4	0	1.00	3	.224	.335	.248
Galarraga, Luis	1b	Red Sox	Bos	R	21	19	37	8	3	0	0	11	6	5	6	0	12	2	0	2	2	0	1.00	3	.216	.340	.297
Gall, John	1b	New Jersey	StL	A-	23	71	259	62	10	0	2	78	28	27	25	0	37	1	0	4	16	5	.76	7	.239	.304	.301
Gallaher, T.T.	of	Columbus	Cle	A	23	72	215	56	6	2	3	75	36	21	34	0	39	1	5	2	18	5	.78	5	.260	.361	.349
		Kinston	Cle	A+	23	20	65	14	4	1	0	20	7	11	7	0	12	1	2	1	1	2	.33	2	.215	.297	.308
Gallo, Ismael*	2b	Vero Beach	LA	A+	24	113	425	144	32	3	0	182	55	68	31	0	25	3	3	5	6	2	.75	10	.339	.384	.428
Gambino, Michael	2b	Red Sox	Bos	R	23	5	14	3	0	0	0	3	2	2	2	0	2	0	0	0	1	1	.50	2	.214	.313	.214
		Augusta	Bos	A	23	20	63	18	2	0	0	20	8	2	5	0	8	1	2	0	2	1	.67	4	.286	.348	.317
Gandolfo, Rob*	2b	Lancaster	Sea	A+	23	55	184	39	4	1	1	48	28	12	16	0	20	7	0	2	4	7	.36	4	.212	.297	.261
Gann, Bryan	2b	Salem-Keizr	SF	A-	23	66	256	70	9	0	0	79	33	15	19	0	40	3	15	1	5	3	.63	2	.273	.330	.309
Garabito, Vianney	3b	Billings	Cin	R+	21	39	157	42	6	1	10	80	26	42	5	0	15	3	0	3	1	0	1.00	5	.268	.298	.510
Garbe, B.J.	of	Quad City	Min	A	20	133	476	111	12	3	5	144	62	51	63	2	91	10	5	3	14	7	.67	10	.233	.333	.303
Garcia, Cip	c	South Bend	Ari	A	22	11	22	1	1	0	0	2	1	3	0	0	7	1	1	0	0	0	.00	1	.045	.087	.091

2000 Batting — Class-A and Rookie Leagues

BATTING																					BASERUNNING				PERCENTAGES		
Player	Pos	Team	Org	Lg	A	G	AB	H	2B	3B	HR	TB	R	RBI	TBB	IBB	SO	HBP	SH	SF	SB	CS	SB%	GDP	Avg	OBP	SLG
Garcia, Cristian	of	Marlins	Fla	R	21	25	66	11	1	1	1	17	10	8	13	0	29	3	0	0	1	0	1.00	3	.167	.329	.258
Garcia, Douglas*	of	Charlotte	Tex	A+	22	56	140	36	7	1	1	48	16	17	8	0	28	0	1	0	3	3	.50	1	.257	.297	.343
Garcia, Hector	1b	Beloit	Mil	A	21	111	436	109	18	4	10	165	43	61	15	1	81	7	3	2	2	2	.50	21	.250	.285	.378
Garcia, Isaac	ss	Athletics	Oak	R	20	52	223	71	13	5	3	103	52	28	23	1	29	2	2	2	18	5	.78	1	.318	.384	.462
Garcia, Jose	of-dh	Great Falls	LA	R+	20	6	19	4	0	0	0	4	2	3	1	0	4	2	0	0	2	1	.67	0	.211	.318	.211
Garcia, Juan-C.#	2b	Marlins	Fla	R	19	34	116	27	9	1	1	41	24	15	23	1	45	0	0	2	3	2	.60	1	.233	.355	.353
		Utica	Fla	A-	19	17	52	10	2	0	0	12	6	6	12	0	28	0	0	2	1	1	.50	1	.192	.333	.231
Garcia, Kevys	2b	Auburn	Hou	A-	20	53	161	39	8	0	0	47	11	15	10	1	42	2	3	0	9	5	.64	4	.242	.295	.292
Garcia, Luis	1b	Augusta	Bos	A	22	128	493	128	27	5	20	225	72	77	51	6	112	1	0	2	8	1	.89	8	.260	.329	.456
Garcia, Nick	ss	Orioles	Bal	R	21	6	24	6	0	0	0	6	0	3	0	0	3	1	0	0	0	1	.00	1	.250	.280	.250
		Bluefield	Bal	R+	21	41	159	45	7	0	2	58	21	13	5	0	31	1	1	0	6	2	.75	5	.283	.309	.365
Garcia, Oscar	3b	Columbus	Cle	A	20	41	138	35	5	1	1	45	22	14	21	0	30	4	0	2	9	2	.82	4	.254	.364	.326
Garcia, Sandy	of	Yankees	NYY	R	21	54	186	55	12	4	6	93	36	29	20	0	54	2	0	1	5	2	.71	5	.296	.368	.500
Garcia, Tony	c	Winston-Sal	CWS	A+	23	77	238	66	14	1	3	91	33	32	20	0	55	14	4	1	5	1	.83	7	.277	.366	.382
Garland, Ross	c-dh	Tigers	Det	R	21	39	127	32	6	1	2	46	20	12	16	0	47	4	0	1	0	0	.00	2	.252	.351	.362
Garrett, Shawn#	of	Fort Wayne	SD	A	22	123	438	119	28	3	10	183	59	55	47	2	79	3	1	7	6	5	.55	8	.272	.341	.418
Garrido, Tomas	3b	Giants	SF	R	19	51	188	44	5	0	0	49	32	11	13	0	29	5	7	0	13	4	.76	3	.234	.301	.261
Garza, Rolando	of	Burlington	CWS	A	21	92	277	67	14	2	0	85	30	24	33	0	63	2	4	1	5	7	.42	4	.242	.326	.307
Gastelum, Carlos	2b	Lk Elsinore	Ana	A+	19	27	67	14	4	0	0	18	11	8	11	0	17	4	5	0	3	4	.43	2	.209	.354	.269
		Boise	Ana	A-	19	66	206	41	5	0	0	46	23	14	14	0	36	7	9	0	13	4	.76	4	.199	.273	.223
Gates, Jeff	c-dh	Staten Ilnd	NYY	A-	22	47	112	35	8	0	0	43	15	12	17	0	23	7	3	0	5	4	.56	3	.313	.434	.384
Gauch, Barry	c	Burlington	CWS	A	24	24	67	11	4	0	0	15	4	7	3	0	14	0	1	1	1	1	.50	1	.164	.197	.224
Gay, Curt*	1b-dh	Columbus	Cle	A	23	97	337	57	14	1	7	94	30	37	30	0	128	1	1	1	2	0	1.00	4	.169	.238	.279
Gearlds, Aaron	of	Rockies	Col	R	21	41	168	55	5	2	1	67	36	20	19	0	28	3	1	1	16	5	.76	2	.327	.403	.399
Gemoll, Justin	3b	Spokane	KC	A-	23	9	35	11	2	0	1	16	8	5	4	0	10	3	0	0	0	0	.00	1	.314	.429	.457
Gentry, Garett*	c-dh	Auburn	Hou	A-	20	62	231	66	15	3	4	99	38	34	26	0	27	1	0	1	5	0	1.00	3	.286	.359	.429
Geraldo, Anulfo	2b	Helena	Mil	R+	21	70	268	75	17	2	2	102	41	32	31	0	50	0	4	2	11	4	.73	1	.280	.352	.381
Gerber, Joe*	1b	Oneonta	Det	A-	22	56	189	43	9	1	3	63	27	23	36	2	43	4	1	1	0	1	.00	6	.228	.361	.333
German, Amado#	of	Princeton	TB	R+	20	48	149	40	9	3	0	55	20	9	18	0	38	1	2	1	8	9	.47	1	.268	.349	.369
German, Franklin	of	Lansing	ChC	A	21	100	308	86	14	2	5	119	42	32	21	1	86	4	2	1	37	10	.79	5	.279	.332	.386
German, Ramon#	1b	Martinsvlle	Hou	R+	21	59	225	72	24	1	7	119	42	44	23	0	64	1	0	1	16	8	.67	1	.320	.384	.529
Gettis, Byron	of	Wilmington	KC	A+	21	30	97	15	2	0	0	17	13	10	13	0	33	2	2	1	2	1	.67	1	.155	.265	.175
		Chston-WV	KC	A	21	94	344	74	18	3	5	113	43	50	31	0	95	11	2	4	11	7	.61	5	.215	.297	.328
Gibbs, Mark	2b	Orioles	Bal	R	23	44	143	37	8	0	1	48	23	12	23	1	33	7	1	2	13	2	.87	1	.259	.383	.336
Gil, Jerry	ss	Missoula	Ari	R+	18	58	227	51	10	2	0	65	24	20	11	1	63	2	0	1	7	3	.70	5	.225	.266	.286
Gillikin, Joe	c-dh	Burlington	CWS	A	24	36	111	25	7	0	5	47	14	13	14	0	33	3	1	1	0	1	.00	0	.225	.326	.423
Gingrich, Troy*	of	Vermont	Mon	A-	24	16	65	19	3	1	1	27	12	5	9	0	16	1	0	1	5	2	.71	4	.292	.382	.415
		Cape Fear	Mon	A	24	44	144	36	8	1	0	46	21	12	31	1	32	4	1	0	13	3	.81	1	.250	.397	.319
Giorgis, David#	of	Padres	SD	R	19	53	206	55	9	1	2	72	26	28	10	1	38	2	0	3	3	2	.60	4	.267	.303	.350
Giron, Alejandro	of	Clearwater	Phi	A+	22	115	433	126	31	7	4	183	59	47	33	2	100	6	3	6	16	7	.70	9	.291	.345	.423
Glassey, Josh*	c	San Berndno	LA	A+	24	20	60	11	7	0	0	18	10	4	18	1	20	1	0	0	0	0	.00	2	.183	.380	.300
		High Desert	Ari	A+	24	23	69	18	7	0	0	25	8	6	11	0	16	0	0	0	0	1	.00	0	.261	.363	.362
Godbolt, Keith	of	Great Falls	LA	R+	20	65	230	65	7	3	1	81	31	25	22	0	49	0	2	0	7	3	.70	8	.283	.345	.352
Goelz, Jim	2b-of	Vero Beach	LA	A+	25	75	241	59	7	2	0	70	36	19	25	1	45	2	4	4	2	4	.33	6	.245	.316	.290
		Yakima	LA	A-	25	1	2	1	0	0	0	1	1	0	0	0	0	1	0	0	0	0	.00	0	.500	.667	.500
Goldbach, Jeff	c	Daytona	ChC	A+	21	119	420	84	15	1	10	131	49	60	31	1	76	8	0	7	6	5	.55	1	.200	.264	.312
Golden, Bryan	c	Cubs	ChC	R	20	16	45	12	3	1	0	17	6	7	5	1	15	1	1	0	0	0	.00	1	.267	.353	.378
Goldfield, Josh*	c	Diamondbcks	Ari	R	21	5	17	4	0	0	1	7	3	2	2	0	2	0	0	0	0	2	.00	1	.235	.316	.412
		High Desert	Ari	A+	21	29	85	20	6	0	1	29	9	10	1	0	17	0	0	1	2	2	.50	2	.235	.241	.341
Gomez, Alexis*	of	Wilmington	KC	A+	20	121	461	117	13	4	1	141	63	33	45	1	121	2	7	1	21	10	.68	8	.254	.322	.306
Gomez, Andre	c	Padres	SD	R	22	28	63	14	1	0	0	15	13	5	13	0	4	7	0	2	6	1	.86	2	.222	.400	.238
		Idaho Falls	SD	R+	22	9	32	8	2	0	2	16	5	5	4	0	6	1	0	0	1	0	1.00	1	.250	.351	.500
Gomez, Francis	ss	Athletics	Oak	R	19	17	62	22	3	1	3	36	17	28	11	0	10	0	0	0	8	1	.89	1	.355	.452	.581
Gomez, Jose	of	Johnson Cty	StL	R+	20	53	162	38	7	1	1	50	25	17	25	2	46	4	2	0	6	4	.60	6	.235	.351	.309
Gomez, Rich	of	Lakeland	Det	A+	23	128	455	126	20	10	8	190	78	57	50	1	102	8	6	3	48	8	.86	4	.277	.357	.418
Gonzalez, Adrian*	1b	Marlins	Fla	R	19	53	193	57	10	1	0	69	24	30	32	3	35	2	0	2	0	0	.00	6	.295	.397	.358
		Utica	Fla	A-	19	8	29	9	3	0	0	12	7	3	7	0	6	0	0	0	0	0	.00	0	.310	.444	.414
Gonzalez, Carlos	c	Mariners	Sea	R	19	16	46	15	3	0	1	21	10	7	5	0	7	0	0	1	0	0	.00	0	.326	.385	.457
Gonzalez, Edgar	3b	Hudson Val	TB	A-	23	41	145	32	4	4	0	44	17	8	12	0	32	0	1	0	5	1	.83	3	.221	.280	.303
		Princeton	TB	R+	23	20	63	17	3	3	0	26	6	8	13	0	14	1	1	0	4	1	.80	2	.270	.403	.413
Gonzalez, Jimmy	3b	San Berndno	LA	A+	22	125	510	145	19	5	6	192	71	66	28	0	54	5	9	4	30	21	.59	9	.284	.325	.376
Gonzalez, Jose#	ss	Rangers	Tex	R	20	33	87	21	3	1	0	26	13	7	11	2	27	0	2	1	4	3	.57	0	.241	.323	.299
Gonzalez, Jose	c	Giants	SF	R	19	2	3	0	0	0	0	0	0	0	0	0	2	0	0	0	0	0	.00	0	.000	.000	.000
		Bakersfield	SF	A+	19	4	4	0	0	0	0	0	0	0	0	0	3	0	0	0	0	0	.00	0	.000	.000	.000
Gonzalez, Julian	of	Chston-WV	KC	A	24	16	57	12	2	0	1	17	6	5	1	0	18	2	1	0	1	0	1.00	1	.211	.250	.298
Gonzalez, Luis	2b-ss	Kinston	Cle	A+	22	79	284	70	11	0	2	87	32	33	21	0	54	6	12	2	6	6	.50	6	.246	.310	.306
Gonzalez, Reggie	2b	Elizabethtn	Min	R+	21	52	189	54	11	1	7	88	28	39	10	0	26	0	2	2	8	1	.89	2	.286	.318	.466
Gonzalez, Reggie*	1b	Yankees	NYY	R	23	21	71	15	3	1	1	23	13	8	7	0	9	5	1	2	1	1	.50	3	.211	.318	.324
Goodeill, Harold	of	Princeton	TB	R+	23	3	9	4	0	0	1	7	1	3	1	0	3	2	0	0	0	0	.00	0	.444	.583	.778
		Hudson Val	TB	A-	23	11	21	4	0	0	1	7	2	4	5	0	5	1	0	0	0	0	.00	2	.190	.370	.333
Goodman, Scott*	of	Kane County	Fla	A	23	129	423	99	27	2	16	178	68	54	73	5	110	15	0	2	1	2	.33	8	.234	.365	.421
Goodson, Steve*	of	St. Pete	TB	A+	22	105	351	76	5	4	0	89	30	23	41	5	85	0	5	1	5	1	.83	10	.217	.298	.254
Goodwin, David	dh	Wilmington	KC	A+	26	89	311	77	21	0	3	107	29	38	26	1	83	8	2	3	1	0	1.00	9	.248	.319	.344
Gordon, Alex*	of	Bluefield	Bal	R+	21	60	223	60	17	3	13	122	36	48	29	0	105	1	0	4	3	0	1.00	5	.269	.350	.547
		Delmarva	Bal	A	21	1	2	0	0	0	0	0	0	0	0	0	2	0	0	0	0	0	.00	0	.000	.000	.000
Gordon, Brian*	of	High Desert	Ari	A+	22	127	476	148	26	13	12	236	98	66	47	1	107	2	0	6	19	14	.58	8	.311	.371	.496
Gosewisch, Chip	of	Cedar Rapds	Ana	A	24	59	177	36	10	0	1	49	20	14	14	0	38	2	4	0	2	0	1.00	7	.203	.269	.277

2000 Batting — Class-A and Rookie Leagues

BATTING																					BASERUNNING				PERCENTAGES		
Player	Pos	Team	Org	Lg	A	G	AB	H	2B	3B	HR	TB	R	RBI	TBB	IBB	SO	HBP	SH	SF	SB	CS	SB%	GDP	Avg	OBP	SLG
Gotauco, David	c	Jamestown	Atl	A-	23	21	59	16	6	0	2	28	5	9	6	0	9	3	0	1	1	0	1.00	1	.271	.362	.475
Goudie, Jaime	2b	Hagerstown	Tor	A	22	116	412	100	19	3	6	143	53	51	36	0	68	9	8	3	26	10	.72	6	.243	.315	.347
Gragg, Shaun*	c	Ogden	Mil	R+	23	50	178	46	13	1	2	67	25	35	13	0	43	0	0	2	1	2	.33	3	.258	.306	.376
Graham, Justin	of	South Bend	Ari	A	23	24	53	7	3	0	0	10	4	7	10	0	21	1	1	2	2	0	1.00	0	.132	.273	.189
Graham, Pete	of	Eugene	ChC	A-	22	46	108	30	9	1	1	44	20	7	14	1	32	4	2	3	7	4	.64	2	.278	.372	.407
Gray, Jason*	of	Rangers	Tex	R	23	52	186	51	10	3	1	70	31	32	23	0	31	6	3	4	2	2	.50	1	.274	.365	.376
Gray, Josh	dh	Butte	Ana	R+	20	40	147	48	11	3	8	89	31	36	19	1	41	3	0	1	1	0	1.00	1	.327	.412	.605
Gredvig, Doug	dh	Orioles	Bal	R	21	2	9	4	0	0	0	4	0	1	0	0	1	0	0	0	0	0	.00	0	.444	.444	.444
		Delmarva	Bal	A	21	56	186	41	12	0	6	71	28	24	35	0	48	1	0	0	3	5	.38	2	.220	.347	.382
Green, Andy	2b	South Bend	Ari	A	23	3	9	0	0	0	0	0	1	0	0	0	1	2	0	0	0	0	.00	0	.000	.182	.000
		Missoula	Ari	R+	23	23	83	19	2	1	0	23	10	16	12	0	9	2	1	5	8	3	.73	1	.229	.324	.277
Green, Kevin	c	Jamestown	Atl	A-	22	17	56	7	1	0	1	11	5	7	5	0	25	1	0	0	0	0	.00	2	.125	.210	.196
Green, Nick	ss	Macon	Atl	A	22	91	339	83	19	4	11	143	47	43	22	0	75	5	1	6	10	4	.71	4	.245	.296	.422
		Myrtle Bch	Atl	A+	22	27	91	22	6	0	1	31	13	6	10	0	23	3	1	0	3	2	.60	0	.242	.337	.341
Greene, Claude#	of	Tampa	NYY	A+	24	78	212	45	7	1	6	72	22	19	14	3	53	9	0	1	1	6	.14	4	.212	.288	.340
Greene, Clay	of	San Jose	SF	A+	26	103	326	82	15	1	2	105	49	35	45	0	63	3	8	4	38	15	.72	4	.252	.344	.322
Gregg, Mitch*	1b	Modesto	Oak	A+	24	52	175	38	6	0	2	50	22	22	30	0	50	3	1	0	2	0	1.00	1	.217	.341	.286
Gregorio, Tom	c	Cedar Rapds	Ana	A	24	106	379	93	17	0	6	128	46	41	35	4	79	7	3	2	2	1	.67	13	.245	.319	.338
Griffin, Daniel	of	Expos	Mon	R	20	13	49	12	1	2	0	17	3	7	2	0	7	0	0	0	0	0	.00	2	.245	.275	.347
Griffin, Justin	ss	Columbus	Cle	A	24	8	13	2	0	1	0	4	0	1	0	0	5	0	1	0	0	0	.00	0	.154	.154	.308
Griggs, Reggie*	1b	Phillies	Phi	R	23	57	206	70	18	2	6	110	35	42	17	1	38	3	2	2	0	1	.00	8	.340	.395	.534
Grindell, Nate	3b	Columbus	Cle	A	24	132	500	143	36	3	18	239	80	98	55	3	74	9	0	7	17	2	.89	8	.286	.363	.478
Gripp, Ryan	3b	Lansing	ChC	A	23	135	498	166	36	0	20	262	87	92	68	2	86	5	0	3	4	0	1.00	13	.333	.416	.526
Griswold, Matt*	of	Frederick	Bal	A+	23	24	68	13	3	1	0	18	5	6	6	0	15	0	0	1	2	2	.50	2	.191	.253	.265
Grummitt, Dan	1b-dh	Chston-SC	TB	A	25	111	410	107	22	2	19	190	70	74	37	1	116	22	0	5	6	3	.67	7	.261	.350	.463
Gsell, Tony	dh-2b	Lansing	ChC	A	24	92	296	57	15	2	11	109	43	37	27	0	95	15	3	2	3	3	.50	2	.193	.291	.368
Guante, Domingo	of	Twins	Min	R	20	37	129	39	8	0	0	47	28	12	17	0	21	0	0	1	13	4	.76	1	.302	.381	.364
Guerrero, Cris	of	Beloit	Mil	A	20	15	55	9	4	0	2	19	5	8	1	0	18	1	0	1	1	0	1.00	2	.164	.190	.345
		Ogden	Mil	R+	20	66	255	87	14	4	12	145	56	54	37	1	42	4	0	1	24	6	.80	8	.341	.431	.569
Guerrero, Hector*	of	Great Falls	LA	R+	19	8	32	10	4	1	0	16	3	5	1	0	9	0	0	1	0	0	.00	1	.313	.324	.500
Guerrero, Jorge	2b	Marlins	Fla	R	20	35	112	26	9	0	1	38	18	11	14	0	25	1	0	3	4	1	.80	2	.232	.315	.339
Guerrero, Julio	of	Lowell	Bos	A-	20	43	146	35	3	2	0	42	21	13	12	0	26	1	1	0	17	4	.81	5	.240	.302	.288
Guerrero, Pedro	2b	Charlotte	Tex	A+	21	85	275	52	6	4	0	66	40	21	36	0	65	6	8	1	7	5	.58	7	.189	.296	.240
Guilliams, Earl	c	Braves	Atl	R	20	23	63	18	2	0	0	20	9	4	2	0	7	0	0	0	0	0	.00	1	.286	.308	.317
		Danville	Atl	R+	20	2	3	1	0	0	0	1	1	1	0	0	0	0	0	0	0	0	.00	0	.333	.333	.333
Gulledge, Kelley	c	Quad City	Min	A	22	39	124	19	4	0	0	23	8	12	16	0	37	6	1	0	0	3	.00	1	.153	.281	.185
Gundrum, Kris*	of	Wisconsin	Sea	A	24	75	256	64	14	0	3	87	40	28	22	1	60	3	4	2	13	2	.87	2	.250	.314	.340
Gustafson, Troy	of	Giants	SF	R	21	49	172	46	6	0	0	52	26	12	20	2	20	5	1	0	21	4	.84	2	.267	.360	.302
		San Jose	SF	A+	21	3	5	1	0	0	0	1	0	1	1	0	0	0	0	0	0	0	.00	0	.200	.333	.200
Gutierrez, Derrick	ss	Delmarva	Bal	A	22	4	8	2	0	0	0	2	1	0	1	0	3	0	0	0	0	0	.00	0	.250	.333	.250
Gutierrez, Ricardo	c	Fort Wayne	SD	A	21	11	37	7	1	0	1	11	5	4	2	0	6	0	0	0	2	0	1.00	2	.189	.231	.297
Gutierrez, Said	dh-c	Idaho Falls	SD	R+	21	17	50	11	1	0	0	12	4	5	9	0	10	0	0	2	1	0	1.00	3	.220	.328	.240
Gutierrez, Vic	ss	Lynchburg	Pit	A+	23	107	339	82	9	4	1	102	42	29	40	0	53	1	6	0	15	8	.65	7	.242	.324	.301
Guyton, Eric	dh	Capital Cty	NYM	A	24	94	323	90	12	4	7	131	44	55	39	0	70	11	2	2	1	2	.33	4	.279	.373	.406
Guzman, Carlos	of	Braves	Atl	R	17	38	114	25	4	1	1	34	14	20	12	0	45	3	0	2	3	1	.75	1	.219	.305	.298
Guzman, Elpidio*	of	Lk Elsinore	Ana	A+	22	135	532	150	20	16	9	229	96	72	61	2	116	3	5	11	53	14	.79	6	.282	.353	.430
Guzman, Javier#	of	Portland	Col	A-	21	33	108	29	8	1	0	39	16	13	5	0	45	1	0	1	2	0	1.00	1	.269	.304	.361
Guzman, Juan#	ss-2b	Spokane	KC	A-	21	34	71	14	1	2	1	22	8	9	10	0	22	1	3	0	0	3	.00	0	.197	.305	.310
		Chston-WV	KC	A	21	19	63	11	2	1	0	15	5	2	10	0	24	1	0	0	2	3	.40	0	.175	.297	.238
Haas, Danny*	of	Sarasota	Bos	A+	25	118	398	101	12	1	4	127	44	39	30	2	63	7	1	2	5	8	.38	5	.254	.316	.319
Haase, Jeff	1b	Mahoning Vy	Cle	A-	23	69	244	61	12	5	4	95	46	45	40	1	72	10	2	3	14	2	.88	6	.250	.374	.389
Hafner, Travis*	1b-dh	Charlotte	Tex	A+	24	122	436	151	34	1	22	253	90	109	67	2	86	18	0	7	0	4	.00	9	.346	.447	.580
Hage, Tom*	1b	Frederick	Bal	A+	26	25	97	22	8	1	0	32	10	15	11	0	17	0	0	1	1	0	1.00	4	.227	.303	.330
Hake, Travis	2b	Ogden	Mil	R+	24	50	210	65	17	4	2	96	53	33	22	0	32	5	1	2	19	2	.90	2	.310	.385	.457
Halgren, Chris	c	Vancouver	Oak	A-	22	43	88	20	1	0	0	21	10	11	32	2	26	2	1	3	0	0	.00	3	.227	.432	.239
Hall, Bill	ss	Beloit	Mil	A	21	130	470	123	30	6	3	174	57	41	18	0	127	1	12	5	10	11	.48	12	.262	.287	.370
Hall, Justin	2b	Modesto	Oak	A+	24	90	341	87	17	3	3	119	59	38	56	0	65	6	2	4	12	3	.80	7	.255	.366	.349
Hall, Victor*	of	South Bend	Ari	A	20	41	164	38	4	5	2	58	19	16	13	0	41	2	1	0	12	5	.71	1	.232	.296	.354
		Missoula	Ari	R+	20	70	241	74	7	9	3	108	70	26	77	0	38	5	3	3	47	14	.77	0	.307	.479	.448
Halloran, Matt	ss-2b	Charlotte	Tex	A+	23	5	14	2	2	0	0	4	1	5	1	0	4	1	0	1	0	0	.00	2	.143	.235	.286
		Savannah	Tex	A	23	35	82	14	3	0	0	17	5	5	8	0	15	1	0	2	2	1	.67	1	.171	.247	.207
Haltiwanger, Garrick	of	Dunedin	Tor	A+	26	100	354	103	27	3	10	166	57	56	37	1	67	3	0	1	18	4	.82	10	.291	.362	.469
Hambrick, Marcus*	of	Jamestown	Atl	A-	22	60	195	52	9	5	3	80	17	25	13	0	44	1	1	4	5	5	.50	1	.267	.310	.410
Hamill, Ryan	c-dh	Johnson Cty	StL	R+	22	59	213	56	11	0	12	103	35	46	28	0	42	4	1	4	7	4	.64	6	.263	.353	.484
Hamilton, Josh*	of	Chston-SC	TB	A	20	96	392	118	23	3	13	186	62	61	26	3	72	2	0	3	14	6	.70	5	.301	.345	.474
Hamilton, Mark*	of-1b	Martinsvlle	Hou	R+	23	56	201	54	11	0	3	74	27	23	19	0	48	3	0	2	11	3	.79	1	.269	.338	.368
Hammond, Derry	of	Mudville	Mil	A+	21	66	210	35	6	0	5	56	23	23	15	0	87	6	1	5	2	2	.50	3	.167	.237	.267
Hammond, Joey	3b	Frederick	Bal	A+	23	126	432	111	22	2	0	137	47	39	65	3	88	5	4	5	5	8	.38	7	.257	.357	.317
Hankins, Ryan	3b	Winston-Sal	CWS	A+	25	96	321	86	27	1	7	136	43	52	57	1	64	2	3	8	6	4	.60	4	.268	.374	.424
Hannahan, Buzz	3b	Piedmont	Phi	A	25	76	240	66	13	0	1	82	47	24	36	0	37	5	6	2	25	1	.96	1	.275	.378	.342
Hargreaves, Brad	c	Daytona	ChC	A+	23	46	103	23	5	0	0	28	18	6	8	0	14	2	2	0	0	1	.00	2	.223	.292	.272
Hargrove, Harvey	of	Lancaster	Sea	A+	25	120	399	103	22	2	3	138	60	58	69	0	76	10	1	3	10	14	.42	10	.258	.378	.346
Harper, Shaun	of	Jamestown	Atl	A-	21	72	257	58	12	5	5	95	33	24	13	1	89	1	1	3	5	4	.56	2	.226	.263	.370
Harriman, Preston	2b	Johnson Cty	StL	R+	21	50	129	28	7	2	0	39	23	9	23	0	33	4	1	0	6	2	.75	3	.217	.353	.302
Harris, Cedrick	of	High Desert	Ari	A+	23	34	129	34	6	4	0	48	27	14	12	0	29	1	1	1	10	4	.71	1	.264	.329	.372
Harris, Corey	of	Pittsfield	NYM	A-	21	61	194	62	17	3	4	97	38	30	34	0	28	4	1	5	23	4	.85	3	.320	.422	.500
Harris, Karl	1b	Expos	Mon	R	20	44	158	42	6	0	2	54	16	24	11	0	21	9	1	4	3	3	.50	4	.266	.341	.342

2000 Batting — Class-A and Rookie Leagues

BATTING																					BASERUNNING				PERCENTAGES		
Player	Pos	Team	Org	Lg	A	G	AB	H	2B	3B	HR	TB	R	RBI	TBB	IBB	SO	HBP	SH	SF	SB	CS	SB%	GDP	Avg	OBP	SLG
Harris, Willie*	2b	Delmarva	Bal	A	23	133	474	130	27	10	6	195	106	60	89	4	89	9	7	4	38	15	.72	3	.274	.396	.411
Hart, Bo	2b	Potomac	StL	A+	24	75	273	70	25	4	0	103	42	20	23	0	42	13	4	1	9	6	.60	2	.256	.342	.377
Hart, Corey#	2b	Wilmington	KC	A+	25	88	243	53	6	2	1	66	45	22	64	0	62	2	6	1	6	6	.50	7	.218	.384	.272
Hart, Jon	1b	Ogden	Mil	R+	19	57	216	62	9	1	2	79	32	30	13	0	27	2	1	1	6	0	1.00	6	.287	.332	.366
Hartley, Will#	c-dh	Burlington	Cle	R+	20	16	52	17	2	0	0	19	11	3	5	0	10	1	0	0	1	0	1.00	0	.327	.397	.365
Harts, Jeremy#	of	Hickory	Pit	A	21	124	459	111	14	2	12	165	75	62	32	0	147	9	7	3	25	7	.78	11	.242	.302	.359
Harvey, Ken	dh-1b	Wilmington	KC	A+	23	46	164	55	10	0	4	77	20	25	14	0	29	7	0	0	0	2	.00	4	.335	.411	.470
Hattenburg, Ray#	3b	Spokane	KC	A-	24	64	202	47	5	0	1	55	28	26	27	0	55	12	0	3	2	2	.50	7	.233	.352	.272
Hattig, John#	3b	Lowell	Bos	A-	21	61	242	70	8	1	0	80	30	28	20	1	43	0	1	1	1	1	.50	1	.289	.342	.331
Hawes, B.J.	ss	Dayton	Cin	A	22	39	136	35	4	1	1	44	23	7	9	0	24	1	2	0	7	2	.78	5	.257	.308	.324
		Billings	Cin	R+	22	4	13	3	0	0	0	3	2	1	0	0	3	0	0	1	0	0	.00	0	.231	.214	.231
Hawpe, Brad*	of-1b	Portland	Col	A-	22	62	205	59	19	2	7	103	38	29	40	2	51	2	0	7	2	0	1.00	1	.288	.398	.502
Hawthorne, Kyle	3b	Fort Myers	Min	A+	23	67	235	55	16	2	2	81	42	18	21	0	52	5	3	0	4	2	.67	5	.234	.310	.345
Haynes, Dee	of	New Jersey	StL	A-	23	64	243	62	18	4	7	109	31	37	16	0	53	1	0	3	4	1	.80	4	.255	.300	.449
Haynes, Larry	of	Wisconsin	Sea	A	23	17	53	11	1	1	0	14	6	2	4	0	17	1	0	0	5	0	1.00	1	.208	.276	.264
		Lancaster	Sea	A+	23	7	27	6	2	0	0	8	3	0	0	0	9	0	1	0	2	0	1.00	0	.222	.222	.296
Headley, Justin*	of	Augusta	Bos	A	26	20	62	13	2	0	3	24	9	3	8	0	10	3	0	0	1	0	1.00	5	.210	.329	.387
Heard, Scott*	c	Rangers	Tex	R	19	31	111	39	16	0	2	61	21	16	20	0	17	4	2	0	1	0	1.00	1	.351	.467	.550
		Savannah	Tex	A	19	2	8	2	0	0	0	2	0	0	0	0	3	0	0	0	0	0	.00	1	.250	.250	.250
Helquist, Jon	3b	Michigan	Hou	A	20	96	320	76	19	2	5	114	59	42	48	0	101	4	1	4	4	6	.40	4	.238	.340	.356
Hemme, Justin*	1b	Salem	Col	A+	25	76	249	55	17	0	6	90	27	30	20	0	59	3	1	1	0	0	.00	8	.221	.286	.361
Henderson, Brad	2b	Vancouver	Oak	A-	24	64	212	54	10	0	1	67	26	33	33	1	41	2	7	4	2	0	1.00	4	.255	.355	.316
Hensley, Anthony	of	Batavia	Phi	A-	23	68	235	65	9	3	2	86	48	28	60	1	52	4	2	1	43	9	.83	2	.277	.430	.366
Hernandez, Javier#	of	Kinston	Cle	A+	20	3	12	2	1	0	0	3	1	2	1	0	5	0	0	0	1	0	1.00	0	.167	.231	.250
		Burlington	Cle	R+	20	38	124	30	6	1	3	47	14	14	8	0	30	1	3	1	4	3	.57	1	.242	.291	.379
		Columbus	Cle	A	20	13	48	13	3	0	0	16	7	8	3	0	18	0	0	1	3	0	1.00	2	.271	.308	.333
Hernandez, Jesus*	of	Kinston	Cle	A+	24	62	222	62	12	5	4	96	30	30	33	0	57	1	1	2	11	7	.61	1	.279	.372	.432
Hernandez, John	c	San Berndno	LA	A+	21	80	273	68	17	0	2	91	30	20	14	1	53	12	7	1	6	2	.75	5	.249	.313	.333
Hernandez, J.#	of	Peoria	StL	A	21	109	379	84	13	2	6	119	47	33	41	2	85	3	6	3	27	12	.69	7	.222	.300	.314
Hernandez, Jose	c	Lynchburg	Pit	A+	20	4	9	3	1	0	0	4	1	1	0	0	4	0	0	1	0	0	.00	0	.333	.300	.444
		Williamsprt	Pit	A-	20	5	17	2	0	0	1	5	2	2	0	0	3	0	1	0	0	0	.00	1	.118	.118	.294
		Hickory	Pit	A	20	9	28	4	0	0	0	4	1	1	0	0	8	1	0	0	0	0	.00	0	.143	.172	.143
Hernandez, Orlando	of	Wisconsin	Sea	A	22	91	331	81	7	1	1	93	31	34	15	2	55	3	2	0	5	11	.31	7	.245	.284	.281
Hernandez, Victor	3b	Sarasota	Bos	A+	24	30	99	23	4	1	1	32	12	7	6	0	30	0	1	1	3	4	.43	2	.232	.274	.323
Hernandez, Yorky	of	Pirates	Pit	R	20	16	55	12	4	1	1	21	7	7	5	0	10	1	0	0	0	0	.00	0	.218	.295	.382
Herr, Aaron	2b	Braves	Atl	R	20	49	175	39	11	0	3	59	27	19	13	0	37	4	0	3	3	1	.75	1	.223	.287	.337
Herrera, Franklyn	dh	New Jersey	StL	A-	20	21	50	14	2	0	0	16	6	1	5	1	12	0	0	0	2	0	1.00	2	.280	.345	.320
Herrick, Jason*	of	Vero Beach	LA	A+	27	28	109	23	4	3	2	39	12	18	8	1	27	0	2	1	3	2	.60	2	.211	.263	.358
Hertel, Brian	1b	Everett	Sea	A-	23	63	199	47	12	3	3	74	29	22	32	1	54	5	2	2	4	4	.50	0	.236	.353	.372
Herzog, Jason	ss	Spokane	KC	A-	23	29	84	22	3	0	1	28	12	8	6	0	29	1	2	0	1	0	1.00	3	.262	.319	.333
Hicks, Brian*	of	Helena	Mil	R+	19	60	213	47	8	1	2	63	41	23	24	0	65	3	2	2	10	6	.63	2	.221	.306	.296
Hicks, Scott*	of	Utica	Fla	A-	21	58	178	36	5	1	1	46	17	18	21	0	43	2	1	1	4	8	.33	1	.202	.292	.258
Higgins, Brett*	1b	Everett	Sea	A-	24	52	181	38	5	0	5	58	19	23	13	1	47	1	0	1	3	2	.60	5	.210	.265	.320
Hilario, Enderson	c	Bristol	CWS	R+	19	22	63	15	1	0	0	16	2	5	2	0	9	1	0	0	0	0	.00	3	.238	.273	.254
Hileman, Jutt	ss	Johnson Cty	StL	R+	19	5	12	3	0	1	1	8	4	4	2	0	4	0	0	0	2	1	.67	0	.250	.357	.667
Hill, Bobby*	2b	St. Lucie	NYM	A+	22	92	290	72	11	1	2	91	41	25	12	0	63	2	11	4	11	9	.55	4	.248	.279	.314
Hill, Jason	c	Lk Elsinore	Ana	A+	24	70	233	58	12	0	4	82	23	33	23	1	44	4	4	2	0	1	.00	5	.249	.324	.352
Hill, Jeremy	c	Wilmington	KC	A+	23	99	299	59	12	2	3	84	33	26	33	1	84	3	6	3	1	2	.33	6	.197	.281	.281
Hill, John	of	Hudson Val	TB	A-	24	56	189	40	6	4	1	57	24	27	28	0	64	2	1	3	13	5	.72	3	.212	.315	.302
Hill, Koyie#	dh	Yakima	LA	A-	22	64	251	65	13	1	2	86	26	29	25	2	47	0	5	2	0	7	.00	7	.259	.324	.343
Hill, Mike	of	Michigan	Hou	A	24	56	198	62	18	4	6	106	38	35	11	0	43	4	0	4	6	1	.86	6	.313	.355	.535
Hill, Willy*	of	Brevard Cty	Fla	A+	24	42	143	45	5	3	0	56	18	15	18	0	11	1	4	1	9	4	.69	4	.315	.393	.392
Hills, Chris	of	Cedar Rapds	Ana	A	23	61	231	51	6	5	0	67	36	17	28	0	54	8	2	0	10	8	.56	3	.221	.326	.290
Hine, Steve*	2b	Savannah	Tex	A	27	95	279	76	15	1	1	96	50	27	43	1	39	2	6	1	13	5	.72	3	.272	.372	.344
Hitchcox, Brian*	2b	Piedmont	Phi	A	22	112	407	109	19	2	3	141	48	42	25	1	35	16	2	3	10	8	.56	5	.268	.333	.346
Hlousek, Rob	2b	W Michigan	Det	A	23	30	89	22	2	2	1	31	15	9	14	0	14	1	3	0	1	1	.50	3	.247	.356	.348
		Lakeland	Det	A+	23	3	8	1	0	0	0	1	0	0	0	0	2	0	1	0	0	0	.00	0	.125	.125	.125
Hobbs, Jay*	of	Lynchburg	Pit	A+	26	98	297	68	22	2	8	118	38	52	44	1	102	2	2	3	2	2	.50	10	.229	.329	.397
Hochgesang, Josh	3b	Visalia	Oak	A+	24	126	443	109	23	3	20	198	78	80	90	4	135	7	2	9	20	9	.69	11	.246	.375	.447
Hodge, Kevin	3b	Fort Myers	Min	A+	24	130	450	125	29	3	10	190	60	56	54	2	91	5	5	4	6	3	.67	12	.278	.359	.422
Hoffpauir, Josh*	2b	Athletics	Oak	R	23	45	172	66	13	2	4	95	51	31	26	1	9	4	0	2	15	4	.79	0	.384	.471	.552
		Vancouver	Oak	A-	23	7	25	7	2	1	0	11	1	5	1	0	0	1	0	0	0	1	.00	0	.280	.333	.440
Holland, Tapley	of	Oneonta	Det	A-	23	46	135	24	4	0	1	31	20	11	23	1	39	4	1	1	2	4	.33	6	.178	.313	.230
Holliday, Josh#	1b	Hagerstown	Tor	A	24	74	218	48	13	1	6	81	46	29	52	1	64	7	3	4	2	0	1.00	2	.220	.381	.372
Holliday, Matt	3b	Salem	Col	A+	21	123	460	126	28	2	7	179	64	72	43	1	74	2	0	5	11	5	.69	12	.274	.335	.389
Holt, Daylan	of	Vancouver	Oak	A-	22	32	118	32	6	0	2	44	17	17	10	0	26	2	0	2	1	0	1.00	3	.271	.333	.373
Holt, Todd	of	Bristol	CWS	R+	23	38	98	22	5	2	2	37	11	10	3	0	32	3	2	1	3	0	1.00	1	.224	.267	.378
Hooper, Clay	ss	Staten Ilnd	NYY	A-	24	64	228	56	15	0	0	71	33	15	25	0	28	1	3	3	6	3	.67	2	.246	.319	.311
Hooper, Kevin	2b	Kane County	Fla	A	24	123	457	114	25	6	3	160	73	38	73	2	83	6	9	1	17	2	.89	6	.249	.359	.350
Hopper, Norris	of	Chston-WV	KC	A	22	116	454	127	20	6	0	159	70	29	51	0	55	4	4	1	24	10	.71	10	.280	.357	.350
House, J.R.	c	Hickory	Pit	A	21	110	420	146	29	1	23	246	78	90	46	2	91	6	0	6	1	2	.33	7	.348	.414	.586
Howe, Matt	1b	Visalia	Oak	A+	24	104	364	93	17	1	13	151	60	55	45	1	77	7	3	7	10	5	.67	8	.255	.343	.415
Hudnall, Josh	ss	Williamsprt	Pit	A-	21	38	117	23	1	1	0	26	13	6	12	0	48	1	1	0	5	1	.83	2	.197	.277	.222
Huguet, J.C.	1b	Reds	Cin	R	23	33	104	25	5	0	0	30	11	17	21	1	16	0	3	1	3	0	1.00	4	.240	.365	.288
Hummel, Tim	ss-3b	Burlington	CWS	A	22	39	144	47	9	1	1	61	22	21	21	0	20	1	0	2	8	3	.73	2	.326	.411	.424
		Winston-Sal	CWS	A+	22	27	98	32	7	0	1	42	15	9	13	1	12	2	0	0	1	1	.50	4	.327	.416	.429
Hunter, David*	1b	Pittsfield	NYM	A-	21	29	94	13	2	0	0	15	6	4	2	0	26	0	1	1	1	1	.50	0	.138	.155	.160

2000 Batting — Class-A and Rookie Leagues

BATTING																					BASERUNNING				PERCENTAGES		
Player	Pos	Team	Org	Lg	A	G	AB	H	2B	3B	HR	TB	R	RBI	TBB	IBB	SO	HBP	SH	SF	SB	CS	SB%	GDP	Avg	OBP	SLG
Hurtado, Omar	of	Clinton	Cin	A	22	125	460	128	31	2	7	184	58	65	47	2	129	4	2	7	19	10	.66	15	.278	.346	.400
Huth, Jason#	2b	Dayton	Cin	A	24	48	127	23	6	0	0	29	16	12	27	0	31	0	2	1	4	3	.57	0	.181	.323	.228
Ide, Antoine	of	Orioles	Bal	R	22	8	29	10	0	0	0	10	4	1	5	0	6	1	2	0	7	2	.78	1	.345	.457	.345
		Delmarva	Bal	A	22	26	67	17	2	1	0	21	13	9	8	0	12	0	0	0	6	0	1.00	1	.254	.333	.313
Illig, Brett	1b	Vero Beach	LA	A+	23	74	234	51	9	1	4	74	34	26	26	2	73	4	1	4	1	1	.50	6	.218	.302	.316
Infante, Franklin	ss	Braves	Atl	R	18	41	131	25	4	0	2	35	16	13	9	0	39	1	0	0	2	2	.50	2	.191	.248	.267
Infante, Juan#	2b	Expos	Mon	R	19	42	143	34	2	1	0	38	26	12	14	0	21	4	3	1	2	4	.33	2	.238	.321	.266
Infante, Omar	ss	Lakeland	Det	A+	19	79	259	71	11	0	2	88	35	24	20	0	29	1	5	4	11	5	.69	4	.274	.324	.340
		W Michigan	Det	A	19	12	48	11	0	0	0	11	7	5	5	0	7	2	0	0	1	0	1.00	2	.229	.327	.229
Infantes, Juan	2b	Padres	SD	R	20	35	96	25	2	0	0	27	20	11	12	0	14	7	2	0	10	0	1.00	0	.260	.383	.281
Inglett, Joe*	2b	Mahoning Vy	Cle	A-	23	56	202	58	12	4	2	84	37	37	31	1	30	5	0	0	4	5	.44	1	.287	.395	.416
Ingram, Darron	dh-of	San Berndno	LA	A+	25	100	396	105	16	6	15	178	58	71	37	1	136	0	0	2	5	5	.50	10	.265	.326	.449
Isenia, Chairon	c	Chston-SC	TB	A	22	102	384	104	21	0	6	143	37	59	16	1	53	6	2	5	5	3	.63	9	.271	.307	.372
Isturiz, Maicer#	ss-dh	Columbus	Cle	A	20	10	29	8	1	0	0	9	4	1	3	0	3	0	0	0	0	0	.00	1	.276	.344	.310
Ivy, Bo	of	White Sox	CWS	R	19	36	129	44	4	2	0	52	35	13	34	0	24	0	0	2	34	11	.76	0	.341	.473	.403
Jackson, Brandon	ss	Hagerstown	Tor	A	25	110	391	122	17	8	5	170	71	52	43	0	83	13	1	8	5	6	.45	6	.312	.391	.435
		Dunedin	Tor	A+	25	6	16	5	2	0	0	7	6	2	3	0	0	1	0	1	2	0	1.00	0	.313	.429	.438
Jackson, Brandon	of	Boise	Ana	A-	24	8	8	1	0	0	0	1	0	0	0	0	3	0	0	0	0	0	.00	0	.125	.125	.125
Jackson, Nic	of	Eugene	ChC	A-	21	74	294	75	12	7	6	119	39	47	22	2	64	1	0	1	25	3	.89	6	.255	.308	.405
Jackson, Steve	1b-dh	Athletics	Oak	R	23	25	80	28	9	1	1	42	13	26	20	0	22	2	0	2	0	1	.00	1	.350	.481	.525
		Vancouver	Oak	A-	23	12	32	4	2	0	0	6	1	3	8	1	12	0	0	0	0	0	.00	0	.125	.300	.188
Jackson, Wilbur	ss	Reds	Cin	R	20	9	34	11	4	0	0	15	3	3	2	0	13	0	0	0	1	1	.50	1	.324	.361	.441
Jacobs, John	of-2b	Chston-SC	TB	A	21	20	61	12	4	1	0	18	5	7	3	0	19	1	0	0	6	0	1.00	1	.197	.246	.295
		Hudson Val	TB	A-	21	40	126	28	7	0	2	41	13	11	9	0	46	0	0	1	7	8	.47	1	.222	.272	.325
Jacobs, Mike*	c	Capital Cty	NYM	A	20	18	56	12	5	0	0	17	1	8	6	1	19	0	0	0	1	1	.50	2	.214	.290	.304
		Kingsport	NYM	R+	20	59	204	55	15	4	7	99	28	40	33	1	62	1	1	2	6	3	.67	3	.270	.371	.485
Jacobson, Russ	c	Piedmont	Phi	A	23	102	348	86	17	0	19	160	43	71	29	0	105	11	2	1	0	1	.00	8	.247	.324	.460
Jaile, Chris	c	Charlotte	Tex	A+	20	4	8	2	0	0	0	2	1	1	4	0	2	0	0	0	0	0	.00	0	.250	.500	.250
		Rangers	Tex	R	20	35	114	22	5	0	2	33	14	16	18	1	23	2	2	3	1	0	1.00	3	.193	.307	.289
Janek, John	of	Billings	Cin	R+	23	2	6	0	0	0	0	0	1	0	1	0	2	0	0	0	0	0	.00	0	.000	.143	.000
		Reds	Cin	R	23	1	0	0	0	0	0	0	0	0	0	0	0	0	0	0	0	0	.00	0	.000	.000	.000
Janowicz, Nate*	of	Mahoning Vy	Cle	A-	23	71	265	90	14	5	3	123	40	43	31	1	34	1	5	3	10	12	.45	5	.340	.407	.464
Jansen, Ardley	of	Braves	Atl	R	18	46	150	40	6	2	0	50	22	16	28	1	36	1	2	0	3	3	.50	2	.267	.385	.333
January, Javerro	of	Ogden	Mil	R+	20	43	101	21	4	1	0	27	19	12	12	0	29	5	1	1	9	5	.64	0	.208	.319	.267
Jaramillo, Frank	ss	Mudville	Mil	A+	26	84	276	66	13	2	5	98	34	27	24	0	63	5	5	1	12	7	.63	4	.239	.310	.355
Jaramillo, Milko#	ss	San Berndno	LA	A+	21	34	105	20	0	1	0	22	11	6	8	0	24	2	6	1	4	1	.80	2	.190	.259	.210
		Yakima	LA	A-	21	10	37	8	1	0	0	9	3	1	4	1	12	1	2	0	4	0	1.00	0	.216	.310	.243
		Great Falls	LA	R+	21	41	144	36	3	1	0	41	25	16	26	0	23	2	6	1	13	4	.76	3	.250	.370	.285
Jaroncyk, Ryan#	dh-of	San Berndno	LA	A+	24	11	38	4	1	0	0	5	4	1	2	0	11	0	3	0	1	0	1.00	1	.105	.150	.132
		Vero Beach	LA	A+	24	1	3	1	0	0	0	1	1	0	0	0	1	0	0	0	0	1	.00	0	.333	.333	.333
Jarvais, Kregg	c	Augusta	Bos	A	24	26	76	14	3	1	1	22	10	14	13	0	30	1	0	1	1	0	1.00	0	.184	.308	.289
Jenkins, Brian	of	Capital Cty	NYM	A	22	60	217	58	12	2	3	83	25	23	14	2	41	3	0	2	5	2	.71	1	.267	.318	.382
Jenkins, Darryl*	3b	Expos	Mon	R	20	11	34	5	1	0	0	6	2	1	5	0	16	0	0	0	1	0	1.00	0	.147	.256	.176
Jenkins, Kevin*	of	Butte	Ana	R+	19	48	143	28	5	0	2	39	26	15	19	0	47	1	1	0	6	3	.67	2	.196	.294	.273
Jenkins, Neil	3b	W Michigan	Det	A	20	112	411	104	16	5	13	169	56	65	38	1	151	1	2	4	0	1	.00	7	.253	.315	.411
Jimenez, Carlos	2b-ss	W Michigan	Det	A	21	102	335	76	18	7	1	111	47	33	35	0	107	2	4	3	13	6	.68	6	.227	.301	.331
Jimenez, Richard#	ss-2b	Queens	Tor	A-	19	9	32	7	1	0	0	8	5	3	3	0	9	1	0	0	0	0	.00	0	.219	.306	.250
Joffrion, Jack	2b	St. Pete	TB	A+	25	67	218	47	13	0	3	69	14	22	12	0	64	4	3	2	4	6	.40	3	.216	.267	.317
Johannes, Todd	c	Cape Fear	Mon	A	24	38	102	20	2	0	0	22	8	10	9	0	20	5	2	1	0	1	.00	1	.196	.291	.216
Johnson, Ben	of	Peoria	StL	A	20	93	330	80	22	1	13	143	58	46	53	0	78	5	0	3	17	6	.74	8	.242	.353	.433
		Fort Wayne	SD	A	20	29	109	21	6	2	3	40	11	13	7	1	25	3	2	0	0	3	.00	5	.193	.261	.367
Johnson, Brian	c	Chston-WV	KC	A	24	61	201	44	13	0	0	57	15	21	8	0	39	10	3	5	1	1	.50	5	.219	.277	.284
Johnson, Chris	2b-of	Billings	Cin	R+	22	51	208	64	8	0	1	75	53	22	38	1	16	4	1	3	15	4	.79	3	.308	.419	.361
Johnson, Eric	of	Columbus	Cle	A	23	67	262	81	11	2	4	108	63	45	37	1	49	7	1	3	41	7	.85	1	.309	.405	.412
		Kinston	Cle	A+	23	55	213	44	4	2	2	58	23	21	27	0	47	5	6	2	15	5	.75	1	.207	.308	.272
Johnson, Erik	of	Salem	Col	A+	24	83	252	61	17	3	5	99	32	26	11	0	38	4	1	3	3	2	.60	5	.242	.281	.393
Johnson, Forrest	dh-c	Oneonta	Det	A-	22	34	110	29	4	2	2	43	20	17	13	0	20	6	0	2	3	2	.60	6	.264	.366	.391
Johnson, Gabe	c-3b	Peoria	StL	A	21	58	197	31	8	0	4	51	20	22	13	1	91	4	4	1	1	2	.33	5	.157	.223	.259
Johnson, Gary	of	Daytona	ChC	A+	24	124	436	126	21	5	15	202	75	65	55	2	74	15	1	7	25	7	.78	11	.289	.382	.463
Johnson, J.J.	3b	Cubs	ChC	R	19	44	177	56	9	4	3	82	27	43	12	0	19	0	0	3	3	2	.60	6	.316	.354	.463
Johnson, Jason	of	Clearwater	Phi	A+	23	95	335	92	18	3	3	125	56	34	32	1	60	10	4	6	22	7	.76	6	.275	.350	.373
Johnson, Jeremy*	of	Medcine Hat	Tor	R+	23	67	245	92	24	3	9	149	66	58	55	3	29	6	1	1	5	3	.63	8	.376	.498	.608
Johnson, Kade	dh	Ogden	Mil	R+	22	28	98	31	7	0	10	68	16	35	14	2	20	4	0	1	2	1	.67	1	.316	.419	.694
Johnson, Kareem	of	Elizabethtn	Min	R+	20	4	12	2	0	0	0	2	0	0	0	0	2	0	0	0	1	0	1.00	0	.167	.167	.167
Johnson, Kelly*	ss	Braves	Atl	R	19	53	193	52	12	3	4	82	27	29	24	0	45	0	1	1	6	1	.86	4	.269	.349	.425
Johnson, Patrick*	of	Red Sox	Bos	R	22	8	28	6	2	0	1	11	2	4	2	0	5	0	0	0	1	0	1.00	3	.214	.267	.393
		Lowell	Bos	A-	22	26	70	14	5	0	2	25	8	4	14	2	20	0	0	0	0	2	.00	2	.200	.333	.357
Johnson, Reed	of	Hagerstown	Tor	A	24	95	324	94	24	5	8	152	66	70	62	1	49	14	2	3	14	2	.88	9	.290	.422	.469
		Dunedin	Tor	A+	24	36	133	42	9	2	4	67	26	28	14	0	27	11	1	3	3	2	.60	1	.316	.416	.504
Johnson, Seth	3b	Expos	Mon	R	19	47	187	56	9	0	1	68	22	18	9	0	21	1	1	0	1	2	.33	5	.299	.335	.364
Johnson, Tripper	3b	Orioles	Bal	R	19	48	180	55	5	3	2	72	22	33	13	0	38	4	2	6	7	5	.58	2	.306	.355	.400
Johnson, Tristan	1b	Pirates	Pit	R	19	11	35	2	0	0	0	2	1	0	2	0	22	0	0	0	0	0	.00	1	.057	.108	.057
Johnstone, Ben	of	Lansing	ChC	A	23	128	512	128	15	4	2	157	82	43	29	1	62	20	10	3	54	21	.72	2	.250	.314	.307
Jones, Aaron*	1b	Tampa	NYY	A+	25	113	365	84	19	0	9	130	41	37	54	4	86	1	2	3	3	4	.43	10	.230	.329	.356
Jones, Brian*	c	Dayton	Cin	A	23	41	122	28	8	0	5	51	14	25	4	0	43	3	1	1	0	0	.00	4	.230	.269	.418
Jones, Damien*	of	Macon	Atl	A	21	126	503	135	18	4	1	164	82	33	63	0	98	1	3	0	44	19	.70	7	.268	.351	.326
Jones, Dwayne*	dh	Pirates	Pit	R	24	14	38	3	1	0	0	4	3	3	2	0	23	1	0	0	0	0	.00	1	.079	.146	.105

2000 Batting — Class-A and Rookie Leagues

BATTING																					BASERUNNING				PERCENTAGES		
Player	Pos	Team	Org	Lg	A	G	AB	H	2B	3B	HR	TB	R	RBI	TBB	IBB	SO	HBP	SH	SF	SB	CS	SB%	GDP	Avg	OBP	SLG
Jones, Garrett*	1b	Danville	Atl	R+	20	40	138	24	7	2	0	35	12	16	13	0	55	0	0	2	0	3	.00	2	.174	.242	.254
Jones, Jared	dh	Mariners	Sea	R	21	6	18	2	0	0	0	2	2	2	3	0	7	0	0	0	1	0	1.00	0	.111	.238	.111
Jones, Jason#	1b	Savannah	Tex	A	24	132	466	125	34	6	9	198	59	61	65	1	97	4	1	5	9	5	.64	15	.268	.359	.425
Jones, Mitch	of	Staten Ilnd	NYY	A-	23	74	284	76	28	3	11	143	46	54	35	0	66	3	0	2	8	2	.80	1	.268	.352	.504
Jordan, Kevin	of	Kissimmee	Hou	A+	24	38	127	32	6	3	4	56	22	19	11	0	23	5	0	1	2	5	.29	7	.252	.333	.441
Jordan, Yustin	of	Quad City	Min	A	22	87	231	54	9	0	7	84	35	28	38	0	67	3	1	3	6	4	.60	2	.234	.345	.364
Jorgensen, Ryan	c	Eugene	ChC	A-	22	41	130	39	10	2	1	56	17	23	17	0	27	1	2	2	2	4	.33	1	.300	.380	.431
Joyce, Jesse	of	Kissimmee	Hou	A+	25	56	154	33	14	1	1	52	17	16	12	0	25	0	2	4	7	0	1.00	3	.214	.265	.338
Joyce, Thomas*	of	Orioles	Bal	R	19	44	129	27	6	2	0	37	13	9	17	1	28	1	6	0	2	3	.40	3	.209	.306	.287
Jung, Young-Jin	1b	Padres	SD	R	23	37	120	22	3	0	0	25	10	3	4	0	28	2	1	0	0	1	.00	4	.183	.222	.208
Kail, Tom	of	Missoula	Ari	R+	21	42	134	33	7	1	0	42	20	9	17	0	23	0	0	3	1	2	.33	7	.246	.325	.313
Kalczynski, Joe	c	South Bend	Ari	A	23	50	115	18	3	0	0	21	12	8	17	0	23	5	3	0	1	2	.33	0	.157	.292	.183
Kasper, Todd*	c	High Desert	Ari	A+	24	45	137	32	6	0	1	41	16	19	19	1	26	1	1	2	2	4	.33	3	.234	.327	.299
		Cape Fear	Mon	A	24	19	58	10	3	0	0	13	1	5	6	0	15	0	0	0	2	1	.67	2	.172	.250	.224
Kata, Matt#	ss	South Bend	Ari	A	23	133	521	133	22	9	6	191	82	59	52	2	58	6	3	5	38	12	.76	10	.255	.327	.367
Katz, Damon	ss	Mahoning Vy	Cle	A-	23	24	76	19	3	3	0	28	11	7	3	0	17	6	3	1	1	1	.50	1	.250	.326	.368
Kaup, Nathan	1b	Hudson Val	TB	A-	23	35	136	45	9	0	2	60	21	22	5	0	25	1	0	2	3	2	.60	4	.331	.354	.441
Kavourias, Jim	of	Utica	Fla	A-	21	15	50	16	4	0	2	26	7	7	10	0	6	0	0	0	1	0	1.00	0	.320	.433	.520
Kawabata, K.#	of	Augusta	Bos	A	22	12	32	4	1	0	0	5	5	2	6	0	14	0	0	0	0	0	.00	1	.125	.263	.156
		Sarasota	Bos	A+	22	44	94	21	2	0	2	29	11	6	12	0	30	2	2	0	2	1	.67	1	.223	.324	.309
Kay, Kevin*	c	Boise	Ana	A-	23	28	50	12	3	1	0	17	9	8	10	0	12	3	0	0	5	0	1.00	2	.240	.397	.340
Kearns, Austin	of	Dayton	Cin	A	21	136	484	148	37	2	27	270	110	104	90	5	93	7	0	9	18	5	.78	14	.306	.415	.558
Keating, Matt*	1b	Salem-Keizr	SF	A-	23	34	114	26	6	0	0	32	12	16	5	0	13	1	0	2	0	0	.00	6	.228	.262	.281
		San Jose	SF	A+	23	10	22	7	1	0	0	8	1	0	1	0	2	0	0	0	0	1	.00	0	.318	.348	.364
Keene, Kurt	1b	Queens	Tor	A-	23	11	46	12	1	0	0	13	10	5	6	0	10	0	0	0	4	1	.80	3	.261	.346	.283
		Hagerstown	Tor	A	23	55	199	52	11	0	1	66	16	25	8	0	33	3	0	1	4	6	.40	3	.261	.299	.332
Keller, G.W.	of	Visalia	Oak	A+	24	28	77	18	3	3	0	27	15	9	9	0	15	1	2	1	3	2	.60	2	.234	.318	.351
		Vancouver	Oak	A-	24	62	217	54	8	3	1	71	32	33	20	0	41	7	3	2	5	2	.71	4	.249	.329	.327
Kelley, Casey*	1b	Cedar Rapds	Ana	A	24	82	256	65	13	1	14	122	39	43	56	1	97	0	3	3	4	3	.57	2	.254	.384	.477
Kelly, Chris	dh-1b	Peoria	StL	A	24	8	16	1	0	0	0	1	0	1	1	0	9	1	1	0	0	0	.00	1	.063	.167	.063
Kelly, Heath	3b	Brevard Cty	Fla	A+	25	50	152	35	8	0	5	58	17	25	9	1	54	2	2	0	2	1	.67	3	.230	.282	.382
Kelly, Shane	of	Chston-SC	TB	A	22	8	26	3	0	0	0	3	2	2	2	0	11	0	0	2	1	0	1.00	1	.115	.167	.115
Kelton, David	3b	Daytona	ChC	A+	21	132	523	140	30	7	18	238	75	84	38	4	120	2	1	5	7	8	.47	9	.268	.317	.455
Kenney, Jeff	3b	Ogden	Mil	R+	23	9	36	11	1	0	0	12	10	9	5	1	6	2	0	2	0	0	.00	1	.306	.400	.333
		Mudville	Mil	A+	23	56	188	50	13	0	0	63	27	16	34	0	34	4	3	1	5	7	.42	3	.266	.388	.335
Kent, Mat*	c	Everett	Sea	A-	20	34	99	21	7	0	1	31	7	7	3	0	39	0	1	0	0	0	.00	0	.212	.235	.313
Keppinger, Billy*	of	Spokane	KC	A-	22	51	152	42	11	0	2	59	22	21	18	0	32	1	0	2	4	2	.67	1	.276	.353	.388
Kerner, Craig*	of	Vermont	Mon	A-	22	33	108	29	1	2	0	34	24	11	15	0	25	5	3	0	12	4	.75	0	.269	.383	.315
Kerrigan, Joe*	2b	Sarasota	Bos	A+	23	83	264	54	14	0	0	68	28	21	51	2	48	1	1	3	4	8	.33	6	.205	.332	.258
		Augusta	Bos	A	23	27	102	30	3	3	0	39	18	10	16	0	21	0	1	1	1	0	1.00	2	.294	.387	.382
Kessick, Jon	c	Delmarva	Bal	A	23	103	294	55	7	1	1	67	40	21	48	0	107	2	5	2	5	1	.83	3	.187	.303	.228
Kidd, Scott	2b	Tampa	NYY	A+	27	88	301	85	16	1	9	130	38	41	19	0	63	5	0	2	1	2	.33	7	.282	.333	.432
Kidwell, Tommy	2b	Potomac	StL	A+	24	9	13	1	0	0	0	1	0	0	0	0	3	0	0	0	0	0	.00	0	.077	.077	.077
Kim, Dave	of	Potomac	StL	A+	25	42	141	34	10	0	5	59	15	18	21	0	31	5	1	0	1	1	.50	4	.241	.359	.418
Kimberley, Glynn	of	Medcine Hat	Tor	R+	19	26	83	19	4	0	1	26	13	13	9	0	32	3	0	1	0	0	.00	2	.229	.323	.313
Kinchen, Jason*	1b	Staten Ilnd	NYY	A-	25	66	231	65	16	1	10	113	39	50	22	1	47	8	0	3	0	1	.00	2	.281	.360	.489
King, Brennan	3b	Yakima	LA	A-	20	61	238	57	10	1	1	72	27	30	29	3	49	5	1	1	14	5	.74	7	.239	.333	.303
King, Jason	3b	Danville	Atl	R+	21	35	122	34	4	0	4	50	14	14	15	0	19	0	1	1	2	1	.67	3	.279	.355	.410
Kison, Robbie	2b-ss	Clinton	Cin	A	24	34	92	19	1	0	0	20	15	6	14	0	17	1	0	0	6	3	.67	1	.207	.318	.217
		Dayton	Cin	A	24	43	115	26	2	1	0	30	14	15	29	0	25	3	1	1	6	2	.75	2	.226	.392	.261
Klatt, Joel	3b	Padres	SD	R	19	51	177	37	12	2	1	56	12	15	10	0	29	5	2	0	1	1	.50	5	.209	.271	.316
Knight, Marcus#	of	Boise	Ana	A-	22	1	3	2	0	0	2	8	2	4	1	0	0	0	0	0	1	0	1.00	0	.667	.750	2.667
		Lk Elsinore	Ana	A+	22	55	192	45	10	2	4	71	26	20	20	1	39	2	4	2	4	4	.50	4	.234	.310	.370
Knox, Matt	2b	Expos	Mon	R	23	23	62	12	1	0	0	13	1	4	3	0	15	2	2	0	2	1	.67	1	.194	.254	.210
Knox, Ryan	of	Beloit	Mil	A	24	125	460	125	19	6	2	162	72	41	34	3	61	17	16	7	42	10	.81	5	.272	.340	.352
Koerner, Mike*	of	Vero Beach	LA	A+	25	21	65	17	2	0	1	22	7	5	5	0	13	2	0	0	0	1	.00	2	.262	.333	.338
Koonce, Gray*	1b	Rancho Cuca	SD	A+	26	137	475	140	40	3	18	240	92	93	107	7	105	4	0	4	0	0	.00	4	.295	.425	.505
Kopitzke, Casey	c	Lansing	ChC	A	23	68	201	45	10	0	1	58	19	22	18	0	28	3	3	3	1	1	.50	8	.224	.293	.289
Koreger, Josh*	of	Diamondbcks	Ari	R	18	54	222	66	9	3	4	93	40	28	21	1	41	1	0	1	5	4	.56	3	.297	.359	.419
Krga, Mike	2b-dh	Princeton	TB	R+	18	35	132	36	4	1	1	45	14	11	8	0	29	0	1	0	1	0	1.00	2	.273	.314	.341
Kropf, Andy#	c	Tigers	Det	R	22	12	34	6	2	0	1	11	3	3	3	0	3	0	0	1	1	1	.50	0	.176	.237	.324
		Lakeland	Det	A+	22	29	87	22	3	0	2	31	7	8	6	0	29	0	0	1	0	0	.00	2	.253	.298	.356
Krynzel, Dave*	of	Ogden	Mil	R+	19	34	131	47	8	3	1	64	25	29	16	3	23	5	1	2	8	4	.67	0	.359	.442	.489
Kubel, Jason*	of	Twins	Min	R	19	23	78	22	3	2	0	29	17	13	10	0	9	1	1	1	0	0	.00	1	.282	.367	.372
Kuzmic, Craig#	1b	Lancaster	Sea	A+	24	136	522	155	27	10	19	259	106	104	71	3	124	10	0	6	5	8	.38	10	.297	.388	.496
Kweon, Yoon-Min	c	Eugene	ChC	A-	22	44	145	37	9	1	5	63	15	18	22	0	29	5	0	0	5	3	.63	5	.255	.372	.434
Lackaff, John	3b	Bristol	CWS	R+	22	59	217	62	9	3	3	86	30	34	14	1	36	9	2	2	9	4	.69	7	.286	.351	.396
LaForest, Pete*	dh-c	St. Pete	TB	A+	23	129	474	128	28	7	14	212	85	70	56	4	108	6	1	5	2	4	.33	4	.270	.351	.447
Laidlaw, Jake	3b	Marlins	Fla	R	19	23	76	19	5	1	2	32	13	14	10	0	14	3	0	3	2	0	1.00	0	.250	.348	.421
Laird, Gerald	c	Athletics	Oak	R	21	14	50	15	2	1	0	19	10	9	6	0	7	1	0	1	2	0	1.00	3	.300	.379	.380
		Visalia	Oak	A+	21	33	103	25	3	0	0	28	14	13	14	0	27	1	0	2	7	2	.78	3	.243	.333	.272
Lake, Josh	dh-c	Helena	Mil	R+	20	4	10	2	0	0	0	2	0	1	1	0	6	1	1	0	0	0	.00	0	.200	.333	.200
		Ogden	Mil	R+	20	4	8	1	0	0	0	1	1	0	2	0	2	0	0	0	0	0	.00	0	.125	.300	.125
Lama, Jesus	of	Princeton	TB	R+	21	54	184	45	10	1	1	60	23	19	19	0	59	1	0	4	4	2	.67	7	.245	.313	.326
Lambert, Shawn	1b	Tigers	Det	R	19	37	118	29	4	0	5	48	15	16	24	0	48	0	0	0	2	3	.40	3	.246	.373	.407
Landaeta, Luis*	of	Salem	Col	A+	24	89	288	73	11	0	9	111	34	33	9	0	51	2	3	3	10	5	.67	8	.253	.278	.385
Landreth, Jason	of	Lynchburg	Pit	A+	25	22	57	11	1	0	1	15	5	6	9	0	23	2	0	1	1	0	1.00	1	.193	.319	.263

2000 Batting — Class-A and Rookie Leagues

BATTING																					BASERUNNING				PERCENTAGES		
Player	Pos	Team	Org	Lg	A	G	AB	H	2B	3B	HR	TB	R	RBI	TBB	IBB	SO	HBP	SH	SF	SB	CS	SB%	GDP	Avg	OBP	SLG
		Hickory	Pit	A	25	72	260	79	16	4	4	115	43	41	49	3	50	3	0	2	21	9	.70	6	.304	.417	.442
Lane, Jason	of	Michigan	Hou	A	24	133	511	153	38	0	23	260	98	104	62	7	91	8	0	13	20	7	.74	9	.299	.375	.509
Lane, Rich*	1b	Cape Fear	Mon	A	21	74	277	86	15	2	4	117	46	47	25	0	46	2	0	2	3	0	1.00	8	.310	.369	.422
Langerhans, Ryan*	of	Myrtle Bch	Atl	A+	21	116	392	83	14	7	6	129	55	37	32	1	104	9	4	0	25	11	.69	3	.212	.286	.329
Langill, Eric	c	Vermont	Mon	A-	22	14	44	6	1	0	0	7	3	7	7	0	14	1	0	2	0	0	.00	0	.136	.259	.159
Langlois, Jean-S.	of	Jamestown	Atl	A-	22	15	41	3	0	0	0	3	5	3	4	0	12	3	0	1	1	1	.50	0	.073	.204	.073
Langs, Ronte	of	Yakima	LA	A-	22	55	170	38	5	1	0	45	26	17	24	2	45	4	4	1	11	6	.65	4	.224	.332	.265
Langston, James#	3b	Hickory	Pit	A	23	113	435	127	23	3	8	180	62	77	27	2	99	2	3	4	3	1	.75	8	.292	.333	.414
Lantigua, Denys	c	Burlington	Cle	R+	21	38	107	22	6	0	1	31	18	13	17	0	14	5	0	1	4	0	1.00	6	.206	.338	.290
Lara, Balmes	dh	W Michigan	Det	A	23	105	372	89	14	1	8	129	64	52	35	1	81	5	0	2	11	1	.92	7	.239	.312	.347
Larned, Drew	c	Augusta	Bos	A	25	59	178	40	9	0	0	49	29	16	36	0	50	2	1	3	3	2	.60	2	.225	.356	.275
LaRoche, Adam*	1b	Danville	Atl	R+	21	56	201	62	13	3	7	102	38	45	24	2	46	2	1	4	4	1	.80	2	.308	.381	.507
Laureano, Wilfredo	of	Royals	KC	R	20	46	147	31	4	0	3	44	9	24	11	1	28	2	1	3	2	0	1.00	6	.211	.270	.299
Lawson, Forrest	of	Kingsport	NYM	R+	20	60	203	55	12	2	2	77	27	22	28	0	43	4	3	0	12	7	.63	4	.271	.370	.379
Layton, Blane*	of	Dayton	Cin	A	24	86	279	64	17	1	6	101	48	27	43	0	70	1	3	0	15	9	.63	3	.229	.334	.362
Leal, Jaeme	1b-dh	Macon	Atl	A	22	107	387	100	20	1	16	170	44	65	35	0	133	10	0	4	0	0	.00	5	.258	.333	.439
Leatherman, Dan*	1b	Fort Myers	Min	A+	25	93	265	54	15	1	5	86	34	31	18	0	40	2	6	4	2	4	.33	6	.204	.256	.325
Leaumont, Jeff*	1b	Greensboro	NYY	A	24	88	323	91	18	3	9	142	45	59	39	1	83	5	0	2	2	1	.67	5	.282	.366	.440
		Staten Ilnd	NYY	A-	24	25	86	23	2	1	0	27	10	9	11	0	17	3	0	1	0	0	.00	4	.267	.366	.314
Lebron, Edgardo	3b	Twins	Min	R	18	32	119	29	3	2	0	36	13	9	8	0	31	1	1	0	2	3	.40	5	.244	.297	.303
Lebron, Francisco	1b	Capital Cty	NYM	A	26	14	43	8	4	0	1	15	4	5	9	0	13	1	1	0	0	1	.00	1	.186	.340	.349
Lee, Eric	of	Auburn	Hou	A-	23	59	199	36	6	2	3	55	27	15	18	0	48	4	0	1	8	7	.53	2	.181	.261	.276
Lee, Monte	of	Savannah	Tex	A	24	44	110	22	2	0	1	27	17	8	18	0	32	8	3	2	10	3	.77	1	.200	.348	.245
Leer, David	of	Oneonta	Det	A-	24	29	115	36	8	0	0	44	20	6	7	0	35	4	0	0	10	5	.67	0	.313	.373	.383
LeFlore, Alex	of	Billings	Cin	R+	20	17	58	13	4	0	1	20	11	5	6	0	10	2	1	0	5	0	1.00	0	.224	.318	.345
Lehr, Ryan	1b-dh	Myrtle Bch	Atl	A+	22	64	207	41	8	1	2	57	15	22	21	0	43	1	2	1	1	1	.50	5	.198	.274	.275
		Macon	Atl	A	22	46	184	60	15	1	2	83	25	36	9	1	22	2	0	0	2	2	.50	6	.326	.364	.451
Lemon, Tim	of	Peoria	StL	A	20	127	466	105	25	5	10	170	64	52	17	0	105	5	8	1	25	10	.71	6	.225	.260	.365
Lentz, Ryan*	dh	Jupiter	Mon	A+	24	7	19	7	2	1	0	11	3	3	7	2	7	0	0	0	0	0	.00	0	.368	.538	.579
Leon, Alfredo	1b	Delmarva	Bal	A	21	8	11	0	0	0	0	0	0	0	0	0	3	0	0	0	0	0	.00	1	.000	.000	.000
		Bluefield	Bal	R+	21	7	26	6	1	1	0	9	5	0	3	0	1	1	0	0	0	0	.00	1	.231	.333	.346
		Frederick	Bal	A+	21	35	117	28	3	0	1	34	8	10	8	0	24	1	0	1	0	1	.00	3	.239	.291	.291
Leon, Omar	c	Marlins	Fla	R	19	22	57	17	2	1	0	21	4	10	2	0	6	2	0	2	0	1	.00	5	.298	.333	.368
Leonardo, Santos	of	Tigers	Det	R	19	26	89	15	1	1	3	27	17	12	7	0	18	5	0	0	12	1	.92	1	.169	.267	.303
Leone, Justin	3b	Wisconsin	Sea	A	24	115	374	100	32	3	18	192	77	63	79	1	107	11	2	3	9	2	.82	3	.267	.407	.513
Lichay, Don	3b	Pittsfield	NYM	A-	24	35	93	18	3	1	1	26	15	8	13	0	32	3	3	0	6	2	.75	1	.194	.312	.280
Lincoln, Justin	ss	Asheville	Col	A	22	126	451	106	22	0	17	179	58	60	35	1	161	5	0	3	18	10	.64	7	.235	.296	.397
Lindsey, Cordell	3b	Cedar Rapds	Ana	A	23	105	409	87	22	1	6	129	42	56	20	0	65	4	3	4	16	9	.64	9	.213	.254	.315
Lindsey, John	dh	Salem	Col	A+	24	104	343	96	23	1	9	148	43	56	37	0	76	15	0	3	5	3	.63	6	.280	.372	.431
Lipowicz, Nathan	of	Great Falls	LA	R+	23	43	145	35	5	3	3	55	22	12	7	0	36	1	0	2	2	2	.50	2	.241	.277	.379
Liriano, Pedro	2b	Mariners	Sea	R	19	43	170	68	15	2	1	90	46	30	21	0	11	2	0	4	18	5	.78	1	.400	.462	.529
		Everett	Sea	A-	19	4	15	3	0	0	0	3	2	2	4	0	4	0	0	0	4	0	1.00	1	.200	.368	.200
Little, Jim	of	Butte	Ana	R+	23	51	184	48	9	3	3	72	33	25	14	0	29	3	3	2	5	2	.71	5	.261	.320	.391
Littleton, Brandon#	of	Bluefield	Bal	R+	21	55	209	61	11	5	2	88	39	25	35	0	42	3	1	0	12	2	.86	3	.292	.401	.421
Llamas, Juan	3b	Reds	Cin	R	21	24	87	26	1	1	1	32	10	11	4	0	15	2	0	0	1	1	.50	1	.299	.344	.368
		Billings	Cin	R+	21	4	19	6	1	0	0	7	1	1	0	0	3	0	1	0	0	0	.00	1	.316	.316	.368
Lockhart, Paul#	of	Auburn	Hou	A-	23	67	231	59	15	3	1	83	20	29	16	1	44	2	0	2	4	6	.40	4	.255	.307	.359
Loeb, Bryan	c	Missoula	Ari	R+	23	32	88	29	9	1	1	43	16	10	11	0	21	6	1	0	0	0	.00	2	.330	.438	.489
Logan, Exavier	ss	Tigers	Det	R	21	43	136	38	2	2	0	44	29	14	31	0	36	1	1	2	20	3	.87	1	.279	.412	.324
		Lakeland	Det	A+	21	11	42	14	1	0	0	15	4	3	2	0	13	0	1	0	2	1	.67	0	.333	.364	.357
Logan, Matt*	1b	Dunedin	Tor	A+	21	124	373	104	26	1	9	159	58	55	36	0	93	7	2	6	4	1	.80	13	.279	.348	.426
Loggins, Josh	c-of	Rancho Cuca	SD	A+	24	78	293	88	13	4	6	127	52	43	30	2	84	6	0	4	9	4	.69	5	.300	.372	.433
Lopez, Aristides	of	Martinsvlle	Hou	R+	22	11	32	11	3	1	0	16	4	4	3	0	3	1	0	0	5	2	.71	0	.344	.417	.500
		Auburn	Hou	A-	22	41	134	27	8	1	1	40	19	16	8	0	27	1	1	0	9	4	.69	2	.201	.252	.299
Lopez, Chuck*	of	Everett	Sea	A-	24	34	121	32	6	0	3	47	18	21	13	2	22	4	0	1	2	0	1.00	1	.264	.353	.388
Lopez, Luis	of	Kissimmee	Hou	A+	23	74	226	46	10	4	5	79	33	25	15	0	67	3	2	1	7	6	.54	3	.204	.261	.350
Lopez, Norberto	c	Lk Elsinore	Ana	A+	24	30	79	3	1	0	0	4	2	2	9	0	29	0	2	0	0	0	.00	3	.038	.136	.051
Lopez, Oliver	ss	Padres	SD	R	19	19	40	7	1	0	0	8	6	3	5	0	14	0	2	0	0	1	.00	0	.175	.267	.200
Lopez, Raul*	1b	Jamestown	Atl	A-	22	72	267	59	15	2	5	93	32	41	26	2	52	3	0	2	0	0	.00	9	.221	.295	.348
Lopez, Willy	c-dh	Lowell	Bos	A-	22	8	28	4	1	0	0	5	3	1	4	0	13	0	0	0	1	0	1.00	0	.143	.250	.179
Lopez, Yovanny	of	Augusta	Bos	A	21	10	33	5	1	0	1	9	3	2	2	0	17	0	0	0	0	0	.00	1	.152	.200	.273
		Red Sox	Bos	R	21	41	124	30	1	0	2	37	10	15	20	1	27	1	0	0	8	5	.62	4	.242	.352	.298
Lora, Thomas#	2b	Chston-WV	KC	A	22	105	359	73	13	1	0	88	39	18	26	0	86	4	5	1	30	12	.71	7	.203	.264	.245
Lorenzo, Juan#	ss	Fort Myers	Min	A+	23	119	431	122	25	1	3	158	57	44	20	0	33	6	7	4	8	3	.73	10	.283	.321	.367
Louisa, Lorvin	of	Expos	Mon	R	18	38	118	16	4	1	0	22	7	6	11	0	49	2	0	0	1	0	1.00	2	.136	.221	.186
Louwsma, Chris	3b	Utica	Fla	A-	22	71	265	63	13	0	2	82	28	34	23	1	55	1	1	0	3	4	.43	10	.238	.301	.309
Love, Marc*	of	Pirates	Pit	R	21	33	108	26	4	0	0	30	11	11	6	0	28	3	2	0	5	1	.83	2	.241	.299	.278
Lowe, Ernesto	of	Bristol	CWS	R+	22	44	130	33	3	1	1	41	21	7	10	0	20	3	2	1	5	3	.63	3	.254	.319	.315
Lowe, Steve	ss	Columbus	Cle	A	24	46	135	36	4	3	1	49	16	19	14	0	43	10	1	3	3	1	.75	0	.267	.370	.363
		Mahoning Vy	Cle	A-	24	41	140	34	1	2	3	48	27	14	21	0	31	10	1	0	1	0	1.00	3	.243	.380	.343
Lucas, Matt	c	Martinsvlle	Hou	R+	22	3	12	1	0	0	0	1	0	0	0	0	5	0	0	0	0	0	.00	0	.083	.083	.083
		Auburn	Hou	A-	22	29	89	27	3	0	0	30	11	10	3	0	19	0	1	1	3	2	.60	1	.303	.323	.337
Lucca, Tony*	1b	Brevard Cty	Fla	A+	26	102	329	78	14	2	3	105	38	31	58	6	54	4	2	2	0	0	.00	10	.237	.356	.319
Ludwick, Ryan	of	Modesto	Oak	A+	22	129	493	130	26	3	29	249	86	102	68	0	128	9	1	7	10	6	.63	6	.264	.359	.505
Lugo, Felix#	3b	Jupiter	Mon	A+	20	2	7	1	0	0	0	1	2	0	0	0	3	0	0	0	0	1	.00	0	.143	.143	.143
		Vermont	Mon	A-	20	39	140	35	13	0	3	57	22	19	7	0	47	6	0	1	11	4	.73	2	.250	.312	.407
		Cape Fear	Mon	A	20	16	59	11	2	0	2	19	7	7	2	0	20	0	1	0	3	1	.75	1	.186	.213	.322

2000 Batting — Class-A and Rookie Leagues

BATTING																					BASERUNNING				PERCENTAGES		
Player	Pos	Team	Org	Lg	A	G	AB	H	2B	3B	HR	TB	R	RBI	TBB	IBB	SO	HBP	SH	SF	SB	CS	SB%	GDP	Avg	OBP	SLG
Lugo, Roberto*	1b	Kingsport	NYM	R+	21	14	22	4	1	1	1	10	2	4	10	0	6	0	1	0	1	2	.33	0	.182	.438	.455
Luna, Hector	ss	Burlington	Cle	R+	19	55	201	41	5	0	1	49	25	15	27	0	35	3	0	1	19	4	.83	4	.204	.306	.244
		Mahoning Vy	Cle	A-	19	5	19	6	2	0	0	8	2	4	1	0	3	0	1	0	0	0	.00	0	.316	.350	.421
Lundquist, Ryan	of	Clinton	Cin	A	24	120	438	110	24	2	15	183	61	61	43	1	106	10	3	2	10	1	.91	7	.251	.331	.418
Lunsford, Trey	c	Salem-Keizr	SF	A-	22	59	215	58	9	0	3	76	23	30	30	2	40	8	0	1	1	0	1.00	6	.270	.378	.353
Luster, Jeremy#	1b	Bakersfield	SF	A+	24	137	517	146	35	5	14	233	86	99	77	6	104	10	0	8	17	2	.89	11	.282	.381	.451
Luther, Ryan	2b	Bakersfield	SF	A+	24	110	414	124	25	2	7	174	78	48	48	1	94	10	5	6	14	8	.64	6	.300	.381	.420
Lutz, David*	1b	Cape Fear	Mon	A	19	11	37	8	0	0	0	8	5	5	5	0	15	0	0	0	0	0	.00	0	.216	.310	.216
		Vermont	Mon	A-	19	35	118	26	1	0	0	27	18	13	25	1	25	0	0	2	9	1	.90	0	.220	.352	.229
Luuloa, Miles#	2b	Oneonta	Det	A-	20	53	169	35	5	1	0	42	28	15	30	0	58	4	4	2	3	4	.43	8	.207	.337	.249
Lydic, Joe	3b	Auburn	Hou	A-	22	67	260	71	16	3	6	111	37	30	11	2	60	5	0	2	1	2	.33	2	.273	.313	.427
Lydon, Wayne	of	Kingsport	NYM	R+	20	55	172	35	4	1	3	50	34	20	24	0	47	1	4	3	35	6	.85	2	.203	.300	.291
Lynn, Brody#	c	Burlington	Cle	R+	20	9	30	3	1	0	0	4	3	0	0	0	13	1	0	0	0	0	.00	0	.100	.129	.133
Macalutas, Jon	of	Mudville	Mil	A+	27	137	483	121	31	1	10	184	79	48	104	1	68	11	0	6	38	16	.70	8	.251	.391	.381
Machado, Albenis#	ss	Jupiter	Mon	A+	22	128	428	105	10	4	1	126	79	39	79	2	67	5	18	9	16	11	.59	6	.245	.363	.294
Machado, Alejandro	2b	Danville	Atl	R+	19	61	217	74	6	2	0	84	45	16	53	0	29	6	2	3	30	12	.71	3	.341	.477	.387
Mack, Antonio	of	Bluefield	Bal	R+	22	41	93	16	3	0	2	25	12	8	10	0	41	0	2	0	5	1	.83	3	.172	.252	.269
Madera, Sandy	c	Athletics	Oak	R	20	28	104	29	6	3	2	47	19	24	17	1	10	0	0	0	4	2	.67	8	.279	.380	.452
		Vancouver	Oak	A-	20	16	57	15	2	0	0	17	7	2	8	0	7	1	0	0	0	0	.00	3	.263	.364	.298
Maduro, Jorge	c	Princeton	TB	R+	20	40	119	30	7	0	0	37	7	15	5	0	30	2	2	1	1	1	.50	5	.252	.291	.311
		Chston-SC	TB	A	20	1	2	0	0	0	0	0	0	0	0	0	1	0	0	0	0	0	.00	0	.000	.000	.000
Magness, Pat*	1b	Utica	Fla	A-	23	50	175	54	18	0	5	87	31	40	30	2	34	2	0	1	2	0	1.00	2	.309	.413	.497
Malave, Dennis*	of	Kinston	Cle	A+	21	19	46	16	4	2	1	27	8	11	6	0	8	0	1	0	4	0	1.00	0	.348	.423	.587
		Mahoning Vy	Cle	A-	21	42	178	53	4	8	2	79	39	26	23	1	30	2	4	1	15	5	.75	3	.298	.382	.444
Maldonado, Ed	ss	Salem-Keizr	SF	A-	22	57	191	36	9	0	1	48	23	16	13	0	46	1	5	3	0	3	.00	4	.188	.240	.251
Mallory, Mike	of	Eugene	ChC	A-	20	70	262	55	12	3	6	91	39	30	16	0	98	8	0	2	9	3	.75	4	.210	.274	.347
Malpica, Martin	3b-dh	Queens	Tor	A-	21	55	216	60	14	0	2	80	30	34	7	0	35	2	1	0	0	3	.00	5	.278	.307	.370
Mann, Derek*	2b	St. Pete	TB	A+	23	65	195	48	7	3	2	67	25	14	21	0	28	2	8	2	5	3	.63	3	.246	.323	.344
Manning, Pat	2b	Macon	Atl	A	21	124	435	88	27	0	7	136	48	49	63	2	82	6	4	5	9	2	.82	9	.202	.308	.313
Manning, Ricky*	of	Twins	Min	R	20	26	69	19	0	0	0	19	20	10	16	1	13	3	3	1	6	3	.67	1	.275	.427	.275
Manuel, Marcello*	of	Winston-Sal	CWS	A+	25	75	246	56	10	1	0	68	18	26	17	0	31	1	3	2	0	1	.00	4	.228	.278	.276
Mapes, Jake	c-p	Giants	SF	R	22	22	33	5	0	0	0	5	5	2	4	0	10	0	0	0	0	1	.00	2	.152	.243	.152
Marciniak, Dave	1b	Fort Myers	Min	A+	24	4	15	5	0	0	0	5	2	3	0	0	4	0	0	0	0	1	.00	0	.333	.333	.333
Marconi, Alex	c	Princeton	TB	R+	23	19	65	22	10	0	0	32	8	9	4	0	10	0	1	0	0	0	.00	5	.338	.377	.492
		Hudson Val	TB	A-	23	24	86	25	1	2	1	33	11	10	7	1	15	0	0	1	2	2	.50	3	.291	.340	.384
Markray, Thad	3b-p	Clinton	Cin	A	21	14	34	4	0	0	0	4	1	4	3	0	9	0	1	1	0	0	.00	3	.118	.184	.118
		Reds	Cin	R	21	10	5	1	0	0	0	1	0	1	0	0	1	0	0	0	0	0	.00	0	.200	.200	.200
Marquie, Craig	3b	Yankees	NYY	R	23	5	12	2	0	0	0	2	3	1	1	0	4	0	0	0	1	0	1.00	0	.167	.231	.167
Marsh, Jason	c	Hudson Val	TB	A-	23	53	194	49	7	0	1	59	20	19	5	0	41	4	1	3	3	6	.33	1	.253	.282	.304
Marsters, Brandon	c	Fort Myers	Min	A+	26	118	407	126	25	4	7	180	46	77	31	6	61	4	2	3	2	1	.67	9	.310	.362	.442
Martin, Billy	dh-1b	South Bend	Ari	A	25	123	415	116	26	4	25	225	78	90	83	6	130	11	0	3	7	1	.88	6	.280	.410	.542
Martin, Brian	of	Chston-SC	TB	A	21	87	279	56	14	4	3	87	37	27	32	1	104	11	0	2	3	0	1.00	7	.201	.306	.312
Martin, Justin#	of	Lynchburg	Pit	A+	25	98	355	93	9	1	0	104	52	26	58	0	70	8	4	1	37	10	.79	6	.262	.377	.293
Martin, Kyle	dh-c	Bluefield	Bal	R+	21	23	71	11	1	1	0	14	5	8	6	0	29	2	0	0	0	1	.00	4	.155	.241	.197
Martin, Tyler#	2b	Pulaski	Tex	R+	23	53	191	54	13	2	3	80	43	30	28	0	42	1	5	5	14	2	.88	5	.283	.369	.419
		Charlotte	Tex	A+	23	6	18	3	0	0	0	3	2	1	4	0	2	0	2	0	0	0	.00	1	.167	.318	.167
Martinez, Abel#	3b	Spokane	KC	A-	21	62	247	76	4	3	1	89	30	31	17	0	29	1	0	1	5	5	.50	5	.308	.353	.360
Martinez, Candido	of	Yakima	LA	A-	21	39	137	37	7	2	3	57	20	14	9	0	53	1	0	2	6	4	.60	3	.270	.315	.416
Martinez, Casey	c	Medcine Hat	Tor	R+	23	9	25	7	3	0	1	13	5	3	6	0	7	1	0	0	0	0	.00	1	.280	.438	.520
		Queens	Tor	A-	23	7	22	3	0	0	0	3	2	0	1	0	7	1	1	0	0	0	.00	0	.136	.208	.136
Martinez, Dionnar#	ss	Eugene	ChC	A-	20	53	172	37	4	0	0	41	23	16	14	0	34	3	2	0	8	2	.80	5	.215	.286	.238
Martinez, Edgar	c	Augusta	Bos	A	19	16	50	5	1	0	1	9	4	4	3	0	13	1	0	0	0	0	.00	2	.100	.167	.180
		Red Sox	Bos	R	19	35	119	20	3	0	3	32	12	14	5	0	23	4	0	1	0	2	.00	4	.168	.225	.269
Martinez, GRob.#	2b	Lancaster	Sea	A+	21	30	96	21	7	3	0	34	11	13	9	0	25	0	2	1	1	2	.33	2	.219	.283	.354
		Everett	Sea	A-	21	46	175	38	5	0	0	43	23	13	10	1	36	1	3	0	10	4	.71	5	.217	.263	.246
Martinez, Hipolito	of	Visalia	Oak	A+	24	113	400	81	16	5	13	146	51	48	46	1	135	6	2	2	8	6	.57	11	.203	.293	.365
Martinez, Octavio	c	Bluefield	Bal	R+	21	49	181	70	14	1	7	107	45	46	19	0	21	8	1	3	0	1	.00	4	.387	.460	.591
		Frederick	Bal	A+	21	2	8	3	0	0	0	3	0	1	0	0	0	1	0	0	0	0	.00	0	.375	.444	.375
Martinez, Peter#	ss-2b	Twins	Min	R	19	39	131	31	6	0	0	37	24	20	22	0	23	3	4	5	4	4	.50	2	.237	.348	.282
Martinez, Ramon#	ss	Charlotte	Tex	A+	21	42	152	44	7	1	1	56	12	20	5	0	28	0	3	1	8	3	.73	2	.289	.310	.368
		Savannah	Tex	A	21	39	164	51	9	0	1	63	19	17	2	0	29	3	6	0	6	5	.55	3	.311	.331	.384
Martinez, Victor#	c	Kinston	Cle	A+	22	26	83	18	7	0	0	25	9	8	11	0	5	1	3	1	1	1	.50	3	.217	.313	.301
		Columbus	Cle	A	22	21	70	26	9	1	2	43	11	12	11	0	6	1	0	2	0	0	.00	1	.371	.452	.614
Martinez, William	of	Orioles	Bal	R	20	38	132	36	6	1	1	47	16	8	7	1	27	3	3	0	6	3	.67	3	.273	.324	.356
Masino, Adam	1b	Twins	Min	R	19	30	96	17	4	0	2	27	12	14	18	1	33	3	0	0	2	0	1.00	3	.177	.325	.281
Massey, John	c	South Bend	Ari	A	22	41	146	39	10	0	0	49	9	13	12	0	30	4	0	1	3	1	.75	5	.267	.337	.336
Massiatte, Danny	c	Chston-SC	TB	A	22	9	26	8	1	0	0	9	5	4	6	0	6	1	0	0	3	0	1.00	1	.308	.455	.346
Matan, James	1b	Dayton	Cin	A	25	72	225	46	7	0	4	65	22	30	28	0	59	1	0	1	0	0	.00	8	.204	.294	.289
Materano, Oscar	3b	Rockies	Col	R	19	31	115	28	3	3	0	37	19	13	10	0	25	5	0	0	5	3	.63	2	.243	.331	.322
Mathews, Del*	3b	Helena	Mil	R+	26	38	100	17	3	0	0	20	10	4	19	0	30	3	0	1	4	3	.57	5	.170	.317	.200
Matos, Angel	c-dh	Savannah	Tex	A	21	31	73	18	1	0	6	37	9	16	3	0	25	0	0	1	0	0	.00	1	.247	.273	.507
		Pulaski	Tex	R+	21	54	199	60	14	2	9	105	41	56	37	0	59	1	1	1	10	3	.77	0	.302	.412	.528
Matos, Cesar	c	Athletics	Oak	R	22	23	79	20	6	0	2	32	10	14	4	0	26	1	0	0	2	1	.67	5	.253	.298	.405
Matos, Watson	1b	Elizabethtn	Min	R+	21	31	88	27	5	1	3	43	18	14	15	0	30	0	1	1	1	4	.20	1	.307	.404	.489
Matthews, Lamont*	of	San Berndno	LA	A+	23	131	473	116	28	9	24	234	79	90	88	2	170	6	1	6	12	13	.48	5	.245	.366	.495
Matthews, Michael#	1b-dh	Royals	KC	R	21	35	120	29	4	1	0	35	11	21	7	1	24	1	2	1	1	0	1.00	2	.242	.287	.292
		Chston-WV	KC	A	21	1	4	0	0	0	0	0	0	0	0	0	1	0	0	0	0	0	.00	0	.000	.000	.000

2000 Batting — Class-A and Rookie Leagues

BATTING																					BASERUNNING				PERCENTAGES		
Player	Pos	Team	Org	Lg	A	G	AB	H	2B	3B	HR	TB	R	RBI	TBB	IBB	SO	HBP	SH	SF	SB	CS	SB%	GDP	Avg	OBP	SLG
Mauck, Matt*	c	Lansing	ChC	A	22	31	99	15	4	1	2	27	6	13	11	0	43	0	0	2	2	0	1.00	2	.152	.232	.273
Maule, Jason*	2b	Michigan	Hou	A	23	68	241	68	11	0	0	79	46	26	48	0	47	2	2	2	26	6	.81	9	.282	.403	.328
Maxwell, Keith	of-dh	Lynchburg	Pit	A+	26	11	28	6	0	0	0	6	1	0	2	0	11	2	0	0	0	0	.00	0	.214	.313	.214
May, Freddy*	dh	San Berndno	LA	A+	25	10	29	6	1	0	0	7	1	3	7	0	3	0	0	1	2	1	.67	0	.207	.351	.241
		Lancaster	Sea	A+	25	76	258	79	11	4	2	104	56	36	45	3	44	3	1	1	7	8	.47	9	.306	.414	.403
Maya, Johan#	2b	Michigan	Hou	A	21	55	155	32	4	1	1	41	19	19	23	0	30	7	6	1	2	1	.67	7	.206	.333	.265
Maynard, Scott	c	Lancaster	Sea	A+	23	94	342	89	15	0	7	125	43	59	39	0	96	2	1	3	4	2	.67	7	.260	.337	.365
Mayo, Terry	of	Helena	Mil	R+	19	58	184	44	13	0	5	72	22	21	24	0	84	6	0	1	10	3	.77	1	.239	.344	.391
Mayorson, Manuel	ss	Medcine Hat	Tor	R+	18	56	218	48	2	1	0	52	39	12	33	0	27	1	2	0	3	2	.60	6	.220	.325	.239
Maza, Luis	ss	Elizabethtn	Min	R+	21	56	210	62	16	3	8	108	40	35	19	1	41	12	7	1	12	4	.75	1	.295	.384	.514
McAuley, Jim	c	Chston-WV	KC	A	23	53	160	39	5	1	1	49	21	23	23	0	44	3	3	1	4	1	.80	7	.244	.348	.306
McCall, Gerard	c	Bristol	CWS	R+	21	47	164	47	10	1	4	71	20	23	14	0	28	1	4	2	1	1	.50	2	.287	.343	.433
McCarty, Brock	of	Missoula	Ari	R+	21	46	117	28	1	5	1	42	18	13	7	1	25	2	2	0	4	4	.50	3	.239	.294	.359
McClanahan, Jonah	of	Ogden	Mil	R+	20	37	117	29	6	2	0	39	20	17	19	0	16	4	1	0	0	1	.00	1	.248	.371	.333
McCool, Lee	2b	Idaho Falls	SD	R+	22	56	236	73	17	3	6	114	62	30	36	0	46	6	1	0	10	5	.67	2	.309	.414	.483
McCorkle, Shawn*	1b	Wisconsin	Sea	A	23	129	432	125	29	4	17	213	77	73	87	4	112	6	2	4	4	6	.40	7	.289	.412	.493
McCrotty, Will	c	Vero Beach	LA	A+	22	76	256	55	10	0	3	74	19	34	31	0	53	3	0	3	0	2	.00	6	.215	.304	.289
McDougall, Marshall	2b	Vancouver	Oak	A-	22	27	102	28	4	2	0	36	17	11	18	0	19	0	0	1	5	3	.63	1	.275	.380	.353
McDowell, Arturo*	of	Bakersfield	SF	A+	21	122	453	97	13	4	7	139	77	53	77	1	129	6	7	6	38	13	.75	5	.214	.332	.307
McGee, Tom	c	Frederick	Bal	A+	26	85	252	56	12	1	2	76	29	27	25	0	74	4	6	2	5	1	.83	9	.222	.300	.302
McGrath, Ryan	c	Auburn	Hou	A-	24	37	106	29	5	0	0	34	13	4	12	0	21	5	1	1	6	2	.75	2	.274	.371	.321
McIntyre, Robert	2b	Pittsfield	NYM	A-	20	5	17	3	0	0	0	3	1	1	3	0	5	0	1	0	0	0	.00	0	.176	.300	.176
		Kingsport	NYM	R+	20	53	197	58	13	3	3	86	33	29	14	0	60	8	1	2	13	13	.50	2	.294	.362	.437
McKee, Mickey	1b	Auburn	Hou	A-	23	51	165	48	11	3	0	65	20	18	5	0	32	0	2	4	6	4	.60	1	.291	.305	.394
McKinley, Josh#	3b	Cape Fear	Mon	A	21	129	480	123	34	3	5	178	73	64	54	3	100	4	1	6	46	14	.77	10	.256	.333	.371
McKinney, Antonio	of	W Michigan	Det	A	23	88	316	88	12	2	7	125	48	44	26	1	70	7	1	1	23	2	.92	8	.278	.346	.396
McKnight, Lukas*	c-1b	Cubs	ChC	R	21	35	107	31	3	1	1	39	16	15	15	0	18	3	1	0	2	2	.50	3	.290	.392	.364
McMillan, Drew	c	Jupiter	Mon	A+	20	8	22	3	0	0	0	3	2	1	2	0	4	0	1	0	1	0	1.00	0	.136	.208	.136
		Cape Fear	Mon	A	20	29	94	10	0	0	0	10	6	4	5	0	19	4	0	0	0	0	.00	1	.106	.184	.106
		Vermont	Mon	A-	20	23	77	11	1	0	0	12	6	4	8	0	22	3	0	0	1	0	1.00	1	.143	.250	.156
McMillin, Brian	of	Fort Myers	Min	A+	24	86	312	70	15	2	3	98	42	28	29	1	67	1	2	1	17	5	.77	4	.224	.292	.314
McNaughton, Troy*	of	Potomac	StL	A+	26	125	458	126	26	2	13	195	63	70	41	2	124	2	2	3	16	9	.64	8	.275	.335	.426
McQueen, Eric	c	Asheville	Col	A	24	61	209	42	12	0	6	72	22	27	12	0	76	5	1	1	5	0	1.00	3	.201	.260	.344
Meadows, Randy	2b	Jupiter	Mon	A+	24	47	142	33	5	1	0	40	16	9	4	0	27	1	3	0	2	1	.67	3	.232	.259	.282
Medina, Luis	1b	Lansing	ChC	A	22	126	476	146	19	2	3	178	53	44	23	2	34	5	4	3	5	4	.56	22	.307	.343	.374
Medrano, Jesus	2b	Brevard Cty	Fla	A+	22	117	466	102	18	3	3	135	56	46	48	2	98	5	3	10	32	8	.80	9	.219	.293	.290
Mejia, Anderson	c	Cubs	ChC	R	19	29	76	26	4	1	0	32	13	15	7	0	11	1	0	2	4	3	.57	0	.342	.395	.421
Mejia, Manuel	c	Pirates	Pit	R	21	34	114	39	8	2	2	57	18	9	13	0	23	2	0	1	1	3	.25	3	.342	.415	.500
Mejia, Max	of	San Berndno	LA	A+	23	82	305	71	13	2	6	106	43	30	29	2	76	7	2	3	19	12	.61	3	.233	.311	.348
Mejias, Aureliano#	of	Johnson Cty	StL	R+	20	11	27	4	1	0	0	5	3	2	2	0	10	0	0	0	0	1	.00	0	.148	.207	.185
Mejias, Erick#	2b-ss	Charlotte	Tex	A+	20	3	12	0	0	0	0	0	1	1	0	0	3	0	0	0	1	0	1.00	0	.000	.000	.000
		Pulaski	Tex	R+	20	45	154	33	4	1	0	39	24	14	16	0	46	3	0	1	7	4	.64	1	.214	.299	.253
Melebeck, Aaron	ss	Spokane	KC	A-	23	47	166	47	6	0	1	56	23	23	26	1	31	6	5	4	8	3	.73	4	.283	.391	.337
Melo, Hanlet	of	Braves	Atl	R	19	44	155	41	4	1	1	50	18	10	15	0	28	2	1	1	6	7	.46	2	.265	.335	.323
		Jamestown	Atl	A-	19	8	23	5	1	0	0	6	1	1	1	0	6	0	0	0	0	0	.00	2	.217	.250	.261
Melton, John	c	Diamondbcks	Ari	R	22	22	59	20	7	1	0	29	12	9	5	0	24	3	0	1	0	1	.00	1	.339	.412	.492
		Missoula	Ari	R+	22	2	5	1	0	0	0	1	2	0	3	0	3	0	0	0	0	0	.00	0	.200	.500	.200
Melucci, Lou	2b	Cape Fear	Mon	A	23	68	198	46	9	2	2	65	27	18	20	0	58	4	0	1	8	0	1.00	1	.232	.314	.328
Mench, Kevin	of	Charlotte	Tex	A+	23	132	491	164	39	9	27	302	118	121	78	3	72	7	0	7	19	7	.73	9	.334	.427	.615
Mendez, Deivi	ss	Yankees	NYY	R	18	56	210	63	20	1	2	91	37	25	26	0	39	3	3	2	4	0	1.00	4	.300	.382	.433
Mendez, Donaldo	ss	Michigan	Hou	A	23	101	370	100	17	0	2	123	65	51	33	1	68	14	6	2	39	10	.80	3	.270	.351	.332
Mendez, Mario	ss	Helena	Mil	R+	19	5	14	6	1	0	0	7	2	3	2	0	3	0	0	0	2	0	1.00	0	.429	.500	.500
Mendoza, Adrian*	1b-of	Great Falls	LA	R+	22	45	140	31	6	1	1	42	17	12	20	2	45	2	2	1	5	2	.71	3	.221	.325	.300
Mendoza, Angel	of	Sarasota	Bos	A+	22	76	280	74	19	6	3	114	35	23	19	2	62	1	0	2	19	6	.76	10	.264	.311	.407
Mendoza, Carlos#	ss	Giants	SF	R	21	6	20	6	2	1	0	10	1	0	2	1	2	0	0	0	1	0	1.00	1	.300	.364	.500
		San Jose	SF	A+	21	112	394	101	16	4	5	140	52	45	49	0	82	9	9	3	25	13	.66	11	.256	.349	.355
Mento, Al	of	Capital Cty	NYM	A	23	48	149	20	8	0	1	31	10	16	21	0	40	3	2	5	12	6	.67	2	.134	.247	.208
Mercado, Onix	c	Reds	Cin	R	21	45	157	36	11	0	0	47	10	20	14	3	39	3	1	2	0	3	.00	1	.229	.301	.299
Mercado, Wilkins	3b	Chston-WV	KC	A	22	42	145	40	8	2	2	58	12	22	15	0	45	2	1	0	0	0	.00	1	.276	.352	.400
Merchan, Jesus	ss	Twins	Min	R	20	36	118	37	5	0	0	42	22	16	11	0	15	5	8	1	1	2	.33	5	.314	.393	.356
Merhoff, Aaron	of	Clearwater	Phi	A+	25	8	26	6	0	1	0	8	3	3	2	0	8	3	0	0	1	0	1.00	0	.231	.355	.308
		Piedmont	Phi	A	25	38	112	20	2	0	1	25	11	11	11	0	37	1	2	1	4	1	.80	3	.179	.256	.223
Merrill, Ron#	ss	Oneonta	Det	A-	22	33	135	42	5	2	1	54	21	21	12	1	23	2	0	0	6	3	.67	1	.311	.376	.400
Merriman, Terrell*	of	Winston-Sal	CWS	A+	23	134	439	102	22	9	12	178	64	67	94	1	109	7	1	5	28	7	.80	6	.232	.372	.405
Meseberg, Seth*	of	Hudson Val	TB	A-	22	29	94	12	1	0	0	13	9	6	10	0	31	0	1	0	2	0	1.00	0	.128	.212	.138
Michaelis, Derek*	1b	Yakima	LA	A-	22	60	211	42	6	1	5	65	23	28	18	0	77	0	1	1	1	2	.33	2	.199	.261	.308
Miles, Aaron#	2b	Kissimmee	Hou	A+	24	75	295	86	20	1	2	114	40	36	28	0	29	0	2	1	11	6	.65	7	.292	.352	.386
Miller, Eric	1b	Vermont	Mon	A-	23	47	160	48	9	2	0	61	25	18	15	3	18	3	0	0	6	2	.75	6	.300	.371	.381
Minges, Tyler	of	Kinston	Cle	A+	21	110	404	90	17	4	6	133	46	51	32	0	78	3	2	5	12	9	.57	12	.223	.282	.329
Minus, Steve	3b	Sarasota	Bos	A+	24	46	147	28	5	1	1	38	14	17	14	0	51	1	2	1	0	2	.00	1	.190	.264	.259
		Augusta	Bos	A	24	71	256	73	14	2	4	103	36	32	27	0	61	0	0	4	2	1	.67	5	.285	.348	.402
Mitchell, Todd	ss-2b	Greensboro	NYY	A	22	53	155	36	8	1	3	55	19	14	22	0	34	3	0	2	1	2	.33	1	.232	.335	.355
Miyamoto, Eij	2b	Expos	Mon	R	21	13	43	10	0	0	0	10	5	4	5	0	3	4	4	0	0	1	.00	1	.233	.365	.233
		Cape Fear	Mon	A	21	3	0	0	0	0	0	0	0	0	0	0	0	0	0	0	0	0	.00	0	.000	.000	.000
Moccia, Mark	3b-2b	Oneonta	Det	A-	24	51	203	47	6	6	0	65	23	20	14	0	40	3	2	3	6	4	.60	1	.232	.287	.320
Mohr, Dustan	of	Fort Myers	Min	A+	25	101	370	98	19	2	11	154	58	75	35	1	65	8	1	4	7	4	.64	11	.265	.338	.416
Molina, Angel	c	Marlins	Fla	R	19	10	27	4	1	0	0	5	3	3	5	0	11	1	0	0	1	0	1.00	1	.148	.303	.185

2000 Batting — Class-A and Rookie Leagues

BATTING																					BASERUNNING				PERCENTAGES		
Player	Pos	Team	Org	Lg	A	G	AB	H	2B	3B	HR	TB	R	RBI	TBB	IBB	SO	HBP	SH	SF	SB	CS	SB%	GDP	Avg	OBP	SLG
Molina, Gustavo	c	White Sox	CWS	R	19	31	115	28	10	0	1	41	15	22	13	0	13	2	1	3	3	1	.75	0	.243	.323	.357
Monegan, Anthony*	of	Bristol	CWS	R+	22	45	119	24	3	0	0	27	12	11	17	1	43	2	3	2	6	2	.75	0	.202	.307	.227
Money, Freddie	of	Lowell	Bos	A-	22	55	203	40	4	4	2	58	28	16	19	0	40	3	1	2	10	5	.67	1	.197	.273	.286
Mongeluzzo, A.	3b	Pulaski	Tex	R+	22	38	142	31	7	0	6	56	18	24	6	0	42	3	2	1	1	1	.50	2	.218	.263	.394
Montanez, Luis	ss	Cubs	ChC	R	19	50	192	66	16	7	2	102	50	37	25	1	42	8	3	1	11	6	.65	5	.344	.438	.531
		Lansing	ChC	A	19	8	29	4	1	0	0	5	2	0	3	0	6	0	0	0	0	1	.00	0	.138	.219	.172
Montero, Esteban	ss	Rockies	Col	R	18	49	175	55	12	4	0	75	41	28	29	0	49	3	0	2	9	3	.75	1	.314	.416	.429
Montgomery, Billy#	of	Pulaski	Tex	R+	21	49	164	36	3	0	1	42	25	9	26	0	44	6	4	0	7	3	.70	1	.220	.347	.256
Mooney, Dan	c	Lowell	Bos	A-	24	34	110	20	4	0	3	33	10	13	5	0	31	3	1	3	2	0	1.00	1	.182	.231	.300
Moore, Chris*	3b	Asheville	Col	A	24	77	292	78	12	0	12	126	43	43	39	2	58	2	0	3	13	8	.62	1	.267	.354	.432
Moore, Frank*	2b	Chston-SC	TB	A	22	96	372	98	18	2	5	135	53	41	16	1	78	5	3	4	12	5	.71	3	.263	.300	.363
Moore, Jason#	ss	Fort Wayne	SD	A	23	123	438	102	18	2	3	133	62	42	47	2	86	3	3	1	10	7	.59	10	.233	.311	.304
Moore, Kevin#	3b	Mudville	Mil	A+	26	20	61	13	2	0	1	18	10	8	9	0	19	0	0	1	0	0	.00	1	.213	.310	.295
Moose, Robert	1b	Danville	Atl	R+	23	3	7	2	0	0	0	2	1	1	1	0	3	0	0	0	0	0	.00	0	.286	.375	.286
Mora, Ruben#	of	Padres	SD	R	18	33	72	13	1	0	0	14	14	4	9	0	25	5	1	0	4	2	.67	1	.181	.314	.194
Moraga, Omar*	2b	Columbus	Cle	A	24	114	424	126	18	4	4	164	53	59	45	1	71	3	1	5	10	4	.71	7	.297	.365	.387
Morban, Dany*	of	Reds	Cin	R	19	53	182	42	7	8	1	68	23	22	30	3	59	3	1	0	11	2	.85	2	.231	.349	.374
Morban, Jose	ss	Savannah	Tex	A	21	80	273	60	8	4	4	88	44	28	41	0	79	4	5	0	27	13	.68	6	.220	.330	.322
		Pulaski	Tex	R+	21	30	120	27	3	2	3	43	21	17	12	2	35	0	3	1	6	3	.67	0	.225	.293	.358
Morency, Vernand	of	Portland	Col	A-	21	48	180	41	6	2	2	57	17	18	18	1	57	4	0	1	6	6	.50	6	.228	.310	.317
Moreno, Jorge	of	Columbus	Cle	A	20	55	211	64	15	2	7	104	37	32	19	0	57	2	1	5	10	2	.83	2	.303	.359	.493
Morneau, Justin*	1b-c	Twins	Min	R	20	52	194	78	21	0	10	129	47	58	30	7	18	0	0	2	3	1	.75	5	.402	.478	.665
		Elizabethtn	Min	R+	20	6	23	5	0	0	1	8	4	3	1	0	6	0	0	0	0	0	.00	0	.217	.250	.348
Morris, Ken#	of	New Jersey	StL	A-	21	63	182	31	2	1	0	35	34	15	50	1	48	3	4	1	42	12	.78	1	.170	.356	.192
Morrissey, Adam	3b	Eugene	ChC	A-	20	73	269	74	16	2	7	115	32	36	42	1	50	3	3	4	12	11	.52	2	.275	.374	.428
Morrow, Alvin	of	Beloit	Mil	A	23	64	204	53	17	1	9	99	32	27	37	2	77	4	0	1	0	3	.00	4	.260	.382	.485
		Hagerstown	Tor	A	23	32	105	22	3	0	4	37	15	8	14	0	42	2	0	0	2	0	1.00	3	.210	.314	.352
Morse, Mike	ss	White Sox	CWS	R	19	45	180	46	6	1	2	60	32	24	15	0	29	1	0	5	5	2	.71	6	.256	.308	.333
Mota, Pedro*	of	San Jose	SF	A+	23	49	154	35	6	4	1	52	17	18	23	2	33	1	3	1	7	3	.70	2	.227	.330	.338
Motooka, Rafael	c	Reds	Cin	R	18	7	12	3	0	0	0	3	0	0	0	0	3	0	0	0	0	0	.00	1	.250	.250	.250
Mott, Bill*	dh	Lk Elsinore	Ana	A+	25	115	396	119	20	9	11	190	83	82	76	5	78	10	1	5	29	8	.78	5	.301	.421	.480
Mounts, J.R.#	of	Burlington	CWS	A	22	50	164	28	3	2	2	41	19	13	23	0	67	1	1	1	13	2	.87	1	.171	.275	.250
		Boise	Ana	A-	22	55	190	47	9	3	4	74	31	28	18	0	69	3	3	1	6	1	.86	4	.247	.321	.389
Moya, Wilson	2b	Rangers	Tex	R	21	35	96	21	2	1	0	25	16	7	10	0	26	3	1	0	2	1	.67	0	.219	.312	.260
Moyer, Kyle*	dh-1b	Columbus	Cle	A	20	52	177	44	4	0	3	57	13	24	19	0	67	1	0	2	0	0	.00	6	.249	.322	.322
Moylan, Dan*	c	New Jersey	StL	A-	22	56	168	46	6	0	0	52	20	14	42	0	28	4	0	2	8	8	.50	6	.274	.426	.310
Mulqueen, Dave#	1b	Rockies	Col	R	20	46	180	55	14	8	6	103	43	48	19	0	43	10	0	2	7	2	.78	2	.306	.398	.572
		Portland	Col	A-	20	13	40	6	1	1	0	9	5	4	2	0	20	0	0	0	1	0	1.00	1	.150	.190	.225
Mulvehill, Chase	of	Capital Cty	NYM	A	23	47	160	37	5	2	2	52	21	11	18	0	55	3	0	1	4	7	.36	1	.231	.319	.325
Murch, Jeremy*	of	St. Pete	TB	A+	22	26	100	23	8	0	2	37	11	9	6	0	25	0	0	0	4	0	1.00	1	.230	.274	.370
		Chston-SC	TB	A	22	56	187	51	15	1	7	89	30	27	14	0	56	1	1	0	3	2	.60	5	.273	.327	.476
Murphy, Tommy	ss	Boise	Ana	A-	21	55	213	48	18	1	2	74	38	25	15	0	52	5	1	1	14	7	.67	1	.225	.291	.347
Muth, Edmund*	of	Asheville	Col	A	23	50	173	41	11	0	1	55	15	13	24	0	57	7	1	1	8	5	.62	2	.237	.351	.318
Muthig, Dean	1b-dh	Batavia	Phi	A-	23	36	120	27	2	1	5	46	13	15	6	0	33	0	0	2	2	0	1.00	3	.225	.258	.383
Myers, Corey	3b	South Bend	Ari	A	21	19	64	8	2	0	0	10	5	4	7	0	23	0	1	1	1	1	.50	3	.125	.208	.156
		Missoula	Ari	R+	21	75	272	59	16	2	6	97	40	49	30	2	62	3	1	5	5	2	.71	5	.217	.297	.357
Myers, Tootie	2b	Jupiter	Mon	A+	22	110	449	109	16	9	7	164	70	43	41	1	111	3	9	2	26	16	.62	3	.243	.309	.365
Napoli, Mike	1b	Butte	Ana	R+	19	10	26	6	2	0	0	8	3	3	8	1	8	0	1	1	1	0	1.00	2	.231	.400	.308
Navarrete, Ray	3b	Williamsprt	Pit	A-	23	66	248	77	13	1	3	101	19	36	20	2	27	3	1	5	1	1	.50	4	.310	.362	.407
Neal, Steve*	1b	High Desert	Ari	A+	24	111	395	117	27	3	15	195	59	70	56	1	92	3	0	1	11	4	.73	8	.296	.387	.494
Negron, Miguel*	of	Medcine Hat	Tor	R+	18	53	190	44	5	0	0	49	26	13	23	3	39	3	2	0	5	3	.63	2	.232	.324	.258
Neill, John	of	Oneonta	Det	A-	23	64	230	63	7	5	5	95	41	39	45	1	74	10	0	4	16	8	.67	3	.274	.408	.413
Nelson, Eric#	2b	Wilmington	KC	A+	24	106	370	78	13	4	1	102	44	28	34	0	94	6	7	4	10	4	.71	2	.211	.285	.276
Nelson, Nate	3b	Martinsvlle	Hou	R+	24	42	158	42	9	0	4	63	19	24	6	0	22	5	2	2	10	5	.67	9	.266	.310	.399
Nelson, Reggie	2b	Lakeland	Det	A+	22	52	159	35	5	2	0	44	17	14	19	0	29	4	1	1	6	8	.43	2	.220	.317	.277
		W Michigan	Det	A	22	56	202	55	5	0	0	60	35	15	26	0	26	1	4	3	19	3	.86	2	.272	.353	.297
Nelson, Tim	1b	Bluefield	Bal	R+	23	1	4	0	0	0	0	0	1	0	0	0	0	0	0	0	0	0	.00	0	.000	.000	.000
Nettles, Jeff	ss-3b	Greensboro	NYY	A	22	84	283	73	14	0	8	111	34	45	22	0	43	6	2	3	2	3	.40	8	.258	.322	.392
Nettles, Tim	of	Staten Ilnd	NYY	A-	24	36	53	13	1	1	0	16	9	5	4	0	12	2	0	0	3	3	.50	2	.245	.322	.302
Neubart, Adam	of	Chston-WV	KC	A	23	34	128	35	4	2	0	43	24	13	14	0	29	4	1	1	9	4	.69	2	.273	.361	.336
Newton, Kimani	of	Vero Beach	LA	A+	22	34	104	22	3	1	1	30	17	16	18	0	31	1	0	1	3	3	.50	3	.212	.331	.288
Nicholson, Derek*	of	Michigan	Hou	A	25	116	408	127	25	4	7	181	62	69	65	2	54	5	0	8	9	7	.56	6	.311	.405	.444
Nicholson, Tommy*	2b	Burlington	CWS	A	21	66	250	65	10	2	0	79	33	24	22	1	33	5	3	2	10	2	.83	10	.260	.330	.316
Nicolas, Jose	of	Williamsprt	Pit	A-	22	55	204	46	9	0	6	73	25	16	19	0	67	1	0	0	3	0	1.00	4	.225	.295	.358
Nieckula, Aaron	c	Visalia	Oak	A+	24	72	212	55	8	0	2	69	45	29	39	1	54	13	0	2	14	6	.70	3	.259	.402	.325
		Modesto	Oak	A+	24	15	48	13	2	0	0	15	6	5	12	0	12	1	0	0	3	1	.75	1	.271	.426	.313
Niekro, Lance	3b	Salem-Keizr	SF	A-	22	49	196	71	14	4	5	108	27	44	11	2	25	4	0	2	2	0	1.00	6	.362	.404	.551
Niemet, Bob	c	San Jose	SF	A+	24	7	11	1	0	0	0	1	0	0	0	0	4	0	0	0	0	0	.00	0	.091	.091	.091
Nieves, Raul#	ss	Lowell	Bos	A-	22	56	202	50	7	1	0	59	23	13	22	1	33	0	4	1	5	2	.71	2	.248	.320	.292
Nina, Amuarys	of	Charlotte	Tex	A+	23	102	354	91	10	9	1	122	52	39	48	1	86	10	5	1	11	7	.61	11	.257	.361	.345
Nix, Laynce*	of	Rangers	Tex	R	20	51	199	45	7	1	2	60	34	25	23	1	37	2	2	4	4	2	.67	3	.226	.307	.302
Noboa, Joel	of	South Bend	Ari	A	21	19	71	16	0	0	0	16	5	1	0	0	30	1	0	0	3	1	.75	0	.225	.236	.225
		Missoula	Ari	R+	21	53	202	43	16	3	6	83	18	34	3	0	67	2	0	2	0	1	.00	4	.213	.230	.411
Nohr, Ryan	of-dh	Ogden	Mil	R+	22	44	146	36	7	0	2	49	27	18	18	0	21	4	2	1	2	2	.50	4	.247	.343	.336
Norrell, Troy	c	Greensboro	NYY	A	24	52	162	24	6	0	2	36	13	15	17	0	76	2	3	2	0	1	.00	4	.148	.235	.222
Nowlin, Cody*	of	Savannah	Tex	A	21	136	501	122	27	3	15	200	66	68	44	1	104	6	2	3	3	0	1.00	7	.244	.310	.399
Nulton, Kevin	2b	Padres	SD	R	18	52	187	59	7	1	1	71	29	23	9	0	25	4	2	4	17	4	.81	4	.316	.353	.380

2000 Batting — Class-A and Rookie Leagues

BATTING																					BASERUNNING				PERCENTAGES		
Player	Pos	Team	Org	Lg	A	G	AB	H	2B	3B	HR	TB	R	RBI	TBB	IBB	SO	HBP	SH	SF	SB	CS	SB%	GDP	Avg	OBP	SLG
Nunez, Felix	1b	Princeton	TB	R+	18	56	200	57	8	4	0	73	20	23	6	0	58	4	0	0	1	2	.33	3	.285	.319	.365
Nunez, Jose	3b	Potomac	StL	A+	22	87	242	61	18	0	2	85	25	24	11	0	36	4	2	0	4	2	.67	5	.252	.296	.351
Nunez, Manuel	ss	Great Falls	LA	R+	21	59	210	48	4	3	1	61	43	24	45	0	70	3	6	3	15	3	.83	1	.229	.368	.290
Nunez, Sergio	2b	Clearwater	Phi	A+	26	105	378	85	18	3	0	109	44	39	40	0	46	1	8	6	23	3	.88	16	.225	.296	.288
Nunn, Jason	of	Yankees	NYY	R	23	47	151	35	9	2	2	54	19	24	14	0	43	2	0	0	7	2	.78	0	.232	.305	.358
Nye, Rodney	3b	St. Lucie	NYM	A+	24	132	464	126	28	1	6	174	70	62	58	4	74	10	0	4	8	8	.50	15	.272	.362	.375
Nykoluk, Kevin	c	Potomac	StL	A+	26	61	177	37	5	0	3	51	16	14	21	0	30	3	7	0	0	0	.00	3	.209	.303	.288
Oborn, Spencer	of	Burlington	CWS	A	23	127	448	112	23	3	7	162	56	52	54	1	94	3	3	5	28	6	.82	1	.250	.331	.362
O'Brien, Kevin*	1b	Hudson Val	TB	A-	20	22	75	16	2	0	1	21	9	7	6	1	23	0	1	0	0	1	.00	1	.213	.272	.280
		Princeton	TB	R+	20	11	39	4	0	0	0	4	2	4	1	0	17	1	0	2	0	0	.00	0	.103	.140	.103
O'Brien, Mike	1b-dh	Oneonta	Det	A-	27	68	241	64	9	3	5	94	34	45	30	2	63	2	0	3	10	2	.83	4	.266	.348	.390
O'Connor, Brian	c	Michigan	Hou	A	24	32	89	15	1	0	1	19	7	11	18	0	34	2	2	1	1	1	.50	3	.169	.318	.213
O'Donnell, Ryan*	of	Padres	SD	R	22	37	141	44	9	3	1	62	24	25	11	1	17	3	1	2	7	3	.70	3	.312	.369	.440
		Idaho Falls	SD	R+	22	14	52	19	0	0	2	25	14	13	5	0	5	1	0	1	1	3	.25	5	.365	.424	.481
Oetting, Todd	c	Phillies	Phi	R	20	20	60	15	4	0	0	19	8	6	6	0	5	1	1	0	0	2	.00	1	.250	.328	.317
Oglesby, Travis	dh	High Desert	Ari	A+	23	88	265	65	16	1	13	122	40	45	37	1	100	1	0	0	0	0	.00	8	.245	.340	.460
Oh, Chul*	of-dh	Red Sox	Bos	R	20	24	70	20	6	0	2	32	8	9	4	0	16	0	0	0	0	0	.00	3	.286	.324	.457
O'Keefe, Mike*	of	Cedar Rapds	Ana	A	23	118	377	82	14	2	12	136	56	45	60	2	72	9	2	4	6	5	.55	5	.218	.336	.361
Olivares, Teuris	ss	Tampa	NYY	A+	22	121	468	118	22	3	7	167	56	47	39	0	70	0	3	5	20	11	.65	10	.252	.307	.357
Oliveros, Luis	c	Mariners	Sea	R	18	28	87	31	5	0	0	36	15	19	1	0	7	2	1	1	3	3	.50	3	.356	.374	.414
Olkowski, Kevin*	1b	Mariners	Sea	R	24	41	154	53	12	1	0	67	32	21	13	0	27	2	0	2	3	3	.50	0	.344	.398	.435
Olmeda, Jose#	ss	Winston-Sal	CWS	A+	23	45	166	34	14	2	3	61	14	20	5	1	45	1	3	2	4	3	.57	4	.205	.230	.367
Olmedo, Ranier	ss	Dayton	Cin	A	20	111	369	94	19	1	4	127	50	41	30	1	70	1	14	4	17	11	.61	11	.255	.309	.344
Olson, David	of	Padres	SD	R	19	19	34	5	0	0	0	5	3	1	8	0	22	0	0	0	2	0	1.00	0	.147	.310	.147
Olson, Eric	3b	Greensboro	NYY	A	24	20	63	9	3	0	1	15	3	6	7	0	29	5	2	0	0	1	.00	2	.143	.280	.238
Olson, Tim	of	South Bend	Ari	A	22	68	261	57	14	2	2	81	37	26	15	0	49	8	0	1	15	3	.83	5	.218	.281	.310
O'Neill, Dan	of	Batavia	Phi	A-	24	29	91	18	2	0	2	26	10	7	15	0	24	0	0	0	0	0	.00	2	.198	.311	.286
		Piedmont	Phi	A	24	12	37	9	3	0	0	12	6	1	9	0	11	0	1	0	0	0	.00	0	.243	.391	.324
Orgill, Pete*	dh	Cedar Rapds	Ana	A	24	25	76	17	5	0	0	22	5	8	6	1	18	1	2	1	0	1	.00	2	.224	.286	.289
Oropeza, Asdrubal	3b	Macon	Atl	A	20	115	397	88	25	2	11	150	54	44	47	1	92	7	3	2	6	6	.50	5	.222	.313	.378
Orr, Peter*	2b-3b	Jamestown	Atl	A-	22	69	265	64	8	1	2	80	40	15	24	0	51	6	0	4	9	5	.64	4	.242	.314	.302
Ortega, Felix	c	Phillies	Phi	R	19	19	50	9	0	0	1	12	6	4	10	0	19	0	0	0	0	0	.00	0	.180	.317	.240
Ortega, Sixto	c	Portland	Col	A-	21	6	20	5	2	0	0	7	1	2	0	0	6	0	0	0	0	0	.00	0	.250	.250	.350
		Rockies	Col	R	21	24	81	26	2	2	0	32	16	13	7	0	18	0	1	0	3	1	.75	2	.321	.375	.395
Ortiz, Daniel	dh	Princeton	TB	R+	20	15	55	12	1	0	2	19	4	2	2	0	18	2	0	0	0	1	.00	0	.218	.271	.345
Ortiz, Jorge	3b	Athletics	Oak	R	20	31	90	19	4	1	0	25	16	9	13	0	36	1	1	0	0	1	.00	3	.211	.317	.278
Ortiz, Matt	dh	New Jersey	StL	A-	23	28	87	16	3	1	2	27	6	8	5	0	16	0	0	0	0	0	.00	2	.184	.228	.310
		Peoria	StL	A	23	9	23	4	0	0	1	7	2	3	2	0	6	0	0	0	0	0	.00	1	.174	.240	.304
Ortiz, Miguel*	3b	Cedar Rapds	Ana	A	22	86	330	87	17	1	6	124	42	50	12	2	51	7	4	6	25	7	.78	14	.264	.299	.376
Osborn, Jason	c	Pittsfield	NYM	A-	21	7	23	4	0	0	0	4	0	3	1	0	7	0	0	0	0	1	.00	1	.174	.208	.174
		Kingsport	NYM	R+	21	11	35	5	2	0	0	7	1	2	1	0	6	1	0	1	0	0	.00	1	.143	.184	.200
Osborne, Mark*	1b	Mahoning Vy	Cle	A-	23	6	20	3	0	1	0	5	1	1	4	0	6	1	0	0	0	0	.00	0	.150	.320	.250
O'Sullivan, Pat	of	Pittsfield	NYM	A-	24	1	4	1	0	0	0	1	0	0	0	0	2	0	0	0	0	0	.00	0	.250	.250	.250
Owens, Jeremy	of	Rancho Cuca	SD	A+	24	138	570	146	29	10	16	243	99	63	63	1	183	5	8	4	54	12	.82	5	.256	.333	.426
Paciorek, Pete*	1b	San Berndno	LA	A+	25	134	499	139	29	9	12	222	80	83	76	6	106	7	1	5	10	10	.50	6	.279	.378	.445
Pack, Branden#	c	Pulaski	Tex	R+	22	57	205	48	10	1	8	84	28	32	27	0	68	2	0	1	2	1	.67	7	.234	.328	.410
Padgett, Matt*	of	Kane County	Fla	A	23	125	446	104	22	2	12	166	60	60	53	5	139	4	0	3	5	3	.63	13	.233	.318	.372
Padilla, Jorge	of	Piedmont	Phi	A	21	108	413	126	24	8	11	199	62	67	26	0	89	2	0	4	8	4	.67	10	.305	.346	.482
Padilla, Juan	of	Expos	Mon	R	20	41	142	36	7	2	2	53	16	17	3	0	35	3	0	1	0	2	.00	2	.254	.282	.373
Pagan, Andres	c	Idaho Falls	SD	R+	20	41	154	48	8	0	4	68	25	24	13	0	41	0	1	2	3	3	.50	4	.312	.361	.442
Pagan, Angel#	of	Kingsport	NYM	R+	19	19	72	26	5	1	0	33	13	8	6	0	8	0	0	0	6	1	.86	1	.361	.410	.458
Pagan, Carlos	c	Wilmington	KC	A+	25	3	4	1	0	1	0	3	1	1	0	0	1	1	0	0	0	0	.00	0	.250	.400	.750
Pagan, Jon	1b	Williamsprt	Pit	A-	20	54	185	38	11	0	5	64	19	14	19	0	75	3	0	0	0	1	.00	6	.205	.290	.346
Pagana, Mike	2b	Rangers	Tex	R	27	4	16	4	0	0	0	4	5	2	2	0	2	0	1	0	1	0	1.00	1	.250	.333	.250
Palmieri, Jon	1b-dh	Cedar Rapds	Ana	A	24	28	85	20	2	1	0	24	10	4	14	0	10	2	0	0	1	0	1.00	1	.235	.356	.282
		Cape Fear	Mon	A	24	49	183	49	12	2	1	68	28	21	28	0	22	5	0	1	8	2	.80	1	.268	.378	.372
Palomares, Luis	dh-of	Helena	Mil	R+	22	8	26	5	0	0	0	5	2	2	2	0	7	1	0	0	0	0	.00	0	.192	.276	.192
Paredes, Reny	of	Eugene	ChC	A-	21	21	48	7	2	1	1	14	2	5	1	0	21	0	0	0	0	0	.00	2	.146	.163	.292
Parker, Chris	c	W Michigan	Det	A	21	6	18	6	2	0	0	8	2	2	4	0	1	1	0	0	0	0	.00	1	.333	.478	.444
		Oneonta	Det	A-	21	34	108	28	4	0	0	32	13	11	20	0	22	2	3	1	2	0	1.00	1	.259	.382	.296
Parnell, Sean	of	Wisconsin	Sea	A	23	95	318	72	16	0	5	103	40	35	27	0	82	6	7	4	5	9	.36	7	.226	.296	.324
Parrish, Dave	c	Staten Ilnd	NYY	A-	22	63	221	53	20	1	4	87	29	29	25	0	54	4	1	0	0	0	.00	4	.240	.328	.394
Parrott, Tom	3b	Braves	Atl	R	20	9	24	6	2	0	0	8	0	3	2	0	6	1	0	1	0	1	.00	1	.250	.321	.333
		Danville	Atl	R+	20	22	72	13	4	1	1	22	13	5	8	0	21	1	0	0	2	2	.50	2	.181	.272	.306
Pascucci, Val	of	Cape Fear	Mon	A	22	20	69	22	4	0	3	35	17	10	16	0	15	0	0	1	5	0	1.00	2	.319	.442	.507
		Jupiter	Mon	A+	22	113	405	115	30	2	14	191	70	66	66	0	98	11	0	5	14	6	.70	9	.284	.394	.472
Patchett, Gary	3b	Reds	Cin	R	22	19	65	19	3	0	0	22	9	5	8	0	11	2	1	0	1	3	.25	3	.292	.387	.338
Patten, Chris	2b	Mudville	Mil	A+	22	118	443	115	28	3	6	167	60	49	31	0	111	9	5	3	10	7	.59	15	.260	.319	.377
Patterson, Sean	1b-dh	Reds	Cin	R	19	17	49	7	1	0	0	8	2	3	8	0	22	0	0	0	0	0	.00	0	.143	.263	.163
Paulino, Dave	2b	Kane County	Fla	A	21	15	20	2	0	0	0	2	2	1	8	0	5	0	0	0	2	2	.50	1	.100	.357	.100
		Utica	Fla	A-	21	2	4	2	0	1	0	4	1	0	0	0	0	0	0	0	2	0	1.00	0	.500	.500	1.000
Paulino, Luis	of	Medcine Hat	Tor	R+	19	62	224	58	14	6	5	99	30	25	20	0	51	4	0	0	6	4	.60	2	.259	.331	.442
Paulino, Miguel#	ss	Cubs	ChC	R	20	10	20	4	0	0	0	4	5	1	6	0	5	0	0	0	3	1	.75	0	.200	.385	.200
		Eugene	ChC	A-	20	18	48	8	0	0	0	8	7	4	7	1	16	1	0	0	7	1	.88	0	.167	.286	.167
Paulino, Ron	c	Hickory	Pit	A	20	88	301	87	16	2	6	125	38	39	27	0	71	4	0	1	3	2	.60	9	.289	.354	.415
Pearson, Shawn	of	Dunedin	Tor	A+	23	4	10	6	1	0	0	7	3	3	1	0	1	0	0	0	0	0	.00	0	.600	.636	.700
		Queens	Tor	A-	23	20	74	26	1	0	0	27	18	3	18	0	8	0	0	2	7	4	.64	1	.351	.468	.365

2000 Batting — Class-A and Rookie Leagues

BATTING																					BASERUNNING				PERCENTAGES		
Player	Pos	Team	Org	Lg	A	G	AB	H	2B	3B	HR	TB	R	RBI	TBB	IBB	SO	HBP	SH	SF	SB	CS	SB%	GDP	Avg	OBP	SLG
		Hagerstown	Tor	A	23	33	92	13	0	1	0	15	9	5	15	1	20	1	1	0	4	2	.67	3	.141	.269	.163
Peck, Bryan	3b	Portland	Col	A-	23	54	196	44	9	1	3	64	21	16	13	1	35	4	1	2	0	3	.00	3	.224	.284	.327
Peguero, Miguel#	ss-3b	Lakeland	Det	A+	20	4	11	2	1	0	0	3	0	1	0	0	4	0	0	0	0	0	.00	0	.182	.182	.273
		Tigers	Det	R	20	41	148	37	5	1	0	44	22	13	11	0	34	2	2	0	9	2	.82	3	.250	.311	.297
		Oneonta	Det	A-	20	22	72	23	0	0	0	23	7	9	6	0	21	0	3	0	1	2	.33	1	.319	.372	.319
Pekar, Jason	dh-of	Salem-Keizr	SF	A-	22	24	65	11	4	0	0	15	10	7	6	0	20	0	0	3	1	0	1.00	2	.169	.230	.231
Pelfrey, Brice	2b	Williamsprt	Pit	A-	21	49	162	37	5	0	0	42	27	10	12	0	27	2	1	2	6	1	.86	3	.228	.287	.259
Pena, Amaury	3b-2b	White Sox	CWS	R	21	17	69	22	7	5	1	42	21	16	11	0	9	3	0	3	8	2	.80	1	.319	.419	.609
		Bristol	CWS	R+	21	37	125	35	7	1	3	53	20	14	11	0	33	2	2	0	4	0	1.00	3	.280	.348	.424
Pena, Jose	of	Augusta	Bos	A	21	32	117	25	7	1	2	40	12	11	8	0	29	5	0	0	4	5	.44	1	.214	.292	.342
Pena, Onesimo	of	Rangers	Tex	R	23	7	22	4	0	0	0	4	3	2	3	0	3	1	2	0	0	0	.00	0	.182	.308	.182
Pena, Pelagio	c	Everett	Sea	A-	21	47	144	26	5	0	2	37	11	8	12	0	56	3	0	0	4	1	.80	4	.181	.258	.257
Pena, Rodolfo	c	Sarasota	Bos	A+	22	78	217	42	9	0	0	51	18	18	15	0	40	8	4	1	3	2	.60	5	.194	.270	.235
Pena, Tony	ss	Danville	Atl	R+	20	55	215	46	5	0	2	57	22	20	5	0	53	0	2	2	6	2	.75	8	.214	.230	.265
Pena, Wilton	c	Vancouver	Oak	A-	22	46	123	23	5	0	2	34	16	13	14	0	44	3	1	0	0	0	.00	2	.187	.286	.276
Pena, Wily Mo	of	Greensboro	NYY	A	19	67	249	51	7	1	10	90	41	28	18	1	91	5	0	4	6	5	.55	9	.205	.268	.361
		Staten Ilnd	NYY	A-	19	20	73	22	1	2	0	27	7	10	2	0	23	4	0	0	2	0	1.00	1	.301	.354	.370
Peralta, John	ss	Columbus	Cle	A	19	106	349	84	13	1	3	108	52	34	59	0	102	2	1	2	7	6	.54	13	.241	.352	.309
Perea, Jean	c	Savannah	Tex	A	22	42	130	27	2	0	4	41	13	15	5	0	25	3	0	1	2	0	1.00	3	.208	.252	.315
Perez, Antonio	ss	Lancaster	Sea	A+	19	98	395	109	36	6	17	208	90	63	58	1	99	8	9	4	28	16	.64	3	.276	.376	.527
Perez, Deivi	3b	Hickory	Pit	A	20	82	224	40	11	2	1	58	32	12	21	0	76	2	1	2	4	2	.67	4	.179	.253	.259
Perez, Felipe	of	Bluefield	Bal	R+	21	27	100	24	2	1	3	37	10	10	3	0	39	4	0	1	1	1	.50	2	.240	.287	.370
Perez, Jay#	c-dh	Martinsvlle	Hou	R+	21	50	173	41	6	2	4	63	25	23	22	1	39	9	0	0	7	1	.88	3	.237	.353	.364
Perez, Jersen	ss	Dunedin	Tor	A+	25	126	509	138	35	7	8	211	69	64	20	0	106	4	8	5	8	4	.67	11	.271	.301	.415
Perez, Juan	of	Johnson Cty	StL	R+	20	23	85	21	3	2	1	31	13	4	9	0	17	3	1	0	6	1	.86	1	.247	.340	.365
Perez, Kenny#	ss	Red Sox	Bos	R	19	43	158	45	7	0	1	55	28	23	12	1	12	1	1	1	3	2	.60	3	.285	.337	.348
Perez, Radhame	of	Athletics	Oak	R	21	40	144	43	5	3	0	54	34	22	16	0	33	0	2	1	3	2	.60	2	.299	.366	.375
Perez-Bermudez,J#	c	Padres	SD	R	19	26	53	11	2	0	0	13	3	7	6	0	5	0	0	0	0	0	.00	3	.208	.288	.245
Perich, Josh	of	Kingsport	NYM	R+	21	24	80	19	1	0	3	29	12	11	8	0	24	0	0	0	2	4	.33	4	.238	.307	.363
		Capital Cty	NYM	A	21	6	19	3	0	0	0	3	0	0	2	0	8	0	0	0	0	0	.00	0	.158	.238	.158
		Pittsfield	NYM	A-	21	21	69	10	1	2	0	15	6	4	8	0	24	0	1	0	1	2	.33	1	.145	.234	.217
Perkins, Kevin	of	Kane County	Fla	A	23	91	255	72	12	0	4	96	34	27	32	4	49	10	2	2	9	5	.64	8	.282	.381	.376
Perkins, Robert	dh-c	Braves	Atl	R	20	38	112	24	5	0	2	35	12	8	14	0	27	5	0	0	0	1	.00	0	.214	.328	.313
Pernalete, Marco#	2b-ss	Bakersfield	SF	A+	22	91	301	77	16	1	5	110	53	27	57	2	88	3	6	1	15	3	.83	5	.256	.378	.365
Peters, Samone	1b	Clinton	Cin	A	22	125	456	93	22	0	21	178	51	64	32	1	198	7	0	1	0	0	.00	6	.204	.266	.390
Peters, Tony	of	Dunedin	Tor	A+	26	127	455	122	30	2	15	201	97	61	71	1	164	7	4	3	23	8	.74	9	.268	.373	.442
Peterson, Brian	c	Burlington	Cle	R+	22	10	35	13	2	0	0	15	5	5	3	0	8	0	0	0	0	0	.00	0	.371	.421	.429
		Mahoning Vy	Cle	A-	22	24	72	16	2	1	0	20	9	6	12	0	20	4	3	1	2	0	1.00	2	.222	.360	.278
Pfister, Billy	2b-ss	Lakeland	Det	A+	21	4	8	3	0	0	0	3	0	0	2	0	1	0	0	0	0	0	.00	0	.375	.500	.375
		Tigers	Det	R	21	15	44	11	0	0	0	11	6	4	8	0	7	0	0	0	0	0	.00	1	.250	.365	.250
		Oneonta	Det	A-	21	26	81	21	1	4	0	30	9	6	15	0	24	0	0	0	6	1	.86	1	.259	.375	.370
Phillips, Brandon	ss	Cape Fear	Mon	A	20	126	484	117	17	8	11	183	74	72	38	3	97	9	0	5	23	8	.74	11	.242	.306	.378
Phillips, Dan	of	Asheville	Col	A	22	123	473	129	32	2	13	204	71	45	18	0	130	8	2	0	39	17	.70	9	.273	.311	.431
Pichardo, Henry	2b	Burlington	Cle	R+	22	49	146	47	12	1	2	67	34	21	23	0	25	3	1	2	8	8	.50	5	.322	.420	.459
		Kinston	Cle	A+	22	16	48	9	2	0	1	14	7	6	3	0	11	0	0	0	4	2	.67	1	.188	.235	.292
		Mahoning Vy	Cle	A-	22	3	10	1	0	0	0	1	2	0	1	0	3	0	0	0	1	0	1.00	1	.100	.182	.100
Pichardo, Maximo	2b	Butte	Ana	R+	22	28	100	28	4	1	0	34	14	13	10	0	8	1	1	0	0	4	.00	4	.280	.351	.340
Pickering, Kelvin	1b-dh	Orioles	Bal	R	21	27	81	17	2	0	2	25	11	6	8	1	25	1	0	0	3	0	1.00	2	.210	.289	.309
Piedra, Jorge*	of	Vero Beach	LA	A+	22	92	360	102	11	6	6	143	59	52	29	1	57	5	3	7	21	5	.81	6	.283	.339	.397
		Daytona	ChC	A+	22	34	139	48	11	1	1	64	24	17	6	0	15	0	2	2	8	4	.67	0	.345	.367	.460
Pietro, Jim	2b	Mahoning Vy	Cle	A-	23	35	119	23	2	0	0	25	19	5	19	0	32	4	4	1	4	2	.67	3	.193	.322	.210
Pilkington, Ross	of	Rockies	Col	R	19	29	107	30	5	5	1	48	19	18	10	0	35	1	0	1	5	1	.83	0	.280	.345	.449
Pimentel, Franklin#	ss-2b	Lakeland	Det	A+	22	46	152	37	7	1	0	46	18	12	18	0	39	1	1	1	1	1	.50	2	.243	.326	.303
Pina, Emmanuel	c	Eugene	ChC	A-	21	1	1	0	0	0	0	0	0	0	0	0	1	0	0	0	0	0	.00	0	.000	.000	.000
		Cubs	ChC	R	21	9	25	8	0	0	0	8	4	5	1	0	4	0	0	0	0	0	.00	0	.320	.346	.320
Pinales, Franklin	of	Elizabethtn	Min	R+	21	40	113	24	8	0	0	32	13	12	20	0	26	2	0	3	10	5	.67	2	.212	.333	.283
Pinango, Ever#	of-1b	Giants	SF	R	19	47	130	31	4	0	0	35	23	11	14	0	17	4	3	0	13	7	.65	5	.238	.331	.269
Pines, Greg	of	Mariners	Sea	R	22	42	156	41	12	0	4	65	32	19	17	0	29	4	0	2	1	1	.50	2	.263	.346	.417
Pini, Ryan*	of	San Jose	SF	A+	24	123	416	88	13	2	6	123	47	47	52	1	124	3	3	4	6	7	.46	10	.212	.301	.296
Pittman, Tom	1b	Jupiter	Mon	A+	21	58	226	55	8	2	1	70	24	31	16	1	60	1	0	5	6	5	.55	8	.243	.290	.310
Poe, Adam	of-dh	Savannah	Tex	A	23	115	383	96	20	0	4	128	37	39	46	3	81	12	3	4	20	4	.83	10	.251	.346	.334
Pogue, Jamie	c	New Jersey	StL	A-	23	28	90	21	6	0	0	27	12	9	24	1	18	1	0	1	1	0	1.00	4	.233	.397	.300
		Peoria	StL	A	23	22	66	11	1	1	1	17	8	6	12	0	20	3	2	0	0	1	.00	2	.167	.321	.258
Pohle, Ike	c	Tampa	NYY	A+	24	1	2	0	0	0	0	0	0	0	0	0	1	0	0	0	0	0	.00	0	.000	.000	.000
		Staten Ilnd	NYY	A-	24	14	21	4	2	0	0	6	0	3	1	0	7	1	0	0	0	0	.00	0	.190	.261	.286
		Greensboro	NYY	A	24	4	12	1	0	0	0	1	1	1	3	0	4	0	0	0	0	0	.00	0	.083	.267	.083
Pollaro, Dallas	2b	New Jersey	StL	A-	21	20	55	8	0	0	0	8	5	3	3	0	10	3	1	0	3	0	1.00	2	.145	.230	.145
Pond, Simon*	3b	Jupiter	Mon	A+	24	19	63	13	1	0	3	23	7	8	9	0	13	1	0	0	1	0	1.00	0	.206	.315	.365
		Kinston	Cle	A+	24	64	237	76	18	0	6	112	40	37	22	1	49	3	0	2	14	3	.82	9	.321	.383	.473
Postell, Matthew*	c	Utica	Fla	A-	24	46	156	47	10	3	1	66	24	15	12	0	29	2	1	0	2	1	.67	3	.301	.359	.423
Powers, Jeff*	2b	High Desert	Ari	A+	25	112	408	126	20	3	2	158	55	52	34	0	29	4	5	4	3	6	.33	2	.309	.364	.387
Pregnalato, Bob	of	Ogden	Mil	R+	23	59	205	57	9	2	1	73	49	25	20	0	37	2	5	0	15	5	.75	2	.278	.348	.356
Pressley, Josh*	1b-dh	Chston-SC	TB	A	21	130	488	148	44	0	6	210	61	60	49	3	62	4	0	3	2	1	.67	17	.303	.369	.430
Preston, Brian	c	Cape Fear	Mon	A	24	18	58	9	4	0	1	16	7	6	7	0	13	0	0	0	1	0	1.00	0	.155	.246	.276
		Jupiter	Mon	A+	24	18	53	11	2	0	1	16	7	6	4	0	6	0	0	1	0	1	.00	1	.208	.259	.302
Price, Jared	c-dh	Great Falls	LA	R+	19	27	89	17	3	1	1	25	13	10	13	0	30	6	0	1	2	2	.50	0	.191	.330	.281
Pride, Josh	c	Portland	Col	A-	23	16	57	7	0	1	0	9	4	4	2	0	15	2	0	0	1	0	1.00	3	.123	.180	.158

2000 Batting — Class-A and Rookie Leagues

BATTING																					BASERUNNING				PERCENTAGES		
Player	Pos	Team	Org	Lg	A	G	AB	H	2B	3B	HR	TB	R	RBI	TBB	IBB	SO	HBP	SH	SF	SB	CS	SB%	GDP	Avg	OBP	SLG
		Salem	Col	A+	23	10	22	5	2	0	0	7	3	2	3	0	8	2	0	1	0	0	.00	1	.227	.357	.318
Prieto, Jon#	2b	Lynchburg	Pit	A+	21	112	392	93	12	6	1	120	61	31	58	0	88	2	9	2	23	5	.82	10	.237	.337	.306
Puccinelli, John	3b	Padres	SD	R	20	8	32	6	4	1	0	12	5	3	0	0	5	0	0	0	0	0	.00	1	.188	.188	.375
		Idaho Falls	SD	R+	20	46	163	44	9	0	4	65	25	11	21	1	38	5	0	1	0	0	.00	2	.270	.368	.399
Puffinbarger, Rusty	c	Columbus	Cle	A	25	19	57	7	0	2	0	11	8	6	5	0	20	2	2	0	2	0	1.00	4	.123	.219	.193
		Kinston	Cle	A+	25	13	33	4	0	0	0	4	4	1	6	0	9	1	0	0	0	0	.00	1	.121	.275	.121
Pugh, Dwayne	of-dh	Queens	Tor	A-	23	8	16	0	0	0	0	0	2	0	1	0	5	0	0	0	1	0	1.00	0	.000	.059	.000
		Hagerstown	Tor	A	23	6	15	2	0	0	0	2	2	0	5	0	0	1	0	0	2	0	1.00	0	.133	.381	.133
Pugh, Josh	c	Macon	Atl	A	23	37	125	35	2	1	3	48	20	19	19	1	30	3	1	1	1	0	1.00	3	.280	.385	.384
		Myrtle Bch	Atl	A+	23	38	115	20	6	0	2	32	11	10	10	0	30	1	0	0	0	1	.00	2	.174	.246	.278
Pujols, Gonzalez	dh-1b	Visalia	Oak	A+	23	117	422	136	16	2	9	183	61	74	50	5	57	1	0	8	11	6	.65	8	.322	.389	.434
Quatraro, Matt	c	St. Pete	TB	A+	27	15	49	10	1	1	1	16	6	3	2	0	14	0	0	0	0	0	.00	4	.204	.235	.327
Quattlebaum, Hugh	3b	Oneonta	Det	A-	23	49	186	56	5	6	0	73	27	26	24	0	28	3	0	2	4	2	.67	4	.301	.386	.392
Quickstad, Barry*	of	Elizabethtn	Min	R+	20	52	178	42	11	4	4	73	28	33	27	1	48	1	5	0	6	1	.86	1	.236	.340	.410
Quinlan, Robb	1b	Lk Elsinore	Ana	A+	24	127	482	153	35	5	5	213	79	85	67	1	82	2	2	9	6	4	.60	7	.317	.396	.442
Quintana, Wilfredo	of	Everett	Sea	A-	23	22	82	25	3	0	7	49	16	26	9	1	24	0	0	1	2	1	.67	1	.305	.370	.598
		Lancaster	Sea	A+	23	33	103	38	7	2	7	70	25	24	9	0	17	1	2	0	3	4	.43	1	.369	.425	.680
Quintero, Humberto	c	Burlington	CWS	A	21	75	248	59	12	2	0	75	23	24	15	1	31	3	4	2	10	6	.63	8	.238	.287	.302
		White Sox	CWS	R	21	15	56	22	2	2	0	28	13	8	0	0	3	2	0	0	1	0	1.00	2	.393	.414	.500
Quintin, Luis	of	Rangers	Tex	R	18	22	71	16	4	0	1	23	6	10	4	0	27	0	2	0	1	1	.50	0	.225	.267	.324
Quiroz, Guillermo	c	Hagerstown	Tor	A	19	43	136	22	4	0	1	29	14	12	16	0	44	4	3	0	0	1	.00	3	.162	.269	.213
		Queens	Tor	A-	19	55	196	44	9	0	5	68	27	29	27	0	48	4	0	1	1	2	.33	4	.224	.329	.347
Rabe, Josh	of	Elizabethtn	Min	R+	22	44	154	34	5	0	3	48	33	11	25	0	34	4	0	0	2	0	1.00	6	.221	.344	.312
Raburn, John#	3b	Burlington	CWS	A	22	61	206	51	10	1	3	72	17	27	14	0	48	3	1	2	3	4	.43	5	.248	.302	.350
		Boise	Ana	A-	22	72	280	71	12	4	0	91	49	34	54	0	72	2	4	3	28	3	.90	2	.254	.375	.325
Rachels, Wes	1b	Delmarva	Bal	A	25	123	373	97	14	1	0	113	58	46	96	0	58	5	7	4	7	1	.88	13	.260	.414	.303
Rafael, Alberto	of	White Sox	CWS	R	19	39	117	28	9	0	1	40	18	20	16	0	33	3	2	1	0	6	.00	2	.239	.343	.342
Raffo, John*	1b	Kingsport	NYM	R+	23	52	158	43	10	0	7	74	28	20	30	2	30	1	3	1	4	0	1.00	2	.272	.389	.468
Raines Jr., Tim#	of	Frederick	Bal	A+	21	127	457	108	21	3	2	141	89	36	67	0	106	13	11	3	81	19	.81	8	.236	.348	.309
Ralph, Brian*	of	Daytona	ChC	A+	25	77	246	56	11	3	1	76	39	23	28	1	22	2	3	2	18	9	.67	0	.228	.309	.309
		Vero Beach	LA	A+	25	33	120	39	2	1	1	46	32	14	30	0	16	2	2	1	13	2	.87	1	.325	.464	.383
Ramirez, Alexander	2b	Giants	SF	R	19	40	70	11	1	2	0	16	15	4	4	0	26	0	0	1	5	5	.50	1	.157	.200	.229
Ramirez, Charlie	of	Chston-WV	KC	A	22	16	54	12	1	1	0	15	3	5	0	0	8	0	0	0	0	0	.00	2	.222	.222	.278
Ramirez, Domingo	c	San Jose	SF	A+	20	5	9	0	0	0	0	0	0	0	1	0	3	0	0	0	0	0	.00	1	.000	.100	.000
		Giants	SF	R	20	19	41	11	2	0	0	13	2	4	2	0	4	1	0	1	1	1	.50	2	.268	.311	.317
Ramirez, Jordy#	2b	Reds	Cin	R	21	40	128	22	2	1	1	29	21	6	25	0	37	0	6	1	4	3	.57	1	.172	.305	.227
Ramirez, Oscar	2b	Wisconsin	Sea	A	22	70	209	49	13	3	1	71	34	24	40	0	34	7	3	1	7	5	.58	3	.234	.374	.340
Ramirez, Wagner#	2b	Cubs	ChC	R	20	39	112	27	3	0	0	30	15	6	8	0	22	2	2	2	5	2	.71	2	.241	.298	.268
Ramos, Ebaldo	1b	Medcine Hat	Tor	R+	20	26	90	21	8	0	0	29	13	11	10	0	24	0	1	0	0	0	.00	2	.233	.310	.322
Ramos, Victor*	c	Pirates	Pit	R	19	27	91	19	2	0	0	21	4	14	5	0	15	0	1	0	1	1	.50	3	.209	.250	.231
Ramsey, Brad	c	Cubs	ChC	R	24	5	15	5	2	1	1	12	5	3	5	0	2	0	0	0	0	0	.00	0	.333	.500	.800
		Lansing	ChC	A	24	4	12	1	0	0	0	1	0	0	3	0	5	0	1	0	0	0	.00	0	.083	.267	.083
Rasmussen, Wes	3b	Danville	Atl	R+	20	19	64	11	2	0	0	13	8	3	6	0	27	0	1	0	3	0	1.00	0	.172	.243	.203
Ravelo, Manny	of	Williamsprt	Pit	A-	19	52	195	59	4	7	0	77	38	17	26	0	30	5	5	0	28	9	.76	2	.303	.398	.395
Raymundo, G.J.	dh	Chston-WV	KC	A	24	85	268	74	11	1	3	96	29	35	34	1	61	8	1	2	0	1	.00	9	.276	.372	.358
Redman, Prentice	of	Capital Cty	NYM	A	21	131	497	129	19	1	3	159	60	46	52	1	90	3	1	2	26	10	.72	5	.260	.332	.320
Reed, Keith	of	Delmarva	Bal	A	22	70	269	78	16	1	11	129	43	59	25	5	56	5	1	3	20	4	.83	3	.290	.358	.480
		Frederick	Bal	A+	22	65	243	57	10	1	8	93	33	31	21	2	58	4	0	3	9	1	.90	4	.235	.303	.383
Reed, Matt	2b-of	Twins	Min	R	20	33	86	22	1	0	0	23	21	12	19	0	17	6	2	0	7	4	.64	3	.256	.423	.267
Reed, Robert	1b	Red Sox	Bos	R	23	17	27	3	1	0	0	4	1	0	2	0	4	0	0	0	0	0	.00	0	.111	.172	.148
Reese, Kevin*	of	Idaho Falls	SD	R+	23	53	201	72	14	4	2	100	51	36	43	2	30	3	0	2	12	3	.80	5	.358	.474	.498
Remekie, Collin	of	Braves	Atl	R	20	13	27	1	0	0	0	1	2	0	5	0	17	0	0	0	0	1	.00	0	.037	.188	.037
Repko, Jason	ss	Yakima	LA	A-	20	8	17	5	2	0	0	7	3	1	1	0	7	0	0	0	0	0	.00	0	.294	.333	.412
Requena, Alex#	of	Columbus	Cle	A	20	126	482	125	6	6	1	146	90	24	66	0	137	6	4	2	87	20	.81	1	.259	.354	.303
Restovich, Mike	of	Fort Myers	Min	A+	22	135	475	125	27	9	8	194	73	64	61	1	100	4	0	3	19	7	.73	11	.263	.350	.408
Reyes, Ambiorix	ss	Piedmont	Phi	A	22	64	204	52	8	0	0	60	28	27	4	0	31	0	8	2	8	2	.80	9	.255	.267	.294
Reyes, Christian#	3b	Vancouver	Oak	A-	23	25	87	28	9	0	1	40	12	14	12	0	20	1	0	0	0	2	.00	0	.322	.410	.460
		Modesto	Oak	A+	23	68	225	50	7	3	0	63	26	19	27	0	62	1	2	1	4	3	.57	15	.222	.307	.280
Reyes, Eduardo	3b	Beloit	Mil	A	21	54	173	36	5	2	1	48	25	15	14	0	39	3	6	0	4	3	.57	1	.208	.279	.277
Reyes, Guillermo#	2b	Bristol	CWS	R+	19	66	257	76	10	2	3	99	45	31	22	0	24	2	4	2	21	10	.68	3	.296	.353	.385
Reyes, Henry#	ss-2b	Giants	SF	R	18	47	151	37	5	2	1	49	30	15	26	0	39	4	4	1	14	7	.67	1	.245	.368	.325
Reyes, Ivan	2b	Tampa	NYY	A+	20	1	3	0	0	0	0	0	0	0	0	0	2	0	0	0	0	0	.00	0	.000	.000	.000
		Yankees	NYY	R	20	54	192	35	13	1	2	56	37	27	30	0	52	3	0	4	4	2	.67	4	.182	.297	.292
Reyes, Jose#	ss	Kingsport	NYM	R+	18	49	132	33	3	3	0	42	22	8	20	0	37	3	3	1	10	4	.71	1	.250	.359	.318
Reyes, Julio*	of	Bristol	CWS	R+	21	41	146	41	12	4	1	64	20	18	7	0	35	0	3	2	2	2	.50	1	.281	.310	.438
Reynoso, Ismael	ss	San Jose	SF	A+	23	51	144	25	2	1	1	32	16	5	12	0	22	5	2	0	1	4	.20	3	.174	.261	.222
		Salem-Keizr	SF	A-	23	18	60	9	4	0	0	13	4	5	1	0	12	0	2	0	0	0	.00	3	.150	.164	.217
Reynoso, Paulino*	1b	White Sox	CWS	R	20	42	129	31	6	1	1	42	19	13	21	0	44	0	0	3	1	0	1.00	0	.240	.340	.326
Rhodes, Dusty*	of	Tampa	NYY	A+	25	65	146	28	6	4	1	45	21	11	29	1	40	2	1	1	2	6	.25	2	.192	.331	.308
		Greensboro	NYY	A	25	14	55	13	3	1	1	21	8	5	8	0	13	1	0	0	0	1	.00	1	.236	.344	.382
Rich, Dominic*	2b	Queens	Tor	A-	21	67	236	62	11	4	0	81	37	25	38	0	33	5	4	3	10	4	.71	8	.263	.372	.343
Richardson, Corey	of	W Michigan	Det	A	24	126	454	120	12	2	1	139	80	50	94	1	124	8	6	2	41	10	.80	1	.264	.398	.306
Richardson, Juan	3b	Batavia	Phi	A-	20	10	39	6	2	0	0	8	0	2	3	0	15	0	0	0	0	0	.00	2	.154	.214	.205
		Piedmont	Phi	A	20	43	149	36	11	0	2	53	19	15	17	0	43	2	0	0	0	1	.00	5	.242	.327	.356
Richardson, Miguel	of	Everett	Sea	A-	20	56	181	39	7	1	7	69	19	25	12	1	77	3	1	2	5	7	.42	5	.215	.273	.381
Ridley, Jeremy#	dh	Medcine Hat	Tor	R+	23	3	7	2	1	0	0	3	3	1	3	0	2	0	0	0	0	0	.00	0	.286	.500	.429
		Queens	Tor	A-	23	1	2	0	0	0	0	0	0	0	0	0	0	0	0	0	0	0	.00	0	.000	.000	.000

2000 Batting — Class-A and Rookie Leagues

BATTING																					BASERUNNING				PERCENTAGES		
Player	Pos	Team	Org	Lg	A	G	AB	H	2B	3B	HR	TB	R	RBI	TBB	IBB	SO	HBP	SH	SF	SB	CS	SB%	GDP	Avg	OBP	SLG
Ridley, Shayne#	3b-dh	Bluefield	Bal	R+	23	41	150	39	7	0	1	49	22	16	18	0	32	1	1	1	3	1	.75	3	.260	.341	.327
Riek, Cliff	1b	Williamsprt	Pit	A-	20	29	86	12	3	0	2	21	9	12	5	0	25	6	0	0	0	0	.00	0	.140	.237	.244
		Pirates	Pit	R	20	10	32	5	3	0	0	8	5	2	6	0	12	2	0	1	1	0	1.00	1	.156	.317	.250
Riepe, Andy	c-dh	Augusta	Bos	A	24	11	40	7	1	0	0	8	5	4	3	0	8	0	1	0	0	0	.00	2	.175	.233	.200
		Sarasota	Bos	A+	24	41	103	21	2	0	1	26	11	9	13	0	21	2	0	0	2	4	.33	2	.204	.305	.252
Riera, Zack#	c-dh	Williamsprt	Pit	A-	22	15	45	6	1	0	0	7	4	2	4	0	11	3	0	0	1	0	1.00	3	.133	.250	.156
Riggins, Auntwan#	of	Hagerstown	Tor	A	25	67	195	43	5	0	0	48	25	9	12	0	56	2	4	0	16	4	.80	4	.221	.273	.246
Rikert, Wade*	of	Medcine Hat	Tor	R+	24	24	97	24	4	0	4	40	27	15	15	2	19	3	1	1	6	1	.86	0	.247	.362	.412
		Queens	Tor	A-	24	36	108	27	5	0	0	32	19	14	18	0	22	1	1	1	8	3	.73	1	.250	.359	.296
Riley, Brett	dh	Boise	Ana	A-	23	1	1	0	0	0	0	0	0	0	0	0	1	0	0	0	0	0	.00	0	.000	.000	.000
		Butte	Ana	R+	23	12	16	4	0	1	0	6	4	1	2	0	9	1	0	0	0	0	.00	0	.250	.368	.375
Rincon, Carlos	of	Auburn	Hou	A-	21	11	23	3	1	0	0	4	3	4	2	0	7	0	0	0	2	0	1.00	0	.130	.200	.174
		Martinsvlle	Hou	R+	21	15	43	6	0	0	2	12	8	4	3	0	17	1	0	0	1	1	.50	0	.140	.213	.279
Rinne, Jim	dh-of	Asheville	Col	A	24	112	385	107	21	1	13	169	66	48	72	1	96	5	1	3	15	12	.56	8	.278	.396	.439
Riordan, Matt	of	Delmarva	Bal	A	23	109	389	110	22	2	4	148	54	51	47	2	74	8	1	1	11	4	.73	5	.283	.371	.380
Rios, Alexis	of-dh	Hagerstown	Tor	A	20	22	74	17	3	1	0	22	5	5	2	0	14	1	0	1	2	3	.40	0	.230	.256	.297
		Queens	Tor	A-	20	50	206	55	9	2	1	71	22	25	11	2	22	4	1	2	5	5	.50	5	.267	.314	.345
Rios, Fernando	of	Clinton	Cin	A	22	30	123	41	12	0	0	53	22	20	11	1	16	1	2	1	2	1	.67	6	.333	.390	.431
		Dayton	Cin	A	22	62	227	52	11	1	1	68	27	26	20	0	27	1	0	1	2	3	.40	8	.229	.293	.300
Risinger, Ben	2b	Rancho Cuca	SD	A+	23	15	50	13	4	0	2	23	5	9	6	0	13	1	0	1	0	0	.00	3	.260	.345	.460
		Fort Wayne	SD	A	23	50	159	28	4	0	0	32	10	8	15	0	31	5	3	0	0	1	.00	3	.176	.268	.201
Rivas, Justo	of	Macon	Atl	A	21	129	504	145	30	2	8	203	67	65	33	2	103	10	4	3	7	8	.47	11	.288	.342	.403
Rivas, Norberto	dh	Expos	Mon	R	19	1	4	0	0	0	0	0	0	0	0	0	1	0	0	0	0	0	.00	0	.000	.000	.000
Rivera, Carlos*	1b	Pirates	Pit	R	23	6	24	7	0	0	0	7	2	0	1	0	2	0	0	0	0	0	.00	1	.292	.320	.292
		Lynchburg	Pit	A+	23	64	233	63	17	0	5	95	20	47	6	1	34	2	0	9	0	1	.00	7	.270	.284	.408
Rivera, Carlos	dh-1b	Phillies	Phi	R	19	26	72	14	2	0	1	19	5	4	8	0	28	2	0	0	0	0	.00	0	.194	.293	.264
Rivera, Erick	of	Phillies	Phi	R	20	43	126	21	2	1	2	31	17	14	11	0	34	9	0	2	2	0	1.00	2	.167	.277	.246
Rivera, Francisco*	c	Clinton	Cin	A	21	67	195	45	4	0	3	58	28	22	32	1	38	2	2	2	0	0	.00	6	.231	.342	.297
Rivera, William*	2b	Medcine Hat	Tor	R+	19	39	124	34	3	1	0	39	22	8	24	0	29	0	4	0	0	0	.00	2	.274	.392	.315
Roberts, Brian#	ss	Orioles	Bal	R	23	9	29	9	1	2	1	17	8	3	7	0	4	0	0	1	7	1	.88	0	.310	.432	.586
		Frederick	Bal	A+	23	48	163	49	6	3	0	61	27	16	27	1	24	1	7	0	13	10	.57	4	.301	.403	.374
Robertson, Matt	of	Sarasota	Bos	A+	24	17	55	9	1	1	1	15	7	5	8	0	10	2	1	1	2	1	.67	2	.164	.288	.273
Robinson, Bo	3b	Lancaster	Sea	A+	25	136	515	161	33	0	10	224	93	97	65	2	69	5	1	9	2	5	.29	23	.313	.389	.435
Robles, Kevin	c	Wisconsin	Sea	A	23	62	223	49	11	2	1	67	16	21	7	0	59	5	2	0	1	2	.33	13	.220	.260	.300
Rock, Jamie	of	Portland	Col	A-	23	57	209	53	14	1	1	72	33	22	16	0	53	4	0	1	7	2	.78	6	.254	.317	.344
Rodgers, Albert	1b	Johnson Cty	StL	R+	22	62	220	48	12	1	6	80	25	20	15	1	68	8	2	2	4	5	.44	3	.218	.290	.364
Rodgers, Mackeel#	3b	Royals	KC	R	20	26	91	19	3	1	1	27	14	6	12	0	18	3	0	0	2	5	.29	1	.209	.321	.297
Rodriguez, Carlos	of	Augusta	Bos	A	24	116	471	144	28	5	18	236	62	94	17	2	108	12	0	4	24	12	.67	9	.306	.343	.501
Rodriguez, G.	c	Bakersfield	SF	A+	23	118	437	105	27	1	10	164	63	58	30	0	101	13	4	3	20	8	.71	11	.240	.306	.375
Rodriguez, Jeff	c	Macon	Atl	A	24	15	39	6	0	0	0	6	3	0	3	0	9	0	1	0	1	0	1.00	0	.154	.214	.154
Rodriguez, Jose#	2b	Orioles	Bal	R	21	1	5	2	0	0	0	2	2	1	0	0	1	0	0	0	1	0	1.00	1	.400	.400	.400
Rodriguez, Luis#	2b	Quad City	Min	A	21	106	342	77	11	2	0	92	35	28	40	1	29	5	19	2	4	5	.44	10	.225	.314	.269
Rodriguez, Mike	3b	Dunedin	Tor	A+	26	73	223	61	11	1	1	77	34	23	28	2	44	4	2	4	1	3	.25	6	.274	.359	.345
Rodriguez, Ricardo	ss	Braves	Atl	R	20	20	67	14	2	0	1	19	11	2	6	1	10	7	0	1	2	2	.50	1	.209	.333	.284
		Danville	Atl	R+	20	11	29	5	1	0	0	6	4	1	2	0	8	1	1	0	0	0	.00	0	.172	.250	.207
Rodriguez, Ronny	2b	Augusta	Bos	A	20	6	19	2	1	0	0	3	5	1	4	0	10	1	0	0	0	0	.00	1	.105	.292	.158
		Lowell	Bos	A-	20	13	38	4	1	0	0	5	7	0	4	0	18	2	2	0	1	2	.33	0	.105	.227	.132
		Sarasota	Bos	A+	20	1	3	0	0	0	0	0	0	0	0	0	2	0	0	0	0	0	.00	0	.000	.000	.000
		Red Sox	Bos	R	20	20	52	13	2	0	0	15	3	2	5	0	17	1	0	0	0	0	.00	1	.250	.328	.288
Rodriguez, Serafin	of	Clinton	Cin	A	22	27	99	23	6	0	0	29	13	6	11	1	11	0	1	1	5	2	.71	2	.232	.306	.293
		Dayton	Cin	A	22	68	270	77	8	1	3	96	29	30	15	0	38	2	1	2	9	3	.75	5	.285	.325	.356
Rodriguez, Wilson	of	Mahoning Vy	Cle	A-	20	3	9	0	0	0	0	0	3	1	1	0	2	0	0	0	0	0	.00	0	.000	.100	.000
Roenicke, Jarett*	of-1b	Padres	SD	R	21	49	171	46	9	0	1	58	22	21	20	3	28	4	1	1	2	2	.50	3	.269	.357	.339
Roger, Omar	2b	Orioles	Bal	R	18	31	78	17	2	0	2	25	16	9	9	1	22	1	3	0	4	2	.67	0	.218	.307	.321
Rogers, Brandon	c	Butte	Ana	R+	23	11	38	12	2	0	2	20	5	5	9	0	8	0	0	1	0	0	.00	1	.316	.438	.526
		Boise	Ana	A-	23	31	89	22	2	0	1	27	9	11	7	0	24	3	0	0	0	0	.00	4	.247	.323	.303
Rogers, Brian*	dh-c	Marlins	Fla	R	23	5	18	7	0	0	1	10	3	3	2	1	4	0	0	0	0	1	.00	0	.389	.450	.556
Rogowski, Casey*	1b	Burlington	CWS	A	20	122	412	95	19	1	6	134	62	41	47	2	89	4	3	1	11	3	.79	10	.231	.315	.325
Rojas, Alex#	2b	Piedmont	Phi	A	23	33	100	17	2	1	0	21	16	11	8	0	26	1	1	0	7	2	.78	3	.170	.239	.210
		Batavia	Phi	A-	23	46	137	23	4	1	0	29	27	13	5	0	31	1	3	3	12	2	.86	4	.168	.199	.212
Romano, Jimmie	c	Charlotte	Tex	A+	24	45	129	42	5	1	1	52	15	12	15	0	24	1	1	1	4	3	.57	2	.326	.397	.403
Rombley, Danny	of	Cape Fear	Mon	A	21	24	89	23	1	2	0	28	8	10	2	0	30	1	1	0	2	1	.67	1	.258	.283	.315
		Vermont	Mon	A-	21	49	192	45	3	2	0	52	32	28	16	0	51	4	1	3	14	8	.64	2	.234	.302	.271
Romero, Flavio*	ss	Mexico	—	R	21	51	178	61	8	4	0	77	40	26	52	0	27	1	0	3	8	7	.53	2	.343	.487	.433
Romero, Gabe	1b	Braves	Atl	R	21	36	116	23	5	0	0	28	12	9	5	0	16	4	0	1	3	4	.43	0	.198	.254	.241
Romero, Nicholas	ss	Padres	SD	R	21	29	102	28	2	3	1	39	19	12	16	1	30	3	1	0	9	5	.64	1	.275	.388	.382
		Idaho Falls	SD	R+	21	5	18	2	0	0	0	2	1	2	0	0	4	0	0	0	0	0	.00	2	.111	.111	.111
Roneberg, Brett*	of	Brevard Cty	Fla	A+	22	125	445	116	18	2	2	144	51	45	77	5	60	1	4	4	4	2	.67	13	.261	.368	.324
Rooi, Vince	3b	Vermont	Mon	A-	19	65	234	54	9	1	6	83	36	43	40	2	60	4	0	4	9	2	.82	3	.231	.348	.355
Roper, Doug#	ss	Hagerstown	Tor	A	23	25	76	13	2	0	0	15	16	9	12	0	31	0	0	0	3	0	1.00	1	.171	.284	.197
Roper, Zachary	3b	Boise	Ana	A-	23	54	195	60	16	0	4	88	36	34	31	0	44	2	0	0	4	1	.80	7	.308	.408	.451
Rosa, Ivan*	of	Athletics	Oak	R	22	36	123	32	3	3	3	50	19	23	10	0	27	2	1	2	2	1	.67	1	.260	.321	.407
Rosa, Wally	c	White Sox	CWS	R	19	17	61	21	4	0	1	28	11	10	8	0	11	0	0	1	1	1	.50	1	.344	.414	.459
		Burlington	CWS	A	19	27	95	20	4	0	0	24	7	9	4	0	25	2	0	1	1	0	1.00	3	.211	.255	.253
Rosamond, Mike	of	Kissimmee	Hou	A+	23	129	446	92	14	7	16	168	60	60	60	3	151	2	2	6	17	13	.57	6	.206	.300	.377
Rosario, Carlos#	2b	Modesto	Oak	A+	21	86	284	67	11	4	2	92	45	38	54	0	93	2	4	0	20	7	.74	4	.236	.362	.324
Rosario, Melvin*	of	Asheville	Col	A	22	78	219	42	2	1	0	46	26	10	23	0	57	3	2	2	8	9	.47	5	.192	.275	.210

2000 Batting — Class-A and Rookie Leagues

BATTING																					BASERUNNING				PERCENTAGES		
Player	Pos	Team	Org	Lg	A	G	AB	H	2B	3B	HR	TB	R	RBI	TBB	IBB	SO	HBP	SH	SF	SB	CS	SB%	GDP	Avg	OBP	SLG
Rosario, Vicente	of	Mariners	Sea	R	23	34	143	49	2	4	2	65	33	16	12	0	27	2	1	4	10	2	.83	1	.343	.391	.455
		Everett	Sea	A-	23	21	78	21	3	1	1	29	11	12	4	0	23	4	1	1	9	6	.60	1	.269	.333	.372
Rosas, Luis	ss	Expos	Mon	R	19	33	94	18	2	0	0	20	8	5	6	0	21	2	1	0	0	1	.00	3	.191	.255	.213
Ross, Cody	of	W Michigan	Det	A	20	122	434	116	17	9	7	172	71	68	55	0	83	9	2	7	11	3	.79	14	.267	.356	.396
Ross, Donovan*	dh	Chston-WV	KC	A	23	105	360	109	20	5	13	178	54	61	56	1	72	7	5	1	1	4	.20	13	.303	.406	.494
Rowan, Chris	ss	Ogden	Mil	R+	22	4	15	4	0	0	0	4	0	1	1	0	5	0	0	1	1	0	1.00	0	.267	.294	.267
		Mudville	Mil	A+	22	39	143	25	5	1	2	38	13	4	3	0	55	1	0	0	0	2	.00	3	.175	.197	.266
Rowden, Monte	c	Lansing	ChC	A	24	6	3	0	0	0	0	0	0	0	1	0	1	1	0	0	0	0	.00	0	.000	.400	.000
Royer, Lissandro	2b	Kingsport	NYM	R+	21	25	56	15	0	1	1	20	14	2	6	0	9	3	4	0	5	5	.50	0	.268	.369	.357
Ruan, Wilken	of	Cape Fear	Mon	A	21	134	574	165	29	10	0	214	95	51	24	1	75	8	2	3	64	10	.86	4	.287	.323	.373
Ruiz, Carlos	c	Phillies	Phi	R	21	38	130	36	7	1	1	48	11	22	9	0	9	2	0	2	3	0	1.00	5	.277	.329	.369
Ruiz, Ramon	3b	San Berndno	LA	A+	25	39	125	28	8	2	2	46	21	23	12	0	28	1	4	2	6	0	1.00	3	.224	.293	.368
Ruiz, Randy	dh	Billings	Cin	R+	23	61	231	88	15	1	10	135	55	55	29	0	56	10	1	2	1	2	.33	6	.381	.467	.584
Ruiz, Willy	2b-ss	Wilmington	KC	A+	22	8	12	2	1	0	0	3	1	1	4	0	3	0	0	0	2	0	1.00	1	.167	.375	.250
		Chston-WV	KC	A	22	77	272	66	4	2	0	74	32	24	28	0	35	2	4	3	18	8	.69	10	.243	.315	.272
Rush, Travis	c	Pirates	Pit	R	19	4	10	2	0	0	0	2	0	0	0	0	0	1	0	0	2	0	1.00	0	.200	.273	.200
Russell, Byron*	1b	Royals	KC	R	20	47	140	28	4	0	3	41	12	19	18	1	35	1	3	0	3	0	1.00	6	.200	.296	.293
Russell, Mike	c	Orioles	Bal	R	19	24	74	21	4	0	1	28	9	9	10	0	14	1	1	1	1	4	.20	1	.284	.372	.378
Ryan, Jeff	of	Lansing	ChC	A	24	55	169	41	9	2	3	63	28	20	28	0	25	5	2	2	11	6	.65	2	.243	.363	.373
		Columbus	Cle	A	24	3	5	2	0	0	0	2	0	1	1	0	1	0	0	0	0	0	.00	0	.400	.500	.400
		Mahoning Vy	Cle	A-	24	2	8	1	0	0	0	1	0	0	0	0	3	0	0	0	0	0	.00	1	.125	.125	.125
Ryan, Kelvin	of	St. Pete	TB	A+	22	84	279	50	11	2	3	74	26	27	13	0	56	4	2	1	5	5	.50	8	.179	.226	.265
Saba, Cesar#	ss	Augusta	Bos	A	19	47	192	51	10	3	2	73	26	30	12	0	33	1	1	4	2	5	.29	4	.266	.306	.380
		Red Sox	Bos	R	19	2	6	1	0	0	0	1	0	1	1	0	3	0	0	0	0	0	.00	0	.167	.286	.167
		Padres	SD	R	19	2	5	1	0	0	0	1	0	0	0	0	0	0	0	0	0	0	.00	0	.200	.200	.200
		Fort Wayne	SD	A	19	35	124	22	6	0	0	28	5	14	8	0	23	0	2	0	2	0	1.00	3	.177	.227	.226
Sadler, Raymond	of	Cubs	ChC	R	20	42	165	56	5	5	1	74	32	27	16	1	27	1	0	3	4	3	.57	1	.339	.395	.448
Salargo, Steve	of	Delmarva	Bal	A	24	72	205	49	11	1	3	71	42	28	33	0	53	4	1	0	5	0	1.00	5	.239	.355	.346
		Frederick	Bal	A+	24	20	51	10	2	0	0	12	3	5	3	0	12	1	0	0	0	0	.00	3	.196	.255	.235
Salas, Jose#	c	Danville	Atl	R+	19	41	156	47	6	0	3	62	17	23	10	1	31	7	0	1	2	1	.67	4	.301	.368	.397
Salas, Juan	3b	Chston-SC	TB	A	19	60	220	53	11	0	1	67	25	26	3	0	50	7	0	3	6	3	.67	4	.241	.270	.305
		Hudson Val	TB	A-	19	38	134	38	7	1	2	53	22	14	9	0	31	1	1	0	3	5	.38	11	.284	.333	.396
Salazar, Jeremy	c	Clearwater	Phi	A+	25	45	164	41	11	1	1	57	18	25	13	0	37	1	1	1	0	0	.00	6	.250	.307	.348
Salazar, Ruben	2b	Fort Myers	Min	A+	23	124	499	155	25	0	11	213	80	64	37	1	81	2	0	3	3	5	.38	18	.311	.359	.427
Salinas, Trey	3b-c	Dayton	Cin	A	26	14	37	7	1	0	0	8	4	4	6	1	10	0	0	0	0	0	.00	2	.189	.302	.216
Salvesen, Matt*	1b	Bristol	CWS	R+	21	39	123	30	8	2	1	45	11	20	5	0	32	2	0	0	0	0	.00	2	.244	.285	.366
Sanchez, Braulio*	of	Diamondbcks	Ari	R	19	14	34	7	1	2	0	12	7	4	8	0	9	0	0	0	1	0	1.00	0	.206	.357	.353
Sanchez, Freddy	ss	Lowell	Bos	A-	23	34	132	38	13	2	1	58	24	14	9	0	16	3	2	0	2	4	.33	1	.288	.347	.439
		Augusta	Bos	A	23	30	109	33	7	0	0	40	17	15	11	0	19	1	4	0	4	0	1.00	1	.303	.372	.367
Sanchez, Tino#	1b	Asheville	Col	A	22	58	187	47	4	1	1	56	15	16	21	0	27	2	0	1	7	1	.88	2	.251	.332	.299
Sandberg, Eric*	1b	Quad City	Min	A	21	128	424	109	11	0	15	165	72	59	95	8	71	8	0	5	0	0	.00	11	.257	.398	.389
Sandoval, Jhensy	of	High Desert	Ari	A+	22	42	148	35	13	0	5	63	17	19	8	0	45	1	0	1	2	5	.29	1	.236	.278	.426
		South Bend	Ari	A	22	18	62	16	4	0	2	26	8	14	5	0	16	1	1	3	3	2	.60	1	.258	.310	.419
		Diamondbcks	Ari	R	22	7	21	6	2	0	0	8	2	5	2	0	2	0	0	2	0	0	.00	1	.286	.320	.381
Sandoval, Michael	3b	Twins	Min	R	19	17	63	19	1	2	1	27	13	10	14	0	8	0	0	0	2	2	.50	3	.302	.429	.429
		Elizabethtn	Min	R+	19	42	149	40	10	2	2	60	27	30	24	0	22	4	0	4	4	0	1.00	1	.268	.376	.403
Santamarina, Juan*	3b-dh	Burlington	CWS	A	21	17	52	10	3	1	0	15	5	2	4	0	11	0	0	0	1	0	1.00	2	.192	.250	.288
Santana, E.*	1b	Chston-WV	KC	A	20	38	129	18	3	0	1	24	13	13	19	0	30	3	1	0	1	0	1.00	1	.140	.265	.186
Santana, Jorge	of	Cubs	ChC	R	19	11	26	3	0	0	1	6	3	3	3	0	10	0	0	0	1	0	1.00	0	.115	.207	.231
Santana, M.	1b	White Sox	CWS	R	19	18	72	29	12	1	0	43	16	23	11	0	6	0	1	1	1	0	1.00	2	.403	.476	.597
		Bristol	CWS	R+	19	34	98	18	4	2	1	29	12	8	19	0	26	1	2	0	2	3	.40	3	.184	.322	.296
Santana, Pedro	of	Tampa	NYY	A+	22	20	71	16	3	0	1	22	8	13	5	1	22	0	0	1	2	1	.67	0	.225	.273	.310
		Greensboro	NYY	A	22	83	309	74	10	1	4	98	29	26	14	0	89	3	1	3	17	9	.65	3	.239	.277	.317
		Staten Ilnd	NYY	A-	22	19	73	22	4	0	1	29	17	13	8	1	16	1	0	2	0	0	.00	3	.301	.369	.397
Santana, Sandy	2b	Johnson Cty	StL	R+	20	35	124	32	7	1	3	50	21	17	11	0	27	3	1	1	9	1	.90	2	.258	.331	.403
Santiago, Daniel#	c	Dayton	Cin	A	22	9	21	2	0	0	0	2	1	0	0	0	7	1	1	0	0	0	.00	1	.095	.136	.095
		Billings	Cin	R+	22	18	66	17	4	0	0	21	11	6	10	1	15	1	0	1	1	0	1.00	1	.258	.359	.318
Santiago, Ramon#	ss	W Michigan	Det	A	19	98	379	103	15	1	1	123	69	42	34	1	60	12	15	6	39	12	.76	11	.272	.346	.325
Santini, Travis	of	Columbus	Cle	A	20	52	185	33	9	0	0	42	10	12	9	0	52	2	0	0	2	0	1.00	6	.178	.224	.227
Santor, John#	1b	Johnson Cty	StL	R+	19	14	46	8	3	0	0	11	3	4	2	0	13	0	0	0	1	0	1.00	0	.174	.208	.239
Santora, Jack#	2b	South Bend	Ari	A	24	102	316	78	16	3	1	103	38	28	59	1	61	4	18	2	20	13	.61	6	.247	.370	.326
Santoro, Pat	2b	Augusta	Bos	A	22	30	113	30	6	1	3	47	13	15	10	1	27	4	0	1	4	2	.67	2	.265	.344	.416
		Red Sox	Bos	R	22	12	43	10	2	0	0	12	4	4	2	0	10	0	0	0	0	0	.00	2	.233	.267	.279
		Sarasota	Bos	A+	22	17	53	12	3	1	0	17	3	5	5	0	9	0	0	2	0	1	.00	0	.226	.283	.321
Santos, Chad*	1b	Chston-WV	KC	A	20	59	187	39	9	2	4	64	16	18	27	3	62	0	2	1	0	1	.00	4	.209	.307	.342
		Spokane	KC	A-	20	73	267	67	18	0	14	127	40	47	36	3	103	2	3	0	1	0	1.00	2	.251	.344	.476
Santos, Deivis*	1b	Giants	SF	R	21	12	43	16	2	1	2	26	13	10	7	0	6	0	0	0	4	1	.80	0	.372	.460	.605
		Salem-Keizr	SF	A-	21	2	7	0	0	0	0	0	0	0	0	0	0	0	0	0	0	0	.00	0	.000	.000	.000
Santos, Jose	3b	Brevard Cty	Fla	A+	23	129	444	96	16	2	7	137	55	54	55	2	125	14	0	5	7	2	.78	14	.216	.319	.309
Santos, Juan#	c	Queens	Tor	A-	23	9	29	7	2	0	0	9	2	3	6	0	6	0	1	0	0	0	.00	0	.241	.371	.310
		Hagerstown	Tor	A	23	14	41	6	1	0	2	13	4	5	5	0	20	1	1	1	1	1	.50	1	.146	.250	.317
Santos, Luis	2b-ss	South Bend	Ari	A	22	22	48	10	2	0	0	12	8	7	10	0	6	0	1	0	1	0	1.00	1	.208	.345	.250
		Missoula	Ari	R+	22	2	7	2	0	0	0	2	0	1	0	0	4	0	0	0	0	0	.00	1	.286	.286	.286
		High Desert	Ari	A+	22	49	145	33	5	1	1	43	12	15	14	0	15	0	2	3	1	3	.25	6	.228	.290	.297
Sarna, Kenny	dh	Spokane	KC	A-	23	1	4	1	0	0	0	1	0	0	0	0	2	0	0	0	0	0	.00	0	.250	.250	.250
Saucke, Casey	2b	Orioles	Bal	R	23	48	187	55	6	1	6	81	29	26	12	1	46	4	2	1	12	3	.80	4	.294	.348	.433
		Delmarva	Bal	A	23	9	15	4	1	0	0	5	1	1	1	0	6	0	0	0	0	0	.00	0	.267	.313	.333

2000 Batting — Class-A and Rookie Leagues

BATTING																				BASERUNNING				PERCENTAGES		
Player	Pos	Team	Org	Lg	A	G	AB	H	2B	3B	HR	TB	R	RBI	TBB	IBB	SO	HBP	SH	SF	SB	CS	SB%	GDP	Avg	OBP	SLG
Scales, Bobby#	2b	Fort Wayne	SD	A	23	81	269	76	14	3	1	99	42	27	39	5	52	3	3	0	14	7	.67	9	.283	.379	.368
Scanlon, Matt*	3b-dh	Quad City	Min	A	23	120	439	113	29	5	7	173	59	58	39	1	61	19	1	6	5	4	.56	12	.257	.340	.394
		Fort Myers	Min	A+	23	5	18	5	1	0	0	6	2	0	3	0	3	0	0	0	1	0	1.00	2	.278	.381	.333
Scarborough, Steve	2b	Beloit	Mil	A	23	127	452	109	24	2	2	143	51	64	55	2	80	3	13	7	8	2	.80	4	.241	.323	.316
Scarcella, Chris	c-p	Athletics	Oak	R	22	31	87	23	2	1	0	27	19	14	14	0	10	1	2	2	1	1	.50	2	.264	.365	.310
		Vancouver	Oak	A-	22	21	0	0	0	0	0	0	0	0	0	0	0	0	0	0	0	0	.00	0	.000	.000	.000
Schader, Troy	3b	Fort Wayne	SD	A	24	77	279	85	23	2	13	151	51	53	29	1	71	6	0	2	5	1	.83	7	.305	.380	.541
Schalick, George*	1b	Orioles	Bal	R	23	22	63	18	5	0	1	26	11	11	17	2	8	1	0	0	1	1	.50	2	.286	.444	.413
Schell, Barry*	of	Utica	Fla	A-	23	44	128	29	5	0	6	52	20	21	18	0	52	1	0	0	0	1	.00	4	.227	.327	.406
Schied, Jeremy*	1b	Vancouver	Oak	A-	25	75	236	55	16	0	2	77	37	28	48	0	51	9	0	4	2	1	.67	1	.233	.377	.326
Schill, Vaughn	3b	Lancaster	Sea	A+	23	6	16	4	0	0	0	4	4	0	5	0	5	0	0	0	2	1	.67	0	.250	.429	.250
Schilling, Chris	c	Ogden	Mil	R+	20	10	21	3	1	0	0	4	1	0	1	0	8	2	1	0	0	0	.00	0	.143	.250	.190
		Helena	Mil	R+	20	8	21	2	1	0	0	3	1	1	2	0	9	0	0	0	0	0	.00	1	.095	.174	.143
Schmidt, J.P.*	3b	Vancouver	Oak	A-	21	48	102	24	4	1	2	36	19	12	15	1	35	0	3	0	1	1	.50	2	.235	.333	.353
Schmitt, Billy	3b	Johnson Cty	StL	R+	18	46	165	53	5	3	2	70	21	21	10	0	23	1	1	1	3	1	.75	6	.321	.362	.424
Schmitt, Brian*	1b	Michigan	Hou	A	22	123	447	129	24	2	9	184	61	71	44	1	94	5	6	4	13	2	.87	9	.289	.356	.412
Schnall, Kevin	c	Dayton	Cin	A	24	2	4	1	0	0	0	1	1	0	1	0	2	0	0	0	0	0	.00	0	.250	.400	.250
Schneider, Matt*	1b	Lynchburg	Pit	A+	23	6	20	4	0	0	0	4	0	0	2	0	7	0	0	0	0	0	.00	0	.200	.273	.200
		Hickory	Pit	A	23	80	305	80	18	0	1	101	35	25	20	0	93	5	0	1	6	2	.75	5	.262	.317	.331
Schneidmiller, Gary	3b	Modesto	Oak	A+	21	77	242	54	11	0	1	68	36	21	61	0	62	1	1	1	4	3	.57	10	.223	.380	.281
Schrager, Tony	2b	Daytona	ChC	A+	24	116	378	87	19	3	9	139	48	49	56	0	83	4	3	3	7	3	.70	2	.230	.333	.368
Schreimann, Eric	c	Piedmont	Phi	A	26	29	110	27	6	0	2	39	7	16	4	0	31	1	0	2	1	1	.50	3	.245	.274	.355
		Clearwater	Phi	A+	26	40	153	36	8	0	2	50	19	21	11	0	29	6	0	1	0	1	.00	5	.235	.310	.327
Schrock, Chris	ss	Chston-SC	TB	A	25	71	216	56	9	0	2	71	28	19	10	0	39	4	3	1	0	1	.00	2	.259	.303	.329
Schuda, Justin*	dh	Hudson Val	TB	A-	20	65	231	62	16	1	3	89	25	27	28	1	70	0	0	3	2	1	.67	2	.268	.344	.385
Schumacher, S.*	c	Peoria	StL	A	24	13	46	13	5	0	0	18	5	5	2	0	6	0	0	0	0	0	.00	0	.283	.313	.391
Scott, Charles	c	Mahoning Vy	Cle	A-	23	1	4	1	0	0	0	1	0	0	1	0	1	0	0	0	0	0	.00	1	.250	.400	.250
Seal, Scott*	of	Salem	Col	A+	25	103	344	92	31	3	6	147	55	35	23	0	75	9	0	1	10	5	.67	6	.267	.329	.427
Seale, Marvin#	of	Capital Cty	NYM	A	22	120	453	132	23	6	6	185	76	37	53	1	125	13	6	1	52	14	.79	7	.291	.381	.408
		St. Lucie	NYM	A+	22	5	17	6	1	0	1	10	5	2	2	0	6	0	1	0	0	1	.00	1	.353	.421	.588
Seestedt, Mike	c	Delmarva	Bal	A	23	59	158	35	6	0	3	50	19	19	16	0	29	1	2	0	2	0	1.00	8	.222	.297	.316
Seever, Brian	of	Cedar Rapds	Ana	A	24	109	380	98	14	5	5	137	74	48	65	4	90	5	4	5	57	11	.84	6	.258	.369	.361
Segar, Jeff	of	Yankees	NYY	R	22	23	83	21	1	0	0	22	11	6	8	0	12	2	0	3	4	0	1.00	0	.253	.323	.265
Segura, Rolando	3b	Lynchburg	Pit	A+	22	108	378	102	19	1	9	150	42	47	25	0	105	8	2	3	0	1	.00	9	.270	.326	.397
Seiber, Antron	of	Red Sox	Bos	R	21	49	196	60	7	1	4	81	36	21	16	0	31	7	0	2	21	5	.81	4	.306	.376	.413
		Lowell	Bos	A-	21	6	21	4	0	1	0	6	2	2	0	0	5	0	0	0	1	0	1.00	0	.190	.190	.286
Sein, Javier*	1b	Billings	Cin	R+	22	57	215	61	11	0	6	90	33	36	13	0	59	1	0	3	1	0	1.00	6	.284	.323	.419
Selander, Craig*	of	Quad City	Min	A	24	45	131	31	7	3	2	50	19	17	13	1	23	0	0	1	1	1	.50	2	.237	.303	.382
Self, Todd*	of	Auburn	Hou	A-	22	52	160	31	3	1	1	39	13	19	28	0	42	4	2	1	10	4	.71	1	.194	.326	.244
Sellier, Brian*	of	Queens	Tor	A-	23	66	209	54	5	4	5	82	34	33	41	0	51	2	1	6	11	2	.85	6	.258	.376	.392
Sena, Sonel	c	Orioles	Bal	R	19	9	28	10	1	0	0	11	3	4	2	0	5	2	0	0	0	0	.00	0	.357	.438	.393
Senjem, Guye*	c	Clinton	Cin	A	26	3	9	4	3	0	1	10	2	2	0	0	3	0	0	0	0	0	.00	0	.444	.444	1.111
Serrano, Eddie	2b	Padres	SD	R	19	29	63	10	0	0	0	10	7	3	9	0	16	1	0	1	4	4	.50	1	.159	.270	.159
Serrano, Raymond	c	Danville	Atl	R+	20	21	67	22	4	0	4	38	16	16	7	0	11	1	0	1	2	0	1.00	0	.328	.395	.567
		Jamestown	Atl	A-	20	21	78	25	4	0	5	44	9	14	2	0	9	1	0	1	1	0	1.00	0	.321	.341	.564
Serrano, Sammy	c	San Jose	SF	A+	24	38	132	24	3	2	2	37	12	17	12	0	30	0	0	1	4	1	.80	5	.182	.248	.280
Shabala, Adam*	of	Salem-Keizr	SF	A-	23	59	176	38	6	3	4	62	27	19	30	0	60	2	0	1	2	1	.67	4	.216	.335	.352
Shackelford, Brian*	of	Wilmington	KC	A+	24	113	423	99	23	1	11	157	44	63	30	4	83	5	2	4	4	1	.80	10	.234	.290	.371
Shaffer, Josh*	ss	Cedar Rapds	Ana	A	21	116	394	94	10	2	1	111	43	36	30	0	73	1	7	4	3	2	.60	4	.239	.291	.282
Sherlock, Jon	c	Diamondbcks	Ari	R	19	26	44	9	2	0	0	11	5	3	10	0	16	1	3	0	0	1	.00	1	.205	.364	.250
Sherrill, J.J.#	dh	Mahoning Vy	Cle	A-	20	24	93	26	6	1	1	37	16	5	14	0	25	3	2	0	9	8	.53	2	.280	.391	.398
Sherrod, Justin	of	Lowell	Bos	A-	23	59	204	46	10	1	5	73	31	20	25	0	74	3	1	2	2	0	1.00	4	.225	.316	.358
Shier, Pete	ss	Orioles	Bal	R	20	6	17	8	3	0	0	11	5	3	11	0	3	2	0	1	2	0	1.00	2	.471	.677	.647
		Bluefield	Bal	R+	20	30	101	20	3	1	2	31	13	10	16	0	32	1	0	1	5	1	.83	3	.198	.311	.307
Shipp, Brian	ss-2b	St. Lucie	NYM	A+	22	42	147	29	4	1	4	47	17	25	6	0	42	4	1	2	8	0	1.00	0	.197	.245	.320
		Capital Cty	NYM	A	22	49	155	28	5	0	2	39	14	6	10	0	57	6	1	1	7	2	.78	5	.181	.256	.252
Sickles, Jeremy	c	Lynchburg	Pit	A+	23	40	115	23	6	0	0	29	8	16	4	0	26	3	2	4	1	0	1.00	4	.200	.238	.252
Silvera, Andrea	2b-3b	Phillies	Phi	R	19	53	193	50	15	2	5	84	27	24	12	0	37	7	1	1	4	5	.44	4	.259	.324	.435
Silvestre, Juan	of	Lancaster	Sea	A+	23	127	506	154	15	3	30	265	104	137	60	1	126	7	0	7	9	6	.60	5	.304	.381	.524
Sing, Brandon	dh-3b	Eugene	ChC	A-	20	61	218	50	11	1	9	90	29	28	35	0	75	2	1	2	4	5	.44	6	.229	.339	.413
Siriveaw, Nom#	3b	Medcine Hat	Tor	R+	20	63	235	57	8	2	8	93	40	40	35	1	64	0	0	0	7	0	1.00	2	.243	.341	.396
Sisk, Aaron	3b-ss	Medcine Hat	Tor	R+	22	59	218	56	10	2	13	109	32	50	34	1	56	3	0	2	4	0	1.00	7	.257	.362	.500
Sitzman, Jim*	of	Piedmont	Phi	A	23	107	418	132	17	8	6	183	95	55	38	3	88	15	2	5	53	12	.82	3	.316	.389	.438
Sizemore, Grady*	of	Expos	Mon	R	18	55	205	60	8	3	1	77	31	14	23	0	24	6	2	0	16	2	.89	1	.293	.380	.376
Skeens, Jeremy	of	Vermont	Mon	A-	23	7	20	2	1	0	0	3	2	0	1	0	8	0	1	0	0	0	.00	0	.100	.143	.150
Sledge, Termel*	of	Wisconsin	Sea	A	24	7	23	5	2	2	0	11	5	3	3	0	3	1	0	0	1	0	1.00	1	.217	.333	.478
		Lancaster	Sea	A+	24	103	384	130	22	7	11	199	90	75	72	3	49	17	1	5	35	11	.76	4	.339	.458	.518
Small, Buster	c	Queens	Tor	A-	23	4	15	2	1	0	0	3	2	1	1	0	5	0	0	0	0	0	.00	0	.133	.188	.200
		Medcine Hat	Tor	R+	23	38	131	29	0	0	0	29	13	6	14	0	23	3	4	1	2	1	.67	2	.221	.309	.221
Smiley, Jermaine*	of	Royals	KC	R	21	6	17	8	1	0	0	9	5	3	9	0	3	1	0	0	3	1	.75	0	.471	.667	.529
		Spokane	KC	A-	21	51	153	34	3	1	0	39	19	17	25	0	56	1	4	1	2	0	1.00	5	.222	.333	.255
Smith, Bradley	ss	Pulaski	Tex	R+	22	35	90	14	2	1	1	21	13	7	13	0	33	6	3	2	1	1	.50	2	.156	.297	.233
Smith, Brett#	of	Chston-SC	TB	A	22	34	103	28	3	0	3	40	14	10	16	0	25	2	2	0	2	2	.50	3	.272	.380	.388
Smith, Corey	3b	Burlington	Cle	R+	19	57	207	53	8	2	4	77	21	39	27	0	50	1	0	4	8	1	.89	4	.256	.339	.372
Smith, Marcus	of	Braves	Atl	R	19	8	16	2	0	0	0	2	1	3	1	0	8	2	0	0	0	0	.00	0	.125	.263	.125
Smith, Nate	dh	Braves	Atl	R	26	1	3	0	0	0	0	0	0	0	0	0	3	0	0	0	0	0	.00	0	.000	.000	.000
Smith, Nestor#	of	Fort Myers	Min	A+	23	106	359	107	21	4	1	139	53	41	34	0	72	5	2	5	6	3	.67	6	.298	.362	.387

2000 Batting — Class-A and Rookie Leagues

BATTING																					BASERUNNING				PERCENTAGES		
Player	Pos	Team	Org	Lg	A	G	AB	H	2B	3B	HR	TB	R	RBI	TBB	IBB	SO	HBP	SH	SF	SB	CS	SB%	GDP	Avg	OBP	SLG
Smith, Ryan	c	Capital Cty	NYM	A	22	26	71	14	2	2	0	20	12	3	19	0	18	4	2	0	1	0	1.00	4	.197	.394	.282
		Pittsfield	NYM	A-	22	16	41	8	3	1	0	13	5	3	10	0	13	0	0	0	0	1	.00	0	.195	.353	.317
Smith, Ryan	of	Billings	Cin	R+	23	48	172	36	9	1	3	56	28	23	36	0	41	6	0	0	13	3	.81	2	.209	.364	.326
Smith, Sam	3b-1b	Salem	Col	A+	22	3	10	1	0	0	0	1	0	1	1	0	3	0	0	0	0	0	.00	1	.100	.182	.100
		Asheville	Col	A	22	94	321	66	14	4	3	97	31	22	22	0	100	14	1	0	6	4	.60	7	.206	.286	.302
Smith, Sean	2b	Pirates	Pit	R	18	21	63	16	2	1	0	20	12	6	9	0	8	1	2	1	3	0	1.00	0	.254	.351	.317
Smith, Will	of	Lowell	Bos	A-	24	51	172	46	5	0	0	51	21	14	38	0	32	5	5	2	20	7	.74	0	.267	.410	.297
Smith, Will*	of	Marlins	Fla	R	19	54	204	75	21	2	2	106	37	34	26	1	24	1	0	1	7	3	.70	3	.368	.440	.520
Smitherman, Steve	of	Billings	Cin	R+	22	70	301	95	16	5	15	166	61	65	23	2	67	6	0	2	14	1	.93	10	.316	.373	.551
Snead, Esix#	of	Potomac	StL	A+	25	132	493	116	14	3	1	139	82	34	72	1	98	7	9	1	109	35	.76	7	.235	.340	.282
Snelling, Chris*	of	Wisconsin	Sea	A	19	72	259	79	9	5	9	125	44	56	34	3	34	6	1	9	7	4	.64	2	.305	.386	.483
Snyder, Earl	1b	St. Lucie	NYM	A+	25	134	514	145	36	0	25	256	84	93	57	6	127	8	0	8	4	4	.50	8	.282	.358	.498
Snyder, Mike*	1b	Hagerstown	Tor	A	20	54	165	30	8	1	1	43	26	13	32	0	48	1	0	0	4	1	.80	2	.182	.318	.261
		Queens	Tor	A-	20	57	227	63	11	3	4	92	28	34	22	1	49	1	0	1	4	3	.57	2	.278	.343	.405
Socarras, Antonio*	c	Boise	Ana	A-	22	55	161	41	9	0	5	65	26	28	24	1	47	4	0	3	0	4	.00	3	.255	.359	.404
Solano, Fausto	dh	Dunedin	Tor	A+	27	50	158	38	8	1	2	54	20	22	19	2	27	3	0	2	6	2	.75	4	.241	.330	.342
Solano, Francisco#	of	Reds	Cin	R	18	33	116	30	6	0	0	36	20	6	21	0	31	2	1	0	11	8	.58	2	.259	.381	.310
Solorzano, Lenin	3b	Burlington	CWS	A	21	70	210	42	2	1	0	46	14	13	11	0	50	4	3	2	6	4	.60	14	.200	.251	.219
Soriano, Carlos	of	Helena	Mil	R+	21	37	123	21	4	1	2	33	16	12	5	0	43	1	0	1	7	2	.78	3	.171	.208	.268
		Beloit	Mil	A	21	9	32	3	1	1	0	6	3	4	2	0	12	0	0	0	0	1	.00	1	.094	.147	.188
Soriano, Jairo#	ss	Orioles	Bal	R	20	36	110	33	4	4	0	45	17	12	19	1	25	2	2	1	10	3	.77	1	.300	.409	.409
Sosa, Francisco	c	Kingsport	NYM	R+	20	32	78	25	2	1	0	29	12	10	2	0	12	2	2	2	12	4	.75	1	.321	.345	.372
Sosa, Jorge#	of	Portland	Col	A-	23	62	200	46	7	5	4	75	24	26	37	0	102	3	0	1	4	6	.40	3	.230	.357	.375
Sosa, Jovanny	of	Hickory	Pit	A	20	117	431	107	16	1	18	179	48	65	40	2	135	7	0	4	3	3	.50	5	.248	.320	.415
Sosa, Nick	1b	Modesto	Oak	A+	23	61	219	61	18	1	6	99	38	44	38	0	64	0	2	2	0	0	.00	6	.279	.382	.452
Soto, Jorge	1b	Visalia	Oak	A+	23	44	119	20	4	0	6	42	17	22	21	0	58	4	1	0	4	1	.80	6	.168	.313	.353
		Vancouver	Oak	A-	23	2	4	0	0	0	0	0	0	0	0	0	2	0	0	0	0	0	.00	0	.000	.000	.000
Soto, Jose#	dh	Marlins	Fla	R	21	42	165	36	9	2	3	58	24	19	12	0	62	4	2	1	8	4	.67	3	.218	.286	.352
Soto, Saul	c	Yakima	LA	A-	22	55	192	49	12	0	6	79	26	26	19	1	46	9	2	0	1	3	.25	5	.255	.350	.411
Soto, T.J.	2b	Auburn	Hou	A-	23	67	235	52	6	4	9	93	40	32	24	0	66	5	0	1	10	2	.83	5	.221	.306	.396
Soules, Ryan*	dh-1b	Tampa	NYY	A+	25	106	336	83	25	1	11	143	50	42	56	1	89	2	0	4	1	0	1.00	7	.247	.354	.426
Southward, D.	of	Quad City	Min	A	23	62	118	21	1	0	0	22	19	12	20	0	34	2	1	3	4	4	.50	3	.178	.301	.186
Sowers, Wil*	1b	Bluefield	Bal	R+	23	59	221	62	14	2	11	113	48	41	37	1	59	1	0	3	4	2	.67	2	.281	.382	.511
Spadt, Eric	3b	Billings	Cin	R+	22	3	12	0	0	0	0	0	1	1	1	0	4	0	0	0	0	0	.00	0	.000	.077	.000
		Clinton	Cin	A	22	13	28	9	1	0	2	16	5	7	7	0	12	1	1	0	0	0	.00	0	.321	.472	.571
Sparks, Stacy	c	Billings	Cin	R+	22	6	22	5	1	0	0	6	2	2	3	1	7	0	0	0	0	0	.00	1	.227	.320	.273
		Dayton	Cin	A	22	6	8	1	0	0	0	1	1	1	1	0	2	0	0	0	0	0	.00	0	.125	.222	.125
		Clinton	Cin	A	22	2	2	0	0	0	0	0	0	0	2	0	1	0	0	0	0	0	.00	0	.000	.500	.000
Specht, Brian#	ss	Lk Elsinore	Ana	A+	20	89	334	90	22	5	2	128	70	35	52	2	80	3	3	3	25	12	.68	6	.269	.370	.383
Spidale, Mike	3b	White Sox	CWS	R	19	21	66	21	2	1	0	25	21	7	17	0	10	2	1	0	16	4	.80	2	.318	.471	.379
Spoerl, Josh	dh	Clinton	Cin	A	22	110	405	116	20	3	10	172	46	57	24	0	106	7	0	5	15	6	.71	6	.286	.333	.425
Sprowl, Jon-Mark*	dh	Lansing	ChC	A	20	2	4	0	0	0	0	0	3	0	3	0	2	0	0	0	0	0	.00	0	.000	.429	.000
		Eugene	ChC	A-	20	40	98	23	2	0	1	28	9	7	14	0	24	0	1	2	3	0	1.00	0	.235	.325	.286
St. Pierre, Maxim	c	W Michigan	Det	A	21	73	229	57	10	1	2	75	41	28	42	1	37	5	2	3	2	2	.50	10	.249	.373	.328
Stanley, Derek	of	Bristol	CWS	R+	21	65	251	64	9	1	1	78	47	33	24	0	39	7	5	3	25	4	.86	3	.255	.333	.311
Stanley, Henry*	of	Martinsvlle	Hou	R+	23	46	165	41	8	6	4	73	34	20	25	0	37	1	0	2	10	4	.71	1	.248	.347	.442
Steele, Alex	of-dh	Lakeland	Det	A+	25	89	286	62	16	0	6	96	43	31	37	0	121	2	0	1	2	1	.67	8	.217	.310	.336
Stegall, Randy	3b	Dayton	Cin	A	26	123	466	144	43	3	5	208	84	60	53	3	81	14	1	1	5	5	.50	13	.309	.395	.446
Sterling, Ivan*	of	Cubs	ChC	R	20	33	98	22	6	1	0	30	19	14	10	0	37	0	1	3	1	1	.50	4	.224	.288	.306
Stevens, Jeff	c	Utica	Fla	A-	24	39	110	22	8	0	0	30	11	9	8	0	29	3	0	1	2	2	.50	3	.200	.270	.273
Stockton, Jeff	ss	Phillies	Phi	R	23	6	16	3	1	0	0	4	2	1	1	1	11	1	0	0	0	0	.00	0	.188	.278	.250
		Butte	Ana	R+	23	51	185	46	11	0	4	69	32	23	16	0	60	2	3	1	3	4	.43	3	.249	.314	.373
Stokes, Greg	3b	Elizabethtn	Min	R+	22	30	76	15	2	0	0	17	10	4	8	0	29	1	0	1	1	2	.33	1	.197	.279	.224
Stone, Jon#	c	Fort Wayne	SD	A	22	12	31	6	0	0	0	6	7	2	6	0	9	2	0	0	1	0	1.00	2	.194	.359	.194
		Padres	SD	R	22	13	30	4	2	0	0	6	2	5	5	0	9	2	0	1	2	0	1.00	1	.133	.289	.200
		Rancho Cuca	SD	A+	22	12	37	9	0	1	0	11	4	2	1	0	13	0	1	0	0	0	.00	0	.243	.263	.297
Stone, Todd	c	Billings	Cin	R+	23	18	47	8	0	0	2	14	8	5	17	0	21	8	1	0	1	1	.50	0	.170	.458	.298
Storey, Eric	3b	Rockies	Col	R	23	47	180	59	13	4	9	107	40	40	36	0	56	3	0	3	10	3	.77	2	.328	.441	.594
		Portland	Col	A-	23	6	20	2	0	0	1	5	3	3	3	0	7	0	1	0	0	0	.00	1	.100	.217	.250
Story-Harden, T.	1b	Great Falls	LA	R+	21	55	177	41	3	3	4	62	27	30	25	0	55	3	1	1	9	1	.90	1	.232	.335	.350
Strange, Mike	3b-2b	Dunedin	Tor	A+	27	16	36	9	2	0	0	11	6	2	11	0	14	0	0	0	0	2	.00	0	.250	.426	.306
Strankman, Elliott	2b	Salem-Keizr	SF	A-	24	3	6	1	0	1	0	3	2	0	0	0	2	0	0	0	0	0	.00	0	.167	.167	.500
Stratton, Rob	of	St. Lucie	NYM	A+	23	108	381	87	18	4	29	200	61	87	60	3	180	8	1	2	3	5	.38	3	.228	.344	.525
Strong, Jamal	of	Everett	Sea	A-	22	75	296	93	7	3	1	109	63	28	52	1	29	4	5	1	60	14	.81	0	.314	.422	.368
Stuart, Rich	of	Lk Elsinore	Ana	A+	24	83	293	72	11	4	9	118	52	39	21	0	56	4	3	3	14	9	.61	5	.246	.302	.403
Suarez, Luis	ss	Winston-Sal	CWS	A+	22	102	346	85	17	3	5	123	39	38	15	0	81	2	8	3	4	4	.50	7	.246	.279	.355
Suarez, Marc	c	Clinton	Cin	A	25	1	2	0	0	0	0	0	0	0	0	0	0	0	0	0	0	0	.00	0	.000	.000	.000
Suarez, Victor#	ss-3b	Royals	KC	R	19	47	127	24	1	2	1	32	10	7	17	1	30	2	1	2	0	3	.00	2	.189	.291	.252
Sulbaran, Orlando	c	Rangers	Tex	R	19	17	36	8	2	0	0	10	9	1	13	0	6	3	1	0	0	0	.00	0	.222	.462	.278
Sullivan, Kevin	c	Batavia	Phi	A-	23	12	34	6	1	0	0	7	4	1	8	0	10	0	2	0	1	0	1.00	0	.176	.333	.206
		Piedmont	Phi	A	23	11	37	12	4	0	0	16	8	4	0	0	4	0	1	1	1	0	1.00	1	.324	.316	.432
Suraci, Scott*	of	Elizabethtn	Min	R+	23	40	130	29	6	0	4	47	22	26	14	1	36	5	0	2	1	2	.33	1	.223	.318	.362
Suriel, Miguel	c	St. Pete	TB	A+	24	94	325	80	14	0	4	106	44	32	31	0	54	2	5	5	3	5	.38	3	.246	.311	.326
Sutter, Tony#	2b	Staten Ilnd	NYY	A-	23	38	72	17	3	0	0	20	14	9	16	1	15	0	0	0	2	1	.67	1	.236	.375	.278
Svihlik, D.J.*	dh	Yankees	NYY	R	23	9	18	6	1	0	0	7	4	3	0	0	3	0	0	1	0	0	.00	0	.333	.316	.389
Swedlow, Sean*	1b-dh	Burlington	Cle	R+	19	36	115	26	5	0	0	31	13	7	23	0	41	2	0	0	1	2	.33	4	.226	.364	.270
Swenson, Leland	3b	Rangers	Tex	R	24	28	70	18	2	0	0	20	8	5	20	1	10	0	2	0	4	1	.80	0	.257	.422	.286

2000 Batting — Class-A and Rookie Leagues

BATTING																					BASERUNNING				PERCENTAGES		
Player	Pos	Team	Org	Lg	A	G	AB	H	2B	3B	HR	TB	R	RBI	TBB	IBB	SO	HBP	SH	SF	SB	CS	SB%	GDP	Avg	OBP	SLG
Tablado, Raul	ss	Queens	Tor	A-	19	52	198	42	8	2	3	63	27	29	31	0	76	1	1	3	1	1	.50	6	.212	.318	.318
Tamburrino, Brett#	2b	Twins	Min	R	19	52	172	42	7	2	0	53	43	25	49	2	27	5	3	1	18	2	.90	3	.244	.423	.308
		Quad City	Min	A	19	8	29	5	0	0	0	5	2	1	2	0	7	2	1	0	1	0	1.00	1	.172	.273	.172
Tapia, Roman	1b-3b	Bristol	CWS	R+	21	13	28	8	1	0	0	9	8	0	6	1	7	0	0	0	1	0	1.00	0	.286	.412	.321
		White Sox	CWS	R	21	27	93	26	7	2	0	37	14	13	10	0	26	1	0	0	1	1	.50	5	.280	.356	.398
Taveras, Frank	3b	Marlins	Fla	R	19	53	182	50	7	0	2	63	25	30	20	0	45	5	0	3	7	2	.78	5	.275	.357	.346
Taveras, Jose	of	Wilmington	KC	A+	24	99	286	62	10	3	0	78	25	15	13	0	73	3	4	2	21	7	.75	4	.217	.257	.273
Taveras, Willy	of	Burlington	Cle	R+	19	50	190	50	4	3	1	63	46	16	23	0	44	6	1	3	36	9	.80	0	.263	.356	.332
Taylor, Seth	2b	Tampa	NYY	A+	23	110	354	73	9	3	4	100	37	32	35	0	53	5	2	5	10	8	.56	11	.206	.283	.282
Teilon, Nilson	2b	Burlington	CWS	A	20	126	466	116	19	2	14	181	61	55	34	0	106	3	1	2	6	9	.40	15	.249	.303	.388
Tejada, Michael#	c	Rockies	Col	R	22	5	17	4	1	0	1	8	4	3	3	0	3	1	0	0	0	0	.00	2	.235	.381	.471
		Portland	Col	A-	22	41	126	29	2	1	2	39	6	19	15	1	42	0	1	2	3	0	1.00	1	.230	.308	.310
Tejero, Armando*	1b	Braves	Atl	R	18	33	93	15	2	0	1	20	9	12	23	0	39	2	0	0	0	0	.00	0	.161	.339	.215
Tellis, Antoine	of-dh	Tigers	Det	R	19	21	59	9	0	0	0	9	6	1	8	0	32	0	1	0	1	1	.50	2	.153	.254	.153
Templeton, Garry	3b	Boise	Ana	A-	22	20	25	4	1	0	0	5	2	1	3	0	11	1	0	0	1	1	.50	0	.160	.276	.200
		Butte	Ana	R+	22	21	80	20	3	2	0	27	19	9	11	0	22	1	1	0	6	1	.86	0	.250	.348	.338
Terni, Chaz	3b-2b	Augusta	Bos	A	22	91	309	65	14	3	3	94	39	24	25	0	91	10	4	2	11	8	.58	7	.210	.289	.304
Terrell, Jeff#	3b	Clearwater	Phi	A+	26	87	317	84	17	3	4	119	27	54	33	3	52	3	3	7	7	5	.58	5	.265	.333	.375
Terrero, Luis	of	High Desert	Ari	A+	21	19	79	15	3	1	0	20	10	1	3	0	16	1	0	0	5	5	.50	2	.190	.229	.253
		Missoula	Ari	R+	21	68	276	72	10	0	8	106	48	44	10	0	75	8	1	1	23	11	.68	5	.261	.305	.384
Terveen, Bryce*	c	Jamestown	Atl	A-	23	55	196	64	11	1	3	86	30	41	23	3	38	2	1	2	0	1	.00	3	.327	.399	.439
Testa, Chris*	of	Rockies	Col	R	20	44	177	61	10	3	2	83	43	30	16	0	24	2	0	2	8	4	.67	0	.345	.401	.469
		Portland	Col	A-	20	5	19	4	1	0	0	5	1	2	0	0	9	0	0	0	1	1	.50	0	.211	.211	.263
Thames, Damon	ss	Peoria	StL	A	24	82	280	65	11	2	3	89	23	29	17	1	59	2	3	4	9	3	.75	4	.232	.277	.318
		Potomac	StL	A+	24	30	104	27	5	0	6	50	12	16	1	0	18	1	2	0	1	0	1.00	3	.260	.274	.481
Thomas, Charles	of	Yakima	LA	A-	21	64	249	75	12	2	2	97	31	28	19	3	59	4	1	2	16	4	.80	5	.301	.358	.390
Thomas, Charles*	of	Jamestown	Atl	A-	22	68	264	80	20	8	1	119	39	25	19	0	58	1	0	1	10	2	.83	7	.303	.351	.451
Thomas, J.J.	dh-1b	Kissimmee	Hou	A+	25	112	380	104	27	1	19	190	58	58	38	0	139	12	1	3	2	5	.29	6	.274	.356	.500
Thomas, Mark*	1b	Jupiter	Mon	A+	25	76	225	54	7	1	0	63	35	17	27	1	58	3	4	1	11	3	.79	5	.240	.328	.280
Thomman, John	of	Twins	Min	R	19	35	107	16	1	2	0	21	15	8	16	0	38	4	3	1	4	1	.80	3	.150	.281	.196
Thompson, Alva	dh	Danville	Atl	R+	24	39	144	46	7	2	6	75	27	26	14	0	31	6	0	4	5	2	.71	6	.319	.393	.521
Thompson, Andy*	c	St. Lucie	NYM	A+	27	38	108	16	4	0	0	20	5	8	10	1	18	3	1	2	0	0	.00	3	.148	.236	.185
Thompson, Craig#	of	Idaho Falls	SD	R+	23	58	218	78	14	1	10	124	52	62	52	3	23	2	2	7	5	2	.71	0	.358	.473	.569
Thompson, Eric*	of	Mahoning Vy	Cle	A-	22	1	3	0	0	0	0	0	0	0	0	0	1	1	0	0	2	0	1.00	0	.000	.250	.000
Thompson, Kevin	dh-2b	Yankees	NYY	R	21	20	75	20	7	1	2	35	13	9	10	0	14	1	0	1	2	3	.40	1	.267	.356	.467
Thompson, Rich*	of	Queens	Tor	A-	22	68	252	66	9	5	1	88	42	27	45	1	57	6	5	0	28	8	.78	0	.262	.386	.349
Thompson, Tyler	of	Dunedin	Tor	A+	25	103	350	98	26	2	11	161	51	57	45	1	93	4	2	2	20	5	.80	5	.280	.367	.460
Thompson, Zach*	of	Helena	Mil	R+	19	43	103	17	3	2	0	24	11	7	17	0	44	6	0	0	1	5	.17	1	.165	.317	.233
Thorman, Scott*	3b	Braves	Atl	R	19	29	97	22	7	1	1	34	15	19	12	0	23	4	0	2	0	1	.00	1	.227	.330	.351
Thornton-Murray, J.#	2b-3b	Cubs	ChC	R	20	50	179	50	10	9	2	84	30	35	14	0	32	1	2	3	3	2	.60	2	.279	.330	.469
Thulin, Tom	of	Butte	Ana	R+	22	7	16	2	0	0	1	5	5	4	6	0	3	0	0	0	1	0	1.00	2	.125	.364	.313
Thurston, Joe*	ss	San Berndno	LA	A+	21	138	551	167	31	8	4	226	97	70	56	1	61	17	9	8	43	25	.63	8	.303	.380	.410
Ticehurst, Brad*	of-dh	Greensboro	NYY	A	24	22	69	17	4	1	0	23	10	10	10	0	26	0	1	1	1	2	.33	0	.246	.338	.333
Tiffee, Terry#	3b-dh	Quad City	Min	A	22	129	493	125	25	0	7	171	59	60	29	0	73	0	0	5	2	0	1.00	14	.254	.292	.347
Timaure, Jesus	of	Marlins	Fla	R	21	20	56	14	4	0	0	18	10	10	6	0	26	0	0	1	0	0	.00	1	.250	.317	.321
		Brevard Cty	Fla	A+	21	1	1	0	0	0	0	0	0	0	0	0	0	0	0	0	0	0	.00	0	.000	.000	.000
		Utica	Fla	A-	21	4	10	3	2	0	0	5	1	1	3	0	2	0	0	0	0	0	.00	1	.300	.462	.500
Tindell, Matt	c	Helena	Mil	R+	21	44	135	27	4	0	0	31	9	7	9	0	35	1	0	0	3	6	.33	4	.200	.255	.230
Toledo, Eduardo#	ss	Mariners	Sea	R	19	36	139	34	3	1	0	39	19	22	11	1	22	1	2	1	3	2	.60	6	.245	.303	.281
Tolli, Barry	of	Lakeland	Det	A+	21	14	40	4	1	1	0	7	4	1	3	0	11	1	0	0	1	1	.50	1	.100	.182	.175
		Oneonta	Det	A-	21	64	242	65	8	3	3	88	29	33	16	0	65	2	2	2	9	5	.64	3	.269	.317	.364
Tomlin, James	of	Twins	Min	R	18	42	145	49	12	0	0	61	24	18	15	0	11	4	1	3	12	3	.80	2	.338	.407	.421
Tommasini, Kevin	of	Bakersfield	SF	A+	26	98	297	76	12	3	8	118	59	47	51	0	81	3	1	3	11	7	.61	8	.256	.367	.397
Tood, Jeremy*	1b	Pittsfield	NYM	A-	27	63	214	53	14	5	5	92	31	47	22	3	52	6	2	3	6	3	.67	3	.248	.331	.430
Toomey, Chris	dh-of	Clinton	Cin	A	23	23	70	13	0	0	0	13	6	6	6	1	16	3	0	0	1	0	1.00	1	.186	.278	.186
Tope, Stephen	dh	Twins	Min	R	19	24	70	17	2	0	1	22	11	10	16	1	20	2	1	0	3	0	1.00	0	.243	.398	.314
Topolski, Jon*	of	Michigan	Hou	A	24	133	475	122	20	12	3	175	84	40	105	1	124	4	12	2	24	22	.52	7	.257	.394	.368
Torrealba, Steve	c	Myrtle Bch	Atl	A+	23	99	334	90	16	0	7	127	43	35	31	0	79	1	4	6	5	1	.83	12	.269	.328	.380
Torres, Digno*	1b	Elizabethtn	Min	R+	21	51	184	46	9	1	5	72	35	31	22	0	32	1	0	0	2	1	.67	3	.250	.333	.391
Torres, Fred	c	Charlotte	Tex	A+	21	80	275	65	18	0	3	92	34	20	19	0	65	4	2	2	1	1	.50	6	.236	.293	.335
Torres, Jason*	c	Savannah	Tex	A	22	94	270	52	15	1	1	72	32	28	29	0	57	4	2	3	2	2	.50	5	.193	.278	.267
Tosca, Dan*	c	Batavia	Phi	A-	20	42	150	39	13	2	0	56	15	16	15	0	34	2	1	3	1	0	1.00	2	.260	.329	.373
Treanor, Matt	c	Brevard Cty	Fla	A+	25	109	350	86	17	0	3	112	51	37	48	0	65	14	4	3	3	3	.50	6	.246	.357	.320
Tritle, Chris	of	Athletics	Oak	R	19	44	150	35	10	1	3	56	30	21	20	0	39	1	1	0	8	1	.89	2	.233	.327	.373
Trout, Casey	3b	Beloit	Mil	A	24	17	57	14	5	0	0	19	8	5	5	0	9	0	3	0	1	0	1.00	2	.246	.306	.333
		Ogden	Mil	R+	24	21	69	14	1	0	0	15	13	10	9	0	10	4	0	1	2	1	.67	9	.203	.325	.217
Truitt, Steve	of	Beloit	Mil	A	23	19	66	12	2	0	2	20	6	4	4	0	20	0	3	0	1	1	.50	0	.182	.229	.303
Trumble, Dan	of	Giants	SF	R	21	42	161	59	15	4	8	106	40	36	15	0	53	6	0	3	9	3	.75	3	.366	.432	.658
		Salem-Keizr	SF	A-	21	15	48	8	1	1	0	11	1	3	6	0	24	1	0	0	1	0	1.00	0	.167	.273	.229
Trzesniak, Nick	c	Idaho Falls	SD	R+	20	36	132	45	6	2	7	76	32	30	23	2	30	4	0	0	4	2	.67	6	.341	.453	.576
Tucker, Mamon	of	Delmarva	Bal	A	21	117	411	98	11	6	1	124	60	54	44	0	88	6	4	4	13	6	.68	5	.238	.318	.302
Turco, Anthony*	c	Salem-Keizr	SF	A-	21	3	12	6	1	0	0	7	3	3	0	0	2	0	0	0	0	0	.00	0	.500	.500	.583
		San Jose	SF	A+	21	28	72	12	2	0	0	14	3	5	6	0	24	0	0	2	0	0	.00	0	.167	.225	.194
Turco, Paul#	2b	Bakersfield	SF	A+	24	33	88	21	0	0	0	21	12	11	21	0	20	0	4	1	1	3	.25	0	.239	.382	.239
Turner, Jason*	1b	Yankees	NYY	R	23	58	207	65	9	2	6	96	35	42	28	0	34	4	0	3	2	2	.50	3	.314	.401	.464
Turnquist, Tyler	3b	Kissimmee	Hou	A+	25	74	246	59	15	1	0	76	25	29	22	1	34	3	2	0	0	1	.00	8	.240	.310	.309
Tyson, Torre#	2b	Greensboro	NYY	A	25	124	475	138	15	3	3	168	87	41	76	2	70	5	7	1	33	14	.70	3	.291	.393	.354

2000 Batting — Class-A and Rookie Leagues

BATTING																					BASERUNNING				PERCENTAGES		
Player	Pos	Team	Org	Lg	A	G	AB	H	2B	3B	HR	TB	R	RBI	TBB	IBB	SO	HBP	SH	SF	SB	CS	SB%	GDP	Avg	OBP	SLG
Ugueto, Luis#	ss	Kane County	Fla	A	22	114	393	92	13	2	1	112	43	32	28	0	83	5	7	4	12	14	.46	10	.234	.291	.285
Umbria, Jose	c	Medcine Hat	Tor	R+	23	14	55	19	2	0	3	30	11	14	11	0	10	0	0	0	0	0	.00	0	.345	.455	.545
		Queens	Tor	A-	23	3	10	5	1	0	0	6	3	4	0	0	0	0	0	0	0	0	.00	0	.500	.500	.600
		Hagerstown	Tor	A	23	27	91	19	2	0	0	21	3	8	8	0	19	1	1	2	0	2	.00	2	.209	.275	.231
Underdown, P.	2b	Batavia	Phi	A-	23	17	56	11	2	0	0	13	6	4	6	0	13	2	0	0	2	0	1.00	1	.196	.297	.232
Uribe, Juan	ss	Salem	Col	A+	20	134	485	124	22	7	13	199	64	65	38	0	100	4	4	2	22	5	.81	11	.256	.314	.410
Uruata, Luis#	1b	Diamondbcks	Ari	R	20	54	183	43	15	2	3	71	31	27	30	0	56	3	1	2	6	1	.86	1	.235	.349	.388
Utley, Chase*	2b	Batavia	Phi	A-	22	40	153	47	13	1	2	68	21	22	18	1	23	2	0	2	5	3	.63	3	.307	.383	.444
Valderrama, Carlos	of	Bakersfield	SF	A+	23	121	435	137	21	5	13	207	78	81	39	1	96	4	5	8	54	11	.83	4	.315	.370	.476
Valdez, Angel	of	Greensboro	NYY	A	23	66	230	71	15	5	3	105	46	29	13	1	58	1	2	3	3	2	.60	3	.309	.344	.457
Valdez, Castulo	c	Chston-SC	TB	A	23	60	126	22	4	1	0	28	13	11	2	0	33	5	1	2	0	0	.00	3	.175	.215	.222
Valdez, Darlin	c	Vermont	Mon	A-	21	12	41	7	1	1	2	16	7	3	7	0	11	0	0	0	2	0	1.00	2	.171	.292	.390
Valdez, Jerry	c	Clearwater	Phi	A+	27	59	218	49	14	1	3	74	24	21	19	1	41	4	0	0	1	1	.50	4	.225	.299	.339
Valdez, Ramon	ss	Butte	Ana	R+	20	30	117	37	7	3	4	62	33	17	15	0	15	1	1	2	11	1	.92	3	.316	.393	.530
Valdez, Tommy	of	Athletics	Oak	R	19	25	54	5	1	1	0	8	8	5	11	0	20	1	1	1	0	1	.00	2	.093	.254	.148
Valdez, Wilson	ss	Cape Fear	Mon	A	21	15	49	12	2	0	0	14	6	3	2	0	9	0	2	0	3	0	1.00	0	.245	.275	.286
		Vermont	Mon	A-	21	65	248	66	8	1	1	79	32	30	17	0	32	1	3	3	16	9	.64	3	.266	.312	.319
Valenzuela, C.	3b	Butte	Ana	R+	20	56	194	58	7	1	1	70	25	26	15	0	31	1	3	5	1	0	1.00	4	.299	.344	.361
Valenzuela, Mario	of	Winston-Sal	CWS	A+	24	138	524	137	31	2	21	235	87	85	59	0	110	2	1	6	11	3	.79	8	.261	.335	.448
Valera, Luis	c	Reds	Cin	R	19	33	114	22	3	0	1	28	8	11	8	0	21	2	0	0	1	1	.50	3	.193	.258	.246
Van Buizen, R.	2b	Yakima	LA	A-	20	48	173	38	4	2	0	46	17	21	13	1	27	3	4	3	4	6	.40	5	.220	.281	.266
Vandemore, Tony*	of	Idaho Falls	SD	R+	24	12	40	10	2	1	0	14	5	5	6	0	10	0	0	1	0	0	.00	1	.250	.340	.350
		Fort Wayne	SD	A	24	10	29	7	2	1	0	11	1	3	4	0	12	1	0	0	0	0	.00	0	.241	.353	.379
Van Horn, Ryan	c	Lansing	ChC	A	23	11	20	4	1	0	0	5	1	2	5	1	3	0	0	0	0	1	.00	0	.200	.360	.250
		Daytona	ChC	A+	23	15	13	2	0	0	0	2	1	1	1	0	2	1	1	0	0	1	.00	0	.154	.267	.154
Van Iten, Bob*	1b	Clearwater	Phi	A+	23	108	390	92	22	0	5	129	52	33	36	4	80	4	4	3	0	0	.00	7	.236	.305	.331
Van Rossum, Chris*	of	Clinton	Cin	A	27	59	216	55	6	2	5	80	28	34	15	0	52	6	0	1	11	3	.79	3	.255	.319	.370
Vargas, Inakel	c	W Michigan	Det	A	23	66	207	51	9	2	2	70	25	19	23	2	31	7	2	1	0	2	.00	6	.246	.340	.338
Varner, Gary	3b	Billings	Cin	R+	20	11	35	9	1	1	0	12	4	3	2	0	10	0	0	0	0	0	.00	1	.257	.297	.343
Vasquez, Alejandro*	of	Kissimmee	Hou	A+	23	61	209	42	5	2	0	51	17	17	11	1	26	4	0	2	8	4	.67	8	.201	.252	.244
		Michigan	Hou	A	23	38	150	36	10	0	1	49	17	17	6	0	16	1	0	3	6	4	.60	4	.240	.269	.327
Vasquez, Jose*	1b-dh	Rockies	Col	R	18	46	177	55	12	5	5	92	37	38	27	0	73	4	0	1	10	2	.83	1	.311	.411	.520
Vasquez, Sandy	of	San Berndno	LA	A+	24	93	331	71	16	3	10	123	55	43	24	0	115	5	5	2	11	8	.58	2	.215	.276	.372
Vega, Jesus	c	Butte	Ana	R+	19	28	91	17	2	0	0	19	0	10	5	0	25	0	1	1	0	1	.00	1	.187	.227	.209
Velazquez, Gil	ss	St. Lucie	NYM	A+	21	125	440	101	16	1	1	122	37	43	25	0	69	9	4	3	3	9	.25	15	.230	.283	.277
Velazquez, Jose*	1b	St. Pete	TB	A+	25	135	513	152	30	2	10	216	60	79	29	5	48	4	0	5	2	2	.50	16	.296	.336	.421
Veleber, Troy#	of	Williamsprt	Pit	A-	22	44	169	40	1	4	1	52	28	15	16	0	31	2	5	0	14	3	.82	5	.237	.310	.308
Venales, Luis	c	Kane County	Fla	A	21	6	13	3	0	0	0	3	1	2	2	0	4	0	0	0	0	0	.00	0	.231	.333	.231
Vento, Mike	of	Tampa	NYY	A+	23	10	30	5	0	0	1	8	1	4	4	0	12	1	1	1	1	0	1.00	0	.167	.278	.267
		Greensboro	NYY	A	23	84	318	83	15	2	6	120	49	52	47	0	66	11	2	3	13	8	.62	11	.261	.372	.377
Ventura, Juan	2b	Portland	Col	A-	20	56	195	43	9	1	1	57	24	15	14	0	36	2	6	2	14	6	.70	6	.221	.277	.292
Victorino, Shane	2b	Yakima	LA	A-	20	61	236	58	7	2	2	75	32	20	20	1	44	3	12	2	21	9	.70	3	.246	.310	.318
Villar, Jose	of	Macon	Atl	A	22	61	216	43	7	1	9	79	36	26	16	0	69	4	1	1	8	6	.57	7	.199	.266	.366
		Jamestown	Atl	A-	22	23	82	14	3	0	1	20	7	8	9	0	23	2	0	0	1	3	.25	1	.171	.269	.244
Villegas, Ernest	1b	Pulaski	Tex	R+	22	47	179	50	16	1	9	95	43	37	22	0	40	9	0	1	11	1	.92	4	.279	.384	.531
Villero, Armando*	of	Beloit	Mil	A	24	6	18	4	0	0	0	4	0	0	0	0	5	0	0	0	0	1	.00	0	.222	.222	.222
		Helena	Mil	R+	24	54	196	60	8	0	2	74	32	18	22	0	26	6	0	0	16	1	.94	8	.306	.393	.378
Vilorio, Miguel	2b	Asheville	Col	A	21	92	363	101	15	3	3	131	47	29	19	0	52	3	7	2	25	17	.60	4	.278	.318	.361
Virgen, Constancio	c	Mexico	—	R	19	39	130	30	6	0	1	39	12	18	12	0	22	2	1	1	0	1	.00	4	.231	.303	.300
Vizcaino, Maximo	ss	Diamondbcks	Ari	R	20	53	211	52	3	3	0	61	27	27	16	0	48	2	2	2	1	3	.25	3	.246	.303	.289
		High Desert	Ari	A+	20	48	160	36	6	2	1	49	11	10	2	0	33	0	1	0	1	2	.33	3	.225	.235	.306
Volquez, Bolivar	ss	St. Pete	TB	A+	19	12	33	5	2	0	0	7	2	4	4	0	9	0	0	0	0	1	.00	3	.152	.243	.212
		Chston-SC	TB	A	19	17	60	8	0	0	0	8	6	4	2	0	12	0	0	0	2	0	1.00	1	.133	.161	.133
		Hudson Val	TB	A-	19	68	217	47	4	0	0	51	16	22	14	0	51	1	9	7	7	9	.44	7	.217	.259	.235
Volquez, Julio#	ss	Rangers	Tex	R	20	42	164	48	10	0	1	61	31	25	17	2	22	2	1	1	10	7	.59	2	.293	.364	.372
Voltz, Robert*	1b	Helena	Mil	R+	23	67	242	69	12	6	12	129	47	53	39	1	66	1	0	3	11	3	.79	4	.285	.382	.533
Voshell, Chase	2b	Peoria	StL	A	24	12	40	12	1	0	1	16	5	5	3	0	6	1	1	0	1	0	1.00	1	.300	.364	.400
Wagner, Jeff	1b	Boise	Ana	A-	24	72	253	64	17	0	12	117	50	53	45	2	62	6	0	5	3	0	1.00	13	.253	.372	.462
Wagner, Mike	of	Fort Wayne	SD	A	23	35	105	19	6	2	1	32	15	5	13	1	53	2	0	0	1	2	.33	2	.181	.283	.305
Wakakuwa, Kenn	dh	Chston-SC	TB	A	23	1	4	2	0	0	0	2	1	0	0	0	0	0	0	0	0	0	.00	0	.500	.500	.500
		St. Pete	TB	A+	23	2	7	2	0	0	0	2	0	0	0	0	2	0	0	0	0	0	.00	0	.286	.286	.286
		Hudson Val	TB	A-	23	7	20	5	1	0	0	6	5	1	1	0	4	0	0	0	1	0	1.00	0	.250	.286	.300
Waldron, Jeff*	c-dh	Augusta	Bos	A	24	16	52	15	1	0	0	16	6	1	8	0	9	0	0	0	0	1	.00	1	.288	.383	.308
		Sarasota	Bos	A+	24	19	38	6	1	0	0	7	4	4	6	0	9	0	0	1	0	0	.00	3	.158	.267	.184
Walker, Mark	of	Salem-Keizr	SF	A-	22	35	95	18	3	1	1	26	12	7	13	0	52	0	0	0	3	1	.75	0	.189	.287	.274
Walker, Matt	of	Oneonta	Det	A-	23	31	115	38	8	0	1	49	16	12	16	0	19	2	0	1	8	1	.89	4	.330	.418	.426
Walkill, Juance	2b	Rockies	Col	R	19	28	120	29	3	3	0	38	26	18	9	0	24	3	0	3	9	3	.75	3	.242	.304	.317
Wallace, Kellen*	of	Butte	Ana	R+	20	34	121	29	5	1	0	36	9	16	8	0	27	1	1	0	0	1	.00	2	.240	.292	.298
Wallis, Jacob	c	Clinton	Cin	A	21	8	14	0	0	0	0	0	0	0	2	1	7	0	0	0	0	0	.00	0	.000	.125	.000
Walter, Scott	c	Spokane	KC	A-	22	13	35	4	1	0	0	5	2	2	1	0	10	0	1	1	1	0	1.00	1	.114	.135	.143
Ward, Brian	2b-dh	Fort Wayne	SD	A	23	106	377	108	24	3	5	153	58	36	56	3	60	5	3	4	4	4	.50	12	.286	.382	.406
Ward, Corey	of	Billings	Cin	R+	22	25	80	21	9	0	3	39	13	11	2	0	32	3	0	0	1	3	.25	0	.263	.306	.488
Ware, Anthony	of	Tigers	Det	R	20	50	147	31	9	2	2	50	21	20	33	0	48	6	0	4	3	1	.75	2	.211	.368	.340
Warner, Bryan*	dh-of	Lansing	ChC	A	26	99	341	93	17	3	10	146	37	52	19	1	45	3	0	5	2	3	.40	9	.273	.313	.428
Warner, J.R.*	of	Boise	Ana	A-	22	74	266	74	14	3	5	109	54	33	42	0	68	4	0	0	6	1	.86	7	.278	.385	.410
Warren, Chris#	3b	Asheville	Col	A	24	77	255	59	15	0	7	95	23	30	29	0	79	2	0	1	12	7	.63	7	.231	.314	.373
Warren, Chris	of	Augusta	Bos	A	24	135	484	125	26	2	15	200	72	61	48	2	152	19	1	2	19	8	.70	11	.258	.347	.413

2000 Batting — Class-A and Rookie Leagues

BATTING																					BASERUNNING				PERCENTAGES		
Player	Pos	Team	Org	Lg	A	G	AB	H	2B	3B	HR	TB	R	RBI	TBB	IBB	SO	HBP	SH	SF	SB	CS	SB%	GDP	Avg	OBP	SLG
Warren, Tom#	1b	Helena	Mil	R+	21	1	3	1	0	0	0	1	1	0	0	0	2	0	1	0	0	0	.00	0	.333	.333	.333
Warriax, Brandon	ss	Rangers	Tex	R	22	7	32	4	2	0	0	6	1	6	3	0	6	0	0	0	1	0	1.00	0	.125	.200	.188
		Charlotte	Tex	A+	22	84	304	63	13	1	4	90	33	39	20	0	74	0	1	1	8	7	.53	7	.207	.255	.296
Warrior, Joseph	of	Mariners	Sea	R	19	7	14	2	0	0	0	2	0	2	1	0	4	0	0	0	0	0	.00	0	.143	.200	.143
Washington, Dion	1b	Greensboro	NYY	A	24	83	279	68	16	0	4	96	31	29	37	1	89	4	0	1	6	1	.86	4	.244	.340	.344
Washington, Kelley	3b	Kane County	Fla	A	21	107	365	75	14	4	1	100	45	30	25	1	113	5	1	4	20	9	.69	6	.205	.263	.274
Watkins, Tommy	2b-ss	Elizabethtn	Min	R+	21	37	114	25	2	1	0	29	15	15	14	0	24	2	2	2	4	1	.80	1	.219	.311	.254
Watson, Brandon*	of	Vermont	Mon	A-	19	69	278	81	9	1	0	92	53	30	25	0	38	3	4	2	26	9	.74	4	.291	.354	.331
Watson, Matt*	dh-of	Jupiter	Mon	A+	22	40	137	24	5	2	0	33	10	8	18	2	23	1	0	0	4	3	.57	6	.175	.276	.241
Weber, Jon*	of	Clinton	Cin	A	23	108	321	71	14	2	6	107	60	34	50	1	50	5	4	2	8	6	.57	5	.221	.333	.333
Weekly, Chris*	3b	Hagerstown	Tor	A	24	66	234	68	15	1	7	106	21	49	22	0	53	1	0	3	2	5	.29	8	.291	.350	.453
		Dunedin	Tor	A+	24	34	120	30	7	0	5	52	23	22	14	0	30	3	1	1	0	2	.00	0	.250	.341	.433
Weichard, Paul#	of	Lynchburg	Pit	A+	21	80	263	66	10	2	5	95	39	26	30	1	84	5	4	1	20	6	.77	9	.251	.338	.361
Welch, Ed*	of	Cedar Rapds	Ana	A	21	32	102	18	0	0	0	18	9	1	9	1	32	0	1	0	9	3	.75	2	.176	.243	.176
		Boise	Ana	A-	21	31	93	20	0	0	0	20	15	11	11	0	27	1	1	0	9	0	1.00	2	.215	.305	.215
Wendt, Justin*	1b-dh	Kingsport	NYM	R+	19	9	33	12	5	0	1	20	4	5	0	0	4	1	0	0	0	1	.00	0	.364	.382	.606
Wenner, Mike	of	Visalia	Oak	A+	22	122	477	113	20	5	3	152	82	53	55	0	91	6	18	6	57	18	.76	6	.237	.320	.319
West, Kevin	of	Quad City	Min	A	21	112	368	88	14	2	6	124	42	54	34	0	85	12	0	5	10	4	.71	8	.239	.320	.337
West, Todd	ss	Helena	Mil	R+	22	57	207	56	6	0	0	62	44	12	28	0	29	7	8	0	7	6	.54	1	.271	.376	.300
		Ogden	Mil	R+	22	5	20	10	3	0	0	13	5	4	2	0	0	1	0	0	1	1	.50	0	.500	.565	.650
Weston, Aron*	of	Hickory	Pit	A	20	82	315	84	13	2	2	107	52	21	36	1	89	1	4	0	28	6	.82	0	.267	.344	.340
White, Greg	1b	Cedar Rapds	Ana	A	25	65	212	48	15	0	5	78	30	35	42	1	63	1	1	0	5	3	.63	4	.226	.357	.368
Whiteman, Tom	ss	Auburn	Hou	A-	21	70	232	58	10	3	1	77	33	22	22	1	52	1	1	0	7	5	.58	7	.250	.318	.332
Whitesides, Jake*	of	Martinsvlle	Hou	R+	20	37	129	23	2	1	1	30	14	6	15	0	49	1	0	1	7	2	.78	0	.178	.267	.233
Wiese, Brian	of	Sarasota	Bos	A+	24	50	165	46	7	1	7	76	28	22	20	0	49	4	1	3	8	4	.67	4	.279	.365	.461
Wigginton, Derek*	dh	Bristol	CWS	R+	22	47	144	52	10	3	5	83	26	26	17	1	23	3	0	3	8	1	.89	2	.361	.431	.576
Wilfong, Nick*	of	Salem-Keizr	SF	A-	22	65	227	64	14	5	5	103	35	31	30	2	83	4	1	1	6	2	.75	3	.282	.374	.454
Wilken, Kris#	3b	Bluefield	Bal	R+	22	58	208	57	10	2	5	86	35	28	34	0	49	1	0	5	1	3	.25	5	.274	.371	.413
William, Jovany	c	Potomac	StL	A+	24	87	314	68	20	1	8	114	37	43	15	2	86	3	4	3	0	3	.00	9	.217	.257	.363
Williams, Brady	dh-3b	Augusta	Bos	A	21	83	267	60	16	1	5	93	41	30	48	0	107	8	1	0	4	1	.80	1	.225	.359	.348
Williams, Charles#	of	Peoria	StL	A	23	82	276	65	12	1	2	85	31	14	36	1	63	5	1	3	11	5	.69	5	.236	.331	.308
Williams, Clyde*	of-1b	Cape Fear	Mon	A	21	72	252	57	12	1	3	80	19	29	14	0	61	3	1	2	2	2	.50	5	.226	.273	.317
Williams, Glenn	2b	Dunedin	Tor	A+	23	107	391	102	26	4	13	175	53	77	33	1	91	6	0	6	4	2	.67	11	.261	.323	.448
Williams, Jason	ss	High Desert	Ari	A+	22	7	27	6	1	0	0	7	4	1	4	0	4	1	0	0	1	0	1.00	1	.222	.344	.259
		Diamondbcks	Ari	R	22	2	5	1	0	0	0	1	1	0	0	0	1	0	0	0	0	0	.00	0	.200	.200	.200
Williams, P.J.	of	Lancaster	Sea	A+	24	51	175	51	3	5	0	64	37	27	28	0	38	1	3	0	20	9	.69	4	.291	.392	.366
Williams, Peanut	1b	Mariners	Sea	R	23	4	17	6	2	0	0	8	6	3	4	1	6	0	0	0	0	0	.00	0	.353	.476	.471
		Lancaster	Sea	A+	23	76	292	74	15	0	8	113	53	55	24	0	109	5	1	1	3	2	.60	6	.253	.320	.387
Williamson, Chris*	of-1b	Dayton	Cin	A	22	21	62	11	2	0	3	22	8	9	7	0	28	4	0	0	1	0	1.00	0	.177	.301	.355
		Billings	Cin	R+	22	25	100	31	10	2	5	60	30	33	22	2	32	0	0	3	2	1	.67	1	.310	.424	.600
Williford, Dan*	dh	High Desert	Ari	A+	24	31	94	18	5	0	0	23	15	5	2	0	31	2	0	0	0	1	.00	0	.191	.224	.245
		Missoula	Ari	R+	24	20	69	16	4	2	0	24	11	2	3	1	16	1	0	0	2	0	1.00	2	.232	.274	.348
Willingham, Josh	of	Utica	Fla	A-	22	65	205	54	16	0	6	88	37	29	39	1	55	9	1	2	9	5	.64	2	.263	.400	.429
Wilson, Brandon	c-dh	Kingsport	NYM	R+	18	8	25	4	0	0	0	4	0	1	1	0	13	1	0	0	0	1	.00	1	.160	.222	.160
Wilson, Heath	c	Burlington	Cle	R+	22	12	32	7	3	1	1	15	4	7	2	0	10	1	0	0	0	0	.00	0	.219	.286	.469
Wilson, Jacob*	3b	Butte	Ana	R+	23	8	15	2	0	0	0	2	2	1	5	0	5	0	0	0	0	0	.00	0	.133	.350	.133
Wilson, John	c-dh	Pittsfield	NYM	A-	22	69	247	80	16	1	0	98	36	48	24	0	30	12	0	5	18	3	.86	4	.324	.403	.397
Wilson, Josh	ss	Utica	Fla	A-	20	66	259	89	13	6	3	123	43	43	29	3	47	5	1	1	9	8	.53	6	.344	.418	.475
		Kane County	Fla	A	20	13	52	14	3	1	1	22	2	6	3	0	14	1	0	1	0	0	.00	2	.269	.316	.423
Wilson, Travis	2b	Myrtle Bch	Atl	A+	23	125	484	133	33	5	12	212	62	63	16	0	111	9	3	4	7	8	.47	9	.275	.308	.438
Winchester, Jeff	c	Asheville	Col	A	21	110	397	104	29	0	17	184	62	73	31	0	109	20	0	5	9	7	.56	7	.262	.342	.463
Winrow, Tommy*	of	Staten Ilnd	NYY	A-	20	63	239	69	7	6	0	88	33	28	21	0	57	3	3	1	5	3	.63	4	.289	.352	.368
Withey, Ryan	of	Boise	Ana	A-	23	16	45	6	2	0	1	11	3	5	5	0	18	8	1	0	3	0	1.00	1	.133	.328	.244
Womack, Robert*	of	Burlington	Cle	R+	22	5	18	2	0	0	0	2	0	3	3	0	6	0	0	0	0	0	.00	1	.111	.238	.111
		Mahoning Vy	Cle	A-	22	31	86	15	2	1	0	19	16	10	20	0	24	3	0	2	9	1	.90	1	.174	.342	.221
Wood, Steve	1b	Medcine Hat	Tor	R+	23	21	88	20	8	0	2	34	14	14	9	2	16	0	0	0	0	0	.00	3	.227	.299	.386
Woodcock, Lance	ss	Mahoning Vy	Cle	A-	24	10	41	7	2	1	0	11	6	3	4	0	19	0	0	1	2	0	1.00	0	.171	.239	.268
Woodrow, Justin*	of	Johnson Cty	StL	R+	19	40	135	38	3	0	0	41	22	14	22	1	29	0	1	0	7	3	.70	3	.281	.382	.304
Woods, Ahmad	of	Braves	Atl	R	19	38	114	21	6	2	1	34	18	16	10	0	30	4	0	1	2	0	1.00	0	.184	.271	.298
Woodward, J.P.*	1b	Idaho Falls	SD	R+	24	68	281	89	26	0	20	175	67	92	43	0	76	5	0	4	9	4	.69	5	.317	.411	.623
Woodward, Steve#	of	High Desert	Ari	A+	23	69	265	69	10	1	2	87	45	25	27	0	74	2	5	4	7	7	.50	3	.260	.329	.328
Woody, Dominic	c-dh	Kane County	Fla	A	22	64	235	55	11	1	5	83	27	22	20	1	54	5	0	2	0	0	.00	4	.234	.305	.353
Wren, Cliff	1b	Vero Beach	LA	A+	24	98	356	88	11	3	6	123	45	40	16	0	55	4	3	3	4	0	1.00	13	.247	.285	.346
Wrenn, Michael	c	Quad City	Min	A	23	52	174	43	9	0	2	58	19	18	9	1	44	9	7	1	4	2	.67	6	.247	.316	.333
Wright, Brad*	of-1b	Capital Cty	NYM	A	25	65	217	60	12	0	2	78	19	23	10	0	37	3	1	3	3	2	.60	6	.276	.313	.359
Wright, Daron*	2b	Batavia	Phi	A-	23	7	20	3	0	0	0	3	0	1	2	0	6	1	0	0	2	0	1.00	0	.150	.261	.150
Wright, Gavin	of	Michigan	Hou	A	22	43	163	47	10	5	2	73	22	19	18	0	37	0	1	2	10	3	.77	2	.288	.355	.448
Wright, Mike	c	San Jose	SF	A+	25	97	299	57	10	1	6	87	29	33	31	0	102	6	10	0	1	0	1.00	6	.191	.280	.291
Wright, Nate	2b-ss	Yakima	LA	A-	23	4	9	2	0	0	0	2	1	2	1	0	4	0	0	0	0	0	.00	0	.222	.300	.222
		Great Falls	LA	R+	23	4	4	0	0	0	0	0	2	0	3	0	0	0	0	0	0	0	.00	0	.000	.429	.000
Yakopich, Joe*	2b	Missoula	Ari	R+	20	48	138	36	9	1	1	50	23	20	27	0	15	3	1	1	6	1	.86	1	.261	.391	.362
Yan, Edwin#	ss	Pirates	Pit	R	19	12	42	15	0	1	0	17	10	1	12	0	8	0	0	0	5	4	.56	1	.357	.500	.405
Yancy, Mike	of	Capital Cty	NYM	A	22	3	11	2	0	0	0	2	1	1	0	0	4	0	0	0	0	1	.00	0	.182	.182	.182
		Pittsfield	NYM	A-	22	18	61	7	1	0	0	8	3	4	3	1	19	1	2	0	1	1	.50	1	.115	.169	.131
Yingling, Joe	1b	Tigers	Det	R	20	16	43	7	1	0	0	8	2	1	5	0	9	0	0	1	0	0	.00	0	.163	.245	.186
Young, Walter*	1b	Pirates	Pit	R	21	45	162	48	11	1	10	91	32	34	8	1	29	9	0	3	3	2	.60	2	.296	.357	.562
		Williamsprt	Pit	A-	21	24	92	17	4	0	2	27	5	12	1	0	26	1	0	1	0	0	.00	1	.185	.200	.293

2000 Batting — Class-A and Rookie Leagues

Player	Pos	Team	Org	Lg	A	G	AB	H	2B	3B	HR	TB	R	RBI	TBB	IBB	SO	HBP	SH	SF	SB	CS	SB%	GDP	Avg	OBP	SLG
Youngbauer, Scott#	ss	Batavia	Phi	A-	22	66	251	59	16	2	6	97	41	35	22	0	40	0	1	4	0	0	.00	9	.235	.292	.386
Zapey, Winton	c	Utica	Fla	A-	21	28	75	7	1	0	1	11	9	7	8	0	21	0	3	0	0	2	.00	0	.093	.181	.147
Zapp, A.J.*	1b	Myrtle Bch	Atl	A+	23	107	385	103	28	1	8	157	59	49	57	3	106	10	0	0	3	2	.60	4	.268	.376	.408
Zaragoza, Joel	2b	Pittsfield	NYM	A-	28	54	163	29	9	1	0	40	18	13	12	1	44	6	8	2	3	0	1.00	2	.178	.257	.245
Zoccolillo, Pete*	of	Lansing	ChC	A	24	109	358	104	22	2	8	154	58	56	46	5	47	8	0	4	5	2	.71	4	.291	.380	.430
Zumwalt, Alec	of	Danville	Atl	R+	20	59	204	48	15	2	3	76	27	28	38	0	67	5	0	0	5	5	.50	4	.235	.368	.373

2000 Pitching — Class-A and Rookie Leagues

HOW MUCH HE PITCHED											WHAT HE GAVE UP												THE RESULTS					
Player	Team	Org	Lg	A	G	GS	CG	GF	IP	BFP	H	R	ER	HR	SH	SF	HB	TBB	IBB	SO	WP	Bk	W	L	Pct.	ShO	Sv	ERA
Abbott, David	Medcine Hat	Tor	R+	23	8	4	0	0	22.2	95	19	11	5	0	1	3	1	6	0	18	1	0	2	1	.667	0	0	1.99
Abbott, Jim	Elizabethtn	Min	R+	21	2	2	0	0	12.1	47	9	4	3	1	0	0	0	1	0	19	2	0	0	0	.000	0	0	2.19
Abell, Joe	Portland	Col	A-	23	24	0	0	12	31.2	128	19	11	11	2	0	3	2	12	1	28	0	0	1	1	.500	0	3	3.13
Abrams, Grant	Danville	Atl	R+	21	18	0	0	10	28.1	128	33	19	15	0	1	0	1	10	0	30	1	0	2	5	.286	0	0	4.76
Abreu, Jonathan*	Giants	SF	R	18	8	0	0	1	14	71	21	16	9	0	2	0	2	7	1	12	1	0	0	1	.000	0	0	5.79
Acevedo, Jose	Dayton	Cin	A	23	25	23	0	2	141	610	135	74	61	16	1	4	6	53	0	123	6	0	11	5	.688	0	0	3.89
Achilles, Matt	Frederick	Bal	A+	24	26	26	0	0	150	667	166	75	57	13	2	5	12	65	0	137	7	0	8	11	.421	0	0	3.42
Acosta, Jhon	Lansing	ChC	A	21	5	0	0	0	10	45	6	7	6	2	0	1	0	10	0	9	0	0	0	0	.000	0	0	5.40
Acosta, Manuel	Yankees	NYY	R	20	12	10	0	1	62.1	270	64	28	24	3	4	0	0	21	0	46	1	0	4	2	.667	0	0	3.47
Adames, Martin	Giants	SF	R	20	10	0	0	5	17.2	86	22	11	8	2	0	0	1	11	1	11	0	2	3	0	1.000	0	0	4.08
Adams, Brian*	Lowell	Bos	A-	23	12	10	0	0	52.2	225	61	30	26	2	2	4	0	13	0	38	1	0	3	4	.429	0	0	4.44
Adams, Dan	Batavia	Phi	A-	23	23	0	0	13	29	124	27	8	7	0	4	3	4	13	4	30	3	1	2	0	1.000	0	5	2.17
Advincola, Jose*	Bluefield	Bal	R+	21	17	0	0	1	30.1	155	43	26	26	6	0	1	6	21	0	22	11	1	1	0	1.000	0	0	7.71
Affeldt, Jeremy*	Wilmington	KC	A+	22	27	26	0	0	147.1	656	158	87	67	7	8	5	10	59	0	92	17	1	5	15	.250	0	0	4.09
Aguilar, Mario*	Mexico	—	R	22	5	5	0	0	25	118	33	20	19	2	0	1	1	11	0	16	0	1	0	1	.000	0	0	6.84
Aguilera, Adrian*	San Berndno	LA	A+	21	9	0	0	6	11.2	56	10	13	13	1	2	0	3	9	1	4	2	0	0	1	.000	0	1	10.03
	Yakima	LA	A-	21	17	0	0	12	36.2	164	36	21	16	1	5	0	1	14	0	36	2	1	0	3	.000	0	5	3.93
Akens, Phil	Marlins	Fla	R	18	18	0	0	7	35.2	162	33	21	19	2	0	0	9	15	0	35	5	0	4	0	1.000	0	3	4.79
Akin, Aaron	Brevard Cty	Fla	A+	24	17	16	0	0	82.1	368	91	56	39	5	2	1	6	33	0	51	4	0	3	8	.273	0	0	4.26
Albers, Mike*	Burlington	Cle	R+	25	6	0	0	2	8.2	42	11	9	8	0	1	2	2	5	0	7	1	1	0	2	.000	0	0	8.31
Albertus, Roberto*	Braves	Atl	R	19	9	8	0	0	35.2	163	52	22	18	1	0	1	1	11	0	27	5	1	3	3	.500	0	0	4.54
	Jamestown	Atl	A-	19	4	1	0	1	11.2	47	7	3	2	0	1	0	0	4	0	13	0	0	2	0	1.000	0	0	1.54
Albin, Scott	Jupiter	Mon	A+	25	49	0	0	25	67	290	66	31	22	2	7	3	2	23	3	51	1	0	4	3	.571	0	2	2.96
Albright, Eric	Eugene	ChC	A-	23	27	0	0	19	42.2	179	45	19	17	4	0	2	0	8	2	36	2	0	1	5	.167	0	6	3.59
Alcala, Jason	Williamsprt	Pit	A-	20	17	8	1	6	63.2	270	67	26	23	3	1	5	0	22	1	49	2	3	2	4	.333	0	1	3.25
Alcantara, Over	Marlins	Fla	R	20	14	10	0	4	54.1	244	66	33	24	1	0	2	4	9	0	32	3	3	2	4	.333	0	2	3.98
Allen, Rodney	Mudville	Mil	A+	27	16	3	0	2	31	151	40	25	17	2	0	2	4	14	0	34	2	2	0	2	.000	0	0	4.94
Almeida, Brian	Braves	Atl	R	19	11	9	0	0	43.2	193	40	22	16	1	0	2	2	20	0	35	4	1	2	6	.250	0	0	3.30
Alston, Travis	Piedmont	Phi	A	24	5	2	0	2	13	62	13	9	7	2	0	0	0	10	0	8	2	0	0	1	.000	0	0	4.85
	Batavia	Phi	A-	24	20	5	1	13	47	218	43	19	14	0	5	0	3	28	2	40	3	0	3	2	.600	1	6	2.68
Altman, Gene	Dayton	Cin	A	22	9	0	0	3	16.2	83	17	10	7	0	1	0	1	13	0	16	0	0	2	0	1.000	0	0	3.78
	Beloit	Mil	A	22	33	0	0	27	37.2	163	32	11	9	1	0	0	6	18	0	42	2	0	4	0	1.000	0	17	2.15
Alvarez, Larry	Eugene	ChC	A-	21	18	0	0	7	32.2	149	33	21	14	0	3	0	2	12	0	34	2	0	1	1	.500	0	0	3.86
Alvarez, Oscar*	Burlington	Cle	R+	20	16	1	0	2	37.2	166	32	29	19	2	1	3	1	19	0	39	3	0	2	3	.400	0	0	4.54
Alvarez, Wilson*	St. Pete	TB	A+	31	1	1	0	0	4	12	0	0	0	0	0	0	0	0	0	2	0	0	0	0	.000	0	0	0.00
Amancio, Jose	Athletics	Oak	R	19	14	6	0	3	34	173	53	46	26	4	2	4	5	12	0	20	2	1	3	3	.500	0	0	6.88
Ammons, Cary*	Wilmington	KC	A+	24	17	9	1	4	80	338	79	34	29	4	4	3	4	30	0	85	7	0	3	4	.429	0	2	3.26
Andersen, Derek*	Chston-SC	TB	A	23	15	0	0	9	19.2	86	25	11	9	3	1	0	0	2	0	22	1	0	1	1	.500	0	0	4.12
Anderson, Craig*	Wisconsin	Sea	A	20	26	26	1	0	157.2	659	161	81	65	14	4	5	6	40	1	131	2	3	11	8	.579	0	0	3.71
Anderson, Jason	Staten Ilnd	NYY	A-	22	15	15	0	0	80.1	342	84	41	36	1	2	2	5	25	0	73	5	4	6	5	.545	0	0	4.03
Anderson, Julius	Princeton	TB	R+	21	11	8	1	0	47.2	223	61	36	26	4	0	5	3	18	0	26	3	0	4	4	.500	0	0	4.91
Anderson, Luke	Salem-Keizr	SF	A-	23	25	0	0	19	31	124	19	5	5	1	2	1	1	10	0	55	3	0	1	0	1.000	0	12	1.45
Anderson, Travis	Michigan	Hou	A	23	27	27	2	0	143	646	142	99	81	14	4	5	9	73	1	106	18	0	8	10	.444	1	0	5.10
Anderson, Wes	Brevard Cty	Fla	A+	21	22	21	0	0	115.2	517	108	55	44	5	2	4	4	66	1	91	5	1	6	9	.400	0	0	3.42
Andrade, Jancy	Delmarva	Bal	A	23	29	19	0	0	114	499	121	76	68	7	2	3	3	43	1	99	3	4	7	7	.500	0	0	5.37
Andrews, Aron	Great Falls	LA	R+	23	19	0	0	14	25	105	19	6	6	0	0	0	3	7	0	25	2	0	5	0	1.000	0	4	2.16
Andujar, Jesse	Phillies	Phi	R	21	2	1	0	0	5	21	3	3	2	0	0	0	1	4	0	4	1	0	0	0	.000	0	0	3.60
Anez, Omar	Orioles	Bal	R	20	15	8	0	3	51	235	55	38	27	5	2	2	1	31	2	45	15	1	3	3	.500	0	0	4.76
Aramboles, Ricardo	Greensboro	NYY	A	21	25	25	2	0	137.2	603	150	81	66	12	3	1	5	47	0	150	9	0	5	13	.278	0	0	4.31
Arellan, Felix*	Great Falls	LA	R+	20	13	0	0	3	17.2	115	25	21	12	0	0	0	2	30	0	24	12	0	0	1	.000	0	0	6.11
Arellano, Salvador	Padres	SD	R	18	14	6	0	1	42	216	69	41	33	2	1	2	5	16	0	34	6	1	0	5	.000	0	0	7.07
Arias, Miguel	Royals	KC	R	21	18	1	0	7	27.1	128	26	20	12	0	0	2	3	17	1	17	7	0	1	3	.250	0	2	3.95
Arias, Pablo	Lakeland	Det	A+	22	5	5	0	0	27.2	120	26	21	18	2	0	5	3	13	0	21	1	1	2	1	.667	0	0	5.86
	W Michigan	Det	A	22	15	13	0	0	84	336	61	26	23	8	1	3	4	30	1	54	2	0	6	3	.667	0	0	2.46
Armitage, Barry	Royals	KC	R	22	5	3	0	0	10	40	9	3	2	0	0	0	0	1	0	10	0	0	0	1	.000	0	0	1.80
Armstrong, Jack	Brevard Cty	Fla	A+	36	4	4	0	0	17	70	15	14	12	3	1	0	3	6	0	13	0	0	1	1	.500	0	0	6.35
Arthurs, Shane	Cape Fear	Mon	A	21	14	14	0	0	70.1	321	88	40	33	5	1	2	6	26	0	40	6	0	4	3	.571	0	0	4.22
Artieta, Corey*	Beloit	Mil	A	24	32	5	0	8	90.1	404	94	48	35	7	1	5	2	38	4	63	5	0	7	3	.700	0	0	3.49
Artiles, Carlos*	Yankees	NYY	R	20	17	0	0	3	25.2	119	26	11	7	0	2	0	0	13	0	33	5	0	1	2	.333	0	0	2.45
Artman, Dane*	Ogden	Mil	R+	19	7	7	0	0	25.1	123	35	18	15	2	0	0	1	11	0	19	1	1	1	0	1.000	0	0	5.33
Ascencio, Miguel	Clearwater	Phi	A+	20	5	5	0	0	33	132	22	10	10	2	0	0	0	17	0	24	1	1	2	1	.667	0	0	2.73
	Batavia	Phi	A-	20	7	7	1	0	39.2	165	32	23	22	3	1	1	3	17	0	28	2	0	2	2	.500	0	0	4.99
Ashlock, Chad	Salem-Keizr	SF	A-	22	2	2	0	0	4	21	5	2	1	0	0	0	0	4	0	2	1	0	0	0	.000	0	0	2.25
Askew, Will*	Padres	SD	R	22	14	0	0	3	16.1	79	16	13	9	2	2	0	0	13	0	17	2	0	0	1	.000	0	0	4.96
Atencio, Donald	Athletics	Oak	R	19	11	5	0	1	34.2	177	46	40	29	2	0	7	6	26	0	23	10	0	1	3	.250	0	1	7.53
Avery, Paul*	Vero Beach	LA	A+	24	22	10	0	8	63.1	313	92	67	50	9	0	5	2	31	1	34	7	1	2	5	.286	0	0	7.11
	High Desert	Ari	A+	24	3	0	0	1	3	20	8	6	6	1	0	1	0	4	0	2	1	0	0	0	.000	0	0	18.00
Axelson, Josh	New Jersey	StL	A-	22	15	14	0	0	73.2	330	79	53	42	2	2	3	4	34	0	63	9	0	3	9	.250	0	0	5.13
Babula, Shaun*	Delmarva	Bal	A	24	9	0	0	4	14	60	13	2	1	0	1	0	2	4	0	11	0	0	1	0	1.000	0	0	0.64
	Frederick	Bal	A+	24	37	0	0	17	46.1	206	40	25	17	4	3	2	3	25	2	47	1	0	3	2	.600	0	2	3.30
Backsmeyer, Justin	Savannah	Tex	A	21	40	0	0	21	72	314	60	37	33	7	1	2	6	35	1	54	2	1	9	1	.900	0	0	4.13
Baek, Cha	Wisconsin	Sea	A	21	24	24	0	0	127.2	547	137	71	56	13	6	2	5	36	0	99	6	0	8	5	.615	0	0	3.95
Baerlocher, Ryan	Chston-WV	KC	A	23	19	19	0	0	113.2	457	88	43	27	6	0	0	3	33	0	139	5	0	5	6	.455	0	0	2.14
	Wilmington	KC	A+	23	8	8	0	0	51.1	206	35	18	17	3	3	1	2	17	0	54	0	1	5	1	.833	0	0	2.98
Bailey, David	Lansing	ChC	A	24	45	0	0	27	57	240	45	16	16	3	4	4	3	25	0	48	0	0	1	3	.250	0	14	2.53
Bailie, Matt	Piedmont	Phi	A	25	44	0	0	17	71.1	285	50	15	11	2	4	6	2	24	0	82	1	0	7	0	1.000	0	6	1.39
Baisley, Brad	Clearwater	Phi	A+	21	16	15	2	1	89	391	95	47	37	9	0	2	3	34	0	60	4	0	3	9	.250	0	1	3.74

2000 Pitching — Class-A and Rookie Leagues

HOW MUCH HE PITCHED											WHAT HE GAVE UP												THE RESULTS					
Player	Team	Org	Lg	A	G	GS	CG	GF	IP	BFP	H	R	ER	HR	SH	SF	HB	TBB	IBB	SO	WP	Bk	W	L	Pct.	ShO	Sv	ERA
Bajenaru, Jeff	Bristol	CWS	R+	23	12	0	0	11	14.1	61	10	6	6	2	0	0	0	5	0	31	2	0	1	1	.500	0	5	3.77
	Winston-Sal	CWS	A+	23	10	0	0	7	12.1	52	7	6	6	1	0	3	2	5	0	15	4	0	2	0	1.000	0	2	4.38
Baker, Brad	Augusta	Bos	A	20	27	27	0	0	137.2	591	125	58	47	3	3	6	15	55	0	126	10	0	12	7	.632	0	0	3.07
Baker, Brett	Marlins	Fla	R	19	1	0	0	0	0	0	0	0	0	0	0	0	0	0	0	0	0	0	0	0	.000	0	0	0.00
Baker, Chris	Dunedin	Tor	A+	23	41	6	0	10	104	440	91	50	37	11	2	1	5	29	2	85	9	1	9	5	.643	0	5	3.20
Baker, Joey	Spokane	KC	A-	22	14	14	0	0	63	291	77	48	38	5	3	0	4	25	0	31	3	0	4	4	.500	0	0	5.43
Baker, Ryan	Jamestown	Atl	A-	23	21	2	0	12	34.1	141	33	14	13	2	1	0	0	13	0	36	1	1	4	2	.667	0	3	3.41
Balbuena, Caleb	Wisconsin	Sea	A	24	12	11	1	1	62	269	51	28	23	1	2	1	10	37	0	46	1	1	5	3	.625	0	1	3.34
	Lancaster	Sea	A+	24	21	3	0	11	39.2	185	47	29	20	3	2	1	3	18	2	24	2	0	3	1	.750	0	3	4.54
Baldassano, Joe	Butte	Ana	R+	21	25	0	0	12	37	212	58	50	42	5	0	3	8	34	1	28	15	0	1	5	.167	0	0	10.22
Balfour, Grant	Fort Myers	Min	A+	23	35	10	0	13	89	392	91	46	42	8	3	1	8	34	2	90	10	1	8	5	.615	0	6	4.25
Baranowski, B.	Chston-WV	KC	A	24	10	0	0	4	17.2	87	22	14	10	4	0	1	0	13	0	19	0	0	1	1	.500	0	0	5.09
	Spokane	KC	A-	24	19	0	0	3	36.2	154	20	14	10	1	1	1	1	24	1	44	5	1	2	0	1.000	0	2	2.45
Barber, Scott	Diamondbcks	Ari	R	22	2	1	0	0	3	11	0	1	1	0	0	0	0	2	0	4	0	0	0	0	.000	0	0	3.00
	High Desert	Ari	A+	22	4	4	0	0	15.2	69	18	15	12	0	0	2	1	5	0	12	0	1	0	2	.000	0	0	6.89
Barnett, Aaron*	W Michigan	Det	A	24	46	0	0	13	62.2	295	68	39	29	1	3	5	3	40	2	33	3	0	2	2	.500	0	4	4.16
Barr, Adam*	Columbus	Cle	A	20	13	13	0	0	59	288	77	46	38	2	2	4	3	48	0	41	4	0	3	5	.375	0	0	5.80
Barreto, Joel	Quad City	Min	A	20	14	0	0	6	24	109	21	12	12	1	1	0	1	19	3	26	5	0	2	1	.667	0	0	4.50
	Elizabethtn	Min	R+	20	22	0	0	15	31.1	140	30	18	15	2	2	0	1	18	1	36	9	0	1	3	.250	0	3	4.31
Barrett, Jimmy	Martinsvlle	Hou	R+	20	13	13	0	0	66.2	294	60	37	35	4	0	1	10	32	0	72	4	1	6	2	.750	0	0	4.73
Bartlett, Richard	Orioles	Bal	R	19	10	9	0	0	39.2	181	46	25	19	2	1	0	6	21	2	32	1	0	0	4	.000	0	0	4.31
Bartosh, Cliff*	Fort Wayne	SD	A	21	50	4	0	18	77	335	50	40	26	6	2	3	5	44	3	94	8	2	8	4	.667	0	1	3.04
Bass, Brian	Royals	KC	R	19	12	9	0	0	44	200	36	27	19	0	1	1	9	18	0	44	10	0	3	5	.375	0	0	3.89
	Chston-WV	KC	A	19	1	1	0	0	4	18	6	3	3	0	0	0	0	0	0	1	0	0	0	0	.000	0	0	6.75
Bastardo, Jose*	Giants	SF	R	20	6	0	0	4	6.1	41	6	14	13	0	0	0	2	14	0	7	1	0	0	0	.000	0	0	18.47
Batchelor, Rich	Tampa	NYY	A+	34	8	0	0	8	7.2	40	10	6	5	0	1	0	0	6	3	7	1	0	0	2	.000	0	2	5.87
Batista, Javier	Mariners	Sea	R	19	12	3	0	2	39	188	54	33	24	2	2	0	3	21	0	14	10	2	3	1	.750	0	0	5.54
Batista, Roberto	Johnson Cty	StL	R+	19	7	7	0	0	37.2	167	42	23	13	2	0	2	1	13	0	12	3	0	1	3	.250	0	0	3.11
Batson, Byron	Ogden	Mil	R+	22	20	0	0	7	51.2	240	54	38	28	3	4	0	5	29	2	45	3	0	0	3	.000	0	3	4.88
Bauer, Greg	Yakima	LA	A-	23	21	0	0	16	33.2	148	26	17	13	2	1	1	2	19	4	50	5	2	2	1	.667	0	9	3.48
Bauer, Pete	Hagerstown	Tor	A	22	9	9	0	0	32	141	37	27	18	2	2	3	3	8	0	22	4	0	1	5	.167	0	0	5.06
Baum, David*	Pirates	Pit	R	21	2	0	0	1	4.1	17	2	0	0	0	0	0	0	0	0	4	0	0	0	0	.000	0	0	0.00
	Williamsprt	Pit	A-	21	14	0	0	5	24.2	121	36	19	16	1	0	2	2	12	0	25	1	0	1	1	.500	0	0	5.84
Bausher, Andy*	Lynchburg	Pit	A+	24	30	5	0	10	66.1	299	77	48	44	8	4	2	6	27	0	44	1	1	1	5	.167	0	0	5.97
	Rancho Cuca	SD	A+	24	5	0	0	2	5.2	28	6	4	2	0	2	0	0	4	1	3	0	0	1	0	1.000	0	0	3.18
Bautista, Denny	Marlins	Fla	R	18	11	11	2	0	63	260	49	24	17	1	1	0	8	17	1	58	3	1	6	2	.750	0	0	2.43
	Utica	Fla	A-	18	1	1	0	0	5	21	4	3	2	0	0	0	1	2	0	5	0	0	0	0	.000	0	0	3.60
Baxter, Gerik	Fort Wayne	SD	A	21	20	19	0	0	100.2	418	81	46	38	5	1	6	6	44	0	103	7	0	5	6	.455	0	0	3.40
Bazan, Juan	Williamsprt	Pit	A-	23	3	1	0	0	12.1	45	6	2	2	1	0	0	1	1	0	10	0	0	0	0	.000	0	0	1.46
	Hickory	Pit	A	23	15	0	0	12	20.2	94	15	8	4	1	4	1	0	14	0	15	0	0	3	4	.429	0	1	1.74
Bazzell, Shane	Modesto	Oak	A+	22	32	5	0	10	72	331	91	57	46	6	1	4	1	30	4	71	7	1	3	4	.429	0	1	5.75
Beal, Andy*	Staten Ilnd	NYY	A-	22	14	14	1	0	92.1	361	72	27	24	6	3	0	2	17	0	87	8	1	9	3	.750	1	0	2.34
Bean, Colter	Staten Ilnd	NYY	A-	24	3	0	0	2	2	14	3	3	1	0	0	0	0	3	1	2	0	1	0	0	.000	0	0	4.50
	Greensboro	NYY	A	24	18	0	0	9	25.2	110	21	16	14	1	0	0	1	11	0	35	4	0	1	0	1.000	0	0	4.91
Bechler, Steve	Frederick	Bal	A+	21	27	27	2	0	162	712	179	98	87	19	3	1	6	57	1	137	6	0	8	12	.400	0	0	4.83
Beckett, Josh	Kane County	Fla	A	21	13	12	0	0	59.1	232	45	18	14	4	5	0	2	15	0	61	1	1	2	3	.400	0	0	2.12
Beckman, Jacob	Modesto	Oak	A+	22	11	0	0	5	14	69	16	8	7	0	0	2	1	15	2	4	0	2	1	0	1.000	0	0	4.50
	Vancouver	Oak	A-	22	12	0	0	8	19.2	81	13	3	2	0	2	0	1	9	2	11	0	0	3	2	.600	0	1	0.92
Bedard, Erik*	Delmarva	Bal	A	22	29	22	1	2	111	466	98	48	44	2	1	0	10	35	0	131	14	0	9	4	.692	1	2	3.57
Beigh, David	Pirates	Pit	R	20	7	4	0	0	22	89	24	15	9	2	0	1	1	4	0	13	3	0	1	1	.500	0	0	3.68
Belanger, Brandon	Idaho Falls	SD	R+	23	31	0	0	26	34	148	35	19	18	5	2	0	1	8	0	27	1	1	3	1	.750	0	12	4.76
Belicic, Adam*	Butte	Ana	R+	22	17	0	0	5	30.2	144	38	24	11	1	0	1	4	12	0	29	3	0	1	2	.333	0	3	3.23
	Cedar Rapds	Ana	A	22	6	0	0	2	10	50	17	8	8	2	0	0	0	7	0	5	1	0	1	0	1.000	0	0	7.20
Belisle, Matt	Macon	Atl	A	21	15	15	1	0	102.1	392	79	37	27	7	2	3	4	18	0	97	7	0	9	5	.643	0	0	2.37
	Myrtle Bch	Atl	A+	21	12	12	0	0	78.2	314	72	32	30	5	3	5	2	11	0	71	9	1	3	4	.429	0	0	3.43
Bell, Casey	Fort Wayne	SD	A	22	3	0	0	0	4.1	20	3	2	1	0	0	0	0	6	0	2	1	0	1	0	1.000	0	0	2.08
	Butte	Ana	R+	22	3	1	0	0	6	31	11	8	6	1	0	0	0	2	0	4	2	0	1	1	.500	0	0	9.00
	Lk Elsinore	Ana	A+	22	3	0	0	1	3.2	21	5	8	5	0	1	2	0	4	0	2	1	0	0	1	.000	0	0	12.27
Bell, Heath	St. Lucie	NYM	A+	23	48	0	0	37	60	241	43	19	17	4	2	2	2	21	2	75	1	0	5	1	.833	0	23	2.55
Bell, Tom	Marlins	Fla	R	20	7	0	0	5	14.2	60	11	4	3	0	1	0	1	8	1	3	0	0	1	0	1.000	0	2	1.84
Bello, Jilberto	Delmarva	Bal	A	24	34	0	0	11	64.1	266	58	27	22	3	1	0	2	18	1	33	7	1	2	2	.500	0	0	3.08
	Frederick	Bal	A+	24	4	0	0	1	8	47	17	10	7	0	1	0	2	5	0	3	0	0	0	0	.000	0	0	7.88
Belovsky, Josh	Sarasota	Bos	A+	27	51	0	0	43	63.1	305	83	36	29	5	5	1	2	31	6	72	5	1	3	8	.273	0	14	4.12
Belson, Greg	Missoula	Ari	R+	22	3	0	0	3	5	18	4	2	1	1	0	0	0	0	0	4	0	0	1	0	1.000	0	1	1.80
	High Desert	Ari	A+	22	22	0	0	21	25.1	107	19	8	7	3	1	0	0	13	0	23	2	0	2	0	1.000	0	8	2.49
Beltran, Francis	Lansing	ChC	A	20	16	0	0	11	17.2	97	24	22	19	0	0	3	4	19	0	16	4	0	1	1	.500	0	0	9.68
	Eugene	ChC	A-	20	25	0	0	13	43.2	180	28	16	13	1	1	1	1	20	2	52	6	0	2	2	.500	0	8	2.68
Beltre, Omar	Rangers	Tex	R	18	13	13	0	0	61	251	54	30	24	2	1	2	6	15	0	44	2	2	5	4	.556	0	0	3.54
Beltre, Sandy	Bristol	CWS	R+	19	4	4	0	0	22	90	19	13	9	3	1	1	1	6	0	15	3	0	2	1	.667	0	0	3.68
Benedetti, John	Hudson Val	TB	A-	23	26	0	0	17	41.1	178	44	26	19	3	2	0	0	17	4	37	0	0	4	3	.571	0	3	4.14
Benitez, Fabricio	Red Sox	Bos	R	20	1	1	0	0	1	8	4	3	2	0	0	0	0	1	0	0	0	0	0	1	.000	0	0	18.00
Bennett, Jamie*	Batavia	Phi	A-	23	25	0	0	12	31.1	133	23	18	13	2	1	1	1	13	1	37	3	1	4	1	.800	0	1	3.73
Bennett, Jeff	Hickory	Pit	A	21	27	27	1	0	171.2	761	189	116	84	14	5	7	16	47	1	126	11	2	10	13	.435	0	0	4.40
Bennett, Steve	Pittsfield	NYM	A-	24	13	13	0	0	54.1	222	42	25	17	1	0	2	8	17	0	50	3	3	4	4	.500	0	0	2.82
Bent, Andy	Danville	Atl	R+	22	16	5	0	6	47.1	197	42	18	14	1	3	1	4	11	1	55	1	4	5	2	.714	0	1	2.66
Bentley, Brian	Lowell	Bos	A-	22	21	0	0	12	38.1	147	28	8	8	0	3	0	1	7	0	48	2	0	4	1	.800	0	3	1.88
Bergman, Dusty*	Cedar Rapds	Ana	A	23	28	25	6	0	163.2	727	174	102	71	12	9	2	5	60	0	108	10	0	4	15	.211	1	0	3.90

2000 Pitching — Class-A and Rookie Leagues

HOW MUCH HE PITCHED											WHAT HE GAVE UP												THE RESULTS					
Player	Team	Org	Lg	A	G	GS	CG	GF	IP	BFP	H	R	ER	HR	SH	SF	HB	TBB	IBB	SO	WP	Bk	W	L	Pct.	ShO	Sv	ERA
	Lk Elsinore	Ana	A+	23	1	1	0	0	4	18	3	4	1	0	0	0	0	1	0	3	0	0	0	1	.000	0	0	2.25
Bermudez, Manny	Bakersfield	SF	A+	24	59	0	0	25	120.1	487	107	41	38	3	9	2	9	27	3	66	4	0	9	7	.563	0	7	2.84
Berney, Scott	Portland	Col	A-	23	15	0	0	6	21.2	102	29	22	21	1	0	0	1	12	0	14	0	2	0	0	.000	0	0	8.72
Berry, Casey	Rangers	Tex	R	20	12	12	0	0	46.2	196	48	26	21	3	0	2	1	13	0	38	0	0	1	2	.333	0	0	4.05
Berry, Jon	San Berndno	LA	A+	23	40	0	0	24	68.2	310	57	33	24	3	6	2	5	47	2	68	6	0	7	4	.636	0	5	3.15
Berryman, Brian	Padres	SD	R	23	9	0	0	6	12.2	74	23	21	16	2	0	0	2	9	0	2	1	0	1	0	1.000	0	1	11.37
Berryman, Chad	Lk Elsinore	Ana	A+	24	25	0	0	8	37	169	46	32	29	4	2	1	1	13	1	22	7	0	0	4	.000	0	2	7.05
	Cedar Rapds	Ana	A	24	11	10	1	1	54.2	259	70	45	38	7	6	0	4	27	0	34	5	0	2	2	.500	1	0	6.26
Berube, Martin	Orioles	Bal	R	19	9	9	0	0	47.1	199	43	21	16	4	1	1	1	13	0	39	1	0	2	1	.667	0	0	3.04
	Bluefield	Bal	R+	19	5	5	0	0	29.1	121	34	15	15	4	0	2	1	4	0	22	0	1	1	1	.500	0	0	4.60
Bess, Steve	Lakeland	Det	A+	24	26	0	0	11	36	178	40	26	22	2	2	2	1	27	2	23	6	0	1	3	.250	0	5	5.50
Betancourt, E.	Princeton	TB	R+	19	13	11	0	0	46.2	232	60	48	38	7	2	1	8	23	0	31	7	1	1	5	.167	0	0	7.33
Bevis, P.J.	Missoula	Ari	R+	20	14	14	0	0	83.2	354	92	50	31	4	1	2	2	22	1	63	8	1	3	6	.333	0	0	3.33
Bimeal, Matt	Medcine Hat	Tor	R+	20	21	0	0	8	43.1	199	55	40	29	8	1	3	1	13	0	50	8	2	1	0	1.000	0	0	6.02
Bingler, Travis*	White Sox	CWS	R	24	19	0	0	12	21.2	103	30	25	16	2	1	1	0	11	1	15	0	0	2	2	.500	0	3	6.65
Birdsong, Tim	Dayton	Cin	A	24	20	13	2	1	78	359	100	56	45	5	2	2	3	24	0	61	3	1	6	6	.500	0	0	5.19
Blackwell, Scott	Elizabethtn	Min	R+	21	4	4	0	0	16.2	66	14	7	6	1	0	0	1	5	1	18	2	0	1	1	.500	0	0	3.24
	Quad City	Min	A	21	11	8	0	2	47	199	40	24	23	3	1	3	5	23	3	27	5	2	3	3	.500	0	0	4.40
Blair, David*	Orioles	Bal	R	23	14	0	0	3	13.2	75	17	17	6	1	1	2	4	18	2	4	3	0	1	3	.250	0	0	3.95
Blake, Peter*	Quad City	Min	A	22	18	0	0	6	26	122	30	18	13	2	1	2	0	18	3	18	5	0	2	2	.500	0	0	4.50
Blanco, Tommy	Padres	SD	R	19	13	0	0	6	20.2	84	23	10	10	0	3	2	1	0	0	10	2	0	1	1	.500	0	1	4.35
Blankenshi, John*	Yankees	NYY	R	22	6	2	0	2	24.2	97	17	4	3	1	0	1	1	4	0	19	0	0	2	0	1.000	0	0	1.09
Blevins, Jeremy	Tampa	NYY	A+	23	42	12	0	26	95.1	417	96	50	47	5	2	2	3	49	2	104	6	1	3	7	.300	0	20	4.44
Blood, Darin	Bakersfield	SF	A+	26	4	2	0	1	3	23	4	5	5	0	0	0	1	10	0	0	1	0	0	1	.000	0	0	15.00
	Giants	SF	R	26	2	0	0	1	3.2	19	3	4	4	0	0	0	2	3	0	3	2	0	0	1	.000	0	0	9.82
	San Jose	SF	A+	26	1	0	0	1	1	9	2	3	3	0	0	0	0	4	0	1	1	0	0	0	.000	0	0	27.00
Bludau, Frank	Reds	Cin	R	24	10	3	0	5	28.1	112	22	9	5	0	3	2	0	6	0	23	2	0	2	4	.333	0	1	1.59
	Dayton	Cin	A	24	2	0	0	1	4	14	2	0	0	0	0	0	0	0	0	1	0	0	1	0	1.000	0	0	0.00
Bluma, Marc	Hagerstown	Tor	A	24	48	0	0	19	67.1	306	75	48	32	3	3	4	5	27	3	52	1	0	2	2	.500	0	1	4.28
Bohannan, Kyle	Bristol	CWS	R+	23	15	0	0	11	24.2	99	16	5	3	0	2	3	3	10	2	29	1	0	4	2	.667	0	4	1.09
	Winston-Sal	CWS	A+	23	4	0	0	3	5.2	22	5	2	2	0	1	1	0	0	0	5	0	0	0	1	.000	0	2	3.18
Bohannon, Gary	St. Lucie	NYM	A+	25	39	3	0	14	90.2	375	81	38	26	5	3	3	7	24	2	63	0	0	6	4	.600	0	2	2.58
Bolson, Mike	Vermont	Mon	A-	23	21	0	0	6	29.2	137	30	25	19	1	1	2	2	19	0	18	2	1	3	3	.500	0	1	5.76
Bond, Aaron	Charlotte	Tex	A+	24	3	1	0	0	7.1	38	13	6	5	0	0	0	0	5	0	4	1	0	0	0	.000	0	0	6.14
Bong, Jung*	Macon	Atl	A	20	20	19	0	0	112.2	500	119	65	53	4	5	3	14	45	0	90	10	2	7	7	.500	0	0	4.23
	Myrtle Bch	Atl	A+	20	7	6	0	0	41.1	163	33	14	10	1	1	0	5	7	0	37	4	0	3	1	.750	0	0	2.18
Bonilla, Ben*	Missoula	Ari	R+	23	2	0	0	0	4.1	18	4	4	3	0	0	0	0	3	0	3	1	0	0	0	.000	0	0	6.23
	South Bend	Ari	A	23	11	9	0	0	45.1	210	65	39	30	3	1	5	2	16	0	23	4	2	1	4	.200	0	0	5.96
	High Desert	Ari	A+	23	1	0	0	1	1	5	1	1	1	0	0	1	0	1	0	0	0	0	0	0	.000	0	0	9.00
Bonilla, Vincente	Quad City	Min	A	22	15	10	1	2	62	277	70	39	31	3	6	3	3	25	1	50	7	0	2	8	.200	0	0	4.50
Bonser, Boof	Salem-Keizr	SF	A-	19	10	9	0	0	33	145	21	23	22	2	1	2	1	29	0	41	4	0	1	4	.200	0	0	6.00
Borne, Matt	Burlington	CWS	A	24	25	5	0	10	56.2	279	78	46	34	9	4	4	6	30	3	41	5	1	1	6	.143	0	0	5.40
Borrell, Danny*	Yankees	NYY	R	22	1	1	0	0	3	11	2	1	0	0	0	0	0	0	0	2	1	0	0	1	.000	0	0	0.00
	Staten Ilnd	NYY	A-	22	10	10	0	0	56.1	224	39	21	20	2	1	1	2	19	0	44	1	0	4	2	.667	0	0	3.20
Bottenfield, Jason	Augusta	Bos	A	24	14	0	0	4	26.1	132	44	28	21	3	2	1	3	6	0	21	2	0	1	2	.333	0	0	7.18
	Lowell	Bos	A-	24	1	0	0	0	2.1	8	0	0	0	0	0	0	0	1	0	0	0	0	0	0	.000	0	0	0.00
Boughey, Bill	Phillies	Phi	R	24	15	2	0	2	38.1	172	46	19	10	1	2	1	0	6	0	33	1	1	2	2	.500	0	0	2.35
Bouie, Aaron	Orioles	Bal	R	22	2	0	0	0	3.2	19	6	4	3	0	0	0	0	3	0	5	1	0	0	0	.000	0	0	7.36
	Bluefield	Bal	R+	22	10	7	0	0	36.2	163	38	24	18	1	0	2	3	18	0	29	6	2	1	4	.200	0	0	4.42
Boutwell, Andy	Billings	Cin	R+	21	23	0	0	11	30	143	22	21	17	3	1	0	1	33	0	24	3	2	4	1	.800	0	4	5.10
Bowe, Brandon	Kane County	Fla	A	25	61	0	0	25	79.2	345	73	36	33	4	2	4	5	32	0	89	5	0	7	3	.700	0	6	3.73
Bowen, Chad	Kingsport	NYM	R+	19	11	11	0	0	63	274	59	22	21	4	2	0	4	23	0	41	2	0	7	2	.778	0	0	3.00
Bowers, Robert	Rangers	Tex	R	23	20	0	0	14	35	157	35	26	18	2	2	0	3	14	2	24	1	0	2	3	.400	0	5	4.63
Bowyer, Travis	Twins	Min	R	19	12	12	1	0	55.1	250	55	31	25	2	2	2	8	22	0	36	5	0	3	5	.375	0	0	4.07
Boyer, Blaine	Braves	Atl	R	19	11	5	0	2	32.1	142	24	16	9	0	0	0	3	19	0	27	3	2	1	3	.250	0	1	2.51
Bradley, Bobby	Hickory	Pit	A	20	14	14	3	0	82.2	336	62	31	21	3	1	4	4	21	0	118	2	0	8	2	.800	0	0	2.29
Bradley, David	Clinton	Cin	A	23	41	4	0	13	88.1	353	61	37	32	3	2	2	4	41	3	84	7	0	3	6	.333	0	4	3.26
Bravo, Franklin	Lynchburg	Pit	A+	22	20	12	0	2	75.2	355	91	60	53	7	2	5	6	34	1	55	6	0	2	9	.182	0	0	6.30
Brazoban, Jose	Helena	Mil	R+	20	24	0	0	13	31.1	166	42	30	27	3	1	0	5	32	2	25	6	2	2	1	.667	0	2	7.76
Brewer, Clint	Dayton	Cin	A	22	16	1	0	4	37	172	53	36	29	5	1	2	3	8	0	26	3	2	1	4	.200	0	0	7.05
Bridenbaugh, C.*	Yakima	LA	A-	21	7	6	0	0	37.2	161	48	19	17	2	0	0	0	10	0	24	1	0	2	3	.400	0	0	4.06
	San Berndno	LA	A+	21	11	0	0	3	20.1	103	29	20	18	6	1	1	1	10	0	18	5	0	2	0	1.000	0	1	7.97
Bridges, Doug*	Lk Elsinore	Ana	A+	24	31	22	1	3	140	626	166	103	89	15	7	9	3	62	0	85	10	2	6	10	.375	0	0	5.72
Brito, Eude*	Phillies	Phi	R	19	9	7	0	1	49.2	205	38	20	14	1	0	1	3	19	0	42	10	0	3	5	.375	0	0	2.54
	Batavia	Phi	A-	19	4	3	0	1	18.1	75	16	14	11	0	0	0	1	3	0	11	5	0	1	1	.500	0	0	5.40
Brito, Jose	Reds	Cin	R	20	4	0	0	0	10	53	16	13	12	3	1	1	1	5	0	8	3	0	1	0	1.000	0	0	10.80
Brito, Juan*	Expos	Mon	R	25	2	0	0	2	5	21	3	2	2	1	0	0	0	2	0	3	0	1	1	0	1.000	0	0	3.60
	Cape Fear	Mon	A	25	14	0	0	11	25	111	30	15	12	2	0	2	4	7	0	15	4	0	2	0	1.000	0	1	4.32
Brookman, Ryan	Batavia	Phi	A-	24	9	1	0	6	22	101	27	11	10	2	0	1	3	8	1	17	0	0	0	2	.000	0	2	4.09
	Piedmont	Phi	A	24	8	1	0	4	17.1	65	12	5	5	2	0	2	0	2	0	7	2	0	2	0	1.000	0	1	2.60
Brooks, Conor	Vancouver	Oak	A-	23	18	8	0	3	62.1	260	60	31	24	3	1	1	1	18	2	56	4	1	2	2	.500	0	0	3.47
Brooks, Frank*	Piedmont	Phi	A	22	29	27	3	1	177.2	734	152	78	68	17	7	8	14	60	0	138	8	1	14	8	.636	2	0	3.44
Brous, David*	San Jose	SF	A+	21	9	7	0	1	33.1	143	26	17	17	1	1	0	0	23	0	25	2	1	1	3	.250	0	0	4.59
Brown, Derek	Frederick	Bal	A+	24	41	0	0	31	51.2	221	52	25	23	4	1	3	2	13	0	39	4	0	2	5	.286	0	8	4.01
Brown, Paul*	Dayton	Cin	A	22	14	1	0	2	33.2	148	42	23	20	2	2	2	4	8	0	11	2	2	1	0	1.000	0	0	5.35
	Billings	Cin	R+	22	5	5	0	0	27.2	126	35	23	22	4	2	4	2	12	1	17	1	0	1	2	.333	0	0	7.16
Bruback, Matt	Lansing	ChC	A	22	9	9	2	0	55.1	237	49	23	18	2	1	0	4	19	0	36	3	1	4	2	.667	0	0	2.93

2000 Pitching — Class-A and Rookie Leagues

HOW MUCH HE PITCHED											WHAT HE GAVE UP												THE RESULTS					
Player	Team	Org	Lg	A	G	GS	CG	GF	IP	BFP	H	R	ER	HR	SH	SF	HB	TBB	IBB	SO	WP	Bk	W	L	Pct.	ShO	Sv	ERA
	Daytona	ChC	A+	22	18	18	0	0	89	409	101	57	48	6	5	4	6	50	1	69	12	0	5	5	.500	0	0	4.85
Brueggemann, D.*	Salem	Col	A+	25	44	0	0	21	52.1	228	51	31	24	1	4	4	3	16	0	41	4	0	3	1	.750	0	1	4.13
Bruney, Brian	Diamondbcks	Ari	R	19	20	2	0	11	25	131	21	23	18	2	0	1	6	29	0	24	5	1	4	1	.800	0	2	6.48
Buchanan, Brian*	Greensboro	NYY	A	24	19	0	0	6	22.1	99	22	9	9	1	0	1	0	15	0	19	3	0	0	0	.000	0	1	3.63
Buchholz, Taylor	Phillies	Phi	R	19	12	7	0	2	44	188	46	22	11	2	0	1	2	14	0	41	3	1	2	3	.400	0	0	2.25
Bucktrot, Keith	Phillies	Phi	R	20	11	7	0	0	37.2	166	39	21	20	5	0	0	1	19	0	40	3	2	3	2	.600	0	0	4.78
Buglovsky, Chris	Portland	Col	A-	21	14	12	0	0	65	273	50	30	19	5	0	2	3	32	1	50	4	2	5	5	.500	0	0	2.63
Buirley, Matt	Lynchburg	Pit	A+	25	11	0	0	3	16.1	85	17	14	10	2	1	0	2	17	0	18	6	0	0	1	.000	0	0	5.51
	Dayton	Cin	A	25	16	0	0	10	20	100	17	14	14	2	0	3	5	20	0	20	8	0	1	1	.500	0	1	6.30
Bukowski, Stan	Cedar Rapds	Ana	A	19	5	5	0	0	19.2	105	26	29	25	2	1	3	4	17	0	15	2	0	0	5	.000	0	0	11.44
	Boise	Ana	A-	19	5	0	0	2	3.2	19	5	3	3	1	0	0	1	2	0	3	3	0	0	0	.000	0	0	7.36
Bukvich, Ryan	Spokane	KC	A-	23	10	0	0	8	14	56	5	1	1	0	1	0	1	9	0	15	1	0	2	0	1.000	0	2	0.64
	Chston-WV	KC	A	23	11	0	0	9	14.1	57	6	3	3	0	2	0	1	7	0	17	1	0	0	0	.000	0	4	1.88
	Wilmington	KC	A+	23	2	0	0	0	2	15	3	4	4	0	1	0	1	5	2	3	1	0	0	1	.000	0	0	18.00
Bullard, Jason	Bakersfield	SF	A+	32	58	0	0	52	65	287	69	33	29	6	3	2	4	26	1	65	5	0	4	4	.500	0	30	4.02
Buller, Sean*	Lakeland	Det	A+	25	29	1	0	13	49.2	212	45	19	11	3	0	1	0	18	1	29	3	0	5	2	.714	0	1	1.99
Bullinger, Trey	Spokane	KC	A-	23	16	0	0	4	22.1	105	23	9	9	2	0	0	1	15	0	38	1	0	2	1	.667	0	0	3.63
Bullock, Jeremiah*	Savannah	Tex	A	21	4	4	0	0	15.1	80	22	18	12	3	2	1	1	6	0	11	2	0	1	3	.250	0	0	7.04
Bullock, Trevor*	Batavia	Phi	A-	24	15	7	1	4	62	264	57	23	18	2	0	0	3	17	3	54	1	0	6	3	.667	0	1	2.61
Bumatay, Mike*	Williamsprt	Pit	A-	21	7	0	0	6	12.2	53	10	4	4	1	0	0	0	7	0	17	2	1	1	0	1.000	0	2	2.84
	Hickory	Pit	A	21	16	0	0	13	25.1	108	20	7	5	1	2	0	2	12	0	32	1	1	3	0	1.000	0	8	1.78
Burch, Matt	Wilmington	KC	A+	24	32	17	0	2	113.2	517	125	82	68	11	8	1	12	59	2	71	5	2	5	9	.357	0	0	5.38
Buret, Jorge	Rockies	Col	R	19	14	9	0	0	52.2	224	50	21	14	2	2	3	4	14	0	29	2	2	5	1	.833	0	0	2.39
Burger, Rob	Asheville	Col	A	25	3	0	0	2	6.1	27	4	3	2	0	0	1	1	2	0	4	0	0	0	0	.000	0	0	2.84
	Salem	Col	A+	25	8	0	0	4	14	68	9	10	9	0	1	0	4	15	0	15	3	1	0	1	.000	0	0	5.79
Burgess, Richie	Johnson Cty	StL	R+	21	9	9	0	0	43.1	203	59	37	34	5	3	3	4	16	0	26	2	0	1	4	.200	0	0	7.06
Burke, Erick*	W Michigan	Det	A	23	21	0	0	16	32	165	45	27	25	4	2	0	0	28	1	32	2	0	1	1	.500	0	0	7.03
	Lakeland	Det	A+	23	12	0	0	3	17.2	91	20	17	10	2	0	2	4	15	1	13	3	0	0	1	.000	0	0	5.09
Burnau, Ryan	Cubs	ChC	R	19	10	5	0	1	37	175	46	27	22	1	0	3	5	14	0	33	4	1	2	2	.500	0	0	5.35
Burnett, Sean*	Pirates	Pit	R	18	8	6	0	1	31	128	31	17	14	0	0	1	0	3	0	24	2	1	2	1	.667	0	0	4.06
Burns, Casey	Fort Wayne	SD	A	23	5	3	0	0	11.2	57	13	13	13	0	0	0	3	9	0	12	2	3	1	1	.500	0	0	10.03
Burns, Mike	Martinsvlle	Hou	R+	22	12	12	0	0	65.2	286	75	52	33	12	4	2	4	9	0	51	2	1	2	7	.222	0	0	4.52
Burton, O.J.	Everett	Sea	A-	24	3	0	0	3	3	12	4	2	1	1	0	0	0	0	0	3	0	0	0	0	.000	0	0	3.00
	Wisconsin	Sea	A	24	17	0	0	8	24.1	109	26	11	8	0	1	2	1	13	0	15	1	0	2	0	1.000	0	1	2.96
Bussard, Jesse	Idaho Falls	SD	R+	23	20	0	0	8	24	118	27	24	17	3	0	1	4	13	0	18	7	0	0	0	.000	0	1	6.38
Bustillos, Oscar	Princeton	TB	R+	21	13	0	0	8	17	65	9	4	3	0	0	0	1	5	0	25	2	0	0	1	.000	0	2	1.59
Butler, John	Everett	Sea	A-	23	30	0	0	25	38	159	22	12	6	0	4	3	4	18	3	39	1	1	5	2	.714	0	10	1.42
Butler, Matt	Macon	Atl	A	21	26	26	2	0	156	661	132	75	51	13	1	10	2	66	0	122	5	1	13	7	.650	2	0	2.94
Button, Sammy*	Columbus	Cle	A	23	3	3	0	0	4.1	36	9	17	17	4	0	1	1	13	0	4	0	0	0	3	.000	0	0	35.31
	Mahoning Vy	Cle	A-	23	11	6	0	0	40.2	178	44	24	19	4	1	3	0	15	0	42	2	1	2	2	.500	0	0	4.20
Byard, Dave	Kingsport	NYM	R+	23	17	0	0	12	20	94	20	10	9	1	1	1	1	12	2	19	2	0	2	1	.667	0	4	4.05
Bye, Chris	Vermont	Mon	A-	23	22	0	0	10	36	159	27	15	9	1	0	0	2	20	0	39	3	0	3	3	.500	0	2	2.25
Bynum, Matt	Reds	Cin	R	20	8	0	0	6	13.1	67	11	5	5	0	2	0	3	14	0	9	4	0	1	1	.500	0	0	3.38
	Billings	Cin	R+	20	8	2	0	3	18.1	100	24	23	16	3	1	2	1	18	1	18	2	0	0	2	.000	0	1	7.85
Byrd, Mike	Columbus	Cle	A	23	2	0	0	0	3	20	7	10	8	2	0	0	0	3	0	0	0	0	0	2	.000	0	0	24.00
Byron, Terence	Kane County	Fla	A	22	6	4	0	0	23.2	102	18	16	11	1	0	1	0	15	0	13	1	0	1	2	.333	0	0	4.18
Cabell, Shannon*	Williamsprt	Pit	A-	22	16	0	0	7	31.1	140	32	20	17	2	0	3	2	12	0	33	0	1	2	1	.667	0	0	4.88
Cabrera, Fernando	Burlington	Cle	R+	19	13	13	0	0	68.1	282	64	42	35	4	2	2	4	20	0	50	14	0	3	7	.300	0	0	4.61
Cabrera, Walin	Burlington	Cle	R+	19	10	0	0	3	13	73	20	20	15	1	0	2	1	10	0	10	3	1	0	1	.000	0	0	10.38
Cabrera, Yunior*	Kingsport	NYM	R+	20	13	7	0	1	45.2	201	44	23	14	1	3	0	1	21	1	44	3	2	4	1	.800	0	0	2.76
Calandriello, D.*	Athletics	Oak	R	25	2	2	0	0	1.2	9	3	1	1	0	0	0	0	1	0	1	0	0	0	0	.000	0	0	5.40
Cali, Carmen*	New Jersey	StL	A-	22	14	14	0	0	70	301	68	45	38	3	2	3	5	30	0	55	11	0	2	7	.222	0	0	4.89
Calvo, Jose	Michigan	Hou	A	21	4	3	0	0	14.2	70	15	13	12	2	0	3	0	11	0	15	1	0	2	1	.667	0	0	7.36
	Auburn	Hou	A-	21	5	5	0	0	22	99	26	12	11	1	1	1	2	6	0	17	2	0	1	1	.500	0	0	4.50
Calzada, Javier	Visalia	Oak	A+	22	31	24	1	2	150	643	149	83	78	25	4	2	6	55	1	127	4	0	7	8	.467	0	2	4.68
Camelia, Aron	Yankees	NYY	R	21	2	0	0	1	1.1	8	1	1	0	0	0	0	0	3	0	1	0	0	0	0	.000	0	0	0.00
Cameron, Ryan	Salem	Col	A+	23	26	26	1	0	160.1	715	152	81	64	9	7	5	9	78	0	168	12	2	13	7	.650	0	0	3.59
Campbell, Dayle	Tigers	Det	R	22	11	8	0	1	45.2	205	39	21	19	0	1	1	8	25	0	32	11	1	1	3	.250	0	0	3.74
Campbell, Jarrett	Hudson Val	TB	A-	21	21	0	0	7	37.2	172	41	25	16	2	3	1	2	20	1	42	4	1	0	2	.000	0	0	3.82
Campos, David*	Brevard Cty	Fla	A+	23	2	0	0	1	6	29	7	3	3	0	0	1	1	4	0	4	2	0	0	0	.000	0	0	4.50
	Utica	Fla	A-	23	15	5	0	4	37.2	160	33	19	15	4	1	1	2	16	0	42	3	0	0	2	.000	0	2	3.58
Campos, Juan	Auburn	Hou	A-	21	29	0	0	13	61	248	44	21	13	1	3	3	4	19	0	59	5	1	3	1	.750	0	7	1.92
Canale, Tom	Mahoning Vy	Cle	A-	21	11	0	0	2	22.1	105	24	9	9	1	0	0	3	5	0	19	0	1	0	1	.000	0	0	3.63
Candelario, Delvis	Bristol	CWS	R+	21	12	12	1	0	59.1	273	63	42	35	4	3	5	10	30	2	59	6	0	2	7	.222	0	0	5.31
Caple, Chance	Potomac	StL	A+	22	22	22	0	0	125	529	128	68	61	11	4	4	6	34	0	97	5	3	7	9	.438	0	0	4.39
Capuano, Chris*	South Bend	Ari	A	22	18	18	0	0	101.2	408	68	35	25	2	4	1	5	45	0	105	2	2	10	4	.714	0	0	2.21
Caraballo, Angel	Bristol	CWS	R+	21	13	13	0	0	77.1	319	67	39	27	8	3	2	2	27	0	61	6	0	7	4	.636	0	0	3.14
Caraccioli, Lance*	San Berndno	LA	A+	23	34	9	0	12	105.2	476	105	56	46	8	3	3	6	68	1	95	4	2	10	3	.769	0	4	3.92
Carbajal, Alex*	Hudson Val	TB	A-	23	21	0	0	7	28	123	26	13	7	1	1	2	1	9	1	32	3	3	1	1	.500	0	0	2.25
Cardwell, Brian	Hagerstown	Tor	A	20	11	6	0	2	31.2	154	41	38	32	7	0	1	1	21	0	29	2	1	0	5	.000	0	0	9.09
	Queens	Tor	A-	20	12	11	1	1	49.2	213	49	32	26	6	2	3	6	19	0	61	4	0	2	4	.333	0	0	4.71
Carr, Tim	Wilmington	KC	A+	23	45	0	0	27	58.2	275	74	35	25	2	3	2	5	27	3	39	2	1	1	2	.333	0	0	3.84
Carter, Justin*	Salem	Col	A+	24	17	17	1	0	106.2	480	113	61	49	4	9	4	3	58	0	75	6	0	5	8	.385	0	0	4.13
Carter, Ryan*	Batavia	Phi	A-	21	13	13	1	0	72	304	63	36	32	2	2	0	2	33	1	67	8	0	5	6	.455	0	0	4.00
Casadiego, Gerardo	Cape Fear	Mon	A	20	30	1	0	10	61.1	271	58	33	30	7	2	2	5	26	2	50	4	0	5	7	.417	0	1	4.40
Casey, Joe	Dunedin	Tor	A+	22	27	27	0	0	158.1	677	151	88	74	7	1	5	14	74	2	96	21	2	10	8	.556	0	0	4.21
Cassel, Jack	Idaho Falls	SD	R+	20	7	0	0	2	12.2	52	10	8	2	1	0	1	0	3	1	13	0	1	0	0	.000	0	0	1.42

2000 Pitching — Class-A and Rookie Leagues

HOW MUCH HE PITCHED											WHAT HE GAVE UP												THE RESULTS					
Player	Team	Org	Lg	A	G	GS	CG	GF	IP	BFP	H	R	ER	HR	SH	SF	HB	TBB	IBB	SO	WP	Bk	W	L	Pct.	ShO	Sv	ERA
	Fort Wayne	SD	A	20	22	0	0	6	36.1	160	42	24	19	2	0	2	2	12	0	25	4	0	2	2	.500	0	0	4.71
Castellanos, Hugo	Hagerstown	Tor	A	21	29	0	0	19	38.1	155	16	11	7	1	2	0	5	18	1	30	5	0	0	3	.000	0	7	1.64
	Dunedin	Tor	A+	20	4	0	0	4	8	37	5	4	4	1	1	1	0	10	1	5	0	0	0	0	.000	0	1	4.50
Castelli, Bobby	Jupiter	Mon	A+	24	11	0	0	5	11.1	66	15	19	17	2	0	0	3	15	0	8	6	0	0	0	.000	0	0	13.50
Castillo, Geraldo	Helena	Mil	R+	19	17	10	0	1	70	323	81	58	52	6	2	4	10	31	2	55	7	2	4	5	.444	0	0	6.69
Castillo, Jose	Lakeland	Det	A+	24	1	0	0	1	1	5	1	0	0	0	0	0	0	1	1	1	0	0	0	0	.000	0	0	0.00
	Tigers	Det	R	24	1	0	0	0	1	7	4	2	2	0	0	0	0	0	0	1	0	0	0	0	.000	0	0	18.00
Castillo, Marcos	Vero Beach	LA	A+	22	25	22	2	2	141	614	150	77	61	18	3	6	12	34	1	91	10	0	7	9	.438	2	0	3.89
Castillo, Ramon	Utica	Fla	A-	22	13	13	0	0	66.1	307	80	44	35	2	1	6	6	31	0	47	3	2	4	4	.500	0	0	4.75
Castro, Eleuterio	Augusta	Bos	A	23	30	0	0	13	58.2	251	57	33	21	2	1	1	3	19	0	41	6	0	3	1	.750	0	1	3.22
	Sarasota	Bos	A+	23	7	0	0	3	12.1	65	18	17	12	3	1	0	1	8	1	9	0	0	0	1	.000	0	0	8.76
Cavazos, Andy	Savannah	Tex	A	20	20	15	0	1	82.1	364	67	49	43	13	2	1	3	55	0	71	10	0	2	5	.286	0	1	4.70
Cedeno, Jovanny	Savannah	Tex	A	21	24	22	0	0	130.1	530	95	40	35	1	1	3	7	53	0	153	5	0	11	4	.733	0	0	2.42
Cento, Tony*	Quad City	Min	A	23	52	1	0	14	82.1	335	56	31	18	3	4	3	2	34	9	72	1	2	6	7	.462	0	5	1.97
Cepeda, Wellington	South Bend	Ari	A	23	26	2	0	7	50.1	231	59	39	33	4	0	4	4	26	1	32	5	0	2	3	.400	0	0	5.90
Cercy, Rick	Asheville	Col	A	24	44	0	0	18	61	236	38	10	8	3	0	0	4	21	0	78	1	0	4	1	.800	0	4	1.18
Cerda, Jaime*	Pittsfield	NYM	A-	22	20	1	0	6	47	176	33	6	3	0	2	0	0	6	1	51	2	0	4	1	.800	0	5	0.57
Cetani, Bryan*	Danville	Atl	R+	19	16	1	0	4	30.1	145	37	18	14	0	0	3	2	17	0	17	3	0	3	1	.750	0	0	4.15
Chacon, Ernesto	Yankees	NYY	R	21	18	0	0	7	18.2	77	15	7	4	0	0	0	1	7	0	13	3	0	0	1	.000	0	1	1.93
Chapman, Dennis	Fort Wayne	SD	A	22	5	0	0	0	6.1	40	9	10	10	0	1	2	1	11	1	5	3	0	0	0	.000	0	0	14.21
	Idaho Falls	SD	R+	22	21	0	0	8	25.1	131	30	31	27	4	1	3	3	20	1	33	8	1	1	2	.333	0	0	9.59
Charron, Eric	Cape Fear	Mon	A	22	26	15	0	2	94	418	113	57	48	4	0	4	7	29	1	71	7	1	5	10	.333	0	0	4.60
Chavez, Carlos	Visalia	Oak	A+	28	34	0	0	11	56	235	51	21	17	4	4	1	2	14	2	66	5	0	5	2	.714	0	5	2.73
Chavez, Chris	Myrtle Bch	Atl	A+	25	35	0	0	14	52.2	224	40	20	14	5	3	4	3	24	2	56	2	0	3	5	.375	0	2	2.39
Chavez, Wilton	Eugene	ChC	A-	20	15	15	0	0	90.1	371	69	28	17	0	4	1	10	25	0	103	4	3	7	1	.875	0	0	1.69
Cheek, Andrew*	Red Sox	Bos	R	23	7	0	0	5	10	47	11	4	3	0	1	1	0	5	1	5	1	0	1	1	.500	0	0	2.70
Chenard, Ken	Capital Cty	NYM	A	22	21	21	0	0	94.1	396	75	39	30	2	1	1	4	48	0	112	9	0	4	5	.444	0	0	2.86
Chiasson, Scott	Visalia	Oak	A+	23	31	23	0	4	156	666	146	66	53	17	3	2	6	57	2	150	8	1	11	4	.733	0	2	3.06
Chiavacci, Ron	Jupiter	Mon	A+	23	28	26	1	2	158	674	145	80	64	12	4	7	7	59	0	131	7	0	11	11	.500	0	0	3.65
Childers, Jason	Mudville	Mil	A+	26	28	28	0	0	157.1	646	140	71	61	12	3	3	0	54	0	177	6	0	12	10	.545	0	0	3.49
Childers, Matt	Beloit	Mil	A	22	12	12	1	0	73	300	64	33	22	4	0	0	1	17	0	47	2	1	8	2	.800	1	0	2.71
	Mudville	Mil	A+	22	15	15	0	0	85.1	388	103	59	45	10	2	2	3	32	0	43	3	2	3	9	.250	0	0	4.75
Chipperfield, Calvin	W Michigan	Det	A	23	24	22	3	0	143.2	588	95	45	34	12	3	1	9	65	0	151	3	0	12	3	.800	3	0	2.13
Chisnall, Wes	Vermont	Mon	A-	20	13	13	1	0	71	296	76	44	34	4	1	4	2	13	0	29	1	0	5	5	.500	0	0	4.31
Christ, John	Burlington	Cle	R+	23	2	0	0	2	2	13	2	2	0	0	0	0	1	2	0	3	1	1	0	0	.000	0	1	0.00
	Mahoning Vy	Cle	A-	23	18	0	0	10	26	112	20	10	9	0	0	0	1	12	1	27	3	0	2	1	.667	0	1	3.12
Christensen, Deryck	Rockies	Col	R	20	17	0	0	3	24	112	22	17	13	0	0	2	2	17	1	14	4	0	3	1	.750	0	0	4.88
Christenson, Ryan	Potomac	StL	A+	24	22	13	0	1	84	362	90	54	50	4	2	4	4	27	0	61	3	1	6	6	.500	0	0	5.36
Chrysler, Clint*	Lynchburg	Pit	A+	25	51	0	0	32	63	260	48	20	18	1	0	1	0	22	2	63	4	0	5	1	.833	0	14	2.57
Chulk, Charlie	Medcine Hat	Tor	R+	22	14	13	0	0	68.2	295	75	36	29	5	0	2	2	20	0	51	3	0	2	4	.333	0	0	3.80
Cimorelli, Brett	Butte	Ana	R+	19	7	4	0	0	24.2	113	23	19	16	3	0	0	6	12	0	11	1	0	1	0	1.000	0	0	5.84
Cisar, Mark	Sarasota	Bos	A+	26	10	0	0	1	16.1	70	15	8	5	1	0	0	1	4	1	14	0	0	0	0	.000	0	0	2.76
Cislak, Chad	Burlington	Cle	R+	22	6	0	0	2	11.1	53	10	11	6	0	3	1	0	8	0	9	6	0	0	1	.000	0	0	4.76
Clackum, Scott	Brevard Cty	Fla	A+	26	33	0	0	12	59	234	53	20	17	2	6	1	1	12	2	39	1	0	6	3	.667	0	1	2.59
Clark, Chris	Jamestown	Atl	A-	23	15	1	0	3	29.1	135	38	20	18	2	0	0	0	11	0	27	0	1	0	3	.000	0	1	5.52
Clark, Jeff	Giants	SF	R	21	11	11	0	0	56.2	247	66	41	35	2	2	2	9	10	0	35	0	0	2	5	.286	0	0	5.56
	San Jose	SF	A+	21	2	0	0	0	4	14	2	1	1	0	0	0	0	0	0	8	1	0	0	0	.000	0	0	2.25
Classen, Ender	Williamsprt	Pit	A-	23	12	12	0	0	60.2	278	60	39	28	4	0	6	5	37	0	41	3	0	2	4	.333	0	0	4.15
Claussen, Brandon*	Greensboro	NYY	A	22	17	17	1	0	97.2	416	91	49	44	9	4	4	1	44	0	98	3	0	8	5	.615	0	0	4.05
	Tampa	NYY	A+	22	9	9	1	0	52.1	220	49	24	18	1	1	0	2	17	0	44	2	1	2	5	.286	1	0	3.10
Clifton, Derek	Jamestown	Atl	A-	21	14	0	0	6	19	85	10	7	2	0	1	0	3	10	3	9	0	2	3	2	.600	0	0	0.95
Coa, Jesus	Chston-WV	KC	A	21	21	12	0	3	81.2	390	98	65	42	9	2	0	3	41	0	34	3	2	4	9	.308	0	1	4.63
Cole, Joey	Pittsfield	NYM	A-	23	10	10	0	0	49.1	221	41	28	25	0	2	0	9	32	0	50	0	2	4	2	.667	0	0	4.56
	Capital Cty	NYM	A	23	4	4	0	0	20.2	99	25	19	15	3	0	0	1	16	0	16	2	0	1	3	.250	0	0	6.53
Collado, Jerry	Rockies	Col	R	21	16	0	0	3	19.2	99	19	18	15	0	1	1	4	20	0	9	5	1	0	1	.000	0	0	6.86
Collazo, Rafael*	Tigers	Det	R	24	6	0	0	2	5.2	24	4	1	1	0	0	0	0	2	0	7	0	0	0	0	.000	0	1	1.59
	Oneonta	Det	A-	24	3	0	0	2	4	17	5	2	2	0	0	0	1	0	0	2	0	0	0	0	.000	0	1	4.50
Collins, Clint	Billings	Cin	R+	22	22	0	0	17	40.2	179	32	24	19	6	1	1	4	25	1	46	6	0	2	5	.286	0	4	4.20
Collins, Pat	Cape Fear	Mon	A	23	24	23	1	0	143.2	636	140	81	61	10	4	1	24	75	1	96	11	1	7	12	.368	0	0	3.82
	Jupiter	Mon	A+	23	2	2	0	0	11	47	10	9	8	1	0	1	0	6	0	3	0	0	0	1	.000	0	0	6.55
Colmenares, Luis	Asheville	Col	A	24	6	0	0	4	7	31	5	2	2	1	0	0	1	5	0	8	0	0	0	0	.000	0	0	2.57
	Salem	Col	A+	24	9	0	0	6	13.2	58	15	6	5	0	1	0	2	2	0	13	1	3	0	1	.000	0	0	3.29
Colon, Jose	Columbus	Cle	A	23	28	0	0	27	32.1	133	23	8	6	1	0	0	1	8	0	31	0	0	1	1	.500	0	19	1.67
	Kinston	Cle	A+	23	17	0	0	13	17.2	92	29	19	16	3	1	1	2	8	2	16	0	0	2	1	.667	0	2	8.15
Colton, Kyle	Danville	Atl	R+	20	8	6	0	1	23	111	19	19	17	0	2	2	3	20	0	13	2	1	0	4	.000	0	0	6.65
Colvard, Ron	Burlington	Cle	R+	23	19	0	0	9	38.2	168	41	24	11	2	0	4	0	12	0	38	6	1	3	2	.600	0	1	2.56
	Mahoning Vy	Cle	A-	23	3	0	0	1	6	26	4	1	1	0	0	0	2	2	0	6	0	0	2	0	1.000	0	0	1.50
Colyer, Steve*	Vero Beach	LA	A+	22	26	18	1	2	95.1	442	97	74	61	9	2	7	7	68	0	80	6	0	5	7	.417	0	0	5.76
Connolly, Keith	San Jose	SF	A+	26	54	0	0	22	77.2	336	66	45	36	12	4	8	3	33	1	71	9	0	3	6	.333	0	1	4.17
Connolly, Mike*	Pirates	Pit	R	19	11	0	0	7	19.2	84	20	6	5	0	2	0	1	6	0	25	2	0	1	2	.333	0	2	2.29
Conroy, Ken	Lansing	ChC	A	22	27	25	1	1	137.1	635	151	90	66	7	6	5	19	78	0	108	17	0	11	6	.647	0	0	4.33
Cook, Aaron	Asheville	Col	A	22	21	21	4	0	142.2	579	130	54	47	10	1	0	16	23	0	118	5	0	10	7	.588	2	0	2.96
	Salem	Col	A+	22	7	7	1	0	43	196	52	33	26	4	1	1	7	12	0	37	3	0	1	6	.143	0	0	5.44
Cook, Andy	St. Lucie	NYM	A+	24	28	16	1	7	126	537	123	51	47	7	3	4	11	37	1	94	2	1	10	4	.714	1	4	3.36
Cook, B.R.	Peoria	StL	A	23	18	18	0	0	97.2	438	90	66	40	7	3	1	3	52	2	83	7	1	5	7	.417	0	0	3.69
	Potomac	StL	A+	23	8	8	0	0	42.1	193	48	31	26	3	3	3	2	27	0	23	3	0	0	4	.000	0	0	5.53
Cook, Jeremy	New Jersey	StL	A-	23	32	0	0	8	49.1	211	51	21	13	3	1	0	2	17	0	34	1	0	2	1	.667	0	1	2.37

2000 Pitching — Class-A and Rookie Leagues

HOW MUCH HE PITCHED											WHAT HE GAVE UP												THE RESULTS					
Player	Team	Org	Lg	A	G	GS	CG	GF	IP	BFP	H	R	ER	HR	SH	SF	HB	TBB	IBB	SO	WP	Bk	W	L	Pct.	ShO	Sv	ERA
Cooke, Andrew*	Twins	Min	R	20	11	5	0	0	26.1	128	36	17	14	1	0	1	0	16	1	26	2	0	2	1	.667	0	0	4.78
Cooper, Eric	Billings	Cin	R+	23	3	3	0	0	7	35	8	9	8	1	0	0	1	6	0	4	3	0	0	1	.000	0	0	10.29
Corbin, John	Cubs	ChC	R	24	17	0	0	11	24	113	24	18	13	1	0	3	3	11	1	31	1	0	3	0	1.000	0	3	4.88
Corcoran, Tim	Capital Cty	NYM	A	23	31	0	0	13	53.1	230	46	28	24	7	0	0	4	27	2	58	11	0	3	5	.375	0	1	4.05
Cordero, Frangil*	Eugene	ChC	A-	20	6	5	0	0	24.1	106	23	10	8	3	0	0	0	15	0	19	3	1	1	1	.500	0	0	2.96
	Lansing	ChC	A	20	23	4	0	9	36.2	174	39	27	25	2	2	2	1	28	1	28	2	1	2	3	.400	0	7	6.14
Cordero, Jesus	Great Falls	LA	R+	22	18	1	0	6	30.1	143	30	15	8	1	0	1	1	21	0	27	6	0	1	1	.500	0	1	2.37
Cordero, Victor	Helena	Mil	R+	21	8	0	0	4	18.2	96	19	12	8	1	1	0	5	12	2	29	3	0	1	2	.333	0	0	3.86
	Beloit	Mil	A	21	15	0	0	4	30	137	26	16	14	5	0	1	4	18	0	31	7	0	1	1	.500	0	1	4.20
Cordova, Jorge	Kane County	Fla	A	23	22	15	1	2	95	395	94	41	41	9	4	2	4	21	1	94	9	0	6	7	.462	0	1	3.88
	Reds	Cin	R	23	1	0	0	0	1.1	5	0	0	0	0	0	0	0	1	0	0	0	0	0	0	.000	0	0	0.00
	Clinton	Cin	A	23	8	8	0	0	48.2	216	48	26	23	1	1	6	0	28	0	50	8	1	3	2	.600	0	0	4.25
Corn, Terry	Elizabethtn	Min	R+	22	19	0	0	8	29.1	123	17	15	13	3	1	2	5	18	0	31	6	0	2	0	1.000	0	3	3.99
Cornejo, Jesse*	Chston-SC	TB	A	24	30	1	0	12	52.2	230	50	22	18	4	6	2	0	21	3	48	3	1	4	1	.800	0	1	3.08
	St. Pete	TB	A+	24	10	0	0	4	15.2	67	13	8	8	1	3	2	0	10	2	14	0	0	0	2	.000	0	0	4.60
Correa, Cristobal	Potomac	StL	A+	21	18	18	0	0	100	419	82	41	36	9	1	3	5	49	0	76	6	0	6	6	.500	0	0	3.24
Correa, Dominic	Greensboro	NYY	A	24	5	0	0	3	7.1	28	2	0	0	0	1	0	2	2	0	7	0	1	1	0	1.000	0	0	0.00
	Staten Ilnd	NYY	A-	24	15	0	0	5	20	78	10	3	3	0	2	0	3	9	0	19	3	0	0	1	.000	0	2	1.35
Correa, Elvis	San Berndno	LA	A+	22	41	0	0	34	67.2	285	74	25	23	5	9	2	2	16	3	58	6	0	3	9	.250	0	14	3.06
Coscia, Tony	Bakersfield	SF	A+	27	21	21	0	0	119.2	503	115	63	55	15	1	2	11	31	0	124	7	4	7	8	.467	0	0	4.14
Cosgrove, Mike	Kissimmee	Hou	A+	25	8	0	0	4	10.2	49	13	9	6	3	0	0	1	3	0	4	1	0	1	1	.500	0	1	5.06
Cotton, Nathan	Reds	Cin	R	21	14	0	0	11	25.2	106	19	10	10	1	4	1	1	11	4	24	0	0	1	3	.250	0	3	3.51
Coughenour, Jory	Auburn	Hou	A-	23	15	15	0	0	74.2	339	90	53	42	7	2	1	8	25	0	34	8	1	4	7	.364	0	0	5.06
Coward, Chad	Princeton	TB	R+	22	6	6	0	0	30.1	130	27	13	7	1	1	1	1	16	0	41	4	0	2	1	.667	0	0	2.08
	Hudson Val	TB	A-	22	6	6	1	0	33.2	153	34	22	16	1	0	4	2	14	0	31	5	0	2	3	.400	0	0	4.28
Cowie, Steve	Columbus	Cle	A	24	14	14	0	0	85	346	77	35	32	12	1	2	2	21	0	64	1	0	7	1	.875	0	0	3.39
	Kinston	Cle	A+	24	12	12	1	0	69.2	313	82	45	35	7	1	4	6	24	1	48	3	0	2	5	.286	0	0	4.52
Cox, Adam*	Burlington	Cle	R+	21	12	12	0	0	46.2	201	42	31	25	5	2	0	6	27	0	50	9	1	2	4	.333	0	0	4.82
Cox, Mike*	Pittsfield	NYM	A-	23	14	12	1	0	61.2	261	43	23	17	3	0	2	5	30	0	81	6	0	2	3	.400	0	0	2.48
Cozier, Vance	Bakersfield	SF	A+	23	28	28	0	0	150.1	665	164	82	65	6	6	7	4	61	0	106	6	2	10	8	.556	0	0	3.89
Cramblitt, Joey	Missoula	Ari	R+	22	5	0	0	0	11.1	44	8	3	2	2	0	0	0	0	0	11	1	1	2	0	1.000	0	0	1.59
	High Desert	Ari	A+	22	22	0	0	7	42	194	62	35	29	8	2	0	2	14	0	28	0	1	4	1	.800	0	0	6.21
Crawford, Chris	Hudson Val	TB	A-	23	2	0	0	1	2	9	2	0	0	0	0	0	0	1	0	2	0	0	0	0	.000	0	0	0.00
Crawford, Tristan	Twins	Min	R	18	8	0	0	6	6.1	34	12	9	7	0	0	0	0	2	0	3	2	0	0	0	.000	0	0	9.95
Crawford, Wes*	Lk Elsinore	Ana	A+	24	27	22	1	0	141.2	625	145	84	69	9	6	5	12	66	1	102	10	4	7	8	.467	0	0	4.38
Crist, Ryan	Oneonta	Det	A-	22	3	0	0	1	5.2	23	3	2	2	0	0	1	0	4	0	3	0	0	0	0	.000	0	0	3.18
Cristobal, Luis	Rangers	Tex	R	21	8	3	0	1	19	93	24	13	10	1	0	1	3	10	0	13	0	0	2	0	1.000	0	0	4.74
Cromer, Jason*	Princeton	TB	R+	20	13	13	0	0	70.2	304	88	36	31	5	4	1	3	15	0	50	4	0	3	4	.429	0	0	3.95
Cromer, Nathan*	Hudson Val	TB	A-	20	13	13	0	0	60.1	280	63	57	40	3	1	3	4	29	0	45	6	0	2	7	.222	0	0	5.97
Crowder, Chuck*	Salem	Col	A+	24	28	28	0	0	168.2	710	124	78	66	6	10	9	10	86	0	154	8	6	14	9	.609	0	0	3.52
Crowell, Kyle	Vancouver	Oak	A-	22	17	9	0	4	65	274	63	28	21	0	4	0	4	12	0	64	5	3	4	4	.500	0	2	2.91
Crowther, Jackson	Cape Fear	Mon	A	24	18	1	0	5	30.2	146	32	22	20	2	0	4	0	20	0	23	6	0	1	2	.333	0	0	5.87
Crudale, Mike	Peoria	StL	A	24	38	0	0	14	50.2	209	40	17	13	2	5	0	3	16	3	45	4	0	6	1	.857	0	5	2.31
	Potomac	StL	A+	24	21	0	0	9	25.2	120	31	17	13	3	2	2	1	11	1	28	0	0	2	4	.333	0	2	4.56
Crump, Joel*	Orioles	Bal	R	19	12	0	0	3	20	97	32	20	18	1	1	2	0	11	3	7	3	0	2	1	.667	0	0	8.10
Cruz, Juan	Lansing	ChC	A	20	17	17	2	0	96	423	75	50	35	6	1	0	13	60	0	106	8	1	5	5	.500	1	0	3.28
	Daytona	ChC	A+	20	8	7	1	0	44.1	182	30	22	16	5	0	0	3	18	0	54	4	0	3	0	1.000	0	0	3.25
Cuello, Manolin	Tigers	Det	R	20	11	5	0	0	47.2	201	37	14	12	0	1	2	7	22	2	41	5	0	6	0	1.000	0	0	2.27
	Lakeland	Det	A+	20	2	1	0	0	6	31	6	7	4	0	0	1	0	4	0	8	2	0	0	1	.000	0	0	6.00
Cueto, Jose	Lansing	ChC	A	22	16	1	0	6	26.2	132	26	19	17	1	3	2	0	25	1	35	9	1	0	4	.000	0	0	5.74
	Eugene	ChC	A-	22	13	7	0	1	44.2	200	43	27	26	1	0	1	4	24	0	51	5	1	2	5	.286	0	1	5.24
Cullen, Ryan*	Savannah	Tex	A	21	48	0	0	36	94.2	389	79	33	32	3	5	2	1	35	2	103	3	1	6	6	.500	0	9	3.04
Culp, Brandon	Billings	Cin	R+	23	7	0	0	2	16.1	78	19	12	12	0	0	0	2	6	0	19	1	0	1	0	1.000	0	0	6.61
Cummings, Frank	Braves	Atl	R	24	3	0	0	2	4	15	3	0	0	0	0	0	0	0	0	5	0	0	0	0	.000	0	1	0.00
	Jamestown	Atl	A-	24	22	0	0	12	32	146	36	25	14	6	2	1	1	14	0	27	0	0	0	3	.000	0	2	3.94
Cummings, Jeremy	Peoria	StL	A	24	3	3	0	0	11.1	51	15	9	8	3	0	0	0	3	0	8	1	0	1	1	.500	0	0	6.35
Cunningham, J.	San Jose	SF	A+	22	34	19	0	6	133.1	625	169	105	88	8	9	4	9	61	0	90	21	4	5	14	.263	0	0	5.94
Curreri, Joe	Burlington	CWS	A	24	41	0	0	29	53.2	237	46	24	22	5	2	4	3	35	5	56	3	1	4	4	.500	0	12	3.69
Curtice, John*	Sarasota	Bos	A+	21	25	23	0	1	112.1	526	114	87	81	5	6	8	12	68	0	83	7	1	4	10	.286	0	0	6.49
Curtin, Brian	Mahoning Vy	Cle	A-	23	4	3	0	0	17	69	16	10	10	1	0	0	0	4	0	9	2	0	1	2	.333	0	0	5.29
Curtis, Bill	Cedar Rapds	Ana	A	23	2	0	0	1	1.2	10	3	4	4	1	0	0	0	2	0	1	0	0	0	0	.000	0	1	21.60
	Butte	Ana	R+	23	7	0	0	4	11.1	46	11	5	5	1	0	0	1	3	1	11	0	0	1	0	1.000	0	0	3.97
Curtis, Dan	Macon	Atl	A	21	7	6	2	0	45.2	171	35	10	10	4	0	1	0	7	0	45	0	0	5	0	1.000	1	0	1.97
	Myrtle Bch	Atl	A+	21	8	8	1	0	50.1	213	48	18	15	5	4	2	3	15	1	34	0	2	3	2	.600	0	0	2.68
Curtiss, Tom*	Macon	Atl	A	24	10	0	0	4	17.1	86	17	16	13	0	1	1	1	17	0	14	0	0	0	1	.000	0	0	6.75
	Jamestown	Atl	A-	24	24	0	0	16	29.1	127	17	6	4	0	1	0	1	15	0	41	5	0	1	1	.500	0	9	1.23
Cyr, Eric*	Padres	SD	R	22	2	1	0	1	3	14	4	1	1	0	0	0	0	2	0	4	0	0	0	0	.000	0	0	3.00
	Fort Wayne	SD	A	22	9	6	0	0	32.2	140	28	18	17	2	0	1	4	15	0	31	1	0	2	2	.500	0	0	4.68
Daigle, Casey	Missoula	Ari	R+	20	15	15	0	0	82.2	390	88	57	45	4	2	0	9	54	0	56	10	3	3	5	.375	0	0	4.90
D'Amico, Leonardo	Butte	Ana	R+	19	7	4	0	0	30	147	40	32	18	5	0	1	4	12	0	19	3	1	0	3	.000	0	0	5.40
Dant, Larry	Daytona	ChC	A+	24	8	0	0	2	10.1	56	18	15	15	0	0	2	1	8	1	3	0	0	0	0	.000	0	0	13.06
	Lansing	ChC	A	24	6	3	0	1	20.2	92	27	17	15	5	1	0	0	6	0	8	0	0	1	0	1.000	0	0	6.53
Darnell, Paul*	Clinton	Cin	A	25	26	25	3	0	161.2	679	131	81	63	11	10	4	7	67	1	164	12	1	9	10	.474	1	0	3.51
Davies, Michael*	Rockies	Col	R	20	15	7	0	2	46.2	208	51	26	21	3	0	2	1	19	0	38	1	2	4	1	.800	0	1	4.05
Davis, Jason	Burlington	Cle	R+	21	10	10	0	0	45	201	48	27	22	5	3	3	5	16	0	35	5	1	4	4	.500	0	0	4.40
Davis, Mikael	Diamondbcks	Ari	R	20	17	0	0	8	25.2	138	34	32	21	0	0	2	2	31	0	14	8	0	0	1	.000	0	0	7.36
Deaton, Kevin	Kingsport	NYM	R+	19	12	0	0	4	20	81	15	7	7	1	1	0	1	4	0	19	1	0	0	1	.000	0	2	3.15

2000 Pitching — Class-A and Rookie Leagues

HOW MUCH HE PITCHED											WHAT HE GAVE UP												THE RESULTS					
Player	Team	Org	Lg	A	G	GS	CG	GF	IP	BFP	H	R	ER	HR	SH	SF	HB	TBB	IBB	SO	WP	Bk	W	L	Pct.	ShO	Sv	ERA
DeHart, Blair	Fort Wayne	SD	A	23	20	10	0	1	73.1	314	85	38	33	7	1	2	5	14	1	64	2	0	5	4	.556	0	1	4.05
	Rancho Cuca	SD	A+	23	9	9	0	0	48	217	55	45	39	5	1	3	4	18	0	36	2	1	0	7	.000	0	0	7.31
DeHart, Casey*	Dayton	Cin	A	23	50	0	0	20	63.1	291	67	39	30	3	4	3	0	38	0	52	9	0	6	3	.667	0	2	4.26
DeJesus, Henky	Diamondbcks	Ari	R	20	20	0	0	8	28.1	152	44	36	26	1	0	0	3	19	0	19	2	0	3	2	.600	0	1	8.26
DeJesus, Rigoberto	Johnson Cty	StL	R+	19	12	0	0	2	15	73	16	16	8	3	0	0	0	11	0	13	4	0	1	1	.500	0	0	4.80
DeJesus, Tony	Everett	Sea	A-	23	15	12	0	1	65	277	60	28	21	5	2	3	0	28	0	72	3	0	4	6	.400	0	0	2.91
de la Cruz, Andres	Greensboro	NYY	A	21	26	0	0	15	27	145	31	28	22	3	0	2	6	30	0	16	3	0	0	1	.000	0	1	7.33
de la Cruz, Carlos	Burlington	Cle	R+	19	19	0	0	13	29.2	143	34	30	23	5	1	2	5	15	0	28	5	1	1	1	.500	0	3	6.98
de la Cruz, Juan	Pirates	Pit	R	21	3	0	0	3	2.1	12	1	2	2	0	0	0	0	4	0	5	0	0	0	1	.000	0	2	7.71
	Williamsprt	Pit	A-	21	13	0	0	10	22	102	24	18	15	4	1	1	1	10	0	24	2	0	2	2	.500	0	1	6.14
de la Cruz, Pedro	Helena	Mil	R+	20	8	4	0	1	19	89	18	15	10	1	1	0	3	13	0	14	2	0	0	1	.000	0	0	4.74
DeLeon, Jose	Potomac	StL	A+	24	11	0	0	5	15	86	28	21	17	4	3	0	0	9	0	6	1	0	0	3	.000	0	0	10.20
Delgado, Danny	Wisconsin	Sea	A	23	37	3	1	15	79.1	324	67	31	28	8	4	1	4	26	0	71	0	1	5	2	.714	0	4	3.18
Delgado, Joseph	Royals	KC	R	21	1	1	0	0	2.1	15	4	3	3	0	0	0	0	4	0	2	0	0	0	1	.000	0	0	11.57
de los Santos, C.	Pirates	Pit	R	20	11	7	0	3	51.2	227	45	24	20	4	0	0	10	23	0	53	5	2	3	5	.375	0	1	3.48
de los Santos, Luis	Yankees	NYY	R	23	4	3	0	0	15	64	15	5	5	0	0	0	0	6	0	19	0	1	2	0	1.000	0	0	3.00
Denney, Kyle	Columbus	Cle	A	23	28	24	0	1	138.2	584	135	55	47	12	4	1	4	46	0	131	5	0	8	6	.571	0	0	3.05
DePaula, Freddy*	Athletics	Oak	R	20	5	0	0	1	11.1	44	7	2	1	0	2	0	1	3	0	9	0	0	1	1	.500	0	0	0.79
DePaula, Julio	Asheville	Col	A	21	28	27	1	0	155	663	151	90	81	16	2	5	13	62	0	187	7	2	8	13	.381	1	0	4.70
DeQuin, Benji*	Vermont	Mon	A-	21	16	14	0	0	74.2	328	60	33	24	2	0	3	4	50	0	79	6	0	6	3	.667	0	0	2.89
Detillion, Jamie*	Tigers	Det	R	23	16	1	0	4	34.2	136	23	11	10	2	3	2	1	10	1	29	3	0	5	3	.625	0	2	2.60
	Lakeland	Det	A+	23	4	0	0	2	5	23	7	6	6	2	0	0	0	2	0	2	1	0	0	0	.000	0	0	10.80
Detwiler, Jim*	Queens	Tor	A-	25	20	0	0	8	35	146	25	12	11	0	2	0	2	19	1	38	3	1	3	1	.750	0	1	2.83
Devey, Phil*	San Berndno	LA	A+	24	29	24	1	1	172.1	737	179	86	72	13	5	7	13	54	1	112	3	1	6	11	.353	0	0	3.76
Devine, Travis	Fort Wayne	SD	A	21	23	16	1	4	99	423	102	57	49	8	5	1	4	35	0	61	10	0	4	7	.364	0	0	4.45
D'Frank, Carlos	Burlington	Cle	R+	18	6	3	0	1	21	97	20	16	11	1	2	2	3	9	0	19	1	0	2	2	.500	0	0	4.71
Diaz, Alex	Visalia	Oak	A+	21	7	0	0	3	7.1	41	18	15	15	2	0	0	0	5	0	3	2	0	0	0	.000	0	0	18.41
	Vancouver	Oak	A-	21	2	0	0	1	3.2	15	2	1	0	0	0	1	0	2	1	4	0	0	0	0	.000	0	0	0.00
	Athletics	Oak	R	21	13	9	0	2	60.2	255	71	27	22	0	3	4	1	4	0	39	2	1	3	1	.750	0	0	3.26
Diaz, Antonio	Fort Wayne	SD	A	22	6	0	0	1	9	33	5	1	1	1	1	0	1	4	2	2	1	0	0	1	.000	0	0	1.00
	Rancho Cuca	SD	A+	22	24	0	0	5	38.2	190	58	40	33	5	5	4	1	17	1	18	7	3	2	4	.333	0	0	7.68
Diaz, Eddy	Cubs	ChC	R	20	5	3	0	0	22.1	102	27	16	12	0	2	1	2	10	1	14	4	0	1	0	1.000	0	0	4.84
Diaz, Elisandy	Expos	Mon	R	20	13	9	0	1	52.2	234	58	35	25	4	0	1	7	12	0	38	2	1	1	1	.500	0	0	4.27
Diaz, Felix	Giants	SF	R	19	11	11	0	0	62.2	270	56	35	29	0	4	4	5	16	0	58	3	3	3	4	.429	0	0	4.16
	Salem-Keizr	SF	A-	19	3	0	0	2	3.1	19	6	6	3	2	2	0	1	1	0	2	0	0	0	1	.000	0	0	8.10
Diaz, Franklin	Athletics	Oak	R	21	1	0	0	0	2.1	13	5	4	4	1	0	0	0	1	0	0	1	0	0	0	.000	0	0	15.43
Dickinson, Rodney	Augusta	Bos	A	26	13	0	0	3	27	103	20	4	3	0	2	1	1	4	1	30	1	0	1	1	.500	0	1	1.00
Digby, Bryan	Braves	Atl	R	19	10	3	0	0	27	133	28	28	22	3	1	0	2	21	0	34	10	1	1	3	.250	0	0	7.33
Dimma, Doug*	Dunedin	Tor	A+	22	43	0	0	17	79.2	361	74	46	34	6	1	3	9	48	4	42	7	0	6	3	.667	0	1	3.84
Dischiavo, John	Princeton	TB	R+	19	11	8	0	0	35	160	39	22	21	3	1	0	6	7	0	27	6	0	0	2	.000	0	0	5.40
Dittfurth, Ryan	Savannah	Tex	A	21	29	29	2	0	158.2	699	127	83	75	8	2	5	17	99	1	158	16	3	8	13	.381	1	0	4.25
Dobis, Jason	Fort Myers	Min	A+	25	37	3	1	13	77.2	321	74	34	28	2	3	3	1	29	1	39	6	0	3	4	.429	0	4	3.24
Dobson, Scott	Cape Fear	Mon	A	24	14	0	0	3	17	98	27	26	21	4	0	1	4	17	0	13	7	0	0	0	.000	0	0	11.12
Dohmann, Scott	Portland	Col	A-	23	5	4	0	0	23	85	14	3	2	0	0	0	1	5	0	23	0	0	2	1	.667	0	0	0.78
	Asheville	Col	A	23	7	7	0	0	32.2	149	43	24	22	3	0	3	3	8	0	36	3	1	1	5	.167	0	0	6.06
Donaghey, Steve	Mahoning Vy	Cle	A-	22	21	0	0	6	49.2	202	43	14	12	1	1	3	3	9	1	21	1	1	3	1	.750	0	1	2.17
Donovan, Kevin*	Batavia	Phi	A-	24	7	0	0	2	10.2	57	17	15	13	2	0	2	1	6	0	13	1	0	0	1	.000	0	0	10.97
Dorman, Rich	Hudson Val	TB	A-	22	14	14	0	0	70	331	71	47	27	0	2	4	4	40	2	46	9	1	2	6	.250	0	0	3.47
Dorn, Grant	Cape Fear	Mon	A	23	17	17	1	0	91.1	404	106	60	53	6	1	7	1	36	1	55	4	0	3	6	.333	0	0	5.22
Dotel, Melido	San Berndno	LA	A+	24	8	0	0	1	9.2	50	7	6	4	0	0	0	4	12	0	11	2	0	1	1	.500	0	0	3.72
Dougherty, Kevin*	Pittsfield	NYM	A-	23	2	0	0	0	2.2	13	5	3	2	1	0	0	0	1	0	1	0	0	0	0	.000	0	0	6.75
Douglas, Rod	Braves	Atl	R	19	13	0	0	4	23.2	123	25	20	14	0	1	0	2	19	0	24	4	2	1	3	.250	0	0	5.32
Douglass, Ryan	Chston-WV	KC	A	22	27	27	2	0	159	668	174	88	71	9	3	1	6	34	0	105	6	1	6	14	.300	0	0	4.02
Doyne, Cory	Martinsvlle	Hou	R+	19	12	8	0	0	39.2	177	25	27	24	1	0	1	1	35	0	54	8	0	3	6	.333	0	0	5.45
Drain, Brad	Mariners	Sea	R	21	4	1	0	0	19	74	18	6	6	2	0	1	0	1	0	15	0	0	2	2	.500	0	0	2.84
	Everett	Sea	A-	21	14	0	0	6	19	79	17	8	5	1	0	1	1	4	0	17	2	0	2	0	1.000	0	1	2.37
Drese, Ryan	Kinston	Cle	A+	25	1	1	0	0	2.1	9	2	1	1	0	1	0	0	1	0	4	1	0	0	1	.000	0	0	3.86
Dubuc, Charles*	Expos	Mon	R	20	12	3	0	2	44	212	46	38	30	6	1	4	7	24	0	44	6	1	1	4	.200	0	0	6.14
Dukeman, Greg	Hickory	Pit	A	22	25	19	0	2	132	606	151	91	67	17	3	3	14	46	0	82	16	1	5	6	.455	0	0	4.57
Dulkowski, Marc	Padres	SD	R	19	4	0	0	2	3.2	20	4	4	1	0	0	1	0	6	0	3	0	0	0	0	.000	0	0	2.45
Dumatrait, Phil*	Red Sox	Bos	R	19	6	6	0	0	16.1	73	10	6	3	0	1	0	2	12	0	12	0	0	0	1	.000	0	0	1.65
Dunn, Keith	Greensboro	NYY	A	23	8	8	0	0	45	201	54	29	22	7	2	1	2	13	0	38	1	1	1	5	.167	0	0	4.40
	Tampa	NYY	A+	23	24	1	0	9	58.1	240	45	16	15	2	1	0	1	26	2	31	0	2	4	4	.500	0	0	2.31
Dunn, Scott	Clinton	Cin	A	23	26	26	2	0	147.2	638	123	78	65	9	2	3	4	89	1	159	20	0	11	3	.786	1	0	3.96
Dunning, Justin	Capital Cty	NYM	A	24	28	26	0	1	120	545	114	91	81	8	1	5	17	71	0	128	31	0	5	11	.313	0	0	6.07
Dunphy, Micah*	Athletics	Oak	R	21	7	0	0	1	11.2	57	9	6	2	1	1	0	4	9	0	11	0	0	2	0	1.000	0	0	1.54
Duprey, Pete*	Wisconsin	Sea	A	22	19	0	0	11	24.1	108	26	17	12	2	1	0	1	8	2	28	0	0	0	0	.000	0	2	4.44
	Daytona	ChC	A+	22	1	0	0	0	1.2	8	2	0	0	0	0	0	0	1	0	1	0	0	0	0	.000	0	0	0.00
	Lansing	ChC	A	22	12	0	0	2	25.2	114	28	9	5	1	0	3	1	9	1	15	3	0	2	1	.667	0	0	1.75
Durbin, J.D.	Twins	Min	R	19	2	0	0	0	2	9	2	0	0	0	0	0	0	0	0	4	0	0	0	0	.000	0	0	0.00
Durkee, Jeremy*	Helena	Mil	R+	20	18	4	0	4	38	194	67	41	31	4	4	4	3	13	2	24	7	1	0	3	.000	0	0	7.34
Duverge, Alcides	Boise	Ana	A-	21	2	0	0	0	1.1	13	4	6	6	0	0	1	1	4	0	0	2	0	0	0	.000	0	0	40.50
	Butte	Ana	R+	21	8	0	0	4	8.1	50	13	13	11	2	0	0	2	10	0	7	6	0	0	1	.000	0	0	11.88
Earey, Ryan	Idaho Falls	SD	R+	22	14	13	0	0	69.1	306	93	47	39	8	3	2	4	14	0	45	1	0	4	3	.571	0	0	5.06
Earl, Ryan*	Oneonta	Det	A-	20	12	12	0	0	57.1	264	61	45	35	5	1	1	5	23	0	53	9	0	2	7	.222	0	0	5.49
Earley, Andrew	Cubs	ChC	R	21	12	6	0	4	45.1	211	37	22	20	0	2	2	8	33	0	29	4	0	2	0	1.000	0	0	3.97
Ebanks, Palmer	Cedar Rapds	Ana	A	24	21	2	0	8	49	224	55	36	25	4	2	2	2	16	1	27	4	0	1	4	.200	0	0	4.59

2000 Pitching — Class-A and Rookie Leagues

HOW MUCH HE PITCHED											WHAT HE GAVE UP												THE RESULTS					
Player	Team	Org	Lg	A	G	GS	CG	GF	IP	BFP	H	R	ER	HR	SH	SF	HB	TBB	IBB	SO	WP	Bk	W	L	Pct.	ShO	Sv	ERA
Echols, Justin	Pulaski	Tex	R+	20	9	5	0	3	32.2	146	34	21	16	2	1	1	1	15	0	39	6	2	0	4	.000	0	0	4.41
Eckenstahler, Eric*	Oneonta	Det	A-	24	8	0	0	4	11	46	7	3	2	0	0	1	2	3	0	13	1	0	0	0	.000	0	0	1.64
	W Michigan	Det	A	24	10	3	0	4	18.2	89	21	15	12	4	1	1	1	11	0	22	0	1	0	2	.000	0	1	5.79
Edwards, Bryan	Billings	Cin	R+	21	4	2	0	1	6	39	5	9	8	0	0	0	1	18	0	4	4	1	0	2	.000	0	0	12.00
	Reds	Cin	R	21	9	0	0	4	9.2	55	10	7	4	0	2	0	4	9	0	7	3	0	0	0	.000	0	0	3.72
Elliott, Chad*	Pittsfield	NYM	A-	23	11	8	0	1	49.2	227	58	33	27	3	2	1	2	22	1	54	3	0	1	4	.200	0	0	4.89
Elmore, Chris*	Lowell	Bos	A-	24	15	10	1	3	71.1	279	55	20	15	0	1	1	6	14	0	46	3	2	3	3	.500	1	2	1.89
Elskamp, Andrew	Phillies	Phi	R	22	11	0	0	2	27	118	23	14	11	1	1	0	1	12	0	20	3	0	5	1	.833	0	0	3.67
Emanuel, Brandon	Lk Elsinore	Ana	A+	25	19	17	2	1	103.1	489	136	89	72	14	2	5	7	43	2	54	12	1	4	10	.286	0	0	6.27
Encarnacion, Luis	Mariners	Sea	R	21	13	4	0	5	27	147	43	39	37	4	0	6	9	16	0	20	10	0	1	2	.333	0	0	12.33
Encarnacion, O.	Pittsfield	NYM	A-	22	8	2	0	1	26.2	100	17	2	1	0	1	0	1	6	0	18	1	0	4	0	1.000	0	1	0.34
	Capital Cty	NYM	A	22	19	0	0	10	41	181	43	31	29	5	1	4	3	14	1	36	5	1	1	2	.333	0	0	6.37
Ennis, John	Macon	Atl	A	21	18	16	0	0	98.2	403	77	37	28	5	2	1	6	25	0	105	3	0	7	4	.636	0	0	2.55
Enochs, Chris	Visalia	Oak	A+	25	18	18	0	0	97	429	116	61	50	6	5	5	0	38	0	75	6	1	2	5	.286	0	0	4.64
Eppeneder, Jim*	Lansing	ChC	A	22	44	1	0	14	81.1	336	66	33	28	9	3	4	2	33	3	59	5	1	7	1	.875	0	3	3.10
Eppolito, Vince	Missoula	Ari	R+	23	20	0	0	8	32.1	153	30	28	26	1	0	1	8	25	0	35	9	0	4	0	1.000	0	0	7.24
Ericks, Dave	Eugene	ChC	A-	21	10	0	0	4	14.2	74	17	18	16	2	1	1	1	13	1	11	3	0	2	1	.667	0	0	9.82
Escamilla, Paco	Clinton	Cin	A	24	2	1	0	1	10	43	9	3	2	0	0	0	0	5	0	10	1	0	0	0	.000	0	1	1.80
Esdaile, Kremlin	Burlington	Cle	R+	20	17	0	0	7	28	145	30	24	17	3	2	2	3	24	0	28	8	0	1	4	.200	0	0	5.46
Espaillat, Ezequiel	Marlins	Fla	R	20	11	1	0	5	31	127	23	6	6	1	1	2	1	14	3	19	3	1	3	0	1.000	0	2	1.74
Esquivia, Manuel	Marlins	Fla	R	21	12	11	0	0	64.2	263	42	20	20	4	1	5	3	24	0	77	5	0	6	1	.857	0	0	2.78
	Utica	Fla	A-	21	2	2	0	0	11	46	9	3	3	0	0	1	0	4	0	14	2	0	1	0	1.000	0	0	2.45
Esslinger, Cam	Asheville	Col	A	24	47	2	0	39	64.2	271	55	23	22	2	2	2	3	23	1	84	4	0	4	2	.667	0	24	3.06
Estel, Justin	Vermont	Mon	A-	23	3	0	0	1	5	21	3	1	1	0	0	0	1	3	0	3	0	1	0	0	.000	0	0	1.80
Evans, Kyle	Mahoning Vy	Cle	A-	22	12	11	0	1	63	259	56	29	22	4	0	4	1	22	0	53	3	1	5	2	.714	0	0	3.14
Everett, Matt	Mahoning Vy	Cle	A-	25	1	0	0	0	1	5	1	0	0	0	0	0	0	1	0	1	0	1	1	0	1.000	0	0	0.00
Eversgerd, Randy	Sarasota	Bos	A+	24	8	2	0	2	21.2	91	23	7	6	1	0	3	0	4	0	19	0	0	2	0	1.000	0	1	2.49
Evert, Brett	Macon	Atl	A	20	7	7	0	0	42.2	190	53	27	22	7	0	0	3	9	0	29	7	1	1	4	.200	0	0	4.64
	Jamestown	Atl	A-	20	15	15	0	0	77.1	344	92	52	29	6	0	1	5	19	0	64	2	0	8	3	.727	0	0	3.38
Ewin, Ryan	Braves	Atl	R	19	10	8	0	0	43.1	185	31	23	13	1	3	0	0	22	0	51	5	0	0	6	.000	0	0	2.70
	Jamestown	Atl	A-	19	2	2	0	0	11	48	10	8	7	0	1	1	0	4	0	10	1	0	0	1	.000	0	0	5.73
Eyre, Willie	Quad City	Min	A	22	26	18	1	3	99.2	457	104	64	51	9	2	3	5	56	0	81	9	0	5	7	.417	1	0	4.61
Faas, Matt	Salem-Keizr	SF	A-	24	23	0	0	8	34	157	32	14	11	3	3	5	5	21	0	18	6	0	3	1	.750	0	0	2.91
Fahrner, Evan	High Desert	Ari	A+	23	45	5	0	15	87.2	411	102	79	52	10	4	3	4	43	1	92	12	3	1	12	.077	0	1	5.34
Fahs, Paul	Peoria	StL	A	23	30	2	0	7	52	234	54	30	27	1	4	4	1	29	1	22	6	1	0	1	.000	0	0	4.67
Faigin, Jason	Staten Ilnd	NYY	A-	22	22	0	0	6	31	137	25	19	14	0	2	0	2	18	0	27	5	2	2	2	.500	0	1	4.06
Farizo, Brad	Brevard Cty	Fla	A+	22	7	2	0	1	26	121	35	24	19	2	0	0	2	8	1	10	2	1	1	2	.333	0	1	6.58
	Kane County	Fla	A	22	10	8	0	1	49.1	209	50	23	20	3	3	0	1	10	0	37	4	1	3	4	.429	0	0	3.65
Farley, Joe*	Salem-Keizr	SF	A-	22	16	14	0	0	76	345	63	42	37	9	1	3	6	56	0	87	3	2	4	4	.500	0	0	4.38
Farmer, Jason	Salem-Keizr	SF	A-	26	16	9	0	0	66.2	287	58	19	12	2	4	2	7	31	0	47	1	1	3	3	.500	0	0	1.62
Farren, Dave	Bluefield	Bal	R+	20	15	5	0	4	37	189	59	45	33	3	2	2	4	17	0	27	4	0	2	4	.333	0	0	8.03
Faust, Wesley	Salem-Keizr	SF	A-	23	15	11	0	1	84.1	363	102	44	36	9	2	0	2	24	0	56	5	1	6	4	.600	0	0	3.84
Fawcett, Mike	Billings	Cin	R+	23	14	0	0	4	16.1	81	28	15	12	1	1	1	0	4	0	7	0	0	2	1	.667	0	1	6.61
Featherstone, D.	San Jose	SF	A+	24	1	0	0	0	3.1	19	7	3	2	0	0	1	1	0	0	2	0	0	0	0	.000	0	0	5.40
	Salem-Keizr	SF	A-	24	12	3	0	2	18.1	111	25	23	19	3	1	0	3	34	0	15	9	0	0	2	.000	0	0	9.33
	Giants	SF	R	24	1	0	0	1	1.1	8	2	2	2	1	0	0	0	2	0	2	1	0	0	0	.000	0	0	13.50
Feleciano, Ruben	Rangers	Tex	R	21	19	0	0	8	37	166	38	17	15	1	2	1	3	21	2	23	7	1	6	2	.750	0	3	3.65
Felix, Miguel	Winston-Sal	CWS	A+	24	27	0	0	10	35.1	167	39	32	30	2	1	2	6	21	0	32	9	0	0	0	.000	0	0	7.64
	Frederick	Bal	A+	24	8	0	0	4	11.1	65	18	17	17	3	0	0	6	11	0	5	0	0	0	0	.000	0	0	13.50
Fereira, Ramon	Martinsvlle	Hou	R+	22	16	2	0	6	35	165	43	36	30	3	0	0	3	16	1	31	3	0	2	3	.400	0	0	7.71
Ferguson, Ian	Spokane	KC	A-	21	15	15	0	0	71.1	312	76	38	26	6	5	2	4	16	0	66	9	1	5	6	.455	0	0	3.28
Ferran, Dario	Bristol	CWS	R+	20	13	12	2	0	82	352	92	39	34	6	2	2	4	20	0	73	9	2	5	5	.500	0	0	3.73
Ferrand, Julian	Rockies	Col	R	21	16	0	0	4	22	96	18	5	5	0	0	1	0	12	0	12	1	1	0	0	.000	0	1	2.05
Ferrari, Anthony*	Vermont	Mon	A-	23	25	0	0	21	47.1	190	31	14	9	2	3	0	5	15	0	37	2	1	2	2	.500	0	5	1.71
Field, Luke	Mahoning Vy	Cle	A-	22	22	1	0	6	49.2	221	56	36	27	3	0	3	3	21	0	31	4	2	2	3	.400	0	0	4.89
Field, Nathan	Chston-WV	KC	A	25	17	0	0	4	36.1	152	28	10	9	2	4	1	2	15	0	31	3	1	1	2	.333	0	0	2.23
Figueroa, Carlos*	Charlotte	Tex	A+	22	33	1	0	7	58	270	53	41	37	0	2	1	5	44	1	51	6	1	6	3	.667	0	1	5.74
Fikac, Jeremy	Rancho Cuca	SD	A+	26	61	0	0	43	75	298	46	19	15	2	4	1	4	24	0	101	6	0	5	3	.625	0	20	1.80
Fingers, Jason	Spokane	KC	A-	22	18	0	0	12	29.1	134	35	18	12	1	0	0	0	11	0	24	4	0	1	2	.333	0	2	3.68
Fiora, Chris	Potomac	StL	A+	22	1	0	0	0	0.1	3	0	1	1	0	0	0	1	1	0	1	0	0	0	0	.000	0	0	27.00
	New Jersey	StL	A-	22	27	0	0	7	28.2	159	33	31	23	0	0	0	5	35	0	30	9	0	2	0	1.000	0	1	7.22
Fischer, Eric*	Winston-Sal	CWS	A+	21	25	12	0	0	69.2	338	91	66	56	8	4	0	1	36	1	49	7	1	4	9	.308	0	0	7.23
Fischer, Mike	San Berndno	LA	A+	24	11	10	0	0	45.1	198	53	24	20	4	0	1	2	17	0	33	3	0	2	2	.500	0	0	3.97
Fischer, Rich	Butte	Ana	R+	20	18	13	1	2	70	335	103	63	46	8	0	1	3	26	0	45	6	0	3	5	.375	0	1	5.91
Fischer, Steve	Vancouver	Oak	A-	23	18	2	0	3	46	186	35	19	15	1	1	2	1	12	1	42	1	0	3	2	.600	0	1	2.93
Fitch, Steve	Mahoning Vy	Cle	A-	23	12	10	0	0	61	255	68	30	29	3	4	1	0	12	0	38	1	0	5	1	.833	0	0	4.28
Fitzgerald, Ryan	Michigan	Hou	A	25	28	0	0	11	50.1	217	44	24	21	6	1	0	3	21	1	43	4	0	3	2	.600	0	1	3.75
Flading, Cameron	Boise	Ana	A-	22	3	0	0	2	4	19	7	4	4	0	0	1	0	1	0	5	0	0	0	0	.000	0	0	9.00
	Butte	Ana	R+	22	4	0	0	2	4.2	22	4	2	1	0	0	2	0	4	1	3	0	0	0	0	.000	0	0	1.93
Flanagan, Jeremy	Cubs	ChC	R	20	9	6	0	1	26.1	120	33	19	17	2	1	1	1	15	0	20	4	0	0	1	.000	0	1	5.81
Flanagan, Ryan	Elizabethtn	Min	R+	22	18	0	0	7	20.2	105	18	21	18	3	1	0	3	23	0	21	5	0	0	0	.000	0	0	7.84
Flannery, Michael	Utica	Fla	A-	21	13	13	0	0	70	304	71	51	38	8	0	4	3	20	0	44	5	1	2	7	.222	0	0	4.89
Fleming, Emar	Charlotte	Tex	A+	24	42	8	1	18	118.2	509	121	53	46	8	5	6	6	39	1	93	4	1	6	6	.500	1	4	3.49
Fleming, John	High Desert	Ari	A+	23	13	7	0	2	42.2	202	53	36	29	3	1	2	1	26	0	39	0	0	2	3	.400	0	0	6.12
Fleming, Travis	Delmarva	Bal	A	24	53	0	0	32	72	308	74	32	31	7	0	0	2	21	3	85	2	0	7	2	.778	0	11	3.88
Fletcher, Dan	Billings	Cin	R+	19	8	4	0	0	18	100	25	31	30	5	0	0	3	22	0	14	4	0	0	2	.000	0	0	15.00
Flohr, Adam*	St. Pete	TB	A+	24	27	27	2	0	173.1	729	173	88	68	7	5	2	9	51	0	134	10	0	6	11	.353	1	0	3.53

2000 Pitching — Class-A and Rookie Leagues

HOW MUCH HE PITCHED											WHAT HE GAVE UP												THE RESULTS					
Player	Team	Org	Lg	A	G	GS	CG	GF	IP	BFP	H	R	ER	HR	SH	SF	HB	TBB	IBB	SO	WP	Bk	W	L	Pct.	ShO	Sv	ERA
Flores, Benito*	San Jose	SF	A+	25	48	2	0	17	108.2	504	131	74	56	9	10	4	4	55	3	62	3	0	2	9	.182	0	0	4.64
Flores, Neomar	Medcine Hat	Tor	R+	19	1	1	0	0	3	14	6	4	4	1	0	0	0	1	0	2	0	0	0	0	.000	0	0	12.00
Flores, Ron*	Vancouver	Oak	A-	21	13	0	0	1	12.1	60	16	10	7	2	0	1	1	4	0	10	1	0	1	1	.500	0	0	5.11
Fontana, Tony	Lowell	Bos	A-	22	14	11	1	1	72.1	294	61	29	20	1	3	2	5	17	0	46	6	1	5	4	.556	1	1	2.49
Forbes, Derek	High Desert	Ari	A+	22	20	2	0	4	40.1	186	37	40	37	9	1	3	0	31	1	38	2	0	0	3	.000	0	0	8.26
Forbes, Keith	Rancho Cuca	SD	A+	24	74	0	0	24	98	437	79	59	44	10	7	5	3	59	0	99	10	5	5	6	.455	0	1	4.04
Ford, Matt*	Hagerstown	Tor	A	20	18	14	1	0	83.2	353	81	42	36	5	0	4	3	36	0	86	5	0	5	3	.625	0	0	3.87
Ford, Thomas*	Bluefield	Bal	R+	24	19	0	0	6	36.2	146	27	19	16	2	1	0	2	15	0	41	1	2	1	0	1.000	0	3	3.93
Fortin, Mike	Williamsprt	Pit	A-	23	16	0	0	7	28.1	137	36	20	15	2	1	2	3	16	0	12	2	0	0	2	.000	0	0	4.76
Fortunato, B.	Princeton	TB	R+	20	17	5	0	2	46.2	223	56	31	24	4	2	1	4	19	0	51	8	0	3	4	.429	0	1	4.63
Forystek, Brian*	Orioles	Bal	R	22	11	0	0	3	19.1	86	18	10	8	1	2	0	1	8	2	28	3	0	4	0	1.000	0	1	3.72
	Frederick	Bal	A+	22	3	0	0	0	6.2	28	5	1	1	0	0	0	0	1	0	7	1	0	1	0	1.000	0	0	1.35
Fossum, Casey*	Sarasota	Bos	A+	23	27	27	3	0	149.1	623	147	71	57	7	2	6	7	36	0	143	3	0	9	10	.474	3	0	3.44
Foster, John*	Myrtle Bch	Atl	A+	23	38	0	0	17	48.2	204	48	13	10	2	4	2	2	14	4	46	4	0	2	1	.667	0	3	1.85
Foster, Kris	San Berndno	LA	A+	26	10	1	0	5	11.2	42	7	2	1	0	0	0	1	1	0	19	0	0	0	0	.000	0	2	0.77
Francisco, Franklin	Red Sox	Bos	R	21	1	0	0	0	1	7	2	3	2	0	0	0	0	2	0	1	1	0	0	0	.000	0	0	18.00
Franco, Jose	Greensboro	NYY	A	23	39	0	0	36	44	185	34	17	15	2	3	0	1	20	2	47	3	0	3	3	.500	0	17	3.07
	Staten Ilnd	NYY	A-	23	5	0	0	2	5.2	24	3	0	0	0	0	0	0	4	1	7	0	0	0	0	.000	0	1	0.00
Franco, Martire	Piedmont	Phi	A	20	24	23	2	0	126.1	573	146	70	58	7	3	4	6	57	0	89	10	2	8	6	.571	2	0	4.13
Franke, Aaron	Boise	Ana	A-	21	6	6	0	0	28.2	129	24	19	17	2	0	3	2	23	1	19	4	0	3	1	.750	0	0	5.34
	Cedar Rapds	Ana	A	21	8	8	0	0	40.2	206	60	46	35	4	2	4	1	30	0	37	3	1	0	6	.000	0	0	7.75
Frasor, Jason	W Michigan	Det	A	23	14	14	0	0	71.1	300	55	32	26	2	0	2	4	29	0	65	5	1	5	3	.625	0	0	3.28
Frederick, Kevin	Quad City	Min	A	24	27	0	0	11	46	193	34	17	12	1	3	1	4	23	4	51	4	0	5	0	1.000	0	4	2.35
	Fort Myers	Min	A+	24	19	0	0	7	30	123	20	11	9	0	1	1	1	14	1	37	4	2	2	1	.667	0	3	2.70
Freed, Mark*	Eugene	ChC	A-	22	15	13	1	1	88	351	77	36	35	3	3	1	1	30	1	66	1	0	9	2	.818	0	0	3.58
Frendling, Neal	Chston-SC	TB	A	21	27	27	4	0	157	654	137	73	59	13	3	6	10	46	0	174	13	1	8	8	.500	0	0	3.38
Frey, Chris	Charlotte	Tex	A+	27	30	0	0	21	51.1	218	43	21	15	2	1	1	2	14	0	40	2	0	5	2	.714	0	7	2.63
Frias, Juan	Chston-SC	TB	A	22	7	0	0	1	10.2	46	13	6	6	1	0	0	0	4	0	9	1	0	2	0	1.000	0	0	5.06
	Hudson Val	TB	A-	22	23	0	0	9	36.2	178	44	32	26	4	2	3	5	19	2	33	4	0	0	4	.000	0	0	6.38
Fries, Scott*	Eugene	ChC	A-	23	26	0	0	10	46	189	35	17	13	1	1	2	1	16	4	51	1	0	2	1	.667	0	3	2.54
Fry, Justin	Piedmont	Phi	A	24	44	0	0	32	57.1	241	40	19	16	2	2	2	5	23	5	77	2	0	4	4	.500	0	13	2.51
Fuell, Jerrod	Tigers	Det	R	20	13	0	0	6	21.2	114	30	23	20	4	0	1	0	19	0	25	2	0	1	2	.333	0	0	8.31
Fugarino, Steve	Mahoning Vy	Cle	A-	23	14	0	0	8	17	78	16	10	10	3	0	0	3	9	0	14	3	0	0	1	.000	0	1	5.29
Gagliano, Steve	Lansing	ChC	A	23	12	2	0	3	32	145	34	18	15	0	0	1	1	13	0	13	1	0	2	0	1.000	0	0	4.22
	Daytona	ChC	A+	23	16	3	0	3	39	161	29	14	12	4	1	0	4	10	0	40	7	1	1	1	.500	0	3	2.77
Gallo, Mike*	Michigan	Hou	A	23	24	13	0	3	90.2	406	104	58	49	6	5	6	3	27	1	56	4	1	8	3	.727	0	0	4.86
Galva, Claudio*	Visalia	Oak	A+	21	48	7	0	30	97.1	421	103	54	39	9	1	3	1	29	0	98	3	1	7	4	.636	0	15	3.61
Galvez, Willy	Red Sox	Bos	R	19	3	2	0	0	14.2	57	11	6	5	0	0	0	1	7	0	11	0	0	2	1	.667	0	0	3.07
Gamble, Jerome	Augusta	Bos	A	21	15	15	0	0	78.2	335	69	26	22	1	0	3	5	32	0	71	9	0	5	3	.625	0	0	2.52
Gandy, Josh*	Kinston	Cle	A+	25	9	0	0	4	18.1	85	22	11	10	3	0	2	1	9	0	18	1	0	1	0	1.000	0	0	4.91
Gangemi, Joe*	Beloit	Mil	A	25	11	4	0	4	25	115	34	20	20	2	1	0	3	8	0	19	4	1	1	1	.500	0	0	7.20
Garcia, Carlos	San Berndno	LA	A+	22	27	27	2	0	182	737	162	61	52	5	5	4	14	49	0	106	2	3	14	7	.667	1	0	2.57
Garcia, Gabe	Kissimmee	Hou	A+	24	40	4	0	12	77.1	358	90	54	48	6	8	2	10	34	1	62	4	0	2	3	.400	0	1	5.59
Garcia, Rafael	Royals	KC	R	23	13	6	0	2	44.1	189	34	22	16	1	1	1	3	24	0	55	4	1	4	4	.500	0	0	3.25
Garcia, Raul	Chston-WV	KC	A	24	40	0	0	15	55.2	253	63	35	29	5	2	2	5	28	0	57	4	0	0	5	.000	0	0	4.69
Garcia, Reynaldo	Savannah	Tex	A	23	49	2	1	35	97	410	87	37	29	6	2	4	5	33	1	82	8	0	6	7	.462	0	14	2.69
Garcia, Rosman	Greensboro	NYY	A	22	23	15	1	1	104.1	454	115	67	53	12	3	1	4	35	0	73	5	1	6	6	.500	0	0	4.57
	Tampa	NYY	A+	22	4	3	0	1	18	77	18	13	11	1	0	3	2	4	0	6	0	1	0	2	.000	0	1	5.50
Garcia, Sonny	Delmarva	Bal	A	24	26	21	1	0	110.2	478	106	55	46	12	2	2	5	38	1	123	2	1	6	7	.462	0	0	3.74
Gardea, Mario	Billings	Cin	R+	21	23	0	0	12	32.1	166	32	27	19	0	0	1	2	40	1	35	13	0	0	3	.000	0	2	5.29
Gardner, Hayden	Rangers	Tex	R	20	17	1	0	10	28	128	28	11	7	1	2	3	0	16	1	23	0	0	0	3	.000	0	3	2.25
Gargano, Mike	Potomac	StL	A+	22	38	3	0	9	63.2	294	71	37	36	6	5	1	7	38	3	23	6	0	1	3	.250	0	0	5.09
Garibaldi, Cecilio	St. Pete	TB	A+	23	25	17	2	2	110	465	101	59	45	9	1	7	10	36	2	73	6	0	5	7	.417	0	0	3.68
Garner, Brandon	Portland	Col	A-	21	18	0	0	2	32	141	33	22	21	3	1	0	1	10	0	23	2	1	0	1	.000	0	0	5.91
Garris, Antonio	Cape Fear	Mon	A	23	1	0	0	1	2	9	2	2	2	1	0	0	0	1	0	2	0	0	0	0	.000	0	0	9.00
	Vermont	Mon	A-	23	24	0	0	18	34.2	144	17	9	7	1	1	1	0	25	0	44	2	0	3	1	.750	0	10	1.82
Garza, Alberto	Kinston	Cle	A+	24	22	15	0	3	78.1	372	61	58	49	8	3	3	11	81	0	85	8	0	4	10	.286	0	0	5.63
Gehrke, Jay	Chston-WV	KC	A	23	43	0	0	28	60	276	50	36	25	3	3	4	2	42	1	38	4	1	1	4	.200	0	4	3.75
Geigel, Rolando	Marlins	Fla	R	21	7	0	0	5	12.1	64	15	15	9	2	1	1	6	3	0	17	3	0	0	2	.000	0	1	6.57
	Brevard Cty	Fla	A+	21	5	0	0	1	10	43	9	5	4	1	1	0	0	4	1	5	2	0	2	0	1.000	0	0	3.60
Generelli, Dan	Red Sox	Bos	R	20	7	1	0	1	17.1	80	12	10	7	1	0	0	1	16	0	17	5	3	1	1	.500	0	1	3.63
Gentile, Mark*	White Sox	CWS	R	20	3	0	0	0	1	12	4	7	7	0	0	0	1	5	0	0	5	0	0	0	.000	0	0	63.00
George, Bradley	Billings	Cin	R+	19	11	8	0	1	47.2	215	51	28	25	2	0	1	6	21	0	55	9	0	2	0	1.000	0	1	4.72
George, Chris	Michigan	Hou	A	23	48	0	0	43	58.2	221	34	12	9	3	1	4	1	21	3	54	3	0	3	2	.600	0	24	1.38
George, Nelson	Reds	Cin	R	19	10	0	0	4	20	113	21	26	21	1	1	1	5	25	1	15	11	0	1	0	1.000	0	0	9.45
Gerk, Jordan*	Oneonta	Det	A-	21	11	7	0	0	42.2	179	42	20	16	1	1	3	0	11	0	31	0	1	1	2	.333	0	0	3.38
Gerlach, Brian	Twins	Min	R	23	25	0	0	14	29.2	110	15	5	3	1	1	0	0	12	3	35	0	0	3	1	.750	0	4	0.91
German, Franklyn	Modesto	Oak	A+	21	17	14	0	2	72	333	88	55	44	4	0	3	6	37	0	52	7	2	5	5	.500	0	0	5.50
	Vancouver	Oak	A-	21	9	2	0	2	20.1	86	13	4	4	0	0	0	1	10	0	20	4	0	1	0	1.000	0	0	1.77
German, Yon*	St. Lucie	NYM	A+	23	14	12	0	0	70.2	297	76	33	21	5	2	1	1	14	0	33	1	0	4	4	.500	0	0	2.67
Germano, Justin	Padres	SD	R	18	17	8	0	4	66.2	277	65	36	34	4	3	1	3	9	0	67	5	1	5	5	.500	0	1	4.59
Giese, Daniel	Lowell	Bos	A-	24	15	0	0	13	19.2	75	12	3	2	1	1	0	0	1	0	20	1	0	0	0	.000	0	9	0.92
	Sarasota	Bos	A+	24	8	0	0	2	14.1	64	19	8	5	2	0	1	0	2	0	13	0	0	1	0	1.000	0	0	3.14
Gilbert, Richard*	Rangers	Tex	R	21	1	1	0	0	4	22	7	6	6	0	0	2	1	4	0	0	0	0	0	0	.000	0	0	13.50
	Pulaski	Tex	R+	21	12	12	1	0	69	300	63	45	37	5	2	5	4	32	0	82	6	1	3	4	.429	0	0	4.83
Gill, Ryan	Yankees	NYY	R	24	10	0	0	5	16.1	60	6	1	0	0	0	0	1	5	0	10	1	1	2	0	1.000	0	3	0.00
Gilmore, Travis*	Boise	Ana	A-	22	3	0	0	3	2.2	11	2	0	0	0	0	0	0	2	0	4	0	0	0	0	.000	0	0	0.00

2000 Pitching — Class-A and Rookie Leagues

HOW MUCH HE PITCHED											WHAT HE GAVE UP												THE RESULTS					
Player	Team	Org	Lg	A	G	GS	CG	GF	IP	BFP	H	R	ER	HR	SH	SF	HB	TBB	IBB	SO	WP	Bk	W	L	Pct.	ShO	Sv	ERA
	Butte	Ana	R+	22	14	1	0	3	27.1	143	32	28	23	2	1	3	0	27	1	24	1	0	1	1	.500	0	0	7.57
Gilpatrick, Tyler	Vancouver	Oak	A-	22	15	2	0	5	21.1	109	34	24	21	0	0	0	0	17	0	17	1	0	2	2	.500	0	0	8.86
Girdley, Josh*	Vermont	Mon	A-	20	14	14	0	0	79.1	321	60	32	26	4	1	6	5	28	0	70	5	0	5	0	1.000	0	0	2.95
Giuliano, Joe	Dayton	Cin	A	25	22	1	0	15	38	179	48	31	23	4	1	2	3	13	0	30	2	2	0	3	.000	0	4	5.45
Glascock, John-P.	Cubs	ChC	R	21	15	1	0	7	30.2	157	38	33	26	0	3	3	8	25	0	20	6	0	2	5	.286	0	0	7.63
Glaser, Eric	Augusta	Bos	A	23	32	16	1	8	124.1	493	103	53	46	14	0	4	3	34	1	120	4	0	9	6	.600	1	1	3.33
Gleason, Mike	Rangers	Tex	R	19	10	0	0	4	14.2	71	12	9	6	0	1	0	2	14	1	9	0	0	2	0	1.000	0	2	3.68
Glidewell, Clifton*	Yakima	LA	A-	23	10	0	0	5	13.2	70	24	18	16	4	1	1	0	6	0	12	2	0	0	1	.000	0	0	10.54
	Great Falls	LA	R+	23	6	0	0	1	10.2	43	8	4	1	1	0	0	1	5	0	10	0	0	1	1	.500	0	0	0.84
Gobble, Jimmy*	Chston-WV	KC	A	19	25	25	3	0	145	604	144	75	59	10	1	2	4	34	0	115	1	1	12	10	.545	2	0	3.66
Gold, J.M.	Beloit	Mil	A	21	7	7	0	0	34	143	27	13	11	0	2	0	1	16	0	33	1	0	3	1	.750	0	0	2.91
Gomer, Jeramy*	Lansing	ChC	A	22	24	24	1	0	135	607	141	84	69	15	6	6	11	55	0	98	12	1	6	8	.429	0	0	4.60
Gomez, Benito*	Princeton	TB	R+	22	25	0	0	1	39.1	179	35	19	17	5	2	2	4	24	0	46	4	0	4	1	.800	0	0	3.89
Gomez, Diogenes	Portland	Col	A-	22	25	0	0	23	24.2	104	22	7	5	1	1	0	0	8	2	17	1	0	2	2	.500	0	6	1.82
Gomez, Hunter	Helena	Mil	R+	23	12	0	0	9	20	96	25	16	14	2	0	0	3	9	1	25	1	4	1	3	.250	0	2	6.30
Gomez, Mariano*	Burlington	Cle	R+	18	13	11	0	0	54.1	247	77	44	26	7	1	3	1	16	0	30	5	3	0	5	.000	0	0	4.31
Gomez, Odalis	Cedar Rapds	Ana	A	22	7	0	0	0	16.1	92	27	20	16	2	0	3	1	19	0	13	10	1	1	0	1.000	0	0	8.82
Gomez, Rafael	Kingsport	NYM	R+	23	5	5	0	0	25	110	26	12	11	2	0	0	1	9	0	20	2	1	1	1	.500	0	0	3.96
	Capital Cty	NYM	A	23	10	0	0	7	20.1	90	25	16	15	4	0	0	1	6	0	18	0	0	1	2	.333	0	1	6.64
Gomez, Ricardo	Staten Ilnd	NYY	A-	23	20	0	0	7	41	165	25	8	8	1	2	1	2	21	0	40	7	1	3	1	.750	0	1	1.76
Gonzalez, Cristian	Modesto	Oak	A+	22	4	0	0	0	8.1	45	16	9	8	1	0	0	1	5	0	4	2	0	0	0	.000	0	0	8.64
	Athletics	Oak	R	22	14	6	0	3	54.2	249	78	45	32	6	5	2	6	8	1	36	0	0	3	1	.750	0	1	5.27
Gonzalez, Giovanni	Pirates	Pit	R	21	7	0	0	4	9	42	8	7	4	0	0	3	2	5	0	5	0	0	1	0	1.000	0	0	4.00
Gonzalez, Jeremi	Cubs	ChC	R	26	4	4	0	0	10	40	8	3	3	0	0	0	0	2	0	15	0	0	0	1	.000	0	0	2.70
	Lansing	ChC	A	26	1	1	0	0	0.2	2	0	0	0	0	0	0	0	0	0	2	0	0	0	0	.000	0	0	0.00
Gonzalez, Jose	Red Sox	Bos	R	21	6	6	0	0	26	114	24	12	10	1	0	0	8	13	0	14	1	0	1	0	1.000	0	0	3.46
Gonzalez, Miguel	Rockies	Col	R	21	15	0	0	6	20.2	91	19	13	11	0	1	1	1	15	0	17	1	1	2	2	.500	0	0	4.79
Gonzalez, Mike*	Pirates	Pit	R	23	2	1	0	1	6	35	8	6	3	1	0	0	1	4	0	7	3	0	1	0	1.000	0	0	4.50
	Lynchburg	Pit	A+	23	12	10	0	1	56	256	57	34	29	6	5	2	3	34	0	53	1	0	4	3	.571	0	0	4.66
Good, Eric*	Cape Fear	Mon	A	21	8	8	0	0	36	157	31	15	11	1	0	3	5	12	0	32	3	1	1	2	.333	0	0	2.75
Gordon, Justin*	Ogden	Mil	R+	22	16	15	0	0	76	337	69	45	36	7	1	2	1	42	0	53	10	0	5	5	.500	0	0	4.26
Gordon, Kevin	Kane County	Fla	A	24	23	0	0	6	36.1	161	31	17	16	3	1	2	2	19	0	43	6	1	2	1	.667	0	1	3.96
Gorman, Pat	Capital Cty	NYM	A	23	30	0	0	27	37.1	163	24	10	8	1	1	1	1	28	2	54	9	0	2	2	.500	0	15	1.93
	Delmarva	Bal	A	23	2	0	0	2	2.2	11	1	0	0	0	0	0	1	1	0	5	0	0	0	0	.000	0	1	0.00
	Frederick	Bal	A+	23	7	0	0	7	7	31	6	1	1	0	0	0	0	4	0	7	0	0	0	0	.000	0	5	1.29
Goure, Sam*	Portland	Col	A-	23	22	3	0	5	29	147	33	24	20	1	1	2	5	24	1	23	3	0	1	1	.500	0	0	6.21
Grace, Bryan	Tampa	NYY	A+	25	5	0	0	2	6	32	10	6	6	0	0	0	0	6	0	1	1	0	0	1	.000	0	0	9.00
	Yankees	NYY	R	25	5	3	0	1	18	79	15	10	7	1	0	1	1	6	0	22	2	0	1	1	.500	0	0	3.50
Gracesqui, F.*	Medcine Hat	Tor	R+	21	8	4	0	0	24	105	15	11	7	1	1	0	2	21	0	20	5	0	0	1	.000	0	0	2.63
	Hagerstown	Tor	A	21	3	1	0	1	7.1	33	4	4	4	1	0	0	1	9	0	6	0	0	0	1	.000	0	0	4.91
Graham, Brian	Bristol	CWS	R+	23	12	12	0	0	65.2	274	63	35	28	3	3	1	2	19	0	52	2	1	5	4	.556	0	0	3.84
	Winston-Sal	CWS	A+	23	1	1	0	0	5.2	27	7	5	2	0	1	0	0	0	0	1	1	0	0	0	.000	0	0	3.18
Graham, Elgin	Salem-Keizr	SF	A-	23	19	2	0	6	35	165	37	24	24	1	1	2	2	25	0	24	3	0	1	1	.500	0	0	6.17
Graham, Frank	Capital Cty	NYM	A	22	27	25	1	0	143.1	636	152	80	69	7	3	5	23	52	0	109	11	0	10	12	.455	0	0	4.33
Graham, Tom	Rangers	Tex	R	23	18	4	0	3	59	236	57	17	15	1	0	2	4	8	1	53	1	0	5	0	1.000	0	2	2.29
Granadillo, Adel	Burlington	Cle	R+	22	3	3	0	0	8.1	34	3	1	1	0	0	0	5	4	0	9	1	1	0	0	.000	0	0	1.08
Granado, Jan*	Reds	Cin	R	18	5	0	0	2	9	39	11	1	1	0	0	0	0	3	0	8	0	0	0	0	.000	0	0	1.00
Granados, Bernie	Rockies	Col	R	22	12	0	0	10	12	61	17	11	6	0	1	0	0	7	0	12	2	1	1	1	.500	0	2	4.50
Grassing, Bryan	Johnson Cty	StL	R+	23	27	0	0	7	39.2	184	53	32	26	3	1	1	2	9	0	36	6	0	1	3	.250	0	0	5.90
Grater, Kevin	Beloit	Mil	A	23	17	7	0	4	60.1	251	51	23	20	8	1	1	3	18	0	52	2	0	2	1	.667	0	2	2.98
Graves, Donovan	Johnson Cty	StL	R+	20	13	12	0	0	56	251	58	42	28	2	0	3	1	33	0	48	3	0	3	4	.429	0	0	4.50
Gray, Brett	Dayton	Cin	A	24	13	4	1	4	47.2	193	37	19	16	6	3	1	3	13	2	43	1	0	5	3	.625	0	0	3.02
Gray, Michael*	Myrtle Bch	Atl	A+	24	30	0	0	17	52.2	212	50	24	22	7	2	2	0	10	1	53	0	0	2	3	.400	0	1	3.76
Gray, Rusty	Ogden	Mil	R+	23	8	0	0	2	15	68	18	9	5	0	1	2	0	4	1	11	2	0	2	0	1.000	0	1	3.00
Green, Sean	Portland	Col	A-	22	22	0	0	4	28.2	155	45	32	27	2	1	2	5	19	2	17	5	0	1	4	.200	0	0	8.48
Grezlovski, Ben	Cedar Rapds	Ana	A	24	11	0	0	10	9.2	45	9	6	4	0	0	0	0	6	1	12	0	0	0	1	.000	0	6	3.72
	Lk Elsinore	Ana	A+	24	43	0	0	33	53.1	241	48	33	31	2	3	1	2	30	4	51	5	0	2	4	.333	0	13	5.23
Griffin, Kirk	Potomac	StL	A+	26	50	0	0	24	61.2	269	64	35	25	4	2	6	6	18	3	34	4	0	2	6	.250	0	2	3.65
Griffiths, Jeremy	Capital Cty	NYM	A	23	26	26	0	0	128.2	548	120	78	62	12	1	4	8	39	0	138	8	0	7	12	.368	0	0	4.34
Grippo, Mike*	New Jersey	StL	A-	25	22	0	0	9	24	118	21	16	13	0	1	0	6	18	0	36	9	0	0	2	.000	0	1	4.88
	Peoria	StL	A	25	5	0	0	2	6.2	28	2	4	2	0	1	0	0	6	0	8	0	0	0	0	.000	0	0	2.70
Griswold, Jordan*	Expos	Mon	R	19	14	4	0	5	32.1	146	22	13	13	0	1	1	0	33	0	30	2	0	1	1	.500	0	1	3.62
Gross, Kyle	Salem-Keizr	SF	A-	22	8	2	0	0	13	75	15	14	11	1	2	2	5	18	0	9	1	0	1	2	.333	0	0	7.62
Gross, Rafael	Columbus	Cle	A	26	8	0	0	7	18	66	11	5	5	3	0	0	0	3	0	23	0	0	1	0	1.000	0	1	2.50
	Kinston	Cle	A+	26	29	0	0	17	52.2	225	50	24	21	7	0	0	1	19	1	42	3	1	2	2	.500	0	5	3.59
Gruban, Jarret	Butte	Ana	R+	22	8	7	0	0	35	162	31	26	16	1	1	1	2	23	0	26	11	0	1	1	.500	0	0	4.11
	Boise	Ana	A-	22	6	6	0	0	26	120	28	20	15	3	1	2	3	17	0	18	3	0	1	2	.333	0	0	5.19
	Cedar Rapds	Ana	A	22	1	1	0	0	6	25	4	2	2	0	0	1	0	5	0	0	0	0	0	1	.000	0	0	3.00
Grunwald, Erik	Wisconsin	Sea	A	24	37	0	0	19	66.1	276	53	24	15	3	3	2	3	18	2	59	5	0	2	1	.667	0	3	2.04
Guerrero, Julio	Pirates	Pit	R	20	11	9	0	1	57	242	56	28	20	2	1	2	4	9	0	25	2	2	5	3	.625	0	0	3.16
Guerrero, Neftali	Kingsport	NYM	R+	21	15	0	0	7	23	109	31	16	12	0	1	1	0	8	0	19	3	0	0	1	.000	0	0	4.70
Gutierrez, Fernando	Orioles	Bal	R	20	17	0	0	13	24	116	22	15	14	1	3	1	1	20	3	28	2	5	3	2	.600	0	1	5.25
Guzman, Alexis	Medcine Hat	Tor	R+	21	27	1	0	6	53	226	49	25	14	3	4	2	6	11	0	35	2	0	6	8	.429	0	0	2.38
Guzman, Ambiorix	Charlotte	Tex	A+	23	31	2	0	16	56.2	234	65	29	26	5	1	2	2	6	2	35	1	0	1	4	.200	0	3	4.13
Gwyn, Marcus	Vancouver	Oak	A-	23	12	2	0	5	28.1	124	29	16	9	0	2	0	4	2	0	31	3	1	2	1	.667	0	1	2.86
Haase, Frank*	Portland	Col	A-	21	5	0	0	0	5	33	9	8	8	0	0	1	3	6	1	4	0	0	0	0	.000	0	0	14.40
	Rockies	Col	R	21	14	1	0	1	18	88	16	21	19	0	1	1	1	16	0	9	2	0	1	2	.333	0	0	9.50

2000 Pitching — Class-A and Rookie Leagues

HOW MUCH HE PITCHED											WHAT HE GAVE UP												THE RESULTS					
Player	Team	Org	Lg	A	G	GS	CG	GF	IP	BFP	H	R	ER	HR	SH	SF	HB	TBB	IBB	SO	WP	Bk	W	L	Pct.	ShO	Sv	ERA
Hadden, Randy	Vero Beach	LA	A+	23	36	5	0	11	95.2	426	113	52	47	12	3	6	6	29	2	52	4	2	9	3	.750	0	1	4.42
Hall, Dan	Ogden	Mil	R+	22	23	0	0	21	26	119	27	13	11	5	2	1	1	11	2	36	0	2	1	3	.250	0	11	3.81
Hall, Josh	Reds	Cin	R	20	6	6	0	0	15.1	84	26	25	18	2	0	1	0	13	0	20	3	0	0	5	.000	0	0	10.57
Hall, Kevin	Pirates	Pit	R	21	13	0	0	11	17	79	21	4	3	0	2	2	1	7	0	20	1	0	1	2	.333	0	4	1.59
Hall, Shane	Red Sox	Bos	R	21	15	3	0	2	45.2	216	47	27	21	2	2	1	3	28	1	31	1	1	4	2	.667	0	0	4.14
Halpin, Jeremy	Frederick	Bal	A+	26	25	0	0	13	40	192	52	37	32	6	3	1	2	17	0	13	4	0	2	2	.500	0	0	7.20
Halvorson, Greg	Capital Cty	NYM	A	24	29	14	0	7	108.1	502	132	82	69	9	2	3	10	49	0	90	17	0	3	8	.273	0	0	5.73
Hamann, Robert	Hagerstown	Tor	A	24	34	1	0	19	58	244	48	25	19	4	3	2	5	21	4	34	9	0	8	4	.667	0	6	2.95
	Dunedin	Tor	A+	24	16	0	0	13	24	91	16	5	4	2	1	1	0	7	3	14	2	1	2	1	.667	0	5	1.50
Hamilton, Charlie	Royals	KC	R	22	3	2	0	0	8	35	10	5	5	1	0	1	1	2	0	7	1	0	0	1	.000	0	0	5.63
Hamilton, Ryan	Martinsvlle	Hou	R+	23	8	8	1	0	50.1	205	45	23	19	2	2	2	3	9	0	31	4	0	3	3	.500	0	0	3.40
	Auburn	Hou	A-	23	5	5	0	0	25	112	28	17	16	1	3	1	2	9	0	15	3	0	0	3	.000	0	0	5.76
Hammons, Matt	Cubs	ChC	R	24	1	1	0	0	1.2	6	1	0	0	0	0	0	0	0	0	4	0	0	0	0	.000	0	0	0.00
Hampson, Justin*	Portland	Col	A-	21	14	13	0	0	68.2	309	74	43	27	5	3	2	4	27	0	44	1	0	1	8	.111	0	0	3.54
Hamulack, Tim*	Kissimmee	Hou	A+	24	41	0	0	20	56	251	67	37	31	3	2	1	1	21	1	54	0	0	3	1	.750	0	1	4.98
Hancock, Josh	Sarasota	Bos	A+	23	26	24	1	0	143.2	628	164	89	71	9	5	6	6	37	0	95	8	2	5	10	.333	0	0	4.45
Handy, Russell	Fort Wayne	SD	A	26	2	0	0	1	1	10	1	6	5	0	0	1	0	5	0	0	1	0	0	0	.000	0	0	45.00
Hannah, Shawn	Oneonta	Det	A-	24	16	1	1	5	41.1	157	31	8	6	0	1	1	0	7	1	25	3	0	6	1	.857	0	0	1.31
	W Michigan	Det	A	24	2	0	0	1	8	27	3	0	0	0	0	0	0	1	0	5	0	0	1	0	1.000	0	1	0.00
Hannaman, Ryan*	Giants	SF	R	19	5	0	0	2	3.1	26	4	8	8	0	0	2	1	11	0	6	4	0	0	1	.000	0	0	21.60
	Salem-Keizr	SF	A-	19	1	0	0	1	1	5	1	0	0	0	0	0	0	1	0	1	0	0	0	0	.000	0	0	0.00
Hanrahan, Joel	Great Falls	LA	R+	19	12	11	0	0	55	240	49	32	29	4	0	0	5	23	0	40	4	0	3	1	.750	0	0	4.75
Hanson, David	Medcine Hat	Tor	R+	20	15	15	0	0	79	352	82	55	51	6	3	2	5	29	0	79	12	1	7	3	.700	0	0	5.81
Harang, Aaron	Charlotte	Tex	A+	23	28	27	3	0	157	642	128	68	58	10	1	3	7	50	0	136	5	1	13	5	.722	2	0	3.32
Harber, Ryan*	Brevard Cty	Fla	A+	24	22	11	1	5	89.2	389	95	53	48	8	2	3	0	34	0	54	4	0	5	4	.556	0	0	4.82
Harrell, Tim	Vero Beach	LA	A+	25	30	18	1	5	117	508	121	77	65	9	1	7	3	44	1	89	8	1	7	7	.500	1	2	5.00
Harrelson, Ralph	Salem-Keizr	SF	A-	22	6	4	0	0	17	95	27	23	23	4	0	0	9	9	0	11	6	0	1	4	.200	0	0	12.18
Harris, J.T.	Cedar Rapds	Ana	A	25	28	6	0	11	63.2	283	75	41	33	6	3	1	1	20	0	43	4	0	3	5	.375	0	1	4.66
Harris, Julian*	Cedar Rapds	Ana	A	23	31	9	0	13	90	416	93	61	43	8	3	6	8	48	0	56	13	0	2	7	.222	0	2	4.30
Harris, Silas*	Cape Fear	Mon	A	24	14	0	0	9	24.2	114	23	23	12	2	0	0	0	17	1	17	7	0	1	2	.333	0	1	4.38
Harris, Toby	High Desert	Ari	A+	24	14	0	0	2	20.1	108	34	28	25	3	0	0	1	15	1	19	0	3	2	2	.500	0	0	11.07
	Beloit	Mil	A	24	11	0	0	3	18	92	22	18	13	4	1	0	4	9	0	9	2	1	1	2	.333	0	0	6.50
Harvey, Ian	Augusta	Bos	A	24	9	0	0	5	13.2	57	12	5	4	2	1	0	0	4	1	17	1	0	2	1	.667	0	0	2.63
Harvey, Victor	White Sox	CWS	R	20	16	2	0	4	22	129	43	35	31	3	0	0	2	20	0	25	3	1	0	2	.000	0	0	12.68
Hassler, Drew	Orioles	Bal	R	20	7	0	0	1	12.1	64	17	16	15	0	0	0	0	10	0	10	1	0	1	0	1.000	0	0	10.95
Hawk, David*	Williamsprt	Pit	A-	22	12	9	0	0	40	199	47	37	30	0	0	1	9	33	0	30	4	1	1	7	.125	0	0	6.75
Hawkins, Chad	Savannah	Tex	A	22	5	1	0	1	9.2	43	7	1	1	1	1	0	0	5	0	11	0	0	0	0	.000	0	1	0.93
Haworth, Brent	Boise	Ana	A-	24	5	0	0	3	11.1	60	17	7	6	1	0	0	2	7	0	6	0	0	0	1	.000	0	2	4.76
	Lk Elsinore	Ana	A+	24	17	0	0	9	33.2	142	42	18	15	5	1	0	0	6	0	13	0	1	3	2	.600	0	0	4.01
Hayden, Terry*	Dayton	Cin	A	26	15	3	0	5	35.1	157	44	23	22	5	2	1	4	7	0	19	3	0	0	1	.000	0	2	5.60
Haynes, Brad	Marlins	Fla	R	19	10	8	0	0	46.1	199	25	19	15	1	1	0	5	34	0	51	7	1	4	1	.800	0	0	2.91
Haynie, Jason*	Lynchburg	Pit	A+	27	23	21	0	1	109.1	487	133	76	67	17	4	4	4	43	1	76	5	0	6	12	.333	0	1	5.52
Hazelton, Justin	Mahoning Vy	Cle	A-	22	4	0	0	4	5	37	11	12	12	2	0	0	0	11	0	5	6	0	0	0	.000	0	0	21.60
Head, Daniel	Everett	Sea	A-	22	10	0	0	3	16	78	21	10	8	1	1	1	2	7	0	17	0	0	0	0	.000	0	0	4.50
Heath, Woody	Dunedin	Tor	A+	24	8	1	0	3	20	97	27	17	14	1	0	2	1	16	0	11	4	0	0	2	.000	0	1	6.30
Hebert, Cedric	Dayton	Cin	A	23	2	0	0	2	2.2	16	2	2	1	0	0	1	1	4	0	2	0	0	0	0	.000	0	0	3.38
	Billings	Cin	R+	23	8	7	0	0	39.1	161	31	17	15	4	0	1	5	18	0	33	2	3	5	2	.714	0	0	3.43
Heck, Chris*	Idaho Falls	SD	R+	24	19	0	0	3	31.1	145	42	19	14	3	2	0	0	9	0	25	2	0	1	1	.500	0	0	4.02
Hee, Aaron*	Pittsfield	NYM	A-	22	18	0	0	2	35.2	169	32	21	16	0	0	3	2	35	1	39	6	0	2	1	.667	0	0	4.04
Heimbach, Andy	Chston-SC	TB	A	23	6	4	0	0	20	94	25	14	13	2	1	0	4	8	1	13	5	0	1	1	.500	0	0	5.85
Henderson, Eric*	Ogden	Mil	R+	21	1	1	0	0	1.2	5	1	0	0	0	0	0	0	1	0	2	0	0	0	0	.000	0	0	0.00
Henderson, Kenny*	Williamsprt	Pit	A-	23	15	6	0	0	53.2	241	58	34	25	4	0	3	1	25	0	35	0	3	2	5	.286	0	0	4.19
Hendricks, John*	Capital Cty	NYM	A	23	7	0	0	3	12.1	63	15	18	12	3	0	1	4	6	0	12	0	0	0	1	.000	0	0	8.76
Hendrickson, Ben	Ogden	Mil	R+	20	13	7	0	2	50.2	237	50	37	32	7	1	2	1	29	0	48	12	0	4	3	.571	0	1	5.68
Henriquez, Hector*	Kane County	Fla	A	22	50	3	0	22	71.1	328	82	52	45	7	2	2	3	36	1	67	8	0	5	5	.500	0	1	5.68
Hensley, Matt	Butte	Ana	R+	22	8	5	0	0	28	132	29	21	8	0	0	0	2	10	0	22	3	3	1	2	.333	0	0	2.57
	Cedar Rapds	Ana	A	22	5	5	1	0	30.1	129	33	16	14	1	0	2	2	10	0	26	1	2	2	2	.500	0	0	4.15
	Lk Elsinore	Ana	A+	22	1	0	0	0	1	4	1	0	0	0	0	0	0	0	0	2	0	0	0	0	.000	0	0	0.00
Herbert, John	Idaho Falls	SD	R+	23	17	0	0	7	21.2	91	17	14	11	2	2	0	0	6	0	24	5	0	2	2	.500	0	0	4.57
Heredia, Nixon	Reds	Cin	R	18	5	0	0	4	5.1	27	8	4	2	0	0	1	0	2	0	3	0	1	0	0	.000	0	0	3.38
Hernandez, Buddy	Jamestown	Atl	A-	22	12	0	0	4	23	90	17	5	4	0	0	1	0	7	0	35	0	1	1	1	.500	0	3	1.57
Hernandez, Carlos*	Michigan	Hou	A	21	22	22	2	0	110.2	490	92	57	47	8	5	3	11	63	0	115	10	1	6	6	.500	1	0	3.82
Hernandez, Fausto	Tigers	Det	R	21	27	0	0	25	32.1	129	20	10	8	2	1	1	1	13	1	31	1	0	1	1	.500	0	17	2.23
Hernandez, John-E.	Oneonta	Det	A-	23	2	0	0	0	1.2	14	3	4	4	0	1	0	0	5	0	1	0	0	0	1	.000	0	0	21.60
Hernandez, Juan	White Sox	CWS	R	21	13	9	0	0	57	285	90	61	45	4	3	3	2	26	0	43	2	1	2	3	.400	0	0	7.11
Hernandez, Yoel	Phillies	Phi	R	19	10	9	2	0	60	237	39	10	9	2	0	0	7	17	0	46	4	1	4	1	.800	1	0	1.35
Herrera, Jose	Everett	Sea	A-	21	14	10	0	1	61	276	63	37	26	3	2	4	7	29	0	31	5	1	1	4	.200	0	0	3.84
Hertzel, Pat	Chston-SC	TB	A	24	14	14	0	0	79.1	352	105	57	47	12	2	1	5	19	0	53	4	0	2	6	.250	0	0	5.33
Hickman, Ben	Kane County	Fla	A	24	8	2	0	5	17.1	74	15	4	3	0	1	0	1	5	0	13	0	0	1	0	1.000	0	0	1.56
Hickman, Jason*	Great Falls	LA	R+	22	12	9	0	0	55.1	250	65	32	30	6	1	1	3	25	0	52	5	1	3	3	.500	0	0	4.88
Hicks, Ralph*	Auburn	Hou	A-	23	26	0	0	8	35.1	159	19	19	17	0	1	3	7	26	1	48	7	1	1	3	.250	0	1	4.33
Higgins, Josh	Williamsprt	Pit	A-	22	23	0	0	18	34.2	137	25	7	4	1	4	0	2	8	0	40	2	1	3	1	.750	0	8	1.04
Hiles, Cary	Clearwater	Phi	A+	25	46	0	0	41	62.2	280	76	27	22	0	5	1	3	22	2	41	3	1	8	3	.727	0	20	3.16
Hill, Jamie*	Yankees	NYY	R	24	2	0	0	0	4.2	23	5	4	4	0	0	0	1	3	0	4	2	0	0	0	.000	0	0	7.71
Hill, Shawn	Expos	Mon	R	20	7	7	0	0	24.1	117	25	17	13	0	0	1	6	10	0	20	3	1	1	3	.250	0	0	4.81
Hoard, Brent*	Quad City	Min	A	24	6	6	1	0	28.1	130	34	22	17	5	0	0	0	11	0	14	2	0	0	3	.000	0	0	5.40
	Fort Myers	Min	A+	24	19	18	0	1	92	412	98	57	44	6	3	2	3	44	2	55	8	0	5	9	.357	0	0	4.30

2000 Pitching — Class-A and Rookie Leagues

HOW MUCH HE PITCHED											WHAT HE GAVE UP												THE RESULTS					
Player	Team	Org	Lg	A	G	GS	CG	GF	IP	BFP	H	R	ER	HR	SH	SF	HB	TBB	IBB	SO	WP	Bk	W	L	Pct.	ShO	Sv	ERA
Hodges, Trey	Jamestown	Atl	A-	23	13	2	0	2	19.2	93	22	14	13	3	1	0	1	12	0	13	1	2	0	2	.000	0	0	5.95
Hoerman, Jared	Wisconsin	Sea	A	24	22	0	0	7	38.1	177	35	25	20	4	2	2	7	22	4	44	8	1	0	4	.000	0	1	4.70
Hoffman, Matt	Rockies	Col	R	24	4	0	0	1	4.1	24	7	4	4	0	0	0	0	4	0	6	2	0	3	0	1.000	0	0	8.31
Hollifield, Alec	White Sox	CWS	R	20	8	8	0	0	52.2	220	58	26	12	1	2	1	4	12	0	34	4	0	4	3	.571	0	0	2.05
	Bristol	CWS	R+	20	5	5	0	0	22	105	32	25	24	6	0	0	1	11	0	20	1	0	0	4	.000	0	0	9.82
Holmes, Mike	Modesto	Oak	A+	25	21	2	0	6	54	237	60	32	27	4	2	5	1	14	1	40	2	0	4	0	1.000	0	1	4.50
Holubec, Ken*	Elizabethtn	Min	R+	22	9	6	0	0	32.2	129	22	11	11	1	1	1	2	12	0	43	2	0	4	1	.800	0	0	3.03
Hopper, Josh*	Capital Cty	NYM	A	23	23	0	0	9	34	160	35	30	26	2	2	2	4	26	3	34	4	0	1	4	.200	0	1	6.88
	Pittsfield	NYM	A-	23	15	0	0	8	30.2	131	27	17	14	2	1	1	2	19	0	24	3	0	1	0	1.000	0	0	4.11
Hopper, Kevin	Braves	Atl	R	23	2	0	0	1	3.2	18	3	3	1	0	0	0	0	2	0	2	1	0	0	0	.000	0	0	2.45
	Danville	Atl	R+	23	16	0	0	7	30.2	128	27	13	12	2	1	0	1	7	0	26	4	0	2	0	1.000	0	3	3.52
Horney, Mike	Clinton	Cin	A	23	15	0	0	6	25.2	121	30	17	13	2	3	2	3	8	2	23	4	0	0	3	.000	0	0	4.56
Hosford, Clinton	Great Falls	LA	R+	20	17	5	0	5	68.1	313	76	50	33	5	2	3	7	25	2	56	7	0	2	7	.222	0	0	4.35
Houston, Ryan	Queens	Tor	A-	21	12	0	0	2	28.2	118	23	11	9	1	1	0	3	8	0	29	1	0	1	2	.333	0	0	2.83
	Hagerstown	Tor	A	21	6	6	0	0	36.2	136	17	9	9	2	0	0	4	13	0	27	1	0	5	1	.833	0	0	2.21
Howard, Ben	Rancho Cuca	SD	A+	22	32	19	0	4	107.1	506	88	87	76	8	2	2	2	111	1	150	14	1	5	11	.313	0	0	6.37
Howington, Ty*	Dayton	Cin	A	20	27	26	0	0	141.2	656	150	91	83	7	3	8	13	86	1	119	19	1	5	15	.250	0	0	5.27
Hoyt, Mike	Idaho Falls	SD	R+	23	16	1	0	3	25	125	27	20	17	2	2	0	4	17	1	20	4	0	1	1	.500	0	0	6.12
Hubbel, Travis	Hagerstown	Tor	A	22	19	19	0	0	113.1	478	103	62	50	7	3	3	10	55	0	75	13	0	8	6	.571	0	0	3.97
	Dunedin	Tor	A+	22	3	0	0	1	5.1	20	4	2	2	2	1	0	0	2	0	3	1	0	0	0	.000	0	0	3.38
Huber, John	Padres	SD	R	23	14	10	0	0	45	223	54	49	33	1	3	3	1	32	0	39	6	0	1	4	.200	0	0	6.60
Hudson, Luke	Salem	Col	A+	24	19	19	2	0	110	462	101	47	40	9	3	4	10	34	0	80	5	1	5	8	.385	2	0	3.27
Huesgen, Danny	Queens	Tor	A-	23	16	0	0	2	26	115	27	9	7	2	3	1	0	10	0	17	1	0	2	1	.667	0	1	2.42
Hughes, Nial*	Yakima	LA	A-	23	16	5	0	4	47.1	211	35	20	15	3	3	2	4	30	2	61	5	1	3	1	.750	0	1	2.85
Hughes, Rocky*	Bristol	CWS	R+	22	16	3	0	4	33.1	144	23	18	14	2	2	0	1	20	1	40	3	1	1	1	.500	0	1	3.78
Hughes, Travis	Charlotte	Tex	A+	23	39	14	1	19	126.1	553	122	76	62	9	6	1	12	54	3	96	11	0	9	9	.500	0	9	4.42
Huie, Bryan*	Everett	Sea	A-	26	10	0	0	2	15.1	75	9	13	13	0	1	1	2	17	0	15	8	0	2	1	.667	0	0	7.63
Huisman, Justin	Portland	Col	A-	22	16	3	0	6	43.2	180	31	16	9	1	2	2	1	17	1	32	0	0	3	6	.333	0	1	1.85
Humrich, Cris	Cape Fear	Mon	A	23	38	0	0	16	66.1	305	72	45	40	9	2	3	5	28	0	51	9	0	4	1	.800	0	2	5.43
Hunt, Jordan	Martinsvlle	Hou	R+	22	14	7	0	2	45	211	56	39	31	5	0	1	2	22	0	42	7	0	1	2	.333	0	1	6.20
Hunter, Johnny	Fort Wayne	SD	A	26	4	0	0	2	7	32	7	5	4	1	1	0	0	4	0	10	1	0	1	1	.500	0	0	5.14
	Rancho Cuca	SD	A+	26	47	8	0	7	106	469	92	68	55	7	3	6	2	65	0	87	14	4	5	5	.500	0	0	4.67
Hurley, Derek*	Hickory	Pit	A	23	18	0	0	12	38.2	194	58	33	25	6	2	1	1	14	2	25	2	0	2	1	.667	0	1	5.82
Hussman, Darrell	Billings	Cin	R+	24	3	3	0	0	11.2	42	5	2	2	0	0	0	1	3	0	9	0	0	0	0	.000	0	0	1.54
	Clinton	Cin	A	24	9	8	0	0	42	181	46	26	24	1	1	0	3	14	0	33	7	0	2	3	.400	0	0	5.14
Igualada, Eric	Greensboro	NYY	A	22	9	0	0	3	13.2	66	17	13	13	1	3	0	0	10	2	9	2	0	0	2	.000	0	0	8.56
Jackson, Brian	Mahoning Vy	Cle	A-	23	30	0	0	29	33.1	151	34	18	12	1	0	1	3	10	0	32	3	0	2	2	.500	0	11	3.24
Jackson, Jeremy*	Capital Cty	NYM	A	25	3	0	0	2	4	17	4	0	0	0	0	0	0	2	0	3	1	0	0	0	.000	0	0	0.00
Jackson, Stosh*	Lansing	ChC	A	25	42	4	0	23	83.2	381	90	58	51	5	3	5	9	40	0	54	9	0	5	6	.455	0	2	5.49
Jacobs, Dwayne	San Berndno	LA	A+	24	21	0	0	11	29	135	23	14	13	2	1	0	1	30	0	41	5	0	3	2	.600	0	4	4.03
Jacobs, Greg*	Lk Elsinore	Ana	A+	24	32	0	0	11	41	205	39	37	31	2	0	3	5	43	2	37	9	1	2	1	.667	0	0	6.80
Jacobsen, Landon	Williamsprt	Pit	A-	22	9	9	0	0	57.1	228	38	15	9	1	1	2	6	17	0	57	1	0	3	2	.600	0	0	1.41
	Hickory	Pit	A	22	5	4	0	0	29.2	141	40	16	12	0	0	3	4	13	0	25	1	0	3	0	1.000	0	0	3.64
Jamison, Ryan	Michigan	Hou	A	23	41	7	0	15	98.2	402	66	32	23	3	4	3	10	38	3	95	8	1	8	3	.727	0	7	2.10
Janke, Cheyenne	Peoria	StL	A	24	28	27	0	0	167	734	169	97	75	8	7	4	10	53	3	90	11	0	10	10	.500	0	0	4.04
Jauregui, Miguel	Columbus	Cle	A	21	29	1	0	8	64.1	287	59	34	30	1	1	2	11	30	1	64	3	0	3	3	.500	0	2	4.20
Jenks, Bobby	Butte	Ana	R+	20	14	12	0	0	52.2	265	61	57	46	2	2	4	5	44	0	42	19	2	1	7	.125	0	0	7.86
Jensen, Jared	Visalia	Oak	A+	27	30	6	0	3	75	345	94	56	41	7	2	1	6	28	1	60	4	2	1	3	.250	0	0	4.92
Jensen, Jason*	High Desert	Ari	A+	25	28	26	0	0	154.1	697	181	115	97	13	2	5	5	82	0	103	13	1	6	12	.333	0	0	5.66
Jimenez, Ronal	Phillies	Phi	R	20	20	0	0	17	26.1	115	19	10	7	3	2	1	0	14	1	23	3	0	2	2	.500	0	6	2.39
Johnson, Adam	Fort Myers	Min	A+	21	13	12	1	0	69.1	267	45	21	19	2	0	2	3	20	1	92	2	1	5	4	.556	1	0	2.47
Johnson, Derrick*	Auburn	Hou	A-	22	21	0	0	7	42	179	32	13	10	1	0	2	5	24	0	44	3	1	0	0	.000	0	1	2.14
Johnson, Eric	San Jose	SF	A+	23	13	0	0	4	26.2	136	37	31	26	4	2	1	2	20	0	15	4	1	0	0	.000	0	0	8.78
	Salem-Keizr	SF	A-	23	8	8	0	0	39.2	172	30	19	14	0	1	3	1	24	0	24	4	0	2	2	.500	0	0	3.18
	Bakersfield	SF	A+	23	5	4	0	0	14.1	73	19	12	11	1	0	2	0	15	0	5	1	0	0	0	.000	0	0	6.91
Johnson, Everrett	Everett	Sea	A-	21	17	8	0	2	69.2	286	51	26	16	1	3	3	2	21	0	88	5	1	5	4	.556	0	0	2.07
Johnson, Jeremy	Oneonta	Det	A-	18	2	2	0	0	9.1	39	8	5	3	0	0	0	0	4	0	5	2	0	0	1	.000	0	0	2.89
	Tigers	Det	R	18	12	7	0	1	39	176	37	24	18	1	0	2	2	19	0	41	3	0	3	1	.750	0	0	4.15
Johnson, Kelly	Johnson Cty	StL	R+	21	22	0	0	12	26	128	24	25	23	3	2	1	3	23	1	21	9	0	2	6	.250	0	1	7.96
Johnston, Clint*	Lynchburg	Pit	A+	23	10	6	0	2	37	167	48	28	22	3	3	3	0	15	0	23	3	1	1	2	.333	0	0	5.35
Johnston, Dave	Marlins	Fla	R	20	14	0	0	8	25.1	110	21	12	9	0	1	1	4	11	0	19	1	0	1	1	.500	0	3	3.20
	Brevard Cty	Fla	A+	20	5	1	0	3	12.1	62	18	13	10	3	2	0	3	6	1	7	1	0	0	2	.000	0	0	7.30
Johnston, Mike*	Hickory	Pit	A	22	26	0	0	7	50.2	245	66	42	35	2	2	2	5	30	0	52	0	2	4	2	.667	0	2	6.22
Johnston, Rikki*	W Michigan	Det	A	20	1	1	0	0	6	30	8	4	1	0	1	0	0	4	0	4	1	0	1	0	1.000	0	0	1.50
	Oneonta	Det	A-	20	15	15	1	0	97.1	417	98	47	44	3	1	5	6	33	0	58	7	0	6	4	.600	0	0	4.07
Johnston, Sean*	Cubs	ChC	R	25	1	1	0	0	2	6	1	0	0	0	0	0	0	0	0	2	0	0	0	0	.000	0	0	0.00
Jolliffe, Brian*	Fort Wayne	SD	A	26	48	0	0	11	70.1	325	64	44	34	6	2	3	7	49	4	47	5	1	5	5	.500	0	0	4.35
Jones, A.J.	Pirates	Pit	R	22	11	1	0	5	44	201	45	28	19	5	1	7	10	14	1	20	2	0	1	3	.250	0	0	3.89
Jones, Alvin	White Sox	CWS	R	19	14	6	0	3	44.1	225	48	49	37	4	2	3	5	41	0	45	17	0	1	3	.250	0	1	7.51
Jones, Chris*	San Jose	SF	A+	21	36	7	0	7	61.1	341	74	89	73	8	0	8	6	85	0	50	20	0	3	6	.333	0	0	10.71
Jones, Fontella	Beloit	Mil	A	26	25	0	0	23	24.1	97	21	10	7	2	1	2	1	5	0	23	2	1	0	3	.000	0	18	2.59
	Mudville	Mil	A+	26	25	0	0	12	30.2	141	30	19	17	5	1	1	1	24	0	35	3	1	1	1	.500	0	3	4.99
Jones, Geoff*	Padres	SD	R	21	20	0	0	3	28.1	149	45	30	25	2	3	1	0	18	1	35	1	1	0	3	.000	0	0	7.94
Jones, Quentin	Danville	Atl	R+	22	21	0	0	18	27	116	27	13	11	1	2	1	1	5	0	32	2	1	4	2	.667	0	9	3.67
Jones, Rob*	Utica	Fla	A-	22	14	0	0	5	18.2	84	18	10	6	0	1	1	1	11	0	17	2	0	0	1	.000	0	0	2.89
Jones, Sean	Frederick	Bal	A+	23	1	0	0	0	2	10	2	2	0	0	0	0	1	0	0	3	0	0	0	0	.000	0	0	0.00
	Delmarva	Bal	A	23	39	3	0	9	68.2	303	72	38	33	2	2	4	8	23	1	65	3	0	8	4	.667	0	0	4.33

2000 Pitching — Class-A and Rookie Leagues

HOW MUCH HE PITCHED											WHAT HE GAVE UP												THE RESULTS					
Player	Team	Org	Lg	A	G	GS	CG	GF	IP	BFP	H	R	ER	HR	SH	SF	HB	TBB	IBB	SO	WP	Bk	W	L	Pct.	ShO	Sv	ERA
Jones, Travis*	Fort Wayne	SD	A	23	8	0	0	1	10.2	50	13	4	4	2	0	0	1	7	1	10	0	0	0	2	.000	0	0	3.38
Joseph, Glen	Reds	Cin	R	20	7	1	0	2	8	55	12	20	15	1	0	0	3	16	0	4	3	0	0	1	.000	0	1	16.88
	Billings	Cin	R+	20	8	0	0	3	12.1	69	15	13	11	1	1	3	0	17	1	10	8	0	0	1	.000	0	0	8.03
Joseph, Jake	Capital Cty	NYM	A	23	15	15	0	0	85.1	365	81	45	27	2	3	0	7	29	0	59	6	0	4	3	.571	0	0	2.85
Journell, Jimmy	New Jersey	StL	A-	23	13	1	0	3	32	136	12	12	7	0	0	2	2	24	0	39	8	0	1	0	1.000	0	0	1.97
Julio, Jorge	Jupiter	Mon	A+	22	21	15	0	3	79.1	363	93	60	52	4	1	5	4	35	0	67	1	3	2	10	.167	0	1	5.90
Junge, Eric	San Berndno	LA	A+	24	29	24	0	2	158	666	159	69	59	8	3	5	9	53	0	116	8	2	8	1	.889	0	1	3.36
Kaanoi, Jason	Royals	KC	R	18	4	4	0	0	16	62	13	2	1	0	0	0	0	2	0	20	2	1	2	1	.667	0	0	0.56
	Chston-WV	KC	A	18	4	4	0	0	21	93	23	13	10	0	0	1	0	11	0	9	1	0	0	1	.000	0	0	4.29
Kalita, Tim*	Lakeland	Det	A+	22	27	25	1	0	149.2	672	146	93	76	7	3	4	16	73	0	107	11	0	7	12	.368	0	0	4.57
Kane, Kyle	Winston-Sal	CWS	A+	25	32	0	0	7	50.2	243	57	39	33	3	2	1	6	31	3	47	1	0	1	2	.333	0	0	5.86
Kearney, Ryan	Columbus	Cle	A	25	2	0	0	2	2	6	0	0	0	0	0	0	0	0	0	2	0	0	0	0	.000	0	0	0.00
	Kinston	Cle	A+	25	32	0	0	20	53.1	231	54	25	25	7	4	1	2	18	1	59	1	0	5	4	.556	0	1	4.22
Keefer, Ryan	Orioles	Bal	R	19	13	1	0	4	22.1	102	26	13	11	0	1	0	3	6	3	21	1	0	1	2	.333	0	0	4.43
Keelin, Chris	Piedmont	Phi	A	24	45	1	0	21	61	255	36	26	22	4	5	0	6	37	0	82	5	1	3	2	.600	0	1	3.25
Kees, Justin	High Desert	Ari	A+	23	32	0	0	9	59	285	75	54	50	6	2	5	6	38	0	34	9	2	4	3	.571	0	0	7.63
	South Bend	Ari	A	23	17	2	0	6	33	145	29	18	18	4	4	1	1	20	1	24	2	0	0	1	.000	0	0	4.91
Kegley, Charlie	Dunedin	Tor	A+	21	23	23	0	0	111.1	490	96	60	48	6	4	4	8	74	1	66	11	5	3	9	.250	0	0	3.88
Keirstead, Michael	Great Falls	LA	R+	20	18	7	0	2	58	262	68	38	31	3	1	3	4	23	0	36	2	0	4	3	.571	0	0	4.81
Kelley, Chris	Mahoning Vy	Cle	A-	23	11	1	0	2	29.1	127	25	15	13	1	2	3	2	15	0	33	5	1	3	2	.600	0	0	3.99
	Columbus	Cle	A	23	8	0	0	5	20	85	15	9	8	0	0	2	4	7	0	28	4	0	1	1	.500	0	2	3.60
Kelly, Dan*	Jamestown	Atl	A-	23	2	0	0	2	5	19	4	1	1	0	0	0	0	1	0	3	1	0	0	1	.000	0	0	1.80
	Macon	Atl	A	23	12	0	0	6	19	78	17	5	5	2	1	1	0	3	0	18	0	0	1	0	1.000	0	0	2.37
Kemp, Bo	Twins	Min	R	20	7	0	0	2	8.2	37	6	5	3	0	0	1	1	3	0	10	3	0	0	1	.000	0	1	3.12
	Elizabethtn	Min	R+	20	17	0	0	16	20.2	81	12	6	5	2	0	1	0	6	0	28	0	0	1	0	1.000	0	7	2.18
Kennedy, Casey	Yakima	LA	A-	22	13	13	0	0	72.1	303	73	33	26	3	2	0	2	10	0	69	2	1	6	4	.600	0	0	3.24
Kennedy, Joe*	Chston-SC	TB	A	22	22	22	3	0	136.1	546	122	59	50	6	2	6	4	29	1	142	9	2	11	6	.647	2	0	3.30
Kent, Nathan	Macon	Atl	A	22	5	1	0	4	9.2	42	9	5	5	0	0	1	1	3	0	5	1	0	1	1	.500	0	0	4.66
	Myrtle Bch	Atl	A+	22	24	20	1	0	137.2	537	97	50	39	3	4	3	4	30	0	89	3	1	10	6	.625	0	0	2.55
Kent, Steve*	Everett	Sea	A-	22	24	3	0	6	52.2	219	38	16	15	5	2	0	2	23	1	61	5	0	4	1	.800	0	2	2.56
Keppel, Bob	Kingsport	NYM	R+	19	8	6	0	0	29	136	31	22	22	1	0	0	4	13	0	29	6	0	1	2	.333	0	0	6.83
Kesten, Mike*	Mariners	Sea	R	19	16	0	0	5	26.1	120	29	16	14	0	0	1	1	13	0	23	1	0	5	0	1.000	0	0	4.78
Ketchner, Ryan*	Mariners	Sea	R	19	9	1	0	2	25.2	104	22	14	12	0	0	3	1	3	0	27	2	1	1	2	.333	0	0	4.21
Key, Chris*	Utica	Fla	A-	23	19	0	0	16	34.1	124	19	3	3	1	3	0	0	5	1	42	3	0	3	2	.600	0	7	0.79
	Kane County	Fla	A	23	5	2	0	1	17	76	21	11	7	0	0	2	1	1	0	18	2	0	0	2	.000	0	0	3.71
Keyser, Jason	Pirates	Pit	R	19	4	0	0	1	7	31	8	4	4	0	1	0	1	2	0	7	0	0	0	0	.000	0	1	5.14
Kibler, Ryan	Asheville	Col	A	20	26	26	0	0	155	711	173	107	76	9	3	1	14	67	0	110	7	0	10	14	.417	0	0	4.41
Kidd, Jake	Asheville	Col	A	23	20	0	0	11	30.2	140	43	16	16	0	1	1	3	9	0	25	3	0	1	1	.500	0	0	4.70
Kimball, Cody	Twins	Min	R	19	18	3	0	1	33.1	138	30	8	5	0	0	0	1	12	1	26	2	0	2	0	1.000	0	0	1.35
King, Jeremy	Yankees	NYY	R	19	11	11	0	0	55.1	252	65	35	27	2	0	5	3	24	0	46	6	1	2	4	.333	0	0	4.39
King, Jim*	Wilmington	KC	A+	23	46	0	0	23	52	207	48	19	19	2	3	2	2	11	0	45	4	0	2	2	.500	0	6	3.29
Kinnie, Gary	Mariners	Sea	R	24	12	10	0	0	52.2	238	55	44	33	3	2	0	2	29	0	44	10	1	3	3	.500	0	0	5.64
Kleine, Victor*	Mahoning Vy	Cle	A-	21	3	1	0	0	4	18	2	2	2	0	0	0	3	4	0	2	1	0	0	0	.000	0	0	4.50
Klepacki, Ed	Cape Fear	Mon	A	23	14	14	0	0	83.2	343	85	39	28	2	3	0	2	17	0	64	4	0	7	4	.636	0	0	3.01
	Jupiter	Mon	A+	23	11	11	0	0	55.2	253	75	37	28	1	2	4	0	14	0	28	1	0	2	2	.500	0	0	4.53
Knapp, Ben	Bluefield	Bal	R+	21	7	6	0	1	29.1	135	37	24	19	4	1	1	2	11	0	26	2	2	1	3	.250	0	0	5.83
Knowles, Mike	Greensboro	NYY	A	21	24	22	0	0	114.1	544	150	98	74	7	4	5	12	53	1	66	15	0	4	14	.222	0	0	5.83
Koeth, Mark	Kinston	Cle	A+	23	1	0	0	1	3	17	5	4	3	0	1	0	0	1	0	1	0	0	0	0	.000	0	0	9.00
	Columbus	Cle	A	23	20	0	0	14	32.2	152	45	25	23	3	0	5	1	13	0	31	1	0	2	1	.667	0	4	6.34
Kofler, Ed	St. Pete	TB	A+	23	28	26	1	1	148.1	658	180	98	87	11	3	9	8	46	0	98	11	2	9	10	.474	0	0	5.28
Kohl, Doug	South Bend	Ari	A	21	11	0	0	7	20.1	91	20	11	10	2	1	2	2	8	0	20	2	1	1	2	.333	0	0	4.43
	Peoria	StL	A	21	25	0	0	6	38	148	29	15	13	4	2	0	1	7	0	28	0	0	1	2	.333	0	1	3.08
Koronka, John*	Clinton	Cin	A	20	20	18	4	0	104	452	123	65	50	7	2	3	0	38	2	74	4	0	4	13	.235	0	0	4.33
Kosderka, Matt	Savannah	Tex	A	25	20	12	0	6	87.2	356	65	36	25	7	1	3	3	27	0	70	5	0	5	4	.556	0	1	2.57
	Charlotte	Tex	A+	25	12	5	0	1	38.2	170	49	28	22	3	1	0	3	10	0	27	0	0	1	3	.250	0	0	5.12
Koutrouba, Tom*	Lakeland	Det	A+	23	40	1	0	20	70.1	299	67	31	25	4	1	2	2	22	2	49	4	0	2	7	.222	0	3	3.20
Koziara, Matt	Clinton	Cin	A	24	38	0	0	17	72	314	80	34	27	2	5	2	0	31	3	42	9	0	3	3	.500	0	2	3.38
Kozlowski, Ben*	Macon	Atl	A	20	15	14	0	0	77	353	76	53	36	6	2	4	6	39	0	67	4	2	3	8	.273	0	0	4.21
Kozlowski, Kris*	Queens	Tor	A-	23	21	0	0	3	44.2	194	38	21	14	2	1	1	0	20	0	58	3	2	4	1	.800	0	0	2.82
Kozol, Anthony	Lowell	Bos	A-	23	16	1	0	14	29	129	32	15	9	1	2	1	4	7	2	30	2	0	1	3	.250	0	6	2.79
Krawiec, Aaron*	Eugene	ChC	A-	22	14	14	0	0	78	323	59	28	22	4	4	1	4	26	0	99	1	2	6	4	.600	0	0	2.54
Kremer, John	Greensboro	NYY	A	24	38	1	0	15	73	335	79	52	43	5	6	2	6	38	4	82	11	0	1	6	.143	0	0	5.30
Krug, Dustin	Daytona	ChC	A+	24	52	1	0	16	79.1	353	82	39	31	6	1	3	4	37	9	64	7	1	5	7	.417	0	0	3.52
Krysa, John	Auburn	Hou	A-	22	21	2	0	7	37	162	27	21	12	1	1	1	2	21	0	28	6	1	3	4	.429	0	1	2.92
Kubes, Greg*	Clearwater	Phi	A+	24	24	24	0	0	136.1	612	158	81	69	6	5	5	5	64	1	70	4	0	5	9	.357	0	0	4.56
Kuo, Hong-Chih*	San Berndno	LA	A+	19	1	1	0	0	3	10	0	0	0	0	0	0	1	0	0	7	0	0	0	0	.000	0	0	0.00
Kurtz-Nicholl, J.*	Wilmington	KC	A+	24	8	0	0	3	9	47	10	9	5	1	1	0	0	8	1	12	0	1	0	1	.000	0	0	5.00
	Chston-WV	KC	A	24	29	0	0	14	38.2	161	29	13	11	2	2	0	2	17	0	31	3	0	3	1	.750	0	1	2.56
Labitzke, Jesse*	Asheville	Col	A	23	36	0	0	9	52.2	248	64	32	29	3	3	2	0	36	0	38	2	0	1	0	1.000	0	0	4.96
LaChapelle, Yan	Dunedin	Tor	A+	25	18	7	0	3	55.1	234	42	22	16	4	2	2	2	27	1	49	2	0	5	1	.833	0	0	2.60
LaCorte, Vince	Cedar Rapds	Ana	A	22	17	9	0	4	69.2	323	94	59	50	13	2	4	2	21	0	54	3	0	5	7	.417	0	0	6.46
Laesch, Mike	Billings	Cin	R+	23	24	3	0	7	56	259	69	47	37	6	0	2	6	21	1	49	6	0	5	2	.714	0	3	5.95
Lajara, Eudy*	Marlins	Fla	R	21	11	1	0	5	28.2	122	22	6	3	1	1	1	1	7	1	35	1	0	4	1	.800	0	1	0.94
	Brevard Cty	Fla	A+	21	6	0	0	2	10	48	12	11	9	2	0	0	0	8	0	6	0	0	0	2	.000	0	0	8.10
LaMattina, Ryan*	Salem	Col	A+	25	27	0	0	8	34	174	42	19	16	2	0	0	2	29	0	41	4	1	0	0	.000	0	2	4.24
Landestoy, Gilbert	Boise	Ana	A-	24	28	0	0	8	64	263	47	27	20	0	1	4	7	21	1	54	2	0	4	2	.667	0	0	2.81
Landkamer, Michael	Dayton	Cin	A	24	3	0	0	1	3	25	13	11	8	1	0	0	1	1	0	2	0	0	0	0	.000	0	0	24.00

2000 Pitching — Class-A and Rookie Leagues

HOW MUCH HE PITCHED											WHAT HE GAVE UP												THE RESULTS					
Player	Team	Org	Lg	A	G	GS	CG	GF	IP	BFP	H	R	ER	HR	SH	SF	HB	TBB	IBB	SO	WP	Bk	W	L	Pct.	ShO	Sv	ERA
	Billings	Cin	R+	24	6	0	0	2	8	36	9	6	6	0	0	1	0	6	0	3	3	1	0	0	.000	0	0	6.75
Langen, Brian*	Potomac	StL	A+	23	31	0	0	6	42.2	181	34	14	9	2	3	1	5	21	0	28	2	0	1	0	1.000	0	0	1.90
Langone, Steve	Yakima	LA	A-	23	15	12	0	1	84.2	335	76	30	29	6	4	2	3	5	0	79	1	0	4	4	.500	0	1	3.08
Lansford, Dustin	Helena	Mil	R+	21	11	6	0	2	37	162	30	20	20	4	1	0	2	32	1	36	5	0	1	3	.250	0	0	4.86
LaPlante, Reggie	Yankees	NYY	R	21	24	0	0	22	26	97	9	4	3	1	0	1	3	9	1	27	1	0	6	0	1.000	0	13	1.04
Lara, Mauricio*	Augusta	Bos	A	22	16	0	0	4	32	133	25	11	5	2	0	1	2	13	0	33	5	0	1	0	1.000	0	0	1.41
	Lowell	Bos	A-	22	15	14	1	0	85	330	70	22	20	0	2	0	3	21	0	83	2	2	4	3	.571	0	0	2.12
Larman, Jayson	Billings	Cin	R+	22	7	2	0	0	11	72	13	16	14	1	0	0	3	27	0	9	4	0	0	1	.000	0	0	11.45
LaRosa, Dancy	Elizabethtn	Min	R+	22	16	8	0	2	55.1	258	71	37	28	2	3	3	2	23	0	33	9	1	6	5	.545	0	1	4.55
Larson, Ryan	Burlington	Cle	R+	22	19	0	0	10	46	189	32	17	13	5	2	0	2	17	0	56	9	0	2	0	1.000	0	2	2.54
Lasose, Enrique	Ogden	Mil	R+	19	13	0	0	12	15	83	23	23	19	3	0	1	2	12	0	10	2	0	0	0	.000	0	0	11.40
Laureano, Edgardo	Padres	SD	R	18	12	0	0	7	11	57	12	12	7	0	1	1	0	7	1	10	1	0	0	1	.000	0	2	5.73
Lavery, Tim*	Cubs	ChC	R	22	5	5	0	0	15	69	17	11	8	1	0	1	2	3	0	13	0	0	0	2	.000	0	0	4.80
Lavigne, Tim	Pittsfield	NYM	A-	22	15	0	0	12	16.2	66	11	5	5	1	1	0	2	7	0	15	2	0	2	1	.667	0	6	2.70
Law, Keith	W Michigan	Det	A	24	33	1	0	13	50.1	237	43	33	27	3	3	2	5	34	1	46	1	0	4	4	.500	0	0	4.83
	Oneonta	Det	A-	24	11	0	0	7	16	75	19	12	7	2	0	0	2	5	2	15	1	0	2	2	.500	0	0	3.94
Lawson, Jarrod	Batavia	Phi	A-	22	4	4	0	0	10.1	52	8	11	11	0	0	0	2	15	0	2	2	0	1	1	.500	0	0	9.58
Lawton, Charles	Padres	SD	R	19	12	6	0	0	36.2	165	37	28	23	2	1	5	3	18	0	25	4	1	1	4	.200	0	0	5.65
Layfield, Scotty	Peoria	StL	A	24	53	0	0	29	54.1	277	65	46	31	4	2	4	2	40	5	50	6	0	2	4	.333	0	15	5.13
Lazo, Rafael	Kingsport	NYM	R+	21	15	0	0	4	24.2	107	17	9	8	3	3	0	3	11	1	30	2	0	0	2	.000	0	1	2.92
Leach, Bryan	Augusta	Bos	A	23	60	0	0	58	72.1	289	45	23	13	4	6	1	2	20	1	87	5	0	3	3	.500	0	40	1.62
Leclair, Aric*	South Bend	Ari	A	23	23	0	0	9	38.2	188	41	29	22	3	1	3	4	30	4	38	5	0	1	1	.500	0	0	5.12
Ledden, Ryan	Hickory	Pit	A	23	30	0	0	24	45.2	204	39	25	17	2	0	2	5	25	0	37	1	0	1	2	.333	0	7	3.35
	Lynchburg	Pit	A+	23	15	0	0	5	20	92	14	12	7	0	2	2	0	16	1	14	3	1	3	0	1.000	0	0	3.15
Ledezma, Wil*	Augusta	Bos	A	20	14	14	0	0	52.2	240	51	33	30	3	1	1	2	36	0	60	5	0	2	4	.333	0	0	5.13
Lee, Adam*	Johnson Cty	StL	R+	23	19	0	0	3	30.1	127	26	14	12	2	1	2	1	13	0	20	6	0	0	0	.000	0	0	3.56
Lee, Clifton*	Cape Fear	Mon	A	22	11	11	0	0	44.2	217	50	39	26	1	1	1	1	36	0	63	3	2	1	4	.200	0	0	5.24
Lee, Fletcher	Bakersfield	SF	A+	25	9	0	0	6	14.2	73	19	6	5	0	0	0	4	9	1	13	0	0	0	1	.000	0	1	3.07
Lee, Kevin	Pirates	Pit	R	19	9	0	0	4	15	69	16	5	3	1	2	0	3	4	0	7	0	0	4	0	1.000	0	0	1.80
Lee, Tymber	Boise	Ana	A-	23	22	0	0	10	29	143	34	28	17	0	1	2	4	21	2	19	5	0	1	2	.333	0	1	5.28
Legette, Richard	Phillies	Phi	R	20	12	2	0	5	18.2	85	14	12	11	2	0	0	2	12	0	20	3	1	0	1	.000	0	0	5.30
Leicester, John	Eugene	ChC	A-	22	17	7	0	1	49.2	224	47	36	30	4	6	4	2	22	1	31	2	0	1	5	.167	0	0	5.44
Lelless, Alex	Jamestown	Atl	A-	21	19	0	0	8	39	179	37	24	18	1	1	3	1	30	1	23	7	0	0	1	.000	0	1	4.15
Leon, Brigmer	Athletics	Oak	R	20	12	1	0	1	32.1	136	28	15	12	3	0	1	4	5	1	15	1	0	1	0	1.000	0	1	3.34
Lesieur, Chris	Missoula	Ari	R+	22	23	0	0	6	25	128	27	24	13	2	1	0	3	19	0	26	5	0	1	0	1.000	0	2	4.68
Leuenberge, Jeff	Oneonta	Det	A-	22	2	0	0	0	2	11	2	0	0	0	0	0	1	2	0	2	0	0	0	0	.000	0	0	0.00
	W Michigan	Det	A	22	12	9	0	1	59.1	255	54	24	18	0	2	2	2	27	0	33	4	0	3	1	.750	0	0	2.73
Levan, Matt*	Brevard Cty	Fla	A+	26	4	0	0	3	8.2	40	10	8	8	1	0	0	0	5	0	12	0	0	0	1	.000	0	2	8.31
Levesque, Ben	Williamsprt	Pit	A-	21	17	0	0	6	29.1	156	31	30	18	1	1	2	4	33	0	23	3	0	3	4	.429	0	0	5.52
Lewis, Colby	Charlotte	Tex	A+	21	28	27	3	0	163.2	692	169	83	74	11	4	7	10	45	0	153	11	2	11	10	.524	1	0	4.07
Lewis, Craig	Tampa	NYY	A+	24	1	0	0	0	2	10	3	3	3	0	0	1	0	1	0	1	0	0	0	0	.000	0	0	13.50
Lewis, Jeremy*	Tigers	Det	R	20	12	10	1	0	57.2	252	52	38	30	1	1	3	2	28	0	57	8	1	2	5	.286	0	0	4.68
	Oneonta	Det	A-	20	2	1	0	1	7	29	6	1	0	0	0	0	0	3	0	6	0	0	1	0	1.000	0	0	0.00
Lewis, Peyton	Hagerstown	Tor	A	25	23	0	0	17	27.2	129	34	17	16	2	1	1	1	12	0	25	2	0	0	3	.000	0	6	5.20
	Cubs	ChC	R	25	5	0	0	5	7	28	6	0	0	0	1	0	0	1	0	8	1	0	1	0	1.000	0	3	0.00
	Lansing	ChC	A	25	15	0	0	5	24	104	21	11	7	2	2	0	1	14	1	23	2	0	2	4	.333	0	2	2.63
Leyva, Julian	Modesto	Oak	A+	23	42	0	0	27	74	312	64	41	36	5	7	6	2	27	4	56	2	0	4	4	.500	0	5	4.38
Lidge, Brad	Kissimmee	Hou	A+	24	8	8	0	0	41.2	164	28	14	13	3	1	0	1	15	0	46	1	2	2	1	.667	0	0	2.81
Lima, Frank	Auburn	Hou	A-	22	5	0	0	0	14.1	53	5	0	0	0	2	0	1	2	0	16	1	0	0	0	.000	0	0	0.00
	Michigan	Hou	A	22	18	0	0	7	29.2	127	26	14	11	2	3	0	1	14	0	31	1	0	3	2	.600	0	1	3.34
Lima, Juan	Expos	Mon	R	19	8	3	0	1	27.2	112	21	13	8	1	1	0	1	9	0	15	1	0	2	1	.667	0	0	2.60
Lindsey, Bart*	Phillies	Phi	R	22	13	0	0	1	20.1	85	23	11	9	1	1	2	0	6	0	17	2	0	1	1	.500	0	1	3.98
Lindsey, David	Johnson Cty	StL	R+	22	19	3	0	4	40	190	46	32	27	3	0	2	2	22	0	25	1	2	2	3	.400	0	0	6.07
Lineweaver, Aaron	High Desert	Ari	A+	27	1	0	0	0	2	9	3	0	0	0	0	0	0	0	0	2	0	0	0	0	.000	0	0	0.00
Litman, Johri	Mahoning Vy	Cle	A-	21	3	0	0	0	6.2	28	5	2	2	0	0	0	1	3	0	3	1	0	0	1	.000	0	0	2.70
Little, Roger	Portland	Col	A-	22	13	0	0	2	15.2	95	31	23	15	3	2	1	4	13	2	6	4	0	1	1	.500	0	0	8.62
Lizarraga, Edgar	Great Falls	LA	R+	20	24	0	0	20	30	138	32	20	18	3	1	0	4	11	0	51	5	1	2	1	.667	0	7	5.40
Lockhart, John	Johnson Cty	StL	R+	22	19	0	0	9	23	107	26	19	13	0	1	0	2	7	0	22	1	0	0	1	.000	0	2	5.09
Lockwood, Luke*	Jupiter	Mon	A+	19	3	3	0	0	14	65	24	17	17	3	0	0	1	5	0	2	0	0	0	1	.000	0	0	10.93
	Vermont	Mon	A-	19	2	2	0	0	12	45	12	3	3	1	1	0	0	1	0	8	1	0	1	0	1.000	0	0	2.25
	Cape Fear	Mon	A	19	9	9	0	0	48	209	49	32	24	3	2	1	5	20	1	33	2	0	2	4	.333	0	0	4.50
Lohrman, Dave	St. Lucie	NYM	A+	25	43	0	0	19	63	310	75	40	34	1	2	3	5	42	2	70	12	0	1	6	.143	0	3	4.86
Lombardi, Justin*	Marlins	Fla	R	21	6	0	0	3	8	35	4	4	1	0	0	1	0	6	0	15	1	0	2	1	.667	0	0	1.13
	Brevard Cty	Fla	A+	21	3	1	0	0	6	37	13	12	10	2	0	1	1	6	0	1	0	1	0	2	.000	0	0	15.00
Longo, Neil	Lancaster	Sea	A+	23	34	0	0	6	50.2	249	76	49	41	11	0	0	3	22	0	34	12	0	2	1	.667	0	1	7.28
Looper, Aaron	Lancaster	Sea	A+	24	51	0	0	8	72.2	357	105	62	46	7	3	5	8	22	1	47	8	1	5	3	.625	0	0	5.70
Lopez, Aquilino	Wisconsin	Sea	A	20	39	5	1	29	68	268	47	16	14	1	0	1	4	20	4	67	3	0	6	1	.857	1	17	1.85
Lopez, Arturo	Mariners	Sea	R	21	10	3	0	1	22	96	23	15	12	1	0	0	2	11	0	20	1	0	2	0	1.000	0	0	4.91
Lopez, Gustavo	Brevard Cty	Fla	A+	22	2	0	0	2	4	14	1	2	0	1	0	0	0	0	0	5	0	0	0	0	.000	0	0	0.00
	Kane County	Fla	A	22	29	15	0	1	97.2	416	99	51	47	4	5	4	2	28	1	73	8	1	5	4	.556	0	1	4.33
Lopez, Javier*	High Desert	Ari	A+	23	30	21	0	4	136.1	602	152	87	79	14	4	7	6	57	0	98	8	2	4	8	.333	0	2	5.22
Lopez, Jose	Hickory	Pit	A	25	29	7	2	10	76.2	315	54	27	20	3	2	3	1	35	3	73	6	1	3	4	.429	1	1	2.35
	Lynchburg	Pit	A+	25	6	6	1	0	37.2	161	29	14	13	2	0	0	1	19	2	38	0	0	4	1	.800	1	0	3.11
Lopez, Juan*	Burlington	CWS	A	21	28	1	0	11	47.2	220	32	29	24	2	6	3	4	48	3	43	4	1	2	7	.222	0	0	4.53
Lopez, Miguel	Princeton	TB	R+	19	21	0	0	13	32.2	139	28	14	11	0	2	1	0	19	0	40	1	0	4	3	.571	0	4	3.03
Lopez, Omar	Reds	Cin	R	19	8	5	0	1	32.2	136	30	18	15	0	1	0	5	12	0	24	2	1	1	1	.500	0	0	4.13
Lopez, Rafael	Kingsport	NYM	R+	20	9	9	1	0	56.1	226	50	20	19	1	0	1	5	9	0	43	4	0	3	3	.500	0	0	3.04

2000 Pitching — Class-A and Rookie Leagues

HOW MUCH HE PITCHED											WHAT HE GAVE UP												THE RESULTS					
Player	Team	Org	Lg	A	G	GS	CG	GF	IP	BFP	H	R	ER	HR	SH	SF	HB	TBB	IBB	SO	WP	Bk	W	L	Pct.	ShO	Sv	ERA
	Pittsfield	NYM	A-	20	4	4	1	0	22	91	22	10	8	0	0	2	0	4	0	23	0	0	3	1	.750	1	0	3.27
Lopez, Samuel	Royals	KC	R	19	23	0	0	21	27.1	123	23	12	10	1	1	1	7	13	0	25	2	0	1	1	.500	0	11	3.29
Lorenzen, Jonathan	Great Falls	LA	R+	19	14	7	0	0	49	217	46	32	29	2	0	3	3	28	0	39	6	0	2	3	.400	0	0	5.33
Lorenzo, Javier	Asheville	Col	A	22	6	0	0	1	8	52	12	15	13	1	1	1	3	11	0	9	2	0	0	0	.000	0	1	14.63
	Portland	Col	A-	22	18	0	0	10	26.2	112	16	10	9	0	2	0	2	13	0	35	1	1	1	1	.500	0	1	3.04
Loudon, Gary	South Bend	Ari	A	25	7	0	0	2	10.1	45	3	5	4	0	0	0	0	11	0	8	1	0	0	0	.000	0	0	3.48
Love, Brandon	Dayton	Cin	A	21	7	7	0	0	34.2	159	33	18	14	1	1	0	4	19	0	32	4	0	2	1	.667	0	0	3.63
	Reds	Cin	R	21	2	2	0	0	6.2	31	4	4	0	0	0	0	1	6	0	8	0	0	0	1	.000	0	0	0.00
Lowe, Matt	Capital Cty	NYM	A	22	2	0	0	0	2	13	5	4	4	0	0	0	0	2	0	1	0	0	0	1	.000	0	0	18.00
	Ogden	Mil	R+	22	2	0	0	1	3	18	2	5	3	0	0	0	1	4	0	6	3	0	0	0	.000	0	0	9.00
	Beloit	Mil	A	22	24	0	0	8	33	147	48	24	20	2	3	0	1	8	0	15	1	0	1	1	.500	0	2	5.45
Lugo, Ruddy	Ogden	Mil	R+	21	16	16	1	0	91.2	397	82	48	35	7	3	6	12	52	1	88	7	0	5	5	.500	0	0	3.44
Lundgren, Wayne	Red Sox	Bos	R	19	11	2	0	1	29	135	39	20	11	1	0	2	1	8	0	12	1	0	2	2	.500	0	1	3.41
Luque, Roger*	Rancho Cuca	SD	A+	21	29	2	0	8	43.2	213	55	35	29	1	3	1	5	27	0	34	13	0	3	3	.500	0	1	5.98
	Fort Wayne	SD	A	21	14	12	0	0	63.2	283	66	37	30	3	1	2	6	20	0	56	1	0	4	3	.571	0	0	4.24
Lutz, Ken	Great Falls	LA	R+	19	7	7	0	0	35.1	158	44	26	24	3	1	1	3	11	0	16	2	0	3	2	.600	0	0	6.11
Lyon, Brandon	Queens	Tor	A-	21	15	13	0	0	60.1	230	43	20	16	1	2	2	2	6	0	55	1	1	5	3	.625	0	0	2.39
Lyons, Jon	Sarasota	Bos	A+	26	33	0	0	11	53	232	64	31	29	5	3	3	3	19	3	30	2	0	4	3	.571	0	0	4.92
Mabry, Barry	Braves	Atl	R	19	8	0	0	5	17.2	68	13	4	4	0	2	0	0	4	0	13	0	0	0	1	.000	0	1	2.04
MacHen, Mike	Braves	Atl	R	19	12	1	0	2	30.1	147	22	15	10	1	1	2	7	26	1	28	7	0	2	1	.667	0	0	2.97
Madril, Steve*	White Sox	CWS	R	23	24	1	0	13	43.2	185	44	25	19	1	2	2	1	7	0	51	6	3	3	2	.600	0	4	3.92
Madritsch, Robert*	Reds	Cin	R	25	6	4	0	0	22.1	90	15	5	5	0	1	0	2	9	0	27	0	0	1	1	.500	0	0	2.01
	Dayton	Cin	A	25	2	2	0	0	10	44	8	1	1	0	0	1	0	7	0	7	1	0	0	0	.000	0	0	0.90
Madson, Ryan	Piedmont	Phi	A	20	21	21	2	0	135.2	564	113	50	39	5	3	0	13	45	0	123	5	1	14	5	.737	1	0	2.59
Magrane, Jim	Chston-SC	TB	A	22	27	27	1	0	173	710	158	64	53	9	3	0	4	43	0	162	14	1	12	5	.706	1	0	2.76
Majewski, Gary	Burlington	CWS	A	21	22	22	3	0	134.2	546	83	53	46	8	3	6	12	68	0	137	2	0	6	7	.462	3	0	3.07
	Winston-Sal	CWS	A+	21	6	6	0	0	37	163	32	21	21	1	2	2	8	17	0	24	2	0	2	4	.333	0	0	5.11
Malaska, Mark*	Chston-SC	TB	A	23	2	0	0	0	2	8	3	2	2	1	0	0	0	0	0	3	0	0	0	0	.000	0	0	9.00
	Hudson Val	TB	A-	23	10	5	0	0	40.1	176	44	27	22	1	0	0	1	14	2	36	8	0	0	2	.000	0	0	4.91
Maldonado, E.	Kissimmee	Hou	A+	25	36	14	0	11	106.1	487	123	76	63	9	2	2	5	46	3	70	16	1	3	12	.200	0	2	5.33
Maleski, Eric	Kinston	Cle	A+	24	5	0	0	3	8	37	9	7	7	0	0	1	0	6	1	3	0	0	0	0	.000	0	0	7.88
Mallette, Brian	Mudville	Mil	A+	26	50	0	0	15	71	316	52	35	26	6	1	3	5	52	1	94	11	0	4	4	.500	0	2	3.30
Malloy, Bill	Bakersfield	SF	A+	26	10	10	0	0	44.2	205	52	27	24	4	0	2	3	26	0	27	5	0	3	3	.500	0	0	4.84
Malone, Corwin*	Burlington	CWS	A	20	38	1	0	16	71.2	345	67	52	39	4	4	4	2	60	4	82	17	2	2	3	.400	0	0	4.90
Mangrum, Micah	Spokane	KC	A-	23	20	0	0	6	39.1	160	35	14	12	2	0	0	2	10	1	39	2	0	0	3	.000	0	0	2.75
Mangum, Mark	Jupiter	Mon	A+	22	20	19	1	1	114	487	109	62	52	11	4	5	12	30	0	55	4	0	6	8	.429	0	0	4.11
Manning, Mike	Columbus	Cle	A	23	5	0	0	3	4.1	25	4	7	6	0	1	2	1	6	0	2	0	0	0	0	.000	0	2	12.46
Mansfield, Monte	Martinsvlle	Hou	R+	20	18	0	0	15	24.1	100	16	7	6	2	2	1	2	14	2	32	6	0	2	1	.667	0	3	2.22
Marceau, Pierre-L.*	Expos	Mon	R	20	6	3	0	1	10.1	62	9	18	8	0	1	1	4	17	0	9	6	0	0	4	.000	0	0	6.97
Marchetti, Dan	Bluefield	Bal	R+	22	22	0	0	9	29.2	137	42	29	19	4	0	1	3	8	0	31	4	0	3	2	.600	0	0	5.76
Marietta, Ron*	Columbus	Cle	A	23	1	0	0	1	0	3	1	1	1	0	0	0	1	1	1	0	1	0	0	1	.000	0	0	0.00
Marin, Willy	Vero Beach	LA	A+	22	1	0	0	0	1	10	5	6	3	0	0	0	0	1	0	1	0	0	0	0	.000	0	0	27.00
	Yakima	LA	A-	22	19	0	0	10	31.1	144	42	23	19	4	0	1	2	11	0	23	2	0	4	1	.800	0	1	5.46
Marini, Anthony*	Kinston	Cle	A+	24	1	0	0	0	2.1	9	1	2	1	0	1	0	0	0	0	2	0	0	0	1	.000	0	0	3.86
	Mahoning Vy	Cle	A-	24	1	0	0	0	5	19	3	1	1	0	0	0	0	0	0	1	1	0	1	0	1.000	0	0	1.80
	Columbus	Cle	A	24	11	10	0	1	62.1	267	63	24	22	2	3	3	4	26	1	44	0	0	4	2	.667	0	0	3.18
Markert, Jackson	Salem-Keizr	SF	A-	22	21	0	0	13	35.2	152	28	9	9	0	1	0	2	15	0	38	4	0	3	1	.750	0	6	2.27
Markwell, D.*	Hagerstown	Tor	A	20	2	0	0	0	2	15	3	2	2	0	1	0	0	5	0	2	0	0	0	1	.000	0	0	9.00
	Queens	Tor	A-	20	14	13	0	1	73.2	306	59	29	25	2	1	4	3	31	0	66	2	0	4	3	.571	0	0	3.05
Marquez, Jose	Diamondbcks	Ari	R	20	13	8	0	0	68	305	71	48	42	2	1	3	4	30	0	33	6	2	2	5	.286	0	0	5.56
Marr, Jason	Potomac	StL	A+	25	48	0	0	46	55.2	235	52	24	22	5	2	2	3	17	0	45	0	1	2	4	.333	0	30	3.56
Marrero, Darwin	Jupiter	Mon	A+	20	1	0	0	0	1.1	10	4	5	2	1	0	0	0	2	0	2	0	0	0	1	.000	0	0	13.50
	Expos	Mon	R	20	11	7	1	0	49.2	231	60	42	35	3	0	1	12	15	0	36	4	2	1	6	.143	0	0	6.34
Marriott, Mike	Brevard Cty	Fla	A+	24	2	1	0	0	2.1	14	4	3	2	0	1	1	0	3	0	0	0	0	0	0	.000	0	0	7.71
Marsonek, Sam	Greensboro	NYY	A	22	18	18	1	0	114.1	510	114	64	54	8	1	3	23	51	0	78	15	2	6	7	.462	0	0	4.25
Martin, Lucas*	Elizabethtn	Min	R+	22	15	8	0	1	61.2	237	58	20	17	3	0	0	0	8	0	53	0	1	7	0	1.000	0	1	2.48
Martin, Scott	San Berndno	LA	A+	23	33	12	0	7	111	451	97	45	41	7	0	4	6	28	1	90	5	1	6	5	.545	0	1	3.32
Martinez, Anastacio	Red Sox	Bos	R	20	2	1	0	0	6.2	38	15	9	7	0	0	1	0	3	0	1	0	0	0	1	.000	0	0	9.45
	Augusta	Bos	A	20	23	23	0	0	120.1	526	130	69	62	8	4	4	2	50	0	107	12	1	9	6	.600	0	0	4.64
Martinez, Antonio	Padres	SD	R	18	3	0	0	2	3.1	13	0	0	0	0	0	0	0	3	0	2	0	0	0	0	.000	0	1	0.00
Martinez, Carlos*	Spokane	KC	A-	22	21	0	0	0	35	159	36	24	24	3	1	3	4	22	0	26	2	2	1	1	.500	0	0	6.17
Martinez, Dan*	Burlington	CWS	A	22	8	0	0	5	9.1	49	12	7	7	0	0	0	1	9	0	6	1	0	0	0	.000	0	0	6.75
	Bristol	CWS	R+	22	12	0	0	3	17.1	86	21	17	12	3	2	1	4	7	2	12	4	0	0	0	.000	0	0	6.23
Martinez, David*	Greensboro	NYY	A	21	8	8	1	0	49.1	207	33	24	16	0	0	0	4	27	0	44	5	1	2	5	.286	0	0	2.92
	Staten Ilnd	NYY	A-	21	6	4	0	1	32.1	129	20	12	9	2	0	0	4	11	0	33	2	0	2	2	.500	0	0	2.51
Martinez, Eduardo*	Martinsvlle	Hou	R+	22	17	0	0	6	38	171	41	27	13	3	2	0	3	16	0	30	4	0	1	1	.500	0	0	3.08
Martinez, Gustavo	Mariners	Sea	R	20	17	1	0	4	42.2	197	42	27	17	0	0	0	3	25	0	53	3	0	6	3	.667	0	1	3.59
Martinez, Javier	Dayton	Cin	A	24	16	1	0	7	17	82	20	13	12	3	0	0	1	10	1	24	1	0	4	1	.800	0	1	6.35
Martinez, Jesus	Yankees	NYY	R	18	3	0	0	2	3	16	4	3	3	0	0	0	0	2	0	3	0	1	0	1	.000	0	0	9.00
Martinez, Luis	Beloit	Mil	A	21	28	13	0	7	92.2	412	71	49	39	8	0	6	5	61	1	77	7	1	5	7	.417	0	0	3.79
Martinez, Mark*	Lowell	Bos	A-	23	17	1	0	2	43	193	28	25	17	0	4	4	1	42	1	29	10	0	2	0	1.000	0	0	3.56
Martinez, Miguel	Johnson Cty	StL	R+	19	13	13	1	0	62.2	280	75	44	37	4	2	1	1	16	0	43	0	1	2	5	.286	0	0	5.31
Martinez, Oscar	Staten Ilnd	NYY	A-	22	26	0	0	22	25	88	11	2	1	0	0	1	0	6	0	40	5	0	2	0	1.000	0	13	0.36
Martinez, Ramon	Great Falls	LA	R+	22	6	0	0	5	5	28	8	6	4	0	0	0	2	4	0	7	2	0	0	0	.000	0	3	7.20
Martinez, Renan*	Cedar Rapds	Ana	A	19	7	5	0	2	31.1	141	37	15	14	4	0	1	2	12	0	18	2	0	1	1	.500	0	0	4.02
Martunas, Matt*	Hudson Val	TB	A-	22	3	0	0	2	5	26	8	7	5	0	1	1	1	2	1	3	0	0	1	0	1.000	0	0	9.00
Marx, Tom*	W Michigan	Det	A	21	18	18	1	0	98.2	416	74	35	30	6	4	4	1	51	0	83	4	1	7	6	.538	1	0	2.74

2000 Pitching — Class-A and Rookie Leagues

HOW MUCH HE PITCHED											WHAT HE GAVE UP												THE RESULTS					
Player	Team	Org	Lg	A	G	GS	CG	GF	IP	BFP	H	R	ER	HR	SH	SF	HB	TBB	IBB	SO	WP	Bk	W	L	Pct.	ShO	Sv	ERA
Massingale, Matt	Utica	Fla	A-	22	6	6	0	0	35.2	133	23	4	2	0	1	0	0	9	0	31	2	0	3	0	1.000	0	0	0.50
Mastrolonardo, D.	Charlotte	Tex	A+	26	8	0	0	1	12.1	65	16	8	7	1	0	1	1	12	0	11	0	0	1	0	1.000	0	0	5.11
Mateo, Julio	Wisconsin	Sea	A	21	36	1	0	15	68.2	295	63	38	32	12	4	1	6	23	1	73	9	0	4	8	.333	0	4	4.19
Matheny, Brandon*	Mahoning Vy	Cle	A-	22	15	15	0	0	76.2	317	70	30	28	3	1	3	3	32	0	69	6	0	6	3	.667	0	0	3.29
Mathews, Dan	Beloit	Mil	A	25	45	1	0	25	68.2	278	54	20	16	0	3	0	4	17	2	58	7	0	4	4	.500	0	8	2.10
Matos, Jesus	Rockies	Col	R	22	15	4	0	6	46	186	40	20	13	2	0	3	1	8	0	41	2	0	5	1	.833	0	0	2.54
Matos, Raymond*	Giants	SF	R	18	10	3	0	2	25.1	128	33	23	17	2	2	2	3	19	0	16	4	0	0	1	.000	0	0	6.04
Matsko, Rick	Columbus	Cle	A	24	26	0	0	10	55	222	37	16	14	1	3	1	4	21	1	68	2	0	3	2	.600	0	3	2.29
Mattioni, Nick	Pittsfield	NYM	A-	22	16	0	0	6	28.1	119	23	16	14	2	1	1	1	11	2	28	4	0	1	1	.500	0	0	4.45
Matzenbacher, B.	South Bend	Ari	A	24	51	0	0	22	65.2	282	56	25	22	3	2	1	3	31	2	61	4	0	5	6	.455	0	5	3.02
Mayfield, James	Phillies	Phi	R	22	11	8	0	2	42	184	48	28	23	2	2	0	0	10	1	25	0	0	4	3	.571	0	1	4.93
Mays, Jarrod	Kinston	Cle	A+	26	14	0	0	11	21	90	17	8	5	1	1	1	1	10	3	19	0	0	2	0	1.000	0	7	2.14
Maysonet, Roberto	Helena	Mil	R+	21	15	13	0	0	78.2	358	78	52	37	5	0	1	7	39	1	84	13	0	3	6	.333	0	0	4.23
	Beloit	Mil	A	21	1	1	0	0	3	18	5	5	5	0	0	0	1	4	0	5	0	0	0	0	.000	0	0	15.00
Mazur, Bryan*	Modesto	Oak	A+	23	36	2	0	19	76.2	333	81	34	31	3	3	2	3	23	3	68	9	0	5	3	.625	0	7	3.64
McAdoo, Duncan	Idaho Falls	SD	R+	23	9	7	0	1	42.1	173	42	17	16	1	2	0	3	6	0	37	1	1	4	1	.800	0	0	3.40
	Rancho Cuca	SD	A+	23	6	6	0	0	26.2	133	41	25	23	3	0	2	1	17	1	21	2	3	1	4	.200	0	0	7.76
McCall, Derell	Athletics	Oak	R	19	13	8	0	1	48.1	217	56	27	22	1	0	4	2	16	0	32	3	3	5	3	.625	0	0	4.10
McCall, Travis*	Visalia	Oak	A+	23	43	0	0	28	52.2	244	58	36	31	7	3	4	3	23	2	40	1	1	2	5	.286	0	7	5.30
McCasland, Ralph*	Expos	Mon	R	22	7	4	1	1	29.1	127	32	13	10	2	1	0	4	3	0	18	3	0	0	3	.000	0	0	3.07
	Vermont	Mon	A-	22	11	0	0	6	26.1	107	19	11	4	1	1	1	1	8	0	23	3	0	0	2	.000	0	1	1.37
McClain, Kevin	Cedar Rapds	Ana	A	23	30	0	0	19	46	187	36	21	16	5	0	3	2	15	0	47	4	0	4	3	.571	0	3	3.13
McClaskey, Tim	Brevard Cty	Fla	A+	25	46	0	0	38	84	333	72	26	21	6	2	2	5	18	4	97	2	1	7	4	.636	0	13	2.25
McClellan, Zach	Spokane	KC	A-	22	13	13	0	0	55.1	244	52	24	22	1	2	2	4	29	0	46	3	1	2	3	.400	0	0	3.58
McClung, Seth	Hudson Val	TB	A-	20	8	8	0	0	43.2	186	37	18	9	0	1	2	3	17	0	38	6	1	2	2	.500	0	0	1.85
	Chston-SC	TB	A	20	6	6	0	0	31	145	30	14	11	0	1	0	3	19	0	26	8	0	2	1	.667	0	0	3.19
McCormick, Terry*	Hudson Val	TB	A-	22	12	0	0	7	27.1	112	23	15	14	2	1	1	5	3	0	26	4	0	2	4	.333	0	3	4.61
	Chston-SC	TB	A	22	5	0	0	1	7	38	11	7	3	0	0	0	0	5	0	7	1	0	0	0	.000	0	0	3.86
McCullem, Ryan*	Medcine Hat	Tor	R+	20	16	6	0	1	54.2	254	64	34	24	5	3	2	2	27	0	53	5	0	2	2	.500	0	0	3.95
McCulloch, Andy	Medcine Hat	Tor	R+	23	27	0	0	24	27	112	24	9	8	3	0	0	0	7	0	26	2	0	0	0	.000	0	15	2.67
McDade, Neal	Lynchburg	Pit	A+	25	7	7	0	0	29	131	35	18	15	2	1	3	1	11	1	24	0	0	1	2	.333	0	0	4.66
McDaniel, Denny*	Lancaster	Sea	A+	24	43	0	0	14	44.1	208	42	29	20	2	0	6	5	25	2	37	5	0	5	0	1.000	0	1	4.06
McDonald, Jon	Fort Myers	Min	A+	23	10	10	0	0	49.2	207	42	24	22	1	1	1	6	16	0	33	3	1	3	3	.500	0	0	3.99
McFarland, Stuart*	Queens	Tor	A-	23	19	0	0	10	26	115	12	9	6	0	2	2	8	22	1	21	1	0	2	2	.500	0	2	2.08
McGerry, Kevin	Vancouver	Oak	A-	21	13	5	0	1	35	155	29	27	23	2	1	2	3	24	0	37	8	1	2	2	.500	0	0	5.91
McGill, Frank	Savannah	Tex	A	21	26	12	1	6	93.1	419	107	65	59	11	1	3	4	32	0	66	2	0	3	6	.333	1	1	5.69
McGinnis, Johnny	Jamestown	Atl	A-	21	11	0	0	2	15	76	11	14	10	0	2	0	5	16	0	13	3	0	0	1	.000	0	0	6.00
McGowan, Brian	St. Pete	TB	A+	24	11	3	0	1	22.2	106	23	19	14	0	0	1	1	17	1	13	8	1	0	2	.000	0	0	5.56
McGowan, Dustin	Medcine Hat	Tor	R+	19	8	8	0	0	25	129	26	21	18	2	1	5	3	25	0	19	8	0	0	3	.000	0	0	6.48
McKay, John	Marlins	Fla	R	24	1	0	0	1	1	4	1	0	0	0	0	0	0	0	0	2	0	0	0	0	.000	0	0	0.00
	Utica	Fla	A-	24	17	4	0	5	37.2	156	35	11	8	3	1	0	0	8	0	42	2	1	2	0	1.000	0	1	1.91
McKey, Dustin	Princeton	TB	R+	23	17	0	0	8	22.2	84	12	3	2	0	2	1	1	6	1	11	1	1	3	1	.750	0	4	0.79
	Hudson Val	TB	A-	23	10	0	0	9	13	65	16	9	6	0	1	0	2	4	1	7	1	1	1	2	.333	0	1	4.15
McKinley, Ryan	Cubs	ChC	R	22	15	0	0	11	26	130	36	27	22	1	4	1	1	13	0	17	4	0	1	3	.250	0	2	7.62
McMillan, Josh*	Medcine Hat	Tor	R+	22	15	15	0	0	64.1	293	72	47	31	5	3	1	2	29	0	56	5	0	3	3	.500	0	0	4.34
McMurray, Heath	Ogden	Mil	R+	22	12	0	0	6	26	116	31	13	13	6	1	1	1	7	0	26	0	2	3	2	.600	0	3	4.50
McNutt, Mike	Utica	Fla	A-	21	15	10	0	2	62	273	68	39	35	4	1	0	5	18	1	38	5	2	2	6	.250	0	0	5.08
McWhirter, Kris	Burlington	CWS	A	22	28	17	2	4	122.1	532	118	67	51	11	7	4	7	46	1	103	6	1	3	9	.250	0	0	3.75
Mead, David	Pulaski	Tex	R+	20	12	12	0	0	62.1	274	57	35	32	2	1	4	12	24	0	66	5	1	6	2	.750	0	0	4.62
Mears, Chris	Lancaster	Sea	A+	23	28	28	0	0	151.1	670	178	92	80	13	4	8	10	54	0	89	6	1	11	8	.579	0	0	4.76
Medina, Carlos*	St. Lucie	NYM	A+	24	11	1	0	2	21.1	87	22	10	8	0	1	0	1	9	0	16	0	2	1	2	.333	0	0	3.38
Medina, Franklin	Diamondbcks	Ari	R	19	13	8	0	1	56	248	43	36	27	2	0	2	4	37	0	53	4	9	3	3	.500	0	1	4.34
	South Bend	Ari	A	19	2	1	0	0	3.1	21	4	5	4	1	0	0	0	7	0	1	0	0	0	1	.000	0	0	10.80
Medlock, Chet	Johnson Cty	StL	R+	22	5	4	0	0	22.2	89	12	7	5	2	0	0	1	11	0	17	1	1	2	0	1.000	0	0	1.99
	New Jersey	StL	A-	22	7	7	0	0	27	131	35	24	21	2	0	0	4	13	0	22	2	0	2	4	.333	0	0	7.00
Meisenheim, Matt	Rangers	Tex	R	19	6	5	0	0	15.2	69	15	5	4	0	0	0	1	7	0	13	1	0	0	1	.000	0	0	2.30
Mejia, Francisco*	Frederick	Bal	A+	21	4	1	0	1	10	43	9	5	5	1	0	1	0	6	0	7	0	0	0	0	.000	0	0	4.50
	Bluefield	Bal	R+	21	4	4	0	0	17.1	78	18	17	12	3	0	0	3	10	0	11	0	0	2	1	.667	0	0	6.23
Meldahl, Todd*	Batavia	Phi	A-	23	18	5	1	4	48.2	205	52	24	18	2	2	1	3	13	1	46	3	0	3	3	.500	0	0	3.33
Melendez, Dave	Tigers	Det	R	25	5	2	1	2	17	68	12	7	4	2	0	0	1	3	0	9	0	0	1	1	.500	0	1	2.12
	Lakeland	Det	A+	25	7	4	0	1	22.2	125	37	30	23	2	0	3	3	17	0	13	2	0	0	4	.000	0	0	9.13
Mendez, David*	Jamestown	Atl	A-	21	15	15	0	0	84.2	360	75	33	27	7	0	1	6	31	0	84	3	0	5	4	.556	0	0	2.87
Mendez, Pastor	Helena	Mil	R+	21	2	1	0	0	6	33	10	12	6	0	1	1	1	4	0	3	1	1	1	1	.500	0	0	9.00
Mendible, Franklin	Twins	Min	R	21	17	0	0	2	20	87	16	6	6	0	1	2	1	14	0	23	3	0	2	2	.500	0	0	2.70
Mendoza, G.	Winston-Sal	CWS	A+	23	31	19	4	4	145	635	146	65	55	7	5	3	4	65	0	117	13	0	11	6	.647	3	0	3.41
Mendoza, Hatuey	High Desert	Ari	A+	21	29	27	0	0	150.2	710	170	140	110	17	1	4	12	98	0	107	19	0	8	12	.400	0	0	6.57
Mendoza, Mario	Cedar Rapds	Ana	A	22	14	14	4	0	98.1	414	101	54	47	10	5	1	4	19	0	67	5	1	6	6	.500	0	0	4.30
	Lk Elsinore	Ana	A+	22	12	8	0	0	51.1	222	51	27	20	4	2	2	1	19	1	35	1	0	1	1	.500	0	0	3.51
Merricks, Charles*	Rockies	Col	R	22	13	10	0	0	49.2	216	47	27	15	0	0	4	4	24	0	37	1	1	2	1	.667	0	0	2.72
Merricks, Matt*	Braves	Atl	R	18	9	0	0	6	21.1	96	21	15	6	0	0	0	1	11	0	28	2	0	1	0	1.000	0	1	2.53
Messenger, Randy	Marlins	Fla	R	19	12	12	0	0	59.2	263	66	37	32	6	1	1	3	22	0	29	7	2	2	2	.500	0	0	4.83
Metzger, Jon*	Spokane	KC	A-	22	13	12	0	0	62	259	46	32	27	0	2	2	3	34	0	64	5	5	2	6	.250	0	0	3.92
Meyer, Dave	San Berndno	LA	A+	25	8	0	0	8	11	46	13	5	5	0	0	1	0	1	0	5	0	1	0	1	.000	0	1	4.09
	Vero Beach	LA	A+	25	11	0	0	7	18	69	12	2	2	1	2	0	1	5	0	12	0	0	1	0	1.000	0	0	1.00
Meyer, John	Idaho Falls	SD	R+	22	17	0	0	0	20	108	19	21	18	1	0	0	4	27	0	15	4	0	0	1	.000	0	0	8.10
Meyer, Mike	New Jersey	StL	A-	23	27	0	0	5	34.1	166	48	29	24	3	2	3	2	15	0	24	7	0	1	1	.500	0	0	6.29
Meza, Nathan	New Jersey	StL	A-	23	12	11	0	0	54.2	254	67	38	35	2	3	3	2	22	1	37	2	1	3	7	.300	0	0	5.76

2000 Pitching — Class-A and Rookie Leagues

HOW MUCH HE PITCHED											WHAT HE GAVE UP												THE RESULTS					
Player	Team	Org	Lg	A	G	GS	CG	GF	IP	BFP	H	R	ER	HR	SH	SF	HB	TBB	IBB	SO	WP	Bk	W	L	Pct.	ShO	Sv	ERA
Middleton, Kyle	Royals	KC	R	21	15	1	0	2	20	109	32	34	33	2	0	1	0	17	0	14	6	0	0	2	.000	0	0	14.85
Mieses, Jose	Beloit	Mil	A	21	21	21	2	0	135	530	107	43	38	8	5	1	3	37	1	132	6	1	13	6	.684	2	0	2.53
	Mudville	Mil	A+	21	6	6	0	0	34	144	25	11	10	1	1	1	2	18	0	40	3	1	4	1	.800	0	0	2.65
Mikels, Jason	Macon	Atl	A	21	31	6	0	10	70.2	329	87	56	47	14	2	2	2	27	0	59	4	1	1	5	.167	0	1	5.99
Miller, Colby	Twins	Min	R	19	14	10	0	0	55.1	231	44	26	19	2	5	0	3	21	0	55	3	0	3	2	.600	0	0	3.09
	Quad City	Min	A	19	2	2	0	0	6.2	39	10	6	5	0	2	0	1	7	0	6	2	0	0	1	.000	0	0	6.75
Miller, Corey	Visalia	Oak	A+	24	47	0	0	23	55	242	56	27	21	2	4	2	3	25	4	59	2	1	6	4	.600	0	7	3.44
Miller, Jason*	Twins	Min	R	18	2	1	0	0	4	15	2	1	0	0	1	0	0	0	0	3	0	0	0	0	.000	0	0	0.00
	Elizabethtn	Min	R+	18	9	5	0	0	26	104	23	16	13	7	0	1	1	5	0	22	0	1	2	1	.667	0	0	4.50
Miller, Jim	Mudville	Mil	A+	25	12	2	0	5	21.2	116	33	21	16	4	1	3	4	15	1	22	5	2	0	4	.000	0	0	6.65
Miller, Matt*	Braves	Atl	R	23	3	0	0	2	5	23	5	2	2	0	0	0	0	3	0	7	0	0	0	0	.000	0	0	3.60
	Jamestown	Atl	A-	23	18	0	0	6	32.1	151	36	23	19	1	0	1	1	16	1	33	0	0	0	2	.000	0	1	5.29
Miller, Ryan	Ogden	Mil	R+	23	15	10	0	2	76.2	318	62	35	31	8	1	7	8	27	0	66	1	3	7	3	.700	0	0	3.64
Miller, Tom*	Bakersfield	SF	A+	26	32	16	0	2	108.2	494	126	71	54	10	2	3	2	53	0	92	17	4	4	2	.667	0	0	4.47
Milo, Tony*	Butte	Ana	R+	23	12	2	0	3	35.2	166	44	25	18	2	1	2	2	10	0	44	2	0	1	3	.250	0	2	4.54
	Boise	Ana	A-	23	9	4	0	0	32	130	26	9	9	2	0	0	2	11	0	51	0	0	4	0	1.000	0	0	2.53
Mims, Brandon*	Red Sox	Bos	R	19	4	2	1	0	13	54	10	3	2	1	1	2	1	8	0	15	2	1	1	1	.500	1	0	1.38
Minaya, Edwin	Vancouver	Oak	A-	21	19	14	0	0	74.2	328	71	46	35	5	7	2	3	28	0	55	7	0	4	6	.400	0	0	4.22
Minaya, Pedro	Dayton	Cin	A	23	16	0	0	12	19.1	103	30	27	24	4	0	1	2	19	0	15	4	0	0	1	.000	0	4	11.17
	Reds	Cin	R	23	6	4	0	0	16.1	80	28	17	14	0	0	2	0	8	0	14	1	0	1	3	.250	0	0	7.71
Miniel, Rene	Red Sox	Bos	R	20	21	1	0	17	36	162	37	21	16	1	5	1	0	21	3	31	3	0	2	4	.333	0	7	4.00
Miniel, Roberto	Ogden	Mil	R+	21	16	14	0	0	83.1	355	84	41	25	7	0	3	4	22	0	80	5	0	9	3	.750	0	0	2.70
Minix, Travis	Chston-SC	TB	A	23	48	1	0	16	78.1	346	85	36	29	5	1	0	2	27	1	73	1	0	4	2	.667	0	2	3.33
Mitchel, Cristobal	Hudson Val	TB	A-	22	19	0	0	11	24	122	30	14	14	1	1	1	3	18	2	27	1	0	0	3	.000	0	3	5.25
Mitchell, Thomas	Expos	Mon	R	20	10	9	0	1	46	201	43	29	19	6	1	1	3	18	0	26	0	0	2	3	.400	0	0	3.72
Montalbano, Greg*	Red Sox	Bos	R	23	4	4	0	0	12	51	13	6	5	1	0	0	0	3	0	14	1	0	0	2	.000	0	0	3.75
	Lowell	Bos	A-	23	2	2	0	0	10.1	39	4	3	2	0	1	1	0	4	0	15	0	0	0	1	.000	0	0	1.74
Montero, Agustin	Vero Beach	LA	A+	23	3	0	0	1	3	17	2	2	2	0	0	0	0	6	0	4	2	0	0	0	.000	0	0	6.00
	San Berndno	LA	A+	23	7	0	0	3	8.1	52	13	14	9	0	0	1	2	12	0	10	2	0	0	2	.000	0	0	9.72
	Great Falls	LA	R+	23	11	0	0	3	18.1	85	16	10	8	1	0	0	2	12	0	21	3	0	2	1	.667	0	0	3.93
	Yakima	LA	A-	23	7	0	0	3	13.1	64	12	9	9	0	1	0	5	7	1	21	3	0	1	0	1.000	0	0	6.08
Montero, Francisco	Clearwater	Phi	A+	25	26	2	0	17	61.2	267	72	32	30	4	1	1	1	15	1	39	2	3	2	1	.667	0	1	4.38
Montero, Jose	Savannah	Tex	A	22	34	0	0	13	61.2	274	44	26	20	1	2	2	9	36	0	62	8	2	5	2	.714	0	3	2.92
Montero, Oscar	Lansing	ChC	A	23	17	0	0	15	24.1	103	18	6	1	0	2	0	1	12	1	27	0	0	4	1	.800	0	6	0.37
Montgomery, Greg	White Sox	CWS	R	26	2	0	0	1	3.2	18	4	5	5	0	0	0	0	3	0	4	1	0	0	0	.000	0	1	12.27
	Winston-Sal	CWS	A+	26	2	0	0	0	3	11	0	1	1	0	0	0	0	2	0	5	2	0	0	0	.000	0	0	3.00
Montgomery, Steve	Red Sox	Bos	R	27	2	0	0	1	4	25	7	10	6	0	0	0	1	4	0	4	2	0	0	1	.000	0	0	13.50
Montilla, Elvis	Orioles	Bal	R	19	16	2	0	4	31	129	24	14	12	3	0	1	3	10	1	15	0	0	3	2	.600	0	0	3.48
Montilla, Felix	Williamsprt	Pit	A-	21	15	15	1	0	83	375	81	49	34	2	2	2	12	43	0	82	5	2	3	5	.375	1	0	3.69
Monzon, Yoel	Asheville	Col	A	24	39	0	0	10	64	271	48	28	23	9	0	2	9	20	0	83	2	0	4	1	.800	0	2	3.23
Moore, Bryan	Kane County	Fla	A	24	58	0	0	54	69.2	291	78	28	24	3	7	2	3	12	1	58	4	0	5	2	.714	0	27	3.10
Moore, Chris	Brevard Cty	Fla	A+	22	4	0	0	1	5.2	31	7	9	8	1	1	1	1	6	1	2	3	0	1	0	1.000	0	1	12.71
	Marlins	Fla	R	22	6	0	0	4	12.2	55	9	3	3	0	0	1	4	4	0	13	1	0	1	0	1.000	0	1	2.13
Moore, Darin	Modesto	Oak	A+	24	3	1	0	0	3.2	30	5	12	9	1	0	0	6	6	0	5	2	0	0	2	.000	0	0	22.09
	Vancouver	Oak	A-	24	18	14	0	0	69.2	312	58	45	37	2	6	1	11	37	1	61	12	0	2	7	.222	0	0	4.78
Moore, Greg	Cedar Rapds	Ana	A	22	15	0	0	2	21.1	93	24	15	13	2	4	2	0	10	0	10	2	1	0	2	.000	0	0	5.48
	Boise	Ana	A-	22	13	0	0	6	29	146	48	29	24	1	1	3	3	6	1	19	1	0	0	3	.000	0	1	7.45
	Butte	Ana	R+	22	7	5	1	0	34	152	44	23	20	3	1	2	0	6	0	19	1	0	3	1	.750	0	0	5.29
Mora, Sergio	Mexico	—	R	20	10	9	2	0	55.1	247	60	35	32	2	0	3	8	28	0	47	10	0	5	3	.625	1	0	5.20
Morban, Domingo*	Kingsport	NYM	R+	19	11	0	0	3	18.2	93	24	18	10	3	1	0	4	9	0	16	5	2	1	0	1.000	0	0	4.82
Morel, Jesus	Twins	Min	R	20	8	0	0	1	9.2	36	6	4	2	1	0	0	1	3	0	11	0	0	0	1	.000	0	0	1.86
Moreno, Darwin	Braves	Atl	R	18	14	1	0	7	30.1	150	35	23	18	2	0	1	0	18	0	25	1	1	4	3	.571	0	0	5.34
Moreno, Edwin	Savannah	Tex	A	20	23	22	1	0	133	562	127	58	48	9	1	2	7	46	0	89	6	0	9	8	.529	0	0	3.25
Morris, Will	Medcine Hat	Tor	R+	23	24	0	0	8	44	192	46	33	27	4	3	3	1	17	1	29	3	0	3	4	.429	0	0	5.52
Morrison, Cody	Lancaster	Sea	A+	26	52	0	0	21	82	342	78	42	39	5	2	1	6	29	3	60	5	2	8	7	.533	0	3	4.28
Morse, Bryan*	Utica	Fla	A-	23	2	0	0	0	2.2	10	1	0	0	0	0	0	0	1	0	2	0	0	1	0	1.000	0	0	0.00
	Kane County	Fla	A	23	16	0	0	2	36.2	152	30	13	11	0	2	0	5	13	0	30	3	0	3	4	.429	0	0	2.70
Moseley, Marcus	Elizabethtn	Min	R+	20	18	5	0	3	38.2	197	41	42	35	3	1	1	4	43	0	38	8	0	2	1	.667	0	0	8.15
Moser, Todd*	Kane County	Fla	A	24	21	21	3	0	136.2	566	136	54	43	6	5	3	9	26	0	101	7	0	9	5	.643	0	0	2.83
Mosher, Andy	Beloit	Mil	A	25	17	0	0	6	25.1	116	28	22	18	1	1	6	4	12	0	18	3	0	1	1	.500	0	0	6.39
Mosley, Eric	Yankees	NYY	R	20	5	0	0	1	4	24	11	7	7	0	0	0	1	2	0	2	0	1	0	0	.000	0	0	15.75
Mottl, Ryan	Clinton	Cin	A	23	9	4	0	1	29	141	41	27	24	4	1	2	2	8	1	28	0	0	1	3	.250	0	0	7.45
Mowday, Chris	Queens	Tor	A-	19	15	13	0	2	71.2	310	61	32	27	1	0	3	4	41	0	65	8	0	5	2	.714	0	0	3.39
Mozingo, Dan*	Burlington	CWS	A	21	10	0	0	3	10.1	68	17	24	22	2	0	0	6	16	0	9	0	0	0	0	.000	0	0	19.16
	Bristol	CWS	R+	21	9	0	0	6	15	63	13	5	5	1	1	1	0	6	0	16	4	0	0	0	.000	0	1	3.00
Muldoon, Tommy	Oneonta	Det	A-	24	12	0	0	5	19	89	14	13	9	0	3	0	2	17	0	19	1	0	1	1	.500	0	0	4.26
Munoz, Arnaldo*	Burlington	CWS	A	19	22	0	0	8	38.1	185	45	34	29	2	1	0	6	25	0	44	7	5	2	3	.400	0	0	6.81
Murphy, Matt*	Daytona	ChC	A+	22	47	2	0	19	60	279	65	38	31	2	4	3	0	41	5	46	3	0	0	7	.000	0	5	4.65
Murray, Brad*	Bristol	CWS	R+	22	16	4	0	5	50.2	215	49	28	24	1	2	1	5	16	0	37	4	1	2	1	.667	0	1	4.26
Musser, Neal*	Kingsport	NYM	R+	20	7	7	0	0	34.1	138	33	10	8	1	0	0	1	6	0	21	3	0	3	2	.600	0	0	2.10
Myers, Aaron	Mudville	Mil	A+	25	50	0	0	19	88.1	374	64	36	35	9	2	3	6	44	0	104	3	0	2	3	.400	0	2	3.57
Myers, Brett	Piedmont	Phi	A	20	27	27	2	0	175.1	738	165	78	62	7	1	4	9	69	0	140	8	0	13	7	.650	1	0	3.18
Nacar, Yimmy	Giants	SF	R	18	12	0	0	6	20.1	107	25	22	22	1	0	2	2	20	0	17	6	0	0	1	.000	0	0	9.74
Nageotte, Clint	Mariners	Sea	R	20	12	7	0	1	50	207	29	15	12	0	0	2	3	28	0	59	2	0	4	1	.800	0	1	2.16
Nakamura, Mike	Fort Myers	Min	A+	24	32	0	0	19	41.1	162	33	9	7	0	2	1	2	11	1	46	2	0	1	0	1.000	0	12	1.52
Nall, T.J.	San Berndno	LA	A+	20	3	3	0	0	12.1	50	10	6	6	2	0	0	2	2	0	11	0	0	1	1	.500	0	0	4.38
Nance, Shane*	Yakima	LA	A-	23	12	9	0	0	58	228	41	19	16	1	2	0	2	22	0	66	2	0	2	4	.333	0	0	2.48

2000 Pitching — Class-A and Rookie Leagues

HOW MUCH HE PITCHED											WHAT HE GAVE UP												THE RESULTS					
Player	Team	Org	Lg	A	G	GS	CG	GF	IP	BFP	H	R	ER	HR	SH	SF	HB	TBB	IBB	SO	WP	Bk	W	L	Pct.	ShO	Sv	ERA
Nanninga, Matt	Clinton	Cin	A	24	1	0	0	0	1.2	13	6	5	5	0	0	0	0	2	0	0	1	0	0	0	.000	0	0	27.00
Nannini, Mike	Michigan	Hou	A	20	15	15	3	0	101.1	411	85	45	40	4	1	3	2	33	0	86	1	0	7	4	.636	0	0	3.55
	Kissimmee	Hou	A+	20	12	12	2	0	78.1	329	83	34	29	3	0	0	0	14	0	56	0	0	7	3	.700	1	0	3.33
Narveson, Chris*	Johnson Cty	StL	R+	19	12	12	0	0	55	247	57	33	20	7	1	1	3	25	0	63	3	0	2	4	.333	0	0	3.27
Natale, Mike	Spokane	KC	A-	21	23	0	0	18	41	162	30	7	6	0	3	1	1	13	0	43	4	0	2	1	.667	0	8	1.32
Neal, Blaine	Brevard Cty	Fla	A+	23	41	0	0	34	54.1	231	40	27	13	1	1	2	4	24	3	65	1	0	2	2	.500	0	11	2.15
Neary, Andrew	Helena	Mil	R+	23	21	0	0	8	47.2	199	43	25	23	7	2	2	1	14	3	27	2	0	4	3	.571	0	1	4.34
	Ogden	Mil	R+	23	1	0	0	1	1	4	0	0	0	0	0	0	0	0	0	2	0	0	0	0	.000	0	0	0.00
Negrette, Richard	Frederick	Bal	A+	25	4	0	0	1	5.2	28	3	5	0	0	1	1	0	4	0	5	0	1	0	1	.000	0	0	0.00
	Orioles	Bal	R	25	7	0	0	3	12.1	61	13	10	10	0	0	0	0	12	2	8	1	0	0	2	.000	0	0	7.30
Negron, Alex	Vancouver	Oak	A-	23	4	0	0	2	6	29	5	5	1	0	0	0	2	3	1	7	0	0	0	1	.000	0	0	1.50
	Cubs	ChC	R	23	9	0	0	7	14.1	62	11	7	6	0	0	1	1	8	0	15	1	0	2	0	1.000	0	2	3.77
	Eugene	ChC	A-	23	8	0	0	2	8.2	39	10	6	6	2	1	1	0	4	0	11	1	0	0	1	.000	0	0	6.23
Neil, Dan*	Columbus	Cle	A	22	33	0	0	10	73.1	313	74	39	31	1	5	2	8	24	2	57	2	0	6	4	.600	0	2	3.80
Nelson, Bubba	Braves	Atl	R	19	12	6	1	4	44.2	190	40	24	21	2	3	1	1	13	0	54	6	0	3	2	.600	0	0	4.23
Nelson, James*	Jamestown	Atl	A-	28	3	0	0	1	4	16	3	3	1	0	0	0	0	1	0	7	0	0	0	0	.000	0	0	2.25
Nelson, Joe	Braves	Atl	R	26	4	0	0	1	4	18	3	1	1	0	0	0	0	3	0	7	0	0	1	0	1.000	0	1	2.25
Neu, Mike	Clinton	Cin	A	23	58	0	0	54	69	306	47	27	24	5	4	3	1	52	8	95	10	0	7	7	.500	0	24	3.13
Newbauer, Marc*	Marlins	Fla	R	23	2	0	0	0	2.1	9	0	0	0	0	0	0	0	2	1	3	0	0	0	0	.000	0	0	0.00
	Kane County	Fla	A	23	17	3	0	1	35	146	40	16	15	4	2	2	1	11	0	14	4	0	6	2	.750	0	0	3.86
Newill, Max*	Spokane	KC	A-	25	19	1	0	7	40	165	32	14	10	0	4	1	3	12	3	35	5	1	3	3	.500	0	2	2.25
Nichols, Brian	Kingsport	NYM	R+	23	12	8	0	2	48.1	230	61	42	33	3	1	1	6	25	0	40	7	1	2	5	.286	0	0	6.14
Nielsen, Brian*	Ogden	Mil	R+	19	10	2	0	2	28	127	39	23	20	6	0	1	0	6	0	25	2	0	1	3	.250	0	1	6.43
Nix, Wayne	Visalia	Oak	A+	24	30	24	1	2	139.1	615	125	99	82	7	3	4	7	76	2	146	19	1	9	5	.643	1	1	5.30
Noel, Todd	Tampa	NYY	A+	22	4	4	0	0	10	55	18	13	12	2	0	0	0	8	0	11	3	0	0	0	.000	0	0	10.80
Norderum, Jason*	Vermont	Mon	A-	19	15	15	0	0	76.1	343	66	44	32	3	0	2	7	47	0	40	7	0	5	3	.625	0	0	3.77
Novoa, Niquel*	Princeton	TB	R+	19	3	0	0	2	2.2	16	7	5	5	1	0	0	0	2	0	2	0	0	0	0	.000	0	0	16.88
Noyce, Dave*	Brevard Cty	Fla	A+	24	18	17	1	0	93	413	91	53	40	12	3	4	12	35	0	63	4	1	6	5	.545	1	0	3.87
	Daytona	ChC	A+	24	3	3	0	0	12.1	56	9	6	3	0	0	0	0	9	0	6	0	0	1	0	1.000	0	0	2.19
Nunez, Franklin	Clearwater	Phi	A+	24	23	14	1	6	112	492	112	54	45	4	1	3	7	57	0	81	9	1	10	4	.714	0	2	3.62
Nunez, Jose*	Capital Cty	NYM	A	22	34	5	0	16	95.1	396	82	36	32	6	2	7	10	23	0	112	4	2	3	4	.429	0	8	3.02
Nunez, Maximo	Red Sox	Bos	R	24	2	0	0	1	6	29	12	3	2	0	0	0	0	0	0	8	0	0	0	0	.000	0	0	3.00
	Lowell	Bos	A-	24	16	0	0	6	33.1	150	39	24	21	1	4	0	1	11	0	39	4	0	3	2	.600	0	1	5.67
Nunez, Severino*	Helena	Mil	R+	20	16	10	0	0	58.2	262	52	33	26	2	1	2	0	32	2	40	12	1	2	1	.667	0	0	3.99
Nunley, Derrick	Medcine Hat	Tor	R+	20	8	0	0	2	13.2	57	10	4	4	0	0	0	2	6	0	11	5	0	1	0	1.000	0	0	2.63
	Queens	Tor	A-	20	11	1	0	2	19.1	88	23	12	11	1	0	2	0	8	0	20	0	0	2	0	1.000	0	0	5.12
Nye, Ryan	Phillies	Phi	R	28	2	2	0	0	4.2	21	6	1	1	1	0	0	0	1	0	7	0	0	0	0	.000	0	0	1.93
Obando, Omar	Lancaster	Sea	A+	24	21	0	0	9	20.1	92	11	10	10	1	0	1	3	17	1	10	0	0	0	1	.000	0	3	4.43
Obermueller, Wes	Chston-WV	KC	A	24	8	7	0	0	31.2	117	19	6	4	0	0	0	3	5	0	29	1	0	3	0	1.000	0	0	1.14
O'Brien, Matt*	Vancouver	Oak	A-	24	13	8	0	1	49.1	209	46	21	14	5	3	0	2	19	0	38	1	1	3	3	.500	0	0	2.55
	Modesto	Oak	A+	24	4	3	0	0	18	70	10	6	3	1	1	0	0	7	0	24	0	0	2	0	1.000	0	0	1.50
O'Brien, Pat	Pirates	Pit	R	20	10	10	1	0	49	235	66	32	27	1	1	3	9	19	0	31	2	0	3	1	.750	0	0	4.96
Odom, Lance	Quad City	Min	A	22	6	0	0	3	7.2	43	14	10	7	0	0	0	0	5	0	6	0	2	0	0	.000	0	0	8.22
O'Gara, Dan	Helena	Mil	R+	23	10	0	0	6	24.2	115	28	13	13	1	0	1	1	16	2	17	4	0	0	3	.000	0	0	4.74
Olean, Chris	Beloit	Mil	A	24	12	5	1	1	40.2	155	28	16	16	3	1	0	1	4	0	27	3	0	2	3	.400	0	0	3.54
Olive, Jesse	Red Sox	Bos	R	23	13	0	0	3	31	153	45	26	24	0	2	1	1	18	3	16	1	0	3	1	.750	0	1	6.97
Oliver, Scott	Greensboro	NYY	A	24	29	7	0	8	96.2	441	108	61	54	7	2	1	5	45	0	71	8	1	4	7	.364	0	1	5.03
Olivero, Pedro	Cubs	ChC	R	19	7	4	0	1	26.1	129	29	21	18	3	0	3	2	16	0	16	5	0	3	1	.750	0	0	6.15
Olivo, Carlos	Johnson Cty	StL	R+	21	24	0	0	7	40	182	41	26	23	5	3	0	4	20	1	40	3	0	1	4	.200	0	0	5.18
Olson, Jason	Yakima	LA	A-	23	18	0	0	8	37.1	170	37	22	18	4	2	1	2	18	1	43	3	2	0	1	.000	0	1	4.34
O'Neal, Brandon	Boise	Ana	A-	22	13	10	0	1	53	248	66	45	33	3	2	1	11	22	1	45	0	0	1	5	.167	0	1	5.60
Orloski, Joe	Queens	Tor	A-	22	22	0	0	8	52	206	32	13	8	2	2	1	2	16	1	66	2	0	4	0	1.000	0	3	1.38
Ormond, Rodney	Frederick	Bal	A+	24	39	0	0	12	67	294	66	38	27	3	5	2	3	25	0	59	4	0	2	5	.286	0	2	3.63
Ortega, Carlos*	Vero Beach	LA	A+	22	14	10	0	2	61.1	279	70	39	31	9	0	4	4	29	0	53	1	2	4	2	.667	0	0	4.55
Ortega, Orlando	Royals	KC	R	21	20	0	0	9	32	153	33	23	19	0	1	1	1	22	2	41	1	2	1	4	.200	0	1	5.34
Ortiz, Javier	Yankees	NYY	R	21	1	0	0	0	2.1	11	3	2	2	0	0	0	0	1	0	2	0	0	0	0	.000	0	0	7.71
Ortiz, Jose	Chston-SC	TB	A	23	46	0	0	27	58.2	267	49	35	25	4	5	3	2	38	4	51	9	0	4	5	.444	0	9	3.84
Ortiz, Omar	Fort Wayne	SD	A	23	6	6	0	0	29.2	134	28	21	15	7	0	1	1	18	1	27	2	0	2	1	.667	0	0	4.55
	Rancho Cuca	SD	A+	23	21	21	0	0	99	485	111	82	70	12	4	6	9	81	0	97	11	3	3	9	.250	0	0	6.36
Osberg, Tanner	Kingsport	NYM	R+	18	12	0	0	5	21.1	89	18	10	5	2	2	1	1	6	1	22	1	1	1	2	.333	0	1	2.11
Ough, Wayne	Kingsport	NYM	R+	22	9	3	1	2	30.1	124	24	13	12	2	0	0	2	14	0	22	3	1	3	2	.600	0	1	3.56
Outlaw, Mark*	Piedmont	Phi	A	24	48	0	0	25	48	197	28	15	5	1	1	3	2	18	2	61	2	0	5	2	.714	0	11	0.94
Ovalles, Juan	Missoula	Ari	R+	19	8	7	0	0	45.2	192	46	21	11	1	1	0	2	7	0	40	0	0	4	2	.667	0	0	2.17
	South Bend	Ari	A	19	8	8	0	0	37.2	181	51	32	27	4	1	5	3	16	0	24	5	1	1	4	.200	0	0	6.45
Ozuna, Benigno	Helena	Mil	R+	22	21	8	0	5	66.2	317	82	51	41	5	3	3	3	36	2	27	9	0	2	5	.286	0	0	5.54
Pace, Adam*	Boise	Ana	A-	21	16	9	0	3	52	238	67	44	41	10	4	2	3	20	0	39	2	1	0	5	.000	0	2	7.10
Pacheco, E.	Asheville	Col	A	21	21	21	0	0	117	508	129	67	48	9	3	4	10	35	0	79	8	0	8	10	.444	0	0	3.69
Padgett, Daniel*	Salem-Keizr	SF	A-	23	20	1	0	11	26.2	113	24	14	13	2	3	0	0	11	0	41	3	2	2	1	.667	0	1	4.39
Padilla, Edgar	Butte	Ana	R+	19	4	0	0	3	5	26	6	6	6	1	1	0	1	4	0	1	0	0	1	0	1.000	0	0	10.80
Pageler, Mick	Brevard Cty	Fla	A+	25	4	0	0	2	7	33	10	5	5	0	1	0	1	3	0	4	0	0	0	1	.000	0	0	6.43
Palki, Jeromy	Fort Myers	Min	A+	25	42	0	0	16	73	314	72	32	26	6	0	2	3	30	1	75	4	0	6	3	.667	0	3	3.21
Palma, Rick*	Daytona	ChC	A+	21	20	19	0	1	99.2	446	109	61	52	9	5	5	0	44	0	72	9	5	4	8	.333	0	1	4.70
Pape, Stace	Billings	Cin	R+	23	4	0	0	0	4.2	27	5	5	4	0	0	0	1	5	0	1	0	0	0	0	.000	0	0	7.71
Paradis, Mike	Delmarva	Bal	A	23	18	18	0	0	97	438	95	53	43	5	1	2	7	49	0	81	10	2	6	5	.545	0	0	3.99
	Frederick	Bal	A+	23	8	8	1	0	45.1	212	55	24	21	1	0	2	4	24	0	32	2	0	2	5	.286	0	0	4.17
Parker, Brandon	Lancaster	Sea	A+	25	52	0	0	45	53.1	235	49	25	22	3	3	2	4	28	2	74	5	0	4	2	.667	0	22	3.71
Parker, Daniel	Auburn	Hou	A-	21	19	10	0	7	58.1	257	59	31	28	3	0	2	6	21	1	50	3	0	4	3	.571	0	1	4.32

2000 Pitching — Class-A and Rookie Leagues

HOW MUCH HE PITCHED											WHAT HE GAVE UP												THE RESULTS					
Player	Team	Org	Lg	A	G	GS	CG	GF	IP	BFP	H	R	ER	HR	SH	SF	HB	TBB	IBB	SO	WP	Bk	W	L	Pct.	ShO	Sv	ERA
Parker, Dwayne*	Royals	KC	R	21	12	0	0	3	21.1	103	22	10	10	0	1	2	2	19	0	31	4	0	0	2	.000	0	0	4.22
Parker, Matt	Peoria	StL	A	22	26	0	0	17	31.1	129	24	9	9	0	3	1	0	13	1	20	5	0	2	2	.500	0	3	2.59
	Beloit	Mil	A	22	14	12	0	1	78	327	72	43	30	10	1	2	3	19	1	54	5	0	4	2	.667	0	0	3.46
Parra, Christian	Myrtle Bch	Atl	A+	23	26	25	2	1	157.2	608	98	46	40	6	2	5	3	56	0	163	8	2	17	4	.810	2	0	2.28
Parris, Matt	Tigers	Det	R	18	9	6	0	1	33.2	148	29	11	8	0	5	0	2	17	1	29	1	1	3	0	1.000	0	0	2.14
Parrish, Wade*	San Berndno	LA	A+	23	29	0	0	12	51	221	39	22	18	3	1	0	0	32	3	56	3	0	2	3	.400	0	2	3.18
Partenheimer, B.*	Brevard Cty	Fla	A+	26	34	3	0	12	86	376	79	44	36	12	2	6	12	26	1	49	2	2	2	5	.286	0	0	3.77
Patten, Lanny	Medcine Hat	Tor	R+	22	17	3	0	5	43.2	196	57	31	18	5	0	1	5	11	0	38	8	0	2	3	.400	0	0	3.71
Patten, Scott	White Sox	CWS	R	20	14	14	0	0	73	344	80	55	41	1	0	8	8	41	0	58	12	1	4	4	.500	0	0	5.05
Patterson, Quenten	Pittsfield	NYM	A-	23	8	6	0	0	29.1	143	41	28	19	0	1	2	5	16	0	9	2	0	3	4	.429	0	0	5.83
Pautz, Brad	Piedmont	Phi	A	24	13	11	1	0	65.2	272	53	20	17	2	0	5	4	24	0	33	3	0	3	2	.600	0	0	2.33
Pavlovich, Tony	Lynchburg	Pit	A+	26	36	0	0	27	40	171	38	18	16	0	1	0	3	13	1	33	1	0	2	1	.667	0	14	3.60
Pavon, Julio	Salem-Keizr	SF	A-	25	15	2	0	4	49	224	63	33	30	5	3	1	2	16	1	50	3	1	5	1	.833	0	1	5.51
	Bakersfield	SF	A+	25	7	0	0	0	13	58	15	11	5	2	1	0	0	5	0	15	1	0	3	0	1.000	0	0	3.46
Payne, Jerrod	Queens	Tor	A-	23	2	0	0	1	2	8	3	2	2	1	0	0	0	0	0	1	1	0	0	0	.000	0	0	9.00
	Hagerstown	Tor	A	23	19	0	0	17	17	70	15	9	7	0	0	2	0	6	0	6	2	0	0	2	.000	0	8	3.71
Paz, Jackson*	Braves	Atl	R	18	8	0	0	5	14	56	12	4	2	0	0	0	0	2	0	11	0	0	2	0	1.000	0	1	1.29
Peavy, Jacob	Fort Wayne	SD	A	20	26	25	0	0	133.2	565	107	61	43	6	4	3	9	53	0	164	8	2	13	8	.619	0	0	2.90
Peck, Brandon*	Peoria	StL	A	24	29	1	0	5	46.2	222	58	33	25	4	2	0	1	23	3	24	4	1	2	2	.500	0	0	4.82
Pederson, Justin	Wilmington	KC	A+	26	47	0	0	27	68.1	304	64	42	36	4	4	1	5	34	0	66	4	2	8	6	.571	0	9	4.74
Peeples, Jim*	Yankees	NYY	R	20	5	0	0	2	4.1	29	9	7	5	0	0	0	4	5	0	4	0	0	0	1	.000	0	0	10.38
Peeples, Ross*	Kingsport	NYM	R+	21	15	2	0	5	31	128	25	15	9	1	1	1	0	10	0	29	1	0	1	2	.333	0	0	2.61
Peguero, Darwin*	Michigan	Hou	A	22	39	3	0	14	77.2	331	67	33	27	4	2	6	4	36	4	62	8	0	3	4	.429	0	0	3.13
Peguero, Radhame	Chston-SC	TB	A	23	4	4	0	0	16	80	16	17	9	2	0	0	3	15	0	13	2	0	0	2	.000	0	0	5.06
Pember, Dave	Beloit	Mil	A	23	17	16	0	0	98	434	118	56	51	9	3	4	8	25	2	70	5	2	2	10	.167	0	0	4.68
Pena, Alex	Hickory	Pit	A	23	3	2	0	0	9	39	8	5	5	0	0	0	1	7	0	3	0	0	0	0	.000	0	0	5.00
Pena, Domingo	Pirates	Pit	R	24	2	2	0	0	4.2	17	4	1	1	0	0	0	0	1	0	4	0	0	0	0	.000	0	0	1.93
Pena, Francisco	Martinsvlle	Hou	R+	21	13	1	0	5	30	130	18	14	8	3	1	1	3	22	0	36	6	0	3	2	.600	0	2	2.40
Pena, Juan*	Modesto	Oak	A+	22	29	27	0	0	154	659	132	85	66	7	5	4	1	75	2	177	16	3	6	9	.400	0	0	3.86
Pepen, Robert	Kingsport	NYM	R+	22	13	0	0	11	15	63	13	3	2	1	2	1	0	4	0	18	1	0	1	1	.500	0	7	1.20
	Pittsfield	NYM	A-	22	7	0	0	4	8.2	40	7	4	3	1	0	0	0	5	0	8	0	0	0	1	.000	0	0	3.12
Peralta, Joel	Butte	Ana	R+	21	10	1	0	8	19	87	24	15	14	2	1	2	2	10	1	17	2	1	2	1	.667	0	1	6.63
	Boise	Ana	A-	21	4	0	0	1	8.1	41	12	6	6	0	0	1	1	5	0	9	0	0	0	0	.000	0	0	6.48
Peres, Luis*	Red Sox	Bos	R	20	9	5	0	2	34.1	139	24	12	9	2	0	0	1	13	0	43	0	0	3	1	.750	0	1	2.36
Perez, Amauris	Giants	SF	R	20	10	0	0	4	18.2	91	25	12	10	0	1	1	2	6	1	13	2	0	1	2	.333	0	0	4.82
Perez, Armando*	White Sox	CWS	R	20	15	8	0	2	43	204	51	38	29	4	2	1	2	26	0	37	3	1	0	3	.000	0	0	6.07
	Reds	Cin	R	20	6	4	0	0	22	103	17	13	6	2	1	0	4	13	0	16	6	3	1	2	.333	0	0	2.45
Perez, Beltran	Diamondbcks	Ari	R	19	11	4	0	0	48	221	61	37	31	1	2	2	2	25	1	47	0	1	5	1	.833	0	0	5.81
	High Desert	Ari	A+	19	2	2	0	0	10	43	8	4	4	3	0	0	0	5	0	11	0	1	0	1	.000	0	0	3.60
Perez, Elvis	Jamestown	Atl	A-	21	15	15	0	0	77.2	331	79	40	36	5	3	3	2	29	0	56	3	1	7	5	.583	0	0	4.17
Perez, Frank	Piedmont	Phi	A	20	36	9	0	12	97.2	410	85	47	33	3	2	4	9	39	1	64	7	0	5	5	.500	0	2	3.04
Perez, Franklin	Tigers	Det	R	21	6	3	1	2	22.1	90	21	9	9	1	0	1	0	4	0	25	3	0	1	2	.333	0	1	3.63
	Lakeland	Det	A+	21	10	8	0	0	50	231	54	34	21	4	0	6	1	34	1	25	2	0	2	3	.400	0	0	3.78
Perez, George	Queens	Tor	A-	22	29	0	0	25	34.2	138	21	3	3	1	2	2	3	15	2	35	3	0	5	1	.833	0	12	0.78
Perez, Henry	Padres	SD	R	18	13	10	0	2	47.2	215	40	32	24	3	2	1	1	36	0	39	5	3	2	5	.286	0	0	4.53
Perez, Julio	Cape Fear	Mon	A	22	41	0	0	27	67.2	284	59	26	24	3	2	1	3	26	1	79	3	0	6	2	.750	0	11	3.19
	Jupiter	Mon	A+	22	7	0	0	4	13.1	58	13	6	5	0	0	1	2	5	1	7	0	0	0	1	.000	0	1	3.38
Perez, Keino	Burlington	Cle	R+	21	21	0	0	14	34.1	161	34	23	13	5	2	2	3	14	0	27	1	0	1	4	.200	0	3	3.41
	Mahoning Vy	Cle	A-	21	1	0	0	0	2	11	4	2	0	0	0	1	0	0	0	2	0	0	0	0	.000	0	0	0.00
Perez, Oliver*	Idaho Falls	SD	R+	19	5	5	0	0	24.1	100	24	14	11	1	0	1	1	9	0	27	3	0	3	1	.750	0	0	4.07
Perez, Randy*	Delmarva	Bal	A	21	25	25	1	0	154	630	147	70	61	4	4	2	1	33	2	123	4	0	10	9	.526	1	0	3.56
Perio, Ian*	Lowell	Bos	A-	23	13	2	0	8	33.1	146	33	20	14	2	5	2	1	11	0	31	2	0	5	2	.714	0	1	3.78
Perkins, Greg	Missoula	Ari	R+	20	6	6	1	0	30.1	127	29	13	12	2	0	1	4	10	0	28	3	2	2	1	.667	1	0	3.56
	Diamondbcks	Ari	R	20	2	0	0	1	3	12	3	0	0	0	0	0	0	0	0	2	0	0	0	0	.000	0	0	0.00
Perkins, Mike	Peoria	StL	A	22	8	6	0	0	23.2	116	31	23	12	1	0	2	0	14	0	28	4	0	2	3	.400	0	0	4.56
	New Jersey	StL	A-	22	15	15	0	0	84.1	376	85	47	40	4	1	4	7	41	0	77	3	0	5	6	.455	0	0	4.27
Persby, Andy	Elizabethtn	Min	R+	23	20	2	0	4	42	158	21	5	5	0	0	1	0	24	0	45	5	2	6	1	.857	0	1	1.07
Pett, Jose	Mahoning Vy	Cle	A-	25	1	0	0	0	1	3	0	0	0	0	0	0	0	0	0	2	0	0	0	0	.000	0	0	0.00
Petty, Chad*	Tigers	Det	R	19	9	7	1	1	39	165	31	18	13	0	0	2	1	20	0	38	1	1	2	3	.400	0	0	3.00
Petulla, Craig	Martinsvlle	Hou	R+	22	13	0	0	5	19.1	88	18	11	10	1	0	2	5	9	1	17	1	0	0	1	.000	0	2	4.66
Pfalzgraf, Chris	Rangers	Tex	R	23	20	0	0	10	30	129	23	17	15	2	2	0	1	17	0	30	2	0	3	0	1.000	0	5	4.50
Phillips, Chase	Bluefield	Bal	R+	20	22	0	0	8	28.1	154	49	38	34	6	3	2	3	22	0	17	1	0	2	3	.400	0	0	10.80
Phillips, Mark*	Idaho Falls	SD	R+	19	10	10	0	0	37	164	35	30	22	2	1	1	0	24	0	37	4	2	1	1	.500	0	0	5.35
Pichardo, Carlos	Chston-WV	KC	A	23	34	9	0	11	91	403	98	52	40	4	2	5	4	35	1	59	5	3	5	6	.455	0	2	3.96
Pignatiell, Carmen*	Cubs	ChC	R	18	9	3	0	1	36.1	169	48	26	18	1	1	1	1	13	0	32	1	2	4	1	.800	0	0	4.46
Pike, Matt	Reds	Cin	R	22	11	3	0	2	31.2	138	26	18	13	2	2	1	1	17	1	42	2	0	0	1	.000	0	0	3.69
	Billings	Cin	R+	22	2	1	0	0	3.2	24	6	6	6	1	0	0	0	8	0	2	1	0	0	1	.000	0	0	14.73
Pike, Tom	Clinton	Cin	A	24	31	0	0	14	46	216	55	26	18	0	2	3	2	24	1	41	4	1	3	1	.750	0	1	3.52
Pillier, Santo	Athletics	Oak	R	20	17	0	0	10	25.2	110	22	13	6	2	3	1	0	9	2	22	3	0	2	3	.400	0	1	2.10
Pimentel, Gregorio	Giants	SF	R	19	9	1	0	3	17.2	67	14	3	2	0	1	0	1	5	0	10	0	0	1	1	.500	0	0	1.02
Pineda, Isauro	Red Sox	Bos	R	22	4	3	0	0	15	65	13	8	7	0	1	0	1	7	0	11	2	0	0	1	.000	0	0	4.20
	Sarasota	Bos	A+	22	7	6	0	0	22.2	105	25	12	9	3	0	1	0	14	0	17	2	0	1	1	.500	0	0	3.57
Pineda, Jairo	W Michigan	Det	A	24	42	1	0	9	68	288	53	29	23	6	3	2	12	25	0	37	1	0	5	2	.714	0	1	3.04
Pineda, Luis	Lakeland	Det	A+	23	18	0	0	13	26.2	122	23	13	10	3	2	1	1	19	0	42	4	1	1	3	.250	0	4	3.38
Pinto, Renyel*	Cubs	ChC	R	18	9	4	0	0	30	152	42	29	21	3	2	0	5	16	0	23	6	3	0	2	.000	0	0	6.30
Pitney, Jim	Oneonta	Det	A-	23	17	1	0	7	34	149	28	15	14	1	2	0	3	15	1	42	3	1	4	1	.800	0	0	3.71
Place, Eric*	Hagerstown	Tor	A	26	4	0	0	3	5	21	6	3	3	0	0	1	0	0	0	6	0	0	0	1	.000	0	0	5.40

2000 Pitching — Class-A and Rookie Leagues

HOW MUCH HE PITCHED											WHAT HE GAVE UP												THE RESULTS					
Player	Team	Org	Lg	A	G	GS	CG	GF	IP	BFP	H	R	ER	HR	SH	SF	HB	TBB	IBB	SO	WP	Bk	W	L	Pct.	ShO	Sv	ERA
	Dunedin	Tor	A+	26	24	1	0	11	46.2	220	47	27	22	3	5	5	2	33	3	32	1	0	5	2	.714	0	0	4.24
Plank, Terry	Delmarva	Bal	A	23	48	0	0	25	74.1	329	74	36	30	2	4	2	5	32	2	73	5	0	3	7	.300	0	5	3.63
Polanco, Elvis	Mudville	Mil	A+	23	35	0	0	14	57.2	260	52	37	27	3	5	3	6	36	3	49	4	0	4	3	.571	0	0	4.21
Polk, Scott	Capital Cty	NYM	A	24	40	0	0	16	69	295	49	28	19	4	3	4	2	40	3	95	9	0	7	2	.778	0	5	2.48
Polo, Bienvenido	New Jersey	StL	A-	22	25	0	0	6	32.1	174	45	36	26	1	2	3	6	26	0	32	7	0	3	0	1.000	0	1	7.24
Ponce de Leon, D.	Johnson Cty	StL	R+	23	20	0	0	17	23.1	94	13	7	7	1	0	1	0	8	0	26	4	1	2	0	1.000	0	8	2.70
	New Jersey	StL	A-	23	2	0	0	1	3	15	6	3	2	0	0	1	0	0	0	1	1	0	0	0	.000	0	0	6.00
Pool, Matt	Vero Beach	LA	A+	27	8	2	0	3	22.2	98	28	9	9	2	0	0	1	7	0	12	1	0	2	1	.667	0	0	3.57
Porter, Scott	Dunedin	Tor	A+	24	24	0	0	12	33.2	135	20	14	10	2	1	0	3	15	3	41	2	0	1	2	.333	0	4	2.67
Portobanco, Luz	Kingsport	NYM	R+	21	16	9	0	2	57	257	62	43	31	3	4	1	8	18	0	38	7	0	3	3	.500	0	0	4.89
Powalski, Rich*	Macon	Atl	A	23	43	0	0	26	58.2	258	57	31	23	3	2	1	6	23	3	58	3	1	2	5	.286	0	8	3.53
Powell, Maurice	Twins	Min	R	20	11	0	0	2	13.2	68	14	12	7	0	3	1	6	5	0	11	3	0	1	1	.500	0	0	4.61
Prata, Danny*	San Jose	SF	A+	22	20	7	0	2	60	273	60	42	35	7	2	2	5	39	0	37	1	0	1	1	.500	0	0	5.25
	Bakersfield	SF	A+	22	3	3	0	0	9	49	14	13	11	1	0	1	1	8	0	5	0	0	1	1	.500	0	0	11.00
Prater, Andy	Fort Wayne	SD	A	23	26	3	0	6	45	204	38	23	21	4	1	3	2	28	0	44	1	0	0	1	.000	0	0	4.20
Prather, Scott*	Potomac	StL	A+	24	42	7	0	7	75.2	339	61	50	42	6	3	6	1	56	0	70	5	0	5	3	.625	0	2	5.00
Pridie, Jon	Quad City	Min	A	21	45	8	0	9	97	421	89	47	37	5	1	3	6	42	4	91	5	0	7	7	.500	0	2	3.43
Proctor, Scott	Vero Beach	LA	A+	24	35	5	0	15	89	413	93	65	51	13	2	4	6	54	1	70	6	1	3	7	.300	0	1	5.16
Prokop, Mike	St. Lucie	NYM	A+	23	38	0	0	21	51.1	236	63	31	23	3	1	1	3	24	5	33	2	0	3	2	.600	0	1	4.03
Pruett, Jason*	Chston-SC	TB	A	22	49	0	0	25	68.2	290	55	30	19	4	6	4	1	20	0	73	2	0	6	4	.600	0	13	2.49
	St. Pete	TB	A+	22	8	0	0	8	10.2	45	11	2	1	0	3	0	0	3	0	7	1	0	2	1	.667	0	2	0.84
Pruitt, Jason*	Delmarva	Bal	A	20	2	0	0	1	1.2	12	5	5	3	0	0	0	0	1	0	2	0	0	0	0	.000	0	0	16.20
Puello, Ignacio	Expos	Mon	R	20	4	3	0	0	16.1	82	20	13	11	0	0	0	0	12	0	13	4	0	1	1	.500	0	0	6.06
Puffer, Brandon	Asheville	Col	A	25	14	0	0	9	14.1	75	19	16	13	3	2	0	3	11	3	15	3	0	0	0	.000	0	5	8.16
	Kissimmee	Hou	A+	25	18	0	0	18	21.1	95	18	6	3	0	3	0	1	11	4	26	3	0	2	3	.400	0	9	1.27
Putz, J.J.	Wisconsin	Sea	A	24	26	25	3	0	142.2	611	130	71	50	4	6	7	9	63	2	105	8	0	12	6	.667	2	0	3.15
Quarnstrom, Rob*	Charlotte	Tex	A+	24	10	0	0	4	20.1	96	30	12	7	0	1	2	1	4	0	11	1	0	2	0	1.000	0	1	3.10
Queen, Mike*	St. Lucie	NYM	A+	23	33	1	0	11	68.2	304	74	39	26	6	4	4	3	24	1	34	5	3	3	5	.375	0	1	3.41
Rada, Gerald	Yankees	NYY	R	19	8	7	0	0	33.1	128	25	8	5	0	0	1	0	4	0	27	0	2	2	1	.667	0	0	1.35
Rajotte, Jason*	San Jose	SF	A+	28	44	1	0	26	61	276	70	42	30	3	2	3	3	23	0	41	4	0	1	4	.200	0	5	4.43
Ramirez, Enrique	Bluefield	Bal	R+	21	25	0	0	21	21.2	104	23	15	11	0	2	0	1	17	0	18	4	1	1	3	.250	0	8	4.57
Ramirez, Eucebio	Marlins	Fla	R	21	3	3	0	0	18.1	71	14	3	3	1	0	0	0	4	0	16	1	3	1	1	.500	0	0	1.47
Ramirez, Hector	Giants	SF	R	21	16	0	0	15	16.2	78	24	12	10	0	1	0	1	6	1	10	2	0	1	2	.333	0	10	5.40
Ramirez, Horacio*	Myrtle Bch	Atl	A+	21	27	26	3	0	148.1	609	136	57	53	14	1	1	2	42	0	125	6	4	15	8	.652	2	0	3.22
Ramirez, Joslin	Diamondbcks	Ari	R	20	15	4	0	2	50.1	245	70	50	36	2	0	1	1	28	0	47	3	1	4	5	.444	0	0	6.44
Ramirez, Santiago	Michigan	Hou	A	20	23	0	0	12	29.2	146	27	28	20	6	1	0	3	32	1	22	3	1	3	3	.500	0	5	6.07
	Auburn	Hou	A-	20	20	9	0	9	53	228	36	34	25	3	0	2	4	39	1	57	9	1	3	6	.333	0	2	4.25
Ramos, Fernando	Clearwater	Phi	A+	25	27	1	0	15	54	240	53	31	26	6	0	2	0	27	0	37	2	1	0	1	.000	0	1	4.33
Ramos, Juan	Wisconsin	Sea	A	25	36	0	0	15	58.1	252	39	25	18	3	4	1	13	30	2	51	2	0	6	3	.667	0	3	2.78
Randazzo, Jeff*	Twins	Min	R	19	13	12	3	0	68.2	283	70	35	24	2	3	2	6	19	0	58	4	1	7	2	.778	1	0	3.15
	Quad City	Min	A	19	2	2	0	0	11.1	49	10	5	5	3	0	0	0	8	0	12	0	0	1	1	.500	0	0	3.97
Rayborn, Kris*	New Jersey	StL	A-	21	11	0	0	4	14.1	71	19	12	8	0	0	0	2	8	0	12	2	0	0	1	.000	0	0	5.02
Reames, Jim	Savannah	Tex	A	26	3	0	0	2	2.2	13	0	0	0	0	0	0	1	5	0	1	0	0	0	0	.000	0	0	0.00
Reece, Dana*	Hagerstown	Tor	A	24	34	1	0	11	43	226	65	47	35	5	1	1	2	31	0	37	11	1	0	0	.000	0	0	7.33
Reese, Josh	Johnson Cty	StL	R+	22	12	3	0	2	19	100	28	21	18	1	0	0	2	12	0	31	6	0	1	4	.200	0	0	8.53
Regilio, Nick	Charlotte	Tex	A+	22	20	20	0	0	85.2	369	94	54	43	8	3	1	7	29	0	63	10	2	4	3	.571	0	0	4.52
Reid, Justin	Hickory	Pit	A	24	27	22	5	4	170	694	146	82	57	12	3	4	3	30	0	176	5	0	9	8	.529	0	3	3.02
Reimers, Cameron	Hagerstown	Tor	A	22	26	26	2	0	154.1	671	158	79	64	10	5	4	21	45	0	112	14	2	7	11	.389	0	0	3.73
Rejean, Rhett	Rangers	Tex	R	23	15	11	0	1	55	249	58	41	35	6	2	3	2	29	0	34	3	0	3	2	.600	0	0	5.73
Rengifo, Nohemar	Expos	Mon	R	18	11	0	0	10	20.1	103	27	27	21	2	3	2	3	17	0	10	8	0	1	3	.250	0	1	9.30
Renteria, Juan	Princeton	TB	R+	21	24	1	0	17	36.1	162	38	20	14	2	0	0	1	20	0	50	8	1	1	0	1.000	0	6	3.47
Renwick, Tyler	Queens	Tor	A-	22	7	7	0	0	35.1	156	26	19	10	1	0	0	1	23	0	31	5	0	2	2	.500	0	0	2.55
	Hagerstown	Tor	A	22	7	7	0	0	35	170	44	28	21	2	2	1	5	21	0	17	11	0	3	2	.600	0	0	5.40
Reyes, Hipolito	Royals	KC	R	20	9	8	0	1	37	162	28	14	9	1	1	0	8	22	0	23	3	0	2	1	.667	0	0	2.19
Reyes, Junior*	Cubs	ChC	R	19	13	3	0	3	41.1	206	57	35	25	2	3	4	6	24	0	39	5	1	4	2	.667	0	2	5.44
Reynolds, Eric*	Yankees	NYY	R	21	9	9	0	0	39.2	166	37	20	17	1	1	1	1	18	0	33	3	0	2	3	.400	0	0	3.86
Reynolds, Jacob	Burlington	Cle	R+	21	10	2	0	0	30	146	34	28	21	1	1	1	1	24	0	25	6	1	0	2	.000	0	0	6.30
Reynolds, Josh	Pittsfield	NYM	A-	21	7	6	0	0	26.2	119	35	13	13	1	0	0	3	11	0	23	0	0	1	1	.500	0	0	4.39
Reynoso, Roberto	Butte	Ana	R+	20	11	8	0	1	41.1	200	59	40	26	1	2	2	0	12	0	37	3	1	1	4	.200	0	1	5.66
Ricciardi, Joe	Missoula	Ari	R+	21	25	1	0	14	31.1	149	30	21	17	0	1	1	7	22	0	36	4	1	0	0	.000	0	2	4.88
Riccobono, Rick	Augusta	Bos	A	21	25	24	0	0	124	548	116	69	45	11	3	4	11	49	0	72	5	0	10	7	.588	0	0	3.27
Rice, Scott*	Orioles	Bal	R	19	13	13	0	0	57	273	61	46	33	0	2	3	8	48	1	34	3	1	1	6	.143	0	0	5.21
Richardson, Jason	Twins	Min	R	21	6	0	0	0	12.1	60	10	6	2	0	1	1	4	9	0	10	4	1	1	1	.500	0	0	1.46
	Elizabethtn	Min	R+	21	10	9	2	0	47.1	194	29	11	9	2	1	0	8	16	0	51	5	0	5	1	.833	0	0	1.71
Richardson, Kasey*	Asheville	Col	A	24	9	0	0	4	12.1	56	16	10	7	3	0	1	0	5	0	9	1	0	0	1	.000	0	0	5.11
Ridgway, Jeff*	Princeton	TB	R+	20	12	12	0	0	54.2	237	47	24	15	2	0	2	1	30	0	60	6	0	3	4	.429	0	0	2.47
Riethmaier, Matt	Batavia	Phi	A-	22	14	9	1	0	69.2	303	67	43	33	3	3	2	8	28	1	47	8	2	4	4	.500	1	0	4.26
Rigueiro, Rafael	Salem-Keizr	SF	A-	24	28	0	0	4	40.2	188	38	24	21	1	2	1	2	31	1	52	9	1	0	1	.000	0	0	4.65
Rijo, Fernando	Yakima	LA	A-	23	3	0	0	2	5.2	26	5	3	2	0	0	0	0	1	0	5	0	0	0	0	.000	0	1	3.18
Rijo, Hector*	Expos	Mon	R	20	18	0	0	15	34	151	39	23	18	3	0	1	1	12	0	21	0	0	0	2	.000	0	6	4.76
Rincones, Rafael	Chston-WV	KC	A	22	6	6	0	0	27	134	42	31	27	6	1	0	1	14	0	24	2	0	0	6	.000	0	0	9.00
	Spokane	KC	A-	22	18	0	0	11	28	126	26	11	9	2	2	0	1	17	3	37	1	1	2	1	.667	0	3	2.89
Rivera, Homero*	W Michigan	Det	A	22	36	0	0	10	47.1	202	45	23	18	4	2	2	3	15	1	40	1	0	3	4	.429	0	2	3.42
Rivera, Jimmy	Mariners	Sea	R	21	7	1	0	0	11	56	12	13	12	0	0	0	0	17	0	7	5	0	0	2	.000	0	0	9.82
Rivera, Ramon*	Butte	Ana	R+	21	15	1	0	7	28	134	33	22	15	3	1	0	0	15	0	16	1	1	0	3	.000	0	4	4.82
Rivera, Samuel	Oneonta	Det	A-	21	9	0	0	1	12.1	65	9	11	11	0	0	3	2	15	0	14	3	0	0	0	.000	0	0	8.03
	W Michigan	Det	A	21	18	0	0	3	21	112	18	14	10	0	1	1	2	29	0	18	5	1	1	2	.333	0	0	4.29

2000 Pitching — Class-A and Rookie Leagues

HOW MUCH HE PITCHED											WHAT HE GAVE UP												THE RESULTS					
Player	Team	Org	Lg	A	G	GS	CG	GF	IP	BFP	H	R	ER	HR	SH	SF	HB	TBB	IBB	SO	WP	Bk	W	L	Pct.	ShO	Sv	ERA
Riviere, Rhett	Pulaski	Tex	R+	21	15	3	0	11	48.2	209	44	20	14	2	1	3	2	18	0	29	6	1	6	0	1.000	0	1	2.59
Rleal, Sendy	Bluefield	Bal	R+	21	13	12	0	1	61	265	61	26	23	5	1	3	8	25	0	55	3	1	6	2	.750	0	0	3.39
	Delmarva	Bal	A	21	1	1	0	0	3.1	18	3	5	4	0	0	0	1	3	0	4	0	0	0	1	.000	0	0	10.80
Roberts, Marquis*	Hudson Val	TB	A-	21	17	0	0	2	38	162	33	20	16	1	1	0	4	14	0	39	2	0	0	2	.000	0	1	3.79
Roberts, Mike	Wilmington	KC	A+	25	31	0	0	18	43.2	185	39	17	16	3	5	2	3	18	1	30	1	1	0	0	.000	0	5	3.30
Roberts, Nick	Michigan	Hou	A	24	22	20	2	1	139.1	587	121	53	48	10	1	5	5	61	1	107	5	1	13	6	.684	1	0	3.10
Roberts, Rick*	San Berndno	LA	A+	22	29	15	0	5	108.2	480	112	66	61	7	3	3	5	53	1	88	8	2	8	5	.615	0	1	5.05
Robertson, Nate*	Kane County	Fla	A	23	6	6	0	0	17.2	81	24	13	10	0	0	0	1	6	0	15	0	0	0	2	.000	0	0	5.09
Robinson, Dustin	Clinton	Cin	A	25	40	4	0	12	89	374	81	49	39	9	3	4	2	30	4	61	5	0	7	4	.636	0	1	3.94
Robinson, Jeff	Beloit	Mil	A	24	17	16	0	0	82.2	357	63	50	43	10	6	1	7	43	1	88	8	1	5	8	.385	0	0	4.68
Robinson, Jeremy*	St. Pete	TB	A+	23	37	0	0	16	57.2	265	60	38	28	1	3	5	4	28	0	28	3	0	3	3	.500	0	0	4.37
Rodarmel, Rich	Vancouver	Oak	A-	24	18	0	0	15	23	90	15	3	3	0	0	1	1	8	0	33	4	0	1	0	1.000	0	10	1.17
Rodney, Fernando	W Michigan	Det	A	20	22	10	0	1	82.2	353	74	34	27	2	5	0	2	35	0	56	3	0	6	4	.600	0	0	2.94
Rodney, Lee	Lakeland	Det	A+	23	1	1	0	0	5.2	23	4	1	1	0	0	0	0	4	0	3	2	2	0	0	.000	0	0	1.59
	Oneonta	Det	A-	23	9	9	1	0	45	204	52	30	23	2	2	0	0	26	0	37	6	1	2	4	.333	0	0	4.60
Rodriguez, Ale.	Phillies	Phi	R	20	3	1	0	0	16	68	15	6	5	1	0	0	1	4	0	21	1	0	1	0	1.000	0	0	2.81
	Batavia	Phi	A-	20	6	4	0	0	31.2	146	37	24	18	4	1	1	3	11	0	14	4	3	2	2	.500	0	0	5.12
Rodriguez, Alf.	Savannah	Tex	A	23	6	0	0	2	9.2	43	10	7	7	2	0	0	2	3	0	6	1	0	1	0	1.000	0	0	6.52
Rodriguez, C.	Cape Fear	Mon	A	22	14	14	1	0	76.1	344	77	53	45	9	5	3	4	35	0	70	7	3	5	6	.455	0	0	5.31
Rodriguez, Eddy	Orioles	Bal	R	19	18	0	0	14	27	116	17	8	6	0	3	0	2	19	1	31	0	0	2	1	.667	0	6	2.00
	Delmarva	Bal	A	19	4	0	0	1	5	21	5	1	1	1	0	0	0	2	0	3	0	0	0	0	.000	0	0	1.80
Rodriguez, F.	Lk Elsinore	Ana	A+	19	13	12	0	0	64	265	43	29	20	2	2	2	1	32	0	79	12	1	4	4	.500	0	0	2.81
Rodriguez, George	Phillies	Phi	R	21	19	0	0	14	22.1	91	17	6	4	0	3	0	1	6	0	30	0	0	0	0	.000	0	7	1.61
Rodriguez, Jose	Chston-SC	TB	A	23	16	3	0	3	38.1	186	49	31	23	2	1	2	5	17	1	29	7	0	1	3	.250	0	0	5.40
Rodriguez, Jose	Danville	Atl	R+	19	12	12	1	0	61.1	280	59	33	27	6	1	2	4	40	0	31	7	1	3	1	.750	0	0	3.96
Rodriguez, Juan	Pirates	Pit	R	20	12	3	0	4	34	154	39	24	14	1	1	2	2	8	0	24	5	1	1	2	.333	0	0	3.71
Rodriguez, Luis	Rangers	Tex	R	19	6	6	0	0	25.2	109	23	11	9	0	0	1	0	13	0	19	2	0	2	0	1.000	0	0	3.16
	Pulaski	Tex	R+	19	10	0	0	7	24.1	100	17	6	3	1	1	0	1	11	1	40	1	0	2	1	.667	0	3	1.11
Rodriguez, Marino*	Marlins	Fla	R	22	7	0	0	5	8.2	40	10	4	4	0	2	1	1	5	0	4	2	0	1	0	1.000	0	1	4.15
Rodriguez, O.*	White Sox	CWS	R	20	16	5	0	4	40.2	190	36	30	19	3	1	1	2	32	0	53	3	1	2	5	.286	0	0	4.20
Rodriguez, Ricardo	Great Falls	LA	R+	22	15	15	2	0	95.2	374	66	32	20	2	3	3	1	23	0	129	4	0	10	3	.769	0	0	1.88
Rogers, Brad	Orioles	Bal	R	19	9	9	0	0	44	183	34	16	14	2	1	1	5	16	0	24	2	0	2	2	.500	0	0	2.86
	Bluefield	Bal	R+	19	4	3	0	0	18.1	80	21	10	9	1	1	0	2	4	0	15	0	0	2	1	.667	0	0	4.42
Rogers, Devin	Columbus	Cle	A	22	20	20	0	0	89.2	409	78	59	45	6	5	2	7	66	0	83	8	0	4	5	.444	0	0	4.52
Rogers, Jon	Braves	Atl	R	19	8	0	0	5	17	69	13	1	1	0	1	1	1	8	1	10	1	0	1	0	1.000	0	2	0.53
Rogers, Lionel	Pittsfield	NYM	A-	23	23	0	0	15	30.2	132	17	11	7	0	2	0	2	20	0	31	5	0	1	3	.250	0	5	2.05
Rohling, Stuart	Burlington	CWS	A	23	26	2	0	7	60	269	42	25	19	3	2	2	2	51	1	58	4	1	2	4	.333	0	0	2.85
Rojas, Chris	Idaho Falls	SD	R+	24	2	2	0	0	9	43	8	5	5	0	0	0	3	4	0	13	4	0	1	0	1.000	0	0	5.00
	Fort Wayne	SD	A	24	15	15	0	0	79.1	339	64	26	24	4	3	2	3	38	0	69	3	4	5	4	.556	0	0	2.72
Rojas, Jose	Yakima	LA	A-	19	13	9	0	2	52.2	222	45	26	19	3	2	1	5	19	0	47	8	1	4	4	.500	0	1	3.25
Rojas, Ramon	Giants	SF	R	20	18	2	0	3	35.1	181	55	38	25	1	5	2	3	15	3	20	2	0	4	3	.571	0	1	6.37
Roller, Adam	Greensboro	NYY	A	23	13	0	0	5	20.2	87	15	6	3	1	1	1	1	5	1	22	6	0	0	1	.000	0	1	1.31
	Tampa	NYY	A+	23	19	0	0	14	25.2	118	29	17	12	1	1	3	3	9	0	26	5	0	1	4	.200	0	1	4.21
Roman, Orlando	Pittsfield	NYM	A-	22	11	8	0	0	33.2	159	40	29	23	1	2	2	2	18	0	27	4	4	3	5	.375	0	0	6.15
Romero, Cesar	Yankees	NYY	R	19	14	0	0	6	19.2	94	16	14	11	1	0	3	3	14	0	13	2	0	3	2	.600	0	0	5.03
Romero, Garvis	Rockies	Col	R	20	20	0	0	9	21.1	104	29	18	12	1	0	2	0	8	0	15	1	2	2	2	.500	0	0	5.06
Romero, Josmir	Elizabethtn	Min	R+	20	13	13	2	0	76.1	319	80	42	38	9	5	3	2	18	0	52	3	2	5	2	.714	1	0	4.48
Romo, Noe	Mexico	—	R	23	7	1	0	4	18.2	95	21	20	16	0	0	3	3	16	0	13	1	4	0	2	.000	0	1	7.71
Rondon, Gabriel	Kingsport	NYM	R+	23	14	0	0	7	18.2	77	14	10	3	2	1	0	0	5	0	10	3	0	2	1	.667	0	1	1.45
Roney, Matt	Portland	Col	A-	21	15	15	0	0	80.1	360	75	35	28	6	1	1	7	44	0	85	8	2	7	5	.583	0	0	3.14
Rooney, Mike	High Desert	Ari	A+	25	17	15	1	0	70.1	326	85	64	59	13	1	5	7	37	0	29	3	1	2	8	.200	0	0	7.55
Roque, Darryll	Vermont	Mon	A-	24	5	0	0	0	7.1	29	9	3	2	1	0	1	0	1	0	4	1	0	0	0	.000	0	0	2.45
	Cape Fear	Mon	A	24	9	1	0	3	28.2	127	32	14	8	1	2	1	2	6	0	23	1	0	1	1	.500	0	1	2.51
Rosa, Elias*	Royals	KC	R	18	6	1	0	0	11	60	15	8	6	0	0	0	2	9	0	4	1	0	1	0	1.000	0	0	4.91
Rosado, Hector*	Royals	KC	R	20	14	1	0	4	25	98	15	12	8	2	0	2	0	8	0	18	0	0	1	3	.250	0	0	2.88
Rosado, Juan*	Lakeland	Det	A+	26	21	0	0	12	26.2	129	26	16	14	0	1	2	2	23	1	17	3	1	2	2	.500	0	0	4.72
Rosario, Andres	Great Falls	LA	R+	21	19	1	0	5	28.2	153	39	27	20	1	0	0	2	26	1	29	8	1	1	1	.500	0	1	6.28
Rosario, Dionis*	White Sox	CWS	R	17	2	2	0	0	3.1	18	2	4	3	0	0	0	0	6	0	3	0	0	0	0	.000	0	0	8.10
Rosario, Hipolito	Padres	SD	R	21	19	0	0	7	36.2	173	50	29	28	0	0	6	4	16	2	24	1	1	3	2	.600	0	2	6.87
Rosario, Rodrigo	Auburn	Hou	A-	21	14	14	0	0	75.2	330	67	36	29	3	2	1	6	32	1	67	2	0	5	6	.455	0	0	3.45
Rose, Mike	Vermont	Mon	A-	24	2	0	0	1	3	13	2	0	0	0	0	0	0	2	0	3	0	0	0	0	.000	0	1	0.00
	Cape Fear	Mon	A	24	1	0	0	0	1	4	1	1	1	0	0	1	0	0	0	1	0	0	0	0	.000	0	0	9.00
Rosengren, Phil	Columbus	Cle	A	24	23	17	1	2	102.1	445	121	56	52	11	1	2	8	19	0	71	11	1	3	5	.375	0	0	4.57
Ross, Brian*	Billings	Cin	R+	23	14	0	0	3	15	70	14	10	8	2	0	0	0	8	0	12	2	0	0	1	.000	0	2	4.80
Ross, Christian	Reds	Cin	R	22	6	3	0	0	21	87	18	14	10	1	0	1	0	7	1	21	1	0	0	3	.000	0	0	4.29
Ross, Lew*	High Desert	Ari	A+	23	23	0	0	9	35.2	160	39	22	17	2	0	4	3	17	1	49	2	0	2	2	.500	0	1	4.29
	Missoula	Ari	R+	23	23	0	0	14	34.1	148	27	16	15	4	1	1	4	11	2	46	3	0	2	4	.333	0	6	3.93
Rossellini, Will	Missoula	Ari	R+	21	5	4	0	0	11.2	75	15	23	16	1	2	1	7	19	0	7	3	0	0	4	.000	0	0	12.34
	Diamondbcks	Ari	R	21	4	1	0	0	8	30	2	2	0	0	0	0	1	6	0	8	1	0	0	1	.000	0	0	0.00
Rowe, Casey	W Michigan	Det	A	22	15	15	2	0	97	400	85	40	33	11	1	3	4	27	1	67	5	0	8	5	.615	1	0	3.06
	Lakeland	Det	A+	22	11	11	0	0	51.2	250	57	46	33	7	1	6	1	37	0	37	5	0	1	7	.125	0	0	5.75
Rowland, Carl	Johnson Cty	StL	R+	24	15	2	0	3	31.2	144	38	24	21	3	1	1	1	11	1	25	1	1	2	2	.500	0	0	5.97
Royer, Jason	High Desert	Ari	A+	22	8	0	0	2	12.2	74	21	20	18	1	0	3	1	14	0	7	0	0	0	1	.000	0	0	12.79
Ruelas, Heriberto*	Mexico	—	R	19	6	4	0	2	22.1	108	33	23	20	2	0	2	1	14	0	24	3	0	0	3	.000	0	0	8.06
Ruhl, Nathan	St. Pete	TB	A+	24	40	5	1	22	72.2	346	82	58	47	5	1	5	3	41	1	53	9	1	4	6	.400	0	7	5.82
Rundles, Richard*	Red Sox	Bos	R	20	9	6	0	0	40.1	158	31	15	11	3	2	0	4	10	0	32	0	1	3	1	.750	0	0	2.45
Runser, Greg	Pulaski	Tex	R+	22	21	0	0	16	48.1	196	35	18	6	2	1	2	0	14	1	47	6	0	3	3	.500	0	6	1.12

2000 Pitching — Class-A and Rookie Leagues

HOW MUCH HE PITCHED											WHAT HE GAVE UP												THE RESULTS					
Player	Team	Org	Lg	A	G	GS	CG	GF	IP	BFP	H	R	ER	HR	SH	SF	HB	TBB	IBB	SO	WP	Bk	W	L	Pct.	ShO	Sv	ERA
Rupp, Mike	Augusta	Bos	A	23	30	1	0	5	64.1	282	65	30	27	4	2	3	3	29	0	44	1	0	6	4	.600	0	0	3.78
Russ, Chris*	Pulaski	Tex	R+	21	6	2	0	1	21.2	85	14	4	2	0	2	0	1	4	0	26	2	0	2	0	1.000	0	0	0.83
	Savannah	Tex	A	21	7	7	0	0	40.2	172	38	14	11	2	0	0	1	14	0	34	8	0	3	1	.750	0	0	2.43
Russo, Dennis	Jamestown	Atl	A-	21	11	10	0	0	49.1	218	56	38	27	4	1	6	2	19	0	17	5	0	4	4	.500	0	0	4.93
Russo, Mike	Everett	Sea	A-	23	6	0	0	2	8.1	44	8	5	5	1	0	1	1	10	0	7	2	0	0	0	.000	0	0	5.40
Russo, Scott*	Vermont	Mon	A-	23	14	0	0	4	25.1	103	25	10	5	1	1	0	0	6	0	21	0	1	2	1	.667	0	0	1.78
Rust, Evan	Princeton	TB	R+	23	26	0	0	5	43.2	184	37	17	14	3	1	3	3	13	0	34	3	0	5	2	.714	0	1	2.89
Ryan, Jeremy	Martinsvlle	Hou	R+	23	7	7	0	0	25.2	116	26	20	14	2	2	0	2	15	0	25	1	0	0	4	.000	0	0	4.91
Sachse, Matt*	Everett	Sea	A-	25	24	0	0	5	40	204	60	43	28	5	6	0	3	20	1	47	6	0	2	3	.400	0	0	6.30
Sadler, Carl*	Mahoning Vy	Cle	A-	24	5	0	0	1	6	25	5	2	2	0	1	0	0	3	0	3	0	0	0	0	.000	0	0	3.00
	Columbus	Cle	A	24	10	0	0	3	16.1	73	20	13	12	0	0	0	0	7	0	21	5	0	1	3	.250	0	0	6.61
Sadowski, Chad	Batavia	Phi	A-	23	20	1	0	6	38.1	168	42	21	14	2	0	2	1	13	0	31	3	0	1	1	.500	0	2	3.29
Saenz, Jason*	St. Lucie	NYM	A+	24	28	28	0	0	153.1	684	165	98	75	7	4	10	8	83	0	107	14	4	6	9	.400	0	0	4.40
Saladin, Miguel	Auburn	Hou	A-	23	27	0	0	16	40	182	32	19	3	0	4	0	6	20	3	42	4	0	2	3	.400	0	4	0.68
Salazar, Luis	Marlins	Fla	R	22	1	0	0	0	2	7	0	0	0	0	0	0	0	1	0	1	0	0	0	0	.000	0	0	0.00
	Utica	Fla	A-	22	19	1	0	9	37	165	28	13	10	0	5	2	1	24	0	38	4	1	2	4	.333	0	2	2.43
Salinas, Sean	Reds	Cin	R	22	2	0	0	1	1.2	10	2	4	4	1	1	0	0	3	0	3	0	0	0	0	.000	0	0	21.60
Salmon, Brad	Clinton	Cin	A	21	22	22	1	0	123.2	538	134	71	59	4	3	4	2	46	0	119	11	0	7	5	.583	0	0	4.29
Samora, Santo	New Jersey	StL	A-	21	32	0	0	27	36.2	157	37	17	16	2	2	0	4	9	0	20	6	0	2	3	.400	0	17	3.93
Sams, Aaron*	Daytona	ChC	A+	25	35	2	0	13	57.2	284	69	49	35	3	9	3	3	40	4	56	8	1	2	4	.333	0	1	5.46
	Lansing	ChC	A	25	6	4	0	1	28.2	128	38	22	19	1	2	4	1	11	0	20	2	0	0	4	.000	0	0	5.97
Sanches, Brian	Wilmington	KC	A+	22	28	27	2	0	158	665	132	77	62	9	5	7	15	69	0	122	11	3	6	12	.333	1	0	3.53
Sanchez, Cade	Visalia	Oak	A+	24	14	0	0	2	11.1	57	14	9	6	0	0	2	1	9	0	8	1	1	4	0	1.000	0	0	4.76
	Vancouver	Oak	A-	24	16	0	0	14	16.1	73	10	5	4	0	1	0	1	13	2	13	3	1	0	2	.000	0	6	2.20
Sanchez, Duaner	South Bend	Ari	A	21	28	28	4	0	165.1	700	152	80	67	6	5	5	11	54	1	121	6	2	8	9	.471	0	0	3.65
Sanchez, Elby	Royals	KC	R	18	19	2	0	7	28.2	137	25	17	16	2	1	2	2	23	0	25	3	0	2	2	.500	0	0	5.02
Sanchez, Pedro*	Twins	Min	R	19	19	0	0	6	13	66	13	8	8	0	0	2	2	11	0	11	0	0	0	1	.000	0	0	5.54
Sanders, David*	Winston-Sal	CWS	A+	21	51	0	0	20	48.1	228	39	35	28	4	2	2	4	39	1	50	12	1	3	2	.600	0	6	5.21
Sandoval, Marcos	Hagerstown	Tor	A	20	28	25	2	0	163.2	721	188	105	83	20	3	3	15	49	3	100	3	2	8	13	.381	1	0	4.56
Sansom, Trevor	Peoria	StL	A	25	44	5	0	13	87.1	378	81	42	28	2	4	2	6	33	4	45	4	0	2	8	.200	0	3	2.89
Santana, Eddy	Yankees	NYY	R	20	17	0	0	4	32.1	143	40	16	13	0	2	2	1	12	0	17	1	0	4	0	1.000	0	1	3.62
Santillan, Manuel	Martinsvlle	Hou	R+	21	19	0	0	13	22.2	110	21	18	12	1	0	0	3	24	0	20	3	2	1	0	1.000	0	1	4.76
Santos, Alex	St. Pete	TB	A+	23	17	16	0	0	88.1	387	86	54	46	6	0	2	6	34	0	69	5	3	3	9	.250	0	0	4.69
Santos, Bernaldo	Martinsvlle	Hou	R+	22	3	0	0	1	4.2	22	6	5	5	0	0	0	0	2	0	5	2	1	0	0	.000	0	0	9.64
	Auburn	Hou	A-	22	15	0	0	6	25.2	121	31	13	10	1	1	1	3	11	0	10	2	1	0	0	.000	0	0	3.51
Santos, Josh*	Columbus	Cle	A	24	28	0	0	17	49	227	54	27	22	4	5	2	5	19	3	53	2	1	3	8	.273	0	0	4.04
Sauer, Danny	Expos	Mon	R	22	14	0	0	8	29.2	151	28	27	16	2	2	3	3	34	0	17	9	1	1	6	.143	0	2	4.85
Sauer, Marc	Kane County	Fla	A	21	28	28	2	0	164	696	177	92	77	21	9	3	8	29	1	95	4	0	8	10	.444	0	0	4.23
Saunders, Tony*	Chston-SC	TB	A	27	2	2	0	0	5	20	2	1	1	0	0	0	1	2	0	3	0	0	0	0	.000	0	0	1.80
	St. Pete	TB	A+	27	2	2	0	0	7	30	7	4	3	1	0	1	0	3	0	3	1	0	0	0	.000	0	0	3.86
Sawyer, Steve	Utica	Fla	A-	22	15	0	0	5	27	110	14	8	6	0	1	1	2	12	0	22	5	0	4	1	.800	0	2	2.00
	Kane County	Fla	A	22	3	0	0	0	4	14	0	0	0	0	0	0	0	3	0	6	0	0	1	0	1.000	0	0	0.00
Saye, Trey	Royals	KC	R	20	8	0	0	4	11.2	57	10	10	9	0	0	1	3	7	0	11	6	0	0	1	.000	0	0	6.94
Schachleit, Jeff	Billings	Cin	R+	19	7	2	0	1	11.2	70	20	23	23	3	1	0	2	18	0	13	5	1	0	1	.000	0	0	17.74
Schilling, Tim*	Utica	Fla	A-	22	10	3	0	0	25.2	121	31	19	16	3	4	0	2	18	0	22	2	0	1	1	.500	0	0	5.61
Schiml, Tony*	Lowell	Bos	A-	24	2	0	0	1	5	22	6	1	1	0	0	0	0	4	0	2	0	1	1	1	.500	0	0	1.80
Schmitt, Eric	Staten Ilnd	NYY	A-	22	15	0	0	9	30	121	21	9	7	0	0	0	1	8	0	35	0	1	2	1	.667	0	1	2.10
Schneider, Scott	Boise	Ana	A-	23	26	0	0	9	51.2	228	44	25	15	2	3	0	4	28	2	44	8	0	5	2	.714	0	5	2.61
Schoening, Brent	Twins	Min	R	23	2	2	0	0	7	25	2	1	1	1	0	0	0	3	0	8	0	0	0	0	.000	0	0	1.29
	Fort Myers	Min	A+	23	12	12	0	0	70	295	61	27	25	3	2	4	4	27	2	57	4	0	6	4	.600	0	0	3.21
Schultz, Bryan	New Jersey	StL	A-	23	4	0	0	2	6	25	4	0	0	0	0	0	1	2	0	8	0	0	0	0	.000	0	0	0.00
	Peoria	StL	A	23	12	0	0	3	15.2	63	9	2	2	1	0	0	0	9	0	14	0	0	1	1	.500	0	0	1.15
Schultz, Jeff	Visalia	Oak	A+	25	35	7	0	11	83.1	390	96	63	54	4	2	6	4	47	0	64	4	1	7	6	.538	0	2	5.83
Schultz, Mike	Diamondbcks	Ari	R	21	2	0	0	0	2.2	17	7	7	2	1	0	1	1	1	0	2	0	0	0	1	.000	0	0	6.75
	High Desert	Ari	A+	21	7	7	0	0	22.1	90	15	9	9	2	0	1	0	11	0	16	1	0	1	2	.333	0	0	3.63
Schurman, Ryan	Clinton	Cin	A	24	22	0	0	9	38	174	29	22	20	2	3	2	3	30	3	21	7	0	1	2	.333	0	1	4.74
Schwager, Matt	Delmarva	Bal	A	23	47	0	0	23	76.2	324	78	35	28	6	5	4	4	21	3	66	4	1	6	5	.545	0	5	3.29
Sclafani, Anthony	Danville	Atl	R+	19	19	0	0	12	27.1	124	27	13	11	1	1	1	2	18	0	25	3	0	1	0	1.000	0	8	3.62
Scott, J.K.	Padres	SD	R	19	15	5	0	6	27	140	39	28	19	1	1	2	1	20	0	21	6	0	1	3	.250	0	2	6.33
Scuglik, Mike*	Charlotte	Tex	A+	24	1	0	0	1	0.2	4	2	0	0	0	0	0	0	0	0	0	0	0	0	0	.000	0	0	0.00
	Pulaski	Tex	R+	24	18	0	0	12	29.2	135	26	19	17	1	2	0	2	22	1	27	5	0	0	2	.000	0	1	5.16
Seabury, Jaron	Mudville	Mil	A+	25	33	21	1	0	150.1	650	135	83	68	6	5	6	19	72	0	97	14	4	10	7	.588	0	0	4.07
Seale, Dustin*	Jupiter	Mon	A+	23	23	0	0	12	27.2	118	23	11	7	3	0	2	3	14	0	14	0	0	0	0	.000	0	0	2.28
	Cape Fear	Mon	A	23	6	0	0	5	11	48	8	3	2	0	1	1	1	7	0	13	0	0	2	1	.667	0	0	1.64
Seaman, John	Eugene	ChC	A-	24	11	0	0	3	19.1	86	16	7	4	0	1	0	0	8	1	22	2	0	1	0	1.000	0	1	1.86
Searles, Jon	Pirates	Pit	R	20	7	6	0	0	37	170	41	23	15	2	1	1	3	10	0	19	7	0	2	2	.500	0	0	3.65
	Williamsprt	Pit	A-	20	6	6	0	0	35	156	44	20	16	1	4	2	1	8	0	21	2	1	0	5	.000	0	0	4.11
Seaver, Mark	Modesto	Oak	A+	26	29	27	0	0	144	657	157	100	87	16	5	13	16	70	3	114	4	1	8	10	.444	0	0	5.44
Sequea, Jacobo	Frederick	Bal	A+	19	23	22	2	0	123.2	544	121	80	70	11	6	6	8	58	0	94	4	5	9	11	.450	1	0	5.09
Sergent, Joe*	Kane County	Fla	A	22	46	10	0	4	101	417	97	34	30	7	1	2	2	20	0	70	5	0	8	3	.727	0	1	2.67
Serrano, Alex	Rockies	Col	R	20	6	0	0	4	6.1	23	2	0	0	0	0	0	0	1	0	5	0	0	0	0	.000	0	1	0.00
Serrano, Elio	Piedmont	Phi	A	22	38	0	0	13	67.1	287	67	26	17	5	4	1	10	15	0	56	3	0	4	2	.667	0	5	2.27
Serrano, Willy	Lakeland	Det	A+	20	26	0	0	11	40.2	190	31	22	14	4	3	3	1	38	4	27	5	1	3	3	.500	0	2	3.10
Severino, Cleris*	Reds	Cin	R	19	13	5	0	1	52	224	46	25	18	3	1	1	4	23	0	36	2	0	1	3	.250	0	0	3.12
Severino, Jose	Tigers	Det	R	22	2	2	0	0	13.1	56	15	8	8	2	0	1	2	3	0	11	1	0	2	0	1.000	0	0	5.40
	Oneonta	Det	A-	22	3	3	0	0	18	79	23	14	12	0	1	1	2	0	0	13	2	2	1	2	.333	0	0	6.00
	Lakeland	Det	A+	22	7	5	1	0	31	134	28	19	14	3	1	0	4	14	0	19	2	1	3	3	.500	0	0	4.06

2000 Pitching — Class-A and Rookie Leagues

Player	Team	Org	Lg	A	G	GS	CG	GF	IP	BFP	H	R	ER	HR	SH	SF	HB	TBB	IBB	SO	WP	Bk	W	L	Pct.	ShO	Sv	ERA
Shabansky, Rob*	High Desert	Ari	A+	24	6	3	0	0	17	98	35	28	25	1	0	2	1	14	0	9	3	0	0	2	.000	0	0	13.24
	Missoula	Ari	R+	24	11	7	0	1	39	175	35	26	17	1	1	3	0	18	0	40	0	0	3	1	.750	0	0	3.92
Shafer, Kurt	Pirates	Pit	R	19	8	1	0	6	13	54	15	4	4	0	1	1	0	3	0	5	2	0	2	1	.667	0	1	2.77
Shaffar, Ben	Lansing	ChC	A	23	19	18	1	0	102	469	127	70	56	7	6	2	10	30	0	72	11	0	6	9	.400	0	0	4.94
Shaw, Elliott	Princeton	TB	R+	21	18	4	0	4	37	181	38	28	19	2	0	1	2	34	0	29	15	1	0	1	.000	0	0	4.62
Sheefel, Adam*	Billings	Cin	R+	23	16	15	0	0	91.1	412	111	53	42	4	2	1	6	27	0	83	5	0	9	1	.900	0	0	4.14
Sheldon, Kyle	Jupiter	Mon	A+	24	40	1	0	13	77	337	87	48	38	8	2	4	4	15	1	46	2	0	5	0	1.000	0	2	4.44
Shelley, Jason	Hickory	Pit	A	24	3	0	0	2	6	29	8	8	6	3	1	0	0	2	0	6	1	0	0	0	.000	0	1	9.00
	Williamsprt	Pit	A-	24	7	6	0	0	31.2	135	25	14	11	3	2	2	3	17	0	34	1	1	2	1	.667	0	0	3.13
Shiell, Jason	Rancho Cuca	SD	A+	24	16	14	0	0	81	356	73	54	48	9	0	3	6	41	0	80	10	2	7	5	.583	0	0	5.33
Shiyuk, Todd*	Fort Wayne	SD	A	24	32	0	0	13	38	166	31	14	9	4	3	1	2	17	1	40	5	0	0	2	.000	0	4	2.13
	Rancho Cuca	SD	A+	24	29	0	0	9	30.1	142	32	19	16	1	0	0	2	19	0	35	6	1	0	1	.000	0	0	4.75
Shorey, Jeremy	Ogden	Mil	R+	20	15	0	0	5	29.2	157	56	37	30	2	1	3	1	12	0	16	4	0	2	1	.667	0	2	9.10
Shortslef, Josh*	Pirates	Pit	R	19	11	3	0	3	31.1	132	26	15	13	1	1	0	4	11	0	19	2	1	3	2	.600	0	0	3.73
Shrout, Kevin	Ogden	Mil	R+	23	14	2	0	5	46	228	73	46	39	6	2	4	2	18	0	39	5	1	1	1	.500	0	3	7.63
	Beloit	Mil	A	23	4	2	0	0	14	54	8	2	0	0	0	0	0	4	0	10	1	0	1	0	1.000	0	0	0.00
Shwam, Mike	Helena	Mil	R+	23	23	0	0	21	27.1	123	26	12	12	2	1	0	2	12	0	34	5	0	1	3	.250	0	9	3.95
Sierra, Auvin*	Tigers	Det	R	23	13	0	0	5	20	77	15	5	3	0	0	0	0	4	0	23	4	1	3	1	.750	0	1	1.35
	Lakeland	Det	A+	23	2	0	0	0	4	16	2	0	0	0	0	0	0	3	0	5	0	0	0	0	.000	0	0	0.00
	Oneonta	Det	A-	23	7	0	0	3	7	26	4	1	1	0	0	0	0	1	0	11	0	0	0	0	.000	0	0	0.00
Sikaras, Pete	South Bend	Ari	A	22	20	0	0	2	29.1	146	33	25	20	1	1	2	2	22	0	17	0	0	0	3	.000	0	1	6.14
Silva, Carlos	Clearwater	Phi	A+	22	26	24	4	0	176.1	778	229	99	70	7	6	5	11	26	1	82	4	2	8	13	.381	0	0	3.57
Silva, Doug	Charlotte	Tex	A+	22	45	0	0	28	67.1	299	74	37	34	7	4	3	1	24	1	55	0	5	5	5	.500	0	10	4.54
Silverio, Carlos	Batavia	Phi	A-	22	1	1	0	0	4	15	3	1	1	0	0	0	0	2	0	1	1	0	0	0	.000	0	0	2.25
Silverio, Marcelino	Idaho Falls	SD	R+	22	25	0	0	8	27	121	33	17	13	3	1	1	1	9	0	22	3	0	1	3	.250	0	2	4.33
Simon, Janewrys	Twins	Min	R	19	9	1	0	4	11.1	57	8	8	8	1	0	0	4	11	0	16	3	0	0	0	.000	0	1	6.35
Simonson, Chris	Mudville	Mil	A+	24	14	5	0	1	40.1	204	65	44	36	3	2	3	5	19	1	20	1	0	1	2	.333	0	0	8.03
	Beloit	Mil	A	24	14	9	0	4	61.1	258	61	37	31	5	0	0	7	14	0	47	1	0	4	4	.500	0	0	4.55
Simpson, Allan	Lancaster	Sea	A+	23	52	0	0	20	52	217	34	17	12	1	0	2	2	27	1	67	2	0	3	2	.600	0	6	2.08
Simpson, Andre	Burlington	CWS	A	20	45	1	0	34	80.2	339	68	34	27	5	5	5	4	32	2	68	5	1	5	6	.455	0	15	3.01
Simpson, Cory	Braves	Atl	R	23	4	1	0	0	6.2	28	6	6	0	1	0	0	0	1	0	12	0	0	0	0	.000	0	0	0.00
	Macon	Atl	A	23	7	3	1	3	17.2	83	16	10	5	0	1	1	0	10	0	16	1	0	0	1	.000	0	0	2.55
Simpson, Joe	Rockies	Col	R	22	11	0	0	4	11.2	55	11	9	6	0	0	1	0	6	0	6	2	0	0	0	.000	0	1	4.63
Sims, Ken	Frederick	Bal	A+	25					81	361	98	44	35	10	3	3	9	27	1	44	6	1	5	3	.625	0	0	3.89
Sirianni, Jay*	Columbus	Cle	A	25	13	3	0	6	38.1	171	41	15	14	2	3	1	1	15	4	28	3	0	1	3	.250	0	0	3.29
	Kinston	Cle	A+	25	7	2	0	3	17.2	81	18	14	9	1	2	1	0	11	1	6	1	0	0	2	.000	0	0	4.58
Sismondo, Bobby*	Clearwater	Phi	A+	24	32	6	0	11	87.2	375	85	49	39	7	2	2	3	35	0	62	5	1	5	7	.417	0	1	4.00
Slaten, Doug*	Diamondbcks	Ari	R	21	9	4	0	3	9.1	40	7	1	1	0	0	2	0	3	0	7	0	0	0	0	.000	0	0	0.96
Sloan, Brandon	Utica	Fla	A-	23	14	14	0	0	73.1	328	89	49	39	5	0	2	1	24	0	50	7	2	4	4	.500	0	0	4.79
Smalley, Mike*	Jamestown	Atl	A-	22	3	2	0	0	10	38	6	1	1	0	0	0	0	2	0	8	1	0	0	0	.000	0	0	0.90
	Macon	Atl	A	22	12	12	0	0	68.1	291	72	37	32	5	2	2	2	29	0	45	3	0	4	4	.500	0	0	4.21
Smart, Richard*	Elizabethtn	Min	R+	21	15	1	0	1	34.1	151	26	20	17	3	1	0	3	24	0	36	8	1	3	2	.600	0	0	4.46
Smith, Clint	Lakeland	Det	A+	23	37	13	0	14	104.2	486	131	76	67	9	1	4	6	50	2	76	10	1	4	11	.267	0	0	5.76
Smith, Hans*	Princeton	TB	R+	22	7	0	0	6	7.1	30	6	7	7	0	1	0	0	4	0	9	2	0	1	1	.500	0	3	8.59
	Chston-SC	TB	A	22	26	0	0	11	31	132	28	6	6	2	0	0	2	6	2	23	2	0	1	2	.333	0	7	1.74
Smith, Jason	Yankees	NYY	R	19	10	10	0	0	57.1	249	57	26	22	2	0	1	4	13	0	54	2	0	6	2	.750	0	0	3.45
Smith, Joe	Giants	SF	R	22	12	11	0	0	63.1	270	69	40	29	1	1	3	6	9	0	55	4	3	1	4	.200	0	0	4.12
	Salem-Keizr	SF	A-	23	3	0	0	0	5	20	3	0	0	0	0	0	0	4	0	5	0	0	0	0	.000	0	0	0.00
Smith, Justin*	Mariners	Sea	R	24	3	3	0	0	5	24	5	1	1	0	0	0	0	2	0	5	0	0	0	0	.000	0	0	1.80
	Lancaster	Sea	A+	24	1	1	0	0	2.2	11	1	2	1	0	0	0	0	2	0	4	0	0	0	1	.000	0	0	3.38
	Everett	Sea	A-	24	6	0	0	1	12	47	8	1	1	1	1	0	1	1	0	11	0	0	1	0	1.000	0	0	0.75
Smith, Matt	Pittsfield	NYM	A-	22	20	0	0	13	27.1	138	35	21	14	0	0	2	0	20	0	23	2	0	0	2	.000	0	0	4.61
Smith, Matt*	Staten Ilnd	NYY	A-	22	14	14	0	0	75.2	308	74	32	20	1	3	0	2	20	0	59	4	0	5	4	.556	0	0	2.38
Smith, Mike	Queens	Tor	A-	22	14	12	0	0	51	205	41	18	13	1	1	1	0	17	0	55	9	1	2	2	.500	0	0	2.29
Smith, Taylor	Dunedin	Tor	A+	22	13	0	0	5	23	101	21	19	9	1	1	0	0	10	1	20	2	0	0	0	.000	0	0	3.52
Smith, Toebius	Danville	Atl	R+	21	19	0	0	4	41	167	37	21	20	4	3	1	0	9	0	35	5	1	2	1	.667	0	1	4.39
Smuin, Shane	Kane County	Fla	A	22	4	0	0	2	5.1	23	3	3	0	0	0	0	0	4	0	4	0	0	1	0	1.000	0	0	0.00
	Brevard Cty	Fla	A+	22	1	0	0	0	4	13	3	0	0	0	0	0	0	0	0	2	0	0	0	0	.000	0	0	0.00
	Utica	Fla	A-	22	26	0	0	13	38	190	50	43	29	6	2	2	5	23	2	34	6	0	2	5	.286	0	1	6.87
Smyth, Steve*	Daytona	ChC	A+	23	24	23	1	0	138.1	589	134	62	50	9	0	2	5	57	0	100	9	1	8	8	.500	0	0	3.25
Snell, Ian	Pirates	Pit	R	19	4	0	0	1	7.2	28	5	2	2	1	1	0	1	1	0	8	0	0	1	0	1.000	0	0	2.35
Snider, Rich	Vancouver	Oak	A-	22	7	0	0	2	9.1	39	11	4	4	1	0	1	1	1	0	7	1	0	1	0	1.000	0	0	3.86
	Athletics	Oak	R	22	9	3	0	2	29	116	30	8	8	0	1	0	0	2	0	30	1	0	2	2	.500	0	1	2.48
Snyder, Kyle	Royals	KC	R	23	1	1	0	0	2	7	1	0	0	0	0	0	0	0	0	4	0	0	0	0	.000	0	0	0.00
	Wilmington	KC	A+						0.1	1	1	0	0	0	0	0	0	0	0	1	0	0	0	0	.000	0	0	0.00
Sobchuk, Justin	Athletics	Oak	R	20	14	8	0	1	43	214	60	44	33	3	1	4	4	26	0	23	8	0	1	4	.200	0	0	6.91
Solano, Alex	Lowell	Bos	A-	21	1	0	0	1	1	3	0	0	0	0	0	0	0	0	0	2	0	0	0	0	.000	0	0	0.00
	Augusta	Bos	A-	21	33	1	0	19	56	259	65	45	34	8	5	2	5	27	1	38	6	0	3	7	.300	0	5	5.46
Sollenberger, Matt*	Capital Cty	NYM	A	24	4	0	0	3	5.2	29	7	5	4	0	1	1	0	4	1	8	2	0	0	0	.000	0	0	6.35
	Pittsfield	NYM	A-	20	20	0	0	5	40	170	33	18	17	3	0	0	1	14	0	39	4	1	2	3	.333	0	2	3.83
Song, Seung	Lowell	Bos	A-	21	13	13	0	0	72.2	293	63	26	21	1	0	2	0	20	0	93	6	1	5	2	.714	0	0	2.60
Soriano, Rafael	Wisconsin	Sea	A	20	21	21	1	0	122.1	500	99	47	39	3	2	5	12	50	0	90	5	2	4	6	.400	0	0	2.87
Sosebee, Chad	Lowell	Bos	A-	23	12	0	0	7	18.2	95	27	15	11	0	0	4	1	11	0	19	1	1	1	2	.333	0	2	5.30
Soto, Darwin	Padres	SD	R	19	17	2	0	5	45.2	219	64	34	23	1	2	1	0	18	0	28	4	1	2	2	.500	0	0	4.53
Southard, Lee	Queens	Tor	A-	23	5	0	0	1	6	37	7	10	8	0	0	1	0	12	0	7	5	0	1	0	1.000	0	0	12.00
Spear, Russell	Tigers	Det	R	23	3	0	0	0	3.2	18	2	1	1	0	0	0	0	5	0	5	0	1	0	0	.000	0	0	2.45
	Lakeland	Det	A+	23	13	2	0	6	34.2	156	24	11	10	0	0	2	2	35	0	21	6	0	1	0	1.000	0	0	2.60

2000 Pitching — Class-A and Rookie Leagues

HOW MUCH HE PITCHED											WHAT HE GAVE UP												THE RESULTS					
Player	Team	Org	Lg	A	G	GS	CG	GF	IP	BFP	H	R	ER	HR	SH	SF	HB	TBB	IBB	SO	WP	Bk	W	L	Pct.	ShO	Sv	ERA
Spencer, Corey*	Augusta	Bos	A	24	53	0	0	11	96.2	423	90	46	28	4	3	4	5	34	0	119	4	0	8	2	.800	0	2	2.61
Sperring, Jayme	Orioles	Bal	R	22	3	0	0	1	5	18	2	0	0	0	0	0	0	1	0	9	0	0	0	0	.000	0	0	0.00
	Bluefield	Bal	R+	22	4	0	0	2	4	16	2	1	0	0	0	0	0	2	0	5	1	0	1	0	1.000	0	1	0.00
	Delmarva	Bal	A	22	13	0	0	6	21.2	92	19	12	10	1	0	0	2	9	0	28	2	0	0	0	.000	0	0	4.15
Spillers, Larry	Orioles	Bal	R	19	3	3	0	0	10	40	5	1	1	0	1	1	2	6	0	8	0	0	0	0	.000	0	0	0.90
Spillman, Jeromie*	Medcine Hat	Tor	R+	22	22	0	0	7	39	169	34	22	18	4	4	1	0	18	3	36	2	2	4	3	.571	0	1	4.15
Spooneybarger, T.	Myrtle Bch	Atl	A+	21	19	6	0	5	49.2	187	18	7	5	0	4	0	1	19	0	57	6	0	3	0	1.000	0	0	0.91
Sprague, Kevin*	Peoria	StL	A	24	24	24	0	0	120.2	520	117	60	54	5	3	4	6	53	1	117	15	1	8	9	.471	0	0	4.03
Spurling, Chris	Tampa	NYY	A+	24	34	0	0	15	57	239	50	27	24	1	2	3	1	22	5	55	3	0	4	6	.400	0	1	3.79
	Lynchburg	Pit	A+	24	9	0	0	6	18.1	66	8	2	2	1	0	1	0	3	0	17	0	0	1	0	1.000	0	5	0.98
St. Amand, Reuben	Queens	Tor	A-	21	17	5	0	3	46	219	65	42	30	1	1	5	2	22	0	28	8	0	2	4	.333	0	0	5.87
St. Amant, John	Phillies	Phi	R	22	11	1	0	7	18	95	25	17	11	1	0	0	3	6	0	18	3	0	0	2	.000	0	0	5.50
Stabile, Paul*	Hickory	Pit	A	25	7	0	0	2	10.2	53	11	10	5	1	0	0	0	9	0	18	0	0	0	0	.000	0	0	4.22
	Lynchburg	Pit	A+	25	10	0	0	5	14.2	75	21	19	16	1	1	1	1	8	0	11	1	0	0	0	.000	0	0	9.82
	High Desert	Ari	A+	25	21	0	0	9	21.1	106	17	10	9	0	0	0	1	24	0	26	4	0	0	0	.000	0	1	3.80
Stafford, Mike*	Tampa	NYY	A+	26	44	0	0	12	46.1	197	51	21	20	3	3	1	1	8	0	38	2	0	4	0	1.000	0	2	3.88
Stahl, Rich*	Delmarva	Bal	A	20	20	20	0	0	89	399	97	47	33	3	2	0	0	51	0	83	9	1	5	6	.455	0	0	3.34
Stamler, Keith	Pulaski	Tex	R+	21	14	9	1	2	66	276	59	32	26	2	5	0	7	15	1	59	2	0	5	4	.556	0	0	3.55
	Savannah	Tex	A	21	1	1	0	0	6	23	5	2	2	1	0	0	0	1	0	3	0	0	0	1	.000	0	0	3.00
Stanford, Derek	Michigan	Hou	A	22	28	25	3	0	169	736	141	85	75	11	8	2	18	92	3	133	15	0	11	6	.647	1	0	3.99
Stanton, Jeff	Staten Ilnd	NYY	A-	24	11	0	0	6	18.2	78	16	8	7	1	1	1	2	3	0	17	1	0	1	2	.333	0	0	3.38
	Greensboro	NYY	A	24	4	0	0	2	11	47	11	1	1	1	2	0	0	3	2	4	1	0	1	0	1.000	0	1	0.82
Stanton, Tim*	South Bend	Ari	A	24	51	0	0	21	65	291	61	33	28	5	5	2	6	33	4	55	4	1	5	5	.500	0	2	3.88
Stasio, Doug	Batavia	Phi	A-	23	18	1	0	7	29.2	133	36	12	12	1	2	2	3	15	3	17	3	3	1	4	.200	0	3	3.64
Staveland, Toby	Danville	Atl	R+	21	5	1	0	0	15	58	10	2	2	1	1	0	0	5	0	12	0	0	2	0	1.000	0	0	1.20
	Jamestown	Atl	A-	21	11	10	0	0	45	210	57	36	26	3	1	1	1	21	0	24	1	1	2	2	.500	0	0	5.20
Steele, Brad	Phillies	Phi	R	23	13	3	0	3	27	126	35	18	12	3	1	1	2	4	0	30	2	1	2	1	.667	0	0	4.00
Steele, Matt	South Bend	Ari	A	24	6	0	0	2	8.1	49	12	11	10	0	0	0	2	9	0	4	2	0	0	0	.000	0	0	10.80
	Missoula	Ari	R+	24	16	1	0	3	26.1	120	17	14	9	1	1	0	4	21	0	32	5	0	2	0	1.000	0	0	3.08
Steele, Michael	Oneonta	Det	A-	22	22	0	0	20	26.2	117	21	11	8	0	1	0	3	11	1	41	4	0	2	1	.667	0	9	2.70
Steffek, Brian	Great Falls	LA	R+	23	21	0	0	10	29.1	132	25	19	16	4	1	2	1	18	0	28	3	0	1	1	.500	0	2	4.91
Stein, Ethan	Wilmington	KC	A+	26	26	2	0	12	41.1	169	35	23	20	3	2	2	0	10	0	25	4	1	2	3	.400	0	2	4.35
Stemle, Steve	Potomac	StL	A+	24	26	26	1	0	150	668	169	89	80	15	2	4	12	59	1	84	16	0	9	10	.474	0	0	4.80
Stephens, John	Frederick	Bal	A+	21	20	20	0	0	118	497	119	45	40	5	3	4	8	22	1	121	6	0	7	6	.538	0	0	3.05
Stephenson, Eric*	Medcine Hat	Tor	R+	18	19	0	0	8	27	134	41	28	25	2	1	2	2	13	0	21	9	0	1	1	.500	0	0	8.33
Stepka, Tom	Asheville	Col	A	25	16	7	1	2	52.1	246	82	43	40	4	4	4	1	12	0	34	2	0	0	5	.000	0	0	6.88
Sterett, Adam	Marlins	Fla	R	18	11	0	0	3	16	86	19	15	12	0	0	2	7	14	0	13	6	0	1	3	.250	0	0	6.75
Stevens, Josh	Hagerstown	Tor	A	22	47	3	0	15	84.1	363	97	42	28	4	3	2	3	19	1	95	9	0	4	4	.500	0	5	2.99
Stewart, John*	Charlotte	Tex	A+	23	11	1	0	4	24.2	114	35	23	19	3	1	4	5	9	0	8	2	0	1	1	.500	0	1	6.93
	Pulaski	Tex	R+	23	21	2	0	13	45	196	45	24	22	2	0	3	2	17	0	42	2	0	0	4	.000	0	3	4.40
Stewart, Josh*	Burlington	CWS	A	22	25	25	1	0	138	617	157	84	70	14	5	3	10	58	2	82	9	0	9	9	.500	1	0	4.57
Stewart, Steve*	Beloit	Mil	A	24	21	1	0	5	29	135	38	23	22	7	0	2	0	10	1	27	1	0	1	3	.250	0	0	6.83
Stiehl, Robert	Auburn	Hou	A-	20	5	0	0	1	9.2	37	4	1	1	0	0	0	0	4	0	19	1	1	1	0	1.000	0	1	0.93
	Michigan	Hou	A	20	1	0	0	1	1	5	1	1	1	0	0	0	0	1	0	1	1	0	0	0	.000	0	0	9.00
Stiles, Brad*	Chston-WV	KC	A	20	6	4	0	0	22.1	103	25	19	16	3	1	3	3	12	0	11	3	0	1	5	.167	0	0	6.45
	Spokane	KC	A-	20	15	15	0	0	78.2	344	76	42	33	3	4	3	7	39	0	44	6	0	8	3	.727	0	0	3.78
Stine, Justin*	Hagerstown	Tor	A	24	41	0	0	9	54.2	229	53	28	19	2	2	1	0	26	1	46	3	0	3	4	.429	0	1	3.13
Stockman, Phil	Diamondbcks	Ari	R	21	14	2	0	5	41.2	194	40	22	12	2	0	0	2	23	0	40	3	1	3	2	.600	0	1	2.59
	Missoula	Ari	R+	21	2	2	0	0	11	46	10	3	3	0	0	0	0	3	0	4	0	0	2	0	1.000	0	0	2.45
Stocks, Nick	Peoria	StL	A	22	25	24	1	0	150	643	133	88	63	4	4	4	15	52	5	118	8	2	10	10	.500	0	0	3.78
Stockstill, Jason*	Cedar Rapds	Ana	A	24	10	1	0	5	22	104	29	18	18	0	0	1	0	9	0	22	4	0	0	2	.000	0	0	7.36
Stodolka, Mike*	Royals	KC	R	19	9	6	0	0	37	157	31	18	11	1	0	1	2	16	0	32	3	1	0	3	.000	0	0	2.68
	Chston-WV	KC	A	19	1	1	0	0	4.2	21	3	4	4	0	0	0	0	4	0	0	0	0	0	0	.000	0	0	7.71
Stokes, Brian	Chston-SC	TB	A	21	46	0	0	16	70.1	293	45	24	20	1	2	1	4	34	2	66	10	0	5	6	.455	0	5	2.56
Stokes, Shaun	New Jersey	StL	A-	22	4	4	0	0	17	60	10	1	1	0	0	0	0	1	0	23	0	0	0	0	.000	0	0	0.53
	Peoria	StL	A	22	8	8	0	0	45.2	192	47	22	18	5	5	0	2	12	2	36	3	0	2	2	.500	0	0	3.55
Stokley, Billy	Boise	Ana	A-	24	25	0	0	5	41	199	52	37	31	4	0	0	5	20	4	33	4	0	5	1	.833	0	0	6.80
Story, Aaron*	Pirates	Pit	R	20	5	3	0	1	23	94	16	5	4	2	0	0	3	7	0	27	2	0	2	0	1.000	0	1	1.57
	Williamsprt	Pit	A-	20	10	1	0	6	19.1	85	17	15	12	2	2	0	0	10	0	16	3	1	2	0	1.000	0	0	5.59
Stumm, Jason	Burlington	CWS	A	20	13	13	2	0	66.1	289	66	46	34	6	4	1	2	30	2	62	3	1	2	7	.222	0	0	4.61
Sullivan, Ted	Mahoning Vy	Cle	A-	24	2	0	0	2	2	7	1	0	0	0	1	0	0	2	0	1	0	0	2	0	1.000	0	0	0.00
	Columbus	Cle	A	24	10	0	0	10	15.1	77	24	16	10	1	2	4	1	4	1	5	1	0	1	0	1.000	0	3	5.87
	Kinston	Cle	A+	24	4	0	0	4	3.1	12	0	1	0	0	0	0	0	0	0	3	0	2	0	0	.000	0	3	0.00
Sullivan, Tom*	Elizabethtn	Min	R+	22	4	0	0	1	4.1	17	2	0	0	0	0	0	0	1	0	1	0	0	1	0	1.000	0	0	0.00
Sunderman, Nick*	Mahoning Vy	Cle	A-	22	18	4	0	4	46.2	220	50	39	36	5	2	2	2	33	1	37	6	1	4	4	.500	0	0	6.94
Surkont, Keith	Visalia	Oak	A+	24	27	22	0	1	125.2	535	104	60	38	6	4	3	11	54	0	122	5	4	8	7	.533	0	1	2.72
Surridge, Lance	Sarasota	Bos	A+	24	20	1	0	11	42.2	197	50	27	23	2	6	3	7	16	3	22	3	0	2	3	.400	0	1	4.85
	Augusta	Bos	A	24	23	4	0	6	60	254	56	24	23	1	6	2	4	19	0	57	5	0	3	1	.750	0	2	3.45
Swanson, Erick*	Everett	Sea	A-	22	18	0	0	8	26	117	18	19	10	1	3	0	2	23	0	24	3	0	3	2	.600	0	1	3.46
Sweeney, James*	Bristol	CWS	R+	21	17	2	0	1	39.1	156	31	10	7	1	0	2	0	16	0	36	3	0	3	1	.750	0	0	1.60
Swindell, Jeremy*	Oneonta	Det	A-	23	18	0	0	6	31.1	136	29	20	14	3	1	1	1	16	0	28	1	1	1	3	.250	0	1	4.02
Sylvester, Billy	Myrtle Bch	Atl	A+	24	32	0	0	27	45.2	172	16	8	4	2	1	1	3	15	1	48	2	0	3	0	1.000	0	16	0.79
Szuminski, Jason	Cubs	ChC	R	22	10	4	0	0	40.2	171	39	15	11	0	1	0	3	13	0	31	2	0	2	1	.667	0	0	2.43
	Lansing	ChC	A	22	4	4	0	0	21.1	89	19	8	8	0	0	1	1	10	0	7	1	1	3	1	.750	0	0	3.38
Takach, Ryan*	South Bend	Ari	A	23	12	0	0	6	17	82	16	13	8	1	1	1	1	14	1	12	1	1	2	1	.667	0	0	4.24
	Missoula	Ari	R+	23	24	1	0	6	40.2	183	39	16	14	0	2	0	1	19	0	37	3	1	3	2	.600	0	0	3.10
Tallet, Brian*	Mahoning Vy	Cle	A-	23	6	6	0	0	15.2	62	10	2	2	0	0	0	1	3	0	20	0	0	0	0	.000	0	0	1.15

2000 Pitching — Class-A and Rookie Leagues

HOW MUCH HE PITCHED											WHAT HE GAVE UP												THE RESULTS					
Player	Team	Org	Lg	A	G	GS	CG	GF	IP	BFP	H	R	ER	HR	SH	SF	HB	TBB	IBB	SO	WP	Bk	W	L	Pct.	ShO	Sv	ERA
Tankersley, Dennis	Augusta	Bos	A	22	15	15	1	0	75.1	326	73	41	34	4	0	0	4	32	0	74	1	1	5	3	.625	1	0	4.06
	Fort Wayne	SD	A	22	12	12	0	0	66.1	265	48	25	21	5	2	2	2	25	0	87	2	0	5	2	.714	0	0	2.85
Taschner, Jack*	San Jose	SF	A+	23	10	2	0	1	26.1	119	23	17	12	0	0	1	4	17	0	22	3	3	2	2	.500	0	1	4.10
Tate, Matt	Orioles	Bal	R	20	9	2	0	2	16	75	16	11	11	1	0	1	1	11	1	13	2	0	0	1	.000	0	1	6.19
	Bluefield	Bal	R+	20	7	5	0	1	26.1	127	40	26	23	3	2	3	5	8	0	16	2	0	1	3	.250	0	0	7.86
Tavarez, David	Bluefield	Bal	R+	19	7	7	0	0	34.1	166	47	30	23	8	0	3	3	14	0	23	2	0	3	2	.600	0	0	6.03
Taylor, Aaron	Everett	Sea	A-	23	15	14	0	1	63	298	76	54	52	5	0	2	9	37	0	57	10	1	1	4	.200	0	0	7.43
Taylor, Brien*	Columbus	Cle	A	29	5	0	0	2	2.2	25	5	11	8	1	0	0	2	9	0	2	7	0	0	0	.000	0	0	27.00
Taylor, John	Queens	Tor	A-	23	10	0	0	4	8.2	47	13	10	9	0	1	2	2	6	0	9	4	0	0	1	.000	0	0	9.35
Teekel, Josh	Johnson Cty	StL	R+	20	4	3	0	0	12.2	53	7	4	2	0	0	0	1	8	0	18	1	0	1	0	1.000	0	0	1.42
Tejada, Franklin	Peoria	StL	A	21	19	17	1	1	106.1	453	100	57	41	4	3	6	5	31	3	64	4	1	6	6	.500	1	0	3.47
Tejada, Sandy	Twins	Min	R	19	15	10	1	0	57.2	243	57	30	29	3	2	2	1	20	0	49	4	0	6	2	.750	0	0	4.53
Tejeda, Robinson	Phillies	Phi	R	19	10	6	1	1	39	178	44	30	24	3	1	2	2	12	0	22	5	1	2	5	.286	1	0	5.54
Tekavec, Nate	Oneonta	Det	A-	22	11	11	0	0	60.2	270	75	38	31	6	1	4	1	9	1	44	4	1	4	4	.500	0	0	4.60
Temple, Jason	Rancho Cuca	SD	A+	26	57	0	0	11	82	433	78	81	73	8	0	6	13	105	1	72	18	0	3	3	.500	0	1	8.01
Tetz, Kris	Cape Fear	Mon	A	22	19	0	0	16	22.1	96	15	19	14	2	1	0	0	18	0	19	1	0	1	0	1.000	0	6	5.64
	Jupiter	Mon	A+	22	25	0	0	18	25.1	124	30	13	11	0	4	0	1	18	3	19	1	0	1	3	.250	0	9	3.91
Thames, Charlie	Boise	Ana	A-	22	17	0	0	17	26	102	18	2	1	0	2	0	1	5	1	30	1	0	1	1	.500	0	11	0.35
	Lk Elsinore	Ana	A+	22	6	0	0	5	9.1	46	15	11	9	2	0	1	0	1	0	6	0	0	0	0	.000	0	2	8.68
Theodile, Simieon	Delmarva	Bal	A	24	36	1	0	15	69	297	75	34	27	4	2	3	3	17	0	58	6	1	3	1	.750	0	3	3.52
Thigpen, Josh	Red Sox	Bos	R	19	2	0	0	0	3	17	3	5	5	1	0	1	0	6	0	2	1	0	0	1	.000	0	0	15.00
Thomas, Adam	Boise	Ana	A-	22	8	8	0	0	37.1	170	47	37	30	3	2	2	2	13	0	28	1	5	2	4	.333	0	0	7.23
	Butte	Ana	R+	22	6	6	0	0	34	159	44	26	17	3	1	0	4	10	0	22	3	2	0	2	.000	0	0	4.50
Thomas, Don*	Michigan	Hou	A	25	43	1	0	14	62.1	279	65	28	21	3	4	1	5	34	2	44	6	1	4	1	.800	0	2	3.03
Thomas, Gaige	Kane County	Fla	A	22	10	0	0	5	9.1	57	10	17	17	0	0	0	1	21	0	5	5	0	0	0	.000	0	0	16.39
	Utica	Fla	A-	22	21	0	0	5	38.2	186	40	23	23	3	1	0	1	35	0	37	11	0	3	0	1.000	0	1	5.35
Thomas, Jeb	Spokane	KC	A-	22	14	1	0	1	21	99	20	16	13	0	0	1	2	19	0	20	9	1	1	0	1.000	0	0	5.57
Thomas, Joe*	Fort Myers	Min	A+	26	22	11	0	5	66.1	294	77	35	33	9	4	1	5	16	1	34	2	1	7	2	.778	0	1	4.48
Thompson, Derek*	Burlington	Cle	R+	20	12	12	0	0	43.1	201	50	38	28	2	0	2	2	14	0	40	4	0	0	4	.000	0	0	5.82
Thompson, Doug	Salem	Col	A+	24	46	0	0	13	62	267	43	29	21	2	3	1	5	35	1	80	3	2	5	3	.625	0	1	3.05
Thompson, Jesse	Reds	Cin	R	21	7	1	0	3	14	67	16	12	8	2	1	1	1	6	0	18	2	0	0	2	.000	0	0	5.14
	Billings	Cin	R+	21	9	0	0	4	19.1	85	18	10	9	2	3	0	0	14	1	18	3	0	1	0	1.000	0	0	4.19
Thompson, Matt	Red Sox	Bos	R	19	12	11	0	0	56.2	258	65	33	23	5	1	3	4	18	0	54	6	0	4	2	.667	0	0	3.65
Thompson, Mike	Fort Wayne	SD	A	20	6	6	0	0	26.1	122	28	19	15	1	2	3	5	15	0	17	3	0	1	3	.250	0	0	5.13
	Idaho Falls	SD	R+	20	14	14	0	0	72.2	339	99	56	48	8	1	1	8	30	0	52	8	0	6	4	.600	0	0	5.94
Thomson, John	Rockies	Col	R	27	3	3	0	0	5.1	29	8	8	8	0	0	1	0	4	0	7	1	0	0	1	.000	0	0	13.50
	Portland	Col	A-	27	1	1	0	0	4	17	4	1	1	0	0	0	0	1	0	3	0	0	0	0	.000	0	0	2.25
Thornton, Matt*	Wisconsin	Sea	A	24	26	17	0	3	103.1	465	94	59	46	2	3	0	6	72	1	88	12	2	6	9	.400	0	0	4.01
Thorpe, Tracy	Medcine Hat	Tor	R+	20	11	6	0	0	26.1	126	28	28	25	3	3	1	3	17	0	15	3	0	0	4	.000	0	0	8.54
Tibbs, Jeff	Great Falls	LA	R+	19	14	13	0	0	47	227	54	46	41	6	4	1	4	41	0	28	6	1	2	5	.286	0	0	7.85
Tillery, Josh	Danville	Atl	R+	22	17	1	0	1	42.1	190	53	23	18	1	3	2	2	14	0	36	1	0	2	1	.667	0	0	3.83
Timm, Dan	Reds	Cin	R	25	1	1	0	0	0.2	9	4	6	6	0	1	0	0	3	0	0	1	0	0	1	.000	0	0	81.00
Timmerman, Heath	Cedar Rapds	Ana	A	23	13	3	0	5	26.2	127	26	16	15	0	0	1	3	20	0	17	6	0	0	0	.000	0	0	5.06
Tisdale, Marlyn	Billings	Cin	R+	23	8	1	0	3	17.1	74	9	6	1	0	2	1	2	11	0	17	1	0	2	1	.667	0	0	0.52
Tomaszewski, Eliot	Bluefield	Bal	R+	21	21	1	0	6	34.1	158	36	22	20	1	0	0	7	15	0	36	4	0	1	1	.500	0	0	5.24
Tomsu, Josh	Billings	Cin	R+	21	12	12	0	0	59.1	276	65	50	43	6	3	2	2	37	0	25	6	1	2	5	.286	0	0	6.52
Toriz, Steve	Cape Fear	Mon	A	24	10	0	0	2	14.2	78	19	19	11	1	0	0	2	14	0	16	1	0	2	1	.667	0	0	6.75
Torres, Alex*	Lakeland	Det	A+	22	1	0	0	1	0.2	4	0	0	0	0	0	0	0	2	0	0	0	0	0	0	.000	0	0	0.00
	Tigers	Det	R	22	3	0	0	2	4.2	29	4	6	2	0	0	0	2	8	0	7	1	0	0	1	.000	0	0	3.86
Torres, Carlos	Reds	Cin	R	20	11	7	0	1	43.1	217	56	42	25	3	3	4	5	26	0	17	13	1	2	3	.400	0	0	5.19
Torres, Joe*	Boise	Ana	A-	18	11	10	0	0	46	186	27	17	13	0	1	2	1	23	0	52	4	1	4	1	.800	0	0	2.54
Torres, Leo*	Daytona	ChC	A+	25	46	0	0	18	76	316	72	35	29	1	3	3	2	24	1	64	2	1	4	5	.444	0	5	3.43
Torres, Luis	Hickory	Pit	A	21	23	21	0	1	110.1	511	121	73	55	10	3	5	12	60	0	68	4	0	5	7	.417	0	0	4.49
Torres, Luis	Vermont	Mon	A-	20	15	15	0	0	86.2	372	82	45	33	6	2	3	3	34	0	56	6	1	7	5	.583	0	0	3.43
Totten, Heath	Yakima	LA	A-	22	13	13	0	0	74.1	292	55	24	19	4	0	2	2	15	0	67	3	0	8	2	.800	0	0	2.30
Tranchina, Scott	Eugene	ChC	A-	24	10	0	0	4	17	69	12	5	3	0	0	2	1	4	0	24	1	0	1	2	.333	0	1	1.59
	Daytona	ChC	A+	24	15	0	0	13	20.1	86	14	5	4	0	0	0	2	9	0	21	3	0	2	0	1.000	0	5	1.77
Treadway, Brion	Salem-Keizr	SF	A-	22	7	7	0	0	29	132	28	17	8	2	0	2	4	15	0	25	0	1	2	3	.400	0	0	2.48
Tremblay, Max*	Kissimmee	Hou	A+	25	13	0	0	1	21.1	95	20	13	10	1	0	1	1	11	0	23	2	0	0	0	.000	0	0	4.22
Tremont, Harold	Rangers	Tex	R	20	16	0	0	4	45.2	191	38	15	14	3	1	1	5	16	0	26	0	0	5	0	1.000	0	4	2.76
	Pulaski	Tex	R+	20	2	1	0	0	6	29	11	5	5	0	0	1	1	1	0	7	1	0	1	0	1.000	0	0	7.50
Trevino, Chris*	Braves	Atl	R	20	4	1	0	1	11	46	10	7	5	1	0	1	0	5	0	10	2	0	0	0	.000	0	0	4.09
	Danville	Atl	R+	20	12	12	1	0	56.1	242	56	28	21	7	2	1	1	23	0	51	5	0	1	4	.200	0	0	3.36
Troilo, Joseph	Red Sox	Bos	R	23	24	0	0	19	30.2	142	31	17	9	2	5	4	4	14	2	25	4	2	1	1	.500	0	4	2.64
	Augusta	Bos	A	23	2	1	0	1	7.2	26	4	1	1	1	0	0	0	1	0	8	0	0	0	0	.000	0	0	1.17
Trosper, Tanner	Athletics	Oak	R	23	17	0	0	14	23	95	17	7	4	0	1	1	1	7	0	24	3	0	0	1	.000	0	6	1.57
Truitt, Derrick	Macon	Atl	A	23	40	0	0	11	73	306	55	29	16	3	2	4	8	27	1	43	4	0	1	2	.333	0	2	1.97
Trujillo, John	Fort Wayne	SD	A	25	63	0	0	59	74.2	286	39	16	11	3	3	0	5	25	1	85	4	2	3	4	.429	0	42	1.33
Truselo, Randy	Rangers	Tex	R	20	8	0	0	1	13.2	62	14	8	6	1	1	0	1	8	0	10	0	0	1	1	.500	0	0	3.95
Tsao, Chin-Hui	Asheville	Col	A	20	24	24	0	0	145	591	119	54	44	8	3	2	5	40	0	187	6	1	11	8	.579	0	0	2.73
Tucker, Ben	Bakersfield	SF	A+	27	12	12	0	0	56	257	73	37	33	4	1	4	8	22	0	41	3	0	5	2	.714	0	0	5.30
Turner, Jess	Twins	Min	R	22	16	0	0	8	11.2	59	14	12	9	1	4	0	2	7	0	15	2	0	1	1	.500	0	2	6.94
Turner, Kyle*	Chston-WV	KC	A	22	8	5	0	1	32	155	42	25	20	1	0	3	2	14	0	29	3	0	2	3	.400	0	0	5.63
	Spokane	KC	A-	22	5	5	0	0	22.2	103	29	16	14	1	0	1	1	11	0	16	1	0	1	3	.250	0	0	5.56
Turuda, Miyoki	San Berndno	LA	A+	22	6	0	0	3	14	65	17	12	12	1	4	0	2	7	1	10	2	0	2	1	.667	0	0	7.71
Ugas, Juan	Vero Beach	LA	A+	21	7	0	0	3	15.2	69	21	13	11	3	0	1	0	2	0	14	0	0	2	2	.500	0	1	6.32
	Yakima	LA	A-	21	20	0	0	13	34.1	142	30	17	14	2	1	1	0	9	0	27	2	0	1	3	.250	0	0	3.67

2000 Pitching — Class-A and Rookie Leagues

HOW MUCH HE PITCHED											WHAT HE GAVE UP												THE RESULTS					
Player	Team	Org	Lg	A	G	GS	CG	GF	IP	BFP	H	R	ER	HR	SH	SF	HB	TBB	IBB	SO	WP	Bk	W	L	Pct.	ShO	Sv	ERA
Ulacia, Dennis*	Burlington	CWS	A	20	28	28	1	0	148.1	671	157	109	78	8	8	6	11	67	0	111	7	0	4	14	.222	0	0	4.73
Urbina, Ulmer	Vermont	Mon	A-	21	25	0	0	6	43	186	30	20	18	2	2	1	5	22	0	57	2	2	2	1	.667	0	0	3.77
Urdaneta, Lino	Vero Beach	LA	A+	21	27	5	0	7	78	351	103	60	47	7	2	5	3	24	1	40	6	0	5	4	.556	0	1	5.42
Urena, Sixto	Pulaski	Tex	R+	20	11	11	1	0	60.1	255	53	24	19	0	0	0	5	25	0	47	3	1	6	2	.750	0	0	2.83
Urrutia, Carlos	Cubs	ChC	R	19	7	5	0	1	31	140	32	20	17	0	1	0	5	12	0	10	6	1	2	2	.500	0	0	4.94
Uzzell, Todd	Salem-Keizr	SF	A-	23	16	2	0	5	39	187	44	31	20	2	5	2	3	22	0	28	9	1	1	5	.167	0	1	4.62
	San Jose	SF	A+	23	2	0	0	1	2.2	14	4	2	2	0	0	0	1	2	0	3	1	0	0	0	.000	0	0	6.75
Valdez, Domingo	Pulaski	Tex	R+	21	11	11	0	0	60.2	250	45	23	11	1	0	0	5	25	0	71	5	2	6	2	.750	0	0	1.63
Valdez, Jose	Clinton	Cin	A	22	14	14	2	0	86	357	63	39	26	7	5	4	3	40	0	76	5	1	5	3	.625	1	0	2.72
	Reds	Cin	R	22	1	1	0	0	2	10	2	1	0	0	0	0	0	3	0	1	0	0	0	0	.000	0	0	0.00
Valenti, Jon	Bakersfield	SF	A+	27	58	0	0	30	95.2	417	87	49	41	9	2	2	6	42	0	89	6	0	13	5	.722	0	7	3.86
Valentin, Emmanuel	Tigers	Det	R	18	9	1	0	2	15.2	89	23	21	21	2	0	1	1	18	0	16	3	0	1	2	.333	0	0	12.06
Valentine, Joe	Bristol	CWS	R+	21	19	0	0	16	25	104	14	10	8	1	2	2	2	12	1	30	9	0	2	1	.667	0	7	2.88
Valenzuela, Ramon	Twins	Min	R	20	18	0	0	5	24	104	27	12	10	3	1	0	1	5	0	13	2	0	2	2	.500	0	1	3.75
Valera, Greg	South Bend	Ari	A	22	29	18	0	5	119	525	119	67	59	9	4	2	6	56	0	93	9	2	5	7	.417	0	0	4.46
Valera, Nelson	St. Pete	TB	A+	22	1	0	0	1	1	6	2	1	1	0	0	0	0	1	0	1	2	0	0	0	.000	0	0	9.00
	Chston-SC	TB	A	22	18	0	0	8	30	150	46	29	25	4	0	3	1	13	1	22	4	0	0	2	.000	0	0	7.50
Valle, Yoiset*	Staten Ilnd	NYY	A-	23	3	1	0	1	5.1	33	13	10	9	1	0	0	1	2	0	4	1	0	0	0	.000	0	1	15.19
	Yankees	NYY	R	23	5	1	0	0	12	60	15	13	9	1	0	0	3	7	0	13	1	0	1	1	.500	0	0	6.75
	Greensboro	NYY	A	23	6	3	0	2	23.2	98	23	10	8	0	0	1	3	8	0	16	5	0	1	0	1.000	0	0	3.04
Valles, Rolando*	Martinsvlle	Hou	R+	21	19	0	0	11	39.1	165	34	17	15	4	1	2	4	20	0	32	2	2	5	2	.714	0	3	3.43
Valverde, Jose	South Bend	Ari	A	21	31	0	0	21	31.2	152	31	20	19	1	2	0	3	25	0	39	8	0	0	5	.000	0	14	5.40
	Missoula	Ari	R+	21	12	0	0	11	11.2	44	3	0	0	0	0	0	0	4	0	24	2	0	1	0	1.000	0	4	0.00
Van Buren, J.	Portland	Col	A-	20	13	13	0	0	69	291	54	27	20	1	4	2	3	30	0	41	3	2	4	5	.444	0	0	2.61
Vance, Cory*	Portland	Col	A-	22	7	3	0	1	24.1	93	11	5	3	1	3	0	2	8	0	26	1	0	0	2	.000	0	0	1.11
Vandermeer, Scott	Hudson Val	TB	A-	20	15	15	0	0	72.2	334	88	54	43	5	2	4	5	24	0	65	4	0	2	6	.250	0	0	5.33
Van Dusen, D.*	Mariners	Sea	R	20	10	2	0	0	41	166	38	14	12	1	0	1	0	6	0	58	2	0	6	0	1.000	0	0	2.63
	Everett	Sea	A-	20	4	2	0	0	15	72	17	13	6	1	0	1	3	5	0	24	5	0	1	1	.500	0	0	3.60
VanHekken, Andy*	W Michigan	Det	A	21	26	25	3	1	158	648	139	48	43	3	3	2	7	37	0	126	3	0	16	6	.727	1	1	2.45
Van Vessen, Josh*	Oneonta	Det	A-	24	15	0	0	9	24.2	114	25	13	8	1	1	3	0	10	1	19	1	3	0	0	.000	0	2	2.92
Vardijan, Dan	High Desert	Ari	A+	24	16	0	0	7	20	99	16	22	17	0	1	0	5	23	1	12	3	0	1	0	1.000	0	0	7.65
Vargas, Jose	Kinston	Cle	A+	24	27	9	0	7	78	326	69	43	37	4	4	2	5	29	0	76	3	1	3	4	.429	0	0	4.27
Vasquez, Luis*	Michigan	Hou	A	21	2	2	0	0	4.1	24	9	8	7	1	0	0	2	2	0	5	1	0	0	1	.000	0	0	14.54
Vazquez, William	Rockies	Col	R	21	13	11	0	0	52.1	236	52	36	24	4	1	1	1	21	0	38	7	1	3	3	.500	0	0	4.13
Vega, Rene*	St. Lucie	NYM	A+	24	27	26	1	0	147.1	648	150	88	72	12	3	4	14	62	1	97	8	2	11	6	.647	0	0	4.40
Vega, Vigri	Medcine Hat	Tor	R+	24	10	0	0	7	11	47	8	4	2	0	1	1	1	2	0	15	2	0	2	0	1.000	0	1	1.64
Velasquez, R.	Royals	KC	R	18	6	2	0	0	16	70	15	11	10	0	0	2	0	8	0	15	0	0	1	0	1.000	0	0	5.63
Velazquez, Elih*	Athletics	Oak	R	21	14	3	0	4	34.1	159	55	34	30	3	1	1	1	6	0	24	2	1	3	2	.600	0	2	7.86
Velazquez, Ernesto	Idaho Falls	SD	R+	19	6	1	0	1	15.1	68	19	9	6	1	0	0	0	2	0	15	1	1	3	0	1.000	0	0	3.52
Vent, Kevin	Bakersfield	SF	A+	24	26	21	0	2	83.2	397	115	65	48	6	4	2	1	44	0	65	6	4	4	7	.364	0	0	5.16
Veras, Enger	Chston-SC	TB	A	20	20	20	1	0	106.2	493	125	74	57	7	2	1	11	41	0	102	11	1	8	8	.500	0	0	4.81
Veronie, Shanin	Macon	Atl	A	24	43	0	0	34	66.1	269	48	22	20	4	3	1	4	26	2	69	2	0	4	4	.500	0	13	2.71
Victoria, Lester*	Fort Myers	Min	A+	25	17	0	0	9	18.1	92	22	17	15	3	0	1	1	15	1	16	3	0	0	0	.000	0	1	7.36
Vigeland, Ole	Charlotte	Tex	A+	24	23	0	0	8	39	176	44	26	26	2	4	3	3	16	1	26	3	0	1	2	.333	0	0	6.00
Villacis, Eduardo	Portland	Col	A-	21	5	0	0	2	4.1	20	4	1	0	0	0	0	0	3	1	4	0	0	0	0	.000	0	1	0.00
	Rockies	Col	R	21	13	9	0	1	48.1	202	39	17	10	0	3	2	2	19	1	37	3	1	4	2	.667	0	1	1.86
Villalon, Julio	Chston-SC	TB	A	23	4	3	0	0	18.1	78	18	14	13	2	0	0	3	6	0	25	0	0	1	0	1.000	0	0	6.38
	St. Pete	TB	A+	23	6	6	0	0	31.1	153	48	30	29	4	1	3	3	11	0	20	2	0	0	2	.000	0	0	8.33
Villanueva, Bill	Kane County	Fla	A	22	13	10	0	0	61.1	267	59	32	25	7	4	3	9	25	0	36	2	0	1	6	.143	0	0	3.67
	Utica	Fla	A-	22	14	3	0	9	22.2	116	20	22	18	3	3	0	2	23	1	20	6	2	1	3	.250	0	0	7.15
Villatoro, Wilmer	Padres	SD	R	18	2	0	0	0	2.1	11	3	4	4	0	0	0	1	2	0	5	0	0	0	0	.000	0	0	15.43
Villegas, Felix	Lowell	Bos	A-	22	16	10	0	3	71.2	318	79	49	40	0	5	4	2	28	0	42	4	1	4	6	.400	0	0	5.02
Vincent, Matt*	Peoria	StL	A	24	58	0	0	19	66.2	303	65	36	29	5	8	4	5	30	3	65	6	2	3	4	.429	0	1	3.92
Viole, Paul	Capital Cty	NYM	A	23	17	0	0	2	19.1	96	18	13	13	0	0	0	1	18	0	25	2	1	1	0	1.000	0	0	6.05
Vitek, Josh	Idaho Falls	SD	R+	21	15	15	0	0	73	343	92	48	41	4	1	5	6	40	0	42	5	1	5	4	.556	0	0	5.05
Volkman, Keith*	Rancho Cuca	SD	A+	25	6	0	0	1	6	42	15	13	10	2	0	1	1	6	0	6	1	0	0	1	.000	0	0	15.00
Voyles, Brad	Myrtle Bch	Atl	A+	24	39	0	0	36	56.2	212	21	8	7	1	1	3	0	25	2	70	8	0	5	2	.714	0	19	1.11
Vriesenga, Matt	New Jersey	StL	A-	23	22	4	0	3	48.2	202	48	22	15	3	2	3	1	12	1	39	1	0	2	3	.400	0	0	2.77
Wade, Matt	Columbus	Cle	A	21	10	10	0	0	40.1	195	61	33	30	0	3	4	3	16	0	24	1	0	2	4	.333	0	0	6.69
Waechter, Doug	Hudson Val	TB	A-	20	14	14	2	0	72.2	302	53	23	19	2	2	1	4	37	0	58	7	3	4	4	.500	2	0	2.35
Wagner, Frank*	Helena	Mil	R+	23	6	4	0	0	19.1	102	28	28	22	2	1	1	5	14	0	12	6	0	1	1	.500	0	0	10.24
Wahlbrink, Steven	Pirates	Pit	R	22	1	0	0	0	0.1	4	3	1	1	0	0	0	0	1	0	0	0	0	0	0	.000	0	0	27.00
Wainwright, Adam	Braves	Atl	R	19	7	5	0	1	32	120	15	5	4	1	0	0	0	10	0	42	1	1	4	0	1.000	0	0	1.13
	Danville	Atl	R+	19	6	6	0	0	29.1	115	28	13	12	3	1	0	1	2	0	39	1	0	2	2	.500	0	0	3.68
Waldron, Brad	Jupiter	Mon	A+	24	44	0	0	12	79	338	89	47	43	8	4	3	2	19	3	50	1	0	3	5	.375	0	0	4.90
Waligora, Tom	Daytona	ChC	A+	24	55	0	0	18	78.2	345	78	51	46	8	5	3	6	29	1	61	7	0	10	4	.714	0	5	5.26
Walk, Mitch*	Giants	SF	R	23	12	12	1	0	63	280	63	37	31	5	2	1	6	17	0	68	7	2	4	4	.500	0	0	4.43
	San Jose	SF	A+	23	1	1	0	0	6	25	7	2	2	0	0	0	0	1	0	6	0	0	0	1	.000	0	0	3.00
Walker, Adam*	Piedmont	Phi	A	25	8	8	0	0	48.1	196	37	11	11	1	1	0	2	14	0	50	3	0	6	1	.857	0	0	2.05
	Clearwater	Phi	A+	25	18	17	1	0	114	486	116	50	39	6	3	6	4	39	1	87	7	1	9	8	.529	0	0	3.08
Wallace, Ben*	Helena	Mil	R+	20	16	14	0	0	69.2	332	78	73	46	10	4	3	3	46	0	44	17	1	3	7	.300	0	0	5.94
Wallace, Chris	Tampa	NYY	A+	25	39	0	0	22	48	217	55	28	24	3	3	0	1	24	4	32	4	0	2	4	.333	0	7	4.50
Wallace, Shane*	Columbus	Cle	A	20	13	8	1	2	54.1	227	53	27	17	6	4	1	3	14	1	40	2	0	2	2	.500	0	1	2.82
Walrond, Les*	Potomac	StL	A+	24	27	27	0	0	151	632	134	66	56	9	1	3	7	54	0	153	12	1	10	5	.667	0	0	3.34
Walton, Sam*	Everett	Sea	A-	22	7	6	0	0	31.1	133	27	6	5	1	1	1	0	10	0	39	4	0	2	0	1.000	0	0	1.44
Wamback, Trevor	Jupiter	Mon	A+	24	19	18	2	1	112.1	471	113	54	48	10	4	0	6	21	0	62	3	0	7	7	.500	0	0	3.85
Wang, Chien-Ming	Staten Ilnd	NYY	A-	21	14	14	2	0	87	358	77	34	24	2	3	1	2	21	1	75	7	1	4	4	.500	1	0	2.48

2000 Pitching — Class-A and Rookie Leagues

HOW MUCH HE PITCHED											WHAT HE GAVE UP												THE RESULTS					
Player	Team	Org	Lg	A	G	GS	CG	GF	IP	BFP	H	R	ER	HR	SH	SF	HB	TBB	IBB	SO	WP	Bk	W	L	Pct.	ShO	Sv	ERA
Ward, Jeremy*	Boise	Ana	A-	23	16	7	0	1	48.1	231	67	35	33	3	1	4	2	27	1	30	4	1	2	2	.500	0	0	6.14
Wardle, Sean	Helena	Mil	R+	23	9	1	0	1	19.2	89	17	12	9	2	1	2	0	14	2	14	1	2	0	1	.000	0	0	4.12
	Ogden	Mil	R+	23	11	0	0	7	17.1	95	24	19	13	3	0	1	1	17	1	15	6	0	0	2	.000	0	0	6.75
Warren, Josh	Butte	Ana	R+	22	23	1	0	10	46.2	252	78	62	42	5	2	1	2	31	2	29	11	0	3	5	.375	0	0	8.10
Washburn, Ben	Vermont	Mon	A-	22	9	2	0	0	18	76	22	11	7	0	0	2	1	2	0	16	1	0	1	0	1.000	0	0	3.50
	Cape Fear	Mon	A	22	7	7	0	0	48.1	188	30	14	7	1	2	0	1	9	0	34	0	0	3	0	1.000	0	0	1.30
Waters, Chris	Danville	Atl	R+	25	13	13	1	0	69	286	64	33	30	4	2	2	2	29	0	73	6	0	5	3	.625	0	0	3.91
Watkins, David	Danville	Atl	R+	19	10	9	0	0	61.1	258	58	28	25	2	1	2	5	16	0	56	5	0	3	3	.500	0	0	3.67
	Macon	Atl	A	19	4	4	0	0	16.1	76	24	17	13	4	0	2	1	5	0	8	1	1	0	2	.000	0	0	7.16
Watkins, Steve	Rancho Cuca	SD	A+	22	27	27	0	0	151	652	118	75	62	10	8	6	1	90	0	163	10	2	7	6	.538	0	0	3.70
Watson, Greg	W Michigan	Det	A	24	62	0	0	59	58.1	256	40	21	14	1	5	1	8	38	1	68	5	1	2	2	.500	0	30	2.16
Wawrzyniak, Alan	Boise	Ana	A-	23	10	0	0	5	9.2	53	9	8	8	0	0	0	1	17	0	15	1	0	0	0	.000	0	0	7.45
Wayne, Hawkeye	Everett	Sea	A-	23	12	4	0	1	21.1	125	29	31	30	3	2	1	9	29	0	22	11	0	0	2	.000	0	0	12.66
Wayne, Justin	Jupiter	Mon	A+	22	5	5	0	0	26.1	112	26	22	17	2	1	1	0	11	0	24	1	0	0	3	.000	0	0	5.81
Weaver, Joe	Savannah	Tex	A	23	22	3	0	8	46.1	198	42	26	23	5	0	2	3	12	0	33	4	0	1	1	.500	0	1	4.47
Webb, Brandon	Diamondbcks	Ari	R	22	1	1	0	0	1	5	2	1	1	0	0	0	0	0	0	3	0	0	0	0	.000	0	0	9.00
	South Bend	Ari	A	22	12	0	0	7	16.2	69	10	7	6	0	0	0	2	9	1	18	1	0	0	0	.000	0	2	3.24
Webb, John	Lansing	ChC	A	22	21	21	1	0	134.2	559	125	53	37	4	3	6	8	40	0	108	9	1	7	6	.538	1	0	2.47
	Daytona	ChC	A+	22	4	2	0	1	17	71	17	11	9	1	0	0	0	3	0	18	2	0	1	1	.500	0	1	4.76
Webb, Nick*	Portland	Col	A-	21	16	6	0	3	43.2	215	52	37	27	3	3	3	1	29	1	52	7	2	0	1	.000	0	0	5.56
Weber, Brett	Yankees	NYY	R	24	4	0	0	3	5.2	19	4	0	0	0	0	0	0	0	0	5	0	0	0	0	.000	0	0	0.00
	Greensboro	NYY	A	24	16	0	0	10	17.1	71	14	5	5	0	0	1	0	6	0	18	1	0	0	0	.000	0	2	2.60
	Tampa	NYY	A+	24	14	0	0	5	15.1	64	15	10	10	0	0	1	0	6	2	19	1	0	0	1	.000	0	2	5.87
Webster, Jeremy*	Idaho Falls	SD	R+	22	21	0	0	2	30	145	31	23	15	3	0	1	4	24	1	28	3	0	5	4	.556	0	1	4.50
Wedel, Jeremy	Clearwater	Phi	A+	24	39	0	0	23	71.2	283	43	19	17	1	7	2	3	30	1	45	4	0	5	4	.556	0	9	2.13
Weis, John*	Quad City	Min	A	23	40	0	0	22	60	255	55	20	17	9	0	3	6	22	5	56	4	1	1	2	.333	0	0	2.55
Wellemeyer, Todd	Eugene	ChC	A-	22	15	15	0	0	76	315	62	35	31	3	1	1	4	33	2	85	3	1	4	4	.500	0	0	3.67
Wells, Carlton*	Missoula	Ari	R+	21	24	0	0	8	43.2	184	42	26	17	2	1	0	0	12	0	39	3	0	6	2	.750	0	1	3.50
Wells, Roy	Everett	Sea	A-	22	14	13	0	0	66	287	74	41	38	9	2	2	7	17	0	59	3	0	3	5	.375	0	0	5.18
Wells, Zach	Bakersfield	SF	A+	24	40	0	0	7	72	305	74	41	38	2	6	4	5	23	1	42	3	0	0	2	.000	0	0	4.75
Werner, Kelly*	Ogden	Mil	R+	24	1	1	0	0	2.1	16	4	6	6	1	0	1	1	5	0	0	0	0	0	0	.000	0	0	23.14
	Helena	Mil	R+	24	7	1	0	1	10.2	53	10	10	4	0	0	2	1	9	0	5	1	0	0	1	.000	0	0	3.38
Weslowski, Robert	Capital Cty	NYM	A	22	39	1	0	18	83.1	362	75	28	23	2	3	4	4	43	3	98	9	0	3	4	.429	0	7	2.48
West, Brian	Burlington	CWS	A	20	24	24	0	0	147.2	654	146	81	62	3	7	6	9	73	1	90	11	0	8	9	.471	0	0	3.78
	Winston-Sal	CWS	A+	20	2	2	0	0	6.1	37	10	12	8	2	0	0	0	6	1	3	1	1	0	1	.000	0	0	11.37
Westmoreland, Ken	Piedmont	Phi	A	26	7	7	0	0	33.2	147	33	23	16	2	1	0	2	18	0	21	2	0	2	2	.500	0	0	4.28
	Clearwater	Phi	A+	26	12	8	1	4	44.2	225	68	51	41	5	0	2	4	20	0	12	5	0	0	6	.000	0	1	8.26
Whatley, Brannon	Winston-Sal	CWS	A+	24	26	1	0	16	41.1	187	49	21	19	7	1	1	3	20	0	31	3	1	1	5	.167	0	2	4.14
Wheatland, Matt	Tigers	Det	R	19	5	4	0	1	21.2	84	14	4	3	1	0	1	1	1	0	21	2	0	2	1	.667	0	0	1.25
	Oneonta	Det	A-	19	5	5	0	0	24.1	107	30	18	15	1	1	1	2	4	0	25	2	2	1	2	.333	0	0	5.55
White, Bill*	Diamondbcks	Ari	R	22	4	1	0	0	6	25	3	4	4	0	0	1	0	5	0	9	3	0	0	1	.000	0	0	6.00
	South Bend	Ari	A	22	1	1	0	0	2.2	14	3	1	1	0	0	0	0	3	0	5	1	0	0	0	.000	0	0	3.38
White, Matt*	Kinston	Cle	A+	23	28	26	2	1	143.2	616	136	76	65	14	7	7	10	63	0	115	7	1	11	9	.550	0	0	4.07
Whiteaker, Gregg	Giants	SF	R	21	12	1	0	3	26.1	120	30	20	16	3	2	1	1	9	4	16	4	0	1	1	.500	0	2	5.47
Whitecotton, Billy	Bluefield	Bal	R+	20	9	8	1	0	49.1	188	35	12	9	2	1	0	3	16	0	33	0	1	2	2	.500	0	0	1.64
	Delmarva	Bal	A	20	6	6	0	0	28.1	125	32	18	18	4	0	2	2	17	0	25	3	0	1	1	.500	0	0	5.72
	Frederick	Bal	A+	20	1	0	0	0	2.2	10	2	0	0	0	0	0	0	1	0	2	0	0	0	0	.000	0	0	0.00
Whitesides, Johnny	Michigan	Hou	A	23	13	0	0	5	25.2	113	25	17	13	2	0	3	0	9	0	17	2	0	0	2	.000	0	1	4.56
	Kissimmee	Hou	A+	23	21	3	0	7	41.2	181	43	25	24	4	1	1	4	13	1	27	4	1	2	3	.400	0	1	5.18
Whitney, Jacob*	Kissimmee	Hou	A+	25	40	11	0	6	104	464	135	55	49	7	2	6	1	29	5	93	4	1	9	7	.563	0	3	4.24
Wiggins, Henry	Lansing	ChC	A	24	24	0	0	7	34.2	171	50	31	26	7	3	4	1	20	0	32	2	1	1	3	.250	0	1	6.75
Wiggins, Scott*	Tampa	NYY	A+	25	28	15	1	1	100.2	444	106	61	46	4	2	3	5	46	0	68	4	1	2	8	.200	1	0	4.11
Wiles, Chad	Mariners	Sea	R	23	17	0	0	15	33.1	133	25	7	5	0	1	0	1	8	1	36	0	0	3	0	1.000	0	7	1.35
	Wisconsin	Sea	A	23	2	0	0	2	2	6	0	0	0	0	0	0	0	0	0	1	0	0	0	0	.000	0	1	0.00
Wiley, Skip	Mariners	Sea	R	19	7	3	0	2	17	69	14	9	7	2	0	1	1	4	0	13	1	0	1	0	1.000	0	0	3.71
Wilkerson, Byron	Kissimmee	Hou	A+	24	30	2	0	18	56.1	264	64	34	27	1	1	2	10	28	1	43	1	0	1	2	.333	0	0	4.31
Wilkerson, George	Spokane	KC	A-	24	12	0	0	5	16.2	87	24	19	18	2	0	2	2	9	0	8	1	0	0	1	.000	0	0	9.72
Williams, Adam*	Vero Beach	LA	A+	22	27	23	0	0	124	593	161	110	92	14	4	7	9	68	0	72	8	3	5	12	.294	0	0	6.68
Williams, Blake	New Jersey	StL	A-	22	6	6	0	0	28.1	112	20	7	5	1	0	1	3	9	0	25	1	0	3	1	.750	0	0	1.59
Williams, Dave*	Hickory	Pit	A	22	24	24	1	0	170	687	145	66	56	14	11	2	9	39	2	193	4	0	11	9	.550	1	0	2.96
	Lynchburg	Pit	A+	22	2	2	0	0	11	51	18	8	8	2	1	0	0	3	0	8	2	0	1	0	1.000	0	0	6.55
Williams, Jerome	San Jose	SF	A+	19	23	19	0	2	125.2	512	89	53	41	6	5	6	10	48	3	115	9	2	7	6	.538	0	0	2.94
Williams, Justin	Idaho Falls	SD	R+	21	25	2	0	5	43	192	43	23	19	2	1	1	3	20	1	47	6	0	3	0	1.000	0	0	3.98
Williams, Larry	Lynchburg	Pit	A+	25	14	0	0	4	21.1	103	25	12	9	1	0	1	0	10	0	21	3	0	1	1	.500	0	0	3.80
Williams, Marcus	Reds	Cin	R	19	9	0	0	5	11	56	14	15	14	3	2	1	0	9	1	8	4	0	0	2	.000	0	0	11.45
Williams, Mike	Winston-Sal	CWS	A+	22	46	1	0	22	70	315	62	39	29	4	5	4	13	37	1	79	14	0	3	4	.429	0	1	3.73
Williams, Ruddy	Martinsvlle	Hou	R+	20	12	8	0	1	53.1	228	40	25	16	3	1	2	6	26	1	26	5	1	1	2	.333	0	1	2.70
Williamson, Charles	High Desert	Ari	A+	23	19	0	0	6	17	80	16	13	13	1	1	0	1	14	0	28	1	1	1	0	1.000	0	0	6.88
	Missoula	Ari	R+	23	1	0	0	0	0.2	5	1	2	2	0	1	0	1	1	1	0	0	0	0	0	.000	0	0	27.00
Willis, Dontrelle*	Cubs	ChC	R	19	9	1	0	3	28	118	26	15	12	0	1	2	1	8	1	22	0	0	3	1	.750	0	0	3.86
Willis, Jason	Staten Ilnd	NYY	A-	22	13	2	0	1	32	141	29	18	16	0	1	1	1	20	0	25	4	0	4	0	1.000	0	1	4.50
Willoughby, Justin*	Macon	Atl	A	23	38	6	0	13	76.1	337	79	46	43	2	3	3	0	35	0	64	3	0	3	6	.333	0	1	5.07
Wilson, Philip	Cedar Rapds	Ana	A	20	21	21	1	0	129.1	544	114	61	49	9	4	4	7	49	0	82	9	1	8	5	.615	0	0	3.41
	Lk Elsinore	Ana	A+	20	6	6	0	0	41.1	165	32	9	9	1	0	2	2	10	0	33	2	0	3	0	1.000	0	0	1.96
Wise, Eric	Expos	Mon	R	21	12	0	0	7	23.1	118	33	22	13	3	4	3	0	10	0	11	0	0	2	2	.500	0	1	5.01
Withelder, Greg*	Yakima	LA	A-	22	10	9	0	0	48.1	202	43	21	20	2	1	1	2	19	1	57	0	0	4	3	.571	0	0	3.72
Withers, Darvin	Vancouver	Oak	A-	21	13	6	0	1	41.1	166	27	10	8	0	1	2	1	16	2	33	3	0	2	1	.667	0	1	1.74

2000 Pitching — Class-A and Rookie Leagues

					HOW MUCH HE PITCHED						WHAT HE GAVE UP												THE RESULTS					
Player	Team	Org	Lg	A	G	GS	CG	GF	IP	BFP	H	R	ER	HR	SH	SF	HB	TBB	IBB	SO	WP	Bk	W	L	Pct.	ShO	Sv	ERA
Witte, Lou	Greensboro	NYY	A	24	31	0	0	15	50.1	232	66	38	27	4	1	2	0	15	3	31	2	0	3	3	.500	0	3	4.83
Wolensky, David	Boise	Ana	A-	21	15	15	0	0	76.1	317	60	29	26	1	0	1	2	35	1	88	3	0	8	3	.727	0	0	3.07
Wolfe, Brian	Quad City	Min	A	20	31	18	0	2	123.1	541	148	73	65	13	2	6	4	34	1	91	7	1	5	9	.357	0	0	4.74
Wombacher, Mike*	Staten IInd	NYY	A-	23	21	0	0	9	19.2	87	20	11	11	2	0	1	2	10	0	15	3	1	2	1	.667	0	1	5.03
Wood, Brandon	Diamondbcks	Ari	R	22	5	0	0	5	6.1	27	5	3	2	0	0	0	1	4	0	5	0	0	0	0	.000	0	2	2.84
	High Desert	Ari	A+	22	35	0	0	18	51.2	242	52	43	34	3	2	3	4	32	0	48	5	1	3	6	.333	0	2	5.92
Woodards, Orlando	Dunedin	Tor	A+	23	41	1	0	16	87.1	353	65	26	22	4	1	3	3	32	1	69	2	0	8	1	.889	0	7	2.27
Woodyard, Mark	Oneonta	Det	A-	22	11	9	0	1	51	243	48	32	26	0	1	0	6	39	0	38	6	0	1	5	.167	0	0	4.59
Wright, Barrett	Chston-SC	TB	A	22	5	5	0	0	26.1	123	34	19	17	1	0	2	1	12	0	10	3	1	0	2	.000	0	0	5.81
	St. Pete	TB	A+	22	3	0	0	2	4	19	5	3	3	0	0	0	1	2	0	3	0	0	0	0	.000	0	0	6.75
Wright, Chris	St. Pete	TB	A+	24	46	1	0	20	72	306	70	40	35	7	3	2	2	24	2	56	8	0	5	5	.500	0	3	4.38
Wright, Matt	Braves	Atl	R	19	12	0	0	10	21	85	8	5	2	0	2	0	1	11	0	30	2	0	2	0	.000	0	4	0.86
Wright, Raymond	Reds	Cin	R	21	3	0	0	1	2	21	4	10	9	0	0	0	1	10	0	3	7	0	0	0	.000	0	0	40.50
Wright, Shane	Hickory	Pit	A	24	32	1	0	14	75.2	352	99	54	42	7	3	4	6	20	1	58	5	0	3	3	.500	0	4	5.00
Wright, Shayne	Butte	Ana	R+	20	15	5	0	4	40	167	33	15	12	1	2	1	5	14	0	43	5	0	5	0	1.000	0	1	2.70
	Boise	Ana	A-	20	1	1	0	0	4.1	21	5	4	2	0	1	0	0	2	0	4	0	0	0	0	.000	0	0	4.15
Wrightsman, Dustin	Royals	KC	R	21	8	5	0	0	22.1	104	25	14	14	3	0	2	0	12	0	15	1	2	1	3	.250	0	0	5.64
Wrigley, Jase	Salem	Col	A+	25	47	0	0	36	61	250	52	26	18	3	5	2	1	22	1	38	4	0	3	2	.600	0	16	2.66
Wuertz, Mike	Daytona	ChC	A+	22	28	28	3	0	171.1	732	166	79	72	15	6	4	3	64	1	142	7	1	12	7	.632	2	0	3.78
Wylie, Mitch	Winston-Sal	CWS	A+	24	17	17	0	0	95.1	422	112	59	46	8	4	4	3	34	0	57	1	2	3	7	.300	0	0	4.34
Yates, Chad	Peoria	StL	A	24	17	0	0	17	15.2	60	7	5	3	0	1	1	1	6	1	13	1	0	1	0	.000	0	6	1.72
Yee, Damon	Auburn	Hou	A-	23	14	14	0	0	71.2	307	69	40	35	6	3	2	8	20	0	56	2	0	5	5	.500	0	0	4.40
Yen, Buddy	Chston-WV	KC	A	24	29	0	0	16	35.1	179	35	30	20	2	1	1	5	29	0	38	6	0	1	1	.500	0	0	5.09
Yoshida, Nobuaki*	Padres	SD	R	19	7	7	0	0	31	118	23	11	8	1	1	1	1	7	0	32	3	1	0	2	.000	0	0	2.32
	Idaho Falls	SD	R+	19	4	4	0	0	18	76	16	8	6	2	0	1	1	3	0	21	1	0	1	0	1.000	0	0	3.00
Young, Colin*	Asheville	Col	A	23	36	0	0	18	64	247	37	10	10	2	3	1	4	22	2	91	1	0	3	1	.750	0	2	1.41
Young, Curtis	Bristol	CWS	R+	21	15	0	0	7	16.2	87	22	19	16	0	0	1	1	16	0	26	6	0	0	1	.000	0	0	8.64
Young, Doug	Fort Wayne	SD	A	25	62	0	0	12	89.2	357	58	34	29	1	2	4	1	40	1	85	5	0	5	2	.714	0	0	2.91
Young, Simon*	Mahoning Vy	Cle	A-	23	14	13	0	0	77	295	62	20	15	1	1	1	4	21	0	56	3	1	7	2	.778	0	0	1.75
Yount, Andy	Lakeland	Det	A+	24	8	0	0	1	12.1	68	16	13	11	0	0	2	1	15	0	14	1	0	0	0	.000	0	0	8.03
Zaug, Kevin	White Sox	CWS	R	22	22	0	0	10	46.2	227	58	41	31	4	1	1	6	26	3	29	1	2	3	6	.333	0	1	5.98
Ziegler, Mike	Vancouver	Oak	A-	21	12	0	0	2	42.2	167	27	10	6	2	2	0	1	8	0	48	3	1	3	0	1.000	0	0	1.27
Zirelli, Mike	Bakersfield	SF	A+	24	40	3	1	5	103.2	453	110	52	47	13	7	1	7	28	1	61	1	1	8	4	.667	0	1	4.08
Zorrilla, Reinaldo	White Sox	CWS	R	19	20	0	0	6	23.1	119	25	18	17	3	0	0	0	28	0	22	7	0	1	0	1.000	0	0	6.56
Zurita, Thomas	Chston-WV	KC	A	21	14	0	0	4	25	116	29	20	16	0	1	3	2	11	0	14	4	1	1	2	.333	0	1	5.76
	Royals	KC	R	21	11	5	0	0	32.1	146	35	17	14	1	1	1	6	10	0	18	2	0	0	1	.000	0	0	3.90

2000 Team Statistics

How do the different leagues at a classification compare? This section answers that question, as team statistics for all 16 minor leagues follow. (A complete list of abbreviations can be found in the back of this book.)

For instance, a quick look at these numbers reveals that Triple-A hitters fare significantly better in the Pacific Coast League than in the International League.

The team stats also can help identify the most extreme parks in the minors. Check out the Texas League numbers, and you'll know why pitchers hate working in El Paso and Midland.

International League Batting - AAA

Team	Org	G	AB	H	2B	3B	HR	TB	R	RBI	TBB	IBB	SO	HBP	SH	SF	SB	CS	SB%	GDP	Avg	OBP	SLG
Louisville	Cin	144	4951	1350	305	28	157	2182	748	701	502	27	854	55	39	48	86	45	.66	126	.273	.343	.441
Durham	TB	143	4888	1387	281	27	143	2151	746	703	494	23	894	48	41	44	167	63	.73	113	.284	.352	.440
Buffalo	Cle	145	4755	1284	238	37	148	2040	743	692	546	10	932	39	37	46	86	40	.68	88	.270	.347	.429
Columbus	NYY	144	4784	1290	272	39	156	2108	729	686	541	21	913	42	30	38	132	60	.69	113	.270	.347	.441
Scranton-WB	Phi	145	4909	1341	270	50	113	2050	717	651	481	28	782	57	59	50	139	61	.70	104	.273	.342	.418
Pawtucket	Bos	143	4704	1163	220	24	185	1986	713	665	554	17	1028	79	42	38	67	31	.68	97	.247	.334	.422
Indianapolis	Mil	144	4860	1299	299	37	117	2023	704	657	531	32	959	41	40	48	121	42	.74	111	.267	.341	.416
Toledo	Det	141	4712	1225	259	20	168	2028	657	617	479	18	867	38	19	42	33	35	.49	124	.260	.330	.430
Norfolk	NYM	144	4841	1281	254	24	96	1871	654	603	529	26	873	60	50	42	152	93	.62	105	.265	.342	.386
Charlotte	CWS	143	4654	1224	227	24	119	1856	644	604	552	19	784	42	59	45	99	43	.70	126	.263	.343	.399
Syracuse	Tor	140	4659	1230	250	36	149	1999	632	609	384	15	798	42	29	36	136	63	.68	89	.264	.323	.429
Richmond	Atl	143	4820	1253	244	30	119	1914	626	598	421	17	943	51	58	32	95	57	.63	95	.260	.324	.397
Rochester	Bal	144	4874	1319	260	35	86	1907	622	578	455	17	856	41	39	41	74	47	.61	126	.271	.335	.391
Ottawa	Mon	141	4602	1187	260	29	80	1745	599	542	519	25	870	55	49	43	73	45	.62	112	.258	.337	.379
Total		1002	67013	17833	3639	440	1836	27860	9534	8906	6988	295	12353	690	591	593	1460	725	.67	1529	.266	.339	.416

International League Pitching - AAA

Team	Org	G	GS	CG	GF	IP	BFP	H	R	ER	HR	SH	SF	HB	TBB	IBB	SO	WP	Bk	W	L	Pct.	ShO	Sv	ERA
Scranton-WB	Phi	145	145	14	131	1281.1	5397	1184	567	517	112	55	30	42	466	25	936	43	6	85	60	.586	10	34	3.63
Syracuse	Tor	140	140	16	124	1208.2	5157	1137	583	523	112	37	37	40	515	10	825	42	5	74	66	.529	9	35	3.89
Charlotte	CWS	143	143	5	138	1230	5277	1233	605	541	149	42	30	51	439	24	847	57	13	78	65	.545	8	42	3.96
Pawtucket	Bos	143	143	11	132	1249.2	5242	1206	637	574	141	39	41	45	388	22	925	40	8	82	61	.573	9	33	4.13
Indianapolis	Mil	144	144	7	137	1270	5511	1239	644	560	132	58	43	54	530	23	879	73	5	81	63	.563	7	45	3.97
Norfolk	NYM	144	144	11	133	1270	5534	1299	647	596	113	42	40	55	508	44	895	75	9	65	79	.451	6	29	4.22
Buffalo	Cle	145	145	5	140	1235	5404	1319	654	589	125	40	41	46	456	21	838	55	6	86	59	.593	7	45	4.29
Rochester	Bal	144	144	6	138	1253.2	5397	1216	675	580	141	36	41	58	483	11	944	53	12	65	79	.451	8	31	4.16
Louisville	Cin	144	144	5	139	1277	5582	1321	698	611	116	41	50	34	529	20	880	62	6	71	73	.493	7	36	4.31
Durham	TB	143	143	0	143	1251	5516	1323	719	636	144	32	25	55	534	23	871	62	6	81	62	.566	8	50	4.58
Columbus	NYY	144	144	17	127	1245	5485	1271	720	623	132	43	52	40	531	26	970	69	22	75	69	.521	8	39	4.50
Richmond	Atl	143	143	3	140	1242	5563	1390	782	701	132	51	61	54	542	21	885	67	11	51	92	.357	2	23	5.08
Ottawa	Mon	141	141	1	140	1195.2	5411	1364	795	699	132	43	46	71	515	12	789	60	12	53	88	.376	5	31	5.26
Toledo	Det	141	141	8	133	1203	5402	1331	808	698	155	32	56	45	552	13	869	59	6	55	86	.390	6	22	5.22
Total		1002	1002	109	893	17412	75878	17833	9534	8448	1836	591	593	690	6988	295	12353	817	127	1002	1002	.500	100	495	4.37

Pacific Coast League Batting - AAA

Team	Org	G	AB	H	2B	3B	HR	TB	R	RBI	TBB	IBB	SO	HBP	SH	SF	SB	CS	SB%	GDP	Avg	OBP	SLG
Salt Lake	Min	143	5064	1580	358	42	185	2577	1016	970	562	13	865	49	34	70	85	36	.70	131	.312	.381	.509
Albuquerque	LA	144	5020	1506	310	44	170	2414	943	855	588	21	945	45	61	34	156	103	.60	106	.300	.376	.481
Sacramento	Oak	144	4956	1410	274	32	152	2204	864	796	691	28	968	54	28	49	161	67	.71	114	.285	.375	.445
Las Vegas	SD	143	4831	1364	333	36	130	2159	830	769	649	15	998	45	49	52	95	43	.69	107	.282	.369	.447
Col. Springs	Col	142	4812	1419	286	53	136	2219	823	764	573	27	959	38	67	57	149	63	.70	110	.295	.370	.461
Memphis	StL	144	4994	1318	266	33	149	2097	771	716	580	25	1001	62	45	40	106	49	.68	111	.264	.345	.420
Calgary	Fla	142	4873	1390	297	30	166	2076	768	710	436	16	1012	47	49	42	117	62	.65	103	.285	.347	.461
Tucson	Ari	141	4843	1399	300	46	95	2076	752	696	400	22	735	49	56	49	69	44	.61	125	.289	.346	.429
Oklahoma	Tex	143	4775	1289	249	40	124	1990	735	671	570	18	909	44	32	42	73	52	.58	131	.270	.350	.417
Iowa	ChC	144	4794	1267	277	20	161	2067	715	681	469	23	921	63	50	40	114	62	.65	104	.264	.335	.431
Tacoma	Sea	143	4835	1342	283	35	117	2046	696	638	510	20	865	58	45	48	120	56	.68	107	.278	.350	.423
Edmonton	Ana	144	4689	1239	260	50	130	1989	695	645	481	20	916	53	30	39	104	65	.62	100	.264	.337	.424
Fresno	SF	141	4793	1255	228	29	162	2027	692	641	484	16	947	34	44	33	100	59	.63	120	.262	.332	.423
Nashville	Pit	142	4821	1246	251	28	138	1967	681	639	458	9	1008	70	38	37	129	58	.69	99	.258	.329	.408
Omaha	KC	143	4741	1266	238	27	132	1954	658	600	446	14	754	57	47	45	135	70	.66	119	.267	.336	.412
New Orleans	Hou	142	4775	1233	210	34	81	1760	633	570	501	28	949	57	44	65	116	63	.65	131	.258	.333	.369
Total		1141	77616	21523	4420	582	2228	33791	12272	11365	8398	315	14752	835	711	720	1829	952	.66	1818	.277	.351	.435

Pacific Coast League Pitching - AAA

Team	Org	G	GS	CG	GF	IP	BFP	H	R	ER	HR	SH	SF	HB	TBB	IBB	SO	WP	Bk	W	L	Pct.	ShO	Sv	ERA
Memphis	StL	144	144	5	139	1301.2	5561	1275	659	574	118	63	40	48	513	19	906	39	7	83	61	.576	12	45	3.97
Tacoma	Sea	143	143	11	132	1244.1	5370	1243	676	579	120	35	31	45	503	25	999	51	12	76	67	.531	12	42	4.19
Sacramento	Oak	144	144	1	143	1273	5462	1291	681	588	133	37	41	36	452	17	940	59	8	90	54	.625	6	42	4.16
New Orleans	Hou	142	142	6	136	1266	5448	1260	688	581	118	54	37	55	462	32	934	43	5	68	74	.479	8	29	4.13
Tucson	Ari	141	141	3	138	1219.1	5448	1369	746	650	137	50	48	36	519	26	876	44	9	68	73	.482	4	34	4.80
Albuquerque	LA	144	144	7	137	1273.1	5664	1368	754	634	115	52	46	72	614	12	950	75	9	86	58	.597	8	36	4.48
Las Vegas	SD	143	143	6	137	1231.1	5501	1359	754	648	142	37	44	59	479	21	1034	47	5	73	70	.510	7	32	4.74
Oklahoma	Tex	143	143	14	129	1227.2	5438	1310	756	653	113	30	60	43	591	22	912	66	11	69	74	.483	8	30	4.79
Nashville	Pit	142	142	4	138	1252.2	5513	1279	758	668	140	61	39	64	577	32	854	91	7	63	79	.444	8	34	4.80
Omaha	KC	143	143	3	140	1230.1	5406	1352	771	687	184	26	45	58	487	22	875	64	9	64	79	.448	3	33	5.03
Edmonton	Ana	141	141	8	133	1214	5442	1316	774	691	124	23	52	49	549	6	828	74	7	63	78	.447	4	35	5.12
Salt Lake	Min	143	143	6	137	1266	5625	1449	795	697	151	30	41	45	465	18	936	67	12	90	53	.629	4	40	4.95
Col. Springs	Col	142	142	9	133	1229.1	5493	1363	811	721	144	52	47	62	482	10	928	73	9	74	68	.521	7	33	5.28
Iowa	ChC	144	144	4	140	1242.1	5600	1358	836	740	155	51	48	51	624	32	980	74	10	57	87	.396	4	29	5.36
Fresno	SF	141	141	1	140	1239	5600	1413	887	765	179	54	44	59	505	7	920	49	9	57	84	.404	1	35	5.56
Calgary	Fla	142	142	6	136	1228.1	5701	1518	926	818	155	56	57	53	576	14	880	76	7	60	82	.423	0	30	5.99
Total		1141	1141	94	1047	19938.2	88300	21523	12272	10694	2228	711	720	835	8398	315	14752	1007	136	1141	1141	.500	96	556	4.83

Eastern League Batting - AA

Team	Org	G	AB	H	2B	3B	HR	TB	R	RBI	TBB	IBB	SO	HBP	SH	SF	SB	CS	SB%	GDP	Avg	OBP	SLG
Portland	Fla	141	4674	1257	232	42	95	1858	736	677	555	17	957	69	45	48	145	78	.65	77	.269	.352	.398
Reading	Phi	142	4797	1269	262	29	138	2003	730	680	530	12	763	75	68	52	98	51	.66	92	.265	.344	.418
Trenton	Bos	142	4832	1314	258	29	108	1954	691	648	421	6	947	60	17	40	83	66	.56	110	.272	.335	.404
Altoona	Pit	142	4764	1257	230	31	113	1888	682	621	527	23	941	48	55	43	75	48	.61	93	.264	.340	.396
New Haven	Sea	142	4778	1274	253	40	95	1892	668	607	526	17	858	63	41	39	91	42	.68	111	.267	.345	.396
Bowie	Bal	142	4733	1255	246	32	87	1826	664	603	487	11	818	66	41	48	117	58	.67	111	.265	.339	.386
Akron	Cle	143	4804	1243	237	41	104	1874	656	609	503	15	948	50	38	41	110	56	.66	83	.259	.333	.390
Norwich	NYY	142	4743	1213	260	32	113	1876	653	617	530	23	1019	42	38	30	106	61	.63	102	.256	.334	.396
Binghamton	NYM	140	4498	1191	239	30	106	1808	650	592	389	15	1021	64	45	34	133	73	.65	93	.265	.330	.402
Harrisburg	Mon	143	4638	1166	217	54	62	1677	644	570	514	14	916	69	60	41	197	80	.71	84	.251	.332	.362
New Britain	Min	142	4721	1244	251	49	84	1845	631	589	484	16	883	63	28	33	67	38	.64	136	.264	.328	.391
Erie	Ana	141	4582	1136	206	39	89	1687	581	531	444	7	1006	76	45	38	125	66	.65	79	.248	.322	.368
Total		851	56564	14819	2891	448	1194	22188	7986	7344	5910	176	11077	745	521	487	1347	717	.65	1171	.262	.337	.392

Eastern League Pitching - AA

Team	Org	G	GS	CG	GF	IP	BFP	H	R	ER	HR	SH	SF	HB	TBB	IBB	SO	WP	Bk	W	L	Pct.	ShO	Sv	ERA
New Haven	Sea	142	142	10	132	1243.1	5224	1172	529	483	76	34	34	73	402	14	1043	70	10	82	60	.577	18	43	3.50
Reading	Phi	142	142	4	138	1269.1	5409	1211	596	535	115	54	28	56	451	16	987	44	9	85	57	.599	10	53	3.79
Binghamton	NYM	140	140	6	134	1184	5125	1140	609	519	86	40	42	58	487	5	957	57	10	82	58	.586	12	49	3.95
Norwich	NYY	142	142	14	128	1241.2	5420	1182	632	504	78	41	39	66	570	26	976	71	21	76	66	.535	11	35	3.65
Akron	Cle	143	143	4	139	1246	5404	1187	639	558	90	55	42	83	497	16	928	73	4	75	68	.524	5	32	4.03
Harrisburg	Mon	143	143	14	129	1229	5317	1230	647	553	115	45	44	61	457	11	775	47	4	76	67	.531	11	30	4.05
Bowie	Bal	142	142	10	132	1222.2	5352	1233	676	583	121	42	45	47	504	26	916	45	2	65	77	.458	9	34	4.29
Altoona	Pit	142	142	16	126	1244	5493	1223	696	561	67	45	43	61	565	20	856	65	11	74	68	.521	8	32	4.06
Trenton	Bos	142	142	8	134	1237	5385	1312	698	600	83	39	45	48	420	16	981	54	9	67	75	.472	8	29	4.37
Portland	Fla	141	141	14	127	1206.2	5342	1282	714	608	130	54	35	61	496	11	864	52	5	71	70	.504	8	34	4.53
Erie	Ana	141	141	10	131	1198.2	5360	1296	757	652	125	36	49	71	557	6	797	58	11	47	94	.333	5	22	4.90
New Britain	Min	142	142	5	137	1206.2	5425	1351	793	673	108	36	41	60	504	9	997	76	4	51	91	.359	4	21	5.02
Total		851	851	115	736	14729	64256	14819	7986	6829	1194	521	487	745	5910	176	11077	712	100	851	851	.500	109	414	4.17

Southern League Batting - AA

Team	Org	G	AB	H	2B	3B	HR	TB	R	RBI	TBB	IBB	SO	HBP	SH	SF	SB	CS	SB%	GDP	Avg	OBP	SLG
Chattanooga	Cin	138	4592	1171	229	37	115	1819	646	587	489	16	994	75	44	36	160	110	.59	81	.255	.334	.396
Tennessee	Tor	140	4686	1241	242	29	107	1862	640	584	494	23	880	70	50	46	105	72	.59	102	.265	.341	.397
Birmingham	CWS	140	4639	1168	224	25	94	1724	629	585	522	20	935	66	40	39	121	62	.66	94	.252	.333	.372
West Tenn	ChC	138	4595	1125	209	41	104	1728	609	549	486	23	1125	66	39	40	147	78	.65	88	.245	.324	.376
Huntsville	Mil	139	4561	1122	222	21	84	1638	603	547	565	19	1018	77	61	40	133	79	.63	84	.246	.336	.359
Jacksonville	Det	140	4628	1131	240	25	98	1715	594	546	518	11	1031	81	39	40	140	47	.75	94	.244	.328	.371
Mobile	SD	139	4707	1185	242	23	98	1767	591	553	492	19	912	56	44	42	71	54	.57	102	.252	.327	.375
Carolina	Col	139	4508	1149	215	28	70	1630	570	510	512	27	907	72	67	37	208	85	.71	95	.255	.338	.362
Greenville	Atl	139	4538	1054	225	16	117	1662	565	508	479	19	1048	55	36	35	126	49	.72	100	.232	.311	.366
Orlando	TB	136	4467	1121	194	30	66	1573	512	450	461	11	869	65	44	40	83	81	.51	88	.251	.327	.352
Total		694	45921	11467	2242	275	953	17118	5959	5419	5018	188	9719	683	464	391	1294	717	.64	928	.250	.330	.373

Southern League Pitching - AA

Team	Org	G	GS	CG	GF	IP	BFP	H	R	ER	HR	SH	SF	HB	TBB	IBB	SO	WP	Bk	W	L	Pct.	ShO	Sv	ERA
West Tenn	ChC	138	138	7	131	1238	5232	1013	493	423	84	58	38	54	546	18	1105	56	5	80	58	.580	15	43	3.08
Birmingham	CWS	140	140	7	133	1235.2	5169	1142	547	433	77	35	32	68	432	22	954	69	4	77	63	.550	13	36	3.15
Orlando	TB	136	136	8	128	1182	5031	1021	549	452	87	37	37	104	478	11	905	64	7	65	71	.478	10	37	3.44
Greenville	Atl	139	139	4	135	1217.1	5256	1184	581	509	92	48	50	41	518	21	961	62	3	68	71	.489	11	38	3.76
Carolina	Col	139	139	12	127	1199.1	5219	1162	605	515	87	45	37	66	500	11	992	89	1	64	75	.460	6	32	3.86
Chattanooga	Cin	138	138	11	127	1227.1	5329	1187	617	504	84	66	34	65	553	47	987	80	8	70	68	.507	7	37	3.70
Jacksonville	Det	140	140	4	122	1222	5253	1195	634	567	112	35	47	59	499	16	931	70	5	69	71	.493	10	33	4.18
Mobile	SD	139	139	3	136	1238	5318	1170	635	544	115	53	30	69	481	12	971	60	7	66	73	.475	10	35	3.95
Huntsville	Mil	139	139	2	137	1221.2	5338	1224	647	549	115	42	40	63	487	15	952	76	5	64	75	.460	13	41	4.04
Tennessee	Tor	140	140	7	133	1227.2	5376	1169	651	543	100	45	46	94	524	15	961	74	9	71	69	.507	8	34	3.98
Total		694	694	67	627	12209	52488	11467	5959	5039	953	464	391	683	5018	188	9719	700	54	694	694	.500	103	366	3.71

Texas League Batting - AA

Team	Org	G	AB	H	2B	3B	HR	TB	R	RBI	TBB	IBB	SO	HBP	SH	SF	SB	CS	SB%	GDP	Avg	OBP	SLG
Tulsa	Tex	141	4830	1335	284	36	136	2099	806	731	661	24	967	48	54	59	162	71	.70	98	.276	.365	.435
Midland	Oak	139	4835	1353	301	27	130	2098	788	738	599	21	937	72	27	58	86	61	.59	124	.280	.364	.434
El Paso	Ari	141	4801	1302	251	52	114	1999	759	690	543	32	1065	42	46	39	142	75	.65	115	.271	.348	.416
Round Rock	Hou	140	4781	1343	274	23	147	2104	745	706	523	30	1079	85	44	38	127	81	.61	102	.281	.359	.440
Wichita	KC	137	4635	1297	218	29	98	1867	725	656	544	26	793	83	50	48	187	87	.68	105	.280	.362	.403
Arkansas	StL	139	4692	1309	243	45	137	2053	696	644	434	27	916	65	44	33	73	61	.54	112	.279	.346	.438
San Antonio	LA	140	4638	1156	203	35	92	1705	612	558	509	25	964	45	69	34	157	72	.69	110	.249	.327	.368
Shreveport	SF	139	4591	1139	221	21	93	1681	572	534	436	21	957	56	52	37	80	52	.61	113	.248	.319	.366
Total		558	37803	10234	1995	268	947	15606	5703	5257	4249	206	7678	496	386	346	1014	560	.64	879	.271	.349	.413

Texas League Pitching - AA

Team	Org	G	GS	CG	GF	IP	BFP	H	R	ER	HR	SH	SF	HB	TBB	IBB	SO	WP	Bk	W	L	Pct.	ShO	Sv	ERA
Shreveport	SF	139	139	3	136	1212.2	5279	1264	631	531	110	61	49	41	466	44	931	41	12	58	81	.417	8	27	3.94
Wichita	KC	137	137	3	134	1204.2	5237	1229	661	565	134	35	30	64	505	32	905	66	11	76	61	.555	4	40	4.22
Round Rock	Hou	140	140	5	135	1245.1	5414	1224	671	569	130	55	40	48	546	19	1003	56	4	83	57	.593	11	38	4.11
San Antonio	LA	140	140	4	136	1231.1	5431	1264	707	601	108	62	48	81	552	21	1007	52	5	64	76	.457	9	29	4.39
Arkansas	StL	139	139	6	133	1196.1	5283	1240	723	627	131	52	47	56	538	35	904	62	7	68	71	.489	9	40	4.72
El Paso	Ari	141	141	1	140	1242.2	5525	1371	740	627	100	50	37	83	498	16	1018	67	7	74	66	.529	3	42	4.54
Midland	Oak	139	139	1	139	1243.2	5506	1307	766	636	110	36	40	61	531	28	981	76	5	70	69	.504	7	40	4.60
Tulsa	Tex	141	141	1	140	1238	5610	1335	804	668	124	35	55	62	613	11	928	91	3	64	76	.457	9	33	4.86
Total		558	558	24	534	9814.2	43285	10234	5703	4824	947	386	346	496	4249	206	7677	511	54	557	557	.500	60	289	4.42

California League Batting - A+

Team	Org	G	AB	H	2B	3B	HR	TB	R	RBI	TBB	IBB	SO	HBP	SH	SF	SB	CS	SB%	GDP	Avg	OBP	SLG
Lancaster	Sea	140	4882	1405	257	53	119	2125	933	860	655	15	1031	87	30	46	178	119	.60	99	.288	.379	.435
Bakersfield	SF	140	4702	1246	238	36	116	1904	807	703	622	14	1144	80	50	58	254	87	.74	77	.265	.357	.405
Lake Elsinore	Ana	140	4808	1296	245	53	81	1890	770	688	551	14	962	58	54	57	244	106	.70	84	.270	.348	.393
Modesto	Oak	140	4721	1211	247	33	88	1788	757	685	741	9	1212	69	45	45	156	69	.69	114	.257	.362	.379
Visalia	Oak	140	4634	1191	217	42	109	1819	754	658	658	22	1061	77	39	52	273	103	.73	91	.257	.355	.393
High Desert	Ari	140	4851	1313	254	50	112	2003	738	657	463	6	1100	46	23	40	128	92	.58	82	.271	.337	.413
San Bernardino	LA	140	4731	1252	228	52	89	1851	713	628	508	16	1006	67	64	48	207	121	.63	74	.265	.341	.391
Rancho Cuca.	SD	140	4825	1294	255	45	92	1915	703	636	472	20	1012	59	24	48	164	83	.66	138	.268	.338	.397
San Jose	SF	140	4744	1208	201	30	50	1646	656	597	569	14	982	76	53	43	196	89	.69	93	.255	.341	.347
Mudville	Mil	140	4606	1122	218	27	88	1658	604	516	487	13	1049	73	33	42	167	94	.64	87	.244	.323	.360
Total		700	47504	12538	2360	421	953	18599	7435	6628	5726	143	10559	692	415	479	1967	963	.67	939	.264	.348	.392

California League Pitching - A+

Team	Org	G	GS	CG	GF	IP	BFP	H	R	ER	HR	SH	SF	HB	TBB	IBB	SO	WP	Bk	W	L	Pct.	ShO	Sv	ERA
San Bernardino	LA	140	140	3	137	1253	5388	1220	604	519	79	43	36	81	519	14	1002	73	12	77	63	.550	5	37	3.73
Mudville	Mil	140	140	1	139	1235.1	5354	1106	638	529	83	35	43	73	605	8	1213	87	15	68	72	.486	9	31	3.85
Modesto	Oak	140	140	2	138	1240.1	5354	1213	668	538	71	49	54	53	493	39	1083	94	15	76	64	.543	7	46	3.90
Bakersfield	SF	140	140	1	137	1237.1	5457	1305	680	569	89	45	39	72	524	7	980	77	17	80	60	.571	7	46	4.14
Lancaster	Sea	140	140	1	139	1254.2	5500	1320	721	585	115	26	46	71	449	17	1064	73	14	89	51	.636	5	39	4.20
Visalia	Oak	140	140	2	138	1235.2	5414	1254	726	597	107	41	37	55	507	16	1143	66	15	78	62	.557	10	46	4.35
Lake Elsinore	Ana	140	140	6	134	1251.2	5515	1266	748	581	85	42	56	59	542	22	955	104	19	70	70	.500	7	29	4.18
Rancho Cuca.	SD	140	140	0	140	1249.2	5635	1153	808	673	93	50	53	71	774	6	1245	142	27	61	79	.436	5	33	4.85
San Jose	SF	140	140	2	138	1237.1	5593	1321	855	691	103	50	61	81	612	9	926	115	15	53	87	.379	4	28	5.03
High Desert	Ari	140	140	1	139	1215.1	5626	1380	987	828	128	34	54	76	701	5	948	100	21	48	92	.343	2	23	6.13
Total		700	700	19	681	12410.1	54836	12538	7435	6110	953	415	479	692	5726	143	10559	931	170	700	700	.500	61	358	4.43

Carolina League Batting - A+

Team	Org	BATTING															BASERUNNING				PERCENTAGES		
		G	AB	H	2B	3B	HR	TB	R	RBI	TBB	IBB	SO	HBP	SH	SF	SB	CS	SB%	GDP	Avg	OBP	SLG
Frederick	Bal	137	4472	1151	220	24	71	1632	658	582	597	19	974	64	60	49	202	82	.71	111	.257	.350	.365
Salem	Col	140	4625	1239	273	45	84	1854	654	595	405	4	866	63	25	44	140	66	.68	95	.268	.332	.401
Winston-Salem	CWS	139	4497	1104	267	33	96	1725	630	568	544	12	978	62	45	44	118	54	.69	97	.245	.332	.384
Kinston	Cle	137	4572	1189	258	31	83	1758	618	562	488	11	973	65	47	36	177	71	.71	96	.260	.338	.385
Potomac	StL	138	4517	1092	241	29	77	1622	597	531	447	6	1019	91	54	32	181	82	.69	94	.242	.320	.359
Lynchburg	Pit	138	4416	1105	213	30	95	1663	594	540	509	9	1128	64	46	43	145	51	.74	102	.250	.333	.377
Wilmington	KC	139	4551	1145	199	30	52	1560	584	519	475	9	981	81	60	37	127	51	.71	105	.252	.331	.343
Myrtle Beach	Atl	140	4502	1069	225	31	92	1632	567	503	431	8	1166	79	32	29	104	57	.65	64	.237	.313	.363
Total		554	36152	9094	1896	253	650	13446	4902	4400	3896	78	8085	569	369	314	1194	514	.70	764	.252	.331	.372

Carolina League Pitching - A+

Team	Org	HOW MUCH THEY PITCHED						WHAT THEY GAVE UP											THE RESULTS					
		G	GS	CG	GF	IP	BFP	H	R	ER	HR	SH	SF	HB	TBB	IBB	SO	WP	Bk	W	L	Pct.	ShO	Sv	ERA
Myrtle Beach	Atl	140	140	8	132	1205.2	4831	908	395	336	68	38	33	38	382	11	1089	64	9	88	52	.629	27	43	2.51
Salem	Col	140	140	9	131	1203	5276	1100	615	510	56	61	42	80	562	2	1088	92	17	73	67	.521	7	37	3.82
Kinston	Cle	137	137	7	130	1194.1	5173	1127	624	531	94	45	38	83	516	13	1105	58	9	68	69	.496	8	25	4.00
Wilmington	KC	139	139	4	135	1189	5146	1128	627	514	62	56	35	80	521	13	951	94	21	63	76	.453	12	27	3.89
Potomac	StL	138	138	2	136	1205.2	5230	1200	642	558	95	37	46	75	491	11	896	72	6	62	76	.449	9	40	4.17
Frederick	Bal	137	137	6	131	1187	5202	1225	658	545	105	36	44	73	441	9	1004	64	8	66	71	.482	1	27	4.13
Lynchburg	Pit	138	138	3	135	1170	5145	1222	668	557	98	50	40	53	460	12	920	66	3	66	72	.478	9	36	4.28
Winston-Salem	CWS	139	139	9	130	1200.1	5303	1184	673	549	72	46	36	87	523	7	1032	123	10	68	71	.489	7	34	4.12
Total		554	554	48	506	9555	41306	9094	4902	4100	650	369	314	569	3896	78	8085	632	86	554	554	.500	80	269	3.86

Florida State League Batting - A+

Team	Org	BATTING															BASERUNNING				PERCENTAGES		
		G	AB	H	2B	3B	HR	TB	R	RBI	TBB	IBB	SO	HBP	SH	SF	SB	CS	SB%	GDP	Avg	OBP	SLG
Dunedin	Tor	138	4642	1294	298	28	125	2023	760	703	529	19	1026	71	32	49	127	57	.69	104	.279	.358	.436
Charlotte	Tex	139	4707	1311	252	57	88	1941	748	663	562	19	863	88	40	37	119	70	.63	94	.279	.364	.412
St. Lucie	NYM	139	4691	1245	235	22	103	1833	702	641	475	31	965	72	41	48	189	85	.69	96	.265	.339	.391
Daytona	ChC	139	4693	1233	247	43	107	1887	696	622	460	17	905	71	38	53	145	86	.63	73	.263	.334	.402
Jupiter	Mon	140	4705	1237	205	40	61	1705	669	595	517	25	870	60	53	52	190	96	.66	93	.263	.340	.362
Vero Beach	LA	137	4590	1238	194	40	61	1695	661	594	417	13	819	69	30	51	177	71	.71	110	.270	.336	.369
Fort Myers	Min	140	4685	1243	254	31	63	1748	641	577	430	14	831	54	33	34	86	43	.67	125	.265	.332	.373
Kissimmee	Hou	139	4532	1147	253	33	87	1727	627	563	453	11	917	57	27	47	131	63	.68	111	.253	.326	.381
Sarasota	Bos	139	4537	1137	206	35	74	1623	596	513	436	18	935	67	31	40	125	91	.58	95	.251	.323	.358
Lakeland	Det	140	4607	1176	214	46	75	1707	589	518	426	18	1120	46	37	30	173	82	.68	92	.255	.323	.371
Brevard County	Fla	140	4630	1121	202	31	60	1565	581	515	552	25	914	64	37	42	128	56	.70	102	.242	.328	.338
Clearwater	Phi	135	4444	1141	237	41	41	1583	562	500	445	16	912	73	38	44	149	76	.66	91	.257	.331	.356
Tampa	NYY	140	4493	1095	229	21	100	1666	551	505	470	19	940	58	16	43	72	60	.55	94	.244	.320	.371
St. Petersburg	TB	139	4555	1162	236	33	57	1635	549	483	346	19	860	54	44	37	75	54	.58	106	.255	.313	.359
Total		972	64511	16780	3262	501	1098	24338	8932	7972	6518	264	12877	904	497	607	1886	990	.66	1386	.260	.334	.377

Florida State League Pitching - A+

Team	Org	HOW MUCH THEY PITCHED						WHAT THEY GAVE UP											THE RESULTS					
		G	GS	CG	GF	IP	BFP	H	R	ER	HR	SH	SF	HB	TBB	IBB	SO	WP	Bk	W	L	Pct.	Sv	ERA
Fort Myers	Min	140	140	5	135	1221	5177	1118	536	436	59	30	32	63	462	27	1037	84	7	83	57	.593	11	43	3.21
Tampa	NYY	140	140	11	129	1193.2	5065	1121	548	452	43	36	30	42	441	28	1023	61	10	70	70	.500	14	37	3.41
Clearwater	Phi	135	135	9	126	1167.2	5062	1227	594	486	61	33	33	49	428	8	750	55	12	64	71	.474	6	36	3.75
Dunedin	Tor	138	138	3	135	1205.2	5192	1089	595	481	87	31	44	62	573	26	887	92	10	84	54	.609	10	47	3.59
Kissimmee	Hou	139	139	6	133	1195.2	5161	1200	605	510	71	35	33	59	415	21	1026	62	10	73	66	.525	9	36	3.84
St. Lucie	NYM	139	139	4	135	1226	5275	1198	613	486	74	37	45	73	475	16	921	60	18	81	58	.583	14	37	3.57
Daytona	ChC	139	139	6	133	1233	5332	1172	615	511	84	46	33	46	532	24	1045	90	15	76	63	.547	7	37	3.73
Charlotte	Tex	139	139	11	128	1210	5263	1212	639	539	80	39	40	75	430	9	946	77	11	78	61	.561	7	36	4.01
Brevard County	Fla	140	140	4	136	1227.1	5263	1174	645	519	91	39	38	78	455	22	972	51	10	66	74	.471	11	34	3.81
St. Petersburg	TB	139	139	10	129	1176	5122	1182	676	553	69	28	51	64	446	12	840	86	7	58	81	.417	10	24	4.23
Sarasota	Bos	139	139	6	133	1198	5277	1296	684	570	85	48	47	77	390	30	977	46	7	60	79	.432	7	27	4.28
Lakeland	Det	140	140	8	132	1194.2	5308	1180	708	552	87	23	63	74	581	16	847	85	11	52	88	.371	3	31	4.16
Jupiter	Mon	140	140	4	136	1227	5358	1305	722	597	82	43	55	69	403	14	784	44	3	61	79	.436	5	27	4.38
Vero Beach	LA	137	137	6	131	1182	5282	1306	752	621	125	29	63	73	487	11	822	69	11	66	71	.482	4	39	4.73
Total		972	972	93	879	16857.2	73072	16780	8932	7313	1098	497	607	904	6518	264	12877	962	142	972	972	.500	118	491	3.90

Midwest League Batting - A

Team	Org	G	AB	H	2B	3B	HR	TB	R	RBI	TBB	IBB	SO	HBP	SH	SF	SB	CS	SB%	GDP	Avg	OBP	SLG
Michigan	Hou	138	4624	1245	255	36	80	1812	747	659	627	20	959	71	42	60	189	78	.71	99	.269	.361	.392
Dayton	Cin	137	4567	1201	271	15	114	1844	730	658	593	22	969	73	33	37	116	54	.68	120	.263	.354	.404
Wisconsin	Sea	138	4538	1126	222	28	90	1674	689	602	554	17	1087	81	48	51	164	85	.66	76	.248	.337	.369
West Michigan	Det	140	4592	1160	179	32	57	1574	685	584	545	14	1073	84	46	41	175	50	.78	98	.253	.343	.343
Clinton	Cin	140	4650	1182	238	19	99	1755	655	591	484	20	1078	71	34	42	149	66	.69	90	.254	.331	.377
South Bend	Ari	138	4520	1142	220	44	84	1702	654	574	582	21	928	65	47	36	192	73	.72	81	.253	.344	.377
Lansing	ChC	138	4616	1209	230	25	104	1801	642	596	456	20	863	81	30	42	156	70	.69	95	.262	.336	.390
Fort Wayne	SD	137	4477	1113	252	25	72	1631	598	528	508	20	992	64	23	33	112	51	.69	112	.249	.332	.364
Beloit	Mil	135	4395	1110	230	31	71	1615	594	527	425	17	943	77	87	38	126	57	.69	92	.253	.332	.367
Peoria	StL	137	4524	1095	240	36	85	1662	590	507	447	18	1078	56	57	29	144	70	.67	83	.242	.316	.367
Cedar Rapids	Ana	139	4530	1060	186	22	68	1494	588	516	542	20	996	62	49	39	160	77	.68	93	.234	.322	.330
Kane County	Fla	139	4446	1070	208	37	84	1604	586	521	538	25	1033	80	29	37	120	62	.66	98	.241	.331	.361
Quad City	Min	139	4535	1081	183	22	68	1512	581	517	489	16	858	97	56	42	77	51	.60	101	.238	.323	.333
Burlington	CWS	139	4501	1112	191	30	45	1498	542	462	427	10	873	46	43	33	215	93	.70	97	.247	.317	.333
Total		967	63515	15906	3105	402	1121	23178	8881	7842	7217	260	13730	1008	624	560	2095	937	.69	1335	.250	.334	.365

Midwest League Pitching - A

Team	Org	G	GS	CG	GF	IP	BFP	H	R	ER	HR	SH	SF	HB	TBB	IBB	SO	WP	Bk	W	L	Pct.	ShO	Sv	ERA
West Michigan	Det	140	140	9	131	1218.2	5205	1023	502	404	69	41	31	70	536	8	975	50	5	88	52	.629	19	40	2.98
Kane County	Fla	139	139	6	133	1188.2	5055	1184	571	489	83	53	32	60	353	5	942	78	4	74	65	.532	10	38	3.70
Fort Wayne	SD	137	137	1	136	1186.2	5083	1011	584	472	78	35	42	76	538	16	1140	80	14	72	65	.526	10	49	3.58
Beloit	Mil	135	135	4	131	1171	4990	1085	586	483	98	30	32	70	409	13	966	75	9	71	64	.526	9	37	3.71
Wisconsin	Sea	138	138	8	130	1204	5138	1087	587	457	74	43	33	93	487	21	1019	63	10	78	60	.565	9	37	3.42
Michigan	Hou	138	138	12	126	1206.2	5211	1064	607	504	85	40	44	77	568	20	992	91	6	82	56	.594	9	41	3.76
Quad City	Min	139	139	9	130	1200.2	5220	1155	620	490	84	42	34	72	509	43	1015	92	12	64	75	.460	8	35	3.67
Clinton	Cin	140	140	13	127	1223	5269	1128	641	522	70	48	44	36	566	29	1122	117	4	71	69	.507	9	34	3.84
South Bend	Ari	138	138	6	132	1183.2	5205	1149	659	534	65	43	45	76	542	23	930	82	13	60	78	.435	4	27	4.06
Peoria	StL	137	137	2	135	1191	5215	1139	665	497	62	57	37	61	484	37	880	89	9	63	74	.460	12	34	3.76
Lansing	ChC	138	138	8	130	1193.2	5320	1204	678	542	80	48	53	93	561	8	932	101	9	70	68	.507	8	35	4.09
Dayton	Cin	137	137	13	124	1199.1	5364	1259	716	595	93	35	41	80	519	5	983	100	9	70	67	.511	3	31	4.46
Burlington	CWS	139	139	9	130	1189.2	5321	1140	718	567	82	58	48	76	650	24	997	86	14	51	88	.367	8	27	4.29
Cedar Rapids	Ana	139	139	15	124	1201	5341	1278	747	595	98	51	44	58	495	8	837	101	9	53	86	.381	5	26	4.46
Total		967	967	115	852	16757.2	72937	15906	8881	7151	1121	624	560	1008	7217	260	13730	1205	127	967	967	.500	124	502	3.84

South Atlantic League Batting - A

Team	Org	G	AB	H	2B	3B	HR	TB	R	RBI	TBB	IBB	SO	HBP	SH	SF	SB	CS	SB%	GDP	Avg	OBP	SLG
Hickory	Pit	141	4935	1359	255	32	130	2068	762	689	456	15	1261	77	27	37	189	77	.70	86	.275	.344	.419
Piedmont	Phi	137	4600	1244	233	38	92	1829	709	626	455	11	1020	76	38	45	209	59	.78	90	.270	.343	.398
Delmarva	Bal	136	4557	1166	201	42	52	1607	700	590	551	12	908	71	55	37	188	68	.73	83	.256	.343	.353
Augusta	Bos	141	4676	1206	248	39	95	1817	692	609	494	16	1131	93	35	31	158	64	.71	105	.258	.339	.389
Charleston-SC	TB	139	4819	1265	266	32	83	1844	670	590	326	12	1079	91	29	43	145	43	.77	79	.263	.319	.383
Columbus	Cle	137	4569	1159	198	37	78	1665	651	562	497	7	1106	69	24	46	237	55	.81	85	.254	.333	.364
Cape Fear	Mon	138	4583	1158	209	37	54	1603	633	567	429	11	931	61	22	36	239	71	.77	87	.253	.323	.350
Greensboro	NYY	137	4605	1153	213	27	90	1690	630	566	483	8	1234	79	29	32	112	66	.63	74	.250	.330	.367
Macon	Atl	139	4675	1168	234	23	104	1760	626	574	473	9	1024	79	27	30	128	67	.66	89	.250	.327	.376
Hagerstown	Tor	137	4444	1088	204	31	67	1555	621	543	525	5	1056	86	30	31	152	65	.70	76	.245	.334	.350
Savannah	Tex	139	4518	1144	209	36	71	1638	585	512	467	11	923	71	51	47	202	79	.72	87	.253	.330	.363
Asheville	Col	135	4444	1085	229	14	114	1684	560	503	435	8	1228	82	18	26	193	105	.62	82	.244	.321	.379
Capital City	NYM	137	4511	1113	225	26	48	1534	533	458	444	11	1039	83	36	33	185	80	.70	71	.247	.323	.340
Charleston-WV	KC	133	4274	1010	179	37	46	1401	505	449	480	6	966	72	42	33	114	56	.67	106	.236	.321	.328
Total		963	64210	16318	3103	451	1124	23695	8877	7838	6515	142	14906	1090	463	507	2420	955	.72	1200	.254	.331	.369

South Atlantic League Pitching - A

Team	Org	G	GS	CG	GF	IP	BFP	H	R	ER	HR	SH	SF	HB	TBB	IBB	SO	WP	Bk	W	L	Pct.	ShO	Sv	ERA
Piedmont	Phi	137	137	10	127	1195.2	5026	1030	492	387	62	34	39	84	455	8	1031	63	5	90	47	.657	13	39	2.91
Savannah	Tex	139	139	7	132	1207.2	5147	1033	551	472	83	23	33	72	507	5	1061	83	7	74	65	.532	12	31	3.52
Delmarva	Bal	136	136	3	133	1189.1	5134	1190	603	512	64	28	24	58	426	15	1100	75	11	74	62	.544	5	27	3.87
Asheville	Col	135	135	6	129	1187.1	5113	1171	605	504	86	28	31	93	413	6	1196	57	4	66	69	.489	9	38	3.82
Augusta	Bos	141	141	2	139	1229	5280	1155	607	471	77	39	38	70	461	5	1125	82	2	83	58	.589	10	47	3.45
Macon	Atl	139	139	6	133	1219.1	5187	1112	613	477	91	33	42	62	442	8	1072	61	9	69	70	.496	9	29	3.52
Charleston-WV	KC	133	133	5	128	1139.2	4949	1134	628	482	72	26	31	57	434	2	895	64	11	53	80	.398	9	29	3.81
Columbus	Cle	137	137	2	135	1196.1	5255	1223	647	540	79	47	47	82	485	16	1049	71	3	59	81	.489	5	39	4.06
Charleston-SC	TB	139	139	9	130	1236.1	5368	1237	648	516	84	36	33	64	427	16	1149	110	7	73	66	.525	7	37	3.76
Hagerstown	Tor	137	137	5	132	1167.2	5087	1184	681	526	85	33	39	90	460	13	896	99	6	63	74	.460	3	34	4.05
Capital City	NYM	137	137	1	136	1179.2	5193	1128	682	563	78	24	42	105	543	15	1206	140	4	56	81	.409	6	34	4.30
Greensboro	NYY	137	137	3	130	1180.2	5222	1222	697	561	87	36	26	77	509	15	1025	113	8	56	81	.409	2	27	4.28
Hickory	Pit	141	141	12	129	1266.2	5554	1270	709	527	96	43	41	90	447	10	1148	62	7	75	66	.532	6	34	3.74
Cape Fear	Mon	138	138	3	135	1195	5291	1229	714	564	80	33	41	86	506	8	953	94	9	64	74	.464	3	33	4.25
Total		963	963	78	885	16790.1	72806	16318	8877	7102	1124	463	507	1090	6515	142	14906	1174	93	963	963	.500	99	473	3.81

New York-Penn League Batting - A-

Team	Org	G	AB	H	2B	3B	HR	TB	R	RBI	TBB	IBB	SO	HBP	SH	SF	SB	CS	SB%	GDP	Avg	OBP	SLG
Mahoning Vlly	Cle	76	2539	633	112	42	39	946	432	359	347	8	578	83	31	20	92	44	.68	49	.249	.356	.373
Vermont	Mon	75	2554	645	101	21	18	842	407	302	309	8	546	56	16	25	184	59	.76	39	.253	.343	.330
Jamestown	Atl	75	2588	702	136	32	47	1043	383	342	236	9	561	30	9	33	56	29	.66	49	.271	.335	.403
Staten Island	NYY	74	2506	662	140	19	40	960	375	325	291	5	560	50	22	24	61	29	.68	48	.264	.349	.383
Queens	Tor	75	2538	637	106	25	25	868	364	321	328	6	530	31	19	24	88	40	.69	52	.251	.341	.342
Utica	Fla	75	2509	635	132	18	35	908	361	311	291	7	589	40	12	18	86	54	.61	45	.253	.338	.362
Oneonta	Det	76	2494	652	88	34	21	871	355	309	326	7	609	49	17	22	88	47	.65	53	.261	.355	.349
Batavia	Phi	76	2557	634	107	19	32	875	354	312	278	3	537	36	18	30	128	26	.83	45	.248	.327	.342
Pittsfield	NYM	75	2409	602	112	26	14	808	336	267	248	9	535	51	37	22	155	50	.76	30	.250	.330	.335
Auburn	Hou	74	2440	584	113	24	27	826	305	260	192	5	553	37	12	15	96	47	.67	38	.239	.303	.339
Hudson Valley	TB	75	2412	576	100	13	22	768	298	251	234	3	647	24	21	27	91	56	.62	49	.239	.309	.318
Lowell	Bos	75	2458	575	93	16	24	772	292	242	272	5	579	28	24	19	68	36	.65	26	.234	.315	.314
Williamsport	Pit	73	2435	566	90	20	27	777	280	240	226	4	547	45	18	19	75	28	.73	51	.232	.307	.319
New Jersey	StL	76	2432	517	90	15	14	679	264	216	280	5	585	32	27	22	156	55	.74	48	.213	.300	.279
Total		525	34871	8620	1520	324	385	11943	4806	4057	3858	84	7956	592	283	320	1424	600	.70	622	.247	.330	.342

New York-Penn League Pitching - A-

Team	Org	G	GS	CG	GF	IP	BFP	H	R	ER	HR	SH	SF	HB	TBB	IBB	SO	WP	Bk	W	L	Pct.	ShO	Sv	ERA
Staten Island	NYY	74	74	3	71	654.1	2688	542	258	207	19	20	9	31	217	3	602	56	12	46	28	.622	5	22	2.85
Lowell	Bos	75	75	3	72	664.2	2763	600	290	227	10	33	22	25	213	3	590	44	8	41	34	.547	7	26	3.07
Queens	Tor	75	75	1	74	671.1	2853	568	304	235	23	21	31	40	295	5	663	62	5	46	29	.613	4	19	3.15
Pittsfield	NYM	75	75	2	73	647.2	2805	580	324	252	19	15	17	50	300	5	620	47	11	38	37	.507	4	19	3.50
Vermont	Mon	75	75	1	74	676.2	2879	572	325	238	31	14	26	40	299	0	548	42	7	45	30	.600	7	20	3.17
Mahoning Vlly	Cle	76	76	0	76	676.1	2892	646	328	279	33	14	26	35	257	3	537	52	10	48	28	.632	5	14	3.71
Auburn	Hou	74	74	0	74	645.1	2813	569	330	250	28	23	20	64	279	7	562	58	8	32	42	.432	2	18	3.49
Batavia	Phi	76	76	8	68	667	2891	633	356	288	29	25	18	52	263	22	500	53	11	39	37	.513	5	20	3.89
Oneonta	Det	76	76	3	73	649.2	2873	644	365	293	25	19	25	39	264	7	545	58	12	35	41	.461	1	13	4.06
Utica	Fla	75	75	0	75	650.1	2860	636	365	289	43	25	21	32	287	5	552	69	11	35	40	.467	3	16	4.00
Jamestown	Atl	75	75	0	75	648.2	2854	646	367	272	40	16	19	29	275	5	543	34	9	37	38	.493	4	20	3.77
Williamsport	Pit	73	73	2	71	639.2	2858	637	369	279	33	19	33	52	311	1	549	33	15	29	44	.397	3	12	3.93
Hudson Valley	TB	75	75	3	72	647.1	2909	659	411	301	26	21	27	47	282	16	567	64	10	29	45	.392	3	11	4.18
New Jersey	StL	76	76	0	76	665.1	3001	688	414	329	26	18	26	56	316	2	578	79	1	31	45	.408	3	21	4.45
Total		525	525	26	499	9204.1	39939	8620	4806	3739	385	283	320	592	3858	84	7956	751	130	525	525	.500	56	251	3.66

Northwest League Batting - A-

Team	Org	G	AB	H	2B	3B	HR	TB	R	RBI	TBB	IBB	SO	HBP	SH	SF	SB	CS	SB%	GDP	Avg	OBP	SLG
Boise	Ana	76	2665	686	146	14	53	1019	440	382	348	7	687	59	22	16	102	29	.78	58	.257	.354	.382
Spokane	KC	76	2559	647	117	12	35	893	389	341	340	8	629	50	36	23	80	30	.73	52	.253	.349	.349
Everett	Sea	76	2610	637	111	15	46	916	376	327	317	18	685	36	23	17	141	60	.70	38	.244	.332	.351
Salem-Keizer	SF	76	2653	667	127	22	26	916	361	313	279	7	584	40	31	21	52	25	.68	46	.251	.329	.345
Vancouver	Oak	76	2511	597	124	11	21	806	344	303	336	12	649	48	25	21	47	28	.63	44	.238	.336	.321
Eugene	ChC	76	2574	627	129	22	47	941	340	306	296	7	615	49	20	26	120	48	.71	43	.244	.330	.366
Yakima	LA	76	2535	646	121	15	34	899	326	294	250	14	583	45	47	19	109	56	.66	52	.255	.330	.355
Portland	Col	76	2531	606	120	22	31	863	317	280	264	8	664	36	16	23	69	41	.63	44	.239	.317	.341
Total		304	20638	5113	995	133	293	7253	2893	2546	2430	81	5096	363	220	166	720	317	.69	377	.248	.335	.351

Northwest League Pitching - A-

Team	Org	G	GS	CG	GF	IP	BFP	H	R	ER	HR	SH	SF	HB	TBB	IBB	SO	WP	Bk	W	L	Pct.	ShO	Sv	ERA
Eugene	ChC	76	76	1	75	688.2	2904	583	314	259	30	26	18	32	264	14	707	37	8	40	36	.526	8	24	3.38
Yakima	LA	76	76	0	76	681.1	2882	628	322	268	41	25	13	32	215	9	687	41	8	41	35	.539	6	20	3.54
Vancouver	Oak	76	76	0	76	671.1	2877	585	322	242	23	31	14	40	260	13	603	67	9	39	37	.513	7	22	3.24
Spokane	KC	76	76	0	76	677	2961	642	347	284	29	28	19	41	315	8	596	62	13	38	38	.500	3	19	3.78
Portland	Col	76	76	0	76	657	2927	621	362	278	35	24	21	47	314	13	541	40	12	32	44	.421	7	12	3.81
Salem-Keizer	SF	76	76	0	76	681.1	3100	669	386	319	49	34	26	56	401	2	631	74	10	36	40	.474	4	21	4.21
Everett	Sea	76	76	0	76	681.1	3095	669	399	310	50	32	26	57	329	7	716	80	5	37	39	.487	4	14	4.03
Boise	Ana	76	76	0	76	685.2	3087	716	441	360	36	20	29	58	332	15	615	48	8	41	35	.539	2	23	4.73
Total		304	304	1	303	5434	23833	5113	2893	2320	293	220	166	363	2430	81	5096	449	73	304	304	.500	41	155	3.84

Appalachian League Batting - R+

Team	Org	G	AB	H	2B	3B	HR	TB	R	RBI	TBB	IBB	SO	HBP	SH	SF	SB	CS	SB%	GDP	Avg	OBP	SLG
Pulaski	Tex	68	2204	560	107	19	57	876	412	346	340	3	568	42	24	20	112	33	.77	34	.254	.361	.397
Elizabethton	Min	64	2137	549	106	16	46	825	378	332	254	4	461	45	22	17	75	28	.73	28	.257	.346	.386
Bluefield	Bal	63	2068	544	100	19	49	829	344	284	265	2	554	32	11	20	61	16	.79	49	.263	.353	.401
Danville	Atl	66	2234	596	108	22	38	862	341	290	235	4	509	36	16	23	95	42	.69	46	.267	.343	.386
Johnson City	StL	68	2221	553	98	13	44	809	335	272	225	6	537	49	19	16	95	46	.67	46	.249	.329	.364
Kingsport	NYM	67	2159	567	114	21	49	870	334	290	254	4	540	41	36	19	145	72	.67	33	.263	.349	.403
Bristol	CWS	67	2211	591	101	27	26	824	319	278	192	4	416	38	30	20	93	33	.74	39	.267	.334	.373
Martinsville	Hou	66	2131	538	125	24	36	819	317	265	225	1	471	50	5	15	114	43	.73	36	.252	.336	.384
Princeton	TB	68	2196	569	108	21	26	797	292	245	191	1	555	33	15	19	53	35	.60	52	.259	.325	.363
Burlington	Cle	67	2195	529	88	10	29	724	282	248	220	0	513	37	10	14	102	37	.73	44	.241	.319	.330
Total		332	21756	5596	1055	192	400	8235	3354	2850	2401	29	5124	403	188	183	945	385	.71	407	.257	.339	.379

Appalachian League Pitching - R+

Team	Org	G	GS	CG	GF	IP	BFP	H	R	ER	HR	SH	SF	HB	TBB	IBB	SO	WP	Bk	W	L	Pct.	ShO	Sv	ERA
Pulaski	Tex	68	68	3	65	574.2	2451	503	276	210	20	16	19	43	223	4	582	50	8	40	28	.588	2	14	3.29
Elizabethton	Min	64	64	4	60	558.1	2365	481	279	236	42	17	13	33	248	2	536	64	8	46	18	.719	7	16	3.80
Danville	Atl	66	66	3	63	589.2	2545	577	294	249	33	24	18	29	226	1	531	46	8	37	29	.561	2	22	3.80
Kingsport	NYM	67	67	2	65	581.1	2537	567	305	236	32	23	8	42	207	5	480	56	8	35	32	.522	1	17	3.65
Bristol	CWS	67	67	3	64	564.2	2428	535	311	252	41	23	22	36	221	8	537	63	5	34	33	.507	1	19	4.02
Princeton	TB	68	68	1	67	571.1	2553	588	327	254	39	18	19	38	256	1	534	74	4	34	34	.500	3	21	4.00
Martinsville	Hou	66	66	1	65	559.2	2468	524	358	271	46	15	15	51	271	5	504	58	8	30	36	.455	3	13	4.36
Bluefield	Bal	63	63	1	62	524.2	2385	612	379	310	53	14	20	56	228	0	428	45	11	31	32	.492	2	12	5.32
Johnson City	StL	68	68	1	67	580.1	2635	625	409	320	46	15	18	29	263	3	489	57	6	24	44	.353	2	11	4.96
Burlington	Cle	67	67	0	67	568	2569	584	416	294	48	23	31	46	258	0	503	88	12	21	46	.313	3	10	4.66
Total		332	332	19	313	5672.2	24936	5596	3354	2632	400	188	183	403	2401	29	5124	601	78	332	332	.500	26	155	4.18

Pioneer League Batting - R+

Team	Org	G	AB	H	2B	3B	HR	TB	R	RBI	TBB	IBB	SO	HBP	SH	SF	SB	CS	SB%	GDP	Avg	OBP	SLG
Idaho Falls	SD	74	2684	850	170	24	75	1293	585	497	395	11	569	38	5	33	78	40	.66	74	.317	.407	.482
Ogden	Mil	75	2696	788	151	26	59	1168	531	454	322	12	460	61	23	24	115	42	.73	50	.292	.377	.433
Billings	Cin	75	2652	749	120	23	68	1119	513	443	308	7	564	67	14	23	93	32	.74	57	.282	.369	.422
Butte	Ana	76	2655	749	137	33	53	1111	486	413	340	4	551	46	26	29	73	32	.70	57	.282	.370	.418
Medicine Hat	Tor	76	2660	703	125	21	58	1044	457	378	382	12	563	43	20	9	50	20	.71	52	.264	.365	.392
Missoula	Ari	76	2567	663	125	34	43	985	429	348	327	6	583	53	11	29	132	49	.73	50	.258	.350	.384
Great Falls	LA	76	2513	629	86	26	33	866	394	341	296	5	598	41	37	21	129	44	.75	41	.250	.336	.345
Helena	Mil	76	2545	637	127	18	36	908	377	298	289	2	644	46	21	18	105	51	.67	41	.250	.335	.357
Total		302	20972	5768	1041	205	425	8494	3772	3172	2659	59	4532	395	157	186	775	310	.71	422	.275	.364	.405

Pioneer League Pitching - R+

Team	Org	G	GS	CG	GF	IP	BFP	H	R	ER	HR	SH	SF	HB	TBB	IBB	SO	WP	Bk	W	L	Pct.	ShO	Sv	ERA
Missoula	Ari	76	76	1	75	668.1	2969	640	396	291	28	20	11	56	303	4	618	65	10	44	32	.579	4	16	3.92
Great Falls	LA	76	76	2	74	658.2	2983	670	416	330	42	14	18	48	333	3	618	77	4	42	34	.553	3	18	4.51
Medicine Hat	Tor	76	76	0	76	669.1	2995	711	443	339	57	29	29	38	273	4	574	83	5	36	40	.474	1	17	4.56
Idaho Falls	SD	74	74	0	74	655	2988	742	453	365	56	19	19	50	288	5	561	71	8	45	29	.608	1	16	5.02
Ogden	Mil	75	75	1	74	667.1	3048	736	456	361	73	17	35	42	309	7	588	63	9	41	34	.547	5	25	4.87
Billings	Cin	75	75	0	75	659.1	3101	702	504	422	59	18	22	53	441	5	557	96	9	39	36	.520	0	18	5.76
Helena	Mil	76	76	0	76	663	3109	734	513	401	57	24	26	55	378	22	515	102	14	26	50	.342	0	14	5.44
Butte	Ana	76	76	2	74	656.1	3181	831	591	426	53	16	26	53	334	7	501	98	11	29	47	.382	1	13	5.84
Total		302	302	6	296	5297.1	24374	5766	3772	2935	425	157	186	395	2659	59	4532	655	70	302	302	.500	15	137	4.99

Arizona League Batting - R

Team	Org	G	AB	H	2B	3B	HR	TB	R	RBI	TBB	IBB	SO	HBP	SH	SF	SB	CS	SB%	GDP	Avg	OBP	SLG
Rockies	Col	54	1917	592	102	50	33	893	417	356	235	0	446	48	5	19	91	33	.73	24	.309	.394	.466
Mariners	Sea	55	2009	634	117	16	29	870	408	341	195	6	330	43	14	32	60	25	.71	27	.316	.383	.433
Athletics	Oak	54	1915	550	106	32	26	798	403	326	298	4	421	27	15	17	87	27	.76	39	.287	.388	.417
White Sox	CWS	55	1919	571	124	27	9	776	381	314	267	4	389	28	7	26	143	53	.73	33	.298	.387	.404
Cubs	ChC	56	1969	582	104	44	25	849	371	328	189	7	411	32	20	25	61	36	.63	32	.296	.363	.431
Diamondbacks	Ari	54	1846	494	92	29	18	698	314	257	217	1	443	27	17	19	58	38	.60	22	.268	.350	.378
Mex. All-Stars	IND	55	1835	480	90	21	14	654	305	223	252	1	333	33	9	27	44	19	.70	41	.262	.356	.356
Giants	SF	54	1840	463	64	19	13	604	273	203	187	3	355	32	29	22	117	63	.65	36	.264	.342	.345
Padres	SD	55	1840	443	78	15	11	584	252	206	173	6	403	52	16	17	71	27	.72	37	.241	.321	.317
Total		246	17001	4809	877	253	178	6726	3124	2554	2013	32	3531	322	132	204	732	321	.70	291	.283	.366	.396

Arizona League Pitching - R

Team	Org	G	GS	CG	GF	IP	BFP	H	R	ER	HR	SH	SF	HB	TBB	IBB	SO	WP	Bk	W	L	Pct.	ShO	Sv	ERA
Rockies	Col	54	54	0	54	461	2054	447	271	196	12	10	25	21	215	2	332	37	13	35	19	.648	2	7	3.83
Mariners	Sea	55	55	0	55	481	2087	457	276	219	17	7	16	29	197	1	478	49	4	39	16	.709	6	14	4.10
Athletics	Oak	54	54	0	54	474	2143	567	336	246	29	20	29	36	140	4	334	38	7	29	25	.537	1	14	4.67
Cubs	ChC	56	56	0	56	495.1	2304	558	344	271	15	22	26	54	237	3	394	54	8	32	24	.571	2	13	4.92
Giants	SF	54	54	1	53	463	2146	531	354	281	19	24	21	50	187	12	364	46	11	22	32	.407	1	13	5.46
Diamondbacks	Ari	54	54	0	54	472.2	2196	507	358	260	13	4	16	35	278	2	394	48	20	27	27	.500	3	9	4.95
Mex. All-Stars	IND	55	55	8	47	467.1	2220	598	383	344	22	8	23	41	243	0	419	59	12	23	32	.418	2	6	6.62
Padres	SD	55	55	0	55	479.2	2247	571	383	298	21	23	27	23	232	4	397	47	10	17	38	.309	2	10	5.59
White Sox	CWS	55	55	0	55	476	2279	573	419	312	30	14	21	33	284	4	419	64	10	22	33	.400	2	10	5.90
Total		246	246	9	237	4270	19676	4809	3124	2427	178	132	204	322	2013	32	3531	442	95	246	246	.500	21	96	5.12

Gulf Coast League Batting - R

Team	Org	G	AB	H	2B	3B	HR	TB	R	RBI	TBB	IBB	SO	HBP	SH	SF	SB	CS	SB%	GDP	Avg	OBP	SLG
Twins	Min	56	1796	495	91	10	16	654	345	273	297	13	320	40	29	19	77	32	.71	46	.276	.387	.364
Rangers	Tex	56	1856	483	100	11	19	662	318	266	280	14	370	45	29	20	51	23	.69	28	.260	.367	.357
Marlins	Fla	60	1987	526	114	18	21	739	316	262	254	6	502	40	4	21	55	17	.76	44	.265	.356	.372
Yankees	NYY	60	1925	510	115	19	35	768	311	278	242	1	399	44	7	28	43	18	.70	34	.265	.356	.399
Red Sox	Bos	55	1832	505	84	8	49	752	297	252	198	7	371	41	1	15	90	27	.77	45	.276	.357	.410
Pirates	Pit	60	1951	494	104	17	29	719	295	250	184	1	428	36	11	16	83	25	.77	33	.253	.326	.369
Phillies	Phi	60	1953	502	93	12	26	697	269	229	163	2	353	43	20	17	72	26	.73	43	.257	.325	.357
Orioles	Bal	56	1810	474	77	18	22	653	266	214	207	11	392	41	33	23	92	34	.73	39	.262	.347	.361
Tigers	Det	60	1852	432	58	15	21	583	265	213	244	3	529	43	10	19	90	25	.78	29	.233	.333	.315
Braves	Atl	60	1890	428	85	11	19	592	251	204	198	2	458	47	5	13	36	25	.59	21	.226	.313	.313
Expos	Mon	60	1961	462	60	16	12	590	270	170	156	0	420	42	18	9	37	22	.63	45	.236	.304	.301
Royals	KC	60	1778	374	47	10	9	468	195	158	227	6	365	34	27	14	50	23	.68	43	.210	.309	.263
Reds	Cin	55	1736	387	67	16	6	504	188	156	201	8	470	25	15	5	59	43	.58	29	.223	.312	.290
Total		379	24327	6072	1095	181	284	8381	3526	2925	2851	74	5377	521	209	219	835	340	.71	479	.250	.338	.345

Gulf Coast League Pitching - R

Team	Org	G	GS	CG	GF	IP	BFP	H	R	ER	HR	SH	SF	HB	TBB	IBB	SO	WP	Bk	W	L	Pct.	ShO	Sv	ERA
Yankees	NYY	60	60	0	60	493.2	2129	465	227	178	13	9	16	28	180	1	429	31	7	38	22	.633	8	18	3.25
Marlins	Fla	60	60	2	58	514.1	2226	440	232	186	20	11	18	57	209	7	450	49	12	40	20	.667	6	16	3.25
Twins	Min	56	56	5	51	470	2040	439	236	179	18	24	14	41	195	5	423	42	2	33	23	.589	3	9	3.43
Tigers	Det	60	60	4	56	488.1	2125	429	245	201	19	12	18	33	224	5	460	49	6	34	26	.567	7	23	3.70
Phillies	Phi	60	60	3	57	503	2186	487	252	187	29	13	10	28	167	2	442	44	8	31	29	.517	6	15	3.35
Rangers	Tex	56	56	0	56	492	2138	476	253	206	23	14	18	34	205	7	363	19	3	38	18	.679	4	24	3.77
Pirates	Pit	60	60	1	59	500.1	2194	504	255	188	23	15	23	56	150	1	365	44	7	26	34	.567	3	12	3.38
Braves	Atl	60	60	1	59	491.1	2179	443	263	182	16	15	10	23	234	2	507	58	9	26	34	.433	5	12	3.33
Red Sox	Bos	55	55	1	54	462.2	2090	482	268	193	22	21	17	34	224	10	367	34	9	26	29	.527	3	15	3.75
Royals	KC	60	60	0	60	479.1	2178	448	287	228	15	8	21	51	256	3	437	56	7	20	40	.333	6	14	4.28
Orioles	Bal	56	56	0	56	476.1	2174	479	307	235	22	19	15	38	284	23	377	42	7	25	31	.446	0	9	4.44
Reds	Cin	55	55	0	55	460.2	2154	468	350	258	27	29	18	45	275	8	393	71	6	14	41	.255	3	5	5.04
Expos	Mon	60	60	3	57	509.1	2321	512	351	259	37	19	21	53	248	0	364	53	7	17	43	.283	0	11	4.58
Total		379	379	20	359	6341.1	28134	6072	3526	2680	284	209	219	521	2851	74	5377	592	90	379	379	.500	54	183	3.80

2000 Leader Boards

It's hard to find leader boards like these. We offer plenty of categories and break them down five different ways. In addition to leader lists for Triple-A, Double-A, full-season Class-A and short-season leagues, you'll find a leader board for all full-season leagues regardless of classification.

The leader board for all full-season leagues will inform you that 22-year-old Jason Hart led all minor leaguers in hits (183), extra-base hits (79) and total bases (327). The Oakland farmhand punished Double-A pitching while playing for Midland and finished the year at Triple-A Sacramento. When his season was over, he also ranked second among all minor leaguers with 125 RBI and finished in the top 10 for doubles and homers.

For short-season ball, the leader board will tell you not only did Anaheim's Sergio Contreras flirt with a .400 average at Butte of the Pioneer League, but that his .399 mark topped all short-season players. And while Cardinals prospect Esix Snead established a new Carolina League record with 109 steals for full-season Potomac, Seattle's Jamal Strong led all short-season leagues with 60 stolen bases at Everett in the Northwest League.

If a player appeared with more than one team in a given breakdown, we list him with his last team in that category. To qualify for leadership, full-season players had to have 383 plate appearances (350 PA for catchers), 112 innings pitched, 18 starts (starting pitchers) or 40 games with fewer than 18 starts (relief pitchers). Short-season players required 150 plate appearances, 55 innings pitched, nine starts (starting pitchers) or 20 games with fewer than nine starts (relief pitchers).

League abbreviations are as follows:

INT—International League (AAA)
PCL—Pacific Coast League (AAA)
EL—Eastern League (AA)
SL—Southern League (AA)
TL—Texas League (AA)
CAL—California League (A+)
CAR—Carolina League (A+)
FSL—Florida State League (A+)
MWL—Midwest League (A)
SAL—South Atlantic League (A)
NYP—New York-Penn League (A-)
NWL—Northwest League (A-)
APP—Appalachian League (R+)
PIO—Pioneer League (R+)
AZL—Arizona League (R)
GCL—Gulf Coast League (R)

Full-Season Batting Leaders

Batting Average

Player, Team	Lg	Org	Avg
John Barnes, Salt Lake	**PCL**	**Min**	**.365**
Mike Kinkade, Rochester	INT	Bal	.358
Carlos Mendoza, Colo Sprngs	PCL	Col	.354
Jose Ortiz, Sacramento	PCL	Oak	.351
J.R. House, Hickory	SAL	Pit	.348
Travis Hafner, Charlotte	FSL	Tex	.346
Billy McMillon, Toledo	INT	Det	.345
Mario Valdez, Sacramento	PCL	Oak	.345
Mike Darr, Las Vegas	PCL	SD	.344
Lyle Overbay, El Paso	TL	Ari	.342

Catchers Batting Average

Player, Team	Lg	Org	Avg
Mike Kinkade, Rochester	**INT**	**Bal**	**.358**
J.R. House, Hickory	SAL	Pit	.348
Toby Hall, Durham	INT	TB	.327
Shawn Wooten, Edmonton	PCL	Ana	.327
Adam Melhuse, Colo Sprngs	PCL	Col	.324
A.J. Pierzynski, Salt Lake	PCL	Min	.313
Brandon Marsters, Fort Myers	FSL	Min	.310
Cody McKay, Sacramento	PCL	Oak	.307
Gary Bennett, Scranton-WB	INT	Phi	.306
Jason Phillips, Binghamton	EL	NYM	.304

First Basemen Batting Average

Player, Team	Lg	Org	Avg
Travis Hafner, Charlotte	**FSL**	**Tex**	**.346**
Mario Valdez, Sacramento	PCL	Oak	.345
Lyle Overbay, El Paso	TL	Ari	.342
Doug Mientkiewicz, Salt Lake	PCL	Min	.334
Nate Rolison, Calgary	PCL	Fla	.330
Sean McGowan, Shreveport	TL	SF	.330
Chris Donnels, Albuquerque	PCL	LA	.328
Jason Hart, Sacramento	PCL	Oak	.324
Shea Hillenbrand, Trenton	EL	Bos	.323
Jay Gibbons, Tennessee	SL	Tor	.321

Second Basemen Batting Average

Player, Team	Lg	Org	Avg
Jose Ortiz, Sacramento	**PCL**	**Oak**	**.351**
Ismael Gallo, Vero Beach	FSL	LA	.339
Keith Ginter, Round Rock	TL	Hou	.333
Hiram Bocachica, Albuquerque	PCL	LA	.322
Willie Bloomquist, Tacoma	PCL	Sea	.313
Ruben Salazar, Fort Myers	FSL	Min	.311
Jeff Powers, High Desert	CAL	Ari	.309
Pablo Ozuna, Portland	EL	Fla	.308
Keith Johnson, Edmonton	PCL	Ana	.307
Marlon Anderson, Scranton-WB	INT	Phi	.305

Third Basemen Batting Average

Player, Team	Lg	Org	Avg
Ryan Gripp, Lansing	**MWL**	**ChC**	**.333**
Luis Lopez, Syracuse	INT	Tor	.328
Tony Torcato, Shreveport	TL	SF	.327
Mike Gulan, Calgary	PCL	Fla	.317
Aubrey Huff, Durham	INT	TB	.316
Albert Pujols, Memphis	PCL	StL	.314
Adam Riggs, Albuquerque	PCL	LA	.313
Bo Robinson, Lancaster	CAL	Sea	.313
Randy Stegall, Dayton	MWL	Cin	.309
Joe Crede, Birmingham	SL	CWS	.306

Shortstops Batting Average

Player, Team	Lg	Org	Avg
Chris Sexton, Louisville	**INT**	**Cin**	**.324**
Esteban Beltre, Tucson	PCL	Ari	.314
Brandon Jackson, Dunedin	FSL	Tor	.312
Victor Rodriguez, Akron	EL	Cle	.305
Joe Thurston, San Berndno	CAL	LA	.303
Mark Ellis, Wichita	TL	KC	.302
Matt Erickson, Portland	EL	Fla	.301
Andy Beattie, Clinton	MWL	Cin	.301
Alex Cintron, El Paso	TL	Ari	.301
Chris Snopek, Tacoma	PCL	Sea	.300

Outfielders Batting Average

Player, Team	Lg	Org	Avg
John Barnes, Salt Lake	**PCL**	**Min**	**.365**
Carlos Mendoza, Colo Sprngs	PCL	Col	.354
Billy McMillon, Toledo	INT	Det	.345
Mike Darr, Las Vegas	PCL	SD	.344
Bobby Darula, Beloit	MWL	Mil	.336
Kevin Mench, Charlotte	FSL	Tex	.334
Pedro Valdes, Oklahoma	PCL	Tex	.332
Terrmel Sledge, Lancaster	CAL	Sea	.332
Juan Pierre, Colo Sprngs	PCL	Col	.331
Carlos Urquiola, El Paso	TL	Ari	.328

Switch-Hitters Batting Average

Player, Team	Lg	Org	Avg
Ruben Sierra, Oklahoma	**PCL**	**Tex**	**.326**
Milton Bradley, Ottawa	INT	Mon	.304
Andy Beattie, Clinton	MWL	Cin	.301
Alex Cintron, El Paso	TL	Ari	.301
Elvis Pena, Carolina	SL	Col	.300
Nestor Smith, Fort Myers	FSL	Min	.298
Kimera Bartee, Louisville	INT	Cin	.298
Pat Burns, St. Lucie	FSL	NYM	.298
Mickey Lopez, Huntsville	SL	Mil	.298
Craig Kuzmic, Lancaster	CAL	Sea	.297

Full-Season Batting Leaders

Hits

Player, Team	Lg	Org	H
Jason Hart, Sacramento	**PCL**	**Oak**	**183**
Jose Ortiz, Sacramento	PCL	Oak	182
Sean McGowan, Shreveport	TL	SF	173
Lyle Overbay, El Paso	TL	Ari	172
Shea Hillenbrand, Trenton	EL	Bos	171
Carl Crawford, Chston-SC	SAL	TB	170
Joe Thurston, San Berndno	CAL	LA	167
Brian Cole, Binghamton	EL	NYM	166
Ryan Gripp, Lansing	MWL	ChC	166
2 tied with			165

Extra-Base Hits

Player, Team	Lg	Org	XBH
Jason Hart, Sacramento	**PCL**	**Oak**	**79**
Kevin Mench, Charlotte	FSL	Tex	75
Ross Gload, Iowa	PCL	ChC	74
Phil Hiatt, Colo Sprngs	PCL	Col	73
Adam Hyzdu, Altoona	EL	Pit	72
Robin Jennings, Louisville	INT	Cin	70
Pedro Feliz, Fresno	PCL	SF	69
Eric Cole, Round Rock	TL	Hou	68
Brad Wilkerson, Ottawa	INT	Mon	68
2 tied with			67

Doubles

Player, Team	Lg	Org	2B
Eric Byrnes, Sacramento	**PCL**	**Oak**	**48**
Robin Jennings, Louisville	INT	Cin	47
Brad Wilkerson, Ottawa	INT	Mon	47
Eric Cole, Round Rock	TL	Hou	46
Jason Hart, Sacramento	PCL	Oak	45
Scott Seabol, Norwich	EL	NYY	45
Josh Pressley, Chston-SC	SAL	TB	44
Randy Stegall, Dayton	MWL	Cin	43
Greg LaRocca, Las Vegas	PCL	SD	42
3 tied with			41

Total Bases

Player, Team	Lg	Org	TB
Jason Hart, Sacramento	**PCL**	**Oak**	**327**
Phil Hiatt, Colo Sprngs	PCL	Col	303
Kevin Mench, Charlotte	FSL	Tex	302
Jose Ortiz, Sacramento	PCL	Oak	298
Ross Gload, Iowa	PCL	ChC	296
Pedro Feliz, Fresno	PCL	SF	287
Chad Mottola, Syracuse	INT	Tor	286
Adam Hyzdu, Altoona	EL	Pit	285
Carlos Pena, Tulsa	TL	Tex	282
Gary Johnson, Erie	EL	Ana	275

Triples

Player, Team	Lg	Org	3B
Elpidio Guzman, Lk Elsinore	**CAL**	**Ana**	**16**
Chone Figgins, Salem	CAR	Col	14
Dan McKinley, Harrisburg	EL	Mon	14
Carlos Mendoza, Colo Sprngs	PCL	Col	14
Marlon Byrd, Piedmont	SAL	Phi	13
Brian Gordon, High Desert	CAL	Ari	13
Ramon Gomez, El Paso	TL	Ari	12
Jon Topolski, Michigan	MWL	Hou	12
10 tied with			11

Runs

Player, Team	Lg	Org	R
Lew Ford, Augusta	**SAL**	**Bos**	**122**
Kevin Mench, Charlotte	FSL	Tex	118
Carlos Pena, Tulsa	TL	Tex	117
Mark Bellhorn, Sacramento	PCL	Oak	111
Austin Kearns, Dayton	MWL	Cin	110
Keith Ginter, Round Rock	TL	Hou	108
John Barnes, Salt Lake	PCL	Min	107
Jose Ortiz, Sacramento	PCL	Oak	107
3 tied with			106

Home Runs

Player, Team	Lg	Org	HR
Alex Cabrera, Tucson	**PCL**	**Ari**	**39**
Phil Hiatt, Colo Sprngs	PCL	Col	36
Ernie Young, Memphis	PCL	StL	35
Pedro Feliz, Fresno	PCL	SF	33
Chad Mottola, Syracuse	INT	Tor	33
Craig Wilson, Nashville	PCL	Pit	33
Jeff Liefer, Charlotte	INT	CWS	32
Jason Hart, Sacramento	PCL	Oak	31
Chris Hatcher, Edmonton	PCL	Ana	31
Adam Hyzdu, Altoona	EL	Pit	31

Runs Batted In

Player, Team	Lg	Org	RBI
Juan Silvestre, Lancaster	**CAL**	**Sea**	**137**
Jason Hart, Sacramento	PCL	Oak	125
Kevin Mench, Charlotte	FSL	Tex	121
Gary Johnson, Erie	EL	Ana	118
Sean McGowan, Shreveport	TL	SF	118
Troy Farnsworth, Potomac	CAR	StL	113
Travis Hafner, Charlotte	FSL	Tex	109
Phil Hiatt, Colo Sprngs	PCL	Col	109
Jose Ortiz, Sacramento	PCL	Oak	108
2 tied with			106

Full-Season Batting Leaders

Walks

Player, Team	Lg	Org	BB
Jack Cust, El Paso	**TL**	**Ari**	**117**
Gray Koonce, Rancho Cuca	CAL	SD	107
Bobby Kielty, Salt Lake	PCL	Min	105
Jon Topolski, Michigan	MWL	Hou	105
Jon Macalutas, Mudville	CAL	Mil	104
Nate Espy, Piedmont	SAL	Phi	101
Carlos Pena, Tulsa	TL	Tex	101
Adam Dunn, Dayton	MWL	Cin	100
Joe Lawrence, Tennessee	SL	Tor	99
Rich Paz, Bowie	EL	Bal	98

Strikeouts

Player, Team	Lg	Org	K
Samone Peters, Clinton	**MWL**	**Cin**	**198**
Jeremy Owens, Rancho Cuca	CAL	SD	183
Andy Brown, Greensboro	SAL	NYY	182
Rob Stratton, St. Lucie	FSL	NYM	180
Mike Hessman, Greenville	SL	Atl	178
J.J. Davis, Lynchburg	CAR	Pit	171
Lamont Matthews, San Berndno	CAL	LA	170
Tony Peters, Dunedin	FSL	Tor	164
Caonabo Cosme, Modesto	CAL	Oak	163
Justin Lincoln, Asheville	SAL	Col	161

Plate Appearances/Strikeout

Player, Team	Lg	Org	PA/K
Juan Pierre, Colo Sprngs	**PCL**	**Col**	**19.46**
Ismael Gallo, Vero Beach	FSL	LA	18.68
Luis Lopez, Syracuse	INT	Tor	16.64
Augie Ojeda, Iowa	PCL	ChC	16.41
Jeff Powers, High Desert	CAL	Ari	15.69
Jason Phillips, Binghamton	EL	NYM	15.64
Omar Ramirez, New Orleans	PCL	Hou	15.36
Luis Medina, Lansing	MWL	ChC	15.03
Shea Hillenbrand, Trenton	EL	Bos	14.31
Juan Lorenzo, Fort Myers	FSL	Min	14.18

Hit By Pitch

Player, Team	Lg	Org	HBP
Corky Miller, Chattanooga	**SL**	**Cin**	**30**
David Eckstein, Edmonton	PCL	Ana	25
Reed Johnson, Dunedin	FSL	Tor	25
Craig Wilson, Nashville	PCL	Pit	25
Keith Ginter, Round Rock	TL	Hou	24
Jesus Basabe, Modesto	CAL	Oak	23
Jeff Auterson, Vero Beach	FSL	LA	22
Dan Grummitt, Chston-SC	SAL	TB	22
4 tied with			20

Stolen Bases

Player, Team	Lg	Org	SB
Esix Snead, Potomac	**CAR**	**StL**	**109**
Alex Requena, Columbus	SAL	Cle	87
Esteban German, Visalia	CAL	Oak	83
Tim Raines Jr., Frederick	CAR	Bal	81
Alfredo Amezaga, Lk Elsinore	CAL	Ana	73
Brian Cole, Binghamton	EL	NYM	69
Andres Torres, Jacksnville	SL	Det	67
Wilken Ruan, Cape Fear	SAL	Mon	64
Chad Durham, Burlington	MWL	CWS	58
2 tied with			57

On-Base Percentage

Player, Team	Lg	Org	OBP
Keith Ginter, Round Rock	**TL**	**Hou**	**.457**
Terrmel Sledge, Lancaster	CAL	Sea	.451
Carlos Mendoza, Colo Sprngs	PCL	Col	.449
Travis Hafner, Charlotte	FSL	Tex	.447
Billy McMillon, Toledo	INT	Det	.446
Mario Valdez, Sacramento	PCL	Oak	.442
Bobby Darula, Beloit	MWL	Mil	.442
Chris Donnels, Albuquerque	PCL	LA	.440
Jack Cust, El Paso	TL	Ari	.440
Mike Kinkade, Rochester	INT	Bal	.440

Slugging Percentage

Player, Team	Lg	Org	SLG
Chris Donnels, Albuquerque	**PCL**	**LA**	**.660**
Kevin Mench, Charlotte	FSL	Tex	.615
Chris Hatcher, Edmonton	PCL	Ana	.608
Craig Wilson, Nashville	PCL	Pit	.604
Phil Hiatt, Colo Sprngs	PCL	Col	.598
Ross Gload, Iowa	PCL	ChC	.586
J.R. House, Hickory	SAL	Pit	.586
Nate Rolison, Calgary	PCL	Fla	.582
Travis Hafner, Charlotte	FSL	Tex	.580
Keith Ginter, Round Rock	TL	Hou	.580

Errors

Player, Team	Lg	Org	E
Jose Castillo, Hickory	**SAL**	**Pit**	**60**
Jorge Nunez, Albuquerque	PCL	LA	58
Angel Berroa, Visalia	CAL	Oak	54
Jeff Brooks, High Desert	CAL	Ari	51
Ricky Bell, Vero Beach	FSL	LA	47
Alex Ahumada, Sarasota	FSL	Bos	46
Nick Green, Myrtle Bch	CAR	Atl	46
Neil Jenkins, W Michigan	MWL	Det	46
Josh McKinley, Cape Fear	SAL	Mon	46
2 tied with			44

Full-Season Pitching Leaders

Earned Run Average

Player, Team	Lg	Org	ERA
Calvin Chipperfield, W Mich.	**MWL**	**Det**	**2.13**
Roy Oswalt, Round Rock	TL	Hou	2.21
Matt Ginter, Birmingham	SL	CWS	2.25
Bud Smith, Memphis	PCL	StL	2.26
Mark Buehrle, Birmingham	SL	CWS	2.28
Christian Parra, Myrtle Bch	CAR	Atl	2.28
Brian Lawrence, Las Vegas	PCL	SD	2.28
Greg Wooten, New Haven	EL	Sea	2.31
Ryan Baerlocher, Wilmington	CAR	KC	2.40
Ben Sheets, Indianapolis	INT	Mil	2.40
Jovanny Cedeno, Savannah	SAL	Tex	2.42
Lance Davis, Louisville	INT	Cin	2.44
Luke Prokopec, San Antonio	TL	LA	2.45
Andy VanHekken, W Michigan	MWL	Det	2.45
Jose Mieses, Mudville	CAL	Mil	2.56

Wins

Player, Team	Lg	Org	W
Jose Mieses, Mudville	**CAL**	**Mil**	**17**
Christian Parra, Myrtle Bch	**CAR**	**Atl**	**17**
Bud Smith, Memphis	**PCL**	**StL**	**17**
Travis Thompson, Dayton	**MWL**	**Cin**	**17**
Greg Wooten, New Haven	**EL**	**Sea**	**17**
Donnie Bridges, Harrisburg	EL	Mon	16
Lindsay Gulin, West Tenn	SL	ChC	16
Jon Rauch, Birmingham	SL	CWS	16
Andy VanHekken, W Michigan	MWL	Det	16
Larry Wimberly, Lynchburg	CAR	Pit	16
6 tied with			15

Losses

Player, Team	Lg	Org	L
Kyle Lohse, New Britain	**EL**	**Min**	**18**
Dusty Bergman, Lk Elsinore	CAL	Ana	16
Jeremy Affeldt, Wilmington	CAR	KC	15
Bryan Hebson, Harrisburg	EL	Mon	15
Ty Howington, Dayton	MWL	Cin	15
Jeff Hundley, Lk Elsinore	CAL	Ana	15
Mike Oquist, Toledo	INT	Det	15
Geraldo Padua, Lynchburg	CAR	Pit	15
Ken Pumphrey, Fort Myers	FSL	Min	15
10 tied with			14

Saves

Player, Team	Lg	Org	S
John Trujillo, Fort Wayne	**MWL**	**SD**	**42**
Bryan Leach, Augusta	SAL	Bos	40
Bob Scanlan, Indianapolis	INT	Mil	35
Jay Tessmer, Columbus	INT	NYY	34
Todd Williams, Tacoma	PCL	Sea	32
Jason Bullard, Bakersfield	CAL	SF	30
Jarrod Kingrey, Tennessee	SL	Tor	30
Jason Marr, Potomac	CAR	StL	30
Maximo Regalado, San Antonio	TL	LA	30
Greg Watson, W Michigan	MWL	Det	30
Bob File, Syracuse	INT	Tor	28
Domingo Jean, Norwich	EL	NYY	28
Jerrod Riggan, Binghamton	EL	NYM	28
3 tied with			27

Games

Player, Team	Lg	Org	G
Keith Forbes, Rancho Cuca	**CAL**	**SD**	**74**
Isabel Giron, Mobile	SL	SD	69
Brent Stentz, Salt Lake	PCL	Min	66
Robbie Crabtree, Fresno	PCL	SF	63
Gus Gandarillas, Salt Lake	PCL	Min	63
John Trujillo, Fort Wayne	MWL	SD	63
Domingo Jean, Norwich	EL	NYY	62
Kris Keller, Jacksnville	SL	Det	62
Bert Snow, Midland	TL	Oak	62
Greg Watson, W Michigan	MWL	Det	62
Doug Young, Fort Wayne	MWL	SD	62
6 tied with			61

Innings Pitched

Player, Team	Lg	Org	IP
Christian Parker, Norwich	**EL**	**NYY**	**204.0**
Donnie Bridges, Harrisburg	EL	Mon	201.1
Josh Fogg, Birmingham	SL	CWS	192.1
Travis Thompson, Dayton	MWL	Cin	188.2
John Lackey, Erie	EL	Ana	188.1
Jason Jennings, Carolina	SL	Col	187.0
Randy Keisler, Columbus	INT	NYY	186.0
Aaron Cook, Salem	CAR	Col	185.2
Brandon Knight, Columbus	INT	NYY	184.2
Brian Reith, Chattanooga	SL	Cin	184.0
Joe Beimel, Altoona	EL	Pit	183.1
Carlos Garcia, San Berndno	CAL	LA	182.0
Matt Belisle, Myrtle Bch	CAR	Atl	181.0
Dave Williams, Lynchburg	CAR	Pit	181.0
Tim Redding, Round Rock	TL	Hou	180.2

Full-Season Pitching Leaders

Walks

Player, Team	Lg	Org	BB
Nick Neugebauer, Huntsville	**SL**	**Mil**	**134**
Ryan Price, Salem	CAR	Col	113
Ben Howard, Rancho Cuca	CAL	SD	111
Damian Moss, Richmond	INT	Atl	106
Jason Temple, Rancho Cuca	CAL	SD	105
Phil Norton, Iowa	PCL	ChC	104
Paul Morse, Edmonton	PCL	Ana	102
Matt Beaumont, Erie	EL	Ana	101
Jason Beverlin, Norwich	EL	NYY	101
Mike Drumright, Calgary	PCL	Fla	101
Ryan Dittfurth, Savannah	SAL	Tex	99
Omar Ortiz, Rancho Cuca	CAL	SD	99
Hatuey Mendoza, High Desert	CAL	Ari	98
Ryan Mills, New Britain	EL	Min	98
Derek Stanford, Michigan	MWL	Hou	92

Strikeouts

Player, Team	Lg	Org	K
Dave Williams, Lynchburg	**CAR**	**Pit**	**201**
Ryan Baerlocher, Wilmington	CAR	KC	193
Tim Redding, Round Rock	TL	Hou	192
Roy Oswalt, Round Rock	TL	Hou	188
Julio DePaula, Asheville	SAL	Col	187
Jon Rauch, Birmingham	SL	CWS	187
Chin-Hui Tsao, Asheville	SAL	Col	187
Zach Day, Akron	EL	Cle	180
Brandon Duckworth, Reading	EL	Phi	178
Jason Childers, Mudville	CAL	Mil	177
Juan Pena, Modesto	CAL	Oak	177
Justin Reid, Hickory	SAL	Pit	176
Neal Frendling, Chston-SC	SAL	TB	174
Nick Neugebauer, Huntsville	SL	Mil	174
2 tied with			172

Strikeouts/9 Innings—Starters

Player, Team	Lg	Org	K/9
Ryan Anderson, Tacoma	**PCL**	**Sea**	**12.63**
Ben Howard, Rancho Cuca	CAL	SD	12.58
Nick Neugebauer, Huntsville	SL	Mil	12.23
Chin-Hui Tsao, Asheville	SAL	Col	11.61
Jacob Peavy, Fort Wayne	MWL	SD	11.04
Julio DePaula, Asheville	SAL	Col	10.86
Ken Chenard, Capital Cty	SAL	NYM	10.69
Erik Bedard, Delmarva	SAL	Bal	10.62
Jovanny Cedeno, Savannah	SAL	Tex	10.57
Ryan Baerlocher, Wilmington	CAR	KC	10.53
Juan Pena, Modesto	CAL	Oak	10.34
Juan Cruz, Daytona	FSL	ChC	10.26
Dennis Tankersley, Fort Wayne	MWL	SD	10.23
Jon Rauch, Birmingham	SL	CWS	10.14
Jason Childers, Mudville	CAL	Mil	10.13

Strikeouts/9 Innings—Relievers

Player, Team	Lg	Org	K/9
Bert Snow, Midland	**TL**	**Oak**	**13.05**
F. Hernandez, New Orleans	PCL	Hou	13.00
Shawn Sonnier, Wichita	TL	KC	12.66
Brandon Parker, Lancaster	CAL	Sea	12.49
Mike Neu, Clinton	MWL	Cin	12.39
Scott Polk, Capital Cty	SAL	NYM	12.39
Jeremy Fikac, Rancho Cuca	CAL	SD	12.12
Chris Keelin, Piedmont	SAL	Phi	12.10
Justin Fry, Piedmont	SAL	Phi	12.09
Maximo Regalado, San Antonio	TL	LA	12.00
Brian Mallette, Mudville	CAL	Mil	11.92
Chris Booker, West Tenn	SL	ChC	11.69
Cam Esslinger, Asheville	SAL	Col	11.69
Justin Kaye, New Haven	EL	Sea	11.63
Doug Thompson, Salem	CAR	Col	11.61

Hits/9 Innings—Starters

Player, Team	Lg	Org	H/9
Nick Neugebauer, Huntsville	**SL**	**Mil**	**5.48**
Christian Parra, Myrtle Bch	CAR	Atl	5.59
Calvin Chipperfield, W Michigan	MWL	Det	5.95
Chris Capuano, South Bend	MWL	Ari	6.02
Gary Majewski, Winston-Sal	CAR	CWS	6.03
Jerome Williams, San Jose	CAL	SF	6.37
Nathan Kent, Myrtle Bch	CAR	Atl	6.48
Jovanny Cedeno, Savannah	SAL	Tex	6.56
Chuck Crowder, Salem	CAR	Col	6.62
Ryan Baerlocher, Wilmington	CAR	KC	6.71
Juan Cruz, Daytona	FSL	ChC	6.73
Tom Marx, W Michigan	MWL	Det	6.75
Jim Lynch, Bakersfield	CAL	SF	6.77
Tyler Walker, Norfolk	INT	NYM	6.78
Tim Redding, Round Rock	TL	Hou	6.92

Hits/9 Innings—Relievers

Player, Team	Lg	Org	H/9
John Trujillo, Fort Wayne	**MWL**	**SD**	**4.70**
Chris George, Michigan	MWL	Hou	5.22
Mark Outlaw, Piedmont	SAL	Phi	5.25
Chris Keelin, Piedmont	SAL	Phi	5.31
Eric Cammack, Norfolk	INT	NYM	5.37
Jeremy Fikac, Rancho Cuca	CAL	SD	5.52
Aaron Rakers, Bowie	EL	Bal	5.56
Bryan Leach, Augusta	SAL	Bos	5.60
Rick Cercy, Asheville	SAL	Col	5.61
Brian Stokes, Chston-SC	SAL	TB	5.76
Shawn Sonnier, Wichita	TL	KC	5.77
Ronni Seberino, Durham	INT	TB	5.82
Doug Young, Fort Wayne	MWL	SD	5.82
Cliff Bartosh, Fort Wayne	MWL	SD	5.84
Allan Simpson, Lancaster	CAL	Sea	5.88

Triple-A Batting Leaders

Batting Average

Player, Team	Lg	Org	Avg
John Barnes, Salt Lake	**PCL**	**Min**	**.365**
Carlos Mendoza, Colo Sprngs	PCL	Col	.354
Jose Ortiz, Sacramento	PCL	Oak	.351
Billy McMillon, Toledo	INT	Det	.345
Mike Darr, Las Vegas	PCL	SD	.344
Mario Valdez, Sacramento	PCL	Oak	.344
Doug Mientkiewicz, Salt Lake	PCL	Min	.334
Pedro Valdes, Oklahoma	PCL	Tex	.332
Nate Rolison, Calgary	PCL	Fla	.330
Chris Donnels, Albuquerque	PCL	LA	.328

Catchers Batting Average

Player, Team	Lg	Org	Avg
Gary Bennett, Scranton-WB	**INT**	**Phi**	**.306**
Robert Machado, Tacoma	PCL	Sea	.300
Carlos Mendez, Toledo	INT	Det	.289
Creighton Gubanich, Indianapolis	INT	Mil	.284
Craig Wilson, Nashville	PCL	Pit	.283
Tom Wilson, Columbus	INT	NYY	.276
Pat Borders, Durham	INT	TB	.273
Guillermo Garcia, Louisville	INT	Cin	.272
A.J. Hinch, Sacramento	PCL	Oak	.266
Vance Wilson, Norfolk	INT	NYM	.260

First Basemen Batting Average

Player, Team	Lg	Org	Avg
Mario Valdez, Sacramento	**PCL**	**Oak**	**.344**
Doug Mientkiewicz, Salt Lake	PCL	Min	.334
Nate Rolison, Calgary	PCL	Fla	.330
Chris Donnels, Albuquerque	PCL	LA	.328
Julio Zuleta, Iowa	PCL	ChC	.311
Ryan Jackson, Durham	INT	TB	.311
Phil Hiatt, Colo Sprngs	PCL	Col	.310
Damon Minor, Fresno	PCL	SF	.290
Brian Lesher, Tacoma	PCL	Sea	.288
Tommy Davis, Rochester	INT	Bal	.287

Second Basemen Batting Average

Player, Team	Lg	Org	Avg
Jose Ortiz, Sacramento	**PCL**	**Oak**	**.351**
Hiram Bocachica, Albuquerque	PCL	LA	.322
Keith Johnson, Edmonton	PCL	Ana	.307
Marlon Anderson, Scranton-WB	INT	Phi	.305
Amaury Garcia, Calgary	PCL	Fla	.292
Brent Butler, Colo Sprngs	PCL	Col	.292
Jon Shave, Oklahoma	PCL	Tex	.290
Brent Abernathy, Durham	INT	TB	.290
Marcos Scutaro, Indianapolis	INT	Mil	.283
Norberto Martin, Indianapolis	INT	Mil	.281

Third Basemen Batting Average

Player, Team	Lg	Org	Avg
Luis Lopez, Syracuse	**INT**	**Tor**	**.328**
Mike Gulan, Calgary	PCL	Fla	.317
Aubrey Huff, Durham	INT	TB	.316
Adam Riggs, Albuquerque	PCL	LA	.313
Pedro Feliz, Fresno	PCL	SF	.298
Greg LaRocca, Las Vegas	PCL	SD	.295
Casey Blake, Salt Lake	PCL	Min	.291
Wes Helms, Richmond	INT	Atl	.288
Jose Fernandez, Indianapolis	INT	Mil	.286
Lou Lucca, Memphis	PCL	StL	.284

Shortstops Batting Average

Player, Team	Lg	Org	Avg
Chris Sexton, Louisville	**INT**	**Cin**	**.324**
Esteban Beltre, Tucson	PCL	Ari	.314
Chris Snopek, Tacoma	PCL	Sea	.300
Juan Melo, Fresno	PCL	SF	.295
Mark DeRosa, Richmond	INT	Atl	.292
Luis Garcia, Memphis	PCL	StL	.290
Alfonso Soriano, Columbus	INT	NYY	.290
Jose Flores, Tacoma	PCL	Sea	.284
Giomar Guevara, Toledo	INT	Det	.282
Ralph Milliard, Las Vegas	PCL	SD	.280

Outfielders Batting Average

Player, Team	Lg	Org	Avg
John Barnes, Salt Lake	**PCL**	**Min**	**.365**
Carlos Mendoza, Colo Sprngs	PCL	Col	.354
Billy McMillon, Toledo	INT	Det	.345
Mike Darr, Las Vegas	PCL	SD	.344
Pedro Valdes, Oklahoma	PCL	Tex	.332
Robin Jennings, Louisville	INT	Cin	.328
Chip Sell, Tucson	PCL	Ari	.326
Ruben Sierra, Oklahoma	PCL	Tex	.326
Jalal Leach, Fresno	PCL	SF	.325
Omar Ramirez, New Orleans	PCL	Hou	.320

Switch-Hitters Batting Average

Player, Team	Lg	Org	Avg
Ruben Sierra, Oklahoma	**PCL**	**Tex**	**.326**
Milton Bradley, Ottawa	INT	Mon	.304
Kimera Bartee, Louisville	INT	Cin	.298
Juan Melo, Fresno	PCL	SF	.295
Giomar Guevara, Toledo	INT	Det	.282
Augie Ojeda, Iowa	PCL	ChC	.280
Abraham Nunez, Nashville	PCL	Pit	.276
Mark Whiten, Buffalo	INT	Cle	.276
Santiago Perez, Indianapolis	INT	Mil	.275
Jimmy Rollins, Scranton-WB	INT	Phi	.274

Triple-A Batting Leaders

Hits

Player, Team	Lg	Org	H
Jose Ortiz, Sacramento	**PCL**	**Oak**	**182**
Jose Herrera, Rochester	INT	Bal	163
Doug Mientkiewicz, Salt Lake	PCL	Min	162
John Barnes, Salt Lake	PCL	Min	161
Luis Lopez, Syracuse	INT	Tor	161
Phil Hiatt, Colo Sprngs	PCL	Col	157
Ryan Jackson, Durham	INT	TB	156
Chad Mottola, Syracuse	INT	Tor	156
3 tied with			155

Extra-Base Hits

Player, Team	Lg	Org	XBH
Phil Hiatt, Colo Sprngs	**PCL**	**Col**	**73**
Robin Jennings, Louisville	INT	Cin	70
Pedro Feliz, Fresno	PCL	SF	69
Hiram Bocachica, Albuquerque	PCL	LA	65
Brady Clark, Louisville	INT	Cin	63
Jose Ortiz, Sacramento	PCL	Oak	63
Nate Rolison, Calgary	PCL	Fla	63
Jeff Liefer, Charlotte	INT	CWS	62
Ozzie Timmons, Durham	INT	TB	62
2 tied with			61

Doubles

Player, Team	Lg	Org	2B
Robin Jennings, Louisville	**INT**	**Cin**	**47**
Greg LaRocca, Las Vegas	PCL	SD	42
Brady Clark, Louisville	INT	Cin	41
Mike Gulan, Calgary	PCL	Fla	40
Hiram Bocachica, Albuquerque	PCL	LA	38
Ryan Jackson, Durham	INT	TB	38
Mike Neill, Tacoma	PCL	Sea	38
John Barnes, Salt Lake	PCL	Min	37
Jose Fernandez, Indianapols	INT	Mil	37
Nate Rolison, Calgary	PCL	Fla	37

Total Bases

Player, Team	Lg	Org	TB
Phil Hiatt, Colo Sprngs	**PCL**	**Col**	**303**
Jose Ortiz, Sacramento	PCL	Oak	298
Pedro Feliz, Fresno	PCL	SF	287
Chad Mottola, Syracuse	INT	Tor	286
Ozzie Timmons, Durham	INT	TB	273
Hiram Bocachica, Albuquerque	PCL	LA	270
Robin Jennings, Louisville	INT	Cin	262
Damon Minor, Fresno	PCL	SF	259
Nate Rolison, Calgary	PCL	Fla	258
Wes Helms, Richmond	INT	Atl	256

Triples

Player, Team	Lg	Org	3B
Carlos Mendoza, Colo Sprngs	**PCL**	**Col**	**14**
Larry Barnes, Edmonton	PCL	Ana	11
Mark Bellhorn, Sacramento	PCL	Oak	11
Wayne Kirby, Rochester	INT	Bal	11
Tike Redman, Nashville	PCL	Pit	11
Jimmy Rollins, Scranton-WB	INT	Phi	11
Kerry Robinson, Columbus	INT	NYY	9
Juan Sosa, Colo Sprngs	PCL	Col	9
3 tied with			8

Runs

Player, Team	Lg	Org	R
Mark Bellhorn, Sacramento	**PCL**	**Oak**	**111**
John Barnes, Salt Lake	PCL	Min	107
Jose Ortiz, Sacramento	PCL	Oak	107
Phil Hiatt, Colo Sprngs	PCL	Col	106
Ozzie Timmons, Durham	INT	TB	100
Hiram Bocachica, Albuquerque	PCL	LA	99
Chris Ashby, Albuquerque	PCL	LA	98
Doug Mientkiewicz, Salt Lake	PCL	Min	96
David Eckstein, Edmonton	PCL	Ana	94
Bo Porter, Sacramento	PCL	Oak	94

Home Runs

Player, Team	Lg	Org	HR
Phil Hiatt, Colo Sprngs	**PCL**	**Col**	**36**
Ernie Young, Memphis	PCL	StL	35
Pedro Feliz, Fresno	PCL	SF	33
Chad Mottola, Syracuse	INT	Tor	33
Craig Wilson, Nashville	PCL	Pit	33
Jeff Liefer, Charlotte	INT	CWS	32
Chris Hatcher, Edmonton	PCL	Ana	31
Damon Minor, Fresno	PCL	SF	30
Israel Alcantara, Pawtucket	INT	Bos	29
Ozzie Timmons, Durham	INT	TB	29

Runs Batted In

Player, Team	Lg	Org	RBI
Phil Hiatt, Colo Sprngs	**PCL**	**Col**	**109**
Jose Ortiz, Sacramento	PCL	Oak	108
Damon Minor, Fresno	PCL	SF	106
Pedro Feliz, Fresno	PCL	SF	105
Ozzie Timmons, Durham	INT	TB	104
Brian Buchanan, Salt Lake	PCL	Min	103
Chad Mottola, Syracuse	INT	Tor	102
Ernie Young, Memphis	PCL	StL	98
Doug Mientkiewicz, Salt Lake	PCL	Min	96
Mario Valdez, Sacramento	PCL	Oak	96

Triple-A Batting Leaders

Walks

Player, Team	Lg	Org	BB
Mark Bellhorn, Sacramento	**PCL**	**Oak**	**94**
Bo Porter, Sacramento	PCL	Oak	88
Ryan McGuire, Norfolk	INT	NYM	87
Damon Minor, Fresno	PCL	SF	87
Cliff Brumbaugh, Oklahoma	PCL	Tex	85
Gabe Alvarez, Las Vegas	PCL	SD	80
Stubby Clapp, Memphis	PCL	StL	80
Mike Byas, Fresno	PCL	SF	78
Adam Everett, New Orleans	PCL	Hou	75
Mike Neill, Tacoma	PCL	Sea	75

Stolen Bases

Player, Team	Lg	Org	SB
Alex Sanchez, Durham	**INT**	**TB**	**52**
Bo Porter, Sacramento	PCL	Oak	39
Dave Roberts, Buffalo	INT	Cle	39
Kerry Robinson, Columbus	INT	NYY	37
Mike Byas, Fresno	PCL	SF	36
Amaury Garcia, Calgary	PCL	Fla	35
Chad Meyers, Iowa	PCL	ChC	34
Jason Tyner, Norfolk	INT	NYM	33
George Lombard, Richmond	INT	Atl	32
Santiago Perez, Indianapols	INT	Mil	31

Strikeouts

Player, Team	Lg	Org	K
Phil Hiatt, Colo Sprngs	**PCL**	**Col**	**149**
Chris Wakeland, Toledo	INT	Det	148
J.R. Phillips, New Orleans	PCL	Hou	142
Kevin Witt, Syracuse	INT	Tor	132
George Lombard, Richmond	INT	Atl	130
Jim Chamblee, Pawtucket	INT	Bos	129
Kelly Dransfeldt, Oklahoma	PCL	Tex	123
Mike Zywica, Oklahoma	PCL	Tex	123
Danny Peoples, Buffalo	INT	Cle	122
2 tied with			121

On-Base Percentage

Player, Team	Lg	Org	OBP
Carlos Mendoza, Colo Sprngs	**PCL**	**Col**	**.449**
Billy McMillon, Toledo	INT	Det	.446
Mario Valdez, Sacramento	PCL	Oak	.441
Chris Donnels, Albuquerque	PCL	LA	.440
John Barnes, Salt Lake	PCL	Min	.439
Curtis Pride, Albuquerque	PCL	LA	.423
Mike Neill, Tacoma	PCL	Sea	.423
Nate Rolison, Calgary	PCL	Fla	.423
Ryan McGuire, Norfolk	INT	NYM	.422
Chris Sexton, Louisville	INT	Cin	.416

Plate Appearances/Strikeout

Player, Team	Lg	Org	PA/K
Luis Lopez, Syracuse	**INT**	**Tor**	**16.64**
Augie Ojeda, Iowa	PCL	ChC	16.41
Omar Ramirez, New Orleans	PCL	Hou	15.36
David Eckstein, Edmonton	PCL	Ana	12.63
Kerry Robinson, Columbus	INT	NYY	12.28
Liu Rodriguez, Charlotte	INT	CWS	12.26
Jamey Carroll, Ottawa	INT	Mon	12.25
Ken Woods, Scranton-WB	INT	Phi	12.02
Tony Medrano, Omaha	PCL	KC	11.82
Brent Abernathy, Durham	INT	TB	11.74

Slugging Percentage

Player, Team	Lg	Org	SLG
Chris Donnels, Albuquerque	**PCL**	**LA**	**.660**
Chris Hatcher, Edmonton	PCL	Ana	.608
Craig Wilson, Nashville	PCL	Pit	.604
Phil Hiatt, Colo Sprngs	PCL	Col	.598
Nate Rolison, Calgary	PCL	Fla	.582
Brian Buchanan, Salt Lake	PCL	Min	.580
Mario Valdez, Sacramento	PCL	Oak	.579
Julio Zuleta, Iowa	PCL	ChC	.579
Jose Ortiz, Sacramento	PCL	Oak	.575
Pedro Feliz, Fresno	PCL	SF	.571

Hit By Pitch

Player, Team	Lg	Org	HBP
David Eckstein, Edmonton	**PCL**	**Ana**	**25**
Craig Wilson, Nashville	**PCL**	**Pit**	**25**
Gene Schall, Scranton-WB	INT	Phi	18
Jon Shave, Oklahoma	PCL	Tex	17
Kit Pellow, Omaha	PCL	KC	16
Hiram Bocachica, Albuquerque	PCL	LA	15
Chris Hatcher, Edmonton	PCL	Ana	13
4 tied with			12

Errors

Player, Team	Lg	Org	E
Esteban Beltre, Tucson	**PCL**	**Ari**	**38**
Luis Garcia, Memphis	PCL	StL	32
Jose Ortiz, Sacramento	PCL	Oak	32
Santiago Perez, Indianapols	INT	Mil	27
Jimmy Rollins, Scranton-WB	INT	Phi	26
Rob Sasser, Toledo	INT	Det	26
Adam Everett, New Orleans	PCL	Hou	25
Greg LaRocca, Las Vegas	PCL	SD	25
Juan Sosa, Colo Sprngs	PCL	Col	25
Pedro Feliz, Fresno	PCL	SF	24

Triple-A Pitching Leaders

Earned Run Average

Player, Team	Lg	Org	ERA
Clint Weibl, Memphis	**PCL**	**StL**	**2.83**
Tomokazu Ohka, Pawtucket	INT	Bos	2.96
Jared Fernandez, Pawtucket	INT	Bos	3.02
Randy Keisler, Columbus	INT	NYY	3.02
Nelson Figueroa, Scranton-WB	INT	Phi	3.11
Cliff Politte, Scranton-WB	INT	Phi	3.12
Rick Krivda, Rochester	INT	Bal	3.12
Damian Moss, Richmond	INT	Atl	3.14
Ariel Prieto, Sacramento	PCL	Oak	3.27
Kerry Taylor, Syracuse	INT	Tor	3.32
Horacio Estrada, Indianapols	INT	Mil	3.33
Grant Roberts, Norfolk	INT	NYM	3.38
Josh Towers, Rochester	INT	Bal	3.47
Evan Thomas, Scranton-WB	INT	Phi	3.53
Larry Luebbers, Louisville	INT	Cin	3.53

Saves

Player, Team	Lg	Org	S
Bob Scanlan, Indianapolis	**INT**	**Mil**	**35**
Jay Tessmer, Columbus	INT	NYY	34
Todd Williams, Tacoma	PCL	Sea	32
Chris Nichting, Buffalo	INT	Cle	26
Gene Stechschulte, Memphis	PCL	StL	26
Billy Taylor, Durham	INT	TB	26
Johnny Ruffin, Tucson	PCL	Ari	20
Brandon Kolb, Las Vegas	PCL	SD	16
Rob Stanifer, Pawtucket	INT	Bos	16
Matt DeWitt, Syracuse	INT	Tor	15
Scott Service, Sacramento	PCL	Oak	13
Brent Stentz, Salt Lake	PCL	Min	13
Eric Weaver, Edmonton	PCL	Ana	13
6 tied with			12

Wins

Player, Team	Lg	Org	W
Horacio Estrada, Indianapolis	**INT**	**Mil**	**14**
Pat Ahearne, Tacoma	PCL	Sea	13
Nelson Figueroa, Scranton-WB	INT	Phi	13
Mike Romano, Salt Lake	PCL	Min	13
Evan Thomas, Scranton-WB	INT	Phi	13
Travis Driskill, New Orleans	PCL	Hou	12
Mickey Callaway, Durham	INT	TB	11
Ryan Franklin, Tacoma	PCL	Sea	11
Sun-Woo Kim, Pawtucket	INT	Bos	11
Rick Krivda, Rochester	INT	Bal	11
Chris Michalak, Albuquerque	PCL	LA	11
Brian Schmack, Charlotte	INT	CWS	11
Aaron Small, Colo Sprngs	PCL	Col	11
11 tied with			10

Games

Player, Team	Lg	Org	G
Robbie Crabtree, Fresno	**PCL**	**SF**	**63**
Gus Gandarillas, Salt Lake	**PCL**	**Min**	**63**
Todd Rizzo, Salt Lake	PCL	Min	61
Jim Dougherty, Memphis	PCL	StL	60
Jay Tessmer, Columbus	INT	NYY	60
Joe Davenport, Charlotte	INT	CWS	59
Pete Walker, Colo Sprngs	PCL	Col	58
Bob Scanlan, Indianapolis	INT	Mil	57
Barry Johnson, Scranton-WB	INT	Phi	56
Cory Bailey, Nashville	PCL	Pit	55
Todd Belitz, Sacramento	PCL	Oak	55
Chad Bradford, Charlotte	INT	CWS	55
Rick Heiserman, Memphis	PCL	StL	55
3 tied with			54

Losses

Player, Team	Lg	Org	L
Mike Oquist, Toledo	**INT**	**Det**	**15**
Pat Daneker, Syracuse	INT	Tor	13
Doug Linton, Colo Sprngs	PCL	Col	13
Phil Norton, Iowa	PCL	ChC	13
Jeremy Powell, Ottawa	INT	Mon	13
Scot Shields, Edmonton	PCL	Ana	13
Brandon Knight, Columbus	INT	NYY	12
Corey Lee, Oklahoma	PCL	Tex	12
Bronswell Patrick, Calgary	PCL	Fla	12
8 tied with			11

Innings Pitched

Player, Team	Lg	Org	IP
Brandon Knight, Columbus	**INT**	**NYY**	**184.2**
Travis Driskill, New Orleans	PCL	Hou	179.1
Doug Linton, Colo Sprngs	PCL	Col	174.0
Evan Thomas, Scranton-WB	INT	Phi	171.0
Pat Ahearne, Tacoma	PCL	Sea	168.0
Gary Glover, Syracuse	INT	Tor	166.2
Ryan Franklin, Tacoma	PCL	Sea	164.0
Scot Shields, Edmonton	PCL	Ana	163.0
Nelson Figueroa, Scranton-WB	INT	Phi	162.0
Mike Oquist, Toledo	INT	Det	161.0
Damian Moss, Richmond	INT	Atl	160.2
Phil Norton, Iowa	PCL	ChC	159.2
Horacio Estrada, Indianapols	INT	Mil	159.1
Mike Romano, Salt Lake	PCL	Min	159.0
R.A. Dickey, Oklahoma	PCL	Tex	158.1

Triple-A Pitching Leaders

Walks

Player, Team	Lg	Org	BB
Damian Moss, Richmond	**INT**	**Atl**	**106**
Phil Norton, Iowa	PCL	ChC	104
Mike Drumright, Calgary	PCL	Fla	101
Corey Lee, Oklahoma	PCL	Tex	87
Scot Shields, Edmonton	PCL	Ana	82
Bart Evans, Toledo	INT	Det	69
Willie Martinez, Buffalo	INT	Cle	67
Heath Murray, Albuquerque	PCL	LA	66
R.A. Dickey, Oklahoma	PCL	Tex	65
Junior Herndon, Las Vegas	PCL	SD	65
Jose Parra, Nashville	PCL	Pit	65
Jamie Arnold, Iowa	PCL	ChC	64
4 tied with			63

Strikeouts

Player, Team	Lg	Org	K
Scot Shields, Edmonton	**PCL**	**Ana**	**156**
Ryan Anderson, Tacoma	PCL	Sea	146
Ryan Franklin, Tacoma	PCL	Sea	142
Brandon Knight, Columbus	INT	NYY	138
Doug Linton, Colo Sprngs	PCL	Col	136
Buddy Carlyle, Las Vegas	PCL	SD	127
Ted Lilly, Columbus	INT	NYY	127
Evan Thomas, Scranton-WB	INT	Phi	127
Phil Norton, Iowa	PCL	ChC	126
Scott Sanders, Sacramento	PCL	Oak	124
Damian Moss, Richmond	INT	Atl	123
Gary Glover, Syracuse	INT	Tor	119
Robbie Crabtree, Fresno	PCL	SF	116
Sun-Woo Kim, Pawtucket	INT	Bos	116
Grant Roberts, Norfolk	INT	NYM	115

Strikeouts/9 Innings—Starters

Player, Team	Lg	Org	K/9
Ryan Anderson, Tacoma	**PCL**	**Sea**	**12.63**
Scot Shields, Edmonton	PCL	Ana	8.61
Cliff Politte, Scranton-WB	INT	Phi	8.47
Ted Lilly, Columbus	INT	NYY	8.32
Rodrigo Lopez, Las Vegas	PCL	SD	8.23
Barry Zito, Sacramento	PCL	Oak	8.06
Mike Riley, Fresno	PCL	SF	8.02
Miguel del Toro, Fresno	PCL	SF	7.85
Ryan Franklin, Tacoma	PCL	Sea	7.79
Sun-Woo Kim, Pawtucket	INT	Bos	7.77
Scott Sanders, Sacramento	PCL	Oak	7.64
Ryan Jensen, Fresno	PCL	SF	7.58
Buddy Carlyle, Las Vegas	PCL	SD	7.57
Rafael Roque, Indianapols	INT	Mil	7.55
John Parrish, Rochester	INT	Bal	7.53

Strikeouts/9 Innings—Relievers

Player, Team	Lg	Org	K/9
Mark Lukasiewicz, Syracuse	**INT**	**Tor**	**11.32**
Chad Harville, Sacramento	PCL	Oak	10.83
Rick Huisman, New Orleans	PCL	Hou	10.60
Johnny Ruffin, Tucson	PCL	Ari	10.36
Erik Hiljus, Toledo	INT	Det	10.32
Chad Ricketts, Albuquerque	PCL	LA	9.98
Paul Spoljaric, Omaha	PCL	KC	9.88
Eric Cammack, Norfolk	INT	NYM	9.47
Brandon Kolb, Las Vegas	PCL	SD	9.43
Billy Taylor, Durham	INT	TB	9.33
Sang-Hoon Lee, Pawtucket	INT	Bos	9.25
Jim Dougherty, Memphis	PCL	StL	9.07
Jack Cressend, Salt Lake	PCL	Min	9.07
Brent Stentz, Salt Lake	PCL	Min	9.06
John Riedling, Louisville	INT	Cin	9.00

Hits/9 Innings—Starters

Player, Team	Lg	Org	H/9
Ryan Anderson, Tacoma	**PCL**	**Sea**	**7.18**
Damian Moss, Richmond	INT	Atl	7.28
Clint Weibl, Memphis	PCL	StL	7.31
John Parrish, Rochester	INT	Bal	7.36
Cliff Politte, Scranton-WB	INT	Phi	7.51
Tomokazu Ohka, Pawtucket	INT	Bos	7.65
Barry Zito, Sacramento	PCL	Oak	7.79
Ryan Franklin, Tacoma	PCL	Sea	8.07
Allen Levrault, Indianapols	INT	Mil	8.14
Bobby M. Jones, Norfolk	INT	NYM	8.24
Aaron Myette, Charlotte	INT	CWS	8.30
Rick Krivda, Rochester	INT	Bal	8.37
Brandon Knight, Columbus	INT	NYY	8.38
Nelson Figueroa, Scranton-WB	INT	Phi	8.39
Amaury Telemaco, Scranton-WB	INT	Phi	8.39

Hits/9 Innings—Relievers

Player, Team	Lg	Org	H/9
Eric Cammack, Norfolk	**INT**	**NYM**	**5.37**
Rick Huisman, New Orleans	PCL	Hou	5.96
Brent Stentz, Salt Lake	PCL	Min	5.98
Scott Eyre, Charlotte	INT	CWS	6.19
Bob Scanlan, Indianapols	INT	Mil	6.27
Chad Bradford, Charlotte	INT	CWS	6.37
Sang-Hoon Lee, Pawtucket	INT	Bos	6.46
Tom Fordham, Indianapols	INT	Mil	6.55
Jim Mann, Norfolk	INT	NYM	6.72
Todd Belitz, Sacramento	PCL	Oak	6.83
Rob Stanifer, Pawtucket	INT	Bos	6.88
Juan Alvarez, Edmonton	PCL	Ana	7.04
Gene Stechschulte, Memphis	PCL	StL	7.17
Craig Dingman, Columbus	INT	NYY	7.33
Barry Johnson, Scranton-WB	INT	Phi	7.33

Double-A Batting Leaders

Batting Average

Player, Team	Lg	Org	Avg
Mike Kinkade, Bowie	**EL**	**Bal**	**.358**
Keith Ginter, Round Rock	TL	Hou	.333
Rick Short, Bowie	EL	Bal	.331
Jason Hart, Midland	TL	Oak	.326
Juan Pierre, Carolina	SL	Col	.326
Pat Hallmark, Wichita	TL	KC	.326
Shea Hillenbrand, Trenton	EL	Bos	.323
Ryan Lane, Tulsa	TL	Tex	.322
Andy Bevins, Arkansas	TL	StL	.321
Jay Gibbons, Tennessee	SL	Tor	.321

Catchers Batting Average

Player, Team	Lg	Org	Avg
Mike Kinkade, Bowie	**EL**	**Bal**	**.358**
Cody McKay, Midland	TL	Oak	.319
Johnny Estrada, Reading	EL	Phi	.295
Yorvit Torrealba, Shreveport	TL	SF	.286
John Pachot, Portland	EL	Fla	.285
Mike Amrhein, West Tenn	SL	ChC	.284
Geronimo Gil, San Antonio	TL	LA	.284
Mike Rose, El Paso	TL	Ari	.284
Carlos Maldonado, Round Rock	TL	Hou	.270
Humberto Cota, Altoona	EL	Pit	.261

First Basemen Batting Average

Player, Team	Lg	Org	Avg
Jason Hart, Midland	**TL**	**Oak**	**.326**
Shea Hillenbrand, Trenton	EL	Bos	.323
Jay Gibbons, Tennessee	SL	Tor	.321
Todd Betts, Portland	EL	Fla	.321
Dan Held, Binghamton	EL	NYM	.312
Aaron McNeal, Round Rock	TL	Hou	.310
Todd Sears, New Britain	EL	Min	.305
Carlos Pena, Tulsa	TL	Tex	.299
David Gibralter, Bowie	EL	Bal	.284
Greg Connors, New Haven	EL	Sea	.279

Second Basemen Batting Average

Player, Team	Lg	Org	Avg
Keith Ginter, Round Rock	**TL**	**Hou**	**.333**
Pablo Ozuna, Portland	EL	Fla	.308
Rob Mackowiak, Altoona	EL	Pit	.297
T.J. Maier, Arkansas	TL	StL	.294
Jermaine Clark, New Haven	EL	Sea	.293
Mike Young, Tulsa	TL	Tex	.291
Marcus Giles, Greenville	SL	Atl	.290
Jackie Rexrode, Birmingham	SL	CWS	.288
Henry Mateo, Harrisburg	EL	Mon	.287
Ty Wigginton, Binghamton	EL	NYM	.285

Third Basemen Batting Average

Player, Team	Lg	Org	Avg
Joe Crede, Birmingham	**SL**	**CWS**	**.306**
Morgan Ensberg, Round Rock	TL	Hou	.300
Scott Seabol, Norwich	EL	NYY	.296
Mike Edwards, Akron	EL	Cle	.295
Rusty McNamara, Reading	EL	Phi	.294
Sean Burroughs, Mobile	SL	SD	.291
Tony DeRosso, Trenton	EL	Bos	.281
Brian Dallimore, El Paso	TL	Ari	.275
Jason Grabowski, Tulsa	TL	Tex	.274
2 tied with			.272

Shortstops Batting Average

Player, Team	Lg	Org	Avg
Matt Erickson, Portland	**EL**	**Fla**	**.301**
Alex Cintron, El Paso	TL	Ari	.301
Elvis Pena, Carolina	SL	Col	.300
Oscar Salazar, Midland	TL	Oak	.300
Ramon Vazquez, New Haven	EL	Sea	.286
Luis Figueroa, Altoona	EL	Pit	.284
Nicky Ortiz, Norwich	EL	NYY	.282
Jack Wilson, Altoona	EL	Pit	.282
Erick Almonte, Norwich	EL	NYY	.271
Wilmy Caceres, Chattanooga	SL	Cin	.268

Outfielders Batting Average

Player, Team	Lg	Org	Avg
Juan Pierre, Carolina	**SL**	**Col**	**.326**
Pat Hallmark, Wichita	TL	KC	.326
Andy Bevins, Arkansas	TL	StL	.321
Joe Caruso, Wichita	TL	KC	.313
Virgil Chevalier, Trenton	EL	Bos	.309
Paul Ottavinia, Norwich	EL	NYY	.302
Jason Michaels, Reading	EL	Phi	.295
Jack Cust, El Paso	TL	Ari	.293
Eric Cole, Round Rock	TL	Hou	.291
Adam Hyzdu, Altoona	EL	Pit	.290

Switch-Hitters Batting Average

Player, Team	Lg	Org	Avg
Alex Cintron, El Paso	**TL**	**Ari**	**.301**
Elvis Pena, Carolina	SL	Col	.300
Henry Mateo, Harrisburg	EL	Mon	.287
Mike Rose, El Paso	TL	Ari	.284
Luis Figueroa, Altoona	EL	Pit	.284
Chris Magruder, Shreveport	TL	SF	.282
Dionys Cesar, Midland	TL	Oak	.277
Fletcher Bates, El Paso	TL	Ari	.276
Demond Smith, Greenville	SL	Atl	.274
Brian Harris, Reading	EL	Phi	.268

Double-A Batting Leaders

Hits

Player, Team	Lg	Org	H
Jason Hart, Midland	**TL**	**Oak**	**178**
Shea Hillenbrand, Trenton	EL	Bos	171
Joe Crede, Birmingham	SL	CWS	163
Eric Cole, Round Rock	TL	Hou	158
Carlos Pena, Tulsa	TL	Tex	158
Alex Cintron, El Paso	TL	Ari	157
Robert Perez, Tennessee	SL	Tor	157
Pat Hallmark, Wichita	TL	KC	156
Rob Mackowiak, Altoona	EL	Pit	156
Mike Young, Tulsa	TL	Tex	155

Extra-Base Hits

Player, Team	Lg	Org	XBH
Jason Hart, Midland	**TL**	**Oak**	**77**
Adam Hyzdu, Altoona	EL	Pit	72
Eric Cole, Round Rock	TL	Hou	68
Scott Seabol, Norwich	EL	NYY	67
Carlos Pena, Tulsa	TL	Tex	66
Morgan Ensberg, Round Rock	TL	Hou	62
Keith Ginter, Round Rock	TL	Hou	59
Craig Monroe, Tulsa	TL	Tex	59
4 tied with			58

Doubles

Player, Team	Lg	Org	2B
Eric Cole, Round Rock	**TL**	**Hou**	**46**
Scott Seabol, Norwich	EL	NYY	45
Jason Hart, Midland	TL	Oak	44
Stoney Briggs, Jacksnville	SL	Det	39
Adam Hyzdu, Altoona	EL	Pit	39
Rick Short, Bowie	EL	Bal	39
Jay Gibbons, Tennessee	SL	Tor	38
Mike Young, Tulsa	TL	Tex	37
Carlos Pena, Tulsa	TL	Tex	36
Brad Wilkerson, Harrisburg	EL	Mon	36

Total Bases

Player, Team	Lg	Org	TB
Jason Hart, Midland	**TL**	**Oak**	**318**
Adam Hyzdu, Altoona	EL	Pit	285
Carlos Pena, Tulsa	TL	Tex	282
Eric Cole, Round Rock	TL	Hou	270
Keith Ginter, Round Rock	TL	Hou	268
Morgan Ensberg, Round Rock	TL	Hou	263
Joe Crede, Birmingham	SL	CWS	261
Scott Seabol, Norwich	EL	NYY	255
Juan Thomas, New Haven	EL	Sea	251
2 tied with			249

Triples

Player, Team	Lg	Org	3B
Dan McKinley, Harrisburg	**EL**	**Mon**	**14**
Henry Mateo, Harrisburg	EL	Mon	11
Luis Saturria, Arkansas	TL	StL	10
Jamie Saylor, El Paso	TL	Ari	10
Jack Wilson, Altoona	EL	Pit	10
Mike Young, Tulsa	TL	Tex	10
Jermaine Clark, New Haven	EL	Sea	9
Eric Hinske, West Tenn	SL	ChC	9
6 tied with			8

Runs

Player, Team	Lg	Org	R
Carlos Pena, Tulsa	**TL**	**Tex**	**117**
Keith Ginter, Round Rock	TL	Hou	108
Mike Curry, Wichita	TL	KC	104
Jack Cust, El Paso	TL	Ari	100
Jason Hart, Midland	TL	Oak	98
Cesar Crespo, Portland	EL	Fla	96
Adam Hyzdu, Altoona	EL	Pit	96
Morgan Ensberg, Round Rock	TL	Hou	95
Jason Grabowski, Tulsa	TL	Tex	93
Elvis Pena, Carolina	SL	Col	92

Home Runs

Player, Team	Lg	Org	HR
Alex Cabrera, El Paso	**TL**	**Ari**	**35**
Adam Hyzdu, Altoona	EL	Pit	31
Jason Hart, Midland	TL	Oak	30
Morgan Ensberg, Round Rock	TL	Hou	28
Carlos Pena, Tulsa	TL	Tex	28
Juan Thomas, New Haven	EL	Sea	27
Keith Ginter, Round Rock	TL	Hou	26
Andy Bevins, Arkansas	TL	StL	25
Alejandro Freire, Jacksnville	SL	Det	25
Todd Mensik, Midland	TL	Oak	23

Runs Batted In

Player, Team	Lg	Org	RBI
Jason Hart, Midland	**TL**	**Oak**	**121**
Adam Hyzdu, Altoona	EL	Pit	106
Carlos Pena, Tulsa	TL	Tex	105
Juan Thomas, New Haven	EL	Sea	100
Aaron Rowand, Birmingham	SL	CWS	98
Eric Cole, Round Rock	TL	Hou	94
Joe Crede, Birmingham	SL	CWS	94
Keith Ginter, Round Rock	TL	Hou	92
Robert Perez, Tennessee	SL	Tor	92
3 tied with			90

Double-A Batting Leaders

Walks

Player, Team	Lg	Org	BB
Jack Cust, El Paso	**TL**	**Ari**	**117**
Carlos Pena, Tulsa	TL	Tex	101
Bobby Kielty, New Britain	EL	Min	98
Mike Curry, Wichita	TL	KC	94
Adam Hyzdu, Altoona	EL	Pit	94
Morgan Ensberg, Round Rock	TL	Hou	92
Todd Sears, New Britain	EL	Min	90
Jason Grabowski, Tulsa	TL	Tex	88
Jermaine Clark, New Haven	EL	Sea	87
Rick Prieto, Birmingham	SL	CWS	86

Stolen Bases

Player, Team	Lg	Org	SB
Mike Curry, Wichita	**TL**	**KC**	**52**
Henry Mateo, Harrisburg	EL	Mon	48
Elvis Pena, Carolina	SL	Col	48
Rod Lindsey, Jacksnville	SL	Det	46
Juan Pierre, Carolina	SL	Col	46
Jaisen Randolph, West Tenn	SL	ChC	46
Cesar Crespo, Portland	EL	Fla	41
Pat Hallmark, Wichita	TL	KC	41
Pedro Santana, Jacksnville	SL	Det	40
Jermaine Clark, New Haven	EL	Sea	38

Strikeouts

Player, Team	Lg	Org	K
Mike Hessman, Greenville	**SL**	**Atl**	**178**
Jack Cust, El Paso	TL	Ari	150
Pete Tucci, Mobile	SL	SD	147
Stoney Briggs, Jacksnville	SL	Det	145
Jacques Landry, Midland	TL	Oak	143
Jason Dellaero, Birmingham	SL	CWS	142
Cody Ransom, Shreveport	TL	SF	141
Joe Pomierski, Orlando	SL	TB	137
Darren Blakely, Erie	EL	Ana	136
Eric Hinske, West Tenn	SL	ChC	133

On-Base Percentage

Player, Team	Lg	Org	OBP
Keith Ginter, Round Rock	**TL**	**Hou**	**.457**
Jack Cust, El Paso	TL	Ari	.440
Mike Kinkade, Bowie	EL	Bal	.434
Todd Sears, New Britain	EL	Min	.423
Jermaine Clark, New Haven	EL	Sea	.421
Ryan Lane, Tulsa	TL	Tex	.416
Matt Erickson, Portland	EL	Fla	.416
Morgan Ensberg, Round Rock	TL	Hou	.416
Todd Betts, Portland	EL	Fla	.416
Cody McKay, Midland	TL	Oak	.414

Plate Appearances/Strikeout

Player, Team	Lg	Org	PA/K
Juan Pierre, Carolina	**SL**	**Col**	**18.81**
Shea Hillenbrand, Trenton	EL	Bos	14.31
Rusty McNamara, Reading	EL	Phi	13.02
Luis Figueroa, Altoona	EL	Pit	12.25
Luis Figueroa, New Haven	EL	Sea	11.97
Virgil Chevalier, Trenton	EL	Bos	11.14
Paul Ottavinia, Norwich	EL	NYY	10.96
Jackie Rexrode, Birmingham	SL	CWS	10.56
Julius Matos, Mobile	SL	SD	10.28
Sean Burroughs, Mobile	SL	SD	10.24

Slugging Percentage

Player, Team	Lg	Org	SLG
Jason Hart, Midland	**TL**	**Oak**	**.582**
Keith Ginter, Round Rock	TL	Hou	.580
Andy Bevins, Arkansas	TL	StL	.577
Mike Kinkade, Bowie	EL	Bal	.561
Adam Hyzdu, Altoona	EL	Pit	.554
Morgan Ensberg, Round Rock	TL	Hou	.545
Carlos Pena, Tulsa	TL	Tex	.533
Jack Cust, El Paso	TL	Ari	.526
Jay Gibbons, Tennessee	SL	Tor	.525
Scott Seabol, Norwich	EL	NYY	.517

Hit By Pitch

Player, Team	Lg	Org	HBP
Corky Miller, Chattanooga	**SL**	**Cin**	**30**
Keith Ginter, Round Rock	TL	Hou	24
Darren Blakely, Erie	EL	Ana	20
Pat Hallmark, Wichita	TL	KC	20
Rusty McNamara, Reading	EL	Phi	18
Eric Munson, Jacksnville	SL	Det	18
Dan Held, Binghamton	EL	NYM	17
David Matranga, Round Rock	TL	Hou	17
Joe Caruso, Wichita	TL	KC	16
Alejandro Freire, Jacksnville	SL	Det	16

Errors

Player, Team	Lg	Org	E
Felipe Lopez, Tennessee	**SL**	**Tor**	**44**
Jason Grabowski, Tulsa	TL	Tex	40
Jason Smith, West Tenn	SL	ChC	37
Cleatus Davidson, New Britain	EL	Min	35
Michael Cuddyer, New Britain	EL	Min	34
Oscar Salazar, Midland	TL	Oak	34
Erick Almonte, Norwich	EL	NYY	33
Steve Lackey, Greenville	SL	Atl	33
Jacques Landry, Midland	TL	Oak	33
Elvis Pena, Carolina	SL	Col	33

Double-A Pitching Leaders

Earned Run Average

Player, Team	Lg	Org	ERA
Roy Oswalt, Round Rock	**TL**	**Hou**	**1.94**
Lance Davis, Chattanooga	SL	Cin	2.18
Matt Ginter, Birmingham	SL	CWS	2.25
Mark Buehrle, Birmingham	SL	CWS	2.28
Greg Wooten, New Haven	EL	Sea	2.31
David Moraga, Carolina	SL	Col	2.34
Donnie Bridges, Harrisburg	EL	Mon	2.39
Brian Lawrence, Mobile	SL	SD	2.42
Luke Prokopec, San Antonio	TL	LA	2.45
Jimmy Osting, Reading	EL	Phi	2.53
Derek Lee, Huntsville	SL	Mil	2.54
Josh Fogg, Birmingham	SL	CWS	2.57
Robert Averette, Carolina	SL	Col	2.58
Tyler Walker, Binghamton	EL	NYM	2.75
Eddie Priest, Chattanooga	SL	Cin	2.80

Wins

Player, Team	Lg	Org	W
Greg Wooten, New Haven	**EL**	**Sea**	**17**
Shawn Sedlacek, Wichita	TL	KC	15
Spike Lundberg, Tulsa	TL	Tex	14
Christian Parker, Norwich	EL	NYY	14
Robert Averette, Carolina	SL	Col	13
Brandon Duckworth, Reading	EL	Phi	13
Dicky Gonzalez, Binghamton	EL	NYM	13
Pasqual Coco, Tennessee	SL	Tor	12
Brandon Leese, Portland	EL	Fla	12
Shane Loux, Jacksnville	SL	Det	12
Brian O'Connor, Altoona	EL	Pit	12
Bud Smith, Arkansas	TL	StL	12
Travis Smith, Huntsville	SL	Mil	12
13 tied with			11

Losses

Player, Team	Lg	Org	L
Kyle Lohse, New Britain	**EL**	**Min**	**18**
Bryan Hebson, Harrisburg	EL	Mon	15
Kevin Gregg, Midland	TL	Oak	14
Mike Maroth, Jacksnville	SL	Det	14
Patrick Coogan, Arkansas	TL	StL	13
Jason Middlebrook, Mobile	SL	SD	13
Brian Fuentes, New Haven	EL	Sea	12
Matt McClellan, Tennessee	SL	Tor	12
Pablo Ochoa, Binghamton	EL	NYM	12
John Sneed, Reading	EL	Phi	12
Kevin Joseph, Shreveport	TL	SF	11
7 tied with			10

Saves

Player, Team	Lg	Org	S
Domingo Jean, Norwich	**EL**	**NYY**	**28**
Jerrod Riggan, Binghamton	**EL**	**NYM**	**28**
Bert Snow, Midland	TL	Oak	27
Kris Keller, Jacksnville	SL	Det	26
Bret Prinz, El Paso	TL	Ari	26
Courtney Duncan, West Tenn	SL	ChC	25
Bo Donaldson, Chattanooga	SL	Cin	24
Bobby Rodgers, Portland	EL	Fla	22
Mike Rossiter, Huntsville	SL	Mil	22
Shawn Sonnier, Wichita	TL	KC	21
Bob File, Tennessee	SL	Tor	20
Jacob Shumate, Greenville	SL	Atl	18
Travis Thompson, Carolina	SL	Col	17
Doug Nickle, Reading	EL	Phi	16
Jim Serrano, Harrisburg	EL	Mon	16

Games

Player, Team	Lg	Org	G
Isabel Giron, Mobile	**SL**	**SD**	**69**
Domingo Jean, Norwich	EL	NYY	62
Kris Keller, Jacksnville	SL	Det	62
Courtney Duncan, West Tenn	SL	ChC	61
Jay Yennaco, West Tenn	SL	ChC	60
Scott Huntsman, Huntsville	SL	Mil	59
Lee Marshall, New Britain	EL	Min	59
Will Ohman, West Tenn	SL	ChC	59
Eddie Oropesa, Shreveport	TL	SF	59
Bert Snow, Midland	TL	Oak	59
Benji Miller, Shreveport	TL	SF	58
Corey Avrard, Arkansas	TL	StL	57
Kevin Crafton, Arkansas	TL	StL	57
Bo Donaldson, Chattanooga	SL	Cin	57
Doug Sessions, Round Rock	TL	Hou	56

Innings Pitched

Player, Team	Lg	Org	IP
Christian Parker, Norwich	**EL**	**NYY**	**204.0**
Josh Fogg, Birmingham	SL	CWS	192.1
Eddie Priest, Chattanooga	SL	Cin	180.0
Denny Wagner, Midland	TL	Oak	180.0
Matt Ginter, Birmingham	SL	CWS	179.2
Eric Ireland, Round Rock	TL	Hou	179.2
Greg Wooten, New Haven	EL	Sea	179.1
Troy Mattes, Harrisburg	EL	Mon	174.1
Shawn Chacon, Carolina	SL	Col	173.2
Brandon Leese, Portland	EL	Fla	173.2
Bryan Hebson, Harrisburg	EL	Mon	171.1
Matt McClellan, Tennessee	SL	Tor	168.2
Pasqual Coco, Tennessee	SL	Tor	167.2
Robert Averette, Carolina	SL	Col	167.1
Kyle Lohse, New Britain	EL	Min	167.0

Double-A Pitching Leaders

Walks

Player, Team	Lg	Org	BB
Matt Beaumont, Erie	**EL**	**Ana**	**92**
Jason Brester, Reading	EL	Phi	89
David Elder, Tulsa	TL	Tex	88
Jason Beverlin, Norwich	EL	NYY	87
Shawn Chacon, Carolina	SL	Col	85
Derrick Lewis, Greenville	SL	Atl	83
Ryan Price, Carolina	SL	Col	76
Pablo Ochoa, Binghamton	EL	NYM	75
John Sneed, Reading	EL	Phi	75
Kevin Gregg, Midland	TL	Oak	73
Lesli Brea, Bowie	EL	Bal	70
Brian Fuentes, New Haven	EL	Sea	70
Brian Rogers, Norwich	EL	NYY	70
3 tied with			69

Strikeouts

Player, Team	Lg	Org	K
Brandon Duckworth, Reading	**EL**	**Phi**	**178**
Shawn Chacon, Carolina	SL	Col	172
Joey Nation, West Tenn	SL	ChC	165
Brian Fuentes, New Haven	EL	Sea	152
Eddie Priest, Chattanooga	SL	Cin	149
Christian Parker, Norwich	EL	NYY	147
Ryan Vogelsong, Shreveport	TL	SF	147
Derrick Lewis, Greenville	SL	Atl	143
Pasqual Coco, Tennessee	SL	Tor	142
Roy Oswalt, Round Rock	TL	Hou	141
Matt McClellan, Tennessee	SL	Tor	140
Dicky Gonzalez, Binghamton	EL	NYM	138
Josh Fogg, Birmingham	SL	CWS	136
Brian Rogers, Norwich	EL	NYY	132
3 tied with			130

Strikeouts/9 Innings—Starters

Player, Team	Lg	Org	K/9
Brian Fuentes, New Haven	**EL**	**Sea**	**9.79**
Roy Oswalt, Round Rock	TL	Hou	9.79
Brandon Duckworth, Reading	EL	Phi	9.71
Wascar Serrano, Mobile	SL	SD	8.97
Joey Nation, West Tenn	SL	ChC	8.95
Shawn Chacon, Carolina	SL	Col	8.91
Travis Phelps, Orlando	SL	TB	8.83
Luke Prokopec, San Antonio	TL	LA	8.67
Ryan Vogelsong, Shreveport	TL	SF	8.52
Justin Miller, Midland	TL	Oak	8.48
Brian Lawrence, Mobile	SL	SD	8.46
Bud Smith, Arkansas	TL	StL	8.45
Dicky Gonzalez, Binghamton	EL	NYM	8.41
Tyler Walker, Binghamton	EL	NYM	8.26
Micah Bowie, West Tenn	SL	ChC	8.13

Strikeouts/9 Innings—Relievers

Player, Team	Lg	Org	K/9
Bert Snow, Midland	**TL**	**Oak**	**13.03**
Shawn Sonnier, Wichita	TL	KC	12.66
Justin Kaye, New Haven	EL	Sea	11.63
Bo Donaldson, Chattanooga	SL	Cin	11.38
Jerrod Riggan, Binghamton	EL	NYM	10.94
Will Ohman, West Tenn	SL	ChC	10.72
Marc Deschenes, Akron	EL	Cle	10.60
Bret Prinz, El Paso	TL	Ari	10.24
Jay Yennaco, West Tenn	SL	ChC	10.06
Matt Duff, Altoona	EL	Pit	9.98
Ray Beasley, Greenville	SL	Atl	9.76
Jim Serrano, Harrisburg	EL	Mon	9.60
Bobby Rodgers, Portland	EL	Fla	9.43
3 tied with			9.00

Hits/9 Innings—Starters

Player, Team	Lg	Org	H/9
Tyler Walker, Binghamton	**EL**	**NYM**	**6.10**
Jason Beverlin, Norwich	EL	NYY	6.89
Micah Bowie, West Tenn	SL	ChC	6.98
Brian Lawrence, Mobile	SL	SD	7.03
Matt White, Orlando	SL	TB	7.05
Travis Phelps, Orlando	SL	TB	7.08
Cedrick Bowers, Orlando	SL	TB	7.17
Matt Beaumont, Erie	EL	Ana	7.23
Donnie Bridges, Harrisburg	EL	Mon	7.31
Roy Oswalt, Round Rock	TL	Hou	7.36
Joey Nation, West Tenn	SL	ChC	7.43
Wascar Serrano, Mobile	SL	SD	7.45
Wilson Guzman, Altoona	EL	Pit	7.47
Justin Miller, Midland	TL	Oak	7.66
Matt Ginter, Birmingham	SL	CWS	7.66

Hits/9 Innings—Relievers

Player, Team	Lg	Org	H/9
Shawn Sonnier, Wichita	**TL**	**KC**	**5.77**
Jerrod Riggan, Binghamton	EL	NYM	5.95
Bobby Rodgers, Portland	EL	Fla	6.18
Kevin Mobley, Jacksnville	SL	Det	6.20
Jacob Shumate, Greenville	SL	Atl	6.31
Doug Nickle, Reading	EL	Phi	6.40
Domingo Jean, Norwich	EL	NYY	6.57
Will Ohman, West Tenn	SL	ChC	6.69
Jay Yennaco, West Tenn	SL	ChC	6.75
Ken Vining, Birmingham	SL	CWS	6.99
Courtney Duncan, West Tenn	SL	ChC	7.00
Brian Bowles, Tennessee	SL	Tor	7.05
Marc Deschenes, Akron	EL	Cle	7.12
Shawn Camp, Mobile	SL	SD	7.13
Bo Donaldson, Chattanooga	SL	Cin	7.30

Class-A Batting Leaders

Batting Average

Player, Team	Lg	Org	Avg
J.R. House, Hickory	**SAL**	**Pit**	**.348**
Travis Hafner, Charlotte	FSL	Tex	.346
Ismael Gallo, Vero Beach	FSL	LA	.339
Kevin Mench, Charlotte	FSL	Tex	.334
Ryan Gripp, Lansing	MWL	ChC	.333
Terrmel Sledge, Lancaster	CAL	Sea	.332
Victor Rodriguez, Kinston	CAR	Cle	.327
Sean McGowan, San Jose	CAL	SF	.327
Tony Torcato, San Jose	CAL	SF	.324
Gonzalez Pujols, Visalia	CAL	Oak	.322

Catchers Batting Average

Player, Team	Lg	Org	Avg
J.R. House, Hickory	**SAL**	**Pit**	**.348**
Brandon Marsters, Fort Myers	FSL	Min	.310
Joe Lawrence, Dunedin	FSL	Tor	.301
Eliezer Alfonzo, Beloit	MWL	Mil	.285
John Buck, Michigan	MWL	Hou	.282
Scott Ackerman, Jupiter	FSL	Mon	.281
Chairon Isenia, Chston-SC	SAL	TB	.271
Steve Torrealba, Myrtle Bch	CAR	Atl	.269
Matt Frick, Kane County	MWL	Fla	.263
Jeff Winchester, Asheville	SAL	Col	.262

First Basemen Batting Average

Player, Team	Lg	Org	Avg
Travis Hafner, Charlotte	**FSL**	**Tex**	**.346**
Sean McGowan, San Jose	CAL	SF	.327
Robb Quinlan, Lk Elsinore	CAL	Ana	.317
Nate Espy, Piedmont	SAL	Phi	.312
Luis Medina, Lansing	MWL	ChC	.307
Josh Pressley, Chston-SC	SAL	TB	.303
Craig Kuzmic, Lancaster	CAL	Sea	.297
Jose Velazquez, St. Pete	FSL	TB	.296
Steve Neal, High Desert	CAL	Ari	.296
Hee Seop Choi, Daytona	FSL	ChC	.296

Second Basemen Batting Average

Player, Team	Lg	Org	Avg
Ismael Gallo, Vero Beach	**FSL**	**LA**	**.339**
Ruben Salazar, Fort Myers	FSL	Min	.311
Jeff Powers, High Desert	CAL	Ari	.309
Mark Burnett, Clinton	MWL	Cin	.301
Ryan Luther, Bakersfield	CAL	SF	.300
Omar Moraga, Columbus	SAL	Cle	.297
Mike Collins, San Berndno	CAL	LA	.292
Torre Tyson, Greensboro	SAL	NYY	.291
Brian Ward, Fort Wayne	MWL	SD	.286
Kevin Connacher, Winston-Sal	CAR	CWS	.286

Third Basemen Batting Average

Player, Team	Lg	Org	Avg
Ryan Gripp, Lansing	**MWL**	**ChC**	**.333**
Tony Torcato, San Jose	CAL	SF	.324
Albert Pujols, Potomac	CAR	StL	.317
Bo Robinson, Lancaster	CAL	Sea	.313
Randy Stegall, Dayton	MWL	Cin	.309
Scott Hodges, Jupiter	FSL	Mon	.306
Shane Hopper, Rancho Cuca	CAL	SD	.302
Hank Blalock, Savannah	SAL	Tex	.299
Royce Huffman, Kissimmee	FSL	Hou	.298
Andrew Beinbrink, St. Pete	FSL	TB	.297

Shortstops Batting Average

Player, Team	Lg	Org	Avg
Victor Rodriguez, Kinston	**CAR**	**Cle**	**.327**
Brandon Jackson, Dunedin	FSL	Tor	.312
Joe Thurston, San Berndno	CAL	LA	.303
Mark Ellis, Wilmington	CAR	KC	.302
Andy Beattie, Clinton	MWL	Cin	.301
Danny Sandoval, Winston-Sal	CAR	CWS	.299
Jose Castillo, Hickory	SAL	Pit	.299
Nate Frese, Daytona	FSL	ChC	.296
Jim Deschaine, Lansing	MWL	ChC	.293
Jorge Nunez, Vero Beach	FSL	LA	.288

Outfielders Batting Average

Player, Team	Lg	Org	Avg
Kevin Mench, Charlotte	**FSL**	**Tex**	**.334**
Terrmel Sledge, Lancaster	CAL	Sea	.332
Rusty Keith, Modesto	CAL	Oak	.316
Jim Sitzman, Piedmont	SAL	Phi	.316
Lew Ford, Augusta	SAL	Bos	.315
Carlos Valderrama, Bakersfield	CAL	SF	.315
Brian Cole, St. Lucie	FSL	NYM	.312
Derek Nicholson, Michigan	MWL	Hou	.311
Brian Gordon, High Desert	CAL	Ari	.311
Marlon Byrd, Piedmont	SAL	Phi	.309

Switch-Hitters Batting Average

Player, Team	Lg	Org	Avg
Andy Beattie, Clinton	**MWL**	**Cin**	**.301**
Nestor Smith, Fort Myers	FSL	Min	.298
Pat Burns, St. Lucie	FSL	NYM	.298
Craig Kuzmic, Lancaster	CAL	Sea	.297
Andres Torres, Lakeland	FSL	Det	.296
Marvin Seale, St. Lucie	FSL	NYM	.294
James Langston, Hickory	SAL	Pit	.292
Torre Tyson, Greensboro	SAL	NYY	.291
Orlando Hudson, Dunedin	FSL	Tor	.285
Juan Lorenzo, Fort Myers	FSL	Min	.283

Class-A Batting Leaders

Hits

Player, Team	Lg	Org	H
Carl Crawford, Chston-SC	**SAL**	**TB**	**170**
Joe Thurston, San Berndno	CAL	LA	167
Ryan Gripp, Lansing	MWL	ChC	166
Wilken Ruan, Cape Fear	SAL	Mon	165
Kevin Mench, Charlotte	FSL	Tex	164
Lew Ford, Augusta	SAL	Bos	162
Bo Robinson, Lancaster	CAL	Sea	161
Matt Cepicky, Jupiter	FSL	Mon	160
Marlon Byrd, Piedmont	SAL	Phi	159
Tony Torcato, San Jose	CAL	SF	159

Doubles

Player, Team	Lg	Org	2B
Josh Pressley, Chston-SC	**SAL**	**TB**	**44**
Randy Stegall, Dayton	MWL	Cin	43
Kevin Burford, Salem	CAR	Col	40
Gray Koonce, Rancho Cuca	CAL	SD	40
Albert Pujols, Potomac	CAR	StL	40
Kevin Mench, Charlotte	FSL	Tex	39
Jason Lane, Michigan	MWL	Hou	38
Austin Kearns, Dayton	MWL	Cin	37
Tony Torcato, San Jose	CAL	SF	37
5 tied with			36

Triples

Player, Team	Lg	Org	3B
Elpidio Guzman, Lk Elsinore	**CAL**	**Ana**	**16**
Chone Figgins, Salem	CAR	Col	14
Marlon Byrd, Piedmont	SAL	Phi	13
Brian Gordon, High Desert	CAL	Ari	13
Jon Topolski, Michigan	MWL	Hou	12
Carl Crawford, Chston-SC	SAL	TB	11
Lew Ford, Augusta	SAL	Bos	11
Andres Torres, Lakeland	FSL	Det	11
6 tied with			10

Home Runs

Player, Team	Lg	Org	HR
Juan Silvestre, Lancaster	**CAL**	**Sea**	**30**
Ryan Ludwick, Modesto	CAL	Oak	29
Rob Stratton, St. Lucie	FSL	NYM	29
Austin Kearns, Dayton	MWL	Cin	27
Kevin Mench, Charlotte	FSL	Tex	27
Billy Martin, South Bend	MWL	Ari	25
Earl Snyder, St. Lucie	FSL	NYM	25
Lamont Matthews, San Berndno	CAL	LA	24
3 tied with			23

Extra-Base Hits

Player, Team	Lg	Org	XBH
Kevin Mench, Charlotte	**FSL**	**Tex**	**75**
Austin Kearns, Dayton	MWL	Cin	66
Albert Pujols, Potomac	CAR	StL	66
Gray Koonce, Rancho Cuca	CAL	SD	61
Jason Lane, Michigan	MWL	Hou	61
Lamont Matthews, San Berndno	CAL	LA	61
Earl Snyder, St. Lucie	FSL	NYM	61
Kevin Burford, Salem	CAR	Col	60
Marlon Byrd, Piedmont	SAL	Phi	59
Antonio Perez, Lancaster	CAL	Sea	59

Total Bases

Player, Team	Lg	Org	TB
Kevin Mench, Charlotte	**FSL**	**Tex**	**302**
Austin Kearns, Dayton	MWL	Cin	270
Marlon Byrd, Piedmont	SAL	Phi	265
Juan Silvestre, Lancaster	CAL	Sea	265
Ryan Gripp, Lansing	MWL	ChC	262
Albert Pujols, Potomac	CAR	StL	262
Jason Lane, Michigan	MWL	Hou	260
Craig Kuzmic, Lancaster	CAL	Sea	259
Earl Snyder, St. Lucie	FSL	NYM	256
Jose Castillo, Hickory	SAL	Pit	254

Runs

Player, Team	Lg	Org	R
Lew Ford, Augusta	**SAL**	**Bos**	**122**
Kevin Mench, Charlotte	FSL	Tex	118
Austin Kearns, Dayton	MWL	Cin	110
Willie Harris, Delmarva	SAL	Bal	106
Craig Kuzmic, Lancaster	CAL	Sea	106
Marlon Byrd, Piedmont	SAL	Phi	104
Juan Silvestre, Lancaster	CAL	Sea	104
Adam Dunn, Dayton	MWL	Cin	101
Carl Crawford, Chston-SC	SAL	TB	99
Jeremy Owens, Rancho Cuca	CAL	SD	99

Runs Batted In

Player, Team	Lg	Org	RBI
Juan Silvestre, Lancaster	**CAL**	**Sea**	**137**
Kevin Mench, Charlotte	FSL	Tex	121
Troy Farnsworth, Potomac	CAR	StL	113
Travis Hafner, Charlotte	FSL	Tex	109
Sean McGowan, San Jose	CAL	SF	106
Austin Kearns, Dayton	MWL	Cin	104
Craig Kuzmic, Lancaster	CAL	Sea	104
Jason Lane, Michigan	MWL	Hou	104
Ryan Ludwick, Modesto	CAL	Oak	102
Jeremy Luster, Bakersfield	CAL	SF	99

Class-A Batting Leaders

Walks

Player, Team	Lg	Org	BB
Gray Koonce, Rancho Cuca	**CAL**	**SD**	**107**
Jon Topolski, Michigan	MWL	Hou	105
Jon Macalutas, Mudville	CAL	Mil	104
Nate Espy, Piedmont	SAL	Phi	101
Adam Dunn, Dayton	MWL	Cin	100
Brett Casper, Bakersfield	CAL	SF	97
Wes Rachels, Delmarva	SAL	Bal	96
Eric Sandberg, Quad City	MWL	Min	95
Terrell Merriman, Winston-Sal	CAR	CWS	94
Corey Richardson, W Michigan	MWL	Det	94

Stolen Bases

Player, Team	Lg	Org	SB
Esix Snead, Potomac	**CAR**	**StL**	**109**
Alex Requena, Columbus	SAL	Cle	87
Tim Raines Jr., Frederick	CAR	Bal	81
Esteban German, Visalia	CAL	Oak	78
Alfredo Amezaga, Lk Elsinore	CAL	Ana	73
Andres Torres, Lakeland	FSL	Det	65
Wilken Ruan, Cape Fear	SAL	Mon	64
Chad Durham, Burlington	MWL	CWS	58
Brian Seever, Cedar Rapds	MWL	Ana	57
Mike Wenner, Visalia	CAL	Oak	57

Strikeouts

Player, Team	Lg	Org	K
Samone Peters, Clinton	**MWL**	**Cin**	**198**
Jeremy Owens, Rancho Cuca	CAL	SD	183
Andy Brown, Greensboro	SAL	NYY	182
Rob Stratton, St. Lucie	FSL	NYM	180
J.J. Davis, Lynchburg	CAR	Pit	171
Lamont Matthews, San Berndno	CAL	LA	170
Tony Peters, Dunedin	FSL	Tor	164
Caonabo Cosme, Modesto	CAL	Oak	163
Justin Lincoln, Asheville	SAL	Col	161
Vince Faison, Fort Wayne	MWL	SD	159

On-Base Percentage

Player, Team	Lg	Org	OBP
Terrmel Sledge, Lancaster	**CAL**	**Sea**	**.451**
Travis Hafner, Charlotte	FSL	Tex	.447
Nate Espy, Piedmont	SAL	Phi	.439
Rusty Keith, Modesto	CAL	Oak	.436
Adam Dunn, Dayton	MWL	Cin	.428
Kevin Mench, Charlotte	FSL	Tex	.427
Gray Koonce, Rancho Cuca	CAL	SD	.425
Bill Mott, Lk Elsinore	CAL	Ana	.421
Reed Johnson, Dunedin	FSL	Tor	.420
Ryan Gripp, Lansing	MWL	ChC	.416

Plate Appearances/Strikeout

Player, Team	Lg	Org	PA/K
Ismael Gallo, Vero Beach	**FSL**	**LA**	**18.68**
Jeff Powers, High Desert	CAL	Ari	15.69
Luis Medina, Lansing	MWL	ChC	15.03
Juan Lorenzo, Fort Myers	FSL	Min	14.18
Luis Rodriguez, Quad City	MWL	Min	14.07
Brian Hitchcox, Piedmont	SAL	Phi	12.94
Danny Sandoval, Winston-Sal	CAR	CWS	12.16
Clay Snellgrove, Rancho Cuca	CAL	SD	12.00
Albert Pujols, Potomac	CAR	StL	11.76
Jose Velazquez, St. Pete	FSL	TB	11.48

Slugging Percentage

Player, Team	Lg	Org	SLG
Kevin Mench, Charlotte	**FSL**	**Tex**	**.615**
J.R. House, Hickory	SAL	Pit	.586
Travis Hafner, Charlotte	FSL	Tex	.580
Austin Kearns, Dayton	MWL	Cin	.558
Albert Pujols, Potomac	CAR	StL	.550
Billy Martin, South Bend	MWL	Ari	.542
Hee Seop Choi, Daytona	FSL	ChC	.533
Nate Espy, Piedmont	SAL	Phi	.531
Brian Cole, St. Lucie	FSL	NYM	.528
Antonio Perez, Lancaster	CAL	Sea	.527

Hit By Pitch

Player, Team	Lg	Org	HBP
Reed Johnson, Dunedin	**FSL**	**Tor**	**25**
Jesus Basabe, Modesto	CAL	Oak	23
Jeff Auterson, Vero Beach	FSL	LA	22
Dan Grummitt, Chston-SC	SAL	TB	22
Ben Johnstone, Lansing	MWL	ChC	20
Jeff Winchester, Asheville	SAL	Col	20
Matt Scanlon, Fort Myers	FSL	Min	19
Chris Warren, Augusta	SAL	Bos	19
Travis Hafner, Charlotte	FSL	Tex	18
Terrmel Sledge, Lancaster	CAL	Sea	18

Errors

Player, Team	Lg	Org	E
Jose Castillo, Hickory	**SAL**	**Pit**	**60**
Jorge Nunez, Vero Beach	FSL	LA	58
Angel Berroa, Visalia	CAL	Oak	54
Jeff Brooks, High Desert	CAL	Ari	51
Ricky Bell, Vero Beach	FSL	LA	47
Alex Ahumada, Sarasota	FSL	Bos	46
Nick Green, Myrtle Bch	CAR	Atl	46
Neil Jenkins, W Michigan	MWL	Det	46
Josh McKinley, Cape Fear	SAL	Mon	46
2 tied with			43

Class-A Pitching Leaders

Earned Run Average

Player, Team	Lg	Org	ERA
Calvin Chipperfield, W Mich.	**MWL**	**Det**	**2.13**
Corey Thurman, Wilmington	CAR	KC	2.26
Christian Parra, Myrtle Bch	CAR	Atl	2.28
Brian Reith, Dayton	MWL	Cin	2.34
Ryan Baerlocher, Wilmington	CAR	KC	2.40
Jovanny Cedeno, Savannah	SAL	Tex	2.42
Andy VanHekken, W Michigan	MWL	Det	2.45
Travis Thompson, Dayton	MWL	Cin	2.54
Jose Mieses, Mudville	CAL	Mil	2.56
Zach Day, Tampa	FSL	NYY	2.56
Brett Jodie, Tampa	FSL	NYY	2.57
Carlos Garcia, San Berndno	CAL	LA	2.57
Ryan Madson, Piedmont	SAL	Phi	2.59
Jose Lopez, Lynchburg	CAR	Pit	2.60
Jason Stanford, Kinston	CAR	Cle	2.66

Wins

Player, Team	Lg	Org	W
Jose Mieses, Mudville	**CAL**	**Mil**	**17**
Christian Parra, Myrtle Bch	**CAR**	**Atl**	**17**
Travis Thompson, Dayton	MWL	Cin	16
Andy VanHekken, W Michigan	MWL	Det	16
Horacio Ramirez, Myrtle Bch	CAR	Atl	15
Adam Walker, Clearwater	FSL	Phi	15
Frank Brooks, Piedmont	SAL	Phi	14
Chuck Crowder, Salem	CAR	Col	14
Carlos Garcia, San Berndno	CAL	LA	14
Jeff Heaverlo, Lancaster	CAL	Sea	14
Joe Horgan, San Jose	CAL	SF	14
Ryan Madson, Piedmont	SAL	Phi	14
Mike Nannini, Kissimmee	FSL	Hou	14
8 tied with			13

Losses

Player, Team	Lg	Org	L
Dusty Bergman, Lk Elsinore	**CAL**	**Ana**	**16**
Jeremy Affeldt, Wilmington	CAR	KC	15
Ty Howington, Dayton	MWL	Cin	15
Jeremy Cunningham, San Jose	CAL	SF	14
Ryan Douglass, Chstn-WV	SAL	KC	14
Ryan Kibler, Asheville	SAL	Col	14
Mike Knowles, Greensboro	SAL	NYY	14
Dennis Ulacia, Burlington	MWL	CWS	14
Jeff Verplancke, San Jose	CAL	SF	14
9 tied with			13

Saves

Player, Team	Lg	Org	S
John Trujillo, Fort Wayne	**MWL**	**SD**	**42**
Bryan Leach, Augusta	SAL	Bos	40
Jason Bullard, Bakersfield	CAL	SF	30
Jason Marr, Potomac	CAR	StL	30
Greg Watson, W Michigan	MWL	Det	30
Bryan Moore, Kane County	MWL	Fla	27
Cam Esslinger, Asheville	SAL	Col	24
Chris George, Michigan	MWL	Hou	24
Mike Neu, Clinton	MWL	Cin	24
Heath Bell, St. Lucie	FSL	NYM	23
Jarrod Kingrey, Dunedin	FSL	Tor	23
Brandon Parker, Lancaster	CAL	Sea	22
5 tied with			21

Games

Player, Team	Lg	Org	G
Keith Forbes, Rancho Cuca	**CAL**	**SD**	**74**
John Trujillo, Fort Wayne	MWL	SD	63
Greg Watson, W Michigan	MWL	Det	62
Doug Young, Fort Wayne	MWL	SD	62
Brandon Bowe, Kane County	MWL	Fla	61
Jeremy Fikac, Rancho Cuca	CAL	SD	61
Todd Shiyuk, Rancho Cuca	CAL	SD	61
Bryan Leach, Augusta	SAL	Bos	60
Manny Bermudez, Bakersfield	CAL	SF	59
Mike Crudale, Potomac	CAR	StL	59
Jason Bullard, Bakersfield	CAL	SF	58
Bryan Moore, Kane County	MWL	Fla	58
Mike Neu, Clinton	MWL	Cin	58
Jon Valenti, Bakersfield	CAL	SF	58
Matt Vincent, Peoria	MWL	StL	58

Innings Pitched

Player, Team	Lg	Org	IP
Aaron Cook, Salem	**CAR**	**Col**	**185.2**
Carlos Garcia, San Berndno	CAL	LA	182.0
Matt Belisle, Myrtle Bch	CAR	Atl	181.0
Dave Williams, Lynchburg	CAR	Pit	181.0
Mike Nannini, Kissimmee	FSL	Hou	179.2
Frank Brooks, Piedmont	SAL	Phi	177.2
Travis Thompson, Dayton	MWL	Cin	177.0
Carlos Silva, Clearwater	FSL	Phi	176.1
Brett Myers, Piedmont	SAL	Phi	175.1
Justin Lehr, Modesto	CAL	Oak	175.0
Adam Flohr, St. Pete	FSL	TB	173.1
Jim Magrane, Chston-SC	SAL	TB	173.0
Phil Devey, San Berndno	CAL	LA	172.1
Jeff Bennett, Hickory	SAL	Pit	171.2
Gary Majewski, Winston-Sal	CAR	CWS	171.2

Class-A Pitching Leaders

Walks

Player, Team	Lg	Org	BB
Ben Howard, Rancho Cuca	**CAL**	**SD**	**111**
Jason Temple, Rancho Cuca	CAL	SD	105
Ryan Dittfurth, Savannah	SAL	Tex	99
Omar Ortiz, Rancho Cuca	CAL	SD	99
Hatuey Mendoza, High Desert	CAL	Ari	98
Derek Stanford, Michigan	MWL	Hou	92
Steve Watkins, Rancho Cuca	CAL	SD	90
Scott Dunn, Clinton	MWL	Cin	89
Nick Neugebauer, Mudville	CAL	Mil	87
Rob Purvis, Winston-Sal	CAR	CWS	87
Chuck Crowder, Salem	CAR	Col	86
Ty Howington, Dayton	MWL	Cin	86
Chris Jones, San Jose	CAL	SF	85
Gary Majewski, Winston-Sal	CAR	CWS	85
Jason Saenz, St. Lucie	FSL	NYM	83

Strikeouts

Player, Team	Lg	Org	K
Dave Williams, Lynchburg	**CAR**	**Pit**	**201**
Ryan Baerlocher, Wilmington	CAR	KC	193
Julio DePaula, Asheville	SAL	Col	187
Chin-Hui Tsao, Asheville	SAL	Col	187
Jason Childers, Mudville	CAL	Mil	177
Juan Pena, Modesto	CAL	Oak	177
Justin Reid, Hickory	SAL	Pit	176
Neal Frendling, Chston-SC	SAL	TB	174
Jose Mieses, Mudville	CAL	Mil	172
Tim Redding, Kissimmee	FSL	Hou	170
Matt Belisle, Myrtle Bch	CAR	Atl	168
Ryan Cameron, Salem	CAR	Col	168
Paul Darnell, Clinton	MWL	Cin	164
Jacob Peavy, Fort Wayne	MWL	SD	164
2 tied with			163

Strikeouts/9 Innings—Starters

Player, Team	Lg	Org	K/9
Nick Neugebauer, Mudville	**CAL**	**Mil**	**13.62**
Ben Howard, Rancho Cuca	CAL	SD	12.58
Chin-Hui Tsao, Asheville	SAL	Col	11.61
Jacob Peavy, Fort Wayne	MWL	SD	11.04
Julio DePaula, Asheville	SAL	Col	10.86
Ken Chenard, Capital Cty	SAL	NYM	10.69
Erik Bedard, Delmarva	SAL	Bal	10.62
Jovanny Cedeno, Savannah	SAL	Tex	10.57
Ryan Baerlocher, Wilmington	CAR	KC	10.53
Juan Pena, Modesto	CAL	Oak	10.34
Zach Day, Tampa	FSL	NYY	10.30
Juan Cruz, Daytona	FSL	ChC	10.26
Dennis Tankersley, Fort Wayne	MWL	SD	10.23
Jon Rauch, Winston-Sal	CAR	CWS	10.15
Jason Childers, Mudville	CAL	Mil	10.13

Strikeouts/9 Innings—Relievers

Player, Team	Lg	Org	K/9
Brandon Parker, Lancaster	**CAL**	**Sea**	**12.49**
Mike Neu, Clinton	MWL	Cin	12.39
Scott Polk, Capital Cty	SAL	NYM	12.39
Jeremy Fikac, Rancho Cuca	CAL	SD	12.12
Chris Keelin, Piedmont	SAL	Phi	12.10
Justin Fry, Piedmont	SAL	Phi	12.09
Brian Mallette, Mudville	CAL	Mil	11.92
Cam Esslinger, Asheville	SAL	Col	11.69
Doug Thompson, Salem	CAR	Col	11.61
Allan Simpson, Lancaster	CAL	Sea	11.60
Rick Cercy, Asheville	SAL	Col	11.51
Brian Brantley, Salem	CAR	Col	11.44
Mark Outlaw, Piedmont	SAL	Phi	11.44
Heath Bell, St. Lucie	FSL	NYM	11.25
Corey Spencer, Augusta	SAL	Bos	11.08

Hits/9 Innings—Starters

Player, Team	Lg	Org	H/9
Nick Neugebauer, Mudville	**CAL**	**Mil**	**5.00**
Christian Parra, Myrtle Bch	CAR	Atl	5.59
Calvin Chipperfield, W Michigan	MWL	Det	5.95
Chris Capuano, South Bend	MWL	Ari	6.02
Gary Majewski, Winston-Sal	CAR	CWS	6.03
Jerome Williams, San Jose	CAL	SF	6.37
Nathan Kent, Myrtle Bch	CAR	Atl	6.48
Jovanny Cedeno, Savannah	SAL	Tex	6.56
Chuck Crowder, Salem	CAR	Col	6.62
Jim Lynch, Bakersfield	CAL	SF	6.64
Ryan Baerlocher, Wilmington	CAR	KC	6.71
Juan Cruz, Daytona	FSL	ChC	6.73
Tom Marx, W Michigan	MWL	Det	6.75
Pablo Arias, W Michigan	MWL	Det	7.01
Jose Mieses, Mudville	CAL	Mil	7.03

Hits/9 Innings—Relievers

Player, Team	Lg	Org	H/9
John Trujillo, Fort Wayne	**MWL**	**SD**	**4.70**
Chris George, Michigan	MWL	Hou	5.22
Mark Outlaw, Piedmont	SAL	Phi	5.25
Chris Keelin, Piedmont	SAL	Phi	5.31
Jeremy Fikac, Rancho Cuca	CAL	SD	5.52
Bryan Leach, Augusta	SAL	Bos	5.60
Rick Cercy, Asheville	SAL	Col	5.61
Brian Stokes, Chston-SC	SAL	TB	5.76
Brian Brantley, Salem	CAR	Col	5.80
Doug Young, Fort Wayne	MWL	SD	5.82
Cliff Bartosh, Fort Wayne	MWL	SD	5.84
Allan Simpson, Lancaster	CAL	Sea	5.88
Ryan Jamison, Michigan	MWL	Hou	6.02
Tony Cento, Quad City	MWL	Min	6.12
Mike Neu, Clinton	MWL	Cin	6.13

Short-Season Batting Leaders

Batting Average

Player, Team	Lg	Org	Avg
Sergio Contreras, Butte	**PIO**	**Ana**	**.399**
Octavio Martinez, Bluefield	APP	Bal	.387
Syketo Anderson, Cubs	AZL	ChC	.387
Pedro Liriano, Everett	NWL	Sea	.384
Justin Morneau, Elizabethtn	APP	Min	.382
Randy Ruiz, Billings	PIO	Cin	.381
Jeremy Johnson, Medcine Hat	PIO	Tor	.376
Josh Hoffpauir, Vancouver	NWL	Oak	.371
Will Smith, Marlins	GCL	Fla	.368
Lance Niekro, Salem-Keizr	NWL	SF	.362

Catchers Batting Average

Player, Team	Lg	Org	Avg
Octavio Martinez, Bluefield	**APP**	**Bal**	**.387**
Nick Trzesniak, Idaho Falls	PIO	SD	.341
Jason Belcher, Helena	PIO	Mil	.333
Bryce Terveen, Jamestown	NYP	Atl	.327
Raymond Serrano, Jamestown	NYP	Atl	.324
John Wilson, Pittsfield	NYP	NYM	.324
Alejandro Fernandez, Staten Ilnd	NYP	NYY	.314
Ryan Doumit, Williamsprt	NYP	Pit	.313
Andres Pagan, Idaho Falls	PIO	SD	.312
Jorge Delgado, Diamondbcks	AZL	Ari	.311

First Basemen Batting Average

Player, Team	Lg	Org	Avg
Sergio Contreras, Butte	**PIO**	**Ana**	**.399**
Justin Morneau, Elizabethtn	APP	Min	.382
Ron Davenport, Medcine Hat	PIO	Tor	.345
Kevin Olkowski, Mariners	AZL	Sea	.344
Reggie Griggs, Phillies	GCL	Phi	.340
Jake Epstein, Butte	PIO	Ana	.336
Ramon German, Martinsvlle	APP	Hou	.320
Jason Botts, Rangers	GCL	Tex	.319
J.P. Woodward, Idaho Falls	PIO	SD	.317
Jason Turner, Yankees	GCL	NYY	.314

Second Basemen Batting Average

Player, Team	Lg	Org	Avg
Pedro Liriano, Everett	**NWL**	**Sea**	**.384**
Josh Hoffpauir, Vancouver	NWL	Oak	.371
Alejandro Machado, Danville	APP	Atl	.341
Elio Ayala, Ogden	PIO	Mil	.338
Ricardo Cordova, Great Falls	PIO	LA	.316
Kevin Nulton, Padres	AZL	SD	.316
Travis Hake, Ogden	PIO	Mil	.310
Lee McCool, Idaho Falls	PIO	SD	.309
Chris Johnson, Billings	PIO	Cin	.308
Henry Pichardo, Mahoning Vy	NYP	Cle	.308

Third Basemen Batting Average

Player, Team	Lg	Org	Avg
Lance Niekro, Salem-Keizr	**NWL**	**SF**	**.362**
Tony Blanco, Lowell	NYP	Bos	.353
Miguel Villilo, Mariners	AZL	Sea	.347
Daryl Clark, Ogden	PIO	Mil	.339
Reinaldo Barrera, Diamondbcks	AZL	Ari	.326
Michael Forbes, Jamestown	NYP	Atl	.321
Billy Schmitt, Johnson Cty	APP	StL	.321
J.J. Johnson, Cubs	AZL	ChC	.316
Edwin Encarnacion, Rangers	GCL	Tex	.311
Ray Navarrete, Williamsprt	NYP	Pit	.310

Shortstops Batting Average

Player, Team	Lg	Org	Avg
Chris Basak, Pittsfield	**NYP**	**NYM**	**.349**
Luis Montanez, Cubs	AZL	ChC	.344
Josh Wilson, Utica	NYP	Fla	.344
J.J. Furmaniak, Idaho Falls	PIO	SD	.343
Flavio Romero, Mexico	AZL	—	.343
Wilson Betemit, Jamestown	NYP	Atl	.331
Ryan Dacey, Yakima	NWL	LA	.323
Isaac Garcia, Athletics	AZL	Oak	.318
Israel Cruz, Mariners	AZL	Sea	.318
Esteban Montero, Rockies	AZL	Col	.314

Outfielders Batting Average

Player, Team	Lg	Org	Avg
Syketo Anderson, Cubs	**AZL**	**ChC**	**.387**
Jeremy Johnson, Medcine Hat	PIO	Tor	.376
Will Smith, Marlins	GCL	Fla	.368
Dave Krynzel, Ogden	PIO	Mil	.359
Kevin Reese, Idaho Falls	PIO	SD	.358
Michael Campo, Butte	PIO	Ana	.358
Craig Thompson, Idaho Falls	PIO	SD	.358
Sneideer Santos, Diamondbcks	AZL	Ari	.342
Cris Guerrero, Ogden	PIO	Mil	.341
Bo Ivy, White Sox	AZL	CWS	.341

Switch-Hitters Batting Average

Player, Team	Lg	Org	Avg
Craig Thompson, Idaho Falls	**PIO**	**SD**	**.358**
Miguel Villilo, Mariners	AZL	Sea	.347
Wilson Betemit, Jamestown	NYP	Atl	.331
Reinaldo Barrera, Diamondbcks	AZL	Ari	.326
Ramon German, Martinsvlle	APP	Hou	.320
Jason Botts, Rangers	GCL	Tex	.319
Ricardo Cordova, Great Falls	PIO	LA	.316
Ryan Doumit, Williamsprt	NYP	Pit	.313
Ron Merrill, Oneonta	NYP	Det	.311
Juan Camacho, Yankees	GCL	NYY	.302

Short-Season Batting Leaders

Hits

Player, Team	Lg	Org	H
Brad Downing, Boise	**NWL**	**Ana**	**96**
Steve Smitherman, Billings	PIO	Cin	95
Jamal Strong, Everett	NWL	Sea	93
Jeremy Johnson, Medcine Hat	PIO	Tor	92
Jason Ellison, Salem-Keizr	NWL	SF	90
Nate Janowicz, Mahoning Vy	NYP	Cle	90
Wilson Betemit, Jamestown	NYP	Atl	89
Josh Wilson, Utica	NYP	Fla	89
J.P. Woodward, Idaho Falls	PIO	SD	89
2 tied with			88

Extra-Base Hits

Player, Team	Lg	Org	XBH
J.P. Woodward, Idaho Falls	**PIO**	**SD**	**46**
Mitch Jones, Staten Ilnd	NYP	NYY	42
Jeremy Johnson, Medcine Hat	PIO	Tor	36
Steve Smitherman, Billings	PIO	Cin	36
Alex Gordon, Bluefield	APP	Bal	33
Ramon German, Martinsvlle	APP	Hou	32
Justin Morneau, Elizabethtn	APP	Min	32
Chad Santos, Spokane	NWL	KC	32
3 tied with			31

Doubles

Player, Team	Lg	Org	2B
Mitch Jones, Staten Ilnd	**NYP**	**NYY**	**28**
J.P. Woodward, Idaho Falls	PIO	SD	26
Ramon German, Martinsvlle	APP	Hou	24
Jeremy Johnson, Medcine Hat	PIO	Tor	24
Kelly Eddlemon, Princeton	APP	TB	21
Justin Morneau, Elizabethtn	APP	Min	21
Will Smith, Marlins	GCL	Fla	21
6 tied with			20

Total Bases

Player, Team	Lg	Org	TB
J.P. Woodward, Idaho Falls	**PIO**	**SD**	**175**
Steve Smitherman, Billings	PIO	Cin	166
Jeremy Johnson, Medcine Hat	PIO	Tor	149
Cris Guerrero, Ogden	PIO	Mil	145
Mitch Jones, Staten Ilnd	NYP	NYY	143
Daryl Clark, Ogden	PIO	Mil	139
Ryan Church, Mahoning Vy	NYP	Cle	137
Justin Morneau, Elizabethtn	APP	Min	137
Randy Ruiz, Billings	PIO	Cin	135
Brad Downing, Boise	NWL	Ana	134

Triples

Player, Team	Lg	Org	3B
Victor Hall, Missoula	**PIO**	**Ari**	**9**
Dave Mulqueen, Portland	**NWL**	**Col**	**9**
Jandin Thornton-Murray, Cubs	**AZL**	**ChC**	**9**
Sergio Contreras, Butte	PIO	Ana	8
Phillip Downing, Vermont	NYP	Mon	8
Dennis Malave, Mahoning Vy	NYP	Cle	8
Dany Morban, Reds	GCL	Cin	8
Charles Thomas, Jamestown	NYP	Atl	8
5 tied with			7

Runs

Player, Team	Lg	Org	R
J.J. Furmaniak, Idaho Falls	**PIO**	**SD**	**72**
Victor Hall, Missoula	PIO	Ari	70
Jason Ellison, Salem-Keizr	NWL	SF	67
J.P. Woodward, Idaho Falls	PIO	SD	67
Jeremy Johnson, Medcine Hat	PIO	Tor	66
Jamal Strong, Everett	NWL	Sea	63
Lee McCool, Idaho Falls	PIO	SD	62
Steve Smitherman, Billings	PIO	Cin	61
Marco Cunningham, Spokane	NWL	KC	58
Elio Ayala, Ogden	PIO	Mil	57

Home Runs

Player, Team	Lg	Org	HR
J.P. Woodward, Idaho Falls	**PIO**	**SD**	**20**
Daryl Clark, Ogden	PIO	Mil	15
Steve Smitherman, Billings	PIO	Cin	15
Chad Santos, Spokane	NWL	KC	14
Bryan Barnowski, Lowell	NYP	Bos	13
Tony Blanco, Lowell	NYP	Bos	13
Charlie Dees, Pulaski	APP	Tex	13
Alex Gordon, Bluefield	APP	Bal	13
Aaron Sisk, Medcine Hat	PIO	Tor	13
5 tied with			12

Runs Batted In

Player, Team	Lg	Org	RBI
J.P. Woodward, Idaho Falls	**PIO**	**SD**	**92**
Ryan Church, Mahoning Vy	NYP	Cle	65
Steve Smitherman, Billings	PIO	Cin	65
Daryl Clark, Ogden	PIO	Mil	64
Craig Thompson, Idaho Falls	PIO	SD	62
Justin Morneau, Elizabethtn	APP	Min	61
Jeremy Johnson, Medcine Hat	PIO	Tor	58
Angel Matos, Pulaski	APP	Tex	56
Randy Ruiz, Billings	PIO	Cin	55
2 tied with			54

Short-Season Batting Leaders

Walks

Player, Team	Lg	Org	BB
Victor Hall, Missoula	**PIO**	**Ari**	**77**
Daryl Clark, Ogden	PIO	Mil	67
Jared Abruzzo, Butte	PIO	Ana	61
Anthony Hensley, Batavia	NYP	Phi	60
Jeremy Johnson, Medcine Hat	PIO	Tor	55
Marco Cunningham, Spokane	NWL	KC	54
John Raburn, Boise	NWL	Ana	54
Alejandro Machado, Danville	APP	Atl	53
5 tied with			52

Stolen Bases

Player, Team	Lg	Org	SB
Jamal Strong, Everett	**NWL**	**Sea**	**60**
Victor Hall, Missoula	PIO	Ari	47
Anthony Hensley, Batavia	NYP	Phi	43
Ken Morris, New Jersey	NYP	StL	42
Chris Amador, White Sox	AZL	CWS	40
Willy Taveras, Burlington	APP	Cle	36
Wayne Lydon, Kingsport	APP	NYM	35
Bo Ivy, White Sox	AZL	CWS	34
Reggie Abercrombie, Great Falls	PIO	LA	32
Chris Basak, Pittsfield	NYP	NYM	32

Strikeouts

Player, Team	Lg	Org	K
Alex Gordon, Bluefield	**APP**	**Bal**	**105**
Chad Santos, Spokane	NWL	KC	103
Jorge Sosa, Portland	NWL	Col	102
Mike Mallory, Eugene	NWL	ChC	98
Shaun Harper, Jamestown	NYP	Atl	89
Luis Candelario, Hudson Val	NYP	TB	85
Terry Mayo, Helena	PIO	Mil	84
Nick Wilfong, Salem-Keizr	NWL	SF	83
3 tied with			77

On-Base Percentage

Player, Team	Lg	Org	OBP
Jeremy Johnson, Medcine Hat	**PIO**	**Tor**	**.498**
Daryl Clark, Ogden	PIO	Mil	.495
Flavio Romero, Mexico	AZL	—	.487
Victor Hall, Missoula	PIO	Ari	.479
Alejandro Machado, Danville	APP	Atl	.477
Alejandro Fernandez, Staten Ilnd	NYP	NYY	.475
Kevin Reese, Idaho Falls	PIO	SD	.474
Craig Thompson, Idaho Falls	PIO	SD	.473
Josh Brack, Athletics	AZL	Oak	.473
Bo Ivy, White Sox	AZL	CWS	.473

Plate Appearances/Strikeout

Player, Team	Lg	Org	PA/K
Josh Hoffpauir, Vancouver	**NWL**	**Oak**	**25.67**
Ralph Flores, Bristol	APP	CWS	17.89
Chris Johnson, Billings	PIO	Cin	15.88
James Tomlin, Twins	GCL	Min	15.27
Elio Ayala, Ogden	PIO	Mil	15.06
Luis Borges, Royals	GCL	KC	14.55
Kenny Perez, Red Sox	GCL	Bos	14.42
Pedro Liriano, Everett	NWL	Sea	14.40
Vic Buttler, Williamsprt	NYP	Pit	12.77
Michael Campo, Butte	PIO	Ana	12.41

Slugging Percentage

Player, Team	Lg	Org	SLG
Daryl Clark, Ogden	**PIO**	**Mil**	**.638**
Justin Morneau, Elizabethtn	APP	Min	.631
J.P. Woodward, Idaho Falls	PIO	SD	.623
Jeremy Johnson, Medcine Hat	PIO	Tor	.608
Tony Blanco, Lowell	NYP	Bos	.606
Josh Gray, Butte	PIO	Ana	.605
Sergio Contreras, Butte	PIO	Ana	.601
Charlie Dees, Pulaski	APP	Tex	.597
Octavio Martinez, Bluefield	APP	Bal	.591
Randy Ruiz, Billings	PIO	Cin	.584

Hit By Pitch

Player, Team	Lg	Org	HBP
Jeff Becker, Mahoning Vy	**NYP**	**Cle**	**20**
Tommy Callen, Medcine Hat	PIO	Tor	12
Jorge Delgado, Diamondbcks	AZL	Ari	12
Ray Hattenburg, Spokane	NWL	KC	12
Luis Maza, Elizabethtn	APP	Min	12
John Wilson, Pittsfield	NYP	NYM	12
Eric Bruntlett, Martinsvlle	APP	Hou	11
Brian Fatur, Johnson Cty	APP	StL	11
9 tied with			10

Errors

Player, Team	Lg	Org	E
Jeff Stockton, Butte	**PIO**	**Ana**	**37**
Jerry Gil, Missoula	PIO	Ari	35
Corey Smith, Burlington	APP	Cle	32
Wilson Betemit, Jamestown	NYP	Atl	29
Landon Brandes, New Jersey	NYP	StL	29
Freddie Bynum, Vancouver	NWL	Oak	29
Christian Valenzuela, Butte	PIO	Ana	29
Bolivar Volquez, Hudson Val	NYP	TB	29
Hector Luna, Mahoning Vy	NYP	Cle	28
3 tied with			27

Short-Season Pitching Leaders

Earned Run Average

Player, Team	Lg	Org	ERA
Yoel Hernandez, Phillies	**GCL**	**Phi**	**1.35**
Landon Jacobsen, Williamsprt	NYP	Pit	1.41
Jason Farmer, Salem-Keizr	NWL	SF	1.62
Domingo Valdez, Pulaski	APP	Tex	1.63
Jason Richardson, Elizabethtn	APP	Min	1.66
Wilton Chavez, Eugene	NWL	ChC	1.69
Simon Young, Mahoning Vy	NYP	Cle	1.75
Ricardo Rodriguez, Great Falls	PIO	LA	1.88
Chris Elmore, Lowell	NYP	Bos	1.89
Juan Campos, Auburn	NYP	Hou	1.92
Everett Johnson, Everett	NWL	Sea	2.07
Mauricio Lara, Lowell	NYP	Bos	2.12
Ralph McCasland, Vermont	NYP	Mon	2.26
Tom Graham, Rangers	GCL	Tex	2.29
Heath Totten, Yakima	NWL	LA	2.30

Saves

Player, Team	Lg	Org	S
Fausto Hernandez, Tigers	**GCL**	**Det**	**17**
Santo Samora, New Jersey	**NYP**	**StL**	**17**
Andy McCulloch, Medcine Hat	PIO	Tor	15
Reggie LaPlante, Yankees	GCL	NYY	13
Oscar Martinez, Staten Ilnd	NYP	NYY	13
Luke Anderson, Salem-Keizr	NWL	SF	12
Brandon Belanger, Idaho Falls	PIO	SD	12
George Perez, Queens	NYP	Tor	12
Dan Hall, Ogden	PIO	Mil	11
Brian Jackson, Mahoning Vy	NYP	Cle	11
Samuel Lopez, Royals	GCL	KC	11
Charlie Thames, Boise	NWL	Ana	11
4 tied with			10

Wins

Player, Team	Lg	Org	W
Ricardo Rodriguez, Great Falls	**PIO**	**LA**	**10**
Andy Beal, Staten Ilnd	NYP	NYY	9
Mark Freed, Eugene	NWL	ChC	9
Roberto Miniel, Ogden	PIO	Mil	9
Adam Sheefel, Billings	PIO	Cin	9
Brett Evert, Jamestown	NYP	Atl	8
Brad Stiles, Spokane	NWL	KC	8
Heath Totten, Yakima	NWL	LA	8
David Wolensky, Boise	NWL	Ana	8
13 tied with			7

Games

Player, Team	Lg	Org	G
Jeremy Cook, New Jersey	**NYP**	**StL**	**32**
Santo Samora, New Jersey	**NYP**	**StL**	**32**
Brandon Belanger, Idaho Falls	PIO	SD	31
John Butler, Everett	NWL	Sea	30
Brian Jackson, Mahoning Vy	NYP	Cle	30
Juan Campos, Auburn	NYP	Hou	29
George Perez, Queens	NYP	Tor	29
Gilbert Landestoy, Boise	NWL	Ana	28
Rafael Rigueiro, Salem-Keizr	NWL	SF	28
9 tied with			27

Losses

Player, Team	Lg	Org	L
Josh Axelson, New Jersey	**NYP**	**StL**	**9**
Alexis Guzman, Medcine Hat	PIO	Tor	8
Justin Hampson, Portland	NWL	Col	8
17 tied with			7

Innings Pitched

Player, Team	Lg	Org	IP
Corey Dagley, Batavia	**NYP**	**Phi**	**102.2**
Rikki Johnston, Oneonta	NYP	Det	97.1
Ricardo Rodriguez, Great Falls	PIO	LA	95.2
Andy Beal, Staten Ilnd	NYP	NYY	92.1
Ruddy Lugo, Ogden	PIO	Mil	91.2
Adam Sheefel, Billings	PIO	Cin	91.1
Wilton Chavez, Eugene	NWL	ChC	90.1
Mark Freed, Eugene	NWL	ChC	88.0
Chien-Ming Wang, Staten Ilnd	NYP	NYY	87.0
Luis Torres, Vermont	NYP	Mon	86.2
Mauricio Lara, Lowell	NYP	Bos	85.0
Steve Langone, Yakima	NWL	LA	84.2
David Mendez, Jamestown	NYP	Atl	84.2
Wesley Faust, Salem-Keizr	NWL	SF	84.1
Mike Perkins, New Jersey	NYP	StL	84.1

Short-Season Pitching Leaders

Walks

Player, Team	Lg	Org	BB
Joe Farley, Salem-Keizr	**NWL**	**SF**	**56**
Casey Daigle, Missoula	PIO	Ari	54
Ruddy Lugo, Ogden	PIO	Mil	52
Benji DeQuin, Vermont	NYP	Mon	50
Scott Rice, Orioles	GCL	Bal	48
Jason Norderum, Vermont	NYP	Mon	47
Ben Wallace, Helena	PIO	Mil	46
Bobby Jenks, Butte	PIO	Ana	44
Matt Roney, Portland	NWL	Col	44
Felix Montilla, Williamsprt	NYP	Pit	43
Marcus Moseley, Elizabethtn	APP	Min	43
Justin Gordon, Ogden	PIO	Mil	42
Mark Martinez, Lowell	NYP	Bos	42
5 tied with			41

Strikeouts

Player, Team	Lg	Org	K
Ricardo Rodriguez, Great Falls	**PIO**	**LA**	**129**
Wilton Chavez, Eugene	NWL	ChC	103
Aaron Krawiec, Eugene	NWL	ChC	99
Tony Milo, Boise	NWL	Ana	95
Seung Song, Lowell	NYP	Bos	93
Manuel Esquivia, Utica	NYP	Fla	91
Everett Johnson, Everett	NWL	Sea	88
Ruddy Lugo, Ogden	PIO	Mil	88
David Wolensky, Boise	NWL	Ana	88
Andy Beal, Staten Ilnd	NYP	NYY	87
Joe Farley, Salem-Keizr	NWL	SF	87
Matt Roney, Portland	NWL	Col	85
Todd Wellemeyer, Eugene	NWL	ChC	85
Roberto Maysonet, Helena	PIO	Mil	84
David Mendez, Jamestown	NYP	Atl	84

Strikeouts/9 Innings—Starters

Player, Team	Lg	Org	K/9
Ricardo Rodriguez, Great Falls	**PIO**	**LA**	**12.14**
Adam Wainwright, Danville	APP	Atl	11.89
Mike Cox, Pittsfield	NYP	NYM	11.82
Seung Song, Lowell	NYP	Bos	11.52
Aaron Krawiec, Eugene	NWL	ChC	11.42
Boof Bonser, Salem-Keizr	NWL	SF	11.18
Brian Cardwell, Queens	NYP	Tor	11.05
Manuel Esquivia, Utica	NYP	Fla	10.82
Greg Withelder, Yakima	NWL	LA	10.61
Domingo Valdez, Pulaski	APP	Tex	10.53
Jordan Zimmerman, Mariners	AZL	Sea	10.50
David Wolensky, Boise	NWL	Ana	10.38
Chris Narveson, Johnson Cty	APP	StL	10.31
Joe Farley, Salem-Keizr	NWL	SF	10.30
Wilton Chavez, Eugene	NWL	ChC	10.26

Strikeouts/9 Innings—Relievers

Player, Team	Lg	Org	K/9
Luke Anderson, Salem-Keizr	**NWL**	**SF**	**15.97**
Edgar Lizarraga, Great Falls	PIO	LA	15.30
Oscar Martinez, Staten Ilnd	NYP	NYY	14.40
Daniel Padgett, Salem-Keizr	NWL	SF	13.84
Michael Steele, Oneonta	NYP	Det	13.84
Mike Grippo, New Jersey	NYP	StL	13.50
Greg Bauer, Yakima	NWL	LA	13.37
Tony Milo, Boise	NWL	Ana	12.64
Tom Curtiss, Jamestown	NYP	Atl	12.58
Dan Hall, Ogden	PIO	Mil	12.46
Juan Renteria, Princeton	APP	TB	12.39
Ralph Hicks, Auburn	NYP	Hou	12.23
Lew Ross, Missoula	PIO	Ari	12.06
Ulmer Urbina, Vermont	NYP	Mon	11.93
Dennis Chapman, Idaho Falls	PIO	SD	11.72

Hits/9 Innings—Starters

Player, Team	Lg	Org	H/9
Jordan Zimmerman, Mariners	**AZL**	**Sea**	**5.25**
Joe Torres, Boise	NWL	Ana	5.28
Boof Bonser, Salem-Keizr	NWL	SF	5.73
Yoel Hernandez, Phillies	GCL	Phi	5.85
Jason Richardson, Elizabethtn	APP	Min	5.88
Landon Jacobsen, Williamsprt	NYP	Pit	5.97
Manuel Esquivia, Utica	NYP	Fla	6.07
Santiago Ramirez, Auburn	NYP	Hou	6.11
Ricardo Rodriguez, Great Falls	PIO	LA	6.21
Danny Borrell, Staten Ilnd	NYP	NYY	6.22
Mike Cox, Pittsfield	NYP	NYM	6.28
Adam Wainwright, Danville	APP	Atl	6.31
Shane Nance, Yakima	NWL	LA	6.36
Brandon Lyon, Queens	NYP	Tor	6.41
Doug Waechter, Hudson Val	NYP	TB	6.56

Hits/9 Innings—Relievers

Player, Team	Lg	Org	H/9
Reggie LaPlante, Yankees	**GCL**	**NYY**	**3.12**
Oscar Martinez, Staten Ilnd	NYP	NYY	3.96
Antonio Garris, Vermont	NYP	Mon	4.41
Andy Persby, Elizabethtn	APP	Min	4.50
Brian Gerlach, Twins	GCL	Min	4.55
Ralph Hicks, Auburn	NYP	Hou	4.84
Lionel Rogers, Pittsfield	NYP	NYM	4.99
John Butler, Everett	NWL	Sea	5.21
Tom Curtiss, Jamestown	NYP	Atl	5.22
Joe Abell, Portland	NWL	Col	5.40
George Perez, Queens	NYP	Tor	5.45
Ricardo Gomez, Staten Ilnd	NYP	NYY	5.49
Luke Anderson, Salem-Keizr	NWL	SF	5.52
Bo Kemp, Elizabethtn	APP	Min	5.52
Joe Orloski, Queens	NYP	Tor	5.54

2000 Triple-A and Double-A Splits

This section features lefty/righty and home/road splits for Triple-A and Double-A players. To be listed in this section, a hitter required 200 at-bats for a single team at a classification, while a pitcher needed either 200 at-bats against (lefty/righty) or 80 innings pitched (home/road).

These statistics will help you identify which hitters can handle all types of pitching, and vice versa. Other hitters might have to be platooned while certain pitchers may be best suited for specialized relief work. You'll also see which players had legitimate big seasons, and which were assisted by their ballparks.

Triple-A Batting vs. Lefthanded and Righthanded Pitchers

			vs Left					vs Right				
Player	Team	Org	AB	H	HR	RBI	Avg	AB	H	HR	RBI	Avg
Brent Abernathy	Syracuse	Tor	63	13	1	2	.206	295	93	3	33	.315
Chad Akers	Tacoma	Sea	92	32	2	7	.348	297	74	4	27	.249
Israel Alcantara	Pawtucket	Bos	75	25	7	15	.333	224	67	22	61	.299
Chad Alexander	Tacoma	Sea	108	27	2	10	.250	332	92	10	45	.277
Chad Allen	Salt Lake	Min	102	32	1	18	.314	287	89	8	49	.310
Dusty Allen	Las Vegas	SD	47	17	3	11	.362	175	52	11	44	.297
Wady Almonte	Rochester	Bal	53	16	0	8	.302	176	44	1	25	.250
Gabe Alvarez	Toledo	Det	61	11	2	11	.180	180	39	6	24	.217
Marlon Anderson	Scranton-WB	Phi	68	21	2	11	.309	329	100	6	42	.304
Danny Ardoin	Sacramento	Oak	55	14	2	7	.255	179	51	4	27	.285
Chris Ashby	Albuquerque	LA	144	41	2	18	.285	321	97	5	41	.302
Jesus Azuaje	Toledo	Det	62	13	1	2	.210	173	38	3	11	.220
Kevin Baez	Norfolk	NYM	100	26	1	12	.260	307	87	4	38	.283
Jeff Ball	Fresno	SF	47	15	2	5	.319	176	39	3	6	.222
Rod Barajas	Tucson	Ari	82	23	3	15	.280	334	71	10	60	.213
Kevin Barker	Indianapolis	Mil	49	11	0	6	.224	237	45	11	38	.190
Andy Barkett	Richmond	Atl	45	9	1	8	.200	215	54	5	30	.251
John Barnes	Salt Lake	Min	105	42	5	25	.400	336	119	8	62	.354
Larry Barnes	Edmonton	Ana	97	29	3	16	.299	300	73	4	38	.243
Kimera Bartee	Louisville	Cin	122	39	3	13	.320	331	96	5	35	.290
Justin Baughman	Edmonton	Ana	69	20	1	16	.290	234	51	0	19	.218
Mike Bell	Louisville	Cin	120	27	8	24	.225	309	88	14	54	.285
Mark Bellhorn	Sacramento	Oak	74	16	1	11	.216	362	100	23	62	.276
Esteban Beltre	Tucson	Ari	94	35	1	18	.372	358	107	2	42	.299
Gary Bennett	Scranton-WB	Phi	64	15	1	9	.234	253	82	11	43	.324
James Betzsold	New Orleans	Hou	112	31	3	18	.277	202	58	5	31	.287
Kurt Bierek	Indianapolis	Mil	78	19	0	9	.244	352	95	19	63	.270
Steve Bieser	Memphis	StL	61	13	0	4	.213	201	54	0	10	.269
Casey Blake	Salt Lake	Min	69	27	2	14	.391	224	66	10	38	.295
Hiram Bocachica	Albuquerque	LA	135	46	8	24	.341	347	109	15	60	.314
Pat Borders	Durham	TB	87	24	3	16	.276	261	71	9	39	.272
Milton Bradley	Ottawa	Mon	69	21	1	6	.304	273	83	5	23	.304
Jeff Branson	Albuquerque	LA	42	12	0	9	.286	290	84	5	32	.290
Russell Branyan	Buffalo	Cle	57	11	4	10	.193	172	45	17	50	.262
Brent Brede	Nashville	Pit	46	16	1	6	.348	223	51	0	17	.229
Kary Bridges	Ottawa	Mon	34	14	1	5	.412	176	57	1	22	.324
Tarrik Brock	Iowa	ChC	101	23	0	13	.228	287	79	12	34	.275
Dee Brown	Omaha	KC	121	32	7	22	.264	358	97	16	48	.271
Emil Brown	Nashville	Pit	51	16	1	6	.314	186	58	4	19	.312
Roosevelt Brown	Iowa	ChC	89	25	4	12	.281	274	87	8	43	.318
Cliff Brumbaugh	Oklahoma	Tex	124	40	3	10	.323	330	86	7	46	.261
Jim Buccheri	Durham	TB	80	24	2	8	.300	236	57	2	18	.242
Brian Buchanan	Salt Lake	Min	91	30	5	24	.330	273	78	22	79	.286
Mark Budzinski	Buffalo	Cle	92	22	0	4	.239	335	102	6	33	.304
Jamie Burke	Edmonton	Ana	48	13	0	4	.271	215	50	0	13	.233
Morgan Burkhart	Pawtucket	Bos	96	23	7	18	.240	257	67	16	59	.261
Brent Butler	Col. Springs	Col	105	31	1	13	.295	333	97	7	41	.291
Mike Byas	Fresno	SF	104	34	2	13	.327	412	102	0	21	.248
Eric Byrnes	Sacramento	Oak	48	19	1	9	.396	195	62	8	38	.318
Javier Cardona	Toledo	Det	51	17	1	8	.333	167	43	10	35	.257
Dustin Carr	Durham	TB	102	29	1	12	.284	263	51	2	24	.194
Jamey Carroll	Ottawa	Mon	58	20	2	4	.345	291	77	0	19	.265
Mike Caruso	Charlotte	CWS	50	7	0	3	.140	259	69	0	23	.266
Nelson Castro	Fresno	SF	36	8	0	2	.222	208	54	5	18	.260
Ramon Castro	Calgary	Fla	71	21	5	11	.296	147	52	9	34	.354
Jim Chamblee	Pawtucket	Bos	104	27	4	13	.260	303	78	13	43	.257
Frank Charles	New Orleans	Hou	119	37	4	19	.311	165	37	1	18	.224
Raul Chavez	New Orleans	Hou	83	26	1	12	.313	220	48	1	24	.218
G. Chiaramonte	Fresno	SF	91	14	2	13	.154	352	99	22	66	.281
McKay Christensen	Charlotte	CWS	65	16	0	4	.246	272	73	6	25	.268
Chris Clapinski	Calgary	Fla	52	9	0	4	.173	162	51	6	20	.315
Stubby Clapp	Memphis	StL	151	46	1	16	.305	354	92	0	36	.260
Brady Clark	Louisville	Cin	138	45	3	23	.326	349	103	13	56	.295
Jason Conti	Tucson	Ari	84	22	3	15	.262	299	95	8	42	.318
Mike Coolbaugh	Columbus	NYY	91	23	5	16	.253	296	82	18	45	.277
Trace Coquillette	Ottawa	Mon	55	10	0	1	.182	212	54	1	26	.255
John Cotton	Col. Springs	Col	39	18	1	15	.462	275	85	15	47	.309
Darron Cox	Col. Springs	Col	74	22	1	11	.297	170	56	2	35	.329
D.T. Cromer	Louisville	Cin	97	17	0	11	.175	318	95	14	56	.299
Tripp Cromer	New Orleans	Hou	61	15	0	3	.246	163	33	4	21	.202
John Curl	Las Vegas	SD	62	19	0	14	.306	230	66	5	39	.287
Mike Darr	Las Vegas	SD	74	22	0	13	.297	292	104	9	52	.356
Ben Davis	Las Vegas	SD	41	12	2	10	.293	180	46	5	30	.256
Tommy Davis	Rochester	Bal	102	25	5	10	.245	354	106	10	54	.299
Steve Decker	Sacramento	Oak	46	10	1	10	.217	197	56	3	33	.284
Tomas de la Rosa	Ottawa	Mon	83	17	0	6	.205	257	52	1	30	.202
Eddy de los Santos	Durham	TB	64	15	1	11	.234	207	53	2	21	.256
Chris Demetral	Oklahoma	Tex	84	16	1	9	.190	271	69	7	38	.255
Mark DeRosa	Richmond	Atl	66	17	0	6	.258	304	91	3	29	.299
Chris Donnels	Albuquerque	LA	81	21	5	21	.259	251	88	22	63	.351
Dave Doster	Scranton-WB	Phi	92	27	1	11	.293	358	95	9	55	.265
Kelly Dransfeldt	Oklahoma	Tex	115	25	2	11	.217	326	84	6	31	.258
Angel Echevarria	Col. Springs	Col	79	25	1	12	.316	205	70	6	38	.341
David Eckstein	Pawtucket	Bos	92	24	0	8	.261	330	80	1	23	.242
Mario Encarnacion	Sacramento	Oak	65	20	3	14	.308	226	61	10	47	.258
Emiliano Escandon	Omaha	KC	44	12	2	4	.273	258	57	5	28	.221
Adam Everett	New Orleans	Hou	143	31	2	12	.217	310	80	3	25	.258
Pedro Feliz	Fresno	SF	97	35	11	30	.361	406	115	22	75	.283
Jeff Ferguson	Salt Lake	Min	66	17	1	12	.258	169	40	1	19	.237
Jose Fernandez	Indianapolis	Mil	124	35	4	20	.282	344	99	7	48	.288
Jose Flores	Tacoma	Sea	59	21	0	7	.356	269	72	3	23	.268
P.J. Forbes	Scranton-WB	Phi	98	28	0	8	.286	236	64	2	24	.271
Ryan Freel	Syracuse	Tor	54	20	3	6	.370	229	61	7	24	.266
Shawn Gallagher	Oklahoma	Tex	70	15	2	7	.214	149	37	4	23	.248
Jamie Gann	Tucson	Ari	47	12	1	8	.255	161	40	4	25	.248
Amaury Garcia	Calgary	Fla	123	38	4	11	.309	356	102	9	36	.287
Carlos Garcia	Columbus	NYY	72	20	1	12	.278	208	56	1	27	.269
Freddy Garcia	Pawtucket	Bos	85	20	5	16	.235	300	81	19	58	.270
Guillermo Garcia	Louisville	Cin	100	21	2	8	.210	227	68	12	47	.300
Jesse Garcia	Rochester	Bal	89	26	0	6	.292	283	64	1	17	.226
Karim Garcia	Rochester	Bal	76	19	3	14	.250	194	56	10	40	.289
Luis Garcia	Memphis	StL	120	46	5	21	.383	266	66	6	23	.248
Steve Gibralter	Charlotte	CWS	55	14	3	6	.255	182	46	8	31	.253
Derrick Gibson	Calgary	Fla	94	28	3	13	.298	246	67	7	30	.272
Shawn Gilbert	Albuquerque	LA	84	33	4	14	.393	213	66	10	35	.310
Eric Gillespie	Toledo	Det	63	19	0	6	.302	176	43	8	33	.244
Charles Gipson	Tacoma	Sea	53	14	1	5	.264	161	39	0	17	.242
Raul Gonzalez	Iowa	ChC	39	7	1	2	.179	202	57	3	31	.282
Charlie Greene	Syracuse	Tor	60	15	2	5	.250	207	45	3	21	.217
Kevin Grijak	Albuquerque	LA	33	6	1	8	.182	304	90	16	71	.296
Creighton Gubanich	Indianapolis	Mil	91	28	3	17	.308	289	80	13	54	.277
Giomar Guevara	Toledo	Det	121	37	1	9	.306	262	71	6	24	.271
Aaron Guiel	Omaha	KC	60	21	4	11	.350	198	53	9	29	.268
Mike Gulan	Calgary	Fla	118	37	3	11	.314	308	98	14	63	.318
Edwards Guzman	Fresno	SF	78	22	1	7	.282	343	96	5	45	.280
Jerry Hairston	Rochester	Bal	36	11	0	4	.306	165	48	4	17	.291
Chris Hatcher	Iowa	ChC	58	17	3	7	.293	230	63	21	64	.274
Wes Helms	Richmond	Atl	101	25	2	8	.248	438	130	18	80	.297
Chad Hermansen	Nashville	Pit	75	17	4	9	.227	219	49	7	29	.224
Alex Hernandez	Nashville	Pit	44	14	1	7	.318	232	62	7	30	.267
Carlos Hernandez	Tacoma	Sea	38	10	0	2	.263	172	40	0	13	.233
Jose Herrera	Rochester	Bal	133	46	2	15	.346	419	117	2	39	.279
Phil Hiatt	Col. Springs	Col	123	43	9	30	.350	384	114	27	79	.297
A.J. Hinch	Sacramento	Oak	95	22	1	11	.232	322	89	5	36	.276
Aaron Holbert	Pawtucket	Bos	62	20	1	9	.323	232	54	2	14	.233
Ray Holbert	Omaha	KC	83	27	0	10	.325	255	59	2	30	.231
Damon Hollins	Indianapolis	Mil	83	23	1	10	.277	204	59	1	22	.289
Mike Hubbard	Richmond	Atl	53	15	1	5	.283	171	51	5	26	.298
Ken Huckaby	Tucson	Ari	53	18	0	8	.340	190	49	4	25	.258
Aubrey Huff	Durham	TB	117	32	1	15	.274	291	97	19	61	.333
Bobby Hughes	Buffalo	Cle	47	14	3	9	.298	177	43	4	23	.243
Torii Hunter	Salt Lake	Min	36	12	3	13	.333	173	65	15	48	.376
Garey Ingram	Pawtucket	Bos	70	13	2	8	.186	241	61	8	28	.253
Cesar Izturis	Syracuse	Tor	103	20	0	4	.194	332	75	0	23	.226
Ryan Jackson	Durham	TB	125	34	4	25	.272	377	122	14	60	.324
Robin Jennings	Salt Lake	Min	77	23	0	7	.299	268	84	11	54	.313
Keith Johns	Iowa	ChC	81	20	1	5	.247	272	66	1	21	.243
Keith Johnson	Edmonton	Ana	94	30	4	12	.319	329	100	9	52	.304
Mark Johnson	Norfolk	NYM	90	29	6	25	.322	225	56	11	35	.249
Chris Jones	Indianapolis	Mil	62	20	1	4	.323	171	51	2	21	.298
Felix Jose	Columbus	NYY	50	13	2	7	.260	160	52	9	31	.325
Brooks Kieschnick	Louisville	Cin	135	38	5	34	.281	305	84	20	56	.275
Wayne Kirby	Rochester	Bal	119	31	0	7	.261	388	113	6	53	.291
Randy Knorr	Oklahoma	Tex	61	14	2	7	.230	191	50	4	34	.262
Scott Krause	Indianapolis	Mil	66	21	3	13	.318	142	35	4	20	.246
Tim Laker	Nashville	Pit	111	31	6	28	.279	310	73	13	47	.235
David Lamb	Norfolk	NYM	76	15	1	8	.197	280	65	1	27	.232
Greg LaRocca	Las Vegas	SD	93	25	2	13	.269	389	117	7	67	.301
Jason LaRue	Louisville	Cin	71	19	5	18	.268	236	59	9	30	.250
Chris Latham	Col. Springs	Col	111	32	4	24	.288	228	51	3	25	.224
Aaron Ledesma	Col. Springs	Col	58	25	0	16	.431	166	52	0	21	.313
Chris Lemonis	Toledo	Det	69	16	1	5	.232	219	46	2	18	.210
Pat Lennon	Ottawa	Mon	85	31	3	14	.365	333	91	11	49	.273
Donny Leon	Columbus	NYY	39	14	1	2	.359	165	37	8	24	.224
Brian Lesher	Tacoma	Sea	115	47	7	28	.409	374	94	18	64	.251
Jeff Liefer	Charlotte	CWS	126	35	7	21	.278	319	90	25	70	.282
Cole Liniak	Iowa	ChC	100	25	4	13	.250	311	72	15	45	.232
Mark Little	Memphis	StL	136	34	6	22	.250	288	86	9	42	.299
Paul Loduca	Albuquerque	LA	75	28	1	11	.373	204	70	3	43	.343
George Lombard	Richmond	Atl	89	23	1	6	.258	335	94	9	42	.281
Luis Lopez	Syracuse	Tor	94	39	2	23	.415	397	122	5	56	.307
Mendy Lopez	Calgary	Fla	46	11	1	2	.239	179	62	6	27	.346
Mickey Lopez	Indianapolis	Mil	43	10	1	3	.233	165	44	1	19	.267
Terrell Lowery	Fresno	SF	74	18	6	12	.243	227	42	10	32	.185
Lou Lucca	Memphis	StL	127	37	1	13	.291	335	94	13	57	.281
Keith Luuloa	Edmonton	Ana	64	20	3	17	.313	206	46	5	27	.223
Scott Lydy	Charlotte	CWS	90	29	6	13	.322	278	71	8	32	.255
Robert Machado	Tacoma	Sea	67	14	2	11	.209	263	85	7	47	.323
Jeff Manto	Buffalo	Cle	68	12	4	14	.176	256	53	9	32	.207
Norberto Martin	Indianapolis	Mil	120	34	0	7	.283	286	80	1	34	.280
Manny Martinez	Calgary	Fla	94	20	2	8	.213	286	81	7	46	.283
Sandy Martinez	Calgary	Fla	49	14	4	17	.286	228	69	11	31	.303
Eric Martins	Sacramento	Oak	45	11	0	6	.244	216	55	2	15	.255
Francisco Matos	Rochester	Bal	84	23	0	6	.274	249	70	1	18	.281
Pascual Matos	Richmond	Atl	45	8	0	1	.178	185	47	4	20	.254
Gary Matthews	Iowa	ChC	50	12	4	8	.240	161	39	1	14	.242
Derrick May	Rochester	Bal	43	6	0	1	.140	170	54	5	33	.318
Scott McClain	Col. Springs	Col	106	28	6	26	.264	332	93	19	61	.280
Quinton McCracken	Durham	TB	95	25	0	6	.263	239	62	2	22	.259
John McDonald	Buffalo	Cle	51	18	0	14	.353	235	59	1	22	.251

Triple-A Batting vs. Lefthanded and Righthanded Pitchers

			vs Left					vs Right				
layer	Team	Org	AB	H	HR	RBI	Avg	AB	H	HR	RBI	Avg
eith McDonald	Memphis	StL	95	31	1	9	.326	171	39	4	21	.228
yan McGuire	Norfolk	NYM	88	20	2	12	.227	304	97	8	50	.319
illy McMillon	Toledo	Det	112	36	2	15	.321	268	95	11	35	.354
ean McNally	Calgary	Fla	84	22	4	11	.262	290	76	8	30	.262
ony Medrano	Omaha	KC	120	31	3	16	.258	365	98	5	39	.268
uan Melo	Fresno	SF	84	24	1	6	.286	333	99	11	44	.297
'arlos Mendez	Toledo	Det	135	37	7	31	.274	239	71	12	41	.297
arlos Mendoza	Col. Springs	Col	88	33	0	12	.375	271	94	0	30	.347
had Meyers	Iowa	ChC	64	23	2	10	.359	237	58	0	16	.245
oug Mientkiewicz	Salt Lake	Min	109	39	7	24	.358	376	123	11	72	.327
yan Miller	New Orleans	Hou	123	31	1	13	.252	176	44	2	22	.250
alph Milliard	Las Vegas	SD	72	21	1	8	.292	299	83	4	32	.278
amon Minor	Fresno	SF	116	26	4	22	.224	366	114	26	84	.311
yan Minor	Rochester	Bal	48	18	4	12	.375	193	53	10	36	.275
like Mitchell	Tucson	Ari	47	15	0	6	.319	232	71	4	34	.306
zzy Molina	Omaha	KC	76	18	2	8	.237	235	55	8	28	.234
ose Molina	Iowa	ChC	55	14	0	5	.255	193	44	1	12	.228
ay Montgomery	Nashville	Pit	61	15	3	7	.246	167	44	4	22	.263
randon Moore	Charlotte	CWS	92	21	0	10	.228	208	50	0	12	.240
Villie Morales	Rochester	Bal	77	17	1	7	.221	172	45	5	16	.262
cott Morgan	Edmonton	Ana	79	26	4	19	.329	241	53	5	35	.220
like Moriarty	Salt Lake	Min	82	23	5	16	.280	308	74	8	39	.240
'ony Mota	Albuquerque	LA	99	24	1	11	.242	273	76	5	36	.278
Chad Mottola	Syracuse	Tor	106	31	11	25	.292	399	125	22	77	.313
like Murphy	Tacoma	Sea	75	19	0	11	.253	285	83	6	27	.291
late Murphy	Edmonton	Ana	77	22	1	10	.286	316	79	7	28	.250
like Neill	Tacoma	Sea	93	32	4	18	.344	304	91	7	45	.299
3ry Nelson	Tucson	Ari	56	20	1	7	.357	205	61	4	24	.298
'om Nevers	Louisville	Cin	61	18	2	6	.295	160	34	3	16	.213
)avid Newhan	Las Vegas	SD	48	12	1	11	.250	196	50	4	24	.255
Kevin Nicholson	Las Vegas	SD	77	21	1	11	.273	249	70	5	33	.281
.es Norman	Omaha	KC	107	28	2	16	.262	304	78	9	47	.257
Abraham Nunez	Nashville	Pit	84	20	1	4	.238	267	77	2	25	.288
Augie Ojeda	Iowa	ChC	103	30	2	11	.291	293	81	6	32	.276
Hector Ortiz	Omaha	KC	48	18	2	7	.375	179	55	4	17	.307
Jose Ortiz	Sacramento	Oak	117	38	7	26	.325	401	144	17	82	.359
.uis Ortiz	Tucson	Ari	78	23	3	21	.295	230	70	7	44	.304
Jeff Patzke	Buffalo	Cle	49	12	0	3	.245	161	40	2	15	.248
Kit Pellow	Omaha	KC	103	28	5	18	.272	318	77	17	57	.242
Angel Pena	Albuquerque	LA	88	30	7	19	.341	227	67	10	42	.295
Tyrone Pendergrass	Richmond	Atl	93	16	0	8	.172	314	68	0	24	.217
Danny Peoples	Buffalo	Cle	76	24	4	12	.316	344	85	17	62	.247
Eduardo Perez	Memphis	StL	71	28	8	28	.394	206	52	11	38	.252
Santiago Perez	Indianapolis	Mil	83	18	0	4	.217	325	94	5	30	.289
Timoniel Perez	Norfolk	NYM	87	33	0	4	.379	204	71	6	33	.348
Tomas Perez	Scranton-WB	Phi	59	19	3	17	.322	220	63	7	39	.286
Chan Perry	Buffalo	Cle	90	25	3	18	.278	272	82	7	47	.301
Chris Petersen	Richmond	Atl	65	15	0	4	.231	187	42	0	17	.225
Ben Petrick	Col. Springs	Col	59	26	4	13	.441	189	52	5	34	.275
J.R. Phillips	New Orleans	Hou	94	26	5	22	.277	175	46	9	30	.263
J.R. Phillips	Charlotte	CWS	48	8	2	6	.167	162	38	8	29	.235
Adam Piatt	Sacramento	Oak	42	13	2	11	.310	212	59	6	31	.278
Bo Porter	Sacramento	Oak	90	26	3	14	.289	391	105	11	50	.269
Dave Post	Ottawa	Mon	75	20	0	11	.267	287	72	4	32	.251
Alonzo Powell	Columbus	NYY	55	17	3	8	.309	184	46	5	19	.250
Alejandro Prieto	Omaha	KC	83	24	1	5	.289	301	77	6	32	.256
Chris Prieto	Albuquerque	LA	56	15	1	7	.268	192	54	7	24	.281
Chris Pritchett	Scranton-WB	Phi	54	16	0	7	.296	337	77	6	53	.228
Ryan Radmanovich	Las Vegas	SD	86	19	0	5	.221	313	90	11	54	.288
Julio Ramirez	Calgary	Fla	79	29	4	15	.367	271	64	3	37	.236
Omar Ramirez	New Orleans	Hou	158	50	2	24	.316	311	100	0	29	.322
.uis Raven	Calgary	Fla	112	37	7	18	.330	308	78	17	63	.253
Tike Redman	Nashville	Pit	145	36	0	17	.248	361	96	4	34	.266
Chris Richard	Memphis	StL	130	33	2	17	.254	245	71	14	58	.290
Brian Richardson	New Orleans	Hou	87	31	1	14	.356	162	34	2	21	.210
Adam Riggs	Albuquerque	LA	141	51	3	21	.362	207	58	9	36	.280
Dave Roberts	Buffalo	Cle	84	24	1	11	.286	378	111	12	44	.294
Mike Robertson	New Orleans	Hou	111	33	5	18	.297	290	64	4	31	.221
Kerry Robinson	Columbus	NYY	80	22	0	7	.275	357	117	0	25	.328
Liu Rodriguez	Charlotte	CWS	95	27	2	12	.284	301	81	2	34	.269
Nate Rolison	Calgary	Fla	106	27	3	10	.255	337	119	20	78	.353
Jimmy Rollins	Scranton-WB	Phi	99	24	3	20	.242	371	105	9	49	.283
John Roskos	Las Vegas	SD	83	24	6	16	.289	294	96	12	58	.327
Toby Rumfield	Richmond	Atl	84	16	5	9	.190	346	100	14	61	.289
Rob Ryan	Tucson	Ari	64	22	3	17	.344	268	80	5	38	.299
Donnie Sadler	Pawtucket	Bos	79	17	0	1	.215	234	46	5	22	.197
Marc Sagmoen	New Orleans	Hou	91	18	0	3	.198	323	93	12	40	.288
Alex Sanchez	Durham	TB	104	32	1	6	.308	342	98	1	27	.287
Anthony Sanders	Tacoma	Sea	103	34	8	27	.330	325	97	12	53	.298
Rob Sasser	Toledo	Det	139	40	12	23	.288	348	91	13	40	.261
Gene Schall	Scranton-WB	Phi	104	28	5	16	.269	326	95	16	64	.291
Brian Schneider	Ottawa	Mon	34	7	1	7	.206	204	52	3	24	.255
Marcos Scutaro	Buffalo	Cle	81	27	2	15	.333	344	90	3	39	.262
Brad Seitzer	Charlotte	CWS	72	21	0	8	.292	191	56	11	34	.293
Bill Selby	Buffalo	Cle	88	19	3	18	.216	296	87	18	68	.294
Chip Sell	Tucson	Ari	85	27	1	9	.318	320	105	3	45	.328
Chris Sexton	Louisville	Cin	86	36	2	9	.419	303	90	5	41	.297
Jon Shave	Oklahoma	Tex	136	40	3	14	.294	374	108	7	40	.289
Andy Sheets	Pawtucket	Bos	61	17	2	13	.279	220	47	6	23	.214
Chris Sheff	Norfolk	NYM	100	29	1	8	.290	240	59	6	35	.246

			vs Left					vs Right				
Player	Team	Org	AB	H	HR	RBI	Avg	AB	H	HR	RBI	Avg
Ruben Sierra	Oklahoma	Tex	134	40	7	26	.299	305	103	11	56	.338
Randall Simon	Columbus	NYY	89	21	1	11	.236	275	76	16	63	.276
Mitch Simons	Norfolk	NYM	106	38	0	9	.358	303	71	0	39	.234
Steve Sisco	Richmond	Atl	53	15	1	2	.283	222	66	11	33	.297
Bobby Smith	Durham	TB	79	22	3	16	.278	182	54	14	42	.297
Chris Snopek	Tacoma	Sea	89	32	3	17	.360	304	86	10	31	.283
Alfonso Soriano	Columbus	NYY	94	35	3	17	.372	365	98	9	49	.268
Juan Sosa	Col. Springs	Col	124	38	4	15	.306	325	85	5	54	.262
Tim Spehr	Pawtucket	Bos	57	5	1	2	.088	170	29	4	23	.171
Dernell Stenson	Pawtucket	Bos	111	28	4	18	.252	269	74	19	53	.275
Mike Stoner	Edmonton	Ana	88	27	3	14	.307	241	63	10	30	.261
Darond Stovall	Edmonton	Ana	60	13	1	3	.217	192	53	8	29	.276
Larry Sutton	Memphis	StL	107	31	4	30	.290	240	58	8	40	.242
Pedro Swann	Richmond	Atl	82	18	0	10	.220	360	117	9	47	.325
Reggie Taylor	Scranton-WB	Phi	93	26	4	10	.280	329	90	11	33	.274
Andy Thompson	Syracuse	Tor	101	30	4	9	.297	325	75	18	56	.231
Ryan Thompson	Columbus	NYY	76	20	5	21	.263	250	73	18	54	.292
Ozzie Timmons	Durham	TB	134	44	5	23	.328	372	108	24	81	.290
Jorge Toca	Norfolk	NYM	123	35	3	20	.285	330	88	8	50	.267
Juan Tolentino	Edmonton	Ana	91	20	2	13	.220	341	86	9	45	.252
Chris Truby	New Orleans	Hou	81	25	2	10	.309	187	51	0	20	.273
Brad Tyler	Indianapolis	Mil	62	14	2	14	.226	309	78	6	35	.252
Josh Tyler	Fresno	SF	45	13	0	4	.289	167	45	0	7	.269
Jason Tyner	Norfolk	NYM	85	25	0	5	.294	242	80	0	23	.331
Tim Unroe	Richmond	Atl	88	21	5	15	.239	330	95	19	72	.288
Pedro Valdes	Oklahoma	Tex	104	29	3	19	.279	248	88	13	59	.355
Mario Valdez	Salt Lake	Min	62	23	3	19	.371	255	93	15	66	.365
Roberto Vaz	Sacramento	Oak	81	23	2	14	.284	345	100	8	58	.290
Jorge Velandia	Sacramento	Oak	54	16	2	9	.296	248	68	7	48	.274
Wilton Veras	Pawtucket	Bos	61	13	2	5	.213	157	33	1	20	.210
Joe Vitiello	Las Vegas	SD	52	26	1	13	.500	222	70	10	33	.315
Chris Wakeland	Toledo	Det	144	45	12	34	.313	348	88	16	42	.253
Todd Walker	Salt Lake	Min	60	21	0	8	.350	189	60	2	29	.317
B.J. Waszgis	Oklahoma	Tex	60	21	6	24	.350	199	47	7	38	.236
Dusty Wathan	Tacoma	Sea	37	15	0	4	.405	166	51	3	25	.307
Pat Watkins	Toledo	Det	97	22	2	8	.227	207	54	6	28	.261
John Wehner	Nashville	Pit	98	32	3	11	.327	329	77	13	52	.234
Vernon Wells	Syracuse	Tor	106	27	4	17	.255	387	93	12	49	.240
Mark Whiten	Buffalo	Cle	66	19	2	5	.288	289	79	8	34	.273
Darrell Whitmore	Memphis	StL	50	11	1	6	.220	206	61	9	28	.296
Luke Wilcox	Columbus	NYY	68	17	3	13	.250	275	58	10	36	.211
Brad Wilkerson	Ottawa	Mon	43	13	3	10	.302	169	40	9	25	.237
Jason Williams	Louisville	Cin	91	19	0	8	.209	300	83	4	25	.277
Craig Wilson	Nashville	Pit	97	22	7	19	.227	299	90	26	67	.301
Craig Wilson	Charlotte	CWS	57	26	1	7	.456	173	59	2	27	.341
Desi Wilson	Charlotte	CWS	85	19	1	6	.224	354	99	2	49	.280
Tom Wilson	Columbus	NYY	92	28	7	21	.304	238	63	13	50	.265
Vance Wilson	Norfolk	NYM	107	28	7	25	.262	293	76	9	37	.259
Randy Winn	Durham	TB	85	32	1	9	.376	218	68	6	31	.312
Kevin Witt	Syracuse	Tor	122	24	6	18	.197	367	97	20	54	.264
Jason Wood	Nashville	Pit	78	23	5	17	.295	238	52	2	28	.218
Ken Woods	Scranton-WB	Phi	110	39	0	4	.355	402	116	2	31	.289
Shawn Wooten	Edmonton	Ana	54	20	4	11	.370	198	69	7	31	.348
Ernie Young	Memphis	StL	139	41	12	33	.295	314	78	23	65	.248
Alan Zinter	Iowa	ChC	51	13	5	9	.255	182	40	9	26	.220
Jon Zuber	Columbus	NYY	62	20	0	7	.323	232	66	1	32	.284
Julio Zuleta	Iowa	ChC	97	30	8	22	.309	295	92	18	72	.312
Mike Zywica	Oklahoma	Tex	124	33	2	13	.266	296	77	7	45	.260

Triple-A Batting at Home and on the Road

			Home					Road				
Player	Team	Org	AB	H	HR	RBI	Avg	AB	H	HR	RBI	Avg
Brent Abernathy	Syracuse	Tor	172	50	3	22	.291	186	56	1	13	.301
Chad Akers	Tacoma	Sea	182	45	1	13	.247	207	61	5	21	.295
Israel Alcantara	Pawtucket	Bos	157	47	17	35	.299	142	45	12	41	.317
Chad Alexander	Tacoma	Sea	207	51	8	27	.246	233	68	4	28	.292
Chad Allen	Salt Lake	Min	195	67	6	42	.344	194	54	3	25	.278
Dusty Allen	Las Vegas	SD	113	41	8	27	.363	109	28	6	28	.257
Wady Almonte	Rochester	Bal	123	34	0	17	.276	106	26	1	16	.245
Gabe Alvarez	Toledo	Det	138	29	3	17	.210	103	21	5	18	.204
Marlon Anderson	Scranton-WB	Phi	182	60	6	29	.330	215	61	2	24	.284
Danny Ardoin	Sacramento	Oak	89	21	2	7	.236	145	44	4	27	.303
Chris Ashby	Albuquerque	LA	245	79	4	40	.322	220	59	3	19	.268
Jesus Azuaje	Toledo	Det	124	30	4	9	.242	111	21	0	4	.189
Kevin Baez	Norfolk	NYM	191	57	3	30	.298	216	56	2	20	.259
Jeff Ball	Fresno	SF	110	23	3	7	.209	113	31	2	4	.274
Rod Barajas	Tucson	Ari	191	43	7	37	.225	225	51	6	38	.227
Kevin Barker	Indianapolis	Mil	136	22	3	15	.162	150	34	8	29	.227
Andy Barkett	Richmond	Atl	122	30	2	15	.246	138	33	4	23	.239
John Barnes	Salt Lake	Min	209	87	8	53	.416	232	74	5	34	.319
Larry Barnes	Edmonton	Ana	189	50	5	29	.265	208	52	2	25	.250
Kimera Bartee	Louisville	Cin	221	68	2	22	.308	232	67	6	26	.289
Justin Baughman	Edmonton	Ana	148	42	1	16	.284	155	29	0	19	.187
Mike Bell	Louisville	Cin	221	62	11	46	.281	208	53	11	32	.255
Mark Bellhorn	Sacramento	Oak	192	47	11	33	.245	244	69	13	40	.283
Esteban Beltre	Tucson	Ari	229	82	1	32	.358	223	60	2	28	.269
Gary Bennett	Scranton-WB	Phi	144	43	9	28	.299	173	54	3	24	.312
James Betzsold	New Orleans	Hou	140	43	2	18	.307	174	46	6	31	.264
Kurt Bierek	Indianapolis	Mil	201	53	8	34	.264	229	61	11	38	.266
Steve Bieser	Memphis	StL	141	30	0	4	.213	121	37	0	10	.306
Casey Blake	Salt Lake	Min	126	41	5	28	.325	167	52	7	24	.311
Hiram Bocachica	Albuquerque	LA	224	84	5	46	.375	258	71	18	38	.275
Pat Borders	Durham	TB	180	52	7	25	.289	168	43	5	30	.256
Milton Bradley	Ottawa	Mon	153	42	1	10	.275	189	62	5	19	.328
Jeff Branson	Albuquerque	LA	175	52	2	29	.297	157	44	3	12	.280
Russell Branyan	Buffalo	Cle	92	23	5	15	.250	137	33	16	45	.241
Brent Brede	Nashville	Pit	143	36	1	15	.252	126	31	0	8	.246
Kary Bridges	Ottawa	Mon	91	33	1	10	.363	119	38	1	17	.319
Tarrik Brock	Iowa	ChC	182	53	9	25	.291	206	49	3	22	.238
Dee Brown	Omaha	KC	240	70	12	36	.292	239	59	11	34	.247
Emil Brown	Nashville	Pit	118	33	3	14	.280	119	41	2	11	.345
Roosevelt Brown	Iowa	ChC	163	49	5	23	.301	200	63	7	32	.315
Cliff Brumbaugh	Oklahoma	Tex	202	61	6	27	.302	252	65	4	29	.258
Jim Buccheri	Durham	TB	152	46	3	11	.303	164	35	1	15	.213
Brian Buchanan	Salt Lake	Min	171	55	11	53	.322	193	53	16	50	.275
Mark Budzinski	Buffalo	Cle	198	62	3	19	.313	229	62	3	18	.271
Jamie Burke	Edmonton	Ana	119	37	0	10	.311	144	26	0	7	.181
Morgan Burkhart	Pawtucket	Bos	183	49	12	42	.268	170	41	11	35	.241
Brent Butler	Col. Springs	Col	221	70	3	28	.317	217	58	5	26	.267
Mike Byas	Fresno	SF	250	67	2	17	.268	266	69	0	17	.259
Eric Byrnes	Sacramento	Oak	143	51	4	25	.357	100	30	5	22	.300
Javier Cardona	Toledo	Det	116	29	6	22	.250	102	31	5	21	.304
Dustin Carr	Durham	TB	174	45	2	19	.259	191	35	1	17	.183
Jamey Carroll	Ottawa	Mon	179	55	2	12	.307	170	42	0	11	.247
Mike Caruso	Charlotte	CWS	148	39	0	10	.264	161	37	0	16	.230
Nelson Castro	Fresno	SF	106	29	4	15	.274	138	33	1	5	.239
Ramon Castro	Calgary	Fla	111	35	8	27	.315	107	38	6	18	.355
Jim Chamblee	Pawtucket	Bos	193	45	6	20	.233	214	60	11	36	.280
Frank Charles	New Orleans	Hou	135	38	3	24	.281	149	36	2	13	.242
Raul Chavez	New Orleans	Hou	152	41	0	24	.270	151	33	2	12	.219
G. Chiaramonte	Fresno	SF	235	55	14	44	.234	208	58	10	35	.279
McKay Christensen	Charlotte	CWS	168	39	2	9	.232	169	50	4	20	.296
Chris Clapinski	Calgary	Fla	110	31	2	15	.282	104	29	4	9	.279
Stubby Clapp	Memphis	StL	220	55	0	16	.250	285	83	1	36	.291
Brady Clark	Louisville	Cin	234	76	7	49	.325	253	72	9	30	.285
Jason Conti	Tucson	Ari	168	50	3	28	.298	215	67	8	29	.312
Mike Coolbaugh	Columbus	NYY	188	48	9	24	.255	199	57	14	37	.286
Trace Coquillette	Ottawa	Mon	133	31	1	12	.233	134	33	0	15	.246
John Cotton	Col. Springs	Col	158	57	9	40	.361	156	46	7	22	.295
Darron Cox	Col. Springs	Col	122	43	0	21	.352	122	35	3	25	.287
D.T. Cromer	Louisville	Cin	211	68	8	45	.322	204	44	6	22	.216
Tripp Cromer	New Orleans	Hou	113	18	2	12	.159	111	30	2	12	.270
John Curl	Las Vegas	SD	166	57	4	39	.343	126	28	1	14	.222
Mike Darr	Las Vegas	SD	175	65	3	30	.371	191	61	6	35	.319
Ben Davis	Las Vegas	SD	110	30	3	18	.273	111	28	4	22	.252
Tommy Davis	Rochester	Bal	235	69	6	33	.294	221	62	9	31	.281
Steve Decker	Sacramento	Oak	143	40	3	33	.280	100	26	1	10	.260
Tomas de la Rosa	Ottawa	Mon	144	33	0	14	.229	196	36	1	22	.184
Eddy de los Santos	Durham	TB	138	34	3	17	.246	133	34	0	15	.256
Chris Demetral	Oklahoma	Tex	162	42	2	18	.259	193	43	6	29	.223
Mark DeRosa	Richmond	Atl	181	61	0	20	.337	189	47	3	15	.249
Chris Donnels	Albuquerque	LA	177	60	9	48	.339	155	49	18	36	.316
Dave Doster	Scranton-WB	Phi	228	65	5	38	.285	222	57	5	28	.257
Kelly Dransfeldt	Oklahoma	Tex	212	49	3	23	.231	229	60	5	19	.262
Angel Echevarria	Col. Springs	Col	155	60	6	34	.387	129	35	1	16	.271
David Eckstein	Pawtucket	Bos	205	52	1	18	.254	217	52	0	13	.240
Mario Encarnacion	Sacramento	Oak	161	43	5	24	.267	140	38	8	37	.271
Emiliano Escandon	Omaha	KC	139	28	6	17	.201	163	41	1	15	.252
Adam Everett	New Orleans	Hou	226	57	2	14	.252	227	54	3	23	.238
Pedro Feliz	Fresno	SF	254	78	20	56	.307	249	72	13	49	.289
Jeff Ferguson	Salt Lake	Min	116	33	0	18	.284	119	24	2	13	.202
Jose Fernandez	Indianapolis	Mil	224	64	3	32	.286	244	70	8	36	.287
Jose Flores	Tacoma	Sea	148	41	1	11	.277	180	52	2	19	.289
P.J. Forbes	Scranton-WB	Phi	160	47	1	19	.294	174	45	1	13	.259
Ryan Freel	Syracuse	Tor	145	43	7	20	.297	138	38	3	10	.275
Shawn Gallagher	Oklahoma	Tex	109	26	3	18	.239	110	26	3	12	.236
Jamie Gann	Tucson	Ari	109	32	0	18	.294	99	20	5	15	.202
Amaury Garcia	Calgary	Fla	250	81	10	34	.324	229	59	3	13	.258
Carlos Garcia	Columbus	NYY	145	38	2	14	.262	135	38	0	25	.281
Freddy Garcia	Pawtucket	Bos	192	51	15	45	.266	193	50	9	29	.259
Guillermo Garcia	Louisville	Cin	164	47	8	34	.287	163	42	6	21	.258
Jesse Garcia	Rochester	Bal	175	40	1	8	.229	197	50	0	15	.254
Karim Garcia	Rochester	Bal	128	36	9	24	.281	142	39	4	30	.275
Luis Garcia	Memphis	StL	182	48	8	24	.264	204	64	3	20	.314
Steve Gibralter	Charlotte	CWS	98	20	5	14	.204	139	40	6	23	.288
Derrick Gibson	Calgary	Fla	156	37	5	19	.237	184	58	5	24	.315
Shawn Gilbert	Albuquerque	LA	161	61	7	30	.379	136	38	7	19	.279
Eric Gillespie	Toledo	Det	119	36	6	28	.303	120	26	2	11	.217
Charles Gipson	Tacoma	Sea	109	25	0	10	.229	105	28	1	12	.267
Raul Gonzalez	Iowa	ChC	121	29	2	16	.240	120	35	2	17	.292
Charlie Greene	Syracuse	Tor	146	33	2	14	.226	121	27	3	12	.223
Kevin Grijak	Albuquerque	LA	165	55	10	44	.333	172	41	7	35	.238
Creighton Gubanich	Indianapolis	Mil	187	48	10	37	.257	193	60	6	34	.311
Giomar Guevara	Toledo	Det	194	52	4	21	.268	189	56	3	12	.296
Aaron Guiel	Omaha	KC	123	31	5	19	.252	135	43	8	21	.319
Mike Gulan	Calgary	Fla	217	75	7	40	.346	209	60	10	34	.287
Edwards Guzman	Fresno	SF	221	68	4	31	.308	200	50	2	21	.250
Jerry Hairston	Rochester	Bal	93	29	2	7	.312	108	30	2	14	.278
Chris Hatcher	Iowa	ChC	135	38	11	32	.281	153	42	13	39	.275
Wes Helms	Richmond	Atl	255	78	11	53	.306	284	77	9	35	.271
Chad Hermansen	Nashville	Pit	147	32	9	22	.218	147	34	2	16	.231
Alex Hernandez	Nashville	Pit	123	25	4	17	.203	153	51	4	20	.333
Carlos Hernandez	Tacoma	Sea	99	26	0	7	.263	111	24	0	8	.216
Jose Herrera	Rochester	Bal	282	82	2	28	.291	270	81	2	26	.300
Phil Hiatt	Col. Springs	Col	256	89	24	67	.348	251	68	12	42	.271
A.J. Hinch	Sacramento	Oak	180	49	2	19	.272	237	62	4	28	.262
Aaron Holbert	Pawtucket	Bos	140	34	0	6	.243	154	40	3	17	.260
Ray Holbert	Omaha	KC	184	47	1	17	.255	154	39	1	23	.253
Damon Hollins	Indianapolis	Mil	142	37	1	9	.261	145	45	1	23	.310
Mike Hubbard	Richmond	Atl	98	29	2	12	.296	126	37	4	19	.294
Ken Huckaby	Tucson	Ari	126	40	1	20	.317	117	27	3	13	.231
Aubrey Huff	Durham	TB	215	67	13	38	.312	193	62	7	38	.321
Bobby Hughes	Buffalo	Cle	109	31	5	18	.284	115	26	2	14	.226
Torii Hunter	Salt Lake	Min	106	39	9	29	.368	103	38	9	32	.369
Garey Ingram	Pawtucket	Bos	126	35	3	15	.278	185	39	7	21	.211
Cesar Izturis	Syracuse	Tor	216	45	0	14	.208	219	50	0	13	.228
Ryan Jackson	Durham	TB	245	79	9	36	.322	257	77	9	49	.300
Robin Jennings	Salt Lake	Min	174	52	7	38	.299	171	55	4	23	.322
Keith Johns	Iowa	ChC	171	42	1	14	.246	182	44	1	12	.242
Keith Johnson	Edmonton	Ana	212	58	4	25	.274	211	72	9	39	.341
Mark Johnson	Norfolk	NYM	156	42	11	33	.269	159	43	6	27	.270
Chris Jones	Indianapolis	Mil	104	34	1	9	.327	129	37	2	16	.287
Felix Jose	Columbus	NYY	128	37	5	19	.289	82	28	6	19	.341
Brooks Kieschnick	Louisville	Cin	221	70	16	59	.317	219	52	9	31	.237
Wayne Kirby	Rochester	Bal	236	55	1	27	.233	271	89	5	33	.328
Randy Knorr	Oklahoma	Tex	123	34	3	26	.276	129	30	3	15	.233
Scott Krause	Indianapolis	Mil	107	31	5	21	.290	101	25	2	12	.248
Tim Laker	Nashville	Pit	206	45	8	28	.218	215	59	11	47	.274
David Lamb	Norfolk	NYM	186	45	2	19	.242	170	35	0	16	.206
Greg LaRocca	Las Vegas	SD	243	78	7	48	.321	239	64	2	32	.268
Jason LaRue	Louisville	Cin	138	38	7	24	.275	169	40	7	24	.237
Chris Latham	Col. Springs	Col	161	34	2	20	.211	178	49	5	29	.275
Aaron Ledesma	Col. Springs	Col	96	36	0	15	.375	128	41	0	22	.320
Chris Lemonis	Toledo	Det	119	23	1	10	.193	169	39	2	13	.231
Pat Lennon	Ottawa	Mon	194	63	7	25	.325	224	59	7	38	.263
Donny Leon	Columbus	NYY	106	28	7	18	.264	98	23	2	8	.235
Brian Lesher	Tacoma	Sea	250	69	10	43	.276	239	72	15	49	.301
Jeff Liefer	Charlotte	CWS	232	62	22	53	.267	213	63	10	38	.296
Cole Liniak	Iowa	ChC	210	51	10	36	.243	201	46	9	22	.229
Mark Little	Memphis	StL	185	54	10	27	.292	239	66	5	37	.276
Paul Loduca	Albuquerque	LA	142	53	2	30	.373	137	45	2	24	.328
George Lombard	Richmond	Atl	230	68	4	29	.296	194	49	6	19	.253
Luis Lopez	Syracuse	Tor	238	83	4	46	.349	253	78	3	33	.308
Mendy Lopez	Calgary	Fla	116	34	5	19	.293	109	39	2	10	.358
Mickey Lopez	Indianapolis	Mil	104	31	2	18	.298	104	23	0	4	.221
Terrell Lowery	Fresno	SF	153	28	8	26	.183	148	32	8	18	.216
Lou Lucca	Memphis	StL	228	58	6	32	.254	234	73	8	38	.312
Keith Luuloa	Edmonton	Ana	122	31	1	17	.254	148	35	7	27	.236
Scott Lydy	Charlotte	CWS	189	49	10	28	.259	179	51	4	17	.285
Robert Machado	Tacoma	Sea	151	39	4	25	.258	179	60	5	33	.335
Jeff Manto	Buffalo	Cle	156	34	9	27	.218	168	31	4	19	.185
Norberto Martin	Indianapolis	Mil	205	59	1	23	.288	201	55	0	18	.274
Manny Martinez	Calgary	Fla	182	50	5	24	.275	198	51	4	30	.258
Sandy Martinez	Calgary	Fla	130	36	9	24	.277	147	47	6	24	.320
Eric Martins	Sacramento	Oak	126	31	0	10	.246	135	35	2	11	.259
Francisco Matos	Rochester	Bal	162	42	0	12	.259	171	51	1	12	.298
Pascual Matos	Richmond	Atl	112	31	2	12	.277	118	24	2	9	.203
Gary Matthews	Iowa	ChC	104	23	4	11	.221	107	28	1	11	.262
Derrick May	Rochester	Bal	102	29	2	16	.284	111	31	3	18	.279
Scott McClain	Col. Springs	Col	205	60	17	47	.293	233	61	8	40	.262
Quinton McCracken	Durham	TB	196	61	1	23	.311	138	26	1	5	.188
John McDonald	Buffalo	Cle	149	40	1	17	.268	137	37	0	19	.270

Triple-A Batting at Home and on the Road

			Home					Road				
Player	Team	Org	AB	H	HR	RBI	Avg	AB	H	HR	RBI	Avg
Keith McDonald	Memphis	StL	148	35	3	12	.236	118	35	2	18	.297
Ryan McGuire	Norfolk	NYM	188	65	4	34	.346	204	52	6	28	.255
Billy McMillon	Toledo	Det	201	69	8	27	.343	179	62	5	23	.346
Sean McNally	Calgary	Fla	196	54	5	26	.276	178	44	7	15	.247
Tony Medrano	Omaha	KC	218	62	5	34	.284	267	67	3	21	.251
Juan Melo	Fresno	SF	224	69	9	33	.308	193	54	3	17	.280
Carlos Mendez	Toledo	Det	201	56	10	39	.279	173	52	9	33	.301
Carlos Mendoza	Col. Springs	Col	208	76	0	26	.365	151	51	0	16	.338
Chad Meyers	Iowa	ChC	150	37	0	13	.247	151	44	2	13	.291
Doug Mientkiewicz	Salt Lake	Min	227	79	7	40	.348	258	83	11	56	.322
Ryan Miller	New Orleans	Hou	130	33	2	17	.254	169	42	1	18	.249
Ralph Milliard	Las Vegas	SD	228	74	4	34	.325	143	30	1	6	.210
Damon Minor	Fresno	SF	242	67	16	54	.277	240	73	14	52	.304
Ryan Minor	Rochester	Bal	116	31	5	20	.267	125	40	9	28	.320
Mike Mitchell	Tucson	Ari	126	38	1	17	.302	153	48	3	23	.314
Izzy Molina	Omaha	KC	145	39	5	17	.269	166	34	5	19	.205
Jose Molina	Iowa	ChC	130	27	1	8	.208	118	31	0	9	.263
Ray Montgomery	Nashville	Pit	85	24	3	12	.282	143	35	4	17	.245
Brandon Moore	Charlotte	CWS	134	34	0	9	.254	166	37	0	13	.223
Willie Morales	Rochester	Bal	127	35	3	10	.276	122	27	3	13	.221
Scott Morgan	Edmonton	Ana	162	43	6	33	.265	158	36	3	21	.228
Mike Moriarty	Salt Lake	Min	194	47	8	22	.242	196	50	5	33	.255
Tony Mota	Albuquerque	LA	162	37	2	20	.228	210	63	4	27	.300
Chad Mottola	Syracuse	Tor	252	77	18	55	.306	253	79	15	47	.312
Mike Murphy	Tacoma	Sea	173	43	4	16	.249	187	59	2	22	.316
Nate Murphy	Edmonton	Ana	205	56	4	21	.273	188	45	4	17	.239
Mike Neill	Tacoma	Sea	204	66	7	35	.324	193	57	4	28	.295
Bry Nelson	Tucson	Ari	132	42	0	17	.318	129	39	5	14	.302
Tom Nevers	Louisville	Cin	85	19	2	12	.224	136	33	3	10	.243
David Newhan	Las Vegas	SD	96	23	2	14	.240	148	39	3	21	.264
Kevin Nicholson	Las Vegas	SD	153	44	1	19	.288	173	47	5	25	.272
Les Norman	Omaha	KC	187	44	6	28	.235	224	62	5	35	.277
Abraham Nunez	Nashville	Pit	141	40	3	13	.284	210	57	0	16	.271
Augie Ojeda	Iowa	ChC	197	55	2	14	.279	199	56	6	29	.281
Hector Ortiz	Omaha	KC	117	39	2	10	.333	110	34	4	14	.309
Jose Ortiz	Sacramento	Oak	256	91	17	62	.355	262	91	7	46	.347
Luis Ortiz	Tucson	Ari	160	51	4	34	.319	148	42	6	31	.284
Jeff Patzke	Buffalo	Cle	116	23	2	10	.198	94	29	0	8	.309
Kit Pellow	Omaha	KC	203	52	12	36	.256	218	53	10	39	.243
Angel Pena	Albuquerque	LA	155	52	10	37	.335	160	45	7	24	.281
Tyrone Pendergrass	Richmond	Atl	180	41	0	12	.228	227	43	0	20	.189
Danny Peoples	Buffalo	Cle	198	49	10	34	.247	222	60	11	40	.270
Eduardo Perez	Memphis	StL	154	42	9	33	.273	123	38	10	33	.309
Santiago Perez	Indianapolis	Mil	203	58	5	24	.286	205	54	0	10	.263
Timoniel Perez	Norfolk	NYM	141	49	0	12	.348	150	55	6	25	.367
Tomas Perez	Scranton-WB	Phi	121	34	7	28	.281	158	48	3	28	.304
Chan Perry	Buffalo	Cle	180	61	7	34	.339	182	46	3	31	.253
Chris Petersen	Richmond	Atl	106	23	0	8	.217	146	34	0	13	.233
Ben Petrick	Col. Springs	Col	117	42	3	23	.359	131	36	6	24	.275
J.R. Phillips	New Orleans	Hou	138	35	8	27	.254	131	37	6	25	.282
J.R. Phillips	Charlotte	CWS	98	24	8	24	.245	112	22	2	11	.196
Adam Piatt	Sacramento	Oak	114	36	4	23	.316	140	36	4	19	.257
Bo Porter	Sacramento	Oak	242	61	9	26	.252	239	70	5	38	.293
Dave Post	Ottawa	Mon	155	36	1	18	.232	207	56	3	25	.271
Alonzo Powell	Columbus	NYY	104	26	1	7	.250	135	37	7	20	.274
Alejandro Prieto	Omaha	KC	175	41	3	15	.234	209	60	4	22	.287
Chris Prieto	Albuquerque	LA	130	40	5	19	.308	118	29	3	12	.246
Chris Pritchett	Scranton-WB	Phi	201	42	2	27	.209	190	51	4	33	.268
Ryan Radmanovich	Las Vegas	SD	188	58	6	30	.309	211	51	5	29	.242
Julio Ramirez	Calgary	Fla	172	42	4	26	.244	178	51	3	26	.287
Omar Ramirez	New Orleans	Hou	229	76	0	19	.332	240	74	2	34	.308
Luis Raven	Calgary	Fla	203	56	10	39	.276	217	59	14	42	.272
Tike Redman	Nashville	Pit	244	58	4	25	.238	262	74	0	26	.282
Chris Richard	Memphis	StL	189	53	11	40	.280	186	51	5	35	.274
Brian Richardson	New Orleans	Hou	113	25	0	16	.221	136	40	3	19	.294
Adam Riggs	Albuquerque	LA	178	62	2	26	.348	170	47	10	31	.276
Dave Roberts	Buffalo	Cle	226	55	6	30	.243	236	80	7	25	.339
Mike Robertson	New Orleans	Hou	196	57	4	30	.291	205	40	5	19	.195
Kerry Robinson	Columbus	NYY	214	66	0	14	.308	223	73	0	18	.327
Liu Rodriguez	Charlotte	CWS	201	63	4	29	.313	195	45	0	17	.231
Nate Rolison	Calgary	Fla	229	84	12	46	.367	214	62	11	42	.290
Jimmy Rollins	Scranton-WB	Phi	228	67	4	33	.294	242	62	8	36	.256
John Roskos	Las Vegas	SD	196	69	8	38	.352	181	51	10	36	.282
Toby Rumfield	Richmond	Atl	209	59	8	36	.282	221	57	11	34	.258
Rob Ryan	Tucson	Ari	106	36	2	16	.340	226	66	6	39	.292
Donnie Sadler	Pawtucket	Bos	152	34	2	9	.224	161	29	3	14	.180
Marc Sagmoen	New Orleans	Hou	208	49	5	16	.236	206	62	7	27	.301
Alex Sanchez	Durham	TB	219	66	2	17	.301	227	64	0	16	.282
Anthony Sanders	Tacoma	Sea	209	53	8	24	.254	219	78	12	56	.356
Rob Sasser	Toledo	Det	240	65	14	31	.271	247	66	11	32	.267
Gene Schall	Scranton-WB	Phi	212	59	9	33	.278	218	64	12	47	.294
Brian Schneider	Ottawa	Mon	108	28	1	12	.259	130	31	3	19	.238
Marcos Scutaro	Buffalo	Cle	202	57	3	30	.282	223	60	2	24	.269
Brad Seitzer	Charlotte	CWS	142	38	7	22	.268	121	39	4	20	.322
Bill Selby	Buffalo	Cle	174	45	10	40	.259	210	61	11	46	.290
Chip Sell	Tucson	Ari	220	77	3	30	.350	185	55	1	24	.297
Chris Sexton	Louisville	Cin	193	69	2	27	.358	196	57	5	23	.291
Jon Shave	Oklahoma	Tex	237	68	3	20	.287	273	80	7	34	.293
Andy Sheets	Pawtucket	Bos	116	25	3	11	.216	165	39	5	25	.236
Chris Sheff	Norfolk	NYM	145	30	3	20	.207	195	58	4	23	.297

			Home					Road				
Player	Team	Org	AB	H	HR	RBI	Avg	AB	H	HR	RBI	Avg
Ruben Sierra	Oklahoma	Tex	201	70	12	55	.348	238	73	6	27	.307
Randall Simon	Columbus	NYY	155	42	9	30	.271	209	55	8	44	.263
Mitch Simons	Norfolk	NYM	193	50	0	26	.259	216	59	0	22	.273
Steve Sisco	Richmond	Atl	156	39	6	17	.250	119	42	6	18	.353
Bobby Smith	Durham	TB	142	38	6	25	.268	119	38	11	33	.319
Chris Snopek	Tacoma	Sea	177	51	6	20	.288	216	67	7	28	.310
Alfonso Soriano	Columbus	NYY	201	60	5	24	.299	258	73	7	42	.283
Juan Sosa	Col. Springs	Col	224	63	4	37	.281	225	60	5	32	.267
Tim Spehr	Pawtucket	Bos	109	13	3	16	.119	118	21	2	9	.178
Dernell Stenson	Pawtucket	Bos	193	47	12	31	.244	187	55	11	40	.294
Mike Stoner	Edmonton	Ana	151	37	4	16	.245	178	53	9	28	.298
Darond Stovall	Edmonton	Ana	123	26	4	12	.211	129	40	5	20	.310
Larry Sutton	Memphis	StL	168	43	6	30	.256	179	46	6	40	.257
Pedro Swann	Richmond	Atl	232	67	4	33	.289	210	68	5	24	.324
Reggie Taylor	Scranton-WB	Phi	215	57	9	22	.265	207	59	6	21	.285
Andy Thompson	Syracuse	Tor	226	57	14	35	.252	200	48	8	30	.240
Ryan Thompson	Columbus	NYY	163	49	13	40	.301	163	44	10	35	.270
Ozzie Timmons	Durham	TB	243	72	16	54	.296	263	80	13	50	.304
Jorge Toca	Norfolk	NYM	224	63	4	34	.281	229	60	7	36	.262
Juan Tolentino	Edmonton	Ana	195	48	2	22	.246	237	58	9	36	.245
Chris Truby	New Orleans	Hou	124	36	1	11	.290	144	40	1	19	.278
Brad Tyler	Indianapolis	Mil	197	52	3	26	.264	174	40	5	23	.230
Josh Tyler	Fresno	SF	99	28	0	7	.283	113	30	0	4	.265
Jason Tyner	Norfolk	NYM	157	57	0	15	.363	170	48	0	13	.282
Tim Unroe	Richmond	Atl	179	54	12	44	.302	239	62	12	43	.259
Pedro Valdes	Oklahoma	Tex	156	47	4	26	.301	196	70	12	52	.357
Mario Valdez	Salt Lake	Min	177	57	11	42	.322	140	59	7	43	.421
Roberto Vaz	Sacramento	Oak	196	52	1	26	.265	230	71	9	46	.309
Jorge Velandia	Sacramento	Oak	184	51	7	39	.277	118	33	2	18	.280
Wilton Veras	Pawtucket	Bos	118	23	1	13	.195	100	23	2	12	.230
Joe Vitiello	Las Vegas	SD	123	45	4	24	.366	151	51	7	22	.338
Chris Wakeland	Toledo	Det	246	64	13	34	.260	246	69	15	42	.280
Todd Walker	Salt Lake	Min	117	43	2	24	.368	132	38	0	13	.288
B.J. Waszgis	Oklahoma	Tex	131	39	8	44	.298	128	29	5	18	.227
Dusty Wathan	Tacoma	Sea	107	33	1	13	.308	96	33	2	16	.344
Pat Watkins	Toledo	Det	151	46	3	12	.305	153	30	5	24	.196
John Wehner	Nashville	Pit	199	51	5	23	.256	228	58	11	40	.254
Vernon Wells	Syracuse	Tor	238	64	8	34	.269	255	56	8	32	.220
Mark Whiten	Buffalo	Cle	185	55	5	21	.297	170	43	5	18	.253
Darrell Whitmore	Memphis	StL	129	38	6	21	.295	127	34	4	13	.268
Luke Wilcox	Columbus	NYY	161	39	11	30	.242	182	36	2	19	.198
Brad Wilkerson	Ottawa	Mon	115	24	6	19	.209	97	29	6	16	.299
Jason Williams	Louisville	Cin	204	54	3	21	.265	187	48	1	12	.257
Craig Wilson	Nashville	Pit	194	56	13	44	.289	202	56	20	42	.277
Craig Wilson	Charlotte	CWS	137	48	3	24	.350	93	37	0	10	.398
Desi Wilson	Charlotte	CWS	218	58	3	23	.266	221	60	0	32	.271
Tom Wilson	Columbus	NYY	162	39	12	40	.241	168	52	8	31	.310
Vance Wilson	Norfolk	NYM	185	47	5	21	.254	215	57	11	41	.265
Randy Winn	Durham	TB	137	38	3	13	.277	166	62	4	27	.373
Kevin Witt	Syracuse	Tor	239	55	12	40	.230	250	66	14	32	.264
Jason Wood	Nashville	Pit	152	32	1	13	.211	164	43	6	32	.262
Ken Woods	Scranton-WB	Phi	243	81	0	21	.333	269	74	2	14	.275
Shawn Wooten	Edmonton	Ana	118	47	5	18	.398	134	42	6	24	.313
Ernie Young	Memphis	StL	206	51	16	44	.248	247	68	19	54	.275
Alan Zinter	Iowa	ChC	114	28	9	20	.246	119	25	5	15	.210
Jon Zuber	Columbus	NYY	158	46	1	24	.291	136	40	0	15	.294
Julio Zuleta	Iowa	ChC	186	60	14	51	.323	206	62	12	43	.301
Mike Zywica	Oklahoma	Tex	215	53	6	35	.247	205	57	3	23	.278

Triple-A Pitching vs. Lefthanded and Righthanded Batters

			vs Left					vs Right				
Player	Team	Org	AB	H	HR	SO	Avg	AB	H	HR	SO	Avg
Pat Ahearne	Tacoma	Sea	272	76	6	41	.279	392	114	5	51	.291
Paul Ah Yat	Nashville	Pit	108	24	3	15	.222	315	86	11	45	.273
Ryan Anderson	Tacoma	Sea	75	27	3	22	.360	305	56	5	124	.184
Clayton Andrews	Syracuse	Tor	92	30	1	14	.326	308	84	7	45	.273
Jamie Arnold	Albuquerque	LA	123	38	2	22	.309	228	56	3	25	.246
Bronson Arroyo	Nashville	Pit	149	35	0	21	.235	178	47	7	31	.264
Justin Atchley	Louisville	Cin	113	31	3	10	.274	398	137	16	59	.344
Jeff Austin	Omaha	KC	187	45	6	22	.241	315	105	10	35	.333
Cory Bailey	Nashville	Pit	106	26	0	32	.245	167	50	2	30	.299
John Bale	Syracuse	Tor	66	16	2	18	.242	225	52	2	52	.231
Travis Baptist	Nashville	Pit	91	28	2	15	.308	417	118	15	78	.283
Lorenzo Barcelo	Charlotte	CWS	153	41	7	29	.268	254	73	13	33	.287
Manny Barrios	Scranton-WB	Phi	78	26	1	8	.333	174	45	5	52	.259
Rigo Beltran	Col. Springs	Col	92	28	1	24	.304	393	104	14	71	.265
Shayne Bennett	Ottawa	Mon	108	31	4	13	.287	214	63	9	41	.294
Sean Bergman	Calgary	Fla	103	38	3	15	.369	232	69	5	33	.297
Brent Billingsley	Ottawa	Mon	94	22	1	19	.234	315	96	13	57	.305
Jaime Bluma	Omaha	KC	83	19	1	8	.229	126	39	7	22	.310
Rod Bolton	Indianapolis	Mil	97	34	5	13	.351	129	32	4	24	.248
Shane Bowers	Scranton-WB	Phi	198	47	6	35	.237	326	82	13	64	.252
Ryan Bradley	Columbus	NYY	105	35	8	18	.333	176	47	3	36	.267
Jim Brower	Buffalo	Cle	141	36	3	18	.255	250	63	4	50	.252
Mark Brownson	Scranton-WB	Phi	191	54	6	41	.283	313	80	9	63	.256
Mike Buddie	Indianapolis	Mil	71	16	1	12	.225	136	24	3	27	.176
Tim Byrdak	Omaha	KC	74	16	3	25	.216	132	43	2	22	.326
Mickey Callaway	Durham	TB	195	55	2	24	.282	287	96	9	40	.334
Eric Cammack	Norfolk	NYM	83	16	0	25	.193	140	22	2	42	.157
Buddy Carlyle	Las Vegas	SD	219	46	10	56	.210	385	119	15	71	.309
Giovanni Carrara	Col. Springs	Col	154	36	2	40	.234	209	53	6	49	.254
Lance Carter	Omaha	KC	117	35	4	10	.299	181	53	9	41	.293
Carlos Castillo	Calgary	Fla	129	45	2	12	.349	134	49	4	25	.366
Mike Cather	Calgary	Fla	67	24	2	17	.358	176	42	4	45	.239
Carlos Chantres	Charlotte	CWS	227	59	7	36	.260	304	77	5	49	.253
Robinson Checo	Albuquerque	LA	110	24	3	23	.218	209	54	8	62	.258
Jin-Ho Cho	Pawtucket	Bos	124	31	8	23	.250	156	46	1	14	.295
Chris Clemons	Buffalo	Cle	79	31	3	10	.392	148	37	5	29	.250
Ken Cloude	Tacoma	Sea	130	41	3	22	.315	171	47	7	40	.275
Steve Connelly	Fresno	SF	72	21	5	14	.292	156	42	4	30	.269
Brian Cooper	Edmonton	Ana	112	37	3	15	.330	151	50	9	22	.331
Bryan Corey	Sacramento	Oak	97	21	1	18	.216	225	67	10	37	.298
Mark Corey	Norfolk	NYM	110	32	6	23	.291	151	48	5	20	.318
Brad Cornett	Durham	TB	148	50	2	19	.338	206	50	5	53	.243
Robbie Crabtree	Fresno	SF	133	40	2	29	.301	362	86	6	87	.238
Paxton Crawford	Pawtucket	Bos	98	23	4	24	.235	118	24	2	23	.203
Jack Cressend	Salt Lake	Min	105	25	0	27	.238	228	62	3	60	.272
Nelson Cruz	Toledo	Det	93	27	7	21	.290	113	27	2	18	.239
Will Cunnane	Las Vegas	SD	151	38	5	43	.252	222	58	2	54	.261
Jeff D'Amico	Omaha	KC	170	49	7	28	.288	182	38	9	38	.209
Pat Daneker	Charlotte	CWS	251	77	10	38	.307	324	91	16	31	.281
David Darwin	Toledo	Det	75	16	3	21	.213	170	54	8	26	.318
Joe Davenport	Charlotte	CWS	114	30	2	23	.263	151	44	4	19	.291
Tom Davey	Tacoma	Sea	149	38	3	31	.255	228	66	7	46	.289
Clint Davis	Tucson	Ari	82	24	2	9	.293	214	56	1	47	.262
Doug Davis	Oklahoma	Tex	52	18	1	10	.346	198	44	7	43	.222
Jason Davis	Fresno	SF	84	22	0	12	.262	246	82	10	27	.333
Javier de la Hoya	Rochester	Bal	159	34	4	34	.214	196	51	8	31	.260
Miguel Del Toro	Fresno	SF	119	34	2	22	.286	325	83	15	76	.255
John DeSilva	Calgary	Fla	209	57	4	27	.273	342	93	17	67	.272
Matt DeWitt	Syracuse	Tor	125	44	3	18	.352	137	34	3	23	.248
R.A. Dickey	Oklahoma	Tex	233	63	5	35	.270	362	104	8	50	.287
Craig Dingman	Columbus	NYY	95	26	1	16	.274	178	34	4	49	.191
Jim Dougherty	Memphis	StL	85	17	0	31	.200	213	59	5	51	.277
Tim Drew	Buffalo	Cle	141	43	4	26	.305	250	79	8	27	.316
Travis Driskill	New Orleans	Hou	268	82	5	44	.306	446	119	10	69	.267
Mike Drumright	Calgary	Fla	214	72	4	40	.336	314	92	6	47	.293
Chad Durbin	Omaha	KC	106	29	4	20	.274	173	46	6	33	.266
Mike Duvall	Durham	TB	92	27	1	12	.293	220	58	7	37	.264
Derrin Ebert	Richmond	Atl	125	41	10	13	.328	486	151	11	78	.311
Joey Eischen	Ottawa	Mon	49	12	2	13	.245	171	43	6	21	.251
Horacio Estrada	Indianapolis	Mil	142	40	2	21	.282	460	109	12	82	.237
Leo Estrella	Syracuse	Tor	150	32	3	25	.213	167	36	5	23	.216
Luis Estrella	Fresno	SF	61	22	4	5	.361	171	53	5	27	.310
Seth Etherton	Edmonton	Ana	73	13	2	13	.178	154	47	4	37	.305
Bart Evans	Toledo	Det	137	36	5	27	.263	187	45	7	45	.241
Dave Evans	Tucson	Ari	104	29	1	21	.279	192	53	10	39	.276
Keith Evans	Ottawa	Mon	80	24	1	10	.300	131	40	2	12	.305
Bryan Eversgerd	Memphis	StL	79	20	4	17	.253	194	47	5	35	.242
Jared Fernandez	Pawtucket	Bos	186	46	3	35	.247	229	57	7	30	.249
Osvaldo Fernandez	Louisville	Cin	100	27	1	26	.270	118	30	2	18	.254
Nelson Figueroa	Tucson	Ari	139	40	6	20	.288	284	61	3	58	.215
Tony Fiore	Durham	TB	102	21	0	15	.206	168	41	3	24	.244
Tom Fordham	Indianapolis	Mil	75	17	0	19	.227	167	31	2	45	.186
Ryan Franklin	Tacoma	Sea	216	49	12	59	.227	396	98	16	83	.247
Eric Gagne	Albuquerque	LA	94	28	3	19	.298	121	28	5	40	.231
Steve Gajkowski	Sacramento	Oak	80	24	3	15	.300	165	49	5	26	.297
Gus Gandarillas	Salt Lake	Min	119	37	5	27	.311	233	68	4	48	.292
Jon Garland	Charlotte	CWS	188	44	2	33	.234	207	55	1	30	.266
Gary Glover	Syracuse	Tor	293	91	10	55	.311	368	90	11	64	.245
Ryan Glynn	Oklahoma	Tex	148	33	0	36	.223	158	39	5	30	.247
Lariel Gonzalez	Norfolk	NYM	85	16	1	22	.188	168	52	3	39	.310
Mike Grace	Rochester	Bal	109	22	2	20	.202	181	44	3	23	.243
Kip Gross	New Orleans	Hou	231	66	10	24	.286	369	90	10	70	.244
Domingo Guzman	Las Vegas	SD	79	21	5	17	.266	151	35	5	37	.232
Luther Hackman	Memphis	StL	210	59	1	25	.281	263	75	10	41	.285
Roy Halladay	Syracuse	Tor	122	40	7	20	.328	171	45	3	18	.263
Chris Haney	Buffalo	Cle	65	15	1	23	.231	291	72	7	47	.247
Tim Harikkala	Indianapolis	Mil	106	33	3	10	.311	150	40	2	12	.267
Travis Harper	Durham	TB	151	35	6	24	.232	248	63	9	24	.254
Chad Harville	Sacramento	Oak	91	21	3	19	.231	148	32	5	58	.216
Derek Hasselhoff	Charlotte	CWS	91	23	2	15	.253	161	39	4	36	.242
Mike Heathcott	Iowa	ChC	110	37	3	10	.336	186	56	5	27	.301
Rick Heiserman	Memphis	StL	121	31	6	29	.256	179	54	4	26	.302
F. Hernandez	New Orleans	Hou	75	15	2	26	.200	144	26	3	62	.181
Junior Herndon	Las Vegas	SD	173	44	9	29	.254	361	107	4	46	.296
Erik Hiljus	Toledo	Det	104	25	1	28	.240	166	42	2	53	.253
Brett Hinchliffe	Edmonton	Ana	102	30	1	14	.294	141	33	5	16	.234
Kevin Hodges	Tacoma	Sea	124	28	0	29	.226	234	59	3	44	.252
Mark Hutton	New Orleans	Hou	84	24	3	13	.286	143	34	5	14	.238
Tom Jacquez	Scranton-WB	Phi	84	24	2	19	.286	116	29	1	15	.250
Ryan Jensen	Fresno	SF	164	55	9	30	.335	384	112	9	84	.292
Barry Johnson	Scranton-WB	Phi	91	21	2	17	.231	209	45	4	40	.215
Jonathan Johnson	Oklahoma	Tex	81	25	1	21	.309	133	30	7	42	.226
Mark Johnson	Toledo	Det	176	56	4	25	.318	240	86	11	23	.358
Bobby Jones	Norfolk	NYM	132	29	2	28	.220	374	93	11	72	.249
Marcus Jones	Sacramento	Oak	131	42	3	9	.321	257	66	4	42	.257
Mike Judd	Albuquerque	LA	203	56	4	43	.276	340	97	8	49	.285
Jason Karnuth	Memphis	StL	139	35	3	14	.252	164	54	4	14	.329
Brad Kaufman	New Orleans	Hou	91	33	5	23	.363	150	41	0	30	.273
Randy Keisler	Columbus	NYY	98	36	2	20	.367	328	68	7	66	.207
Sun-Woo Kim	Pawtucket	Bos	229	69	8	39	.301	321	101	9	77	.315
Brandon Knight	Columbus	NYY	318	75	11	62	.236	389	97	10	76	.249
Brian Knoll	Fresno	SF	69	19	3	10	.275	175	57	10	26	.326
Brandon Kolb	Las Vegas	SD	74	23	0	23	.311	149	30	2	36	.201
Rick Krivda	Rochester	Bal	127	32	4	30	.252	443	110	11	69	.248
Tim Kubinski	Sacramento	Oak	64	22	3	12	.344	217	62	7	39	.286
Denny Lail	Columbus	NYY	237	64	12	57	.270	329	85	11	57	.258
Frank Lankford	Sacramento	Oak	81	25	1	9	.309	172	43	3	24	.250
Brett Laxton	Omaha	KC	186	59	0	35	.317	230	59	4	53	.257
Corey Lee	Oklahoma	Tex	108	35	4	23	.324	366	128	11	61	.350
Sang Lee	Pawtucket	Bos	81	23	3	24	.284	178	28	2	49	.157
Allen Levrault	Indianapolis	Mil	180	51	7	23	.283	215	47	2	55	.219
Ted Lilly	Columbus	NYY	133	47	5	43	.353	414	110	9	84	.266
Mike Lincoln	Salt Lake	Min	102	25	1	12	.245	184	47	3	25	.255
Scott Linebrink	Fresno	SF	78	22	3	12	.282	162	32	7	37	.198
Doug Linton	Col. Springs	Col	290	80	6	58	.276	388	109	9	78	.281
Johan Lopez	Oklahoma	Tex	80	21	3	12	.262	125	23	3	30	.184
Rodrigo Lopez	Las Vegas	SD	137	50	6	32	.365	289	73	3	68	.253
Andrew Lorraine	Buffalo	Cle	90	22	3	12	.244	260	75	5	39	.288
Eric Ludwick	Indianapolis	Mil	111	24	1	26	.216	124	31	2	26	.250
Larry Luebbers	Louisville	Cin	182	42	1	25	.231	240	55	8	44	.229
Alan Mahaffey	Salt Lake	Min	87	25	2	20	.287	313	93	14	54	.297
Jim Mann	Norfolk	NYM	103	28	4	27	.272	183	33	4	47	.180
David Manning	Iowa	ChC	99	33	4	16	.333	174	49	7	24	.282
Robert Marquez	Ottawa	Mon	134	45	4	22	.336	246	71	3	41	.289
Jose Martinez	Oklahoma	Tex	100	36	7	13	.360	125	41	3	10	.328
Willie Martinez	Buffalo	Cle	221	60	5	30	.271	296	72	11	65	.243
Rob Mattson	Nashville	Pit	166	45	6	27	.271	206	58	7	39	.282
Tony McKnight	New Orleans	Hou	164	49	4	27	.299	296	80	6	36	.270
Brian McNichol	Iowa	ChC	128	38	4	33	.297	327	93	16	72	.284
Rusty Meacham	New Orleans	Hou	82	20	1	21	.244	123	23	4	35	.187
Hector Mercado	Louisville	Cin	83	15	0	25	.181	200	54	2	42	.270
Mike Meyers	Iowa	ChC	100	30	3	22	.300	134	44	6	22	.328
Chris Michalak	Albuquerque	LA	119	34	3	27	.286	399	132	15	56	.331
Justin Miller	Sacramento	Oak	74	17	1	13	.230	126	25	2	21	.198
Matt Miller	Oklahoma	Tex	87	21	1	26	.241	144	40	5	43	.278
Trever Miller	Albuquerque	LA	55	13	2	11	.236	169	47	3	28	.278
Wade Miller	New Orleans	Hou	153	44	3	37	.288	235	51	3	44	.217
Dean Mitchell	Oklahoma	Tex	89	32	1	10	.360	143	37	4	29	.259
Scott Mitchell	Ottawa	Mon	134	45	6	24	.336	221	64	7	28	.290
Greg Mix	Indianapolis	Mil	78	24	4	12	.308	132	33	4	30	.250
Eric Moody	Calgary	Fla	63	21	2	12	.333	153	54	10	14	.353
Trey Moore	Ottawa	Mon	54	14	1	12	.259	171	42	3	31	.246
Paul Morse	Edmonton	Ana	102	27	6	11	.265	181	46	3	20	.254
Damian Moss	Richmond	Atl	132	34	3	30	.258	453	96	11	93	.212
Guillermo Mota	Ottawa	Mon	85	17	0	19	.200	138	32	4	16	.232
Tony Mounce	Oklahoma	Tex	73	27	2	13	.370	175	47	2	35	.269
Bobby Munoz	Louisville	Cin	133	38	3	24	.286	182	39	3	40	.214
Peter Munro	Syracuse	Tor	100	26	0	21	.260	121	26	1	24	.215
Dan Murray	Omaha	KC	241	71	13	37	.295	299	77	9	65	.258
Heath Murray	Albuquerque	LA	111	27	0	29	.243	507	157	8	81	.310
Aaron Myette	Charlotte	CWS	183	55	7	31	.301	238	48	11	54	.202
Alan Newman	Buffalo	Cle	62	20	1	16	.323	213	51	8	47	.239
Eric Newman	Iowa	ChC	105	31	6	14	.295	183	43	6	54	.235
Chris Nichting	Buffalo	Cle	85	18	2	25	.212	168	47	4	35	.280
Ben Norris	Tucson	Ari	45	10	0	6	.222	192	78	7	22	.406
Phillip Norton	Iowa	ChC	127	33	1	29	.260	485	133	15	97	.274
Vladimir Nunez	Calgary	Fla	105	32	4	33	.305	233	60	5	62	.258
Mark Nussbeck	Memphis	StL	168	44	4	26	.262	316	83	7	50	.263
Tomo Ohka	Pawtucket	Bos	238	59	7	33	.248	240	52	8	45	.217
Mike Oquist	Toledo	Det	314	98	10	41	.312	347	116	8	56	.334

Triple-A Pitching vs. Lefthanded and Righthanded Batters

Player	Team	Org	vs Left					vs Right				
			AB	H	HR	SO	Avg	AB	H	HR	SO	Avg
Ramon Ortiz	Edmonton	Ana	128	28	4	29	.219	204	46	3	47	.225
Delvis Pacheco	Richmond	Atl	72	22	0	12	.306	139	39	6	32	.281
Jose Parra	Nashville	Pit	154	41	3	31	.266	233	65	4	37	.279
John Parrish	Rochester	Bal	113	30	2	32	.265	248	55	8	55	.222
Bronswell Patrick	Calgary	Fla	209	77	6	28	.368	329	97	12	44	.295
Dave Pavlas	Nashville	Pit	100	30	2	20	.300	174	41	6	41	.236
Dan Perkins	Salt Lake	Min	225	77	12	37	.342	378	130	14	60	.344
Chris Peters	Nashville	Pit	30	12	1	9	.400	192	59	5	23	.307
Rafael Pina	Rochester	Bal	91	26	3	17	.286	129	38	6	17	.295
Joel Pineiro	Tacoma	Sea	80	21	1	15	.262	148	32	2	26	.216
Cliff Politte	Scranton-WB	Phi	164	35	0	34	.213	251	59	8	72	.235
Brian Powell	New Orleans	Hou	147	39	2	23	.265	244	64	7	34	.262
Jeremy Powell	Ottawa	Mon	131	58	4	32	.304	332	102	13	67	.307
Ariel Prieto	Sacramento	Oak	161	33	2	29	.205	272	77	7	50	.283
Tim Pugh	Richmond	Atl	162	46	6	34	.284	209	71	4	35	.340
Bill Pulsipher	Tucson	Ari	40	10	0	10	.250	228	63	7	41	.276
Ruben Quevedo	Iowa	ChC	107	21	2	31	.196	176	47	5	46	.267
Jason Rakers	Omaha	KC	106	31	6	23	.292	193	52	8	45	.269
Scott Randall	Oklahoma	Tex	107	35	4	14	.327	186	61	4	21	.328
Scott Randall	Salt Lake	Min	113	36	3	19	.319	206	69	6	35	.335
Fred Rath	Memphis	StL	88	25	2	14	.284	155	47	7	19	.303
Jon Ratliff	Sacramento	Oak	138	31	5	26	.225	264	71	7	46	.269
Britt Reames	Memphis	StL	88	23	1	22	.261	172	32	1	55	.186
Brandon Reed	Toledo	Det	117	36	5	23	.308	170	44	8	33	.259
Chad Ricketts	Albuquerque	LA	83	25	0	19	.301	163	34	7	56	.209
John Riedling	Louisville	Cin	111	34	5	24	.306	168	29	2	51	.173
Brad Rigby	Ottawa	Mon	150	42	1	19	.280	204	75	7	32	.368
Paul Rigdon	Buffalo	Cle	95	22	2	18	.232	174	50	2	23	.287
Mike Riley	Fresno	SF	81	23	1	16	.284	430	118	20	98	.274
Todd Rizzo	Salt Lake	Min	94	25	0	20	.266	190	51	1	23	.268
Grant Roberts	Norfolk	NYM	277	69	1	48	.249	330	85	5	67	.258
Mark Roberts	Charlotte	CWS	96	27	1	17	.281	139	31	6	21	.223
Willis Roberts	Louisville	Cin	243	64	10	28	.263	237	74	9	38	.312
Mike Romano	Syracuse	Tor	119	26	2	16	.218	111	27	5	18	.243
Mike Romano	Salt Lake	Min	145	40	5	19	.276	247	82	6	35	.332
J.C. Romero	Salt Lake	Min	46	11	0	7	.239	200	49	6	31	.245
Rafael Roque	Indianapolis	Mil	122	32	2	21	.262	376	95	16	90	.253
Johnny Ruffin	Tucson	Ari	59	14	3	18	.237	160	34	1	48	.213
Jason Ryan	Salt Lake	Min	137	36	6	20	.263	242	58	10	46	.240
Matt Ryan	Rochester	Bal	67	17	2	15	.254	164	38	3	20	.232
Erik Sabel	Tucson	Ari	150	61	8	17	.407	275	88	8	44	.320
Mike Saipe	Col. Springs	Col	98	35	6	14	.357	144	59	12	23	.410
Benj Sampson	Salt Lake	Min	73	31	5	13	.425	239	83	10	34	.347
Scott Sanders	Sacramento	Oak	75	26	4	17	.347	125	37	5	21	.296
Julio Santana	Pawtucket	Bos	123	35	6	26	.285	122	26	1	29	.213
Rich Sauveur	Sacramento	Oak	84	20	0	21	.238	241	68	7	38	.282
Bob Scanlan	Indianapolis	Mil	86	19	0	8	.221	132	23	4	15	.174
Brian Schmack	Charlotte	CWS	142	30	3	35	.211	202	52	7	49	.257
Jason Secoda	Charlotte	CWS	192	54	10	37	.281	212	68	10	38	.321
Chris Seelbach	Richmond	Atl	190	49	4	41	.258	264	69	8	55	.261
Jason Sekany	Pawtucket	Bos	83	27	2	13	.325	123	32	6	16	.260
Dan Serafini	Las Vegas	SD	75	32	2	9	.427	144	42	4	36	.292
Ben Sheets	Indianapolis	Mil	111	29	2	22	.261	196	48	2	37	.245
Scot Shields	Edmonton	Ana	252	61	7	70	.242	379	97	9	86	.256
Brian Shouse	Rochester	Bal	83	28	3	17	.337	143	35	1	35	.245
Anthony Shumaker	Norfolk	NYM	98	29	2	20	.296	301	92	10	35	.306
Brian Sikorski	Oklahoma	Tex	210	46	5	37	.219	308	85	4	62	.276
Steve Sinclair	Tacoma	Sea	80	22	0	14	.275	152	46	6	31	.303
Aaron Small	Col. Springs	Col	218	55	5	24	.252	315	97	9	61	.308
Cam Smith	Albuquerque	LA	79	23	3	18	.291	147	38	0	38	.259
Chuck Smith	Oklahoma	Tex	106	32	1	25	.302	150	41	2	48	.273
Dan Smith	Pawtucket	Bos	211	51	7	29	.242	280	83	8	41	.296
Dan Smith	Richmond	Atl	106	24	0	22	.226	189	59	2	36	.312
Steve Soderstrom	Louisville	Cin	243	81	3	20	.333	294	79	5	47	.269
Steve Sparks	Toledo	Det	148	39	3	23	.264	196	47	5	21	.240
Dennis Springer	Norfolk	NYM	183	48	7	11	.262	270	72	8	24	.267
Kennie Steenstra	Tucson	Ari	175	53	6	18	.303	340	106	9	44	.312
Dave Stevens	Richmond	Atl	111	25	3	16	.225	167	48	7	34	.287
Scott Stewart	Norfolk	NYM	95	27	0	20	.284	190	53	3	37	.279
Ricky Stone	Albuquerque	LA	196	61	2	34	.311	277	85	7	41	.307
Everett Stull	Indianapolis	Mil	152	36	2	36	.237	232	59	1	38	.254
Brendan Sullivan	Las Vegas	SD	107	37	4	14	.346	221	64	5	38	.290
Kerry Taylor	Syracuse	Tor	204	39	1	39	.191	298	80	15	44	.268
Amaury Telemaco	Scranton-WB	Phi	161	48	7	27	.298	303	67	8	61	.221
Jay Tessmer	Columbus	NYY	97	32	3	8	.330	166	41	2	32	.247
Evan Thomas	Scranton-WB	Phi	220	55	4	47	.250	440	108	13	80	.245
Brian Tollberg	Las Vegas	SD	120	31	1	23	.258	175	41	4	33	.234
Josh Towers	Rochester	Bal	235	71	5	40	.302	348	86	12	62	.247
Dave Tuttle	Tucson	Ari	123	32	4	22	.260	187	53	3	40	.283
Brandon Villafuerte	Toledo	Det	156	60	3	26	.385	206	52	4	59	.252
Mike Villano	Nashville	Pit	109	29	6	24	.266	178	48	7	32	.270
Ismael Villegas	Richmond	Atl	93	25	2	14	.269	149	41	5	37	.275
Jamie Walker	Omaha	KC	103	37	7	14	.359	308	101	18	38	.328
Pete Walker	Col. Springs	Col	81	26	2	17	.321	196	38	1	44	.194
Doug Walls	Toledo	Det	135	34	1	27	.252	187	54	9	34	.289
Scott Watkins	Col. Springs	Col	95	24	2	19	.253	216	69	4	23	.319
Ben Weber	Fresno	SF	88	33	2	11	.375	206	39	5	55	.189
Clint Weibl	Memphis	StL	197	40	6	45	.203	237	58	5	47	.245
Kip Wells	Charlotte	CWS	105	28	4	14	.267	141	39	6	24	.277
Don Wengert	Richmond	Atl	174	42	3	35	.241	255	75	6	48	.294

Player	Team	Org	vs Left					vs Right				
			AB	H	HR	SO	Avg	AB	H	HR	SO	Avg
Jake Westbrook	Columbus	NYY	171	46	2	25	.269	175	48	1	36	.274
Dan Wheeler	Durham	TB	261	80	15	31	.307	350	103	20	60	.294
Jeff Williams	Albuquerque	LA	73	21	3	15	.288	160	43	3	23	.269
Shad Williams	Edmonton	Ana	74	22	2	9	.297	146	45	3	25	.308
Paul Wilson	Norfolk	NYM	115	30	4	20	.261	204	55	3	36	.270
Scott Winchester	Louisville	Cin	96	27	1	17	.281	132	40	3	16	.303
Matt Wise	Edmonton	Ana	186	41	4	40	.220	287	81	6	42	.282
S. Wojciechowski	Calgary	Fla	59	15	1	5	.254	141	49	9	22	.348
Bryan Wolff	New Orleans	Hou	97	24	2	12	.247	138	39	4	34	.283
Bryan Wolff	Salt Lake	Min	73	16	2	22	.219	130	37	6	21	.285
Ed Yarnall	Louisville	Cin	81	20	2	20	.247	186	52	5	39	.280
Carlos Zambrano	Iowa	ChC	69	19	2	14	.275	139	35	1	32	.252
Victor Zambrano	Durham	TB	102	22	3	22	.216	151	50	6	33	.331
Dave Zancanaro	Iowa	ChC	88	22	3	13	.250	366	109	16	54	.298
Chad Zerbe	Fresno	SF	57	18	0	8	.316	263	76	5	33	.289
Barry Zito	Sacramento	Oak	54	12	1	20	.222	328	76	3	71	.232

Triple-A Pitching at Home and on the Road

			Home					Road				
Player	Team	Org	G	IP	W	L	ERA	G	IP	W	L	ERA
Pat Ahearne	Tacoma	Sea	13	80.0	6	4	3.71	16	88.0	7	4	3.99
Paul Ah Yat	Nashville	Pit	10	56.2	2	4	3.81	9	54.0	1	5	4.33
Ryan Anderson	Tacoma	Sea	10	57.0	2	3	3.79	10	47.0	3	5	4.21
Clayton Andrews	Syracuse	Tor	11	62.0	4	4	4.50	8	40.0	4	3	5.40
Jamie Arnold	Albuquerque	LA	12	58.2	2	5	5.52	8	33.2	2	2	4.28
Bronson Arroyo	Nashville	Pit	7	52.0	4	0	2.42	6	36.2	4	2	5.40
Justin Atchley	Louisville	Cin	14	52.0	3	2	5.54	16	70.0	5	4	6.17
Jeff Austin	Omaha	KC	12	67.0	5	3	4.16	11	59.2	2	6	4.83
Travis Baptist	Nashville	Pit	18	73.0	0	8	6.41	16	60.0	4	2	4.65
Lorenzo Barcelo	Charlotte	CWS	10	60.0	2	4	3.60	7	39.0	3	2	5.31
Rigo Beltran	Col. Springs	Col	15	79.1	4	4	5.45	10	45.0	2	6	6.80
Sean Bergman	Calgary	Fla	6	31.1	1	2	10.05	7	50.0	3	1	3.06
Brent Billingsley	Ottawa	Mon	9	53.0	4	4	4.25	11	50.0	4	5	7.20
Shane Bowers	Scranton-WB	Phi	17	76.0	5	2	3.67	19	61.0	3	5	5.90
Jim Brower	Buffalo	Cle	8	50.2	5	2	2.84	8	50.2	4	2	3.38
Mark Brownson	Scranton-WB	Phi	14	44.2	1	4	4.84	17	88.0	9	4	4.40
Mickey Callaway	Durham	TB	14	66.0	5	4	5.32	12	51.0	6	2	5.29
Buddy Carlyle	Las Vegas	SD	15	86.1	5	3	4.38	12	64.1	3	3	4.20
Giovanni Carrara	Col. Springs	Col	8	39.0	3	1	4.38	10	57.0	4	1	2.53
Carlos Chantres	Charlotte	CWS	11	52.2	4	1	3.93	18	90.0	6	3	3.30
Robinson Checo	Albuquerque	LA	7	41.0	3	2	3.51	9	45.0	5	1	3.80
Bryan Corey	Sacramento	Oak	21	41.0	2	0	2.20	26	43.2	6	3	6.18
Brad Cornett	Durham	TB	9	34.0	1	2	4.24	10	54.0	3	3	4.33
Robbie Crabtree	Fresno	SF	35	69.0	4	2	4.30	28	58.2	1	4	3.22
Jack Cressend	Salt Lake	Min	32	48.0	0	3	3.75	22	38.0	4	1	3.08
Will Cunnane	Las Vegas	SD	9	49.0	3	2	3.49	8	48.0	4	2	4.50
Jeff D'Amico	Omaha	KC	9	50.0	2	2	3.96	7	41.0	1	1	3.73
Pat Daneker	Charlotte	CWS	14	71.0	3	7	6.97	13	72.1	5	5	4.60
Tom Davey	Tacoma	Sea	13	42.0	4	2	3.64	15	51.2	4	4	5.40
Javier de la Hoya	Rochester	Bal	11	52.2	6	2	4.27	7	39.2	1	4	4.31
Miguel Del Toro	Fresno	SF	11	56.0	3	5	8.52	10	56.0	3	1	3.54
John DeSilva	Calgary	Fla	13	63.0	4	6	5.71	16	77.0	6	3	3.86
R.A. Dickey	Oklahoma	Tex	18	98.0	7	3	3.77	12	60.0	1	6	5.70
Jim Dougherty	Memphis	StL	31	45.0	3	3	2.20	29	36.0	0	4	4.75
Tim Drew	Buffalo	Cle	9	58.0	6	3	3.88	7	37.0	1	5	9.00
Travis Driskill	New Orleans	Hou	16	110.0	7	6	2.95	12	69.0	5	5	5.74
Mike Drumright	Calgary	Fla	17	61.0	4	5	7.23	17	70.0	5	3	5.40
Mike Duvall	Durham	TB	18	46.0	4	2	5.09	12	34.0	2	0	3.97
Derrin Ebert	Richmond	Atl	16	84.0	4	4	4.71	16	66.0	1	5	4.91
Horacio Estrada	Indianapolis	Mil	12	78.0	5	3	3.46	13	81.0	9	1	3.22
Leo Estrella	Syracuse	Tor	6	33.0	2	2	5.73	9	56.0	3	2	3.05
Bart Evans	Toledo	Det	11	38.0	2	1	4.97	13	45.0	3	3	7.40
Jared Fernandez	Pawtucket	Bos	16	60.0	5	3	3.60	15	53.0	5	1	2.38
Nelson Figueroa	Tucson	Ari	8	50.0	5	3	3.42	9	62.0	4	1	2.32
Ryan Franklin	Tacoma	Sea	15	87.1	4	3	3.09	16	76.0	7	2	4.86
Gus Gandarillas	Salt Lake	Min	33	42.2	7	2	5.70	30	47.0	2	2	3.06
Jon Garland	Charlotte	CWS	7	49.0	4	1	2.02	9	54.0	5	1	2.50
Gary Glover	Syracuse	Tor	15	95.1	5	6	5.19	12	71.0	4	3	4.82
Ryan Glynn	Oklahoma	Tex	6	26.1	2	0	3.76	9	57.0	2	2	3.47
Kip Gross	New Orleans	Hou	15	95.0	7	4	4.45	10	62.2	1	3	3.16
Luther Hackman	Memphis	StL	9	52.2	2	6	4.61	12	67.0	6	3	4.84
Chris Haney	Buffalo	Cle	8	52.2	4	1	1.71	7	39.2	4	2	3.40
Travis Harper	Durham	TB	9	53.0	4	3	4.08	8	50.2	3	1	4.44
Junior Herndon	Las Vegas	SD	13	66.0	6	7	5.59	13	69.0	4	4	4.70
Kevin Hodges	Tacoma	Sea	18	65.1	3	3	3.58	12	32.0	1	0	1.13
Ryan Jensen	Fresno	SF	11	62.2	3	1	3.59	15	72.1	2	7	7.71
Barry Johnson	Scranton-WB	Phi	30	45.0	4	2	2.60	26	36.0	3	2	2.75
Mark Johnson	Toledo	Det	12	71.0	2	8	5.70	5	29.0	0	3	8.69
Bobby Jones	Norfolk	NYM	10	69.0	4	4	2.61	12	64.0	6	4	6.19
Marcus Jones	Sacramento	Oak	8	47.2	4	0	3.40	9	53.2	2	4	5.20
Mike Judd	Albuquerque	LA	11	62.0	4	1	4.79	13	79.0	3	5	4.33
Randy Keisler	Columbus	NYY	9	57.0	5	2	4.26	8	56.0	3	1	1.77
Sun-Woo Kim	Pawtucket	Bos	11	60.0	5	4	4.95	15	74.0	6	3	6.93
Brandon Knight	Columbus	NYY	16	104.1	5	8	4.83	12	80.0	5	4	3.94
Rick Krivda	Rochester	Bal	16	92.1	6	6	3.02	10	60.0	5	3	3.30
Denny Lail	Columbus	NYY	15	75.1	3	3	4.54	12	71.1	4	4	4.79
Brett Laxton	Omaha	KC	11	55.2	2	5	6.14	10	52.2	3	4	4.44
Corey Lee	Oklahoma	Tex	13	49.0	0	5	11.39	13	63.0	2	7	6.71
Allen Levrault	Indianapolis	Mil	10	52.0	3	4	4.67	11	56.0	3	4	3.86
Ted Lilly	Columbus	NYY	10	56.0	2	6	5.63	12	81.0	6	5	3.22
Doug Linton	Col. Springs	Col	14	86.1	5	7	6.05	14	87.1	5	6	4.74
Rodrigo Lopez	Las Vegas	SD	9	55.2	5	0	2.91	11	53.2	3	7	6.54
Andrew Lorraine	Buffalo	Cle	6	41.0	5	0	1.76	8	49.0	3	3	4.96
Larry Luebbers	Louisville	Cin	10	63.0	5	2	2.57	8	51.0	2	4	4.76
Alan Mahaffey	Salt Lake	Min	19	55.0	4	2	6.05	15	47.0	3	1	4.40
Jim Mann	Norfolk	NYM	23	39.0	2	2	3.46	26	42.2	1	2	2.53
Robert Marquez	Ottawa	Mon	25	46.2	0	2	3.28	28	49.0	4	2	6.80
Willie Martinez	Buffalo	Cle	12	56.0	1	2	4.98	16	79.0	7	3	4.10
Rob Mattson	Nashville	Pit	12	65.0	3	7	6.51	5	32.2	3	1	3.86
Tony McKnight	New Orleans	Hou	8	53.2	2	2	3.02	11	64.1	2	6	5.88
Brian McNichol	Iowa	ChC	24	79.0	2	5	4.44	19	36.0	1	3	9.00
Chris Michalak	Albuquerque	LA	10	56.2	5	1	3.65	13	76.0	6	2	4.74
Wade Miller	New Orleans	Hou	8	55.2	3	2	2.43	8	49.2	1	3	5.07
Scott Mitchell	Ottawa	Mon	12	46.2	4	2	4.44	16	42.2	2	3	7.80
Damian Moss	Richmond	Atl	15	83.0	5	2	3.04	14	77.1	4	4	3.26
Bobby Munoz	Louisville	Cin	11	37.0	4	2	5.35	10	47.2	2	6	4.34
Dan Murray	Omaha	KC	16	84.1	4	6	6.08	11	56.0	6	3	4.82
Heath Murray	Albuquerque	LA	14	83.1	5	4	4.43	15	72.0	2	6	5.13
Aaron Myette	Charlotte	CWS	13	83.0	3	4	4.23	6	28.2	2	1	4.71
Phillip Norton	Iowa	ChC	16	89.1	5	6	3.43	12	70.0	3	7	6.94
Vladimir Nunez	Calgary	Fla	8	47.2	4	3	3.97	7	42.0	2	4	4.29
Mark Nussbeck	Memphis	StL	10	68.0	5	1	2.65	11	56.2	4	3	5.56
Tomo Ohka	Pawtucket	Bos	9	61.2	4	4	3.65	10	69.0	5	2	2.35
Mike Oquist	Toledo	Det	13	73.0	3	7	4.32	16	87.1	4	8	5.98
Ramon Ortiz	Edmonton	Ana	8	51.0	4	4	4.94	7	38.0	2	2	4.03
Jose Parra	Nashville	Pit	10	46.0	2	3	4.11	13	55.2	4	2	6.14
John Parrish	Rochester	Bal	7	43.0	4	1	2.51	11	60.2	2	6	5.49
Bronswell Patrick	Calgary	Fla	14	61.2	1	7	9.19	13	66.1	4	5	5.16
Dan Perkins	Salt Lake	Min	18	73.0	5	4	7.64	15	68.0	4	6	7.01
Cliff Politte	Scranton-WB	Phi	9	55.0	5	1	2.78	12	57.0	3	3	3.47
Brian Powell	New Orleans	Hou	7	42.0	4	1	4.07	11	61.2	5	3	5.55
Jeremy Powell	Ottawa	Mon	13	63.2	4	7	7.35	12	62.2	1	6	6.46
Ariel Prieto	Sacramento	Oak	10	62.0	5	2	2.03	10	50.2	3	2	4.80
Tim Pugh	Richmond	Atl	7	38.2	2	2	5.59	11	50.0	4	2	4.86
Jon Ratliff	Sacramento	Oak	11	57.0	6	1	2.68	9	50.0	2	3	4.32
Brad Rigby	Ottawa	Mon	10	35.0	2	3	4.89	14	48.0	1	7	8.06
Mike Riley	Fresno	SF	14	72.0	1	5	6.50	10	56.0	5	3	5.14
Grant Roberts	Norfolk	NYM	13	85.0	5	4	3.28	12	72.0	2	4	3.50
Willis Roberts	Louisville	Cin	10	51.2	4	4	7.14	15	72.0	3	4	4.63
Mike Romano	Salt Lake	Min	7	37.0	2	3	8.51	9	58.0	5	3	4.66
Rafael Roque	Indianapolis	Mil	11	60.0	4	2	4.80	14	72.0	5	2	3.63
Jason Ryan	Salt Lake	Min	7	39.0	2	0	2.77	10	57.2	7	2	5.46
Erik Sabel	Tucson	Ari	16	52.0	4	5	6.92	13	46.0	0	6	7.63
Rich Sauveur	Sacramento	Oak	11	40.2	1	2	5.31	14	42.0	4	0	3.86
Brian Schmack	Charlotte	CWS	28	53.0	7	3	3.23	23	37.2	4	4	2.15
Jason Secoda	Charlotte	CWS	17	58.0	1	3	5.28	15	42.0	1	4	7.07
Chris Seelbach	Richmond	Atl	12	50.0	1	3	4.50	17	68.0	4	6	5.03
Ben Sheets	Indianapolis	Mil	7	43.0	2	2	2.93	7	38.2	1	3	2.79
Scot Shields	Edmonton	Ana	14	82.0	3	7	6.37	13	80.1	4	6	4.48
Anthony Shumaker	Norfolk	NYM	12	53.0	2	2	5.43	9	47.2	2	3	4.53
Brian Sikorski	Oklahoma	Tex	11	73.1	7	3	2.21	13	66.1	3	6	6.11
Aaron Small	Col. Springs	Col	18	57.0	7	2	5.68	18	74.0	4	4	5.59
Dan Smith	Pawtucket	Bos	11	56.2	3	3	3.97	13	68.0	4	7	5.56
Steve Soderstrom	Louisville	Cin	19	81.0	7	6	4.22	12	56.0	2	5	5.95
Steve Sparks	Toledo	Det	10	56.2	3	3	2.70	6	34.0	2	4	5.56
Dennis Springer	Norfolk	NYM	12	58.0	2	3	4.34	13	59.0	3	2	4.42
Kennie Steenstra	Tucson	Ari	11	63.2	6	1	3.25	13	66.1	2	4	4.75
Ricky Stone	Albuquerque	LA	25	60.0	6	3	6.00	23	60.0	3	2	3.90
Everett Stull	Indianapolis	Mil	9	61.2	3	3	2.92	7	42.0	4	2	3.00
Brendan Sullivan	Las Vegas	SD	22	39.0	1	2	5.77	23	43.0	1	3	6.70
Kerry Taylor	Syracuse	Tor	17	76.0	5	2	2.96	16	59.2	4	6	3.77
Amaury Telemaco	Scranton-WB	Phi	10	60.0	3	2	4.65	11	63.0	5	1	3.14
Evan Thomas	Scranton-WB	Phi	16	88.1	10	4	4.08	13	82.0	3	6	2.96
Josh Towers	Rochester	Bal	9	55.0	3	2	2.62	15	92.1	5	6	4.00
Dave Tuttle	Tucson	Ari	9	43.0	2	1	3.14	11	37.2	1	3	6.69
Brandon Villafuerte	Toledo	Det	21	44.2	2	5	7.86	25	43.0	2	4	5.44
Jamie Walker	Omaha	KC	12	52.2	1	7	6.49	12	49.0	2	3	3.86
Doug Walls	Toledo	Det	11	49.0	3	2	4.22	7	36.0	1	4	6.50
Scott Watkins	Col. Springs	Col	20	36.0	1	1	5.25	23	45.0	2	0	3.60
Clint Weibl	Memphis	StL	8	53.0	4	1	2.38	11	67.0	5	3	3.22
Don Wengert	Richmond	Atl	15	61.0	2	6	5.75	14	49.2	2	1	2.36
Jake Westbrook	Columbus	NYY	9	51.0	4	2	4.24	7	37.2	1	5	5.26
Dan Wheeler	Durham	TB	12	72.0	2	5	6.38	14	78.0	3	6	4.96
Paul Wilson	Norfolk	NYM	9	52.2	3	3	3.93	6	30.1	2	2	4.75
Matt Wise	Edmonton	Ana	9	64.0	4	3	2.95	10	60.0	5	3	4.50
Dave Zancanaro	Iowa	ChC	12	55.2	2	5	5.66	13	59.2	2	5	4.83
Chad Zerbe	Fresno	SF	6	29.1	3	1	5.22	11	52.0	4	2	3.81
Barry Zito	Sacramento	Oak	9	53.0	4	2	3.06	9	48.2	4	3	3.33

Double-A Batting vs. Lefthanded and Righthanded Pitchers

			vs Left					vs Right				
Player	Team	Org	AB	H	HR	RBI	Avg	AB	H	HR	RBI	Avg
Chuck Abbott	Erie	Ana	91	28	1	16	.308	239	54	4	23	.226
Kurt Airoso	Jacksonville	Det	81	18	1	8	.222	245	60	3	33	.245
Jeff Allen	Shreveport	SF	123	28	1	18	.228	324	78	6	34	.241
Luke Allen	San Antonio	LA	76	18	1	9	.237	263	72	6	51	.274
Erick Almonte	Norwich	NYY	100	28	6	26	.280	354	95	9	51	.268
Rafael Alvarez	New Britain	Min	33	8	0	4	.242	241	63	7	42	.261
Jose Amado	Wichita	KC	65	18	0	9	.277	253	75	5	47	.296
Mike Amrhein	West Tenn	ChC	90	24	3	9	.267	262	76	6	40	.290
Brooks Badeaux	Orlando	TB	68	15	0	5	.221	192	53	1	22	.276
Ryan Balfe	Mobile	SD	149	38	4	26	.255	313	83	8	40	.265
Blake Barthol	New Haven	Sea	55	16	2	5	.291	193	58	5	25	.301
Fletcher Bates	El Paso	Ari	95	29	4	20	.305	260	69	6	42	.265
Eric Battersby	Birmingham	CWS	100	17	2	7	.170	311	81	6	36	.260
Brian Becker	Orlando	TB	154	44	3	13	.286	349	96	6	45	.275
Todd Betts	Portland	Fla	117	29	3	15	.248	304	106	6	56	.349
Andy Bevins	Arkansas	StL	114	38	9	23	.333	316	100	16	65	.316
Darren Blakely	Erie	Ana	141	30	5	16	.213	298	74	11	38	.248
Papo Bolivar	New Britain	Min	95	34	0	15	.358	311	79	2	27	.254
Justin Bowles	Midland	Oak	109	37	6	23	.339	334	83	10	42	.249
Danny Bravo	Birmingham	CWS	97	24	2	8	.247	243	55	1	21	.226
Stoney Briggs	Jacksonville	Det	120	27	3	12	.225	376	99	14	53	.263
Ben Broussard	Chattanooga	Cin	70	12	2	10	.171	216	61	12	41	.282
Jason Brown	Orlando	TB	91	24	2	9	.264	139	36	6	20	.259
Rich Brown	Norwich	NYY	83	26	3	15	.313	236	50	1	15	.212
Mo Bruce	Binghamton	NYM	68	18	1	4	.265	246	68	1	19	.276
Gary Burnham	Reading	Phi	57	12	1	6	.211	298	83	12	55	.279
Kevin Burns	Round Rock	Hou	41	12	2	10	.293	214	69	6	36	.322
Andy Burress	Chattanooga	Cin	103	26	0	9	.252	297	74	6	32	.249
Sean Burroughs	Mobile	SD	129	43	1	17	.333	263	71	1	25	.270
Darren Burton	Altoona	Pit	36	13	1	4	.361	193	62	4	29	.321
Eric Byrnes	Midland	Oak	54	13	1	4	.241	205	65	4	33	.317
Alex Cabrera	El Paso	Ari	52	19	11	19	.365	160	62	24	63	.387
Wilmy Caceres	Chattanooga	Cin	122	31	0	10	.254	412	112	2	23	.272
Jason Camilli	Harrisburg	Mon	69	14	2	7	.203	171	37	1	12	.216
Aaron Capista	Trenton	Bos	82	17	0	5	.207	352	86	2	31	.244
Joe Caruso	Wichita	KC	99	33	4	20	.333	301	92	9	46	.306
Carlos Casimiro	Bowie	Bal	72	18	2	8	.250	218	58	4	24	.266
Dionys Cesar	Midland	Oak	98	19	0	5	.194	335	101	4	32	.301
Chin-Feng Chen	San Antonio	LA	123	40	2	19	.325	393	103	4	48	.262
Virgil Chevalier	Trenton	Bos	80	24	3	15	.300	266	83	4	52	.312
Alex Cintron	El Paso	Ari	143	50	0	16	.350	379	107	4	43	.282
Doug Clark	Shreveport	SF	122	30	3	20	.246	370	104	7	55	.281
Jermaine Clark	New Haven	Sea	115	26	0	8	.226	332	105	2	36	.316
Ivanon Coffie	Bowie	Bal	123	33	1	14	.268	218	58	8	30	.266
Eric Cole	Round Rock	Hou	114	39	6	25	.342	429	119	16	69	.277
Javier Colina	Carolina	Col	133	32	0	5	.241	296	61	2	30	.206
Greg Connors	New Haven	Sea	116	30	1	14	.259	336	96	8	44	.286
Chris Coste	Akron	Cle	82	32	0	7	.390	158	48	2	24	.304
Humberto Cota	Altoona	Pit	106	25	2	13	.236	323	87	6	31	.269
Joe Crede	Birmingham	CWS	128	39	5	21	.305	405	124	16	73	.306
Cesar Crespo	Portland	Fla	143	33	1	12	.231	339	91	8	48	.268
Mike Cuddyer	New Britain	Min	109	40	2	18	.367	381	89	4	43	.234
Mike Curry	Wichita	KC	102	27	0	15	.265	359	106	4	37	.295
Jack Cust	El Paso	Ari	128	28	3	18	.219	319	103	17	57	.323
Brian Dallimore	El Paso	Ari	98	37	0	15	.378	258	62	4	38	.240
Cleatus Davidson	New Britain	Min	97	23	0	6	.237	348	79	0	25	.227
Glenn Davis	San Antonio	LA	82	15	2	5	.183	295	63	7	35	.214
Travis Dawkins	Chattanooga	Cin	85	26	0	6	.306	283	59	6	25	.208
Tim DeCinces	Mobile	SD	38	7	2	7	.184	169	49	9	37	.290
Jorge DeLeon	Trenton	Bos	99	32	0	11	.323	240	72	2	27	.300
Jason Dellaero	Birmingham	CWS	119	22	4	8	.185	319	59	3	34	.185
Darrell Dent	Bowie	Bal	79	15	0	4	.190	283	79	0	21	.279
Tony DeRosso	Trenton	Bos	111	30	5	20	.270	338	96	15	65	.284
Jason Dewey	Carolina	Col	97	31	3	13	.320	221	41	6	31	.186
Alejandro Diaz	Chattanooga	Cin	120	24	4	15	.200	371	107	9	51	.288
Joe Dillon	Wichita	KC	48	22	2	8	.458	172	48	8	35	.279
Allen Dina	Binghamton	NYM	108	33	1	14	.306	311	75	6	32	.241
Jeremy Dodson	Wichita	KC	100	18	2	12	.180	350	89	16	45	.254
Andy Dominique	Reading	Phi	114	24	4	18	.211	213	54	9	32	.254
Jeb Dougherty	Erie	Ana	105	24	1	13	.229	162	40	0	19	.247
Kevin Eberwein	Mobile	SD	100	26	2	19	.260	272	72	16	52	.265
Alex Eckelman	Arkansas	StL	75	16	1	10	.213	205	71	3	23	.346
Mike Edwards	Akron	Cle	144	34	0	9	.236	337	108	11	54	.320
Morgan Ensberg	Round Rock	Hou	92	29	5	21	.315	391	116	23	69	.297
Matt Erickson	Portland	Fla	88	29	0	8	.330	247	72	2	33	.291
Mark Ernster	Huntsville	Mil	81	20	2	7	.247	124	30	3	19	.242
Alex Escobar	Binghamton	NYM	110	26	2	17	.236	327	100	14	50	.306
Johnny Estrada	Reading	Phi	116	38	4	22	.328	240	67	8	20	.279
Ethan Faggett	Mobile	SD	101	22	0	3	.218	269	67	2	20	.249
Cordell Farley	Arkansas	StL	60	11	1	5	.183	189	46	6	19	.243
Alex Fernandez	New Haven	Sea	72	16	0	4	.222	278	73	4	36	.263
Luis Figueroa	New Haven	Sea	118	37	0	10	.314	309	79	1	27	.256
Luis Figueroa	Altoona	Pit	86	30	1	9	.349	256	67	0	19	.262
Jason Fitzgerald	Akron	Cle	54	13	1	9	.241	154	45	3	21	.292
Tim Flaherty	Shreveport	SF	73	18	4	17	.247	191	36	4	17	.188
Franklin Font	West Tenn	ChC	95	26	0	7	.274	234	60	0	19	.256
Quincy Foster	Portland	Fla	69	19	0	2	.275	179	58	2	19	.324
David Francia	Reading	Phi	28	4	0	4	.143	182	57	3	22	.313
Alejandro Freire	Jacksonville	Det	129	34	3	18	.264	342	95	22	59	.278
Eddy Furniss	Altoona	Pit	80	21	3	11	.262	268	62	8	41	.231

			vs Left					vs Right				
Player	Team	Org	AB	H	HR	RBI	Avg	AB	H	HR	RBI	Avg
Bryon Gainey	Binghamton	NYM	47	13	1	5	.277	298	57	10	44	.191
Eddy Garabito	Bowie	Bal	143	35	3	14	.245	339	86	3	38	.254
Matt Garrick	Arkansas	StL	74	16	0	6	.216	251	60	4	29	.239
Marty Gazarek	Greenville	Atl	67	24	5	15	.358	135	34	2	13	.252
Jody Gerut	Carolina	Col	125	32	1	16	.256	237	71	2	41	.300
Jay Gibbons	Tennessee	Tor	143	47	5	20	.329	331	105	14	55	.317
David Gibralter	Bowie	Bal	140	38	6	20	.271	357	103	13	67	.289
Geronimo Gil	San Antonio	LA	86	26	5	18	.302	266	74	6	40	.278
Marcus Giles	Greenville	Atl	129	40	6	18	.310	329	93	11	44	.283
Tim Giles	Tennessee	Tor	113	30	2	13	.265	284	75	11	43	.264
Keith Ginter	Round Rock	Hou	98	37	5	22	.378	364	117	21	70	.321
Mike Glavine	Greenville	Atl	107	27	2	23	.252	316	72	9	58	.228
Mike Glendenning	Shreveport	SF	80	25	4	17	.313	211	51	12	37	.242
Ross Gload	Portland	Fla	122	38	2	16	.311	279	76	14	49	.272
Ramon Gomez	El Paso	Ari	87	23	1	11	.264	177	52	1	26	.294
Jimmy Gonzalez	Binghamton	NYM	50	14	1	6	.280	184	51	7	24	.277
Steve Goodell	Carolina	Col	74	23	5	18	.311	155	36	6	24	.232
Robb Gorr	San Antonio	LA	73	16	2	7	.219	207	57	6	34	.275
Jason Grabowski	Tulsa	Tex	132	26	0	11	.197	361	109	19	79	.302
Jess Graham	Trenton	Bos	36	6	0	4	.167	220	55	5	29	.250
Chad Green	Huntsville	Mil	78	10	0	3	.128	239	64	3	24	.268
Jeff Guiel	Erie	Ana	115	27	2	12	.235	295	77	14	47	.261
Chris Haas	Arkansas	StL	72	16	4	11	.222	219	63	13	48	.288
Toby Hall	Orlando	TB	66	27	4	20	.409	205	66	5	30	.322
Pat Hallmark	Wichita	KC	109	48	5	30	.440	370	108	5	49	.292
Jon Hamilton	Akron	Cle	158	44	4	22	.278	335	79	3	34	.236
Kip Harkrider	San Antonio	LA	25	4	0	1	.160	261	62	4	34	.238
Brian Harris	Reading	Phi	116	36	6	16	.310	235	58	4	25	.247
Jason Hart	Midland	Oak	106	35	6	26	.330	440	143	24	95	.325
Nathan Haynes	Erie	Ana	139	34	2	13	.245	318	82	4	30	.258
Chris Heintz	Birmingham	CWS	71	15	1	9	.211	168	49	1	25	.292
Dan Held	Binghamton	NYM	100	30	1	10	.300	281	89	10	59	.317
Bret Hemphill	Erie	Ana	62	15	1	8	.242	145	33	3	16	.228
Drew Henson	Norwich	NYY	46	15	2	8	.326	177	49	5	31	.277
Mike Hessman	Greenville	Atl	123	25	1	10	.203	314	55	18	40	.175
Shea Hillenbrand	Trenton	Bos	128	49	2	22	.383	401	122	9	57	.304
Eric Hinske	West Tenn	ChC	117	30	6	16	.256	319	83	14	57	.260
Jay Hood	Erie	Ana	60	15	2	9	.250	180	36	2	20	.200
Paul Hoover	Orlando	TB	115	33	1	16	.287	245	57	2	28	.233
Jim Horner	New Haven	Sea	71	15	0	5	.211	174	44	9	28	.253
B.J. Huff	Binghamton	NYM	62	16	2	8	.258	146	28	2	16	.192
Larry Huff	Wichita	KC	63	22	1	8	.349	227	65	2	35	.286
Jason Huisman	Erie	Ana	135	37	2	18	.274	306	84	1	24	.275
Steve Huls	New Britain	Min	59	14	0	4	.237	190	37	0	11	.195
Scott Hunter	Akron	Cle	120	28	2	12	.233	227	51	3	21	.225
Norm Hutchins	Carolina	Col	69	17	0	6	.246	212	51	4	23	.241
Adam Hyzdu	Altoona	Pit	114	34	10	30	.298	400	115	21	76	.287
Anthony Iapoce	Huntsville	Mil	76	20	0	5	.263	171	35	0	15	.205
Brandon Inge	Jacksonville	Det	72	25	2	17	.347	226	52	4	36	.230
Jeff Inglin	Birmingham	CWS	50	16	2	15	.320	194	55	3	25	.284
Bucky Jacobsen	Huntsville	Mil	69	21	4	14	.304	199	53	14	36	.266
Kenny James	Harrisburg	Mon	114	25	1	10	.219	207	52	1	22	.251
Adam Johnson	Birmingham	CWS	67	14	2	12	.209	312	74	9	48	.237
Gary Johnson	Erie	Ana	79	22	2	18	.278	179	52	8	38	.291
Rontrez Johnson	Trenton	Bos	128	37	2	11	.289	396	104	4	42	.263
Ryan Jones	Akron	Cle	74	25	2	14	.338	135	29	7	24	.215
Brian Keck	Carolina	Col	61	17	1	4	.279	142	36	2	24	.254
Kenny Kelly	Orlando	TB	132	36	3	14	.273	357	87	0	15	.244
Bobby Kielty	New Britain	Min	120	34	3	17	.283	331	84	11	48	.254
Mike Kinkade	Binghamton	NYM	72	25	3	19	.347	245	91	7	48	.371
Scott Kirby	Huntsville	Mil	118	19	6	16	.161	226	56	6	29	.248
Josh Klimek	Huntsville	Mil	77	20	3	13	.260	301	86	11	49	.286
Jason Knupfer	Reading	Phi	103	29	0	6	.282	176	46	4	18	.261
Toby Kominek	Huntsville	Mil	129	28	5	17	.217	298	83	5	51	.279
Steve Lackey	Greenville	Atl	141	38	2	10	.270	348	76	1	23	.218
Jacques Landry	Midland	Oak	107	33	3	12	.308	363	87	15	68	.240
Ryan Lane	Tulsa	Tex	107	32	1	12	.299	318	105	15	67	.330
Selwyn Langaigne	Tennessee	Tor	47	8	0	6	.170	166	44	0	16	.265
Derrick Lankford	Altoona	Pit	75	21	2	8	.280	239	71	8	32	.297
Brandon Larson	Chattanooga	Cin	106	24	6	16	.226	321	92	14	48	.287
Nick Leach	Norwich	NYY	62	18	1	9	.290	292	80	6	40	.274
Juan Lebron	Binghamton	NYM	54	14	2	4	.259	184	40	4	21	.217
A.J. Leday	Mobile	SD	129	33	5	19	.256	278	82	7	51	.295
Jose Leon	Arkansas	StL	72	20	3	8	.278	225	60	11	33	.267
Marc Lewis	Trenton	Bos	58	15	1	9	.259	149	43	4	21	.289
Rodney Lindsey	Jacksonville	Det	108	21	0	4	.194	285	67	0	16	.235
David Lindstrom	Jacksonville	Det	57	12	2	13	.211	165	40	5	23	.242
Mike Lockwood	Midland	Oak	68	21	1	13	.309	168	52	3	18	.310
Kyle Logan	Round Rock	Hou	46	6	0	4	.130	297	69	6	27	.232
Steve Lomasney	Trenton	Bos	37	6	0	3	.162	196	51	8	24	.260
Ryan Long	Birmingham	CWS	94	24	3	12	.255	221	52	7	27	.235
Felipe Lopez	Tennessee	Tor	161	45	5	16	.280	302	74	4	25	.245
Mickey Lopez	Huntsville	Mil	71	27	3	12	.380	141	44	1	14	.312
Rafael Lopez	West Tenn	ChC	57	17	0	5	.298	170	42	1	21	.247
Rob Mackowiak	Altoona	Pit	131	36	1	21	.275	395	120	12	66	.304
Garry Maddox Jr.	Trenton	Bos	93	24	1	15	.258	270	76	3	25	.281
Chris Magruder	Shreveport	SF	122	36	1	4	.295	374	104	3	35	.278
T.J. Maier	Arkansas	StL	84	21	1	10	.250	280	86	5	32	.307
Carlos Maldonado	Round Rock	Hou	94	27	4	14	.287	329	87	1	38	.264
Dwight Maness	New Haven	Sea	100	30	4	13	.300	307	63	8	39	.205

Double-A Batting vs. Lefthanded and Righthanded Pitchers

Player	Team	Org	AB	H	HR	RBI	Avg	AB	H	HR	RBI	Avg
Belvani Martinez	Carolina	Col	121	26	3	14	.215	285	75	0	22	.263
Henry Mateo	Harrisburg	Mon	173	54	2	21	.312	357	98	3	42	.275
Jared Mathis	Huntsville	Mil	110	33	2	6	.300	241	58	0	15	.241
Julius Matos	Mobile	SD	163	42	1	6	.258	383	102	4	29	.266
David Matranga	Round Rock	Hou	92	26	0	9	.283	281	61	6	35	.217
Brian McClure	Jacksonville	Det	30	11	0	2	.367	216	59	1	16	.273
Darnell McDonald	Bowie	Bal	136	33	1	9	.243	323	78	5	34	.241
Cody McKay	Midland	Oak	111	34	3	21	.306	316	102	2	68	.323
Walt McKeel	Carolina	Col	66	23	5	11	.348	161	28	3	15	.174
Dan McKinley	Harrisburg	Mon	172	42	2	19	.244	345	103	2	38	.299
Rusty McNamara	Reading	Phi	147	43	6	32	.293	319	94	8	44	.295
Aaron McNeal	Round Rock	Hou	73	27	5	22	.370	288	85	6	47	.295
Tydus Meadows	West Tenn	ChC	80	21	1	5	.262	169	44	4	27	.260
Ryan Medrano	New Haven	Sea	55	14	1	10	.255	161	38	1	16	.236
Jackson Melian	Norwich	NYY	88	18	3	5	.205	227	55	6	33	.242
Todd Mensik	Midland	Oak	96	24	6	17	.250	318	85	17	67	.267
Rod Metzler	Wichita	KC	76	18	0	10	.237	285	78	5	34	.274
Jason Michaels	Reading	Phi	150	55	5	33	.367	287	74	5	41	.258
Corky Miller	Chattanooga	Cin	69	13	3	8	.188	248	61	6	36	.246
Marc Mirizzi	Norwich	NYY	66	17	1	9	.258	252	59	5	20	.234
Derek Mitchell	Jacksonville	Det	83	18	0	8	.217	247	47	1	19	.190
Craig Monroe	Tulsa	Tex	118	40	6	31	.339	346	91	14	58	.263
Brian Moon	Huntsville	Mil	80	16	0	4	.200	232	41	1	29	.177
Ramon Moreta	San Antonio	LA	123	38	7	11	.309	345	74	4	20	.214
Cesar Morillo	Round Rock	Hou	70	22	1	9	.314	211	61	2	28	.289
Bobby Morris	Chattanooga	Cin	53	9	0	6	.170	192	58	5	29	.302
Billy Munoz	Akron	Cle	85	27	5	22	.318	196	50	9	26	.255
Juan Munoz	Arkansas	StL	49	16	0	10	.327	198	69	5	21	.348
Eric Munson	Jacksonville	Det	111	24	6	24	.216	254	68	9	44	.268
Adrian Myers	New Haven	Sea	100	26	1	11	.260	233	69	1	23	.296
Scott Neuberger	Orlando	TB	124	29	1	3	.234	294	62	7	37	.211
Wilbert Nieves	Mobile	SD	64	18	3	11	.281	150	39	1	19	.260
Dax Norris	Greenville	Atl	151	43	6	25	.285	333	79	7	47	.237
Chris Norton	Portland	Fla	55	20	4	18	.364	151	37	6	25	.245
Abraham Nunez	Portland	Fla	63	16	1	10	.254	158	45	5	32	.285
Talmadge Nunnari	Harrisburg	Mon	110	23	1	14	.209	207	62	4	40	.300
Bill Ortega	Arkansas	StL	72	19	1	7	.264	260	89	11	55	.342
Nick Ortiz	Wichita	KC	77	28	3	16	.364	304	84	7	46	.276
Paul Ottavinia	Norwich	NYY	104	30	2	14	.288	373	114	6	44	.306
Lyle Overbay	El Paso	Ari	67	21	1	14	.313	177	65	7	35	.367
Ryan Owens	El Paso	Ari	53	9	1	6	.170	155	36	4	18	.232
Pablo Ozuna	Portland	Fla	134	43	2	20	.321	330	100	5	39	.303
John Pachot	Portland	Fla	97	32	2	20	.330	226	62	1	37	.274
Corey Patterson	West Tenn	ChC	117	23	5	18	.197	327	93	17	64	.284
Eddie Pearson	Arkansas	StL	56	14	2	10	.250	201	63	8	28	.313
Jay Pecci	Midland	Oak	90	21	2	15	.233	263	66	0	21	.251
Mike Peeples	Tennessee	Tor	154	37	5	17	.240	321	96	13	56	.299
Carlos Pena	Tulsa	Tex	161	49	5	25	.304	368	109	23	80	.296
Elvis Pena	Carolina	Col	158	43	1	12	.272	319	100	2	25	.313
Jhonny Perez	Round Rock	Hou	93	27	2	14	.290	180	54	5	17	.300
Nestor Perez	Orlando	TB	72	10	0	3	.139	168	39	0	11	.232
Robert Perez	Tennessee	Tor	162	49	11	39	.302	385	108	8	53	.281
Tommy Peterman	New Britain	Min	55	16	1	7	.291	339	91	8	36	.268
Paul Phillips	Wichita	KC	54	14	0	3	.259	237	71	4	27	.300
Wynter Phoenix	Portland	Fla	94	23	1	16	.245	291	76	9	46	.261
Jeff Pickler	Huntsville	Mil	50	15	0	4	.300	204	62	0	22	.304
Juan Pierre	Carolina	Col	125	46	0	11	.368	314	97	0	21	.309
A.J. Pierzynski	New Britain	Min	68	16	1	12	.235	160	52	3	22	.325
Juan Piniella	Tulsa	Tex	84	23	1	7	.274	363	87	4	33	.240
Joe Pomierski	Orlando	TB	129	29	5	15	.225	330	79	11	50	.239
Colin Porter	Round Rock	Hou	104	28	2	14	.269	331	91	12	43	.275
John Powers	Mobile	SD	89	26	0	7	.292	216	54	3	15	.250
Scott Pratt	Akron	Cle	156	31	0	7	.199	344	87	7	44	.253
Rick Prieto	Birmingham	CWS	110	34	0	6	.309	322	76	1	34	.236
Nick Punto	Reading	Phi	145	35	2	15	.241	311	81	3	32	.260
Dan Ramirez	Carolina	Col	131	36	2	14	.275	251	62	0	25	.247
Jaisen Randolph	West Tenn	ChC	121	24	1	7	.198	369	95	0	24	.257
Cody Ransom	Shreveport	SF	109	23	3	11	.211	350	69	4	36	.197
Josh Reding	Harrisburg	Mon	151	35	1	17	.232	306	65	1	31	.212
Jackie Rexrode	Birmingham	CWS	97	24	0	7	.247	240	73	0	7	.304
Eric Riggs	San Antonio	LA	110	25	1	12	.227	311	69	6	27	.222
Brian Rios	Jacksonville	Det	71	18	0	7	.254	244	64	5	29	.262
Luis Rivas	New Britain	Min	89	22	2	7	.247	239	60	1	33	.251
Roberto Rivera	Bowie	Bal	84	20	3	14	.238	188	41	1	20	.218
Cito Rodriguez	Erie	Ana	90	20	1	3	.222	148	38	0	11	.257
Jason Romano	Tulsa	Tex	116	33	1	12	.284	419	112	7	58	.267
Mandy Romero	Akron	Cle	81	23	3	14	.284	199	64	9	32	.322
Mel Rosario	Birmingham	CWS	74	21	1	9	.284	215	54	5	33	.251
Mike Rose	El Paso	Ari	80	21	1	15	.262	272	79	9	47	.290
Pete Rose	Reading	Phi	102	33	4	19	.225	254	65	4	37	.256
Jason Ross	Greenville	Atl	80	18	2	6	.225	171	45	10	20	.263
Aaron Rowand	Birmingham	CWS	143	29	0	20	.203	389	108	20	78	.278
Mike Ryan	New Britain	Min	118	25	2	9	.212	363	108	9	60	.298
Rich Saitta	San Antonio	LA	100	30	2	16	.300	251	58	1	20	.231
Oscar Salazar	Midland	Oak	93	20	0	3	.215	334	108	13	54	.323
Wellington Sanchez	Huntsville	Mil	40	7	0	3	.175	204	56	1	25	.275
Jared Sandberg	Orlando	TB	80	22	2	14	.275	164	41	3	21	.250
Pedro Santana	Jacksonville	Det	110	27	2	11	.245	338	99	4	42	.293
Angel Santos	Trenton	Bos	68	21	1	9	.309	207	50	2	23	.242
Damian Sapp	Trenton	Bos	53	13	0	4	.245	169	35	6	22	.207

Player	Team	Org	AB	H	HR	RBI	Avg	AB	H	HR	RBI	Avg
Luis Saturria	Arkansas	StL	106	36	4	19	.340	372	95	16	57	.255
Chris Saunders	Chattanooga	Cin	45	12	3	8	.267	155	58	6	29	.374
Jamie Saylor	El Paso	Ari	51	7	0	7	.137	235	54	1	21	.230
Tony Schifano	Tennessee	Tor	99	26	0	11	.263	176	38	1	13	.216
Scott Seabol	Norwich	NYY	105	42	9	29	.400	388	104	11	49	.268
Todd Sears	Carolina	Col	87	25	4	16	.287	212	65	8	56	.307
Rick Short	Bowie	Bal	134	42	4	20	.313	313	106	5	62	.339
Demond Smith	Greenville	Atl	130	39	7	19	.300	301	79	6	29	.262
Jason Smith	West Tenn	ChC	122	29	3	21	.238	359	85	9	40	.237
Rod Smith	Orlando	TB	73	20	0	5	.274	133	30	0	7	.226
Danny Solano	Tulsa	Tex	83	21	3	9	.253	276	69	4	24	.250
Scott Sollmann	Tennessee	Tor	138	28	0	7	.203	247	63	0	20	.255
Zach Sorensen	Akron	Cle	111	32	2	9	.288	271	67	4	29	.247
John Tamargo	Binghamton	NYM	56	16	0	6	.286	235	59	1	23	.251
Luis Taveras	Tulsa	Tex	65	15	1	12	.231	220	51	4	25	.232
Marcus Thames	Norwich	NYY	113	33	4	19	.292	361	81	11	60	.224
Nick Theodorou	San Antonio	LA	59	14	0	6	.237	207	50	1	19	.242
Juan Thomas	New Haven	Sea	116	30	8	22	.259	379	106	19	78	.280
Yorvit Torrealba	Shreveport	SF	96	31	1	4	.323	302	83	3	28	.275
Pete Tucci	Mobile	SD	142	32	8	26	.225	334	71	9	47	.213
Dave Ullery	Wichita	KC	33	6	0	9	.182	169	52	5	33	.308
Carlos Urquiola	El Paso	Ari	43	12	0	6	.279	182	56	0	12	.308
Brant Ust	Jacksonville	Det	110	26	3	11	.236	273	57	1	17	.209
Vic Valencia	Norwich	NYY	66	14	3	8	.212	190	37	5	28	.195
Eric Valent	Reading	Phi	135	43	9	40	.319	334	78	13	50	.234
Yohanny Valera	Harrisburg	Mon	91	24	3	13	.264	190	42	0	21	.221
Ramon Vazquez	New Haven	Sea	100	23	2	10	.230	305	93	6	49	.305
Scott Vieira	West Tenn	ChC	96	23	2	9	.240	226	48	5	25	.212
Chris Walther	Erie	Ana	98	27	0	9	.276	153	37	1	10	.242
Jeremy Ware	Harrisburg	Mon	132	44	2	21	.333	310	79	8	42	.255
Rico Washington	Altoona	Pit	116	21	0	13	.181	387	109	8	46	.282
Jake Weber	New Haven	Sea	124	29	0	10	.234	349	92	5	46	.264
Jayson Werth	Bowie	Bal	81	24	2	9	.296	195	39	3	17	.200
Chad Whitaker	Akron	Cle	103	31	3	21	.301	264	55	4	29	.208
Ty Wigginton	Binghamton	NYM	113	38	9	26	.336	340	91	11	51	.268
Brad Wilkerson	Harrisburg	Mon	66	19	1	11	.288	163	58	5	33	.356
Dave Willis	Wichita	KC	83	15	3	10	.181	219	51	4	27	.233
Jack Wilson	Arkansas	StL	76	21	3	7	.276	267	80	3	27	.300
Ron Wright	Chattanooga	Cin	61	17	5	12	.279	176	46	7	38	.261
Mike Young	Tennessee	Tor	88	34	3	16	.386	257	61	3	31	.237
Travis Young	Shreveport	SF	87	21	1	6	.241	247	62	5	25	.251
Tony Zuniga	Shreveport	SF	90	20	4	9	.222	317	86	13	53	.271

Double-A Batting at Home and on the Road

			Home					Road				
Player	Team	Org	AB	H	HR	RBI	Avg	AB	H	HR	RBI	Avg
Chuck Abbott	Erie	Ana	161	48	5	26	.298	169	34	0	13	.201
Kurt Airoso	Jacksonville	Det	191	45	1	21	.236	135	33	3	20	.244
Jeff Allen	Shreveport	SF	216	51	3	25	.236	231	55	4	27	.238
Luke Allen	San Antonio	LA	170	45	3	29	.265	169	45	4	31	.266
Erick Almonte	Norwich	NYY	212	55	5	41	.259	242	68	10	36	.281
Rafael Alvarez	New Britain	Min	130	31	4	24	.238	144	40	3	22	.278
Jose Amado	Wichita	KC	169	54	4	38	.320	149	39	1	18	.262
Mike Amrhein	West Tenn	ChC	177	53	3	26	.299	175	47	6	23	.269
Brooks Badeaux	Orlando	TB	113	38	1	16	.336	147	30	0	11	.204
Ryan Balfe	Mobile	SD	228	59	8	33	.259	234	62	4	33	.265
Blake Barthol	New Haven	Sea	125	36	1	7	.288	123	38	6	23	.309
Fletcher Bates	El Paso	Ari	186	54	5	30	.290	169	44	5	32	.260
Eric Battersby	Birmingham	CWS	192	48	3	23	.250	219	50	5	20	.228
Brian Becker	Orlando	TB	246	57	0	22	.232	257	83	9	36	.323
Todd Betts	Portland	Fla	212	74	6	42	.349	209	61	3	29	.292
Andy Bevins	Arkansas	StL	219	71	10	43	.324	211	67	15	45	.318
Darren Blakely	Erie	Ana	209	52	6	31	.249	230	52	10	23	.226
Papo Bolivar	New Britain	Min	194	63	1	26	.325	212	50	1	16	.236
Justin Bowles	Midland	Oak	241	70	12	46	.290	202	50	4	19	.248
Danny Bravo	Birmingham	CWS	169	36	1	17	.213	171	43	2	12	.251
Stoney Briggs	Jacksonville	Det	241	64	13	40	.266	255	62	4	25	.243
Ben Broussard	Chattanooga	Cin	124	37	5	17	.298	162	36	9	34	.222
Jason Brown	Orlando	TB	112	34	5	17	.304	118	26	3	12	.220
Rich Brown	Norwich	NYY	178	45	3	19	.253	141	31	1	11	.220
Mo Bruce	Binghamton	NYM	162	46	1	15	.284	152	40	1	8	.263
Gary Burnham	Reading	Phi	160	48	6	27	.300	195	47	7	34	.241
Kevin Burns	Round Rock	Hou	118	37	3	18	.314	137	44	5	28	.321
Andy Burress	Chattanooga	Cin	196	43	3	17	.219	204	57	3	24	.279
Sean Burroughs	Mobile	SD	189	51	1	19	.270	203	63	1	23	.310
Darren Burton	Altoona	Pit	120	36	1	18	.300	109	39	4	15	.358
Eric Byrnes	Midland	Oak	139	44	3	23	.317	120	34	2	14	.283
Alex Cabrera	El Paso	Ari	103	44	16	39	.427	109	37	19	43	.339
Wilmy Caceres	Chattanooga	Cin	256	61	1	19	.238	278	82	1	14	.295
Jason Camilli	Harrisburg	Mon	129	27	3	12	.209	111	24	0	7	.216
Aaron Capista	Trenton	Bos	215	57	1	19	.265	219	46	1	17	.210
Joe Caruso	Wichita	KC	175	57	5	32	.326	225	68	8	34	.302
Carlos Casimiro	Bowie	Bal	145	38	4	15	.262	145	38	2	17	.262
Dionys Cesar	Midland	Oak	210	61	1	16	.290	223	59	3	21	.265
Chin-Feng Chen	San Antonio	LA	267	71	2	35	.266	249	72	4	32	.289
Virgil Chevalier	Trenton	Bos	199	56	2	32	.281	147	51	5	35	.347
Alex Cintron	El Paso	Ari	278	87	1	38	.313	244	70	3	21	.287
Doug Clark	Shreveport	SF	232	60	3	34	.259	260	74	7	41	.285
Jermaine Clark	New Haven	Sea	212	62	1	23	.292	235	69	1	21	.294
Ivanon Coffie	Bowie	Bal	155	35	6	24	.226	186	56	3	20	.301
Eric Cole	Round Rock	Hou	253	63	12	42	.249	290	95	10	52	.328
Javier Colina	Carolina	Col	211	51	2	17	.242	218	42	0	18	.193
Greg Connors	New Haven	Sea	198	49	5	26	.247	254	77	4	32	.303
Chris Coste	Akron	Cle	97	31	2	15	.320	143	49	0	16	.343
Humberto Cota	Altoona	Pit	207	54	4	21	.261	222	58	4	23	.261
Joe Crede	Birmingham	CWS	262	76	3	29	.290	271	87	18	65	.321
Cesar Crespo	Portland	Fla	240	59	4	25	.246	242	65	5	35	.269
Mike Cuddyer	New Britain	Min	240	66	1	30	.275	250	63	5	31	.252
Mike Curry	Wichita	KC	208	67	3	28	.322	253	66	1	24	.261
Jack Cust	El Paso	Ari	203	65	9	41	.320	244	66	11	34	.270
Brian Dallimore	El Paso	Ari	158	50	1	27	.316	198	49	3	26	.247
Cleatus Davidson	New Britain	Min	217	51	0	18	.235	228	51	0	13	.224
Glenn Davis	San Antonio	LA	190	35	2	19	.184	187	43	7	21	.230
Travis Dawkins	Chattanooga	Cin	195	49	4	17	.251	173	36	2	14	.208
Tim DeCinces	Mobile	SD	104	33	6	26	.317	103	23	5	18	.223
Jorge DeLeon	Trenton	Bos	157	52	2	19	.331	182	52	0	19	.286
Jason Dellaero	Birmingham	CWS	217	37	2	15	.171	221	44	5	27	.199
Darrell Dent	Bowie	Bal	189	57	0	15	.302	173	37	0	10	.214
Tony DeRosso	Trenton	Bos	206	51	10	40	.248	243	75	10	45	.309
Jason Dewey	Carolina	Col	150	35	5	22	.233	168	37	4	22	.220
Alejandro Diaz	Chattanooga	Cin	246	62	4	32	.252	245	69	9	34	.282
Joe Dillon	Wichita	KC	110	36	4	21	.327	110	34	6	22	.309
Allen Dina	Binghamton	NYM	199	48	4	23	.241	220	60	3	23	.273
Jeremy Dodson	Wichita	KC	231	58	9	27	.251	219	49	9	30	.224
Andy Dominique	Reading	Phi	162	40	6	27	.247	165	38	7	23	.230
Jeb Dougherty	Erie	Ana	125	34	1	17	.272	142	30	0	15	.211
Kevin Eberwein	Mobile	SD	182	54	9	34	.297	190	44	9	37	.232
Alex Eckelman	Arkansas	StL	125	43	3	17	.344	155	44	1	16	.284
Mike Edwards	Akron	Cle	231	68	3	23	.294	250	74	8	40	.296
Morgan Ensberg	Round Rock	Hou	244	67	16	55	.275	239	78	12	35	.326
Matt Erickson	Portland	Fla	157	45	2	20	.287	178	56	0	21	.315
Mark Ernster	Huntsville	Mil	101	27	1	14	.267	104	23	4	12	.221
Alex Escobar	Binghamton	NYM	207	66	11	45	.319	230	60	5	22	.261
Johnny Estrada	Reading	Phi	176	54	8	29	.307	180	51	4	13	.283
Ethan Faggett	Mobile	SD	179	41	1	9	.229	191	48	1	14	.251
Cordell Farley	Arkansas	StL	107	24	4	12	.224	142	33	3	12	.232
Alex Fernandez	New Haven	Sea	170	41	2	14	.241	180	48	2	26	.267
Luis Figueroa	New Haven	Sea	201	52	1	10	.259	226	64	0	27	.283
Luis Figueroa	Altoona	Pit	154	43	1	11	.279	188	54	0	17	.287
Jason Fitzgerald	Akron	Cle	93	27	2	13	.290	115	31	2	17	.270
Tim Flaherty	Shreveport	SF	124	21	3	15	.169	140	33	5	19	.236
Franklin Font	West Tenn	ChC	162	43	0	7	.265	167	43	0	19	.257
Quincy Foster	Portland	Fla	141	46	1	7	.326	107	31	1	14	.290
David Francia	Reading	Phi	117	33	3	17	.282	93	28	0	9	.301
Alejandro Freire	Jacksonville	Det	229	59	15	38	.258	242	70	10	39	.289
Eddy Furniss	Altoona	Pit	169	40	4	22	.237	179	43	7	30	.240

			Home					Road				
Player	Team	Org	AB	H	HR	RBI	Avg	AB	H	HR	RBI	Avg
Bryon Gainey	Binghamton	NYM	171	41	6	29	.240	174	29	5	20	.167
Eddy Garabito	Bowie	Bal	225	50	3	29	.222	257	71	3	23	.276
Matt Garrick	Arkansas	StL	170	39	1	17	.229	155	37	3	18	.239
Marty Gazarek	Greenville	Atl	97	29	4	18	.299	105	29	3	10	.276
Jody Gerut	Carolina	Col	164	47	1	24	.287	198	56	2	33	.283
Jay Gibbons	Tennessee	Tor	227	75	10	41	.330	247	77	9	34	.312
David Gibralter	Bowie	Bal	237	52	8	28	.219	260	89	11	59	.342
Geronimo Gil	San Antonio	LA	165	46	6	25	.279	187	54	5	33	.289
Marcus Giles	Greenville	Atl	208	65	10	29	.313	250	68	7	33	.272
Tim Giles	Tennessee	Tor	177	44	5	31	.249	220	61	8	25	.277
Keith Ginter	Round Rock	Hou	237	70	13	43	.295	225	84	13	49	.373
Mike Glavine	Greenville	Atl	205	54	7	46	.263	218	45	4	35	.206
Mike Glendenning	Shreveport	SF	134	28	9	20	.209	157	48	7	34	.306
Ross Gload	Portland	Fla	187	54	7	35	.289	214	60	9	30	.280
Ramon Gomez	El Paso	Ari	126	45	0	22	.357	138	30	2	15	.217
Jimmy Gonzalez	Binghamton	NYM	114	36	5	19	.316	120	29	3	11	.242
Steve Goodell	Carolina	Col	98	31	6	27	.316	131	28	5	15	.214
Robb Gorr	San Antonio	LA	127	33	1	16	.260	153	40	7	25	.261
Jason Grabowski	Tulsa	Tex	236	68	9	44	.288	257	67	10	46	.261
Jess Graham	Trenton	Bos	99	21	1	12	.212	157	40	4	21	.255
Chad Green	Huntsville	Mil	164	40	2	10	.244	153	34	1	17	.222
Jeff Guiel	Erie	Ana	212	53	9	37	.250	198	51	7	22	.258
Chris Haas	Arkansas	StL	148	39	11	37	.264	143	40	6	22	.280
Toby Hall	Orlando	TB	113	35	1	22	.310	158	58	8	28	.367
Pat Hallmark	Wichita	KC	220	64	2	35	.291	259	92	8	44	.355
Jon Hamilton	Akron	Cle	251	64	2	31	.255	242	59	5	25	.244
Kip Harkrider	San Antonio	LA	134	30	0	16	.224	152	36	4	19	.237
Brian Harris	Reading	Phi	154	43	3	14	.279	197	51	7	27	.259
Jason Hart	Midland	Oak	281	94	15	64	.335	265	84	15	57	.317
Nathan Haynes	Erie	Ana	224	59	4	20	.263	233	57	2	23	.245
Chris Heintz	Birmingham	CWS	114	27	1	11	.237	125	37	1	23	.296
Dan Held	Binghamton	NYM	199	74	3	43	.372	182	45	8	26	.247
Bret Hemphill	Erie	Ana	91	20	0	9	.220	116	28	4	15	.241
Drew Henson	Norwich	NYY	117	35	1	20	.299	106	29	6	19	.274
Mike Hessman	Greenville	Atl	233	44	10	28	.189	204	36	9	22	.176
Shea Hillenbrand	Trenton	Bos	254	79	5	37	.311	275	92	6	42	.335
Eric Hinske	West Tenn	ChC	211	55	7	34	.261	225	58	13	39	.258
Jay Hood	Erie	Ana	115	23	3	17	.200	125	28	1	12	.224
Paul Hoover	Orlando	TB	186	53	0	26	.285	174	37	3	18	.213
Jim Horner	New Haven	Sea	105	24	5	17	.229	140	35	4	16	.250
B.J. Huff	Binghamton	NYM	125	35	4	17	.280	83	9	0	7	.108
Larry Huff	Wichita	KC	140	45	2	22	.321	150	42	1	21	.280
Jason Huisman	Erie	Ana	206	58	2	23	.282	235	63	1	19	.268
Steve Huls	New Britain	Min	114	24	0	7	.211	135	27	0	8	.200
Scott Hunter	Akron	Cle	146	34	0	9	.233	201	45	5	24	.224
Norm Hutchins	Carolina	Col	146	26	1	12	.178	135	42	3	17	.311
Adam Hyzdu	Altoona	Pit	242	73	16	57	.302	272	76	15	49	.279
Anthony Iapoce	Huntsville	Mil	119	32	0	10	.269	128	23	0	10	.180
Brandon Inge	Jacksonville	Det	152	45	4	36	.296	146	32	2	17	.219
Jeff Inglin	Birmingham	CWS	124	34	2	19	.274	120	37	3	21	.308
Bucky Jacobsen	Huntsville	Mil	126	30	7	20	.238	142	44	11	30	.310
Kenny James	Harrisburg	Mon	158	38	2	20	.241	163	39	0	12	.239
Adam Johnson	Birmingham	CWS	179	33	3	22	.184	200	55	8	38	.275
Gary Johnson	Erie	Ana	132	35	1	20	.265	126	39	9	36	.310
Rontrez Johnson	Trenton	Bos	244	60	2	23	.246	280	81	4	30	.289
Ryan Jones	Akron	Cle	109	36	6	23	.330	100	18	3	15	.180
Brian Keck	Carolina	Col	91	23	1	13	.253	112	30	2	15	.268
Kenny Kelly	Orlando	TB	244	59	1	12	.242	245	64	2	17	.261
Bobby Kielty	New Britain	Min	234	58	7	38	.248	217	60	7	27	.276
Mike Kinkade	Binghamton	NYM	154	56	5	31	.364	163	60	5	36	.368
Scott Kirby	Huntsville	Mil	173	34	6	25	.197	171	41	6	20	.240
Josh Klimek	Huntsville	Mil	174	52	9	29	.299	204	54	5	33	.265
Jason Knupfer	Reading	Phi	121	37	2	13	.306	158	38	2	11	.241
Toby Kominek	Huntsville	Mil	221	60	4	40	.271	206	51	6	28	.248
Steve Lackey	Greenville	Atl	241	58	1	19	.241	248	56	2	14	.226
Jacques Landry	Midland	Oak	235	71	11	51	.302	235	49	7	29	.209
Ryan Lane	Tulsa	Tex	210	76	11	50	.362	215	61	5	29	.284
Selwyn Langaigne	Tennessee	Tor	96	22	0	10	.229	117	30	0	12	.256
Derrick Lankford	Altoona	Pit	135	37	0	13	.274	179	55	10	27	.307
Brandon Larson	Chattanooga	Cin	197	56	8	38	.284	230	60	12	26	.261
Nick Leach	Norwich	NYY	168	48	3	21	.286	186	50	4	28	.269
Juan Lebron	Binghamton	NYM	112	28	3	13	.250	126	26	3	12	.206
A.J. Leday	Mobile	SD	209	59	6	35	.282	198	56	6	35	.283
Jose Leon	Arkansas	StL	119	33	4	16	.277	178	47	10	25	.264
Marc Lewis	Trenton	Bos	106	29	1	8	.274	101	29	4	22	.287
Rod Lindsey	Jacksonville	Det	185	41	0	12	.222	208	47	0	8	.226
David Lindstrom	Jacksonville	Det	114	24	4	17	.211	108	28	3	19	.259
Mike Lockwood	Midland	Oak	96	33	2	11	.344	140	40	2	20	.286
Kyle Logan	Round Rock	Hou	156	38	3	15	.244	187	37	3	16	.198
Steve Lomasney	Trenton	Bos	126	31	3	14	.246	107	26	5	13	.243
Ryan Long	Birmingham	CWS	147	38	5	22	.259	168	38	5	17	.226
Felipe Lopez	Tennessee	Tor	200	46	3	20	.230	263	73	6	21	.278
Mickey Lopez	Huntsville	Mil	111	33	3	12	.297	101	38	1	14	.376
Rafael Lopez	West Tenn	ChC	109	27	1	9	.248	118	32	0	17	.271
Rob Mackowiak	Altoona	Pit	260	84	5	41	.323	266	72	8	46	.271
Garry Maddox Jr.	Trenton	Bos	173	56	3	25	.324	190	44	1	15	.232
Chris Magruder	Shreveport	SF	238	70	2	20	.294	258	70	2	19	.271
T.J. Maier	Arkansas	StL	181	54	3	22	.298	183	53	3	20	.290
Carlos Maldonado	Round Rock	Hou	213	54	2	24	.254	210	60	3	28	.286
Dwight Maness	New Haven	Sea	203	51	4	29	.251	204	42	8	23	.206

Double-A Batting at Home and on the Road

Player	Team	Org	Home AB	H	HR	RBI	Avg	Road AB	H	HR	RBI	Avg
Belvani Martinez	Carolina	Col	209	54	2	22	.258	197	47	1	14	.239
Henry Mateo	Harrisburg	Mon	258	78	3	38	.302	272	74	2	25	.272
Jared Mathis	Huntsville	Mil	170	41	0	9	.241	181	50	2	12	.276
Julius Matos	Mobile	SD	274	69	1	13	.252	272	75	4	22	.276
David Matranga	Round Rock	Hou	181	32	3	19	.177	192	55	3	25	.286
Brian McClure	Jacksonville	Det	110	31	1	10	.282	136	39	0	8	.287
Darnell McDonald	Bowie	Bal	206	53	3	24	.257	253	58	3	19	.229
Cody McKay	Midland	Oak	226	75	3	47	.332	201	61	2	42	.303
Walt McKeel	Carolina	Col	106	24	6	18	.226	121	27	2	8	.223
Dan McKinley	Harrisburg	Mon	260	72	3	20	.277	257	73	1	37	.284
Rusty McNamara	Reading	Phi	221	74	8	43	.335	245	63	6	33	.257
Aaron McNeal	Round Rock	Hou	174	55	6	37	.316	187	57	5	32	.305
Tydus Meadows	West Tenn	ChC	132	40	3	23	.303	117	25	2	10	.214
Ryan Medrano	New Haven	Sea	107	25	1	13	.234	109	27	1	13	.248
Jackson Melian	Norwich	NYY	154	38	4	21	.247	136	35	5	17	.257
Todd Mensik	Midland	Oak	207	54	12	42	.261	207	55	11	42	.266
Rod Metzler	Wichita	KC	190	56	4	28	.295	171	40	1	16	.234
Jason Michaels	Reading	Phi	214	64	2	29	.299	223	65	8	45	.291
Corky Miller	Chattanooga	Cin	152	32	2	19	.211	165	42	7	25	.255
Marc Mirizzi	Norwich	NYY	152	39	3	16	.257	166	37	3	13	.223
Derek Mitchell	Jacksonville	Det	159	28	1	14	.176	171	37	0	13	.216
Craig Monroe	Tulsa	Tex	221	66	12	46	.299	243	65	8	43	.267
Brian Moon	Huntsville	Mil	165	33	0	15	.200	147	24	1	18	.163
Ramon Moreta	San Antonio	LA	236	68	10	22	.288	232	44	1	9	.190
Cesar Morillo	Round Rock	Hou	144	48	2	26	.333	137	35	1	11	.255
Bobby Morris	Chattanooga	Cin	118	36	3	14	.305	127	31	2	21	.244
Billy Munoz	Akron	Cle	126	35	6	22	.278	155	42	8	26	.271
Juan Munoz	Arkansas	StL	116	39	4	14	.336	131	46	1	17	.351
Eric Munson	Jacksonville	Det	149	48	6	32	.254	176	44	9	36	.250
Adrian Myers	New Haven	Sea	149	42	0	12	.282	185	53	3	22	.286
Scott Neuberger	Orlando	TB	212	46	4	17	.217	206	45	4	23	.218
Wilbert Nieves	Mobile	SD	103	30	3	16	.252	95	27	1	14	.284
Dax Norris	Greenville	Atl	231	53	5	30	.229	253	69	8	42	.273
Chris Norton	Portland	Fla	121	38	8	28	.314	85	19	1	11	.224
Abraham Nunez	Portland	Fla	116	30	1	19	.259	105	31	5	23	.295
Talmadge Nunnari	Harrisburg	Mon	151	44	4	31	.291	166	41	1	23	.247
Bill Ortega	Arkansas	StL	167	51	5	29	.305	165	57	7	33	.345
Nick Ortiz	Wichita	KC	180	51	6	24	.283	201	61	4	38	.303
Paul Ottavinia	Norwich	NYY	237	74	4	31	.312	240	70	4	27	.292
Lyle Overbay	El Paso	Ari	122	44	4	31	.361	122	42	4	18	.344
Ryan Owens	El Paso	Ari	117	24	3	12	.205	91	21	2	12	.231
Pablo Ozuna	Portland	Fla	235	73	4	31	.311	229	70	3	28	.306
John Pachot	Portland	Fla	161	47	2	26	.292	162	47	1	30	.290
Corey Patterson	West Tenn	ChC	203	50	11	32	.246	241	66	11	50	.274
Eddie Pearson	Arkansas	StL	127	42	7	26	.331	130	35	3	12	.269
Jay Pecci	Midland	Oak	167	44	2	15	.263	186	43	0	21	.231
Mike Peeples	Tennessee	Tor	240	82	12	50	.342	235	51	6	23	.217
Carlos Pena	Tulsa	Tex	267	81	15	63	.303	262	77	13	42	.294
Elvis Pena	Carolina	Col	208	67	1	16	.322	269	76	2	21	.283
Jhonny Perez	Round Rock	Hou	156	56	6	20	.359	117	25	1	11	.214
Nestor Perez	Orlando	TB	122	21	0	8	.172	118	28	0	6	.237
Robert Perez	Tennessee	Tor	261	85	9	46	.326	286	72	10	46	.252
Tommy Peterman	New Britain	Min	189	55	1	19	.291	205	52	8	24	.254
Paul Phillips	Wichita	KC	171	54	3	15	.316	120	31	1	15	.258
Wynter Phoenix	Portland	Fla	184	43	6	28	.234	201	56	4	34	.279
Jeff Pickler	Huntsville	Mil	120	36	0	14	.300	134	41	0	12	.306
Juan Pierre	Carolina	Col	213	68	0	16	.319	226	75	0	16	.332
A.J. Pierzynski	New Britain	Min	119	37	3	19	.311	109	31	1	15	.284
Juan Piniella	Tulsa	Tex	221	57	2	16	.258	226	53	3	24	.235
Joe Pomierski	Orlando	TB	226	58	6	29	.257	233	50	10	36	.215
Colin Porter	Round Rock	Hou	228	61	8	24	.268	207	58	6	33	.280
John Powers	Mobile	SD	148	39	0	11	.264	157	41	3	11	.261
Scott Pratt	Akron	Cle	241	61	5	28	.253	259	57	2	23	.220
Rick Prieto	Birmingham	CWS	197	55	0	18	.279	235	55	1	22	.234
Nick Punto	Reading	Phi	237	64	1	23	.270	219	52	4	24	.237
Dan Ramirez	Carolina	Col	175	42	0	21	.240	207	56	2	18	.271
Jaisen Randolph	West Tenn	ChC	231	51	1	11	.221	259	68	0	20	.263
Cody Ransom	Shreveport	SF	217	49	6	29	.226	242	43	1	18	.178
Josh Reding	Harrisburg	Mon	228	55	2	22	.241	229	45	0	26	.197
Jackie Rexrode	Birmingham	CWS	162	41	0	7	.253	175	56	0	7	.320
Eric Riggs	San Antonio	LA	223	47	2	16	.211	198	47	5	23	.237
Brian Rios	Jacksonville	Det	146	35	3	18	.240	169	47	2	18	.278
Luis Rivas	New Britain	Min	175	51	3	26	.291	153	31	0	14	.203
Roberto Rivera	Bowie	Bal	126	26	2	14	.206	146	35	2	20	.240
Cito Rodriguez	Erie	Ana	122	35	1	10	.287	116	23	0	4	.198
Jason Romano	Tulsa	Tex	267	72	6	35	.270	268	73	2	35	.272
Mandy Romero	Akron	Cle	145	45	3	24	.310	135	42	9	22	.311
Mel Rosario	Birmingham	CWS	150	37	3	20	.247	139	38	3	22	.273
Mike Rose	El Paso	Ari	183	55	5	36	.301	169	45	5	26	.266
Pete Rose	Reading	Phi	175	44	5	29	.251	181	44	3	27	.243
Jason Ross	Greenville	Atl	114	32	6	15	.281	137	31	6	11	.226
Aaron Rowand	Birmingham	CWS	248	62	7	43	.250	284	75	13	55	.264
Mike Ryan	New Britain	Min	242	68	5	35	.281	239	65	6	34	.272
Rich Saitta	San Antonio	LA	161	40	2	12	.248	190	48	1	24	.253
Oscar Salazar	Midland	Oak	210	66	12	35	.314	217	62	1	22	.286
Wellington Sanchez	Huntsville	Mil	133	35	0	14	.263	111	28	1	14	.252
Jared Sandberg	Orlando	TB	116	33	0	17	.284	128	30	5	18	.234
Pedro Santana	Jacksonville	Det	220	54	4	26	.245	228	72	2	27	.316
Angel Santos	Trenton	Bos	131	32	1	13	.244	144	39	2	19	.271
Damian Sapp	Trenton	Bos	110	22	3	13	.200	112	26	3	13	.232

Player	Team	Org	Home AB	H	HR	RBI	Avg	Road AB	H	HR	RBI	Avg
Luis Saturria	Arkansas	StL	234	63	10	35	.269	244	68	10	41	.279
Chris Saunders	Chattanooga	Cin	117	39	3	17	.333	83	31	6	20	.373
Jamie Saylor	El Paso	Ari	145	42	1	19	.290	141	19	0	9	.135
Tony Schifano	Tennessee	Tor	142	32	0	8	.225	133	32	1	16	.241
Scott Seabol	Norwich	NYY	256	81	9	42	.316	237	65	11	36	.274
Todd Sears	Carolina	Col	134	45	6	39	.336	165	45	6	33	.273
Rick Short	Bowie	Bal	229	74	6	36	.323	218	74	3	46	.339
Demond Smith	Greenville	Atl	213	58	7	26	.272	218	60	6	22	.275
Jason Smith	West Tenn	ChC	233	53	7	37	.227	248	61	5	24	.246
Rod Smith	Orlando	TB	114	32	0	5	.281	92	18	0	7	.196
Danny Solano	Tulsa	Tex	180	43	3	17	.239	179	47	4	16	.263
Scott Sollmann	Tennessee	Tor	195	46	0	9	.236	190	45	0	18	.237
Zach Sorensen	Akron	Cle	161	50	3	20	.311	221	49	3	18	.222
John Tamargo	Binghamton	NYM	156	45	1	20	.288	134	30	0	9	.224
Luis Taveras	Tulsa	Tex	149	37	4	21	.248	136	29	1	16	.213
Marcus Thames	Norwich	NYY	245	54	5	38	.220	229	60	10	41	.262
Nick Theodorou	San Antonio	LA	126	29	0	11	.230	140	35	1	14	.250
Juan Thomas	New Haven	Sea	227	56	10	39	.247	268	80	17	61	.299
Yorvit Torrealba	Shreveport	SF	182	52	4	15	.286	216	62	0	17	.287
Pete Tucci	Mobile	SD	229	44	8	32	.192	247	59	9	41	.239
Dave Ullery	Wichita	KC	109	31	4	28	.284	93	27	1	14	.290
Carlos Urquiola	El Paso	Ari	113	38	0	13	.336	112	30	0	5	.268
Brant Ust	Jacksonville	Det	197	51	1	16	.259	186	32	3	12	.172
Vic Valencia	Norwich	NYY	130	29	3	17	.223	126	22	5	19	.175
Eric Valent	Reading	Phi	246	63	9	49	.256	223	58	13	41	.260
Yohanny Valera	Harrisburg	Mon	140	29	0	20	.207	141	37	3	14	.262
Ramon Vazquez	New Haven	Sea	201	52	5	25	.259	204	64	3	34	.314
Scott Vieira	West Tenn	ChC	159	44	4	23	.277	163	27	3	11	.166
Chris Walther	Erie	Ana	116	27	0	6	.233	135	37	1	13	.274
Jeremy Ware	Harrisburg	Mon	207	59	4	30	.285	235	64	6	33	.272
Rico Washington	Altoona	Pit	234	59	2	18	.252	269	71	6	41	.264
Jake Weber	New Haven	Sea	213	48	1	29	.225	260	73	4	27	.281
Jayson Werth	Bowie	Bal	133	29	3	11	.218	143	34	2	15	.238
Chad Whitaker	Akron	Cle	174	36	2	23	.207	193	50	5	27	.259
Ty Wigginton	Binghamton	NYM	204	63	12	44	.309	249	66	8	33	.265
Brad Wilkerson	Harrisburg	Mon	106	40	5	26	.377	123	37	1	18	.301
Dave Willis	Wichita	KC	139	31	3	23	.223	163	35	4	14	.215
Jack Wilson	Arkansas	StL	159	50	1	15	.314	184	51	5	24	.277
Ron Wright	Chattanooga	Cin	123	32	2	18	.260	114	31	10	32	.272
Mike Young	Tennessee	Tor	170	54	6	29	.318	175	41	0	18	.234
Travis Young	Shreveport	SF	172	41	4	18	.238	162	42	2	13	.259
Tony Zuniga	Shreveport	SF	193	53	12	31	.275	214	53	5	31	.248

Double-A Pitching vs. Lefthanded and Righthanded Batters

			vs Left					vs Right				
Player	Team	Org	AB	H	HR	SO	Avg	AB	H	HR	SO	Avg
B. Agamennone	Harrisburg	Mon	197	60	6	23	.305	172	42	4	32	.244
Kurt Ainsworth	Shreveport	SF	215	48	6	33	.223	377	90	6	97	.239
Jeff Andra	Shreveport	SF	64	18	0	15	.281	291	88	6	49	.302
Jeff Andrews	El Paso	Ari	93	27	3	16	.290	160	61	9	19	.381
Angel Aragon	Mobile	SD	113	30	3	27	.265	188	54	6	34	.287
Luis Arroyo	Portland	Fla	54	14	0	5	.259	154	36	2	42	.234
J.D. Arteaga	Binghamton	NYM	117	27	0	25	.231	330	98	6	51	.297
Robert Averette	Chattanooga	Cin	207	53	3	34	.256	313	73	3	53	.233
Corey Avrard	Arkansas	StL	95	23	4	24	.242	163	41	6	33	.252
Julio Ayala	New Haven	Sea	59	20	1	9	.339	172	35	3	32	.203
Mike Ayers	Altoona	Pit	63	16	2	18	.254	151	31	0	31	.205
Mike Bacsik	Akron	Cle	49	9	1	9	.184	215	52	2	35	.242
Benito Baez	Midland	Oak	61	14	1	18	.230	155	47	3	32	.303
Danys Baez	Akron	Cle	141	35	1	21	.248	237	63	5	56	.266
Jason Baker	Wichita	KC	80	29	5	7	.363	199	58	3	42	.291
Brian Barkley	Trenton	Bos	57	17	0	10	.298	215	68	1	55	.316
Rick Bauer	Bowie	Bal	277	83	11	46	.300	249	71	5	41	.285
Ray Beasley	Greenville	Atl	64	16	1	28	.250	159	38	1	36	.239
Matt Beaumont	Erie	Ana	126	23	2	39	.183	299	72	9	45	.241
Greg Beck	Huntsville	Mil	105	31	0	20	.295	226	66	8	40	.292
Tom Becker	Jacksonville	Det	79	23	0	12	.291	150	42	5	35	.280
Joe Beimel	Altoona	Pit	57	17	1	8	.298	193	55	7	20	.285
Adam Benes	Arkansas	StL	124	43	4	20	.347	200	50	4	35	.250
Joel Bennett	Trenton	Bos	91	22	1	20	.242	143	38	3	34	.266
Joaquin Benoit	Tulsa	Tex	107	33	1	20	.308	201	40	5	52	.199
Adam Bernero	Jacksonville	Det	92	23	2	18	.250	136	31	4	28	.228
Bobby Bevel	San Antonio	LA	85	21	3	32	.247	222	65	5	43	.293
Jason Beverlin	Norwich	NYY	238	41	1	47	.172	276	69	6	53	.250
Rocky Biddle	Birmingham	CWS	231	56	6	49	.242	321	82	4	69	.255
Cedrick Bowers	Orlando	TB	67	17	2	10	.254	323	68	6	82	.211
Micah Bowie	West Tenn	ChC	76	14	2	16	.184	346	77	4	90	.223
Brian Bowles	Tennessee	Tor	95	16	0	20	.168	199	48	1	52	.241
Bryan Braswell	Round Rock	Hou	71	16	3	16	.225	210	62	10	22	.295
Lesli Brea	Binghamton	NYM	155	42	6	33	.271	191	43	4	53	.225
Jason Brester	Reading	Phi	114	27	1	17	.237	310	80	6	57	.258
Donnie Bridges	Harrisburg	Mon	251	49	4	47	.195	213	55	1	37	.258
Corey Brittan	Binghamton	NYM	113	28	0	12	.248	159	39	1	36	.245
Elliot Brown	Orlando	TB	88	22	0	11	.250	196	53	5	28	.270
Jamie Brown	Akron	Cle	166	39	3	24	.235	213	56	9	33	.263
Mark Buehrle	Birmingham	CWS	71	14	0	12	.197	357	81	8	56	.227
Nate Bump	Portland	Fla	263	90	10	42	.342	326	79	6	56	.242
Adrian Burnside	San Antonio	LA	85	16	0	22	.188	242	57	6	60	.236
Enrique Calero	Wichita	KC	192	63	5	37	.328	370	78	11	93	.211
Jeremy Callier	Erie	Ana	105	25	3	27	.238	104	27	2	17	.260
Shawn Camp	Mobile	SD	84	19	1	13	.226	133	28	3	40	.211
Matt Carnes	New Britain	Min	148	41	1	19	.277	196	58	6	44	.296
Blas Cedeno	Reading	Phi	86	27	1	10	.314	116	20	3	24	.172
Juan Cerros	Binghamton	NYM	112	35	4	13	.313	178	36	4	39	.202
Chris Cervantes	El Paso	Ari	96	28	2	20	.292	281	80	11	52	.285
Shawn Chacon	Carolina	Col	223	56	3	66	.251	416	95	7	106	.228
Jake Chapman	Harrisburg	Mon	109	21	1	32	.193	154	52	3	21	.338
Jin Ho Cho	Trenton	Bos	137	44	5	18	.321	107	32	3	14	.299
Chris Clark	Portland	Fla	114	27	2	16	.237	211	56	3	38	.265
Pasqual Coco	Tennessee	Tor	236	50	1	68	.212	396	104	15	74	.263
Jesus Colome	Midland	Oak	155	36	2	30	.232	260	63	8	65	.242
Scott Comer	Portland	Fla	108	39	5	10	.361	448	141	23	50	.315
Patrick Coogan	Arkansas	StL	222	75	14	26	.338	356	89	7	53	.250
Derrick Cook	Tulsa	Tex	149	35	2	23	.235	284	76	10	49	.268
Michael Corey	Greenville	Atl	68	19	1	22	.279	188	48	5	44	.255
Nate Cornejo	Jacksonville	Det	122	37	1	19	.303	214	54	5	41	.252
Edwin Corps	Shreveport	SF	169	52	3	21	.308	270	68	7	42	.252
Marino Cota	Binghamton	NYM	127	43	5	28	.339	161	31	4	29	.193
Joe Cotton	Reading	Phi	112	18	3	26	.161	139	30	2	25	.216
Kevin Crafton	Arkansas	StL	90	27	2	11	.300	174	42	3	37	.241
Paxton Crawford	Trenton	Bos	113	29	1	32	.257	91	21	2	22	.231
Chuck Crumpton	Harrisburg	Mon	162	50	3	13	.309	149	40	4	21	.268
Ryan Cummings	Erie	Ana	201	59	5	20	.294	207	63	9	33	.304
John Daniels	Reading	Phi	151	33	3	36	.219	167	45	7	39	.269
Allen Davis	San Antonio	LA	140	42	3	24	.300	497	145	15	99	.292
Lance Davis	Chattanooga	Cin	90	24	2	20	.267	332	72	2	78	.217
Fernando de la Cruz	Trenton	Bos	120	41	0	16	.342	141	39	4	26	.277
Doug Dent	Mobile	SD	136	38	4	18	.279	193	59	4	29	.306
Mark DiFelice	Carolina	Col	198	68	7	31	.343	334	84	8	67	.251
Glenn Dishman	Huntsville	Mil	65	15	1	16	.231	184	52	11	43	.283
Bo Donaldson	Chattanooga	Cin	66	17	3	11	.258	161	33	4	67	.205
Randey Dorame	San Antonio	LA	40	9	1	8	.225	173	44	4	20	.254
Brian Doughty	Mobile	SD	207	48	3	32	.232	332	106	10	35	.319
Sean Douglass	Bowie	Bal	304	82	7	60	.270	318	73	10	58	.230
Justin Duchscherer	Trenton	Bos	239	46	2	59	.192	305	88	5	67	.289
Brandon Duckworth	Reading	Phi	264	64	8	69	.242	358	81	9	109	.226
Matt Duff	Altoona	Pit	84	20	1	19	.238	126	30	0	42	.238
Courtney Duncan	West Tenn	ChC	79	23	2	17	.291	188	34	0	55	.181
Sean Duncan	Tulsa	Tex	66	12	1	22	.182	234	57	9	35	.244
Adam Eaton	Mobile	SD	88	18	1	23	.205	127	29	2	35	.228
Geoff Edsell	San Antonio	LA	125	29	0	26	.232	200	55	9	48	.275
Scott Eibey	Bowie	Bal	90	21	4	12	.233	131	38	4	20	.290
David Elder	Tulsa	Tex	178	56	3	37	.315	276	65	6	67	.236
Jamie Emiliano	Carolina	Col	67	17	1	10	.254	151	35	0	27	.232
Trevor Enders	Orlando	TB	46	14	1	8	.304	205	49	6	33	.239
Rendy Espina	Tennessee	Tor	61	22	0	11	.361	158	27	1	30	.171

			vs Left					vs Right				
Player	Team	Org	AB	H	HR	SO	Avg	AB	H	HR	SO	Avg
Leo Estrella	Tennessee	Tor	112	27	0	26	.241	164	41	6	37	.250
Luis Estrella	Shreveport	SF	82	20	2	16	.244	125	31	0	15	.248
Jeff Farnsworth	New Haven	Sea	154	44	1	27	.286	222	47	5	43	.212
Juan Figueroa	Birmingham	CWS	93	25	3	20	.269	114	32	1	22	.281
Steve Fish	Erie	Ana	115	33	1	16	.287	135	43	6	28	.319
Peter Fisher	New Britain	Min	128	41	1	21	.320	135	48	3	15	.356
Brian Fitzgerald	New Haven	Sea	94	24	2	23	.255	213	60	5	39	.282
Jason Flach	Greenville	Atl	129	40	4	18	.310	228	55	8	46	.241
Randy Flores	Norwich	NYY	135	27	1	33	.200	397	111	7	64	.280
Josh Fogg	Birmingham	CWS	314	81	2	59	.258	414	109	5	77	.263
Kevin Foster	Trenton	Bos	85	16	0	12	.188	143	33	0	40	.231
Zach Frachiseur	Greenville	Atl	116	37	4	17	.319	222	55	4	41	.248
Aaron France	Altoona	Pit	156	39	1	27	.250	166	44	3	30	.265
Lance Franks	Arkansas	StL	130	39	8	19	.300	210	51	8	37	.243
Kai Freeman	Birmingham	CWS	78	28	2	8	.359	130	29	3	23	.223
Brian Fuentes	New Haven	Sea	116	25	3	31	.216	400	102	4	121	.255
Randy Galvez	San Antonio	LA	104	37	2	13	.356	141	37	3	22	.262
Jose Garcia	Huntsville	Mil	165	51	4	30	.309	232	56	4	48	.241
Geoff Geary	Reading	Phi	259	74	7	51	.286	259	67	8	61	.259
Chris George	Wichita	KC	64	16	2	12	.250	299	76	3	68	.254
Matt Ginter	Birmingham	CWS	274	73	4	49	.266	384	80	2	77	.208
Isabel Giron	Mobile	SD	104	29	4	22	.279	190	42	5	55	.221
Chris Gissell	West Tenn	ChC	128	29	3	19	.227	215	51	3	46	.237
Dicky Gonzalez	Binghamton	NYM	248	54	5	66	.218	308	76	9	72	.247
Arnold Gooch	Chattanooga	Cin	208	49	3	35	.236	307	84	10	45	.274
Jason Gooding	Wichita	KC	55	15	2	13	.273	263	82	10	33	.312
Randy Goodrich	Shreveport	SF	105	35	3	12	.333	201	55	7	36	.274
John Grabow	Altoona	Pit	134	40	1	21	.299	426	105	9	88	.246
Steve Green	Erie	Ana	162	32	3	35	.198	129	39	4	31	.302
Kevin Gregg	Midland	Oak	207	54	5	43	.261	356	117	13	54	.329
Junior Guerrero	Wichita	KC	190	58	10	25	.305	333	95	15	54	.285
Rick Guttormson	Mobile	SD	134	36	6	15	.269	181	52	3	21	.287
Brad Guy	Altoona	Pit	148	35	0	13	.236	177	47	3	24	.266
Juan Guzman	Bowie	Bal	194	58	3	29	.299	200	56	2	28	.280
Leiby Guzman	Tulsa	Tex	166	57	5	32	.343	307	86	10	52	.280
Wilson Guzman	Altoona	Pit	125	27	2	32	.216	309	72	4	45	.233
Jeff Hafer	Binghamton	NYM	91	33	3	18	.363	114	31	3	11	.272
Jimmy Hamilton	Bowie	Bal	83	18	1	23	.217	134	35	5	26	.261
Brett Haring	Chattanooga	Cin	109	34	2	17	.312	310	99	3	52	.319
Al Hawkins	Huntsville	Mil	140	30	4	29	.214	219	58	8	37	.265
Andy Hazlett	Trenton	Bos	114	26	2	26	.228	241	59	7	58	.245
Bryan Hebson	Harrisburg	Mon	320	82	12	40	.256	343	93	11	50	.271
Scott Henderson	Portland	Fla	83	19	3	29	.229	155	28	2	44	.181
Russ Herbert	Round Rock	Hou	117	29	4	34	.248	199	55	6	49	.276
Dave Hooten	New Britain	Min	90	23	3	23	.256	139	36	3	41	.259
Scott Huntsman	Huntsville	Mil	99	27	3	15	.273	187	54	3	28	.289
Brent Husted	San Antonio	LA	101	21	1	21	.208	165	43	6	27	.261
Mario Iglesias	Bowie	Bal	82	26	3	14	.317	139	37	3	35	.266
Eric Ireland	Round Rock	Hou	306	66	7	58	.216	368	105	7	65	.285
Domingo Jean	Norwich	NYY	142	29	4	31	.204	166	34	4	42	.205
James Johnson	Huntsville	Mil	51	11	1	13	.216	223	63	8	61	.283
Doug Johnston	West Tenn	ChC	174	39	0	23	.224	257	67	6	59	.261
Kevin Joseph	Shreveport	SF	145	49	2	14	.338	244	67	6	57	.275
Jason Karnuth	Arkansas	StL	66	17	2	8	.258	136	42	1	23	.309
Justin Kaye	New Haven	Sea	130	39	0	35	.300	191	41	3	74	.215
Randy Keisler	Norwich	NYY	67	19	1	16	.284	210	44	3	54	.210
Kris Keller	Jacksonville	Det	88	23	0	17	.261	161	35	0	43	.217
Rich Kelley	Erie	Ana	122	42	4	27	.344	260	78	8	45	.300
Jason Kershner	Reading	Phi	129	33	3	19	.256	335	92	12	61	.275
Kyle Kessel	Round Rock	Hou	55	18	3	8	.327	208	50	9	35	.240
Matt Kinney	New Britain	Min	132	33	3	25	.250	188	41	4	68	.218
Brian Knoll	Shreveport	SF	97	30	5	20	.309	208	50	3	42	.240
Gary Knotts	Portland	Fla	294	76	5	54	.259	315	85	10	59	.270
Mike Kusiewicz	Tennessee	Tor	96	20	2	24	.208	507	129	12	91	.254
John Lackey	Erie	Ana	98	27	4	18	.276	125	31	2	25	.248
Justin Lamber	Wichita	KC	62	20	2	15	.323	198	65	6	28	.328
Otoniel Lanfranco	Arkansas	StL	182	51	10	23	.280	279	72	7	47	.258
Brian Lawrence	Mobile	SD	172	38	5	36	.221	285	61	1	83	.214
Clint Lawrence	Tennessee	Tor	48	18	2	2	.375	171	45	5	29	.263
Derek Lee	Huntsville	Mil	105	27	2	22	.257	385	94	4	65	.244
Brandon Leese	Portland	Fla	264	70	7	43	.265	397	109	11	53	.275
Derrick Lewis	Greenville	Atl	231	65	1	46	.281	378	81	4	97	.214
Joe Lisio	Norwich	NYY	78	27	2	14	.346	122	28	2	28	.230
Kyle Lohse	New Britain	Min	282	93	8	43	.330	391	103	15	81	.263
Alex Lontayo	Erie	Ana	72	20	3	15	.278	138	35	4	22	.254
Shane Loux	Jacksonville	Det	232	57	4	58	.246	359	93	8	72	.259
Matt Lubozynski	Erie	Ana	113	27	3	29	.239	212	61	6	37	.288
Spike Lundberg	Tulsa	Tex	196	54	1	38	.276	369	94	8	64	.255
Scott MaCrae	Chattanooga	Cin	81	20	2	21	.247	204	55	2	40	.270
Tim Manwiller	Midland	Oak	174	49	5	26	.282	270	73	11	54	.270
Mike Maroth	Jacksonville	Det	132	32	1	16	.242	478	144	13	69	.301
Jason Marquis	Greenville	Atl	111	29	4	18	.261	149	39	6	31	.262
Lee Marshall	New Britain	Min	98	23	0	19	.235	170	59	4	33	.347
Jason Martines	El Paso	Ari	113	25	1	21	.221	204	47	2	56	.230
Jose Martinez	Tulsa	Tex	140	40	2	14	.286	262	57	5	65	.218
Josue Matos	New Haven	Sea	141	33	5	29	.234	175	44	6	31	.251
Troy Mattes	Harrisburg	Mon	334	90	11	46	.269	327	80	9	63	.245
Brian Matz	Harrisburg	Mon	138	33	3	24	.239	226	62	7	33	.274
Blake Mayo	El Paso	Ari	212	63	1	44	.297	328	94	4	76	.287
Jon McBride	Tennessee	Tor	71	14	1	13	.197	152	37	4	24	.243

Double-A Pitching vs. Lefthanded and Righthanded Batters

Player	Team	Org	vs Left					vs Right				
			AB	H	HR	SO	Avg	AB	H	HR	SO	Avg
Matt McClellan	Tennessee	Tor	228	69	6	43	.303	429	105	10	97	.245
Matt McClendon	Greenville	Atl	162	48	3	27	.296	328	76	3	63	.232
Sam McConnell	Altoona	Pit	120	24	0	23	.200	270	59	3	38	.219
Paul McCurtain	Portland	Fla	117	27	4	25	.231	219	71	5	31	.324
Marty McLeary	Trenton	Bos	170	43	2	30	.253	216	71	3	23	.329
Joe Messman	Shreveport	SF	64	12	2	10	.188	155	39	5	36	.252
Mike Meyers	West Tenn	ChC	88	19	1	22	.216	117	22	3	29	.188
Jason Middlebrook	Mobile	SD	185	48	7	40	.259	283	85	8	35	.300
Benji Miller	Shreveport	SF	124	27	2	21	.218	201	54	8	50	.269
Justin Miller	Midland	Oak	126	24	3	31	.190	196	50	5	51	.255
Matt Miller	Jacksonville	Det	68	17	1	14	.250	401	109	9	85	.272
Kevin Mobley	Jacksonville	Det	118	24	2	22	.203	201	38	3	50	.189
Matt Montgomery	San Antonio	LA	116	39	3	23	.336	231	59	2	59	.255
David Moraga	Harrisburg	Mon	72	18	0	12	.250	199	49	2	27	.246
David Moraga	Carolina	Col	17	3	0	3	.176	208	49	3	50	.236
Robbie Morrison	Wichita	KC	77	19	2	17	.247	155	39	4	32	.252
Paul Morse	Erie	Ana	152	42	3	22	.276	142	38	1	24	.268
Ryan Moskau	Portland	Fla	71	21	1	15	.296	254	75	8	38	.295
Scott Mullen	Wichita	KC	53	16	1	15	.302	215	49	4	46	.228
Joey Nation	West Tenn	ChC	97	25	3	23	.258	515	112	14	142	.217
Scott Navarro	Round Rock	Hou	60	19	3	8	.317	205	57	6	22	.278
Doug Nickle	Reading	Phi	121	29	2	22	.240	159	26	2	36	.164
Randy Niles	Midland	Oak	111	26	1	18	.234	192	61	5	27	.318
Elvin Nina	Erie	Ana	105	27	2	14	.257	106	24	1	16	.226
Maximo Nunez	San Antonio	LA	99	29	0	19	.293	162	50	8	40	.309
Pablo Ochoa	Binghamton	NYM	268	79	4	55	.295	297	92	6	51	.310
Brian O'Connor	Altoona	Pit	110	27	1	27	.245	377	93	3	49	.247
Will Ohman	West Tenn	ChC	63	12	1	24	.190	202	41	2	61	.203
Kevin Olsen	Portland	Fla	96	29	3	23	.302	114	25	5	24	.219
Eddie Oropesa	Shreveport	SF	84	16	2	30	.190	210	54	4	46	.257
Jimmy Osting	Reading	Phi	73	16	0	10	.219	134	37	1	21	.276
Jimmy Osting	Greenville	Atl	53	11	0	14	.208	217	56	6	38	.258
Roy Oswalt	Round Rock	Hou	174	35	2	47	.201	316	71	3	94	.225
Delvis Pachecho	Greenville	Atl	87	19	5	18	.218	134	36	4	33	.269
Christian Parker	Norwich	NYY	405	112	4	72	.277	370	84	4	75	.227
Josh Pearce	Arkansas	StL	180	58	6	21	.322	212	59	7	42	.278
Dario Perez	Trenton	Bos	116	38	5	24	.328	193	44	4	43	.228
Mark Persails	Round Rock	Hou	103	32	1	22	.311	217	69	4	41	.318
Tommy Phelps	Jacksonville	Det	90	26	2	12	.289	311	85	15	50	.273
Travis Phelps	Orlando	TB	140	35	0	29	.250	247	50	5	77	.202
Chris Piersoll	West Tenn	ChC	70	14	0	17	.200	153	37	4	37	.242
Rafael Pina	El Paso	Ari	105	32	2	24	.305	184	50	4	41	.272
Chad Poeck	Tulsa	Tex	97	24	1	23	.247	203	63	5	42	.310
Trey Poland	Tulsa	Tex	59	13	1	15	.220	334	102	11	52	.305
Mike Porzio	Carolina	Col	81	18	2	18	.222	376	93	9	72	.247
Andy Pratt	Tulsa	Tex	26	9	2	7	.346	192	57	5	35	.297
Ryan Price	Carolina	Col	113	32	1	24	.283	212	54	4	43	.255
Eddie Priest	Chattanooga	Cin	155	38	3	36	.245	533	144	2	113	.270
Bret Prinz	El Paso	Ari	93	32	3	29	.344	149	39	3	40	.262
Luke Prokopec	San Antonio	LA	180	45	4	56	.250	307	73	4	68	.238
Ken Pumphrey	New Britain	Min	112	34	3	16	.304	136	34	4	23	.250
Erasmo Ramirez	Shreveport	SF	73	20	2	18	.274	162	60	5	28	.370
Jon Rauch	Birmingham	CWS	65	10	0	20	.154	136	26	4	43	.191
Chris Reitsma	Trenton	Bos	140	34	2	24	.243	196	44	5	34	.224
Todd Revenig	El Paso	Ari	96	31	5	14	.323	154	59	2	36	.383
Eddy Reyes	Orlando	TB	65	13	4	11	.200	154	39	1	33	.253
Jerrod Riggan	Binghamton	NYM	93	17	0	34	.183	134	26	2	45	.194
Matt Riley	Bowie	Bal	65	26	4	14	.400	217	48	5	52	.221
Juan Rincon	New Britain	Min	151	42	4	24	.278	208	54	5	55	.260
Joe Roa	Akron	Cle	174	43	5	21	.247	213	48	2	38	.225
Jake Robbins	Norwich	NYY	100	21	1	16	.210	175	47	3	37	.269
Mark Roberts	Birmingham	CWS	101	31	2	12	.307	135	34	2	34	.252
Jeriome Robertson	Round Rock	Hou	46	7	0	10	.152	195	55	8	20	.282
Neiro Rodriguez	Trenton	Bos	189	50	4	39	.265	231	65	5	54	.281
Wilfredo Rodriguez	Round Rock	Hou	47	13	2	13	.277	165	41	8	42	.248
Brian Rogers	Norwich	NYY	260	64	5	58	.246	365	91	5	74	.249
Mark Rutherford	Reading	Phi	228	65	7	27	.285	215	56	6	35	.260
C.C. Sabathia	Akron	Cle	61	11	0	18	.180	275	64	6	72	.233
Martin Sanchez	El Paso	Ari	161	45	6	26	.280	272	67	9	62	.246
Frankie Sanders	Akron	Cle	111	38	6	21	.342	158	39	3	29	.247
Brian Scott	El Paso	Ari	78	17	0	12	.218	169	56	6	31	.331
Bobby Seay	Orlando	TB	62	16	0	9	.258	436	116	13	97	.266
Shawn Sedlacek	Wichita	KC	194	50	3	23	.258	356	103	7	58	.289
Ryan Seifert	Carolina	Col	133	36	1	33	.271	241	61	5	62	.253
Jim Serrano	Harrisburg	Mon	138	33	1	39	.239	136	31	5	41	.228
Wascar Serrano	Mobile	SD	177	45	2	41	.254	241	48	9	71	.199
Doug Sessions	Round Rock	Hou	116	31	4	32	.267	190	47	3	48	.247
Jeff Sexton	Carolina	Col	91	33	3	15	.363	177	45	0	43	.254
Tom Sheam	Round Rock	Hou	215	60	8	44	.279	303	74	6	58	.244
Ben Sheets	Huntsville	Mil	104	23	1	27	.221	152	32	3	33	.211
Ben Simon	San Antonio	LA	157	37	5	41	.236	244	65	10	50	.266
Bud Smith	Arkansas	StL	70	14	0	22	.200	332	79	5	80	.238
Travis Smith	Huntsville	Mil	248	61	6	52	.246	335	80	7	61	.239
John Sneed	Tennessee	Tor	177	51	4	34	.288	294	73	5	66	.248
Bert Snow	Midland	Oak	78	16	0	28	.205	133	42	6	70	.243
Matt Snyder	Bowie	Bal	151	39	4	27	.258	181	45	5	50	.249
Shawn Sonnier	Wichita	KC	69	11	0	28	.159	162	30	6	62	.185
Steve Sparks	Altoona	Pit	197	43	0	34	.218	214	60	6	32	.280
Corey Spiers	New Britain	Min	75	22	0	7	.293	194	72	6	21	.371
Jason Standridge	Orlando	TB	119	32	1	13	.269	239	53	3	42	.222

Player	Team	Org	vs Left					vs Right				
			AB	H	HR	SO	Avg	AB	H	HR	SO	Avg
Rod Stevenson	Harrisburg	Mon	106	26	0	23	.245	109	37	3	15	.339
Pat Strange	Binghamton	NYM	97	26	0	14	.268	119	36	2	22	.303
Jeff Taglienti	Trenton	Bos	92	30	2	12	.326	114	29	1	21	.254
Nate Teut	West Tenn	ChC	79	21	0	17	.266	444	112	13	89	.252
Brad Thomas	New Britain	Min	78	18	0	19	.231	211	62	3	47	.294
Eric Thompson	Midland	Oak	152	43	2	42	.283	247	64	3	37	.259
Travis Thompson	Carolina	Col	89	30	2	17	.337	147	40	6	26	.272
Todd Thorn	El Paso	Ari	111	24	1	26	.216	247	89	3	39	.360
Jason Turman	New Haven	Sea	156	43	3	39	.276	230	59	4	55	.257
Martin Vargas	Akron	Cle	139	46	2	28	.331	195	50	2	34	.256
Leo Vasquez	Midland	Oak	50	13	0	18	.260	150	35	3	41	.233
Ryan Vogelsong	Shreveport	SF	216	46	4	70	.213	372	107	11	77	.288
Denny Wagner	Midland	Oak	241	68	3	38	.282	471	141	10	71	.299
Tyler Walker	Binghamton	NYM	182	29	1	56	.159	248	53	2	55	.214
Dave Walling	Norwich	NYY	127	42	5	26	.331	213	59	5	44	.277
Doug Walls	Jacksonville	Det	96	31	1	19	.323	119	35	7	19	.294
Neil Weber	Bowie	Bal	101	29	0	22	.287	134	39	2	29	.291
Clint Weibl	Arkansas	StL	60	13	3	22	.217	161	44	7	29	.273
Matt Weimer	Tennessee	Tor	70	19	2	7	.271	172	49	4	24	.285
Allan Westfall	New Haven	Sea	165	36	1	37	.218	167	44	1	27	.263
Matt White	Orlando	TB	161	32	3	37	.199	264	62	7	61	.235
Jeff Wilson	Bowie	Bal	129	33	3	24	.256	289	68	3	55	.235
Kris Wilson	Wichita	KC	152	38	6	27	.250	241	61	6	42	.253
Hank Woodman	Tulsa	Tex	139	43	1	25	.309	246	87	11	35	.354
Greg Wooten	New Haven	Sea	322	92	8	52	.286	353	74	1	63	.210
L.J. Yankosky	Greenville	Atl	200	55	2	22	.275	328	84	5	78	.256
Jay Yennaco	West Tenn	ChC	80	20	3	19	.250	174	33	2	60	.190
Carlos Zambrano	West Tenn	ChC	91	13	2	13	.143	125	26	0	30	.208
Pete Zamora	Reading	Phi	134	34	2	36	.254	265	71	4	58	.268

Double-A Pitching at Home and on the Road

Player	Team	Org	Home G	IP	W	L	ERA	Road G	IP	W	L	ERA
B. Agamennone	Harrisburg	Mon	14	42.2	4	4	5.06	16	53.0	4	3	3.40
Kurt Ainsworth	Shreveport	SF	13	74.1	5	3	2.42	15	83.0	5	6	4.12
Jeff Andra	Shreveport	SF	7	37.2	3	3	2.87	10	53.2	3	3	4.53
J.D. Arteaga	Binghamton	NYM	15	50.2	5	4	4.62	19	61.2	5	3	2.48
Robert Averette	Chattanooga	Cin	12	86.1	6	5	2.40	7	50.0	6	1	2.52
Danny Baez	Akron	Cle	10	54.2	3	5	3.46	8	48.0	1	4	3.94
Rick Bauer	Bowie	Bal	13	73.1	4	4	2.95	13	55.0	2	4	8.51
Matt Beaumont	Erie	Ana	18	70.0	1	7	4.24	12	48.0	4	3	3.19
Greg Beck	Huntsville	Mil	27	51.0	3	4	4.94	21	32.0	0	2	5.06
Adam Benes	Arkansas	StL	11	41.0	1	2	4.83	15	42.0	1	3	3.86
Joaquin Benoit	Tulsa	Tex	8	30.2	2	3	5.28	8	51.2	2	1	2.96
Jason Beverlin	Norwich	NYY	15	91.1	6	4	2.17	9	52.0	2	5	3.98
Rocky Biddle	Birmingham	CWS	10	64.0	4	4	2.81	13	82.0	7	2	3.29
Cedrick Bowers	Orlando	TB	8	45.0	1	4	1.80	12	61.2	4	4	3.50
Micah Bowie	West Tenn	ChC	9	58.0	3	3	4.50	9	59.0	4	3	2.44
Brian Bowles	Tennessee	Tor	25	41.2	3	2	2.81	24	40.0	1	2	3.15
Lesli Brea	Binghamton	NYM	9	39.2	1	5	6.13	10	53.2	4	3	2.85
Jason Brester	Reading	Phi	12	53.2	6	2	4.02	13	62.0	5	4	4.50
Donnie Bridges	Harrisburg	Mon	10	62.0	5	4	2.76	9	65.1	6	3	2.07
Jamie Brown	Akron	Cle	10	55.0	4	4	4.25	7	41.0	3	2	4.61
Mark Buehrle	Birmingham	CWS	10	78.0	6	1	1.85	6	40.0	2	3	3.15
Nate Bump	Portland	Fla	11	69.1	4	4	4.67	15	80.0	4	5	4.50
Adrian Burnside	San Antonio	LA	8	42.0	2	2	1.93	9	51.0	4	3	3.71
Enrique Calero	Wichita	KC	11	61.0	5	1	2.95	17	92.1	5	6	4.09
Matt Carnes	New Britain	Min	7	43.2	1	3	5.15	7	45.0	0	5	5.20
Chris Cervantes	El Paso	Ari	7	46.0	3	3	4.70	9	49.0	4	2	4.04
Shawn Chacon	Carolina	Col	14	85.1	4	6	3.38	13	88.0	6	4	2.97
Chris Clark	Portland	Fla	17	42.0	2	1	3.21	15	44.2	5	2	4.43
Pasqual Coco	Tennessee	Tor	15	102.0	8	3	3.44	12	65.1	4	4	4.27
Jesus Colome	Midland	Oak	11	59.0	5	1	3.36	9	51.0	4	3	3.88
Scott Comer	Portland	Fla	14	72.1	2	5	6.97	11	57.2	2	5	5.77
Patrick Coogan	Arkansas	StL	13	67.0	4	7	5.78	14	82.1	5	6	4.59
Derrick Cook	Tulsa	Tex	10	57.0	2	3	3.95	11	56.2	3	5	5.24
Nate Cornejo	Jacksonville	Det	7	44.0	3	2	3.48	9	47.0	2	5	5.74
Edwin Corps	Shreveport	SF	19	71.0	3	2	2.03	17	41.0	2	4	5.05
Ryan Cummings	Erie	Ana	13	47.0	1	5	6.32	13	52.2	3	4	6.15
John Daniels	Reading	Phi	22	49.0	5	3	4.04	19	35.0	2	2	3.09
Allen Davis	San Antonio	LA	14	88.0	5	3	3.48	15	75.0	5	5	5.76
Lance Davis	Chattanooga	Cin	14	63.0	4	2	2.43	11	52.0	3	3	1.90
Doug Dent	Mobile	SD	9	42.0	1	6	6.21	9	40.0	3	3	5.63
Mark DiFelice	Carolina	Col	13	81.0	3	2	3.44	10	52.0	4	3	3.81
Brian Doughty	Mobile	SD	13	68.1	4	4	2.90	18	65.0	5	6	5.54
Sean Douglass	Bowie	Bal	14	86.0	4	5	3.66	13	74.1	5	3	4.48
Justin Duchscherer	Trenton	Bos	14	91.0	5	5	2.37	10	52.0	2	4	5.19
Brandon Duckworth	Reading	Phi	15	96.0	8	4	3.28	12	69.0	5	3	3.00
Geoff Edsell	San Antonio	LA	14	52.2	4	3	4.10	11	30.1	1	2	5.04
David Elder	Tulsa	Tex	20	72.1	4	2	3.48	13	44.0	3	4	7.36
Jeff Farnsworth	New Haven	Sea	23	68.0	8	1	3.18	16	33.0	1	2	4.09
Jason Flach	Greenville	Atl	14	49.0	2	1	4.41	14	46.0	2	5	4.30
Randy Flores	Norwich	NYY	15	51.0	5	2	1.59	16	89.1	5	7	3.73
Josh Fogg	Birmingham	CWS	13	96.0	3	5	2.25	14	96.1	8	2	2.90
Zach Frachiseur	Greenville	Atl	17	41.2	1	3	4.75	25	45.0	1	4	4.80
Aaron France	Altoona	Pit	11	40.0	2	2	4.05	11	40.2	3	0	2.88
Lance Franks	Arkansas	StL	18	42.0	2	2	4.29	25	46.2	4	2	5.98
Brian Fuentes	New Haven	Sea	12	68.0	5	5	3.57	14	71.0	2	7	5.45
Jose Garcia	Huntsville	Mil	11	60.0	1	5	3.60	8	43.0	3	3	3.98
Geoff Geary	Reading	Phi	9	53.0	3	2	4.08	13	76.0	4	4	4.14
Chris George	Wichita	KC	10	58.0	6	3	3.10	8	39.0	2	2	3.23
Matt Ginter	Birmingham	CWS	17	115.1	8	4	1.64	10	64.0	3	4	3.38
Chris Gissell	West Tenn	ChC	9	54.2	4	3	2.63	7	38.0	3	2	3.79
Dicky Gonzalez	Binghamton	NYM	16	94.1	9	1	3.72	10	53.0	4	4	4.08
Arnold Gooch	Chattanooga	Cin	10	65.0	3	6	4.85	11	70.0	6	1	3.47
Jason Gooding	Wichita	KC	15	46.0	3	2	3.91	14	35.0	3	1	4.11
John Grabow	Altoona	Pit	13	81.0	4	4	4.00	11	64.0	4	3	4.78
Kevin Gregg	Midland	Oak	13	72.0	5	6	5.75	15	68.1	0	8	7.11
Junior Guerrero	Wichita	KC	13	63.2	1	8	6.64	15	67.0	3	2	4.84
Rick Guttormson	Mobile	SD	8	41.0	3	2	3.07	9	40.0	1	2	4.95
Brad Guy	Altoona	Pit	25	41.0	2	1	3.07	29	40.0	2	5	4.05
Juan Guzman	Bowie	Bal	8	45.0	4	2	4.40	10	51.2	1	7	4.88
Leiby Guzman	Tulsa	Tex	15	70.0	4	6	5.40	9	45.0	3	3	6.20
Wilson Guzman	Altoona	Pit	8	55.2	5	1	1.78	10	63.2	5	3	4.10
Brett Haring	Chattanooga	Cin	11	47.0	2	5	5.17	12	59.2	4	2	5.13
Al Hawkins	Huntsville	Mil	9	46.2	4	5	4.82	9	50.0	3	2	2.70
Andy Hazlett	Trenton	Bos	24	55.0	2	3	2.45	18	37.0	4	3	4.62
Bryan Hebson	Harrisburg	Mon	14	90.0	5	6	4.00	15	81.0	2	9	5.22
Russ Herbert	Round Rock	Hou	15	34.2	1	1	4.67	23	52.2	3	1	3.93
Eric Ireland	Round Rock	Hou	12	83.0	6	2	2.82	17	96.1	5	7	3.92
Domingo Jean	Norwich	NYY	36	52.0	6	2	2.42	26	34.0	3	2	4.24
Doug Johnston	West Tenn	ChC	15	55.0	1	4	5.24	15	61.0	3	0	2.66
Kevin Joseph	Shreveport	SF	13	48.0	0	6	6.38	14	54.2	3	5	4.12
Justin Kaye	New Haven	Sea	23	41.2	1	0	1.51	27	42.2	1	5	3.80
Rich Kelley	Erie	Ana	24	53.0	3	1	4.25	20	44.0	2	5	4.70
Jason Kershner	Reading	Phi	10	46.0	3	0	3.13	17	72.1	6	2	3.98
Matt Kinney	New Britain	Min	7	41.2	4	1	3.24	8	44.2	2	0	2.22
Gary Knotts	Portland	Fla	15	90.0	6	4	4.90	12	66.0	3	4	4.36
Mike Kusiewicz	Tennessee	Tor	12	66.1	4	3	3.93	15	89.1	3	6	3.43
Otoniel Lanfranco	Arkansas	StL	15	65.1	5	2	4.41	18	54.0	4	4	5.83
Brian Lawrence	Mobile	SD	10	62.0	3	2	2.47	11	64.0	4	4	2.39
Derek Lee	Huntsville	Mil	15	75.0	8	1	2.28	13	56.0	3	2	2.89
Brandon Leese	Portland	Fla	13	84.1	5	4	3.31	14	89.0	7	5	3.64

Player	Team	Org	Home G	IP	W	L	ERA	Road G	IP	W	L	ERA
Derrick Lewis	Greenville	Atl	13	81.0	4	4	2.89	14	82.0	3	5	3.73
Kyle Lohse	New Britain	Min	14	84.0	2	8	5.68	14	82.1	1	1	6.45
Shane Loux	Jacksonville	Det	13	78.0	7	2	4.04	13	79.0	5	7	3.65
Matt Lubozynski	Erie	Ana	12	40.0	1	3	5.40	11	43.0	0	5	3.56
Spike Lundberg	Tulsa	Tex	21	66.1	7	3	2.31	19	84.0	7	4	3.64
Tim Manwiller	Midland	Oak	13	62.0	1	4	5.23	12	52.0	3	1	3.46
Mike Maroth	Jacksonville	Det	12	72.0	5	5	4.00	15	92.1	4	9	3.90
Jason Martines	El Paso	Ari	28	51.0	6	1	3.18	27	35.0	3	0	2.31
Jose Martinez	Tulsa	Tex	11	65.1	3	3	3.17	7	37.2	2	3	3.11
Josue Matos	New Haven	Sea	6	39.2	1	2	2.72	8	44.2	3	3	4.43
Troy Mattes	Harrisburg	Mon	15	93.0	5	5	4.35	13	81.0	6	4	4.00
Brian Matz	Harrisburg	Mon	22	40.0	3	3	5.18	19	53.2	4	3	4.19
Blake Mayo	El Paso	Ari	22	79.0	4	0	4.10	16	57.0	4	3	4.11
Matt McClellan	Tennessee	Tor	15	92.1	3	8	4.48	13	76.0	3	4	5.21
Matt McClendon	Greenville	Atl	12	72.0	5	3	3.00	10	58.2	2	3	4.76
Sam McConnell	Altoona	Pit	11	60.0	5	2	1.50	9	46.0	4	0	1.76
Paul McCurtain	Portland	Fla	21	46.2	3	0	4.05	20	38.2	3	1	4.19
Marty McLeary	Trenton	Bos	23	50.0	1	3	3.78	20	46.2	1	6	5.40
Jason Middlebrook	Mobile	SD	12	58.2	3	6	6.60	12	61.0	2	7	5.75
Benji Miller	Shreveport	SF	29	49.0	3	5	3.49	29	37.0	1	4	3.16
Justin Miller	Midland	Oak	10	52.0	3	3	4.67	8	35.0	2	1	4.37
Matt Miller	Jacksonville	Det	10	59.0	3	2	2.90	10	62.2	5	3	3.45
Kevin Mobley	Jacksonville	Det	24	47.0	3	0	2.87	19	42.2	3	0	2.53
Matt Montgomery	San Antonio	LA	21	49.2	3	2	2.90	20	39.0	2	3	5.31
Paul Morse	Erie	Ana	5	21.0	1	4	9.86	9	59.0	2	4	2.44
Ryan Moskau	Portland	Fla	7	33.0	1	4	5.73	9	51.2	2	4	5.40
Joey Nation	West Tenn	ChC	12	76.1	5	3	2.83	15	89.1	6	7	3.73
Pablo Ochoa	Binghamton	NYM	11	62.2	4	6	5.46	15	84.0	5	6	5.04
Brian O'Connor	Altoona	Pit	11	65.0	7	2	2.49	11	64.0	5	2	5.06
Roy Oswalt	Round Rock	Hou	12	84.1	6	2	1.71	7	45.0	5	2	2.40
Christian Parker	Norwich	NYY	13	91.1	5	2	3.15	15	112.1	9	4	3.12
Josh Pearce	Arkansas	StL	9	53.0	4	3	4.42	8	44.0	1	3	6.75
Tommy Phelps	Jacksonville	Det	23	68.1	4	5	4.35	15	33.0	2	1	6.27
Travis Phelps	Orlando	TB	9	45.0	5	4	2.20	12	62.2	2	4	3.59
Trey Poland	Tulsa	Tex	13	45.0	3	5	8.20	17	53.2	3	3	5.37
Mike Porzio	Carolina	Col	11	67.0	4	1	3.22	9	54.0	3	3	3.67
Ryan Price	Carolina	Col	8	35.0	3	3	6.17	12	50.2	3	4	6.22
Eddie Priest	Chattanooga	Cin	14	92.0	6	3	3.33	13	88.0	5	4	2.25
Luke Prokopec	San Antonio	LA	9	49.2	2	1	1.27	13	79.0	5	2	3.19
Chris Reitsma	Trenton	Bos	7	42.2	2	2	2.32	7	48.0	5	0	2.81
Juan Rincon	New Britain	Min	8	46.0	0	5	4.30	7	43.0	3	4	5.02
Joe Roa	Akron	Cle	8	39.2	2	4	2.95	11	63.0	4	1	3.71
Neiro Rodriguez	Trenton	Bos	8	47.0	2	4	4.40	11	62.0	5	3	5.08
Brian Rogers	Norwich	NYY	15	86.1	6	3	3.86	12	77.1	5	3	4.07
Mark Rutherford	Reading	Phi	17	63.2	4	5	4.52	12	50.0	3	4	4.14
C.C. Sabathia	Akron	Cle	8	43.0	1	5	3.14	9	47.0	2	2	4.02
Martin Sanchez	El Paso	Ari	13	43.2	3	2	6.39	15	67.0	4	4	4.03
Bobby Seay	Orlando	TB	13	74.1	7	2	2.18	11	57.2	1	5	6.09
Shawn Sedlacek	Wichita	KC	17	74.0	10	1	3.04	18	66.0	5	5	4.36
Ryan Seifert	Carolina	Col	16	53.2	3	2	3.35	16	44.0	0	4	4.91
Wascar Serrano	Mobile	SD	8	44.0	3	2	2.45	12	68.0	6	2	3.04
Doug Sessions	Round Rock	Hou	30	46.0	2	2	1.37	26	36.0	4	2	6.00
Tom Shearn	Round Rock	Hou	14	83.1	6	4	3.46	11	52.2	3	2	6.66
Ben Simon	San Antonio	LA	16	67.0	6	5	3.76	13	41.0	2	3	5.71
Bud Smith	Arkansas	StL	7	44.0	5	0	1.43	11	64.1	7	1	2.94
Travis Smith	Huntsville	Mil	13	68.0	3	5	4.37	14	86.1	9	2	3.23
John Sneed	Tennessee	Tor	10	56.2	4	4	4.45	11	64.0	1	5	4.64
Matt Snyder	Bowie	Bal	13	54.2	0	5	3.29	10	35.0	2	2	4.89
Steve Sparks	Altoona	Pit	11	50.0	3	3	3.96	12	59.0	3	4	5.49
Jason Standridge	Orlando	TB	7	45.0	4	2	1.80	10	51.2	2	6	5.23
Nate Teut	West Tenn	ChC	13	69.0	6	3	2.87	14	69.0	5	3	3.26
Eric Thompson	Midland	Oak	9	50.2	3	2	3.73	9	50.2	3	4	4.09
Todd Thorn	El Paso	Ari	11	43.2	2	2	3.92	12	44.0	1	6	6.14
Jason Turman	New Haven	Sea	21	47.2	2	3	4.53	18	53.0	1	1	4.25
Martin Vargas	Akron	Cle	29	44.0	5	2	5.11	24	37.0	5	6	5.84
Ryan Vogelsong	Shreveport	SF	12	75.0	3	5	3.36	15	80.0	3	5	5.06
Denny Wagner	Midland	Oak	15	86.0	2	5	5.97	14	94.0	5	4	3.26
Tyler Walker	Binghamton	NYM	11	59.0	1	3	2.14	11	61.2	6	3	3.36
Dave Walling	Norwich	NYY	9	57.0	2	6	4.89	5	28.0	1	3	6.11
Allan Westfall	New Haven	Sea	9	47.0	3	3	2.49	9	41.0	4	2	2.85
Matt White	Orlando	TB	10	60.0	3	4	5.10	10	59.2	4	2	2.41
Jeff Wilson	Bowie	Bal	8	43.0	2	3	3.14	11	67.1	4	4	3.48
Kris Wilson	Wichita	KC	12	57.0	4	1	3.16	9	45.2	3	2	3.94
Hank Woodman	Tulsa	Tex	23	53.0	4	2	4.75	19	38.0	1	4	7.11
Greg Wooten	New Haven	Sea	13	91.1	7	3	2.27	13	88.0	10	0	2.35
L.J. Yankosky	Greenville	Atl	12	57.0	6	2	3.00	14	83.0	4	6	3.80
Pete Zamora	Reading	Phi	22	50.0	1	1	4.86	21	51.0	1	2	3.35

2000 Major League Equivalencies

When Bill James first devised Major League Equivalencies 15 years ago, he said it was easily the most important research he ever had done. That's quite a statement, considering how much he has contributed to the study of baseball.

An MLE translates a Double-A or Triple-A hitter's statistics into big league numbers. It does this by making a series of adjustments for a player's minor league home ballpark, his minor league and his future major league home park. If he plays in a pitcher's league, his MLE will get a boost. If he's a Rockies prospect, then his numbers will be inflated, just like they are for all hitters at Coors Field. The MLE also recognizes that it's significantly tougher to hit in the majors than in the upper minors, and makes a further adjustment.

The end result is an estimation of what the hitter would have done had he gotten similar playing time in the major leagues with his parent club in 2000. Please understand that an MLE is not a projection for the future. If a player's MLE gives him 30 homers, that doesn't mean he'll hit 30 homers in the majors if given a chance to play in 2001. Treat an MLE as a single season in the major league career of a player. It's quite possible that a player with a banner MLE had the misfortune of spending his career year in Triple-A or Double-A.

The MLE can't tell you if a player is going to get a chance to play in the majors. But it can show you, with a high degree of accuracy, what he would have done with that opportunity in 2000. Ages are as of June 30, 2000.

Major League Equivalencies for 2000 AAA/AA Batters

ANAHEIM ANGELS		Age	Avg	G	AB	R	H	2B	3B	HR	RBI	BB	SO	SB	CS	OBP	SLG
Abbott,Chuck	2B	25	.224	102	335	34	75	12	2	4	37	16	107	2	3	.259	.307
Barnes,Larry	1B	25	.228	103	382	44	87	18	8	5	42	37	85	2	6	.296	.356
Baughman,Justin	SS	25	.222	111	414	47	92	6	2	0	32	28	64	28	9	.271	.246
Blakely,Darren	OF	23	.219	122	429	63	94	17	5	14	47	22	145	9	5	.257	.380
Burke,Jamie	3B	28	.209	75	253	19	53	10	0	0	13	14	44	0	1	.251	.249
Dougherty,Jeb	OF	24	.219	76	260	29	57	8	2	0	28	26	44	14	5	.290	.265
Eckstein,David	2B	25	.235	134	460	74	108	25	0	2	30	54	48	10	11	.315	.302
Guiel,Jeff	DH	26	.235	118	400	48	94	22	2	14	51	36	103	1	4	.298	.405
Hatcher,Chris	OF	31	.268	116	388	51	104	19	3	25	75	27	92	2	4	.316	.526
Haynes,Nathan	OF	20	.235	118	446	49	105	14	3	5	37	24	114	27	10	.274	.314
Hemphill,Bret	C	28	.227	100	343	44	78	13	2	7	37	32	72	0	1	.293	.338
Hood,Jay	SS	23	.192	71	234	22	45	14	0	3	25	11	53	2	0	.229	.291
Huisman,Jason	1B	24	.252	120	428	45	108	20	3	2	37	29	80	10	4	.300	.327
Johnson,Gary	OF	24	.267	71	251	38	67	9	3	8	49	26	67	2	4	.336	.422
Johnson,Keith	2B	29	.273	109	403	49	110	26	1	10	50	14	74	5	8	.297	.417
King,Brett	2B	27	.142	86	218	14	31	5	1	3	18	27	78	2	5	.237	.216
Morgan,Scott	OF	26	.229	101	340	45	78	23	1	7	45	31	84	5	3	.294	.365
Murphy,Nate	OF	25	.228	119	378	47	86	14	4	6	29	40	95	4	4	.301	.333
Rodriguez,Juan	1B	25	.224	68	232	21	52	8	0	0	12	14	70	0	1	.268	.259
Stovall,DaRond	OF	27	.231	79	242	27	56	5	5	7	25	27	79	7	4	.309	.380
t'Hoen,E.J.	SS-3B	24	.191	101	309	31	59	16	0	7	29	23	94	4	2	.247	.311
Tolentino,Juan	OF	24	.216	122	416	45	90	25	2	8	45	29	111	11	14	.267	.344
Walther,Chris	3B	23	.234	71	244	17	57	9	0	0	16	14	26	0	3	.275	.270
Wooten,Shawn	C	27	.296	117	423	61	125	27	3	16	63	26	71	2	1	.336	.487

ARIZ. DIAMONDBACKS		Age	Avg	G	AB	R	H	2B	3B	HR	RBI	BB	SO	SB	CS	OBP	SLG
Barajas,Rod	C	24	.201	110	403	33	81	22	0	10	58	10	68	2	3	.220	.330
Bates,Fletcher	OF	26	.249	109	342	41	85	21	3	7	49	23	78	9	9	.296	.389
Beltre,Esteban	SS	32	.282	129	432	40	122	20	2	2	46	21	74	4	9	.316	.352
Brown,Vick	2B	27	.213	98	230	34	49	9	1	0	13	24	42	6	3	.287	.261
Cabrera,Alex	1B	28	.322	74	276	58	89	20	1	30	73	19	74	2	2	.366	.728
Carvajal,Jhonny	SS	25	.243	91	267	29	65	13	1	0	19	21	53	3	4	.299	.300
Cintron,Alex	SS	21	.271	125	501	65	136	26	4	3	46	19	59	6	9	.298	.357
Conti,Jason	OF	25	.275	93	367	58	101	17	3	8	44	17	59	7	3	.307	.403
Cust,Jack	OF	21	.265	129	430	79	114	28	4	15	59	78	160	7	9	.378	.453
Dallimore,Brian	3B	26	.246	112	353	39	87	14	0	3	43	16	61	12	3	.279	.312
Gann,Jamie	OF	25	.203	107	349	42	71	14	1	6	32	6	83	4	3	.217	.301
Gomez,Ramon	OF	24	.256	74	254	33	65	7	6	1	29	17	53	12	2	.303	.343
Huckaby,Ken	C	29	.245	76	233	24	57	9	0	3	25	7	31	1	2	.267	.322
Nelson,Bry	3B	26	.280	69	250	26	70	18	0	3	24	12	21	2	2	.313	.388
Newstrom,Doug	3B	28	.230	97	243	19	56	14	0	0	19	18	51	3	2	.284	.288
Ortiz,Luis	3B	30	.271	92	295	38	80	22	2	7	50	12	17	0	0	.300	.431
Overbay,Lyle	1B	23	.319	62	232	33	74	14	1	6	38	18	41	2	2	.368	.466
Owens,Ryan	3B	22	.193	60	202	23	39	6	3	3	18	14	64	3	4	.245	.297
Rose,Mike	C	23	.257	117	339	45	87	19	0	7	49	45	74	5	11	.344	.375
Ryan,Rob	OF	27	.277	92	318	43	88	16	0	6	42	35	36	0	1	.348	.384
Saylor,Jamie	2B	25	.196	115	337	41	66	14	7	0	28	36	93	9	4	.273	.279
Sell,Chip	OF	29	.295	112	387	50	114	20	5	3	42	21	74	5	6	.331	.395
Urquiola,Carlos	OF	20	.273	68	216	26	59	7	0	0	14	13	18	9	8	.314	.306
White,Walt	2B	28	.250	76	204	18	51	11	0	0	22	13	49	2	2	.295	.304
Zinter,Alan	1B	32	.222	101	261	28	58	14	1	11	31	37	89	0	0	.319	.410

Major League Equivalencies for 2000 AAA/AA Batters

ATLANTA BRAVES		Age	Avg	G	AB	R	H	2B	3B	HR	RBI	BB	SO	SB	CS	OBP	SLG
Barkett,Andy	1B	25	.207	88	295	20	61	15	0	4	30	13	44	2	2	.240	.298
DeRosa,Mark	SS	25	.262	101	355	48	93	19	2	2	27	30	37	9	4	.319	.344
Giles,Marcus	2B	22	.265	132	442	59	117	25	1	13	50	50	76	17	6	.339	.414
Glavine,Mike	1B	27	.212	128	411	30	87	23	0	8	66	25	88	0	1	.257	.326
Helms,Wes	3B	24	.259	136	518	58	134	23	5	15	69	21	96	0	6	.288	.409
Hessman,Mike	3B	22	.164	127	427	42	70	20	0	14	41	25	190	2	1	.210	.309
Hubbard,Mike	C	29	.266	78	222	26	59	7	0	4	24	17	29	2	3	.318	.351
Lackey,Steve	SS	25	.212	129	476	50	101	8	0	2	27	27	101	17	6	.254	.242
Lombard,George	OF	24	.248	112	408	56	101	21	5	7	37	43	136	23	9	.319	.375
Matos,Pascual	C	25	.194	94	304	21	59	13	1	3	20	9	95	0	1	.217	.273
Miller,David	1B-OF	26	.222	96	315	36	70	23	0	7	43	28	52	6	1	.286	.362
Moore,Mike	OF	29	.174	79	236	20	41	7	0	7	21	11	120	0	0	.211	.292
Norris,Dax	C	27	.228	132	469	46	107	24	0	10	59	34	79	0	1	.280	.343
Pendergrass,T.	OF	23	.184	115	396	37	73	12	2	0	25	37	87	9	7	.254	.225
Petersen,Chris	2B-SS	29	.188	88	261	9	49	8	0	0	16	12	49	1	4	.223	.218
Ross,Jason	OF	26	.226	73	243	26	55	14	0	9	21	15	97	9	5	.271	.395
Rumfield,Toby	1B	27	.242	127	414	48	100	15	0	14	55	25	61	2	7	.285	.379
Sisco,Steve	2B	30	.265	75	264	36	70	14	0	9	27	16	48	2	2	.307	.420
Smith,Demond	OF	27	.249	117	417	64	104	29	5	10	39	46	99	21	8	.324	.415
Swann,Pedro	OF	29	.276	125	424	55	117	19	1	6	45	42	71	4	5	.341	.368
Unroe,Tim	OF	29	.249	121	402	46	100	24	1	18	68	21	119	1	4	.286	.448
BALTIMORE ORIOLES		Age	Avg	G	AB	R	H	2B	3B	HR	RBI	BB	SO	SB	CS	OBP	SLG
Almonte,Wady	OF	25	.239	73	222	22	53	15	3	0	29	9	36	2	5	.268	.333
Brinkley,Darryl	OF	31	.304	69	224	28	68	8	0	1	30	18	42	6	2	.355	.353
Casimiro,Carlos	3B	23	.233	111	361	47	84	13	1	8	37	20	87	1	4	.273	.341
Clark,Howie	2B	26	.274	67	234	31	64	13	0	2	26	25	20	2	1	.344	.355
Coffie,Ivanon	SS	23	.236	108	407	46	96	19	2	7	48	27	79	0	4	.283	.344
Davis,Tommy	1B	27	.270	122	445	59	120	23	0	14	58	40	98	1	1	.330	.416
Dent,Darrell	OF	23	.239	115	352	46	84	9	0	0	22	41	68	14	5	.318	.264
Garabito,Eddy	2B	21	.220	125	504	65	111	17	1	5	46	21	69	16	6	.251	.288
Garcia,Jesse	SS	26	.225	106	364	39	82	10	1	0	20	24	63	7	4	.273	.258
Garcia,Karim	OF	24	.259	116	410	58	106	20	1	21	78	38	107	3	4	.321	.466
Gibralter,David	1B	25	.264	134	484	62	128	17	0	17	77	29	87	2	1	.306	.405
Herrera,Jose	OF	27	.273	132	535	71	146	31	4	3	49	33	77	9	8	.315	.363
Kinkade,Mike	C	27	.326	113	380	66	124	24	2	9	68	35	59	12	5	.383	.471
Kirby,Wayne	OF	36	.262	129	492	69	129	21	7	5	54	41	64	7	4	.319	.364
Leon,Jose	3B	23	.247	108	356	41	88	14	2	12	40	13	83	4	3	.274	.399
Matos,Francisco	2B	30	.259	91	324	33	84	16	2	0	21	11	36	5	3	.284	.321
Matos,Luis	OF	21	.230	61	209	24	48	6	3	1	29	14	32	11	8	.278	.301
May,Derrick	DH	31	.261	56	207	24	54	14	0	4	30	25	26	1	2	.341	.386
McDonald,Darnell	OF	21	.223	116	448	52	100	11	3	5	38	21	94	8	4	.258	.295
Minor,Ryan	3B	26	.277	68	235	29	65	7	0	13	43	28	60	0	4	.354	.472
Morales,Willie	C	27	.230	73	243	19	56	10	0	5	20	10	61	0	3	.261	.333
Richard,Chris	OF	26	.253	95	363	52	92	21	0	13	60	40	72	6	3	.328	.419
Rivera,Roberto	OF	23	.204	80	265	27	54	10	1	3	30	23	67	7	2	.267	.283
Short,Rick	DH	27	.301	129	468	57	141	34	0	8	74	35	62	2	3	.350	.425
Werth,Jayson	C	21	.208	85	269	41	56	14	1	4	23	40	54	6	3	.311	.312
BOSTON RED SOX		Age	Avg	G	AB	R	H	2B	3B	HR	RBI	BB	SO	SB	CS	OBP	SLG
Alcantara,Israel	OF-DH	27	.281	78	288	47	81	16	0	22	60	19	88	1	1	.326	.566
Burkhart,Morgan	1B	28	.233	105	343	47	80	17	0	16	61	55	93	0	0	.339	.423

Major League Equivalencies for 2000 AAA/AA Batters

BOSTON RED SOX		Age	Avg	G	AB	R	H	2B	3B	HR	RBI	BB	SO	SB	CS	OBP	SLG
Capista,Aaron	SS	21	.217	126	423	41	92	20	2	1	28	24	72	5	4	.260	.281
Chamblee,Jim	OF	25	.237	127	396	57	94	25	3	13	44	39	135	5	3	.306	.414
Chevalier,Virgil	OF	26	.274	97	358	45	98	24	0	5	52	22	37	2	2	.316	.383
DeLeon,Jorge	2B	25	.274	93	343	37	94	15	0	1	30	16	58	0	8	.306	.327
DeRosso,Tony	3B	24	.257	120	435	60	112	26	3	15	67	30	97	0	1	.305	.434
Diaz,Juan	1B	24	.280	63	232	36	65	13	0	18	54	10	68	0	0	.310	.569
Figga,Mike	C	29	.207	68	208	18	43	7	0	6	22	9	61	0	0	.240	.327
Garcia,Freddy	DH-3B	27	.241	105	374	41	90	26	1	18	59	21	86	0	3	.281	.460
Graham,Jess	OF	24	.217	75	249	22	54	10	2	3	26	13	65	0	3	.256	.309
Hillenbrand,Shea	1B	24	.299	135	511	60	153	33	2	8	62	12	41	2	3	.315	.419
Holbert,Aaron	SS	27	.230	109	383	42	88	15	1	4	30	17	68	6	10	.263	.305
Ingram,Garey	OF	29	.218	103	303	35	66	16	1	7	28	35	55	3	2	.299	.347
Johnson,Rontrez	OF	23	.248	134	509	65	126	20	1	4	41	36	78	19	8	.297	.314
Lewis,Marc	OF	25	.259	63	201	20	52	13	2	3	23	6	47	2	2	.280	.388
Lomasney,Steve	C	22	.225	66	227	23	51	15	0	6	21	16	86	2	6	.276	.370
Maddox Jr.,Garry	OF	25	.253	100	352	45	89	12	2	2	31	24	93	4	5	.301	.315
Pride,Curtis	OF	31	.262	101	302	62	79	15	3	10	38	52	77	14	8	.370	.430
Sadler,Donnie	OF-SS	25	.183	91	306	35	56	5	3	3	18	35	62	6	1	.267	.248
Santos,Angel	2B	20	.239	80	268	25	64	17	1	2	25	21	64	11	8	.294	.332
Sapp,Damian	C	24	.194	74	227	23	44	9	0	4	20	22	87	0	0	.265	.286
Sheets,Andy	SS	28	.208	83	274	30	57	8	2	6	28	30	50	2	2	.286	.318
Spehr,Tim	C	33	.135	77	223	19	30	6	0	3	19	28	89	0	1	.231	.202
Stenson,Dernell	1B	22	.245	98	368	47	90	13	0	16	56	35	103	0	0	.310	.410
Veras,Wilton	3B	22	.192	60	213	14	41	8	0	2	19	9	18	0	1	.225	.258
CHICAGO CUBS		Age	Avg	G	AB	R	H	2B	3B	HR	RBI	BB	SO	SB	CS	OBP	SLG
Amrhein,Mike	C	25	.280	104	350	44	98	17	0	9	48	29	42	0	3	.335	.406
Brock,Tarrik	OF	26	.239	104	376	48	90	16	3	9	38	34	114	10	7	.302	.370
Brown,Roosevelt	OF	24	.283	100	350	54	99	28	0	9	44	30	62	7	3	.339	.440
Font,Franklin	2B	22	.255	104	326	38	83	8	2	0	25	22	47	7	4	.302	.291
Gload,Ross	OF-1B	24	.274	128	481	65	132	31	4	22	81	26	69	2	2	.312	.493
Gonzalez,Raul	OF	26	.240	69	233	28	56	11	0	3	26	17	21	3	5	.292	.326
Hinske,Eric	3B	22	.256	131	434	75	111	20	7	19	72	66	142	11	5	.354	.465
Johns,Keith	2B	28	.219	115	342	40	75	21	0	1	21	26	78	2	4	.274	.289
Liniak,Cole	3B	23	.215	123	400	51	86	21	0	16	47	31	80	3	3	.271	.388
Lopez,Pee Wee	C	23	.253	69	225	18	57	11	0	1	25	11	35	0	1	.288	.316
Luuloa,Keith	SS	25	.222	80	275	33	61	14	1	6	37	24	32	1	4	.284	.345
Mahoney,Mike	C	27	.281	87	249	34	70	18	0	5	28	17	46	1	1	.327	.414
Matthews Jr.,Gary	OF	25	.220	60	205	21	45	9	2	4	17	14	43	4	1	.269	.341
Meadows,Tydus	OF	22	.255	80	247	32	63	13	3	5	31	16	77	3	2	.300	.393
Meyers,Chad	2B	24	.244	80	291	43	71	8	0	1	21	34	43	24	9	.323	.282
Molina,Jose	C	25	.212	76	241	17	51	7	0	0	13	18	64	0	4	.266	.241
Ojeda,Augie	SS	25	.256	113	383	45	98	20	1	6	34	26	28	11	6	.303	.360
Patterson,Corey	OF	20	.256	118	441	72	113	25	4	21	81	38	123	21	8	.315	.474
Randolph,Jaisen	OF	21	.238	126	487	75	116	14	3	1	30	47	102	36	14	.305	.285
Smith,Jason	SS	22	.234	119	479	54	112	21	5	11	60	18	139	13	10	.262	.367
Stoner,Mike	DH	27	.255	111	396	49	101	14	1	11	47	16	50	0	2	.284	.379
Vieira,Scott	1B	26	.214	99	323	43	69	15	1	7	33	37	121	0	3	.294	.331
Zuleta,Julio	1B	25	.286	107	378	61	108	22	0	22	76	25	80	3	4	.330	.519
CHICAGO WHITE SOX		Age	Avg	G	AB	R	H	2B	3B	HR	RBI	BB	SO	SB	CS	OBP	SLG
Battersby,Eric	1B	24	.231	127	407	58	94	19	2	7	42	46	88	4	8	.309	.339

424

Major League Equivalencies for 2000 AAA/AA Batters

CHICAGO WHITE SOX		Age	Avg	G	AB	R	H	2B	3B	HR	RBI	BB	SO	SB	CS	OBP	SLG
Bravo,Danny	2B	23	.226	96	337	47	76	11	0	2	28	35	58	8	9	.298	.276
Brumfield,Jacob	OF	35	.196	80	276	31	54	15	0	1	18	23	39	5	3	.258	.261
Caruso,Mike	SS	23	.228	88	302	33	69	10	4	0	23	19	23	3	7	.274	.288
Christensen,M.	OF	24	.246	90	329	43	81	11	1	5	25	28	53	21	8	.305	.331
Crede,Joe	3B	22	.299	138	528	82	158	34	0	20	92	46	117	2	4	.355	.477
Dellaero,Jason	SS	23	.179	122	435	35	78	17	0	6	41	16	149	7	6	.208	.260
Gibralter,Steve	OF	27	.237	65	232	29	55	8	1	9	32	15	56	5	0	.283	.397
Heintz,Chris	C	25	.262	73	237	26	62	14	0	1	33	17	34	3	1	.311	.333
Inglin,Jeff	OF-DH	24	.282	110	383	58	108	18	2	8	66	38	62	5	2	.347	.402
Johnson,Adam	DH	24	.224	105	375	41	84	20	1	10	59	35	78	2	5	.290	.363
Liefer,Jeff	1B	25	.261	120	433	66	113	26	0	27	80	46	111	1	3	.332	.508
Long,Ryan	OF	27	.227	92	321	36	73	13	0	9	38	19	97	0	0	.271	.352
Lydy,Scott	OF	31	.256	116	360	58	92	13	3	12	39	61	72	11	2	.363	.408
Moore,Brandon	2B-3B	27	.221	96	294	30	65	9	1	0	19	34	34	2	4	.302	.259
Prieto,Rick	OF	27	.248	118	428	64	106	14	2	0	39	72	62	23	9	.356	.290
Rexrode,Jackie	2B	21	.279	90	333	59	93	9	2	0	13	56	41	14	11	.383	.318
Rodriguez,Liu	2B-SS	23	.256	126	387	38	99	18	2	3	40	47	40	2	7	.336	.336
Rosario,Mel	C	27	.252	83	286	33	72	22	2	5	41	17	66	1	2	.294	.395
Rowand,Aaron	OF	22	.252	139	528	78	133	25	4	19	96	31	124	17	6	.293	.422
Seitzer,Brad	3B	30	.273	80	256	37	70	18	0	9	37	40	48	0	1	.372	.449
Wilson,Craig	3B-SS	29	.350	62	223	38	78	12	1	2	30	28	27	0	1	.422	.439
Wilson,Desi	OF	31	.250	124	428	51	107	21	0	2	48	45	82	13	4	.321	.313
CINCINNATI REDS		**Age**	**Avg**	**G**	**AB**	**R**	**H**	**2B**	**3B**	**HR**	**RBI**	**BB**	**SO**	**SB**	**CS**	**OBP**	**SLG**
Bartee,Kimera	OF	27	.264	119	432	52	114	17	2	6	36	38	67	21	7	.323	.354
Bell,Mike	3B	25	.238	115	412	52	98	26	1	16	58	35	79	0	0	.298	.422
Broussard,Ben	OF	23	.231	87	277	51	64	7	2	11	41	51	83	10	1	.351	.390
Burress,Andy	OF	22	.225	123	387	43	87	14	5	4	33	36	83	10	13	.291	.318
Caceres,Wilmy	SS-2B	21	.242	130	516	55	125	22	2	1	26	27	76	27	9	.280	.298
Clark,Brady	OF	27	.271	132	465	67	126	37	4	12	59	56	53	8	7	.349	.445
Cromer,D.T.	1B-DH	29	.239	106	398	43	95	23	2	10	50	25	88	4	3	.284	.382
Dawkins,Travis	SS-2B	21	.209	95	358	43	75	18	4	4	25	28	76	15	5	.267	.316
Diaz,Alejandro	OF	21	.242	122	475	55	115	17	5	10	53	10	82	13	19	.258	.362
Garcia,Guillermo	C	28	.242	102	314	28	76	21	1	10	41	19	56	1	1	.285	.411
Henson,Drew	3B	20	.237	75	278	38	66	15	1	5	40	16	106	1	5	.279	.353
Jennings,Robin	OF	28	.286	123	440	59	126	40	4	10	60	30	63	2	3	.332	.464
Kieschnick,B.	OF-1B	28	.248	113	423	51	105	31	0	19	67	29	112	1	0	.296	.456
Larson,Brandon	3B	24	.247	128	473	57	117	30	0	17	54	25	146	11	4	.285	.419
LaRue,Jason	C	26	.226	82	296	40	67	19	0	10	36	17	54	2	1	.268	.392
Melian,Jackson	OF	20	.226	83	287	29	65	7	2	7	32	13	73	12	1	.260	.338
Miller,Corky	C	24	.211	103	308	32	65	16	0	7	35	29	54	3	7	.279	.331
Monahan,Shane	OF	25	.227	85	264	28	60	12	1	5	40	14	50	3	5	.266	.337
Morris,Bobby	2B	27	.249	87	237	27	59	13	0	4	28	22	44	4	1	.313	.354
Nevers,Tom	SS	28	.207	76	213	21	44	8	0	3	16	15	61	1	1	.259	.286
Saunders,Chris	1B	29	.275	87	258	28	71	14	0	7	30	22	68	0	5	.332	.411
Sexton,Chris	SS	28	.289	99	370	59	107	17	0	5	37	49	47	5	3	.372	.376
Williams,Jason	2B	26	.229	121	375	37	86	14	0	3	24	34	50	1	1	.293	.291
Wright,Ron	1B	24	.229	97	288	36	66	20	0	10	49	32	92	1	1	.306	.403
CLEVELAND INDIANS		**Age**	**Avg**	**G**	**AB**	**R**	**H**	**2B**	**3B**	**HR**	**RBI**	**BB**	**SO**	**SB**	**CS**	**OBP**	**SLG**
Branyan,Russ	3B	24	.238	64	227	42	54	8	1	19	55	26	97	0	1	.316	.533
Budzinski,Mark	OF	26	.274	136	492	69	135	21	5	5	38	49	106	11	6	.340	.368

Major League Equivalencies for 2000 AAA/AA Batters

CLEVELAND INDIANS		Age	Avg	G	AB	R	H	2B	3B	HR	RBI	BB	SO	SB	CS	OBP	SLG
Coste,Chris	DH	27	.314	96	331	43	104	20	3	4	36	14	47	0	3	.342	.429
Edwards,Mike	3B	23	.288	136	476	68	137	24	1	10	59	54	92	5	3	.360	.405
Fitzgerald,Jason	OF	24	.272	56	206	25	56	7	3	3	28	18	40	5	6	.330	.379
Hamilton,Jon	OF	22	.243	137	489	54	119	27	2	6	53	49	125	9	6	.312	.344
Hughes,Bobby	C	29	.244	69	221	27	54	12	0	6	29	13	46	1	2	.286	.380
Hunter,Scott	OF	24	.217	102	364	34	79	16	2	4	33	11	71	8	6	.240	.305
Manto,Jeff	DH	35	.193	94	321	36	62	13	0	11	42	47	100	0	0	.296	.336
McDonald,John	SS	25	.261	75	283	34	74	16	1	0	33	19	30	3	3	.308	.325
Munoz,Billy	1B	25	.266	74	278	38	74	14	3	13	45	23	70	0	0	.322	.478
Patzke,Jeff	SS	26	.243	76	226	39	55	13	1	1	17	39	64	3	2	.355	.323
Peoples,Danny	1B	25	.251	124	415	63	104	18	1	18	69	58	128	1	4	.342	.429
Perry,Chan	OF	27	.286	92	357	44	102	17	0	9	60	19	57	0	2	.322	.409
Post,Dave	3B	26	.234	120	367	37	86	20	4	3	36	50	48	6	2	.326	.335
Pratt,Scott	2B	23	.225	133	507	63	114	17	4	6	48	31	108	17	6	.270	.310
Roberts,Dave	OF	28	.284	120	457	86	130	15	2	12	51	55	71	31	12	.361	.405
Romero,Mandy	C	32	.307	83	293	52	90	20	1	11	46	34	38	0	1	.379	.495
Selby,Bill	3B	30	.268	100	380	64	102	20	4	19	80	44	64	0	1	.344	.492
Sorensen,Zach	SS	23	.252	108	416	62	105	17	3	5	37	35	75	12	6	.310	.344
Whitaker,Chad	OF	23	.228	104	364	41	83	10	2	6	47	32	102	2	4	.290	.316
Whiten,Mark	OF	33	.268	98	351	55	94	26	0	9	36	30	75	4	2	.325	.419
COLORADO ROCKIES		Age	Avg	G	AB	R	H	2B	3B	HR	RBI	BB	SO	SB	CS	OBP	SLG
Butler,Brent	2B	22	.294	122	439	60	129	34	0	8	44	36	44	0	3	.347	.426
Colina,Javier	3B	21	.242	130	443	36	107	13	1	2	37	40	80	4	2	.304	.289
Cotton,John	OF	29	.326	103	313	48	102	20	4	15	51	24	94	9	0	.374	.559
Cox,Darron	C	32	.322	78	245	30	79	13	0	3	38	22	33	2	3	.378	.412
Dewey,Jason	C	23	.252	96	329	31	83	27	0	12	47	31	100	0	3	.317	.444
Gerut,Jody	OF	22	.307	109	374	51	115	36	3	3	61	69	53	14	11	.415	.444
Goodell,Steve	1B	25	.289	76	239	42	69	14	1	15	45	44	47	1	1	.399	.544
Hiatt,Phil	1B	31	.318	136	513	87	163	35	0	39	90	52	145	10	2	.381	.614
Hutchins,Norm	OF	24	.263	92	335	39	88	16	7	7	34	20	78	16	7	.304	.415
Keck,Brian	SS	26	.289	63	211	23	61	11	1	4	30	16	43	7	5	.339	.408
Latham,Chris	OF	27	.247	126	340	63	84	16	6	8	40	58	97	20	8	.357	.400
Ledesma,Aaron	3B	29	.347	59	225	25	78	8	0	0	30	14	29	7	1	.385	.382
Martinez,Belvani	2B	21	.277	115	422	53	117	20	4	4	38	10	62	20	8	.294	.372
McClain,Scott	3B	28	.283	123	442	63	125	24	2	27	72	51	86	5	9	.357	.529
McKeel,Walt	C	28	.251	72	235	31	59	16	0	11	28	28	44	2	3	.331	.460
Melhuse,Adam	C	28	.294	94	293	46	86	16	1	4	34	38	63	5	5	.375	.396
Mendoza,Carlos	OF	25	.352	107	358	65	126	15	13	0	34	49	48	18	7	.430	.466
Pena,Elvis	SS	23	.329	126	498	99	164	19	9	4	39	63	72	38	15	.405	.428
Petrick,Ben	C	23	.317	63	249	31	79	21	2	9	38	26	39	5	2	.382	.526
Pierre,Juan	OF	22	.354	111	472	69	167	18	4	0	34	30	25	37	16	.392	.409
Ramirez,Dan	OF	26	.285	110	397	43	113	9	2	2	42	12	88	14	13	.306	.332
Sosa,Juan	SS	24	.279	118	452	55	126	24	8	9	57	25	52	16	6	.317	.427
Walker,Todd	2B	27	.279	63	233	33	65	11	0	1	24	21	34	5	3	.339	.339
DETROIT TIGERS		Age	Avg	G	AB	R	H	2B	3B	HR	RBI	BB	SO	SB	CS	OBP	SLG
Airoso,Kurt	OF	25	.218	98	317	36	69	13	0	3	34	35	73	4	1	.295	.287
Allen,Dusty	OF	27	.247	92	296	44	73	15	2	11	48	43	81	1	2	.342	.422
Azuaje,Jesus	SS	27	.189	61	227	25	43	8	0	2	10	18	17	2	2	.249	.251
Briggs,Stoney	OF	28	.232	134	482	55	112	36	1	12	55	43	153	12	6	.295	.386
Cardona,Javier	C	24	.244	56	209	22	51	9	0	7	33	11	34	0	1	.282	.388

426

Major League Equivalencies for 2000 AAA/AA Batters

DETROIT TIGERS		Age	Avg	G	AB	R	H	2B	3B	HR	RBI	BB	SO	SB	CS	OBP	SLG
Freire,Alejandro	DH-1B	25	.248	135	455	61	113	15	0	18	65	49	117	1	4	.321	.400
Gillespie,Eric	1B	25	.234	69	231	19	54	15	0	5	30	14	50	0	2	.278	.364
Guevara,Giomar	SS	27	.253	109	368	48	93	21	1	4	26	34	67	2	5	.316	.348
Inge,Brandon	C	23	.222	133	474	51	105	31	2	7	59	29	128	8	4	.266	.340
Lemonis,Chris	2B	26	.193	84	280	23	54	19	2	2	18	13	55	0	1	.229	.296
Lindsey,Rod	OF	24	.204	114	383	48	78	10	3	0	16	27	106	33	13	.256	.245
Lindstrom,David	C	25	.216	80	250	26	54	10	0	6	34	14	21	0	0	.258	.328
McClure,Brian	OF	26	.267	97	285	32	76	16	0	0	17	35	56	1	1	.347	.323
McMillon,Billy	OF	28	.314	105	363	48	114	27	0	9	39	55	67	2	1	.404	.463
Mendez,Carlos	C	26	.257	100	358	38	92	19	0	13	56	9	38	0	0	.275	.419
Mitchell,Derek	SS	25	.180	116	323	32	58	13	0	0	22	38	80	2	3	.266	.220
Munson,Eric	1B	22	.231	98	355	44	82	19	3	11	57	28	101	3	2	.287	.394
Rios,Brian	SS	25	.239	95	306	35	73	21	2	3	30	20	62	0	1	.285	.350
Santana,Pedro	2B	23	.258	112	434	51	112	18	3	4	44	27	88	29	11	.302	.341
Sasser,Rob	3B	25	.238	137	467	60	111	26	0	17	49	40	110	5	5	.298	.403
Ust,Brant	3B	21	.198	111	374	31	74	14	3	3	23	23	100	1	4	.244	.275
Wakeland,Chris	OF	26	.243	141	474	51	115	22	1	20	59	47	153	2	5	.311	.420
Watkins,Pat	OF	27	.233	110	408	51	95	13	0	5	40	20	51	3	5	.269	.301
FLORIDA MARLINS		Age	Avg	G	AB	R	H	2B	3B	HR	RBI	BB	SO	SB	CS	OBP	SLG
Betts,Todd	1B-3B	27	.283	120	400	57	113	22	1	6	55	42	61	2	3	.351	.388
Castro,Ramon	C	24	.279	67	201	29	56	17	0	8	30	10	39	0	0	.313	.483
Clapinski,Chris	SS	28	.234	62	201	27	47	7	2	3	16	22	37	1	3	.309	.333
Crespo,Cesar	OF	21	.227	134	463	74	105	17	5	6	46	51	126	28	11	.304	.324
Erickson,Matt	SS-3B	24	.266	100	319	43	85	19	3	1	31	39	66	5	3	.346	.354
Foster,Quincy	OF	25	.275	65	236	46	65	5	3	1	16	15	44	17	6	.319	.335
Garcia,Amaury	2B	25	.243	120	448	55	109	20	2	8	31	27	82	23	9	.286	.350
Gibson,Derrick	OF	25	.232	100	319	28	74	9	1	6	28	12	88	8	7	.260	.323
Gulan,Mike	3B-OF	29	.265	119	396	44	105	31	1	10	49	18	98	3	1	.297	.424
Lopez,Mendy	SS	25	.273	56	209	22	57	15	0	4	19	8	39	0	1	.300	.402
Martinez,Manny	OF	29	.221	126	358	38	79	15	0	5	36	20	60	13	5	.262	.304
Martinez,Sandy	C	27	.248	86	258	30	64	15	0	9	32	10	59	1	1	.276	.411
McNally,Sean	3B	27	.216	112	352	38	76	17	3	7	27	28	109	1	4	.274	.341
Norton,Chris	1B-DH	29	.223	94	305	42	68	11	0	8	48	33	85	0	0	.299	.338
Nunez,Abraham	DH	20	.242	74	211	30	51	14	2	4	32	29	68	5	6	.333	.384
Ozuna,Pablo	2B	21	.274	118	442	57	121	21	4	5	45	26	58	24	9	.314	.373
Pachot,John	C	25	.249	102	321	27	80	16	0	2	44	14	44	0	4	.281	.318
Phoenix,Wynter	OF	25	.225	121	369	53	83	19	4	7	48	40	101	6	7	.301	.355
Ramirez,Julio	OF	22	.221	94	330	30	73	14	2	4	34	14	90	13	5	.253	.312
Raven,Luis	OF	31	.226	115	394	45	89	18	1	15	54	22	102	2	1	.267	.391
Rolison,Nate	1B	23	.276	123	410	58	113	29	2	13	58	47	122	1	1	.350	.451
HOUSTON ASTROS		Age	Avg	G	AB	R	H	2B	3B	HR	RBI	BB	SO	SB	CS	OBP	SLG
Bautista,Juan	SS	25	.219	90	269	29	59	12	0	4	25	11	54	7	7	.250	.309
Betzsold,James	OF	27	.269	93	308	41	83	16	0	7	43	25	106	12	7	.324	.390
Burns,Kevin	1B	24	.294	91	262	42	77	16	1	7	38	19	64	0	2	.342	.443
Charles,Frank	C	31	.247	84	279	25	69	9	2	4	32	18	65	0	3	.293	.337
Chavez,Raul	C	26	.232	99	298	27	69	12	0	1	31	29	46	2	0	.300	.282
Cole,Eric	OF	24	.274	132	530	75	145	43	0	19	78	30	104	15	6	.313	.462
Cromer,Tripp	2B	32	.204	66	221	18	45	6	2	3	21	14	49	0	0	.251	.290
Ensberg,Morgan	3B	24	.282	137	471	79	133	32	0	24	75	65	114	6	12	.369	.503
Everett,Adam	SS	23	.233	126	446	72	104	24	1	4	32	65	104	9	4	.331	.318

Major League Equivalencies for 2000 AAA/AA Batters

HOUSTON ASTROS		Age	Avg	G	AB	R	H	2B	3B	HR	RBI	BB	SO	SB	CS	OBP	SLG
Ginter,Keith	2B	24	.314	125	449	90	141	28	2	22	76	58	136	16	6	.393	.532
Logan,Kyle	OF	24	.205	109	337	36	69	16	0	5	25	24	67	9	5	.258	.297
Maldonado,Carlos	C	21	.252	116	413	38	104	22	1	4	43	24	76	3	4	.293	.339
Matranga,David	SS	23	.219	120	366	41	80	13	2	5	36	34	106	3	5	.285	.306
McNeal,Aaron	1B	22	.293	97	352	33	103	19	1	9	57	17	97	0	4	.325	.429
Miller,Ryan	2B	27	.238	111	294	27	70	17	0	2	30	15	60	0	5	.275	.316
Morillo,Cesar	SS	26	.269	98	294	35	79	14	0	2	30	17	65	6	7	.309	.337
Perez,Jhonny	OF	23	.278	79	266	36	74	8	0	6	25	12	42	10	4	.309	.376
Phillips,J.R.	1B-OF	30	.232	132	470	49	109	15	0	21	76	39	147	2	0	.291	.398
Porter,Colin	OF	24	.258	124	426	63	110	23	4	12	47	39	139	12	9	.320	.415
Ramirez,Omar	OF	29	.307	133	460	64	141	23	1	1	46	60	37	14	13	.387	.367
Richardson,Brian	3B	24	.235	119	392	42	92	13	4	2	41	21	102	1	0	.274	.304
Robertson,Mike	1B	29	.232	121	396	50	92	22	4	8	43	39	58	0	3	.301	.369
Sagmoen,Marc	OF	29	.257	122	408	57	105	14	6	11	37	35	86	15	6	.316	.402
Truby,Chris	3B	26	.270	64	263	27	71	10	2	1	26	14	33	4	2	.307	.335
KANSAS CITY ROYALS		Age	Avg	G	AB	R	H	2B	3B	HR	RBI	BB	SO	SB	CS	OBP	SLG
Amado,Jose	1B	25	.274	88	310	36	85	15	0	4	49	29	26	4	1	.336	.361
Brown,Dee	OF	22	.254	125	469	65	119	22	6	19	60	31	112	14	5	.300	.448
Caruso,Joe	OF	25	.295	108	390	61	115	23	1	11	58	25	46	7	4	.337	.444
Curry,Mike	OF	23	.276	123	453	92	125	16	6	3	46	70	101	36	14	.373	.358
Dillon,Joe	3B	24	.286	107	360	46	103	23	4	8	47	43	65	0	0	.362	.439
Dodson,Jeremy	OF	23	.226	128	443	61	100	14	4	15	50	38	114	12	7	.287	.377
Escandon,E.	2B	25	.213	103	296	30	63	10	0	6	27	42	56	2	0	.311	.307
Guiel,Aaron	OF	27	.270	73	252	40	68	13	2	11	34	29	54	4	0	.345	.468
Hallmark,Pat	OF	26	.308	132	467	70	144	23	3	8	69	38	76	29	11	.360	.422
Holbert,Ray	SS	29	.236	94	330	35	78	10	1	1	34	29	49	10	8	.298	.282
Huff,Larry	3B	28	.283	83	283	42	80	12	1	2	38	37	49	9	7	.366	.353
Medrano,Tony	SS	25	.247	128	473	56	117	20	1	6	47	28	45	13	7	.289	.332
Metzler,Rod	2B	25	.251	111	354	44	89	13	3	4	38	20	74	4	7	.291	.339
Molina,Izzy	C	29	.217	90	304	33	66	8	1	8	31	11	55	3	3	.244	.329
Norman,Les	OF	31	.241	109	402	45	97	19	4	9	54	25	62	5	3	.286	.376
Ortiz,Hector	C	30	.300	68	220	25	66	10	0	5	20	18	18	2	2	.353	.414
Pellow,Kit	1B	26	.233	117	412	52	96	15	3	19	64	32	89	4	3	.288	.422
Phillips,Paul	C	23	.277	82	285	43	79	10	5	3	26	15	22	2	4	.313	.379
Prieto,Alejandro	SS-2B	24	.245	118	375	46	92	17	0	6	31	22	40	10	5	.287	.339
Roberge,J.P.	DH	27	.193	71	218	26	42	10	0	0	15	10	30	0	0	.228	.239
Willis,Dave	1B	25	.205	87	297	32	61	15	2	6	32	17	56	5	6	.248	.330
LA DODGERS		Age	Avg	G	AB	R	H	2B	3B	HR	RBI	BB	SO	SB	CS	OBP	SLG
Allen,Luke	3B	21	.229	90	323	43	74	12	2	5	47	26	76	9	5	.287	.325
Ashby,Chris	OF	25	.245	134	433	67	106	25	1	4	40	36	77	10	11	.303	.335
Bocachica,Hiram	2B	24	.268	124	447	67	120	28	2	15	57	26	104	6	14	.309	.441
Branson,Jeff	3B	33	.239	108	310	30	74	17	1	3	28	18	74	3	4	.280	.329
Chen,Chin-Feng	OF	22	.242	133	492	51	119	22	1	4	52	40	140	15	6	.299	.315
Davis,Glenn	1B	24	.176	113	363	42	64	13	2	6	31	37	121	1	0	.253	.273
Donnels,Chris	1B	34	.274	105	307	54	84	20	0	18	57	44	54	3	1	.365	.515
Gil,Geronimo	C	24	.255	115	380	39	97	18	0	9	60	24	77	2	3	.300	.374
Gilbert,Shawn	SS	35	.277	86	274	45	76	14	2	9	33	40	72	7	10	.369	.442
Gorr,Robb	1B	23	.228	87	268	25	61	11	0	6	32	13	57	2	3	.263	.336
Grijak,Kevin	1B	29	.235	112	315	41	74	15	1	11	54	20	57	6	9	.281	.394
Harkrider,Kip	SS	24	.200	97	275	22	55	7	0	3	27	11	41	0	0	.231	.258

Major League Equivalencies for 2000 AAA/AA Batters

LA DODGERS		Age	Avg	G	AB	R	H	2B	3B	HR	RBI	BB	SO	SB	CS	OBP	SLG
LoDuca,Paul	C	28	.293	78	256	32	75	20	1	2	37	22	14	5	5	.349	.402
Metcalfe,Mike	2B	27	.225	87	325	48	73	7	2	1	33	25	35	28	20	.280	.268
Moreta,Ramon	OF	24	.207	126	449	48	93	13	1	8	24	24	92	18	7	.247	.294
Mota,Tony	OF	22	.221	102	349	39	77	7	1	4	32	18	64	5	6	.259	.281
Pena,Angel	C	25	.256	87	293	35	75	9	1	11	41	18	78	1	1	.299	.406
Powell,Dante	OF	26	.193	82	233	33	45	8	0	4	18	21	70	14	7	.260	.279
Prieto,Chris	OF	27	.228	85	232	36	53	9	1	5	21	33	44	16	6	.325	.341
Riggs,Adam	3B	27	.260	124	323	48	84	18	2	8	39	23	70	7	7	.309	.402
Riggs,Eric	SS	23	.193	117	405	44	78	14	1	5	30	34	91	12	6	.255	.269
Saitta,Rich	2B	24	.215	106	335	37	72	11	2	2	28	17	69	6	2	.253	.278
Theodorou,Nick	OF	25	.205	113	254	22	52	10	1	0	19	31	41	1	3	.291	.252
MILWAUKEE BREWERS		Age	Avg	G	AB	R	H	2B	3B	HR	RBI	BB	SO	SB	CS	OBP	SLG
Barker,Kevin	1B	24	.176	85	279	33	49	8	0	8	36	42	78	0	0	.283	.290
Bierek,Kurt	1B	27	.240	128	416	50	100	19	1	14	59	46	79	0	0	.316	.392
Brown,Kevin L.	C	27	.287	74	254	28	73	19	0	6	31	11	72	0	0	.317	.433
Collier,Lou	3B	26	.243	67	222	30	54	6	1	1	34	31	55	6	3	.336	.293
Echevarria,Angel	OF	29	.337	74	285	38	96	22	1	7	41	21	42	0	1	.382	.495
Ernster,Mark	SS	22	.225	57	200	23	45	8	0	4	22	26	48	7	5	.314	.325
Fernandez,Jose	3B	25	.261	133	452	57	118	33	2	8	55	40	95	7	2	.321	.396
Green,Chad	OF	25	.207	128	430	52	89	27	2	4	31	29	124	18	6	.257	.307
Gubanich,C.	C	28	.259	109	367	39	95	30	0	12	58	28	97	0	0	.311	.439
Hollins,Damon	OF	26	.263	87	278	27	73	14	2	1	26	17	36	3	2	.305	.338
Iapoce,Anthony	OF	26	.200	97	280	23	56	6	0	0	17	20	69	12	3	.253	.221
Jacobsen,Bucky	1B	24	.257	81	261	38	67	12	0	14	43	37	72	2	1	.349	.464
Jones,Chris	OF	34	.273	77	249	30	68	16	4	2	24	10	68	3	3	.301	.394
Kirby,Scott	OF	22	.202	118	337	47	68	10	0	9	39	49	117	5	4	.303	.312
Klimek,Josh	OF-3B	26	.261	108	368	46	96	20	0	11	54	21	74	2	3	.301	.405
Kominek,Toby	OF-1B	27	.242	130	417	49	101	16	4	8	59	46	109	11	6	.317	.357
Krause,Scott	OF	26	.250	78	228	24	57	15	0	5	31	12	66	0	0	.288	.382
Lopez,Mickey	2B	26	.273	120	406	67	111	32	3	4	40	52	59	21	12	.356	.397
Martin,Norberto	2B	33	.257	117	393	41	101	23	2	0	33	18	39	7	2	.290	.326
Mathis,Jared	OF	24	.242	101	343	42	83	21	0	1	18	8	51	3	8	.259	.312
Moon,Brian	C	22	.169	106	307	29	52	11	0	0	28	33	50	1	3	.250	.205
Perez,Santiago	SS	24	.251	106	395	60	99	23	5	3	27	36	97	23	8	.313	.357
Pickler,Jeff	2B	24	.282	127	429	56	121	15	0	0	38	41	56	21	13	.345	.317
Sanchez,W.	SS	23	.243	85	239	22	58	8	1	0	24	25	49	0	5	.314	.285
Scutaro,Marcos	2B	24	.273	128	432	66	118	19	4	4	52	56	57	7	6	.357	.363
Tyler,Brad	OF	31	.225	113	360	48	81	14	2	6	40	55	64	9	2	.328	.325
MINNESOTA TWINS		Age	Avg	G	AB	R	H	2B	3B	HR	RBI	BB	SO	SB	CS	OBP	SLG
Allen,Chad	OF	25	.266	96	365	47	97	17	3	5	44	20	77	6	2	.304	.370
Alvarez,Rafael	OF	23	.237	97	266	28	63	13	1	5	37	24	71	2	1	.300	.350
Ardoin,Danny	C	25	.248	70	234	34	58	14	0	4	28	29	78	4	0	.331	.359
Barnes,John	OF	24	.315	120	409	71	129	31	4	8	57	38	51	4	6	.374	.469
Blake,Casey	3B	26	.251	110	378	48	95	24	1	8	40	33	87	4	5	.311	.384
Bolivar,Papo	OF	21	.254	117	393	37	100	17	5	1	33	16	75	10	8	.284	.331
Buchanan,Brian	OF	26	.251	95	342	54	86	16	0	17	68	27	80	3	1	.306	.447
Cuddyer,Michael	3B	21	.240	138	475	57	114	27	6	4	49	38	101	3	4	.296	.347
Davidson,Cleatus	SS	23	.208	119	433	33	90	12	5	0	24	19	102	11	7	.241	.259
Ferguson,Jeff	2B	27	.205	78	224	30	46	11	1	1	20	19	54	2	0	.267	.277
Huls,Steve	2B	25	.185	102	243	19	45	3	1	0	12	22	55	2	2	.253	.206

Major League Equivalencies for 2000 AAA/AA Batters

MINNESOTA TWINS		Age	Avg	G	AB	R	H	2B	3B	HR	RBI	BB	SO	SB	CS	OBP	SLG
Kielty,Bobby	OF	23	.235	138	468	68	110	31	2	11	53	72	130	4	4	.337	.380
LeCroy,Matthew	C	24	.257	70	249	35	64	15	0	10	39	22	48	0	0	.317	.438
Marcinczyk,T.R.	DH-1B	26	.198	71	222	19	44	8	0	5	20	21	64	0	2	.267	.302
Mientkiewicz,Doug	1B	26	.289	130	454	63	131	27	2	12	63	41	72	5	5	.347	.436
Moriarty,Mike	SS	26	.210	127	371	48	78	19	2	8	36	42	62	0	2	.291	.337
Peterman,Tommy	1B	25	.249	118	382	43	95	16	0	7	34	23	58	1	1	.291	.346
Pierzynski,A.J.	C	23	.279	103	365	42	102	26	1	5	43	8	47	0	1	.295	.397
Rivas,Luis	2B	20	.242	123	466	66	113	32	4	3	48	32	66	11	8	.291	.348
Ryan,Mike	OF	22	.251	125	474	51	119	21	6	9	56	25	88	2	3	.289	.378
Sears,Todd	1B	24	.314	129	455	71	143	30	0	17	91	78	120	9	3	.415	.492
Smith,Jeff	C-DH	26	.315	62	213	24	67	15	0	5	29	5	39	0	1	.330	.455
MONTREAL EXPOS		Age	Avg	G	AB	R	H	2B	3B	HR	RBI	BB	SO	SB	CS	OBP	SLG
Bradley,Milton	OF	22	.281	88	331	48	93	19	0	4	24	37	58	7	14	.353	.375
Bridges,Kary	2B	27	.315	61	203	29	64	11	2	1	22	22	7	7	2	.382	.404
Camilli,Jason	3B	24	.181	86	310	28	56	12	2	2	25	19	76	2	5	.228	.252
Carroll,Jamey	2B-3B	25	.259	136	502	63	130	20	3	1	34	35	46	10	3	.307	.317
Coquillette,Trace	OF	26	.219	75	260	25	57	18	0	0	22	20	60	0	1	.275	.288
de la Rosa,Tomas	SS	22	.184	103	332	22	61	9	0	0	30	25	45	7	2	.241	.211
Gallagher,Shawn	DH-1B	23	.225	114	391	47	88	17	2	9	50	33	89	2	3	.285	.348
James,Kenny	OF	23	.223	139	489	61	109	17	5	1	36	37	86	28	8	.278	.284
Lennon,Patrick	DH	32	.267	118	404	57	108	19	1	11	52	43	115	0	5	.338	.401
Mateo,Henry	2B	23	.267	140	516	78	138	24	9	3	54	42	103	35	13	.323	.366
McKinley,Dan	OF	24	.263	131	505	56	133	19	11	3	49	18	80	17	6	.289	.362
Nunnari,Talmadge	1B	25	.254	136	441	53	112	26	1	4	56	54	102	7	5	.335	.345
Patterson,Jarrod	3B	26	.235	106	315	26	74	14	0	3	39	15	66	0	1	.270	.308
Reding,Josh	SS	23	.201	137	447	49	90	10	4	1	41	42	117	18	6	.270	.248
Schneider,Brian	C	23	.228	67	232	18	53	20	2	3	25	13	44	0	0	.269	.371
Valera,Yohanny	C	23	.197	113	340	29	67	7	2	3	37	20	78	0	2	.242	.256
Ware,Jeremy	OF	24	.258	123	430	53	111	22	1	8	54	28	93	8	10	.303	.370
Wilkerson,Brad	OF	23	.275	129	429	78	118	44	1	13	66	67	102	8	6	.373	.473
NEW YORK METS		Age	Avg	G	AB	R	H	2B	3B	HR	RBI	BB	SO	SB	CS	OBP	SLG
Baez,Kevin	SS	33	.250	122	392	43	98	23	0	3	41	41	52	2	11	.321	.332
Bruce,Mo	3B-SS	25	.232	124	448	60	104	17	2	2	26	26	106	19	8	.274	.292
Dina,Allen	OF	26	.230	121	404	47	93	19	3	5	37	15	83	14	5	.258	.329
Escobar,Alex	OF	21	.258	122	419	64	108	21	5	12	55	39	122	16	6	.321	.418
Gainey,Bryon	1B	24	.182	106	336	29	61	15	0	8	40	15	141	0	2	.217	.298
Gonzalez,Jimmy	C	27	.249	73	225	26	56	11	0	6	24	14	55	0	2	.293	.378
Held,Dan	1B	29	.278	117	370	54	103	20	0	8	56	19	78	2	3	.314	.397
Huff,B.J.	OF	24	.184	73	201	14	37	6	0	3	19	15	84	0	2	.241	.259
Johnson,Mark P.	OF-1B	32	.243	94	304	40	74	18	0	13	49	54	56	9	2	.358	.431
Lamb,David	SS	25	.200	109	345	37	69	19	0	1	29	32	51	5	3	.268	.264
LeBron,Juan	OF	23	.200	72	230	21	46	14	0	4	20	11	87	1	4	.237	.313
Martinez,Gabby	SS	26	.198	86	263	26	52	3	2	3	17	9	38	10	11	.224	.259
McGuire,Ryan	OF	28	.272	122	378	52	103	20	0	7	51	71	88	4	3	.388	.381
Perez,Timoniel	OF	23	.327	72	278	37	91	14	3	4	30	13	26	9	7	.357	.442
Sheff,Chris	OF	29	.232	114	328	38	76	15	0	5	35	36	76	6	4	.308	.323
Simons,Mitch	2B	31	.239	113	394	43	94	19	3	0	39	30	57	11	13	.292	.302
Tamargo,John	2B	25	.227	100	291	39	66	15	0	0	23	30	51	3	7	.299	.278
Toca,Jorge	1B	25	.238	123	446	48	106	21	2	8	58	13	75	6	8	.259	.348
Velandia,Jorge	SS	25	.243	87	300	46	73	17	0	7	47	27	54	2	3	.306	.370

Major League Equivalencies for 2000 AAA/AA Batters

NEW YORK METS		Age	Avg	G	AB	R	H	2B	3B	HR	RBI	BB	SO	SB	CS	OBP	SLG
Wigginton,Ty	2B-3B	22	.253	122	434	52	110	23	2	15	63	16	114	3	5	.280	.419
Wilson,Vance	C	27	.231	111	385	38	89	20	0	12	51	19	68	7	6	.267	.377
NEW YORK YANKEES		Age	Avg	G	AB	R	H	2B	3B	HR	RBI	BB	SO	SB	CS	OBP	SLG
Almonte,Erick	SS	22	.251	131	442	48	111	16	2	12	66	25	138	8	2	.291	.378
Brown,Rich	OF	23	.214	92	346	45	74	14	2	3	27	18	43	11	7	.253	.292
Coolbaugh,Mike	SS	28	.242	117	372	49	90	24	0	17	47	52	100	4	3	.335	.444
Frank,Mike	OF	25	.229	115	350	40	80	18	4	5	34	27	41	8	3	.284	.346
Garcia,Carlos	2B	32	.242	93	269	27	65	14	0	1	30	21	55	5	6	.297	.305
Jose,Felix	DH	35	.275	59	200	24	55	14	1	8	29	18	62	2	3	.335	.475
Leach,Nick	1B	22	.256	113	344	38	88	21	0	6	42	41	84	3	3	.335	.369
McDonald,Donzell	OF	25	.221	68	240	32	53	9	3	1	12	43	49	17	7	.339	.296
Mirizzi,Marc	2B	25	.222	93	311	34	69	14	0	5	25	29	78	3	4	.288	.315
Orie,Kevin	3B	27	.261	95	314	39	82	20	2	7	33	32	53	2	2	.329	.404
Ortiz,Nicky	SS	26	.267	122	409	55	109	17	2	8	54	43	75	10	5	.336	.377
Ottavinia,Paul	OF	27	.281	127	463	69	130	24	5	6	50	41	53	11	5	.339	.393
Powell,Alonzo	OF-DH	35	.240	85	288	33	69	14	0	7	24	23	61	0	2	.296	.361
Robinson,Kerry	OF	26	.285	119	417	55	119	14	6	0	25	32	42	26	10	.336	.348
Seabol,Scott	3B	25	.274	132	478	71	131	41	1	16	67	30	115	1	4	.317	.464
Simon,Randall	1B	25	.237	116	413	43	98	19	2	13	65	27	47	4	5	.284	.387
Soriano,Alfonso	SS-2B	22	.259	111	440	70	114	27	4	9	51	19	89	10	7	.290	.400
Thames,Marcus	OF	23	.221	131	462	62	102	27	1	12	68	36	95	0	5	.277	.361
Thompson,Ryan	OF	32	.253	86	312	35	79	19	2	17	58	21	75	7	3	.300	.490
Valencia,Vic	C	23	.189	99	297	23	56	10	0	9	38	30	98	0	1	.263	.313
Wilcox,Luke	OF	26	.203	124	400	45	81	17	1	11	53	36	70	5	4	.268	.333
Wilson,Tom	C	29	.246	104	317	49	78	17	0	15	55	57	119	1	2	.361	.442
Zuber,Jon	1B	30	.262	87	282	28	74	13	0	0	40	29	6	2	.354	.309
OAKLAND ATHLETICS		Age	Avg	G	AB	R	H	2B	3B	HR	RBI	BB	SO	SB	CS	OBP	SLG
Bellhorn,Mark	3B	25	.240	117	421	91	101	14	8	18	60	73	122	14	6	.352	.439
Bowles,Justin	OF	26	.235	124	422	55	99	20	4	11	47	24	116	4	6	.276	.379
Byrnes,Eric	OF	24	.282	134	478	80	135	40	1	10	65	49	69	22	10	.349	.433
Cesar,Dionys	OF	23	.240	111	412	45	99	17	1	2	27	22	67	8	10	.279	.301
Decker,Steve	1B	34	.254	110	389	40	99	19	0	9	62	58	64	0	2	.351	.373
Encarnacion,Mario	OF	22	.241	81	290	42	70	14	2	10	50	28	97	11	7	.308	.407
Espada,Josue	2B	24	.215	63	233	29	50	11	0	0	13	28	35	6	4	.299	.262
Hart,Jason	1B	22	.282	140	531	74	150	36	2	21	91	42	124	2	0	.335	.476
Hinch,A.J.	C	26	.241	109	403	53	97	20	1	4	38	36	68	3	5	.303	.325
Landry,Jacques	3B	26	.219	127	448	60	98	26	2	12	58	28	150	6	5	.265	.366
Lockwood,Mike	OF	23	.255	92	345	43	88	15	0	2	32	25	48	0	3	.305	.316
Martins,Eric	3B	27	.229	76	253	28	58	8	0	1	17	29	32	0	5	.309	.273
McKay,Cody	C	26	.268	131	459	57	123	32	1	3	70	44	70	0	5	.332	.362
Mensik,Todd	DH	25	.226	124	394	41	89	20	1	16	61	43	119	0	0	.302	.404
Ortiz,Jose	2B-SS	23	.321	131	495	88	159	30	3	19	89	37	65	16	6	.368	.509
Pecci,Jay	2B	23	.213	102	338	38	72	12	2	1	26	26	51	3	7	.269	.269
Piatt,Adam	OF	24	.257	65	245	29	63	13	0	6	34	20	58	2	2	.313	.384
Porter,Bo	OF	27	.247	129	465	77	115	18	2	11	52	70	120	28	11	.346	.366
Salazar,Oscar	SS	22	.255	115	416	51	106	22	0	9	41	23	75	2	4	.294	.373
Valdez,Mario	1B-DH	25	.299	105	354	59	106	22	0	13	65	45	62	0	1	.378	.472
Vaz,Roberto	OF	25	.263	114	411	46	108	19	2	7	59	39	74	14	6	.327	.370
PHIL. PHILLIES		Age	Avg	G	AB	R	H	2B	3B	HR	RBI	BB	SO	SB	CS	OBP	SLG
Anderson,Marlon	2B	26	.289	103	388	49	112	18	6	7	45	34	46	18	7	.346	.420

Major League Equivalencies for 2000 AAA/AA Batters

PHIL. PHILLIES		Age	Avg	G	AB	R	H	2B	3B	HR	RBI	BB	SO	SB	CS	OBP	SLG
Bennett,Gary	C	28	.290	92	310	40	90	24	0	10	44	35	47	0	0	.362	.465
Burnham,Gary	1B	25	.251	111	347	44	87	27	0	11	51	29	51	0	1	.309	.424
Dominique,Andy	C-1B	24	.222	104	320	38	71	26	0	10	41	25	61	0	1	.278	.397
Doster,David	3B	29	.256	124	441	59	113	28	5	8	57	34	74	9	4	.309	.397
Estrada,Johnny	C	24	.275	95	346	35	95	18	0	10	35	7	22	0	0	.289	.413
Forbes,P.J.	OF	32	.260	99	327	44	85	22	0	1	27	26	31	5	2	.314	.336
Francia,David	OF	25	.270	104	318	43	86	16	2	3	33	22	49	16	11	.318	.362
Harris,Brian	2B	25	.251	110	343	38	86	22	2	8	34	27	53	8	5	.305	.397
Knupfer,Jason	2B	25	.250	84	272	44	68	13	0	3	20	28	50	4	6	.320	.331
McNamara,Rusty	3B	25	.274	125	453	66	124	23	4	11	63	31	44	2	3	.320	.415
Michaels,Jason	OF	24	.275	113	425	59	117	29	3	8	61	20	95	5	4	.308	.414
Newhan,David	2B	26	.220	91	313	37	69	6	1	5	31	35	80	7	4	.299	.294
Perez,Tomas	3B	26	.278	77	273	38	76	16	1	8	48	14	52	3	1	.314	.432
Pritchett,Chris	1B	30	.224	117	384	47	86	18	1	5	51	49	69	3	2	.312	.315
Punto,Nick	SS	22	.236	121	445	64	105	15	3	4	39	50	78	23	9	.313	.310
Rollins,Jimmy	SS	21	.260	133	461	57	120	29	9	10	59	43	59	18	7	.323	.427
Rose Jr.,Pete	3B	30	.230	109	348	46	80	21	0	6	46	40	51	5	2	.309	.342
Schall,Gene	DH	30	.271	124	421	62	114	25	0	18	69	43	100	0	5	.338	.458
Taylor,Reggie	OF	23	.259	98	413	51	107	10	6	13	37	18	93	17	6	.290	.407
Valent,Eric	OF	23	.240	128	458	67	110	21	4	18	75	50	97	1	3	.315	.421
Woods,Ken	OF	29	.286	133	500	76	143	28	5	1	30	34	50	15	5	.331	.368
PITTSBURGH PIRATES		Age	Avg	G	AB	R	H	2B	3B	HR	RBI	BB	SO	SB	CS	OBP	SLG
Brede,Brent	OF	28	.223	101	260	29	58	14	0	0	18	27	54	1	0	.296	.277
Brown,Emil	OF	25	.285	70	228	34	65	18	0	3	19	31	46	18	7	.371	.404
Burton,Darren	OF	27	.293	77	249	36	73	12	1	4	27	22	53	3	0	.351	.398
Cota,Humberto	C	21	.242	112	418	40	101	19	0	6	36	14	86	4	3	.266	.330
Figueroa,Luis	SS	26	.254	117	393	41	100	10	3	2	29	26	42	11	4	.301	.310
Furniss,Eddy	1B	24	.221	121	340	41	75	15	0	9	43	48	88	2	3	.317	.344
Hermansen,Chad	OF	22	.203	78	286	36	58	11	0	8	29	19	94	11	3	.252	.325
Hernandez,Alex	OF-1B	23	.277	126	459	45	127	30	1	9	57	17	108	4	3	.303	.405
Hyzdu,Adam	OF	28	.270	142	500	79	135	37	1	26	88	66	110	2	6	.355	.504
Laker,Tim	C	30	.225	121	409	54	92	26	3	15	58	42	77	3	0	.297	.413
Lankford,Derrick	OF	25	.272	96	305	34	83	15	1	8	33	33	64	2	0	.343	.407
Mackowiak,Rob	2B	24	.276	134	511	68	141	31	3	10	72	15	103	13	4	.297	.407
Montgomery,Ray	OF	29	.232	71	220	28	51	9	0	5	22	14	40	2	4	.278	.341
Nunez,Abraham	SS	24	.249	90	338	38	84	10	0	2	22	28	49	14	5	.306	.296
Redman,Tike	OF	23	.237	121	490	48	116	22	8	3	40	25	77	17	6	.274	.333
Washington,Rico	3B-2B	22	.239	135	490	61	117	21	5	6	49	38	80	2	8	.294	.339
Wehner,John	2B	33	.230	121	413	44	95	21	0	12	49	43	68	10	4	.303	.368
Wilson,Craig	C	23	.257	124	382	65	98	22	1	26	67	34	128	0	1	.317	.524
Wilson,Jack	SS	22	.262	121	469	71	123	24	6	5	42	35	80	1	5	.313	.371
Wood,Jason	3B-SS	30	.215	88	307	31	66	16	0	5	35	21	89	1	1	.265	.316
ST. LOUIS CARDINALS		Age	Avg	G	AB	R	H	2B	3B	HR	RBI	BB	SO	SB	CS	OBP	SLG
Bevins,Andy	OF	24	.294	130	439	73	129	26	2	22	79	25	95	0	4	.332	.513
Bieser,Steve	OF	32	.232	94	254	33	59	9	2	0	11	28	30	7	3	.309	.283
Clapp,Stubby	2B	27	.248	129	488	72	121	25	5	0	42	65	91	7	5	.336	.320
Eckelman,Alex	2B	25	.293	91	287	37	84	14	2	3	28	17	29	3	1	.332	.387
Farley,Cordell	OF	27	.213	96	244	32	52	6	0	6	21	16	80	12	8	.262	.311
Garcia,Luis	SS	25	.263	112	372	43	98	15	2	9	35	10	67	3	5	.283	.387
Garrick,Matt	C	24	.217	101	318	28	69	15	0	3	30	26	75	0	2	.276	.292

Major League Equivalencies for 2000 AAA/AA Batters

ST. LOUIS CARDINALS		Age	Avg	G	AB	R	H	2B	3B	HR	RBI	BB	SO	SB	CS	OBP	SLG
Haas,Chris	3B	23	.245	105	339	50	83	13	1	15	58	36	100	0	1	.317	.422
Little,Mark	OF	27	.257	107	409	56	105	26	5	12	52	41	101	16	6	.324	.433
Lucca,Lou	3B	29	.258	122	446	56	115	27	1	11	56	26	63	5	4	.299	.397
Maier,T.J.	2B	25	.276	110	355	51	98	14	2	5	36	36	44	9	7	.343	.369
Martinez,Pablo	SS	31	.192	93	271	18	52	8	0	0	21	18	67	9	3	.242	.221
McDonald,Keith	C	27	.237	83	257	27	61	13	0	4	24	22	61	0	2	.297	.335
Mitchell,Mike	1B	27	.277	97	311	40	86	26	1	3	34	33	51	1	3	.346	.395
Munoz,Juan	1B-OF	26	.293	100	317	39	93	19	0	4	32	12	26	4	3	.319	.391
Ortega,Bill	OF	24	.304	86	322	44	98	16	3	10	54	20	44	0	5	.345	.466
Pearson,Eddie	1B	26	.280	74	250	24	70	14	0	9	33	16	35	0	0	.323	.444
Perez,Eduardo	1B	30	.262	77	267	46	70	10	2	15	53	34	49	7	3	.346	.483
Saturria,Luis	OF	23	.255	129	466	68	119	23	7	17	66	33	131	13	11	.305	.444
Sutton,Larry	1B	30	.234	95	337	49	79	18	1	10	56	54	58	2	1	.340	.383
Tebbs,Nate	2B	27	.233	108	377	35	88	13	1	3	34	14	78	5	7	.261	.297
Whitmore,Darrell	OF	31	.255	89	247	29	63	12	1	8	27	10	66	2	2	.284	.409
Woolf,Jay	SS	23	.218	77	261	36	57	11	1	2	15	26	65	8	11	.289	.291
Young,Ernie	OF	30	.239	124	439	61	105	14	0	28	79	53	121	8	1	.321	.462
SAN DIEGO PADRES		**Age**	**Avg**	**G**	**AB**	**R**	**H**	**2B**	**3B**	**HR**	**RBI**	**BB**	**SO**	**SB**	**CS**	**OBP**	**SLG**
Alvarez,Gabe	1B	26	.210	112	366	52	77	17	1	11	45	60	101	1	1	.322	.352
Balfe,Ryan	OF	24	.232	130	444	47	103	16	2	8	51	29	130	2	3	.279	.331
Burroughs,Sean	3B	19	.255	108	373	36	95	23	2	1	32	37	48	4	8	.322	.335
Curl,John	OF	27	.247	111	275	30	68	19	2	3	38	24	84	1	1	.308	.364
Darr,Mike	OF	24	.296	91	341	56	101	18	3	6	46	31	58	8	6	.355	.419
Davis,Ben	C	23	.224	59	210	27	47	12	0	4	28	26	45	3	2	.309	.338
Eberwein,Kevin	1B	23	.232	100	357	44	83	13	1	14	55	29	83	1	2	.290	.392
Faggett,Ethan	OF	25	.215	131	484	58	104	21	3	5	28	38	122	12	18	.272	.302
LaRocca,Greg	3B	27	.251	137	454	64	114	33	4	6	57	38	65	8	4	.309	.381
Leday,A.J.	OF	27	.251	117	390	35	98	16	1	9	54	16	90	2	2	.281	.367
Matos,Julius	SS	25	.234	135	525	47	123	24	0	3	27	20	61	7	9	.262	.297
Milliard,Ralph	SS-2B	26	.239	108	351	43	84	20	1	3	28	44	66	11	9	.324	.328
Nicholson,Kevin	SS	24	.237	91	308	34	73	19	1	4	31	24	66	2	4	.292	.344
Nieves,Wilbert	C	22	.237	69	207	14	49	3	0	3	23	10	23	0	1	.272	.295
Powers,John	2B	26	.229	93	292	47	67	18	0	2	17	32	60	3	3	.306	.312
Radmanovich,R.	OF	28	.231	120	377	53	87	24	1	7	42	42	89	2	3	.308	.355
Roskos,John	OF	25	.276	99	355	53	98	22	0	12	53	37	71	1	5	.344	.439
Soliz,Steve	C	29	.179	78	246	21	44	10	0	1	12	20	55	0	1	.241	.232
Tucci,Pete	OF	24	.187	133	459	49	86	28	1	13	57	25	159	12	4	.229	.338
Vitiello,Joe	1B	30	.302	77	255	30	77	24	0	7	33	19	62	1	0	.350	.478
SF GIANTS		**Age**	**Avg**	**G**	**AB**	**R**	**H**	**2B**	**3B**	**HR**	**RBI**	**BB**	**SO**	**SB**	**CS**	**OBP**	**SLG**
Allen,Jeff	OF	24	.229	128	442	39	101	22	1	6	50	21	102	6	9	.263	.324
Ball,Jeff	OF	31	.210	72	214	23	45	6	0	3	8	11	46	0	0	.249	.280
Byas,Mike	OF	24	.229	135	493	62	113	8	0	1	25	57	91	24	9	.309	.252
Castro,Nelson	SS	24	.219	67	233	20	51	5	1	3	14	10	52	7	3	.251	.288
Chiaramonte,G.	C	24	.222	122	424	52	94	25	4	17	59	34	84	1	0	.279	.420
Clark,Doug	OF	24	.262	131	485	66	127	19	5	9	73	35	108	9	3	.312	.377
Feliz,Pedro	3B	23	.262	128	478	63	125	28	1	24	78	22	97	0	0	.294	.475
Flaherty,Tim	1B	23	.195	92	261	28	51	12	0	7	33	25	102	6	1	.266	.322
Glendenning,Mike	OF	23	.225	125	422	61	95	18	0	19	65	38	134	0	0	.289	.403
Guzman,Edwards	2B	23	.243	115	400	38	97	20	0	4	38	12	44	0	4	.265	.323
Leach,Jalal	OF	31	.292	116	360	45	105	22	4	11	51	29	65	8	7	.344	.467

Major League Equivalencies for 2000 AAA/AA Batters

SF GIANTS		Age	Avg	G	AB	R	H	2B	3B	HR	RBI	BB	SO	SB	CS	OBP	SLG
Lowery,Terrell	OF	29	.172	84	291	35	50	7	0	11	32	26	91	4	0	.240	.309
Magruder,Chris	OF	23	.272	134	489	83	133	31	2	3	38	54	78	14	9	.344	.362
Marval,Raul	2B	24	.189	103	301	19	57	4	0	2	22	14	37	2	4	.225	.223
Melo,Juan	SS-2B	23	.258	123	396	43	102	21	4	8	37	25	91	9	12	.302	.391
Minor,Damon	1B	26	.252	133	457	62	115	22	0	21	79	64	100	0	0	.344	.438
Ransom,Cody	SS	24	.193	130	455	56	88	20	1	6	46	33	149	7	2	.248	.281
Torrealba,Yorvit	C	21	.277	108	393	49	109	20	0	3	31	28	58	1	2	.325	.351
Tyler,Josh	OF	26	.238	78	202	17	48	8	0	0	8	17	30	8	3	.297	.277
Williams,Keith	OF	28	.207	96	295	32	61	8	0	5	31	27	85	2	0	.273	.285
Young,Travis	2B	25	.230	110	361	41	83	13	3	5	30	22	76	11	6	.274	.324
Zuniga,Tony	3B	25	.251	125	402	52	101	23	0	16	60	40	53	2	3	.319	.428
SEATTLE MARINERS		Age	Avg	G	AB	R	H	2B	3B	HR	RBI	BB	SO	SB	CS	OBP	SLG
Akers,Chad	3B	28	.249	103	377	50	94	27	3	5	30	21	43	10	4	.289	.377
Alexander,Chad	OF	26	.248	120	427	52	106	24	1	10	49	35	74	4	2	.305	.379
Barthol,Blake	C	27	.287	74	244	43	70	8	0	6	30	22	48	0	0	.346	.393
Clark,Jermaine	2B	23	.279	133	438	80	122	21	7	2	44	75	75	30	11	.384	.372
Connors,Greg	1B	25	.267	123	445	64	119	27	2	8	58	40	90	0	0	.328	.391
Fernandez,Alex	OF	19	.241	101	344	32	83	20	0	4	40	9	55	8	3	.261	.334
Figueroa,Luis	3B	23	.261	117	421	49	110	22	0	0	37	29	42	0	0	.309	.314
Flores,Jose	SS	27	.251	103	355	52	89	14	2	2	28	54	52	15	6	.350	.318
Gipson,Charles	OF	27	.226	67	208	24	47	5	4	0	19	28	40	12	6	.318	.288
Hernandez,C. E.	2B	24	.216	62	204	18	44	9	0	0	13	13	40	7	0	.263	.260
Horner,Jim	C	26	.228	65	241	36	55	10	1	8	33	17	45	3	0	.279	.378
Lesher,Brian	1B	29	.266	132	474	69	126	29	2	21	83	63	111	3	3	.352	.468
Machado,Robert	C	27	.276	92	319	37	88	18	0	7	52	25	46	0	4	.328	.398
Maness,Dwight	OF	26	.217	114	401	54	87	19	3	11	52	25	107	7	4	.263	.362
Medrano,Ryan	3B	26	.230	77	213	25	49	8	0	1	26	33	49	1	0	.333	.282
Murphy,Mike	OF	28	.261	97	349	48	91	16	2	5	34	29	92	7	2	.317	.361
Myers,Adrian	OF	25	.274	92	329	60	90	18	2	1	34	51	75	6	9	.371	.350
Neill,Mike	OF	30	.285	112	383	62	109	34	0	9	56	68	112	7	3	.392	.444
Sanders,Anthony	OF	26	.283	114	414	65	117	18	2	17	72	30	116	7	7	.331	.459
Snopek,Chris	SS	29	.276	104	380	68	105	21	1	11	43	40	42	9	5	.345	.424
Thomas,Juan	DH	28	.263	127	487	66	128	26	2	25	100	38	139	4	0	.316	.478
Vazquez,Ramon	SS	23	.272	124	397	58	108	23	3	8	59	44	83	0	5	.345	.406
Weber,Jake	OF	24	.243	129	465	71	113	20	5	5	56	51	61	8	3	.318	.340
TAMPA BAY DEVIL RAYS		Age	Avg	G	AB	R	H	2B	3B	HR	RBI	BB	SO	SB	CS	OBP	SLG
Abernathy,Brent	2B	22	.273	119	439	53	120	26	1	3	43	32	44	17	14	.323	.358
Badeaux,Brooks	2B	23	.256	106	347	41	89	8	4	0	26	31	53	1	1	.317	.303
Becker,Brian	1B	25	.264	132	493	40	130	26	1	8	52	30	94	0	2	.306	.369
Borders,Pat	C	37	.240	96	333	32	80	14	0	8	40	14	69	4	1	.271	.354
Brown,Jason	C-DH	26	.244	69	225	18	55	11	0	7	26	10	56	0	0	.277	.387
Buccheri,Jim	OF	31	.224	84	303	27	68	8	0	2	19	19	55	12	3	.270	.271
Butler,Rich	OF	27	.198	70	268	28	53	8	0	7	35	17	59	1	0	.246	.306
Carr,Dustin	2B	25	.191	113	362	28	69	12	1	2	26	35	66	6	1	.262	.246
de los Santos,E.	SS	22	.220	126	428	28	94	8	0	2	30	18	79	3	3	.251	.252
Hall,Toby	C	24	.303	115	439	48	133	26	0	13	69	14	44	2	1	.325	.451
Hoover,Paul	3B	24	.235	110	362	48	85	19	3	2	39	50	75	6	7	.328	.320
Huff,Aubrey	3B	23	.283	108	389	53	110	31	2	15	56	37	75	1	2	.345	.488
Jackson,Ryan	1B	28	.276	139	478	50	132	33	1	14	62	36	117	4	3	.327	.437
Kelly,Kenny	OF	21	.238	124	480	65	114	16	6	2	26	44	127	22	8	.302	.308

Major League Equivalencies for 2000 AAA/AA Batters

TAMPA BAY DEVIL RAYS		Age	Avg	G	AB	R	H	2B	3B	HR	RBI	BB	SO	SB	CS	OBP	SLG
McCracken,Q.	OF	30	.228	85	320	39	73	15	1	1	20	24	59	8	6	.282	.291
Neuberger,Scott	OF	22	.204	118	411	32	84	14	0	7	35	23	80	2	4	.247	.290
Perez,Nestor	SS	23	.191	75	236	13	45	3	0	0	12	10	42	0	2	.224	.203
Pomierski,Joe	DH-OF	26	.223	131	452	53	101	24	2	15	58	53	146	0	2	.305	.385
Sanchez,Alex	OF	23	.259	127	509	66	132	16	2	1	27	21	82	36	19	.289	.305
Sandberg,Jared	3B	22	.249	70	253	27	63	16	0	5	36	24	64	3	2	.314	.372
Smith,Bobby	2B	26	.257	66	249	35	64	17	1	12	42	16	64	10	1	.302	.478
Smith,Rod	2B	24	.216	78	236	22	51	9	0	0	10	26	57	8	10	.294	.254
Timmons,Ozzie	DH-OF	29	.266	137	482	73	128	28	0	21	76	53	110	3	3	.338	.454
Tyner,Jason	OF	23	.295	84	315	44	93	4	1	0	23	24	33	23	9	.345	.314
Winn,Randy	OF	26	.293	79	287	49	84	21	3	5	29	34	55	11	4	.368	.439

TEXAS RANGERS		Age	Avg	G	AB	R	H	2B	3B	HR	RBI	BB	SO	SB	CS	OBP	SLG
Brumbaugh,Cliff	OF-1B	26	.259	134	471	75	122	26	3	9	51	80	84	6	11	.367	.384
Demetral,Chris	2B	30	.229	106	350	48	80	8	4	7	41	48	55	1	2	.322	.334
Dransfeldt,Kelly	SS	25	.233	117	433	52	101	20	2	7	36	33	127	7	4	.288	.337
Grabowski,Jason	3B	24	.259	135	483	79	125	30	4	17	76	63	112	5	6	.344	.443
Knorr,Randy	C	31	.224	83	286	33	64	15	0	5	39	23	62	0	0	.282	.329
Lane,Ryan	OF-DH	25	.303	117	413	63	125	26	1	13	67	49	99	10	6	.377	.465
Monroe,Craig	OF	23	.265	120	453	75	120	31	4	17	75	46	96	8	12	.333	.464
Pena,Carlos	1B	22	.282	138	517	99	146	33	1	25	89	72	114	8	0	.370	.495
Piniella,Juan	OF	22	.231	126	438	57	101	15	0	4	34	48	111	16	6	.307	.292
Romano,Jason	2B	21	.254	131	523	73	133	32	1	6	59	40	89	17	6	.307	.354
Shave,Jon	2B	32	.276	131	500	74	138	19	4	8	47	35	67	9	4	.323	.378
Sierra,Ruben	OF	34	.310	112	429	61	133	24	3	16	72	48	65	3	1	.379	.492
Solano,Danny	SS	21	.234	109	351	30	82	11	2	5	28	28	69	6	5	.290	.319
Taveras,Luis	C	22	.215	82	279	37	60	12	2	4	31	24	77	2	1	.277	.315
Valdes,Pedro	OF	27	.319	92	345	56	110	28	1	15	68	39	42	1	0	.388	.536
Waszgis,B.J.	C	29	.248	77	254	39	63	10	2	11	54	48	70	1	1	.368	.433
Young,Mike	2B	23	.279	134	524	73	146	35	8	5	71	41	106	18	7	.331	.405
Zywica,Mike	OF	23	.253	131	430	55	109	23	3	7	57	41	129	5	6	.318	.370

TORONTO BLUE JAYS		Age	Avg	G	AB	R	H	2B	3B	HR	RBI	BB	SO	SB	CS	OBP	SLG
Freel,Ryan	OF	24	.274	92	321	67	88	17	4	9	34	38	52	25	12	.351	.436
Gibbons,Jay	1B	23	.310	132	467	80	145	38	0	17	71	49	71	2	1	.376	.501
Giles,Tim	DH-1B	24	.255	115	392	40	100	18	0	12	53	42	104	0	6	.327	.393
Greene,Charlie	C	29	.213	77	263	21	56	12	0	4	24	15	48	0	3	.255	.304
Izturis,Cesar	SS	20	.207	132	429	50	89	16	4	0	25	18	46	17	6	.239	.263
Langaigne,Selwyn	OF	24	.231	92	255	26	59	9	0	0	20	17	54	0	6	.279	.267
Lopez,Felipe	SS	20	.247	127	457	49	113	18	3	8	39	25	117	9	11	.286	.352
Lopez,Luis	3B-DH	26	.315	130	482	59	152	27	0	6	73	44	34	2	1	.373	.409
Loyd,Brian	C	26	.252	80	242	21	61	10	0	0	24	25	32	5	5	.322	.293
Mottola,Chad	OF	28	.295	134	495	79	146	25	2	30	95	34	103	24	9	.340	.535
Peeples,Mike	OF	23	.271	123	469	66	127	26	3	16	69	37	76	8	8	.324	.441
Perez,Robert	OF	31	.278	136	540	62	150	33	0	17	87	21	87	6	7	.305	.433
Schifano,Tony	3B	25	.224	87	272	22	61	11	0	0	22	15	56	4	4	.265	.265
Sollmann,Scott	OF	25	.226	114	380	62	86	16	4	0	25	42	62	14	10	.303	.289
Thompson,Andy	OF	24	.236	121	420	54	99	27	1	20	60	46	99	7	2	.311	.448
Wells,Vernon	OF	21	.233	127	486	70	113	31	5	14	61	44	92	18	7	.296	.403
Witt,Kevin	1B	24	.235	135	481	54	113	24	4	23	67	41	138	0	1	.295	.445

2000 Olympic Baseball Wrap Up

On the following pages you'll find game-by-game coverage of Team USA as it shook the baseball world in Sydney, ultimately defeating Cuba to bring home the gold. We lead off with a composite box for the players representing the United States in Australia. We follow with complete boxscores for the 8-1 Team USA. Finally, we give you the statistics for players affiliated with major league clubs who participated in the Olympic games for other countries.

The following abbreviations are used in this section:

Ana—Anaheim Angels
AUS—Australia
CUB—Cuba
Det—Detroit Tigers
Fla—Florida Marlins
Hou—Houston Astros
ITA—Italy
JPN—Japan
KOR—Korea
LA—Los Angeles Dodgers
Min—Minnesota Twins
Mon—Montreal Expos
NED—Netherlands
NYM—New York Mets
NYY—New York Yankees
Pit—Pittsburgh Pirates
RSA—South Africa
SD—San Diego Padres
Sea—Seattle Mariners
TB—Tampa Bay Devil Rays
Tor—Toronto Blue Jays

Team USA Composite Statistics

PLAYER	AVG	G	AB	R	H	2B	3B	HR	RBI	BB	SO	SB	PO	A	E
Abernathy, Brent—2b	.385	9	*39	4	*15	*6	0	0	4	1	4	3	21	20	0
Borders, Pat—c	.429	4	14	0	6	2	0	0	2	1	0	0	36	1	0
Burroughs, Sean—3b	.375	4	8	1	3	1	0	0	1	0	3	0	0	3	1
Cotton, John—dh	.185	8	27	3	5	3	*1	0	6	3	7	0	0	0	0
Dawkins, Travis—ss, 2b	.000	7	6	2	0	0	0	0	0	1	3	1	2	10	0
Everett, Adam—ss, 3b	.043	8	23	1	1	0	0	0	0	3	6	0	9	27	2
Jensen, Marcus—c	.167	5	18	2	3	0	0	1	6	0	4	0	30	6	0
Kinkade, Mike—3b, 1b	.207	9	29	4	5	1	0	0	3	2	7	0	9	21	1
Mientkiewicz, Doug—1b	.414	9	29	6	12	1	0	2	8	4	2	2	88	3	2
Neill, Mike—lf	.219	9	32	*9	7	0	0	*3	5	*8	11	1	13	0	1
Sanders, Anthony—cf	.167	5	6	3	1	0	0	0	1	1	4	1	5	0	0
Wilkerson, Brad—cf, rf	.216	9	37	7	8	1	*1	1	1	1	3	12	2	15	0	0
Young, Ernie—rf, dh	.385	9	26	7	10	1	0	1	8	7	4	1	10	0	1
Pitchers	—	—	—	—	—	—	—	—	—	—	—	—	2	13	0
TEAM TOTALS	.262	9	294	49	77	16	2	8	45	34	67	11	240	104	8

* = Led Tournament

PITCHER	W-L	ERA	G	GS	CG	SHO	SV	IP	H	R	ER	BB	SO
Ainsworth, Kurt	2-0	1.54	2	2	0	0	0	11.2	10	1	1	2	3
Franklin, Ryan	*3-0	0.00	4	0	0	0	0	8.1	0	0	0	3	7
George, Chris	0-0	0.00	3	0	0	0	0	3.2	2	0	0	1	3
Heams, Shane	0-0	7.71	3	0	0	0	0	2.1	5	2	2	1	1
Krivda, Rick	0-1	18.00	1	1	0	0	0	2.0	5	4	4	1	1
Oswalt, Roy	0-0	1.38	2	2	0	0	0	13.0	10	2	2	3	10
Rauch, Jon	1-0	0.82	2	1	1	0	0	11.0	6	2	1	0	21
Seay, Bobby	0-0	0.00	1	0	0	0	0	0.2	0	0	0	0	0
Sheets, Ben	1-0	0.41	3	3	1	1	0	22.0	11	2	1	1	11
Williams, Todd	1-0	0.00	4	0	0	0	1	5.0	3	1	0	1	6
Young, Tim	0-0	0.00	2	0	0	0	0	0.1	1	0	0	2	1
TEAM TOTALS	8-1	1.35	9	9	2	1	1	80.0	53	16	12	15	67

* = Led Tournament

USA Game 1, September 17, 2000

Japan

No. Player, Pos	AB	R	H	RBI	BB	SO	PO	A
1 So Taguchi, lf	6	1	2	0	0	0	0	0
24 Tomohiro Iizuka, cf	2	0	0	0	0	1	5	0
8 Yoshinori Okihara, ph-ss	3	0	0	1	0	0	1	1
3 Nobuhiko Matsunaka, 1b	4	0	2	0	0	0	5	0
26 Norihiro Akahoshi	2	0	0	0	0	1	1	0
5 Norihiro Nakamura, 3b	4	0	2	0	0	0	1	0
9 Osamu Nogami, pr-2b	1	1	0	0	0	0	1	2
6 Yukio Tanaka, ss-1b	4	0	0	0	1	2	7	3
21 Shinnosuke Abe, dh	4	0	0	0	0	0	—	—
10 Yoshihiko Kajiyama, rf	3	0	0	0	0	0	3	0
25 Jun Hirose, ph-rf	2	0	1	0	0	1	2	0
4 Jun Heima, 2b-3b	5	0	0	0	0	1	1	3
2 Fumihiro Suzuki, c	5	0	0	0	0	1	9	0
Totals	45	2	7	1	1	7	36	11

United States

No. Player, Pos	AB	R	H	RBI	BB	SO	PO	A
5 Brent Abernathy, 2b	6	0	2	0	0	0	2	6
12 Brad Wilkerson, cf-rf	5	1	0	0	1	0	2	0
17 Mike Neill, lf	4	1	2	2	2	0	2	0
19 Ernie Young, rf	4	0	1	0	0	0	1	0
26 Anthony Sanders, cf	1	0	0	0	0	0	2	0
22 John Cotton, dh	5	1	1	0	0	2	—	—
18 Mike Kinkade, 3b-1b	5	1	2	1	0	0	4	5
16 Doug Mientkiewicz, 1b	4	0	2	0	0	1	16	1
7 Travis Dawkins, pr-ss	1	0	0	0	0	1	0	2
15 Marcus Jensen, c	5	0	0	1	0	1	7	3
8 Adam Everett, ss-3b	5	0	0	0	0	2	3	5
Totals	45	4	10	4	3	7	39	25

	1	2	3	4	5	6	7	8	9	10	11	12	13	R	H	E
JPN	0	0	0	0	0	0	0	1	1	0	0	0	0	2	7	1
USA	0	0	0	0	0	0	2	0	0	0	0	0	2	4	10	3

E—Everett, Mientkiewicz, Suzuki. DP—JPN 1 (Matsuzaka, Nogami, Okihara), USA 1 (Everett, Mientkiewicz). 3B—Cotton, Taguchi. HR—Neill. SB—Dawkins, Neill. S—Abe, Iizuka.

Japan

No. Pitcher	IP	H	R	ER	BB	SO	HR
18 Daisuke Matsuzaka	10.0	8	2	2	2	5	0
17 Toshiya Sugiuchi, L	2.0	2	2	2	1	2	1
Totals	12.0	10	4	4	3	7	1

United States

No. Pitcher	IP	H	R	ER	BB	SO	HR
28 Ben Sheets	7.0	4	0	0	0	3	0
36 Shane Heams	0.1	1	1	1	0	0	0
27 Bobby Seay	0.2	0	0	0	0	0	0
29 Todd Williams	1.0	2	1	0	0	1	0
31 Ryan Franklin, W	4.0	0	0	0	1	3	0
Totals	13.0	7	2	1	1	7	0

WP—Sugiuchi. T—3:33. A—13,404. Umpires—HP, Anibal Rosario (PUR). 1B, Cesar Valdes (CUB). 2B, Pierfranco Leone (ITA). 3B, Humberto Castillo (VEN).

USA Game 2, September 18, 2000

South Africa

No. Player, Pos	AB	R	H	RBI	BB	SO	PO	A
6 Paul Bell, ss	3	0	0	0	0	2	0	1
7 Clint Alfino, lf	3	0	0	0	0	2	0	0
24 Ian Holness, rf	3	1	1	0	0	2	1	0
29 Nick Dempsey, 1b	3	0	1	1	0	1	6	0
33 Jason Cook, cf	3	0	0	0	0	2	4	0
31 Bles Kemp, c	2	0	1	0	0	0	3	0
20 Darryl Gonsalves, c	1	0	0	0	0	0	2	0
16 Neil Adonis, dh	3	0	0	0	0	1	—	—
2 Francisco Alfino, 3b	1	0	0	0	0	1	0	1
9 Errol Davis, ph	1	0	0	0	0	0		
11 Kevin Johnson, 2b	2	0	0	0	0	1	2	2
Totals	25	1	3	1	0	13	18	5

United States

No. Player, Pos	AB	R	H	RBI	BB	SO	PO	A
5 Brent Abernathy, 2b	2	1	1	1	0	0	0	0
8 Adam Everett, ph-ss	1	0	0	0	0	0	0	1
12 Brad Wilkerson, cf-rf	3	3	2	0	1	0	2	0
17 Mike Neill, lf	3	3	1	1	1	1	1	0
19 Ernie Young, rf	1	2	1	1	2	0	0	0
26 Anthony Sanders, cf	1	0	0	0	0	1	0	0
22 John Cotton, dh	4	0	2	5	0	1	—	—
18 Mike Kinkade, 3b	2	0	0	0	0	1	0	2
10 Sean Burroughs, 3b	1	0	0	0	0	0	0	1
16 Doug Mientkiewicz, 1b	3	1	1	0	0	0	7	0
14 Pat Borders, c	3	0	1	0	0	0	11	1
7 Travis Dawkins, ss-2b	2	1	0	0	0	1	0	2
Totals	26	11	9	9	4	5	21	7

	1	2	3	4	5	6	7	8	9	R	H	E
RSA	1	0	0	0	0	0	0			1	3	1
USA	2	5	0	3	0	1	x			11	9	1

E—Cook, Neill. 2B—Abernathy, Borders, Cotton. 3B—Wilkerson. HR—Neill. SB—Abernathy, Mientkiewicz, Wilkerson.

South Africa

No. Pitcher	IP	H	R	ER	BB	SO	HR
22 Liall Mauritz, L	3.0	7	10	7	3	3	0
44 Ashley Dove	3.0	2	1	1	1	2	1
Totals	6.0	9	11	8	4	5	1

United States

No. Pitcher	IP	H	R	ER	BB	SO	HR
23 Jon Rauch, W	7.0	3	1	0	0	13	0
Totals	7.0	3	1	0	0	13	0

Mauritz faced 3 batters in the 4th.

HBP—Dawkins by Mauritz, F.Alfino by Rauch. WP—Mauritz 2, Rauch. T—2:01. A—3,474. Umpires—HP, Iain Rouse (AUS). 1B, Pierfranco Leone (ITA). 2B, Katsuhito Koyama (JPN). 3B, Liang-Kuei Hsieh (TPE).

USA Game 3, September 19, 2000

United States

No. Player, Pos	AB	R	H	RBI	BB	SO	PO	A
5 Brent Abernathy, 2b	4	1	2	0	1	0	3	4
12 Brad Wilkerson, cf	5	2	2	1	0	2	3	0
17 Mike Neill, lf	4	0	0	0	0	2	1	0
19 Ernie Young, rf	4	2	3	3	0	0	0	0
22 John Cotton, dh	1	1	0	0	2	0	—	—
18 Mike Kinkade, 3b	3	0	0	0	0	2	1	2
7 Travis Dawkins, ss	0	0	0	0	0	0	0	2
16 Doug Mientkiewicz, 1b	2	0	1	2	1	0	14	0
15 Marcus Jensen, c	4	0	0	0	0	0	4	0
8 Adam Everett, ss-3b	3	0	0	0	1	0	1	7
Totals	30	6	8	6	5	6	27	16

Netherlands

No. Player, Pos	AB	R	H	RBI	BB	SO	PO	A
15 Rikkert Faneyte, cf	4	1	1	0	0	0	3	0
7 Ralph Milliard, 2b	4	0	1	0	0	1	4	4
12 Sharnol Adriana, dh	3	1	1	1	1	0	—	—
32 Hensley Meulens, lf	4	0	2	1	0	0	2	0
26 Percy Isenia, 1b	4	0	0	0	0	0	8	0
6 Robert Eenhoorn, ss	4	0	0	0	0	0	3	4
23 Johnny Balentina, c	3	0	0	0	0	1	7	0
30 Ken Brauckmiller, ph	1	0	0	0	0	0	—	—
18 Dirk Van t'Klooster, rf	2	0	2	0	2	0	0	0
3 Evert-Jan t'Hoen, 3b	3	0	1	0	0	2	0	0
24 Remy Maduro, ph	1	0	0	0	0	0	0	0
Totals	33	2	8	2	3	4	27	9

	1	2	3	4	5	6	7	8	9	R	H	E
USA	2	0	1	0	0	1	1	1	0	6	8	0
NED	1	0	0	0	0	0	0	1	0	2	8	0

DP—USA 2 (Abernathy 2, Everett 2, Mientkiewicz 2), NED 3 (Eenhoorn 2, Isenia 2, Milliard 3). 2B—Abernathy, Mientkiewicz, Young. 3B—Van t'Klooster. HR—Adriana, Wilkerson, Young. GDP—Isenia 2, Jensen.

United States

No. Pitcher	IP	H	R	ER	BB	SO	HR
20 Kurt Ainsworth, W	6.2	5	1	1	2	3	0
30 Tim Young	0.1	0	0	0	1	1	0
36 Shane Heams	1.0	2	1	1	0	0	1
29 Todd Williams	1.0	1	0	0	0	0	0
Totals	9.0	8	2	2	3	4	1

Netherlands

No. Pitcher	IP	H	R	ER	BB	SO	HR
19 Rob Cordemans, L	6.1	6	4	4	4	5	1
5 Ferenc Jongejan	0.2	2	2	2	0	1	1
20 Eelco Jansen	2.0	0	0	0	1	1	0
Totals	9.0	8	6	6	5	6	2

HBP—Cotton by Jongejan. WP—Ainsworth, Cordemans, Jansen. PB—Jensen. T—2:42. A—3,352. Umpires—HP, Pierfranco Leone (ITA). 1B, Katsuhito Koyama (JPN). 2B, Paul Begg (AUS). Ian McCabe (RSA).

USA Game 4, September 20, 2000

Korea

No. Player, Pos	AB	R	H	RBI	BB	SO	PO	A
9 Byung-Kyu Lee, lf	5	0	2	0	0	2	4	1
31 Jong-Ho Park, 2b	5	0	1	0	0	1	1	2
62 Jae-Hong Park, rf	3	0	0	0	1	2	1	0
11 Ki-Tai Kim, 1b	4	0	0	0	0	1	9	0
36 Seung-Yuop Lee, dh	2	0	0	0	1	1	—	—
1 Sung-Ho Jang, pr	0	0	0	0	0	0	—	—
5 Han-Soo Kim, 3b	2	0	0	0	0	1	1	0
18 Dong-Joo Kim, 3b	2	0	1	0	0	1	0	2
7 Jin-Man Park, ss	3	0	1	0	1	0	1	3
22 Sung-Heon Hong, c	4	0	1	0	0	0	6	0
8 Soo-Keun Jung, cf	2	0	1	0	0	0	0	0
Totals	32	0	7	0	4	9	24	11

United States

No. Player, Pos	AB	R	H	RBI	BB	SO	PO	A
5 Brent Abernathy, 2b	4	0	1	0	0	0	3	0
12 Brad Wilkerson, cf	4	0	1	0	0	0	1	0
17 Mike Neill, lf	4	1	1	0	0	1	2	0
19 Ernie Young, rf	3	1	1	0	1	1	1	0
22 John Cotton, dh	3	0	0	0	0	0	—	—
26 Anthony Sanders, ph	1	0	0	0	0	1	—	—
18 Mike Kinkade, 3b	3	1	0	0	1	1	1	4
16 Doug Mientkiewicz, 1b	4	1	3	4	0	0	9	1
14 Pat Borders, c	4	0	1	0	0	0	9	0
8 Adam Everett, ss	3	0	0	0	0	2	0	5
Totals	33	4	8	4	2	6	27	10

	1	2	3	4	5	6	7	8	9	R	H	E
KOR	0	0	0	0	0	0	0	0	0	0	7	2
USA	0	0	0	0	0	0	0	4	x	4	8	0

E—Chong, K.Kim. DP—KOR 1 (B.Lee, Jo.Park), USA 1 (Kinkade, Mientkiewicz). 2B—Abernathy. HR—Mientkiewicz. SB—Wilkerson, Young. S—Jung. GDP—Ji.Park.

Korea

No. Pitcher	IP	H	R	ER	BB	SO	HR
19 Tae-Hyon Chong	7.0	6	0	0	0	5	0
21 Jin-Woo Song, L	0.1	1	2	2	1	0	0
35 Pil-Jung Jin	0.2	1	2	2	1	1	1
Totals	8.0	8	4	4	2	6	1

United States

No. Pitcher	IP	H	R	ER	BB	SO	HR
25 Roy Oswalt	7.0	7	0	0	2	6	0
32 Chris George	0.2	0	0	0	0	1	0
31 Ryan Franklin, W	0.1	0	0	0	0	1	0
30 Tim Young	0.0	0	0	0	1	0	0
29 Todd Williams	1.0	0	0	0	1	1	0
Totals	9.0	7	0	0	4	9	0

HBP—S.Lee by George. IBB—S.Lee by Oswalt. A—13,818. Umpires—HP, Katsuhito Koyama (JPN). 1B, Liang-Kuei Hsieh (TPE). 2B, Robert Bellerose (CAN). 3B, Neil Poulton (AUS).

USA Game 5, September 22, 2000

Italy

No. Player, Pos	AB	R	H	RBI	BB	SO	PO	A
5 Claudio Liverziani, rf	3	0	1	0	0	0	0	0
8 Roberto de Franceschi, cf	4	0	0	0	0	1	2	0
53 Christopher Madonna, c	3	1	1	0	1	0	6	0
29 David Sheldon, 3b	4	0	1	1	0	2	2	0
22 Daniel DiPace, 1b	3	1	1	0	1	0	7	2
23 Alberto D'Auria, 2b	4	0	0	0	0	1	0	4
50 Luigi Carrozza, dh	4	0	1	1	0	1	—	—
21 Daniele Frignani, lf	3	0	0	0	0	0	2	0
47 Daniel Newman, ph	1	0	0	0	0	0	—	—
9 Seth LaFera, ss	2	0	0	0	1	1	1	0
Totals	31	2	5	2	3	6	24	7

United States

No. Player, Pos	AB	R	H	RBI	BB	SO	PO	A
5 Brent Abernathy, 2b	4	1	2	0	0	0	4	2
12 Brad Wilkerson, cf	4	0	1	0	0	1	2	0
17 Mike Neill, lf	3	1	0	1	1	0	3	0
19 Ernie Young, rf	3	1	2	1	1	0	1	0
22 John Cotton, dh	3	1	0	0	1	0	—	—
18 Mike Kinkade, 3b	4	0	0	0	0	1	1	5
7 Travis Dawkins, ss	0	0	0	0	0	0	0	1
16 Doug Mientkiewicz, 1b	4	0	1	0	0	0	8	0
15 Marcus Jensen, c	3	0	0	0	0	2	6	2
8 Adam Everett, ss-3b	2	0	0	1	1	0	2	0
Totals	30	4	6	2	4	4	27	13

	1	2	3	4	5	6	7	8	9	R	H	E
ITA	0	0	0	2	0	0	0	0	0	2	5	2
USA	2	0	0	0	0	0	0	2	x	4	6	1

E—Everett, Perri, Simontacchi. DP—ITA 1 (DiPace, Perri). 2B—Madonna. SB—Abernathy. S—Liverziani.

Italy

No. Pitcher	IP	H	R	ER	BB	SO	HR
11 Battista Perri, L	7.2	6	4	2	4	4	0
55 Jason Simontacchi	0.1	0	0	0	0	0	0
Totals	8.0	6	4	2	4	4	0

United States

No. Pitcher	IP	H	R	ER	BB	SO	HR
28 Ben Sheets	6.0	4	2	1	1	3	0
31 Ryan Franklin, W	2.0	0	0	0	2	1	0
30 Tim Young	0.0	1	0	0	0	0	0
29 Todd Williams, S	1.0	0	0	0	0	2	0
Totals	9.0	5	2	1	3	6	0

Young faced 1 batter in the 9th.

IBB—Madonna by Franklin. PB—Jensen. T—2:33. A—13,912. Umpires—HP, Liang-Kuei Hsieh (TPE). 1B, Ian McCabe (RSA). 2B, Neil Poulton (AUS). 3B, Katsuhito Koyama (JPN).

USA Game 6, September 23, 2000

United States

No. Player, Pos	AB	R	H	RBI	BB	SO	PO	A
5 Brent Abernathy, 2b	5	0	1	0	0	2	2	2
12 Brad Wilkerson, cf	4	0	0	0	0	4	0	0
16 Doug Mientkiewicz, 1b	4	0	1	0	0	0	10	1
19 Ernie Young, rf	2	0	0	0	1	0	0	0
22 John Cotton, dh	4	0	0	0	0	3	—	—
17 Mike Neill, lf	3	0	0	0	1	3	0	0
10 Sean Burroughs, 3b	4	1	2	0	0	2	0	2
14 Pat Borders, c	4	0	2	1	0	0	11	0
7 Travis Dawkins, pr	0	0	0	0	0	0	0	0
8 Adam Everett, ss	3	0	0	0	0	0	0	2
18 Mike Kinkade, ph	1	0	1	0	0	0	0	0
Totals	34	1	7	1	2	14	24	10

Cuba

No. Player, Pos	AB	R	H	RBI	BB	SO	PO	A
1 Luis Ulacia, lf	4	1	1	0	0	1	1	0
5 Yasser Gomez, cf	3	0	0	0	0	1	1	0
10 Omar Linares, 3b	3	1	0	0	1	2	0	1
46 Orestes Kindelan, 1b	4	0	1	0	0	2	7	1
24 Yobal Duenas, pr-1b	0	1	0	0	0	0	0	0
6 Antonio Pacheco, dh	2	1	2	1	0	0	—	—
25 Antonio Scull, ph-dh	1	0	0	0	0	0	0	0
38 Oscar Macias, 2b	4	1	1	0	0	2	1	2
18 Miguel Caldes, rf	4	1	2	2	0	1	1	0
13 Ariel Pestano, c	4	0	1	1	0	2	15	0
11 German Mesa, ss	2	0	2	1	2	0	1	2
Totals	31	6	10	6	3	11	27	7

	1	2	3	4	5	6	7	8	9	R	H	E
USA	0	0	0	0	0	0	0	0	1	1	7	2
CUB	4	0	0	1	0	0	0	1	x	6	10	0

E—Burroughs, Young. DP—USA 1 (Abernathy, Everett, Mientkiewicz). 2B—Burroughs, Caldes. 3B—Mesa. S—Gomez, Scull, Ulacia. GDP—Ulacia.

United States

No. Pitcher	IP	H	R	ER	BB	SO	HR
33 Rick Krivda, L	2.0	5	4	4	1	1	0
23 Jon Rauch	4.0	3	1	1	0	8	0
32 Chris George	1.0	0	0	0	1	1	0
36 Shane Heams	1.0	2	1	0	1	1	0
Totals	8.0	10	6	5	3	11	0

Cuba

No. Pitcher	IP	H	R	ER	BB	SO	HR
36 Jose Ibar, W	7.0	3	0	0	2	10	0
99 Pedro Luis Lazo	2.0	4	1	1	0	4	0
Totals	9.0	7	1	1	2	14	0

HBP—Young by Ibar. WP—Rauch 2. A—14,010. Umpires—HP, Carlos Rey (PUR). 1B, Pierfranco Leone (ITA). 2B, Myung-Hoon Yoon (KOR). 3B—Bernardo Contreras (DOM).

USA Game 7, September 24, 2000
United States

No. Player, Pos	AB	R	H	RBI	BB	SO	PO	A
5 Brent Abernathy, 2b	5	0	4	3	0	0	4	2
12 Brad Wilkerson, rf	5	0	1	0	0	2	2	0
17 Mike Neill, lf	3	2	1	0	2	0	2	0
19 Ernie Young, dh	2	1	0	1	1	1	—	—
16 Doug Mientkiewicz, 1b	2	2	1	1	1	0	2	0
10 Sean Burroughs, 3b	2	0	1	0	0	0	0	0
18 Mike Kinkade, 3b-1b	5	1	2	2	0	1	1	0
26 Anthony Sanders, cf	3	3	1	1	1	2	3	0
15 Marcus Jensen, c	4	2	3	4	0	0	5	0
7 Travis Dawkins, ss	3	1	0	0	1	1	2	3
Totals	34	12	14	12	6	7	21	5

Australia

No. Player, Pos	AB	R	H	RBI	BB	SO	PO	A
35 Glenn Reeves, rf	3	0	0	0	0	1	0	0
25 Chris Snelling, cf	3	0	0	0	0	0	1	0
14 David Nilsson, dh	2	1	1	0	0	0	—	—
43 Ron Johnson, ph-dh	1	0	1	0	0	0	—	—
45 Clayton Byrne, lf	3	0	1	0	0	2	2	0
36 Paul Gonzalez, 3b	2	0	0	1	0	0	1	2
6 Rod. Van Buizen, ph-3b	1	0	1	0	0	0	0	0
42 Michael Moyle, c	3	0	0	0	0	1	4	1
15 Gary White, c	0	0	0	0	0	0	2	1
17 Brett Roneberg, 1b	3	0	1	0	0	0	7	0
18 Glenn Williams, 2b	3	0	0	0	0	0	3	3
9 Mathew Buckley, ss	3	0	2	0	0	0	1	0
Totals	27	1	7	1	0	4	21	7

	1	2	3	4	5	6	7	8	9	R	H	E
USA	0	4	1	5	0	1	1			12	14	0
AUS	0	0	0	1	0	0	0			1	7	2

E—Ettles, Reeves. DP—USA 1 (Abernathy, Dawkins, Kinkade). AUS 2 (Gonzalez, Moyle, Roneberg 2, Williams 2). 2B—Abernathy 2, Johnson, Kinkade, Nilsson. HR—Jensen. SB—Abernathy, Mientkiewicz, Sanders. GDP—Kinkade, Williams, Young.

United States

No. Pitcher	IP	H	R	ER	BB	SO	HR
20 Kurt Ainsworth, W	5.0	5	1	1	0	3	0
32 Chris George	2.0	2	0	0	0	1	0
Totals	7.0	7	1	1	0	4	0

Australia

No. Pitcher	IP	H	R	ER	BB	SO	HR
39 Mark Hutton, L	2.0	5	4	4	4	0	0
37 David White	1.0	5	5	5	0	1	0
29 Mark Ettles	3.0	2	2	2	1	3	1
38 Adrian Meagher	1.0	2	1	1	1	3	0
Totals	7.0	14	12	12	6	7	1

HBP—Sanders by White, Young by Ettles. WP—White, Ettles. A—14,018. Umpires—HP, Robert Bellerose (CAN). 1B, Bernardo Contreras (DOM). 2B, Pierfranco Leone (ITA). 3B, Carlos Rey (PUR).

USA Game 8, September 26, 2000
Korea

No. Player, Pos	AB	R	H	RBI	BB	SO	PO	A
9 Byung-Kyu Lee, rf	4	0	1	1	0	0	1	0
31 Jong-Ho Park, 2b	4	0	0	0	0	2	0	1
36 Seung-Yuop Lee, 1b	4	0	0	0	0	2	12	0
18 Dong-Joo Kim, 3b	4	0	0	0	0	1	1	2
11 Ki-Tai Kim, dh	3	0	0	0	0	0	—	—
22 Sung-Heon Hong, c	3	0	0	0	0	0	7	2
1 Sung-Ho Jang, lf	2	1	0	0	1	2	0	0
7 Jin-Man Park, ss	3	1	1	0	0	1	2	1
8 Soo-Keun Jung, cf	2	0	1	0	0	0	2	0
Totals	29	2	3	2	1	8	25	10

United States

No. Player, Pos	AB	R	H	RBI	BB	SO	PO	A
5 Brent Abernathy, 2b	4	0	1	0	0	0	3	2
12 Brad Wilkerson, cf	3	1	1	0	0	0	2	0
17 Mike Neill, lf	3	0	0	0	1	1	1	0
19 Ernie Young, rf	3	0	0	0	0	2	4	0
22 John Cotton, dh	4	0	1	0	0	1	—	—
18 Mike Kinkade, 3b	2	1	1	0	0	0	1	1
7 Travis Dawkins, pr	0	0	0	0	0	0	0	0
16 Doug Mientkiewicz, 1b	3	1	2	1	1	0	6	0
15 Marcus Jensen, c	2	0	0	1	0	1	8	1
8 Adam Everett, ss	3	0	0	0	0	1	2	0
Totals	27	3	6	3	3	6	27	5

	1	2	3	4	5	6	7	8	9	R	H	E
KOR	0	0	2	0	0	0	0	0	0	2	3	0
USA	0	0	0	1	0	0	1	0	1	3	6	1

E—Kinkade. DP—KOR 1 (Hong, D.Kim, S.Lee). 2B—Abernathy, Cotton, B.Lee, Ji.Park, Wilkerson. HR—Mientkiewicz. SB—Jung. GDP—Cotton.

Korea

No. Pitcher	IP	H	R	ER	BB	SO	HR
19 Tae-Hyon Chong	6.1	3	2	2	2	6	0
21 Jin-Woo Song	0.1	1	0	0	0	0	0
59 Seok-Jin Park, L	1.2	2	1	1	1	0	1
Totals	8.1	6	3	3	3	6	1

United States

No. Pitcher	IP	H	R	ER	BB	SO	HR
25 Roy Oswalt	6.0	3	2	2	1	4	0
31 Ryan Franklin	2.0	0	0	0	0	2	0
29 Todd Williams, W	1.0	0	0	0	0	2	0
Totals	9.0	3	2	2	1	8	0

HBP—Wilkerson by Chong, Young by Park, Kinkade by Park. IBB—Neill by S.Park. A—14,002. Umpires—HP, Cesar Valdes (CUB). 1B, Paul Begg (AUS). 2B, Anton Bodaan (NED). 3B, Humberto Castillo (VEN). LF, Ian McCabe (RSA). RF, Neil Poulton (AUS).

USA Game 9, September 27, 2000

United States

No. Player, Pos	AB	R	H	RBI	BB	SO	PO	A
5 Brent Abernathy, 2b	5	1	1	0	0	2	0	2
12 Brad Wilkerson, cf-rf	4	0	0	0	1	3	1	0
17 Mike Neill, lf	5	1	2	1	0	3	1	0
19 Ernie Young, rf	4	0	2	2	1	0	3	0
26 Anthony Sanders, pr-cf	0	0	0	0	0	0	0	0
22 John Cotton, dh	3	0	1	0	0	0	—	—
10 Sean Burroughs, ph-dh	1	0	0	0	0	1	—	—
18 Mike Kinkade, 3b	4	0	0	0	0	1	0	2
16 Doug Mientkiewicz, 1b	3	1	0	0	1	1	16	0
14 Pat Borders, c	3	0	2	1	1	0	5	0
8 Adam Everett, ss	3	1	1	0	1	1	1	7
Totals	35	4	9	4	5	12	27	13

Cuba

No. Player, Pos	AB	R	H	RBI	BB	SO	PO	A
1 Luis Ulacia, lf	4	0	0	0	0	1	0	0
5 Yasser Gomez, cf	4	0	0	0	0	1	1	0
10 Omar Linares, 3b	3	0	2	0	0	0	3	2
46 Orestes Kindelan, 1b	3	0	0	0	0	2	6	1
6 Antonio Pacheco, dh	3	0	0	0	0	0	—	—
38 Oscar Macias, 2b	3	0	1	0	0	0	3	1
18 Miguel Caldes, rf	3	0	0	0	0	0	0	0
13 Ariel Pestano, c	2	0	0	0	0	0	10	1
45 Juan Manrique, ph-c	1	0	0	0	0	0	2	0
11 German Mesa, ss	2	0	0	0	0	0	1	1
17 Javier Mendez, ph	1	0	0	0	0	1	—	—
Totals	29	0	3	0	0	5	27	9

	1	2	3	4	5	6	7	8	9	R	H	E
USA	1	0	0	0	3	0	0	0	0	4	9	0
CUB	0	0	0	0	0	0	0	0	0	0	3	0

DP—USA 1 (Everet, Mientkiewicz, Sheets). 2B—Borders, Cotton. HR—Neill. GDP—Pacheco.

United States

No. Pitcher	IP	H	R	ER	BB	SO	HR
28 Ben Sheets, W	9.0	3	0	0	0	5	0
Totals	9.0	3	0	0	0	5	0

Cuba

No. Pitcher	IP	H	R	ER	BB	SO	HR
99 Pedro Luis Lazo, L	1.0	3	1	1	0	2	1
36 Jose Ibar	3.1	2	3	3	2	3	0
44 Maels Rodriguez	4.2	4	0	0	3	7	0
Totals	9.0	9	4	4	5	12	1

HBP—Cotton by Rodriguez. T—2:37. A—14,107. Umpires—HP, Anibal Rosario (PUR). 1B, Katsuhito Koyama (JPN). 2B, Bernardo Contreras (DOM). 3B, Humberto Castillo (VEN). LF, Paul Begg (AUS). RF, Gerard Tancred (AUS).

Other Minor Leaguers in the Olympics

Player	Tm	Org	AVG	G	AB	R	H	2B	3B	HR	RBI	SB	BB	SO	SLG	OBP
Sharnol Adriana	NED	Pit	.115	7	26	2	3	1	0	2	4	0	3	8	.385	.207
Mike Crouwel	NED	Pit	.000	1	1	0	0	0	0	0	0	0	0	0	.000	.000
Rikkert Faneyte	NED	Pit	.269	7	26	4	7	1	0	0	1	0	4	6	.308	.367
Chairon Isenia	NED	TB	.000	2	3	0	0	0	0	0	0	0	0	1	.000	.000
Remy Maduro	NED	Pit	.000	6	4	0	0	0	0	0	0	0	0	0	.000	.000
Ralph Milliard	NED	SD	.174	6	23	2	4	0	*1	0	1	1	1	6	.261	.240
Dave Nilsson	AUS	NYY	*.565	7	23	6	13	*6	0	1	6	3	7	5	*.957	*.667
Brett Roneberg	AUS	Fla	.333	6	15	1	5	0	0	0	2	0	1	2	.333	.375
Chris Snelling	AUS	Sea	.071	5	14	1	1	0	0	0	0	1	1	0	.071	.133
E.J. t'Hoen	NED	Ana	.091	6	11	1	1	0	0	0	0	0	1	5	.091	.167
Rodney Van Buizen	AUS	LA	.333	4	6	1	2	0	0	0	0	0	0	0	.333	.333
Glenn Williams	AUS	Tor	.111	5	9	0	1	0	0	0	0	0	1	2	.111	.200

* = Led Tournament

Player	Tm	Org	W	L	SV	ERA	IP	H	R	ER	BB	SO	HR
Craig Anderson	AUS	Sea	1	1	0	1.29	7.0	3	2	1	3	6	1
Grant Balfour	AUS	Min	0	0	1	4.15	4.1	3	2	2	1	9	1
Tom Becker	AUS	Det	0	0	0	0.00	4.1	4	2	0	1	3	0
Shayne Bennett	AUS	Mon	0	*2	0	0.75	12.0	15	5	1	2	7	1
Radhames Dykhoff	NED	NYM	0	0	0	0.00	1.0	3	0	0	0	0	0
Tim Harrell	RSA	LA	1	1	0	4.05	13.1	10	8	6	*9	7	1
Mark Hutton	AUS	Hou	0	1	0	9.00	7.0	10	7	7	6	1	0
Mike Nakamura	AUS	Min	0	0	0	4.15	4.1	3	2	2	1	5	1
Brad Thomas	AUS	Min	0	0	0	4.15	8.2	12	4	4	6	3	0

* = Led Tournament

Appendix

Minor League Team	Organization	League	Level	Minor League Team	Organization	League	Level
Akron Aeros	Indians	EL	AA	Frederick Keys	Orioles	CAR	A+
Albuquerque Dukes	Dodgers	PCL	AAA	Fresno Grizzlies	Giants	PCL	AAA
Altoona Curve	Pirates	EL	AA	Fort Myers Miracle	Twins	FSL	A+
Arkansas Travelers	Cardinals	TL	AA	Fort Wayne Wizards	Padres	MWL	A
Asheville Tourists	Rockies	SAL	A	Giants (Scottsdale)	Giants	AZL	R
Athletics (Phoenix)	Athletics	AZL	R	Great Falls Dodgers	Dodgers	PIO	R+
Auburn Doubledays	Astros	NYP	A-	Greensboro Bats	Yankees	SAL	A
Augusta GreenJackets	Red Sox	SAL	A	Greenville Braves	Braves	SL	AA
Bakersfield Blaze	Giants	CAL	A+	Hagerstown Suns	Blue Jays	SAL	A
Batavia Muckdogs	Phillies	NYP	A-	Harrisburg Senators	Expos	EL	AA
Beloit Snappers	Brewers	MWL	A	Helena Brewers	Brewers	PIO	R+
Billings Mustangs	Reds	PIO	R+	Hickory Crawdads	Pirates	SAL	A
Binghamton Mets	Mets	EL	AA	High Desert Mavericks	Diamondbacks	CAL	A+
Birmingham Barons	White Sox	SL	AA	Hudson Valley Renegades	Devil Rays	NYP	A-
Bluefield Orioles	Orioles	APP	R+	Huntsville Stars	Brewers	SL	AA
Boise Hawks	Angels	NWL	A-	Idaho Falls Braves	Padres	PIO	R+
Bowie Baysox	Orioles	EL	AA	Indianapolis Indians	Brewers	IL	AAA
Braves (Orlando)	Braves	GCL	R	Iowa Cubs	Cubs	PCL	AAA
Brevard County Manatees	Marlins	FSL	A+	Jacksonville Suns	Tigers	SL	AA
Bristol Sox	White Sox	APP	R+	Jamestown Jammers	Braves	NYP	A-
Buffalo Bisons	Indians	IL	AAA	Johnson City Cardinals	Cardinals	APP	R+
Burlington Bees	White Sox	MWL	A	Jupiter Hammerheads	Expos	FSL	A+
Burlington Indians	Indians	APP	R+	Kane County Cougars	Marlins	MWL	A
Butte Copper Kings	Angels	PIO	R+	Kingsport Mets	Mets	APP	R+
Calgary Cannons	Marlins	PCL	AAA	Kinston Indians	Indians	CAR	A+
Cape Fear Crocs	Expos	SAL	A	Kissimmee Cobras	Astros	FSL	A+
Capital City Bombers	Mets	SAL	A	Lake Elsinore Storm	Angels	CAL	A+
Carolina Mudcats	Rockies	SL	AA	Lakeland Tigers	Tigers	FSL	A+
Cedar Rapids Kernels	Angels	MWL	A	Lancaster JetHawks	Mariners	CAL	A+
Charleston (S.C.) RiverDogs	Devil Rays	SAL	A	Lansing Lugnuts	Cubs	MWL	A
Charleston (W.Va.) Alley Cats	Royals	SAL	A	Las Vegas Stars	Padres	PCL	AAA
Charlotte Knights	White Sox	IL	AAA	Louisville RiverBats	Reds	IL	AAA
Charlotte Rangers	Rangers	FSL	A+	Lowell Spinners	Red Sox	NYP	A-
Chattanooga Lookouts	Reds	SL	AA	Lynchburg Hillcats	Pirates	CAR	A+
Clearwater Phillies	Phillies	FSL	A+	Macon Braves	Braves	SAL	A
Clinton LumberKings	Reds	MWL	A	Mahoning Valley Scrappers	Indians	NYP	A-
Colorado Springs Sky Sox	Rockies	PCL	AAA	Mariners (Peoria)	Mariners	AZL	R
Columbus Clippers	Yankees	IL	AAA	Marlins (Melbourne)	Marlins	GCL	R
Columbus RedStixx	Indians	SAL	A	Martinsville Astros	Astros	APP	R+
Cubs (Mesa)	Cubs	AZL	R	Medicine Hat Blue Jays	Blue Jays	PIO	R+
Danville Braves	Braves	APP	R+	Memphis Redbirds	Cardinals	PCL	AAA
Dayton Dragons	Reds	MWL	A	Mexico All-Stars (Tucson)	—	AZL	R
Daytona Cubs	Cubs	FSL	A+	Michigan Battle Cats	Astros	MWL	A
Delmarva Shorebirds	Orioles	SAL	A	Midland RockHounds	Athletics	TL	AA
Diamondbacks (Tucson)	Diamondbacks	AZL	R	Missoula Osprey	Diamondbacks	PIO	R+
Dunedin Blue Jays	Blue Jays	FSL	A+	Mobile BayBears	Padres	SL	AA
Durham Bulls	Devil Rays	IL	AAA	Modesto A's	Athletics	CAL	A+
Edmonton Trappers	Angels	PCL	AAA	Mudville Nine	Brewers	CAL	A+
El Paso Diablos	Diamondbacks	TL	AA	Myrtle Beach Pelicans	Braves	CAR	A+
Elizabethton Twins	Twins	APP	R+	Nashville Sounds	Pirates	PCL	AAA
Erie SeaWolves	Angels	EL	AA	New Britain Rock Cats	Twins	EL	AA
Eugene Emeralds	Cubs	NWL	A-	New Haven Ravens	Mariners	EL	AA
Everett AquaSox	Mariners	NWL	A-	New Jersey Cardinals	Cardinals	NYP	A-
Expos (Jupiter)	Expos	GCL	R	New Orleans Zephyrs	Astros	PCL	AAA

Minor League Team	Organization	League	Level	Minor League Team	Organization	League	Level
Norfolk Tides	Mets	IL	AAA	Salem-Keizer Volcanoes	Giants	NWL	A-
Norwich Navigators	Yankees	EL	AA	Salt Lake Buzz	Twins	PCL	AAA
Ogden Raptors	Brewers	PIO	R+	San Antonio Missions	Dodgers	TL	AA
Oklahoma Redhawks	Rangers	PCL	AAA	San Bernardino Stampede	Dodgers	CAL	A+
Omaha Golden Spikes	Royals	PCL	AAA	San Jose Giants	Giants	CAL	A+
Oneonta Tigers	Tigers	NYP	A-	Sarasota Red Sox	Red Sox	FSL	A+
Orioles (Sarasota)	Orioles	GCL	R	Savannah Sand Gnats	Rangers	SAL	A
Orlando Rays	Devil Rays	SL	AA	Scranton/Wilkes-Barre Red Barons	Phillies	IL	AAA
Ottawa Lynx	Expos	IL	AAA	Shreveport Captains	Giants	TL	AA
Padres (Peoria)	Padres	AZL	R	South Bend Silver Hawks	Diamondbacks	MWL	A
Pawtucket Red Sox	Red Sox	IL	AAA	Spokane Indians	Royals	NWL	A-
Peoria Chiefs	Cardinals	MWL	A	Staten Island Yankees	Yankees	NYP	A-
Phillies (Clearwater)	Phillies	GCL	R	Syracuse SkyChiefs	Blue Jays	IL	AAA
Piedmont Boll Weevils	Phillies	SAL	A	Tacoma Rainiers	Mariners	PCL	AAA
Pirates (Bradenton)	Pirates	GCL	R	Tampa Yankees	Yankees	FSL	A+
Pittsfield Mets	Mets	NYP	A-	Tennessee Smokies	Blue Jays	SL	AA
Portland Sea Dogs	Marlins	EL	AA	Tigers (Lakeland)	Tigers	GCL	R
Portland Rockies	Rockies	NWL	A-	Toledo Mud Hens	Tigers	IL	AAA
Potomac Cannons	Cardinals	CAR	A+	Tucson Sidewinders	Diamondbacks	PCL	AAA
Princeton Devil Rays	Devil Rays	APP	R+	Trenton Thunder	Red Sox	EL	AA
Pulaski Rangers	Rangers	APP	R+	Tulsa Drillers	Rangers	TL	AA
Quad City River Bandits	Twins	MWL	A	Twins (Fort Myers)	Twins	GCL	R
Queens Kings	Blue Jays	NYP	A-	Utica Blue Sox	Marlins	NYP	A-
Rancho Cucamonga Quakes	Padres	CAL	A+	Vancouver Canadians	Athletics	NWL	A-
Rangers (Port Charlotte)	Rangers	GCL	R	Vermont Expos	Expos	NYP	A-
Reading Phillies	Phillies	EL	AA	Vero Beach Dodgers	Dodgers	FSL	A+
Red Sox (Fort Myers)	Red Sox	GCL	R	Visalia Oaks	Athletics	CAL	A+
Reds (Sarasota)	Reds	GCL	R	West Michigan Whitecaps	Tigers	MWL	A
Richmond Braves	Braves	IL	AAA	West Tenn Diamond Jaxx	Cubs	SL	AA
Rochester Red Wings	Orioles	IL	AAA	White Sox (Tucson)	White Sox	AZL	R
Rockies (Tucson)	Rockies	AZL	R	Wichita Wranglers	Royals	TL	AA
Round Rock Express	Astros	TL	AA	Williamsport Crosscutters	Pirates	NYP	A-
Royals (Baseball City)	Royals	GCL	R	Wilmington Blue Rocks	Royals	CAR	A+
St. Lucie Mets	Mets	FSL	A+	Winston-Salem Warthogs	White Sox	CAR	A+
St. Petersburg Devil Rays	Devil Rays	FSL	A+	Wisconsin Timber Rattlers	Mariners	MWL	A
Sacramento RiverCats	Athletics	PCL	AAA	Yakima Bears	Dodgers	NWL	A-
Salem Avalanche	Rockies	CAR	A+	Yankees (Tampa)	Yankees	GCL	R

About STATS, Inc.

STATS, Inc. is the nation's leading sports information and statistical analysis company, providing detailed sports services for a wide array of commercial clients. In January 2000, STATS was purchased by News Digital Media, the digital division of News Corporation. News Digital Media engages in three primary activities: operating FOXNews.com, FOXSports.com, FOXMarketwire.com and FOX.com; developing related interactive services; and directing investment activities and strategy for News Corporation, as they relate to digital media.

As one of the fastest growing companies in sports, STATS provides the most detailed, up-to-the-minute sports information to professional teams, print and broadcast media, software developers and interactive service providers around the country. STATS recently was recognized as "one of Chicago's 100 most influential technology players" by *Crain's Chicago Business* and has been one of 16 finalists for KPMG/Peat Marwick's Illinois High Tech Award for three consecutive years. Some of our major clients include Fox Sports, the Associated Press, America Online, *The Sporting News*, ESPN, Electronic Arts, MSNBC, SONY and Topps. Much of the information we provide is available to the public via STATS On-Line. With a computer and a modem, you can follow action in the four major professional sports, as well as NCAA football and basketball and other professional and college sports.

STATS Publishing, a division of STATS, Inc., produces 12 annual books, including the *Major League Handbook*, *The Scouting Notebook*, the *Pro Football Handbook*, the *Pro Basketball Handbook* and the *Hockey Handbook*. In 1998, we introduced two baseball encyclopedias, the *All-Time Major League Handbook* and the *All-Time Baseball Sourcebook*. Together they combine for more than 5,000 pages of baseball history. Also available is *From Abba Dabba to Zorro: The World of Baseball Nicknames*, a wacky look at monikers and their origins. A new football title was launched in 1999, the *Pro Football Scoreboard*, and we added the *Pro Football Sourcebook* in 2000. All of our publications deliver STATS' expertise to fans, scouts, general managers and media around the country.

In addition, STATS Fantasy Sports is at the forefront of the booming fantasy sports industry. We develop fantasy baseball, football, basketball, hockey, golf and auto racing games for FOXSports.com. We also feature the first historical baseball simulation game created specifically for the Internet—FOX Diamond Legends. No matter what time of year, STATS Fantasy Sports has a fantasy game to keep even the most passionate sports fan satisfied.

Information technology has grown by leaps and bounds in the last decade, and STATS will continue to be at the forefront as both a vendor and supplier of the most up-to-date, in-depth sports information available. For those of you on the information superhighway, you always can catch STATS in our area on America Online or at our Internet site.

For more information on our products, or on joining our reporter network, contact us via:

America Online — Keyword: STATS

Internet — www.stats.com

Toll Free in the USA at 1-800-63-STATS (1-800-637-8287)

Outside the USA at 1-847-470-8798

Or write to:

STATS, Inc.
8130 Lehigh Ave.
Morton Grove, IL 60053

About Howe Sportsdata

Howe Sportsdata has been compiling statistics on professional baseball since 1910. Currently, Howe is the official statistician for all 17 U.S.-based National Association professional baseball leagues. Howe also compiles statistics for the Arizona Fall League, the Hawaiian Winter League and winter leagues located in Mexico, Puerto Rico, the Dominican Republic, Venezuela and Australia. In addition, Howe keeps the official statistics of the Continental Basketball Association, all professional minor hockey leagues and the National Professional Soccer League.

Originally based in Chicago, Howe Sportsdata is now located in Boston, MA and is under the ownership of SportsTicker Enterprises, L.P., the instant sports news and information service of ESPN, Inc. All told, Howe is responsible for maintaining statistics for more than 300 teams who collectively play more than 14,000 games per year.

Howe also provides statistical information to all 30 major league teams and to major media outlets such as *USA Today*, *The Sporting News*, *Baseball America*, the Associated Press and *Sports Illustrated*. Howe also counts as its customers many leading newspapers, of which the following are a small representative sample: the *Los Angeles Times*, the *Detroit Free Press*, the *Miami Herald* and both the *Chicago Sun-Times* and *Chicago Tribune*. For more information about Howe, write to:

Howe Sportsdata
Boston Fish Pier, West Building #1, Suite 302
Boston, Massachusetts 02110

STATS Power Hitters

Bill James Presents:

<u>STATS Major League Handbook 2001</u>

- Career stats for every 2000 major leaguer
- Bill James' & STATS' exclusive player projections for 2001
- Complete fielding stats for every player at every position
- Expanded and exclusive leader boards
- Managerial performances and tendencies

"STATS consistently provides a thorough and innovative analysis of the game of baseball."
—Ron Schueler, GM, Chicago White Sox

Item #HB01, $19.95, Available Now
Comb-bound #HC01, $24.95, Available Now

<u>STATS Player Profiles 2001</u>

Extensive season and five-year breakdowns including:
- Lefty-righty splits for hitters and pitchers
- Breakdowns for clutch situations
- Home vs. road, day vs. night, grass vs. turf...
- Batting in different lineup spots for hitters
- Pitching after various days of rest

"*Player Profiles* is my companion on all road trips."
—Rod Beaton, *USA Today*

Item #PP01, $19.95, Available Now
Comb-bound #PC01, $24.95, Available Now

Order From STATS INC. Today!
1-800-63-STATS   847-470-8798   www.stats.com

Free First-Class Shipping for Books Over $10
Order form in back of this book

Hot Coverage of the Winter Sports

STATS Hockey Handbook 2000-01

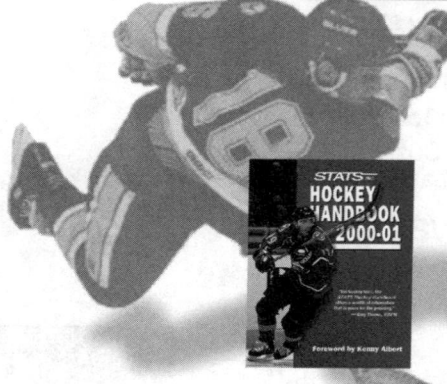

- Career stats for every NHL player who made an appearance in 1999-2000
- In-depth player profiles identifying strengths and weaknesses
- Leader boards for forwards, defensemen and goaltenders
- Team game logs

"STATS scores again with the *Hockey Handbook*."
– Bill Clement, *ESPN* Hockey Analyst

Item #HH01, $19.95, Available Now

STATS Pro Basketball Handbook 2000-01

- Career stats for every player who logged minutes during the 1999-2000 season
- Team game logs with points, rebounds, assists and much more
- Leader boards from points per game to triple-doubles
- 1999-2000 and five-year player splits

"A great guide for the dedicated NBA fan."
– Rick Telander, *ESPN Magazine*

Item #BH01, $19.95, Available Now

Order From **STATS INC.** Today!

1-800-63-STATS   847-470-8798   www.stats.com

Free First-Class Shipping for Books Over $10
Order form in back of this book

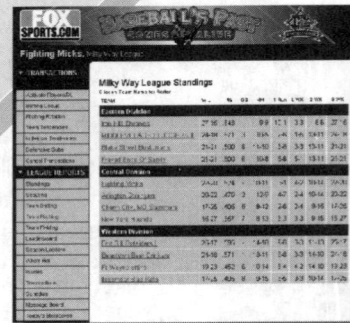

SPORTS TEAM ANALYSIS & TRACKING SYSTEMS

Phone:
1-800-63-STATS
(847) 677-3322

Mail:
STATS, Inc.
8130 Lehigh Avenue
Morton Grove, IL 60053

Fax:
(847) 470-9140

Bill To:
Company_____
Name_____
Address_____
City_____State_____Zip_____
Phone (   )_____Ext.____Fax (   )_____
E-mail Address_____

Ship To: *(Fill in this section if shipping address differs from billing address)*
Company_____
Name_____
Address_____
City_____State_____Zip_____
Phone (   )_____Ext.____Fax (   )_____
E-mail Address_____

Method of payment:
All prices stated
in U.S. Dollars

❑ Charge to my *(circle one)*
  Visa
  MasterCard
  American Express
  Discover

❑ Check or Money Order
  (U.S. funds only)

Please include credit card number
and expiration date with charge orders!

[ ][ ][ ][ ][ ][ ][ ][ ][ ][ ][ ][ ][ ][ ][ ][ ]

Exp. Date [____/____]
     Month Year

X_____
  Signature *(as shown on credit card)*

Totals for STATS Products:	
Books	
Books Under $10 *	
Prior Book Editions *	
order 2 or more books/subtract: $1.00/book *(Does not include prior editions)*	
Illinois residents add 8.5% sales tax	
Sub Total	

Shipping Costs		
Canada	Add $4.00/book	
* All books under $10	Add $2.00/book	
	Grand Total	
	(No other discounts apply)	

(Orders subject to availability)

Free First-Class Shipping for Books Over $10

Books (Free first-class shipping for books over $10)

Qty	Product Name	Item Number	Price	Total
	STATS Major League Handbook 2001	HB01	$ 19.95	
	STATS Major League Handbook 2001 (Comb-bound)	HC01	$ 24.95	
	The Scouting Notebook 2001	SN01	$ 19.95	
	The Scouting Notebook 2001 (Comb-bound)	SC01	$ 24.95	
	STATS Minor League Handbook 2001	MH01	$ 19.95	
	STATS Minor League Handbook 2001 (Comb-bound)	MC01	$ 24.95	
	STATS Player Profiles 2001	PP01	$ 19.95	
	STATS Player Profiles 2001 (Comb-bound)	PC01	$ 24.95	
	STATS Minor League Scouting Notebook 2001	MN01	$ 19.95	
	STATS Batter Vs. Pitcher Match-Ups! 2001	BP01	$ 24.95	
	STATS Ballpark Sourcebook: Diamond Diagrams	BSDD	$ 24.95	
	STATS Baseball Scoreboard 2001	SB01	$ 19.95	
	STATS Pro Football Handbook 2000	FH00	$ 19.95	
	STATS Pro Football Handbook 2000 (Comb-bound)	FC00	$ 24.95	
	STATS Pro Football Scoreboard 2000	SF00	$ 19.95	
	STATS Pro Football Sourcebook 2000	PF00	$ 19.95	
	STATS Hockey Handbook 2000-01	HH01	$ 19.95	
	STATS Pro Basketball Handbook 2000-01	BH01	$ 19.95	
	STATS All-Time Major League Handbook, 2nd Edition	ATHB	$ 79.95	
			Total	

Books Under $10 (Please include $2.00 S&H for each book/magazine)

Qty	Product Name	Item Number	Price	Total
	From Abba Dabba to Zorro: The World of Baseball Nicknames	ABBA	$ 9.95	
	STATS Baseball's Terrific 20	KID1	$ 9.95	
	STATS Player Projections Update 2001	PJUP	$ 9.95	
			Total	

Previous Editions (Please Circle appropriate years and include $2.00 S&H for each book)

Qty	Product Name	Years	Price	Total
	STATS Major League Handbook	'91 '92 '93 '94 '95 '96 '97 '98 '99 '00	$ 9.95	
	The Scouting Notebook/Report	'94 '95 '96 '97 '98 '99 '00	$ 9.95	
	STATS Player Profiles	'93 '94 '95 '96 '97 '98 '99 '00	$ 9.95	
	STATS Minor League Handbook	'92 '93 '94 '95 '96 '97 '98 '99 '00	$ 9.95	
	STATS Minor League Scouting Notebook	'95 '96 '97 '98 '99 '00	$ 9.95	
	STATS Batter Vs. Pitcher Match-Ups!	'94 '95 '96 '97 '98 '99 '00	$ 9.95	
	STATS Diamond Chronicles	'97 '98 '99 '00	$ 9.95	
	STATS Baseball Scoreboard	'92 '93 '94 '95 '96 '97 '98 '99 '00	$ 9.95	
	Pro Football Revealed: The 100-Yard War	'94 '95 '96 '97 '98	$ 9.95	
	STATS Pro Football Handbook	'95 '96 '97 '98 '99	$ 9.95	
	STATS Pro Football Scoreboard	'99	$ 9.95	
	STATS Hockey Handbook	'96-97 '97-98 '98-99 '99-00	$ 9.95	
	STATS Pro Basketball Handbook	'93-94 '94-95 '95-96 '96-97 '97-98 '98-99 '99-00	$ 9.95	
	All-Time Major League Handbook (Slightly dinged)	First Edition	$ 45.00	
	All-Time Major League Sourcebook (Slightly dinged)	First Edition	$ 45.00	
			Total	

TOTAL [   ]